THE *Virgin* ENCYCLOPEDIA OF

FIFTIES MUSIC

Virgin

IN ASSOCIATION WITH MUZE UK LTD

Still dedicated to Guy Mitchell, of course

First published in Great Britain in 1998 by
VIRGIN BOOKS
an imprint of Virgin Publishing Ltd
332 Ladbroke Grove, London W10 5AH

ISBN 0 7535 0268 2

Written, edited and produced by
MUZE UK Ltd
to whom all editorial enquiries should be sent
Iron Bridge House, 3 Bridge Approach, Chalk Farm, London NW1 8BD

Editor In Chief: Colin Larkin
Production Editor: Susan Pipe
Editorial and Research Assistant: Nic Oliver
Copy Editor: Sarah Lavelle
Typographic Design Consultant: Roger Kohn
Special thanks to Trev Huxley, Tony Laudico, Paul Zullo
and all the Klugettes at Muze Inc.,
and to Rob Shreeve of Virgin Publishing.
Typeset by Peggy Sue at True Love Ways Studios
Printed and bound in Great Britain by Butler & Tanner Ltd, Frome and London

INTRODUCTION

The fabulous fifties. Were they? Or were we swept along with the tidalwave of optimism now that war had truly ended. The music of the day was attempting to be cosmopolitan. In the USA, pop lived side by side with R&B. The cheese in the middle of the sandwich was Rock 'n' Roll, and it tasted like nothing on earth. Grand theft was made from Fats Domino and Ruth Brown, and sparkling white crooners attempted Rock 'n' Roll. Few would argue that Elvis Presley, Jerry Lee Lewis and Dion did a pretty fine job. Others stayed with their own roots, which were firmly welded to the great American songbook. Forty years later we are still basking in the genius of Ella Fitzgerald and Frank Sinatra. Their output of classic songs on albums of the fifties is untouchable. Thank goodness Ella and Frankie gave a titanic wide berth to Rock 'n' Roll, and stayed with what they knew.

I was fortunate in having the best of both worlds. I spent much of my first six years living on a travelling fairground. My parents badly needed work and most weekends and public holidays were spent in a chrome mobile home, and at night sleeping on the top floor of a converted double-decker bus that doubled as a tyre store. While they worked, I would wander from noon to midnight through a technicolour Wurlitzer juke-box of image and sound. All rides had their own turntable and boxes of 78s, together with a heavenly sounding, ripped Tannoy speaker. Each ride played its own music, and as you wandered, loud, distorted Little Richard or Lloyd Price would give way to a passive Doris Day, who would become LaVern Baker a few yards later. Imagine turning a radio dial and finding just about every station playing a fantastic song simultaneously. The fairground was just like that, only in colour and with the smell of fried onions and candy floss.

The fairground certainly taught me to love and appreciate most pop, R&B and rock, and when I returned home to the quiet calm of my older brother's bedroom, I would be fed a diet of Sinatra, Ella, *Oklahoma* and *Carousel*. I did draw the line when it came to 'How Much Is That Doggy In The Window' or 'Gilly Gilly Ossenfeffer Katzenellen Bogen By The Sea'. Few would argue that the glut of cover versions of American pop hits in the early fifties were mainly horrendous. Denmark Street publishers sought out unremarkable UK crooners to 'get a cover' of the American hit. In the UK charts between May and June 1955 were three 'Cherry Pink And Apple Blossom Time', three 'Stranger In Paradise' and three 'Unchained Melody'. Those cigar-puffing buffoons could have killed the industry stone dead had it continued. They didn't, and the fifties' apprentices became the sixties' mastercraftsmen. For now, just wallow and fantasize about pink Vauxhall Crestas, Mecca Ballrooms, white suits with two-inch turn-ups, Sinatra hats, Alma Cogan frocks and real nylon stockings with fine point heels. Nostalgia is just not what it used to be.

The Virgin Encyclopedia Of Fifties Music is one in the major series of books taken from the *Encyclopedia Of Popular Music*. Other titles already available are:

The Virgin Encyclopedia Of Sixties Music
The Virgin Encyclopedia Of Seventies Music
The Virgin Encyclopedia Of Eighties Music
The Virgin Encyclopedia Of Popular Music
The Virgin Encyclopedia Of Indie & New Wave
The Virgin Encyclopedia Of The Blues
The Virgin Encyclopedia Of Country Music
The Virgin Encyclopedia Of Soul And R&B
The Virgin Encyclopedia Of Reggae

ENTRY STYLE

Albums, EPs (extended play 45s), newspapers, magazines, television programmes, films and stage musicals are referred to in italics. All song titles appear in single quotes. We spell rock 'n' roll like this. There are two main reasons for spelling rock 'n' roll with 'n' as opposed to 'n'. First, historical precedent: when the term was first coined in the 50s, the popular spelling was 'n'. Second, the 'n' is not simply an abbreviation of 'and' (in which case 'n' would apply) but a phonetic representation of n as a sound. The ' ', therefore, serve as inverted commas rather than as apostrophes. The further reading section at the end of each entry has been expanded to give the reader a much wider choice of available books. These are not necessarily recommended titles but we have attempted to leave out any publication that has little or no merit.

We have also started to add videos at the ends of the entries. Again, this is an area that is expanding faster than we can easily cope with, but there are many items in the videography and further items in the filmography, which is another new section we have decided to include. Release dates in keeping with albums attempt to show the release date in the country of origin. We have also tried to include both US and UK titles where applicable.

ALBUM RATING

Due to many requests from our readers we have now decided to rate all albums. All new releases are reviewed either by myself or by our team of contributors. We also take into consideration the review ratings of the leading music journals and critics' opinions.

Our system is slightly different to most 5 Star ratings in that we rate according to the artist in question's work. Therefore, a 4 Star album from Peggy Lee may have the overall edge over a 4 Star album by Dennis Lotis. Sorry Den.

Our ratings are carefully made, and consequently you will find we are very sparing with 5 Star and 1 Star albums.

Outstanding in every way. A classic and therefore strongly recommended. No comprehensive record collection should be without this album.

Excellent. A high standard album from this artist and therefore highly recommended.

Good. By the artist's usual standards and therefore recommended.

Disappointing. Flawed or lacking in some way.

★

Poor. An album to avoid unless you are a completist.

PLAGIARISM

In maintaining the largest text database of popular music in the world we are naturally protective of its content. We license to approved licensees only. It is both flattering and irritating to see our work reproduced without credit. Time and time again over the past few years I have read an obituary, when suddenly: hang on, I wrote that line. Secondly, it has come to our notice that other companies attempting to produce their own rock or pop encyclopedias use our material as a core. Flattering this might also be, but highly illegal. We have therefore dropped a few more textual 'depth charges' in addition to the original ones. Be warned.

ACKNOWLEDGEMENTS

Our in-house editorial team is lean and efficient. Our Database is now a fully grown child and needs only regular food, attention and love. Thanks to my team for carrying out their task with great responsibility and humour: Susan Pipe, Nic Oliver and Sarah Lavelle are the best. Our outside contributors are further reduced in number, as we now write most of and amend all our existing text. However, we could not function without the continuing efforts and dedication of 50s stalwart and genius Big John Martland, 'Oor' Alex Ogg and Brian Hogg. America's premier R&B authority Robert Pruter continues to supply his

specialist knowledge and experience. Mike Kaye is still our Database doctor, Jon Staines came back to us for about ten minutes, Charlie Furniss is with us full-time and the Hoboken bundle Dawn Eden joined for the long haul, in between her duties as secretary of the John Carter fan club.

Other past contributors' work may appear in this volume and I acknowledge once again; Simon Adams, David Ades, Mike Atherton, Gavin Badderley, Alan Balfour, Michael Barnett, Johnny Black, Chris Blackford, Keith Briggs, Michael Ian Burgess, Paul M. Brown, Tony Burke, John Child, Rick Christian, Alan Clayson, Paul Cross, Norman Darwen, Roy Davenport, Peter Doggett, Kevin Eden, John Eley, Lars Fahlin, Ian Garlinge, Mike Gavin, Andy Hamilton, Mike Hughes, Arthur Jackson, Mark Jones, Simon Jones, Dave Laing, Steve Lake, Paul Lewis, Graham Lock, Chris May, Dave McAleer, Greg Moffitt, Nick Morgan, Michael Newman, Pete Nickols, Lyndon Noon, Zbigniew Nowara, James Nye, Ken Orton, Ian Peel, Dave Penny, Lionel Robinson, Johnny Rogan, Alan Rowett, Dave Sissons, Neil Slaven, Chris Smith, Steve Smith, Mitch Solomons, Mike Stephenson, Jeff Tamarkin, Ray Templeton, Gerard Tierney, John Tobler, Pete Wadeson, Pete Watson, Dave Wilson and Barry Witherden.

Record company press offices are often bombarded with my requests for biogs and review copies. Theirs is a thankless task, but thanks anyway, especially to Alan Robinson of Demon, Sue and Dave Williams at Frontier, Julia Honeywell at Ace, Richard Wooton and his colleagues at the Manor House and Pat Naylor and Nicola Powell at Ryko/Hannibal.

Thanks for the continuing enthusiasm and co-operation of all our new colleagues at Virgin Publishing under the guidance of the consistently inconsistent Rob Shreeve, in particular to the sensual yet efficient Roz Scott who is so efficient and sensual. Also to the quite great Pete Bassett.

To our colleagues at Muze Inc., who are the business partners I always knew I wanted but never knew where to find, and many of them are becoming good friends. To everyone at the offices on 304 Hudson Street in New York. In particular to the handsome new CEO Tony Laudico, the well turned-out Paul Zullo, Steve 'Binary' Figard, Marc 'Moony' Miller, Mike Nevins, the shy Gary Geller, Sylvia and all other Klugettes, and of course, the hugely loveable Trev Huxley. And lastly to my reelin' and rockin' tin lids, who quite like Little Richard but are not sure about Guy Mitchell (yet).

Colin Larkin, April 1998

ABRAMSON, HERB

b. c.1920, Brooklyn, New York, USA. A record collector from his teens, Abramson staged jazz concerts with Ahmet Ertegun and his brother Nesuhi in New York and Washington in the early 40s, while training as a dentist. He was also a part-time producer for National from 1944-47, working with Billy Eckstine and the Ravens. Abramson briefly ran the Jubilee and Quality labels with Jerry Blaine before he and Ahmet Ertegun set up Atlantic in 1947. Over the next five years, he and Ertegun worked as producers, promoters and distributors in building up the company into a leading R&B label. From 1953-55, Abramson did military service and on his return launched the Atco subsidiary, working with the Coasters, Clyde McPhatter, Bobby Darin and Wynonie Harris. However, tensions between the Atlantic team, which by then included his wife Miriam, caused Abramson to sell his interest in Atlantic in 1957 for $300,000. He then set up labels such as Triumph, Festival and Blaze, which provided his only big pop hit, 'Tennessee Waltz' by Bobby Comstock (1959). After those companies failed, Abramson continued as an independent producer, supervising tracks by Gene Pitney, Don Covay and others. In the R&B field, he recorded sessions by Elmore James, Tommy Tucker ('Hi Heel Sneekers,' 1964), Titus Turner and Louisiana Red (Atco, 1971).

ACE, JOHNNY

b. John Marshall Alexander Jnr., 9 June 1929, Memphis, Tennessee, USA, d. 24 December 1954. Ace began his professional career as an R&B singer in 1949, playing piano in a band that eventually evolved into the Beale Streeters, which included at various times B.B. King, Bobby Bland, Roscoe Gordon and Earl Forest. The Beale Streeters established a considerable reputation and toured Tennessee and the surrounding states, giving Ace the experience to develop into an outstanding blues ballad singer. In 1952, he was signed by Duke Records and secured a number 1 R&B hit with his debut, 'My Song' (a hit for Aretha Franklin in 1968). The languid song, sung with Ace's distinctive blues-flavoured smoothness and a touch of sadness in his voice, determined his direction for seven subsequent hits in the USA, notably 'Saving My Love' (number 2 R&B 1953), 'Please Forgive Me' (number 2 R&B 1954), 'Cross My Heart' (number 3 R&B 1953), 'The Clock' (number 1 R&B 1953) and 'Never Let Me Go' (number 9 R&B 1954). Ace, by committing suicide playing Russian Roulette backstage at a concert on Christmas Eve 1954, made his death his claim to fame, unfairly obscuring the fine music of his legacy. He had two posthumous hits, 'Pledging My Love' (number 1 R&B 1955) and 'Anymore' (number 7 R&B 1955); the former was Ace's only mainstream success, reaching number 17 on *Billboard*'s national pop chart. Duke Records released a 10-inch and 12-inch album, and both became perennial sellers.
● ALBUMS: *The Johnny Ace Memorial Album* 10-inch album (Duke 1955)★★★, *The Johnny Ace Memorial Album* 12-inch album (Duke 1957)★★★.

ADAMS, FAYE

b. Fayle Tuell, c.1925, New Jersey, USA. Adams exploded onto the R&B scene in the early 50s with a series of gospel-infused hits that foreshadowed soul music years before its time. She began her career in gospel at the age of five when she and her siblings formed a group called the Tuell Sisters. She joined the Joe Morris Orchestra in 1952, and as part of that organization recorded the three songs that established her name in the R&B world, 'Shake A Hand' (number 1 R&B, number 22 pop), 'I'll Be True' (number 1 R&B), and 'Hurts Me To My Heart' (number 1 R&B). Her last chart record was 'Keeper Of My Heart' in 1957. Adams later returned to the church, abandoning her R&B career.
● COMPILATIONS: *Softly He Speaks* (Savoy 1976)★★★, *I'm Goin' To Leave You* (Mr. R&B 1990)★★★.

ADAMS, MARIE

b. Ollie Marie Givens, 19 October 1925, Linden, Texas, USA. Known affectionately as 'TV Mama' (the one with the big wide screen), by her colleagues in the Johnny Otis band, singer Marie Adams began her recording career in Houston, Texas, for the local Peacock label in 1952, accompanied by the bands of Bill Harvey, Chuck Dillon and Pluma Davis, finding success with her first release, 'I'm Gonna Play The Honky Tonks'. Covering Johnny Ace's 'My Song' in 1953 at a Peacock session in New York City with the Cherokee Conyers Orchestra (a cut-down Buddy Johnson unit), she joined Johnny Otis's band, staying until the late 50s and appearing on Otis recordings for Peacock and, as lead singer with the Three Tons Of Joy, for Capitol Records on such pop rock 'n' roll classics as 'Ma, He's Making Eyes At Me', 'In The Dark', and 'What Do You Want To Make Those Eyes At Me For'. In the early 60s she made records in Los Angeles for Sure Play and Encore Artists. She was back performing with the Three Tons Of Joy and was on a world tour with Otis in 1972, but she is believed to have died shortly afterwards.

ADAMS, WOODROW

b. Woodrow Wilson Adams, 9 April 1917, Tchula, Mississippi, USA. Although he earned his living driving a tractor in rural Mississippi, Woodrow Adams made enough records to offer a fascinating insight into the music of a non-professional Delta blues musician. He learned both harmonica and guitar during childhood, but was 35 years old before he made his first record. In all, he released three singles between 1952 and 1961. The first was an extremely rough, unpolished performance in the Mississippi-based Chicago blues style of the time, but by the time the third was released, there was an attempt to update his sound to a more commercial R&B. None of these records enjoyed any success and Adams was still working on a plantation when researcher David Evans recorded a session with his band in 1967, part of which was later issued on an album.
● ALBUMS: *Lowdown Memphis Harmonica Jam* (1976)★★★.

ADDISON, JOHN

b. John Mervin Addison, 16 March 1920, Cobham, Surrey, England. A composer for the theatre and films, Addison studied composition and several instruments, including the piano, oboe and clarinet, at the Royal College of Music shortly before, and after, World War II. He was Professor of Composition at the college from 1950-57; his own classical compositions included music for the ballet, chamber orchestra and a trumpet concerto. For the theatre, in the 50s he collaborated with *avant garde* choreographer John Cranko on shows such as *Cranks* and *Keep Your Hair On*, and much later, in the early 70s, wrote the music to lyrics by David Heneker for *The Amazons* and *Popkiss*. He also contributed music to several plays, including *Luther*, *A Patriot For Me*, *Bloomsbury*, *The Entertainer* and *Antony And Cleopatra*. In the film world he was among the leading British composers, particularly during the 60s, with scores such as *Seven Days To Noon*, *The Man Between*, *Private's Progress*, *Reach For The Sky* (the popular biopic of flying ace Douglas Bader, starring Kenneth More), *Lucky Jim*, *I Was Monty's Double*, *Look Back In Anger*, *A French Mistress*, *The Entertainer*, *School For Scoundrels*, *A Taste Of Honey*, *The Girl In The Headlines*, *Girl With Green Eyes*, *The Loneliness Of The Long Distance Runner*, *Tom Jones* (1963, starring Albert Finney, and for which Addison won an Academy Award), *Guns At Batasi*, *The Amorous Adventures of Moll Flanders*, *The Loved Ones*, *Torn Curtain*, *A Fine Madness*, *The Honey Pot*, *Smashing Time*, *The Charge Of The Light Brigade*, *Start The Revolution Without Me*, *Country Dance*, *Mr. Forbush And The Penguins*, *Sleuth* (nominated for an Academy Award), *Dead Cert*, *A Bridge Too Far*, *The Seven Per Cent Solution*, *The Pilot*, *Strange Invaders*, *The Ultimate Solution of Grace Quigley*, and *Code Name: Emerald* (1985). Addison has also composed extensively for television programmes, which have included *Sambo And The Snow Mountain*, *The Search For Ulysses*, *Grady* series (NBC), *Black Beauty*, *The Bastard*, *Centennial*, *Like Normal People*, *Love's Savage Fury* and *The French Atlantic Affair*, *Charles And Diana*, *A Royal Love Story*, *Eleanor-First Lady Of The World*, *Mistress Of Paradise*, *Mail Order Bride*, *Ellis Island* and *Murder She Wrote* (series), *Something In Common*, *Thirteen At Dinner*, *Deadman's Folly*, *Bigger Than A Breadbox*, *The Pumpkin Competition*, *Mr. Boogedy*, *Something In Common*, *Bridge Of Boogedy*, *Strange Voices*, *Beryl Markham*, *A Shadow Of The Sun* and *The Phantom Of The Opera*.

ADLER, LARRY

b. Lawrence Cecil Adler, 10 February 1914, Baltimore, Maryland, USA. Adler prefers to be described simply as a 'mouth-organist' - yet he is arguably the most accomplished and celebrated exponent of the instrument there has ever been. His orthodox Judaism gave him the opportunity to train in religious music, and he became a cantor at the age of 10. He sang, and learned to play the piano and mouth-organ by ear from listening to phonograph records, and could not actually read music until 1941. After being expelled from the Peabody Conservatory of Music, he won the Maryland Harmonica Championship in 1927. Shortly afterwards, he ran away to New York and joined one of the Paramount units, playing in movie theatres between features. He was also presented as a 'ragged urchin' ('just in from the street, folks!') in vaudeville, and in Lew Leslie's revue, *Clowns In Clover* (1928). He also served as Eddie

Cantor's stooge for a time, and accompanied Fred Astaire in Florenz Ziegfeld's *Smiles*.

His lifelong admiration and appreciation of George Gershwin began when he was introduced to the composer by Paul Whiteman, and his interpretations of Gershwin's works, especially *Porgy And Bess* and 'Rhapsody In Blue' (on which Adler is sometimes accompanied by a piano-roll made by Gershwin himself), are definitive. Many years later in 1981, Adler's haunting version of Gershwin's 'Summertime' played a significant role in the success of the enormously popular UK ice dancers Torvill and Dean. In 1934, after further speciality roles on stage in *Flying Colors* and on film in Paramount's *Many Happy Returns* (the first of his five movies), in which he was backed by Duke Ellington's Orchestra, Adler was spotted at New York's Palace Theatre by the English producer Charles B. Cochran, who engaged him for the London revue *Streamline*. Shortly after the show opened, sales of mouth-organs in the UK increased by several thousand per cent, and fan clubs proliferated. Adler played the top nightclubs, and the 1937 revue *Tune Inn* was built around him. After marrying top model Eileen Walser, he toured South Africa and Australia before returning to the USA in 1939, where he gained national recognition in the classical field when he appeared as a soloist with the Chicago Women's Symphony Orchestra. During the 40s, Adler appeared at Carnegie Hall with the dancer Paul Draper, and toured with him extensively in the USA, Africa and the Middle East, entertaining troops, and insisting on a non-segregation policy between whites and blacks at concerts. Adler also entertained in the South Pacific with artists such Carol Landis, Martha Tilton and comedian Jack Benny, and worked consistently for the war effort and the Allied forces. He was 'on duty' again in 1951 during the Korean conflict. By then, as a high-profile liberal, he had been included on McCarthy's 'communist' blacklist, and moved to live and work in England, only for the 'red spectre' to follow him even there. In 1954, he was forced by the Rank film organization to give up his billing rights on US prints of the classic comedy film *Genevieve*, for which he had written the gentle but highly distinctive score. The music was duly nominated for an Academy Award, and an embarrassed Rank could only offer orchestra conductor Muir Mathieson's name as composer. Fortunately for them it did not win the Oscar - voters preferred Dimitri Tiomkin's music for *The High And The Mighty* - and Adler had to wait until 1986 for the Academy's official recognition of his work. In 1952, Adler experienced 'the highlight of his musical life' at a Royal Albert Hall Promenade Concert, when he was 'forced' to encore Ralph Vaughan Williams' 'Romance For Mouth-Organ, Piano And Strings', a piece that had been written especially for him. In the 50s, although domiciled in the UK, Adler made frequent, although often difficult, trips to the USA and worked in many other countries of the world with major symphony orchestras. In 1963 as a soloist at the Edinburgh Festival, Adler gave the first performance of 'Lullaby Time', a string quartet written by George Gershwin in 1921, and presented to Adler by Ira Gershwin. That piece, and several other unpublished works by composers such as Cole Porter, Harold Arlen and Richard Rodgers, were included on his RCA album *Discovery*. His own most familiar composition is the music for *Genevieve*, but he has composed the music for other films, including *The Hellions*, *King And*

Country, *High Wind In Jamaica* and *The Great Chase*. His work for television programmes and plays includes *Midnight Men*, along with concert pieces such as 'Theme And Variations'. Works have been specially written for him by Malcolm Arnold, Darius Milhaud, Arthur Benjamin, Gordon Jacobs, and others. In 1965 Adler was back at the Edinburgh Festival with his one-man show, *Hand To Mouth*, and in 1967 and 1973, gave his services to Israel in aid of those affected by the Six Day and Yom Kippur wars. In 1988, as busy as ever, he appeared at New York's Ballroom club with Harold Nicholas, one half of the legendary dance team the Nicholas Brothers. To many, the engagement brought back memories of Adler's tours in the 40s with his friend, tap-dancer Paul Draper. As usual on these occasions, Adler skilfully blended classical selections with a 'honky-tonk jazz' approach to numbers written by the great popular songwriters of the past. The following year he performed in concert at London's Royal Albert Hall, marking his 75th birthday, accompanied by pianist John Ogden, and the Wren Orchestra conducted by Stanley Black. During the early 90s he played regularly at the Pizza on the Park, sometimes accompanied by 'The Hot Club Of London', and recalled numbers forever associated with him. In 1994, at the age of 80, Adler released *The Glory Of Gershwin*, on which he was joined by stars from the rock world such as Sting, Meat Loaf, Kate Bush, Peter Gabriel and Sinead O'Connor. The media interest generated by this project - the album just failed to reach the top of the UK album chart - led to Adler making sell-out appearances at venues such as the Jazz Café and the Café Royal. He also embarked on *A Living Legend-The Final Tour* late in 1994. As a musician and a journalist, Larry Adler seems to have met and worked with almost everyone who is (or has ever been) anyone in showbusiness, politics, and many other walks of life. A tennis fanatic, he once played in a doubles match with Charlie Chaplin, Greta Garbo and Salvador Dali, and is always prepared to talk about it.

● ALBUMS: with Morton Gould *Discovery* (RCA 1969)★★★★, *Plays Gershwin, Porter, Kern, Rodgers, Arlen And Gould* (RCA 1985)★★★★, *Golden Age Of Larry Adler* (Golden Age 1986)★★★, *Works For Harmonica And Orchestra* (Accordion 80s)★★★, *The Mouth Organ Virtuoso* (EMI 1994)★★★, with others *The Glory Of Gershwin* (Mercury 1994)★★.

● FURTHER READING: All titles by Larry Adler *How I Play*, *Larry Adler's Own Arrangements*. *Jokes And How To Tell Them*. *It Ain't Necessarily So: His Autobiography*. *Me And My Big Mouth*.

● FILMS: *St Martin's Lane* (1938), *Music For Millions* (1944), *Genevieve* (composer) (1953), *The Hellions* (composer) (1961), *King And Country* (composer) (1963), *The Hook* (composer) (1963), *High Wind In Jamaica* (composer) (1964).

ADLER, RICHARD

b. 3 August 1921, New York, USA. This composer, lyricist, and producer had two hit Broadway shows in the 50s, but has since been unable to produce another one. The son of a concert pianist, Adler was not attracted to classical music, and studied to be a writer at the University of North Carolina before spending three years in the US Navy. After his discharge he went into the advertising business, and composed the occasional song in his spare time. In the early 50s he met Jerry Ross (b. Jerold Rosenberg, 9 March 1926, The Bronx, New York, USA, d. 11 November 1955, New York, USA), and they began to write songs together. In 1953, contracted to Frank Loesser's publishing company Frank Music, they had a hit with 'Rags To Riches', which became a US chart-topper for Tony Bennett. After contributing several numbers to the revue *John Murray Anderson's Almanac*, Adler and Ross wrote the complete score for *The Pajama Game*, which opened on Broadway in May 1954 and ran for 1,063 performances. Several of the songs became popular outside the show, including 'Hernando's Hideaway', 'Hey There' (a US number 1 for Rosemary Clooney) and 'Small Talk'. Almost exactly one year later they returned with the highly entertaining baseball musical *Damn Yankees*, which once again was full of lively and tuneful songs such as 'Heart', which became successful for Eddie Fisher and the Four Aces, and 'Whatever Lola Wants', a chart hit for Sarah Vaughan and Dinah Shore. The show was settling in for a run of 1,019 performances when Ross died of leukaemia in November 1955. Three years later, 'Everybody Loves A Lover', another Adler-Ross song, which does not appear to have been included in a show or film, became a hit for Doris Day. After Ross's death Adler turned his hand to producing, but without success: *The Sin Of Pat Muldoon*, Richard Rodgers' *Rex*, and *Music Is* (for which Adler also wrote the music) were major disappointments. In the 60s he wrote both music and lyrics for *Kwamina* and *A Mother's Kisses*, but neither took off. His score for *Kwamina*, a show whose theme was a plea for racial tolerance in Africa and starred his then-wife Sally Ann Howes, was regarded as a fine piece of work, and can now be reassessed following the re-release of the Original Cast recording by Broadway Angel. Adler has also been actively writing for television commercials, and directing business conventions and political rallies.

● FURTHER READING: *You Gotta Have Heart*, Richard Adler with Lee Davis.

AINSWORTH, ALYN

b. 24 August 1924, Bolton, Lancashire, England, d. 4 October 1990, London, England. A highly respected musical director and arranger for records, television and the West End stage, Ainsworth studied guitar from the age of seven, left school at 14 to join Herman Darewski's Orchestra as a boy soprano, and sang at the London Palladium. When his voice broke, he returned to Bolton and became an assistant golf professional, playing guitar in his own band, the Falcons, while also studying musical arranging. In the late 40s he worked as a staff arranger for Oscar Rabin, and then Geraldo, one of the top UK dance bands. In 1951 he began to arrange for the newly formed BBC Northern Variety Orchestra, and, when its conductor, Vilem Tausky, moved to the Northern Symphony Orchestra, Ainsworth was offered the job of resident conductor with the NVO. In December 1952, BBC Television launched *The Good Old Days* from the City Variety Theatre in Leeds - this music-hall show ran for over 30 years - and Ainsworth and the Northern Variety Orchestra provided the appropriate musical setting. Economics, it is said, obliged the BBC to prune the orchestra, removing all the members of the string section, bar one, and renaming it the Northern Dance Orchestra. With the help of musicians such as trumpeter Syd Lawrence, Ainsworth welded the NDO into one of the finest units of its kind in the world.

Based in Manchester for a decade, Ainsworth and the NDO appeared on numerous radio and television programmes, accompanying singers such as Frankie Vaughan, Ronnie Hilton, and David Whitfield. Together with singer Sheila Buxton and laid-back announcer Roger Moffat, they had their own highly acclaimed late-night UK television show, *Make Way For Music*. In 1961 Ainsworth moved from Manchester to London to serve as musical director for the imported American musical *Bye Bye Birdie*, which starred Chita Rivera and UK rock 'n' roller Marty Wilde. Between 1958 and 1965, the Alyn Ainsworth Orchestra also recorded a number of orchestral pieces for George Martin. During the 60s Ainsworth became a leading conductor and arranger for West End shows such as *Gentlemen Prefer Blondes, Hello, Dolly!, A Funny Thing Happened On The Way To The Forum, She Loves Me* and *Sweet Charity*. He also orchestrated Leslie Bricusse and Anthony Newley's *The Roar Of The Greasepaint-The Smell Of The Crowd*. The 60s also saw the start of his long and successful collaboration with singer Shirley Bassey, during which time he acted as her musical director for many cabaret seasons in the UK and abroad. Back home in Britain, Ainsworth's television credits included Val Parnell's *Sunday Night At The London Palladium, International Cabaret From the Talk Of The Town, The David Nixon Show, Dee Time, The Cannon And Ball Show, Search For A Star, Night Of Hundred Stars, The BAFTA Awards, Live From Her Majesty's, Bruce's Big Night Out*, more than 10 *Royal Command Performances*, and many 'specials' featuring artists such as Cilla Black, Russ Abbott, Stanley Baxter, Vera Lynn, and Lulu. He also composed the theme music for several of the shows. His other compositions included 'Bedtime For Drums', 'Italian Sunset', 'Mi Amor', 'Pete's Party' and 'If I Were A Buddy Rich Man'. Ainsworth was also associated with the Brotherhood Of Man, and conducted for them at the Eurovision Song contest which they won in 1976 with 'Save Your Kisses For Me'. He also worked with many visiting Americans, including Johnny Mathis, Neil Sedaka, and Barry Manilow. Ainsworth also collaborated with the Beverley Sisters on their recording of 'Triplets', among others, and was engaged for a time to one of the twins, Teddy. His own records included a rare excursion into rock 'n' roll with '18th Century Rock', credited to 'Alyn Ainsworth with The Rock-A-Fellas', and the more typically smooth *Themes And Dreams* and *True Love*. The ultimate professional, Ainsworth would often conduct the first house of one West End show, and the second house of another, after rehearsing for television during the day. He was capable of producing his best work under extreme pressure, while also motivating others, and was the man on whom producers could rely for the big occasion.

● ALBUMS: *Themes And Dreams* (Pickwick 1982)★★★, *True Love* (Hallmark 1982)★★★.

ALBERT, EDDIE

b. Edward Albert Heimberger, 22 April 1908, Rock Island, Illinois, USA. A singer and actor in theatre and films, with a range that extends from 'amiable, best friend' parts, through to overbearing, thoroughly nasty character roles. Albert began his career as a singer, and worked in theatres and on radio with the Threesome, and then teamed with Grace Bradt to form the Honeymooners - Grace and Eddie. He made his Broadway debut at the Empire Theatre in the play *O Evening Star* (1935), which was followed by *Brother Rat*

(1936), and *Room Service* (1937). A year later, he played Antipholus of Syracuse and introduced 'This Can't Be Love' in *The Boys From Syracuse*. During World War II, Albert served as a lieutenant in the US Navy, and it was 1949 before he returned to the Broadway musical theatre in *Miss Liberty* (1949), in which he sang the appealing 'Let's Take An Old-Fashioned Walk'. Nine years later he took over from David Wayne in *Say, Darling*, and then succeeded Robert Preston as Professor Harold Hill in *The Music Man*, in January 1960. In between, he continued to perform in serious plays on Broadway and in regional theatre. He also carved out an impressive career in films, which total more than 70 to date. These have included several musicals such as *On Your Toes* (1939), *Hit Parade Of 1947, Meet Me After The Show* (1951), and *The Girl Rush* (1955). In the 50s he had two particularly good roles, firstly in *Oklahoma!* (1955), in which he played pedlar-man Ali Hakim, and then in *The Joker Is Wild* (1957), where, as the accompanist of comedian Joe E. Lewis (played by Frank Sinatra), he was outstanding. Albert has been seen on the screen in dramatic roles in films such as *Brother Rat* (1938), *Four Wives* (1939), *Smash Up* (1947), *Carrie* (1952), *Roman Holiday* (1953), *I'll Cry Tomorrow* (1955), *Attack!* (1956), *The Teahouse Of The August Moon* (1956), *The Roots Of Heaven* (1958), *Orders To Kill* (1958), *The Longest Day* (1962), *Captain Newman MD* (1963), *The Heartbreak Kid* (1972), and *The Longest Yard* (1974), continuing into the 90s. His extensive television credits include many films and series, including *Leave It To Larry* (1952), *Green Acres* (1965-70), *Switch* (1975-76) and *The Chocolate Soldier* (1984). In the 50s Albert appeared in a television adaptation of *A Connecticut Yankee*, and had a sophisticated nightclub act with his wife Margo. Their son, Edward Albert, is a film and television actor.

● ALBUMS: *Eddie Albert* (Columbia 50s)★★★, *One God* (Kapp 1954)★★★, *Eddie Albert And Margo* (Kapp 1956)★★★★, Original Broadway Cast *Miss Liberty* (Columbia 50s)★★★.

ALBERY, DONALD

b. Donald Arthur Rolleston Albery, 19 June 1914, London, England, d. 14 September 1988, Monte Carlo. A producer and theatre-owner, Albery came from a family steeped in theatrical history - his paternal grandfather was the playwright James Albery, and his father was Sir Bronson Albery who founded what became the Society of West End Theatres. Donald Albery was educated in Switzerland before serving as general manager of Sadlers Wells Ballet from 1941-45. He started out as a producer in 1953, and throughout the 50s and 60s presented or co-presented several notable plays, such as *The Living Room, Waiting For Godot, A Taste Of Honey* and *Who's Afraid Of Virginia Woolf?* His first musical production was *Grab Me A Gondola* in 1956, and this was followed by a mixture of smash hits and minor flops, which included *Zuleika* (1957), *Irma La Douce* (1958), *Make Me An Offer* (1959), *Fings Ain't Wot They Used T'Be* (1960), *Oliver!* (1960), *The Art Of Living* (1960), *Not To Worry* (1962), *Blitz!* (1962), *Fiorello!* (1962), *Oliver!* (New York 1963), *Instant Marriage* (1964), *Jorrocks* (1966), *Oliver!* (London revival 1967), *Man Of La Mancha* (1968), *Mandrake* (1970) and *Popkiss* (1972). Albery also enjoyed a long-runner with the revue *Beyond The Fringe* in 1961. In 1962 he took over the Wyndham Group of London theatres from his father,

consisting of Wyndham's, the New (later renamed the Albery) and the Criterion; Albery later also acquired the Piccadilly Theatre. Albery was knighted in 1977, and sold his Group to Associated Newspapers a year later, when he retired. His son Ian took over as manager.
● FURTHER READING: *All On Stage: Charles Wyndham And The Alberys*, W. Trewin.

ALDA, ROBERT

b. Alphonso Giuseppe Giovanni Robert D'Abruzzo, 26 February 1914, New York, USA, d. 3 May 1986, Los Angeles, California, USA. An actor and singer who, although he enjoyed a long career in many areas of showbusiness, is remembered mainly for his first film role, when he portrayed the composer George Gershwin in the 1945 Warner biopic *Rhapsody In Blue*. The son of a barber, Alda was educated at New York University, and worked as an architectural draughtsman before making his stage debut in vaudeville in 1933 with an act called Charlie Ahearn And His Millionaires. He subsequently worked on radio, toured in burlesque, and performed in summer stock in numerous straight plays, such as *Tobacco Road*, *The Postman Always Rings Twice*, *Room Service* and *The Time Of Your Life*. Alda made his Broadway debut in 1950, creating the role of gambler Sky Masterson in the Abe Burrows-Jo Swerling-Frank Loesser musical *Guys And Dolls*. He stayed with the show for nearly two years, and his performance gained him a Tony Award, as well as Donaldson and New York Drama Critics Poll honours. While touring Italy and Sicily in the mid-50s in *La Padrona Di Raggio Di Luna*, he received the Golden Wing Award for his performance as an Italian, and in the early 60s settled in Rome for some years. He continued to work occasionally in the USA, and in 1963 toured with *Can-Can*, before returning to Broadway in the following year, co-starring with Steve Lawrence and Sally Ann Howes in a musical spoof on Hollywood's Golden Age of the 30s, *What Makes Sammy Run?* Alda's own movie career never lived up to the promise of *Rhapsody In Blue*. He made only two more musicals, *Cinderella Jones* (1946) and *April Showers* (1948), along with some 20 or so other films, which included *The Beast With Five Fingers* (1947), *The Man I Love* (1947), *Tarzan And The Slave Girl* (1950), *Two Gals And A Guy* (1951), *Beautiful And Dangerous* (1958), *Imitation Of Life* (1959), *Cleopatra's Daughter* (1961), *The Girl Who Knew Too Much* (1968), *I Will, I Will, I Will ... For Now* (1976), *Bittersweet Love* (1976), and *The Squeeze* (1980). Alda also appeared frequently on US television, in programmes such as *By Popular Demand*, *The Milton Berle Show*, *The Kids From Fame*, *Police Story*, *Perfect Gentlemen*, *Days Of Our Lives*, *Supertrain* and *The Robert Alda Show*. He also starred on Italian radio and television, and played in cabaret throughout most of his career. In 1984, Alda suffered a stroke from which he never fully recovered. His son is the famous actor-director Alan Alda.

ALLEN, RED

b. Harley Allen, 12 February 1930, Hazard, Perry County, Kentucky, USA, d. 3 April 1993, Dayton, Ohio, USA. Greatly influenced in his early years by Charlie Monroe, whom he regularly heard on WNOX Knoxville, he developed a great love for bluegrass music. During his career, Allen, an outstanding vocalist and competent rhythm guitarist (he also played banjo and mandolin), established himself as one of the leading exponents of the genre. After service with the US Marine Corps in the late 40s, he began to play with various musicians, including banjoist Noah Crase (with whom he made his first recordings for a minor label in 1953), around Dayton, Ohio. Between 1954 and 1958, he worked with the Osborne Brothers, the act being very popular on the WWVA *Wheeling Jamboree* and also for some MGM recordings, especially 'Once More' which, in 1958, reached number 13 in the US country charts. In 1960, he relocated to the Washington area where, in partnership with Frank Wakefield, he formed his noted bluegrass band, the Kentuckians. During the next few years, he made many fine recordings for several major labels, including his version of 'Beautiful Brown Eyes'. In 1967, when Lester Flatt was hospitalized by a heart attack, Allen moved to Nashville to deputize for him. The following year, he relocated to Lexington, where he formed the Kentucky Mountain Boys with J.D. Crowe. By 1970, he had returned to Dayton, where he worked with a band consisting of four of his sons. They became very popular on WWVA *Jamboree* and also recorded for Lemco and King Bluegrass. (His sons have also recorded less traditional bluegrass music as the Allen Brothers but they should not to be confused with the old-time country act of same name.) In the late 70s, Allen recorded an album on Folkways Records as his tribute to the memory of Lester Flatt and he even had two albums released in Japan. In the late 80s, failing health limited his contributions, but he continued to make appearances at various festivals until he finally lost his battle with cancer on 3 April 1993.
● ALBUMS: with the Osborne Brothers *Country Pickin' & Hillside Singin'* (MGM 1959)★★★, *Red Allen, Frank Wakefield & The Kentuckians* (Folkways 1964)★★★, *The Solid Bluegrass Sound Of The Kentuckians* (Melodeon 1966)★★★, *Bluegrass Country* (County 1966)★★★, *Bluegrass Country Volume 2* (County 1967)★★★, with J.D. Crowe And The Kentucky Mountain Boys *Bluegrass Holiday* (Lemco 1969)★★★, *My Old Kentucky Home* (King Bluegrass 1973)★★★, *Allengrass* (Lemco 1973)★★★, *Red Allen Favorites* (King Bluegrass 1975)★★★, *Red Allen & Frank Wakefield* (Red Clay 1976)★★★, *Live And Let Live* (Folkways 1979)★★★, *In Memory Of The Man* (Folkways 1980)★★★, *Family & Friends* (Folkways 1982)★★★, *The Red Allen Tradition* (Folkways 1983)★★★.
● COMPILATIONS: with Osborne Brothers *The Osborne Brothers & Red Allen* (Rounder 1977)★★★, *Classic Recordings 1954-69* reissue of 45s (Collector Classics 1984)★★★, *Bluegrass Special - 1960s Radio Shows* (Storyville)★★★.

ALLEY CATS

This R&B vocal group from Los Angeles, California, USA, comprised Billy Storm (lead), Chester Pipkin, Ed Wallis, and Bryce Caulfield. A classic one-hit-wonder, the Alley Cats had just one chart record, 'Puddin N' Tain (Ask Me Again, I'll Tell You The Same)' (number 21 R&B, number 43 pop) in 1963, and nobody ever heard of them again. The record was produced by legendary producer Phil Spector and was released on his Philles label, but apparently Spector was not interested in continuing the association, and he never again worked with the group. The unit first recorded on Keen in 1957, and recorded as the Untouchables for Madison in 1960, on both occasions without success.

ALLYSON, JUNE

b. Ella Geisman, 7 October 1917, The Bronx, New York, USA. An attractive actress and singer with a distinctive husky voice, Allyson was often cast as the archetypal cute girl-next-door, and is probably best remembered for her portrayal of the bandleader's wife (opposite James Stewart) in *The Glenn Miller Story* (1954). Allyson was raised by her mother who worked as a waitress to make ends meet. At the age of nine she was confined to a wheelchair for a time after being injured by a falling tree, and took up dancing to strengthen her back. In the late 30s and early 40s she had small roles in the Broadway musicals *Sing Out The News*, *Very Warm For May*, *Higher And Higher* and *Panama Hattie*, and had a leading part in *Best Foot Forward* (1941). She recreated her role in the latter show for the 1943 film version, and in the same year appeared on screen in *Girl Crazy* and the multi-star extravaganza *Thousands Cheer*. From that point, she starred in a string of mostly MGM musicals, including *Meet The People*, *Two Girls And A Sailor*, *Music For Millions*, *Two Sisters From Boston*, *Till The Clouds Roll By*, *Good News*, *Words And Music*, *The Glenn Miller Story*, *You Can't Run Away From It*, and *The Opposite Sex* (1956). In addition, she appeared in an equal number of straight, and rather sugary, films such as the 1949 remake of *Little Women* and the dramatic and highly emotional *The Shrike* (1955), with Jose Ferrer. She and her husband, actor Dick Powell, were active on US television throughout the 50s and early 60s - they both had their own shows - but after his death in 1963 Allyson withdrew from public life for a time. Later she continued to work in films, nightclubs, and on stage and television.

ALTON, ROBERT

b. Robert Alton Hart, 28 January 1897, Bennington, Vermont, USA, d. 12 June 1957, Hollywood, California, USA. A particularly innovative and stylish choreographer for the musical stage and Hollywood, Alton appeared on Broadway as a dancer in *Take It From Me* (1919) and *Greenwich Village Follies* (1924) before staging the dance scenes for comedian Joe Cook's last Broadway musical, *Hold Your Horses* (1933). Thereafter, during the rest of the 30s through to the early 50s, he choreographed a mixture of revues and musical comedies, among which were some of the biggest hits of the day. They included *Ziegfeld Follies* (1934), *Life Begins At 8:40* (1934), *Anything Goes* (1934), *Thumbs Up!* (1934), *Parade* (1935), *Ziegfeld Follies* (1936), *Hooray For What!* (1937), *Between The Devil* (1937), *You Never Know* (1938), *Leave It To Me!* (1938), *One For The Money* (1939), *The Streets Of Paris* (1939), *Too Many Girls* (1939), *Du Barry Was A Lady* (1939), *Two For The Show* (1940), *Panama Hattie* (1940), *Higher And Higher* (1940), *Pal Joey* (1940), *Sons O' Fun* (1941), *By Jupiter* (1942), *Count Me In* (1942), *Ziegfeld Follies* (1943), *Laffing Room Only* (1944), *Hazel Flagg* (1953) and *Me And Juliet* (1953). Alton also served as both choreographer and director on *Early To Bed* (1943), the 1952 Broadhurst Theatre revival of *Pal Joey* (with David Alexander), and *The Vamp* (1955).

In parallel with his stage work, Alton created some classic dance scenes in a number of highly successful and fondly remembered movie musicals, such as *You'll Never Get Rich* (1941, the 'Wedding Cake Walk' sequence), *The Harvey Girls* (1946, the Oscar-winning 'On The Atcheson, Topeka And The Santa Fe'), *Ziegfeld Follies* (1946, 'This Heart Of Mine'), *Good News* (1947, with Charles Walters, 'Varsity Drag'),

Easter Parade (1948, 'The Girl On The Magazine Cover', 'Shaking The Blues Away', 'A Couple Of Swells'), *The Pirate* (1948, with Gene Kelly, 'Be A Clown'), *Annie Get Your Gun* (1950, 'I'm An Indian Too'), *Show Boat* (1951, 'I Might Fall Back On You', 'Life Upon The Wicked Stage'), and many more. His other film credits, mostly for MGM, included *Strike Me Pink* (1936), *Bathing Beauty* (1944, with Jack Donohue), *Till The Clouds Roll By* (1946), *Words And Music* (1948, with Kelly), *The Barkleys Of Broadway* (1949), *In The Good Old Summertime* (1949), *Pagan Love Song* (1950, also directed), *The Belle Of New York* (1952), *I Love Melvin* (1953), *Call Me Madam* (1953), *White Christmas* (1954), *There's No Business Like Show Business* (1955), and *The Girl Rush* (1955). In many cases, stars such as Gene Kelly and Fred Astaire would stage one or more of the numbers in their own movies, and there were other occasions when additional choreographers were called in to work alongside Alton, such as on *There's No Business Like Show Business*, when all Marilyn Monroe's dance routines were created by Jack Cole. In a varied and distinguished career, Allen also directed *Merton Of The Movies* (1947), the second film remake of Harry Leon Wilson's endearing novel, which starred Red Skelton, Virginia O'Brien, Alan Mowbray, Gloria Grahame and Leon Ames.

AMERICAN IN PARIS, AN

One of the most enchanting of all film musicals, *An American In Paris* was released in 1951 and became one of the top money-makers of the decade. It has endured simply because of the all-round high-class talent involved. Alan Jay Lerner's screenplay is set in Paris, where Jerry Mulligan (Gene Kelly) is gaining far more personal fulfilment as a painter than he did in his former occupation as a GI. Other areas of his life are not so satisfying: a wealthy American, the rather more mature Milo Richards (Nina Foch), seems more interested in him than in his canvases; and the girl with whom he falls in love, Lise Bourvier (the delightful dancer Leslie Caron in her screen debut), is promised to another, Henri Baurel (Georges Guetary), who happens to be Jerry's best friend. Naturally, it all ends happily, with Jerry keeping his friend and getting the girl. In any case, the story was subservient to the songs - a great collection from George and Ira Gershwin that included 'By Strauss', 'I'll Build A Stairway To Paradise', 'Embraceable You', 'Love Is Here To Stay', 'Tra-La-La', and ''S Wonderful'. The film's climax was a spectacular 18 minute-long ballet, during which Kelly (who choreographed the complete film) found himself in various Parisian locations, each of which was presented in the style of a famous painter. Among the other highlights were Kelly's French lesson for an eager and engaging bunch of kids via 'I Got Rhythm', and a dream sequence during which Oscar Levant conducts part of the 'Piano Concerto In F', and every member of the orchestra appears to be him! A Technicolor production from Arthur Freed's MGM unit, *An American In Paris* was directed with supreme style and flair by Vincente Minnelli. It won Academy Awards for best picture, screenplay, musical arrangements (Saul Chaplin and Johnny Green), cinematography and art/set direction. At the same awards ceremony - in 1952 - Gene Kelly received a special Oscar for his versatility as an actor, singer, director, dancer - and especially - choreographer.

AMES BROTHERS

This family group from Malden, Massachusetts, USA, featured Joe Urick (b. 3 May 1924), Gene Urick (b. 13 February 1925), Vic Urick (b. 20 May 1926, d. 23 January 1978, Nashville, Tennessee, USA) and Ed Urick (b. 9 July 1927). The group were consistently popular from the late 40s through the 50s. The brothers started singing together in high school and won several amateur contests in their home-town. They first sang professionally in Boston, and later in clubs and theatres in New York, Chicago and Hollywood. After recording 'A Tree In A Meadow' with Monica Lewis, for the independent Signature label, they signed for Coral, later switching to RCA Victor. After minor successes with 'You, You, You Are The One' and 'Cruising Down The River', they hit number 1 in 1950 with the novelty 'Rag Mop'/'Sentimental Me' (a million-seller). During the 50s they were extremely popular in stage shows and on US television, with their skilful blend of comedy and an uncomplicated singing style on bouncy numbers and ballads. They also had four more million-selling records: 'Undecided' (backed by Les Brown and his orchestra), 'You You You', 'The Naughty Lady Of Shady Lane' and 'Melodie D'Amour'. Their other US Top 20 hits were 'Can Anyone Explain? (No, No, No!)', 'Put Another Nickel In (Music! Music! Music!)', 'Stars Are The Windows Of Heaven', 'Oh Babe!', 'Wang Wang Blues', 'I Wanna Love You', 'Auf Wiederseh'n Sweetheart', 'String Along', 'My Favorite Song', 'The Man With The Banjo', 'My Bonnie Lassie', 'It Only Hurts For A Little While', 'The Naughty Lady Of Shady Lane', 'Tammy', 'A Very Precious Love' and 'Pussy Cat'. Around 1960, the group disbanded, but Ed Ames continued as a solo act, appearing frequently on US television. He also had hit singles in 1967 with 'My Cup Runneth Over' and 'Who Will Answer?', plus several 60s US chart albums.
● ALBUMS: *Sing A Song Of Christmas* (Coral 1950)★★, *In The Evening By The Moonlight* (Coral 1951)★★★★, *Sentimental Me* (Coral 1951)★★★, *Hoop-De-Hoo* (Coral 1951)★★★, *Sweet Leilani* (Coral 1951)★★★, *Favorite Spirituals* (Coral 1952)★★★, *Home On The Range* (Coral 1952)★★★, *Merry Christmas 1952* (Coral 1952)★★★, *Favorite Songs* (Coral 1954)★★★★, *It Must Be True* (RCA Victor 1954)★★★, *Ames Brothers Concert* (Coral 1956)★★, *Love's Old Sweet Song* (Coral 1956)★★★, *Exactly Like You* (RCA Victor 1956)★★★, *Four Brothers* (RCA Victor 1956)★★★★, *The Ames Brothers With Hugo Winterhalter* (RCA Victor 1956)★★, *Sounds Of Christmas Harmony* (Coral 1957)★★★, *Love Serenade* (Coral 1957)★★★★, *Sweet Seventeen* (RCA Victor 1957)★★★, *There'll Always Be A Christmas* (RCA Victor 1957)★★★, *With Roy Smeck Serenaders* (1958)★★★, *Destination Moon* (RCA Victor 1958)★★★, *Smoochin' Time* (RCA Victor 1958)★★★, *Words & Music With The Ames Brothers* (RCA Victor 1959)★★★★, *Ames Brothers Sing Famous Hits Of Famous Quartets* (RCA Victor 1959)★★★, *Sing The Best In Country* (RCA Victor 1959)★★, *Sing The Best Of The Bands* (RCA Victor 1960)★★★, *The Blend And The Beat* (RCA Victor 1960)★★★, *Hello Amigos* (RCA Victor 1960)★★★, *Sweet & Swing* (RCA Victor 1960)★★★, *Knees Up!* (RCA Victor 1963)★★★.
● COMPILATIONS: *The Best Of The Ames Brothers* (RCA Victor 1958)★★★★, *Our Golden Favorites* (Coral 1960)★★★★.

ANDERSON, PINKNEY 'PINK'

b. 12 February 1900, Laurens, South Carolina, USA, d. 12 October 1974, Spartanburg, South Carolina, USA. For much of his life, Anderson was Spartanburg's most famous songster and medicine show huckster. He was 10 when he first learned to play the guitar in open tuning from Joe Wicks. He also earned money as a buck dancer on the streets of Laurens. In 1917 he joined 'Doctor' W.R. Kerr's medicine show, learning every facet of the calling, and stayed with the show, with Peg Leg Sam as his straight man, until it ceased in 1945. When not on the road, he partnered Simmie Dooley, a blind guitarist from whom he learned to tune his guitar and play chords. In 1928 the pair recorded four titles for Columbia Records in Atlanta. One of the songs, 'Every Day In In The Week', also featured on a May 1950 session, recorded while Anderson was performing at the State Fair in Charlottesville, and released in conjunction with titles by another Laurens musician, Blind Gary Davis. Anderson continued to work the medicine shows, teaming up with Baby Tate, until heart trouble forced his retirement in 1957. In 1961 he recorded three albums for Bluesville, each with a theme: blues, medicine show songs and folk ballads. Gradually, deteriorating health prevented him from working. An album project for Trix, begun in 1970, was never realized.
● ALBUMS: with Rev. Gary Davis *Carolina Street Ballads/Harlem Street Spirituals* (Riverside 1951)★★★, *Carolina Blues Man* (Bluesville 1962)★★★★, *Medicine Show Man* (Bluesville 1962)★★★, *Ballad And Folksinger* (Bluesville 1963)★★★.

ANGELO, BOBBY, AND THE TUXEDOS

A late 50s/early 60s US rock 'n' roll act led by Bobby Angelo (b. Robert Hemmings). They were best known for the track 'Baby Sittin'', although it was not a major hit either in the UK or USA. The track was reissued in the UK in the late 70s on an EP that also featured the songs 'Skinny Lizzie', 'I Gotta Have You' and 'Don't Stop'.

ANKA, PAUL

b. 30 July 1941, Ottawa, Ontario, Canada. A prolific songwriter and child prodigy, Anka was one of the major teen-idols of the 50s. He burst onto the scene in 1957 with the self-written 'Diana', an intense ballad describing the frustration and unrequited love of a young teenager for a slightly older female. With its distinctive rhythm pattern, the song was powerfully evocative and stayed at the top of the UK charts for a lengthy nine weeks, as well as reaching number 1 in the USA. It sold a reported 10 million copies worldwide. Anka followed it with a series of hits such as 'You Are My Destiny', 'Lonely Boy', 'Put Your Head On My Shoulder' and 'Puppy Love'. Pubescent worries and the desire to be taken seriously by condescending parents were familiar themes in those songs and contributed greatly to his success. As the 50s drew to a close, he wisely moved away from teen ballads and planned for a long-term future as a songwriter and cabaret artist. His moving 'It Doesn't Matter Anymore' was a posthumous UK number 1 for Buddy Holly in 1959 and during the same year Anka starred in his first film, *Girls' Town*. This prepared him for the more serious *The Longest Day* three years later. During the 60s the former teen star was a regular at New York's Copacabana and Los Angeles'

Coconut Grove, and was much in demand on the nightclub circuit. Additionally, he attempted an acting career, making an appearance in *The Longest Day*. For much of the decade, however, he was earning large sums of money appearing at Las Vegas hotels The success of Donny Osmond, meanwhile, who took 'Puppy Love' to the top in Britain, kept Anka's early material alive for a new generation. Songwriting success continued, most notably with Frank Sinatra's reading of his lyric to 'My Way' and Tom Jones's million-selling 'She's A Lady'. In the 70s, Anka himself returned to number 1 in the USA courtesy of a risqué duet with his protégée Odia Coates, with the song '(You're) Having My Baby'. A spree of hits followed, punctuated by regular supper-club appearances. As late as 1983, the former 50s teen star was back in the charts with 'Hold Me Till The Mornin' Comes'. He continued to play lucrative seasons in Las Vegas and Atlantic City, and toured Europe in 1992 for the first time in 25 years. The following year he threatened to sue Dulux, a UK house-paint manufacturer, when their television commercial portrayed a sheepdog apparently singing a parody of 'My Way'. In 1996 he released his first album aimed at the Latin market, with some of his greatest hits sung in Spanish and duets with artists including Celine Dion, Julio Iglesias and Jose Luis Rodriguez.

● ALBUMS: *Paul Anka* (ABC 1958)★★★, *My Heart Sings* (ABC 1959)★★★, *Paul Anka Swings For Young Lovers* (ABC 1960)★★★★, *Anka At The Copa* (ABC 1960)★★★, *It's Christmas Everywhere* (ABC 1960)★★★, *Strictly Instrumental* (ABC 1961)★★, *Diana* (ABC 1962)★★★★, *Young, Alive And In Love!* (RCA Victor 1962)★★★★, *Let's Sit This One Out!* (RCA Victor 1962)★★★, *Our Man Around The World* (RCA Victor 1963)★★★, *Songs I Wished I'd Written* (RCA Victor 1963)★★, *Excitement On Park Avenue* (RCA Victor 1964)★★★, *Strictly Nashville* (RCA Victor 1966)★★, *Paul Anka Alive* (RCA Victor 1967)★★, *Goodnight My Love* (RCA Victor 1969)★★★, *Life Goes On* (RCA Victor 1969)★★★, *Paul Anka* (Buddah 1971)★★, *Jubilation* (Buddah 1972)★★, *Anka* (United Artists 1974)★★★, *Feelings* (United Artists 1975)★★★, *The Painter* (United Artists 1976)★★★, *The Music Man* (United Artists 1977)★★★, *Listen To Your Heart* (RCA 1978)★★, *Both Sides Of Love* (RCA 1981)★★, *Walk A Fine Line* (Columbia 1983)★★★, *Italiano* (Crescent 1987)★★★, *Amigos* (Globo/Sony 1996)★★★.

● COMPILATIONS: *Paul Anka Sings His Big 15* (ABC 1960)★★★★, *Paul Anka Sings His Big 15, Volume 2* (ABC 1961)★★★, *Paul Anka Sings His Big 15, Volume 3* (ABC 1961)★★, *Paul Anka's 21 Golden Hits* (RCA 1963)★★★, *Paul Anka Gold* (Sire 1974)★★★★, *Times Of Your Life* (United Artists 1975)★★★, *Essential Paul Anka* (1976)★★★★, *Vintage Years, 1957-61* (1977)★★★★, *Paul Anka At His Best* (United Artists 1979)★★★★, *The Original Hits Of Paul Anka* (Columbia 1987)★★★, *Gypsy Ways* (1988)★★★, *30th Anniversary Collection* (Rhino 1989)★★★, *The Ultimate Collection* (1992)★★★★.

● FILMS: *Girl's Town* aka *The Innocent And The Damned* (1959), *Lonely Boy* (1962), *The Longest Day* (1962).

ANNIE GET YOUR GUN (FILM MUSICAL)

Like many other films boasting Irving Berlin scores, *Annie Get Your Gun* is rarely seen nowadays, owing to the composer's original financial demands over any performance or broadcasting of his work. The film was released in 1950, five years after Ethel Merman's triumphant opening night in the original Broadway show. Unlike many other Broadway-to-Hollywood transfers, *Annie Get Your Gun*'s screen debut for MGM was generally regarded as being highly faithful to the stage show. Judy Garland was the first choice to play the lead, but a recurrence of the latter's personal problems gave Betty Hutton the best role of her career. She played sharpshooter Annie Oakley, who deliberately loses a shooting match with her rival, Frank Butler (Howard Keel), so that he will not consider her a threat to his masculinity, and they can be married. Naturally, this scenario took place long before the rise of feminism, in the days when men were men, and women were expected to be grateful. Although he had made a previous screen appearance in the UK while appearing in the West End in *Oklahoma!*, this was Keel's first Hollywood musical and he was in fine voice, giving an impressive performance. Among the rest of the cast were Louis Calhern (Buffalo Bill), J. Carrol Naish (Sitting Bull), Keenan Wynn, Edward Arnold and Benay Venuta. Berlin's stage score survived practically intact in its screen incarnation, the main casualty being the lovely ballad 'Moonshine Lullaby'. All the major hits were present, including 'Doin' What Comes Natur'lly', 'I Got The Sun In The Morning', 'You Can't Get A Man With A Gun', 'The Girl That I Marry', 'They Say It's Wonderful', 'My Defenses Are Down', 'Anything You Can Do', along with Hutton's highly amusing 'I'm An Indian, Too', and the rousing 'There's No Business Like Show Business'. *Annie Get Your Gun* was photographed in Technicolor and directed by George Sidney, with choreography by Robert Alton. It was the top musical money-spinner of 1950, and won Academy Awards for 'scoring of a musical picture' for Adolph Deutsch and Roger Edens.

ANTHONY, RAY

b. Raymond Antonini, 20 January 1922, Bentleyville, Pennsylvania, USA. After playing in local bands in Cleveland, Anthony spent brief spells in the trumpet sections of the Al Donahue, Glenn Miller and Jimmy Dorsey orchestras. Following a four-year period in the US Navy, where he led a services orchestra, Anthony formed his own band in 1946 and signed with Capitol Records. The band became one of the top attractions of the 50s, touring colleges and universities, producing hit singles such as 'At Last', 'Harbour Lights', the television themes from *Dragnet* and *Peter Gunn*, plus novelty dance numbers, such as 'The Bunny Hop' and 'I Can't Tell A Waltz From A Tango'. From the start, the band had always had a Millerish reed sound, so when the Miller 'revival' happened they participated more successfully than most. Anthony appeared with his band in two movies, Fred Astaire's *Daddy Long Legs* and *This Could Be The Night*. He appeared on his own in the Jayne Mansfield/Tom Ewell rock 'n' roll spoof *The Girl Can't Help It*, and in an eerie piece of Hollywood casting, featured as the saxophone-playing Jimmy Dorsey in the Red Nichols biopic *The Five Pennies*. In the 60s, with a limited market for 16-piece bands, Anthony formed a sextet, with a female vocal duo, playing clubs and lounges throughout the USA. He was also active in preserving big-band music for schools and radio stations. In 1986 the Aerospace label relaunched a series of Ray Anthony titles.

● ALBUMS: *Ray Anthony's Orchestra* (Capitol 1953)★★★★, *Sweet And Lovely* (Capitol 1953)★★★★, *House Party*

(Capitol 1953)★★★★, *I Remember Glenn Miller* (Capitol 1954)★★★★, *Arthur Murray Swing Foxtrots* (Capitol 1955)★★★, *Golden Horn* (Capitol 1955)★★★★, *Jam Session At The Tower* (Capitol 1956)★★★, *Dream Dancing* (Capitol 1956)★★★★, *Star Dancing* (Capitol 1957)★★★, *Young Ideas* (Capitol 1957)★★★★, *The Dream Girl* (Capitol 1958)★★★★, *Dances in Love* (Capitol 1958)★★★, *Dancing Over The Waves* (Capitol 1959)★★★, *Anthony Plays Allen* (Capitol 1959)★★★, *Sound Spectacular* (Capitol 1960)★★★, *Worried Mind* (Capitol 1962)★★★★, *More Dream Dancing* (Capitol 1983)★★★, *Plays For Dream Dancing* (Capitol 1984)★★★, *Swingin' On Campus* (Capitol 1985)★★★, *Dream Dancing Medley* (Capitol 1985)★★★, *House Party Hop* (Capitol 1985)★★★, *Dancing Alone Together* (Capitol 1986)★★★, *Sweet And Swingin' 1949-53* (Circle 1987)★★★, *Hooked On Big Bands - Live On Radio* (Aerospace 1988)★★★★, *For Dancers Only* (Capitol 1988)★★★, *Glenn Miller - Then And Now* (Aerospace 1988)★★★★, *I Get The Blues When It Rains* (Ranwood 1989)★★★, *Dancers In Love* (Memoir 1989)★★★.
● COMPILATIONS: *The Sampler* (Aerospace 1986)★★★★, *The Hits Of Ray Anthony* (Aerospace 1986)★★★★, *Show And Dance And Party* (Aerospace 1986)★★★★, *Capitol Collectors Series* (Capitol 1991)★★★★.
● FILMS: *The Girl Can't Help It* (1956).

ARBELLO, FERNANDO

b. 30 May 1907, Ponce, Puerto Rico, d. 26 July 1970. Arbello was playing the trombone before he entered his teenage years and played with bands in his homeland, mostly working in the fields of popular and classical music. In the mid-20s he went to New York where he played with many bands including that led by Wilbur De Paris. He worked with June Clark and then with a succession of bands before settling in with Claude Hopkins for three years. After this he was with Chick Webb, Fletcher Henderson, Lucky Millinder, and others. In the early 40s he was mostly with small New York-based groups, including those led by Zutty Singleton and Marty Marsala, but then returned to big bands with spells under the leadership of Benny Carter, Henderson again, and a number of years with Jimmie Lunceford. In the 50s he briefly led his own small band and also played with Rex Stewart, and in the following decade worked with Machito. In the late 60s he returned to his homeland and led a band there for a short time before his death. Arbello was a strong and reliable section player, only rarely soloing, and was content to provide the much needed body of the big bands of his era.

ARCHIBALD

b. Leon T. Gross, 14 September 1912, New Orleans, Louisiana, USA, d. 8 January 1973, New Orleans, Louisiana, USA. With a reputation that rests on his first and only hit, Archibald is best remembered for the impression he made upon younger piano players such as Fats Domino, James Booker and Allen Toussaint. Self-taught but influenced by Burnell Santiago, he gained the nickname 'Archie Boy' during years of playing at parties and brothels. After serving in the army during World War II, he was spotted and signed by Imperial talent scout Al Young. His first release, a two-part version of 'Stack-O-Lee', was an immediate hit, but subsequent records for Imperial and its subsidiary, Colony,

failed to maintain his popularity. For many years, he was the resident pianist at the Poodle Patio club, but by the 70s his career was all but over. Nevertheless, his music typified the syncopated piano style with which others achieved more success.
● COMPILATIONS: *The New Orleans Sessions 1950-52* (Krazy Kat 1983)★★★.

ARMSTRONG, LILLIAN

b. Lillian Hardin, 3 February 1898, Memphis, Tennessee, USA, d. 27 August 1971, Chicago, Illinois, USA. A classically trained pianist, Hardin worked extensively in Chicago in the 20s, becoming highly popular both as a solo performer and also playing with the bands of Sugar Johnny, Freddie Keppard and Joe 'King' Oliver. It was while she was with Oliver that she met and married the band's newest recruit, Louis Armstrong. Aware of her new husband's massive talent, and being hugely ambitious for him, she persuaded Louis to start his own band, and was herself a crucial presence in his classic Hot Five and Hot Seven groups. Personality clashes later made their marriage untenable and they were divorced. Lillian Armstrong's subsequent career found her leading bands for club work and on numerous radio and recording dates. From the 50s onwards she worked mostly as a solo pianist and singer, usually in Chicago, although she sometimes played at festivals in the USA and Europe, where she also appeared in clubs. An occasional composer, one of her songs, 'Just For A Thrill', was recorded in the 50s by Ray Charles. She died in 1971 while taking part in a memorial concert for Louis, who had died a few weeks earlier.
● ALBUMS: *Satchmo And Me* (Riverside 1956)★★★, *Lil Armstrong And Her Orchestra* (Riverside 1962)★★★.
● COMPILATIONS: *Louis Armstrong Hot Five/Hot Seven* (1926-27)★★★★, *Born To Swing* (1936-37)★★★★, *Harlem On A Saturday Night* (1936-38)★★★★, *The Swing Orchestra* (1936-40)★★★★.

ARNAZ, DESI

b. Desiderio Alberto Arnez y de Acha III, 2 March 1917, Santiago, Cuba, d. 2 December 1986, Del Mar, California, USA. Arnaz came to the USA in the early 20s and began singing and playing bongo and conga drums with Xaviar Cugat and others before forming his own band. Arnaz achieved sufficient popularity to be offered musical spots in films. While working on one of these, *Dance, Girl, Dance* (1940), he met and subsequently married Lucille Ball. In the late 40s Ball appeared on radio in a popular series, *My Favourite Husband*, in which she co-starred with film actor Richard Denning. In the early 50s Ball decided to adapt the show for television with her real-life husband as producer, and she also decided that Arnaz should play her television husband - two decisions frowned upon by executives at CBS Records and Philip Morris (cigarette makers and potential sponsors for the show). Their reluctance stemmed from the fact that as a producer Arnaz was an unknown quantity and as an actor he was a potential liability because of his pronounced Cuban accent. In the event, Ball and Arnaz prevailed but had to make concessions. These included taking a salary reduction, though as compensation CBS made the multi-million-dollar blunder of allowing the couple to retain 100% residuals. The new show, *I Love Lucy*, was a runaway success and made a fortune for Desilu, the company Ball and Arnaz had formed to produce the show. *I Love Lucy* ran until 1959 and the following year the couple were divorced, although they continued as business partners. After *I Love Lucy*, Ball starred in *The Lucy Show* which was produced by Arnaz. In 1962 Ball bought out Arnaz's share of their company and for a while ran Desilu on her own, producing such popular television shows as *Star Trek* and *Mission: Impossible*. Arnaz made a few film appearances in the mid-50s, including the popular *The Long, Long Trailer* with Ball, but then drifted into retirement. Later, he returned for occasional cameo roles, produced the NBC television series *The Mothers-In-Law* (1967), which starred Eve Arden and Kaye Ballard, and published his autobiography. His daughter, Lucie Arnaz, was gaining favourable reviews for her singing in New York clubs in the early 90s. In 1993, she, and her husband, Laurence Luckinbill, were the executive producers of *Lucy And Desi: A Home Movie*, 'their own version of Lucy and Desi's entwined careers', which was shown in the USA on NBC Television.

● FURTHER READING: *The Book*, Desi Arnaz. *Desilu: The Story Of Lucille Ball And Desi Arnaz*, Coyne Steven Sanders and Tom Gilbert.

● FILMS: *The Long Long Trailer* (1954), *Forever Darling* (1956), *The Escape Artist* (1982).

ARNOLD, BILLY BOY

b. 16 March 1935, Chicago, Illinois, USA. Arnold first played blues harmonica with Bo Diddley's group in 1950 and became a well-known figure in Chicago blues throughout the following two decades. Among those he accompanied were Johnny Shines and Otis Rush. With a serviceable singing voice and a harmonica style influenced by John Lee 'Sonny Boy' Williamson, Arnold recorded as a solo artist for local labels Cool (1953) and Vee Jay (1955). In 1958 he led a group that included Mighty Joe Young and recorded for Mighty H. However, none of Arnold's records were as successful as the mid-50s hits of Bo Diddley such as 'Pretty Thing' and 'Hey Bo Diddley', to which he contributed the keening harp phrases. The most renowned of Arnold's own tracks is 'I Wish You Would' (Vee Jay), which was adopted by British R&B group the Yardbirds, appearing on *Five Live Yardbirds* (1964). During the mid-60s blues boom, he cut an album for Prestige/Bluesville (1964), recorded with pianist Johnny Jones (a 1963 session that remained unreleased for 17 years), and there was also a later album for Vogue. Not forgotten by European blues enthusiasts, Arnold toured there in 1975 as part of the Blues Legends package, when he recorded two albums for Peter Shertser's UK-based Red Lightnin'.

● ALBUMS: *More Blues On The South Side* (Prestige/Bluesville 1964)★★★, *Blow The Back Off It* (Red Lightnin' 1975)★★★, *Sinner's Prayer* (Red Lightnin' 1976)★★★, *Checkin' It Out* (Red Lightnin' 1979)★★★, *Johnny Jones & Billy Boy Arnold* (Alligator 1980)★★★, *Crying & Pleading* reissue (1980)★★★, *I Wish You Would* mid-50s recordings (1993)★★★, *Back Where I Belong* (Alligator 1993)★★, *Ten Million Dollars* (Evidence 1995)★★★, *Eldorado Cadillac* (Alligator 1996)★★★.

ARNOLD, EDDY

b. Richard Edward Arnold, 15 May 1918, on a farm near Madisonville, Chester County, Tennessee, USA. Arnold's father and mother played fiddle and guitar, respectively, and he learned guitar as a child. His father died on Eddy's 11th birthday and he left school to work on the farm. By the end of the year the bank foreclosed, and the farm was sold but the family stayed as sharecroppers. Deciding that such a thing would not happen to him again he turned his thoughts to music and began playing at local dances. In 1936, working with a fiddle-playing friend, Speedy McNatt, he made his debut on local radio WTJS Jackson and during the next few years played various venues including Memphis, Louisville and St. Louis. Between 1940 and 1943 he was a member of Pee Wee King's Golden West Cowboys, appearing with them on the *Grand Ole Opry* and touring with the *Opry*'s travelling *Camel Caravan Show*. Late in 1943, as 'The Tennessee Plowboy', he launched his solo career, playing six days a week on WSM. Signed by RCA Records he made his country chart debut in 1945 with 'Each Minute Seems A Million Years' and soon replaced Roy Acuff as country music's most popular and prolific singer. Between 1945 and 1955 he had 21 number 1 singles among his 68 US country chart hits. Sentimental ballads, incorporating the plaintive steel guitar work of Little Roy Wiggins, were the norm and many, such as the million-sellers 'I'll Hold You In My Heart Till I Can Hold You In My Arms', 'Anytime', 'Bouquet Of Roses' and 'Just A Little Lovin' Will Go A Long Way', also became Top 30 US pop chart hits. Perhaps his best-remembered recording from this decade is 'Cattle Call'. During the late 40s he varied his image: although still retaining the nickname he became a country crooner wearing a tuxedo and bow tie. Colonel Tom Parker became his manager and was so successful with his promotion that Arnold was soon a nationally known star. Some of Parker's publicity stunts were unique for their time, such as the occasion when he travelled to a disc jockey convention in Nashville astride an elephant, bearing a cloth saying 'Never Forget Eddy Arnold'. Arnold began his solo *Opry* career as host of the *Ralston Purina* segment in 1946 but in 1948, due to Parker's unacceptable demands on the WSM management for shares of gate receipts, he left, being replaced on the *Opry* roster by another country crooner, George Morgan. In 1948, with the exception of Jimmy Wakely's recording of 'One Has My Heart', Arnold's recordings held the number 1 position in the country charts for the whole year. Arnold eventually tired of Parker's management and apparently sacked him; he has said it was because 'I am a very conservative man', but few believed that was the sole reason.

During the 50s, he appeared on all major radio and television shows and became the first country singer to host his own network television show, *Eddy Arnold Time*. He also became one of the first country singers to play at Carnegie Hall and later appeared in concerts with major symphony orchestras. It is impossible to categorize his new style as either country or pure pop. Many of his early fans objected to it but the television and cabaret performances won him countless new fans from the wider audience and he easily maintained his popularity and chart successes. After 1954, his nickname no longer appeared on the records and he moved to MGM in 1972, but returned to RCA four years later. Between 1956 and 1983 he took his tally of US country chart hits to 145, and his number 1 singles to 28 (and 92 of the entries had made the Top 10!). Again, many recordings achieved crossover success, including 'Tennessee Stud', 'What's He Doing In My World' and 'Make The World Go Away', which reached number 6 in 1965 and the next year repeated the feat in the UK pop charts. Several of his albums have also achieved Top 10 status in the US album charts. He appeared in several films, including starring roles in *Feudin' Rhythm* and *Hoedown*, and he even received a mention in *Jailhouse Rock*. He was elected to the Country Music Hall Of Fame in 1966 and by the 80s he had semi-retired to his home near Nashville. RCA have assessed that his record sales are in excess of 85 million. It is quite astonishing that Elvis Presley *et al.* are automatically regarded as the most successful chart acts. Arnold's chart success eclipses everybody and is unlikely ever to be beaten.

● ALBUMS: *Anytime* (RCA 1952)★★★, *All-Time Hits From The Hills* (RCA 1952)★★★★, *All Time Favorites* (RCA 1953)★★★★, *An American Institution (10th Anniversary Album)* (RCA 1954)★★★, *Chapel On The Hill* (RCA 1954)★★★, *Wanderin' With Eddy Arnold* (RCA 1955)★★★, *Anytime* (RCA 1955)★★★★, *A Dozen Hits* (RCA 1956)★★★, *A Little On The Lonely Side* (RCA 1956)★★★, *When They Were Young* (RCA 1957)★★★, *My Darling, My Darling* (RCA 1957)★★★, *Praise Him, Praise Him (Fanny Crosby Hymns)* (RCA 1958)★★, *Have Guitar, Will Travel* (reissued as *Eddy Arnold Goes Travelin'*) (RCA 1959)★★★★, *Eddy Arnold* (RCA 1959)★★★★, *Thereby Hangs A Tale* (RCA 1959)★★★, *Eddy Arnold Sings Them Again* (RCA 1960)★★★, *More Eddy Arnold* (RCA 1960)★★★★, *You Gotta Have Love* (RCA 1960)★★★, *Christmas With Eddy Arnold* (RCA 1961)★★, *Let's Make Memories Tonight* (RCA 1961)★★★, *One More Time* (RCA 1962)★★★★, *Our Man Down South* (RCA 1963)★★★, *Country Songs I Love To Sing* (RCA 1963)★★★, *Faithfully Yours* (RCA 1963)★★★, *Cattle Call* (RCA 1963)★★★★, *Pop Hits From The Country Side* (RCA 1964)★★★, *Eddy's Songs* (RCA 1964)★★★, with Needmore Creek Singers *Folk Song Book* (RCA 1964)★★★, *Sometimes I'm Happy, Sometimes I'm Blue* (RCA 1964)★★★, *The Easy Way* (RCA 1965)★★★, *I'm Throwing Rice (At The Girl I Love)* (RCA 1965)★★★, *My World* (RCA 1965)★★★, *Somebody Liked Me* (RCA 1966)★★★, *I Want To Go With You* (RCA 1966)★★★, *The Last Word In Lonesome* (RCA 1966)★★★, *Lonely Again* (RCA 1967)★★★, *Turn The World Around* (RCA 1967)★★★, *The Everloving World Of Eddy Arnold* (RCA 1968)★★★★, *Romantic World Of Eddy Arnold* (RCA 1968)★★★★, *Walkin' In Love Land* (RCA 1968)★★★, *Songs Of The Young World* (RCA 1969)★★★, *The Warmth Of Eddy Arnold* (RCA 1969)★★★, *The Glory Of Love* (RCA 1969)★★★, *This Is Eddy Arnold* (RCA 1970)★★★★, *Standing Alone* (RCA 1970)★★★, *Love And Guitars* (RCA 1970)★★★, *Then You Can Tell Me Goodbye* (RCA 1971)★★★, *Welcome To My World* (RCA 1971)★★★, *Loving Her Was Easier* (RCA 1971)★★★, *Portrait Of My Woman* (RCA 1971)★★★, *Chained To A Memory* (MGM 1972)★★★, *Eddy Arnold (Sings For Housewives & Other Lovers)* (MGM 1972)★★, *Lonely People* (MGM 1972)★★★, *I Love How You Love Me* (MGM 1973)★★★, *The World Of Eddy Arnold* (MGM 1973)★★★★, *Christmas Greetings From Nashville* (MGM 1973)★★★, *So Many Ways/If The Whole World Stopped Lovin'* (MGM 1973)★★★, *Eddy Arnold Sings Love Songs* (MGM 1974)★★★, *I Wish That I Had Loved You Better*

(MGM 1974)★★★, *Misty Blue* (MGM 1974)★★★, *She's Got Everything I Need* (MGM 1974)★★★, *The Wonderful World Of Eddy Arnold* (MGM 1975)★★★★, *Eddy* (MGM 1976)★★★, *Eddy Arnold's World Of Hits* (MGM 1976)★★★★, *I Need You All The Time* (RCA 1977)★★★, *Somebody Loves You* (RCA 1979)★★★, *A Legend And His Lady* (RCA 1980)★★★, *Man For All Seasons* (RCA 1981)★★★, *Country Music - Eddy Arnold* (RCA 1981)★★★, *Don't Give Up On Me* (RCA 1982)★★★, *Close Enough To Love* (RCA 1983)★★★, *Anytime* (RCA 1988)★★★, *Christmas With Eddy Arnold* (RCA 1990)★★, *Hand-Holdin' Songs* (RCA 1990)★★★, *You Don't Miss A Thing* (RCA 1991)★★★, *Last Of The Love Song Singers: Then & Now* (RCA 1993)★★★.

● COMPILATIONS: *The Best Of Eddy Arnold* (RCA 1967)★★★, *Living Legend* (K-Tel 1974)★★★, *Country Gold* (RCA 1975)★★★, *Pure Gold-Eddy Arnold* (RCA 1975)★★★, *Eddy Arnold's Best* (RCA 1979)★★★, *20 Of The Best* (RCA 1982)★★★, *Eddy Arnold - A Legendary Performer* (RCA 1983)★★★, *Collector's Series* (RCA 1987)★★★, *All Time Favourites* (RCA 1987)★★★★, *Best Of Eddy Arnold* (Curb 1990)★★★, *The Essential Eddy Arnold* (RCA 1996)★★★★.

● FURTHER READING: *It's A Long Way From Chester County*, Eddy Arnold.

ARNOLD, HARRY

b. Harry Arnold Persson, 7 August 1920, Hälsingborg, Sweden, d. 11 February 1971. From the early 40s Arnold became well known as a bandleader, and for his big band who played on radio and made records. He wrote many of the band's charts and also played saxophone. Rooted in the swing era style that was already fading in the USA, Arnold capitalized upon the continuing demand for this kind of music in Europe. In the 50s and 60s he continued to lead a big band and also played in and usually directed studio bands for records and radio. Notably, he led the Swedish Radio Big Band, which became known in the USA as the Jazztone Mystery Band, and which featured in its ranks many fine Swedish musicians including Arne Domnérus, Åke Persson and Georg Riedel. The band was also host to numerous visiting Americans, several of whom recorded and broadcast while in Sweden. Among them were Coleman Hawkins, Benny Bailey and Quincy Jones, who also arranged for the band. Although slightly out of its time, Arnold's band was always highly professional and its members played to the highest standards.

● ALBUMS: *Quincy's Home Again* (Metronome 1958)★★★, *Harry Arnold Guest Book* (Metronome 1960-61)★★★

ARNOLD, MALCOLM

b. 21 October 1921, Northampton, England. A composer, conductor, arranger and trumpet player. Arnold became aware of music at the age of four, and taught himself to play trumpet - his inspiration was Louis Armstrong. He began his career in 1941 as an instrumentalist with the London Philharmonic Orchestra, and returned to the orchestra in 1946 after brief service in World War II, and a spell with the BBC Symphony Orchestra. During these times he was also composing; one of his best-known pieces, 'Sea Shanties', was written in 1943. He became a full-time composer in the early 50s, and soon won much critical acclaim as 'one of the great hopes of British music'. His work schedule was exhausting; from 1951-56 he is said to have written the

music for over 70 films, as well as three operas, ballet music, concertos and other classical and light works. One of his more unusual compositions was the 'Grand Overture' for a Gerald Hoffnung concert, in which the more conventional instruments of the orchestra were augmented by three vacuum cleaners and an electric polisher. His film scores, many of which complemented classic British productions, include *The Sound Barrier* (1952), *The Holly And The Ivy*, *The Captain's Paradise*, *Hobson's Choice*, *Prize Of Gold*, *I Am A Camera*, *Trapeze*, *Tiger In The Smoke*, *The Deep Blue Sea*, *Island In The Sun*, *The Bridge On The River Kwai* (one of the film's six Oscars went to Arnold), *Blue Murder At St. Trinians*, *The Inn Of The Sixth Happiness* (the film theme won an Ivor Novello Award in 1959), *The Key*, *The Root Of Heaven*, *Dunkirk*, *Tunes Of Glory*, *The Angry Silence*, *No Love For Johnnie*, *The Inspector*, *Whistle Down The Wind*, *The Lion*, *Nine Hours To Rama*, *The Chalk Garden*, *The Heroes Of Telemark*, *The Thin Red Line*, *Sky West And Crooked*, and *The Reckoning* (1969). During the 60s Arnold was ignored, even reviled, by critics and sections of the concert and broadcasting establishment. He was dismissed as 'a clown', and his work was criticized as being 'out of phase' with contemporary trends in music. Arnold developed alcohol problems, suffered several nervous breakdowns, and attempted suicide more than once. He continued to write, when he was able, and was particularly interested in brass band music, but his work generally remained unappreciated. His ninth and final symphony, written in 1986, still had not received an official premiere by 1991, when low-key celebrations for his 70th birthday involved a concert at London's Queen Elizabeth Hall, which included his double violin concerto, commissioned by Yehudi Menuhin in 1962. In 1993 Malcolm Arnold received a knighthood in the Queen's New Year honours list.
● ALBUMS: *Malcolm Arnold Film Music* (Chandos 1992)★★★★, *Arnold Overtures* (Reference Recordings 1992)★★★★.
● FURTHER READING: *Malcolm Arnold: A Catalogue Of His Music*, A. Poulton.

AROUND THE WORLD IN 80 DAYS - VARIOUS ★★★★★

Producer Mike Todd persuaded more than 40 major stars, including Frank Sinatra, Marlene Dietrich and Ronald Colman, to contribute cameo roles to this 1957 widescreen treatment of Jules Verne's classic story, in which David Niven as Phileas Fogg and his 'man', Passepartout, played by the Mexican comedian Cantiflas, circumnavigate the globe. They were accompanied by veteran composer Victor Young's breathtakingly beautiful musical themes, which thrilled record-buyers to such an extent that this album stayed at number 1 in the USA for 10 weeks, although it did not reach the UK charts. The composer's Academy Award for his work was a fitting end to a distinguished career that ended a few months after the film's release.
● TRACKS: *Around The World* (main theme); *Around The World Part II*; *Entrance Of The Bull March* (medley); *Epilogue*; *India Country Side*; *Invitation To A Bull Fight* (medley); *Land Ho*; *Pagoda Of Pillagi*; *Paris Arrival*; *Passepartout*; *Prairie Sail Car*; *Sky Symphony*.

ARTHUR, BEATRICE

b. Bernice Frankel, 13 May 1926, New York, USA. A stylish, droll, acid-tongued actress, comedienne and singer, with an attractive dark-brown voice, Bea Arthur came to prominence playing the role of Lucy Brown in Marc Blitzstein's adaptation of Kurt Weill and Bertholt Brecht's *The Threepenny Opera* - the second US version - which opened off-Broadway at the Theatre De Lys in March 1954, and ran for 2,706 performances. She then appeared in Ben Bagley's 1955 *Shoestring Revue*, and in the same year took the part of Mme. Suze in *Seventh Heaven*, a musicalized version of the Oscar-winning 1927 silent film classic, which starred Janice Gaynor and Charles Farrell. In 1960 Arthur was off-Broadway again, this time as Hortense in a brief revival of the 1932 Fred Astaire musical *Gay Divorce*. In direct contrast to that disappointment, Arthur's next appearance on Broadway in 1964 was in one of the best-loved musicals of all time, *Fiddler On The Roof*. She created the role of the village matchmaker, Yente, in a production which ran for 3,242 performances. Another blockbuster followed in 1966 when Arthur won a Tony Award for her portrayal of the superbly bitchy Vera Charles in Jerry Herman's *Mame*. Her duet with star Angela Lansbury, 'Bosom Buddies' (Mame: 'I've been meaning to tell you for years, you should keep your hair natural like mine.' Vera: 'If I kept my hair natural like yours, I'd be bald.'), regularly brought the house down. Unfortunately, although the number was filmed as part of the 1974 film version of *Mame*, in which Arthur recreated her role opposite Lucille Ball, it was cut from most prints. In 1968, she led a cast that included Carl Ballantine and Bill Callaway in *A Mother's Kisses* (1968), with a score by Richard Adler, but it folded out of town. She was married to Gene Saks, the show's director, for some years. He also directed *Generation* (1965), *Half A Sixpence* (1965), *I Love My Wife* (1977) and *Rags* (1986), among others. Apart from *Mame*, Arthur made several more films, including *That Kind Of Woman* (1958), *Lovers And Other Strangers* (1969) and *History Of The World: Part One* (1981). She has also appeared extensively on television. Her telling performances in *All In The Family* led to *Maude*, her own series (1972-76), and eventually to the part of Dorothy in *The Golden Girls* situation comedy (1985), which is still enjoyed by television audiences round the world in the 90s.

AT THE DROP OF A HAT

(see Flanders And Swann)

ATWELL, WINIFRED

b. 1914, Tunapuna, Trinidad, d. February 1983, Sydney, Australia. Atwell began playing piano at the age of four, gave classical recitals when six and played concerts at the Services Club, Trinidad. She went to New York and studied with Alexander Borovsky before moving to London for tuition with Harold Craxton. Supplementing her income from classical music by playing boogie-woogie gained her a contract with Decca Records and throughout the 50s she had great success with a series of 'knees up', singalong medleys and 'rags', mostly on her old honky-tonk, 'other' piano. The first of these, 'Black And White Rag', was later selected as the signature tune for *Pot Black*, BBC Television's first regular snooker programme. Other 50s Top 10 hits were 'Britannia Rag', 'Coronation Rag', 'Flirtation Waltz', 'Let's Have A Party',

'Let's Have A Ding Dong', 'Make It A Party', 'Let's Have A Ball', 'Piano Party', and two chart-toppers, 'Poor People Of Paris' and 'Let's Have Another Party'. Atwell's dubbing of John Mills' piano playing in the 1956 movie *It's Great To Be Young*, included a jumping version of 'The Original Dixieland One Step'. Interrupting the pop, there was also the 'back to her roots' single, 'Rachmaninov's 18th Variation On A Theme By Paganini', which went to number 9 in the UK chart. Thereafter, she continued to combine the two musical forms. At her peak she was a huge UK star, but in the 60s her career declined and in the 70s she went to live in Australia, where she died in 1983.

● ALBUMS: *Boogie With Winifred Atwell* (Decca 1955)★★★, *Around The World Of Winifred Atwell In Eighty Tunes* (Decca 1972)★★★, *Seven Rags, Seven Boogies* (Eclipse 1975)★★★, *It's Ragtime* (RCA 1982)★★★, *Winifred Atwell Plays 50 All-Time Greats* (President 1983)★★★★, *Winifred Atwell, Piano Party* (Flashback 1984)★★★★, *Winnie's Piano Party* (President 1989)★★★, *Big Ben Boogie* (Gema 1995)★★★★.

AUGUST, JAN

b. Jan Augustoff, 1912, New York, USA, d. 17 January 1976. In the early 30s August played piano in Manhattan nightclubs, but later adopted vibes and xylophone as second instruments for a spell with Paul Whiteman's orchestra. Returning to nightclub work as a cocktail pianist, he had only moderate success until adopting a percussive Latin-American style for 'Misirlou', a Top 10 US hit on the Mercury label in 1946. This became a long-time popular 'Family Favourite' on BBC radio, where announcers persisted in calling him 'Yan Owgoost', although his name was pronounced as spelled. He had no other hits as a soloist, but in 1950 teamed up with Jerry Murad's Harmonicats for 'Bewitched' (US number 8 1950) and in 1956 with Richard Hayman's Orchestra for 'Moritat', aka 'Mack The Knife'. In the late 50s and early 60s he built up an impressive library of solo piano albums, all with great variation in style and content. By the time of his death in January 1976, there were none left in the catalogue.

● ALBUMS: *Piano Roll Blues* (Mercury 1955)★★★★, *Music For The Quiet Hour* (Mercury 1956)★★★★, *Songs To Remember* (Mercury 1956)★★★, *Latin Rhythms,* (Mercury 1957)★★, *For Cocktails And Conversations* (Mercury 1957)★★★, *Keyboard Waltzes* (Mercury 1958)★★★, *Piano Wizardry* (Mercury 1958)★★★★, *Cha-Cha Charm* (Mercury 1959)★★, *Accent! Latin Piano* (Mercury 1961)★★★, *Great Pop Piano Classics* (Mercury 1962)★★★.

AURIC, GEORGES

b. 15 February 1899, Lodève, Hérault, France, d. 23 July 1983, Paris, France. A composer of many classical pieces including an opera and ballet, and choral and instrumental music. From 1930 until the early 60s he contributed the scores to French films such as *Quand J'étais*, *A Nous La Liberté*, *Orphée* and *Belles De Nuit*. He also wrote the music for numerous English-speaking movies, including several classic Ealing comedies. His scores included *Dead Of Night* (1945), *Caesar And Cleopatra*, *Hue And Cry*, *It Always Rains On Sunday*, *Another Shore*, *Corridors Of Mirrors*, *Silent Dust*, *Passport To Pimlico*, *The Queen Of Spades*, *The Spider And The Fly*, *Cage Of Gold*, *The Galloping Major*, *The Lavender Hill*

Mob, *Moulin Rouge*, *Roman Holiday*, *The Wages Of Fear*, *Father Brown*, *Rififi*, *The Witches Of Salem*, *Gervaise*, *The Picasso Mystery*, *Bonjour Tristesse*, *Heaven Knows Mr Allison*, *Heaven Fell That Night*, *The Innocents*, *The Mind Benders*, *Thomas The Impostor*, *Therese And Isabelle* and *The Christmas Tree* (1969). The haunting theme from *Moulin Rouge* (1952), with a lyric by Bill Engvick ('Whenever we kiss, I worry and wonder/Your lips may be here, but where is your heart?'), became a hit in the USA for Percy Faith and his Orchestra, with the vocal by Felicia Sanders; and a record of the title music from *Bonjour Tristesse* (1957), with words added by the film's screenwriter, Arthur Laurents, was popular for Gogi Grant. Auric published his autobiography in 1974.

AUTRY, GENE

b. Orvin Gene Autry, 29 September 1907, near Tioga, Texas, USA. The eldest of four children of Delbert Autry, a poor tenant farmer, who moved his family many times over the years, before eventually arriving at Ravia, Oklahoma. His grandfather, a Baptist minister, taught him to sing when he was a child so that he could perform in his church choir and at other local events. Autry also learned to ride at an early age and worked the fields with his father. He grew up listening to cowboy songs and received his first guitar at the age of 12 (initially he studied the saxophone but chose the guitar so that he could sing as well). He graduated from school in 1924 and found work as a telegraph operator for the Frisco Railroad in Chelsea, Oklahoma. He used to take his guitar to work and one night his singing was heard by the famous entertainer Will Rogers, who stopped to send a telegram. He suggested that Autry should look for a job in radio. After trying unsuccessfully to find work in New York, he returned to Oklahoma and began to appear on KVOO Tulsa as The Oklahoma Yodeling Cowboy. After hearing recordings of Jimmie Rodgers, he became something of a Rodgers clone as he tried to further his career. In 1929, he made his first RCA Victor recordings, 'My Dreaming Of You' and 'My Alabama Home', on which he was accompanied by Jimmy Long (a fellow telegrapher) and Frankie and Johnny Marvin. Further recordings followed for ARC Records under the direction of Art Satherley, some being released on various labels for chain store sales. It was because of releases on Conqueror for Sears that Autry found himself given the opportunity to join WLS in Chicago. In 1931, he became a featured artist on the *National Barn Dance*, as well as having his own *Conqueror Record Time*. Before long, Gene Autry 'Roundup' guitars and songbooks were being sold by Sears. Interestingly, WLS portrayed him as a singing cowboy even though, at this time, few of his songs were of that genre. Between 1931 and 1934, he was a hillbilly singer, who still at times sounded like Rodgers. In fact, most experts later rated him the best of the Rodgers impersonators. He began to include his own songs and such numbers as 'The Gangster's Warning' and 'My Old Pal Of Yesterday' became very popular.

Late in 1931, he recorded 'That Silver Haired Daddy Of Mine' as a duet with Jimmy Long, with whom he had co-written the song. The song eventually became Autry's first million-selling record. By 1934, he was well known as a radio and recording personality. Having for some time been portrayed as a singing cowboy by the publicity departments of his record companies, he now took his first steps to make the publicity come true. He was given a small part in the Ken Maynard film *In Old Santa Fe*, and soon afterwards starred in a strange 12-episode western/science fiction serial called *The Phantom Empire*. In 1935, Republic Pictures signed him to a contract and *Tumbling Tumbleweeds* became his first starring western film. His previous singing cowboy image was now reality. He sang eight songs in the film including the title track, 'That Silver Haired Daddy' and 'Ridin' Down The Canyon'. Further films followed in quick succession and by 1940 Autry ranked fourth among all Hollywood money-making stars at the box office. In January 1940, Gene Autry's *Melody Ranch* radio show, sponsored by the Wrigley Gum Company, first appeared on CBS and soon became a national institution, running until 1956. Helped out by such artists as Pat Buttram, Johnny Bond and the Cass County Boys, Autry regularly righted wrongs, sang his hits and as a result of the programme, built himself a new home in the San Fernando Valley called Melody Ranch.

Quite apart from the radio shows and films, he toured extensively with his stage show. It featured roping, Indian dancers, comedy, music, fancy riding from Autry, and smart horse tricks by Champion. By 1941, he was respected and famous all over the USA The little town of Berwyn, Oklahoma, even changed its name to Gene Autry, Oklahoma. His songs such as 'Be Honest With Me', 'Back In The Saddle Again' (which became his signature tune), 'You're The Only Star In My Blue Heaven', 'Goodbye, Little Darlin' Goodbye' (later recorded by Johnny Cash) and many more, became tremendously popular. In 1942, his income took a severe cut when he enlisted in the Air Force, being sworn in live on a *Melody Ranch* programme. He spent some time working on recruitment but then became a pilot in Air Ferry Command and saw service in the Far East, India and North Africa. During this period, he co-wrote with Fred Rose his classic song 'At Mail Call Today'. After his release from the services, he resumed his acting and recording career. Between 1944 and 1951, he registered 25 successive Top 10 country hits, including 'Here Comes Santa Claus' (later recorded by Elvis Presley), 'Rudolph, The Red-Nosed Reindeer', 'Peter Cottontail' and 'Frosty The Snow Man', which each sold one million copies. He also had Top 20 US pop chart success with 'Buttons And Bows'. He left Republic in 1947 and formed his own Flying A Productions, which produced his later films for release by Columbia. When he made his last B-movie western, *Last Of The Pony Riders*, in 1953, he had 89 feature films to his credit. Contrary to prevailing belief, there never was a feud between Autry and his replacement at Republic, Roy Rogers - it was purely the invention of Republic's publicity department.

During the 50s, he became very successful in business and purchased many radio and television stations. Between 1950 and 1956, he produced 91 episodes of *The Gene Autry Show* for CBS-TV. His company also produced many other television series, including *The Range Rider, The Adventures Of Champion* and *Annie Oakley*. His business interest became even more involved during the 60s, when apart from owning various radio and television companies, he became the owner of the California Angels major league baseball team. *Melody Ranch* reappeared as a television programme in the 60s and ran for seven years on Autry's KTLA station. It was syndicated to stations across the country and although Autry

did not appear as a regular, he did make guest appearances. In 1986, Nashville Network decided to screen his Republic and Columbia B-movie westerns under the title of *Melody Ranch Theatre* with Autry himself doing opening and closing announcements. During his long career, Autry had three horses to fill the role of Champion. The original died in 1947. Champion III, who appeared in the Gene Autry television series and also as the star of the *Adventures Of Champion* television series, died in 1991 at the age of 42. There was also a personal appearance Champion and a pony known as Little Champ. During his career he regularly sported a custom-made C.F. Martin guitar, with beautiful ornamental pearl inlay, together with his name.

Autry was elected to the Country Music Hall Of Fame in 1969 for his songwriting abilities as well as his singing and acting. In 1980, he was inducted into the Cowboy Hall Of Fame Of Great Westerners. At the time of his induction, he was described as 'one of the most famous men, not only in America but in the world'. Autry sold the final 10 acres of his Melody Ranch film set in 1991. The ranch, in Placerita Canyon, California, which was used for the making of such classic westerns as *High Noon* and the television series *Gunsmoke*, is scheduled to become a historical feature. His last US country chart entry was 'Old Soldiers Never Die' in 1971 - judging by the popularity of his old films and recordings, it is probably true to say that neither do old cowboys.

● ALBUMS: *Western Classics* (Columbia 1949)★★★, *Western Classics Volume 2* (Columbia 1949)★★★, *Easter Favorites* (Columbia 1949)★★, *Champion* (Columbia 1950)★★★, *Merry Christmas with Gene Autry* (Columbia 1950)★★, *The Story Of The Nativity* (Columbia 1955)★★, *Little Johnny Pilgrim & Guffy The Goofy Gobbler* (Columbia 1955)★, *Rusty The Rocking Horse & Bucky, The Bucking Bronco* (Columbia 1955)★, *Sings Peter Cottontail* (Columbia 1955)★, *Stampede* (Columbia 1955)★★★, *Gene Autry & Champion Western Adventures* (Columbia 1955)★★, *At The Rodeo* (Columbia 1958)★★★, *Christmas With Gene Autry* (Challenge 1958)★★, with Rosemary Clooney and Art Carney *Christmas Favorites* (Harmony 1964)★★★★, *Great Western Hits* (Harmony 1965)★★★, *Melody Ranch* (Melody Ranch 1965)★★★, with Clooney, Art Carney *Sings Peter Cottontail (First Easter Record For Children)* (Harmony 1965)★, *Back In The Saddle Again* (Harmony 1966)★★★, *Gene Autry Sings* (Harmony 1966)★★★, *Rudolph The Red-Nosed Reindeer* (Grand Prix 1968)★, *Live From Madison Square Garden* (Republic 1968)★★, *Christmas Time* (1974)★★★, *Melody Ranch - A Radio Adventure* (Radiola 1975)★★, *Cowboy Hall Of Fame* (1976)★★★, *Murray Hill Record Theatre Presents Gene Autry's Melody Ranch* (1977)★★★, *50th Anniversary Album* (Republic 1978)★★★, *Songs Of Faith* (1978)★★, *Christmas Classics* (Starday 1978)★★, *Sounds Like Jimmie Rodgers* (1985)★★★.

● COMPILATIONS: *Greatest Hits* (Columbia 1961)★★★, *Golden Hits* (RCA Victor 1962)★★★★, *Country Music Hall Of Fame* (Columbia 1970)★★★, *Back In The Saddle Again* (Sony 1977)★★★, *22 All Time Favorites* (GRT 1977)★★★, *Columbia Historic Edition* (Columbia 1982)★★★, *Golden Hits* (Good Music 1985)★★★, *Christmas Favorites* (Columbia 1989)★★★, *Greatest Hits* (Sony 1992)★★★★, *The Essential 1933-46* (Columbia/Legacy 1992)★★★★, *South Of The Border* (Castle 1994)★★★, *Portrait Of An Artist* (Sound Exchange 1995)★★★★, *Blues Singer 1929-1931: Booger*

Rooger Saturday (1996)★★★, *Sing, Cowboy, Sing! The Gene Autry Collection* 3-CD box set (Rhino 1997)★★★★.
● FURTHER READING: *Back In The Saddle Again*, Gene Autry with Mickey Herskowitz. *The Gene Autry Book*, David Rothel.

AVALON, FRANKIE

b. Francis Avallone, 18 September 1939, Philadelphia, Pennsylvania, USA. The photogenic 50s teen-idol started as a trumpet-playing child prodigy. His first recordings in 1954 were the instrumentals 'Trumpet Sorrento' and 'Trumpet Tarantella' on X-Vik Records (an RCA Records subsidiary). In the mid-50s, he appeared on many television and radio shows including those of Paul Whiteman, Jackie Gleason and Ray Anthony. He joined Rocco & The Saints and was seen singing with them in the 1957 film *Jamboree* (*Disc Jockey Jamboree* in the UK). Avalon signed to Chancellor Records and in 1958 his third single for them, 'Dede Dinah', reached the US Top 10. It was the first of his 25 US chart entries, many of which were written by his hard-working manager, Bob Marucci. Despite the fact that he had a weak voice, he quickly became one of the top stars in the USA and managed two chart-toppers in 1959, 'Venus' and 'Why', which were his only UK Top 20 entries. He has had an astonishing 25 hits in the USA, astonishing because his musical talent was often in question. He had to wait until his 21st birthday in 1961 to receive the $100,000 he had earned to date, and by that time he had passed his peak as a singer and turned his attention to acting. His acting career was also successful, with appearances in many films, including a string of beach movies alongside fellow 50s pop star Annette. He also appeared in the highly successful 1978 film *Grease*. He later recorded with little success on United Artists, Reprise, Metromedia, Regalia, Delite, Amos and Bobcat. Apart from his film and occasional television appearances, Avalon still performs on the supper-club circuit, and in 1986 toured in *Golden Boys Of Bandstand*. Alongside fellow Chancellor Records artist Fabian, he is often dismissed by rock critics, yet remains one of the American public's best-loved 50s teen-idols.
● ALBUMS: *Frankie Avalon* (Chancellor 1958)★★, *The Young Frankie Avalon* (Chancellor 1959)★★, *Swingin' On A Rainbow* (Chancellor 1959)★★, *Young And In Love* (Chancellor 1960)★★, *Summer Scene* (Chancellor 1960)★★, *And Now About Mr. Avalon* (Chancellor 1961)★★, *Italiano* (Chancellor 1962)★, *You Are Mine* (Chancellor 1962)★★, *Frankie Avalon's Christmas Album* (Chancellor 1962)★★, *Songs From Muscle Beach Party* film soundtrack (United Artists 1964)★★, *I'll Take Sweden* film soundtrack (United Artists 1965)★★, *I Want You Near Me* (1970)★, *Bobby Sox To Stockings* (Ace 1984)★★.
● COMPILATIONS: *A Whole Lotta Frankie* (Chancellor 1961)★★, *15 Greatest Hits* (United Artists 1964)★★★, *Best Of Frankie Avalon* (Creole 1984)★★★, *Frankie Avalon: Collection* (Castle 1990)★★, *The Fabulous Frankie Avalon* (Ace 1991)★★★, *Venus And Other Hits* (1993)★★★, *Venus: The Best Of Frankie Avalon* (Varese Vintage 1995)★★★, *Greatest Hits* (Curb 1995)★★★.
● FILMS: *Jamboree* aka *Disc Jockey Jamboree* (1957), *Beach Party* (1963), *Bikini Beach* (1964), *How To Stuff A Wild Bikini* (1965), *Beach Blanket Bingo* (1965), *Fireball 500* (1966), *Grease* (1978)

BADDELEY, HERMIONE

b. Hermione Clinton-Baddeley, 13 November 1906, Broseley, Shropshire, England, d. 19 August 1986, Los Angeles, California, USA. A distinguished actress and singer, Baddeley joined Margaret Morrison's School of Dancing when she was quite young, and then travelled with the Arts League of Service for three years. She had already established herself as a fine dramatic actress when she made her musical stage debut in May 1924 at London's Duke of York's Theatre in Archie de Bear's revue *Punch Bowl*. From then on, as well as continuing to appear in the straight theatre, she became one of the finest, and funniest, intimate revue artists ever seen in the West End. In September 1924 she joined the *Co-Optimists* at the Palace Theatre, and a few months later was in Noël Coward's *On With The Dance* (1925). This was followed by *Still Dancing* (1925), *Cochran's Revue* (1926), *Queen High* (a book show by Buddy De Sylva and Lawrence Schwab), *The Five O'Clock Girl* (1929, a Guy Bolton-Fred Thompson book show), *After Dinner* (1932), *Ballyhoo* (1932), and *Floodlight* (1937). She is thought to have reached her peak during the next few years in two supremely witty Herbert Farjeon revues, *Nine Sharp* (1938) and *The Little Revue* (1939), as well as *Rise Above It* (1941), in which she 'sparked off' another mistress of the genre, Hermione Gingold. After World War II, during which Baddeley spent long periods abroad entertaining the troops with ENSA, she returned to the London stage in *The Gaieties* (1945) with Leslie Henson, and then bid farewell to revue in great style with Alan Melville's *A La Carte* (1948) and *At The Lyric* (1953, later revised as *Going To Town*). In 1961 she went to America, and played on Broadway, toured with plays such as *Canterbury Tales* (1969), in which she played the Wife of Bath, and appeared in cabaret. She spent most of the rest of her life in the USA, returning occasionally to Britain, where she was in a revival of *The Threepenny Opera* (1972) as Mrs. Peachum. In America, Baddeley also starred frequently on television, and was particularly successful in *The Good Life* (1971) and *Maude* (1974-77). She also extended a film career that had begun with her taking the role of Calamity Kate in the comedy *A Daughter In Revolt* (1927), and eventually included the musicals *Expresso Bongo* (1959), *The Unsinkable Molly Brown* (1964), *Mary Poppins* (1964), *The Happiest Millionaire* (1967), and an Oscar nomination for Best Supporting Actress in 1959 for her role in *Room At The Top*. She was renowned for her portrayal of cheerful, yet somewhat eccentric, 'ordinary' women, who were able to rise above their problems. One of her elder sisters was actress Angela Baddeley (b. 4 July 1904, d. 22 February 1976), who is probably best remembered as housekeeper Mrs. Bridges in the 70s television series *Upstairs Downstairs*.
● FILMS: *A Daughter In Revolt* (1927), *The Guns Of Loos*

(1928), *Caste* (1930), *Love Life And Laughter* (1934), *Royal Cavalcade* (1935), *Kipps* (1941), *Brighton Rock* (1947), *It Always Rains On Sunday* (1947), *Quartet* (1948), *No Room At The Inn* (1948), *Passport To Pimlico* (1949), *Dear Mr. Prohack* (1949), *The Woman In Question* (1950), *Scrooge* (1951), *There Is Another Sun* (1951), *Hell Is Sold Out* (1951), *Tom Brown's Schooldays* (1951), *The Pickwick Papers* (1952), *Song Of Paris* (1952), *Time Gentlemen Please* (1952), *Counterspy* (1953), *Cosh Boy* (1953), *Women Without Men* (1954), *The Belles Of St. Trinian's* (1954), *Expresso Bongo* (1959), *Jetstorm* (1959), *Room At The Top* (1959), *Midnight Lace* (1960), *Let's Get Married* (1960), *Rag Doll* (1961), *Information Received* (1961), *The Unsinkable Molly Brown* (1964), *Mary Poppins* (1964), *Harlow* (1965), *Do Not Disturb* (1965), *Marriage On The Rocks* (1965), *Bullwhip Griffin* (1967), *The Happiest Millionaire* (1967), *Up the Front* (1972), *The Black Windmill* (1974), *C.H.O.M.P.S.* (1979), *There Goes The Bride* (1980), voice only *The Secret Of Nimh* (1982).
● FURTHER READING: *The Unsinkable Hermione Baddeley*, Hermione Baddeley.

BAILEY, PEARL

b. 29 March 1918, Newport News, Virginia, USA, d. 17 August 1990, Philadelphia, Pennsylvania, USA. Pearlie Mae, as she was known, was an uninhibited performer, who mumbled her way through some songs and filled others with outrageous asides and sly innuendoes. She entered the world of entertainment as a dancer but later sang in vaudeville, graduating to the New York nightclub circuit in the early 40s. After working with the Noble Sissle Orchestra, she became band-vocalist with Cootie Williams, with whom she recorded 'Tessa's Torch Song', previously sung by Dinah Shore in the movie *Up In Arms*. Bailey received strong critical acclaim after substituting for Rosetta Tharpe in a show, and was subsequently signed to star in the 1946 Harold Arlen/Johnny Mercer Broadway musical *St. Louis Woman*. A year later her slurred version of 'Tired' was the highlight of the movie *Variety Girl*, and she gave several other outstanding performances in films such as *Carmen Jones* (1954), *St. Louis Blues* (1958) and *Porgy And Bess* (1959). During her stay with Columbia Records (1945-50) Bailey recorded a series of duets with Frank Sinatra, trumpeter Oran 'Hot Lips' Page and comedienne Moms Mabley. She also recorded some solo tracks with outstanding arrangers/conductors, including Gil Evans and Tadd Dameron. Upon joining the Coral label in 1951, she employed Don Redman as her regular musical director, the association lasting for 10 years. In 1952, she had her biggest hit record 'Takes Two To Tango'. In that same year she married drummer Louie Bellson and he took over from Redman as her musical director in 1961. Although few of her records sold in vast quantities, Bailey had always been a crowd-pulling live performer and, following her early stage triumph in *St. Louis Woman*, was later cast in other shows including *The House Of Flowers*, *Bless You All*, *Arms And The Girl* and an all-black cast version of *Hello, Dolly!*. She also starred in several US television specials, playing down the double-entendre that caused one of her albums, *For Adults Only*, to be 'restricted from air-play'. In 1991 Pearl Bailey was posthumously inducted into the New York Theater Hall Of Fame.
● ALBUMS: *Pearl Bailey Entertains* 10-inch album (Columbia 1950)★★★, *Say Si Si* 10-inch album (Coral 1953)★★★, *I'm With You* 10-inch album (Coral 1953)★★★, *House Of Flowers* film soundtrack (Columbia 1954)★★★, *St Louis Woman* film soundtrack (Capitol 1955)★★★, *The One And Only Pearl Bailey* (Mercury 1956)★★★★, *Birth Of The Blues* (Coral 1956)★★★★, *The One And Only Pearl Bailey Sings* (Mercury 1957)★★★, *The Intoxicating Pearl Bailey* (Mercury 1958)★★★★, *Cultured Pearl* (Coral 1958)★★★, *For Adults Only* (1958)★★★★, *Gems By Pearl Bailey* (Vocalion 1958)★★★★, *Pearl Bailey Sings!* (1959)★★★★, *St. Louis Blues* (1959)★★★★, *Porgy & Bess & Others* (Columbia 1959)★★★★, *More Songs For Adults* (1960)★★★, *Songs Of Bad Old Days* (1960)★★★, *Naughty But Nice* (1961)★★★, *Songs She Loves By Arlen* (1962)★★★★, *All About Good Little Girls And Bad Little Boys* (Roulette 1962)★★★, *Come On Let's Play With Pearlie Mae* (Roulette 1962)★★★, *Songs By Jimmy Van Heusen* (1964)★★★★, *Les Poupees De Paris* (RCA Victor 1964)★★★, *Hello Dolly* film soundtrack (RCA Victor 1964)★★★, *For Adult Listening* (60s)★★★, *C'est La Vie* (60s)★★★, *Risque World* (60s)★★★.
● COMPILATIONS: *The Definitive* (1965)★★★★, *The Best Of - The Roulette Years* (Roulette 1991)★★★★.
● FURTHER READING: *The Raw Pearl*, Pearl Bailey. *Talking To Myself*, Pearl Bailey.
● FILMS: *Variety Girl* (1947), *Isn't It Romantic* (1948), *Carmen Jones* (1954), *That Certain Feeling* (1955), *St. Louis Blues* (1957), *Porgy And Bess* (1959), *All The Fine Young Cannibals* (1960), *The Landlord* (1969).

BAKER, ETTA

b. Etta Reid, 31 March 1915, Caldwell County, North Carolina, USA. From a black family that was proficient in blues, pop, hymns, rags, ballads, dance music and, through intermarriage, white country music, Etta Reid learned guitar, banjo, fiddle and piano, playing alongside her father, Boone Reid, and her elder sister Cora. She married in 1936, from which time her husband, though himself a pianist, discouraged public performance. She was recorded in 1956 and her fluent, raggy guitar became something of a cult among urban folk revivalists, particularly on 'One Dime Blues'. (Her father and Cora's husband Lacey Phillips were also recorded, on banjo, in 1956.) Baker took up her career only after her husband had died, resuming public performances and showing that she was still a magnificent guitarist and banjo player.
● ALBUMS: *Instrumental Music Of The Southern Appalachians* (1956)★★★★, *Music From The Hills Of Caldwell County* (70s)★★★, *One Dime Blues* (1991)★★★.

BAKER, KENNY

b. 1 March 1921, Withernsea, Yorkshire, England. After taking up the trumpet and playing in brass bands, Baker moved to London in the late 30s, to become a professional musician. During the next few years he established himself as an outstanding technician capable of playing in any jazz or dance band. In the early 40s, he played in the bands of Lew Stone and George Chisholm before joining Ted Heath in 1944. He remained with Heath until 1949, and was featured on many recording sessions and countless concerts. In the early 50s he was regularly on the radio, leading his own band, the Baker's Dozen, on a weekly late-night show that lasted throughout the decade. In the 60s he led his own groups and recorded film soundtracks, all the time building his reputation as one of the best trumpet players in the world, even though he only rarely played outside the UK. At the end of the decade he was featured in Benny Goodman's British band. Baker's career continued throughout the 70s, with appearances as co-leader of the Best of British Jazz touring package, and with Ted Heath recreations and the bands led by Don Lusher and other former colleagues. In the early 80s, Baker turned down an invitation to take over leadership of the Harry James band after the latter's death. He could still be regularly heard playing concerts and club dates and also featured on television, usually off-camera, playing soundtracks for Alan Plater's popular UK television series *The Beiderbecke Affair* and *The Beiderbecke Tapes*. In 1989, he took part in a major recording undertaking that set out to recreate the classic recordings of Louis Armstrong using modern recording techniques. Baker took the Armstrong role, comfortably confounding the date on his birth certificate with his masterful playing. A fiery soloist with a remarkable technical capacity that he never uses simply for effect, Baker is one of the UK's greatest contributions to the international jazz scene.

● ALBUMS: *Kenny Baker's Half-Dozen* (Dormouse 1957)★★★, *Date With The Dozen* (Dormouse 1957)★★★, *Presents The Half-Dozen* (Dormouse 1958)★★★, *Baker Plays McHugh* (1958)★★★, with Benny Goodman *London Date* (1969)★★★, *George Chisholm* (1973)★★★, *The Phase 4 World Of Kenny Baker* (Decca 1977)★★★, *The Very Best Of British Jazz* (1983)★★★, with Don Lusher *The Big Band Sound Of Ted Heath* (1986), *The Louis Armstrong Connection Volumes 1-7* (1989)★★★★, *Tribute To The Great Trumpeters* (1993)★★★, *The Boss Is Home* (Big Bear 1994)★★★.

BAKER, LAVERN

b. Delores Williams, 11 November 1929, Chicago, Illinois, USA, d. 10 March 1997, New York, USA. Baker was a pioneering voice in the fusion of R&B and rock 'n' roll in the 50s. In 1947 she was discovered in a Chicago nightclub by bandleader Fletcher Henderson. Although still in her teens, the singer won a recording contract with the influential OKeh Records, where she was nicknamed 'Little Miss Sharecropper' and 'Bea Baker'. Having toured extensively with the Todd Rhodes Orchestra, Baker secured a prestigious contract with Atlantic Records, with whom she enjoyed a fruitful relationship. 'Tweedle Dee' reached both the US R&B and pop charts in 1955, selling in excess of one million copies, and the artist was awarded a second gold disc two years later for 'Jim Dandy'. In 1959, she enjoyed a number 6 pop hit with 'I Cried A Tear' and throughout the decade Baker remained one of black music's leading performers. Although eclipsed by newer acts during the 60s, the singer enjoyed further success with 'Saved', written and produced by Leiber And Stoller, and 'See See Rider', both of which inspired subsequent versions, notably by the Band and the Animals. Baker's final chart entry came with 'Think Twice', a 1966 duet with Jackie Wilson, as her 'classic' R&B intonation grew increasingly out of step with the prevalent soul/Motown boom. After leaving Atlantic, Baker is probably best known for 'One Monkey Don't Stop The Show'. In the late 60s, while entertaining US troops in Vietnam, she became ill, and went to the Philippines to recuperate. She stayed there in self-imposed exile for 22 years, reviving her career at New York's Village Gate club in 1991. During the

following year she undertook a short UK tour, but audience numbers were disappointing for the only female, along with Aretha Franklin, who had, at that time, been elected to the US Rock And Roll Hall Of Fame. She replaced Ruth Brown in the Broadway musical *Black And Blue* in the early 90s but ill health from diabetes, together with amputation of both her legs, made her final years miserable. Baker had a stunning voice that with little effort could crack walls, and yet her ballad singing was wonderfully sensitive.

● ALBUMS: *LaVern* (Atlantic 1956)★★★, *LaVern Baker* (Atlantic 1957)★★★★, *Rock And Roll With LaVern* (Atlantic 1957)★★★★, *LaVern Baker Sings Bessie Smith* (Atlantic 1958)★★★, *Blues Ballads* (Atlantic 1959)★★★★, *Precious Memories* (Atlantic 1959)★★★, *Saved* (Atlantic 1961)★★★, *See See Rider* (Atlantic 1963)★★★, *I'm Gonna Get You* (1966)★★.

● COMPILATIONS: *The Best Of LaVern Baker* (Atlantic 1963)★★★★, *Real Gone Gal* (Charly 1984)★★★, *Soul On Fire - The Best Of* (Atlantic 1993)★★★★, *Blues Ballads* with 6 extra tracks (Sequel 1997)★★★★, *Rock & Roll* (Sequel 1997)★★★★.

BAKER, MICKEY

b. McHouston Baker, 15 October 1925, Louisville, Kentucky, USA. After spells in reform school and a children's home, he moved to New York in 1941. He lived on the fringes of the criminal world but took up the guitar and quickly became a virtuoso, equally adept at jazz and blues styles. From the late 40s, Mickey 'Guitar' Baker played on hundreds of recording sessions, accompanying such artists as Ray Charles, the Coasters, Ivory Joe Hunter, Ruth Brown and Screaming Jay Hawkins. Baker occasionally recorded under his own name and in 1956 teamed up with guitarist/vocalist Sylvia Vanderpool. After an unsuccessful version of 'Walking In The Rain', the atmospheric 'Love Is Strange' (co-written by Bo Diddley) by Mickey And Sylvia was a US Top 20 hit on RCA/Groove in 1956. Later singles on Vik and RCA were only minor hits, although the duo contributed to Ike And Tina Turner's 'It's Gonna Work Out Fine' (1961), where Baker's is the male voice answering Tina's. Some of Baker's solo recordings were collected on a 1959 album for Atlantic Records. In the early 60s, he emigrated to Paris and joined the expatriate community of jazz musicians in the French capital. He toured Europe with such artists as Memphis Slim and Champion Jack Dupree, and performed at the 1973 Montreux Jazz Festival. Baker also arranged the strings for Fleetwood Mac's version of 'Need Your Love So Bad' (1968). During the 70s, he recorded several albums in Europe, including two for Stefan Grossman's guitar-instructional label, Kicking Mule.

● ALBUMS: *The Wildest Guitar* (Atlantic 1959)★★★, *But Wild* (King 1963)★★★, *The Blues In Me* (Black & Blue 1974)★★★, *Take A Look Inside* (1975)★★★, *Up On The Hill* (1975)★★★, *Blues And Jazz Guitar* (Kicking Mule 1977)★★★, *Jazz-Rock Guitar* (Kicking Mule 1978)★★★, *Rock A With A Sock* (1993)★★★.

BALL, LUCILLE

b. Lucille Désirée Ball, 6 August 1911, Celeron, near Jamestown, New York, USA, d. 26 April 1989, Los Angeles, California, USA. An actress and singer, with a trademark mop of red hair, Ball was one of the all-time great American comediennes. Her influence on US television, both as a performer and an executive, was immense. Her father was an electrician and her mother a concert pianist. Ball left high school at the age of 15 in order to join the John Murray Anderson-Robert Milton Dramatic School in New York, and subsequently worked in the chorus of several stage productions; she also featured on giant billboards as the Chesterfield Cigarette Girl, before becoming bed-ridden with rheumatoid arthritis for two years. In 1933, Ball secured the role of a Goldwyn Girl in the Eddie Cantor movie *Roman Scandals*, and she continued with Goldwyn until 1935, when she signed a seven-year contract with RKO. In addition to comedy and more serious assignments, Ball played numerous minor roles in movie musicals such as *Broadway Thru A Keyhole*, *Bottoms Up*, *Hold That Girl*, *Kid Millions*, *Broadway Bill*, *Roberta*, *Old Man Rhythm*, *Top Hat*, *I Dream Too Much* and *Follow The Fleet*, before taking more substantial, and then leading roles, in other musical features, including *Joy Of Living*, *Room Service*, *That's Right-You're Wrong*, *Dance Girl Dance*, *Seven Days Leave*, *Du Barry Was A Lady*, *Best Foot Forward*, *Meet The People* and *Ziegfeld Follies*. After she met the Cuban bandleader Desi Arnaz in 1940 on the set of *Too Many Girls*, in which she was top-billed for the first time, they were married in November of that year. During the 40s, as well as working consistently in movies for a variety of studios, Ball guested frequently on radio and gained her own network show, *My Favorite Husband*, in 1950. This concept transferred to television as *I Love Lucy* in 1951, with Arnaz playing the role of the fictional bandleader Ricky Ricardo to Ball's scatter-brained wife. As part of the deal, Arnaz and Ball's company Desilu Productions attained ownership of all 180 episodes of the series, which it sold back to CBS for $4.3 million in 1956. Playing an important part in the success of the show, which topped the ratings and won five Emmys, were William Frawley and Vivian Vance as the Ricardos' neighbours. It continued to thrive in various formats during the next few years, but came to halt in 1960 after Ball divorced Arnaz. Desilu, which had expanded rapidly, was split evenly between them. Two years later, Ball bought out Arnaz's holdings in Desilu, and in 1967 she sold the company, which was then producing several top-rated series such as *Star Trek* and *Mission: Impossible*, for $17 million to Gulf & Western. Shortly after her divorce, Ball appeared on Broadway in the Cy Coleman-Dorothy Fields musical *Wildcat* (1960), in which she introduced the exuberant 'Hey, Look Me Over'. During the show's run she met comedian Gary Morton and they were married in November 1961. Ball returned to television with *The Lucy Show* (1962-68), *Here's Lucy* (1968-73) and *Life With Lucy* (1986), without recreating the magic of that first series. She also co-starred with Robert Preston in the much-maligned film version of Jerry Herman's stage hit *Mame* (1973). As well as several Emmys, her many awards included membership of the Television Academy's Hall of Fame, the Academy's special citation as First Lady Of Television, and Kennedy Center Honours.

Ball's children, Desi Arnaz Jnr. (b. Desidario Arnaz, 19 January 1953, Los Angeles, California, USA) and Lucie Arnaz (b. Lucy Désirée Arnaz, 17 July 1951, Los Angeles, California, USA) are both television and feature film actors. Lucie is also a singer and cabaret performer. In 1979, she co-starred with Robert Klein in the Neil Simon-Marvin Hamlisch-Carole Bayer Sager Broadway musical *They're Playing Our Song*, and released her first solo album *Just In Time* in 1993. In the same year she and her husband, Laurence Luckinbill, were executive producers on the NBC television documentary film *Lucy And Desi: A Home Movie*. Desi Arnaz Jnr. played the part of his father in the movie *The Mambo Kings* (1992).

● FURTHER READING: *The Lucille Ball Story*, J. Gregory. *Desilu: The Story Of Lucille Ball And Desi Arnaz*, Coyne Steven Sanders and Tom Gilbert.

● FILMS: *Stage Door* (1937), *Don't Tell The Wife* (1937), *Joy Of Living* (1938), *Go Chase Yourself* (1938), *Having Wonderful Time* (1938), *Affairs Of Annabel* (1938), *Room Service* (1938), *Annabel Takes A Tour* (1938), *The Next Time I Marry* (1938), *Beauty For The Asking* (1939), *Twelve Crowded Hours* (1939), *Panama Lady* (1939), *Five Came Back* (1939), *That's Right-You're Wrong* (1939), *The Marines Fly High* (1940), *Dance Girl Dance* (1940), *You Can't Fool Your Wife* (1940), *Too Many Girls* (1940), *A Girl, A Guy And A Gob* (1941), *Look Who's Laughing* (1941), *Valley Of The Sun* (1942), *The Big Street* (1942), *Seven Days Leave* (1943), *Du Barry Was A Lady* (1943), *Thousands Cheer* cameo (1943), *Best Foot Forward* as herself (1943), *Meet The People* (1944), *Without Love* (1945), *Abbott And Costello In Hollywood* (1945), *Easy To Wed* (1946), *Ziegfeld Follies* (1946), *The Dark Corner* (1946), *Lover Come Back* (1946), *Two Smart People* (1946), *When Lovers Meet* (1946), *Personal Column* (1947), *Lured* (1947), *Her Husband's Affair* (1947), *Sorrowful Jones* (1949), *Interference* (1949), *Easy Living* (1949), *Miss Grant Takes Richmond* (1949), *The Fuller Brush Girl* (1950), *Fancy Pants* (1950), *The Magic Carpet* (1951), *The Long Trailer* (1954), *Forever Darling* (1956), *The Facts Of Life* (1960), *Critic's Choice* (1963), *Big Parade Of Comedy* (1964), *A Guide For The Married Man* cameo (1967), *Yours, Mine And Ours* (1968), *Diamond Jim Brady* (1969), *Mame* (1974).

BALLARD, HANK, AND THE MIDNIGHTERS

b. Henry Ballard, 18 November 1936, Detroit, Michigan, USA. His truck-driving father died when Ballard was seven years old and he was sent to Bessemer, Alabama, to live with relations. The strict religious and gospel upbringing caused him to run away, and by the age of 15, Ballard was working on an assembly line at Ford Motors in Detroit. His cousin, Florence Ballard, became a member of the Detroit girl group the Supremes. Hank Ballard's singing voice was heard by Sonny Woods of the Royals, who was amused by his mixture of Jimmy Rushing and Gene Autry. He was asked to replace frontman Lawson Smith during the latter's army service. The Royals had been recommended to King Records by Johnny Otis and had previously recorded 'Every Beat Of My Heart', later an R&B hit for Gladys Knight And The Pips. In 1953, Ballard's first session with the Royals led to their first US R&B Top 10 entry, 'Get It', which he also wrote. Ballard composed their 1954 R&B chart-topper, 'Work With Me, Annie', although its sexual innuendoes were too strong for some radio stations to broadcast. Its popularity spawned sequels ('Annie's Aunt Fanny', 'Annie Had A Baby') as well as answer records (the Platters' 'Annie Doesn't Work Here Anymore'). Etta James's 'Roll With Me, Henry' was modified by Georgia Gibbs to 'Dance With Me, Henry', while Hank himself responded with 'Henry's Got Flat Feet'! The group also had success with 'Sexy Ways', 'Don't Change Your Pretty Ways', 'Open Up Your Back Door' and 'Tore Up Over You'. In 1955, the Drifters had converted a gospel song into 'What'cha Gonna Do?' and, in 1957, Hank Ballard And The Midnighters used the same melody for 'Is Your Love For Real?'. They then modified the arrangement and changed the lyrics to 'The Twist'. Not realizing the song's potential, it was released as the b-side of 'Teardrops On Your Letter', a number 4 US R&B hit. Shortly afterwards, 'The Twist' was covered by Chubby Checker, who added dance steps and thus created a new craze. As a result of 'The Twist', Hank Ballard And The Midnighters received exposure on pop radio stations and made the US pop charts with such dance hits as 'Finger Poppin' Time' (number 7), 'Let's Go, Let's Go, Let's Go' (number 6), 'The Hoochi Coochi Coo' (number 23), 'Let's Go Again (Where We Went Last Night)' (number 39), 'The Continental' (number 33) and 'The Switch-A-Roo' (number 26). On the strength of Chubby Checker's success, their original version of 'The Twist' made number 28 on the US pop charts. In 1963, Hank Ballard split with the Midnighters, but he retained the group's name, which has enabled him to work with numerous musicians using that name. For some years he worked with James Brown, who has paid tribute to him on record. He recorded a double album at the Hammersmith Palais in London and he also recorded 'Two Bad Boys (Just Out Makin' Noise)', with Tim Hauser of Manhattan Transfer.

● ALBUMS: *Their Greatest Hits* (1954)★★, *The Midnighters, Volume 2* (1957)★★, *Greatest Juke Box Hits* (1958)★★★, *Singin' And Swingin'* (King 1959)★★★, *The One And Only Hank Ballard* (King 1960)★★★, *Mr. Rhythm And Blues* (King 1960)★★★, *Finger Poppin' Time* (King 1960)★★★★, *Spotlight On Hank Ballard* (King 1961)★★★★, *Sing Along* (King 1961)★★★, *Let's Go Again* (King 1961)★★★★, *Jumpin' Hank Ballard* (King 1962)★★★, *The Twistin' Fools* (King 1962)★★★, *The 1963 Sound* (King 1963)★★★, *A Star In Your Eyes* (King 1964)★★, *Those Lazy Lazy Days* (King 1965)★★, *Glad Songs, Sad Songs* (King 1966)★★, *24 Hit Tunes* (King 1966)★★★, *24 Great Songs* (King 1968)★★★, *You Can't Keep A Good Man Down* (King 1969)★★, *Hank Ballard Live At The Palais* (Charly 1987)★★, *Naked In The Rain* (1993)★★.

● COMPILATIONS: *Biggest Hits* (King 1963)★★★, *What You Get When The Gettin' Gets Good* (Charly 1985)★★★.

BALLARD, KAYE

b. Catherine Gloria Balotta, 20 November 1926, Cleveland, Ohio, USA. An actress and singer with a long and distinguished career in the theatre and on television and film, Ballard came from Italian descent, and entered showbusiness when she was 14 years old, appearing in a US production of *Stage Door Canteen* in Cleveland. She began her professional career in vaudeville in 1943, and three years later was in the revue *Three To Make Ready* in New York. In the late 40s she toured in various stock productions including *Look Ma, I'm Dancin'* and *Annie Get Your Gun*, and was in the cast of the 1948 Harold Rome revue *That's The Ticket*, which closed out of town in the dreaded 'graveyard' for Broadway-bound shows, Philadelphia. In 1950 Ballard made her London debut at the Prince of Wales's Theatre in the revue *Touch And Go*, and also starred in that year's *Royal Variety Performance*, before joining the US tour of *Top Banana*. In

1954, she was back on Broadway as Helen of Troy in *The Golden Apple* in which she introduced Jerome Moss and John Latouche's languorous 'Lazy Afternoon'. This was followed by *Reuben Reuben*, a Marc Blitzstein show that closed in Boston in 1955, and good roles in Broadway productions of *Carnival* (1961, Rosalie), the revue *The Beast In Me* (1963), and *Molly* (1973, Molly Goldberg). She also appeared in the *Ziegfeld Follies* (1956, Canada), a revival of *Wonderful Town* at the New York City Center (1963), and the revue *The Decline And Fall Of The Entire World As Seen Through The Eyes Of Cole Porter Revisited* (1965, off-Broadway). In the 70s she was appearing in cabaret at prestige rooms such as Mr. Kelly's in Chicago, and the St. Regis and Hotel Plaza in New York. She made her only film musical, *The Girl Most Likely* (1958), with Jane Powell, Tommy Noonan, Cliff Robertson and Keith Andes, having entered television via *The Mel Tormé Show* some six years earlier. She was in the original television production of *Cinderella* (1957, starring Julie Andrews), and starred with Eve Arden in the fondly remembered series *The Mothers-In-Law* in the late 60s. Other frequent television work has included *The Love Boat*, *The Robber Bridegroom*, numerous guest appearances, and her own specials such as *Hello Kaye Ballard, Welcome To Las Vegas* (1980). In more recent times, she joined the Big Band Era 4 Girls 4 tour with Kay Starr, Margaret Whiting and Helen O'Connell, delighting audiences not only with her singing and comedy, but with added burlesque impressions and some sensitive flute playing. In the early 90s she was in the casts of the Long Beach Civic Light Opera production of *Chicago* with Juliet Prowse and Bebe Neuwirth, and the New York Festival's *Pirates Of Penzance*; at the Rainbow And Stars in New York with Jason Graae, Liz Callaway and Ron Raines in an Irving Berlin revue entitled *Say It With Music*; and with Jaye P. Morgan and Marcia Lewis in *Nunsense* in Florida. She also made a fleeting visit to London in 1992 and presented her one-woman show at the Lyric Theatre. She has continued to record occasionally, and in 1958 made the album *The Fanny Brice Story In Song*, which she sent to producer Ray Stark suggesting that she star in a film of the great entertainer's life. Stark rejected her offer, but eventually produced the biopic under the title of *Funny Girl*, starring Barbra Streisand.

● ALBUMS: *The Fanny Brice Story In Song* (MGM 1958)★★★★, *Kaye Ballard Swings* (United Artists 1959)★★★, *Kaye Ballard Live?* (United Artists 1960)★★★, *Ha-Ha Boo-Hoo* (United Artists 1960)★★★, *Kaye Ballard & Arthur Siegel* (1967)★★★, *Then And Again* (Original Cast Records 1994)★★★, with Jaye P. Morgan *Long-Time Friends* (Original Cast Records 1996)★★.

● FILMS: *The Girl Most Likely* (1958), *A House Is Not A Home* (1964), *The Ritz* (1976), *Freaky Friday* (1977), *Falling In Love Again* (1980), *Tiger Warsaw* (1987), *Modern Love* (1990), *Fate* (1990), *Eternity* (1990), *Ava's Magical Adventure* (1994).

BALLEN, IVIN

Ballen formed his 20th Century Records label in Philadelphia during World War II, specializing in a diverse range of music from Jewish humour to gospel. In January 1948, he purchased Sam Goody's Gotham Records and S-G Music Publishing, adding a strong R&B and jazz label to its roster, with artists such as Tiny Grimes, Leo Parker, Jimmy Preston, Johnny Sparrow, Jimmy Rushing and David

'Panama' Francis. In the early 50s, leasing arrangements were made with a network of various independent labels throughout the country - from Washington, DC, to New York, Los Angeles, Chicago and Tulsa. The range of styles was enlarged to encompass hillbilly, vocal group R&B and even the down-home blues of Dan Pickett, John Lee Hooker and Eddie Burns. Ballen entered the rock 'n' roll and rockabilly market of the mid-50s, and like many of the small independents found that he could not compete with the big-selling majors such as RCA and Decca. He wound down the label in the late 50s.

BAND WAGON, THE

Taking the title from a highly successful 1931 Broadway revue that had a score by Arthur Schwartz and Howard Dietz, but no plot, Betty Comden and Adolph Green provided the screenplay for arguably the best and wittiest backstage film musical of them all. Released in 1953, the film's story dealt with an ageing, has-been hoofer, Tony Hunter (Fred Astaire), whose New York comeback is being masterminded and written by Lily and Lester Marton (Oscar Levant and Nanette Fabray), two characters reputedly based on Comden and Green themselves. Ballerina Gabrielle Gerard (Cyd Charisse) reluctantly agrees to become Hunter's co-star, and Jeffrey Cordova (Jack Buchanan), the reigning theatrical virtuoso and super-egotist, is called in to direct, but his extravagant efforts result in something nearer *Faust* than *Funny Face*. However, all is not lost: after the cast have revamped the show (with the help of Cordova, who turns out to be a nice, modest - even insecure - guy underneath), it promises to run for years. Schwartz and Dietz's score was full of marvellous songs, including 'A Shine On Your Shoes', 'By Myself' (Astaire), 'I Guess I'll Have To Change My Plan' (Astaire-Buchanan), the ingenious 'Triplets' (Astaire-Buchanan-Fabray), 'New Sun In The Sky' (Charisse, dubbed by India Adams), and several others involving the principals and chorus, such as 'I Love Louisa', 'Louisiana Hayride', 'You And The Night And The Music', 'Dancing In The Dark' and 'Something To Remember Me By'. The one new number was 'That's Entertainment', which, along with Irving Berlin's 'There's No Business Like Show Business', attempts to explain why, despite Noël Coward's reservations, the show must always go on. Charisse and Astaire's dancing was a dream, especially in the ethereal 'Dancing In The Dark' sequence and the 'Girl Hunt' ballet. Much of the credit for the film's oustanding success was due to director Vincente Minnelli, choreographer Michael Kidd, and producer Arthur Freed, whose special musicals unit at MGM had created yet another winner.

BARBER, BILL

b. John William Barber, 21 May 1920, Hornell, New York, USA. While at school Barber was persuaded to try out for the school orchestra on tuba. Very impressed with the instrument, he studied at the Manhattan and Juilliard schools of music, then was drafted during World War II. After the war he joined the Kansas City Philharmonic Orchestra and also played in several theatre pit bands. By this time, however, he was becoming deeply interested in jazz and joined Claude Thornhill's band. Later, he gigged in New York and was on hand when Miles Davis and Gil Evans were planning *Birth Of The Cool*. The band worked in New York for two weeks,

playing at the Royal Roost, with Barber spending the first part of the evening in the pit band for *Magdalena*, by Villa-Lobos. Despite the latter-day popularity of the album, the Davis nonet was not especially successful and with few other jazz groups having room for a tuba, Barber continued to work in pit bands, including three years with the Broadway production of *The King And I*. During this period he performed occasional sessions with jazz musicians both live and on record, among them Charlie Ventura, the Sauter-Finegan Orchestra and Pete Rugolo. From time to time he rejoined Davis for recording dates, including *Sketches Of Spain* and *At Carnegie Hall*. He also rejoined Evans for *Out Of The Cool*. In later years, Barber began teaching on Long Island, eventually retiring. He was lured out of retirement, however, to record with Gerry Mulligan on *Rebirth Of The Cool*. Although he began playing bass in the 90s, Barber's first love remains the tuba, and the fact that this instrument is rarely used in jazz had meant that this fine musician has never been accorded his due.
● ALBUMS: with Gil Evans *Out Of The Cool* (Impulse 1960)★★★★★, with Gerry Mulligan *Re-Birth Of The Cool* (GRP 1992)★★★.

BARBER, CHRIS

b. 17 April 1930, Welwyn Garden City, Hertfordshire, England. In the 40s Barber studied trombone and bass at the Guildhall School of Music, eventually choosing the former as his principal instrument (although he occasionally played bass in later years). In the late 40s he formed his first band, which, unusually, was formed as a co-operative. Also in the band were Monty Sunshine, Ron Bowden and Lonnie Donegan. By the early 50s the band had gained a considerable following but it was nevertheless decided to invite Ken Colyer to join. The move was musically promising but proved to be unsuccessful when the personalities involved clashed repeatedly. Eventually, Colyer left and was replaced by Pat Halcox. With a remarkably consistent personnel the Barber band was soon one of the UK's leading traditional groups and was well placed to take advantage of the surge of interest in this form of jazz in the late 50s and early 60s. The decline in popularity of 'trad', which came on the heels of the rock explosion, had a dramatic effect on many British jazz bands but Barber's fared much better than most. This was owing in part to his astute business sense and also his keen awareness of musical trends and a willingness to accommodate other forms without compromising his high musical standards. In the 60s Barber changed the name of the band to the Chris Barber Blues and Jazz Band. Into the traditional elements of the band's book he incorporated ragtime but also worked with such modern musicians as Joe Harriott. Among his most important activities at this time was his active promotion of R&B and the blues, which he underlined by bringing major American artists to the UK, often at his own expense. Through such philanthropy he brought to the attention of British audiences the likes of Sister Rosetta Tharpe, Brownie McGhee, Louis Jordan and Muddy Waters. Not content with performing the older blues styles, Barber also acknowledged the contemporary interest in blues evinced by rock musicians and audiences and hired such players as John Slaughter and Pete York (ex-Spencer Davis Group), who worked happily beside long-serving sidemen Halcox, Ian Wheeler, Vic Pitt and others. In the 70s,

Barber focused more on mainstream music, showing a special affinity for small Duke Ellington-styled bands, and toured with visitors such as Russell Procope, Wild Bill Davis, Trummy Young and John Lewis. He also maintained his contact with his jazz roots and, simultaneously, the contemporary blues scene by touring widely with his *Take Me Back To New Orleans* show, which featured Dr. John. As a trombone player, Barber's work is enhanced by his rich sound and flowing solo style. It is, however, as bandleader and trendspotter that he has made his greatest contribution to the jazz scene, both internationally and, especially, in the UK. In the early 90s he was happily entering his fifth decade as a bandleader with no discernible flagging of interest, enthusiasm, skill or, indeed, of his audience. In 1991 he was awarded the OBE, the same year as *Panama!* was released, which features the excellent trumpet playing of Wendell Brunious.

● ALBUMS: *Live In 1954-55* (London 1955)★★★, *Ragtime* (1960)★★★, *Chris Barber At The London Palladium* (1961)★★★, *Trad Tavern* (Philips 1962)★★★★, *Getting Around* (1963)★★★, *Battersea Rain Dance* (1968)★★★, *Live In East Berlin* (Black Lion 1968)★★★, *Get Rolling!* (1971)★★★, *Sideways* (1974)★★★, *Echoes Of Ellington* (1976)★★★, *The Grand Reunion Concert* (Timeless 1976)★★★, *Take Me Back To New Orleans* (Black Lion 1980)★★★, *Creole Love Call* (Timeless 1981)★★★, *Mardi Gras At The Marquee* (Timeless 1983)★★★, *Live In 85* (Timeless 1986)★★★, *Concert For The BBC* (Timeless 1986)★★★, *In Budapest* (Storyville 1987)★★★, *When Its Thursday Night In Egypt* (Sonet 1988)★★★, *Classics Concerts In Berlin* 1959 recording (Chris Barber Collection 1988)★★★, *Stardust* (Timeless 1988)★★★, *Mardi Gras At The Marquee* (Timeless 1989)★★★, *Get Yourself To Jackson Square* (Sonet 1990)★★★, *Echoes Of Ellington Volume I* (Timeless 1991)★★★, *Echoes Of Ellington Volume II* (Timeless 1991)★★★, *In Concert* (Timeless 1991)★★★, with Wendell Brunious *Panama!* (Timeless 1991)★★★, *Who's Blues* (L&R 1991)★★★, *Elite Syncopations* 1960 recording (Lake 1994)★★★.

● COMPILATIONS: *30 Years, Chris Barber* (Timeless 1985)★★★★, *Can't We Get Together? (1954-84)* (Timeless 1986)★★★★, *Best Sellers* (Storyville 1987)★★★, *Everybody Knows* (Compact Collection 1987)★★★, *The Best Of Chris Barber (1959-62)* (PRT 1988)★★★★, *The Entertainer* (Polydor 1988)★★★★, *The Ultimate* (Kaz 1989)★★★★, *Essential Chris Barber* (Kaz 1990)★★★★, *Chris Barber 40 Years Jubilee* (Timeless 1995)★★★★, *Petite Fleur* (Spectrum 1995)★★★★.

● VIDEOS: *Music From The Land Of Dreams Concert* (Storyville 1990), *In Concert* (Virgin Vision 1991).

BARNES, ROOSEVELT 'BOOBA'

b. 25 September 1936, Longwood, Mississippi, USA, d. 3 April 1996, Chicago, Illinois, USA. A self-taught singer, guitarist and harmonica player, Barnes played 'unvarnished gut level blues', strongly influenced by Howlin' Wolf. His first instrument was the harmonica, which he began to play at the age of eight, and he sat in with many of the local blues musicians around Greenville, Mississippi, in the 50s. He formed his first band in 1956 or 1957 and started playing guitar in 1960. In 1964 he moved to Chicago, Illinois, living there until 1971, and then returning two years later to record

as a backing musician with the Jones Brothers; these recordings remain unissued. In 1990 Barnes became the first Mississippi-based performer to record an album for the Rooster Blues label.

● ALBUMS: *The Heartbroken Man* (Rooster Blues 1990)★★★.

BART, LIONEL

b. Lionel Begleiter, 1 August 1930, London, England. The comparative inactivity of Bart for many years has tended to cloud the fact that he is one of the major songwriters of 20th-century popular song. The former silk-screen printer was at the very hub of the rock 'n' roll and skiffle generation that came out of London's Soho in the mid-50s. As a member of the Cavemen with Tommy Steele he later became Steele's main source of non-American song material. In addition to writing the pioneering 'Rock With The Cavemen' he composed a series of glorious singalong numbers, including 'A Handful Of Songs', 'Water Water' and the trite but delightfully innocent 'Little White Bull'. Much of Bart's work was steeped in the English music-hall tradition, diffused with a strong working-class pride, and it was no surprise that he soon graduated into writing songs for full-length stage shows. *Lock Up Your Daughters* and *Fings Ain't Wot They Used T'Be* were two of his early successes, both appearing during 1959, the same year he wrote the classic 'Living Doll' for Cliff Richard. Bart was one of the first writers to introduce mild politics into his lyrics, beautifully transcribed with topical yet humourously ironic innocence, for example: 'They've changed our local Palais into a bowling alley and fings ain't wot they used to be.' As the 60s dawned Bart unconsciously embarked on a decade that saw him reach dizzy heights of success and made him one of the musical personalities of the decade. During the first quarter of the year he topped the charts with 'Do You Mind' for Anthony Newley, a brilliantly simple and catchy song complete with Bart's own finger-snapped accompaniment. The best was yet to come when that year he launched *Oliver!*, a musical based on Dickens' *Oliver Twist*. This became a phenomenal triumph, and remains one of the most successful musicals of all time. Bart's knack of simple melody combined with unforgettable lyrics produced many classics, including the pleading 'Who Will Buy', the rousing 'Food Glorious Food' and the poignant 'As Long As He Needs Me' (also a major hit for Shirley Bassey, although she reputedly never liked the song). Bart was a pivotal figure throughout the swinging London scene of the 60s, although he maintains that the party actually started in the 50s. Bart befriended Brian Epstein, the Beatles, the Rolling Stones, became an international star following *Oliver!*'s success as a film (winning six Oscars) and was romantically linked with Judy Garland and Alma Cogan. Following continued, although lesser, success with *Blitz!* and *Maggie May*, Bart was shaken into reality when the London critics damned his 1965 musical *Twang!!*, based upon the life of Robin Hood. Bart's philanthropic nature made him a prime target for business sharks and he lost much of his fortune as a result. By the end of the 60s the cracks were beginning to show; his dependence on drugs and alcohol increased and he watched many of his close friends die in tragic circumstances - Cogan with cancer, Garland through drink and drugs and Epstein's supposed suicide. In 1969, *La Strada* only had a short run in New York before Bart retreated into himself, and for many years maintained a relatively low profile, watching the 70s and 80s pass almost as a blur, only making contributions to *The Londoners* and *Costa Packet*. During this time the gutter press were eager for a kiss-and-tell story but Bart remained silent, a credible action considering the sums of money he was offered. During the late 80s Bart finally beat his battle with alcohol and ended the decade a saner, wiser and healthier man. His renaissance started in 1989 when he was commissioned by a UK building society to write a television jingle. The composition became part of an award-winning advertisement, featuring a number of angelic children singing with Bart, filmed in pristine monochrome. The song 'Happy Endings' was a justifiable exhumation of a man who remains an immensely talented figure and whose work ranks with some of the greatest of the American 'musical comedy' songwriters. In the early 90s his profile continued to be high, with revivals by the talented National Youth Theatre of *Oliver!*, *Maggie May* and *Blitz!* (the latter production commemorating the 50th anniversary of the real thing), and the inclusion of one of his early songs, 'Rock With The Caveman', in the movie *The Flintstones*, in a version by Big Audio Dynamite. In December 1994 Bart's rehabilitation was complete when producer Cameron Mackintosh presented a major new production of *Oliver!* at the London Palladium, starring Jonathan Pryce. In a gesture rare in the cut-throat world of showbusiness, Mackintosh returned a portion of the show's rights to the composer (Bart had sold them during the bad old days), thereby assuring him an 'income for life'.

● FURTHER READING: *Bart!: The Unauthorized Life & Times, Ins & Outs, Ups & Downs Of Lionel Bart*, David Roper.

BARTHOLOMEW, DAVE

b. 24 December 1920, Edgard, Louisiana, USA. Dave Bartholomew was one of the most important shapers of New Orleans R&B and rock 'n' roll during the 50s. A producer, arranger, songwriter, bandleader and artist, Bartholomew produced and co-wrote most of Fats Domino's major hits for Imperial Records. Bartholomew started playing the trumpet as a child, encouraged by his father, a Dixieland jazz tuba player. He performed in marching bands throughout the 30s and then on a Mississippi riverboat band led by Fats Pichon beginning in 1939, and learned songwriting basics during a stint in the US Army. Upon his return to New Orleans in the late 40s he formed his first band, which became one of the city's most popular. He also backed Little Richard on some early recordings. Bartholomew worked for several labels, including Specialty, Aladdin and De Luxe, for whom he had a big hit in 1949 with 'Country Boy'. In the same year he started a long-term association with Imperial as a producer and arranger. The previous year Bartholomew had discovered Domino in New Orleans' Hideaway Club and he introduced him to Imperial. They collaborated on 'The Fat Man', which, in 1950, became the first of over a dozen hits co-authored by the pair and produced by Bartholomew. Others included 'Blue Monday', 'Walking To New Orleans', 'Let The Four Winds Blow', 'I'm In Love Again', 'Whole Lotta Loving', 'My Girl Josephine' and 'I'm Walkin'', the latter also becoming a hit for Ricky Nelson. Bartholomew's other credits included Smiley Lewis's 'I Hear You Knocking' (later a hit for Dave Edmunds) and 'One Night' (later a hit for Elvis

Presley, with its lyrics tamed), Lloyd Price's 'Lawdy Miss Clawdy', and records for Shirley And Lee, Earl King, Roy Brown, Huey 'Piano' Smith, Bobby Mitchell, Chris Kenner, Robert Parker, Frankie Ford and Snooks Eaglin. In 1963, Imperial was sold to Liberty Records, and Bartholomew declined an invitation to move to their Hollywood base, preferring to stay in New Orleans. In 1972, Chuck Berry reworked 'My Ding-A-Ling', a song Bartholomew had penned in 1952, and achieved his only US number 1 single. Although Bartholomew, who claims to have written over 4,000 songs, recorded under his own name, his contribution was primarily as a backstage figure. He recorded a Dixieland album in 1981 and in the early 90s was still leading a big band at occasional special events such as the New Orleans Jazz & Heritage Festival.

● ALBUMS: *Fats Domino Presents Dave Bartholomew* (Imperial 1961)★★★, *New Orleans House Party* (Imperial 1963)★★★, *Jump Children* (Pathe Marconi 1984)★★, *The Monkey* (Pathe Marconi 1985)★★, *Heritage* (1986)★★, *Graciously* (1987)★★, *The Spirit Of New Orleans* (1993)★★★.

● COMPILATIONS: *The Best Of Dave Bartholomew: The Classic New Orleans R&B Band Sound* (Stateside 1989)★★★★.

BASIN STREET BOYS

This four-piece vocal group was formed in 1945 in Los Angeles, California, USA, by Ormand Wilson. Wilson had originally been taught the guitar by Steve Gibson, whose band was called the Basin Street Boys, and so when Wilson formed his own band he named it after Gibson's as a mark of respect. The other three singers in Wilson's band were Gene Price, Reuben Saunders and Arthur Rainwater (aka Artie Waters), and they performed in a style in keeping with the nascent R&B boom. They signed with the local Exclusive Records label and their debut release was backing Judy Carroll on 'I Want To Love And Be Loved'. Their first effort under their own name, 'Jumpin' At The Jubilee', earned them a local following, but it was the ballad 'I Sold My Heart To The Junkman' that established their name (Patti Labelle And The Blue Belles later took the song into the charts). With a great deal of radio support for the single, the Basin Street Boys toured the USA during 1947, including a date at the Apollo Theatre in New York. In the meantime, singles such as 'This Is The End Of A Dream', 'I'm Gonna Write A letter To My Baby', 'I'll Get Along Somehow' and 'Summertime Gal' also failed to chart, but the group maintained a strong local following. In 1948 the group was renamed Ormand Wilson And The Basin Street Boys and moved to Mercury Records, but, starved of any commercial success, the Basin Street Boys broke up in 1951.

BASS, RALPH

b. 1 May 1911, New York City, New York, USA. A pivotal figure in the history of R&B, Bass began his career during the 40s, promoting live jazz shows in Los Angeles. He subsequently worked for Black And White Records, producing 'Open The Door, Richard' for Jack McVea, but later left to found several small-scale outlets with releases by Errol Garner and Dexter Gordon. Bass also recorded (Little) Esther Phillips, the Robins and Johnny Otis for the Savoy label, and in 1951 became one of the era's first independent producers through the aegis of the Cincinnati-based King company. Armed with his own outlet, Federal, and its Armo publishing wing, he built an impressive roster of acts around Hank Ballard And The Midnighters, the Dominoes and James Brown, whom Bass signed in 1955 on hearing a demo disc at an Atlanta radio station. Although initially unimpressed by the singer's untutored delivery, King managing director Syd Nathan changed his mind when 'Please Please Please' became a bestseller. Brown remained a Federal artist until 1960 but was switched to the parent outlet when Bass departed for Chess Records. The producer brought Etta James and Pigmeat Markham to his new employers, and in turn, worked with several established acts, including Muddy Waters, Howlin' Wolf and Ramsey Lewis. Bass remained with the label until the mid-70s when its Chicago office was closed. He continued to record R&B acts, the masters from which were latterly compiled on a series of albums under the generic title *I Didn't Give A Damn If Whites Bought It*.

BAXTER, LES

b. 14 March 1922, Mexia, Texas, USA, d. 15 January 1996, Palm Springs, California, USA. Baxter studied piano at the Detroit Conservatory before moving to Los Angeles for further studies at Pepperdine College. Abandoning a concert career as a pianist he turned to popular music as a singer, and at the age of 23 he joined Mel Tormé's Mel-Tones, singing on Artie Shaw records such as 'What Is This Thing Called Love'. He then turned to arranging and conducting for Capitol Records in 1950 and was responsible for early Nat 'King' Cole hits 'Mona Lisa' and 'Too Young'. In 1953 he scored his first film, the sailing travelogue *Tanga Tika*. With his own orchestra he released a number of hits including 'Ruby' (1953), 'Unchained Melody' (1955) and 'Poor People Of Paris' (1956). He also achieved success with concept albums of his own orchestral suites, *Le Sacre Du Sauvage*, *Festival Of The Gnomes*, *Ports Of Pleasure* and *Brazil Now*, the first three for Capitol and the fourth on Gene Norman's Crescendo label. Baxter had obvious skill in writing Latin music for strings, but he did not restrict his activities to recording. As he once told *Soundtrack!* magazine, 'I never turn anything down'. In the 60s he formed the Balladeers, a besuited and conservative folk group that at one time featured a slim and youthful David Crosby. He operated in radio as musical director of *Halls Of Ivy* and the Bob Hope and Abbott & Costello shows; he also worked on films and later composed and conducted scores for Roger Corman's Edgar Allan Poe films and other horror stories and teenage musicals, including *Comedy Of Terrors* (1963), *Muscle Beach Party* (1964), *The Dunwich Horror* (1970) and *Frogs* (1972). When soundtrack work reduced in the 80s he scored music for theme parks and seaworlds. In the 90s Baxter was widely celebrated, alongside Martin Denny (for whom he had written 'Quiet Village') and Arthur Lyman, as one of the progenitors of what had become known as the 'exotica' movement. In his 1996 appreciation for *Wired* magazine, writer David Toop remembered Baxter thus: 'Baxter offered package tours in sound, selling tickets to sedentary tourists who wanted to stroll around some taboo emotions before lunch, view a pagan ceremony, go wild in the sun or conjure a demon, all without leaving home hi-fi comforts in the white suburbs.'

● ALBUMS: *Le Sacre Du Sauvage* 10-inch album (Capitol

1952)★★★, *Music Of Prince Di Candriano* (1953)★★★, *Festival Of The Gnomes* (Capitol 1953)★★★, *Music Out Of The Moon* 10-inch album (Capitol 1953)★★★, *Music For Peace Of Mind* 10-inch album (Capitol 1953)★★★, *Le Sacre Du Savage* (Capitol 1954)★★★, *Thinking Of You* (Capitol 1954)★★★, *The Passions* (Capitol 1954)★★★, *Arthur Murray Modern Waltzes* (1955)★★★, *Kaleidoscope* (Capitol 1955)★★★, *Tamboo!* (Capitol 1956)★★★, *Caribbean Moonlight* (Capitol 1956)★★★, *Skins!* (Capitol 1957)★★★, *Round The World* (Capitol 1957)★★★, *Midnight On The Cliffs* (Capitol 1957)★★★, *Ports Of Pleasure* (Capitol 1957)★★★, *Space Escapade* (Capitol 1958)★★★, *Selections From South Pacific* (Capitol 1958)★★★, *Love Is A Fabulous Thing* (Capitol 1958)★★★, *Wild Guitars* (Capitol 1959)★★★, *African Jazz* (Capitol 1959)★★★, *Young Pops* (Capitol 1960)★★★, *The Sacred Idol* film soundtrack (Capitol 1960)★★, *Cry Of Teen Drums* (Capitol 1960)★★★, *Barbarian* film soundtrack (American International 1960)★★, *Broadway '61* (1961)★★★, *Alakazam The Great* film soundtrack (Vee Jay 1961)★★, *Jewels Of The Sea* (Capitol 1961)★★★, *The Sensational! Les Baxter* (Capitol 1962)★★★, *Academy Award Winners 1963 (And Other Outstanding Motion Picture Themes)* (Reprise 1963)★★★, *Brazil Now!* (1967)★★★, *Hell's Belles* film soundtrack (Sidewalk 1969)★★★, *The Dunwich Horror* film soundtrack (American International 1970)★★★, *Bora Bora* film soundtrack (American International 1970)★★, *The Banshee* (Citadel 1970)★★★.

● COMPILATIONS: *Baxter's Best* (Capitol 1960)★★★, *Lost Episodes* (Dionysus 1996)★★★.

BAY BOPS

This vocal quartet was formed in Brooklyn, New York, USA, in 1957 by Barney Zarzana, Danny Zipfel, Bobby Serrao and George Taylor Jnr. 'Joannie', arranged by a young Neil Sedaka, was their debut Coral single in March 1958 and it went on to sell over a quarter of a million copies. Appearances on Dick Clark's television show and the *Dean Martin Telethon*, plus tours with the Drifters and Flamingos, helped to make the Bay Bops perhaps the most well-known white doo-wop group of the time. After their second single, 'My Darling, My Sweet'/'To The Party', in May 1958, the group broke up when Zipfel started another vocal group. The three remaining Bay Bops used the Ravens' Lou Frazier as lead for brief time. In the mid-60s Zipfel recorded for MGM Records without a great deal of success. In 1958 a new version of the Bay Bops was formed by Barney Zarzana and his brothers Michael, Vinnie and Sal, but they did not record.

BEAVERS

This four-piece vocal group was formed in 1949 in New York, USA, when a music school voice teacher, Joe Thomas, encouraged four of his most talented students, Fred Hamilton (tenor), John Wilson (baritone), Raymond Johnson (bass) and Dick Palmer (tenor), to form a group, and secured them a recording contract with Coral Records. The group released two beautiful singles for Coral, 'If You See Tears In My Eyes' and 'I'd Rather Be Wrong Than Blue', neither of which were hits. The Beavers' success did not come under their own name but as the Hamptones, with Lionel Hampton And His Orchestra, featuring Wes

Montgomery on guitar, when they reached number 4 in the R&B charts in 1950 with a cover version of the Ames Brothers' 'Ragmop'. The Beavers also backed Herb Lance on 'That Lucky Old Son' (number 6 R&B, 1949). The Beavers broke up in 1950 when Johnson and Palmer left to join the Blenders. Johnson joined the Marshall Brothers in 1951.

BECAUD, GILBERT

b. Francois Silly, 24 October 1927, Toulon, France. A popular singer-songwriter in France in the 50s and 60s, rivalling other popular balladeers such as Charles Trenet and Charles Aznavour, Becaud studied music in Nice and started writing songs around 1946. His first collaborator was lyricist Pierre Delanoe, and one of their first successes was 'Je T'ai Dans La Peau' for Edith Piaf in 1950. He served as an accompanist for Piaf, and other artists such as Jacques Pills. Later he sang in cabaret, and made his first stage appearance in 1952 at Versailles. Two years later a dramatic performance at the Olympia Music Hall gained him the title of 'Monsieur 1000 Volts', and elevated him to national stardom. In the early 50s Becaud had hit records with 'Les Croix', 'Quand Tu Danses' and 'Mes Mains'. Subsequent successes included 'Dimanche A Orly', 'Le Jour Ou La Pluie Viendra', 'Couventine', 'Heureusement, Y'a Les Copains', 'Viens Danser' and 'Tu Le Regretteras'. In 1958, 'The Day The Rains Came', written with Delanoe and Carl Sigman, became a UK number 1 for Jane Morgan, and in 1962 Morgan also recorded their 'What Now My Love', although it was Shirley Bassey's dramatic version which had the most chart impact. The song was revived by Sonny And Cher in 1966 and was later covered by many other artists including Frank Sinatra. In the following year, Vikki Carr's emotive rendering of 'It Must Be Him' ('Seul Sur Son Etoile'), written with veteran lyricist Mack David, made both the US and UK Top 5. A few years earlier, Becaud's 'Je T'Appartiens' became an international success for the Everly Brothers under the title of 'Let It Be Me' (with Delanoe and Mann Curtis). Becaud himself had a UK hit in 1975 with 'A Little Love And Understanding', written with Marcel Stellman. His other collaborators have included Louis Amade, Maurice Vidalin and the English librettist and lyricist Julian More, with whom he worked on *Roza*, the 1987 Broadway musical based on Romain Gary's novel *La Vie Devant Soi'*. Georgia Brown starred as a 'crusty, retired prostitute who raises the illegitimate offsprings of hookers', but not for long - the show closed after only 12 performances.

● ALBUMS: *Et Maintenant ... Gilbert Becaud* (1964)★★★★, *Gilbert Becaud* (EMI 1968)★★★, *Becaud Olympia '70* (EMI 1970)★★, *A Little Love And Understanding* (Decca 1975)★★★.
● COMPILATIONS: *Collection* (EMI Germany 1983)★★★, *Disque D'or, Volumes 1 & 2* (EMI France 1983)★★★.

BELAFONTE, HARRY

b. Harold George Belafonte, 1 March 1927, Harlem, New York, USA. In recent years, the former 'King Of Calypso' has become better known for his work with UNICEF and his enterprise with USA For Africa. Prior to that, Belafonte had an extraordinarily varied life. His early career was spent as an actor, until he had time to demonstrate his silky smooth and gently relaxing singing voice. He appeared as Joe in Oscar Hammerstein's *Carmen Jones*; an adaptation of *Carmen* by Bizet, and in 1956 he was snapped up by RCA Victor. Belafonte was then at the forefront of the calypso craze, which was a perfect vehicle for his happy-go-lucky folk songs. Early hits included 'Jamaica Farewell', 'Mary's Boy Child' and the classic transatlantic hit 'Banana Boat Song' with its unforgettable refrain: 'Day-oh, dayyy-oh, daylight come and me wanna go home'. *Calypso* became the first ever album to sell a million copies, and spent 31 weeks at the top of the US charts. Belafonte continued throughout the 50s with incredible success. He was able to cross over into many markets appealing to pop, folk and jazz fans, as well as to the ethnic population with whom he became closely associated, particularly during the civil rights movement. He appeared in many films including *Island In The Sun*, singing the title song, and *Odds Against Tomorrow*. His success as an album artist was considerable; between 1956 and 1962 he was hardly ever absent from the album chart. *Belafonte At Carnegie Hall* spent over three years in the charts, and similar success befell *Belafonte Returns To Carnegie Hall*, featuring Miriam Makeba, the Chad Mitchell Trio and Odetta, with a memorable recording of 'There's A Hole In My Bucket'. Throughout the 60s Belafonte was an ambassador of human rights and a most articulate speaker at rallies and on television. His appeal as a concert hall attraction was immense; no less than seven of his albums were recorded in concert. Although his appearances in the bestseller lists had stopped by the 70s he remained an active performer and recording artist, and continued to appear on film, although in lightweight movies such as *Buck And The Preacher* and *Uptown Saturday Night*. In the mid-80s he was a leading light in the USA For Africa appeal and sang on 'We Are The World'. His sterling work continued into the 90s with UNICEF. Belafonte was one of the few black artists who broke down barriers of class and race, and should be counted alongside Dr. Martin Luther King as a major figure in achieving equal rights for blacks in America through his work in popular music.

● ALBUMS: *Mark Twain And Other Folk Favorites* (RCA Victor 1955)★★★, *Belafonte* (RCA Victor 1956)★★★★, *Calypso* (RCA Victor 1956)★★★★, *An Evening With Belafonte* (RCA Victor 1957)★★★★, *Belafonte Sings Of The Caribbean* (RCA Victor 1957)★★★, *Belafonte Sings The Blues* (RCA Victor 1958)★★★, *Love Is A Gentle Thing* (RCA Victor 1959)★★★, with Lena Horne *Porgy And Bess* film soundtrack (RCA Victor 1959)★★★★, *Belafonte At Carnegie Hall* (RCA Victor 1959)★★★★, *My Lord What A Mornin'* (RCA Victor 1960)★★★, *Belafonte Returns To Carnegie Hall* (RCA Victor 1960)★★★, *Swing Dat Hammer* (RCA Victor 1960)★★★, *At Home And Abroad* (RCA Victor 1961)★★★, *Jump Up Calypso* (RCA Victor 1961)★★★★, *The Midnight Special* (RCA Victor 1962)★★★, *The Many Moods Of Belafonte* (RCA Victor 1962)★★★, *To Wish You A Merry Christmas* (RCA Victor 1962)★★★, *Streets I Have Walked* (RCA Victor 1963)★★★, *Belafonte At The Greek Theatre* (RCA Victor 1964)★★★, *Ballads Blues And Boasters* (RCA 1964)★★, with Miriam Makeba *An Evening With Belafonte/Makeba* (RCA 1965)★★★, with Nana Mouskouri *An Evening With Belafonte/Mouskouri* (RCA 1966)★★★★, *In My Quiet Room* (RCA 1966)★★★, *Calypso In Brass* (RCA 1967)★★, *Belafonte On Campus* (RCA 1967)★★, *Homeward Bound* (RCA 1970)★★, *Play Me* (RCA 1976)★★★, *Turn The World Around* (Columbia 1977)★★, *Loving You Is Where I*

Belong (Columbia 1981)★★, *Paradise In Gazankulu* (EMI-Manhattan 1988)★★, *Belafonte '89* (EMI 1989)★★.
● COMPILATIONS: *Pure Gold* (RCA 1975)★★★★, *A Legendary Performer* (RCA 1978)★★★, *The Very Best Of Harry Belafonte* (RCA 1982)★★★, *20 Golden Greats* (Deja Vu 1985)★★★, *Collection* (Castle 1987)★★★, *Banana Boat Song* (Entertainers 1988)★★★, *All Time Greatest Hits, Volume 1* (RCA 1989)★★★★, *All Time Greatest Hits, Volume 2* (RCA 1989)★★★, *All Time Greatest Hits, Volume 3* (RCA 1989)★★★, *Day-O And Other Hits* (RCA 1990)★★★.
● FURTHER READING: *Belafonte*, A.J. Shaw.
● FILMS: *Carmen Jones* (1955), *Island In The Sun* (1957), *The World, The Flesh And The Devil* (1958), *Odds Against Tomorrow* (1959), *The Angel Levine* (1969).

BELAFONTE AT CARNEGIE HALL - HARRY BELAFONTE ★★★★

In 1959, Belafonte was probably at the peak of his popularity when he made this double-album set in a venue that, in the 50s, was usually the home of classical performers rather than pop artists. His magnetic personality, and an impressive mixture of material that ranges from international folk songs such as 'Hava Nageela', 'Sylvie', 'Day-O' and 'Jamaican Farewell', to the traditional 'Danny Boy' and even a sea shanty, 'Shenandoah', ensured a stay of 86 weeks in the US chart (peaking at number 3) and a Gold Disc award. The album also won a Grammy award for Best Engineering Contribution.
● TRACKS: *Darlin' Cora*; *Sylvie*; *John Henry*; *Take My Mother Home*; *Jamaican Farewell*; *Man Piaba, All My Trials, Man Smart*; *Matilda*.

BELL, FREDDIE, AND THE BELLBOYS

This early US rock 'n' roll six-piece outfit was led by singer Freddie Bell (b. 29 September 1931, South Philadelphia, Pennsylvania, USA). Their slightly 'big band' style of rock 'n' roll included a version of Willie Mae Thornton's 'Hound Dog' for the Teen label in 1955. Elvis Presley saw them performing the song live in April 1956 and recorded his own version in July. The Bellboys achieved another landmark by appearing in the first rock 'n' roll movie - *Rock Around The Clock* - in 1956. They were also the first US rock act to tour the UK, supporting Tommy Steele in 1956. Their best-known number was also released that year, 'Giddy Up A Ding Dong', and became a number 4 hit in the UK. Other singles included 'The Hucklebuck', 'Teach You To Rock' and 'Rockin' Is My Business'. Another film appearance was in the 1964 pop exploitation movie *The Swingin' Set* (*Get Yourself A College Girl* in the USA), where Roberta Linn sang with them. The Animals, the Dave Clark Five and the Standells also featured. On the strength of a few hits Bell has sustained a career for over 40 years. Now performing as the Freddie Bell Show, he has a residency in Las Vegas for most of the year and tours the world in the remaining weeks.
● ALBUMS: *Rock 'n' Roll All Flavours* (Mercury 1958)★★★, *Bells Are Swinging* (20th Century 1964)★★.

BELL, T.D.

b. 26 December 1922, Lee County, Texas, USA. Bell did not take up blues guitar until his early twenties, following military service. The major influence on his style was 'T-Bone' Walker. His band was one of the major attractions on the Austin scene, and backed visiting artists at the Victory Grill, and on tour through west Texas, Arizona and New Mexico. Bell gave up playing in the early 70s when disco made live musicians uneconomical, but resumed in the late 80s in partnership with his long-time associate Erbie Bowser; they were still an impressive team.
● ALBUMS: *It's About Time* (1992)★★★.

BELLS ARE RINGING

Despite its unlikely setting, a telephone answering service, the stage musical *Bells Are Ringing* benefited from a strong and original book, by Betty Comden and Adolph Green (they also wrote the lyrics) and some delightful tunes by Jule Styne. The show, which opened at the Shubert Theatre in New York on 29 November 1956, was created by Comden and Green for Judy Holliday, with whom they had worked in the past. Holliday played the role of Ella Peterson, an employee of Susanswerphone, who becomes romantically involved with one of her unseen clients and also solves the problems of others. She won a Tony Award for her delicious performance, and another Tony went to Sydney Chaplin as best actor. Among the show's songs were two that have become standards, 'The Party's Over' and 'Just In Time', along with several other entertaining numbers such as 'Long Before I Knew You', 'Drop That Name', 'I'm Going Back', 'It's A Simple Little System' and 'Is It A Crime?'. *Bells Are Ringing* ran on Broadway for 924 performances, and a further 292 in London. A 1987 West End revival starred Lesley Mackie, and the Goodspeed Opera House in Connecticut mounted a production in 1990. Judy Holliday recreated her role for the 1960 screen version.

BELLSON, LOUIS

b. Louis Paul Balassoni, 6 July 1924, Rock Falls, Illinois, USA. Drummer Bellson first gained public attention by winning a Gene Krupa talent contest in 1940 and one of his early professional jobs was with Krupa's old boss, Benny Goodman. Bellson also worked with the big bands of Tommy Dorsey, Harry James and in 1951 joined Duke Ellington, where his dynamic and aggressive style was startlingly different to that of his sometimes lackadaisical predecessor, Sonny Greer. Ellington used a number of Bellson's compositions, including 'The Hawk Talks' (written for James) and 'Skin Deep', a marathon drum feature. After leaving Ellington, Bellson recorded and toured with small groups and sporadic big bands. In the mid-50s he returned briefly to Tommy Dorsey and also recorded for Norman Granz, accompanying Louis Armstrong, Benny Carter, Ella Fitzgerald, Oscar Peterson, Art Tatum and others. In these settings he proved to be a restrained accompanist, thus confounding those who had considered him merely a thunderer. From the early 60s until her death he was musical director/accompanist to his wife, singer Pearl Bailey, but continued to record and tour with small and large bands under his own name and (in the mid-60s) made brief return visits to Ellington and James. Apart from his jazz compositions, Bellson has also written for the ballet and for jazz and symphony orchestra combinations. He is wholly ambidextrous, displays remarkable finger control, and is one of the most technically accomplished drummers jazz has known. A sought-after teacher and clinician, he is greatly admired by fellow musicians. When on tour Bellson frequently searches out orphanages and the like, putting on free shows. Onstage, he is a spectacular and exciting performer. Offstage, he is quiet, sincere and shy, and is one of the best-liked musicians of his era of jazz.

● ALBUMS: *Duke Ellington's Coronets* (1951)★★★, *Just Jazz All Stars* 10-inch album (Capitol 1952)★★★, *Ellington Uptown* (1952)★★★, *The Exciting Mr Bellson And His Big Band* 10-inch album (Norgran 1954)★★★, *Louis Bellson With Wardell Gray* 10-inch album (Norgran 1954)★★★, *Louis Bellson Quintet* (1954)★★★, *Journey Into Love* (Norgran 1954)★★★, *Louis Bellson And His Drums* reissued as *Skin Deep* (Norgran 1954)★★★, *The Driving Louis Bellson* reissued as *The Hawk Talks* (Norgran 1955)★★★, *Concerto For Drums* (Norgran 1956)★★★, *Drumorama!* (Verve 1957)★★★, *Louis Bellson At The Flamingo* (Verve 1958)★★★, *Lets Call It Swing* (Verve 1958)★★★, *Music Romance And Especially Love* (Verve 1958)★★★, *Drummers Holiday* (Verve 1959)★★★, *The Brilliant Bellson Sound* (Verve 1960)★★★, *Louis Bellson Swings Jules Styne* (Verve 1960)★★★, *Big Band Jazz AtThe Summit* (Roulette 1962)★★★, *With Bells On* (Vogue 1962)★★★, with Gene Krupa *The Mighty Two* (Roulette 1962)★★★, *Around The World In Percussion* (Roulette 1962)★★★, *Thunderbird* (Impulse 1963)★★★, with Lalo Schifrin *Explorations* (Roulette 1964)★★★, *The Dynamic Drums Of Louie Bellson* (1968)★★★, *Louie In London* (1970)★★★, with Duke Ellington *Duke's Big 4* (1973)★★★, *150 MPH* (1974)★★★, *The Louie Bellson Explosion* (1975)★★★, *Louie Bellson's 7* (1976)★★★, *Ecué - Ritmos Cubanos* (1977)★★★, *Prime Time* (1977)★★★, *Sunshine Rock* (Pablo 1977)★★★, *Note Smoking* (1978)★★★, *Raincheck* (1978)★★★, *Intensive Care* (1978)★★★, *Louie Bellson Jam* (Pablo Jazz 1978)★★★, *Matterhorn* (Pablo 1978)★★★, *Side Track* (Concord Jazz 1979)★★★, *Dynamite!* (1979)★★★, *Originals* (Stash 1979)★★★, *Louie Bellson's Big Band Explosion Live* (PRT 1979)★★★, *London Scene* (Concord Jazz 1980)★★★, *The London Concert* (1981)★★★, *Cool Cool Blue* (Pablo 1982)★★★, *The London Gig* (Pablo 1982)★★★, *Louis Bellson Jam* (Pablo 1982)★★★, *East Side Suite* (Music Masters 1987)★★★, *Live At Jazz Showcase* (Concord 1987)★★★, *Hot* (Music Masters 1987)★★★, *Jazz Giants* (Limelight 1989)★★★, *1959 At The Flamingo Hotel* (Jazz Hour 1993)★★★, *Raincheck* (Concord 1995)★★★, *Their Time Was The Greatest* (Concord 1996)★★★.

BELMONTS

The Belmonts were one of the leading American doo-wop groups of the late 50s and comprised Angelo D'Aleo (b. 3 February 1940, Bronx, New York, USA), Carlo Mastrangelo (b. 5 October 1938, Bronx, New York, USA) and Freddie Milano (b. 22 August 1939, Bronx, New York, USA). Their leader was Dion DiMucci, who left for a solo career in 1960. The band soldiered on for three more years after being signed to a new record label, Sabina, with Frank Lyndon replacing Mastrangelo in 1962. They had enough fans to give them six further hits, including a smooth version of the Ink Spots' hit 'Don't Get Around Much Anymore'. They reformed briefly with Dion in 1967, 1972 and 1973. Their most memorable work remains in the 50s with Dion.

● COMPILATIONS: *The Belmonts' Carnival Of Hits* (Sabina 1962)★★★, *Laurie, Sabrina & United Artists Sides Volume 1* (Ace 1995)★★★★.

BELTRAN, LOLA

b. Maria Lucial Beltran Ruiz, 7 March 1932, El Rosario, Sinaloa, Mexico, d. 23 March 1996, Mexico City, Mexico. Long hailed as 'the queen of Mexican ranchera', by the time of her death in 1996 Beltran had appeared in over 50 movies and recorded over 100 albums. One of seven children born to Maria de los Angeles Ruiz del Beltran and Pedro Beltran Felix, her singing carer began at church. Her teacher, Maestro Gallardo, recognized her restless spirit and encouraged her to address songs outside of the church lexicon. Through him she learned the ballads and romances of composers such as Pedro Infante and Augustin Lara. She subsequently began to perform with a variety of local mariachi groups, also working with the group Calavera and the Mexican composer José Alfredo Jimenez. Her enormous popularity has much to do with her constant championing of the underdog in Mexican society, with songs describing the hardships of the country's millions of peasants and migrant workers. A passionate vocalist, Beltran's emotive delivery has influenced generations of her compatriots, from those recording traditional music to contemporary pop artists. Indeed, Linda Ronstadt once called her 'the greatest voice to come out of Mexico.' She began her career in the 50s, quickly earning the sobriquet Lola La Grande (Lola The Great) for her pioneering of ranchera music. As she once told the press, 'The composer writes the words and music. I simply put in the passion and feeling.' Among Beltran's most famous performances have been for US presidents - from Eisenhower to Nixon, as well as French president Charles De Gaulle and Ethiopian emperor Haile Selassie.

BELVIN, JESSE

b. 15 December 1932, San Antonio, Texas, USA, d. 6 February 1960. Raised in Los Angeles, Belvin became a part of the city's flourishing R&B scene while in his teens. He was featured on 'All The Wine Is Gone', a 1950 single by Big Jay McNeely, but his career was then interrupted by a spell in the US Army. 'Earth Angel', a collaboration with two fellow conscripts, was recorded successfully by the Penguins, while Belvin enjoyed a major hit in his own right with 'Goodnight My Love', a haunting, romantic ballad adopted by disc jockey Alan Freed as the closing theme to his highly influential radio show. He also recorded with fellow songwriter Marvin Phillips as Jesse & Marvin, achieving a Top 10 R&B hit in 1953 with 'Dream Girl'. In 1958 Belvin formed a vocal quintet, the Shields, to record for Dot Records the national Top 20 hit 'You Cheated'. That same year the singer was signed to RCA Records, who harboured plans to shape him in the mould of Nat 'King' Cole and Billy Eckstine. Further hits, including 'Funny' and 'Guess Who' - the latter of which was written by his wife and manager Jo Ann - offered a cool, accomplished vocal style suggestive of a lengthy career, but Belvin died, along with his wife, following a car crash in February 1960.

● ALBUMS: *The Casual Jesse Belvin* (Crown 1959)★★★★, *The Unforgettable Jesse Belvin* (Crown 1959)★★★★, *Just Jesse Belvin* (RCA Victor 1959)★★★, *Mr. Easy* (RCA Victor 1960)★★★, *True To Myself* (Warners 1996)★★★.

● COMPILATIONS: *Yesterdays* (RCA 1975)★★★, *Memorial Album* (Ace 1984)★★★★, *Hang Your Tears Out To Dry* (Earth Angel 1987)★★★, *Jesse Belvin: The Blues Balladeer* (Specialty 1990)★★★★.

BENNETT, ROBERT RUSSELL

b. 15 June 1894, Kansas City, Missouri, USA, d. 18 August 1981. A composer, arranger, conductor, and the leading orchestrator of Broadway musicals from the 20s through until 1960. At the age of 10 Bennett was giving piano recitals, and in his teens he studied harmony, counterpoint and composition, and also played in dancehalls and movie houses. While serving in the US Army during World War I, he conducted and scored the music for various bands, and on his release, secured a job with the music publishers T.B. Harms & Company. From then on, for more than 30 years, he orchestrated over 300 scores for Broadway's leading composers, including *Rose-Marie, Show Boat, Roberta, Very Warm For May, Of Thee I Sing, Girl Crazy, The Band Wagon, Porgy And Bess, Anything Goes, Carmen Jones, Bloomer Girl, Kiss Me, Kate, Finian's Rainbow, Lady In The Dark, Annie Get Your Gun, Bloomer Girl, Music In The Air, On A Clear Day You Can See Forever, Gay Divorce, Jumbo, Bells Are Ringing, Camelot, My Fair Lady*, and Richard Rodgers and Oscar Hammerstein II's blockbusters *Oklahoma!, Carousel, South Pacific* and *The Sound Of Music*. Bennett also worked on some 30 films, and won an Oscar for his scoring of *Oklahoma!* in 1955. Three years earlier he had orchestrated Richard Rodgers' music for *Victory At Sea*, presented on US television. He also composed classical music, several operas, symphonies, and many other orchestral, solo and chamber pieces, but it is for his work for Broadway that he will be best remembered. Although composers including Jerome Kern, Cole Porter, George Gershwin, Arthur Schwartz, Harold Arlen and Frederick Loewe wrote the music, the form in which it was heard in the theatre depended on Robert Russell Bennett, with his orchestral colourings, his empathy with lyrics and the book, and the inspired selection of *tempi* - particularly impressive in the overtures to *My Fair Lady* and *Oklahoma!*.
● FURTHER READING: *Instrumentally Speaking*, Robert Russell Bennett.

BENNETT, WAYNE

b. 1934, Sulpher, Oklahoma, USA, d. 28 November 1992. A skilful blues guitarist, Bennett came to prominence in the mid-50s as a member of Otis Rush's Chicago-based band. From there he was picked by Joe Scott to join the touring and recording orchestra of Bobby Bland. With arrangements by Scott and scintillating solos by Bennett, Bland became the leading live attraction on the chitlin' circuit in the late 50s and early 60s. Bennett's playing also contributed to Bland's numerous hits of the era, such as 'I Pity The Fool' (1961) and 'Stormy Monday Blues' (1962). During this period, Bennett was also a session player for other Duke/Peacock artists such as Junior Parker and Gatemouth Brown. He left Bland's group in the late 60s and subsequently appeared on records by such blues artists as Buddy Guy, Fenton Robinson, Jimmy Reed and Jimmy Rogers. In 1981, Bennett was named Blues Guitarist of the Year by the National Blues Foundation and in the early 90s he was based in Louisiana performing with Willie Lockett and the Blues Krewe. Bennett died in November 1992 from heart failure.

BENNY GOODMAN STORY, THE

Hollywood biopics almost always present the same paradox: if the subject is interesting enough to make a film of his/her life, why meddle with the facts? Goodman, portrayed by Steve Allen, but providing his own playing for the soundtrack, had a rags-to-riches life story that simultaneously fulfilled the American Dream and every screenwriter's wildest fantasy. Unfortunately, in real life, Goodman was a single-minded perfectionist who became a household name and a millionaire before he had reached 30. In other words, all he did was practise obsessively and perform, which did not make for good visual drama. Hence, the reality of his dedication was jettisoned in favour of a sloppy story about a home-loving boy who made good. In the course of the film, Goodman periodically whines to his Ma, 'Don't be that way'. This allows the introduction of the tune of that name as the dutiful son's grateful acknowledgement to his mother, thus overlooking the fact that Edgar Sampson wrote the song for another bandleader, Chick Webb. Goodman's not inconsiderable streak of ruthlessness was also overlooked. Nevertheless, the film has some nice musical moments from Allen/Goodman, Teddy Wilson, Lionel Hampton and Gene Krupa in the small group numbers. The specially assembled big band includes Buck Clayton, Stan Getz, Conrad Gozzo, Urbie Green, Manny Klein and Murray McEachern and plays very well, even though it does not sound much like the real Goodman band of the late 30s. Ben Pollack and Kid Ory also appear, as does Harry James (in a close-up solo feature but not in long-shot - contractual reasons were suggested, specifically, too little money). For all this 1955 film's flaws, among which is the famous 1938 Carnegie Hall concert attended by 'longhairs' - in real life the seats were packed with swing-era fans and jitterbugs - it remains one of the least embarrassing of the earlier jazz biopics.

BENSON, AL

b. Arthur Leaner, 30 June 1908, Jackson, Mississippi, USA, d. 6 September 1978, Berrien Springs, Michigan, USA. By the age of seven, Benson was tap-dancing with his father's jazz band, and he went on to work in minstrel shows and to produce musicals. His restless energy led to a number of widely varying jobs, including Chief of Recreation for Jackson's black schools, a railroad cook, probation officer and storefront preacher. His radio career began on Chicago's WGES with a religious programme and then an R&B show that lasted until 1962. In the late 40s and early 50s he started a number of record labels, Old Swingmaster (one of his radio tags), Parrot and Blue Lake, recording such artists as J.B. Lenoir, Sunnyland Slim, Albert King, Willie Mabon and Little Willie Foster. Crash and The Blues each had a brief life during the 60s, releasing material by Magic Sam, Shakey Jake, Johnny 'Big Moose' Walker and others. Benson's flamboyant and self-willed character eventually undermined his status in the black community, although he was active in the civil rights movement, once hiring a plane to drop 5,000 copies of the US Constitution over Mississippi. In later years, he owned a record store in Michigan City before losing both legs due to ill health, which also eventually led to his death from heart failure.

BENTLEY, GLADYS ALBERTA

(aka Fatso Bentley) b. 12 August 1907, Pennsylvania, USA, d. 18 January 1960, Los Angeles, California, USA. A blues singer, pianist and male impersonator, Bentley moved to New York in her late teens to work at various Harlem nightspots, and was soon recording solo for OKeh Records

and with the Washboard Serenaders for RCA Victor. In the early 30s, she opened a nightspot, the Exclusive Club, and began arranging and directing her own shows, including the successful Ubangi Club Revue. In the early 40s, Bentley moved to California and started a fresh career as a blues shouter, recording in the style for small independents such as Excelsior, Flame, Top Hat and Swingtime. She was much in demand throughout the 50s until her death at home of pneumonia.
● COMPILATIONS: one track only *Boogie Blues - Women Sing And Play Boogie Woogie* (1983)★★, one track only *Tough Mamas* (1989)★★.

BENTON, BUSTER

b. Arley Benton, 19 July 1932, Texarkana, Arkansas, USA, d. 20 January 1996. Benton sang in a gospel choir as a young-ster, before moving in 1952 to Toledo, Ohio, where he began playing guitar and turned to the blues, influenced by Sam Cooke and B.B. King. Around the end of the 50s he settled in Chicago, where he led his own band and recorded for the Melloway, Twinight and Alteen labels. He owned the Stardust Lounge for some time in the early 70s but spent several years as guitarist with Willie Dixon. Benton had a hit for Jewel Records with 'Spider In My Stew' in the mid-70s, and recordings he made later for Ralph Bass were issued on several labels worldwide. In the 80s he recorded for Blue Phoenix, and despite some serious health problems he con-tinued to perform and record until his death in 1996.
● ALBUMS: *Spider In My Stew* (Ronn 1979)★★★, *Bluesbuster* (Red Lightnin 1980)★★★, *Buster Benton Is The Feeling* (Ronn 1980)★★★, *First Time In Europe* (Blue Phoenix 1985)★★★, *Blues At The Top* (Blue Phoenix 1987)★★★★, *Why Me?* (Ichiban 1988)★★★, *Money's The Name Of The Game* (Ichiban 1989)★★★, *I Like To Hear My Guitar Sing* (Ichiban 1992)★★★.

BERNABEI, MEMO

Bandleader Memo Bernabei had formerly worked with Ray Pearl, Arvin Dale, Jan Garber and Don Reid before forming his own musical congregation in 1958. Although this group proved highly popular in his native Los Angeles, California, USA, the chances of nationwide fame in the face of rock 'n' roll's onslaught had receded dramatically. Providing a diet of songs in the classic dance band tradition, including 'Bernabei's Bounce' and 'Memories Of You', the group secured dates at many ballrooms and hotels. Bernabei's main contracts came from the Chateau Ballroom (Los Angeles) and Golden West Ballroom (Norwalk), finding more permanent employment at the latter emporium as manager and leader of the house band. He would remain there for the rest of his professional musical career.

BERRY, CHUCK

b. Charles Edward Anderson Berry, 18 October 1926, San Jose, California, USA (although Berry states that he was born in St. Louis, Missouri). A seminal figure in the evolution of rock 'n' roll, Chuck Berry's influence as songwriter and gui-tarist is incalculable. His cogent songs captured adolescent life, yet the artist was 30 years old when he commenced recording. Introduced to music as a child, Berry learned guitar while in his teens, but this period was blighted by a three-year spell in Algoa Reformatory following a conviction

for armed robbery. On his release Berry undertook several blue-collar jobs while pursuing part-time spots in St. Louis bar bands. Inspired by Carl Hogan, guitarist in Louis Jordan's Timpani Five, and Charlie Christian, he continued to hone his craft and in 1951 purchased a tape recorder to capture ideas for compositions. The following year Berry joined Johnnie Johnson (piano) and Ebby Hardy (drums) in the house band at the Cosmopolitan Club. Over the ensuing months the trio became a popular attraction, playing a mix-ture of R&B, country/hillbilly songs and standards, particu-larly those of Nat 'King' Cole, on whom Berry modelled his cool vocal style. The guitarist also fronted his own group, the Chuck Berry Combo, at the rival Crank Club, altering his name to spare his father's embarrassment at such worldly pursuits.

In 1955, during a chance visit to Chicago, Berry met bluesman Muddy Waters, who advised the young singer to approach the Chess label. Berry's demo of 'Ida May', was suf-ficient to win a recording contract and the composition, reti-tled 'Maybellene', duly became his debut single. This ebul-lient performance was a runaway success, topping the R&B chart and reaching number 5 on the US pop listings. Its lustre was partially clouded by a conspiratorial publishing credit that required Berry to share the rights with Russ Fratto and disc jockey Alan Freed, in deference to his repeated air-play. This situation remained unresolved until 1986. Berry enjoyed further US R&B hits with 'Thirty Days' and 'No Money Down', but it was his third recording session that proved even more productive, producing a stream of clas-sics, 'Roll Over Beethoven', 'Too Much Monkey Business' and 'Brown-Eyed Handsome Man'. The artist's subsequent releases read like a lexicon of pop history - 'School Days' (a second R&B number 1), 'Rock And Roll Music' (all 1957), 'Sweet Little Sixteen', 'Reelin' And Rockin', 'Johnny B. Goode' (1958), 'Back In The USA', 'Let It Rock' (1960) and 'Bye Bye Johnny' (1960) are but a handful of the peerless songs written and recorded during this prolific period. In common with contemporary artists, Berry drew from both country and R&B music, but his sharp, often piquant, lyrics, clarified by the singer's clear diction, introduced a new dis-cipline to the genre. Such incomparable performances not only defined rock 'n' roll, they provided a crucial template for successive generations. Both the Beatles and Rolling Stones acknowledged their debt to Berry. The former recorded two of his compositions, taking one, 'Roll Over Beethoven', into the US charts, while the latter drew from his empirical catalogue on many occasions. This included 'Come On', their debut single, 'Little Queenie', 'You Can't Catch Me' and 'Around And Around', as well as non-Berry songs that nonetheless aped his approach. The Stones' read-ings of 'Route 66', 'Down The Road Apiece' and 'Confessin' The Blues' were indebted to their mentor's versions, while Keith Richards' rhythmic, propulsive guitar figures drew from Berry's style. Elsewhere, the Beach Boys rewrote 'Sweet Little Sixteen' as 'Surfin' USA' to attain their first mil-lion-seller, while countless other groups scrambled to record his songs, inspired by their unique combination of imme-diacy and longevity.

Between 1955 and 1960, Berry seemed unassailable. He enjoyed a run of 17 R&B Top 20 entries, appeared in the films *Go Johnny Go*, *Rock, Rock, Rock* and *Jazz On A Summer's Day*, the last of which documented the artist's performance at the 1958 *Newport Jazz Festival*, where he demonstrated the famed 'duckwalk' to a bemused audience. However, personal impropriety undermined Berry's personal and professional life when, on 28 October 1961, he was convicted under the Mann Act of 'transporting an under-age girl across state lines for immoral purposes'. Berry served 20 months in prison, emerging in October 1963 just as 'Memphis Tennessee', recorded in 1958, was providing him with his first UK Top 10 hit. He wrote several compositions during his incarceration, including 'Nadine', 'No Particular Place To Go', 'You Never Can Tell' and 'Promised Land', each of which reached the UK Top 30. Such chart success soon waned as the R&B bubble burst, and in 1966 Berry sought to regenerate his career by moving from Chess to Mercury Records. However, an ill-advised *Golden Hits* set merely featured re-recordings of old material, while attempts to secure a contemporary image on *Live At The Fillmore Auditorium* (recorded with the Steve Miller Band) and *Concerto In B. Goode* proved equally unsatisfactory. He returned to Chess Records in 1969 and immediately re-established his craft with the powerful 'Tulane'. *Back Home* and *San Francisco Dues* were cohesive selections and in-concert appearances showed a renewed purpose. Indeed, a UK performance at the 1972 Manchester Arts Festival not only provided half of Berry's *London Sessions* album, but also his biggest-ever hit. 'My Ding-A-Ling', a mildly ribald *double entendre* first recorded by Dave Bartholomew, topped both the US and UK charts, a paradox in the light of his own far superior compositions, which achieved lesser commercial plaudits. It was his last major hit, and despite several new recordings, including *Rockit*, a much-touted release on Atco, Berry became increasingly confined to the revival circuit. He gained an uncomfortable reputation as a hard, shrewd businessman and disinterested performer, backed by pick-up bands with whom he refused to rehearse. Tales abound within the rock fraternity of Berry's refusal to tell the band which song he was about to launch into. Pauses and changes would come about by the musicians watching Berry closely for an often disguised signal. Berry has insisted for years upon pre-payment of his fee, usually in cash, and he will only perform an encore after a further negotiation for extra payment. Berry's continued legal entanglements resurfaced in 1979 when he was sentenced to a third term of imprisonment following a conviction for income tax evasion. Upon release he embarked on a punishing world tour, but the subsequent decade proved largely unproductive musically and no new recordings were undertaken. In 1986, the artist celebrated his 60th birthday with gala performances in St. Louis and New York. Keith Richards appeared at the former, although relations between the two men were strained, as evinced in the resultant documentary *Hail! Hail! Rock 'N' Roll*, which provided an overview of Berry's career. Berry was inducted into the Rock And Roll Hall Of Fame the same year. Sadly, the 90s began with further controversy and allegations of indecent behaviour at the singer's Berry Park centre. Although these serve to undermine the individual, his stature as an essential figure in the evolution of popular music cannot be underestimated.

● ALBUMS: *After School Session* (Chess 1958)★★★★, *One Dozen Berrys* (Chess 1958)★★★★★, *Chuck Berry Is On Top* (Chess 1959)★★★★, *Rockin' At The Hops* (Chess 1960)★★★★, *New Juke-Box Hits* (Chess 1961)★★★, *Chuck Berry Twist* (Chess 1962)★★★, *More Chuck Berry* UK release (Pye 1963)★★★, *Chuck Berry On Stage* (Chess 1963)★★, *The Latest And The Greatest* (Chess 1964)★★★, with Bo Diddley *Two Great Guitars* (Chess 1964)★★★, *St. Louis To Liverpool* (Chess 1964)★★★★★, *Chuck Berry In London* (Chess 1965)★★★, *Fresh Berrys* (Chess 1965)★★★, *Golden Hits* new recordings (Mercury 1967)★★, *Chuck Berry In Memphis* (Mercury 1967)★★★, *Live At The Fillmore Auditorium* (Mercury 1967)★★, *From St. Louis To Frisco* (Mercury 1968)★★, *Concerto In B. Goode* (Mercury 1969)★★, *Back Home* (Chess 1970)★★, *San Francisco Dues* (Chess 1971)★★, *The London Chuck Berry Sessions* (Chess 1972)★★, *Bio* (Chess 1973)★★, *Chuck Berry* (Chess 1975)★★, *Live In Concert* (Magnum 1978)★★★, *Rockit* (Atco 1979)★★★, *Rock! Rock! Rock 'N' Roll!* (Atco 1980)★★, *Hail, Hail Rock 'N' Roll* film soundtrack (Chess 1987)★★, *On The Blues Side* (1993)★★.

● COMPILATIONS: *Chuck Berry's Greatest Hits* (Chess 1964)★★★★★, *Chuck Berry's Golden Decade* (Chess 1967)★★★★★, *Golden Decade, Volume 2* (Chess 1973)★★★★, *Golden Decade, Volume 3* (Chess 1974)★★★★, *Motorvatin'* (Chess 1977)★★★, *Spotlight On Chuck Berry* (PRT 1980)★★★, *The Great Twenty-Eight* (Chess/MCA 1982)★★★★★, *Chess Masters* (Chess 1983)★★★, *Reelin' And Rockin' (Live)* (Aura 1984)★★, *Rock 'N' Roll Rarities* (Chess/MCA 1986)★★, *More Rock 'N' Roll Rarities* (Chess/MCA 1986)★★, *Chicago Golden Years* (Vogue 1988)★★★, *Decade '55 To '65* (Platinum 1988)★★★, *Chess Box* 3-CD box set (Chess/MCA 1989)★★★★, *Missing Berries: Rarities, Volume 3* (Chess/MCA 1990)★★★, *The Chess Years* 9-CD box set (Charly 1991)★★★, *Oh Yeah!* (Charly 1994)★★★, *Poet Of Rock 'N' Roll* 4-CD box set (Charly 1995)★★★★★.

● VIDEOS: *The Legendary Chuck Berry* (Channel 5 1987), *Hail Hail Rock 'N' Roll* (CIC Video 1988), *Live At The Roxy* (Old Gold 1990), *Rock 'N' Roll Music* (BMG Video 1991).

● FURTHER READING: *Chuck Berry: Rock 'N' Roll Music*, Howard A. De Witt. *Chuck Berry: Mr Rock 'N' Roll*, Krista Reese. *Chuck Berry: The Autobiography*, Chuck Berry.

● FILMS: *Go Johnny Go* (1958), *American Hot Wax* (1976).

BERTELMANN, FRED

b. 7 October 1925, Germany. Teutonic opposite number to Britain's David Whitfield, his light operatic tenor was omnipresent on German radio and television in the late 50s. Darkly handsome and engaging before the cameras, he was briefly, if arguably, Germany's most popular singer - though commercial penetration into other territories was minor at most. Signed to Electrola, he enjoyed domestic chart success until the end of the decade, his biggest hit being 1958's 'Der Lachend Vagabund (The Laughing Vagabond)', on which he was accompanied by the vocal harmonies of the Hansen Quartet. Selling over two million copies, 'Der Lachend Vagabund' was one of Germany's all-time bestsellers. Between 1955 and 1963 he had 12 Top 40 hits in his homeland.

BEVERLEY SISTERS

This close-harmony UK vocal group consisted of three sisters; Joy Beverley (b. 1929) and twins Teddie and Babs (b. 1932) were all born in London, England, daughters of the singing comedy duo Coram and Mills. The girls discovered they could sing harmony on school hymns, with Teddie singing the low parts, ('down in her boots', as she puts it). They started recording in the early 50s with songs such as 'Ferry Boat Inn', 'My Heart Cries For You', and 'Teasin'', and later had hits with 'I Saw Mommy Kissing Santa Claus', 'Little Drummer Boy' and 'Little Donkey'. During 1953 they performed in the USA, appeared in a record-breaking theatre season in Blackpool, played at the London Palladium with Bob Hope and presented their own television series, *Three Little Girls In View*. Their act was particularly suited to cabaret because of its risqué element ('sassy, but classy', according to Ed Sullivan). Songs such as 'We Like To Do Things Like That', 'It's Illegal, It's Immoral Or It Makes You Fat' and 'He Like It, She Like It', inevitably led to one entitled 'We Have To Be So Careful All The Time'. They wore identical outfits, on and off stage, and at one time bought the house next door to their own in order to store all their clothes. Enormously popular in the UK during the 50s, they were still a top act into the 60s, until they retired in 1967 to raise their children. Joy, who was married to ex-England football captain Billy Wright, had two daughters, Vicky and Babette, and Teddie had one girl, Sasha. In the 80s, the three young girls formed a pop group, the Little Foxes. In 1985, while watching their daughters perform at Peter Stringfellow's Hippodrome nightspot in London, the Beverley Sisters themselves were booked to appear there on Mondays, the 'Gay Night'. They received extraordinary receptions, with the audience singing along on the old specialities such as 'Sisters' and 'Together'. Personal appearances and cabaret dates followed; a new album, *Sparkle*, was issued and some of their stage outfits were exhibited at the Victoria & Albert museum in London. The comeback endured into the 90s, with two more albums and a 30-date UK tour in 1995.

● ALBUMS: *A Date With The Bevs* (Philips 1955)★★★, *The Enchanting Beverley Sisters* (Columbia 1960)★★★, *Those Beverley Sisters* (Ace Of Clubs 1960)★★★, *The World Of The Beverley Sisters* (Decca 1971)★★★★, *Together* (MFP 1985)★★★, *Sparkle* (K-Tel 1985)★★★, *Sisters Sisters - An Evening With The Beverley Sisters* (1993)★★★, *Bless 'Em All* (1995)★★★.

BIG BEAT, THE

One of several films made at the advent of rock 'n' roll, *The Big Beat* contained one of the genre's most expansive casts. The wafer-thin plot, wherein a record company executive, who hates rock 'n' roll, employs his pop music-loving son, allowed scope for a variety of acts. Establishment stars including Harry James, George Shearing and the Mills Brothers, were featured alongside emergent talent, notably the Del Vikings and Fats Domino. This 1957 film is of interest because, whether by accident or design, it showed how the 'new' music was an extension of the 'old', rather than an aberration. Rock 'n' roll's roots in jazz are clearly seen and doo-wop is shown as a successor to 40s vocal harmony groups. The inclusion of white act the Diamonds, who specialized in 'clean-cut' cover versions of songs originally recorded by black singers, demonstrated another facet of the era. Although stilted in its presentation, *The Big Beat* puts 50s music into a historical context.

BIG BOPPER

b. Jiles Perry Richardson, 24 October 1930, Sabine Pass, Texas, USA, d. 3 February 1959. After working as a disc jockey in Beaumont, Richardson won a recording contract with Mercury Records, releasing two unsuccessful singles in 1957. The following year, under his radio moniker 'The Big Bopper', he recorded the ebullient 'Chantilly Lace', a rock 'n' roll classic, complete with blaring saxophone and an insistent guitar run. However, it was scheduled to be the b-side, backed with the satirical 'The Purple People Eater Meets The Witch Doctor'; the disc was a transatlantic hit. The follow-up, 'Big Bopper's Wedding', underlined the singer's love of novelty and proved popular enough to win him a place on a tour with Buddy Holly and Ritchie Valens. On 3 February 1959, a plane carrying the three stars crashed, leaving no survivors. Few of Richardson's recordings were left for posterity, though there was enough for a posthumous album, *Chantilly Lace*, which included the rocking 'White Lightning'. In 1960, Johnny Preston offeriold the ultimate valediction by taking the Big Bopper's composition 'Running Bear' to number 1 on both sides of the Atlantic.

● ALBUMS: *Chantilly Lace* (Mercury 1959)★★★.
● COMPILATIONS: *Hellooo Baby! The Best Of The Big Bopper 1954-1959* (Rhino 1989)★★★.
● FURTHER READING: *Chantilly Lace: The Life & Times Of J.P. Richardson*, Tim Knight.

BIG MAYBELLE

b. Mabel Louise Smith, 1 May 1924, Jackson, Tennessee, USA, d. 23 January 1972, Cleveland, Ohio, USA. Maybelle was discovered singing in church by Memphis bandleader Dave Clark in 1935. When Clark disbanded his orchestra to concentrate on record promotion, Smith moved to Christine Chatman's orchestra with whom she first recorded for Decca in 1944. Three years later, Smith made solo records for King and in 1952 she recorded as Big Maybelle when producer Fred Mendelsohn signed her to OKeh, a subsidiary of CBS Records. Her blues shouting style (a female counterpart to Big Joe Turner) brought an R&B hit the next year with 'Gabbin' Blues' (a cleaned-up version of the 'dirty dozens' on which she was partnered by songwriter Rose Marie McCoy). 'Way Back Home' and 'My Country Man' were also bestsellers. In 1955, she made the first recording of 'Whole Lotta Shakin' Goin' On', which later became a major hit for Jerry Lee Lewis. Big Maybelle was also a star attraction on the chitlin' circuit of black clubs, with an act that included risqué comedy as well as emotive ballads and brisk boogies. Leaving OKeh for Savoy, her 'Candy' (1956) brought more success and in 1958, she appeared in *Jazz On A Summer's Day*, the film of that year's Newport Jazz Festival. Despite her acknowledged influence on the soul styles of the 60s, later records for Brunswick, Scepter and Chess made little impact until she signed to the Rojac label in 1966. There she was persuaded to record some recent pop hits by the Beatles and Donovan and had some minor chart success of her own with versions of 'Don't Pass Me By' and '96 Tears'. The latter was composed by Rudy Martinez who also recorded it with his band ? And The Mysterians. Maybelle's career was marred by frequent drug problems which contributed to her early death from a diabetic coma.

● ALBUMS: *Big Maybelle Sings* (Savoy 1958)★★★★, *Blues, Candy And Big Maybelle* (Savoy 1958)★★★★, *What More*

Can A Woman Do? (Brunswick 1962)★★★, *The Gospel Soul Of Big Maybelle* (Brunswick 1964)★★★★, *The Great Soul Hits Of Big Maybelle* (Brunswick 1964)★★★★, *Gabbin' Blues* (Scepter 1965)★★★, *Saga Of The Good Life And Hard Times* (Rojac 1966)★★★, *Got A Brand New Bag* (Rojac 1967)★★★, *The Last Of Big Maybelle* (Paramount 1973)★★★.
● COMPILATIONS: *The OKeh Sessions* (Charly 1983)★★★★, *Roots Of R&B And Early Soul* (Savoy Jazz 1985)★★★★, *Candy* (Savoy 1995)★★★, *The Last Of Big Maybelle* (Muse 1996)★★★.

BIHARI BROTHERS
The Bihari family moved in 1941 from Oklahoma to Los Angeles where eldest brother Jules went into business as a supplier and operator of juke-boxes for the black community. The next step was to ensure the supply of suitable blues and R&B recordings to feed the juke-boxes and with Joe and Saul, he founded the Modern Music Company in 1945. As well as recording west coast artists such as Jimmy Witherspoon and Johnny Moore's Three Blazers, the brothers worked with local producers in Houston, Detroit and Memphis who supplied Modern with more rough-hewn blues material by such artists as Lightnin' Hopkins, John Lee Hooker and B.B. King. In 1951, the fourth Bihari brother, Lester, set up the Meteor label in Memphis. Meteor was responsible for some of Elmore James's earliest records as well as rockabilly by Charlie Feathers. Other Modern group labels included RPM (for which Ike Turner produced Howlin' Wolf), Blues & Rhythm and Flair. During the early 50s, the Bihari brothers released a wide range of material, even aiming at the pop charts by covering R&B titles from other labels. Among its successes were Etta James's 'Wallflower', 'Stranded In The Jungle' by the Cadets, 'Eddie My Love' by the Teen Queens and Jessie Belvin's 'Goodnight My Love'. The arranger/producer of many Modern tracks was Maxwell Davis. However, by the late 50s, the Modern group turned its attention towards reissuing material on the Crown budget-price label, which also included a series of big-band tribute albums masterminded by Davis. When the company found itself in financial difficulties, the Biharis released recordings by Z.Z. Hill, Lowell Fulson and B.B. King on the Kent label, but the death of Saul Bihari in 1975 and Joe's departure from the company led to a virtual cessation of recording, and the remaining brothers concentrated on custom pressing at their vinyl record plant. In 1984, the year of Jules Bihari's death, the family sold the catalogues of Modern, Flair, Kent, Crown and RPM. Seven years later, the labels passed into the hands of a consortium of Virgin Records (USA), Ace (Europe) and Blues Interactions (Japan). These companies continued an extensive reissue programme that the Ace label had initiated as licensee of the Modern group in the early 80s.

BILLIE AND LILLIE
Based in the New York area, this vocal duo comprised Billie (b. Billy Ford, 9 March 1925, Bloomfield, New Jersey, USA) and Lillie (b. Lillie Bryant, 14 February 1940, Newburg, New York, USA). In late 1957 they recorded the bouncy 'La Dee Dah' - written by songwriters Frank C. Slay Jnr. and Bob Crewe, who had recently penned 'Silhouettes' - which became a Top 10 smash in the US charts and sold over a million copies. 'La Dee Dah' was covered in the UK by Scottish teen star Jackie Dennis, whose version reached the Top 5. Billy played the trumpet and also had his own backing group the Thunderbirds. Most of their singles were released on London in the UK.

BINGE, RONALD
b. 15 July 1910, Derby, England, d. 6 September 1979, Ringwood, Hampshire, England. Binge was responsible for creating in 1951 the 'cascading strings' sound that made the Mantovani Orchestra famous throughout the world. This was achieved purely by clever scoring, dividing the violins into several parts, each allotted a different melody-note in turn, which they sustain and then fade out, until called upon to move elsewhere. Binge's inspiration came from his love of church music, particularly Monteverdi. Composers of sacred music had to allow for the long reverberation inevitable in cathedrals, and this is reflected in their writing. The first big success was 'Charmaine', followed by many others that made Mantovani's albums million-sellers, especially in the USA. Binge's association with Mantovani dates from 1935 when he played in, and did all the arrangements for, Mantovani's Tipica Orchestra. During war service in the RAF he spent some time in Blackpool, teaming up with Sidney Torch and his RAF Orchestra to present concerts for recruits. In later years Binge often provided arrangements for Torch's many broadcasts. Much of Binge's post-war work involved orchestrating numerous popular songs of the day for broadcasting, as well as theatrical assignments; Binge scored Noël Coward's musical *Pacific 1860* which opened at London's Theatre Royal Drury Lane in December 1946, with Mary Martin in the starring role. Binge gradually began to concentrate more on composing, and an early success was 'Elizabethan Serenade', first recorded by Mantovani in 1951, and later a big seller for other orchestras, notably Ron Goodwin. It won an Ivor Novello Award in 1957. In 1954 Binge adapted his 'cascade' effect with solo cornets for his 'Concert Carillon'. Like many of his contemporaries, he contributed numerous works to the London publishers' mood music libraries, which serve the special requirements of radio, television and films. Other compositions of note include 'Miss Melanie', 'Madrugado', 'The Red Sombrero', 'Faire Frou Frou', 'Caribbean Calypso', 'Dance Of The Snowflakes', 'The Fire God', 'Song Of Canterbury', 'Tales Of The Three Blind Mice', 'Thames Rhapsody', 'Trade Winds', 'Venetian Carnival', 'Man In A Hurry', 'The Watermill', 'High Stepper' and 'Sailing By', which for many years was the close-down music on BBC Radio 4. The BBC International Festival Of Light Music in 1956 commissioned Binge to compose his 'Concerto For Saxophone', which received its first performance with Michael Krein as soloist. Another major work was 'Saturday Symphony' (1966-68). Binge conducted them both in a recording by the South German Radio Orchestra. His scores for the cinema include *Desperate Moment* (1953), *Our Girl Friday* (1953), *The Runaway Bus* (1954) and *Dance Little Lady* (1954).
● ALBUMS: *Concerto For Saxophone And Orchestra/Saturday Symphony* (Rediffusion 1971)★★★, *British Light Music - Ronald Binge* (Marco Polo 1994)★★★★.

BIRTH OF THE COOL · MILES DAVIS
★★★★★

Although this album is credited to Davis, the importance of Gerry Mulligan's playing and, especially, his stellar compositions 'Jeru', 'Rocker' and the gorgeous 'Venus De Milo' make this 1956 album special. Although it is generally considered to be less accomplished than *Kind Of Blue*, this album is, arguably, in some ways more important. It would be churlish to say this was the birth of the cool, but the songs recorded by the legendary nonet and collected together here certainly mark the birth of something significant. Hearing all the tracks on the newly available CD version makes it more complete, and therefore, more necessary than ever. It is an utterly indispensable album.

● TRACKS: Move; Jeru; Moon Dreams; Venus De Milo; Budo; Deception; Godchild; Boplicity; Rocker; Israel; Rouge.

BLACK, STANLEY

b. 14 June 1913, London, England. At the age of seven he began learning the piano and later studied at the Mathay School of Music. His first composition, when he was aged 12, was broadcast by the BBC Symphony Orchestra. In 1929 he won an arranging contest sponsored by the then jazz weekly, *Melody Maker*, and became known as a promising jazz pianist, recording with visiting Americans Coleman Hawkins, Louis Armstrong and Benny Carter, plus the British bands of Lew Stone and Harry Roy. In 1938, he went to South America with Roy's orchestra, and became fascinated with Latin-American music, a subject on which he became an expert. He started recording for Decca in 1944, and in the same year became conductor of the BBC Dance Orchestra, a position that lasted until 1952. Black took part in many vintage radio shows including *Hi Gang* and *Much Binding In The Marsh*. He also composed signature tunes for several radio programmes, including the legendary *Goon Show*. He also broadcast with ensembles ranging from full symphony orchestras and the BBC Dance Orchestra, to a quartet or sextet in his own programmes such as *Black Magic* and *The Musical World Of Stanley Black*. Black has worked on over a hundred films either as score composer or musical director and in many cases as both. His credits include *It Always Rains On Sunday* (1948), *The Long And The Short And The Tall* (1961), the Cliff Richard musicals *The Young Ones* (1961) and *Summer Holiday* (1962), and all of the late Mario Zampi's screwball comedies, such as *Laughter In Paradise* (1951), *The Naked Truth* (1957) and *Too Many Crooks* (1958). His albums have sold in huge quantities, not only in the UK, but also in the USA, New Zealand and Japan. In 1994 he joined Stéphane Grappelli in a Charity Gala Performance at the Barbican Hall in London. His many honours include an OBE and Life Fellowship of the International Institute of Arts and Letters. In 1995 he was made life president of the Celebrities Guild of Great Britain.

● ALBUMS: *Exotic Percussion* (Phase 4 1962)★★★, *Spain* (Phase 4 1962)★★★, *Film Spectacular* (Phase 4 1963)★★★★, *Film Spectacular, Volume Two* (Phase 4 1963)★★★★, *'Bolero'/Polovtsian Dances* (Phase 4 1964)★★, *Grand Canyon Suite* (Phase 4 1964)★★★, *Music Of A People* (Phase 4 1965)★★★, *Russia* (Phase 4 1966)★★★, *Capriccio* (Phase 4 1965)★★★, *Film Spectacular, Volume Three* (Phase 4 1966)★★★★, *Broadway Spectacular* (Phase 4 1966)★★★, *Gershwin Concert* (Phase 4 1966)★★★, *Blockbusters From Broadway* (Phase 4 1967)★★★★, *Tchaikovsky Concert* (Phase 4 1967)★★, *Sputniks For Orchestra* (Phase 4 1967)★★★, *Spectacular Dances For Orchestra* (Phase 4 1967)★★★, *France* (Phase 4 1967)★★★, *Dimensions In Sound* (Phase 4 1968)★★★★, *Overture* (Phase 4 1968)★★★, *Cuban Moonlight* (Eclipse 1969)★★★, *Great Rhapsodies For Orchestra* (Phase 4 1970)★★★, *Plays For Latin Lovers* (Eclipse 1970)★★★, with the London Symphony Orchestra *Grieg Concert* (Phase 4 1971)★★, *Tribute To Charlie Chaplin* (Phase 4 1972)★★★, *Tropical Moonlight* (Eclipse 1972)★★★, *Film Spectacular, Volume Four - The Epic* (Phase 4 1973)★★★, *Cuban Moonlight, Volume Two* (Eclipse 1973)★★★, with the London Festival Orchestra *Spirit Of A People* (Phase 4 1974)★★★, *Film Spectacular, Volume Five - The Love Story* (Phase 4 1975)★★★★, *Twelve Top Tangos* (Eclipse 1976)★★, *Black Magic* (Phase 4 1976)★★★, *Film Spectacular, Volume Six - Great Stories From World War II* (Phase 4 1976)★★★, *Sounds Wide Screen* (Phase 4 1977)★★★, *Satan Superstar* (Phase 4 1978)★★★, *Digital Magic* (Decca 1979)★★★, *Great Love Stories* (Decca 1988)★★★, *ITV Themes* (Hallmark 1988)★★★, *S'Wonderful* (President 1990)★★★, *Nice 'N' Easy* (Decca 1992)★★★.

● COMPILATIONS: *Film World Of Stanley Black* (Decca 1970)★★★★, *Latin World Of Stanley Black* (Decca 1973)★★★, *Focus On Stanley Black* (Decca 1978)★★★★.

BLACKWELL, OTIS

b. 1931, Brooklyn, New York, USA. The author of 'Great Balls Of Fire', 'Fever' and 'All Shook Up', Blackwell was one of the greatest songwriters of the rock 'n' roll era. He learned piano as a child and grew up listening to both R&B and country music. Victory in a talent contest at Harlem's Apollo Theatre led to a recording contract with the Joe Davis label. His first release was his own composition 'Daddy Rolling Stone', which became a favourite in Jamaica where it was recorded by Derek Martin. The song later became part of the Who's 'Mod' repertoire. During the mid-50s, Blackwell also recorded in a rock 'n' roll vein for RCA Records and Groove before turning to writing songs for other artists. His first successes came in 1956 when Little Willie John's R&B hit with the sultry 'Fever' was an even bigger pop success for Peggy Lee. Subsequently, 'All Shook Up' (first recorded by David Hill on Aladdin Records) began a highly profitable association with Elvis Presley, who was credited as co-writer. The rhythmic tension of the song perfectly fitted Elvis's stage persona and it became his first UK number 1. It was followed by 'Don't Be Cruel' (1956), 'Paralysed' (1957), and the more mellow 'Return To Sender' (1962) and 'One Broken Heart For Sale'. There was a distinct similarity between Blackwell's vocal style and Presley's, which has led to speculation that Elvis adopted some of his songwriter's mannerisms. The prolific Blackwell (who wrote hundreds of songs) also provided hits for Jerry Lee Lewis ('Breathless' and his most famous recording, 'Great Balls Of Fire', 1958), Dee Clark ('Hey Little Girl' and 'Just Keep It Up', 1959), Jimmy Jones ('Handy Man', 1960) and Cliff Richard ('Nine Times Out Of Ten', 1960). As the tide of rock 'n' roll receded, Blackwell reorded R&B material for numerous labels including Atlantic, MGM and Epic. In later years, he was in semi-retirement, making only occasional live appearances.

● ALBUMS: *Singin' The Blues* (Davis 1956)★★, *These Are My Songs* (Inner City 1978)★★.

BLAINE, VIVIAN

b. Vivian Stapleton, 21 November 1921, Newark, New Jersey, USA. A vivacious actress and singer who created one of the American musical theatre's best-loved characters, Miss Adelaide, in Frank Loesser's *Guys And Dolls*. Vivian Blaine appeared on stage at her local theatre, and later attended the American Academy of Dramatic Art. She subsequently toured in various musicals and in vaudeville before making her Broadway debut in *Guys And Dolls* in 1950. She gave a delightful performance as the dancegirl who has been waiting for 14 years in the hope that her fiancé, Nathan Detroit, will finally abandon his floating crap game and marry her. Her frustration boils over in 'Sue Me', and she is splendid in the ensemble numbers with the girls at the 'Hot Box', 'Take Back Your Mink' and 'A Bushel And A Peck', but the stand-out song is 'Adelaide's Lament' in which she shares the knowledge, just gleaned from a book, that there is a direct relationship between long engagements and ill health: 'In other words just from waiting around for that plain little band of gold/A person - can develop a cold.' In 1953 she repeated her success at the London Coliseum, and was back on Broadway five years later with *Say, Darling* in which she starred with Robert Morse, David Wayne and Johnny Desmond. She subsequently toured extensively in a wide range of straight plays and musical revivals including *Zorba*, *Follies*, *Hello, Dolly!*, *Gypsy* and *I Do! I Do!*. She succeeded Jane Russell in the role of Jo Anne in the Broadway production of *Company*, and has also performed in cabaret. In addition to her stage work, Blaine has appeared in several film musicals including *Jitterbugs*, *Something For The Boys*, *Nob Hill*, *State Fair* (1945 version), *Doll Face*, *If I'm Lucky*, *Three Little Girls In Blue*, *Skirts Ahoy* and *Guys And Dolls* (1955).
● ALBUMS: *Vivian Blaine Sings Songs From The Ziegfeld Follies* (Mercury 1957)★★★, *Vivian Blaine Sings Songs From 'The Great White Way'* (Mercury 1957)★★★, *Vivian Blaine Sings Songs From 'Pal Joey'* (Mercury 1958)★★★★, *Broadway's All Time Hits* (Wing 1963)★★★★.

BLENDERS

This four-piece vocal group was formed in 1949 in New York, USA, and consisted of Ollie Jones (tenor), James DeLoache (bass), Abel DeCosta (tenor) and Tommy Adams (baritone). One single was released on the National label, 'I Can Dream Can't I', in November 1949, with Adams singing lead. Their second single 'Gone' was released on Decca in May 1950 and featured a lead vocal from Jones, before DeLoach led for the follow-up, 'Count Every Star'. Both singles were distinguished by the group's elegant harmonies, which bridged the gospel sound of the 40s with the fast-approaching rock 'n' roll beat of the new decade. Adams was replaced by Dick Palmer and DeLoach also left, because of illness, and was replaced by Ray Johnson. Johnson and Palmer had previously worked together as part of Joe Thomas's short-lived but influential Beavers. DeLoach soon returned to the group and Johnson switched to baritone, before he and Palmer left, and Napoleon 'Snaggs' Allen joined as baritone. After eight singles but no hits, Decca's patience ran out, and the group moved to MGM Records. When MGM's Joe Davis set up his own label, Jay-Dee, the Blenders moved with him, following a two single stay at MGM ('I Don't Miss You Anymore' and 'Please Take Me Back'). The change of scene resulted in the Blenders' most successful recording, 'You'll Never Be Mine Again'/'Don't Play Around With Love'. The Blenders broke up in 1954. The posthumous release of 'Somebody's Lying' was credited to the Millionaires, but was actually taken from a Blenders session dating from 1953. Jones and DeCosta later re-emerged in the Cues.

BLEYER, ARCHIE

b. 12 June 1909, Corona, New York, USA, d. 20 March 1989, Sheboygan, Wisconsin, USA. A bandleader, musical arranger and founder of Cadence Records, Bleyer began playing the piano at the age of seven. He enlisted at Columbia College in 1927, intending to become an electrical engineer, but switched to music in his second year, afterwards leaving to become a musical arranger. After organizing a local band, he went to New York in the late 30s and conducted for several Broadway shows. He also composed the jazz piece 'Business In Q', which was performed by various 'hot' bands in the 30s, and he became one of the best-known writers of stock arrangements for music publishers. In the 40s Bleyer joined CBS radio as a musical conductor, and worked extensively on the *Arthur Godfrey Show*, remaining with it when it transferred to television in the 50s. He left the show in 1953, and formed Cadence Records. He had immediate success with artists such as Julius LaRosa ('Eh Cumpari'), the Chordettes ('Mr Sandman', number 1), several chart-toppers for the Everly Brothers and Andy Williams ('Canadian Sunset', 'Butterfly' and 'Are You Sincere'). He also provided the orchestral backing for several of his artists, including Janette Davis, Marion Marlowe, Alfred Drake, and Arthur Godfrey, whose husky baritone can be heard on the album *Arthur Godfrey's TV Calendar Show*. Bleyer also had Top 20 hits with his own orchestra, including 'Hernando's Hideaway' (from *The Pajama Game*), and the novelty number 'The Naughty Lady Of Shady Lane'. He continued to work into the early 60s, but retired from showbusiness in the late 60s, dissolving the Cadence label.

BLUE JAYS

An R&B vocal group from Los Angeles, California, USA, the Blue Jays perfectly embody the transitional era between 50s R&B and 60s soul in their renditions of doo-wop-styled songs with a gospel-style lead vocal. Comprising lead singer Leon Peels (b. 1936, Newport, Arkansas, USA), Alex Manigo, Van Earl Richardson, and Leonard Davidson, the group came together in 1961, and the same year were signed by country singer Werly Fairburn to his Milestone label. The Blue Jays' first record, 'Lovers Island' (number 31 in the US pop chart) in 1961, was at the time considered to be one of the last gasps of doo-wop, yet in retrospect, one can hear the first glimmerings of soul in Peels' gospel-edged vocals. Peculiarly, the song only made the local R&B charts. The group followed the hit with some excellent numbers, notably 'Tears Are Falling' (1961) and 'The Right To Love' (1962), but achieved little success; they disbanded in early 1962.
● ALBUMS: *The Blue Jays Meet Little Caesar* (Milestone 1962)★★★.
● COMPILATIONS: *Lovers Island* (Relic 1987)★★★.

BLUE TRAIN - JOHN COLTRANE ★★★★★

Although it would seem that Alfred Lion's Blue Note label would have been the perfect home for a Bluetrane, this is his only record for the label. Notwithstanding, this 1957 recording shows a confident Coltrane before he became a giant in the field. The opening track is the leader; although a straightforward blues, it is a warming and familiar song. He is supported adequately by Lee 'Sidewinder' Morgan (trumpet), Kenny Drew (piano), Paul Chambers (bass), Curtis Fuller (trombone) and Philly Joe Jones (drums). Coltrane may have made more important albums, but none swung as effectively as this one.

● TRACKS: *Blue Train, Moment's Notice; The Locomotion; I'm Old Fashioned; Lazy Bird.*

BLUEBIRD RECORDS

This influential label was founded in 1933 in Chicago, Illinois, USA, as a blues-based subsidiary of RCA Victor. It achieved prominence the following year under the aegis of Lester Melrose. A successful businessman, Melrose had operated a music store during the early 20s from where he developed publishing interests. Among those whose compositions he administered were King Oliver and Jelly Roll Morton. Melrose then became an agent for several blues performers, including Tampa Red and Big Bill Broonzy, many of whom he introduced to the Bluebird label. Some such signings, notably Bo Carter, opted to record in the traditional manner, accompanying themselves, but others showcased a tight band sound comprised of piano, bass and drums, with occasional harmonica or saxophone. This combination often proved highly recognizable; indeed, many signings backed each other, resulting in what blues scholar Samuel Charters dubbed 'the Bluebird Beat'. Among those Melrose recorded for the label were Big Joe Williams, John Lee Sonny Boy Williamson and Arthur 'Big Boy' Crudup. The last-named composed 'That's All Right' and 'My Baby Left Me', later popularized by Elvis Presley. By the 40s Bluebird was pioneering the 'combo' style, adopted the following decade by Muddy Waters and Little Walter, but the shortage of shellac and the recording ban engendered by World War II caused the label's progress to falter. In 1945 Bluebird had success with Big Maceo's 'Things Have Changed', and that same year the outlet enjoyed a number 1 R&B hit with 'I Wonder' by Roosevelt Sykes. This was succeeded by the same artist's 'signature' tune, 'The Honeydripper' (number 3 R&B), but by 1948 RCA had virtually ceased recording blues. Melrose, who also introduced other acts to the equally renowned Vocalion label, took newer performers elsewhere. Bluebird was discontinued during the early 50s; its once pre-eminent position was taken up by newly established independents, including Chess, Vee Jay and Cobra.

BLUEJEAN BOP! · GENE VINCENT ★★★★

In May 1956, the two and a half minutes of 'Be Bop A Lula' marked the astonishing recording debut of Gene Vincent, and the following month Vincent was back in Owen Bradley's studio in Nashville for his first album, *Bluejean Bop!*. Producer Ken Nelson flipped the echo switch to maximum and created a space-age sound for 'Who Slapped John?', in particular. Vincent's voice was softer than most rock 'n' rollers and his tender versions of 'Ain't She Sweet?' and 'Up A Lazy River' demonstrated his potential as an all-round entertainer. His country roots are covered in 'Waltz Of The Wind', but it is the extraordinary rock 'n' roll numbers such as 'Bluejean Bop' and 'Bop Street' (don't be fooled by the slow start!) that make the album so remarkable and cre-

ated a guitar hero out of Cliff Gallup. Gene Vincent rocks, the Bluecaps roll, and the result is uninhibited magic. The album reached number 16 in the US charts.

● TRACKS: *Bluejean Bop; Jezebel; Who Slapped John?; Ain't She Sweet?; I Flipped; Waltz Of The Wind; Jump Back, Honey, Jump Back; That Old Gang Of Mine; Jumps, Giggles, And Shouts; Up A Lazy River; Bop Street; Peg O' My Heart.*

BLYTH, ANN

b Ann Marie Blyth, 16 August 1928, Mount Kisco, New York, USA. An actress and singer with a fine soprano voice and a fresh, engaging style, Blyth starred in several important movie musicals in the 50s. After voice training, Blyth spent some time with the San Carlo Opera Company, and made her Broadway debut at the age of 13 in the play *Watch On The Rhine*. She began her film career in 1944 when she was just 16, joining song and dance man Donald O'Connor in the musicals *Chip Off The Old Block, The Merry Monahans* and *Bowery To Broadway*. Having made a good impression with those less than serious affairs, she proved her dramatic ability the following year when she was nominated for an Academy Award for her performance as Joan Crawford's selfish daughter in *Mildred Pierce*. From then on, she mixed non-singing roles with 40s musicals, including *Babes On Swing Street* and *Top O' The Morning*. She eventually came into her own in the major 50s screen musicals *The Great Caruso, Rose Marie, The Student Prince* and *Kismet*. Many felt that she was miscast as torch singer Helen Morgan in her last film to date, *The Helen Morgan Story*, and indeed her singing voice was dubbed by Gogi Grant. In more recent years, Blyth has appeared frequently in the musical theatre, and received excellent reviews in November 1992 when she partnered Bill Hayes in an elegant tribute to the songs of Broadway and Hollywood at the Rainbow & Stars nightspot in New York.

● FILMS: *Chip Off The Old Block* (1944), *The Merry Monahans* (1944), *Babes On Swing Street* (1944), *Bowery To Broadway* (1944), *Mildred Pierce* (1945), *Swell Guy* (1946), *Brute Force* (1947), *Killer McCoy* (1947), *A Woman's Vengeance* (1947), *Mr. Peabody And The Mermaid* (1948), *Another Part Of The Forest* (1948), *Red Canyon* (1949), *Free For All* (1949), *Top O' The Morning* (1949), *Once More, My Darling* (1949), *Our Very Own* (1950), *The Great Caruso* (1951), *Katie Did It* (1951), *Thunder On The Hill* (1951), *The Golden Horde* (1951), *I'll Never Forget You* (1951), *One Minute To Zero* (1952), *The World In His Arms* (1952), *Sally And Saint Anne* (1952), *All The Brothers Were Valiant* (1953), *Rose Marie* (1954), *The Student Prince* (1954), *Kismet* (1955), *The King's Thief* (1955), *Slander* (1956), *The Buster Keaton Story* (1957), *Jazz Age* (1957), *The Helen Morgan Story* (1957).*

BOBBETTES

The first all-female R&B group to have a major pop hit record was not the Chantels, as is popularly believed, but the Bobbettes. Their 'Mr. Lee' beat the Chantels' 'He's Gone' to the charts by one month and outranked it in the US pop charts. The Bobbettes formed in 1955 in Harlem, New York City, USA, at PS 109, where they attended school. Consisting of Emma Pought (b. 1944), her sister Jannie (b. 1945), Laura Webb (b. 1943), Helen Gathers (b. 1944) and Reather Dixon (b. 1945), the group was originally called the Harlem Queens. The girls were aged between 11 and 13 years old at the time of the group's formation. In 1957 they appeared on a local television programme, which led to an audition for Atlantic Records. 'Mr. Lee' was a song the girls had written in honour of their fifth-grade teacher, although the lyrics were not as kind in their original version (in fact, their second chart single was titled 'I Shot Mr. Lee'). The infectious 'Mr. Lee' was released in the summer of 1957 and ascended to number 6 in the US chart. Follow-up singles on Atlantic did not chart; the Bobbettes' subsequent singles were issued on the Triple-X, Gone, Jubilee, Diamond and RCA Records labels. Although their last chart success was in 1961, four of the original members were still performing together in the late 80s.

● COMPILATIONS: *Mr Lee & Other Big Hits* (Revival 1989)★★★.

BOCK, JERRY

b. Jerrold Lewis Bock, 23 November 1928, New Haven, Connecticut, USA. An important composer for the musical theatre, Bock studied the piano from an early age and was soon able to play quite complicated compositions by ear. He wrote the music for various shows while studying at high school and the University of Wisconsin in the 40s, and subsequently worked on revues at summer camps and for television. In 1955 Bock and lyricist Larry Holofcener contributed some songs to the Broadway revue *Catch A Star*, and a year later, with George Weiss, they provided the complete score for *Mr. Wonderful*, a musical vehicle for Sammy Davis Jnr., which ran for 383 performances. Bock and Holofcener's last assignment together was for the *Ziegfeld Follies Of 1956*, which closed before it reached New York. Shortly afterwards, Bock met lyricist Sheldon Harnick (b. 30 April 1924, Chicago, Illinois, USA), and they formed what is arguably the most important musical partnership of the 60s. Harnick had been a danceband violinist before moving to New York in 1950 where he had several of his songs performed in revues such as *New Faces Of 1952* ('Boston Beguine') and *Shoestring Revue*. Bock and Harnick's first effort, *The Body Beautiful* (1958), was a failure, but *Fiorello!* (1959) ran for 795 performances. Next came the underrated *Tenderloin* (1960), a humorous exposé of vice in New York with some good songs including 'Little Old New York', 'The Picture Of Happiness' and 'How the Money Changes Hands'. In 1963 the team wrote several numbers for the critically acclaimed marionette show *Man In The Moon*, and later in the same year, came up with what is considered to be their best score, for *She Loves Me*. With delightful songs such as 'Will He Like Me?', 'Ice Cream', 'A Trip To The Library' and 'She Loves Me', plus Broadway's favourite ingénue, Barbara Cook, it warranted a longer stay than just 302 performances. Bock and Harnick's next show clocked up more than 10 times that total in New York, and was a smash hit around the world. *Fiddler On The Roof* (1964), starring Zero Mostel, became one of the most cherished of all Broadway musicals, and gave the world of popular music (and Jewish functions of all kinds) hit songs such as 'Matchmaker, Matchmaker', 'Sunrise, Sunset' and the immortal 'If I Was A Rich Man'. It proved impossible to follow, and for the remainder of the decade the composers worked on a variety of projects including a 'Sherlock Holmes' musical, *Baker Street*, *The Apple Tree*, which was based on stories by Mark Twain and others, and ran for 463 performances, and *Her First Roman*, based on

George Bernard Shaw's play *Caesar And Cleopatra*, to which they contributed a few songs. After *The Rothschilds* (1970), which had a strong Jewish theme and was similar in a way to *Fiddler On The Roof*, Bock and Harnick ended their partnership. Bock has been inactive for over 20 years, with no apparent musical work forthcoming. In 1971, Harnick gave his 'observations on the fine art and craft of lyric writing' at a recital in the *Lyrics And Lyricists* series at the 92nd Street 'Y' in New York, and since then his projects have included *Pinocchio* (1973) with music by Mary Rodgers, *Rex* (1976) with music by Richard Rodgers, and an English translation of the *Umbrellas Of Cherbourg* with composer Michel Legrand for an 1979 off-Broadway production. In the 80s there was a projected musical, *Dragons*, that did not materialize, and in the 90s Harnick collaborated with Joe Raposo on *A Wonderful Life*, and with Thomas Z. Shepard on *Love In Two Countries*, neither of which opened on Broadway following their out-of-town try-outs.

● ALBUMS: *An Evening With Sheldon Harnick* (Laureate 1977)★★★.

BODY AND SOUL · COLEMAN HAWKINS
★★★★

This release features Hawkins' definitive interpretation of the title track. Although he did not write 'Body And Soul', he managed to engrave his own soul into it, and on the strength of this recording, should be entitled to claim it as his own. Regardless of recording techniques and location, the sparse, breathy tone produced by Hawkins is breathtaking. Without denigrating the other tracks on this record, the title track alone justifies its importance (as significant as *Kind Of Blue*) in any record collection. Beautifully preserved from 10-inch disc and recorded in 1939, also included on this album is the 1956 recording, on which even the subtle clicks of the saxophone keys are discernible.

● TRACKS: *Meet Doctor Foo; Fine Dinner; She's Funny That Way; Body And Soul; When Day Is Done; The Sheik Of Araby; My Blue Heaven; Bouncing With Bean; Say It Isn't So; Spotlight; April In Paris; How Strange; Half Step Down Please; Jumping For Jane; I Love You; There Will Never Be Another You; Little Girl Blue; Dinner For One, Please James; I Never Knew; His Very Own Blues; Thirty Nine Inches; Bean Stalks Again; I'm Shooting High; Have You Met Miss Jones?; The Day You Came Along; The Essence Of You.*

BOLLIN, A.D. 'ZUZU'

b. 5 September 1922, Frisco, Texas, USA, d. 19 October 1990, Dallas, Texas, USA. One of the legion of guitarists who embraced the innovatory style of 'T-Bone' Walker, for decades Bollin's reputation rested on two records made in Dallas for Bob Sutton's Torch label in 1951/2. He did not take up music until 1947, after service in the US Navy. He received help in his guitar technique from 'T-Bone' himself, while singing with the E.X. Brooks Band in Omaha, Nebraska. His first band, formed in 1949, included jazzmen Booker Ervin and David 'Fathead' Newman, and he also worked with Ernie Fields, Milton (Brother Bear) Thomas and Percy Mayfield. His first record, 'Why Don't You Eat Where You Slept Last Night'/'Matchbox Blues', featured Newman and Leroy Cooper, both later to work with Ray Charles. The second single, 'Stavin' Chain'/'Cry, Cry, Cry', used members of Jimmy McCracklin's band. Both records

were later reissued. During the 50s, Bollin worked with Joe Morris and Jimmy Reed before retiring from music at the end of the decade. Apart from two untraced 1954 titles, Bollin did not record again until he was rediscovered in 1988 by Chuck Nevitt, and then recorded the album *Texas Bluesman*, sponsored by the Dallas Blues Society. He toured Europe in 1989 and was in the process of recording a second album at the time of his death. Two titles from these sessions were added to a reissue of the first album.
● ALBUMS: *Texas Bluesman* (Antone's 1991)★★★.

BONNIE SISTERS
This three-piece vocal group was formed at New York's Bellevue Hospital in 1955 by three nurses, Sylvia, Jean and Pat. Rainbow Records released their first single, 'Cry Baby', with the seasonal 'I Saw Mommy Cha-Cha-Cha With You-Know-Who' on the b-side, backed by Mickey Baker and his orchestra. The single reached number 18 in the US charts, but their next two singles, 'Wandering Heart' and 'Confess', failed to chart and the group broke up.

BOOKER, CHARLEY
b. 3 September 1925, Quiver Valley, near Sunflower, Mississippi, USA, d. 20 September 1989, South Bend, Indiana, USA. While some singers left Mississippi to seek wider recognition, others like Charley Booker remained, their music retaining traditions that urban sophistication expunged. Booker learned the guitar from his father, Lucius, and uncle, Andrew Shaw. Boyd Gilmore was a childhood friend. He moved to Greenville in 1947, playing in drummer Jesse 'Cleanhead' Love's band, and broadcasting over WGVM radio. In January 1952, along with Gilmore and harmonica player Houston Boines, he recorded four titles with Ike Turner, released on the Modern and Blues & Rhythm labels. 'Rabbit Blues', 'Moonrise Blues', 'No Ridin' Blues' and 'Charley's Boogie Woogie', sung in a distinctive voice with natural vibrato, revealed the influence of Charley Patton. Within a year, he recorded in Memphis for Sam Phillips, but the trenchantly rhythmic 'Walked All Night' and 'Baby I'm Coming Home' were not released until 1977. Booker moved to South Bend, Indiana, in 1953, where he remained, performing only rarely, until his death in 1989.

BOOKER, JAMES
b. 17 December 1939, New Orleans, Louisiana, USA, d. 8 November 1983, New Orleans, Louisiana, USA. As an exceptionally talented child, Booker studied classical piano, but balanced his virtuosity with blues and boogie learned from Isidore 'Tuts' Washington and Edward Frank. In his early teens he appeared on radio WMRY and formed a band he called Booker Boy And The Rhythmaires. He made his first record for Imperial in 1954, 'Doin' The Hambone', and 'Thinkin' 'Bout My Baby', produced by Dave Bartholomew, led to sessions for Fats Domino, Smiley Lewis and Lloyd Price, among others. Booker made just two more singles during the 50s, 'Heavenly Angel' for Chess and 'Open The Door' for Ace. In 1959 he enrolled at Southern University to study music. A year later, he signed to Peacock and had the only hit of his career, an organ instrumental called 'Gonzo', which reached number 3 in the R&B charts. Further singles such as 'Tubby' and 'Big Nick' failed to achieve similar success. By this point, however, drugs had added to his psycho-

logical problems and his work became erratic. In 1970 he served time in Angola State Penitentiary for drug possession. His appearance at the 1975 Jazz Fest led to a recording contract for Island Records. Other records appeared sporadically but his deteriorating mental state and an inability to control his drug problem led to a fatal heart attack. His highly individual style can sometimes be heard in the work of Harry Connick Jnr., who was a student and friend of Booker's.
● ALBUMS: *Junco Partner* (Island/Hannibal 1975/1993)★★★, *New Orleans Piano Wizard Live!* (Rounder 1981)★★★, *Classified* (Rounder 1982)★★★, *Mr Mystery* (Sundown 1985)★★★.
● COMPILATIONS: *Spirit Of New Orleans: The Genius Of Dave Bartholomew* (EMI America 1992)★★★★, *Resurrection Of The Bayou Maharajah* (Rounder 1993)★★★, *Spiders On The Keys* (Rounder 1993)★★★.

BOOTH, SHIRLEY
b. Thelma Booth Ford, 30 August 1898, New York City, USA, d. 16 October 1992, North Chatham, Massachusetts, USA. A distinguished actress and singer, who was once described by the *New York Post* as 'one of the wonders of the American stage; a superb actress, a magnificent comedienne, and an all-round performer of seemingly endless variety', Booth started to act at an early age, and made her professional stage debut in 1923 and her first Broadway appearance two years later. In the Broadway musical theatre she played a gossip columnist in *Hollywood Pinafore* (1945), and excelled as the wonderfully wistful Aunt Cissy with 'Love Is The Reason' and the magnificent 'He Had Refinement', in *A Tree Grows In Brooklyn* (1951). She was a vaudeville star-turned-theatrical boarding house proprietor in *By The Beautiful Sea* (1954), took the title role in *Juno* (1959), a musical version of Sean O'Casey's play *Juno And The Paycock*, with a Marc Blitzstein score, and played the Mother Superior in the short-lived *Look To The Lilies* (1970). In the latter, she introduced Sammy Cahn and Jule Styne's 'I, Yes Me! That's Who!' with Al Freeman Jnr. In non-musical areas, Booth won Tony and Academy Awards for her roles in both stage and film versions of *Come Back, Little Sheba*, and two more Tonys for her work in *Goodbye, My Fancy* and *Time Of The Cuckoo*. She also created the role of Dolly Levi in *The Matchmaker*, the play that Jerry Herman musicalized into *Hello, Dolly!* She was probably best known to the public at large for her performance as the gossipy maid Hazel Burke in the sitcom *Hazel* (1961-66), for which she won two Emmys. The first of her two husbands was actor Edward Gardner with whom she appeared in the popular radio series *Duffy's Tavern*. Until her death, most reference works recorded her date of birth as 1907, but since then sources say that she was born nine years earlier, and was 94 when she died.
● FILMS: *Come Back, Little Sheba* (1952), *Main Street To Broadway* (1953), *About Mrs. Leslie* (1954), *The Matchmaker* (1958), *Hot Spell* (1958).

BOP CHORDS
This vocal quintet was formed in 1955 in Harlem, New York, USA, by Ernest Harriston (lead), Leon Ivey (bass), Morris 'Mickey' Smarr (baritone), William Dailey (first tenor) and Ken 'Butch' Hamilton (second tenor). Having built themselves a formidable local reputation with their good looks

and tight harmonies, they signed to Holiday Records. The first single, 'Castle In The Sky', was an enormous local success in the spring of 1956. After a residency at the Apollo Theatre, their second single, 'When I Woke Up This Morning', was released. Like its predecessor, it sold over 100,000 copies on the east coast without becoming a national hit. However, their fortunes waned after this. Dailey and Smarr were replaced by Skip Boyd on baritone and Peggy Jones on first tenor. The new line-up released 'So Why' in 1957, but they could not recapture their former popularity and broke up shortly afterwards. Harriston went on to a brief solo career (as Eric Johnson) and also worked as backing vocalist for Shep And The Limelites. In 1971 the group reunited for a series of concerts, but no recordings were issued.

BOSWELL, EVE

b. 11 May 1924, Budapest, Hungary. A singer with a vivacious style, who was especially popular in the UK during the 50s, Boswell was also an accomplished pianist and ballet dancer, and speaks four languages fluently. Educated in Lausanne, Switzerland, Boswell later studied music at the Budapest Academy. She came from a vaudeville family with whom she appeared as a teenager in an act known as the Three Hugos. After working in South Africa in Boswell's Circus, and marrying the owner, she went to the UK in 1949 and replaced Doreen Lundy as the star vocalist in Geraldo's Orchestra. After featuring on several of the orchestra's records, including 'Again', 'Best Of All' and, somewhat curiously, 'Confidentially' (the composition and theme song of comedian Reg Dixon), she left Geraldo in 1951, and toured the UK with George & Alfred Black's revue *Happy-Go-Lucky*, and was their leading lady in the musical *The Show Of Shows*, at the Opera House, Blackpool. She also toured Korea and the Far East, entertaining British Forces, appearing regularly in the UK on the radio, television and variety circuit, and at the 1953 Royal Command Performance. Signed to Parlophone Records in 1950, her first record, 'Bewitched', was followed by several other successful titles, including 'Beloved Be Faithful', 'The Little Shoemaker' and 'Ready, Willing And Able'. Her biggest hits were two up-tempo South African songs, 'Sugarbush' (1952) and 'Pickin' A Chicken', which entered the UK chart in 1955, and resurfaced twice during the following year. Although well known for lively, up-tempo material, her album *Sentimental Eve* revealed that she could handle ballads equally well, with such tracks as 'I'll Buy That Dream' and 'You'll Never Know'. She remained active in the UK during the 50s and into the 60s, then faded from the scene.
● ALBUMS: *Sugar And Spice* (Parlophone 1956)★★★★, *Sentimental Eve* (Parlophone 1957)★★★, *Following The Sun Around* (Parlophone 1959)★★★, *Sugar Bush 76* (EMI 1976)★★.
● COMPILATIONS: *Sentimental Journey* (Conifer 1988)★★★, *The EMI Years* (EMI 1989)★★★.

BOWYER, BRENDAN

b. 12 October 1938, Waterford, Eire. Inspired by the rock 'n' roll boom of the late 50s, Bowyer came to prominence in his homeland after joining the newly formed Royal Showband in 1957. The rugby-playing Bowyer was known for his acrobatics onstage which included jumping over his partner Tom Dunphy in mid-song. Bowyer sang lead on the majority of the band's songs, including the Irish number 1 hits 'Kiss Me Quick', 'No More', 'Bless You', 'The Hucklebuck' and 'Don't Lose Your Hucklebuck Shoes'. Unquestionably the most popular vocalist in Eire during the 60s, Bowyer was acclaimed as the showband's answer to Elvis Presley. During the summer of 1971, Bowyer left the Royal to join the Big 8 and followed his mentor Presley onto the Las Vegas circuit. His valedictory tribute to Presley, 'Thank You Elvis', returned him to the Irish Top 10 during 1977. In the meantime, he slipped inexorably into alcoholism, before drying out in the early 80s. He still plays the Vegas circuit, often in the company of the frequently changing Big 8.
● ALBUMS: *Live At Clontarf Castle* (Harmac 1989)★★★.
● VIDEOS: *Irish Showband In Concert* (Unknown 1988).

BOY FRIEND, THE

Despite a quiet opening at London's Players' Theatre in April 1953, Sandy Wilson's stage musical *The Boy Friend* became a huge popular success after transferring to Wyndham's Theatre in the West End on 14 January 1954. An affectionate pastiche of the musical theatre of the 20s, the show starred Anthony Hayes, Hugh Paddick, Denise Hurst, Joan Gadsdon, Juliet Hunt, Beryl Cooke, Joan Sterndale Bennett, Larry Drew, John Rutland, and Anne Rogers, who came in 48 hours before it was due to open. Wilson wrote the book as well as the delightful score, which included several memorable numbers such as 'It's Never Too Late To Fall In Love', 'Won't You Charleston With Me', 'I Could Be Happy With You', 'Fancy Forgetting', 'The Boy Friend', 'Poor Little Pierrette' and the wistful 'A Room In Bloomsbury'. While *The Boy Friend* settled in for a run of 2,084 performances in London, Julie Andrews made her Broadway debut in the US production which opened at the Royale Theatre on 30 September 1954 and ran for well over a year. A major New York revival was mounted in 1958, and London audiences enjoyed the show again in 1967 and 1984. A 40th anniversary revival opened at the Players' Theatre in April 1994, before embarking on a UK tour. It was directed by Maria Charles who played the role of Dulcie in the 1954 production. Another survivor from the original show was John Rutland, who recreated the part of Lord Brockhurst. The 'disastrous' 1971 film version, which starred Twiggy and future Broadway star Tommy Tune, was directed by Ken Russell.

BOYD, EDDIE

b. Edward Riley Boyd, 25 November 1914, Stovall, Mississippi, USA, d. 13 July 1994, Helsinki, Finland. Boyd was a half-brother of Memphis Slim and a cousin of Muddy Waters. He spent his early years on Stovall's Plantation but ran away after a dispute with an overseer. Self-taught on guitar and piano, he worked around the south during the 30s, as both 'Little Eddie' and 'Ernie' Boyd, from a base in Memphis, before settling in Chicago where he worked in a steel-mill. He was active in music, performing with Waters, Johnny Shines and John Lee 'Sonny Boy' Williamson before he had his first big hit under his own name with 'Five Long Years', on the Job label in 1952. He recorded extensively for Chess Records, having successes with '24 Hours' and '3rd Degree'. He journeyed to Europe during the 'Blues Boom' of the 60s and took up residence first in Paris and later in Finland. During this period he appeared with artists as diverse as Buddy Guy and John Mayall and recorded in England, Sweden, Switzerland, Germany, France and Finland. His piano-playing was steadily functional rather than spectacular and his main strength was his ability to put together lyrics that were pithy and acidic. 'Five Long Years' has become a popular blues standard and features in the repertoires of many singers including Muddy Waters and B.B. King.

● ALBUMS: *Legacy Of The Blues Volume 10* (Sonet 1975)★★★, *Rattin' And Running Around* (Crown Prince 1982)★★★, *No More Of This Third Degree* (1982)★★★, *Live* (Storyville 1990)★★★.

BRADDY, PAULINE

b. c.1920, Mississippi, USA. Braddy attended Piney Woods Country Life School where her musical inclinations were encouraged. She started out playing clarinet but had her heart set on the alto saxophone. When the school's founder formed an all-girl jazz orchestra she was included, but was asked to switch to drums when the intended drummer dropped out. Although she was unhappy with the move she proved to be a natural, playing with enormous flair and swing. Braddy admired many of the popular drummers of the day, including 'Big' Sid Catlett, Gene Krupa and Jo Jones, and was by no means a second-division player. Indeed, had she been a man her reputation would have soared. Listening to records by the band, which eventually became known as the International Sweethearts Of Rhythm, it is hard to realize that this is not one of the leading swing bands of the day, and much of the verve of the band stems from Braddy's powerful drumming. With the Sweethearts Braddy toured Europe to entertain US Army personnel during World War II, and later recorded, made movie shorts, and appeared at New York's Apollo Theatre. By the end of the 40s the Sweethearts' day had passed and the band broke up. Braddy remained outside music for some time, but in 1950 she played in a trio with former Sweetheart Carline Ray and bass player Edna Smith. In 1956 Braddy was in a band formed by former Sweethearts frontwoman Anna Mae Winburn. Much admired by many male jazz musicians, including Jones, Braddy appeared always to take a sanguine view of the fact that her name is barely known outside a few *cognoscenti* of women's jazz groups. The reality is that jazz lost a great deal by not giving this fine musician and superbly swinging drummer an opportunity to play and record with leading jazzmen of her era.

● COMPILATIONS: *The International Sweethearts Of Rhythm* (Rosetta 1945-46)★★★★.

BRANDWYNNE, NAT

b. 23 July 1910, New York, USA. A pianist and the leader of a number of sophisticated society and hotel bands, early on in his career Brandwynne played piano for Leo Reisman and Eddy Duchin, and was hired as the musical director for Russ Columbo's band in the early 30s. He also worked with Kate Smith before forming his own ensemble to play at the luxurious Waldorf Astoria Hotel in New York. Over the years he became a firm favourite at that venue, and his orchestra (conducted by Lennie Hayton) contributed considerably to Lena Horne's dynamic performance there in 1956, which was recorded live and released on RCA/Victor Records as *Lena Horne At The Waldorf Astoria* in 1957. In 1936, billed as

Nat Brandwynne And His Stork Club Orchestra, he had US hit records with 'Take My Heart', 'These Foolish Things' and 'Until Today' (all three with vocals by Buddy Clark), as well as the instrumental 'If We Never Meet Again'. His other sides included 'Amapola', 'The Glory Of Love', 'Just One Of Those Things', 'My Heart And I', 'Easy To Love', 'I Dream Of San Marino', 'There's Always A Happy Ending', 'That Lovely Night In Budapest', 'I'd Rather Lead A Band', and a series of 78 rpm albums such as *Songs Of Our Times-1920* and *Songs Of Our Times - 1941*. He also made several long-playing albums and was reported to be leading orchestras well into the 70s, often in Las Vegas. Among his own relatively few compositions were 'Stars Over Bahia', 'If Stars Could Talk' and 'Peacock Alley'. His albums, which were released in the 50s, included *The Smart Set, Cole Porter Dance Book, Songs Of Our Times-Song Hits Of 1935, Dancing At The Waldorf* and *Piano Moods*.

BRENNAN, ROSE

This popular Irish band singer joined Joe Loss, the leader of one of Britain's most enduring dance bands, for a trial period of two weeks, and stayed for 15 years during the 40s and 50s. One of the many who benefited from Loss's policy of generously featuring his vocalists, Brennan was voted the top girl singer in the *New Musical Express* annual poll. Her records with Loss, on several of which she was accompanied by his vocal quintet, the Loss Chords, included 'Tulips And Heather', 'Then I'll Be There', 'Somewhere Along The Way', 'The Isle Of Innisfree', 'Why Don't You Believe Me?', 'Got You On My Mind' (with the Kordites), 'Seven Lonely Days' and 'The Spinning Wheel'. Under her own name, in the 50s, she released several cover versions of hits such as Edith Piaf's 'If You Love Me - I Won't Care (Hymn A L'Amour)', 'Let Me Go, Lover' (which was successful for several artists, including Joan Weber, Dean Martin and Teresa Brewer), and Don Cherry's 'Band Of Gold'. In 1961 she had a UK Top 40 hit of her own with 'Tall Dark Stranger'.

BRENSTON, JACKIE

b. 15 August 1930, Clarksdale, Mississippi, USA, d. 15 December 1979, Memphis, Tennessee, USA. Credited with making the 'first' rock 'n' roll record, Brenston's career quickly reached a peak as a result and then entered a 25-year decline. He had returned from army service in 1947 and learned to play saxophone from local musician Jesse Flowers. Shortly afterwards, he met Ike Turner who was recruiting for his band the Kings Of Rhythm. Their local fame prompted B.B. King to recommend them to Sam Phillips in Memphis. Both Turner and Brenston made singles on 5 March 1951 and both were sold to Chess Records, but it was 'Rocket 88' that became a hit, due in part to the distorted sound of Willie Kizart's guitar. Subsequent singles, including 'My Real Gone Rocket' and 'Hi-Ho Baby', failed to reproduce that sound and after two solid years of touring behind his hit, Brenston's career began to languish. He worked in Lowell Fulson's band for a couple of years and then rejoined Turner's Kings Of Rhythm, with whom he recorded two singles for Federal Records and, in 1961, one for Sue Records. Brenston recorded one last single, 'Want You To Rock Me', with Earl Hooker's band. Jackie Brenston worked for a time in the Shakers, the band of St. Louis bassist Sid Wallace, but by then alcohol had taken over his life and was a contribu-

tory factor to his fatal heart attack. In an interview, he spoke his own epitaph: 'I had a hit record and no sense.'
● COMPILATIONS: *Rocket 88* (Chess 1989)★★★, with Ike Turner *Trailblazer* (Charly 1991)★★★.

BRENT, TONY

b. Reginald Bretagne, 13 August 1926, Bombay, India, d. 19 June 1993, Sydney, Australia. Brent was a popular singer in the UK during the 50s, having moved there on Boxing Day 1947. Two years later he won a talent contest at the Kingston Regal Theatre singing 'Some Enchanted Evening', which led to work with Ambrose and Cyril Stapleton's BBC Showband. Contrary to disinformation spread at the time by his agent, and subsequently repeated by his record company, he had not arrived in England from the USA, nor had he sang with former Glenn Miller accompanist Tex Beneke and his band. In 1952 he made his chart debut with a cover version of one of Sammy Kaye's last hits, 'Walkin' To Missouri', and began to tour the variety circuit and appear on television. His other chart entries through until 1959 included 'Make It Soon', 'Got You On My Mind', 'Cindy, Oh Cindy', 'Dark Moon', 'The Clouds Will Soon Roll By', 'Girl Of My Dreams' and 'Why Should I Be Lonely?'. He additionally duetted with Billie Anthony on a recording of the similarly titled 'I Get So Lonely'. Brent also released two sets of standards, *Off Stage* and *Tony Takes Five*. His EPs included *Time For Tony* and *Tony Calls The Tune*. He was subsequently overwhelmed by the 60s beat group scene and retreated to the clubs. Eventually, he resumed his travels, and left the UK for Australia, where he died of a heart attack in 1993.
● ALBUMS: *Off Stage* (Columbia 1958)★★★★, *Tony Takes Five* (Columbia 1960)★★★.

BREWER, TERESA

b. Theresa Breuer, 7 May 1931, Toledo, Ohio, USA. A child prodigy, Brewer first appeared on radio at the age of two and sang on the *Major Bowes Amateur Hour* between 1938 and 1943. She was a veteran radio and club performer by the time she joined London Records in 1949. The attractive and strong-voiced teenager topped the US chart in 1950 with her debut hit 'Music Music Music', on which she was backed by the Dixieland All Stars. She joined Coral Records in 1952 and continued hitting the US Top 10 with records such as 'Ricochet', 'Jilted' and the number 1 'Till I Waltz Again With You'. In 1953 she made her film debut in *Those Redheads From Seattle* with Guy Mitchell. Her first transatlantic Top 10 hit was her version of 'Let Me Go Lover' in 1955, which she followed with two more in 1956, 'A Tear Fell' and 'Sweet Old-Fashioned Girl'. As rock 'n' roll took over, Brewer's sales declined and like many other MOR pop stars of the time she reverted to covering R&B hits for the white record-buying public. In this vein she had some success with tracks including 'Pledging My Love', 'Tweedle Dee' and 'You Send Me'. Brewer had a brief flirtation with country-styled material in the early 60s and then joined the lucrative nightclub and Las Vegas circuit. She later recorded for Philips, Signature, Project Three and Amsterdam, the latter label being owned by her producer husband Bob Thiele. In all, Brewer accumulated 38 US chart hits, but by the late 50s, when rock was firmly established, there was no place in the charts for this sweet, old-fashioned girl.
● ALBUMS: *Teresa Brewer* 10-inch album (London 1952)★★★★, *A Bouquet Of Hits* 10-inch album (Coral 1952)★★★★, *Till I Waltz Again With You* 10-inch album (Coral 1954)★★★★, *Music, Music, Music* (Coral 1956)★★★, *Teresa* (Coral 1956)★★★★, *For Teenagers In Love* (Coral 1957)★★★, *Teresa Brewer At Christmas Time* (Coral 1957)★★★, *Miss Music* (Coral 1958)★★★, *Time For Teresa* (Coral 1958)★★★, *Teresa Brewer And The Dixieland Band* (Coral 1959)★★★, *When Your Lover Has Gone* (Coral 1959)★★★, *Heavenly Lover* (Coral 1959)★★★, *Ridin' High* (Coral 1960)★★★, *Naughty, Naughty, Naughty* (Coral 1960)★★★, *My Golden Favorites* (Coral 1960)★★★, *Songs Everybody Knows* (Coral 1961)★★★, *Aloha From Teresa* (Coral 1961)★★★, *Don't Mess With Tess* (Coral 1962)★★★, *Terrific Teresa* (Wing 1963)★★★, *Moments To Remember* (1964)★★★, *Golden Hits Of 1964* (1964)★★★, *Goldfinger And Other Great Movie Songs* (1965)★★, *Songs For Our Fighting Men* (1966)★★, *Gold Country* (1966)★★★, *Texas Leather And Mexican Lace* (1967)★★★, *I Dig Big Band Singers* (Doctor Jazz 1983)★★, *Good News* (Doctor Jazz 1984)★★, with Stephane Grappelli *On The Road Again* (Doctor Jazz 1984)★★★, *Teresa Brewer In London* (Signature 1984)★★, *When Your Lover Has Gone* (Jasmine 1984)★★, *Live At Carnegie Hall & Montreux* (Doctor Jazz 1985)★★, *Teenage Dance Party* (Bear Family 1989)★★, *The Songs Of Bessie Smith* (Dillion 1992)★★★, *Chicago Style* (1994)★★.
● COMPILATIONS: *World Of Teresa Brewer* (Decca 1978)★★★, *The Best Of Teresa Brewer* (MCA 1981)★★★★, *Teresa Brewer* (Audio Fidelity 1984)★★★, *Golden Greats* (MCA 1985)★★★★, *Golden Hits* (Pickwick 1989)★★★★.

BRIGADOON

Despite the acknowledged brilliance of the MGM team that transferred the 1947 Broadway musical *Brigadoon* to the big screen (notably producer Arthur Freed and director Vincente Minnelli), for many, the magic touch so evident in their other creations was absent in this 1954 film. Alan Jay Lerner's mystical tale is set in a Scottish Highlands village that only comes to life once every hundred years, and where two Americans, Tommy Albright (Gene Kelly) and Jeff Douglas (Van Johnson), happen to stray during a hunting holiday. Albright falls in love with Fiona (Cyd Charisse), one of the townspeople; initially, the thoughts of his life and girl back home in the USA draw him away and he is unable to make the sacrifice and remain part of the sleeping village. It is only a minor miracle brought about by the strength of Kelly's love that reawakens the village temporarily so he can once again, and forever, be with his true love. Many reasons have been cited for the rather staged *Brigadoon* not working as effectively as other Freed creations. These include the decisions to photograph the film in Ansco Color and CinemaScope and not on location, owing to financial restraints, which resulted in the use of artificial-looking studio backdrops; the proliferation of highly unconvincing Scottish accents; and the exclusion of some of the show's most endearing numbers such as 'There But For You Go I' and 'Come To Me, Bend To Me'. However, despite these factors, the film, released in September 1954, certainly has its enchanting moments. Some sequences are widely considered to be misjudged, but it is hard to fault Charisse and Kelly (also the film's choreographer) when they are dancing to 'Heather On The Hill' (Charisse dubbed by Carole

Richards), or Kelly's expression of joy in 'Almost Like Being In Love'. Other songs in what is a lovely score, written by Frederick Loewe, with charming lyrics from Alan Jay Lerner, included 'Brigadoon', 'Waitin' For My Dearie', 'Once In The Highlands', and the rousing ensemble piece 'I'll Go Home With Bonnie Jean'. Most of the comic moments are left to Van Johnson, who, as Kelly's cynical companion, prefers to dream with the help of alcohol rather than women. Despite its flaws, *Brigadoon*, with its romantic and fairytale atmosphere, is still fondly regarded by many admirers of film musicals.

BRIM, GRACE

b. *c*.1924. One of the few female musicians active on the post-war Chicago blues scene, Brim appeared with her husband John Brim's group, the Gary Kings. At her first recording session in 1950, she played harmonica and sang, demonstrating a pleasant, though not especially expressive, vocal style. Later she took to the drums, although on at least one record she also sang and played harmonica. Some records appeared under her own name, some as Mrs John Brim, but mostly she played a subordinate role on John's records, and can be heard lending very solid support on his fine topical blues, 'Tough Times', with Eddie Taylor and Jimmy Reed. She continued to play for many years, both with her husband and with other groups, and they appeared together on a single in the 70s.
● COMPILATIONS: *Chicago Slickers* (1981)★★★.

BRIM, JOHN

b. 10 April 1922, Hopkinsville, Kentucky, USA. Born on a farm, Brim played blues guitar from an early age. In the mid-40s, he relocated to Chicago, where he joined the burgeoning post-war blues scene, playing with artists such as John Lee 'Sonny Boy' Williamson, Muddy Waters and later Jimmy Reed. The tough sound of his music placed him firmly in the Chicago style of the day; his vocals were raw and convincing and his guitar-playing rough yet effective. His records, some of which featured his wife Grace Brim singing and playing drums, appeared on a variety of labels, but the best were probably the later 50s tracks, such as 'Rattlesnake' (which was based on Big Mama Thornton's 'Hound Dog' and featured the superb harmonica work of Little Walter), 'Lifetime Blues' and the topical 'Tough Times'. Brim has continued to play, issuing an interesting if rather rough single in the 70s, and a fine half-album of tough Chicago blues in the late 80s. Van Halen's cover version of his classic 'Ice Cream Man' led to renewed interest in the late 70s and into the 90s.
● ALBUMS: *Whose Muddy Shoes* (1970)★★★, *Chicago Blues Sessions* (Wolf 1989)★★★, *The Ice Cream Man* (Tone-Cool 1994)★★★.

BRISSON, FREDERICK

b. Carl Frederick Brisson, 17 March 1913, Copenhagen, Denmark, d. 8 October 1984, New York, USA. Brisson, the son of Carl Brisson, was a stage and film producer. He grew up in England, and after attending the Rossall College in Lancashire, began his career as a theatrical manager, He co-produced his father's 1930 hit show *Wonder Bar*, and in 1937 moved into films, first as an associate producer. Brisson also opened a talent agency which eventually had offices in

London, Paris and Hollywood. Finding himself more or less permanently based in the USA, he served in the American Air Force during World War II, attaining the rank of Lieutenant Colonel. After the war he formed Independent Artists Pictures, and in 1954 turned his attention to Broadway, co-producing the hit musicals *The Pajama Game* (1954), *Damn Yankees* (1955) and *New Girl In Town* (1957). He also mounted numerous straight plays, and was instrumental in introducing several important British writers to American audiences, such as Harold Pinter, Peter Shaffer and Tom Stoppard. His projects during the 60s included two more musicals, *Passion Flower Hotel* (1965, London) and *Coco* (1969, New York). Brisson also produced the film musicals *The Girl Rush* (1955) and the acclaimed screen adaptation of *The Pajama Game* (1958). The former starred Rosalind Russell, who was married to Brisson from 1941 until her death in 1976. Brisson's honours included the US Legion of Merit, the King Christian V Medal (Denmark), and the New York Drama Critics Award for his work on Shaffer's *Five Finger Exercise*.

BROCK, 'BIG' GEORGE

b. Mississippi, USA. Brock's father gave him a harmonica as a Christmas present when he was aged eight. At the age of 12, he sang at a 'fish fry' and later worked in many clubs in his native state. He settled in St. Louis, Missouri, in 1953, and after playing in a club for some time, he took it over temporarily. He subsequently became a bandleader again, working with Ike Turner, and employed Albert King as his lead guitarist. Brock refused an opportunity to record in 1963, and eventually made his first single in 1990, followed by an album on his own label later the same year. Brock describes himself as 'a low down pure blues singer', strongly influenced by Howlin' Wolf, B.B. King, Muddy Waters, Elmore James and Jimmy Reed. He is the proud possessor of a gold belt, successfully defended in numerous harmonica championships.
● ALBUMS: *Should Have Been There* (1990)★★★.

BRODSZKY, NICHOLAS

b. 1905, Odessa, Russia, d. 24 December 1958, Hollywood, California, USA. After some musical training in Russia as a child, Brodszky continued his studies in Rome, Vienna and Budapest. From 1930 onwards he wrote music for European films and operetta, and in 1937 travelled to England and collaborated with lyricist A.P. Herbert on the score for the West End revue *Home And Beauty*, which starred Gitta Alpar and Binnie Hale. During the next 10 years he composed the scores for several British movies, including *French Without Tears*, *Freedom Radio*, *Quiet Wedding*, *Unpublished Story*, *Tomorrow We Live*, *The Way To The Stars*, *English Without Tears*, *Carnival*, and *A Man About The House* (1947). In this phase of his career, it has been remarked that he relied heavily on collaborators such as Clive Richardson, Charles Williams, Sidney Torch, Philip Green and Roy Douglas. Brodszky experienced major success when he moved to the USA and teamed with popular lyricist Sammy Cahn on 'Be My Love' for the Mario Lanza picture *The Toast Of New Orleans* (1950). It was the first of five of his songs to be nominated for an Oscar. Three of the others were with Cahn: 'Wonder Why' (from *Rich, Young And Pretty*), the title song for another Lanza vehicle, *Because You're Mine*, and 'I'll

Never Stop Loving You' which was introduced in the Ruth Etting biopic *Love Me Or Leave Me* by Doris Day. The other nominee was 'My Flaming Heart' from *Small Town Girl*, which had a lyric by Leo Robin. There were several other appealing songs in *Rich, Young And Pretty*, including 'How Do You Like Your Eggs In The Morning?', which was sung by Jane Powell, Vic Damone and the Four Freshmen, and 'We Never Talk Much', a delightful number performed in the movie by Danielle Darrieux and Fernando Lamas and later recorded with some success by Dean Martin and Line Renaud. Brodszky's other work for pictures included 'Beloved', 'Summertime In Heidelberg' and 'I'll Walk With God', all with Paul Francis Webster for *The Student Prince*; 'Hell Hath No Fury' (*Meet Me In Las Vegas*); 'Now, Baby, Now' and others (*The Opposite Sex*); and 'You I Love', 'Money Is A Problem', 'Only Trust Your Heart' and the title song for *Ten Thousand Bedrooms* (all with Cahn). Brodszky died in 1958, shortly after that score was completed.

BROOKS, 'BIG' LEON
b. 19 November 1933, Rabbit Foot Farm, near Sunflower, Mississippi, USA, d. 22 January 1982, Chicago, Illinois, USA. Brooks began playing blues harmonica when he was six years old. His original inspiration was Sonny Boy 'Rice Miller' Williamson, but after moving to Chicago in the 40s he met Little Walter Jacobs, described by Brooks as 'my coach' - a fact evident to anyone who has heard both men's music. In the 50s, Brooks led his own band on a sporadic basis, and supplied accompaniment to Jimmy Rogers, Otis Rush, Robert Nighthawk, and others. He was disillusioned by the changes in the blues in the early 60s and left music until 1976, when he once again began to sing and play in Chicago's blues clubs. He died of a heart attack in January 1982.
● COMPILATIONS: four tracks only *Living Chicago Blues, Volume 5* (1980)★★.

BROONZY, 'BIG' BILL
b. William Lee Conley Broonzy, 26 June 1893 (or 1898), Scott, Mississippi, USA, d. 14 August 1958, Chicago, Illinois, USA. Broonzy worked as a field hand, and it was behind the mule that he first developed his unmistakable, hollering voice, with its remarkable range and flexibility. As a child he made himself a violin, and learned to play under the guidance of an uncle. For a time, he worked as a preacher, before settling finally into the secular life of the blues singer. fter service in the army at the end of World War I, he moved to Chicago, where he learned to play guitar from Papa Charlie Jackson. Despite his late start as a guitarist, Broonzy quickly became proficient on the instrument, and when he first recorded in the late 20s, he was a fluent and assured accompanist in both ragtime and blues idioms. His voice retained a flavour of the countryside, in addition to his clear diction, but his playing had the up-to-date sophistication and assurance of the city dweller. The subjects of his blues, too, were those that appealed to blacks who, like him, had recently migrated to the urban north, but retained family and cultural links with the south. As such, Broonzy's music exemplifies the movement made by the blues from locally made folk music to nationally distributed, mass media entertainment. He was sometimes used as a talent scout by record companies, and was also favoured as an accompanist; up to

1942 he recorded hundreds of tracks in this capacity, as well as over 200 issued, and many unissued, titles in his own right. His own records followed trends in black tastes; by the mid-30s they were almost always in a small-group format, with piano, and often brass or woodwind and a rhythm section, but his mellow, sustained guitar tones were always well to the fore. Despite his undoubted 'star' status - not until 1949 was it necessary to put his full name on a race record: just 'Big Bill' was enough - the questionable financial practices of the record industry meant that his income from music did not permit a full-time career as a musician until late in his life. After World War II, Broonzy had lost some of his appeal to black audiences, but by this time he had shrewdly moved his focus to the burgeoning white audience, drawn from jazz fans and the incipient folk song revival movement. He had played Carnegie Hall in 1938 (introduced as a Mississippi ploughhand!), and in 1951 was one the blues' first visitors to Europe. He recorded frequently, if from a narrowed musical base, changing his repertoire radically to emphasize well-known, older blues such as 'Trouble In Mind', blues ballads such as 'John Henry', popular songs such as 'Glory Of Love' and even protest numbers, including the witty 'When Do I Get To Be Called A Man'. He became a polished raconteur, and further developed his swinging, fluent guitar playing, although on slow numbers he sometimes became rather mannered, after the fashion of Josh White. Broonzy was greatly loved by his new audience, and revered by the younger Chicago blues singers. In 1955 he published an engaging, anecdotal autobiography, compiled by Yannick Bruynoghe from his letters. It should be noted that Broonzy had learned to write only in 1950, taught by students at Iowa State University, where he was employed as a janitor. Broonzy was a proud, determined man, and a pivotal figure in blues, both when it was the music of black Americans, and as it became widely available to whites the world over. His reputation suffered after his death, as his later recordings were deemed as having pandered to white tastes. The importance of his earlier contribution to black music was not fully understood. 'Big' Bill Broonzy was an intelligent and versatile entertainer, and his immense talent was always at the service of his audience and their expectations.
● ALBUMS: *Blues Concert* (Dial 1952)★★, *Folk Blues* (EmArcy 1954)★★★, *Big Bill Broonzy Sings* (Period 1956)★★★, *Big Bill Broonzy* (Folkways 1957)★★★★, *Country Blues* (Folkways 1957)★★★★, *Big Bill Broonzy Sings And Josh White Comes A-Visiting* (Period 1958)★★★, *Last Session Parts 1-3* (Verve 1959)★★★, *Remembering ... The Greatest Minstrel Of The Authentic Blues* (1963)★★★.
● COMPILATIONS: *The Big Bill Broonzy Story* 5-LP box set (Verve 1959)★★★★, *Memorial* (Mercury 1963)★★★★, *Remembering Big Bill Broonzy* (Mercury 1964)★★★★, *Big Bill And Sonny Boy* (1964)★★★★, *Trouble In Mind* (1965)★★★, *Big Bill's Blues* (Epic 1969)★★★★, *Feelin' Low Down* (GNP Crescendo 1973)★★★, *Midnight Steppers* (Bluetime 1986)★★★, *Big Bill Broonzy Volumes 1-3* (Document 1986-88)★★★★, *The Young Bill Broonzy 1928-1935* (Yazoo 1988)★★★★, *Sings Folk Songs* (1989)★★★★, *The 1955 London Sessions* (Sequel 1990)★★★, *Remembering Big Bill Broonzy* (Beat Goes On 1990)★★★★, *Good Time Tonight* (Columbia 1990)★★★, *Do That Guitar Rag 1928-35* (Yazoo 1992)★★★, *I Feel So Good* (Indigo 1994)★★★, *Baby*

Please Don't Go (Drive Archive 1995)★★★, *Black, Brown & White* (Evidence 1995)★★★.
● FURTHER READING: *Big Bill Blues: Big Bill Broonzy's Story As Told To Yannick Bruynoghe*, Yannick Bruynoghe. *Hit The Right Lick: The Recordings Of Big Bill Broonzy*, Chris Smith.

BROWN DOTS

A vocal group formed in 1944 by Ivory 'Deek' Watson (tenor singer for the Ink Spots, who left because of personality clashes), the Brown Dots' style, modelled on the Ink Spots, featured a high tenor lead and a talking deep bass. In contrast to the Ink Spots, however, the emphasis was more on the jive jump numbers - reflecting the interests of Watson - rather than the ballads. Original members, besides Watson, were Joe King (tenor), Pat Best (baritone and guitar), and Jimmy Gordon (bass), but within a few months King was replaced by Jimmie Nabbie. At first the group went by the name 'Ink Spots', but the courts, at the behest of the original group, prevented Watson from using the name, so he adopted the simple variation 'Brown Dots'. Recording for the New Jersey-based Manor Records, the Brown Dots produced some outstanding tracks, notably 'Let's Give Love Another Chance' and 'Just In Case You Change Your Mind', both led by Best, and 'For Sentimental Reasons', led by Nabbie. In 1948 Best, Gordon, and Nabbie left Watson and formed another group, the Sentimentalists. Watson recruited a new Brown Dots group, but was never able to sustain the group at its previous level of artistry and commercial appeal. Meanwhile, the Sentimentalists changed their name to the Four Tunes, and became one of the more popular vocal ensembles of the early 50s.

BROWN'S FERRY FOUR

The original group was founded at WLW Cincinnati, in June 1943, and went on to achieve legendary status as one of the finest quartets to have recorded country gospel music. The founding members, all active performers and following other careers as well as singing with the group, were Grandpa Jones, Merle Travis and the Delmore Brothers (Alton and Rabon). They took their name from the Delmores' hit song of the time, 'Brown's Ferry Blues'. They commenced a regular half-hour daily spot, with Alton singing lead, Rabon tenor, Jones baritone and Travis bass, and their fine harmonies quickly established them with the station's listeners. Unfortunately, military service for Travis, Jones and Alton Delmore saw the break-up of the original four. The station kept the name and the programme, entering the early 50s with other singers. In March 1946, the four original members had resumed their careers but with Travis in California, the Delmores in Memphis and Jones in Nashville, they never resumed their WLW association. However, when all were in California for recordings, Sid Nathan of King Records decided to record some of the gospel numbers that they had popularized, the first two being 'Will The Circle Be Unbroken' and 'Just A Little Talk With Jesus'. The recordings proved popular and the following year, Nathan flew all four to Hollywood for further recordings. A change in line-up was enforced when Travis became a Capitol recording artist and Red Foley replaced him on 1947 recordings, which produced their noted 'I'll See You In The Morning'. In 1948, the national ban on all recordings saw the

Delmores incorporate a version of the group within their stage act, with Wayne Raney and Lonnie Glosson replacing Jones and Foley. In the early 50s, Red Turner and Clyde Moody also sang with the Delmores. In 1956, Alton Delmore organized a group to record for Acme. In 1965, Grandpa Jones recorded *Grandpa Jones Remembers The Brown's Ferry Four* for Monument, which featured himself, Merle Travis, Red Rector and Ramona Jones. In the early 80s, Jones with Roy Clark, Buck Owens and Kenny Price recreated the sound of the original group, recording an album as the Hee Haw Gospel Quartet, for the label owned by the popular television *Hee Haw* programme, on which they also appeared. The original four's recordings enjoyed several reissues, going from 78s to 45s, a series of three EPs in 1957 and eventually to albums with reissues on Starday and Pine Mountain.
● ALBUMS: *Sacred Songs* (King 1957)★★★★, *Sacred Songs Volume 2* (King 1958)★★★ *Wonderful Sacred Songs* (King 1964)★★★, *16 Sacred Gospel Songs* (King 1963)★★★.

BROWN, BUSTER

b. Wayman Glasco, 15 August 1911, Cordele, Georgia, USA, d. 31 January 1976, Brooklyn, New York, USA. Brown played harmonica at local clubs and made a few recordings, including 'I'm Gonna Make You Happy' in 1943. Brown moved to New York in 1956 where he was discovered by Fire Records owner Bobby Robinson while working in a chicken and barbecue joint. In 1959, he recorded the archaic-sounding blues, 'Fannie Mae', whose tough harmonica riffs took it into the US Top 40. His similar-sounding 'Sugar Babe' (1961) was covered in the UK by Jimmy Powell. In later years he recorded for Checker and for numerous small labels including Serock, Gwenn and Astroscope.
● ALBUMS: *New King Of The Blues* (Fire 1959)★★★, *Get Down With Buster Brown* (Fire 1962)★★★, *Raise A Ruckus Tonite* (1976)★★★, *Good News* (Charly 1988)★★★.

BROWN, CHARLES

b. 13 September 1922, Texas City, Texas, USA. Brown's mother died only six months after he was born and he was raised by his grandparents. Despite learning piano and church organ at the insistence of his grandparents while a child, Brown became a teacher of chemistry. In 1943, living in Los Angeles, he realized that he could earn more money working as a pianist-singer. At that time, the top small group in Los Angeles was the Nat 'King' Cole Trio, but when Cole moved on, the Three Blazers, led by Johnny Moore (guitarist brother of Oscar Moore) and whom Brown had just joined, moved into the top spot. By 1946 the band was a national favourite, with hit records including 'Driftin' Blues', and appearances at New York's Apollo Theatre. In 1948 the group broke up, although Moore continued to lead a band with the same name, but he was now on his own and virtually unknown as a solo performer. In the early 50s a string of successful records, many featuring his own compositions, boosted his career. Additionally, his work was recorded by such artists as B.B. King, Ray Charles, Sam Cooke, Amos Milburn and Fats Domino, with whom Brown recorded 'I'll Always Be In Love With You' and 'Please Believe Me'. He was heavily influenced by Robert Johnson, Louis Jordan, and especially by Pha Terrell, the singer with the Andy Kirk band. Brown's singing evolved into a highly melodic ballad style that still showed signs of his blues roots. He aptly defined himself as a 'blue ballad singer'. His singing combines the velvety sound of Cole with the tough cynicism of Leroy Carr and Lonnie Johnson. In contrast to Cole, Brown's star waned, although he had successful records with songs such as 'Christmas Comes But Once A Year'. One follower was Ray Charles, who, early in his career, modelled his singing on an amalgam of Brown's and Cole's styles. By the end of the 60s Brown was working in comparative obscurity at Los Angeles nightspots. An appearance at the 1976 San Francisco Blues Festival boosted his reputation, but the pattern remained pretty much unaltered into the 80s and early 90s. He can still be found constantly touring the USA and Europe, providing superb live entertainment, backed by his outstanding guitar player and musical director, Danny Caron.

● ALBUMS: *Race Track Blues* (50s)★★★, *Mood Music* 10-inch album (Aladdin 1955)★★★★, *Driftin' Blues* (Score 1958)★★★, *More Blues With Charles Brown* (Score 1958)★★★★, *Music, Maestro, Please* (60s)★★★, *Charles Brown Sings Million Sellers* .(Imperial 1961)★★★, *Charles Brown Sings Christmas Songs* (King 1961)★★★★, *The Great Charles Brown* (King 1963)★★★, *Ballads My Way* (Mainstream 1965)★★★, *One More For The Road* (Alligator 1986)★★★, *All My Life* (Rounder/Bullseye 1990)★★★, *Someone To Love* (1992)★★★, *Blues And Other Love Songs* (1993)★★★, *Just A Lucky So And So* (Bullseye Blues 1994)★★★, *These Blues* (Verve 1994)★★★, *Charles Brown's Cool Christmas Blues* (Bullseye Blues 1994)★★★, *Blues N' Brown* 1971 recording (Jewel 1995)★★★, *Honey Dripper* (Verve 1996)★★★★.

● COMPILATIONS: *Legend* (Bluesway 1970)★★★★, with Johnny Moore's Three Blazers *Sunny Road* (Route 66 1980)★★★, with Johnny Moore's Three Blazers *Race Track Blues* (Route 66 1981)★★★, with Johnny Moore's Three Blazers *Sail On Blues* (Jukebox Lil 1989)★★★, *Driftin' Blues (The Best Of Charles Brown)* (Capitol 1992)★★★, *The Complete Aladdin Recordings Of Charles Brown* (Mosaic 1994)★★★★, with Johnny Moore's Three Blazers *Drifting And Dreaming* (Ace 1995)★★★.

BROWN, CLARENCE 'GATEMOUTH'

b. 18 April 1924, Vinton, Louisiana, USA (some sources give Orange, Texas, where he was raised from the age of three weeks). Brown's father was a musician who taught him to play guitar and fiddle, and during his youth he heard the music of Tampa Red, Bob Wills, Count Basie, and others. He toured the south as a drummer with a travelling show before being drafted into the army. On his discharge he worked as a musician in San Antonio, Texas, where he honed his guitar skills sufficiently to impress Don Robey, who offered him a spot at his club in Houston. It was here that Gatemouth's big break came, when he took over a show from T-Bone Walker, after Walker was taken ill. He was so well received that Robey took him to Los Angeles to record for the Aladdin Label on 21 August 1947. In 1948 he set up his own Peacock label, for which Brown recorded until 1961. Many of these records are classics of Texas guitar blues, and were enormously influential. During the 60s Gatemouth broadened his stylistic base to include jazz and country, best exemplified by his 1965 Chess recordings made in Nashville. These were pointers to the direction in which Brown's music was

later to develop. In the 70s he recorded a mixed bag of albums for the French Black And Blue label (including a Louis Jordan tribute set), a couple of Cajun/country/rock hybrids and a good blues album for Barclay Records. In the 80s, Rounder successfully showcased Gatemouth's versatile approach by matching him with a big, brassy band, and he has also recorded for Alligator. In recent years Brown has tended to showcase his fiddle-playing to the detriment of his still excellent blues guitar picking, but he remains a fine singer and an extremely talented instrumentalist, whatever genre of music he turns his attention to. On his recent Verve recordings he has begun to put the fiddle in the background.

● ALBUMS: *The Blues Ain't Nothing* (Black And Blue 1971)★★★★, *Sings Louis Jordan* (Black And Blue 1972)★★★, *The Drifter Rides Again* (Barclay 1973)★★★, *The Bogalusa Boogie Man* (Barclay 1974)★★★, *San Antonio Ballbuster* (Red Lightnin' 1974)★★★, *Cold Strange* (Black And Blue 1977)★★★, *Blackjack* (Music Is Medicine 1977)★★★, *Double Live At The Cowboy Bar* (Music Is Medicine 1978)★★★, with Roy Clark *Makin' Music* (MCA 1979)★★★, *Alright Again* (Rounder 1981)★★★, *One More Mile* (Rounder 1983)★★★, *Atomic Energy* (Blues Boy 1983)★★★, *Pressure Cooker* 70s recording (Alligator 1985)★★★, *Texas Guitarman - Duke-Peacock Story, Vol. 1* (Ace 1986)★★★★, *Real Life* (Rounder 1987)★★★, *Texas Swing* early 80s recording (Rounder 1987)★★★, *The Nashville Session 1965* (Chess 1989)★★★, *Standing My Ground* (Alligator 1989)★★★, *No Looking Back* (Alligator 1992)★★★, *Just Got Lucky* Black And Blue recordings (Evidence 1993)★★★★, *The Man* (Gitanes Jazz/Verve 1994)★★★, *Long Way Home* (Verve 1995)★★★, *Live* 1980 recordings (Charly 1995)★★★, *Gate Swings* (Verve 1997)★★★★.

● COMPILATIONS: *Original Peacock Recordings* (Rounder 1988)★★★★, *The Best Of Clarence 'Gatemouth' Brown: A Blues Legend* (Verve 1995)★★★★.

BROWN, DUSTY

b. 11 March 1929, Tralake, Mississippi, USA. A self-taught blues harmonica player, Brown enjoyed a certain amount of success after moving to Chicago in the 40s. He started by sitting in with artists such as Muddy Waters, but soon formed his own band. In 1955, he had a record issued on the local Parrot label (there were also other tracks that remained unissued until over 30 years later), his accompanists featuring, among others, the pianist Henry Gray. Later in the decade, he recorded for Bandera, but again there can have been little commercial success (although, again, a couple of unissued sides have appeared in subsequent years). He gave up attempting to make a living from music until the 70s, when he made a comeback, taking advantage of the renewed interest in the music, in particular from the European market.

● ALBUMS: *Hand Me Down Blues* (1990)★★★.

BROWN, LILLYN

b. 24 April 1885, Atlanta, Georgia, USA, d. 8 June 1969, New York City, New York, USA. Brown was in showbusiness from 1894-1934 (at one time billed as 'the Kate Smith of Harlem'), returning for a period in the 50s. A singer, dancer and male impersonator, she added blues to her act in 1908. In 1921 she recorded four titles with her Jazz-bo Syncopators. The

music, as her background and the group's name imply, was a hybrid of blues, jazz, and the ragtime-influenced pop of a decade earlier, with 'If That's What You Want Here It Is' being a particularly impressive, spirited performance. In the 50s, she operated an acting and singing school, and from 1956 was secretary to the Negro Actors' Guild, also writing and directing plays for her church as late as 1965.
● COMPILATIONS: *Female Blues Singers B/C* (1990)★★.

BROWN, NAPPY

b. Napoleon Brown Culp, 12 October 1929, Charlotte, North Carolina, USA. Brown began his career as a gospel singer, but moved to R&B when an appearance in Newark, New Jersey, led to a recording contract with Savoy in 1954. A deep-voiced, highly individual R&B singer, he had a number of hits during the 50s, including 'Don't Be Angry' (1955), the Rose Marie McCoy/Charlie Singleton song 'Pitter Patter' (a pop hit in Patti Page's cover version), 'It Don't Hurt No More' (1958) and 'I Cried Like A Baby' (1959). He also made the original version of 'The Night Time Is The Right Time', a 1958 hit for Ray Charles. A prison term kept Brown inactive for much of the 60s. He returned to music with an album for Elephant V in 1969 and recorded gospel music in the 70s with the Bell Jubilee Singers for Jewel and as Brother Napoleon Brown for Savoy. In the 80s, Brown was rediscovered by a later generation of blues enthusiasts. He performed at festivals and recorded for Black Top and Alligator, with guitarist Tinsley Ellis accompanying him on *Tore Up*. Brown also appeared on a live album recorded at Tipitina's in New Orleans in 1988. He has continued recording in the 90s, although his most recent albums have not managed to recapture the power of his work of the 50s.
● ALBUMS: *Nappy Brown Sings* (London 1955)★★★★, *The Right Time* (London 1958)★★★★, *Thanks For Nothing* (Elephant V 1969)★★★, *Tore Up* (Alligator 1984)★★★, *Something Gonna Jump Out The Bushes* (Black Top 1988)★★★, *Apples & Lemons* (Ichiban 1990)★★, *Aw, Shucks* (Ichiban 1991)★★, *I'm A Wild Man* (New Moon 1994)★★, *Don't Be Angry* (Savoy 1995)★★, *Who's Been Foolin' You* (New Moon 1997)★★★.

BROWN, RUTH

b. 30 January 1928, Portsmouth, Virginia, USA. Brown started her musical career singing gospel at an early age in the church choir led by her father. In 1948 she was singing with a band led by her husband Jimmy in Washington, DC, when Willis Conover (from the radio show *Voice Of America*) recommended her to Ahmet Ertegun of the newly formed Atlantic Records. Ertegun signed her, despite competition from Capitol, but on the way up to New York for an appearance at the Apollo Theatre, she was involved in a car crash. Hospitalized for nine months, her medical bills were paid by Atlantic and she rewarded them handsomely with her first big hit, 'Teardrops From My Eyes', in 1950. More hits followed with '5-10-15 Hours' (1952) and 'Mama, He Treats Your Daughter Mean' (1953). Atlantic's first real star, Brown became a major figure in 50s R&B, forming a strong link between that music and early rock 'n' roll. Her records were characterized by her rich and expressive singing voice (not unlike that of Dinah Washington) and accompaniment by breathy saxophone solos (initially by Budd Johnson, later by Willie Jackson). Between 1949 and 1955 her songs were on

the charts for 129 weeks, including five number 1s. Brown's concentration upon R&B has not kept her from associations with the jazz world; very early in her career she sang briefly with the Lucky Millinder band, and has recorded with Jerome Richardson and the Thad Jones-Mel Lewis big band. She also brought a distinctively soulful treatment to varied material such as 'Yes, Sir, That's My Baby', 'Sonny Boy', 'Black Coffee' and 'I Can Dream, Can't I?'. In 1989 she won a Tony Award for her performance in the Broadway show *Black And Blue*, and was receiving enthusiastic reviews for her nightclub act in New York, at Michael's Pub and the Blue Note, into the 90s. In 1993 Brown was to be heard broadcasting on a New York radio station, and was inducted into the Rock And Roll Hall Of Fame. In 1994 she undertook a European tour, much to the delight of her small but loyal group of fans. On that tour she was recorded live at Ronnie Scott's club for an album that appeared on their own Jazzhouse label.
● ALBUMS: *Ruth Brown Sings Favorites* 10-inch album (Atlantic 1952)★★★, *Ruth Brown* (Atlantic 1957)★★★★, *Late Date With Ruth Brown* (Atlantic 1959)★★★★, *Miss Rhythm* (Atlantic 1959)★★★★, *Along Comes Ruth* (Philips 1962)★★★★, *Gospel Time* (Philips 1962)★★★, *Ruth Brown '65* (Mainstream 1965)★★★, *Black Is Brown And Brown Is Beautiful* (Rhapsody 1969)★★★, *The Real Ruth Brown* (70s)★★★, *You Don't Know Me* (70s)★★, *Touch Me In The Morning* (70s)★★, *Sugar Babe* (President 1977)★★★, *Takin' Care Of Business* (1980)★★★, *The Soul Survives* (1982)★★, *Brown Sugar* (Topline 1986)★★★, *Sweet Baby Of Mine* (Route 66 1987)★★, *I'll Wait For You* (Official 1988)★★, *Blues On Broadway* (Fantasy 1989)★★★, with Linda Hopkins, Carrie Smith *Black And Blue* (1989)★★★, *Fine And Mellow* (1992)★★★, *The Songs Of My Life* (Fantasy 1993)★★★, *Live In London* (Jazzhouse 1995)★★★.
● COMPILATIONS: *The Best Of Ruth Brown* (Atlantic 1963)★★★★, *Rockin' With Ruth* 1950-60 recordings (Charly 1984)★★★★, *Brown Black And Beautiful* (SDEG 1990)★★★, *Miss Rhythm, Greatest Hits And More* (Atlantic 1993)★★★★, *Blues On Broadway* (Ace 1994)★★★★, *You Don't Know Me* (Indigo 1997)★★★★, *R + B = Ruth Brown* (Bullseye 1997)★★★★.
● FURTHER READING: *Miss Rhythm*, Ruth Brown with Andrew Yule.

BROWNS

Ella Maxine Brown (b. 27 April 1932, Sampti, Louisiana, USA), Jim Edward Brown (b. 1 April 1934, Sparkman, Arkansas, USA) and Bonnie Brown (b. 31 July 1937, Sparkman, Arkansas, USA). In 1953, greatly influenced by WSM broadcasts of the *Grand Ole Opry*, Maxine and her brother began singing as a duo. They first featured on *Barnyard Hayride* on KLRA Little Rock, before being signed to the *Louisiana Hayride* on KWKH Shreveport. They recorded some duet tracks for Fabor and in 1954 registered a Top 10 US country hit with their own song, 'Looking Back To See' (Jim Reeves actually played rhythm guitar on the recording). In 1955, after being joined by sister Bonnie, they became a featured act on Red Foley's *Ozark Jubilee* and their recording of 'Here Today And Gone Tomorrow' became their first country hit as a trio. In 1956, with help from Jim Reeves, they moved to RCA, where they immediately had a US country number 2 hit with their recording of the Louvin's

'I Take The Chance'. The following year they had major success with 'I Heard The Bluebirds Sing', but it was in 1959 that they enjoyed their biggest hit with their million-selling recording of 'The Three Bells'. Based on a song called 'While The Angelus Was Ringing' and sometimes known as 'The Jimmy Brown Song' or 'Les Trois Cloches', the song was popularized in Europe by both Les Compagnons de la Chanson and Edith Piaf. The Browns' recording topped both the US country and pop charts and even reached number 6 on the UK pop charts. Between 1959 and 1967, 12 further hits followed including 'Scarlet Ribbons', 'The Old Lamplighter', 'Then I'll Stop Loving You' and 'I'd Just Be Fool Enough'. In the early 60s, they appeared on all major television shows and toured extensively including trips to Europe and Japan, as well as running their own club in Pine Bluff, Arkansas. They joined the *Grand Ole Opry* in 1963, but in 1967, with Maxine and Bonnie wishing to spend more time with their families, they disbanded. In 1968, Maxine had a minor hit as a solo artist on the Chart label with 'Sugar Cane County', while Jim Ed continued his career as a solo artist with RCA Records. The Browns reunited in 1996 for the gospel set, *Family Bible*.

● ALBUMS: *Jim Edward, Maxine & Bonnie Brown* (RCA Victor 1957)★★★, *Sweet Sounds By The Browns* (RCA Victor 1959)★★★, *Town & Country* (RCA Victor 1960)★★★, *The Browns Sing Their Hits* (RCA Victor 1960)★★★★, *Our Favorite Folk Songs* (RCA Victor 1961)★★★, *Songs From The Little Brown Church Hymnal* (RCA Victor 1961)★★★, *Grand Ole Opry Favorites* (RCA Victor 1964)★★★, *This Young Land* (RCA Victor 1964)★★★, *Three Shades Of Brown* (RCA Victor 1965)★★★, *I Heard The Bluebirds Sing* (RCA Camden 1965)★★★, *Our Kind Of Country* (RCA Victor 1966)★★★, *The Browns Sing The Big Ones From The Country* (RCA Victor 1967)★★★, *The Old Country Church* (RCA Victor 1967)★★★★, *A Harvest Of Country Songs* (RCA Camden 1968)★★★, *Family Bible* (Step One 1996)★★★.
Solo: Maxine Brown *Sugar Cane County* (Chart 1969)★★.
● COMPILATIONS: *Best Of The Browns* (RCA Victor 1966)★★★★, *Rockin' Rollin' Browns* (Bear Family 1984)★★★, *20 Of The Best* (RCA 1985)★★★★, *Looking Back To See* (Bear Family 1986)★★★, *Three Bells* 8-CD box set (Bear Family 1993)★★★★.

BRUBECK, DAVE

b. David Warren Brubeck, 6 December 1920, Concord, California, USA. Initially taught piano by his mother, Brubeck showed an immediate flair for the instrument, and was performing with local professional jazz groups throughout northern California at the age of 15 while still at high school. Enrolling at the College of the Pacific in Stockton, California, as a vetinary major, he transferred to the music conservatory at the suggestion of his college advisor. His involvement in jazz continued by establishing a 12-piece band, but most of his time was spent in the study of theory and composition. After he graduated from Pacific, Brubeck decided to continue his formal classical training. His studying was interrupted by military service in World War II. Returning from Europe in 1946, he went to Mills College as a graduate student under the tutorship of Darius Milhaud, and at about this time he formed his first serious jazz group - the Jazz Workshop Ensemble, an eight-piece unit that recorded some sessions, the results of which were

issued three years later on Fantasy Records as the *Dave Brubeck Octet*.

He began a more consistent professional involvement in the jazz scene in 1949, with the creation of his first trio, with Cal Tjader and Ron Crotty. It was with the addition of alto saxophonist Paul Desmond in 1951 that Brubeck's group achieved major critical acclaim, even though the trio had won the Best Small Combo award in *Downbeat*. Replacing Tjader and Crotty with Gene Wright (in 1958) and Joe Morello (in 1956) towards the end of the 50s, Brubeck led this celebrated and prolific quartet as a unit until 1967, when he disbanded the group. Brubeck toured as the Dave Brubeck Trio with Gerry Mulligan, together with Alan Dawson (drums) and Jack Six (bass) for seven years to widespread critical acclaim. He began using a new group in 1972 involving his three sons, touring as the Darius Brubeck Ensemble and the Dave Brubeck Trio, with either Mulligan or Desmond as guest soloists, until 1976. From 1977 to 1979 the New Brubeck Quartet consisted of four Brubecks, Dave, Darius, Chris and Dan. Apart from a brief classic quartet reunion in 1976, most of his now rare concert appearances have since been in this setting, with the addition at various times of Randy Jones (drums), Jack Six, Bill Smith (clarinet) and Bobby Militello (alto saxophone).

Brubeck's musical relationship with Desmond was central to his success. The group's 1959 classic 'Take Five' was composed by Desmond, and it was the saxophonist's extraordinary gift for melodic improvisation that gave the group much of its musical strength. Always seeing himself primarily as a composer rather than a pianist, Brubeck, in his own solos, tended to rely too much on his ability to work in complex time-signatures (often two at once). His work in the field of composition has produced over 300 pieces, including several jazz standards such as the magnificent 'Blue Rondo A La Turk', as well as 'In Your Own Sweet Way' and 'The Duke'. Additionally, he has composed two ballets, a musical, a mass, works for television and film, an oratorio and two cantatas. However, Brubeck will always be primarily associated with his pivotal quartet recordings with Paul Desmond, and with 'Take Five', in particular. Throughout the 60s, when jazz was able to cross over into other territories, it was primarily Miles Davis, John Coltrane and Brubeck that were quoted, cited and applauded. His band was a central attraction at almost all the major international jazz festivals, and during the 50s and 60s, he frequently won both *Downbeat* and *Metronome* polls. As early as 1954, Brubeck appeared on the cover of *Time* magazine, and 10 years later was invited to play at the White House by Ronald Reagan (which he repeated on numerous occasions, including the 1988 Gorbachev Summit in Moscow). He later received the National Medal of the Arts from President Clinton. Brubeck remains a household name in modern jazz, and was still working on projects during the 90s. His family of talented musicians presently touring with him are Darius Brubeck (piano), Dan Brubeck (drums), Matthew Brubeck (cello) and Chris Brubeck (bass, bass trombone). His resurgence continued in 1995 with his 75th birthday and the release of *Young Lions & Old Tigers*, featuring Jon Hendricks, Gerry Mulligan, Joshua Redman, George Shearing, Joe Lovano and Michael Brecker.

By making pop charts all over the world, Dave Brubeck has brought jazz to unsuspecting ears. He has done much to popularize jazz to the masses and is both a legend and jazz icon. In later years his work will surely be added to classical music reference books, notably his mass *To Hope! A Celebration*, his cantata *La Fiesta De La Posada* and his Bach-influenced *Chromatic Fantasy Sonata*.

● ALBUMS: *Dave Brubeck Octet* (Fantasy 1949/56)★★★, *Dave Brubeck Trio* (Fantasy 1951/56)★★★, *Dave Brubeck Trio* reissued as *Distinctive Rhythm Instrumentals* (Fantasy 1951/56)★★★, *Dave Brubeck Trio* (Fantasy 1952)★★★, *Dave Brubeck Quartet* reissued as *Brubeck Desmond* (Fantasy 1952/56)★★★, *Dave Brubeck Quartet* (Fantasy 1952/56)★★★, *Jazz At Storyville* (Fantasy 1953/57)★★★, *Jazz At The Blackhawk* (Fantasy 1953/56)★★★, *Jazz At Oberlin* (Fantasy 1953/57)★★★, *Stardust* (Fantasy 1953)★★★★, *Jazz At The College Of Pacific* (Fantasy 1954/56)★★★★, *Old Sounds From San Fransisco* (Fantasy 1954)★★★, *Jazz Goes To College* (Columbia 1954)★★★★★, *Jazz Goes To College, Volume 2* (Columbia 1954)★★★, *Dave Brubeck At Storyville: 1954* (Columbia 1954)★★★, *Interchanges '54* (Columbia 1954)★★★, *Paul And Dave's Jazz Interwoven* (Fantasy 1955)★★★, *Brubeck Time* (Columbia 1955)★★★, *Jazz: Red Hot And Cool* (Columbia 1955)★★★, *Brubeck Plays Brubeck* (Columbia 1956)★★★, with J.J. Johnson and Kai Winding *American Jazz Festival At Newport '56* (Columbia 1956)★★★, *Brubeck And Desmond At Wilshire-Ebell* (Fantasy 1957)★★★, *Jazz Impressions Of The USA* (Columbia 1957)★★★, *Jazz Goes To Junior College* (Columbia 1957)★★★, *Dave Digs Disney* (Columbia 1957)★★, *Dave Brubeck Plays And Plays And Plays . . .* (Fantasy 1958)★★★, *Re-union* (Fantasy 1958)★★★, *Dave Brubeck Quartet In Europe* (Columbia 1958)★★★, *Newport 1958* (Columbia 1958)★★★, *Jazz Impressions Of Eurasia* (Columbia 1958)★★★, *Two Nights At The Black Hawk* (Fantasy 1959)★★★, *Gone With The Wind* (Columbia 1959)★★★, *Time Out Featuring 'Take Five'* (Columbia 1959)★★★★, *Brubeck A La Mode* (Fantasy 1960)★★★, *Southern Scene* (Columbia 1960)★★★, *The Riddle* (Columbia 1960)★★★, with the New York Philharmonic Orchestra *Bernstein Plays Brubeck Plays Bernstein* (Columbia 1960)★★★, *Brubeck And Rushing* (Columbia 1960)★★★, *Near-Myth* (Fantasy 1961)★★★, with Carmen McRae *Tonight Only!* (Columbia 1961)★★★, *Time Further Out* (Columbia 1961)★★★, *Countdown - Time In Outer Space* (Columbia 1962)★★★, *Bossa Nova USA* (Columbia 1963)★★★, *Dave Brubeck Quartet At Carnegie Hall* (Columbia 1963)★★★, *Brandenburg Gate: Revisited* (Columbia 1963)★★★, *The Great Concerts* (Columbia 1963)★★★★, *Time Changes* (Columbia 1964)★★★, *Jazz Impressions Of Japan* (Columbia 1964)★★★, *Jazz Impressions Of New York* (Columbia 1965)★★★★, *Take Five* (Columbia 1965)★★★, *Angel Eyes* (Columbia 1965)★★★, *My Favorite Things* (Columbia 1966)★★★, *Time In* (Columbia 1966)★★★, *Anything Goes! Dave Brubeck Quartet Plays Cole Porter* (Columbia 1966)★★★, *Bravo! Brubeck!* (Columbia 1967)★★★, *Jackpot* (Columbia 1967)★★★, *The Last Time We Saw Paris* (Columbia 1968)★★★, with Gerry Mulligan *Compadres* (Columbia 1969)★★★, *Brubeck In Amsterdam* (Columbia 1969)★★★, *Brubeck/Mulligan/Cincinnati* (MCA 1971)★★★★, *Adventures In Time* (1972)★★★, *Two Generations Of Brubeck* (Atlantic 1973)★★★, *We're All Together For The First Time* (Atlantic 1973)★★★, with Paul Desmond *Brubeck And Desmond -*

1975: The Duets (Horizon 1975)★★★, *All The Things We Are* (Atlantic 1975)★★★, *The Dave Brubeck Quartet 25th Anniversary Reunion* (A&M 1976)★★★, *Live At Montreaux* (Tomato 1978)★★★, *Paper Moon* (Concord 1982)★★★, *Concord On A Summer Night* (Concord 1982)★★, *For Iola* (Concord 1985)★★★, *Reflections* (Concord 1986)★★★, *Blue Rondo* (Concord 1987)★★★, *Moscow Night* (Concord 1987)★★★, *New Wine* (Limelight 1988)★★★, *Trio Brubeck* (Limelight 1988)★★★, *Quiet As The Moon* (Limelight 1991)★★★, *Once When I Was Very Young* (Limelight 1992)★★★, *Nightshift* (Telarc 1994)★★★, *Young Lions & Old Tigers* (Telarc 1995)★★★, *A Dave Brubeck Christmas* (Telarc 1996)★★★.

● COMPILATIONS: *Dave Brubeck's Greatest Hits* (Columbia 1966)★★★★, *Twenty-Four Classic Early Recordings* (Fantasy 1982)★★★★, *Collection: Dave Brubeck* (Deja Vu 1985)★★★, *The Essential Dave Brubeck* (Sony 1991)★★★★, *Time Signatures: A Career Retrospective* 4-CD box set (Columbia/Legacy 1993)★★★★★, *This Is Jazz No. 3* (Columbia/Legacy 1996)★★★.

● VIDEOS: *Musical Portrait* (BBC Video 1988).

BRYANT, BEULAH

b. Blooma Walton, 20 February 1918, Dayton, Alabama, USA, d. 31 January 1988, New York City, New York, USA. Bryant frequently sang with local church groups before moving to California in 1936 where she heard, and was influenced by, Ella Fitzgerald. After winning a networked radio show amateur contest the following year, she formed her own trio and began making regular appearances on the west coast. In 1945 she moved to New York and began working as a solo artist. Her recording career began in the late 40s on the tiny Do-Kay-Lo label, switching to MGM (many of the masters being provided by Joe Davis), and making a final session for Excello in 1955. Throughout the 50s, 60s and 70s Bryant was used extensively in radio, films and television. She also maintained an exhaustive touring schedule. In 1979 she belatedly resumed her recording career with a fine session for Victoria Spivey's label.

● ALBUMS: with Irene Redfield, Millie Bosman *Blues Women* (1985)★★★.

BRYANT, BOUDLEAUX

b. Diadorius Boudleaux Bryant, 13 February 1920, Shellman, Georgia, USA, d. 30 June 1987. With his wife Felice Bryant, he formed one of the greatest songwriting teams in country music and pop history. From a musical family, Boudleaux learned classical violin and piano from the age of five. During the early 30s his father organized a family band with Boudleaux and his four sisters and brothers, playing at county fairs in the Midwest. In 1937 Boudleaux moved to Atlanta, playing with the Atlanta Symphony Orchestra as well as jazz and country music groups. For several years he went on the road, playing in radio station bands in Detroit and Memphis before joining Hank Penny's Radio Cowboys, who performed over the airwaves of WSB Atlanta. In 1945 he met and married Felice Scaduto and the pair began composing together. The earliest recordings of Bryant songs included the Three Sons with 'Give Me Some Sugar, Sugar Baby, And I'll Be Your Sweetie Pie', but the first break came when they sent 'Country Boy' to Nashville publisher Fred Rose of Acuff-Rose. When this became a hit for Jimmy

Dickens, the duo moved to Nashville as staff writers for Acuff-Rose. Among their numerous successes in the 50s were 'Have A Good Time' (a pop success for Tony Bennett in 1952), 'Hey Joe' (recorded by Carl Smith and Frankie Laine in 1953) and the Eddy Arnold hits 'I've Been Thinking' and 'The Richest Man' (1955). In 1957, Rose's son Wesley Rose commissioned the Bryants to switch to teenage material for the Everly Brothers. Beginning with 'Bye Bye Love', they supplied a stream of songs that were melodramatic vignettes of teen life. Several of them were composed by Boudleaux alone. These included the wistful 'All I Have To Do Is Dream', the tough and vengeful 'Bird Dog', 'Devoted To You' and 'Like Strangers'. At this time he wrote what has become his most recorded song, 'Love Hurts'. This sorrowful, almost self-pitying ballad has been a favourite with the country rock fraternity, through notable versions by Roy Orbison and Gram Parsons. There have also been less orthodox rock treatments by Jim Capaldi and Nazareth. From the early 60s, the Bryants returned to the country sphere, composing the country standard 'Rocky Top' as well as providing occasional hits for artists such as Sonny James ('Baltimore', country chart number 6 in 1964) and Roy Clark ('Come Live With Me', country chart number 1 in 1973). Shortly before Boudleaux's death in June 1987, the Bryants were inducted into the Songwriters' Hall Of Fame.

● ALBUMS: *Boudleaux Bryant's Best Sellers* (Monument 1963)★★★, *All I Have To Do Is Dream* aka *A Touch Of Bryant* (CMH 1979)★★, *Surfin' On A New Wave* (1979)★★.

BRYANT, CLORA

b. c.1929, Denison, Texas, USA. Bryant began playing trumpet when her brother was away in the army and his instrument was available to her. She played in a school dance band and then in an all-girl orchestra at Prairie View College in Houston, Texas. Later, she attended UCLA, then left music and education behind for a short time to work in domestic service. This quickly palled and she returned to playing trumpet and sometimes drums in and around Los Angeles. She accompanied singer Billy Daniels, and played in the Darlings Of Rhythm, an all-female band, and various other groups. In 1947, during Dizzy Gillespie's engagement at Billy Berg's club, where he was with Charlie Parker, Bryant heard the frequent broadcasts made from the club. Entranced by Gillespie's playing, she redirected her musical career from this point onwards. However, marriage and the birth of her first child kept her from music for a couple of years, but she was soon active again, sitting in at after-hours sessions with musicians such as Lee Morgan. She appeared on television in the 50s and made an album, but the decade was difficult in Los Angeles and she drifted into regular employment with bands in Denver, Colorado, and on tour, notably a two-year gig with Billy Williams. In 1964 she formed a double act with her brother, but for most of the rest of the decade and into the 70s she freelanced, spending much time bringing up her four children. By the late 70s she was studying music and playing whenever she had the opportunity, including gigs with Bill Berry's LA Band. A lively and engaging entertainer, doing Louis Armstrong and Rose Murphy impersonations when the fancy takes her, Bryant is a thoroughly convincing bop trumpeter. Her admiration for Gillespie has not wavered since she first heard him in 1947, although there has never been any hint that in her

trumpet playing she needs to fall back upon mimicry; hers is too rich a talent for that.

● ALBUMS: *The Gal With The Horn* (Mode 1957)★★★.

BRYANT, FELICE

b. Felice Scaduto, 7 August 1925, Milwaukee, Wisconsin, USA. The lyricist of some of the Everly Brothers' biggest hits, Felice Bryant was a member of one of the most famous husband-and-wife songwriting teams in pop and country music. Recordings of their 750 published songs have sold over 300 million copies in versions by over 400 artists as diverse as Bob Dylan and Lawrence Welk. Of Italian extraction, Felice was already writing lyrics when she met Boudleaux Bryant while working as an elevator attendant in a Milwaukee hotel. A violinist with Hank Penny's band, Boudleaux had composed instrumental pieces and after their marriage in 1945 the duo began to write together. The success of 'Country Boy' for Jimmy Dickens led them to Nashville where they were the first full-time songwriters and pluggers. During the 50s, the Bryants' country hits were often covered by pop artists such as Al Martino, Frankie Laine and Tony Bennett. Then, in 1957, they switched to composing teenage pop material for the Everly Brothers. Felice and Boudleaux proved to have a sharp eye for the details of teen life and among the hits they supplied to the close-harmony duo were 'Bye Bye Love', 'Wake Up Little Susie', 'Problems', 'Poor Jenny' and 'Take A Message To Mary'. They also composed 'Raining In My Heart' (for Buddy Holly) and the witty 'Let's Think About Livin'' (Bob Luman). After the rock 'n' roll era had subsided, the Bryants returned to the country scene, composing prolifically throughout the 60s and 70s in bluegrass and American Indian folk material. Their most enduring song from this period has been 'Rocky Top', a hymn of praise to the state of Tennessee. First recorded by the Osborne Brothers in 1969, it was adopted as a theme song by the University of Tennessee. In the late 70s, Felice and Boudleaux recorded their own compositions for the first time.

● ALBUMS: *All I Have To Do Is Dream* aka *A Touch Of Bryant* (CMH 1979)★★, *Surfin' On A New Wave* (1979)★★.

BRYANT, JIMMY

b. 5 March 1925, Moultrie, Georgia, USA, d. 22 September 1980, Moultrie, Georgia, USA. Bryant grew up on the road, playing fiddle or guitar behind his fiddle-playing father. In 1941, he joined the army and was wounded on active service. Finding little work for a fiddle player, he began paying more attention to the guitar, playing country but becoming more interested in the fast jazz styles of Tony Mottola, a fellow soldier. When discharged, he used his release pay to buy an electric guitar and amplifier and began to play with a small group in Moultrie. In 1948, he moved to Los Angeles, where he found radio work, soon becoming the lead guitarist with Cliffie Stone's band on the Hometown Jamboree. He was also soon in great demand as a session guitarist. During the time he spent with Capitol Records, he recorded with country artists such as Roy Rogers, Tennessee Ernie Ford and Tex Williams, and many non-country stars including Bing Crosby, Kay Starr and Stan Kenton, and in later years, he even recorded with the Monkees. Bryant once estimated that between 1955 and 1956, he recorded with 124 different artists. Steel guitarist Speedy West, who had previously

played western swing with Spade Cooley and Hank Penny was also a member of Stone's band. West was a dazzling and versatile musician whose playing was the perfect match for Bryant's extraordinary, rapid guitarwork, prompting Stone to dub them 'the Flaming Guitars'. They became firm friends and their musical improvisations of western swing and jazz/country left other musicians dumbfounded in admiration. They subsequently appeared together on many recordings, and in 1954, they recorded an album together that has become rated as a classic. In 1967, Bryant recorded a guitar tutor album, complete with instruction book, although it is doubtful that any purchaser came even remotely near the tutor's brilliance. In 1973 he recorded with the legendary steel guitarist Noel Boggs. He moved to Nashville in the mid-70s, working for Hohner Guitars, and in 1976 he was reunited with West, although the recordings they made were never released. In 1979 Bryant, a heavy smoker, was found to have lung cancer and he returned to Los Angeles, even playing at a benefit concert organized for him. Soon afterwards, his health worsening, he moved back to Moultrie, where he died in September 1980. Legendary jazz guitarist Barney Kessel once said, 'of all the guitar players I have known, Jimmy Bryant is the fastest and the cleanest, and has more technique than any other'. Bryant, who was an inspiration for England's guitar great Albert Lee, owned the first Fender Broadcaster guitar, which carried his name and the serial number 1.
● ALBUMS: with Speedy West *Two Guitars Country Style* 10-inch album (Capitol 1954)★★★, *Country Cabin Jazz* (Capitol 1960)★★★, *Bryant's Back In Town* (Imperial 1966)★★★, *Laughing Guitar, Crying Guitar* (Imperial 1966)★★★, *We Are Young* (Imperial 1966)★★★, *The Fastest Guitar In The Country* (Imperial 1967)★★, *Play Country Guitar With Jimmy Bryant* (Dolton 1967)★★.
● COMPILATIONS: *Guitar Take-Off* (See For Miles 1989)★★★, with West *Flamin' Guitars* 4-CD box set (Bear Family 1997)★★★★.

BRYNNER, YUL

b. Youl Bryner, 11 July 1920, Sakhalin, Russia, d. 10 October 1985, New York, USA. Sakhalin is a Siberian island north of Japan, and the date of Brynner's date of birth there is a matter for negotiation; it probably lies somewhere between 1915 and 1920. He spent his early childhood in Peking but was brought up in Paris where he sang in clubs before moving to America in 1941. There he worked in radio and toured as an actor until his Broadway debut with Mary Martin in the short-lived musical *Lute Song* in 1946. Two years later he reprised his role for London and subsequently worked as an actor and director in US television, before creating one of the all-time great roles in Richard Rodgers and Oscar Hammerstein II's *The King And I* in 1951. He shaved his head for the character of the King of Siam, and the completely bald dome became his lifelong trademark - although some said it limited his choice of future parts. His striking, sensual performance opposite the 'terribly English' Gertrude Lawrence earned him a Tony Award, and their duet, 'Shall We Dance?', remains one of the most memorable moments in American musical theatre. Deborah Kerr, another delightful English actress, was his partner in the 1956 film version for which he won an Oscar. For most of the rest of his career he worked in films, and was highly acclaimed for

his performances in many of them, particularly *Anastasia*, *The Brothers Karamazov*, *The Magnificent Seven*, *Taras Bulba*, *Westworld* and *Invitation To A Gunfighter*. In the early 60s he settled in Switzerland and spent a good deal of his time making documentary films about refugee children for the United Nations. He returned to America in 1972 and appeared with the English actress Samantha Eggar in the television series *Anna And The King Of Siam*. Five years later came a triumphant Broadway revival of *The King And I* which was also seen in London in 1979. He brought it back to New York again in 1985 even though he was suffering from lung cancer, which entailed regular radiation treatment. It was the biggest hit of the season with Brynner's curtain calls lasting so long that they became known as 'the third act'. In June 1985 he received a special Tony Award in recognition of his 4,525 performances in *The King And I*. He increased that figure by another 100 before he died at the Cornell Medical Centre in New York in October of that year.
● ALBUMS: *The Gypsy And I* (Vanguard 1967)★★★.

BUCCANEERS

This vocal quartet was formed in 1952 in Philadelphia, USA, by Ernest Smith (lead), Richard Gregory (tenor), Julius Robinson (tenor) and Donald Marshall (bass). They were spotted playing in their home-town in November 1952 by Ed Kresnel and Jerry Halperin, two white teenagers who saw in them the potential for great things. Krensel and Halperin persuaded the Buccaneers that they had music business connections, which was not, in fact, true. They did, however, finance a recording session at Reco-Art Studios in Philadelphia, where the group recorded 'Dear Ruth' (written by Halperin for his girlfriend) and 'Fine Brown Fame'. Placing the single proved difficult, so Krensel and Halperin started their own label, Southern Records, in January 1953, and soon 'Dear Ruth' began to sell well. Rainbow Records then distributed it nationally, but it failed to repeat its local success. Halperin moved the group to Rama Records, who released 'In The Mission Of St. Augustine' backed by 'You Did Me Wrong'. However, the simultaneous release of the same song by the Orioles killed any chance the Buccaneers' version might have had. After the similarly unsuccessful release of 'The Stars Will Remember' / 'Come Back My Love' in 1954, the Buccaneers broke up.

BUCKLEY, LORD

b. Richard Myrle Buckley, 5 April 1906, Stockton, California, USA, d. 12 November 1960. A celebrated humorist and raconteur, Lord Buckley began his career in Chicago's speakeasys where, it is said, he enjoyed the patronage of mobster Al Capone. He assimilated the patois of Black America, infusing his monologues with a bewildering succession of images and phrases that owed their inspiration to jazz or bop prose. The artist sustained comprehension by adapting well-known subject matter - Mark Anthony's eulogy in Shakespeare's *Julius Caesar* began 'Hipsters, Flipsters and Finger-Poppin' Daddies', while in another sketch Jesus Christ was referred to as 'The Naz'. Buckley was a true eccentric. Resplendent with his waxed moustache and sporting a pith helmet, the comedian challenged contemporary convention and even founded his own religion, the Church Of The Living Swing. For a time his career was overseen by later Byrds manager Jim Dickson. The enterprise substituted belly dancers for altar boys and was raided by the Chicago vice squad. A voracious appetite for artificial stimulants eventually took its toll, and despite rumours that the cause of his death was a beating by Black Muslims, Lord Buckley's death in 1960 is recorded as the result of prolonged drug and alcohol abuse. In the early 80s, Chris 'C.P.' Lee, the leading member of UK comic rock group Alberto Y Lost Trios Paranioas, staged a one-man show in tribute to Buckley's legacy.

● ALBUMS: *Hipsters, Flipsters And Finger-Poppin' Daddies, Knock Me Your Lobes* 10-inch album (RCA Victor 1955)★★★, *Euphoria* 10-inch album (Vaya 1955)★★★, *Euphoria, Volumes 1 & 2* (Vaya 1957)★★★, *Gettysburg Address And James Dean* (mid-50s)★★★, *The Way Out Humour Of Lord Buckley* reissued as *Lord Buckley In Concert* (World Pacific 1959)★★★.

● COMPILATIONS: *The Best Of Lord Buckley* (Crestview 1963)★★★★, *Blowing His Mind (And Yours, Too)* (World Pacific 1966)★★★, *Buckley's Best* (World Pacific 1968)★★★, *Bad Rapping Of The Marquis De Sade* (World Pacific 1969)★★★, *A Most Immaculately Hip Aristocrat* (Straight 1970)★★★.

● FURTHER READING: *The Hiparama Of The Classics*, Lord Buckley.

BUFORD, 'MOJO' GEORGE

b. 10 November 1929, Hernando, Mississippi, USA. Buford began to dabble with the harmonica at the age of 12 while living in Memphis, but he started playing seriously after hearing Little Walter's 'Juke'. He moved to Chicago in 1952 and formed the Savage Boys, a band 'adopted' by Muddy Waters to maintain his club residency while he was on tour. Buford recorded behind Joseph 'Jo Jo' Williams in 1959 and in the same year joined Waters' band for the first of several spells. In 1962, Buford left and moved to Minneapolis where he acquired his nickname by fulfilling requests for 'Got My Mojo Working'. While there, he recorded sporadically under his own name until the late 70s. In 1967 he recorded with several of Muddy Waters' sidemen and later played on several of Waters' recording sessions. Buford returned to Chicago in 1978, making an album for Rooster Blues, and in the 80s moved back to Memphis. He has also recorded sessions in Europe for Isabel and JSP Records. Buford's vocals and his approach to blues still remain close to the Waters sound.

● ALBUMS: *Mojo Buford's Chicago Blues Summit* (Rooster 1978)★★★, *State Of The Blues Harp* (JSP 1990)★★★, *Harpslinger* (Blue Loon 1993)★★★, *Juice Machine* (Taxim 1995)★★★, *Still Blowin' Strong* (Blue Loon 1996)★★★★.

BURGESS, SONNY

b. Albert Burgess, 28 May 1931, Newport, Arkansas, USA. As a child Burgess earned the name 'Sonny' as a result of his father also being called Albert. Inspired by the *Grand Ole Opry* show transmitted over WSM's airwaves, he set about learning to play a catalogue-purchased guitar. He joined his first country band while at high school, eventually moving from the role of supporting guitarist to lead the band. After graduation, Burgess joined the backing band of local singer Fred Waner (later a successful solo singer as Freddie Hart), along with Johnny Ray Hubbard (bass) and Gerald Jackson (drums) who had been with his high school group. Military

service in Germany then intervened, but Burgess still found an opportunity to perform, eventually forming a band that successfully auditioned for the overseas forces' version of the *Grand Ole Opry*. Returning to Arkansas after his discharge in 1953, he found work at a box factory but also formed a new group, the Moonlighters, with Hubbard, Kern Kennedy and Russ Smith. After their first handful of performances at local venues the young mandolin player Joe Lewis also joined. Although their original sound was up-tempo country, the rise of Elvis Presley in the mid-50s soon led them to incorporate many of his best-known songs into their set. In 1955 the Moonlighters supported Presley at Newport's Silver Moon club. Jack Nance then joined the group in time for its name change to the Pacers. Finally, in May 1956, Burgess decided it was time to record the band, journeying to Sun Studios in Memphis to audition for Sam Phillips. 'Red Headed Woman'/'We Wanna Boogie' duly became their first single release for Sun Records, selling a respectable 90,000 copies, its popularity spreading outside of the local community. Their first major tour of the Midwest followed, before the Pacers took an engagement as Roy Orbison's backing band. Their second single, 'Restless'/'Ain't Got A Thing', followed in January 1957. Shortly afterwards, they slimmed to a trio when Lewis left to join Conway Twitty and Smith departed for Jerry Lee Lewis's band. Further singles, including 'One Broken Heart' and 'Ain't Gonna Do It', followed, as did touring engagements with Orbison. The Pacers continued to release singles, including 'My Bucket's Got A Hole In It', but were unable to secure that elusive hit. The line-up also shifted again. The 1958 model of the band saw Burgess supported by J.C. Caughron (guitar), Bobby Crafford (drums) and Kern Kennedy on piano. Further recording sessions took place, resulting in the release of several singles including 'Oh Mama!', 'What'cha Gonna Do' and 'One Night'. Burgess later cited the recording of the latter song as the main inspiration behind Presley's version - certainly the similarities between their respective interpretations are remarkable. However, by the end of 1957 the Pacers were out of contract with Sun, and the group had to content itself with touring commitments. A final single, 'Sadie's Back In Town', was released on Sam Phillips' Phillips International, after which the Pacers broke up. Burgess remained in the music business with a new, but largely unrecorded group, Kings IV, until 1970, at which time he returned home to Newport. Between 1974 and 1986 he stayed away from the music business, preferring to work as a travelling salesman. Renewed interest in the 90s led to Rounder Records signing him and in 1996 a remarkably fresh-sounding Burgess was heard on *Sonny Burgess* (subtitled *has still got it*). An excellent choice of tracks included 'Bigger Than Elvis' and Bruce Springsteen's 'Tiger Rose'. His vital contributions to both the development of rockabilly and the Sun Records' story offers a testimony to his status denied him in simple chart placings. It would appear that recognition is coming 40 years too late.

● ALBUMS: *We Wanna Boogie* (Rounder 1990)★★★, with Dave Alvin *Tennessee Border* (Hightone 1992)★★★, *Sonny Burgess (has still got it)* (Rounder 1996)★★★.

● COMPILATIONS: *The Classic Recordings 1956-1959* (Bear Family 1991)★★★, *The Arkansas Wild Man* 1956-60 recordings (Charly 1995)★★★★.

BURNETT, CAROL

b. 26 April 1933, San Antonio, Texas, USA. An actress, comedienne and singer, Burnett was raised by her maternal grandmother in Los Angeles and studied theatre arts and English at the University of California. After graduating she worked in summer stock before moving to New York in 1954. Unable to find work as an actress, she staged a show at the Rehearsal Club hotel in which she sang Eartha's Kitt's hit song 'Monotonous' from *New Faces Of 1953*. In 1957 she caused a stir at the Blue Angel nightclub with her rendition of 'I Made A Fool Of Myself Over John Foster Dulles'. This parody aimed at teenage rock 'n' roll groupies was written by Ken Welch, a songwriter and vocal coach. Years later, he and his wife Mitzi wrote medleys for Burnett's television specials with Julie Andrews and others. In 1959 Burnett made an impressive Broadway debut as Princess Winnifred in *Once Upon A Mattress*, a musical based on the fairytale *The Princess And The Pea*. At around the same time she began appearing on *The Garry Moore Show*, and in the early 60s won an Emmy and several awards as the most popular female performer on television. In 1962 Burnett and Julie Andrews won more Emmys for the special *Julie And Carol At Carnegie Hall*. The two performers were teamed again in similar concerts at the Lincoln Centre (1971) and in Los Angeles (1989). Signed to CBS in 1962, Burnett's television career failed to take off during the next few years, and it was not until she returned to Broadway in the musical *Fade Out-Fade In* (1965) that her fortunes began to improve. Although the show itself - an affectionate look at the Hollywood of the 30s - was not well received, Burnett's 'genial comic impudence' and 'cheerful gaucherie' were singled out for praise, and her impression of Shirley Temple on 'You Mustn't Be Discouraged' was hilarious. From 1967 CBS aired *The Carol Burnett Show*, a weekly prime-time variety show that featured a stellar line-up of guest stars and won 22 Emmys. In 1978, after appearing in approximately 1,500 sketches, Burnett had tired of the weekly grind and turned more to the theatre and feature films. In 1985 she was Carlotta Campion for two nights in the Stephen Sondheim tribute *Follies In Concert*, and performed marvellous renditions of the composer's 'survival anthem' 'I'm Still Here'. She returned to weekly television again in 1990 and chose an anthology format for her new series *Carol And Company*, which added to her list of honours that already included People's Choice, Critics Circle, Photoplay and Golden Globe Awards, along with her induction into the Television Academy Hall of Fame. In 1993 she starred in a new musical production *From The Top*, staged by the Long Beach Civic Light Opera. It was conceived and written by Ken Welch and Mitzi, and consisted of three one-act musicals. The first, *My Walking Stick*, was a backstage vaudeville story set at the time of World War I, with songs by Irving Berlin; the second, called *One Night In Marrakech*, had words and music by Cole Porter; and the third and final piece, *That Simpson Woman*, was an attempt to find a new angle on the famous Duke and Duchess of Windsor-in-exile saga, with a background of songs with lyrics by Ira Gershwin and. music by a variety of composers.

● ALBUMS: *Remembers How They Stopped The Show* (Columbia 1962)★★★★, *Let Me Entertain You* (Columbia 1964)★★★, *Sings* (Columbia 1967)★★★.
● FURTHER READING: *One More Time*, Carol Burnett. *Laughing Till It Hurts*, J. Randy Taraborrelli.

BURNETTE, DORSEY

b. 28 December 1932, Memphis, Tennessee, USA, d. 19 August 1979. He was a member of a classic 50s rock 'n' roll act, had his own hit soloist act in the 60s and became a country singer in the 70s. He helped to form the highly respected Johnny Burnette Trio with younger brother Johnny in 1953. After appearing in the film *Rock, Rock, Rock* in 1956, Dorsey left the trio. He recorded with Johnny as The Texans (on Infinity and Jox) and wrote major hits for Ricky Nelson, including 'It's Late' and 'Waitin' In School'. As a soloist, he recorded for Abbott, Cee-Jam, and then Era, where he had his two biggest solo hits, 'Tall Oak Tree' and 'Hey Little One', in 1960, both classics of their kind and both showcasing his deep, rich, country-style voice. He then recorded without luck on Lama, Dot, Imperial, Reprise, Mel-O-Day, Condor, Liberty, Merri, Happy Tiger, Music Factory, Smash (where he re-recorded 'Tall Oak Tree'), Mercury and Hickory. In the 70s he had 15 Top 100 country hits (none making the Top 20) on Capitol, Melodyland, Calliope and Elektra, with whom he had only recently signed when he died of a heart attack in August 1979. His son Billy Burnette is also a recording artist.

● ALBUMS: *Tall Oak Tree* (Era 1960)★★, *Dorsey Burnette Sings* (Dot 1963)★★, *Dorsey Burnette's Greatest Hits* (Era 1969)★★★, *Things I Treasure* (Calliope 70s)★★.
● COMPILATIONS: *Great Shakin' Fever* (Bear Family 1992)★★★.
● FILMS: *Rock, Rock, Rock* (1956).

BURNETTE, JOHNNY

b. 28 March 1934, Memphis, Tennessee, USA, d. 1 August 1964, Clear Lake, California, USA. Having attended the same high school as Elvis Presley, Johnny moved into the rockabilly genre by forming a trio with his brother Dorsey Burnette on string bass and schoolfriend Paul Burlison on guitar. Allegedly rejected by Sun Records supremo Sam Phillips, the group recorded 'Go Mule Go' for Von Records in New York and were subsequently signed to Coral, where they enjoyed a minor hit with 'Tear It Up'. After touring with Carl Perkins and Gene Vincent, the trio underwent a change of personnel in November 1956 with the recruitment of drummer Tony Austin. That same month, the trio were featured in Alan Freed's movie *Rock, Rock, Rock*. During this period, they issued a number of singles, including 'Honey Hush', 'The Train Kept A-Rollin'', 'Lonesome Train', 'Eager Beaver Baby', 'Drinkin' Wine', 'Spo-Dee-O-Dee' and 'If You Want It Enough', but despite the quality of the songs their work was unheralded. By the autumn of 1957, the trio broke up and the Burnette brothers moved on to enjoy considerable success as songwriters. Writing as a team, they provided Ricky Nelson with the hits 'It's Late', 'Believe What You Say' and 'Just A Little Too Much'. After briefly working as a duo, the brothers parted for solo careers. Johnny proved an adept interpreter of teen ballads, whose lyrics conjured up innocent dreams of wish-fulfilment. Both 'Dreamin'' and 'You're Sixteen' were transatlantic Top 10 hits, perfectly suited to Burnette's light but expressive vocal. A series of lesser successes followed with 'Little Boy Sad', 'Big Big World', 'Girls' and 'God, Country And My Baby'. With his recording career in decline, Burnette formed his own label Magic Lamp in 1964. In August that year, he accidentally fell from his boat during a fishing trip in Clear Lake, California and drowned.

Among the family he left behind was his son Rocky Burnette, who would subsequently achieve recording success at the end of the 70s.

● ALBUMS: as the Johnny Burnette Trio *Rock 'N' Roll Trio* (Coral 1957)★★★, *Dreamin'* (Liberty 1961)★★★, *You're Sixteen* (Liberty 1961)★★★, *Johnny Burnette* (Liberty 1961)★★★, *Johnny Burnette Sings* (Liberty 1961)★★★, *Burnette's Hits And Other Favourites* (Liberty 1962)★★★, *Roses Are Red* (Liberty 1962)★★★.

● COMPILATIONS: *The Johnny Burnette Story* (Liberty 1964)★★★★, with the Rock 'n' Roll Trio *Tear It Up* (Solid Smoke/Coral 1968)★★★, *Tenth Anniversary Album* (United Artists 1974)★★★, *We're Having A Party* (Rockstar 1988)★★★, *Rock 'N' Roll Masters: The Best Of Johnny Burnette* (Liberty 1989)★★★★, *You're Sixteen: The Best Of Johnny Burnette* (Capitol 1992)★★★★.

BURNS, EDDIE

b. 8 February 1928, Mississippi, USA. Inspired by John Lee 'Sonny Boy' Williamson and self-taught, Burns was a stalwart of the immediate post-war Detroit blues scene, being first recorded in 1948 by Bernie Bessman. The latter was responsible for giving John Lee Hooker his break and used Burns as a session musician for Hooker in 1949. This session produced four tracks, including the fast shuffle 'Burnin' Hell', which was notable for Burns's powerful harmonica playing. Throughout the 50s and 60s he periodically recorded for Joseph Van Battle, who either released the material on his own JVB and Von labels or else sold the masters to concerns such as Gotham and Checker. Rarely straying from his home state of Michigan, Burns briefly visited Europe in 1972 under the billing Eddie 'Guitar' Burns, recording an album in London for Action. He returned three years later for a more intensive tour under the 'American Blues Legends '75' banner. Since then Eddie Burns has stayed mostly in Detroit, working day-jobs, playing clubs in the evenings and occasionally appearing at festivals.

● ALBUMS: *Detroit Black Bottom* (Big Bear 1975)★★★, *Treat Me Like I Treat You* (Moonshine 1985)★★★, with John Lee Hooker *Detroit* (Krazy Kat 1987)★★★.

BURNS, RAY

A popular singer in the UK in the 50s, Burns entered show-business straight after demobilization from the RAF in 1945. In the early days he was encouraged by Issy Bonn, and was spotted by Ambrose at the Blue Lagoon Club, and recorded with his Orchestra in 1949. After singing with Jack Nathan's band at the Coconut Grove and other nightspots such as Selby's and the Stork Club, he spent some time with Dave Shand's Orchestra, before signing for Columbia Records in 1953. His early sides included 'Mother Nature And Father Time' and 'Lonely Nightingale'. He had two chart entries in 1955, 'Mobile' (written by US songwriters Bob Wells and David Holt) and 'That's How A Love Song Was Born' (composed by the British team of record producer Norman Newell and Philip Green). His other releases during the 50s included 'Begorrah', 'Rags To Riches', 'I Can't Tell A Waltz From A Tango', 'Why?', 'A Smile Is Worth A Million Tears', 'Blue Star', 'Wonderful! Wonderful!', 'Meanwhile, Back In My Arms' and 'Condemned For Life (With A Rock And Roll Wife)'.

BURRAGE, HAROLD

b. 30 March 1931, Chicago, Illinois, USA, d. 26 November 1966, Chicago, Illinois, USA. A great singer and pianist in the city blues tradition, Burrage was a well-known face on Chicago's west side R&B scene by his late teens. In 1950 he made his first recordings for Decca backed by Horace Henderson's septet, resulting in Claude Trenier's suggestive 'Hi Yo Silver', which spawned several cover versions. He completed one-off sessions for Aladdin (1951) and States (1954) before hitting his stride between 1956 and 1958 with Cobra Records, with whom he recorded in his own right in a soul-blues vein, as well as backing artists such as Magic Sam, Otis Rush and Ike Turner. He continued in the same style in his brief associations for Vee Jay Records, Paso and Foxy, but in 1962 he joined One-Derful's M-Pac subsidiary and over the following four years produced his prime work, including his only real hit, 'Got To Find A Way', which reached number 31 in the August 1965 R&B charts. He died of a heart attack at the age of 35, at the home of his friend Tyrone Davis.

● COMPILATIONS: *Harrold Burrage: The Pioneer Of Chicago Soul* (P-Vine 1979)★★★, *She Knocks Me Out* (Flyright 1981)★★★.

BURRELL, KENNY

b. 31 July 1931, Detroit, Michigan, USA. Coming from a family that encouraged music (all his three brothers were musicians), Burrell studied classical guitar for a mere 18 months (1952-53). In 1955 he received a Bachelor of Music degree from Detroit's Wayne University. He played guitar with the Candy Johnson Sextet in 1948, with Count Belcher in 1949 and Tommy Barnett in 1950. In 1951 Dizzy Gillespie visited Detroit and they recorded together. In March 1955 he stood in for Herb Ellis in the Oscar Peterson trio and in 1957 saw work with Benny Goodman. Discovered by the prestigious Blue Note label, he formed an association with organist Jimmy Smith, and recorded with John Coltrane under the name The Cats. Like all jazz guitarists of his generation Burrell was primarily influenced by Charlie Christian, but developed his own particular playing style. His series of 60s albums for Blue Note and Verve contain his classic work. Arguably, *Midnight Blue*, featuring Stanley Turrentine (with its famous Reid Miles typography and the inspiration behind Elvis Costello's *Almost Blue* sleeve), is his best album. The track 'Midnight Blue' has been cited as the influence for Van Morrison's 'Moondance'. The excellent *Guitar Forms* with Gil Evans in 1965 is another important work, the ambitious suite demonstrating wide influences. Along with Grant Green, there is no finer exponent of 'smokey guitar jazz'. In the late 80s his encouragement of young black talent - especially the drummer Kenny Washington - gave his trio an edge that belied his reputation for classy easy listening. In 1994 he was once again touring with the Jimmy Smith Trio.

● ALBUMS: *Introducing Kenny Burrell* (Blue Note 1956)★★★, *Kenny Burrell, Volume 2* (Blue Note 1957)★★★, *Kenny Burrell* reissued as *Blue Moods* (Prestige 1957)★★★★, *Blue Lights, Volumes 1 and 2* (Blue Note 1959)★★★★, *Night At The Village Vanguard* reissued as *Man At Work* (Argo 1959)★★★, *On View At The Five Spot Cafe, Volume 1* (Blue Note 1960)★★★, *Weaver Of Dreams* (Columbia 1961)★★, *Lotsa Bossa Nova* (Kapp 1962)★★, with John Coltrane *Kenny Burrell With John Coltrane* (New Jazz 1962)★★★★,

Bluesy Burrell reissued as *Out Of This World* (Moodsville 1963)★★★, *All Day Long* (Prestige 1963)★★★, *All Night Long* (Prestige 1963)★★★, *Blue Bash* (Verve 1963)★★★★, *Midnight Blue* (Blue Note 1963)★★★★★, *Soul Call* (Prestige 1964)★★★, *Crash* (Prestige 1964)★★★, *Guitar Forms* (Verve 1965)★★★★, *A Generation Ago Today* (Verve 1966)★★★, *The Tender Gender* (Cadet 1966)★★, *Have Yourself A Soulful Little Christmas* (Cadet 1966)★★, *For Charlie Christian And Benny Goodman* (Verve 1967)★★, *Ode To 52nd Street* (Cadet 1967)★★, *Blues - The Common Ground* (Verve 1968)★★★, *Night Song* (Verve 1968)★★★, *Asphalt Canyon Suite* (Verve 1969)★★★, *Ellington Is Forever Volume 1* (Fantasy 1975)★★★★, *Ellington Is Forever Volume 2* (Fantasy 1976)★★★★, *Handcrafted* (Muse 1978)★★★, *Kenny Burrell In New York* (Muse 1981)★★★, *Listen To The Dawn* (Muse 1983)★★★, *Bluesin' Around* (Columbia 1984)★★★, *Al La Carte* (Muse 1986)★★★, *Generations* (Blue Note 1987)★★★, *Groovin' High* (Muse 1987)★★★, with Grover Washington Jr. *Togethering* (Blue Note 1989)★★, *Recapitulation* (Charly 1989)★★, *Guiding Spirit* (Contemporary 1990)★★★, *Sunnup To Sundown* (Contemporary 1992)★★★, with Jimmy Smith Trio *The Master* (Blue Note 1994)★★★, *Lotus Blossom* (Concord 1995)★★★, *Midnight At The Village Vanguard* (Evidence 1996)★★★, *Live At The Blue Note* (Concord 1997)★★★.
● COMPILATIONS: *The Best Of Kenny Burrell* (Prestige 1967)★★★.

BURRIS, J.C.

b. 1928, Selby, North Carolina, USA, d. 15 May 1988, Greensboro, North Carolina, USA. Burris learned harmonica from his uncle Sonny Terry. He left farm work in his early 20s and moved to New York, where between 1955 and 1960 he made some recordings with Granville 'Sticks' McGhee, Brownie McGhee and Terry. At the turn of that decade, he moved out to the west coast, eventually settling in San Francisco, where he began to make a name for himself on the local folk-blues scene. A stroke disabled him for some years, but he eventually returned to music, performing regularly and making an album in 1975. His style owed much to Terry's, but he added his own distinctive touches, performing solo, playing bones as well as his harmonica, and sometimes appearing with a wooden dancing doll.
● ALBUMS: *One Of These Mornings* (Arhoolie 1975)★★★.

BURTON, JAMES

b. 21 August 1939, Shreveport, Louisiana, USA. One of the most distinguished of rock and country rock guitar players, Burton toured and recorded with Ricky Nelson, Elvis Presley and numerous other artists. His first recording was the highly influential 'Suzie Q', sung by Dale Hawkins in 1957. Burton also performed with country singer Bob Luman before moving to Los Angeles where he was hired to work with Nelson, then the latest teen sensation. For six years he toured and recorded with Nelson, perfecting a guitar sound known as 'chicken pickin''. This was achieved by damping the strings for staccato-sounding single-string riffs and solos. Among the best examples of this style are 'Hello Mary Lou', 'Never Be Anyone Else But You' and the more frantic, rockabilly-flavoured 'Believe What You Say'. During the late 60s and early 70s, Burton was much in demand as a session guitarist, working with Dale Hawkins on a comeback album as

well as various artists including Buffalo Springfield, Judy Collins, John Phillips, Joni Mitchell, Michael Nesmith and Longbranch Pennywhistle, a group featuring future Eagles member Glenn Frey. Burton also played dobro on albums by P.F. Sloan and John Stewart. In addition, Burton's powerful, rockabilly-influenced guitarwork made a major contribution to the harsher country sound developed at this time by Merle Haggard. Burton made two albums of his own during these years, one in collaboration with steel guitarist Ralph Mooney. During the 70s, Burton's work took him in contrasting directions. With pianist Glen D. Hardin (a former Crickets member), he was a mainstay of Elvis Presley's touring and recording band from 1969-77, but he also played a leading role in the growing trend towards country/rock fusion. Burton's most significant performances in this respect came on the albums of Gram Parsons. After Parsons' death, Burton and Hardin toured with Emmylou Harris and backed her on several solo albums. More recently he has toured with Jerry Lee Lewis. As a session guitarist, Burton played on albums by Jesse Winchester, Ronnie Hawkins, Rodney Crowell, Phil Everly, J.J. Cale and Nicolette Larson. As a result of an accident in 1995, Burton lost the use of his hands and has been receiving treatment to enable him to play the guitar again. He had no medical insurance and faced bankruptcy after financing his own treatment. A fund has been set up to help him and benefit concerts are being held.
● ALBUMS: with Ralph Mooney *Corn Pickin' And Slick Slidin'* (1969)★★, *The Guitar Sound Of James Burton* (A&M 1971)★★.

BYGRAVES, MAX

b. Walter Bygraves, 16 October 1922, London, England. Performing as a soloist in his school choir and employing Max Miller impressions in the RAF, with music hall dates in the late 40s, led Bygraves quickly to his recording debut and first Royal Command Performance in 1950. His debut record, with the Carrol Gibbons Band, contained impressions of Al Jolson, and was followed by a string of novelty hits through the 50s such as 'Cowpuncher's Cantata', 'Heart Of My Heart', 'Gilly Gilly Ossenfeffer Katzenellen Bogen By The Sea', 'Meet Me On The Corner', 'You Need Hands'/'Tulips From Amsterdam', 'Jingle Bell Rock' and 'Fings Ain't Wot They Used To Be'. On the popular BBC radio show *Educating Archie*, scripted by comedian Eric Sykes, he gave a receptive nation catchphrases such as 'a good idea son!' and 'bighead!'. Bygraves became enormously popular on stage and television with his clever mix of song and patter, defying the dramatic changes in music and entertainment taking place in the 60s. In the early 70s with Pye Records musical director Cyril Stapleton and the Tony Mansell Singers, Bygraves recorded an album of standard songs in medley form, called *Sing Along With Max*. It was the first of an amazingly successful series for which he has now earned over 30 Gold Discs. Surprisingly, he has never successfully adapted his 'song and dance' image to films, although he has played several, mainly dramatic, roles to substantial critical acclaim, including *A Cry From The Streets* and *Spare The Rod*. As early as the late 50s he formed his own music publishing company, Lakeview Music. It was intended to publish his own songs, including 'You Need Hands'. However, he bought the publishing rights to a 16-

song show score for £350 because he liked one of the numbers. The show was Lionel Bart's *Oliver*, and in the 80s Bygraves is said to have sold the rights to Essex Music for a quarter of a million pounds. In 1982 he received the OBE, and 10 years later, celebrated his 70th birthday by attending a lunch given in his honour by the Variety Club, and including in his theatre act a cheeky topical parody of the old number 'They're Changing Guard At Buckingham Palace', entitled 'They're Changing *Wives* At Buckingham Palace'. In 1994 Max Bygraves released 'The Bells Of Arnheim', a powerful and emotional 50th anniversary commemoration of the men in Britain's World War II Airborne Forces who were defeated in the nine-day massacre that came to be known as 'A Bridge Too Far'. The song was written by Les Reed and Geoff Stephens, and all proceeds from the recording went to Airborne Forces charities.

● ALBUMS: *Songs For Young In Heart* (Decca 1959)★★★, *Max Bygraves* (Hallmark 1971)★★★, *Max* (Hallmark 1972)★★★, *Sing Along With Max* (Pye 1972)★★★★, *Sing Along With Max, Volume 2* (Pye 1972)★★★★, *Singalongamax, Volume 3* (Pye 1973)★★★★, *Singalongamax, Volume 4* (Pye 1973)★★★★, *Singalongapartysong* (Pye 1973)★★★, *You Make Me Feel Like Singing A Song* (Pye 1974)★★★, *Singalongaxmas* (Pye 1974)★★, *I Wanna Sing You A Story* (Pye 1975)★★★, *Viva Congalongamax* (Pye 1975)★★, *Singalongamovies* (Pye 1975)★★, *Smile* (Pye 1976)★★★, *Golden Greats Of The 20s* (Pye 1977)★★★, *Golden Greats Of The 30s* (Pye 1977)★★, *Golden Greats Of The 40s* (Pye 1977)★★★, *Golden Greats Of The 50s* (Pye 1977)★★★, *Lingalongamax* (Ronco 1978)★★, with Victor Silvester *Song And Dance Men* (Pye 1978)★★★, *Golden Greats Of The 60s* (Pye 1979)★★, *Discolongamax* (Pye 1979)★★, *Lingalongamax, Volume 2* (Pye 1980)★★, with Acker Bilk *Twogether* (Piccadilly 1980)★★, *Maximemories* (Celebrity 1981)★★★, *You're My Everything* (Monarch 1982)★★, *Max Sings While Ted Swings* (President 1983)★★★★, with Silvester *Together: Max Bygraves And Victor Silvester* (PRT 1985)★★★, *Singalong A Christmas* (Hallmark 1988)★★, *Singalongawaryears* (Parkfield 1989)★★★, *Singalongawaryears, Volume 2* (Parkfield 1989)★★★.

● COMPILATIONS: *World Of Max Bygraves* (Decca 1969)★★★, *World Of Max Bygraves, Volume 2* (Decca 1969)★★★, *Unbeatable Bygraves* (Decca 1974)★★★, *100 Golden Greats* (Ronco 1976)★★★★, *Focus On Max Bygraves* (Decca 1978)★★★, *Max Bygraves At His Very Best* (Golden Hour 1979)★★★, *Spotlight On Max Bygraves, Volume 1* (PRT 1981)★★★, *Spotlight On Max Bygraves, Volume 2* (PRT 1982)★★★, *100 Minutes Of Max Bygraves* (PRT 1982)★★★, *Happy Hits* (Spot 1983)★★★, *Best Of Max* (Spot 1984)★★★, *Classics* (MFP 1984)★★★, *Collection* (PRT 1986)★★★, *The Singalong Collection* (PRT 1987)★★★, *An Hour Of Max Bygraves* (Hour Of Pleasure 1988)★★★★, *Singalong Years* (Ariola 1990)★★★, *Tulips From Amsterdam* (Deram 1990)★★★★, *The EMI Years* (EMI 1991)★★★.

● VIDEOS: *Singalongawaryears* (Parkfield Publishing 1989).

● FURTHER READING: *I Wanna Tell You A Story*. Max Bygraves, *I Wanna Tell You A Funny Story*, Max Bygraves.*After Thoughts*, Max Bygraves.

CADETS/JACKS

An R&B vocal group from Los Angeles, California, USA. This unit, who recorded for Modern as the Cadets and for RPM as the Jacks, is an example of a house group, used by a record company to record cover hits or songs in styles of other groups. As the Cadets, the group had a hit with the novelty jump 'Stranded In The Jungle' (number 4 R&B, number 15 pop), in 1956, and as the Jacks with the ballad 'Why Don't You Write Me' (number 4 R&B, number 82 pop) in 1955. 'Stranded' was a cover of a record by the original Jayhawks and 'Why Don't You Write Me' was a cover of a record by the Feathers. The unit came together as a gospel group in 1947, and by the time they were signed to Modern in 1955 the members were Willie Davis (first tenor), Ted Taylor (first tenor), Aaron Collins (second tenor), Lloyd McGraw (baritone), and Will 'Dub' Jones (bass). When the group left Modern in 1957, Ted Taylor dropped out of the group and established a successful solo career as a hard soul singer during the 60s. Davis and Collins kept the group together under the name Cadets, recording several singles for minor labels without success. In 1961 Collins and Davis, with several new members, recorded as the Flares and had a hit with 'Foot Stompin''.

● ALBUMS: as the Cadets *Rockin' 'N' Rollin' With The Cadets* (Crown 1957)★★★, *The Cadets* (Crown 1963)★★★; as the Jacks *Jumpin' With The Jacks* (RPM 1956)★★★, *Jumpin' With The Jacks* (Crown 1960)★★★, *The Jacks* (1963)★★★.

● COMPILATIONS: *The Best Of The Jacks* (Relic 1975)★★★, *The Best Of The Cadets* (Relic 1975)★★★, *The Cadets Meet The Jacks* (Ace 1987)★★★.

CADILLACS

This vocal quintet, initially called the Carnations, was formed in 1953 in New York, USA, and consisted of Earl Carroll (b. 2 November 1937, New York, USA), LaVerne Drake, Bobby Phillips, Johnny Willingham and James Clark, who also sang with the Five Crowns. The Cadillac's debut single, 'Gloria', was released by Josie Records in July 1954, and although it did not chart at the time, it was later considered a doo-wop classic. Clark and Willingham were then replaced by Earl Wade (ex-Crystals) and Charles Brooks. Their next two singles, 'No Chance'/'Sympathy' and 'Down The Road', failed to chart, but 'Speedoo', released in October 1955, did reach number 17 in the *Billboard* R&B charts. Meanwhile, the group's dance steps were being choreographed by Charles Atkinson (aka Cholly Atkins), who later worked with a number of Motown Records' acts. Following lucrative tours with Ray Charles, Fats Domino and others, in May 1956 Drake was replaced by James Bailey (ex-Crickets), and after two more unsuccessful singles the Cadillacs returned to the charts (number 11) with 'Rudolph The Red

Nosed Reindeer'. They returned to their roots with the wonderful 'Sugar Sugar' (not the song later made famous by the Archies) but by this time their original audience was confused about their direction. The group split in two early in 1957, with both parties continuing to use the name Cadillacs and remaining on Josie Records. Caroll, Phillips, Wade and Brooks became known as the Original Cadillacs, while Bailey hired Bobby Spencer (Harptones), Bill Lindsey (Starlings) and Champ Rollow to join his version of the group. After Bailey's group flopped with 'My Girlfriend' and the Original Cadillacs flopped with 'Lucy', Bailey rejoined Caroll, Phillips Wade and new member Caddy Spencer, and together they recorded 'Speedo Is Back'. Their next single, 'Peek-A-Boo', reached number 28 in the *Billboard* R&B chart in October 1958, but the next year Caroll left the group (later recording as Speedo And The Pearls) and was replaced by a string of ex-members of the Solitaires. The Cadillacs then signed to Mercury Records, and in the next decade Curtis Williams, Ray Brewster and Irving Lee Gails all sang with the group, as did Earl Caroll and Roland Martinez. They could not, however, match their former achievements. Reunions of the various formations of the Cadillacs have occurred from time to time.

● COMPILATIONS: *The Best Of The Cadillacs* (Rhino 1990)★★★★.

● FILMS: *Go Johnny Go* (1958).

CAHN, SAMMY

b. Samuel Cohen, 18 June 1913, New York, USA, d. 15 January 1993, Los Angeles, California, USA. The son of Jewish immigrant parents from Galicia, Poland, Cahn grew up on Manhatten's Lower East Side. Encouraged by his mother, he learned to play the violin, joined a small orchestra that played at bar mitzvahs and other functions, and later worked as a violinist in Bowery burlesque houses. At the age of 16 he wrote his first lyric, 'Like Niagrara Falls, I'm Falling For You', and persuaded a fellow member of the orchestra, Saul Chaplin, to join him in a songwriting partnership. Their first published effort was 'Shake Your Head From Side To Side', and in the early 30s they wrote special material for vaudeville acts and bands. In 1935 they had their first big hit when the Jimmy Lunceford orchestra recorded their 'Rhythm Is Our Business'. The following year Andy Kirk topped the US Hit Parade with the duo's 'Until The Real Thing Comes Along', and Louis Armstrong featured their 'Shoe Shine Boy' in the revue *Connie's Hot Chocolates Of 1936*. In the following year Cahn and Chaplin had their biggest success to date when they adapted the Yiddish folk song 'Beir Mir Bist Du Schöen'. It became the top novelty song of the year and gave the Andrews Sisters their first million-seller. The team followed this with 'Please Be Kind', a major seller for Bob Crosby, Red Norvo and Benny Goodman. During this time Cahn and Chaplin were also under contract to Warner Brothers Records, and soon after that commitment ended they decided to part company. In 1942, Cahn began his very productive partnership with Jule Styne, with their first chart success, 'I've Heard That Song Before'. Just as significant was Cahn's renewed association with Frank Sinatra, whom he had known when the singer was with Tommy Dorsey. Cahn and Styne wrote the score for the Sinatra films *Step Lively* (1944), ('Come Out Wherever You Are' and 'As Long As There's Music'), *Anchors*

Aweigh (1945) ('I Fall In Love Too Easily', 'The Charm Of You' and 'What Makes The Sunset?') and *It Happened In Brooklyn* (1947) ('Time After Time', 'It's The Same Old Dream' and 'It's Gotta Come From The Heart'). Sinatra also popularized several other 40s Cahn/Styne songs, including 'I'll Walk Alone', 'Saturday Night Is The Loneliest Night In The Week', 'The Things We Did Last Summer', 'Five Minutes More', and the bleak 'Guess I'll Hang My Tears Out To Dry', which appeared on his 1958 album *Only The Lonely*. Some of their other hits included 'It's Been A Long, Long Time', associated with Harry James and his vocalist Kitty Kallen, 'Let It Snow! Let It Snow! Let It Snow!' (Vaughan Monroe) and 'There Goes That Song Again' (Kay Kyser and Russ Morgan). Cahn and Styne wrote the scores for several other films, including *Tonight And Every Night* (1945), two Danny Kaye vehicles, *Wonder Man* (1945) and *The Kid From Brooklyn* (1946), and *West Point Story* (1950). They also provided the songs for *Romance On The High Seas* (1948), the film in which Doris Day shot to international stardom, singing 'It's Magic' and 'Put 'Em In A Box, Tie It With A Ribbon, And Throw 'Em In The Deep Blue Sea'. The two songwriters also wrote the Broadway show *High Button Shoes* (1947), starring Phil Silvers (later Sgt. Bilko) and Nanette Fabray, which ran for 727 performances and introduced songs such as 'I Still Get Jealous', 'You're My Girl' and 'Papa, Won't You Dance With Me'. After *High Button Shoes* Cahn went to California, while Styne stayed in New York. Cahn collaborated with Nicholas Brodszky for a time in the early 50s, writing movie songs for Mario Lanza including 'Be My Love', 'Wonder Why', 'Because You're Mine', 'Serenade' and 'My Destiny'. The collaboration also composed 'I'll Never Stop Loving You' for the Doris Day film *Love Me Or Leave Me* (1955). Cahn and Styne reunited briefly in 1954, ostensibly to write the score for the film *Pink Tights*, to star Sinatra and Marilyn Monroe, but the project was shelved. Soon afterwards, Cahn and Styne were asked to write the title song for the film *Three Coins In The Fountain*. The result, a big hit for Sinatra and for the Four Aces, gained Cahn his first Academy Award. Cahn and Styne eventually worked with Monroe when they wrote the score for the comedy *The Seven Year Itch* (1955). In the same year Cahn started his last major collaboration - with Jimmy Van Heusen and, some would say, with Frank Sinatra as well. They had immediate success with the title song of the Sinatra movie *The Tender Trap* (1955), and won Academy Awards for songs in two of his movies, 'All The Way', from *The Joker Is Wild* (1957) and 'High Hopes', from *A Hole In The Head* (1959). A parody of 'High Hopes' was used as John F. Kennedy's presidential campaign song in 1960. Among the many other numbers written especially for Sinatra were 'My Kind Of Town' (from *Robin And The Seven Hoods*, 1964) and the title songs for his bestselling albums *Come Fly With Me*, *Only The Lonely*, *Come Dance With Me!*, *No One Cares*, *Ring-A-Ding-Ding!* and *September Of My Years*. Cahn and Van Heusen also produced his successful Timex television series during 1959-60. They won another Oscar for 'Call Me Irresponsible' (from *Papa's Delicate Condition*, 1963), Cahn's fourth Academy Award from over 30 nominations, and contributed to many other films including 'The Second Time Around' (from *High Time*) and the title songs from *A Pocketful Of Miracles*, *Where Love Has Gone*, *Thoroughly Modern Millie* and *Star*. The songwriters also supplied the score for a television musical version of Thorton

Wilder's play *Our Town*, which introduced 'Love And Marriage' and 'The Impatient Years'. In the mid-60s they wrote the scores for two Broadway musicals, *Skyscraper* ('Everybody Has The Right To Be Wrong') and 'I'll Only Miss Her When I Think Of Her') and *Walking Happy*, while in 1969 Cahn worked with Styne again on another musical, *Look To The Lilies* ('I, Yes, Me! That's Who!'). Cahn's other collaborators included Axel Stordahl and Paul Weston ('Day By Day' and 'I Should Care'), Gene De Paul ('Teach Me Tonight'), Arthur Schwartz ('Relax-Ay-Voo'), George Barrie ('All That Love To Waste' and 'That's What Makes Paris Paree', and 'I'm Gonna Ring The Bell Tonight'). In 1972 Cahn was inducted into the Songwriters Hall Of Fame after claiming throughout his lifetime that he only wrote songs so that he could demonstrate them. Two years later he mounted his 'one man show', *Words And Music*, on Broadway, and despite his voice being described by a New York critic as that of 'a vain duck with a hangover', the nostalgic mixture of his songs, sprinkled with amusing memories of the way they were created, won the Outer Circle Critics Award for the best new talent on Broadway. Later in 1974, he repeated his triumph in England, and then restaged the whole show all over again in 1987. After over six decades of 'putting *that* word to *that* note', as he termed it, he died in January 1993.

● ALBUMS: *I've Heard That Song Before* (EMI 1977)★★.
● FURTHER READING: *I Should Care: The Sammy Cahn Story*, Sammy Cahn.

CAIOLA, AL

b. Alexander Emil Caiola, 7 September 1920, Jersey City, New Jersey, USA. A highly respected studio guitarist, Caiola played with many renowned musical directors such as Percy Faith, Hugo Winterhalter and Andre Kostelanetz. After serving as musical arranger and conductor for United Artists Records, Caiola released several singles on RCA during the 50s, including 'Delicado', a Brazilian song written by Walter Azevedo, which became a hit for Percy Faith, Stan Kenton, Ralph Flanagan and Dinah Shore. Caiola also released *Serenade In Blue* and *Deep In A Dream*, recorded by his Quintet. In 1961 he entered the US Top 40 charts with the movie theme *The Magnificent Seven* and *Bonanza*, the title music from the popular western television series; he had his own television show for a short time in the USA.

● ALBUMS: *Deep In A Dream* (Savoy/London 1955)★★, *Serenade In Blue* (Savoy/London 1956)★★★, *High Strung* (RCA Victor 1959)★★★, *Music For Space Squirrels* (Atco 1960)★★, with Don Arnone *Great Pickin'* (Chancellor 1960)★★★, *Salute Italia* (Roulette 1960)★★, *Percussion Espanol* (Time 1960)★★★, *Spanish Guitars* (Time 1960)★★★, *Gershwin And Guitars* (Time 1961)★★★, *Soft Guitars* (60s)★★★, *Guitar Of Plenty* (60s)★★★, *Cleopatra And All That Jazz* (United Artists 1963)★★★, *Tough Guitar* (United Artists 1964)★★, *Music To Read James Bond By* (1965)★★★, *Sounds For Spies And Private Eyes* (United Artists 1965)★★★.

CALAMITY JANE

Straying from her girl-next-door image, and employing all her substantial wisecracking and musical talents, Doris Day was the definitive Calamity Jane in this Warner Brothers 1953 release. The story of one the most famous characters from the days of the Old West has been filmed several times over the years, but this version was as good as any of them. In James O'Hanlon's screenplay, the residents of Deadwood, right in the heart of good ol' cowboy and Injun territory, drool over cigarette pictures of stage star Adelaide Adams. As a result, naïve but good-hearted Calamity Jane takes the stagecoach to Chicago to persuade Adams to perform at Deadwood's humble theatre - but mistakenly returns with the star's maid instead. Rather conveniently, Katie Brown (Allyn McLerie) proves to be quite an entertainer and wins the hearts of the Deadwood people. Howard Keel is in fine voice as Wild Bill Hickock, a reminder of his performance in *Annie Get Your Gun*, to which *Calamity Jane* was quite naturally compared. However, this film does not match the excellence of that classic, although Day and Keel's wrangling on the song 'I Can Do Without You' was very reminiscent of Keel and Betty Hutton's performance of 'Anything You Can Do' in the earlier film. Sammy Fain and Paul Francis Webster's refreshing score contained several comic uptempo moments, such as 'The Deadwood Stage' and 'Just Blew In From The Windy City', along with 'Higher Than A Hawk', ''Tis Harry I'm Planning To Marry', 'I've Got A Heart Full Of Honey', 'A Woman's Touch' and 'The Black Hills Of Dakota'. The tender 'Secret Love' won the Oscar for best song and went on to become a US number 1 for Doris Day. Also among the cast were Paul Harvey, Dick Wesson, Phil Carey and Chubby Johnson. Jack Donohue staged the dance sequences, and Wilfred M. Cline was in charge of the superb Technicolor photography. The director was David Butler. In 1995, two stage adaptations of *Calamity Jane* were mounted in the UK, at the Leicester Haymarket Theatre and the Battersea Arts Centre.

CALL ME MADAM (STAGE MUSICAL)

With advance ticket sales exceeding $1,000,000, the stage musical *Call Me Madam* was a guaranteed hit when it opened at the Imperial Theatre in New York on 12 October 1950. With a score by Irving Berlin, the book by Russell Crouse and Howard Lindsay was based loosely upon the life and career of Perle Mesta, a famous Washington, DC, hostess who became the US Ambassador to Luxembourg. Ethel Merman played the dedicated diplomat Sally Adams, belting out her personal calling-card, 'The Hostess With The Mostes' On The Ball'. The remainder of a bunch of great numbers included 'The Best Thing For You', 'It's A Lovely Day Today', 'They Like Ike' (about US Army General Dwight D. Eisenhower, who attended the opening night), 'Marrying For Love', 'Can You Use Any Money Today?' and 'Something To Dance About'. There was also the delightful 'You're Just In Love', an engaging contrapuntal song performed by Merman and Russell Nype. The show won Tony Awards for best score, actress (Merman), and featured actor (Nype). It ran for almost 650 performances on Broadway and 485 in London, and was filmed in 1953 with Merman, George Sanders and Donald O'Connor.

CALL ME MADAM (FILM MUSICAL)

Ethel Merman enjoyed her greatest film triumph when she recreated her original role in this 1953 adaptation of Irving Berlin's hit Broadway show. Although she was never considered to be as effective on the screen as she was on stage, the part of the extrovert oil-heiress Sally Adams, the brand new

Ambassador to the mythical Duchy of Lichtenburg, suited her down to the ground. In Arthur Sheekman's screenplay, based on Howard Lindsay and Russell Crouse's witty and sometimes satirical libretto, Merman flirted with one of the tiny principality's highest officials, Cosmo Constantine (George Sanders), while enquiring 'Can You Use Any Money Today?'. This was only one of the charming and amusing numbers in a Berlin score that arrived in Hollywood from New York almost intact, although inevitably the reference to 'panties' in Merman's *tour de force*, 'The Hostess With The Mostes", which had presumably been acceptable to Broadway theatregoers, was removed for worldwide consumption. Merman was also firing on all cylinders with 'That International Rag', 'You're Just In Love' (with Donald O'Connor, who played her press attaché Ken Gibson) and 'The Best Thing For You' (with Sanders). The latter artist was more than adequate on the gentle 'Marrying For Love', and O'Connor had his moments on 'What Chance Have I With Love?', 'Something To Dance About' and 'It's A Lovely Day Today', the last two with Vera-Ellen, whose singing was dubbed by Carole Richards. O'Connor and Vera-Ellen made a charming couple, and their dances together, which were choreographed by Robert Alton, were sublime. The rest of the cast included the always watchable duo Walter Slezak and Billy De Wolfe. Musical Director Alfred Newman won an Oscar for his 'scoring of a musical picture' which was directed by Walter Lang and released by 20th Century-Fox.

CALLENDER, RED

b. George Sylvester Callender, 6 March 1916, Haynesville, Virginia, USA, d. 8 March 1992, Saugus, California, USA. Callender began performing in jazz groups, playing bass, while still in his teens. By the mid-30s he had settled in California and during the next few years worked with a succession of bands, including those led by Buck Clayton, Louis Armstrong, Erroll Garner and Lester Young. From the early 40s Callender was deeply involved in bebop, adapting comfortably to the new concept. He recorded extensively with prominent beboppers such as Charlie Parker, Wardell Gray and Dexter Gordon. As well as appearing in the Nat 'King' Cole trio during this period, Callender also led his own small groups, usually a trio, one of which included Lester Young. In the 50s Callender's skilled musicianship led to his becoming a sought-after studio player; he subsequently worked on record dates with artists as diverse as Frank Sinatra and Stevie Wonder, but also continued to work with jazzmen. A particularly noteworthy set of recordings came in the mid-50s when he was signed by Norman Granz to accompany Art Tatum. In later years Callender frequently turned to playing tuba, an instrument on which he proved to possess remarkable dexterity. In addition to his playing, Callender has also composed and arranged, and in 1985 published his autobiography, *Unfinished Dream*.

● ALBUMS: *Swinging Suite* (Modern 1956)★★★, *Red Callender Speaks Low* (Crown 1957)★★★★, *The Lowest* (Metrojazz 1958)★★★, *Basin Street Blues* (1973)★★★, with Gerry Wiggins *Night Mist Blues* (1983)★★★, with Jeannie and Jimmy Cheatham *Homeward Bound* (Concord 1987)★★.

● FURTHER READING: *Unfinished Dream: The Musical World Of Red Callender*, Red Callender with Elaine Cohen.

CALLOWAY, CAB

b. Cabell Calloway, 25 December 1907, Rochester, New York, USA, d. 8 November 1994, Cokebury Village, Delaware, USA. Involved in showbusiness from an early age, vocalist Calloway was an occasional drummer and MC, working mostly in Baltimore, where he was raised, and Chicago, where he relocated in the late 20s. He worked with his sister Blanche, and then, in 1929, he became frontman for the Alabamians. Engagements with this band took him to New York; in the same year he fronted the Missourians, a band for which he had briefly worked a year earlier. The Missourians were hired for New York's Savoy Ballroom; although the band consisted of proficient musicians, there is no doubt that it was Calloway's flamboyant leadership that attracted most attention. Dressing outlandishly in an eye-catching 'Zoot Suit' - knee-length drape jacket, voluminous trousers, huge wide-brimmed hat and a floor-trailing watch chain - he was the centre of attraction. His speech was peppered with hip phraseology and his catchphrase, 'Hi-De-Hi', echoed by the fans, became a permanent part of the language. The popularity of the band and of its leader led to changes. Renamed as Cab Calloway And His Orchestra, the band moved into the Cotton Club in 1931 as replacement for Duke Ellington, allegedly at the insistence of the club's Mafia-connected owners. The radio exposure this brought helped to establish Calloway as a national figure. As a singer Calloway proved difficult for jazz fans to swallow. His eccentricities of dress extended into his vocal style, which carried echoes of the blues, crass sentimentality and cantorial religiosity. At his best, however, as on 'Geechy Joe' and 'Sunday In Savannah', which he sang in the 1943 film *Stormy Weather*, he could be highly effective. His greatest popular hits were a succession of songs, the lyrics of which were replete with veiled references to drugs that, presumably, the record company executives failed to recognize. 'Minnie The Moocher' was the first of these, recorded in March 1931 with 'Kicking The Gong Around', an expression that means smoking opium, released in October the same year. Other hits, about sexual prowess, were Fats Waller's 'Six Or Seven Times' and the Harold Arlen-Ted Koehler song 'Triggeration'. For the more perceptive jazz fans who were patient enough to sit through the razzmatazz, and what one of his sidemen referred to as 'all that hooping and hollering', Calloway's chief contribution to the music came through the extraordinary calibre of the musicians he hired. In the earlier band he had the remarkable cornetist Reuben Reeves, trombonist Ed Swayzee, Doc Cheatham and Bennie Payne. As his popularity increased, Calloway began hiring the best men he could find, paying excellent salaries and allowing plenty of solo space, even though the records were usually heavily orientated towards his singing. By the early 40s the band included outstanding players such as Chu Berry, featured on 'Ghost Of A Chance' and 'Tappin' Off', Hilton Jefferson ('Willow Weep For Me'), Milt Hinton ('Pluckin' The Bass'), Cozy Cole ('Ratamacue' and 'Crescendo In Drums') and Jonah Jones ('Jonah Joins The Cab'). Further musicians included Ben Webster, Shad Collins, Garvin Bushell, Mario Bauza, Walter 'Foots' Thomas, Tyree Glenn, J.C. Heard and Dizzy Gillespie, making the Calloway band a force with which to be reckoned and one of the outstanding big bands of the swing era. In later years Cab worked on the stage in *Porgy And Bess* and *Hello, Dolly!*, and took acting roles in films such as *The Blues Brothers* (1980). His other films over the years included *The Big Broadcast* (1932), *International House*, *The Singing Kid*, *Manhattan Merry Go Round*, *Sensations Of 1945*, *St. Louis Blues*, *The Cincinnati Kid* and *A Man Called Adam* (1966). Calloway enjoyed a resurgence of popularity in the 70s with a Broadway appearance in *Bubbling Brown Sugar*. In the 80s he was seen and heard on stages and television screens in the USA and UK, sometimes as star, sometimes as support but always as the centre of attraction. In 1993 he appeared at London's Barbican Centre, and in the same year celebrated his honorary doctorate in fine arts at the University of Rochester in New York State by leading the 9,000 graduates and guests in a singalong to 'Minnie The Moocher'. Calloway died the following year.

● ALBUMS: *Cab Calloway* 10-inch album (Brunswick 1954)★★★★, *Cab Calloway* ii (Epic 1956)★★★, *Hi De Hi, Hi De Ho* (RCA Victor 1958)★★★★, *The Cotton Club Revue Of 1958* (Gone 1959)★★★, *Blues Make Me Happy* (Coral 1962)★★★.

● COMPILATIONS: *Club Zanzibar Broadcasts* (Unique Jazz 1981)★★★, *Kicking The Gong Around* (Living Era 1982)★★★, *The Hi-De-Ho Man* (RCA 1983)★★★★, *Cab & Co.* (RCA 1985)★★★, *Cab Calloway Collection - 20 Greatest Hits* (Deja Vu 1986)★★★★, *Missourians* (1986)★★★, *The Cab Calloway Story* (Deja Vu 1989)★★★★, *Best Of The Big Bands* (Columbia 1991)★★★, *Classics 1941-42* (1993)★★★★.

● FURTHER READING: *Of Minnie The Moocher And Me* (his autobiography). *The New Cab Calloway's Hepster's Dictionary*, Cab Calloway.

● FILMS: *The Big Broadcast* (1932), *International House* (1933), *Stormy Weather* (1943), *Sensations Of 1945* (1945), *St. Louis Blues* (1958), *A Man Called Adam* (1966), *The Blues Brothers* (1980).

CALVERT, EDDIE

b. 15 March 1922, Preston, Lancashire, England, d. 7 August 1978, Johannesburg, South Africa. Calvert's father taught him to play the trumpet, and at the age of 11, he joined the Preston Town Silver Band. In the 40s he played with Billy Ternent and Geraldo before forming his own group for night-club engagements. By the early 50s he was touring the British variety circuit, and became known as 'The Man With The Golden Trumpet'. In 1953 he recorded a Swiss tune 'O Mein Papa' which went to number 1 in the UK and made the Top 10 in the USA. Two years later he topped the UK charts again with a cover version of the Perez Prado hit 'Cherry Pink And Apple Blossom White', and in the late 50s had more success with 'Zambesi', 'Mandy' and the theme from the Peter Sellers film *John And Julie*. Calvert had enormous success in theatres and clubs in the UK, including the London Palladium and major regional venues, until he moved to South Africa in 1968, where he was appointed liaison officer between the government and the Bantu tribe. He died there from a heart attack in 1978.

● ALBUMS: *Latin Carnival* (Columbia 1960)★★★, *All In The Summer Evening (And Other Songs Of Faith)* (1965)★★★, *Eddie Calvert Salutes The Trumpet Greats* (1967)★★★.

● COMPILATIONS: *The Man With The Golden Trumpet* (One-Up 1978)★★★, *20 Golden Trumpet Greats* (Note 1979)★★★, *The EMI Years* (EMI 1992)★★★★.

CALYPSO - HARRY BELAFONTE ★★★★

Belafonte's third and most successful chart album was full of the kind of folksy and calypso-style songs that made him one of the showbusiness sensations of the 50s. Two of them, 'The Banana Boat Song (Day-O)' and 'Jamaica Farewell', were also singles hits. This 1956 album spent 72 weeks in the US Top 40, 31 of them at number 1, and made history by becoming the first 33 1/3 rpm record by a solo artist to sell a million copies. It marked only the beginning of Belafonte's phenomenal career on record, television and film.

● TRACKS: *The Banana Boat Song (Day-O)*; *Jack-ass Song*; *Hosanna*; *Come Back Liza*; *I Do Adore Her*; *Dolly Dawn*; *Jamaica Farewell*; *Will His Love Be Like His Rum?*; *Man Smart*; *Star O*; *Brown Skin Girl*.

CAMPBELL, IAN, FOLK GROUP

This highly respected British folk group were formed in Birmingham, West Midlands, in 1956, and were originally called the Clarion Skiffle Group. With his parents, Campbell had moved from his home-town of Aberdeen, Scotland, to Birmingham in 1946. The original line-up was Ian Campbell (b. 10 June 1933, Aberdeen, Scotland; guitar, vocals), his sister Lorna Campbell (b. 1939, Aberdeen, Scotland; vocals), Dave Phillips (guitar) and Gordon McCulloch (banjo). In 1958, they became the Ian Campbell Folk Group. McCulloch departed in 1959 and was replaced by John Dunkerley (b. 1942; d. 1977; banjo, guitar, accordion). In 1960, Dave Swarbrick (b. 5 April 1941, New Malden, Surrey, England; fiddle, mandola) joined the group. Issued in 1962, it is notable that *Ceilidh At The Crown* was the first ever live folk club recording to be released. In 1963, the group were signed to Transatlantic Records and Brian Clark (guitar, vocals) joined the line-up as a replacement for Phillips. Clark also became a long-term member, staying until 1978. During the early 60s, the group appeared on television programmes such as the *Hootenanny Show*, *Barn Dance* and *Hullabaloo*. In addition, they regularly played to full houses in concert at venues such as the Royal Albert Hall, and the Royal Festival Hall in London. In 1964, they were invited to perform at the Newport Folk Festival in the USA, and in 1965, they became the first non-US group to record a Bob Dylan song; their version of 'The Times They Are A-Changin'' reached the UK Top 50 in March 1965. The group added bass player Mansell Davies in 1966, but he emigrated to Canada three years later, and he later became an organizer of Canadian festivals such as Calgary. After Swarbrick's departure in 1966, the group worked with George Watts (flute), who appeared on only two albums, *New Impressions* and *The Ian Campbell Folk Group*, the latter recorded in Czechoslovakia. Unfortunately, due to the prevailing political climate of the time, the record was never released outside the country, and the group did not receive royalties. Watts left in 1968, but a year earlier the group took on bassist Dave Pegg, who remained with them for three years before joining Fairport Convention. In 1969, Andy Smith (banjo, mandolin, guitar, fiddle) joined, leaving in 1971. That same year, Mike Hadley (bass) joined the ever-changing line-up, leaving in 1974. *Adam's Rib* was a suite of 12 songs written by Ian for his sister Lorna; the songs dealt with the different crisis points in a woman's life. John Dunkerley left the group, owing to ill health, in 1976, and died the following year from Hodgkinson's disease, aged just 34. The group disbanded in 1978, with Campbell having taken a place at university as a mature student, but the group still had bookings to honour. Various session players were recruited for live performances, including Aiden Ford (b. 1960; banjo, mandola) and Colin Tommis (b. 1960; guitar), who stayed for 18 months, touring Scandinavia. In 1984, Neil Cox (guitar) was added, and the group were booked by former bass player Mansell Davies to play dates in Canada. Cox then left, but Ian and Lorna Campbell, Cox and Ford played occasionally for special dates. An album recorded in Denmark in 1977 has never been released because there was no group to promote it. The sessions included Luke Kelly of the Dubliners, Dave Swarbrick and Martin Carthy. Many of Ian Campbell's songs are often thought of as traditional, but those such as 'The Sun Is Burning' have been covered by countless others, including Simon And Garfunkel.

● ALBUMS: *Ceilidh At The Crown* (1962)★★★, *Songs Of Protest* (1962)★★★, *This Is The Ian Campbell Folk Group* (Transatlantic 1963)★★★, *The Ian Campbell Folk Four* (Transatlantic 1964)★★★, *Across The Hills* (Transatlantic 1964)★★★, *Coaldust Ballads* (1965)★★★, *The Ian Campbell Folk Group* (1965)★★★, *The Singing Campbells* (1965)★★★, *Contemporary Campbells* (1966)★★, *New Impressions Of The Ian Campbell Folk Group* (1967)★★★, *Circle Game* (1968)★★★, *The Cock Doth Crow* (1968)★★★, Ian Campbell and John Dunkerley *Tam O'Shanter* (1968)★★★, *Ian Campbell - With The Ian Campbell Folk Group And Dave Swarbrick* (1969)★★★, *The Sun Is Burning* (Argo 1970)★★★, *Something To Sing About* (1972)★★★, *The Ian Campbell Folk Group Live* (1974)★★, *Adam's Rib* (1976)★★★.

● COMPILATIONS: *The Ian Campbell Folk Group Sampler Volume 1* (1969)★★★★, *The Ian Campbell Folk Group Sampler Volume 2* (1969)★★★, *And Another Thing* (Celtic Music 1994)★★★.

CAN-CAN

For *Can-Can*, his penultimate Broadway stage musical, which opened at the Shubert Theatre in New York on 7 May 1953, Cole Porter chose the setting of turn-of-the-century Paris. Abe Burrows' book was essentially a love story, in which the participants become involved with an attempt by the city authorities to close down a Montmartre nightclub that stages the outrageous can-can dance. Judge Aristide Forestier (Peter Cookson) investigates allegations of impropriety at the nightclub operated by La Mome Pistache (Lilo). However, the real show-stopping star was Gwen Verdon as the dancer Claudine. With splendid choreography by Michael Kidd, *Can-Can* was a great success and ran for more than two years on Broadway. Verdon and Kidd both won Tony Awards, and there were fine all-round performances from the rest of the cast. However, the show's greatest strength lay in Porter's music and lyrics. The songs included 'It's All Right With Me', 'Allez-Vous-En', 'Come Along With Me', 'Maidens Typical of France', 'I Am In Love', Never Give Anything Away', 'Montmart'', 'Live And Let Live', and two major hits, 'C'est Magnifique' and 'I Love Paris'. In 1988, *Can-Can* was revived in Chicago with Chita Rivera, and in New York and London with Donna McKechnie. The outstanding Original Cast album was re-released on CD in 1993. A 1960 film version starred Frank Sinatra, Shirley MacLaine and Maurice Chevalier.

CAPRIS

This R&B vocal group from Philadelphia, Pennsylvania, USA, comprised Rena Hinton, Bobby Smart, Eddie Warner, Harrison Scott, and Reuben White. Their one claim to fame was 'God Only Knows' (not the Beach Boys' hit) in 1954, which featured the quivering and fetching lead of Hinton. His vocals typified the delicate high-pitched lead work of Philadelphia doo-wop groups. The Capris originally formed in the early 50s in west Philadelphia, and in 1953 established their recording configuration when original member Charlie Stroud left the group to be replaced by Hinton. The Capris signed with Gotham in June 1954. 'God Only Knows' attracted considerable east coast play and they made radio and television appearances. The follow-ups, 'It's A Miracle' and 'It Was Moonglow', both ballads featuring the same vocal approach did not sustain the group's commercial success. When some of the members entered the Air Force in early 1955, the Capris were forced to disband. The group re-formed in 1958, with Fred Hale replacing Harrison Scott. They recorded 'My Weakness', but its lack of success served to break up the group for good. Some members of the Capris later formed the Moniques.

● COMPILATIONS: *Gotham Recording Stars: The Capris* (Collectables 1990)★★★.

CARMEN JONES

This was at least the fifth manifestation of a story that began as a novel by Frenchman Prosper Mérimeé, then became a grand opera by Bizet, Meilhac and Halévy, a 1943 Broadway musical, a 1948 film *The Loves Of Carmen* starring Rita Hayworth and Glenn Ford, and eventually this, a full-blown film musical that was produced and directed by Otto Preminger for 20th Century-Fox in 1954. Harry Kleiner's screenplay, which was based on Oscar Hammerstein II's libretto for that 1943 musical, follows the dramatic action of its operatic source, but changes the setting of the cigarette factory in Seville to a parachute factory in Chicago, and updates the story to World War II. Don José becomes Joe (Harry Belafonte), a soldier destined for flying school before being ruined by Carmen (Dorothy Dandridge); Escamillo, the toreador, is now Husky Miller (Joe Adams), a champion heavyweight prizefighter; Micaëla, the village maid, is transformed into Cindy Lou (Olga James), a small-town maiden who always remains faithful to her Joe; and Frasquita and the smuggler friends of Carmen are now Frankie (Pearl Bailey), Myrt (Diahann Carroll), Dink (Nick Stewart) and Rum (Roy Glenn). The singing voices of Carmen, Joe, Husky, Myrt, Rum and Dink are dubbed by Marilyn Horne, LeVerne Hutcherson, Marvin Hayes, Bernice Peterson, Brock Peters and Joe Crawford, respectively. The score, with music by Georges Bizet and lyrics by Oscar Hammerstein, was comprised of 'Dat's Love', 'You Talk Jus' Like My Maw', 'Dere's A Cafe On De Corner', 'Dis Flower', 'Beat Out Dat Rhythm On A Drum', 'Stan' Up And Fight', 'Whizzin' Away Along De Track', 'Card Song' and 'My Joe'. Herbert Ross was the choreographer and *Carmen Jones* was photographed by Sam Leavitt in Delux Color and CinemaScope.

CARNATIONS

R&B vocal group the Carnations were formed in 1954 in Bridgeport, Connecticut, USA, by leads Matthew Morales and Carl Hatton, with Harvey Arrington, Alan Mason and

Arthur Blackwell. Based in the Yellow Mill River ghetto school Watersville Junior High, they started singing together aged 13 and initially took the name Startones. Under this name they recorded two singles, 'Betty', from 1954, and 'I Love You So Dearly', in 1956. The following year their career was interrupted when two members, Hatton and Arrington, joined and Blackwell's younger brother, Tommy, took his place. In 1959 Edward Kennedy stepped in for Mason, who had joined another group. At this stage a further name change was required, and the Startones became the Teardrops. As such they made the acquaintance of Bo Diddley, who took them on tour and in 1959 asked them to back him on the recording of his R&B hit I'm Sorry'. Also recorded at the same sessions was 'Crackin' Up', which became Diddley's first record to reach the *Billboard* Top 100, though on neither of the releases were the Teardrops properly credited. By 1960 the group had moved on to a near-residency at the Apollo Theatre in New York, winning its famed talent contests for six weeks in a row. They still remained without a contract, however, despite their treks through New York's music industry corridors. After one particularly frustrating day, the group retired to a toilet in one record company building to revive their spirits by practising harmony. Joe René, A&R director of Beltone Records, was in the vicinity, and a contract was arranged with subsidiary label Lescay Records. However, Beltone insisted on a change of name from the generic Teardrops, and the quartet became the Carnations. Their October 1961 debut single, 'Long Tall Girl', sold well locally (and has become a major doo-wop favourite for later generations), but not enough to establish them as serious chart contenders. Lescay pulled the plug quickly, leaving two proposed singles, 'Arlene' and 'Crying Shame', unreleased.

CAROLINA SLIM

b. Edward P. Harris, 22 August 1923, Leasburg, North Carolina, USA, d. 22 October 1953, Newark, New Jersey, USA. Little is known about Harris, but it seems that he started his musical career in North Carolina and moved to Newark about the time of his first recordings in 1950. Records followed on three different labels, under four different pseudonyms; Carolina Slim, Jammin' Jim, Country Paul and Lazy Slim Jim. These records are unusual for their time in that many of them feature solo country blues, either in the Carolina style of Blind Boy Fuller, or blatant copies of Lightnin' Hopkins, although all are skilful and convincing performances. At his best, Slim could synthesize his influences to produce a satisfyingly distinctive sound, but unfortunately he did not live long enough to develop a real style of his own.
● COMPILATIONS: *Carolina Blues And Boogie* (Travelin' Man 1985)★★★, *1950-52* (1993)★★★.

CAROLLONS

The Carollons were formed in New York, USA, in the mid-50s. Originally called the Emeralds, the quintet featured Robert Dunson, Irving Brodsky, Artie Levy, Jimmy Laffey and Tyler Volks. Volks and Dunson were shortly replaced by Richard Jackson and Eric Nathonson. Inspired by the Moonglows and the Dells, they wrote much of their own material. 'Chapel Of Tears' was their debut release on Mohawk in 1958 and was a considerable local success. They

toured the north-east throughout the year and appeared on Clay Cole's television show. The more pop-orientated 'Hold Me Close' followed but failed to build on their initial breakthrough. When 'You Say' was also ignored the group disappeared with it.

CAROLS

Originally formed as a gospel group called United Baptist Five, in Detroit, Michigan, USA, in 1949, the Carols consisted of Tommy Evans (bass lead), Wilbert Tindle (baritone), James Worthy (piano), Richard Coleman (first tenor) and William Davis (second tenor). They met while working in a car factory, before discovering a shared love of harmony singing and spirituals. However, as the Carols, they sang secular songs and started to make an impression performing live in Harlem, New York. Columbia Records released their debut single, 'Please Believe In Me', in June 1950. Neither this nor the follow-up 'If I Could Steal You From Somebody Else' was a success on the charts and the Carols moved to Savoy Records. By this time, Kenneth Duncan had replaced Coleman, but their only Savoy issue, 'Fifty Million Women' flopped and the Carols broke up when Evans joined the Ravens.

CAROUSEL

It took more than 10 years for Richard Rodgers and Oscar Hammerstein II's second musical to transfer from Broadway to Hollywood in 1956, but the wait was more than worthwhile. The story, with its inherent dark undertones, was always going to be tricky to film, but Henry Ephron and his wife Phoebe wrote a fine screenplay. It was based on the original stage libretto, which itself had been adapted from Ferenc Molnar's play *Liliom*. It was set in Maine, New England, in 1873, and told of the tragic love affair between carousel barker Billy Bigelow (Gordon MacRae) and mill worker Julie Jordan (Shirley Jones). Out of work, and desperate to earn enough money to support his pregnant wife, Billy is persuaded by sly Jigger Craigin (Cameron Mitchell) to take part in a robbery that goes awry. He is killed in the ensuing scuffle when he falls on his own knife. Fifteen years later he is allowed to return to earth for just one day so that he can make his peace with his lovely teenage daughter. An admirable supporting cast included Barbara Ruick and Robert Rounseville as the delightful Carrie Pipperidge and Enoch Snow, Claramae Turner, Susan Luckey, Audrey Christie, Gene Lockhart and Jacques d'Amboise. The classic score remained more or less intact, from the majestic 'Carousel Waltz' through to the inspirational 'You'll Never Walk Alone'. Along the way there are other memorable numbers such as 'You're A Queer One, Julie Jordan', 'If I Loved You', 'Mr. Snow', 'June Is Bustin' Out All Over', 'When The Children Are Asleep', 'Soliloquy', 'Stonecutters Cut It On Stone', 'What's The Use Of Wond'rin'?' and 'A Real Nice Clambake'. Roger Alexander and the legendary Agnes de Mille staged the dances, and the film, which was produced by Henry Ephron for 20th Century-Fox, was photographed by Charles Clarke in DeLuxe Color and CinemaScope. The director was Henry King. Frank Sinatra was the original choice to play Billy Bigelow but he withdrew soon after filming began. However, he did record an impressive version of 'Soliloquy' which stretched to both sides of a 12-inch 78 rpm record.

CARR, VALERIE

b. 1936, New York City, New York, USA. Carr started by studying classical piano, which she eventually dropped in the mid-50s in favour of singing. She attended New York's High School of Performing Arts and the Berklee College Of Music in Boston and also studied under noted singing tutor Lee Daniels. Roulette Records signed her in 1957 and her debut single, 'You're The Greatest' was narrowly beaten into the chart by the Billy Scott version of the song. Her follow-up, 'When The Boys Talk About The Girls' a teen-orientated beat ballad from the pen of the 50s top tunesmith Bob Merrill, was a big US hit and reached both the US Top 100 and the UK Top 30. Neither her next release, 'Bad Girl', nor her later records made any impression. This could have been due to the fact that this strong-voiced artist's records were aimed towards the older MOR market too early in her career.

CARROLL, DAVID, AND HIS ORCHESTRA

b. Nook Schrier, 15 October 1913, Chicago, Illinois, USA. David Carroll became orchestra arranger/conductor for Mercury Records in 1951, and from 1953-62, he and the Jack Halloran Singers appeared on 36 US Top 100 hits including the Crew-Cuts' 'Sh-Boom' (1954, a number 1 hit) and 'Earth Angel' (1955); Rusty Draper's 'Shifting, Whispering Sands' (1955), covered in the UK by Eamonn Andrews; and several Vic Damone hits. Carroll's biggest success was an instrumental version of 'Melody Of Love', which peaked at number 8 in 1955.
● ALBUMS: *Let's Dance* (Mercury 1959)★★★★, *Let's Dance Again* (Mercury 1959)★★.

CARROLL, RONNIE

b. Ronald Cleghorn, 18 August 1934, Belfast, Northern Ireland. A singer with an extremely high baritone voice, who became known as 'The Minstrel'. Carroll has been a baker, plumber, greengrocer, milkman, car mechanic and auctioneer's assistant. He began his career in shows promoted by Ruby Murray's father, then joined Eddie Lee's *Hollywood Doubles Show*, blacking up to provide Nat 'King' Cole impressions. Cole attended his performance in Liverpool and asked, 'What are you trying to do, cripple me?'. Carroll toured the UK Variety circuit with the show, adding Billy Eckstine material to his repertoire. After BBC producer Albert Stevenson gave him his television debut, he met singer and actress Millicent Martin on a show and they were married in 1959. Carroll was signed to Philips by A&R manager Johnny Franz who had seen him at the London Metropolitan, Edgware Road. In the late 50s he had UK hits with 'Walk Hand In Hand' (1956) and 'The Wisdom Of A Fool' (1957), and in the early 60s with 'Footsteps' (1960), 'Roses Are Red' (1962 - a number 3 hit), 'If Only Tomorrow' (1962) and two songs with which he won the British heats of the *Eurovision Song Contest*, 'Ring-A-Ding Girl' (1962) and 'Say Wonderful Things' (1963 - Top 10). He was still working in the 80s, but the recession in the UK northern club business forced him to seek work in holiday camps and in Singapore and Kuala Lumpur hotels. In 1989, Carroll was discharged from bankruptcy with reported debts of many thousands of pounds. In 1997 he stood as a parliamentary candidate at the general election.
● ALBUMS: with Bill McGuffie *From Ten Till One* (Philips 1956)★★★, *Lucky Thirteen* (Philips 1959)★★★, *Sometimes I'm Happy, Sometimes I'm Blue* (Philips 1963)★★★, with Millicent Martin *Mr & Mrs Is The Name* (Philips 1964)★★, *Carroll Calling* (1965)★★★, *Wonderful Things And Other Favourites* (Wing 1967)★★★, with Anna Pollack *Phil The Fluter* (Fontana 1969)★★, with Aimi McDonald *Promises Promises* (Fontana 1970)★★.
● COMPILATIONS: *Roses Are Red: The Ronnie Carroll Story* (Diamond 1996)★★★★.

CARSON, MINDY

b. 16 July 1927, New York City, New York, USA. After singing on bandleader Paul Whiteman's 40s radio show, female pop vocalist Mindy Carson first hit the US Top 20 in 1946 with a duet with Harry Cool, with a version of Frankie Carle's number 1 'Rumors Are Flying'. She continued to have chart successes until the mid-50s - including two with Guy Mitchell - by covering the big hits of the day, including Dean Martin's 1956 UK and US chart-topper 'Memories Are Made Of This' and R&B singer Ivory Joe Hunter's 'Since I Met You Baby' She also hosted her own radio and television programmes.

CARTER, BENNY

b. Bennett Lester Carter, 8 August 1907, New York City, New York, USA. Carter was born and raised in the area of New York known as San Juan Hill, a tough neighbourhood. His working-class parents encouraged their children to take up music and Carter and his two sisters received piano tuition from their mother, Sadie Bennett Carter. A cousin, Theodore 'Cuban' Bennett, was a well-known trumpeter in New York jazz clubs in the 20s, while another cousin, Darnell Howard, played clarinet with the bands of W.C. Handy, Joe 'King' Oliver and Carroll Dickerson in the 20s. Apart from his mother's tuition, Carter took early lessons on the C-melody saxophone from a succession of teachers, among them Harold Proctor and Lt. Eugene Mickell Snr. Musician neighbours of Carter, in his youth, included Bubber Miley, Freddy Johnson, Rudy Powell, Russell Procope and Bobby Stark. Carter was already familiar with the Harlem jazz scene when, in 1923, his family settled there. By the late 20s, Carter, who had by then switched to the alto saxophone, was becoming known as a reliable and dedicated young musician who had gained valuable experience in bands led by Billy Fowler, Duke Ellington and Fletcher Henderson. In 1928 he was working in the band led by Fletcher's brother, Horace Henderson. When Horace left, Carter took over as leader. Despite engagements at top dancehalls, the band proved short-lived, owing, in part, to Carter's personal manner and attitude towards music. A naturally elegant man and musically a perfectionist and utter professional, Carter refused to resort to the kind of flash and showmanship audiences expected. After the band folded, Carter worked as musical director of McKinney's Cotton Pickers, a period during which he began to develop his interest in arranging. During the early 30s Carter also played trumpet, surprising fellow musicians with the ease at which he switched from reeds to brass and back again. By this time he was also adept on clarinet, tenor saxophone, trombone and piano. He pursued his interest in writing, providing arrangements for many leading bands of the day, including those of Chick Webb, for whom he also played alto, and Benny

Goodman. In 1933 he formed a new big band, which featured Chu Berry and Dicky Wells. In this same year he also played on recording dates organized by British composer-bass player Spike Hughes. In 1935 Carter joined Willie Lewis's band, with which he visited Europe. In all, Carter was away for three years, working in several countries including France, Holland and Denmark. At the urging of writer Leonard Feather, Carter was hired by Henry Hall as staff arranger for the BBC Dance Orchestra in London. In 1938, aware of the commercial successes of the swing era back in the USA, he returned home and formed a new big band. Once again, his refusal to compromise his standards meant that the band enjoyed little commercial success. He also recorded extensively on small group sessions, such as Lionel Hampton's RCA recordings, for some of which he wrote arrangements. Other bands included the Chocolate Dandies, in which he played alongside Coleman Hawkins and Roy Eldridge, and the Varsity Seven. In 1942 Carter settled in California, formed a new big band and signed with agent Carlos Gastel, who also handled Nat 'King' Cole, Sonny Dunham and Stan Kenton. Employed to write for films, Carter proved a fast learner and, although he was sometimes uncredited, because blacks had yet to achieve full status in Hollywood, he worked on numerous scores for 20th Century-Fox, Warner Brothers and MGM. In the winter of 1946/7 Carter folded his big band for the last time but continued to re-form it for special recording dates. In the early 50s he began touring with Jazz At The Philharmonic and made numerous records for Norman Granz. He also arranged and provided orchestral backing for a host of singers, notably Peggy Lee, Ella Fitzgerald and Mel Tormé. A heart attack in January 1956 barely slowed him down and he remained active in his writing and playing; the same year he married for the fourth time. The late 50s and early 60s were especially fruitful times and he composed, arranged and played on a succession of important albums, including Aspects, Further Definitions and Additions To Further Definitions. He also wrote a major work for Count Basie, the Kansas City Suite. By now he was also working in television and touring the international festival circuit. In the early 70s Carter began a continuing association with Princeton University, where he became Visiting Lecturer in the Council of Humanities and the African-American Studies Programme. His personal contact with Morroe Berger at Princeton led to the appearance of Berger's major biography, Benny Carter: A Life In American Music (1982). During the 70s Carter began a regular string of visits to Japan, where he became extremely popular, and also continued to record, again for Norman Granz. In the 80s Carter toured and recorded, on many occasions scoring and composing extensively.

As a player, on any of his many instruments, Carter is skilled and always inventive and delightful to hear. It is on alto saxophone, however, that he has made his greatest contribution. A liquid player in the tradition of Johnny Hodges and Willie Smith, the two contemporary giants with whom he is usually grouped, Carter displays a striking pungency and an effortless capacity for creating solos of interest and fascination. As a composer of tunes such as 'Doozy' and 'When Lights Are Low' he has contributed greatly to the jazz catalogue. As an arranger in the 30s he was a major force in shaping big band music and has continued to demonstrate

his skills in this area and in small group settings to lasting effect. His longevity and the fact that neither his playing nor writing skills have shown any signs of diminishing are truly remarkable. In 1987 he joined forces with John Lewis and the All-American Jazz Orchestra, an occasionally assembled repertory dedicated to the performance of music especially written for big bands. For a concert and subsequent recording date, Carter composed and arranged a new major work, Central City Sketches. Additionally, Carter rehearsed the orchestra, conducted, played solo alto and drew from the musicians taking part admiration, enthusiasm and a sparkling performance. In the late summer of 1989 the Classical Jazz series of concerts at New York's Lincoln Center celebrated Carter's 82nd birthday with a set of his songs, sung by Ernestine Anderson and Sylvia Syms. In the same week, at the Chicago Jazz Festival, he presented a recreation of his Further Definitions album, using some of the original musicians. In February 1990, Carter led an all-star big band at the Lincoln Center in a concert tribute to Ella Fitzgerald. Events such as these added to the endless and imperishable catalogue of achievements of this remarkable man. In 1995 a tribute album of sorts was issued, and unusually, Carter was present on the project. It featured some beautiful vocal treatments of Carter's work, including tracks from Ruth Brown, Diana Krall, Dianne Reeves and Peggy Lee. It was probably Ben Webster who first dubbed Carter 'The King', a name that stuck because, unlike titles bestowed by outsiders, this one was offered in tribute to qualities that jazz musicians themselves esteemed.

● ALBUMS: Jazz Off The Air (1944)★★★, Cosmopolite 10-inch album (Clef 1953)★★★, The Urbane Mr Carter 10-inch album (Norgran 1954)★★★, The Formidable Benny Carter 10-inch album (Norgran 1954)★★★, Benny Carter Plays Pretty reissued as Moonglow - Love Songs By Benny Carter (Norgran 1955)★★★, Benny Carter (Norgran 1955)★★★★, New Jazz Sounds (Norgran 1955)★★★, Alone Together (Norgran 1956)★★★, Sessions, Live (1957)★★★, Jazz Giant (Contemporary 1958)★★★, Swingin' The Twenties (Contemporary 1959)★★★, 'Can Can' And 'Anything Goes' (United Artists 1959)★★★, Aspects (United Artists 1959)★★★★, The Fabulous Benny Carter (Audio Lab 1959)★★★, Jazz Calendar (United Artists 1960)★★★, Sax A La Carter (United Artists 1960)★★★, Further Definitions (Impulse 1962)★★★★, B.B.B. & Co. (1962)★★★, The World Of Sight And Sounds (1963)★★★, Benny Carter In Paris (20th Century Fox 1963)★★★, Additions To Further Definitions (Impulse 1966)★★★★, Benny Carter 1933 (Prestige 1969)★★★, The King (Pablo 1976)★★★, Carter, Gillespie Inc. (1976)★★★, Wonderland (Pablo 1976)★★★, Benny Carter At Montreux '77 (Original Jazz Classics 1977)★★★, Live And Well In Japan (Original Jazz Classics 1977)★★★, Jazz Allstar Orchestra Live In Japan '79 (1979)★★★, Summer Serenade (Storyville 1980)★★★, Gentlemen Of Swing (1980)★★★, Skyline Drive (1982)★★★, The Benny Carter All Stars Featuring Nat Adderley And Red Norvo (Sonet 1985)★★★, Benny Carter Meets Oscar Peterson (Pablo 1986)★★★, A Gentleman And His Music (Concord 1986)★★★, with the All-American Jazz Orchestra Central City Sketches (Limelight 1987)★★★, In The Mood For Swing (Limelight 1987)★★★, My Kind Of Trouble (Pablo 1988)★★★, Cooking At Carlos 1 (Limelight 1989)★★★, My Man Benny, My Man Phil (Limelight 1990)★★★, All That

Jazz Live At Princeton (Limelight 1991)★★★, *Harlem Renaissance* (1993)★★★, *Songbook* (Music Masters 1996)★★★.
● COMPILATIONS: *The Best Of Benny Carter* (Pablo 1982)★★★★, *Benny Carter 1928-52* (RCA 1983)★★★★, *The Benny Carter Collection - 16 Golden Greats* (Deja Vu 1987)★★★★, *When Lights Are Low* (Happy Days 1987)★★★, *3,4,5 - The Verve Small Group Sessions* (1991)★★★★, *The Complete Recordings* (Affinity/Charly 1992)★★★★, *These Foolish Things* (Tring 1993)★★★, *New Jazz Sounds: The Urbane Sessions* 2-CD set (Verve 1996)★★★★.
● VIDEOS: *Symphony In Riffs* (Rhapsody 1995).
● FURTHER READING: *The Alto Saxophone, Trumpet And Clarinet Of Benny Carter, 1927-1946*, Jan Evensmo. *Benny Carter: A Life In American Music*, M. and E. Berger.

CARTER, BIG LUCKY

b. Levester Carter, 1920, Weir, Mississippi, USA. Although he had played spirituals on his grandmother's piano, Carter did not take up the guitar until he was serving in the Pacific during World War II. When he returned to Mississippi, he took instruction from local musicians James Henry and Big Boy Anderson. In 1949, he joined a band that also featured pianist Ford Nelson. In Memphis the following year he joined his cousin, saxophonist Ed Kirby (who worked as Prince Gabe), in his band the Rhythmaires. He remained with the band (its name having been changed to the Millionaires) for eight years. In January 1957 they recorded a session for Sun Records under his cousin's real name, from which some titles were issued during the 70s. Carter led his own band during the 60s but continued to record with Kirby for Savoy, Westside and Bandstand USA. In 1969 he made two singles for Willie Mitchell's M.O.C. label, one of which, 'Goofer Dust', is regarded as his principal achievement, and on which he was backed by members of Al Green's band, including guitarist Mabon 'Teenie' Hodges. These and two further titles were issued on *River Town Blues* two years later. Although he continued to write and perform, nothing was heard from Carter until his appearance at the 1993 Burnley Blues Festival.
● ALBUMS: *River Town Blues* (Hi 1971)★★★, *River Town Blues Plus!* (Hi 1991)★★★.

CARTER, VIVIAN, AND JAMES BRACKEN

Vivian 'Vee' Carter (b. 1920, Tunica, Mississippi, USA, d. 12 June 1989, Gary, Indiana, USA) and James 'Jay' C. Bracken (b. 1909, Kansas City, Missouri, USA, d. 1972), founded the US independent record label Vee Jay Records in 1953, and controlled its rise from regional obscurity to a position as one of black music's leading outlets. Their initial signings included the Spaniels, who provided the company's first major success when their haunting doo-wop ballad, 'Goodnite Sweetheart, Goodnite', was a hit in the R&B and pop chart. The couple, now married, established their offices in Chicago's East 47th Street. Vivian's brother, Calvin Carter, also joined the company; this intuitive individual was responsible for attracting several important acts, including vocal groups the El Dorados and the Dells, as well as gospel artists the Staple Singers and the Swan Silvertones. Vee Jay's staff was considerably bolstered by the addition of Ewart Abner, whose business acumen did much to facilitate the

label's meteoric rise. By the early 60s the Vee Jay roster included Jerry Butler, Dee Clark and Gene Chandler, each of whom enjoyed popular success, while influential blues performers Jimmy Reed and John Lee Hooker recorded their best-known material for the outlet. However, by 1963 the label was encountering financial difficulties. Vee Jay had diversified into white pop by securing the Four Seasons, and had won the rights to the Beatles' early releases when Capitol Records declined their option. When the former act had several hits, the label was unable to meet royalty payments and a protracted lawsuit ensued. Capitol then rescinded their Beatles agreement; although Vee Jay latterly retained material already licensed, the rights to future recordings were lost. This controversial period also saw Abner's departure, while the label moved its operations to Los Angeles. However, by 1965 Vee Jay was back in Chicago, with Abner reinstated in his former position. Such upheavals proved fatal. Unsettled artists moved to other outlets, and when interim manager Randy Wood sued for breach of contract, Vee Jay filed for bankruptcy. In May 1966, the company closed its offices and released its remaining employees. Arguably capable of rivalling Tamla/Motown had they overcome their internal problems, Vee Jay nonetheless holds an important place in the development of black music. Abner eventually rose to become president of Motown, while James Bracken died in 1972, the owner of a record shop. Calvin Carter died in 1986, while Vivian Carter ran a radio station in her home-town of Gary, Indiana.

CASONOVAS

Originally called the Jubilee Kings, this vocal quartet was formed in High Point, North Carolina, USA, shortly after the end of World War II as a gospel quartet. Brothers Frank and Willie McWilliams teamed with cousins L.D. and Chester Mayfield to sing in local churches. After a spell as paratroopers in the Korean war, they returned in 1954 and changed tempo to R&B, recording demos that earned them a session with Apollo Records in November. 'That's All' was their debut release in April 1955, followed two months later by 'Hush-A-Meca'. Of more interest was their third release, 'I Don't Want You To Go'. This song's melody (written by Chester Mayfield) was later reprised by Lowman Pauling for his 'Dedicated To The One I Love', which became a Top 3 *Billboard* hit twice over when later covered by the Shirelles in 1961 and the Mamas And The Papas in 1967. After one further ballad at the end of 1955, 'My Baby's Love', the group retired to the local club scene for the next two years. 'Please Be Mine' was eventually released in November 1957, by which point the group's fortunes were in terminal decline. 'You Are My Queen' became their final release a year later.

CASSIDY, JACK

b. John Cassidy, 5 March 1927, Richmond Hill, New York, USA, d. 12 March 1976, Los Angeles, California, USA. A versatile actor and singer who, even in his later years, seemed to retain his youthful appearance, Cassidy made his Broadway debut at the age of 17 in the chorus of the 1943 Cole Porter-Ethel Merman hit musical *Something For The Boys*. More chorus work followed in *Sadie Thompson*, *The Firebrand Of Florence*, *Around The World*, *Music In My Heart*, and *Inside USA*, before Cassidy played a more prominent

role, along with others on the brink of success such as Tom Ewell and Alice Pearce, in the stylish revue *Small Wonder* (1948). He was in the short-lived *Alive And Kicking* in 1950, and two years later took over the part of Seabee Richard West in *South Pacific*. Also in 1952, Cassidy had his first leading role as the suave Chick Miller in *Wish You Were Here*, a show that attracted a great deal of publicity owing to the fact that it had a swimming-pool built into the stage. Cassidy introduced the appealing title song, and also sang the underrated 'Where Did The Night Go?'. He subsequently played opposite Betty Oakes in the offbeat *Sandhog* (1954), co-starred with Carol Lawrence in a musical adaptation of James Hilton's novel *Lost Horizon* called *Shangri-La*, and appeared in various musical productions in the US regions and Europe, before returning to Broadway in 1963 with the charming *She Loves Me*. While Barbara Cook and Daniel Massey resolved their complicated relationship, Cassidy, playing the unctuous 'resident ladies man' Steven Kodaly, pursued Barbara Baxley with 'Ilona' and 'Grand Knowing You'. His performance was rewarded with the 1964 Tony Award for Supporting/Featured Actor in a musical. During the remainder of the 60s, Cassidy had another ultra-smooth role as Hollywood leading man Byron Prong in *Fade Out-Fade In* (1964), was egotistical columnist Max Mencken in the comic strip spoof *It's A Bird, It's A Plane, It's Superman* (1966), and played Irishman Phineas Flynn in the Civil War musical *Maggie Flynn* (1968). In the title role of the latter show was Shirley Jones, the former star of films such as *Oklahoma!*, *Carousel* and *The Music Man*, who was Cassidy's second wife. Cassidy himself also appeared in a number of films, notably as John Barrymore in *W.C. Fields And Me* and as Damon Runyon in *The Private Files Of J. Edgar Hoover*. After his Broadway career declined, he worked in regional theatre, both straight and musical, and appeared on television and in nightclubs. He died at the age of 49 in a fire at his Los Angeles apartment. His sons, Patrick, Shaun and David Cassidy, are also in showbusiness. David began his career in the theatre and on television in *The Partridge Family* before becoming a teen-idol recording artist in the 70s. He later appeared in a Broadway production of *Joseph And The Amazing Technicolor Dreamcoat* in 1983, replaced Cliff Richard in *Time* (London, 1987), and he and Shaun took over the roles of the twins Mickey and Eddie in Willy Russell's *Blood Brothers* on Broadway in 1993. David reprised his role in London's West End two years later. Patrick Cassidy appeared as Frederic in *The Pirates Of Penzance* on Broadway in 1982, and as Jeff Barry in Ellie Greenwich's *Leader Of The Pack* (1985).
● FILMS: *Look In Any Window* (1961), *The Chapman Report* (1962), *FBI Code 98* (1964), *Guide For The Married Man* (1967), *The Cockeyed Cowboys Of Calico County* (1970), *Bunny O'Hare* (1971), *The Eiger Sanction* (1975), *W.C. Fields And Me* (1976), *The Private Files Of J. Edgar Hoover* (1978).

CASTELLES

An R&B vocal group from Philadelphia, Pennsylvania, USA, comprising lead George Grant, Octavious Anthony, William Taylor, Frank Vance, and Ronald Everett. The Castelles, featuring the delicate and quivering falsetto tenor of Grant, perfectly exemplified the Philadelphia vocal group sound of the 50s. The group joined Herb Slotkin's Grand Records in 1954, and under the production aegis of an up-and-coming pro-

ducer, Jerry Ragovoy, achieved a hit with their very first effort, 'My Girl Awaits Me' (1954), which sold well in Philadelphia, New York, and Washington, DC. The follow-up, 'This Silver Ring', composed by Ragovoy, was a commercial disappointment, but artistically it was as evocative and pristine as their debut The third release, 'Do You Remember', had little impact, but the b-side, a version of the old standard 'If You Were The Only Girl', sold well in Philadelphia. Other notable songs followed, 'Heavenly Father' (a remake of the Edna McGriff hit from 1952), and 'Over A Cup Of Coffee' (1955). The group moved to Atlantic Records, and had one Coasters-styled release before breaking up in 1956. Members of the Atco-based group were Grant, Anthony, Taylor, and new member, lead Clarence Scott.
● COMPILATIONS: *The Sweet Sound Of The Castelles* (Collectables 1990)★★★.

CASTON, LEONARD 'BABY DOO'

b. 2 June 1917, Sumrall, near Hattisburg, Mississippi, USA, d. 22 August 1987, Minneapolis, Minnesota, USA. More than just a blues pianist, Baby Doo Caston was a musician whose range included popular and light classical music. His early influence and mentor was his cousin Alan Weathersby, who taught him to play guitar at an early age. After several moves they began playing around the Natchez area and were managed by Leonard's mother Minda. Baby Doo took up the piano around 1936 and moved to Chicago, where he heard the likes of Earl Hines, Big Bill Broonzy and T-Bone Walker, but he was most influenced by Leroy Carr. He played with the Five Breezes and his own group, the Rhythm Rascals Trio, before the war found him on a United States Overseas entertainment tour with Alberta Hunter. He worked through China, Burma, India, Egypt, Africa and Europe, a high spot being a command performance for Generals Eisenhower, Montgomery and Zhukov in Germany in 1945. Returning to Chicago, he formed the Big Three Trio with Willie Dixon and Ollie Crawford, with whom he recorded for Bullet, Columbia and OKeh, as well as working as a soloist (recording an album on his own Hot Shot label) and supporting many blues artists. His final job was a long-standing engagement in Minneapolis where he died of heart failure.
● ALBUMS: *Hot Shot* (Hot Shot 1986)★★★, *I Feel Like Steppin' Out* (1986)★★★, *Willie Dixon And The Big Three Trio* (Columbia 1990)★★★.
● FURTHER READING: *From Blues To Pop: The Autobiography Of Leonard 'Baby Doo' Caston*, Jeff Todd Titon.

CAT IRON

b. William Carradine, c.1896, Garden City, Louisiana, USA, d. c.1958, Natchez, Mississippi, USA. A folklorist's mishearing of his surname resulted in the evocative billing given to this singer and guitarist's only album. Recorded on a single day in 1958, at first he would play only stirring versions of old hymns with slide accompaniment, but later consented to record a number of fine blues, including the important blues ballad 'Jimmy Bell'. Cat Iron made a television appearance that year, but is believed to have died soon afterwards.
● ALBUMS: *Cat Iron Sings Blues & Hymns* (1960)★★★.

CATES, GEORGE

b. 19 October 1911, New York City, New York, USA. A composer, arranger, conductor and record producer, Cates was educated at New York University. He became a producer for Coral and Dot Records, and was music supervisor for bandleader Lawrence Welk's extremely successful 50s and 60s television shows. In 1955 he provided the accompaniment for Steve Allen's piano solo on a hit recording of 'Autumn Leaves', shortly after Allen founded the famous *Tonight Show*. He also made records with his own orchestra, mainly of film songs and themes, including 'Moonglow And Theme From *Picnic*' in 1955 (which sold over a million copies), 'Whatever Will Be, Will Be (Que Sera, Sera)', from the Doris Day film *The Man Who Knew Too Much*, and the title songs from *Friendly Persuasion* (1956) and the fairly obscure Bing Crosby movie *Man On Fire* (1957).
● ALBUMS: *Polynesian Percussion* (1961)★★, *Take Five* (1961)★★★★, *3rd Man Theme* (1962)★★★, *Twistin' Twelve Great Hits* (1962)★★, *Great Hit Sounds* (1964)★★★, *Hit Songs - Hit Sounds* (1964)★★★, *1965's Greatest Hits* (1966)★★★.

CATHCART, DICK

b. 6 November 1924, Michigan City, Indiana, USA, d. 8 November 1993, Woodland Hills, California, USA. A fine trumpeter, his first major band appearance was with Ray McKinley. He later played in bands in the US Army during World War II, and after the war was with Bob Crosby before a spell in the Hollywood studios. Among the film soundtracks on which he can be heard are *Dragnet* (1954), *Battle Stations* (1955), *Nightmare* (1956), in which he dubbed for the on-screen Billy May, who was more than capable of blowing his own trumpet, and *The Five Pennies* (1959). Cathcart played in other name bands in the late 40s and 50s but became best known, by sound if not by name, when he played trumpet for the leading character in a 1952 US radio series entitled *Pete Kelly's Blues*. When the programme also became a feature film in 1955 and transferred to television later in the decade, Cathcart again ghosted for the star (Jack Webb in the film, William Reynolds on television), although he also appeared on-camera in the small-screen version. Cathcart made a series of successful small-group jazz albums, not surprisingly taking the sound marketing step of naming his band 'Pete Kelly's Big Seven'. Apart from playing trumpet with a bell-like tone, Cathcart also sang; it was in this capacity that he was most active in the 60s and 70s. During the 80s he returned to jazz stages, playing trumpet as well as ever.
● ALBUMS: *Pete Kelly At Home* (1956)★★★★, *Bix MCMLIX* (Warners 1959)★★★.

CELLOS

This vocal quintet was formed in 1955 at Charles Evan Hughes High School in Manhattan, New York, USA, by Alton Campbell (lead), Bobby Thomas (baritone), Alvin Williams (bass), Billy Montgomery (first tenor) and Clifford Williams (second tenor). Influenced by the Coasters and Crests, they originally took the name Marcals while singing on New York street corners. Their first recording was a demo of one of Alvin Williams' compositions, 'Rang Tang Ding Dong'. Apollo Records released a re-recorded version of the track as a single in January 1956 that reached number 62 in *Billboard*'s R&B chart. With the debut single considered something of a novelty (it was about a Japanese man who had lots of success with women), they continued their offbeat approach to songwriting with 'Juicy Crocodile'. However, it failed to chart, as did 'Be-Bop Mouse' (September 1957) and 'What's The Matter For You' (January 1958), the latter derived from Italian immigrant vernacular. It was their final release, and Campbell and Montgomery joined the Channels.
● COMPILATIONS: *Rang Tang Ding Dong* (Relic 1992)★★★.

CHACKSFIELD, FRANK

b. 9 May 1914, Battle, Sussex, England, d. 9 June 1995. After early training on the piano and organ, Chacksfield led small groups in the late 30s before becoming arranger for the *Stars In Battledress* entertainment unit in World War II. His first radio broadcast was *Original Songs At The Piano* from Glasgow, and during the late 40s he worked with comedian Charlie Chester's *Stand Easy*, making his recording debut accompanying Chester's resident singer, Frederick Ferrari. He also conducted for the Henry Hall and Geraldo orchestras, and later formed his own band, the Tunesmiths. In 1953, he had a hit with the novelty 'Little Red Monkey', with composer Jack Jordan on the clavioline. Later that year, with a 40-piece orchestra featuring a large string section, Chacksfield made the Top 10 in the UK and US charts with Charles Chaplin's 'Terry's Theme From *Limelight*', repeating the process in 1954 with his version of 'Ebb Tide'. Both records, with their richly scored arrangements, became million-sellers. He had further success in the 50s with 'In Old Lisbon', 'Donkey Cart', 'Flirtation Waltz', 'Memories Of You', and another Chaplin theme, 'Smile'. He had his own weekly radio programme for a time, and in later years continued to broadcast regularly in programmes such as *Friday Night Is Music Night*. His many albums reflected music from all over the world, as well as featuring the work of various popular composers.
● ALBUMS: *The Ebb Tide* (Decca 1960)★★★, *The New Ebb Tide* (Decca 1964)★★★, *New Limelight* (Phase 4 1965)★★★, *All Time Top TV Themes* (Phase 4 1965)★★★, *Beyond The Sea* (Phase 4 1965)★★★★, *Great Country And Western Hits* (Phase 4 1966)★★, *Film Festival* (Phase 4 1968)★★★, *South Sea Island Magic* (Eclipse 1969)★★, *Tango* (Eclipse 1970)★★★, *New York* (Phase 4 1970)★★★★, *Plays The Beatles Songbook* (Phase 4 1970)★★★, *Plays Simon And Garfunkel/Jim Webb* (Phase 4 1971)★★, *Mediterranean Moonlight* (Eclipse 1971)★★★, *Plays Bacharach* (Phase 4 1972)★★★, *The World Of Immortal Classics* (Decca 1972)★★★, *Music Of Cole Porter* (Phase 4 1972)★★★, *Opera's Golden Moments* (Phase 4 1973)★★, *Music For Christmas* (Decca 1973)★★★, *The World Of Immortal Serenades* (Decca 1973)★★★, *Music Of Noël Coward* (Eclipse 1974)★★★, *Romantic Europe* (Eclipse 1974)★★★, *The Glory That Was Gershwin* (Phase 4 1974)★★★★, *The Incomparable Jerome Kern* (Phase 4 1975)★★★★, *Plays Rodgers And Hart* (Phase 4 1975)★★★★, *The World Of Immortal Strauss Waltzes* (Decca 1975)★★★, *The World Of Operatic Melodies* (Decca 1976)★★★, *Plays Lerner And Loewe* (Phase 4 1976)★★★, *Plays Irving Berlin* (Phase 4 1976)★★★, *Vintage '52* (Phase 4 1977)★★★, *Plays Hoagy Carmichael* (Phase 4 1977)★★★, *Hawaii* (Goldcrown 1978)★★★, *The Unmistakeable Frank Chacksfield* (Rim

1979)★★★, *Could I Have This Dance?* (Dansan 1981)★★★, *Chariots Of Fire* (Premier 1984)★★★, *Love Is In The Air* (Premier 1984)★★★, *Nice 'N' Easy* (Premier 1984)★★★, *A Little More Love* (Premier 1987)★★★, *Thanks For The Memories (Academy Award Winners 1934-55)* (Eclipse 1991)★★★.

● COMPILATIONS: *The World Of Frank Chacksfield* (Decca 1969)★★★, *The World Of Frank Chacksfield, Volume Two* (Decca 1971)★★★★, *Focus On Frank Chacksfield* (Decca 1977)★★★, *Stardust* (Contour 1981)★★★, *Limelight And Other Favourites* (President 1985)★★★.

CHAMPION, GOWER

b. 22 June 1920, Geneva, Illinois, USA, d. 25 August 1980, New York City, New York, USA. One of the most distinguished and influential directors and choreographers in the American musical theatre, Champion was brought up in Los Angeles and took dancing lessons from an early age. When he was 15, he and his friend, Jeanne Tyler, toured nightclubs as 'Gower and Jeanne America's youngest dance team'. After serving in the US Coast Guard during World War II, Champion found another dance partner, Marge Belcher, and they were married in 1947. In the 50s they appeared together on numerous television variety programmes and in their own situation comedy, *The Marge And Gower Champion Show*. They also made several film musicals including *Mr. Music, Lovely To Look At, Give A Girl A Break, Jupiter's Darling, Three For The Show*, and the autobiographical *Everything I Have Is Yours*. Their exuberant dancing to 'I Might Fall Back On You' and 'Life Upon The Wicked Stage' were two of the highlights of the 1951 remake of *Show Boat*, which starred Howard Keel and Kathryn Grayson. During the late 30s and 40s Champion worked on Broadway as a solo dancer and choreographer. In 1948 he began to direct as well, and won a Tony Award for his staging of the musical *Lend An Ear*, the show that introduced Carol Channing to New York theatre audiences. From then on he choreographed and directed a mixture of smash hits and dismal flops in a list that included *Three For Tonight, Bye Bye Birdie, Carnival, Hello, Dolly!, I Do! I Do!, The Happy Time, Sugar, Irene, Mack And Mabel* (1974) and *Rockabye Hamlet* (1976). They earned him another three Tonys and New York Critics and Donaldson Awards. After some years away from Broadway, he returned (uncredited) to 'doctor' *The Act* (1977), but could do nothing to prevent *A Broadway Musical* (1978) folding after only one night. He finished with a smash hit, however, when he choreographed and directed a 1980 stage adaptation of the movie classic *42nd Street*. During the show's try-out in Washington, Champion learnt that he had a rare form of blood cancer, and after the first curtain call on the New York opening night, producer David Merrick informed the cast and the audience that Gower Champion had died that afternoon.

CHAMPS

Best known for the classic 1958 rock 'n' roll near-instrumental 'Tequila', a US number 1 song, the Champs were formed in Los Angeles, California, USA, in December 1957. The five musicians initially comprising the group were Dave Burgess (rhythm guitar), Danny Flores (saxophone, piano), Cliff Hills (bass), Buddy Bruce (lead guitar) and Gene Alden (drums). The musicians were united by Joe Johnson, co-owner of Challenge Records, for the purpose of providing backing for the Kuf-Linx vocal group. With time left after that session, the musicians recorded three instrumentals written by Burgess. Flores, who also went under the name Chuck Rio, as he was already contracted to the RPM label, taught the others 'Tequila' from a riff on which he had worked for performance at club dates in Los Angeles. The recording was considered a 'throwaway' by the musicians, who did not even stay to hear the final playback. Issued in January 1958 under the name Champs (in honour of Champion, a horse owned by Challenge founder Gene Autry), 'Tequila' was planned as the b-side to 'Train To Nowhere'. Radio stations preferred 'Tequila' and the Champs' version battled for chart positions with a cover version of the song by Eddie Platt; the latter's version reached number 20 in the US charts while the Champs' made number 1. With the song a success, there was a need for them to tour, so a new line-up was formed including Flores, Burgess, Alden and new members Dale Norris (guitar) and Joe Burnas (bass). Flores and Alden left in late 1958 and were replaced by Jim Seals (saxophone), Dash Crofts (drums) and Dean Beard (piano). Seals And Crofts remained with the group until its termination, before forming the Dawnbreakers and then re-emerging in the late 60s as a popular acoustic music duo. The Champs placed a further seven singles in the charts through 1962, none of which came close to matching the debut's success. Further personnel changes occurred throughout their history, most notably the replacement of Burgess by young guitarist Glen Campbell in 1960. The Champs disbanded in 1964.

● ALBUMS: *Go Champs Go* (Challenge 1958)★★★, *Everybody's Rockin' With The Champs* (Challenge 1959)★★★, *Great Dance Hits Of Today* (Challenge 1962)★★★, *All American Music With The Champs* (Challenge 1962)★★★.

● COMPILATIONS: *Wing Ding!* (Ace 1994)★★★, *The Early Singles* (Ace 1996)★★★.

CHANNING, CAROL

b. 31 January 1921, Seattle, Washington, USA. An actress and singer with a style and appearance that are difficult to define, she has been described as 'a blonde, wide-eyed, long-legged, husky voiced, scatty personality' - among other things. The daughter of a Christian Science teacher, Channing moved with her family to San Franciso at an early age, and later attended Bennington College in Vermont, where she majored in drama and dance. In 1941 she appeared in Marc Blitzstein's labour opera *No For An Answer*, but only for three Sunday nights. In the same year she served as an understudy in *Let's Face It!* on Broadway, and had a small part in *Proof Through The Night* (1942). After playing nightclubs around New York, she returned to San Francisco in 1946 and won a part in the Hollywood revue *Lend An Ear*. Her performance in the Broadway version of the show led to her triumph as Lorelei Lee in *Gentlemen Prefer Blondes*, in which she introduced several memorable numbers including 'A Little Girl From Little Rock' and 'Diamonds Are A Girl's Best Friend'. In 1954, she replaced Rosalind Russell in *Wonderful Town*, and in the next year, had her first big flop with *The Vamp*. In the late 50s her nightclub act was so successful that it was turned into a one-woman revue entitled *Show Girl*, which played on Broadway in 1961. Three years later, she had her biggest success in *Hello, Dolly!*, as the matchmaker Dolly Levi, with a Jerry Herman score that included 'So Long, Dearie', 'Before The Parade Passes By', and the insinuating title song. She won a Tony Award for outstanding performance, but Barbra Streisand was preferred for the movie version. Channing's larger-than-life personality is perhaps more suited to the stage than film, although she was hilarious in *Thoroughly Modern Millie* (1967). Other film credits include *Paid In Full*, *The First Travelling Saleslady*, *Skidoo* and *Shinbone Alley* (voice only). In 1974 she was back on Broadway in *Lorelei*, which, as the title suggests, was a compilation of the best scenes from *Gentlemen Prefer Blondes*. It lasted for 320 performances and had a reasonable life on the road. At that stage of her career, with suitable musical comedy roles hard to come by, Channing continued to work mostly on US television and in nightclubs, but in 1987 she co-starred with Mary Martin in James Kirkwood's aptly named show *Legends!*. A year later she embarked on a concert tour of locations such as Kansas City and San Diego, accompanied at each stop by the local symphony orchestra. In 1990 she appeared at the Desert Inn, Las Vegas, and two years later she toured with Rita Moreno in *Two Ladies Of Broadway*. In 1995, Carol Channing was back where she belonged, starring in a major revival of her greatest success, *Hello, Dolly!*

● ALBUMS: *Carol Channing* (Vanguard 1959)★★★, *Previous Hits* (Vanguard 1959)★★★, *Carol Channing Entertains* (1965)★★★★, *Jazz Baby* (DRG 1994)★★★, and Original Cast and soundtrack recordings.

● FILMS: *Paid In Full* (1950), *The First Travelling Saleslady* (1956), *Thoroughly Modern Millie* (1967).

CHARLES, RAY

b. Ray Charles Robinson, 23 September 1930, Albany, Georgia, USA. Few epithets sit less comfortably than that of genius; Ray Charles has borne this title for over 30 years. As a singer, composer, arranger and pianist, his prolific work deserves no other praise. Born in extreme poverty, Charles was slowly blinded by glaucoma until, by the age of seven, he had lost his sight completely. Earlier, he had been forced to cope with the tragic death of his brother, whom he had seen drown in a water tub. He learned to read and write music in braille and was proficient on several instruments by the time he left school. His mother Aretha died when Charles was 15, and he continued to have a shared upbringing with Mary Jane (the first wife of Charles's absent father). Charles drifted around the Florida circuit, picking up work where he could, before moving across the country to Seattle. Here he continued his itinerant career, playing piano at several nightclubs in a style reminiscent of Nat 'King' Cole. Charles began recording in 1949 and this early, imitative approach was captured on several sessions. Three years later, Atlantic Records acquired his contract, but initially the singer continued his 'cool' direction, revealing only an occasional hint of the passions later unleashed. 'It Should've Been Me', 'Mess Around' and 'Losing Hand' best represent this early R&B era, but Charles's individual style emerged as a result of his work with Guitar Slim. This impassioned, almost crude blues performer sang with a gospel-based fervour that greatly influenced Charles's thinking. He arranged Slim's million-selling single, 'Things That I Used To Do', on which the riffing horns and unrestrained voice set

the tone for Charles's own subsequent direction. This effect was fully realized in 'I Got A Woman' (1954), a song soaked in the fervour of the Baptist Church, but rendered salacious by the singer's abandoned, unrefined delivery. Its extraordinary success, commercially and artistically, inspired similarly compulsive recordings, including 'This Little Girl Of Mine' (1955), 'Talkin' 'Bout You' (1957) and the lush and evocative 'Don't Let The Sun Catch You Crying' (1959), a style culminating in the thrilling call and response of 'What'd I Say' (1959). This acknowledged classic is one of the all-time great encore numbers performed by countless singers and bands in stadiums, clubs and bars all over the world. However, Charles was equally adept at slow ballads, as his heartbreaking interpretations of 'Drown In My Own Tears' and 'I Believe To My Soul' (both 1959) clearly show. Proficient in numerous styles, Charles's recordings embraced blues, jazz, standards and even country, as his muscular reading of 'I'm Movin' On' attested.

In November 1959 Charles left the Atlantic label for ABC Records, where he secured both musical and financial freedom. Commentators often cite this as the point at which the singer lost his fire, but early releases for this new outlet simply continued his groundbreaking style. 'Georgia On My Mind' (1960) and 'Hit The Road Jack' (1961) were, respectively, poignant and ebullient, and established the artist as an international name. This stature was enhanced further in 1962 with the release of the massive-selling album *Modern Sounds In Country And Western*, a landmark collection that produced the million-selling single 'I Can't Stop Loving You'. Its success defined the pattern for Charles's later career; the edges were blunted, the vibrancy was stilled as Charles's repertoire grew increasingly inoffensive. There were still moments of inspiration: 'Let's Go Get Stoned' and 'I Don't Need No Doctor' brought glimpses of a passion now too often muted, while *Crying Time*, Charles's first album since kicking his heroin habit, compared favourably with any Atlantic release. This respite was, however, temporary and as the 60s progressed so the singer's work became less compulsive and increasingly MOR. Like most artists, he attempted cover versions of Beatles songs and had substantial hits with versions of 'Yesterday' and 'Eleanor Rigby'. Two 70s releases, *A Message From The People* and *Renaissance*, did include contemporary material in Stevie Wonder's 'Living In The City' and Randy Newman's 'Sail Away', but subsequent releases reneged on this promise.

Charles's 80s work included more country-flavoured collections and a cameo appearance in the film *The Blues Brothers*, but the period is better marked by the singer's powerful appearance on the USA For Africa release, 'We Are The World' (1985). It brought to mind a talent too often dormant, a performer whose marriage of gospel and R&B laid the foundations for soul music. His influence is inestimable, and his talent widely acknowledged and imitated by formidable white artists such as Steve Winwood, Joe Cocker, Van Morrison and Eric Burdon. Charles has been honoured with countless awards during his career including induction into the Rock And Roll Hall Of Fame in 1986, and receiving the Grammy Lifetime Achievement Award in 1987. He has performed rock, jazz, blues and country with spectacular ease, but it is 'father of soul music' that remains his greatest title; it was fitting that, in 1992, an acclaimed documentary, *Ray Charles: The Genius Of Soul*, was broadcast by PBS television.

My World was a sparkling return to form, and was one of his finest albums in many years, being particularly noteworthy for his version of Leon Russell's 'A Song For You', a song that sounds as if it has always been a Charles song, such is the power of his outstanding voice. *Strong Love Affair* continued in the same vein with a balance of ballads matching the up-tempo tracks; however, it was clear that low-register, slow songs such as 'Say No More', 'Angelina' and 'Out Of My Life' should be the focus of Charles's concentration.

● ALBUMS: *Hallelujah, I Love Her So* aka *Ray Charles* (Atlantic 1957)★★★, *The Great Ray Charles* (Atlantic 1957)★★★★, with Milt Jackson *Soul Brothers* (Atlantic 1958)★★★, *Ray Charles At Newport* (Atlantic 1958)★★★, *Yes Indeed* (Atlantic 1959)★★★★, *Ray Charles* (Hollywood 1959)★★★★, *The Fabulous Ray Charles* (Hollywood 1959)★★★, *What'd I Say* (Atlantic 1959)★★★, *The Genius Of Ray Charles* (Atlantic 1959)★★★★, *Ray Charles In Person* (Atlantic 1960)★★★, *The Genius Hits The Road* (ABC 1960)★★★, *Dedicated To You* (ABC 1961)★★★, *Genius + Soul = Jazz* (Impulse! 1961)★★★★★, *The Genius After Hours* (Atlantic 1961)★★★★, with Betty Carter *Ray Charles And Betty Carter* (ABC 1961)★★★★, *The Genius Sings The Blues* (Atlantic 1961)★★★★, with Jackson *Soul Meeting* (Atlantic 1961)★★★, *Do The Twist With Ray Charles* (Atlantic 1961)★★★, *Modern Sounds In Country And Western* (ABC 1962)★★★★★, *Modern Sounds In Country And Western Volume 2* (ABC 1962)★★★★, *Ingredients In A Recipe For Soul* (ABC 1963)★★★★, *Sweet And Sour Tears* (ABC 1964)★★★, *Have A Smile With Me* (ABC 1964)★★★, *Ray Charles Live In Concert* (ABC 1965)★★★, *Country And Western Meets Rhythm And Blues* aka *Together Again* (ABC 1965)★★★, *Crying Time* (ABC 1966)★★★, *Ray's Moods* (ABC 1966)★★★, *Ray Charles Invites You To Listen* (ABC 1967)★★★, *A Portrait Of Ray* (ABC 1968)★★, *I'm All Yours, Baby!* (ABC 1969)★★, *Doing His Thing* (ABC 1969)★★★, *My Kind Of Jazz* (Tangerine 1970)★★★, *Love Country Style* (ABC 1970)★★, *Volcanic Action Of My Soul* (ABC 1971)★★, *A Message From The People* (ABC 1972)★★, *Through The Eyes Of Love* (ABC 1972), *Jazz Number II* (Tangerine 1972)★★★, *Ray Charles Live* (Atlantic 1973)★★★, *Come Live With Me* (Crossover 1974)★★, *Renaissance* (Crossover 1975)★★, *My Kind Of Jazz III* (Crossover 1975)★★, *Live In Japan* (1975)★★★, with Cleo Laine *Porgy And Bess* (RCA 1976)★★★, *True To Life* (Atlantic 1977)★★, *Love And Peace* (Atlantic 1978)★★, *Ain't It So* (Atlantic 1979)★★, *Brother Ray Is At It Again* (Atlantic 1980)★★, *Wish You Were Here Tonight* (Columbia 1983)★★, *Do I Ever Cross Your Mind* (Columbia 1984)★★, *Friendship* (Columbia 1985)★★, *The Spirit Of Christmas* (Columbia 1985)★★, *From The Pages Of My Mind* (Columbia 1986)★★, *Just Between Us* (Columbia 1988)★★, *Seven Spanish Angels And Other Hits* (Columbia 1989)★★, *Would You Believe* (Warners 1990)★★, *My World* (Warners 1993)★★★★, *Strong Love Affair* (Qwest 1996)★★, *Berlin, 1962* (Pablo 1996)★★★★.

● COMPILATIONS: *The Ray Charles Story* (Atlantic 1962)★★★, *Ray Charles' Greatest Hits* (ABC 1962)★★★★, *A Man And His Soul* (ABC 1967)★★★, *The Best Of Ray Charles 1956-58* (Atlantic 1970)★★★★, *A 25th Anniversary In Show Business Salute To Ray Charles* (ABC 1971)★★★★, *The Right Time* (Atlantic 1987)★★★, *A Life In Music 1956-59* (Atlantic 1982)★★★★, *Greatest Hits Volume 1 1960-67* (Rhino 1988)★★★★, *Greatest Hits Volume 2 1960-72* (Rhino

1988)★★★★, *Anthology* (Rhino 1989)★★★★, *The Collection* ABC recordings (Castle 1990)★★★, *Blues Is My Middle Name* 1949-52 recordings (Double Play 1991)★★★, *The Birth Of Soul 1952-59* (Atlantic 1991)★★★★★, *The Complete Atlantic Rhythm And Blues Recordings* 4-CD box set (Atlantic 1992)★★★★★, *The Living Legend* (1993)★★★, *The Best Of The Atlantic Years* (Rhino/Atlantic 1994)★★★, *Classics* (Rhino 1995)★★★, *Genius & Soul* 5-CD box set (Rhino 1997)★★★.

● FURTHER READING: *Ray Charles*, Sharon Bell Mathis. *Brother Ray, Ray Charles' Own Story*, Ray Charles and David Ritz.

● FILMS: *Blues For Lovers* aka *Ballad In Blue* (1964), *The Blues Brothers* (1980).

CHARMS

A popular R&B group of the mid-50s, the Charms were formed in Cincinnati, USA, by Otis Williams (lead), Richard Parker (bass), Joseph Penn (baritone), Donald Peak (tenor) and Rolland Bradley (tenor). 'Heaven Only Knows' was released by Deluxe Records, followed by 'Happy Are We', 'Bye-Bye Baby', 'Quiet Please' and 'My Baby Dearest Darling', all of which failed to secure significant success. However, their September 1954 cover version of the Jewels' 'Hearts Of Stone' took them into the US charts and by January of the following year the song had peaked at number 15 (number 1 in the R&B charts), despite competing versions by both the Jewels and the Fontane Sisters. December 1954 produced two follow-ups: 'Mambo Sha-Mambo' and another cover version, this time the Five Keys' 'Ling, Ting, Tong', were released concurrently, the latter keeping stride with the Five Keys' original version and reaching number 26 on the *Billboard* charts. The policy of outgunning the opposition over 'hot new songs' soon became a Charms trait, but it was not always so successful. An attempt to hijack Gene And Eunice's 'Ko Ko Mo' in February 1955 failed, and saw the group return to writing originals. 'Two Hearts' was written by Otis Williams and King Records' A&R head Henry Glover, but was in turn covered within a week by Pat Boone, who took it to US number 16. The Charms then toured as part of the Top Ten R&B Show package with the Moonglows, Clovers and others. After asking for a pay rise from Deluxe the entire band, with the exception of Otis Williams, was sacked. Williams was joined by Rollie Willis, Chuck Barksdale (ex-Dells) and Larry Graves. This version of the Charms was imaginatively renamed 'Otis Williams And His New Group'. Some things, though, did not change. The success of 'Gum Drop' was usurped by a *Billboard* Top 10 version by the Crewcuts. Meanwhile, the remaining four-fifths of the original Charms had left for Miami, where they filed suit against Deluxe over their continued use of the brand name. Deluxe countered by issuing two singles under the name Otis Williams And His Charms, while Parker, Penn, Peak and Bradley released 'Love's Our Inspiration' for their new label, Chart Records. Without Otis Williams there was little residual interest, especially as Williams' incarnation of the Charms went on to score two significant hits in 'That's Your Mistake' and 'Ivory Tower'. However, both Barksdale (back to the Dells) and Graves quit, with Winfred Gerald, Matt Williams (no relation) and Lonnie Carter taking their places. A poor chart run was then ended with the release of another cover version, this time of the Lovenotes' 'United', in June 1957. It was their last significant success, despite a continuing and prolific relationship with Deluxe, and then King Records, until 1963. Only 'Little Turtle Dove' and 'Panic', both from 1961, scraped the lower reaches of the charts. Ironically, by this time Lonnie Carter had joined the original Charms, who had now become the Escos. Williams then transferred to Okeh Records but without success, before signing to Stop Records as a solo country artist. The Charms' complicated but fascinating history ended with the move.

CHARISSE, CYD

b. Tulla Ellice Finklea, 8 March 1923, Amarillo, Texas, USA. An elegant, long-legged dancer who appeared in several outstanding film musicals of the 40s and 50s, she took ballet classes from an early age, and was enrolled in the renowned Fanchon and Marco Dance Studio in Hollywood at the age of 12. One of the teachers there was Frenchman Nico Charisse, and four years later, during which time she performed at intervals with the famed Ballet Russes, they were married. Her connections with the Ballet Russes gained Charisse a part in the Columbia film *Something To Shout About* (1943), which led to a contract with MGM. One of the studio's top producers, Arthur Freed, is said to have been responsible for changing her name to Cyd (she had been known as Sid by her friends since childhood). During the late 40s and early 50s she made effective contributions to several straight films, and a number of musicals, which included *Ziegfeld Follies*, *The Harvey Girls*, *Till The Clouds Roll By*, *Fiesta* (in which Ricardo Montalban made his debut), *The Unfinished Dance*, *On An Island With You*, *Words And Music*, *The Kissing Bandit*, *Singin' In The Rain* (with Gene Kelly) and *Easy To Love* (1953). Also in 1953 she had what was arguably her best role in *The Band Wagon* with Fred Astaire and Jack Buchanan. By this time she was at her peak both as an actress and a dancer (although her singing was invariably dubbed in films), and her excellent work during the remaining years of the 50s included *Brigadoon*, *It's Always Fair Weather* and *Invitation To The Dance* (all with Kelly), *Meet Me In Las Vegas* (with Dan Dailey), and *Silk Stockings* (with Astaire). The latter was her last musical, although she did appear in the occasional dance sequence in films such as *Black Tights* (1960) and *The Silencers* (1966). Her screen work since then has been confined to guest appearances and television features. After the break-up of her first marriage in the early 40s, she married the popular singer Tony Martin in 1948, and he travelled with her to London in 1986 when she played the role of Lady Hadwell in a new production of David Heneker's musical *Charlie Girl*. Even then, when she was in her 60s, those famous legs were still the main subject of discussion. Impresario Harold Fielding said: 'They are her trademark, so we're going to insure them for a million, maybe two.' A substantial sum of money must also have changed hands in 1988 when Cyd Charisse agreed to appear in a video to promote a pop single by the two-man group the Blue Mercedes. Their record of 'I Want To Be Your Property' reached the top of the US dance charts. In a rather different vein, four years later Miss Charisse made her Broadway debut when she took over the role of fading ballerina Grushinskaya in the hit musical *Grand Hotel*. Asked about her age, which has always been a subject of some dispute (born 1921 or 1923), she would only say: 'Oh, I feel young!'

● FURTHER READING: *The Two Of Us*, Tony Martin and Cyd Charisse.

CHARTS

An R&B vocal group from Harlem, New York City, New York, USA, the Charts were one of the finest examples of the 'greasy' style of doo-wop for which New York was famed in the late 50s, in which harsh leads, piercing tenors, deep basses, and exotic changes produced a rather unwholesome sound and a predominant image of greasy-haired young hoodlums. The members were lead Joe Grier, first tenor Steve Brown, second tenor Glenmore Jackson, baritone Leroy Binns and bass Ross Buford, who had formed the group in 1957 on a street corner on 115th Street. They were a classic one-hit-wonder group; their 'Deserie', recorded for Danny Robinson's Everlast label, became a perennial as an oldies standard after becoming a hit in 1957. 'Deserie' was distinctive in that it featured no bridge between the second and third verse. Grier, as the principal songwriter of the group, came up with equally appealing songs for the group, notably 'Dance Girl' and 'My Diane', both from 1957, but like so many vocal groups of the day, could not repeat their initial success. By 1958 the Charts had broken up. Grier took up saxophone and was the featured player on Les Cooper's 1962 instrumental hit, 'Wiggle Wobble'. A re-formed Charts, with Brown and Binns, and new members Frankie Harris and Tony Pierce, appeared with an updated version of 'Deserie' in 1967, but their career was short-lived. During the 70s and 80s several members of the group worked the doo-wop east coast revival circuit. Grier played saxophone behind many such groups, and Brown and Binns formed a revival Charts as well as working in groups such as the Coasters, Cadillacs, and Del-Vikings.

● COMPILATIONS: *The Charts Greatest Hits* (Collectables 1990)★★★.

CHAVIS, WILSON 'BOOZOO'

b. 23 October 1930, Lake Charles, Louisiana, USA. 'Boozoo' Chavis was one of the first artists to perform zydeco music in the 50s and enjoyed renewed popularity in the 80s and 90s. Chavis had learned to play accordion and harmonica by the age of nine and performed around Lake Charles while in his teens. In 1954 he was signed to Folk-Star Records by owner Eddie Shuler. Chavis recorded a traditional song, 'Paper In My Shoe' (for which he and Shuler took writing credit), backed by the local Classie Ballou's Tempo Kings. The session marked the first time Chavis had played with a band. The record sold well regionally and was picked up for national distribution by Imperial Records of Los Angeles. Chavis continued to record for Folk-Star and Shuler's Goldband label sporadically through the early 60s, then retreated from the music industry until 1984, when he began performing again in Louisiana. He quickly became a local favourite and began recording for the small Maison de Soul, Rounder Records and Antones labels.

● ALBUMS: *Lousiana Zydeco Music* (1986)★★★, *Boozoo Zydeco* (Maison De Soul 1987)★★★, *Paper In My Shoe* (Ace 1987)★★★, *La Zydeco Music* (Maison De Soul 1987)★★★, *Live At Richard's Zydeco Dance Hall, Volume One* (Rounder 1988)★★★, *Nathon And The Zydeco Cha Cha's* (1989)★★★, *Boozoo's Breakdown* (Sonet 1991)★★★, with the Majic Sounds *Live! At The Habibi Temple, Lake Charles, Louisiana*

(Rounder 1994)★★★, *Hey Do Right!* (Antones 1996)★★★.
● COMPILATIONS: *The Lake Charles Atomic Bomb* (1990)★★★.

CHERRY, DON

b. 11 January 1924, Wichita, Texas, USA. Cherry sang briefly with the post-war orchestras of Jan Garber, Victor Young and Tommy Dorsey. His first solo hits for Decca Records in 1950/51 were 'Thinking Of You' from the Fred Astaire/Vera-Ellen movie *Three Little Words*, 'Vanity' and 'Belle, Belle, My Liberty Belle', the latter beaten to the upper reaches of the US chart by Guy Mitchell's version. Switching to Columbia Records, Cherry had a massive seller in 1955 with the Bob Musel and Jack Taylor ballad, 'Band Of Gold' (not to be confused with another song with the same title which was a hit in 1970 for Freda Payne). The unusual choral backing on the Cherry record signified trombonist/arranger Ray Conniff's first arrangement for Columbia. After further US success in 1956 with 'Wild Cherry', 'Ghost Town' and 'Namely You', Cherry, always a keen amateur golfer, launched an assault on the US professional circuit, but was still recording occasionally on the Monument label well into the 60s. In the mid-80s, he was still telling golf stories in-between songs such as 'Wind Beneath My Wings' and 'Band Of Gold', in his Las Vegas nightclub act.
● ALBUMS: with Ray Conniff And His Orchestra *Swingin' For Two* (Columbia 1956)★★★, *Don Cherry* (Monument 1967)★★.

CHESTNUTS

Formed in 1955 in New Haven, Connecticut, USA, this powerful, underrated R&B quintet consisted of Leroy Griffin (lead), Jimmy Curtis (baritone), Reuben White (bass), Lymon Hopkins (fist tenor) and Frank Hopkins (second tenor). Unable to secure a recording contract in their locality, the group travelled to New York where they found a sympathetic ear in Joe Davis of Jay Dee and Davis Records. He encouraged them to recruit a female lead, which they accomplished by finding fellow New Haven native Ruby Whitaker (losing Griffin in the process). The group made their recording debut with 'Love Is True', a song that they had earlier attempted to hawk around the New York music industry. Affectionately recalled by fans of 50s vocal music, it nevertheless failed to chart. A second single, 'Forever I Vow', again hinged on the group's ability to produce a stirring ballad, but received scant attention. Davis's patience wore thin, and the group was forced to return to New Haven to record with a local company before a fourth single for New York's El Dorado Records. Whitaker departed at this point to be replaced by ex-Five Satins member Bill Baker, with a third Hopkins brother, Arthur, also joining the fold, in place of Jimmy Curtis (who would, ironically, go on to an extended tenure in the Five Satins). Two 1959 releases under this formation, 'Won't You Tell My Heart' and 'Wonderful Girl', failed to revive their fortunes.

CHEVALIER, MAURICE

b. Maurice Auguste Chevalier, 12 September 1888, Menilmontant, nr. Paris, France, d. 1 January 1972, Paris, France. The ninth of 10 children eventually reduced by death to three males, Chevalier's early ambitions to become an acrobat were thwarted by injury. He toured local cafes and music halls as a singer and broad comedian, and later performed at the Eldorado in Paris. His big break came when he signed a three-year contract with the *Folies Bergère*, and worked with his idol, Mistinguett. In 1913 he was drafted into the French Army, was captured, and then sent to Alten Grabow prisoner-of-war camp where he learnt to speak English. After the war he developed a more sophisticated act, wearing a tuxedo for his solo spot, and the straw boater that soon became his trademark. In-between the triumphs at the Folies Bergère, Casino de Paris and the Empire in Paris, Chevalier suffered a serious mental breakdown. When he recovered he went to England in 1927 and appeared in the revue *White Birds*. Two years later he made his first Hollywood film, *Innocents Of Paris*, in which he introduced 'Louise', a song forever associated with him ('every little breeze seems to whisper Louise'). He also sang his famous French version of 'Yes, We Have No Bananas'. He then starred in several films, directed by Ernst Lubitsch including Lubitsch's first talkie, *The Love Parade* (1929). It was also the first of four films that Chevalier made with Jeanette MacDonald. Following *The Smiling Lieutenant* (1931) with Claudette Colbert, and *One Hour With You* (1932), Chevalier made what has been described as 'one of the great films of the decade'. *Love Me Tonight*, directed by Rouben Mamoulian and co-starring MacDonald, was innovative in several ways, especially in its integration of plot and music. It also contained 'Mimi', another speciality Chevalier song. He then appeared in *The Merry Widow* (1934, MGM) and *Folies Bergère* (1935, United Artists) in 1935 before returning to France, as one of the world's leading entertainers. During World War II Chevalier lived mostly in seclusion, emerging twice to perform in response to German demands, once in exchange for the release of 10 French prisoners. Rumours and accusations of collaboration with the enemy were emphatically disproved. After the war he projected a more mature image in the film *Le Silence Est D'or* (1947) directed by René Clair, which won the Grand Prize at the Brussels Film Festival. During the same period, Chevalier toured Europe and the USA with his 'one man show'. Semi-retired during the early 50s, he returned to Hollywood to play a series of character roles in films such as *Love In The Afternoon* (1957), *Gigi* (1958), *Can-Can* (1959), *Fanny* (1961), *In Search Of The Castaways* (1962) and *I'd Rather Be Rich* (1964). *Gigi* was one of the highlights of Chevalier's career. His idiosyncratic versions of 'Thank Heaven For Little Girls', 'I'm Glad I'm Not Young Any More', and a duet with Hermione Gingold, 'I Remember It Well', charmed the Academy of MPAS into awarding *Gigi* nine Oscars, including Best Picture. At the age of 70, Chevalier received a special Academy Award for his contribution to the world of entertainment for over half a century. During the 60s he appeared frequently on US television with his own 'specials' such as *The World Of Maurice Chevalier*, and travelled widely with his 'one man show' until 1968, when, from the stage of the Theatre des Champs Elysees in Paris, he announced his retirement. His honours included the Croix de Guerre (1917), the Belgian Order of Leopold (1943), the Légion d'Honneur (1938) and the Order Mérite National (1964).
● ALBUMS: *Maurice Chevalier Sings Broadway* (MGM 1959)★★★★, *A Tribute To Al Jolson* (MGM 1959)★★★, *Life Is Just A Bowl Of Cherries* (MGM 1960)★★★★, *Thank*

Heaven For Little Girls (MGM 1960)★★★, *Thank Heaven For Maurice Chevalier* (RCA Victor 1960)★★★, *Maurice Chevalier Sings Lerner, Loewe And Chevalier* (MGM 1962)★★★, *Paris To Broadway* (MGM 1963)★★★★, *Maurice Chevalier* (Time 1963)★★★.
● COMPILATIONS: *Sings* (Retrospect 1969)★★★★, *The World Of Maurice Chevalier* (Decca 1971)★★★★, *You Brought A New Kind Of Love To Me* (Monmouth Evergreen 1979)★★★, *Encore Maurice* (Living Era 1982)★★★, *Bonjour D'Amour* (Karussell 1982)★★★, *Ma Pomme* (EMI France 1983)★★★, *The Golden Age Of Maurice Chevalier* (Golden Age 1984)★★★★, *Bravo Maurice* (Living Era 1986)★★★, *The Maurice Chevalier Collection* (Deja Vu 1987)★★★★, *Maurice Chevalier's Paris* (Compact Selection 1988)★★★, *On Top Of The World* (Flapper 1990)★★★.
● FURTHER READING: *The Man In The Straw Hat*, Maurice Chevalier. *With Love*, Maurice Chevalier. *I Remember It Well*, Maurice Chevalier. *Maurice Chevalier: His Life 1888-1972*, James Harding. *Thank Heaven For Little Girls: The True Story Of Maurice Chevalier's Life*, Edward Behr.
● FILMS: *Trop Crédule* (1908), *Par Habitude* (1911), *Un Mariée Récalcitrante* (1911), *Une Mariée Qui Se Fait Attendre* (1911), *La Valse Renversante* (1914), *Une Soirée Mondaine* (1917), *Le Mauvais Garçon* (1921), *Le Match Criqui-Ledoux* (1922), *L'Affaire De La Rue Lourcine* (1923), *Gonzague* (1923), *Jim Bougne Boxeur* (1924), *Par Habitude* remake (1924), *Bonjour New York!* (1928), *Innocents Of Paris* (1929), *The Love Parade* (1929), *Playboy Of Paris* (1930), *The Big Pond* (1930), *Paramount On Parade* (1930), *The Smiling Lieutenant* (1931), *The Stolen Jools (The Slippery Pearls)* (1931), *El Cliente Seductor* (1931), *Love Me Tonight* (1932), *Make Me A Star* (1932), *One Hour With You* (1932), *Toboggan (Battling Georges)* (1932), *The Way To Love* (1933), *Bedtime Story* (1933), *The Merry Widow* (1934), *Folies Bergère* (1935), *The Beloved Vagabond* (1936), *Avec Le Sourire* (1936), *L'Homme Du Jour* (1936), *Break The News* (1938), *Pièges* (1939), *Le Silence Est D'Or* (1945), *Le Roi* (1946), *Paris 1900* (1950), *Ma Pomme* (1950), *Schlager-Parade* (1953), *J'Avais Sept Filles* (1954), *Cento Anni D'Amore* (1954), *Love In The Afternoon* (1957), *Rendezvous With Maurice Chevalier* series of six (1957), *Gigi* (1958), *Count Your Blessings* (1959), *Can-Can* (1959), *Pepe* (1960), *A Breath Of Scandal* (1960), *Un, Deux, Trois, Quatre!* (1960), *Fanny* (1961), *In Search Of The Castaways* (1962), *Jessica* (1962), *A New Kind Of Love* (1963), *I'd Rather Be Rich* (1964), *Panic Button* (1964), *Monkeys Go Home!* (1966).

CHIPS

Formed in the Bedford-Stuyvesant district of Brooklyn, New York, USA, in 1956, the Chips drew their membership from teenage friends Charles Johnson (lead), Nathaniel Epps (baritone), Paul Fulton (bass), Sammy Strain (first tenor) and Shedwick Lincoln (second tenor). The group's first recording would be their most enduring; 'Rubber Biscuit' started life as Johnson's answer to the marching rhythms of the Warwick School For Delinquent Teenagers while he was an intern there. When Josie Records heard the tune they signed the band and issued the record in September 1956. Although it did not chart, 'Rubber Biscuit' became an instant east coast R&B radio favourite, and saw its authors joining touring bills alongside the Dells, Cadillacs and Bo Diddley. Appearances

at the Apollo and Empire Theaters followed, but the momentum gained by their debut single was waning rapidly. The group broke up at the end of 1957, with Fulton joining the Velours and the Poets, and Strain working with the Fantastics, Little Anthony And The Imperials and O'Jays. Johnson joined the Platters while Lincoln became part of the Invitations. This might well have signalled the end of the Chips story, had it not been for the Dan Aykroyd and John Belushi (aka the Blues Brothers) cover version of 'Rubber Biscuit' in 1979, which made the US Top 40. The resultant interest saw the Chips (minus Strain, replaced by Dave Eason) reunite in the same year. One record was released, which coupled two cover versions, 'Everyone's Laughing' (Spaniels) and 'When I'm With You' (Moonglows).

CHORDETTES

Formed in 1946 in Sheboygan, Wisconsin, USA, the Chordettes were a female singing group whose career extended into the rock era. Initially envisioning themselves as a female barbershop quartet the members were Dorothy Schwartz (lead), Janet Ertel (d. 4 November 1988, Black River, Wisconsin, USA; bass), Carol Buschman (baritone) and Jinny Lockard (tenor). In 1949 the group came to the attention of Arthur Godfrey, whose national *Talent Scouts* radio programme was a popular means for acts to break through to a wider audience. Godfrey offered the Chordettes a permanent spot on the show and they were signed to Columbia Records, for whom they recorded a series of 10-inch EPs. In 1953 the group left Godfrey and signed to Cadence Records, operated by Godfrey's musical director, Archie Bleyer (Ertel married Bleyer in 1954). Their first recording for Cadence, 'Mr. Sandman', in 1954, became a million-seller, logging seven weeks at number 1 in the US charts. It featured Lynn Evans, who had replaced Schwartz, as lead singer, and Margie Needham, who had replaced Lockard. The Chordettes remained with Cadence until the early 60s, gaining three other Top 10 hits: 'Born To Be With You' (1956), 'Just Between You And Me' (1957) and 'Lollipop' (1958). The group disbanded in the mid-60s.
● ALBUMS: *Harmony Time* 10-inch album (Columbia 1950)★★★★, *Harmony Time, Volume 2* 10-inch album (Columbia 1951)★★, *Harmony Encores* 10-inch album (Columbia 1952)★★★, *Your Requests* 10-inch album (Columbia 1953)★★★, *Listen* (Columbia 1956)★★, *The Chordettes* (Cadence 1957)★★★, *Close Harmony* (Cadence 1957)★★★, *Never On Sunday* (Cadence 1962)★★.
● COMPILATIONS: *The Chordettes* (Ace 1983)★★★, *The Best Of The Chordettes* (1985)★★★, *Mainly Rock 'N' Roll* (Ace 1990)★★★★, *The Fabulous Chordettes* (Ace 1991)★★★.

CHORDS

The original members were brothers Carl (d. 23 January 1981; lead tenor) and Claude Feaster (baritone), Jimmy Keyes (d. 22 July 1995; tenor), Floyd McRae (tenor), William Edwards (bass) and pianist Rupert Branker, all schoolfriends from the Bronx, New York, USA. The Chords, who evolved out of three other groups, the Tunetoppers, the Keynotes and the Four Notes, were one of the first acts signed to the Atlantic subsidiary label Cat. Their debut disc was a doo-wop version of the then current Patti Page hit 'Cross Over The Bridge'. On the b-side of this 1954 release, Cat grudgingly issued one of the group's own songs, 'Sh-Boom', which became a milestone in rock 'n' roll music. This fun piece of nonsense took the USA by storm and featured the joyous but contentious lyric, 'Ah, life could be a dream, sh-boom, sh-boom!'. Some claim that this was rock 'n' roll's first 'drug song'! It shot into the US Top 10, a unique occurrence in those days for an R&B record, while a watered-down cover version by Canada's Crew-Cuts had the honour of being America's first number 1 rock 'n' roll hit. The song created such a furore that even ace satirist Stan Freberg's cruel take-off of the Chords' record also made the Top 20. Since a group on Gem Records was already using the same name, the group quickly became the Chordcats. They tried to follow the monster novelty hit with other similar tracks, such as the follow-up 'Zippety-Zum', but with no success. Some personnel changes and another new name, the inevitable Sh-Booms, also failed to return them to the charts. The Chords, who were probably the first R&B group to appear on USA television nationwide, also recorded on Vik, Roulette (under the name Lionel Thorpe), Atlantic and Baron, among others. They occasionally reunited to play 'oldies' shows until lead singer Carl died on 23 January 1981.

CHRISTY, JUNE

b. Shirley Luster, 20 November 1925, Springfield, Illinois, USA, d. 21 June 1990. Christy first came to prominence with the bands of Boyd Raeburn and Stan Kenton, although her chirpy singing style sometimes sat oddly with the earnestly progressive experiments of her employers. Her bright, bubbling personality glowed through her performances and she was especially effective on up-tempo swingers. However, she was also adept on reflective ballads and was never afraid to have fun with a song. With Kenton she had successes in all of these areas. One of her first recordings with the band was 'Tampico', which became a million-seller; another was 'How High The Moon'. During the late 40s she was one of the band's main attractions. Kenton and his chief arranger, Pete Rugolo, responded by providing effective settings for her voice which, while of limited range, was engaging and her performances were always highly professional. In January 1947 she married Kenton's tenor saxophonist Bob Cooper, with whom she made some fine recordings backed by his small group. After leaving Kenton in 1948 Christy worked as a solo artist, making many successful recordings for Capitol Records, including three US Top 20 albums, *Something Cool* (imaginatively arranged for her by Rugolo), *The Misty Miss Christy* and *June - Fair And Warmer!*. After many years in retirement, she died in June 1990 of kidney failure.
● ALBUMS: *Something Cool* 10-inch album (Capitol 1954)★★★★, with Stan Kenton *Duets* (Capitol 1955)★★★★, *The Misty Miss Christy* (Capitol 1956)★★★★, *June - Fair And Warmer!* (Capitol 1957)★★★, *Gone For The Day* (Capitol 1957)★★★, *June's Got Rhythm* (Capitol 1958)★★★★, *The Song Is June!* (Capitol 1959)★★★★, *June Christy Recalls Those Kenton Days* (Capitol 1959)★★★, *Ballads For Night People* (Capitol 1959)★★★, with Kenton *The Road Show, Volumes 1 & 2* (Capitol 1960)★★★, with Kenton *Together Again* (Capitol 1960)★★★, *The Cool School* (Capitol 1960)★★★, *Off Beat* (Capitol 1961)★★★, *Do-Re-Mi* film soundtrack (Capitol 1961)★★, *That Time Of Year* (Capitol 1961)★★★, *Big Band Specials* (Capitol 1962)★★, *The Intimate June Christy* (Capitol 1962)★★★★, *Something*

Broadway, Something Latin (Capitol 1965)★★, *Impromptu* (Interplay 1977)★★★, *Willow Weep For Me* (1979)★★★, *Interlude* (Discovery 1985)★★★.
● COMPILATIONS: *This Is June Christy!* (Capitol 1958)★★★★, *The Best Of June Christy* (Capitol 1962)★★★★, *The Capitol Years* (Capitol 1989)★★★★, *A Lovely Way To Spend An Evening* (Jasmine 1989)★★★.

CHURCH, EUGENE

b. 23 January 1938, Los Angeles, California, USA, d. 16 April 1993. Church first recorded with Jesse Belvin in a duo called the Cliques; their 1956 song 'Girl Of My Dreams' was classic Los Angeles-styled R&B, featuring a dreamy, smooth sound. His debut solo record, 'Open Up Your Heart', was in essence a group record, since on it he was backed by the Turks. This was followed by 'Rock & Roll Show', on which Church sang as a member of the Saxons. Church had his biggest hit in 1958 with 'Pretty Girls Everywhere' (number 6 R&B, number 36 pop), which featured backing from Jesse Belvin and members of the Turks. Subsequent chart successes were 'Miami' (number 24 R&B, number 67 pop) in 1959 and 'Mind Your Own Business' (number 19 R&B) in 1961. With the exception of a one-off record in 1986, his recording career was essentially over by 1963. Church died from AIDS in 1993.

CLARK, DAVE

b. 6 March 1909, Jackson, Tennessee, USA, d. 22 July 1995, Madison, Mississippi, USA. Although not a star of America's R&B period, Clark's work on promotion, spanning 50 years, was central to the music's development. Growing up in Chicago, he graduated from Lane College in Jackson in 1934, then the Juilliard School Of Music in New York five years later. During this period he had already started writing his own compositions, and 'plugged' these for sale to local bands. His first success in this capacity was with Jimmy Lunceford's recording of 'St. Paul's Walking Through Heaven With You' in 1938. He had already established his name in the Chicago music community by starting a jazz column for *Downbeat* magazine in 1934. Having worked in promotion for several small Chicago labels before the war, after its end he began a contract with Aristocrat Records and its successor, Chess Records. He then joined Star Maid and Ronel Records in 1955. However, much of the time he operated on a piece-work basis, simultaneously pushing records for several companies in a manner that anticipated the later trend for freelance promotion and plugging. By 1954 he had joined Duke/Peacock Records in Houston with whom he would later work exclusively. Playing a large hand in the establishment of such artists as Bobby Bland, Junior Parker and O.V. Wright, Clark stayed with Duke until the early 70s. In this period he also worked as a songwriter, co-writing 'Why I Sing The Blues' (1969) and 'Chains And Things (1970) with B.B. King. He moved to Stax Records in 1971 for five years, working with Little Milton and the Staple Singers. TK Records was his next stop, an association that included promoting such artists as KC And The Sunshine Band and Betty Wright. By now Clark had built up strong loyalties within the music community, and when he moved to Malaco Records in 1980 he was able to attract artists including Z.Z. Hill, Johnnie Taylor, Bobby Bland and Denise LaSalle. While in his 70s, he scored a major success by pushing Z.Z. Hill's blues back to the black radio community, with his album *Down Home* (1982) becoming one of the decade's biggest blues successes. In the 90s his health failed, and he was confined to a nursing home until his death in 1995.

CLARK, DICK

b. Richard Wagstaff Clark, 30 November 1929, Mount Vernon, New York, USA. Clark became a showbusiness giant via the US television dance programme *American Bandstand*, the longest-running variety show in television history. As its host for over 30 years, Clark brought rock 'n' roll music and dancing into millions of American homes. He has been nicknamed 'America's Oldest Living Teenager'. Clark's career began in 1947, upon his graduation from high school. After working at minor jobs at his uncle's radio station, WRUN (Utica, New York), Clark debuted on the air at WAER, the radio station at Syracuse University, which he attended. Further radio jobs followed, until Clark took his first television job, as a newscaster, in 1951. He returned to radio upon moving to Philadelphia's WFIL, but by 1956 WFIL's television outlet needed a replacement host for its *Bandstand* show. Clark was offered the position and started his new job on 9 July 1956. *Bandstand*'s format was simple: play current hit records and invite local teenagers to come in and dance to them. The programme was a surprise success and a year later the ABC network decided to broadcast it nationally, changing the name to *American Bandstand* on 5 August 1957. Clark continued to host, bringing in guest artists - particularly top rock 'n' roll performers of the day - and the programme became a national phenomenon. Record promoters coveted airplay on *Bandstand*, as its power to 'break' records was unparalleled, and managers clamoured to land their artists on the programme to 'lip-sync' their latest hits. Many artists, particularly such Philadelphia-based singers as Fabian, Bobby Rydell, Chubby Checker and Frankie Avalon, largely owed their success to *Bandstand* exposure. Bobby Darin, Paul Anka and Connie Francis were also regulars. By this time Clark's own power within the music industry had grown, and when in 1959-60 the US government cracked down on so-called 'payola', the practice of disc jockeys accepting money or gifts in exchange for airplay, Clark was called to Washington to testify. He claimed innocence and was cleared with his reputation intact, although he divested himself of some $8 million in music business-related investments.

Clark had formed a production company early in his career, and in the mid-60s began producing other music television programmes, such as *Where The Action Is* and *Happening*. He also produced television game shows and films (including *Psych-Out* and *Because They're Young*). Clark's later creations include the *American Music Awards*, the *Country Music Awards* and television films about the Beatles and Elvis Presley - ironically, the only two major pop artists never to appear on *American Bandstand*. He also arranged tours called the Caravan of Stars, which took top musical stars on one-night-stand concerts throughout the USA in the early 60s. In 1964 *Bandstand* moved to Los Angeles from Philadelphia, and eventually it was scaled down from a daily to a weekly show. It continued until the late 80s, featuring contemporary artists such as Madonna, Prince and Cyndi Lauper. Clark remained an enormously powerful and influential figure in the entertainment industry into the 90s.

● FURTHER READING: *Rock, Roll & Remember*, Dick Clark and Richard Robinson.
● FILMS: *Because They're Young* (1960).

CLAY, W.C.

b. 1927, Jonestown, Mississippi, USA. Along with a number of Mississippi- and Arkansas-based blues artists, Clay played with the *King Biscuit* radio show entertainers, including Sonny Boy 'Rice Miller' Williamson. After 1950, and following Williamson's death in 1965, Clay regularly featured on the show playing Williamson favourites such as 'Keep It To Yourself'. In 1976 he was living in Elaine, near Helena, Arkansas.
● COMPILATIONS: with various artists *Keep It To Yourself - Arkansas Blues, Volume 1* (1983)★★★.

CLEARWATER, EDDY

b. Eddy Harrington, 10 January 1935, Macon, Mississippi, USA. Clearwater grew up hearing C&W records and began playing guitar in church after moving to Birmingham, Alabama, when he was 13 years old. He settled in Chicago in 1950 and was playing blues within a few years. Although primarily a powerful blues singer and guitarist in the west side Chicago style, he has also displayed, both on record and stage, a penchant for Chuck Berry-influenced rock 'n' roll, soul and country. He is a popular performer, both in the USA and Europe and is often seen performing in a spectacular native American headdress and feathers. He has made numerous recordings for a variety of labels, although it is his very versatility that often results in the failure completely to satisfy any listener, despite the fact that he can perform in almost any musical genre. His cousin is Carey Bell.
● ALBUMS: *The Chief* (Rooster 1980)★★, *Two Times Nine* (Charly 1981)★★★, *Flim Doozie* (Rooster 1987)★★, *Blues Hangout* (Black & Blue 1991)★★★, *Help Yourself* (Blind Pig 1992)★★, *Live At The Kingston Mines, Chicago, 1978* (1992)★★★, *Boogie My Blues Away* (Delmark 1995)★★★, *Mean Case Of The Blues* (Bullseye 1996)★★★★, *Black Night* (Storyville 1996)★.

CLEFS

Formed at high school in Arlington, Virginia, USA, in 1951 by Scotty Mansfield (lead), Fred Council (baritone), Gerald Bullock (bass), Pavel Bess (tenor) and Frank Newman (second tenor), this R&B vocal group's early performances were limited to fraternity parties and school hops. For the recording of their first demo a year later, Leroy Flack (brother of Roberta Flack) had replaced Bullock on bass, with James Sheppard adding further tenor support. Through manager Lillian Claiborne they were brought to the attention of Chess Records, who subsequently released their cover version of the Ink Spots' 'We Three'. Afterwards they returned to the local club circuit, losing one member (Flack) in 1955, at which time Bess took over bass duties. One further single emerged before they were offered a contract with Peacock Records in Houston, Texas. However, the Clefs declined, opting to pursue their fortunes with the more musically sympathetic Vee Jay Records. However, 1955's 'I'll Be Waiting' failed to provide any degree of success. Their name was then changed to Scotty Mann And The Masters, but 'Just A Little Bit Of Loving' also failed to work the miracle for them, in light of which they returned solely to live performances and, finally, more secure day jobs. This turn of events had become inevitable when Vee Jay failed to release them from contract, despite not wishing to release any new material by the band in either incarnation.

CLEFTONES

This R&B vocal group from Queens, New York, USA, consisted of Herb Cox (b. 6 May 1939, Cincinnati, Ohio, USA; lead), Charlie James (b. 1940; first tenor), Berman Patterson (b. 1938; second tenor), William McClain (b. 1938; baritone), and Warren Corbin (b. 1939; bass). The group came together at Jamaica High School in 1955. After joining George Goldner's Gee label, the group launched their recording career with 'You Baby You', a regional hit in late 1955. The record, with Cox's dry lead, Warren Corbin's effective bass-fills, and session musician Jimmy Wright's frantic saxophone blowing, set the tenor of the group's subsequent records. With their second record, 'Little Girl Of Mine', another peppy number, the group became nationally known as the record went to number 8 R&B and number 57 pop in 1956. Two excellent follow-ups the same year, 'Can't We Be Sweethearts' and 'String Around My Heart', were superbly representative of the Cleftones' exuberant style, but both remained regional hits. A move to a ballad in 1957, the outstanding 'See You Next Year', did not restore the Cleftones to national prominence. In 1959 Gene Pearson (from the Rivileers) replaced McClain, and the following year Patricia Spann was added to the group. The addition of the female to the group also signalled a slight change in style; the leads began to take greater prominence over the ensemble sound as doo-wop was beginning to fade. 'Heart And Soul', a rock 'n' roll remake of an evergreen, typified the new approach and proved to be the group's biggest hit, going to number 10 R&B and number 18 pop in 1961. Other important tracks from this era included the album cut 'Please Say You Want Me' (featuring Pat Spann in a beautiful remake of the Schoolboys' hit) and another evergreen remake, 'For Sentimental Reasons'. The Cleftones' recording career came to an end in 1964.

● ALBUMS: *Heart And Soul* (Gee 1961)★★★, *For Sentimental Reasons* (Gee 1962)★★★.
● COMPILATIONS: *The Best Of The Cleftones* (Rhino 1990)★★★, *For Collectors Only* (Collectables 1992)★★★.

CLIFF SINGS - CLIFF RICHARD ★★★★

Britain's greatest hit-maker has never been critically acclaimed for making a great album and his monumental contribution remains his dozens of memorable pop singles. It is fitting to note that this, released in 1959, was his second album, and strangely, his most appealing. *Cliff Sings* reached number 2 in the UK chart, and showcased Cliff as the cute, sneering rocker, whizzing through tried and tested rock 'n' roll classics. Most of the tracks evoke a 'beat group' sound and images of bad British B-movies are brought to mind. Hefty helpings of Bigsby tremelo arms and echo from the Drifters make this a timeless period piece.

● TRACKS: *Blue Suede Shoes; The Snake And The Bookworm; Here Comes Summer; I'll String Along With You; Embraceable You; As Time Goes By; The Touch Of Your Lips; Twenty Flight Rock; Pointed Toe Shoes; Mean Woman Blues; I'm Walking; I Don't Know Why; Little Things Mean A Lot; Somewhere Along The Way; That's My Desire.*

CLINE, PATSY

b. Virginia Patterson Hensley, 8 September 1932, Gore, near Winchester, Virginia, USA, d. 5 March 1963, Camden, Tennessee, USA. Her father, Sam Hensley, already had two children from a previous marriage when he married Hilda, Patsy's mother - a woman many years his junior. Hilda was only 16 when Patsy was born and they grew up like sisters. At the age of four, Patsy was influenced by a film of Shirley Temple and, without tuition, learned tap-dancing and showed an interest in music that was encouraged by the piano-playing of her step-sister. In spite of financial hardships, her parents gave her a piano for her seventh birthday, which she soon learned to play by ear. Hilda could never understand her daughter's affinity with country music, since neither she nor Sam was interested in the genre. At the age of 10, Patsy was eagerly listening to broadcasts from the *Grand Ole Opry* and informing everyone that one day she too would be an *Opry* star. In the early 40s, the Hensleys relocated to Winchester, where Patsy became interested in the country show on WINC presented by Joltin' Jim McCoy. Apart from playing records, he also fronted his own band in live spots on the show. At the age of 14, Patsy contacted McCoy and told him she wanted to sing on his show. He was impressed by her voice and Virginia Hensley quickly became a regular singer with his Melody Playboys. She also became associated with pianist William 'Jumbo' Rinker with whom she sang at local venues, and she left school to work in Gaunt's Drug Store to help the family finances. In 1948, Wally Fowler, a noted *Opry* artist whose gospel show was broadcast live on WSM, appeared at the Palace Theatre in Winchester. Patsy brazenly manoeuvred herself backstage on the night and confronted Fowler. Taken aback by her approach, he sarcastically suggested that perhaps she was 'Winchester's answer to Kitty Wells', but nevertheless let her sing for him. She sang unaccompanied and impressed Fowler so much that he included her in that night's show. Having sought Hilda's permission for her to audition for WSM in Nashville, a few weeks later, Patsy went to see Jim Denny, the manager of the *Opry*. Accompanied by the legendary pianist Moon Mullican, Patsy impressed Denny who asked her to remain in Nashville so that he could arrange an *Opry* appearance. However, without money, although too embarrassed to admit it, and accompanied by the two younger children, Hilda pleaded that they must return to Winchester that day. Before they left, Roy Acuff, who had heard Patsy's singing from an adjoining studio, asked her to sing on his *Noon Time Neighbours* broadcast that day. Her hopes that she would hear from Denny, however, were not realized and Patsy returned to the drug store and singing locally. In 1952, she met Bill Peer, a disc jockey and musician, who had run bands for some years, and who was at the time touring the Tri-State Moose Lodge circuit with his band, the Melody Boys and Girls. He hired Patsy as lead vocalist and on 27 September 1952, she made her first appearance with him at the Brunswick Moose Club in Maryland. Peer did not think the name Virginia was suitable and, wrongly assuming that her second name was Patricia, he billed her as Patsy Hensley. On 27 February 1953, Patsy married Gerald Cline, whom she had met at a show only a few weeks earlier. On the night of her marriage, Patsy appeared on stage for the first time as Patsy Cline. Although Cline's name was known over a considerable area, Peer was aware that she needed national exposure, and concentrated his efforts on seeking a recording contract for her. A demo tape attracted attention and on 30 September 1954, she signed a two-year contract with Four-Star, a Pasadena-based independent company, once owned by Gene Autry, whose president was now William A. McCall, a man not highly regarded by many in the music business. The contract stated that all Patsy Cline's recordings would remain Four-Star property - in effect, she could only record songs that McCall published and, being a non-writer herself, she was obliged to record any material he chose. Cline made her first four recordings on 1 June 1955 under the production of pianist, guitarist and arranger Owen Bradley, in his 'Quonset' hut studios in Nashville. 'A Church, A Courtroom And Then Goodbye', penned by Eddie Miller and W.S. Stevenson, was the chosen song, but it failed to reach the country charts (W.S. Stevenson was a pseudonym used by McCall, seemingly for his own songs, but it is known that, on occasions, he applied the name to songs that were written by other writers, such as Donn Hecht, who were under contract to his label). Cline made further recordings on 5 January and 22 April 1956, including the toe-tapping 'I Love You Honey' and the rockabilly 'Stop, Look And Listen'. The anticipated country chart entries did not occur and she became despondent. Her private life took a new turn in April 1956, when she met Charlie Dick, who became her second husband when her marriage to Gerald Cline ended in 1957. In an effort to secure a country hit, McCall commissioned songwriter Hecht, who suggested 'Walking After Midnight', a blues-styled number that he had initially written for Kay Starr, who had turned it down. Cline did not like the song either, claiming it was 'nothing but a little old pop song'. Under pressure from Decca (who leased her records from Four-Star), she recorded it, on 8 November 1956, in a session that also included 'A Poor Man's Roses (Or A Rich Man's Gold)' and 'The Heart You Break May Be Your Own'. On 28 January 1957, although preferring 'A Poor Man's Roses', she sang 'Walking After Midnight' on the Arthur Godfrey *Talent Scouts* show. On 11 February, Decca released the two songs in a picture sleeve on 78 rpm and it immediately entered both country and pop charts. Cline first sang 'Walking After Midnight' on the *Opry* on 16 February. The song finally peaked as a number 2 country and number 12 pop hit, while 'A Poor Man's Roses' also reached number 14 on the country chart. It was later estimated that the record sold around three-quarters of a million copies. In July 1959, she recorded two fine gospel numbers, 'Life's Railroad To Heaven' and 'Just A Closer Walk With Thee', but although Decca released various records the follow-up chart hit did not materialize. In truth, Decca had only 11 songs, recorded between February 1958 and November 1960, from which to choose. It was possible Cline chose to record the minimum number necessary under the terms of her Four-Star contract in the hope McCall would drop her, thus enabling her to pick up a promised Decca contract. The first song she recorded under her new association with Decca, on 16 November 1960, was 'I Fall To Pieces' by Hank Cochran and Harlan Howard. It quickly became a country number 1 and also peaked at number 12 on the pop charts. In August 1961 she completed a four-day recording session that included 'True Love', 'The Wayward Wind', 'San Antonio Rose' and her now legendary version of 'Crazy'. Willie Nelson, who had written the song, had demoed it

almost as a narration. With Owen Bradley's persuasion, she produced her own stunning interpretation in one take. The recording was a number 2 country and a number 9 pop hit. In 1962, 'She's Got You' was an even bigger country hit, spending five weeks at number 1, while peaking at number 14 in the pop charts. It also became her first entry in the Top 50 UK pop charts. Meanwhile, her marriage to Charlie Dick was becoming more stormy. Her wild and promiscuous lifestyle included an enduring affair with Faron Young. Her last recording session took place on 7 February 1963, when she recorded 'He Called Me Baby', 'You Took Him Off My Hands' and 'I'll Sail My Ship Alone'. The latter, ironically, was a song written by Moon Mullican, the pianist who had played for her *Opry* audition in 1948. Cline appeared in Birmingham, Alabama, with Tex Ritter and Jerry Lee Lewis on 2 March 1963, following which she agreed with other artists to appear in a charity show in Kansas City the next day, a show staged for the widow of Jack Call, a noted disc jockey on KCMK, known as Cactus Jack, who had died in a car crash. The weather was bad on 4 March but early on the afternoon of 5 March, in spite of further adverse weather forecasts, Cline, together with country singers Cowboy Copas and Hawkshaw Hawkins, set off on the five-hundred-mile flight to Nashville in a small aircraft piloted by Randy Hughes, the son-in-law of Copas and Cline's lover and manager. Hughes first landed at Little Rock to avoid rain and sleet and then at Dyersburg to refuel, where he was warned of bad weather in the area. They encountered further bad weather and, although the exact reason for the crash is unknown, the life of Patsy Cline came to an end some 50 minutes later, when the aircraft came down in woodland about a mile off Highway 70, near Camden, Tennessee. At the time of her death, Cline's recording of 'Leaving On Your Mind' was in both country and pop charts and before the year was over, both 'Sweet Dreams' and 'Faded Love' became Top 10 country and minor pop hits. It has been suggested that Patsy Cline was not an outstanding performer of up-tempo material, but it is an undisputed fact that she could extract every possible piece of emotion from a country weepie. Her versions of 'Walking After Midnight', 'I Fall To Pieces', 'Crazy', 'She's Got You' and 'Sweet Dreams' represent five of the greatest recordings ever made in country music. Those in any doubt of her standing should consult the *Billboard* back-catalogue country chart - her *Greatest Hits* stood at number 1 for over four years.

● ALBUMS: *Patsy Cline* (Decca 1957)★★★, *Patsy Cline Showcase* (Decca 1961)★★★★, *Sentimentally Yours* (Decca 1962)★★★★, *In Memoriam* (Everest 1963)★★★★, *Encores* (Everest 1963)★★★, *A Legend* (Everest 1963)★★★, *Reflections* (Everest 1964)★★★, *A Portait Of Patsy Cline* (Decca 1964)★★★★, *That's How A Heartache Begins* (Decca 1964)★★★, *Today, Tomorrow, Forever* (Hilltop 1964)★★★, *Gotta Lot Of Rhythm In My Soul* (Metro 1965)★★★, *Stop The World And Let Me Off* (Hilltop 1966)★★★, *The Last Sessions* (MCA 1980)★★★★, *Try Again* (Quicksilver 1982)★★★, *Sweet Dreams* film soundtrack (1985)★★★, *Live At The Opry* (MCA 1988)★★★, *Live - Volume Two* (MCA 1989)★★★, *The Birth Of A Star* (Razor & Tie 1996)★★★, *Live At The Cimarron Ballroom* recorded 1961 (MCA 1997)★★★.

● COMPILATIONS: *Patsy Cline's Golden Hits* (Everest 1962)★★★, *The Patsy Cline Story* (Decca 1963)★★★★, *Patsy*

Cline's Greatest Hits (Decca 1967)★★★, *Country Great* (Vocalion 1969)★★★, *Greatest Hits* (MCA 1973)★★★★★, *Golden Greats* (MCA 1979)★★★★★, *20 Golden Greats* (Astan 1984)★★★, *20 Classic Tracks* (Starburst 1987)★★★, *12 Greatest Hits* (MCA 1988)★★★, *Dreaming* (Platinum Music 1988)★★★, *20 Golden Hits* (Deluxe 1989)★★★, *Walkin' Dreams: Her First Recordings, Volume One* (Rhino 1989)★★★★, *Hungry For Love: Her First Recordings, Volume Two* (Rhino 1989)★★★★, *Rockin' Side: Her First Recordings, Volume Three* (Rhino 1989)★★★★, *The Patsy Cline Collection* 4-CD box set (MCA 1991)★★★★★, *The Definitive* (1992)★★★, *Discovery* (Prism Leisure 1994)★★★, *Premier Collection* (Pickwick 1994)★★★, *The Patsy Cline Story* (MCA 1994)★★★★, *Thinking Of You* (Summit 1995)★★★, *Today, Tomorrow And Forever* 2-CD set (Parade 1995)★★★.

● VIDEOS: *The Real Patsy Cline* (Platinum Music 1989), *Remembering Patsy* (1993).

● FURTHER READING: *Patsy Cline: Sweet Dreams*, Ellis Nassour. *Honky Tonk Angel: The Intimate Story Of Patsy Cline*, Ellis Nassour. *Patsy: The Life And Times Of Patsy Cline*, Margaret Jones. *I Fall To Pieces: The Music And The Life Of Patsy Cline*, Mark Bego.

CLOONEY, ROSEMARY

b. 23 May 1928, Maysville, Kentucky, USA. While very young, Rosemary and her sister Betty sang at political rallies in support of their paternal grandfather. When Rosemary was 13 the Clooney children moved to Cincinnati, Ohio, and appeared on radio station WLW. In 1945 they auditioned successfully for tenor saxophonist Tony Pastor and joined his band as featured vocalists, travelling the country doing mainly one-night shows. Rosemary made her first solo record in 1946 with 'I'm Sorry I Didn't Say I'm Sorry When I Made You Cry Last Night'. After around three years of touring, Betty quit, and Rosemary stayed on as a soloist with the band. She signed for Columbia Records in 1950 and had some success with children's songs such as 'Me And My Teddy Bear' and 'Little Johnny Chickadee', before coming under the influence of A&R manager Mitch Miller, who had a penchant for folksy, novelty dialect songs. In 1951 Clooney's warm, husky melodious voice registered well on minor hits, 'You're Just In Love', a duet with Guy Mitchell, and 'Beautiful Brown Eyes'. Later that year she topped the US chart with 'Come On-A-My House' from the off-Broadway musical *The Son*, with a catchy harpsichord accompaniment by Stan Freeman. During the next four years Clooney had a string of US hits including 'Tenderly', which became her theme tune, 'Half As Much' (number 1), 'Botcha-Me', 'Too Old To Cut The Mustard' (a duet with Marlene Dietrich), 'The Night Before Christmas Song' (with Gene Autry), 'Hey There' and 'This Ole House' (both number 1 hits), and 'Mambo Italiano'. UK hits included 'Man', with the b-side, 'Woman', sung by her husband, actor/producer/director Jose Ferrer, and the novelty, 'Where Will The Dimple Be'. Her last singles hit was 'Mangos', in 1957. Her own US television series regularly featured close harmony vocal group the Hi-Lo's, leading to their communal album *Ring Around Rosie*. Clooney's film career started in 1953 with *The Stars Are Singing* and was followed by three films the next year, *Here Come The Girls* with Bob Hope, *Red Garters* (1954) with Guy Mitchell and the Sigmund Romberg biopic, *Deep In My Heart*. In the same year she teamed with Bing Crosby in

White Christmas. Highly compatible, with friendly, easy-going styles, their professional association was to last until Crosby died, and included, in 1958, the highly regarded album *Fancy Meeting You Here*, a musical travelogue with special material by Sammy Cahn and James Van Heusen, arranged and conducted by Billy May. Semi-retired in the 60s, her psychiatric problems were chronicled in her autobiography, *This For Remembrance*, later dramatized on television as *Escape From Madness*. Her more recent work has been jazz-based, and included a series of tributes to the 'great' songwriters such as Harold Arlen, Cole Porter and Duke Ellington, released on the Concorde Jazz label. In 1991 Clooney gave an 'assured performance' in concert at Carnegie Hall, and duetted with her special guest artist, Linda Ronstadt. Throughout the early 90s she has continued to play US clubs, including her much appreciated annual stint at the Rainbow & Stars in New York.

● ALBUMS: *Hollywood's Best* (Columbia 1952/55)★★★, *Deep In My Heart* film soundtrack (MGM 1954)★★★, *Rosemary Clooney* 10-inch album (Columbia 1954)★★★, *White Christmas* 10-inch album (Columbia 1954)★★★★, *Red Garters* film soundtrack (Columbia 1954)★★★, *Tenderly* 10-inch album (Columbia 1955)★★★★, *Children's Favorites* 10-inch album (Columbia 1956)★★, *Blue Rose* (Columbia 1956)★★★, *A Date With The King* 10-inch album (Columbia 1956)★★★, *On Stage* 10-inch album (Columbia 1956)★★, *My Fair Lady* 10-inch album (Columbia 1956)★★, *Clooney Tunes* (Columbia 1957)★★★, with the Hi-Lo's *Ring A Round Rosie* (Columbia 1957)★★★★, *Swing Around Rosie* (Coral 1958)★★★, with Bing Crosby *Fancy Meeting You Here* (RCA Victor 1958)★★★★, *Rosemary Clooney In Hi-Fidelity* (Harmony 1958)★★★, *The Ferrers At Home* (1958)★★★, *Hymns From The Heart* (MGM 1959)★★, *Oh Captain!* (MGM 1959)★★, *Rosemary Clooney Swings Softly* (MGM 1960)★★★★, *A Touch Of Tabasco* (RCA Victor 1960)★★★, *Clap Hands, Here Comes Rosie* (RCA Victor 1960)★★★, *Rosie Solves The Swingin' Riddle* (RCA Victor 1961)★★★★, *Country Hits From The Heart* (RCA Victor 1963)★★★, *Love* (Reprise 1963)★★★, *Thanks For Nothing* (Reprise 1964)★★★, with Crosby *That Travelin' Two Beat* (Capitol 1965)★★★, *Look My Way* (United Artists 1976)★★★, *Nice To Be Around* (United Artists 1977)★★★, *Here's To My Lady* (Concord 1979)★★★, *With Love* (Concord 1981)★★★, *Sings The Music Of Cole Porter* (Concord 1982)★★★★, *Sings Harold Arlen* (Concord 1983)★★★★, *My Buddy* (Concord 1983)★★★, *Sings The Music Of Irving Berlin* (Concord 1984)★★★★, *Rosemary Clooney Sings Ballads* (Concord 1985)★★★, *Our Favourite Things* (Dance Band Days 1986)★★★, *Mixed Emotions* (Columbia 1986)★★★, *Sings The Lyrics Of Johnny Mercer* (Concord 1987)★★★★, *Sings The Music Of Jimmy Van Heusen* (Concord 1987)★★★★, *Show Tunes* (Concord 1989)★★★, *Everything's Coming Up Rosie* (Concord 1989)★★★, *Sings Rodgers, Hart And Hammerstein* (Concord 1990)★★★, *Sings The Lyrics Of Ira Gershwin* (Concord 1990)★★★★, *For The Duration* (Concord 1991)★★★, *Girl Singer* (Concord 1992)★★★, *Do You Miss New York?* (Concord 1994)★★★, *Still On The Road* (Concord 1994)★★★★, *Demi-Centennial* (Concord 1995)★★★, *Dedicated To Nelson* (Concord 1995)★★★★, *Mothers And Daughters* (Concord 1997)★★★.

● COMPILATIONS: *Rosie's Greatest Hits* (Columbia

1957)★★★★, *Rosemary Clooney Showcase Of Hits* (Columbia 1959)★★★★, *Greatest Hits* (Columbia 1983)★★★★, *The Best Of Rosemary Clooney* (Creole 1984)★★★★, *The Rosemary Clooney Songbook* (Columbia 1984)★★★★.
● FURTHER READING: *This For Remembrance*, Rosemary Clooney.

CLOVERS

This US R&B vocal ensemble formed in Washington, DC, in 1946, and built a career recording smooth ballads and bluesy jumps for New York independent Atlantic Records, in the process becoming one of the most popular vocal groups of the 50s. By the time the group first recorded for Rainbow Records in early 1950, the Clovers consisted of John 'Buddy' Bailey (b. 1930, Washington, DC, USA; lead), Matthew McQuater (tenor), Harold Lucas (baritone) and Harold Winley (bass), with instrumental accompaniment from Bill Harris (b. 14 April 1925, Nashville, North Carolina, USA, d. 5 December 1988; guitar). Later in the year the Clovers joined the fledgling Atlantic label. In 1952 Charles White (b. 1930, Washington, DC, USA), who had earlier experience in the Dominoes and the Checkers, became the Clovers' new lead, replacing Buddy Bailey who was drafted into the US Army. In late 1953 Billy Mitchell took over from White. Bailey rejoined the group in 1954 but Mitchell remained and the two alternated the leads. Whoever was the lead, from 1951-56 the Clovers achieved a consistent sound and remarkably consistent success. They had three US number 1 R&B hits with 'Don't You Know I Love You', 'Fool, Fool, Fool' (both 1951) and 'Ting-A-Ling' (1952), plus four number 2 R&B hits with 'One Mint Julep', 'Hey, Miss Fannie' (both 1952), 'Good Lovin'' (1953) and 'Lovey Dovey' (1954). The best-known of the remaining 11 other Top 10 hits for Atlantic was 'Devil Or Angel', a song frequently covered, most notably by Bobby Vee. The Clovers only made the US pop charts with 'Love Love Love' (number 30, 1956) and 'Love Potion No. 9' (number 23, 1959). The latter, one of Leiber And Stoller's best songs, was recorded for United Artists, the only label other than Atlantic that saw the Clovers reach the charts. In 1961 the Clovers split into rival groups led, respectively, by Buddy Bailey and Harold Lucas, and the hits dried up. Various permutations of the Clovers continued to record and perform for years afterwards, particularly in the Carolinas where their brand of music was popular as 'beach music'.
● ALBUMS: *The Clovers* (Atlantic 1956)★★★★, *Dance Party* (Atlantic 1959)★★★★, *In Clover* (Poplar 1959)★★, *Love Potion Number Nine* (United Artists 1959)★★★, *Clovers Live At CT's* (1989)★★.
● COMPILATIONS: *The Original Love Potion Number Nine* (Grand Prix 1964)★★★★, *Their Greatest Recordings - The Early Years* (Atco 1975)★★★★, *The Best Of The Clovers: Love Potion Number Nine* (EMI 1991)★★★★, *Down In The Alley* (Atlantic 1991)★★★, *Dance Party* (Sequel 1997)★★★★.

COASTERS

This R&B vocal group hailed from Los Angeles, USA. The illustrious career of the Coasters, the pre-eminent vocal group of the early rock 'n' roll era, was built on a remarkable body of cleverly comic R&B songs by their producers, Leiber And Stoller. Under their direction, the Coasters exchanged the crooning of ballads favoured by most groups of the era

for robust and full-throated R&B shouting. The group came together in 1955 from remnants of the Robins, who had a dispute with their producers/songwriters, Leiber and Stoller. The original Coasters consisted of two ex-Robins, Carl Gardner (b. 29 April 1928, Tyler, Texas, USA; lead) and Bobby Nunn (b. 1925, Birmingham, Alabama, USA, d. 5 November 1986; bass), plus Leon Hughes (b. 1938; tenor), Billy Guy (b. 20 June 1936, Itasca, Texas, USA; lead and baritone) and Adolph Jacobs (b. Oakland, California, USA; guitar). Hughes was replaced in 1956 by Young Jessie, who in turn was replaced by ex-Flairs Cornell Gunther (b. 14 November 1936, Los Angeles, California, USA, d. 26 February 1990). In 1958 Nunn was replaced by ex-Cadets Will 'Dub' Jones (b. 1939, Los Angeles, California, USA). Ex-Cadillacs Earl Carroll (b. Gregory Carroll, 2 November 1937, New York, New York, USA) replaced Gunther in 1961. The Coasters first charted with 'Down In Mexico' (US R&B Top 10) in 1956, but the double-sided hit from 1957, 'Searchin'' (US R&B number 1 and pop number 3) and 'Young Blood' (US R&B number 2 and pop Top 10) established the group as major rock 'n' roll stars (in the UK, 'Searchin'' reached number 30). Three more giant hits sustained the Coasters' career, namely 'Yakety Yak' (US R&B and pop number 1 in 1958), 'Charlie Brown' (US R&B and pop number 2 in 1959), and 'Poison Ivy' (US R&B number 1 and pop Top 10 in 1959). In the UK, 'Yakety Yak' went to number 12, 'Charlie Brown' to number 6, and 'Poison Ivy' to number 15, the group's last chart record in the UK. By this time, they were generally regarded as one of the wittiest exponents of teenage growing problems to emerge from the rock 'n' roll era. By the early 60s the lustre had worn off, as the hits increasingly emphasized the comic lyrics to the detriment of the music. The group continued for decades as an oldies act, and fractured into two different groups playing the oldies circuit. Bobby Nunn died in 1986; Cornell Gunther in 1990. The group was inducted into the Rock And Roll Hall Of Fame in 1987.
● ALBUMS: *The Coasters* (Atco 1958)★★★★, *One By One* (Atco 1960)★★★★, *Coast Along With The Coasters* (Atco 1962)★★★, *That's Rock And Roll* (Clarion 1964)★★, *On Broadway* (King 1973)★★.
● COMPILATIONS: *The Coasters' Greatest Hits* (Atco 1959)★★★★, *Their Greatest Recordings: The Early Years* (Atco 1971)★★★, *20 Great Originals* (Atlantic 1978)★★★, *What Is The Secret Of Your Success?* (Mr R&B 1980)★★★, *Thumbin' A Ride* (Edsel 1985)★★★, *The Ultimate Coasters* (Warners 1986)★★★, *Let's Go To The Dance* (Harmony 1988)★★★, *Poison Ivy* (1991)★★★★, *50 Coastin' Classics: The Coasters Anthology* (Rhino/Atlantic 1992)★★★★, *Yakety Yak* (Pickwick 1995)★★★★.
● FURTHER READING: *The Coasters*, Bill Millar.

COBBS, WILLIE

b. 15 July 1940, Monroe, Arkansas, USA. As a youngster, Cobbs was deeply involved in gospel music in his local area. He moved to Chicago in 1951, where he received tuition in the blues harmonica from Little Walter. After his national service from 1953-57 he returned to Chicago and recorded (as a singer only) in 1958. In 1961 he made 'You Don't Love Me', now a much-covered standard which has overshadowed Cobbs' musical career. Since the 60s he has been based in the south, recording down-home blues singles (sometimes with backing vocals as a nod to the soul market) for a

number of small labels, although in 1991 he did record for collector label Rooster Records.
● ALBUMS: *Down To Earth* (Rooster 1995)★★★.
● COMPILATIONS: *Hey Little Girl* (1991)★★★.

COCHRAN, EDDIE

b. Edward Cochrane, 3 October 1938, Oklahoma City, Oklahoma, USA, d. 17 April 1960, Chippenham, Wiltshire, England. Although Cochran's career was brief, during which time he topped the charts only once, he is now regarded as one of the finest ever rock 'n' roll artists. Originally one half of the Cochran Brothers (with non-relative Hank) he started as a country singer, and demonstrated an early prowess as an outstanding rockabilly guitarist with his trademark Gretsch guitar. In 1956 his cameo performance of 'Twenty Flight Rock' in the film *The Girl Can't Help It* gave this handsome James Dean lookalike the career boost he needed and he was signed by Liberty Records. Strangely, his new record company decided to release a ballad, 'Sittin' In The Balcony', which became a US Top 20 hit. The following year the first of his classic anthems was released. The song 'Summertime Blues' has been recorded and performed by dozens of artists, and is now one of the most famous rock songs of all time. This lyric of teenage angst is timeless and features many perceptive observations of frustration, for example: 'Well my ma and papa told me son, you gotta make some money, if you wanna use the car to go a-riding next Sunday'. The repeated chorus 'Sometimes I wonder what I'm a gonna do, but there ain't no cure for the Summertime Blues' perfectly encapsulated American teenage feelings. Additionally, the infectious riff has been copied down the ages, as the simple chord progression EABE sounds *great* to every guitar novice. The Who's lengthy and gutsy version is probably the most famous other than Cochran's. The following year, another timeless classic appeared, 'C'mon Everybody', with a similarly infectious riff; this time Cochran brilliantly conveyed the relief of finishing a hard day's work and preparing for a night out: 'Well c'mon everybody and lets get together tonight, I've got some money in my jeans and I'm really gonna spend it right', followed by the repeated and long-anticipated chorus, 'Whooah c'mon everybody'. This gem of a record ably showed how 50s rock 'n' roll could be uplifting, musically brilliant and yet contain simple, honest and enduring lyrics. The following year during a package tour in Britain, Cochran was killed in Chippenham, Wiltshire, when his taxi suffered a burst tyre and crashed after veering off the road. Gene Vincent was a badly injured passenger, as was Sharon Sheeley, co-writer of his posthumous hit 'Something Else', which became a major hit for the Sex Pistols in 1979. His biggest record was the inappropriately titled 'Three Steps To Heaven', which topped the UK chart shortly after his untimely death. 'Weekend' was the last of his classics, another tale of simple youthful enthusiasm for life: 'Friday night and everything's right for the weekend, boy its great for staying out late at the weekend'. In 1963 ex-Tornados bassist Heinz launched his solo career with the Joe Meek-produced tribute 'Just Like Eddie'. Heinz was only one of the many artists who have been influenced by Cochran. His reputation continues to grow as his slim catalogue of recordings is constantly repackaged to a perennial audience, eager to hear one of the greatest exponents of 'progressive' rock 'n' roll.

● ALBUMS: *Singing To My Baby* (Liberty 1957)★★★, *The Eddie Cochran Memorial Album* (Liberty 1960)★★★, *Never To Be Forgotten* (Liberty 1962)★★★, *Cherished Memories* (Liberty 1962)★★★★, *My Way* (Liberty 1964)★★★, *On The Air* (United Artists 1972)★★★, *The Many Sides Of Eddie Cochran* (Rockstar 1975)★★★, *The Young Eddie Cochran* (Rockstar 1982)★★★, *Words And Music* (Rockstar 1985)★★★, *Portrait Of A Legend* (Rockstar 1985)★★★, *The Many Styles Of Eddie Cochran* (Conifer 1985)★★★, *The Hollywood Sessions* (Rockstar 1986)★★★, *Thinkin' About You* (Rockstar 1989)★★★, with Hank Cochran *Eddie And Hank: The Cochran Brothers* (Rockstar 1991)★★★, *L.A. Sessions* (Rockstar 1994)★★★, *Mighty Mean* (Rockstar 1995)★★★.
● COMPILATIONS: *Summertime Blues* (Sunset 1966)★★★★, *The Very Best Of Eddie Cochran* (Liberty 1970)★★★★, *Legendary Masters* (United Artists 1971)★★★★, *The Very Best Of Eddie Cochran: 15th Anniversary Album* (United Artists 1975)★★★, *The Singles Album* (United Artists 1979)★★★★, *20th Anniversary Album* 4-LP box set (United Artists 1980)★★★★, *The 25th Anniversary Album* (Liberty 1985)★★★★, *Rock 'N' Roll Legend* (Rockstar 1987)★★★, *The Early Years* (Ace 1988)★★★★, *C'mon Everybody* (Liberty 1988)★★★★, *The Eddie Cochran Box Set* 6-LP box set (Liberty 1988)★★★★, *The EP Collection* (See For Miles 1989)★★★★, *Greatest Hits* (Curb 1990)★★★★.
● FURTHER READING: *The Eddie Cochran Nostalgia Book*, Alan Clark. *Eddie Cochran: Never To Be Forgotten*, Alan Clark. *The Legend Continues*, Alan Clark.
● FILMS: *The Girl Can't Help It* (1956), *Go Johnny Go* (1958).

COGAN, ALMA

b. 19 May 1932, London, England, d. 26 October 1966, London, England. After appearing in the stage shows *Sauce Tartare* and *High Button Shoes*, Cogan was spotted by A&R representative Wally Ridley and signed to HMV Records. Although she began her career as a balladeer, her breakthrough came with the novelty hit 'Bell Bottom Blues', which reached the Top 5 in the UK in 1954. A cover version of Kitty Kallen's 'Little Things Mean A Lot' followed quickly and during that same year Cogan appeared with Frankie Vaughan on a couple of unsuccessful singles. Her lone UK number 1 occurred in the spring of 1955 with 'Dreamboat' and the following Christmas she was back with the novelty 'Never Do A Tango With An Eskimo'. A duet with Ronnie Hilton appeared on the b-side of his chart-topper 'No Other Love', and throughout this period Cogan earnestly covered a string of US hits including Jewel Akens' 'The Birds And The Bees' and Frankie Lymon And The Teenagers' 'Why Do Fools Fall In Love?'. By the end of the 50s, she had notched up 18 UK chart entries, more than any female singer of her era. The press were fascinated by her amazing collection of dresses; at one time it was rumoured that she never wore any dress more than once, and her home in Essex was reputedly full of hundreds of voluminous frocks. Meanwhile, she was succeeding as a top variety star and enjoyed the luxury of her own television programme. Another duet, this time with Ocher Nebbish, appeared on one of her b-sides. Nebbish was, in fact, famed composer Lionel Bart, who not only cast Alma in *Oliver!*, but planned to marry her, much to the astonishment of the showbiz community. The unlikely nuptials never occurred, and by the 60s, Cogan was no longer a chart regular. Always a candidate for the cover version game, she recorded the bouncy 'Tell Him' but lost out to Billie Davis. Paul McCartney made a surprise appearance playing tambourine on the b-side of one of her singles and she repaid the compliment by cutting 'Eight Days A Week', a belated shot at chart fame that narrowly missed. In March 1966, doctors discovered that the singer had cancer. During a period of convalescence she wrote a number of songs under the pseudonym Al Western, including Ronnie Carroll's 'Wait For Me' and Joe Dolan's 'I Only Dream Of You'. At the peak of the popularity of the *Man From UNCLE* television series, she recorded a tribute disc to its star, David McCallum. 'Love Ya Illya', by the pseudonymous Angela And The Fans, received extensive airplay and only narrowly missed the charts in 1966. That autumn, while working in Sweden, Cogan collapsed and was sent home. On 26 October 1966, she lost her fight against cancer and died at London's Middlesex Hospital. In 1992, she was the subject of a 30-minute documentary as part of BBC Television's *The Lime Grove Story*.

● ALBUMS: *I Love To Sing* (HMV 1958)★★★, *With You In Mind* (Columbia 1961)★★★, *How About Love* (Columbia 1962)★★★.
● COMPILATIONS: *The Alma Cogan Collection* (One-Up 1977)★★★, *The Second Collection* (One-Up 1978)★★★, *The Very Best Of Alma Cogan* (MFP 1984)★★★, *With Love In Mind* (MFP 1986)★★★, *A Celebration* (Capitol 1987)★★★, *The Almanac* (MFP 1990)★★★, *The EMI Years* (EMI 1991)★★★★, *The A-Z Of Alma* 3-CD box set (1994)★★★★.
● FURTHER READING: *Alma Cogan*, Sandra Caron. *Alma Cogan*, Gordon Burn.

COLE, ANN

b. Cynthia Coleman, 24 January 1934, Newark, New Jersey, USA. Cole is best known for recording the original version of 'Got My Mojo Working' (1957), which Muddy Waters later placed on the charts and practically made his signature song. Her father sang with the family gospel group the Coleman Brothers, and young Cynthia began singing in her grandfather's church as a child. In 1949, after absorbing the diverse influences of Billie Holiday and Mahalia Jackson, she formed a gospel group with her cousins, the Colemanaires, who recorded for Timely Records in 1953 and 1954. She began a solo career in 1954 under the name of Ann Cole, recording obscure sides for Timely and Mor-Play before switching to Baton Records in 1956. There she had some success with the original versions of two famous blues songs, 'Easy Easy, Baby' (made famous by Magic Sam) and 'Got My Mojo Working'. She had chart success with 'Are You Satisfied' (number 10 R&B) in 1956 and 'In The Chapel' (number 14 R&B) in 1957. After leaving Baton in 1959, her only subsequent hit was for Roulette in 1962, 'House Fun' (number 21 R&B) backed with 'Don't Stop The Wedding' (number 99 pop), the latter an answer to Etta James's 'Stop The Wedding'. Cole suffered a serious accident that eventually resulted in her being confined to a wheelchair, and she returned to performing the spirituals and hymns that were her first inspiration.

● COMPILATIONS: *Got My Mojo Working: Original Baton Recordings: 1956-1959* (Krazy Kat 1984)★★★.

COLE, NAT 'KING'

b. Nathaniel Adams Coles, 17 March 1916, Montgomery, Alabama, USA, d. 15 February 1965. Cole was born into a family that held a key position in the black community; his father was pastor of the First Baptist Church. In 1921 the family migrated to Chicago, part of the mass exodus of blacks seeking a better life in the booming industrial towns of the north. He learned piano by ear from his mother, who was choir director in the church, from the age of four. When he was 12 years old he took lessons in classical piano, 'everything from Bach to Rachmaninoff'. Jazz was all-pervasive in Chicago, and Cole's school was a musical hotbed, producing musicians of the stature of Ray Nance, Eddie South and Milt Hinton. Cole's first professional break came touring with the show *Shuffle Along*, a revival of the first all-black show to make it to Broadway, which he joined with his bass-playing brother, Eddie. Stranded in Los Angeles when the show folded, Cole looked for club work and found it at the Century Club on Santa Monica Boulevard. It was a hangout for musicians and the young pianist made a splash: 'All the musicians dug him,' said Robert 'Bumps' Blackwell, 'that cat could play! He was unique.' In 1939 Cole formed an innovative trio with Oscar Moore on guitar and Wesley Prince on bass, eschewing the noise of drums. Like Fats Waller in the previous generation, Cole managed to combine pleasing and humorous ditties with piano stylings that were state-of-the-art. Times had moved on, and Cole had a suave sophistication that expressed the new aspirations of the black community. In 1943 he recorded his 'Straighten Up And Fly Right' for Capitol Records - it was an instant hit and Cole's future as a pop success was assured. In 1946 'The Christmas Song' added strings, starting a process that would lead to Cole emerging as a middle-of-the-road singer, accompanied by leading arrangers and conductors including Nelson Riddle, Gordon Jenkins, Ralph Carmichael, Pete Rugolo and Billy May. In the 40s Cole made several memorable sides with the Trio, including 'Sweet Lorraine', 'It's Only A Paper Moon', '(Get Your Kicks) On Route 66' and '(I Love You) For Sentimental Reasons'. By 1948, and 'Nature Boy' (a US number 1), on which Cole was accompanied by Frank DeVol's Orchestra, the move away from small-group jazz, towards his eventual position as one of the most popular vocalists of the day, was well underway. Absolute confirmation came in 1950, when Cole, with Les Baxter conducting Nelson Riddle's lush arrangement of 'Mona Lisa', spent eight weeks at the top of the US chart with what was to become one of his most celebrated recordings. Throughout the 50s the singles hits continued to flow, mostly with ballads such as 'Too Young', 'Faith Can Move Mountains', 'Because You're Mine', 'Unforgettable', 'Somewhere Along The Way', 'Funny (Not Much)', 'Pretend', 'Can't I?', 'Answer Me, My Love', 'Smile', 'Darling Je Vous Aime Beaucoup', 'The Sand And The Sea', 'A Blossom Fell', 'When I Fall In Love' and 'Stardust' (said to be composer Hoagy Carmichael's favourite version of his song). No doubt because of his jazz grounding, Cole was equally at home with the more up-tempo 'Orange Coloured Sky', backed by Stan Kenton And His Orchestra, 'Walkin' My Baby Back Home', 'Night Lights' and 'Ballerina'. In the same period, his bestselling albums included *After Midnight* (with the Trio), *Love Is The Thing*, which was at the top of the US chart for eight weeks, *Just One Of Those Things*, *Cole Espanol* and *The Very Thought Of You*. During the 50s he was urged to make films, but his appearances were few and far between, including character parts in *Blue Gardenia*, *China Gate* and *Night Of The Quarter Moon*. Cole's most effective film role came in 1958 when he played W.C. Handy in *St. Louis Blues*. He also appeared on screen with Stubby Kaye, singing the linking ballads in the spoof western *Cat Ballou* (1965), but it was clear that his enormous appeal lay in concerts and records. One of his lesser-known albums, *Welcome To The Club*, featured the [Count] Basie Orchestra, without the Count himself (for contractual reasons), and included Cole's superior readings of 'She's Funny That Way', 'Avalon' and 'Look Out For Love'. The title track was composed by Noel Sherman, who, with his brother Joe, wrote 'Mr Cole Won't Rock And Roll', an amusing piece performed by the singer in his concert show, 'Sights And Sounds', which played over 100 cities in the early 60s. It was not so much rock 'n' roll that concerned Cole's purist fans around that time: they had acute reservations about another of the Sherman Brothers' numbers, 'Ramblin' Rose' (1962), the singer's first big hit in four years, which came complete with a 'twangy C&W feeling'. They also objected to 'Those Lazy Hazy Crazy Days Of Summer' ('unabashed corn'), which also made the Top 10 in the following year. Cole himself felt that he was 'just adjusting to the market: as soon as you start to make money in the popular field, they scream about how good you were in the old days, and what a bum you are now'. As part of his most agreeable musical association during the early 60s, *Nat King Cole Sings/George Shearing Plays*, Cole went back to 1940 for Ian Grant and Lionel Rand's 'Let There Be Love'. His version became a hit single in many parts of the world, and remains a particularly fondly remembered performance. During the years of Cole's enormous popularity in the 'easy listening' field, jazz fans had to turn out to see him in the clubs to hear his glorious piano - an extension of the Earl Hines style that had many features of the new, hip sounds of bebop. If Cole had not had such an effective singing voice he might well have been one of bebop's leaders. Bebop was an expression of black pride, but so was Cole's career, creating opportunities for all kinds of 'sepia Sinatras' (Charles Brown, Sammy Davis Jnr., etc.) who proved that whites had no monopoly on sophistication. Cole bore the brunt of racism, meeting objections when he bought a house in Beverly Hills, and becoming the first black television presenter (he abandoned the role in 1957, protesting that the agencies would not find him a national sponsor). Though his position entailed compromises that gained him the hostility of civil rights activists in the early 60s, he was a brave and decent figure in a period when racial prejudice was at its most demeaning. Before his death from lung cancer in 1965, he was planning a production of James Baldwin's play *Amen Corner*, showing an interest in radical black literature at odds with his image as a sentimental crooner. Nat Cole's voice, which floats butter-won't-melt vowel sounds in an easy, dark drawl, is one of the great moments of black music, and no matter how sugary the arrangements he always managed to sing as if it mattered. In 1991 his daughter Natalie Cole revived his 'Unforgettable', singing a duet with his recorded vocal. Despite the questionable taste of beyond-the-grave duets, Cole's piano intro was a startling reminder of the extraordinary harmonic creativity he brought to the pop music of his time. Perhaps, like Louis Armstrong, the most moving aspect of his legacy is the

way his music cuts across the usual boundaries - chart-watchers and jazzheads, rock 'n' rollers and MOR fans can all have a good time with his music.

● ALBUMS: *The King Cole Trio* 10-inch album (Capitol 1950)★★★, *The King Cole Trio Volume 2* 10-inch album (Capitol 1950)★★★, *The King Cole Trio Volume 3* 10-inch album (Capitol 1950)★★★, *At The Piano* 10-inch album (Capitol 1950)★★★, *The King Cole Trio Volume 4* 10-inch album (Capitol 1950)★★★, *Harvest Of Hits* 10-inch album (Capitol 1950)★★★, *Penthouse Serenade* 10-inch album (Capitol 1952)★★★, *Unforgettable* (Capitol 1952)★★★★, *Nat 'King' Cole Sings For Two In Love* 10-inch album (Capitol 1953)★★★, *8 Top Pops* (Capitol 1954)★★★, *Tenth Anniversary Album* (Capitol 1955)★★★, *Vocal Classics* (Capitol 1955)★★★, *Instrumental Classics* (Capitol 1955)★★★, *The Piano Style of Nat King Cole* (Capitol 1956)★★★, *In The Beginning* (Decca 1956)★★, *Ballads Of The Day* (Capitol 1956)★★★, *After Midnight* (Capitol 1957)★★★, *Love Is The Thing* (Capitol 1957)★★★★, *This Is Nat 'King' Cole* (Capitol 1957)★★★★, *Just One Of Those Things* (Capitol 1957)★★★, *St. Louis Blues* film soundtrack (Capitol 1958)★★, *Cole Espanol* (Columbia 1958)★★, *The Very Thought Of You* (Capitol 1958)★★★★, *Welcome To The Club* (Capitol 1959)★★★, *To Whom It May Concern* (Capitol 1959)★★★, *A Mis Amigos* (Capitol 1959)★★, *Tell Me All About Yourself* (Capitol 1960)★★★, *Every Time I Feel The Spirit* (Capitol 1960)★★★, *Wild Is Love* (Capitol 1960)★★★, *The Magic Of Christmas* (Capitol 1960)★★★, *The Touch Of Your Lips* (Capitol 1961)★★★★, *String Along With Nat 'King' Cole* (Capitol 1961)★★★★, *Nat 'King' Cole Sings/George Shearing Plays* (Capitol 1962)★★★★, *Ramblin' Rose* (Capitol 1962)★★★, *Sings The Blues* (Capitol 1962)★★★, *Dear Lonely Hearts* (Capitol 1962)★★★, *Where Did Everyone Go?* (Capitol 1963)★★★, *Those Lazy-Hazy-Crazy Days Of Summer* (Capitol 1963)★★★, *Sings The Blues Volume 2* (Capitol 1963)★★★, *The Christmas Song* (Capitol 1963)★★★, *I Don't Want To Be Hurt Anymore* (Capitol 1964)★★★, *My Fair Lady* (Capitol 1964)★★★, *L-O-V-E* (Capitol 1965)★★★, *Songs From 'Cat Ballou' And Other Motion Pictures* (Capitol 1965)★★★, *Looking Back* (Capitol 1965)★★★, *Nat 'King' Cole At The Sands* (Capitol 1966)★★★, *At JATP* (Verve 1966)★★★, *At JATP 2* (Verve 1966)★★★, *The Great Songs!* 1957 recording (Capitol 1966)★★★, with Dean Martin *White Christmas* (Capitol 1971)★★★, *Christmas With Nat 'King' Cole* (Stylus 1988)★★★.

● COMPILATIONS: *The Nat King Cole Story* 3-LP box set (Capitol 1961)★★★★, *The Best Of Nat King Cole* (Capitol 1968)★★★★, *20 Golden Greats* (Capitol 1978)★★★★, *Greatest Love Songs* (Capitol 1982)★★★★, *Trio Days* (Affinity 1984)★★★, *The Complete Capitol Recordings Of The Nat King Cole Trio* 18-CD box set (Mosiac 1990)★★★★, *The Unforgettable Nat 'King' Cole* (EMI 1991)★★★★, *The Nat King Cole Gold Collection* (1993)★★★★, *World War II Transcriptions* (1994)★★★.

● VIDEOS: *Nat King Cole* (Missing In Action 1988), *Unforgettable* (PMI 1988), *Nat King Cole Collection* (Castle Music Pictures 1990), *Nat King Cole 1942-1949* (Verve Video 1990), *Nat King Cole* (Virgin Vision 1992).

● FURTHER READING: *Nat King Cole: The Man And His Music*, Jim Haskins and Kathleen Benson. *Unforgettable: The Life and Mystique of Nat King Cole*, Leslie Gourse.

COLEMAN, CY

b. Seymour Kaufman, 14 June 1929, New York, USA. A pianist, singer, producer and composer of popular songs and scores for films and the Broadway stage. The youngest of the five sons of emigrants from Russia, Coleman was born and brought up in the Bronx, where his mother owned two tenement buildings. He began to pick out tunes on the piano when he was four years old, irritating his father, a carpenter, to such an extent that he nailed down the lid of the instrument. However, a local teacher was so impressed by Coleman's piano playing that she provided free lessons in classical music. Between the ages of six and nine, Coleman performed in New York at the Town Hall, Steinway Hall and Carnegie Hall. While continuing his classical studies at the High School of Music and Art and the New York College of Music, from which he graduated in 1948, Coleman decided to change course and pursue a career in popular music. After a stint at Billy Reed's Little Club, he spent two years as a cocktail-lounge pianist at the exclusive Sherry Netherland Hotel in Manhattan, and played piano for several television programmes, including *The Kate Smith Show* and *A Date In Manhattan*. In 1950 he appeared with his trio, and singer Margaret Phelan, in the RKO short *Package Of Rhythm*. During the early 50s Coleman began to play in jazz clubs in New York and elsewhere, developing what he called a 'kind of bepoppy style'. By then he had been composing songs for several years. One of his earliest collaborators was Joseph Allen McCarthy, whose father, also named Joseph, wrote the lyrics for shows such as *Irene*, *Kid Boots* and *Rio Rita*. One of their first efforts, 'The Riviera', was included several years later on Johnny Mathis's *Live It Up*, while 'I'm Gonna Laugh You Right Out Of My Life' was recorded by singer-pianist Buddy Greco. Another, 'Why Try To Change Me Now?', received a memorable reading from Frank Sinatra in 1952. In the following year Coleman contributed 'Tin Pan Alley' to the Broadway show *John Murray Anderson's Almanac*, and around the same time, he wrote several songs for a Tallulah Bankhead vehicle, *Ziegfeld Follies*, which never made it to Broadway. From the late 50s until 1962, Coleman had a 'stormy' working relationship with lyricist Carolyn Leigh. Together they wrote several popular numbers such as 'Witchcraft' (Frank Sinatra), 'The Best Is Yet To Come' (Mabel Mercer), 'A Moment Of Madness' (Sammy Davis Jnr.), 'When In Rome (I Do As The Romans Do)' (Vikki Carr/Barbra Streisand), 'You Fascinate Me So' (Mark Murphy), 'Playboy's Theme', 'The Rules Of The Road', 'It Amazes Me', 'I Walk A Little Faster' and 'Firefly'. The latter was written in 1958 for Coleman and Leigh's musical based on the memoirs of stripper Gypsy Rose Lee. The project was later abandoned, but the song became a hit for Tony Bennett, who was instrumental in bringing their work before the public, and included two of their songs in his famous Carnegie Hall concert in 1962. Two years before that, the team wrote the music and lyrics for the Broadway musical *Wildcat*. The score included the show-stopper 'What Takes My Fancy', plus 'That's What I Want For Janie', 'Give A Little Whistle', 'You've Come Home', 'El Sombrero', and the march 'Hey, Look Me Over'. The latter became a hit for Peggy Lee. Coleman and Lee collaborated to write 'Then Is Then And Now Is Now'.

In 1962, Coleman and Leigh were back on Broadway with *Little Me*. The libretto, by Neil Simon, was based on a suc-cessful novel by Patrick Dennis, and traced the life of Belle Poitrine. Sid Caesar played all seven of her lovers, from the 16-year-old Noble Eggleston to the geriatric skinflint Mr. Pinchley. The score included 'Love You', 'Deep Down Inside', 'The Other Side Of The Tracks', 'Real Live Girl' and the show-stopper 'I've Got Your Number'. Despite a favourable reception from the critics, *Little Me* did not fulfil its potential, and folded after only 257 performances. In 1964, it was acclaimed in London, where comedian and song and dance man Bruce Forsyth played the lead, and a revised version was presented in the West End in 1984, starring the UK television comic Russ Abbott. After *Little Me*, Coleman and Leigh went their separate ways, collaborating briefly again in 1964 for 'Pass Me By', which was sung by the British writer-performer Digby Wolfe, over the opening titles of the Cary Grant movie *Father Goose*. In the same year, Coleman wrote the catchy 'Take a Little Walk' with Buddy Greco, before teaming with the lyricist and librettist Dorothy Fields. Fields was 25 years older than Coleman, with an impressive track record of standard songs for films and shows, written with composers such as Jimmy McHugh, Jerome Kern and Arthur Schwartz, plus the book for Irving Berlin's smash hit musical *Annie Get Your Gun*. In 1966 the new combination had their own Broadway hit with the score for *Sweet Charity*, a musical version of Federico Fellini's film *Nights Of Cabiria*. The accent was very much on dancing in this 'sentimental story of a New York dancehall hostess, and her desperate search for love'. The Coleman-Fields score included 'Baby, Dream Your Dream', 'Big Spender', 'If My Friends Could See Me Now', 'There's Gotta Be Something Better Than This', 'Where Am I Going?' and 'I'm A Brass Band'. The show ran for 608 performances on Broadway, and for 14 months in London, where it starred Juliet Prowse. The lead in the 1969 movie version was taken by Shirley Maclaine, and it also featured Sammy Davis Jnr. as a hippie evangelist singing 'The Rhythm Of Life', and Stubby Kaye leading the ensemble in 'I Love To Cry At Weddings'. Coleman was nominated for an Academy Award for his musical score. After failing to have several other projects mounted, such as a biography of Eleanor Roosevelt and a stage adaptation of the 1939 James Stewart movie *Mr. Smith Goes To Washington*, Coleman and Fields were back on Broadway in 1973 with *Seesaw*, based on William Gibson's 50s comedy *Two For The Seesaw*. The score included 'Welcome To Holiday Inn', 'Poor Everybody Else' and the blockbusters 'It's Not Where You Start (It's Where You Finish)' and 'Nobody Does It Like Me'. The latter became successful outside the show as a cabaret number for artists such as Shirley Bassey and comedienne Marti Caine. After Dorothy Fields' death in 1974, it was another three years before Coleman returned to Broadway with *I Love My Wife*, with book and lyrics by Michael Stewart. Adapted from Luis Rego's farce 'about two suburban couples and their bumbling attempt to engage in wife swapping', the production ran for 857 performances. It featured a small onstage orchestra whose members sang, dressed in fancy clothes, and commented on the show's action. Coleman won the Drama Desk Award for a score which included 'Hey There, Good Times', 'Something Wonderful I Missed', 'Sexually Free', 'Lovers On Christmas Eve', 'Everybody Today Is Turning On' and the title song. Less than a year after the opening of *I Love My Wife*, Coleman contributed to *On The Twentieth Century*, which was based on a 30s play by Ben

Hecht and Charles MacArthur, with lyrics and libretto by Betty Comden and Adolph Green. The production included the songs 'I Rise Again', 'Together', 'Never', 'She's A Nut' and 'Our Private World'. The show ran for over a year, and earned six Tony Awards, including best score of a musical. Coleman's next project, with lyricist Barbara Fried, was *Home Again*, which 'followed an Illinois family from the Depression to the Watergate scandal'. It closed in Toronto during April 1979, two weeks before it was set to open on Broadway. In complete contrast, *Barnum* (1980), a musical treatment of the life of showman P.T. Barnum, was a smash hit. Coleman's music and Michael Stewart's lyrics were 'catchy and clever, and occasionally very beautiful'. British actor Jim Dale received rave notices for his endearing performance in the title role, which called for him to sing and be a clown, ride a unicycle and walk a tightrope. The part of his wife was played by Glenn Close, on the brink of her 80s movie stardom. The score included 'There's A Sucker Born Ev'ry Minute', 'One Brick At A Time', 'The Colours Of My Life' and 'Come Follow The Band'. *Barnum* ran for 854 performances and captured three Tonys and two Grammies for the Broadway Cast album. Its subsequent run of almost two years at the London Palladium was a triumph for Michael Crawford. During the early 80s Coleman mounted Broadway revivals of *Little Me* and *Sweet Charity* which won four Tonys, including best revival of a play or musical. In 1988 Coleman wrote the music and lyrics, in collaboration with A.E. Hotchner, for *Let 'Em Rot*. It failed to reach New York, and when Coleman did return to Broadway in April 1989 with *Welcome To The Club*, that show was censured by the critics, and only ran for a few performances. It proved to be a temporary setback, for in December of that year, Coleman had one of the biggest hits of his career with *City Of Angels*, utilizing David Zippel's lyrics, and a book by Larry Gelbart that 'both satirized and celebrated the film *noir* genre and the hard boiled detective fiction of the 1940s'. The show garnered six Tonys, three Outer Critics Circle Awards and eight Drama Desk Awards, among them those for best musical, best music and lyrics. The production included the songs 'With Every Breath I Take', 'The Tennis Song', 'What You Don't Know About Women', 'You're Nothing Without Me' and 'Double Talk'. *City Of Angels* ran at the Virginia Theatre in New York for 878 performances. Meanwhile, Coleman had turned his attention to *The Will Rogers Follies*, which related 'the life story of America's favourite humorist in the style of a *Ziegfeld Follies*' (1991). With Keith Carradine in the title role, Peter Stone's book called for 'a mutt act, a world champion roper, four kids, 12 sisters, a ranchful of cowboys, Gregory Peck (his voice only), and girls wearing spangles, and, of course, girls wearing not much of anything at all', which was put together by director-choreographer Tommy Tune. For the lyrics to his pastiche melodies, Coleman turned again to Comden and Green for 'Never Met A Man I Didn't Like', 'Let's Go Flying', 'Willamania', 'It's A Boy!', 'The Powder Puff Ballet', 'Give A Man Enough Rope' and 'Marry Me Now/I Got You'. Despite initial notices citing 'lapses of taste' and 'a paltry case for a cultural icon', the show ran for 1,420 performances, and gained Tony Awards for best musical and original score. In parallel with his Broadway career, Coleman has written several film scores, although they have generally failed to match the critical acclaim of his stage work. His music for *Family Business* was termed by one critic as 'one of the most appalling music scores in recent memory'. Coleman's other film work has included *Father Goose* (1964), *The Troublemaker* (1964), *The Art Of Love* (1965), *The Heartbreak Kid* (1972), *Blame It On Rio* (1984), *Garbo Talks* (1984) and *Power* (1986). He has also worked in television, where he conceived and co-produced Shirley Maclaine's special *If They Could See Me Now* (1974), and produced her *Gypsy In My Soul* (1976), both Emmy-winning presentations. Coleman has also performed with many symphony orchestras, including those of Milwaukee, Detroit, San Antonio, Indianapolis and Fort Worth, and has been a director of ASCAP, and a governor of the Academy of Television Arts And Sciences and the Dramatists Guild. He was inducted into the Songwriters' Hall of Fame, and has served as a member of the Academy of Motion Picture Arts and Sciences and the New York State Advisory Committee on Music. His honours include the La Guardia Award for Outstanding Achievement in Music and the Irvin Feld Humanitarian award from the National Conference of Christians and Jews.

● ALBUMS: as a pianist and vocalist *Cy Coleman* 10-inch album (Benida 1955)★★★, *Jamaica*, *Playboy's Penthouse*, *Piano Artistry* (all 50s)★★★, *Cool Coleman* (Westminster 1958)★★★★, *Flower Drum Song* (1959)★★★, *Why Try To Change Me* (1959)★★★, *If My Friends Could See Me Now* (1966)★★★, *Barnum* (Rhapsody 1981)★★★, *Coming Home* (DRG 1988)★★★.

COLLINS KIDS

A brother and sister rockabilly act, Larry Collins (b. 4 October 1944, Tulsa, Oklahoma, USA) and Lorrie Collins (b. Lawrencine Collins, 7 May 1942, Tahlequah, Oklahoma, USA) recorded numerous singles for Columbia Records in the 50s and early 60s that are revered by fans and collectors of early rock 'n' roll but never dented the charts. The duo gained what little recognition it had through frequent television appearances. Lorrie Collins was the first of the siblings to enter showbusiness. At the age of eight she won a singing contest and two years later the family moved to Los Angeles. Guitarist Larry joined his sister's act in 1954, after having won contests on his own through his prodigious musicianship. After the pair won a talent contest together, they were hired to perform for a television programme called *Town Hall Party* on which they soon became regulars, appearing on every programme. The Collins Kids, as they became known professionally, were signed to Columbia in 1955. As Columbia at that time was not primarily a rock 'n' roll label, poor promotion doomed the Collins Kids to failure. When Lorrie married in 1959, the act temporarily split up. They reunited briefly but with the birth of Lorrie's first child in 1961, the team was effectively terminated. Larry Collins recorded a handful of solo records, which also failed to chart, and later became a country songwriter, whose credits included co-writing the Tanya Tucker hit 'Delta Dawn' and David Frizzell and Shelly West's 'You're The Reason God Made Oklahoma'. In later life, he became a professional golfer and Lorrie retired to raise her family.

● COMPILATIONS: *Introducing Larry And Lorrie* (Columbia 1958)★★★, *Rockin' Rollin' Collins Kids* (Bear Family 1983)★★★, *Rockin' Rollin' Collins Kids, Volume 2* (Bear Family 1983)★★, *Hop, Skip & Jump* 2-CD set (Bear Family 1991)★★★★, *Rockin' On T.V.* (Krazy Kat 1993)★★★.

COLTRANE, JOHN

b. John William Coltrane, 23 September 1926, Hamlet, North Carolina, USA, d. 17 July 1967. Coltrane grew up in the house of his maternal grandfather, Rev. William Blair (who gave him his middle name), a preacher and community spokesman. While he was taking clarinet lessons at school, his school band leader suggested his mother buy him an alto saxophone. In 1939 his grandfather and then his father died, and after finishing high school he joined his mother in Philadelphia. He spent a short period at the Ornstein School of Music and the Granoff Studios, where he won scholarships for both performance and composition, but his real education began when he started gigging. Two years' military service was spent in a navy band (1945-46), after which he toured in the King Kolax and Eddie 'Cleanhead' Vinson bands, playing goodtime, rhythmic big-band music. It was while playing in the Dizzy Gillespie Big Band (1949-51) that he switched to tenor saxophone. Coltrane's musical roots were in acoustic black music that combined swing and instrumental prowess in solos, the forerunner of R&B. He toured with Earl Bostic (1952), Johnny Hodges (1953-54) and Jimmy Smith (1955). However, it was his induction into Miles Davis's band of 1955 - rightly termed the Classic Quintet - that brought him to notice. Next to Davis's filigree sensitivity, Coltrane sounds awkward and crude, and Davis received criticism for his choice of saxophonist. The only precedent for such modernist interrogation of tenor harmony was John Gilmore's playing with Sun Ra. Critics found Coltrane's tone raw and shocking after years in which the cool school of Lester Young and Stan Getz had held sway. It was generally acknowledged, however, that his ideas were first rate. Along with Sonny Rollins, he became New York's most in-demand hard bop tenor player: 1957 saw him appearing on 21 important recordings, and enjoying a brief but fruitful association with Thelonious Monk. That same year he returned to Philadelphia, kicking his long-time heroin habit, and started to develop his own music (Coltrane's notes to the later A Love Supreme refer to a 'spiritual awakening'). He also found half of his 'classic' quartet: at the Red Rooster (a nightclub that he visited with trumpeter Calvin Massey, an old friend from the 40s) he discovered pianist McCoy Tyner and bassist Jimmy Garrison.

After recording numerous albums for the Prestige label, Coltrane signed to Atlantic Records and, on 15 August 1959, he recorded Giant Steps. Although it did not use the talents of his new friends from Philadelphia, it featured a dizzying torrent of tenor solos that harked back to the pressure-cooker creativity of bebop, while incorporating the muscular gospel attack of hard bop. Pianist Tommy Flanagan (later celebrated for his sensitive backings for singers such as Ella Fitzgerald and Tony Bennett) and drummer Art Taylor provided the best performances of their lives. Although this record is rightly hailed as a masterpiece, it encapsulated a problem: where could hard bop go from here? Coltrane knew the answer; after a second spell with Davis (1958-60), he formed his best-known quartet with Tyner, Garrison and the amazing polyrhythmic drummer Elvin Jones. Jazz has been recovering ever since.

The social situation of the 60s meant that Coltrane's innovations were simultaneously applauded as avant garde statements of black revolution and efficiently recorded and marketed. The Impulse! label, to which he switched from Atlantic in 1961, has a staggering catalogue that includes most of Coltrane's landmark records, plus several experimental sessions from the mid-60s that still remain unreleased (although they missed My Favourite Things, recorded in 1960 for Atlantic, in which Coltrane established the soprano saxophone as an important instrument). Between 1961 and his death in 1967, Coltrane made music that has become the foundation of modern jazz. For commercial reasons, Impulse! Records had a habit of delaying the release of his music; fans emerged from the live performances in shock at the pace of his evolution. A record of Ballads and an encounter with Duke Ellington in 1962 seemed designed to deflect criticisms of coarseness, although Coltrane later attributed their relatively temperate ambience to persistent problems with his mouthpiece. A Love Supreme was more hypnotic and lulling on record than in live performance, but nevertheless a classic. After that, the records became wilder and wilder. The unstinting commitment to new horizons led to ruptures within the group. Elvin Jones left after Coltrane incorporated a second drummer (Rashied Ali). McCoy Tyner was replaced by Alice McLeod (who married Coltrane in 1966). Coltrane was especially interested in new saxophone players and Ascension (1965) made space for Archie Shepp, Pharoah Sanders, Marion Brown and John Tchicai. Eric Dolphy, although he represented a different tradition of playing from Coltrane (a modernist projection of Charlie Parker), had also been a frequent guest player with the quartet in the early 60s, touring Europe with them in 1961. Interstellar Space (1967), a duet record, pitched Coltrane's tenor against Ali's drums, and provides a fascinating hint of new directions.

Coltrane's death in 1967 robbed avant garde jazz of its father figure. The commercial ubiquity of fusion in the 70s obscured his music and the 80s jazz revival concentrated on his hard bop period. Only Reggie Workman's Ensemble and Ali's Phalanx carried the huge ambition of Coltrane's later music into the 90s. As soloists, however, few tenor players have remained untouched by his example. It is interesting that the saxophonists Coltrane encouraged did not sound like him; since his death, his 'sound' has become a mainstream commodity, from the Berklee College Of Music style of Michael Brecker to the 'European' variant of Jan Garbarek. New stars such as Andy Sheppard have established new audiences for jazz without finding new ways of playing. Coltrane's music - like that of Jimi Hendrix - ran parallel with a tide of mass political action and consciousness. Perhaps those conditions are required for the creation of such innovative and intense music. Nevertheless, Coltrane's music reached a wide audience, and was particularly popular with the younger generation of listeners who were also big fans of rock music. A Love Supreme sold sufficient copies to win a gold disc, while the Byrds used the theme of Coltrane's tune 'India' as the basis of their hit single 'Eight Miles High'. Perhaps by alerting the rock audience to the presence of jazz, Coltrane can be said to have - inadvertently - prepared the way for fusion.

● ALBUMS: with Elmo Hope Informal Jazz reissued as Two Tenors (Prestige 1956)★★★, with various artists Tenor Conclave (Prestige 1957)★★★, Dakar (Prestige 1957)★★★, Coltrane reissued as The First Trane (Prestige 1957)★★★, John Coltrane With The Red Garland Trio reissued as Traneing In (Prestige 1957)★★★, with various artists

Wheelin' And Dealing (Prestige 1957)★★★, *Blue Train* (Blue Note 1957)★★★★★, with Thelonious Monk *Thelonious Monk With John Coltrane* (Jazzland 1957)★★★★, with Miles Davis *Miles And Coltrane* (Columbia 1958)★★★★, *Lush Life* (Prestige 1958)★★★, *Soultrane* (Blue Note 1958)★★★★, *John Coltrane* (Prestige 1958)★★★, *Settin The Pace* (Prestige 1958)★★★, *Cattin' With Coltrane And Quinichette* (Prestige 1959)★★★, *Coltrane Plays For Lovers* (Prestige 1959)★★★, *The Believer* (Prestige 1959)★★★, *Black Pearls* (Prestige 1959)★★★, *The Stardust Session* (Prestige 1959)★★★, *Standard Coltrane* (Prestige 1959)★★★, *Bahia* (Prestige 1959)★★★, *Giant Steps* (Atlantic 1959)★★★★★, *Coltrane Jazz* (Atlantic 1960)★★★★, with Don Cherry *The Avant-Garde* (Atlantic 1960)★★★, with Milt Jackson *Bags And Trane* (Atlantic 1961)★★★, *My Favourite Things* (Atlantic 1961)★★★★, *Olé Coltrane* (Atlantic 1961)★★★, *Africa/Brass: Volumes 1 & 2* (Impulse 1961)★★★★, with Kenny Burrell *Kenny Burrell With John Coltrane* (New Jazz 1962)★★★★, *Live At The Village Vanguard* (Impulse 1962)★★★, *Coltrane Plays The Blues* (Atlantic 1962)★★★★, *Coltrane Time* originally released as Cecil Taylor's *Hard Driving Jazz* (United Artists 1962)★★★, *Coltrane* (Impulse 1962)★★★★, with Duke Ellington *Duke Ellington And John Coltrane* (MCA/Impulse 1962)★★★★, *Ballads* (Impulse 1962)★★★★, *John Coltrane And Johnny Hartman* (Impulse 1963)★★★, *Coltrane Live At Birdland* (Impulse 1963)★★★, *Impressions* (Impulse 1963)★★★★, *Coltrane's Sound* (Atlantic 1964)★★★★, *Crescent* (Impulse 1964)★★★, *The Last Trane* (Prestige 1965)★★★, *A Love Supreme* (Impulse 1965)★★★★★, *The John Coltrane Quartet Plays* (Impulse 1965)★★★, with Archie Shepp *New Thing At Newport* (Impulse 1965)★★★, *Ascension - Edition 1* (Impulse 1965)★★★★, *Transition* (Impulse 1965)★★★★, *Ascension - Edition 2* (Impulse 1966)★★★★, *Kulu Se Mama* (Impulse 1966)★★★, *Meditations* (Impulse 1966)★★★★, *Expression* (Impulse 1967)★★★, *Live At The Village Vanguard Again!* (Impulse 1967)★★★, *Om* (Impulse 1967)★★★, *Selflessness* 1963, 1965 recordings (Impulse 1969)★★★, *Sun Ship* 1965 recording (1971)★★★, *Dear Old Stockholm* (Impulse 1965)★★★, *Live In Seattle* 1965 recording (Impulse 1971)★★★, *Africa Brass, Volume Two* 1961 recording (1974)★★★★, *Interstellar Space* 1967 recording (Impulse 1974)★★★, *First Meditations - For Quartet* 1965 recording (Impulse 1977)★★★, *The Other Village Vanguard Tapes* 1961 recording (1977)★★★, *Afro-Blue Impressions* 1962 recording (Pablo 1977)★★★, *The Paris Concert* 1962 recording (Pablo 1979)★★★, *The European Tour* 1962 recording (Pablo 1980)★★★, *Bye Bye Blackbird* 1962 recording (1981)★★★, *Live At Birdland - Featuring Eric Dolphy* 1962 recording (1982)★★★, *Stellar Regions* 1967 recording (Impulse 1995)★★.
● COMPILATIONS: *The Best Of John Coltrane* (Atlantic 1969)★★★★, *The Best Of John Coltrane - His Greatest Years (1961-1966)* (MCA/Impulse 1972)★★★★, *The Best Of John Coltrane - His Greatest Years, Volume 2 (1961-1967)* (MCA/Impulse 1972)★★★★, *The Mastery Of John Coltrane, Volumes 1-4* (1978)★★★★, *The Art Of John Coltrane (The Atlantic Years)* (Pablo 1983)★★★★, *The Gentle Side Of John Coltrane* (Impulse 1992)★★★★, *The Major Works Of John Coltrane* (Impulse 1992)★★★★, *The Impulse! Years* (Impulse 1993)★★★★, *The Heavyweight Champion* 7-CD box set (Rhino/Atlantic 1995)★★★★★, *The Complete 1961 Village Vanguard Recordings* (Impulse 1997)★★★★.
● VIDEOS: *The World According To John Coltrane* (1993).
● FURTHER READING: *Trane 'N' Me*, Andrew Nathaniel White. *About John Coltrane*, Tim Gelatt (ed.). *John Coltrane, Discography*, Brian Davis. *The Artistry Of John Coltrane*, John Coltrane. *The Style Of John Coltrane*, William Shadrack Cole. *Chasin' The Trane*, J.C. Thomas. *Coltrane*, Cuthbert Ormond Simpkins. *John Coltrane*, Brian Priestley. *John Coltrane*, Bill Cole. *Ascension: John Coltrane And His Quest*, Eric Nisenson.

COLTS

R&B vocal group the Colts honed their act in front of truck drivers at a drive-in eatery in Bakersfield, California, USA. At the core of the group were brothers Ruben (lead) and Joe Grundy, plus Carl Moland, accompanied by several part-time contributors. It was not until the trio started attending Los Angeles City College that the line-up was finalized with the addition of former New Jersey boxer Leroy Smith. They then secured the management and writing services of Buck Ram, a veteran of work with the Platters and Penguins. Through Ram they signed to Vita Records in Pasadena and recorded one of Ram's compositions, 'Adorable', in August 1955, backed by 'Lips Like Red Wine'. It became a staple of clubs and radio stations throughout California, leading to the Drifters recording a version that went to number 1 in *Billboard*'s R&B chart (the Colts' own take on 'Adorable' stalled at number 11). Touring slots with the Platters, Penguins and Dinah Washington ensued, as well as an appearance at New York's Apollo Theatre. If the Drifters' hijacking of their tune had put the Colts in the shade, then Ram's decision to spend more time with the Platters (after they had enjoyed a US number 1 with his song 'The Great Pretender') eclipsed them completely. 'Sweet Sixteen' and 'Never No More' were their final two releases before Ram switched them to his new Antler Records label. However, neither 'Sheik Of Araby' (1957) nor 'I Never Knew' (for Delco Records in 1959) returned them to the limelight.

COLYER, KEN

b. 18 April 1928, Great Yarmouth, Norfolk, England, d. 8 March 1988, south of France. Of all the musicians involved in the British Revivalist movement of the late 40s and early 50s, trumpeter Colyer was the only one to achieve the status of a jazz legend. He achieved this through a gritty determination to adhere to what he believed to be the true spirit of jazz. Colyer first demonstrated his obsession with the great traditions of New Orleans jazz in the early 50s. He joined the Merchant Navy in order to visit the USA, where he promptly jumped ship and headed for the Crescent City. In New Orleans he sat in with local grandmasters, including George Lewis and Emile Barnes, before the authorities caught up with him and he was deported. Before his visit to the USA, Colyer had already worked with the Crane River Jazz Band and the Christie Brothers Stompers, but his American exploits had made him a big name in the UK and he was invited to front the co-operative band formed a little earlier by Chris Barber and Monty Sunshine. Although this unit was working regularly and building a reputation, Barber and Sunshine felt that Colyer's fame would be an asset. For a while this assumption proved correct, but personality clashes developed, particularly when Colyer appeared to lose sight of the fact that the band he was leading was not his own but was a collective venture. In 1954 Barber took over the reins and Colyer formed his own band, which, with various personnel changes, he continued to lead for the next 30 years. Among the many musicians who worked under Colyer's leadership were Acker Bilk, Diz Disley, Ian Wheeler and Sammy Rimington. Conceding that his technique was limited, Colyer overcame any deficiencies in style through an unflinching determination not to be swayed by changing public tastes or commercial considerations, although he did play guitar and sing in a skiffle group in the mid-50s. In 1957 he returned to the USA and joined the George Lewis band, arranging their trips to Europe. His last significant work was as part of the touring jazz show *New Orleans Mardi Gras*. Colyer defeated cancer, and the temporary retirement this necessitated, playing on into the 80s. A year after he died, a commemorative blue plaque was placed on the wall of the 100 Club in London, and many of his former colleagues took part in a concert organized by the Ken Colyer Trust.

● ALBUMS: *Ken Colyer In New Orleans* (Vogue 1954)★★★★, *New Orleans To London* (Decca 1954)★★★★, *In The Beginning ...* (1954)★★★★, *Back To The Delta* (Decca 1954)★★★★, *Ken Colyer's Jazzmen* (Tempo 1956)★★★, *Club Session With Colyer* (Decca 1957)★★★, *A Very Good Year* (1957)★★★, *In Gloryland* (Decca 1958)★★★, *In Hamburg* (Decca 1959)★★★, *Plays Standards* (Decca 1959)★★★, *Sensation* (Lake 1960)★★★, *This Is Jazz* (Columbia 1960)★★★, *This Is Jazz Volume 2* (Columbia 1961)★★★, *When I Leave The World Behind* (Lake 1963)★★★, *Out Of Nowhere* (1965)★★★, *Wandering* (KC 1965)★★★, *Live At The Dancing Slipper* (1969)★★★, *Ken Colyer And His Handpicked Jazzmen* (1972)★★★, *Watch That Dirty Tone Of Yours* (Joy 1974)★★★, *Spirituals, Volumes 1 & 2* (Joy 1974)★★★, *Swinging And Singing* (1975)★★★, *Painting The Clouds With Sunshine* (Black Lion 1979)★★★, *Darkness On The Delta* (Black Lion 1979)★★★, *Ken Colyer With John Petters' New Orleans Allstars* (1985)★★★, with Max Collie, Cy Laurie *New Orleans Mardi Gras* (1985)★★★, *Too Busy* (CMJ 1985)★★★, with Acker Bilk *It Looks Like A Big Time Tonight* (Stomp 1988)★★★.

● COMPILATIONS: *The Decca Years, Volume 1 (1955-59)* (Lake 1985)★★★★, *The Decca Years, Volume 2 (1955-59)* (Lake 1986)★★★★, *The Decca Years, Volume 3 (1955-59)* (Lake 1987)★★★★, *The Decca Years, Volume 4 (Skiffle Sessions 1954-57)* (Lake 1987)★★★★, *The Decca Years, Volume 5 (Lonesome Road)* (Lake 1988)★★★★, *The Decca Years, Volume 6 (In The Beginning)* (Lake 1988)★★★★, *The Guv'nor (1959-61)* (Polydor 1989)★★★★.

● FURTHER READING: *When Dreams Are In The Dust (The Path Of A Jazzman)*, Ken Colyer.

COMDEN, BETTY

b. 3 May 1915, New York City, New York, USA. After graduating with a degree in science, Betty Comden strove to find work as an actress. During this period, the late 30s, she met Adolph Green (b. 2 December 1915, New York, USA), who was also seeking work in the theatre. Unsuccessful in their attempts to find acting jobs, Comden and Green formed their own troupe, together with another struggling actress, Judy Holliday. In the absence of suitable material, Comden and Green began creating their own and discovered an ability to write librettos and lyrics. At first their success was

only limited, but in the early 40s they were invited by a mutual friend, Leonard Bernstein, to work on the book and lyrics of a musical he planned to adapt from his ballet score *Fancy Free*. The show, in which Comden and Green also appeared, was retitled *On The Town* (1944), and became a huge success; Comden and Green never looked back. *On The Town* was followed by *Billion Dollar Baby* (1945, music by Morton Gould) and an assignment in Hollywood for the musical films *Good News* (1947), *The Barkleys Of Broadway* (1949), *On The Town* and *Take Me Out To The Ball Game* (both 1949). In the 50s and 60s Comden and Green were back on Broadway, collaborating with Bernstein again on *Wonderful Town* (1953), and with Jule Styne on *Two On The Aisle*, *Peter Pan*, *Say, Darling*, *Do Re Mi*, *Subways Are For Sleeping*, *Fade Out-Fade In*, *Halleluja, Baby!*, and most notably, *Bells Are Ringing* (1956), in which the leading role was played by their former associate Judy Holliday. Among their films were *Singin' In The Rain* (1952), for which they wrote the screenplay, incorporating the songs of Nacio Herb Brown, and *The Band Wagon* (1953), again contributing the screenplay which was peppered with the songs of Arthur Schwartz and Howard Dietz. For *It's Always Fair Weather* (1955) they wrote screenplay and lyrics (music by André Previn) and later in the 50s and into the 60s wrote screenplays for *Auntie Mame* (1958) and *Bells Are Ringing* (1960), among others. From the late 50s they also performed their own accomplished two-person stage show. After writing the libretto for *Applause* (1970) they continued to make sporadic returns to the musical stage with *Lorelei* (1974), *On The Twentieth Century* (1978), *A Doll's Life* (1982) and *The Will Rogers Follies* (1991). Among their best-known songs are 'Just In Time', 'Make Someone Happy', 'Lonely Town', 'Some Other Time', 'Never-Never Land', 'It's Love', 'Long Before I Knew You', 'Lucky To Be Me', 'New York, New York', 'The Party's Over' and The Right Girl For Me'. Regarded as the longest-running creative partnership in theatre history, Comden and Green have gained several Tony Awards, a Grammy and Kennedy Center Awards. They have also been elected to the Songwriters' Hall of Fame and the Theatre Hall of Fame. Albums celebrating their work have been released by Sally Mayes and Blossom Dearie, among others. In 1993, 40 years after they wrote one of their most famous numbers, 'Ohio', for *On The Town*, the Governor of that US State threw an opulent anniversary party, *The Show Must Go On: Fifty Years Of Comden And Green*, in their honour.

● ALBUMS: *A Party With Betty Comden And Adolph Green* (Broadway Angel 1993)★★★★.

● FURTHER READING: *Betty Comden And Adolph Green: A Bio-Bibliography*, Alice M. Robinson. *Off Stage*, Betty Comden.

COME DANCE WITH ME - FRANK SINATRA ★★★★★

On Sinatra's great records of the 50s and early 60s, equal billing should be given to the excellent conductors and arrangers. Through their skills, Sinatra was free to concentrate solely on his own interpretation, and was therefore able to blossom with the confidence that the great songs he had chosen, together with his voice, would be enhanced by the orchestration. This 1959 album is another in a series of quite brilliant arrangements, giving new life to Johnny Mercer's 'Something's Gotta Give', Irving Berlin's 'Cheek To

Cheek' and George Weiss's 'Too Close For Comfort'. It reached number 2 in both the USA and UK. In keeping with other reissues, the CD features four bonus tracks, including 'It All Depends On You'.

● TRACKS: *Come Dance With Me; Something's Gotta Give; Just In Time; Dancing In The Dark; Too Close For Comfort; I Could Have Danced All Night; Saturday Night Is The Loneliest Night Of The Week; Day In, Day Out; Cheek To Cheek; Baubles, Bangles And Beads; The Song Is You; Last Dance.*

COME FLY WITH ME · FRANK SINATRA
★★★★★

Come Fly With Me is a concept album that has endured, featuring a selection of songs that takes the listener around the world in 45 minutes. Some of Sinatra's finest moments are on this 1958 release, notably with Sammy Cahn and Jimmy Van Heusen's uplifting 'Come Fly With Me' and 'It's Nice To Go Trav'ling'. This was Sinatra's first album to be arranged and conducted by Billy May, a relationship that produced further classic orchestrations. Once again, the CD purchaser in the 90s will greatly benefit from three bonus tracks with Nelson Riddle in charge: 'Chicago', South Of The Border' and 'I Love Paris'. Successful in both the USA (peaking at number 1) and UK (number 2), this album simply delivers happy-go-lucky fare that we all need from time to time.

● TRACKS: *Come Fly With Me; Around The World; Isle Of Capri; Moonlight In Vermont; Autumn In New York; On The Road To Mandalay; Let's Get Away From It All; April In Paris; London By Night; Brazil; Blue Hawaii; It's Nice To Go Trav'ling.*

COMO, PERRY

b. Pierino Como, 18 May 1912, Canonsburg, Pennsylvania, USA. An accomplished popular singer with a warm baritone voice, whose repertoire has included ballads, novelty numbers and singalongs, Como left his home-town barber shop in 1933 and toured with the local band of Freddie Carlone. His big break came in 1936 when he joined trombonist Ted Weems' band and featured on their *Beat The Band* radio show. He left the band when it broke up in 1942, and the following year signed for RCA Records. After minor hits with 'Long Ago And Far Away', 'I'm Gonna Love That Gal' and 'If I Loved You', he topped the US charts in 1945 with 'Till The End Of Time', based on Chopin's 'Polonaise In A-Flat Major'. A comparatively late starter in hit parade terms, he made up for lost time in the late 40s with a string of US hits including 'Did You Ever Get That Feeling In The Moonlight?', 'Dig You Later (A Hubba-Hubba-Hubba)', 'I'm Always Chasing Rainbows' (adapted from another Chopin theme), 'You Won't Be Satisfied (Until You Break My Heart)', 'Prisoner Of Love' (number 1), 'All Through The Day', 'They Say It's Wonderful', 'Surrender' (number 1), 'Chi-Baba, Chi-Baba, (My Baby Go To Sleep)' (number 1), 'When You Were Sweet Sixteen', 'I Wonder Who's Kissing Her Now' (a 1939 recording when Como was with Ted Weems), 'Because' (a 1902 song, originally sung by Enrico Caruso), 'Far Away Places', 'Forever And Ever', 'A-You're Adorable' (a number 1, with the Fontane Sisters), 'Some Enchanted Evening' (number 1) and 'A Dreamer's Holiday'. He also featured regularly on radio programmes, such as his own *Supper Club* series, and made four films, *Something for The Boys* (1944), loosely based on the Cole Porter Broadway show, *Doll Face,*

If I'm Lucky (1946), and the star-studded Richard Rodgers/Lorenz Hart biopic, *Words And Music* (1948). The 50s were even more fruitful years for Como, mainly because of the apparent ease with which he adapted to television. His easy, relaxed singing style coupled with an engaging sense of humour proved ideal for the relatively new medium, and his weekly *Music Hall*, with its theme, 'Dream Along With Me', ran from 1955-63 and is still regarded as the best of its kind. It also inspired the albums *We Get Letters* and *Dear Perry*. In the early 50s, despite the onset of rock 'n' roll, the hits continued with Hoop-Dee-Doo' (number 1) and 'You're Just In Love' (both with the Fontane Sisters), 'Patricia', 'A Bushel And A Peck', 'If', 'Maybe' (with Eddie Fisher), 'Don't Let The Stars Get In Your Eyes' (number 1 in the USA and UK), 'Wild Horses' (adapted From Robert Schumann's 'Wild Horseman'), 'Say You're Mine Again', 'No Other Love' (based on the theme from the 1954 documentary *Victory At Sea*), 'You Alone', 'Wanted' (number 1) and 'Papa Loves Mambo'. During the latter half of the 50s, with the advantage of the television showcase, he still registered strongly in the USA with 'Ko Ko Mo (I Love You So)', 'Tina Marie', 'Hot Diggity (Dog Ziggitty Boom)' (number 1), 'Juke Box Baby', 'More', 'Glendora', 'Round And Round' (number 1), 'Catch A Falling Star' (number 1), 'Magic Moments' (UK number 1 - an early Burt Bacharach and Hal David song) and 'Kewpie Doll'. He also made the UK Top 10 with 'Love Makes The World Go Round', 'Tomboy' and 'Delaware'. Semi-retired during the 60s, he emerged in 1970 to play 'live' for the first time for over 20 years, an event celebrated by the album *Live At The International Hotel Las Vegas*. He then, somewhat surprisingly, embarked on a series of world tours, and had his first hit singles for over a decade with the Mexican song 'It's Impossible', composed by Armando Manzanero, with a new lyric by Sid Wayne, 'And I Love You So' and 'For The Good Times'. At this time Como's record sales were estimated at over 60 million, including 20 gold discs. To many, Como's laid-back approach and many popular television specials, particularly at Christmas, bordered on parody, and yet his immense commercial success is undeniable, and is perhaps one of the reasons when male song stylists are discussed, that he is too often underrated. In the late 80s he was still performing occasionally in Las Vegas, and received media tributes in 1992 on the occasion of his 80th birthday.

● ALBUMS: *Merry Christmas* 10-inch album (RCA Victor 1951)★★★, *TV Favorites* 10-inch album (RCA Victor 1952)★★★, *A Sentimental Date With Perry Como* 10-inch album (RCA Victor 1952)★★★, *Supper Club Favorites* 10-inch album (RCA Victor 1952)★★★, *Hits From Broadway Shows* 10-inch album (RCA Victor 1953)★★★, *Around The Christmas Tree* 10-inch album (RCA Victor 1953)★★★, *I Believe* 10-inch album (RCA Victor 1954)★★★, *So Smooth* (RCA Victor 1955)★★★, *Relaxing With Perry Como* (RCA Victor 1956)★★★, *We Get Letters* (RCA Victor 1957)★★★, *We Get Letters Volume 2* (RCA Victor 1957)★★★, *Merry Christmas Music* (RCA Victor 1957)★★★, *Dream Along With Me* (RCA Camden 1957)★★★, *Saturday Night With Mr. C.* (RCA Victor 1958)★★★, *Dear Perry* (RCA Victor 1958)★★★, *When You Come To The End Of The Day* (RCA Victor 1958)★★★, *Como Swings* (RCA Victor 1959)★★★, *Season's Greetings* (RCA Victor 1959)★★★, *Sing To Me Mr. C.* (RCA 1961)★★★, *For The Young At Heart* (RCA 1961)★★★, *By Request* (RCA 1962)★★★, *The Best Of Irving Berlin's Songs*

From 'Mr. President' (RCA 1962)★★★, *The Songs I Love* (RCA 1963)★★★, *The Scene Changes* (RCA 1965)★★, *Lightly Latin* (RCA 1966)★★, *Perry Como In Italy* (RCA 1966)★★★, *Seattle* (RCA 1969)★★★, *It's Impossible* (RCA 1970)★★★, *I Think Of You* (RCA 1971)★★★, *And I Love You So* (RCA 1973)★★★, *Perry* (RCA 1974)★★★, *Just Out Of Reach* (RCA 1975)★★, *Best Of British* (RCA 1977)★★★, *Something Special* (RCA 1978)★★★, *Especially For You* (RCA 1980)★★★, *Perry Como* (RCA 1980)★★★, *Live On Tour* (RCA 1981)★★, *So It Goes* (RCA 1983)★★, *Perry Como Today* (RCA 1987)★★★, *Take It Easy* (RCA 1990)★★★.

● COMPILATIONS: *Como's Golden Records* (RCA Victor 1954/58)★★★★, *Memories Are Made Of Hits* (RCA 1975)★★★★, *40 Greatest Hits* (K-Tel 1975)★★★★, *A Legendary Performer* (RCA 1976)★★★, *The First Thirty Years* 4-LP box set (RCA 1979)★★★, *The Perry Como Christmas Collection* (Pickwick 1979)★★★, *20 Greatest Hits (Volume 1)* (RCA 1982)★★★, *20 Greatest Hits (Volume 2)* (RCA 1982)★★★, *For The Good Times* (Telstar 1983)★★★★, *16 Million Hits* (RCA Germany 1983)★★★★, with the Ted Weems Orchestra *The Young Perry Como (1936-41)* (MCA 1984)★★, *Pure Gold* (RCA 1984)★★★★, *The Best Of Times* (RCA 1986)★★★, *Jukebox Baby* (Bear Family 1988)★★★, *Collection* (Castle 1988)★★★★, *The Living Legend* (1992)★★★.

● VIDEOS: *The Best Of Perry Como Volume 2* (Warner Music Video 1992), *Perry Como's Christmas Concert* (Teal 1994), *Perry Como's Christmas Classics* (Haber Video 1996).

COMPAGNONS DE LA CHANSON

This French male vocal group were Edith Piaf's original accompanists, and featured on one of her best-known numbers, 'Les Trois Cloches', composed by Jean Villard in 1945. Later, they recorded it under their own name, and when an English lyric by Bert Reisfeld was added in 1948, the song was retitled 'The Three Bells (The Jimmy Brown Song)'. Their re-recorded Anglicized version reached the UK chart in 1959. Apparently, it was their version, sung on the *Ed Sullivan Show* in 1951, that inspired US group the Browns to record it, thereby giving themselves a number 1 hit. Composer Jean Villard used the same melody in 1945 for 'While The Angelus Was Ringing', which had a lyric by the American songwriter Dick Manning.

CONCERT BY THE SEA - ERROLL GARNER ★★★★★

Garner's place in the history of jazz piano is unusual. He demonstrates no obvious influences of any other pianist, he appears to have influenced no-one, and yet his is such a thoroughly engaging, happy, always enjoyable style. On this 1956 recording, he deftly picks his way through a sprightly selection of songs. Throughout, 'the Elf' happily indulges his penchant for lengthy introductions that defy listeners to identify the coming tune, yet, when he finally arrives at the song as the composer wrote it, everything seems just right. This release offers ageless music in an impishly droll style that defies categorization, in Garner's own inimitable style. *Concert By The Sea* reached number 12 in the US chart.

● TRACKS: *I'll Remember April; Teach Me Tonight; Mambo Carmel; It's Alright With Me; Red Top; April In Paris; They Can't Take That Away From Me; Where Or When; Erroll's Theme.*

CONWAY, RUSS

b. Trevor Stanford, 2 September 1925, Bristol, Avon, England. Conway not only played the piano as a young boy, but won a scholarship to join the choir at the Bristol Cathedral School. He was conscripted into the Royal Navy in 1942 and, during a varied career, was awarded the DSM for service during campaigns in the Mediterranean and Aegean sea and lost part of a finger while using a bread slicer. In 1955, following spells in the post-war Merchant Navy, Conway played piano in nightclubs, worked as rehearsal pianist for choreographer Irving Davies and audition pianist for Columbia (UK) record producer Norman Newell. He later served as accompanist for star singers such as Dennis Lotis, Gracie Fields and Joan Regan. Signed to Columbia, his first hit, 'Party Pops', in 1957, was an instrumental medley of standard songs. It was the first of 20 UK chart entries featuring his catchy piano-playing through to 1963, including two number 1 singles, 'Side Saddle' and 'Roulette', and Top 10 entries 'China Tea' and 'Snowcoach', all of which were his own compositions. He headlined several times at the London Palladium, had his own television show and regularly guested on others, including the Billy Cotton Band Show on BBC television where his cross-talk and vocal duets with the host revealed a genuine flair for comedy and an acceptable light baritone voice. During the 60s his career was marred by ill health, a nervous breakdown while on stage and a mild stroke which prevented him from working during 1968-1971. Since then, still an anachronism, his combination of lively tunes, light classical themes and shy smile have consistently proved a big draw abroad and in the UK, where he promotes his own nostalgia package shows and charity concerts. After fighting stomach cancer for five years, in June 1994 Conway was told by doctors that he was in good health. Two years earlier he had been awarded the Lord Mayor of Bristol's Medal for his contributions to popular music and the cancer fund he set up after learning that he had the disease. Early in 1995, Conway's career was under threat once more after he trapped a thumb in the door of his Rolls Royce car.

● ALBUMS: *Pack Up Your Troubles* (Columbia 1958)★★★, *Songs To Sing In Your Bath* (Columbia 1958)★★★, *Family Favourites* (Columbia 1959)★★★, *Time To Celebrate* (Columbia 1959)★★★, *My Concerto For You* (Columbia 1960)★★★, *Party Time* (Columbia 1960)★★★, *At The Theatre* (Columbia 1961)★★★, *At The Cinema* (Columbia 1961)★★★, *Happy Days* (Columbia 1961)★★★, *Concerto For Dreamers* (Columbia 1962)★★★, *Russ Conway's Trad Party* (Columbia 1962)★★★, *Something For Mum* (Columbia 1963)★★★, *Enjoy Yourself* (Columbia 1964)★★★, *Concerto For Lovers* (Columbia 1964)★★★, *Once More It's Party Time* (Columbia 1965)★★★, *Pop-A-Conway* (Columbia 1966)★★★, *Concerto For Memories* (Columbia 1966)★★★, *Russ Hour* (Columbia 1966)★★★, *New Side Of Russ Conway* (Chapter 1 1971)★★★, *The One And Only* (MFP 1979)★★★, *Always You And Me* (MFP 1981)★★★, *A Long Time Ago* (Churchill 1986)★★★.

● COMPILATIONS: *Songs From Stage And Screen* (Golden Hour 1974)★★★, *The Very Best Of Russ Conway* (EMI 1976)★★★★, *24 Piano Greats* (Ronco 1977)★★★, *Russ Conway Playing Great Piano Hits* (1980)★★★, *The Two Sides Of Russ Conway* (Platinum 1986)★★★, *Greatest Hits* (Hour Of Pleasure 1986)★★★★, *The Magic Piano Of Russ Conway*

(Ditto 1988)★★★, *The EMI Years: The Best Of Russ Conway* (EMI 1989)★★★★, *The EP Collection* (See For Miles 1991)★★★.
● FILMS: *It's All Happening* (1963).

COOK, BARBARA

b. 25 October 1927, Atlanta, Georgia, USA. A celebrated actress and singer, with a style that, as one critic expressed it, 'marries a beautiful and undiminished soprano voice to nuance-rich phrasing and a skilled actress's emotional interpretation'. Cook's first professional engagement was at New York's Blue Angel club in 1950, where she sang mainly standards by the likes of George Gershwin, Jerome Kern and Rodgers And Hart. A year later she was starring on Broadway as Sandy in the offbeat, short-lived musical *Flahooley*. In 1953 she played Ado Annie in a City Centre revival of *Oklahoma!*, followed by a national tour. The following year her performance as Carrie Pipperidge in another Richard Rodgers/Oscar Hammerstein II revival, *Carousel*, gained her the role of Hilda Miller in *Plain And Fancy* which ran for over 400 performances. In 1956 she introduced Leonard Bernstein and Richard Wilbur's 'Glitter And Be Gay' in *Candide*, 'the season's most interesting failure', and, soon afterwards, played the lead in yet another New York revival of *Carousel*, with Howard Keel. The highlight of her early career came in 1957 when she appeared with Robert Preston in Meredith Willson's *The Music Man*, which ran for over 1,300 performances. In the role of Marian Paroo, the stern librarian, for which she won a Tony Award, Cook excelled with numbers such as 'Till There Was You', 'Goodnight My Someone' and 'Will I Ever Tell You', and is reported to have been 'devastated' when Shirley Jones played Marian in the 1962 movie version. After gaining good reviews as a youthful Anna in *The King And I* at the City Centre, *The Gay Life* (1961) gave Cook her most prestigious role to date, with a superior Arthur Schwartz and Howard Dietz score containing 'Something You Never Had Before', 'Is She Waiting There For You?' and 'Magic Moment'. Two years later, she appeared in *She Loves Me*. Bock and Harnick's score gave her the delightful 'Will He Like Me?', 'Dear Friend' and 'Ice Cream', and was released on a double album. This was Cook's final major Broadway musical, although she did appear in the less successful *Something More!* (1964) and *The Grass Harp* (1971). She had been Broadway's favourite ingénue for 10 years and, for a while, continued to tour in well-received revivals such as *Showboat* (1966). She also appeared in several straight plays including *Any Wednesday* and *Little Murders*. In 1973, after starring in a stage show entitled *The Gershwin Years*, she started playing clubs again, including the Brothers & Sisters in New York. In 1975 she made her concert debut at Carnegie Hall in New York, and received a rapturous reception that was repeated in large cities throughout the USA. In complete contrast, on her first visit to the UK in the late 70s she performed at the small Country Cousin club in London, where she had to compete with interference on the PA system from an adjoining taxi cab company. She was back at Carnegie Hall again in 1980 (*It's Better With A Band*) with a programme that included some contemporary material along with the show tunes, and an amusing item co-written by her musical director, Wally Harper, called 'The Ingenue' ('The parts for boys you play against, they bring out all the clones to

do/And movie roles you live to play, they give to Shirley Jones to do!'). In 1985 Cook's career received an enormous boost when she appeared in two performances of *Follies In Concert With The New York Philharmonic*, along with other Broadway luminaries such as Lee Remick, George Hearn, Elaine Stritch and Carol Burnett. She scored a personal triumph with the Stephen Sondheim numbers 'Losing My Mind', 'The Girl Upstairs', 'Who's That Woman?' and 'In Buddy's Eyes'. In September 1986, her one-woman show, *Wait 'Til You See Her*, reached London's West End and was acclaimed by critics and public alike. In the following year, she was back on Broadway in *A Concert For The Theatre*, for which she received a Drama Desk Award, and continued to play other US venues. Also in 1987, on a recording of *Carousel* produced by Thomas Z. Shepard, she was joined by Sarah Brightman and opera singers Maureen Forrester, David Rendall and Samuel Ramey, and accompanied by the Royal Philharmonic Orchestra. A hiccup occurred in the UK in 1988 when she withdrew from the Royal Shakespeare Company's touring production of the Broadway-bound musical *Carrie*, but she continues to delight international concert and cabaret audiences well into the 90s. In 1994 Barbara Cook was inducted into Broadway's Hall Of Fame.
● ALBUMS: *Songs Of Perfect Propriety* (Urania 1958)★★★, *From The Heart* (Urania 1959)★★★, *Barbara Cook At Carnegie Hall* (Columbia 1975)★★★★, *As Of Today* (Columbia 1977)★★★, *It's Better With A Band* (MMG 1981)★★★, *Sings The Walt Disney Song Book* (MCA 1988)★★★, *Close As Pages In A Book* (DRG 1993)★★★, *A Cabaret Christmas* (DRG 1993)★★★, *Thumbelina* (SBK 1994)★★★, *Live From London* (DRG 1994)★★★, *The Broadway Years* (Kock 1995)★★★, *Oscar Winners: The Lyrics Of Oscar Hammerstein II* (DRG 1997)★★★, and Original Cast and Ben Bagley 'Revisited' albums.

COOPER, TRENTON

b. 1923, Hope, Arkansas, USA. This talented blues pianist played in his college orchestra before joining an R&B band led by Jay Franks. The band also featured Nelson Carson on guitar, and Cooper co-wrote Franks's 'Fish Tail'. After 1950 Cooper played in the Drops Of Joy, the R&B combo led by Jimmy Liggins. When he was traced by blues historian Jim O'Neal in 1976, he was the director of the Co-operative Education office at the University of Arkansas in Pine Bluff.
● COMPILATIONS: with various artists *Keep It To Yourself - Arkansas Blues, Volume 1* (1983)★★★.

COPELAND, KEN

b. 1937, Texas, USA. Ken Copeland placed one single, 'Pledge Of Love', at number 12 in the *Billboard* chart in 1957, before resurfacing in the late 60s as a successful evangelist. Copeland was leading his band, the Minits, in Gainesville, Texas, USA, when approached by a small record label owner to make some recordings. The group's first single failed but the second, 'Pledge Of Love', was a local success, and was picked up by the national Imperial Records label. Although first pressings of the record credited the Minits, the hit version went out solely under Copeland's name. His subsequent recordings failed and in 1968 he established the Kenneth Copeland Ministries in Fort Worth, Texas. His television broadcasts, gospel recordings and even a magazine are said to have millions of followers in the USA.

CORAL RECORDS

Founded in 1949, Coral was a wholly owned subsidiary of the American Decca Records. It was inaugurated as an outlet for R&B, but rather than initiate material, the label became known for its cover versions. MOR-styled recordings by the McGuire Sisters, Steve Lawrence and Teresa Brewer brought Coral a string of US chart entries while Johnny Desmond enjoyed a US smash with 'The Yellow Rose Of Texas' in 1955. However, in 1956 A&R director Dick Jacobs, who recorded several minor hits for the label under his own name, made his first crucial rock 'n' roll signing: the Johnny Burnette Trio. Employing a rockabilly sound similar to that of the Sun label, Burnette recorded a mixture of standards and original material, investing them with an almost uninhibited fervour. These seminal releases were not a commercial success and Burnette was dropped in 1958. By that point Coral had joined Brunswick Records in signing a tape-lease agreement with Norman Petty, an independent producer from Clovis, New Mexico. His protégé, Buddy Holly, recorded for Coral as a solo act, while as a member of the Crickets, his releases appeared on Brunswick. Holly's hits under his own name included 'Peggy Sue' (1957), 'Rave On' (1958) and 'It Doesn't Matter Anymore' (1959), the last of which was a posthumous success following the singer's death in a plane crash. In the UK, recordings by both Holly and the Crickets appeared on Coral. The British outlet was initially aligned with the semi-autonomous Vogue as Vogue-Coral, but achieved an identity in its own right when the former became an outlet for recordings aimed at the West Indian market. However, the era of Coral as an active force was drawing to a close. Holly's death was followed by the defection of the Crickets for Liberty. Label producer Bob Thiele switched from pop to jazz at Impulse! Records and although repackages kept the Coral name afloat, the halcyon days were ending. Pop singer Bobbi Martin gave Coral three minor hits during 1964/5 but Coral ceased trading when the entire US Decca group was taken over by MCA in 1968.

CORNELL, DON

b. 1924, New York City, New York, USA. During the late 30s Cornell sang and played guitar with several bands, including Lennie Hayton, Red Nichols and Mickey Alpert, before joining Sammy Kaye, mainly as a guitar player, in 1942. He stayed with Kaye until 1950, with a break for military service, and sang on several of the band's hits, including 'I Left My Heart At The Stage Door Canteen', 'Tell Me A Story' and 'It Isn't Fair' (a million-seller), all for RCA Victor. His first solo success, 'I Need You So', was also on that label, but his move to Coral in 1951 produced several winners including 'I'll Walk Alone', 'I', (the shortest song title ever charted), 'Heart Of My Heart', accompanied by Alan Dale and ex-Glenn Miller vocalist Johnny Desmond, and two more gold discs with 'I'm Yours' and 'Hold My Hand'. The latter song was featured in the 1954 movie *Susan Slept Here* and was nominated for an Academy Award, only to be beaten by 'Three Coins In The Fountain'. Later in the 50s Cornell had several US Top 30 entries including 'Stranger In Paradise', 'Most Of All', 'The Bible Tells Me So', 'Love Is A Many Splendoured Thing' and 'Young Abe Lincoln'. After that the hits dried up, but Cornell's high baritone voice remained in demand for club and theatre work.
● ALBUMS: *Don Cornell For You* (Vogue Coral 1954)★★★,

Let's Get Lost (Coral 1956)★★★, *For Teenagers Only!* (Coral 1957)★★★, *Don Cornell* (1959)★★, *Don Cornell Sings Love Songs* (Signature 1962)★★, *I Wish You Love* (1966)★★★.
● COMPILATIONS: *Don Cornell's Great Hits* (Dot 1959)★★★.

CORONETS

This vocal group from Cleveland, Ohio, USA, comprised Charles Carruthers (lead), Lester Russaw (first tenor), Sam Griggs (second tenor), George Lewis (second tenor), William Griggs (bass) and Tony King (guitarist). The Coronets, like the Moonglows, tried to grab the brass ring of success, but unlike their more famous Cleveland counterparts never went beyond one-hit-wonderdom. Their lone success, the languorous ballad, 'Nadine' (number 3 R&B), became a staple of Chess anthology albums and in 1970 was revived by the Dells for Chess Records with great success. The Coronets have their origin in Thomas Edison High School in Cleveland, and began their foray into the entertainment world in early 1953 with only four songs in their repertoire. One was an original, 'Nadine' (written by Carruthers). They took the demo to Alan Freed, who then introduced them to Chess. The failure of subsequent releases and the draft served to splinter the group. The Coronets in later regroupings released records in Stirling and RCA's Groove subsidiary in 1955, and on the Job label in 1960, but the group could not recapture the magic that made 'Nadine' a memorable hit.

COSTA, DON

b. 10 June 1925, Boston, Massachusetts, USA, d. 19 January 1983, New York, USA. The youngest of five children, Costa taught himself to play the guitar by the age of eight, and at 15 was a member of the CBS radio orchestra in Boston. In his spare time he loved to dance the jitterbug. After starting as a musical arranger in radio in the 40s, Costa moved into the recording business as an A&R executive, working with new and established artists, and choosing their material. In 1957, while at ABC-Paramount, he launched Paul Anka's career, and later worked with a variety of artists including Little Anthony, Dean Martin, Frankie Avalon, Barbra Streisand, Steve Lawrence and the Osmonds. In the 60s he formed DCP (Don Costa Productions) and collaborated with Frank Sinatra as producer, arranger and conductor on several albums including *Sinatra & Strings*, *My Way* and *Cycles*. In 1973, with Gordon Jenkins, Costa conducted Sinatra's television special *Ol' Blue Eyes Is Back*. He is reputed to have conducted and arranged over 200 hit records in his career, working with many kinds of music including C&W, jazz, rock, disco and film music. In 1960 he entered the US Top 30 singles chart with 'Theme From *The Unforgiven* (The Need For Love)' and the Academy Award-winning song 'Never On Sunday'. His own film scores include *Rough Night In Jericho* (1967), *Madigan* (1968) and *The Impossible Years* (1968). Among his many successful albums were *101 Strings Play Million Seller Hits*, *Theme From The Misfits*, *I'll Walk The Line* and *Never On Sunday*. One of his last albums, *Out Here On My Own*, was recorded with his daughter Nikka, and they were also working on another at the time of his death.
● ALBUMS: *Don Costa Conducts His 15 Hits* (ABC-Paramount 1961)★★★.

COTTON, BILLY

b. 6 May 1899, Westminster, London, England, d. 25 March 1969, London, England. The youngest of 10 children, Cotton sang solo treble in the choir of St. Margaret's Church, Westminster. In 1914 he joined the army as a bugler-drummer and served in the Dardanelles Campaign in Gallipoli before returning to the UK and spending the rest of World War I in the Royal Flying Corps. After the war he drove London buses, played for Brentford Football Club as an amateur (and later, for the then Athenian league club Wimbledon), and raced motorcycles and cars. In the early 20s he played drums for various groups, including the Laurie Johnson Band at the 1924 British Empire Exhibition at Wembley and then formed his own London Savannah Band. Cotton gave up the drumstool to front the band in 1925 when Clem Bernard joined the organization as pianist/arranger and stayed for over 40 years as the musical brain behind the Cotton band. Initially they played the big dancehalls, including the Astoria in London's Charing Cross Road, and top nightclubs such as Ciro's, in both London and Paris. During the 30s they played in cine-variety before becoming a theatre showband and introducing broad visual humour and saucy songs. Their records reflected the change with such songs as 'Bessie Couldn't Help It', 'She Was Only Somebody's Daughter' and 'They All Start Whistling At Mary', besides the 'hotter' numbers, 'New Tiger Rag', 'Truckin'' and 'Shine', which featured Nat Gonella, Teddy Foster and the American trombonist and skilful tap-dancer Ellis Jackson. Sixteen examples of Cotton's 30s style can be found on *The Golden Age Of Billy Cotton*. During World War II, Cotton toured France with ENSA and was put in charge of Air Training Corps entertainment, besides touring the music halls. After the war he boosted his declining variety theatre bookings with *Wakey Wakey!!*, a Sunday lunchtime BBC radio programme that became a national institution and ran for over 20 years. The material was much the same as ever, including 'Oh, Oh, Oh, Oh, What A Referee', 'Oh, Nicholas, Don't Be So Ridiculous', 'Forty Fousand Fevvers On A Frush', 'The Dambusters March', 'The Sunshine Of Your Smile', 'Fall In And Follow Me', 'Maybe It's Because I'm A Londoner', all heralded by his theme, 'Somebody Stole My Gal'. These tunes were played and sung by regulars Doreen Stevens, Johnny Johnson, Rita Williams and the Highlights, Kathy Kaye, trumpeter Grisha Farfel and vocalist/general all-rounder Alan Breeze, ever-present with Cotton since the early 30s. During the 50s he had chart hits with 'In A Golden Coach' (to celebrate the 1953 Coronation), 'I Saw Mommy Kissing Santa Claus', 'Friends And Neighbours' and 'Puttin' On The Style'. In 1957, following an unsatisfactory flirtation with commercial television, *The Billy Cotton Band Show* came to BBC Television. At 60 years of age and substantially built, Cotton danced with the Silhouettes, a line of dancing girls, sang with and insulted his favourite guest stars, Russ Conway, Alma Cogan and Max Bygraves, conducted the band, and joined in throwing cotton-wool balls into the audience during one of their favourite numbers, 'I've Got A Lovely Bunch Of Coconuts'. By now he was one of the most popular figures in UK light entertainment. Some of the shows were produced by Cotton's son, Bill Jnr., who later became Controller of BBC Television. In 1962 Cotton Snr. was voted 'Show Business Personality Of The Year'. He also suffered a stroke, which slowed him down, although he did

work again during the 60s until his untimely death while watching a boxing match at Wembley in March 1969. He was buried at St. Margaret's Church where he had once been a choirboy.

● ALBUMS: *Soldiers Of The Queen* (Decca 1953)★★, *Wakey Wakey!* i (Decca 1954)★★★, *Wakey Wakey!* ii (Columbia 1961)★★★.
● COMPILATIONS: *The World Of Billy Cotton* (Decca 1969)★★★, *The World Of Billy Cotton, Volume Two* (Decca 1971)★★★, *Billy Cotton* (EMI 1971)★★★, *That Rhythm Man 1928-31* (Saville 1982)★★★, *Rock Your Cares Away* (Joy 1983)★★★, *Let's All Join In* (Bulldog 1983)★★★, *Sing A New Song 1930-32* (Saville 1983)★★★, *The Golden Age Of Billy Cotton* (Golden Age 1984)★★★, *Wakee Wakee!* (Living Era 1985)★★★, *Somebody Stole My Gal* (Old Bean 1986)★★★, *Crazy Weather* (Happy Days 1986)★★★, *Nobody's Sweetheart* (1987)★★★, *The Things I Love* (1994)★★★.
● FURTHER READING: *I Did It My Way*, Billy Cotton.

COUNTRY JIM

b. Jim Bledsoe, *c.*1925, near Shreveport, Louisiana, USA. A somewhat obscure character, Bledsoe made several records in Shreveport, in 1949-50. As the pseudonym suggests, his music was down-home country blues, accompanied only by his guitar, a string bass, and occasional drums. His first record was issued on the local Pacemaker label, under the name Hot Rod Happy, but the later ones appeared on Imperial and had wider distribution. A year or so later, he completed a couple of long sessions for the Specialty company, but nothing was issued at the time, although a few sides appeared on albums in the 70s.
● COMPILATIONS: *Country Blues* (1973)★★★, *Down South Blues* (1977)★★★.

COURTNEIDGE, CICELY

b. Esmeralda Cicely Courtneidge, 1 April 1893, Sydney, Australia, d. 26 April 1980, London, England. Her father, actor, producer and writer Robert Courtneidge, was appearing in the operetta *Esmeralda* when she was born, hence the name. Back in Britain she trained for the stage and at the age of 10 appeared as Fairy Peaseblossom in *Midsummer Night's Dream*, followed by her father's production of *The Arcadians* in 1909. She made her first records in 1911, singing selections from the show in which she was appearing, *(The) Mousme*. Courtneidge married musical comedy star Jack Hulbert in 1914, and while he was engaged in World War I she toured the music halls as a male impersonator and somewhat risqué comedienne. After appearing in several shows together, Courtneidge and Hulbert made their first big impact as a team in the 1925 revue *By The Way*, with music by Vivian Ellis. It ran for over 300 performances before transferring to New York. *Lido Lady*, in 1926, with a Richard Rodgers/Lorenz Hart score, and *Clowns In Clover*, which opened in 1927 and ran for two years, confirmed their enormous popularity in London's West End. By now, Hulbert was also writing and producing. The team split up temporarily, and while he was appearing with Sophie Tucker in the musical play *Follow A Star*, Courtneidge was considered to be at her best in the Vivian Ellis revue *Folly To Be Wise*. For most of the 30s Courtneidge concentrated on making films such as *Ghost Train*, *Jack's The Boy*, *Aunt Sally*, *Soldiers Of The King*, *Me And Marlborough* and *Take My Tip*.

She returned to the stage in 1937 in *Hide And Seek* and in the following year the Hulberts reunited for one of their biggest successes, *Under Your Hat*, yet again with music and lyrics by Vivian Ellis. It ran for over two years and was filmed in 1940. During World War II the team had substantial runs in *Full Swing* and their last musical show on the London stage together, *Something In The Air*, as well as undertaking extensive ENSA tours. After the war Courtneidge starred in *Her Excellency*, and *Under The Counter* in London and New York, where it attracted extremely hostile reviews. In 1951 she undertook probably the best role of her career, playing Gay Davenport in the satirical backstage musical play *Gay's The Word*, by Ivor Novello and Alan Melville. It presented her with several good songs including 'Guards Are On Parade', 'It's Bound To Be Right On The Night' and 'Vitality', a number that epitomized her stage persona throughout her long career. The show ran at the Saville Theatre for 504 performances, and was Novello's last - he died three weeks after the opening. Courtneidge's final West End musical was *High Spirits* in 1964, a musical version of Noël Coward's 1941 play *Blithe Spirit*. Its songs did not suit her as well as others she had introduced over the years, such as 'The King's Horses', 'Home', 'There's Something About A Soldier', 'We'll All Go Riding On A Rainbow' and 'I Was Anything But Sentimental'. During the 60s and 70s she toured in plays and revues including, with Hulbert, the semi-autobiographical *Once More With Music*. She also appeared in several more films including a critically acclaimed character part in Bryan Forbes' *The L-Shaped Room* (1963), and cameos in *Those Magnificent Men In Their Flying Machines* (1965), *The Wrong Box* (1966) and *Not Now Darling* (1972). The latter was released when she was aged 80. In the same year she was created a Dame of the British Empire. In 1986, Courtneidge's history reached a new generation when her 'Take Me Back To Dear Old Blighty' was used as the opening for the Smiths' album *The Queen Is Dead*. In 1995 a tribute show entitled *Vitality*, written by and starring Helen Fraser, was presented on the London Fringe.

● ALBUMS: *The Golden Age Of Jack Hulbert And Cicely Courtneidge* (Golden Age 1984)★★★★.

● FURTHER READING: *The Little Woman's Always Right*, Jack Hulbert. *Cicely: An Autobiography*, Cicely Courtneidge.

COX, HARRY

b. 10 October 1885, Barton Turf, near Great Yarmouth, Norfolk, England, d. 6 May 1971, Catfield, Norfolk, England. One of a family of 13, he learned many of his songs from his father, a singer and dancer. His grandfather had been a farm worker, like Cox, but his father went to sea as a young man, learning many of his songs there, and living till the age of 92. Cox started singing in pubs all over Broadland (the area in Norfolk known as the Norfolk Broads) when he was about 11 years old, along with his father who played fiddle. Gradually, he learned more songs and was asked to sing more often. Over the years, Cox collected something over 100 local songs, which would otherwise have been lost. It was partly due to this that Cox was acclaimed as 'The Father of East Anglian Folk Music'. He recorded numerous tracks for compilation folk albums including *Folk Song Today*, released by EMI in 1956, on which he sang 'Foggy Dew'. EMI also released an EP of Cox, *Foggy Dew*, in 1960. *Seventeen Come Sunday* consisted of recordings made by Peter Kennedy

between 1953 and 1956. In 1970, Cox was honoured with the Gold Badge of the English Folk Dance and Song Society (EFDSS) for his services to folk music. He died the following year.

● ALBUMS: *Folk Songs-England* (BBC 1956)★★★★, *Harry Cox English Folk Singer* (EFDSS 1965)★★★★, *Harry Cox Sings English Love Songs* (DTS Records 1965)★★★, *Seventeen Come Sunday* (Folktracks 1975)★★★, *The Barley Straw* (Folktracks 1975)★★★★.

CRAWFORD, SUGARBOY

b. James Crawford, 12 October 1934, New Orleans, Louisiana, USA. Responsible for one of the two anthems of New Orleans' Mardi Gras festival, Crawford's career was cut short when he was assaulted by a policeman. A self-taught pianist, his career began when he and some schoolfriends started an informal band that came to the attention of disc jockey Dr. Daddy-O. He named them the Chapaka Shaweez, after the Creole title of one of their tunes, which translated as 'We are not raccoons'. He also introduced them to Dave Bartholomew, who produced them as the Sha-Weez for Aladdin in November 1952. A year later, Crawford And His Cane Cutters, featuring a young Snooks Eaglin on guitar, recorded 'Jock-O-Mo' for Checker, which with the Hawketts' 1955 hit, 'Mardi Gras Mambo', helped to define the city's festivities. Further Checker sessions only produced one more single, after which Bartholomew signed Crawford to Imperial. None of his four singles made much impression and he made just three singles between 1959 and 1962, for Jin, Ace and Peacock. He and his band were in Monroe on the way to a gig when the police accused him of drink-driving. In the altercation that followed, he was pistol-whipped about the head; the blow rendered him paralysed for a year and effectively ended his career. In 1965, three high-school students called the Dixie-Cups appropriated his finest moment, called it 'Iko Iko', and thereby mugged Crawford a second time.

● COMPILATIONS: *Sugarboy Crawford* (Chess 1976)★★★, *New Orleans Classics* (Pathe Marconi 1985)★★★.

CRESTS

Formed in New York City, USA, in 1956, the Crests soon became one of the most successful of the 'integrated' doo-wop groups of the period, after being discovered by Al Browne. Headed by the lead tenor of Johnny Mastro (b. Johnny Mastrangelo, 7 May 1930, USA), the rest of the band comprised Harold Torres, Talmadge Gough, J.T. Carter and Patricia Van Dross. By 1957 they were recording for Joyce Records and achieved their first minor pop hit with 'Sweetest One'. Moving to the new Coed label, the Crests (without Van Dross) recorded their signature tune and one of doo-wop's enduring classics, '16 Candles', a heartfelt and beautifully orchestrated ballad. It became a national pop hit at number 2 in the *Billboard* charts, paving the way for further R&B and pop successes such as 'Six Nights A Week', 'The Angels Listened In' and 'Step By Step'. At this time the band were almost permanently on the road. Following 'Trouble In Paradise' in 1960, the band's final two chart singles would be credited to The Crests featuring Johnny Mastro. However, this was evidently not enough to satisfy their label, Coed, whose priority now was to launch the singer as a solo artist. Mastro's decision to go solo in 1960 (subsequently calling himself Johnny Maestro) weakened the band, although they did continue with James Ancrum in his stead. Their former vocalist made the charts with 'Model Girl', still for Coed, in the following year, before re-emerging as leader of Brooklyn Bridge, an 11-piece doo-wop group who are best remembered for their 1968 single 'Worst That Could Happen'. After 'Little Miracles' failed to break the *Billboard* Top 100 (the first such failure for the Crests in 10 singles), Gough moved to Detroit and a job with General Motors. He was replaced by Gary Lewis. However, the Crests were now entangled in legal disputes with Coed over the ownership of their name. They eventually moved to Selma, although the songs made available to the group were now of significantly inferior quality, including 'You Blew Out The Candles', a blatant attempt to revisit the success of '16 Candles'. The band continued to tour throughout the 60s, though Torres had left to become a jeweller, leaving a core of Carter, Lewis and Ancrum. Later line-ups were organized by Carter for lounge sessions (although there are no recordings from this period), and in June 1987 the original line-up (minus Van Dross) was re-formed for a show in Peepskill, New York.

● COMPILATIONS: *The Best Of The Crests* (Coed 1960)★★★★, *Crests Sing All Biggies* (Coed 1985)★★★, *16 Fabulous Hits* (Coed 1988)★★★, *Best Of The Crests* (Rhino 1990)★★★★, *Best Of The Rest* (Coed 1991)★★★.

CREW-CUTS

Formed in Toronto, Ontario, Canada, in 1952, the Crew-Cuts were a white vocal quartet that had success in the early 50s by covering black R&B songs. Their version of 'Sh-Boom', originally a number 2 R&B hit for the Chords in 1954, became a number 1 pop hit for the Crew-Cuts, staying in that position for nine weeks and helping to usher in the rock 'n' roll era. The group was comprised of Rudi Maugeri (b. 21 January 1931; baritone), Pat Barrett (b. 15 September 1931; tenor), John Perkins (b. 28 August 1931; lead) and his brother Ray Perkins (b. 28 November 1932; bass), all born in Toronto. The group met at Toronto's Cathedral School, where they all sang in the choir, and decided to form a barber shop-style group. Initially called the Canadaires, the group received its first break in Cleveland, Ohio, USA, where they appeared on Gene Carroll's television programme. After that show they were introduced to the influential local disc jockey Bill Randle, who suggested the name change (after a popular short-cropped hairstyle). Randle introduced the group to Mercury Records, who signed them. Their first recording, an original composition called 'Crazy 'Bout Ya Baby', made the Top 10 in the US charts. Mercury suggested covering 'Sh-Boom' and its massive success led to further cover versions of R&B records by the group, including the Penguins' 'Earth Angel', Nappy Brown's 'Don't Be Angry' and the Nutmegs' 'A Story Untold'. The success of the Crew-Cuts and other white cover artists helped pave the way for recognition and acceptance of the black originators. In addition to 'Sh-Boom', other Top 10 placings were 'Earth Angel' (1955), 'Ko Ko Mo (I Love You So)' (1955) and 'Gum Drop' (1955). The Crew-Cuts placed 14 singles in the charts throughout 1957, moving to RCA Records in 1958; they disbanded in 1963.

● ALBUMS: *The Crew-Cuts On The Campus* (Mercury 1954)★★★, *The Crew-Cuts Go Longhair* (Mercury 1956)★★★, *Crew-Cut Capers* (Mercury 1957)★★★, *Music*

Ala Carte (Mercury 1957)★★★, *Rock And Roll Bash* (Mercury 1957)★★★, *Surprise Package* (RCA Victor 1958)★★★, *The Crew-Cuts Sing!* (RCA Victor 1959)★★★, *You Must Have Been A Beautiful Baby* (RCA Victor 1960)★★★, *The Crew Cuts Sing Out!* (RCA Victor 1960)★★★, *The Crew Cuts Have A Ball And Bowling Tips* (RCA Victor 1960)★★★, *The Crew Cuts* (RCA Victor 1962)★★★, *High School Favorites* (RCA Victor 1962)★★★, *Sing The Masters* (RCA Victor 1962)★★★, *The Crew-Cuts Sing Folk* (RCA Victor 1963)★★.

CRICKETS

An R&B vocal group from the Bronx section of New York City, New York, USA, the members were Grover 'Dean' Barlow (lead), Harold Johnson (tenor, guitar), Eugene Stapleton (tenor), Leon Carter (baritone) and Rodney Jackson (bass). The Crickets' only hit was with 'You're Mine' (number 10 R&B) on the MGM label in 1953. Their lack of success probably stemmed from their pop sound, a sound that was typical for black groups during the 40s when the Ink Spots, Deep River Boys, and Charioteers held sway. However, during 1953-55, when the Crickets were recording, the more bluesy Clovers, Dominoes, and Five Royales were storming up the charts, so to both listeners and radio programmers the Crickets, with their pretty singing and tasteful but thin arrangements, may have sounded dated. Veteran record man Joe Davis produced their sessions both for the MGM label and for his own Davis label. It is fortunate for posterity that Davis was there, because what may not have been commercial in 1953 sounded fabulous decades later to record collectors, making Crickets records prized collector items. The ballads, such as 'Be Faithful', 'You're Mine' and the jump 'My Little Baby's Shoes', were the most desired and the most rewarding.

● COMPILATIONS: *Dreams & Wishes* (Relic 1992)★★★.

CROCKETT, G.L.

b. c.1929, Carrollton, Mississippi, USA, d. 14 February 1967. In the late 50s George L. Crockett was living on Chicago's west side and sitting in as a singer with Magic Sam, Freddie King and others. He made his first record for the Chief label in 1958, later reissued by USA and Checker: 'Look Out Mabel' was a much sought-after item in the late 70s, often cited as the original black rockabilly record. In 1965 he recorded the Jimmy Reed soundalike 'It's A Man Down There' for Four Brothers Records and it was the company's biggest hit (a US R&B Top 10 and pop Top 100). There were two less successful singles before Crockett died of a cerebral haemorrhage in 1967.

● COMPILATIONS: *Chess Rockabillies* one track only (Chess 1978)★★.

CROSBY, BING

b. Harry Lillis Crosby, 3 May 1903, Tacoma, Washington, USA, d. 14 October 1977. One of the most popular vocalists of all time, Crosby picked up his nickname through a childhood love of a strip-cartoon character in a local newspaper. After first singing with a jazz band at high school, he sang at university with a friend, Al Rinker. The duo decided to take a chance on showbusiness success, quit school and called on Rinker's sister, Mildred Bailey, in the hope that she could help them find work. Their hopes were fulfilled and they were soon hired by Paul Whiteman. With the addition of Harry Barris they formed the singing trio the Rhythm Boys, and quickly became one of the major attractions of the Whiteman entertainment package. The popularity of the trio on such recordings as 'Mississippi Mud' and 'I'm Coming Virginia', and an appearance in the film *The King Of Jazz* (1930), gave Crosby an edge when he chose to begin a solo career. The late 20s saw a great increase in the use of microphones in public auditoriums and the widespread use of more sophisticated microphones in recording studios. This allowed singers to adopt a more confidential singing style, which became known as 'crooning'. Of the new breed of crooners, Crosby was by far the most popular and successful. Although never a jazz singer, Crosby worked with many jazzmen, especially during his stint with Whiteman, when his accompanists included Jimmy and Tommy Dorsey, Joe Venuti and Bix Beiderbecke. This early experience, and a sharp awareness of the rhythmic advances of Louis Armstrong, brought Crosby to the forefront of popular American singers in an era when jazz styles were beginning to reshape popular music. Another contributory factor to his rise was the fact that the new singing style was very well suited to radio, which at the time dominated the entertainment industry. He made numerous film appearances and many hundreds of records, several of them massive hits. Indeed, sales of his records eclipsed those of any earlier recording artist and by the 40s, these had helped to establish Crosby as the world's biggest singing star. In contrast, his films were usually frothy affairs and he displayed only limited acting ability. However, in the early 40s his film career took an upswing with a series of comedies in which he co-starred with Bob Hope and Dorothy Lamour, while some good light dramatic roles advanced his career still further. Throughout the 50s Crosby continued to work in radio and television, and made regular concert appearances and still more records. During his radio and television career Crosby often worked with other leading entertainers, among them Al Jolson, Connee Boswell, Dinah Shore, Judy Garland, Armstrong, Hope and his brother, Bob Crosby. By the mid-60s he was content to take things a little easier, although he still made records and personal appearances. Despite his carefree public persona, Crosby was a complex man, difficult to know and understand. As a singer, his seemingly lazy intonation often gave the impression that anyone could sing the way he did, itself a possible factor in his popularity. Nevertheless, his distinctive phrasing was achieved by a good ear, selective taste in building his repertoire, and an acute awareness of what the public wanted. Although his countless fans may well regard it as heresy, Crosby's way with a song was not always what songwriters might have wanted. Indeed, some of Crosby's recordings indicate scant regard for the meanings of lyrics and, unlike Frank Sinatra, for instance, he was never a major interpreter of songs. Despite this casual disregard for the niceties of music and lyrics, many of Crosby's best-known recordings remain definitive by virtue of the highly personal stylistic stamp he placed upon them. Songs such as 'Pennies From Heaven', 'Blue Skies', 'White Christmas', 'The Bells Of St Mary's', 'Moonlight Becomes You', 'Love In Bloom', 'How Deep Is The Ocean', 'The Blue Of The Night' and 'Temptation' became his own. Although Sinatra is the major male song-stylist of American popular music, and also the one who

most influenced other singers, every vocalist who followed Crosby owes him a debt for the manner in which his casual, relaxed approach completely altered audience perceptions of how a singer should behave. Towards the end of his life, Crosby's star had waned but he was still capable of attracting sell-out crowds for his occasional public appearances, even though he preferred to spend as much time as he could on the golf course. It was while playing golf in Spain that he collapsed and died.

● ALBUMS: *Merry Christmas* (Decca 1945)★★★, *Going My Way* film soundtrack (Decca 1945)★★★, *The Bells Of St. Mary's* film soundtrack (Decca 1946)★★★, *Don't Fence Me In* (Decca 1946)★★★, *The Happy Prince* (Decca 1946)★★★, *Road To Utopia* (Decca 1946)★★★, *Stephen Foster Songs* (Decca 1946)★★★, *What So Proudly We Hail* (Decca 1946)★★★, *Favorite Hawaiian Songs Volumes 1 & 2* (Decca 1946)★★★, *Blue Skies* (Decca 1946)★★★, *St. Patrick's Day* (Decca 1947)★★★, *Merry Christmas* (Decca 1948)★★★, *Emperor Waltz* (Decca 1948)★★★, *St. Valentine's Day* (Decca 1948)★★★, *Stardust* (Decca 1948)★★★, *A Connecticut Yankee* (Decca 1949)★★★, *South Pacific* (Decca 1949)★★★, *Christmas Greetings* (Decca 1949)★★★, *Hits From Musical Comedies* (Decca 1949)★★★, *Jerome Kern Songs* (Decca 1949)★★★, with Andrews Sisters *Merry Christmas* (Decca 1949)★★★, *El Bingo* (Decca 1950)★★★, *Drifting And Dreaming* (Decca 1950)★★★, *Auld Lang Syne* (Decca 1950)★★★, *Showboat Selections* (Decca 1950)★★★, *Cole Porter Songs* (Decca 1950)★★★, *Songs By Gershwin* (Decca 1950)★★★, *Holiday Inn* film soundtrack (Decca 1950)★★★, *Blue Of The Night* (Decca 1950)★★★, *Cowboy Songs* (Decca 1950)★★★, *Cowboy Songs, Volume 2* (Decca 1950)★★★, *Bing Sings Hits* (Decca 1950)★★★, *Top O' The Morning* (Decca 1950)★★★, *Mr. Music* (Decca 1950)★★★, *The Small One/The Happy Prince* film soundtrack (Decca 1950)★★★, with Connee Boswell *Bing And Connee* (Decca 1951)★★★, *Hits From Broadway Shows* (Decca 1951)★★★, *Go West, Young Man* (Decca 1951)★★★, *Way Back Home* (Decca 1951)★★★, *Bing Crosby* (Decca 1951)★★★, *Bing And The Dixieland Bands* (Decca 1951)★★★, *Yours Is My Heart Alone* (Decca 1951)★★★, *Country Style* (Decca 1951)★★★, *Down Memory Lane* (Decca 1951)★★★, *Down Memory Lane, Volume 2* (Decca 1951)★★★, *Beloved Hymns* (Decca 1951)★★★, *Bing Sings Victor Herbert* (Decca 1951)★★★, *Ichabod Crane* (Decca 1951)★★★, *Collector's Classics* (Decca 1951)★★★, *Two For Tonight* (Decca 1951)★★★, *Rhythm Of The Range* film soundtrack (Decca 1951)★★★, *Waikiki Wedding* film soundtrack (Decca 1951)★★★, *The Star Maker* film soundtrack (Decca 1951)★★★, *The Road To Singapore* film soundtrack (Decca 1951)★★★, *When Irish Eyes Are Smiling* (Decca 1952)★★★, *Just For You* (Decca 1952)★★★, *The Road To Bali* film soundtrack (Decca 1952)★★, *Song Hits Of Paris/Le Bing* (Decca 1953)★★★, *Country Girl* (Decca 1953)★★★, *Some Fine Old Chestnuts* (Decca 1954)★★★, *A Man Without A Country* (Decca 1954)★★★, *White Christmas* film soundtrack (Decca 1954)★★★★, *Lullabye Time* (Decca 1955)★★★, *Shillelaghs And Shamrocks* (Decca 1956)★★★, *Home On The Range* (Decca 1956)★★★, *Blue Hawaii* (Decca 1956)★★★, *High Tor* film soundtrack (Decca 1956)★★★, *Anything Goes* film soundtrack (Decca 1956)★★★, *Songs I Wish I Had Sung The First Time Around* (Decca 1956)★★★, *Twilight On The Trail* (Decca 1956)★★★, *A Christmas Sing With Bing Around The World*

(Decca 1956)★★★, *High Society* film soundtrack (Capitol 1956)★★★★, *Bing Crosby Sings While Bergman Swings* (Verve 1956)★★★, *New Tricks* (Decca 1957)★★★, *Ali Baba And The Forty Thieves* (Grand Award 1957)★★★, *Christmas Story* (Grand Award 1957)★★★, *Bing With A Beat* (RCA Victor 1957)★★★, *Around The World* (Decca 1958)★★★, *Bing In Paris* (Decca 1958)★★★, *That Christmas Feeling* (Decca 1958)★★★, with Rosemary Clooney *Fancy Meeting You Here* (RCA Victor 1958)★★★★, *Paris Holiday* film soundtrack (United Artists 1958)★★★, *In A Little Spanish Town* (Decca 1959)★★★, *Ichabod* (Decca 1959)★★★, *Young Bing Crosby* (RCA Victor 1959)★★★, with Louis Armstrong *Bing And Satchmo* (MGM 1960)★★★, *High Time* film soundtrack (RCA Victor 1960)★★★, *Join Bing And Sing Along: 33 Great Songs* (Warners 1960)★★★, *Join Bing And Sing Along: 101 Gang Songs* (Warners 1960)★★★, *Join Bing In A Gang Sing Along* (Warners 1961)★★★, *My Golden Favorites* (Decca 1961)★★★, *Easy To Remember* (Decca 1962)★★★, *Pennies From Heaven* (Decca 1962)★★★, *Pocket Full Of Dreams* (Decca 1962)★★★, *East Side Of Heaven* (Decca 1962)★★★, *The Road Begins* (Decca 1962)★★★, *Only Forever* (Decca 1962)★★★, *Swinging On A Star* (Decca 1962)★★★, *Accentuate The Positive* (Decca 1962)★★★, *But Beautiful* (Decca 1962)★★★, *Sunshine Cake* (Decca 1962)★★★, *Cool Of The Evening* (Decca 1962)★★★, *Zing A Little Zong* (Decca 1962)★★★, *Anything Goes* (Decca 1962)★★★, *Holiday In Europe* (Decca 1962)★★★, *The Small One* (Decca 1962)★★★, *The Road To Hong Kong* film soundtrack (Liberty 1962)★★★, *A Southern Memoir* (London 1962)★★★, *Join Bing And Sing Along: 51 Good Time Songs* (Warners 1962)★★★, *On The Happy Side* (Warners 1962)★★★, *I Wish You A Merry Christmas* (Warners 1962)★★★, *Bing Sings The Great Standards* (MGM 1963)★★★, *Songs Everybody Knows* (Decca 1964)★★★, *Return To Paradise Islands* (Reprise 1964)★★★, with Frank Sinatra, Fred Waring *America, I Hear You Singing* (Reprise 1964)★★, *Robin And The Seven Hoods* film soundtrack (Reprise 1964)★★★, with Clooney *That Travellin' Two-Beat* (Capitol 1965)★★★, *Bing Crosby* (MGM 1965)★★★, *Great Country Hits* (Capitol 1965)★★★, *Thoroughly Modern Bing* (Stateside 1968)★★★, *Hey Jude/Hey Bing!!* (Amos 1969)★★★, *Wrap Your Troubles In Dreams* (RCA 1972)★★★, *Bingo Viejo* (London 1975)★★★, *The Dinah Shore-Bing Crosby Shows* (Sunbeam 1975)★★★, *That's What Life Is All About* (United Artists 1975)★★★, with Fred Astaire *A Couple Of Song And Dance Men* (United Artists 1975)★★★, *Feels Good, Feels Right* (Decca 1976)★★★, *Live At The London Palladium* (K-Tel 1976)★★★, *"On The Air"* (Spokane 1976)★★★★, *At My Time Of Life* (United Artists 1976)★★★★, *Beautiful Memories* (United Artists 1976)★★★★, *Kraft Music Hall December 24, 1942* (Spokane 1978)★★★.

● COMPILATIONS: *Crosby Classics, Volume 1* (Columbia 1949)★★★, *Crosby Classics, Volume 2* (Columbia 1950)★★★, *Bing Crosby Volumes 1 & 2* (Brunswick 1950)★★★, *Bing - A Musical Autobiography* 5-LP box set (Decca 1954)★★★, *Old Masters* 3-LP set (Decca 1954)★★★, *Der Bingle* (Columbia 1955)★★★, *Crosby Classics* (Columbia 1955)★★★, *The Voice Of Bing In The 30s* (Brunswick 1955)★★★, *A Musical Autobiography Of Bing Crosby 1927-34* (Decca 1958)★★★, *A Musical Autobiography Of Bing Crosby 1934-41* (Decca 1958)★★★, *A Musical Autobiography Of Bing*

Crosby 1941-44 (Decca 1958)★★★, *A Musical Autobiography Of Bing Crosby 1944-47* (Decca 1958)★★★, *A Musical Autobiography Of Bing Crosby, 1947-53* (Decca 1958)★★★, *The Very Best Of* (MGM 1964)★★★, *The Best Of Bing Crosby* (Decca 1965)★★★, *The Bing Crosby Story - Volume 1: Early Jazz Years 1928-32* (Columbia 1968)★★★, *Bing Crosby Remembered: A CSP Treasury* (Fairway 1977)★★★, *Bing Crosby's Greatest Hits* (MCA 1977)★★★★, *Seasons* (Polydor 1977)★★★, *A Legendary Performer* (RCA 1977)★★★★, *Crosby Classics Volume 3* (Capitol 1977)★★★★, *A Bing Crosby Collection Volumes 1 & 2* (Columbia 1978)★★★★, *Christmas With Bing* (Reader's Digest 1980)★★★, *Bing In The Hall* (Spokane 1980)★★★, *Music Hall Highlights* (Spokane 1981)★★★, *Rare 1930-31 Brunswick Recordings* (MCA 1982)★★★, *Bing In The Thirties Volumes 1-8* (Spokane 1984-88)★★★★, *The Radio Years Volumes 1-4* (GNP Crescendo 1985-87)★★★★, *Bing Crosby Sings Again* (MCA 1986)★★★, *10th Anniversary Album* (Warwick 1987)★★★★, *Bing Crosby 1929-34, Classic Years Volume 1* (BBC 1987)★★★★, *Chronological Bing Crosby Volumes 1-10* (Jonzo 1985-88)★★★★, *The Crooner: The Columbia Years 1928-34* (Columbia 1988)★★★★, *The Victor Masters Featuring Bing Crosby (Paul Whiteman And His Orchestra)* (RCA 1989)★★★★, *The All Time Best Of* (Curb 1990)★★★, *Bing Crosby And Some Jazz Friends* (MCA/GRP 1991)★★★★, *The Jazzin' Bing Crosby* (Charly 1992)★★★★, *16 Most Requested Songs Legacy* (Columbia 1992)★★★★, *The Quintessential Bing Crosby* (1993)★★★★, *The EP Collection* (1993)★★★★, *Bing Crosby And Friends* (1993)★★★, *His Legendary Years* 4-CD box set (MCA 1993)★★★★, *Only Forever* (Empress 1994)★★★.

● VIDEOS: *A Bing Crosby Christmas* (VCI 1997).

● FURTHER READING: *Bing: The Authorized Biography*, Charles Thompson. *The One & Only Bing*, Bob Thomas. *The Complete Crosby*, Charles Thompson. *Bing Crosby: The Hollow Man*, Donald Shepherd. *Bing Crosby: A Discography, Radio Programme List & Filmography*, Timothy A. Morgereth.

● FILMS: *King Of Jazz* (1930), *Reaching For The Moon* (1930), *Confessions Of A Co-Ed* (1931), *The Bif Broadcast* (1932), *College Humor* (1933), *Too Much Harmony* (1933), *Going Hollywood* (1933), *Here Is My Heart* (1934), *She Loves Me Not* (1934), *We're Not Dressing* (1934), *The Big Broadcast Of 1936* (1935), *Two For Tonight* (1935), *Mississippi* (1935), *Pennies From Heaven* (1936), *Rhythm On The Range* (1936), *Anything Goes* (1936), *Double Or Nothing* (1937), *Waikiki Wedding* (1937), *Sing You Sinners* (1938), *Doctor Rhythm* (1938), *The Star Maker* (1939), *East Side Of Heaven* (1939), *Paris Honeymoon* (1939), *Rhythm On The River* (1940), *If I Had My Way* (1940), *Road To Singapore* (1940), *Birth Of The Blues* (1941), *Road To Zanzibar* (1941), *My Favorite Blonde* cameo (1942), *Star-Spangled Rhythm* (1942), *Road To Morocco* (1942), *Holiday Inn* (1942), *Dixie* (1943), *The Princess And The Pirate* (1944), *Here Comes The Waves* (1944), *Going My Way* (1944), *The Bells Of St. Mary's* (1945), *Duffy's Tavern* (1945), *Blue Skies* (1946), *Road To Utopia* (1946), *My Favorite Brunette* cameo (1947), *Variety Girl* (1947), *Road To Rio* (1947), *Welcome Stranger* (1947), *The Emperor Waltz* (1948), *Top O' The Morning* (1949), *A Connecticut Yankee In King Arthur's Court* (1949), *Mr. Music* (1950), *Riding High* (1950), *Here Comes The Groom* (1951), *Son Of Paleface* cameo (1952), *The Greatest Show On Earth* cameo (1952), *Road To Bali* (1952), *Just For You* (1952), *Scared Stiff* cameo (1953), *Little Boy Lost* (1953), *The Country Girl* (1954), *White Christmas* (1954), *High Society* (1956), *Anything Goes* remake (1956), *Man On Fire* (1957), *Alias Jesse James* cameo (1959), *Say One For Me* (1959), *Pepe* cameo (1960), *Let's Make Love* cameo (1960), *High Time* (1960), *The Road To Hong Kong* (1962), *Robin And The Seven Hoods* (1964), *Stagecoach* (1966).

CROSBY, BOB

b. George Robert Crosby, 25 August 1913, Spokane, Washington, USA, d. 9 March 1993, La Jolla, California, USA. For most of his early career, Crosby was inevitably over-shadowed by his older brother, Bing Crosby. Nevertheless, he achieved modest success thanks to a pleasant voice and a matching personality. In the immediate pre-swing era years he sang with Anson Weeks and then joined the band co-led by brothers Jimmy and Tommy Dorsey. In 1935 the disaffected musicians who had left the Ben Pollack band decided to form a co-operative group but wanted a frontman. They approached Crosby, who accepted the job, bringing a casual, relaxed air to one of the swing era's liveliest bands. Unusually, the band favoured an energetic, two-beat Dixieland style that became extremely popular. The leading musicians in the band were trumpeters Billy Butterfield and Yank Lawson, saxophonists Eddie Miller, Irving Fazola and Matty Matlock and rhythm players Bob Zurke, Hilton 'Nappy' Lamare, Bob Haggart and Ray Bauduc. After the band folded in 1942 Crosby continued to make films and personal appearances, sometimes as leader of reconstituted Dixieland-style bands, sometimes of more contemporary-sounding bands. Generally, by the 70s and 80s, these groups bore little resemblance to the original Bob Crosby band, but the fans loved it all. Crosby died of cancer in 1993.
● ALBUMS: *One Night Stand* (1946)★★★, *Swinging At The Sugar Bowl* 10-inch album (Coral 1950)★★★, *Dixieland Jazz 1* 10-inch album (Coral 1950)★★★, *Marches In Dixieland Style* 10-inch album (Coral 1950)★★★, *St. Louis Blues* 10-inch album (Coral 1950)★★★, *Bob Crosby And His Bobcats* (Capitol 1952/54)★★★, *The Golden Days Of Jazz* (1954)★★★★, *Five Feet Of Swing* (Decca 1954)★★★, *Bob Crosby's Bobcats* (Decca 1954)★★★, *The Bobcats' Ball* (Coral 1955)★★★, *Bobcats' Blues* (Coral 1956)★★★, *Bobcats On Parade* (Coral 1956)★★★, *Bob Crosby In Hi Fi* (Coral 1956)★★★, *The Bobcats In Hi Fi* (Coral 1958)★★★, *Petite Fleur* (Dot 1959)★★, *The Sounds Of The Swing Years* (1960)★★★, *Live At The Rainbow Grill* (1960)★★, *Mardi Gras Parade* (1960)★★★.
● COMPILATIONS: *Bob Crosby 1936 - 1956* (Coral 1957)★★★, *The Hits Of Bob Crosby's Bobcats* (Capitol 1961)★★★, *Bob Crosby's Bobcats - Their Greatest Hits* (Decca 1966)★★★★, *Bob Crosby On The Air, 1940* (Aircheck 1979)★★★, *Bob Crosby And His Orchestra, 1935-36* (Rarities 1981)★★★★, *20 Golden Pieces* (Bulldog 1981)★★★★, *Camel Caravans - The Summer Of '39* (Giants Of Jazz 1985)★★★, *Suddenly It's 1939* (Giants Of Jazz 1985)★★★★, *Accent On Swing* (Giants Of Jazz 1986)★★★, *The Big Apple, 1936-40* (Bandstand 1988)★★★, *Sugar Foot Strut (1936-42)* (Bandstand 1988)★★★★, *Bob Crosby - Jazz Classics In Digital Stereo* (BBC 1988)★★★.
● FURTHER READING: *Stomp Off, Let's Go! The Story Of Bob Crosby's Bob Cats & Big Band*, John Chilton.

CRUDUP, ARTHUR 'BIG BOY'

b. 24 August 1905, Forest, Mississippi, USA, d. 28 March 1974, Nassawadox, Virginia, USA. During the 40s and early 50s Arthur Crudup was an important name in the blues field, his records selling particularly well in the south. For much of his early life Crudup worked in various rural occupations, not learning to play the guitar until he was 32. His teacher was one 'Papa Harvey', a local bluesman, and although Crudup's guitar style never became adventurous, it formed an effective backdrop for his high, expressive voice. Allegedly, Crudup was playing on the sidewalk in Chicago when he was spotted by the music publisher and general 'Mr Fixit' for the blues in the Windy City, Lester Melrose. Like many others with his background, Big Boy's first recordings were his most countrified; 'If I Get Lucky' and 'Black Pony Blues' were recorded in September 1941 and probably sold largely to the same group of resident and ex-patriot southerners who were buying records by Tommy McClennan and Sleepy John Estes. During the next 12 years he recorded approximately 80 tracks for Victor, including songs that became blues standards. 'Mean Old Frisco' was later picked up by artists as diverse as Brownie McGhee (1946) and B.B. King (1959), and was one of the first blues recordings to feature an electric guitar. He recorded 'Dust My Broom' in 1949 and the following year moonlighted for the Trumpet label in Jackson, Mississippi, under the name 'Elmer James'. Despite attempts to update his sound by the introduction of piano, harmonicas and saxophones, by 1954 Big Boy's heyday was over. When he was contracted to record an album of his hits for Fire in 1962, the project had to be delayed until the picking season was over, Crudup having given up music and gone back to working on the land. Two of Crudup's compositions, 'That's All Right' and 'My Baby Left Me' were recorded by Elvis Presley, who also sang his 'I'm So Glad You're Mine', but it is not likely that Crudup benefited much from this. A second career bloomed for Big Boy with the interest in blues among the white audience in the mid-60s, beginning with an album for Bob Koester's Delmark label. This prompted appearances at campuses and clubs in the USA and Crudup even journeyed to Europe - always encouraged to perform in a country style. It appears likely that, with his superior lyrics and wide cross-racial popularity, Big Boy Crudup gave more to the blues than he ever received in return.
● ALBUMS: *Mean Ol' Frisco* (Fire 1957)★★★★, *Look On Yonders Wall* (Delmark 1968)★★★, *Crudup's Mood* (Delmark 1970)★★★, *Meets The Master Blues Bassists* (Delmark 1994)★★★.
● COMPILATIONS: *The Father Of Rock And Roll* (RCA Victor 1971)★★★.

CRUTCHFIELD, JAMES

b. 25 May 1912, Baton Rouge, Louisiana, USA. A self-taught pianist, Crutchfield left home when young and found work in the sawmills and lumber camps of Louisiana and Texas. In a logging camp in Bogalusa he met pianist Little Brother Montgomery who taught him to play '44 Blues'. In the late 40s Crutchfield moved to St. Louis where he worked in clubs, coming into contact with many of the city's celebrated pianists such as Henry Brown and Roosevelt Sykes. Around 1955, Charlie O'Brien, blues fan and policeman, introduced Crutchfield to John Bentley, who included four of his songs in a series of albums devoted to St. Louis jazz and blues pianists. Crutchfield resurfaced in the early 80s, toured parts of Europe and recorded an album for the Swingmaster label in Holland.

● ALBUMS: *Original Barrelhouse Blues* (Swingmaster 1985)★★★.

CUES

The Cues' marvellous harmonizing underpinned many of the great records of the 50s. The group was in effect an in-house vocal harmony group created by Atlantic Records' arranger Jesse Stone to accompany a variety of his artists in the studio. They were built around vocalist and songwriter Ollie Jones (ex-Blenders), with Robie Kirk (baritone), Abel DeCosta (tenor; also ex-Blenders), Jimmy Breedlove (second tenor) and Eddie Barnes (bass). As well as backing other artists the Cues were to have a second function: demoing potential songs for name acts to choose from. Soon their work in this vein also came from outside the label, with various writers and publishers learning of the Cues' abilities to animate new material. Their first backing engagement came on Ruth Brown's 'Oh What A Dream' in July 1954, a number 1 *Billboard* R&B success, which stayed at the top for eight weeks. Their first own-name recording (they were given a variety of names on record labels, including the title Rhythm Makers in the case of Ruth Brown) came when Stone moved to Aladdin Records. October 1954 saw 'Scoochie Scoochie' released on Aladdin's Lamp subsidiary to little fanfare. In the wake of its lack of success the Cues returned to their former employment, backing artists including Ivory Joe Hunter, Joe Turner, Carmen Taylor, LaVern Baker, Ray Charles, Nat King Cole and Bobby Darin. They became so busy, in fact, that a 'second team' of Cues was started by Stone, which included members of the Ravens, Four Buddies and Shirelles. Eventually the Cues were offered a contract in their own right by Capitol Records. Their debut release was 'Burn That Candle', which charted but lost sales due to a competing version from Bill Haley. Neither 'Charlie Brown' nor 'Destination 2100 And 65' did particularly well. Their final brace of releases for Capitol, 'The Girl I Love' (later recorded by the Cadillacs) and 'Why', flopped. They switched to subsidiary label Prep for May 1957's 'I Pretend', but continued to find more success as backing singers. After a final single, 'Old Man River', in 1960, the group dispersed to concentrate on separate projects. Ollie Jones joined the Billy Williams Quartet and Breedlove joined the Ink Spots.

DADDY LONG LEGS

Previously filmed in 1919, 1931 and 1935, this 1955 adaptation of Jean Webster's classic novel, by Phoebe and Henry Ephron, strayed somewhat from the original because of the presence of the delightful French actress Leslie Caron.

In this version of the story, a wealthy US businessman, played by Fred Astaire, sponsors the education of a French orphan-girl (Caron) - on the strict understanding that he remains anonymous. After his office receives fulsome letters of gratitude from her school, his secretary (a beautifully 'hard-bitten' performance by Thelma Ritter) persuades him to visit her. He is captivated by the charming young woman and they fall in love, although she still has no idea that he is her mysterious benefactor, even when she continues her education in the USA. Their romance blossoms, and Astaire and Caron proved to be a perfect dancing team, accompanied by a score by Johnny Mercer containing two songs that went on to become standards, 'Something's Gotta Give' and 'Dream'. The former gave Astaire the opportunity to convey a perfect lyrical illustration of the difficulties inherent in the 'generation gap' ('When an irresistible force such as you/Meets an old immovable object like me'), and the latter, a lovely ethereal ballad that enhanced the film's dream sequences, was subsequently used for many years by Frank Sinatra as his closing theme. One of the many highlights in *Daddy Long Legs* came in 'Sluefoot', when Astaire demonstrated to a group of college students how this dance business really should be done, backed by trumpeter Ray Anthony And His Orchestra. Astaire also gave a good account of himself on the drums. The rest of a lively and highly entertaining set of songs included 'History Of The Beat', 'C-A-T Spells Cat' and 'Welcome Egghead'. Legendary film composer Alex North was responsible for much of the film's orchestral music. Also in the cast were Terry Moore, Fred Clark, Ralph Dumke and Larry Keating. The film, which was choreographed by David Robel and Roland Petit, and directed by Jean Negulesco, was photographed in DeLuxe Color and CinemaScope and released by 20th Century-Fox.

DAILEY, DAN

b. 14 December 1914 (or 1917), New York City, New York, USA, d. 1978. An elegant and versatile song-and-dance-man with a genial personality, who starred in some of the most entertaining musicals of the 40s and 50s, often as a vaudeville performer or similar. As a youngster, Dailey worked in minstrel shows and vaudeville. In 1937 he got a job in the chorus of Richard Rodgers and Lorenz Hart's Broadway show *Babes In Arms*, and, two years later, played a supporting role in another stage musical, *Stars In Your Eyes*, which starred Ethel Merman and Jimmy Durante. His first appearance in a movie musical came in 1941 with the lavish *Ziegfeld Girl*, which was followed by *Lady Be Good* and *Panama Hattie*. After service in World War II, Dailey signed for 20th Century-Fox and began to play the lead in films such as *Mother Wore Tights* (the first of several he made with Betty Grable), *You Were Meant For Me*, *Give My Regards To Broadway*, *When My Baby Smiles At Me* (for which he was nominated for the best actor Oscar, only to be beaten by Laurence Olivier!), *You're My Everything*, *I'll Get By*, *My Blue Heaven*, and *Call Me Mister*. In 1952 his portrayal of baseball star Dizzy Dean in *The Pride Of St. Louis* was highly acclaimed. As well as these occasional, but skilfully played straight roles, he continued to devote most of his time to musicals such as *The Girl Next Door*, *There's No Business Like Show Business*, *It's Always Fair Weather*, *The Best Things In Life Are Free*, *Meet Me In Las Vegas*, and *Pepe* (1960). By then, the lavish, big budget musicals had become old fashioned, and Dailey subsequently worked on stage and in the big US cabaret rooms. In the late 50s he co-starred with Vittorio De Sica, Jack Hawkins and Richard Conte in *The Four Just Men*, a television series which was popular in the US and UK, and his other small screen work included *The Governor And J.J.* in the 60s, and *Faraday And Company* in the 70s.

● FILMS: *The Mortal Storm* (1940), *Dulcy* (1940), *Ziegfeld Girl* (1941), *Moon Over Her Shoulder* (1941), *Lady Be Good* (1941), *Panama Hattie* (1942), *Give Out Sisters* (1942), *Mother Wore Tights* (1947), *Give My Regards To Broadway* (1948), *You Were Meant For Me* (1948), *When My Baby Smiles At Me* (1948), *Chicken Every Sunday* (1949), *My Blue Heaven* (1950), *When Willie Comes Marching Home* (1950), *I Can Get It For You Wholesale* (1951), *Call Me Mister* (1951), *The Pride Of St. Louis* (1952), *What Price Glory* (1952), *Meet Me At The Fair* (1953), *There's No Business Like Show Business* (1954), *It's Always Fair Weather* (1955), *Meet Me In Las Vegas* (1956), *The Wings Of Eagles* (1956), *Oh Men, Oh Women* (1957), *The Wayward Bus* (1957), *Pepe* (1960), *Hemingway's Adventures Of A Young Man* (1962).

DAILY, PAPPY

b. Harold W. Daily, 8 February 1902, Yoakum, Texas, USA, d. 5 December 1987, Houston, Texas, USA. After lying about his age, he saw service with the US Marines in World War I. He became involved in several successful business ventures but his involvement in country music did not really start until 1953, when he and Jack Starnes formed the Starday label in Beaumont, Texas. The label launched the career of George Jones and, by doing so, ensured its own success. When Starnes left, Daily and Don Pierce worked together, until parting amicably in 1961. Daily had also formed his own D label, in 1958, and apart from the Starday work, he successfully recorded several artists, including Eddie Noack, Claude Gray and James O'Gwynn. In 1961, he joined United Artists Records, where he continued to record George Jones, who had moved to the label with him. He produced a series of solo hits for Jones, including 'The Race Is On', and also for Melba Montgomery. His foresight in recording them as a duo produced several hits, especially a number 3 hit with 'We Must Have Been Out Of Our Minds'. In 1965, when Daily and Art Talmadge formed the Musicor label, Jones joined them and charted almost 30 hits for the label, including Top 3s with 'Walk Through This World With Me', 'When The Grass Grows Over Me' and 'I'll Share My World With You'. In

1971, the close relationship with Jones encountered problems when, for some reason regarding the way he was being handled, the singer demanded his release in order to move to Epic and record with Tammy Wynette. It has been stated that Talmadge may have been the cause of the problem but Jones departed and his relationship with Daily from that point was never more than casual. Daily continued in the business for some time but never achieved further success to match that gained early in his career. He later managed the distribution companies Big State and H.W. Daily. He died following a heart attack in 1987.

DALE, ALAN

b. Aldo Sigismondi, 9 July 1926, Brooklyn, New York, USA. Formerly with Carmen Cavallaro, Alan Dale first graced the US charts when his rich baritone vocal style provided Ray Bloch And His Orchestra with the 'swing' hit 'Kate (Have I Come Too Early Too Late)' in 1947. In the following year he duetted with Connie Haines on 'At The Darktown Strutters' Ball'. In 1951 he hosted his own US television series, which led to more success, most notably with 'Heart Of My Heart' (with Johnny Desmond and Don Cornell) and 'East Side, West Side' (with Desmond and Buddy Greco). In 1955 he again made the US Top 20 with 'Cherry Pink (And Apple Blossom White)' and an adaptation of a Cuban mambo-cha-cha 'Me Lo Dijo Adela', entitled 'Sweet And Gentle'.

● FILMS: *Don't Knock The Rock* (1956).

DALE, JIM

b. Jim Smith, 15 August 1935, Kettering, Northamptonshire, England. Dale, a failed impressionist, who wanted to be an all-round entertainer, had a two-year stint with Carrol Levis's touring show as part of a comedy tumbling act. He then became a solo comedian and only turned to singing when he found people preferred his finale song to his tame comedy. He joined the BBC Television series *6.5 Special* in April 1957, and shortly afterwards signed to Parlophone Records, where he was produced by George Martin. His only Top 20 hit came with his second single, a cover version of Johnny Madara's 'Be My Girl', which reached number 2 in late 1957. He had three more UK Top 40 entries, the last being a version of the McGuire Sisters' US hit 'Sugartime' in 1958. In the 60s Dale pursued his acting career, and appeared in a string of successful *Carry On* films, and others, such as *Lock Up Your Daughters*. He made his West End debut in a musical, *The Wayward Way*, and appeared at the Edinburgh Festival in a pop version of *The Winter's Tale*. He also co-wrote the Seekers' smash hit 'Georgy Girl', for which he was nominated for an Academy Award, and contributed to the music for movies such as *Shalako* and *Lola*. In the late 60s and early 70s, as member of the National Theatre Company, he appeared in several productions at the Old Vic and the Young Vic. He also made more films, including *Adolph Hitler - My Part In His Downfall* and *Digby, The Biggest Dog In The World*. In 1973, Dale played for six months at the Queen's Theatre, London, in the musical *The Card*, and around the same time, hosted the popular television show, Sunday Night At The London Palladium. In 1974 he went to the USA with the National Theatre Company and created a stir with his performance as an 'ingratiating scamp' in the Molière farce *Scapino*, which brought him Drama Desk and Outer Critics Circle Awards, and a Tony nomination. During the

late 70s, by now domiciled in the USA, he appeared in stage productions of *Comedians* and *Privates On Parade*, as well as making several other movies, three of them for the Disney Studio. In 1980 Dale found the ideal vehicle for his talents in *Barnum*, a musical about the life of the famed US showman, which involved juggling, trampolining and tightrope walking, among other skills. He won a Tony Award for his performance and stayed with the show for over a year, following ecstatic opening reviews. In the 80s he made more films, and appeared on the New York stage in productions as diverse as Peter Nichol's *Joe Egg* (1985), *Me And My Girl* (1987), and a revival of *Privates On Parade* (1989). In 1992 he returned to the UK, and to his 60s roots, to play the title role in the film *Carry On Columbus*. In 1995 he played the leading role in *The Music Man* in a recording for BBC Radio 2.
● ALBUMS: *Jim!* (Parlophone 1958)★★.

DALLAS, REX

b. 6 November 1938, Wallerawang, New South Wales, Australia. Dallas inherited a love of bush poetry through a close friendship with his grandfather, who regularly read poems to him. He first appeared on local radio, on 2LT Lithgow, at the age of 15 but a year later, he relocated to Sydney. His appearance on *Australia's Amateur Hour* led to him becoming a regular on 2SM's *On The Trail And Hall Shows* for the next three years. He later toured with Lee Gordon and made his first recordings for EMI in the early 60s, his first single being 'Bicycle Wreck'. His versatility has seen him perform material varying from country to rock 'n' roll and even light operetta. Like many Australian artists, he is a very fine yodeller, being so especially devoted to Harry Torrani that in 1975, he recorded an album of Torrani songs. Its immediate success led to a second album and 20 of the tracks found subsequent release in the UK (*Yodelling Songs Of Harry Torrani* - Westwood 1978). Although an excellent yodeller, he does not use the art on all his recordings, in fact, he is perhaps best known to many of his Australasian fans for his ability to follow in the footsteps of Buddy Williams and Slim Dusty as a leading performer of bush ballads. He has, in fact, even won awards for his self-penned bush ballads. One of these, 'Old Wallerawang', a tribute to his grandfather, won him a Gold Guitar at the Tamworth awards, as did 'His Spurs Are Rusty Now', which he co-wrote with his son Colin in 1982 ('Old Wallerawang' was also recorded by several other artists, including Rolf Harris). His albums also include selections of horse songs, war songs, mother songs and even one on the theme of coalmining. From the early 70s, he toured extensively, accompanied by his band, the Dallas Cowboys, which included his two sons, Brett (b. 16 January 1963, Sydney, New South Wales, Australia; lead guitarist) and Colin (b. 8 November 1965, Cooma, New South Wales, Australia; drums). During the 80s, his two younger sons, Jeffrey (b. 27 August 1970, Sydney, New South Wales, Australia; bass, mandolin) and Shannan, began to make appearances on his show, Shannan being only three when he made his debut. In 1981, Dallas featured in a television documentary about his touring show. He holds the distinction of being the first artist ever to take the title from constant winners Slim Dusty or Reg Lindsay, when he was voted best male vocalist at Tamworth in 1976. He has his own venue, Gully Park, in Moonbi, New South Wales, where he

regularly entertains, when not touring with his country show. Dallas has been a stalwart of Australian country music for more than three decades, but so far he has not toured the UK.
● ALBUMS: *Harry Torrani Yodelling Album* (Hadley 1975)★★★★★★, *Harry Torrani Yodelling Album Volume 2* (Hadley 1975)★★★, *In The Days When I Was Me* (Hadley 1976)★★★, *I Love The Old Bush Ballad Songs* (Hadley 1978)★★★, *Old Wallerawang* (Hadley 1979)★★★, *Here's To The Songwriter* (Hadley 1979)★★, *Yodelling Mad* (Hadley 1980)★★★, *Buckjump And Saddle Tales* (Hadley 1981)★★★, *Remembering Those Hillbilly Hits* (Hadley 1982)★★★★, *Mother's Flower Garden* (Hadley 1982)★★★, *Born To The Saddle* (Hadley 1983)★★★, *Easy Loving* (Hadley 1984)★★, *For Valour* (Hadley 1985)★★★, *Rex Dallas & Sons* (Briar 1986)★★★, *Yodels Harry Torrani Classics Volume 3* (Briar 1986)★★★, with Owen Blundell *Duelling Yodellers* (Selection 1988)★★★★, *We Dig Coal* (Sundown 1990)★★★, *Heartland* (Hadley 1994)★★★.

DAMN YANKEES (STAGE MUSICAL)

Combining the improbable ingredients of a Faustian plot with a baseball setting, itself a notoriously jinx-ridden subject, the stage musical *Damn Yankees* was an unexpected hit following its opening at the 46th Street Theatre in New York on 5 May 1955. With a book by George Abbott and Douglass Wallop, and a score by Jerry Ross and Richard Adler, the show starred the remarkable Gwen Verdon as the lovely Lola, a lady who gets what she wants (most of the time). The storyline of *Damn Yankees* follows hapless Joe Boyd (Robert Shafer), a middle-aged baseball fan, who announces that he would willingly sell his soul to the Devil if only his team, the Washington Senators, could win the pennant. The Devil promptly appears and grants his wish, although Joe believes he can outsmart 'Old Nick' if he remains faithful to his wife, Meg (Shannon Bolin). In a flash, Boyd turns into Joe Hardy, a handsome young ballplayer who steers the Senators to victory in almost every match, while successfully fending off the advances of Lola, the Devil's glamorous reincarnation of an ugly old hag. Eventually, after his team has won the pennant, Joe returns to plump middle-age and his nice, ordinary wife, while Lola gets back on her broomstick. Stephen Douglass was the hard-hitting Joe Hardy, and Ray Walston played 'Mr Applegate', the name by which the Devil was known in his earthly manifestations. The show was full of entertaining numbers including 'Shoeless Joe From Hannibal, Mo', 'A Little Brains-A Little Talent', 'Who's Got The Pain?', 'Those Were The Good Old Days', 'Two Lost Souls' and 'Whatever Lola Wants (Lola Gets)' Another of the songs, 'Heart', was a big hit in the USA for Eddie Fisher and the Four Aces, and in Britain for the Johnston Brothers and Max Bygraves. *Damn Yankees* scooped the 1956 Tony Awards, winning for best musical, actress (Verdon), actor (Walston), supporting actor (Russ Brown), choreographer (Bob Fosse) and director (Hal Hastings). Gwen Verdon's powerful and sexy performance swept her to stardom in this show which ran on Broadway for 1,019 performances, and a further 258 in London. Verdon and Walston were joined by pop heart-throb Tab Hunter in the 1958 film version. An acclaimed Broadway revival opened in March 1994, starring Bebe Neuwirth (Lola), Jarrod Emick (Joe Hardy) and Victor Garber (Applegate). Emick won a Tony Award for featured actor, and Garber was succeeded as Applegate by comedian Jerry Lewis, making his Broadway debut. Lewis also led the touring production, which reached London's West End in June 1997.

DAMN YANKEES (FILM MUSICAL)

Although the original 1955 Broadway show kept that title for the London stage production, the 1958 film version was released in the UK as *What Lola Wants*. Regardless of its title, this story of Joe Boyd (Robert Shafer), an ageing American baseball fan, whose frustration with his team, the Washington Senators, leads him to make a Faustian pact with the Devil, turned out to be a highly entertaining movie musical. Joe's musings along the lines of 'I'd sell my soul for just one long-ball hitter' bring forth a Mr. Applegate (Ray Walston), who, after casually flashing his red socks and lighting a cigarette by spontaneous combustion ('I'm handy with fire'), agrees to turn Joe into a young athlete for one season only in return for his soul. The deal is done, and, sure enough, as the Senators' amazing new discovery Joe Hardy (Tab Hunter), he galvanizes the team into action and leads them to glory, after which he reverts to his former self (his contract with Applegate contains an escape clause), and returns to his humdrum life and wife Meg (Shannon Bolin). Walston was marvellous, as always, and former pop heart-throb Hunter also gave an appealing performance. However, the star of the film without any doubt was the red-headed, long-legged dancer Gwen Verdon. She plays Lola, Applegate's apprentice, whose mission is to retain Joe's soul forever. Her attempt to seduce him in the locker-room to the sexy strains of 'Whatever Lola Wants', was a hilarious send-up of every vamp scene in the history of stage and screen. Verdon was one of the original Broadway team - not including Hunter - who recreated their roles for the screen. Russ Brown, as the Senators' coach, and Rae Allen in the role of Gloria, the nosy, hard-bitten newspaper reporter, were also in the film cast, along with Nathaniel Frey, Jimmie Komack, Jean Stapleton and Albert Linville. Richard Adler and Jerry Ross's splendid score included 'Goodbye, Old Girl', 'Heart' ('You gotta have . . .'), 'Shoeless Jo From Hannibal, Mo', 'A Little Brains-A Little Talent', 'There's Something About An Empty Chair', 'Two Lost Souls', 'Those Were The Good Old Days' and 'Six Months Out Of Every Year'. Bob Fosse was again responsible for the brilliant choreography, and he also joined Gwen Verdon for the mambo-styled 'Who's Got The Pain?'. George Abbott's screenplay was based on his own stage libretto which was adapted from the novel *The Year The Yankees Lost The Pennant* by Douglass Wallop. Abbott also co-directed the film with Stanley Donen. It was shot in Technicolor for Warner Brothers.

DAMONE, VIC

b. Vito Farinola, 12 June 1928, Brooklyn, New York, USA. A romantic balladeer with a strong, smooth baritone voice, Damone took singing lessons while working as an usher and elevator operator at New York's Paramount Theater. After appearing with *Arthur Godfrey's Talent Scouts*, he sang at La Martinique Club, a venue known as a nursery for young vocalists. When he started recording for Mercury Records in 1947, his first chart successes included 'I Have But One Heart', 'You Do' and 'Say Something Sweet To Your Sweetheart' (with Patti Page). In 1949 he had two million-

sellers: 'Again', from the Ida Lupino film *Roadhouse*; and 'You're Breaking My Heart'. In the late 40s Damone also had his own CBS radio show, *Saturday Night Serenade*. His film career started in 1951 when he featured in *Rich, Young And Pretty*, the first in a series of musicals with soprano Jane Powell. These included *Athena* (1953), the Sigmund Romberg biopic *Deep In My Heart* (1954) and *Hit The Deck* (1955). Damone also appeared in *The Strip* (1951), a musical mystery melodrama, which featured Mickey Rooney, and jazz stars Jack Teagarden, Louis Armstrong, Earl 'Fatha' Hines and Barney Bigard; and a screen adaptation of the stage musical *Kismet* (1955), co-starring with Howard Keel, Anne Blythe and Dolores Gray. His many record hits during the 50s included 'Tzena, Tzena, Tzena' (adapted from an Israeli song), 'Cincinnati Dancing Pig', 'My Heart Cries for You', 'My Truly, Truly Fair', 'Here In My Heart' (a UK number 1 for Al Martino), 'April In Portugal', 'Eternally' (the theme from Charlie Chaplin's film *Limelight*), 'Ebb Tide', 'On The Street Where You Live' (Damone's third million-seller) and 'An Affair To Remember' (one of prolific film composer Harry Warren's last songs). He was also in the album charts with *That Towering Feeling*, and had his own television series in 1956-57. Like many other singers of his kind, Damone suffered from the changing musical climate of the 60s and 70s, although he did make some well-regarded albums such as *Linger Awhile* and *On the South Side*, and had a US Top 30 single in 1965 with 'You Were Only Fooling (While I Was Falling In Love)'. He made a remarkable comeback in the UK in the early 80s, chiefly because his back-catalogue was plugged incessantly by BBC Radio 2 presenter David Jacobs. Suddenly, he was in fashion again. Most of his old albums were reissued, and many of his hit singles, and others, were repackaged on *Vic Damone Sings The Great Songs*. Throughout the 80s he recorded several new albums, promoting them in the UK via regular concert tours. In 1987 he was married, for the third time, to actress Diahann Carroll. In 1991 Damone played Michael's Pub in New York, his first club appearance in the city for more than 10 years.

● ALBUMS: *Vic Damone* 10-inch album (Mercury 1950)★★★, *Song Hits* 10-inch album (Mercury 1950)★★★, *Christmas Favorites* 10-inch album (Mercury 1951)★★★, *Rich, Young And Pretty* film soundtrack (MGM 1951)★★★, *Vic Damone And Others* 10-inch album (Mercury 1952)★★★, *The Night Has A Thousand Eyes* 10-inch album (Mercury 1952)★★★, *Vocals By Vic* 10-inch album (Mercury 1952)★★★, *April In Paris* 10-inch album (Mercury 1952)★★★, *Athena* film soundtrack (Mercury 1954)★★★, *Deep In My Heart* film soundtrack (MGM 1954)★★★, *The Voice Of Vic Damone* (1956)★★★, *That Towering Feeling!* (Columbia 1956)★★★, *The Stingiest Man In The World* film soundtrack (Columbia 1956)★★★, *Yours For A Song* (Mercury 1957)★★★, *All Time Song Hits* (Mercury 1957)★★★, *My Favorites* (Mercury 1957)★★★, *The Gift Of Love* film soundtrack (Columbia 1958)★★★, *Closer Than A Kiss* (Philips 1958)★★★, *Angela Mia* (1959)★★★, *This Game Of Love* (Philips 1959)★★★, *On The South Side Of Chicago* (1961)★★★★, *Linger Awhile With Vic Damone* (Capitol 1962)★★★, *Strange Enchantment* (Capitol 1962)★★★, *The Lively Ones* (Capitol 1962)★★★, *My Baby Loves To Swing* (Capitol 1963)★★★★, *The Liveliest* (Capitol 1963)★★★, *On The Street Where You Live* (Capitol 1964)★★★, *You Were Only Fooling* (Warners 1965)★★★,

Arrivederci Baby film soundtrack (RCA Victor 1966)★★★, *Stay With Me* (RCA 1976)★★★, *Damone's Feeling 1978* (Rebecca 1979)★★★, *Now* (RCA 1981)★★★, *Make Someone Happy* (RCA 1981)★★★, *Now And Forever* (RCA 1982)★★★, *Vic Damone Sings The Great Songs* (Columbia 1983)★★★, *The Damone Type Of Thing* (RCA 1984)★★★, *Christmas With Vic Damone* (Audio Fidelity 1984)★★★, *The Best Of Vic Damone, Live* (Ranwood 1989)★★★.
● COMPILATIONS: *Vic Damone's Best* (RCA 1980)★★★★, *20 Golden Pieces* (Bulldog 1982)★★★★, *Magic Moments With Vic Damone* (RCA 1985)★★★★, *Didn't We?* (Castle 1986)★★★, *The Capitol Years* (Capitol 1989)★★★, *16 Most Requested Songs* (1992)★★★★.
● FILMS: *Rich, Young And Pretty* (1951), *The Strip* (1951), *Athena* (1953), *Deep In My Heart* (1954), *Hit The Deck* (1955), *Kismet* (1955), *Hell To Eternity* (1960).

DANCER, PRANCER AND NERVOUS
Los Angeles-based Russ Regan was the mastermind behind the fictitious reindeer trio Dancer, Prancer & Nervous, whose single 'The Happy Reindeer' was one of 1959's biggest US Christmas hits. It combined the elements of two previous Christmas successes, having a similar storyline to 'Rudolph the Red Nosed Reindeer' and using the speeded-up voice gimmick of 'The Chipmunk Song'. Regan, who like the Chipmunks' mentor David Seville, was of Armenian descent, started as a solo singer and also sang with groups including the Check Mates and the Rowdies. Often cited as the man who renamed Carl & The Passions the Beach Boys, he went on to become a very successful record company executive. He first signed Elton John in the USA when at UNI, and signed Barry White when running 20th Century Records. He was later a vice president at Phonogram and Motown and currently heads the successful indie label Quality, who topped the US chart in 1991 via Timmy T. The reindeers' only other release was the unsuccessful 'I Wanna Be An Easter Bunny', released simply under the name the Singing Reindeers.

DANDERLIERS
This R&B vocal group was formed in 1955 in Chicago, Illinois, USA. The Danderliers were not a big-selling group, having only one national hit to their credit, 'Chop Chop Boom' (number 10 R&B 1955), but they had a pioneering influence in their home-town of Chicago. Eugene Record of the Chi-Lites was inspired to form a vocal group after hearing Danderliers songs. The members were Dallas Taylor (tenor and jump lead), James Campbell (tenor and ballad lead), first tenor Bernard Dixon, baritone Walter Stephenson, and bass Richard Thomas (replaced by Louis Johnson in 1956). 'Chop Chop Boom' was also a hit by a Canadian cover group, the Crew-Cuts, the same year. The song was a great jump number and unfairly obscured the Danderliers' tremendous reputation as masters of romantic ballads, notably 'My Autumn Love' (the flip-side to 'Chop Chop Boom'), 'May God Be With You' (1956) and 'My Love' (1956). The group broke up in 1957.

DANIELS, BILLY
b. 12 September 1915, Jacksonville, Florida, USA, d. 7 October 1988. Daniels began his career as a singing waiter before working with dance bands and in vaudeville. In the late 30s he became popular in clubs and on radio. In 1943, during a club appearance, he performed 'That Old Black Magic', giving the song a highly dramatic, visually exciting treatment it had never before received, and from that time onwards, the singer and the song were inseparable. At his best in a cabaret setting, Daniels was a natural for television and from 1950, in partnership with pianist Bennie Payne, appeared regularly in the USA and UK. He made a few film appearances and was also in the television production of *Night Of The Quarter Moon*. P.J. Proby used much of Daniels' vocal technique with his epic ballads during the 60s. In 1975 he worked with Pearl Bailey in *Hello, Dolly!* and two years later starred in London in the UK version of *Bubbling Brown Sugar*. He also appeared with Sammy Davis Jnr. in the revival of *Golden Boy*. Offstage, Daniels frequently associated with underworld characters. He was stabbed in one incident and was once charged with a shooting. Late in his life he suffered ill health and twice underwent heart bypass surgery before his death in 1988.
● ALBUMS: *Around That Time* (50s)★★★, *At The Stardust Las Vegas* (50s)★★, *Love Songs For A Fool* (50s)★★★, *You Go to My Head* (1957)★★★★, *The Masculine Touch* (1958)★★★, *At the Crescendo* (1959)★★★, *Dance To The Magic* (1959)★★★, *Bubbling Black Magic* (Polydor 1978)★★★.
● COMPILATIONS: *The Magic Of Billy Daniels* (MFP 1976)★★★.

DANIELS, MAXINE
b. Gladys Lynch, 2 November 1930, Stepney, London, England. The sister of entertainer Kenny Lynch, and an accomplished and affectionately regarded jazz singer, Maxine Daniels won a local talent contest held at her local cinema when she was only 14 years old. Later, she enjoyed a long residency with the Denny Boyce Band at the Orchid Room, Purley, and took first place on UK television's *Youth Takes A Bow* in 1953. Signed to the Delfont Agency and Oriole Records, she played smart London cabaret venues such as Churchill's, the Stork Club and the Savoy, toured the Moss Empires circuit, and appeared frequently on top-rated UK television programmes, including the legendary *Sunday Night At The London Palladium*. In 1962 Maxine Daniels suffered a severe nervous breakdown, and it was several years before she was ready to return to work. Her gradual rehabilitation was completed in the 80s when she made two fine albums, appeared with Humphrey Lyttelton and the Dutch Swing College Band, and sang at legendary trumpeter Nat Gonella's 80th birthday celebrations. In the early 90s she toured with George Chisholm in Swinging Down Memory Lane, and with Terry Lightfoot And His Band in *Basin Street To Broadway*. In 1995 she was appearing with artists such as Buddy Greco, Humphrey Lyttelton, Helen Shapiro, Dave Shepherd and Digby Fairweather, in the first UK Jazz And Swing Festival. She was also featured on Laurie Johnson's *London Big Band Volume One*.
● ALBUMS: *A Beautiful Friendship* (Maxam 1985)★★★, *Every Night About This Time* (Calligraph 1986)★★★.

DANKWORTH, JOHN
b. 20 September 1927, London, England. Dankworth started playing clarinet as a child and in the early 40s was a member of a traditional jazz band. In the mid-40s he studied at the

Royal Academy of Music and extended his knowledge of jazz by taking work on transatlantic liners, so that he could hear leading jazzmen in New York. Among his influences at this time was Charlie Parker, and Dankworth began to concentrate on alto saxophone. He was an active participant in the London bebop scene of the late 40s and early 50s, often playing at the Club 11. In 1950 he formed his own band, the Johnny Dankworth Seven, which included Jimmy Deuchar and Don Rendell. Three years later he formed a big band, playing his own, sometimes innovative, arrangements. The band's singer was Cleo Laine whom Dankworth married in 1958. For his big band Dankworth drew upon the best available modern jazzmen; at one time or another, artists such as Dick Hawdon, Kenny Wheeler, Rendell, Danny Moss, Peter King, Dudley Moore and Kenny Clare were in its ranks. Dankworth's writing, especially for the big band, demonstrated his considerable arranging skills, although for many fans it is the performances by the Seven that linger longest in fond memory. In the 60s Dankworth was in demand for film work, which, together with the growing popularity of Laine, led to a shift in policy. In the early 70s Dankworth became Laine's musical director, touring extensively with her and making many records. Dankworth's musical interests extend beyond jazz and he has composed in the classical form, including a nine-movement work, 'Fair Oak Fusions', written for cellist Julian Lloyd Webber. He has also experimented with third-stream music. His deep interest in music education led in 1969 to the founding of the Wavendon Allmusic Plan, which has continued to attract performers, students and audiences from around the world to concerts, classes, courses and lectures. Although a reliable performer on alto, it is as an arranger and tireless promoter of music that Dankworth has made his greatest contributions to the international jazz scene. In 1974, in recognition of his work, he became a Companion of the British Empire.
● ALBUMS: Five Steps To Dankworth (Parlophone 1957)★★★★, London To Newport (Top Rank 1960)★★★, Jazz Routes (Columbia 1961)★★★, Curtain Up (Columbia 1963)★★★, What The Dickens! (Fontana 1963)★★, Zodiac Variations (Fontana 1965)★★★, Shakespeare - And All That Jazz (1965)★★★, Fathom film soundtrack (Stateside 1967)★★, The $1,000,000 Collection (Fontana 1968)★★★, Full Circle (1972)★★★, Lifeline (1973)★★★, Movies 'N' Me (1974)★★, . . . And The Philharmonic (Boulevard 1974)★★, with Cleo Laine Lover And His Lass (Esquire 1976)★★★, Sepia (1979)★★★, Fair Oak Fusions (1982)★★★, Metro (Repertoire 1983)★★★, Zodiac Variations (Sepia 1983)★★★, Gone Hitchin' (Sepia 1983)★★★, What The Dickens? (Sepia 1983)★★★, Octavius (Sepia 1983)★★★, Symphonic Fusions (Pickwick 1985)★★★, Innovations (Pickwick 1987)★★★, Live At Ronnie Scott's (Total 1992)★★★, with Alec Dankworth Generation Big Band (Jazz House 1994)★★★★.
● COMPILATIONS: Johnny Dankworth Seven And Orchestra 1953-57 recordings★★★★, Featuring Cleo Laine 1953-58 recordings (Retrospect 1984)★★★, with others Bop At Club 11 1949 recordings (Esquire 1986)★★, The John Dankworth Big Band, Vintage Years 1953-1959 (Sepia 1990)★★★★, with Humphrey Lyttelton All That Jazz (MFP 1990)★★★★, The Roulette Years (Roulette 1991)★★★★.

DANNY AND THE JUNIORS

This Philadelphia-based, Italian-American vocal quartet comprised lead vocalist Danny Rapp (b. 10 May 1941, d. 4 April 1983), first tenor Dave White, second tenor Frank Mattei and baritone Joe Terranova. Formed in 1955 as the Juvenairs, their song 'Do The Bop' came to the attention of Dick Clark, who suggested the title change 'At The Hop'. They took his advice and released the song in 1957, initially with few sales. However, after they sang it on Clark's television show Bandstand, it was picked up by ABC-Paramount and shot to the top of the US chart for five weeks. Despite comments from the British music press that the group was amateur and imitative, it made the UK Top 3 and sold over two million copies worldwide. They followed it with their only other US Top 20 hit, the similar-sounding and prophetically titled 'Rock 'n' Roll Is Here To Stay'. In 1960 they signed to Dick Clark's Swan Records where they gained their fourth and last US Top 40 hit, 'Twistin' USA' (they re-recorded it unsuccessfully for the UK as 'Twistin England'). They recorded songs about such dance crazes as the Mashed Potato, Pony, Cha Cha, Fish, Continental Walk and Limbo, but could not repeat their earlier success, even when they released 'Back To The Hop' in 1961. Later in the 60s they also appeared on Guyden, Mercury and Capitol, where they re-recorded 'Rock 'n' Roll Is Here To Stay' in 1968. Dave White left the group in the early 60s to concentrate on writing and production and composed a number of hits, including 'You Don't Own Me' for Lesley Gore and '1-2-3' and 'Like A Baby' for Len Barry, before recording a solo album on Bell in 1971. In the 70s they played the 'oldies' circuit with a line-up that included Fabian's ex-backing singer Jimmy Testa. In 1976 a reissue of their classic 'At The Hop' returned them to the UK Top 40. After a few quiet years, leader Rapp was found dead in Arizona in 1983, having apparently committed suicide.
● COMPILATIONS: Rockin' With Danny And The Juniors (MCA 1983)★★, Back To Hop (Roller Coaster 1992)★★.

DARNELL, LARRY

b. Leo Edward Donald, 1929, Columbus, Ohio, USA, d. 3 July 1983, Columbus, Ohio, USA. Darnell began singing in Columbus gospel choirs and started sneaking into local clubs in the early 40s to sing for cash. At the age of 15 he joined the travelling show Irwin C. Miller's Brownskin Models, which he left in New Orleans after being offered a residency at the famous Dew Drop Inn. Something of a heart-throb, he became known as 'Mr Heart & Soul' and secured a recording contract with Regal in 1949, with whom he enjoyed big hits with 'For You My Love' and the two-part 'I'll Get Along Somehow', backed by Paul Gayten's band. Moving to New York in 1950, Darnell's later tracks for Regal, OKeh, Savoy and DeLuxe failed to live up to the early successes. Having made occasional recordings in the 60s for Warwick, Argo and Instant, he retired from popular music in 1969, although he continued to sing for the church and contribute to benefit shows until two years before his death from cancer in 1983.
● COMPILATIONS: I'll Get Along Somehow (Route 66 1987)★★★.

DAVIS, CEDELL 'BIG G'

b. 1926, Halena, Arkansas, USA. An excellent slide guitar and harmonica player, Davis performed briefly as a member of the King Biscuits Time entertainers in the early 50s with

Sonny Boy 'Rice Miller' Williamson, before joining guitarist Robert Nighthawk's band. In 1961 he moved to Pine Bluff, Arkansas, and continued to work locally and occasionally with Nighthawk, who along with Tampa Red, influenced his slide guitar playing. Because of the effects of childhood polio which denied him the full use of his hands, Davis played the guitar upside down and used a butter knife for a slide. He was last reported to be living in a nursing home in Pine Bluff.
● COMPILATIONS: *Keep It To Yourself, Arkansas Blues Volume 1* (1983)★★★, *Feel Like Doin' Something Wrong* (Demon 1994)★★★, *The Best Of CeDell Davis* (Capricorn/Fat Possum 1995)★★★.

DAVIS, LARRY

b. 4 December 1936, Kansas City, Missouri, USA, d. 19 April 1994, Los Angeles, California, USA. One of many blues artists to be remembered solely for one early record, Larry Davis continued to make distinctive albums for the contemporary market until his death. Moving to Little Rock, Arkansas, with his father in 1944, he learned to play drums in the school band. His first gig was with harmonica player Sunny Blair, although he was not present on Blair's sessions for RPM and Meteor in 1952. He also played with guitarist Sammy Lawhorn and Gilbert Cables. Fenton Robinson and Charles McGowan visited Little Rock in 1955 and Davis joined their band before moving on to St. Louis. In 1957, Davis, McGowan, Billy Gayles and pianist Ernest Lane travelled to California, working there for a year, and the following year Davis recorded with Robinson for Duke Records in Houston. 'Texas Flood' was his first and best-known recording, followed by 'Angels In Houston' and 'Will She Come Home'. Davis did not record again until the late 60s, cutting Robinson's 'The Years Go Passing By' for B.B. King's Virgo label and completing various sessions from which tracks were issued on Kent and Pieces. Further recordings for Hub City and True Soul in the 70s, on which Davis played guitar, went unnoticed. He was recorded live at J.B. Hutto's St. Louis club in 1980 but the album was only issued in Japan. Davis's first studio album, *I Ain't Beggin' Nobody*, was made in 1988, and in 1992 he recorded *Sooner Or Later*, an album that mixed Southern Soul in the Bobby Bland manner with more straighforward guitar blues.
● ALBUMS: *I Ain't Beggin' Nobody* (Pulsar 1988)★★★, *Sooner Or Later* (Bullseye Blues 1992)★★★.

DAVIS, MILES

b. 25 May 1926, Alton, Illinois, USA, d. 28 September 1991. Davis was born into a comparatively wealthy middle-class family and both his mother and sister were capable musicians. He was given a trumpet for his thirteenth birthday by his dentist father, who could not have conceived that his gift would set his son on the road to becoming one a giant in the development of jazz. Notwithstanding his outstanding talent as master of the trumpet, Davis's versatility encompassed flügelhorn and keyboards together with a considerable gift as a composer. This extraordinary list of talents earned Davis an unassailable reputation as the greatest leader/catalyst in the history of jazz. Such accolades were not used lightly, and he can justifiably be termed a 'musical genius'. Davis quickly progressed from his high school band into Eddie Randall's band in 1941, after his family had moved to

St. Louis. He studied at the Juilliard School of Music in New York in 1945 before joining Charlie 'Bird' Parker, with whom he had previously played in the Billy Eckstine band. By 1948 Davis had played or recorded with many jazz giants, most notably Coleman Hawkins, Dizzy Gillespie, Benny Carter, John Lewis, Illinois Jacquet and Gerry Mulligan. That year was to be a landmark for jazz; Davis, in collaboration with Gil Evans, made a series of 78s that were eventually released in 1956 as the highly influential album *Birth Of The Cool*. Davis had now refined his innovative style of playing, which was based upon understatement rather than the hurried action of the great bebop players.
During the early 50s Davis became dependent on heroin and his career was put on hold for a lengthy period. This spell of inactivity lasted until as late as 1954. The following year his seminal quintet included, variously, Red Garland, John Coltrane, Charles Mingus, Paul Chambers, Philly Joe Jones, Bill Evans and Sonny Rollins. Among their output was the acclaimed series of collections *Cookin'*, *Relaxin'*, *Workin'* and *Steamin'*. During this time Miles was consistently voted the number 1 artist in all the major jazz polls. No longer dependent on drugs by this time, he set about collaborating with Gil Evans once again. The orchestral albums made with Evans between 1957 and 1959 have all become classics: *Miles Ahead*, *Porgy And Bess* and the sparsely beautiful *Sketches Of Spain* (influenced by composer Joaquin Rodrigo). Evans was able to blend lush and full orchestration with Davis's trumpet - allowing it the space and clarity it richly deserved. Davis went on further, assembling a sextet featuring a spectacular line-up including Coltrane, Chambers, Bill Evans, Jimmy Cobb and Cannonball Adderley. Two further landmark albums during this fertile period were the aptly titled *Milestones*, followed by *Kind Of Blue*. The latter album is cited by many critics as the finest in jazz history. More than 30 years later his albums are still available, and form an essential part of any jazz record collection, with *Kind Of Blue* at the top of the list. 'So What', the opening track, has been covered by dozens of artists, the most recent offerings from guitarist Ronnie Jordan, Larry Carlton, saxophonist Candy Dulfer and reggae star Smiley Culture, who added his own lyrics and performed it in the film *Absolute Beginners*. Ian Carr, Davis's leading biographer, perceptively stated of *Kind Of Blue* in 1982: 'The more it is listened to, the more it reveals new delights and fresh depths'.
In 1959, following the bizarre arrest and beating he received at the hands of the New York Police, Davis took out a lawsuit, which he subsequently and wisely dropped. Davis entered the 60s comfortably, still the leading innovator in jazz, and shrugged off attempts from John Coltrane to dethrone him in the jazz polls. Davis chose to keep to his sparse style, allowing his musicians air and range. In 1964 while the world experienced Beatlemania, Davis created another musical landmark when he assembled arguably his finest line-up. The combination of Herbie Hancock, Wayne Shorter, Ron Carter and Tony Williams delivered the monumental *E.S.P.* in 1965. He continued with this acoustic line-up through another three recordings, including *Miles Smiles* and ending with *Nefertiti*. By the time of *Filles De Kilimanjaro*, Davis had gradually electrified his various groups and took bold steps towards rock music, integrating multiple electric keyboards and utilizing a wah-wah pedal

connected to his electrified trumpet. Additionally, his own fascination with the possibilities of electric guitar, as demonstrated by Jimi Hendrix, assumed an increasing prominence in his bands. Young American west coast rock musicians had begun to produce a form of music based upon improvisation (mostly through the use of hallucinogenics). This clearly interested Davis, who recognized the potential of blending traditional rock rhythms with jazz, although he was often contemptuous of some white rock musicians at this time. The decade closed with his band being accepted by rock fans. Davis appeared at major festivals with deliriously stoned audiences appreciating his line-up, which now featured the brilliant electric guitarist John McLaughlin, of whom Davis stated in deference to black musicians: 'Show me a black who can play like him, and I'd have him instead'. Other outstanding musicians Davis employed included Keith Jarrett, Airto, Chick Corea, Dave Holland, Joe Zawinul, Billy Cobham and Jack DeJohnette. Two major albums from this period were *In A Silent Way* and *Bitches Brew*, which unconsciously invented jazz rock and what was later to be called fusion. These records were marketed as rock albums, and consequently appeared in the regular charts. By the early 70s Davis had alienated himself from the mainstream jazz purists by continuing to flirt with rock music. In 1975, after a succession of personal upheavals including a car crash, further drug problems, a shooting incident, more police harassment and eventual arrest, Davis, not surprisingly, retired. During this time he became seriously ill, and it was generally felt that he would never play again, but, unpredictable as ever, Davis returned healthy and fit six years later with the comeback album, *The Man With The Horn*. He assembled a new band and received favourable reviews for live performances. Among the personnel were guitarist John Scofield and saxophonist Bill Evans. On the predominantly funk-based *You're Under Arrest*, he tackled pure pop songs, and although unambitious by jazz standards, tracks such as Cyndi Lauper's 'Time After Time' and Michael Jackson's 'Human Nature' were given Davis's brilliant master touch. The aggressive disco album *Tutu* followed, featuring his trumpet played through a synthesizer. A soundtrack recording for the Dennis Hopper film *The Hot Spot* found Davis playing the blues alongside Taj Mahal, John Lee Hooker, Tim Drummond and Roy Rogers. During his final years Davis settled into a comfortable pattern of touring the world and recording, able to dictate the pace of his life with the knowledge that ecstatic audiences were waiting for him everywhere. Following further bouts of ill health, during which times he took to painting, Davis was admitted to hospital in California and died in September 1991. The worldwide obituaries were neither sycophantic nor morose; great things had already been said about Davis for many years. Django Bates stated that his own favourite Davis recordings were those between 1926 and mid-1991. Ian Carr added, in his impressive obituary, with regard to Davis's music: 'unflagging intelligence, great courage, integrity, honesty and a sustained spirit of enquiry always in the pursuit of art - never mere experimentation for its own sake'. Miles Davis's influence on rock music is considerable; his influence on jazz is inestimable.

● ALBUMS: *Bopping The Blues* 1946 recording (Black Lion)★★★, *Cool Boppin'* 1948-49 recordings (Fresh Sounds)★★★, *Young Man With A Horn* 10-inch album (Blue Note 1952)★★★, *The New Sounds Of Miles Davis* 10-inch album (Prestige 1952)★★★, *Miles Davis Volume 2* (Blue Note 1953/55)★★★★, *Blue Period* 10-inch album (Prestige 1953)★★★, *Miles Davis Plays Al Cohn Compositions* 10-inch album (Prestige 1953)★★★, *Miles Davis Quintet* 10-inch album (Prestige 1953)★★★, *Miles Davis Quintet Featuring Sonny Rollins* 10-inch album (Prestige 1953)★★★, *Miles Davis Volume 3* (Blue Note 1954)★★★, *Miles Davis Sextet* 10-inch album (reissued as *Walkin'*) (Prestige 1954)★★★★, *Jeru* 10-inch album (Capitol 1954)★★★★★, *Miles Davis All Stars Volume1* 10-inch album (Prestige 1955)★★★★, *Miles Davis All Stars Volume 2* 10-inch album (Prestige 1955)★★★★, *Blue Moods* (Debut 1955)★★★, *Musings Of Miles* reissued as *The Beginning* (Prestige 1955)★★★, with Sonny Rollins *Dig Miles Davis/Sonny Rollins* reissued as *Diggin'* (Prestige 1956)★★★, *Collectors Item* (Prestige 1956)★★★, *Miles - The New Miles Davis Quintet* reissued as *The Original Quintet* (Prestige 1956)★★★, *Blue Haze* (Prestige 1956)★★★, *Birth Of The Cool* 1949-50 recordings (Capitol 1956)★★★★★, *Miles* (Original Jazz Classics 1956)★★★, *Miles Davis And Horns* reissued as *Early Miles* (Prestige 1956)★★★, *Miles Davis And Milt Jackson Quintet/Sextet* reissued as *Odyssey* (Prestige 1956)★★★, *Cookin' With The Miles Davis Quintet* (Prestige 1957)★★★★, *Relaxin' With The Miles Davis Quintet* (Prestige 1957)★★★★, *Bags Groove* (Prestige 1957)★★★★, *Round About Midnight* (Columbia 1957)★★★★, *Miles Ahead* (Columbia 1957)★★★★★, *Miles Davis And The Modern Jazz Giants* (Prestige 1958)★★★, with John Coltrane *Miles And Coltrane* (Columbia 1958)★★★★, *Milestones* (Columbia 1958)★★★★★, *Porgy And Bess* (Columbia 1958)★★★★, *'58 Miles* (Columbia 1958)★★★★, *Jazz Track* (Columbia 1958)★★★, *Workin' With The Miles Davis Quintet* (Prestige 1959)★★★★, *Kind Of Blue* (Columbia 1959)★★★★★, *Sketches Of Spain* (Columbia 1960)★★★★, *On Green Dolphin Street* 1960 recording (Jazz Door 1960)★★★, *Live In Zurich* (Jazz Unlimited 1960)★★★, *Live In Stockholm 1960* (Royal Jazz 1960)★★★, *Steamin' With The Miles Davis Quintet* (Prestige 1961)★★★★, *Miles Davis In Person (Friday And Saturday Nights At The Blackhawk, San Fransisco)* (Columbia 1961)★★★★, *Someday My Prince Will Come* (Columbia 1961)★★★★, *Miles Davis At Carnegie Hall* (Columbia 1962)★★★, *Quiet Nights* (Columbia 1962)★★★, *Seven Steps To Heaven* (Columbia 1963)★★★, *Miles Davis In Europe* (Columbia 1963)★★★, *Miles In Antibes* (Columbia 1964)★★★, with Thelonious Monk *Miles And Monk At Newport* (Columbia 1964)★★★, *My Funny Valentine* (Columbia 1964)★★★★, *E.S.P.* (Columbia 1965)★★★★, *Miles Davis Plays For Lovers* (Prestige 1965)★★★, *Jazz Classics* (Prestige 1965)★★★, *'Four' And More - Recorded Live In Concert* (Columbia 1966)★★★, *Miles Smiles* (Columbia 1966)★★★, *Milestones* (Columbia 1967)★★★★, *Sorcerer* (Columbia 1967)★★★, *Nefertiti* (Columbia 1967)★★★, *Miles In The Sky* (Columbia 1968)★★★, *Filles De Kilimanjaro* (Columbia 1968)★★★★, *Miles Orbits* (Columbia 1968)★★★, *In A Silent Way* (Columbia 1969)★★★★★, *Double Image* (Moon 1969)★★★, *Paraphernalia* (JMY 1969)★★★, *Bitches Brew* (Columbia 1970)★★★★★, *Miles Davis At The Fillmore* (Columbia 1970)★★★★, *A Tribute To Jack Johnson* (Columbia 1971)★★★★, *What I Say? Volumes 1 & 2* (JMY 1971)★★★, *Live-Evil* (Columbia 1971)★★★★, *On The Corner* (Columbia

1972)★★★, *Tallest Trees* (Prestige 1973)★★★, *In Concert* (Columbia 1973)★★★★, *Black Beauty* (Columbia 1974)★★★★, *Big Fun* (Columbia 1974)★★★, *Get Up With It* (Columbia 1974)★★★, *Jazz At The Plaza Volume 1* (1974)★★★, *Agharta* (Columbia 1976)★★★★, *Pangaea* (Columbia 1976)★★★, *Live At The Plugged Nickel* (Columbia 1976)★★★★, *Water Babies* (Columbia 1977)★★★, *The Man With The Horn* (Columbia 1981)★★★, *A Night In Tunisia* (Star Jazz 1981)★★★, *We Want Miles* (Columbia 1982)★★★, *Star People* (Columbia 1983)★★★, *Blue Christmas* (Columbia 1983)★★★, *Heard 'Round the World* 1964 concert recordings (Columbia 1983)★★★, with the Lighthouse All Stars *At Last* (Boplicity 1985)★★★, *Decoy* (Columbia 1984)★★★, *You're Under Arrest* (Columbia 1985)★★★★, *Tutu* (Warners 1986)★★★★, *Blue Haze* (Prestige 1988)★★★, *Music From Siesta '88* (Warners 1988)★★★, *Amandla* (Warners 1989)★★★, *Aura* (Columbia 1989)★★★★, *The Hot Spot* (1990)★★★, with Michel Legrand *Dingo* (Warners 1991)★★★, *Doo-Bop* (Warners 1992)★★★, *The Complete Concert: 1964* (Columbia 1992)★★★★, *Live In Europe 1988* (1993)★★★, with Quincy Jones *Miles And Quincy Jones Live At Montreux* 1991 recording (Reprise 1993)★★★★, *The Complete Live At The Plugged Nickel 1965* 8-CD box set (Columbia 1995)★★★★, *Highlights From The Plugged Nickel* (Columbia 1995)★★★★, *Live Around The World* (Warners 1996)★★★.

● COMPILATIONS: *Miles Davis' Greatest Hits* (Prestige 1957)★★★★, *Greatest Hits* (Columbia 1969)★★★★, *Basic Miles - The Classic Performances Of Miles Davis* recordings (Columbia 1973)★★★★, *Circle In The Round* 1955-70 recordings (Columbia 1979)★★★, *Directions* unreleased recordings 1960-70 (Columbia 1981)★★★, *Chronicle: The Complete Prestige Recordings* (Prestige 1987)★★★★, *The Columbia Years 1955-1985* (Columbia 1988)★★★★, *Ballads* 1961-63 recordings (Columbia 1988)★★★★, *Mellow Miles* 1961-63 recordings (Columbia 1989)★★★, *First Miles* (Savoy 1989)★★★, *The Collection* (1990)★★★★, *The Essence Of Miles Davis* (Columbia 1991)★★★★, *Gold Collection* (1993)★★★★, *Ballads And Blues* (Blue Note 1996)★★★★, *This Is Jazz No. 8 - Miles Davis Acoustic* (Legacy 1996)★★★, with Gil Evans *Miles Davis - Gil Evans: The Complete Columbia Studio Recordings* 6-CD box set (Columbia/Legacy 1996)★★★★★, *Miles Davis Plays Ballads; This Is Jazz No. 22* (Legacy 1997)★★★★, *Miles Davis Live And Electric: Live Evil* (Legacy 1997)★★★★, *Miles Davis Live And Electric: Miles Davis At The Fillmore East* (Legacy 1997)★★★★, *Miles Davis Live And Electric: Black Beauty, Miles Davis Live At The Fillmore West* (Legacy 1997)★★★★, *Miles Davis Live And Electric: Dark Magus, Live At Carnegie Hall* (Legacy 1997)★★★★, *Miles Davis Live And Electric: Miles Davis In Concert, Live At The Philharmonic Hall* (Legacy 1997)★★★★, *Quintet 1965-1968: The Complete Columbia Studio Recordings* box set (Columbia 1998)★★★, remix collection by Bill Laswell *Panthalassa: The Music Of Miles Davis 1969-1974* (Columbia 1998)★★★★.

● VIDEOS: *Miles Davis And Jazz Hoofer* (Kay Jazz 1988), *Miles In Paris* (Warner Music Video 1990), *Miles Davis And Quincy Jones: Live At Montreux* (1993).

● FURTHER READING: *Miles Davis Transcribed Solos*, Miles Davis. *Miles: The Autobiography*, Miles Davis. *Milestones: 1. Miles Davis, 1945-60*, J. Chambers. *Milestones: 2. Miles Davis Since 1960*, J. Chambers. *Miles Davis*, Barry McRae. *Miles*

Davis: A Critical Biography, Ian Carr. *Miles Davis For Beginners*, Daryl Long. *The Man In The Green Shirt: Miles Davis*, Richard Williams. *Miles Davis: The Early Years*, Bill Cole. *The Miles Davis Companion*, Gary Carner.

DAVIS, SAMMY, JR.

b. 8 December 1925, Harlem, New York, USA, d. 16 May 1990, Los Angeles, California, USA. A dynamic and versatile all-round entertainer, Davis was a trouper in the old-fashioned tradition. The only son of two dancers in a black vaudeville troupe, called Will Mastin's Holiday In Dixieland, Davis made his professional debut with the group at the age of three, as 'Silent Sam, The Dancing Midget'. While still young he was coached by the legendary tap-dancer Bill 'Bojangles' Robinson. Davis left the group in 1943 to serve in the US Army, where he encountered severe racial prejudice for the first, but not the last, time. After the war he rejoined his father and adopted uncle in the Will Mastin Trio. By 1950 the Trio were headlining at venues such as the Capitol in New York and Ciro's in Hollywood with stars including Jack Benny and Bob Hope, but it was Davis who was receiving the standing ovations for his singing, dancing, drumming, comedy and apparently inexhaustible energy. In 1954 he signed for Decca Records, and released two albums, *Starring Sammy Davis Jr.* (number 1 in the US chart), featuring his impressions of stars such as Dean Martin, Jerry Lewis, Johnnie Ray and Jimmy Durante, and *Just For Lovers*. He also made the US singles chart with 'Hey There' from *The Pajama Game*, and in the same year he lost his left eye in a road accident. When he returned to performing in January 1955 wearing an eyepatch, he was greeted even more enthusiastically than before. During that year he reached the US Top 20 with 'Something's Gotta Give', 'Love Me Or Leave Me' and 'That Old Black Magic'. In 1956 he made his Broadway debut in the musical *Mr Wonderful*, with music and lyrics by Jerry Bock, Larry Holofcener and George Weiss. Also in the show were the rest of the Will Mastin Trio, Sammy's uncle and Davis Snr. The show ran for nearly 400 performances and produced two hits, 'Too Close For Comfort', and the title song, which was very successful for Peggy Lee. Although generally regarded as the first popular American black performer to become acceptable to both black and white audiences, Davis attracted heavy criticism in 1956 over his conversion to Judaism, and later for his marriage to Swedish actress Mai Britt. He described himself as a 'one-eyed Jewish nigger'. Apart from a few brief appearances when he was very young, Davis started his film career in 1958 with *Anna Lucasta*, and was critically acclaimed the following year for his performance as Sporting Life in *Porgy And Bess*. By this time Davis was a leading member of Frank Sinatra's 'inner circle', called, variously, the 'Clan' or the 'Rat Pack'. He appeared with Sinatra in three movies, *Ocean's Eleven* (1960), *Sergeants Three* (1962), and *Robin And The Seven Hoods* (1964), but made, perhaps, a greater impact when he co-starred with another member of the 'Clan', Shirley MacLaine, in the Cy Coleman and Dorothy Fields film musical *Sweet Charity*. The 60s were good times for Davis, who was enormously popular on records and television, but especially 'live', at Las Vegas and in concert. In 1962 he made the US chart with the Anthony Newley/Leslie Bricusse number 'What Kind Of Fool Am I?', and thereafter featured several of their songs in his act. He sang Bricusse's nominated song, 'Talk To The Animals', at the 1967 Academy Awards ceremony, and collected the Oscar on behalf of the songwriter when it won. In 1972, he had a million-selling hit record with another Newley/Bricusse song, 'The Candy Man', from the film *Willy Wonka And The Chocolate Factory*. He appeared again on Broadway in 1964 in *Golden Boy*, Charles Strouse and Lee Adams' musical adaptation of Clifford Odet's 1937 drama of a young man torn between the boxing ring and his violin. Also in the cast was Billy Daniels. The show ran for 569 performances in New York, and went to London in 1968. During the 70s Davis worked less, suffering, allegedly, as a result of previous alcohol and drug abuse. He entertained US troops in the Lebanon in 1983, and five years later undertook an arduous comeback tour of the USA and Canada with Sinatra and Dean Martin. In 1989 he toured Europe with the show *The Ultimate Event*, along with Liza Minnelli and Sinatra. By this time he was already ill, although it was not apparent to audiences. After his death in 1990 it was revealed that his estate was almost worthless. In 1992, an all-star tribute, led by Liza Minnelli, was mounted at the Royal Albert Hall in London. Proceeds from the concert went to the Royal Marsden Cancer Appeal.

● ALBUMS: *Starring Sammy Davis Jr.* (Decca 1955)★★★, *Just For Lovers* (Decca 1955)★★★, *Mr. Wonderful* film soundtrack (Decca 1956)★★, *Here's Looking At You* (Decca 1956)★★★, with Carmen McRae *Boy Meets Girl* (1957)★★★, *Sammy Swings* (Decca 1957)★★★★, *It's All Over But The Swingin'* (Decca 1957)★★★★, *Mood To Be Wooed* (Decca 1958)★★★, *All The Way And Then Some* (Decca 1958)★★★★, *Sammy Davis Jr. At Town Hall* (Decca 1959)★★★★, *Porgy And Bess* (Decca 1959)★★★, *I Got A Right To Swing* (Decca 1960)★★★★, *Sammy Awards* (Decca 1960)★★★, *What Kind Of Fool Am I And Other Show-Stoppers* (Reprise 1962)★★★★, *Sammy Davis Jr. At The Cocoanut Grove* (Reprise 1963)★★★★, *Johnny Cool* film soundtrack (United Artists 1963)★★★, *As Long As She Needs Me* (Reprise 1963)★★★, *Sammy Davis Jr. Salutes The Stars Of The London Palladium* (Reprise 1964)★★★, *The Shelter Of Your Arms* (Reprise 1964)★★★, *Golden Boy* film soundtrack (Capitol 1964)★★, with Count Basie *Our Shining Hour* (Verve 1965)★★★, *Sammy's Back On Broadway* (Reprise 1965)★★★, *A Man Called Adam* film soundtrack (Reprise 1966)★★, *I've Gotta Be Me* (Reprise 1969)★★★, *Sammy Davis Jr. Now* (MGM 1972)★★★, *Portrait Of Sammy Davis Jr.* (MGM 1972)★★★, *It's A Musical World* (MGM 1976)★★★, *The Song And Dance Man* (20th Century 1977)★★★★, *Sammy Davis Jr. In Person 1977* (RCA 1983)★★★, *Closest Of Friends* (Vogue 1984).

● COMPILATIONS: *The Best Of Sammy Davis Jr.* (MCA 1982)★★★, *Collection* (Castle 1989)★★★, *The Great Sammy Davis Jr.* (MFP 1989)★★★, *Capitol Collectors Series* (Capitol 1990)★★★.

● VIDEOS: *Mr Bojangles* (Decca/Polygram Music Video 1991).

● FURTHER READING: *Yes I Can: The Story Of Sammy Davis Jr.*, Sammy Davis Jr. *Hollywood In A Suitcase*, Sammy Davis Jr. *Why Me: The Autobiography Of Sammy Davis Jr.*, Sammy Davis Jr. with Burt Boyar.

● FILMS: *The Benny Goodman Story* (1956), *Anna Lucasta* (1958), *Porgy And Bess* (1959), *Pepe* (1960), *Ocean's Eleven* (1960), *Convicts Four* (1962), *Sergeants Three* (1962), *Johnny Cool* (1963), *The Threepenny Opera* (1963), *Robin And The Seven Hoods* (1964), *Nightmare In The Sun* (1964), *A Man Called Adam* (1966), *Salt And Pepper* (1968), *Man Without Mercy* (1969), *Sweet Charity* (1969), *One More Time* (1970), *Diamonds Are Forever* (1972), *Save The Children* concert film (1973), *Stop The World - I Want To Get Off* (1978), *The Cannonball Run II* (1984), *Moon Over Parador* (1988), *Tap* (1989).

DAWN, BILLY, QUARTETTE

One of many groups who started their careers harmonizing in the Crown Heights district of Brooklyn, New York, USA, this ill-fated doo-wop/R&B concern was initiated by Billy Dawn Smith (lead), his brother Tommy Smith (baritone), plus Donnie Myles (tenor) and Sonny Benton (bass). Future producer Al Browne also added piano and occasional baritone. 'This Is The Real Thing Now' was their debut release for the small Decatur Records label in 1952. It failed to sell, and as a result the quartet moved to Duke Records. Their single for the label, 'Why Can't I Have You', was released in the summer of 1952, but saw the band credited as the Mighty Dukes instead of the Billy Dawn Quartette. They then became the Four Dukes for their next single, a sprightly version of 'Crying In The Chapel' released in September 1953. Despite competition from a version by the Orioles, it achieved significant local sales. It was much to the group's surprise then, that Duke Records did not renew their option. A fourth single and a fourth name eventually arrived when they found a sympathetic ear at Herald Records. 'Eternal Love' was credited to the Heralds, and released in September 1954. Meanwhile, Billy Dawn Smith had secured himself an A&R position at this, the group's third label, through which he was able to find work backing several Ember and Herald Records artists in the studio. Eventually he saw his future as more in writing than in performance, and the Heralds broke up in 1956 without recording again (though in the interim they had enjoyed a regular slot on the *Spotlight On Harlem* television show). Billy Dawn found success with compositions for the Crests, Five Satins and Passions, as well as being a co-founder of Hull Records. Myles went on to work with the Victorians.

DAY, BOBBY

b. Robert Byrd, 1 July 1932, Fort Worth, Texas, USA, d. 27 July 1990. He moved to Los Angeles in 1947 and shortly afterwards formed the Flames, who recorded under a variety of names on numerous labels throughout the 50s. Oddly, it took until 1957 before they achieved their first and biggest hit as the Hollywood Flames with Day's song 'Buzz, Buzz, Buzz'. Simultaneously, the group were climbing the US charts as Bobby Day And The Satellites with another of his songs, 'Little Bitty Pretty One' on Class Records, although a cover version by Thurston Harris became a bigger hit. Day, who first recorded solo in 1955, took lone billing again in 1958 for the double-sided US number 2 hit 'Rockin' Robin' and 'Over And Over'. Despite releasing a string of further outstanding R&B/rock singles in the 50s, this distinctive singer-songwriter never returned to the Top 40. In the early 60s he formed Bob And Earl with ex-Hollywood Flame Earl Nelson, although he was replaced before the duo's hit 'Harlem Shuffle'. He later recorded without success under various names on Rendezvous, RCA and Sureshot and his own Bird Land label. He temporarily relocated to Australia before settling in Florida. Although his records were no longer selling, his songs were often revived, with Dave Clark taking 'Over And Over' to the top in 1965, Michael Jackson taking 'Rockin' Robin' to number 2 in 1972 and the Jackson Five reaching the Top 20 with the catchy 'Little Bitty Pretty One' in 1972. Day's long-awaited UK debut in 1989 was warmly received, although sadly he died of cancer in July 1990.

● ALBUMS: *Rockin' With Robin* (Class 1958)★★★.

DAY, DORIS

b. Doris Von Kappelhoff, 3 April 1922, Cincinnati, Ohio, USA. One of popular music's premier post-war vocalists and biggest names, Kappelhoff originally trained as a dancer, before turning to singing at the age of 16. After changing her surname to Day, she became the featured singer with the Bob Crosby Band. A similarly successful period with the Les Brown Band saw her record a single for Columbia, 'Sentimental Journey', which sold in excess of a million copies. Already an accomplished businesswoman, it was rumoured that she held a substantial shareholding in her record company. After securing the female lead in the 1948 film *Romance On The High Seas*, in which she introduced Sammy Cahn and Jule Styne's 'It's Magic', she enjoyed a stupendous movie career. Her striking looks, crystal-clear singing voice and willingness to play tomboy heroines, as well as romantic figures, brought her a huge following. In common with other female singers of the period, she was occasionally teamed with the stars of the day and enjoyed collaborative hits with Frankie Laine ('Sugarbush') and Johnnie Ray ('Let's Walk That A-Way'). She appeared in nearly 40 movies over two decades, including *It's A Great Feeling* (1949), *Young Man With A Horn* (1950), *Tea For Two* (1950), *West Point Story* (1950), *Lullaby Of Broadway* (1951), *On Moonlight Bay* (1951), *Starlift* (1951), *I'll See You In My Dreams* (1951), *April In Paris* (1952), *By The Light Of The Silvery Moon* (1953), *Calamity Jane* (1953), *Young At Heart* (1954), *Love Me Or Leave Me* (1955), *The Man Who Knew Too Much* (1956), *The Pajama Game* (1957), *Pillow Talk* (1959) and *Jumbo* (1962). These films featured some of her best-known hits. One of her finest performances was in the uproarious romantic western *Calamity Jane*, which featured her enduringly vivacious versions of 'The Deadwood Stage' and 'Black Hills Of Dakota'. The movie also gave her a US/UK number 1 single with the yearningly sensual 'Secret Love' (later a lesser hit for Kathy Kirby). Day enjoyed a further UK chart topper with the romantically uplifting 'Whatever Will Be Will Be (Que Sera, Sera)'. After a gap of nearly six years, she returned to the charts with the sexually inviting movie theme 'Move Over Darling', co-written by her producer son Terry Melcher. Her Hollywood career ended in the late 60s and thereafter she was known for her reclusiveness. After more than 20 years away from the public's gaze, she emerged into the limelight in 1993 for a charity screening of *Calamity Jane* in her home-town of Carmel, California. Two years later she made further appearances to promote *The Love Album*, which was recorded in 1967 but had been 'lost' since that time and never released. History has made her an icon; her fresh-faced looks and strikingly pure vocal style effectively summed up an era of American music.

● ALBUMS: *You're My Thrill* (Columbia 1949)★★, *Young*

Man With A Horn film soundtrack (Columbia 1950/54)★★, *Tea For Two* film soundtrack (Columbia 1950)★★, *Lullaby Of Broadway* film soundtrack (Columbia 1951)★★, *On Moonlight Bay* film soundtrack (Columbia 1951)★★★, *I'll See You In My Dreams* film soundtrack (Columbia 1951)★★★, *By The Light Of The Silvery Moon* film soundtrack (Columbia 1953)★★★, *Calamity Jane* film soundtrack (Columbia 1953)★★★★, *Young At Heart* (Columbia 1954)★★★★, *Lights Camera Action* (Columbia 1955)★★★, *Boys And Girls Together* (Columbia 1955)★★★, with Peggy Lee *Hot Canaries* (Columbia 1955)★★★, *Lullaby Of Broadway* (Columbia 1955)★★★★, *Day Dreams* (Columbia 1955)★★★, *Day In Hollywood* (Columbia 1955)★★★, *Love Me Or Leave Me* film soundtrack (Columbia 1955)★★★★, *Day By Day* (Columbia 1957)★★★★, *Day By Night* (Columbia 1957)★★★, *The Pajama Game* film soundtrack (Columbia 1957)★★★★, *Hooray For Hollywood* (Columbia 1958)★★★, *Cuttin' Capers* (Columbia 1959)★★★, *Show Time* (Columbia 1960)★★★, *What Every Girl Should Know* (Columbia 1960)★★★, *Listen To Day* (Columbia 1960)★★★, *Bright & Shiny* (Columbia 1961)★★, *I Have Dreamed* (Columbia 1961)★★★, *Love Him!* (Columbia 1964)★★★, *Sentimental Journey* (Columbia 1965)★★★, *Latin For Lovers* (Columbia 1965)★★, *The Love Album* 1967 recordings (1994)★★★★.

● COMPILATIONS: *Doris Day's Greatest Hits* (Columbia 1958)★★★★, *Golden Greats* (Warwick 1978)★★★, *The Best Of Doris Day* (Columbia 1980)★★★★, *It's Magic* 6-CD box set (Bear Family 1993)★★★★, *Hit Singles Collection* (Telstar 1994)★★★★, *The Vintage Years* (1994)★★★, *Personal Christmas Collection* (1994)★★★, *Best Of Doris Day* (1994)★★★,*The Magic Of Doris Day* (Sony 1994)★★★★.

● VIDEOS: *Magic Of Doris Day* (1989).

● FURTHER READING: *Doris Day: Her Own Story*, Doris Day and A.E. Hotcher. *Doris Day*, Eric Braun.

● FILMS: *Romance On The High Seas* (1948), *It's A Great Feeling* (1949), *My Dream Is Yours* (1949), *West Point Story* (1950), *Tea For Two* (1950), *Young Man With A Horn* (1950), *Starlift* cameo (1951), *I'll See You In My Dreams* (1951), *On Moonlight Bay* (1951), *Lullaby Of Broadway* (1951), *Storm Warning* (1951), *April In Paris* (1952), *The Winning Team* (1952), *Calamity Jane* (1953), *By The Light Of The Silvery Moon* (1953), *Lucky Me* (1954), *Young At Heart* (1954), *Love Me Or Leave Me* (1955), *Julie* (1956), *The Man Who Knew Too Much* (1956), *The Pajama Game* (1957), *Teacher's Pet* (1958), *Tunnel Of Love* (1958), *Pillow Talk* (1959), *It Happened To Jane* (1959), *Midnight Lace* (1960), *Please Don't Eat The Daisies* (1960), *That Touch Of Mink* (1962), *Jumbo* (1962), *Lover Come Back* (1962), *Move Over Darling* (1963), *The Thrill Of It All* (1963), *Send Me No Flowers* (1964), *Do Not Disturb* (1965), *The Glass Bottom Boat* (1966), *Caprice* (1967), *With Six You Get Eggroll* (1968), *Where Were You When The Lights Went Out?* (1968), *The Ballad Of Josie* (1968).

DAY, JILL

b. Yvonne Page, 5 December 1930, Brighton, Sussex, England, d. 16 November 1990, Kingston, Surrey, England. Originally a band singer, Day graduated to become the main vocalist in the Geraldo orchestra. By 1954 she had topped the bill at the London Palladium and co-starred in the West End production of *The Talk Of The Town*. Screen appearances followed in *Always The Bride* and *All For Mary*. Although she registered no chart hits, her name became synonymous with a number of ballads including 'I'm Old Fashioned', 'Mangoes', 'A Holiday Affair' and 'I've Got My Love To Keep Me Warm'. Diminutive but tough, she was known for her fierce temper, made worse by her inexorable slide into alcoholism. Although various comebacks were mooted, including a prestigious part in the musical *Follies*, her singing career declined during the 60s. In 1963 she made the headlines when she emptied a tureen of peas over a waiter at the Pigalle theatre-restaurant, complaining that he clattered plates and cutlery during her act. Later she owned racehorses, and her business ventures included a theatrical agency and a baby-clothes company. She died of cancer in 1990.

DAY, MARGIE

b. Margaret Hoeffler, 1926, Norfolk, Virginia, USA. Day had a giant impact in the R&B market for two years, 1950-51, when she hit with 'Street-Walkin' Daddy' (number 7 R&B) and 'Little Red Rooster' (number 5 R&B) as lead singer of the Griffin Brothers Orchestra. In 1952 she left the Griffin Brothers and joined the Paul Williams band. In 1964 she briefly retired from the music business and returned to Norfolk. There she joined the Dick Morgan Trio, and in the late 60s made two albums of standards for RCA. In 1969 after becoming ill she retired permanently from showbusiness.
● COMPILATIONS: *Riffin With The Griffin Brothers Orchestra* (Ace 1985)★★★, *I'll Get A Deal* (Mr. R&B 1986)★★★.

DE BERRY, JIMMY

b. 17 November 1911, Gumwood, Arkansas, USA, d. 17 January 1985, Sikeston, Missouri, USA. De Berry was an active if peripheral member of the Memphis blues community from its heyday during the 20s until the early 50s. He grew up in Arkansas and Mississippi before moving to Memphis to live with his aunt in 1927. Teaching himself to play ukulele and then banjo and guitar, he associated with the likes of Will Shade, Charlie Burse, Jack Kelly, Frank Stokes and a very young Walter Horton. While in East St. Louis in 1934, he lost the lower part of his right leg in a train accident. Five years later, he recorded for Vocalion with his Memphis Playboys in a style that updated the hokum music from the earlier part of the decade. Over the next 15 years De Berry spent time in St. Louis and Jackson, Tennessee, returning to Memphis to make radio appearances with Willie Nix and Walter Horton. In 1953 he recorded two sessions for Sun Records; at the first session, he and Horton recorded the classic 'Easy', an instrumental adaptation of Ivory Joe Hunter's 'I Almost Lost My Mind'. The blues ballad 'Time Has Made A Change', with accompaniment from pianist Mose Vinson, came from the second session. In 1972 producer Steve LaVere reunited De Berry and Horton for sessions designed to recreate their earlier partnership, an endeavour that met with little success.
● COMPILATIONS: *Sun Records Harmonica Classics* (Rounder 1989)★★★, with Charlie Burse *Complete Recordings* (Old Tramp 1989)★★★, with Walter Horton *Easy* (Crosscut 1989)★★★, *Back* (Crosscut 1989)★★★.

DE CASTRO SISTERS

Peggy De Castro (b. Dominican Republic), Babette De Castro (b. Havana, Cuba) and Cherie De Castro (b. New York, USA) formed this close-harmony vocal trio who were extremely popular on record in the USA during the 50s, with a mixture of ballads and novelty numbers, and also in nightclubs, with a slick and flamboyant (some say flashy) act. They were raised in Cuba, on their father's sugar plantation, and began singing as a group when they moved to New York. Signed to the small Abbott label, they had a smash hit in 1954 with 'Teach Me Tonight', written by Sammy Cahn and Gene De Paul, which sold over five million copies. In 1955 they made the US charts again, with 'Boom Boom Boomerang'. Other important 50s titles included 'Too Late Now', 'Snowbound For Christmas', 'It's Yours', 'Who Are They To Say', 'Cuckoo In The Clock', 'Give Me Time' and 'Cowboys Don't Cry'. In 1959, they re-recorded their original hit as 'Teach Me Tonight Cha Cha', perhaps a sign that their appeal, at least on record, was fading. Despite the rapidly changing musical climate, they released *Sing* and *Rockin' Beat* in the early 60s. More than 25 years later, in 1988, the De Castro Sisters hit the comeback trail at Vegas World, Las Vegas. Reliving 50s joys while also strutting to later anthems such as 'New York, New York', they made up for tired vocal cords with an abundance of showbiz flair.
● ALBUMS: *The DeCastros Sing* (Capitol 1960)★★★, *The DeCastro Sisters* (Abbott 1960)★★, *The Rockin' Beat* (Capitol 1961)★★★, *At The Stardust* (1965)★★.

DEE, LENNY

b. c.20s, Illinois, USA. Dee was an organist who achieved one Top 20 single in 1955 and four charting albums during his career. He was raised in Florida, learning to play piano at the age of seven. Dee later took up the banjo and accordion. He studied music in Chicago and subsequently began performing his unique organ style, which reportedly demonstrated his ability to match perfectly the sound of a wide range of other instruments. Following a Nashville performance, Dee was approached by country star Red Foley, who introduced him to Decca, where he remained until the 70s. His first single for the label was 'Plantation Boogie', which reached number 19 in the US charts. Four albums also charted for Dee, including his first, *Dee-lightful!*, which narrowly missed the US Top 10.
● ALBUMS: *Dee-lightful!* (Decca 1955)★★★★, *Gentle On My Mind* (Decca 1968)★★, *Turn Around, Look At Me* (Decca 1969)★★, *Spinning Wheel* (Decca 1969)★★.

DEEMS, BARRETT

b. 1 March 1914, Springfield, Illinois, USA. Throughout the 30s Deems worked with Paul Ash and led his own small bands. Towards the end of the decade he worked extensively with Joe Venuti, an association that lasted until the mid-40s. Thereafter, Deems played in bands led by Red Norvo, Charlie Barnet and Muggsy Spanier. Billed as the 'World's Fastest Drummer', Deems had an eccentric onstage personality that was captured on film during a solo-feature in *Rhythm Inn* (1951). In 1954 he joined Louis Armstrong's All Stars, touring several countries and again appearing on film, this time in a feature, *High Society*, and the Ed Morrow television documentary *Satchmo The Great* (both 1956). In the 60s he worked with Jack Teagarden and the Dukes Of

Dixieland before settling in Chicago, where he played in clubs, often backing visiting jazzmen. In 1976 he toured with Benny Goodman, and in the 80s worked with Wild Bill Davison and as a member of Keith Smith's package celebrating the music of Louis Armstrong. At this time, Deems' eccentricity was enhanced by his wild, bearded appearance and his offstage volubility. He referred to himself as the oldest teenager in the business and ruined countless recorded interviews with his irreverent and frequently unbroadcastable wit. Despite the flamboyance of his appearance, Deems played with a powerful attack and his spell with Armstrong included the album of W.C. Handy tunes, which proved to be a classic of the leader's later work.
● ALBUMS: *Louis Armstrong Plays W.C. Handy* (Columbia 1954)★★★★, *Louis Armstrong At The Pasadena Civic Auditorium* (Decca 1956)★★★, with the Dukes Of Dixieland *World's Fair* (1964)★★★, *Deems* (Champion 1979)★★★.

DEEP IN MY HEART

This film biography of Sigmund Romberg, the composer of more than 50 American stage musicals, was released by MGM in 1954. José Ferrer, who had distinguished himself in movies such as *Joan Of Arc*, *Cyrano De Bergerac*, and *Moulin Rouge*, played Romberg with Doe Avedon as his wife. The screenplay, by Leonard Spigelgass, traced the composer's life from his early days as a musician in a New York café run by Anna Mueller (Helen Traubel), through to his many and varied Broadway triumphs. Among the cast were Walter Pidgeon as J.J. Shubert, the youngest brother of the powerful trio of theatrical producers, Merle Oberon as lyricist Dorothy Donnelly, one of Romberg's principal collaborators, and Paul Henreid, who played impresario Florenz Ziegfeld. Other parts were taken by Tamara Toumanova, Jim Backus and Paul Stewart. What must have been an almost impossible task of selecting musical highlights from such a prolific output, resulted in sequences in which Gene Kelly and his brother, Fred, dance together for the first time on film in 'I Love To Go Swimmin' With Wimmen''; Ann Miller's scintillating dance to 'It'; Ferrer and his real-life wife, actress-singer Rosemary Clooney, with 'Mr. And Mrs.'; Ferrer again in another duet, this time with Helen Traubel, on 'Leg Of Mutton'; and Tony Martin and Joan Weldon's lovely version of 'Lover, Come Back To Me'. One particularly memorable scene had Ferrer taking all the roles in an hilarious musical comedy spoof, *Jazz A Doo*. Squeezed into the film's running time of more than two hours were many more of Romberg's wonderful songs, including 'The Road To Paradise', 'Softly, As In a Morning Sunrise', 'Stouthearted Men', 'Serenade', 'One Alone', 'Your Land And My Land', 'You Will Remember Vienna', 'When I Grow Too Old To Dream', 'One Kiss', 'Auf Wiedersehn', and of course, 'Deep In My Heart'. The list of guest artists featured such illustrious names as Howard Keel, Vic Damone, Jane Powell, Cyd Charisse, James Mitchell and William Ovis. The choreographer was Eugene Loring, and the film, which was shot in Eastman Color, was directed by Stanley Donen. Not a box-office blockbuster by any means, but a diverting film for all that.

DEEP RIVER BOYS

A leading black vocal quartet of the 40s and 50s who, like their counterparts, the Charioteers, the Golden Gate Quartet, and the Delta Rhythm Boys, represented the jubilee and smooth ballad styles of the period. The Deep River Boys were formed by students at Hampton Institute in 1936 and consisted of lead Harry Douglass (b. 6 May 1916, Bridgeville, Delaware, USA), bass Edward Ware, second tenor George Lawson and first tenor Vernon Gardner. Pianist Charlie Ford joined the group in 1937 and with his coaching and arrangements, the Deep River Boys proved a sensation, becoming regulars on network radio for the next few years. Ford was replaced in 1940 by Ray Duran (b. Horacio Duran, 1910, d. 1980), who in turn was replaced by Cameron Williams in 1943. The Deep River Boys began recording in 1940, and continued regularly for the next 15 years to record alternately for Victor and for Joe Davis's Beacon and Jay Dee labels. Appearances in 'soundies' (the 40s version of videos) further spread their name to the public. Although hit records proved elusive, songs associated with the group included 'That Chick's Too Young To Fry' (1946), 'Recess In Heaven' and 'Truthfully' (1952). The Deep River Boys' first visit to the UK was in 1949, launching their popularity in Europe, which in the 50s superseded their success in the USA, where the rise of R&B made their music seem dated. In the UK they achieved a chart record in 1956 with 'That's Right', which went to number 29 for one week. In 1950 Lawson left the group, and in 1955 Duran came back to replace Williams as pianist. Following the departure in 1956 of originals Ware and Gardner, Harry Douglass kept the group going through a bewildering number of personnel changes, but following the death of Duran in 1980, he retired.
● ALBUMS: *The Deep River Boys Sing Songs Of Jubilee* 10-inch album (Waldorf Music Hall 1955)★★★★, *The Deep River Boys Sing Spirituals* 10-inch album (Waldorf Music Hall 1955)★★★, *Presenting The Deep River Boys* (X 1956)★★★★, *Midnight Magic* (Que 1957)★★★, *The Amazing The Deep River Boys*, *The Sensational Voices Of The Deep River Boys*, *Presenting Harry Douglass & The Deep River Boys*, *The International Inn Presents...*, *Old And New Songs*, *Golden Negro Spirituals*.
● COMPILATIONS: *Rock A Beatin' Boogie* (See For Miles 1985)★★★★.

DEJOHN SISTERS

Dux (b. 21 January 1933) and Julie DeGiovanni (b. 18 March 1931, both in Chester, Pennsylvania, USA), as the DeJohn Sisters, placed one record, '(My Baby Don't Love Me) No More', in the *Billboard* Top 10 in 1955. They began singing together in their teens. Their first professional engagement was as a replacement for the Four Aces, also of Chester, at a local social club. After becoming popular at the club, the sisters were spotted by a representative of Epic Records, and their debut recording became a US hit. Only one other Epic single, 'C'est La Vie', charted in 1955, and a 1958 single for Sunbeam Records, 'Straighten Up And Fly Right', marked the end of their chart run, although they continued to record for other labels.
● ALBUMS: *The DeJohn Sisters* (Epic 1955)★★★.

DEL-FI RECORDS

Bob Keane founded Del-Fi Records in Los Angeles, California, USA, in 1958. The fledgling label enjoyed almost immediate success with Ritchie Valens, who achieved US hits with 'C'mon, Let's Go', 'Donna' and 'La Bamba', each of which Keane produced. Valens' death in the 1959 plane

crash that also claimed Buddy Holly and the Big Bopper, robbed Del-Fi of its brightest star, but Keane had hits with other discoveries Ron Holden ('Love You So'), Little Caesar And The Romans ('Those Oldies But Goodies') and Johnny Crawford ('Cindy's Birthday', 'Your Nose Is Gonna Grow'). These were issued either on Del-Fi itself, or its Donna subsidiary, named after Valens' plaintive hit. Keane also released Chan Romero's original version of 'Hippy Hippy Shake', which became a huge UK hit in the hands of the Swinging Blue Jeans. By the early 60s Del-Fi had become an important outlet for surf and hot rod music. Bruce Johnston made some of his earliest records for the label, and other formative talents recording for Keane included Frank Zappa, David Gates and Arthur Lee, later of Love. Del-Fi was wound down as an active concern in 1964, after which Keane founded Mustang Records for new protégés the Bobby Fuller Four. However, Fuller died before his potential could fully flourish. Keane, nevertheless, has remained active in the US music industry, overseeing his considerable music catalogue.
● COMPILATIONS: *The Del-Fi And Donna Story* (Ace 1992)★★★★, *The Return Of The Del-Fi And Donna Story* (Ace 1994)★★★, *The Del-Fi Story* (Repertoire 1995)★★★★.

DEL-VIKINGS

Formed by members of the US Air Force in 1955 at their social club in Pittsburg, Ohio, the Del-Vikings' place in history is primarily secured by their status as the first successful multiracial rock 'n' roll band, but their recorded legacy also stands the test of time. Another fact overlooked by many archivists is that they were in fact, at inception, an all-black troupe. They were formed at Pittsburgh airport in 1956 by Clarence Quick (bass), Corinthian 'Kripp' Johnson (b. 1933, USA, d. 22 June 1990; lead and tenor), Samuel Patterson (lead and tenor), Don Jackson (baritone) and Bernard Robertson (second tenor). They were invited to record by producer Joe Averback, but Air Force assignments in Germany dragged away both Patterson and Robertson, who were replaced by Norman Wright and Dave Lerchey, the latter the band's first white member. 'Come Go With Me' became the lead-off track on their debut single for Averback's Fee Bee Records, but was then nationally licensed to Dot Records. It reached number 4 in the *Billboard* charts in February 1957, the highest position thus far achieved by a mixed-race group. That mix was further refined when Jackson became the third member to be transferred to Air Force duties in Germany, at which time he was replaced by a second white member, Donald 'Gus' Backus. The group's second record, 'Down In Bermuda', was ignored, but 'Whispering Bells' was afforded a better reception, reaching number 9 in the US charts. Strange circumstances surrounded the subsequent disappearance of Johnson from the group; when their manager Al Berman took the Del-Vikings to Mercury Records, he was able to break their contract with Fee Bee because the musicians were under-age when they signed, apart from Johnson, who was legally bound being 21 years of age. William Blakely replaced him in the new line-up, which debuted with 'Cool Shake' in May 1957 (this entered the charts at about the same time as 'Whispering Bells', causing considerable confusion). Kripp Johnson retaliated by forming his own Del-Vikings with Arthur Budd, Eddie Everette, Chuck Jackson

and original member Don Jackson, who had returned from his service endeavours in Germany. They released two singles, 'Willette' and 'I Want To Marry You', to little commercial recognition. Luniverse Records also muddied the picture by releasing an album of eight Del-Vikings songs that the group had originally placed with them in 1956 before Averback had signed them to Fee Bee. In order to clarify the situation, the next release on Dot Records was credited to the Dell-Vikings And Kripp Johnson, but this did not prevent Mercury Records suing to ensure that any use of the Del-Vikings name, whatever its spelling, belonged to it. Some of the confusion was abated when Kripp Johnson was able to rejoin the Del-Vikings when his contract with Fee Bee ran out in 1958 (by which time Donald Backus had become the fourth member of the group to lose his place due to an Air Force posting to Germany). Kripp sang lead on the group's last two Mercury singles, 'You Cheated' and 'How Could You'. Although recordings by the 'original Del-Vikings' were less forthcoming from this point, the group, now all discharged from the Air Force, toured widely throughout the 60s. They signed to a new label, ABC Paramount Records, in 1961, and began in promising style with 'Bring Back Your Heart'. Several excellent releases followed, but none revisited the chart action of old. The 70s saw them record a handful of one-off singles as they toured widely, including stints in Europe and the Far East.
● ALBUMS: *Come Go With The Del Vikings* (Luniverse 1957)★★★, *They Sing - They Swing* (Mercury 1957)★★★, *A Swinging, Singing Record Session* (Mercury 1958)★★, *Newies And Oldies* (1959)★★★, *The Del Vikings And The Sonnets* (Crown 1963)★★★, *Come Go With Me* (Dot 1966)★★★.
● COMPILATIONS: *Del Vikings* (Buffalo Bop 1988)★★★, *Cool Shake* (Buffalo Bop 1988)★★★, *Collectables* (Mercury 1988)★★★.

DELANEY, ERIC

b. 22 May 1924, London, England. Delaney came from a musical family and learnt to play the piano while still at school. He switched to the drums at the age of 10, and studied tympani at the Guildhall School of Music in London during 1946-47. After playing in other bands, including the one led by Geraldo, Delaney formed his own unit in 1954, which was built around his 'Siamese twin drum kit', revolving stage, and a distinctive percussion sound. The record catalogues of the day listed him as a 'swing drummer'. His novel recording of 'Oranges And Lemons' gave the band its first boost, and it toured the UK Variety circuit in 1955, and in the following year played in the Royal Command Performance at the London Palladium, besides visiting the USA. Typical of the band's repertoire were 'Roamin' In The Gloamin'', 'Hornpipe Boogie', 'Cockles And Muscles', 'Say Si Si', 'Fanfare Jump' and the album *Cha-Cha-Cha Delaney*, all of which appeared on the UK Pye label. In 1960 Delaney switched to Parlophone Records and made an album *Swingin' Thro' The Shows*, produced by George Martin. In the 80s he was still touring with a small group, predominantly in the north of England. In 1991, sporting a 'Yul Brynner' haircut, Delaney announced his return to work following a three-month hiatus prompted by a condition he described as 'Lumbar Sacral Spondylosis'.
● ALBUMS: *Cha-Cha-Cha Delaney* (Pye 1959)★★★, *Swingin' Thro' The Shows* (Parlophone 1960)★★★.

DELROYS

The Delroys were formed in the Queensbridge Housing Projects of Long Island City, New York, USA, in 1956, out of several groups who sang on the neighbourhood's street corners. Reggie Walker joined with Ronnie and Bobby Coleman, plus John Blount and a vocalist dubbed Snookie. Their performances attracted the attention of manager Ernest Kelly and he secured them a contract with Apollo Records as a consequence of Apollo's desire to sign another artist he represented, Milton Sparks. Apollo were clearly not as impressed with the young band (average age still 14), and issued their first recording, 'Bermuda Shorts', only as a b-side to Sparks' debut release, 'Time'. It proved as popular as the more heavily promoted a-side, and gave the Delroys the chance to embark on major east coast touring. Unfortunately, this experience was somewhat traumatic, with the band left stranded after a concert in Washington when their tour manager absconded with the takings. By the time they found their way back to Long Island, Blount left the band and was replaced by Bobby Taylor of the Uniques (manager Junior Talbot would also become a participating member of the band). However, the group's second release, 'Wise Old Owl', for Sparkell Records, failed to capture the public's imagination. The group was disbanded in 1961, though Ronnie Coleman did resuscitate the name with Ray Pain (lead), Norman Boquie (second tenor) and Cliff Davis (baritone). One single, 'Love Me Tenderly', was released for Carol Records, before the members dispersed once more. Three original members of the Delroys then reunited as the First Three in 1979 (the Coleman brothers plus Reggie Walker). A further reunification of the same personnel followed in 1982, this time back under the Delroys banner. Five years later they issued only their fifth single, 'Talk To Me', on their own label.

DENE, TERRY

b. Terence Williams, 20 December 1938, London, England. Dene was discovered singing in the famous Soho coffee bar the 2 I's. His big break came when he appeared on the BBC Television show *6.5 Special* in April 1957. After being rejected by EMI, he was signed by Decca A&R man Dick Rowe and his version of Marty Robbins' 'A White Sport Coat' became the first of his three UK Top 20 hits between 1957 and 1958. His other big hits were 'Start Movin'', a cover version of the Sal Mineo original, and another Marty Robbins song, 'The Stairway Of Love'. Fame brought him many problems and in 1958 he was fined for both drunkenness and vandalism. A one-time screen extra, he also starred in the unsuccessful 1958 British pop film *The Golden Disc*. Often referred to as 'Britain's Elvis', this singer - with an admitted history of mental disturbance - was inducted into the army with the full press treatment in 1959. A large battalion of media representatives was also present when he was released as 'medically unfit' just two months later. The end of his short marriage to singer Edna Savage continued to give him the kind of publicity that destroyed what was left of his career. He next joined Larry Parnes' stable of stars, but the legendary impresario could not salvage Dene's career. After abandoning pop music, he became a street-singing evangelist, recording three gospel albums. He spent five years living in Sweden and in 1974 a book and album, both called *I Thought Terry Dene Was Dead*, were issued. In the 80s he returned to singing and rock 'n' roll with members of his original group, the Dene-Aces, which included Brian Gregg, writer of the classic 'Shakin' All Over'. Despite the fact that Dene was not a great rock 'n' roll original, he was welcomed back like a true legend by many UK fans.

● ALBUMS: *I Thought Terry Dene Was Dead* (Decca 1974)★★★.
● FURTHER READING: *I Thought Terry Dene Was Dead*, Dan Wooding.
● FILMS: *The Golden Disc* (1958).

DENNIS, JACKIE

b. 1942, Edinburgh, Scotland. Dennis was discovered by UK comedians Mike and Bernie Winters, when he was performing at an American Air Force base in Prestwick. They brought him to the attention of top agent Eve Taylor and she instantly booked him on the *6.5 Special* television show. Dennis's impact was immediate and he was quickly added to the cast of the *6.5 Special* film; it was even announced that he was to start filming *The Jackie Dennis Story*. The future looked very bright indeed in 1958 for the lively, kilt-wearing, 15-year-old pop singer, whose first record 'La Dee Dah', a cover version of Billy And Lillie's US hit, had leapt into the UK Top 20 just two weeks after its release. Television and live bookings flooded in and he was even invited to the USA to appear in Perry Como's top-rated television show, where he was introduced as 'Britain's Ricky Nelson'. Despite all this, record buyers did not purchase his subsequent releases in any quantity and he faded from the public eye just as quickly as he had arrived.

DENNIS, MATT

b. 11 February 1914, Seattle, Washington, USA. A composer, singer and pianist, Dennis was born into a musical family. His father was a well-known singer and his mother played the violin; at one stage they were both part of a vaudeville act called the Five Musical Lovelands. Early in Dennis's life the family moved to Los Angeles, California, where he attended San Rafael High School, eventually directing the school's dance orchestra. In 1933 he joined Horace Heidt's band as a pianist, and sang with Alice King, one of the King Sisters. Some years later he formed a band with Dick Haymes, and subsequently served as an arranger and accompanist for Martha Tilton, Margaret Whiting and the Stafford Sisters. In 1940, when Jo Stafford became a member of the Pied Pipers with the famed band of Tommy Dorsey, she recommended Dennis as a staff arranger and composer. His compositions for the band, with lyrics by Tom Adair, included 'Everything Happens To Me', 'Violets For Your Furs' and 'Free For All', all recorded by Dorsey's young vocalist Frank Sinatra; 'Will You Still Be Mine?' was sung by Connie Haines and 'Let's Get Away From It All', which spanned both sides of a 78 rpm disc, was sung by Sinatra, Jo Stafford, Connie Haines and the Pied Pipers. Stafford and the Dorsey band also performed Dennis's 'Little Man With A Candy Cigar' (lyric by Frank Kilduff). After three and a half years with the Radio Production Unit of the US Army Air Force during World War II, Dennis was much in demand, writing and performing on radio shows such as the *The Alan Young Show*, *The Chesterfield Supper Club* and the *Seven-Up Show*. He was also a regular performer at the smart Hollywood nightclubs, including the Tally-Ho, Encore and

Captain's Table, and had his own NBC television show for a time. When Sinatra began his series of classic albums with Capitol Records in the early 50s, he gave the definitive reading of the Dennis/Adair ballad 'Violets For Your Furs', on *Songs For Young Lovers*, and the singer continued to include several more of the composer's works in his repertoire, such as 'The Night We Called It A Day' (Adair; the song featured in the 1944 Allan Jones picture *Sing A Jingle* - UK title *Lucky Days*), and 'Angel Eyes' (Earl Brent). Dennis himself sang the latter song in the Ida Lupino/Howard Duff film *Jennifer* (1953). His first album, *Matt Dennis Plays And Sings*, was an early on-site recording at the Tally-Ho club, and featured his own songs, including 'Compared To You' (lyric by Paul Herrick), 'Tired Routine Called Love' (Ted Steele), 'It Wasn't In The Stars' (Dave Gillam), 'Junior And Julie' (Adair) and some of the other numbers he wrote for the Dorsey band, such as 'Will You Still Be Mine?', a 'list' song, which was amusingly updated in 1955 on *Buddy Greco At Mr. Kelly's*. Dennis's other compositions include 'Relax', 'Music', 'Show Me The Way To Get Out Of This World', 'Love Turns Winter To Spring', 'Blues For Breakfast', 'Who's Yehoodi?' (a 1940 novelty hit for both Kay Kyser and Jerry Colonna) and 'We Belong Together'. Among his many collaborators have been Jerry Gladstone, Sammy Cahn, Bob Russell, and his wife, Ginny Maxey Dennis, who also produced *Matt Dennis Is Back!* in 1981. For some years before that he had concentrated on his music publishing interests and piano tutorials such as *The Matt Dennis Popular Piano Method*. On his 1981 album he retained the inimitable touch and style that has, throughout his life, endeared him to the musical cognoscenti, but has not made him even moderately famous. His melodies continue to surface, and one of the best of them, 'Violets For Your Furs', was performed by pianist Kenny Clayton at the 1993 memorial service for the celebrated entertainer Bernard Braden.

Dennis's chief collaborator, Tom Adair (b. 15 June 1913, Newton, Kansas, USA), wrote lyrics with several other composers, including Al D'Artega, with whom he worked on 'In The Blue Of Evening', a tender ballad that became a best-seller in 1943 for the Dorsey band with a vocal by Sinatra. After military service during World War II, Adair contributed special material to radio - and later, television shows - and nightclub acts and shows. In 1949 he worked with the composer-conductor Gordon Jenkins on the score for the Broadway revue *Along Fifth Avenue*. Although the show enjoyed only a modest run, it did contain some appealing numbers, including 'The Best Time Of Day', 'I Love Love In New York', 'Weep No More' and 'The Skyscraper Blues', which subsequently received an impressive reading on record by Tony Bennett. Adair also wrote for movies, and his 'Hail The Princess Aurora' and 'The Sleeping Beauty Song' (with George Bruns) were a feature of the Walt Disney animated film *Sleeping Beauty* (1959).

● ALBUMS: *Matt Dennis Plays And Sings* (1954)★★★, *Dennis, Anyone?* (1956)★★★, *Welcome, Matt Dennis!* (1958)★★★, *Melancholy Baby* (1959)★★★, *Some Of My Favourites* (1960)★★, *Matt Dennis Is Back!* (1981)★★.

DIAMOND, LEO

b. 29 June 1915, New York City, New York, USA, d. 15 September 1966, Los Angeles, California, USA. After spending 1930-46 as the arranger and lead harmonica player

for the Borrah Minevitch Harmonica Rascals, Leo Diamond attempted a solo career. His debut, and biggest, single was the instrumental 'Off Shore', which reached the US Top 20 in late 1953. The follow-up, however, 'Sadie Thompson's Song (Blue Pacific Blues)', taken from the original film soundtrack of *Miss Sadie Thompson*, failed to chart. His only other hit was a version of 'Melody Of Love', which spent one week at number 30 in the US charts in February 1955.

DIAMONDS (CANADA)

The group comprised Dave Somerville (lead), Ted Kowalski (tenor), Bill Reed (bass) and Phil Leavitt (baritone), all born in Toronto, Canada. A white vocal group that specialized in cover versions of black R&B hits, the Diamonds were formed in 1953, and during the next two years, attracted a good deal of attention on the club circuit in America's Midwest states. In 1955 they recorded several sides for Decca's Coral label, including a cover version of the Cheers' Top 10 single, 'Black Denim Trousers And Motor Cycle Boots'. Early in the following year they moved to Mercury, a label already highly skilled in recreating existing hits, such as the Crew-Cuts' version of 'Sh-Boom' (1954), which was first released by the Chords. The Diamonds made their initial impact for Mercury with 'Why Do Fools Fall In Love', a Top 10 hit for Frankie Lymon And The Teenagers in 1956. The Diamonds' version made the US Top 20, and was followed in the same year by further successful substitutes for the originals, such as 'Church Bells May Ring' (Willows), 'Little Girl Of Mine' (Cleftones), 'Love, Love, Love' (Clovers), 'Ka Ding Dong' (G-Clefs)', 'Soft Summer Breeze' (Eddie Heywood) and 'A Thousand Miles Away' (Heartbeats). 'Little Darlin'' (1957), written by Maurice Williams when he was lead singer with the Gladiolas and before he went on to the Zodiacs, gave the Diamonds their highest US chart entry (number 2). The group's remaining Top 40 hits in the 50s were 'Words Of Love', 'Zip Zip', 'Silhouettes', 'The Stroll', 'High Sign', 'Kathy-O' (a ballad, in a more easy-listening style), 'Walking Along' and 'She Say Oom Dooby Doom'. In 1958 Phil Leavitt retired and was replaced by Michael Douglas, and, in the following year, two Californians, Evan Fisher and John Felton, took over from Bill Reed and Ted Kowalski. The 'new' Diamonds continued to record throughout the early 60s and had one Top 30 entry with 'One Summer Night' in 1961. After the group split up, Dave Somerville formed a double act with ex-Four Prep Bruce Belland, until the Diamonds re-formed in the early 70s. Despite Felton's death in an air crash in 1982, the group continued to tour, and was especially popular on the county fair circuit into the 90s.

● ALBUMS: *Collection Of Golden Hits* (Mercury 1956)★★★, *The Diamonds* (Mercury 1957)★★★, *The Diamonds Meet Pete Rugolo* (Mercury 1958)★★★, *The Diamonds Sing The Songs Of The Old West* (Mercury 1959)★★, *America's Famous Song Stylists* (Wing 1962)★★★, *Pop Hits By The Diamonds* (Wing 1962)★★.

● COMPILATIONS: *The Best Of The Diamonds* (Rhino 1984)★★★.

● FILMS: *The Big Beat* (1957).

DIAMONDS (USA)

The members of this vocal group from New York, USA, were lead Harold Wright (d. April 1996), first tenor Myles Hardy and bass Daniel Stevens. The Diamonds had moderate success in the early 50s specializing in deep-sounding ballads. The group was formed in 1948 as a trio - Wright, Hardy and Stevens - but in 1950 they added a guitarist, Ernest Ward, who also sang tenor. The group was discovered by Bobby Schiffman of the Apollo Theatre and he gave them their start by having them play the amateur shows at his theatre. As their manager he helped them to sign with Atlantic Records, which was enjoying great success with the Clovers at the time. The company released three singles by the group, the best-remembered being 'A Beggar For Your Kisses'. The unit broke up by 1954, and Wright joined the Regals, who recorded four tracks for Aladdin. When the other Regals became Sonny Till's new Orioles group, Wright formed the Metronones, who recorded four tracks for Cadence.

DILLARD, VARETTA

b. 3 February 1933, Harlem, New York, USA, d. 4 October 1993, Brooklyn, New York, USA. Dillard was known for several hits of poppish R&B in a style very reminiscent of Ruth Brown. As the result of a bone deficiency she spent most of her childhood years in a hospital, where she discovered singing as a therapy. Encouraged and inspired by Carl Feaster, lead singer with the Chords, Dillard began entering talent shows, which led to two consecutive wins at the Apollo's amateur show. Signed to Savoy Records in 1951, she made her own records and duetted with H-Bomb Ferguson, enjoying success with 'Easy, Easy Baby' (number 8 R&B, 1952), 'Mercy Mr. Percy' (number 6 R&B, 1953), and after Johnny Ace's untimely demise, 'Johnny Has Gone' (number 6 R&B, 1955). In 1956 Dillard switched to the RCA subsidiary label Groove, where, much to her distaste, she was coerced into capitalizing on James Dean's death with 'I Miss You Jimmy'. Later recordings for Triumph and MGM's Cub subsidiary failed to match her Savoy successes, and she ended her solo recording career in 1961, although she continued singing into the late 60s by joining her husband's group, the Tri-Odds, who were active in the Civil Rights movement, performing jazz, a cappella, and black-centric poetry.
● COMPILATIONS: *Double Crossing Daddy* (Mr. R&B 1984)★★★, *Mercy Mr. Percy* (Savoy Jazz 1988)★★★, *Got You On My Mind* (Bear Family 1989)★★★, *The Lovin' Bird* (Bear Family 1989)★★★.

DINNING SISTERS

This versatile close harmony vocal trio, popular in the late 40s and 50s, consisted of Lou (b. Lucille Dinning, 29 September 1922, Kentucky, USA; alto) and twins Ginger (b. Virginia Dinning; lead) and Jean (b. Eugenia Dinning; soprano - both b. 29 March 1924, Oklahoma, USA). The trio, from a family of five daughters and four sons, were blessed with perfect pitch, and sang together in their church choir from an early age. In their teens, the girls had their own 15-minute local radio show, and later toured clubs and theatres in the Midwest with Herbie Holmes's orchestra. After moving to Chicago in 1939, they won a five-year contract with NBC, and during the early 40s were regulars on programmes such as the *Bowman Musical Milkwagon*, *Gary Moore's Club Matinee* and the *National Barn Dance*, and headlined at venues such as the Chez Paree, the Chicago Theatre and the Latin Quarter. A trip to Hollywood led to an appearance with Ozzie Nelson's band in the movie *Strictly In The Groove*. They also provided vocals for two Walt Disney films,

Fun And Fancy Free and *Melody Time*, in the latter of which they sang 'Blame It On The Samba', accompanied by organist Ethel Smith. While on the west coast they signed for Capitol Records, and had several hits in the late 40s, including 'My Adobe Hacienda', 'I Wonder Who's Kissing Her Now', 'Beg Your Pardon' and the million-seller 'Buttons And Bows' (1948), accompanied by accordionist Art Van Damme's Quintet. Lou Dinning also made some solo records, including 'The Little White Cloud That Cried', 'Trust In Me', 'Just Friends' and 'Nobody Else But Me', with Paul Weston's Orchestra. By the mid-50s the Dinning Sisters' appeal had waned, and they subsequently retired. In 1960 their brother, Mark Dinning, topped the US chart in a very different style, with 'Teen Angel'.
● ALBUMS: *Songs By The Dinning Sisters* (Capitol 1957)★★★.
● COMPILATIONS: *The Dinning Sisters, Volume 1* (Capitol 1984)★★★, *The Dinning Sisters, Volume 2* (Capitol 1986)★★★.

DISC JOCKEY JAMBOREE

Arguably the most anodyne film of the rock 'n' roll era, this 1957 feature starred Kay Medford and Robert Pastine as two theatrical agents. Once married, now separated, they individually represent 'Pete' and 'Honey', two singers who begin to work together and become 'America's Sweethearts'. During the course of this, the Medford and Pastine characters are reconciled. Amid this sugary plot are performances by rock 'n' roll and rockabilly stars Jerry Lee Lewis ('Great Balls Of Fire'), Buddy Knox ('Hula Love'), Charlie Gracie ('Cool Baby') and Carl Perkins ('Glad All Over'). Fats Domino, Connie Francis and Frankie Avalon - later the star of innumerable 'beach' films - are also featured in this film that at best showcases acts rarely enshrined on celluloid.

DIXON, REGINALD

b. 1905, Sheffield, England, d. 9 May 1985, Blackpool, Lancashire, England. The son of a craftsman in the local Sheffield steel industry, as a teenager Dixon played the organ in a Methodist church and provided the accompaniment for silent films. In 1930 he accepted the position of organist at the Tower Ballroom in Blackpool, and stayed there - except for a spell in the RAF during World War II - for 40 years, until his retirement. Heralded by his much-loved signature tune 'Oh, I Do Like To Be Beside The Seaside', he came to be known as 'Mr. Blackpool', and was almost as famous as the Tower itself. However, his reputation also reached other areas of the UK through his frequent broadcasts and recordings of medleys of familiar popular tunes and light classical pieces.
● ALBUMS: *Presenting Reginald Dixon* (Columbia 1963)★★★★, *Happy Memories Of Blackpool* (Encore 1964)★★★, *Mr. Blackpool* (Columbia 1964)★★★★, *Sing Along At The Tower* (Columbia 1966)★★★, *Gala Night At The Tower* (Encore 1966)★★★, *Great Organ Favourites* (Columbia 1967)★★★, *At Your Request* (Columbia 1967)★★★, *Meet Mr. Blackpool* (Columbia 1968)★★★, *Beside The Seaside* (Columbia 1969)★★★★, *Farewell Mr. Blackpool* (Columbia 1970)★★★, *At The Movies* (One-Up 1976)★★★, *Isn't This A Lovely Day* (EMI 1980)★★★, *At The Wurlitzer Organ* (Ideal 1981)★★★★, *Over The Waves* (EMI 1981)★★★, *Blackpool Nights* (EMI 1985)★★★★, *Fascinating*

Rhythm (Burlington Records 1988)★★★, *At The Organ Of The Tower Ballroom, Blackpool* (Ideal 1991)★★★.
● COMPILATIONS: *World Of Reginald Dixon* (Decca 1969)★★★★, *Magic Of Reginald Dixon* (MFP 1987)★★★.

DIXON, WILLIE

b. 1 July 1915, Vicksburg, Mississippi, USA, d. 29 January 1992. At an early age Dixon was interested in both words and music, writing lyrics and admiring the playing of Little Brother Montgomery. As an adolescent, Dixon sang bass with local gospel groups, had some confrontation with the law, and hoboed his way to Chicago, where he became a boxer. He entered music professionally after meeting Baby Doo Caston, and together they formed the Five Breezes, whose 1940 recordings blend blues, jazz, pop and the vocal group harmonies of the Inkspots and the Mills Brothers. During World War II, Dixon resisted the draft, and was imprisoned for 10 months. After the war, he formed the Four Jumps Of Jive before reuniting with Caston in the Big Three Trio, who toured the Midwest and recorded for Columbia Records. The trio featured vocal harmonies and the jazz-influenced guitarwork of Ollie Crawford. Dixon's performing activities lessened as his involvement with Chess Records increased. By 1951 he was a full-time employee, as producer, A&R representative, session musician, talent scout, songwriter, and occasionally, name artist. Apart from an interlude when he worked for Cobra in a similar capacity, Dixon remained with Chess until 1971. The relationship, however, was ultimately complex; he was forced to regain control of his copyrights by legal action. Meanwhile, Dixon was largely responsible for the sound of Chicago blues on Chess and Cobra, and of the black rock 'n' roll of Chuck Berry and Bo Diddley. He was also used on gospel sessions by Duke/Peacock, and his bass playing was excellent behind Rev. Robert Ballinger. Dixon's productions of his own songs included Muddy Waters' 'I'm Your Hoochie Coochie Man', Howlin' Wolf's 'Spoonful', Diddley's 'You Can't Judge A Book By Its Cover', Otis Rush's 'I Can't Quit You Baby' (a triumph for Dixon's and Rush's taste for minor chords), and Koko Taylor's 'Wang Dang Doodle', among many others. In the early 60s, Dixon teamed up with Memphis Slim to play the folk revival's notion of blues, and operated as a booking agent and manager, in which role he was crucial to the American Folk Blues Festival Tours of Europe. Many British R&B bands recorded his songs, including the Rolling Stones and Led Zeppelin, who adapted 'You Need Love'. After leaving Chess, Dixon went into independent production with his own labels, Yambo and Spoonful, and resumed a recording and performing career. He also administered the Blues Heaven Foundation, a charity that aimed to promote awareness of the blues, and to rectify the financial injustices of the past. Willie Dixon claimed, 'I am the blues'; and he was, certainly, hugely important in its history, not only as a great songwriter, but also as a producer, performer and mediator between artists and record companies.
● ALBUMS: *Willie's Blues* (Bluesville 1959)★★★, *Memphis Slim & Willie Dixon At The Village Gate* (1960)★★★★, *I Am The Blues* (Columbia 1970)★★, *Peace* (1971)★★★, *Catalyst* (Ovation 1973)★★★, *Mighty Earthquake And Hurricane* (1983)★★★, *I Feel Like Steppin' Out* (1986)★★★, *Gene Gilmore & The Five Breezes* (1989)★★, *Hidden Charms* (Bug 1988)★★★, *The Big Three Trio* (Columbia 1990)★★★, *Blues*

Dixonary (1993)★★★, *Across The Borderline* (1993)★★★.
● COMPILATIONS: *Collection* (Deja Vu 1987)★★★, *The Chess Box* box set (Chess 1988)★★★, *The Original Wang Dang Doodle - The Chess Recordings & More* (MCA/Chess 1995)★★★★.
● FURTHER READING: *I Am The Blues*, Willie Dixon.

DJANGO REINHARDT

A good examination of the work of the first European to achieve international status in jazz. Directed by Paul Paviot, this 1958 film features several musicians associated with Reinhardt, including his brother, Joseph, and Stéphane Grappelli.

DOGGETT, BILL

b. 16 February 1916, Philadelphia, Pennsylvania, USA, d. 13 November 1996. In 1938 pianist Doggett formed his first band, partly drawing his sidemen from the band of Jimmy Goreham, with whom he had played for the past few years. Later that year he worked with Lucky Millinder, with whom he also played in the early 40s - Millinder having taken over leadership of Doggett's band. During this period Doggett wrote many arrangements for various bands, including Lionel Hampton and Count Basie, and also worked as staff arranger and accompanist with the popular vocal group the Ink Spots. He made a number of recordings with Buddy Tate and Illinois Jacquet, then worked with Willie Bryant, Johnny Otis and Louis Jordan. In the mid-40s he began playing organ, and when he formed his own R&B band in 1951, concentrated on this instrument. He had big hits with 'Honky Tonk', which reached number 1 in the R&B charts and number 2 in the US charts in 1956, and was in the Top 10 for 14 weeks with 'Slow Walk'. He showed his versatility by arranging and conducting Ella Fitzgerald's 1963 album *Rhythm Is Our Business*. Doggett continued leading a swinging R&B-orientated band into the 80s.
● ALBUMS: *Bill Doggett - His Organ And Combo* 10-inch album (King 1955)★★★, *Bill Doggett - His Organ And Combo Volume 2* 10-inch album (King 1955)★★★, *All-Time Christmas Favorites* 10-inch album (King 1955)★★, *Sentimentally Yours* 10-inch album (King 1956)★★, *Moondust* (King 1957)★★, *Hot Doggett* (King 1957)★★, with Earl Bostic *C'mon And Dance With Earl Bostic* (King 1958)★★★, *As You Desire* (King 1958)★★★, *A Salute To Ellington* (King 1958)★★★, *Goin' Doggett* (1958)★★★, *The Doggett Beat For Dancing Feet* (King 1958)★★★, *Candle Glow* (King 1958)★★★, *Dame Dreaming* (King 1958)★★★, *Everybody Dance To The Honky Tonk* (King 1958)★★★, *Man With A Beat* (1958)★★★, *Swingin' Easy* (King 1959)★★★, *Dance Awhile With Doggett* (King 1959)★★, *Hold It* (King 1959)★★★, *High And Wide* (King 1959)★★★, *Big City Dance Party* (King 1959)★★★, *Bill Doggett On Tour* (King 1959)★★★, *Bill Doggett Christmas* (King 1959)★★, *For Reminiscent Lovers, Romantic Songs* (King 1960)★★★, *Back Again With More Bill Doggett* (King 1960)★★★, *Focus On Bill Doggett* (1960)★★, *Bonanza Of 24 Songs* (King 1960)★★★, *The Many Moods Of Bill Doggett* (King 1963)★★, *American Songs In The Bossa Nova Style* (King 1963)★★, *Impressions* (King 1964)★★★, *Honky Tonk Popcorn* (King 1969)★★★, *Bill Doggett* (1971)★★★, *Lionel Hampton Presents Bill Doggett* (1977)★★★, *Midnight Shows Volume 9* (1978)★★★.
● COMPILATIONS: with Buddy Tate *Jumpin' On The West*

Coast (1947)★★★, *The Best Of Bill Doggett* (King 1964)★★★, *Bonanza Of 24 Hit Songs* (King 1966)★★★, *14 Original Greatest Hits* (King 1988)★★★.

DOMINO, FATS

b. Antoine Domino, 26 February 1928, New Orleans, Louisiana, USA. From a large family, he learned piano from local musician Harrison Verrett who was also his brother-in-law. A factory worker after leaving school, Domino played in local clubs such as the Hideaway. It was there in 1949 that bandleader Dave Bartholomew and Lew Chudd of Imperial Records heard him. His first recording, 'The Fat Man', became a Top 10 R&B hit the next year and launched his unique partnership with Bartholomew who co-wrote and arranged dozens of Domino tracks over the next two decades. Like that of Professor Longhair, Domino's playing was derived from the rich mixture of musical styles to be found in New Orleans. These included traditional jazz, Latin rhythms, boogie-woogie, Cajun and blues. Domino's personal synthesis of these influences involved lazy, rich vocals supported by rolling piano rhythms. On occasion his relaxed approach was at odds with the urgency of other R&B and rock artists and the Imperial engineers would frequently speed up the tapes before Domino's singles were released. During the early 50s, Domino gradually became one of the most successful R&B artists in America. Songs such as 'Goin' Home' and 'Going To The River', 'Please Don't Leave Me' and 'Don't You Know' were bestsellers and he also toured throughout the country. The touring group included the nucleus of the band assembled by Dave Bartholomew for recordings at Cosimo Matassa's studio. Among the musicians were Lee Allen (saxophone), Frank Field (bass) and Walter 'Papoose' Nelson (guitar).

By 1955, rock 'n' roll had arrived and young white audiences were ready for Domino's music. His first pop success came with 'Ain't That A Shame' in 1955, although Pat Boone's cover version sold more copies. 'Bo Weevil' was also covered, by Teresa Brewer, but the catchy 'I'm In Love Again', with its incisive saxophone phrases from Allen, took Domino into the pop Top 10. The b-side was an up-tempo treatment of the 20s standard, 'My Blue Heaven', which Verrett had sung with Papa Celestin's New Orleans jazz band. Domino's next big success also came with a pre-rock 'n' roll song, 'Blueberry Hill'. Inspired by Louis Armstrong's 1949 version, Domino used his creole drawl to perfection. Altogether, Fats Domino had nearly 20 US Top 20 singles between 1955 and 1960. Among the last of them was the majestic 'Walking To New Orleans', a Bobby Charles composition that became a string-laden tribute to the sources of his musical inspiration. His track record in the *Billboard* R&B lists, however, is impressive, with 63 records reaching the charts. He continued to record prolifically for Imperial until 1963, maintaining a consistently high level of performance. There were original compositions such as the jumping 'My Girl Josephine' and 'Let the Four Winds Blow' and cover versions of country songs (Hank Williams' 'Jambalaya') as well as standard ballads such as 'Red Sails In The Sunset', his final hit single in 1963. The complex off-beat of 'Be My Guest' was a clear precursor of the ska rhythms of Jamaica, where Domino was popular and toured in 1961. The only unimpressive moments came when he was persuaded to jump on the twist bandwagon, recording a number titled 'Dance With Mr

Domino'. By now, Lew Chudd had sold the Imperial company and Domino had switched labels to ABC Paramount. There he recorded several albums with producers Felton Jarvis and Bill Justis, but his continuing importance lay in his tours of North America and Europe, which recreated the sound of the 50s for new generations of listeners. The quality of Domino's touring band was well captured on a 1965 live album for Mercury from Las Vegas with Roy Montrell (guitar), Cornelius Coleman (drums) and the saxophones of Herb Hardesty and Lee Allen. Domino continued this pattern of work into the 70s, breaking it slightly when he gave the Beatles' 'Lady Madonna' a New Orleans treatment. He made further albums for Reprise (1968) and Sonet (1979), the Reprise sides being the results of a reunion session with Dave Bartholomew.

In 1986 Domino was inducted into the Rock And Roll Hall Of Fame, and won Hall Of Fame and Lifetime Achievement awards at the 1987 Grammys. In 1991 EMI, which now owns the Imperial catalogue, released a scholarly box set of Domino's remarkable recordings. Two years later, Domino was back in the studio recording his first sessions proper for 25 years, resulting in his *Christmas Is A Special Day* set. 'People don't know what they've done for me', he reflected. 'They always tell me, "Oh Fats, thanks for so many years of good music". And I'll be thankin' them before they're finished thankin' me!' He remains a giant figure of R&B and rock 'n' roll, both musically and physically.

● ALBUMS: *Carry On Rockin'* (Imperial 1955)★★★★, *Rock And Rollin' With Fats* (Imperial 1956)★★★★, *Rock And Rollin'* (Imperial 1956)★★★★, *This Is Fats Domino!* (Imperial 1957)★★★★, *Here Stands Fats Domino* (Imperial 1958)★★★★, *Fabulous Mr D* (Imperial 1958)★★★★, *Let's Play Fats Domino* (Imperial 1959)★★★★, *Fats Domino Swings* (Imperial 1959)★★★★, *Million Record Hits* (Imperial 1960)★★★★, *A Lot Of Dominos* (Imperial 1960)★★★★, *I Miss You So* (Imperial 1961)★★★, *Let The Four Winds Blow* (Imperial 1961)★★★★, *What A Party* (Imperial 1962)★★★, *Twistin' The Stomp* (Imperial 1962)★★★, *Just Domino* (Imperial 1962)★★★, *Here Comes Fats Domino* (ABC-Paramount 1963)★★★, *Walkin' To New Orleans* (Imperial 1963)★★★★, *Let's Dance With Domino* (Imperial 1963)★★★, *Here He Comes Again* (Imperial 1963)★★★, *Fats On Fire* (ABC 1964)★★★, *Fats Domino '65* (Mercury 1965)★★★, *Getaway With Fats Domino* (ABC 1965)★★★, *Fats Is Back* (Reprise 1968)★★★, *Cookin' With Fats* (United Artists 1974)★★★, *Sleeping On The Job* (Sonet 1979)★★★, *Live At Montreux* (Atlantic 1987)★★★, *Christmas Is A Special Day* (Right Stuff/EMI 1994)★★★.
● COMPILATIONS: *The Very Best Of Fats Domino* (Liberty 1970)★★★★, *Rare Domino's* (Liberty 1970)★★★, *Rare Domino's Volume 2* (Liberty 1971)★★★, *Fats Domino - His Greatest Hits* (MCA 1986)★★★, *My Blue Heaven - The Best Of Fats Domino* (EMI 1990)★★★★, *They Call Me The Fat Man: The Legendary Imperial Recordings* 4-CD box set (EMI/Imperial 1991)★★★★★, *Out Of Orleans* 8-CD box set (Bear Family 1993)★★★★★, *The EP Collection Volume 1* (See For Miles 1995)★★★★, *The Early Imperial Singles 1950-52* (Ace 1996)★★★★, *The EP Collection Volume 2* (See For Miles 1997)★★★★.
● FILMS: *The Girl Can't Help It* (1956), *Jamboree* aka *Disc Jockey Jamboree* (1957), *The Big Beat* (1957).

DON'T KNOCK THE ROCK

The same production team responsible for Rock Around The Clock made this 1956 film. Alan Dale played the part of rock 'n' roll singer Arnie Haynes, accused by parents of corrupting impressionable minds when he returns to his hometown. Disc jockey Alan Freed enjoyed a prominent role as Haynes' agent. When a riot breaks out at a concert headlined by Bill Haley And His Comets, the pair stage another show to convince the adults the music is no more controversial than previous fashions. The Treniers and Dave Appell And His Applejacks make appearances, but the film's highlight comes courtesy of Little Richard who contributes explosive versions of 'Long Tall Sally', 'Tutti Frutti' and 'Rip It Up'. His performances saved this hurriedly produced film from oblivion.

DONEGAN, LONNIE

b. Anthony Donegan, 29 April 1931, Glasgow, Scotland. Donegan, as 'The King Of Skiffle', became a more homogeneous UK equivalent to Elvis Presley than Tommy Steele. Steeped in traditional jazz and its by-products, he was a guitarist in a skiffle band before a spell in the army found him drumming in the Wolverines Jazz Band. After his discharge, he played banjo with Ken Colyer and then Chris Barber. With his very stage forename a tribute to a black bluesman, both units allowed him to sing a couple of blues-tinged American folk tunes as a 'skiffle' break. His version of Lead Belly's 'Rock Island Line', issued from Barber's New Orleans Joys in 1954 as a single after months in the domestic hit parade, was also a US hit. Donegan's music inspired thousands of teenagers to form amateur skiffle combos, with friends playing broomstick tea-chest bass, washboards and other instruments fashioned from household implements. The Beatles, playing initially as the Quarrymen, were the foremost example of an act traceable to such roots.

With his own group, Donegan was a prominent figure in skiffle throughout its 1957 prime; he possessed an energetic whine far removed from the gentle plumminess of other native pop vocalists. Donegan could dazzle with his virtuosity on 12-string acoustic guitar and his string of familiar songs has rarely been surpassed: 'Don't You Rock Me Daddy-O', 'Putting On The Style' ('putting on the agony, putting on the style'), 'Bring A Little Water Sylvie', 'Grand Coulee Dam', 'Does Your Chewing Gum Lose Its Flavour On The Bedpost Over Night' and 'Jimmy Brown The Newsboy', were only a few of Donegan's gems. He arguably made the traditional song 'Cumberland Gap' his own (his first UK number 1), and 1959's 'Battle Of New Orleans' was the finest ever reading. He delved more deeply into Americana to embrace bluegrass, spirituals, Cajun and even Appalachian music, the formal opposite of jazz. However, when the skiffle boom diminished, he broadened his appeal - to much purist criticism - with old-time music hall/pub singalong favourites, and a more pronounced comedy element. His final chart-topper was with the uproarious 'My Old Man's A Dustman', which sensationally entered the UK charts at number 1 in 1960. The hit was an adaptation of the ribald Liverpool folk ditty 'My Old Man's A Fireman On The Elder-Dempster Line'. He followed it with further comedy numbers including 'Lively' in 1960. Two years later, Donegan's Top 20 run ended as it had started, with a Lead Belly number ('Pick A Bale Of Cotton'). However, between 1956 and 1962 he had num-

bered 34 hits. He finished the 60s with huge sales of two mid-price Golden Age Of Donegan volumes, supplementing his earnings in cabaret and occasional spots on BBC Television's The Good Old Days. The most interesting diversion of the next decade was Adam Faith's production of Putting On The Style. Here, at Paul McCartney's suggestion, Donegan remade old smashes backed by an extraordinary glut of artists who were lifelong fans, including Rory Gallagher, Ringo Starr, Leo Sayer, Zoot Money, Albert Lee, Gary Brooker, Brian May, Nicky Hopkins, Elton John and Ron Wood. While this album brushed 1978's UK album list, a 1982 single, 'Spread A Little Happiness', was also a minor success - and, as exemplified by the Traveling Wilburys' 'skiffle for the 90s', the impact of Donegan's earliest chart entries continues to exert an influence on pop music. Although no longer enjoying the best of health, Donegan continues to entertain. He has long been an influential legend and the man who personifies British skiffle music. In the early 90s he was touring occasionally with his old boss, Chris Barber, and in 1995 he was presented with an Ivor Novello Award for Outstanding Contribution To British Music. In 1997 Donegan was working on his long-awaited autobiography.

● ALBUMS: Showcase (Pye Nixa 1956)★★★, Lonnie (Pye Nixa 1957), Tops With Lonnie (Pye 1958)★★★★, Lonnie Rides Again (Pye 1959)★★★, More Tops With Lonnie (Pye 1961)★★★, Sings Hallelujah (Pye 1962)★★★, The Lonnie Donegan Folk Album (Pye 1965)★★★★, Lonniepops-Lonnie Donegan Today (Decca 1970)★★★, Lonnie Donegan Meets Leineman (1974)★★, Lonnie Donegan (1975)★★, Lonnie Donegan Meets Leineman-Country Roads (1976)★★, Putting On The Style (Chrysalis 1978)★★, Sundown (Chrysalis 1979)★★, Jubilee Concert (Cube 1981)★★.

● COMPILATIONS: Golden Age Of Donegan (Golden Guinea 1962)★★★★, Golden Age Of Donegan Volume 2 (Golden Guinea 1963)★★★★, Golden Hour Of Golden Hits (Golden Hour 1973)★★★, Golden Hour Of Golden Hits, Volume 2 (Golden Hour 1974)★★★, The Lonnie Donegan File (Pye 1977)★★★★, The Hits Of Lonnie Donegan (MFP 1978)★★★, Greatest Hits: Lonnie Donegan (Ditto 1983)★★★★, Rare And Unissued Gems (Bear Family 1985)★★★, Rock Island Line (Flashback 1985)★★★★, The Hit Singles Collection (PRT 1987)★★★★, The Best Of Lonnie Donegan (Pickwick 1989)★★★★, The Collection: Lonnie Donegan (Castle 1989)★★★★, The EP Collection (See For Miles 1992)★★★, Putting On The Styles 3-CD box set (1992)★★★★, More Than 'Pye In The Sky' 8-CD box set (Bear Family 1994)★★★.

● FURTHER READING: Skiffle: The Inside Story, Chas McDevitt.

DONEN, STANLEY

b. 13 April 1924, Columbia, South Carolina, USA. The director and choreographer for a string of classic MGM musicals of the 50s, Donen was fascinated by film and theatre from an early age. After graduating from high school he worked on Broadway in the chorus of the Richard Rodgers and Lorenz Hart musical Pal Joey (1940), which starred Gene Kelly, and he assisted Kelly on the choreography for Best Foot Forward (1941) and also appeared in the chorus. Signed to MGM, during the 40s he worked as choreographer, co-choreographer and/or co-director of occasional sequences (often uncredited) on musicals such as *Cover Girl*, *Hey Rookie*, *Jam Session*, *Kansas City Kitty*, *Anchors Aweigh*, *Holiday In Mexico*, *No Leave, No Love*, *Living In A Big Way*, *This Time For Keeps*, *A Date With Judy*, *The Kissing Bandit* and *Take Me Out To The Ball Game*. In 1949 Donen made his official directorial debut as Gene Kelly's co-director on the acclaimed, ground-breaking musical *On The Town*, and they worked together on several more memorable films, including *Singin' In The Rain*, *It's Always Fair Weather* and *The Pajama Game*. Donen also brought his skill as a director of breathtakingly fresh and exuberant sequences to pictures such as *Wedding Bells*, *Give A Girl A Break* (also choreographed with Gower Champion), *Deep In My Heart*, *Seven Brides For Seven Brothers*, *Funny Face* and *Damn Yankees* (1958). By that time the golden age of movie musicals was over, and, with the exception of *The Little Prince* (1974), Donen concentrated on directing (and producing) dramatic and light-comedy films such as *Indiscreet*, *The Grass Is Greener*, *Arabesque*, *Two For The Road*, *Bedazzled*, *Staircase*, *Lucky Lady*, *Movie, Movie*, *Saturn 3*, and *Blame It On Rio* (1984). In 1988 he produced the Academy Awards show, and five years later made his directorial debut on Broadway in the Jule Styne musical *The Red Shoes*. After the original director, Susan Schulman, bowed out in the early stages of production, Donen took over. Unfortunately, unlike those earlier MGM musicals, there was no happy ending and the show closed after three days.

DOOTONES

The origins of vocal group the Dootones can be traced to Fremont High School in Los Angeles, California, USA, where singer and multi-instrumentalist H.B. Barnum played in a jazz band with his drumming friend Ronald Barrett. The Dootones were subsequently formed in 1954 when the duo added Charles Gardner and Marvin Wilkins. Their initial employment was as backing singers/musicians to the Meadowlarks and Penguins. They were titled the Dootones in 1955 by their manager, Dootsie Williams, and made their debut with 'Teller Of Fortune' in April. A pop-orientated take on R&B, it attracted local airplay, while further exposure came with Californian tours with Etta James and Jackie Wilson. Afterwards, Williams put the quartet together with Vernon Green, formerly of the Medallions, for a Canadian tour, and made his intentions to remodel the band as the new Medallions clear. The existing Dootones were evidently unhappy with this turn of events, and disbanded without issuing any further recordings. Barrett teamed up with the Meadowlarks, Gardner persevered with Green as yet another version of the Medallions, while Barnum joined the Robins, later working as an arranger with artists including Ray Charles and Lou Rawls. Charles Gardner became a minister in Pasadena. The Dootones recorded 'Down The Road' in 1962. Originally recorded in 1955, it backed a track entitled 'Sailor Boy' by a second, entirely different version of the Dootones assembled by Dootsie Williams. That formation had earlier released a single entitled 'Strange Love Affair'.

DOTSON, BIG BILL

An obscure figure, Big Bill Dotson is known only for one record, made around 1952, possibly in Houston, Texas, and issued on the Black & White label. Singing accompanied only by his guitar, his style on this very limited evidence was reminiscent of Lightnin' Hopkins, and indeed, his two tracks have appeared on a Hopkins album, credited to that artist. His vocals were somewhat lighter and his guitarwork more rudimentary than those of the more famous artist, but he deserves his own small place in blues history.

● COMPILATIONS: *Blues From The Deep South* (1969)★★★.

DOUGLAS, JOHNNY

b. 9 June 1920, London, England. A prolific composer and arranger, who has composed numerous film and television scores, Douglas has also recorded with many top singers and has sold millions of albums, including 80 made for RCA. An injury during wartime service in the RAF forced him to give up piano playing for a time, and concentrate on composing and arranging. After the war he was in demand from Bert Ambrose, Ted Heath, Edmundo Ros, Cyril Stapleton, Billy Cotton, Joe Loss, Mantovani, Jack Parnell and other top British bands. He also accompanied Howard Keel, Shirley Jones, Moira Anderson, Shirley Bassey, Max Bygraves, Al Martino, John Hanson, Dennis Lotis, Barbra Streisand, Vera Lynn, Tex Ritter (Johnny was on the 1952 hit 'High Noon'), Harry Secombe and Frankie Vaughan, among many others. In 1958 for the first time Douglas was given the chance to conduct a large orchestra playing his own arrangements. The RCA album *Living Strings Play Music Of The Sea* was the start of a long and successful association; his album *Feelings* won a gold disc. Douglas has scored 36 feature films, the best-known of which, *The Railway Children*, received a British Academy nomination. Others included *Touch Of Death*, *The Hi-Jackers*, *Strictly For The Birds*, *Mozambique*, *City Of Fear*, *Circus Of Fear*, *Dateline Diamonds*, *Day Of The Triffids*, *Crack In The World*, *Kid Rodelo*, *Bikini Paradise*, *Run Like A Thief*, *The Bay Of Saint Michael*, *The Gun Fighters Of Casa Grande*, *The Stalkers* and 21 films in the *Scales Of Justice* series. In the 80s Douglas formed his own record company, Dulcima.

● ALBUMS: *Living Strings Play Music Of The Sea* (RCA Victor 1958)★★★, *Many Sides Of Johnny Douglas And His Orchestra* (Cambra 1983)★★★, *More Romance With The Classics* (Dulcima 1988)★★★, *On Stage* (Dulcima 1990)★★★★, *On Stage* (Dulcima 1991)★★★★, *It's Magic* (Dulcima 1994)★★.

DREAM WEAVERS

A vocal group consisting of three college students, two men and a women, based in Miami, Florida, USA. The Dream Weavers were born out of necessity when Wade Buff and Eugene Atkinson were unable to find an artist to record their composition 'It's Almost Tomorrow'. After exposure on the college radio station, their own self-financed recording was picked up by Decca Records and entered the US Top 10 in 1955. It did even better in the UK, climbing to the top of the charts in the following year. Subsequently, the Dream Weavers had a minor hit with Sammy Fain and Paul Francis Webster's 'A Little Love Can Go A Long, Long Way', from the film *Ain't Misbehavin'*, but then disappeared without a trace. 'It's Almost Tomorrow' also charted in the USA for Jo Stafford, Snooky Lanson and David Carroll in the 50s, and reached number 12 in the UK charts for Mark Wynter in 1963.

DRIFTING SLIM

b. Elmon Mickle, 24 February 1919, Keo, Arkansas, USA, d. 17 September 1977. He was inspired to sing and play harmonica by John Lee 'Sonny Boy' Williamson, whose style he successfully emulated on local radio stations in the 40s. Mickle formed his first band in 1951 and recorded for the Modern/RPM company; he learned to play guitar and drums and worked occasionally as a one-man band. In 1957 he moved to Los Angeles, where he recorded for several small labels (including Elko, E.M., J Gems, Wonder, Magnum and Styletone, using the pseudonym Model T. Slim for the latter), and in 1966 he made an album for Milestone Records. Poor health prevented him playing many club dates in the 70s; he died of cancer in September 1977.
● ALBUMS: as Model T. Slim *Somebody Done Voodoo The Hoodoo Man* (1980)★★★.

DU DROPPERS

Although the Du Droppers formed in Harlem, New York, USA, in 1952, each member of the vocal quartet had already sung within their local gospel communities. Indeed, while doo-wop was primarily a young man's concern, the Du Droppers - J.C. 'Junior' Caleb Ginyard (b. 15 January 1910, St. Matthews, South Carolina, USA, d. 11 August 1978; lead), Harvey Ray (tenor/baritone), Willie Ray (tenor/baritone) and Eddie Hashew (bass) - had an average age of well over 40 at formation. Ginyard's previous experience was the most extensive, having sung with the Royal Harmony Singers, Jubalaires and Dixieaires. As the Du Droppers they rehearsed in basements until Paul Kapp, manager of the Delta Rhythm Boys, took over. They made their debut at the end of 1952 with a single for Bobby Robinson's Red Robin Records in Harlem, 'Can't Do Sixty No More'. This was an answer record to the Dominoes' 'Sixty Minute Man', but failed to replicate its success. After replacing Hashew with Bob Kornegay the group passed an audition for RCA Records, making their debut with 'I Want To Know (What You Do When You Go Round There)'. Released in March 1953, it made number 3 in the *Billboard* R&B charts. In retaliation Red Robin issued a single from masters that they still held, 'Come On And Love Me Baby'. However, its arrival was eclipsed by the Du Droppers' second release on RCA, 'I Found Out (What You Do When You Go Round There)', which continued firmly in the vein of their label debut. Continuing the parallels, it too hit number 3 in the R&B charts. 'Whatever You're Doin' was also an extension of the theme, but failed to break the charts, nor did their first ballad, 'Don't Pass Me By'. RCA then initiated a new R&B subsidiary, Groove Records, and the Du Droppers gave the label its first release, 'Speed King'. For the subsequent 'How Much Longer', Prentice Moreland expanded the group to a quintet. He soon departed for spells in the Dominoes and Cadets, while the Du Droppers regrouped with the addition of Ravens singer Joe Van Loan. He did not last long, and was forced to 'leave' following record company politicking between Herald Records (who wanted to sign the Du Droppers, and who had Van Loan under contract anyway) and RCA (who wished to exercise their option for another year). Harvey Ray also left the fold. From then on the lead role was handled by Charlie Hughes (later of the Drifters) in the studio and Van Loan live. Hughes made his debut on the April 1955 single 'Give Me Some Consideration', after which

Harvey Ray rejoined for a Canadian tour. One final single emerged amid all the confusion caused by the shifting personnel, 'You're Mine Already', before Ginyard left to join the Golden Gate Quartet. Though the other members struggled to carry on, this signalled the death knell for the Du Droppers.
● COMPILATIONS: *Can't Do Sixty No More* (Dr. Horse 1987)★★★.

DUBS

The original members of this vocal group from Harlem, New York, USA, were lead Richard Blandon, first tenor Billy Carlisle, tenor Cleveland Still, baritone James 'Jake' Miller, and bass Thomas Gardner. They came together in 1957 and were an amalgamation of members of two previous groups. Blandon and Carlisle had previously been with the Five Wings who had recorded for King (notably 'Teardrops Are Falling'), and Still, Miller and Gardner had come from the Scale-Tones, who had recorded for Jay-Dee. (Shortly after their first recordings, the Dubs replaced Gardner with former Five Wing Tommy Grate.) The Dubs never had any national hits, but several of their songs still resonate today as 'golden oldies', primarily because of their popularity on the east coast doo-wop scene. The group had five consecutive regional hits; 'Don't Ask Me To Be Lonely' (1957), 'Could This Be Magic' (1957), 'Beside My Love' (1958), 'Be Sure My Love' (1958) and 'Chapel Of Dreams' (1958). The group broke up in 1958, but like many such groups there were sporadic reunions and break-ups in subsequent years. In the 80s there were two different Dubs groups playing the east coast oldies circuit.
● ALBUMS: *The Dubs Meet The Shells* (Josie 1962)★★★.
● COMPILATIONS: *The Best Of The Dubs* (Collectables 1991)★★★, *The Unavailable 24 Tracks* (Juke Box Treasures 1993)★★.

DUKE WORE JEANS, THE

Taking its cue from the plot of *The Prince And The Pauper*, this 1958 film starred Tommy Steele as the son of a Cockney pearly king who trades lifestyles with his double, the Hon. Tony Whitecliffe. Inevitably, the former falls in love with an aristocrat. *The Duke Wore Jeans* has little to commend it other than being a vehicle for Steele's chirpy personality. He contributed eight songs to the soundtrack, including 'Happy Guitar', which reached number 20 in the UK charts when issued as a single. If Steele was ever a bona fide rock 'n' roll singer, this film marked his transformation into an all-round entertainer. *The Duke Wore Jeans* was retitled *It's All Happening* for the US market. The same title was used for a British 1963 feature film starring Steele, which was known as *The Dream Maker* in America.

DUKES, 'LITTLE' LAURA

b. 10 June 1907, Memphis, Tennessee, USA. An early start in music led Little Laura Dukes to a lifetime of involvement with entertainment in Memphis. Her father had been a drummer with W.C. Handy's band, but it was a less sophisticated idiom that Dukes chose, playing blues with the jug bands for which that city is so well known. She sang and played banjo and ukelele with the Will Batts Novelty Band, and although they made two recordings in the early 50s, these were not issued until 20 years later. She made some more records with the revival of interest in blues and related music in the 70s, and also appeared in a BBC Television series. As late as the 80s, she was still performing in Memphis, at the Blues Alley club, set up to showcase the city's blues talent.

● ALBUMS: *South Memphis Jug Band* (1975)★★★.

DUNCAN, JOHNNY, AND THE BLUE GRASS BOYS

b. John Franklin Duncan, 7 September 1932, Oliver Springs, near Knoxville, Tennessee, USA. Duncan sang from an early age in a church choir and then, when aged 13, he joined a gospel quartet. At 16, he left Tennessee for Texas and while there, he formed a country group. Duncan was drafted into the US army in 1952 and posted in England. He married an English woman, Betty, in 1953. After his demobilization, they went to the USA. Betty returned home for Christmas 1955 and, as she fell ill and needed an operation, Duncan worked in the UK for his father-in-law. He met jazz band-leader Chris Barber, who was looking to replace Lonnie Donegan. Donegan had formed his own skiffle group, a fashion he had started with Barber's band. Barber was impressed by Duncan's nasal vocal delivery and physical resemblance to Donegan and immediately recruited him, and he joined them the following night at London's Royal Festival Hall. In 1957 Duncan left the band and called his own group the Blue Grass Boys in homage to Bill Monroe, but they were all British - Denny Wright (guitar), Jack Fallon (bass), Danny Levan (violin) and Lennie Hastings (drums). Although promoted as a skiffle artist, Duncan was a straight country performer, both in terms of arrangements and repertoire. 'Last Train To San Fernando', a Trinidad calypso he re-arranged, steamed up the UK charts, but the commu-nication cord was pulled just before it reached the top. The b-side, 'Rock-A-Billy Baby', was equally strong. Duncan was featured on BBC Television's *6.5 Special* and hosted radio programmes for the BBC and Radio Luxembourg, but he only had two more Top 30 entries, 'Blue Blue Heartache' and 'Footprints In The Snow', which both reached number 27. Duncan subsequently worked as a country singer in UK clubs and encouraged local talent. In 1974 he emigrated to Melbourne, Australia, where he has since worked as a country singer.

● ALBUMS: *Johnny Duncan's Tennessee Songbag* (1957)★★★, *Johnny Duncan Salutes Hank Williams* (1958)★★★, *Beyond The Sunset* (1961)★★★, *Back In Town* (1970)★★, *The World Of Country Music* (Decca 1973)★★★.

● COMPILATIONS: *Last Train To San Fernando* 4-CD box set (Bear Family 1997)★★★★.

DUNCAN, TREVOR

b. Leonard Charles Trebilco, 27 February 1924, Camberwell, London, England. Duncan is a talented composer whose unique style has been in great demand from many pub-lishers for their mood music libraries. At the age of 18 he joined the BBC as a sound and balance engineer, and wartime service in the RAF (allowing him to play with many different bands) increased his awareness of the needs of musicians. Back at the BBC he paid great attention to mun-dane matters such as microphone placings, but all this was invaluable experience for the recording career that was to follow. Encouraged by conductor Ray Martin, in 1949

Duncan showed his composition 'High Heels' to publishers Boosey & Hawkes, and it was immediately accepted. The next year Sidney Torch recorded it for Parlophone, and it was a great success (Duncan privately admitted the influ-ence of David Rose's 'Holiday For Strings'). A conflict arose between Duncan's BBC career (which did not allow the exploitation of his own music) and the natural wishes of his publishers to promote his undoubted composing talents. In 1956 he accepted the inevitable, and decided to concentrate solely on writing. Such was his output that Boosey & Hawkes could not handle everything he wrote, so his works began to appear in the recorded music libraries of other London publishers. In 1959 Ron Goodwin recorded 'The Girl From Corsica', and soon afterwards BBC Television chose Duncan's march from 'A Little Suite' as the theme music for *Dr. Finlay's Casebook*. Both pieces made a great impact on the public, and they remain popular standards of light music. Other works of note included 'Tomboy', 'Panoramic Splendour', 'Overland To Oregon', 'Twentieth Century Express', 'Enchanted April', 'Little Debbie', 'Still Waters', 'A Vision In Velvet', 'The Unwanted', 'The Challenge Of Space', 'Children In The Park', 'The House Of Tranquility', 'The Visionaries', 'The Spirit Of Industry', 'Meadow Mist', 'The Wine Festival', 'Schooner Bay', 'Broad Horizons' and 'Passage To Windward'. Many of his pieces convey his love of sailing. 'Citizens Of The World' was used in an early ITV series *The Planemakers*, and one of Duncan's short works, 'Grand Vista', was used with great effect on Pearl and Dean advertising fea-tures in the cinema. His most serious orchestral work is 'Sinfonia Tellurica' (1970), depicting the Elements measured against mankind's endeavours and achievements. In his later career he has combined his interest in mathematics with electronic music.

● ALBUMS: *British Light Music - Trevor Duncan* (Marco Polo 1995)★★★★.

DUNING, GEORGE

b. 25 February 1908, Richmond, Indiana, USA. A composer and conductor for films, from the 40s through to the 80s. Duning studied at the University of Cincinnati, and the Cincinnati Conservatory Of Music, becoming a jazz and symphonic trumpet player. He was a sideman and chief arranger for the Kay Kyser Band in the early 40s. Around the same time, he began to arrange and orchestrate music for films, and in 1946 he collaborated with Irving Gertz to write the score for *The Devil's Mask*. Between then and 1950, he scored some 21 features for Columbia, a mixture of thrillers, melodramas, westerns and comedies. These included *Mysterious Intruder*; *Johnny O'Clock* and *To The Ends Of Earth*, starring Dick Powell, *The Guilt Of Janet James*; *I Love Trouble*; *The Man From Colorado*; *Shockproof*; *The Dark Past*; *The Undercover Man* and *And Baby Makes Three*. Duning also scored *Down To Earth* and *The Gallant Blade*, both starring Larry Parks, and Parks appeared once more in *Jolson Sings Again*, for which Duning gained the first of five Oscar nom-inations. Three of the others came to Duning in the 50s for his work on *From Here To Eternity*, *The Eddie Duchin Story* and *Picnic* (1955). The latter's theme music, used extremely effectively on the soundtrack in conjunction with the 1934 melody 'Moonglow', became a US number 1 for Morris Stolloff and his orchestra, and a substantial hit for pianist George Cates. A lyric was added by Steve Allen. Duning's other scores during the 50s and 60s included *Lorna Doone, Man In The Saddle, Scandal Sheet; Last Of The Commanches, Salome, Houseboat; Bell, Book And Candle, Cowboy, The World Of Suzie Wong, The Devil At 4 O'Clock, Toys In The Attic, My Blood Runs Cold* and *Any Wednesday*. In the 60s and 70s, apart from the occasional feature such as *Arnold* (1973), *Terror In The Wax Museum* (1976) and *The Man With Bogart's Face* (1980), which was George Raft's last film, Duning concentrated on writing for television. He scored several films such as *Then Came Bronson, Quarantined, But I Don't Want To Get Married!, Yuma, Black Noon, Climb An Angry Mountain, The Woman Hunter, Honour Thy Father, The Abduction Of Saint Anne, The Top Of The Hill, The Dream Merchants* and *Goliath Waits* (1981); he also contributed music to numerous television series, including *Star Trek, The Partridge Family* and *Houseboat*.

DVORKIN, JUDITH

b. 1928, USA, d. 24 July 1995, New York, USA. A composer, lyricist and songwriter, Dvorkin published most of her music under the pseudonym Judy Spencer. She enjoyed a varied and prolific career, starting as one of the songwriters for the children's television programme *Captain Kangaroo*. Arguably her best known song was 'Soft Summer Breeze', a radio standard that achieved more than one million plays in her lifetime. She wrote a musical play, *Cyrano*, which was performed at the Brooklyn Academy Of Music and off-Broadway. As well as her one-act opera for children, *What's In A Name*, she also wrote commercially available classical pieces, such as *Three Letters, John Keats To Fanny Brawne, Maurice: A Madrigal* and *Suite For Violin And Clarinet*. Before dying of cancer at the age of 67, she guided the careers of several young composers, while her work has been included in two American song anthologies: J.T. Howard's *Our American Music* and M. Stewart-Green's *Women Composers' Work*.

EAGER, VINCE

One of the many UK rock/pop artists of the late 50s Eager was one of the more promising singers in the Larry Parnes stable of stars. Launched in the spring of 1958 and christened Eager because of his enthusiastic personality, the vocalist was featured on several prestigious television shows, most notably Jack Good's pioneering *Oh Boy*. He seemed a strong bet to follow Parnes' other acts, Tommy

Steele and Marty Wilde, into the UK charts but, despite a series of singles written by such name writers as Floyd Robinson, Marty Robbins, Conway Twitty and Gene Pitney, chart success proved elusive. Eager also received regular star billing on the BBC Television series *Drumbeat*, but his career prospects receded when he split with Parnes. In later years, he featured in the musical *Elvis*.

● ALBUMS: *Vince Eager Plays Tribute To Elvis Presley* (Avenue 1972)★.

EARL-JEAN

b. Ethel 'Earl-Jean' McCrea, North Carolina, USA. Together with Margie Hendrix and Pat Lyles she formed the Cookies, who first recorded on Lamp in 1954. They joined Atlantic in 1955 and were heard singing backing vocals on many hits on that label in the mid-50s. They had their own Top 10 R&B hit in 1956 with 'In Paradise' and shortly afterwards went to work with Ray Charles under the name the Raelettes. Earl-Jean re-formed the group with new members Dorothy Jones and Margaret Ross in 1962, and signed to Goffin And King's Dimension label as both artists and session singers. They had US Top 20 hits with 'Chains' (later recorded by the Beatles) and 'Don't Say Nothin' Bad (About My Baby)'. In 1964 Earl-Jean went solo on Colpix and her first single, 'I'm Into Something Good', another Goffin and King composition, became her only US hit, reaching the bottom of the Top 40. A year later, the song became a UK number 1 hit for Herman's Hermits. Earl-Jean's follow-up, 'Randy', failed to chart, and although she continued to record as Darlene McCrae, she was unable to achieve consistent success.

ECKSTINE, BILLY

b. William Clarence Eckstein, 8 July 1914, Pittsburgh, Pennsylvania, USA, d. 8 March 1993, Pittsburgh, Pennsylvania, USA. Eckstine possessed one of the most distinctive voices in popular music, a deep tone with a unique vibrato. He began singing at the age of 11 but until his late teens was undecided between a career as a singer or football player. He won a sporting scholarship but soon afterwards broke his collar bone and decided that singing was less dangerous. He worked mostly in the north-eastern states in the early 30s and towards the end of the decade joined the Earl Hines band in Chicago. Although far from being a jazz singer, opting instead for a highly sophisticated form of balladry, Eckstine clearly loved working with jazz musicians and in particular the young experimenters who drifted into the Hines band in the early 40s, among them Wardell Gray, Dizzy Gillespie and Charlie Parker. While with Hines he developed into a competent trumpeter and, later, valve trombonist, having first mimed as a trumpet player in order to circumvent union rules. In 1943, acting on the advice and encouragement of Budd Johnson, Eckstine formed his own band. Although his original intention was to have a band merely to back his vocals, Eckstine gathered together an exciting group of young bebop musicians and thus found himself leader of what constituted the first true bebop big band. During the band's four-year existence its ranks were graced by Gray, Parker, Gillespie, Gene Ammons, Dexter Gordon, Miles Davis, Kenny Dorham, Fats Navarro and Art Blakey, playing arrangements by Gillespie, Johnson, Tadd Dameron, Gil Fuller and Jerry Valentine. Eckstine also hired the Hines band's other singer, Sarah Vaughan. In 1947 the band folded but had already served as an inspiration to Gillespie, who formed his own bebop big band that year. Eckstine's commercial recordings during the life of the big band were mostly ballads which he wrapped in his deep, liquid baritone voice, and with his bandleading days behind him he continued his career as a successful solo singer. He gained a huge international reputation as a stylish balladeer. During his long career Eckstine had many hit records, including 'Jelly, Jelly', recorded in 1940 with Hines, 'Skylark', 'Everything I Have Is Yours', 'I Apologize' (stylistically covered by P.J. Proby to great success), 'Prisoner Of Love', 'Cottage For Sale', 'No One But You' (number three in the UK charts in 1954), 'Gigi' (number eight in 1959), and several duets with Vaughan, the best-known being 'Passing Strangers', which, although recorded a dozen years earlier, reached number 17 in the 1969 charts. He went on to record for Motown, Stax and A&M. In later years Eckstine recorded a new single with Ian Levine as part of his Motown revival project on the Motor City label.

● ALBUMS: *Live At Club Plantation, Los Angeles* (1945)★★★, *Billy Eckstine Sings* (National 1949)★★★, *Songs By Billy Eckstine* (MGM 1951)★★★, *Favorites* (MGM 1951)★★★, *Billy Eckstine Sings Rogers And Hammerstein* (MGM 1952)★★★★, *The Great Mr B* (King 1953)★★★, *Tenderly* (MGM 1953)★★★★, *I Let A Song Go Out Of My Heart* (MGM 1954)★★★, *Blues For Sale* (EmArcy 1954/55)★★★★, *The Love Songs Of Mr B* (EmArcy 1954/55)★★★, *Mr B With A Beat* (MGM 1955)★★★, *Rendezvous* (MGM 1955)★★★, *I Surrender Dear* (EmArcy 1955)★★★, *That Old Feeling* (MGM 1955)★★★★, *Prisoner Of Love* (Regent 1957)★★★, *The Duke the Blues And Me* (Regent 1957)★★★, *My Deep Blue Dream* (Regent 1957)★★★★, *You Call It Madness* (Regent 1957)★★★, *Billy Eckstine's Imagination* (EmArcy 1958)★★★★, *Billy's Best* (Mercury 1958)★★★, with Sarah Vaughan *Sarah Vaughan And Billy Eckstine Sing The Best Of Irving Berlin* (Mercury 1958)★★★★, with Vaughan *Billy And Sarah* (Lion 1959)★★★★, with Count Basie *Basie, Eckstine Inc.* (Roulette 1959)★★★, *Golden Saxophones* (London 1960)★★★, *I Apologize* (1960)★★★★, *Mr B* (Audio Lab 1960)★★★, *Broadway Bongos And Mr B* (Mercury 1961)★★★, *No Cover No Minimum* (Mercury 1961)★★★, with Quincy Jones *Billy Eckstine & Quincy Jones At Basin St. East* (Mercury 1962)★★★, *Don't Worry 'Bout Me* (Mercury 1962)★★★, *Once More With Feeling* (Mercury 1962)★★★, *Everything I Have Is Yours* (Metro 1965)★★★, *Prime Of My Life* (Motown 1965)★★, *My Way* (Motown 1966)★★, *For Love Of Ivy* (Motown 1969)★★, *Gentle On My Mind* (Motown 1969)★★, *Feel The Warm* (1971)★★, *Stormy* (Stax 1971)★★, *If She Walked Into My Life* (Stax 1974)★★, *Something More* (Stax 1981)★★, *Billy Eckstine Sings With Benny Carter* (1986)★★★, *I'm A Singer* (Kim 1987)★★.

● COMPILATIONS: *The Best Of Billy Eckstine* (Lion 1958)★★★, *The Golden Hits Of Billy Eckstine* (Mercury 1963)★★★★, *Golden Hour: Billy Eckstine* (Golden Hour 1975)★★★★, *Greatest Hits* (Polydor 1984)★★★★, *Mr B And The Band - Savoy Sessions* (Savoy 1986)★★★.

EDWARDS, CLARENCE

b. 25 March 1933, Linsey, Louisiana, USA, d. 20 May 1993, Scotlandville, Louisiana, USA. Edwards began playing blues guitar at around the age of 12, when he moved to Baton Rouge. In the 50s and 60s, he was working the same local blues circuit as the likes of Lightnin' Slim, in bands with names such as the Boogie Beats and the Bluebird Kings. His first experience of recording was in a traditional setting, in sessions for folklorist Harry Oster between 1959 and 1961, with his brother Cornelius and violinist James 'Butch' Cage. Nine years later, he recorded again, this time with a more contemporary sound, and from the mid-80s, when the blues scene revived with the help of Tabby Thomas's Blues Box club, he was playing regularly. In 1990, he recorded his first album, a powerful mixture of acoustic and electric sounds in the swamp blues style. After his death an excellent compilation, *I Looked Down That Railroad*, was released.

● ALBUMS: *Swamp's The Word* (Red Lightnin' 1991)★★★★, with Henry Gray and Short Fuse *Thibodeaux's Cafe* (Sidetrack 1995)★★★.

● COMPILATIONS: *I Looked Down That Railroad* (Last Call 1996)★★★★.

EDWARDS, TOMMY

b. 17 February 1922, Richmond, Virginia, USA, d. 22 October 1969, Virginia, USA. This jazz/pop/R&B singer-songwriter began his professional career in 1931. He wrote the hit 'That Chick's Too Young To Fry' for Louis Jordan in 1946. A demo recording of his own 'All Over Again' later won Edwards an MGM contract. Early releases included 'It's All In The Game' (US number 18 in 1951), a tune based on a 1912 melody by future US Vice-President Charles Gates Dawes. Edwards re-recorded the song in 1958 in a 'beat-ballad' arrangement, hitting number 1 on both sides of the Atlantic and eventually selling 3.5 million. The song was an indisputable classic of its era, highlighted by Edwards' strong, masterful vocal. The song was covered many times and provided hits for Cliff Richard (1963-64) and the Four Tops (1970) and was a notable album track by Van Morrison (1979). Edwards himself enjoyed five more hits during the next two years, including 'Love Is All We Need' and remakes of earlier successes 'Please Mr. Sun' and 'The Morning Side Of The Mountain'.

● ALBUMS: *For Young Lovers* (MGM 1958)★★★, *Tommy Edwards Sings* (Regent 1959)★★, *It's All In The Game* (MGM 1959)★★★★, *Step Out Singing* (MGM 1960)★★★, *You Started Me Dreaming* (MGM 1960)★★★, *Tommy Edwards In Hawaii* (MGM 1960)★, *Golden Country Hits* (MGM 1961)★, *Stardust* (MGM 1962)★★★, *Soft Strings And Two Guitars* (MGM 1962)★★★, *Tommy Edwards* (1965)★★.

● COMPILATIONS: *Tommy Edwards' Greatest Hits* (MGM 1961)★★★, *The Very Best Of Tommy Edwards* (MGM 1963)★★★, *It's All In The Game: The Complete Hits* (Epic 1995)★★★★.

EL DORADOS

This Chicago, Illinois R&B vocal group achieved fame with one of the great jump tracks of the early rock 'n' roll era, 'At My Front Door', also called 'Crazy Little Mama'. Members on that hit were Pirkle Lee Moses (lead), Louis Bradley (second tenor), Jewel Jones (first tenor), James Maddox (baritone) and Richard Nickens (d. 1991; bass). The group was formed in 1952, and signed with Vee Jay Records in 1954. The El Dorados achieved nothing but local hits until finding success with 'At My Front Door' in 1955, when it went to number 2 R&B and number 17 pop. The group's only other chart

record was the mid-tempo 'I'll Be Forever Loving You' (number 8 R&B 1956). The group reorganized in 1958, when Pirkle Lee Moses was abandoned by the other members and recruited new singers from another Vee Jay group, the Kool Gents, whose lead, Dee Clark, had just deserted them. The new El Dorados besides Moses were Doug Brown, John McCall and Teddy Long (d. 1991), but having no luck with further releases, this group broke up in 1959. Despite the El Dorados' meagre chart success most of their records have been cherished by doo-wop fans, who find the group not only one of the more soulful-sounding of the 50s doo-wop ensembles but equally adept at both ballads (notably 'I Began To Realize') and jumps (typically 'Bim Bam Boom'). The group took, perhaps unconsciously, a music that most observers consider nothing more than a commercial entertainment and created a profound and genuine folk art. Both Teddy Long and Richard Nickens died in 1991.
● ALBUMS: *Crazy Little Mama* (Vee Jay 1957)★★★, *Bim Bam Boom* (Charly 1981)★★★, *Low Milage - High Octane* (1984)★★★.

EL VENOS

A rare sextet in the 50s R&B scene, this Pittsburgh group's ranks featured Leon Daniels (lead), sister Anna Mae Jackson (lead), brother Joey Daniels (baritone), Daniel Jackson (first tenor), Leon Taylor (second tenor) and Bernard Palmer (bass). They began on the familiar street-corner career route in 1955, eventually signing with RCA Records, where they were placed on their Groove Records R&B subsidiary. A few months later 'Geraldine', written by Taylor, was released to instant favour. The song was played on Dick Clark's *American Bandstand* television show, but the possibility of a live appearance was lost when the members were unable to raise the finance for the journey to Philadelphia. Instead the El Venos were forced to content themselves with local shows, often conducted with major artists such as the Heartbeats who were passing through Pittsburgh. They transferred to a second RCA affiliate, Vik Records, for their second single, 'You Must Be True', but this failed to match the impact of their debut. The next two years were spent raising money in order to travel to New York for auditions. However, Calico Records chose not to release the two songs the El Venos recorded with them. The same fate befell two more songs recorded for Mercury Records' Amp 3 subsidiary. Dispirited, the group broke up, with Anna Mae Jackson changing her name to Anne Keith and releasing a solo record, backed by the Altairs (the band formed by their erstwhile sponsor, Pittsburgh disc jockey Bill Powell).

ELLA FITZGERALD SINGS THE COLE PORTER SONGBOOK ▪ ELLA FITZGERALD ★★★★★

One of Fitzgerald's great assets was also, paradoxically, one of her failings as a jazz singer. Throughout her long career, her voice always sounded like that of an innocent girl. This immaturity of sound, allied as it was to consummate musical mastery, weakened her jazz performances, especially in the blues, where emotional intensity is of paramount importance. As if sensing this, Norman Granz heard in Fitzgerald's voice the ideal vehicle for a selection of readings from the Great American Songbook. Her coolly detached approach to lyrics is nowhere better displayed than on these 1956 record-

ings of songs by one of the most sophisticated American songwriters. The album reached number 15 in the US chart.
● TRACKS: *All Through The Night; Anything Goes; Miss Otis Regrets; Too Darn Hot; In The Still Of The Night; I Get A Kick Out Of You; Do I Love You; Always True To You In My Fashion; Let's Do It; Just One Of Those Things; Every Time We Say Goodbye; All Of You; Begin The Beguine; Get Out Of Turn; I Am In Love; From This Moment On; I Love Paris; You Do Something To Me; Riding High; Easy To Love; It's Alright With Me; Why Can't You Behave; What Is This Thing Called Love; You're The Top; Love For Sale; It's D'Lovely; Night And Day; Ace In The Hole; So In Love; I've Got You Under My Skin; I Concentrate On You; Don't Fence Me In.*

ELLA FITZGERALD SINGS THE RODGERS AND HART SONGBOOK ▪ ELLA FITZGERALD ★★★★★

Richard Rodgers' tuneful music and Lorenz Hart's witty and amusing lyrics form a very special part of American popular music. So too does Ella Fitzgerald, and their meeting - under the benign influence of Norman Granz - is a high-water mark in the story of popular singing. The singer's unworldly and ingenuous charm perfectly suits the material and transports the listener to times without care; until, that is, the occasional tartness of a Hart lyric reminds us that life is not always a song. Along with the rest of the *Songbook* series, this 1956 release represents popular music at its best and sets standards never previously attained, and never since beaten. It reached a peak position of number 11 in the US chart.
● TRACKS: *Have You Met Miss Jones?; You Took Advantage Of Me; Ship Without A Sail; To Keep My Love Alive; Dancing On The Ceiling; The Lady Is A Tramp; With A Song In My Heart; Manhattan; Johnny One Note; I Wish I Were In Love Again; Spring Is Here; It Never Entered My Mind; This Can't Be Love; Thou Swell; My Romance; Where Or When; Little Girl Blue; Give It Back To The Indians; Ten Cents A Dance; There's A Small Hotel; I Don't Know What Time It Was; Everything I've Got; I Could Write A Book; Blue Room; My Funny Valentine; Bewitched; Mountain Greenery; Wait Till You See Her; Lover; Isn't It Romantic?; Here In My Arms; Blue Moon; My Heart Stood Still; I've Got Five Dollars.*

ELLINGTON, DUKE

b. Edward Kennedy Ellington, 29 April 1899, Washington, DC, USA, d. 24 May 1974. Ellington began playing piano as a child but, despite some local success, took up a career as a signpainter. In his teens he continued to play piano, studied harmony, composed his first tunes and was generally active in music in Washington. Among his childhood friends were Sonny Greer, Artie Whetsol and Otto Hardwicke; from 1919 he played with them in various bands, sometimes working outside the city. In 1923 he ventured to New York to work with Elmer Snowden, and the following year formed his own band, the Washingtonians. Also in 1924, in collaboration with lyricist Joe Trent, he composed the *Chocolate Kiddies* revue. By 1927, Ellington's band had become established in east coast states and at several New York nightclubs. At the end of the year he successfully auditioned for a residency at Harlem's Cotton Club. The benefits arising from this engagement were immeasurable: regular radio broadcasts from the club ensured a widespread audience and Ellington's tours and recording sessions during the period of the residency, which ended early in 1931, built upon the band's popularity. In the early 30s the band consolidated its reputation with extended tours of the USA, appearances in films and visits to Europe, which included performances in London in 1933. Towards the end of the decade the band returned for further seasons at the Cotton Club. Throughout the 30s and early 40s the band recorded extensively and to great acclaim; they continued to tour and record with little interruption during the rest of the 40s and into the early 50s but, although the quality of the music remained high, the band became significantly less popular than had once been the case. An appearance at the 1956 Newport Jazz Festival revived their popularity, and during the rest of the 50s and the following decade Ellington toured ceaselessly, playing concerts around the world. Ellington had always been a prolific writer, composing thousands of tunes including 'It Don't Mean A Thing (If It Ain't Got That Swing)', 'Sophisticated Lady', 'In A Sentimental Mood', 'Prelude To A Kiss', 'Concert For Cootie (Do Nothin' Till You Hear From Me)', 'Cotton Tail', 'In A Mellotone', 'I Got It Bad And That Ain't Good', 'Don't Get Around Much Anymore', 'I'm Beginning To See The Light' and 'Satin Doll'. In later years he also composed film scores, among them *The Asphalt Jungle* (1950), *Anatomy Of A Murder* (1959), *Paris Blues* (1960) and *Assault On A Queen* (1966). More importantly, he began to concentrate upon extended works, composing several suites and a series of sacred music concerts, the latter mostly performed in churches and cathedrals. Over the years the personnel of Ellington's orchestra proved remarkably stable, several of his sidemen remaining with him for decades. The ceaseless touring continued into the early 70s, with Ellington making few concessions to the advancing years. After his death in 1974 the orchestra continued for a time under the direction of his son, Mercer Ellington, but despite the continuing presence of a handful of survivors, such as Harry Carney, who had been in the band virtually without a break for 47 years, the spirit and guiding light was gone. From this moment, Ellington lived on through an immense recorded legacy and in the memories of musicians and an army of fans.

Ellington was born into relatively comfortable circumstances. His father had been a butler, even working for some time at the White House. The family was deeply religious and musical, and Ellington himself was very close to his parents. He reported that he was 'pampered and spoiled rotten', and of his parents he wrote: 'My mother was beautiful but my father was only handsome.' His mother was a piano player; under her influence, Ellington had music lessons from a teacher called Mrs. Clinkscales. In later life, he whimsically commented that one of the first things she taught him was never to share the stage with Oscar Peterson. Perhaps more influential than Mrs. Clinkscales were the piano players he heard in the pool-rooms, where, like any self-respecting, under-age, sharp-suited adolescent-about-town, he found his supplementary education among a diversity of gamblers, lawyers, pickpockets, doctors and hustlers. 'At heart,' he said, 'they were all great artists.' He paid special tribute to Oliver 'Doc' Perry, a pianist who gave him lessons of a less formal but more practical nature than those of Mrs. Clinkscales - 'reading the leads and recognizing the chords'. Ellington became a professional musician in his teens. One of his first engagements was playing 'mood' music for a trav-

elling magician and fortune teller, improvising to suit the moment, whether serious or mystical. In 1914 he wrote his first compositions: 'Soda Fountain Rag' and 'What You Gonna Do When The Bed Breaks Down?'. By the age of 18 he was leading bands in the Washington area, having quickly learned that the bandleader, as 'Mr. Fixit', generally earned more money than the other members of the band. Thus, by the age of 20, he was pianist, composer and bandleader: the essential Duke Ellington was formed, and would later blossom into one of the most influential musicians in jazz, although with characteristic perversity, he insisted that he wrote folk music, not jazz.

By the time of the band's debut at the Cotton Club, in addition to Greer and Hardwicke, Ellington had recruited key players such as James 'Bubber' Miley, his first great 'growling' trumpet player; the trombonist Joe 'Tricky Sam' Nanton; the bassist Wellman Braud and Carney, whose baritone saxophone formed the rich and sturdy foundation of the band's reed section for its entire history. Perhaps just as crucial was Ellington's meeting with Irving Mills, who became his manager. For a black musician to survive, let alone prosper, in the America of the 20s and 30s, a tough white manager was an essential safeguard. In 1927 came the first classic recordings of 'Black And Tan Fantasy' and 'Creole Love Call', the latter with the legendary vocal line by Adelaide Hall. In these, and in up-tempo numbers such as 'Hot And Bothered', the Ellington method was fully formed. The conventional way to praise a big band was to say that they played like one man. The quality of the Ellington bands was that they always played like a bunch of highly talented and wildly disparate individuals, recalling the 'great artists' of the pool-room. The Cotton Club provided an ideal workshop and laboratory for Ellington. Situated in Harlem, its performers were exclusively black, its clientele exclusively white and in pursuit of dusky exotic pleasures. Ellington, who enjoyed being a showman, gave the audience what it wanted: music for showgirls and boys to dance to, in every tempo from the slow and sultry to the hot and hectic, coloured with so-called 'jungle sounds'. Although this was a racial slur, Ellington had the skill and wit to transcend it, creating music that met the specification but disarmingly turned it inside-out. The music winked at the audience. Moving into the 30s, the band's repertoire was enriched by pieces such as 'Rocking' In Rhythm', 'Old Man Blues', 'The Mooche' and, of course, 'Mood Indigo'. Its personnel now included Juan Tizol on trombone, Cootie Williams, de facto successor to Miley on trumpet, and the sublime Johnny Hodges on alto saxophone, whose lyricism, tempered with melancholy, became a crucial element in the Ellington palette. Hodges became the most striking example of the truism 'once an Ellingtonian, always an Ellingtonian'. Like Williams and Tizol, he would leave the band to become a leader in his own right or briefly a sideman in another band, only to return. The 30s saw the first attempts at compositions longer than the conventional three minutes (the length of a gramophone record), starting with 'Creole Rhapsody' in 1931. The period also saw, to oversimplify the situation, a move into respectability. Critics and musicians from the serious side of the tracks had begun to take notice. People as diverse as Constant Lambert, Percy Grainger, Leopold Stokowski and Igor Stravinsky recognized the extraordinary and unique gifts of Ellington. Phrases such as 'America's greatest living composer' crept into print. Ellington continued to refer to himself, gracefully and demurely, as 'our piano player'. To be sure, his composing methods, from all accounts, were radically different from those of other title contenders. He would scribble a few notes on the back of an envelope, or memorize them, and develop the piece in rehearsal. The initial themes were often created by musicians in the band - hence the frequent shared composer credits: 'The Blues I Love To Sing' with Miley, 'Caravan' with Tizol, and 'Jeep's Blues' with Hodges. 'Bluebird Of Delhi', from the 1966 'Far East Suite', was based on a phrase sung by a bird outside Billy Strayhorn's room. Strayhorn joined the band in 1939, as arranger, composer, occasional piano player, friend and musical alter ego. A small, quiet and gentle man, he became a vital element in the Ellington success story. His arrival coincided with that of the tenor saxophone player Ben Webster, and the brilliant young bass player Jimmy Blanton, who died in 1943, aged 23. By common consent, the Webster/Blanton band produced some of the finest music in the Ellington canon, exemplified by 'Jack The Bear', with Blanton's innovative bass solo, and 'Just A-Settin' And A-Rockin', where Webster demonstrates that the quality of jazz playing lies in discretion and timing rather than vast numbers of notes to the square inch.

Duke Ellington was elegantly dismissive of analysis; too much talk, he said, stinks up the place. However, he was more than capable of sensitive examination of his own music. Of the haunting and plaintive 'Mood Indigo', he said: 'Just a story about a little girl and a little boy. They are about eight and the girl loves the boy. They never speak of it, of course, but she just likes the way he wears his hat. Every day he comes to her house at a certain time and she sits in her window and waits. Then one day he doesn't come. "Mood Indigo" just tells how she feels.' The story, and the tune it describes, are characteristically Ellingtonian: they bear the hallmark of true sophistication, which is audacious simplicity. His music is never cluttered, and travels lightly and politely.

Ellington's output as a composer was immense. The late Derek Jewell, in his indispensable biography of the man, estimated that he wrote at least 2000 pieces, but, because of his cavalier way with pieces of paper, it may have been as many as 5000. Among them were many tunes that have become popular standards - 'Sophisticated Lady', 'In A Sentimental Mood', 'Don't Get Around Much Anymore' and 'I'm Beginning To See The Light' are just a selected handful. Their significance, aside from the musical, was that their royalty income effectively subsidized the band, particularly during the post-war period when the big bands virtually disappeared under successive onslaughts from inflation, the growth of television, the decline of the dancehalls and, most significantly, the arrival of rock 'n' roll. Even Ellington was not immune to these pressures and in the early 50s, looking handsome suddenly became hard work. The turning-point came at the Newport Jazz Festival on 7 July 1956, when morale was low. The previous year had seen embarrassing attempts at cashing in on commercial trends with recordings of 'Twelfth Street Rag Mambo' and 'Bunny Hop Mambo', plus a summer season at an aquashow, with a string section and two harpists. The first set at Newport was equally embarrassing. Ellington arrived onstage to find four of his musicians missing. The band played a few numbers, then

departed. They returned around midnight, at full strength, to play the 'Newport Jazz Festival Suite', composed with Strayhorn for the occasion. Then Ellington, possibly still rankled by the earlier behaviour of the band, called 'Diminuendo And Crescendo In Blue', a piece written almost 20 years earlier and by no means a regular item on their usual concert programme. In two sections, and linked by a bridge passage from, on this occasion, the tenor saxophone player Paul Gonsalves, the piece was a revelation. Gonsalves blew 27 choruses, the crowd went wild, the band played four encores, and the news travelled around the world on the jazz grapevine; it was also reported in detail in *Time* magazine, with a picture of the piano player on the cover. After Newport and until his death, Ellington's life and career became a triumphal and global procession, garlanded with awards, honorary degrees, close encounters with world leaders and, more importantly, further major compositions. 'Such Sweet Thunder', his Shakespearian suite written with Strayhorn, contains gems such as 'Lady Mac' - 'Though she was a lady of noble birth, we suspect there was a little ragtime in her soul' - and 'Madness In Great Ones', dedicated to Hamlet with the laconic remark 'in those days crazy didn't mean the same thing it means now'. Further collaborations with Strayhorn included an enchanting reworking of Tchaikovsky's 'Nutcracker Suite' and 'The Far East Suite' - still adorned with dazzling contributions from various of the now-elder statesmen in the band: Hodges, Gonsalves and Carney in the reeds, Lawrence Brown, Britt Woodman and Tizol among the trombones, and Ray Nance and Cat Anderson in the trumpet section. Astonishingly, the band that recorded the *70th Birthday Concert* in England in 1969 included Carney, Hodges and Williams 40 years after they first joined Ellington, and on the record they still sounded like a group of kids having a good night on the town. The freshness and energy of the band as it tackled material played hundreds of times before, was extraordinary.

There was another side to the story. Ellington had always been a religious man, and in his later years he turned increasingly to the writing and performance of sacred music. The origins of this can be traced back to 'Come Sunday', from the 1945 suite 'Black, Brown And Beige', and beyond that to 'Reminiscing In Tempo', written 10 years earlier, following the death of his mother, of which he said: 'My mother's death was the greatest shock. I didn't do anything but brood. The music is representative of all that. It begins with pleasant thoughts. Then something awful gets you down. Then you snap out of it and it ends affirmatively.' From a man who was dismissive of analysis, this represented a very shrewd assessment not only of the piece in question, but of his entire output. Working within the framework of the conventional big band line-up he produced music of extraordinary diversity. His themes were startling in their simplicity, as if he had picked them off trees, and in a way, he did. The tonal qualities of the band - the unique Ellington sound - were based on a celebration of its individuals. The music might be lyrical or triumphant, elegiac or celebratory and the blues were never far away, yet it always ended affirmatively. To borrow a phrase from Philip Larkin, writing about Sidney Bechet, Duke Ellington's life and music added up to A Resounding Yes. He was a giant influence and one of the most important figures in popular music.

● ALBUMS: *Carnegie Hall Concert* (1943)★★★★, *The*

Hollywood Bowl Concert Volumes 1 & 2 (1947)★★★, *Mood Ellington* 10-inch album (Columbia 1949)★★★, *Liberian Suite* 10-inch album (Columbia 1949)★★★, *Ellingtonia, Volume 1* 10-inch album (Brunswick 1950)★★★★, *Ellingtonia, Volume 2* 10-inch album (Brunswick 1950)★★★★, *Masterpieces By Ellington* (Columbia 1951)★★★, *Ellington Uptown* (Columbia 1951)★★★, *Duke Ellington Volumes 1-3* 10-inch albums (Jazz Panorama 1951)★★★, *Duke Ellington* (RCA Victor 1951)★★★★, *The Duke Is On The Air - From The Blue Note* (1952)★★★★, *This Is Duke Ellington And His Orchestra* (RCA Victor 1952)★★★, *Duke Ellington Plays the Blues* (RCA Victor 1953)★★★★, *Premiered By Ellington* 10-inch album (Capitol 1953)★★★, *Ellington Plays Ellington* 10-inch album (Capitol 1953)★★★★, *Early Ellington* (Brunswick 1954)★★★, *The Music Of Duke Ellington* (Columbia 1954)★★★, *Duke Ellington Plays* 10-inch album (Allegro 1954)★★★, *Ellington '55* (Capitol 1954)★★★, *The Duke Plays Ellington* (Capitol 1954)★★★★, *Seattle Concert* (RCA Victor 1954)★★★, *Dukes Mixture* 10-inch album (Columbia 1955)★★★, *Dance To The Duke* (Capitol 1955)★★★, *Duke And His Men* (RCA Victor 1955)★★★, *Blue Light* (Columbia 1955)★★★★, *Here's The Duke* 10-inch album (Columbia 1956)★★★, *Historically Speaking, The Duke* (Bethlehem 1956)★★★, *Duke Ellington Presents* (Bethlehem 1956)★★★, *Birth Of Big Band Jazz* (Riverside 1956)★★★★, *Al Hibbler With the Duke* 10-inch album (Columbia 1956)★★★, with Johnny Hodges *Ellington At Newport '56* (Columbia 1956)★★★★★, *Ellington Showcase* (Capitol 1956)★★★, *A Drum Is A Woman* (Columbia 1957)★★★, *Such Sweet Thunder* (Columbia 1957)★★★, *In A Mellotone* (RCA Victor 1957)★★★★, *Ellington Indigos* (Columbia 1958)★★★★, *Duke Ellington At His Very Best* (RCA Victor 1958)★★★, *Newport 1958* (Columbia 1958)★★★★★, *Brown Black And Beige* (Columbia 1958)★★★★, *The Cosmic Scene* (Columbia 1958)★★★, *Duke Ellington At The Bal Masque* (Columbia 1959)★★★, *Duke Ellington Jazz Party* (Columbia 1959)★★★, with Hodges *Back To Back: Duke Ellington And Johnny Hodges Play The Blues* (Verve 1959)★★★★, with Hodges *Side By Side* (Verve 1959)★★★, *Festival Session* (Columbia 1959)★★★, *Ellington Moods* (SeSac 1959)★★★, *Anatomy Of A Murder* (1959), *The Ellington Suites: The Queen's Suite* (1959)★★★, *Swinging Suites By Edward E. And Edward G. (Suite Thursday/Peer Gynt)* (Columbia 1960)★★★, with Hodges *The Nutcracker Suite* (Columbia 1960)★★★, *Piano In The Background* (Columbia 1960)★★★, *Blues In Orbit* (Columbia 1960)★★★★, *Paris Blues* (1961)★★★, *The Indispensible Duke Ellington* (RCA Victor 1961)★★★, with Count Basie *Ellington/Basie - First Time! The Count Meets The Duke* (Columbia 1962)★★★, *Afro Bossa* (Reprise 1962)★★★, with Charles Mingus, Max Roach *Money Jungle* (United Artists 1962)★★★★, *All American* (Columbia 1962)★★★, *Duke Ellington And His Orchestra Featuring Paul Gonsalves* (1962)★★★, *Midnight In Paris* (Columbia 1962)★★★, with John Coltrane *Duke Ellington And John Coltrane* (MCA/Impulse 1962)★★★★, with Coleman Hawkins *Duke Ellington Meets Coleman Hawkins* (MCA/Impulse 1963)★★★★, *Symphonic Ellington* (1963)★★★, *My People* (1963)★★★, *Piano In The Foreground* (Columbia 1963)★★★, with Billy Strayhorn *Piano Duets: Great Times!* (Riverside 1963)★★★, *Duke Ellington's Concert Of Sacred Music* (RCA Victor 1964)★★★,

The Symphonic Ellington (Reprise 1964)★★★, *Hit's Of The 60s* (Reprise 1964)★★, *Daybreak Express* (RCA Victor 1964)★★★, *Jumpin' Pumpkins* (RCA Victor 1965)★★, *Johnny Come Lately* (RCA Victor 1965)★★, *Mary Poppins* (Reprise 1965)★, *Pretty Woman* (RCA Victor 1965)★★, *Flaming Youth* (RCA Victor 1965)★★, *Ellington '66* (Reprise 1965)★★★, *Will Big Bands Ever Come Back?* (Reprise 1965)★★★, *Concert In The Virgin Islands* (Reprise 1965)★★★, with Boston Pops Orchestra *The Duke At Tanglewood* (RCA Victor 1966)★★★, with Ella Fitzgerald *Ella At Duke's Place* (Verve 1966)★★★★, with Fitzgerald *The Stockholm Concert* (1966)★★★, with Fitzgerald *Ella And Duke At The Côte D'Azure* (Verve 1966)★★★, *The Popular Duke Ellington* (RCA Victor 1966)★★★, *Concert Of Sacred Music* (RCA Victor 1966)★★★, with Hodges *Far East Suite* (RCA Victor 1967)★★★★, *Soul Call* (Verve 1967)★★★, *And His Mother Called Him Bill* (RCA Victor 1968)★★★★, with Frank Sinatra *Francis A. And Edward K.* (Reprise 1968)★★★, *Second Sacred Concert* (Prestige 1968)★★★, *70th Birthday Concert* (1969)★★★, *The Latin American Suite* (Fantasy 1969)★★★, *The New Orleans Suite* (Atlantic 1970)★★★, *Afro-Eurasian Eclipse* (Fantasy 1971)★★★, with Ray Brown *This One's For Blanton* (Pablo 1972)★★★, *Third Sacred Concert* (Prestige 1973)★★★, *Eastbourne Performance* (RCA 1973)★★, *Yale Concert* (Fantasy 1973)★★★, with Teresa Brewer *It Don't Mean A Thing . . .* (Columbia 1973)★★★★, *The Duke's Big 4* (Pablo 1974)★★★★, *The Duke Ellington Carnegie Hall Concerts-January, 1943* (Prestige 1977)★★★★, *The Duke Ellington Carnegie Hall Concerts-December, 1944* (Prestige 1977)★★★★, *The Duke Ellington Carnegie Hall Concerts-January, 1946* (Prestige 1977)★★★★, *The Duke Ellington Carnegie Hall Concerts-December, 1947* (Prestige 1977)★★★★, *The Unknown Session* 1960 recording (Columbia 1979)★★★, *In Concert At The Pleyel Paris* 1958 recording (Magic 1990)★★★.

● COMPILATIONS: *Ellington's Greatest* (RCA Victor 1954)★★★★, *Duke Ellington Volume 1 - In The Beginning* (Decca 1958)★★★★, *Duke Ellington Volume 2 - Hot In Harlem* (Decca 1959)★★★★, *Duke Ellington Volume 3 - Rockin' In Rhythm* (Decca 1959)★★★★, *The Best Of Duke Ellington* (Capitol 1961)★★★★, *The Ellington Era Volume 1* 3-LP box set (Columbia 1963)★★★★, *The Ellington Era Volume 2* 3-LP box set (Columbia 1964)★★★★, *Duke Ellington's Greatest Hits* (Reprise 1966)★★★★, *Duke Ellington - The Pianist* 1966-74 recordings (Fantasy 1974)★★★★, *The Ellington Suites* (Pablo 1976)★★★★, *The Intimate Ellington* (Pablo 1977)★★★, *The All-Star Road Band, Volume 1* (Columbia 1983)★★★★, *The All-Star Road Band, Volume 2* (Columbia 1983)★★★★, *The Indispensable Duke Ellington Volumes 1-12* (RCA 1983-87)★★★, *The Intimacy Of The Blues* 1970 recordings (Fantasy 1986)★★★★, *The Blanton-Webster Band* (RCA Bluebird 1987)★★★★★, *Black, Brown And Beige* (RCA Bluebird 1988)★★★★, *Four Symphonic Works* (MusicMasters 1989)★★★★, *The Best Of Duke Ellington* (Columbia 1989)★★★, *Braggin' In Brass - The Immortal 1938 Year* (Portrait 1989)★★★★, *The Brunswick Era, Volume 1* (MCA 1990)★★★★, with Blanton and others *Solos, Duets And Trios* 1932-67 recordings (RCA Bluebird 1990)★★★★, *The OKeh Ellington* (Columbia 1991)★★★★, *Small Groups, Volume 1* (Columbia/Legacy 1991)★★★★, *The Essence Of Duke Ellington* (Columbia/Legacy 1991)★★★★★.

● VIDEOS: *Duke Ellington* (Virgin Vision 1992), *On The Road With Duke Ellington* (Direct Cinema 1995).
● FURTHER READING: *Duke Ellington: Young Music Master*, Martha E. Schaaf. *Sweet Man, The Real Duke Ellington*, Don R. George. *Duke Ellington*, Ron Franki. *Duke Ellington*, Barry Ulanov. *The World Of Duke Ellington*, Stanley Dance. *Music Is My Mistress*, Duke Ellington. *Celebrating The Duke*, Ralph J. Gleason. *Duke: A Portrait Of Duke Ellington*, Derek Jewell. *Duke Ellington In Person*, Mercer Ellington. *Duke Ellington: His Life And Music*, Peter Gammond. *Duke Ellington: Life And Times Of A Restless Genius Of Jazz*, James Lincoln Collier. *Duke Ellington: The Early Years*, Michael Tucker. *Duke Ellington: Jazz Composer*, Ken Rattenbury. *The Duke Ellington Reader*, Mark Tucker. *Beyond Category: The Life And Genius Of Duke Ellington*, John Edward Hasse. *The Duke Ellington Primer*, Dempsey J. Travis.

ELLINGTON, RAY
b. 1915, London, England, d. 28 February 1985. Ellington began playing drums as a teenager and by 1937 was proficient enough to replace Joe Daniels in Harry Roy's popular band. He remained with Roy for almost five years, although his personal musical taste tended more towards the new jazz styles, and soon after the end of World War II he was playing bop in London clubs. He led his own quartet at this time and made a number of records, and sometimes accompanied visiting American jazzmen. He began to incorporate comedy and novelty material into his repertoire but the group's musical base was always strongly bop-influenced. Throughout the 50s the quartet was regularly featured on *The Goon Show* on BBC Radio, usually with Ellington singing, and he also took small acting roles in the programme. By the 60s and with the passing of *The Goon Show*, Ellington was much less in demand, but he continued playing until shortly before his death in 1985. His son, Lance Ellington, played trombone with the National Youth Jazz Orchestra and also sang as a member of the pop duo Coffee And Cream.
● ALBUMS: *Goon Show Hits* (BBC 1958)★★★, *You're The Talk Of The Town* (Gold Star 1975)★★.

ELLIS, WILBERT 'BIG CHIEF'
b. 10 November 1914, Birmingham, Alabama, USA, d. 20 December 1977, Birmingham, Alabama, USA. A part-time musician, Ellis also worked as a taxi driver, bartender and gambler. His blues piano was rooted in the rolling, hard-hitting styles of Birmingham, to which was added a strong influence from Walter Davis. Resident in New York from 1936, he made a few splendid records under his own name in the 50s, and accompanied Tarheel Slim, Brownie McGhee, Jack Dupree and others. Rediscovered in Washington in the 70s, he returned to performing, enthusiastically and with unimpaired skills, until his death.
● ALBUMS: *Big Chief Ellis* (1976)★★★, *Let's Have A Ball* (1978)★★★.

EMERSON, BILLY 'THE KID'
b. William Robert Emerson, 21 December 1929, Tarpon Springs, Florida, USA. Emerson's father was a blues singer and the young Emerson played piano with the Billy Battle Band and other local groups before serving in the forces in 1952-54. On his return, he joined Ike Turner's band in Memphis. Here, Emerson made his first records for Sun which displayed his talent for wordplay and included 'No Teasing Around', the jive-talking 'The Woodchuck' and 'Red Hot', a song later taken up by rockabilly singer Billy Lee Riley and by Bob Luman. He moved to Chicago soon afterwards, playing piano or organ on numerous recording sessions and releasing singles under his own name from 1955-57 for Vee Jay ('Every Woman I Know Is Crazy About An Automobile', later revived by Ry Cooder) and from 1958-59 for Chess ('I'll Get You Too'). There were later records for Mad (1960), M-Pac (the dance craze song 'The Whip', 1963) and USA (1963) before Emerson formed his own Tarpon label in the mid-60s. Among his Tarpon singles was 'I Dig The Funky Broadway'.
● ALBUMS: (reissues) *Little Fine Healthy Thing* (Charly 1980)★★★, *Crazy 'Bout Automobiles* (Charly 1982)★★★.

ENGLISH, LOGAN
Born and raised in Kentucky, USA, English was exposed to traditional music at an early age. He was drawn into the folk and coffee-house circuit of the 50s following a brief spell as an actor, and became a regular performer on the east and west coast clubs circuit Several successful appearances at New York's Town and Carnegie Halls predated the Greenwich Village boom of the early 60s. Sceptical of the newer generation of singers, English continued to work with traditional material and was subsequently surpassed by those embracing more contemporary forms. He remained a fixture on the folk scene, albeit in a lessened role, but despite enjoying the respect of his peers, commercial success proved elusive.
● ALBUMS: *Kentucky Ballads* 10-inch album (Folkways 50s)★★★, *The Days Of '49* (Folkways 50s)★★★★, *Gambling Songs* (Riverside 50s)★★★★, *American Folk Ballads* (1962)★★★★.

ENNIS, SKINNAY
b. Robert Ennis, 13 August 1909, Salisbury, North Carolina, USA, d. 3 June 1963, Beverley Hills, California, USA. Ennis joined the Hal Kemp band as a singer/drummer in the late 20s while still at the University of North Carolina. He became the band's leading attraction because of his unique 'out of breath' vocal style. Ennis left Kemp in 1938 and, after working with Gil Evans and Claude Thornhill, formed his own band with its theme song 'Got A Date With An Angel', and gained maximum exposure with a prestigious residency on Bob Hope's *Pepsodent Show*. Ennis also featured in the show's comedy routines and became a personality in his own right. After World War II, during which he led a service band, Ennis rejoined Hope until 1946, and then worked on radio with Abbott And Costello in the late 40s. He made several diverting appearances in films including *College Swing* (with Bob Hope), *Follow The Band*, *Swing It Soldier*, *Sleepytime Gal*, *Let's Go Steady* and *Radio Stars On Parade*. During the 50s his band toured the USA, playing the hotel circuit, including, from 1958, a five-year residency at the Statler-Hilton, Los Angeles. During the early 60s he recorded the album *Skinnay Ennis Salutes Hal Kemp*, using many of the musicians who had played in the original Kemp band. He died after choking on a bone while dining in a restaurant.
● ALBUMS: *Skinnay Ennis, 1947-1948* (Hindsight 1989)★★★.

EVERLY BROTHERS

Don (b. 1 February 1937, Brownie, Kentucky, USA) and Phil (b. 19 January 1939, Chicago, Illinois, USA), the world's most famous rock 'n' roll duo, had already experienced a full career before their first record 'Bye Bye Love' was released. As sons of popular country artists Ike and Margaret, they were pushed into the limelight from an early age. They regularly appeared on their parents' radio shows throughout the 40s and accompanied them on many tours. In the mid-50s, as rockabilly was evolving into rock 'n' roll, the boys moved to Nashville, the mecca for such music. Don had a minor hit when Kitty Wells recorded his composition 'Thou Shalt Not Steal' in 1954.

In 1957 they were given a Felice and Boudleaux Bryant song that was finding difficulty being placed. They took 'Bye Bye Love' and made it their own; it narrowly missed the US number 1 position and reached number 6 in the UK. The brothers then embarked on a career that made them second only to Elvis Presley in the rock 'n' roll popularity stakes. Their blend of country and folk did much to sanitize and make respectable a phenomenon towards which many parents still showed hostility. America, then a racially segregated country, was not ready for its white teenagers to listen to black-based rock music. The brothers' clean looks and even cleaner harmonies did much to change people's attitudes. They quickly followed this initial success with more irresistible Bryant songs, 'Wake Up Little Susie', 'All I Have To Do Is Dream', 'Bird Dog', 'Problems', 'So Sad' and the beautiful 'Devoted To You'. The brothers were supremely confident live performers, both with their trademark Gibson Dove and later, black J50 guitars. By the end of the 50s they were the world's number 1 vocal group. Amazingly, their career gained further momentum when, after signing with the newly formed Warner Brothers Records for $1 million, they delivered a song that was catalogued WB1. This historical debut was the superlative 'Cathy's Clown', written by Don. No Everly record had sounded like this before; the echo-laden production and the treble-loaded harmonies ensured that it stayed at number 1 in the USA for five weeks. In the UK it stayed on top for over two months, selling several million and making it one of the most successful records of all time. The brothers continued to release immaculate records; many of them reached the US Top 10, although in England their success was even greater, with two further number 1 hits during 1961. Again the echo and treble dominated in two more classics, 'Walk Right Back' and a fast-paced reworking of the former Bing Crosby hit 'Temptation'. At the end of 1961 they were drafted into the US Marines, albeit for only six months, and resumed by embarking on a European tour. Don became dependent on drugs, and the pressures from constant touring and recording began to show; during one historic night at London's East Ham Granada, England, a nervous Phil performed solo. The standard 'food poisoning/exhaustion' excuse was used. What was not known by the doting fans was that Don had attempted a suicidal drug overdose twice in 48 hours. Phil completed the tour solo. Don's addiction continued for another three years, although they were able to work during part of this time.

The advent of the beat boom pushed the brothers out of the spotlight and while they continued to make hit records, none approached their previous achievements. The decline was briefly halted in 1965 with two excellent major UK hits,

'The Price Of Love' and 'Love Is Strange'. The former, a striking chart-topper, sounded like their early Warner sound, while the latter harked back even earlier, with a naïve but infectious call-and-answer spoken segment. In 1966 they released *Two Yanks In England*, a strong album that contained eight songs by Nash/Clarke/Hicks of the Hollies; surprisingly, the album failed to chart. The duo were recognized only for their superb singles, and many of their albums were less well received. *Stories We Could Tell*, recorded with an array of guest players, threatened to extend their market into the rock mainstream, but it was not to be. After a few years of declining fortunes and arrival at the supper-club circuit, the brothers parted acrimoniously. Following a show at Knotts Berry Farm, California, in 1973, during which a drunken Don had insulted Phil, the latter walked off, smashed one of his beloved Gibsons and vowed, 'I will never get on a stage with that man again'. The only time they met over the next 10 years was at their father's funeral.

Both embarked on solo careers with varying degrees of accomplishment. Their country-flavoured albums found more favour with the Nashville audience of their roots. Don and his band, the Dead Cowboys, regularly played in Nashville, while Phil released the critically acclaimed *Star Spangled Springer*. Inexplicably, the album was a relatively poor seller, as were several follow-ups Phil made a cameo appearance in the film *Every Which Way But Lose*, performing with actress Sondra Locke. While Don maintained a steady career, playing with ex-Heads, Hands And Feet maestro Albert Lee, Phil concentrated on writing songs. 'She Means Nothing To Me' was a striking duet with Cliff Richard which put the Everly name back in the UK Top 10. Rumours began to circulate of a reunion, which was further fuelled by a UK television advertisement for an Everly Brothers compilation. In June 1983 they hugged and made up and their emotional reconciliation was made before an ecstatic, wet-eyed audience at London's Royal Albert Hall. The following year *EB84* was released and gave them another major hit with Paul McCartney's 'Wings Of A Nightingale'. In 1986 they were inducted into the Rock And Roll Hall Of Fame and the following year Phil gave Don a pound of gold and a hand-made guitar for his 50th birthday. The Everly Brothers' influence on a generation of pop and rock artists is inestimable; they set a standard for close harmony singing that has rarely been bettered. They now perform regularly together, with no pressure from record companies. Don lives quietly in Nashville and tours with his brother for a few months every year. To date, the ceasefire has held.

● ALBUMS: *The Everly Brothers* (Cadence 1958)★★★, *Songs Our Daddy Taught Us* (Cadence 1959)★★★, *The Everly Brothers' Best* (Cadence 1959)★★★, *It's Everly Time* (Warners 1960)★★★, *The Fabulous Style Of The Everly Brothers* (Cadence 1960)★★★★, *A Date With The Everly Brothers* (Warners 1961)★★★★, *Both Sides Of An Evening* (Warners 1961)★★★, *Folk Songs of the Everly Brothers* (Cadence 1962)★★★, *Instant Party* (Warners 1962)★★★, *Christmas With The Everly Brothers And The Boys Town Choir* (Warners 1962)★★★, *The Everly Brothers Sing Great Country Hits* (Warners 1963)★★★, *Gone Gone Gone* (Warners 1965)★★★★, *Rock 'N' Soul* (Warners 1965)★★★, *Beat 'N' Soul* (Warners 1965)★★★, *In Our Image* (Warners 1966)★★★, *Two Yanks In England* (Warners 1966)★★★, *The*

Hit Sound Of The Everly Brothers (Warners 1967)★★★, *The Everly Brothers Sing* (Warners 1967)★★★, *Roots* (Warners 1968)★★★, *The Everly Brothers Show* (Warners 1970)★★★, *End Of An Era* (Barnaby/Columbia 1971)★★★, *Stories We Could Tell* (RCA Victor 1972)★★★, *Pass The Chicken And Listen* (RCA Victor 1973)★★, *The Exciting Everly Brothers* (RCA 1975)★★★, *Living Legends* (Warwick 1977)★★★, *The New Album* previously unissued Warners material (Warners 1977)★★★, *The Everly Brothers Reunion Concert* (Impression 1983)★★★★, *Nice Guys* previously unissued Warners material (Magnum Force 1984)★★, *EB84* (Mercury 1984)★★★, *In The Studio* previously unissued Cadence material (Ace 1985)★★★, *Born Yesterday* (Mercury 1985)★★★, *Some Hearts* (Mercury 1989)★★★, *Live In Paris* (Big Beat 1997)★★★.

Solo: Don Everly *Don Everly* (A&M 1971)★★, *Sunset Towers* (Ode 1974)★★, *Brother Juke Box* (Hickory 1976)★★★. Phil Everly *Star Spangled Springer* (RCA 1973)★★★, *Phil's Diner (There's Nothing Too Good For My Baby)* (Pye 1974)★★, *Mystic Line* (Pye 1975)★★, *Living Alone* (Elektra 1979)★★, *Phil Everly* (Capitol 1983)★★.

● COMPILATIONS: *The Golden Hits Of The Everly Brothers* (Warners 1962)★★★★, *15 Everly Hits* (Cadence 1963)★★★, *The Very Best Of The Everly Brothers* (Warners 1964)★★★★, *The Everly Brothers' Original Greatest Hits* (Columbia 1970)★★★★, *The Most Beautiful Songs Of The Everly Brothers* (Warners 1973)★★★, *Don's And Phil's Fabulous Fifties Treasury* (Janus 1974)★★★, *Walk Right Back With The Everlys* (Warners 1975)★★★★, *The Everly Brothers Greatest Hits Collection* (Pickwick 1979)★★★, *The Sensational Everly Brothers* (Reader Digest 1979)★★, *Cathy's Clown* (Pickwick 1980)★★★, *The Very Best Of The Everly Brothers* (Marks & Spencer 1980)★★, *The Everly Brothers* (Warners 1981)★★★, *Rock 'N' Roll Forever* (Warners 1981)★★★, *Love Hurts* (K-Tel 1982)★★, *Rip It Up* (Ace 1983)★★★, *Cadence Classics (Their 20 Greatest Hits)* (Rhino 1985)★★★★, *The Best Of The Everly Brothers* (Rhino 1985)★★★, *All They Had To Do Is Dream* US only (Rhino 1985)★★★, *Great Recordings* (Ace 1986)★★★, *The Everly Brothers Collection* (Castle 1988)★★★, *The Very Best Of The Everly Brothers* (Pickwick 1988)★★★, *Hidden Gems* Warners material (Ace 1989)★★★, *The Very Best Of The Everly Brothers Volume 2* (Pickwick 1990)★★, *Perfect Harmony* box set (Knight 1990)★★★, *Classic Everly Brothers* 3-CD box set (Bear Family 1992)★★★★, *The Golden Years Of The Everly Brothers* (Warners 1993)★★★★, *Heartaches And Harmonies* 4-CD box set (Rhino 1995)★★★★★, *Walk Right Back: On Warner Bros. 1960 To 1969* 2-CD set (Warners 1996)★★★★, *All I Have To Do Is Dream* (Carlton 1997)★★★, *The EP Collection* (See For Miles 1998)★★★.

● VIDEOS: *Rock 'N' Roll Odyssey* (MGM 1984).

● FURTHER READING: *Everly Brothers: An Illustrated Discography*, John Hosum. *The Everly Brothers: Walk Right Back*, Roger White. *Ike's Boys*, Phyllis Karpp. *The Everly Brothers: Ladies Love Outlaws*, Consuelo Dodge. *For-Everly Yours*, Peter Aarts and Martin Alberts.

EXPRESSO BONGO (STAGE MUSICAL)

Considered by many to be 'the most important and original British musical of its time', *Expresso Bongo* opened at the Saville Theatre on 23 April 1958. The book, by Wolf Mankowitz and Julian More, was taken from a newspaper piece by Mankowitz, and is said to have been based on the true-life story of the young ex-merchant seaman Thomas Hicks. He had been discovered in 1956, playing the guitar and singing in a Soho coffee-bar called the 2I's, by his future manager John Kennedy. He, and the agent Larry Parnes, changed Hicks' name to Tommy Steele, and moulded him into Britain's first rock 'n' roller. In this show, Herbert Rudge is also discovered at a trendy coffee-bar, but he is playing bongo drums, not guitar, hence his eventual stage name of Bongo Herbert. With the aid of a crafty agent, Johnnie (Paul Schofield), he quickly climbs the chart with 'Expresso Party', and then, just like Steele, shrewdly broadens his image, in Bongo's case with a magnificently ghastly hymn to his old mum, 'The Shrine On The Second Floor' ('There's a beautiful grey-haired Madonna/Who once taught me what life had in store'). The show was full of accurately drawn, colourful characters such as the stripper who wants to be a singer, Maisie King (Millicent Martin), a recording executive, Mr. Mayer (Meir Tzelniker), and a well-to-do, ageing actress, Dixie Collins (Hy Hazell), who gives Bongo a taste of the high life, and arranges for him to be represented by an 'establishment' agent. Johnnie cannot compete, looks around for new talent, and decides to promote Maisie as a singer. The score, by David Heneker and Monty Norman, both of whom also collaborated on the lyrics with Julian More, was a match for the book. The songs were witty and satirical, including Bongo's wry 'Don't You Sell Me Down The River', and Johnnie's charting of his ups and downs with 'I've Never Had It So Good' and 'The Gravy Train', while Maisie ground her hips (and a good deal more) to 'Spoil The Child'. She also had two poignant ballads, 'Seriously' and 'I Am'. Dixie reflected on her life in and out of the theatre with the touching 'Time', and joined Johnnie and Mr. Mayer for 'Nothing Is For Nothing'. Opinions as to the show's value were mixed, and ran along the lines of 'an adult approach', 'wit, bite and topicality' and 'a raucous paeon of disgust aimed at the shoddy side of society'. It was certainly very different in style from that other British musical, Sandy Wilson's *Valmouth* (set in an English spa town inhabited by centenarians), which came to the Lyric when *Expresso Bongo* closed after a run of 316 performances. Even then, the Tommy Steele connections continued: his brother, Colin Hicks, played the lead in the touring version of *Expresso Bongo*, and the show's co-composer and lyricist, David Heneker, wrote the score for Steele's smash-hit musical *Half A Sixpence*, in 1963. The 1959 film of *Expresso Bongo* starred Laurence Harvey, Cliff Richard, Yolande Dolan and Sylvia Syms. Changes in the score resulted in the inclusion of 'A Voice In The Wilderness', written by Norrie Paramor and Bunny Lewis, which Richard took to number 2 in the UK chart.

EXPRESSO BONGO (FILM MUSICAL)

This 1959 comedy feature began life as a stage play loosely based on the rise of British rock 'n' roll star Tommy Steele. Written by Wolf Mankowitz and directed by Val Guest, *Expresso Bongo* starred Laurence Harvey as an unscrupulous Soho agent, determined to make his protégé, ably played by Cliff Richard, into an international success. The film manages to convey some of the exploitative nature of early pop and the nascent teenage subculture spearheaded by the legendary 2I's coffee bar. However, the cynicism of Mankowitz meant the funny moments lacked warmth and the film now merely offers period charm. Although mild-mannered by the standards of today, *Expresso Bongo* was given an X-certificate, confirming the moody, threat-to-society image Richard initially bore. It did nothing to hinder his popularity, however, and in 1960 a soundtrack EP reached the number 14 position in the UK singles chart while the film's finest song, 'Voice In The Wilderness', peaked at number 2.

FABIAN

b. Fabiano Forte Bonaparte, 6 February 1943, Philadelphia, USA. Fabian, almost despite himself, was among the more endurable products of the late 50s when the North American charts were infested with a turnover of vapid boys-next-door - all hair spray, doe eyes and coy half-smiles - groomed for fleeting stardom. Fabian was 'discovered' by two local talent scouts, Peter De Angelis and Bob Marucci, in Frankie Avalon's Teen And Twenty youth club in 1957. Enthralled by the youth's good looks, the pair shortened his name and contracted him to their Chancellor Records where a huge budget was allocated to project him as a tamed Elvis Presley. Accompanied by the Four Dates, Fabian's first two singles - 'I'm In Love' and 'Lilly Lou' - were only regional hits, but a string of television performances on Dick Clark's nationally-broadcast *American Bandstand* plus a coast-to-coast tour had the desired effect on female teenagers, and Fabian found himself suddenly in *Billboard*'s Top 40 with 'I'm A Man,' composed by the songwriting team Doc Pomus/Mort Shuman, who also delivered more lucrative hits in 'Turn Me Loose' and 'Hound Dog Man', the main theme from Fabian's screen debut of the same name. More substantial movie roles came his way after his recording career peaked with 1959's million-selling 'Tiger' and *Hold That Tiger*. As well as the predictable teen-pics he coped surprisingly well as John Wayne's sidekick in 1960's *North To Alaska* and with Bing Crosby and Tuesday Weld in *High Time*. Fabian's decline was as rapid as his launch after Congress pinpointed him as an instance of one of the exploited puppets in the payola scandal. Questioned at the time, Fabian made matters worse by outlining the considerable electronic doctoring necessary to improve his voice on record. His first serious miss came in 1960 with 'About This Thing Called Love' and an irredeemable downward spiral mitigated by 1962's 'Kissin' And Twistin'' and other small hits. Nevertheless, he could be seen in films such as 1962's *The Longest Day*, but more commen-

surate with his talent were productions such as *Fireball 500* (a 1966 epic with his friend Frankie Avalon) and 1965's *Ride The Wild Surf*. Fabian's limited vocal range should not be held against him: he became a puppet and he danced; out of it he traded a doomed musical career for a credible movie career.

● ALBUMS: *Hold That Tiger* (Chancellor 1959)★★, *The Fabulous Fabian* (Chancellor 1959)★★, *The Good Old Summertime* (Chancellor 1960)★★, *Fabian Facade* (Chancellor 1961)★★, *Rockin' Hot* (Chancellor 1961)★★, *Fabian's 16 Fabulous Hits* (Chancellor 1962)★★, *All The Hits* (1993)★★.

● COMPILATIONS: *The Best Of ...* (Varese Sarabande 1996)★★.

● FILMS: *Hound Dog Man* (1959), *North To Alaska* (1960), *High Time* (1960), *Mr Hobbs Takes A Vacation* (1962), *The Longest Day* (1962), *Dear Brigitte* (1965), *Fireball 500* (1966), *Dr Goldfoot And The Girl Bomb* (1966), *American Pop* (1981).

FAITH, PERCY

b. 7 April 1908, Toronto, Ontario, Canada, d. 9 February 1976, Ericino, California, USA. During the 30s Faith worked extensively on radio in Canada, and moved to the USA in 1940 to take up a post with NBC. During the 50s he was musical director for Columbia Records, for whom he made a number of popular albums, mostly of mood music. He worked with Tony Bennett, with whom he had three million-selling singles, and, from 1950, also had several hits in his own right, including 'Cross My Fingers', 'All My Love', 'On Top Of Old Smoky' (vocal by Burl Ives), 'Delicado', 'Song From The Moulin Rouge (Where Is Your Heart)' (US number 1 in 1953), 'Return To Paradise' (1953), and 'Theme From A Summer Place', which reached number 1 in the US and number 2 in the UK charts in 1960. In Hollywood in the 50s Faith had composed several background film scores, including *Love Me Or Leave Me* (1955), the highly acclaimed biopic of singer Ruth Etting, which starred Doris Day. His film credits in the 60s included *Tammy Tell Me True* (1961), *I'd Rather Be Rich* (1964), *The Third Day* (1965) and *The Oscar* (1966). For *The Love Goddesses*, Faith wrote the title song with Mack David. His other compositions included 'My Heart Cries For You' (with his main collaborator Carl Sigman), which was a big hit for Guy Mitchell, Dinah Shore, Vic Damone and others in 1951. Faith died of cancer in February 1976.

In the mid-90s there has been a renewed interest in Faith's work, particularly in Japan, where many of his albums have been reissued. New performances of his arrangements have been conducted by Nick Perito for a series of CDs.

● ALBUMS: *Continental Music* (Columbia 1956)★★★, *Passport To Romance* (Columbia 1956)★★★, *Music From My Fair Lady* (Columbia 1957)★★★★, *Touchdown!* (Columbia 1958)★★★, *North & South Of The Border* (Columbia 1958)★★★, *Music Of Victor Herbert* (Columbia 1958)★★★, *Viva!* (Columbia 1959)★★★, *Hallelujah* (Columbia 1959)★★★, *Porgy And Bess* (Columbia 1959)★★★, *Music Of George Gershwin* (Columbia 1959)★★★★, *A Night With Sigmund Romberg* (Columbia 1959)★★★, *Malaguena* (Columbia 1959)★★★, *Bouquet* (Columbia 1959)★★★★, *Music From South Pacific* (Columbia 1960)★★, *Bon Voyage!* (Columbia 1960)★★★, *Continental Souvenirs* (Columbia 1960)★★★, *Jealousy* (Columbia 1960)★★★★, *A Night With*

Jerome Kern (Columbia 1960)★★★, *Camelot* (Columbia 1961)★★★★, *Carefree* (Columbia 1961)★★★, *Mucho Gusto! More Music Of Mexico* (Columbia 1961)★★, *Tara's Theme* (Columbia 1961)★★★, *Bouquet Of Love* (Columbia 1962)★★★, *Subways Are For Sleeping* (Columbia 1962)★★★, *The Music Of Brazil!* (Columbia 1962)★★★, *Hollywood's Themes* (Columbia 1963)★★★★, *American Serenade* (Columbia 1963)★★★, *Exotic Strings* (Columbia 1963)★★★, *Shangri-La!* (Columbia 1963)★★★, *Great Folk Themes* (Columbia 1964)★★★, *More Themes For Young Lovers* (Columbia 1964)★★★, *Latin Themes* (Columbia 1965)★★★, *Broadway Bouquet* (Columbia 1965)★★★, *Themes For The 'In' Crowd* (Columbia 1966)★★★, *The Academy Award Winner And Other Great Movie Themes* (Columbia 1967)★★★★, *Today's Themes For Young Lovers* (Columbia 1967)★★★, *For Those In Love* (Columbia 1968)★★★, *Angel Of The Morning (Hit Themes For Young Lovers)* (Columbia 1968)★★, *Those Were The Days* (Columbia 1969)★★, *Windmills Of Your Mind* (Columbia 1969)★★, *Love Theme From 'Romeo And Juliet'* (Columbia 1969)★★★, *Forever Young* (Columbia 1970)★★, *Leaving On A Jet Plane* (Columbia 1970)★★, *Held Over! Today's Great Movie Themes* (Columbia 1970)★★★, *The Beatles Album* (Columbia 1970)★★, *A Time For Love* (Columbia 1971)★★★, *I Think I Love You* (Columbia 1971)★★, *Black Magic Woman* (Columbia 1971)★★, *Jesus Christ, Superstar* (Columbia 1971)★★, *Joy* (Columbia 1972)★★★, *Day By Day* (Columbia 1972)★★★.
● COMPILATIONS: *Moods* (Ditto 1983)★★★, *Images* (Knight 1990)★★★, *Music From the Movies* (1994)★★★.

FAWKES, WALLY

b. 21 June 1924, Vancouver, British Columbia, Canada. Fawkes moved to the UK while still very young and in the mid-40s was recruited by George Webb, leader of one of the first bands to attract popular attention during the trad-jazz boom. In 1947 he left Webb along with fellow sideman Humphrey Lyttelton to become a founder-member of the latter's new band. This musical relationship lasted until 1956 and was rewarding for musicians and fans alike. After leaving Lyttelton, Fawkes played with several other leaders, including Bruce Turner and Sandy Brown, with whom he recorded in 1954 and 1956, respectively (both sessions being reissued on a single 1989 album), and he also led his own semi-professional band, the Troglodytes, a more loosely swinging band than many of his contemporaries in the sometimes staid UK trad scene. Later, Fawkes, a gifted, Sidney Bechet-influenced clarinettist, whose musical abilities have made him a major name on the trad circuit, chose to play freelance, usually showing a marked preference for obscure pubs in the London area. For several decades, Fawkes, using the byline 'Trog', drew the strip-cartoon 'Flook' in the *Daily Mail*, the script for which was written by singer George Melly. Fawkes continued his sporadic jazz career into the 80s with several excellent records, including reunions with Lyttelton and Ian Christie, another sparring partner from the heyday of British trad jazz.
● ALBUMS: *Wally Fawkes And The Neo-Troglodytes* (Dawn 1979)★★★, with Humphrey Lyttelton *It Seems Like Yesterday* (Calligraph 1983)★★★, with Ian Christie *That's The Blues Old Man* (1984)★★★, *Wally Fawkes And The Rhythm Kings* (Stomp Off 1985)★★★, *Whatever Next!*

(Stomp Off 1986)★★★, *October Song* (Calligraph 1986)★★★, with Bruce Turner, Sandy Brown *Juicy And Full Toned 1954-56 recordings* (Lake 1989)★★★★, *Fidgety Feet* (Stomp Off 1993)★★★.
● COMPILATIONS: with Lyttelton *A Tribute To Humph, Volume 1* (Dormouse 1984)★★★.

FEATHER, LEONARD

b. 13 September 1914, London, England, d. 22 September 1994, Los Angeles, California, USA. After studying piano, Feather advanced his musical interests by teaching himself arranging and in the early 30s produced a number of record sessions, contributing charts and scores. Among the musicians for whom he worked in such capacities was Benny Carter and he was instrumental in persuading Henry Hall to hire Carter for the BBC Dance Orchestra. In the mid-30s Feather went to the USA and during the next decade he continued to work in record production, sometimes supplying original material for artists such as Louis Armstrong, Lionel Hampton ('Blowtop Blues') and Dinah Washington ('Evil Gal Blues'). Feather also branched into concert promotion and produced numerous recording sessions. Additionally, he continued to compose songs for artists such as Sarah Vaughan, Ella Fitzgerald, Cannonball Adderley and Sonny Stitt. Despite all these endeavours, most of his considerable efforts in the cause of jazz were gradually concentrated into writing on the subject for several magazines, including *Esquire* and *Downbeat*, and he also wrote a jazz column for the *Los Angeles Times*. He was the author of several jazz books, notably *Encyclopedia Of Jazz* and his autobiography, *The Jazz Years: Ear Witness To An Era*. He was also a frequent broadcaster on jazz on radio and television. His daughter Lorraine is an accomplished singer.
● ALBUMS: all as producer *Leonard Feather's Swinging Swedes* (1951-54)★★★, *Winter Sequence* 10-inch album (MGM 1954)★★★, *Swingin' On The Vibories* (ABC-Paramount 1956)★★, *Leonard Feather Presents Bop* reissued as *Leonard Feather Presents 52nd Street* (Mode 1957)★★★, *Hi-Fi Suite* (MGM 1957)★★★, *Oh, Captain!* (MGM 1958)★★★, *Seven Ages Of Jazz* (1958)★★★, *Swedish Punch* (1959)★★★, *Leonard Feather's Encyclopedia Of Jazz All Stars* (1967)★★★★, *Leonard Feather Presents* (VSOP 1988)★★★, *Night Blooming* (Mainstream 1991)★★★.
● FURTHER READING: *The Jazz Years: Ear Witness To An Era*, Leonard Feather. *The Encyclopedia Of Jazz* (various editions), Leonard Feather.

FEATHERS, CHARLIE

b. Charles Arthur Feathers, 12 June 1932, Holly Springs, Mississippi, USA. The work of rockabilly legend Feathers becomes more elevated during each revival of interest in the genre. Feathers is now an enigmatic superstar, although in reality his influence totally overshadows his commercial success. His upbringing on a farm, being taught guitar by a cotton-picking black bluesman and leaving home to work on an oilfield, gave Feathers a wealth of material for his compositions. In the early 50s, together with Jody Chastain and Jerry Huffman, he performed as the Musical Warriors. He was an early signing to Sam Phillips' Sun Records. He recorded his first song, 'Defrost Your Heart', in 1955, and claimed to have co-written Elvis Presley's debut, 'Blue Moon Of Kentucky'. He did, however, co-write Presley's first hit, 'I

Forgot To Remember To Forget'. Over the years he has continued to record for a number of labels, still unable to break through the barrier between 'cult' and 'star'. Among his early rockabilly sides was 'One Hand Loose' on King, regarded by many collectors as one of the finest examples of its kind. His highly applauded performance at London's famous Rainbow theatre in 1977 gave his career a significant boost and brought him a new audience, notably the fans who were following Dave Edmunds and his crusade for 'rockabilly'. Feathers' recent recordings have suffered from the problem of being helped out by younger musicians who are merely in awe of his work, and his best material is from the 50s. Influential but spartan, full of whoops and growls, but ultimately, irresistible country rock, Feather's 'light comedy' style has been an 'invisible influence' over many decades, from Big Bopper in the 50s to Hank Wangford in the 80s. His 1991 release contained a reworked version of his classic 'I Forgot To Remember To Forget'. He now performs with his son and daughter on guitar and vocals, respectively. A remarkable crop of unissued demos appeared in 1995 as *Tip Top Daddy* and further highlighted the originality of the man who defined country rockabilly long before Garth Brooks was born, and yet has never received widespread recognition for his contribution.

● ALBUMS: *Live In Memphis* (Barrelhouse 1979)★★★, *Charlie Feathers* (Elektra 1991)★★★.

● COMPILATIONS: *Rockabilly Mainman* (Charly 1978)★★★, *Honky Tonk Man* (1982)★★★, *Rockabilly Kings* (1984)★★★, *The Legendary 1956 Demo Session* (Zu Zazz 1986)★★, *Jungle Fever* (Kay 1987)★★★, *Wild Wild Party* (Rockstar 1987)★★★, *The Living Legend* (Redita 1988)★★★, *Rock-A-Billy* (Zu Zazz 1991)★★★, *Tip Top Daddy* (Norton 1995)★★★.

FERGUSON, H-BOMB

b. Robert Ferguson. In the fall-out that succeeded the acquisition of his stage name, Ferguson obliterated all knowledge of his past, beyond the fact that his father was a minister who disapproved of his son playing blues and boogie-woogie on the church piano. In later years, his identity has been further masked by a bewildering array of gaudy wigs. He first took the stage at the age of 16, having persuaded Cat Anderson to let him sing with his band. A year later, Anderson hired him. He first recorded as Bob Ferguson with Jack Parker's Orchestra for Derby in 1950. Around this time, manager Chet Patterson suggested he call himself The Cobra Kid, but his 1951 records for Atlas billed him as H-Bomb, as celebrated in 'Rock H-Bomb Rock'. After a single for Prestige, he signed to Savoy and singles such as 'Good Lovin'' and 'Preachin' The Blues' (based on 'Bloodshot Eyes') were full-blown imitations of the Wynonie Harris shouting style. In 1953 he recorded two titles for Specialty that remained unissued for some 40 years. Further singles for Sunset, Finch, Big Bang and ARC failed to sell and his 1960 session for Federal marked the end of his recording career at the time. In recent years, he has made a comeback, but his energetic live performances and outlandish headwear are insufficient compensation for a wayward talent long since spent.

● ALBUMS: *Life Is Hard* (Savoy Jazz 1987)★★★, *Bad Times Blues* (Papa Lou Recordings 1990)★★, *Wiggin' Out* (Earwig 1993)★★.

● COMPILATIONS: *Roots Of Rock'n'Roll Volume 9, The Shouters* (Savoy 1980)★★★, *Shouting The Blues* (Specialty 1993)★★★.

FERRARI, FREDERICK

b. 20 July 1912, Manchester, Lancashire, England, d. 19 April 1994, London, England. Usually known simply as 'the voice' because of his superb tenor, Ferrari was among the most popular of the post-war variety club and radio acts. He took his name - and his love for singing - from his Italian father. After appearing in small concert parties around the Manchester area, his career began in earnest when he joined the army in 1941. Although ultimately the army life helped to advance his singing ambitions (via the khaki entertainment troupe *Stars In Battledress*), his call-up actually scotched an engagement with the Carl Rosa Opera Company. Together with top comedian Charlie Chester, Ferrari went on to appear in over 2,000 service shows both at home and overseas, performances often highlighted by the rendering of his signature tune, 'Love Descended Like An Angel', written for him by Chester. After the war, Ferrari joined Chester in his popular radio show *Stand Easy*, before returning to variety (still as a huge star) in the early 50s. In addition to seaside residencies, he regularly performed at the London Palladium and made an appearance in front of the Queen. Alongside charity work he continued to be a popular attraction at functions and shows long after the variety halls closed.

FIELDS, ERNIE

b. 26 August 1905, Nacogdoches, Texas, USA. This trombonist, arranger and bandleader fronted his own outfit in the Tulsa, Oklahoma area from the 30s, and recorded for various labels, including Vocalian, Frisco, Bullet and Gotham. During the 50s he became an arranger for pop and rock sessions, and ran his own R&B band. In 1958 he became co-founder of the Rendezvous label, and had a million-seller with his swinging revival of the 1939 Glenn Miller favourite, 'In The Mood'. He followed that with his own individual interpretations of other standards, such as 'Chattanooga Choo Choo' and 'The Charleston', but without the same success. He was also involved with the Rendezvous act, B. Bumble And The Stingers, who had hits with 'Bumble Boogie' and 'Nut Rocker', before Rendezvous folded in the early 60s.

FINEGAN, BILL

b. 3 April 1917, Newark, New Jersey, USA. Pianist Finegan's first successes were the arrangements he wrote for the Tommy Dorsey band, but his real breakthrough came in 1938 when he became a staff arranger for Glenn Miller. Throughout the late 30s and early 40s, Finegan wrote extensively for films, but continued to provide charts for Miller, Dorsey, Horace Heidt and others. At the start of the 50s Finegan was studying at the Paris Conservatoire and began corresponding with fellow-arranger Eddie Sauter, who was then hospitalized with tuberculosis. Out of this correspondence emerged a decision to form an orchestra of their own that would play music other leaders might well regard as uncommercial. In 1952 the 21-piece Sauter-Finegan Orchestra made its appearance. With so many musicians, several of whom doubled and even trebled on other instruments, the tonal palette was huge and the two arrangers took full advantage of this. The band was hugely successful with memorable records such as 'The Doodletown Fifers' and 'Sleigh Ride' (based upon music by Prokofiev). On this latter title the sound effect of horses' hooves on hard-packed snow was created by Finegan beating his chest. Later, he wryly remarked, 'this is probably my finest effort on wax - or snow'. In the late 50s Finegan worked mostly in radio and television, but in the 70s returned to big band arranging with charts for the Glenn Miller reunion orchestra and for Mel Lewis, who continued to use his work into the 80s.

● ALBUMS: all by Sauter-Finegan Orchestra *New Directions In Music* 10-inch album (RCA Victor 1953)★★★★, *Inside Sauter-Finegan* (RCA Victor 1954)★★★, *The Sound Of Sauter-Finegen* (RCA Victor 1954)★★★, *Sons Of Sauter-Finegan* (RCA Victor 1955)★★★, *Concert Jazz* (RCA Victor 1955)★★★, *New Directions In Music* (RCA 1956)★★★★★, *Adventure In Time* (RCA Victor 1956)★★★, *Under Analysis* (RCA Victor 1957)★★★★, *One Night Stand With The Sauter-Finegan Orchestra* (RCA Victor 1957)★★★, *Straight Down The Middle* (RCA Victor 1957)★★★, *Inside Sauter-Finegan Revisited* (RCA Victor 1961)★★★, *Sleigh Ride* (RCA Victor 1961)★★★★, *The Return Of The Doodletown Fifers* (Capitol 1985)★★★.

FINGS AIN'T WOT THEY USED T'BE

This show originally opened on 17 February 1959 at the Theatre Royal, Stratford East, London, home of the *avant garde* director Joan Littlewood and her 'repertory company'. During two separate runs there it was completely revised and remodelled, and transferred to the Garrick Theatre in the West End on 11 February 1960. Set in the drab and dreary world of London's Soho district, with its prostitutes, pimps and small-time criminals, Frank Norman's book (Norman was an ex-convict) told of Fred Cochran (Glynn Edwards), one of life's losers, who runs a sleazy gambling club - a haven for the local low-life. He can only dream of owning a big-time venue, but a large win on the horses means that he can at least have his place decorated by the camp decorator Horace Seaton (Wallas Eaton). Unfortunately, the reopening night party is ruined when Fred is beaten up for not providing the police with their usual slice of payola. There is a good deal more trouble and strife before Fred ends up with a knees-up *al fresco* wedding to his girlfriend Lily Smith (Miriam Karlin). The local milieu is populated by a variety of characters such as the crooked copper Sergeant Collins (Tom Chatto), plus two more members of the constabulary, played by Yootha Joyce and George Sewell, a civilian crook, Redhot (Edward Carrick), Tosher (James Booth), the area's premier ponce, and several 'ladies of the night', including Rosie (Barbara Windsor) and Betty (Toni Palmer). Lionel Bart, who had provided just the lyrics for *Lock Up Your Daughters* at the Mermaid Theatre in 1959, wrote both words and music for this exhilarating piece. His songs, which so accurately captured the show's spirit and atmosphere, included 'G'Night Dearie', 'Layin' Abaht', 'Where It's Hot', 'Contempery', 'Meatface', 'The Ceilin's Comin' Dahn', 'Where Do Little Birds Go?', 'The Student Ponce', 'Big Time', 'Polka Dots', 'Cop A Bit Of Pride' and 'Cochran Will Return'. The popular comedian-singer Max Bygraves took a cleaned-up version of the title song into the UK Top 5, and the personality pianist Russ Conway also had a minor hit with the tune. The critics were not enthusiastic about the show, but

audiences loved it, and *Fings Ain't Wot They Used T'Be* enjoyed a two-year run of 897 performances. This established Lionel Bart as a real force in the London musical theatre, and won the *Evening Standard Award* for best musical.

FIREFLIES

Formed in 1957 in Philadelphia, Pennsylvania, USA, the Fireflies placed two singles on the charts in 1959-60, and then disappeared from view. The group was started by Gerry Granahan (b. 17 June 1939, Pittston, Pennsylvania, USA) and Lee Reynolds and Vinnie Rodgers, who were each on their way to separate auditions for a singing job at a resort in upstate New York. Learning that the club wanted a group, they decided to form one on the spot and were hired. The group lasted long enough to record a demo called 'The Crawl', which was released on Roulette Records in 1958 (under the spelling Fireflys) but did not chart. The group then disbanded while Granahan went on to chart as a solo artist with 'No Chemise, Please'. Granahan decided to reactivate the group in 1959 when he heard the song 'You Were Mine', written by Paul Giacalone. Granahan then recorded the song in his studio, singing lead. But he was unsatisfied with his vocal and hired Ritchie Adams to re-do the vocal (Granahan sang all background vocals). It was released on Ribbon Records, which Granahan co-owned, and reached number 21. Granahan and Adams then teamed up with Lee Reynolds and toured. One follow-up single, 'I Can't Say Goodbye', also charted, in early 1960, but the group disbanded, with Adams going on to write the number 1 hit 'Tossin' And Turnin'' for Bobby Lewis and Granahan going on to record with other groups (such as Dicky Doo And The Don'ts) as well as producing for other artists.

● ALBUMS: *You Were Mine* (Taurus 1961)★★★.

FISHER, EDDIE

b. Edwin Jack Fisher, 10 August 1928, Philadelphia, Pennsylvania, USA. Fisher was a 'bobby sox idol', one of the most popular US singers of the 50s, with a strong, melodic voice. He sang with the bands of Buddy Morrow and Charlie Ventura at the age of 18, and his nickname was 'Sonny Boy' because of his affection for Al Jolson songs. In 1949 he gained nationwide exposure on Eddie Cantor's radio show. Signed to RCA Victor Records, and accompanied by Hugo Winterhalter, Fisher had a string of US Top 10 hits through to 1956, including 'Thinking Of You', 'Turn Back The Hands Of Time', 'Tell Me Why', 'I'm Yours', 'Maybe'/'Watermelon Weather' (duets with Perry Como), 'Wish You Were Here' (number 1), 'Lady Of Spain', 'I'm Walking Behind You' (number 1), 'Oh My Pa-Pa' (number 1), 'I Need You Now' (number 1), 'Count Your Blessings', 'Heart', 'Dungaree Doll' and 'Cindy, Oh Cindy'. Five of those won gold discs. He also made the US Top 40 album charts in 1955 with *I Love You*. His career was interrupted from 1952-53 when he served in the US Armed Forces Special Services, and spent some time in Korea. After his discharge he became immensely popular singing in top nightclubs, and on his own television series, *Coke Time* and *The Chesterfield Supper Club*, with George Gobel. In 1956 he co-starred with his first wife, Debbie Reynolds, in the film musical *Bundle Of Joy*; and had a straight role in *Butterfield 8* (1960), in which his second wife, Elizabeth Taylor, won an Academy Award for Best Actress. During the 60s, beset by drug and financial problems, he switched record labels and recorded *Eddie Fisher At The Winter Garden* for his own Ramrod Records, and *Eddie Fisher Today!* for Dot Records. He returned to RCA and had a minor singles hit in 1966 with 'Games That Lovers Play', which became the title of a bestselling album. His last album for RCA was a Jolson tribute, *You Ain't Heard Nothing Yet*. During the late 60s he married and divorced actress Connie Stevens, and in the 70s attempted several unsuccessful comebacks. In 1990, following extended periods of treatment at the Betty Ford Centre, Fisher announced that he was finally cured of his drug problems and intended to resume work. His daughter by Debbie Reynolds, actress Carrie Fisher, appeared in the hit movies *Star Wars*, *The Empire Strikes Back*, *Return Of The Jedi*, and *When Harry Met Sally*. The film *Postcards From The Edge*, reputedly based on her drug problems and her life with Debbie Reynolds, was released in 1990.

● ALBUMS: *Fisher Sings* 10-inch album (RCA Victor 1952)★★★, *I'm In The Mood For Love* (RCA Victor 1952/55)★★★, *Christmas With Fisher* 10-inch album (RCA Victor 1952)★★, *Irving Berlin Favorites* 10-inch album (RCA Victor 1954)★★★, *May I Sing To You?* (RCA Victor 1954/55)★★★, *I Love You* (RCA Victor 1955)★★★, *Academy Award Winners* (RCA Victor 1955)★★★, *Bundle Of Joy* film soundtrack (RCA Victor 1956)★★, *Thinking Of You* (RCA Victor 1957)★★★, *As Long As There's Music* (RCA Victor 1958)★★★, *Scent Of Mystery* film soundtrack (Ramrod 1960)★★, *Eddie Fisher At The Winter Garden* (Ramrod 1963)★★, *Eddie Fisher Today!* (Dot 1965)★★, *When I Was Young* (1965)★★, *Games That Lovers Play* (RCA 1966)★★, *People Like You* (RCA 1967)★★, *You Ain't Heard Nothing Yet* (RCA 1968)★★.

● COMPILATIONS: *The Best Of Eddie Fisher* 10-inch album (RCA Victor 1954)★★★, *Eddie Fisher's Greatest Hits* (RCA Victor 1962)★★★, *His Greatest Hits* (RCA 1965)★★★, *The Very Best Of Eddie Fisher* (MCA 1988)★★★.

● VIDEOS: *A Singing Legend* (1994).

● FURTHER READING: *The Eddie Fisher Story*, Myrna Greene. *My Life, My Loves*, Eddie Fisher.

● FILMS: *All About Eve* (1950), *Bundle Of Joy* (1956), *Butterfield 8* (1960).

FISHER, MISS TONI

b. 1931, Los Angeles, California, USA. Miss Toni Fisher is best remembered for her one US Top 10 hit, 'The Big Hurt', from 1959, but little is known of her background. She was a torch singer who recorded the Wayne Shanklin-penned hit for the small Signet label, backed by Heine Beau And His Orchestra. The single featured a 'phasing' effect that would become popular on psychedelic recordings nearly a decade later, and Fisher's album, named after the hit single, was notable in that it was an early stereo recording. Fisher had two more chart singles, a remake of Irving Berlin's 'How Deep Is The Ocean', and 'West Of The Wall', the latter a reference to the Berlin Wall, a newsworthy topic when the song was issued in 1962, on Big Top Records. Fisher went on to record for Columbia Records, Capitol Records and Smash Records in the 60s and then disappeared from the music scene.

● ALBUMS: *The Big Hurt* (Signet 1959)★★★.

FITZGERALD, ELLA

b. Ella Jane Fitzgerald, 25 April 1917, Newport News, Virginia, USA, d. 15 June 1996. Following the death of her father, Fitzgerald was taken to New York City by her mother. At school she sang with a glee club and showed early promise, but preferred dancing to singing. Even so, chronic shyness militated against her chances of succeeding as an entertainer. Nevertheless, she entered a talent contest as a dancer, but owing to last-minute nerves, she was unable to dance and was therefore forced to sing. Her unexpected success prompted her to enter other talent contests, and she began to win frequently enough to persevere with her singing. Eventually, she reached the top end of the talent show circuit, singing at the Harlem Opera House where she was heard by several influential people. In later years many claimed to have 'discovered' her, but among those most likely to have been involved in trying to establish her as a professional singer with the Fletcher Henderson band were Benny Carter and Charles Linton. These early efforts were unsuccessful, however, and she continued her round of the talent shows. An appearance at Harlem's Apollo Theatre, where she won, was the most important stepping-stone in her career. She was heard by Linton, who sang with the Chick Webb band at the Savoy Ballroom. Webb took her on, at first paying her out of his own pocket, and for the fringe audience she quickly became the band's main attraction. She recorded extensively with Webb, with a small group led by Teddy Wilson, with the Ink Spots and others, and even recorded with Benny Goodman. Her hits with Webb included 'Sing Me A Swing Song', 'Oh, Yes, Take Another Guess', 'The Dipsy Doodle', 'If Dreams Come True', 'A-Tisket, A-Tasket' (a song on which she collaborated on the lyric), 'F.D.R. Jones' and 'Undecided'. After Webb's death in 1939 she became the nominal leader of the band, a position she retained until 1942. Fitzgerald then began her solo career, recording numerous popular songs, sometimes teaming up with other artists, and in the late 40s signing with Norman Granz. It was Granz's masterly and astute control of her career that helped to establish her as one of America's leading jazz singers. She was certainly the most popular jazz singer with non-jazz audiences, and through judicious choice of repertoire, became the foremost female interpreter of the Great American Popular Song Book. With Granz she worked on the 'songbook' series, placing on record definitive performances of the work of America's leading songwriters, and she also toured extensively as part of his Jazz At The Philharmonic package.

Fitzgerald had a wide vocal range, but her voice retained a youthful, light vibrancy throughout the greater part of her career, bringing a fresh and appealing quality to most of her material, especially 'scat' singing. However, it proved less suited to the blues, a genre that, for the most part, she wisely avoided. Indeed, in her early work the most apparent musical influence was Connee Boswell. As a jazz singer, Fitzgerald performed with elegantly swinging virtuosity and her work with accompanists such as Ray Brown, to whom she was married for a time (they had an adopted son, Ray Brown Jnr, a drummer), Joe Pass and Tommy Flanagan was always immaculately conceived. However, her recordings with Louis Armstrong reveal the marked difference between Fitzgerald's approach and that of a singer for whom the material is secondary to his or her own improvisational skills. For all the enviably high quality of her jazz work, it is as a singer of superior popular songs that Fitzgerald is most important and influential. Her respect for her material, beautifully displayed in the 'songbook' series, helped her to establish and retain her place as the finest vocalist in her chosen area of music. Due largely to deteriorating health, by the mid-80s Fitzgerald's career was at a virtual standstill, although a 1990 appearance in the UK was well received by an ecstatic audience. In April 1994 it was reported that both her legs had been amputated because of complications caused by diabetes. She lived a reclusive existence at her Beverly Hills home until her death in 1996. Her most obvious counterpart among male singers is Frank Sinatra and, with Fitzgerald's death, and Sinatra aged and infirm, questions inevitably arise about the fate of the great popular songs of the 30s and 40s. While there are still numerous excellent interpreters in the 90s, and many whose work has been strongly influenced by Fitzgerald, the social and artistic conditions that helped to create America's First Lady of Song no longer exist, and it seems highly unlikely, therefore, that we shall ever see or hear her like again.

● ALBUMS: *Ella And Ray* (1948)★★★, *The Ella Fitzgerald Set* (1949)★★★, *Souvenir Album* 10-inch album (Decca 1950)★★★, *Ella Fitzgerald Sings Gershwin Songs* 10-inch album (Decca 1950)★★★★, *Songs In A Mellow Mood* (Decca 1954)★★★★, *Lullabies Of Birdland* (Decca 1955)★★★, *Sweet And Hot* (Decca 1955)★★★, *Ella Fitzgerald Sings The Cole Porter Songbook* (Verve 1956)★★★★★, *Ella Fitzgerald Sings The Rodgers And Hart Songbook* (Verve 1956)★★★★★, with Count Basie, Joe Williams *One O' Clock Jump* (Columbia 1956)★★★★, with Louis Armstrong *Ella And Louis* (Verve 1956)★★★★★, with Armstrong *Porgy And Bess* (Verve 1956)★★★★, with Armstrong *Ella And Louis Again* (Verve 1956)★★★★★, *Like Someone In Love* (Verve 1957)★★★★★, *Ella Fitzgerald Sings The Duke Ellington Songbook* 4-LP box set (Verve 1957)★★★★★, *Ella Fitzgerald Sings The Gershwin Songbook* (Verve 1957)★★★★, *Ella Sings Gershwin* (Decca 1957)★★★★, *Ella And Her Fellas* (Decca 1957)★★★, *Ella Fitzgerald At The Opera House* (Verve 1958)★★★, *Ella Fitzgerald Sings The Irving Berlin Songbook* (Verve 1958)★★★★★, *First Lady Of Song* (Decca 1958)★★, *Miss Ella Fitzgerald And Mr Nelson Riddle Invite You To Listen And Relax* (Decca 1958)★★★, with Billie Holiday *Ella Fitzgerald And Billie Holiday At Newport* (Verve 1958)★★★, *For Sentimental Reasons* (Decca 1958)★★★, *Ella Fitzgerald Sings The George And Ira Gershwin Songbook* 5-LP box set (Verve 1959)★★★★★, *Ella Swings Lightly* (Verve 1959)★★★★, *Ella Sings Sweet Songs For Swingers* (Verve 1959)★★★, *Hello Love* (Verve 1959)★★★, *Get Happy!* (Verve 1959)★★★★, *Mack The Knife - Ella In Berlin* (Verve 1960)★★★, *Ella Wishes You A Swinging Christmas* (Verve 1960)★★★★, *The Intimate Ella* (Decca 1960)★★★★, *Golden Favorites* (Decca 1961)★★★, *Ella Returns To Berlin* (Verve 1961)★★★, *Ella Fitzgerald Sings The Harold Arlen Songbook* (Verve 1961)★★★★★, *Clap Hands, Here Comes Charlie!* (Verve 1962)★★★, *Ella Swings Brightly With Nelson* (Verve 1962)★★★★★, *Ella Swings Gently With Nelson* (Verve 1962)★★★★★, *Rhythm Is My Business* (Verve 1962)★★★, *Ella Fitzgerald Sings The Jerome Kern Songbook* (Verve 1963)★★★★, *These Are The Blues* (Verve 1963)★★★★, *Ella Sings Broadway* (Verve 1963)★★★, with Basie *Ella And Basie!* (Verve 1963)★★★★, *Ella At Juan-Les-Pins* (Verve 1964)★★★, *Hello, Dolly!* (Verve 1964)★★★, *Stairway To The Stars* (Decca 1964)★★★, *Early Ella* (Decca 1964)★★★, *A Tribute To Cole Porter* (Verve 1964)★★★, *Ella Fitzgerald Sings The Johnny Mercer Songbook* (Verve 1965)★★★★★, with Duke Ellington *Ella At Duke's Place* (Verve 1966)★★★★, with Ellington *The Stockholm Concert* (1966)★★★, with Ellington *Ella And Duke At The Côte D'Azure* (Verve 1966)★★★, *Ella In Hamburg* (Verve 1966)★★★, *The World Of Ella Fitzgerald* (Metro 1966)★★★, *Whisper Not* (Verve 1966)★★★, *Brighten The Corner* (Capitol 1967)★★★, *Misty Blue* (Columbia 1968)★★★, *Ella 'Live'* (Verve 1968)★★★, *30 By Ella* (Columbia 1968)★★★, *Sunshine Of Your Love/Watch What Happens* (Prestige 1969)★★★, *Ella* (Reprise 1969)★★★, *Things Ain't What They Used To Be* (Reprise 1970)★★★, *Ella A Nice* (1971)★★★, *Ella Fitzgerald At Carnegie Hall* (Columbia 1973)★★★, with Joe Pass *Take Love Easy* (Pablo 1974)★★★, *Ella In London* (Pablo 1974)★★★, *Fine And Mellow* (Pablo 1974)★★★, *Ella - At The Montreux Jazz Festival 1975* (Pablo 1975)★★★, with Oscar Peterson *Ella And Oscar* (Pablo 1975)★★★, with Pass *Fitzgerald And Pass . . . Again* (Pablo 1976)★★★, with Tommy Flanagan *Ella Fitzgerald With The Tommy Flanagan Trio* (Pablo 1977)★★★, *Lady Time* (Pablo 1978)★★★, *Dream Dancing* (Pablo 1978)★★★, with Basie *A Classy Pair* (Pablo 1979)★★★, with Basie *A Perfect Match: Basie And Ella* (Pablo 1979)★★★, with Pass *Digital III At Montreux* (Pablo 1980)★★★, *Ella Fitzgerald Sings The Antonio Carlos Jobim Songbook* (Pablo 1981)★★★, *The Best Is Yet To Come* (Pablo 1982)★★★, with Pass *Speak Love* (Pablo 1983)★★★, *Nice Work If You Can Get It* (Pablo 1983)★★★, *Easy Living* (Pablo 1986)★★★, *All That Jazz* (Pablo 1990)★★★, *A 75th Birthday Tribute* (1993)★★★.

● COMPILATIONS: *The Best Of Ella* (Decca 1958)★★★, *The Best Of Ella Fitzgerald* (Verve 1964)★★★★, *The Best Of Ella Fitzgerald Volume 2* (Verve 1969)★★★, shared with Billie Holiday, Lena Horne and Sarah Vaughan *Billie, Ella, Lena, Sarah!* (Columbia 1980)★★★★, *The Best Of Ella Fitzgerald* (Pablo 1988)★★★★, *The Pablo Years* (1993)★★★★, *Oh Lady Be Good! Best Of The Gershwin Songbook* (Verve 1995)★★★★, *Ella: The Legendary Decca Recordings* 4-CD box set (Decca 1995)★★★, *Ella Fitzgerald: Priceless Jazz* (GRP 1997)★★★.

● FURTHER READING: *Ella: The Life And Times Of Ella Fitzgerald*, Sid Colin. *Ella Fitzgerald: A Life Through Jazz*, Jim Haskins. *Ella Fitzgerald*, Stuart Nicholson. *First Lady Of Song*, Mark Fidelman.

FIVE BLIND BOYS OF MISSISSIPPI

This vocal gospel group, consisting of Archie Brownley (lead), Joseph Ford, Lawrence Abrams and Lloyd Woodard, was formed in 1936 by blind students of the Piney Woods School, Jackson, Mississippi. They began singing together in their school grounds and called themselves the Cotton Blossom Singers. By the mid-40s the group had moved to New Orleans and had added Melvin Henderson as their second lead. He was in turn replaced by (the sighted) Percell Perkins, whereupon the band became the Five Blind Boys Of Mississippi. Ford left the group in 1948 and was replaced by J.T. Clinkscales (also blind). The group moved to Houston, Texas, in the 50s and signed to Peacock Records. 'Our Father' was their biggest hit, and became a gospel classic. It also reached number 10 in the R&B chart. Dozens of 45s and at least five albums emerged on Peacock during the 60s as the group toured constantly. Perkins left in order to devote himself to the ministry and became Reverend Perkins. His replacements included Reverend Samy Lewis, Reverend George Warren and Tiny Powell. Brownley died in New Orleans in 1960 and Roscoe Robinson took over as lead, and Willmer 'Little Axe' Broadnax joined as second lead. Woodard died in the mid-70s and Lawrence Abrams in 1982, but the Five Blind Boys continued to tour with new members. Brownley is one of the pivotal influences in the development of black soul music in the 50s and 60s, with both Ray Charles and James Brown taking their cue from his strident vocal performances.

● ALBUMS: *My Desire* (Peacock *c.*60s)★★★, *There's A God* (Peacock *c.*60s)★★★, *Best Of The Five Blind Boys Of Mississippi Volume 1* (MCA *c.*70s)★★★, *Best Of The Five Blind Boys Of Mississippi Volume 2* (MCA *c.*70s)★★★ *Soon I'll Be Done* (MCA *c.*70s)★★★.

FIVE CROWNS

The Five Crowns were formed at Wadleigh Junior High School in Harlem, New York, USA, in 1952. The group comprised Wilbur 'Yunkie' Paul (lead), brothers James 'Poppa' Clark, Claudie 'Nicky' Clark and John 'Sonny Boy' Clark (all tenor) and Doc Green (bass/baritone). Their distinctive sound (not least because of the presence of four tenors) brought them to the attention of Rainbow Records in July 1952. They found instant success in October when 'You're My Inspiration' became a major regional R&B hit. However, they failed to follow up this breakthrough, with successive singles such as 'Who Can Be True', 'Why Don't You Believe Me' and 'Alone Again' faring poorly. Finding themselves in dispute with an evidently disappointed Rainbow Records, they moved to the Old Town label in July 1953. However, neither 'You Could Be My Love' nor 'Lullaby Of The Bells' revived fortunes. In the aftermath they returned to Rainbow on its subsidiary label Riviera Records. A creative renaissance was witnessed by the powerful 'You Came To Me', but this again failed to translate into commercial sales. The group disbanded later that year. Green then put together a new Five Crowns who released one single, 'God Bless You', for Gee Records. He was also the only original member remaining in the reshuffled line-up who released 'I Can't Pretend' for Transworld Records. Titled simply the Crowns by 1958, the formation that recorded 'Kiss And Make Up' was ironically closer to the original Five Crowns, with James Clark rejoining, plus the presence of Benjamin Nelson (later known as Ben E. King), Elsbury Hobbs and Charlie Thomas. This was the only record ever to be released on Doc Pomus's R&B Records label. Afterwards, they performed at the Apollo Theatre and so impressed George Treadwell that he immediately sacked the members of his band the Drifters, and replaced them in a straight swap with the Crowns.

FIVE DISCS

The Five Discs were one of several doo-wop groups (Carollons, Chips, etc.) to trace their origins to the Bedford-Stuyvesant district of Brooklyn, New York, USA. They were formed in 1954 by Joe Brocco (lead), Joe Barsalona (baritone), Paul Albano (first tenor) and Tony Basile (second tenor). Composed of Italian-descended young men and orig-

inally titled the Flames, they subsequently shuffled the pack by adding black singers Mario deAndrade and Andrew Jackson from the Love Notes. This produced a new line-up of deAndrade (lead), Jackson (bass), Albano (first tenor), Basile (second tenor) and Barsalona (baritone), though membership remained fluid over ensuing years. After recording demos at Bell Sound studios in New York the group started to offer these to interested parties. There were no takers until songwriter Billy Martin introduced them to the proprietors of the Emge Records label. They were still titled the Flames when they cut deAndrade's song 'I Remember', but when it was released they had chosen a new name, the Five Discs. Despite achieving strong popularity in the local New York and Boston markets, the group felt dissatisfied with the label's promotion of the single, and looked elsewhere. 'My Chinese Girl', released on Dwain Records in 1959, failed to improve their standing. Jackson and deAndrade then left, and were replaced by Lenny Hutter of the Chalets on lead and John Russell on bass. 'Come On Baby' emerged to little fanfare in 1961, and Hutter left immediately, to be replaced by John Carbone. Calo Records took over the promotion of Carbone's debut on 'Adios', an old deAndrade song. However, the band moved on again, this time to Cher Records, with Russell replaced by Charlie DiBella. 'Never Let You Go' was the last single to feature Carbone, as Eddie Parducci of the Delvons took his place. It was their most successful project for some time, but still failed to breach the national charts. As a result the group changed tack to become the Boyfriends, releasing a solitary single on Kapp Records titled 'Let's Fall In Love'. Numerous line-up changes ensued before the group became Dawn in 1968 (not of 'Tie A Yellow Ribbon' fame), their sole release under this guise being a cover version of Sam Cooke's 'Bring It On Home To Me'. Ironically, the last Five Discs record would see them return to the Schwarz brothers and Laurie Records for 1972's 'Rock & Roll Revival', though throughout the 70s several archive singles were also released as interest in 50s doo-wop escalated. A typically *ad hoc* line-up reunited in 1991 for the Doo-wop Society Show.

FIVE KEYS

This US R&B vocal group helped shape the rhythm and blues revolution of the early 50s. The ensemble was formed as the Sentimental Four in Newport News, Virginia, USA, in the late 40s, and originally consisted of two sets of brothers - Rudy West (b. 25 July 1932, Newport News, Virginia, USA) and Bernie West (b. 4 February 1930, Newport News, Virginia, USA), and Ripley Ingram (b. 1930, d. 23 March 1995, Newport News, Virginia, USA) and Raphael Ingram. After Raphael Ingram left and Maryland Pierce (b. 1933) and Dickie Smith became members in 1949, the name of the group was changed to Five Keys. With Pierce doing the lead work, the Five Keys joined Los Angeles-based Aladdin Records in 1951, and the same year had a hit with a remake of the old standard 'Glory Of Love', which became a US R&B number 1. Despite recording an appealing combination of old standards and R&B originals, further chart success on Aladdin eluded the Five Keys. In 1952 Rudy West went into the army, and was replaced by Ulysses K. Hicks, and in 1954 Dickie Smith left and was replaced with Ramon Loper. This new line-up of Five Keys was signed to Capitol Records, which brought the group to stardom, albeit with some modification in their style from a deep rhythm and blues sound to a more pop vein with greater instrumentation in support. The group's first hit for Capitol Records was the novelty pop jump 'Ling Ting Tong' (US R&B number 5 and pop Top 30 in 1955). Following the first Capitol recording session, Rudy West rejoined the Five Keys in October 1954, replacing the ailing Hicks, who died a few months later. Further successes on Capitol included some spectacular R&B ballads: the Chuck Willis-composed 'Close Your Eyes' (R&B number 5, 1955), 'The Verdict' (R&B number 13, 1955) and 'Out Of Sight, Out Of Mind' (R&B number 12 and pop Top 30 in 1956). The Capitol material also featured old standards, such as a marvellous remake of the Ink Spots' 'The Gypsy' (1957). Rudy West retired in 1958. An unsuccessful period at King Records from 1958-61 produced more personnel changes and no hits, and few songs that could compete with the new rock 'n' roll sounds. Periodic sessions were recorded by various reunion groups in subsequent years, but the basic legacy of the Five Keys rests in their Aladdin, Capitol and King sessions.

● ALBUMS: *The Best Of The Five Keys* (Aladdin 1956)★★★, *The Five Keys On The Town* (Score 1957)★★, *The Five Keys On Stage* (Capitol 1957)★, *The Five Keys* (King 1960)★★★, *Rhythm And Blues Hits Past And Present* (King 1960)★★★, *The Fantastic Five Keys* (Capitol 1962)★★★.

● COMPILATIONS: *The Five Keys* (King 1978)★★, *The Five Keys And The Nitecaps* (Detour 1988)★★★, *The Five Keys: Capitol Collector's Series* (Capitol 1989)★★★, *Dream On* (Charly 1991)★★★, *The Five Keys: The Aladdin Years* (EMI 1991)★★★.

FIVE PENNIES, THE

This schmaltzy biopic of 20s cornet player Red Nichols was released by Paramount in 1959. Danny Kaye plays Nichols, and Barbara Bel Geddes is the wife who, following his early success, stays with him through the emotional traumas of their daughter's illness, until he re-emerges from depression and returns to his beloved world of jazz. On-screen musicians include Shelly Manne (in the role of Dave Tough, the second time in the same year he played the part of a drummer), Bobby Troup, Ray Anthony (in the role of Jimmy Dorsey, despite his being a trumpet player), and Louis Armstrong and his All Stars, who at that time included Peanuts Hucko, Billy Kyle and Trummy Young. Kaye and Armstrong mug their way through a vocal and trumpet duet of 'When the Saints Go Marching In', with Nichols himself dubbing for Kaye. Period songs such as 'Runnin' Wild' (Joe Grey-Leo Wood-A. Harrington Gibbs), 'Out Of Nowhere' (Edward Heyman-Johnny Green), 'After You've Gone' (Henry Creamer-Turner Layton), and 'Indiana' (Ballard MacDonald-James F. Hanley), are supplemented by three new ones written by Kaye's wife, Sylvia Fine - 'The Five Pennies', 'Lullaby In Ragtime' and 'Goodnight Sleep Tight', the last two of which are presented in a charming contrapuntal setting. Leith Stevens won an Oscar nomination for his 'scoring for a musical film', and there were other nominations for Daniel L. Fapp's impressive Vistavision and Technicolor cinematography, and Fine's title song. Melville Shavelson directed the picture, and he and Jack Rose wrote the script.

5 ROYALES

The 5 Royales were hugely successful exponents of southern vocal R&B throughout the 50s, although they started their career in a different style as the Royal Sons Gospel Group of Winston-Salem, North Carolina, USA. This quintet variously featured the brothers Clarence, Curtis and Lowman Pauling (d. 26 December 1973, Brooklyn, New York, USA), Otto Jeffries, Johnny Tanner, Obadiah Carter (d. July 1994, Winston-Salem, North Carolina, USA), James Moore and William Samuels. The Pauling brothers had started out supporting their father, Lowman Pauling Snr., on local North Carolina stages, while his namesake son reputedly built his first guitar out of cigar-boxes. Lowman Pauling Jnr. was the group's musical arranger and springboard, while Johnny Tanner usually handled lead vocals. At the suggestion of local radio producer Robert Woodward, the group contacted New York label Apollo Records, headed by Bess Berman and Carl Le Bowe. There the group sang spirituals as the Royal Sons Quintet, until Le Bowe rechristened them 5 Royales for the purposes of recording R&B music. Having elected to pursue the latter style, Johnny Holmes, the final member of the Royal Sons who graced their 'Bedside Of A Neighbour' debut, departed. This left a core 5 Royales line-up of Lowman Pauling (guitar), Johnny Tanner (lead), Moore (tenor), Carter (tenor) and Jeffries (baritone). Typical of their background, their first single, 'Give Me One More Chance' (coupled with 'Too Much Of A Little Bit'), was a spiritual standard energized into a raunchy R&B number. By 1953 Eugene Tanner (b. 1936, d. 29 December 1994, Winston-Salem, North Carolina, USA; baritone/bass) had replaced Jeffries (who became the group's manager). Together they achieved their first major success with 'Baby Don't Do It', which made number 1 in the US R&B charts in January 1953. The follow-up single, 'Help Me Somebody', stayed at number 1 on the same chart for five weeks, while the band's powerful and frequent live performances, now completely divorced from their gospel background, built them a formidable reputation. Their new-found fame also resulted in a lawsuit when they discovered that the Royals of Detroit were the first of several groups to impersonate them. The band's first appearance at the Apollo followed in January 1953, appearing for a week alongside Willy Mabon and Gene Ammons. In August 'Too Much Lovin'' became another sizeable R&B hit, although it was the b-side, 'Laundromat Blues', with its sexually suggestive lyric, that provoked most attention. By 1954 the group had signed to King Records, following Le Bowe's defection to that label. However, the 5 Royales were never as successful again. Though over 40 singles were issued under their name up to 1965, usually of good quality, they seldom reached the charts. 'Tears Of Joy' and 'Think', from 1957 and 1959, respectively, were two notable exceptions. 'Think' was their first national US pop chart success, at number 66, although 'Dedicated To The One I Love', later covered by the Shirelles and Mamas And The Papas, also reached number 81 on the same chart in 1961. This was a revised version of a Chester Mayfield composition, 'I Don't Want You To Go', which Mayfield had written while a member of fellow North Carolina R&B group the Casanovas, also signed to Apollo. Their membership included William Samuels, Lowman Pauling's brother-in-law and formerly of the Royal Sons himself. However, after leaving King Records in 1960 the band failed to reach the charts again, despite recording for several labels with variable line-ups. Lowman Pauling left the group between stints at Home Of The Blues Records and Todd Records, replaced by Robert 'Pee Wee' Burris on guitar. Tanner also departed in December 1963, and was replaced by Eudell Graham. Graham, who became the focus of the touring 5 Royales, was later jailed for armed robbery. After the group broke up, Clarence Pauling rechristened himself Clarence Paul, and became the A&R director at Motown Records. The 5 Royales' influence on R&B, meanwhile, proved fundamental to the music of James Brown, with whom the band had frequently worked. Lowman Pauling, whose uninhibited guitar style was also a major influence on the style of Eric Clapton, died in 1973 while working as a custodian at a Brooklyn synagogue.

● ALBUMS: *The Five Royales* (Apollo 1953)★★★, *The Five Royales Sing For You* (King 1959)★★★.

● COMPILATIONS: *Sing Baby Don't Do It* (Relic 1987)★★, *Sing Laundromat Blues* (Relic 1987)★★, *Monkey, Hips And Rice: The 5 Royales Anthology* (Rhino 1997)★★★.

FIVE SATINS

This R&B vocal group was formed in New Haven, Connecticut, USA, in 1955. The Five Satins' first hit, 'In The Still Of The Night' (US R&B number 3 and pop Top 30 in 1956), was one of the definitive songs of the early rock 'n' roll era, with its strong chanting of doo-wop riffs in the background and impassioned lead work. The group on this record consisted of lead Fred Parris, Al Denby, Ed Martin, bass Jim Freeman and pianist Jessie Murphy. Parris, who wrote the song, brought valuable experience to the Five Satins, having formed the Scarlets (Parris, Denby, Bill Powers, Sylvester Hopkins and Nate Mosely) in 1953, a group that hit regionally with 'Dear One' in 1954. The long-cherished national success for Parris was initially denied him, as he was in the army stationed in Japan when 'In The Still Of The Night' became a hit, and the wonderful follow-up, 'To The Aisle' (US R&B number 5 and pop Top 30 in 1957), featured a reorganized group with Bill Baker (b. Auburn, Alabama, USA, d. 10 August 1994, New Haven, Connecticut, USA) as lead. Parris returned from Japan in 1958 and again reorganized the Five Satins, recruiting tenor Richie Freeman (b. December 1940), second tenor West Forbes (b. 1937), Sylvester Hopkins (b. 1938) and Lou Peeples. This group was not able to secure another big hit, although 'Shadows' (US R&B number 27, 1959) kept their name visible. Their profile was significantly enhanced with the release of Art Laboe's first *Oldies But Goodies*, which included 'In The Still Of The Night'. As a result, the song helped to create the doo-wop revival in the early 60s and re-entered the national pop chart in 1961. The Five Satins broke up in the early 60s, but re-formed and became a perennial on the oldies circuit in the 70s. The new group consisted of Fred Parris, Richie Freeman, Jimmy Curtis and Nate Marshall. Under the name Black Satin, they had a number 49 R&B hit in 1975 with 'Everybody Stand And Clap Your Hands (For The Entertainer)'.

● ALBUMS: *The Five Satins Sing* (Ember 1957)★★★, *Encore, Volume 2* (Ember 1960)★★★.

● COMPILATIONS: *The Best Of The Five Satins* (Celebrity Show 1971)★★★, *In The Still Of The Night* (1990)★★★.

FIVE SHARPS

Formed in the early 50s in Jamaica, New York, USA, the Five Sharps were a vocal harmony group whose sole claim to fame is the fact that their only record, Harold Arlen's 'Stormy Weather', is acknowledged by collectors to be the rarest in the world. The group consisted of Ronald Cuffey (lead vocals), Clarence Bassett and Robert Ward (both tenors), Mickey Owens (bass vocals) and Tom Duckett (piano). In late 1952 the group recorded the standard 'Stormy Weather' for Jubilee Records. The record failed to gain any significant airplay or sales and the Five Sharps broke up. Virtually no one remembered their recording until a collector found a 78 rpm copy at a Brooklyn record store in 1961. When no others turned up, the value of the surviving original rose steadily; a second copy was finally located in 1977 and sold for nearly $4,000. No 45s were ever discovered and should another 78 appear in the 90s, its value is now estimated by experts to be over $10,000.

FLAMINGOS

This R&B vocal group, formed in Chicago, Illinois, USA, in 1951, was renowned for producing the tightest and most gorgeous harmonies of the rock 'n' roll era. For much of their history they consisted of Zeke Carey (b. 24 January 1933, Bluefield, Virginia, USA), Jake Carey (b. 9 September 1926, Pulaski, Virginia, USA), Paul Wilson (b. 6 January 1935, Chicago, Illinois, USA, d. May 1988) and Johnny Carter (b. 2 June 1934, Chicago, Illinois, USA). The group's first lead was Sollie McElroy (b. 16 July 1933, Gulfport, Mississippi, USA, d. 15 January 1995), who brought the group regional fame on 'Golden Teardrops' for the Chance label in 1954. He was replaced by Nate Nelson (b. 10 April 1932, Chicago, Illinois, USA, d. 10 April 1984) who brought the group into the rock 'n' roll era with the magnificent ballad 'I'll Be Home', a number 5 R&B hit in 1956 on the Chess label. There then followed a period of disarray, in which Carter and Zeke Carey were lost to the draft. The Flamingos brought into the group Tommy Hunt (b. 18 June 1933, Pittsburgh, Pennsylvania, USA) and Terry Johnson (b. 12 November 1935, Baltimore, Maryland, USA) and moved to New York where they signed with End Records in 1958. At End the Flamingos had their biggest US hits, 'Lovers Never Say Goodbye' (R&B number 25 in 1958), 'I Only Have Eyes For You' (R&B number 3 and pop number 11 in 1959), 'Nobody Loves Me Like You' (R&B number 23 and pop Top 30 in 1960), the latter song written by Sam Cooke. One of the group's last outstanding records was 'I Know Better' (1962), a Drifters' sound-alike that captured top spots in many markets. During the early 60s the Flamingos lost the rest of their original members, except for Jake and Zeke Carey. The cousins managed to achieve some minor hits during the soul era, notably 'Boogaloo Party', which was the group's only UK chart hit when it reached number 26 in 1969 (three years earlier it was a US R&B number 22 hit). The Flamingos' last US chart record was 'Buffalo Soldier' 1970 (R&B Top 30). Nate Nelson died in 1984 and Paul Wilson in 1988. Sollie McElroy, after leaving the Flamingos in 1955, joined the Moroccos, with whom he recorded for three years, and Johnny Carter joined the Dells in 1960.

● ALBUMS: *The Flamingos* (Checker 1959)★★★, *Flamingos Serenade* (End 1959)★★★, *Flamingos Favorites* (End 1960)★★★, *Requestfully Yours* (End 1960)★★★, *The Sound*

Of The Flamingos (End 1962)★★★, *The Spiritual And Folk Moods Of The Flamingos* (1963)★★, *Their Hits - Then And Now* (Philips 1966)★★, *Flamingos Today* (1971)★★.
● COMPILATIONS: *Collectors Showcase: The Flamingos* (Constellation 1964)★★★, *Golden Teardrops* (1982)★★★, *Flamingos* (Chess 1984)★★★★, *The Chess Sessions* (Chess 1987)★★★, *The Best Of The Flamingos* (Rhino 1990)★★★★, *The Flamingos: I Only Have Eyes For You* (Sequel 1991)★★★, *The Flamingos Meet The Moonglows: The Complete 25 Chance Recordings* (Vee Jay 1993)★★★.
● FILMS: *Go Johnny Go* (1958).

FLANAGAN, RALPH

b. 7 April 1919, Loranie, Ohio, USA. Flanagan played piano with several local bands during his teen years, eventually becoming pianist-arranger with Sammy Kaye in 1940. He was a member of the Merchant Marines during World War II and later provided arrangements for Charlie Barnet, Sammy Kaye, Gene Krupa, Blue Barron, Alvino Rey, Tony Pastor and many other bands. He also worked with a number of singers including Mindy Carson and Perry Como. He struck lucky when Herb Hendler, who worked for a minor record label, commissioned him to provide an album devoted to cover versions of Glenn Miller favourites. The resulting record sold so well that when Hendler moved to a job at RCA Victor, he persuaded that company (which owned all the original Miller masters) to release further tracks by Flanagan. This time, he grafted Miller-style arrangements onto material not formerly associated with the Miller band. The ploy paid off and the records sold prolifically, encouraging Flanagan to form a full-time orchestra in early 1950 and to take it out on the road. The band was heavily influenced by Miller, and their vocal group, the Singing Winds, emulated the sounds of the Pied Pipers. Flanagan's band also boasted a good male vocalist named Harry Prime, filling the Ray Eberle role. As a result, the band quickly became one of the biggest crowd-pullers on the big-band circuit, hit records coming with 'Rag Mop', 'Nevertheless' and 'Harbour Lights' in 1950, followed by 'Slow Poke', and his own composition 'Hot Toddy'. The success of the Flanagan band sparked off a whole Miller revival, with such former Miller-men as Ray Anthony and Jerry Gray, plus many others who had never even met Miller, organizing bands that echoed the Miller sound. Most of these imitators gradually faded, although Flanagan was still an active leader/arranger in the early 60s.
● COMPILATIONS: *Hot Toddy* (1988)★★★, *On The Beat* (Golden Era 1989)★★★.

FLANDERS AND SWANN

The son of an actor father, and a mother who had been a concert-violinist before she married, Michael Flanders (b. 1 March 1922, London, England, d. 14 April 1975), was brought up in a musical household. He learned to play the clarinet and made his stage debut at the age of seven in a singing contest with *Uncle Mac's Minstrel Show*. At Westminster School in London, where Peter Ustinov was one of his classmates, he started to write and stage revues. His search for a pianist led him to Donald Swann (b. Donald Ibrahim Swann, 30 September 1923, Llanelli, Wales, d. 23 March 1994, London, England), and their first revue together was *Go To It*. At Oxford University in 1940 Flanders played in and directed several productions for the Dramatic

Society and made his professional debut as Valentine in Shaw's *You Never Can Tell*, at the Oxford Playhouse. In 1943, while serving in the Royal Navy Volunteer Reserve, having survived the infamous convoys to Russia, he was struck down by poliomyelitis. Three years later he was discharged from hospital, in a wheelchair, and with a full beard which he retained for the rest of his life. Unable to resume a normal acting career, Flanders turned to writing and broadcasting. He contributed lyrics to several West End revues, in collaboration with Swann, including *Penny Plain* (1951), *Airs On A Shoestring* (1953) and *Fresh Airs* (1956). Flanders also appeared extensively on radio, and later, television, in programmes ranging from sports commentary to poetry readings, and including a spell of two years as chairman of *The Brains Trust*. His translation of Stravinsky's *Soldier's Tale* (with Kitty Black) became the standard English version, and his concert performance of it with Peter Ustinov and Sir Ralph Richardson was a surprise sell-out at the Royal Festival Hall in 1956. After successfully entertaining their friends at parties with their own songs, Flanders and Swann decided to perform professionally, so on New Year's Eve 1956, they opened their own two-man show, *At The Drop Of A Hat*, at the intimate New Lindsey Theatre, Notting Hill, west London, moving three weeks later into the West End's Fortune Theatre. The show was a smash hit and ran for over two years. It was reported that Princess Margaret attended a performance, and returned the following week with the Queen and the Duke of Edinburgh. With Flanders' urbane image contrasting with Swann's almost schoolboy enthusiasm, they introduced songs such as 'The Hippopotamus ('Mud, Mud, Glorious Mud')', 'Misalliance', 'A Gnu', and 'Madeira M'Dear?'. Two albums from the show were released, the earlier mono recording being preferable to the later stereo issue from the last night of the London run. In 1959 the show opened on Broadway, billed as 'An After-Dinner Farrago', and later toured the USA, Canada and the UK. In 1963 at the Haymarket Theatre, London, they presented a fully revised version entitled *At The Drop Of Another Hat*, which included songs such as 'The Gas-Man Cometh', 'First And Second Law' and 'Bedstead Men'. During 1964/5 they toured Australia, New Zealand and Hong Kong, before returning to the West End in 1965, and yet again, to New York in the following year. Meanwhile, Flanders was still continuing with his other work, writing, broadcasting and performing theatrical speech recitals. He published *Creatures Great And Small*, a children's book of verses about animals and, together with Swann, released an album of animal songs entitled *The Bestiary Of Flanders And Swann*. Flanders was awarded the OBE in 1964. After the partnership broke up in 1967, Swann, who was born of Russian parents, continued to compose. In the 50s he had written the music for revues such as *Pay The Piper* and *Wild Thyme*, but in later years his music reflected his religious beliefs (he was a Quaker) and his love of Greece, and many other interests. He was working up to the time he died from cancer in 1994. In that same year, a musical celebration of the works of Michael Flanders and Donald Swann, entitled *Under Their Hats*, was presented at the King's Head Theatre in London.
● ALBUMS: *At The Drop Of A Hat* (Parlophone 1957)★★★★, *The Bestiary Of Flanders And Swann* (Parlophone 1961)★★★, *At The Drop Of Another Hat* (Parlophone 1964)★★★.

● COMPILATIONS: *A Review Of Revues* (EMI 1975)★★★, *Tried By Centre Court* (Note 1977)★★★, *The Complete Flanders & Swann* 3-CD set (EMI 1991)★★★★.
● VIDEOS: *The Only Flanders And Swann Video* (PMI 1992).
● FURTHER READING: all by Donald Swann *The Space Behind The Bars. Swann's Way Out. Swann's Way-A-Life In Song* (autobiography).

FLATT AND SCRUGGS

Lester Flatt (b. 28 June 1914, Overton County, Tennessee, USA, d. 11 May 1979, Nashville, Tennessee, USA; guitar) and Earl Scruggs (b. 6 January 1924, Cleveland County, North Carolina, USA; banjo). These influential musicians began working together in December 1945 as members of Bill Monroe's Bluegrass Boys. In February 1948 they left to form the Foggy Mountain Boys with Jim Shumate (fiddle), Howard Watts aka Cedric Rainwater (bass fiddle) - both ex-Bill Monroe - and, latterly, Mac Wiseman (tenor vocals, guitar). They became an established feature of Virginia's WCYB radio station and undertook recording sessions for the Mercury label before embarking on a prolonged tour of the south. Here they forged a more powerful, ebullient sound than was associated with their chosen genre and in November 1950 Flatt and Scruggs joined Columbia/CBS Records, with whom they remained throughout their career together. Three years later they signed a sponsorship agreement with Martha White Mills which engendered a regular show on Nashville's WSM and favoured slots on their patron's television shows. Josh Graves (dobro) was then added to the line-up which in turn evolved a less frenetic sound and reduced the emphasis on Scruggs' banjo playing. Appearances on the nationally syndicated *Folk Sound USA* brought the group's modern bluegrass sound to a much wider audience, while their stature was further enhanced by an appearance at the 1960 Newport Folk Festival. Flatt and Scruggs were then adopted by the college circuit where they were seen as antecedents to a new generation of acts, including the Kentucky Colonels, the Hillmen and the Dillards. The Foggy Mountain Boys performed the theme song, 'The Ballad Of Jed Clampett', to the popular *Beverly Hillbillies* television show in the early 60s while their enduring instrumental, 'Foggy Mountain Breakdown', was heavily featured in the film *Bonnie And Clyde*. Bluegrass students suggested that this version lacked the sparkle of earlier arrangements and declared that the group lacked its erstwhile vitality. By 1968 Earl Scruggs' sons, Randy and Gary, had been brought into the line-up, but the banjoist nonetheless grew dissatisfied with the constraints of a purely bluegrass setting. The partnership was dissolved the following year. While Flatt formed a new act, the Nashville Grass, his former partner added further members of his family to found the Earl Scruggs Revue. Plans for a reunion album were thwarted by Flatt's death in May 1979. The duo were inducted into the Country Music Hall Of Fame in 1985.
● ALBUMS: *Foggy Mountain Jamboree* (Columbia 1957)★★★★, *Country Music* (Mercury 1958)★★★, *Lester Flatt And Earl Scruggs* (Mercury 1959)★★★★, *Songs Of Glory* (Columbia 1960)★★★, *Flatt And Scruggs And The Foggy Mountain Boys* (Harmony 1960)★★★, *Foggy Mountain Banjo* (Columbia 1961)★★★★, *Songs Of The Famous Carter Family* (Columbia 1961)★★★, *Folk Songs Of Our Land* (Columbia 1962)★★★★, *Flatt And Scruggs At Carnegie Hall* (Columbia 1962)★★★, *The Original Sound Of Flatt And Scruggs* (Mercury 1963)★★★, *Hard Travelin'/The Ballad Of Jed Clampett* (Columbia 1963)★★★★, *Recorded Live At Vanderbilt University* (Columbia 1964)★★★, *The Fabulous Sound Of Flatt And Scruggs* (Columbia 1964)★★★, *The Versatile Flatt And Scruggs* (Columbia 1965)★★★, *Pickin' Strummin' And Singin'* (Columbia 1965)★★★, one side is Jim And Jesse *Stars Of The Grand Ol' Opry* (Starday 1966)★★, *Town & Country* (Columbia 1966)★★★, *When The Saints Go Marching In* (Columbia 1966)★★★, with Doc Watson *Strictly Instrumental* (Columbia 1967)★★, *Hear The Whistle Blow* (Columbia 1967)★★, *The Original Theme From Bonnie & Clyde* (Mercury 1968)★★, with Bill Monroe *Bill Monroe With Lester Flatt & Earl Scruggs:The Original Bluegrass Band* (Decca 1978)★★★.
● COMPILATIONS: *Flatt And Scruggs Greatest Hits* (Columbia 1966)★★★, *The Original Foggy Mountain Breakdown* (Mercury 1968)★★★★, *World Of Flatt And Scruggs* (Columbia 1973)★★★, *The Golden Era 1950-1955* (Rounder 1977)★★★★, *Foggy Mountain Banjo* (1978)★★★★, *Blue Ridge Cabin Home* (Rebel 1979)★★★★, *Columbia Historic Edition* (Columbia 1982)★★★, *20 All Time Great Recordings* (Columbia 1983)★★★, *Country And Western Classics* 3-LP box set (Time-Life 1982)★★★, *Mercury Sessions, Volume 1* (Mercury 1987)★★★★, *Mercury Sessions, Volume 2* (Mercury 1987)★★★, *You Can Feel It In Your Soul* (County 1988)★★★, *Don't Get Above Your Raisin'* (Rounder 1992)★★★, *The Complete Mercury Sessions* (Mercury 1992)★★★★, *1949 -1959* 4-CD box set (Bear Family 1992)★★★★, *1959 - 1963* 5-CD box set (Bear Family 1992)★★★★, *1964 - 69, Plus* 6-CD box set (Bear Family 1996)★★★★, *'Tis Sweet To Be Remembered: The Essential* (Legacy/Columbia 1997)★★★★.

FLEETWOODS

One of America's most popular doo-wop groups in the late 50s comprised Gary Troxell (b. 28 November 1939, Centralia, Washington, DC, USA), Gretchen Christopher (b. 29 February 1940, Olympia, Washingtion, DC, USA) and Barbara Ellis (b. 20 February 1940, Olympia, Washington, USA). They met while seniors at high school in the girls' home-town. Originally a female duo, they recruited Troxell initially to play trumpet. The girls had composed a song, while independently, Troxell had written a hook that went something like: 'Mmm Dooby Doo, Dum Dim Dum Doo Dum'; they put them together and 'Come Softly To Me' was born. Their first moniker, Two Girls And A Guy, was changed by a Seattle record distributor Bob Reisdorff, who became their manager and founded Dolphin Records (later called Dolton) which released the single. Chart fame was instant for the distinctive trio and the haunting and catchy song (on which the vocal was recorded a cappella) shot to the top of the US charts and made the UK Top 10 despite a hit cover version by Frankie Vaughan and the Kaye Sisters. Their third release, 'Mr. Blue', a Dwayne Blackwell song originally written for the Platters, was also a US number 1 (in the UK two cover versions took the honours) and made Troxell one of the leaders in the teen-idol stakes. In the midst of their success he was drafted into the navy, his place being taken when necessary by subsequent solo star Vic Dana. Despite Troxell's absence, the US hits continued and they totalled nine Top 40 hits between 1959 and 1963, including the number 10 hit 'Tragedy', a revival of the Thomas Wayne song. The unmistakable close-harmony trio surfaced again in 1973 when they signed with the noted producer Jerry Dennon, but no hits resulted from this collaboration.

● ALBUMS: *Mr. Blue* (Dolton 1959)★★★, *The Fleetwoods* (Dolton 1960)★★★★, *Softly* (Dolton 1961)★★★★, *Deep In A Dream* (Dolton 1961)★★★, *The Best Of The Oldies* (Dolton 1962)★★★, *Goodnight My Love* (Dalton 1963)★★★, *The Fleetwoods Sing For Lovers By Night* (Dolton 1963)★★★, *Before And After* (Dolton 1965)★★, *Folk Rock* (Dolton 1966)★★.

● COMPILATIONS: *The Fleetwoods' Greatest Hits* (Dolton 1962)★★★★, *In A Mellow Mood* (Sunset 1966)★★★, *The Best Of ...* (Rhino 1990)★★★★, *Come Softly To Me: The Best Of ...* (EMI 1993)★★★★.

FLEMONS, WADE

b. 25 September 1940, Coffeyville, Kansas, USA, d. 13 October 1993. Flemons made a brief impact on the R&B scene in the late 50s and early 60s, recording hits for the Chicago-based Vee Jay Records. He was raised in Wichita, Kansas, until the age of 15, when he moved with his parents to Battle Creek, Michigan. There he formed a vocal group, the Newcomers, and was discovered by Vee Jay Records in 1958. On Flemons's first hit, 'Here I Stand' (number 19 R&B, number 80 pop), the company billed the act as Wade Flemons And The Newcomers. As a solo artist, he charted again in 1960 with 'Easy Lovin'' (number 10 R&B, number 70 pop), but the b-side, 'Woops Now', received solid airplay in many areas. Flemons's remake of the Percy Mayfield song 'Please Send Me Someone To Love' (number 20 R&B), in 1961, was his last chart record. Flemons deserved to chart in 1964 with his definitive version of 'I Knew You When', which Billy Joe Royal put high on the pop charts a year later. Flemons was a co-writer for one of the Dells' biggest hits, 'Stay In My Corner'. In the early 70s he played keyboards for Earth, Wind And Fire, who then recorded for Warner Brothers, but was not a part of the group after they signed with Columbia in 1973.

● ALBUMS: *Wade Flemons* (Vee Jay 1960)★★★.

FLOOD, DICK

b. 13 November 1932, Philadelphia, Pennsylvania, USA. Pop singer-songwriter Flood performed with US singer Billy Graves as 'The Country Lads' on Jimmy Dean's CBS television show in 1957. Flood achieved his only hit in 1959 when his cover version of the French-adapted 'The Three Bells (The Jimmy Brown Song)' reached number 23 in the US charts. It was released in the UK on the short-lived Felsted label in September 1959, but failed to chart due to versions from US vocal group the Browns and a re-release of the US 1954 hit from French group Compagnons De La Chanson, both of which made the UK Top 30.

FLOWER DRUM SONG

Most of Richard Rodgers and Oscar Hammerstein's blockbuster musicals were adapted from existing works, and this show was based on a novel by Chin Y. Lee. It opened at the St. James Theatre in New York on 1 December 1958, and was the only Broadway show that Gene Kelly directed. Hammerstein's book, written in collaboration with Joseph

Fields, is set in San Francisco's Chinatown, and deals in a warm-hearted way with the problems of the Chinese, the Chinese-Americans, and their Americanized children. The difficulties posed by the various generation-gaps and cultures are sympathetically presented in a story of mail-order brides, marriage contracts, and fiendishly clever plot-lines, resulting in the inevitable wedding ceremony. Mei Li (Miyoshi Umeki) is the lady who was delivered via by the US Mail, but she is not the bride. Linda Low (Pat Suzuki) is the lucky married lady, and has one of the show's most popular numbers, 'I Enjoy Being A Girl', as well as the duet 'Sunday', with her groom Sammy Fong (Larry Blyden). The rest of Rodgers and Hammerstein's lovely score included 'You Are Beautiful', 'A Hundred Million Miracles', 'I Am Going To Like It Here', 'Like A God', 'Chop Suey', 'Don't Marry Me', 'Grant Avenue', 'Love Look Away', 'Gliding Through My Memories' and 'The Other Generation'. Juanita Hall played Madame Liang, 'an enthusiastic candidate for American citizenship'. She also starred in Rodgers and Hammerstein's film of *South Pacific*, which was released in the same year as *Flower Drum Song* began its Broadway run of 600 performances. The popular vocalist Anita Ellis was also in the show's cast. She played a nightclub singer, and had the novelty number 'Fan Tan Fannie'. That scene, and the rest of the production, was choreographed by Carol Haney, who introduced 'Hernado's Hideaway' in *The Pajama Game*. The 1960 London production of *Flower Drum Song* had different principal cast members, but Miyoshi Umeki recreated her role for the 1961 film version, which also starred Nancy Kwan.

FLOYD, FRANK

b. 11 October 1908, Toccopola, Mississippi, USA, d. 7 August 1984, Memphis, Tennessee, USA. Having spent many of his earlier years travelling the southern states of the USA, playing in carnivals and street shows, Floyd, aka Harmonica Frank, developed a solo guitar and harmonica style much influenced by black country blues. This led to his first recordings - made by Sam Phillips in Memphis in 1951 - being issued on the Chess label, at that time orientated entirely towards a black audience. These, along with later recordings that Phillips issued in 1954 on his own Sun label, in particular 'Rocking Chair Daddy', stand as direct precursors to the first Elvis Presley records, also on Sun, in their mixture of white and black styles, although Floyd enjoyed no similar commercial success. In the late 50s, he recorded again for a self-owned label, and there was also an album for Barrelhouse in 1975.

● ALBUMS: *The Great Original Recordings Of Harmonica Frank* (Puritan 1974)★★★, *Harmonica Frank Floyd* (Barrelhouse 1975)★★★.

● COMPILATIONS: *Harmonica Frank Floyd: The Great Medical Menagerist* (Edsel 1997)★★★.

● FURTHER READING: *Mystery Train: Images Of America In Rock And Roll Music*, Greil Marcus.

FOLEY, RED

b. Clyde Julian Foley, 17 June 1910, in a log cabin between Blue Lick and Berea, Kentucky, USA, d. 19 September 1968, Fort Wayne, Indiana, USA. The son of a fiddle player, he learned guitar as a child and was encouraged to sing by his parents. After high school, he attended Georgetown College, Kentucky, where he was discovered by a scout for the noted

WLS National Barn Dance in Chicago. In 1930, he joined John Lair's Cumberland Ridge Runners and returned to Kentucky with Lair in 1937, to help him establish the now famous Renfro Valley Barn Dance. He returned to Chicago in 1941, co-starred with Red Skelton in the network country radio show *Avalon Time* and signed with Decca. The first number he recorded was 'Old Shep', a song he had written in 1933, about a dog he had owned as a child (in reality, the dog, sadly poisoned by a neighbour, had been a German shepherd named Hoover). The song, later recorded by many artists including Hank Snow and Elvis Presley, has become a country classic. His first chart success came in 1944, when the patriotic wartime song 'Smoke On The Water' was a US pop chart number 7 and a 13-week occupant of the number 1 position in the country charts. On 17 January 1945, Foley had the distinction of making the first modern country records recorded in Nashville. In April 1946, Foley became a regular member of the *Grand Ole Opry*, replacing Roy Acuff as the star of NBC's prestigious *Prince Albert Show*. When he left Chicago for Nashville, he took with him a young guitar player called Chet Atkins, one of the many artists he helped. During the next eight years Foley established himself as one of the most respected and versatile performers in country music. He acted as master of ceremonies, the straight man for *Opry* comedians Rod Brasfield and Minnie Pearl, and proved himself a vocalist who could handle all types of material. In 1954, he moved to KWTO Springfield, as the host of the *Ozark Jubilee*, which, in 1956, became one of the first successful network television shows. Between 1944 and 1959, Foley charted 41 solo country entries of which 38 were Top 10 hits. There were six more country number 1s, including his 1950 million-selling 'Chattanoogie Shoe Shine Boy', which also topped the pop charts. Several others achieved crossover pop chart success. During this time he also had many major hit duets with various artists including Evelyn Knight, his daughter Betty Foley, Ernest Tubb, ('Goodnight Irene') and six with Kitty Wells, including their country number 1, 'One By One', which remained on the charts for 41 weeks. His performances of gospel numbers were so popular that recordings of 'Steal Away' (1950) (recorded by Hank Williams as 'The Funeral'), 'Just A Closer Walk With Thee' (1950) and 'Peace In The Valley' (1951) all became million-sellers. He also recorded with the Andrews Sisters and in the late 50s, even cut some rock 'n' roll recordings such as 'Crazy Little Guitar Man'. Although he continued to tour and appear on network television shows, he also moved into acting in the early 60s and co-starred with Fess Parker in the ABC-TV series *Mr. Smith Goes To Washington*. His daughter Shirley married one-time pop and later gospel singer Pat Boone, and some ten years after Foley's death, his granddaughter Debby Boone had both country and pop success. Foley never lost his love for country music and, unlike Eddy Arnold, never sought success as a pop artist, even though many of his recordings did attain pop chart status. His voice was mellow and had none of the raw or nasal style associated with many of his contemporaries; some have even likened it to Bing Crosby. His importance to the country music scene is often overlooked and little has been written about him, but he was rightfully elected to the Country Music Hall of Fame in 1967. He was headlining a touring *Opry* show when, after playing the matinée and evening shows, Foley suffered a heart attack and

died in his sleep at Fort Wayne, Indiana, on 19 September 1968. This prompted Hank Jnr., seemingly the last person to speak to him, to write and record (as Luke The Drifter Jnr) the tribute narration 'I Was With Red Foley (The Night He Passed Away)', which charted in November 1968. In the song, Hank Jnr. relates that after reminiscing about the problems faced by country singers such as himself and Hank Snr., Red's final words were: 'I'm awful tired now, Hank, I've got to go to bed'.

● ALBUMS: *Red Foley Souvenir Album* (Decca 1951)★★★★, *Lift Up Your Voice* (Decca 1954)★★★, with Ernest Tubb *Red & Ernie* (Decca 1956)★★★★, *My Keepsake Album* (Decca 1958)★★★, *Beyond The Sunset* (Decca 1958)★★★★, *He Walks With Thee* (Decca 1958)★★, *Red Foley's Dickies Souvenir Album* (Decca 1958)★★★, *Let's All Sing To Him* (Decca 1959)★★, *Let's All Sing With Red Foley* (Decca 1959)★★★, *Company's Comin'* (Decca 1961)★★★, *Red Foley's Golden Favorites* (Decca 1961)★★★★, *Songs Of Devotion* (Decca 1961)★★★, with Kitty Wells *Kitty Wells & Red Foley's Greatest Hits* (Decca 1961)★★★★, *Dear Hearts And Gentle People* (Decca 1962)★★★, *The Red Foley Show* (Decca 1963)★★★, *The Red Foley Story* (Decca 1964)★★★★, *Songs Everybody Knows* (Decca 1965)★★★, *I'm Bound For The Kingdom* (Vocalion 1965)★★★, *Red Foley* (Vocalion 1966)★★★, *Songs For The Soul* (Decca 1967)★★★, with Kitty Wells *Together Again* (Decca 1967)★★★, *I Believe* (1969)★★★, *The Old Master* (1969)★★★, *Red Foley Memories* (1971)★★★★.

● COMPILATIONS: *Gospel Favorites* (1976)★★★, *Beyond The Sunset* (MCA 1981)★★★★, *Tennessee Saturday Night* (Charly 1984)★★★, *The Red Foley Story* (MCA 1986)★★★★, *Red Foley: Country Music Hall Of Fame Series* (MCA 1991)★★★★.

FOLKWAYS RECORDS

Founded in New York, USA, in 1948 by Moe Asch and Marion Distler, Folkways has grown from informal origins to become the embodiment of America's divergent traditions. Initial releases included square-dance tunes, Cuban music and jazz, but the venture was primarily devoted to folk styles. Recordings by Lead Belly established the label nationally and his prodigious output - over 900 songs were committed to tape - included several now recognized as standards, notably 'Goodnight Irene', 'Midnight Special', 'Cottonfields' and 'Rock Island Line'. Folkways also recorded Woody Guthrie, Cisco Houston and Pete Seeger; the latter completed over 60 albums for the label, and embraced the urban folk revival of the late 50s and early 60s with releases by Dave Van Ronk, Len Chandler, Paul Clayton, Logan English and the New Lost City Ramblers. Asch also established several subsidiary outlets, including RBF and Broadside, the latter of which evolved out of a mimeographed publication devoted to the topical song. Bob Dylan, Phil Ochs and Eric Andersen were among those contributing to attendant albums. However, Folkways was not solely confined to folk and its ever-increasing catalogue included language instruction, science, spoken-word and documentary material, of which *We Shall Overcome*, an audio-vérité recording of the 1963 civil rights march on Washington, was particularly impressive. In 1965, Asch founded Verve-Folkways, in an effort to secure national distribution for selected repackages from his extensive library. New recordings, by Tim Hardin, the Blues Magoos and Blues Project, were also undertaken but the label's title was altered to Verve-Forecast in 1967 as electric styles prevailed over acoustic. Excellent albums by, among others, Richie Havens, Janis Ian, Odetta and James Cotton ensued, but the venture folded when parent company MGM incurred financial difficulties. Asch continued to maintain the original Folkways which, by retaining its small-scale origins, has avoided the trappings of commercialization. Between 1,500 and 2,000 titles remain in circulation at all times and the company's peerless position within America was recognized in 1988 with *Folkways: A Vision Shared*, a star-studded recording undertaken to celebrate the label's 40th anniversary. Bruce Springsteen, U2, Brian Wilson, Little Richard, Taj Mahal, Emmylou Harris and Bob Dylan were among those gathering to pay tribute through interpretations of compositions by Lead Belly and Woody Guthrie.

● COMPILATIONS: *Folkways: A Vision Shared* (1988)★★★.

FONTANE SISTERS

The line-up of this close-harmony 50s US vocal group, whose initial success was achieved by making cover versions of black R&B records, comprised Marge Rosse (b. New Milford, New Jersey, USA; lead), Bea Rosse (b. New Milford, New Jersey, USA; low harmony) and Geri Rosse (b. New Milford, New Jersey, USA; harmony). Their mother was a choral director and organist. After leaving high school they joined an all-girl troupe and went on an eight-month tour. Later, they were joined by their brother Frank on guitar, and appeared on radio and in theatres and clubs. After Frank was killed in World War II, the girls re-formed in 1944 as a trio and worked for several years on Perry Como's radio and television shows; they also backed him on several records, including the US number 1 hits 'You're Adorable' and 'Hoop-Dee-Doo'. Signed for RCA-Victor in 1949, they had several minor hits in the early 50s, including 'Tennessee Waltz', 'Let Me In' (with Texas Jim Robertson) and 'Cold, Cold Heart'. In 1954 they switched to Dot Records, a label that specialized in making cover versions of established hits, and came under the influence of Dot's musical director, Billy Vaughn, who, with his orchestra, provided the backing for most of their successful records. Early that year, they made the US charts with 'Happy Days And Lonely Nights', a 1929 song by Fred Fisher and Billy Rose, and in December 1954 they went to number 1 with 'Hearts Of Stone'. The original version was the debut disc of the R&B Cincinnati group Otis Williams And The Charms. Other successful cover versions of black artists' records included 'Rock Love', 'Rollin' Stone' (original by the Marigolds) and 'Eddie, My Love' (originally by the sisters Betty and Rosie Collins' group, the Teen Queens). Other 'white' cover versions included Boyd Bennett And His Rockets' 'Seventeen', which the Fontanes took to number 3 in the US chart, and 'Daddy-O', a song said to have been inspired by a character in the movie *Blackboard Jungle*, and which was originally a US Top 20 hit for Bonnie Lou. The Fontanes' version of 'Banana Boat Song' also made the Top 20, but was prevented from rising higher by a version by the Tarriers; another version, by Steve Lawrence, was his first chart entry. By the late 50s, with more black artists reaching the charts themselves, the Fontanes faded from their position as one of the top girl groups of the 50s. Their last two hits, 'Chanson D'Amour' and 'Jealous Heart', came in 1958.

● ALBUMS: *The Fontanes Sing* (Dot 1956)★★★, *A Visit With The Fontane Sisters* (Dot 1957)★★★, *Tips Of My Fingers* (1963)★★.

● COMPILATIONS: *Rock Love* (Charly 1984)★★★, *Rock Again Love* (Charly 1986)★★★, *Hearts Of Stone* (Varese Sarabande 1994)★★★★.

FORD, FRANKIE

b. Francis Guzzo, 4 August 1939, Gretna, Louisiana, USA. A rocker from a suburb of New Orleans, Frankie Ford is second cousin to that other New Orleans legend Dr. John. His first major appearance was on *Ted Mack's Amateur Hour Talent Show*, where he sang with Carmen Miranda and Sophie Tucker. After winning a scholarship to South Eastern College, Hammond, he started his first band with schoolfriends. By 1958 he was singing with the Syncopators, when he was asked to audition for Ace Records. Subsequently, he released his first single, 'Cheatin' Woman', as Frankie Ford. Fellow musician Huey 'Piano' Smith (b. 26 January 1934, New Orleans, Louisiana, USA) had previously recorded with his group the Clowns a self-penned song called 'Sea Cruise', but Ace persuaded him to let Ford record a new vocal over Bobby Marcham's original. They also added a few extra effects such as paddle-steamer whistle blows, which altered the song enough for Ford to claim a co-writing credit. Released under the title Frankie Ford with Huey 'Piano' Smith and his Clowns, it sold over a million copies and docked in the national Top 20. It was perceived in retrospect as a rock 'n' roll classic, and was revived by Jerry Lee Lewis, Herman's Hermits, Sha Na Na, John Fogerty and Shakin' Stevens. Both 'Sea Cruise' and its follow-up, 'Alimony', were taken from original tapes recorded by composer Huey Smith with the Clowns; the lead vocals were then erased and Ford's singing superimposed. As Morgus And The Ghouls, Ford and the Clowns also recorded 'Morgus The Magnificent', a novelty tribute to a local television personality. There was also an unissued homage to Fats Domino, written and recorded by Ford and Dave Bartholomew. Ford left Ace in 1960 to form his own Spinet Records and signed to Liberty in 1960, but never repeated the success of 'Sea Cruise'. He also formed a 'supergroup' with Huey Smith, Robert Parker (hitmaker of 'Barefootin'') and Dr. John (under various pseudonyms due to contractual problems), and they recorded various New Orleans favourites. He continued to record for obscure labels throughout the 70s. In 1971, he opened a club in New Orleans' French Quarter where he became a cabaret fixture and tourist attraction. Moreover, he still looked youthful enough to play his younger self in the 1978 movie *American Hot Wax*, set in the late 50s. As part of a package, he toured the UK in 1985 along with Rick Nelson, Bobby Vee and Bo Diddley. Ford resents the term one-hit-wonder, and rightly pointed out that his four recordings of 'Sea Cruise' have now sold over 30 million copies worldwide.

● ALBUMS: *Let's Take A Sea Cruise* (Ace 1959)★★, *Frankie Ford* (1976)★★.

● COMPILATIONS: *New Orleans Dynamo* (Ace 1989)★★★.

● FILMS: *American Hot Wax* (1978).

FORD, TENNESSEE ERNIE

b. Ernest Jennings Ford, 13 February 1919, Bristol, Tennessee, USA, d. 17 October 1991, Reston, Virginia, USA. It is difficult to categorize a performer with so many varied achievements, but Ford can be summarized as a master interpreter of melodic songs and hymns. The fact that he has been able to combine singing with his strong faith gives America's best-loved gospel singer great satisfaction. When only four years old, he was singing 'The Old Rugged Cross' at family gatherings, and from an early age, he wanted to be an entertainer. He pestered the local radio station until they made him a staff announcer in 1937 and he also took singing lessons. He subsequently worked for radio stations WATL in Atlanta and WROL in Knoxville, where he announced the attack on Pearl Harbor. He joined the US Army Air Corps in 1942 and married a secretary, Betty Heminger, whom he met at the bombardier's school. After the war, they moved to California and he worked as an announcer and a disc jockey of hillbilly music for KXFM in San Bernardino. He rang cowbells and added bass harmonies to the records he was playing and so developed a country yokel character, Tennessee Ernie. He continued with this on KXLA Pasadena and he became a regular on their *Hometown Jamboree*, which was hosted by bandleader Cliffie Stone. He was also known as the Tennessee Pea-Picker, using the catchphrase 'Bless your pea-pickin' hearts' and appearing on stage in bib overalls and with a blacked-out tooth. Lee Gillette, an A&R man for Capitol Records, heard Ford singing along with a record on air and asked Stone about him. His first record, in 1949, was 'Milk 'Em In The Morning Blues'. Ford began his chart success with 'Tennessee Border', 'Country Junction' and 'Smokey Mountain Boogie', a song he wrote with Stone. 'Mule Train', despite opposition from Frankie Laine, Gene Autry and Vaughn Monroe, was a national hit and a US country number 1. An attempt to write with Hank Williams did not lead to any completed songs, but Ford wrote 'Anticipation Blues' about his wife's pregnancy and it reached the US charts in 1949. Capitol teamed him with many of their female artists including Ella Mae Morse, Molly Bee and the Dinning Sisters, and his most successful duets were 'Ain't Nobody's Business But My Own' and 'I'll Never Be Free', a double-sided single with Kay Starr. The duet just missed gold record status, but he secured one, also in 1950, with his own song, 'Shotgun Boogie', which capitalized on the boogie craze and can be taken as a forerunner of rock 'n' roll. Its UK popularity enabled him to top a variety bill at the London Palladium in 1953. Ford recalls, 'When somebody told me that "Give Me Your Word" was number 1 in your charts, I said, "When did I record that?' because it wasn't big in America and I had forgotten about it!"'. Ford also had success with 'The Cry Of The Wild Goose' and the theme for the Marilyn Monroe film *The River Of No Return*, while the superb musicians on his records included Joe 'Fingers' Carr, who was given equal billing on 'Tailor Made Woman' in 1951, Speedy West and Jimmy Bryant. Ford hosted a US daytime television show for five days a week and, in 1955, Capitol informed him that he would be in breach of contract if he did not record again soon. He chose a song he had been performing on the show, Merle Travis's 'Sixteen Tons'. Ford says, 'The producer, Lee Gillette, asked me what tempo I would like it in. I snapped my fingers and he said, "Leave that in." That snapping on the record is me.' 'Sixteen Tons' topped both the US and the UK charts, and Ford was also one of many who recorded 'The Ballad Of Davy Crockett', the theme of a Walt Disney western starring Fess Parker, which made number 3 in the UK. His half-hour US television show,

The Ford Show (guess the sponsor), ran from 1956-61. He closed every television show with a hymn, which led to him recording over 400 gospel songs. One album, *Hymns*, made number 2 in the US album charts and was listed for over five years. He has shared his billing with the Jordanaires on several albums including *Great Gospel Songs*, which won a Grammy in 1964. Ford says, 'Long before I turned pro, it was a part of my life. There are many different types of gospel music, ranging from black music to the plain old Protestant hymns. I've shown that you don't have to sing them with a black robe on.' Ford had further US hits with 'That's All', 'In The Middle Of An Island' and 'Hicktown' but, for many years, he concentrated on gospel. In 1961 he decided to spend more time with his family and moved to a ranch in the hills of San Francisco. He recorded albums of well-known songs, both pop and country, and he rates *Country Hits - Feelin' Blue* and *Ernie Sings And Glen Picks*, an album that showcases his deep, mellow voice alongside Glen Campbell's guitar, among his best work. Many collectors seek original copies of his albums of Civil War songs. Ford, who was elected to the Country Music Hall of Fame in 1990, remarked, 'People say to me, "Why don't you record another 'Sixteen Tons'?" And I say, "There is no other 'Sixteen Tons'"'.
● ALBUMS: *This Lusty Land* (Capitol 1956)★★★, *Hymns* (Capitol 1956)★★★, *Spirituals* (Capitol 1957)★★★, *C-H-R-I-S-T-M-A-S* (Capitol 1957)★★, *Tennessee Ernie Ford Favourites* (Capitol 1957)★★★, *Ol' Rockin' 'Ern* (Capitol 1957)★★★, *The Folk Album* (Capitol 1958)★★★, *Nearer The Cross* (Capitol 1958)★★★, *The Star Carol* (Capitol 1958)★★★, with the Jordanaires *Gather 'Round* (Capitol 1959)★★★★, with the Jordanaires *A Friend We Have* (Capitol 1960)★★★, *Sing A Hymn With Me* (Capitol 1960)★★★, *Sixteen Tons* (Capitol 1960)★★★★, *Sing A Spiritual With Me* (Capitol 1960)★★, *Come To The Fair* (Capitol 1960)★★★, *Sings Civil War Songs Of The North* (Capitol 1961)★★★★, *Sings Civil War Songs Of The South* (Capitol 1961)★★★★, *Ernie Ford Looks At Love* (Capitol 1961)★★, *Hymns At Home* (Capitol 1961)★★★, *Here Comes The Tennessee Ernie Ford Mississippi Showboat* (Capitol 1962)★★, *I Love To Tell The Story* (Capitol 1962)★★★, *Book Of Favourite Hymns* (Capitol 1962)★★, *Long, Long Ago* (Capitol 1963)★★★, with the San Quentin Prison Choir *We Gather Together* (Capitol 1963)★★★, with the Roger Wagnor Chorale *The Story Of Christmas* (Capitol 1963)★★, with the Jordanaires *Great Gospel Songs* (Capitol 1964)★★, *Country Hits - Feeling Blue* (Capitol 1964)★★★★, *Let Me Walk With Thee* (Capitol 1965)★★, *Sing We Now Of Christmas* (Capitol 1965)★★★, *My Favourite Things* (Capitol 1966)★★★, *Wonderful Peace* (Capitol 1966)★★, *God Lives* (Capitol 1966)★★, *Aloha From Tennessee Ernie Ford* (Capitol 1967)★★★, *Faith Of Our Fathers* (Capitol 1967)★★, with Marilyn Horne *Our Garden Of Hymns* (Capitol 1967)★★, with Brenda Lee *The Show For Christmas Seals* (Decca 1968)★★★, *The World Of Pop And Country Hits* (Capitol 1968)★★★, *O Come All Ye Faithful* (Capitol 1968)★★★, *Songs I Like To Sing* (Capitol 1969)★★★, *New Wave* (Capitol 1969)★★★, *Holy Holy Holy* (Capitol 1969)★★★, *America The Beautiful* (Capitol 1970)★★★, *Sweet Hour Of Prayer* (Capitol 1970)★★★, *Tennessee Ernie Ford Christmas Special* (Capitol 1970)★★★, *Everything Is Beautiful* (Capitol 1970)★★★, *Abide With Me* (Capitol 1971)★★★, *Mr. Words And Music* (Capitol 1972)★★★, *It's Tennessee Ernie Ford* (Capitol 1972)★★★, *Country Morning* (Capitol 1973)★★★,

Ernie Ford Sings About Jesus (Capitol 1973)★★, *Precious Memories* (Capitol 1975)★★★, with Glen Campbell *Ernie Sings And Glen Picks* (Capitol 1975)★★★, *Tennessee Ernie Ford Sings His Great Love* (Capitol 1976)★★★, *For The 83rd Time* (Capitol 1976)★★★, *He Touched Me* (Capitol 1977)★★, with the Jordanaires *Swing Wide Your Golden Gate* (Capitol 1978)★★★★, *Tell The Old, Old Story* (Capitol 1981)★★★, *There's A Song In My Heart* (Word 1982)★★★, *Sunday's Still A Special Day* (Capitol 1984)★★★, *Keep Looking Up* (Word 1985)★★★.
● COMPILATIONS: *Tennessee Ernie Ford Deluxe Set* (Capitol 1968)★★★, *The Very Best Of Tennessee Ernie Ford* (MFP 1983)★★★, *16 Tons Of Boogie/The Best Of Tennessee Ernie Ford* (Rhino 1989)★★★★, *All Time Greatest Hymns* (Curb 1990)★★★★, *Capitol Collectors Series* (Capitol 1991)★★★, *Country Gospel Classics, Volumes 1 & 2* (Capitol 1991)★★★, *Sings Songs Of The Civil War* (Capitol 1991)★★★, *Red, White & Blue* (Capitol 1991)★★★, *Sixteen Tons* (Capitol 1995)★★★★, *The Tennessee Ernie Ford Collection (1949-1965)* (Razor & Tie 1997)★★★★.

FOSSE, BOB

b. Robert Louis Fosse, 23 June 1927, Chicago, Illinois, USA, d. 23 September 1987, Washington, DC, USA. A director, choreographer, dancer and actor for films and stage, Fosse was renowned particularly for his innovative and spectacular staging, with the emphasis very firmly on the exhilarating dance sequences. He studied ballet, tap and acrobatic dance from an early age, and, while still a youngster, performed with a partner as the Riff Brothers in vaudeville and burlesque houses. After graduating from high school in 1945, he spent two years in the US Navy before moving to New York and studying acting at the American Theatre Wing. He then toured in the chorus of various productions before making his Broadway debut as a dancer in the revue *Dance Me A Song* (1950). He worked on television and in theatres and clubs for a time until Hollywood beckoned, and he moved to the west coast to appear in three films, *Give A Girl A Break*, *The Affairs Of Dobie Gillis* and *Kiss Me, Kate* (1953). On his return to New York, he gained his big break when author and director George Abbott hired him as a choreographer for *The Pajama Game* (1954). The show was a massive hit, and Fosse was much in demand - for a time at least. He met Gwen Verdon while working on *Damn Yankees* in 1955, and they were married in 1960. He choreographed *Bells Are Ringing* in 1956, and worked with Verdon again on *New Girl In Town* a year later. From then on, with the exception of *How To Succeed In Business Without Really Trying* (1961), he directed his shows as well as staging the dancing. Fosse's dual role is considered by critics to be a major factor in the success of highly popular productions such as *Redhead* (1959), *Little Me* (1962), *Sweet Charity* (1966), *Pippin* (1972), *Chicago* (1975) and *Dancin'* (1978). Throughout all this time he moved back and forwards between New York and Hollywood, working on films such as *My Sister Eileen* (1955), *The Pajama Game* (1957) and *Damn Yankees* (1958), all three of which were well received. However, *Sweet Charity* (1968), which Fosse controlled completely in his role as director and choreographer, was hammered by many critics for Shirley MacLaine's over-the-top performance, and particularly for the director's self-indulgent cinematography, with its looming close-ups, zooms and blurred focus effects. Fosse

was in the wilderness for some time, but all was forgiven four years later when *Cabaret*, starring Liza Minnelli and Joel Grey, won eight Academy Awards, one of which went to Fosse. It was a box-office smash, and Fosse also satisfied most of the purists by confining the dance sequences to appropriate locations such as a beer garden and nightclub, rather than flooding the streets of Berlin with terpsichorean tourists. In the early 70s Fosse was applauded for his direction of *Lenny*, a film biography of the comedian Lennie Bruce, which starred Dustin Hoffman. In the light of Fosse's recent heart problems, his record as a workaholic, and his lifelong obsesssion with perfection, many observers thought that *All That Jazz* (1979) was intended to be Fosse's own film autobiography, with its ghoulish, self-indulgent examination of life and death. However, no one denied the brilliance of the dance routines or the outstanding performance of Roy Scheider in the leading role. In 1983 Fosse wrote and directed his last movie, *Star 80*, which also had a lurid, tragic theme. Three years later, he wrote, staged and choreographed his final Broadway musical, *Big Deal* - which was, in fact, far less than its title suggested. It represented an inappropriate end to a brilliant career, in which Fosse had created some of the most imaginative and thrilling dance routines ever seen on Broadway or in Hollywood, winning eight Tony Awards in the process. In 1987 he revived one of his most successful shows, *Sweet Charity*, and died shortly before the curtain went up on the night of 23 September. A fascinating documentary entitled *Bob Fosse - Steam Heat*, was made by the US company WNET/Thirteen in 1990. His widow, dancer and actress Anne Reinking, instigated a phenomenally successful revival of *Chicago* on Broadway and in London in 1997/8.
● FURTHER READING: *Razzle Dazzle: The Life And Works Of Bob Fosse*, Kevin Boyd Grubb.

FOSTER, LITTLE WILLIE

b. 5 April 1922, Clarksdale, Mississippi, USA. Foster came to Chicago in 1941, already playing guitar, piano and harmonica. Tutored on the latter instrument by Walter Horton, he played on Maxwell Street, and in a band with Homesick James, Floyd Jones and Moody Jones. Foster recorded two singles in the mid-50s, and 'Crying The Blues', one of the titles, reflected both his emotional singing and his wailing, swooping harmonica. Shortly thereafter, he was shot and semi-paralyzed; he improved slowly, and remained able to play and sing, but only rarely in public. Floyd Jones stated that Foster fatally shot a man, and was placed in a mental hospital early in 1974, but as he was photographed in Chicago in September of that year, this information is somewhat dubious. His 1996 debut album was produced by Bobby Mack, who played the guitar parts.'.
● ALBUMS: *I Found Joy* (Palindrome 1996)★★★.
● COMPILATIONS: *Chicago Blues - The Early 1950s* (1965)★★★, *King Cobras* (1980)★★★.

FOUR ACES

A close-harmony vocal group of the pre-rock 'n' roll era, the quartet was founded in Pennsylvania, USA, in 1949 by baritone lead singer Al Alberts (b. Chester, Pennsylvania, USA). With Dave Mahoney, Lou Silvestri and Sol Vocare, he recorded a single on the local Victoria label in 1951. 'Sin (Not a Sin)' sold a million copies and the Four Aces were signed

to Decca Records. Alberts and Martin Gold co-wrote 'Tell Me Why', which began a string of hit singles during the mid-50s. Among them were the 1952 revival of Hoagy Carmichael and Frank Loesser's 1938 song 'Heart And Soul', 'Stranger In Paradise' (from the stage musical *Kismet*), 'Mister Sandman' (1954), 'Heart' and 'Melody Of Love' (1955). The group's only number 1 record was the Oscar-winning 'Love Is A Many Splendoured Thing', the title song from the 1955 film starring Jennifer Jones and William Holden. The Four Aces also recorded versions of the theme from *Three Coins In The Fountain* and 'The World Outside' from the film *Suicide Squadron*. In 1956, the group suffered a double blow as Alberts left to follow a solo career and rock 'n' roll arrived. The Four Aces tried various strategies to survive, including covering a Pat Boone song ('Friendly Persuasion') and jumping on the calypso and rock bandwagons with 'Bahama Mama' and 'Rock And Roll Rhapsody'. However, few of these records were even minor hits and by the end of the 50s the Four Aces had disappeared from view. Alberts did little better, although 'Willingly' (1958) was only a minor success.
● ALBUMS: *The Four Aces* 10-inch album (Decca 1952)★★★★, *The Mood For Love* (Decca 1955)★★★, *Merry Christmas* (Decca 1956)★★★, *Sentimental Souvenirs* (Decca 1956)★★★, *Heart And Soul* (Decca 1957)★★★, *She Sees All The Hollywood Hits* (Decca 1957)★★★, *Written On The Wind* film soundtrack (Decca 1957)★★, *Shuffling Along* (Decca 1957)★★, *Hits From Hollywood* (Decca 1958)★★★, *The Swingin' Aces* (Decca 1958)★★, *Hits From Broadway* (Decca 1959)★★, *Beyond The Blue Horizon* (Decca 1959)★★.
● COMPILATIONS: *The Golden Hits Of The Four Aces* (Decca 1960)★★★★, *Record Oldies* (United Artists 1963)★★★.
● FILMS: *The Big Beat* (1957).

FOUR BLAZES

The most famous line-up of this group from Chicago, Illinois, USA, was Tommy Braden (d. 1957; lead vocals, bass), William 'Shorty' Hill (vocals, guitar), Floyd McDaniels (vocals, guitar), and Paul Lindsley 'Jelly' Holt (vocals, drums). The Four Blazes became hit-makers in the early 50s with a mélange of jive, ballad, and jazz sounds that combined vocal harmony with their own instrumental support. This type of group was common in the 40s, when acts such as Cats And The Fiddle and Five Red Caps held sway, and the Four Blazes were one of the last of this breed to have R&B hits. The group was formed in 1940 by Holt, who recruited Hill, McDaniels, and bassist Prentice Butler, and they soon became perennials in Chicago clubs. They became the Five Blazes when they added pianist and lead vocalist Ernie Harper in 1946. They first recorded for Aristocrat in 1947, but were unable to garner more than a few local plays for their records. In 1950, after Butler died and Harper left the group, Holt recruited Tennessee bassist Tommy Braden, who became the new lead singer of the renamed Four Blazes. In 1952 they signed with United and immediately achieved a number 1 R&B hit in 1952 with the Braden-composed 'Mary Jo'. Tenor saxophonist Eddie Chamblee was prominently featured on the record and in effect became a part of the group both while touring and recording. 'Mary Jo' was followed with two more charting records, 'Please Send Her Back To Me' (number 7 R&B) and

'Perfect Woman' (number 5 R&B), both from 1953. Another record that received strong regional sales was 'My Hat's On The Side Of My Head' (1953). Braden left the group in late 1954, and neither he nor the group could return to the charts. Holt recruited new members and continued to play Chicago clubs as the Five Blazes until disbanding the group in 1957. Braden died in 1957.
● COMPILATIONS: *Swingin' & Singin'* six tracks, remainder by the Dozier Boy (P-Vine 1982)★★★.

FOUR BUDDIES

The Four Buddies, from Baltimore, Maryland, USA, were one of the best representatives of the smooth, deep-sounding vocal harmony style that was popular in the early 50s. The group members were Leon Harrison (lead, first tenor), Gregory Carroll (second tenor), Bert Palmer (baritone) and Tommy Smith (bass). The group was discovered and signed by Savoy Records in 1951 and managed by Friz Pollard (the famed All-American football star from Brown in 1915). They first recorded as the Metronomes with Johnny Otis on Savoy. Then as the Four Buddies they had one R&B hit, 'I Will Wait' (number 2 R&B), in 1951, but other outstanding songs included 'My Summer's Gone' and 'Don't Leave Me Now'. The group toured extensively from Las Vegas to the chitlin' circuit theatres of the Apollo and the Howard. When the Four Buddies' contract at Savoy expired in 1953, the group broke up. Gregory joined the Orioles a year later, but Harrison formed a new group, the Buddies, which included second tenor Luther Dixon (who later produced and wrote for Scepter and Wand), baritone Roger Wainwright and bass Danny Ferguson. In 1954 the Buddies recorded for Glory and as the Barons for Decca, but without any chart success.

FOUR COINS

Formed in Canonsburg, Pennsylvania, USA, in 1952, the vocal harmony group the Four Coins consisted of George Mantalis, James Gregorakis and brothers George and Michael Mahramas. Originally the quartet were horn players in an orchestra with Bobby Vinton, who was an unknown at the time. At the end of 1952 the foursome began harmonizing together, and in January 1953 appeared on an 'amateur hour' radio programme, which they won. They left Vinton in 1953 and began a residency at a Pittsburgh club called the Blue Ridge Inn, naming themselves the Four Keys. They recorded their first singles in November 1953 for Corona Records, which led to a contract with Epic Records, a branch of the larger Columbia Records. Taking their cue from another quartet, the Four Aces, the group changed its name to the Four Coins. The group's first Epic single, 'We'll Be Married (In The Church In The Wildwood)', sold well but it was not until 1957 that they recorded their biggest hit, 'Shangri-La', which reached number 11 in the US charts and earned a gold record. The group had charted seven times by 1959. In 1960 they changed labels to MGM Records and continued to record for Jubilee Records, Vee Jay Records and Roulette Records, undergoing personnel changes along the way. They disbanded in 1970.
● ALBUMS: *The Four Coins* (Epic 1955)★★★★, *The Four Coins In Shangri-La* (Epic 1958)★★, *Greek Songs By The Four Coins* (1961)★★★, *Greek Songs Mama Never Taught Me* (1964)★★.
● FILMS: *Jamboree* a.k.a. *Disc Jockey Jamboree* (1957).

FOUR ESQUIRES

Bill Courtney (lead singer) and backing vocalists Walter Gold, Robert Golden and Frank Mahoney were students at the University of Boston, Massachusetts, USA, in the early 50s who harmonized for their own amusement to whatever instrumental accompaniment they could muster. Though popular locally, they waited until they were sufficiently schooled before becoming professional entertainers. After London Records signed them in March 1956, 'Look Homeward Angel' was a turntable hit, but it was eclipsed by Johnnie Ray's version. Their workmanlike 'Love Me Forever' (augmented with a female session vocalist's obligato), was overshadowed by a US cover version by Eydie Gorme and one in Britain by Marion Ryan. Nevertheless, it clawed into each country's Top 30 and, unhindered by competition, so did 1958's 'Hideaway' in the USA. While able to fill moderate-sized auditoriums and becoming a reliable support act in bigger venues, the Esquires clocked up no further chart entries and had disbanded by the early 60s.

FOUR FELLOWS

Formed in Brooklyn, New York, USA, the group consisted of Jimmy McGowan, Larry Banks, Davy Jones and Teddy Williams. McGowan and Williams began their careers in the late 40s when they were a part of a gospel and jubilee group, the Starlight Toppers. That unit broke up around 1951, but in 1953 McGowan and Williams joined Banks and Jones to form the Four Fellows. The group's debut for Derby went unnoticed, and they next signed with Glory Records. They recorded a fine record, 'I Wish I Didn't Love You', but it, too, went unnoticed. The Four Fellows' third record was a song that Banks had written while serving in the Korean War, 'Soldier Boy' (not be confused with the Shirelles' later hit of the same title), and it finally reached number 4 R&B in 1955. The following year, after the group recorded the fine ballad 'Darling You', Jones left and joined the Rays. He was replaced by Jimmy Mobley. The Four Fellows never returned to the charts and broke up in 1957. Banks later wrote the hit 'Go Now', which was first recorded by his wife, Bessie Banks, and became a hit for the Moody Blues in 1964. McGowan wrote and published his memoirs in 1983 under the title *Here Today! Here To Stay!*.

FOUR FRESHMEN

Formed at Arthur Jordan Conservatory of Music in Indianapolis, Indiana, USA, in 1948, the Four Freshmen were a ground-breaking vocal group who influenced the Hi-Lo's, the Beach Boys, Manhattan Transfer and countless other close-harmony outfits. The group originally consisted of lead vocalist Bob Flanigan (b. 22 August 1926, Greencastle, Indiana, USA), his cousins Ross Barbour (b. 31 December 1928, Columbus, Indiana, USA) and Don Barbour (b. 19 April 1929, Columbus, Indiana, USA, d. 5 October 1961), and Hal Kratzsch (b. Warsaw, Indiana, USA, d. 18 November 1970). Prior to the formation of the Four Freshmen, the Barbour brothers and Kratzsch, along with lead singer Marvin Pruitt, had been in a barbershop quartet called Hal's Harmonizers, each member playing an instrument. The same line-up formed a more jazz-oriented second group, called the Toppers, in 1948. Pruitt left that same year, at which point Flanigan returned from Florida, where he had spent the summer. Inspired by Mel Tormé's Mel-Tones,

the new group, renamed the Four Freshmen, was discovered in September 1949 by Woody Herman. In 1950 Stan Kenton saw the quartet in concert in Dayton, Ohio, and arranged for them to audition for Capitol Records, who signed them. Their first hit single came in 1952, 'It's A Blue World', which reached number 30 in the USA. Spring 1953 saw a personnel change when Kratzsch left, replaced by Ken Errair (b. 23 January 1930, d. 14 June 1968). Errair also departed in 1955, replaced by Ken Albers. By that time the group had logged two more Top 40 hits, 'It Happened Once Before' and 'Mood Indigo'. Three final chart singles were issued in 1955-56, including the number 17 'Graduation Day', later covered by the Beach Boys. The group had seven album hits, including the Top 10 *Four Freshmen And 5 Trombones* in 1956 and *4 Freshmen And 5 Trumpets* the following year. Further personnel changes marked the group's career. Don Barbour left in 1960, replaced by Bill Comstock (who left in 1972). Ross Barbour stayed on until 1977 and Ken Albers in 1982. Flanigan remained with the group into the early 90s. Don Barbour was killed in a car crash in 1961, Kratzsch died of cancer in 1970 and Errair died in a plane crash in 1968. The latest Four Freshman line-up toured the UK in 1992, backed by Ray McVay's UK All-Star Big Band.

● ALBUMS: *Voices In Modern* (Capitol 1955)★★★, *Four Freshmen And 5 Trombones* (Capitol 1956)★★★, *Freshmen Favorites* (Capitol 1956)★★★, *4 Freshmen And 5 Trumpets* (Capitol 1957)★★★, *Four Freshmen And Five Saxes* (Capitol 1957)★★★, *Voices In Latin* (Capitol 1958)★★, *The Four Freshmen In Person* (Capitol 1958)★★★, *Voices In Love* (Capitol 1958)★★★, *Freshmen Favorites Volume 2* (Capitol 1959)★★★, *Love Lost* (Capitol 1959)★★, *The Four Freshmen And Five Guitars* (Capitol 1960)★★, *Voices And Brass* (Capitol 1960)★★, *Road Show* (Capitol 1960)★★, *First Affair* (Capitol 1960)★★, *Freshmen Year* (Capitol 1961)★★, *Voices In Fun* (Capitol 1961)★★, *Stars In Our Eyes* (Capitol 1962)★★, *Got That Feelin'* (Capitol 1963)★★, *More With 5 Trombones* (Capitol 1964)★★, *Time Slips Away* (Capitol 1964)★★.
● COMPILATIONS: *The Best Of The Four Freshmen* (Capitol 1962)★★★★.

FOUR KNIGHTS

The singing of Gene Alford was framed by the backing harmonies of Oscar Broadway, Clarence Dixon and John Wallace (who also strummed guitar). From regular performances in the late 40s on radio stations local to their native Charlotte, North Carolina, USA, the Knights graduated to television, providing musical interludes on nationally broadcast situation comedies starring Arthur Godfrey and Red Skelton. The group signed to Capitol Records and received much airplay for their debut single, 1951's 'It's No Sin'. In 1953, they reached the national hit parade with 'Oh Happy Day' - lush with orchestral accompaniment - and the following year, came up with the million-selling 'I Get So Lonely', a clever up-tempo reworking of a hillbilly ballad. After 'O Falling Star' slipped from the charts, the quartet teamed up with Nat 'King' Cole for a 1956 smash with 'That's All There Is To That' - and so it was for the Four Knights, who never had another hit.

● ALBUMS: *Spotlight Songs* (Capitol 1953/56)★★★, *The Four Knights* (Coral 1959)★★★, *Million $ Baby* (Coral 1960)★★★.

FOUR LADS

The line-up comprised Frank Busseri (b. Toronto, Canada; baritone), Bernard Toorish (b. Toronto, Canada; second tenor), James Arnold (b. Toronto, Canada; first tenor) and Connie Codarini (b. Toronto, Canada; bass). A versatile vocal quartet, popular in US clubs and theatres, and on television and records, especially during the 50s. The Lads formed their group while attending St. Michael's Choir School in Toronto. Aided by 'Dad' Wilson, a member of the Golden Gate Quartet, the Lads played a try-out engagement at Le Ruban Bleu in New York, stayed for some 30 weeks, and then toured extensively. They were signed by Columbia Records as a background group, and in 1951 accompanied Johnnie Ray on his first big hit, 'Cry'. Their first solo success was in 1952 with 'Mocking Bird', followed by 'He Who Has Love', 'Down By The Riverside', 'Istanbul (Not Constantinople)', 'Gilly, Gilly, Ossenfeffer, Katzenellen Bogen By The Sea' and 'Skokiian', a South African song. In 1955 they had a big hit with 'Moments To Remember', written by Robert Allen and Al Stillman. The songwriters also provided the Lads with 'No, Not Much', 'Who Needs You', 'Enchanted Island' and 'There's Only One Of You'. Allen and Stillman also contributed to Johnny Mathis's early success with numbers such as 'Chances Are' and 'It's Not For Me To Say'. Other Four Lads' US Top 20 entries, through until 1958, included 'The Bus Stop Song (A Paper Of Pins)', 'A House With Love In It', 'Put A Light At The Window' and 'Standing On The Corner', from Frank Loesser's Broadway show *The Most Happy Fella*. In 1957, the group recorded *The Four Lads Sing Frank Loesser*, which featured medleys from three of his successful scores: *Where's Charley?*, *Hans Christian Andersen* and *Guys And Dolls*. Other successful albums were their US Top 20 entry, *On The Sunny Side*, with the Claude Thornhill Orchestra, *Breezin' Along*, conducted by Ray Ellis and *Four On The Aisle*, a collection of extended medleys from the musical shows *Annie Get Your Gun*, *Babes In Arms* and *Kiss Me, Kate*. A modified version of the group was still working in the 80s, Arnold and Busseri performing with two new members. Toorish was to be found singing with the Vince Mastro Quartet.
● ALBUMS: *Stage Show* 10-inch album (Columbia 1954)★★★, *On The Sunny Side* (Columbia 1956)★★★★, *The Stingiest Man In Town* film soundtrack (Columbia 1956)★★, with Frankie Laine *The Four Lads With Frankie Laine* (Columbia 1956)★★★, *The Four Lads Sing Frank Loesser* (Columbia 1957)★★★, *Breezin' Along* (Columbia 1959)★★★★, *Four On The Aisle* (Columbia 1959)★★★, *The Four Lads Swing Along* (Columbia 1959)★★★, *High Spirits!* (Columbia 1959)★★, *Love Affair* (Columbia 1960)★★★, *Everything Goes* (Columbia 1960)★★★, *Dixieland Doin's* (1961)★★★, *Hits Of The 60's* (1962)★★★, *Oh, Happy Day* (1963)★★★, *This Year's Top Movie Hits* (1964)★★★, *Songs Of World War I* (1964)★★.
● COMPILATIONS: *The Four Lads' Greatest Hits* (Columbia 1958)★★★★, *Twelve Hits* (Columbia 1961)★★★★.

FOUR LOVERS

Under the name the Variatones, this New Jersey, USA quartet originally encompassed country, pop and rockabilly in their repertoire. Comprising Francis Castelluccio (aka Frankie Valli, who had already recorded solo as Frankie Valley), Tommy DeVito, Nick DeVito and Hank Majewski, they formed in 1955 and played the local club circuit before attracting the attention of RCA Records. By the time they recorded for their new employers in April 1956 they had switched names to the Four Lovers and changed their style to a firm R&B direction. Two potent singles emerged as the result of these sessions, 'You're The Apple Of My Eye' and 'Honey Love'. The former release made the *Billboard* charts at number 62, and resulted in an appearance on Ed Sullivan's television show. Sadly, their next three releases for RCA, 'Jambalaya', 'Happy Am I' and 'Shake A Hand', failed to match their debut's impact. They switched to Epic Records in 1957 but attracted little interest. A change of direction was required - this coincided with the replacement of Nick DeVito by Charlie Callelo, and with a change of name, giving their lead vocalist improved status in its label credits, which now read Frankie Valle And The Romans. Eventually success did come their way, but not until the Four Lovers were reborn as Valli's backing band, the Four Seasons (with only Tommy DeVito surviving the transition).
● ALBUMS: *The Four Lovers* (RCA 1957)★★★.

FOUR PREPS

Formed in the early 50s in Hollywood, California, USA, the Four Preps were a vocal group consisting of Bruce Belland, Glen Larson, Marvin Inabnett and Ed Cobb. Recording for Capitol Records, they placed 13 singles in the US charts between 1956 and 1964, two of which made the Top 5 in 1958. The quartet began singing together during their high-school years, influenced by the Mills Brothers, Four Aces, and Four Freshmen acts. Impressed by a demo tape the group recorded Mel Shauer, manager of Les Paul And Mary Ford, took the group under his wing and arranged a recording contract with Capitol. Their first session, in late 1956, yielded 'Dreamy Eyes', which was a minor hit, but the follow-up, '26 Miles (Santa Catalina)', written by Belland and Larson years earlier, reached number 2, and their next single, 'Big Man', made number 3. Subsequent singles failed to reach the US Top 10 although the group did achieve a Top 10 album, *Four Preps On Campus*, in 1961 during the height of the folk music revival in the USA. The group's final charting single, 1964's 'A Letter To The Beatles', parodied Beatlemania but was allegedly withdrawn from distribution by Capitol upon the request of the Beatles' management. The group continued until 1967. Cobb went on to join the group Piltdown Men, and later to produce such records as the Standells' 'Dirty Water'; he also wrote 'Tainted Love', a hit for Soft Cell in 1982. In 1988, the Four Preps were back on the road, with two of the original members, Belland and Cobb, being joined by David Somerville, former lead singer of the Diamonds and Jim Pike, founder of the Lettermen.
● ALBUMS: *The Four Preps* (Capitol 1958)★★★★, *The Things We Did Last Summer* (Capitol 1958)★★★★, *Dancing And Dreaming* (Capitol 1959)★★★, *Early In The Morning* (Capitol 1960)★★, *Those Good Old Memories* (Capitol 1960)★★★, *Four Preps On Campus* (Capitol 1961)★★★, *Campus Encore* (Capitol 1962)★★★, *Campus Confidential* (Capitol 1963)★★, *Songs For A Campus Party* (Capitol 1963)★★, *How To Succeed In Love!* (Capitol 1964)★★.
● COMPILATIONS: *Best Of The Four Preps* (Capitol 1967)★★★★, *Capitol Collectors Series* (Capitol 1989)★★★★.

FOUR TUNES

The Four Tunes, like many African-American groups of the 40s and early 50s, were a pop rather than a R&B ensemble. The group had its origin in the Brown Dots, and were formed by Ivory 'Deek' Watson after he left the Ink Spots in 1945. The remainder of the group was Pat Best, Jimmy Gordon and Jimmy Nabbie. While still with the Brown Dots, Best, Gordon and Nabbie joined with Danny Owens in 1946 to record on the Manor label as the Sentimentalists, changing their name shortly afterwards to the Four Tunes. They backed Savannah Churchill on her 1947 hit 'I Want To Be Loved (But Only By You)', but did not attain any national hits of their own while with Manor. In 1948 they finally left the Brown Dots and a year later signed with RCA. Their two big chart hits came after they signed with Jubilee in 1953 with 'Marie' (number 2 R&B, number 13 pop) from 1953, and 'I Understand (Just How You Feel)' (number 7 R&B, number 6 pop) from 1954. The Four Tunes made their last recordings in 1956 and finally broke up in 1963. Their musical legacy was remembered in 1961 when the G-Clefs had a big hit with 'I Understand (Just How You Feel)' and in 1965 when the Bachelors reached number 9 in the UK charts with 'Marie'.
● ALBUMS: *The Four Tunes: 12 X 4* (Jubilee 1957)★★★.
● COMPILATIONS: *The Complete Jubilee Sessions* (Sequel 1992)★★★.

FOUR VOICES

Formed in the USA during the mid-50s, the Four Voices were Allan Chase (tenor), Sal Mayo (tenor), Bill McBride (baritone) and Frank Fosta (bass baritone). The group appeared on the *Arthur Godfrey* television programme and were seen by Columbia Records' A&R executive Mitch Miller, who signed them in 1955. The quartet placed one single, 'Lovely One', in the Top 20 in 1956 and a second at number 50. They then had an uneventful five years, but by the early 60s Chase left and the others tried to carry on for another year before resigning themselves to anonymity. They recorded no albums.

FRANKLIN, C.L., REV.

b. Clarence LaVaughn Franklin, 22 January 1915, Sunflower County, Mississippi, USA, d. 24 July 1984. Although his own career was eclipsed by that of his daughter, Aretha Franklin, the Rev. C.L. Franklin was a popular religious recording artist in his own right. Franklin began singing in church at the age of 12 and began preaching two years later. He attended college and gained a ministerial degree, preaching in Mississippi, New York and Tennessee before being named pastor of the New Bethel Baptist Church in Detroit, Michigan, USA, in 1946. He began recording 78s featuring his sermons, for the J-V-B label in 1953, some of which were leased to Chess Records for more widespread distribution. He recorded over a dozen singles for the label. Each summer, daughter Aretha would accompany her father on the road, where he participated in gospel revues; much of her exposure to the gospel singing style came during those tours. In the 60s the Rev. Franklin became active in the civil rights movement and helped organize the 1963 March on Washington, at which Dr. Martin Luther King delivered his famous 'I have a dream' speech. Also the father of Erma Franklin and Carolyn Franklin, the Rev. Franklin was shot by burglars entering his home in 1979. He lapsed into a coma from which he never recovered.
● ALBUMS: *A Wild Man Meets Jesus* (1968)★★★, *Man On The Moon* (1970)★★★.

FRANZ, JOHNNY

b. John Charles Franz, 23 February 1922, London, England, d. 29 January 1977, London, England. An extremely successful and highly regarded pianist, and A&R producer for Philips Records in the UK. Franz began to study the piano when he was 13, and two years later, he joined the music publishers Francis, Day and Hunter. In parallel with his day job, Franz worked in the evenings with artists such as Jack Jackson, George Elrick and Nat Allen. He also served as accompanist to harmonica soloist Ronald Chesney, on the latter's radio series. In 1940 Franz played the piano for the band singer Bernard Hunter's first stage appearance, at Collins Music Hall, and, by the late 40s, had established a reputation as one of the leading accompanists in Britain, working with Adelaide Hall, Benny Lee and visiting American star Vivian Blaine. One of his most enduring associations was with Anne Shelton, and they were part of an entertainment 'package' that was flown on a round trip of 1,500 miles to play three dates in the American zone of Nurembourg, West Germany, in 1950. Ironically, not long afterwards, Franz was a passenger in a Rapide small aircraft that up-ended on a runway in Jersey, and he was reluctant ever to fly again. In 1954, after spending 17 years with Francis, Day and Hunter, while also discovering and coaching new talent, Franz was appointed the A&R Manager of Philips Records in 1954. His previous background meant that he was ideally suited to the job. He was able to select the right kind of material for his roster of artists, routine them, and explain to the musical arrangers precisely the sound that he wanted to hear on the finished records. Blessed with perfect pitch, he could also spot a clinker in the string section from the other side of the control room. In the late 50s Franz was responsible for the output of some of the most successful artists in the UK, such as Frankie Vaughan, Shirley Bassey, Harry Secombe, the Beverley Sisters, the Kaye Sisters, Robert Earl, Ronnie Carroll, Susan Maughan, Julie Rogers and, of course, Anne Shelton. It was his idea, when recording Shelton's 1956 chart-topper 'Lay Down Your Arms', to add the sound of martial marching feet by having one of the studio staff shuffle about in a sand tray. In complete contrast, he worked with the risqué American cabaret star Ruth Wallis, and also produced the sophisticated *Mel Tormé Meets The British*, which was arranged by Wally Stott, one of Franz's key conductor-arrangers along with Ivor Raymonde and Peter Knight. In the late 50s, Marty Wilde was at the forefront of Philips's assault on the charts, as Franz adapted to the radical musical changes that were happening all around him. Early in the 60s he nurtured the vocal instrumental group the Springfields, from which emerged one of the decade's superstars, Dusty Springfield, with a string of hits that included the million-sellers 'I Only Want To Be With You' (written by her musical director, Ivor Raymonde, with Mike Hawker) and 'You Don't Have To Say You Love Me'. The Four Pennies were another successful Franz act around that time, with their UK number 1 'Juliet'; so too were the Walker Brothers, who introduced the pop world to another 60s icon, Scott Walker. The sound that

Franz created for Walker Brothers hits such as 'Make It Easy On Yourself', 'My Ship Is Coming In' and 'The Sun Ain't Gonna Shine Any More', is sometimes called 'Phil Spectorish'. This had shades of truth, although the two producers were very different in appearance and style: Franz could easily have been mistaken for a bank manager - albeit one who chain-smoked and devoured copious amounts of tea. As well as producing Scott Walker's chart hits 'Jackie', 'Joanna' and 'Lights Of Cincinatti', Franz's influence was also apparent on *Sings Songs From His T.V. Series*, which, with show numbers such as 'I Have Dreamed', 'The Song Is You' and 'If She Walked Into My Life', showed Walker to be a romantic balladeer of the old school. In a way, it was the 'old pals' act' that brought much of the best commercial material Franz's way. His contacts in the music publishing business, such as Cyril Shane, ensured that Philips were offered many potential hit songs, some of them from abroad. Dusty Springfield's 'I Only Want To Be With You' came to London from the 1965 San Remo Song Festival, and in 1973, Franz placed 'Welcome Home' ('Vivre'), a French number with an English lyric by Bryan Blackburn, with *Opportunity Knocks* winners Peters And Lee. It gave them a UK number 1, and they hit the top spot again in the same year with *We Can Make It*, the first of their four Top 10 albums in the 70s. Among the most fondly remembered television and recording performers of the decade, the duo were a part of the final flourish in the life of a man who has been called 'the last of the great pro's'. Johnny Franz died in 1977 at the age of 55, in a Chelsea hospital.

FREED, ALAN

b. 15 December 1926, Johnstown, Pennsylvania, USA, d. 20 January 1965. Freed was one of several key individuals who helped to create the audience for rock 'n' roll. As an influential disc jockey, he made enemies among the music business establishment by championing the cause of black artists but his career ended tragically when he was found to be guilty of payola in 1962. The son of European immigrants, he played trombone in a high school band named the Sultans Of Swing. After US Army service, he secured his first radio job in 1946, playing classical records. He moved on to Akron, Ohio, to play contemporary pop material and in 1951 joined WJW Cleveland. There Freed hosted a show sponsored by local record store owner Leo Mintz, consisting of R&B originals rather than white pop cover versions. Entitled *Moondog's Rock 'N' Roll Party*, the show attracted large audiences of white teenagers who swamped a 1952 concert by the Moonglows, a group Freed had discovered and signed to his own short-lived Champagne label. His local success led him to New York and WINS in 1953. He was stopped from using the Moondog title after litigation with the blind Manhattan street musician Moondog (Louis Hardin). Still a champion of black artists such as Chuck Berry and Fats Domino, Freed hosted major live shows at the Paramount Theatre and in 1956-58 appeared in the films *Rock Around The Clock*, *Rock Rock Rock*, *Don't Knock The Rock* and *Go Johnny Go*. However, with the rise of Bill Haley, Elvis Presley and Pat Boone (whose cover versions he frequently ignored), Freed's power as a disc jockey was weakened. In particular, he became a target of opponents of rock 'n' roll such as Columbia's A&R chief Mitch Miller, and when Freed refused to play Columbia releases he was fired by WINS. He

then joined WABC and hosted a televised *Dance Party* show on WNEW-TV based on Dick Clark's *American Bandstand*. Freed's arrest on a charge of inciting a riot at a Boston concert left him ill prepared to deal with the accusations of payola levelled by a Congressional investigation in 1959. It emerged that independent labels had offered cash or publishing rights to Freed in return for the airplay they were denied by the prejudices of other radio stations. In 1962 Freed was found guilty of bribery and this was followed by charges of tax evasion. He died of uremic poisoning in January 1965.
● ALBUMS: *The Big Beat* 10-inch album (MGM 1956)★★★, *Alan Freed's Rock 'N Roll Dance Party, Volume 1* (Coral 1956)★★★, *Alan Freed's Rock 'N Roll Dance Party, Volume 2* (Coral 1956)★★★, *Go Go Go - Alan Freed's TV Record Hop* (Coral 1957)★★★, *Rock Around The Block* (Coral 1958)★★★, *Alan Freed Presents The King's Henchmen* (Coral 1958)★★★, *The Alan Freed Rock & Roll Show* (Brunswick 1959)★★★, *Alan Freed's Memory Lane* (End 1962)★★.
● FURTHER READING: *Big Beat Heat: Alan Freed And The Early Years Of Rock 'n' Roll*, John A. Jackson.
● FILMS: *Rock Around The Clock* (1956), *Don't Knock The Rock* (1956), *Rock Rock Rock* (1957), *Go Johnny Go* (1958).

FREEMAN, BOBBY

b. 13 June 1940, San Francisco, California, USA. Freeman is generally recognized as his home city's first rock 'n' roll star by virtue of 'Do You Want To Dance'. This 1958 smash hit was later immortalized by the Beach Boys and Cliff Richard. The singer enjoyed further success in 1964 with 'C'mon And Swim', a dance-craze novelty song produced, and co-written, by Sly Stone. Freeman later elected to pursue his singing career at a local topless club, but more recent appearances at the annual San Francisco Bay Area Music ('Bammy') awards showed him an able performer.
● ALBUMS: *Do You Wanna Dance?* (Jubilee 1958)★★, *Twist With Bobby Freeman* (Jubilee 1962)★★, *C'mon And S-W-I-M* (Autumn 1964)★★, *The Lovable Style Of Bobby Freeman* (King 1965)★★, *Get In The Swim With Bobby Freeman* (Josie 1965)★★.
● COMPILATIONS: *The Best Of Bobby Freeman* (1992)★★★.

FREEMAN, ERNIE

b. 16 August 1922, Cleveland, Ohio, USA, d. 16 May 1981. A noted pianist, arranger and producer, Freeman enjoyed a series of minor hits during the late 50s and early 60s. His chart entries included 'Dumplins' (1957) and 'Indian Love Call' (1959), but his biggest success came with a cover version of Bill Justis's smash 'Raunchy'. Although the original reached the US Top 3, Freeman's interpretation peaked at number 12. He recorded as B. Bumble And The Stingers on all of this act's releases, bar 'Nut Rocker', before embarking on a successful session career. Freeman appeared on material by Frank Sinatra, Dean Martin and Connie Francis, and later became musical director with the Reprise Records label, a post he held for 10 years. Freeman retired during the 70s and died as the result of a heart attack.
● ALBUMS: *Ernie Freeman Plays Irving Berlin* (Imperial 1957)★★★, *Jivin' Around* (Imperial 1957)★★★, *Ernie Freeman* (Imperial 1958)★★★, *Dark At The Top Of The Stairs* (Imperial 1959)★★★, *Twistin' Time* (Imperial

1960)★★★, *The Stripper* (Imperial 1962)★★, *Limbo Dance Party* (Liberty 1963)★★, *Comin' Home, Baby* (Liberty 1963)★★★.

FRIZZELL, LEFTY

b. William Orville Frizzell, 31 March 1928, Corsicana, Navarro County, Texas, USA, d. 19 July 1975. The eldest of eight children of an itinerant oilfield worker, he was raised mainly in El Dorado, Arkansas, but also lived in sundry places in Texas and Oklahoma. Greatly influenced by his parents' old 78s of Jimmie Rodgers, he sang as a young boy and when aged 12, he had a regular spot on KELD El Dorado. Two years later he was performing at local dances at Greenville and further exposure on other radio stations followed as the family moved around. At the age of 16, he was playing the honky tonks and clubs in places such as Waco and Dallas and grew into a tough character himself, performing the music of Jimmie Rodgers, plus some of his own songs. Some accounts suggest that it was at this time that he became known as Lefty after fighting in a Golden Gloves boxing match, but this appears to have been later publicity hype by Columbia Records. Both his father and his wife have steadfastly denied the story, maintaining that Lefty actually gained the nickname when he beat the school bully during his schooldays. It is further claimed that it was a schoolfriend and guitarist called Gene Whitworth who first called him Lefty (he was actually always known as Sonny to his family). In 1945, he was married, and his wife Alice became the inspiration for several of his songs over the 30 years the marriage lasted. More and more frequently, his drinking landed him in trouble with the authorities, and he was inspired to write his famous song, 'I Love You A Thousand Ways', while spending a night in a Texas country jail. He made his first recordings for Columbia in 1950, and had immediate success when 'If You've Got The Money, I've Got The Time' and 'I Love You A Thousand Ways' both became US country number 1 hits. He became close friends with Hank Williams, who suggested Frizzell should join the *Grand Ole Opry*. Frizzell replied, 'Look, I got the number-one song, the number-two song, the number-seven song, the number-eight song on the charts and you tell me I need to join the *Opry*'; Williams thought for a while, and commented, 'Darned if you ain't got a hell of an argument'. The following year he had seven Top 10 entries, which included three more number 1 hits, 'I Want To Be With You Always' (which also gained Top 30 status in the US pop charts), 'Always Late (With Your Kisses)' and 'Give Me More More More (Of Your Kisses)'. Further Top 10s followed and as Merle Haggard later sang in his song 'The Way It Was in '51', 'Hank and Lefty crowded every jukebox'. In 1952, Frizzell did join the *Opry* but left after a few months, stating that he did not like it. In 1953, Frizzell moved from Beaumont, Texas, to Los Angeles, where he became a regular on *Town Hall Party*. He had by now become accepted as a national entertainer and he recorded regularly, although the hits became less frequent. His hard-drinking lifestyle was partly to blame, and certainly he and Williams suffered similar troubles. Charles Wolfe quotes Frizzell as once saying: 'All Hank thought about was writing. He did record a number he wrote because I was having trouble with my better half, called "I'm Sorry for You, My Friend".' Some time later, the friendship between the two men was damaged when Frizzell

refused to allow Williams to record 'What Am I Gonna Do With All This Love I Have For You', Frizzell intending to record it himself, although, for some reason, he never did so. Lefty Frizzell became upset about material not being released by Columbia and in 1954, he broke up his band and stopped writing songs; tired of the way he had been exploited, his behaviour became more unpredictable. He was joined in California by his brother David Frizzell, and for a time they toured together. Eventually he charted again with his version of Marty Robbins' 'Cigarettes And Coffee Blues' and in 1959, he enjoyed a number 6 US country hit with 'The Long Black Veil'. The *Town Hall Party* had closed in 1960 and late in 1961, Frizzell decided to move to Nashville. He played bookings wherever he could and made further recordings, achieving minor hits that included 'Don't Let Her See Me Cry'. His career received a welcome boost in 1964 when 'Saginaw, Michigan' became a country number 1 and also entered the US pop charts. This song must rate as one of country music's finest ballads and Frizzell's version has rightly become a standard and worthy of a place in any collection. Twelve more chart entries followed between 1964 and 1972, but only 'She's Gone Gone Gone' reached the Top 20. In the late 60s, he became despondent that Columbia were not releasing his material; the label issued some albums but released few singles that were potential chart hits. In 1968, he even recorded with June Stearns as Agnes And Orville but, concerned at the lack of promotion of his own material, his drinking worsened. In 1972, after 22 years with the label, he left Columbia and joined ABC. The change seemed to work wonders - he set about recording material for albums, resumed playing concerts all over the USA and appeared on network television. He charted with such songs as 'I Can't Get Over You To Change My Life', 'I Never Go Around Mirrors' and 'Railroad Lady', and his album releases proved very popular. His superb song 'That's The Way Love Goes' (his own recording was only issued as a b-side) became a US country number 1 for Johnny Rodriguez in 1974 and Merle Haggard in 1984. Frizzell developed high blood pressure, but refused to take medication to treat the condition since he thought the medicine would interfere with his alcohol consumption. Even in the depths of his drinking, he remained humorous, which led writer Bob Oermann to describe him as 'a lovable, punch-drunk, boozy, puddin'-headed, bear-like kind of a guy who never really got along with Nashville or the *Opry*'. He spent much time between concerts fishing at his home just outside Nashville, and maintained daily contact with his wife despite their recent separation. He was 47 (although he looked older), and aside from the blood pressure, seemed to be in reasonable health. It therefore came as a surprise to most when, on the morning of 19 July 1975, he suffered a massive stroke, and though rushed to Nashville's Memorial Hospital, he died later that evening of the resulting haemorrhage. Ironically, at the time of his death, he had a chart hit with the song 'Falling'.

Lefty Frizzell was a great songwriter and one of the best stylists that the world of country music has ever seen. His singing was distinctive, with a unique style of pronunciation and a laid-back delivery and gentle vibrato that may have appeared lazy, but was in fact part of a carefully designed pattern that he alone mastered. The bending of words as emphasized in 'Alway-yayys Lay-yate' (Always Late) and similar songs led to him being described as a genius for phrasing. John Pugh once described his singing as 'a compelling, ethereal, transcendent vocal quality that has produced some of the most hauntingly beautiful sounds ever to emanate from a pair of human vocal chords'. His influence is evident on later performers such as Merle Haggard, John Anderson, Stoney Edwards, Randy Travis and George Strait, who, although not perhaps intentionally trying to imitate their mentor, are readily identifiable as students of Frizzell. Since his death many artists have recorded tribute songs, while some have even recorded complete albums, including Willie Nelson (*To Lefty From Willie*) and brother David Frizzell (*David Sings Lefty*). Lefty Frizzell was elected to the Nashville Songwriters' Association International Hall Of Fame in 1972 and inducted into the Country Music Hall Of Fame in 1982.

● ALBUMS: *The Songs Of Jimmie Rodgers* 10-inch album (Columbia 1951)★★★★, *Listen To Lefty* 10-inch album (Columbia 1952)★★★★, shared with Carl Smith and Marty Robbins *Carl, Lefty & Marty* (Columbia 1956)★★★★, *The One And Only Lefty Frizzell* (Columbia 1959)★★★★, *Lefty Frizzell Sings The Songs Of Jimmie Rodgers* (Harmony 1960)★★★★, *Saginaw, Michigan* (Columbia 1964)★★★, *The Sad Side Of Love* (Columbia 1965)★★★, *Lefty Frizzell's Country Favorites* (Harmony 1966)★★★, *Lefty Frizzell Puttin' On* (Columbia 1967)★★★, *Mom And Dad's Waltz (& Other Great Country Hits)* (Harmony 1967)★★★, *Signed Sealed And Delivered* (Columbia 1968)★★★, *The Legendary Lefty Frizzell* (ABC 1973)★★★, *The Classic Style Of Lefty Frizzell* (1975)★★★, *Lefty Frizzell In 1951* (1982)★★★, *The Legend Lives On* (1983)★★★, *The Legendary Last Sessions* (MCA 1986)★★★ *Lefty Goes To Nashville* (Rounder 1988)★★★.

● COMPILATIONS: *Lefty Frizzell's Greatest Hits* (Columbia 1966)★★★★, *Remembering . . . The Greatest Hits Of Lefty Frizzell* (Columbia 1975)★★★, *The ABC Collection-Lefty Frizzell* (ABC 1977)★★★★, *Treasures Untold: The Early Recordings Of Lefty* (Rounder 1980)★★★, *Lefty Frizzell* (Columbia Historic Edition 1982)★★★, *American Originals* (Columbia 1990)★★★, *The Best Of Lefty Frizzell* (Rhino 1991)★★★★, *His Life - His Music* 14-LP box set (Bear Family 1984)★★★★ reissued as *Life's Like Poetry* 12-CD box set (Bear Family 1992)★★★★, *That's The Way Love Goes: The Final Recordings Of Lefty Frizzell* (Varese Sarabande 1997)★★★, *Look What Thoughts Will Do: The Essential, 1950-1963* (Columbia 1997)★★★★.

● FURTHER READING: *Lefty Frizzell His Life - His Music*, Charles Wolfe. *The Honky Tonk Life Of Country Music's Greatest Singer*, Daniel Cooper.

FULLER, JESSE 'LONE CAT'

b. 12 March 1896, Jonesboro, Georgia, USA, d. 29 January 1976, Oakland, California, USA. A veteran of tent shows, Fuller fashioned himself a unique one-man band of six-string bass (played with his right foot), a combination of kazoo, harmonica and microphone fixed to a harness around his neck, a hi-hat cymbal (played with the left foot) and a 12-string guitar. He came to fame in the late 50s as a result of appearances on US television, where he followed Ramblin' Jack Elliot's lionization via his recording of 'San Francisco Bay Blues'. In the 50s he made three albums of original and traditional material and by the mid-60s became a darling of the 'coffee-house circuit' after Bob Dylan cited him as one of

his influences. Similar success followed in Britain resulting from Donovan's performance of 'San Francisco Bay Blues' on UK Independent Television's *Ready Steady Go* music programme in 1965. Although Fuller's output is meagre his influence is considerable. Eric Clapton provoked renewed interest with his excellent version of 'San Francisco Bay Blues' on his *MTV Unplugged* album in 1992. Original Blues Classics have reissued his albums on CD with the original covers.

● ALBUMS: *Workin' On The Railroad* 10-inch album (World Songs 1954)★★★, *'Frisco Bound* (Cavalier 1955/58)★★★, *Work Songs Blues And Spirituals* (Good Time Jazz 1958)★★★, *The Lone Cat* (Good Time Jazz 1961)★★★, *San Francisco Bay Blues* (Folklore 1964)★★★★, *Railroad Worksong* (1993)★★★★.

FULLER, JOHNNY

b. 20 April 1929, Edwards, Mississippi, USA. Major Fuller moved his family west to Vallejo, California, in 1935, possibly drawn by work in the shipyards. Johnny was a largely self-taught musician and played guitar, his first interest being C&W music, particularly the songs of Ernest Tubb and Gene Autry. At the age of 15, he was singing in church, later forming the Teenage Gospel Singers, who became the Golden West Gospel Singers. In about 1948 he made solo gospel records for Jackson, and for several years performed every Sunday on stations KWBR in Oakland and KRE in Berkeley. In the early 50s he learned piano and organ and played blues in a style reminiscent of Charles Brown, but with less sophistication. This was evident on his first record, 'Train, Train Blues', for Bob Geddins' Rhythm label. Subsequent sessions were sold to Flair and Hollywood. His tribute, 'Johnny Ace's Last Letter', leased to Aladdin, became his first success and put him on the package tour circuit for several years. His 1956 single for Imperial, 'Don't Slam That Door', was later covered by Snooks Eaglin. Later records for Irma and Specialty strayed into rock 'n' roll and rockabilly. He spent much of the 60s outside music, returning to the clubs of Oakland and Richmond at the end of the decade. In 1973 he recorded an album, released in Australia, combining new material with older songs such as 'Fools Paradise', 'Bad Luck Overtook Me' and 'Strange Land', with a band that also featured Philip Walker. Further club and festival work continued through the 70s, since which time nothing further has been reported.

● ALBUMS: *Fuller's Blues* (Diving Duck 1974/1988)★★★.

FULSON, LOWELL

b. 31 March 1921, Tulsa, Oklahoma, USA. Blues guitarist Lowell Fulson (whose surname is often mistakenly misspelled Fulsom) recorded steadily from 1946 until the late 70s and still performs regularly on the US and European club circuits. He began his career in his native Oklahoma, performing with string bands and backing country blues vocalist Alger 'Texas' Alexander in the late 30s. During World War II he was stationed in Oakland, California, where he met record producer Bob Geddins. Following his discharge from the US Navy, Fulson recorded for several labels under the direction of Geddins, including Big Town, Down Beat, Gilt Edge and Trilon. His first hit came in 1950 on the Swing Time label when he reworked Memphis Slim's 'Nobody Loves Me' into 'Every Day I Have The Blues'. At that time his

12-piece orchestra included Ray Charles on piano. Also playing with Fulson around this time was tenor saxophonist Stanley Turrentine. Fulson recorded for Aladdin Records in 1953 and then switched to Checker Records, a subsidiary of Chess Records, the following year. His first side for that company, 'Reconsider Baby', was covered by Elvis Presley. Fulson stayed with Checker Records into the early 60s and then moved to Kent Records, who changed the spelling of his name. Among his biggest hits for Kent were 'Black Nights' in 1965 and 'Tramp' the next year. The latter song, co-written with Jimmy McCracklin, was later a hit for Otis Redding and Carla Thomas. In 1968 Fulson signed with Jewel Records and then recorded for a succession of small labels including Crazy Cajun and Granite. By the early 90s his early work often appeared on reissues, while some of his new material was only being released on minor labels, such as France's Blue Phoenix Records. However, in 1993 the artist received five W.C. Handy Awards, and was inducted into the Blues Hall Of Fame, both for himself and his song, 'Reconsider Baby'.

● ALBUMS: *In A Heavy Bag* (Jewell 1965)★★★, *I've Got The Blues* (Jewell 1965)★★★, *Lowell Fulson* (Kent 1965)★★★★, *Soul* (Kent 1966)★★★★, *Tramp* (Kent 1967)★★★, *Lowell Fulson Now!* (Kent 1969)★★★, *Let's Go Get Stoned* (1971)★★★, *The Ol' Blues Singer* (Jet 1976)★★★, *Lovemaker* (1978)★★★, *Think Twice Before You Speak* (JSP 1984)★★★, *Blue Days, Black Nights* (Ace 1986)★★★, *I Don't Know My Mind* (Bear Family 1987)★★★, *Baby Won't You Jump With Me* (Crown Prince 1988)★★★, *Back Home Blues* (1992)★★★, *Hold On* (Bullseye 1993)★★★, *River Blues* (1993)★★★, *Them Update Blues* (Bullseye 1995)★★★.

● COMPILATIONS: *Man Of Motion* (Charly 1981)★★★, *Everyday I Have The Blues* (1984)★★★★, *Lowell Fulson 1946-57* (Blues Boy 1987)★★★, *San Francisco Blues* (1993)★★★, *Reconsider Baby* (1993)★★★, *Every Day I Have The Blues* (Night Train 1996)★★★★, *Sinner's Prayer* (Night Train 1996)★★★★.

● VIDEOS: *John Lee Hooker/Lowell Fulson/Percy Mayfield* (1992).

FUNNY FACE

George and Ira Gershwin's 1927 Broadway hit *Funny Face* took 30 years to travel from New York to Hollywood, but the wait was well worthwhile. Screenwriter Leonard Gershe discarded the original story entirely and adapted the plot from his own unproduced musical *Wedding Day*. Five songs survived the trip - and so did Fred Astaire, who had co-starred with his sister Adele in *Funny Face* in both New York and London. In this new scenario, Fred played a fashion photographer who transforms a shy, intellectual Greenwich Village librarian (Audrey Hepburn) into a cover girl for a sophisticated magazine. She agrees to go with him to Paris for the photo-shoot so that she can meet her intellectual mentor, who is portrayed in the film as a Jean-Paul Sartre figure, the founder of the then popular Existentialist movement. However, he and his philosophies are soon forgotten shortly after the elegant Astaire takes her in his arms and the magical music begins. Although Astaire was in his late 50s, the years seemed to fall away as he recreated the wonderful numbers from 30 years earlier, such as 'Funny Face', ''S Wonderful', 'He Loves And She Loves', and 'Let's Kiss And Make Up'. Hepburn, too, was charming on 'How Long Has

This Been Going On?', which had been written for the original show but was cut before the New York opening night. Kay Thompson gave an outstanding performance as the magazine editor with lots of pizzazz, and duetted with Astaire on another Gershwin song, 'Clap Yo' Hands', which had been used previously in the musical *Oh, Kay!* (1926). Leonard Gershe and Roger Edens contributed 'Bonjour Paris', 'On How To Be Lovely' and 'Think Pink', which was the opening number in what is generally regarded as a visually gorgeous movie. Much of the credit for that aspect of the production was owing to fashion photographer Richard Avedon's work as visual consultant. Ray June photographed the film in Technicolor and VistaVision. *Funny Face* was originally conceived by the Arthur Freed Unit at MGM, who, for various reasons, decided not to proceed with it themselves and sold it to Paramount, along with the services of MGM stalwarts such as Edens, Gershe, director Stanley Donen, dance director Eugene Loring, and music arranger Adolph Deutsch. In 1992 *Funny Face* was released on laserdisc with its colour enhanced and in a slightly 'letterboxed' format.

G-CLEFS

This US doo-wop-styled vocal group consisted of brothers Teddy, Chris, Timmy and Arnold Scott and friend Ray Gibson, all from Roxbury, Massachusetts, USA. The quintet, who began singing gospel, were spotted by Pilgrim Records' Jack Gould and in 1956 their first release, 'Ka Ding Dong' (on which Freddy Cannon is reputed to have played guitar), reached the R&B Juke Box Top 10 and the US Top 40 pop chart. It probably would have been a bigger hit but for cover versions by two name acts, the Diamonds and Hilltoppers. Following another release on Pilgrim and two on Paris they decided to put their singing careers on ice and finish their schooling. After the youngest member Arnold left school in 1960 they re-formed and, with help from Gould, joined Terrace Records. Their first release, a version of the Four Tunes' song 'I Understand' cleverly combined with the chorus of 'Auld Lang Syne', gave them their only US Top 10 entry and five months later (around New Year) their sole UK Top 20 hit. The follow-up 'A Girl Has To Know' charted, but later releases including ones on Loma, Regina and Veep brought them no further success. Freddie And The Dreamers had a UK Top 5 hit with a cover version of their arrangement of 'I Understand' in 1964.

GADDY, BOB

b. 4 February 1924, Vivian, West Virginia, USA. Gaddy took a childhood interest in the piano from watching his minister, Clayton Jones, playing in church. Gospel music remained his musical focus until he was drafted into the army in 1943. Transferred to the San Francisco area, he frequented the local clubs and bars, encouraged by his friends to play the latest boogie hits. Demobbed in 1946, he made his way to New York, where he met Brownie McGhee and sat in with his band, the Three B's. Soon afterwards, he and McGhee formed the Mighty Houserockers and played a four-year residency at Billy's Tavern, a New Jersey nightclub. Through McGhee, Gaddy made records for Jackson, Jax, Dot and Harlem, before signing with Old Town in 1955. Over the next five years, records such as 'Operator', 'Paper Lady' and 'Woe, Woe Is Me' achieved success principally in the New York area, but were popular enough for him to tour the Midwest and the south. Other tracks from his nine singles tended to be disguised rewrites of more popular songs by artists such as Chuck Willis and Ray Charles. As the 50s ended, Gaddy formed a new partnership with guitarist Larry Dale which lasted until the 70s. When rediscovered in 1986, he was working as a cook in a Madison Avenue restaurant.
● ALBUMS: *Rip'n'Run* (Ace 1986)★★★, *Bob Gaddy And Friends* (Moonshine 1986), *Harlem Hit Parade* (Ace 1987)★★★, *Harlem Blues Operator* (Ace 1993)★★★, *Old Town Blues Volume 1 Downtown Sides* (Ace 1993)★★★.

GAINES, ROY

b. 12 August 1934, Houston, Texas, USA. The brother of Grady Gaines, Roy became interested in the electric guitar at an early age and began fraternizing with other local young blues guitarists such as Clarence Hollimon and Johnny Copeland. Gaines made his debut with an obscure release on the Miami-based Chart label before coming to the attention of local Houston bandleader and head of Duke Records' house band, Bill Harvey. Gaines was featured with Harvey's band on various releases by Big Mama Thornton and Bobby Bland in 1955 for the Duke and Peacock labels, before being enticed away by an impressed Chuck Willis. After moving to New York City, Gaines recorded with Willis for Atlantic as well as signing to RCA Victor's Groove subsidiary under his own name. This resulted in two releases in 1956. The following year he signed to DeLuxe, returned to Victor in 1958 and experienced a lean decade in the 60s with only two releases on the small Del-Fi and Uni labels. In the 70s, Gaines was again in demand, both for public appearances and as guitarist with the celebrated Crusaders. In 1981, Red Lightnin Records interrupted his busy touring schedule and recorded a fine album, *Gainelining*, which underlined Gaines' four decades of musical influence.
● ALBUMS: *Gainelining* (Red Lightnin 1981)★★★★.

GAMLEY, DOUGLAS

b. 13 September 1924, Melbourne, Australia. Composer, pianist, musical director and arranger - Douglas Gamley has played an important part in the musical scene of Britain and Australia since the early 50s. Initially he specialized in film work, and he acknowledges the valuable guidance he received from Robert Farnon who assisted him on several projects. More recently he has concentrated on concert work, especially with the Melbourne-based Australian 'Pops'

Orchestra, which he frequently conducts. He also had a spell (from 1976 onwards) as assistant musical director for the Vancouver Opera. Like many composers working in films, Gamley spent much of his time collaborating with other composers, often not receiving any screen credit. It is not uncommon for major writers to hire 'assistants' who often score the majority of the music in the film. In this capacity Gamley has worked with Richard Addinsell, John Hollingsworth, Bruce Montgomery (who did the early *Carry On* films), Kenneth V. Jones, Miklos Rozsa (Gamley orchestrated half of *El Cid*) and Henry Mancini. His list of scores is impressive: *Jumping For Joy* - orchestrator for Larry Adler (1955), *One Wish Too Many* (1956), *High Flight* - with Kenneth V. Jones, title march by Eric Coates (1957), *The Prince And The Showgirl* - orchestrator for Richard Addinsell (1957), *The Admirable Crichton* - dances by Richard Addinsell (1957), *Fire Down Below* - with Kenneth V. Jones (1957), *Gideon's Day* - also known as *Gideon Of Scotland Yard* (1958), *A Tale Of Two Cities* - orchestrator for Richard Addinsell (1958), *Cry From The Streets* - orchestrator for Larry Adler (1958), *Another Time, Another Place* (1958), *Tom Thumb* - dance sequences by Ken Jones (1958), *Beyond This Place* aka *Web Of Evidence* (1959), *The Rough And The Smooth* aka *Portrait Of A Sinner* (1959), *Tarzan's Greatest Adventure* (1959), *The Ugly Duckling* (1959), *City Of The Dead* - with Kenneth V. Jones (1960), *Foxhole In Cairo* - period music by Ken Jones (1960), *Light Up The Sky* (1960), *Watch It Sailor* (1960), *Carry On Cruising* - theme and two cues by Bruce Montgomery (1961), *Macbeth* - orchestrator for Richard Addinsell (1961), *The Roman Spring Of Mrs Stone* - orchestrator for Richard Addinsell (1961), *The Canadians* (1961), *The War Lover* - orchestrator for Richard Addinsell (1962), *Charade* - orchestrator for Henry Mancini (1964), *A Shot In The Dark* - orchestrator for Henry Mancini (1964), *The Return Of Mr. Moto* (1965), *Rotten To The Core* - musical director (score by Michael Dress) (1966), *The Family Way* - musical director (score Paul McCartney) (1966), *The Deadly Affair* - musical director (score Quincy Jones) (1966), *Arabesque* - orchestrator for Henry Mancini (1966), *Two For The Road* - orchestrator for Henry Mancini (1966), *Girl On A Motorcycle* - musical director (score Les Reed) (1968), *Spring And Port Wine* (1970), *Sunday Bloody Sunday* - with Ron Geesin (1971), *Tales From The Crypt* (1972), *Asylum* (1972), *And Now The Screaming Starts* (1972), *Vault Of Horror* (1973), *The Beast Must Die* (1974), *The Little Prince* - musical director (score Alan Jay Lerner and Frederick Loewe) (1974), *Return Of The Pink Panther* - orchestrator for Henry Mancini (1974), *The Land That Time Forgot* (1974), *From Beyond The Grave* (1974), *Madhouse* - also known as *The Return Of Dr. Death* (1974), *The Monster Club* (1975), *Enigma* with Marc Wilkinson (1983). Douglas Gamley's own compositions include 'London Bridge March', 'Souvenir de Granada' and 'Prater Fest'. As a pianist he has recorded an album of Robert Farnon compositions (Delyse Envoy 1960). By far his most extensive work in the recording studios has been numerous titles arranged and conducted for *Reader's Digest*, including some under the pseudonym Eric Hammerstein.

GARLAND, JUDY

b. Frances Gumm, 10 June 1922, Grand Rapids, Minnesota, USA, d. 22 June 1969. The Gumms were a theatrical family. Parents Frank and Ethel had appeared in vaudeville as Jack and Virginia Lee, and later, with the addition of their first two daughters, Mary Jane and Virginia, they appeared locally as 'The Four Gumms'. 'Baby Frances' joined the troupe when she was just over two years of age, and it was quickly apparent that with her arrival, even at that early age, the Gumm family had outgrown their locale. The family moved to Los Angeles, where all three girls were enrolled in a dance school. When Frank Gumm bought a run-down theatre in Lancaster, a desert town north of Los Angeles, the family moved again. Domestic problems beset the Gumm family throughout this period and Frances's life was further disrupted by Ethel Gumm's determined belief in her youngest daughter's showbusiness potential. The act had become the Gumm Sisters, although Baby Frances was clearly the one audiences wanted to see and hear. In 1933 Ethel Gumm returned to Los Angeles, taking the girls with her. Frances was again enrolled in a theatrical school. A visit to Chicago was an important step for the girls, with the youngest once more attracting the most attention; here too, at the urging of comedian George Jessell, they changed their name to the Garland Sisters. On their return to Los Angeles in 1934 the sisters played a successful engagement at Grauman's Chinese Theater in Hollywood. Soon afterwards, Frances was personally auditioned by Louis B. Mayer, head of MGM. Deeply impressed by what he saw and heard, Mayer signed the girl before she had even taken a screen test. With another adjustment to her name, Frances became Judy Garland. She made her first film appearance in *Every Sunday* (1936), a short musical film that also featured Deanna Durbin. Her first major impact on audiences came with her third film, *Broadway Melody Of 1938*, in which she sang 'Dear Mr Gable' (to a photograph of Clark Gable), seguing into 'You Made Me Love You'. She was then teamed with MGM's established child star Mickey Rooney, a partnership that brought a succession of popular films in the 'Andy Hardy' series. By now, everyone at MGM knew that they had a star on their hands. This fact was triumphantly confirmed with her appearance in *The Wizard Of Oz* (1939), in which she sang 'Over The Rainbow', the song with which she would subsequently always be associated. Unfortunately, this period of frenzied activity came at a time when she was still developing physically. Like many young teenagers, she tended to put on weight, which was something film-makers could not tolerate. Undoubtedly, they did not want a podgy celebrity, and continuity considerations could not allow their star to change appearance during the course of the film. Regardless of the reason, she was prescribed some drugs for weight control, others to ensure she was bright and perky for the long hours of shooting, and still more to bring her down at the end of the day so that she could sleep. This was long before the side effects of amphetamines (which she took to suppress her appetite) were understood, and no one at the time was aware that the pills she was consuming in such huge quantities were highly addictive. Added to the growing girl's problems were emotional difficulties that had begun during her parents' stormy relationship and were exacerbated by the pressures of her new life. In 1941, against the wishes and advice of her mother and the studio, she married David Rose and soon afterwards became pregnant, but was persuaded by her mother and Mayer to have an abortion. With her personal life already on a downward spiral, Garland's successful film career conversely took a further upswing. In 1942 she appeared in *For Me And My Gal*, then made *Presenting Lily Mars*, *Thousands Cheer*, *Girl Crazy* (all 1943), *Meet Me In St Louis* (1944), *The Harvey Girls*, *Ziegfeld Follies* and *Till The Clouds Roll By* (all 1946). Garland's popularity extended beyond films into radio and records, but her private life was still in disarray. In 1945 she divorced Rose and married Vincente Minnelli, who had directed her in *Meet Me In St Louis*. In 1946 her daughter, Liza Minnelli, was born. The late 40s brought more film successes with *The Pirate*, *Easter Parade*, *Words And Music* (all 1948) and *In The Good Old Summertime* (1949). Although Garland's career appeared to be in splendid shape, in 1950 her private life was fast deteriorating. Pills, alcohol and severe emotional disturbances led to her failing to appear before the cameras on several occasions and resulted in the ending of her contract with MGM. In 1951 her marriage to Minnelli also dissolved and she attempted suicide. Her subsequent marriage to Sid Luft and his handling of her career brought an upturn both emotionally and professionally. She made a trip to Europe, appearing at the London Palladium to great acclaim. On her return to the USA she played the Palace Theater in New York for a hugely successful 19-week run. Her film career resumed with a dramatic/singing role in *A Star Is Born* (1954), for which she was nominated for an Oscar. By the late 50s, her problems had returned, and in some cases, had worsened. She suffered nervous and emotional breakdowns, and made further suicide attempts. A straight dramatic role in *Judgement At Nuremberg* (1961), for which she was again nominated for an Oscar, enhanced her reputation. However, her marriage was in trouble, although she and Luft made repeated attempts to hold it together (they had two children, Lorna and Joey). Despite the personal traumas and the professional ups and downs, Garland achieved another huge success with a personal appearance at New York's Carnegie Hall on 23 April 1961, the subsequent album of the concert winning five Grammy Awards. A 1963 television series was disappointing and, despite another good film performance in a dramatic role in *A Child Is Waiting*, and a fair dramatic/singing appearance in *I Could Go On Singing* (both 1963), her career remained plagued with inconsistencies. The marriage with Luft ended in divorce, as did a subsequent marriage. Remarried again in 1969, Garland attempted a comeback in a season at London's Talk Of The Town nightclub, but suffered the indignity of having bread sticks and other objects thrown at her when she turned up late for some performances. On 22 June 1969 she was found dead, apparently from an accidental overdose of sleeping pills. She was at her best in such films as *Meet Me In St Louis* and *The Wizard Of Oz* and on stage for the superb Carnegie Hall concert, and had she done nothing else, she would have earned a substantial reputation as a major singing star. To her powerful singing voice she added great emotional depths, which came not only through artifice but from the often cruel reality of her life. When the catalogue of personal tragedies was added to Garland's performing talent she became something else, a cult figure, and a showbusiness legend. She was a figure that only Hollywood could have created and yet, had she been a character in a melodrama, no one would have believed such a life was possible.

● ALBUMS: *Till The Clouds Roll By* film soundtrack (MGM 1950/55)★★★, *Easter Parade* film soundtrack (MGM

1950/55)★★★, *Words And Music* film soundtrack (MGM 1950/55)★★★, *Summer Stock/The Pirate* film soundtracks (MGM 1950/55)★★★, *Judy Garland Sings* (MGM 1951)★★★, *Judy At The Palace* (Decca 1951)★★★, *The Wizard Of Oz* (Decca 1951)★★★★, *Girl Crazy* film soundtrack (Decca 1953)★★★, *If You Feel Like Singing Sing* (MGM 1955)★★★, *Judy Garland's Greatest Performances* (Decca 1955)★★★, *Miss Show Business* (Capitol 1955)★★★, *Judy Garland With The MGM Orchestra* (MGM 1956)★★★, *The Wizard Of Oz* (MGM 1956)★★★★, *Judy* (Capitol 1956)★★★, *Meet Me In St Louis/The Harvey Girls* film soundtracks (Decca 1957)★★★, *Alone* (Capitol 1957)★★★, *A Star Is Born* (Columbia 1958)★★★★, *Judy In Love* (Capitol 1958)★★★, *In Love* (Capitol 1958)★★★, *Garland At The Grove* (Capitol 1959)★★★, with John Ireland *The Letter* (Capitol 1959)★★★, *Judy! That's Entertainment* (Capitol 1960)★★★, *Judy At Carnegie Hall* (Capitol 1961)★★★★★, *Pepe* film soundtrack (Colpix 1961)★★, *The Star Years* (MGM 1961)★★★, *The Magic Of Judy Garland* (Decca 1961)★★★, *The Hollywood Years* (MGM 1962)★★★, *Gay Purr-ee* film soundtrack (Warners 1962)★★, *The Garland Touch* (Capitol 1962)★★★, *I Could Go On Singing* film soundtrack (Capitol 1963)★★★★, *Our Love Letter* (Capitol 1963)★★★, *Just For Openers* (Capitol 1964)★★★, with Liza Minnelli *Live At The London Palladium* (Capitol 1965)★★★, *Judy Garland* (1965)★★★, *Judy Garland At Home At The Palace* (ABC 1967)★★★, *The Last Concert 20-7-68* (Paragon 1984)★★★, *Judy Garland Live!* recorded 1962 (Capitol 1989)★★★, *Judy Garland On Radio: 1936-44, Volume One* (Vintage Jazz Classics 1993)★★★.

● COMPILATIONS: *The Very Best Of Judy Garland* (MGM 1962)★★★, *The Hits Of Judy Garland* (Capitol 1963)★★★★, *The Best Of Judy Garland* (Decca 1964)★★★, *The Judy Garland Deluxe Set* 3-LP box set (Capitol 1957)★★★★, *The ABC Years* (1976)★★★, *The Beginning* (1979)★★★, *The Young Judy Garland 1938-42* (MCA 1983)★★★, *Golden Greats* (MCA 1985)★★★, *Collection* (Castle 1986)★★★, *The Capitol Years* (Capitol 1989)★★★★, *Great MGM Stars* (MGM 1991)★★★, *The One And Only* 3-CD box set (Capitol 1991)★★★, *The Complete Decca Masters (Plus)* 4-CD box set (1994)★★★★, *Child Of Hollywood* (CDS 1994)★★★, *Collectors' Gems From The M-G-M Films* (R2 1997)★★★.

● VIDEOS: *Best Of Judy Garland* (World Of Video 1988), *Judy Garland In Concert* (RCA/Columbia 1988).

● FURTHER READING: *Judy: The Films And Career Of Judy Garland*, Joe Morella and Edward Epstein. *The Other Side Of The Rainbow: With Judy Garland On The Dawn Patrol*, Mel Tormé. *Weep No More, My Lady: An Intimate Biography Of Judy Garland*, Mickey Deans. *Judy With Love*, Lorna Smith. *Judy*, Gerold Frank. *Rainbow: The Stormy Life Of Judy Garland*, Christopher Finch. *Judy Garland: A Mortgaged Life*, Anne Edwards. *Little Girl Lost: The Life And Hard Times Of Judy Garland*, Al DiOrio. *The Young Judy*, David Dahl and Barry Kehoe. *Judy & Liza*, James Spada and Karen Swenson. *Judy: Portrait Of An American Legend*, Thomas J. Watson and Bill Chapman. *The Complete Judy Garland*, Emily R. Coleman. *Rainbow's End: The Judy Garland Show*, Coyne Stephen Sanders. *Judy Garland*, David Shipman.

● FILMS: *Every Sunday* (1936), *Pigskin Parade* (1936), *Broadway Melody Of 1938* (1938), *Thoroughbreds Don't Cry* (1938), *Everybody Sing* (1938), *Listen Darling* (1938), *Love Finds Andy Hardy* (1938), *The Wizard Of Oz* (1939), *Babes In Arms* (1939), *Andy Hardy Meets A Debutante* (1939), *Strike Up The Band* (1940), *Little Nellie Kelly* (1940), *Ziegfeld Girl* (1941), *Life Begins For Andy Hardy* (1941), *Babes On Broadway* (1941), *For Me And My Gal* (1942), *We Must Have Music* (1942), *Presenting Lily Mars* (1943), *Girl Crazy* (1943), *Thousands Cheer* (1943), *Meet Me In St. Louis* (1944), *Under The Clock* (1945), *The Harvey Girls* (1946), *Till The Clouds Roll By* (1946), *Ziegfeld Follies* (1946), *The Pirate* (1948), *Easter Parade* (1948), *Words And Music* (1948), *In The Good Old Summertime* (1949), *Summer Stock* (1950), *A Star Is Born* (1954), *Pepe* (1960), *Judgment At Nuremberg* (1961), *A Child Is Waiting* (1962), *I Could Go On Singing* (1963).

GARNER, ERROLL

b. 15 June 1921, Pittsburgh, Pennsylvania, USA, d. 2 January 1977. A self-taught pianist, Garner played on the radio at the age of 10 and within a few more years was playing professionally in his home-town. Among the bands with which he played during this period were those led by Leroy Brown and, reputedly, Fate Marable. In 1944 Garner moved to New York and began working in nightclubs, including the Rendezvous and the Melody Bar. He became a popular and successful performer in these establishments, but also enjoyed playing at the more jazz-orientated venues along 52nd Street, such as Tondelayo's and the Three Deuces. For a short time, he worked in a trio led by Slam Stewart, but soon formed his own trio. For the rest of his life, with only occasional exceptions, Garner worked as leader of a trio or as a soloist. Throughout the 50s, 60s and early 70s, he toured the USA, playing prestigious club and hotel engagements, appearing at festivals and on radio and television. He also visited Europe and the UK, where he appeared on television, and in 1962 he had an album in the UK charts. During these years, Garner recorded numerous albums, some of them, such as the classic *Concert By The Sea*, becoming virtual fixtures in the catalogue. Although Garner taught himself to play, he never learnt to read music, yet he contrived to create several jazz tunes, including one, 'Misty', that became a standard when Johnny Burke added a lyric. Slight echoes of the full sound of Earl 'Fatha' Hines occasionally appear in Garner's playing, as do touches that suggest he had absorbed the work of the stride piano players, yet throughout the bulk of his vast output, Garner remains unique. Playing consistently to a very high standard, he developed certain characteristics that bear few resemblances to other pianists. Notably, these include a plangent left-hand, block-chorded pulse, a dancing pattern of seemingly random ideas played with the right hand in chords or single notes, and playful introductions, which appear as independent miniature compositions, only to sweep suddenly, with apparent spontaneity and complete logic, into an entirely different song. Sumptuously romantic on ballads, and fleet and daring on up-tempo swingers, Garner's range was wide. Nicknamed 'The Elf', more, perhaps, for his diminutive stature than for the impish good humour of those introductions, Garner was the first jazz pianist since Fats Waller to appeal to the non-jazz audience, and the first jazzman ever to achieve popular acclaim from this audience without recourse to singing or clowning. Dudley Moore acknowledges much of his style to Garner, and 'swinging 60s piano jazz' owes a massive debt to him. Stylistically, Garner is in a category of which he is, so far, the only member. Since his death in January 1977, there has been no sign that any other pianist other than Keith Jarrett is following his independent path in jazz.

● ALBUMS: *Free Piano Improvisations Recorded By Baron Timme Rosenkrantz At One Of His Famous Gaslight Jazz Sessions* reissued as *Early Erroll* (Dial 1949),★★★ *Piano Moods* (Columbia 1950)★★, *Rhapsody* (Atlantic 1950)★★, *Erroll Garner Volume 1* (Dial 1950)★★★, *Erroll Garner Playing Piano Solos, Volume 1* (Savoy 1950)★★★, *Erroll Garner Playing Piano Solos, Volume 2* (Savoy 1950)★★★, *Erroll Garner Playing Piano Solos, Volume 3* (Savoy 1950)★★★, *Erroll Garner Playing Piano Solos, Volume 4* (Savoy 1951)★★★, *Gone With Garner* (Mercury 1951)★★★, *Gems* (Columbia 1951)★★, *Erroll Garner At The Piano* (Mercury 1951)★★★, *Erroll Garner At The Piano* (Atlantic 1951)★★★, *Passport To Fame* (Atlantic 1952)★★★, *Solo Flight* (Columbia 1952)★★★, *Piano Solos Volume 2* (Atlantic 1952)★★★, *Overture To Dawn Volume 1* (Blue Note 1952)★★★★, *Overture To Dawn Volume 2* (Blue Note 1952)★★★★, *Piano Stylist* reissued as *Piano Variations* (King 1952)★★★, *Separate Keyboards* (Savoy 50s)★★, *Long Ago And Far Away* (Columbia 50s)★★★, *Erroll Garner At The Piano* (Savoy 1953)★★★, *Erroll Garner At The Piano* (Columbia 1953)★★★, *Overture To Dawn Volume 3* (Blue Note 1953)★★★, *Overture To Dawn Volume 4* (Blue Note 1953)★★★, *Overture To Dawn Volume 5* (Blue Note 1953)★★★, *Erroll Garner Plays For Dancing* (Columbia 1953)★★★, *Body And Soul* (Columbia 1953)★★★★, *Mambo Moves Garner* (Mercury 1954)★★, *Solitaire* (Mercury 1954)★★★, *Garnering* (EmArcy 1954)★★★★, *Contrasts* (EmArcy 1954)★★★, *Afternoon Of An Elf* (Mercury 1955)★★, *Garnerland* (Columbia 1955)★★★, *Penthouse Serenade* (Savoy 1955)★★★, *Serenade To Laura* (Savoy 1955)★★★, *Gone Garner Gonest* (Columbia 1955)★★★, *Erroll!* (EmArcy 1956)★★★★, *The Greatest Garner* (Atlantic 1956)★★★★, *He's Here! He's Gone! He's Garner* (Columbia 1956)★★★, *Concert By The Sea* (Columbia 1956)★★★★★, *Most Happy Piano* (Columbia 1957)★★★, *Other Voices* (Columbia 1957)★★, *Soliloquy* (Columbia 1957)★★★, *Erroll Garner* (Ron-lette 1958)★★★, *Encores In Hi-Fi* (Columbia 1958)★★★, *Paris Impressions* (Columbia 1958)★★★★, *Paris Impressions Volume 2* (Columbia 1958)★★★★, *Perpetual Motion* (Atlantic 1959)★★★, *The One And Only Erroll Garner* (Columbia 1960)★★★, *Swinging Solos* (Columbia 1960)★★★, *Dreamstreet* (ABC-Paramount 1961)★★★, *The Provocative Erroll Garner* (Columbia 1961)★★★★, *Closeup In Swing* (ABC-Paramount 1961)★★★, *Informal Piano Improvisations* (Baronet 1962)★★★, *Misty* (Mercury 1962)★★★★, *The Concert Garner In England* (1963)★★★★, *One World Concert* (Reprise 1963)★★★, *Seeing Is Believing* (Mercury 1964)★★★, *A Night At The Movies* (1965)★★★, *Now Playing* (MGM 1966)★★★, *Campus Concert* (MGM 1966)★★★, *That's My Kick* (MGM 1967)★★★, *Up In Erroll's Room* (MGM 1967)★★★.

● COMPILATIONS: *Historical First Recordings* (1944)★★★★, *Overture To Dawn* (1944)★★★, *Passport To Fame* (1944)★★★, *Early Erroll: 1945 Stride Volumes 1 & 2* (1945)★★★★, *Gemini* (Decca 1978)★★★, *The Great Garner* (Atlantic 1979)★★★, *Complete Savoy Sessions Volume 1 1945-49 recordings* (RCA 1986)★★★, *Yesterdays* (1945-49)★★★, *The Elf* (1945-49)★★★, *Cocktail Time* (1947)★★★, *Body & Soul* (1951-52)★★★★, *Erroll Garner Plays Gershwin And Kern* (1958-65)★★★, *Complete Savoy Sessions Volume 2 1949 recordings* (RCA 1986)★★★, *Jazz Portraits* (Jazz Portraits 1993)★★★.

● FURTHER READING: *Erroll Garner: The Most Happy Piano*, James M. Doran.

GATEWAY SINGERS

Like many groups formed during the popular commercial folk explosion of the late 50s, the Gateway Singers had a relatively short life. The line-up consisted of Jerry Walter (vocals, banjo), Elmerlee Thomas (vocals), Lou Gottleib (bass) and Travis Edmondson (guitar). Following a path started by others, such as the Almanac Singers and the Weavers, they became one of the better-known US groups in the field at the time. Gottleib left the group in 1959, after the group's two releases on Decca, and was replaced by Ernie Sheldon as lead guitar player. The group split up in 1961, at the height of the folk boom. For a time, the Gateway Trio, comprising Jerry Walter, Milt Chapman (bass, vocals), Betty Mann (guitar, vocals), continued performing. After releasing albums for Capitol Records, the trio broke up.

● ALBUMS: *The Gateway Singers At The Hungry i* (Decca 1956)★★★, *The Gateway Singers In Hi Fi* (Decca 1958)★★★★, *The Gateway Singers On The Lot* (Warners 1959)★★★, *Wagons West* (Warners 1960)★★★, *Down In The Valley* (MGM 1961)★★★, *Hootenanny* (MGM 1963)★★★.

GAY, CONNIE B.

b. Connie Barriot Gay, 22 August 1914, Lizard Lick, North Carolina, USA, d. 3 December 1989. After local education, Gay attended the State University and graduated in 1935. He first worked as a salesman in Washington DC, but in the early 40s, his interest in radio led to his joining the Department of Agriculture and becoming involved with its *National Farm And Home Hour*. In 1946, he became the presenter of *Town And Country*, a one-hour country music show on WARL Arlington, Virginia, working only for a percentage of the advertising monies, but he was shrewd enough to register 'Town And Country' as a trademark. Listener reaction soon saw the show increased to three hours and renamed *Gay Time*. In 1947, after promoting two major sell-out country shows starring Eddy Arnold, Gay moved on towards promotional work. His friendship with Jim Denny, a fellow promoter but also the manager of the *Grand Ole Opry*, led to Gay promoting *Opry* acts and quickly establishing himself as a major promoter. His shows gained network coverage on radio and television and he was never short of promotional gimmicks. He arranged train tours to Nashville, river cruises on the Potomac, country concerts starring the major acts at many prestigious 'intown' venues and even Special Service Road Shows, which toured to US bases overseas. In the late 50s, an alcohol problem ended his marriage and saw him disappear for a time when he entered Alcoholics Anonymous. In 1961, he remarried and with his wife's financial help, he relaunched his promotional activities. He promoted major radio and television shows, including *Town And Country Jamboree*, *Town And Country Time* and *Country Style*. His investments, at one time, made him the owner of nine radio stations. He was involved in the discovery of Patsy Cline and promoting Roy Clark and Jimmy Dean to major stardom. In 1960, after failing to become the Governor of the Virgin Islands, he relocated to McLean, Virginia. He was inducted into the Country Music

Hall Of Fame in 1980. His plaque notes that he was an advisor to five Presidents and states: 'His pioneer use of the term country music and registered trademark "Town and Country" were instrumental in bringing country music "uptown". He has served as founding President of the Country Music Association and President of the Country Music Foundation'. Gay died of cancer, at his home in McLean, in 1989.

GAYNOR, MITZI

b. Francesca Mitzi Gerber, 4 September 1930, Chicago, Illinois, USA. This vivacious and extremely talented actress, singer and dancer, reputedly of Hungarian descent, graced several good movie musicals in the 50s, and is probably best remembered as the girl who tried to 'wash that man (Rossano Brazzi) right out of her hair' in *South Pacific* (1958). After taking ballet lessons from an early age, Gaynor danced with the Los Angeles Civic Light Opera while in her early teens, and made a strong impression with Betty Grable and Dan Dailey in her first movie, *My Blue Heaven* (1950). This was followed by one or two straight parts, and a few musicals such as *Golden Girl*, *Bloodhounds Of Broadway*, *Down Among The Sheltering Palms* and *The 'I Don't Care' Girl* (1953), which were not as satisfying. The situation improved as the 50s progressed and she had excellent roles in *There's No Business Like Show Business*, *Anything Goes*, *The Birds And The Bees*, *The Joker Is Wild* and *Les Girls* (1957). She was good, too, in *South Pacific*, but although it remains, to date, the fourth highest-grossing screen musical of the period in the USA, she was reportedly personally disaffected with the experience. Her particular genre of film musicals was becoming extinct, and she worked more often in television and had her own top-rated specials during the 60s. She also toured in stage musical revivals, and, as an accomplished actress, continued to play the occasional comic or dramatic movie role. Gaynor also built up a polished and highly regarded concert and cabaret act. In 1987 she was acclaimed for her nightclub performances, which included a section devoted to Irving Berlin and Fred Astaire, a satirical version of Harry Von Tilzer and Arthur Lamb's nineteenth-century song 'A Bird In A Gilded Cage', and a rousing 'God Bless America' finale. Two years later she embarked on an 11-month, 36-city tour of the USA in a revival of Cole Porter's 1934 show *Anything Goes*, the first time in her long career that she had been on the road in a book musical.
● ALBUMS: *Mitzi* (Verve 1959)★★★, *Mitzi Gaynor Sings The Lyrics Of Ira Gershwin* (Verve 1959)★★★, and soundtrack recordings.

GELDRAY, MAX

b. Max van Gelder, 1916, Amsterdam, Netherlands. Geldray was born into a musical family and reputed to be one of the first harmonica players in Europe. His mother was a classically trained pianist, and the young Geldray inherited his father's ability to play an instrument by ear. He bought his first harmonica when he was aged 16, and taught himself to play it. Influenced by hearing jazz greats such as Louis Armstrong on the radio, Geldray formed his own eight-piece group, which soon evolved into a quartet, the Hollander Boys. They were spotted by the English comedian and impresario Tom Moss, and travelled to the UK where they toured the variety theatres. On his return to Holland Geldray went solo, and played at the Boeuf sur la Toit Club in Brussels, and with the Johnny Fresco Band in Ostend. It was there that he met the French bandleader Ray Ventura, who took him to Paris in the late 30s. Geldray was billed as the 'special attraction' with Ventura's orchestra, which was considered to be one of the top bands in Europe, and he became something of a celebrity, often jamming with the legendary jazz guitarist Django Reinhardt. Just after the outbreak of World War II, Geldray fled to Britain and joined the Princess Irene Brigade. He also did numerous broadcasts for the BBC, and appeared in a special Royal Command Performance at Windsor Castle to celebrate Princess Elizabeth's 16th birthday. In 1945 he rejoined Ray Ventura in Paris for a time, and then returned to Britain and subsequently provided the musical interludes (and, as 'the world's worst actor', spoke a few lines) in the radio series that started out as *Crazy People*, but was soon retitled *The Goon Show*, starring Spike Milligan, Harry Secombe, Peter Sellers and (initially) Michael Bentine. Geldray and his harmonica were ever-present in more than 200 episodes from 1951 until the series ended in 1960. In the early 60s, after working in Australia and on cruise ships, Geldray moved to the USA, but was reunited with his former colleagues in *The Last Goon Of All* in 1972. On returning to America, he took work outside the music business before eventually retiring to Palm Springs, California, emerging only to play the occasional gig. In more recent years Geldray has done extensive voluntary work for the local Stroke Centre and the Betty Ford Centre for drugs and alcohol rehabilitation.
● ALBUMS: *Goon With The Wind* (Parlophone *c*.60s)★★★.
● FURTHER READING: *Goon With The Wind*, Max Geldray with John R. Vance.

GENE KRUPA STORY, THE

This film, made in 1959, is another jazz biopic that misses its target by a mile. Sal Mineo portrays Gene Krupa as a sulky rebel, quite unlike the real-life drummer. Despite other shortcomings, Mineo convincingly played on-screen drums to Krupa's ghosted backing, and, to his credit, the actor later acknowledged the film's mediocrity. On the strength of this telling of Krupa's tale, no one could have imagined that he was a heart-throb idol of millions and one of the greatest showbiz attractions of his era; but then, any film on Krupa that manages to omit Benny Goodman is more than a little short on veracity. Shot in black and white, the film's director was Don Weis. Musically, there are low and high points. Among the former is a scrappy jam session with Red Nichols; the best of the latter is a wonderful version of 'Memories Of You' sung by Anita O'Day. Shelly Manne appears as Dave Tough (he also played the late drummer in *The Five Pennies*). Krupa's return to the stage after a drugs bust that put him in jail and cost him his highly popular band is quite well represented, with Tommy Pederson playing the role of Tommy Dorsey who hired Krupa in 1944. In 1989 a projected remake was abandoned when a leading Hollywood star, interested in the role of Krupa, had to bow out to meet other obligations.

GENIES

From Long Beach, Long Island, New York, USA, the Genies comprised Roy Hammond (lead and tenor), Bill Gains (second tenor), Alexander 'Buddy' Faison (baritone) and

Fred Jones (bass). Claude Johnson was added on lead shortly after the group's formation in 1956. Shad Records released 'Who's That Knockin'' in June 1958. Its placing at number 71 in the *Billboard* charts failed adequately to reflect its enormous east coast popularity. Bill Gains eloped to Canada during a week of performances at the Apollo Theatre supporting the Channels and the Cadillacs, which forced the remaining members to improvise parts of their act to cover the vacated second tenor role. The theme of their debut was then reprised with 'No More Knockin'' for Hollywood Records in 1959. However, three singles for Warwick Records during 1960 and 1961, 'There Goes The Train', 'Just Like The Bluebird' and 'Crazy Feeling', failed to impress, and in truth the band members had long since gone their separate ways. Johnson enjoyed subsequent success as part of a duo with Roland Trone as Don And Juan. Their 'What's Your Name' single reached number 7 in the *Billboard* charts early in 1962 but they, too, were unable to build on their initial success.

GENTLEMEN PREFER BLONDES (FILM MUSICAL)

Carol Channing really started something in 1949 when she created the role of diamond-loving Lorelei Lee in the hit Broadway musical *Gentlemen Prefer Blondes*. Ever since then - even into the early 90s - actresses all over the world have endeavoured to purvey the right mixture of sexiness and vulnerability that was Lorelei, and one of them who achieved it, in this 1953 screen version, was Marilyn Monroe. The concept started with Anita Loos' novel, which she turned into a stage show with the help of Joseph Fields. Charles Lederer's screenplay followed the same familiar path: thoroughly modern 20s girls Lorelei and her best friend, Dorothy Shaw (Jane Russell), travel to Paris with the intention of improving Lorelei's finances and Dorothy's marriage prospects. After causing a certain amount of havoc amongst the city's male population, they return to New York having accomplished their aims (and celebrate with a double wedding). The supporting cast was exceptionally fine, and included Charles Coburn, Tommy Noonan, Elliot Reid, Taylor Holmes, Norma Varden, Steven Geray, the seven-year-old 'frog-voiced' George Winslow, and the 20-year-old George (*West Side Story*) Chakiris. Only three of Jule Styne and Leo Robin's songs survived from the original show: the delicious 'Diamonds Are A Girl's Best Friend' (Monroe), 'A Little Girl From Little Rock' - or rather, 'Two Girls From Little Rock' (Monroe-Russell) - and 'Bye, Bye Baby'. Hoagy Carmichael and Harold Adamson contributed two more: 'Ain't There Anyone Here For Love?', Jane Russell's touching plea to a gymnasium full of muscular males, and the reflective 'When Love Goes Wrong' (Monroe-Russell). The whole affair was a delight, with both Monroe and Russell giving marvellous performances. Jack Cole designed the spirited choreography, and the director was Howard Hawks. Sol C. Seigel produced the film in Technicolor for 20th Century-Fox. A sequel, *Gentlemen Marry Brunettes*, was released in 1955. Jeanne Crain replaced Marilyn Monroe and played Jane Russell's sister in a lacklustre, pale shadow of the original, which, apart from the title song by Herbert Spencer and Earle Hagen, featured a score consisting of old standards.

GERARD, DANYEL

b. 7 March 1939, Paris, France. Gerard spent much of his childhood in South America but he was a Parisian student when taken under the wing of Lucien Morisse, a Gallic equivalent of UK svengali Larry Parnes. Gerard's debut single, a 1958 adaptation (in French) of the nursery rhyme 'Billy Boy', can be cited as the country's first original attempt at rock 'n' roll. Its singer's continued commercial prosperity was stifled by national service in Great Kubylie. During this two-year absence, he was overtaken by Johnny Hallyday, Eddy Mitchell and other newer icons. After Gerard was demobbed, he regained lost ground with 'La Leçon De Twist' and a translation of Pat Boone's 'Speedy Gonzales'. The adoration of his female fans might have palled when he became engaged to chanteuse Christine LeBail, as his subsequent cover version of Ben E. King's 'I (Who Have Nothing)' followed by 'Il Pleut Dans Ma Maison' and 'D'Accord D'Accord' were only moderate hits. Nevertheless, self-managed by that point, he ploughed back his earnings into a lucrative production company, and forged a second career as a songwriter, with Marie LaForet's 'Les Vendanges De L'Amour' and Herve Villand's 'Mourir Ou Vivre' being among his successes.

GIBBS, GEORGIA

b. Freda Gibbons, 17 August 1920, Worcester, Massachusetts, USA. Gibbs has been unfairly maligned by rock critics for building her career in the 50s by covering R&B hits of LaVern Baker and Etta James. In reality, she was a genuinely talented pop vocalist, whose jazz-tinged approach reflected years of experience in the big band era, a period when there was no stigma attached to cover versions. Her big break in showbusiness came in 1936 when she joined the Hudson-DeLange Orchestra, recording for Brunswick Records. That led to a radio career in 1937, including *Your Hit Parade*. There were also recording stints with the bands of Frankie Trumbauer (1940), Artie Shaw (1942) and Tommy Dorsey (1944). On the *Jimmy Durante Camel Caravan* radio show 1943-47, she received her trademark nickname when host Garry Moore dubbed her 'Her Nibs, Miss Gibbs'. Gibbs first entered the charts in 1950 with a cover version of Eileen Barton's 'If I Knew You Were Comin' I'd've Baked A Cake' (number 5 pop), and had her first number 1 hit with 'Kiss Of Fire', a vocal version of the 30s tango instrumental 'El Choclo'. After gaining another hit with 'Seven Lonely Days' (number 5 pop 1953), Gibbs achieved notoriety in 1955 when she hit with two note-for-note cover versions of R&B tunes - 'Tweedledee' (US pop number 2) by Baker and 'Dance With Me Henry' (US pop number 1) by James. 'Kiss Me Another' (US pop number 30) and 'Tra La La' (US pop number 24) kept her in the public eye in 1956, but not for long. Her last chart record was 'The Hula Hoop Song' (US pop Top 40, 1958), which tried to ride the success of the silly toy fad. In the UK, Gibb's chart success was minuscule, constituting two one-week appearances by 'Tweedle Dee' and 'Kiss Me Another', respectively.

● ALBUMS: *Ballin' The Jack* 10-inch album (Coral 1951)★★★★, *Georgia Gibbs Sings Oldies* 10-inch album (Mercury 1953)★★★★, *The Man That Got Away* 10-inch album (Mercury 1954)★★★, *Music And Memories* (Mercury 1956)★★★, *Song Favorites* (Mercury 1956)★★★, *Swingin' With Her Nibs* (Mercury 1956)★★★, *Her Nibs* (Coral

1957)★★★, *Something's Gotta Give* (1964)★★★★, *Call Me* (1966).★★★
● COMPILATIONS: *Georgia Gibbs' Greatest Hits* (1963)★★★★, *Her Nibs Miss Georgia Gibbs* (1994)★★★★.

GIGI

The golden era of MGM film musicals was drawing to a close when this most delightful of films was released in 1958. The original story, by the French novelist Colette, had previously been adapted into a non-musical film in 1948 starring Daniele Delormé and Gaby Morlay, and a play that was subsequently performed in New York and London. Alan Jay Lerner's screenplay for this musical treatment was set in Paris at the turn of the century and tells of the young, strong-willed Gigi (Leslie Caron), who is being brought up by her grandmother, Mamita (Hermione Gingold), and her great-aunt Alicia (Isabel Jeans) to be a courtesan, but breaks with that family tradition - and actually marries her suitor, Gaston Lachailles (Louis Jourdan). Watching over this somewhat shocking situation is Honoré Lachailles (Maurice Chevalier), Gaston's grandfather and a good friend of Mamita. He is also a gentleman with much experience in the delights of romance, and, therefore, is appalled when Gaston, his well-heeled grandson, who, permanently surrounded by lovely ladies and all the other good things in life, suddenly declares that 'It's A Bore'. This was just one of Alan Jay Lerner and Frederick Loewe's memorable songs that were so skilfully integrated into the charming story. Other highlights included Chevalier's 'Thank Heaven For Little Girls' ('Those little eyes so helpless and appealing/One day will flash, and send you crashing through the ceiling'), 'The Parisians' (Caron), 'Waltz At Maxim's (She Is Not Thinking Of Me)' (Jordan), 'The Night They Invented Champagne' (Caron-Jourdan-Mamita), 'Say A Prayer For Me Tonight' (Caron), 'I'm Glad I'm Not Young Anymore' (Chevalier) and 'Gigi (Gaston's Soliloquy)' (Jourdan). For many, the most endearing moment came when Honoré and Mamita reminisced about old times with 'I Remember It Well' (He: 'You wore a gown of gold.' She: 'I was all in blue.' He: 'Am I getting old?' She: 'Oh, no - not you.'). Vincente Minnelli directed the film which was mostly shot on location in Paris, and the producer was Arthur Freed. It was photographed in Metrocolor and CinemaScope by Joseph Ruttenberg, and he won one of the picture's Academy Awards, along with those for Cecil Beaton's sumptuous costumes and best picture, director, writer (Lerner), art direction-set direction (William A. Horning and Preston Ames; Henry Grace and Keogh Gleason), film editing (Adrienne Fazan), best song ('Gigi'), and scoring of a musical picture (André Previn). At the same awards ceremony Maurice Chevalier received a special Oscar 'for his contributions to the world of entertainment for more than half a century'. *Gigi* was one of the Top 10 highest-grossing films of the 50s in the USA, but subsequent stage productions did not appeal. The 1973 Broadway production starring Alfred Drake, Agnes Moorhead, Maria Karnilova and Daniel Massey only ran for three months, and West End audiences saw *Gigi* for seven months in 1985-86.

GIRL CAN'T HELP IT, THE

Perhaps the finest film of the rock 'n' roll era, this 1956 outing has much to recommend it. In a plot illiberally borrowed from Judy Holliday's *Born Yesterday*, struggling agent Tom Ewell is charged by mobster Edmund O'Brien to further the career of his girlfriend (Jayne Mansfield). Risqué (for 1956) references to the latter's physical attributes aside - a running gag throughout - the film is fired by comedy veteran Frank Tashlin's script and direction which, for once, matches the pace and rhythm of the musical interludes. Gene Vincent contributes a memorable 'The Girl Can't Help It', the fledgling talent of Eddie Cochran is heard on 'Twenty Flight Rock' and Fats Domino adds a superb 'Blue Monday'. However, the star is undoubtedly Little Richard, who tears through the title song, 'She's Got It' and 'Ready Teddy'. *The Girl Can't Help It* not only showcased such acts without condescension, it was the first rock 'n' roll film shot in colour. However, the film's strength does not solely rest on these pivotal figures. Tom Ewell is superb as the long-suffering agent, and his hallucinations about a former client immortalized Julie London's 'Cry Me A River'. Edmund O'Brien relished his rare excursion into comedy and the gangster-inspired composition he sang, 'Rock Around The Rock Pile', acted as a thinly veiled sideswipe at exploitative releases made to cash in on fads. Few films embraced rock 'n' roll with similar understanding and respect.

GLAHE, WILL

b. Elberfeld, Germany, 12 February 1902, d. 21 November 1989. This European accordionist-bandleader, in conjunction with his Musette Orchestra, had a big hit in the USA in 1939 with 'Beer Barrel Polka'. The song was based on an original Czechoslovakian melody, 'Skoda Lasky' ('Lost Love'), by Jaromir Vejvoda and Wladimir Timm, with an English lyric by Lew Brown. It sold over a million copies for Glahe, who followed it in the USA with other hits such as 'Hot Pretzels', 'W.P.A. Polka', 'Woodpecker', 'Bartender Polka' and 'You Can't Be True Dear'. It was almost 10 years before Glahe, with his Orchestra and Chorus, made the US charts again, with 'Liechtensteiner Polka' in 1957. The number also had some success in the UK, along with 'The Crazy Otto Rag', which was credited to 'Will Glahe and his Sunshine Quintet'.
● ALBUMS: *In Bavaria* (Decca 1979)★★★, *Golden Will Glahe Album* (Teldec 1986)★★★.

GLEASON, JACKIE

b. Herbert John Gleason, 26 February 1916, Brooklyn, New York, USA, d. 24 June 1987. Gleason was primarily a comedian, starring on stage, screen and television, but he also recorded a number of albums in the 50s and 60s. He established his persona with early films such as *Orchestra Wives* (1942) and several appearances on Broadway (*Artists And Models*, *Follow The Girls* and *Along Fifth Avenue*). However, stardom came with the dawn of the 50s. The formative television series *The Life Of Riley* led to *Cavalcade Of Stars* in 1949, from which Gleason, alongside Art Carney, launched a series of sketches and basic comedy routines. He then fronted a variety/new talent CBS programme *Stageshow* before Tommy and Jimmy Dorsey took over. The programme was notable for introducing Elvis Presley to a television audience. The enormously popular television show *The Honeymooners* followed in 1955, before a series of films leading into the 60s. Notable among these were *The Hustler* (1961), alongside Paul Newman, for which Gleason was nominated for an Oscar as Best Supporting Actor, and *Requiem For A Heavyweight*, the first major play by *The*

Twilight Zone's creator Rod Serling. Gleason also appeared as Buford T. Ford, a law officer prone to mishap in the Burt Reynolds vehicle *Smokey And The Bandit* in 1977. By this time his recording career had largely ended. He had previously written the score for *Gigot* (1962), and his own television theme, 'Melancholy Serenade'. In addition there were several 'mood music' albums on Capitol, which represented his most successful material, and a projected ballet. A string of Top 10 US albums between 1956 and 1957 featured Bobby Hackett and Pee Wee Erwin in his studio orchestras.

● ALBUMS: *Music For Lovers Only* (Capitol 1952/53)★★★, *Lover's Rhapsody* 10-inch album (Capitol 1953)★★★, *Music To Make You Misty* (Capitol 1954)★★★★, *Tawny* (Capitol 1954)★★, *And Awaaay We Go!* TV soundtrack (Capitol 1954/55)★★, *Music Martinis And Memories* (Capitol 1954)★★★, *Music To Remember Her* (Capitol 1955)★★, *Lonesome Echo* (Capitol 1955)★★★★, *Romantic Jazz* (Capitol 1955)★★★, *Music To Change Her Mind* (Capitol 1956)★★★, *Night Winds* (Capitol 1956)★★★★, *Merry Christmas* (Capitol 1956)★★, *Music For The Love Hours* (Capitol 1957)★★★★, *Velvet Brass* (Capitol 1957)★★★★, *Jackie Gleason Presents 'Oooo!'* (Capitol 1957)★★★, *The Torch With The Blue Flame* (Capitol 1958)★★★, *Riff Jazz* (Capitol 1958)★★★, *Take Me Along* film soundtrack (RCA Victor 1959)★★★, *Aphrodisia* (Capitol 1960)★★★, *The Gentle Touch* (Capitol 1961)★★★, *Gigot* film soundtrack (Capitol 1962)★★★, *Movie Themes - For Lovers Only* (Capitol 1963)★★, *Today's Romantic Hits: For Lovers Only* (Capitol 1963)★★, *Today's Romantic Hits: For Lovers Only, Volume 2* (Capitol 1964)★★, *Silk 'N' Brass* (Capitol 1966)★★★, *How Sweet It Is For Lovers* (Capitol 1966)★★★, *A Taste Of Brass For Lovers Only* (Capitol 1967)★★.

● COMPILATIONS: *Close-Up* (Capitol 1969)★★★, *The Romantic Moods Of ...* (Capitol 1997)★★★.

● FURTHER READING: *The Great One: The Life And Legend Of Jackie Gleason*, William A. Henry III. *Jackie Gleason: An Intimate Portrait Of The Great One*, W.J. Weatherby.

● FILMS: *The Hustler* (1961), *Blood Money* (1962), *Gigot* (1962), *Requiem For A Heavyweight* (1963), *Soldier In The Rain* (1964), *Skidoo* (1968), *How To Commit Marriage* (1969), *Don't Drink The Water* (1969), *Smokey And The Bandit* (1977).

GLENN MILLER STORY, THE

Competently directed by Anthony Mann, and featuring a fine James Stewart performance as Miller (portrayed as much more warm-hearted than the real man), this 1953 biopic does not pass up any opportunity for a cliché. Miller's search for a 'new sound' is hounded to death (scratch any ex-sideman of Miller and one would hear a different version of how he achieved it), but the storyline omits the obvious, if dull, solution that it was all a matter of a workmanlike arranger sticking to his trade. The cross-country slogs on a tour of one-night shows are well presented and the studio-assembled band accurately recreates Miller's music. Stewart copes well with his on-screen trombone miming, and off-screen, Joe Yukl (and possibly Murray McEachern) provides the sound. Miller's disappearance, just before Christmas 1944, is tied into a mythical 'gift' to his wife of an arrangement of her favourite tune, 'Little Brown Jug'. In fact, Miller's hit recording of this tune came some years before

his death, but in this way, the film can end without a dry eye in the house. In a jazz club sequence, the 1953 edition of the Louis Armstrong All Stars, including Barney Bigard, William 'Cozy' Cole and Trummy Young, teams up with a handful of 30s swing stars, including Gene Krupa and Babe Russin, to knock spots off 'Basin Street Blues'.

GO JOHNNY GO

Disc jockey Alan Freed, who reputedly coined the phrase 'rock 'n' roll', took part in several 50s genre films, including *Rock Around The Clock* and *Rock Rock Rock*. He assumed the lead role in this 1958 feature, playing to type as a DJ searching for singer Johnny Melody, whose demo recordings proved highly popular with Freed's audience. Chuck Berry also enjoys a (brief) acting part, but is clearly more comfortable performing the title song, plus 'Little Queenie' and 'Memphis, Tennessee', the last of which became a UK Top 10 entry five years later. Rising star Richie Valens contributes 'Ooh My Head' in what would be his only film appearance, while other notable cameos include the Flamingos' 'Jump Children', Eddie Cochran's 'Teenage Heaven', Jackie Wilson's 'You'd Better Know It' and Harvey Fuqua's 'Don't Be Afraid To Love Me'. New Orleans-based singer Jimmy Clanton, who played Melody, provides four songs for the soundtrack, including 'My Own True Love', a US Top 40 entry in 1959. The film did not propel Clanton to stardom, although the singer did enjoy several subsequent hit singles, including 'Go Jimmy Go' (clearly based on his starring feature) and 'Venus In Blue Jeans'.

GOLDEN APPLE, THE

Following its enthusiastic reception at the off-Broadway Phoenix Theatre, New York, USA, in March 1954, *The Golden Apple* was rapidly moved uptown to the Alvin Theatre where it reopened on 20 April. Based on Homer's *Iliad* and *The Odyssey*, John Latouche (book and lyrics) and Jerome Moross (music) transported those epic tales to the state of Washington in the early part of the 20th century. The story concerns the consternation caused in the town of Angel's Roost when a travelling salesman named Paris (Jonathan Lucas) arrives unannounced in a balloon, and takes Helen (Kaye Ballard), the impressionable wife of old Sheriff Menelaus (Dean Michener), off to Rhododendron by-the-sea (not entirely against her will). For some reason, the intrepid Ulysses (Stephen Douglass), who has just returned from the Spanish-American war, leaves his wife Penelope (Priscilla Gillette), and sets off to retrieve the errant Helen. After a decade of excitement and adventure - during which time he engages successfully in fisticuffs with Paris - Ulysses is finally reunited with his incredibly patient spouse. As for the songs - which carried the story almost on their own - Kaye Ballard's languid reading of 'Lazy Afternoon' was one of the high points of a delicious score that is treasured in recordings by stage musical buffs the world over. The other numbers, a mixture of witty spoofs and appealing ballads, included 'Goona-Goona', 'It's The Going Home Together', 'Come Along, Boys', 'Doomed, Doomed Doomed', 'My Picture In The Papers', 'Store-Bought Suit', 'Helen Is Always Willing', 'My Love Is On The Way' and 'Scylla And Charybdis'. This 'brilliant, innovative theatre experience', which was just pipped for a Tony Award by *The Pajama Game*, but which won the New York Drama Critics Award best musical, closed after only 127 performances. It was revived off-Broadway in 1962 (112 performances), and is regarded as something of a musical theatre legend.

GOLDEN DISC, THE

Titled *The In-Between Age* for the USA, *The Golden Disc* starred ill-fated British rock 'n' roll star Terry Dene. This Jack Good discovery was briefly touted as a bona fide star, although none of his three UK chart entries reached the Top 10. A former record packer, Dene briefly enjoyed the limelight upon joining the army, but praise turned to derision when the singer was discharged following a nervous breakdown. The fiancée who 'would wait for him' promptly broke off their engagement and his recording career was left in tatters. He later joined the Salvation Army. Real-life events were certainly more interesting than the plot of this 1957 film, in which the owners of a café turn it into an expresso bar before founding a record label to showcase the acts performing there. With skiffle the fad of the moment, acts including Nancy Whiskey and Sonny Stewart And The Skiffle Kings featured in the cast alongside disc jockey David Jacobs, crooner Dennis Lotis and the exceptional Phil Seamen Jazz Group. Other performers included future impresario Terry Kennedy, Sheila Buxton and Murray Campbell. *The Golden Disc* is not an auspicious feature, but serves as a timely reminder of Terry Dene's all too brief ascendancy.

GONELLA, NAT

b. 7 March 1908, London, England. This great pioneer of British jazz began playing trumpet as a child and toured music halls in a youth band. At the age of 20, Gonella began a seven-year stint in several leading dancebands, including those of Billy Cotton, Roy Fox, Ray Noble and Lew Stone. His 1932 recording of 'Georgia On My Mind' proved immensely popular and later became his theme tune, providing the name for his own band, the Georgians. Heavily influenced by Louis Armstrong, Gonella modelled his playing and singing style on that of the master. In the post-war years, Gonella led his own big and small bands, benefiting from the trad-jazz boom of the early 50s but finally losing out to the subsequent rise of pop music. After several years in obscurity, in the 70s Gonella reappeared on the music scene with a hit record in Holland and, in the 80s, with club and concert engagements, record dates, television appearances and a biography.

● ALBUMS: *Runnin' Wild* (1958)★★★, *The Nat Gonella Story* (1961)★★★★, *Nat Gonella And His Trumpet* (Ace Of Clubs 1967)★★★, *When You're Smiling* (1970)★★★★, *The Music Goes 'Round And 'Round* (1975)★★★★, *My Favourite Things* (1975)★★★, *Wishing You A Swinging Christmas* (1975)★★.

● COMPILATIONS: *Nat Gonella Story* (Note 1978)★★★, *Georgia On My Mind* 1931-46 recordings (Decca 1981)★★★★, *Mister Rhythm Man* 1934-35 recordings (Retrospect 1984)★★★, *Nat Gonella Scrapbook* (Joy 1985)★★★, *Naturally Gonella* 1935 recordings (Happy Days 1986)★★★★, *How'm I Doin'* (Old Bean 1987)★★★, *Yeah Man* 1935-37 recordings (Harlequin 1988)★★★, *Running Wild* (Harlequin 1988)★★★, *Crazy Valves* 1934-35 recordings (Living Era 1988)★★★★, *Nat Gonella Volume 1 1934-35* (Neovox 1990)★★★, *Nat Gonella Volume 2 1932-35* (Neovox 1990)★★★, *The Cream Of Nat Gonella* (Flapper 1991)★★★★, *Hold Tight* (Memoir 1991)★★★.

● FURTHER READING: *The Nat Gonella Story*, Ron Brown and Cyril Brown.

GOODWIN, RON

b. 17 February 1925, Plymouth, Devon, England. An important composer, conductor and arranger, from an early age Goodwin was deeply interested in all things musical, but began his working life outside the business. Eventually, he took a job as a music copier with a firm of music publishers. He also studied trumpet and arranging at the Guildhall School of Music in London, and played trumpet professionally with Harry Gold and wrote arrangements for the bands of Ted Heath and Geraldo. Goodwin made several records, arranging and conducting the backing music for singers, including Petula Clark, and also worked in radio. He has composed music in the classical form, including his 'Drake 400 Concert Suite' and 'New Zealand Suite', but it is as a writer for films that he made his greatest impact. After first writing for documentaries, from the 60s through to the 80s he composed the scores - and generally served as the musical director - for numerous feature films, including *Whirlpool*, *The Witness*, *I'm All Right Jack*, *In The Nick*, *Village Of The Damned*, *The Trials Of Oscar Wilde*, *The Man With The Green Carnation*, *The Man At The Carleton Tower*, *The Clue Of The New Pin*, *Partners In Crime*, *Invasion Quartet*, a series of 'Miss Marple' films starring Margaret Rutherford (*Murder, She Said*, *Murder At The Gallop*, *Murder Most Foul* and *Murder Ahoy*), *The Day Of The Triffids*, *Follow The Boys*, *Of Human Bondage*, *Children Of The Damned*, *633 Squadron*, *A Home Of Your Own*, *Those Magnificent Men In Their Flying Machines*, *Operation Crossbow*, *The Alphabet Murders*, *That Riviera Touch*, *The Trap* (used as the theme for the London Marathon), *Mrs. Brown, You've Got A Lovely Daughter*, *Where Eagles Dare*, *Battle Of Britain*, *The Executioner*, *Frenzy*, *One Of Our Dinosaurs Is Missing*, *Escape From The Dark*, *Ride A Wild Pony*, *Candleshoe*, *Force 10 From Navarone*, *The Spaceman And King Arthur*, *Clash Of Loyalties* and *Valhalla* (1986). He has won several Ivor Novello Awards, including the Entertainment Music Award in 1972, and a Life Achievement Award in 1993. In the 70s Goodwin made concert tours of the UK with an orchestra performing his own film scores. He has continued to broadcast on radio, and has worked extensively in Canada.

● ALBUMS: *Film Favourites* (Parlophone 1954)★★★★, *Music To Set You Dreaming* (Parlophone 1956)★★★, *Out Of This World* (Parlophone 1958)★★★★, *Adventure And Excitement/Music For An Arabian Night* (Parlophone 1958)★★★, *Decline And Fall ... Of A Birdwatcher* film soundtrack (Stateside 1968)★★, *Monte Carlo Or Bust* film soundtrack (Paramount 1969)★★★, *Legend Of The Glass Mountain* (Studio 2 1970)★★★, *Spellbound* (Studio 2 1973)★★★, *Elizabethan Serenade* (MFP 1975)★★★, *I'll See You In My Dreams* (Studio 2 1976)★★★, *Escape From The Dark* film soundtrack (EMI 1976)★★, *Rhythm And Romance* (Studio 2 1977)★★★, with the New Zealand Symphony Orchestra *Going Places* (Studio 2 1978)★★★, *Christmas Wonderland* (One-Up 1978)★★★, with the Bournemouth Symphony Orchestra *Ron Goodwin And The Bournemouth Symphony Orchestra* (Chandos 1980)★★★, *Drake 400 Concert Suite* (Chandos 1980)★★★, *Sounds Superb* (MFP 1981)★★★, with the Royal Philharmonic Orchestra *Projections* (EMI 1983)★★★, *Fire And Romance* (EMI 1984)★★★, with the New Zealand Symphony Orchestra *New Zealand Suite* (Columbia 1984)★★★, *Ron Goodwin Plays Bacharach And David* (Ideal 1984)★★★, *The Love Album* (MFP 1985)★★★, with the Bournemouth Symphony Orchestra *My Kind Of Music* (Chandos 1989)★★★.

● COMPILATIONS: *This Is Ron Goodwin* (EMI 1973)★★★, *Very Best Of Ron Goodwin* (Studio 2 1977)★★★, *First 25 Years* (Studio 2 1978)★★★★.

GOONS

Mutating from Britain's radio show *Crazy People* in 1951, the high summer of the BBC Home Service's *Goon Show* was reflected in UK hit parade entries in 1956 for its spin-off double a-sides, 'I'm Walking Backwards For Christmas'/'Bluebottle Blues' and 'Bloodnok's Rock 'N' Roll'/'Ying Tong Song' - which encapsulated the offbeat humour, topical parodies and musical interludes (under the baton of bandleader Ray Ellington) of the radio series starring Spike Milligan, Peter Sellers, Harry Secombe and, briefly, Michael Bentine. As well as ushering in the strata of comedy that culminated in the late 60s with *Monty Python's Flying Circus*, aspects of the Goons became apparent in the stylistic determination of the Scaffold, the Bonzo Dog Doo-Dah Band and, less directly, the Beatles - particularly in their first two films and in John Lennon's literary output. In reciprocation, a cod-Shakespearian recitation of 'A Hard Day's Night' was among Sellers' solo successes. However, Secombe - whose chart career began before that of the Goons - enjoyed greater success with sonorous ballads, almost topping the British list in 1967 with 'This Is My Song'. Nevertheless, Secombe's next - and last - Top 10 entry came six years later with a reissue of the Goons' 'Ying Tong Song', shortly after the troupe's one-off radio and television reunion during the BBC's 50th anniversary celebrations.

● ALBUMS: *The Best Of The Goon Shows* (Parlophone 1959)★★★★, *The Best Of The Goon Shows Volume 2* (Parlophone 1960)★★★★, *The Last Goon Show Of All* (BBC 1972)★★★, there are also many BBC spoken word cassettes of *The Goon Show*.

GORDON, ARCHIE 'STOMP'

Singer and pianist Gordon led a fine jump quintet throughout the 50s that included Billy Brooks on trumpet and 'Little' Hiawatha Edmundson on tenor saxophone. Beginning with Decca's 48000 R&B series in 1952, with whom the band recorded the insulting 'Damp Rag', the Gordon band recorded excellent tracks for Mercury in 1953 - including an uproarious celebration of the then recent Kinsey Sex Report in 'What's Her Whimsey Dr Kinsey?' - and later recorded for Chess and Savoy in the mid-50s.

GORDON, BARRY

b. 21 December 1948, Brookline, Massachusetts, USA, A precocious Barry Gordon found himself at the number 6 position in the US charts at the age of seven with a novelty song, 'Nuttin' For Christmas'. His first television appearance came at the age of three, followed by numerous other guest slots on programmes hosted by stars such as Jackie Gleason. MGM Records signed Gordon to sing the 'Christmas Song', written by Sid Tepper and Roy Bennett, which quickly

reached the Top 10. Within weeks cover versions were released by such artists as Stan Freberg, Homer And Jethro, Fontane Sisters and Joe Ward, who reached number 20 with his version. Gordon placed only one other single in the charts, another novelty tune called 'Rock Around Mother Goose', in 1956. He went on to act on television and the stage and was still active in those areas in the mid-80s.

GORDON, ROSCO

b. 23 December 1933, Memphis, Tennessee, USA. A self-taught pianist with no acknowledged influences other than a presumed awareness of the work of Amos Milburn and Little Willie Littlefield. Gordon was part of the Beale Streeters group in the late 40s, alongside Johnny Ace, B.B. King and later, Bobby Bland. Ike Turner, then a freelance producer and talent scout, recognized the potential of Gordon's powerful singing and recorded him for Modern. He was still a teenager when he first recorded at Sam Phillips' Memphis Recording Service in January 1951. Phillips sold masters to both Chess Records in Chicago and RPM in Los Angeles, and thus, Gordon's 'Booted' appeared on both labels, a possible factor in its becoming the number 1 R&B hit in the spring of 1952. The follow-up, 'No More Doggin'', was another Top 10 R&B hit and typified what became known as 'Rosco's Rhythm', a loping boogie shuffle rhythm that predated and perhaps influenced Jamaican ska and blue-heat music. Gordon signed to Phillips' own Sun label in 1955, recording a regional hit, 'The Chicken', which led to his appearance in the film *Rock Baby, Rock It* two years later. Moving to New York, he formed the duo Rosco and Barbara, making singles for Old Town. Many tracks recorded during this time remained unissued until the 70s and 80s. His most well-known song reached number 2 in the R&B charts and was recorded in 1960 for the Chicago-based label Vee Jay. With its catchy sax-driven riff, 'Just A Little Bit' captured the imaginations of British R&B groups as well as black record buyers. A version by Merseybeat band the Undertakers was a minor hit in 1964. Further records for ABC, Old Town, Jomada, Rae-Cox and Calla made little impression and in 1970, Gordon created his own label, Bab-Roc, issuing records by himself and his wife Barbara. An album of new compositions plus remakes of his hits was recorded for Organic Productions in 1971 but never released. A brief visit to England in 1982 brought an onstage reunion with B.B. King at London's 100 Club. At that time he was financing recordings from his own cleaning business.

● COMPILATIONS: *The Legendary Sun Performers: Rosco Gordon* (Charly 1977)★★★, *Best Of Rosco Gordon Volume 1* (Ace 1980)★★★, *Rosco Gordon Volume 2* (Ace 1982)★★★, *Keep On Diggin'* (Mr R&B 1981)★★★, *The Memphis Masters* (Ace 1982)★★★, *Rosco Rocks Again* (JSP 1983)★★★, *Bootin' Boogie* (1990)★★★, *Lets Get High* (Charly 1990)★★★.

● FILMS: *Rock Baby, Rock It* (1957).

GORME, EYDIE

b. Edith Gorme, 16 August 1931, New York City, New York, USA. The youngest of three children, Gorme's parents were of Turkish and Spanish origin, and since Spanish was the family language, she grew up speaking it fluently. At the age of three she made her radio debut, singing in a children's programme from a department store. While at the William Howard Taft High School in the Bronx, Gorme was voted 'the prettiest, peppiest cheerleader', starred in the school musicals, and sang with her friend Ken Greengrass's band at the weekends. On leaving school, she worked as a Spanish interpreter with the Theatrical Supply Export Company, before deciding to concentrate on a singing career, with Greengrass as her manager. Her first break came in 1950 when she successfully auditioned for bandleader Tommy Tucker, and toured with him for two months. When that tour ended she spent a year with Tex Beneke before going out on her own, appearing in nightclubs, and on radio and television. After being turned down several times by Arthur Godfrey's talent scouts ('the fourth time I tried, they locked the office door when they saw me coming up the stairs'), Gorme signed for Coral Records in 1952. Her singles included 'Frenesi', 'I've Gotta Crow', 'Tea For Two' and 'Fini', which entered the US Top 20. She also hosted her own radio show, *Cita Con Eydie* (*A Date With Eydie*), which was transmitted to Spanish-speaking countries via the *Voice Of America*. In September 1953, she became a permanent member of Steve Allen's top-rated *Tonight* show, on which she sang, and wrote and performed sketches with another regular, Steve Lawrence. They also introduced Allen's composition 'This Could Be The Start Of Something', which became associated with them as their singing partnership blossomed into romance. Steve Lawrence (b. Stephen Leibowitz, 8 July 1935, Brooklyn, New York, USA), was the son of Eastern European parents and had sung in the choir at his cantor father's synagogue. Lawrence *did* make it onto the *Arthur Godfrey Talent Show*, in 1952, and had made an impression with his version of Tony Martin's hit 'Domino'. An important and influential figure in both Gorme and Lawrence's recording careers was conductor, arranger and producer Don Costa. In February 1956, Gorme deputized at short notice for Billy Daniels at New York's Copacabana nightclub, and was so well received that she returned in July to headline with her own show. In January 1957, she made her Broadway debut in the *Jerry Lewis Stage Show* at the Palace Theatre, and in December, Gorme and Lawrence were married in Las Vegas. Gorme's success in the US singles chart up to this period had included 'Too Close For Comfort', 'Mama, Teach Me To Dance' (both 1956), 'Love Me Forever' (1957) and the number 11 hit 'You Need Hands' (1958). During the summer of 1958 the couple starred in their own weekly one-hour musical variety television show, as a replacement for Steve Allen. Shortly afterwards, Lawrence was inducted into the US Army for two years. Gorme embarked on a country-wide nightclub tour until 1960 when she was reunited with Lawrence at the Copacabana and the Coconut Grove, Los Angeles, and the Sands and Sahara Hotels in Las Vegas. In 1960 they won a Grammy Award for *We Got Us*, their first complete duet album, which was followed by several others, including *Two On The Aisle*, a set of Broadway show numbers and *At The Movies*. In the singles chart, the couple's most successful joint efforts included 'I Want To Stay Here' (1963) and 'I Can't Stop Talking About You' (1964). Eydie received a Grammy Award for Best Popular Female Vocalist for her version of 'If He Walked Into My Life', from Jerry Herman's musical *Mame*. In 1968, the couple appeared on Broadway in *Golden Rainbow*, a musical adaptation of Arnold Schulman's play *A Hole In the Head*, with words and music by Walter Marks. One of the songs, 'I've Gotta Be Me', became the title of a Lawrence album, and also became a

regular part of Sammy Davis Jnr.'s repertoire. In 1969, Gorme and Lawrence recorded their first musical, *What It Was, Was Love*, written for them by Gordon Jenkins. During the 70s and 80s, the couple continued to record and appear regularly on television. Several of their 'specials', commemorating the music of composers such as Cole Porter and George and Ira Gershwin, won awards; *Steve And Eydie Celebrate Irving Berlin* gained a record-breaking seven Emmys. In 1987, they were in a television production of *Alice In Wonderland*, written by Steve Allen, playing the parts of Tweedledum and Tweedledee. In 1989, they released *Alone Together*, on their own GL label. It was for their live performances, however, that they received the most applause. During the 80s, they appeared at venues such as Carnegie Hall in 1981 and 1983, the Universal Amphitheatre, in Los Angeles, Harrah's, Tahoe, and the 1,400-seater Bally's at Las Vegas. Their skilful blend of classy songs (or, as they put it, 'no punk, no funk, no rock, no schlock'), coupled with a brand of humour that has been honed for over 30 years, make them one of the few consistently successful acts of their kind in the world. In 1991, they saw quite a lot of that world, when they joined Frank Sinatra on his year-long *Diamond Jubilee Tour*, to commemorate his 75th birthday.

● ALBUMS: *Delight* (Coral 1957)★★, *Eydie Gorme* (ABC-Paramount 1957)★★★, *Eydie Swings The Blues* (ABC-Paramount 1957)★★★★, *Eydie Gorme Vamps The Roaring '20s* (ABC-Paramount 1958)★★★★, *Eydie In Love ...* (ABC-Paramount 1958)★★★★, *Love Is A Season* (ABC-Paramount 1958)★★★, *Eydie Sings Showstoppers* (ABC-Paramount 1959)★★★★, *Eydie Gorme On Stage* (ABC-Paramount 1959)★★★★, *Eydie Gorme In Dixieland* (ABC-Paramount 1960)★★, *Come Sing With Me* (1961)★★★, *I Feel So Spanish* (1962)★★★, *Blame It On The Bossa Nova* (Columbia 1963)★★★★, *Let The Good Times Roll* (1963)★★★, *Gorme Country Style* (Columbia 1964)★, *Amor* (Columbia 1964)★★★, *More Amor* (Columbia 1965)★★, *Don't Go To Strangers* (Columbia 1966)★★★, with the Trio Los Panchos *Navidad Means Christmas* (1966)★★, *Softly, As I Love You* (Columbia 1967)★★★, *Tonight I'll Say A Prayer* (RCA 1970)★★★, *Tomame O Dejame* (President 1985)★★★, *Come In From The Rain* (President 1985)★★★, *Sings/Canta* (Sound 1987)★★★.

With Steve Lawrence *We Got Us* (ABC-Paramount 1960)★★★★, *Steve And Eydie Sing The Golden Hits* (ABC-Paramount 1960)★★★, *Cozy* (United Artists 1961)★★★, *Two On The Aisle* (United Artists 1963)★★★, *Our Best To You* (ABC-Paramount 1964)★★★, *Together On Broadway* (Columbia 1967)★★★, *What It Was, Was Love* (RCA 1969)★★★, *Real True Lovin'* (RCA 1969)★★★, *Tonight I'll Say A Prayer* (RCA 1970)★★★, *We Can Make It Together* (Ember 1975)★★★, *Our Love Is Here To Stay* (United Artists 1977)★★★, *I Still Believe In Love* (President 1985)★★★, *Alone Together* (GL 1989)★★★, *Since I Fell For You* (1993)★★★.

● COMPILATIONS: *The Very Best Of Eydie Gorme* (1961)★★★, *Eydie Gorme's Greatest Hits* (Columbia 1967)★★★.

With Steve Lawrence *The Very Best Of Eydie And Steve* (United Artists 1962)★★★, *The Golden Hits Of Eydie And Steve* (United Artists 1962)★★★, *The Best Of Steve And Eydie* (Columbia 1977)★★★, *20 Golden Performances* (1977)★★★.

GOULD, MORTON

b. 10 December 1913, Richmond Hill, New York, USA, d. 21 February 1996. Gould was one of the most important figures in American music in the twentieth century, and his composition 'Pavane' (from his 'American Symphonette No. 2') has become a light-music standard. By the age of 21 he was conducting and arranging a weekly series of orchestral radio shows, which allowed him to introduce many of his lighter works to a wider public. Equally at home in the popular and classical fields, his compositions included 'American Salute', 'Latin-American Symphonette', 'Spirituals For Orchestra', 'Interplay For Piano And Orchestra', 'Tap Dance Concerto', 'Dance Variations For Two Pianos And Orchestra', 'Jekyll And Hyde Variations', plus five symphonies and numerous works for symphonic band. Among many special commissions were 'Fall River Legend', 'Inventions For Four Pianos And Wind Orchestra', 'Declaration', 'St Lawrence Suite', 'Festive Music', 'Venice', 'Columbia', 'Soundings', 'Cheers' (commissioned by the Boston Symphony for Arthur Fiedler's 50th anniversary), 'Burchfield Gallery', 'Celebration '81', 'Housewarming', 'Cello Suite', 'Concerto Concertante', 'Centennial Symphony For Band' and 'Troubador Music For Four Guitars'. Gould's musical scores for Broadway included *Billion Dollar Baby* (1945) and *Arms And The Girl* (1950). For the cinema he scored *Delightfully Dangerous*, *Cinerama Holiday* and *Windjammer*. Ballets included Jerome Robbins' *Interplay*, Agnes De Mille's *Fall River Legend*, George Balanchine's *Clarinade* and Eliot Field's *Santa Fe Saga* and *Halftime*. His television work included a *CBS World War 1* documentary series, *F. Scott Fitzgerald In Hollywood* for ABC, the four-part mini-series *Holocaust* (1978) and a role as musical host for the National Educational Network series *The World Of Music With Morton Gould*. His list of recordings is extensive and he received many 'Grammy' nominations. In 1966 his RCA Red Seal recording of Charles Ives with the Chicago Symphony won the NARAS Grammy Award as the best classical recording of the year. In lighter vein, Gould's mood albums by his own orchestra from the 40s and 50s are collector's items. He also recorded with the London Symphony, London Philharmonic, the American Symphony Orchestra and the Louisville Orchestra. Gould travelled widely in the USA and throughout the world as a guest conductor, and was the recipient of numerous awards from fellow musicians. In March 1986 he became President of the American Society of Composers, Authors and Publishers (ASCAP), holding the post until 1994. Much of his music featured a strong patriotic American flavour, partly explaining why his own compositions were not better known outside the USA. In 1995, at the age of 81, Morton Gould won his first Pulitzer Prize in music for his work 'Stringmusic'. He died suddenly at a hotel in Orlando, Florida, while attending the Disney Institute as artist-in-residence.
● ALBUMS: *South Of The Border* (Columbia)★★★, *Soft Lights And Sweet Music* (Columbia)★★★, *Christmas Music For Orchestra* (Columbia)★★★, *Manhattan Moods* (Columbia)★★★, *Music At Midnight* (Columbia)★★★, *Morton Gould Showcase* (Columbia)★★★, *Music Of Morton Gould* (Columbia)★★★, *Curtain Time* (Columbia)★★★, *The Months (Tchaikovsky)* (Columbia)★★★, *Movie Time* (Columbia)★★★, *Memories* (Columbia)★★★, *Wagon Wheels* (Columbia)★★★, *Famous Operettas* (Columbia)★★★, *Jungle Drums* (RCA)★★★, *Music For Summertime* (RCA)★★★, *World's Best Loved Waltzes* (RCA)★★★, *Brass And Percussion* (RCA)★★★, *Coffee Time* (RCA)★★★, *Blues In The Night* (RCA)★★★, *Temptation* (RCA)★★★, *Batons And Bows* (RCA)★★★, *Doubling In Brass* (RCA)★★★, *Living Strings* (RCA)★★★, *Ballet Music by Gould* (RCA)★★★, *Beyond The Blue Horizon* (RCA)★★★, *Kern And Porter Favorites* (RCA)★★★, *Sousa Forever!* (RCA)★★★, *Love Walked In* (RCA)★★★, *Goodnight Sweetheart* (RCA)★★★, *Spirituals For Strings* (RCA)★★★, *Latin Lush And Lovely* (RCA)★★★, *Discovery* (RCA)★★★, *Holocaust* (RCA)★★★, *The Louisville Orchestra First Edition Series - Morton Gould* (Albany 1988)★★★.

GRACIE, CHARLIE

b. Charles Anthony Graci, 14 May 1936, Philadelphia, Pennsylvania, USA. When guitarist and songwriter Charlie Gracie recorded the original version of the rock 'n' roll song 'Butterfly' in 1957, he faced stiff competition from Andy Williams' cover version. Gracie's 'Elvis Presley-like vocal' took the song to number 5 in the US charts and Top 20 in the UK, but Williams' charted higher, number 1 in the UK and USA. They both sold over a million copies. He started out appearing as a teenager on Paul Whiteman's top-rated American television show. Gracie's subsequent singles were styled to suit his voice, including the ballads 'Fabulous' and 'Wanderin' Eyes', both Top 10 smashes in the UK in the same year. For many years he has been a legend rather than a performing artist. Often controversial, he has changed record labels countless times and still regularly performs in the USA and Europe. In the UK he has a fiercely loyal following, probably owing to the fact that he was the first ever rock 'n' roller to tour the UK in the 50s.
● ALBUMS: *The Cameo Parkway Sessions* (London 1978)★★★, *Charlie Gracies's Early Recordings* (Revival 1979)★★★, *Rockin' Philadelphia* (Magnum Force 1982)★★★, *Amazing Gracie* (Charly 1982)★★★, *Live At The Stockton Globe 1957* (Rollercoaster 1983)★★, *Boogie Boogie Blues And Other Rarities* (Revival 1990)★★.
● COMPILATIONS: *Best Of Charlie Gracie* (Revival 1988)★★★, *It's Fabulous* (Stomper Time 1995)★★★, *It's Fabulous It's Charlie Gracie* (Cotton Town Jubilee 1995)★★★.
● FILMS: *Jamboree* aka *Disc Jockey Jamboree* (1957).

GRAHAM, KENNY

b. Kenneth Thomas Skingle, 19 July 1924, London, England, d. 17 February 1997. Graham first played professionally at the age of 15, making his debut on alto saxophone with the Nottingham-based Rube Sunshine band. He later moved to London to join Billy Smith at the Cricklewood Palais but used his spare time to good effect, by touring London clubs where he met and played with well-known British jazzmen such as Jack Parnell and Nat Gonella. He spent some time with Johnny Claes's Claepigeons, a band that included drummer Carlo Krahmer (who later founded Esquire Records). After military service during World War II he worked with a variety of bands, including Ambrose and Macari and his Dutch Serenaders and was by that point usually heard on tenor saxophone. In April 1950 Graham introduced his own band, the Afro-Cubists, who successfully fused bebop with Latin and Caribbean rhythms. The band

was home to pianist Ralph Dollimore, Phil Seamen and at one time, a five-man saxophone section that included Derek Humble and Joe Temperley. The band folded in 1958 and thereafter Graham concentrated on arranging, his charts being played and recorded by jazz artists as diverse as Ted Heath and Humphrey Lyttelton. Graham proved especially adept at building interesting arrangements on unusual tonal effects, a good example being his 'Moondog Suite', which developed the ethereal sounds of Louis Hardin, the legendary blind street musician who was recorded on the streets of New York in the early 50s. In the 80s Graham was still writing, and the incorporation of synthesizers and other electronic instruments into his work showed that he had lost none of the enthusiasm for new sounds that had marked his early career. In the 80s he had to supplement his income by taking on extra work, and in his last years he was a warden at an apartment block.
● ALBUMS: *Mango Walk* (Esquire 1953)★★★★, *Caribbean Suite/Afro Kadabra* (Esquire 1953)★★, *Moondog And Suncat Suites* (1956)★★★, *Kenny Graham And His Orchestra* (1957)★★★.

GRANAHAN, GERRY

b. 17 June 1939, Pittston, Pennsylvania, USA. Granahan was associated with the 50s groups Dicky Doo And The Don'ts and the Fireflies and also recorded under his own name. Granahan started out as a disc jockey in his home-town before switching to a music career. At the age of 17 he began recording demos for Elvis Presley at the latter's Gladys Music firm. He recorded an unreleased single under the name Jerry Grant in 1957. The following year he co-wrote a song called 'No Chemise, Please' and recorded it under his name for Sunbeam Records; it reached number 23 in the summer of 1958. That same year Granahan also reached the US charts as a member of the Fireflies, who just missed the Top 20 with the ballad 'You Were Mine', on Ribbon Records, and led Dicky Doo And The Don'ts, a quintet that charted five times on Swan Records, first and most notably with 'Click Clack', a novelty rock 'n' roll song Granahan co-wrote with Dave Alldred, ex-drummer of Jimmy Bowen and the Rhythm Orchids. In later years Granahan became a producer for such artists as Shirley Ellis, Linda Scott, the Dave Clark Five, Jay And The Americans, Patty Duke and Farrante And Teicher, and ran his own Caprice label, whose roster at one time included Linda Scott, the Angels, James Ray and Santo And Johnny (the latter actually signed to the related Canadian-American label). In the early 90s he was running his own GPG Studios in Warwick, Rhode Island.
● ALBUMS: *Gerry Granahan's King-Sized Hits Volumes 1 and 2.*

GRANT, GOGI

b. Myrtle Audrey Arinsberg, 20 September 1924, Philadelphia, Pennsylvania, USA. Pop vocalist Grant was apparently named after a New York restaurant called Gogi's La Rue, which was frequented by Dave Kapp, head of A&R at RCA Records. She had previously recorded, without success, as Audrey Brown and Audrey Grant, but as Gogi Grant she hit the US Top 10 in 1955 with the ballad 'Suddenly There's A Valley'. Her biggest hit came a year later with a sad ballad about lost love, 'The Wayward Wind', which shot to number 1 in the USA and reached the Top 10 in the UK.

After signing to RCA Victor she was heavily marketed as an easy-listening singer. She provided all the vocals for actress Ann Blyth's portrayal of 1920s torch singer Helen Morgan in the 1957 biopic *The Helen Morgan Story*.
● ALBUMS: *Suddenly There's Gogi Grant* (Era 1956)★★★, *The Helen Morgan Story* film soundtrack (RCA Victor 1957)★★★, *Welcome To My Heart* (RCA Victor 1958)★★★, *Torch Time* (RCA Victor 1959)★★, *Kiss Me Kate* (RCA Victor 1959)★★, *Granted . . . It's Gogi* (RCA Victor 1960)★★, *If You Want To Get To Heaven, Shout* (Liberty 1960)★★, *The Wayward Wind* (Era 1960)★★★.
● FILMS: *The Big Beat* (1957).

GRANZ, NORMAN

b. 6 August 1918, Los Angeles, California, USA. A lifelong love of jazz led to Granz's early involvement in music as both film-maker and concert promoter. Together with photographer Gjon Mili, he made *Jammin' The Blues* (1944), still regarded as one of the best jazz short films ever made. Granz also promoted jazz sessions at Los Angeles clubs, insisting upon desegregated audiences. In 1944 he staged a jazz concert at the Philharmonic Auditorium in Los Angeles, an event whose title was shortened to fit the available advertising space. The abbreviated version, Jazz At The Philharmonic, or JATP, became synonymous with concert-hall jam sessions featuring the very best jazz talent. A few of the saxophonists who played at JATP in its formative years were Lester Young, Coleman Hawkins, Charlie Parker, Benny Carter, Charlie Ventura, Illinois Jacquet, Willie Smith and Joe 'Flip' Phillips. Granz insisted on desegregated audiences and first-class travel and hotel accommodation - things of which jazz musicians, especially those who were black, had previously only dreamed. From the start, Granz recorded his concerts and eventually began releasing them, often on labels he owned or controlled, among them Clef, Norgran, Verve and, more recently, Pablo. On record dates, Granz arranged for the return to the studios of several musicians who had been neglected by the major record companies. Among those whose careers were resuscitated was Art Tatum, whom Granz recorded with a wide range of musical partners and also in an extensive series of solo albums. Granz became personal manager for some of the artists he promoted, notably Ella Fitzgerald, with whom he recorded the remarkable 'Songbook' sequence of albums, and Oscar Peterson. Granz was also responsible for recording much of Billie Holiday's later work.

GRAY, GLEN

b. Glen Gray Knoblaugh, 7 June 1906, Roanoke, Illinois, USA, d. 23 August 1963, Plymouth, Massachusetts, USA. Educated at Illinois Westleyan College, Gray played the saxophone with one of the Jean Goldkette outfits, the Orange Blossom Band. In 1928 the group played the Casa Loma hotel in Toronto, which later folded, and adopted the name Casa Loma Orchestra for its gigs around the Detroit area. Gray was the president and leader when the co-operative band was formed in 1929; it was headed by Henry Biagini, then by violinist Mel Jenssen, who remained its leader for several years. The band recorded for Brunswick Records in the early 30s with Gene Gifford shaping the band's arrangements and style. A fine swing unit with catchy riffs and attractive ballads, the Casa Loma orchestra gained a spot on the *Camel Caravan* radio show during 1934-36 and was later signed for the *George Burns And Gracie Allen Show*. Glen Gray was elected leader by popular vote in 1937 until his retirement in 1950; he and the Casa Loma appeared in such movies as *Time Out For Rhythm* (1941) and *Gals, Inc* (1943). During the mid-50s he began recording a series of extremely successful albums for Capitol Records, recreating the sounds of the Casa Loma and other bands of the swing era. He was still engaged on this project when he became a victim of cancer in 1963. Highly regarded by pundits and swing fans alike, the Casa Loma orchestra had a large number of best-selling discs on Brunswick and Decca Records, including 'Blue Moon', 'When I Grow Too Old To Dream', 'Smoke Rings' (the Casa Loma theme), 'Heaven Can Wait', 'My Heart Tells Me', 'It's The Talk Of The Town', 'Sophisticated Lady', 'Out In The Cold Again', 'Fare Thee Well, Annabelle', 'My Shining Hour' and 'Sunrise Serenade', which featured its composer Frankie Carle on piano. Many of them had romantic vocals by Kenny Sargent. The band also recorded instrumentals such as 'Blue Jazz', 'White Jazz', 'Black Jazz' and 'No Name Jive'.

● ALBUMS: *The Great Recordings Of Glen Gray* (50s)★★★, *Musical Smoke Rings* (50s)★★★, *Hoagy Carmichael Songs* (50s)★★★★, *Casa Loma In Hi Fi!* (Capitol 1957)★★★, *Sounds Of The Great Bands!* (Capitol 1959)★★★, *Please, Mr Gray* (1961)★★★, *Glen Gray: Shall We Swing?* (1961)★★★, *Themes Of The Great Bands* (Capitol 1963)★★, *Today's Best* (Capitol 1963)★★.

● COMPILATIONS: *Glen Gray And The Casa Loma Orchestra 1943-46* (London-American 1979)★★★★, *Solo Spotlight* (Capitol 1986)★★, *Glen Gray And The Casa Loma Orchestra 1939-40* (Hindsight 1988)★★★★, *Glen Gray And The Casa Loma Orchestra 1943-46* (Hindsight 1988)★★★★, *Glen Gray And The Casa Loma Orchestra* (Columbia 1990)★★★.

GRAYSON, KATHRYN

b. Zelma Kathryn Hedrick, 9 February 1922, Winston-Salem, North Carolina, USA. An actress and singer with a spectacular soprano voice and a charming and ingenuous personality, who was popular in MGM musicals in the 40s and 50s. She is said to have been discovered while singing on Eddie Cantor's radio show in the late 30s, and made her film debut in 1941 with Mickey Rooney in *Andy Hardy's Private Secretary*. After being teamed with the comedy duo Bud Abbott and Lou Costello in *Rio Rita* (1942), during the rest of the 40s and in the 50s, she co-starred with major stars such as Frank Sinatra, Mario Lanza and Howard Keel in a string of musicals that included *Seven Sweethearts*, *Thousands Cheer*, *Two Sisters From Boston*, *Ziegfeld Follies*, *Till The Clouds Roll By*, *It Happened In Brooklyn*, *The Toast Of New Orleans*, *Show Boat*, *Lovely To Look At*, *The Desert Song*, *Kiss Me Kate* and *The Vagabond King* (1956). In *So This Is Love* (1953), she portrayed opera singer Grace Moore, and in some of her other films, she again played characters attempting to audition for maestros, such as José Iturbi, with the intention of making a career as a classical singer. As the golden age of movie musicals drew to a close in the late 50s, Grayson played concerts and clubs for a time, and subsequently toured in revivals of well-known stage musicals.

● ALBUMS: *Kathryn Grayson* 10-inch album (MGM 1952)★★★, *Kathryn Grayson Sings* (MGM 1956)★★★,

Kathryn Grayson (Lion 1959)★★★, and film soundtracks.

● COMPILATIONS: *20 Golden Favourites* (Bulldog 1984)★★★.

GREAT CARUSO, THE

This lavishly produced biopic of the celebrated Italian opera singer was released by MGM in 1951. Mario Lanza, making his third screen appearance, was the perfect choice to play the lead in a screenplay by Sonia Levian and William Ludwig that, in certain areas of Caruso's life, was somewhat economical with the truth. For instance, the existence of one of his wives was totally ignored in the haste to condense drastically his rise to fame, and to feature as much music on the screen as possible. It was all rather false, and even the hit song that emerged from the film, 'The Loveliest Night Of The Year', was not actually associated with Caruso, being a Mexican instrumental piece, 'Over The Waves' (Juventino Rosas), adapted by Irving Aaronson and lyricist Paul Francis Webster. As for the remainder of the musical fare, it was a collection of songs and operatic excerpts that included 'Last Rose Of Summer' (Thomas Moore-Richard Alfred Milliken), 'Sextet' (Donizetti), 'La Donna E Mobile' (Verdi), 'Celeste Aida' (Verdi), 'Ave Maria' (Bach-Charles Gounod), 'Sweethearts' (Victor Herbert-Robert B. Smith), 'Vesti La Guibba' (Leoncavallo) and 'M'Appari' (Flotow). Anne Blyth played Dorothy Benjamin, Caruso's wife, and among the rest of the cast were Dorothy Kirsten, Jarmila Novotna, Richard Hageman, Eduard Franz, Carl Benton, Ludwig Donath, Ian Wolfe and Mae Clarke. Joseph Ruttenbergs' Technicolor photography enhanced the whole spectacular affair, which was produced by Joe Pasternak and directed by Richard Thorpe. Musical directors Johnny Green and Peter Herman Adler were nominated for Oscars, and Douglas Shearer won one for sound recording. *The Great Caruso* grossed over $4.5 million in North America (a great deal of money in those days), and proved to be the most popular of Mario Lanza's brief film career (he made only seven films).

GRECO, BUDDY

b. Armando Greco, 14 August 1926, Philadelphia, Pennsylvania, USA. A singer and pianist known for his swinging, ultra-hip interpretations of classy songs. The son of a music critic who had his own radio show on station WPEN, Buddy himself appeared on WPEN at the age of five, initially making his mark as a singer and actor. Later on, like his two brothers, he studied to become a pianist, practising and playing at the Philadelphia Settlement House, a 10-block complex of recreational and hobby facilities, where so many of the city's youthful musicians congregated. Greco led his own trio during 1944-49, and recorded a major hit version of Carmen Lombardo's 'Ooh, Look-A There Ain't She Pretty', though the singer received only $32 for recording the single. Heard by Benny Goodman while playing at Philadelphia's Club 13, he was offered a job by the bandleader and subsequently became pianist-vocalist-arranger with the Goodman orchestra, appearing with Goodman's sextet at the London Palladium in 1949, embarking on several tours with the band and his vocals gracing such Goodman Capitol sides as 'It Isn't Fair', 'Don't Worry 'Bout Me', 'The Land of Oo-Bla-Dee' and 'Brother Bill'. By 1951 Greco had become a solo act once more, gaining a regular spot on the *Broadway Open House* television show and providing Coral with a hit record in 'I

Ran All The Way Home'. He also won many lucrative nightclub engagements, one of which provided the bestselling album *Buddy Greco At Mister Kelly's*, a superb document of his appearances at the Chicago club in 1955. Greco's biggest hit was still to come, a non-stop, grab-at-the-lyrics version of Richard Rodgers and Lorenz Hart's 'The Lady Is A Tramp', cut for Epic Records in 1960. This track sold over a million copies worldwide and gave Buddy his first UK chart entry. During the late 60s and 70s Greco became increasingly associated with the British showbusiness scene, playing dates at London's Talk Of The Town, appearing on the Royal Command Performance and recording an instrumental album with the London Symphony Orchestra. This well-travelled and appreciated performer claims to have played every major club in the world on at least two occasions, and was still touring round some of them again in the late 80s. In the early 90s he re-established himself in Britain with well-received cabaret appearances at London's Café Royal.
● ALBUMS: *Buddy Greco At Mister Kelly's* (Coral 1956)★★★, *Broadway Melodies* (Kapp 1956)★★★, *My Buddy* (Fontana 1960)★★★, *Songs For Swinging Losers* (Columbia 1960)★★★, *Buddy's Back In Town* (1961)★★★, *I Like It Swinging* (Columbia 1961)★★★, *Let's Love* (Columbia 1962)★★★, *Buddy And Soul* (Columbia 1963)★★★, *Buddy's Back In Town* (Columbia 1963)★★★, *Sings For Intimate Moments* (Columbia 1963)★★★, *Soft And Gentle* (Columbia 1963)★★★, *One More Time* (Columbia 1964)★★★, *On Stage* (Columbia 1964)★★★, *Modern Sounds Of Hank Williams* (Columbia 1965)★★, *I Love A Piano* (Columbia 1966)★★★, *Let The Sunshine In* (Wand 1970)★★, *Live At Pullen's Talk Of North, April 1974* (Pye 1974)★★★, *For Once In My Life* (Bulldog 1982)★★★, *Moving On (It's Magic)* (Prestige 1990)★★★, *Route 66* (1994)★★★, *MacArthur Park* (1995)★★★.
● COMPILATIONS: *Golden Hour Presents Buddy Greco* (Golden Hour 1978)★★★, *Greatest Hits* (Columbia 1984)★★★, *I Had A Ball* (1993)★★★.

GRÉCO, JULIETTE

b. 1927, Montpelier, France. An actress and inimitable singer of the *chanson*, Gréco was born the daughter of a police chief and a Resistance worker. After spending some time in prison during the Occupation when she was 15, Gréco took acting lessons, and began to dress in men's black clothing - heavy overcoats and trousers, with polo neck sweaters - and cut her hair in a fringe. In the mid-40s she became a leading member of the philosopher Jean-Paul Sartre's intellectual Existentialist movement, which flourished in cafés such as Le Boeuf sur le Toit and Café Flore on Paris's Left Bank. Sartre encouraged her to sing, and with her slightly raw-edged voice, attractive appearance and impressive stage presence, she soon became immensely popular in the world of cabaret. Among her most memorable - and usually sad - songs are Hubert Giraud and Jean Drejec's 'Sous Le Ciel De Paris' ('Under Paris Skies'), Jacques Brel's 'J'arrive' and 'Je Suis Bien', along with several written by Joseph Kosma and Jacques Prevert, including 'Les Feuilles Mortes', which, with an English lyric by Johnny Mercer, became the wistful 'Autumn Leaves'. After appearing in a few French films from 1949 onwards, in the late 50s she embarked on a brief Hollywood career sponsored by Darryl F. Zanuck, starring in *The Sun Also Rises*, *Roots Of Heaven*, *Crack In The Mirror* and

The Big Gamble. Afterwards, she returned to her *chansons*, and has continued to sing ever since. Her popularity in Britain has waned since the 50s, but she did perform in London in 1989 for the first time in 10 years. In the previous year, she married her musical director and accompanist Gérard Jouannest. Her previous husbands, Philippe Lemaire and Michel Piccoli, were both actors.
● ALBUMS: *Juliette Greco* (Philips 1954)★★★, *Gréco* (Philips 1957)★★, *Les Grandes Chansons* (Philips 1961)★★★★, *Juliette Gréco Showcase* (Philips 1962)★★★, *La Femme* (Philips 1968)★★, *Juliette Gréco* (French Decca 1972)★★★, *Je Vous Attends* (French Decca 1974)★★, *Le Disque D'Or* (Phonogram 1974)★★.
● COMPILATIONS: *Greatest Hits* (Impact 1977)★★★.
● FILMS: including *Au Royaume Des Cieux* (1949), *Orpheus* (1950), *The Green Glove* (1952), *Quand Tu Liras Cette Lettre* (1953), *Paris Does Strange Things* (1956), *The Sun Also Rises* (1957), *Bonjour Tristesse* (1958), *Naked Earth* (1958), *Roots Of Heaven* (1959), *Whirlpool* (1959), *Crack In The Mirror* (1960), *The Big Gamble* (1961), *Where The Truth Lies* (1962), *Uncle Tom's Cabin* (1965), *The Night Of The Generals* (1967).

GREEN, CLARENCE

b. 15 March 1929, Galveston, Texas, USA. A self-taught blues piano player, Clarence 'Candy' Green performed on radio and in the numerous clubs of Galveston, a naval town known as the 'Playground Of the South'. His first record was 'Green's Bounce', made in Houston for Eddie's in 1948. His brother Cal Green was a guitarist who also recorded. Clarence recorded 'Hard Headed Woman' (Peacock) before starting army service in 1951. Returning to Texas two years later, he remained a familiar figure in local clubs throughout the 50s, sometimes recording as Galveston Green and working with Clarence 'Gatemouth' Brown. In 1966 he recorded the soulful 'I Saw You Last Night' for Duke Records.
● ALBUMS: *Lady in Red* (1982)★★★.

GREEN, L.C.

b. 23 October 1921, Minter City, Mississippi, USA, d. 24 August 1985, Pontiac, Michigan, USA. Vocally and for his repertoire, L.C. Greene, whose records were issued without the final 'e' to his name, was indebted to John Lee 'Sonny Boy' Williamson. His amplified guitar playing is clearly Mississippi Delta-derived, but probably owes something to the popularity of fellow Detroit blues singer John Lee Hooker. Greene recorded in the early 50s (often with his cousin Walter Mitchell on harmonica) for Joe Von Battle's shoestring operation, which leased a few sides to Dot Records, but he never matched the fortunes of Hooker, whom he equalled in guitar talent and power, although not in songwriting ability.
● COMPILATIONS: *Detroit Blues Guitar Killers!* (1977)★★★.

GREER, 'BIG' JOHN

b. John Marshall Greer, 21 November 1923, Hot Springs, Arkansas, USA, d. 12 May 1972. Greer, who performed both as a vocalist and a tenor saxophonist, is a perfect representative of the flowering of the saxophone in the post-World War II era as an R&B instrument. He first made his mark in the music business leading his own quintet in 1948 and made some favourably received recordings. In late 1948 he joined the Lucky Millinder Band, with whom he recorded as both a vocalist and sax soloist, but in April 1949 he was again making solo recordings for the RCA label. Over the following years he had releases both as a member of the Millinder band and as a solo artist. 'Got You On My Mind' from 1952 was his only national R&B hit. RCA released him from his contract in 1955, and after a short stay at King Records in 1956, he never made another recording.

● COMPILATIONS: *R&B In New York City* (Official 1988)★★★, *Rockin' With Big John* (Bear Family 1992)★★★.

GRENFELL, JOYCE

b. Joyce Irene Phipps, 10 February 1910, London, England, d. 30 November 1979, London, England. An actress, singer and author, and a brilliant exponent of the monologue and witty song. The daughter of American parents - her mother's sister was Nancy Astor - Joyce Phipps used to describe herself as 'three fourths American'. She became interested in the theatre at an early age, and spent a term at RADA before marrying Reginald Grenfell in 1929. Subsequently, she worked for a time in commercial art, contributed to *Punch* and *Country Life*, and spent over three years as radio critic for the *Observer*. After impressing the humorist Steven Potter with her own charming recollection of a lecture that she had recently attended at a Women's Institute, she was engaged by the theatrical producer Herbert Farjeon for *The Little Revue* (1939). In the early 40s she appeared in other Farjeon revues, *Diversion*, *Diversion No. 2* and *Light And Shade*, and then, in 1944, toured extensively with ENSA, in the Near and Far East, and in India, entertaining the troops in British forces' hospitals, with comic monologues and songs. Two years later she was awarded the OBE. In *Sigh No More* (1945), at London's Piccadilly Theatre, Grenfell dressed as a schoolgirl for Noël Coward's witty 'That Is The End Of The News', and, in the same show, introduced 'Du Maurier', a song she had written with composer Richard Addinsell. They collaborated again on material for the revues, *Tuppence Coloured* (1947) and *Penny Plain* (1951), in which Grenfell also appeared. It was the beginning of a significant and enduring professional relationship. By the late 40s and early 50s, Grenfell was working more and more in radio - as a panellist on *We Beg To Differ*, and as the British host of *Transatlantic Quiz*. She made a couple of propaganda films during the war, but her movie career proper began in 1943 with a comedy, *The Demi-Paradise*, which starred Laurence Olivier and Margaret Rutherford. Grenfell appeared with Rutherford again, in *The Happiest Days Of Your Life* (1949), which also starred the lugubrious Alastair Sim. He and Grenfell managed to emerge unscathed from the *St. Trinians* film series. during the late 50s. Grenfell's other film roles, some of them highly telling cameos, included appearances in *Here Comes The Bride*, *The Galloping Major*, *Pickwick Papers*, *The Million Pound Note* and *The Americanization Of Emily*. It was on stage, however, that she really came into her own. In 1954 she wrote the book and lyrics, with Addinsell's music, for *Joyce Grenfell Requests The Pleasure*, which ran for nearly a year in London before transferring to Broadway in the following year. In America, Grenfell developed her one-woman show, toured US cities, and appeared on the *Ed Sullivan Show* several times in the late 50s. One Sullivan date saw her on the same bill with Elvis Presley ('a pasty-faced plump boy', as she recalled). She presented her solo effort in London for the first time in 1957, at the Lyric theatre, under

the title of *Joyce Grenfell - A Miscellany*, and later took the show to Australia where it was called *Meet Joyce Grenfell*. Throughout the 60s she continued to tour extensively at home and abroad, and went back to Australia three times. In the early 70s she lost the sight in one eye and retired from the stage. During the next six years she published two volumes of autobiography, *Joyce Grenfell Requests The Pleasure* and *In Pleasant Places*, before cancer affected her other eye, and she died in 1979. Always an effective broadcaster, from 1966 she was an essential panel-member on television's *Face The Music*, a general knowledge quiz about music, and had her own series on BBC2 for a time. As a performer she was unique, and impossible to pigeonhole. Despite her 'terribly English' image, she was incredibly popular around the world, particularly in America. With the gentle 'I'm Going To See You Today', which became her theme, the pomp of 'Stately As A Galleon', and many other favourites such as 'Maude', 'Nursery School', 'A Terrible Worrier', 'Time', 'Three Brothers', 'It's Almost Tomorrow', and two recorded duets with Norman Wisdom, 'Narcissus' and 'I Don't 'Arf Love You', she presented a refined, humorous, perceptive, yet never unkind, view of society. One of her best-remembered pieces is 'I Like Life', which accords with her own philosophy: 'I am not interested in the pursuit of happiness, but only in the discovery of joy'. Her companion on that journey, Reginald Grenfell, who edited some of her books, died in 1993. In 1988, the revue *Re: Joyce!*, 'a diverting and engaging mixture of anecdotal biography and quintessential sketch material', starring Maureen Lipman with Denis King, opened in London and continued to be presented at intervals into the 90s.

● ALBUMS: *Requests The Pleasure* (1955)★★★★, *At Home* (1957)★★★★,

● COMPILATIONS: *The Collection* (One-Up 1976)★★★★, *George Don't Do That* (Starline 1977)★★★★, *The New Collection* (EMI 1978)★★★, *The Second Collection* (Encore 1979)★★★★, *Joyce Grenfell Talking* (Cube 1981)★★★★, *Keepsake* (Retrospect 1986)★★★, *Re: Joyce* (EMI 1988)★★★, Maureen Lipman and Denis King *Re: Joyce!* stage cast (EMI 1989)★★, *Songs And Monologues Of Joyce Grenfell* (EMI 1991)★★★★, *Joyful Joyce* (1991)★★★★, *Requests The Pleasure* 3-CD Set (BBC 1992)★★★★, *More Joyful Joyce* (1994)★★★.

● FURTHER READING: *George - Don't Do That...* (sketches and songs). *Stately As A Galleon* (sketches and songs). *Time Of My Life - Entertaining The Troops: Her Wartime Journals*, Joyce Grenfell. *Joyce Grenfell Requests The Pleasure*, Joyce Grenfell. *In Pleasant Places*, Joyce Grenfell. *Darling Ma: Letters To Her Mother, 1932-1944*, edited by James Roose-Evans. *Joyce: By Herself And Her Friends*, edited by Reggie Grenfell and Richard Garnett.

GRIFFIN BROTHERS

Based in Washington, DC, around Jimmy and Ernest 'Buddy' Griffin from Norfolk, Virginia, the Griffin Brothers Orchestra comprised Jimmy on trombone, Buddy on piano, Wilbur Dyer and Virgil Wilson on saxophone, with Jimmy Reeves and Emmett 'Nab' Shields on bass and drums. Introduced to Randy Wood in 1950, the band began recording for his label Dot Records; their biggest hits were the songs of their vocalists Margie Day - 'Street Walkin' Daddy' and 'Little Red Rooster', among others - and Tommy Brown - 'Tra-La-La' and

'Weepin' And Cryin". During a tour of the south in April 1950, Jimmy and Buddy were asked to participate in the Roy Brown session for DeLuxe that resulted in his biggest hit, 'Hard Luck Blues'. However, they returned to their own band, which now included Noble 'Thin Man' Watts on tenor saxophone, and recorded with Dot Records until they split up in 1954. The brothers each made their own solo recordings for Dot after the split, and subsequently Jimmy went to Atco Records in New York, while Buddy had some success in Chicago on the Chess label with vocalist Claudia Swann.

● COMPILATIONS: with Margie Day *Riffin' With The Griffin Brothers Orchestra* (Ace 1985)★★★, with Margie Day *I'll Get A Deal* (Mr R&B 1986)★★★.

GUESNON, CREOLE GEORGE

b. 25 May 1907, New Orleans, Louisiana, USA, d. 5 May 1968, New Orleans, Louisiana, USA. A jazz banjoist and guitarist, Guesnon worked in many 'Crescent City' bands from 1927 to 1965, often recording as a sideman from 1951. He also toured with Little Brother Montgomery's Jackson-based Southland Troubadours in the mid-30s, and it may have been this experience that prompted 'Mississippi Town', a blues tribute to Jackson recorded in 1940. ('Iberville And Franklin' did the same for New Orleans.) Guesnon did not play on these recordings, which show him to have been a likeable, clear-voiced singer, as adept at ballads as with the blues.

● COMPILATIONS: *Blues Bands* (1990)★★★.

GUITAR GABLE

b. Gabriel Perrodin, 17 August 1937, Bellvue, Louisiana, USA. Learning guitar in his teens, Gable was influenced by the ringing, melodic style of Guitar Slim. He recorded for Jay Miller with his band the Musical Kings in 1956-57, and several successful singles were issued on Excello Records. The music was very much in the south Louisiana R&B mould, with a touch of New Orleans rock 'n' roll; Gable's distinctive guitar effectively complemented the lead vocals of King Karl. Guitar Gable's band retained its popularity in local clubs throughout the rest of the 50s, but it appears that he retired from performing when he joined the army around 1959.

● COMPILATIONS: *Cool, Calm, Collected* (Flyright 1984)★★★.

GUNTER, ARTHUR

b. 23 May 1926, Nashville, Tennessee, USA, d. 16 March 1976, Port Huron, Michigan, USA. Gunter wrote and recorded 'Baby Let's Play House' for Excello in the summer of 1954. That December, the Thunderbirds vocal group recorded their version, issued on DeLuxe, in Miami. Three months later, it was one side of Elvis Presley's fourth Sun single. This marked the point at which Gunter realized that he had no ambition to write another hit. His father was a preacher; he and his brothers, Jimmy and Junior, and cousin Julian, sang spirituals as the Gunter Brothers Quartet. He learned guitar from another brother, Larry, and absorbed blues old and new - Blind Boy Fuller and Big Boy Crudup, Jimmy Reed and Blind Lemon Jefferson. He frequented the record store run by Ernie Young, founder of Excello and Nashboro. There he met pianist Skippy Brooks, and played gigs with Brooks' band, the Kid King Combo. Most of the time he performed just with cousin Julian on drums. 'Baby

Let's Play House' was his first record, and a hit in the Nashville area. None of his succeeding 11 singles did as well, and Excello dropped him in 1961. His brother Little Al also made two singles for the company. Gunter moved to Port Huron, Michigan, in 1966 and completely abandoned music. In 1973 he won $50,000 in the Michigan State Lottery, and played as part of the Ann Arbor Blues Festival's 'Music Of Detroit' afternoon.

● COMPILATIONS: *Black And Blues* (Excello 1987)★★★, *Baby Let's Play House: The Best Of Arthur Gunter* (Excello 1995)★★★.

GUYS AND DOLLS (STAGE MUSICAL)

Opening at the 46th Street Theatre in New York on 24 November 1950, the stage musical *Guys And Dolls* was a predicted success. With a book by Abe Burrows and Jo Swerling, and music and lyrics by Frank Loesser, out-of-town try-outs were hugely successful and by the time of its opening night on Broadway, the word was out that the show was a winner. Based upon the risqué yarns of Damon Runyon, the dialogue and lyrics effectively captured the speech patterns of Runyon's larger-than-life characters and the music perfectly matched the show's mood. The story tells of two love affairs, the first between compulsive gambler Nathan Detroit and the leading dancer at the 'Hot Box', Miss Adelaide, and the second between another - far more successful - gambler, Sky Masterson, and Miss Sarah Brown, a member of the 'Save A Soul Mission'. Other Runyonesque characters complete the cast, notably Benny Southstreet, Big Jule, Harry the Horse, and Nicely-Nicely Johnson. During the course of the show true love eventually triumphs, despite many obstacles, not least of which is police lieutenant Brannigan's desperate attempts to locate and close down Nathan's floating crap game, the oldest established in New York. By the time the curtain falls, Masterson is a reformed character and has married Sarah, while Nathan and Miss Adelaide are about to marry after a 14-year-long courtship. Loesser's marvellous songs included 'Fugue For Tinhorns', 'The Oldest Established' 'Take Back Your Mink', 'A Bushel And A Peck', 'Adelaide's Lament', 'Marry The Man Today', 'Sue Me', 'If I Were A Bell', 'I've Never Been In Love Before', 'More I Cannot Wish You' and 'Luck Be A Lady'. Complementing the show's strong characterization and dramatic storyline, the producers cast actors rather than singers in the key roles, among them Sam Levene as Nathan, Vivian Blaine, who had worked in Hollywood musicals, as Miss Adelaide, Robert Alda as Sky, Isabel Bigley as Sarah, and Stubby Kaye as Nicely-Nicely, who stopped the show every night with his exuberant singing of 'Sit Down, You're Rockin' The Boat'. Critics and public loved the show and it ran for some 1,200 performances, winning Tony Awards for best musical, actor (Alda), featured actress (Bigley), director (George S. Kaufman) and choreographer (Michael Kidd). A London production opened in 1953, and the show was revived in 1982 by the National Theatre, and again in 1985 with pop singer Lulu as Miss Adelaide. An accaimed Broadway revival, starring Nathan Lane, Faith Prince, Peter Gallagher and Josie de Guzman, opened in April 1992 and ran for 1,143 performances. It won Tonys for best revival, actress (Prince), and director (Jerry Zaks). The 1955 film version starred Marlon Brando, Frank Sinatra, Vivian Blaine and Stubby Kaye.

GUYS AND DOLLS (FILM MUSICAL)

Producer Sam Goldwyn pulled off quite a coup when he cast Frank Sinatra and Marlon Brando in this 1955 screen version of the smash-hit Broadway show. In Joseph L. Mankiewicz's screenplay, which was based on Abe Burrows' libretto and Damon Runyan's short story *The Idyll Of Miss Sarah Brown*, Sinatra plays Nathan Detroit, the operator of the oldest established permanent floating crap game in New York. Constantly harassed by Inspector Brannigan (Robert Keith), and his fiancé of 14 years, Miss Adelaide (Vivian Blaine), Nathan bets 'the highest roller in town', Sky Masterson (Brando), that he cannot transport Salvation Army stalwart Sarah Brown (Jean Simmons), from the Save Our Souls Mission in New York, to Havana. Against all the odds, Sky and Sarah make the trip, but Nathan subsequently loses nothing - except his precious freedom - when he and Adelaide, along with Sky and Sarah, make it a double wedding in Times Square. There was a rumour that Sinatra wanted to play the Brando role because, in the original, Nathan does not have a solo number. In the event, composer Frank Loesser gave him a new song, 'Adelaide', and he also wrote another new one for Brando, 'A Woman In Love', because the actor reportedly could not handle the tender 'I've Never Been In Love Before'. In fact, both he and Jean Simmons were surprisingly good on 'I'll Know' and 'If I Were A Bell'. The rest of the magnificent score - arguably Loesser's masterpiece - included 'Fugue For Tinhorns' (Sinatra-Silver-Danny Dayton), 'The Oldest Established' (Sinatra-Silver-Kaye-ensemble), 'Pet Me Poppa' (which replaced 'A Bushel And A Peck') (Blaine and chorus), 'Adelaide's Lament' (Blaine), 'Guys And Dolls' (Sinatra-Silver-Kaye), 'Take Back Your Mink' (Blaine and chorus), 'Luck Be A Lady' (Brando), 'Sue Me' (Sinatra-Blaine) and 'Sit Down, You're Rockin' The Boat'. The latter number was performed by the irrepressible Stubby Kaye, recreating his Broadway role of Nicely-Nicely Johnson. Other veterans of the stage show, playing two of the loveable Runyanesque rogues, were Johnny Silver (Benny Southstreet) and B.S. Pully (Big Jule), along with the marvellous Vivian Blaine and choreographer Michael Kidd. Also in the cast were Sheldon Leonard, George E. Stone, Regis Toomey, Kathryn Givney, Veda Ann Borg and Alan Hokanson. Directed by Mankiewicz, and photographed in Eastman Color and CinemaScope for MGM, *Guys And Dolls* was derided by the critics, but welcomed by the cinema-going public who made it one of the top box-office successes of the 50s.

GYPSY

With a book by Arthur Laurents, which was based on stripper Gypsy Rose Lee's autobiography, and music and lyrics by Jule Styne and Stephen Sondheim, this show opened at the Broadway Theatre in New York on 21 May 1959. Director and choreographer Jerome Robbins gave the production added strength and *Gypsy* looked promising from the start, but the story's construction demanded a powerful lead in the role of Mamma Rose. She was the tough, ambitious mother of the two aspiring entertainers who grew up to be 'Louise' and 'June'; in real life, Gypsy Rose Lee and her much more talented younger sister, screen actress June Havoc. In casting Ethel Merman, the producers not only secured the best woman for the job, they also had an artist audiences would flock to see. The score is one of the most

highly regarded in Broadway musical history, and included 'Let Me Entertain You', 'Together Wherever We Go', 'Small World', 'If Mamma Was Married', 'All I Need Is The Girl', 'You Gotta Have A Gimmick', 'Mr. Goldstone', and Merman's blockbusters, 'Everything's Coming Up Roses' and 'Rose's Turn'. Other cast members included Sandra Church as Louise, and Jack Klugman as Rose's manager and would-be husband. The show ran for 702 performances, and was revived in 1974 with Angela Lansbury as Rose. This acclaimed production also played in London during 1973. In 1989 *Gypsy* returned to Broadway in triumph, with television star Tyne Daly as Mamma Rose. She won a Tony Award for best actress, and the show won another for best musical revival. A unique opportunity to view at leisure one of the greatest musicals in the history of the American theatre came in 1993, when *Gypsy*, starring Bette Midler, was shown on US television and later released on video. It purported to be the first film of a complete stage musical to retain the complete text, with no material added or altered. The 1962 film version starred Natalie Wood as Louise and Rosalind Russell as Rose.

HALEY, BILL, AND HIS COMETS

b. William John Clifton Haley, 6 July 1925, Highland Park, Michigan, USA, d. 9 February 1981, Harlingen, Texas, USA. Haley was one of the great pioneers of rock 'n' roll and was the first artist to take the new musical form to the world stage. His roots were in country music and he began his career as a yodelling cowboy. After playing in such country groups as the Downhomers and the Range Drifters, he formed the Four Aces Of Western Swing in 1948. At that point, his repertoire included compositions by both Red Foley and Hank Williams. His next group was the Saddlemen, who played a stirring mixture of western swing, mixed with polka. In 1951, he recorded the R&B hit 'Rocket 88', which indicated how far he had already travelled in assimilating the styles of rock 'n' roll. Haley's fusion of country, R&B and a steady beat was to provide the backbone of the musical genre that he immortalized. The jive talk used on the following year's 'Rock The Joint', coupled with the distinctive slap bass playing on the record, continued the experiment.

In 1953, Haley abandoned the cowboy image and formed a new group, Bill Haley And His Comets. The line-up of the group would change frequently over the years, but Haley himself was a constant. Their first single, the exuberant 'Crazy Man Crazy', crossed over into the national charts and was the first rock 'n' roll Top 20 US hit. After signing to Decca Records in May 1954, Haley recorded a series of songs with Danny Cedrone (d. 1954; lead guitar), Joey D'Ambrosia (sax), Billy Williamson (steel guitar), Johnny Grande (piano), Marshall Lytle (bass) and Dick Richards (drums) that were historically crucial in bringing rock 'n' roll to the world. 'Rock Around The Clock' was a staggering achievement, a single whose timing, vocal, spine-tingling guitar breaks and inspired drumming were quite unlike any other commercial recordings up until that time. Amazingly, it was initially issued as a b-side and, even when the sides were flipped, it initially became only a minor hit. Haley returned to the studio to record a follow-up: 'Shake Rattle And Roll'. This was another seminal work, whose jive-style lyrics and brilliant employment of saxophone and upright bass brought a new sound into the US Top 20. Haley enjoyed further, though less important hits, during the next year with 'Dim Dim The Lights' and 'Mambo Rock'. Then, in the spring of 1955, his career took a dramatic upswing when the previously issued 'Rock Around The Clock' was included in the controversial film The Blackboard Jungle. Suddenly, the world woke up to the importance of 'Rock Around The Clock' and it became a veritable rock 'n' roll anthem and rallying cry. It soared to the top of the US charts for a lengthy spell and achieved the same feat in the UK. When The Blackboard Jungle was shown in Britain, enthusiastic youths jived in the aisles and ripped up their seats in excitement. Haley was crowned the king of rock 'n' roll and dominated the US/UK chart listings throughout 1955/6 with such songs as 'Rock-A-Beatin' Boogie', 'See You Later Alligator', 'The Saints Rock 'N' Roll', 'Razzle Dazzle', 'Burn That Candle', 'Rip It Up' and 'Rudy's Rock'. The latter was an instrumental that focused attention on Haley's saxophone player, the excellent Rudy Pompilli (d. 5 February 1976), who often played onstage lying on his back. His brother, Al Pompilli, was another important component in the group, renowned for his acrobatic displays on the stand-up bass. Haley's exciting stage act provoked hysteria among the youth population, which soon became pandemic. In February 1957, he travelled to England, the first rock 'n' roll star to tour abroad. He was mobbed when his train arrived in London and there were rabid scenes of fan mania when he performed at the Dominion Theatre, London. Inevitably, the moral pundits criticized such performances but Haley proved himself an adept apologist and emphasized the point by recording the protest 'Don't Knock The Rock', the title theme of an Alan Freed film.

Haley's star burned brightly for a couple of years, but his weakness was his age and image. At the age of 32, he was a little too old to be seen as the voice of teendom and his personality was more avuncular than erotic. Once Elvis Presley exploded onto the scene, Haley seemed a less authentic rock 'n' roll rebel and swiftly lost his standing among his young audience. He was still respected as a kind of elder statesman of rock - the man who first brought the music to the masses. Not surprisingly, he maintained his popularity by constantly touring, and his recordings veered from Latin dance excursions to novelty and straight country. He was always called upon to carry the rock 'n' roll mantle whenever there was a nostalgic outbreak of 50s revivalism. It is a testament to the

power of Haley's influence that 'Rock Around The Clock' returned to the UK Top 20 on two separate occasions: in 1968 and 1974. His music effectively transcended the generation gap by reaching new listeners over three decades. By the late 70s, Haley was reportedly ill and drinking heavily. He returned to England in November 1979 for a memorable performance at the Royal Variety Show. The following year reports filtered through that he was suffering from a brain tumour. On 9 February 1981, he died of a heart attack in Harlingen, Texas, USA. His inestimable influence on rock 'n' roll still continues, and he was posthumously inducted into the Rock And Roll Hall Of Fame in 1987.

● ALBUMS: Rock With Bill Haley And The Comets (Essex 1955)★★, Shake, Rattle And Roll 10-inch album (Decca 1955)★★★, Rock Around The Clock (Decca 1956)★★★★, with various artists Music For The Boyfriend (Decca 1956)★★, Rock 'N Roll Stage Show (Decca 1956)★★★★, Rocking The Oldies (Decca 1957)★★, Rockin' Around The World (Decca 1958)★★★, Rocking The Joint (Decca 1958)★★★, Bill Haley's Chicks (Decca 1959)★★★, Strictly Instrumental (Decca 1960)★★, Bill Haley And His Comets (Warners 1960)★★★, Bill Haley's Jukebox (Warners 1960)★★★, Twistin' Knights At The Round Table (Roulette 1962)★★★, Bill Haley And The Comets (Vocalion 1963)★★, Rip It Up (MCA 1968)★★★, Scrapbook/Live At The Bitter End (Kama Sutra 1970)★, Travelin' Band (Janus 1970)★★, Golden King Of Rock (Hallmark 1972)★★★, Just Rock And Roll Music (Sonet 1973)★★★, Live In London '74 (Atlantic 1974)★★, Rock Around The Country (Hallmark 1974)★★.

● COMPILATIONS: Bill Haley's Greatest Hits (Decca 1967)★★★, King Of Rock (Ember 1968)★★★, Mister Rock 'n' Roll (Ember 1969)★★★, The Bill Haley Collection (Pickwick 1976)★★★, R-O-C-K (Sonet 1976)★★★, Armchair Rock 'N' Roll (MCA 1978)★★★, Everyone Can Rock 'N' Roll (Sonet 1980)★★★, A Tribute To Bill Haley (MCA 1981)★★★, The Essential Bill Haley (Charly 1984)★★★, Hillbilly Haley (Rollercoaster 1984)★★★, Boogie With Bill Haley (Topline 1985)★★★, Greatest Hits (MCA 1985)★★★, Golden Greats (MCA 1985)★★★, From The Original Master Tapes (MCA 1985)★★★, The Original Hits '54-'57 (Hallmark 1987)★★★, Greatest Hits (Connoisseur 1988)★★★, Rip It Up Rock 'N' Roll (Connoisseur 1988)★★★, Golden CD Collection (Bulldog 1989)★★★, Bill Haley's Rock 'N' Roll Scrapbook (Sequel 1990)★★★, The Decca Years And More 5-CD box set (Bear Family 1991)★★★.

● FURTHER READING: Sound & Glory, John Von Hoelle and John Haley.

● FILMS: Don't Knock The Rock (1956).

HALL, ROBIN, AND JIMMIE MACGREGOR

This well-known folk duo from Scotland featured Robin Hall (b. 27 June 1937, Edinburgh, Scotland; vocals, bodhran) and Jimmie MacGregor (b. 10 March 1930, Springburn, Glasgow, Scotland; vocals, guitar). Hall had studied at the Royal Scottish Academy Of Music And Dramatic Art from 1955-58. There followed a brief spell as an actor in repertory theatre, plus some solo gigs and radio work. He met and teamed up with MacGregor at the World Youth Festival in Vienna. In contrast, MacGregor came from a working-class family, and was involved in the folk revival of the 50s. He learned a great number of songs at the famous house parties that took place at the time, with everyone singing and harmonizing. MacGregor's first influences were not Scottish at all, and were, in fact, Burl Ives and black American blues man Josh White. MacGregor built up a repertoire of Ives songs with the first guitar he bought. His next big influence was Ewan MacColl and 'Ballads And Blues'. MacGregor graduated after four years at art school, and worked as a studio potter and teacher. He often hitch-hiked to London to visit what few folk clubs there were at the time. Eventually, he settled in London, joining Chas McDevvitt's skiffle group, but he left a few weeks before they had the hit record 'Freight Train'. There followed a series of solo performances and membership of various groups, including the Steve Benbow Folk Four. After meeting Hall in Vienna, the two were given much encouragement by Paul Robeson who was playing at the same concert. Hall's solo album of child ballads from the Gavin Greig collection, *Last Leaves Of Traditional Ballads*, is now a collector's item. The duo were popular on television, making their first appearance on BBC's *Tonight*, and appeared five nights weekly for 14 years. In 1960, Decca released the single 'Football Crazy', which received a great deal of airplay and attendant publicity. Hall and MacGregor also appeared regularly on radio, and are remembered for the series *Hullabaloo*, which started on 28 September 1963, on ABC television.

They went on to tour the world, and record more than 20 albums, appearing on countless radio and television programmes. One series for which they became known was *The White Heather Club*, which they hosted for five years. After 21 years together, it was Hall who called a halt to the duo's career. He had always been nervous and had never really liked performing. After the split, Hall went into broadcasting for the BBC World Service, as well as writing, arranging and producing records. In addition to scriptwriting, he also took up journalism as a music and drama critic. In 1977, he won two national radio awards, best presenter and best documentary, for a documentary on Radio Clyde, *The Sing Song Streets*, a programme about Glasgow told through songs, stories and children's games. The programme was written, produced and presented by Hall. MacGregor wrote three folk songbooks, did some solo work, and wrote a book on the West Highland Way, which became the basis of a successful television series. Subsequently, he has made six outdoor television series, and written five accompanying books. His own radio show for BBC Scotland, *MacGregor's Gathering*, has been running now for many years. In 1993 MacGregor was awarded an OBE.

● ALBUMS: Robin Hall *Last Leaves Of Traditional Ballads* (1959)★★★, the Galliards *Scottish Choice* (1961)★★★★, the Galliards *A Rovin'* (1961)★★★, *Scotch And Irish* (Eclipse 1962)★★★★, *Tonight And Every Night* (1962)★★★★, *Two Heids Are Better Than Yin* (Eclipse 1963)★★★, the Galliards *The Next Tonight Will Be-Robin Hall And Jimmie MacGregor* (1964)★★★★, *By Public Demand* (1964)★★★ *The Red Yo-Yo* (1966)★★★, *Songs Of Grief And Glory* (1967)★★★, *One Over Eight* (1969)★★, *We Belong To Glasgow* (1970)★★, *Scottish Choice* (Eclipse 1971)★★★, *Kids Stuff* (Eclipse 1974)★★★, *Scotland's Best* (Decca 1975)★★★, *Songs For Scotland* (Beltona 1977)★★★.

HAMILTON, ROY

b. 16 April 1929, Leesburg, Georgia, USA, d. 20 July 1969. Hamilton's booming baritone voice made him a 50s hit-maker singing gospel-flavoured pop songs. In the late 40s Hamilton honed his singing skills in a church choir and as a member of its offshoot quartet, the Searchlight Singers. He won a talent contest at the Apollo Theatre in 1947, but it was not until 1953 that he was discovered singing in a New Jersey club by Bill Cook, an influential local disc jockey who became the singer's manager. Hamilton's very first record for Columbia's subsidiary Epic, 'You'll Never Walk Alone', became an R&B number 1 and national US Top 30 hit in 1954, and it shot Hamilton to fame (the song would also later become a UK hit for Gerry And The Pacemakers in 1963). There followed for Hamilton a long string of singles that reached both R&B and pop audiences, notably 'If I Loved You', 'Ebb Tide' and 'Hurt' (all three 1954), and 'Unchained Melody' (an R&B number 1, 1955). Hamilton's songbook was built from the most popular entertainments of the day; 'You'll Never Walk Alone' and 'If I Loved You' were two Rodgers And Hammerstein songs taken from their musical *Carousel*, and 'Unchained Melody' came from a Warner Brothers film, *Unchained*. Hamilton retired during 1956-58 due to exhaustion, but when he came back he had adopted the harder gospel sound of his youth to compete with rock 'n' roll and the emerging soul sound. Best reflecting the change in style were the singles 'Don't Let Go' (1958) and his last hit record, 'You Can Have Her' (1961), plus the album *Mr. Rock And Soul* in 1962. The Epic label treated Hamilton as a major pop star and issued 16 albums by the artist. During the mid-60s, his career sank while recording with MGM and then RCA.

● ALBUMS: *Roy Hamilton* (Epic 1956)★★★, *You'll Never Walk Alone* (Epic 1956)★★★, *The Golden Boy* (Epic 1957)★★★, *With All My Love* (Epic 1958)★★★, *Why Fight The Feeling?* (Epic 1959)★★, *Come Out Swingin'* (Epic 1959)★★★, *Have Blues, Must Travel* (Epic 1959)★★, *Roy Hamilton Sings Spirituals* (Epic 1960)★★★, *Soft 'N' Warm* (Epic 1960)★★★, *You Can Have Her* (Epic 1961)★★★, *Only You* (Epic 1961)★★★, *Mr. Rock And Soul* (Epic 1962)★★★, *The Great Golden Grooves* (1963)★★, *Warm Soul* (1963)★★★, *Sentimental, Lonely And Blue* (1964)★★, *The Impossible Dream* (1966)★★★.

● COMPILATIONS: *Roy Hamilton At His Best* (Epic 1960)★★★, *Roy Hamilton's Greatest Hits* (Epic 1962)★★★, *The Voice Of Roy Hamilton* (1967)★★★, *Unchained* (Charly 1988)★★★, *Golden Classics* (1991)★★★.

HAMILTON, RUSS

b. Ronald Hulme, 1933, Liverpool, England. This singer-songwriter was the first Liverpool artist to make the US Top 10 in the 50s. In 1956, this Korean War veteran (he was in the Royal Air Force) entertained children as a Redcoat at Butlins Holiday Camps in Blackpool and Brighton, and when at the latter, he formed a skiffle group and recorded his first single for Oriole. The a-side, 'We Will Make Love', written after splitting up with girlfriend Pat Hichin, made number 2 in the UK, staying in the Top 10 for 15 weeks. The b-side, 'Rainbow', which he says took only a couple of minutes to write, made him a US one-hit-wonder and shot to number 7, becoming the biggest hit to date there by a UK male artist. In the summer of 1957 he was a transatlantic star, commuting between the USA and Clacton, Essex, where he was entertaining Butlins holidaymakers at one of their camps. His follow-up, 'Wedding Ring', again written about Miss Hitchin, gave him his last UK chart entry. He joined MGM Records in 1960, but even recording in Nashville did not help him return to the charts. Despite having such a spectacular start to his career, it seemed that either Hamilton's face, distinctive lisp, or seemingly unfashionable ballad singing style, no longer fitted.

● ALBUMS: *Rainbow* (Kapp 1957)★★, *We Will Make Love* (Oriole 1959)★★.

HAMMERSTEIN, OSCAR, II

b. 12 July 1895, New York City, New York, USA, d. 23 August 1960. Hammerstein was born into a family with long-standing theatrical associations. His father, William Hammerstein, was manager of New York's Victoria theatre, and an uncle, Arthur Hammerstein, was a Broadway producer. Most famous of all his ancestors was his grandfather, Oscar Hammerstein I, who had made a fortune in industry before becoming one of New York's leading theatrical impresarios and founder of the Manhattan Opera. Although he studied law, the young Oscar's background inevitably affected him and, while still at school, he wrote for shows. He was doubtless also influenced by some of his fellow students, who included future songwriters Lorenz Hart and Howard Dietz. Oscar's showbusiness career began when he was employed by his uncle as assistant stage manager. Soon afterwards, he collaborated with Otto Harbach, Frank Mandel, and composer Herbert Stothart on *Tickle Me* (1920). Subsequently, he and Harbach teamed up again to write the book and lyrics to the season's biggest hit, *Wildflower* (1923), which had music by Stothart and Vincent Youmans. Hammerstein, Harbach and Stothart then had further success, working with Rudolph Friml on *Rose-Marie* (1924), which proved to be a classic of American operetta. Two of the show's most memorable songs were 'Rose-Marie' and 'Indian Love Call'. Hammerstein and Harbach's next composing partner was Jerome Kern, and their liaison resulted in *Sunny* (1925), which had the appealing 'Sunny' and 'Who?' in its score.

In the following year, Hammerstein worked with George Gershwin on *Song Of The Flame*, and the year after that with Harbach and Sigmund Romberg on *The Desert Song*, which produced lasting successes such as 'The Desert Song' and 'One Alone'. Hammerstein teamed up again with Kern in 1927 for *Show Boat*, writing lyrics for such immortal numbers as 'Why Do I Love You?', 'Can't Help Lovin' Dat Man', 'Only Make Believe' and 'Ol' Man River'. In 1928 he rejoined Harbach and Friml to gain further acclaim with *The New Moon*, which featured 'Lover Come Back To Me' and 'Softly As In A Morning Sunrise'. He continued to work with Kern, and during the next few years their shows were full of songs that became standards, among them 'The Song Is You', 'I've Told Ev'ry Little Star' and 'All The Things You Are'.

In the early 30s Hammerstein was lured to Hollywood, where he met with only limited success. Although some of the films on which he worked were box-office failures, he nevertheless co-authored several timeless songs, including 'When I Grow Too Old To Dream' (with Romberg) and 'I Won't Dance' (with Harbach and Kern), the latter for the 1935 Fred Astaire-Ginger Rogers film *Roberta*. Other songs

written with Kern for films were 'Can I Forget You', 'The Folks Who Live On The Hill', 'I'll Take Romance' and 'The Last Time I Saw Paris', which won an Oscar in 1941. In the early 40s Hammerstein's career took a new direction, and the ups and downs of the past were forgotten with the first of a series of smash-hit Broadway shows written with a new partner. He had worked briefly with Richard Rodgers in 1928 and again in 1935, but now, with Rodgers' regular collaborator Lorenz Hart a victim of alcoholism and depression, a new partnership was formed. Rodgers and Hammerstein's first score was for *Oklahoma!* (1943), which was followed by *Carousel* (1945), *Allegro* (1947), *South Pacific* (1949), *The King And I* (1951), *Me And Juliet* (1953), *Pipe Dream* (1955), *Flower Drum Song* (1958) and *The Sound Of Music* (1959). Collectively, these shows were among the most successful in the history of the American musical theatre, with *Oklahoma!* running for 2,212 performances and winning a Pulitzer Prize - as did *South Pacific*, which ran for 1,925 performances. In addition to their stage successes, Rodgers and Hammerstein wrote the score for the film *State Fair* (1945), which included the Oscar-winning song 'It Might As Well Be Spring', and the television show *Cinderella* (1957). A brief list of songs from their stage musicals includes such well-loved hits as 'Oh, What A Beautiful Morning', 'People Will Say We're In Love', 'The Surrey With The Fringe On Top', 'If I Loved You', 'You'll Never Walk Alone', 'Some Enchanted Evening', 'Younger Than Springtime', 'Bali Ha'i', 'Hello, Young Lovers', 'Shall We Dance?', 'No Other Love' and 'Climb Ev'ry Mountain'. Between *Oklahoma!* and *Carousel*, Hammerstein wrote a new book and lyrics for Georges Bizet's opera *Carmen*. The new show, *Carmen Jones*, opened on Broadway in 1943 and was a great success. It was transferred to the screen in 1954 and, most recently, was revived in London's West End in 1991. Hammerstein's remarkable contribution to America's theatrical tradition was profound, and his irreproachable standards represented the culmination of the traditional, operetta-based style of musical comedy. In 1993, the 50th anniversary of Rodgers and Hammerstein's first collaboration on 'America's most loved musical' was celebrated by the publication of *OK! The Story Of Oklahoma!* and *The Rodgers And Hammerstein Birthday Book*. In addition, the revue *A Grand Night For Singing*, which was packed with their songs, played for a brief spell in New York.

● FURTHER READING: *Some Enchanted Evening: The Story Of Rodgers and Hammerstein*, J.D. Taylor. *The Rodgers And Hammerstein Story*, Stanley Green. *The Sound Of Their Music: The Story Of Rodgers And Hammerstein*, Frederick Nolan. *OK! The Story Of Oklahoma!*, Max Wilk. *Rodgers And Hammerstein Birthday Book*, compiled by Bert Fink. *The Wordsmiths: Oscar Hammerstein & Alan Jay Lerner*, Stephen Citron.

HAMMOND, JOHN, JNR.

b. John Henry Hammond II, 15 December 1910, New York City, USA, d. July 1987. Hammond became a jazz fan as a child and in the early 30s was a record reviewer for *Melody Maker*. He used his inherited wealth to finance recordings at a time when economic depression had made record companies unwilling to invest in jazz, and produced Billie Holiday's first session as well as tracks by Teddy Wilson, Bessie Smith, Mildred Bailey and Artie Shaw. In 1936 a chance hearing of a broadcast by Count Basie from Kansas

City (Hammond was listening on his car radio outside a Chicago hotel where Benny Goodman was appearing) led him actively to promote Basie's career. In 1938/9, Hammond devised and organized the *Spirituals To Swing* concerts at New York's Carnegie Hall. These were designed to show the full breadth of black American music and featured gospel (Rosetta Tharpe), blues (Big Bill Broonzy), New Orleans jazz (Sidney Bechet) and contemporary dance music (Benny Goodman, who married Hammond's sister, Alice). In the early 40s, he worked for Columbia Records and after army service moved to Keynote, Mercury and Vanguard as a staff producer. Hammond returned to Columbia in 1958 and was chiefly responsible for signing such folk revival artists as Pete Seeger and Bob Dylan, who was known at the company as 'Hammond's folly' in the early years of his contract. Hammond was the producer of Dylan's first two albums. While chiefly involved with jazz and blues - he supervised reissues of Bessie Smith and Robert Johnson, and was a founder of the Newport Jazz Festival - Hammond continued to bring new artists to Columbia during the 60s and 70s, most notably Leonard Cohen, George Benson and Bruce Springsteen. His son, John Hammond III (often confusingly titled John Hammond Jnr. himself, which leads to his father being mistakenly identified as Hammond Snr.), is a noted white blues singer whose recording career began in the mid-60s.

HANS CHRISTIAN ANDERSEN

This extremely popular, but critically slated, musical biopic of the legendary Danish storyteller was produced by Samuel Goldwyn in 1952. Estimates vary as to how many prospective screenplays were rejected by the producer (and the Danish authorities) before Moss Hart came up with the final draft. Eschewing all pretensions of biographical accuracy, this 'fairy tale about a great spinner of fairy tales' set in 1830, told of a simple cobbler (Danny Kaye) who falls in love with a beautiful ballerina (Jeanmaire) after he has made some shoes for her. When his love is rejected, he returns to his home-town and eventually makes a fortune from writing children's stories. Kaye, whose renowned zany style had made him a controversial choice for the leading role, toned down the histrionics and gave a brilliant performance. He was assisted in no small part by a marvellous Frank Loesser score, much of which was inspired by Andersen's original tales. It included several endearing numbers, such as 'Thumbelina', 'No Two People', 'I'm Hans Christian Andersen', 'The King's New Clothes', 'Wonderful Copenhagen', 'Anywhere I Wander', 'The Ugly Duckling' and 'The Inchworm'. The delightful ballet sequences were choreographed by Roland Petit, who made an appearance in one of them. Also in the cast were Farley Granger, Joey Walsh, John Brown, Philip Tonge, Erik Bruhn and John Qualen. The director was Charles Vidor, and the film was beautifully photographed in Technicolor by Harry Stradling. It grossed $6 million in the USA, and went on to become one of the most celebrated film musicals of the decade. A successful stage production, entitled *Hans Andersen*, with a new book by Beverley Cross and additional songs by Marvin Laird, was presented in London's West End. It starred Tommy Steele, who was also in the 1977 revival.

HANSON, JOHN

b. John Stanley Watts, 31 August 1922, Oshawa, Ontario, Canada. A singer, actor and producer, Hanson moved to the UK with his parents in 1925 and was brought up in Scotland. He sang as a boy soprano in his local choir and made several broadcasts in the early 30s. When he left school he became a production engineer before making his professional debut in 1946 at a concert in Birmingham. He made his name initially on radio programmes such as *Songs From The Shows*, accompanied by the orchestras of Geraldo and Mantovani, and Troise And His Mandoliers, and later became a regular on *Friday Night Is Music Night*, *Fred Hartleys' Hour* and *Ray's A Laugh*. It was Mantovani who gave Hanson his first opportunity on television and he eventually had his own series, *John Hanson Sings*, which was introduced by 'A Song Of Romance', one of his own compositions. In 1957 he began to organize and appear in touring revivals of romantic musicals from the past. He played the Red Shadow in *The Desert Song*, and the role became indelibly associated with him. It was followed by *The Student Prince*, *The Vagabond King*, *Lilac Time*, *Rose Marie*, and *Maid Of The Mountains*. In Britain the beat boom was well under way, but Hanson - who by then was being termed 'the last of the matinee idols' - continued to bring a glorious taste of nostalgia to eager and appreciative audiences throughout the UK. In 1965 he took the leading role in *The World Of Ivor Novello* and a year later appeared in *When You're Young*, for which he wrote the book, music, and lyrics. In 1967 he made his West End debut in *The Desert Song* which was succeeded by *The Student Prince*. Both London productions transferred to Blackpool for summer seasons in 1969/70. In 1972 at the Prince of Wales Theatre he played John Carteret in *Smilin' Through*, his own musical adaptation of the film of the same name. Over the next few years he continued to tour in nostalgic productions such as *Lilac Time*, *Rose Marie*, *The Dancing Years*, and *Glamorous Night*. After producing and directing a farewell tour of *The Desert Song* in 1976/7, he devoted most of his time to concerts and summer seasons, and was still active until the mid-80s when he was forced to retire through ill health.

● ALBUMS: *The Student Prince-Vagabond King* (1961)★★★★, *Lilac Time-Maid Of the Mountains* (1964)★★★, *In Musical Comedy* (1964)★★★, *Music Of Ivor Novello* (1965)★★★★, *Songs Of Romance* (1965)★★★, with Vanessa Lee *This Is London* (1966)★★★, *Encores* (1966)★★★, *When You're Young* (1966)★★★, *The Desert Song-New Moon* (1967)★★, *Rodgers And Hammerstein Favourites* (1968)★★★, *My Songs Of Love For You* (1969)★★★, *Desert Song-Student Prince* (1970)★★★, *Great Songs From Great Films* (1970)★★★, *Smilin' Through* (1972)★★★, *Lilac Time-Maid Of The Mountain* (1973)★★★, *Sings Friml Favourites* (1973)★★★, *I'll Sing You A Thousand Love Songs* (1973)★★★, *The Dancing Years-White Horse Inn* (Philips 1975)★★, *Sings 20 Showtime Greats* (K-Tel 1977)★★★.

● COMPILATIONS: *Showcase* (1968)★★★, *Favourites* (Philips 1974)★★★, *Sings Songs From His Hit Shows* (Philips 1976)★★★, *Spotlight On John Hanson* (Philips 1977)★★★.

● FURTHER READING: *Me And My Red Shadow, The Autobiography* John Hanson.

HARPTONES

An R&B vocal group formed in 1953 in Harlem, New York City, New York, USA. The members were lead Willie Winfield, first tenor Nick Clark, second tenor William Dempsey, baritone Bill 'Dicey' Galloway, bass Billy Brown and pianist/arranger Raoul J. Cita. The Harptones were one of the smoothest and most polished R&B vocal groups to emerge during the early rock 'n' roll era. Although considered a part of the doo-wop phenomenon, they rarely employed nonsense syllables. Instead, the chorus would answer in words employing a special 'opened mouth harmony' devised by Cita. The Harptones were giants on the east coast but virtually unknown elsewhere in the country. Among their best numbers (all ballads) are 'Sunday Kind Of Love' (1954), 'My Memories Of You' (1954) and 'Life Is But A Dream'' (1955); none of their jump songs were particularly convincing. By 1956, with the death of Brown, the group was beginning to break up, and during this time Jimmy Beckum appeared on many of the tracks recorded for George Goldner's Rama/Gee complex. Top notch songs during this period included 'On Sunday Afternoon' and 'Shrine Of St. Cecilia'. Their final recordings were released in 1957. During the 70s and 80s Winfield and Cita made up various permutations of a Harptones group to play the east coast oldies circuit.

● COMPILATIONS: *The Paragons Meet The Harptones* (Musicnote 1963)★★★, *The Harptones Featuring Willie Winfield* (Relic 1971)★★★, *Echoes Of A Rock Era* 12 tracks by the Harptones, 12 by the Crows (Roulette 1972)★★★, *The Harptones Featuring Willie Winfield Volume 2* (Relic 1973)★★★, *Golden Classics: The Goldner Recordings, 1956-57* (Collectables 1991)★★★★, *A Sunday Kind Of Love* (Relic 1992)★★★.

HARRIS, MAX

b. 15 September 1918, Bournemouth, Dorset, England. A pianist, composer and prolific conductor-arranger for radio and television programmes. As a boy, he had private tuition on the piano up to the Royal Academy Of Music Advanced Grade, and gave piano lessons himself, while still a teenager. He served as pianist-arranger with the Jack Parnell orchestra, played gigs with top sidemen such as Tommy Whittle and George Chisholm, and made his first broadcast in 1950 on the BBC's *Jazz Club*. During the 50s he arranged for BBC Radio's *Show Band Show*, conducted by Cyril Stapleton, which featured top US artists such as Frank Sinatra. He has also worked on many of Britain's top-rated radio and television comedy shows, with such artists as Frankie Howerd, Arthur Askey, Russell Harty, Dave Allen and Peter Goodwright, and was involved in a special radio tribute to the Queen Mother on her 80th birthday. His compositions have included the title themes and/or incidental music for radio and television programmes such as *Round The Horne*, *Young At Heart*, *Father Charlie*, *Mickey Dunne*, *Doomwatch*, *Poldark*, *Horseman Riding By*, *The Spies*, *Open All Hours*, *Mind Your Language*, *Porridge*, *Sherlock Holmes*, *On The Buses* and *Doctor's Daughters*. His 'Gurney Slade Theme', from ATV's quirky *The Strange World Of Gurney Slade* (1960-61), starring Anthony Newley, made the UK Top 20, and won an Ivor Novello Award. Harris gained another 'Ivor' in 1964, when his 'Bombay Duck', from the *Kipling* television series, was adjudged 'The Year's Outstanding Orchestral /

Instrumental Composition'. He also won the Designer and Graphics Association Award in 1980 for his work on *The Pink Medicine Show*. Besides his own recordings, he has served as arranger and musical director for many top artists, such as Ted Heath, Ella Fitzgerald, Dick Haymes, Owen Brannigan, and a series of four albums which brought legendary musicians Yehudi Menuhin and Stéphane Grappelli together on record for the first time.

HARRIS, WEE WILLIE

'Discovered' in London's famous coffee bar club the 2I's - shrine of early UK pop - he was promoted by his manager as the kingdom's very own Jerry Lee Lewis - though he was less a teen-idol than a television gimmick in loud attire and hair dyed a funny colour - usually shocking pink, green or orange - for regular appearances on the television pop show *6.5 Special*. Nor was he above banal publicity stunts, including a 'feud' with blue-rinsed Larry Page, another 50s hopeful. Though Harris composed 'Rockin' At the 2 I's' as a debut single, he relied mostly on US cover versions - albeit delivered with more enthusiasm than many other native contemporaries. Nevertheless, home consumers preferred the original versions of 'Riot In Cell Block Number Nine' (the Robins) and 'Wild One' (Bobby Rydell), though they were unlikely to have heard Timmie Rogers' 'Back To School Again' or Gerry Granahan's 'No Chemise Please' before Harris rehashed them. Although a less enduring clown than Screaming Lord Sutch, he resurfaced as a nostalgia act in the late 70s after Ian Dury mentioned his name in the lyrics of 1979's 'Reasons To Be Cheerful (Part Three)'.

● COMPILATIONS: *Goes Ape* (Ace 1986)★★.

HARRISON, WILBERT

b. 5 January 1929, Charlotte, North Carolina, USA, d. 26 October 1994, Spencer, North Carolina, USA. Although Harrison first recorded as early as 1953, it was not until the end of the decade that the singer established his reputation with a superb jump blues-styled adaptation of the perennial 'Kansas City'. This memorable single eventually rose to number 1 in the US pop and R&B charts, despite the attention of several competing versions. The singer then unleashed a series of similarly excellent releases including the compulsive 'Let's Stick Together', which was revived many years later by Bryan Ferry. Harrison continued to record, rather unsuccessfully, throughout the 60s, until 'Let's Work Together', a regenerated reading of that former release, returned him to the public eye. Harrison subsequently appeared in London with Creedence Clearwater Revival, but the song ultimately became better known with Canned Heat's hit version, a number 2 in the UK and a number 17 in the USA. Its originator, meanwhile, made several excellent albums in the wake of his new-found popularity, but was unable to gain any consistent commercial appeal.

● ALBUMS: *Kansas City* (Sphere Sound 1965)★★★, *Let's Work Together* (Sue 1970)★★★, *Shoot You Full Of Love* (Juggernaut 1971)★★, *Anything You Want* (1971)★★, *Wilbert Harrison* (Buddah 1971)★★, *Soul Food Man* (Chelsea 1976)★★, *Lovin' Operator* (Charly 1985)★★, *Small Labels* (Krazy Kat 1986)★★, *Listen To My Song* (Savoy Jazz 1987)★★.

● COMPILATIONS: *Kansas City* (Relic 1990)★★★★.

HART, MOSS

b. 24 October 1904, New York, USA, d. 20 December 1961, Palm Springs, California, USA. A distinguished librettist, director, and playwright who was particularly renowned for his work with George S. Kaufman. Hart is reported to have written the book for the short-lived *Jonica* in 1930, but his first real Broadway musical credit came three years later when he contributed the sketches to the Irving Berlin revue *As Thousands Cheer*. Subsequent revues for which he co-wrote sketches included *The Show Is On*, *Seven Lively Arts* and *Inside USA*. During the remainder of the 30s Hart wrote the librettos for *The Great Waltz* (adapted from the operetta *Waltzes Of Vienna*), *Jubilee*, *I'd Rather Be Right* (with Kaufman) and *Sing Out The News* (which he also co-produced with Kaufman and Max Gordon). In 1941 he wrote one of his wittiest and most inventive books for *Lady In Dark*, which starred Gertrude Lawrence, and gave Danny Kaye his first chance on Broadway. Thereafter, as far as the musical theatre was concerned, apart from the occasional revue, Hart concentrated mostly on directing, and sometimes producing, shows such as Irving Berlin's *Miss Liberty*, and Alan Jay Lerner and Frederick Loewe's smash hits *My Fair Lady* and *Camelot*. He won a Tony Award for his work on *My Fair Lady*. His considerable output for the straight theatre included *Light Up The Sky*, *The Climate Of Eden*, *Winged Victory*, and (with Kaufman) *Once In A Lifetime*, *You Can't Take It With You* (for which they both won the Pulitzer Prize) and *The Man Who Came To Dinner*. Hart also wrote the screenplays for two film musicals, *Hans Christian Andersen* (1952) and the 1954 remake of *A Star Is Born*, starring Judy Garland. His absorbing autobiography, *Act One*, was filmed in 1963 with George Hamilton as Hart and Jason Robards as Kaufman.

● FURTHER READING: *Act One*, Moss Hart.

HAVER, JUNE

b. June Stovenour, 10 June 1926, Rock Island, Illinois, USA. A vivacious singer and actress in several 20th Century-Fox musicals of the 40s and early 50s, who gave up her career after marrying the highly successful film actor Fred MacMurray. A talented all-round entertainer as a youngster - she is said to have played the piano with the Cincinnati Symphony Orchestra - Haver sang with dance bands before landing the part of a hat-check girl in the Alice Faye movie *The Gang's All Here* in 1943. A year later, when she co-starred with crooner Dick Haymes in *When Irish Eyes Are Smiling*, she was being tipped as the successor to Betty Grable. During the course of *Where Do We Go From Here?* (1945), she lost Fred MacMurray to Joan Leslie - but they were reunited (in real life) some years later. Before then, Haver decorated a series of period musicals - mostly set around the turn of the century - which included *The Dolly Sisters*, *Three Little Girls In Blue*, *Wake Up And Dream*, *I Wonder Who's Kissing Her Now*, *Look For The Silver Lining*, *Oh You Beautiful Doll*, *The Daughter Of Rosie O'Grady* and *I'll Get By* (1950). *The Girl Next Door* (1953), in which Haver co-starred with Dan Dailey, was her last film (and one of her best), and the only one with contemporary costumes and setting. Her decision to leave the movie business while she was still at her peak and enter The Sisters of Charity Convent at Xavier, Kansas, in February 1953, was branded by many as a publicity stunt. This conclusion seemed the more credible when she re-emerged into the outside world after only seven and a half months. However, she claimed that she 'did not have the physical strength to withstand the strain of religious life', and after meeting up with Fred MacMurray again, and marrying him in June 1954, she has not made another motion picture since. Even that union, in view of the difference in their ages (he was 45, she 28), came in for a fair amount of criticism, but they raised their twin daughters and were still together when MacMurray died in 1991 at the age of 83.

HAWKINS, COLEMAN

b. Coleman Randolph Hawkins, 21 November *c*.1901, St. Joseph, Missouri, USA, d. 19 May 1969. Coleman Hawkins (aka 'Bean' and 'Hawk') is the colossus of the tenor saxophone, and hence of modern jazz. He was the first to use the instrument as a serious means of expression and continued to be open to new developments for 40 years. Starting piano lessons at the age of five, he later learned cello and took up tenor saxophone when he was nine years old. Within a few years he was playing dances and appearing in Kansas and Chicago. He attended Washburn College in Topeka and toured as a member of Mamie Smith's Jazz Hounds in 1921. He joined Fletcher Henderson's Orchestra in 1924, a sophisticated New York dance band then coming to terms with the new jazz music - hot and improvised - that Louis Armstrong, who had also joined Henderson in 1924, had brought from New Orleans by way of Chicago. Released in 1926, 'The Stampede' featured Hawkins' first notable solo. In his ten years with the band he transformed the tenor sax - previously a novelty instrument for blues and hokum records - from rather quaint imitations of Armstrong's staccato style into a vehicle for the powerful and suave solos that were the essence of swing. 'St Louis Shuffle' (1927), 'Sugar Foot Stomp' (1931) and 'Hocus Pocus' (1934) are three brilliant sides that trace this evolution. By 1934 jazz had become a global music. Coleman Hawkins left Fletcher Henderson and travelled to Europe, where he was welcomed by the local players. He recorded with Jack Hylton in England. Excluded from a Hylton tour of Germany in 1935 by the Nazis' new racial laws, he joined Theo Masman's Ramblers Dance Orchestra and recorded with them for Decca. In 1937 he met up with Django Reinhardt and recorded some memorable music (Stéphane Grappelli was relegated to piano), and he also played with fellow exile Benny Carter. When war broke out in 1939 Hawkins returned to the USA. There his supremacy on tenor sax had been challenged by the languid yet harmonically sophisticated playing of Lester Young, but his recording of 'Body & Soul' (on 11 October 1939) was a massive hit and established him as a national figure, his confessional, tender-but-tough tenor the epitome of jazz. In 1940 he toured with his own 16-piece, appearing at premier New York jazz spots the Arcadia and the Savoy Ballroom, but the days of the big band were numbered. In December 1943 his small combo recordings - 'How Deep Is The Ocean', 'Stumpy' and an irresistible swinger called 'Voodte' - represented the apex of swing, though the sense of headlong abandon was akin to the new music of bebop. Bebop was black America's first *avant garde* art form, featuring innovations many established musicians felt moved to denounce, but Hawkins loved it. He led an early bebop recording session in February 1944 - featuring Don Byas, Dizzy Gillespie and Max Roach. In 1943 he had formed a sextet with

Thelonious Monk, Don Byas and trumpeter Benny Harris and a year later gave Monk his recording debut. Most of 1944 and 1945 were spent on the west coast with a band that included Sir Charles Thompson and Howard McGhee. As featured soloist on Norman Granz's *Jazz At The Philharmonic* tours, trips to Europe followed in 1950 and 1954.

The popularity of Stan Getz's interpretation of Lester Young made Hawkins and his ripe sound unfashionable in the 50s, but his strength as a player - and his openness of mind - never left him. In 1957 Thelonious Monk repaid the compliment by inviting him to join his septet, and the application of Hawkins' big, swinging tenor to Monk's paradoxical compositions yielded wonderful results on tunes such as 'Off Minor'. Playing next to young turks such as John Coltrane, Hawkins showed that he still had something to contribute. The classic *The Hawk Flies High* (1957) showed what Hawkins could accomplish in a mainstream setting, while a reunion with his ex-Henderson colleague Henry 'Red' Allen in the same year showed he could also shine in a more traditional context. In the 60s Hawkins kept playing, recording with new tenor star Sonny Rollins. The list of his engagements in that decade is testament to the catholic taste that an established elder statesman can afford: Pee Wee Russell, Duke Ellington, Bud Powell, Tommy Flanagan, Eric Dolphy, even an appearance on Max Roach's inflammatory *We Insist! Freedom Now* suite and at a 1966 'Tenors Titan' concert that also featured Rollins, Coltrane, Zoot Sims and Yusef Lateef. He played on the last JATP tour (1967) and toured with pianist Oscar Peterson in 1968, although by that point he was increasingly prone to bouts of depression and drinking, exacerbated by a refusal to eat. His death from pneumonia in 1969 marked the end of an era; he was a jazz master whose life-work stretched across six decades of the music's history.

● ALBUMS: *Originals With Hawkins* 10-inch album (Stinson 1950)★★★, *Coleman Hawkins All Stars* 10-inch album (Apollo 1951)★★★, *Coleman Hawkins Favorites* 10-inch album (Advance 1951)★★★, *King Of The Tenor Sax* reissued as *Meditations* (Commodore 1952)★★★★, *Classics In Jazz* 10-inch album (Capitol 1952)★★★, *Tenor Sax* 10-inch album (Brunswick 1953)★★★, *The Bean* 10-inch album (EmArcy 1954)★★★, *The Hawk Talks* 10-inch album (Savoy 1954)★★★, *Improvisations Unlimited* (Concert Hall 1955)★★★, *Accent On The Tenor Sax* (Urania 1955)★★★, *Hawk in Flight* (RCA Victor 1955)★★★★, *The Hawk Returns* (Savoy 1955)★★★, *Coleman Hawkins And His Orchestra* (American Record Society 1956)★★★, *Coleman Hawkins: A Documentary* (Riverside 1956)★★★, *Hawk In Hi-Fi* (RCA Victor 1956)★★★, *The Hawk In Paris* (Vik 1957)★★★, *Gilded Hawk* (Capitol 1957)★★★, *The Hawk Flies High* (Riverside 1957)★★★, with Roy Eldridge *At The Opera House* (Verve 1957)★★★★, *The High And The Mighty Hawk* (Felsted 1958)★★★, *Coleman Hawkins With The Basie Sax Section* (World Wide 1958)★★★, *Soul* (Prestige 1959)★★★★, *Hawk Eyes* (Prestige 1959)★★★, with Ben Webster *Coleman Hawkins Encounters Ben Webster* (Verve 1959)★★★★, with Oscar Peterson *Coleman Hawkins And His Confreres With The Oscar Peterson Trio* (Verve 1959)★★★★, *Coleman Hawkins Plus The Red Garland Trio* (Swingville 1960)★★★, *At Ease With Colman Hawkins* (Moodsville 1960)★★★, *The Coleman Hawkins All Stars* (Swingville 1960)★★★, *Night Hawk* (Swingville 1961)★★★, *Night Hawk* (Prestige

1961)★★★, *The Hawk Swings* (Crown 1961)★★★, *Things Ain't What They Used To Be* (Swingville 1961)★★★, *The Hawk Blows At Midnight* (Decca 1961)★★★, *Years Ago* (Swingville 1961)★★★, *The Hawk Relaxes* (Moodsville 1961)★★★, *Good Old Broadway* (Moodsville 1962)★★★, *The Jazz Version Of No Strings* (Moodsville 1962)★★★, *On The Bean* (Continental 1962)★★★, *In A Mellow Tone* (Original Jazz Classics 1962)★★★, *Jazz At The Metropole* (Philips 1962)★★★, with Duke Ellington *Duke Ellington Meets Coleman Hawkins* (MCA/Impulse 1963)★★★★, *Desafinado: Bossa Nova & Jazz Samba* (Impulse 1963)★★★, *Septet Today And Now* (Impulse 1963)★★★, *Make Someone Happy* (Moodsville 1963)★★★, *Hawkins! Alive! At The Village Gate* (Verve 1963)★★★, with Sonny Rollins *Sonny Meets Hawk* (RCA Victor 1963)★★★★,*Wrapped Tight* (Impulse 1965)★★★, with Frank Hunter *The Hawk And The Hunter* (Mira 1965)★★★, *Sirius* (1966)★★★, *Supreme* 1966 concert recording (Enja 1995)★★★.

● COMPILATIONS: with the Ramblers *The Hawk In Holland* (1935)★★★, one side only *Classic Tenors* (1943)★★★, *The Genius Of Coleman Hawkins* (Verve 1958)★★★★, *The Essential Coleman Hawkins* (Verve 1964)★★★★, *Body And Soul* (Bluebird 1988)★★★★, *1927-39* (1990)★★★★, *The Complete Recordings 1929-31* (1992)★★★★, *April In Paris* 1939-56 recordings (Bluebird 1992)★★★★, *Body And Soul* 1961 recordings (1993)★★★★, *Rainbow Mist* (1993)★★★, *Lady Be Good* (Tring 1993)★★, *The Complete Recordings 1929-1940* (Charly 1993)★★★, *A Retrospective 1929-1963* (Bluebird 1995)★★★★, *In The Groove* (Indigo 1996)★★★.

● FURTHER READING: *Coleman Hawkins Volume 1 1922-44, Volume 2 1945-57*, Jean François Villetard. *The Song Of The Hawk*, John Chilton. *Coleman Hawkins*, Burnett James.

HAWKINS, DALE

b. Delmar Allen Hawkins, 22 August 1938, Goldmine, Louisiana, USA. One of the earliest exponents of rockabilly, singer-guitarist Hawkins was discovered in 1955 by Shreveport record distributor Stan Lewis and signed by the Chicago-based Chess label. Among his earliest singles was the Bobby Charles composition 'See You Soon Baboon', an answer record to Bill Haley's 'See You Later Alligator' (which was also written by Charles), but Hawkins' biggest hit was the Howlin' Wolf-influenced 'Suzie Q', with Roy Buchanan on guitar. It reached the US Top 30 in 1957 and was later covered by numerous artists, including the Everly Brothers, Rolling Stones and Creedence Clearwater Revival, for whom the song was a Top 20 hit in 1968. Hawkins recorded further hard-rocking tracks such as 'La Do-Dada' and 'Class Cutter' over the next few years, featuring guitarists Scotty Moore and James Burton. Hawkins left Chess in 1961 and made occasional records for other labels, but during the 60s he concentrated on production, creating Top 10 hits for Bruce Channel ('Hey Baby', 1962) and the Five Americans ('Western Union', 1967). Hawkins returned to recording with a pleasant country-rock album for Bell in 1969 which contained versions of Leiber And Stoller's 'Hound Dog' and Jimmy Reed's 'Baby What You Want Me To Do'. Among the artists Hawkins produced in the 70s was Texas rock band Rio Grande.

● ALBUMS: *Susie Q* (Chess 1958)★★★, *Let's Twist At The Miami Beach Peppermint Lounge* (Roulette 1962)★★, *L.A.,*

Memphis & Tyler, Texas (Bell 1969)★★, *Oh Susie Q* (Checker 1973)★★★, *Daredevil* (Norton 1997)★★★.
● COMPILATIONS: *Oh! Suzy Q, The Best Of Dale Hawkins* (MCA 1995)★★★.

HAWKINS, 'SCREAMIN' JAY'

b. Jalacy Hawkins, 18 July 1929, Cleveland, Ohio, USA. Reportedly raised in Cleveland by a tribe of Blackfoot Indians, young Jalacy became interested in music at an early age, teaching himself piano at the age of six and, having mastered the keyboard, he then learned to play sax-ophone in his early teens. Hawkins was also an adept young boxer, winning an amateur *Golden Gloves* contest at the age of 14 and becoming Middleweight Champion of Alaska in 1949. He judged music to be the easier option, and became a professional musician, playing piano with artists such as Gene Ammons, Arnett Cobb, Illinois Jacquet, James Moody, Lynn Hope, and on one occasion, Count Basie. In 1950, Hawkins began developing an act based more on his almost operatic bass-baritone voice, and the following year he joined Tiny Grimes' Rocking Highlanders as pianist and occasional vocalist, making his recording debut with the band for Gotham Records in 1952 (the record was withdrawn after three weeks) and for Atlantic Records in 1953 (the results remain unissued). Leaving Grimes, Hawkins was befriended by blues shouter Wynonie Harris, who brought the young musician to New York City as his protégé. At this point, Hawkins' fortunes began to take an upswing, first with his debut records under his own name for the Timely label, followed by superior efforts for Mercury/Wing and Grand Records. In 1956, Screamin' Jay (as he was now known) signed with Columbia's reactivated OKeh subsidiary and enjoyed enormous success with his manic - and appar-ently drunken - rendition of his own 'I Put A Spell On You', which he had recorded earlier as a ballad for Grand Records. Released in October 1956, the original version was quickly withdrawn as a result of the public outrage caused by the 'suggestive and cannibalistic' sound effects provided by Hawkins. A suitably truncated substitution was soon made. Despite these efforts, an air-play ban remained in force, but the record sold over a million copies regardless, becoming a classic of rock music and invoking hundreds of cover ver-sions from Nina Simone to the Alan Price Set and Creedence Clearwater Revival. Remaining with OKeh until 1958, Hawkins ran the gamut of his weird-but-wonderful reper-toire with recordings of straight R&B songs such as 'Little Demon' and 'Person To Person', tongue-in-cheek, semi-oper-atic standards such as 'I Love Paris' and 'Temptation', and the unclassifiable and uniquely bizarre 'Hong Kong', 'Alligator Wine' and 'There's Something Wrong With You'. To enhance this ghoulish strangeness, on his tours with rock 'n' roll package shows, Hawkins was encouraged by Alan Freed to use macabre props such as skulls, snakes and shrunken heads and to begin his act from the inside of a coffin. Again, uproar followed, resulting in a largely unrepresentative album release and, worse still, Hawkins' only 50s film appearance in *Mister Rock 'N' Roll* being cut out in case par-ents boycotted the film's release. Shunned by the mass media, Hawkins spent most of the 60s playing one-nighters and tired rock 'n' roll revival gigs, making the occasional one-off recording agreement with tiny independent labels. *The Night And Day Of Screaming Jay Hawkins*, recorded in

London for producer Shel Talmy's Planet label, was more conservative in tone. A brace of late 60s albums extended his idiosyncratic reputation and it was during these sessions that Hawkins recorded the original 'Constipation Blues', a lavatorial performance destined to become an intrinsic part of his stage act. He enjoyed a cameo role in the much-praised film *American Hot Wax*, and later won a starring role as the laconic hotel desk clerk in Jim Jarmusch's *Mystery Train*. Hawkins later collaborated with modern garage band the Fleshtones. A 1991 release, *Black Music For White People*, which included readings of two Tom Waits compositions, 'Ice Cream Man' and 'Heart Attack And Vine', as well as a rap interpretation of 'I Put A Spell On You', revealed a largely undiminished power. His influence on other performers, notably Screaming Lord Sutch, Arthur Brown and Alice Cooper, should not be underestimated. Touring and recording steadily through the 70s and 80s, Hawkins has recently formed a new band, the Fuzztones, and has made successful tours of Europe and the USA.
● ALBUMS: *At Home With Screamin' Jay Hawkins* (Epic 1958)★★★, *I Put A Spell On You* (Epic 1959)★★★★, *The Night & Day Of Screamin' Jay Hawkins* (Planet 1965)★★★, *What That Is* (Philips 1969)★★, *Screamin' Jay Hawkins* (Philips 1970)★★★, *A Portrait Of A Man & His Woman* (1972)★★★, *I Put A Spell On You* (1977)★★★, *Frenzy* (Edsel 1982)★★, *Real Life* (Charly 1983)★★, *Midnight* (1985)★★, *Live And Crazy* (Midnight Music 1986)★★★, *Feast Of The Mau Mau* (Edsel 1988)★★, *Real Life* (Charly 1989)★★★, *I Is* (1989)★★★, *I Want To Do It In A Cave!* (1990)★★★, *Voodoo Jive* (1990)★★★, *Black Music For White People* (Demon 1991)★★★, *Stone Crazy* (Demon 1993)★★★, *Somethin' Funny Goin' On* (Demon 1994)★★★.
● COMPILATIONS: *I Put A Spell On You* (Direction 1969)★★★, *Screamin' The Blues* (Red Lightnin' 1982)★★★, *Frenzy* (Edsel 1986)★★★, *I Put A Spell On You* (Charly 1989)★★★, *Spellbound 1955-1974* (Bear Family 1990)★★★, *Voodoo Jive: The Best Of Screamin' Jay Hawkins* (Rhino 1990)★★★, *Cow Fingers And Mosquito Pie* (Epic 1991)★★★, *Screamin' Jay Hawkins - 1952-1955* (Magpie 1991)★★★, *From Gotham And Grand* (SJH 1992)★★★, *Portrait Of A Man* (Edsel 1995)★★★.
● FILMS: *American Hot Wax* (1976), *Mystery Train* (1989).

HAYES, BILL

b. 5 June 1926, Harvey, Illinois, USA. Pop vocalist Bill Hayes was already known to American audiences via his regular appearances on comedian Sid Caesar's 50s US television series *Your Show Of Shows*, when his recording of 'The Ballad Of Davy Crockett' shot to number 1 in the US charts in March 1955, despite three other versions, two of which also made the Top 5. The song also reached number 2 in the UK. He had a minor follow-up, 'Wringle, Wrangle', from the 1956 movie *Westward Ho, The Wagons* in the USA, before turning to acting and playing Doug Williams in the US NBC televi-sion soap *Days Of Our Lives*.

HEARTBEATS

This doo-wop vocal quartet was formed in Queens, New York, USA, in 1954, originally named simply the Hearts. Three of the band members, Albert Crump (lead), Wally Roker (bass) and Vernon Seavers (baritone), met while attending Woodrow Wilson High School. They completed the line-up with Robby Tatum from a neighbouring school. They acquired a new lead in the shape of James Sheppard (d. 24 January 1970, Long Island, New York, USA) and Crump then sang first tenor. The group made their recording debut on Philadelphia's Network Records with Sheppard's 'Tormented'. Receiving scant promotion, it brought the group little exposure and fewer sales. More productive would be a liaison with Hull Records. This began in September 1955 with 'Crazy For You', a strong regional seller, and continued with 'Darling How Long' in February of the following year. One of the most fondly remembered records of the whole doo-wop era, 'Your Way', like all their previous releases was written by Sheppard. Though it did not chart at the time, it has subsequently become one of the most popular songs of the period. Their star rising, the group's next recording was 'Oh Baby Don't', but it sold mainly on the strength of Sheppard's plangent b-side composition, 'A Thousand Miles Away'. This quickly became a nationwide hit, peaking at number 53 in the *Billboard* charts. The Heartbeats sought to confirm their popularity with nationwide tours in the company of Ray Charles, B.B. King and others. After a publishing dispute with Hull Records, the Heartbeats' next single emerged on Rama Records in 1957. 'I Won't Be The Fool Anymore' was followed by 'Everybody's Somebody's Fool', which returned them to the lower reaches of the charts. Spells at Gee and Roulette Records (two singles each) preceded the band's break-up in 1958, at which time the members divided into two factions. The rest of the band were allegedly none too impressed when Sheppard fell asleep at the microphone one night in Philadelphia, and other bouts of unshackled egotism exacerbated the situation. The momentum was lost, and all bar Sheppard returned to regular employment. Their erstwhile lead put together Shep And The Limelites, who released a number of singles, though only one, 'Daddy's Home', enjoyed major success (US number 2 in 1961). Sheppard was found dead in his car in 1970 after being shot and robbed.

● COMPILATIONS: *The Best Of The Heartbeats Including Shep & The Limelites* (Rhino 1990)★★★★.

HEATH, TED

b. 30 March 1900, Wandsworth, London, England, d. 18 November 1969, Surrey, England. After playing tenor horn at the age of six, Heath later switched to trombone and throughout the 20s and 30s played with top orchestras such as Jack Hylton, Al Sarita, Sydney Lipton, and in the early 40s with Geraldo. On 7 May 1945, (VJ Day), he formed his own band, some of the early finance being provided by royalties from the songs 'That Lovely Weekend' and 'I'm Gonna Love That Guy', written by Heath and his wife Moira. Kenny Baker, Jack Parnell, Ronnie Chamberlain and Don Lusher were just some of the top musicians who played for him, plus vocalists Paul Carpenter and Beryl Davis. In 1946 the band provided the musical background for the first major British movie musical, *London Town*. Taking a big chance, Heath hired the London Palladium for a *Sunday Night Swing Session*, which proved to be so successful, that it ran for several years. The addition of singers Lita Roza, Dennis Lotis and Dickie Valentine in the early 50s gave the band more teenage appeal, and they appeared in three more films, *Dance Hall* (1950), *It's A Wonderful World* (1956) and *Jazz Boat* (1960). Their theme, 'Listen To My Music', introduced many

specialities including 'Opus One', 'The Champ', 'Dragnet', 'Skin Deep', 'Hot Toddy' and 'Swingin' Shepherd Blues'. The Heath band was the first unit to go to the USA when Musicians' Union restrictions were relaxed in 1955, and subsequently toured there many times. The band compared favourably with even America's top units, and is generally accepted as the best swing band that Britain ever produced. Heath died in 1969. Many of his original personnel still play together, usually under the direction of Jack Parnell or Don Lusher. A three-part series of biographical programmes was broadcast on BBC Radio 2 in 1993.

● ALBUMS: *Ted Heath And His Orchestra* 10-inch album (London 50s)★★★, featuring Winifred Atwell *Black And White Magic* 10-inch album (London 50s)★★★, *Tempo For Dancers* (Decca 1951)★★★, *Listen To My Music* (Decca 1952)★★★, *Selection* (Decca 1952)★★★, *At The London Palladium* (Decca 1953)★★★★, *Strike Up The Band* (Decca 1953)★★★★, *Ted Heath's Fats Waller Album* (Decca 1954)★★★, *100th London Palladium Concert* (Decca 1954)★★★★, *Gershwin For Moderns* (Decca 1954)★★★, *Kern For Moderns* (Decca 1956)★★★, *At The London Palladium Volume 4* (Decca 1956)★★★, *Rodgers For Moderns* (Decca 1956)★★★, *A Yank In Europe* (London 1956)★★★, *Spotlight On Sidemen* (London 1957)★★★, *Showcase* (London 1957)★★★, *Tribute To The Fabulous Dorseys* (London 1957)★★★, featuring Winifred Atwell *Rhapsody In Blue* (London 1957)★★★, *At Carnegie Hall* (Decca 1957)★★★, *First American Tour* (Decca 1957)★★★, *Hits I Missed* (Decca 1958)★★★, *Olde Englyshe* (Decca 1958)★★, *Swings In Hi-Fi Stereo* (Decca 1958)★★★★, *Things To Come* (London 1958)★★★, *Shall We Dance* (London 1959)★★★, *Pop Hits From The Classics* (London 1959)★★★, *Big Band Blues* (London 1959)★★★, *Swing Session* (Decca 1959)★★★★, *Plays The Great Film Hits* (Decca 1959)★★★, *My Very Good Friends The Band Leaders* (Decca 1960)★★★, *The Big Band Dixie Sound* (London 1960)★★★, *The Hits Of The Twenties* (London 1960)★★★, *Ted Heath In Concert* (London 1960)★★★, *Songs For The Young At Heart* (London 1960)★★★, *The Hits Of The 30s* (London 1960)★★★, *Latin Swingers* (London 1961)★★★, *Big Band Beat* (Richmond 60s)★★★, featuring Winifred Atwell *Ted Heath Plays Gershwin* (Richmond 60s)★★★, *Ted Heath Plays The Music Of Fats Waller* (Richmond 60s)★★★, *Big Band Gershwin* (Richmond 60s)★★★, *Big Band Kern* (Richmond 60s)★★★, *Big Band Rodgers* (Richmond 60s)★★★, *Big Band Percussion* (Phase 4 1962)★★★, *Big Band Bash* (Phase 4 1963)★★★, *Satin Saxes And Bouncing Brass* (Phase 4 1963)★★★, *Big Band Spirituals* (Phase 4 1964)★★★, *Coast To Coast* (Phase 4 1964)★★★, *Palladium Revisited* (Phase 4 1964)★★★, with Edmundo Ros *Heath Versus Ros* (Phase 4 1964)★★★, *The Sound Of Music* (Phase 4 1965)★★, with Ros *Heath Versus Ros, Round Two* (Phase 4 1967)★★, *Ted Heath Recalls The Fabulous Dorseys* (Eclipse 1969)★★★★, *Fever* (Phase 4 1966)★★★, *Beatles, Bach And Bacharach* (Phase 4 1971)★★, *Salute To Glenn Miller* (Phase 4 1973)★★★★, *Big Band Themes Remembered, Volume One* (Phase 4 1974)★★★★, *Big Band Themes Remembered, Volume Two* (Phase 4 1974)★★★, *Salutes The Duke* (Phase 4 1975)★★★★, *Ted Heath At The London Palladium 1953* (Eclipse 1976)★★★★, *Salutes Benny Goodman* (Decca 1976)★★★, *Smooth 'N' Swinging 1959-62* recordings (Decca 1981)★★★.

● COMPILATIONS: *Big Band World Of Ted Heath* (Decca

1970)★★★, *The World Of Big Band Blues* (Decca 1972)★★★, *Swing Meets Latin* (Decca 1974)★★★, with Dennis Lotis, Lita Roza *The Ted Heath Years* (Decca 1977)★★★★, *Focus On Ted Heath* (Phase 4 1978)★★★★, *All Time Top Twelve* (Decca 1979)★★★, *Ted Heath At The BBC* (BBC 1983)★★★★, *Big Band Favourites* (Decca 1984)★★★★, *Big Band Bash, Volumes 1-4* (Echo Jazz 1988)★★★★, *The Golden Age Of Ted Heath Volumes 1-3* (Horatio Nelson 1990)★★★★, *The Very Best Of Ted Heath Volume 1* (Horatio Nelson 1995)★★★★.

HEFTI, NEAL

b. 29 October 1922, Hastings, Nebraska, USA. One of the most influential big band arrangers of the 40s and 50s, Hefti's early charts were played by the Nat Towles band in the late 30s. His material was also used by Earl Hines; however, his first real taste of the big time came when he joined Charlie Barnet in 1942 and then moved into the Woody Herman band in 1944. Both engagements were as a member of the trumpet section, but his writing became steadily more important than his playing. For Herman he arranged many of the band's most popular recordings, including 'The Good Earth' and 'Wild Root', and was co-arranger with Ralph Burns of 'Caldonia'. In 1946 Hefti's charts were among those used by the ill-fated Billy Butterfield big band and by Charlie Ventura's equally short-lived band. In the late 40s he wrote for what was one of the best of Harry James's bands; in the mid-50s, along with Ernie Wilkins and Nat Pierce, he helped to give the Count Basie band the new distinctive, tighter style that led to a wholesale re-evaluation of big band music, especially in the UK. *Atomic Basie* was composed by Hefti and it features the glorious 'Lil' Darlin'' and 'Splanky'. The album remains one of Basie's finest works and Hefti's peak. Throughout the 50s and 60s Hefti was heavily involved in composing for films and television (including the theme for the US *Batman* television series), and while much of his work in these quarters was geared to the demands of the medium, there were many moments when he was able to infuse his work with echoes of his jazz heritage. Throughout those years and into the 70s Hefti periodically formed big bands either for club, concert or record dates. The tradition of precise, disciplined arranging, of which Hefti was one of the more important exponents, continues to make itself heard in the work of Sam Nestico, which has proved immensely popular with college and university bands on both sides of the Atlantic.
● ALBUMS: *Swingin' On A Coral Reef* 10-inch album (Coral 1953)★★★, *Music Of Rudolph Frimil* 10-inch album (X 1954)★★★, *Pardon My Doo-wah* (1954)★★, *Hot 'N' Hearty* (1955)★★★, *Singing Instrumentals* (Epic 1956)★★★, *Light And Right!!* (Columbia 1960)★★, *Themes From TV's Top 12* (Reprise 1962)★★, *Boeing Boeing* film soundtrack (RCA Victor 1966)★★, *Batman Theme* (RCA Victor 1966)★★★, *Hefti In Gotham City* (RCA Victor 1966)★★★, *Duel At Diablo* film soundtrack (United Artists 1966)★★★, *Barefoot In The Park* film soundtrack (London 1967)★★★, *The Odd Couple* film soundtrack (Dot 1968)★★★.

HENDERSON, JOE 'MR PIANO'

b. 2 May 1920, Glasgow, Scotland, d. 4 May 1980, London, England. A pianist and composer, Henderson formed his own band to play at school dances before turning profes-sional at the age of 13. In the early 50s he served as accompanist for former child actress and singer Petula Clark, who featured frequently in the UK charts, and subsequently recorded several of her ex-pianist's compositions. Henderson himself became extremely popular on the UK variety circuit, alongside other solo piano acts, such as Winifred Atwell, Russ Conway and - much later - Bobby Crush. He survived the radical changes in popular music that began to take place in the 50s, and still retained an audience. He also featured in *Bumper Bundle* on Radio Luxembourg, and had his own television series *Sing Along With Joe* and *Mr. Piano Plays*. Henderson's first hits came in 1955 with 'Sing It With Joe' and 'Sing It Again With Joe'. These consisted of short piano medleys of jolly standards, such as 'Margie' and 'Somebody Stole My Gal'. In 1958 he had another UK Top 20 hit with 'Trudie', accompanied by the Beryl Stott Chorus. It was the best-known of his mostly bright, catchy compositions, and won an Ivor Novello Award for 'The Year's Best Selling And Most Performed Item'. He earned another 'Ivor' the following year for the movie title song 'Jazzboat', 'The Year's Most Outstanding Composition In The "Jazz" Or "Beat" Idiom'. *Jazzboat* was one of three films that Henderson scored that starred Anthony Newley. The others were *Idle On Parade*, the film that launched Newley's singing career (he co-wrote some of the songs) and *Let's Get Married*. Henderson's other compositions, published by his own company, included 'Why Don't They Understand?' (a US and UK chart hit for country singer George Hamilton IV), 'Chick', 'Treble Chance' (his last Top 30 entry, in 1959), 'Dear Daddy' (with lyrics by Jack Fishman, featured on *Ruby Murray Successes*), 'Matchbox Samba', 'Coffee Bar Jive', 'What A Day We'll Have', 'I'd Have A Long Way To Go', 'When You're Away', 'Dream Of Paradise', 'First Theme', 'I Need You', 'Somebody' and 'Crinoline Waltz'. His other recordings included Charles Chaplin's 'Smile', Leroy Anderson's 'Forgotten Dreams', 'The Theme From the Threepenny Opera (Moritat)' and a lively version of the novelty 'Don't Ring-A Da Bell'. On the latter he played harpsichord, while the vocal was by the British actress Shani Wallis, who went on to play Nancy in the movie of Lionel Bart's *Oliver!* Henderson continued to entertain for many years after the hits dried up, particularly in that very British institution, the seaside summer season.
● ALBUMS: *Joe 'Mr. Piano' Henderson* (1961)★★★★, *Dancing Cheek To Cheek* (60s)★★★, *Bumper Bundle* (60s)★★★★, *The Hits Of 1968* (1968)★★, *Secret Love Hits Of The 50s* (Columbia 1972)★★★, *Sing-A-Long With Joe* (Spark 1973)★★, *Swing-A-Long With Joe 'Mr. Piano' Henderson* (Spark 1974)★★★, *40 All Time Singalong Party Hits* (Warwick 1975)★★★, *Joe Henderson Recalls The Unforgettable 50s* (One-Up 1975)★★★★.

HENDERSON, LYLE 'SKITCH'

b. 27 January 1918, Halstad, Minnesota, USA. After studying at the Juilliard School of Music in New York, Henderson undertook further studies with Arnold Schoenberg. Despite his classical training, Henderson began playing piano in dance bands, some of which he also led. In the early 40s he accompanied leading artists such as Judy Garland and Bing Crosby, for whom he acted as musical director on radio. In the late 40s Henderson had his own big band, but by the early 50s had become Frank Sinatra's MD. Later, he went into the studios of NBC. In the mid-50s he was musical director for the Steve Allen television show and thereafter for the *Tonight* show. His sidemen in the bands he led on these shows included leading session musicians, among them Doc Severinson, Snooky Young and Clark Terry, and he used arrangements by distinguished writers such as Neal Hefti and Ernie Wilkins. In 1971 Henderson returned to his musical roots, becoming conductor of the Tulsa Symphony Orchestra; he was later musical director for the New York production of Kurt Weill's *Street Scene*.

● ALBUMS: *Skitch...Tonight!* (1965)★★★, *Sketches By Skitch* (60s)★★★, *A Tribute To Irving Berlin* (60s)★★.

HENRY, HAYWOOD

b. Frank Haywood Henry, 7 January 1909, Birmingham, Alabama, USA. Haywood began playing clarinet while still a schoolboy, and at the Alabama State Teachers College he joined the college band with classmate Dud Bascomb. This band, the 'Bama State Collegians, was also home to Erskine Hawkins, who eventually took over the band when it turned professional. This was in 1935 and Haywood stayed with the group, playing clarinet and baritone saxophone, for the next two decades. In the 50s he was often on record dates playing jazz with other leaders, including Rex Stewart, and he also played R&B. In the 60s he spent time with Wilbur De Paris and Earl Hines and in the 70s was regularly called upon as a member of bands accompanying artists such as Ella Fitzgerald. Henry was a good clarinet soloist and his baritone playing was solid and workmanlike, providing as it did a resonant foundation for the reed sections in which he appeared. He continued to perform into the 80s.

● COMPILATIONS: *The Chronological Erskine Hawkins 1939-1940* (Classics 1939-40)★★★★.

HERE'S LITTLE RICHARD · LITTLE RICHARD ★★★★★

The enigmatic Little Richard turned rock 'n' roll inside-out with a succession of highly expressive recordings during the mid-50s. Fuelled by an unfettered New Orleans backbeat, he combined gospel fervour and orgasmic delight in equal doses, singing without recourse to convention, and hammering the piano keys with a barely checked passion. *Here's Little Richard* (1957) abounds with essential performances that define an era, and few other collections offer such unremitting excitement. The pace rarely relents, while almost every track has become an integral part of pop history, either in its own right, or through the countless cover versions the songs inspired. It is an exceptional album from an exceptional talent. It reached a peak position of number 13 in the US album chart.

● TRACKS: *Tutti Frutti; True, Fine Mama; Ready Teddy; Baby; Slippin' And Slidin'; Long Tall Sally; Miss Ann; Oh Why?; Rip It Up; Jenny Jenny; She's Got It; Can't Believe You Wanna Leave.*

HERFURT, SKEETS

b. Arthur Herfurt, 28 May 1911, Cincinnati, Ohio, USA. As a young man Herfurt played various reed instruments, mostly in the south-west and especially in Colorado, where he grew up and was educated. His first name-band engagement was with Smith Ballew, the popular singer. This was in 1934 and in the same year he joined the Dorsey Brothers band,

remaining in its ranks after the brothers split up, when the band continued under Jimmy Dorsey's name. Later in the 30s, Herfurt played with bands led by Ray Noble, George Stoll and Tommy Dorsey. Tiring of travelling, he settled in the Los Angeles area, and was briefly with the mid-40s band led by Alvino Rey before military service towards the end of World War II. After the war Herfurt worked in film studios, but had a short spell with Benny Goodman. During the 50s and beyond, he worked in studios, led his own band, and played in numerous recording studio orchestras under many different leaders. He had a further spell with Goodman in the early 60s and again in the middle of the decade. Herfurt's tenor saxophone and clarinet playing was of a very high standard and he was one of countless unsung stalwarts of the swing era's big bands.

● COMPILATIONS: *The Dorsey Brothers Orchestra* (MCA 1934-35)★★★★, *The Uncollected Alvino Rey* (Hindsight 1944-45)★★★.

HERMAN, LENNY

Although largely uncelebrated during his career as a bandleader, Lenny Herman made a significant contribution to the dance band music of New York, USA, from the early 50s onwards. Based in hotels such as the Astor, Edison, Roosevelt, Waldorf-Astoria and New Yorker, his compact band, often dubbed 'The Mightiest Little Band In The Land', etched a definite impression on the evening dancers of those establishments with songs such as 'No Foolin''. Led by Herman's accordion playing, the band, which never numbered more than ten and frequently less than eight, also found engagements further afield in Philadelphia (the Warwick Hotel), Atlantic City (the Straymore Hotel), Virginia Beach (the Cavalier Hotel) and Dallas (the Baker Hotel). By the mid-60s the band had moved permanently to the Lake Tahoe area, where the now five or six strong ensemble earned its living playing to mixed audiences at the resort hotels. They continue to do so to this day.

HEY BOY! HEY GIRL!

This slight 1959 feature starred husband and wife team Keely Smith and Louis Prima. The latter was renowned as a jazz vocalist, trumpeter, composer and bandleader, whose rhythmic style provided a stepping-stone towards rock 'n' roll. After their marriage, the pair embraced Smith's MOR inclinations, enjoying residencies in Las Vegas clubs where they were backed by Sam Butera And The Witnesses. The group appeared with the couple in *Hey Boy! Hey Girl!*, in which Smith plays Dorothy Spencer, a singer who joins Prima and the Witnesses on the understanding that the band will help her with a church bazaar. The film featured such numbers as 'Autumn Leaves', 'Fever', 'When The Saints Go Marching In' and 'Lazy River', although it does not include the duo's 1959 US hit, 'That Old Black Magic'. The couple separated in 1961; Smith later enjoyed a UK hit with 'You're Breaking My Heart' (1965), while Prima enjoyed greater acclaim by providing the voice for King Louis in the Walt Disney cartoon *The Jungle Book*.

HI-LO's

The name of this outstanding North American vocal unit derived from the contrast in height between its tallest members - leader/arranger Eugene Thomas Puerling (b. 31 March

1929, Milwaukee, Wisconsin) and Robert Morse (b. 27 July 1927, Pasadena, Texas) - and diminutive Clark Burroughs (b. 3 March 1930, Los Angeles, California) and Robert Strasen (b. 1 April 1928, Strasbourg, France). While developing their sophisticated close-harmony style, they lived in the same Chicago house, making ends meet with menial jobs and engagements at weekends and evenings. Through the offices of bandleader Jerry Fielding, they recorded for several labels while building a reputation as a versatile, technically accomplished act via a Las Vegas hotel season, a tour supporting Judy Garland and replacing the Four Esquires as resident musical turn on comedian Red Skelton's networked television series. Before Strasen was replaced by Dan Shelton in 1958, the four teamed up on disc with the Marty Paich Dektette - and Rosemary Clooney with whom they notched up a US hit with 1957's 'Ring Around Rosie' (with Morse's counter-tenor prominent). This breakthrough assisted the passage of *Now Hear This* into the album Top 20. Further collections - some devoted to specific stylistic genres - sold steadily if less remarkably.

After the Hi-Lo's disbanded in 1964, Puerling and Shelton found employment producing advertising jingles with vocalists Len Dresslar and Bonnie Herman with whom they formed Singers Unlimited in 1966. An impressed Oscar Peterson recommended them to Germany's BASF/MPS company, which released several Singers albums including *Sentimental Journey* and, accompanied by Robert Farnon's orchestra, 1978's *Eventide*. That same year, the Shelton line-up of the Hi-Lo's re-formed as a recording entity and were affectionately welcomed at performances in nostalgia revues. The Hi-Lo's had a profound influence on the harmony sound of the Four Freshmen and the Beach Boys.

● ALBUMS: *Listen!* (Starlite 1955/56)★★★, *The Hi-Lo's, I Presume* (Starlite 1955/56)★★★, *The Hi-Lo's Under Glass* (Starlite 1956)★★★, *The Hi-Lo's On Hand* (Starlite 1956)★★★, *The Hi-Lo's And The Jerry Fielding Band* (Kapp 1956)★★★, *The Hi-Lo's In Stereo* (Omega 50s)★★★★, *Suddenly It's The Hi-Lo's* (Columbia 1957)★★★, *Now Hear This* (Columbia 1957)★★★, with Rosemary Clooney *Ring A Round Rosie* (Columbia 1957)★★★★, *The Hi-Lo's And All That Jazz*, (Columbia 1959)★★★, *Broadway Playbill* (Columbia 1959)★★, *All Over The Place* (Columbia 1960)★★★, *The Hi-Lo's Happen To Folk* (Columbia 1962)★★★, *This Time It's Love* (Columbia 1962)★★★, *The Hi-Lo's Happen To Bossa Nova* (Reprise 1963)★★, *Back Again* (1978)★★.

HIGGINS, CHUCK

b. Charles Williams Higgins, 17 April 1924, Gary, Indiana, USA. Higgins was an R&B singer best known for his recording 'Pachuko Hop' in 1952. The son of a preacher who also played trombone, Higgins learned to play the trumpet at the age of 10. In 1940 he moved to Los Angeles, where he played the trumpet in his high-school band. While attending the Los Angeles Music Conservatory, Higgins formed a band with pianist Frank Dunn, saxophonist Johnny Parker and others on bass and drums. After a series of personnel changes, Higgins took over the saxophone position and wrote 'Pachuko Hop', featuring a squealing solo on that instrument. It became a highlight of his stage show and was heard by Vernon 'Jake' Porter, owner of Combo Records. Porter released the single ('pachuko' was a slang word

denoting a Mexican-American dressed fashionably in baggy pants, with a long key chain), with the b-side 'Motorhead Baby', another raw R&B rocker (and later the inspiration for the nickname of Frank Zappa sideman James 'Motorhead' Sherwood, and subsequently, the heavy metal band Motorhead). Although the record was not a big seller outside the Los Angeles area, it made Higgins a local favourite and he secured concert bookings with Charlie Parker, Nat 'King' Cole, Johnny Ace, Little Richard and the Orioles. Among Higgins' band members at the time was Johnny 'Guitar' Watson, who then left for a successful blues solo career. Higgins never signed an exclusive recording contract, so his records were released on numerous labels, including Aladdin Records, Caddy, Lucky, Recorded in Hollywood, Specialty Records and Dootone. Primarily an instrumentalist, Higgins also recorded some music featuring singers. He retired from performing in the early 60s and went on to teach music at Los Angeles high schools and colleges. He attempted a comeback briefly in the mid-70s, performing in a disco style, but achieved no success. Two albums recorded in the late 70s returned him to his earlier style and attracted a small European following. In 1983 he toured the UK and later returned to performing in his original style at Los Angeles nightclubs during the 80s. A collection of his early rare singles, *Yak A Dak*, was released on the Swedish Saxophonograph label in 1990.

● ALBUMS: *Pachuko Hop* (Combo 1956)★★★, *Rock 'N' Roll Versus Rhythm And Blues* (Dootone 1959)★★★, *Motor Head Chuck* (1977)★★★, *Chuck Higgins Is A Ph.D.* (1979)★★.

● COMPILATIONS: *Yak A Dak* (Saxophonograph 1990)★★★, *Pachuko Hop* (Ace/Specialty 1992)★★★.

HIGGINS, LIZZIE

b. Elizabeth Ann Youlden, 20 September 1929, Aberdeen, Scotland, d. 20 February 1993. Higgins is the only daughter of Scottish ballad singer Jeannie Robertson and piper Donald Higgins. She left school at the age of 15 and worked for a while as a fish filleter. After the 'discovery' of her mother by the song collector Hamish Henderson, she occasionally accompanied Robertson on her travels around Scotland and England, collecting and performing songs. In the wake of their growing reputation, Lizzie took up singing full-time. It was only after her mother's death in 1975 that she started to perform with regularity. Her technique included what she herself called 'the pipe singing'. In this she would embellish a tune in much the same way a piper might. She is often remembered for her contribution to the double album of ballad recordings made by the School of Scottish Studies, *The Muckle Sangs*, and is widely regarded as one of the greatest Scottish traditional singers. Although Higgins appeared on a number of recordings, she only made two albums in her own right. She died of cancer in 1993.

● ALBUMS: *Princess Of The Thistle* (Topic 1969)★★★, *Up And Awa' Wi' The Laverock* (Topic)★★★, with various artists *The Muckle Sangs* (1973)★★, *What A Voice!* (Lismor 1985)★★★.

● FURTHER READING: *Lizzie Higgins And The Oral Transmission Of Ten Child Ballads*, Ailie Munro. *A Study Of Lizzie Higgins As A Transitional Figure In The Development Of The Oral Tradition In The Northeast Of Scotland*, Stephanie Perrin.

HIGH SOCIETY

This enjoyable musical adaptation of Philip Barry's stylish play, *The Philadephia Story*, which was filmed (without songs) in 1940 with Katharine Hepburn, Cary Grant and James Stewart, was released by MGM in 1956. Apart from some changes in characterization and locales, John Patrick's screenplay, which was set in swanky Newport, Rhode Island, stayed fairly close to the original and concerns Tracey Lord (Grace Kelly), who is set to marry an insufferable snob, George Ketteridge (John Lund), when her former husband, C.K. Dexter Haven (Bing Crosby), returns to his house next door, ostensibly to organize a jazz festival. This situation is further complicated by the arrival of Mike Connor (Frank Sinatra) and Liz Imbrie (Celeste Holm), two reporters from *Spy* Magazine, which has been allowed access to the wedding because it is in possession of certain information regarding the (alleged) philandering of Tracey's father, Seth Lord (Sidney Blackmer). Louis Calhern is especially amusing as Tracey's Uncle Willie, and also in the cast were Lydia Reed, Margalo Gillmore, Richard Keene, Hugh Boswell, and jazz giant Louis Armstrong who played - who else but himself? By the end of the film Tracey comes to her senses, sends George off in a huff, and remarries Dexter. It is obvious that Mike and Liz will be making their own arrangements soon. Cole Porter's score contained several pleasing numbers such as 'High Society Calypso' (Armstrong), 'Now You Has Jazz' (Crosby-Armstrong), 'Little One' (Crosby), 'Who Wants to Be A Millionaire?' (Sinatra-Holm), 'You're Sensational' (Sinatra), 'I Love You, Samantha' (Crosby) and 'Well, Did You Evah?' (Crosby-Sinatra). Bing Crosby and Grace Kelly's record of 'True Love' made the Top 5 in both UK and US charts, and Sinatra's version of 'Mind If I Make Love To You?' remains one of his most endearing recorded performances. The director-choreographer was Charles Walters, and, in a decade that produced a feast of film musicals, *High Society* grossed nearly six million dollars. A 1986 UK stage adaptation of the movie, starring Trevor Eve, Stephen Rea, Natasha Richardson and Angela Richards, interpolated some of Porter's other numbers into the score.

HIGHLIGHTS

The Highlights had one US Top 20 single in 1956 and never again approached similar success. The group, formed in the Chicago area, comprised singers Frank Pizani, Frank Calzaretta, Tony Calzaretta, Jerry Oleski and Bill Melshimer. The group's first recording was of a song called 'Jingle-lo', which they took to the local Bally Records. The label liked the group but not the song, and gave them one called 'City Of Angels' instead. It reached number 19 in the USA but when it was time to record a follow-up, the group, unsatisfied at being merely a backing group for Pizani, wanted a more equitable arrangement, causing Pizani to leave. Bally issued one song they had recorded with Pizani before his exit, and it hit the lower regions of the charts. The group soon broke up when its only subsequent single failed to chart; Pizani, meanwhile, had one last minor chart hit, 'Indiana Style'. He spent the 80s acting as a Tony Bennett impersonator. The others retired from the entertainment business.

HILL, ERNEST

b 14 March 1900, Pittsburgh, Pennsylvania, USA, d. 16 September 1964. In his earlier years Hill played brass bass as well as string bass, eventually concentrating on the latter. In the early 20s he was with the orchestra led by Claude Hopkins that visited Europe as part of a show featuring Joséphine Baker. In New York he again played with Hopkins, then several other bands in the city, and in the early 30s was with Chick Webb, Benny Carter, Willie Bryant and Rex Stewart. Towards the end of the 30s he again travelled to Europe where he worked until the start of World War II. In 1940 he returned to New York, again spent time with Hopkins, then toured with Zutty Singleton, Louis Armstrong, Hopkins yet again, and Cliff Jackson. He also toured with the globe-trotting band Herbie Cowens took on USO tours. Towards the end of the 40s, Hill was again in Europe, playing with Bill Coleman, Frank 'Big Boy' Goudie and others. In the early 50s he was back in the USA, performing with several bands including that led by Happy Caldwell. As his career suggests, Hill was not only footloose but also held in high regard by bandleaders who welcomed his presence in their bands for the solidity he brought to rhythm sections.

HILLIARD, BOB

b. 21 January 1918, New York, USA, d. 1 February 1971, Hollywood, California, USA. A prolific lyricist from the mid-40s into the 60s, the first of many Hilliard hit songs came in 1946 when he collaborated with Dick Miles on 'The Coffee Song'. It became successful for Frank Sinatra, who remembered it again many years later, and included it on *Ring-A-Ding-Ding*, the first album for his own Reprise label. In 1947, Hilliard and Carl Sigman contributed 'The Big Brass Band From Brazil' and 'Civilization' to the Broadway musical *Angel With Wings*. 'Civilization' was sung by Elaine Stritch in the show, and became a massive hit for Danny Kaye and the Andrews Sisters, Ray McKinley and Louis Prima. Hilliard's other 40s successes included 'A Strawberry Moon', 'Careless Hands' (with Sigman - revived by Des O'Connor in 1967) and 'Dear Hearts And Gentle People' (with Sammy Fain), which was a hit for Bing Crosby, Dennis Day, Gordon MacRae and others. In the 50s Hilliard collaborated with Jule Styne on the scores for two Broadway musicals, *Michael Todd's Peep Show* ('Stay With The Happy People') and *Hazel Flagg* ('Every Street's A Boulevard In Old New York' and 'How Do You Speak To An Angel?'). His film work around this time included several songs, with Sammy Fain, for Walt Disney's *Alice In Wonderland* (1952, 'It's Late', 'Very Good Advice'). Among Hilliard's other 50s songs were 'Dearie' (with Dave Mann), 'Be My Life's Companion', 'Jealous Eyes', 'Bouquet Of Roses', 'Downhearted' (a hit for Eddie Fisher), 'Sweet Forgiveness', 'Somebody Bad Stole De Wedding Bells' (with Mann) and 'Moonlight Gambler' (with Phil Springer). In 1959 Hilliard had a hit with another novelty song, 'Seven Little Girls Sitting In The Back Seat' (with Lee Pockriss), recorded by Paul Evans in the US, and the Avons in the UK. In the early 60s, with the advent of the beat boom, his output declined, although he had some success with 'Tower Of Strength' (with Burt Bacharach), 'You're Following Me', 'My Summer Love', 'My Little Corner Of The World' (with Pockriss) and 'Our Day Will Come' (with Mort Garson), which was a US number 1 for Ruby And The Romantics.

Hilliard's other songs included 'Don't You Believe It', 'Any Day Now', 'Red Silk Stockings And Green Perfume', 'The Thousand Islands Song', 'Chocolate Whiskey And Vanilla Gin', 'Castanets And Lace', and 'Baby Come Home'. Among his many collaborators were Dick Sanford and Sammy Mysels.

HILLTOPPERS

This vocal quartet formed at the Western Kentucky College in Bowling Green, Kentucky, USA, comprised lead Jimmy Sacca (b. Hazard, Kentucky, USA), baritone Billy Vaughn (b. 12 April 1931, Glasgow, Kentucky, USA), tenor Seymour Speigelman and bass Don McGuire. Sacca and Vaughn formed the group to record 'Trying' in 1952 and named it after their college nickname. Dot Records signed the band, re-recorded 'Trying' in the college auditorium, and it reached the US Top 10 (making the UK charts in 1956). Over the next five years the group, who wore college sweaters and beanies on stage, scored a further nine US Top 20 singles, the biggest being 'P.S. I Love You' in 1953, 'Only You' in 1955 and 'Marianne' in 1957. Vaughn left in 1955 and had a very successful career as musical director for Dot and as an orchestra leader. In the UK, where the Platters' original version of 'Only You' was not released until 1956, they reached number 3 with their recording and were in the Top 20 for six months. They were one of the most successful early 50s vocal groups, but like many other acts they could not survive in a rock 'n' roll world and disbanded in 1963. Since then Sacca has occasionally played dates with new sets of Hilltoppers.
● ALBUMS: *Tops In Pops* (London 1957)★★★, *The Towering Hilltoppers* (London 1957)★★★, *Love In Bloom* (Dot 1958)★★.
● COMPILATIONS: *P.S. I Love You - The Best Of* (Varese Vintage 1994)★★★.

HILTON, RONNIE

b. Adrian Hill, 26 January 1926, Hull, England. Hilton left school at the age of 14 and worked in an aircraft factory during the war before joining the Highland Light Infantry. He was demobilized in 1947 and returned to factory work in Leeds. He sang with the Johnny Addlestone band at the Starlight Roof in Leeds from 1950 and was heard by A&R manager Wally Ridley and signed to HMV. At this point he underwent surgery for a hair lip, changed his name, and in July 1954 made his debut as Ronnie Hilton. His first appearance on stage was at the Dudley Hippodrome in 1955, and soon afterwards he had his own radio series. For the next 10 years he was one of the most popular vocalists in the UK and specialized in romantic ballads. His hits included 'I Still Believe', 'Veni Vidi Vici', 'A Blossom Fell', 'Stars Shine In Your Eyes', 'Yellow Rose Of Texas', 'Young And Foolish', 'No Other Love' (a UK number 1 in 1956), 'Who Are We', 'Two Different Worlds', 'Around The World', 'The World Outside', and the novelty, 'A Windmill In Old Amsterdam'. He still performs summer seasons and tours with nostalgia packages that include contemporaries such as Russ Conway, Dennis Lotis and Rosemary Squires. For several years he presented *Sounds Of The 50s* for BBC Radio Two.
● ALBUMS: *I'm Beginning To See The Light* (EMI 1959)★★★.
● COMPILATIONS: *The Very Best Of Ronnie Hilton - 16 Favourites Of The 50s* (MFP 1984)★★★, *The EMI Years: The Best Of Ronnie Hilton* (EMI 1989)★★★, *Ronnie Hilton* (Hour Of Pleasure 1990)★★★.

HIPP, JUTTA

b. 4 February 1925, Leipzig, Germany. Although her musical career was quite brief, Hipp made a big impression in post-war Europe. She studied piano formally as a small child, taking an interest in jazz in her mid-teens. At the end of the war she formed her own small band, mostly playing bop. After playing throughout Europe, in the mid-50s she visited the USA where she led a trio that was completed by Peter Ind and Ed Thigpen. By the late 50s, however, Hipp had decided to concentrate upon what had thus far been a complementary career as a painter. On the evidence of her few recordings, Hipp's decision to abandon professional music was purely a matter of personal choice and by no means an indication of either technical inability or lack of imaginative talent.
● ALBUMS: *Jutta Hipp At The Hickory House* (Blue Note 1956)★★.

HIT THE DECK

Considering the wealth of talent on board, this 1955 screen adaptation of the 1927 Broadway musical proved to be a disappointing affair, mainly owing to a lacklustre screenplay by Sonya Levien and William Ludwig. It told the familiar story of three off-duty sailors (Tony Martin, Russ Tamblyn and Vic Damone) and their search for three lovely gals (Ann Miller, Debbie Reynolds and Jane Powell) with whom to embark on the voyage of life. Fortunately, there were plenty of musical highlights in composer Vincent Youmans' score, such as the lovely 'More Than You Know' (Tony Martin; lyric: Billy Rose-Edward Eliscu), 'Sometimes I'm Happy' (Vic Damone-Jane Powell; lyric: Clifford Grey-Irving Caesar), 'Hallelujah' (Martin-Tamblyn-Damone; lyric: Grey-Leo Robin), 'I Know that You Know' (Damone-Powell; lyric: Anne Caldwell) and 'Keepin' Myself For You' (Martin-Ann Miller; lyric: Sidney Clare). Other songs included 'Join The Navy', 'Why, Oh Why' and 'Lucky Bird' (all with lyrics by Robin and Grey), 'Lady From The Bayou' and 'A Kiss Or Two' (lyrics: Robin), and 'Ciribiribin' (Albert Pestalozza). Hermes Pan staged the dance sequences with his usual imagination and flair (especially in the sequences that involved Ann Miller) and Roy Rowland directed a cast that also included Walter Pidgeon, Kay Armen, Gene Raymond, J. Carrol Naish and Allan King. *Hit The Deck* was photographed in Eastman Color and Cinemascope, and produced for MGM by Joe Pasternak. Hubert Osborne's play *Shore Leave*, which was the basis for this film and the original Broadway musical, had previously been filmed in 1930 with Jack Oakie, Polly Walker and Roger Gray.

HODGES, EDDIE

b. 5 March 1947, Hattiesburg, Mississippi, USA. In the mid-50s child star Hodges appeared in television programmes *The Jackie Gleason Show* and *Name That Tune* and was seen on Broadway 405 times in the hit musical *The Music Man*. In 1959 he starred alongside Frank Sinatra and Edward G. Robinson in the film *A Hole In The Head* and can be heard on Sinatra's hit from the film, 'High Hopes'. He also had a major role in the film of *Huckleberry Finn*, starred with Hayley Mills in *Summer Magic* and even had his own television show, *The Secret World of Eddie Hodges*. His youthful revival of the Isley Brothers' 'I'm Gonna Knock On Your Door' on Cadence, not only took him into the US Top 20 in 1961 but also gave the 14-year-old an Australian and Canadian chart-topper and a small UK hit. He returned to the US Top 20 with an endearing song written by Phil Everly, '(Girls, Girls, Girls) Made To Love' in 1962. He had releases on Columbia in 1963 and MGM in 1964 before 'New Orleans' on Aurora in 1965 gave him his last US chart entry. It seems that, for Hodges, maturity brought a halt to his recording career.

HODGES, JOHNNY

b. 25 July 1907, Cambridge, Massachusetts, USA, d. 11 May 1970. One of the greatest alto saxophonists in jazz, Hodges first tried other instruments before settling upon the one that would best serve his glorious romanticism. Largely self-taught, Hodges played in a number of minor bands in Boston and New York in the early 20s but also spent a little time with Willie 'The Lion' Smith, in whose band he replaced Sidney Bechet - who had given him some of the little instruction he ever received. In 1926 he joined Chick Webb, where his brother-in-law, Don Kirkpatrick, was pianist-arranger. Two years later Hodges began an association with Duke Ellington that would continue virtually uninterrupted for the rest of his life. Apart from playing on hundreds of records with Ellington, soloing magnificently on many, Hodges also originated several tunes that Ellington developed, among them 'Jeep's Blues' and 'The Jeep Is Jumpin'' ('Jeep' was one of Hodges' nicknames; others were 'Rabbit' and 'Squatty Roo'). From 1951-55 Hodges led his own band, which briefly included John Coltrane in its ranks, and had a hit record with 'Castle Rock'. In 1958 and again in 1961 he worked outside the Ellington orchestra but always in an Ellingtonian style. Although capable of playing low-down blues, Hodges was in his true element as a balladeer. The lush beauty of his playing was perfectly exhibited on compositions created for his special talents by Ellington and by Billy Strayhorn. Among the many tunes on which he played, and frequently recorded, were 'I Let A Song Go Out Of My Heart', 'Warm Valley', 'Black Butterfly', 'Isfahan' (from the 'Far East Suite') and 'Empty Ballroom Blues'. Hodges recorded several albums for Norman Granz, including a 1952 jam session that teamed him with fellow altoists Benny Carter and Charlie Parker and organist Wild Bill Davis. Despite the excellence of all his other forays, however, it is for his work with Ellington that he will be remembered. The liquid beauty of Hodges' contribution to the sound of the Ellington band, and especially to the manner in which it played ballads, was so crucial that his death in May 1970 marked the end of an era: as Ellington himself observed, 'our band will never sound the same'. Throughout his long career Hodges was indisputably among the finest alto players in jazz. Even though, after the early 40s, Charlie Parker took the alto saxophone in other directions, Hodges remains one of the giants of the instrument.

● ALBUMS: *Johnny Hodges, Volume 1* 10-inch album (Mercer 1951)★★★, *Johnny Hodges, Volume 2* 10-inch album (Mercer 1951)★★★, with Benny Carter, Charlie Parker *Norman Granz Jam Session* (1952)★★★★, *Alto Sax* 10-inch album (RCA Victor 1952)★★★, *Johnny Hodges Collates* 10-inch album (Mercury 1952)★★★, *Swing With Johnny Hodges* 10-inch album (Norgran 1954)★★★, *Memories Of Ellington* reissued as *In A Mellow Tone* (Norgran 1954)★★★, *More Of Johnny Hodges* (Norgran 1954)★★★, *Johnny Hodges Dance Bash* reissued as *Perdido* (Norgran 1955)★★★, *Creamy* (Norgran 1955)★★★, *Castle Rock* (Norgran 1955)★★★, *Hodge Podge* (Epic 1955)★★★, *Ellingtonia '56* (Norgran 1956)★★★★, with Duke Ellington *Ellington At Newport '56* (Columbia 1956)★★★★★, *In A Tender Mood* (Norgran 1956)★★★, *Used To Be Duke* (Norgran 1956)★★★, *The Blues* (Norgran 1956)★★★, *Duke's In Bed* (Verve 1957)★★★, *The Big Sound* (Verve 1958)★★★, *The Prettiest Gershwin* (Verve 1959)★★★, with Ellington *Back To Back: Duke Ellington And Johnny Hodges Play The Blues* (Verve 1959)★★★★, with Ellington *Side By Side* (Verve 1959)★★★, *The Smooth One* (Verve 1960)★★★, *Not So Dukish* (Verve 1960)★★★, with Ellington *The Nutcracker Suite* (Columbia 1960)★★★, *Master Of Jazz* (1960)★★★, *Blues-A-Plenty* (Verve 1960)★★★★, *The Johnny Hodges All Stars/The Johnny Hodges-Harry Carney Sextet* (1961)★★★, *Johnny Hodges At The Sportspalast, Berlin* (1961)★★★, *Johnny Hodges In Scandinavia* (1961)★★★, with Wild Bill Davis *Johnny Hodges And Wild Bill Davis* (Verve 1961)★★★, with Billy Strayhorn *Johnny Hodges With Billy Strayhorn And His Orchestra* (Verve 1962)★★★★, *Johnny Hodges With Claus Ogermann's Orchestra* (1963)★★★, with Davis *Mess Of Blues* (Verve 1964)★★★★, with Davis *Blue Rabbit* (Verve 1964)★★★, *Everybody Knows Johnny Hodges* (Impulse 1964)★★★, with Davis *Blue Pyramid* (Verve 1965)★★★★, with Davis *Wings And Things* (Verve 1965)★★★, with Lawrence Welk *Johnny Hodges With Lawrence Welk's Orchestra* (Dot 1965)★★★, *Johnny Hodges And All The Dukesmen* (Verve 1966)★★★, *Alto Blue* (Verve 1966)★★★, with Earl Hines *Stride Right* (Verve 1966)★★★, *In A Mellotone* (Bluebird 1966)★★★★, *Things Ain't What They Used To Be* (RCA Victor 1966)★★★, with Ellington *Far East Suite* (RCA Victor 1967)★★★★, *Triple Play* (RCA Victor 1967)★★★, *Don't Sleep In The Subway* (Verve 1967)★★★, with Hines *Swing's Our Thing* (Verve 1967)★★★★, *Rippin' And Runnin'* (Verve 1968)★★★, *3 Shades Of Blue* (1970)★★★.

● COMPILATIONS: *The Indispensable Duke Ellington Volumes 1-12* (RCA 1983-87)★★★, with Ellington *The Blanton-Webster Band* (RCA Bluebird 1987)★★★★★, *Love In Swingtime (1938-39)* (Tax 1988)★★★, *The Complete Johnny Hodges Sessions 1951-1955* 6-LP box set (1989)★★★★★, *Rarities And Private Recordings* (Suisa 1992)★★★.

HOLLIDAY, JUDY

b. Judith Tuvim, 21 June 1922, New York, USA, d. 7 June 1965, New York, USA. An actress and singer with an endearing quality and a warm, unique comic style, Holliday's first attempt to break into showbusiness was with Orson Welles and John Houseman at the Mercury Theatre, but she only succeeded in getting a job there as a telephone operator - ironic considering her later memorable role in the musical theatre. Holliday joined some more young hopefuls, Betty Comden, Adolph Green, John Frank and Alvin Hammer, in a nightclub act called the Revuers, who attracted a good deal of attention. In 1945 she made her Broadway debut in the play *Kiss Them For Me*, and a year later was acclaimed for her performance in the Garson Kanin comedy *Born Yesterday*. She had taken over the dizzy blonde role after the producers' original choice, Jean Arthur, withdrew during the Philadelphia try-out. In 1950 Holliday won an Academy Award when she recreated her part for the Columbia film version. In the previous year she had almost stolen the glory from stars Katharine Hepburn and Spencer Tracey in *Adam's Rib*, which also had a screenplay by Kanin and his wife Ruth Gordon. In 1956 Holliday returned to Broadway in the musical *Bells Are Ringing*. The book and lyrics were by her old friends, Comden and Green (music by Jule Styne), and Holliday played Ella Peterson, a telephone operator who cannot help becoming emotionally involved with the clients who subscribe to Susansanswerphone, the answering service where she works. *Bells Are Ringing* was a smash hit, and Holliday introduced several of its delightful songs, including 'The Party's Over', 'Drop That Name', 'Just In Time' and 'Long Before I Knew You' (both with Sydney Chaplin), and the immortal 'I'm Goin' Back (To The Bonjour Tristesse Brassiere Company)'. Her unforgettable performance won her Tony and New York Drama Critics awards.

In 1948 she had married musician David Oppenheim, who became head of the classical division of Columbia Records, but they divorced in 1957. Holliday's subsequent partner was another musician, a giant of the jazz world, Gerry Mulligan. He played one of her boyfriends in the 1960 screen adaptation of *Bells Are Ringing*, in which she co-starred with Dean Martin, and they also wrote songs together. Four of the best of these, 'What's The Rush?', 'Loving You', 'It Must Be Christmas' and 'Summer's Over', were included among the standards on an album they recorded in 1961. In spite of its tender and poignant quality, and the presence of accompanying luminaries such as Bob Brookmeyer, Mel Lewis and Al Klink, Holliday was reported to be unhappy with the result, and the album was not released until 1980. In 1960 she was out of town with the play *Laurette*, based on the life of the former Broadway star Laurette Taylor, when she found that she was unable to project her voice properly. It was the first sign that she had cancer. After surgery, she returned to New York in 1963 with the musical *Hot Spot*, but it folded after only 43 performances. She died just two weeks before her forty-third birthday.

● ALBUMS: with Gerry Mulligan *Holliday With Mulligan* 1961 recording (DRG 1980)★★★★, and Original Cast and soundtrack recordings.
● FURTHER READING: *Judy Holliday*, W. Holtzman. *Judy Holliday*, G. Carey.
● FILMS: *Greenwich Village* (1944), *Something For The Boys* (1944), *Winged Victory* (1944), *Adam's Rib* (1949), *Born Yesterday* (1950), *The Marrying Kind* (1952), *It Should Happen To You* (1954), *Phffft* (1954), *The Solid Gold Cadillac* (1956), *Full Of Life* (1956), *Bells Are Ringing* (1960).

HOLLIDAY, MICHAEL

b. Michael Milne, 26 November 1928, Liverpool, England, d. 29 October 1963, Croydon, Surrey, England. A popular singer in the UK during the 50s, influenced by, and very similar in style and tone to Bing Crosby. After entertaining his shipmates in the Merchant Navy, Holliday made his first public appearance as a singer when his ship docked in New York. He won a talent contest on the stage of Radio City Music Hall, one of the world's largest theatres. In the absence of offers to star in a big Broadway musical, he

returned to the UK, was released from the navy, and obtained work as a singer-guitarist with the Eric Winstone Band, touring UK holiday camps. He was signed for Columbia by Norrie Paramor in 1955, and during the next couple of years, covered several US artists' hits such as 'The Yellow Rose Of Texas' (Mitch Miller), 'Sixteen Tons' (Tennessee Ernie Ford) and 'Hot Diggity' (Perry Como), while also reaching the UK Top 30 with 'Nothin' To Do', 'Ten Thousand Miles' and 'The Gal With The Yaller Shoes', from the 1956 movie *Meet Me In Las Vegas*. In 1958 he had some success with 'In Love', 'Stairway Of Love' and the 1929 number 'I'll Always Be In Love With You', and topped the UK chart with 'The Story Of My Life', an early composition by Burt Bacharach and Hal David. On the b-side of that record was one of Holliday's own compositions, 'Keep Your Heart'. Early in 1960 he had another number 1 with 'Starry Eyed', but after 'Skylark' and 'Little Boy Lost' later in the year, the singles hits dried up. On his albums such as *Mike* and *Holliday Mixture*, he ignored the contemporary music scene, and sang old standards - as he did on television. With his casual, easy-going style, he was a natural for the small screen, and had his own *Relax With Mike* series, on which he duetted with himself on a tape recorder, in the days when those machines were a domestic novelty in the UK. His only appearance on the larger screen was in the movie *Life Is A Circus* (1962), with one of Britain's best-loved comedy teams, the Crazy Gang. Unfortunately, his relaxed image seems to have been a façade, concealing professional and personal problems. When Holliday died in a Croydon hospital the cause of death was reported to be have been an overdose of drugs.
● ALBUMS: *Hi!* (Columbia 1958)★★★, *Mike* (Columbia 1959)★★★, *Holliday Mixture* (Columbia 1960)★★★, *Happy Holiday* (Columbia 1961)★★, *To Bing From Mike* (Columbia 1962)★★★.
● COMPILATIONS: *The Best Of Michael Holliday* (Columbia 1964)★★★, *Story Of My Life* (One-Up 1973)★★★, *The Very Best Of Michael Holliday* (MFP 1984)★★★, with Edna Savage *A Sentimental Journey* (See For Miles 1988)★★★, *The EMI Years: The Best Of Michael Holliday* (EMI 1989)★★★★, *30th Anniversary Collection* (1994)★★★★.

HOLLY, BUDDY

b. Charles Hardin Holley, 7 September 1936, Lubbock, Texas, USA, d. 3 February 1959. Holly was one of the first major rock 'n' roll groundbreakers, and one of its most influential artists. He wrote his own songs, recorded with a self-contained guitar-bass-drums combo, experimented in the studio and even changed the image of what a rock singer could look like: until he came along, the idea of a bespectacled rock idol was unthinkable. Holly's hiccupping vocal style and mature, melodic compositions inspired many of the rockers who would emerge in the 60s and 70s, from the Beatles and Bob Dylan to the Hollies. Later, British singer-songwriter Elvis Costello would emerge with an unabashed Holly-inspired physical appearance. Like many other early rock 'n' rollers, Holly's musical influences included both C&W music and 'race' music, or R&B. He made his first stage appearance at the age of five, joining with his brothers Larry and Travis in a talent contest; he won $5. During his childhood, Holly learned to play guitar, violin and piano, taking formal lessons but teaching himself boogie-woogie rhythms on the piano. At 12 years old he was entertaining friends with Hank Williams songs and in 1949 formed a bluegrass duo, Buddy And Bob, with friend Bob Montgomery. He learned to play banjo and mandolin during this period. Holly made his first recording on a home tape recorder in 1949, a song called 'My Two Timin' Woman'.

By 1952 Buddy And Bob had become popular around Lubbock; recording two songs together at Holly's home that year and another in 1953. In September of that year Buddy And Bob appeared on KDAV radio, performing two numbers. Adding Larry Welborn on bass, they were given their own programme, *The Buddy And Bob Show*. They performed country material primarily, but occasionally included an R&B song by artists such as Hank Ballard. KDAV disc jockey Hipockets Duncan became the trio's manager and secured work for them in the West Texas area. Further recording took place at KDAV but none of it was released. In 1954 the trio added fiddler Sonny Curtis and steel guitarist Don Guess to the group, and together made more recordings in Lubbock and at Nesman Recording Studio in Wichita Falls, Texas. That year the group, now including drummer Jerry Allison, opened concerts for Bill Haley And His Comets and Elvis Presley in Texas. Holly was impressed by Presley and began thinking about performing in the new rock 'n' roll style. However, in the meantime he continued to play country.

In December 1955 Nashville agent Eddie Crandall requested of KDAV disc jockey Dave Stone that Holly and his group record four demo songs, believing he could secure them a contract with Decca Records. The group, now minus Montgomery, sent five songs, and Decca brought them to Nashville where they recorded four songs produced by Owen Bradley at Bradley's Barn Studio on 26 January 1956. Decca issued 'Blue Days, Black Nights', backed with 'Love Me', under the name Buddy Holly And The Three Tunes (the Crickets were not contracted to Decca at this time), in April. Several other records were recorded in two sessions for Decca during the autumn of 1956, but Holly, dissatisfied with Decca's insistence that he continue to play country music, together with the loss of his group to insensitive sessionmen, left the label in September. Later that year, Holly, Allison and Welborn went to Clovis, New Mexico, where they recorded two songs with Norman Petty at his NorVaJak studio. Upon returning to Lubbock, Holly formed the Crickets with Allison and Niki Sullivan on rhythm guitar. On 25 February 1957 they went back to Clovis and recorded a rock 'n' roll version of Holly's 'That'll Be The Day', a song from their period in Nashville. The song was a revelation and contained one of the most gripping vocals and distinctive galloping riffs of any record released during the 50s. Joe B. Mauldin joined as the Crickets' bassist following those sessions. A number of record companies turned down the song until it was issued by Brunswick Records in May, ironically a division of Decca, of which Coral Records was another subsidiary, although artistically independent. With Petty as manager, the single underwent heavy promotion until it reached number 1 in September 1957. It also reached number 1 in the UK. Just as the record was being released, the Crickets performed at such venues as the Apollo Theatre in New York and the Howard Theater in Washington, DC, winning over predominantly black audiences and helping to further break down racial barriers in rock. They spent the next three months touring the USA. The group recorded prolifically in

1957, including such indisputable classics as 'Words Of Love', 'Maybe Baby', 'Not Fade Away', 'Everyday', 'Peggy Sue' (named after Allison's girlfriend) and 'Oh Boy'. Holly was innovative in the studio, making much use of newly available production techniques, such as overdubbing vocals and double-tracking guitar parts. The vocals on 'Peggy Sue' were a typical example of Holly's technique. Although simple in structure and execution, Holly somehow managed to recite the words 'Peggy Sue' differently in every line, as if fascinated by the very syllables of her name. A seemingly straightforward song like 'Everyday' is similarly transformed by the ingenious use of a celeste (played by Petty's wife, Vi) and the decision to include Jerry Allison slapping his knee, in place of drums. Brunswick continued to issue recordings under the Crickets name while Holly signed on as a solo artist to Coral Records. Despite this, most releases featured the entire group, often with other musicians (Vi Petty on piano) and a vocal group (the Picks). Of these releases, 'Peggy Sue' reached number 3 in the USA and 'Oh Boy' number 10 during 1957. Contrary to the legend, Holly and the Crickets only charted 11 times in the USA during their brief career. No albums charted during Holly's lifetime. The Crickets closed 1957 with an appearance on the influential *Ed Sullivan Show* and again in January 1958, by which time Holly had left the group. In late January the Crickets recorded 'Rave On' in New York and then toured Australia for six days. Further Clovis recording sessions, including 'Well...All Right' occupied February. This was followed by a UK tour beginning on 2 March at the Trocadero in London, which also included appearances on the UK television programmes *Sunday Night At The London Palladium* and *Off The Record*. The UK tour finished on 25 March at the Hammersmith Gaumont. Holly and the group enjoyed immense popularity in Britain, with nine top 10 singles. 'Maybe Baby' became the fourth Holly/Crickets single to chart in the USA in March, eventually peaking at number 17 (and number 4 in the UK). The group returned to the USA in late March and immediately embarked on a US tour instigated by disc jockey Alan Freed, also featuring such popular artists as Jerry Lee Lewis and Chuck Berry. Coral released the frantic 'Rave On' in May and although it reached only number 37 in the USA, it made number 5 in the UK. Following the tour, on 19 June, Holly recorded two songs written by Bobby Darin in New York without the Crickets; they remained unreleased but signalled an impending rift between Holly and the group. While in New York Holly met Maria Elena Santiago, whom he married two months later. During that summer Holly returned to Petty's studio in Clovis and recorded 'Heartbeat', 'Love's Made A Fool Of You' and 'Wishing'. Guitarist Tommy Allsup played on the latter two and was subsequently asked to join the Crickets. During September sessions in Clovis, extra musicians including saxophonist King Curtis and guitarist Phil Everly joined Holly. Waylon Jennings, then unknown, provided backing vocals on one track; during the same period, Holly produced Jennings' debut single. By September three more Holly/Crickets singles had charted in the USA, but none fared very well.

Holly and the Crickets toured the north-east and Canada during October, by which time there was apparently friction between the Hollys and the Pettys. Buddy and Maria Holly travelled separately from the group between dates. During the trip, Holly decided to try recording with strings, but prior to returning to New York for that session in October 1958, he announced to manager/producer Petty that he was leaving him. To Holly's surprise the other Crickets chose to leave Holly and remain with Petty; Holly allowed them use of the group's name and they continued to record without him (Sonny Curtis joined the group after Holly's death). Meanwhile, on 21 October, Holly, producer Dick Jacobs and studio musicians (including a string section) recorded 'True Love Ways', 'It Doesn't Matter Anymore' (written by Paul Anka), 'Raining In My Heart' and 'Moondreams'. They were held for later release while 'It's So Easy' was released; it failed to chart in the USA. 'Heartbeat' was issued in December and became the last Holly single to chart in the USA during his lifetime. The superb 'It Doesn't Matter Anymore' was released posthumously and its lyrics betrayed an unintended elegiac mood in light of the singer's fate. The song provided Holly with his only UK number 1 hit and served as a perfect memorial. The flip-side, 'Raining In My Heart', was equally inventive, with a touching melody reinforced by the orchestral arrangement in which strings were used to startling effect to suggest tearful raindrops.

In December 1958 Holly, now living in New York with his wife, recorded six songs at home on his tape recorder, presumably to be re-recorded in the studio at a later date. During Christmas Holly returned to Lubbock and appeared on radio station KLLL with Jennings. Back in New York during January 1959 he made other demos at home by himself. That month he began assembling a band to take on the 'Winter Dance Party' tour of the US Midwest. Allsup was hired on guitar, Jennings on bass and Carl Bunch on drums. They were billed as the Crickets despite the agreement to give Holly's former bandmates that name. Also starring Ritchie Valens, the Big Bopper, Dion And The Belmonts and the unknown Frankie Sardo, the tour began on 23 January 1959 in Milwaukee, Wisconsin. On the afternoon of 1 February the tour played in Green Bay, Wisconsin, but an evening show was cancelled owing to bad weather. The 2 February date at the Surf Ballroom in Clear Lake, Iowa, went ahead. It was following this show that Holly, Valens and the Big Bopper chartered a small plane to take them to the next date in Moorhead, Minnesota, rather than travel on the tour bus, which had a defective heater and had previously broken down several times. In the dark early hours of a freezing cold morning and as a result of the snowy weather, the plane crashed minutes after take-off, killing all three stars and the pilot. (The tour actually continued after their deaths, with Bobby Vee, Jimmy Clanton and Frankie Avalon filling in.)

Holly's popularity increased after his death, and his influence continues to this day. Even as late as the 80s unreleased material was still being released. Several of the posthumous releases fared particularly well in the UK. In 1962 Norman Petty took the demos Holly had recorded at home in 1958 and had the instrumental group the Fireballs play along to them, creating new Buddy Holly records from the unfinished tapes. In 1965, Holly In The Hills, comprised of the early Buddy and Bob radio station recordings, was released and charted in the UK. Compilation albums also charted in both the USA and the UK, as late as the 70s. During the 70s the publishing rights to Holly's song catalogue were purchased by Paul McCartney, who began sponsoring annual Buddy Holly Week celebrations. A Buddy

Holly Memorial Society was also formed in the USA to commemorate the singer. In 1978, a film called The Buddy Holly Story, starring actor Gary Busey as Holly, premiered; members of the Crickets, in particular, denounced it as containing many inaccurate scenes. The following year, a six-record boxed set called The Complete Buddy Holly was released in the UK (it was issued in the USA two years later). A 1983 release, For The First Time Anywhere, contained original Holly recordings prior to overdubbing. As of the early 90s a group called the Crickets, which included at least one original member (and usually more), was still touring. In 1990, Buddy, a musical play that had previously been staged in London, opened on Broadway in New York. Buddy Holly's legacy lives on, not only with tributes such as these, but in the dozens of cover versions of his songs that have been recorded over the years. Holly was an initial inductee into the Rock And Roll Hall of Fame in 1986. To have a catalogue of songs of this calibre behind him at the age of 22 was remarkable. How would he have approached the 60s and subsequent decades? Such was the quality of his work that few could doubt that he would have lasted the course.

● ALBUMS: The 'Chirping' Crickets (Brunswick 1957)★★★★, Buddy Holly (Coral 1958)★★★★, That'll Be The Day (Decca 1958)★★★★, The Buddy Holly Story (Coral 1959)★★★★★, The Buddy Holly Story, Volume 2 (Coral 1960)★★★★★, Buddy Holly And The Crickets (Coral 1963)★★★★, Reminiscing (Coral 1963)★★★★, Showcase (Coral 1964)★★★★, Holly In The Hills (Coral 1965)★★★★, The Great Buddy Holly (Vocalion 1967)★★★★, Giant (Coral 1969)★★★★, Remember (Coral 1971)★★★, Good Rockin' (Vocalion 1971)★★★, A Rock And Roll Collection (Decca 1972)★★★, The Nashville Sessions (MCA 1975)★★★★, Western And Bop (Coral 1977)★★★, For The First Time Anywhere (MCA 1983)★★★, From The Original Master Tapes (MCA 1985)★★★★★, Something Special From Buddy Holly (Rollercoaster 1986)★★★★, Buddy Holly And The Picks Original Voices Of The Crickets (1993)★★★★.

● COMPILATIONS: The Best Of Buddy Holly (Coral 1966)★★★★, Buddy Holly's Greatest Hits (Coral 1967)★★★★, Rave On (MFP 1975)★★★, 20 Golden Greats (MCA 1978)★★★★★, The Complete Buddy Holly 6-LP box set (Coral 1979)★★★★★, Love Songs (MCA 1981)★★★, Legend (MCA 1985)★★★★, Buddy Holly Rocks (Charly 1985)★★★, Buddy Holly (Castle 1986)★★★, True Love Ways (Telstar 1989)★★★★, Words Of Love (Polygram 1993)★★★★, The Singles Collection 1957-1960 (Pickwick 1994)★★★, The Very Best Of Buddy Holly (Dino 1996)★★★★.

● FURTHER READING: Buddy Holly, Dave Laing. Buddy Holly: A Biography In Words Photographs And Music, Elizabeth Peer and Ralph Peer. Buddy Holly: His Life And Music, John Goldrosen. The Buddy I Knew, Larry Holley. The Buddy Holly Story, John Goldrosen. Buddy Holly And The Crickets, Alan Clark. Buddy Holly: 30th Anniversary Memorial Series No 1, Alan Clark. The Legend That Is Buddy Holly, Richard Peters. Buddy Holly, Alan Mann's A-Z, Alan Mann. Buddy Holly: A Biography, Ellis Amburn. Remembering Buddy, John Goldrosen and John Beecher. Buddy The Biography (UK) Rave On (USA), Phillip Norman. Memories Of Buddy Holly, Jim Dawson and Spencer Leigh.

HOLLYWOOD FLAMES

Formed as the Flames in 1949, this R&B group went through a variety of name changes - Four Flames, Hollywood Four Flames, Jets, Ebbtides and Satellites - during its career. However, it was as the Hollywood Flames that they had their biggest success, the 1957 hit 'Buzz, Buzz, Buzz'. The song was written by founding member Bobby Byrd, who also had a solo career as Bobby Day. The vocal on the song was not by Day, however, but by group member Earl Nelson, who also recorded as Jackie Lee and as half of Bob And Earl. The other members of the group at the time of the hit, which reached number 11 in the US pop charts and number 5 in the R&B charts, were founding member David Ford and baritone Curtis Williams, co-writer of the hit 'Earth Angel' and a former member of the group that recorded it, the Penguins. 'Buzz, Buzz, Buzz' was released on Ebb Records in November 1957, the single spent 17 weeks in the charts. Follow-up singles were issued under Day's name, but by 1959 Ebb had folded. The group continued to record with various personnel for several years.
● COMPILATIONS: *The Hollywood Flames* (Specialty 1992)★★★.

HOMER AND JETHRO

Homer (b. Henry D. Haynes, 27 July 1920, d. 7 August 1971, Chicago, Illinois, USA) and Jethro (b. Kenneth C. Burns, 10 March 1920, d. 4 February 1989, Evanston, Illinois, USA) were both from Knoxville, Tennessee, USA. They went to the same school and learned to play stringed instruments as young children. In 1932, they began to work together as musicians on WNOX Knoxville, where they performed in a quartet known as the String Dusters. With Homer on guitar and Jethro on mandolin, they mainly played instrumental pop music and any vocals were usually performed as a trio. Somewhat bored with the regular format, they developed a comedy act that they used backstage. They began to present comedy versions of popular songs by maintaining the melody but changing the lyrics, and before long, they were encouraged to perform them live on the radio. They were given the names of Homer and Jethro by the programme director, Lowell Blanchard. The act quickly proved a popular part of the String Dusters' routine. In 1936, they left the group to work solely as Homer and Jethro but stayed at WNOX until 1939. They then became regulars on the *Renfro Valley Barn Dance* in Kentucky, but in 1941, they were both called up for military service. In 1945, they were back together as regulars on the *Midwestern Hayride* on WLW Cincinnati, and between 1946 and 1948, they recorded their humorous songs for the local King label. In 1949, after a move to RCA Records, they had Top 10 US country chart success with a recording with June Carter of 'Baby It's Cold Outside'. In the late 1940s, they toured with their own tent show but eventually joined Red Foley on KWTO Springfield. In 1949, they toured the USA as part of orchestra leader Spike Jones' show and in 1951, while in Chicago with Jones, they were invited to become regulars on the *National Barn Dance* on WLS, where they remained until 1958. During the 50s and 60s, they toured extensively, their humour proving very popular in many varied venues, including Las Vegas. Their biggest country chart hit came in 1953, when 'How Much Is That Hound Dog In The Window' reached number 2. In 1959, they had a US pop Top 20 hit with 'The Battle Of

Kookamonga', their parody of Johnny Horton's hit 'Battle Of New Orleans'. Proving that no song was safe from the couple's attentions in 1964, they had their last chart entry with their version of the Beatles' 'I Want To Hold Your Hand'. They also made commercials for Kellogg's Cornflakes during the 60s, which made them household names in the USA, but might have prompted a drop in sales had they been shown in Britain. The zany comedy tended to overshadow the fact that the duo were fine musicians. They made instrumental albums and in 1970, they recorded with Chet Atkins (Jethro's brother-in-law) as the Nashville String Band (it was not until the album had reached the charts that RCA revealed the identities of the musicians). Atkins rated Homer as one of the best rhythm guitarists he ever knew. He was also a good enough vocalist to have pursued a singing career but had no interest in doing so. Jethro was also noted as an excellent mandolin player and one who, even in his early days, did much to make the instrument acceptable in jazz music. The partnership came to an end after 39 years on 7 August 1971, when Homer suffered a heart attack and died. Jethro was deeply affected by Homer's death but eventually returned to work as a musician. In the late 70s, he toured and recorded with Steve Goodman. Jethro died of cancer at his home in February 1989. Homer and Jethro's parodies included such titles as 'The Ballad Of Davy Crew-Cut' and 'Hart Brake Motel', and few could match album titles such as *Songs My Mother Never Sang*, *Ooh! That's Corny* (named after their catchphrase) or, bearing in mind they had been steadily turning out albums for 16 years, to suddenly decide to call one simply *Homer & Jethro's Next Album*.
● ALBUMS: *Homer & Jethro Fracture Frank Loesser* 10-inch album (RCA Victor 1953)★★★, *The Worst Of Homer & Jethro* (RCA Victor 1957)★★★★, *Barefoot Ballads* (RCA Victor 1957)★★★, *Life Can Be Miserable* (RCA Victor 1958)★★★★, *Musical Madness* (Audio Lab 1958)★★★, *They Sure Are Corny* (King 1959)★★★★, *At The Country Club* (RCA Victor 1960)★★★, *Songs My Mother Never Sang* (RCA Victor 1961)★★★, *Homer & Jethro At The Convention* (RCA Victor 1962)★★★, *Homer & Jethro Strike Back* (Camden 1962)★★★, *Playing It Straight* (RCA Victor 1962)★★★, *Cornier Than Corn* (King 1963)★★★★, *Zany Songs Of The 30s* (RCA Victor 1963)★★★, *Homer & Jethro Go West* (RCA Victor 1963)★★★, *Ooh, That's Corny!* (RCA Victor 1963)★★★, *The Humorous Side Of Country Music* (Camden 1963)★★★, *Cornfucius Say* (RCA Victor 1964)★★★, *Fractured Folk Songs* (RCA Victor 1964)★★★, *Homer & Jethro Sing Tenderly And Other Love Ballads* (RCA Victor 1965)★★★, *The Old Crusty Minstrels* (RCA Victor 1965)★★★, *Songs To Tickle Your Funny Bone* (Camden 1966)★★★, *Wanted For Murder* (RCA Victor 1966)★★★, *Any News From Nashville* (RCA Victor 1966)★★★, *It Ain't Necessarily Square* (RCA Victor 1967)★★★, *Nashville Cats* (RCA Victor 1967)★★★, *24 Great Songs In The Homer & Jethro Style* (King 1967)★★★, *Something Stupid* (RCA Victor 1967)★★★, *Songs For The 'Out' Crowd* (RCA Victor 1967)★★★, *The Playboy Song* (Camden 1968)★★★, *There's Nothing Like An Old Hippie* (RCA Victor 1968)★★, *Homer & Jethro Live At Vanderbilt University* (RCA Victor 1968)★★★, *Cool Crazy Christmas* (RCA Victor 1968)★★, *Homer & Jethro's Next Album* (RCA Victor 1969)★★★, *The Far Out World Of Homer & Jethro* (RCA Victor 1972)★★★. With The

Nashville String Band *Down Home* (RCA Victor 1970)★★★, *Identified* (RCA Victor 1970)★★★, *Strung Up* (RCA Victor 1971)★★★.

By Jethro Burns: with Joe Venuti, Curly Chalker, Eldon Shamblin *S'Wonderful (4 Giants Of Swing)* (Flying Fish 1977)★★★, *Jethro Burns* (Flying Fish 1977)★★★, *Jethro Burns Live* (Flying Fish 1978)★★★, with Tiny Moore *Back To Back* (Flying Fish 1980)★★★, *Tea For One* (Flying Fish 1982)★★★, with Red Rector *Old Friends* (Flying Fish 1983)★★★.

● COMPILATIONS: *The Best Of Homer & Jethro* (RCA Victor 1966)★★★, *Country Comedy* (Camden 1971)★★★, *Assault On The Rock 'N' Roll Era* (Bear Family 1989)★★★, *The Best Of* (RCA 1992)★★★, *America's Favorite Song Butchers: The Weird World Of Homer & Jethro* (Razor & Tie 1997)★★★★.

HORNE, LENA

b. 30 June 1917, Brooklyn, New York, USA. A dynamic performer, of striking appearance and elegant style. The daughter of an actress and a hotel operator, she was brought up mainly by her paternal grandmother, Cora Calhoun Horne. She made her professional debut at the age of 16 as a singer in the chorus at Harlem's Cotton Club, learning from Duke Ellington, Cab Calloway, Billie Holiday and Harold Arlen, the composer of a future big hit, 'Stormy Weather'. From 1935-36 she was featured vocalist with the all-black Noble Sissle's Society Orchestra (the same Noble Sissle who, with Eubie Blake, wrote several hit songs including 'Shuffle Along' and 'I'm Just Wild About Harry') and later toured with the top swing band of Charlie Barnet, singing numbers such as 'Good For Nothin' Joe' and 'You're My Thrill'. Sometimes, when Barnet's Band played the southern towns, Horne had to stay in the band bus. She made her Broadway debut in 1934 as 'A Quadroon Girl' in *Dance With Your Gods*, and also appeared in Lew Leslie's *Blackbirds Of 1939*, in which she sang Mitchell Parish and Sammy Fain's 'You're So Indifferent' - but only for the show's run of nine performances.

After a spell at the Café Society Downtown in New York, she moved to Hollywood's Little Troc Club and was spotted by Roger Edens, musical supervisor for MGM Pictures, and former accompanist for Ethel Merman, who introduced her to producer Arthur Freed. In her first film for MGM, *Panama Hattie* (1942), which starred Merman, Horne sang Cole Porter's 'Just One Of Those Things', and a rhumba number called 'The Sping'. To make her skin appear lighter on film, the studio used a special make-up called 'Light Egyptian'. Horne referred to herself as 'a sepia Hedy Lamarr'. Her next two films, *Cabin In The Sky* and *Stormy Weather*, both made in 1943, are generally regarded as her best. In the remainder of her 40s and 50s movie musicals (which included *Thousands Cheer, Swing Fever, Broadway Rhythm, Two Girls And A Sailor, Ziegfeld Follies, Till The Clouds Roll By, Words And Music, Duchess Of Idaho* and *Meet Me In Las Vegas*), she merely performed guest shots that were easily removable, without spoiling the plot, for the benefit of southern-state distributors.

Her 40s record hits included her theme song, 'Stormy Weather', and two other Arlen songs, ''Deed I Do' and 'As Long As I Live'. She also recorded with several big swing era names such as Artie Shaw, Cab Calloway and Teddy Wilson. During World War II, she became the pin-up girl for many thousands of black GIs and refused to appear on US tours unless black soldiers were admitted to the audience. In 1947 she married pianist, arranger and conductor Lennie Hayton, who also became her manager and mentor until his death in 1971. For a time during the 50s Lena Horne was blacklisted, probably for her constant involvement with the Civil Rights movement, but particularly for her friendship with alleged Communist sympathizer Paul Robeson. Ironically, she was at the peak of her powers at that time, and although she was unable to appear much on television and in films, she continued to make records and appear in nightclubs, which were regarded as her special forte. Evidence of that was displayed on *Lena Horne At The Waldorf Astoria*. The material ranged from the sultry 'Mood Indigo', right through to the novelty 'New Fangled Tango' and *Lena At The Sands*, with its medleys of songs by Richard Rodgers/Oscar Hammerstein II, Jule Styne and E.Y. 'Yip' Harburg. Other US Top 30 chart albums included *Give The Lady What She Wants* and *Porgy And Bess*, with Harry Belafonte. Horne also made the US Top 20 singles charts in 1955 with 'Love Me Or Leave Me', written by Gus Kahn and Walter Donaldson for Ruth Etting to sing in the 1928 Broadway show *Whoopee*. In 1957 Horne had her first starring role on Broadway when she played Savannah, opposite Ricardo Montalban, in the Arlen/Harburg musical *Jamaica*. In the 60s, besides the usual round of television shows and records, she appeared in a dramatic role, with Richard Widmark, in *Death Of A Gunfighter* (1969). After Hayton's death in 1971 she worked less, but did feature in *The Wiz*, an all-black film version of *The Wizard Of Oz*, starring Diana Ross and Michael Jackson, and in 1979 she received an honorary doctorate degree from Harvard University. In May 1981, she opened on Broadway in her own autobiographical show, *Lena Horne: The Lady And Her Music*. It ran at the Nederland Theatre to full houses for 14 months, a Broadway record for a one-woman show. Horne received several awards including a special Tony Award for 'Distinguished Achievement In The Theatre', a Drama Desk Award, New York Drama Critics' Special Award, New York City's Handel Medallion, Dance Theatre of Harlem's Emergence Award, two Grammy Awards and the NAACP Springarn Award. She took the show to London in 1984, where it was also acclaimed. In 1993, after not having sung in public for several years, Lena Horne agreed to perform the songs of Billy Strayhorn at the US JVC Jazz Festival. She included several of the same composer's songs on her 1994 album *We'll Be Together Again*, and, in the same year, surprised and delighted her fans by appearing in concert at Carnegie Hall.

● ALBUMS: *Lena Horne Sings* 10-inch album (MGM 1952)★★★, *This Is Lena Horne* 10-inch album 10-inch album (RCA Victor 1952)★★★★, *Moanin' Low* 10-inch album (Tops 1954)★★★, *It's Love* (RCA Victor 1955)★★★, *Stormy Weather* (RCA Victor 1956)★★★★, *Lena Horne At The Waldorf Astoria* (RCA Victor 1957)★★★★, *Jamaica* film soundtrack (RCA Victor 1957)★★, *Lena And Ivie* (Jazztine 1957)★★★, *Give The Lady What She Wants* (RCA Victor 1958)★★★, with Harry Belafonte *Porgy And Bess* film soundtrack (RCA Victor 1959)★★★★, *Songs Of Burke And Van Heusen* (RCA Victor 1959)★★★, *Lena Horne At The Sands* (RCA Victor 1961)★★★★, *Lena On The Blue Side* (RCA Victor 1962)★★★, *Lena ... Lovely And Alive* (RCA Victor 1963)★★★, *Lena Goes Latin* (RCA Victor 1963)★★★,

with Gabor Szabo *Lena And Gabor* (Skye 1970)★★★, *Lena* (1974)★★★, *Lena, A New Album* (RCA 1976)★★★, *Lena Horne: The Lady And Her Music* stage cast (Qwest 1981)★★★, *A Song For You* (1992)★★★, *We'll Be Together Again* (Blue Note 1994)★★★, *An Evening With Lena Horne* (Blue Note 1995)★★★.
● COMPILATIONS: *Twenty Golden Pieces Of Lena Horne* (Bulldog 1979)★★★, *Lena Horne* (Jazz Greats 1979)★★★, *Lena Horne And Pearl Bailey* (Jazz Greats 1979)★★★, shared with Billie Holiday, Ella Fitzgerald and Sarah Vaughan *Billie, Ella, Lena, Sarah!* (Columbia 1980)★★★★, *Lena Horne And Frank Sinatra* (Astan 1984)★★★, *The Fabulous Lena Horne* (Cambra 1985)★★★.
● FURTHER READING: *In Person*, Lena Horne. *Lena*, Lena Horne with Richard Schikel. *Lena: A Personal And Professional Biography*, J. Haskins and K. Benson.
● FILMS: *The Duke Is Tops* (1938), *Panama Hattie* (1942), *I Dood It* (1943), *Swing Fever* (1943), *Stormy Weather* (1943), *Thousands Cheer* (1943), *Cabin In The Sky* (1943), *Two Girls And A Sailor* (1944), *Broadway Rhythm* (1944), *Till The Clouds Roll By* (1946), *Ziegfeld Follies* (1946), *Words And Music* (1948), *Duchess Of Idaho* (1950), *Meet Me In Las Vegas* (1956), *Death Of A Gunfighter* (1969), *The Wiz* (1978).

HORTON, JOHNNY

b. 3 April 1925, Los Angeles, California, USA, d. 5 November 1960, Texas, USA. Horton was raised in Tyler, Texas, where his sharecropping family settled in search of work. He learned the guitar from his mother and, due to his athletic prowess, won scholarships at Baylor University and later the University of Seattle. For a time he worked in the fishing industry but began his singing career on KXLA Pasadena in 1950, quickly acquiring the nickname of 'The Singing Fisherman'. He recorded for Cormac in 1951 and then became the first artist on Fabor Robinson's Abbott label. In 1952 he moved to Mercury Records but was soon in conflict with the company about the choice of songs. He married Hank Williams' widow, Billie Jean, in September 1953, who encouraged him to better himself. With Tillman Franks as his manager, Horton moved to Columbia Records, and their co-written 'Honky Tonk Man' marked his debut in the US country charts. Horton recorded 'Honky Tonk Man' the day after Elvis Presley recorded 'Heartbreak Hotel' and Presley's bass player, Bill Black, was on the session. The song was successfully revived by Dwight Yoakam in 1986, while George Jones revived another song recorded that day, 'I'm A One Woman Man', in 1989. Other fine examples of Horton's rockabilly talents are 'All Grown Up' and the hard-hitting 'Honky Tonk Hardwood Floor'.
In 1959, Horton switched direction and concentrated on story songs, often with an historical basis, and had his first US country number 1 with a Tillman Franks song, 'When It's Springtime In Alaska'. This was followed by his version of Jimmie Driftwood's 'The Battle Of New Orleans', which became a number 1 pop and country hit in the USA. Lonnie Donegan's 'Battle Of New Orleans' made number 2 in the UK, but Horton's number 16 was respectable, especially in view of the fact that this version was banned by the BBC for referring to 'the bloody British'. Horton's next record was another historical song, 'Johnny Reb', backed with the up-tempo novelty, 'Sal's Got A Sugar Lip'. Told simply to cover Horton's latest record, Donegan mistakenly covered 'Sal's

Got A Sugar Lip' - and still managed to have a hit! Horton's 'Sink The Bismarck', inspired by the film, made number 3 in the US charts, while he sang the title song of the John Wayne film *North To Alaska* and took it to number 4 in the USA and number 23 in the UK. It also topped the US country charts for five weeks.
On 5 November 1960, Horton died on the way to hospital after a head-on collision with a pick-up truck near Milano, Texas. Tillman Franks received head and chest injuries that required hospital treatment and guitarist Tommy Tomlinson suffered a very serious leg injury which, because of his diabetes, failed to heal and a few months later the leg was amputated. He later played guitar for a time with Claude King but never really recovered from the crash (the driver of the other vehicle, James Davis, aged 19, also died). Billie Jean (who later stated that before he left for the last time, Horton kissed her on exactly the same place on the same cheek that Hank Williams had kissed her when he set off for his final trip) became a country star's widow for the second time in 10 years. Horton, who has been described as the last major star of the *Louisiana Hayride*, is buried in Hillcrest Cemetery, Bossier City, Louisiana. Much of his up-tempo material did not appeal to the traditionalists. However, his 'saga' songs have certainly guaranteed that he is not forgotten.
● ALBUMS: *Honky Tonk Man* (Columbia 1957)★★★, *Done Rovin'* (Briar Internatonal 1958)★★, *Free And Easy Songs* (Sesac 1959)★★, *The Fantastic Johnny Horton* (Mercury 1959)★★★, *The Spectacular Johnny Horton* (Columbia 1960)★★★, *Johnny Horton Makes History* (Columbia 1960)★★★, *Honky Tonk Man* (Columbia 1962)★★★, *Johnny Horton* (Dot 1962)★★★, *I Can't Forget You* (Columbia 1965)★★★, *The Voice Of Johnny Horton* (Hilltop 1965)★★★, *Johnny Horton On The Louisiana Hayride* (Columbia 1966)★★★, *All For The Love Of A Girl* (Hilltop 1968)★★, *The Unforgettable Johnny Horton* (Harmony 1968)★★★, *Johnny Horton On The Road* (Columbia 1969)★★, *The Battle Of New Orleans* (Harmony 1971)★★★.
● COMPILATIONS: *Johnny Horton's Greatest Hits* (Columbia 1961)★★★, *America Remembers Johnny Horton* (Columbia Special Products 1980)★★★, *Rockin' Rollin' Johnny Horton* (Bear Family 1981)★★★★, *American Originals* (Columbia 1989)★★★, *The Early Years* 7-LP box set (Bear Family 1991)★★★, *Johnny Horton 1956-1960* 4-CD box set (Bear Family 1991)★★★★, *Honky Tonk Man: The Essential Johnny Horton 1956-1960* (Columbia/Legacy 1996)★★★★, *Somebody's Rockin'* (Bear Family 1996)★★★.
● FURTHER READING: *Johnny Horton: Your Singing Fisherman*, Michael LeVine.

HOT ROD GANG

Retitled *Fury Unleashed* for UK audiences, *Hot Rod Gang* was a low-budget film notable only for the appearance of Gene Vincent in its cast. This 1958 feature starred John Ashley as John Abernethy III, who is unable to inherit a considerable fortune in time to finance his entry to a hot-rod race. He attempts to secure the cash required to build a car by joining Vincent's group, the Blue Caps. Although not credited, rock singer Eddie Cochran also appears as a member of the band, cementing a friendship with Vincent that culminated in their joint 1960 UK tour. This fateful visit ended with the car crash in which Cochran was killed. Although both artists are seen to better effect in *The Girl Can't Help It*, *Hot Rod Gang* does at least afford another opportunity to see two of rock 'n' roll's seminal performers.

HOUND-DOG MAN

Fabian was one of several 50s rock 'n' roll singers styled on Elvis Presley, but boasting only a slim resemblance to their role model. 'Turn Me Loose' and 'Tiger' were among his US Top 10 entries, but the sexual bravura of their titles was undermined by unconvincing vocals. However, he was quickly plucked from the singles chart and presented in a series of blithe Hollywood films. Released in 1959, *Hound-Dog Man* provided Fabian's first starring role, in which he plays one of two teenagers star-struck by a wayward acquaintance. The light comedy feature was set in 1912, demanding that Fabian act rather than simply perform, while rising director Don Seigel, later famed for Clint Eastwood's *Dirty Harry* series, brought a sharper focus to the proceedings than many contemporary releases of its type. The title song became one of Fabian's five US Top 30 entries during 1959, but the appeal of his recordings waned as quickly as it arose.

HOUSTON, JOE

b. 1927, Austin, Texas, USA. Joe Houston was inspired to take up the saxophone after seeing Count Hastings playing with Tiny Bradshaw's Orchestra, and lists Joe Thomas, Charlie Parker and Arnett Cobb among his other influences. By 1949 he became associated with Big Joe Turner, and made his recording debut on Turner's sole release on the Rouge label and probably played on Turner's first Freedom session. Houston's own recording career began in 1949 with Freedom Records, although his biggest successes were with 'Worry-Worry-Worry' (recorded by Bob Shad for his Sittin In With label, but actually issued on Mercury in 1951), 'Cornbread And Cabbage Greens' and 'Blow, Joe, Blow' (both for Macy's Records, also in 1951), and with 'All Night Long' (recorded for both the Money and Caddy labels, after Houston relocated to Los Angeles in 1955). Other recordings were issued on a gamut of labels: Modern/RPM/Crown, Imperial/Bay'ou, Combo, Lucky, Recorded In Hollywood, Cas, Dooto and other independent Los Angeles labels. In recent years, Houston has made a comeback with numerous personal appearances.
● ALBUMS: *Kicking Back* (1983)★★★, *Rockin' At The Drive In* (Ace 1984)★★★, *Earthquake* (Pathe Marconi 1985)★★★, *Rockin' 'N' Boppin'* (Saxophonograph 1989)★★★, *Cornbread And Cabbage Greens* (Ace 1992)★★★, with Otis Grand *The Return Of Honk* (JSP 1994)★★★.

HOWARD, DON

b. Donald Howard Koplow, 11 May 1935, Cleveland, Ohio, USA. Pop vocalist Don Howard was 17 years old when he first heard a particular folk song recited by a girlfriend. After playing it on his guitar he adjusted the lyrics and copyrighted it under the title 'Oh Happy Day'. With his booming voice and the song's slow, chanting rhythm, it was released in the USA in December 1952 and rose to number 4 in the charts without any promotion or plugging, selling over a million copies. Some time afterwards, Nancy Binns Reed (the girlfriend), an amateur songwriter, claimed ownership of the tune. Howard gave her a credit as co-writer and

agreed to share the royalties. A cover version by vocal quartet the Johnston Brothers also reached number 4 in the UK in mid-1953.

HOWLIN' WOLF

b. Chester Arthur Burnett, 10 June 1910, West Point, Mississippi, USA, d. 10 January 1976, Hines, Illinois, USA. Howlin' Wolf was one of the most important of the southern expatriates who created the post-war blues out of their rural past and moulded it into the tough 'Chicago sound' of the 50s. He was one of six children born to farmer Dock Burnett and his wife Gertrude, and spent his earliest years around Aberdeen, Mississippi, where he sang in the local baptist church. In 1923 he relocated to Ruleville, Mississippi, and 10 years later moved again to work on Nat Phillips' plantation at Twist, Arkansas. By this time he was working in music, appearing at local parties and juke-joints. He had been inspired by performers such as Charley Patton and Tommy Johnson, both of whom he had met, and he took much of the showmanship of his act from them, although his hoarse, powerful voice and eerie 'howling' were peculiarly his own. Other seminal Mississippi figures, Robert Johnson and Son House, also proved influential. During this period he enjoyed many nicknames such as 'Big Foot' and 'Bull Cow' but it was as Howlin' Wolf that his fame grew. He was a huge man with a commanding presence and threatening aspect, whom contemporary Johnny Shines once likened to a wild animal, saying that he (Shines) was scared to lay his hand on him.

Throughout the 30s Wolf combined farming with working in music, sometimes travelling in the company of people such as Shines, Robert Johnson, and Sonny Boy 'Rice Miller' Williamson. Williamson, who courted and married Wolf's half-sister Mary, taught his new brother-in-law to play some harmonica and Wolf also experimented with the guitar. Wolf's first marriage had been to a sister of singer Willie Brown and it was during this time that he married his second wife, Lillie Handley. It was a union that lasted until his death. During 1941-44 Wolf was drafted into the army but once he had left, he formed his own group and gained sufficient fame to be approached by KWEM, a west Memphis radio station that was competing for local black listeners and recognized Wolf's potential. For KWEM, Wolf worked as a disc jockey as well as performing himself, and this brought him to the attention of Sam Phillips, who was recording material in Memphis and leasing it to others for sale in the black communities of the northern and western areas of the USA. Phillips, who considered Wolf to be one of the greatest talents he knew, originally made separate agreements with the Bihari Brothers in California and the Chess Brothers of Chicago to issue Wolf's recordings. The success of the early recordings led to something of a war between these two camps, with each trying to attract him under their own aegis. On the evidence of some of the songs that he recorded at the time, it seems that Wolf was tempted to take a 'stroll out west', but in the event he went to Chicago, 'the onliest one who drove out of the south like a gentleman'.

In Memphis, Wolf, whose recording sessions were often under the direction of Ike Turner, had been lucky to employ the talents of guitarist Willie Johnson, who refused to move north, and in Chicago that good fortune continued as he worked first with Jody Williams and then the unique Hubert

Sumlin. The raw delta sound of Wolf's earlier records assured him of a ready-made audience once he reached Chicago, and he quickly built a powerful reputation on the club circuit, extending it with such classic records as 'Smokestack Lightning' and 'Killing Floor'. Like his great rival Muddy Waters, he maintained his audience, and a Chess recording contract, through the lean times of rock 'n' roll and into the blues boom of the 60s. He came to Europe with the AFBF in 1964 and continued to return over the next ten years. The Rolling Stones and the Yardbirds did much to publicize Wolf's (and Waters') music, both in Europe and white America, and as the 60s progressed, the newer artists at Chess saw their target audience as the emerging white 'love and peace' culture and tried to influence their material to suit it. Wolf's music was a significant influence on rock and many of his best-known songs - 'Sitting On Top Of The World', 'I Ain't Superstitious', 'Killin' Floor', 'Back Door Man' and 'Little Red Rooster' - were recorded by acts as diverse as the Doors, Cream, the Rolling Stones, the Yardbirds and Manfred Mann. Few, however, rivalled the power or sexual bravura displayed on the originals and only Don Van Vliet (Captain Beefheart) came close to recapturing his aggressive, raucous voice. A compelling appearance on the teen-oriented *Shindig* television show (at the behest of the Rolling Stones) was a rare concession to commerciality. His label's desire for success, akin to the white acts he influenced, resulted in the lamentable *The Howlin' Wolf Album*, which the artist described as 'dog shit'. This ill-conceived attempt to update earlier songs was outshone by *The London Howlin' Wolf Sessions*, on which Wolf and long-serving guitarist Hubert Sumlin were joined by an array of guests, including Eric Clapton, Steve Winwood, and Rolling Stones members Bill Wyman and Charlie Watts. Wolf, along with others like Muddy Waters, resisted this move but were powerless to control it. They were, of course, men in their 50s, set in their ways but needing to maintain an audience outside the dwindling Chicago clubs. Fortunately, Wolf outlived this trend, along with that for piling well-known artists together into 'super bands'. Wolf continued to tour but his health was declining. After a protracted period of illness Howlin' Wolf died of cancer in the Veterans Administration Hospital in 1976. His influence has survived the excesses of the 'swinging 60s' and is to be seen today in the work of many of the emerging bluesmen such as Roosevelt 'Booba' Barnes.
● ALBUMS: *Moaning In The Moonlight* (Chess 1959)★★★★, *Howlin' Wolf* aka *The Rocking Chair Album* (Chess 1962)★★★★, *Howlin' Wolf Sings The Blues* (Crown 1962)★★★, *The Real Folk Blues* (Chess 1966)★★★★, *Big City Blues* (Custom 1966)★★★, *Original Folk Blues* (Kent 1967)★★★, *More Real Folk Blues* (Chess 1967)★★★★, *This Is Howlin' Wolf's New Album* aka *The Dog Shit Album* (Cadet 1969)★★, *Evil* (Chess 1969)★★★, *Message To The Young* (Chess 1971)★★, *The London Sessions* (Chess 1971)★★★, *Live And Cookin' At Alice's Revisited* (Chess 1972)★★, *Howlin' Wolf AKA Chester Burnett* (Chess 1972)★★★, *The Back Door Wolf* (Chess 1973)★★★★, *Change My Way* (Chess 1975)★★★, *Ridin' In The Moonlight* (Ace 1982)★★★, *Live In Europe 1964* (Sundown 1988)★★★, *Memphis Days Volume 1* (Bear Family 1989)★★★, *Memphis Days Volume 2* (Bear Family 1990)★★★, *Howlin' Wolf Rides Again* (Ace 1991)★★★.
● COMPILATIONS: *Going Back Home* (1970)★★★, *Chess Blues Masters* (Chess 1976)★★★, *The Legendary Sun Performers* (Charly 1977)★★★, *Chess Masters* (Chess 1981)★★★★, *Chess Masters 2* (Chess 1982)★★★★, *Chess Masters 3* (Chess 1983)★★★, *The Wolf* (Blue Moon 1984)★★★, *Golden Classics* (Astan 1984)★★★, *The Howlin' Wolf Collection* (Deja Vu 1985)★★★★, *His Greatest Hits* (Chess 1986)★★★, *Cadillac Daddy: Memphis Recordings, 1952* (Rounder 1987)★★★, *Howlin' For My Baby* (Sun 1987)★★★, *Shake For Me - The Red Rooster* (Vogue 1988)★★★, *Smokestack Lightnin'* (Vogue 1988)★★★, *Red Rooster* (Joker 1988)★★★, *Moanin' And Howlin'* (Charly 1988)★★★, *Howlin' Wolf* 5-LP box set (Chess 1991)★★★★, *Going Down Slow* 5-CD box set (Roots 1992)★★★★, *Gold Collection* (1993)★★★, *The Wolf Is At Your Door* (Fan 1994)★★★, *The Complete Recordings 1951-1969* 7-CD box set (Charly 1994)★★★★, *The Genuine Article - The Best Of* (MCA 1994)★★★★, *The Very Best Of Howlin' Wolf* 3-CD set (Charly 1995)★★★★, *His Best* (Chess 1997)★★★★.

HUNTER, TAB
b. Arthur Andrew Kelm, 11 July 1931, New York City, New York, USA. This blond-haired, blue-eyed pop vocalist/actor used his mother's maiden name, Gelien, until he was spotted in 1948, working at a stable, by talent scout Dick Clayton. He introduced him to Rock Hudson's Hollywood agent Harry Wilson, who said 'We've got to tab you something', then named him Tab Hunter. He made his screen debut in the 1950 film *The Lawless* and two years later co-starred with Linda Darnell in the British film *Saturday Island* (US title: *Island Of Desire*). In late 1956 he received a phone call from Randy Wood, president of Dot Records, asking him to record a song recently cut by US country star Sonny James, the lilting ballad 'Young Love'. Both versions made the US charts, Hunter reaching number 1 and James peaking at number 2. Hunter also topped the UK chart, but James lagged behind at number 11. He continued recording for Dot and hit with the slightly up-tempo '99 Ways', which narrowly missed the US Top 10 but made the UK Top 5 (1957). In the following year he appeared in the film version of the Broadway show *Damn Yankees*, with Gwen Verdon and Ray Walston. As Warner Brothers had him under contract to make films, they resented him recording for Dot and established their own record label in 1958. He signed, with moderate success, and in 1960 starred in his own NBC US television series. He continued his acting and appeared opposite Fabian in the 1964 'beach party' film *Ride The Wild Surf*. He was still acting in the 80s, notably with the late Divine in *Polyester* and *Lust In The Dust*, and also in the *Grease* sequel, *Grease 2*. In the latter part of the decade Hunter moved to Mexico to write, and set up a film production company, one of the fruits of which was the 'family' picture *Dark Horse* (1992).
● ALBUMS: *Tab Hunter* (Warners 1958)★★, *When I Fall In Love* (Warners 1959)★★, *R.F.D. Tab Hunter* (Warners 1960)★★, *Young Love* (Dot 1961)★★.
● FILMS: *The Lawless* (1950), *Saturday Island* (1952), *Damn Yankees* (1958), *Ride The Wild Surf* (1964).

HUTTON, BETTY
b. 26 February 1921, Battle Creek, Michigan, USA. A dynamic and vivacious singer and actress, while still a small child Hutton began singing in the streets to help support her

impoverished family. By her early teens she was already beginning to make a name for herself when she was hired by Vincent Lopez, then leader of a popular radio band. In 1940, by then known as 'The Blonde Bombshell' in recognition of her fizzing vitality, Hutton appeared on Broadway in *Panama Hattie*, and the following year was snapped up by Hollywood. During the 40s she appeared in a string of popular musicals including *Star Spangled Rhythm*, *Happy Go Lucky*, *Let's Face It*, *And The Angels Sing*, *Here Comes The Waves*, *Incendiary Blonde*, *Duffy's Tavern*, *The Stork Club*, *Cross My Heart*, *The Perils Of Pauline*, *Dream Girl* and *Red Hot And Blue*. However, it was her sensational performance in the title role of *Annie Get Your Gun* in 1950 that established her as a major star. It gained her an international reputation, which she enhanced with roles in *Let's Dance* (1950), *The Greatest Show On Earth* and *Somebody Loves Me* (both 1952). Subsequent contractual difficulties with the studio resulted in her career coming to an abrupt halt, and although she made a brief appearance in the 1957 film *Spring Reunion*, she was declared bankrupt in 1967. In 1971, the last of her four marriages, to trumpeter Pete Candoli, ended in divorce, and after suffering a nervous breakdown and problems with drugs and alcohol, she worked for several years as a cook and housekeeper in a rectory in Portsmouth, Long Island. She made a triumphant comeback in 1980 when she took over the role of Miss Hannigan in the hit Broadway musical *Annie*. Later, she enrolled as a student at a New England college, before settling in Los Angeles. Her sister, Marion, two years her senior, was also a singer who worked with Glenn Miller's civilian band. In 1994 Capitol issued a collection of some of her most entertaining tracks, and a year later ex-Sugarcubes lead singer Björk included one of Hutton's specialities, 'It's Oh So Quiet', on her *Post* album.

● ALBUMS: *Square In The Social Circle* 10-inch album (Capitol 1950)★★★, *Annie Get Your Gun* film soundtrack (MGM 1950/55)★★★, *Somebody Loves Me* film soundtrack (RCA 1952)★★★, *Satins And Spurs* TV soundtrack (Capitol 1954)★★, *At The Saints And Sinners Ball* (Warners 1959)★★★.

● COMPILATIONS: *Great Ladies Of Song: Spotlight On Betty Hutton* (Capitol 1994)★★★.

● FILMS: *The Fleet's In* (1942), *Star Spangled Rhythm* (1942), *The Miracle Of Morgan's Creek* (1943), *Let's Face It* (1943), *Here Comes The Waves* (1944), *And The Angels Sing* (1944), *Incendiary Blonde* (1945), *The Stork Club* (1946), *Cross My Heart* (1946), *The Perils Of Pauline* (1947), *Dream Girl* (1948) *Annie Get Your Gun* (1950), *Let's Dance* (1951), *Somebody Loves Me* (1952), *The Greatest Show On Earth* (1952), *Spring Reunion* (1957).

HYMAN, DICK

b. 8 March 1927, New York City, New York, USA. After studying classical music, Hyman broadened his interests to encompass jazz and many other areas of music. In the late 40s he played piano in and around his home-town, working with leading bop musicians, including founding fathers Charlie Parker and Dizzy Gillespie. Early in the 50s he began a long career as a studio musician, playing piano, arranging, composing and leading orchestras. His work in the studios did not keep him from actively participating in jazz dates, many of which he himself organized. He also became deeply interested in the history of jazz and especially the develop-

ment of jazz piano. He demonstrated his interest in radio broadcasts and concert performances. His enormously eclectic taste allowed him to range from ragtime to freeform with complete confidence. Through performances and recordings with the New York Jazz Repertory Company, he encouraged interest in the music of Jelly Roll Morton, Fats Waller, James P. Johnson and Louis Armstrong. He also formed a small group, the Perfect Jazz Repertory Quintet. During his freeform period he played electric piano and later added the organ to the instruments at his command, recording *Cincinnati Fats*, *New School Concert* and other duo albums with Ruby Braff. Later still, Hyman recorded with Braff using, however improbably in a jazz context, a Wurlitzer organ. Unusual though it might have been, *A Pipe Organ Recital Plus One* was a critical and popular success. As a composer, Hyman has written for large and small ensembles and composed the score for the film *Scott Joplin* in 1976. A master of jazz piano, his performances not only display his extraordinary virtuoso technique but also demonstrate his deep understanding and abiding love for the great traditions of the music.

● ALBUMS: *60 Great All Time Songs, Volume 3* (MGM 1957)★★★, *Electrodynamics* (Command 1963)★★★, *Fabulous* (Command 1964)★★★, *Mirrors - Reflections Of Today* (Command 1968)★★★, *Moog -The Electric Eclectics Of Dick Hyman* (Command 1969)★★★, *The Age Of Electronicus* (Command 1969)★★★, *The Happy Breed* (1972)★★★, *Genius At Play* (1973)★★★, *Some Rags, Some Stomps And A Little Blues* (1973)★★★★, with NYJRC *Satchmo Remembered* (1974)★★★, *Scott Joplin: The Complete Works For Piano* (1975)★★★★, *A Waltz Dressed In Blue* (1977)★★★, *Charleston* (1977)★★, *Sliding By* (1977)★★★, *Ragtime, Stomp And Stride* (1977)★★★, with NYJRC *The Music Of Jelly Roll Morton* (1978)★★★, *Dick Hyman And The Perfect Jazz Repertory Quintet Plays Irving Berlin* (World Jazz 1979)★★★, *Dick Hyman Piano Solos* (Monmouth 1979)★★★, with Ruby Braff *Cincinnati Fats* (1981)★★★★, with Braff *A Pipe Organ Recital Plus One* (1982)★★★, *The New School Concert 1983* (1983)★★★, *Kitten On The Keys: The Music Of Zez Confrey* (1983)★★, with Braff *The New School Concert 1983* (1983)★★★, *Eubie* (1984)★★★, *Manhattan Jazz* (Limelight 1985)★★★, *Music Of 1937* (Concord 1990)★★★, with Braff *Younger Than Swingtime* (1990)★★★.

IDLE ON PARADE

Taking inspiration from Elvis Presley's induction into the US Army, Anthony Newley starred as the drafted pop star Jeep Jones in this 1959 British feature. Comedy stalwarts Sid James and Lionel Jeffries were also cast, but this jaundiced film owed more to television's *The Army Game* than rock 'n' roll. The soundtrack material, including 'Idle Rock-A-Boogie' and 'Saturday Night Rock-A-Boogie', consisted of little more than poorly formed pastiches, lacking neither the charm of Newley's Goons-inspired hits, 'Strawberry Fair' and 'That Noise', nor the wistfulness of his two UK chart-toppers, 'Why' and 'Do You Mind'. The four-track *Idle On Parade* EP nonetheless reached number 13 in the UK singles chart, reflecting the singer's popularity rather than the success of the film itself. Newley later became a celebrated songwriter for West End and Broadway productions, having bade farewell to his pop-styled inclinations.

IMPALAS

With sweet-voiced lead singer Joe 'Speedo' Frazier (b. 5 September 1943, New York City, New York, USA), this New York doo-wop group had an overnight success with their first record, '(Sorry) I Ran All The Way Home'. From the Carnesie section of Brooklyn, the rest of the Impalas were Richard Wagner, Lenny Renda and Tony Calouchi. They were discovered by disk jockey Alan Freed and Artie Zwirn, who co-wrote the bright, brash novelty tune with Gino Giosasi (of the Gino and Gina vocal duo). With an arrangement by Ray Ellis, '(Sorry) I Ran All The Way Home' was released in 1959 on the MGM subsidiary label Cub, reaching number 2 in America and entering the UK Top 30. The follow-up, 'Oh What A Fool' was a smaller hit. The Impalas made later records for Hamilton and 20th Century Fox before splitting up. Frazier went on to sing with Love's Own in 1973.
● ALBUMS: *Sorry I Ran All The Way Home* (Cub 1959)★★★.

IN THE WEE SMALL HOURS - FRANK SINATRA ★★★★★

As ever, Sinatra's collaboration with Nelson Riddle on this 1955 album is wholly successful. An emotional and romantic Sinatra gently eases himself through another 16 classics of American popular song, and although he fails to swing, he never ceases to move the listener, evoking images of comfy sofas, scotch on the rocks and radiograms. The songs, by Duke Ellington, Rodgers and Hart, Van Heusen, Arlen and Harburg, and Cole Porter, combine to create a mellow, rich and pure collection, but certainly not an album to follow Jimi Hendrix in playing order. It reached number 2 in the US album chart.
● TRACKS: *In the Wee Small Hours Of The Morning; Mood Indigo; Glad To Be Unhappy; I Get Along Without You Very Well; Deep In A Dream; I See Your Face Before Me; Can't We Be Friends?; When Your Lover Has Gone; What Is This Thing Called Love; Last Night When We Were Young; I'll Be Around; Ill Wind; It Never Entered My Mind; Dancing On The Ceiling; I'll Never Be The Same; This Love Of Mine.*

INK SPOTS

The original line-up consisted of Jerry Franklin Daniels (b. 1916, d. 7 November 1995, Indianapolis, Indiana, USA; lead tenor, guitar), Orville 'Hoppy' Jones (b. 17 February 1905, Chicago, Illinois, USA, d. 18 October 1944; bass), Charlie Fuqua (d. 1979; baritone, guitar) and Ivory 'Deek' Watson (d. 1967; second tenor). Most sources state that this enormously popular black vocal quartet was formed in the early 30s when they were working as porters at the Paramount Theatre in New York. Early in their career the Ink Spots played 'hot' numbers, and travelled to England in the mid-30s where they performed with the Jack Hylton Band. When they returned to the USA, Daniels became ill and was replaced by Bill Kenny (b. 1915, d. 23 March 1978). The new combination changed their style, slowed down the tempos, and had a big hit in 1939 with 'If I Didn't Care', which featured Kenny's impressive falsetto and a deep-voiced spoken chorus by bass singer Jones. This record set the pattern for their future success, mixed with only a few slightly more up-tempo items, such as 'Java Jive', 'Your Feet's Too Big', and two of several collaborations with Ella Fitzgerald, 'Cow-Cow-Boogie' and 'Into Each Life Some Rain Must Fall'. The latter sold more than a million copies.

Throughout the 40s their US hits included 'Address Unknown' (number 1), 'My Prayer', 'Bless You', 'When The Swallows Come Back To Capistrano', 'Whispering Grass', 'We Three' (number 1), 'Do I Worry?', 'I Don't Want To Set The World On Fire', 'Don't Get Around Much Any More', 'I'll Get By', 'Someday I'll Meet You Again', 'I'm Making Believe' (number 1) and 'I'm Beginning To See The Light' (both with Ella Fitzgerald), 'The Gypsy' (number 1 and a million-seller), 'Prisoner Of Love', 'To Each His Own' (number 1 and another million-seller), 'It's A Sin To Tell A Lie', 'You Were Only Fooling (While I Was Falling In Love)' and 'You're Breaking My Heart' (1949). The group were also popular on radio, in theatres, and made guest appearances in movies such as *The Great American Broadcast* and *Pardon My Sarong*. Orville Jones died in 1944 and was replaced by Bill Kenny's twin brother Herb (b. Herbert Cornelius Kenny, 1915, d. 11 July 1992, Columbia, Maryland, USA). A year later, founder-member Watson recruited Jimmie Nabbie (b. 1920, Tampa, Florida, USA, d. 15 September 1992, Atlanta, Georgia, USA) as lead tenor, and then Watson himself was replaced by Billy Bowen. Subsequent personnel changes were many and varied. There was some confusion in 1952 when two different groups began using the Ink Spots' name, Charlie Fuqua and Bill Kenny each owning 50 per cent of the title. Fuqua's Inkspots consisted of himself, Watson, Harold Jackson, and high tenor Jimmy Holmes. Other members included Isaac Royal, Leon Antoine and Joseph Boatner (d. 8 May 1989, Laconia, New Hampshire, USA). In the early 50s the Ink Spots had further chart success with 'Echoes', 'Sometime' and 'If', and Bill Kenny also had US hits in his own name, including 'It Is No Secret' (with the Song Spinners) and '(That's Just My Way Of) Forgetting You'. It is said that, over the years, many other groups worked under the famous name, including one led by Al Rivers (d. 17 February 1993, aged 65) who sang with the Ink Spots in the late 40s and 50s, and another fronted by Stanley Morgan (d. 21 November 1989, aged 67), an occasional guitar player with the quartet in the 30s.

In 1988 the original group's first hit, 'If I Didn't Care', was awarded a Grammy, and a year later the Inkspots were inducted into the Rock And Roll Hall Of Fame. Jimmie Nabbie's Inkspots appeared extensively worldwide for many years through to the early 90s, until Nabbie's death in 1992 following double bypass heart surgery. Gregory Lee took over as frontman when the group co-starred with Eartha Kitt in the UK tour of *A Night At The Cotton Club*, during which, according to one critic, 'they reproduced the sedate four-part harmonies with skill and just enough spontaneity to satisfy their long-term fans'. In 1995, when the Inkspots were in cabaret at London's Café Royal, the line-up was Grant Kitchings (lead tenor), Sonny Hatchett (second lead tenor), Ellis Smith (baritone and guitar) and Harold Winley (bass). The latter is said to have worked with the group for more than 40 years.

● ALBUMS: *Americas Favorite Music* 10-inch album (Waldorf Music 1950)★★★, *The Ink Spots Volume 1* 10-inch album (Decca 1950)★★★★, *The Ink Spots Volume 2* 10-inch album (Decca 1950)★★★★, *Precious Memories* 10-inch album (Decca 1951)★★★, *Street Of Dreams* 10-inch album (Decca 1954)★★★★, *The Ink Spots* (Decca 1955)★★★, *Time Out For Tears* (Decca 1956)★★★, *Torch Time* (Decca 1958)★★★, *Something Old, Something New* (King 1958)★★★, *Sincerely Yours* (1958)★★★, *Songs That Will Live Forever* (King 1959)★★★, *The Ink Spots Favorites* (Verve 1960)★★★, *Lost In A Dream* (1965)★★★, *Stanley Morgan's Ink Spots In London* (1977)★★★, *Just Like Old Times* (Open Sky 1982)★★★.

● COMPILATIONS: *Golden Favourites* (Decca 1962)★★★★, *The Best Of The Ink Spots* (Decca 1965)★★★★, *The Ink Spots Greatest, Volumes. 1 & 2* (Grand Award 1956)★★, *The Best Of The Ink Spots* (MCA 1980)★★★★, *Golden Greats: Ink Spots* (MCA 1986)★★★, *Swing High! Swing Low!* (Happy Days 1989)★★★. In addition, there are a great many compilations available under the title of *Greatest Hits* or *Best Of*.

INVITATION TO THE DANCE

Filming began on this ambitious Gene Kelly project in 1952, but the finished product was only presented to the public four years later. Produced by Arthur Freed for MGM, the picture was a gallant but unsuccessful attempt by Kelly to bring ballet to the cinema-going masses. There was no dialogue, and the film consisted of three individual ballet sequences (another, featuring several popular songs, had been cut prior to release). The first, 'Circus', in which Kelly plays a Pierrot character whose love for a ballerina (Claire Sombert) ends in tragedy, had music by Jacques Ibert. The second, 'Ring Around The Rosy', with music by André Previn, had overtones of La Ronde in its story of a bracelet which, after being presented by a husband to his wife, then passed through the hands of an artist, a nightclub singer, and a whore, among others, is finally returned to the husband. The final sequence, 'Sinbad The Sailor', composed by Rimsky-Korsakov, revived memories of Kelly's innovative dance with Jerry the cartoon mouse in *Anchors Aweigh* (1945).

This time he was a sailor once more, involved with animated characters as well as the real-life Carol Haney and David Kasday. Other artists featured in the first two scenes were Igor Youskevitch, Claude Bessey, Tommy Rall, Tamara Toumanova, Belita, Irving Davies, Diana Adams and David Paltenghi. Gene Kelly was also the overall director-choreographer, and the film was beautifully photographed in Technicolor by Freddie Young and Joseph Ruttenberg, and shot mostly in England. Although it was critical and financial flop, the picture became something of a cult item, especially in Europe where it was awarded the Grand Prize in the 1958 West Berlin film festival. It is invariably included in Gene Kelly retrospectives.

IT'S ALWAYS FAIR WEATHER

As the opening titles fade in this entertaining and somewhat satirical musical, released by MGM in 1955, three US soldier buddies, back home in New York after serving together in World War II, have a final drink and sing the poignant 'The Time For Parting' as they pledge to meet again in 10 years later. However, when the threesome, played by Gene Kelly, Dan Dailey and Michael Kidd, reunite in their favourite bar after 10 years, things have changed. Dailey is conceited, continually stressed and hates his job in advertising; Kelly has turned into a tough city dweller with one eye on the fight scene and the other looking over his shoulder; and Kidd is the only one who seems reasonably content with his life as the owner of a provincial diner grandly named the Cordon Bleu. High-powered executive (and boxing fan) Cyd Charisse deviously manoeuvres them and their 'fascinating' story onto the tacky television show *The Throb Of Manhattan*, which is hosted by the gorgeously over-the-top Dolores Gray. When Kelly is threatened by some unsavoury colleagues in the fight racket and Dailey and Kidd jump in to defend him with all fists blazing, the years roll back and it is just like old times for the three pals again. Originally conceived by screenwriters Betty Comden and Adolph Green as a sequel to *On The Town* (1949), *It's Always Fair Weather* turned out to be quite different from that project, with a marked cynical edge, especially in regard to the burgeoning US television industry. The basic creative team remained the same, however, with Arthur Freed producing and Gene Kelly and Stanley Donen sharing the director-choreographer credit. The score, by composer André Previn and Comden and Green (lyrics), had some marvellous moments, such as 'Situation-Wise', Dailey's exposé of the advertising industry; Kelly's escape from a gang of hoodlums via a song, dance and a pair of roller skates in 'I Like Myself'; Gray's magnificently syrupy and effusive 'Thanks A Lot But No Thanks'; and Charisse boxing clever in 'Baby You Knock Me Out'. The three male stars come together for a split screen rendition of 'Once Upon A Time' (the Cinemascope effect is generally destroyed when shown on television), and for an exhilarating dance routine through the streets, at one point using dustbin lids as improvised tap shoes. The other numbers included 'March, March' (Kelly-Dailey-Kidd), 'Stillman's Gym' (Charisse and boxers), and 'Music Is Better Than Words' (lyric: Comden-Green-Roger Edens; ensemble). Also featured were Jay C. Flippen, David Burns, Hal March and Lou Lubin.

IVES, BURL

b. Burl Icle Ivanhoe Ives, 14 June 1909, Hunt Township, Jasper County, Illinois, USA, d. 14 April 1995, Anacortes, Washington, USA. One of the world's most celebrated singers of folk ballads, with a gentle, intimate style, Ives was also an actor on the stage and screen, and an anthologist and editor of folk music. The son of tenant farmers in the 'Bible Belt' of Illinois, he was singing in public for money with his brothers and sisters when he was four years old. Many of the songs they sang originated in the British Isles, and were taught to them by their tobacco-chewing grandmother. After graduating from high school in 1927 Ives went to college with the aim of becoming a professional football coach. Instead, he left college early, in 1930, and hitch-hiked throughout the USA, Canada and Mexico, supporting himself by doing odd jobs and singing to his own banjo accompaniment, picking up songs everywhere he went. After staying for a time in Terre Haute, Indiana, attending the State Teachers College, he moved to New York and studied with vocal coach Ekka Toedt, before enrolling for formal music training at New York University. Despite this classical education, he was determined to devote himself to folk songs. In 1938 he played character roles in several plays, and had a non-singing role on Broadway in the Richard Rodgers and Lorenz Hart musical The Boys From Syracuse, followed by a four-month singing engagement at New York's Village Vanguard nightclub. He then toured with another Rodgers and Hart show, I Married An Angel. In 1940 Ives performed on radio, singing his folk ballads to his own guitar accompaniment on programmes such as Back Where I Come From, and was soon given his own series entitled Wayfaring Stranger. The introductory 'Poor Wayfaring Stranger', one of America's favourite folk songs, and by then already over 100 years old, became his long-time theme. Drafted into the US Army in 1942, Ives sang in Irving Berlin's military musical revue This Is The Army, both on Broadway and on tour. In 1944, after medical discharge from the forces, Ives played a long stint at New York's Cafe Society Uptown nightclub, and also appeared on Broadway with Alfred Drake in Sing Out Sweet Land, a 'Salute To American Folk And Popular Music'. For his performance, Ives received the Donaldson Award as Best Supporting Actor. During the following year, he made a concert appearance at New York's Town Hall, and played a return engagement in 1946. Also in that year he made his first film, Smoky, with Fred McMurray and Anne Baxter, and appeared with Josh White in a full-length feature about folk music. Ives' other movies, in which he played characters ranging from villainous to warmly sympathetic, included So Dear To My Heart (1948), East Of Eden (1955) and Cat On A Hot Tin Roof (1958), in which he played Big Daddy, recreating his highly acclaimed Broadway performance in the Tennessee Williams play; he also appeared in Wind Across The Everglades (1958), Desire Under The Elms (1958) and The Big Country (1958), for which he received an Oscar as the Best Supporting Actor; and Our Man In Havana (1960). In 1954 Ives appeared as Cap'n Andy Hawkes in a revival of Jerome Kern and Oscar Hammerstein II's Show Boat at the New York City Center. In the 60s and 70s he appeared regularly on US television, sometimes in his dramatic series, such as OK Crackerby and The Bold Ones, and several musical specials. In the 80s, he continued to contribute character roles to feature films and television, and performed in concerts around the world. Back in 1948, his first chart record, 'Blue Tail Fly', teamed him with the Andrews Sisters. The song, written by Dan Emmett in 1846, had been in the Ives repertoire for some years. Other US Top 30 hits through to the early 60s included 'Lavender Blue (Dilly Dilly)', 'Riders In The Sky (Cowboy Legend)', 'On Top Of Old Smokey', 'The Wild Side Of Life', 'True Love Goes On And On', 'A Little Bitty Tear', 'Funny Way Of Laughin' and 'Call Me Mr In-Between'. Many other songs became associated with him, such as 'Foggy Foggy Dew', 'Woolie Boogie Bee', 'Turtle Dove', 'Ten Thousand Miles', 'Big Rock Candy Mountain', 'I Know An Old Lady (Who Swallowed A Fly)', 'Aunt Rhody' and 'Ballad Of Davy Crockett'. Ives published several collections of folk ballads and tales, including America's Musical Heritage - Song Of America, Burl Ives Song Book, Tales Of America, Burl Ives Book Of Irish Songs, and for children, Sailing On A Very Fine Day. In 1993, in the distinguished company of Tom Paxton, Pete Seeger, Theodore Bikel, the Chad Mitchell Trio, Oscar Brand and Paul Robeson Jnr., Burl Ives performed in an emotional and nostalgic concert at the 92nd Street 'Y' Theatre in New York. Ives died in April 1995.

● ALBUMS: The Wayfaring Stranger 10-inch album (Stinson 1949)★★★★, Ballads And Folk Songs Volume 1 10-inch album (Decca 1949)★★★★, Ballads And Folk Songs Volume 2 10-inch album (Decca 1949)★★★★, The Return Of The Wayfaring Stranger 10-inch album (Columbia 1949)★★★★, Ballads, Folk And Country Songs 10-inch album (Decca 1949)★★★★, More Folksongs 10-inch album (Columbia 1950)★★★, Christmas Day In The Morning 10-inch album (Decca 1952)★★★, Folk Songs Dramatic And Dangerous 10-inch album (Decca 1953)★★★★, Women: Folk Songs About The Fair 10-inch album (Decca 1954)★★★, Children's Favorites 10-inch album (Columbia 1954)★★★, Coronation Concert (Decca 1956)★★★, The Wild Side Of Life (Decca 1956)★★★, Men (Decca 1956)★★★, Down To The Sea In Ships (Decca 1956)★★★★, Women (Decca 1956)★★, In The Quiet Of Night (Decca 1956)★★★, Burl Ives Sings For Fun (Decca 1956)★★, Burl Ives Sings Songs For All Ages (Columbia 1957)★★, Christmas Eve With Ives (Decca 1957)★★, Songs Of Ireland (Decca 1958)★★★, Old Time Varieties (Decca 1958)★★★, Captain Burl Ives' Ark (Decca 1958)★★★, Australian Folk Songs (Decca 1958)★★★, Cheers (Decca 1959)★★★, Little White Duck (Fontana 1960)★★, Burl Ives Sings Irving Berlin (1961)★★, The Versatile Burl Ives! (Decca 1962)★★, It's Just My Funny Way Of Laughin' (Decca 1962)★★★, Songs Of The West (Brunswick 1962)★★★, Sunshine In My Soul (Brunswick 1963)★★★, Singin' Easy (Brunswick 1963)★★★, Walt Disney Presents Burl Ives - Animal Folk (1964)★★, Pearly Shells (Decca 1964)★★★, Rudolph The Red Nosed Reindeer (Decca 1966)★, Something Special (Brunswick 1966)★★★, Times They Are A-Changin' (Columbia 1968)★★, Animal Folk (Castle Music 1974)★, Chim Chim Cheree (Castle Music 1974)★, with the Korean Children Choir Faith And Joy (Sacred/Word 1974)★, How Great Thou Art (Word 1974)★★, Songs I Sang In Sunday School (Sacred/Word 1974)★★, I Do Believe (Word 1974)★★★, Shall We Gather At The River (Sacred/Word 1978)★★★, Talented Man (Bulldog 1978)★★★, Live In Europe (Polydor 1979)★★★, Bright And Beautiful (Word 1979)★★, Christmas At The White House (Caedmon 1979)★★, Stepping In The Light (Word 1984)★★★, Love And

Joy (Word 1984)★★★, and the 50s film and audio series *Historical America In Song* for *Encyclopedia Britannica*.
● COMPILATIONS: *The Best Of Burl Ives* (MCA 1965)★★★, *Junior Choice* (MFP 1979)★★, *The Best Of Burl's For Boys And Girls* (MCA 1980)★★, *The Very Best Of* (1993)★★★, *A Little Bitty Tear: The Nashville Years 1961-65* (1993)★★★.
● FURTHER READING: *Wayfaring Stranger*, Burl Ives.
● FILMS: *Smoky* (1946), *So Dear To My Heart* (1948), *East Of Eden* (1955), *Cat On A Hot Tin Roof* (1958), *Wind Across The Everglades* (1958), *Desire Under The Elms* (1958), *The Big Country* (1958), *Our Man In Havana* (1960), *The Brass Bottle* (1964), *Rocket To The Moon* (1967).

JACKSON, AUNT MOLLY

b. Mary Magdalene Garland, 1880, Clay County, Kentucky, USA, d. 1 September 1960. Her mother died of starvation when she was six, at 10 she was imprisoned due to her family's unionist campaign for better conditions for miners, and she was married at 14. Her husband and son were both killed in mining accidents and her father and brother blinded. In the early 30s, she served as a nurse but consolidated her work for improving conditions in the mines. She acquired a considerable repertoire of local songs, some of which she adapted as her own protest songs, such as 'Kentucky Miner's Wife', which she recorded for Columbia Records in 1932. She also used the melody of 'Precious Memories' for her melancholy ballad of the death of a child from starvation, in her song 'Dreadful Memories'. In 1931, the authorities, because of her unionist activities, forced her to leave Kentucky. She settled in New York, where her work attracted the attention of both folk song collectors and historians. In 1939, she began to record some of her songs for the Library of Congress, although few actually gained a public release at the time. The folk music revival, in the late 50s, saw her songs gain popularity and in 1960, arrangements were made for her, at the age of 80, to record an album. When ill health rendered her incapable of singing, it was decided that she should introduce the songs and her friend John Greenway would sing them. On 1 September 1960, a few days before the scheduled recording day, she died in poverty and relative obscurity. Greenway continued with the project and recorded *The Songs And Stories Of Aunt Molly Jackson* (Folkways 1961). In the 70s, Aunt Molly Jackson's 1939 recordings were finally released on an album by Rounder. Her half-sister, Sarah Ogan Gunning (b. Sarah Elizabeth Garland, 28 June 1910, Ely Branch, Knox County, Kentucky, USA), who had endured similar hardships, also moved to New York and in 1937 made recordings for the Library of Congress, including her popular 'I Am A Girl Of Constant Sorrow'. In 1963, she came out of retirement to appear at concerts, union meetings and even the Newport Folk Festival. She also recorded many of her songs on *Girl Of Constant Sorrow* (Folk-Legacy 1975).
● ALBUMS: *Aunt Molly Jackson Library Of Congress Recordings* (Rounder 1976)★★★.

JACKSON, MAHALIA

b. 26 October 1911, New Orleans, Louisiana, USA, d. 27 January 1972, Chicago, Illinois, USA. For many commentators, Mahalia Jackson remains the definitive exponent of gospel music. At the age of four she sang at the Plymouth Rock Baptist Church and later joined the Mount Moriah Baptist Church junior choir. She mixed the singing styles of the Baptists with the Sanctified Church, which produced a powerful rhythm and beat, and fell under the influence of gospel artists Roberta Martin and Willie Mae Ford Smith. Coupled with the expressions of Bessie Smith and Ma Rainey, which in her teens Jackson had begun to observe, she developed the beginnings of a deep soulful blues style. In 1927, Mahalia moved from New Orleans to Chicago; after her first Sunday church service, where she had given a impromptu performance of her favourite song, 'Hand Me Down My Favourite Trumpet, Gabriel', she was invited to join the Greater Salem Baptist Church Choir and began touring the city's churches and surrounding areas with the Johnson Singers.

After several years with the Johnsons, Mahalia began to forge a solo career. During this time, as well as singing in church, she sang at political rallies and in 1937 became a song demonstrator of the talents of gospel songwriter Thomas A. Dorsey. That same year she recorded four tracks for Decca, to little commercial success, and was dropped soon afterwards. Jackson then toured extensively - in the intervening time she qualified as a beautician to safeguard her future - and recorded again, this time for the Apollo label in 1946, which included the first use in gospel music of the Hammond organ rather than the usual lone piano. These recordings, most of which feature a simple backdrop, show a singer of peerless quality, whose prudent use of slow hymns allowed space for her voice to develop its seemingly effortless inflections. Pianist Mildred Falls, who remained with Jackson throughout her career, added a measured, complimentary background. The success of the Apollo pressings, in particular 'Move On Up A Little Higher', culminated in 1954 with Jackson hosting and starring in her own Sunday night radio show for CBS, bringing black gospel music to a mass white audience. That same year she began recording for CBS which resulted in a number of tight productions and a departure from the almost improvisational feel of previous sessions. Although these releases lacked the simplicity of earlier work, they became a huge success; in 1956 she brought the studio audience at the *Ed Sullivan Show* to its feet. She later triumphed at the rain-soaked Newport Jazz Festival in 1958. Jackson became an ambassador for gospel music, and embarked on several successful European tours. Despite endless entreaties, she resisted crossing over into jazz or blues and pop for many years, although she did perform with Duke Ellington in his 'Black, Brown And Beige Fantasy' suite. She sang at one of the inaugural balls for President John F. Kennedy in 1960, and often performed at Dr. Martin Luther King's rallies. In 1968 she sang at King's funeral, where she gave an emotional rendition of Dorsey's 'Precious Lord, Take My Hand'. Towards the end of her career Jackson did bow to pressure to record more secular songs and included, among others, 'What The World Needs Now' and Dion's classic anthem, 'Abraham Martin And John'. She gave her last public performance in Germany in October 1971, and died of heart failure in 1972.

● ALBUMS: *Mahalia Jackson* (Vogue 1952)★★★, *Newport 1958* (1958)★★★★, *Great Gettin' Up Morning* (Columbia 1959)★★★, *Just As I Am* (Kenwood 1960)★★★★, *The Power And The Glory* (Columbia 1960)★★, *Come On Children Let's Sing* (1960)★★★, *I Believe* (Columbia 1961)★★★, *Sweet Little Jesus Boy* (Columbia 1961)★★★, *Every Time I Feel The Spirit* (1961)★★★, *Recorded Live In Europe* (1962)★★, *Great Songs Of Love And Faith* (1962)★★★, *Silent Night - Songs For Christmas* (1962)★★, *Make A Joyful Noise Unto The Lord* (1962)★★★, *Bless This House* (Columbia 1963)★★★, *Let's Pray Together* (1964)★★★, *In The Upper Room* (Kenwood 1965)★★★, *Mahalia* (1965)★★★★, *No Matter How You Pray* (1965)★★★, *Mahalia Sings* (1966)★★★★, *The Old Rugged Cross* (1966)★★★, *My Faith* (Columbia 1967)★★★, *In Concert* (Columbia 1968)★★★, *A Mighty Fortress* (Columbia 1968)★★★, *Sings The Best-Loved Hymns Of Dr. Martin Luther King, Jr.* (Columbia 1968)★★★, *You'll Never Walk Alone* (1968)★★★, *Christmas With Mahalia* (Columbia 1968)★★, *Sings America's Favorite Hymns* (Columbia 1971)★★★, *Right Out Of The Church* (Columbia 1976)★★★.

● COMPILATIONS: *Best Of Mahalia Jackson* (Kenwood)★★★★, *1911 - 1972* (Kenwood)★★★★, *Mahalia Jackson's Greatest Hits* (Columbia 1963)★★★, *The Great Mahalia Jackson* (Columbia 1972)★★, *The World's Greatest Gospel Singer* (Columbia 1975)★★★, *How I Got Over* (Columbia 1976)★★★★, *Gospel* (Vogue 1977)★★★, *The Warm And Tender Soul Of Mahalia Jackson* (Joker 1981)★★★, *20 Greatest Hits* (Astan 1984)★★★, *The Mahalia Jackson Collection* (Deja Vu 1985)★★★, *When The Saint's Go Marching In* (Columbia 1987)★★★★, *The Mahalia Jackson Story* (Deja Vu 1989)★★★, *Gospels, Spirituals And Hymns* (Columbia/ Legacy 1991)★★★.

● VIDEOS: *Mahalia* (Hendring Video 1990).

● FURTHER READING: *Just Mahalia, Baby*, Laurraine Goreau. *Got To Tell It: Mahalia Jackson Queen Of Gospel*, Jules Schwerin.

JAFFA, MAX

b. 28 December 1911, London, England, d. 30 July 1991, London, England. A classically trained violinist, inspired and influenced by Jascha Heifetz and Fritz Kreisler, who had a long and successful career in British popular music. Born into a non-musical family, Jaffa's father presented him with a violin on his sixth birthday. At the age of nine he made his first concert appearance at the Palace Pier Theatre, Brighton, and later studied at the Guildhall School Of Music. To supplement his income, he formed a trio to play for silent movies. When he was 17 years old, he worked at the Piccadilly Hotel in London and, during a five-year stay, formed his Salon Orchestra, which made its first broadcast from the hotel in August 1929. Later that year he was

released for a season to become the youngest ever leader of the Scottish Symphony Orchestra, and went on a concert tour of Scotland with Joseph Hislop. During World War II, Jaffa flew with the Royal Air Force, and afterwards found that he was physically unable to play the violin. After reverting to the basics of the instrument, assisted by one of his original tutors, he joined the Mantovani Orchestra, eventually becoming its leader, and played on the original version of the 1951 multi-million-selling record of 'Charmaine'. Around this time, Jaffa's meeting with cellist Reginald Kilbey and pianist Jack Byfield led to the formation of the renowned Max Jaffa Trio. It was a professional association lasting over 30 years. For 27 years, from 1959-86, Max Jaffa served as musical director at Scarborough in Yorkshire, conducting the Spa Orchestra in two concerts a day, during the 17-week summer season. His wife, contralto Jean Grayston, was a regular guest artist. A prolific broadcaster, his radio and television programmes included *Music At Ten*, *Music For Your Pleasure*, *Melody On Strings*, *Max Jaffa Trio*, and the long-running, affectionately remembered *Grand Hotel*, in which he presided over the Palm Court Orchestra. A film he made in 1959, entitled *Music With Max Jaffa*, was billed intriguingly as: 'Musical: Violin, Songs and *Sword Dance*'. His honours included the Gold Medal and Principal's Prize from the Guildhall School of Music, the Freedom of Scarborough, and the OBE, which he received in 1982 for services to music. After a career lasting 70 years, he announced his retirement in 1990. A humorous and enlightened attitude to life and music was reflected in his autobiography, which was published in 1991.

● ALBUMS: *Palm Court Concert* (Columbia 1958)★★★, *Reflections In Gold* (1980)★★★, *Prelude To Romance* (Valentine 1983)★★★, *Music For A Grand Hotel* (Valentine 1986)★★★, *Relax With The Music Of Max Jaffa* (MFP 1987)★★★, *The Way You Look Tonight* (Warwick 1987)★★★, *Favourite Violin Melodies* (Pickwick 1992)★★★.

● FURTHER READING: *A Life On The Fiddle*, Max Jaffa.

● FILMS: *Music With Max Jaffa* (1959).

JAGUARS

An R&B vocal group from Los Angeles, California, USA. The Jaguars were one of the few Los Angeles groups that could sing standards in the spirit and style of pop music, but added a hard rock 'n' roll edge. The members of this black-white-Hispanic group were Sonny Chaney (lead), Val Poliuto (tenor), Manual Chavez (baritone) and Charles Middleton (bass). The group began recording for a small label in Los Angeles in 1955, and the following year found success with a doo-wop remake of the Jerome Kern standard 'The Way You Look Tonight'. The group lost Middleton in 1958, and the following year the remaining three, with freelance vocalists Tony Allen and Richard Berry, recorded as the Velvetones. The record was not a success and the group disbanded. Chavez and Chaney went on to record as a duo.

● COMPILATIONS: *The Way You Look Tonight* (Earth Angel 1988)★★★.

JAILHOUSE ROCK

Although hamstrung by mediocre films throughout much of his Hollywood career, Elvis Presley did complete some outstanding early features. In *Jailhouse Rock* he was aided by a superior plot in which the singer is taught to play guitar while serving in prison for manslaughter. Fame and egotism follow suit until his former cell-mate returns to haunt him and, eventually, prick his conscience. The film also provides an insight into record company practices during the 50s and has a visual impact many other contemporary works lacked. The highly choreographed scene that the title track accompanies has passed into pop cinema history. The Leiber And Stoller songwriting team, famed for their work with the Coasters, provided all of the soundtrack material, which ranges from the electric 'Baby I Don't Care' to the ballad-styled 'Young And Beautiful'. Taken together, the album and film represent a high-water mark in Presley's output.

JARRE, MAURICE

b. 13 September 1924, Lyons, France. An important composer for films for over 40 years, as a youngster Jarre intended to become an electrical engineer, but changed his mind and studied music at the Paris Conservatoire in 1944. He joined the orchestra of the Jean Louise Barrault Theatre, and in 1951, composed the music for Kleist's *Le Prince De Homburg*. Soon afterwards he moved into films, and during the 50s, wrote the scores for such French productions as *Hotel Des Invalides*, *Le Grand Silence*, *Le Tetre Contre Les Murs* and *Les Yeux Sans Visage (Eyes Without A Face)*. During the early 60s, he began to score the occasional non-Gallic movie, such as *Crack In The Mirror*, starring Orson Welles, *The Big Gamble* and 'the last great epic of World War II', *The Longest Day* (1962). In the same year, Jarre won his first Academy Award for his memorable score for *Lawrence Of Arabia*, and was honoured again, three years later, for his music to *Doctor Zhivago*, featuring the haunting 'Lara's Theme' ('Somewhere, My Love'), which, with a lyric by Paul Francis Webster, became a Top 10 singles hit for the Ray Conniff Singers, and was the title track of one of their million-selling albums. Jarre's other 60s scores for English-speaking films included *Behold A Pale Horse*, *The Collector*, *Is Paris Burning?*, *The Professionals*, *Grand Prix*, *Gambit*, *The Night Of The Generals*, *Villa Rides!*, *Five Card Stud*, *The Fixer*, *Isadora*, *The Damned* and Alfred Hitchcock's *Topaz* (1969). He continued to write prolifically in the 70s for films such as director George Steven's swan-song, *The Only Game In Town*, one of Neil Simon's funniest comedies, *Plaza Suite*, and many others, such as *The Effect Of Gamma Rays On Man-In-The-Moon Marigolds*, *The Life And Times Of Judge Roy Bean*, in which Andy Williams sang Jarre's 'Marmalade, Molasses And Honey' (lyric by Alan and Marilyn Bergman), *The Mackintosh Man*, *Great Expectations*, *Posse*, *The Man Who Would Be King*, *The Last Tycoon*, *Mohammed, Messenger Of God*, *March Or Die* and *Winter Kills*. His third Oscar came in 1984 for his 'anachronistic' score for David Lean's *A Passage To India*, and he was nominated in the following year for his work on *Witness*, starring Harrison Ford. His other 80s scores included *Resurrection*, *Lion Of The Desert*, *Taps*, *The Year Of Living Dangerously*, *Dreamscape*, *The Bride*, *Mad Max And The Thunderdrome*, *Enemy Mine*, *The Mosquito Coast*, *No Way Out*, *Fatal Attraction*, *Distant Thunder*, *Gorillas In The Mist* (another Academy Award nomination for Jarre), *Moon Over Parador*, *Chances Are*, *Dead Poets Society* (BAFTA Award, 1989), *Prancer* and *Enemies, A Love Story*. In 1991, Jarre received an ASCAP Award as the composer of the music for *Ghost*, the 'top box office film of 1990'. His other early 90s work included *After Dark, My Sweet*, *School Ties*, *Shadow Of*

The Wolf (aka *Agaguk*), *Only The Lonely*, *Fearless* and *Mr. Jones* (1994). Apart from feature films, Jarre also wrote extensively for television. His credits included *The Silence*, *Jesus Of Nazareth* (mini-series), *Ishi, The Last Of His Tribe*, *Shogun* (mini-series), *Enola Gay*, *Coming Out Of The Ice*, *The Sky's No Limit*, *Samson And Delilah*, *Apology*, *The Murder Of Mary Phagan* (mini-series) and *Robinson Crusoe And Man Friday*.

● ALBUMS: *Jarre By Jarre* (Silva Screen 1989)★★★, *Only The Lonely* (Colosseum 1991)★★.

JENKINS, GORDON

b. 12 May 1910, Webster Groves, Missouri, USA, d. 24 April 1984, Malibu, California, USA. A distinguished songwriter, arranger and conductor, as a child Jenkins occasionally played organ at the Chicago movie theatre where his father was the regular organist. During Prohibition he played piano in a St. Louis speakeasy and was later employed by a radio station in the same city. In 1936 he became chief staff arranger for Isham Jones, producing skilful charts for this superior dance orchestra, and later composed and arranged for Woody Herman, Lennie Hayton, Vincent Lopez, Benny Goodman and André Kostalanetz. He composed Herman's theme, 'Blue Prelude' (with Joe Bishop), and 'Goodbye', which Goodman used as the closing music to hundreds of radio shows. In 1936 he conducted the orchestra for *The Show Is On* on Broadway, and in the following year settled on the west coast, working for Paramount. In 1939 he began a five-year tenure as musical director for NBC in Hollywood. In the mid-40s he worked on the Dick Haymes show and in 1945 became staff conductor for Decca Records. In the same year Jenkins wrote and recorded a long work, in effect a personal love song to New York City, entitled 'Manhattan Tower'. This piece for orchestra and singers has been performed by the Atlanta Symphony Orchestra, in revues and on television. In 1949 Jenkins was back in New York, working on the score for the Broadway show *Along Fifth Avenue*, and at the Capitol and Paramount theatres. Among his song credits, several of which have attracted the attention of jazz musicians, are 'Homesick - That's All', 'Blue Evening', 'Married I Can Always Get', 'New York's My Home', and 'You Have Taken My Heart', 'P.S. I Love You' and 'When A Woman Loves A Man' (the last three with Johnny Mercer). In 1952 Jenkins wrote the score for *Bwana Devil*, the first 3-D feature film, and, through the years, accompanied many top artists on record, such as Martha Tilton, Louis Armstrong and Peggy Lee. His work with Frank Sinatra received much critical acclaim, notably the albums *Where Are You?* (1957) and *No One Cares* (1959), and his scores for Nat 'King' Cole included the definitive vocal arrangement of 'Stardust' for *Love Is The Thing* (1957). Gordon Jenkins and his Orchestra had their own series of hits from 1942-53, often with various vocalists, which included 'I Don't See Me In Your Eyes Anymore', 'Again', 'Don't Cry Joe', 'My Foolish Heart', 'Bewitched', two with the Weavers, 'Tzena, Tzena, Tzena' and 'Goodnight, Irene' (US number 1 in 1950), 'I'm Forever Blowing Bubbles', and 'So Long (It's Been Good To Know Ya)'. He won a Grammy Award in 1965 for his arrangement of Frank Sinatra's 'It Was A Very Good Year', and served as arranger and conductor on the singer's 1973 television comeback.

● ALBUMS: *The Complete Manhattan Tower* (Capitol

1956)★★★, *Dreamer's Holiday* (1958)★★★, *Hawaiian Wedding* (1962)★★, *I Live Alone* (1965)★★★, *Soft Soul* (1966)★★★, *My Heart Sings* (1966)★★★, *Blue Prelude* (1967)★★, *Paris I Wish You Love* (60s)★★, *In The Still Of The Night* (60s)★★★, *P.S. I Love You* (60s)★★.

JESTERS

The Jesters were representative of the classic New York style of doo-wop characterized as 'greasy', in which the vocal harmony was in a rock 'n' roll style, extremely expressive, loaded with exotic flourishes, and usually supporting a falsetto lead. The members of the Jesters were Lenny McKay (lead), Adam Jackson (d. 21 February 1995; lead), Anthony 'Jimmy' Smith (second tenor), Leo Vincent (baritone) and Noel Grant (bass). The group came together in 1955, and was signed by Paul Winley for his Winley label in 1957. They were regularly teamed with another local group, the Paragons, in live mock-competitions. Their first release, 'So Strange'/'Love No One But You', was a double-sided hit in the New York area in the summer of 1957. In the autumn they hit again locally with 'Please Let Me Love You'. 'The Plea', a remake of the Chantels' hit, made it to number 74 of the *Billboard* pop chart in 1958, but, like the other records, it mainly sold in New York. 'I Laughed'/'Now That You're Gone' from the summer of 1958 was the last record to feature the original group. In 1960 a new line-up of Jackson, Smith, Melvin Lewis and Don Lewis recorded the Jesters' most successful song, 'The Wind', a remake of the 1954 Diablos hit.
● COMPILATIONS: *The Paragons Meet The Jesters* (Jubilee 1959)★★★, *The Paragons Meet The Jesters* (Collectables 1990)★★★, *'War': The Paragons Vs The Jesters* (Sting Music Ltd. 1993)★★★, *The Best Of The Jesters* (Collectables 1993)★★★.

JIVE BOMBERS

This New York R&B group was formed in 1948 from elements of two earlier acts, the Tinney Brothers (founded during the mid-30s) and the Palmer Brothers (founded late 20s). The group, recording for Coral as the Sparrows in 1949 and as the Jive Bombers after 1952, were from the same era as the Mills Brothers and Ink Spots. Thus, their age and repertoire of old songs kept them in staid nightclubs during most of their career, and their appearance in the teen rock 'n' roll market was very brief. When the group had a hit with 'Bad Boy' in 1957, the members were Earl Johnson (b. 30 November 1932, New York City, New York, USA; tenor vocals), Al Tinney (b. 28 May 1929, Ansonia, Connecticut, USA; piano), William 'Pee Wee' Tinney (b. 25 September 1930, New York City, New York, USA; drums, guitar) and Clarence Palmer (b. 2 January 1919, Pawtucket, Rhode Island, USA; bass fiddle). 'Bad Boy' went to number 7 on the R&B chart and number 36 on the pop chart. It was written and recorded by Lillian Armstrong as 'Brown Gal' in 1936, and had been recorded by the Jive Bombers twice before, in 1949 and 1952, as 'Brown Boy'. The Jive Bombers failed to reach the charts again, despite recording excellent material such as a remake of 'Cherry', a Don Redman composition from 1928. Although Palmer left the group in 1959, the Jive Bombers stayed together until 1968.
● ALBUMS: *Bad Boy* (Savoy Jazz 1984)★★★★.

JOHNSON, JOHNNIE

b. 1924, Fairmont, West Virginia, USA. Johnson's name may not be well known but his sound has been heard by millions: he was the piano player on most of Chuck Berry's classic Chess Records tracks. Johnson began learning to play piano at the age of seven without the benefit of lessons, influenced by jazz and boogie-woogie musicians such as Earl Hines, Meade 'Lux' Lewis and Clarence 'Pinetop' Smith. After a spell in the US Army Johnson began performing professionally in 1946, and in 1952, leading the Sir John Trio, he hired the young Berry as his guitarist. Berry soon began writing the group's songs and became its leader. Chess artist Muddy Waters suggested the group audition for that label and Berry was signed in 1955. Johnson can be heard on Berry hits such as 'Maybellene', 'Roll Over Beethoven' and 'Johnny B. Goode', which Berry has stated was written for Johnson. Johnson also played in Berry's road band but in the 60s left, working with blues guitarist Albert King, among others. Johnson led his own band in the 70s but still worked with Berry on occasion. He was featured in the 1986 Berry concert film *Hail! Hail! Rock And Roll* and later appeared as a guest on Keith Richards' debut solo album, *Talk Is Cheap*. Johnson has recorded sparingly under his own name, releasing his first solo album in 1987.
● ALBUMS: *Blue Hand Johnnie* (1987)★★★, *Rockin' Eighty-Eights* (1991)★★★, *Johnnie B. Bad* (Elektra 1992)★★★, with the Kentucky Headhunters *That'll Work* (1993)★★★, *Johnnie Be Back* (Music Masters 1995)★★★.
● COMPILATIONS: *Complete Recorded Works Volumes 1-3* (Document 1995)★★★.

JOHNSON, KEG

b. Frederic H. Johnson, 19 November 1908, Dallas, Texas, USA, d. 8 November 1967. Born into a musical family (Johnson's father played cornet and his younger brother was tenor saxophonist Budd Johnson), he began playing trombone as his principal instrument when in his late teens. With his brother, he performed in local bands before they moved to Kansas City, playing there with Jesse Stone and George E. Lee, then to Chicago where, in the early 30s, they played with various bands including the Zilner Randolph-organized band fronted by Louis Armstrong. In 1933 Johnson moved to New York where he played briefly with Benny Carter and Fletcher Henderson before joining Cab Calloway with whom he remained for almost 15 years. In the early 50s he played with several bands, usually for short periods, sometimes deputizing for regular sidemen, and also sometimes playing guitar. This was mostly on the west coat but he eventually returned to New York where he played with Gil Evans, then joined Ray Charles' touring band where he remained until his death. A fluid, light-toned player with a great feeling for the blues, Johnson's musicianship was of a very high order and his solos show imagination allied to unforced technique.

JOHNSON, LAURIE

b. 7 February 1927, England. A bandleader, musical director, and composer for the stage, television and films, Johnson studied at the Royal College Of Music in London, and spent four years in the Coldstream Guards, before establishing himself on the UK entertainment scene in the late 50s and 60s. One of his first major projects early in 1959, was to write

203

the music, and act as musical director, for *Lock Up Your Daughters*, a musical adaptation of Henry Fielding's *Rape Upon Rape*, which opened Bernard Miles's Mermaid Theatre in the City of London. Johnson's score, in collaboration with lyricist Lionel Bart, won an Ivor Novello Award. The show returned to the Mermaid in 1969 for a 10th anniversary season, and also played around the world, including a spell at the Godspeed Opera House in Connecticut, USA. The film version omitted the songs and featured a score by Ron Grainer. Johnson's other work for the West End stage has included music for the Peter Cook revue *Pieces Of Eight* (1959), and the score, with lyrics by Herbert Kretzmer, to *The Four Musketeers* (1967), which starred singer-comedian Harry Secombe. Despite attracting venomous reviews, *The Four Musketeers* ran for over a year. In September 1961 the Laurie Johnson Orchestra had a UK Top 10 chart entry with the Latin-styled 'Sucu Sucu', written by Tarateno Rosa, the theme from the UK television series *Top Secret*. On the b-side was a Johnson composition, the title theme for another television production, *Echo Four-Two*. This is one of over 50 themes and scores that he wrote for television, a list that included *No Hiding Place*, *When The Kissing Had To Stop*, *Jason King*, *Shirley's World*, *The Adventurers*, *Thriller*, *The Avengers*, *The New Avengers* and *The Professionals*. The latter two were produced by Johnson's company, Avengers (Film And TV) Enterprises, formed with Albert Fennell and Brian Clemens. Johnson has also composed extensively for the cinema, from the late 50s. His film scores include *The Moonraker* (1958), *No Trees In The Street* (1958), *Tiger Bay* (1959), *I Aim At The Stars* (1960), *Spare The Rod* (1961), *Dr Strangelove - Or: How I Learned To Stop Worrying And Love The Bomb* (1964), *The First Men In The Moon* (1964), *The Beauty Jungle* (1966), *East Of Sudan* (1966), *Hot Millions* (1968), *And Soon The Darkness* (1970), *The Belstone Fox* (1976), *Diagnosis: Murder* (1976), *It's Alive II (It Lives Again)* (1978), *It Shouldn't Happen To A Vet* (1979) and *Bitter Harvest* (1981). Among his other works was the music for the television movie *Jericho*, which involved many of the original *Avengers* team, including Patrick MacNee. Late in 1994, Laurie Johnson announced the formation of the London Big Band, 'the largest band in Britain', consisting of the 'cream' of the music business, and led by veteran jazzman Jack Parnell.

● ALBUMS: *Operation Orchestra* (1959)★★★, *Songs Of Three Seasons* (1959)★★, *A Brass Band Swinging* (1961)★★★★, *Top Secret* (1962)★★★, *Two Cities Suite* (1963)★★★, *The Avengers* (1963)★★★★, *The New Big Sound Of Johnson* (1964)★★★, *Something's Coming* (1968)★★★, *Themes And...By Laurie Johnson* (1969)★★★, with Sir Bernard Miles *The Conquistadors* (1971)★★, *Laurie Johnson With The London Philharmonic And London Jazz Orchestras* (1973)★★★★, with the London Studio Orchestra *Music From the Avengers, New Avengers & The Professionals* (KPM 1980)★★★★, *Film Music Of Laurie Johnson* (Unicorn-Kanchana 1981)★★★, *Digital Film Scores Volumes 1-3* (1981)★★★, with the London Studio Symphony Orchestra *Rose And The Gun - The Music Of Laurie Johnson* (Unicorn-Kanchana 1992)★★★, *Laurie Johnson's London Big Band* (1994)★★.

JOHNSON, SYL

b. Sylvester Thompson, 1 July 1936, Holly Springs, Mississippi, USA. Johnson was the youngest of three children and his family moved to Chicago during the late 40s. An elder brother, Mac Thompson, played bass with the Magic Sam Blues Band. Having learned guitar and harmonica, Johnson began frequenting the city's southside blues clubs, playing alongside Howlin' Wolf, Muddy Waters and Junior Wells. His first recordings were made in 1956 accompanying Billy Boy Arnold, after which Johnson appeared on sessions for Shakey Jake, Junior Wells and Jimmy Reed. In 1959 Federal released Johnson's first solo single, 'Teardrops', and he recorded unsuccessfully for several independents until signing with Twilight (later changed to Twinight) in 1967. His debut there, 'Come On Sock It To Me', reached number 12 in the R&B chart. Johnson's musical activities, however, were not solely confined to performing. He also produced several local acts including Tyrone Davis and Otis Clay, while the Deacons, his backing group, featuring brother Jimmy Johnson on guitar, enjoyed a minor hit on the singer's Shama label. Johnson was then spotted by Willie Mitchell and 'Dresses Too Short' (1968) was recorded with the Mitchell's Hi Records house band. The remaining Twinight sessions were divided between Memphis and Chicago. Johnson remained with the label until 1971, recording two albums in the process. Free to sign with Hi, he began a series of releases that matched for excellence those of labelmate Al Green. Brash, up-tempo topsides, including 'Back For A Taste Of Your Love' and 'We Did It', contrasted with the often-reflective couplings, of which 'Anyway The Wind Blows' and 'I Hear The Love Chimes' were particularly emotive. The third of his exemplary albums for Hi, *Total Explosion*, produced Johnson's only substantial R&B hit when his version of 'Take Me To The River' (1975) reached number 7. However, his final years at Hi were dogged by internal problems and towards the end of the decade he reactivated his Shama label. A contemporary blues/soul collection, *Ms Fine Brown Frame*, was licensed to Boardwalk, while a French album, *Suicide Blues*, followed in 1984. By the mid-80s, he had semi-retired from the music business and opened a string of fast-food fish restaurants. He returned to performing in 1992 and in 1994 with an excellent album *Back In The Game*.

● ALBUMS: *Dresses Too Short* (Twinight 1968)★★★, *Is It Because I'm Black?* i (Twinight 1970)★★★, *Back For A Taste Of Your Love* (Hi 1973)★★★★, *Diamond In The Rough* (Hi 1974)★★★, *Total Explosion* (Hi 1976)★★★★, *Uptown Shakedown* (Shama 1979)★★★, *Brings Out The Blues In Me* (Shama 1980)★★★, *Ms Fine Brown Frame* (Boardwalk 1983)★★★, *Suicide Blues* (1984)★★★, *Foxy Brown* (Shama 1988)★★★, *Back In The Game* (Delmark 1994)★★★.

● COMPILATIONS: *Brings Out The Blues In Me* (Flyright 1986)★★★, *Is It Because I'm Black?* ii (Charly 1986)★★★★, *The Love Chimes* (Hi 1986)★★★, *Stuck In Chicago* (Hi 1989)★★★.

JOHNSON, WILLIE

b. Willis Lee Johnson, 4 March 1923, Memphis, Tennessee, USA, d. 26 February 1995, Chicago, Illinois, USA. Johnson was the musical linchpin behind one of the most enduring artists of the twentieth century - Howlin' Wolf. He began playing with Wolf as a teenager. He was there at the

Memphis Recording Service studios when the former Chester Arthur Burnett cut his first record, 'Moanin' At Midnight', in the spring of 1951. However, when that record became a huge hit and Wolf moved to Chicago, Johnson initially remained in Memphis, where he accompanied other stellar blues artists including Bobby Bland, Elmore James and Sonny Boy Williamson. He cut his own records alongside harmonica player Little Sammy Lewis for Sun Records as well as sessions with Willie Nix for RPM and Checker Records. Johnson's side of the Lewis single 'So Long Baby Goodbye' remains his only issued vocal. Within three years, however, Wolf returned to Memphis to bring his erstwhile guitarist back with him to Chicago. Johnson remained with Wolf throughout his residencies at clubs such as the 708 Club, the Zanzibar and Silvio's, and also made memorable studio appearances on singles such as 'Who's Been Talkin'?' (1957) and 'Smokestack Lightning' (1956). His performance on the latter was particularly stunning, his easy, evocative style matching tempos beautifully with Wolf's emphatic delivery. However, his relationship with Wolf was precarious, given that Wolf insisted on an alcohol ban for members of his band and Johnson's capacity for drinking was already reaching legendary proportions. There were many disputes, but Johnson finally left Wolf's company for good in 1959 after a show at Theresa's Lounge. That was effectively the end of his creative musical career as alcohol gained increasing control over his life, although he did continue his long service at the 'Mag Wheel' factory. He did, however, continue to make sporadic appearances at local clubs, relying on his versatility and adapting to whatever artist he was supporting. Various blues aficionados tempted him out of semi-retirement during the 80s and 90s, though he would often fail to arrive or be too drunk to play. However, he played one acclaimed set at the Earwig Music's 15th Anniversary Party at Buddy Guy's Legends venue on 2 June 1994, appearing alongside old friends Sunnyland Slim and Homesick James. Plans to record for Earwig were aborted when he died at home in February 1995. Ironically, his death came at the exact moment that his classic guitar-playing on 'Smokestack Lightning' was being aired daily on a television advert.

JOKER IS WILD, THE

One of the first artists that Frank Sinatra signed to his own new Reprise label in the early 60s was nightclub comedian Joe E. Lewis. Before then, the two had been close friends, so it seemed logical, when Paramount decided in 1957 to make the film biography of a singer with a slick line in patter, that Sinatra's name would be to the fore. Shot in black and white, presumably to heighten the dramatic effect, the film turned out to be a hard-hitting, realistic account as to the likely fate of a young man in the Roaring 20s if he declined to co-operate with men in dark overcoats carrying violin cases. Young Lewis's career is progressing well in one particular nightspot, singing songs such as 'At Sundown' (Walter Donaldson) and 'I Cried For You' (Arthur Freed-Gus Arnheim-Abe Lyman). After ignoring warnings against moving elsewhere, he manages to impress audiences in the new venue ('where they carry the drunks out - they don't just toss 'em out into the street') with 'If I Could Be With You One Hour Tonight' (Henry Creamer-Jimmy Johnson) and 'All The Way' (Sammy Cahn-Jimmy Van Heusen), before his

vocals cords are slashed and he finds a new career as a comedian. Subsequent fractured vocalizing is confined to parodies of songs such as 'Out Of Nowhere' (music-John Green), 'Swinging On A Star' (music-Van Heusen), and 'Naturally' (music-Flotow), all with new lyrics by Harry Harris. Before he finally kicks the bottle, Lewis has become a physical wreck and ruined the lives of the two women who love him, played by Jeanne Crain and Mitzi Gaynor. Eddie Albert plays Lewis's accompanist, whose wife (Beverly Garland) forces him to give up on the comedian, and the cast also included Jackie Coogan, Barry Kelley, Ted de Corsia, Valerie Allen, Hank Henry and Sophie Tucker. Oscar Saul's screenplay was adapted from a book by Art Cohn, and the film, which was photographed in VistaVision, was directed by Charles Vidor. The song 'All The Way' won an Academy Award, and gave Frank Sinatra a number 2 hit in the USA.

JONES, EDDIE 'GUITAR SLIM'

b. 10 December 1926, Greenwood, Mississippi, USA, d. 7 February 1959, New York City, New York, USA. Jones took the stage styles of his heroes T-Bone Walker and Gatemouth Brown and added his own particular flamboyance to become the first truly outrageous blues performer of the modern era. Along the way, he wrote and recorded some blues that remain standards to this day. Raised in Mississippi, he combined the intensity associated with singers from that area with the flair of his Texan models. He sang in church choirs in his home state before forming a trio with pianist Huey Smith working around New Orleans. A lean six-footer, he took on the persona of 'Guitar Slim', building a reputation for his extravagant stage antics and offstage drinking problem. One of the first performers to turn to the solid-bodied electric guitar, he began the experimentation with feedback control that reached its apogee with Jimi Hendrix in the late 60s. He combined this with garish stage-wear in fantastic colours (including matching dyed hair) and a gymnastic act that would see him leave the stage and prowl the audience - and even the street outside - with the aid of a guitar cable that could extend to 350 feet, and was connected to a PA system rather than to an amplifier, thereby reaching high volume levels. The reputation that he built up in the clubs led Imperial Records to record him, as Eddie Jones, in 1951; although not successful at the time, Imperial later fared better when they recredited the recordings to Guitar Slim. Slim's break came when he recorded in 1952 for the Bullet label in Nashville. The hit 'Feelin' Sad' aroused the interest of Specialty Records and sparked off Slim's most productive period. His first release for the new label was to become his anthem, 'The Things That I Used To Do', arranged by his pianist Ray Charles and featuring a distinctive guitar signature that has been reproduced almost as often as the Elmore James 'Dust My Broom' riff. The record made Slim a blues force across the nation. In 1956 he left Specialty for Atco who hoped to sell him to the teenage public as Chess had done with Chuck Berry. This approach was not a success and before Slim could make a comeback, he died from the combined effects of drinking, fast living and pneumonia.
● COMPILATIONS: *The Things That I Used To Do* (Specialty 1970)★★★, *The Atco Sessions* (Atlantic 1987)★★★, *Sufferin' Mind* (Specialty 1991)★★★★, *The Slaves Eat First* (Mysoundworks 1995)★★★.

JONES, SHIRLEY

b. 31 March 1934, Smithton, Pennsylvania, USA. An actress and singer whose film portrayals of sweet and wholesome ingénues in the 50s contrasted sharply with her Academy Award-winning performance as Burt Lancaster's prostitute girlfriend in *Elmer Gantry* (1960). After taking singing lessons from an early age, Jones performed in stage productions before making her film debut opposite Gordon MacRae in the excellent film version of Richard Rodgers and Oscar Hammerstein II's *Oklahoma!* (1955). So successful was the collaboration that the two stars came together again a year later for another Rodgers and Hammerstein project, *Carousel*. After appearing with Pat Boone in *April Love* (1957), Jones turned in an impressive acting performance alongside James Cagney in the musical comedy-drama *Never Steal Anything Small*, joined a host of other stars in *Pepe*, and made one or two lacklustre features before partnering Robert Preston in another fine screen adaptation of a Broadway show, *The Music Man* (1962). From then on, Shirley Jones eschewed musical films for dramatic roles in big-screen features and on television. She was married for a time to the actor and singer Jack Cassidy, and she co-starred with her step-son, David Cassidy, in the top-rated television series *The Partridge Family* in the early 70s. Later in the decade she had her own show entitled *Shirley*. She continued to sing in nightclubs and concerts, and in the late 80s undertook a 14-week tour of the USA in *The King And I* with David Carradine. In the summer of 1994 she appeared with Marty Ingels in a provincial production of A.R. Gurney's two-hander *Love Letters*, and also starred in a Detroit revival of *The King And I*.

JORDANAIRES

This renowned harmony-vocal quartet is best known for their lengthy working relationship with Elvis Presley. The group first accompanied the youthful rock 'n' roll star in 1956 during a performance on the pivotal *Louisiana Hayride*. Lead vocalist Gordon Stoker was subsequently featured on Presley's first recordings for RCA Victor, notably 'Heartbreak Hotel', while the remaining trio - Neal Matthews (tenor), Hoyt Hawkins (baritone) and Hugh Jarrett (bass) - joined him on the session that produced 'Hound Dog' and 'Don't Be Cruel'. The Jordanaires also supported Presley on the *Steve Allen* and *Milton Berle* television shows, where their clean-cut, conservative appearance contrasted with the impact of the singer's explosive persona. The quartet continued to accompany him throughout the 50s and 60s, although they were noticeably absent from the 'comeback' NBC-TV spectacular, *Elvis* (1968), where their role was taken by girl-group the Blossoms. The Jordanaires did not feature on the fruitful sessions spawning 'Suspicious Minds' and 'In The Ghetto', nor the subsequent live appearances, but returned to the fold for recordings undertaken in Nashville during June and September 1970. These marked the end of the Jordanaires' relationship with Presley, but the group remained an integral part of the city's music industry. In 1972 they contributed to *Guitar That Shook The World*, the solo debut by long-time Presley guitarist Scotty Moore, and were heavily featured on sessions with Johnny Cash, Kris Kristofferson, Don McLean, Tracy Nelson and Billy Swan. The Jordanaires - by this point consisting of Stoker, Hawkins, Matthews and new bass player Lovis Nunley - also released several albums

in their own right, many of which featured gospel material, but their career remains inextricably linked to that of Elvis Presley. In 1996 they added harmonies to alternative US rock band Ween's album *12 Golden Country Greats*. They continue to tour the world knowing that the audience wants to hear that remarkable smooth harmonic sound, one that has barely changed over five decades.

● ALBUMS: *Beautiful City* 10-inch album (RCA Victor 1953)★★★, *Peace In The Valley* (Decca 1957)★★★★, *Of Rivers And Plants* (Sesac 1958)★★★, *Heavenly Spirit* (Capitol 1958)★★★, *Gloryland* (Capitol 1959)★★★, *Land Of Jordan* (Capitol 1960)★★★★, *To God Be The Glory* (Capitol 1961)★★★, *Spotlight On The Jordanaires* (Capitol 1962)★★★, *We'd Like To Teach The World To Sing* (1972)★★★, *The Jordanaires Sing Elvis' Favourite Spirituals* (Rockhouse 1985)★★★, *The Jordanaires Sing Elvis' Gospel Favourites* (Magnum Force 1986)★★★.

● FILMS: *Jailhouse Rock* (1957), *G.I. Blues* (1960), *Blue Hawaii* (1961), *Girls Girls Girls* (1962), *Fun In Acapulco* (1963), *Elvis - The Movie* (1979).

KARAS, ANTON

b. 7 July 1906, Vienna, Austria, d. 9 January 1985, Vienna, Austria. The man who arguably did more to popularize the zither than anyone before or after him, is best remembered as the sound behind the famous 'Third Man Theme' (Harry Lime). Carol Reed's classic 1949 film, *The Third Man*, utilized Karas's music throughout, and it was no surprise that film-goers made the song and its accompanying album a number 1 hit in 1951. Although Karas was a virtuoso, he remains one of the more famous one-hit-wonders of our time.

● ALBUMS: *Anton Karas* (Decca 1951)★★★.

● COMPILATIONS: *World Of Anton Karas* (Decca 1971)★★★, *Folk Songs Of Austria* (1974)★★★, *Harry Lime Theme (The Third Man)* (1974)★★★, *Bons Bons De Vienne* (1977)★★★.

KAYE SISTERS

This UK pop trio comprised Sheila Jones (b. 21 October 1936, Lewisham, London, England), Shirley 'Shan' Palmer (b. 15 August 1938, Hull, England) and Carole Young (b. 12 April 1930, Oldham, Lancashire, England). Formed in 1954 by Carmen Kaye and originally known as the Three Kayes, their big break came when they appeared on television's *In*

Town Tonight in 1956. They followed this with two weeks at the London Palladium and then their debut single, a cover version of the Charms' 'Ivory Tower' on HMV, made the UK Top 20. They joined the Philips label in 1957 and their first two Top 10 hits, which came in the company of Frankie Vaughan, were cover versions of Bob Jaxon's 'Gotta Have Something In The Bank Frank' (their royalties going to the Boys Clubs, an organization with which Vaughan has been involved for many years) and the Fleetwoods' 'Come Softly To Me'. Of the many singles they released, their only solo Top 10 hit was their version of Anita Bryant's US hit 'Paper Roses' in 1960. Jones retired in the late 60s and was replaced by Gilly. They continued to work, often supporting Max Bygraves. Young left in the late 70s to pursue an acting career, and appeared in the ITV series *Albion Market* and top soap opera *Coronation Street*. 'Shan and Gilly Kaye' appeared at the 1978 Royal Command Performance, and sang together in theatres and cabaret during the 80s. The original three members were reunited in 1992 and 1993, singing numbers made famous by the Andrews Sisters in UK tours of *In The Mood*, a tribute to Glenn Miller.
● ALBUMS: *Shan, Gill And Carole* (1973)★★.

KAYE, DANNY

b. David Daniel Kominsky, 18 January 1913, Brooklyn, New York, USA, d. 3 March 1987, Los Angeles, California, USA. Kaye was an extraordinary entertainer and an apparently inexhaustible comedian, mimic and dancer who seemed to be able to twist his face and body into any shape he wanted. As a singer, he specialized in very fast double talk and tongue-twisters, but could present a gentle ballad equally well. He was also an indefatigable ambassador for numerous charities, especially the United Nations International Children's Emergency Fund (now UNICEF), for which he travelled and worked for many years. A son of Jewish immigrant parents from Russia, Kominsky originally wanted to join the medical profession, but dropped out of high school when he was 14 years old, and hitch-hiked to Florida with his friend, Louis Eilson, where they sang for money. On their return to New York, they formed an act called Red And Blackie, and performed at private functions. During the day, Kominski worked as a soda-jerk, and then as an automobile appraiser with an insurance company. The latter job was terminated after he made a mistake which is said to have cost the company some $40,000. Kominski and Eilson then obtained summer work as 'toomlers', creators of tumult or all-round entertainers, in the Borscht Circuit summer hotels and camps in the Catskill Mountains. After five years, Kominski was earning $1,000 per season.
In 1933, he joined David Harvey and Kathleen Young on the vaudeville circuit in their dancing act, the Three Terpsichoreans, and was billed for the first time as Danny Kaye. An early onstage accident in which he split his trousers, elicited much laughter from the audience and was incorporated into the act. Signed by producer A.B. Marcus, the group toured the USA for five months in the revue *La Vie Paree*, before sailing for the Orient in February 1934. It is often said that this period of playing to non-English speaking audiences in Japan, China and Malaya, was when Kaye first developed his face-making and pantomiming techniques, and his 'gibberish' singing with the occasional recognized word. Back in the USA in 1936, Kaye worked with comedian

Nick Long Jnr. and toured with Abe Lyman's Band, before being booked by impresario Henry Sherek, to appear in cabaret at London's Dorchester Hotel. The engagement, in 1938, was not a success. Kaye commented: 'I was too loud for the joint'. (Ten years later in London, it would be an entirely different story.) While appearing in Max Liebman's *Sunday Night Varieties* in New York, Kaye met pianist-songwriter Sylvia Fine (b. 29 August 1913, New York, USA, d. 28 October 1991, New York, USA), who had been raised in the same Brooklyn neighbourhood, and majored in music at Brooklyn College. She became a powerful influence throughout his career, as his director, coach and critic. Working with Liebman's Saturday night revues at Camp Taimiment in the Pennsylvania Hills, during the summer of 1939, they started their collaboration, with Fine accompanying Kaye on the piano, and writing special material that included three of his most famous numbers, 'Stanislavsky', 'Pavlova' and the story of the unstable chapeau designer, 'Anatole Of Paris'. The best of the material was assembled in *The Straw Hat Revue* in which Kaye appeared with Imogene Coca, and which opened on Broadway in September 1939. The show also featured a young dancer named Jerome Robbins. After Fine and Kaye were married in January 1940, Kaye appeared in a smash hit engagement at La Martinique nightclub in New York, which led to a part in *Lady In The Dark*, starring Gertrude Lawrence. On the first night, Kaye stopped the show with the Kurt Weill and Ira Gershwin tongue-twister 'Tchaikovsky', in which he reeled off the names of 50 real, or imagined, Russian composers in 38 seconds. After playing a return engagement at La Martinique, and a five-week stint at the Paramount Theatre, Kaye appeared again on Broadway, starring in the Cole Porter musical *Let's Face It!*, which opened in October 1941. Porter allowed Sylvia Fine and Max Liebman to interpolate some special material for Kaye, which included a 'jabberwocky of song, dance, illustration and double-talk' called 'Melody In 4F'. Kaye had to leave the show early in 1942, suffering from nervous exhaustion, but having recovered, he toured on behalf of the war effort and is said to have sold a million dollars' worth of government bonds in six months. Rejected by the US Army because of a back ailment, he entertained troops with his two-hour shows in many theatres of operations including the South Pacific.
In 1944, Kaye made his feature film debut in *Up In Arms*, the first in a series of five pictures for Sam Goldwyn at RKO. His performance as a hypochondriac elevator boy, involving yet another memorable Fine-Liebman piece, 'Manic Depressive Pictures Presents: Lobby Number', moved one critic to hail his introduction as 'the most exciting since Garbo's'. Goldwyn was criticized, however for having Kaye's red hair dyed blonde. His remaining films for the studio included *Wonder Man*, in which he gave his impression of a sneezing Russian baritone with 'Orchi Tchornya'. This was the first of several films in which he played more than one character; *The Kid From Brooklyn* (1946), which featured 'Pavlova', *The Secret Life Of Walter Mitty* (1947), one of his best-remembered roles (six of them), and *A Song Is Born* (1948), one of his least remembered. In 1945, Kaye appeared for a year on his own CBS radio show with Harry James and Eve Arden, and during the following year the Kayes' daughter, Dena, was born. When Kaye recorded the old standard 'Dinah', he changed some of the 'i' sounds to 'e', so that the song ran:

'Denah, is there anyone fener? In the State of Carolena . . .', etc. His other hit songs included 'Tubby The Tuba', 'Minnie The Moocher', 'Ballin' The Jack', 'Bloop Bleep', 'Civilization' and 'The Woody Woodpecker Song', both with the Andrews Sisters; 'C'est Si Bon'; and 'Blackstrap Molasses', recorded with Jimmy Durante, Jane Wyman and Groucho Marx. In 1948, Kaye returned to England to appear at the London Palladium. His enormously successful record-breaking performances began an affectionate and enduring relationship with the British public. He is said to have received over 100,000 letters in a week. His shows were attended by the Royal Family; he met both Winston Churchill and George Bernard Shaw, and was cast in wax for London's Madame Tussaud's Museum. He returned in 1949 for the first of several Royal Command Performances, and also toured provincial music-halls throughout 1952. He endeared himself to the British by singing some of their parochial songs such as the novelty 'I've Got A Lovely Bunch Of Coconuts' and 'Maybe It's Because I'm A Londoner'. During one performance at the Palladium, when a member of the audience enquired after the state of Kaye's ribs following a car accident, he ordered the lights to be lowered while he displayed the actual X-ray plates! Kaye went to Canada in 1950 and became the first solo performer to star at the Canadian National Exhibition, where he sold out the 24,000-seater stadium for each of his 14 performances.

He returned to his multiple roles in films such as *The Inspector General* (1949) and *On The Riviera* (1951), before embarking on the somewhat controversial *Hans Christian Andersen* (1952). After 16 different screenplays over a period of 15 years, and protests in the Danish press about the choice of Kaye to play their national hero, the film, with a final screenplay by Moss Hart, became a huge money-spinner. Frank Loesser's score produced several appealing songs, including 'No Two People', 'Anywhere I Wander', 'Inchworm', 'Thumbelina', 'The Ugly Duckling' and 'Wonderful Copenhagen', the latter reaching the UK Top 5. Kaye's other films during the 50s and early 60s included *Knock On Wood* (1954), said to be his favourite, in which he sang two more Fine numbers, the title song, and 'All About Me', *White Christmas* (1954), co-starring with Bing Crosby, Rosemary Clooney and Vera-Ellen, *The Court Jester* (1956), *Me And The Colonel* (1958), *Merry Andrew* (1958), *The Five Pennies* (1959), a biopic of 20s cornet player Red Nichols (including a rousing version of 'When The Saints Go Marching In' with Louis Armstrong), *On The Double* (1961) and *The Man From The Diners' Club* (1963). After a break, he came back for *The Madwoman Of Challiot* (1969), and the following year, returned to Broadway in the role of Noah, in the Richard Rodgers and Martin Charnin musical *Two By Two*. Shortly after the show opened, Kaye tore a ligament in his leg during a performance, and subsequently appeared on crutches or in a wheelchair, in which he tried to run down the other actors, adapting the show to his injury, much to the distaste of producer and composer Richard Rodgers.

During the 70s and 80s, Kaye conducted classical orchestras and appeared on several television shows including *Peter Pan*, *Pinocchio* and *Danny Kaye's Look At The Metropolitan Opera*. He also played dramatic roles on television in *Skokie* and *The Twilight Zone*, but concentrated mainly on his charity work. He had started his association with UNICEF in the early 50s, and in 1955 made a 20-minute documentary,

Assignment Children. He eventually became the organization's ambassador-at-large for 34 years, travelling worldwide on their behalf, and entering the *Guinness Book Of Records* by visiting 65 US and Canadian cities in five days, piloting himself in his own jet plane. During his career he received many awards including the French Légion d'Honneur, the Jean Hersholt Humanitarian Award, and the Knight's Cross of the First Class of the Order of Danneborg, given by the Danish Government. Other awards included a special Academy Award in 1954, along with Tonys for his stage performances, plus Emmys for his successful 60s television series. He died in 1987, following a heart attack.

● ALBUMS: *Danny Kaye* (Columbia 1949)★★, *Danny Kaye Entertains* (Columbia 1949)★★★, *Gilbert And Sullivan And Danny Kaye* (Decca 1949)★★, *Hans Christian Andersen* film soundtrack (1953)★★★★, *Danny At The Palace* (Decca 1953)★★★, *Mommy, Gimme A Drink Of Water* (Capitol 1958)★★★, *Merry Andrew* film soundtrack (Capitol 1958)★★★, with Louis Armstrong *The Five Pennies* film soundtrack (1958)★★★, *The Court Jester* (Decca 1959)★★★, *For Children* (Decca 1959)★★, with Ivor Moreton *Happy Fingers* (1977)★★★.

● COMPILATIONS: *The Best Of Danny Kaye* (Decca 1962)★★★, *The Very Best Of Danny Kaye - 20 Golden Greats* (MCA 1987)★★★.

● FURTHER READING: *The Danny Kaye Saga*, Kurt Singer. *Nobody's Fool - The Secret Lives Of Danny Kaye*, Martin Gottfried. *The Life Story Of Danny Kaye*, D. Richards. *Fine And Danny*, Sylvia Fine.

● FILMS: *Up In Arms* (1944), *Wonder Man* (1945), *The Kid From Brooklyn* (1946), *The Secret Life Of Walter Mitty* (1947), *A Song Is Born* (1948), *The Inspector General* (1949), *On The Riviera* (1951), *Hans Christian Anderson* (1952), *Knock On Wood* (1953), *White Christmas* (1954), *Assignment Children* (1954), *The Court Jester* (1956), *Me And The Colonel* (1957), *Merry Andrew* (1958), *The Five Pennies* (1959), *On The Double* (1962), *The Man From The Diner's Club* (1963), *The Madwoman Of Chaillot* (1969).

KAYE, STUBBY

b. 18 November 1918, New York City, New York, USA, d. 15 December 1997. An actor and singer who carved himself an instant slice of musical history by stopping the show as Nicely-Nicely Johnson in the original Broadway production of *Guys And Dolls* - and then doing it all over again three years later in London. Kaye had his first break when he came first on the Major Bowes Amateur Hour on US radio in 1939. During the late 30s and early 40s he toured as a comedian in vaudeville, and made his London debut in USO shows during World War II. His role in *Guys And Dolls* (1950) was not a leading one, but he was outstanding in numbers such as 'Fugue For Tinhorns', 'The Oldest Established', 'Guys And Dolls', and the rousing 'Sit Down You're Rockin' The Boat'. He had one more big success on Broadway in 1956 as Marryin' Sam in *Li'l Abner*, and subsequently toured in revivals, played nightclubs as a comedian, and appeared on the television series *Love And Marriage* and *My Sister Eileen*. Unlike many stage performers he moved easily into films, and appeared in a variety features including *Guys And Dolls*, *Li'l Abner*, *40 Pounds Of Trouble*, *Cat Ballou* (with Nat King Cole), *Sweet Charity*, *The Cockeyed Cowboys Of Calico County*, *The Dirtiest Girl I Ever Met*, *Six Pack Annie* and *Who Framed*

Roger Rabbit?. The ample figure and sunny disposition he displayed as Nicely-Nicely in 1953 endeared him to London audiences and he made frequent appearances in the UK, including one in the musical *Man Of Magic* in 1956. Eventually he settled in Britain and married Angela Bracewell, who came to fame in the 50s as the hostess of the audience participation game 'Beat The Clock' in the top-rated television variety show *Sunday Night At The London Palladium*. After appearing in the West End in 1983 in the short-lived musical *Dear Anyone*, Kaye returned to Broadway two years later and won the only good notices in the musical *Grind*, a complete disaster that was described by one critic as 'art slaughter'. He continued to work in the UK and in 1986 starred as Ring Lardner in the radio play *Some Like Them Cold*.

● ALBUMS: *Music For Chubby Lovers* (1962)★★★, and Original Cast and film soundtrack recordings.

KEEL, HOWARD

b. Harold C. Leek, 13 April 1917, Gillespie, Illinois, USA. A popular singer in films and on the musical stage, with a rich, powerful baritone voice and commanding presence. After starting his career as a singing waiter in Los Angeles, Keel became an 'in-house entertainer' for the huge Douglas aircraft manufacturing company. In 1945, he appeared in *Carousel* on the west coast and then travelled to the UK to appear in the London production of *Oklahoma!*. At this time he was known as Harold Keel, having reversed the spelling of his last name. He subsequently changed his first name and after making a non-singing appearance in the film *The Small Voice* (1948), he returned to the USA where he landed the role of Frank Butler in the film *Annie Get Your Gun* (1950). He continued to make films, mostly musicals, including *Show Boat* (1951), *Kiss Me Kate* and *Calamity Jane* (both 1953), *Rose Marie* and *Seven Brides For Seven Brothers* (both 1954) and *Kismet* (1955). By the 60s he was touring the USA in revivals of popular shows, and appearing in non-musical low-budget western movies. In 1981 his acting career received a boost when he started to appear in the long-running television soap opera *Dallas*. This revived interest in his singing, particularly in the UK, and in 1984 he recorded his first solo album. In 1993, with his tongue firmly in his cheek, he announced his farewell tour of the UK.

● ALBUMS: *And I Love You So* (Warwick 1984)★★★★, *Reminiscing* (Telstar 1985)★★★, *Live In Concert* (BBC 1988)★★★, *The Collection* (Castle 1989)★★★, *The Great MGM Stars* (MGM 1991)★★★, *An Enchanted Evening With Howard Keel* (Music Club 1991)★★★, *Close To My Heart* (Premier 1991)★★★, and the soundtrack albums from the above musicals.

● VIDEOS: *Close To My Heart* (PMI 1991).

● FILMS: *The Small Voice* (1948), *Pagan Love Song* (1950), *Annie Get Your Gun* (1950), *Texas Carnival* (1951), *Three Guys Named Mike* (1951), *Show Boat* (1951), *Lovely To Look At* (1952), *Desperate Search* (1952), *Callaway Went Thataway* (1952), *Calamity Jane* (1953), *Fast Company* (1953), *I Love Melvin* (1953), *Kiss Me Kate* (1953), *Ride Vaquero!* (1953), *Deep In My Heart* (1954), *Seven Brides For Seven Brothers* (1954), *Rose Marie* (1954), *Jupiter's Darling* (1955), *Kismet* (1955), *Floods Of Fear* (1958), *The Big Fisherman* (1959), *Armoured Command* (1961), *Day Of The Triffids* (1963), *The Man From Button Willow* voice only (1965), *Waco* (1966),

Red Tomahawk (1967), *The War Wagon* (1967), *Arizona Bushwackers* (1968).

KEISKER, MARION

b. 23 September 1917, Memphis, Tennessee, USA, d. 29 December 1989. Marion Keisker was Sam Phillips' assistant at Sun Records in the 50s, and as such was the employee who first recorded the young Elvis Presley in 1953. In 1946, she began working for radio station WREC. Phillips joined as an announcer a year later and when he launched the Memphis Recording Service in 1950, Keisker went along as his assistant, continuing to work part-time for the station until 1955. Phillips started Sun in 1952 and Keisker arranged sessions for the blues musicians who recorded there. She kept a log of all activities at the company, which provided future historians with interesting details. Keisker was on duty in 1953 when Presley arrived at Memphis Recording Service to record two songs as a gift for his mother. She took his fee, ran the recording machines and made a note of the boy's potential. It was she who suggested to Phillips that he record Presley on Sun the following year and she who took Presley around to visit disc jockeys and the press. Presley called her his 'first fan'. As Sun grew, Keisker performed such duties as handling accounts with distributors and pressing plants. All of the aspiring artists who wanted to record for Sun had to speak to Keisker before they were accepted or rejected by Phillips. Keisker left Sun in 1957 to join the US Air Force, with which she worked until 1969. She died of cancer in December 1989.

KELLY, GENE

b. Eugene Curran Kelly, 23 August 1912, Pittsburgh, Pennsylvania, USA, d. 1 February 1996, Los Angeles, California, USA. An actor, dancer, singer, choreographer, director, producer, and one of the most innovative and respected figures in the history of the screen musical. Kelly took dance lessons at the age of eight - albeit against his will - and excelled at sports when he was at high school. During the Depression he had a variety of jobs, including gymnastics instructor, and, with his brother Fred, performed a song-and-dance act at local nightclubs. In the early 30s, he spent a few months at law school before opening the Gene Kelly Studios of the Dance, and discovering that he had a real aptitude for teaching, which would manifest itself throughout his career in some of the most creative choreography ever seen on the big screen. In 1937 Kelly moved to New York, and gained a small part as a dancer in the musical comedy *Leave It To Me!*, in which Mary Martin also made her Broadway debut. A larger role followed in the revue *One For The Money*, and he also played Harry, the 'good natured hoofer', in the Pulitzer prize-winning comedy, *The Time Of Your Life*. In 1940, after working in summer stock, and serving as a dance director at Billy Rose's Diamond Horseshoe club, Kelly won the title role in the new Richard Rodgers and Lorenz Hart musical, *Pal Joey*. His portrayal of the devious, unscrupulous nightclub entertainer made him a star overnight in New York, but, after choreographing another Broadway hit show, *Best Foot Forward*, he moved to Hollywood in 1942, and made his screen debut with Judy Garland in *For Me And My Gal*. He appeared in two more musicals for MGM, *DuBarry Was A Lady* and *Thousands Cheer*, before the company loaned him to Columbia for

Cover Girl (1944). Co-starring with Rita Hayworth and Phil Silvers, the film was a major landmark in Kelly's career, and an indication of the heights he would achieve during the next 10 years. It was memorable in many respects, particularly for Kelly's sensitive rendering of Jerome Kern and Ira Gershwin's 'Long Ago And Far Away', and the 'Alter Ego' dance, during which Kelly danced with his own reflection in a shop window. Back at MGM, he was called upon to play several dramatic roles as well as appearing in *Anchors Aweigh* (1945), for which he received an Oscar nomination for best actor. In the film, as a couple of sailors on leave, Kelly and Frank Sinatra were accompanied by Kathryn Grayson, a Sammy Cahn and Jule Styne score - and Jerry - an animated mouse, who joined Kelly in a live-action/cartoon sequence that is still regarded as a classic of its kind. After spending two years in the real US Navy during World War II, supervising training films, Kelly resumed at MGM with *Ziegfeld Follies* (1946), in which he sang and danced with Fred Astaire for the first time on screen, in 'The Babbitt And The Bromide'. Two years later he was reunited with Judy Garland for *The Pirate*, a somewhat underrated film, with a score by Cole Porter that included 'Be A Clown'. He then choreographed the 'Slaughter On Tenth Avenue' sequence in the Rodgers and Hart biopic *Words And Music*, in which he danced with Vera-Ellen, before joining Sinatra and Jules Munshin, first for the lively *Take Me Out To The Ball Game* (1949), and again for *On The Town*, 'the most inventive and effervescent movie musical Hollywood had thus far produced'. Although criticized for its truncation of the original Broadway score, *On The Town*, with its integrated music and plot, and the athletic dance sequences on the streets of New York, was acclaimed from all sides. After his triumph in *On The Town*, Kelly went on to *Summer Stock*, with Judy Garland again, before turning to what many consider to be the jewel in MGM's musical crown - *An American In Paris* (1951). Directed by Vincente Minnelli, and set in an idealized version of Paris, Kelly and his partner, Leslie Caron, danced exquisitely to a Gershwin score that included 'I Got Rhythm', 'Our Love Is Here To Stay', ''S Wonderful' and 'I'll Build A Stairway To Paradise'. The film ended with a 17-minute ballet sequence, a 'summation of Gene Kelly's work as a film dancer and choreographer, allowing him his full range of style - classical ballet, modern ballet, Cohanesque hoofing, tapping, jitterbugging, and sheer athletic expressionism'. It won eight Academy Awards, including one for best picture. Kelly received a special Oscar 'in appreciation of his versatility as an actor, singer, director, and dancer, and specifically for his brilliant achievements in the art of choreography on film'. If *An American In Paris* was MGM's jewel, then *Singin' In The Rain* (1952), was probably its financial plum - arguably the most popular Hollywood musical of them all. Produced by Arthur Freed, who also wrote the songs with Nacio Herb Brown, the film's witty screenplay, by Betty Comden and Adolph Green, dealt with the Hollywood silent movie industry trying to come to terms with talking pictures. Debbie Reynolds and Donald O'Connor joined Kelly in the joyous spoof, and sang and danced to a score that included 'You Were Meant For Me', 'Make 'Em Laugh', 'Good Mornin'' and 'Moses Supposes'. The scene in which Kelly sings the title song, while getting completely drenched, is probably the most requested film clip in the history of the musical cinema.

For *Deep In My Heart* (1955), the Sigmund Romberg biopic, Kelly went back to his roots and danced with his younger brother, Fred, in one of the film's high spots, 'I Love To Go Swimmin' With Wimmen'. Kelly's final major musical projects for MGM were *Brigadoon* (1954) and *It's Always Fair Weather* (1955). In the former, 'the magical story of a Scottish village long lost to history and coming to life once every hundred years for a single day', Kelly co-starred with Cyd Charisse and Van Johnson in a production that was criticized for being shot in Cinemascope, and in the studio, rather than on location. For the latter film in 1955, Kelly co-starred with Dan Dailey and Michael Kidd for what was essentially a satirical swipe at the cynical commercialism of the US television industry - with music. His next project, *Invitation To The Dance* (1956), with script, choreography, and direction by Kelly, consisted of three unrelated episodes, all entirely danced, with Kelly accompanied by a classically trained troupe. A commercial failure in the USA, it was acclaimed in some parts of Europe, and awarded the grand prize at the West Berlin film festival in 1958. Following its success there, Kelly choreographed a new ballet for the Paris Opera's resident company, and was made a Chevalier of the Legion of Honor by the French government. *Les Girls* (1957) was Kelly's final MGM musical, and Cole Porter's last Hollywood score - the golden era of screen musicals was over. Subsequently, Kelly played several straight roles in films such as *Marjorie Morningstar* and *Inherit The Wind*, but spent much of his time as a director on projects such as Richard Rodgers and Oscar Hammerstein's Broadway musical *Flower Drum Song*, and 20th Century Fox's $20,000,000 extravaganza, *Hello, Dolly!* (1969), which starred Barbra Streisand, Walter Matthau and a young Michael Crawford. In 1974, he was back on the screen in *That's Entertainment!*, 'a nostalgia bash, featuring scenes from nearly 100 MGM musicals'. It became a surprise hit, and two years later, Kelly and Fred Astaire hosted the inevitable sequel, *That's Entertainment, Part 2*. After viewing all that vintage footage, it would be interesting to know Kelly's real opinions on a more modern musical film, such as *Xanadu* (1980), in which he appeared with Olivia Newton-John. By then, together with director Stanley Donen, the complete Arthur Freed Unit, and the rest of the talented personnel who produced most of his musicals at MGM, Kelly, with his athletic performance, choreography and direction, had completed a body of work that was only equalled by the other master of dance on film, Fred Astaire - but in a very different style. Whereas Astaire purveyed the image of a smooth man about town, with top hat, white tie and tails, Kelly's preferred to appear casual in sports shirt, slacks and white socks. As he said himself: 'Astaire represents the aristocracy when he dances - I represent the proletariat!'.

● ALBUMS: *Song And Dance Man* (1954)★★★★, *Singin' In The Rain Again* (Decca 1978)★★, *Best Of Gene Kelly - From MGM Films* (MCA 1988)★★★, *Great MGM Stars* (MGM 1991)★★★, *Gotta Dance! The Best Of Gene Kelly* (1994)★★★, and film soundtracks.

● FURTHER READING: *Gene Kelly: A Biography*, Clive Hirschhorn. *The Films Of Gene Kelly*, Tony Thomas. *Gene Kelly*, J. Basinger.

● FILMS: *For Me And My Gal* (1942), *Pilot No. 5* (1943), *Du Barry Was A Lady* (1943), *Thousands Cheer* (1943), *The Cross Of Lorraine* (1943), *Cover Girl* (1944), *Christmas*

Holiday (1944), *Anchors Aweigh* (1945), *Ziegfeld Follies* (1946), *Living In A Big Way* (1947), *The Pirate* (1948), *The Three Musketeers* (1948), *Words And Music* (1948), *Take Me Out To The Ball Game* (1949), *On The Town* (1949), *The Black Hand* (1950), *Summer Stock* (1950), *An American In Paris* (1951), *It's A Big Country* (1952), *Singin' In The Rain* (1952), *The Devil Makes Three* (1952), *Brigadoon* (1954), *Crest Of The Wave* (1954), *Deep In My Heart* (1955), *It's Always Fair Weather* (1955), *Invitation To The Dance* (1956), *The Happy Road* (1957), *Les Girls* (1957), *Marjorie Morningstar* (1958), *The Tunnel Of Love* as director (1958), *Inherit The Wind* (1960), *Gigot* as director (1962), *Let's Make Love* (1960), *What A Way To Go* (1964), *The Young Girls Of Rochefort* (1968) *A Guide For The Married Man* as director (1967), *Hello, Dolly!* as director (1969), *The Cheyenne Social Club* as director and producer (1970), *40 Carats* (1973), *That's Entertainment!* as narrator (1974), *That's Entertainment, Part 2* as narrator (1976), *Viva Knievel!* (1977), *Xanadu* (1980), *Reporters* (1981), *That's Dancing!* (1985).

KELLY, PAULA

b. 1920, USA, d. 2 April 1992, Costa Mesa, California, USA. An excellent band and ensemble singer with a vivacious personality, Kelly began her career in 1937 with top saxophonist Dick Stabile's band, and then spent two years with Al Donahue. She joined Glenn Miller in 1941 as a featured singer with the Modernaires vocal group; her husband, Hal Dickinson, was founder-leader. Early in 1941 Kelly appeared in the first Glenn Miller movie, *Sun Valley Serenade*, in which the Modernaires sang classics such as 'Chattanooga Choo Choo' and 'I Know Why'. Later in the year she left Miller when former vocalist Marion Hutton rejoined the band. For a while Kelly sang with Artie Shaw, and then for Bob Allen's band. In the mid-40s she rejoined the Modernaires when the group expanded to five. In the 50s they appeared in clubs and theatres, toured with Bob Crosby, and sang on his radio and television shows. They also featured with Crosby, Frankie Laine and Billy Daniels in the movie *When You're Smiling* (1950), and in *The Glenn Miller Story* (1954). After Dickinson died on 18 November 1970, Kelly and the Modernaires worked with ex-Miller sideman Tex Beneke's band and Miller's original boy vocalist, Ray Eberle, riding on the nostalgia boom of the 70s. Kelly's records with the Modernaires included 'Jukebox Saturday Night', 'There, I've Said It Again', 'You Belong To My Heart', 'Goody Goody', 'Margie' and 'Stop, Look And Listen'. With Dick Stabile she recorded 'Lost And Found' and 'My Heart Is Taking Lessons'; with Al Donahue, 'Jeepers Creepers', 'Moon Love', 'The Lambeth Walk', 'Stairway To The Stars' and 'South American Way'; and with Artie Shaw, 'Someone's Rocking My Dreamboat' and 'I Don't Want To Walk Without You'. Kelly retired in 1978, and in the late 80s her daughter, Paula Kelly Jnr., was reported to be singing an updated version of 'Jukebox Saturday Night' with the Modernaires, accompanied by a 15-piece band led by the same Tex Beneke.

KENNEDY, JIMMY

b. 20 July 1902, Omagh, Co. Tyrone, Northern Ireland, d. 6 April 1984, Cheltenham, England. One of Britain's leading songwriters from the mid-30s through to the 50s, Kennedy's collaboration with Michael Carr, in particular, produced some of the most popular songs of the day. After graduating from Trinity College, Dublin, Kennedy spent brief periods as a teacher and a civil servant before deciding to concentrate on songwriting. His first big break came when he signed a contract with music publisher Bert Feldman, which led to him writing lyrics for songs such as 'Oh, Donna Clara' (music by J. Petersburski, 1930), 'The Teddy Bear's Picnic' (a new lyric to John Bratton's 1907 melody), 'My Song Goes Round The World' (Hans May, Ernst Neubach), 'Beside My Caravan' (Karel Vacek), 'Café In Vienna' (Vacek), 'Little Valley In The Mountains' (J. Dvoracek, K. Zeleny), 'Play To Me, Gypsy' (Vacek) and 'Isle Of Capri' (Will Grosz). The latter number has proved to be an enduring all-time standard: Gracie Fields' version, in particular, is fondly remembered. In 1934 Kennedy began his five-year association with Michael Carr, which resulted in several mostly memorable compositions, including 'Ole Faithful', 'Misty Islands Of The Highlands', 'The General's Fast Asleep', 'Did Your Mother Come From Ireland?', 'The Sunset Trail', 'Why Did She Fall For The Leader Of The Band?', 'Waltz Of The Gypsies', 'Cinderella, Stay In My Arms', 'A Handsome Territorial', 'Two Bouquets', and probably their best-known song, 'South Of The Border'.

Kennedy and Carr also contributed to films, and London Palladium shows such as *O-Kay For Sound* ('There's A New World'), *The Little Dog Laughed* ('There's Danger In The Waltz'), and the Flanagan And Allen revue *London Rhapsody* ('Home Town' and 'Sing A Song Of London'). Towards the end of their partnership, they wrote one of the biggest morale-boosting hits of World War II, 'We're Gonna Hang Out The Washing On The Siegfried Line'. During this comparatively brief but highly productive period, Kennedy continued to collaborate with other composers on songs such as 'Red Sails In The Sunset' (Hugh Williams, 1935), 'At The Café Continental', 'Bird On The Wing' and 'Ten Pretty Girls' (all three: Will Grosz), 'Serenade In The Night' (C.A. Bixio, B. Cherubini), 'Harbour Lights' (Hugh Williams), 'The Chestnut Tree' (Tommie Connor, Hamilton Kennedy), 'My Prayer' (Georges Boulanger) and 'Oh Nicholas, Don't Be So Ridiculous' (Harry Castling, 1939). He also wrote both words and music for 'Roll Along Covered Wagon' (1935), 'The Coronation Waltz', 'There's A Boy Coming Home On Leave', 'Saint Mary's In The Twilight', 'All Our Tomorrows', and 'An Hour Never Passes' (1944), among many others, and his lyrical addition to a traditional tune resulted in 'The Cokey Cokey' (often called 'The Hokey Cokey') becoming one of the most popular party dances of all time. After serving in the army during the war, in the late 40s and early 50s Kennedy's prolific and varied output continued with songs such as 'An Apple Blossom Wedding' (Nat Simon), 'Down The Old Spanish Trail' (Kenneth Leslie Smith), 'And Mimi' (Simon), 'Pigalle' (George Ulmer, George Koger), 'French Can-Can Polka' (Jacques Offenbach), 'Down The Trail Of Aching Hearts' (Simon), 'April In Portugal (Coimbra)' (Raul Ferrao, Jose Galhardo) and 'Istanbul (Not Constantinople)' (Simon, 1953). Later, although he was still able to come up with occasional hits such as 'Love Is Like A Violin (Mon Coeur Est Un Violin)' (Miarka Laparcerie) and 'Romeo' (Robert Stolz) for Ken Dodd and Petula Clark, respectively, like so many others, Kennedy's style of songs were swamped by the rock 'n' roll revolution. In the early 60s he retreated to Switzerland, but eventually moved back home to Ireland where he devoted much of his time to writing music for dramatic plays. During his long and distinguished career, his honours included two ASCAP Awards, and Ivor Novello Awards - for Outstanding Services To British Music (1971) and Life Achievement (1980). He was also awarded an honorary doctorate by the University of Ulster (1978), and an OBE (1983). In 1984, the year of his death, the British Academy of Songwriters, Composers and Authors (BASCA) inaugurated a special annual Jimmy Kennedy Award. Further recognition came in 1997, when Kennedy was inducted into the American Songwriters' Hall Of Fame.

Like his sometime partner, Michael Carr (b. 1904, Leeds, England, d. 16 September 1968) was one of Tin Pan Alley's great characters. He spent much of his early life in Dublin before moving to America where he worked at a variety of jobs. Soon after he returned to the UK he was introduced to Jimmy Kennedy and their historic partnership began. Over the years, Carr also collaborated with others on songs such as 'Fonso My Hot Spanish (K)Night' (Leo Tower, Will Haines, 1930), 'Getting Around And About' and 'Old Timer' (both Lewis Ilda), 'The Girl With The Dreamy Eyes' (Eddie Pola), 'The Wheel Of The Wagon Is Broken' (Elton Box, Desmond Cox), 'The Little Boy That Santa Claus Forgot' (Tommie Connor, Jimmy Leach), 'Merrily We Roll Along' (Raymond Wallace), 'A Pair Of Silver Wings' (Eric Maschwitz), 'The First Lullaby' (Jack Popplewell), 'I Love To Sing' (Tommie Connor, Paul Misraki) and 'Lonely Ballerina' (Paul Lambrecht). Early in his career, he wrote, unaided, 'Dinner For One Please, James', 'Cowboy' and 'On The Outside Looking In', and in the early 60s provided the Shadows with the highly successful 'Man Of Mystery' and 'Kon-Tiki'. Just before he died in 1968, Carr wrote Des O'Connor's Top 5 hit 'One-Two-Three O'Leary' with Barry Mason, and Jackie Lee's first chart entry, 'White Horses', with Ben Nisbet.

KENTON, STAN

b. 15 December 1911, Wichita, Kansas, USA, d. 25 August 1979. After playing piano in various dance bands, including those of Everett Hoagland and Vido Musso, mostly on the west coast, Kenton decided to form his own band in 1941. Although geared partially to the commercial needs of the dancehall circuit of the time, Kenton's band, which he termed the 'Artistry In Rhythm' orchestra, also featured powerful brass section work and imaginative saxophone voicings, unlike those of his more orthodox competitors. The band developed a substantial following among the younger elements of the audience who liked their music brash and loud. During the remainder of the 40s Kenton's popularity increased dramatically, seemingly immune to the declining fortunes that affected other bands. A succession of exciting young jazz musicians came into the band, among them Buddy Childers, Art Pepper, Kai Winding, Shelly Manne, Bob Cooper and Laurindo Almeida, playing arrangements by Kenton, Gene Roland and Pete Rugolo. His singers included Anita O'Day, June Christy and Chris Connor. In the 50s, his enthusiasm undimmed, Kenton introduced a 43-piece band, his 'Innovations In Modern Music' orchestra, again featuring Pepper and Manne as well as newcomers such as Maynard Ferguson and Bud Shank. Complex, quasi-classical arrangements by Bob Graettinger and others proved less appealing, but a 1953 tour of Europe ensured Kenton's international reputation. Reduced to a more manageable 19-piece, his

New Concepts In Artistry In Rhythm band continued playing concerts and recording, using arrangements by Roland, Gerry Mulligan and Johnny Richards. Always eager to try new ideas, and to clearly label them, in the 60s Kenton introduced his 'New Era In Modern Music' orchestra, a 23-piece band using mellophoniums, and the 'Neophonic' orchestra, five pieces larger and tempting fate with neo-classical music. In the 70s, he embraced rock rhythms and looked as if he might go on forever. By 1977, however, his health had begun to deteriorate and although he returned from hospitalization to lead his band until August 1978, his bandleading days were almost over. He died in August 1979. More than most bandleaders, Kenton polarized jazz fans, inspiring either love or hatred and only rarely meeting with indifference. Almost half a century after the event it is hard to understand what all the fuss was about. Certainly the band did not swing with the grace of, for example, the Jimmie Lunceford band, but it was equally wrong to declare, as many critics did, that Kenton never swung at all. Although some of the arrangements were too monolithic for effective jazz performances, the abilities of his key soloists were seldom buried for long. Kenton's band was important in bringing together many excellent musicians and for allowing arrangers free rein to experiment in big band concepts, a practice that few other leaders of the period would tolerate.

● ALBUMS: *Stan Kenton At The Hollywood Palladium* (1945)★★★, *Progressive Jazz* (1946-47)★★★, *One Night Stand With Nat 'King' Cole And Stan Kenton* (1947)★★★, *One Night Stand At The Commodore* (1947)★★★, *Stan Kenton And His Orchestra With June Christy* (1949)★★★★, *Encores* 10-inch album (Capitol 1950)★★★, *Innovations In Modern Music* 10-inch album (Capitol 1950)★★★, *Milestones* 10-inch album (Capitol 1950)★★★, *Artistry In Rhythm* 10-inch album (Capitol 1950)★★★★, *A Presentation Of Progressive Jazz* 10-inch album (Capitol 1950)★★★, *One Night Stand With Stan Kenton* i (1950)★★★, *Stan Kenton Presents* 10-inch album (Capitol 1950)★★★★, *Nineteen Fifty-One* (1951)★★★, *One Night Stand With Stan Kenton* ii (1951)★★★, *Carnegie* (1951)★★★★, with Charlie Parker *Kenton And Bird* (1951-54)★★★, *Artistry In Tango* (1951-52)★★★, *Concert In Miniature* (1952)★★★, *Classics* 10-inch album (Capitol 1952)★★★, *City Of Glass* 10-inch album (Capitol 1952)★★★, *Concert In Miniature No 9 And 10* (1952)★★★, *Concert In Miniature No 11 And 12* (1952)★★★, *Concert In Miniature No 13 And 14* (1952)★★★, *New Concepts Of Artistry In Rhythm* (Capitol 1953)★★★★, *Concert Encores* (1953)★★★, *Prologue This Is An Orchestra* 10-inch album (Capitol 1953)★★★, *Popular Favorites* 10-inch album (Capitol 1953)★★★, *The Definitive Stan Kenton With Charlie Parker And Dizzy Gillespie* (1953-54)★★★, *Stan Kenton In Berlin* (1953)★★★, *Europe Fifty Three Part One and Two* (1953)★★★, *Paris, 1953* (1953)★★★, *Sketches On Standards* 10-inch album (Capitol 1953)★★★, *This Modern World* 10-inch album (Capitol 1953)★★★, *Stan Kenton Radio Transcriptions* 10-inch album (MacGregor 1953)★★★, *Portraits Of Standards* 10-inch album (Capitol 1953)★★★, *Artistry In Kenton* (1954)★★★, *Kenton Showcase - The Music Of Bill Russo* 10-inch album (Capitol 1954)★★★, *Kenton Showcase - The Music Of Bill Holman* 10-inch album (Capitol 1954)★★★, *Stan Kenton Festival* (1954)★★★, with June Christy *Duet* (Capitol 1955)★★★★, *Contemporary Concepts*

(Capitol 1955)★★★, *Stan Kenton In Hi-Fi* (Capitol 1956)★★★★, *Kenton In Concert* (1956)★★★, *Kenton In Stereo* (1956)★★★, *In Stockholm* (1956)★★★, *Cuban Fire!* (Capitol 1956)★★★★, *Kenton '56* (1956)★★★, *Rendez-vous With Kenton/At The Rendezvous Volume 1* (Capitol 1957)★★★, *Kenton With Voices* (Capitol 1957)★★★, *Back To Balboa* (Capitol 1958)★★★, *Lush Interlude* (Capitol 1958)★★★, *The Stage Door Swings* (Capitol 1958)★★★, *On The Road* (1958)★★★, *The Kenton Touch* (Capitol 1958)★★★, *The Ballad Style Of Stan Kenton* (Capitol 1958)★★★, *Stan Kenton At The Tropicana* (Capitol 1959)★★★, *In New Jersey* (1959)★★★, *At Ukiah* (1959)★★★, *Viva Kenton* (Capitol 1959)★★★, with Christy *The Road Show, Volumes 1 & 2* (Capitol 1960)★★★, with Ann Richards *Two Much* (1960)★★★, with Christy *Together Again* (Capitol 1960)★★★, *Standards In Silhouette* (Capitol 1960)★★★, *Stan Kenton's Christmas* (1961)★★★, *The Romantic Approach* (Capitol 1961)★★★, *Stan Kenton's West Side Story* (Capitol 1961)★★★★, *Mellophonium Magic* (1961)★★★, *Sophisticated Approach* (1961)★★★, *Adventures In Standards* (1961)★★★, *Adventures In Blues* (Capitol 1961)★★★, *Adventures In Jazz* (Capitol 1961)★★★, *The Sound Of Sixty-Two* (1962)★★★, *Adventures In Time* (Capitol 1962)★★★, *Stan Kenton's Mellophonium Band* (Capitol 1962)★★★, *Artistry In Bossa Nova* (Capitol 1963)★★★, *Artistry In Voices And Brass* (Capitol 1963)★★★, *The Best Of Brant Inn* (1963)★★, *Kenton In England* (1963)★★★, *Wagner* (1964)★★★, *Stan Kenton Conducts The Los Angeles Neophonic Orchestra* (Capitol 1965)★★★, *Rhapsody In Blue* (1965)★★★, *Stan Kenton Conducts The Jazz Compositions Of Dee Barton* (Capitol 1968)★★★, *Live At Redlands University* (Creative World 1970)★★, *Live At Brigham Young University* (Creative World 1971)★★, *Live At Fairfield Hall, Croydon* (1972)★★, *Live At Butler University* (Creative World 1972)★★, *National Anthems Of The World* (1972)★★, *Stan Kenton Today* (London Philharmonic 1972)★★★, *Birthday In Britain* (Creative World 1973)★★, *7.5 On The Richter Scale* (Creative World 1973)★★, *Solo: Stan Kenton Without His Orchestra* (1973)★★, *Stan Kenton Plays Chicago* (Creative World 1974)★★, *Fire, Fury And Fun* (Creative World 1974)★★, *Kenton 1976* (Creative World 1976)★★, *Journey Into Capricorn* (Creative World 1976)★★, *Stan(dard) Kenton: Stan Kenton In Warsaw* (1976)★★★, *Stan Kenton In Europe* (1976)★★★, *Live At Sunset Ridge Country Club Chicago* (Magic 1977)★★, *Live In Cologne 1976 Vols. 1 and 2* (Magic 1977)★★, *Street Of Dreams* (Creative World 1977)★★.

● COMPILATIONS: *The Kenton Era (1940-53)* (Capitol 1955)★★★★, *Stan Kenton's Greatest Hits* (Capitol 1965)★★★★, *Stan Kenton's Greatest Hits (1943-51)* (1983)★★★★, *The Christy Years (1945-47)* (Creative World 1985)★★★★, *The Fabulous Alumni Of Stan Kenton (1945-56)* (Creative World 1985)★★★★, *Collection: 20 Golden Greats* (Deja Vu 1986)★★★★, *Retrospective 1943-1968* 4-CD box set (Capitol 1992)★★★★, *Best Of* (Capitol 1995)★★★★.

● VIDEOS: *Stan Kenton And Frank Rosolino* (Kay Jazz 1988), *Stan Kenton And His Orchestra* (Kay Jazz 1988).

● FURTHER READING: *Straight Ahead: The Story Of Stan Kenton*, Carol Easton. *Stan Kenton: Artistry In Rhythm*, William F. Lee. *Stan Kenton: The Man And His Music*, Lillian Arganian.

KEYES, JIMMY

b. c.30s, Kentucky, USA, d. 22 July 1995, New York City, New York, USA. After growing up in Kentucky, Keyes moved to the Bronx, New York, in 1947, where he formed his first vocal group, the Four Notes. This band eventually evolved into the Tunestoppers, with Carl Feaster, Claude Feaster, Floyd McCrae, James Edwards and Rupert Branker appearing alongside him. They signed to the Atlantic Records subsidiary label Cat, and in March 1954, now billed as the Chords, recorded 'Sh-Boom', co-written by Keyes. An R&B/doo-wop song that also crossed over into the pop charts, it was considered by many as one of the first rock 'n' roll hits. It reached number 5 on the *Billboard* charts, while a cover version by the Crewcuts made number 1. However, the Chords never enjoyed another hit single, and in the late 60s Keyes joined soul band the Popular Five. Again, success eluded him, despite several singles for Mr Chand and Minit Records. However, recurrent interest in 'Sh-Boom' led to Keyes re-forming the Chords with Carl Feaster in the late 70s. When Feaster died in 1981 Keyes opted to keep the group on the oldies circuit, employing various sidemen. He suffered a brain aneurysm in 1995, and died following an operation in New York.

KIDD, MICHAEL

b. Milton Greenwald, 12 August 1919, New York City, New York, USA. An important choreographer and director who pioneered a joyful and energetic style of dancing. Kidd was a soloist with the Ballet Theatre (later called the American Ballet Theatre) before making his Broadway debut as choreographer with *Finian's Rainbow* in 1947. He won a Tony Award for his work on that show, and earned four more during the 50s for *Guys And Dolls* (1950), *Can-Can* (1953), *Li'l Abner* (1956) and *Destry Rides Again* (1959). His other shows around that time were *Hold It, Love Life* and *Arms And The Girl*. From *Li'l Abner* onwards he also directed, and sometimes produced, most of the shows on which he worked, but it was as a choreographer of apparently limitless invention that he dominated the Broadway musical during the 50s. In the 60s and early 70s he worked on productions such as *Wildcat, Subways Are For Sleeping, Here's Love, Ben Franklin In Paris, Skyscraper, Breakfast At Tiffany's* (which closed during previews), *The Rothschilds* (1970), *Cyrano*, and a revival of *Good News* (1974). Kidd also filled the big screen with his brilliant and exuberant dance sequences in classic Hollywood musicals such as *The Band Wagon, Seven Brides For Seven Brothers, It's Always Fair Weather* and *Hello, Dolly!* He co-starred with Gene Kelly and Dan Dailey in *It's Always Fair Weather*, and appeared in several other films, including *Movie Movie*, an affectionate parody of a typical 30s double-feature that went largely unappreciated in 1979. However, recognition of his immense contribution to the screen musical came in 1997 when he received a special Honorary Academy Award.

● FILMS: *It's Always Fair Weather* (1955), *Movie Movie* (1979).

KING AND I, THE (STAGE MUSICAL)

With music by Richard Rodgers and book and lyrics by Oscar Hammerstein II, *The King And I* opened at the St. James Theatre in New York on 29 March 1951. It starred Yul Brynner as the King of Siam and Gertrude Lawrence as

Anna Leonowens, a schoolteacher engaged to educate the royal children. Set in the 1860s, the story of *The King And I* was based on Anna Leonowens' book *The English Governess At The Siamese Court* (Margaret Landon's novel *Anna And The King Of Siam* was also based upon the same source material). The project was Lawrence's brainchild and once she had set the wheels in motion and Rodgers and Hammerstein were hired to write it, the show was scheduled to become one of the greatest money-spinners in Broadway history. The strong storyline highlighted an Oriental nation's attempts to advance towards the progressive ideologies of the west, while still being shackled to the concept of a slave-owning, male-dominated society. With settings of Oriental opulence, a masterly score and superb central performances, *The King And I* was a great success, and ran for 1,246 performances. Among the songs were 'I Whistle A Happy Tune', 'Hello, Young Lovers', 'Getting To Know You', 'My Lord And Master', 'Shall We Dance?', 'I Have Dreamed', 'A Puzzlement', 'We Kiss In A Shadow' and 'Something Wonderful', which was sung by Dorothy Sarnoff in the role of Lady Thiang. Additionally, there was the engaging 'March Of The Siamese Children', in which Rodgers effectively captured an Oriental flavour while using orthodox western musical forms. Fittingly, given her involvement in its creation, *The King And I* was a triumph for Lawrence. It was also her swan-song; she died 18 months after the show's opening, to be succeeded by Constance Carpenter. A London production opened in 1953, starring Herbert Lom and Valerie Hobson. Brynner reprised the greatest role of his career for Broadway in 1977 and London two years later. He was touring the show in the USA in 1983 when he first discovered that he had cancer. Over the years, the show has proved to be a convenient vehicle for artists from different branches of showbusiness. In 1989 a Baltimore production starred Alan Jay Lerner's widow, Liz Robertson, and the ballet superstar Rudolph Nureyev, and in the same year Stacy Keach and Mary Beth Pell starred in an acclaimed Pittsburgh production. In 1990 and 1991 Susan Hampshire was teamed with David Yip and Koshiro Matsumoto IX at Sadlers Wells for limited seasons, and a 1991/92 tour with Hayley Mills and Tony Marinyo grossed $13.5 million in 35 weeks. Liz Robertson and ballet star Irek Mukhamedov brought the show back to London as part of the Covent Garden Festival in 1995. In the following year, a ravishing Broadway revival, starring Donna Murphy and Lou Diamond Phillips (who came to prominence in the 1987 film *La Bamba*), won four Tony Awards for best musical revival, leading actress (Murphy), scenic design (Brian Thompson) and costume design (Roger Kirk). In 1992, Julie Andrews, whom many consider would have been the perfect Anna, sang the role for a studio cast CD, with British actor Ben Kingsley as the King. The 1956 film version starred Yul Brynner and Deborah Kerr.

KING AND I, THE (FILM MUSICAL)

Yul Brynner became a legend in the 1951 Broadway show, and no other actor could even have been considered for the leading role in this 1956 screen version. Brynner's stage partner, Gertrude Lawrence, died during the Broadway run, and his co-star for this film, the British actress Deborah Kerr, proved to be an ideal replacement. She plays Anna, the widowed English governess, who is engaged by King Mongkut of Siam (Brynner) to educate his many children. In spite of their fundamental differences and principles, they fall in love, but are parted by the King's death. The film's other love story is that between one of the King's daughter's, Tuptim (Rita Moreno) and Lun Tha (Carlos Rivas), but that romance, too, is destined to end unhappily. Other parts were taken by Martin Balsam, Rex Thompson, Terry Saunders, Alan Mowbray, Patrick Adiarte, Yuriko, Michiko, Geoffrey Toone, and Charles Irwin. The highly emotional story was complemented by Richard Rodgers and Oscar Hammerstein II's magnificent score, which included 'I Whistle A Happy Tune' (Kerr), 'March Of The Siamese Children' (instrumental), 'Hello, Young Lovers' (Kerr), 'A Puzzlement' (Brynner), 'Getting To Know You' (Kerr with the children), 'We Kiss In A Shadow' (Moreno-Rivas), 'Something Wonderful' (Saunders), 'The Small House Of Uncle Thomas' (ballet) and 'Song Of The King' (Brynner). Perhaps the film's most memorable moment comes when Anna tries to teach the King how to dance, and they - awkwardly at first - and then exuberantly, whirl around the floor to the sublime 'Shall We Dance?'. Deborah Kerr's singing voice was dubbed by Marni Nixon. Ernest Lehman's screenplay was based on Hammerstein's original libretto and Margaret Landon's novel *Anna And The King Of Siam*. Jerome Robbins was the choreographer and the film, which was directed by Walter Land, was superbly photographed by Leon Shamroy in DeLuxe Color and CinemaScope. It won Oscars for best actor (Brynner), its sumptuous costumes (Irene Shariff), sound recording, art-set decoration and scoring of a musical picture (Alfred Newman and Ken Darby), and went on to gross well over $8 million in the USA, ranking high in the Top 10 musical films of the 50s.

KING BROTHERS

Brothers Michael (b. 25 April 1935, Barking, Essex, England; guitar), Tony (b. 31 January 1937, Barking, Essex, England; bass and bass guitar) and Denis King (b. 25 July 1939, Hornchurch, Essex, England; piano, guitar) were one of Britain's top groups in the 50s. The trio, fronted by Denis, made their television debut in 1953 on *Shop Window* and were often seen on mid-50s children's programmes. In 1954, they appeared at London's famous Astor and Embassy clubs, played a season at the Windmill Theatre and performed at the Palladium in 1955. After recording unsuccessfully for World Record Club and Conquest, the old-styled young trio, who were mistakenly tagged 'Britain's Rock 'n' Roll Kids', joined Parlophone. In 1957, they charted with cover versions of 'A White Sport Coat', 'In The Middle Of An Island' and even the Everly Brothers' 'Wake Up Little Susie' and were voted Britain's Top Vocal Group by *New Musical Express* readers. They had four more Top 40 hits in 1960-61, again with Norman Newell-produced cover versions of songs popular in the USA. The biggest of these was 'Standing On The Corner', from the musical *The Most Happy Fella*, which reached number 4 in 1960. Their final chart hit came a year later with '76 Trombones'. In those days, when UK vocal groups were rare, these successes helped them to regain the *NME* Vocal Group award in 1960 and collect *Melody Maker*'s similar award a year later. When they decided to record their own compositions, the hits stopped for the trio, who disliked being associated with rock 'n' roll. They were the last of the old-school vocal groups to be successful in the UK, and were

perhaps fortunate to be on the scene when Britain badly needed a vocal group to call its own. They recorded for Pye in 1963, Oriole in 1964 and CBS and Page One in 1966. Denis King has since become one of the best-known television music writers in the UK, composing the themes for such successful television series as *Bouquet Of Barbed Wire*, *The Fenn St. Gang*, *Within These Walls* and *Black Beauty*, among many others.
● ALBUMS: with Geoff Love *Three Kings And An Ace* (Decca 1959)★★★, *Kings Of Song* (1962)★★★.

KING CREOLE

This 1958 film is, for many, the best of Elvis Presley's Hollywood career. Based on the Harold Robbins novel *A Stone For Danny Fisher*, it afforded him a first-rate plot - that of a singer performing in a New Orleans club owned by mobsters - providing Presley with a dramatic role equal to the memorable soundtrack. 'Trouble', 'Crawfish' and the title track itself rank among the finest tracks he recorded and the content ranged from compulsive rock 'n' roll numbers to melodic ballads. Presley's singing is self-assured yet unmannered and only his induction into the US Army thwarted the direction both his acting and music were taking.

KING, SID

b. Sidney Erwin, 1936, Denton, Texas, USA. King was one of the foremost rockabilly singers of the 50s. As a teenager he formed the Western Melodymakers, which became Sid King And The Five Strings when he signed to Starday in 1954. Among the group's earliest recordings was 'Who Put The Turtle In Myrtle's Girdle', but after joining Columbia, King concentrated on more hard-rocking material. Recording in Dallas, he released a version of Roy Orbison's 'Ooby Dooby' in 1955 but though King's record was issued first, Orbison himself had the hit. He also recorded 'Sag, Drag And Fall' as well as versions of R&B hits including 'Drinkin' Wine Spoo-De-O-Dee'.
● COMPILATIONS: *Gonna Shake This Shack Tonight* (Bear Family 1984)★★★, *Rockin' On The Radio* (Rollercoaster 1984)★★, *Let's Get Loose* (Rockhouse 1987)★★★.

KING, TEDDI

b. Theodora King, 18 September 1929, Boston, Massachusetts, USA, d. 18 November 1977. Teddi King was a jazz-pop singer who enjoyed some crossover success on the 50s pop charts. Her singing career began upon graduation from high school. After working with the bands of Jack Edwards and George Graham she joined Nat Pierce's band in 1951, with which she made her recording debut. She also recorded with George Shearing during this period before going solo in 1953. After setting out on her own, King was signed to RCA Records, who had her recording pop songs, much to the artist's own dismay. Nevertheless, 'Mr. Wonderful', a 1956 single, reached the US Top 20, and two subsequent singles also charted. She then returned to pure jazz singing. Albums she recorded during the 50s for RCA, Storyville and Coral Records all became collectors' items in later years.
● ALBUMS: *'Round Midnight* (1954)★★★★, *Storyville Presents* (1954)★★★, *Now In Vogue* (1956)★★★, *Bidin' My Time* (1956)★★★, *To You From Teddi King* (1957)★★★★, *A Girl And Her Songs* (1957)★★.

KINGSTON TRIO

An influential part of America's folk revival, the Kingston Trio was formed in San Francisco in 1957 and was popular in the late 50s. The group consisted of Bob Shane (b. 1 February 1934, Hilo, Hawaii), Nick Reynolds (b. 27 July 1933, Coronado, California, USA) and Dave Guard (b. 19 October 1934, San Francisco, California, USA, d. 22 March 1991). The Kingston Trio had limited singles successes and are most often remembered for 'Tom Dooley' which reached number 5 in the UK charts, and number 1 in the US chart in 1958. The song, written by Guard, was based on an old folk tune from the 1800s called 'Tom Dula'. *The Kingston Trio*, from which 'Tom Dooley' came, also reached number 1 in the USA. The group had a run of successful albums in 1959, with *From The Hungry i*, a live recording, reaching number 2, and *The Kingston Trio At Large* and *Here We Go Again* both achieving top placings. Further chart-toppers followed with *Sold Out* and *String Along*. Their fresh harmonies and boyish enthusiasm endeared the trio to an America suspicious of the genre's New Left sympathies, but in the process paved the way for a generation of more committed performers. Guard was replaced by John Stewart (b. 5 September 1939, San Diego, California, USA) in May 1961, having left to pursue a solo career and form the Whiskeyhill Singers. *Close-Up* was the first release featuring Stewart, who had previously been with the Cumberland Three, and it reached number 3 in the US charts. 'San Miguel', the follow-up to 'Tom Dooley', only just managed to reach the Top 30 in the UK the following year. 'The Reverend Mr Black' achieved a Top 10 placing in the US chart in 1963. The line-up with Stewart continued until 1967. Shane later re-formed the group, as the New Kingston Trio, with Roger Gamble and George Grove. The group continued to enjoy widespread popularity and their output, if stylistically moribund, was certainly prolific. However, the success of more exciting folk and folk-rock acts rendered them increasingly old-fashioned, and the Trio was disbanded in 1968. A group reunion was hosted on television, by Tom Smothers in 1981, when all six members were brought together for the first time. Stewart went on to a solo career, and continues to record and perform. In 1987 the Trio was on the road again, with Shane, Grove, and new member Bob Haworth.
● ALBUMS: *The Kingston Trio* (Capitol 1958)★★★, *From The Hungry i* (Capitol 1959)★★★, *The Kingston Trio At Large* (Capitol 1959)★★★★, *Here We Go Again!* (Capitol 1959)★★★★, *Sold Out* (Capitol 1960)★★★, *String Along* (Capitol 1960)★★★, *Stereo Concert* (Capitol 1960)★★★, *The Last Month Of The Year* (Capitol 1960)★★★, *Make Way!* (Capitol 1961)★★★, *Goin' Places* (Capitol 1961)★★★, *Close-Up* (Capitol 1961)★★★, *College Concert* (Capitol 1962)★★★, *Something Special* (Capitol 1962)★★★, *New Frontier* (Capitol 1962)★★★, *The Kingston Trio No. 16* (Capitol 1963)★★, *Sunny Side!* (Capitol 1963)★★, *Sing A Song With The Kingston Trio* (Capitol 1963)★★, *Time To Think* (Capitol 1963)★★★, *Back In Town* (Capitol 1964)★★★, *Nick-Bob-John* (Decca 1965)★★, *Stay Awhile* (Decca 1965)★★, *Somethin' Else* (Decca 1965)★★, *Children Of The Morning* (Decca 1966)★★, *Once Upon A Time* 1966 live recording (Tetragrammaton 1969)★★, *American Gold* (Longines 1973)★★★★, *The World Needs A Melody* (1973)★★★, *Aspen Gold* (1979)★★★, *Best Of The Best* (Proarté 1986)★★.
● COMPILATIONS: *Encores* (Capitol 1961)★★★★, *The Best*

Of The Kingston Trio (Capitol 1962)★★★, *The Folk Era* 3-LP box set (Capitol 1964)★★★, *The Best Of The Kingston Trio Vol. 2* (Capitol 1965)★★★★, *The Best Of The Kingston Trio Vol. 3* (Capitol 1966)★★★, *The Kingston Trio* (1972)★★★, *Where Have All The Flowers Gone* (1972)★★★★, *The Historic Recordings Of The Kingston Trio* (1975)★★★★, *The Very Best Of The Kingston Trio* (Capitol 1987)★★★★, *Capitol Collectors Series* (Capitol 1991)★★★, *Greatest Hits* (Curb 1991)★★★, *The EP Collection* (See For Miles 1997)★★★★.
● FURTHER READING: *The Kingston Trio On Record*, Kingston Korner.

KISMET (STAGE MUSICAL)

This was by no means the first time George Forrest and Robert Wright had raided the world of classical music in an effort to devise a hit Broadway musical. They had 'borrowed' elements of Grieg for their highly successful *Song Of Norway* (1944), and for *Kismet* they turned to the work of Alexander Borodin. Forrest and Wright adapted the music and wrote the lyrics, and the book was by Charles Lederer and Luther Davis. When *Kismet* opened at the Ziegfeld Theatre in New York on 3 December 1953, it was met with a measure of indifference from the critics. However, by a fortuitous quirk of fate, there was a newspaper strike at the time and before the reviews were printed, the show had already become a success. Audiences liked this lavish production, and *Kismet*, with its Arabian Nights setting, ran for 583 performances. Several of the songs became popular, including 'Stranger In Paradise', 'Baubles, Bangles And Beads' and 'And This Is My Beloved', but there were other attractive numbers too, such as 'Not Since Ninevah', 'Rhymes Have I', 'Fate', 'Gesticulate', 'The Olive Tree', 'He's In Love', 'Sands Of Time' and 'Night Of My Nights'. Original cast members included Alfred Drake, Richard Kiley and Doretta Morrow. The show won Tony Awards for best musical, actor (Drake) and musical conductor (Louis Adrian). Drake and Morrow recreated their roles for the 1955 London production which ran for 648 performances. In the same year, a film version was released starring Howard Keel, Ann Blyth, Dolores Gray and Vic Damone. A 1978 version of the show, retitled *Timbuktu*, featured an all-black cast.

KISMET (FILM MUSICAL)

This opulent but rather unsatisfying adaptation of the hit Broadway musical reached the screen in 1955, courtesy of Arthur Freed's renowned MGM production unit. Although the show's librettists, Charles Lederer and Luther Davis, were entrusted with the screenplay, much of the magic in this Arabian Nights saga was somehow lost in the transfer. For some strange reason, Alfred Drake, who had enjoyed such a triumph in the stage production, was replaced by Howard Keel. He plays the public poet-turned-beggar Hajj, who lives on the streets of old Baghdad, and embarks on a hectic day-long adventure during which his daughter (Ann Blyth) is married to the young Caliph (Vic Damone), while he elopes with the lovely Lalume (Dolores Gray) after getting rid of her husband, the evil Wazir (Sebastian Cabot). Robert Wright and George Forrest's majestic score was based on themes by Alexander Borodin, and there were several memorable songs in the score, including 'Baubles, Bangles, And Beads', 'The Olive Tree', 'Stranger In Paradise', 'And

This Is My Beloved', 'Not Since Ninevah', 'Fate', 'Bored', 'Sands Of Time', 'Night Of My Nights', 'Rhymes Have I' and 'Gesticulate'. While perhaps regretting the absence of Drake (he only ever made one film), there is no doubt that Keel was in fine voice and he made an adequate substitute. Also taking part were Jay C. Flippen, Monty Woolley, Jack Elam, Ted De Corsia and Aaron Spelling. Jack Cole was the choreographer, and the film was directed by Vincente Minnelli. Whatever its faults, the film did at least look beautiful, owing in no small part to the Eastman Color and Cinemascope photography of Joseph Ruttenberg. The source of *Kismet* - the 1911 play by Edward Knoblock - has also been adapted into three other, non-musical films, in 1920, 1930 and 1944.

KISS ME KATE

This film had most of the elements of a great screen musical - an outstanding score, a witty screenplay, and a fine cast. The original Broadway show from which it was adapted is generally considered to be Cole Porter's masterpiece, and this 1953 version only served to emphasize and reaffirm that view. The story of thespians Fred Graham (Howard Keel) and his ex-wife, Lilli Vanessi (Kathryn Grayson), who allow their onstage conflict in an out-of-town production of *The Taming Of The Shrew* to spill over into their own tempestuous private lives, was both hilarious and musically thrilling. The dance sequences, which were choreographed by Hermes Pan and his assistant Bob Fosse, were stunning, involving high-class hoofers such as Ann Miller, Bobby Van, Tommy Rall and Carol Haney. Most observers cite Miller's scintillating 'Too Darn Hot' as the film's high spot, but all the songs were performed memorably, including 'I Hate Men' (Grayson), 'So In Love', 'Wunderbar' and 'Kiss Me Kate' (Grayson-Keel), 'I've Come To Wive It Wealthily In Padua', 'Were Thine That Special Face' and 'Where Is The Life That Late I Led?' (Keel), 'Always True To You In My Fashion' and 'Why Can't You Behave?' (Miller-Rall), 'We Open In Venice' (Keel-Grayson-Miller-Rall), and 'From This Moment On' (Miller-Rall-Haney-Van-Fosse-Jeannie Coyne). One other item, which would have stopped the show every night if it had been performed in a similar fashion on stage, was 'Brush Up Your Shakespeare', in which James Whitmore and Keenan Wynn, as a couple of affable debt-collecting gangsters, mangle the Bard, courtesy of Porter, in lines such as 'If your blonde won't respond when you flatter 'er/Tell her what Tony told Cleopaterer'. George Sidney directed, and the film was photographed in Ansco Color. Dorothy Kingsley's screenplay was based on Bella and Sam Spewack's original libretto. Some sequences appear slightly puzzling and unnerving - even unnatural - until one realizes that certain effects, such as characters throwing items towards the camera, were inserted to take advantage of the 3-D process in which the film was originally shot.

KITT, EARTHA

b. 26 January 1928, Columbia, South Carolina, USA. Raised in New York's Harlem, Kitt attended the High School for Performing Arts before joining Katharine Dunham's famed dancing troupe. At the end of a European tour Kitt decided to stay behind, taking up residence in Paris. Having added singing to her repertoire, she was a success and on her return to New York appeared at several leading nightclubs. She appeared on Broadway in *New Faces Of 1952* introducing

'Monotonous', and was later seen more widely in the film version of the show. Her other Broadway shows around this time included *Mrs. Patterson* (1954) and *Shinbone Alley* (1957). She continued to work in cabaret, theatre and television, singing in her uniquely accented manner and slinkily draping herself across any available object, animate or otherwise. She made a few more films over the years, playing a leading role in *St Louis Blues* (1958), with Nat 'King' Cole, and in an all-black version of *Anna Lucasta* (1959), opposite Sammy Davis Jnr. Although her highly mannered presentation of songs is best seen rather than merely heard, Kitt has made some songs virtually her own property, among them 'I Want To Be Evil', 'An Englishman Needs Time', 'Santa Baby' and 'I'm Just An Old-Fashioned Girl', a claim which is patently untrue. Her other record successes over the years have included 'Uska Dara - A Turkish Tale', 'C'est Si Bon', 'Somebody Bad Stole De Wedding Bell', 'Lovin' Spree', 'Under The Bridges Of Paris', 'Where Is My Man', 'I Love Men' and 'This Is My Life'. In 1978 Kitt appeared on Broadway with Gilbert Wright and Melba Moore in an all-black version of *Kismet* entitled *Timbuktu*. Her career has continued along similar lines on both sides of the Atlantic throughout the 80s and into the 90s, although she was courted by a much younger audience (witness her collaboration on 'Cha Cha Heels' with Bronski Beat in 1989) who were suitably impressed by her irreverent coolness. In 1988 Kitt played the role of Carlotta Campion in the London production of *Follies* and sang Stephen Sondheim's legendary anthem to survival, 'I'm Still Here', which, appropriately, became the title of her second volume of autobiography. In the early 90s she performed her one-woman show in London and New York and appeared as a witch in the comedy/horror movie *Ernest Scared Stupid*. She also toured Britain with the Ink Spots in the revue *A Night At The Cotton Club*. In 1993 Kitt appeared in cabaret at several international venues, including London's Café Royal, and in the following year she played the role of Molly Bloom, the heroine of James Joyce's novel *Ulysses*, in 'an erotic monologue punctuated with songs by the French crooner, Charles Aznavour', which proved to be a cult hit at the Edinburgh Festival.

● ALBUMS: *New Faces Of 1952* original cast (RCA Victor 1952)★★★, *Songs* 10-inch album (RCA Victor 1953)★★★, *That Bad Eartha* 10-inch album (RCA Victor 1953)★★★★, *Down To Eartha* (RCA Victor 1955)★★★, *Thursday's Child* (RCA Victor 1956)★★★, *St. Louis Blues* (RCA Victor 1958)★★★, *The Fabulous Eartha Kitt* (Kapp 1959)★★★, *Eartha Kitt Revisited* (Kapp 1960)★★★, *Bad But Beautiful* (MGM 1962)★★★, *At The Plaza* (1965)★★★, *Eartha Kitt Sings In Spanish* (Decca 1965)★★★, *C'est Si Bon* (IMS 1983)★★★, *I Love Men* (Record Shack 1984)★★★, *Love For Sale* (Capitol 1984)★★, *The Romantic Eartha Kitt* (Pathe Marconi 1984)★★, *St. Louis Blues* (RCA Germany 1985)★★★, *That Bad Eartha* (RCA Germany 1985)★★★, *Eartha Kitt In Person At The Plaza* (GNP 1988)★★★★, *I'm A Funny Dame* (Official 1988)★★★, *My Way* (Caravan 1988)★★★, *I'm Still Here* (Arista 1989)★★★, *Live In London* (Arista 1990)★★★★, *Thinking Jazz* (1992)★★★, *Back In Business* (1994)★★★.

● COMPILATIONS: *At Her Very Best* (RCA 1982)★★★, *Songs* (RCA 1983)★★★, *Diamond Series: Eartha Kitt* (Diamond 1988)★★★, *Best Of Eartha Kitt* (MCA 1990)★★★.

● FURTHER READING: *Thursday's Child*, Eartha Kitt. *Alone With Me: A New Biography*, Eartha Kitt. *I'm Still Here*, Eartha Kitt.

KITTRELL, CHRISTINE

b. 11 August 1929, Nashville, Tennessee, USA. Kittrell made a number of attractive and moderately successful records for local labels during the 50s. A choir member as a child, her voice lacked the distinctive nuance that might have brought her more durable success. Her first record, 'Old Man You're Slipping' (Tennessee 117), was backed by tenor saxophonist Louis Brooks and his band, with whom she had made her professional debut six years earlier in 1945. Fats Domino sidemen Buddy Hagans and Wendell Duconge played on her first and biggest hit, 'Sittin' Here Drinking' (Tennessee 128), which brought her a six-week engagement at the Pelican Club in New Orleans. Kittrell had toured with the Joe Turner band in 1951 but she preferred to work around Nashville, at clubs such as the New Era and the Elks. Engaged as singer with Paul 'Hucklebuck' Williams' band in December 1952, *Billboard* noted that the 'five-foot-six chirp' was the 'blues find of the decade'. She made her west coast debut in 1954 with Earl Bostic and later Johnny Otis. Several releases on the Republic label at this time led to only regional success. One session, which included 'Lord Have Mercy' (Republic 7096), is reputed to feature Little Richard on piano. In August 1954, *Billboard* announced her departure from the R&B field to sing with the Simmons Akers spiritual singers. In the early 60s she recorded for Vee Jay Records but her original version of 'I'm A Woman' was covered by Peggy Lee. She re-recorded an old Republic song, 'Call His Name' (Federal 12540), in 1965, and spent the next few years touring army bases in south-east Asia entertaining US troops. Subsequently, she retired to her Ohio home.

● COMPILATIONS: *Nashville R&B, Vol 2* (1986)★★★.

KNOX, BUDDY

b. Buddy Wayne Knox, 14 April 1933, Happy, Texas, USA. Knox was one of the first 'pop-abilly' hit-makers in the 50s. With bassist Jimmy Bowen, he formed the country band the Rhythm Orchids in 1956, adding Don Lanier (guitar) and Dave Alldred (drums). The following year Knox sang lead vocals on 'Party Doll', recorded at Norman Petty's Oklahoma studio. First issued locally on the Triple-D label, it became the first release on Roulette, formed by New York nightclub owner Maurice Levy. 'Party Doll' went to number 1 in the USA. At the same session Bowen recorded another hit, 'I'm Stickin' With You'. With his light voice skimming over the insistent rhythms, Knox was the first in a line of Texan rockers that included Buddy Holly and Roy Orbison. Both 'Rock Your Little Baby To Sleep' and the gimmicky 'Hula Love' were Top 20 hits later in 1957, when he also appeared in the film *Disc Jockey Jamboree*. Although he toured frequently with Alan Freed's package shows, 'Somebody Touched Me' (1958) was his only later hit and in 1960, Knox and Bowen moved to Los Angeles. There, Knox turned to 'teenbeat' material such as 'Lovey Dovey', 'Ling Ting Tong' and 'She's Gone' (a minor UK hit in 1962) with producer Snuff Garrett. During the mid-60s he returned to country music, recording in Nashville for Reprise and had a hit with 'Gypsy Man', composed by ex-Crickets' Sonny Curtis. This led to film appearances in *Travellin' Light* (with Waylon

Jennings) and *Sweet Country Music* (with Boots Randolph and Johnny Paycheck). Knox was now based in Canada, where he set up his own Sunnyhill label. He also visited Europe with rockabilly revival shows during the 70s and early 80s. Jimmy Bowen became one of Nashville's most powerful A&R men, working for Dot, MCA and latterly Capitol.

● ALBUMS: *Buddy Knox* (Roulette 1958)★★★, with Jim Bowen *Buddy Knox And Jimmy Bowen* (Roulette 1959)★★★, *Buddy Knox In Nashville* (1967)★★★, *Gypsy Man* (United Artists 1969)★★★, *Four Rock Legends* (1978)★★, *Sweet Country Music* (Rockstar 1981)★★, *Texas Rockabilly Man* (Rockstar 1987)★★, *Travellin' Light* (Rundell 1988)★★.
● COMPILATIONS: *Buddy Knox's Golden Hits* (Liberty 1962)★★★, *Rock Reflections* (Sunset 1971)★★★, *Party Doll* (Pye 1978)★★★, *Greatest Hits* (Rockhouse 1985)★★★, *Liberty Takes* (Charly 1986)★★★, *Party Doll And Other Hits* (Capitol 1988)★★★, *The Best Of Buddy Knox* (Rhino 1990)★★★★, with Jim Bowen *The Complete Roulette Recordings* (Sequel 1996)★★★★.
● FILMS: *Jamboree* aka *Disc Jockey Jamboree* (1957).

LAINE, FRANKIE

b. Frank Paul LoVecchio, 30 March 1913, Chicago, Illinois, USA. Laine had been a chorister at the Immaculate Conception Church in his city's Sicilian quarter before entering showbusiness proper on leaving school. For nearly a decade he travelled as a singing waiter, dancing instructor (with a victory in a 1932 dance marathon as his principal qualification) and other lowly jobs, but it was as a member of a New Jersey nightclub quartet that he was given his first big break - replacing Perry Como in Freddie Carlone's touring band in 1937. This was a springboard to a post as house vocalist with a New York radio station until migration to Los Angeles, where he was 'discovered' entertaining in a Hollywood spa by Hoagy Carmichael. The songwriter persuaded him to adopt an Anglicized *nom de theatre*, and funded the 1947 session that resulted in 'That's My Desire', Laine's first smash. This was followed by 'Shine' (written in 1924) and a revival again in Louis Armstrong's 'When You're Smiling'. This was the title song to a 1950 movie starring Laine, the Mills Brothers, Kay Starr and other contributors of musical interludes to its 'backstage' plot. His later career on celluloid focused largely on his disembodied voice carrying main themes of cowboy movies such as *Man With A Star*, the

celebrated *High Noon*, *Gunfight At The OK Corral* and the *Rawhide* television series. Each enhanced the dramatic, heavily masculine style favoured by Laine's producer, Mitch Miller, who also spiced the artist's output with generous pinches of C&W. This was best exemplified in the extraordinary 1949 hit 'Mule Train', one of the most dramatic and impassioned recordings of its era. Other early successes included 'Jezebel', 'Jalousie' and 'Rose Rose, I Love You', an adaptation by Wilfred Thomas of Hue Lin's Chinese melody 'Mei Kuei'.

Laine proved a formidable international star, particularly in the UK, where his long chart run began in 1952 with 'High Noon'. The following year he made chart history when his version of 'I Believe' topped the charts for a staggering 18 weeks, a record that has never been eclipsed since, despite a valiant run of 16 weeks by Bryan Adams 28 years later. Laine enjoyed two further UK chart-toppers in 1953 with 'Hey Joe' and 'Answer Me'. Incredibly, he was number 1 for 27 weeks that year, another feat of chart domination that it is difficult to envisage ever being equalled. No less than 22 UK Top 20 hits during the 50s emphasized Laine's popularity, including such memorable songs as 'Blowing Wild', 'Granada', 'The Kid's Last Fight', 'My Friend', 'Rain Rain Rain', 'Cool Water', 'Hawkeye', 'Sixteen Tons', 'A Woman In Love' and 'Rawhide'. Laine was also a consummate duettist and enjoyed additional hits with Johnnie Ray, Doris Day and Jimmy Boyd. After his hit-parade farewell with 1961's 'Gunslinger', he pursued a full-time career commuting around the world as a highly paid cabaret performer, with a repertoire built around selections from hit compilations, one of which (*The Very Best Of Frankie Laine*) climbed into international charts as late as 1977. New material tended to be of a sacred nature - though in the more familiar 'clippetty-clop' character was 'Blazing Saddles', featured in Mel Brooks' (the lyricist) 1974 spoof-western of the same name. By the mid-80s, he was in virtual semi-retirement in an opulent ocean-front dwelling in San Diego, California, with his wife, former actress Nanette Gray. With sales in excess of 100 million copies, Laine was one of the most important solo singers of the immediate pre-rock 'n' roll period.

● ALBUMS: *Favorites* (Mercury 1949)★★★, *Songs From The Heart* (Mercury 1949)★★, *Frankie Laine* (Mercury 1950)★★★, *Mr Rhythm Sings* (Mercury 1951)★★★, *Christmas Favorites* (Mercury 1951)★★, *Listen To Laine* (Mercury 1952)★★★, *One For My Baby* (Columbia 1952)★★★★, with Jo Stafford *Musical Portrait Of New Orleans* (Columbia 1954)★★, *Mr Rhythm* (Columbia 1954)★★★, *Songs By Frankie Laine* (Mercury 1955)★★★★, *That's My Desire* (Mercury 1955)★★★★, *Lovers Laine* (Columbia 1955)★★★, *Frankie Laine Sings For Us* (Mercury 1955)★★★, *Concert Date* (Mercury 1955)★★★, *With All My Heart* (Mercury 1955)★★★, *Command Performance* (Columbia 1956)★★★, *Jazz Spectacular* (Columbia 1956)★★, *Rockin'* (Columbia 1957)★★, *Foreign Affair* (Columbia 1958)★★★, *Torchin'* (Columbia 1960)★★★, *Reunion In Rhythm* (Columbia 1961)★★★, *You Are My Love* (Columbia 1961)★★★, *Frankie Laine, Balladeer* (Columbia 1961)★★★, *Hell Bent For Leather!* (Columbia 1961)★★★, *Deuces Wild* (Columbia 1962)★★★, *Call Of The Wild* (1962)★★★, *Wanderlust* (1963)★★, *I'll Take Care Of Your Cares* (ABC 1967)★★★, *I Wanted Someone To Love* (ABC 1967)★★★, *To Each His Own* (ABC 1968)★★, *You Gave Me*

A Mountain (ABC 1969)★★★, with Erich Kunzel And The Cincinnati Pops Orchestra *Round Up* (1987)★★★.
● COMPILATIONS: *Greatest Hits* (Columbia 1959)★★★★, *Golden Hits* (Mercury 1960)★★★★, *Golden Memories* (Polydor 1974)★★★, *The Very Best Of Frankie Laine* (Warwick 1977)★★★★, *American Legend* (Columbia 1978)★★★, *Songbook* (World Records 1981)★★★★, *All Of Me* (Bulldog 1982)★★★, *Golden Greats* (Polydor 1983)★★★, *The Golden Years* (Phillips 1984)★★★, *His Greatest Hits* (Warwick 1986)★★★, *The Uncollected* (Hindsight 1986)★★★, *Rawhide* (Castle 1986)★★★, *20 Of His Best* (The Collection 1987)★★★, *Sixteen Evergreens* (Joker 1988)★★★, *Country Store: Frankie Laine* (Country Store 1988)★★★, *Portrait Of A Song Stylist* (Masterpiece 1989)★★★, *21 Greatest Hits* (Westmoor 1989)★★★, *Memories In Gold* (Prestige 1990)★★★, *All Time Hits* (MFP 1991)★★★, with Jo Stafford *Goin' Like Wildfire* (Bear Family 1992)★★★, *On The Trail Again* (1993)★★★.
● FURTHER READING: *That Lucky Old Son*, Frankie Laine and Joseph F. Laredo.

LAMBERT, HENDRICKS AND ROSS

In the late 50s a group of singers began informal 'vocalese' jam sessions at the New York apartment of Dave Lambert (b. 19 June 1917, Boston, Massachusetts, USA, d. 3 October 1966). At these sessions singers would improvise vocal lines in much the same manner as jazz instrumentalists. Ten years previously, Lambert had worked as arranger and singer in Gene Krupa's band, recording 'What's This?', an early example of a bop vocal. In 1955, Lambert teamed up with Jon Hendricks (b. 16 September 1921, Newark, Ohio, USA) to record a vocalized version of 'Four Brothers'. In 1958, Lambert and Hendricks added to their duo the highly distinctive singer Annie Ross (b. Annabelle Short Lynch, 25 July 1930, Mitcham, Surrey, England) to record the album *Sing A Song Of Basie*. The concept of the Lambert, Hendricks And Ross recordings was simple, although highly complex in execution. The singers performed wordless vocal lines, matching the brass and reed section parts of the Count Basie band's popular recordings. With this formula they enjoyed great success in the late 50s and early 60s. In 1962, Ross left the trio and was replaced by Yolande Bavan (b. 1 June 1940, Colombo, Ceylon). Two years later Lambert also left and soon thereafter the trio concept was abandoned. Lambert worked briefly as a studio arranger before his death in 1966.
● ALBUMS: *Sing A Song Of Basie* (ABC 1957)★★★★, *Sing Along With Basie* (Roulette 1958)★★★★, *The Swingers* (Affinity 1959)★★★, *The Hottest Group In Jazz* (Columbia 1959)★★★★, *Lambert, Hendricks And Ross Sing Ellington* (Columbia 1960)★★★★, *High Flying* (Columbia 1960)★★★★. As Lambert, Hendricks And Bavan *Lambert, Hendricks And Bavan: Having A Ball At The Village Gate* (RCA 1963)★★★, *Live At Basin Street East* (RCA Victor 1963)★★★, *At Newport* (RCA Victor 1963)★★★, *At The Village Gate* (RCA Victor 1964)★★★.
● COMPILATIONS: *Twisted: The Best Of Lambert , Hendricks And Ross* (Rhino 1992)★★★★.

LAMPLIGHTERS

This vocal R&B outfit was formed in 1952 at Jordan High School in Los Angeles, California, USA, but was always too erratic and plagued with personal problems to be destined for success in the long haul. Leon Hughes, Matthew Nelson and Willie Ray Rockwell comprised the initial trio, who entered a talent show at Johnny Otis's Barrell House but came second to singer Thurston Harris (b. 11 July 1931, Indianapolis, Indiana, USA, d. 1990, California, USA). They set about convincing him to join forces with them, and he eventually agreed. Al Frazier, formerly vocalist with the Mellomoods, helped to choreograph their rough stage act. Their performances soon evolved into some of the most exciting and wild events on the west coast R&B circuit, with acrobatics and audience participation that predated the rock 'n' roll boom. Frazier, too, was persuaded to join the group. After losing Leon Hughes, the unit secured a contract at Federal Records, having been once more reduced to a quartet. Their debut single, a powerful ballad titled 'Part Of Me', failed to garner its just reward, though it did introduce them as the Lamplighters (Federal boss Ralph Bass had chosen the name in the absence of any band decision). A second single emerged, 'Bee Bop Wino', but its title ironically mirrored the slide of several members of the band into alcoholism. Indeed, Rockwell later died after drunkenly crashing his car into a telephone pole. In 1954, following the release of 'Sad Life', 'Smootchie', 'I Used To Cry Mercy, Mercy' and 'Salty Dog', the group embarked on a major tour, with Eddie Jones and Harold Lewis deputizing for Rockwell and Nelson. Harris quit halfway through the tour because of a disagreement over money, and that appeared to be the end of the story. However, back in Los Angeles, Frazier put together a new version of the band with Carl White, Sonny Harris and a returning Matthew Nelson. The new formation christened itself the Tenderfoots. Four singles, beginning with 'Kissing Bug' in March 1955, failed to bring any success, and they returned to the Lamplighters name after renewing their friendship with Thurston Harris. Three final singles emerged on Federal between 1955 and 1956. However, Thurston Harris's old behaviour problems resurfaced and he was soon replaced by Turner Wilson III. After this, the group changed names again to the Sharps, while Thurston Harris enjoyed one major solo single, 'Little Bitty Pretty One' (which featured the Sharps as uncredited backing band).

LANZA, MARIO

b. Alfredo Arnold Cocozza, 31 January 1921, Philadelphia, Pennsylvania, USA, d. 7 October 1959. An enormously popular star in film musicals and on records during the 50s, with a magnificent operatic tenor voice. The son of Italian immigrants, he took his stage name from the masculine version of his mother's maiden name, Maria Lanza. From the age of 15, Lanza studied singing with several teachers, and was introduced into society circles with the object of gaining a patron. He was signed to Columbia Artistes Management as a concert singer, but their plans to send him on an introductory tour were quashed when Lanza was drafted into the US Army in 1943. He appeared in shows, billed as 'the Service Caruso', and sang in the chorus of the celebratory Forces show *Winged Victory*. After release, he lived in New York, gave concerts and worked on radio shows. One of the audition recordings that he made for RCA found its way to the MGM Film Studios, and when he deputized for another tenor at the Hollywood Bowl, MGM chief Louis B. Mayer was in the audience. Soon afterwards Lanza was signed to a seven-year MGM contract by Hungarian producer Joe

Pasternak, who was quoted as saying: 'It was the most beautiful voice I had ever heard - but his bushy hair made him look like a caveman!' Lanza's contract allowed him to continue with his concert career, and in April 1948 he made his first, and last, appearance on the professional operatic stage, in two performances of *Madame Butterfly*, with the New Orleans Opera. In Lanza's first film in 1949 for MGM, *That Midnight Kiss*, he co-starred with Kathryn Grayson and pianist Jose Iturbi; the musical contained a mixture of popular standards as diverse as 'They Didn't Believe Me' and 'Down Among The Sheltering Palms', and classical pieces, including 'Celeste Aida' (from Verdi's *Aida*), which gave Lanza one of his first record hits. The film was a big box-office success, and was followed by *The Toast Of New Orleans*, also with Grayson, which, along with the operatic excerpts, contained some songs by Sammy Cahn and Nicholas Brodszky, including one of Lanza's all-time smash hits, the million-seller, 'Be My Love'. Lanza starred in the biopic *The Great Caruso* (1951), performing several arias associated with his idol. He also introduced 'The Loveliest Night Of The Year', a song adapted by Irving Aaronson from 'Over the Waves', by Juventino Rosas, with a new lyric by Paul Francis Webster; it gave Lanza his second million-selling record.

By this point, he was one of Hollywood's hottest properties, and as his career blossomed, so did his waistline. There were rumours of breakfasts consisting of four steaks and six eggs, washed down with a gallon of milk, which caused his weight to soar to 20 stone. He claimed that 'nervousness' made him eat. In 1951, Lanza embarked on a country-wide tour of 22 cities, and also appeared on his own CBS radio series. Back in Hollywood, he initially rejected MGM's next project, *Because You're Mine*, because of its 'singer-becomes-a-GI' storyline. After some difficulties, the film was eventually completed, and was chosen for the 1952 Royal Film Premiere in the UK. The title song, by Cahn and Brodszky, was nominated for an Academy Award in 1952, and became Lanza's third, and last, million-selling single. He had already recorded the songs for his next MGM project, *The Student Prince*, when he walked out on the studio following a disagreement with the director. He avoided damaging breach of contract lawsuits by allowing MGM to retain the rights to his recordings for the film. British actor Edmund Purdom took his place, miming to Lanza's singing voice. Ironically, Lanza's vocal performances for the film were considered to be among his best, and *Songs From The Student Prince And Other Great Musical Comedies* (containing 'The Drinking Song'), was number 1 in the USA for several weeks. Beset by problems with alcohol, food, tranquillizers and the US tax authorities, Lanza became a virtual recluse, not performing for over a year, before appearing on CBS Television with Betty Grable and Harry James. He was criticized in the press for miming to his old recordings on the show, but proved the voice was still intact by resuming his recording career soon afterwards. In 1956, Lanza returned to filming, this time for Warner Brothers. *Serenade*, adapted from the novel by James M. Cain, in which Lanza co-starred with Joan Fontaine, was considered by the critics to be one of his best movies. Once again, the operatic excerpts were interspersed with some romantic songs by Cahn and Brodszky, including 'Serenade' and 'My Destiny'. In 1957, tired of all the crash diets, and disillusioned by life in the USA, Lanza moved to Italy, and settled in Rome. He made one film there, *The Seven Hills Of Rome* (1958). Apart from the sight of Lanza playing an American entertainer doing impersonations of Dean Martin, Frankie Laine and Louis Armstrong, the film is probably best remembered for the inclusion of the 1955 hit song 'Arrivederci, Roma', written by Renato Rascel (Ranucci) and Carl Sigman, impressively sung in the film by Lanza, and which has become the accompaniment to many a backward glance by tourists ever since. In 1958, Lanza visited the UK, making his first stage appearances for six years, in concert at London's Royal Albert Hall and on the Royal Variety Show. From there, he embarked on a European tour. While on the Continent, he made *For The First Time* (1959), which was the last time he was seen on film. He appeared relatively slim, and was still in excellent voice. In the autumn of 1959 he went into a Rome clinic; a week later, he died of a heart attack. Much later it was alleged that he was murdered by the Mafia because he refused to appear at a concert organized by mobster Lucky Luciano. The city of Philadelphia officially proclaimed 7 October as 'Mario Lanza Day', and subsequently established a museum that still preserves his memory in the 90s. Opinions of his voice, and its potential, vary. José Carreras is quoted as saying that he was 'turned on' to opera at the age of 16 by seeing Lanza in *The Great Caruso*, and he emphasized the singer's influence by presenting his *Homage To Mario Lanza* concert at London's Royal Albert Hall in March 1994. Arturo Toscannini allegedly described it as the greatest voice of the twentieth century. On the other hand, one critic, perhaps representing the majority, said: 'He just concentrated on the big "lollipops" of the opera repertoire, he had a poor musical memory, and would never have been an opera star.' Ironically, it was one of the world's leading contemporary opera singers, Placido Domingo, who narrated the 1981 television biography *Mario Lanza - The American Caruso*.

● ALBUMS: *The Great Caruso* (HMV 1953)★★★★, *Operatic Arias* (HMV 1954)★★★, *Songs Of Romance* (HMV 1955)★★★, *Serenade* (HMV 1956)★★★★, *Songs From The Student Prince* film soundtrack (RCA 1956)★★★★, *Lanza On Broadway* (HMV 1957)★★★★, *The Touch Of Your Hand* (HMV 1957)★★★, *In A Cavalcade Of Show Tunes* (RCA 1957)★★★, *Seven Hills Of Rome* film soundtrack (RCA 1958)★★★, *Songs From The Student Prince/The Great Caruso* (1958)★★★★, *Sings A Kiss And Other Love Songs* (RCA 1959)★★★, *For The First Time* film soundtrack (RCA 1959)★★★, *Lanza Sings Christmas Carols* (RCA 1959)★★★, *Mario Lanza Sings Caruso Favourites/The Great Caruso* (RCA 1960)★★★★, *You Do Something To Me* (RCA 1969)★★★.

● COMPILATIONS: *I'll Walk With God* (1962)★★, *His Greatest Hits, Volume 1* (RCA 1971)★★★★, *Art And Voice Of Mario Lanza* (RCA 1973)★★★, *Pure Gold* (RCA 1980)★★★, *His Greatest Hits From Operettas And Musicals, Volumes One, Two & Three* (RCA Classics 1981)★★★★, *The Legendary Mario Lanza* (K-Tel 1981)★★★★, *Collection* (RCA Red Seal 1982)★★★, *20 Golden Favourites* (RCA 1984)★★★★, *Magic Moments With Mario Lanza* (RCA 1985)★★★, *Forever* (RCA 1986)★★★, *A Portrait Of Mario Lanza* (Stylus 1987)★★★★, *Diamond Series: Mario Lanza* (Diamond Series 1988)★★★★, *Be My Love* (RCA 1991)★★★, *The Ultimate Collection* (1994)★★★★, *With A Song In My Heart: The Love: Collection* (Camden 1997)★★★★.

● FURTHER READING: *Mario Lanza*, Matt Bernard. *Mario*

Lanza, Michael Burrows. *Lanza - His Tragic Life*, R. Strait and T. Robinson. *Mario Lanza*, Derek Mannering.

LARKS

An R&B vocal group from Raleigh, North Carolina, USA. The members were Eugene Mumford (tenor, lead), Thurmon Ruth (baritone, lead), Alden Bunn (baritone, lead, guitar), Raymond Barnes (tenor), Hadie Rowe Jnr. (baritone) and David McNeil (bass). The group began as a gospel ensemble, the Jubilators, who were formed in 1950 by Ruth and Bunn after they had withdrawn from the Selah Jubilee Singers (a New York City gospel group that Ruth had formed and led since 1927). The Jubilators went to New York City and to obtain seed money, immediately recorded gospel with four different companies under four different names; the Selah Singers for Jubilee, Jubilators for Regal, Four Barons for Savoy and Southern Harmonaires for Apollo. The latter wanted the group to record some secular tracks and so the group became the Larks to record R&B. It was with the Larks' tracks that the group obtained lasting success and fame. They made their first impact with romantic ballads, using as lead the beautiful voice of Mumford, and initial hits in early 1951 were 'Hopefully Yours' (backed with the masterful 'When I Leave These Prison Walls') and 'My Reverie'. The blues side of the group, with Bunn as lead and on guitar, came to the forefront on their next tracks, when in the last half of 1951 they had hits with a Sonny Boy Williamson song, 'Eyesight To The Blind' (number 5 R&B), and 'Little Side Car' (number 10 R&B). These were the group's last hits, and in 1952 the Larks disbanded. Mumford joined the Golden Gate Quartet, and in 1954 formed a new Larks group, but the magic was gone and the records they made were poor. The new Larks disbanded in 1955, and Mumford joined Billy Ward And The Dominoes and sang lead on their 'Stardust' and 'Deep Purple' hits. Alden Bunn organized the Wheels ('My Heart's Desire') before later carving out a career as blues singer Tarhill Slim. He also made some successful duet recordings with Little Ann.
● COMPILATIONS: *My Reverie* (Relic 1988)★★★, *When I Leave These Prison Walls* (Relic 1988)★★★.

LAWRENCE, ELLIOT

b. Elliot Lawrence Broza, 14 February 1925, Philadelphia, Pennsylvania, USA. A precociously talented pianist, at the age of four Lawrence participated in his father's children's shows on the radio and in his teens he led an orchestra of children for a local broadcast. He continued to be active in music during his university days, and his early professional work was in dance bands and with radio orchestras, some of which he led himself. Lawrence wrote many arrangements for his own bands, accommodating contemporary shifts in jazz. He also used arrangements by other young men who were testing the boundaries of big band music, notably Gerry Mulligan, Al Cohn and Tiny Kahn. As times became harder for big bands, Lawrence eventually abandoned his full-time bandleading career, but occasionally re-formed the group for special engagements and record dates. On such sessions his choice of musicians reflected his determination to look ahead, and soloists included Cohn, Red Rodney, Zoot Sims and Urbie Green. Subsequently, Lawrence's career took him into television and theatrical work.
● ALBUMS: *One Night Stand With Elliot Lawrence*

(1947)★★, *Elevation* (1947)★★, *College Prom* 10-inch album (Decca 1950)★★, *Moonlight On The Campus* 10-inch album (Decca 1950)★★, *Elliot Lawrence Plays Tiny Kahn And Johnny Mandel Arrangements* (Fantasy 1956)★★★, *Dream* (Fantasy 1956)★★★, *Swinging At The Steel Pier* (Fantasy 1956)★★★, *The Four Brothers Together Again!* (Fantasy 1957)★★★, *Elliot Lawrence And His Orchestra* i (Fantasy 1957)★★★, *Elliot Lawrence And His Orchestra* ii (Fantasy 1957)★★, *Elliot Lawrence And His Orchestra* iii (Fantasy 1958)★★★, *Elliot Lawrence And His Orchestra* iv (Fantasy 1958)★★★, *Elliot Lawrence And His Orchestra* v (Fantasy 1958)★★★, *Elliot Lawrence And His Orchestra* vi (Fantasy 1959)★★, *Elliot Lawrence And His Orchestra* vii (Fantasy 1960)★★.

LAWRENCE, JACK

b. 7 April 1912, New York, USA. Although mainly a lyricist, as well as a singer and conductor, Lawrence wrote both words and music for some of his most popular songs. He studied at Long Island University, and sang on various radio stations, before having his first efforts published in the early 30s. One of these, 'Play, Fiddle, Play' (1932, written with Emery Deutsch and Arthur Altman), was made popular in the USA by the bands of George Olsen and Ted Lewis, and in the UK by Al Bowlly with the New Mayfair Dance Orchestra. During the remainder of the 30s, Lawrence's output resulted in record success for artists such as Glen Gray and the Casa Loma Orchestra and Glenn Miller ('Sunrise Serenade', 1938, with Frankie Carle), Ella Fitzgerald ('All Over Nothing At All', 1937), Ella Fitzgerald with the Mills Brothers ('Big Boy Blue', 1937), Andy Kirk And His Clouds Of Joy and Bing Crosby ('What's Your Story, Morning Glory?', 1938, with Paul Francis Webster-Mary Lou Williams), Horace Heidt and Crosby with Jimmy Dorsey ('What Will I Tell My Heart?' (1937, with Peter Tinturin-Irving Gordon), Heidt, the Andrews Sisters and Dick Barrie ('Tu-li-Tulip Time', 1938, with Maria Grever), Raymond Scott ('Huckleberry Duck', with Scott), and Guy Lombardo ('In An Eighteenth Century Drawing Room', 1939, with Scott). One of the songs for which Lawrence composed both words and music was the enduring ballad 'If I Didn't Care', which was a big hit in 1939 for the Ink Spots, and later revived by the Hilltoppers (1954), Connie Francis (1961), the Platters (1970), and David Cassidy (UK 1974). Lawrence was also solely responsible for 'It's Funny To Everyone But Me', and collaborated with Arthur Altman on 'All Or Nothing At All'. Both of those numbers were recorded by Frank Sinatra in 1939 when he was with the Harry James band, but they only entered the US Hit Parade in the early 40s after the singer began to attract a lot of attention during his stint with Tommy Dorsey.
Glenn Miller made the bestseller lists in 1940 with two Lawrence numbers, 'Vagabond Dreams' (with Hoagy Carmichael) and 'Handful Of Stars' (Ted Shapiro), while in the same year Larry Clinton had a hit with 'Johnson Rag' (Guy H. Hall-Henry Kleinkauf), and Kay Kyser and Bob Chester, did well with 'With The Wind And Rain In Your Hair' (Clara Edwards). In the following year Lawrence wrote 'Yes, My Darling Daughter', which was introduced in the revue *Crazy With The Heat* by Gracie Barrie. It subsequently became popular for Dinah Shore and Glenn Miller, and was revived by Eydie Gorme in 1962. Also in 1941, Lawrence adapted Tchaikovsky's 'Piano Concerto Number 1' for

'Concerto For Two', and wrote the English lyric for Toots Camarata and Isaac Albeniz's adaptation of Albeniz's 'Tango In D', which was entitled 'Moonlight Masquerade'. He also provided a lyric for the old Eric Coates composition '(By The) Sleepy Lagoon', which was then recorded by Harry James and Dinah Shore, and became the title number of a 1943 movie starring Judy Canova and Ruth Donnelly. During World War II, Lawrence served in the US Coastguard and the US Navy-US Maritime Service. He wrote the official song for the latter organization, 'Heave Ho, My Lads, Heave Ho', which subsequently appeared in the 1944 film *Moonlight And Cactus*. Lawrence also organized various service bands, welfare and morale units, and worked overseas for a time. After the war, he provided the English lyrics for European numbers such as 'Symphony' (1945, music: Alex Alstone), 'Beyond The Sea' (1947, adapted from Charles Trenet's 'La Mer', and a big hit in 1960 for Bobby Darin), 'Choo Choo Train' (1953, music: Marc Fontenoy), and 'The Poor People Of Paris' (1954, music: Marguerite Monnet). In 1946, with composer Walter Gross, Lawrence produced what is arguably his most enduring song, the lovely ballad 'Tenderly', which Rosemary Clooney adopted as her signature number. There were also many other popular items, such as 'Hand In Hand' (1947), 'Linda' (1947), 'Hold My Hand' (1950, with Richard Myers, sung in the film *Susan Slept Here* by Don Cornell, and nominated for an Academy Award), 'Delicado' (1952, Waldyr Azevado, a US number 1 for Percy Faith), and 'No One But You', written with Nicholas Brodszky for the 1954 Lana Turner movie *The Flame And The Flesh*, and given a memorable recording by Billy Eckstine. Lawrence's work was featured in several other films, including *Outside Of Paradise* (1938, 'A Little Bit Of Everything', 'All For One', 'Outside Of Paradise', 'A Sweet Irish Sweetheart Of Mine', 'Doing Shenanigans', with Peter Tinturin), *Hullabaloo* (1940, 'A Handful Of Stars', with Ted Shapiro), *The Great American Broadcast* (1941), *Doughboys In Ireland* (1943), *Stars On Parade* (1944, 'My Heart Isn't In It'), *Weekend Pass* (1944), *This Is The Life* (1944), *Peter Pan* (1953, 'Never Smile At A Crocodile', with Frank Churchill), *So This Is Love* (1953, 'Ciribiribin', with Harry James), and *Sleeping Beauty* ('Once Upon A Dream', with Sammy Fain). He was also represented on Broadway with the musicals *Courtin' Time* (1951, 'Heart In Hand', with Don Walker), *Torch Song* (1953), and *I Had A Ball* (1964, 'The Fickle Finger Of Fate', 'The Other Half Of Me', with Stan Freeman), starring Buddy Hackett, as well as the aforementioned *Crazy With The Heat*. Among his other collaborators have been John Green, John Barry and Victor Young.
● ALBUMS: *Come To The Circus* (50s)★★★.

LAWRENCE, LEE

b. Leon Siroto, c.1921, Salford, Lancashire, England, d. February 1961. This former ENSA entertainer's quasi-operatic tenor was similar to that of Ronnie Hilton, whom he rivalled as the BBC Light Programme's most featured vocalist in the early 50s. Both of his parents were members of the Carl Rosa Opera Company, and, at the age of 16, Lawrence went to Italy to study opera. After service in World War II he sang with various bands, and made his broadcasting debut on *Beginners Please*. After his 1953 cover version of Rex Allen's 'Crying In The Chapel' peaked at number 7 in the UK Top 10, Lawrence's chart career slumped until a

transfer from Decca to EMI in 1955 brought a second - and final - entry with a version of 'Suddenly There's A Valley' (1955). This, like many other of his recordings, was produced by Ray Martin, and followed a false dawn with an arrangement of Tennessee Ernie Ford's 'Give Me Your Word'. He is fondly remembered for his powerful versions of songs such as 'Fascination', 'The Story Of Tina', 'Lonely Ballerina', 'Falling In Love With Love' and his theme, 'The World Is Mine Tonight'. In the late 50s he moved to the USA and played in cabaret and appeared on television. Before his death, among the more interesting of Lawrence's later releases were 'Don't Nobody Move' and 1956's 'Rock 'N' Roll Opera', a spoof that mentioned Elvis Presley, Gene Vincent, Tommy Steele and other newcomers who were lessening the chances of Lawrence ever returning to the charts.
● ALBUMS: *Presenting Lee Lawrence* (Decca 1953)★★★, *Fascination* (President 1983)★★★.

LAWRENCE, STEVE

b. Stephen Leibowitz, 8 July 1935, Brooklyn, New York, USA. The son of a cantor in a Brooklyn synagogue, Lawrence was in the Glee club at Thomas Jefferson High School, where he began studying piano, saxophone, composition and arranging. He made his recording debut for King Records at the age of 16. The record, 'Mine And Mine Alone', based on 'Softly Awakes My Heart' from *Samson & Delilah*, revealed an amazingly mature voice and style. He got his first break on Steve Allen's *Tonight* television show, where he met, sang with and later married Eydie Gorme. He recorded for Coral Records and had his first hit in 1957 with 'The Banana Boat Song'. It was the infectious 'Party Doll' which gave him a Top 5 hit in 1957 and he followed that same year with four further, although lesser successes, namely 'Pum-Pa-Lum', 'Can't Wait For Summer', 'Fabulous' and 'Fraulein'. During his US Army service (1958-60) he sang with military bands on recruiting drives and bond rallies. Back home he and Eydie embarked on a double act, their most memorable hit being 'I Want To Stay Here' in 1963. As Steve And Eydie they made albums for CBS, ABC and United Artists, including *Steve And Eydie At The Movies*, *Together On Broadway*, *We Got Us*, *Steve And Eydie Sing The Golden Hits* and *Our Love Is Here To Stay*, the latter a double album of George Gershwin songs, which was the soundtrack of a television special. Lawrence, on his own, continued to have regular hits with 'Portrait Of My Love' and 'Go Away Little Girl' in 1961/2, and enjoyed critical success with albums such as *Academy Award Losers* and *Portrait Of My Love*. As an actor he starred on Broadway in *What Makes Sammy Run?*, took the lead in *Pal Joey* in summer stock, and has acted in a crime series on US television. During the 70s and 80s he continued to record and make television appearances with Gorme, with the couple gaining a record-breaking seven Emmys for their *Steve And Eydie Celebrate Irving Berlin* special. The couple also joined Frank Sinatra on his year-long *Diamond Jubilee Tour* in 1991.
● ALBUMS: *About That Girl* (Coral 1956)★★★, *Songs By Steve Lawrence* (Coral 1957)★★★, *Here's Steve Lawrence* (Coral 1958)★★★, *All About Love* (Coral 1959)★★★, *Steve Lawrence* (King 1959)★★★, *Swing Softly With Me* (ABC-Paramount 1960)★★★★, *The Steve Lawrence Sound* (United Artists 1960)★★★★, *Steve Lawrence Goes Latin* (United Artists 1960)★★, *Portrait Of My Love* (United Artists 1961)★★★★, *Winners!* (Columbia 1963)★★★, *Come Waltz*

With Me (Columbia 1963)★★★, *People Will Say We're In Love* (United Artists 1963)★★★, *Steve Lawrence Conquers Broadway* (United Artists 1963)★★★, *Songs Everybody Knows* (Coral 1963)★★★, *Academy Award Losers* (Columbia 1964)★★★★, *What Makes Sammy Run* film soundtrack (Columbia 1964)★★, *The Steve Lawrence Show* (Columbia 1965)★★★, *We're All Alone* (President 1985)★★★.
With Eydie Gorme *We Got Us* (ABC-Paramount 1960)★★★★, *Steve And Eydie Sing The Golden Hits* (ABC-Paramount 1960)★★★, *Cozy* (United Artists 1961)★★★, *Two On The Aisle* (United Artists 1963)★★★, *Our Best To You* (ABC-Paramount 1964)★★★, *Together On Broadway* (Columbia 1967)★★★, *What It Was, Was Love* (RCA 1969)★★★, *Real True Lovin'* (RCA 1969)★★★, *Tonight I'll Say A Prayer* (RCA 1970)★★★, *We Can Make It Together* (Ember 1975)★★★, *Our Love Is Here To Stay* (United Artists 1977)★★★, *I Still Believe In Love* (President 1985)★★★, *Alone Together* (GL 1989)★★★, *Since I Fell For You* (1993)★★★.
● COMPILATIONS: *The Best Of Steve Lawrence* (ABC-Paramount 1960)★★★, *The Very Best Of Steve Lawrence* (United Artists 1962)★★★, *The Best Of Steve Lawrence* (Taragon 1995)★★★.
With Eydie Gorme *The Very Best Of Eydie And Steve* (United Artists 1962)★★★, *The Golden Hits Of Eydie And Steve* (United Artists 1962)★★★, *The Best Of Steve And Eydie* (Columbia 1977)★★★, *20 Golden Performances* (1977)★★★.

LAYNE, JOY

b. late 30s, Chicago, Illinois, USA. Layne had only one US Top 20 single in 1957, 'Your Wild Heart', and never returned to the charts. Managed by her mother, the young girl auditioned for Mercury Records in Chicago. She was given a song that had already been recorded by the Poni-Tails. 'Your Wild Heart' was released in early 1957 and the record reached number 20 in the USA. With a dynamic voice comparable to Brenda Lee's, great things were predicted for Layne. Unfortunately, her mother would not let her tour or promote her recordings, and by 1961 her career was over.

LEE, PEGGY

b. Norma Deloris Egstrom, 26 May 1920, Jamestown, North Dakota, USA. Lee is of Scandinavian descent, her grandparents being Swedish and Norwegian immigrants. She endured a difficult childhood and her mother died when she was four; when her father remarried she experienced a decidedly unpleasant relationship with her stepmother. Her father took to drink, and at the age of 14 she found herself carrying out his duties at the local railroad depot. Despite these and other hardships, she sang frequently and appeared on a local radio station. She took a job as a waitress in Fargo, where the manager of the radio station changed her name to Peggy Lee. In 1937, she took a trip to California to try her luck there but soon returned to Fargo. Another California visit was equally unsuccessful and she then tried Chicago where, in 1941, as a member of a vocal group, The Four Of Us, she was hired to sing at the Ambassador West Hotel. During this engagement she was heard by Mel Powell, who invited Benny Goodman to hear her. Goodman's regular singer, Helen Forrest, was about to leave and Lee was hired as her replacement. She joined the band for an engagement at the College Inn and within a few days

sang on a record date. A song from this period, 'Elmer's Tune', was a huge success. Among other popular recordings she made with Goodman were 'How Deep Is The Ocean?', 'How Long Has This Been Going On?', 'My Old Flame' and 'Why Don't You Do Right?'. Later, Lee married Goodman's guitarist, Dave Barbour. After she left Goodman's band in 1943, she had more successful records, including 'That Old Feeling' and three songs of which she was co-composer with Barbour, 'It's A Good Day', 'Don't Know Enough About You' and 'Mañana'. She also performed on radio with Bing Crosby. In the 50s she made several popular recordings for Capitol, the orchestral backings for many of which were arranged and conducted by Barbour, with whom she maintained a good relationship despite their divorce in 1952. Her 1958 hit single 'Fever' was also a collaboration with Barbour. Her *Black Coffee* album of 1953 was particularly successful, as was *Beauty And The Beat* a few years later. On these and other albums of the period, Lee was often accompanied by jazz musicians, including Jimmy Rowles, Marty Paich and George Shearing. During the 50s Lee was also active in films, performing the title song of *Johnny Guitar* (1954), and writing songs for others including *Tom Thumb* (1958). She also made a number of on-screen appearances in acting roles, including *The Jazz Singer* (1953), and for one, *Pete Kelly's Blues* (1955), she was nominated for an Academy Award as Best Supporting Actress. However, her most lasting fame in films lies in her off-screen work on Walt Disney's *Lady And The Tramp* (1955), for which Lee wrote the song 'He's A Tramp' and provided the voice for the characters of 'Peg', the Siamese cats, and one other screen feline. Her recording successes continued throughout this period even if, on some occasions, she had to fight to persuade Capitol to record them. One such argument surrounded 'Lover', which executives felt would compete directly with the label's then popular version by Les Paul. Lee won out and her performance of her own arrangement, played by a studio orchestra under the direction of Gordon Jenkins, was a sensation. Towards the end of the 50s, the intense level of work began to take its toll and she suffered a period of illness. Throughout the 60s and succeeding decades Lee performed extensively, singing at concerts and on television and, of course, making records, despite being frequently plagued with poor health. Her voice is light with a delicate huskiness, offering intriguing contrasts with the large orchestral accompaniment that is usually a part of a Lee performance. Over the years her repeated use of previously successful settings for songs has tended to make her shows predictable but she remains a dedicated perfectionist in everything that she does. In the early 80s she attempted a stage show, *Peg*, but it proved unpopular and closed quickly. In the late 80s she again suffered ill health and on some of her live performances her voice was starting to betray the ravages of time. For her many fans, it did not seem to matter: to paraphrase the title of one of her songs, they just loved being there with Peg. In 1992, wheelchair-bound for the previous two years, Lee was persisting in a lawsuit, begun in 1987, against the Walt Disney Corporation for her share of the video profits from *Lady And The Tramp*. A year later, dissatisfied with the 'paltry' £2 million settlement for her six songs (written with Sonny Burke) and character voices, she was preparing to write a book about the whole affair. Meanwhile, she continued to make occasional cabaret appearances at New York venues such as Club 53. In 1993 she recorded a duet with Gilbert O'Sullivan for his album *Sounds Of The Loop*. Lee is one of the greatest 'classy' vocalists of the century, alongside Ella Fitzgerald, Billie Holiday, Sarah Vaughan and Betty Carter.

● ALBUMS: with Benny Goodman *Benny Goodman And Peggy Lee* (Columbia 1949)★★★, *Rendezvous* (Capitol 1952)★★★, *My Best To You* (Capitol 1952)★★★, *Song In Intimate Style* (Decca 1953)★★★, *Black Coffee* (Decca 1953)★★★★★, *White Christmas* film soundtrack (Decca 1954)★★★★, *The Lady And The Tramp* film soundtrack (Decca 1955)★★★★, with Ella Fitzgerald *Songs From Pete Kelly's Blues* film soundtrack (Decca 1955)★★★, *Dream Street* (Decca 1956)★★★, *The Man I Love* (Capitol 1957)★★★★, *Jump For Joy* (Capitol 1958)★★★, *Sea Shells* (Decca 1958)★★★, *Things Are Swingin'* (Capitol 1958)★★★★, with George Shearing *Beauty And The Beat* (Capitol 1959)★★★★, *I Like Men* (Capitol 1959)★★★, *Miss Wonderful* (Capitol 1959)★★★, *Pretty Eyes* (Capitol 1960)★★★, *Alright, Okay, You Win* (Capitol 1960)★★★, *Latin A La Lee!* (Capitol 1960)★★★, *All Aglow Again* (Capitol 1960)★★★, *Olé A La Lee* (Capitol 1960)★★★, *Christmas Carousel* (Capitol 1960)★★★, *At Basin Street East* (Capitol 1960)★★★, *Blues Cross Country* (Capitol 1961)★★★, *If You Go* (Capitol 1961)★★★, *Sugar 'N' Spice* (Capitol 1962)★★★, *I'm A Woman* (Capitol 1963)★★★, *Mink Jazz* (Capitol 1963)★★★, *In Love Again* (Capitol 1963)★★★, *Lover* (Decca 1964)★★★, *In The Name Of Love* (Capitol 1964)★★★, *Pass Me By* (Capitol 1965)★★★, *That Was Then, This Is Now* (Capitol 1965)★★★, *Big Spender* (Capitol 1966)★★★, *Extra Special* (Capitol 1967)★★★, *Guitars A La Lee* (Capitol 1967)★★★, *Is That All There Is?* (Capitol 1969)★★★, *Bridge Over Troubled Water* (Capitol 1970)★★★, *Make It With You* (Capitol 1970)★★★, *Let's Love* (Atlantic 1974)★★★, *Mirrors* (A&M 1976)★★★, *Close Enough For Love* (DRG 1979)★★★, *Miss Peggy Lee Sings The Blues* (Music Masters 1988)★★★, *The Peggy Lee Songbook: There'll Be Another Spring* (Musicmasters 1990)★★★, with Quincy Jones *P'S & Q'S* (1992)★★★, *Love Held Lightly* (1993)★★★, *Moments Like This* (1993)★★★, *If I Could Be With You* 1951-52 recordings (1993)★★★.

● COMPILATIONS: *Bewitching-Lee!* (Capitol 1962)★★★★, *The Best Of Peggy Lee* (MCA 1980)★★★★, *Peggy Lee Sings With Benny Goodman (1941-43)* (Columbia 1984)★★★★, *The Peggy Lee Collection - 20 Golden Greats* (MCA 1985)★★★★, *Unforgettable: Peggy Lee* (Unforgettable/Castle 1987)★★★, *The Capitol Years* (Capitol 1988)★★★★, *Capitol Collectors Series: The Early Years* (Capitol 1990)★★★, *All-Time Greatest Hits* (Curb 1990)★★★, *Peggy Lee - Fever* (1992)★★★★, *The Best Of* (1993)★★★★, with Bing Crosby *It's A Good Day* (1993)★★★, *The Best Of Peggy Lee, 1952-1956* (Music Club 1994)★★★★.

● VIDEOS: *Quintessential* (Hendring 1989).

● FURTHER READING: *Miss Peggy Lee*, Peggy Lee.

LEHRER, TOM

b. Thomas Andrew Lehrer, 9 April 1928, New York City, New York, USA. Lehrer was a song satirist who also recorded a number of albums during the 50s and 60s. Having graduated from Harvard University, Lehrer then taught mathematics there. Having trained on piano, he began to perform song satires of his own for colleagues at the college. They enjoyed his songs, so Lehrer recorded a dozen of them in 1953 and had 400 copies pressed on a 10-inch album, on his own Lehrer label. An instant success on campus, Lehrer was forced to press more copies to meet the demand. He then began entertaining in clubs and writing songs for television programmes. Before the end of the 50s he had recorded three more albums on his own label and had begun to tour extensively, even gaining a following in Europe. His sense of black humour is encapsulated in the titles 'Poisoning Pigeons In The Park', 'The Old Dope Peddler' and 'The Masochism Tango' - which could be described as falling somewhere between *Mad* magazine and Lenny Bruce. He stopped making live appearances in 1960 but continued to record, signing with Reprise Records in 1965. He also wrote for the US editions of the television programme *That Was The Week That Was* in 1964-65, lampooning current news events. His album *That Was The Year That Was* collected songs that had featured on the programme. He largely stopped writing in the late 60s although he did contribute songs to the television show *The Electric Company* in 1972. A British musical revue, *Tomfoolery*, in 1980, was based on his songs. He returned to teaching in the late 70s.

● ALBUMS: *Songs By Tom Lehrer* 10-inch album (Lehrer 1953)★★★★, *More Of Tom Lehrer* (Lehrer 1959)★★★★, *An Evening Wasted With Tom Lehrer* (Lehrer 1959)★★★★, *Tom Lehrer Revisited* (Lehrer 1960)★★, *That Was The Year That Was* (Reprise 1965)★★★, *Songs By Tom Lehrer* re-recorded versions of first album's songs (Reprise 1966)★★.

● COMPILATIONS: *Too Many Songs By Tom Lehrer* (1981)★★★★.

LEIBER AND STOLLER

Jerry Leiber (b. 25 April 1933, Baltimore, Maryland, USA) and Mike Stoller (b. 13 March 1933, New York City, New York, USA) began their extraordinary songwriting and production partnership at the age of 17. Leiber was a blues enthusiast and record store assistant, while Stoller played jazz piano. Based in Los Angeles, they provided numerous songs for the city's R&B artists during the early 50s. 'Hard Times' by Charles Brown was the first Leiber and Stoller hit, but their biggest songs of the era were 'Hound Dog' and 'K.C. Lovin'' (later renamed 'Kansas City'). Originally recorded by Big Mama Thornton, 'Hound Dog' was one of the songs that came to define rock 'n' roll after Elvis Presley performed it. 'Kansas City' had its greatest success in a version by Wilbert Harrison, and went on to become part of every UK beat group's repertoire. In 1954, the duo set up their own Spark label to release material by the Robins, a vocal group they had discovered. Renamed the Coasters a year later, when Leiber and Stoller moved to New York, the group was given some of the songwriters' most clever and witty compositions. Songs such as 'Smokey Joe's Cafe', 'Searchin'', 'Yakety Yak' and 'Charlie Brown' bridged the gap between R&B and rock 'n' roll, selling millions in the mid to late 50s, while Leiber And Stoller's innovative production techniques widened the scope of the R&B record, prompting hosts of imitators. In New York, Leiber and Stoller had a production contract with Atlantic Records, where they created hits for numerous artists. They wrote 'Lucky Lips' for Ruth Brown and 'Saved' for LaVern Baker, but their most notable productions were for the Drifters and the group's lead singer Ben E. King. Among these were 'On Broadway', 'Spanish Harlem',

'There Goes My Baby', 'I (Who Have Nothing)' and 'Stand By Me', which was an international hit when reissued in 1986. Away from Atlantic, Leiber and Stoller supplied Elvis Presley with songs including 'Jailhouse Rock', 'Baby I Don't Care', 'Loving You', 'Treat Me Nice' and 'His Latest Flame'. They also wrote hits for Perry Como, Peggy Lee ('I'm A Woman') and Dion. In 1964, the duo set up the Red Bird and Blue Cat record labels with George Goldner. Despite the quality of many of the releases (Alvin Robinson's 'Down Home Girl' was later covered by the Rolling Stones), the only big hits came from the Shangri-Las, who were produced by George 'Shadow' Morton rather than Leiber and Stoller. Subsequently, the duo took several years away from production, purchasing the King Records group and creating the *Cabaret*-like songs for Peggy Lee's album *Mirrors* (1976). They returned to the pop world briefly in 1972, producing albums for UK acts including Stealer's Wheel and Elkie Brooks, for whom they part-wrote 'Pearl's A Singer'. During the 70s, they were in semi-retirement, developing *Only In America*. Another musical based on their work - *Yakety Yak* - was presented in London with oldies band Darts. During the 80s Leiber and Stoller's songs were featured in the cartoon film *Hound Dog* and they were reported to be working on a musical. However, their public appearances seemed to be confined to awards ceremonies where they were made members of several Halls of Fame, including that of Rock 'n' Roll in 1987. In 1979, Robert Palmer wrote a highly praised biography of the duo. The stage musical *Smokey Joe's Cafe: The Songs Of Leiber And Stoller*, which opened to rave reviews in March 1995 at New York's Virginia Theatre, featured nearly 40 songs by the duo.

● FURTHER READING: *Baby, That Was Rock & Roll: The Legendary Leiber And Stoller*, Robert Palmer.

LEIGH, CAROLYN

b. Carolyn Paula Rosenthal, 21 August 1926, New York, USA, d. 19 November 1983, New York, USA. An important lyricist in the late 50s and 60s, Leigh began writing verse and doggerel when she was only nine. After graduating from high school, she studied at Queens College and New York University. She began her career by writing announcements for radio station WQXR and working as a copywriter for an advertising agency. By the time she was 25 years old Leigh is reputed to have written about 200 songs, although none had been published. In 1951, she wrote 'I'm Waiting Just For You' (with Lucky Millinder and Henry Glover), which was modestly successful for Millinder, Rosemary Clooney, and later, Pat Boone. Her first big hit came in 1954, when Frank Sinatra took 'Young At Heart', written with Johnny Richards, to number 2 in the USA, and it became the title and theme of a film in which he co-starred with Doris Day. This led to Leigh being offered the chance to write most of the songs, with composer Mark 'Moose' Charlap, for the Broadway show *Peter Pan* (1954, 'I'm Flying', 'I've Gotta Crow' and 'I Won't Grow Up'). She also contributed to the off-Broadway revue *Shoestring '57*. Leigh's other work around this time included 'The Day The Circus Left Town' (with E.D. Thomas), which was recorded by Eartha Kitt, 'Stowaway' (with Jerry Livingston, a UK Top 20 entry for Barbara Lyon), '(How Little It Matters) How Little We Know' (Philip Springer) and 'Witchcraft' (Cy Coleman). The last two songs

were chart hits for Frank Sinatra. Leigh's fruitful - and, apparently, stormy - collaboration with the composer Cy Coleman lasted from the late 50s into the early 60s. During that time they wrote the scores for the Broadway musicals *Wildcat*, a Lucille Ball vehicle (1960, 'Hey, Look Me Over', 'Give A Little Whistle', 'You've Come Home', 'What Takes My Fancy'), and the marvellous *Little Me* (1962, 'I've Got Your Number', 'Real Live Girl', 'On The Other Side Of The Tracks', 'Deep Down Inside'). Another number intended for *Little Me*, 'When In Rome', was recorded by Barbra Streisand and Vikki Carr. The team also worked on an abortive musical adaptation of the memoirs of stripper Gypsy Rose Lee (later immortalized as *Gypsy* with a score by Jule Styne and Stephen Sondheim), from which came 'Firefly'. It gave Tony Bennett a bestselling record, and he included the song, along with Leigh and Coleman's sensitive ballad 'It Amazes Me', on his 2-LP set *Tony Bennett At Carnegie Hall*. After they split up, Leigh and Coleman worked together again on the charming 'Pass Me By', which was sung over the titles of the 1964 Cary Grant movie *Father Goose*; and 'A Doodlin' Song', which was recorded by Peggy Lee. In 1967, Leigh teamed with composer Elmer Bernstein on the score for *How Now, Dow Jones* ('Live A Little', 'Walk Away', 'He's Here!' and 'Step To The Rear'), and in later years continued to write occasionally for the stage, television and films. She wrote the lyrics for the Bicentennial show *Something To Do*, and for the television special *Heidi*. Her other songs included 'Stay With Me', 'Love Is A Melody (Short And Sweet)', 'Disenchanted Castle', 'Playboy Theme', 'On Second Thought', 'In The Barrio', 'Westport' and 'Bouncing Back For More'. Among her collaborators were Morton Gould, Lee Pockriss and Marvin Hamlisch. She was working on a musical adaptation of *Smiles* with Hamlisch when she died from a heart attack in 1983.

LERNER, ALAN JAY

b. 31 August 1918, New York, USA, d. June 1986. A lyricist and librettist, and one of the most eminent and literate personalities in the history of the Broadway musical theatre, Lerner played the piano as a child, and studied at the Juilliard School of Music, the Bedales public school in England, and Harvard University, where he took a Bachelor of Science degree in the late 30s. After working as a journalist and radio scriptwriter, he met composer Frederick Loewe at the Lamb's Club in 1942. Also a pianist, Loewe had moved to the USA in 1924, and had previously been involved in some unsuccessful musical shows. The new team's first efforts, *What's Up?* and *The Day Before Spring* (1945; 'A Jug Of Wine', 'I Love You This Morning'), did not exactly set Broadway alight, but two years later, they had their first hit with *Brigadoon*. Lerner's whimsical fantasy about a Scottish village that only comes to life every 100 years, contained 'Waitin' For My Dearie', 'I'll Go Home To Bonnie Jean', 'The Heather On The Hill', 'Come To Me, Bend To Me', 'From This Day On', and the future standard, 'Almost Like Being In Love'. A film version was made in 1954, starring Gene Kelly, Cyd Charisse and Van Johnson.

After *Brigadoon*, Lerner collaborated with Kurt Weill on the vaudeville-style *Love Life* (1948), and then spent some time in Hollywood writing the songs, with Burton Lane, for *Royal Wedding* (1951). Among them was one of the longest-ever titles, 'How Could You Believe Me When I Said I Loved You

(When You Know I've Been A Liar All My Life?)', expertly manipulated by Fred Astaire and Jane Powell. Another of the numbers, 'Too Late Now', sung by Powell, was nominated for an Academy Award. In the same year, Lerner picked up an Oscar for his story and screenplay for George and Ira Gershwin's musical film *An American In Paris* (1951). Also in 1951, Lerner reunited with Loewe for the 'Gold Rush' Musical, *Paint Your Wagon*. The colourful score included 'They Call The Wind Maria', 'I Talk To The Trees', 'I Still See Elisa', 'I'm On My Way' and 'Wand'rin' Star', which, in the 1969 movie, received a lugubrious reading from Lee Marvin. Precisely the opposite sentiments prevailed in *My Fair Lady* (1956), Lerner's adaptation of *Pygmalion* by George Bernard Shaw, which starred Rex Harrison as the irascible Higgins, and Julie Andrews as Eliza ('I'm a good girl, I am'). Sometimes called 'the most perfect musical', Lerner and Loewe's memorable score included 'Why Can't The English?', 'Wouldn't It Be Loverly?', 'The Rain In Spain', 'I Could Have Danced All Night', 'On The Street Where You Live', 'Show Me', 'Get Me To The Church On Time', 'A Hymn To Him', 'Without You' and 'I've Grown Accustomed To Her Face'. 'Come To The Ball', originally written for the show, but discarded before the opening, was, subsequently, often performed, particularly by Lerner himself. After a run of 2,717 performances on Broadway, and 2,281 in London, the show was filmed in 1964, when Andrews was replaced by Audrey Hepburn (dubbed by Marni Nixon). The Broadway Cast album went to number 1 in the US charts, sold over five million copies, and stayed in the Top 40 for 311 weeks. In 1958 Lerner was back in Hollywood, with a somewhat reluctant Loewe, for one of the last original screen musicals, the charming *Gigi*. Lerner's stylish treatment of Colette's turn-of-the-century novella, directed by Vincente Minnelli, starred Maurice Chevalier, Leslie Caron, Louis Jourdan and Hermione Gingold, and boasted a delightful score that included 'The Night They Invented Champagne', 'Say A Prayer For Me Tonight', 'I'm Glad I'm Not Young Anymore', 'Thank Heaven For Little Girls', 'Waltz At Maxim's', 'She Is Not Thinking Of Me' and the touching 'I Remember It Well', memorably performed by Chevalier and Gingold. Lerner won one of the film's nine Oscars for his screenplay, and another, with Loewe, for the title song.

Two years later, Lerner and Loewe returned to Broadway with *Camelot*, a musical version of the Arthurian legend, based on T.H. White's *The Once And Future King*. With Julie Andrews, Richard Burton and Robert Goulet, plus a fine score that included 'C'Est Moi', 'The Lusty Month Of May', 'If Ever I Would Leave You', 'Follow Me', 'How To Handle A Woman' and the title song, the show ran on Broadway for two years. During that time it became indelibly connected with the Kennedy presidency: 'for one brief shining moment, that was known as Camelot'. The 1967 movie version was poorly received. In the early 60s, partly because of the composer's ill health, Lerner and Loewe ended their partnership, coming together again briefly in 1973 to write some new songs for a stage presentation of *Gigi*, and, a year later, for the score to the film *The Little Prince*. Lerner's subsequent collaborators included Burton Lane for *On A Clear Day You Can See Forever* (1965) ('Come Back To Me', 'On The S.S. Bernard Cohn', and others). Lerner won a Grammy award for the title song, and maintained that it was his most frequently recorded number. He wrote with Lane again in

1979 for *Carmelina*. In the interim he collaborated with André Previn for *Coco* (1969), which had a respectable run of 332 performances, mainly due to its star, Katherine Hepburn, and with Leonard Bernstein for *1600 Pennsylvania Avenue* (1976). Lerner's last musical, *Dance A Little Closer* (1983), which starred his eighth wife, English actress Liz Robertson, closed after one performance. They had met in 1979 when he directed her, as Eliza, in a major London revival of *My Fair Lady*. Shortly before he died of lung cancer in June 1986, he was still working on various projects, including a musical treatment of the 30s film comedy *My Man Godfrey*, in collaboration with pianist-singer Gerard Kenny, and *Yerma*, based on the play by Federico Garcia Lorca. Frederick Loewe, who shared in Lerner's triumphs, and had been semi-retired since the 60s, died in February 1988. In 1993, New Yorkers celebrated the 75th anniversary of Lerner's birth, and his remarkable and fruitful partnership with Loewe, with *The Night They Invented Champagne: The Lerner And Loewe Revue*, which played a season at the Rainbow and Stars.

● ALBUMS: *An Evening With Alan Jay Lerner* (Laureate 1977)★★★.

● FURTHER READING: *The Musical Theatre: A Celebration*, Alan Jay Lerner. *The Street Where I Live: The Story Of My Fair Lady, Gigi And Camelot*, Alan Jay Lerner. *A Hymn To Him: The Lyrics Of Alan Jay Lerner*, Benny Green (ed.). *The Wordsmiths: Oscar Hammerstein & Alan Jay Lerner*, Stephen Citron.

LEROLE, ELIAS, AND HIS ZIG ZAG JIVE FLUTES

This studio band was one of the most popular penny-whistle jive outfits in South Africa in the mid-50s, and released the first version of the evergreen and hypnotic 'Tom Hark' in 1956. Although a massive international hit for the group - spawning countless cover versions from Ted Heath in the 50s through to the present day - the members of the Zig Zag Jive Flutes are reputed to have received only $10 each for their efforts, while composer Aaron Lerole, Elias's brother, received the princely sum of $15 and the added accolade of having his song credited to producer Ernest Bopape. However, that was showbusiness, 50s-style, in South Africa.

LES GIRLS

To many it must have seemed like the end of an era when Gene Kelly completed his very last MGM musical. The string of hits he left behind are firmly registered in the vaults of film musical history. His last project, *Les Girls*, released in October 1957, and adapted by John Patrick from a Vera Caspery story, struggles to live up to Kelly's own high standards, but there are enough entertaining sequences to maintain the momentum. Directed by George Cukor and produced by Sol C Siegel, the film is set in Paris 1949. It follows the adventures of Kelly, a musical performer, and his female trio, Les Girls, played by Mitzi Gaynor, Kay Kendall and Taina Elg. The unusual story is revealed in a series of flashbacks. The first of them concerns the courtroom battle between two of the girls that opens the film. Lady Wren (Kay Kendall) has included an account of her experiences with Les Girls in her memoirs, and stands in the dock defending her words, while furious Taina Elg refuses to accept any of the book as the truth. As the film continues, the viewer begins to wonder who is really telling the truth, and with which one of the girls Kelly is in love. Or did he have flings with all of them? It is only towards the conclusion of the movie that it is revealed that Mitzi Gaynor is the girl he truly desires. Indeed, during one of the flashbacks he reveals a whole wall of photos of Gaynor, and pretends he is terribly ill in order to win his way into her affections. In the aftermath of the court case, she demands Kelly's assurance that his flings with the other girls were purely fictional. With all these complications, it is hardly surprising that the film becomes rather weighed down, but one or two individual performances and the words and music of Cole Porter save the day (*Les Girls* was his last original score for the big screen). The musical highlights included Kelly and Gaynor's tongue-in-cheek send-up of Marlon Brando in 'Why Am I So Gone About That Gal?' and Kendall's almost music-hall routine with Kelly, 'You're Just Too, Too'. Other songs were 'Ladies In Waiting' and 'Ca, C'est L'Amour'. Among the supporting cast, which had a definite European flavour, were Leslie Phillips, Jacques Bergerac, Henry Daniell and Patrick MacNee. Jack Cole was the choreographer, and it was photographed in Metrocolor and CinemaScope. Not an MGM classic for Kelly and Porter to end with, but amusing and enjoyable all the same.

LET THE GOOD TIMES ROLL

Perhaps one of the finest paeans to classic rock 'n' roll, *Let The Good Times Roll* is a sumptuous amalgamation of documentary footage and memorable concert performances. At its core was a 1972 marathon, hosted at Madison Square Gardens by New York impresario Richard Nader. Directors Sid Levin and Robert Abel blended footage from that event with television appearances, newsreels, interviews and demonstration films. Scenes from 50s genre movies *The Wild One* and *I Was A Teenage Werewolf* help to place the music in a broader cultural context, while intelligent use of split-screen techniques facilitated then-and-now scenarios. One particular clip of Little Richard, in monochrome from the 50s and in colour from the 70s, is particularly memorable. 'Good Golly Miss Molly', 'Rip It Up' and 'Lucille' are among the songs he performs as part of a cast that also includes Fats Domino, Chuck Berry, the Coasters, Danny And The Juniors, the Five Satins, Shirley And Lee, Bo Diddley, the Shirelles, Chubby Checker and Bill Haley And His Comets. 'Blueberry Hill', 'Reelin' And Rockin'', 'At The Hop', 'Poison Ivy', 'I'm A Man' and, of course, 'Rock Around The Clock', are among the songs featured in this endearing tribute to rock's first golden era.

LEWIS, JERRY LEE

b. 29 September 1935, Ferriday, Louisiana, USA. The 'Killer' is the personification of 50s rock 'n' roll at its best. He is rowdy, raw, rebellious and uncompromising. The outrageous piano-pounder has a voice that exudes excitement and an aura of arrogance that becomes understandable after witnessing the seething hysteria and mass excitement at his concerts. As a southern boy, Lewis was brought up listening to many musical styles in a home where religion was as important as breathing. In 1950, he attended a fundamentalist bible school in Waxahachie, Texas, but was expelled. The clash between the secular and the religious would govern Lewis's life and art for the remainder of his career.

He first recorded on the *Louisiana Hayride* in 1954 and decided that Elvis Presley's label, Sun Records, was where he wanted to be. His distinctive version of country star Ray Price's 'Crazy Arms' was his Sun debut, but it was his second single, a revival of Roy Hall's 'Whole Lotta Shakin' Goin' On' in 1957 that propelled him to international fame. The record, which was initially banned as obscene, narrowly missed the top of the US chart, went on to hit number 1 on the R&B and country charts and introduced the fair-haired, one-man piano wrecker to a world ready for a good shaking up. He stole the show from many other stars in the film *Jamboree* in which he sang the classic 'Great Balls Of Fire', which became his biggest hit and topped the UK chart and made number 2 in the USA. He kept up the barrage of rowdy and unadulterated rock with the US/UK Top 10 single 'Breathless', which, like its predecessor, had been written by Otis Blackwell.

Problems started for the flamboyant 'god of the glissando' when he arrived in Britain for a tour in 1958, accompanied by his third wife, Myra, who was also his 13-year-old second cousin. The UK media stirred up a hornet's nest and the tour had to be cancelled after only three concerts, even though the majority of the audience loved him. The furore followed Lewis home and support for him in his homeland also waned; he never returned to the Top 20 pop chart in the USA. His last big hit of the 50s was the title song from his film *High School Confidential*, which made the UK Top 20 in 1959 and number 21 in the USA. Despite a continued high standard of output, his records either only made the lower chart rungs or missed altogether. When his version of Ray Charles' 'What'd I Say' hit the UK Top 10 in 1960 (US number 30) it looked like a record revival was on the way, but it was not to be. The fickle general public may have disowned the hard-living, hellraiser, but his hardcore fans remained loyal and his tours were sell-outs during the 60s. He joined Smash Records in 1963 and although the material he recorded with the company was generally unimaginative, there were some excellent live recordings, most notably *The Greatest Live Show On Earth* (1964).

In 1966, Lewis made an unexpected entry into rock music theatre when he was signed to play Iago in Jack Good's *Catch My Soul*, inspired by *Othello*. After a decade playing rock 'n' roll, Lewis decided to concentrate on country material in 1968. He had often featured country songs in his repertoire, so his new policy did not represent an about-face. This changeover was an instant success - country fans welcomed back their prodigal son with open arms. Over the next 13 years Lewis was one of country's top-selling artists and was a main attraction wherever he put on his 'Greatest Show On Earth'. He first appeared at the *Grand Ole Opry* in 1973, playing an unprecedented 50-minute set. He topped the country chart with records such as 'There Must Be More To Love Than This' in 1970, 'Would You Take Another Chance On Me?' in 1971 and a revival of 'Chantilly Lace' a year later. The latter also returned him briefly to the transatlantic Top 40. However, he also kept the rock 'n' roll flag flying by playing revival shows around the world and by always including his old 50s hits in his stage shows. In fact, long-time fans have always been well catered for - numerous compilations of top-class out-takes and never previously issued tracks from the 50s have regularly been released over the last 20 years. On the personal front, his life has never been short of tragedies, often compounded by his alcohol and drug problems. His family has been equally prone to tragedy. In November 1973, his 19-year-old son, Jerry Lee Jnr., was killed in a road accident following a period of drug abuse and treatment for mental illness. Lewis's own behaviour during the mid-70s was increasingly erratic. He accidentally shot his bass player in the chest - the musician survived and sued him. Late in 1976, Lewis was arrested for waving a gun outside Elvis Presley's Gracelands home. Two years later, Lewis signed to Elektra Records for the appropriately titled *Rockin' My Life Away*. Unfortunately, his association with the company ended with much-publicized lawsuits. In 1981, Lewis was hospitalized and allegedly close to death from a haemorrhaged ulcer. He survived that ordeal and was soon back on the road. In 1982, his fourth wife drowned in a swimming pool. The following year, his fifth wife was found dead at his home following a methodone overdose. The deaths brought fresh scandal to Lewis's troubled life. Meanwhile, the IRS were challenging his earnings from the late 70s in another elongated dispute. A sixth marriage followed, along with more bleeding ulcers and a period in the Betty Ford Clinic for treatment for his pain-killer addiction. Remarkably, Lewis's body and spirit have remained intact, despite these harrowing experiences. During his career he has released dozens of albums, the most successful being *The Session* in 1973, his sole US Top 40 album, on which many pop names of the period backed him, including Peter Frampton and Rory Gallagher. Lewis was one of the first people inducted into the Rock And Roll Hall Of Fame in 1986. In 1989, a biopic of his early career, *Great Balls Of Fire*, starring Dennis Quaid, brought him briefly back into the public eye. In 1990, a much-awaited UK tour had to be cancelled when Lewis and his sixth wife (who was not even born at the time of his fateful first tour) failed to appear. He moved to Dublin, Eire, to avoid the US taxman, but eventually returned to Memphis. In 1995, he jammed with Bruce Springsteen at the opening of the Rock And Roll Hall Of Fame building in Cleveland.

His cousin Mickey Gilley is an accomplished country artist, while another cousin, Jimmy Lee Swaggart, has emerged as one of America's premier television evangelists. Any understanding of the career of Jerry Lee Lewis is inextricably linked with the parallel rise and fall of Swaggart. They were both excellent piano players, but whereas Lewis devoted his energies to the 'devil's music', Swaggart damned rock 'n' roll from the pulpit and played gospel music. Lewis has often described his career as a flight from God, with Swaggart cast in the role of his conscience and indefatigable redeemer. The relationship, however, was more complex than that, and the spirits of these two American institutions were latterly revealed as more complementary than antithetical. When Swaggart was discovered with a prostitute in a motel, the evangelist created a scandal that surpassed even his cousin's series of dramas. Tragedy, scandal and, above all, rock 'n' roll have seldom played such an intrinsic role in one musician's life.

● ALBUMS: *Jerry Lee Lewis* (Sun 1957)★★★★, *Jerry Lee Lewis And His Pumping Piano* (London 1958)★★★, *Jerry Lee's Greatest* (Sun 1961)★★★★, *Rockin' With Jerry Lee Lewis* (Design 1963)★★★, *The Greatest Live Show On Earth* (Smash 1964)★★★, with the Nashville Teens *Live At The Star Club, Hamburg* (Philips 1965)★★, *The Return Of Rock* (Smash 1965)★★★, *Country Songs For City Folks* (Smash 1965)★★★, *Whole Lotta Shakin' Goin' On* (London 1965)★★★★, *Memphis Beat* (Smash 1966)★★★, *By Request - More Greatest Live Show On Earth* (Smash 1966)★★★, *Breathless* (London 1967)★★★, *Soul My Way* (Smash 1967)★★★, *Got You On My Mind* (Fontana 1968)★★★, *Another Time, Another Place* (Mercury 1969)★★★, *She Still Comes Around* (Mercury 1969)★★★, *I'm On Fire* (Mercury 1969)★★★, *Jerry Lee Lewis' Rockin' Rhythm And Blues* (Sun 1969)★★★, with Linda Gail Lewis *Together* (Mercury 1970)★★★, *She Even Woke Me Up To Say Goodbye* (Mercury 1970)★★★, *A Taste Of Country* (Sun 1970)★★★, *There Must Be More To Love Than This* (Mercury 1970)★★★, *Johnny Cash And Jerry Lee Lewis Sing Hank Williams* (Sun 1971)★★★, *Touching Home* (Mercury 1971)★★★, *In Loving Memories* (Mercury 1971)★★★, *Would You Take Another Chance On Me* (Mercury 1972)★★★, *The Killer Rocks On* (Mercury 1972)★★★, *Old Tyme Country Music* (Sun 1972)★★★, with Johnny Cash *Sunday Down South* (Sun 1972)★★, *The Session* (Mercury 1973)★★★, *Live At The International, Las Vegas* (Mercury 1973)★★★, *Great Balls of Fire* (Hallmark 1973)★★★, *Southern Roots* (Mercury 1974)★★★, *Rockin' Up A Storm* (Sun 1974)★★★, *Rockin' And Free* (Sun 1974)★★★, *I'm A Rocker* (Mercury 1975)★★★, *Odd Man In* (Mercury 1975)★★★, *Jerry Lee Lewis* (Elektra 1979)★★★, *Killer Country* (Elektra 1980)★★★, *When Two Worlds Collide* (Elektra 1980)★★★, with Johnny Cash, Carl Perkins *The Survivors* (Columbia 1982)★★★, *My Fingers Do The Talking* (MCA 1983)★★★, *I Am What I Am* (MCA 1984)★★★, with Webb Pierce, Mel Tillis, Faron Young *Four Legends* (1985)★★★, with Johnny Cash, Carl Perkins, Roy Orbison *Class Of '55* (America 1986)★★★, *Interviews From The Class Of '55 Recording Sessions* (America 1986)★★, *Keep Your Hands Off It* (Zu Zazz 1987)★★★, *Don't Drop It* (Zu Zazz 1988)★★★, *Live In Italy* (Magnum Force 1989)★★, *Great Balls Of Fire!* film soundtrack (Polydor 1989)★★★, with Carl Perkins and Elvis Presley *The Million Dollar Quartet* (RCA 1990)★★★, *Rocket* (Instant 1990)★★★, *Live At The Vapors Club* (Ace 1991)★★★, *Young Blood* (Sire/Elektra 1995)★★★, *Jerry Lee Lewis At Hank Cochran's* recorded 1987 (Trend 1996)★★★.
● COMPILATIONS: *Golden Hits* (Smash 1964)★★★★, *Country Music Hall Of Fame Hits Vol. 1* (Smash 1969)★★★★, *Country Music Hall Of Fame Hits Vol. 2* (Smash 1969)★★★★, *Original Golden Hits Vol. 1* (Sun 1969)★★★★, *Original Golden Hits Vol. 2* (Sun 1969)★★★, *The Best Of Jerry Lee Lewis* (Smash 1970)★★★★, *Original Golden Hits Vol. 3* (Sun 1971)★★★, *Monsters* (Sun 1971)★★★, *Rockin' With Jerry Lee Lewis* (Mercury 1972)★★★★, *Fan Club Choice* (Mercury 1974)★★★, *Whole Lotta Shakin' Goin' On* (Hallmark 1974)★★★★, *Good Rockin' Tonight* (Hallmark 1975)★★★, *Jerry Lee Lewis And His Pumping Piano* (Charly 1975)★★★, *Rare Jerry Lee Lewis Vol. 1* (Charly 1975)★★★, *Rare Jerry Lee Lewis Vol. 2* (Charly 1975)★★★, *The Jerry Lee Lewis Collection* (Hallmark 1976)★★★★, *Golden Hits* (Mercury 1976)★★★★, *The Original Jerry Lee Lewis* (Charly 1976)★★★★, *Nuggets* (Charly 1977)★★★★, *Nuggets Vol. 2* (Charly 1977)★★★, *The Essential Jerry Lee Lewis* (Charly 1978)★★★★, *Shakin' Jerry Lee* (Arcade 1978)★★★, *Back To Back* (Mercury 1978)★★★, *Duets* (Sun 1979)★★★, *Jerry Lee Lewis* (Hammer 1979)★★★, *Good Golly Miss Molly* (Bravo

1980)★★★, *Trio Plus* (Sun 1980)★★★, *Jerry Lee's Greatest* (Charly 1981)★★★★, *Killer Country* i (Elektra 1981)★★★★, *Jerry Lee Lewis* (Mercury 1981)★★★, *The Sun Years* 12-LP box set (Sun 1984)★★★★, *18 Original Sun Greatest Hits* (Rhino 1984)★★★★, *Milestones* (Rhino 1985)★★★★, *The Collection* (Deja Vu 1986)★★★★, *The Pumpin' Piano Cat* (Sun 1986)★★★, *Great Balls Of Fire* (Sun 1986)★★★★, *The Wild One* (Sun 1986)★★★, *At The Country Store* (Starblend 1987)★★★, *The Very Best Of Jerry Lee Lewis* (Philips 1987)★★★★, *The Country Sound Of Jerry Lee Lewis* (Pickwick 1988)★★, *The Classic Jerry Lee Lewis* 8-CD box set (Bear Family 1989)★★★★, *The Classic Jerry Lee Lewis* (Ocean 1989)★★★, *Killer's Birthday Cake* (Sun 1989)★★★, *Killer's Rhythm And Blues* (Sun 1989)★★★★, *Killer: The Mercury Years, Volume One, 1963-1968* (Mercury 1989)★★★, *Killer: The Mercury Years, Volume Two, 1969-1972* (Mercury 1989)★★★, *Killer: The Mercury Years, Volume Three, 1973-1977* (Mercury 1989)★★★, *Great Balls Of Fire* (Pickwick 1989)★★, *The EP Collection* (See For Miles 1990)★★★★, *The Jerry Lee Lewis Collection* (Castle 1990)★★★, *The Best Of Jerry Lee Lewis* (Curb 1991)★★★, *Pretty Much Country* (Ace 1992)★★★, *All Killer, No Filler: The Anthology* (Rhino 1993)★★★★, *The Complete Palamino Club Recordings* (1993)★★★, *The EP Collection Vol. 2 ... Plus* (See For Miles 1994)★★★★, *The Locust Years . . . And The Return To The Promised Land* 8-CD box set (Bear Family 1995)★★★★, *Sun Classics* (Charly 1995)★★★★, *Killer Country* ii (Mercury 1995)★★★.

● VIDEOS: *Carl Perkins & Jerry Lee Lewis Live* (BBC Video 1987), *Jerry Lee Lewis* (Fox Video 1989), *I Am What I Am* (Charly Video 1990), *The Killer* (Telstar Video 1991), *Killer Performance* (Virgin Vision 1991), *The Jerry Lee Lewis Show* (MMG Video 1991).

● FURTHER READING: *Jerry Lee Lewis: The Ball Of Fire*, Allan Clark. *Jerry Lee Lewis*, Robert Palmer. *Whole Lotta Shakin' Goin' On: Jerry Lee Lewis*, Robert Cain. *Hellfire: The Jerry Lee Lewis Story*, Nick Tosches. *Great Balls Of Fire: The True Story Of Jerry Lee Lewis*, Myra Lewis. *Rockin' My Life Away: Listening To Jerry Lee Lewis*, Jimmy Guteman. *Killer!*, Jerry Lee Lewis And Charles White.

● FILMS: *Jamboree* aka *Disc Jockey Jamboree* (1957), *Beach Ball* (1964), *Be My Guest* (1965), *American Hot Wax* (1976).

LEWIS, VIC

b. 29 July 1919, London, England. Lewis began playing a four-string banjo while still a child, later switching to guitar. In his teens he formed his own quartet, having developed an interest in jazz through listening to records. His quartet appeared on a talent show and soon obtained radio work on the BBC and Radio Luxembourg and also in London theatres. In the London jazz clubs Lewis met and played with artists such as Django Reinhardt, Stéphane Grappelli, George Shearing and George Chisholm. In 1938, he visited New York where he played with Joe Marsala, Marty Marsala, Joe Bushkin, Buddy Rich, Pee Wee Russell, Bobby Hackett and other noted jazzmen, even sitting in with Tommy Dorsey, Jack Teagarden and Louis Armstrong. He also made a handful of records during this trip with Hackett, Eddie Condon and Zutty Singleton in the band. He returned to England and with the outbreak of war served in the RAF where he played in a band whenever the opportunity presented itself. After the war, Lewis formed a new unit,

teaming up with Jack Parnell to co-lead a small group. When Parnell moved on, Lewis continued to lead the band, which proved very popular and broadcast frequently on the BBC. In the late 40s Lewis formed a big band, employing musicians such as Ronnie Chamberlain, Bob Efford and Gordon Langhorn, that emulated the music of Stan Kenton. He also formed an orchestra that backed visiting American artists including Armstrong and Johnny Ray. On occasion, Lewis sat in with Armstrong and Kenton, playing trombone. In the 60s, Lewis switched tracks, becoming a manager and agent, handling tours by Count Basie, whom he had met in New York in 1938, Dudley Moore (his first client), Judy Garland, Carmen McRae, Johnny Mathis, Andy Williams and Nina Simone. Lewis was also deeply involved with NEMS Enterprises, working with Brian Epstein, the Beatles and Cilla Black. Lewis's activities in these areas continued through the 70s when he organized tours for Shirley Bassey and Elton John. He retained his jazz links, however, recording a bossa nova album in 1963, half in the USA with several Kenton alumni and half in London with a band featuring Tubby Hayes and Ronnie Scott. In the early 80s he began to form occasional big bands for jazz dates. He recruited visiting American stars such as Shorty Rogers and Bud Shank to perform on a series of records. As a bandleader and promoter, Lewis has been active for many decades and has brought to the UK jazz scene a great deal of enthusiasm; his activities on the pop scene were also of much value. For all that, as his autobiography hints, he would probably have given away his entire musical career for a chance to play cricket for England.

● ALBUMS: *Mulligan's Music And At The Royal Festival Hall* (1955)★★★★, *Vic Lewis And His Bossa Nova All Stars* (1963)★★★★, *Vic Lewis At The Beaulieu Jazz Festival* (1965)★★★, *Vic Lewis Plays The Music Of Donovan Leith* (1968)★★, *Vic Lewis With Maynard Ferguson* (1969)★★★, *Don't Cry For Me Argentina* (1974)★★, *Vic Lewis And R.P.O.* (RCA 1977)★★★, *Back Again* (1984)★★★, *Vic Lewis Big Bands* (1985)★★★, *Tea Break* (1985)★★★, *Vic Lewis And The West Coast All Stars* (1989)★★★★, *Know It Today, Know It Tomorrow* (1993)★★★, *Shake Down The Stars* (Candid 1993)★★★, *Play Bill Holman* (Candid 1994)★★★.

● COMPILATIONS: *My Life, My Way* 4-LP box set (1975)★★★, *New York, 1938* (Esquire 1986)★★★, *Vic Lewis Jam Sessions, Vol. 1-6 (1938-49)* (Harlequin 1986)★★★, *Vic Lewis Plays Stan Kenton (1948-54)* (Harlequin 1987)★★★★, *The EMI Years* (EMI 1991)★★★★.

● FURTHER READING: *Music And Maiden Overs: My Show Business Life*, Vic Lewis with Tony Barrow.

LIBERACE

b. Wladziu Valentino Liberace, 16 May 1919, West Allis, Wisconsin, USA, d. 4 February 1987, Palm Springs, Florida, USA. This larger-than-life pianist had no major chart hits - but had an indefinable charm and talent that gave delight to multitudes of fans across the globe. Of Polish-Italian extraction, he was raised in a household where there was always music - particularly from father Salvatore who played French horn in both John Philip Sousa's Concert Band and the Milwaukee Symphony Orchestra. George and the younger Wladziu were, likewise, both eager to become professional players. Wladziu's piano skills were praised by no less than Paderewski, and he won a place at Wisconsin

College of Music at the age of seven. During his 17-year scholarship - the longest ever awarded by the academy - he made his concert debut as a soloist at the age of 11 and was fronting renowned symphony orchestras while still an adolescent. A fulfilling career of classical recitals and university master classes might have beckoned but for the artist's innate sense of humour and flair for self-promotion. In 1934, he had elocution lessons to dilute his Polish accent. After service in an overseas entertainments unit during World War II, he played and sang in club dance bands and it was during a residency at the Wunderbar in Warsaw, Wisconsin, that he was first introduced as 'Liberace'. At New York's Persian Rooms, an experiment whereby he performed counterpoints to records - including his own one-shot single for the Signature label - played on the venue's sound system, was curtailed by a Musicians Union ban. A happier season in a Californian hotel resulted in a Decca contract, for which he was visualized as a second Frankie Carle. However, wishing to develop a more personal style, he moved to Columbia Records where, supervised by Mitch Miller, he recorded a flamboyant version of 'September Song' which, supplemented by an in-concert album, brought Liberace to a national audience.

By the early 50s, his repertoire embraced George Gershwin favourites, cocktail jazz, film themes ('Unchained Melody'), boogie-woogie and self-composed pieces ('Rhapsody By Candlelight'), as well as adaptations of light classics such as 'Story Of Three Loves' - borrowed from a Rachmaninov variation on a tune by Paganini. Nevertheless, Liberace struck the most popular chord with his encores, in which doggerel such as 'Maizy Doats' or 'Three Little Fishes' were dressed in arrangements littered with twee arpeggios and trills. He also started garbing himself from a wardrobe that stretched to rhinestone, white mink, sequins, gold lamé and similar razzle-dazzle. Crowned with a carefully waved coiffeur, he oozed charm and extravagant gesture, with a candelabra-lit piano as the focal point of the epic vulgarity that was *The Liberace Show*, televised coast-to-coast from Los Angeles; the show established a public image that he later tried in vain to modify. His fame was such that he was name-checked in 'Mr. Sandman', a 1954 million-seller by the Chordettes, and a year later, starred (as a deaf concert pianist) in a film, *Sincerely Yours*, with brother George (future administrator of the Liberace Museum in Las Vegas) as musical director. Another spin-off was the publication of a Liberace cookbook. Following the celebration of his quarter century in showbusiness with a Hollywood Bowl spectacular in 1956, Liberace crossed to England (where a vocal outing, 'I Don't Care', was lodged in the Top 30) for the first of three Royal Command Performances. While in the UK, he instigated a High Court action, successfully suing the *Daily Mirror*, whose waspish columnist Cassandra had written an article on the star laced with sexual innuendo. During the next decade, a cameo in the film satire *The Loved One* was reviewed not unfavourably, as was one of his early albums for RCA Records in which he aimed more directly at the contemporary market. This, however, was a rare excursion, as his work generally maintained a certain steady consistency - or 'squareness', in the words of his detractors - that deviated little from the commercial blueprint wrought in the 50s. Nonetheless, Liberace's mode of presentation left its mark on stars such as Gary Glitter, Elton John and Queen.

Although attendant publicity boosted box office takings on a world tour, embarrassing tabloid newspaper allegations by a former employee placed his career in a darker perspective. When the singer died on 4 February 1987 at his Palm Springs mansion, the words 'kidney complaint' were assumed to be a euphemism for an AIDS-related illness. For a 75th Birthday Celebration in 1994, fans from all over America gathered to pay their respects at Liberace Plaza in Las Vegas.

● ALBUMS: *Piano* (Advance 1951)★★★, *Liberace At the Piano* (Columbia 1952)★★★, *An Evening With Liberace* (Columbia 1953)★★★★, *Liberace By Candlelight* (Columbia 1953)★★★, *Concertos For You* (Columbia 1953)★★★, *Concertos For You Vol. 2* (Columbia 1954)★★★, *Plays Chopin* (Columbia 1954)★★★, *Plays Chopin Vol. 2* (Columbia 1954)★★★, *Sincerely Yours* film soundtrack (Columbia 1953)★★★, *Piano Reverie* (Columbia 1955)★★★, *Kiddin' On The Keys* (Columbia 1956)★★★, *My Inspiration* (Coral 1960)★★★, *Liberace At The Palladium* (Coral 1961)★★★, *My Parade Of Golden Favourites* (Coral 1961)★★★, *As Time Goes By* (Coral 1962)★★★, *Rhapsody By Candlelight* (Coral 1962)★★★, *Mr. Showmanship* (1963)★★★, *Christmas* (1963)★★, *My Most Requested* (1964)★★★, *Liberace At The American* (1964)★★★, *Golden Hits Of Hollywood* (Coral 1965)★★★, *Liberace Now* (1967)★★★, *A Brand New Me* (Warners 1970)★★, *Candlelight Classics* (Ember 1973)★★★, *Piano Gems* (Pye 1976)★★★, *Mr. Showmanship - Live* (Pye 1978)★★★, *New Sounds* (Dot 1979)★★★.

● COMPILATIONS: *Just For You* (PRT 1976)★★★, *Best Of Liberace* (MCA 1983)★★★, *The Collection* (Castle 1988)★★★.

● VIDEOS: *Liberace In Las Vegas* (Virgin Vision 1988), *Liberace Live* (Vestron Music 1988).

● FURTHER READING: *Liberace*, Liberace. *Liberace: The True Story*, B. Thomas.

LIEBERSON, GODDARD

b. 5 April 1911, Hanley, Staffordshire, England, d. 29 May 1977, New York City, New York, USA. A record company executive, composer, author, and musician, Lieberson was four years old when his family moved to Seattle, Washington, USA. After graduating from the local university, he studied at the Eastman School of Music in New York, and originally intended to pursue a career as a composer. Financial reality intervened, and in 1939, he became the assistant director of the Masterworks division of Columbia Records, part of the CBS group. During the 40s he recorded plays, operas, and other classical works, while at the same time rising to the position of executive vice-president of Columbia. In the late 40s, he was influential in the decision to select the 33 1/3 speed as the standard for the new long-playing record. The development also contributed directly towards his greatest success as a pioneering producer of original cast recordings of hit Broadway shows. He began in 1949 with *South Pacific*, for which he won the first of seven Gold Discs. The other award winners were *Flower Drum Song*, *Camelot*, *West Side Story*, *Mame*, *The Sound Of Music* and *My Fair Lady*. He was so impressed by the score for the latter show that he persuaded CBS to become the sole investor - and, with sales of over six million units, they made a fortune. His 'amazing ear, his enthusiasm for theatre music, and his respect for the work he was doing' made him a legendary figure in the industry. Lieberson also recorded many shows when they had closed after only a few performances, convinced, quite rightly in most cases, that the scores were worth preserving. He was responsible for recording the vast majority of the shows that have been re-released in CD form on the Sony Broadway label. During a long and distinguished career, Lieberson is credited with having signed many important artists, including Simon And Garfunkel and Bob Dylan. He rose to become the president of Columbia Records (1955-56), of the CBS/Columbia Group (1966-71 and 1973-75), but he will be remembered mainly for his sensitive and brilliant work in preserving so much wonderful Broadway music. His final recordings, in the early 70s, were *A Little Night Music*, *Billy* and the record-breaking *A Chorus Line* (1975).

LIGGINS, JOE

b. 9 July 1916, Guthrie, Oklahoma, USA, d. 26 July 1987, Los Angeles, California, USA. After attempting to learn various brass instruments, Joe Liggins settled down to study musical composition and piano arrangement. After moving to California, he began writing for and playing with local bands, graduating in the 40s to the respected units of Cee Pee Johnson and Sammy Franklin; he was working with the latter when, in 1945, he left to form his own group, the Honeydrippers. Joe Liggins And His Honeydrippers first recorded for Exclusive, with whom they had 10 hits between 1945 and 1949 - including the huge crossover hits 'The Honeydripper' and 'I've Got A Right To Cry'; he followed his brother Jimmy to Specialty Records in 1950 where the hits continued with 'Rag Mop' and the hugely successful 'Pink Champagne' (*Billboard*'s number 1 blues record of the year). Leaving Specialty in 1954, Liggins went briefly to Mercury (1954) and Aladdin Records (1956) before returning to Mercury to record an album in 1962. Later singles appeared on tiny independents such as his own Honeydripper label and Jimmy Liggins' Duplex Records, and he was enjoying something of a renaissance at the time of his death in 1987.
● ALBUMS: *Honeydripper* (Mercury 1962)★★★★, *Great R&B Oldies* (1972)★★★, with Jimmy Liggins *Saturday Night Boogie Woogie Man* (Sonet 1974)★★★.
● COMPILATIONS: *Darktown Strutters' Ball* (Jukebox Lil 1981)★★★, *The Honeydripper* (Jukebox Lil 1988)★★★, *Joe Liggins & The Honeydrippers* (Ace 1989)★★★★, *Vol. 2: Drippers Boogie* (Ace 1993)★★★★.

LIGHTNIN' SLIM

b. Otis Hicks, 13 March 1913, St. Louis, Missouri, USA, d. 27 July 1974, Detroit, Michigan, USA. It is as a Louisiana blues stylist that Hicks is best known, having settled in that state in his early teens. He learned guitar from his father and his brother, and made a name for himself on the Baton Rouge blues circuit during the 40s. In 1954, he recorded for J.D. 'Jay' Miller's Feature label, and began that producer's long and fruitful relationship with the blues. These early recordings had a tough, spare sound that helps to place them alongside the very finest down-home blues of the 50s, and the quality was largely maintained over much of the next decade, with many singles leased to Excello Records. His partnership with harmonica player Lazy Lester was particularly effective and releases such as 'Mean Old Lonesome Train', 'Hoodoo Blues' and, especially, 'Rooster Blues', provided him with commercial success and kept him in

demand for tours both locally and further afield. Many of his releases demonstrate his particular facility for taking raw material from the work of other popular bluesmen, such as Muddy Waters and Lightnin' Hopkins, and turning it into something entirely his own. The relationship with Miller finally came to an end in 1965, but within a few years, Slim found a wider forum for his music when he became a regular visitor to Europe.
● ALBUMS: *Rooster Blues* (Excello 1960)★★★★, *Lightnin' Slim's Bell Ringer* (Excello 1965)★★★★, *High And Lowdown* (Excello 1971)★★★, *Over Easy* (Excello 1971)★★.
● COMPILATIONS: *The Early Years* (1976)★★★, *London Gumbo* (Sonet 1978)★★, *The Feature Sides* (Flyright 1981)★★★, *We Gotta Rock Tonight* (Flyright 1986)★★★, *Blue Lightnin'* (Indigo 1992)★★★, *King Of The Swamp Blues* 1954 recording (Flyright 1992)★★★, *It's Mighty Crazy* 1954-58 recordings (Ace 1995)★★★★, *Nothing But The Devil* (Ace 1996)★★★★, *Winter Time Blues* (Ace 1998)★★★★.

LITTLE RICHARD

b. Richard Wayne Penniman, 5 December 1935, Macon, Georgia, USA. The wildest and arguably the greatest and most influential of the 50s rock 'n' roll singers and songwriters. He first recorded in late 1951 in Atlanta for RCA, cutting eight urban blues tracks with his mentor Billy Wright's Orchestra, 'Taxi Blues' being the first of four unsuccessful single releases on the label. He moved to Houston, Texas, in 1953, and with the Tempo Toppers (vocals) and the Duces of Rhythm (backing), he recorded four R&B tracks including 'Ain't That Good News'. Eight months later he recorded another four with Johnny Otis's Orchestra but none of these were released at the time. In February 1955, at the suggestion of Lloyd Price, he sent a demo to Specialty Records who realized his potential, and in September, under the guidance of producer Robert 'Bumps' Blackwell, recorded a dozen tracks in New Orleans. The classic 'Tutti Frutti', which was among them, gave him his first R&B and pop hit in the USA. The follow-up, 'Long Tall Sally', topped the R&B chart and was the first of his three US Top 10 hits, despite being covered by Pat Boone, whose previous record, a cover version of 'Tutti Frutti', was still charting. Richard's string of Top 20 hits continued with the double-sider 'Rip It Up'/'Ready Teddy', the former being his first UK release and chart entry in late 1956. Richard's frantic, unrestrained performance of his first two hits, 'Long Tall Sally' and 'Tutti Frutti', in the film *Don't Knock The Rock*, undoubtedly helped to push his subsequent UK single, which coupled the tracks, into the Top 3.
His next film and single was *The Girl Can't Help It*, the title song of which missed the US Top 40 but together with its b-side, 'She's Got It' (a reworking of his earlier track 'I Got It'), gave him two more UK Top 20 hits. The remainder of 1957 saw him notch up three more huge transatlantic hits with the rock 'n' roll classics 'Lucille', 'Keep A Knockin'' (he featured both in the movie *Mr. Rock & Roll*) and 'Jenny Jenny' and a Top 20 album with *Here's Little Richard*. At the very height of his career, the man with the highest pompadour in the business shocked the rock world by announcing, during an Australian tour, that he was quitting music to go into a theological college. In 1958, previously recorded material such as the transatlantic Top 10 hit 'Good Golly Miss Molly' kept his name on the chart, and a year later he had his biggest UK hit with a 1956 recording of the oldie 'Baby Face',

which reached number 2. Between 1958 and 1962 Richard recorded only gospel music for Gone, Mercury (with producer Quincy Jones) and Atlantic. In late 1962, Richard toured the UK for the first time and the now short-haired wild man who pounded pianos and pierced eardrums with his manic falsetto was a huge success. In 1963, he worked in Europe with the Beatles and the Rolling Stones, who were both great admirers of his music. His first rock recordings in the 60s were made back at Specialty and resulted in the UK Top 20 hit 'Bama Lama Bama Loo'. In 1964, he signed with Vee Jay where he re-recorded all his hits, revived a few oldies and cut some new rockers - but the sales were unimpressive. In the mid-60s, soul music was taking hold worldwide and Richard's soulful Vee Jay tracks, 'I Don't Know What You've Got But It's Got Me' (which featured Jimi Hendrix on guitar) and 'Without Love', although not pop hits, were among the best recordings of the genre. For the rest of the 60s he continued to draw the crowds, singing his old hits, and in the studios he mixed 50s rock and 60s soul for Modern in 1965, OKeh a year later and Brunswick in 1967. The best of these were his OKeh tracks, which included 'Poor Dog', 'Hurry Sundown' and the UK-recorded 'Get Down With It' (which gave Slade their first hit in the 70s).

Reprise Records, whom he joined in 1970, tried very hard to return him to the top, and under the expertise of producer Richard Perry he managed minor US hits 'Freedom Blues' and 'Greenwood, Mississippi', but his three albums sold poorly. The rest of the 70s was spent jumping from label to label, recording in supergroup-type projects and playing oldies shows. When he desired, he could still 'out-rock' anyone, but there was often too much Las Vegas glitter, excessive posturing and an element of self-parody. In 1976, he rejoined the church and for the next decade preached throughout America. In 1986, Richard was one of the first artists inducted into the Rock And Roll Hall of Fame and he successfully acted in the film *Down And Out In Beverly Hills*, which included the rocking 'Great Gosh A'Mighty', which narrowly missed the US Top 40. Renewed interest spurred WEA to sign him and release *Lifetime Friend*, which included the chart record 'Operator'. Since the mid-80s he has become a frequent visitor on chat shows, an in-demand guest on other artist's records and a familiar face in videos (by acts ranging from Hank Williams Jnr. to Living Colour to Cinderella). He even has his own star on the Hollywood Walk of Fame and a boulevard named after him in his hometown. Nowadays a regular presenter of music awards, he has also been the star of Jive Bunny hits. The leader of rebellious 50s rock 'n' roll, and the man who shook up the music business and the parents of the period, is now a much-loved personality accepted by all age groups.

● ALBUMS: *Little Richard* (Camden 1956)★★★, *Here's Little Richard* (Specialty 1957)★★★★★, *Little Richard Volume 2* (Specialty 1957)★★★★★, *The Fabulous Little Richard* (Specialty 1958)★★★★★, *Sings Gospel* (20th Century 1959)★★, *It's Real* (Mercury 1961)★★, *Little Richard Sings Freedom Songs* (Crown 1963)★★, *Coming Home* (Coral 1963)★★, *King Of The Gospel Singers* (Wing 1964)★, *Little Richard Is Back* (Vee Jay 1965)★★, *The Explosive Little Richard* (Columbia 1967)★★★, *Good Golly Miss Molly* (Specialty 1969)★★★, *The Little Richard Story* (Joy 1970)★★★, *Well Alright* (Specialty 1970)★★★, *Rock Hard*

Rock Heavy (Specialty 1970)★★, *You Can't Keep A Good Man Down* (Union Pacific 1970)★★, *The Rill Thing* (Reprise 1970)★★, *Mr Big* (Joy 1971)★★, *Cast A Long Shadow* (Epic 1971)★★, *King Of Rock 'n' Roll* (Reprise 1971)★★★, *The Original Little Richard* (Specialty 1972)★★★, *The Second Coming* (Warners 1973)★★★, *Rip It Up* (Joy 1973)★★, *Slippin' And Slidin'* (Joy 1973)★★, *Good Golly Miss Molly* (Hallmark 1974)★★★, *Greatest Hits Recorded Live* (Embassy 1974)★★★, *Keep A Knockin'* (Rhapsody 1975)★★, *Dollars Dollars* (Charly 1975)★★, *The Great Ones* (MFP 1976)★★, *Little Richard And Jimi Hendrix Together* (Ember 1977)★, *Whole Lotta Shakin' Goin' On* (DJM 1977)★★★, *Little Richard Now* (Creole 1977)★★, *The Georgia Peach* (Charly 1980)★★★, *Little Richard And His Band* (Specialty 1980)★★, *Ooh! My Soul* (Charly 1982)★★★, *Whole Lotta Shakin'* (Bulldog 1982)★★★, *Get Down With It* (Edsel 1982)★★, *The Real Thing* (Magnum Force 1983)★★★, *Little Richard* (Cambra 1983)★★★, *He's Got It* (Topline 1984)★★, *Lifetime Friend* (Warners 1986)★★★.

● COMPILATIONS: *His Biggest Hits* (Specialty 1963)★★★★, *Little Richard's Greatest Hits* (Vee Jay 1965)★★★★, *Little Richard's Greatest Hits* (OKeh 1967)★★★★, *Little Richard's Greatest Hits* (Joy 1968)★★★, *Little Richard's Grooviest 17 Original Hits* (Specialty 1968)★★★★, *20 Original Greatest Hits* (Specialty 1976)★★★★, *The Essential Little Richard* (Specialty 1985)★★★, *18 Greatest Hits* (Rhino 1985)★★★★, *20 Classic Cuts* (Ace 1986)★★★★, *Shut Up! A Collection Of Rare Tracks (1951 - 1964)* (Rhino 1988)★★★, *The Collection* (Castle 1989)★★★★, *The Specialty Sessions* 6-CD box set (Specialty 1990)★★★★★, *The Formative Years, 1951-53* (Bear Family 1989)★★★, *The EP Collection* (See For Miles 1993)★★★★★.

● FURTHER READING: *The Life And Times Of Little Richard: The Quasar Of Rock*, Charles White.

● FILMS: *The Girl Can't Help It* (1956), *Don't Knock The Rock* (1956), *Catalina Caper* (1967).

LITTLE WALTER

b. Marion Walter Jacobs, 1 May 1930, Marksville, Louisiana, USA, d. 15 February 1968. A major figure of post-war blues, Little Walter is credited for bringing the harmonica, or 'French harp', out from its rural setting and into an urban context. His career began at the age of 12 when he left home for New Orleans, but by 1946 Jacobs was working in Chicago's famed Maxwell Street. Early recordings for the Ora Nelle label were the prelude to his joining the Muddy Waters band, where he helped to forge what became the definitive electric Chicago blues group. The harmonica player emerged as a performer in his own right in 1952 when 'Juke', an instrumental recorded at the end of a Waters session, topped the R&B chart, where it remained for eight consecutive weeks. Little Walter And The Night Caps - David Myers (guitar), Louis Myers (guitar) and Fred Below (drums) - enjoyed further success when 'Sad Hours' and 'Mean Old World' reached the Top 10 in the same chart. The group then became known as Little Walter And The Jukes and, although obliged to fulfil recording agreements with Waters, Jacobs actively pursued his own career. He enjoyed further R&B hits with 'Blues With A Feeling' (1953), 'Last Night' (1954) and the infectious 'My Babe' (1955). The last song, patterned on a spiritual tune, 'This Train', was a second number 1 single and became much covered during later years. Other notable releases included 'Mellow Down Easy' and 'Boom Boom (Out Go The Lights)' which were later recorded, respectively, by Paul Butterfield and the Blues Band. A haunting version of 'Key To The Highway' (1958), previously recorded by Big Bill Broonzy, gave Walter his final Top 10 entry. He nonetheless remained a pivotal figure, undertaking several tours, including one of Britain in 1964. His career, however, was undermined by personal problems. A pugnacious man with a quick temper and a reputation for heavy drinking, he died on 15 February 1968 as a result of injuries sustained in a street brawl. This ignominious end should not detract from Little Walter's status as an innovative figure. The first musician to amplify the harmonica, his heavy, swooping style became the lynchpin for all who followed him, including Norton Buffalo, Butterfield and Charlie Musselwhite.

● ALBUMS: *The Best Of Little Walter* (Checker 1958)★★★★, *Little Walter* (Pye International 1964)★★★★, *Hate To See You Go* (Chess 1969)★★★, *Thunderbird* (Syndicate Chapter 1971)★★★, *On The Road Again* (Xtra 1979)★★★, *Quarter To Twelve* (Red Lightnin' 1982)★★★.

● COMPILATIONS: *Chess Masters* (Charly 1983)★★★★, *Boss Blues Harmonica* (Vogue 1986)★★★★, *Confessin' The Blues* (Chess 1986)★★★★, *Windy City Blues* (Blue Moon 1986)★★★, *Collection: Little Walter 20 Blues Greats* (Deja Vu 1987)★★★, *The Blues World Of Little Walter* (Delmark 1988)★★★★, *The Best Of Little Walter Volume 2* (Chess 1989)★★★, *The Chess Years 1952 - '63* 4-CD box set (Chess 1993)★★★★, *Blues With A Feeling* (MCA/Chess 1995)★★★★.

LIVING IT UP

One of the best films that Dean Martin and Jerry Lewis made together in the mid-50s, this 1954 Paramount release was twice blessed - with an amusing story and a set of good songs. Jack Rose and Melville Shavelson's screenplay was based on James Street's story *Letter To The Editor* and the 1937 movie *Nothing Sacred*, which starred Fredric March and Carole Lombard. Proving that nothing *is* sacred in Hollywood, Lombard's role was played this time by Jerry Lewis, who gave a typically zany performance as a man who thinks he has had a hefty dose of radiation poisoning. Encouraged by his doctor (Martin), who knows very well it is only a sinus condition, and a newspaper reporter (Janet Leigh), who believes he is going to die and knows a good story when she sees one, Lewis takes a press-sponsored trip to New York for one final all-out binge. It was all very entertaining, but much of the original film's bite and satire seemed to be lost on the way. Two of Jule Styne and Bob Hilliard's songs, 'How Do You Speak To An Angel?' and 'Money Burns A Hole In My Pocket', became popular record hits, and Martin's relaxed and easy manner was ideal for the engaging 'That's What I Like' and a duet with Lewis, 'Ev'ry Street's A Boulevard (In Old New York)'. The other songs were 'Champagne And Wedding Cake' and 'You're Gonna Dance With Me, Baby'. Also featured were Edward Arnold, Fred Clark, Sheree North, Sig Ruman and Sammy White. Norman Taurog was the director and the film was shot in Technicolor. Styne and Hilliard also wrote the score for a 1953 Broadway musical based on this story. It was called *Hazel Flagg*, and ran for just 190 performances.

LLOYD, A.L.

b. February 1908, London, England. Bert Lloyd was one of the prime movers of the 50s folk song revival in Britain. He had collected some 500 songs by 1935 and was determined to study and conduct research into folk music. In 1937, he sailed to Antarctica with a whaling fleet, adding further songs to his repertoire. On his return he joined BBC Radio as a scriptwriter. During the 40s he wrote *The Singing Englishman*, the first general book on folk song since Cecil Sharp's in 1909. He also compiled the *Penguin Book Of English Folk Song* with the composer Ralph Vaughan Williams. By the 50s, Lloyd was a full-time folklorist, making several field trips to record material in Bulgaria and Albania as well as publishing a selection of coalfield ballads, which provided repertoire for young singers in the growing number of folk song clubs. At this time he met Ewan MacColl, with whom he made his own first recordings, as part of the *Radio Ballads* series. During the 60s he made a series of solo albums for Topic Records, with accompanists including singers Anne Briggs and Frankie Armstrong, Alf Edwards (accordion), Martin Carthy (guitar, mandolin), Dave Swarbrick (fiddle) and actor and singer Harry H. Corbett. They covered drinking songs, industrial songs and selections from his sheep-shearing and whaling exploits. Lloyd also arranged compilation albums of sea shanties, industrial songs (*The Iron Muse*) and recordings from the Balkan field trips.

● ALBUMS: *Selections From The Penguin Book Of English Folk Songs* (Topic 1960)★★★, *The Iron Muse* (Topic 1963)★★★, with Ewan MacColl *English And Scottish Popular Ballads* (Topic 1964)★★★★, *All For Me Grog* (Topic 1964)★★★, *The Bird In The Bush* (Topic 1965)★★★, *First Person* (Topic 1966)★★★, *Leviathan* (Topic 1968)★★★, *The Great Australian Legend* (Topic 1969)★★★, *Sea Songs And Shanties* (1981)★★★★.

● COMPILATIONS: *Classic A.L. Lloyd* (Fellside 1995).

● FURTHER READING: *The Singing Englishman*, A.L. Lloyd.

LOCK UP YOUR DAUGHTERS

This show was the first to be presented at the new Mermaid Theatre in the City of London, on 28 May 1959, and was, appropriately enough, the brainchild of the Mermaid's founder, Bernard (later, Sir Bernard) Miles. His adaptation of Henry Fielding's *Rape Upon Rape* was an extremely bawdy tale in which a gentle maiden, Hilaret (Stephanie Voss), and her would-be rapist, Ramble (Frederick Jaeger), appear before the lecherous Justice Squeezum (Richard Wordsworth). Squeezum's efforts to inflict his own individual brand of custodial sentence on Hilaret lead to highly complicated manoeuvres that involve the far-from-innocent Mrs Squeezum (Hy Hazell), and result in the Justice himself going to prison. The object of his affections is then reunited with her true love, Captain Constant (Terence Cooper). The score, by two young newcomers, composer Laurie Johnson and lyricist Lionel Bart (Bart's *Fings Ain't Wot They Used T'Be* was just starting out at the Theatre Royal Stratford), complemented perfectly the lusty outrages of the story, in songs such as 'Lock Up Your Daughters' ('Here comes a rake!'), 'When Does The Ravishing Begin?', 'Red Wine And A Wench' and 'I'll Be There'. Hilaret *almost* seduces Squeezum in 'On A Sunny Sunday Morning', and the other delights included

'Lovely Lover', 'Kind Fate', 'A Proper Man', 'It Must Be True', ''Tis Plain To See' and 'Mr. Jones'. The show ran for 330 performances, and subsequently had its US premiere in New Haven in April 1960. *Lock Up Your Daughters* returned to the Mermaid two years later before transferring to the Her Majesty's theatre in the West End for a stay of some 16 months; it returned to the Mermaid in 1969 for a brief stay. Another American production, with 50s film star Carleton Carpenter as Squeezum, was presented at the Goodspeed Opera House in 1982.

LOESSER, FRANK

b. Frank Henry Loesser, 29 June 1910, New York City, New York, USA, d. 28 July 1969. A leading songwriter for the stage, films and Tin Pan Alley from the 30s through to the 60s. Initially, he only wrote lyrics, but later in his career he provided both words and music, and sometimes co-produced through his Frank Productions. Born into a musical family (his father was a music teacher, and his brother a music critic and pianist), Loesser rejected a formal musical education, and trained himself. During the Depression years of the early 30s, following a brief spell at City College, New York, Loesser worked in a variety of jobs including city editor for a local newspaper, jewellery salesman and waiter. His first published song, written with William Schuman in 1931, was 'In Love With A Memory Of You'. Loesser also wrote for vaudeville performers and played piano in nightclubs around New York's 52nd Street. In 1936, he contributed some lyrics to *The Illustrators Show*, with music by Irving Actman, including 'Bang-The Bell Rang!' and 'If You Didn't Love Me', but the show closed after only five Broadway performances. In 1937, Loesser went to Hollywood and spent the next few years writing lyrics for movies such as *Cocoanut Grove* ('Says My Heart'), *College Swing* ('Moments Like This' and 'How'dja Like To Make Love To Me?'), *Sing You Sinners* (Bing Crosby singing 'Small Fry'), *Thanks For The Memory* (Bob Hope and Shirley Ross singing 'Two Sleepy People'), *The Hurricane* (Dorothy Lamour singing 'Moon Of Manakoora'), *Man About Town* ('Fidgety Joe' and 'Strange Enchantment'), *Some Like It Hot* (1939 film starring Bob Hope and Shirley Ross singing 'The Lady's In Love With You'), *Destry Rides Again* (Marlene Dietrich with a memorable version of 'See What The Boys In The Backroom Will Have'), *Dancing On A Dime* ('I Hear Music'), *Las Vegas Nights* ('Dolores'), *Kiss The Boys Goodbye* ('I'll Never Let A Day Pass By', 'Sand In My Shoes' and the title song), *Sweater Girl* ('I Don't Want To Walk Without You' and 'I Said No'), *Forest Rangers* ('Jingle Jangle Jingle'), *Happy-Go-Lucky* ('Let's Get Lost' and ''Murder' She Says'), *Seven Days Leave* ('Can't Get Out Of This Mood') and *Thank Your Lucky Stars* ('They're Either Too Young Or Too Old', sung by Bette Davis, and featuring one of Loesser's most amusing lyrics, including the couplet: 'I either get a fossil, or an adolescent pup/I either have to hold him off, or have to hold him up!'). These songs were written in collaboration with composers Burton Lane, Hoagy Carmichael, Alfred Newman, Matty Malneck, Frederick Hollander, Louis Alter, Victor Schertzinger, Jule Styne, Joseph Lilley, Jimmy McHugh and Arthur Schwartz. The first song for which Loesser wrote both music and lyrics is said to be 'Praise The Lord And Pass The Ammunition', and when he left Hollywood for military service during World War II he added some more service

songs to his catalogue, including 'First Class Private Mary Brown', 'The Ballad Of Roger Young', 'What Do You Do In The Infantry?' and 'Salute To The Army Service Forces'. He also continued to write for films such as *Christmas Holiday* (1944, 'Spring Will Be A Little Late This Year') and *The Perils Of Pauline* (1947), the biopic of silent-movie queen Pearl White, with Loesser's songs 'Poppa Don't Preach To Me' and 'I Wish I Didn't Love You So', the latter of which was nominated for an Academy Award. Loesser finally received his Oscar in 1949 for 'Baby It's Cold Outside', from the Esther Williams/Red Skelton movie *Neptune's Daughter*. In 1948, Loesser wrote 'On A Slow Boat To China', which became a hit for several US artists including Kay Kyser, Freddy Martin, Eddy Howard and Benny Goodman. In the same year he again turned his attention to the Broadway stage, writing the score for a musical adaptation of Brandon Thomas's classic English farce, *Charley's Aunt*. *Where's Charley?*, starring Ray Bolger, included the songs 'My Darling, My Darling', 'Once In Love With Amy', 'The New Ashmoleon Marching Society And Student Conservatory Band' and 'Make A Miracle'. The show ran for a creditable 792 performances.

Far more successful, two years later, was *Guys And Dolls*, a musical setting of a Damon Runyon fable, starring Robert Alda, Vivian Blaine, Sam Levene, Isabel Bigley and Stubby Kaye. It ran for 1,200 performances, and is generally considered to be Loesser's masterpiece. As with *Where's Charley?*, he was now writing both music and lyrics, and the show is such a legend that it is worth listing the principal songs: 'Fugue For Tinhorns', 'The Oldest Established', 'I'll Know', 'A Bushel And A Peck', 'Adelaide's Lament', 'Guys And Dolls', 'If I Were A Bell', 'My Time Of Day', 'I've Never Been In Love Before', 'Take Back Your Mink', 'More I Cannot Wish You', 'Luck Be A Lady', 'Sue Me', 'Sit Down, You're Rockin' The Boat' and 'Marry The Man Today'. The original cast album is still available in the 90s, and among the other associated issues was an all-black cast album, released on the Motown label, and *Guys And Dolls: The Kirby Stone Four*. A film adaptation of *Guys And Dolls* was released in 1955, starring Frank Sinatra, Marlon Brando, Jean Simmons and Vivian Blaine. The movie version left out some of the original songs, and Loesser replaced them with 'A Woman In Love' and 'Adelaide'. In 1952, *Where's Charley?* was released as a film version, and the same year saw a movie of *Hans Christian Andersen*, starring Danny Kaye in the title role, and featuring a Loesser score that included 'Wonderful Copenhagen', 'No Two People', 'Anywhere I Wander', 'Inchworm' and 'Thumbelina'. Loesser's next Broadway project was *The Most Happy Fella*, for which he also wrote the libretto. The show was adapted from the original story *They Knew What They Wanted*, by Sidney Howard, which told the tale of an elderly Italian winegrower living in California, who falls in love at first sight with a waitress. Loesser created what has been called 'one of the most ambitiously operatic works ever written for the Broadway musical theatre'. Arias such as 'Rosabella' and 'My Heart Is So Full Of You' contrast with more familiar Broadway fare such as 'Standing On the Corner', 'Big D' and 'Happy To Make Your Acquaintance'. The show ran for 676 performances, far more than Loesser's 1960 production of the folksy *Greenwillow*, which closed after less than three months. It starred Anthony Perkins in his first musical, and contained a religious hymn, the baptism of a cow, and wistful ballads such as 'Faraway Boy' and

'Walking Away Whistling', along with 'Never Will I Marry' and 'Summertime Love', both sung by Perkins. A three-album set was issued, containing the complete score. In terms of number of performances (1,417), Loesser's last Broadway show, which opened in 1961, was his most successful. *How To Succeed In Business Without Really Trying* was a satire on big business that starred Robert Morse as the aspiring executive J. Pierpont Finch, and Rudy Vallee as his stuffy boss, J.B. Biggley. The songs, which, most critics agreed, fitted the plot neatly, included 'The Company Way', 'A Secretary Is Not A Toy', 'Grand Old Ivy', 'Been A Long Day', 'I Believe In You' and 'Brotherhood Of Man'. The show became one of the select band of American musicals to be awarded a Pulitzer Prize; a film version was released in 1967. Loesser died of lung cancer on 28 July 1969, with cigarettes by his side. A lifelong smoker, with a contentious, volatile temperament, he is regarded as one of the most original, innovative men of the musical theatre. In the early 90s *The Most Happy Fella*, *Guys And Dolls* and *How To Succeed In Business Without Really Trying*, were all revived on Broadway, and Loesser's second wife, Jo Sullivan, and one of his daughters, Emily Loesser, appeared in a provincial production of *Where's Charley?* In 1993, the two ladies also featured on the album *An Evening With Frank Loesser*, singing medleys of songs from his shows. Of even more interest, in the same year a fascinating album consisting of demo recordings by Loesser himself was released.

● ALBUMS: *An Evening With Frank Loesser* (1993)★★★, *Loesser By Loesser* (DRG 1993)★★★★.
● FURTHER READING: *A Most Remarkable Fella*, Susan Loesser.

LOEWE, FREDERICK

b. 10 June 1901, Vienna, Austria, d. 14 February 1988, Palm Springs, Florida, USA. A distinguished composer for the musical theatre, Loewe was born into a musical family (his father was a professional singer). He studied piano as a child, appearing with the Berlin Symphony Orchestra in 1917. In 1924, he visited the USA, but was unable to find work in a classical enviroment. Instead, he eked out a living playing piano in restaurants and bars, then roamed throughout the USA, tackling a variety of jobs, including boxing, prospecting and cowpunching. As a young teenager he had written songs and he resumed this activity in New York in the early 30s. Later in the decade he contributed to various musical shows, and in 1942 began to collaborate with lyricist Alan Jay Lerner. Their first Broadway score was for *What's Up?* in 1943, which was followed two year later with *The Day Before Spring*. From that point onwards, they wrote the music and lyrics (Lerner also contributed the librettos) for some of the most memorable productions in the history of the American musical theatre. They had their first hit in 1947 with *Brigadoon*, from which came 'The Heather On The Hill', 'From This Day On' and 'Almost Like Being In Love', and the association was renewed in 1951 with *Paint Your Wagon*, containing such lovely songs as 'They Call The Wind Maria', 'I Talk To The Trees' and 'Wand'rin' Star'. In 1956, the team had a major triumph with the legendary *My Fair Lady*, which ran on Broadway for 2,717 performances. The score included such lasting favourites as 'On The Street Where You Live', 'Get Me To The Church On Time', 'With A Little Bit Of Luck', 'Wouldn't It Be Loverly?', 'The Rain In Spain',

'Why Can't The English?', 'I'm An Ordinary Man' and 'I Could Have Danced All Night'. After the huge success of *My Fair Lady*, Lerner and Loewe were invited to write the script, music and lyrics for a musical film, and while Lerner was enthusiastic about the idea, Loewe was somewhat reluctant. Eventually he agreed, and together they created the incomparable *Gigi* (1958), one of the final flourishes of the old-style Hollywood musical. The magnificent score included 'Thank Heaven For Little Girls', 'I'm Glad I'm Not Young Anymore', 'I Remember It Well', 'The Night They Invented Champagne', and the charming title song. After being hospitalized with serious heart trouble, Loewe collaborated with Lerner on *Camelot*, which opened in 1960, and ran for over two years. Although the show's pre-production was marred with problems, the result was another success, with such outstanding songs as 'If Ever I Would Leave You' and 'How To Handle A Woman'. Afterwards, Loewe decided to retire, emerging briefly in the early 70s to work with Lerner on two unsuccessful projects - a stage adaptation of *Gigi* (1973) and the film *The Little Prince* (1974).

LONDON, JULIE

b. June Webb, 26 September 1926, Santa Rosa, California, USA. Actress-singer London is inextricably linked to the sultry Andy Hamilton song 'Cry Me A River', which gave the artist her sole million-seller in 1955. Her memorable performance of the song in the film *The Girl Can't Help It*, showcased a lachrymose delivery best exemplified on *Julie Is Her Name*, which also featured the talent of jazz guitarist Barney Kessel. London continued to record prodigiously throughout the late 50s to the mid-60s, but this aspect of her career vied with roles in films, notably *The Great Man* and *A Question Of Adultery*. She later appeared in several television series, often alongside her second husband and long-time producer and songwriter Bobby Troup. Her popularity underwent a revival in the UK in the early 80s after Mari Wilson gained a hit with London's classic lament. London oozed style, but unfortunately she did not possess the vocal range or expression to make her a truly great singer.

● ALBUMS: *Julie Is Her Name* (Liberty 1956)★★★, *Lonely Girl* (Liberty 1956)★★★, *Calendar Girl* (Liberty 1956)★★★, *About The Blues* (Liberty 1957)★★, *Make Love To Me* (Liberty 1957)★★, *Julie* (Liberty 1957)★★, *Julie Is Her Name, Volume 2* (Liberty 1958)★★, *London By Night* (Liberty 1958)★★, *Swing Me An Old Song* (Liberty 1959)★★, *Your Number Please* (Liberty 1959)★★, *Julie London At Home* (Liberty 1959)★★, *Around Midnight* (Liberty 1960)★★, *Send For Me* (Liberty 1960)★★, *Whatever Julie Wants* (Liberty 1961)★★, *Sophisticated Lady* (Liberty 1962)★★, *Love Letters* (Liberty 1962)★★, *Latin In A Satin Mood* (Liberty 1963)★★, *The End Of The World* (Liberty 1963)★★, *Love On The Rocks* (Liberty 1963)★★, *The Wonderful World Of Julie London* (Liberty 1963)★★, *Julie London* (Liberty 1964)★★, *In Person At The Americana* (Liberty 1964)★★, *Our Fair Lady* (Liberty 1965)★★, *Feelin' Good* (Liberty 1965)★★, *All Through The Night* (Liberty 1965)★★, *For The Night People* (Liberty 1966)★★, *Nice Girls Don't Stay For Breakfast* (Liberty 1967)★★, *With Body And Soul* (Liberty 1967)★★, *Easy Does It* (Liberty 1968)★★, *Yummy Yummy Yummy* (Liberty 1969)★★, *By Myself* (Liberty 1969)★★.
● COMPILATIONS: *The Best Of* (Liberty 1962)★★★, *Julie's*

Golden Greats (Liberty 1963)★★★, *Great Performances* (Liberty 1968)★★★, *The Best Of Julie London* (Liberty 1984)★★★, *The Best Of Julie London: The Liberty Years* (Liberty 1988)★★★.
● FILMS: *The Girl Can't Help It* (1956).

LONDON, LAURIE

b. 19 January 1944, London, England. At the age of 13, this pop singer, who had the confidence and showmanship of a veteran, appeared in a closed circuit transmission of *6.5 Special* at the BBC stand at the 1958 Radio Show. He so impressed producer John Warrinton that he was invited back every day and thereby came to the attention of EMI, who put him in the studio with producer Norman Newell. The result was a Geoff Love-arranged revival of the spiritual 'He's Got The Whole World In His Hands'. The record climbed to number 12 in the UK and went on to become the most successful record by a British male in the 50s in the USA, topping the *Billboard* chart. Fame forced London to leave school and his father Will gave up his sales management job to manage him, but he refused the chance of a US tour in 1958 for the 14-year-old. London recorded a handful of other pop/gospel singles including 'Joshua', 'The Gospel Train' and 'I Gotta Robe', but the adolescent, who for all too brief a time had the whole world in his hands, never charted again. He released one album for Capitol Records. He was later reported to be successfully working in the clothing industry in London.
● ALBUMS: *Laurie London* (Parlophone 1958)★★.
● COMPILATIONS: *He's Got The Whole World In His Hands* (Bear Family 1984)★★.

LONE PINE, HAL, AND BETTY CODY

Harold John Breau (b. 5 June 1916, Pea Cove, Maine, USA, d. 26 March 1977; guitar, vocals) and Rita M. Coté (b. 17 August 1921, Sherbrooke, Quebec, Canada; guitar, vocals). In the mid-30s, Breau sang on radio in his native state and became the leader of the Lone Pine Mountaineers. He first met Coté in 1938, after her family had relocated to Aubourn, Maine, where, greatly influenced by Patsy Montana, she started her singing career as the vocalist with Curly And The Country Boys on WCOU Lewiston. They were married in June 1940 and, changing her name from the French to the English spelling, they worked together for over 10 years with the Lone Pine Mountaineers, on radio and shows in the New England area and over the border to Canada's Maritime Provinces. In the early 50s, they recorded both solo and duet numbers for RCA Records, achieving particular success with their duets 'It's Goodbye And So Long To You' and 'Trail Of The Lonesome Pine'. In 1953, Cody's 'Tom Tom Yodel' was a Canadian hit, while 'I Found Out More Than You Ever Knew' reached number 10 in the US country chart (the song was the 'answer' version of the Davis Sisters' hit 'I Forgot More Than You'll Ever Know'). In June 1953, the couple became regulars on the *Wheeling Jamboree*, where they remained for several years. After relocating to Manitoba in the late 50s, they divorced. Breau, usually only known then as Hal Lone Pine, later recorded for Arc Records, including duets with Jean Ward. He eventually returned to Maine, where he remarried and continued to play in the area where he had started his career years earlier, until his death in 1977. Cody retired for a time to look after her family, but in the early

70s, she toured with Dick Curless and between 1972 and 1982, she played a residency. She eventually returned to Lisbon Falls, Maine, where she made occasional appearances with her son, Dennis. The Breaus' eldest son, Leonard, was the noted jazz guitarist Lenny Breau, who was sadly murdered in 1984. Lone Pine is remembered as the writer of two very popular Canadian country songs, 'When It's Apple Blossom Time In Annapolis Valley' and 'Prince Edward Island Is Heaven To Me', both of which have been recorded by many artists, including Wilf Carter and George Hamilton IV. In the 80s, Cattle Records of Germany released albums of their recordings.
● ALBUMS: *Lone Pine & His Mountaineers* (RCA 60s)★★★, *Hal Lone Pine* (Arc 60s)★★★, *More Show Stoppers* (Arc 60s)★★, *Songs Everyone Remembers* (Arc 60s)★★, *Coast Of Maine* (Arc 60s)★★★, *Betty Cody Sings Again* (1979)★★★, *Hal Lone Pine & His Mountaineers* i (Cattle 1979)★★★, *Betty Cody's Country Souvenir Album* (Cattle 1985)★★★, *Duets & Memories* (Elmwood Station 1992)★★★, *Hal Lone Pine & His Mountaineers* ii (Castle 1995)★★★.

LORD ROCKINGHAM'S XI

Scottish bandleader Harry Robinson and his band assumed the pseudonym of Lord Rockingham's XI (after a genuine historical character) to appear on the Jack Good UK television pop programme *Oh Boy*, playing 'novelty' rock instrumentals. Other key members were Chery Wainer (organ), and Red Price (saxophone) as well as renowned British rock 'n' roll drummer Rory Blackwell, the former two of which would feature in their own spots on *Oh Boy*. The first release was 'Fried Onions' in May 1958, but in September Decca released the Robinson-penned 'Hoots Mon', complete with Scottish cries of 'Hoots mon, there's a moose in the hoose!'. It was a UK number 1 hit but the follow-up, 'Wee Tom', only made number 16. They featured on an *Oh Boy* EP but after a further attempt to have a hit with 'Ra Ra Rockingham' failed, Robinson reverted to more straightforward orchestra names such as Harry Robinson's XV and the Robinson Crew. He later revived the Lord Rockingham moniker in an attempt to cash in on the 1962 Twist phenomenon with 'Newcastle Twist'/'Rockingham Twist'. Benny Green played tenor sax with Rockingham before he realized he could make more money writing and talking about jazz than performing. He is now a respected author and broadcaster, but still plays saxophone semi-professionally. Robinson was later involved with another UK number 1 when he provided the musical accompaniment to Millie's 'My Boy Lollipop'.

LOSS, JOE

b. Joshua Alexander Loss, 22 June 1909, Spitalfields, London, England, d. 6 June 1990, London, England. One of the most popular bandleaders in the UK over a period of many years, Loss was taught to play the violin with a view to pursuing a classical career. He won a scholarship to the Trinity College of Music, and later studied at the London School of Music before forming his own band at the age of 16, playing local halls and accompanying silent movies. In 1930 he moved into London's Astoria Ballroom, and played at the Kit-Kat Club a year later. His band made its broadcasting debut in 1933, and, early in 1934, topped the variety bill at the Holborn Empire. Later that year, he returned to the Astoria for a long residency, and while there adopted

'Let's Dance At The Make Believe Ballroom' as his first proper signature tune. Also in 1934, he started recording for the Regal-Zonophone label, later part of EMI, and stayed with the company for over 50 years. A large part of the Loss band's popularity during the 30s was due to the many featured vocalists including Paula Greene, Betty Dale, Adelaide Hall, Shirley Lenner, Elizabeth Batey, Marjorie Kingsley, Monte Rey (with his big hit 'The Donkey Serenade') and especially Chick Henderson, later killed while in the Royal Navy, who recorded the very popular 'Begin The Beguine'. Some of the band's other successes were 'Woodchopper's Ball' and 'Honky Tonk Train Blues'. Loss also gave Vera Lynn her first broadcasting opportunity in 1935, when she sang 'Red Sails In The Sunset'. In 1940, Loss left the Astoria and went to France to play for the British Expeditionary Forces before returning to the UK, and spending the rest of World War II successfully touring the UK's ballrooms. After the war he was resident at the Hammersmith Palais, and later, during the 50s, survived the onslaught of rock 'n' roll. By this time, he also had a successful band agency. In the early 60s he had chart hits with 'Wheels Cha Cha', 'Sucu Sucu', 'The Maigret Theme', 'Must Be Madison', 'The March Of The Mods', and many bestselling albums. During the war Loss had adopted the Glenn Miller favourite 'In The Mood' as his theme tune, and it was his recording that featured on the Jive Bunny And The Mastermixers novelty single in 1989. His series of *World Championship Ballroom Dances* albums reflected his many appearances on BBC Television's *Come Dancing*, and the 14 Carl Alan Awards presented by the industry. During one of his annual working holidays on the QE2 in 1978, he became the first dance bandleader to play in communist China. His post-war singers included Howard Jones (the vocalist on the 1948 Loss US hit 'A Tree In A Meadow'), Larry Gretton, Rose Brennan (who stayed with the band for over 15 years) and Ross McManus (father of Elvis Costello). (McManus and Costello sang together for the first time on stage in a charity tribute to Joe Loss that was presented at the Barbican Theatre in London in 1994.) Loss played at many royal functions, including the Queen's 50th birthday celebrations and the Queen Mother's 80th birthday. The most energetic and mobile of bandleaders officially retired in 1989 after 60 years at the top. Among his awards were Her Majesty's Silver Medal (1977), an OBE (1978), and a Lieutenancy in the Royal Victorian Order (1984).

● ALBUMS: *Dancing Time For Dancers, Number 11* (HMV 1957)★★★, *Dancing Time For Dancers, Number 12* (HMV 1957)★★★, *Dancing Time For Dancers, Number 13* (HMV 1958)★★★, *Dancing Time For Dancers, Number 14* (HMV 1958)★★★, *36 All-Time Hits* (HMV 1960)★★★, *Come Dancing* (HMV 1960)★★★, *Party Dance Time - Another 36 All-Time Hits* (HMV 1961)★★★, *Dancing Party* (HMV 1962)★★★, *Must Be Madison - Must Be Twist* (HMV 1963)★★★★, *Go Latin With Loss* (HMV 1964)★★★, *Latin A La Loss* (Columbia 1968)★★★, *Joe Loss Plays Glenn Miller* (MFP 1969)★★★, *Latin Like Loss* (Columbia 1970)★★★, *Play It Latin* (Starline 1971)★★★, *All-Time Party Hits* (MFP 1971)★★★, *The Loss Concertium* (1972)★★★, *Dances For The World Ballroom Championship* (Columbia 1972)★★★, *Non-Stop Latin Lovelies* (EMI 1973)★★★, *Joe Loss Hits The Road To Songland* (EMI 1974)★★★, *Dance At Your Party* (Columbia 1975)★★★, *Top Pop Party Time* (Columbia 1975)★★★, *Jitterbug And Jive With Joe Loss* (EMI 1976)★★★, *Swing Is The Thing* (MFP 1976)★★★, *World Ballroom Championship Dances* (Note 1977)★★★, *Championship Dances For The World Ballroom* (Columbia 1978)★★★, *New World Championship Ballroom Dances* (Columbia 1979)★★★.

● COMPILATIONS: *The Very Best Of Joe Loss And His Big Band* (Studio 2 1976)★★★, *Let's Dance At The Make-Believe Ballroom 1934-40* (Retrospect 1977)★★★, *50 Fabulous Years* (Note 1980)★★★, *The Golden Age Of Joe Loss* (Golden Age 1985)★★★, *Isn't It Heavenly* (Happy Days 1986)★★★, *In A Romantic Mood* (EMI 1987)★★★, *The Joe Loss Story* (EMI 1990)★★★.

LOTIS, DENNIS

b. 8 March 1925, Johannesburg, South Africa. An extremely popular singer in the UK, particularly in the 50s, with a sophisticated style that was particularly attractive to the young female population. Lotis trained for four years as a boy soprano, and won several cups and medals. He made his first stage appearance at the age of seven, and his first broadcast when he was nine. After leaving school, he worked as a bus conductor and electrician, and sang in cinemas and nightclubs in Johannesburg. When he moved to the UK in the early 50s, he carried with him a letter of introduction to Ted Heath from the former London saxophonist and bandleader Don Barrigo. Following a couple of broadcasts with Henry Hall, Lotis joined the Heath band, and, together with the other resident vocalists Lita Roza and Dickie Valentine, became one of the most popular singers on the circuit. Lotis's vocal talents were evident on such records as 'Sam's Song', 'Goodnight Irene', 'Nevertheless' and 'She's A Lady' (with Roza and Valentine). After enjoying a hit with 'Cuddle Me', he went solo, and during the late 50s toured the UK variety circuit, appeared in his first Royal Command Performances, and rejoined the Heath band for a tour of the USA, including an appearance at Carnegie Hall. He was also voted Top Male Singer in the 1957 *Melody Maker* poll. In 1956 he appeared in a touring production of the stage musical *Harmony Close*, and two years later, starred in John Osborne's *The World Of Paul Slickey*, a 'musical comedy of manners' that was poorly received in Britain. Lotis also made several films, a mixture of drama, comedy, musicals and horror, including *The Extra Day*, *It's A Wonderful World*, *City Of The Dead* and *She'll Have To Go*. Among his other stage roles was an appearance as Lucio in John Neville's Playhouse Production of Shakespeare's *Measure For Measure*. Adversely affected by the changing face of popular music, he played the working men's clubs, and ran his own antiques and restaurant businesses for a time. Eventually, in the 80s and 90s, he returned to the theatres, singing in nostalgia shows with contemporaries such as Joan Regan and Russ Conway. He also frequently joined Lita Roza and some of Britain's top musicians in concerts commemorating the great Ted Heath band.

● ALBUMS: *How About You?* (1958)★★★, *Bidin' My Time* (1959)★★★, *Night And Day* (1983)★★, *Get Happy* (1994)★★★.

LOVE ME OR LEAVE ME

This realistic biopic of the popular 20s and 30s torch singer Ruth Etting was produced by Joe Pasternak for MGM in 1955. Daniel Fuchs won an Oscar for his original story which he and Isobel Lennart adapted for the absorbing screenplay. Doris Day shrugged off her 'goody-goody' image and gave a fine performance as the singer whose dramatic rise from dancehall hostess to nightclub and Ziegfeld star was masterminded by her gangster husband Martin 'Moe the Gimp' Snyder. James Cagney was outstanding as the domineering Snyder, whose response to his wife's relationship with her pianist (Cameron Mitchell) is to shoot him. Although cinematic convention (and box office returns) required a happy ending, there was enough reality left to make this a distinctive film. Most of the songs were authentic Etting favourites, and included 'Ten Cents A Dance' (Richard Rodgers-Lorenz Hart), 'Shaking The Blues Away' (Irving Berlin), 'It All Depends On You' (De Sylva, Brown And Henderson), 'You Made Me Love You' (Jimmy Monaco-Joseph McCarthy), 'Everybody Loves My Baby' (Jack Palmer-Spencer Williams), 'Mean To Me' (Roy Turk-Fred Ahlert), 'Sam The Old Accordion Man' (Walter Donaldson), 'My Blue Heaven' (Donaldson-George Whiting), 'At Sundown' (Donaldson) and the singer's theme song, 'Love Me Or Leave Me' (Donaldson-Gus Kahn). One of the new songs, 'I'll Never Stop Loving You', which was written by Nicholas Brodszky and Sammy Cahn, became a US Top 20 record hit for Doris Day. The strong supporting cast featured Robert Keith, Tom Tully, Harry Bellaver, Claude Stroud, Richard Gaines, Peter Leeds and Audrey Young. Alex Romero was the choreographer and Charles Vidor directed this popular, and sometimes intriguing, film that grossed over $4 million in the USA alone.

LOVE ME TENDER

Elvis Presley's first feature, released in 1956, cast the singer as one of three brothers who rob a bank. Strife over a share of the spoils is compounded by conflicting love interests, culminating with the Presley character's slaying, although he appears as a wraith in the final reel. Although cast as a miscreant, the singer had opted for a more conservatively styled film, a western, rather than embracing contemporary teen subcultures in the manner of *Rebel Without A Cause*. Indeed, he did not enjoy top billing - Richard Egan was the star - but interest naturally focused on Presley's performance. Critics were generally impressed, citing great potential, something tossed to the wind by much of the singer's subsequent film output. Although not a musical, the film's mournful title track gave the singer his third US chart-topper and *Love Me Tender* also featured the well-known 'weepie' 'Old Shep'. Again, by avoiding 'controversial' musical content, the Presley industry showed that, even at this early stage, a wider audience was being courted.

LUKE, ROBIN

b. 20 March 1942, Los Angeles, California, USA. Luke was a rockabilly-style singer who had one Top 5 success, 'Susie Darlin'', in 1958. His family moved frequently, and in 1953 settled in Hawaii, where he learned to play guitar and ukulele. He was discovered by entertainer Kimo McVay, who introduced him to Bob Bertram, who then recorded Luke in his own Bertram International studio. The simplistic 'Susie Darlin'', named after Luke's younger sister, was recorded using a great deal of echo, with Bertram singing behind him and percussion created by simply banging two pens on a box (Bertram later reported that some 75 takes of

the song were recorded). The single was issued on the Bertram International label and became a local favourite. It was then picked up by the larger Dot Records and began its 1958 ascent to number 5 (a few other singles were issued on Bertram while the Dot contract was already in effect). In 1959, Luke moved to California and continued to record, now backed by top session musicians such as Glen Campbell and Barney Kessel. Luke remained with Dot until 1962, but never had another hit, possibly because the more elaborate productions lacked the charm of the minimal Bertram record. In the early 60s, Luke moved to Missouri to complete his education and he subsequently became a university tutor. His only recording after leaving Dot was a remake of 'Susie Darlin'' for K-Tel Records in the 70s.
● ALBUMS: *Susie Darlin'* (Dot 1958)★★★.
● COMPILATIONS: *Susie Darlin'* (Bear Family 1984)★★★.

LUTCHER, NELLIE

b. 15 October 1915, Lake Charles, Louisiana, USA. A singer and pianist, notable for her percussive piano-playing and distinctive scat-vocal approach, Lutcher initially played in a big band with her bass-playing father before moving on to join the Southern Rhythm Boys band. She played clubs on the west coast during the late 30s/early 40s and signed to Capitol Records in 1947 following an appearance on a *March Of Dimes* charity show. Her first release, the R&B-styled 'Hurry On Down', became a US Top 20 hit that same year and was followed by 'He's A Real Gone Guy', 'The Song Is Ended' and 'Fine Brown Frame'. The latter was a cover version of an earlier hit by bandleader Buddy Johnson. She later moved on to Liberty Records, recording a highly rated album, *Our New Nellie*. However, her popularity had faded, and during the late 60s and early 70s she took a staff job with the Hollywood Local Branch of the Musicians' Union, still occasionally playing clubs such as the New York Cookery.
● ALBUMS: *Real Gone* (Capitol 1954)★★★, *Our New Nellie* (Liberty 1955)★★★★.
● COMPILATIONS: *Real Gone Gal* (Stateside 1985)★★★, *My Papa's Got To Have Everything* (Jukebox Lil 1985)★★★, *Ditto From Me To You* (Jukebox Lil 1987)★★★.

LYMAN, ARTHUR, GROUP

b. 1936, Kauai, Hawaii, USA. Lyman popularized a jazzy style of Hawaiian music during the 50s, and gathered a following as a purveyor of so-called exotic music. As a child, Lyman moved to the large Hawaiian city of Honolulu, where he became interested in the music of Benny Goodman and Lionel Hampton. He learned to play along with their records on a toy marimba. At the age of 14, he joined a jazz group and by his early 20s was performing with 'mood music' king Martin Denny. Lyman was signed to the Hi-Fi record label in 1957 and released his debut, *Taboo*, the following year. It ultimately reached number 6 in the USA and remained on the chart for over a year. Lyman led a quartet, with himself on four-mallet vibes, guitar and percussion, John Kramer (bass, ukulele, guitar, flute, clarinet, percussion), Alan Soares (piano, celeste, guitar, glockenspiel, chimes, clavinet, percussion) and Harold Chang (percussion). Because of its superior production - all of their music was recorded at the Henry J. Kaiser Aluminum Dome in Hawaii - and the unusual orchestral sounds created by the group, the record was particularly popular among consumers purchasing the then-new stereo equipment. In 1961, Lyman's single 'Yellow Bird' reached number 4 in the USA, one of the most uncharacteristic hits of the era. The album of the same name reached number 10. Lyman's last charting album in 1963 was *I Wish You Love* but he continued to record.

● ALBUMS: *Taboo* (Hifi 1958)★★★, *Bahia* (Hifi 1959)★★★, *Leis Of Jazz* (Hifi 1959)★★, *On Broadway* (Hifi 1960)★★★, *Yellow Bird* (Hifi 1961)★★, *Many Moods Of Arthur Lyman* (Hifi 1962)★★★★, *The Colourful Percussions Of Arthur Lyman* (Hifi 1962)★★★, *I Wish You Love* (Hifi 1963)★★★, *Blowin' In The Wind* (Hifi 1963)★★, *Merry Christmas* (Hifi 1963)★★, *Midnight Sun* (Hifi 1964)★★, *Cast Your Fate* (GNP Crescendo 1988)★★★, *Pearly Shells* (GNP Crescendo 1988)★★★, *Puka Shells* (GNP Crescendo 1988)★★★.

● COMPILATIONS: *The Exotic Sound Of The Arthur Lyman Group* (1991)★★★★, *The Best Of The Arthur Lyman Group* (DCC 1996)★★★★, *More Of The Best Of The Arthur Lyman Group* (DCC 1996)★★★, *Sonic Sixties* (Tradition 1997)★★★.

LYMON, FRANKIE, AND THE TEENAGERS

b. 30 September 1942, Washington Heights, New York, USA, d. 28 February 1968, New York City, New York, USA. Often billed as the 'boy wonder', Lymon first entered the music business after teaming up with a local all-vocal quartet, the Premiers. The latter comprised Jimmy Merchant (b. 10 February 1940, New York, USA), Sherman Garnes (b. 8 June 1940, New York, USA, d. 26 February 1977), Herman Santiago (b. 18 February 1941, New York, USA) and Joe Negroni (b. 9 September 1940, New York, USA, d. 5 September 1978). Lymon joined them in 1954 and soon afterwards they were signed to the Gee label as the Teenagers. Their debut, the startling 'Why Do Fools Fall In Love?', was issued on 1 January 1956 and soon climbed into the US Top 10, alongside the early recordings of Elvis Presley and Carl Perkins. The song went on to reach number 1 in the UK and sold two million copies. Lymon soon left school and the group toured extensively. For their second single, 'I Want You To Be My Girl', the 13-year-old boy wonder was given superior billing to the group. With their use of high tenor, deep bass and soprano, and teen-orientated lyrics, the Teenagers boasted one of the most distinctive sounds in 50s pop. After registering chart entries in the USA with 'I Promise To Remember' and 'The ABCs Of Love', they found greater acclaim in England. The soaring 'I'm Not A Juvenile Delinquent' (from the film *Rock Rock Rock*) hit the UK Top 12 and Lymon was afforded the honour of appearing at the London Palladium. So strong was his appeal at this point that the single's b-side, 'Baby Baby', received separate promotion and outshone the a-side by climbing to number 4. During his celebrated UK tour, Lymon recorded as a soloist with producer Norrie Paramor and the resulting 'Goody Goody' reached the Top 30 on both sides of the Atlantic. By the summer of 1957, he had split from the Teenagers, and thereafter, his career prospects plummeted. He enjoyed the excesses of stardom, smoking cigars, drinking heavily and enjoying under-age sex with women old enough to be his mother. Despite recording a strong album, his novelty appeal waned when his voice broke. By 1961, the teenager was a heroin addict and entered Manhattan General Hospital on a drug rehabilitation programme. Although he tried to reconstruct his career with the help of Dizzy Gillespie and even took dancing lessons and studied as a jazz

drummer, his drug habit endured. In 1964, he was convicted of possessing narcotics and his finances were in a mess. His private life was equally chaotic and was punctuated by three marriages. In February 1968, he was discovered dead on the bathroom floor of his grandmother's New York apartment with a syringe by his side. The Teenager who never grew up was dead at the tragically young age of 25. His former group continued to record sporadically and in the 80s, surviving members Santiago and Merchant formed a new Teenagers and Pearl McKinnon took Lymon's part. They were inducted into the Rock And Roll Hall Of Fame in 1993.

● ALBUMS: *The Teenagers Featuring Frankie Lymon* (Gee 1957)★★★, *The Teenagers At The London Palladium* (Roulette 1958)★★, *Rock 'N' Roll Party With Frankie Lymon* (Guest 1959)★★★.

● COMPILATIONS: *Frankie Lymon And The Teenagers* 61-track set (Murray Hill 1987)★★★, *The Best Of Frankie Lymon And The Teenagers* (Roulette 1990)★★★.

LYNN, GLORIA

b. 23 November 1930 or 1931, New York City, New York, USA. Lynn began singing at the local Mother African Methodist Episcopal Zion church and also sang at amateur talent contests, then studied for five years in the hope of having a career on the concert platform. Following a successful talent contest appearance at the Apollo Theatre in 1951, she began singing professionally, sometimes as a member of a group, sometimes as soloist. she developed a wide stylistic range that drew upon the inspiration of Ella Fitzgerald, gospel singer Mahalia Jackson, and Marian Anderson, the classical contralto. Lynn's rich and measured voice is a fine vehicle for her chosen repertoire. Surprisingly, given her undoubted qualities, her career never attained the high profile achieved by many less talented contemporaries.

● ALBUMS: *Miss Gloria Lynn* (Evidence 1958)★★★.

LYTTELTON, HUMPHREY

b. 23 May 1921, Eton, Buckinghamshire, England. Raised in an academic atmosphere (his father was a Housemaster at Eton College), he taught himself to play a variety of instruments including the banjolele. His prodigious talent was spotted early and he was given formal lessons on piano and, a little later, in military band drumming. Eventually, his education took him back to Eton College, this time as a pupil. He joined the school orchestra as a timpanist but after a while drifted away from the orchestra and the instrument. At the age of 15 he discovered jazz, thanks to records by trumpeters Nat Gonella and, decisively, Louis Armstrong. By this time Lyttelton had switched to playing the mouth-organ, but, realizing the instrument's limitations, he acquired a trumpet, which he taught himself to play. Forming his own small jazz band at the college, he developed his playing ability and his consuming interest in jazz. With the outbreak of World War II he joined the Grenadier Guards, continuing to play whenever possible. After the war he resumed playing, this time professionally, and in 1947 became a member of George Webb's Dixielanders. The following year he formed his own band and quickly became an important figure in the British revivalist movement. In the late 40s and through to the mid-50s Lyttelton's stature in British jazz increased. Significantly, his deep interest in virtually all aspects of jazz meant that he was constantly listening to other musicians, many of whom played different forms of the music. Although he was never to lose his admiration for Armstrong, he refused to remain rooted in the revivalist tradition. His acceptance and absorption of music from the jazz mainstream ensured that when the trad boom fizzled out, Lyttelton continued to find an audience. In the mid-50s he added alto saxophonist Bruce Turner to his band, outraging some reactionary elements in British jazz circles, and a few years later added Tony Coe, Joe Temperley and other outstanding and forward-thinking musicians.

In the early 60s Lyttelton's reputation spread far beyond the UK and he also developed another important and long-term admiration for a trumpet player, this time, Buck Clayton. By this time, however, Lyttelton's personal style had matured and he was very much his own man. He was also heavily involved in many areas outside the performance of music. In 1954, he had published his first autobiographical volume and in the 60s he began to spread his writing wings as an essayist, journalist and critic. He also broadcast on radio and television, sometimes as a performer but also as a speaker and presenter. These multiple activities continued throughout the next two decades, his UK BBC Radio 2 series, *The Best Of Jazz*, running for many years. His writings included further autobiographical work and his ready wit found outlets in seemingly unlikely settings, such as his role as quizmaster on the long-running radio comedy-panel series, *I'm Sorry I Haven't A Clue*. During this time he continued to lead a band, employing first-rate musicians with whom he toured and made numerous records. Among the sidemen of the 70s and 80s were Dave Green, Mick Pyne, John Surman, John Barnes, Roy Williams and Adrian Macintosh. He also toured and recorded with singers Helen Shapiro, Carol Kidd and Lillian Boutté. Back in the late 40s Lyttelton had recorded with Sidney Bechet and in the 70s and 80s he occasionally made albums with other American jazz stars, including Buddy Tate on *Kansas City Woman*, and Kenny Davern on *Scatterbrains* and *This Old Gang Of Ours*. In the early 80s Lyttelton formed his own recording company, Calligraph, and by the end of the decade numerous new albums were available. In addition to these came others, mostly on the Dormouse label, which reissued his earlier recordings and were eagerly snapped up by fans of all ages. Although he has chosen to spend most of his career in the UK, Lyttelton's reputation elsewhere is extremely high and thoroughly deserved. As a trumpet player and bandleader, and occasional clarinettist, he has ranged from echoing early jazz to near-domination of the British mainstream. For more than 40 years he has succeeded in maintaining the highest musical standards, all the time conducting himself with dignity, charm and good humour. In the early 90s, touring with Kathy Stobart, he showed no signs of letting up and barely acknowledged the fact that he had sailed past his 70th birthday.

● ALBUMS: *Jazz Concert* (Parlophone 1953)★★★★, *Humph At The Conway* (Parlophone 1954)★★★★, *Jazz At The Royal Festival Hall* (Parlophone 1955)★★★★, *Jazz Session With Humph* (Parlophone 1956)★★★★, *Humph Swings Out* (Parlophone 1956)★★★★, *Here's Humph* (Parlophone 1957)★★★★, *I Play As I Please* (Decca 1958)★★★★, with Kathy Stobart *Kath Meets Humph* (Parlophone 1958)★★★★, *Humph In Perspective* (Parlophone 1958)★★★, *Triple Exposure* (Parlophone 1959)★★★, *Triple Exposure* (Parlophone 1959)★★★, *Back To The 60s* 1960-63 recordings (Philips 60s)★★★, *Humphrey Lyttelton And His Band 1960-63* (Philips 60s)★★★★, *21 Years On* (1969)★★★, *South Bank Swing Session* (1973)★★★, with Buddy Tate *Kansas City Woman* (Black Lion 1974)★★★, *Spreadin' Joy* (Black Lion 1978)★★★, *One Day I Met An African* (Black Lion 1980)★★★, *In Canada* (Sackville 1980)★★★, *It Seems Like Yesterday* (Calligraph 1983)★★★, *Movin' And Groovin'* (Black Lion 1983)★★★, with Kenny Davern *Scatterbrains* (Stomp Off 1984)★★★, *Humph At The Bull's Head* (Calligraph 1985)★★★★, with Davern ... *This Old Gang Of Ours* ... (Calligraph 1985)★★★, with Helen Shapiro *Echoes Of The Duke* (Calligraph 1985)★★★★, *Gonna Call My Children Home: The World Of Buddy Bolden* (Calligraph 1986)★★★, *Gigs* (Calligraph 1987)★★★, *Doggin Around* (Wam 1987)★★★, *The Dazzling Lillian Boutté* (1988)★★★, *The Beano Boogie* (Calligraph 1989)★★★, with Shapiro *I Can't Get Started* (Calligraph 1990)★★★★, *Rock Me Gently* (Calligraph 1991)★★★, *Hook Line And Sinker* (Angel 1991)★★★, *At Sundown* (Calligraph 1992)★★★, *Rent Party* (Stomp Off 1992)★★★, *Movin' And Groovin'* (1993)★★★, *Hear Me Talkin' To Ya* (Calligraph 1994)★★★★.

● COMPILATIONS: *Delving Back And Forth With Humph* 1948-86 recordings (Esquire 1979)★★★, *Bad Penny Blues: The Best Of Humph* 1949-56 recordings (Cube 1983)★★★★, *Tribute To Humph Vols 1-8* 1949-56 recordings (Dormouse 1984-88)★★★, *The Parlophone Years* 1949-56 recordings (Dormouse 1989)★★★★, *Jazz At The Royal Festival Hall & Jazz At The Conway Hall* 1951-54 recordings (Dormouse 1991)★★★★, *Dixie Gold* 1960-63 recordings (1991)★★★.

● FURTHER READING: *I Play As I Please*, Humphrey Lyttelton. *Second Chorus*, Humphrey Lyttelton. *Take It From The Top*, Humphrey Lyttelton. *Humph*, Julian Purser.

MacColl, Ewan

b. Jimmie Miller, 25 January 1915, Salford, Manchester, England, d. 22 October 1989. The singing talents of his parents enabled MacColl to learn many of their songs while he was still young. He subsequently wrote many classic and regularly covered songs of his own, including 'Dirty Old Town', which was inspired by his home-town of Salford. The song was later made popular by the Pogues and the Dubliners, among others. Having left school at the age of 14,

MacColl joined the Salford Clarion Players, and by the age of 16 he was already actively involved in street theatre. His life-long allegiance to the Communist Party was influenced by his first-hand experiences during the Depression years, and by seeing the effects of the era on his own father and others around him. As a result of his early involvement in political theatre, MacColl, as playwright, actor, director and singer, co-founded the Theatre Workshop at Stratford, London, with Joan Littlewood, who became his first wife. A meeting with folklorist and collector Alan Lomax in the 50s persuaded MacColl to become involved in the revival of British folk songs, which at the time took a back seat to the wealth of American folk material that had arrived via the skiffle boom. The Critics Group was formed by MacColl in 1964, in an effort to analyze folk song and folk-singing technique. This had its critics, who felt that MacColl and the group were set-ting themselves up as an élitist authority on folk music. It was in the Critics Group that he met Jean Newlove, who became his second wife. They had two children, Hamish and Kirsty MacColl. In 1965, a series of programmes called *The Song Carriers* was broadcast on Midlands Radio. Later, the innovative *Radio Ballads* was formulated, combining the voice of the ordinary working man with songs and music rel-evant to their work. The first series, *The Ballad Of John Axon*, was broadcast in 1958. This brought together Peggy Seeger and radio producer Charles Parker. Despite the success of these programmes, no more were commissioned by the BBC on the grounds of expense. It is more likely, however, that the views and opinions expressed in the series did not con-form to prevailing ideas on what was suitable for broadcast. Unlike many, MacColl believed that it was not sufficient to perform only old songs, but that new material should be aired, and 'The Travelling People' emerged from these ideas. Both Seeger and MacColl continued to perform profession-ally throughout the 70s and 80s, having married following the break-up of MacColl's second marriage. Together they set up Blackthorne Records. They were particularly notice-able during the UK miners' strike of 1984, recording and appearing at benefits.

Outside folk music circles, MacColl is probably best remem-bered for the beautiful 'The First Time Ever I Saw Your Face', which he wrote in 1957 for Peggy Seeger. Roberta Flack reached the top of the US charts with the song in 1972, as well as the UK Top 20. MacColl received an Ivor Novello Award for the song in 1973. He died in October 1989, having only recently completed an autobiography. *Black And White* is a compilation of live and studio recordings from 1972-86 and was compiled by his sons, Calum and Neill. In addition to the three children born to him and Seeger, songs such as 'My Old Man' and 'The Joy Of Living', and a pride in British traditional song, are just part of the considerable legacy he left behind.

● ALBUMS: *Shuttle And Cage* (Topic 1957)★★★, *Barrack Room Ballads* 10-inch album (Topic 1958)★★★★, *Still I Love Him* (Topic 1958)★★★, *Bad Lads And Hard Cases* (Riverside 1959)★★★, with Dominic Behan *Streets Of Song* (1959)★★★★, with Peggy Seeger *Chorus From The Gallows* (Topic 1961)★★★★, *Haul On The Bowlin'* (1962)★★★, with Seeger *Jacobite Songs* (Topic 1962)★★★★, *Off To Sea Once More* (1963)★★★★, *Fourpence A Day-British Industrial Folk Songs* (1963)★★★, with A.L. Lloyd *English And Scottish Folk Ballads* (Topic 1964)★★★★, *The Ballad Of John Axon*

(1965)★★★, *The Long Harvest 1* (Topic 1966)★★★, with Seeger *The Amorous Muse* (1966)★★★, *A Sailor's Garland* (1966)★★★, with Seeger *The Manchester Angel* (1966)★★★★, *Bundook Ballads* (Topic 1967)★★★, *The Long Harvest 2* (1967)★★★, *Blow Boys Blow* (1967)★★★, *Singing The Fishing* (1967)★★★, *The Big Hewer* (1967)★★★, *The Fight Game* (1967)★★★, *The Long Harvest 3* (1968)★★★, *The Wanton Muse* (1968)★★, with Seeger *The Angry Muse* (1968)★★★, *Paper Stage 1* (1969)★★★, *Paper Stage 2* (1969)★★★, *The Long Harvest 4* (1969)★★★, *The Travelling People* (1969)★★★, *The Long Harvest 5* (1970)★★★, *On The Edge* (1970)★★★, *The Long Harvest 6* (1971)★★★, *Solo Flight* (Topic 1972)★★★, *The Long Harvest 7* (1972)★★★, *The Long Harvest 8* (1973)★★★, *The Long Harvest 9* (1974)★★★, *The Long Harvest 10* (1975)★★★, with Seeger *Saturday Night At The Bull And Mouth* (Blackthorne 1977)★★, with Seeger *Cold Snap* (Blackthorne 1977)★★★, with Seeger *Hot Blast* (Blackthorne 1978)★★★, *Blood And Roses* (Blackthorne 1979)★★★★, with Seeger *Kilroy Was Here* (Blackthorne 1980)★★★, *Blood And Roses Vol.2* (Blackthorne 1981)★★★, *Blood And Roses Vol.3* (Blackthorne 1982)★★★, *Blood And Roses Vol.4* (Blackthorne 1982)★★★, *Blood And Roses Vol.5* (Blackthorne 1983)★★★, *Daddy, What Did You Do In The Strike?* (Blackthorne 1985)★★★★, *Items Of News* (Blackthorne 1986)★★★, with Seeger *Naming Of Names* (Cooking Vinyl 1990)★★★.

● COMPILATIONS: *The Best Of* (PRE 1961)★★★★, with Peggy Seeger *The World Of Ewan MacColl And Peggy Seeger* (1970)★★★★, with Seeger *The World Of Ewan MacColl And Peggy Seeger 2* (1972)★★★★, *Black And White - The Definitive Collection* (Cooking Vinyl 1990)★★★★, *The Real MacColl* (1993)★★★★.

● FURTHER READING: *Journeyman*, Ewan MacColl. *Traveller's Songs From England And Scotland*, Ewan MacColl and Peggy Seeger.

MACKINTOSH, KEN

b. 4 September 1919, Liversedge, West Yorkshire, England. Mackintosh began playing alto saxophone as a child and worked with various bands in Yorkshire in his teens. In 1939, he joined the army and towards the end of the war was playing in military bands. He formed his own unit in 1948 and enjoyed a measure of local popularity in dancehalls and on regional radio. In 1950, his band was booked to open the Wimbledon Palais in London and met with immediate suc-cess. The band broadcast regularly and won a recording con-tract with HMV. The Wimbledon engagement lasted three years. During the last year, Mackintosh had a record hit with 'The Creep', his own composition, and this led to a bill-top-ping tour of the UK. Throughout the 50s the band toured, recorded, broadcast extensively on radio and television, where it headlined its own show, *Flying Standards*, and was featured in the film *An Alligator Named Daisy* (1955). Mackintosh was able to give an early career boost to Frankie Vaughan and Alma Cogan, making records with both artists. Among the band's record successes of the 50s were 'Harlem Nocturne' and 'Raunchy', which reached number 8 in 1958. In 1963, Mackintosh was hired to open the new Empire Ballroom in London's Leicester Square, at the time billed as the world's greatest and most expensive ballroom. This engagement lasted for seven years, after which the band moved to the Hammersmith Palais for a further seven-year stint. Late in the 70s, Mackintosh took his band on the road where he frequently backed touring singers, including Matt Monro, Pat Boone, Tom Jones and Shirley Bassey. Throughout the 80s and into the 90s, Mackintosh continued on the road with his band, playing dances at which he acknowledged contemporary sounds while nostalgically recreating the best popular dance music of earlier years. His son is Andy Mackintosh.

● ALBUMS: *Skyliner* (1980)★★, *The Very Thought Of You* (President 1985)★★★, *Blue Skies* (1990)★★★.

MacRae, Gordon

b. 12 March 1921, East Orange, New Jersey, USA, d. 24 January 1986, Lincoln, Nebraska, USA. A popular singer on record, radio and in films during the 50s, MacRae was the son of local radio celebrity Wee Willie MacRae, and often worked on radio as a child actor before joining the Millpond Playhouse in New York. There he met actress Sheila Stephens who became his first wife in 1941. After winning an amateur singing contest at the 1939/40 New York World's Fair, he sang for two weeks with the Harry James and Les Brown bands. While working as a pageboy at NBC Radio, he was heard by bandleader Horace Heidt who signed him for two years, during which time he appeared with Heidt, James Stewart and Paulette Goddard in a movie about Heidt's radio giveaway show, *Pot O' Gold*. After serving in the US Army Air Force Corps in World War II, MacRae returned to New York to take a singing role in the 1946 Broadway revue *Three To Make Ready*, starring Ray Bolger. In 1947, he signed to Capitol Records and had a string of hits up to 1954, including 'I Still Get Jealous', 'At The Candlelight Cafe', 'It's Magic', 'Hair Of Gold, Eyes Of Blue', 'So In Love', 'Mule Train'/'Dear Hearts And Gentle People' and 'Rambling Rose'. After a four-year gap, he entered the US charts again in 1958 with 'The Secret'. MacRae also made a series of successful singles with ex-Tommy Dorsey singer Jo Stafford. These included 'Say Something Sweet To Your Sweetheart', 'Bluebird Of Happiness', 'My Darling, My Darling' (a US number 1), 'A-You're Adorable', 'Need You', 'Whispering Hope', 'Bibbidi-Bobbidi-Boo' and 'Dearie'.

MacRae's film career, mostly for Warner Brothers, started in 1948 with a non-singing role in *The Big Punch*. This was followed by a series of musicals that included *Look For The Silver Lining* (1949) and *The Daughter Of Rosie O'Grady* (1950), both co-starring June Haver, and four films in which he was partnered by Doris Day: *Tea For Two* (1950), *West Point Story* (1950), *On Moonlight Bay* (1951) and *By The Light Of The Silvery Moon* (1953). Among his other screen appearances were roles in *The Desert Song* (1953), co-starring Kathryn Grayson, and *Three Sailors And A Girl* (1953), with Jane Powell. In 1955 and 1956 he had the two most satisfying film parts of his career, when he played opposite Shirley Jones in highly successful adaptations of the Broadway shows *Oklahoma!* and *Carousel*. Also in 1956, MacRae appeared in his last film musical as Buddy De Sylva in *The Best Things In Life Are Free*, a biopic of the 20s/30s songwriting team of De Sylva, Brown And Henderson. In 1979, he made one final film appearance, in a dramatic role in *The Pilot*. In the mid-50s, MacRae was also popular on US television as the singing host of *The Railroad Hour*, *The Colgate Comedy Hour*, and his own *Gordon MacRae Show*.

After divorcing his first wife, he was remarried in 1967 to Elizabeth Lambert Schrafft. In the same year, he made his first Broadway musical appearance since 1946, replacing Robert Preston in *I Do! I Do!* In the 70s he struggled with alcoholism and, in the early 80s, claimed that he had won the battle. He died from cancer of the mouth and jaw in January 1986.

● ALBUMS: with Jo Stafford *Songs Of Faith* 10-inch album (Capitol 1950)★★, *Prisoner Of Love* film soundtrack (MGM 1952)★★★, with various artists *Roberta* 10-inch album (Capitol 1952)★★★, with various artists *Merry Widow* 10-inch album (Capitol 1952)★★★, with Lucille Norman *New Moon/Vagabond King* film soundtrack (Capitol 1952)★★★, with Stafford *Sunday Evening Songs* 10-inch album (Capitol 1953)★★★, with various artists *The Desert Song* (Capitol 1953)★★★★, with various artists *Student Prince* 10-inch album (Capitol 1953)★★★, *By The Light Of The Silvery Moon* film soundtrack (Capitol 1953)★★, *The Red Mill* film soundtrack (Capitol 1954)★★★, with Stafford *Memory Songs* (Capitol 1954)★★★, *Romantic Ballads* (Capitol 1955)★★★, *Oklahoma!* film soundtrack (Capitol 1955)★★★★★, *Carousel* film soundtrack (Capitol 1956)★★★★★, *Operetta Favourites* (Capitol 1956)★★★★, *The Best Things In Life Are Free* (Capitol 1956)★★★, *Motion Picture Soundstage* (Capitol 1957)★★★, *Cowboy's Lament* (Capitol 1957)★★★, *Gordon MacRae In Concert* (Capitol 1958)★★, *This Is Gordon MacRae* (Capitol 1958)★★★★, *Seasons Of Love* (Capitol 1959)★★★, with Stafford *Whispering Hope* (Capitol 1962)★★★, with Stafford *Peace In The Valley* (Capitol 1963)★★, with Stafford *Old Rugged Cross* (Capitol 1963)★★★.

● COMPILATIONS: *Best Of The Capitol Years* (Capitol 1990)★★★★.

● FURTHER READING: *Hollywood Mother Of The Year: Sheila MacRae's Own Story*, Sheila MacRae with Paul Jeffers.

MAGNIFICENTS

Formed in 1953 in Chicago, Illinois, USA, the group members were Johnny Keyes, Thurman 'Ray' Ramsey, Fred Rakestraw and Willie Myles. In their up-tempo songs, the Magnificents brought rock 'n' roll to their doo-wop, and in their ballads they stayed true to their R&B roots. Singing as the Tams, they were discovered by disc jockey Magnificent Montague, who gave them their name and became their manager. Their one hit, 'Up On The Mountain' (number 9 R&B), in 1956, has come to be remembered as a golden oldie, but equally outstanding was their great ballad b-side, 'Why Did She Go', led by Ramsey. However, Ramsey left to be replaced by L.C. Cooke (brother of Sam Cooke), and Barbara Arrington was added to the group as lead. The successful sound of the group was subsequently lost on the next record, 'Caddy Bo'. The third single, 'Off The Mountain', deserved to restore the group to prominence, but it was not to be. Keyes and the rest of the group broke from Montague, who then formed a new Magnificents, the identity of whose members remains unknown. Their 'Don't Leave Me' is one of the most beloved of the doo-wop oldies that were never actually hits.

● COMPILATIONS: *Magnificents & Rhythm Aces: 15 Cool Jewels* (Solid Smoke 1984)★★★.

MANNING, BOB

b. Manny Levin, 1 February 1926, Philadelphia, Pennsylvania, USA. A highly accomplished, but underrated ballad singer, whose career has probably suffered because his voice bore an uncanny similarity to that of the more popular Dick Haymes. Influenced by the singers and bands of the 'Swing Era', Manning sang in Philadephia hotels and had his own show on a local radio station before joining the newly formed Ziggy Elman outfit in 1947. He then worked for short periods with Art Mooney and Tommy Dorsey, and made an impressive appearance on the *Arthur Godfrey Talent Scouts* programme. Unable to secure a contract with a major record company, Manning persuaded a friend to finance a recording session, out of which came 'The Nearness Of You', a classic performance, and reportedly composer Hoagy Carmichael's favourite version of his song. It was picked up by Capitol Records, and entered the US Top 20 in 1953. The singer had further success with 'All I Desire' and 'Venus De Milo', and also released a tasteful collection of standards entitled *Lonely Spell*. Most of the tracks on that album were re-released in 1994. Like so many other classy singers, Manning was overtaken by the advent of rock 'n' roll in the late 50s, and faded into the background.
● ALBUMS: *Lonely Spell* (Capitol 1955)★★★, *Our Wedding Songs* (Everest *c*.50s)★★★, *Great Gentlemen Of Song-Spotlight On Bob Manning*, (Capitol 1994)★★★.

MANTOVANI

b. Annunzio Paolo Mantovani, 15 November 1905, Venice, Italy, d. 30 March 1980, Tunbridge Wells, Kent, England. A violinist, pianist, musical director, conductor, composer and arranger, Mantovani was one of the most successful orchestra leaders and album sellers in the history of popular music. His father was principal violinist at La Scala, Milan, under Arturo Toscanini, and also served under Mascagni, Richter and Saint-Saens, and subsequently, led the Covent Garden Orchestra. It is said that Mantovani received encouragement to become a professional musician from his mother, rather than his father. He began his musical training on the piano, and later learned to play the violin. After the family moved to England in 1912, he made his professional debut at the age of 16, playing the Bruch Violin Concerto Number 1. Four years later he had installed his own orchestra at London's Hotel Metropole, and began his broadcasting career. In the early 30s he formed the Tipica Orchestra and began a series of lunchtime broadcasts from the famous Monseigneur Restaurant in Piccadilly, London, and started recording for Regal Zonophone. He had two US hits in 1935-36, with 'Red Sails In The Sunset' and 'Serenade In The Night'. In the 40s, Mantovani served as musical director for several London West End shows, including *Lady Behave, Twenty To One, Meet Me Victoria, And So To Bed, Bob's Your Uncle* and *La-Di-Da-Di-Da*. He was also involved in Noël Coward's *Pacific 1860* and *Ace Of Clubs*; conducting from the theatre pit for artists such as Lupino Lane, Pat Kirkwood, Mary Martin, Sally Gray, Leslie Henson and many others. His records for UK Decca included 'The Green Cockatoo', 'Hear My Song, Violetta' and 'Tell Me, Marianne' (vocal by Val Merrall). Experimenting with various arrangements with which to target the lucrative US market, he came up with what has been variously called the 'cascading strings', 'cascading violins', or 'tumbling strings' effect, said to be an original idea of arranger Ronald Binge. It became the Orchestra's trademark and was first used to great effect in 1951, on Mantovani's recording of 'Charmaine', a song originally written to promote the 1926 silent film classic *What Price Glory?*. The Mantovani recording was the first of several million-selling singles for his orchestra, which included 'Wyoming', (another 20s number), 'Greensleeves', 'Song From Moulin Rouge' (a UK number 1), 'Swedish Rhapsody' and 'Lonely Ballerina'. Mantovani's own compositions included 'Serenata d'Amore', 'A Poem To The Moon', 'Royal Blue Waltz', 'Dance Of The Eighth Veil', 'Toy Shop Ballet' (Ivor Novello Award 1956), 'Red Petticoats', 'Brass Buttons', 'Tango In the Night' and 'Cara Mia', written with UK record producer/manager Bunny Lewis. David Whitfield's 1954 recording of 'Cara Mia', with Mantovani's orchestra accompaniment, sold over a million copies, and stayed at number 1 in the UK charts for a record (at the time) 10 weeks. It also made Whitfield one of the earliest UK artists to break into the US Top 10. Mantovani issued an instrumental version of the number, featuring himself on piano. This was most unusual in that the instrument was rarely a part of his 40-piece orchestral set-up. Singles apart, it was as an album artist that Mantovani excelled around the world, and especially in the USA. He is said to have been the first to sell over a million stereo units, aided in no small measure by the superb quality of sound obtained by Decca. Between 1955 and 1966 he had 28 albums in the US Top 30. Although he toured many countries of the world, including Russia, his popularity in the USA, where his style of orchestral offerings were often referred to as 'the beautiful music', was unique. An indication of the US audience's devotion can be gained from a claim by George Elrick, Mantovani's manager of 21 years, that at the beginning of one tour of the USA, the maestro was taken ill and a few concerts had to be cancelled; the prospective capacity audience at one of them, the University of Minnesota and Minneapolis, refused to claim refunds, preferring to retain their tickets for the following year. Mantovani continued to perform throughout the 60s and 70s. He was awarded a special Ivor Novello Award in 1956 for services to popular music.
● ALBUMS: *Mantovani Plays Tangos* (Decca/London 1953)★★★, *Strauss Waltzes* (Decca/London 1953)★★★, *Christmas Carols* (Decca/London 1953)★★★, *The Music Of Rudolph Friml* (Decca/London 1955)★★★, *Waltz Time* (Decca/London 1955)★★★, *Song Hits From Theatreland* (Decca/London 1955)★★★, *Ballet Memories* (Decca/London 1956)★★★, *Waltzes Of Irving Berlin* (Decca/London 1956)★★★, *Film Encores* (Decca/London 1957)★★★, *Gems Forever* (Decca/London 1958)★★★, *Continental Encores* (Decca/London 1959)★★★, *Film Encores, Volume 2* (Decca/London 1959)★★★, *The American Scene* (Decca/London 1960)★★★, *Songs To Remember* (Decca/London 1960)★★★, *Mantovani Plays Music From Exodus And Other Great Themes* (Decca/London 1960)★★★, *Concert Spectacular* (Decca/London 1961)★★★, *Operetta Memories* (Decca/London 1961)★★★, *Italia Mia* (Decca/London 1961)★★★, *Themes From Broadway* (Decca/London 1961)★★★, *Songs Of Praise* (Decca/London 1961)★★★, *American Waltzes* (Decca/London 1962)★★★, *Moon River And Other Great Film Themes* (Decca/London 1962)★★★, *Stop The World - I Want To Get Off/Oliver!* (Decca/London 1962)★★★, *Latin Rendezvous*

(Decca/London 1963)★★★, *Classical Encores* (Decca/London 1963)★★★, *Mantovani/Manhattan* (Decca/London 1963)★★★, *Christmas Greetings From Mantovani* (Decca/London 1963)★★, *Kismet* (Decca/London 1964)★★★, *Folk Songs Around The World* (Decca/London 1964)★★★, *The Incomparable Mantovani* (Decca/London 1964)★★★, *The Mantovani Sound - Big Hits From Broadway And Hollywood* (Decca/London 1965)★★★★, *Mantovani Olé* (Decca/London 1965)★★★, *Mantovani Magic* (Decca/London 1966)★★★, *Mr. Music ... Mantovani* (Decca/London 1966)★★★, *Mantovani Hollywood* (Decca/London 1967)★★★, *Old And New Fangled Tangos* (Decca/London 1967)★★★, *The Mantovani Touch* (Decca/London 1968)★★★, *Mantovani/Tango* (Decca/London 1968)★★★, *Mantovani Memories* (Decca/London 1968)★★★, *The Mantovani Scene* (Decca/London 1969)★★★, *Mantovani Today* (Decca/London 1970)★★★, *Mantovani Presents His Concert Successes* (Decca/London 1970)★★★, *To Lovers Everywhere USA* (Decca/London 1971)★★★, *From Monty With Love* (Decca/London 1971)★★★, *Annunzio Paolo Mantovani* (Decca/London 1972)★★★, *Cascade Of Praise* (Word 1985)★★★.
● COMPILATIONS: *Mantovani Stereo Showcase* (Decca/London 1959)★★★, *All-American Showcase* (Decca/London 1959)★★★, *Mantovani's Golden Hits* (Decca/London 1967)★★★, *The World Of Mantovani* (Decca/London 1969)★★★, *The World Of Mantovani, Volume 2* (Decca/London 1969)★★★, *Focus On Mantovani* (Decca 1975)★★★, *Twenty Golden Greats* (Warwick 1979)★★★, *A Lifetime Of Music* (Decca 1980)★★★, *The Golden Age Of The Young Mantovani 1935-1939* (Retrospect 1980)★★★, *The Unforgettable Sounds Of Mantovani* (Decca 1984)★★★, *Mantovani Magic* (Telstar 1985)★★★, *Love Themes* (Horatio Nelson 1985)★★★, *Sixteen Golden Classics* (Unforgettable 1986)★★★, *The Incomparable Mantovani* (K-Tel 1987)★★★, *Collection: Mantovani* (Castle 1987)★★★, *Golden Hits* (Decca 1988)★★★, *The Love Album* (Platinum 1988)★★★, *Film Themes* (Horatio Nelson 1989)★★★, *The Golden Age Of Mantovani* (Horatio Nelson 1995)★★★.

MANUEL AND HIS MUSIC OF THE MOUNTAINS

Orchestra leader Geoff Love (b. 4 September 1917, Todmorden, Yorkshire, England, d. 8 July 1991, London, England) initially used the above name pseudonymously. He took to music at an early age and by the late 50s/early 60s joined Joe Loss and Ted Heath as one of the country's leading bandleaders. Love's Manuel appellation allowed him an artistic freedom to draw influence from South American music and, although early releases did not reveal its creator's identity (Love was 'unmasked' during a cameo appearance on BBC television's *Juke Box Jury*), such recordings later became the natural outlet for his talents. A prodigious output, notably for EMI's *Studio Two* stereo series, ensured that the band remained one of Britain's most popular light orchestral attractions throughout the 60s and 70s.
● ALBUMS: *Manuel And His Music Of The Mountains* (Columbia 1960)★★★★, *Mountain Carnival* (c.60s)★★★★, *Ecstasy* (c.60s)★★★, *Mountain Fiesta* (c.60s)★★★, *Blue Waters* (1966)★★★, *Reflections* (1969)★★★, *This Is Manuel* (Studio 2 1971)★★★★, *Carnival* (Studio 2 1971)★★★★,

Mardi Gras (1972)★★★, *Shangri-La* (1973)★★★, *Sun, Sea And Sky* (1973)★★★, *Y Viva Espana* (1974)★★★★, *You, The Night And Music* (1975)★★★, *El Bimbo* (1975)★★, *Manuel And The Voices Of Mountains* (1975)★★★, *Masquerade* (1976)★★★, *Mountain Fire* (1977)★★★, *Blue Tangos* (Note 1977)★★, *Bossa Nova* (1978)★★, *Cha Cha* (1978)★★★, *Music Of Manuel* (1978)★★★★, *Supernatural* (EMI 1979)★★★, *Viva Manuel* (1979)★★★★, *Manuel Movie Hits* (Note 1979)★★, *Fiesta* (EMI 1980)★★★★, *Digital Spectacular* (EMI 1981)★★★★.
● COMPILATIONS: *The Very Best Of Manuel* (Columbia 1976)★★★★, *Bolero* (MFP 1984)★★★, *Magic Of Manuel And The Music Of The Mountains* (MFP 1986)★★★, *Latin Hits* (EMI 1988)★★★.

MARATHONS

The brief history of the Marathons is shrouded in mystery and confusion. Long thought to be a pseudonym for the Olympics, the US R&B group that had recorded 'Western Movies' in 1958, the Marathons was actually a pseudonym for the Vibrations, a Los Angeles vocal group who had a 1961 dance hit with 'The Watusi', and in a previous incarnation, as the Jayhawks who hit the US singles charts in 1956 with 'Stranded In The Jungle'. The convoluted story of the Marathons' only hit, 1961's 'Peanut Butter', is that the Olympics' record company, Arvee, needed a new release from the group while they were on the road. In the Olympics' place, Arvee hired the Vibrations to record 'Peanut Butter', a virtual soundalike of the Olympics' own '(Baby) Hully Gully'. 'Peanut Butter' reached number 20 on Arvee, but when the Vibrations' own label discovered that its group had been moonlighting, it took over distribution of the record, issuing it on both the Chess and Argo labels. With that decision, the career of the non-existent Marathons came to an end. However, an attempt by Arvee to cash in on the success of the group resulted in a bogus version of the Marathons, along with an album and singles including 'C. Percy Mercy Of Scotland Yard' and 'Tight Sweater'.
● COMPILATIONS: *The Olympics Meet The Marathons* (Ace 1985)★★★.

MARDI GRAS

Pat Boone forged his career by recording antiseptic cover versions of R&B hits. He became the clean-cut face of rock 'n' roll, acceptable to a moral majority fearful of black musicians and the ebullient talent of, for example, Elvis Presley and Jerry Lee Lewis. Boone was thus quickly embraced by Hollywood, but his ventures into pop films proved equally insubstantial. *Mardi Gras*, released in 1958, co-starred aspiring singers Gary Crosby (the son of Bing Crosby) and Tommy Sands, the first husband of Nancy Sinatra. Boone portrays a cadet who wins a date with a movie star; the film's title is inspired by footage of the New Orleans festival which provides momentary relief from this anodyne plot. The soundtrack includes the risible 'A Fiddle, A Rifle, An Axe And A Bible', the last of which Boone grasped in real life when he opted to record religious material.

MARINERS

This four-piece gospel group consisted of two white and two black singers and was formed in 1942 at the Coast Guard in Manhattan Beach in New York, USA. The group consisted of

Thomas Lockard, James O. Lewis, Nathaniel Dickerson and Martin Karl (who had previously performed with the Chicago Opera). The group toured the New York State area and visited several Pacific force bases during 1945. Radio broadcasts brought them to the attention of Arthur Godfrey, and they were regulars on his radio show for several years after the war. They recorded 'On The Island Of Oahu' for Columbia Records in 1949, but their first hit was 'Sometime' in 1950. The run of successes continued with 'They Call The Wind Mariah' and 'I See The Moon', their last and biggest hit, at number 14 in 1952. Still best known through their appearances on Godfrey's shows, they moved to the Cadence label in the late 50s, to diminishing acclaim. By the advent of the 50s more contemporary outfits had seized their mantle, and they disappeared from both the charts and the New York radio scene which had been their most effective medium.

MARSALA, MARTY

b. Mario Salvatore Marsala, 2 April 1909, Chicago, Illinois, USA, d. 27 April 1975. As a young man Marsala first played drums but then switched to trumpet. He played this instrument in various bands in and around Chicago in the late 20s and early 30s. In the middle of the decade he came to New York to team up with his brother, Joe Marsala, who led a band there. With side visits to other bands, he stayed with his brother into the early 40s, then joined Chico Marx and also led a band of his own before military service intervened. After the war he was briefly back with his brother and also played in bands led by Miff Mole and others but mainly led his own bands into the middle of the next decade. On the west coast he played occasionally with Kid Ory and Earl 'Fatha' Hines and also led his own bands through into the 60s. From this date onwards Marsala's career was constantly interrupted by illness. Marsala played with a rich, gutsy tone, delivering pungent solos with wit and fire. His long periods spent in Chicago and San Francisco, allied to his latter-day poor health, kept him in undeserved obscurity.
● ALBUMS: with Earl 'Fatha' Hines *At The Club Hangover Vol. 5* (Storyville 1955)★★★.

MARTERIE, RALPH

b. Ralph Martin, 24 December 1914, Accerra, near Naples, Italy, d. 10 October 1978, Dayton, Ohio, USA. While Marterie was still a child his parents emigrated to the USA, where his father joined the orchestra of the Chicago Civic Opera. Ralph was still a teenager when he started playing trumpet with Dan Russo's Otriole Orchestra. He went on to play in local theatres and with other bands in Chicago, which was at that time the country's largest musical centre outside New York. Consequently, Marterie never had to leave the city to find work, joining the NBC staff orchestra where he played under conductors such as Percy Faith and André Kostelanetz. During World War II Marterie led a US Navy band, then after the war he returned to Chicago as a leader with ABC radio. In 1949 he started recording for Mercury with his own band, which featured his brassy open trumpet. He did not achieve instant success but in 1952 the band spent 10 weeks in the US charts with 'Caravan', earning a second Gold Disc the following year with 'Pretend'. His album and singles output varied between swing standards, novelties and pop instrumentals that highlighted his trademark of trumpet and guitar voiced together (compare his temporary partnership

with guitarist/musical director Al Caiola on a cover version of 'Acapulco 22'). There were moderate hits with 'Guaglione', 'Skokiaan' and 'Tequila', which were successful enough to maintain his reputation and keep him working through changing fashions in pop music. Marterie was still touring with a band until his death in Dayton, where he had just played a one-nighter in October 1978.

MARTIN, DEAN

b. Dino Paul Crocetti, 7 June 1917, Steubenville, Ohio, USA, d. 25 December 1995. An extremely popular ballad singer and light comedian with a relaxed and easy style, who developed into an accomplished dramatic actor. After leaving school in the 10th grade, he worked as a shoe-shine boy and a gas station attendant before becoming an 'amateur' welterweight boxer, 'Kid Crochet', earning 10 dollars a fight. When he retired from the boxing arena, he became a croupier at a local casino. His first singing job is said to have been with the Sammy Watkins band in 1941, when he was initially billed as Dino Martini, but the name was soon changed to Dean Martin. His earliest recordings were for the Diamond label, and included 'Which Way Did My Heart Go'/'All Of Me' and 'I Got the Sun In The Morning'/'Sweetheart Of Sigma Chi'. He also recorded some tracks for the Apollo label, well known for its impressive roster of black talent. The Martin recordings included 'Walkin' My Baby Back Home', 'Oh Marie', 'Santa Lucia', 'Hold Me', 'Memory Lane' and 'Louise'. In 1946, Martin first worked with comedian Jerry Lewis at the 500 Club in Atlantic City. Together they developed an ad-libbing song and comedy act that became very popular on US television and radio in the late 40s. In 1949, they appeared in supporting roles in the film *My Friend Irma*, and in the sequel, *My Friend Irma Goes West*, the following year. The team then starred in another 14 popular comedies, with Martin providing the songs and romantic interest, and Lewis contributing the zany fun. These films included *At War With The Army* (1950), *Jumping Jacks* (1952), *Sailor, Beware!, The Stooge, Scared Stiff* (1953), *The Caddy* (1953), *Living It Up* (1954), *Pardners* (1956) and *Hollywood Or Bust* (1956). Their parting was somewhat acrimonious, and it was widely felt that Martin would be the one to suffer most from the split. In fact, they both did well. After a shaky start in the comedy movie *Ten Thousand Bedrooms* (1957), Martin blossomed as a dramatic actor in *The Young Lions* (1958), *Some Came Running* (1958), *Rio Bravo* (1959), *Ada* (1961), *Toys In The Attic* (1963), *The Sons Of Katie Elder* (1965) and *Airport* (1970). He still retained his comic touch in *Who Was That Lady?* (1960) and *What A Way To Go* (1964), but made surprisingly few musicals. The most notable were *Bells Are Ringing* (1960), with Judy Holliday, and *Robin And The Seven Hoods* (1964). Meanwhile, Martin had signed to Capitol Records in 1948, and for the next 10 years had a series of US Top 30 chart entries, including 'That Certain Party' (duet with Jerry Lewis), 'Powder Your Face With Sunshine', 'I'll Always Love You', 'If', 'You Belong To Me', 'Love Me, Love Me', 'That's Amore', 'I'd Cry Like A Baby', 'Sway', 'Money Burns A Hole In My Pocket, 'Memories Are Made Of This' (number 1), 'Innamorata', 'Standing On The Corner', 'Return To Me', 'Angel Baby' and 'Volare' ('Nel Blu Dipinto Di Blu'). Martin's version of 'That's Amore' resurfaced when it was featured in the 1987 hit movie *Moonstruck*.

Although Martin was still a big attraction on film and in nightclubs, his records found difficulty in making the singles charts during the early part of the 60s. In 1961, Frank Sinatra, who had also been with Capitol Records, started his own Reprise Records. Martin, who was a member of Sinatra's 'Clan', or 'Ratpack', was one of the first recruits to the new label. In 1964, Martin returned to the US singles charts with a bang. His recording of 'Everybody Loves Somebody', produced by Jimmy Bowen, had a commercial country 'feel' to it, and knocked the Beatles' 'A Hard Day's Night' off the top of the chart. Martin's subsequent Top 30 entries were all in the same vein - records such as 'The Door Is Still Open To My Heart', 'You're Nobody Till Somebody Loves You', 'Send Me The Pillow You Dream On', 'Houston', 'In The Chapel In The Moonlight' and 'Little Ole Wine Drinker, Me'. The latter number was a fitting selection for an artist whose stage persona was that of a man more than slightly inebriated. 'Everybody Loves Somebody' became the theme song for *The Dean Martin Show* on NBC TV which started in 1964, ran for nine seasons and was syndicated worldwide. As well being a showcase for Martin's singing talents, the show gave him the opportunity to display his improvisational skills in comedy. He continued to be a big draw in clubs, especially in Las Vegas, and played the London Palladium in the summer of 1987 to favourable reviews. Later that year, he joined ex-Rat Pack colleagues Sinatra and Sammy Davis Jnr. in the 'Together Again' tour, involving 40 performances in 29 cities, but had to withdraw at an early stage because of a kidney ailment. In the autumn of 1993 it was reported that Martin had lung cancer and he died on Christmas Day 1995.

● ALBUMS: *Capitol Presents Dean Martin* (Capitol 1953)★★★, *Swingin' Down Yonder* (Capitol 1955)★★★, *Dean Martin Sings, Nicolini Lucchesi Plays* (Britone 1956)★★, *The Stooge* film soundtrack (Capitol 1956)★★, *Pretty Baby* (Capitol 1957)★★★, *This Is Dean Martin* (Capitol 1958)★★★, *Sleep Warm* (Capitol 1959)★★★, *Winter Romance* (Capitol 1959)★★★, *Bells Are Ringing* film soundtrack (Capitol 1960)★★★, *This Time I'm Swingin'* (Capitol 1961)★★★, *Dino Goes Dixie* (Encore 1961)★★, *Dean Martin* (Capitol 1961)★★★, *Dino - Italian Love Songs* (Capitol 1962)★★★, *French Style* (Reprise 1962)★★★, *Cha Cha De Amor* (Capitol 1962)★★★, *Dino Latino* (Reprise 1963)★★★, *Dean Martin Country Style* (Reprise 1963)★★, *Dean 'Tex' Martin Rides Again* (Reprise 1963)★★, *Everybody Loves Somebody* (Reprise 1964)★★★, *Hey Brother, Pour The Wine* (Reprise 1964)★★★, *Dream With Dean* (Reprise 1964)★★★, *The Door Is Still Open To My Heart* (Reprise 1964)★★★, *Dean Martin Hits Again* (Reprise 1965)★★★, *Dean Martin Sings, Sinatra Conducts* (1965)★★★, *Southern Style* (1965)★★★, *Dean Martin Month* (Reprise 1965)★★★, *Holiday Cheer* (1965)★★★, *I'm Yours* (Sears 1965)★★★, *Lush Years* (1965)★★★, *(Remember Me) I'm The One Who Loves You* (Reprise 1965)★★★, *Houston* (Reprise 1965)★★★, *Somewhere There's A Someone* (Reprise 1966)★★★, *Relaxin'* (1966)★★★, *Happy In Love* (1966)★★★, *Sings Songs From The Silencers* (Reprise 1966)★★★, *The Hit Sound Of Dean Martin* (Reprise 1966)★★★, *The Dean Martin TV Show* (Reprise 1966)★★★, *The Dean Martin Christmas Album* (Reprise 1966)★★★, *At Ease With Dean* (Reprise 1967)★★★, *Happiness Is Dean Martin* (Reprise 1967)★★★, *Love Is A Career* (Stateside 1967)★★★, *Welcome To My World* (Reprise 1967)★★★, *Gentle On My Mind* (Reprise 1969)★★★, *I Take A Lot Of Pride In What I Am* (Reprise 1969)★★★, *My Woman, My Wife* (Reprise 1970)★★★, *For The Good Times* (Reprise 1971)★★★, *Dino* (Reprise 1972)★★★, *Sittin' On Top Of The World* (Reprise 1973)★★★, *You're The Best Thing That Ever Happened To Me* (Reprise 1974)★★★, *Once In A While* (Reprise 1978)★★★, *The Nashville Sessions* (Warners 1983)★★.

● COMPILATIONS: *The Best Of Dean Martin* (Capitol 1966)★★★, *Deluxe Set* 3-LP box set (Capitol 1967)★★★, *Dean Of Music* (MFP 1967)★★★, *Dean Martin's Greatest Hits! Volume 1* (Reprise 1968)★★★, *Dean Martin's Greatest Hits! Volume 2* (Reprise 1968)★★★, *The Best Of Dean Martin* (Capitol 1969)★★★, *The Best Of Dean Martin, Volume 2* (Capitol 1970)★★★, *One More Time* (World Record Club 1970)★★★, *20 Original Dean Martin Hits* (Reprise 1976)★★★, *The Classic Dino* (Capitol 1979)★★★, *Dean Martin* 4-LP box set (World Record Club 1981)★★★, *The Very Best Of Dean Martin* (Capitol 1983)★★★, *20 Love Songs* (Black Tulip 1988)★★★, *The Dean Martin Collection* (Deja Vu 1989)★★★, *The Collection* (Castle 1988)★★★, *That's Amore* (Entertainers 1988)★★★, *The Best Of The Capitol Years* (Capitol 1989)★★★, *Capitol Collectors Series* (Capitol 1990)★★★, *Singles* (1994)★★★, *The Capitol Years* (Capitol 1996)★★★.

● FURTHER READING: *Everybody Loves Somebody*, Arthur Marx. *Dino: Living High In The Dirty Business Of Dreams*, Nick Tosches.

MARTIN, RAY

b. Raymond Stuart Martin, 11 October 1918, Vienna, Austria, d. February 1988, South Africa. A composer, arranger, musical director and author, after studying violin, composition and orchestration at the State Academy for Music and Fine Arts in Vienna, Martin moved to Britain in 1937. He joined the *Carroll Levis Discoveries* show as a solo violin act, touring the UK variety circuit, and was then chosen as the 'New Voice' in the popular BBC radio series *Bandwaggon*, which starred Arthur Askey and Richard Murdoch. After appearing in several editions of *Sidney Torch's Half Hour*, he enlisted in the British Army in 1940 and worked in the Intelligence Corps, aided by his fluency in German, French and English. Later, he became musical director of the Variety Department for the British Forces Network in Hamburg, Germany. He started broadcasting his *Melody From The Sky* programme from there, with a German string orchestra culled from the Hamburg Philharmonic Orchestra, and transferred the show to the BBC in December 1946, where it ran for over 500 broadcasts. Martin was also instrumental in founding the BBC Northern Variety Orchestra, and, from 1949-51, conducted at least six shows a week. He started recording for Columbia Records in 1949 with his own Concert Orchestra accompanying other artists including Julie Andrews, Steve Conway and Jimmy Young. Eventually he became the company's recording manager. His 50s instrumental hits included Leroy Anderson's 'Blue Tango', 'Swedish Rhapsody' and 'Carousel Waltz'. Some of his many compositions and film scores are difficult to locate because, besides his own name, he wrote under several pseudonyms, such as Tony Simmonds, Buddy Cadbury, Lester Powell and Marshall Ross. In 1956 he wrote the background score, and served as musical director, for a British musical film called *It's Great To Be Young*, starring John Mills. In addition to the title track, written under his own name, the film contained Martin's (as Marshall Ross) 1952 composition 'Marching Strings'; and his (as Lester Powell) romantic ballad 'You Are My First Love' (in collaboration with Paddy Roberts). Martin's other compositions included 'Melody From The Sky', 'Once Upon A Winter Time', 'Muriella', 'Begorra', 'Parlour Game', 'Blue Violins' (a US hit for Hugo Winterhalter's Orchestra), 'Any Old Time', 'Waltzing Bugle Boy', 'Airborne', 'Ballet Of The Bells', 'Tango Of The Bells', 'Big Ben Blues', 'Never Too Young' and 'Sounds Out Of Sight'. He composed the incidental music for over 20 BBC Sound cartoons, and wrote the scores for several films, including *Yield To The Night*, a prison melodrama in which ex-'glamour girl' Diana Dors gave a highly acclaimed dramatic performance, and the 1956 version of *My Wife's Father*. In 1957 Martin moved to America to work in New York and Hollywood. His US film scores included *The Young Graduates* and *The Hoax*. In 1972 he returned to work in the UK and, in 1980, appeared as himself in *The Baltimore Bullit*. During the 80s he settled in South Africa, and died there in 1988.

● ALBUMS: *Music In The Ray Martin Manner* (Columbia 1953)★★★★, *Music In The Ray Martin Manner Volume 2* (Columbia 1954)★★★★, *Lehar, Strauss And Novello Melodies* (Columbia 1956)★★★, *High Barbaree-12 Famous Sea Shanties* (Columbia 1957)★★, *Olives, Almonds And Raisins* (Columbia 1958)★★, *Million Dollar Melodies* (Columbia 1959)★★★, *Melodies D'Amour* (Columbia 1961)★★★, *Boots And Saddles* (Columbia 1961)★★, *I Could Have Danced All Night* (1961)★★★, *Dynamica* (RCA 1961)★★★, *We* (1962)★★★, *Spotlight On Strings* (1962)★★★, *Sounds Out Of Sight* (1963)★★★, *The Sound Of Sight* (Phase 4 1964)★★★, *London Under The Stars* (1966)★★★, *Favourite TV Themes* (Decca 1973)★★★, *Favourite TV Themes, Volume 2* (Decca 1975)★★★, *Viva Mariachi* (Gold Star 1975)★★★, *Welcome Home* (Goldstar 1975)★★★.

MARTIN, VINCE

A folk singer who first surfaced in the mid-50s on the east coast club circuit, little is known about Vince Martin's background. His major claim to fame was as the singer on the 1956 Top 10 hit 'Cindy, Oh Cindy', on Glory Records. The folk song, written by Bob Baron and Burt Long, featured Martin backed by the folk group the Tarriers, which included Alan Arkin (who went on to become a successful actor), Erik Darling (who became a member of the folk group the Rooftop Singers) and Bob Carey. Martin made other recordings into the 70s, including singles for ABC Paramount and Elektra Records, and he recorded a self-titled album for Capitol Records in 1973.

● ALBUMS: *Vince Martin* (Capitol 1973)★★★.

MARTINO, AL

b. Alfred Cini, 7 October 1927, Philadelphia, Pennsylvania, USA. The son of Italian immigrants, a fact that was evident in his style and manner, Martino worked as bricklayer in his father's construction business before being encouraged to become a singer by his friend Mario Lanza. After singing in local clubs, and winning Arthur Godfrey's *Talent Scouts*, he recorded 'Here In My Heart' for the small BBS record label. It shot to number 1 in the US chart, and reputedly sold over

a million copies. This disc was also the first ever record to top the *New Musical Express* UK listings, inaugurated in 1952. Martino's success led to a contract with Capitol Records, and more hits in 1953 with 'Take My Heart', 'Rachel' and 'When You're Mine'. For several years after that, the US record buyers apparently tired of Martino's soulful ballads, although he remained popular in Europe for a time - particularly in the UK, where he made the Top 20 with 'Now', 'Wanted', 'The Story Of Tina' and 'The Man From Laramie'. After some telling performances on US television, he made his recording comeback in 1963 with country singer Leon Payne's 'I Love You Because', followed by 'Painted, Tainted Rose', 'Living A Lie', 'I Love You More And More Every Day', 'Tears And Roses', 'Always Together', 'Think I'll Go And Cry Myself To Sleep' and 'Mary In The Morning'. His second million-seller, 'Spanish Eyes' (1965), was originally an instrumental piece, 'Moon Over Naples', written by the popular German orchestra leader, Bert Kaempfert. With lyrics by Charles Singleton and Eddy Snyder, Martino's version became, particularly in Europe, a dreamy dance favourite to rival Charles Aznavour's 'Dance In The Old Fashioned Way'. In 1964, Martino sang the title song for the Bette Davis/Olivia De Havilland film *Hush ... Hush Sweet Charlotte*, and this led to his playing singer Johnny Fontane in the smash hit movie *The Godfather* (1972). In the film, Martino sang the Italian number 'O Marenariello' ('I Have But One Heart'). He also recorded the film's love theme, 'Speak Softly Love', and had chart success with further Italian songs, 'To The Door Of The Sun' ('Alle Porte Del Sole') and the old Dean Martin hit, Domenico Modugno's 'Volare'. In vogue once more, Martino played top nightclubs and theatres, and continued to record with Capitol who have reissued many of his early albums on CD. In 1992 he played some UK dates, mixing selections from *Cats* and *The Phantom Of The Opera* with much requested favourites such as 'Granada'.

● ALBUMS: *Al Martino* (20th Century 1959)★★★, *Sing Along With Al Martino* (20th Century 1959)★★★, *Al Martino Sings* (20th Century 1962)★★★, *The Exciting Voice Of Al Martino* (Capitol 1962)★★★, *The Italian Voice Of Al Martino* (Capitol 1963)★★★, *Love Notes* (20th Century 1963)★★★, *I Love You Because* (Capitol 1963)★★★★, *Painted, Tainted Rose* (Capitol 1963)★★★★, *Living A Lie* (Capitol 1964)★★★, *I Love You More And More Every Day/Tears And Roses* (Capitol 1964)★★★, *We Could* (Capitol 1965)★★★, *Somebody Else Is Taking My Place* (Capitol 1965)★★★, *My Cherie* (Capitol 1965)★★★★, *Spanish Eyes* (Capitol 1966)★★★★, *Think I'll Go Somewhere And Cry Myself To Sleep* (Capitol 1966)★★★, *This Is Love* (Capitol 1966)★★★, *This Love For You* (Capitol 1967)★★★, *Daddy's Little Girl* (Capitol 1967)★★★, *Mary In The Morning* (Capitol 1967)★★★, *This Is Al Martino* (Capitol 1968)★★★, *Love Is Blue* (Capitol 1968)★★★, *Sausalito* Capitol 1969)★★★, *Jean* (Capitol 1969)★★★, *Can't Help Falling In Love* (Capitol 1970)★★★, *My Heart Sings* (Capitol 1970)★★★, *Love Theme From 'The Godfather'* (Capitol 1972)★★, *Country Style* (Capitol 1974)★, *To The Door Of The Sun* (Capitol 1975)★★, *Sing My Love Songs* (Capitol 1977)★★★, *The Next Hundred Years* (Capitol 1978)★★★.

● COMPILATIONS: *The Best Of Al Martino* (Capitol 1968)★★★, *The Very Best Of Al Martino* (Capitol 1974)★★★, *Love Songs: Al Martino* (MFP 1983)★★★, *The*

Hits Of Al Martino (MFP 1985)★★★, *Greatest Hits* (Prism 1991)★★★, *Capitol Collectors Series: Al Martino* (Capitol 1992)★★★.

MARVIN AND JOHNNY

From Los Angeles, California, USA, Marvin Phillips (b. 23 October 1931, Guthrie, Oklahoma, USA) and Emory 'Johnny' Perry (b. 1 March 1928, Sherman, Texas, USA) made a brief impact on the rock 'n' roll scene when Los Angeles was a major centre of the R&B recording scene during the late 40s and early 50s. Phillips and Perry had known each other since 1949, when they both played saxophones in the Richard Lewis Band. When Phillips formed the Marvin Phillips And His Men From Mars combo, Perry joined him. Meanwhile, Phillips gained his first success in the recording business when he teamed with Jesse Belvin in a duo called Marvin And Jesse, reaching the charts with the dreamy ballad 'Dream Girl' (number 2 R&B) in 1952 for Specialty Records. After Belvin was drafted into the army in 1953, Phillips, at the behest of Specialty, recruited a new partner, his old friend Perry, to form Marvin And Johnny. The duo immediately had a hit with 'Baby Doll' (number 9 R&B) in 1953. They moved to Modern in 1954 and released 'Tick Tock' (number 9 R&B). However, they are best remembered for 'Cherry Pie', the b-side to 'Tick Tock', which, although not making any national charts, possibly achieved more radio airplay. The song was revived by Skip And Flip in 1960, putting it high on the pop charts.
● ALBUMS: *Marvin And Johnny* (Crown 1963)★★★.
● COMPILATIONS: *Flipped Out* (Specialty 1992)★★★.

MASTERS, VALERIE

b. 24 April 1940, London, England. This red-headed pop singer from London's East End sang during her childhood in the local underground station during air raids and later became the private secretary to the Mayor of Stepney. She received her big musical break when she replaced Marion Ryan in the popular Ray Ellington Quartet. Masters made her first recording, 'Ding Dong', for Fontana in 1958 and was first seen on television on the *Hughie Green Show*. She was given her own series on Radio Luxembourg in 1959, which ran for over two years. Her only chart success came in 1960 with her sixth single on Fontana, a version of the European song 'Banjo Boy'. This was the same song that gave much-loved singer/comedian George Formby his last chart hit. Masters represented Britain in the European (not Eurovision) Song Contest in Belgium in 1960, and this led to her working in Scandinavia, Germany and the Netherlands. She recorded for HMV in 1963, Columbia in 1964, Polydor in 1966 and once more on Columbia in 1969 but has not graced the chart since.

MATASSA, COSIMO

Of Italian ancestry, Matassa ran a New Orleans juke-box company and a record store, J&M Amusement Services, in the early 40s. In 1945 he opened a small recording studio behind the shop. For the next 20 years, Cosimo's studios were the focus of recording activity in the city. Among the first to produce at Cosimo's was Dave Bartholomew, who recorded Roy Brown for De Luxe and Tommy Ridgley for Imperial. In 1949, Bartholomew began recording Fats Domino at the studio, and in 1952, he recorded Lloyd Price.

There were other hits from J&M by Shirley And Lee. By the mid-50s, a studio band had emerged to accompany the growing number of singers working there. Led by saxophonists Red Tyler and Lee Allen, its members included Earl Palmer (drums) and Frank Fields (bass). In 1956, the studio moved to larger premises and was renamed Cosimo's. Soon afterwards, Little Richard made some of his most famous recordings there. During this time, Matassa had been engineer and studio owner but in 1957 he moved into management with white pop singer Jimmy Clanton. Two years later he started his own, short-lived label, Rex. Among its roster of artists was Mickey Gilley, Earl King, Jerry McCain and Mac Rebennack (Dr. John). Matassa returned to his recording work on hits such as Barbara Lynn's 'You'll Lose A Good Thing' (1962) until 1966, when he set up Dover Records, an ambitious distribution company for local New Orleans labels. There were big successes with Robert Parker ('Barefootin'') and Aaron Neville ('Tell It Like It Is'), but by 1968 Dover too had become bankrupt. Afterwards, Matassa remained a part-owner of the Jazz City Studios in New Orleans, as well as working at Sea-Saint studios and forming the Jefferson Jazz company with Marshall Sehorn.

MATCHUKI, COUNT

b. Winston Cooper, c.1939, Kingston, Jamaica, West Indies, d. 1995. Matchuki, whose nickname came from his habit of chewing matchsticks, is widely acknowledged as the first Jamaican DJ. In the 50s the popular sound was R&B and he would simply add local phraseology to enhance the tunes. R&B is acknowledged to have influenced many Jamaican musicians and in the 50s Coxsone Dodd made frequent visits to secure new releases for his Downbeat Sound System. While on his visits he heard the US DJs' jive talk and felt that the style would augment his status as the top sound man on the island. Following the departure of Dodd's resident DJ Duke Vin, Matchuki was offered and accepted the role, where he attempted to emulate the US radio hosts. By the late 50s, although initially influenced by the American sound, Jamaican musicians had begun to establish their own identity. The Skatalites performed a number of ska instrumentals for Dodd and the Count was invited to add his vocals on a number of recordings, although he often remained uncredited. However, he certainly appeared on the Sound Dimension's 'More Scorcher', 'Doctor Sappa Too' and 'Pepper Pot'. By the late 60s, disillusioned with the lack of recognition and financial rewards, he decided to abandon his career as a DJ. He resurfaced 10 years later in the television series *Deep Roots Music*. Interviewed with the pre-eminent DJ Sir Lord Comic, the duo spent most of the interview in a heated debate relating to the Jiving Juniors' 'Lollipop Girl'. Matchuki's appearance enabled him to set the record straight as to the formative role he played in the DJ phenomenon.

MATHIS, JOHNNY

b. John Royce Mathis, 30 September 1935, San Francisco, California, USA. In 1956, the 19-year-old Mathis was signed to Columbia Records where he began his career with a jazz-tinged album. A US Top 20 hit with 'Wonderful! Wonderful!' saw him move adroitly towards the balladeer market, and before long he was a major concert attraction, with regular appearances on highly rated American television shows. In

1957, together with his first hit, Mathis was barely absent from the US bestseller lists, and that year had a further five hits, including the number 1 'Chances Are', 'The Twelfth Of Never' and 'It's Not For Me To Say'. Mathis had become a phenomenon; his popularity at that time ranked alongside that of Frank Sinatra. By May 1958, he was scraping the UK charts with 'Teacher, Teacher', and soon established himself with major hits such as 'A Certain Smile', 'Winter Wonderland', 'Someone', 'Misty' and 'My Love For You'. His appeal to the adult market ensured spectacular album success, and *Johnny's Greatest Hits* stayed a record 490 weeks in the US chart. With the beat boom and 60s pop explosion making it more difficult for visiting American balladeers to infiltrate the singles chart, Mathis concentrated increasingly on releasing albums. Indeed, he seemed willing to tackle a variety of concepts presented by his various producers and arrangers. *Away From Home*, produced by Norman Newell, saw the singer concentrating on the songs of European composers; *Olé*, the Latin-American outing, was sung in Portuguese and Spanish; *Wonderful World Of Make Believe* consisted entirely of songs based on fairytales; and there were tribute albums to such composers as Burt Bacharach and Bert Kaempfert. Meanwhile, Mathis was suffering from serious drug addiction, but fortunately he managed to kick the habit. By the late 60s, Mathis seemed equally adept at tackling MOR standards and John Lennon/Paul McCartney songs, as well as hoping to update his image. He returned to the UK singles chart in 1974 for the first time in a decade with 'I'm Stone In Love With You' and, two years later, secured the Christmas number 1 with 'When A Child Is Born'. Back in the USA, he was still searching for new ideas and in 1978, collaborated with Deniece Williams on 'Too Much, Too Late'. This, his first duet, became a surprise number 1, his first US chart-topper since 1957. Since then, Mathis has duetted incessantly with a list that includes Gladys Knight, Paulette McWilliams, Stephanie Lawrence, Jane Oliver, Dionne Warwick, Angela Bofill, Natalie Cole, Barbara Dickson and Nana Mouskouri. What has been overlooked is Mathis's incredible commercial success: he is one of the most successful recording artists of all time, although behind Sinatra and Elvis Presley. His remarkable durability and unfailing professionalism demand admiration.

● ALBUMS: *Johnny Mathis* (Columbia 1957)★★★, *Wonderful! Wonderful!* (Columbia 1957)★★★, *Warm* (Columbia 1957)★★★, *Wild Is The Night* film soundtrack (Columbia 1957)★★, *Good Night, Dear Lord* (Columbia 1958)★★, *Swing Softly* (Columbia 1958)★★★, *Merry Christmas* (Columbia 1958)★★★★, *A Certain Smile* film soundtrack (Columbia 1958)★★★, with Al Caiola *Open Fire, Two Guitars* (Columbia 1959)★★★, *Heavenly* (Columbia 1959)★★★★, *Faithfully* (Columbia 1960)★★★★, *Ride On A Rainbow* (Columbia 1960)★★★, *Johnny's Mood* (Columbia 1960)★★★★, *The Rhythms And Ballads Of Broadway* (Columbia 1960)★★★, *I'll Buy You A Star* (Columbia 1961)★★★, *Portrait Of Johnny* (Columbia 1961)★★★★, *Live It Up!* (Columbia 1962)★★★, *Rapture* (Columbia 1962)★★★★, *Johnny* (Columbia 1963)★★★, *Romantically* (Columbia 1963)★★★, *Tender Is The Night* (Mercury 1964)★★★★, *I'll Search My Heart And Other Great Hits* (Columbia 1964)★★★, *The Wonderful World Of Make Believe* (Mercury 1964)★★★, *The Great Years* (Columbia 1964)★★★, *This Is Love* (Mercury 1964)★★★, *Sounds Of Christmas* (Columbia 1964)★★★, *Love Is Everything* (Mercury 1965)★★★, *The Sweetheart Tree* (Mercury 1965)★★★, *Away From Home* (Columbia 1965)★★★, *Olé* (Columbia 1965)★★★, *The Shadow Of Your Smile* (Mercury 1966)★★★★, *So Nice* (Mercury 1966)★★★, *Johnny Mathis Sings* (Mercury 1967)★★★, *Up, Up And Away* (Columbia 1967)★★★, *Love Is Blue* (Columbia 1968)★★★, *Those Were The Days* (Columbia 1968)★★★, *The Impossible Dream* (Columbia 1969)★★★★, *People* (Columbia 1969)★★★, *Love Theme From 'Romeo And Juliet'* (Columbia 1969)★★★, *Johnny Mathis Sings The Music Of Bert Kaempfert* (Columbia 1969)★★★, *Raindrops Keep Fallin' On My Head* (Columbia 1970)★★★★, *The Long And Winding Road* (Columbia 1970)★★★, *Close To You* (Columbia 1970)★★★, *Johnny Mathis Sings The Music Of Bacharach And Kaempfert* (Columbia 1971)★★★, *Love Story* (Columbia 1971)★★★, *You've Got A Friend* (Columbia 1971)★★★, *Christmas With Johnny Mathis* (Columbia 1972)★★★, *Johnny Mathis In Person* (Columbia 1972)★★★, *The First Time Ever (I Saw Your Face)* (Columbia 1972)★★★★, *Make It Easy On Yourself* (Columbia 1972)★★★, *Song Sung Blue* (Columbia 1972)★★★, *Me And Mrs Jones* (Columbia 1973)★★★, *Killing Me Softly With Her Song* (Columbia 1973)★★★, *I'm Coming Home* (Columbia 1973)★★★, *Johnny Mathis Sings The Great Songs* (Columbia 1974)★★★, *The Heart Of A Woman* (Columbia 1974)★★★, *When Will I See You Again* (Columbia 1975)★★★, *Feelings* (Columbia 1975)★★★, *I Only Have Eyes For You* (Columbia 1976)★★★, *Sweet Surrender* (Columbia 1977)★★★, *Mathis Is ...* (Columbia 1977)★★★, *You Light Up My Life* (Columbia 1978)★★★★, with Deniece Williams *That's What Friends Are For* (Columbia 1978)★★★, *When A Child Is Born* (Columbia 1978)★★★, *The Best Days Of My Life* (Columbia 1979)★★★, *Mathis Magic* (Columbia 1979)★★★, *Tears And Laughters* (Columbia 1980)★★★, *All For You* (Columbia 1980)★★★, *Different Kinda Different* (Columbia 1980)★★, *Friends In Love* (Columbia 1982)★★★, *A Special Part Of Me* (Columbia 1984)★★★, *Johnny Mathis Live* (Columbia 1985)★★★, *Right From The Heart* (Columbia 1985)★★★, with Henry Mancini *The Hollywood Musicals* (Columbia 1987)★★★, *In A Sentimental Mood: Mathis Sings Ellington* (Columbia 1990)★★★, *Better Together - The Duet Album* (Columbia 1992)★★★, *How Do You Keep The Music Playing?* (Columbia 1993)★★★, *The Christmas Music Of Johnny Mathis - A Personal Collection* (Legacy 1993)★★★, *All About Love* (Columbia 1996)★★★.

● COMPILATIONS: *Johnny's Greatest Hits* (Columbia 1958)★★★★, *More Of Johnny's Greatest Hits* (Columbia 1959)★★★★, *Johnny's Newest Hits* (Columbia 1963)★★★★, *Johnny Mathis' All-Time Greatest Hits* (Columbia 1972)★★★★, *The Best Of Johnny Mathis 1975-1980* (Columbia 1980)★★★, *The First 25 Years - The Silver Anniversary Album* (Columbia 1981)★★★★, *The Love Songs* (Columbia 1997)★★★, *The Global Masters* (Legacy 1997)★★★.

● VIDEOS: *Johnny Mathis In Concert* (Video Collection 1987), *Home For Christmas* (CMV Enterprises 1990), *Chances Are* (Sony Music Video 1991)

● FURTHER READING: *Johnny: The Authorized Biography Of Johnny Mathis*, Tony Jasper.

MATTHEWS, DAVE

b. 6 June 1911, Chagrin Falls, Ohio, USA. As a young man Matthews studied music in Oklahoma and Chicago. He became proficient on alto and tenor saxophones and also developed skills as an arranger. Caught up in the swing era, he played (mostly alto) with Ben Pollack, Jimmy Dorsey and Benny Goodman. In 1939 he left Goodman to go with Harry James who had formed a new band. Matthews contributed some fine swinging charts for the band and over the next few years continued to write for and also play with (now mostly on tenor) bands led by Hal McIntyre, Woody Herman, Stan Kenton and Charlie Barnet. With the latter, his admiration for the stylings of Duke Ellington were allowed to go unfettered. From time to time he led his own bands but it was as an arranger that he became best known during the 50s. Skilled though he was as a player, and with original thoughts on the occasions when he performed solos, Matthews was usually content to remain an anonymous sideman in the bands in which he played and which he helped to achieve popularity through his writing. (This artist should not be confused with the similarly named pianist, arranger and bandleader active in New York in the mid-70s.)
● COMPILATIONS: with Oran 'Hot Lips' Page *Tooting Through The Roof* (Onyx 1945-46)★★★.

MAY, BILLY

b. 10 November 1916, Pittsburgh, Pennsylvania, USA. May's first impact on the big band scene came in 1938, when he joined the trumpet section of the Charlie Barnet Band and, most notably, began contributing arrangements. Among his best-known charts was Barnet's hit record of the old Ray Noble song 'Cherokee'. In 1939, he joined Glenn Miller, bringing a previously absent vitality to the trumpet section and more fine arrangements. In 1942, he also wrote arrangements for Les Brown and Alvino Rey. The early 40s found him in great demand in radio and film studios, but he continued to write for popular bands of the day. When Capitol Records was formed, with a policy that called for the highest standards of musicianship, May was employed to write and direct for many major singing stars, including Frank Sinatra, Peggy Lee and Nat 'King' Cole. During the 50s, May also began making big band albums, on which he gave full rein to his highly distinctive arranging style. Although adept at all kinds of big band music, he had a particular fondness for voicing the reed section in thirds, creating a so-called 'slurping' saxophone sound. Among his band's successes were arrangements of 'All Of Me', 'Lulu's Back In Town', 'Charmaine', 'When My Sugar Walks Down The Street', 'Lean Baby' and 'Fat Man Boogie' (the last two also his own compositions). His recording of the movie theme 'The Man With The Golden Arm' made the UK Top 10 in 1956. For his studio band, May called upon such reliable sidemen as Murray McEachern, Ted Nash and Alvin Stoller. He also wrote for television, lending musical quality to series such as *Naked City* and to the occasional commercial. He was also musical director on the recording dates on which swing era music was recreated for a series of albums issued by *Time-Life*.
● ALBUMS: *A Band Is Born* (1951)★★★, *Capitol Presents Billy May And His Orchestra* (Capitol 1953)★★★★, *Big Band Bash* (Capitol 1953)★★★★, *Sorta May* (Capitol 1954)★★★★, *Bacchanalia* (Capitol 1954)★★★, *Naughty Operetta* (Capitol 1954)★★★, *Sorta Dixie* (Capitol 1955)★★,

Billy May And His Orchestra i (Capitol 1956)★★★, *The Great Jimmie Lunceford* (1957)★★★, *Billy May And His Orchestra* ii (1958)★★★, *The Girls And Boys On Broadway* (1958)★★★, *Billy May And His Orchestra* iii (1963)★★★, *Billy May And His Orchestra* iv (1966)★★★, *I Believe In You* (1975)★★★, *You May Swing* (Intersound 1980)★★★.
● COMPILATIONS: *20 Golden Pieces* (Bulldog 1981)★★★, *Best Of Billy May And His Orchestra* (MFP 1983)★★★, *The Capitol Years* (Capitol 1987)★★★★.

McDEVITT, CHAS

b. 1935, Glasgow, Scotland. McDevitt was the banjo player with the Crane River Jazz Band in 1955, before forming a skiffle group that won a talent contest organized by Radio Luxembourg. Another contestant, vocalist Nancy Whiskey (b. 1936, Glasgow, Scotland) joined the McDevitt group, which included guitarists Tony Kohn and Bill Branwell (from the Cotton Pickers skiffle group), Marc Sharratt (d. May 1991; washboard) and Lennie Hanson (bass). The group appeared in the film *The Tommy Steele Story* in 1957, performing 'Freight Train', a song introduced to Britain by Peggy Seeger who had learned it from its composer, black American folk singer Elizabeth Cotten. Issued by Oriole, the McDevitt/Whiskey version was a Top 10 hit in the UK and reached the US charts, although McDevitt was the object of a US lawsuit over the ownership of the copyright. After the release of a version of 'Greenback Dollar' and an EP as follow-ups, Whiskey left the group. With a studio group, the Skifflers, she made a series of singles for Oriole from 1957-59, including 'He's Solid Gone' and the folk song 'I Know Where I'm Going' and also released *The Intoxicating Miss Whiskey*. Having opened a Freight Train coffee bar in London, McDevitt continued to perform and record with new vocalist Shirley Douglas (b. 1936, Belfast, Northern Ireland), whom he later married. He briefly followed the rock 'n' roll trend with a conspicuous lack of success, and later performed duets with Douglas after the manner of Nina And Frederik. Among his later efforts were 'It Takes A Worried Man' (Oriole 1957), 'Teenage Letter' (1959) and 'One Love' (HMV 1961). Both McDevitt and Douglas recorded for Joy Records in the 70s enlisting session support from Joe Brown and Wizz Jones.
● ALBUMS: with Nancy Whiskey *Chas And Nancy* (Oriole 1957)★★★, with Whiskey *The Intoxicating Miss Whiskey* (Oriole 1957)★★★, *The Six-Five Special* (50s)★★★★, *Sing Something Old, New, Borrowed & Blue* (1972)★★, *Takes Ya Back Don't It* (Joy 1976)★★.

McGUIRE SISTERS

b. Middletown, Ohio, USA. This close-harmony vocal group, popular in the 50s and early 60s, consisted of three sisters, Chris (Christine) (b. 30 July 1929), Dorothy (Dotty) (b. 13 February 1930) and Phyllis (b. 14 February 1931). While in their teens the sisters sang with church choirs, and won an amateur talent contest at their local cinema for three consecutive weeks. After singing on their local radio station, the McGuires had their first big break, entertaining at army camps and hospitals during a nine-month tour in 1950-51. They then played club and radio dates in Cincinnati before moving to New York in 1952, and successfully auditioning for the *Arthur Godfrey Talent Scouts* contest. They subsequently became regulars on the show, and also appeared for eight weeks on singer Kate Smith's top-rated radio programme. Signed to the Coral label, they had their first minor hit in 1954 with 'Pine Tree, Pine Over Me', in collaboration with Johnny Desmond and Eileen Barton. During the rest of that year they had further successes with their version of the Spaniels' R&B hit 'Goodnight Sweetheart, Goodnight', followed by 'Muskrat Ramble', 'Lonesome Polecat' and 'Christmas Alphabet'. In 1955 the sisters had their first million-seller with another cover version, 'Sincerely', originally recorded by the Moonglows. The McGuires' version stayed at number 1 in the USA for 10 weeks, and accelerated their breakthrough into the big time in clubs, theatres and on television. They sang on the *Red Skelton Show* and the *Phil Silvers Show* and appeared at the Waldorf Astoria, the Desert Inn, Las Vegas and the Coconut Grove in Los Angeles. They made their first visit to London in 1961, and played a season at the Talk Of The Town. Their other hits, up until 1961, included 'No More', 'It May Sound Silly', 'Something's Gotta Give', 'He', 'Moonglow And The Theme From *Picnic*', 'Delilah Jones'; 'Weary Blues' (with Lawrence Welk), 'Ev'ry Day Of My Life', 'Goodnight My Love, Pleasant Dreams', 'Sugartime', 'Ding Dong', 'May You Always' and 'Just For Old Times Sake'. When the McGuires' sweet style was overtaken by the harder sounds of the Crystals, Shirelles and Supremes during the 60s, they turned to cabaret, and eventually disbanded. Phyllis continued solo, appearing regularly in Las Vegas and other cities. In 1985 the McGuire Sisters re-formed and, in the following year, undertook a national tour, stopping off at Bally's Reno to headline in Donn Arden's lavish revue *Hello, Hollywood, Hello*. Their well-received act continued into the 90s, leaning heavily on their old catalogue, along with more contemporary material from *Cats* and *Les Miserables*, and an a cappella version of 'Danny Boy'. In January 1986, Murray Kane, their personal manager and arranger since 1952, died in Las Vegas. He was responsible for writing the arrangements that won the sisters a spot on the *Arthur Godfrey Show*, their first break in New York. Prior to that, Kane had worked with Fred Waring, and had been a member of the Crew Chiefs, Glenn Miller's vocal group during World War II.

● ALBUMS: *By Request* (Coral 1955)★★★★, *Children's Holiday* (Coral 1956)★★★, *Do You Remember When?* (Coral 1956)★★★, *He* (Coral 1956)★★★, *Sincerely* (Coral 1956)★★★, *Teenage Party* (Coral 1957)★★★, *When The Lights Are Low* (Coral 1958) *Musical Magic* (Coral 1957)★★★, *Sugartime* (Coral 1958)★★★★, *Greetings From The McGuire Sisters* (Coral 1958)★★★, *May You Always* (Coral 1959)★★★, *In Harmony With Him* (Coral 1959)★★★, *His And Her's* (Coral 1960)★★★, *Just For Old Times Sake* (Coral 1961)★★★, *Our Golden Favourites* (Coral 1961)★★★, *Subways Are For Sleeping* (Coral 1962)★★★, *Songs Everybody Knows* (1962)★★★, *Showcase* (1963)★★★, *The McGuire Sisters Today* (1966)★★★.

● COMPILATIONS: *The Best Of The McGuire Sisters* (MCA 1982)★★★, *Greatest Hits* (MCA 1989)★★★.

McRae, Carmen

b. 8 April 1920, New York City, New York, USA, d. 10 November 1994, Beverly Hills, California, USA. One of the best American jazz singers, McRae was also an accomplished pianist and songwriter. Early in her career she sang with bands led by Benny Carter, Mercer Ellington, Charlie Barnet and Count Basie (sometimes under the name of Carmen Clarke, from her brief marriage to Kenny Clarke). Although a familiar figure on the New York jazz club scene, including a spell in the early 50s as intermission pianist at Minton's Playhouse, her reputation did not spread far outside the jazz community. In the 60s and 70s she toured internationally and continued to record - usually accompanied by a small group - but she was joined on one occasion by the Clarke-Boland Big Band. By the 80s, she was one of only a tiny handful of major jazz singers whose work had not been diluted by commercial pressures. One of her early songs, 'Dream Of Life', written when she was just 16 years old, was recorded in 1939 by Billie Holiday. Although very much her own woman, McRae occasionally demonstrated the influence of Holiday through her ability to project a lyric with bittersweet intimacy. She also sang with remarkable rhythmic ease and her deft turns-of-phrase helped to conceal a relatively limited range, while her ballad singing revealed enormous emotional depths. Her repertoire included many popular items from the Great American Songbook, but her jazz background ensured that she rarely strayed outside the idiom. Relaxed and unpretentious in performance and dedicated to her craft, McRae secured a place in the history of jazz singing.

● ALBUMS: *Carmen McRae* i 10-inch album (Bethlehem 1954)★★★, *By Special Request* (Decca 1955)★★★, *Torchy!* (Decca 1956)★★★, *Blue Moon* (Decca 1956)★★★, *After Glow* (Decca 1957)★★★, *Carmen For Cool Ones* (Decca 1957)★★★★, *Mad About The Man* (Decca 1957)★★★★, with Sammy Davis Jnr. *Boy Meets Girl* (1957)★★★, *Book Of Ballads* (Kapp 1958)★★★★, *Birds Of A Feather* (Decca 1958)★★★, *When You're Away* (Kapp 1958)★★★, *Something To Swing About* (Kapp 1959)★★★★, *Carmen McRae Live At Sugar Hill* (Time 1960)★★★, *Carmen McRae Sings Lover Man And Other Billie Holiday Classics* (Columbia 1961)★★★★, *Carmen McRae Live At The Flamingo Club, London* (1961)★★★, *Carmen McRae* iii (Vocalion 1962)★★★, *Something Wonderful* (Columbia 1962)★★★, *Carmen McRae* ii (Vocalion 1963)★★★, *In Person* (1963)★★★, *Bittersweet* (Focus 1964)★★★, *Woman Talk: Carmen McRae Live At The Village Gate* (Mainstream 1965)★★★★, *Second to None* (Mainstream 1965)★★★, *Live And Doin' It* (1965)★★★, *Haven't We Met?* (Mainstream 1965)★★★, *Alfie* (Mainstream 1966)★★★, *Portrait Of Carmen* (Atlantic 1967)★★★, *This Is Carmen McRae* (Kapp 1967)★★★★, *For Once In My Life* (Atlantic 1967)★★★, *Yesterday* (Harmony 1968)★★★, with Kenny Clarke, Francy Boland *November Girl* (1970)★★★, *Just A Little Lovin'* (1970)★★★, *The Great American Songbook* (1971)★★★, *As Time Goes By* (1973)★★★, *It Takes A Whole Lot Of Human Feeling* (1973)★★★, *Carmen McRae And Zoot Sims* (1973)★★★, *I Am Music* (1975)★★★, *Can't Hide Love* (Blue Note 1976)★★, *Carmen McRae At The Great American Music Hall* (1976)★★★, *Live At The Roxy* (1976)★★★, *Ronnie Scott Presents Carmen McRae 'Live'* (Pye/Ronnie Scott 1977)★★★, *For Carmen McRae* (1977)★★★, *I'm Coming Home Again* (1978)★★★, with George Shearing *Two For The Road* (Concord Jazz 1980)★★★, *Recorded Live At Bubba's* (1981)★★★, *Heat Wave* (Concord Jazz 1982)★★★, *You're Lookin' At Me (A Collection Of Nat 'King' Cole Songs)* (Concord Jazz 1983)★★★, *Any Old Time* (Denon 1986)★★★, *Fine And Mellow: Live At Birdland West*

(Concord Jazz 1987)★★★, *Velvet Soul* 1973 recording (Denon 1988)★★★, *Carmen Sings Monk* (Novus 1989)★★★, *Sarah Dedicated To You* (Novus 1991)★★★.
● COMPILATIONS: *The Ultimate Carmen McRae* (Mainstream 1991)★★★★, *Sings Great American Songwriters* 1955-59 recordings (GRP 1994)★★★★
● VIDEOS: *Live* (Verve Video 1990).

ME AND JULIET

Perhaps because it emerged into the bright lights of Broadway in the same season as hits such as *Wish You Were Here*, *Wonderful Town*, and *Can-Can*, Richard Rodgers and Oscar Hammerstein's *Me And Juliet* was regarded by critics and public alike to be well below their par. Certainly, after blockbusters such as *Oklahoma!*, *Carousel*, and *The King And I*, a run of 358 performances was not remarkable by their standards. Unlike those three shows, *Me And Juliet* was not adapted from an existing work, but had an original book by Hammerstein. It opened at the Majestic Theatre in New York on 28 May 1953. The setting is a theatre, onstage and off, where a musical entitled *Me And Juliet* is playing. Jeannie (Isabel Bigley), a singer in the chorus, is being pleasantly pursued by Larry (Bill Hayes), the assistant stage manager, until electrician Bob (Mark Dawson), a nasty hard-drinking character, tries to muscle in on the romance to such an extent that he tries to murder her. The traditional 'fun-romance' situation that usually crops up in these kind of shows, in this case involves a dancer, Betty (Joan McCracken) and the stage manager, Mac (Ray Walston). The latter artist proved to be a memorable Luther Billis in the film of Rodgers and Hammerstein's *South Pacific*, and he also gave a 'devil' of a good performance in *Damn Yankees* on both stage and screen. The score for *Me And Juliet* was light, and contained none of the composers' 'deeply meaningful songs' (such as 'You'll Never Walk Alone', 'Carefully Taught', etc.), but there were some pleasant songs, including 'Keep It Gay', 'It's Me', 'The Big Black Giant', 'A Very Special Day', 'I'm Your Girl', and 'Do I Love You Because You're Beautiful' and 'Marriage-Type Love', both of which achieved some modest popularity. Rodgers had used the melody of one of the other numbers, 'No Other Love', before, as part of the background score for the television documentary series, *Victory At Sea* (1952). The song became a big hit for Perry Como in America, and a UK number 1 for Ronnie Hilton. Rodgers remembered the song again, in 1957, and interpolated it into a US television version of *Cinderella*, which starred Julie Andrews. It was also present when *Cinderella* was adapted for the stage, and played the London Coliseum as a Christmas-time entertainment in 1958, with a cast that included Tommy Steele, Bruce Trent, Yana, Jimmy Edwards, Betty Marsden, and Kenneth Williams. Exactly 35 years after that, *Cinderella* was staged in America by the New York City Opera.

MEDALLIONS

The Medallions were formed by lead singer Vernon Green (b. Denver, Colorado, USA) in Los Angeles, California, USA, after record company boss Dootsie Williams commented on the quality of his voice as he was walking down the street one day. The rest of the group - Andrew Blue (tenor), Randolph Bryant (baritone) and Ira Foley (bass) - were built around Green's strong vocal abilities, and took their collec-tive name from their leader's fondness for jewellery. Williams was as good as his word and signed the group to Dootone Records, a relationship that began with the release of 'The Letter'. The b-side, 'Buick 59', was particularly well received on Los Angeles radio, and started a trend of naming singles after car types ('Coupe De Ville Baby', '59 Volvo', etc.). Willy Graham replaced Andrew Blue, while the group expanded to a quintet in 1955 with the addition of Donald Woods. However, the group broke up after the release of their third single, 'Speedin''. Abandoning Green, the other four members formed the Vel-Aires and signed with Flip Records. Green responded by putting together a new Medallions featuring Kenneth Williams and Frank Marshall, issuing 'Only For You'. This formation did not last, however, and Williams then placed Green as singer with another of his groups, the Dootones (who shared the name of the label). They were still titled the Medallions, but their first release together was as back-up group to Johnny Morisette on October 1955's 'My Pretty Baby'. However, a month later they debuted in their own right with 'Dear Darling', then 'I Want A Love'. Their next release saw their billing extended to Vernon Green And The Medallions. They released three singles for Dootone's Dooto subsidiary between 1956 and 1957 in this manner. None of these singles, which again featured fluctuating line-ups, were successful. Green left to form the Phantoms, a masked group who recorded briefly for Specialty Records, but then returned in 1957 to front another version of the Medallions. Five further singles emerged (three for Dooto, one for Minit and one for Pan World Records), while the band continued to tour widely. The most interesting of these singles was the second, 'Magic Mountain'/'59 Volvo'. The latter track was expressly commissioned by a local disc jockey whose brother owned a Volvo dealership. The band was then put on hold for nine years following an automobile accident that incapacitated Green. He returned to front the Medallions for a final 1973 single for Dooto, 'Can You Talk', and again in 1989 at the inaugural Doo-wop Society show.

MEDITATION SINGERS

Originally titled Moments Of Meditation, this all-female gospel group was formed in April 1950 at the New Liberty Missionary Baptist Church in Detroit, Michigan, USA. Ernestine Rundless (lead soprano), Dellareese Early (lead and first soprano), Marie Waters (alto) and DeLillian Mitchell (tenor) were moulded by church directors Pastor E. Alan Rundless II and pianist Emory Radford. Their performances quickly brought them a sizeable local following, as did numerous appearances on radio shows. In 1952 they won the Golden Cup Jubilee, but by this time Early had left for a solo pop and acting career. Her replacement was Laura Lee Newton, while Carrie Williams expanded the group to a quintet. Newton, under the name Laura Lee, also found consistent success as a soul singer in the late 60s and early 70s, reaching number 36 in the US charts with 'Woman's Love Rights' in 1967. At this point Reverend James Cleveland took a hand in the Meditation Singers' fortunes as arranger and writer. With the name abbreviated to Meditation Singers they released a series of records for Hob and Specialty Records that sold steadily in the gospel market. They were still going strong in the 90s (with Waters, Rundless and Newton all surviving the intervening decades).

MELACHRINO, GEORGE

b. George Militiades, 1 May 1909, London, England, d. 18 June 1965, London, England. An orchestra leader, composer, arranger, multi-instrumentalist and singer, Melachrino was the son of Greek parents. He learned to play a miniature violin, and wrote his first composition when he was five years old. He was already an accomplished musician by the age of 14 when he enrolled at the Trinity College Of Music, where he specialized in chamber music and the use of strings. At the age of 16, he wrote a string sextette that was performed in London. He resolved to learn to play every instrument in the orchestra, and succeeded, with the exception of the harp and piano. In 1927, he began his broadcasting career, playing and singing from the BBC studio at Savoy Hill. He strayed further and further away from his initial ambition to be a classical musician, playing jazz instead, and working in dance bands for leaders such as Bert Firman, Harry Hudson, Ambrose and Carroll Gibbons' Savoy Hotel Orchestra. In 1939, Melachrino formed his own dance band to play at the prestigious London venue the Café de Paris, until 1940. During the period of the 'Battle of Britain', he joined the British Army as a military policeman, eventually becoming a Regimental Sergeant-Major. He later toured in the *Stars Of Battledress* and was musical director of the Army Radio Unit, as well as the leader of the British Band of the Allied Expeditionary Forces. He also led the 50-piece 'Orchestra in Khaki', recruited from professional musicians serving in the ranks, who were much amused when he was introduced on broadcasts as 'the Sentimental Sergeant-Major'. The unit held its own against the American band led by Glenn Miller and the Canadian combination led by Robert Farnon, with both of whom Melachrino guested as vocalist on occasions during the war years.

While in the forces, he experimented with large string sounds, and after the war he ran two outfits, the Melachrino Strings and the George Melachrino Orchestra, both purveying the sentimental mood music so popular in the 50s, especially in the USA. The full orchestra consisted of 30 strings, 10 reeds, seven brass, two percussion, a harp and a piano. He formed the Melachrino Music Organization, creating work in concerts, broadcasting, recordings and film music. His film scores included *Woman To Woman* (1946), *Code Of Scotland Yard* (1948), *No Orchids For Miss Blandish* (1948), *Story Of Shirley Yorke* (1948), *Dark Secret* (1949), *The Gamma People* (1956) and *Odongo* (1956). In 1947, he contributed the music, with book and lyrics by Eric Maschwitz and Matt Brooks, to the revue *Starlight Roof*, which starred Fred Emney, Pat Kirkwood and Vic Oliver, and introduced Julie Andrews to London audiences. He also wrote the music for the ill-fated *Lucky Boy*, with lyrics by Ian Douglas. His other compositions included 'First Rhapsody' (his theme tune), 'Winter Sunshine', 'Vision D'Amour', 'Woodland Revel' and 'Portrait Of A Lady'. He had a UK chart entry in 1956 with the Italian melody 'Autumn Concerto' but, like Mantovani, who also specialized in lush string arrangements, his albums sold more in the USA than in the UK. His US hits included *Christmas In High Fidelity*, *Under Western Skies* and *Immortal Ladies*, a set of standards with girls' names as their titles, such as 'Laura', 'Dolores', 'Chloe' and 'Dinah'. Also popular was his series of mood records designed for various times of the day, such as *Music For Daydreaming*, *Music For Relaxation*, *Music For Two People*

Alone, *Music For Dining*, *Music for Reading*, *Music To Help You Sleep*, and others. He died in 1965 following an accident at his home in Kensington, London. The Melachrino Strings and Orchestra continued to record into the 80s, conducted by Robert Mandell.

● ALBUMS: *Soft Lights And Sweet Music* (1954)★★★★, *Christmas In High Fidelity* (RCA 1954)★★, *Music For The Nostalgic Traveller* (1956)★★★, *Famous Themes For Piano And Orchestra* (1957)★★★★, *Moonlight Concerto* (1958)★★★★, *Great Show Tunes - Medleys* (1958)★★★, *Under Western Skies* (RCA 1959)★★★, *The World's Greatest Melodies* (1962)★★★★, *The World Of George Melachrino* (1969)★★★★, *The World Of George Melachrino, Volume Two* (1972)★★★, *Strauss Waltzes* (1973)★★★, *The Immortal Melodies Of Victor Herbert And Sigmund Romberg* (1974)★★★, *Great British Light Orchestras George Melachrino* (EMI 1993)★★★★.

MELLO-KINGS

The Mello-Kings were responsible for one of the most durable doo-wop hits of the 50s. Despite the fact that their only hit, 'Tonite Tonite', never climbed higher than number 77 in the US charts, the single is still considered one of the most popular group harmony recordings of the era, more than three decades after its initial release. The group consisted of brothers Jerry and Bob Scholl, Eddie Quinn, Neil Arena and Larry Esposito. The quintet was formed in 1956 at a high school in Mount Vernon, New York, USA, under the guidance of manager Dick Levister. Originally named the Mellotones, the group was signed to the Herald label. 'Tonite Tonite' was written by Billy Myles, a staff composer for the label. The group was forced to change its name after the single's release, as another group had already claimed Mellotones. The record lasted only 10 weeks in the US charts, and the group was never able to repeat this success, although 'Tonite Tonite' returned in 1961, reaching number 95, due to a resurgence of interest in the doo-wop sound, and has been consistently voted among the top five doo-wop records of all time in radio polls, particularly in the New York area. A new Mello-Kings led by Jerry Scholl, whose brother Bob died on 27 August 1975, was still touring the rock 'n' roll revival circuit in the early 90s.

● COMPILATIONS: *Tonite, Tonite* (Relic 1991)★★★, *Greatest Hits* (Collectables 1992)★★★.

MELLOWS

One of the rare 50s R&B groups to be led by a female vocalist, the Mellows comprised Lillian Leach (lead), Johnny 'Tiny' Wilson (first tenor), Harold Johnson (second tenor) and Norman 'Polecat' Brown (bass). The three boys had met as teenagers at the Morris High School in the Bronx, New York, USA. They encountered Leach at a party in 1954 when she joined their harmonizing. The revised blend was an instant hit, and the sound it produced gave the quartet their name (having learned that their original choice, the Mello-Tones, had already been employed elsewhere). Johnson started seeking a contract, eventually finding one with Jay Dee Records (he had previously worked for that label with Dean Barlow and the Crickets). Johnson also penned their first single, 'How Sentimental Can I Be?', but this pop-orientated ballad failed to find a suitable audience due to a lack of promotion and airplay. They had more success with their second record, the seductive 'Smoke From Your Cigarette', which became a regional hit. However, neither 'I Still Care' nor 'Yesterday's Memories' were substantial enough to build on this impact, and the group was also weakened by the loss of Norman Brown (replaced on bass by Gary Morrison). They then added a fifth member, Arthur Crier of the Chimes. The Mellows moved over to Celeste Records in 1955, but both the singles released on the label flopped. Candlelight Records was their next port of call, although 'You're Gone'/'Men Of Silver' marked the end of their career. They broke up in 1957. Johnson and Crier went on to the Halos, who backed several notable artists and enjoyed a hit under their own steam with 'Nag'. A reunion of the Mellows took place in 1984 with three of the original members, and the group have continued to peddle sweet R&B pop on the nostalgia circuit ever since.

MERRILL, BOB

b. H. Robert Merrill Levan, 17 May 1921, Atlantic City, New Jersey, USA, d. 17 February 1998. A popular songwriter, for Tin Pan Alley and the musical theatre, Merrill worked at a number of jobs in various parts of the USA, before he began singing in clubs and on the stage, where he was also an effective mimic. After military service during World War II, he spent some time in Hollywood as a dialogue director and also made a handful of acting appearances. It was while working on a film that he was asked by comedienne Dorothy Shay to write some songs for her forthcoming album. Merrill did as she suggested, and the financial rewards this brought encouraged him to pursue songwriting as a career. Among the early songs he wrote were 'Lover's Gold' (music by Morty Nevins), 'Fool's Paradise' and 'The Chicken Song' (with Terry Shand). In 1950 Merrill had his first hit with 'If I Knew You Were Coming I'd've Baked A Cake' (Al Hoffman and Clem Watts), which was followed by numerous others, such as 'Sparrow In The Treetop', 'My Truly, Truly Fair', 'She Wears Red Feathers', 'Pittsburgh, Pennsylvania', 'Chicka Boom', 'Feet Up', Belle Belle My Liberty Belle', 'Look At That Girl', 'Cuff Of My Shirt', (all successful for Guy Mitchell), '(How Much Is That) Doggie In The Window?' (a US number 1 for Patti Page), 'Let Me In', 'Walkin' To Missouri', 'Mambo Italiano', 'Where Will The Dimple Be?' and 'A Sweet Old-Fashioned Girl'. Despite the success of these songs, Merrill wanted to write for the musical theatre, and in 1956 he composed the score for New Girl In Town, a musical adaptation of Eugene O'Neill's novel Anna Christie, which opened on Broadway in May 1957. Two years later Merrill wrote the music and lyrics for Take Me Along, which was based on another O'Neill piece, Ah, Wilderness! Both productions enjoyed runs in excess of 400 performances, but Merrill's next show, Carnival (1961), did even better, staying at the Imperial Theatre in New York for 719 performances. The score included several appealing songs such as 'Love Makes The World Go Round', 'Yes, My Heart' and 'Her Face'. In 1964 Merrill wrote two songs, 'Elegance' and 'Motherhood March', with Jerry Herman for Hello, Dolly!, before collaborating with composer Jule Styne on the smash hit Funny Girl, which elevated Barbra Streisand to stardom when it was later filmed. However, Breakfast At Tiffany's (1966) closed during previews, and Henry, Sweet Henry folded after only 80 performances. He subsequently worked with Styne again on Prettybelle (1971), which failed to reach Broadway, and

Sugar, based on the highly successful Billy Wilder film Some Like It Hot. Despite mixed reviews, it ran for 505 performances, and, retitled Some Like it Hot, became a short-lived vehicle for the popular UK entertainer Tommy Steele in 1992. In 1984 Merrill made 37 of his songs into a four-character musical called We're Home. Merrill teamed with Styne once more in 1993 (under the pseudonym of Paul Stryker) to provide extra lyrics for The Red Shoes, which lasted for just three days. In contrast, however, a new career as a screenwriter beckoned, and he also taught at the University of California in Los Angeles. However depression, brought on by a number of illnesses, led Merrill to take his own life in February 1998. A sad end to a man who once said of his songs "they were all wholesome, and they are all happy."

MIGHTY SPARROW

b. Francisco Slinger, Grenada. Having moved to Trinidad as a child, calypso singer Mighty Sparrow first rose to domestic prominence in the 50s. He earned his underwhelming nickname (most calypso singers dealt in more self-aggrandizing names such as Executor and Lion) by virtue of his stage performances, which involved him moving around rapidly while most other singers were stationary. He was rewarded with the Calypso Crown of 1956 for his song 'Jean And Dinah', which complained at what Americans had left behind after leaving Trinidad's military bases. At the same time he lent his support to Eric Williams' People's National Movement, writing many calypso songs in praise of the nationalist leader. His anthem 'Cricket Lovely Cricket' was a particularly painful reminder to UK cricket fans after the humiliating drubbing West Indian star batsman Garfield Sobers gave to the English team in the early 50s. In politics, however, he subsequently revised his position in the 60s as the initial optimism of the PNP soured into disillusionment. Despite his earlier recordings, calypso was ironically just beginning to secure a large following in the USA. His popularity was such that in the 50s and 60s he was capable of filling a venue such as New York's Madison Square Gardens. With the development of soca, Sparrow became a willing convert, although he faced some opposition from calypso purists who despised the new hybrid.
● ALBUMS: The Slave (Island 1963)★★★, Sparrow Come Back (RCA 1966)★★★, Hotter Than Ever (Trojan 1972)★★★, Only A Fool (Trojan 1981)★★★, Peace & Love (Trojan 1981)★★★, King Of The World (Dynamic 1986)★★★, Calypso Carnival (La Records 1990)★★★, with Lord Kitchener Carnival Hits (Ice 1991)★★★.
● COMPILATIONS: Party Classics Volume 1 And 2 (Charlie 1987)★★★.

MILBURN, AMOS

b. 1 April 1927, Houston, Texas, USA, d. 3 January 1980, Houston, Texas, USA. After service in the US Navy in World War II, Milburn formed his own blues and R&B band in Houston in which he played piano and sang, and in 1946 he was offered a contract by the Aladdin label. Between November 1948 and February 1954 he and his band, the Aladdin Chicken Shackers, had an extraordinary run of 19 consecutive Top 10 hits on the Billboard R&B chart, including four number 1s ('Chicken Shack Boogie', 'A&M Blues', 'Roomin' House Boogie' and 'Bad, Bad Whiskey'). His romping boogies about drinking and partying were hugely popular and for two years (1949 and 1950) he was voted Top R&B Artist by *Billboard*. Following the break-up of his band in 1954 he never achieved the same level of success, and he left Aladdin in 1956. He then recorded as part of a duo with Charles Brown for the Ace label, and in 1963 recorded an album for Motown Records. In the 60s he played clubs around Cincinnati and Cleveland, Ohio, drawing heavily on his catalogue of old hits, but did not have any more hit records. In 1970 he suffered the first of a series of strokes. In 1972 he retired and returned to his home-town of Houston where he died eight years later.

● ALBUMS: with Wynonie Harris *Party After Hours* (Aladdin 1955)★★★, *Rockin' The Boogie* (Aladdin 1955)★★★, *Let's Have A Party* (Score 1957)★★★, *Amos Milburn Sings The Blues* (Score 1958)★★★, *The Blues Boss* (Motown 1963)★★★, *13 Unreleased Masters* (Pathé-Marconi 1984)★★.

● COMPILATIONS: *Million Sellers* (Imperial 1962)★★★★, *Greatest Hits* Aladdin recordings (Official Records 1988)★★★★, *Blues & Boogie: His Greatest Hits* (Sequel 1991)★★★★, *Down The Road Apiece: The Best Of ...* (EMI 1994)★★★★, *The Complete Aladdin Recordings Of Amos Milburn* (Mosaic 1995)★★★★.

MILLER, CHUCK

b. California, USA. Miller was a boogie-woogie piano player who had a 1955 Top 10 single with 'The House Of Blue Lights', a rocking version of an Andrews Sisters song that had previously been a hit in 1946 for its co-author, Frank Slack. Recorded for Mercury Records, the cover version was Miller's only major hit. Prior to his biggest recording, Miller had recorded some tracks for Capitol Records and, following the US number 9 hit, he continued to try for others, with no luck. His only other chart record was 'The Auctioneer', a country song that reached number 59 later in 1956.

● ALBUMS: *Goin' Goin' Gone* (Revival 1987)★★★.

MILLER, GARY

b. Neville Williams, 1924, Blackpool, Lancashire, England, d. 15 June 1968, London, England. Miller was a popular singer in the UK during the 50s and early 60s, with a smooth and polished style. As a young man, Miller was a talented soccer player and played for Blackpool Football Club as an amateur. During World War II, he served as a lieutenant in the Royal Navy Volunteer Reserve and, on release, enrolled as a student at London University with the intention of becoming a teacher of languages. After performing in college concerts, and with the experience of singing at a Welsh Eisteddfod festival as a schoolboy, Miller embarked on the learning process of small-time cabaret and concert tours, and made his first radio broadcast on *Beginners, Please*. As well as singing, he also included dancing in his act, and was involved in negotiations for a small part in the Ray Bolger movie *Where's Charley?*, when it was being made in England, but nothing materialized. His first real break came when he was discovered by record executive and songwriter Norman Newell during a Variety appearance at Northampton, which led to him making a few tracks for Columbia. He also made regular appearances, singing and dancing, on television in *Shop Window*, and appeared on the fortnightly *Kaleidoscope* series. By 1954, he was headlining in variety on the Moss Empires circuit. After a spell with Newell at the newly

formed Philips Records in 1953, during which he released mostly romantic ballads, Miller switched to another new label, Pye Nixa, and started recording more up-tempo material. His first hit, 'Yellow Rose Of Texas', in 1955, was overtaken by the US Mitch Miller version, but 'Robin Hood' made the Top 10 despite opposition from Dick James, who benefited by having his version played over the titles during the weekly television show. During that era it was commonplace for several versions of the same song to jostle each other in the singles chart. This was the case with Miller's 'Garden Of Eden', which lost out to Frankie Vaughan. There was also strong competition on 'Wonderful, Wonderful' from Ronnie Hilton, and on 'The Story Of My Life' from Michael Holliday. Miller's record of the latter song is said to have suffered in popularity because he was touring North Africa at the time of its release. Perhaps in an effort to avoid the competition, Miller reached back to 1945 for his final chart entry, 'I've Heard That Song Before' (1961); it proved to be one of his best vocal performances. His first album, *Meet Mister Miller*, contained standards such as 'Manhattan', 'April Showers' and 'Stella By Starlight'. This was followed by *Gary On The Ball*, with the Kenny Ball Jazz Band. In 1964, Miller appeared in the West End production of *She Loves Me*, Jerry Bock and Sheldon Harnick's musical based on the Hungarian play *Perfumerie*. He returned to the London stage in 1966 to play the role of the crooning Agent VO3 in Bryan Blackburn's comedy musical, *Come Spy With Me*, starring female impersonator Danny La Rue, at London's 'home of farce', the Whitehall Theatre. Two years later he died of a heart attack at his south London home.

MILLER, MITCH

b. Mitchell William Miller, 4 July 1911, Rochester, New York, USA. An oboist, record producer, arranger and one of the most commercially successful recording artists of the 50s and early 60s. He learned to play the piano at the age of six, and began studying the oboe when he was 12, and later attended Rochester's Eastman School of Music. After graduating in 1932, Miller played oboe with symphony orchestras in the area, before joining CBS Radio in 1932. For the next 11 years he was a soloist with the CBS Symphony, and played with André Kostelanetz, Percy Faith, the Saidenburg Little Symphony and the Budapest String Quartet. In the late 40s he became director of Mercury Records' 'pop' division, and then in 1950, was appointed head of A&R at Columbia Records. While at Mercury, Miller was responsible for producing several big hits, including Frankie Laine's 'That Lucky Old Sun', 'Mule Train' and 'The Cry Of The Wild Goose'. Miller also conducted the orchestra on Laine's 'Jezebel' and 'Rose, Rose, I Love You'. Shortly after he left the label, Patti Page released 'The Tennessee Waltz', which became one of the biggest-selling singles ever. The original was by R&B singer Erskine Hawkins, and the Page disc is sometimes credited as being the first really successful example of 'crossover' from country to pop, although Miller had already fashioned Hank Williams' 'Hey, Good Lookin'' into a minor hit for Frankie Laine and Jo Stafford. Miller developed this policy when he moved to Columbia, and recorded Guy Mitchell ('Singing The Blues' and 'Knee Deep In The Blues'), Tony Bennett ('Cold, Cold Heart'), Rosemary Clooney ('Half As Much'), Jo Stafford ('Jambalaya') and the little-known Joan Weber ('Let Me Go Lover'). Miller's roster at Columbia also included Johnnie Ray ('Cry', 'The Little White Cloud That Cried', 'Just Crying In The Rain') and Frank Sinatra. There was little empathy between Miller and Sinatra, and the singer rejected several songs that eventually became successful for Guy Mitchell. After he left Columbia, Sinatra sent telegrams to judiciary and senate committees, accusing Miller of presenting him with inferior songs, and of accepting money from writers whose songs he (Miller) had used. Certainly, Sinatra recorded some unsuitable material under Miller's auspices during his final years with the label, although 'American Beauty Rose' and 'Goodnight, Irene', both with Miller's accompaniment, and 'Bim Bam Baby', paled in comparison with perhaps the most bizarre item of all, 'Mama Will Bark', on which Sinatra made barking and growling noises, and duetted with Miller's latest signing, a female named Dagmar.

Miller's own hit recordings, mostly credited to 'Mitch Miller And His Gang', began in 1950 with his adaptation of the Israeli folk song 'Tzena, Tzena, Tzena', complete with a happy vocal chorus that would typify his later work. After 'Meet Mr. Callaghan', 'Without My Lover', 'Under Paris Skies' and 'Napoleon' in the early 50s, he spent six weeks at number 1 with the million-selling 'The Yellow Rose Of Texas', one of the great marching songs from the American Civil War. This was followed by three instrumentals: 'Lisbon Antigua', 'Song For A Summer Night (Parts 1 & 2)' and 'March From The River Kwai And Colonel Bogey'. There was also the novelty 'The Children's Marching Song' from the 1959 film *The Inn Of The Sixth Happiness*. The previous year, Miller had started his series of *Sing Along With Mitch* albums, which featured an all-male chorus singing old favourites, many from before the turn of the century. Nineteen variations on the theme made the US Top 40 between 1958 and 1962, of which seven titles achieved million-selling status. The phenomenally successful *Sing Along* formula was developed as a popular television series which ran from 1961-66, and featured several solo singers such as Victor Griffin, Leslie Uggams and Louise O'Brien. Despite the obvious financial gain to Columbia from his record sales, Miller was constantly criticized for his negative attitude towards rock 'n' roll. He turned down Buddy Holly, among others, and was blamed for his company's relatively small market share in the rapidly changing music scene during his tenure as an influential executive. On the other hand, his promotion of the artists already mentioned, plus Doris Day ('Que Sera, Sera'), Johnny Mathis, Percy Faith, and many more, substantially aided Columbia Records. Out of place in the 'swinging 60s', he nevertheless emerged occasionally to conduct the orchestra on various light and classical music recordings.

● ALBUMS: *Sing Along With Mitch* (Columbia 1958)★★★★, *More Sing Along ...* (Columbia 1958)★★★, *Christmas Sing Along ...* (Columbia 1958)★★★★, *Still More! Sing Along ...* (Columbia 1959)★★★, *Folk Songs Sing Along ...* (Columbia 1959)★★★, *Party Sing Along ...* (Columbia 1959)★★★, *Fireside Sing Along...* (Columbia 1959)★★★, *Saturday Night Sing Along ...* (Columbia 1960)★★★, *Sentimental Sing Along ...* (Columbia 1960)★★★, *March Along ...* (Columbia 1960)★★★, *Memories Sing Along ...* (Columbia 1960)★★★, *Happy Times! Sing Along ...* (Columbia 1961)★★★, *TV Sing Along ...* (Columbia 1961)★★★, *Your Request Sing Along ...* (Columbia 1961)★★★, *Holiday Sing Along ...* (Columbia 1961)★★★, *Rhythm Sing Along ...* (Columbia 1962)★★★, *Family Sing Along ...* (Columbia 1962)★★★.

● COMPILATIONS: *Mitch's Greatest Hits* (Columbia 1961)★★★★.

MILLS BROTHERS

The three permanent members of the group were Herbert Mills (b. 2 April 1912, d. 12 April 1989, Las Vegas, Nevada, USA), Harry Mills (b. 9 August 1913, d. 28 June 1982) and Donald Mills (b. 29 April 1915). John Mills Jnr. (b. 11 February 1911, d. 1935) added vocal notes in string bass form and played guitar. All the brothers were born in Piqua, Ohio, USA, sons of a barber who had been a successful concert singer. By the mid-20s, they were singing in sweet, close harmony in local vaudeville, providing their own backing by accurately imitating saxophones, trumpets, trombones and bass. With the main trio still teenagers, they had their own show on Cincinnati radio before moving to New York in 1930. The brothers signed to Brunswick Records and had a hit in 1931 with their first disc, 'Tiger Rag', which they also sang in the movie *The Big Broadcast*, featuring Bing Crosby and many other stars of US radio. They appeared in several other musical montage movies such as *Twenty Million Sweethearts* (1934), *Broadway Gondolier* (1935) and *Reveille With Beverly* (1943), *Rhythm Parade* (1943), *Cowboy Canteen* (1944) and *When You're Smiling* (1950). In the early 30s, Crosby featured on several of the brothers' record hits, including 'Dinah'/'Can't We Talk It Over', 'Shine' and 'Gems From George White's Scandals', which also included the Boswell Sisters. On later tracks, the Mills Brothers were also joined by Louis Armstrong, Ella Fitzgerald and Cab Calloway. Their early records were labelled: 'No musical instruments or mechanical devices used on this recording other than one guitar'. Other 30s hits included 'You Rascal, You', 'I Heard', 'Good-Bye, Blues', 'Rockin' Chair', 'St. Louis Blues', 'Sweet Sue', 'Bugle Call Rag', 'It Don't Mean A Thing (If It Ain't Got That Swing)', 'Swing It Sister', 'Sleepy Head' and 'Sixty Seconds Together'.

In 1935, John Mills died suddenly and the brothers' father, John Snr., took over as bass singer, and ex-bandleader Bernard Addison joined the group on guitar. During the late 30s, the Mills Brothers toured the USA and abroad, appearing in two UK Royal Command Performances. Their popularity peaked in 1943 with the record 'Paper Doll', which sold over six million copies. They had consistent chart success throughout the 40s with titles on the Decca label such as 'You Always Hurt The One You Love', 'Til Then', 'I Wish', 'I Don't Know Enough About You', 'Across The Alley From The Alamo', 'I Love You So Much It Hurts', 'I've Got My Love To Keep Me Warm', 'Someday (You'll Want Me To Want You)' and 'Put Another Chair At The Table'. By 1950, the instrumental impressions having generally been discarded, the brothers were accompanied by ex-Tommy Dorsey arranger Sy Oliver's orchestra on their hit 'Nevertheless (I'm In Love With You)' and again in 1952 on 'Be My Life's Companion'. That same year, 'The Glow Worm', gave them another blockbuster. This was a 1908 song from the German operetta *Lysistrata*, with a new lyric by Johnny Mercer. Other 50s favourites from the brothers included Sy Oliver's own composition 'Opus Number One', 'Say 'Si-Si', 'Lazy River' and 'Smack Dab In The Middle'. In 1956, John Snr. retired, and the brothers continued as a trio. Their last hit on Decca was

'Queen Of The Senior Prom' in 1957. The switch to the Dot label gave them two US Top 30 entries, 'Get A Job' and their final chart success, 'Cab Driver', in 1968. After Harry Mills' death in 1982, Herbert and Donald continued to perform their brand of highly polished, humorous entertainment with a substitute singer. However, when Herbert died seven years later, Donald, now walking with a cane, gained excellent reviews and favourable audience reaction when he played nightclubs with his son John, using mainly the old Mills Brothers catalogue, but with additional new material.

● ALBUMS: *Barber Shop Ballads* 10-inch album (Decca 1950)★★★★, *Souvenir Album* 10-inch album (Decca 1950)★★★, *Wonderful Words* 10-inch album (Decca 1951)★★★, *Meet The Mills Brothers* 10-inch album (Decca 1954)★★★★, *Louis Armstrong And The Mills Brothers* 10-inch album (Decca 1954)★★★★, *Four Boys And A Guitar* 10-inch album (Decca 1954)★★★, *Singin' And Swingin'* (Decca 1956)★★★, *Memory Lane* (Decca 1956)★★★★, *One Dozen Roses* (Decca 1957)★★★, *The Mills Brothers In Hi-Fi* (Decca 1958)★★★★, *Glow With The Mills Brothers* (Decca 1959)★★★, *Barbershop Harmony* (Decca 1959)★★★, *Harmonizing With The Mills Brothers* (Decca 1959)★★★, *Mmmm, The Mills Brothers* (Dot 1958)★★★, *Great Barbershop Hits* (Dot 1959)★★★, *Merry Christmas* (Dot 1959)★★★, *The Mills Brothers Sing* (Dot 1960)★★★, *Yellow Bird* (Dot 1961)★★★, *San Antonio Rose* (Dot 1961)★★★, *Great Hawaiian Hits* (Dot 1961)★★, *The Beer Barrel Polka And Other Hits* (Dot 1962)★★, *The End Of The World* (Dot 1963)★★, *Gems By The Mills Brothers* (Dot 1964)★★, *Hymns We Love* (Dot 1964)★★, *Say Si Si, And Other Great Latin Hits* (Dot 1964)★★, *The Mills Brothers Sing For You* (Dot 1964)★★★, *These Are The Mills Brothers* (Dot 1966)★★★, *That Country Feelin'* (Dot 1966)★★, *The Mills Brothers Live* (Dot 1967)★★, *Fortuosity* (Dot 1968)★★★, with Count Basie *The Board Of Directors* (Dot 1968)★★★, *My Shy Violet* (Dot 1968)★★★, *Dream* (Dot 1969)★★★.

● COMPILATIONS: *The Mills Brothers Greatest Hits* (Dot 1958)★★★, *Ten Years Of Hits 1954-1964* (Dot 1965)★★★, *Greatest Hits* (MCA 1982)★★★, *Golden Greats* (MCA 1986)★★★, in addition, there are a great many compilations available.

● VIDEOS: *Mills Brothers* (Virgin Vision 1992).

● FILMS: *The Big Beat* (1957).

MILLS, GARRY

b. 13 October 1941, West Wickham, Kent, England. Mills was the nephew of jazz band leader Nat Gonella. Like many other UK pop singers of the late 50s, he started at London's 2 Is coffee bar and this led to his signing with Dick Rowe at Top Rank. He covered major US hits such as 'Running Bear', 'Teen Angel', 'Hey, Baby', 'Seven Little Girls' and 'Footsteps' before charting with the b-side of the last single. The song 'Look For A Star' had been written for the Norman Wisdom film *Follow A Star* but was actually used in the Hammer movie *Circus Of Horrors*. In America, Gary's (he dropped one 'r' for the USA) original soundtrack version was joined on the charts by three local cover versions, and, although he made the Top 40 in 1960, the biggest hit was by his near namesake Garry Miles (aka Buzz Cason). The record was not only Mills' biggest success, it was also the first hit for composer Mark Anthony, better known as Tony Hatch. Mills, who was backed on the road by the Flee-Rekkers, had two smaller UK

hits with the follow-up 'Top Teen Baby' and 'I'll Step Down' on Decca in 1961, and also appeared in the long-forgotten films *London Nights* and *Treasure Island W.C.2.*

MINEO, SAL

b. Salvatore Mineo, 10 January 1939, New York City, New York, USA, d. 12 February 1976. Mineo studied dancing and made his Broadway debut in *The Rose Tattoo*. He followed this with an appearance in *The King And I* in 1952. In the mid-50s he went to Hollywood and began making films, usually appearing as a troubled teenager. Among his best-known films were *Rebel Without A Cause* (1955), for which he was nominated for an Oscar as Best Supporting Actor, *Somebody Up There Likes Me* and *Giant* (both 1956), and *Exodus* (1960), another unsuccessful Oscar nomination. He also played the title role in *The Gene Krupa Story* (1959). In the late 50s, Mineo made a number of records, including 'Love Affair', 'Start Moving (In My Direction)', 'Lasting Love' and 'You Shouldn't Do That'. He continued making films during the 60s and also returned to stage work. He directed and starred in *Fortune And Men's Eyes*, a play that reflected his own homosexuality. He was returning home from the theatre when he was stabbed to death in a Hollywood street.

● ALBUMS: *Sal* (Epic 1958)★★.

MINNELLI, VINCENTE

b. 28 February 1903, Chicago, Illinois, USA, d. 25 July 1986, Los Angeles, California, USA. A distinguished film director with a sophisticated style and flair, particularly in the use of colour and the innovative filming of the most exquisite dance sequences. Minnelli is credited, in collaboration with Gene Kelly, with being the main influence on the classic MGM musicals of the 50s. As a young child Minnelli appeared in plays produced by the family Minnelli Bros. Tent Theatre, which toured the American Midwest. After leaving school at 16 he studied at the Art Institute of Chicago, and worked as a window and costume designer before moving to New York to design the scenery and costumes for two 1932 Broadway shows, the *Earl Carroll Vanities* and *The DuBarry*. From 1933-35 Minnelli was art director at the Radio City Music Hall where he staged a series of ballets and musicals. In 1935 he directed as well as designed the Beatrice Lillie musical *At Home Abroad*, and throughout the 30s worked successfully on productions such as *Ziegfeld Follies*, *The Show Is On*, *Hooray For What!* and *Very Warm For May* (1939). From 1940-42, under the aegis of MGM producer Arthur Freed, Minnelli trained in various aspects of Hollywood film techniques and supervised speciality numbers in a number of films including *Strike Up The Band*, *Babes On Broadway* and *Panama Hattie*. He made his debut as a director in 1943 with the all-black musical *Cabin In The Sky*, which was followed by *I Dood It* a year later. Then came *Meet Me In St. Louis* (1944), a delightful piece of nostalgic Americana that became one of the most beloved musicals of all time. Minnelli married its star, Judy Garland, in 1945 (divorced 1951), and in the following year their daughter, Liza Minnelli, was born. Over the next 25 years Minnelli directed a number of musicals that met with varying degrees of success. *Yolande And The Thief* (1945), which starred Fred Astaire, was followed by the all-star spectacular *Ziegfeld Follies* (1946), and two films with Gene Kelly, the underrated *The Pirate* (1948), and *An American In Paris* (1951), which is often considered to be Minnelli's masterpiece. However, many would argue that another of the director's collaborations with Fred Astaire, *The Band Wagon* (1953), or the delightful *Gigi* (1958), were equally important events in the director's distinguished career. Certainly, whatever their merits - and they were not inconsiderable - few would suggest *Brigadoon* (1954), *Kismet* (1955), *Bells Are Ringing* (1960) or *On A Clear Day You Can See Forever* (1970) as being prime examples of Vincente Minnelli's art. The latter film was made for Paramount after he had ended an association with MGM that had lasted for more than 25 years. However, the majority of Minnelli's films were not musicals. Over the years he made many other pictures in a wide variety of styles and moods, and finally achieved his ambition to work with daughter Liza Minnelli in 1976 on his last film, *A Matter Of Time*. By then, Minnelli's style of films - particularly musicals - were anachronistic, and he lived quietly in retirement until his death at his home in Beverly Hills in 1986. The year of his birth has always been the subject of speculation. The one cited above is that which was printed in the excellent obituary notice in *Variety*. In 1993 the young cabaret entertainer Jeff Harnar presented his solo revue *Dancing In The Dark - Vincente Minnelli's Hollywood* in New York.

● FURTHER READING: *I Remember It Well*, Vincente Minnelli.

● FILMS: as director *I Dood It* (1943), *Cabin In The Sky* (1943), *Meet Me In St. Louis* (1944), *Yolande And The Thief* (1945), *The Clock* (1945), *Till The Clouds Roll By (Judy Garland's sequences only)* (1946), *Ziegfeld Follies* (1946), *Undercurrent* (1946), *The Pirate* (1948), *Madame Bovary* (1949), *Father Of The Bride* (1950), *An American In Paris* (1951), *Father's Little Dividend* (1951), *The Story Of Three Loves (Mademoiselle Sequence)* (1952), *The Bad And The Beautiful* (1952), *The Band Wagon* (1953), *Brigadoon* (1954), *The Long Long Trailer* (1954), *The Cobweb* (1955), *Kismet* (1955), *Lust For Life* (1956), *Tea And Sympathy* (1956), *Designing Woman* (1957), *Some Came Running* (1958), *The Reluctant Debutante* (1958), *Gigi* (1958), *Bells Are Ringing* (1960), *Home From The Hill* (1960), *Two Weeks In Another Town* (1962), *The Four Horsemen Of The Apocalypse* (1962), *The Courtship Of Eddie's Father* (1963), *Goodbye Charlie* (1964), *The Sandpiper* (1965), *On A Clear Day You Can See Forever* (1970), *A Matter Of Time* (1976).

MISTER ROCK AND ROLL

US DJ Alan Freed was a pivotal figure in the development of 50s rock 'n' roll. His radio programmes helped to expose the emergent music to a generation of teenagers and he later showcased many acts live in revue-styled concerts. A cavalcade of performers populated the films with which Freed was involved, including *Rock Around The Clock* and *Rock Rock Rock*, a premise equally prevalent on this 1957 feature. *Mister Rock And Roll* boasted a plot wherein Freed pondered why the record industry had hit a slump. Salvation arrived in the shape of R&B, but Freed must first incur parental wrath, before trying to convert his denigrators. 'Young people. Show your parents how exciting your music is. Take them to see this picture,' ran the publicity blurb for a film showcasing Little Richard, Chuck Berry, Frankie Lymon, LaVern Baker and the Moonglows. Each performance was meritorious in itself, inspiring continued interest in the feature, but the notion of grafting memorable performances to witless plots was already undermining the true potential of celluloid pop.

MITCHELL, GUY

b. Albert Cernick, 22 February 1927, Detroit, Michigan, USA. An enormously popular singer in the USA and especially the UK, particularly during the 50s, with a straightforward style and affable personality. Although his birthplace is often given as Yugoslavia, his parents' homeland, Mitchell confirmed in a 1988 UK interview that he was born in Detroit, and was brought up there until the family moved to Colorado, and then to Los Angeles, California, when he was 11 years old. In Los Angeles, he successfully auditioned for Warner Brothers and, for the next few years, was groomed for a possible movie career as a child star, in addition to singing on the Hollywood radio station KFWB. The possibility of the world having another Mickey Rooney was averted when the family moved again, this time to San Francisco. Mitchell became an apprentice saddle-maker, and worked on ranches and in rodeos in the San Joaquin Valley, and also sang on cowboy singer Dude Martin's radio show. His affection for country music stayed with him for the remainder of his career. After a spell in the US Navy, Mitchell joined pianist Carmen Cavallero, and made his first records with the band, including 'I Go In When The Moon Comes Out' and 'Ah, But It Happens'. He then spent some time in New York, making demonstration records, and also won first place on the *Arthur Godfrey Talent Show*. In 1949, he recorded a few tracks for King Records, which were subsequently reissued on *Sincerely Yours* when Mitchell became successful.

In 1950, he was signed to Columbia Records by Mitch Miller, who is said to have been responsible for changing Cernick to Mitchell, Miller's full Christian name. Their first success came in 1950, with 'My Heart Cries For You' and 'The Roving Kind', which were followed by a string of hits throughout the decade, mostly jaunty novelty numbers, usually with Miller arrangements that used French horns to considerable effect. Several of the songs were written by Bob Merrill, including 'Sparrow In The Tree Top', 'Pittsburgh, Pennsylvania', 'My Truly, Truly Fair', 'Feet Up (Pat Him On The Po-Po)', 'Belle, Belle, My Liberty Belle' and 'She Wears Red Feathers', which contained the immortal Merrill couplet: 'An elephant brought her in, placed her by my side/While six baboons got out bassoons, and played "Here Comes The Bride"!' Other US Top 30 entries during this period included 'You're Just In Love', a duet with another Miller protégée, Rosemary Clooney, 'Christopher Columbus', 'Unless' (a 30s Tolchard Evans number), 'Sweetheart Of Yesterday', 'There's Always Room At Our House', 'I Can't Help It', 'Day Of Jubilo', ''Cause I Love You, That's A-Why', 'Tell Us Where The Good Times Are' (the latter two duets with Mindy Carson) and 'Ninety-Nine Years (Dead Or Alive)'. 'Singing The Blues' (with Ray Conniff And His Orchestra) became his most successful record, staying at number 1 in the US charts for 10 weeks in 1956. In the UK, Tommy Steele had a hit with his cover version, but Mitchell also succeeded by reaching number 1. Further infectious hits followed: 'Knee Deep In The Blues', the irritatingly catchy 'Rock-A-Billy' ('rock-a-billy, rock-a-billy, rock-a-billy rock, rock-a-billy rock-a-billy, ooh rock rock'), and his last US chart entry in 1959,

'Heartaches By The Number' (number 1). Of the aforementioned singles, six sold over a million copies. Most of Mitchell's US hits were also successful in the UK, where he was highly popular, touring regularly, appearing at the London Palladium for the first time in 1952, and performing at the 1954 Royal Variety Performance. Additional chart entries in the UK included 'Pretty Little Black-Eyed Susie', 'Look At That Girl' (number 1), 'Cloud Lucky Seven', 'Cuff Of My Shirt', 'Dime And A Dollar' and 'Chicka Boom'. The latter was featured in Mitchell's first movie, a 3-D musical entitled *Those Redheads From Seattle* (1953), with Rhonda Fleming, Gene Barry and Teresa Brewer. Brewer and Mitchell proved a pleasant combination on the Johnny Mercer/Hoagy Carmichael song 'I Guess It Was You All The Time'. In 1954, Mitchell appeared with Gene Barry again, in the spoof western movie *Red Garters*, which also starred Rosemary Clooney, and contained another Mitchell 'special', 'A Dime And A Dollar'. In contrast to the somewhat perky style, so effective on his singles, some of Mitchell's albums revealed him to be an excellent ballad singer, particularly *A Guy In Love*, with Glenn Osser and his Orchestra, which contained standards such as 'The Moon Got In My Eyes', 'Allegheny Moon', 'East Of The Sun' and 'East Side Of Heaven'. *Sunshine Guitar*, with its guitar choir, was 'carefree and breezy, full of infectious gaiety', with a country 'feel' on several of the numbers. With the 60s beat boom imminent, Mitchell's contract with Columbia ended in 1962, and he released some singles on the Joy and Reprise labels. In 1967, he signed for the Nashville-based Starday label, but shortly after his *Travelling Shoes* and *Singing Up A Storm* were released, the company went out of business. During some periods of the 60s and 70s, Mitchell ceased performing. He issued only a few tracks on his own GMI label - partly because of poor health and serious alcohol problems. In 1979, he toured Australia, and started to play nightclubs in the USA. In the 80s he made several appearances in the UK, and released the old Elvis Presley favourite 'Always On My Mind', backed with 'Wind Beneath My Wings' from the Bette Midler hit movie *Beaches*. This was followed by *A Garden In The Rain*, a set of British numbers that included 'My Kind Of Girl', 'Yesterday', 'I Hadn't Anyone Till You' and Noël Coward's theme tune, 'I'll See You Again'. In the 90s the old hits were still being repackaged and sold to a younger audience following Mitchell's appearance in John Byrne's UK television drama *Your Cheatin' Heart*, in 1990. During the filming in the UK he took the opportunity to play a number of country festival gigs. In 1991 during a tour of Australia he had a horse-riding accident that resulted in serious internal injuries. He spent some time in intensive care but made a complete recovery. He has a loyal following in the UK (where arguably he was more popular); these devotees of 50s nostalgia subscribe to a regular magazine *Mitchell Music* - it is remarkable that their enthusiasm remains as strong 40 years after his heyday. Mitchell typified 50s pop more than any other performer, and his catalogue of hits remains formidable. His work is destined to endure.

● ALBUMS: *Songs Of The Open Spaces* 10-inch album (Columbia 1952)★★★ UK title *Guy Mitchell Sings* (Columbia 1954)★★★, *Red Garters* film soundtrack (Columbia 1954)★★★, *The Voice Of Your Choice* (Philips 1955)★★★, *A Guy In Love* (Columbia/Philips 1959)★★★, as Al Grant *Sincerely Yours* (1959)★★★, *Sunshine Guitar* (Columbia 1960)★★★, *Traveling Shoes* (Starday 1967)★★★, *Singin' Up A Storm* (Starday 1968)★★★, *Heartaches By The Number* (Nashville 1970)★★★, *The Roving Kind* (1981)★★★, *A Garden In The Rain* (President 1985)★★★.

● COMPILATIONS: *Guy Mitchell's Greatest Hits* (Columbia 1958)★★★★, *Showcase Of Hits* (Philips 1958)★★★★, *The Best Of Guy Mitchell* (Columbia 1966)★★★, *American Legend - 16 Greatest Hits* (1977)★★★★, *20 Golden Greats* (1979)★★★★, *Hit Singles 1950-1960* (Columbia 1981)★★★★, *20 Golden Pieces Of Guy Mitchell* (Bulldog 1984)★★★★, *Guy's Greatest Hits* (Columbia 1984)★★★★, *Singing The Blues* (Castle 1986)★★★★, *Portrait Of A Song Stylist* (Masterpiece 1989)★★★, *Sweep Your Blues Away* (1989)★★★, *Heartaches By The Number* (Bear Family 1990)★★★★, *Your Cheatin' Heart* film soundtrack (1990)★★★, *20 All Time Hits* (MFP 1991)★★★★, *16 Most Requested Songs* (Columbia/Legacy 1992)★★★★, *The Essential Collection* (1993)★★★★.

● FURTHER READING: *Mitchell Music*, privately published UK fanzine.

MODERN RECORDS

Modern Records was founded in Los Angeles, California, USA, in 1945 by brothers Jules, Saul And Joe Bihari. They secured early success with Hadda Brooks and Johnny Moore's Three Blazers, and within two years Modern had become one of the leading post-war R&B labels on the west coast, alongside Imperial Records and Aladdin Records. The Biharis manufactured their own records, building one of the largest pressing plants in the region, and an agreement with a network of independent distributors ensured Modern's releases enjoyed national distribution. Etta James's 'Wallflower', Jessie Belvin's 'Goodnight My Love' and the Cadets' 'Stranded In The Jungle' were some of the label's most successful recordings during the early 50s. John Lee Hooker, Lightnin' Hopkins and Willie 'Smokey' Hogg also recorded for Modern but its eminent position was undermined by its practice of 'covering' other R&B hits. Nevertheless, the Biharis were able to establish several subsidiary companies, including RPM, founded in 1950, and Flair, founded in 1953. B.B. King was RPM's most important signing, as this seminal blues singer/guitarist remained with the company until the 60s. Rosco Gordon ('No More Doggin') and Johnny 'Guitar' Watson ('Those Lonely, Lonely Nights') were among the other artists enjoying success on this outlet. Meanwhile, Richard Berry's influential 'Louie Louie' was first issued on Flair. In 1951, armed with a Magnechord tape recorder, Joe Bihari undertook the first of several field trips to Mississippi. He made several important juke-joint blues recordings on location, notably with impassioned slide guitarist Elmore James. In 1952 Modern set up the Meteor label in Memphis, Tennessee, USA. It was managed by a fourth Bihari brother, Lester. By the end of the 50s the Modern group was being eclipsed by newer independent companies, notably Atlantic Records. The Biharis opted to concentrate on a newly founded budget line, Crown Records, which, following bankruptcy, was succeeded by Kent Records. These outlets revived recordings from Modern's halcyon era, but the entire operation ceased trading during the 80s following the death of Jules Bihari. The best of its catalogue has since been repacked for compact disc by Ace Records.

MODUGNO, DOMENICO

b. 9 January 1928, Polignano a Mare, Italy, d. 6 August 1994, Lampeduso. Modugno disappointed his father, a civic dignitary, by rejecting higher education to seek a career as a film actor in Rome. However, although he passed an entrance examination to drama college, National Service postponed entry for two years. Among the parts he gained on graduation was that of a balladeer in 1955's *Il Mantello Rosso*. More conspicuous than expected in this role, he was contracted by both national radio and Fonit Records as a vocalist, with accompaniment that varied from his own lone guitar or accordion to full orchestra. In a developing repertoire were self-composed pieces such as 'Ninna Nanna', 'Lu Piscispada' and - recorded by many other Latinate artists - 'La Donna Riccia'. While he was runner-up in 1957's Neapolitan Song Festival with 'Lazzarella', 'Nel Blu Dipinto Di Blu' (written with Franco Migliacci) was placed first at the more prestigious San Remo event the following year, and thus flung Modugno into a lucrative round of appearances in venues beyond Italy - including North America. With English lyrics by Mitchell Parish, the opus became better known as 'Volare', a Grammy-earning US chart-topper that also reached the UK Top 10 - despite cover versions by Charlie Drake, Marino Marini and Dean Martin. 1959's 'Piove' - another San Remo winner - was an international smash, too - if overtaken in Britain by a version from Marini - when translated by Parish (as 'Ciao Ciao Bambino'). This and lesser triumphs, such as 'Addio Addio' and 1966's 'Dio Come Ti Amo', blessed Modugno with the dubious title of 'genius', though many claim that his most enduring work was his earliest, as demonstrated by periodic revivals of 'Volare', from Bobby Rydell in 1960 to David Bowie in 1986's *Absolute Beginners* movie.

MONDELLO, TOOTS

b. Nuncio M. Mondello, 1912, Boston, Massachusetts, USA, d. 15 November 1992. Mondello began playing saxophone as a youth, as did his brother, both becoming professional musicians. His first name-band job was with Mal Hallett's popular dance band where he remained fairly consistently for five years, playing alto. He then went into a number of bands including those led by Buddy Rogers, Benny Goodman and Ray Noble before turning to studio work. He broadcast and recorded with many diverse musicians including André Kostelanetz, Chick Bullock, Bunny Berigan, Larry Clinton, Louis Armstrong and Lionel Hampton. In 1939 he rejoined Goodman after a spell leading his own band. He recorded with the Metronome All Stars in 1940/1 before being inducted into the US Army. After the war he resumed freelance recording work, playing on sessions with Sarah Vaughan, Billie Holiday and others in the 40s and with Billy Butterfield, Artie Shaw and Goodman in the 50s and 60s. A highly skilled musician with the necessary qualities of playing lead alto in big bands, Mondell's occasional recorded solos display proficiency and intelligence. In later years he continued his studio work.

● COMPILATIONS: *Benny Goodman And His Music Hall Orchestra* (Saville 1934)★★★, with Lionel Hampton *Historic Recording Sessions* (RCA 1937-41)★★★★.

MONOTONES

Formed in 1955 in Newark, New Jersey, USA, the Monotones recorded one of the most memorable doo-wop novelty songs of the 50s, 'Book Of Love'. The group was a sextet, Warren Davis, George Malone, Charles Patrick, Frank Smith, and John and Warren Ryanes. They had sung in the same church choir as Dionne Warwick and Cissy Houston before forming their own group. In 1956, they appeared on the *Ted Mack's Amateur Hour* television programme, singing the Cadillacs' 'Zoom'. They won first prize and began to think more seriously about a career in music. Inspired by a television commercial for toothpaste ('You'll wonder where the yellow went when you brush your teeth with Pepsodent'), Patrick, Malone and Davis wrote 'Book Of Love' to a similar melody. They recorded it at Bell Studio in New York and it was released on the small Mascot label, a subsidiary of Hull Records. It was then picked up by Argo Records for national distribution and ultimately reached number 5 in the USA. The group was touring when their record entered the charts, and months passed before they had a chance to record a follow-up. A single called 'Tom Foolery' was released but failed to chart; the third, 'The Legend Of Sleepy Hollow', was a fine record and is still played on doo-wop radio programmes today, but it also failed to chart in its own time. After a few more singles, the Monotones gave up, although some of the original members performed under that name in the 90s. John Ryanes died on 30 May 1972.

● COMPILATIONS: *Who Wrote The Book Of Love?* (Collectables 1992)★★★.

MONROE, MARILYN

b. Norma Jean Mortenson, 1 June 1926, Los Angeles, California, USA, d. 5 August 1962, Brentwood, California, USA. As well as being a talented comedienne and the number 1 sex symbol in movies during the 50s, Monroe proved to be an appealing interpreter of flirtatious ballads in several of her most popular films. As one of the *Ladies Of The Chorus* (1948), she made a promising start with Lester Lee and Allan Roberts' 'Every Baby Needs A Da-Da-Daddy', which, with its reference to 'Tiffany's', was a precursor to one of her most celebrated performances a few years later, when the same New York store cropped up in 'Diamonds Are A Girl's Best Friend', from Jule Styne and Leo Robin's score for *Gentlemen Prefer Blondes* (1953). In that film Monroe duetted with another of Hollywood's top glamour girls, Jane Russell, on 'Two Little Girls From Little Rock', 'Bye Bye Baby' and a Hoagy Carmichael/Harold Adamson number, 'When Loves Goes Wrong'. Co-starring with Robert Mitchum in *River Of No Return* (1954), Monroe's role as a saloon singer conveniently gave her the opportunity to perform the title song and 'I'm Gonna File My Claim', among others, and, in the same year, she registered strongly with a bundle of Irving Berlin numbers in *There's No Business Like Show Business*. These included 'A Man Chases A Girl' (with Donald O'Connor), 'After You Get What You Want You Don't Want It', 'Heatwave', 'Lazy' and 'You'd Be Surprised'. In 1959 she made what became her most commercially successful film - and arguably the highlight of her career. The classic *Some Like It Hot*, with Tony Curtis, Jack Lemmon and Joe E. ('nobody's perfect') Brown, featured some of Monroe's most effective vocal performances, such as 'I'm Through With

Love', 'I Wanna Be Loved By You' and 'Running Wild'. She sang for the last time on screen in *Let's Make Love* (1960). Apart from contributing the film's high spot, a compelling version of 'My Heart Belongs To Daddy', Monroe duetted with two European heart-throbs, Yves Montand and Frankie Vaughan, on Sammy Cahn and Jimmy Van Heusen's 'Specialization', 'Incurably Romantic' and the title song. Her final performance, a sultry rendering of 'Happy Birthday Mr. President' and 'Thanks For The Memory', was given in May 1962 for President Kennedy's birthday celebrations in Madison Square Garden. Just over two months later she died as the result of an overdose of barbiturates, at the age of 36 (Monroe's death has since been the subject of numerous conspiracy theories, most of which concern her alleged affair with John F. Kennedy). One of the musical selections chosen for her funeral service was a recording of 'Over The Rainbow' sung by Judy Garland, another showbusiness legend who met a tragic end. Since her death, it has been estimated that over 100 Monroe biographies have been published. She was also the subject of several songs, the most famous being Elton John's 'Candle In the Wind'. Others included James Cunningham's 'Norma Jean Wants To Be A Movie Star' and 'Elvis And Marilyn' by Leon Russell.

● COMPILATIONS: *Marilyn* (20th Century Fox 1962)★★★, *Collection: 20 Golden Greats* (Deja Vu 1985)★★★★, *Marilyn Monroe -The Complete Recordings* (Rare 1988)★★★, *The Marilyn Monroe Story* (Deja Vu 1989)★★★.

● FURTHER READING: *Marilyn*, Norman Mailer. *Marilyn Monroe: The Biography*, Donald Spoto. *Goddess: Secret Lives Of Marilyn Monroe*, Anthony Summers. *The Complete Films Of Marilyn Monroe*, Mark Ricci and Michael Conway, *Young Marilyn Becoming The Legend* James Haspiel.

● FILMS: *Dangerous Years* (1948), *Ladies Of The Chorus* (1948), *Love Happy* (1950), *A Ticket To Tomahawk* (1950), *The Asphalt Jungle* (1950), *All About Eve* (1950), *The Fireball* (1950), *Right Cross* (1950), *Home Town Story* (1951), *As Young As You Feel* (1951), *Love Nest* (1951), *Let's Make It Legal* (1951), *We're Not Married* (1952), *Clash By Night* (1952), *Full House* (1952), *Monkey Business* (1952), *Don't Bother To Knock* (1952), *Niagara* (1952), *Gentlemen Prefer Blondes* (1953), *How To Marry A Millionaire* (1953), *River Of No Return* (1954), *There's No Business Like Show Business* (1954), *The Seven-Year Itch* (1955), *Bus Stop* (1956), *The Prince And The Showgirl* (1957), *Some Like It Hot* (1959), *Let's Make Love* (1960), *The Misfits* (1960).

MOONDOG

b. Louis Hardin, 26 May 1916, Marysville, Kansas, USA. This idiosyncratic composer lost his sight at the age of 16 following an accident with a dynamite cap. He was introduced to classical music at the Iowa School for the Blind, studying violin, viola and piano, but having moved to New York, opted for a life as a 'street musician'. He took the name Moondog in 1947 and established a pitch on the city's fabled Times Square. Such was his notoriety, Hardin successfully retained this sobriquet after issuing legal proceedings against disc jockey Alan Freed, who had claimed the 'Moondog' name for his radio show.

In a manner similar to fellow maverick Harry Partch, Moondog constructed his own instruments, claiming conventional scales could not reproduce the sounds heard in his head. This was immediately apparent on his first release, *On*

The Streets Of New York (1953), a 45 rpm EP issued by Epic and London/American. Percussive devices, named the 'oo' and 'trimba', were at the fore of albums recorded for the Prestige label, notably *More Moondog* and *The Story Of Moondog*, although a distinctive jazz influence can also be detected. Further releases ensued, including *Moondog And His Honking Geese*, which the composer financed and distributed. Hardin also arranged an album of Mother Goose songs for singer Julie Andrews. During the 1960s Moondog continued to perform and beg on the city's streets, but his unconventional lifestyle and appearance - he wrapped himself in army surplus blankets and wore a Viking-styled helmet - found succour in the emergent counter-culture. He performed with anti-establishment comedian Lenny Bruce and eccentric singer Tiny Tim, while several groups, including Big Brother and the Holding Company and the Insect Trust, recorded his distinctive musical rounds. In 1969, James Guercio, producer of the highly successful Chicago, introduced Moondog to CBS. Buoyed by a full orchestra, *Moondog* encapsulates twenty years of compositions, showing musical references to such diverse figures as Stravinsky and Charlie Parker, the latter of whom often conversed with Moondog. One particular selection, 'The Witch Of Endor', stands as one of his finest pieces. *Moondog 2* was a collection of rounds, inspired by the recognition afforded the composer by the hip cognoscenti. In 1974 Moondog undertook a tour of Germany where he opted to settle. 'I am a European at heart', he later stated. A further series of albums maintained his unique musical vision, but although he has ceased recording, interest in this fascinating individual continues to flourish.

● ALBUMS: *Moondog And His Friends* 10-inch album (Epic 1954)★★★, *Moondog* (Prestige 1955)★★★, *More Moondog* (Prestige 1956)★★★, *The Story Of Moondog* (Prestige 1957)★★★, *Moondog* (Columbia 1969)★★★★, *Moondog 2* (Columbia 1970)★★★, *Moondog In Europe* (1978)★★★, *H'Art Songs* (1979)★★★, *A New Sound Of An Old Instrument* (1980)★★★, *Selected Works* (1980)★★★, *Big Band* (Trimba 1996)★★★.

MOONGLOWS

This R&B vocal group was formed in Cleveland, Ohio, USA, in 1952. If there were any group that best signalled the birth of rock 'n' roll - by which R&B emerged out of its black sub-culture into mainstream teen culture - it was the Moonglows. The group's career paralleled that of their mentor, legendary disc jockey Alan Freed, who in his rise in rock 'n' roll made the Moonglows the mainstays of his radio programmes, motion pictures and stage shows. Their membership comprised lead singer Bobby Lester (b. 13 January 1930, Louisville, Kentucky, USA, d. 15 October 1980), Harvey Fuqua (b. 27 July 1929, Louisville, Kentucky, USA), Alexander 'Pete' Graves (b. 17 April 1930, Cleveland, Ohio, USA), and Prentiss Barnes (b. 12 April 1925, Magnolia, Mississippi, USA). After recording for Freed's Champagne label in 1953, the group signed with Chicago-based Chance, where they managed to secure a few regional hits, most notably a cover version of Doris Day's 'Secret Love' in 1954. Freed used his connections to sign the Moonglows to a stronger Chicago label, the fast-rising Chess Records, and the group enjoyed a major hit with 'Sincerely' (number 1 R&B/number 20 pop 1954). Joining the group at this time was guitarist Billy Johnson (b. 1924, Hartford, Connecticut, USA, d. 1987). Using a novel technique they called 'blow harmony', other great hits followed: 'Most Of All' (number 5 R&B 1955), 'We Go Together' (number 9 R&B 1956), 'See Saw' (number 6 R&B/number 25 pop 1956), all of which featured Lester on lead; and a remake of Percy Mayfield's 'Please Send Me Someone To Love' (number 5 R&B/number 73 pop 1957) and 'Ten Commandments Of Love' (number 9 R&B/number 22 pop 1958), which featured Fuqua on lead. The original Moonglows disbanded in 1958, and Fuqua put together a new group that included Marvin Gaye. In 1960 Fuqua disbanded this group and he and Gaye went to Detroit to work in the industry there. Fuqua worked with Berry Gordy's sister, Gwen Gordy, on the Anna label and Gaye joined Berry Gordy's Motown operation. Fuqua carved out a very successful career as a producer and record executive, working with Motown artists in the 60s and a stable of Louisville artists in the 70s on the RCA label.

● ALBUMS: *Look! It's The Moonglows* (Chess 1959)★★★, *The Return Of The Moonglows* (RCA Victor 1972)★★★, *The Moonglows On Stage* (Relic 1992)★★.

● COMPILATIONS: *The Best Of Bobby Lester And The Moonglows* (Chess 1962)★★★, *The Flamingos Meet The Moonglows* (Vee Jay 1962)★★★, *The Moonglows* (Constellation 1964)★★★, *Moonglows* (Chess 1976)★★★, *Their Greatest Sides* (Chess 1984)★★★, *Blue Velvet: The Ultimate Collection* (MCA/Chess 1993)★★★, *The Flamingos Meet The Moonglows: The Complete 25 Chance Recordings* (Vee Jay 1993)★★★, *Their Greatest Hits* (MCA 1997)★★★.

MOORE, MARILYN

b. 16 June 1931, Oklahoma City, Oklahoma, USA, d. March 1992. Born into a showbiz family, Moore began performing at the age of three, singing and dancing in the finale of her family's vaudeville act. As a teenager, she decided to concentrate on singing and soon turned to jazz, working in clubs in Oklahoma City and Chicago. In 1949 she sang with Woody Herman, then with Charlie Ventura and by the early 50s had settled in New York. She sang with various groups, including those led by Ray McKinley, Boyd Raeburn and Al Cohn, whom she married in 1953. They had two children, Lisa and Joe Cohn (now a leading jazz guitarist), and Moore's life became focused upon her home and family. In 1957, however, she was invited to record for Bethlehem and the resulting album, on which she is backed by Cohn, Joe Wilder, Don Abney, Barry Galbraith and other leading jazzmen, attracted a great deal of interest. The following year, she was cast in a jazz show, *Oh Captain!*, recorded by MGM Records in which Coleman Hawkins, Art Farmer, Oscar Pettiford and Harry 'Sweets' Edison also appeared. Soon afterwards, Moore and Cohn were divorced and once again she was tied to home-making and family-raising. Despite a deep desire to return to professional singing and to make more records, she never did make it back. A warm and sensitive voice marked Moore's work and in her phrasing and overall style there is evidence of her affinity for Billie Holiday. Overlooked and under-recorded (the MGM album was swiftly deleted and never reissued), the quality of Moore's singing on her first album, reissued on CD in 1990, marks her out as one of the great losses to the world of jazz.

● ALBUMS: *Moody Marilyn Moore* (Affinity 1957)★★★, with others *Oh Captain!* (MGM 1958)★★.

MOORE, SCOTTY

b. Winfield Scott Moore, 27 December 1931, Gadsden, Tennessee, USA. Guitarist Moore started playing at the age of eight and formed his first band while in the US Navy in 1948. After he left the service he joined the Memphis group Doug Poindexter And His Starlite Wranglers who also included bass player Bill Black. The band recorded Moore's 'My Kind Of Carryin' On' for Sam Phillips' Sun label and both Moore and Black played on several other Sun artists' recordings. In June 1954 Phillips invited a young singer he was trying out to Moore's apartment to rehearse some songs: that man was Elvis Presley. A week later, Moore, Presley and Black went into Sun studios to record together for the first time. As a trio (later a quartet with drummer D.J. Fontana) they recorded some of Elvis's finest recordings. When Presley was sold to RCA for a 'king's ransom', Moore and Black were taken on as his sidemen on a relatively meagre salary. Moore had acted as a kind of unpaid manager before Bob Neal and then Colonel Tom Parker took over the role. While Presley was busy filming *Loving You*, Moore and Black headed for the Dallas State Fair where they performed as Scotty And Bill, Elvis's Original Backing Group. Scotty also went to work for the small Memphis label Fernwood Records, whose most successful record was Thomas Wayne's 'Tragedy'. Moore himself released a solo single called 'Have Guitar Will Travel'. During the same period he also played on some sessions for Dale Hawkins at Chess. Unlike Black, Moore returned to play with Presley when he came out of the army in 1960, but not for long. Over the next few years he recorded infrequently with Presley and went back to Sun as production manager. Later in the 60s he went to Nashville to start his own studio. Presley invited him back for the 1968 television special, which was the last time Moore played with, or even saw, him. In 1970 Moore recorded an album with D.J. Fontana but by now he had virtually retired from playing to concentrate on production (most notably engineering Ringo Starr's *Beaucoups Of Blues*). He was enticed out of retirement by Billy Swan to play on his self-titled 1976 album and later played on Ral Donner's Elvis tribute album. By the 80s Moore had established a successful tape copying service in Nashville and rarely picked up his guitar. In 1997 Moore recorded with Fontana again.

● ALBUMS: *The Guitar That Changed The World* (Epic 1964)★★★, *What's Left* (1970)★★, with Carl Perkins *706 Reunion - A Sentimental Journey* (Belle Meade 1993)★★★, with D.J. Fontana *All The King's Men* (Sweetfish 1997)★★.

● FURTHER READING: *That's Alright Elvis*, Scotty Moore and James Dickerson.

MORE, JULIAN

b. 1929, England. A librettist and lyricist for some of the most successful British hit musical shows of the late 50s, More became interested in the theatre while at Cambridge University. He was involved as a performer and writer in undergraduate revues, and contributed the occasional item to the Watergate Theatre. In 1953 he wrote some material for the West End revue *Airs On A Shoestring*, which starred Max Adrian, Moyra Fraser and Betty Marsden. Two years later, he collaborated with composer James Gilbert for the Windsor Theatre production of a 'revusical', *The World's The Limit*, and in the following year, they had a smash hit with *Grab Me A Gondola*. Set at the Venice Film Festival, with the character of the film star heroine 'moulded' on Britain's Diana Dors, the show starred Joan Heal, Denis Quilley and June Wenham. It featured numbers such as 'That's My Biography', 'Cravin' For The Avon', 'A Man, Not a Mouse' and 'New To Me'. Even more successful was *Irma La Douce* (1958) for which More, with Monty Norman and David Heneker, provided the English book and lyrics translation to Marguerite Monnot's music. The story included such songs as 'Our Language Of Love' and 'Dis-Donc', and ran for 1,512 performances in London, and over 500 in New York. The More-Heneker-Norman team combined with Wolfe Mankowitz later in 1958 for *Expresso Bongo*. The 'most important British musical for years' starred Paul Schofield, Hy Hazell and James Kenny, and ran for nine months. The score, which included 'The Shrine On The Second Floor' and 'I've Never Had It So Good', virtually disappeared from the innovative 1960 film version starring Cliff Richard and Laurence Harvey. The lead in the road version was taken by Colin Hicks, the brother of Tommy Steele. London's theatrical scene was changing and More was unable to match previous achievements. Throughout the 60s and 70s his offerings included *The Golden Touch* (with Gilbert), *The Art Of Living* (his last collaboration with both Norman and Heneker), *The Perils Of Scobie Prilt* (with Norman), *The Man From The West* (with David Russell), *Quick, Quick, Slow* (Norman), *Good Time Johnny* (Gilbert), *R Loves J* (with Alexander Ferris) and *Bordello* (with Americans Al Frisch and Bernard Spiro). In 1979 he was back with Monty Norman for *Songbook*, 'a burlesque tale' of the work of the prolific songwriter Mooney Shapiro. Subsequently, More settled in France, with homes in Paris and Provence, and became a successful writer of travel books. Since then, he has re-emerged occasionally, and wrote the book and lyrics to Gilbert Becaud's music for the Broadway show *Roza* (1987), 'a maudlin and awkwardly constructed story with inferior songs'. He also adapted Abe Burrows' original book for a London revival of Cole Porter's *Can-Can* in 1988.

MORLEY, ANGELA

In the 50s, 60s and into the 70s, Wally Stott was a highly respected conductor, arranger and composer on the UK music scene. In the early 70s he underwent a sex-change operation, and was subsequently known professionally as Angela Morley. Stott was born in 1924 in Sheffield, England. He attended the same Mexboro school as Tony Mercer, who went on to become one of the principal singers with the *Black And White Minstrel Show*. Mercer sang and played the piano accordion, while Stott concentrated on the saxophone. On leaving school, they each spent some time with Archie's Juveniles and Oscar Rabin's Band. Stott's route to Rabin was via the bands of Billy Merrin and Bram Martin. By 1944, after some years with the Rabin Band, Stott was leading the saxophone section on alto, and had become the band's sole arranger: a great future was already being forecast for him. Stott's next move was to Geraldo, with whom he stayed for about four years, leaving in late 1948 to 'pursue arranging and film music work, which he is to make his future career'. He still managed to find the time to play the saxophone for outfits such as Jack Nathan's Coconut Grove Orchestra. In the early 50s Stott joined Philips Records, and soon became one of their key arrangers, along with Peter Knight and Ivor Raymonde. During the next 20 years he arranged and con-

ducted for some of the UK's most popular artists, such as Frankie Vaughan ('Green Door', 'The Garden Of Eden' and 'The Heart Of A Man'), Anne Shelton ('Lay Down Your Arms' and *My Heart Sings*), Harry Secombe ('This Is My Song'), the Beverley Sisters ('Somebody Bad Stole De Wedding Bell' and 'Happy Wanderer'), Roy Castle (*Newcomer*), Ronnie Carroll ('Say Wonderful Things' and *Carroll Calling*), the Kaye Sisters ('Paper Roses'), Shirley Bassey ('Banana Boat Song' and 'As I Love You'), Muriel Smith ('Hold Me, Thrill Me, Kiss Me'), the Polka Dots (*Nice Work & You Can Buy It*) and many more, plus a few 'foreigners', too, as on *Mel Tormé Meets The British* (1959). Stott also made several of his own instrumental albums, sometimes augmented by a vocal chorus. He began writing music early in his career, and his first significant piece came to light in November 1954, when *Hancock's Half Hour* began. It proved to be one of BBC Radio's most popular programmes, later moving to television, and its opening theme, played on a tuba over Tony Hancock's stuttering introduction, was composed by Stott. He also wrote and arranged the show's instrumental links, and conducted the orchestra for many other radio programmes, including *The Last Goon Show Of All*. Stott composed numerous pieces of mood music for London publishers, especially Chappell's, which included 'A Canadian In Mayfair' (dedicated to Robert Farnon, who gave Stott valuable advice on arranging and composition), 'Mock Turtles', 'Quiz', 'Travelling Along', 'Miss Universe', 'Flight By Jet', 'Casbah', 'Commenwealth March', 'Practice Makes Perfect', 'China', 'Focus On Fashion' and 'Skylight'. In the late 60s and early 70s, Stott wrote the music for several films, including *The Looking Glass War*, *Captain Nemo And The Underwater City* and *When Eight Bells Toll*, and for television productions such as *Hugh And I*, and the *The Maladjusted Busker*. Around that time, credits began to be given in the name of Angela Morley, and these include two Academy Award nominations, for her arrangements of Alan Jay Lerner and Frederick Loewe's score for *The Little Prince* (1974), and Richard M. and Robert B. Shermans' score for *The Slipper And The Rose* (1977). Morley also composed for the animated feature *Watership Down*, the Italian production *La Colina Dei Comali*, and for televison films such as *Friendships*, *Secrets And Lies*, *Madame X*, *Summer Girl*, *Two Marriages* and *Threesome* (1984). Most of this work has been completed in the USA, where Morley is reported to have been living for most of the last 20 years.
● ALBUMS: *Wally Stott Tribute To George Gershwin* (Parlophone 1955)★★★★, *Tribute To Irving Berlin* (Parlophone 1956)★★★, *Tribute To Jerome Kern* (Parlophone 1957)★★★★, *London Pride* (1959)★★★, *Chorale In Concert* (1967)★★, *Christmas By The Fireside* (1969)★★.

MOROSS, JEROME

b. 1 August 1913, Brooklyn, New York, USA, d. 25 July 1983, Miami, Florida, USA. A highly regarded composer who wrote symphonic works as well as scores for films and Broadway shows. After graduating from New York University at the age of 18, Moross contributed some incidental music to the theatre, and then composed most of the score for the short-lived Broadway revue *Parade* in 1935. Later in that same year he was engaged by George Gershwin as assistant conductor and pianist for the last few weeks of the New York run of *Porgy And Bess*, and subsequently for the west coast production. Moross moved to Hollywood in 1940 and spent the next decade orchestrating scores for a great many films, including *Our Town*, *Action In The North Atlantic* and *Conflict*. He also worked on Hugo Friedhofer's Oscar-winning score for *The Best Years Of Our Lives* (1946). In 1948 he was given the opportunity to compose his own original score for *Close-Up*, which was followed during the 50s and 60s by others such as *When I Grow Up*, *Captive City*, *The Sharkfighters*, *Hans Christian Andersen* (ballet music only), *Seven Wonders Of The World* (with David Raksin and Sol Kaplan), *The Proud Rebel*, *The Jayhawkers*, *The Adventures Of Huckleberry Finn* (1960), *The Mountain Road*, *Five Finger Exercise*, *The Cardinal*, *The War Lord*, *Rachel Rachel*, *Valley Of The Gwang!* and *Hail, Hero!* (1969). His most acclaimed work during that time was undoubtedly for William Wyler's dramatic western, *The Big Country* (1958), for which he was nominated for an Academy Award. The music, and particularly its electrifying main theme, is considered to be among the most memorable in the history of the cinema. His work was also heard regularly on television in such popular programmes as *Lancer* and *Wagon Train*. On Broadway, Moross collaborated twice with the author and librettist John Latouche, firstly in 1948 for *Ballet Ballads*, a musical adaptation of three one-act plays, and again in 1954, for the innovative *The Golden Apple*, which, although it folded after only 127 performances, won the New York Drama Critics Circle Award for best musical, and has since become a cult piece. One of its songs, the ballad 'Lazy Afternoon', has been recorded by several artists, including Tony Bennett. During his long and distinguished career, Moross also won two Guggenheim fellowship awards, in 1947 and 1948. He brought his own individual brand of folksy homespun Americana to his music for ballets such as *American Patterns*, *The Last Judgement* and *Frankie And Johnny*, along with numerous orchestral works which included 'Biguine', 'A Tall Story', 'Paeans', 'Those Everlasting Blues' and 'First Symphony'. His last completed work was a one-act opera, *Sorry, Wrong Number!*

MOST HAPPY FELLA, THE

Any show that opened in the same season as *My Fair Lady* was bound to be somewhat overshadowed by Alan Jay Lerner and Frederick Loewe's masterpiece, which was destined to be a smash hit. However, *The Most Happy Fella* was, in some ways, a more ambitious work than its female counterpart, and enjoyed a satisfactory run of 676 performances on Broadway. The show opened on 3 May 1956 at the Imperial Theatre, and immediately confused many of the critics: was it an opera? A play with music, perhaps? Frank Loesser, who wrote the music, lyrics, and libretto, settled on 'an extended musical comedy'. His adaptation of Sidney Howard's 1924 Pulitzer Prize-winning play, *They Knew What They Wanted*, was set in Napa Valley, California, and tells of an Italian vintner, Tony (Robert Weede, a former opera singer, making his Broadway debut), who is maturing rather more quickly than the grapes in his vineyard. He longs for a wife, and proposes by post to Rosabella (Jo Sullivan, who later became Loesser's wife), a waitress he has noticed in a San Francisco restaurant. To increase his chances of success, he includes a photograph of his handsome young foreman, Joey (Art Lund), and she hurried there to meet him. Even though he has deceived her, she still marries Tony - but tar-

ries with Joey. When she discovers that she is pregnant with Joey's child she is determined to leave, but Tony forgives her and adopts the child as his own. With spoken dialogue at a minimum, *The Most Happy Fella* is a virtually sung-through show, and Loesser's score has moments of high emotion in songs such as 'Somebody Somewhere', My Heart Is Full Of You', and 'Joey, Joey'. Rosabella's friend Cleo (Susan Johnson), who follows her out from San Francisco, becomes fairly friendly herself with one of the ranch hands, Herman (Shorty Long), and leads the company in a hymn to Dallas, the rousing 'Big D'. The show's big hit song was 'Standing On The Corner', which became popular in the USA for Dean Martin, and the Four Lads who repeated their success in the UK, in competition with the King Brothers. Another of the show's lighter numbers, 'Happy To Make Your Acquaintance', also entered the UK chart in a version by Sammy Davis Jnr. and Carmen McRae. The rest of Loesser's highly distinguished score, which contained well over 30 songs in a wide variety of musical styles such as arias and choral pieces, included 'Ooh! My Feet', 'Mama, Mama', 'Warm All Over', 'I Like Everybody', 'Song Of A Summer Night', 'Sposalizio', 'How Beautiful The Days', 'Rosabella', 'The Most Happy Fella' and 'Abbondanza'. *The Most Happy Fella* was not everybody's idea of what a Broadway musical should be, but during a 20-month stay on Broadway, it won the New York Drama Critics Award for best musical, and subsequently ran for 288 performances at the London Coliseum. Lund reprised his role in the West End, during which time he became a favourite of audiences there, and returned with Richard Rogers' *No Strings* in 1963. *The Most Happy Fella* was revived on Broadway in 1979, and presented by the New York City Opera in 1991, with Giorgio Tozzi in the lead. In the following year the show was back on Broadway again, via the Goodspeed Opera House and Los Angeles, this time with just a two-piano orchestration, which Loesser himself had commissioned some years previously. Although critically acclaimed, the production ran for only 229 performances and lost most of its $1.4 million investment. It was nominated for four Tony Awards, but won just one - Scott Waara for best featured actor - being pipped at the post for 'best revival' by *Guys And Dolls*, which is, of course, another Frank Loesser show. Unusually, the Original Cast album was recorded in 'real time' - in two long takes - just as the show was performed in the theatre. Even with part-retakes, the recording took only one day to complete, in comparison with the 1956 three-album set which needed a week of session time. In 1993, a concert performance of *The Most Happy Fella* became 'the first of its kind to be broadcast on BBC radio in England'.

MUDDY WATERS

b. McKinley Morganfield, 4 April 1915, Rolling Fork, Mississippi, USA, d. 30 April 1983, Chicago, Illinois, USA. One of the dominant figures of post-war blues, Muddy Waters was raised in the rural Mississippi town of Clarksdale, in whose juke-joints he came into contact with the legendary Son House. Having already mastered the rudiments of the guitar, Waters began performing and this early, country blues period was later documented by Alan Lomax. Touring the south making field recordings for the Library Of Congress, this renowned archivist taped Waters on three occasions between 1941-42. The following year Waters moved to Chicago where he befriended Big Bill Broonzy, whose influence and help proved vital to the younger performer. Waters soon began using amplified, electric instruments and by 1948 had signed a recording contract with the newly founded Aristocrat label, the name of which was later changed to Chess Records. Waters' second release, 'I Feel Like Goin' Home'/'I Can't Be Satisfied', was a minor R&B hit and its understated accompaniment from bassist Big Crawford set a pattern for several further singles, including 'Rollin' And Tumblin'', 'Rollin' Stone' and 'Walking Blues'. By 1951 the guitarist was using a full backing band and among the musicians who passed through its ranks were Otis Spann (piano), Jimmy Rogers (guitar), Little Walter, Walter 'Shakey' Horton and James Cotton (all harmonica). This pool of talent ensured that the Muddy Waters Band was Chicago's most influential unit and a score of seminal recordings, including 'Hoochie Coochie Man', 'I've Got My Mojo Working', 'Mannish Boy', 'You Need Love' and 'I'm Ready', established the leader's abrasive guitar style and impassioned singing. Waters' international stature was secured in 1958 when he toured Britain at the behest of jazz trombonist Chris Barber. Although criticized in some quarters for his use of amplification, Waters' effect on a new generation of white enthusiasts was incalculable. Cyril Davies and Alexis Korner abandoned skiffle in his wake and their subsequent combo, Blues Incorporated, was the catalyst for the Rolling Stones, the Graham Bond Organisation, Long John Baldry and indeed British R&B itself. Paradoxically, while such groups enjoyed commercial success, Waters struggled against indifference. Deemed 'old-fashioned' in the wake of soul music, he was obliged to update his sound and repertoire, resulting in such misjudged releases as *Electric Mud*, which featured a reading of the Rolling Stones' 'Let's Spend The Night Together', the ultimate artistic *volte-face*. The artist did complete a more sympathetic project in *Fathers And Sons* on which he was joined by Paul Butterfield and Mike Bloomfield, but his work during the 60s was generally disappointing. *The London Sessions* kept Waters in the public eye, as did his appearance in the Band's *The Last Waltz*, but it was an inspired series of collaborations with guitarist Johnny Winter that signalled a dramatic rebirth. This pupil produced and arranged four excellent albums that recaptured the fire and purpose of Muddy's early releases and bestowed a sense of dignity to this musical giant's legacy. Waters died of heart failure in 1983, his status as one of the world's most influential musicians secured.

● ALBUMS: *Muddy Waters Sings Big Bill Broonzy* (Chess 1960)★★★, *Muddy Waters At Newport, 1960* (Chess 1963)★★★★, *Muddy Waters, Folk Singer* (Chess 1964)★★★★, *Muddy, Brass And The Blues* (Chess 1965)★★, *Down On Stovall's Plantation* (Testament 1966)★★★, *Blues From Big Bill's Copacabana* (Chess 1968)★★★, *Electric Mud* (Cadet 1968)★★, *Fathers And Sons* (Chess 1969)★★★, *After The Rain* (Cadet 1969)★★, *Sail On* (Chess 1969)★★★, *The London Sessions* (Chess 1971)★★★, *Live At Mister Kelly's* (1971)★★★, *Experiment In Blues* (1972)★★★, *Can't Get No Grindin'* (Chess 1973)★★★, *Mud In Your Ear* (Musicor 1973)★★★, *London Revisited* (Chess 1974)★★, *The Muddy Waters Woodstock Album* (Chess 1975)★★, *Unk In Funk* (Chess 1977)★★, *Hard Again* (Blue Sky 1977)★★★, *I'm Ready* (Blue Sky 1978)★★★, *Muddy Mississippi Waters Live* (Blue Sky 1979)★★★, *King Bee* (Blue Sky 1981)★★★,

Muddy Waters In Concert 1958 (1982)★★★, *Paris 1972* (Pablo 1997)★★★.

● COMPILATIONS: *The Best Of Muddy Waters* (Chess 1957)★★★★★, *The Real Folk Blues Of Muddy Waters* (Chess 1966)★★★★, *More Real Folk Blues* (Chess 1967)★★★★, *Vintage Mud* (Sunnyland 1970)★★★, *They Call Me Muddy Waters* (Chess 1970)★★★, *McKinley Morganfield* aka *Muddy Waters* (Chess 1971)★★★★, *Back In The Early Days* (Red Lightnin' 1977)★★★, *Chess Masters* 3 volumes (Chess 1981-83)★★★★, *Rare And Unissued* (Chess 1982)★★★, *Rolling Stone* (Chess 1982)★★★, *Trouble No More (Singles, 1955-1959)* (Chess/MCA 1989)★★★, *Muddy Waters* 6-LP box set (Chess 1989)★★★★★, *The Chess Box 1947-67* 9-CD box set (Charly 1990)★★★★★, *Funky Butt* recorded early 70s (1993)★★★, *Gold Collection* (1993)★★★★, *The King Of Chicago Blues* (Charly 1995)★★★★.

● VIDEOS: *Messin' With The Blues* (BMG 1991), *Live* (BMG 1993).

● FURTHER READING: *The Complete Muddy Waters Discography*, Phil Wight and Fred Rothwell. *Muddy Waters Biographie*, Francis Hofstein. *Muddy Waters: Mojo Man*, Sandra B. Tooze.

MUDLARKS

Soprano Mary Mudd, baritone Fred Mudd and tenor Jeff Mudd were the Mudlarks: a clean-cut family pop trio from Bedford, Bedfordshire, England. They started singing in public as the Mudd Trio in 1951 when they were just 12, 14 and 16 years old. Discovered by disc jockey David Jacobs and produced on Columbia Records by Norrie Paramor, they had a hit in 1958 with their second single, 'Lollipop', a cover version of the Chordettes' US hit. Their follow-up, 'Book Of Love', originally by the Monotones, also made the UK Top 10. They were often seen on the pioneering UK television series *6.5 Special*, and won the *New Musical Express* poll award as Top British Vocal Group for both 1958 and 1959. Jeff was called up by the army in early 1959 and David Lane replaced him until his return two years later. One of the few UK pop groups in the 50s, they recorded several more cover versions of US hits without further chart success.

MULLIGAN, GERRY

b. 6 April 1927, New York City, New York, USA, d. 19 January 1996, Darien, Connecticut, USA. Raised in Philadelphia, Mulligan started out on piano before concentrating on arranging. He also took up the saxophone, first the alto and a few years later the baritone. Among the name bands that used his arrangements were those led by Gene Krupa and Claude Thornhill and he occasionally played in their reed sections. While writing for Thornhill he met and began a musical association with fellow-arranger Gil Evans. In New York in 1948 Mulligan joined Evans and Miles Davis, for whom he wrote and played, by now almost exclusively on baritone. In the early 50s Mulligan led his own groups but continued to arrange on a freelance basis. In this capacity his work was performed by Stan Kenton (these charts also being performed in the UK by Vic Lewis). In 1952 Mulligan began a musical association that not only attracted critical acclaim but also brought him widespread popularity with audiences. This came about through the formation with Chet Baker of a quartet that was unusual for the absence of a piano. When Baker quit in 1953, Mulligan subsequently led other quartets, notably with Bob Brookmeyer in the mid-50s. Although the quartet format dominated Mulligan's work during this part of his career he occasionally formed larger groups and early in the 60s formed his Concert Jazz Band. This band was periodically revived during the decade and beyond. He interspersed this with periods of leading groups of various sizes, working and recording with other leaders, including Dave Brubeck, in frequently rewarding partnerships with musicians such as Paul Desmond, Stan Getz, Johnny Hodges, Zoot Sims and Thelonious Monk, and writing arrangements on a freelance basis. In the early 70s Mulligan led big bands, some of which used the name Age Of Steam, and small groups for worldwide concert tours, recording sessions and radio and television appearances. The 80s and early 90s saw him following a similar pattern, sometimes expanding the size of the big band, sometimes content to work in the intimate setting of a quartet or quintet. As an arranger, Mulligan was among the first to attempt to adapt the language of bop for big band and achieved a measure of success with both Krupa and Thornhill. For all the variety of his later work, in many ways his music, as writer and performer, retains the colours and effects of his 50s quartets. In these groups Mulligan explored the possibilities of scoring and improvising jazz in a low-key, seemingly subdued manner. In fact, he thoroughly exploited the possibilities of creating interesting and complex lines which always retained a rich, melodic approach. His classic compositions from the 50s, including 'Night At The Turntable', 'Walkin' Shoes', 'Venus De Milo', 'Soft Shoe' and 'Jeru', and his superb arrangements for 'Bernie's Tune', 'Godchild' and others helped to establish the sound and style of the so-called 'cool school'. The intimate styling favoured in such settings was retained in his big-band work and his concert band recordings from the 60s retained interest for the manner in which they contrasted with most other big-band writing of the same and other periods. As a player, the lightness of touch Mulligan used in his writing was uniquely brought to the baritone saxophone, an instrument which in other, not always lesser, hands sometimes overpowers the fragility of some areas of jazz. It is hard to see in Mulligan's work, whether as writer or performer, a clearly discernible influence. Similarly, despite the enormous popularity he enjoyed over more than five decades, few, if any, writers or players seem to have adopted him as a role model. At the least, this must be something to regret and maybe in time his contribution to jazz, especially in the pioneering decade of the 50s will be seen as 'great'.

● ALBUMS: with Miles Davis *Birth Of The Cool* (Capitol 1951)★★★★★, *Gerry Mulligan* 10-inch album (Prestige 1951)★★★★, *Mulligan Plays Mulligan* (Prestige 1951)★★★★, *Jazz Superstars* (1952)★★★, *The Gerry Mulligan Quartet With Chet Baker* (Pacific 1952-53)★★★★, with Lee Konitz *Konitz Meets Mulligan* 10-inch album (Pacific Jazz 1953)★★★, *Gerry Mulligan And His Ten-tette* 10-inch album (Capitol 1953)★★★, *The Fabulous Gerry Mulligan Quartet: Paris Concert 1954* (Vogue 1954)★★★★, *Gerry Mulligan And His Quartet, Featuring Guests Zoot Sims And Bob Brookmeyer: California Concerts* (World Pacific 1954)★★★, *California Concerts Vols 1 & 2* (Pacific Jazz 1955)★★★, *Presenting The Gerry Mulligan Sextet* (EmArcy 1955)★★★★, *Gerry Mulligan Live In Stockholm* (1955)★★★, *The Original Gerry Mulligan Quartet* (Pacific Jazz 1955)★★★★, *Mainstream Of Jazz* (EmArcy 1955)★★★, *The Vibes Are On* (Chazzer 1955)★★★, *Paris Concert* (Pacific Jazz 1956)★★★★, *Recorded Live In Boston At Storyville* (Pacific Jazz 1956)★★★, *Lee Konitz With The Gerry Mulligan Quartet* (Pacific Jazz 1956)★★★★, with Paul Desmond *Gerry Mulligan Quartet/Paul Desmond Quintet* (Fantasy 1956)★★★★, *Gerry Mulligan, The Arranger* (Columbia 1957)★★★, *Quartet Live In Stockholm* (Moon 1957)★★★, *The Mulligan Songbook* (World Pacific 1957)★★★, *Blues In Time* (Verve 1957)★★★, with Thelonious Monk *Mulligan Meets Monk* (Riverside 1957)★★★★, with Monk *Alternate Takes* (1957)★★★, *Gerry Mulligan With Vinnie Burke's String Jazz Quartet* (Pacific Jazz 1957)★★★, *At Storyville* (Pacific Jazz 1957)★★★★, with Chet Baker *Reunion With Baker* (Pacific Jazz 1957)★★★, *Gerry Mulligan Quartet At Newport* (1958)★★★★, *I Want To Live* (United Artists 1958)★★★, with Paul Desmond *The Gerry Mulligan-Paul Desmond Quartet* (Verve 1958)★★★★, with Annie Ross *Annie Ross Sings A Song With Mulligan!* (World Pacific 1958)★★★, with Stan Getz *Getz Meets Gerry Mulligan In Hi-Fi* (Verve 1958)★★★★, *What Is There To Say?* (Columbia 1959)★★★★★, with Ben Webster *Gerry Mulligan Meets Ben Webster* (Verve 1959)★★★★★, *A Profile Of Gerry Mulligan* (Mercury 1959)★★★, *The Subterraneans: Original Soundtrack* (MGM 1959)★★★, *Gerry Mulligan And The Concert Band On Tour* (1960)★★★, *New York-December 1960* (Jazz Anthology 1960)★★★, *Gerry Mulligan And The Concert Jazz Band* (Verve 1960)★★★, *Nightwatch* (United Artists 1960)★★★, *Mulligan* Columbia 1960)★★★, with Johnny Hodges *Gerry Mulligan Meets Johnny Hodges* (Verve 1960)★★★, *Gerry Mulligan Presents A Concert In Jazz* (Verve 1961)★★★, *Gerry Mulligan And The Concert Jazz Band Live At The Village Vanguard* (Verve 1961)★★★★, with Judy Holliday *Holliday With Mulligan* (DRG 1961)★★★, *The Gerry Mulligan Quartet* (Verve 1962)★★★, *Jeru* (Columbia 1962)★★★★, *Gerry Mulligan And The Concert Jazz Band Presents A Concert In Jazz* (Verve 1962)★★★, with Paul Desmond *Two Of A Kind* (RCA Victor 1962)★★★★★, *Gerry Mulligan And The Concert Jazz Band On Tour With Guest Soloist Zoot Sims* (Verve 1962)★★★, *Blues In Time* (Verve 1962)★★★, *Historically Speaking* (Prestige 1963)★★★, *Timeless* (Pacific Jazz 1963)★★★, *Gerry Mulligan '63-The Concert Jazz Band* (Verve 1963)★★★, *Spring Is Sprung* (Philips 1963)★★★, *Night Lights* (Philips 1963)★★★, *The Essential Gerry Mulligan* (Verve 1964)★★★, *Butterfly With Hiccups* (Limelight 1964)★★★, *If You Can't Beat 'Em, Join Em'* (Limelight 1965)★★★, with Kai Winding and Red Rodney *Broadway* (Status 1965)★★★, *The Gerry Mulligan Quintet* (1965)★★★, *Feelin' Good* (Limelight 1965)★★★, *Gerry Mulligan Meets Zoot Sims* (1966)★★★, *Gerry's Time* (Verve 1966)★★★, *Something Borrowed Something Blue* (Limelight 1966)★★★, *Concert Days* (Sunset 1966)★★★, *Gerry Mulligan With The Dave Brubeck Quartet* (1968)★★★, *Live In New Orleans* (1968)★★★, *The Age Of Steam* (A&M 1971)★★★★, *The Shadow Of Your Smile* (Moon 1971)★★★★, *Summit* (1974)★★★, *Astor Piazzolla Summit Tango Nuevo* (Atlantic 1974)★★★, *Carnegie Hall Concert* (CTI 1974)★★★, *Gerry Mulligan Meets Enrico Intra* (Pausa 1975)★★★, *Idle Gossip* (Chiaroscuro 1976)★★★, *Lionel Hampton Presents Gerry Mulligan* (1977)★★★, *Mulligan* (LRC 1977)★★★, with Benny Carter *Benny Carter/Gerry Mulligan* (LRC 1977)★★★, with Judy Holliday *Holliday*

With Mulligan 1961 recording (DRG 1980)★★★, *Walk On The Water* (DRG 1980)★★★, *LA Menace* film soundtrack (DRG 1982)★★★, *Little Big Horn* (GRP 1983)★★★, with Barry Manilow *2 am Paradise Cafe* (Arista 1984)★★★, with Scott Hamilton *Soft Lights & Sweet Music* (Concord 1986)★★★, *Symphonic Dream* (Sion 1988)★★★, *Lonesome Boulevard* (A&M 1990)★★★, *Re-Birth Of The Cool* (GRP 1992)★★★, *Dream A Little Dream* (Telarc 1995)★★★, *Dragonfly* (Telarc 1995)★★★.

● COMPILATIONS: *Gerry Mulligan And Chet Baker* 1951-65 recordings (GNP Crescendo 1988)★★★★, *The Best Of The Gerry Mulligan Quartet With Chet Baker* 1952-57 recordings (Pacific Jazz 1991)★★★★, *The Complete Pacific Jazz Recordings Of The Gerry Mulligan Quartet With Chet Baker* 4-CD box set (Pacific Jazz 1996)★★★★.

● FURTHER READING: *Gerry Mulligan's Ark*, Raymond Horricks. *Listen: Gerry Mulligan: An Aural Narrative In Jazz*, Jerome Klinkowitz.

● FILMS: *The Subterraneans* (1959), *The Fortune Cookie* (1966).

MURRAY, RUBY

b. 29 March 1935, Belfast, Northern Ireland, d. 17 December 1996. One of the most popular singers in the UK during the 50s, Murray toured Ulster as a child singer in various variety shows, and, after being spotted by producer Richard Afton, made her television debut at the age of 12. Stringent Irish laws regarding child performers held her back for two years, and she returned to school in Belfast until she was 14. In 1954 she travelled to London in comedian Tommy Morgan's touring revue, *Mrs. Mulligan's Hotel*, and was again seen by Afton, at the famous Metropolitan Theatre, Edgware Road. He offered her a position as resident singer on BBC Television's *Quite Contrary*, replacing Joan Regan who was about to leave. Signed to UK Columbia by recording manager and musical director Ray Martin, Murray's first release, 'Heartbeat', made the UK Top 5 in 1954, and was followed by 'Softly, Softly'. The latter reached number 1 in 1955, and became an ideal theme song, reflecting her shy image. In the early part of 1955 Murray had five singles in the Top 20 at the same time, an extraordinary record that lasted until the emergence of Madonna in the 80s. Murray's hits included 'Happy Days And Lonely Nights', 'Let Me Go Lover', 'If Anyone Finds This, I Love You' (with Anne Warren), 'Evermore', 'I'll Come When You Call', 'Real Love', 'Goodbye Jimmy, Goodbye' and 'You Are My First Love'. She sang the last number over the opening titles of the film musical *It's Great To Be Young*. Murray's own film appearances included the comedy, *A Touch Of The Sun*, with Frankie Howerd and Dennis Price. During a hectic period in the mid-50s, she had her own television show, starred at the London Palladium in *Painting The Town* with Norman Wisdom, appeared in a Royal Command Performance, and toured the USA, Malta and North Africa. In 1957, while appearing in a summer season at Blackpool, she met Bernie Burgess, a member of the vocal group the Jones Boys. They married in secret 10 days later. Burgess became her personal manager and, during the early 60s, they toured as a double act. In 1970 Murray had some success with 'Change Your Mind', and released an album with the same title, which included contemporary songs such as 'Raindrops Keep Falling On My Head', and revamped some of her hits. In

1989 *Ruby Murray's EMI Years* included other songs regularly featured in her act. In the 90s, based in Torquay, Devon, with her second husband, impresario Ray Lamar, she still performed in cabaret and in nostalgia shows with other stars of the 50s right up to her death in 1996.

● ALBUMS: *When Irish Eyes Are Smiling* (Columbia 1955)★★★, *Endearing Young Charms* (Columbia 1958)★★★, *Ruby* (Columbia 1960)★★★, *Ruby Murray Successes* (1962)★★★, *Irish-And Proud Of It* (1962)★★★, with various artists *St. Patrick's Day* (1964)★★★, *Your Favourite Colleen* (1965)★★★, *The Spinning Wheel* (1967)★★★, *This Is Ireland* (1968)★★★, *Change Your Mind* (1970)★★★.

● COMPILATIONS: *Best Of Ruby Murray* (EMI 1975)★★★, *Very Best Of Ruby Murray* (MFP 1984)★★★, *Ruby Murray's EMI Years* (EMI 1989)★★★.

MUSIC MAN, THE

This musical came to the Majestic Theatre in New York on 19 December 1957 after experiencing a good many difficulties out of town. With book, music and lyrics by Meredith Willson, the show had undergone several rewrites but the author's persistence paid off, and on the opening night the audience was caught up in the revivalist enthusiasm of the show's characters. The story concerns Harold Hill, an itinerant con man who persuades the citizens of River City, Iowa, that what they need is a boys' band. He offers to teach them to play - and even to supply the instruments. Naturally, not even a penny whistle materializes. *The Music Man* was filled with engaging old-fashioned charm with songs ranging from the soulful 'Goodnight, My Someone' and 'Till There Was You' to the rousing 'Seventy-Six Trombones', by way of 'Marian The Librarian', 'Shipoopi', 'My White Knight', 'The Sadder-But-Wiser Girl', 'Pick-A-Little, Talk-A-Little', 'Gary, Indiana', 'Wells Fargo Wagon', 'Sincere' ('How can there be any sin in sincere?/Where is the good in goodbye'), 'Piano Lesson' and 'Lida Rose'/'Will I Ever Tell You'. In casting film actor Robert Preston, who had never before danced or sung, in the central role of Harold Hill, the producers took a big chance, as many of Willson's songs were far more complex than they appeared on the surface. As it turned out, it was inspired casting, with Preston ably charming his way through a minefield of counter-melodies, rhythmic dialogue and strutting dance routines to earn rapturous applause and critical praise. He had a *tour de force* with 'Trouble', a grim warning regarding the moral danger of introducing a pool table into the community ('That game with the fifteen numbered balls is the Devil's tool'). Co-starring with Preston was Barbara Cook as Marion Paroo; other cast members included David Burns, Iggie Wolfington, Helen Raymond, Pert Kelton, and The Buffalo Bills. The show enjoyed success, and won Tony Awards for best musical, actor (Preston), featured actress (Cook), featured actor (Burns) and musical director (Herbert Green). Several companies toured the USA, and the show was also staged in Europe; the 1961 London production, which ran for 395 performances, starred Hollywood heart-throb Van Johnson. Revivals were presented on Broadway in 1965, 1980 and 1993. A film version was released in 1962 with Shirley Jones as Marian and, thankfully, Robert Preston, thus allowing millions to appreciate the exuberance of his magnificent performance as Professor Harold Hill.

MUSSOLINI, ROMANO

b. Full Mussolini, 26 September 1927, Carpena, Forli, Italy. The son of the fascist dictator Benito Mussolini, who was executed by partisans at the end of World War II, he played piano under a pseudonym in his early years. By the early 50s he was becoming known outside Italy thanks to festival appearances and his work as an accompanist to visiting jazzmen. Among the visitors were Lars Gullin and Chet Baker (reportedly, Baker, worried over how to handle his first meeting with Mussolini, stuck out his hand and blurted out, 'Sorry to hear about your Dad!'). Mussolini regularly led his own small groups, usually playing in a boppish mode; he also developed a technically accomplished solo style.
● ALBUMS: *Topsy* (RCA 1957)★★★.

MY FAIR LADY (STAGE MUSICAL)

One of the most successful shows in the history of the American musical theatre, *My Fair Lady* opened to rave reviews at the Mark Hellinger Theatre in New York on 15 March 1956. The book, by Alan Jay Lerner, was based on George Bernard Shaw's play *Pygmalion*, and told of the attempts by Professor Henry Higgins (Rex Harrison) to transform a Cockney flower girl, Eliza Doolittle (Julie Andrews), into a society lady simply by teaching her to speak correctly. In the course of the story Higgins and Eliza fall in love and all ends happily, if a little differently from the way Shaw ended his play. Alan J. Lerner and Frederick Loewe's score was full of marvellous songs, including 'Wouldn't It Be Loverly?', 'I Could Have Danced All Night', 'On The Street Where You Live', 'Get Me To The Church On Time', 'With A Little Bit Of Luck', 'Show Me', 'I'm An Ordinary Man', 'Without You', 'Just You Wait', 'A Hymn To Him', 'Why Can't The English?' 'Ascot Gavotte' and 'I've Grown Accustomed To Her Face'. Harrison and Andrews were both superb. Their delight and joy when they realize that Eliza has finally 'got it', celebrating their triumph with 'The Rain In Spain', remains a memorable and endearing moment. A strong supporting cast included Stanley Holloway (Alfred P. Doolittle, Eliza's father), Robert Coote (Colonel Pickering), Michael King (Freddy Eynsford-Hill) and Cathleen Nesbitt (Mrs. Higgins). *My Fair Lady* ran on Broadway for six-and-a-half years, a total of 2,717 performances, and won Tony Awards for best musical, actor (Harrison), director (Moss Hart), musical director (Franz Allers), and for Oliver Smith (scenic design) and Cecil Beaton (costumes), both of whom made outstanding contributions to the lavish and spectacular production. Numerous road companies toured the show across the USA and it was subsequently presented in many other countries around the world. Four of the principals, Harrison, Andrews, Holloway and Coote, recreated their roles for the London production, which stayed at the Drury Lane Theatre Royal for five and a half years. The Broadway cast album spent over 300 weeks in the US chart, many of them at number 1. The 1981 US revival with the 73-year-old Harrison and Catherine Nesbitt, who by then was 92, toured the USA before spending some time in New York. By all accounts it attempted to stay true to the original version, which is more than can be said for some later efforts. A 1991 UK provincial production, with a cast headed by Edward Fox, was described by its director Simon Callow, as 'a politically correct' version, and the 1993 Broadway revival, directed by Howard Davies, with Richard Chamberlain as Higgins and Stanley Holloway's son, Julian, as Doolittle, was 'stripped almost entirely of its romanticism and honed to a provocative post-modern edge', according to the *Variety* theatre critic. He went on: 'The famous "Ascot Gavotte" scene is recreated as a living Magritte canvas, the actors in colourful finery descending from the flies to hover above the action against a field of brilliant blue'. The 1964 film version was reasonably faithful to the original stage show though, and starred Harrison, Holloway, and - somewhat controversially - Audrey Hepburn as Eliza. In recent times, the American musical historian David Ewen suggested that one way or another *My Fair Lady* has generated approximately $800 million.

MY FAIR LADY · ORIGINAL BROADWAY CAST ★★★★★

First released in 1956, by the early 90s this superb album of what some still consider to be the most perfect stage musical ever, had spent a record-breaking 292 weeks in the US Top 40 - 15 of them at number 1. It also stayed in the upper reaches of the UK chart for 129 weeks, peaking at number 2. The album was recorded in mono, and Alan Jay Lerner and Frederick Loewe's wonderful score, and the cast headed by Rex Harrison, Julie Andrews and Stanley Holloway, were not nearly as effective in the subsequent stereo version. Just 10 years after its initial release sales were estimated to be well over six million, and the album was inducted into the NARAS Hall of Fame in 1977.
● TRACKS: *Overture; Why Can't The English; Wouldn't It Be Loverly?; With A Little Bit Of Luck; I'm An Ordinary Man; Just You Wait; The Rain In Spain; I Could Have Danced All Night; Ascot Gavotte; On The Street Where You Live; You Did It; Show Me; Get Me To The Church On Time; Hymn To Him; Without You; I've Grown Accustomed To Her Face.*

NEAGLE, ANNA

b. Marjorie Robertson, 20 October 1904, Forest Gate, London, England, d. 3 June 1986, Surrey, England. One of the most beloved and durable artists in the history of British showbusiness, Neagle was an actress, dancer and singer in West End musicals and British films, with a career spanning more than 60 years. She took dancing lessons as a child, and appeared in the chorus of *Charlot's Revue* and a similar production, *Tricks*, in 1925. In the late 20s she undertook more chorus work in *Rose Marie*, *The Charlot Show Of 1926*, *The*

Desert Song and two London Pavilion revues as one of 'Mr Cochran's Young Ladies'. Up until then she had been primarily a dancer, but she developed further in 1931 when she took the ingenue lead opposite Jack Buchanan in the hit musical comedy *Stand Up And Sing*, duetting with him on the lovely 'There's Always Tomorrow'. Herbert Wilcox produced and directed her first film musical, *Goodnight Vienna*, in 1932, and most of her subsequent pictures, and the two were married in 1943. As well as making a number of acclaimed dramatic films during the 30s, Anna Neagle continued to appear in screen musicals such as *The Little Damozel*, *Bitter Sweet*, *The Queen's Affair*, *Limelight* and *London Melody* (1939). From 1940-41 she and Wilcox were in America to make films such as *Irene* (in which she sang and danced to the delightful 'Alice Blue Gown'), *No, No, Nanette* and *Sunny*. They returned to England to make a series of light and frothy romantic comedies, with the occasional musical number, which included *Spring In Park Lane*, *The Courtneys Of Curzon Street* and *Maytime In Mayfair* (1949). Anna Neagle's leading man was Michael Wilding, and this magical partnership ensured that the films were among the British cinema's top box office attractions of the time. In the 50s Anna Neagle returned to the stage for *The Glorious Days* (1953), co-starred with Errol Flynn (of all people) in the film version of that show, *Lilacs In The Spring*; and also appeared in the screen adaptation of *King's Rhapsody*. She then kicked up her heels with popular singer Frankie Vaughan in *The Lady Is A Square* (1958). That was her last appearance on screen, although she did produce three more of Vaughan's films, *These Dangerous Years*, *Wonderful Things!* and *Heart Of A Man*. In the early 60s Wilcox went bankrupt when his film company and several of the couple's other business ventures failed. Part of their salvation came in the form of David Heneker's smash hit musical *Charlie Girl* (1965). Neagle stayed with the show - apart from the occasional holiday - for the duration of its run of over 2,000 performances and subsequent tours. On the day it was announced that she was to be made a Dame of the British Empire, the cast of *Charlie Girl* surprised her by singing 'There Is Nothing Like A Dame' at the end of the evening's performance. In 1973 the new Broadway production of *No, No, Nanette* arrived in London, and Anna Neagle played the role that had been taken by Ruby Keeler in New York. Four years later Herbert Wilcox died, but Anna Neagle continued to work. In 1977 she was back in the West End with the musical *Maggie*; in 1978 she toured as Henry Higgins' mother in a revival of *My Fair Lady*, and in 1982 she played in the pantomime *Cinderella* at the Richmond Theatre. It was as the Fairy Godmother in *Cinderella* that she made her final stage bow at the London Palladium at Christmas 1986. A few weeks after it closed she went into a Surrey nursing home to rest, and died there in June.

● FURTHER READING: *It's Been Fun*, Anna Neagle. *There's Always Tomorrow*, Anna Neagle.

NEIGHBORS, PAUL

b. 1918, USA, d. 26 August 1983, Houston, Texas, USA. Formed in Los Angeles, California, USA, in 1948, Paul Neighbors And His Orchestra took their first engagement at the Mapes Hotel in Reno, Nevada, shortly afterwards. From there the band, fronted by Neighbors' own vocals and occasionally those of Ralph Anthony, toured many west coast

locations. Their regular engagements included frequent visits to the Claremont in Berkeley. In the early 50s the group relocated to Houston, Texas, from where they toured the Midwest extensively, taking in such renowned nightspots as the Peabody, the Chase, Milwaukee's Schroeder Hotel and the Dallas Shamrock Hilton. There were also excursions to the Roseland Ballroom and Pennsylvania Hotel in New York, while the group appeared regularly on a radio broadcast from New Orleans sponsored by Ford Motors. However, the group's first home remained the Shamrock, where they returned between tours for regular six-month engagements. A recording contract with Capitol Records made songs such as 'Love Thy Neighbor', their theme tune, available to a wider public, but their last contract at the Shamrock ended in 1956. Neighbors continued to play low-key engagements around Texas until his death in 1983.

NELSON, GENE

b. Leander Berg, 24 March 1920, Seattle, Washington, USA, d. 16 September 1996, Woodland Hills, California, USA. An actor, director and athletic dancer in the Gene Kelly style who was in several popular musicals of the 50s. Nelson grew up in Los Angeles and attended the renowned Fanchon and Marco dancing school there. After graduating from high school when he was 18, he took up ice-skating and joined Sonja Henie's touring company and appeared in two of her films, *Second Fiddle* and *Everything Happens At Night*. After enlisting in the US Signals Corps early in World War II, he became a member of the cast of Irving Berlin's celebrated wartime musical *This Is The Army*, which opened on Broadway in 1942 and was then filmed before touring the UK and US military bases throughout the world. Following his discharge, Nelson went to Hollywood in 1947 and made the musical, *I Wonder Who's Kissing Her Now*, with June Haver. Ironically, it was while he was starring in the hit Broadway revue *Lend An Ear* (1949), that Nelson was noticed by a representative of Warner Brothers Pictures. After playing a minor role in *The Daughter Of Rosie O'Grady*, he was signed to a long-term contract and given the third-lead to Doris Day and Gordon MacRae in *Tea For Two* (1950). From then on, he appeared in a string of musicals for the studio, including *The West Point Story*, *Lullaby Of Broadway* (his first starring role, opposite Doris Day), *Painting The Clouds With Sunshine*, *She's Working Her Way Through College*, *She's Back On Broadway*, *Three Sailors And A Girl*, *So This Is Paris*, and *Oklahoma!* (1955). In the latter film he had the best role of his career - and two great numbers, 'Kansas City' and 'All Er Nothin'' (with Gloria Grahame as Ado Annie). In the late 50s Nelson appeared on television until he suffered a horse-riding accident that put an end to his dancing - at least for a while. He turned to directing, and in the 60s worked on some melodramas, and two musical films starring Elvis Presley, *Kissin' Cousins* (which he also co-wrote) and *Harum Scarum*. He also directed *Your Cheatin' Heart*, a film biography of country singer Hank Williams. In 1971 he was back on Broadway with other veteran entertainers such as Yvonne De Carlo and Alexis Smith in Stephen Sondheim's *Follies*. Nelson played Buddy Plummer and performed one of the show's outstanding numbers, the rapid-fire 'Buddy's Blues'. He continued to direct in the 70s and 80s, mostly for television, and worked on the top-rated series *Washington*

Behind Closed Doors. In 1993 his projects included staging a US provincial production of Richard Harris's comedy *Stepping Out*.

● FILMS: *I Wonder Who's Kissing Her Now* (1947), *Apartment For Peggy* (1948), *Tea For Two* (1950), *The West Point Story* (1950), *The Daughter Of Rosie O'Grady* (1950), *Painting The Clouds With Sunshine* (1951), *Lullaby Of Broadway* (1951), *She's Back On Broadway* (1952), *She's Working Her Way Through College* (1952), *Three Sailors And A Girl* (1953), *Crime Wave* (1954), *The Way Out* UK title *Dial 999* (1955), *The Atomic Man* UK title *Timeslip* (1955), *Oklahoma!* (1955), *So This Is Paris* (1955), *20,000 Eyes* (1961), *The Purple Hills* (1961), as director *Hand Of Death* (1962), as director *Hootenanny Hoot* (1963), *Thunder Island* (1963), as director *Your Cheatin' Heart* (1964), as director *Kissin' Cousins* (1964), as director *Harum Scarum* (1965), as director *The Cool Ones* (1967), *S.O.B.* (1981).

NELSON, OZZIE

b. 20 March 1906, Jersey City, New Jersey, USA, d. 3 June 1975. While studying for a career in the legal profession, Nelson ran a dance band as a hobby, but it was so successful that he abandoned law for music. He played many of the east coast's more prestigious venues, including Glen Island Casino and the New Yorker Hotel. Nelson's extremely relaxed singing style proved remarkably popular, as did the work of the band's female singer, Harriet Hilliard (b. 1909, d. 1994). Ozzie and Harriet married in 1935 and their romantic duets, coupled with their real-life romance, gave fans something to coo over. In the early 40s Nelson and the band appeared in a number of films, and he made a great impact with a US radio series, *The Adventures Of Ozzie And Harriet*, which began in 1944. In 1952, the show transferred to television and ran until 1966. Nelson's interests expanded into other areas of showbusiness; he worked on the stage and also produced and directed on television. Also in the cast of the television show, when they were old enough, were Ozzie and Harriet's sons, David and Ricky Nelson. After the show's run finished, Ozzie Nelson continued to work in many different facets of showbusiness.

● COMPILATIONS: *Young America's Favorite* (Aircheck 1986)★★★, *Ozzie Nelson (1940-42)* (Hindsight 1988)★★★, *Ozzie Nelson 1937* (Circle 1988)★★★, *Satan Takes A Holiday 1936-41* (Bandstand 1988)★★★, with Harriet *The Nelson Touch* (ASV 1996)★★★.

● FURTHER READING: *Ozzie*, Ozzie Nelson.

NEW GIRL IN TOWN

Bob Merrill, previously known for writing novelty songs such as 'Sparrow In The Treetop', 'Feet Up (Pat Him On the Po-Po)', 'If I Knew You Were Comin' I'd've Baked A Cake' and '(How Much Is That) Doggie In The Window?', some of which became hits for Guy Mitchell, made his Broadway debut with this show, which opened at the 46th Street Theatre in New York on 14 May 1957. George Abbott's book, which was based on Eugene O'Neill's 1921 play, *Anna Christie*, was set in New York at the turn of the century and told of a prostitute, Anna (Gwen Verdon), who returns to live with her bargee father (Chris Christopherson). He is unaware of her occupation, but is soon informed by his unsavoury ladyfriend, Marthy (Thelma Ritter). Matt Burke (George Wallace), a sailor with whom Anna falls in love,

leaves her when he, too, discovers the truth about her lifestyle, but he eventually returns in the hope that they can enjoy a more conventional life together. The lively score included 'It's Good To Be Alive', 'Sunshine Girl', 'Did You Close Your Eyes?', 'If That Was Love', 'You're My Friend Ain'tcha?', 'Look At 'Er', 'At the Check Apron Ball', 'Roll Yer Socks Up' and 'There Ain't No Flies On Me'. The engaging and reflective 'Flings' ('Are meant to be flung' . . . 'As a girl, you start seethin'/Over guys just finished teethin'/Now if they're alive and breathin'/That's enough!') was given an amusing treatment on record from Carol Burnett and Martha Raye. When she starred in this piece, Gwen Verdon, one of the American musical theatre's favourite gypsies (dancers), was in the middle of a purple patch with shows such as *Can-Can*, *Damn Yankees* and *Redhead* - with *Sweet Charity* and *Chicago* in the future. She shared the 1958 Tony Award for best actress with Thelma Ritter. *New Girl In Town* ran for 431 performances - an encouraging start for Merrill, who followed it in 1959 with *Take Me Along*, another adaptation of an O'Neill play, *Ah, Wilderness*.

NEWMAN, LIONEL

b. 4 January 1916, New Haven, Connecticut, USA, d. 3 February 1989, California, USA. A distinguished composer, musical director, conductor and arranger for movies for more than 30 years, Newman was a talented pianist as a child, and while in his teens started as a rehearsal pianist for *Earl Carroll's Vanities*, graduating to the position of musical director. He toured with other shows, played piano for Mae West for a while, and performed the same function at 20th Century-Fox when he joined them in 1943. Earlier in 1938, he had composed the title song (lyric by Arthur Quenzer) for the movie *The Cowboy And The Lady*, which had a score by his elder brother, Alfred Newman. In the late 40s Newman's songs included 'As If I Didn't Have Enough On My Mind' (with Harry James), sung by Dick Haymes in *Do You Love Me?*, as well as 'The Morning Glory Road', 'Ramblin' Around' and 'Sentimental Souvenirs'. He had a smash hit in 1948 with the romantic ballad 'Again' (lyric by Dorcas Cochrane), from the film *Road House*. It was successful at the time for Doris Day, Gordon Jenkins and Vic Damone, among others. Another of his numbers, *Never* (lyric by Eliot Daniel), sung by Dennis Day in *Golden Girl* (1951), was nominated for an Oscar. In his career as a musical director, Newman worked on such films as *Cheaper By The Dozen* (1950), *The Jackpot* (1950), *Mother Didn't Tell Me* (1950), *I'll Get By* (1950), *Dangerous Crossing* (1953), *Love Me Tender* (1956, Elvis Presley's first film), *The Best Things In Life Are Free* (1956), *Mardi Gras* (1958), *Doctor Dolittle* (1967), *The Great White Hope* (1970) and *The Saltzburg Connection* (1972). He supervised all Marilyn Monroe's movies for 20th Century-Fox, such as *Gentlemen Prefer Blondes* (1953), *River Of No Return* (1954) and *There's No Business Like Show Business* (1954). As the studio's general music director, and senior vice-president in 1982, he was a powerful influence on the Fox output. His original music scores included *Don't Bother To Knock* (1952), *The Proud Ones* (1956), *A Kiss Before Dying* (1956), *Compulsion* (1959), *North To Alaska* (1960), *Move Over Darling* (1963), *The Pleasure Seekers* (1964, with Alexander Courage) and *Do Not Disturb* (1965). He was nominated for 11 Academy Awards, and won the Oscar, with Lennie Hayton, in 1969 for his adaptation of Jerry Herman's score for the film version of *Hello, Dolly!*. During the early 80s he conducted the Boston Pops Orchestra in the USA, and performed at London's Royal Albert Hall. He retired in 1985, but was persuaded by MGM to return to the business in 1987. He died two years later.

NORTH, ALEX

b. 4 December 1910, Chester, Pennsylvania, USA, d. 8 September 1991, Pacific Palisades, California, USA. An important composer for films, theatre, television, ballet and classical music, whose career stretched from the late 30s through to the 80s. After studying at Juilliard with the distinguished composer Aaron Copland, as well as at the Moscow Conservatory (1933-35), North composed for the Federal Theatre Project in the late 30s. During those years, through to 1950, he wrote the scores for government documentary and information films, and served in the US Army in World War II. In 1948 he composed the incidental score for Arthur Miller's landmark play *Death Of A Salesman*, on Broadway, and repeated the role for the film version in 1951. For that, and for his innovative jazz-tinged score to *A Streetcar Named Desire* (1951), he gained the first two of his 15 Academy Award nominations. Other early 50s film music included *The 13th Letter*, *Viva Zapata!* (considered an early milestone in his career), *Les Miserables*, the ballet music for Fred Astaire and Leslie Caron in *Daddy Long Legs*, and *Unchained* (1955). The latter featured 'Unchained Melody' (lyric by Hy Zaret), a ballad of yearning that was nominated for an Academy Award, and became popular at the time for Les Baxter (US number 1), Al Hibbler and Jimmy Young (UK number 1), among others, and through the years was constantly remembered and revived. The Righteous Brothers' 1965 smash-hit version accompanied an erotic scene in the popular 1990 movie *Ghost*, and in 1995 the song topped the UK chart once again in a version by Robson Green and Jerome Flynn, two actors from the popular television series *Soldier, Soldier*. North's other 50s scores included *The Man With The Gun* (1955), *I'll Cry Tomorrow* (1955), *The Rose Tattoo* (1955), *The Bad Seed* (1956), *The Rainmaker* (1956), *Four Girls In Town* (1956), *The King And Four Queens* (1956), *The Bachelor Party* (1957), *The Long Hot Summer* (1958), *Stage Struck* (1958), *Hot Spell* (1958), *The Sound And The Fury* (1959) and *The Wonderful Country* (1959).

Early in the 60s North began an association with director John Huston that lasted until Huston's death in 1987. Together they worked on such films as *The Misfits* (1961), *Wise Blood* (1979), *Under The Volcano* (1984), *Prizzi's Honor* (1985) and *The Dead* (1987), Huston's swan-song. North's 60s film work began with the epic *Spartacus* ('magnificent score, staggering battle scenes'), followed, in complete contrast, by *The Children's Hour*. His other scores of the decade included another epic, *Cleopatra*, John Ford's *Cheyenne Autumn*, *The Agony And The Ecstasy*, *Who's Afraid Of Virginia Woolf?*, *The Shoes Of The Fisherman*, *Hard Contract* and *A Dream Of Kings*. In the 70s, as his style of spectacular, dramatic scores went out of fashion, North worked less for the big screen. However, in later years he composed the music for movies such as *Pocket Money*, *Once Upon A Scoundrel*, *Bite The Bullet* and *Somebody Killed Her Husband*. In the 80s, besides his collaborations with Huston, North was still being critically acclaimed for scores such as *Carny*, *Dragonslayer*, *Under The Volcano*, *Good Morning Vietnam*, and his final film, *The*

Penitent (1988). In 1986 he became the first composer to receive an honorary Academy Award 'in recognition of his brilliant artistry in the creation of memorable music for a host of distinguished motion pictures'. He died, five years later, in 1991. As well as films, his occasional television work included the feature documentary *Africa* (1967), music for the mini-series *The Word*, which was nominated for an Emmy, and *Rich Man, Poor Man*, which won two, the tele-feature *Death Of A Salesman* (again), and music for other programmes, such as *Your Show Of Shows*, *77 Sunset Strip*, *Playhouse 90* and *The F.D.R. Story*. Many of his scores were made available on albums, and several individual items such as the title themes from *I'll Cry Tomorrow* and *The Long Hot Summer*, and 'Unchained Melody', of course, endure.

NUDIE

b. Nudie Cohen, 1902, Kiev, Russia, d. May 1984. The surname has also been given as Cohn but he is usually referred to as just 'Nudie'. His father was a bootmaker in the Russian army and as a boy he began to learn the trade of a tailor. Around 1911, because of anti-Jewish purges in Russia, he and an elder brother emigrated to the USA, where they initially settled in Brooklyn. Around 1920, he began travelling around the USA, struggling to make a living. He had a brief and financially unrewarding career as a flyweight boxer, appeared as a Hollywood film extra and did tailoring work in the costume department of Warner Brothers. In New York, he even worked on costumes for striptease acts. In the early 40s, in Los Angeles, he became friendly with country singer Tex Williams, and persuaded Williams that he could make stage costumes for him and his band that would attract attention. Williams was delighted with the result, ordered further costumes and widely advertised their designer. The popularity of his suits quickly spread and soon other West Coast artists, especially singing cowboys such as Gene Autry, Roy Rogers and Rex Allen were wearing brightly coloured, rhinestone-studded Nudie creations. Nudie designed a 'free' suit, whose pattern included wagon wheels and cacti, for Porter Wagoner, then a struggling young hopeful. It was a very shrewd investment on Nudie's part. Wagoner, who continued to wear Nudie suits on the *Grand Ole Opry* for a great many years, became Nudie's best and longest-running advert. The attraction soon passed on to other country singers and during the 40s and 50s, most of Nashville's major stars were dressed by Nudie. His first cowboy designs were mainly elaborately decorated western wear, but for the country stars, he designed the clothes for the individual, as he had done with the wagon wheels for Wagoner. Hawkshaw Hawkins' jacket had a large hawk on the back, Ferlin Husky had husky dogs and Jimmy C. Newman had alligators (after his hit 'Alligator Man'). Hank Williams regularly wore Nudie-designed drape suits and was actually buried in one. Nudie also designed the stage costumes of Bill Anderson and his band, and Hank Snow, another long-time flamboyant dresser, regularly wore his rhinestone-studded creations. It was Nudie who created the $10,000 gold lamé tuxedo worn by Elvis Presley and later the flashy suits worn by the Flying Burrito Brothers, which had marijuana leaves embroidered on them, and stage costumes for the Rolling Stones. However, not all of his creations were so brightly coloured, since it was Nudie who was responsible for Johnny Cash's Man in Black image. Nudie inevitably became a wealthy man and his own suits usually attracted considerable interest, as did his penchant for jewellery, which often saw him wearing $25,000 worth of gold (he was once described as 'a caricature of an American cowboy drawn by an enraged Russian cartoonist'). He was also noted for his famous white Pontiac convertible. The hood had giant Texas longhorn horn ornaments, while the interior contained patterned hand tool leather, with a silver saddle between the rear seats. There were 14 guns mounted in varying positions, which included Colt revolvers that worked as arm rests and door handles, gear lever and direction indicators and three rifles on the rear boot lid. The interior was decorated with hundreds of silver dollars, the front bumper had chrome quarter horses and the tape player could blast out a recording of a cattle stampede, while the horn played Dale Evans singing 'Happy Trails'. It seems that when they were going out together, Nudie's wife, not surprisingly, used to suggest that they took her car. Naturally, the car was at one point stolen, but the police appear to have had little trouble finding it again. Later there were several other Nudie-designed cars, which over the years have had several owners, including Webb Pierce and Hank Williams Jnr. Nudie died from natural causes in May 1984 but his wife continued to operate their store. Nudie, who was once quoted as saying, 'If Tom Mix got out of his grave and saw my clothes, he'd get back in again', was always proud of his achievements but never forgot the early days of struggle. A reminder was the photograph sent to him by famous American strip artist Lili St. Cyr, and autographed with: 'If I ever wear clothes, they'll be yours', which he proudly displayed in his store. For many years, clothes bearing a label that said 'Nudie's Rodeo Tailors, North Hollywood, California', were very much a status symbol to country artists. Nudie also played mandolin and apparently recorded an album featuring himself on that instrument, but recording data is seemingly not readily available. (In 1974, Manual Cuevas, who had started to work for Nudie in the late 50s, left to form his own Manual's Western Wear in North Hollywood, from which he carried on the traditions of dressing film stars and singers, including Dolly Parton, Marty Stuart and Dwight Yoakam, in the styles that he had learned during his years with Nudie.)

NUTMEGS

The Nutmegs comprised lead Leroy Griffin, first tenor James 'Sonny' Griffin, second tenor James Tyson, baritone Billy Emery and bass Leroy McNeil. The group was formed in New Haven, Connecticut, USA, in 1954. The Nutmegs are famed for just two records, 'Story Untold' (number 2 R&B) and the follow-up, 'Ship Of Love' (number 13 R&B), both from 1955. The songs, with their exotic warbling, are a working definition of 'rockaballad', a valuable term of the era that anticipated the rock 'n' roll revolution. Most notable among the lesser songs are 'Whispering Sorrows', 'My Story', and the west coast-sounding 'My Sweet Dream'. Surviving less well in the Nutmegs' canon were the rock 'n' roll jumps, which were mostly routine. After several years of declining fortunes and many personnel changes, the group broke up in 1962. The Nutmegs were one of the cult groups of the east coast collecting scene, and during the early 60s, a cappella practice versions of their songs launched a craze for a cappella doo-wop recordings. The group, without lead Leroy

Griffin (who died years earlier), worked the doo-wop revival circuit on the east coast during the 70s.
● COMPILATIONS: *The Nutmegs Featuring Leroy Griffin* (Relic 1971)★★★, *Story Untold* (Relic 1993)★★★.

O'FLYNN, BRIDGET

b. 1923, Berkely, California, USA. O'Flynn taught herself to play drums as a small child, eventually taking lessons while attending school. Fighting against the automatic resistance towards women in jazz, especially as a drummer, she eventually joined an all-female band, led by Sally Banning. This was in 1939 and she later played in an otherwise all-male band co-led by Sally and George Banning. O'Flynn then formed her own all-male big band, which she led until the USA's entry into World War II. After the war, and by that time based in New York, she played in various clubs, eventually becoming a member of a trio led by Mary Lou Williams that also included June Rotenberg. In the mid-50s O'Flynn became progressively more discouraged with the entrenched attitudes that militated against her as a woman in jazz, and also when racism affected the mixed-race bands with whom she sometimes worked. Early in the following decade, she quit the business. In the early 80s, however, she reportedly told Sally Placksin that she was tempted to return. A fine, supportive drummer with a fine ear for those she is accompanying, O'Flynn always preferred brushes, providing a discreet and subtle rhythmic underpinning to the bands in which she worked.
● COMPILATIONS: included on *Café Society* (Onyx 1948)★★★, included on *Women In Jazz: All-Women Groupos* (Stash various dates).

ODETTA

b. Odetta Holmes Felious Gorden, 31 December 1930, Birmingham, Alabama, USA. A classically trained vocalist, Odetta sang in the chorus of the 1947 Broadway production of *Finian's Rainbow*, before opting for a career in folk music. Successful residencies in San Francisco clubs, the Hungry i and Tin Angel, inspired interest in New York circles although her early releases revealed a still maturing talent. Odetta had been brought up in the blues tradition, but moved increasingly towards folk during the late 50s. Odetta had sung jazz and blues for the RCA and Riverside labels, and, only occasionally, folk for the Tradition label. Her blues was sung in the Bessie Smith tradition, but without the same level of emotion. Nevertheless, she recorded standards including 'House Of The Rising Sun' and 'Make Me A Pallet On Your Floor'. In 1960 she took to the solo acoustic guitar and moved to Vanguard. Possessed of a powerful voice, her style embraced gospel, jazz and blues, but eventually Odetta fell foul of changing trends and fashions in music, and much was forgotten of her early work from the 50s and 60s. The singer was championed by Pete Seeger and Harry Belafonte, the latter of whom Odetta accompanied on a 1961 UK hit, 'Hole In The Bucket', while her solo career flourished with a succession of albums for the Vanguard label. The artist's emotional mixture of spiritual, ethnic and jazz styles is best captured in person, and, therefore, *Odetta At Town Hall* and *Odetta At Carnegie Hall* remain her most representative sets in their showcasing of the full extent of her varied repertoire.

● ALBUMS: *Odetta And Larry* 10-inch album (Fantasy 1955)★★★, *Odetta Sings Ballads And Blues* (Tradition 1956)★★★, *Odetta At The Gate Of Horn* (Tradition 1957)★★★, *My Eyes Have Seen* (Vanguard 1959)★★★, *Ballads For Americans* (Vanguard 1960)★★★, *Odetta At Carnegie Hall* (Vanguard 1961)★★★★, *Christmas Spirituals* (Vanguard 1961)★★★, *Odetta And The Blues* (Riverside 1962)★★★, *Sometimes I Feel Like Crying* (RCA Victor 1962)★★★, *Odetta At Town Hall* (Vanguard 1962)★★★★, *Odetta* (1963)★★★, *Odetta Sings Folk Songs* (RCA 1963)★★★, *One Grain Of Sand* (Vanguard 1963)★★★, *It's A Mighty World* (1964)★★★, *Odetta Sings Of Many Things* (1964)★★★, *Odetta Sings Dylan* (1965)★★★, *Odetta In Japan* (1965)★★★★, *Odetta* (1967)★★★, *Odetta Sings The Blues* (1968)★★★, *Odetta Sings* (1971)★★★, *It's Impossible* (Four Leaf Clover 1978)★★★.

● COMPILATIONS: *Best Of Odetta* (1967)★★★, *The Essential Odetta* (Start 1989)★★★.

OKLAHOMA!

The show that opened on Broadway in 1943, and is credited with being a significant turning point in the history of the musical theatre, was transferred to the screen in the less than glorious Todd-AO widescreen process in 1955. The skilful integration of Richard Rodgers and Oscar Hammerstein II's wonderful songs into the sentimental but sincere story for which the stage production was so rightly admired, was equally impressive in this celluloid version. The action takes place just after the turn of the century, on and around a ranch in the Oklahoma Territory, where Laurey (Shirley Jones) lives with her Aunt Eller (Charlotte Greenwood). The handsome and decent Curly (Gordon MacRae) and the evil-looking and devious Jud (Rod Steiger) both want to take Laurey to the 'box social'. Her decision to spite Curly (with whom she actually wants to go) by accepting Jud's invitation, sets off a train of events that culminates in Jud's death, for which Curly is immediately blamed, but just as swiftly exonerated. Jones and MacRae were perfect together, and the supporting cast was exceptionally fine, with Gene Nelson as Will Parker and Gloria Grahame as his girlfriend Ado Annie, who 'just cain't say no'. Eddie Albert played a travelling pedlar-man, Ali Akim, whose indiscriminate use of a kissing technique known in his native country as 'A Persian Goodbye', results in a shotgun wedding. Other parts were taken by James Whitmore, Marc Platt, Barbara Lawrence and Roy Barcroft.

Dancers James Mitchell and Bambi Lynn were stunning in the ballet sequence to the music of 'Out Of My Dreams'. Most of the rest of Rodgers and Hammerstein's rich and varied score was retained, and included all the favourites such as 'Oh, What A Beautiful Mornin'', 'The Surrey With The Fringe On Top', 'Kansas City', 'I Cain't Say No', 'Many A New Day', 'People Will Say We're In Love', 'Poor Jud Is Dead', 'The Farmer And The Cowman', 'All Er Nothin'', and the rousing 'Oklahoma'. Choreographer Agnes de Mille and musical arranger Robert Russell Bennett adapted their original stage work for the film, and Russell Bennett, together with Jay Blackton and Adolph Deutsch, won Oscars for 'scoring of a musical picture'. It was photographed in Technicolor and produced for Magna by Arthur Hornblow Jnr. The director was Fred Zinnemann. Sonya Levian and William Ludwig's screenplay was adapted from the original libretto by Oscar Hammerstein II, which, in turn, was based on Lynn Riggs' play *Green Grow The Lilacs*.

ONE DOZEN BERRYS • CHUCK BERRY ★★★★★

Popular music is almost unthinkable without the influence of Chuck Berry. He combined the economy of R&B with a brilliant gift for lyricism that encapsulated adolescent spirit in a manner no other performer has matched. The three opening tracks on this 1958 album embody Berry's gifts: each one is now an integral part of the pop lexicon. Intriguingly, these compositions can be heard in the early work of the Beach Boys, Rolling Stones and Beatles, which in itself is tribute to Berry's enormous influence. His unique guitar style is showcased on 'Blue Ceiling' and 'Guitar Boogie', resulting in a set that demonstrates the artist's talents to the full.

● TRACKS: *Sweet Little Sixteen; Blue Feeling; La Jaunda; Guitar Boogie; Oh Baby Doll; In-Go; Rock At The Philharmonic; Reelin' And Rockin; Rock & Roll Music; It Don't Take But A Few Minutes; Low Feeling; How You've Changed*.

ORBACH, JERRY

b. 20 October 1935, Bronx, New York, USA. An actor and singer who created a handful of important roles for the Broadway musical theatre, before turning mostly to films and television. Orbach studied acting with Lee Strasberg, and singing with Mazel Schweppe. After making his professional debut as the Typewriter Man in a 1952 Illinois version of *Room Service*, he continued to work in regional theatre, appearing in stock productions of musicals such as *The King And I* and *The Student Prince*. He made his Broadway debut taking over the roles of the Streetsinger (1957) and Macheath (1958), in the long-running revival of *The Threepenny Opera* that opened at the Theatre De Lys in 1955. In 1960 he played the dual role of the Narrator and the bandit El Gallo off-Broadway in Harvey Schmidt and Tom Jones's historic epic *The Fantasticks*, introducing the show's hit song, 'Try To Remember'. During the 60s he created the character of cynical puppeteer Paul Berthalet in *Carnival* (1961) on Broadway and on tour, played in revivals of *The Cradle Will Rock* (1964 as Larry Foreman), *Guys And Dolls* (1965 as Sky Masterson, with Alan King and Sheila MacRae), *Carousel* (1965 as Jigger Craigin), and *Annie Get Your Gun* (1966 as Charlie Davenport), as well as appearing in several straight plays. In 1969 Orbach won a Tony Award for his portrayal of Chuck Baxter, the sad, lowly office worker who lends out his apartment to senior executives in *Promises, Promises*, and introduced (with Jill O'Hara) Burt Bacharach and Hal David's 'I'll Never Fall In Love Again'. In 1974, he played in the Neil Simon revue *The Trouble With People ... And Other Things* in Miami. Orbach subsequently returned to Broadway, full of assurance, singing 'All I Care About' and 'Razzle Dazzle', as Gwen Verdon and Chita Rivera's smart lawyer, the silver-tongued prince of the courtroom, Mr. Billy Flynn, in *Chicago* (1975). Orbach's last major stage musical role to date came in 1980, when he portrayed tough producer Julian Marsh in the long-running Broadway adaptation of the famous 1932 Busby Berkeley movie *42nd Street*. Since then, he has continued to appear in dramatic parts in the theatre, but seems to have concentrated mostly on television (*Perry Mason, Murder, She Wrote, Law And Order*, etc.) and films. The music connection has continued though, and in more recent years moviegoers have seen him as the disapproving doctor/father figure in the hit film *Dirty Dancing* (1987), and heard his voice behind the hospitable candelabra, Lumiere, singing Alan Menken and Howard Ashman's Oscar-nominated 'Be Our Guest', in Walt Disney's animated feature *Beauty And The Beast* (1991).

● FILMS: *Cop Hater* (1958), *Mad Dog Coll* (1961), *John Goldfarb, Please Come Home* (1964), *The Gang That Couldn't Shoot Straight* (1971), *A Fan's Notes* (1972), *Foreplay* (1975), *The Sentinel* (1977), *Prince Of The City* (1981), *Brewster's Millions* (1985), *F/X* (1986), *The Imagemaker* (1986), *I Love N.Y.* (1987), *Dirty Dancing* (1987), *Someone To Watch Over Me* (1987), *Last Exit To Brooklyn* (1989), *Crimes And Misdemeanors* (1989), *Dead Women In Lingerie* (1990), *Toy Soldiers* (1991), *Out For Justice* (1991), *Delusion* (1991), voice of Lumiere *Beauty And The Beast* (1991), *Delirious* (1992), *Straight Talk* (1992), *Mr. Saturday Night* (1992), *Universal Soldier* (1992), *Quiet Killer* (1992).

OSSER, GLENN

b. 28 August 1914, Munising, Michigan, USA. The son of Russian immigrants, Osser has had a successful career arranging and conducting for many leading bands and singers. He has also achieved a distinctive string sound through his clever scoring, which he describes as 'voicing register, and composition of the counterpoint'. In his early career Osser concentrated on arranging, and his scores were accepted by Bob Crosby, Charlie Barnet, Bunny Berigan, Paul Whiteman, Les Brown and Red Nichols. During the 50s, while still regularly working with Whiteman (who was Musical Director of the ABC Network at that time), Osser was in demand to back many singers for albums, including Georgia Gibbs, Vic Damone, Jack Jones, Frankie Laine, John Raitt, Maurice Chevalier and Guy Mitchell. Osser was also recording his own instrumental albums, notably some with Bobby Hackett and Joe Bushkin. Further albums found Osser backing Johnny Mathis, Jerry Vale, Tony Bennett, Robert Goulet and Leslie Uggams. Leaving US Columbia and moving to RCA, Osser worked with Della Reese and Sam Cooke. Until 1987 he was Music Director and arranger for the *Miss America Beauty Pageant* on television, with Osser and his wife contributing various original songs including 'Miss America, You're Beautiful' and 'Look At Her'. He has also written many works for concert bands that are still performed by many high school and college bands in the USA.

● ALBUMS: as Glenn Osser Orchestra *But Beautiful* (Kapp 1956)★★★, with Joe Bushkin *Midnight Rhapsody* (Capitol 1957)★★★, *March Along Sing Along (Marching Band And Chorus)* (United Artists 1960)★★★, *Be There At Five* (Mercury 1960)★★★.

As accompanist: Marian McPartland *With You In Mind* (Capitol 1957)★★★, Georgia Gibbs *Swingin' With Her Nibs* (Mercury 1957)★★★, Vivian Blaine *Songs From Ziegfeld Follies* (Mercury 1957)★★★★, Jerry Vale *I Remember Buddy* (Columbia 1958)★★, Red Buttons, Barbara Cook *Hansel And Gretel* (MGM 1958)★★★, Maurice Chevalier *Maurice Chevalier Sings Songs Of Yesterday/Today* (MGM 1958)★★★, Guy Mitchell *A Guy In Love* (Columbia/Philips 1959)★★★, Vic Damone *Angela Mia* (Columbia 1959)★★★, Johnny Mathis *Heavenly* (Columbia 1959)★★★★, Leslie Uggams *The Eyes Of God* (Columbia 1959)★★★, Della Reese *Della By Starlight* (RCA 1960)★★★★, Sam Cooke *Cooke's Tour* (RCA 1960)★★★, Tony Bennett *Tony Bennett Sings A String Of Harold Arlen* (Columbia 1960)★★★, Diana Trask *Diana Trask* (Columbia 1961)★★★★, Dona Jacoby *Swinging Big Sound* (Decca 1962)★★★, Bobby Hackett *The Most Beautiful Horn In The World* (Columbia 1962)★★★, Jack Jones *Gift Of Love* (Kapp 1962)★★★, George Maharis *Portrait In Music* (Epic 1962)★★★, Robert Goulet *Two Of Us* (Columbia 1962)★★★, Jerry Vale *Arrivederci Roma* (Columbia 1963)★★★★, Barbara Carroll *Fresh From Broadway* (Warners 1964)★★★, Brook Benton *That Old Feeling* (RCA 1966)★★★, Jerry Vale *The Impossible Dream* (Columbia 1967)★★★, Johnny Mathis *Up Up And Away* (Columbia 1967)★★★, Bob Thiele *Those Were The Days* (Flying Dutchman 1972)★★★.

OTIS, JOHNNY

b. 28 December 1921, Vallejo, California, USA. Born into a family of Greek immigrants, Otis was raised in a largely black neighbourhood where he thoroughly absorbed the prevailing culture and lifestyle. He began playing drums in his mid-teens and worked for a time with some of the locally based jazz bands, including, in 1941, Lloyd Hunter's orchestra. In 1943 he gained his first name-band experience when he joined Harlan Leonard for a short spell. Some sources suggest that, during the difficult days when the draft was pulling musicians out of bands all across the USA, Otis then replaced another ex-Leonard drummer, Jesse Price, in the Stan Kenton band. In the mid-40s Otis also recorded with several jazz groups, including Illinois Jacquet's all-star band and a septet led by Lester Young. In 1945 Otis formed his own big band in Los Angeles. In an early edition assembled for a recording session, he leaned strongly towards a blues-based jazz repertoire and hired such musicians as Eli Robinson, Paul Quinichette, Teddy Buckner, Bill Doggett, Curtis Counce and singer Jimmy Rushing. This particular date produced a major success in 'Harlem Nocturne'. He also led a small band, including McGhee and Teddy Edwards, on a record date backing Wynonie Harris. However, Otis was aware of audience interest in R&B and began to angle his repertoire accordingly. He quickly became one of the leading figures in the R&B boom of the late 40s and early 50s. Otis also enjoyed credit for writing several songs, although, in some cases, this was an area fraught with confusion and litigation. Among his songs was 'Every Beat Of My Heart', which was a minor hit for Jackie Wilson in 1951 and a massive hit a decade later for Gladys Knight. Otis was instrumental in the discovery of Etta James and Willie Mae 'Big Mama' Thornton. A highly complex case of song co-authorship came to light with 'Hound Dog', which was recorded by Thornton. Otis, who had set up the date, was listed first as composer, then as co-composer with its originators, Leiber And Stoller. After the song was turned into a multi-million dollar hit by Elvis Presley, other names appeared on the credits and the lawyers stepped in. Otis had a hit record in the UK with an updated version of 'Ma, He's Making Eyes At Me' in 1957. During the 50s Otis broadcast daily in the USA as a radio disc jockey, and had a weekly television show with his band and also formed several recording companies, all of which helped to make him a widely recognized force in west coast R&B. During the 60s and 70s, Otis continued to appear on radio and television, touring with his well-packaged R&B-based show. His son, Johnny 'Shuggie' Otis Jnr., appeared with the show and at the age of 13 had a hit with 'Country Girl'. In addition to his musical career, Otis wrote a book, *Listen To The Lambs*, written in the aftermath of the Watts riots of the late 60s.

● ALBUMS: *Mel Williams And Johnny Otis* (1955)★★★, *Rock 'N' Roll Parade, Volume 1* (Dig 1957)★★★, *The Johnny Otis Show* (Capitol 1958)★★★★, *Cold Shot* (Kent 1968)★★★★, *Cuttin' Up* (Epic 1970)★★, *Live At Monterey* (Epic 1971)★★, *The New Johnny Otis Show* (Alligator 1981)★★, *Spirit Of The Black Territory Bands* (1993)★★.

● COMPILATIONS: *The Original Johnny Otis Show* (Savoy1985)★★★★, *The Capitol Years* (Capitol 1989)★★★★, *The Greatest Johnny Otis Show* (Ace 1998)★★★.

● FURTHER READING: *Upside Your Head! Rhythm And Blues On Central Avenue*, Johnny Otis.

OWEN, REG

b. February 1928, England. Owen was a British bandleader who reached the US and UK charts in 1959 with 'Manhattan Spiritual', written by Billy Maxted. The song was issued on the small Palette label in the USA and began its climb in December 1958, ultimately reaching number 10 in February 1959. Meanwhile, the record was issued in England on Pye International, where it reached number 20. Owen placed one other single on the English chart, 'Obsession', in 1960, and although he continued to record, there were no further chart successes on either side of the Atlantic. None of his albums, including those recorded for RCA Records prior to the 'Manhattan Spiritual' success, charted in either country.

● ALBUMS: *I'll Sing You A Thousand Love Songs* (RCA 1958)★★★, *Girls Were Made To Take Care Of Boys* (RCA 1959)★★, *Cuddle Up A Little Closer* (RCA 1959)★★★, *Manhattan Spiritual* (RCA 1959)★★, *Fiorello* (RCA 1959)★★★.

OZARK JUBILEE, THE

The show was the brainchild of four Springfield, Missouri men, led by a promoter named Ely E. 'Si' Siman, who was initially connected with KWTO Springfield radio. In the early 50s, KWTO broadcast country radio programmes and Siman recognized the potential success of a networked televised country show. When KYTV Springfield began to televise local country shows, Siman and his three associates, Ralph Foster, Lester Cox and John Mahaffey, formed

Crossroads Television Productions, Inc. and gave up their interest in the purely local radio shows. On 26 December 1953, the first of the new televised shows was broadcast and the following year, Siman succeeded in talking Red Foley, an established *Grand Ole Opry* star in Nashville, into becoming the MC and star of the Springfield show. In September 1954, the show was transmitted from the Jewell Theatre, Springfield, back to KYTV's studio and then relayed from there. Siman soon succeeded in selling the show to ABC-TV and on 22 January 1955, part of it was broadcast live on that network. There were some initial transmission difficulties and for 22 Saturdays, the show was transmitted from KOMU Columbia, Missouri. In April 1955, the *Jubilee* returned to Springfield, where it ran until its final show in January 1961 (Red Foley's departure because of income tax problems with the IRS has been cited as one reason for the show's demise). It was then replaced by the *Five Star Jubilee*, a colour show, which made KYTV the first station outside of Los Angeles, Chicago and New York, to have a regular colour programme. It broadcast 29 shows from the Landers Theatre, Springfield, before the series ended. Many future stars benefited from their appearances on the *Jubilee* programme including Porter Wagoner, Bobby Lord, Wanda Jackson, Jean Shepard, Carl Smith and Billy Walker. Amusingly, Willie Nelson, then the frontman and bass guitarist in Ray Price's band, was once told by the show's producers that he was 'not yet ready for national television'. *The Ozark Jubilee*, sometimes referred to as *Jubilee USA*, did not survive for as long as some of its contemporaries, nor did it ever attain the popularity of the *Opry* or the *Louisiana Hayride*, but it did establish its place in the history of country music by the fact that it was the first to be aired on network television. Siman died of cancer in Springfield on 16 December 1994.

PAGE, PATTI

b. Clara Ann Fowler, 8 November 1927, Tulsa, Oklahoma, USA. A popular singer who is said to have sold more records during the 50s than any other female artist, Page's total sales (singles and albums) are claimed to be in excess of 60 million. One of eight girls in a family of 11, Clara Fowler started her career singing country songs on radio station KTUL in Tulsa, and played weekend gigs with Art Klauser and his Oklahomans. She successfully auditioned for KTUL's *Meet Patti Page* show, sponsored by the Page Milk Company, and took the name with her when she left. Jack Rael, who was

road manager and played baritone saxophone for the Jimmy Joy band, heard her on the radio and engaged her to sing with them; he later became her manager for over 40 years. In 1948 Page appeared on the top-rated *Breakfast Club* on Chicago radio, and sang with the Benny Goodman Septet. In the same year she had her first hit record, 'Confess', on which, in the cause of economy, she overdubbed her own voice to create the effect of a vocal group. In 1949, she used that revolutionary technique again on her first million-seller, 'With My Eyes Wide Open I'm Dreaming'. The song was re-released 10 years later with a more modern orchestral backing. Throughout the 50s, the hits continued to flow: 'I Don't Care If The Sun Don't Shine', 'All My Love' (US number 1), 'The Tennessee Waltz' (said to be the first real 'crossover' hit from country music to pop, and one of the biggest record hits of all time), 'Would I Love You (Love You, Love You)', 'Mockin' Bird Hill' (a cover version of the record made by Les Paul and Mary Ford, who took multi-tracking to the extreme in the 50s), 'Mister And Mississippi', 'Detour' (recorded for her first country music album), 'I Went To Your Wedding', 'Once In Awhile', 'You Belong To Me', 'Why Don't You Believe Me', '(How Much Is) That Doggie In The Window', written by novelty song specialist Bob Merrill, and recorded by Page for a children's album, 'Changing Partners', 'Cross Over The Bridge', 'Steam Heat', 'Let Me Go, Lover', 'Go On With The Wedding', 'Allegheny Moon', 'Old Cape Cod', 'Mama From The Train' (sung in a Pennsylvanian Dutch dialect), 'Left Right Out Of Your Heart', and many more. Her records continued to sell well into the 60s, and she had her last US Top 10 entry in 1965 with the title song from the Bette Davis-Olivia De Havilland movie *Hush, Hush, Sweet Charlotte*. Page also appeared extensively on US television during the 50s, on shows such as the *Scott Music Hall*, the *Big Record* variety show, and her own shows for NBC and CBS. She also made several films, including *Elmer Gantry* (1960), *Dondi* (1961, a comedy-drama, in which she co-starred with David Janssen) and *Boys Night Out* (1962). In the 70s, she recorded mainly country material, and in the 80s, after many successful years with Mercury and Columbia Records, signed for the Nashville-based company Plantation Records, a move that reunited her with top record producer Shelby Singleton. In 1988, Page gained excellent reviews when she played the Ballroom in New York, her first appearance in that city for nearly 20 years.
● ALBUMS: *Songs* (Mercury 1950)★★★, *Folksong Favorites* 10-inch album (Mercury 1951)★★★, *Christmas* (Mercury 1951)★★★, *Tennessee Waltz* 10-inch album (Mercury 1952)★★★, *Patti Sings For Romance* (Mercury 1954)★★★, *Song Souvenirs* (Mercury 1954)★★★, *Just Patti* (Mercury 1954)★★★, *Patti's Songs* (Mercury 1954)★★★, *And I Thought About You* (Mercury 1954)★★★, *So Many Memories* (Mercury 1954)★★★, *Romance On The Range* (Mercury 1955)★★★, *Page I* (Mercury 1956)★★★, *Page II* (Mercury 1956)★★★, *Page III* (Mercury 1956)★★★, *You Go To My Head* (Mercury 1956)★★★, *In The Land Of Hi Fi* (EmArcy 1956)★★★, *Music For Two In Love* (Mercury 1956)★★★, *The Voices Of Patti Page* (Mercury 1956)★★★, *Page IV* (Mercury 1956)★★★, *Let's Get Away From It All* (Mercury 1956)★★★, *I've Heard That Song Before* (Mercury 1956)★★★, *My Song* (1956)★★★, *The East Side* (EmArcy 1956)★★★, *Manhattan Tower* (Mercury 1956)★★★, *The Waltz Queen* (Mercury 1957)★★★, *The West Side* (EmArcy

1958)★★★, *Patti Page On Camera* (Mercury 1959)★★★, *I'll Remember April* (Mercury 1959)★★★, *Indiscretion* (Mercury 1959)★★★, *Sings And Stars In 'Elmer Gantry'* (Mercury 1960)★★★, *Three Little Words* (Mercury 1960)★★★, *Just A Closer Walk With Thee* (Mercury 1960)★★, *Country And Western Golden Hits* (Mercury 1961)★★, *Go On Home* (1962)★★★, *Golden Hit Of The Boys* (Mercury 1962)★★★, *Patti Page On Stage* (1963)★★★, *Say Wonderful Things* (Columbia 1963)★★, *Blue Dream Street* (1964)★★, *The Nearness Of You* (1964)★★★, *Hush, Hush, Sweet Charlotte* (Columbia 1965)★★★, *Gentle On My Mind* (Columbia 1968)★★, *Patti Page With Lou Stein's Music, 1949* (Hindsight 1988)★★★.
● COMPILATIONS: *Patti Page's Golden Hits* (Mercury 1961)★★★, *Patti Page's Golden Hits, Volume 2* (Mercury 1963)★★★, *The Best Of Patti Page* (Creole 1984)★★★, *The Mercury Years, Vol. 1* (Mercury 1991)★★★★, *The Mercury Years, Vol. 2* (Mercury 1991)★★★★.

PAICH, MARTY

b. 23 January 1925, Oakland, California, USA, d. 12 August 1995, Hidden Hills, California, USA. While still undergoing a long and thorough academic training, Paich began writing arrangements. After military service, during which he was able to continue his musical career, he returned to his studies and by the end of the 40s had gained numerous qualifications. In the early 50s he worked with a number of dance bands and also with Shelly Manne and Shorty Rogers, with whom he appeared on *Cool And Crazy*. Also in the early 50s he was, for a while, pianist and arranger for Peggy Lee and wrote arrangements for Mel Tormé. He also wrote charts for another highly successful west coast album, *Art Pepper Plus Eleven*. An inventive and inquiring mind was clearly at work in all Paich's writing, whether as arranger or composer, and he proved particularly adept at creating material for small to medium-sized groups that allows the bands to sound as though they involve many more musicians. His work with such singers as Ella Fitzgerald, Ray Charles, Anita O'Day, Sammy Davis, Lena Horne and Sarah Vaughan, whether as arranger or musical director and conductor, demonstrated an acute appreciation of the particular needs of interpreters of the Great American Songbook. Paich also composed for films and television but the late 80s saw him back on the road with Tormé and some of his former Dek-tette sidemen, reunions that resulted in some remarkable record albums. He died of cancer of the colon in 1995.
● ALBUMS: *Marty Paich Octet* (GNP 1956)★★★, with Mel Tormé *Mel Tormé With The Marty Paich Dek-tette* (Bethlehem 1956)★★★★, *What's New?* (1957)★★★, *Jazz For Relaxation* (Tampa 1957)★★★, *Marty Paich Quintet Featuring Art Pepper* (Tampa 1958)★★★, *The Picasso Of Big Band Jazz* (Candid 1958)★★★, *I Get A Boot Out Of You* (Warners 1959)★★★, *The Broadway Bit* (Warners 1959)★★★, *Piano Quartet* (RCA Victor 1960)★★★, with Tormé *Reunion* (Concord Jazz 1988)★★★★, *Hot Piano* (VSOP 1988), with Tormé *In Concert Tokyo* (Concord Jazz 1989)★★★★, *Moanin'* (1993)★★★★.

PAINT YOUR WAGON

Despite having music by Frederick Loewe and a book and lyrics by Alan Jay Lerner, *Paint Your Wagon* enjoyed only modest success. It opened at the Shubert Theatre in New

York on 12 November 1951, and ran for only 289 performances. Well staged by Daniel Mann, and with some exhilarating choreography by Agnes de Mille, the show was set in California during the 1850s gold rush. James Barton, Tony Bavaar, Olga San Juan, Rufus Smith and James Mitchell played in a cast of hard-bitten prospectors and their equally tough girlfriends. Lerner and Loewe's score, which perfectly complemented this rough-and-tumble situation, contained several appealing songs, including 'They Call The Wind Maria', 'I Still See Elisa', 'There's A Coach Comin' In', 'I Talk To The Trees', 'I'm On My Way', 'Another Autumn', 'Hand Me Down That Can O' Beans' and 'Wand'rin' Star'. In 1953, London audiences were delighted with the show and it ran at Her Majesty's Theatre for over a year with Bobby Howes and his real-life daughter Sally Ann Howes. In 1992, the Goodspeed Opera House in Connecticut gave theatregoers another chance to hear what is now - over 40 years on - regarded as an outstanding score.

PAJAMA GAME, THE (STAGE MUSICAL)

This show opened at the St. James Theatre in New York on 13 May 1954 with only limited expectations. Richard Adler and Jerry Ross, who wrote the music and lyrics, were relatively unknown to Broadway audiences, as was choreographer Bob Fosse. However, the witty book was the work of veteran George Abbott and Richard Bissell, and the score was full of amusing and romantic numbers, such as 'I'll Never Be Jealous Again', 'There Once Was Man', 'Once A Year Day', 'Small Talk', 'I'm Not At All In Love' 'Hernando's Hideaway', 'Steam Heat' and 'Hey, There'. Set against the unlikely backdrop of a factory manufacturing pajamas, with an industrial dispute as its central dramatic device, there were strong performances from Janis Paige, John Raitt and Carol Haney. It won Tony Awards for best musical, featured actress (Haney), and Bob Fosse's choreography, which was an outstanding feature of the show. The 1955 London production, which ran for 501 performances and is remembered with great affection, starred Max Wall, Joy Nichols, Edmund Hockridge, and Elizabeth Seal. Hockridge was subsequently always associated with 'Hey, There', although in fact the song was a UK hit for Rosemary Clooney, Johnnie Ray, Lita Roza and Sammy Davis Jnr. *The Pajama Game* was revived briefly on Broadway in 1973 with Barbara McNair, Hal Linden and Cab Calloway. The 1957 film version achieved the impossible and actually improved upon the original with dazzling performances from Doris Day, Raitt, Haney, and Eddie Foy Jnr. In 1958, the musical *Say Darling*, which was based on Richard Bissell's experiences with *The Pajama Game*, opened on Broadway and ran for 332 performances. The cast was headed by Vivian Blaine, David Wayne and Johnny Desmond, and the score was by Betty Comden and Adolph Green.

PAJAMA GAME, THE (FILM MUSICAL)

Hardly any screen version of a hit Broadway musical is considered to be better than the original, but this one in 1957 was an exception. This was possibly because several members of the original stage team made the trip to Hollywood to recreate their original roles. Two of them, George Abbott and Richard Bissell, adapted their libretto (which had been based on Bissell's novel *Seven And A Half Cents*) for the screenplay. Based in and around the Sleep Tite Pajama Factory in Iowa, it concerns the efforts of union leader Babe Williams (Doris Day) and her Grievance Committee to extract a rise in pay of seven and a half cents for their members, from the new (and extremely dishy) superintendent, Sid Sorokin (John Raitt). Naturally, Babe falls for Sid, in spite of her protests ('I'm Not At All In Love'), and the negotiations are satisfactorily concluded. This was one of only two scores that Richard Adler and Jerry Ross wrote together (the other was *Damn Yankees*) before the latter's tragic death, and it was a complete joy. Not only did the principals, Day and Raitt, share 'Hey, There', 'Small Talk' and 'There Once Was A Man', but the gifted singer and dancer Carol Haney dazzled with 'Steam Heat' and 'Hernando's Hideaway', while Eddie Foy Jnr. was delightfully unconvincing as he assured Reta Shaw 'I'll Never Be Jealous Again'. In addition, there were pleasing ensemble pieces such as 'Once-A-Year-Day' and 'Racing With The Clock'. Also in the cast were Buzz Miller, Peter Gennaro, Barbara Nicholls, Thelma Pelish and Kenneth LeRoy. Bob Fosse, a veteran of the stage show, was responsible for the lively and imaginative choreography (much of it alfresco), and the producer-directors were George Abbott and Stanley Donen. The film was shot in WarnerColor.

PAL JOEY

This somewhat sanitized version of the 1940 Broadway show and John O'Hara's witty essays on which it was based, came to the screen in 1957. Frank Sinatra proved to be the ideal choice for the role of 'the heel of all-time', Joey Evans, the nightclub singer and compere, whose apparent mission in life is to seduce each 'mouse' in the chorus with the offer of 'shrimp cocktail, a steak, french fries, a little wine - the whole mish-mosh', so that he can 'help her with her arrangements'. The ingenuous Linda English (Kim Novak) accepts his offer, and, after the usual complications, and to the surprise of many who had read O'Hara's original short stories, goes off with him into the sunset. The musical high spot comes when Joey sings an electrifying version of 'The Lady Is A Tramp' to the wealthy widow Vera Simpson (Rita Hayworth), who had been known as 'Vanessa The Undresser' in her former life as a stripper. London film critics at the time thought it slightly ridiculous when some of their number actually applauded a piece of celluloid, but it was that kind of performance. Hank Henry, as the grumpy owner of the Barbary Coast nightspot where Joey 'operates', and Bobby Sherwood as the leader of its orchestra, headed a supporting cast that also included Barbara Nicholls and Elizabeth Patterson. The majority of Richard Rodgers and Lorenz Hart's fine stage score was retained, with four additional songs from their other shows. Sinatra was in great voice on 'I Could Write A Book', 'There's a Small Hotel' and 'What Do I Care For A Dame?', while Hayworth shimmied her way through 'Zip' and 'Bewitched' (vocals dubbed by Jo Ann Greer). Trudy Erwin's voice was behind Novak's sultry rendering of 'My Funny Valentine' and 'That Terrific Rainbow'. Hermes Pan was the choreographer, and Dorothy Kingsley's screenplay was adequate - O'Hara's version of events would never have been acceptable even in the late 50s - and this entertaining film grossed nearly $5 million in US rentals alone. It was produced in Technicolor for Columbia by Fred Kohlmar. The director was George Sidney.

PALMER, EARL

b. 25 October 1924, New Orleans, Louisiana, USA. Palmer's mother was a vaudeville performer, and from an early age he began entertaining as a singer and dancer. Playing drums in his school band, he started listening to jazz drummers such as Big Sid Catlett and Panama Francis, and joined Dave Bartholomew's band in 1947. He recorded with the Bartholomew band and went on to play on many of his productions for Imperial Records, notably Fats Domino's classic records. Palmer is probably featured on virtually every other Crescent City classic, including those Specialty rockers by Little Richard and Lloyd Price, but in 1956 Aladdin Records hired him as a session arranger to handle their New Orleans sessions. In February 1957, he moved out to Los Angeles to work for Aladdin until the company was liquidated. He remained one of the busiest session drummers on the west coast throughout the 60s and 70s, recording with everyone from Lightnin' Hopkins to Marvin Gaye and subsequently wrote movie scores and advertising jingles.

PARAMOR, NORRIE

b. 1913, London, England, d. 9 September 1979. The most prolific producer of UK pop chart-toppers was a mild, bespectacled gentleman who had studied piano and worked as an accompanist, prior to playing and arranging with a number of London dance bands, among them Maurice Winnick's Orchestra. During his time in the RAF during World War II, Paramor entertained servicemen in the company of artists such as Sidney Torch and Max Wall, served as a musical director for Ralph Reader's Gang Shows, and scored music for Noël Coward, Mantovani and Jack Buchanan. After the war he was the featured pianist with Harry Gold And His Pieces Of Eight, and toured with the lively Dixieland unit for five years. In 1950 he recorded some sides for the Oriole label with Australian singer Marie Benson, and two years later, joined Columbia Records, an EMI subsidiary, as arranger and A&R manager. In 1954, he produced the first of two UK number 1 hits for Eddie Calvert, and another for Ruby Murray the following year. Although quoted as believing that rock 'n' roll was 'an American phenomenon - and they do it best', he still provided Columbia with such an act in Tony Crombie's Rockets, but had better luck with the mainstream efforts of Michael Holliday and the Mudlarks - both backed by the Ken Jones Orchestra. Then, in 1958, a demo tape by Cliff Richard And The Drifters arrived on his desk. With no rock 'n' roller currently on his books, he contracted Richard, intending to play it safe with a US cover version with the Jones band, until he was persuaded to stick with the Drifters (soon renamed the Shadows) and push a group original ('Move It') as the a-side. Partly through newspaper publicity engineered by Paramor, 'Move It' was a huge hit, and a subsequent policy was instigated of Richard recording singles of untried numbers - among them, at Paramor's insistence, Lionel Bart's 'Living Doll'. Columbia was also successful with the Shadows - even though Paramor initially wished to issue 'Apache' - their first smash - as a b-side. Later, he offended Shadows purists by augmenting the quartet on disc with horn sections and his trademark lush string arrangements.

Other Paramor signings were not allowed to develop to the same idiosyncratic extent as Richard and his associates. Ricky Valance achieved his sole chart-topper with a cover version of Ray Peterson's US hit 'Tell Laura I Love Her', while Helen Shapiro was visualized as a vague 'answer' to Brenda Lee; Paramor even booked and supervised some Shapiro sessions in Nashville in 1963. His greatest success during this period, however, was with Frank Ifield, who dominated the early 60s' UK pop scene with three formidable number 1 hits. Even as late as 1968, Paramor notched up another number 1 with Scaffold's 'Lily The Pink'. Throughout his career, Paramor wrote, and co-wrote, many hit songs, several of them for films, such as *Expresso Bongo* ('A Voice In The Wilderness', Cliff Richard), *The Young Ones* ('The Savage') and *The Frightened City* (title song), both performed by the Shadows, *Play It Cool* ('Once Upon A Dream', Billy Fury), *It's Trad, Dad!* ('Let's Talk About Love', Helen Shapiro) and *Band Of Thieves* ('Lonely', Acker Bilk). He also composed several complete movie scores, and some light orchestral works such as 'The Zodiac' and 'Emotions', which he recorded with his Concert Orchestra, and released several 'mood' albums in the USA, including *London After Dark*, *Amore, Amore!*, *Autumn* and *In London, In Love*, which made the US Top 20. In complete contrast, the Big Ben Banjo, and Big Ben Hawaiian Bands, along with similar 'happy-go-lucky' 'trad jazz' line-ups, were originally formed in 1955 purely as recording units, utilizing the cream of UK session musicians. Paramor was in charge of them all, and their popularity was such that 'live' performances had to be organized. The Big Ben Banjo Band appeared at the Royal Variety Performance in 1958, and were resident on BBC Radio's *Everybody Step* programme, as well as having their own Radio Luxembourg series. Two of the band's 'Let's Get Together' singles, and *More Minstrel Melodies*, reached the UK Top 20. One of the highlights of Paramor's career came in 1960 when he arranged and conducted for Judy Garland's British recording sessions, and was her musical director at the London Palladium and subsequent dates in Europe. In the same year, with his Orchestra, he made the UK singles chart with 'Theme From A Summer Place' and in 1962, registered again with 'Theme From Z Cars'.

From 1972-78 Paramor was the Director of the BBC Midland Radio Orchestra, but he continued to dabble in independent production for acts such as the Excaliburs, and his publishing company was still finding material for Cliff in the 70s. Paramor remains one of the most underrated figures in the history of UK pop and a posthumous reappraisal of his work is overdue.

● ALBUMS: *Just We Two* (Columbia 1955)★★★, *In London, In Love ...* (1956)★★★, *The Zodiac* (1957)★★★, *New York Impressions* (1957)★★★, *Emotions* (1958)★★★, *Dreams And Desires* (1958)★★★, *The Wonderful Waltz* (1958)★★★, *My Fair Lady* (1959)★★★, *Paramor In Paris* (1959)★★★, *Jet Flight* (1959)★★★, *Lovers In Latin* (1959)★★★, *Staged For Stereo* (1961)★★★, *Autumn* (1961)★★★, *The Golden Waltz* (1961)★★★, *Lovers In London* (1964)★★★, with Patricia Clark *Lovers In Tokyo* (1964)★★, *Warm And Willing* (1965)★★★, *Shadows In Latin* (1966)★★★, *Norrie Paramor Plays The Hits Of Cliff Richard* (Studio Two 1967)★★★, *Soul Coaxing* (1968)★★★, *BBC Top Tunes* (BBC 1974)★★★, *Radio 2 Top Tunes, Volume 1* (BBC 1974)★★★, *Radio 2 Top Tunes, Volume 2* (BBC 1975)★★★, *Radio 2 Top Tunes, Volume 3* (BBC 1975)★★★, *Love* (Pye 1975)★★★, *My Personal Choice* (BBC 1976)★★★, *Norrie Paramor Remembers ... 40 Years Of TV Themes* (BBC 1976)★★★, *Silver Serenade* (BBC

1977)★★★, *By Request* (BBC 1978)★★★, *Temptation* (Pye 1978)★★★, *Rags And Tatters* aka *Ragtime* (Pye 1978)★★, *Classical Rhythm* (Pye 1979)★★, *Thank You For The Music* (BBC 1979)★★★.
● COMPILATIONS: *Paramagic Pianos* (Golden Hour 1977)★★★, *The Best Of Norrie Paramor* (BBC 1984)★★★.

PARKER, 'COLONEL' TOM

b. Andreas Cornelius van Kuijk, 26 June 1909, Breda, The Netherlands, d. 21 January 1997. Since his death, there still remains bitter division about Parker. Was he Sam Katzman's 'biggest con artist in the world' or merely an unsophisticated fairground barker sucked into a vortex of circumstances he was unwilling to resist? Arguments supporting either view might be construed from the icy ruthlessness formidable to those accustomed to Tin Pan Alley's glib bonhomie, and his blunt stance in negotiation on behalf of Elvis Presley, his most famous managerial client. 'Don't criticize what you can't understand, son', Presley said in the Colonel's defence. 'You never walked in that man's shoes.' Parker was an illegal immigrant, without passport or papers, who settled into carnival life in the 20s. Over the next decade, he evolved into a cigar-chewing huckster of spectacular amorality - exemplified by his practice of snaring sparrows, painting them yellow and selling them as canaries. With duties that included palm reading, he served the Royal American, the Union's top travelling show, for a while before a seemingly steady job as promoter for a charity organization in Tampa, Florida. Extremely potent fund-raisers, he discovered, were shows headlined by a popular C&W artist - and so it was that Parker came to commit himself full-time to the genre by moving to Nashville, where he became Eddy Arnold's personal manager. Once, when this vocalist was indisposed, an unruffled Parker allegedly offered a substitute attraction of two unhappy 'dancing chickens' who high-stepped around a cage to ease feet scorched by an electric hot plate hidden under their straw.

After Arnold left him, the Colonel (an honorary title conferred by the Tennessee Militia in 1953) took on Hank Snow - and it was in a support spot on a Snow tour of the deep south that 19-year-old Presley was noticed by his future svengali. Via connections nurtured during proceedings concerning Arnold and Snow, Parker persuaded RCA to contract his new find. A few months later in March 1956, the boy committed himself formally to Parker for life - and beyond. From that month, 'Elvis has required every minute of my time, and I think he would have suffered had I signed anyone else'. While facilitating Presley's captivation of a global 'youth market', the Colonel's instinct for the commercial and economic machinations of the record industry obliged RCA to accede to his every desire, such as the pressing of one million copies of every Elvis release, regardless of positioning research. Moreover, to the team fell an average of eight per cent of approved merchandise associated with Presley - and, when the time came for the King to act in films, producer Hal Wallis grew to 'rather try and close a deal with the Devil' than Parker. To publicize one Presley movie, Parker was not above hiring dwarfs to parade through Hollywood as 'The Elvis Presley Midget Fan Club'. He was also behind the taming of Presley via the stressing of a cheerful diligence while on national service; the post-army chart potboilers; the overall projection of Presley as an 'all-round entertainer', and, arguably, the moulding of his reactionary leanings. Nor did Parker object to Katzman dashing off a Presley vehicle in less than a month, each one a quasi-musical of cheery unreality usually more vacuous and streamlined than the one before. This was almost all fans saw of the myth-shrouded Elvis until his impatient return to the stage in 1968, whether the Colonel liked it or not.

After Presley's death in 1977, there were rumours that Parker would be devoting himself professionally to Rick Nelson, but only Presley's posthumous career interrupted a virtual retirement in Palm Springs. Parker was a consummate showman and media manipulator, who clearly enjoyed turning down million of dollars whenever his charge was asked to headline some grand concert package. His handling of merchandising rights during the early part of Presley's career has been compared favourably to the business dealings of later starmakers such as Brian Epstein. The obsession with commerce and disavowal of artistry dominated the Colonel's thinking, however, which mainly explains the singer's appalling film-related output during the early/mid-60s. After Presley's death, Parker's business empire was threatened by the star's estate - in the form of Elvis's ex-wife Priscilla and daughter Lisa Marie. Parker fought tenaciously to protect his empire before settling in June 1983. Thereafter, he surrendered claims to all future Elvis income, but received two million dollars from RCA, and 50 per cent of all Presley's record royalties prior to September 1982. In January 1993, Parker made one of his rare public appearances, signing autographs to promote the newly issued Elvis Presley postage stamp. He spent the last years of his life in his beloved Las Vegas, where he could feed his gambling addiction.
● FURTHER READING: *Elvis*, Albert Grossman. *Elvis And The Colonel*, Dirk Vallenga and Mick Farren.

PARKER, FESS

b. 16 August 1925, Fort Worth, Texas, USA. An actor and singer, Parker did some stage work before making his film debut in 1952 in *Untamed Frontier*, a western starring Joseph Cotton and Shelley Winters. Two years later he appeared as the famous Indian scout-legislator-Alamo defender Davy Crockett, in three episodes of the television series *Disneyland*. The shows were extremely popular, and the theme, 'The Ballad Of Davy Crockett', written by scriptwriter Tom Blackburn and George Bruns, became a US number 1 hit for Bill Hayes, well known on television himself for *Show Of Shows*. Subsequently, Parker's own version of the song made the US Top 10. When the big screen version, *Davy Crockett, King Of The Wild Frontier!*, was made in 1955, coonskin caps abounded, nationwide and beyond; the inevitable sequel, *Davy Crockett And The River Pirates*, was released in 1956. In the same year, Parker starred in Walt Disney's *Westward Ho, The Wagons!*, which featured five new songs, including 'Wringle Wrangle', Parker's second, and last, chart success. His other movies, through to the 60s, included *The Great Locomotive Chase* (1956), *Old Yeller* (1957 - the first of the many Disney films about a boy and his dog), *The Hangman* (1959) and *Hell Is For Heroes* (1962), an exciting World War II drama, with Steve McQueen and Bobby Darin. Parker was also prominent on US television; in 1962 he co-starred with country singer Red Foley in a series based on Lewis R. Foster's classic, *Mr. Smith Goes To Washington*. Two years later he returned to the backwoods and portrayed yet another legendary American pioneer in *Daniel Boone*, which ran until 1968. In 1972 he played a tough sheriff in the US television movie *Climb An Angry Mountain*. After he retired from showbusiness, Parker moved to Santa Barbara, California, and initially concentrated on a career in real estate. Since then, as the owner of Santa Barbara's Red Lion Resort and Parker Winery, he has become something of a tycoon, and by the early 90s his products were selling in over 30 states.

● ALBUMS: with Marion Marlowe *TV Sweethearts* (Columbia 1955)★★, *The Adventures Of Davy Crockett* (Columbia 1955)★★★, *Yarns And Songs* (Disneyland 1959)★★, *Cowboy And Indian Songs* (Disneyland 1960)★★, *Fess Parker Sings About Daniel Boone, Davy Crockett And Abe Lincoln* (RCA Victor 1964)★.

PASTELS

This R&B vocal group formed at a US Air Force base in Narsarssuak, Greenland, in 1954, and comprised Big Dee Irwin, Richard Travis, Tony Thomas and Jimmy Willingham. Members were later transferred to Washington, DC, and the Pastels were discovered by the New York-based Hull Records in 1957. They were signed to the company's subsidiary label, Mascot, but after their first hit, 'Been So Long', all their records were leased to the Chess (Records) brothers' Argo label in Chicago. 'Been So Long', an R&B number 5 and pop Top 30 hit, was an utterly sublime doo-wop with haunting chorusing, and for decades later was a staple on oldies radio shows. By 1958 all the Pastels had left the service, and the group was ready to exploit the success of their hit with follow-ups; however, they instead suffered a severe failure, with a lack of national chart success in 1958 for the sublime 'So Far Away', their third and final release. The following year the Pastels disbanded but Dee Irwin continued in the music business. In 1964 he enjoyed a Top 40 national pop hit with 'Swingin' On A Star', accompanied by the uncredited Little Eva. He continued behind the scenes as a songwriter, composing for artists such as Ray Charles, Arthur Prysock, Esther Phillips and Isaac Hayes.

PATTERSON, OTTILIE

b. Anna-Ottilie Patterson, 31 January 1932, Comber, County Down, Northern Ireland. Patterson is perhaps best known for her long-time association with Chris Barber, her husband, in the 50s and 60s. With Barber she sang jazz and blues but she was also an accomplished folk singer. Ranging outside popular fields, she has also composed music to accompany poetry. For some years she was obliged through ill health to abandon her singing career, but later returned to the stage to the delight of her many fans. An engaging singer, with a strong, earthy delivery that lends itself well to the blues and some aspects of the jazz songbook, for her folk singing she was always able to adjust to a more pensive approach. A bright and bubbling personality, she is at her best in live performances and has been captured in splendid form on a number of live albums by the Barber band.

● ALBUMS: with Chris Barber *Chris Barber At The London Palladium* (Columbia 1961)★★★★.

● COMPILATIONS: with Barber *40 Years Jubilee Volumes 1 and 2* (Timeless 1990)★★★★.

PAUL, LES

b. 9 June 1915, Wankesha, Wisconsin, USA. Paul began playing guitar and other instruments while still a child. In the early 30s he broadcast on the radio and in 1936 was leading his own trio. In the late 30s and early 40s he worked in New York, where he was featured on Fred Waring's radio show. He made records accompanying singers such as Bing Crosby and the Andrews Sisters. Although his work was in the popular vein, with a strong country leaning, Paul was highly adaptable and frequently sat in with jazz musicians. One of his favourites was Nat 'King' Cole, whom he knew in Los Angeles, and the two men appeared together at a Jazz At The Philharmonic concert in 1944, on which Paul played some especially fine blues. Dissatisfied with the sound of the guitars he played, Paul developed his own design for a solid-bodied instrument, which he had made at his own expense. Indeed, the company, Gibson, were so cool towards the concept that they insisted their name should not appear on the instruments they made for him. In later years, when it seemed that half the guitarists in the world were playing Les Paul-style Gibson guitars, the company's attitude was understandably a little different. Paul's dissatisfaction with existing techniques extended beyond the instrument and into the recording studios. Eager to experiment with a multi-tracking concept, he built a primitive studio in his own home. He produced a succession of superb recordings on which he played multi-track guitar, among them 'Lover', 'Nola', 'Brazil' and 'Whispering'. During the 50s Paul continued his experimentation with other, similar recordings, while his wife, Mary Ford (b. 7 July 1928, d. 30 September 1977), sang multiple vocal lines. Other major record successes were 'The World Is Waiting For The Sunrise', 'How High The Moon', which reached number 1, and 'Vaya Con Dios', another US number 1 hit. By the early 60s Paul had tired of the recording business and retired. He and Ford were divorced in 1963 and he spent his time inventing and helping to promote Gibson guitars. In the late 70s he returned to the studios for two successful albums of duets with Chet Atkins, but by the end of the decade he had retired again.

A television documentary in 1980, *The Wizard Of Wankesha*, charted his life and revived interest in his career. In 1984 he made a comeback to performing and continued to make sporadic appearances throughout the rest of the decade. He was even performing at the guitar festival in Seville, Spain, in 1992. A remarkably gifted and far-sighted guitarist, Paul's contribution to popular music must inevitably centre upon his pioneering work on multi-tracking and his creation of the solid-bodied guitar. It would be sad, however, if his efforts in these directions wholly concealed his considerable abilities as a performer.

● ALBUMS: with Mary Ford *Hawaiian Paradise* (Decca 1949)★★, *Galloping Guitars* (Decca 1952)★★★, with Ford *New Sound, Volume 1 & 2* (Capitol 1950)★★★, *Bye, Bye Blues* (Capitol 1952)★★★★, with Ford *The Hitmakers* (Capitol 1955)★★★, with Ford *Les And Mary* (Capitol 1955)★★★★, with Ford *Time To Dream* (Capitol 1957)★★★, *More Of Les* (Decca 1958)★★★, with Ford *Lover's Luau* (Columbia 1959)★★★, with Ford *Warm And Wonderful* (Columbia 1962)★★★, with Ford *Bouquet Of Roses* (Columbia 1962)★★★, with Ford *Swingin' South* (Columbia 1963)★★★, *Les Paul Now* (Decca 1968)★★★, with Chet

Atkins *Chester And Lester* (RCA Victor 1976)★★★, with Atkins *Guitar Monsters* (RCA Victor 1978)★★★.
● COMPILATIONS: with Ford *The Hits Of Les And Mary* (Capitol 1960)★★★★, with Ford *The Fabulous Les Paul And Mary Ford* (Columbia 1965)★★★, *The Very Best Of Les Paul And Mary Ford* (1974)★★★★, with Ford *The Capitol Years* (Capitol 1989)★★★★, *The Legend And The Legacy* 4-CD box set (Capitol 1991)★★★★.
● VIDEOS: *He Changed The Music* (Excalibur 1990), *Living Legend Of The Electric Guitar* (BMG 1995).
● FURTHER READING: *Les Paul: An American Original*, Mary Alice Shaughnessy. *Gibson Les Paul Book: A Complete History Of Gibson Les Paul Guitars*, Tony Bacon and Paul Day.

PEIFFER, BERNARD

b. 23 October 1922, Epinal, France, d. 7 September 1976. Following intensive training as a classical pianist, Peiffer began playing jazz in distinguished company. While still a young man he played with Django Reinhardt, Hubert Rostaing and other European jazzmen and also with visiting Americans such as Rex Stewart, Don Byas and Sidney Bechet. By the end of the 40s he had become very well known in his native land, leading small groups and also working alone. Persuaded to visit the USA, he moved there in the mid-50s and thereafter commuted between the USA and Europe. An exceptionally accomplished technician, Peiffer's solo playing was rich and sometimes florid. He was forward thinking in his style, despite the swing era resonances of his early associations. He also composed much of his repertoire.
● ALBUMS: *Bernie's Tunes* (EmArcy 1956)★★★, *Modern Jazz For People Who Like Original Music* (Laurie 1960)★★★.

PEMBERTON, BILL

b. William McLane Pemberton, 5 March 1918, New York, USA, d. 13 December 1984. After first playing violin, he switched to bass in his late teens. In the early and mid-40s he played in bands led by Frankie Newton and Herman Chittison, finding time also to play with Mercer Ellington, Billy Kyle and others. In the 50s he worked with Art Tatum and Rex Stewart, the latter association being with the acclaimed Fletcher Henderson reunion band. In the mid- to late 60s he had a long spell with Earl 'Fatha' Hines and then formed the JPJ Quartet with Budd Johnson, Oliver Jackson and Dill Jones. This band was active until the mid-70s but Pemberton also played and sometimes recorded with many other musicians, including Ruby Braff and Vic Dickenson. He continued freelancing during the late 70s, then joined David 'Panama' Francis And The Savoy Sultans. He stayed with this band until shortly before his death, his last formal recording date being with Doc Cheatham. A secure and dynamic player, Pemberton displayed a strong rhythmic approach to his instrument. His rich sound added texture to the rhythm sections of the bands in which he played.
● ALBUMS: with Fletcher Henderson *All Stars The Big Reunion* (Jazztone 1957)★★★, with the JPJ Quartet *Montreux '71* (MJR 1971)★★★, with David 'Panama' Francis *Gettin' In The Groove* (Black And Blue 1979)★★★, with Doc Cheatham *The Fabulous Doc Cheatham* (Parkwood 1983)★★★.

PENGUINS

Formed in 1954 in Fremont High School, Los Angeles, California, USA, the Penguins were one of the most important R&B vocal groups from the west coast in the early 50s. Their hit ballad 'Earth Angel' remains one of the most fondly recalled 'doo-wop' recordings. The group consisted of lead vocalist Cleveland 'Cleve' Duncan (b. 23 July 1935, Los Angeles, California, USA), Bruce Tate (baritone), Curtis Williams (first tenor) and Dexter Tisby (second tenor). Williams learned 'Earth Angel' from Los Angeles R&B singer Jesse Belvin, and passed it on to his group. Some sources give co-writing credit to Williams, Belvin and Gaynel Hodge, a member of vocal group the Turks. Hodge won a 1956 lawsuit recognizing his role in the writing of the song. However, most reissues of 'Earth Angel' still list only either Belvin, Williams or both. The Penguins, who took their name from a penguin on a cigarette packet, signed with the local DooTone Records, owned by Dootsie Williams. Their first recording date was as a backing group for a blues singer, Willie Headon. They next recorded 'Hey Sinorita', an up-tempo number. 'Earth Angel' was chosen as their first single's b-side but when both sides were played on LA radio station KGJF, listeners called in to request that 'Earth Angel' be played again. It ultimately reached number 1 in the US *Billboard* R&B chart. It also reached the pop Top 10, but was eclipsed by a cover version by the white group the Crew-Cuts. The song has also charted by Gloria Mann (1955), Johnny Tillotson (1960), the Vogues (1969) and New Edition (1986). The Penguins continued to record other singles for DooTone (plus one album for the related Dooto label) and then Mercury Records, before disbanding in 1959. Members Williams and Tate have since died, Tisby retired from music, and Duncan later formed new bands under the name Penguins; he was still performing under that name in the early 90s.
● ALBUMS: *The Cool, Cool Penguins* (Dooto 1959)★★★, side 1 only *The Best Vocal Groups: Rhythm And Blues* (Dooto 1959)★★★, *Big Jay McNeely Meets The Penguins* (Ace 1984)★★★, *Earth Angel* (Ace 1988)★★★, *The Authentic Golden Hits Of The Penguins* (Juke Box 1993)★★★.

PEPPER, ART

b. 1 September 1925, Gardena, Los Angeles, California, USA, d. 15 June 1982. Pepper started out on clarinet at the age of nine, switching to alto saxophone four years later. After appearing in school groups, he first played professionally with Gus Arnheim's band. During his mid-teens he developed his jazz style sitting in with otherwise all-black bands along Los Angeles's Central Avenue. After leaving Arnheim he worked with Dexter Gordon in Lee Young's band at the Club Alabam. He then joined Benny Carter, playing alongside artists such as Gerald Wilson, Freddie Webster and J.J. Johnson. In 1943 Pepper joined Stan Kenton but soon afterwards was drafted into the US Army, spending most of his wartime service in England. In 1946 he rejoined Kenton, staying with the band until 1951. That year he also recorded with Shorty Rogers, playing a marvellous version of 'Over The Rainbow', a tune he would regularly play over the years. Later, he appeared on Rogers's *Cool And Crazy* album. Pepper subsequently freelanced around Los Angeles, performing many record dates, some under his own name, and usually playing extremely well. Nevertheless, his career in the 50s and 60s was marred by his drug addiction and interrupted by several prison sentences. At the end of the 60s Pepper began a slow, uphill fight against his addiction, a struggle that was eventually successful and heralded his re-emergence in the mid-70s as a major figure on the international jazz scene. In the last years of his life, he produced a rich crop of recordings, including *Winter Moon*, an album with strings (a long-held ambition of Pepper's), the three-album set *Live At The Village Vanguard* (a fourth volume appeared posthumously) and two records recorded live in London under the name of pianist Milcho Leviev, *Blues For The Fisherman* and *True Blues*. Early in his career Pepper played with a light airy tone, through which burned a rare intensity of emotion that reflected his admiration for Charlie Parker and the lessons he learned playing with Carter. After his rehabilitation and a period playing tenor saxophone, on which instrument he showed both the influence of Lester Young and an awareness of John Coltrane, Pepper developed a strong, bop-rooted alto style that retained much of the richly melodic elements of his earlier playing. Pepper's life story was memorably recounted in his candid autobiography and a subsequent film, *Art Pepper: Notes From A Jazz Survivor* (1982), which offered a potent and harshly unsentimental lesson for any young musician contemplating the use of addictive drugs.

● ALBUMS: *Art Pepper Quartet* 10-inch album (Discovery 1952) reissued as *Surf Ride* (Savoy 1956)★★★, *The Way It Was* (1956)★★★, *The Return Of Art Pepper* (Jazz West 1956)★★★, with Chet Baker *The Route* (Pacific Jazz 1956)★★★, with Baker *Playboys* (Pacific Jazz 1957)★★★, *The Artistry Of Pepper* (Pacific 1957)★★★★, *Modern Art* (Intro 1957)★★★★, *The Art Of Pepper* (Blue Note 1957)★★★★, *Art Pepper Meets The Rhythm Section* (Contemporary 1957)★★★, *Art Pepper Quartet* (Tampa 1958)★★★, *Art Pepper + Eleven: Modern Jazz Classics* (Contmporary 1959)★★★★, *Gettin' Together!* (Contemporary 1960)★★★★, *Smack Up!* (Contemporary 1961)★★★★, *Modern Jazz Classics* (Contemporary 1961)★★★★, *Intensity* recorded 1960 (Contemporary 1963)★★★★, *The Way It Was* (Contemporary 1966)★★★★, *Live At Donte's Vol. 1* (1968)★★★, *The Omega Man* recorded 1968 (1974)★★★, *I'll Remember April* (Storyville 1975)★★★, *Living Legend* (Original Jazz Classics 1976)★★★, *The Trip* (Original Jazz Classics 1977)★★★, *A Night In Tunisia* (Storyville 1977)★★★, *No Limit* (Original Jazz Classics 1978)★★★, *Among Friends* (Interplay 1978)★★★, *Live In Japan* (1978)★★★, *Art Pepper Today* (1978)★★★, *Straight Life* (Galaxy 1979)★★★, *Landscape* (Galaxy 1980)★★★, *Omega Alpha* 1957 recording (Liberty 1980)★★★, *So Much In Love* (1980)★★★, *Live At The Village Vanguard* 1977 recording (Contemporary 1981)★★★, *Winter Moon* (Galaxy 1981)★★★, *Besame Mucho* 1979 recording (1981)★★★, *One September Afternoon* (Galaxy 1982)★★★, *Darn That Dream* (1982)★★★, *Road Game* (Galaxy 1982)★★★, *Goin' Home* (Original Jazz Classics 1982)★★★, *Art Lives* 1981 recording (1983)★★★, *Art Works* 1979 recording (1984)★★★, *Live At The Village Vanguard, Volume 4* 1977 recording (Carrere 1985)★★★.

● COMPILATIONS: *Early Art* 1956-57 recordings (1976)★★★, *Artistry In Jazz* (JVC 1987)★★★, *The Art Of Pepper, Volumes 1 & 2* (VSOP 1988)★★★★, *The Complete Galaxy Recordings* 16-CD box set (Galaxy 1989)★★★★, *Memorial Collection Vols 1-4* (Storyville 1990)★★★, *The Best Of Art Pepper* (Blue Note 1993)★★★★, *The Complete Vanguard Sessions* 9-CD box set (Contemporary 1995)★★★★.

● FURTHER READING: *Straight Life: The Story Of Art Pepper*, Art and Laurie Pepper.

PERKINS, CARL

b. Carl Lee Perkins, 9 April 1932, Ridgely, Tennessee, USA (his birth certificate misspelled the last name as Perkings), d. 19 January 1998, Nashville, Tennessee, USA. Carl Perkins was one of the most renowned rockabilly artists recording for Sun Records in the 50s and the author of the classic song 'Blue Suede Shoes'. As a guitarist, he influenced many of the next generation of rock 'n' rollers, most prominently, George Harrison and Dave Edmunds. His parents, Fonie 'Buck' and Louise Brantley Perkins, were sharecroppers during the Depression and the family was thus very poor. As a child Perkins listened to the *Grand Ole Opry* on the radio, exposing him to C&W (or hillbilly) music, and he listened to the blues being sung by a black sharecropper named John Westbrook across the field from where he worked. After World War II the Perkins family relocated to Bemis, Tennessee, where he and his brothers picked cotton; by that time his father was unable to work due to a lung infection. Having taught himself rudimentary guitar from listening to such players as Butterball Page and Arthur Smith, Perkins bought an electric guitar and learned to play it more competently. In 1953 Carl, his brothers Jay (rhythm guitar) and Clayton (upright bass), and drummer W.S. 'Fluke' Holland formed a band that worked up a repertoire of hillbilly songs performing at local honky tonks, primarily in the Jackson, Tennessee area, where Carl settled with his wife Valda Crider in 1954. His borrowing of some techniques from the black musicians he had studied set Perkins apart from the many other country guitarists in that region at that time; his style of playing lead guitar fills around his own vocals was similar to that used in the blues. Encouraged by his wife, and by hearing a record by Elvis Presley on the radio, Perkins decided in 1954 to pursue a musical career. That October the Perkins brothers travelled to Memphis to audition for Sam Phillips at Sun Records. Phillips was not overly impressed, but agreed that the group had potential. In February 1955 he issued two songs from that first Perkins session, 'Movie Magg' and 'Turn Around', on his new Flip label. Pure country in nature, these did not make a dent in the market. Perkins' next single was issued in August, this time on Sun itself. One track, 'Let The Jukebox Keep On Playing', was again country, but the other song, 'Gone! Gone! Gone!' was pure rockabilly. Again, it was not a hit. That November, after Phillips sold Presley's Sun contract to RCA Records, Phillips decided to push the next Perkins single, an original called 'Blue Suede Shoes'. The song had its origins when Johnny Cash, another Sun artist, suggested to Perkins that he write a song based on the phrase 'Don't step on my blue suede shoes'. It was recorded at Sun on 19 December 1955, along with three other songs, among them the b-side 'Honey Don't', later to be covered by the Beatles. 'Blue Suede Shoes' entered the US *Billboard* chart on 3 March 1956 (the same day Presley's first single entered the chart), by which time several cover versions had been recorded, by a range of artists from Presley to Lawrence Welk. Perkins' version quickly became a huge hit and was also the first country record to appear on both the R&B chart and the pop chart, in addition to the country chart. Just as Perkins was beginning to enjoy the fruits of his labour, the car in which he and his band were driving to New York was involved in a severe accident near Dover, Delaware, when their manager, Stuart Pinkham, fell asleep at the wheel. Perkins and his brother Clayton suffered broken bones; brother Jay suffered a fractured neck; and the driver of the truck they hit, Thomas Phillips, was killed. 'Blue Suede Shoes' ultimately reached number 2 on the pop chart, a number 1 country hit and an R&B number 2. Owing to the accident, Perkins was unable to promote the record, the momentum was lost, and none of his four future chart singles would climb nearly as high. In the UK, 'Blue Suede Shoes' became Perkins' only chart single, and was upstaged commercially by the Presley cover version. Perkins continued to record for Sun until mid-1958, but the label's newcomers, Johnny Cash and Jerry Lee Lewis, occupied most of Sam Phillips' attention. Perkins' follow-up to 'Blue Suede Shoes', 'Boppin' The Blues', only reached number 70, and 'Your True Love' number 67. While still at Sun, Perkins did record numerous tracks that would later be revered by rockabilly fans, among them 'Everybody's Trying To Be My Baby' and 'Matchbox', both of which were also covered by the Beatles. On 4 December 1956, Perkins was joined by Lewis and a visiting Presley at Sun in an impromptu jam session which was recorded and released two decades later under the title 'The Million Dollar Quartet'. (Johnny Cash, despite having his photograph taken with Presley, Lewis and Carl, did not take part in the 'million dollar session' - he went shopping instead.) One of Perkins' last acts while at Sun was to appear in the film *Jamboree*, singing a song called 'Glad All Over'. In January 1958, Perkins signed with Columbia Records, where Cash would soon follow. Although some of the songs he recorded for that label were very good, only two, 'Pink Pedal Pushers' and 'Pointed Toe Shoes', both obvious attempts to recapture the success of his first footwear-oriented hit, had a minor impression on the charts. Later that year Jay Perkins died of a brain tumour, causing Carl to turn alcoholic, an affliction from which he would not recover until the late 60s.

In 1963 Perkins signed with Decca Records, for whom there were no successful releases. He also toured outside of the USA in 1963-64; while in Britain, he met the Beatles, and watched as they recorded his songs. Perkins, who, ironically, was becoming something of a legend in Europe (as were many early rockers), returned to England for a second tour in October 1964. By 1966 he had left Decca for the small Dollie Records, a country label. In 1967 he joined Johnny Cash's band as guitarist and was allotted a guest singing spot during each of Cash's concerts and television shows. In 1969, Cash recorded Perkins' song 'Daddy Sang Bass', a minor hit in the USA. By 1970, Perkins was back on Columbia, this time recording an album together with new rock revival group NRBQ. In 1974 he signed with Mercury Records. Late that year his brother Clayton committed suicide and their father died. Perkins left Cash in 1976 and went on the road with a band consisting of Perkins' two sons, with whom he was still performing in the 90s. A tribute single to the late Presley, 'The EP Express', came in 1977 and a new album, now for the Jet label, was released in 1978. By the 80s Perkins' reputation as one of rock's pioneers

had grown. He recorded an album with Cash and Lewis, *The Survivors* (another similar project, with Cash, Lewis and Roy Orbison, *Class Of '55*, followed in 1986). Perkins spent much of the 80s touring and working with younger musicians who were influenced by him, among them Paul McCartney and the Stray Cats. In 1985 he starred in a television special to mark the 30th anniversary of 'Blue Suede Shoes'. It co-starred Harrison, Ringo Starr, Dave Edmunds, two members of the Stray Cats, Rosanne Cash and Eric Clapton. In 1987 Perkins was elected to the Rock And Roll Hall of Fame. He signed to the Universal label in 1989 and released *Born To Rock*. His early work has been anthologized many times in several countries. He was unwell for much of the 90s and suffered from a heart condition that took its toll in January 1998.

● ALBUMS: *The Dance Album Of Carl Perkins* (Sun 1957)★★★★, *Whole Lotta Shakin'* (Columbia 1958)★★★, *Country Boy's Dream* (Dollie 1967)★★★, *Blue Suede Shoes* (Sun 1969)★★★, *Carl Perkins On Top* (Columbia 1969)★★★, with the NRBQ *Boppin' The Blues* (Columbia 1970)★★★, *My Kind Of Country* (Mercury 1973)★★★, *The Carl Perkins Show* (Suede 1976)★★★, *Ol' Blue Suede's Back* (Jet 1978)★★, *Rock 'N' Gospel* (Koala 1979)★★, *Sing A Song With Me* (Koala 1979)★★, *Country Soul* (Koala 1979)★★, *Cane Creek Glory Church* (Koala 1979)★★, *Live At Austin City Limits* (Suede 1981)★★★, with Jerry Lee Lewis, Johnny Cash *The Survivors* (Columbia 1982)★★★, *Carl Perkins* (Dot 1985)★★★, *Turn Around* Decca demos (Culture Press 1985)★★, with Jerry Lee Lewis, Johnny Cash, Roy Orbison *Class Of '55* (America 1986)★★★, *Interviews From The Class Of '55 Recording Sessions* (America 1986)★★, *Born To Rock* (Universal/MCA 1989)★★★, with Elvis Presley and Jerry Lee Lewis *The Million Dollar Quartet* (RCA 1990)★★★, *Friends, Family & Legends* (Platinum 1992)★★★, with Scotty Moore *706 Reunion - A Sentimental Journey* cassette only (Belle Meade 1993)★★★, *Hound Dog* (Muskateer 1995)★★★, with various artists *Go Cat Go!* (Dinosaur 1996)★★★.

● COMPILATIONS: *King Of Rock* (Columbia 1968)★★★, *Carl Perkins' Greatest Hits* re-recorded Sun material (Columbia 1969)★★, *Original Golden Hits* (Sun 1970)★★★, *Blue Suede Shoes* (Sun 1971)★★★, *Carl Perkins* (Harmony 1970)★★★, *The Sun Years* 3-LP box set (Sun 1982)★★★★, *Carl Perkins* (Cambra 1983)★★★, *The Heart And Soul Of Carl Perkins* (Allegiance 1984)★★★, *Dixie Fried* (Charly 1986)★★★, *Up Through The Years, 1954-1957* (Bear Family 1986)★★★★, *Original Sun Greatest Hits* (Rhino 1986)★★★, *The Country Store Collection* (Country Store 1988)★★, *Honky Tonk Gal: Rare And Unissued Sun Masters* (Rounder 1989)★★, *Matchbox* (Tring 1990)★★, *Jive After Five: Best Of Carl Perkins (1958-1978)* (Rhino 1990)★★★, *The Classic Carl Perkins* 5-CD box set (Bear Family 1990)★★★★, *Restless: The Columbia Recordings* (Columbia 1992)★★★, *Country Boy's Dream: The Dollie Masters* (Bear Family 1994)★★★, *Best Of Carl Perkins* (Castle 1995)★★★, *Boppin' Blue Suede Shoes* (Charly 1995)★★★, *The Rockabilly King* (Charly 1995)★★★, *The Unissued Carl Perkins* (Charly 1995)★★, *The Masters* (Eagle 1997)★★★.

● VIDEOS: *Rockabilly Session* (Virgin Vision 1986), *Carl Perkins & Jerry Lee Lewis Live* (BBC Video 1987), *This Country's Rockin'* (1993).

● FURTHER READING: *Disciple In Blue Suede Shoes*, Carl

Perkins. *Go, Cat, Go: Life And Times Of Carl Perkins The King Of Rockabilly*, Carl Perkins with David McGee.
● FILMS: *Jamboree* aka *Disc Jockey Jamboree* (1957).

PERSIANY, ANDRÉ

b. André Paul Stephane Persiani, 19 November 1927, Paris, France. Persiany began playing piano as a child and by his early twenties was an accomplished leader of small groups playing swing-style jazz. He worked with numerous touring American jazz artists including Bill Coleman, Buck Clayton and Lionel Hampton through the late 40s and early 50s. In the mid-50s he moved to New York where he played with several bands before becoming a member of the Jonah Jones quartet in 1961. He remained with Jones for most of the decade before returning to his homeland. In the 70s he again played with visiting Americans, including Milt Buckner in whose playing style Persiany found qualities he liked and chose to emulate. He plays with a strong rhythmic pulse for the swing era style of jazz piano.
● ALBUMS: *Swinging Here And There* (Pathé 1956-58)★★★.

PETER PAN

A musical adaptation of J.M. Barrie's classic story was presented in New York as early as 1905 when Maude Adams and Ernest Lawford starred in a Charles Frohman production. It was revived in 1924, with Marilyn Miller in the leading role, and included two Jerome Kern songs, 'The Sweetest Thing In Life' and 'Just Because You're You'. The 1950 version, which ran for 321 performances, starred Jean Arthur and Boris Karloff. Leonard Bernstein wrote the music and lyrics for several songs, such 'Who Am I?', 'Never-Land', 'Peter, Peter' and 'My House', and Alec Wilder also provided some incidental music. In the fourth interpretation, which opened at the Winter Garden in New York on 20 October 1954, Mary Martin, returning to Broadway for the first time since her triumph in *South Pacific*, played a spirited, high-flying Peter, to Cyril Ritchard's amusingly degenerate Captain Hook. The initial score, which was written by Moose Charlap and Carolyn Leigh, contained songs such as 'Tender Shepherd', 'I've Got To Crow', 'I'm Flying', and 'I Won't Grow Up'. Before the show reached Broadway, director and choreographer Jerome Robbins asked Jule Styne, Betty Comden and Adolph Green to provide the music and lyrics for several additional numbers, including 'Captain Hook's Waltz', 'Wendy', 'Mysterious Lady', and the lovely 'Never Never Land', which is still sung occasionally, and received a sensitive reading from Lena Horne on her *Lena At The Sands*. Mary Martin received the Tony Award for best actress, and this version ran for 152 performances before it was taped and shown on US television, giving non theatre-going audiences a rare opportunity to see a Broadway show. A 1979 New York revival, starring Sandy Duncan and George Rose, beat all the previous versions and lasted for 551 performances. Six years later, the same production played London's West End, with Joss Ackland, Judith Bruce and Bonnie Langford. In 1990, Cathy Rigby and Stephan Hanon played Peter and Hook when *Peter Pan* briefly returned to Broadway for a limited six-week engagement as part of its nationwide tour. Numerous, quite different, adaptations of J.M. Barrie's *Peter Pan* have been presented in the UK, including two major London productions - one with music and lyrics by Stephen Oliver at the Barbican Theatre in 1982, and another, *Peter Pan: The British Musical*, with a score by Piers Chater-Robinson, which starred Ron Moody and played at the Cambridge Theatre in 1994.
● FURTHER READING: *The Peter Pan Chronicles*, Bruce K. Hanson.

PETTY, NORMAN

b. 1927, Clovis, New Mexico, USA, d. 15 August 1984, Lubbock, Texas, USA. Petty studied piano during his youth but became a recording engineer on local radio in Texas until his Norman Petty Trio - with wife Violet (organ) and Jack Vaughn (guitar) - achieved moderate record success in 1954 with an arrangement of Duke Ellington's 'Mood Indigo'. In similar cocktail lounge-style were smaller sellers, notably 'On The Alamo' and 1957's self-composed 'Almost Paradise' (revived in the 70s by Roger Whittaker). More immediate proceeds from these discs enabled him to build a private studio, NorVaJak, in Clovis for the sole use of the Trio, until Petty realized that he was unwittingly the owner of the only such facility in New Mexico and West Texas. Confident in his own technical abilities as both engineer and producer, he went public in 1955 - with Roy Orbison's Teen Kings among early customers. Petty was amenable to working at a paper loss in exchange for first refusal on publishing rights (for the Trio's own Nor Vi Jak Music) on items recorded. With a foot in various doors via 'Mood Indigo' *et al.*, he next tried to interest labels in those tracks he considered marketable. Through a leasing agreement with Roulette Records, the studio's first million-seller was Buddy Knox's 'Party Doll', but the most famous of its clients was Buddy Holly, who, with his Crickets, showed sufficient promise for Petty to offer to manage them. Furthermore, he (and Violet) received writing and arranging credits for certain Holly smashes - including 'That'll Be The Day' - and, until their sale to Paul McCartney in 1973, Petty retained rights to all items recorded by Holly. Indeed, in the years after Holly's fatal aircraft accident in 1958, Petty felt entitled to overdub fuller backings onto often sketchy material for commercial release. Although after Holly's death, Petty continued to record the Crickets, further hits were sporadic. In 1961 he secured an international chartbuster in the String-A-Longs' 'Wheels', while Jimmy Gilmer And The Fireballs topped *Billboard*'s Hot 100 in 1963 with 'Sugar Shack'. In the mid-60s, Petty assisted on two of Brian Poole And The Tremeloes' UK chart entries. He maintained an interest in his studio until his death in 1984 in Lubbock, home-town of Buddy Holly - with whom Petty's name will always be synonymous.
● COMPILATIONS: *15 Classic Memories* (Ace 1994)★★★.

PHILLIPS, DON

b. 18 December 1913, d. 24 February 1994. A popular figure in the worlds of both theatre and music, Phillips made his reputation in the 50s and 60s as a musical arranger for Shirley Bassey, Joan Regan, Donald Peers, Anne Shelton, Dickie Valentine, Alan Jones and others. He also played piano on stage for the Marx Brothers, and toured Cyprus with Harry Secombe to entertain troops. Phillips left school at the age of 14 with no musical training, but by the following year had begun his career playing the piano in London pubs. Almost immediately he was spotted by music publisher Lawrence Wright, who bought his songs. Among his many noteworthy compositions were 'Old Piano Rag',

'Skyscraper Fantasy', 'Concerto In Jazz' and 'A Live Show Is The Best Show', which became the theme tune to literally thousands of summer-season seaside shows. He was granted a Royal Command Performance in 1954. 'Melody Of The Sea' brought him an Ivor Novello award in 1958, while many of his songs were entered in the Eurovision Song Contest, the best-known pair being 'Love Is The Same Everywhere' (Matt Monro) and 'Girl With The Curl' (Ronnie Carroll). He went on to become musical director of several travelling shows and pantomimes, maintaining an office in Denmark Street ('Tin Pan Alley') until he became ill with Parkinson's Disease in the late 80s.

PHILLIPS, SAM

b. 1923, Florence, Alabama, USA. Although harbouring ambitions towards a career in criminal law, Phillips was obliged to drop out of high school to support his family. In 1942 he took up a post as disc jockey at station WLAY in Muscle Shoals, before moving to WREC in Memphis as an announcer four years later. In 1950 he opened Sam's Memphis Recording Studio at 706 Union Avenue, and although initial work largely consisted of chronicling weddings and social gatherings, Phillips' main ambition was to record local blues acts and license the resultant masters. Howlin' Wolf, Bobby Bland, Ike Turner, B.B. King and Roscoe Gordon were among the many acts Phillips produced for independent outlets Chess, Duke and RPM. Their success inspired the founding of Sun Records in February 1952, a venture that flourished the following year when Rufus Thomas achieved a notable R&B hit with 'Bear Cat'. Success was maintained by 'Little' Junior Parker and Billy 'The Kid' Emerson, while Phillips looked to expand the label's horizons by recording country acts. His wish to find a white singer comfortable with R&B was answered in 1954 with the arrival of Elvis Presley. The singer's five singles recorded with Phillips rank among pop's greatest achievements, and although criticized for allowing his protégé to sign for RCA Records, the producer used the settlement fee to further the careers of Carl Perkins, Johnny Cash and, later, Jerry Lee Lewis. Phillips' simple recording technique - single track, rhythmic string bass and judicious echo - defined classic rockabilly and for a brief period the label was in the ascendant. The style, however, proved too inflexible and by the beginning of the 60s new Memphis-based studios, Stax and Hi Records, challenged Sun's pre-eminent position. Phillips also became increasingly distracted by other ventures, including mining concerns, radio stations and, more crucially, his share of the giant Holiday Inn hotel chain. In 1969 he sold the entire Sun empire to country entrepreneur Shelby Singleton, thus effectively ending an era. Sam Phillips is nonetheless still revered as one of the leading catalysts in post-war American music and, if nothing else, for launching the career of Elvis Presley.

PHILLIPS, SID

b. 14 June 1902, London, England, d. 23 May 1973. Deeply involved in the music business from childhood, Phillips played clarinet in various bands, including one led by his brothers, and also worked in music publishing and for record companies. In the early 30s he was staff arranger for the popular band led by Bert Ambrose and later became a member of the band. He also began leading his own small

group in the 30s, but it was the bands he led from 1949 onwards that built his reputation. Broadcasting regularly on the radio, Phillips also recorded, and his band became one of the best-known Dixieland groups in the UK. Among the many fine musicians he employed at one time or another were George Shearing, Kenny Ball and Tommy Whittle. A gutsy, full-toned clarinettist, Phillips was also a skilful arranger and composed jazz-orientated dance tunes and several classical works. Changes in popular taste meant that from the 60s onwards his music was not in great demand, but he continued working until his death in 1973.
● ALBUMS: Sid Phillips And His Band i (1960)★★★★, Stardust (60s)★★★, Sid Phillips And His Band ii (1962)★★★★, Sid Phillips And His Band iii (1964)★★★, Rhythm Is Our Business (1970)★★★, Clarinet Marmalade (Rediffusion 1975)★★★, Sid Phillips And His Great Band Play Stomps, Rags And Blues (Rediffusion 1975)★★★, Sid Phillips Plays Barrelhouse Piano (Rediffusion 1975)★★★.
● COMPILATIONS: Golden Hour Presents Sid Phillips H'ors D'Ouvres (Golden Hour 1976)★★★, Anthology, Volume 1 - Chicago (Gold Star 1976)★★★★, Anthology, Volume 2 - Lonesome Road (Gold Star 1977)★★★, Anthology, Volume 3 - Way Down Yonder In New Orleans (Gold Star 1978)★★★, The Best Of Sid Phillips (EMI 1977)★★★★.

PHILLIPS, WOOLF

b. c.1920, London, England. At the age of 14 Phillips worked in the arranging department of music publisher Lawrence Wright, then went to Campbell Connolly where his older brother, Sid Phillips, was also arranging. Among the bands for whom the brothers arranged was one led by Bert Ambrose. Phillips began playing trombone and eventually joined Ambrose. Soon, he moved to the Joe Loss band, playing trombone and writing arrangements, played with other less well-known bands, then joined Jack Hylton. During World War II Phillips played in the band of the Royal Army Medical Corps and also performed with and arranged for Harry Roy. Phillips was a member of the original Ted Heath band on radio and records. After the war he played with Ambrose again and with Geraldo, formed his own big band, and was also leader of the Skyrockets at the London Palladium. Phillips continued to play and arrange in a variety of musical styles and settings. In 1967 he moved to the USA, continuing to arrange and also compose symphonic music. He has also conducted the Camarillo symphony orchestra.

PIAF, EDITH

b. Edith Giovanna Gassion, 19 December 1915, Paris, France, d. 11 October 1963. Born into desperate poverty, Piaf survived desertion by her mother and temporary childhood blindness, to eke out a living singing on the streets of Paris. After a brief period living in the country she sang in the streets with her father, an impoverished entertainer. The owner of Cerny's cabaret, Louis Leplée, heard the little girl and not only encouraged her but, struck by her diminutive stature, nicknamed her 'piaf', Parisian argot for 'little sparrow'. Piaf's dramatic singing style and her anguished voice appealed to French audiences and by the outbreak of World War II she had become a star. She proved her capacity for survival when she maintained her popularity despite being held as a material witness to Leplée's murder and facing accusations of collaboration with the German occupying forces. After the war Piaf's reputation spread internationally and she appeared in New York, singing at Carnegie Hall. In her private life Piaf was as tormented as the heroines of her songs and she had many relationships, most causing her severe emotional damage. She collapsed in 1959 but came back to sing with renewed vigour, even though her physical condition was visibly deteriorating. Among her many hits were several songs that she made her own, 'Les Tres Cloches, 'Milord', 'La Vie En Rose' and, above all others, if only because the sentiment expressed in the title and lyric so eloquently expressed her attitude to life, 'Non, Je Ne Regrette Rien'.

● ALBUMS: *Chansons De Cafe De Paris* (Decca 1951)★★★, *Chansons* (Columbia 1951)★★★, *La Vie En Rose* (Columbia 1956)★★★, *Sincerely* (Columbia 1960)★★★, *Piaf At The Paris Olympia* (Columbia 1961)★★★, *C'est La Piaf* (1962)★★★, *La Reine De La Chanson* (1963)★★★, *Ses Plus Belles Chansons* (Contour 1969)★★★, *I Regret Nothing* (Columbia 1971)★★★, *Her Legendary Live Recordings* (Columbia 1979)★★★, *De L'Accordeoniste A Milord* (EMI 1983)★★★, *De L'Accordeoniste A Milord (Volume 2)* (EMI 1986)★★★, *Heart And Soul* (Stylus 1987)★★★.

● COMPILATIONS: *Deluxe Set* 3-LP box set (Capitol 1968)★★★, *Edith Piaf, Volumes 1-4* (EMI 1986)★★★, *The Best Of Edith Piaf, Volumes 1 & 2* (Philips 1986)★★★, *Collection: Edith Piaf (20 Golden Greats)* (Deja Vu 1986)★★★, *25th Anniversaire, Volumes 1 & 2* (EMI 1988)★★★, *30eme Anniversaire* (1993)★★★, *Edith Piaf 1946-1963* 10-CD box set (1993)★★★, *L'Immortelle* (1994)★★★, various artists *Edith Piaf Tribute* (D# Records 1994)★★★.

● FURTHER READING: *The Wheel Of Fortune: The Autobiography Of Edith Piaf*, Edith Piaf. *Piaf*, Monique Lange. *The Piaf Legend*, David Bret. *Piaf*, Margaret Crosland. *Piaf*, Simone Berteaut. *Edith Piaf: My Life*, Edith Piaf and Jean Noli.

PIANO RED

b. William Lee Perryman, 19 October 1911, Hampton, Georgia, USA, d. 8 January 1985. The younger brother of blues artist Rufus 'Speckled Red' Perryman, this powerful keyboard player enjoyed several R&B bestsellers from 1950-51, including 'Rockin' With Red' and 'Red's Boogie'. He subsequently assumed another identity, Dr. Feelgood, and with his backing group, the Interns, secured further success in a series of pounding performances. His most influential releases included 'Right String Baby But The Wrong Yo Yo', the eponymous 'Doctor Feelgood', beloved of British beat groups, and 'Mister Moonlight', which was recorded by both the Beatles and the Merseybeats. Another of Perryman's whimsical offerings, 'Bald Headed Lena', was covered by the Lovin' Spoonful, but none of these versions matched the wry insistency of the originals. Perryman remained a popular live attraction, particularly in Europe, until his death in 1985.

● ALBUMS: *Piano Red In Concert* (Groove 1956)★★★, as Dr. Feelgood *Doctor Feelgood And The Interns* (OKeh 1962)★★★, *Happiness Is Piano Red* (King 1970)★★★, *All Alone With His Piano* (1972)★★★, *Piano Red - Ain't Going To Be Your Low-Down Dog No More* (Black Lion 1974)★★, as Dr. Feelgood *All Alone* (Arhoolie 1975)★★★, *Percussive Piano* (Euphonic 1979)★★, *Dr. Feelgood* (Black Lion

1979)★★★, with the Interns *What's Up Doc* (1984)★★, *Music Is Medicine* (1988)★★.

PIERCE, DON

b. 10 October 1919, Seattle, Washington, USA. Although destined to become a very respected record company director and producer, Pierce had no interest in music throughout his school years or his military service in World War II. During these years, golf held a great attraction and his interest in music came only after he became friendly with Hoagy Carmichael. In 1947, he risked his $12,000 savings by investing in the new 4 Star Record Company and (probably to help to safeguard his money at an uncertain time for the label) he also worked as a salesman. He became friendly with country singer T. Texas Tyler and began to take an active part in the production of some of the singer's very successful recordings. In October 1953, he profitably sold his 4 Star interest and, apparently for $333, purchased a third share in the recently formed Starday label, of Jack Starnes Jnr. and Pappy Daily, and its connected Starrite Publishing. Two years later, Starnes left and Pierce became co-owner of the label. A shrewd businessman, with an eye for a hit record and many contacts from his 4 Star days, Pierce soon attracted attention to the label with George Jones's recording of 'Why Baby Why'. For five years Starday, while maintaining all copyrights, operated an agreement with Mercury Records, but in 1958, the agreement ended and Daily and Pierce parted amicably. Pierce, by then the actual owner of the label, moved to Nashville to relaunch Starday. He found immediate success with hit recordings by several artists, including Red Sovine and Cowboy Copas. During the 60s, after also turning his attention to bluegrass music, Flatt And Scruggs, Jim Eanes, Bill Clifton, Carl Story and the Stanley Brothers were some of the stars of that genre to record successfully for Starday. Realizing that the major labels were ignoring the public demand for recordings by old-time artists who were still active, he also recorded Sam And Kirk McGee, Lew Childre and the Blue Sky Boys. Pierce organized mail-order supplies and also caused some controversy by reissuing early recordings of some of the top stars of the day. There were complaints by some artists that such action was not in their best interests. In 1968, when his friend Syd Nathan of King Records died, he made arrangements to merge the two labels. In 1969, realizing that he was fighting a losing battle against the major labels, he sold Starday to LIN Broadcasting, a wise move, as, within two years, the label went into liquidation and changed hands. Pierce, who later went into the real estate business, was a founder-member of the Country Music Association. His love of golf saw him become a founder of the Pro-Celebrity Tournament, which raises money for needy Nashville causes, and he also initiated his Golden Eagle Master Achievement Award (the eagle was Starday's motif), which is presented at the annual Reunion Of Professional Entertainers.

PIERCE, NAT

b. 16 July 1925, Somerville, Massachusetts, USA, d. 10 June 1992, Los Angeles, California, USA. After studying and playing in local bands in his home state, Pierce worked with a handful of name bands, including Larry Clinton's, then briefly led his own band in 1949-51, instigating what is commonly regarded among fellow musicians as being the birth of the so-called 'rehearsal band' concept. In 1951 he joined Woody Herman, in whose band he played piano, arranged, and acted as straw boss until 1955. Thereafter, he arranged for several bands and singers, including Count Basie and Ella Fitzgerald. In great demand as a session musician, he made countless record dates, on which he played with almost everyone who was anyone in the upper echelons of jazz. In 1957 he appeared in the television programme *The Sound Of Jazz*, on which he was responsible for several of the arrangements, including the classic performance of 'Dickie's Dream' that featured Basie, Roy Eldridge, Coleman Hawkins, Ben Webster, Joe Newman, Vic Dickenson and Gerry Mulligan among many others. In the late 50s he led a band that included Buck Clayton and that had the dubious honour of being the last band to play at Harlem's 'Home of Happy Feet', the Savoy Ballroom, before it closed forever. Also in the late 50s he worked with Pee Wee Russell, Quincy Jones, Fitzgerald, Hawkins and others. In 1960 he returned to Herman for a brief spell as road manager and was back again the following year, this time in his former capacities, remaining until 1966. In the early 70s Pierce relocated to the west coast where he played in several bands, including those led by Louie Bellson and Bill Berry. In 1975 he joined Frank Capp as co-leader of a big band that mostly played his arrangements, many of which were in the Basie/Kansas City tradition. This band, which became known as Juggernaut, continued to play through the 80s and on into the 90s. Pierce also continued to write for other musicians and to appear on record dates. He toured extensively, appearing in the UK and Europe with several Basie-alumni bands and other concert packages. A superb pianist in his own right, Pierce's eclecticism was such that at various times he appeared at the piano as substitute for three of the best-known piano-playing bandleaders in big band history: Basie, Duke Ellington and Stan Kenton. In small groups he proved the lynchpin of the rhythm section, swinging with unflagging enthusiasm. As an arranger, especially for big bands, Pierce made an invaluable contribution to jazz, effortlessly creating swinging charts that underscored the 60s success stories of both Herman and Basie. Apart from his performing and arranging, Pierce was also a major source of information on many aspects of jazz history, a history that, through his extensive contributions, he helped to create.

● ALBUMS: *The Nat Pierce-Dick Collins Nonet* 10-inch album (Fantasy 1954)★★★, *Nat Pierce Bandstand* 10-inch album (Vanguard 1955)★★★, *Kansas City Memories* (Coral 1956)★★★, *The Nat Pierce Octet And Tentette* (Keynote 1957)★★★, *The Nat Pierce Big Band At The Savoy Ballroom* (RCA Victor 1957)★★★, with various artists *The Real Sound Of Jazz* television soundtrack (1957)★★★★, *The Ballad Of Jazz Street* (Hep 1961)★★★★, *Juggernaut* (Concord 1977)★★★★, *Juggernaut Live At Century Plaza* (Concord 1978)★★, *5400 North...In Concert With Mary Ann McCall* (Hep 1978)★★★, *Juggernaut Strikes Again* (Concord 1981)★★★, *Boston Bustout* (Hep Jazz 1981)★★★, *Juggernaut Live At The Alleycat* (Concord 1986)★★★★.

PIERCE, WEBB

b. 8 August 1921, near West Monroe, Louisiana, USA, d. 24 February 1991, Nashville, Tennessee, USA. His father died when Pierce was only three months old, his mother remarried and he was raised on a farm seven miles from Monroe. Although no one in the family performed music, his mother had a collection of country records which, together with Gene Autry films, were his first country music influences. He learned to play guitar and when he was 15, he was given his own weekly radio show on KMLB Monroe. During World War II he served in the army, married Betty Jane Lewis in 1942 and after his discharge, they relocated from Monroe to Shreveport where, in 1945, he found employment in the men's department of the Sears Roebuck store. In 1947, he and his wife appeared in an early morning KTBS show as 'Webb Pierce with Betty Jane, the Singing Sweetheart'. He also sang at many local venues and developed the style that became so readily identifiable and was later described as 'a wailing whiskey-voiced tenor that rang out every drop of emotion'. He recorded for 4-Star in 1949 and soon afterwards moved to KWKH, where he became a member of the *Louisiana Hayride* on its inception that year. In 1950, he and Betty Jane were divorced and Pierce began building his solo career. He founded Pacemaker Records and a publishing company with Horace Logan, the director of the *Hayride*. His recording of 'Drifting Texas Sands', labelled as 'Tillman Franks and the Rainbow Valley Boys', due to Pierce still being under contract to 4-Star, attracted attention. His growing popularity brought him to the notice of US Decca and in March 1951 he made his first recordings for that label. His third Decca release, 'Wondering', a song from the 30s by Joe Werner and the Riverside Ramblers, began a phenomenal success when, in March 1952, it spent four weeks at number 1 in the US country charts and gave Pierce his nickname of 'The Wondering Boy'. Two more number 1s, 'That Heart Belongs To Me' (a self-penned song) and 'Back Street Affair', followed - all three remaining charted in excess of 20 weeks. (The latter song also led to Kitty Wells' second chart hit with the 'answer' version, 'Paying For That Back Street Affair', early in 1953.) In November 1952 he married again, this time to Audrey Grisham, and finally gave up his job at Sears Roebuck. He left the *Hayride* and replaced Hank Williams on the *Grand Ole Opry*. During his days at Shreveport his band included such future stars as Goldie Hill, Floyd Cramer, Jimmy Day, the Wilburn Brothers and Faron Young. He remained a member of the *Opry* roster until 1955, leaving because of his heavy touring commitments, but he rejoined briefly in 1956 before a disagreement with the management caused him to leave once again. The problem concerned the fact that Pierce was having to turn down lucrative Saturday concerts elsewhere to return to Nashville to meet his *Opry* commitments, for which he received only the standard *Opry* fee. Pierce's chart successes during the 50s and 60s totalled 88 country hits. Further number 1 singles included 'It's Been So Long', 'Even Tho'', 'More And More', 'I Don't Care', 'Love Love Love' and a duet with Red Sovine of George Jones's song 'Why Baby Why'. Arguably his best-remembered number 1 hits are his version of the old Jimmie Rodgers song 'In The Jailhouse Now', which held the top spot for 21 weeks, and his co-written 'Slowly', which remained there for 17, both songs charting for more than 35 weeks. The recording of 'Slowly' is unique because of Bud Isaacs' electric pedal steel guitar, which created a style that was copied by most other country bands. He also had nine US pop chart hits, the biggest being 'More And More', which reached number 22 in 1954. Pierce recorded rockabilly and rock 'n' roll numbers, having Top 10 country chart success with the first recorded version of 'Teenage Boogie' and with the Everly Brothers' 'Bye Bye Love', but his vocal version of 'Raunchy' failed to chart. In the mid-50s Pierce and the *Opry* manager, Jim Denny, formed Cedarwood Music, which handled other artists' songs as well as Pierce's own, and also bought three radio stations. When Denny died in 1963, Pierce retained the radio stations and left the publishing company to his late partner's family (he later acquired two more stations but eventually sold all five for a sum reputed to be almost $3 million). He toured extensively and appeared in the films *Buffalo Guns* (his co-stars being Marty Robbins and Carl Smith), *Music City USA*, *Second Fiddle To A Steel Guitar* and *Road To Nashville*, and during his career, dressed in rhinestone-studded suits; he became known as one of the most flamboyant, even by country standards, of the singers of his era. During the 60s he had two Pontiac cars fancily studded with silver dollars, large cattle horns mounted as a decoration on the radiator, ornamental pistols and rifles and even leather seats that resembled saddles. Later, his expensive Oak Hill, Nashville home, with its guitar-shaped swimming pool, attracted so many tourist buses to the usually quiet area that he had problems with his neighbours, particularly Ray Stevens. Pierce totally ignored suggestions that he was bringing country music into disrepute, maintaining that the fans had paid for his pool and were therefore entitled to see it. After heated court proceedings he was forced to erect a sign warning fans to stay away. His comment on Stevens, who had been the organizer of the objectors, was: 'That's what he gets for livin' across the street from a star'. Johnny Cash mentions the event in his song 'Let There Be Country', when he sings: 'Pierce invites the tourists in and Ray keeps them away'.

After 'Honky Tonk Song' in 1957, Pierce never gained another number 1 record but he did add eight further country hits during the 70s on Decca and Plantation. When the Columbia duet version of 'In The Jailhouse Now', which he recorded with Willie Nelson, charted in 1982 to register his 97th and last country hit, it gave him the distinction of having charted records in four decades. In the early 1980s he sold his Oak Hill home and retired to the Brentwood area of Nashville. He retired from touring but made special appearances when it pleased him, and, reflecting on his career, he said, 'I've been blessed with so much. I guess it turned out the way I wanted it'. In 1985 he made a goodtime album with his friends Jerry Lee Lewis, Mel Tillis and Faron Young, but contractual problems led to it being withdrawn shortly after issue. Asked about recording again in 1986, he commented, 'Hell, I might get a hit and then everybody would be botherin' me again'. Late in the 80s his health began to fail; he survived open-heart surgery, but early in 1990 it was diagnosed that he was suffering from cancer. He underwent several operations but finally died in Nashville on 24 February 1991. He had been nominated for membership of the Country Music Hall of Fame in August 1990: most authorities expected that he would be elected but it was not to be. The honour may be bestowed before long but, sadly, it will come too late for him to know. Pierce was, without any doubt, one of country music's most successful and popular honky-tonk singers.

● ALBUMS: *That Wondering Boy* 10-inch album (Decca 1953)★★★★, *Webb Pierce* (Decca 1955)★★★, *That Wondering Boy* (Decca 1956)★★★★, *Just Imagination* (Decca 1957)★★★, *Webb!* (Decca 1959)★★★, *Bound For The Kingdom* (Decca 1959)★★★, *The One & Only Webb Pierce* (King 1959)★★★, *Walking The Streets* (Decca 1960)★★★, *Webb With A Beat* (Decca 1960)★★★★, *Fallen Angel* (Decca 1961)★★★, *Cross Country* (Decca 1962)★★★, *Hideaway Heart* (Decca 1962)★★★, *Bow Thy Head* (Decca 1963)★★★, *I've Got A New Heartache* (Decca 1963)★★★, *Sands Of Gold* (Decca 1964)★★★★, *Country Music Time* (Decca 1965)★★★, *Just Webb Pierce* (Hilltop 1965)★★★, *Memory Number One* (Decca 1965)★★★, *Sweet Memories* (Decca 1966)★★★, *Webb Pierce* (Vocalion 1966)★★★, *Webb's Choice* (Decca 1966)★★★, *Where'd Ya Stay Last Night?* (Decca 1967)★★★, *Fool, Fool, Fool* (Decca 1968)★★★, *Country Songs* (Vocalion 1969)★★★, *Saturday Night* (Decca 1969)★★★, *Webb Pierce Sings This Thing* (Decca 1969)★★★, *Love Ain't Never Gonna Be No Better* (Decca 1970)★★★, *Merry Go Round World* (Decca 1970)★★★, *Country Favorites* (Vocalion 1970)★★★, *Webb Pierce Road Show* (Decca 1971)★★, *I'm Gonna Be A Swinger* (Decca 1972)★★★, *Without You* (Decca 1973)★★★, *Carol Channing & Webb Pierce-Country & Western* (Plantation 1976)★★, *Faith, Hope And Love* (Plantation 1977)★★★, with Willie Nelson *In The Jailhouse Now* (Columbia 1982)★★★, with Jerry Lee Lewis, Mel Tillis, Faron Young *Four Legends* (1985)★★★.
● COMPILATIONS: *Golden Favorites* (Decca 1961)★★★, *The Webb Pierce Story* (Decca 1964)★★★, *Webb Pierce's Greatest Hits* (Decca 1968)★★★★, *Golden Hits Volume 1* (Plantation 1976)★★★, *Golden Hits Volume 2* (Plantation 1976)★★★, *The Living Legend Of Webb Pierce* (1977)★★★, *Webb 'The Wondering Boy' Pierce 1951-1958* 4-CD box set (Bear Family 1990)★★★★, *The One And Only...* (1993)★★★, *Webb Pierce: King Of The Honky Tonk: From The Original Master Tapes* (Country Music Foundation 1994)★★★★.

PILGRIM TRAVELERS

Primarily known today as one of soul singer Lou Rawls' first groups, the close-harmony group the Pilgrim Travelers was formed in 1936 in Houston, Texas, USA, as an offshoot of the Pleasantgrove Baptist Church. The founder-members were Joe Johnson, Kylo Turner, Keith Barber and Rayfield Taylor. They won a talent contest in 1944, the prize for which was a national tour with the Soul Stirrers. After the tour the group moved to Los Angeles, California, and added J.W. Alexander as tenor, and Jessie Whitaker as baritone. After brief spells with Big Town and Swing Time, the Pilgrim Travelers moved to Specialty Records in the late 40s. In addition to gospel standards such as 'The Old Rugged Cross', their most fondly remembered track from this period was 'Jesus Met The Woman At The Well'. When Rayfield Taylor departed in the 50s he was replaced by George McCurn. By 1957 Kylo Turner and Keith Barber had also left, and they were replaced by Ernest Booker and Lou Rawls (ex-Teenage Kings Of Harmony and Holy Wonders). With Rawls, Whitaker and Booker alternating leads the group released a string of singles for Andex Records in the 50s, with Sam Cooke guesting on recording sessions and some touring dates. However, after Booker left in 1957 the group abbreviated their name to simply the Travelers and recorded more secular material for a time. The group ground to a halt two years later, with Lou Rawls going on to a successful R&B career and J.W. Alexander partnering Sam Cooke in the formation of Sar Records.

PLATER, BOBBY
b. Robert Plater, 13 May 1914, Newark, New Jersey, USA, d. 20 November 1982. Plater began playing alto saxophone while still a child and in his early teens was talented enough to work with several noted musicians, including Don Lambert. He became a full-time professional musician in the late 30s, working with Tiny Bradshaw and others. After military service during World War II, he returned to gigging but then joined Lionel Hampton in 1946 where he remained until 1964. With Hampton, Plater played lead alto and was also an important soloist. He also wrote arrangements for the band, showing a special aptitude for writing for singers, notably Sonny Parker. He had also taken the time to teach some basic principles to Dinah Washington during her first major professional engagement with Hampton. After leaving Hampton, Plater moved into the Count Basie band, becoming lead alto there, too, and also musical director of the band. A highly skilled instrumentalist with a wide musical knowledge, Plater's sound was rich and creamy, suggesting an influence of Johnny Hodges but overlaid with a slightly acerbic touch that gave his solos added poignancy. He was co-composer of 'Jersey Bounce', a 40s hit.
● ALBUMS: with Lionel Hampton *Lionel Hampton And His Orchestra: Apollo Hall Concert* (Epic 1954)★★★★, with Count Basie *Basie Big Band* (Pablo 1975)★★★, with Basie *Farmer's Market Barbecue* (Pablo 1982)★★★.

PLATT, EDDIE
Very little is known about this Cleveland-born bandleader and saxophonist who reached the US Top 20 in 1958 with his version of 'Tequila', the rock 'n' roll dance number made popular by the Champs. He released one further single, a cover version later that same year of 'Cha-Hua-Hua' by the Pets, which scraped into the lower end of the charts. He apparently never recorded again.

PLATTERS
One of the leading R&B vocal groups of the 50s, they were the first black group to be accepted as a major chart act and, for a short time, were the most successful vocal group in the world. The Platters were formed in Los Angeles in 1953 by entrepreneur/songwriter Buck Ram (b. 21 November 1907, Chicago, Illinois, USA, d. 1 January 1991). Through his ownership of the Platters' name, Ram was able to control the group throughout their career, and his talent for composing and arranging enabled the Platters to make a lasting impression upon popular music. Their original line-up, Tony Williams (b. 5 April 1928, Elizabeth, New Jersey, USA, d. 14 August 1992, New York, USA; lead tenor), David Lynch (b. 1929, St. Louis, Missouri, USA, d. 2 January 1981; tenor), Alex Hodge (baritone) and Herb Reed (b. 1931, Kansas City, Missouri, USA; bass), recorded unsuccessfully in 1954, precipitating the arrival of two new members, Paul Robi (b. 1931, New Orleans, Louisiana, USA, d. 2 January 1989), who replaced Hodge, and Zola Taylor (b. 1934; contralto). Signed to Mercury Records, the Platters secured their first hit in 1955 when 'Only You' reached the US Top 5, an effortlessly

light performance that set the pattern for subsequent releases, including 'The Great Pretender', 'My Prayer' and 'Twilight Time', each of which reached number 1 in the US charts. 'Smoke Gets In Your Eyes' (previously a hit for Paul Whiteman in 1934), which was an international number 1 hit single in 1958-59, highlighted their smooth delivery and arguably remains the group's best-loved release. Lead singer Williams left for a solo career in 1961, taking with him much of the Platters' distinctive style. His departure led to further changes, with Sandra Dawn and Nate Nelson replacing Taylor and Robi. With Sonny Turner as the featured voice, the group began embracing a more contemporary direction, evidenced in such occasional pop hits as 'I Love You 1000 Times' (1966) and 'With This Ring' (1967). During the late 60s, and for a long time afterwards, personnel changes brought much confusion as to who were the legitimate Platters. Sonny Turner and Herb Reed formed their own version, while Tony Williams did likewise. The Platters' legacy has since been undermined by the myriad of line-ups performing under that name, some of which had no tangible links to the actual group. This should not detract from those seminal recordings that bridged the gap between the harmonies of the Mills Brothers and the Ink Spots and the sweet soul of the ensuing decade. In the late 80s, Buck Ram continued to keep an eagle eye on the Platters' sold-out appearances at Las Vegas and other US cities. The group were inducted into the Rock And Roll Hall Of Fame in 1990, but Ram died the following year.
● ALBUMS: *The Platters* (Federal 1955)★★★★ also released on King as *Only You* and Mercury labels, *The Platters, Volume 2* (Mercury 1956)★★★★, *The Flying Platters* (Mercury 1957)★★★, *The Platters On Parade* (Mercury 1959)★★★, *Flying Platters Around The World* (Mercury 1959)★★★, *Remember When* (Mercury 1959)★★★, *Reflections* (Mercury 1960)★★★, *Encore Of Golden Hits* (Mercury 1960)★★★, *More Encore Of Golden Hits* (Mercury 1960)★★★, *The Platters* (Mercury 1960)★★★, *Life Is Just A Bowl Of Cherries* (Mercury 1961)★★★, *The Platters Sing For The Lonely* (Mercury 1962)★★★, *Encore Of The Golden Hits Of The Groups* (Mercury 1962)★★★, *Moonlight Memories* (Mercury 1963)★★★, *Platters Sing All The Movie Hits* (Mercury 1963)★★, *Platters Sing Latino* (Mercury 1963)★★, *Christmas With The Platters* (Mercury 1963)★★★, *New Soul Campus Style Of The Platters* (Mercury 1965)★★, *I Love You 1000 Times* (Musicor 1966)★★, *Going Back To Detroit* (Stateside 1967)★★★, *I Get The Sweetest Feeling* (1968)★★★, *Sweet Sweet Lovin'* (1968)★★, *Our Way* (Pye International 1971)★★★, *Encore Of Broadway Golden Hits* (1972)★★★, *Live* (1974)★★.
● COMPILATIONS: *The Original Platters - 20 Classic Hits* (Mercury 1978)★★★★, *Platterama* (Mercury 1982)★★★★, *The Platters: Anthology* (Rhino 1986)★★★★, *Smoke Gets In Your Eyes* (Charly 1991)★★★★, *Magic Touch: An Anthology* (Polygram 1992)★★★★, *Greatest Hits* (1993)★★★★.
● FILMS: *Carnival Rock* (1957), *Girl's Town* aka *The Innocent And The Damned* (1959).

PLAYMATES
This humorous US pop trio comprised Donny Conn (b. 29 March 1930), Morey Carr (b. 31 July 1932) and Chic Hetti (b. 26 February 1930), all from Waterbury, Connecticut, USA. They formed the comedy and music trio the Nitwits while

studying at the University of Connecticut and started touring in 1952 with an act that relied more on humour than singing ability. Renamed the Playmates, they made their first record, 'I Only Have Myself To Blame', on Rainbow in 1956. They moved to Roulette Records in 1957 and their third single on that label, 'Jo-Ann', a cover version of the Twin Tones' record, hit the US Top 20 in 1958. Over the next four years the clean-cut vocal group chalked up another nine US chart entries including the Top 20 hits 'What Is Love?' and 'Beep Beep', which reached number 4 in the USA. They later recorded on ABC-Paramount, Colpix, Congress and Bell but their sound proved too dated to sell in the 60s.

PONI-TAILS

A US female trio known for the 1958 Top 10 hit 'Born Too Late', the Poni-Tails - who, naturally, sported that hairstyle - were lead vocalist Toni Cistone, Patti McCabe (d. 1989; low harmony - replacing original member Karen Topinka) and LaVerne Novak (high harmony). The group met at their high school in Lyndhurst, Ohio, USA, in 1957. They first recorded for Point Records, an RKO Pictures division, but their two singles for that label were not successful. The members were then signed to ABC-Paramount Records, and their first single for that company fared badly. The next one, 'Born Too Late', an innocent ballad about being passed over by an older boy, catapulted to number 7 in the US chart the following year. Two further singles for ABC reached the charts but did not approach hit status and the group disbanded, each member retiring from the music business.
● COMPILATIONS: *Born Too Late* (South Bay 1994)★★.

PORGY AND BESS

The last film of producer Sam Goldwyn's illustrious career, released by Columbia in 1959, proved to be an expensive and troubled affair. After various disputes with his first choice director, Rouben Mamoulian (who had staged the original 1935 Broadway production), Goldwyn replaced him with Otto Preminger, whose work on this occasion was considered to be somewhat laboured and uninspired. For some reason, the well-known story of the crippled beggar Porgy (Sidney Poitier), who lives in the Catfish Row slum area and loves the tempestuous Bess (Dorothy Dandridge), did not transfer successfully to the big screen. The supporting cast was excellent, with Sammy Davis Jnr. (Sportin' Life), Pearl Bailey (Maria), Brock Peters (Crown), Diahann Carroll (Clara) and Ruth Attaway (Serena) all turning in outstanding performances. Other roles were taken by Leslie Scott, Clarence Muse and Joel Fluellen. Because of the extremely demanding operatic score by composer George Gershwin and lyricists DuBose Heyward and Ira Gershwin, several of the principals were dubbed, including Poitier (Robert McFerrin), Dandridge (Adele Addison), Carroll (Loulie Jean Norman), and Attaway (Inez Matthews). Even so, there were some reservations regarding the vocal quality of the production, but these were swept aside by the sheer magnificence of the songs, which included 'Summertime', 'Bess, You Is My Woman', 'There's A Boat Dat's Leavin' Soon For New York', 'I Loves You Porgy', 'A Woman Is A Sometimes Thing', 'I Got Plenty O' Nuttin'', 'It Ain't Necessarily So', 'My Man's Gone Now' and 'Oh Bess, Oh Where's My Bess'. André Previn and Ken Darby both won Oscars for 'scoring a dramatic picture', and Leo Shamroy was nominated for his superb photog-

raphy in Technicolor and Panavision. Hermes Pan, who had been associated with many top musical films in his long career including the Fred Astaire and Ginger Rogers RKO series, staged the dances. The screenplay, by N. Richard Nash, was based on the original Broadway libretto and novel by Heyward, and his and Dorothy Heyward's play *Porgy*. In the early 90s, this film remained one of the few major musicals not to have been released on video. Cinema distribution has also been curtailed; the Gershwin estate has had this film firmly under lock and key for some years now.

POTTER, DALE

b. Allen Dale Potter, 28 April 1930, Puxico, Missouri, USA, d. 13 March 1996, USA. A regular at the *Grand Ole Opry*, fiddle player Dale Potter contributed to records by many of the stellar country artists of the post-war period, including Hank Williams, Little Jimmy Dickens, Bill Monroe and Cowboy Copas. Taught fiddle and guitar by his father from an early age, Potter gravitated to country music after listening to Bob Wills's KVOO Tulsa radio performances. This event proved axiomatic in the development of his style - unaware that Wills' Texas Playboys featured more than one fiddle player, he adapted his technique to enable him to play both harmony and melody. Potter soon landed a regular radio spot himself, before being summoned to Nashville to join Milton Estes' Musical Millers. He was only 18 when he made his stage debut at the *Grand Ole Opry*, playing a version of Tex Owens' 'Cattle Call'. Zeb Turner then engaged him in recording work to boost his income. His first session was with Hank Williams in 1949, resulting in songs including 'Wedding Bells' and 'Lost Highway'. He subsequently became an in-demand session player, working on Red Foley's Top 10 hit, 'Sugarfoot Rag', and a series of hits by Webb Pierce, Ray Price, Johnny Paycheck and Faron Young. Potter also appeared on the very first Everly Brothers recording session in 1955. Later he joined the Country All-Stars, which featured Chet Atkins, who described him as 'the best all-round fiddler in the business.' He worked with Judy Lynn in 1960, then the Sons Of The West in Dallas, before ill health curtailed his career.

POWELL, JANE

b. Suzanne Burce, 1 April 1929, Portland, Oregon, USA. A petite, vivacious, actress and singer with a thrilling soprano voice who excelled in several popular MGM musicals of the 50s. After singing a mixture of classical and popular songs on local radio, she won a film contract with MGM when she was just 15 years old. Her debut in *Song Of The Open Road* was followed in the 40s and early 50s by *Delightfully Dangerous*, *Holiday In Mexico*, *Three Daring Daughters*, *A Date With Judy*, *Luxury Liner*, *Nancy Goes To Rio*, *Two Weeks With Love*, *Rich, Young And Pretty*, *Small Town Girl* and *Three Sailors And A Girl* (1953). In 1951 she co-starred with Fred Astaire in *Royal Wedding*, and they duetted on one of the longest song titles ever - 'How Could You Believe Me When I Said I Love You When You Know I've Been A Liar All My Life?'. Their recording became a million-seller. Later, in 1956, Powell made the US Top 20 on her own with 'True Love' from *High Society*. Her best film role was in 1954 when she joined Howard Keel in the marvellous *Seven Brides For Seven Brothers*, and she continued to appear on the screen into the late 50s, in musicals such as *Athena*, *Deep In My*

Heart, Hit The Deck and *The Girl Most Likely* (1957). The golden era of movie musicals was drawing to a close by then, and Powell turned to provincial theatre and nightclubs. In the 70s she was active on US television in programmes such as *Murdoch, The Letters* and *Mayday At 40,000 Feet.* She also succeeded Debbie Reynolds in the leading role of the 1973 Broadway revival of *Irene.* In 1988 Powell married her fifth husband, Dick Moore, who was a child star himself, and is an authority on the genre, having written a book entitled *Twinkle, Twinkle Little Star (But Don't Have Sex Or Take The Car).* In the same year she appeared in concert at Carnegie Hall with Skitch Henderson and the New York Pops.

● ALBUMS: *Romance* 10-inch album (Columbia 1949)★★★, *A Date With Jane Powell* 10-inch album (Columbia 1949)★★★, *Alice In Wonderland* (Columbia 1950)★★, *Nancy Goes To Rio* film soundtrack (MGM 1950)★★, *Two Weeks With Love* film soundtrack (MGM 1950)★★★, *Royal Wedding* film soundtrack (MGM 1951)★★★, *Rich, Young And Pretty* film soundtrack (MGM 1951)★★★, *Three Sailors And A Girl* film soundtrack (MGM 1953)★★★, *Seven Brides For Seven Brothers* film soundtrack (MGM 1954)★★★, *Athena* film soundtrack (Mercury 1954)★★, *Can't We Be Friends?* (Verve 1956)★★★, *Something Wonderful* (MGM 1957)★★★.

● COMPILATIONS: *Songs From Her Films* (1989)★★★★.

PRADO, PEREZ

b. Damaso Perez Prado, 11 December 1916, Mantanzas, Cuba, d. 14 September 1989, Mexico City, Mexico. Prado played organ and piano in cinemas and clubs before becoming an arranger for mambo-style local bands in 1942. He formed his own unit in 1948 in Mexico when the mambo beat was becoming very popular. Prado was 'King of the Mambo' in Latin America with his scorching brass and persuasive percussion, exemplified in his 1950 recording of 'Mambo Jambo'. He had some modest US success in 1953-54 with the title theme from the Italian movie *Anne,* and a South African song, 'Skokiaan'. Strong indications that the mambo craze was beginning to catch on in the USA came in 1954, when Perry Como with 'Papa Loves Mambo', and 'Mambo Italiano' by Rosemary Clooney, both reached the Top 10. Prado made his worldwide breakthrough in 1955 when RCA Records released 'Cherry Pink And Apple Blossom White', with an exciting trumpet solo by Billy Regis. It stayed at number 1 in the US charts for 10 weeks and was featured in the Jane Russell/Richard Egan film *Underwater!* (1955). In Britain, Eddie Calvert and the Ted Heath orchestra had their own bestselling versions. Prado's follow-up in 1958 was another instrumental, his own composition, 'Patricia'. Another chart-topper, it contained more than a hint of the current burgeoning pop sounds with its heavy bass and rocking organ rhythms, along with the cha-cha-cha beat, and was used by Federico Fellini as the theme song for the movie *La Dolce Vita* in 1960. By then Prado was out of the limelight, but in 1981 he featured in a musical revue entitled *Sun,* which enjoyed a long run in Mexico City. Persistent ill health led to the amputation of one leg, and he eventually died from a stroke in 1989. Six years later, he narrowly failed to reach the top of the UK chart with the exciting 'Guaglione', following its use in a television commercial for Guinness beer.

● ALBUMS: *Mambo By The King* 10-inch album (RCA Victor 1953)★★★, *Mambo Mania* (RCA Victor 1955)★★★, *Voodoo Suite (And Six All Time Greats)* (RCA Victor 1955)★★★, *Havana 3 am* (RCA Victor 1956)★★★, *Latin Satin* (RCA Victor 1957)★★★, *Prez* (RCA Victor 1958)★★★★, *Dilo Ugh!* (RCA Victor 1958)★★★, *Pops And Prado* (RCA Victor 1959)★★★, *Big Hits By Prado* (RCA Victor 1959)★★★, *A Touch Of Tabasco* (RCA Victor 1960)★★★, *Rockambo* (RCA Victor 1961)★★★, *The New Dance La Chunga* (RCA Victor 1961)★★★, *The Twist Goes Latin* (RCA Victor 1962)★★★, *Exotic Suite* (RCA Victor 1962)★★★, *Our Man In Latin America* (RCA Victor1963)★★★, *A Cat In Latin* (RCA Victor 1964)★★★.

● COMPILATIONS: *Perez Prado* (Bright Orange 1979)★★★, *Perez Prado And Orchestra* (Joker 1988)★★★, *Guantanamera* (W.S. Latino 1989)★★★, *King Of Mambo* (RCA 1991)★★★★, *Go Go Mambo* (1993)★★★★, *Mondo Mambo: The Best Of ...* (Rhino 1995)★★★★.

PRESLEY, ELVIS

b. Elvis Aaron Presley, 8 January 1935, Tupelo, Mississippi, USA, d. 16 August 1977, Memphis, Tennessee. The most celebrated popular music phenomenon of his era and, for many, the purest embodiment of rock 'n' roll, Elvis Presley's life and career have become part of rock legend. The elder of twins, his younger brother, Jesse Garon, was stillborn, a tragedy that partly contributed to the maternal solicitude dominating his childhood and teenage years. Presley's first significant step towards a musical career took place at the age of eight when he won $5 in a local song contest performing the lachrymose Red Foley ballad, 'Old Shep'. His earliest musical influence came from attending the Pentecostal Church and listening to the psalms and gospel songs. He also had a strong grounding in country and blues and it was the combination of these different styles that was to provide his unique musical identity.

By the age of 13, Presley had moved with his family to Memphis, and during his later school years began cultivating an outsider image, with long hair, spidery sideburns and ostentatious clothes. After leaving school he took a job as a truck driver, a role in keeping with his unconventional appearance. In spite of his rebel posturing, Presley remained studiously polite to his elders and was devoted to his mother. Indeed, it was his filial affection that first prompted him to visit Sun Records, whose studios offered the sophisticated equivalent of a fairground recording booth service. As a birthday present to his mother, Gladys, Presley cut a version of the Ink Spots' 'My Happiness', backed with the Raskin/Brown/Fisher standard 'That's When Your Heartaches Begin'. The studio manager, Marion Keisker, noted Presley's unusual but distinctive vocal style and informed Sun's owner/producer Sam Phillips of his potential. Phillips nurtured the boy for almost a year before putting him together with country guitarist Scotty Moore and bassist Bill Black. Their early sessions showed considerable promise, especially when Presley began alternating his unorthodox low-key delivery with a high-pitched whine. The amplified guitars of Moore and Black contributed strongly to the effect and convinced Phillips that the singer was startlingly original. In Presley, Phillips saw something that he had long dreamed of discovering: a white boy who sang like a negro. Presley's debut disc on Sun was the extraordinary 'That's All Right (Mama)', a showcase for his rich, multi-textured vocal dexterity, with sharp, solid backing from his compatriots. The b-side, 'Blue Moon Of Kentucky', was a country song, but the arrangement showed that Presley was threatening to slip into an entirely different genre, closer to R&B. Local response to these strange-sounding performances was encouraging and Phillips eventually shifted 20,000 copies of the disc. For his second single, Presley recorded Roy Brown's 'Good Rockin' Tonight' backed by the zingy 'I Don't Care If The Sun Don't Shine'. The more roots-influenced 'Milkcow Blues Boogie' followed, while the b-side, 'You're A Heartbreaker', had some strong tempo changes that neatly complemented Presley's quirky vocal. 'Baby Let's Play House'/'I'm Left, You're Right, She's Gone' continued the momentum and led to Presley performing on the *Grand Old Opry* and *Louisiana Hayride* radio programmes. A series of live dates commenced in 1955 with drummer D.J. Fontana added to the ranks. Presley toured clubs in Arkansas, Louisiana and Texas billed as 'The King Of Western Bop' and 'The Hillbilly Cat'. Audience reaction verged on the fanatical, which was hardly surprising given Presley's semi-erotic performances. His hip-swivelling routine, in which he cascaded across the stage and plunged to his knees at dramatic moments in a song, was remarkable for the period and prompted near-riotous fan mania. The final Sun single, a cover version of Junior Parker's 'Mystery Train', was later acclaimed by many as the definitive rock 'n' roll single, with its chugging rhythm, soaring vocal and enticing lead guitar breaks. It established Presley as an artist worthy of national attention and ushered in the next phase of his career, which was dominated by the imposing figure of Colonel Tom Parker. The Colonel was a former fairground huckster who managed several country artists ,including Hank Snow and Eddy Arnold. After relieving disc jockey Bob Neal of Presley's managership, Parker persuaded Sam Phillips that his financial interests would be better served by releasing the boy to a major label. RCA Records had already noted the commercial potential of the phenomenon under offer and agreed to pay Sun Records a release fee of $35,000, an incredible sum for the period. The sheer diversity of Presley's musical heritage and his remarkable ability as a vocalist and interpreter of material enabled him to escape the cultural parochialism of his R&B-influenced predecessors. The attendant rock 'n' roll explosion, in which Presley was both a creator and participant, ensured that he could reach a mass audience, many of them newly affluent teenagers.

It was on 10 January 1956, a mere two days after his 21st birthday, that Presley entered RCA's studios in Nashville to record his first tracks for a major label. His debut session produced the epochal 'Heartbreak Hotel', one of the most striking pop records ever released. Co-composed by Hoyt Axton's mother Mae, the song evoked nothing less than a vision of absolute funereal despair. There was nothing in the pop charts of the period that even hinted at the degree of desolation described in the song. Presley's reading was extraordinarily mature and moving, with a determined avoidance of any histrionics in favour of a pained and resigned acceptance of loneliness as death. The economical yet acutely emphatic piano work of Floyd Cramer enhanced the stark mood of the piece, which was frozen in a suitably minimalist production. The startling originality and intensity of 'Heartbreak Hotel' entranced the American public and

pushed the single to number 1 for an astonishing eight weeks. Whatever else he achieved, Presley was already assured a place in pop history for one of the greatest major label debut records ever released. During the same month that 'Heartbreak Hotel' was recorded, Presley made his national television debut displaying his sexually enticing gyrations before a bewildered adult audience whose alleged outrage subsequently persuaded producers to film the star exclusively from the waist upwards. Having outsold his former Sun colleague Carl Perkins with 'Blue Suede Shoes', Presley released a debut album that contained several of the songs he had previously recorded with Sam Phillips, including Little Richard's 'Tutti Fruitti', the R&B classic 'I Got A Woman' and an eerie, wailing version of Richard Rodgers/Lorenz Hart's 'Blue Moon', which emphasized his remarkable vocal range.

Since hitting number 2 in the UK lists with 'Heartbreak Hotel', Presley had been virtually guaranteed European success and his profile was increased via a regular series of releases as RCA took full advantage of their bulging back catalogue. Although there was a danger of overkill, Presley's talent, reputation and immensely strong fanbase vindicated the intense release schedule and the quality of the material ensured that the public was not disappointed. After hitting number 1 for the second time with the slight ballad 'I Want You, I Need You, I Love You', Presley released what was to become the most commercially successful double-sided single in pop history, 'Hound Dog'/'Don't Be Cruel'. The former was composed by the immortal rock 'n' roll songwriting team of Leiber And Stoller, and presented Presley at his upbeat best with a novel lyric, complete with a striking guitar solo and spirited handclapping from his backing group the Jordanaires. Otis Blackwell's 'Don't Be Cruel' was equally effective with a striking melody line and some clever and amusing vocal gymnastics from the hiccupping King of Western Bop, who also received a co-writing credit. The single remained at number 1 in the USA for a staggering 11 weeks and both sides of the record were massive hits in the UK.

Celluloid fame for Presley next beckoned with *Love Me Tender*, produced by David Weisbert, who had previously worked on James Dean's *Rebel Without A Cause*. Presley's movie debut received mixed reviews but was a box-office smash, while the smouldering, perfectly enunciated title track topped the US charts for five weeks. The spate of Presley singles continued in earnest through 1957 and one of the biggest was another Otis Blackwell composition, 'All Shook Up', which the singer used as a cheekily oblique comment on his by now legendary dance movements. By late 1956 it was rumoured that Presley would be drafted into the US Army and, as if to compensate for that irksome eventuality, RCA, Twentieth Century Fox and the Colonel stepped up the work-rate and release schedules. Incredibly, three major films were completed in the next two-and-a-half years. *Loving You* boasted a quasi-autobiographical script with Presley playing a truck driver who becomes a pop star. The title track became the b-side of '(Let Me Be Your) Teddy Bear' which reigned at number 1 for seven weeks. The third movie, *Jailhouse Rock*, was Presley's most successful to date with an excellent soundtrack and some inspired choreography. The Leiber and Stoller title track was an instant classic that again topped the US charts for seven weeks and made pop history by entering the UK listings at number 1. The fourth celluloid outing, *King Creole* (adapted from the Harold Robbins novel, *A Stone For Danny Fisher*), is regarded by many as Presley's finest film and a firm indicator of his sadly unfulfilled potential as a serious actor. Once more the soundtrack album featured some surprisingly strong material such as the haunting 'Crawfish' and the vibrant 'Dixieland Rock'. By the time *King Creole* was released in 1958, Elvis had already been inducted into the US Forces. A publicity photograph of the singer having his hair shorn symbolically commented on his approaching musical emasculation. Although rock 'n' roll purists mourned the passing of the old Elvis, it seemed inevitable in the context of the 50s that he would move towards a broader base appeal and tone down his rebellious image. From 1958-60, Presley served in the US Armed Forces, spending much of his time in Germany where he was regarded as a model soldier. It was during this period that he first met 14-year-old Priscilla Beaulieu, whom he later married in 1967. Back in America, the Colonel kept his absent star's reputation intact via a series of films, record releases and extensive merchandising. Hits such as 'Wear My Ring Around Your Neck', 'Hard Headed Woman', 'One Night', 'I Got Stung', 'A Fool Such As I' and 'A Big Hunk O' Love' filled the long, two-year gap and by the time Presley reappeared, he was ready to assume the mantle of all-round entertainer. The change was immediately evident in the series of number 1 hits that he enjoyed in the early 60s. The enormously successful 'It's Now Or Never', based on the Italian melody 'O Sole Mio', revealed the King as an operatic crooner, far removed from his earlier raucous recordings. 'Are You Lonesome Tonight?', originally recorded by Al Jolson as early as 1927, allowed Presley to quote some Shakespeare in the spoken-word middle section as well as showing his ham-acting ability with an overwrought vocal. The new clean-cut Presley was presented on celluloid in *GI Blues*. The movie played upon his recent army exploits and saw him serenading a puppet on the charming chart-topper 'Wooden Heart', which also allowed Elvis to show off his knowledge of German. The grandiose 'Surrender' completed this phase of big ballads in the old-fashioned style. For the next few years Presley concentrated on an undemanding spree of films, including *Flaming Star*, *Wild In The Country*, *Blue Hawaii*, *Kid Galahad*, *Girls! Girls! Girls!*, *Follow That Dream*, *Fun In Acapulco*, *It Happened At The World's Fair*, *Kissin' Cousins*, *Viva Las Vegas*, *Roustabout*, *Girl Happy*, *Tickle Me*, *Harem Scarem*, *Frankie And Johnny*, *Paradise Hawaiian Style* and *Spinout*. Not surprisingly, most of his album recordings were hastily completed soundtracks with unadventurous commissioned songs. For his singles he relied increasingly on the formidable Doc Pomus/Mort Shuman team who composed such hits as 'Mess Of Blues', 'Little Sister' and 'His Latest Flame'. More and more, however, the hits were adapted from films and their chart positions suffered accordingly. After the 1963 number 1 'Devil In Disguise', a bleak period followed in which such minor songs as 'Bossa Nova Baby', 'Kiss Me Quick', 'Ain't That Lovin' You Baby' and 'Blue Christmas' became the rule rather than the exception. Significantly, his biggest success of the mid-60s, 'Crying In The Chapel', had been recorded five years earlier, and part of its appeal came from the realization that it represented something ineffably lost.

In the wake of the Beatles' rise to fame and the beat boom explosion, Presley seemed a figure out of time. Nevertheless, in spite of the dated nature of many of his recordings, he could still invest power and emotion into classic songs. The sassy 'Frankie And Johnny' was expertly sung by Presley, as was his moving reading of Ketty Lester's 'Love Letters'. His other significant 1966 release, 'If Everyday Was Like Christmas', was a beautiful festive song unlike anything else in the charts of the period. By 1967, however, it was clear to critics and even a large proportion of his devoted following that Presley had seriously lost his way. He continued to grind out pointless movies such as *Double Trouble*, *Speedway*, *Clambake* and *Live A Little, Love A Little*, even though the box office returns were increasingly poor. His capacity to register instant hits, irrespective of the material was also wearing thin, as such lowly placed singles as 'You Gotta Stop' and 'Long Legged Woman' demonstrated all too alarmingly. However, just as Elvis's career had reached its all-time nadir he seemed to wake up, take stock, and break free from the artistic malaise in which he found himself. Two songs written by country guitarist Jerry Reed, 'Guitar Man' and 'US Male', proved a spectacular return to form for Elvis in 1968, such was Presley's conviction that the compositions almost seemed to be written specifically for him. During the same year, Colonel Tom Parker had approached NBC-TV about the possibility of recording a Presley Christmas special in which the singer would perform a selection of religious songs similar in feel to his early 60s album *His Hand In Mine*. However, the executive producers of the show vetoed that concept in favour of a one-hour spectacular designed to capture Elvis at his rock 'n' rollin' best. It was a remarkable challenge for the singer, seemingly in the autumn of his career, and he responded to the idea with unexpected enthusiasm. The *Elvis TV Special* was broadcast in America on 3 December 1968 and has since become legendary as one of the most celebrated moments in pop broadcasting history. The show was not merely good but an absolute revelation, with the King emerging as if he had been frozen in time for 10 years. His determination to recapture past glories oozed from every movement and was discernible in every aside. With his leather jacket and acoustic guitar strung casually round his neck, he resembled nothing less than the consummate pop idol of the 50s who had entranced a generation. To add authenticity to the proceedings he was accompanied by his old sidekicks Scotty Moore and D.J. Fontana. There was no sense of self-parody in the show as Presley joked about his famous surly curled-lip movement and even heaped passing ridicule on his endless stream of bad movies. The music concentrated heavily on his 50s classics but, significantly, there was a startling finale courtesy of the passionate 'If I Can Dream' in which he seemed to sum up the frustration of a decade in a few short lines. The critical plaudits heaped upon Elvis in the wake of his television special prompted the singer to undertake his most significant recordings in years. With producer Chips Moman overseeing the sessions in January 1969, Presley recorded enough material to cover two highly praised albums, *From Elvis In Memphis* and *From Memphis To Vegas/From Vegas To Memphis*. The former was particularly strong with such distinctive tracks as the eerie 'Long Black Limousine' and the engagingly melodic 'Any Day Now'. On the singles front, Presley was back in top form and finally coming to terms with contemporary issues, most notably on the socially aware 'In The Ghetto', which hit number 2 in the UK and number 3 in the USA. The glorious 'Suspicious Minds', a wonderful song of marital jealousy, with cascading tempo changes and an exceptional vocal arrangement, gave him his first US chart-topper since 'Good Luck Charm' back in 1962. Subsequent hits such as the maudlin 'Don't Cry Daddy', which dealt with the death of a marriage, ably demonstrated Presley's ability to read a song. Even his final few films seemed less disastrous than expected. In 1969's *Charro*, he grew a beard for the first time in his portrayal of a moody cowboy, while *A Change Of Habit* dealt with more serious subject matter than usual. More importantly, Presley returned as a live performer at Las Vegas, with a strong backing group including guitarist James Burton and pianist Glen D. Hardin. In common with John Lennon, who also returned to the stage that same year with the Plastic Ono Band, Presley opened his set with Carl Perkins' 'Blue Suede Shoes'. His comeback was well received and one of the live songs, 'The Wonder Of You', stayed at number 1 in Britain for six weeks during the summer of 1970. There was also a revealing documentary film of the tour - *That's The Way It Is* - and a companion album that included contemporary cover versions, such as Tony Joe White's 'Polk Salad Annie', Creedence Clearwater Revival's 'Proud Mary' and Neil Diamond's 'Sweet Caroline'.

During the early 70s Presley continued his live performances, but soon fell victim to the same artistic atrophy that had bedevilled his celluloid career. Rather than re-entering the studio to record fresh material he relied on a slew of patchy live albums that saturated the marketplace. What had been innovative and exciting in 1969 swiftly became a tedious routine and an exercise in misdirected potential. The backdrop to Presley's final years was a sordid slump into drug dependency, reinforced by the pervasive unreality of a pampered lifestyle in his fantasy home, Gracelands. The dissolution of his marriage in 1973 coincided with a further decline and an alarming tendency to put on weight. Remarkably, he continued to undertake live appearances, covering up his bloated frame with brightly coloured jump suits and an enormous, ostentatiously jewelled belt. He collapsed onstage on a couple of occasions and finally on 16 August 1977 his tired, burnt-out body expired. The official cause of death was a heart attack, undoubtedly brought on by barbiturate usage over a long period. In the weeks following his demise, his record sales predictably rocketed and 'Way Down' proved a fittingly final UK number 1.

The importance of Presley in the history of rock 'n' roll and popular music remains incalculable. In spite of his iconographic status, the Elvis image was never captured in a single moment of time like that of Bill Haley, Buddy Holly or even Chuck Berry. Presley, in spite of his apparent creative inertia, was not a one-dimensional artist clinging to history but a multi-faceted performer whose career spanned several decades and phases. For purists and rockabilly enthusiasts it is the early Presley that remains of greatest importance and there is no doubting that his personal fusion of black and white musical influences, incorporating R&B and country, produced some of the finest and most durable recordings of the century. Beyond Elvis 'The Hillbilly Cat', however, there was the face that launched a thousand imitators, that black-haired, smiling or smouldering presence who stared from the front covers of numerous EPs, albums and film posters of the late 50s and early 60s. It was that well-groomed, immaculate pop star who inspired a generation of performers and second-rate imitators in the 60s. There was also Elvis the Las Vegas performer, vibrant and vulgar, yet still distant and increasingly appealing to a later generation brought up on the excesses of 70s rock and glam ephemera. Finally, there was the bloated Presley who bestrode the stage in the last months of his career. For many, he has come to symbolize the decadence and loss of dignity that is all too often heir to pop idolatry. It is no wonder that Presley's remarkable career so sharply divides those who testify to his ultimate greatness and those who bemoan the gifts that he seemingly squandered along the way. In a sense, the contrasting images of Elvis have come to represent everything positive and everything destructive about the music industry. Twenty years after his death, in August 1997, there was no waning of his power and appeal. Television, radio, newspapers and magazines all over the world still found that, whatever was happening elsewhere, little could compare to this anniversary.

● ALBUMS: *Elvis Presley* (RCA Victor 1956)★★★★, *Elvis* (RCA Victor 1956)★★★★★, *Rock 'N' Roll* UK release (HMV 1956)★★★★, *Rock 'N' Roll No. 2* UK release (HMV 1957)★★★★, *Loving You* film soundtrack (RCA Victor 1957)★★★★, *Elvis' Christmas Album* (RCA Victor 1957)★★★, *King Creole* (RCA Victor 1958)★★★★, *For LP Fans Only* (RCA Victor 1959)★★★★, *A Date With Elvis* (RCA Victor 1959)★★★★, *Elvis Is Back!* (RCA Victor 1960)★★★★, *G.I. Blues* (RCA Victor 1960)★★★, *His Hand In Mine* (RCA Victor 1961)★★★, *Something For Everybody* (RCA Victor 1961)★★★, *Blue Hawaii* (RCA Victor 1961)★★★, *Pot Luck* (RCA Victor 1962)★★★, *Girls! Girls! Girls!* (RCA Victor 1963)★★★, *It Happened At The World's Fair* (RCA Victor 1963)★★, *Fun In Acapulco* (RCA Victor 1963)★★, *Kissin' Cousins* (RCA Victor 1964)★★, *Roustabout* (RCA Victor 1964)★★, *Girl Happy* (RCA Victor 1965)★★, *Harem Scarum* (RCA Victor 1965)★★, *Frankie And Johnny* (RCA Victor 1966)★★, *Paradise, Hawaiian Style* (RCA Victor 1966)★★, *Spinout* (RCA Victor 1966)★★, *How Great Thou Art* (RCA Victor 1967)★★★, *Double Trouble* (RCA Victor 1967)★★, *Clambake* (RCA Victor 1967)★★, *Speedway* (RCA Victor 1968)★★, *Elvis - TV Special* (RCA Victor 1968)★★★, *From Elvis In Memphis* (RCA Victor 1969)★★★★, *From Memphis To Vegas/From Vegas To Memphis* (RCA Victor 1969)★★★, *On Stage February 1970* (RCA Victor 1970)★★★★, *Elvis Back In Memphis* (RCA Victor 1970)★★★, *That's The Way It Is* (RCA 1970)★★★, *Elvis Country (I'm 10,000 Years Old)* (RCA 1971)★★★, *Love Letters From Elvis* (RCA 1971)★★★, *Elvis Sings The Wonderful World Of Christmas* (RCA 1971)★★★, *Elvis Now* (RCA 1972)★★★, *He Touched Me* (RCA 1972)★★★, *Elvis As Recorded At Madison Square Garden* (RCA 1972)★★★, *Aloha From Hawaii Via Satellite* (RCA 1973)★★★, *Elvis* (RCA 1973)★★★, *Raised On Rock/ For Ol' Times Sake* (RCA 1973)★★★, *Good Times* (RCA 1974)★★★, *Elvis Recorded Live On Stage In Memphis* (RCA 1974)★★★★, *Having Fun With Elvis On Stage* (RCA 1974)★, *Promised Land* (RCA 1975)★★★, *Elvis Today* (RCA 1975)★★★, *From Elvis Presley Boulevard, Memphis, Tennessee* (RCA 1976)★★★, *Welcome To My World* (RCA 1977)★★★, *Moody Blue* (RCA 1977)★★★, *Guitar Man* (RCA 1980)★★★, *The Ultimate Performance* (RCA 1981)★★★, *The Sound Of Your Cry* (RCA 1982)★★★,

The First Year (Sun 1983)★★★, *Jailhouse Rock/Love In Las Vegas* (RCA 1983)★★★, *Elvis: The First Live Recordings* (Music Works 1984)★★★, *The Elvis Presley Interview Record: An Audio Self-Portrait* (RCA 1984)★★, with Carl Perkins and Jerry Lee Lewis *The Million Dollar Quartet* (RCA 1990)★★★, *The Lost Album* (RCA 1991)★★★, *If Every Day Was Like Christmas* (RCA 1994)★★★, *Elvis Presley '56* (RCA 1996)★★★★★, *Essential Elvis, Volume 4: A Hundred Years From Now* (RCA 1996)★★★.

● COMPILATIONS: *The Best Of Elvis* UK release (HMV 1957)★★★★, *Elvis' Golden Records* (RCA Victor 1958)★★★★★, *50,000,000 Elvis Fans Can't Be Wrong: Golden Records, Volume 2* (RCA Victor 1960)★★★★★, *Elvis' Golden Records, Volume 3* (RCA Victor 1963)★★★★, *Elvis For Everyone!* (RCA Victor 1965)★★★, *Elvis' Golden Records, Volume 4* (RCA Victor 1968)★★★★, *Elvis Sings 'Flaming Star' And Other Hits From His Movies* (RCA Camden 1969)★★, *Let's Be Friends* (RCA Camden 1970)★★★, *Almost In Love* (RCA Camden 1970)★★, *Worldwide 50 Gold Award Hits, Volume 1 - A Touch Of Gold* 4-LP box set (RCA Victor 1970)★★★★★, *You'll Never Walk Alone* (RCA Camden 1971)★★★, *C'mon Everybody* (RCA Camden 1971)★★★, *The Other Sides - Worldwide 50 Gold Award Hits, Volume 2* 4-LP box set (RCA Victor 1971)★★★★, *I Got Lucky* (RCA Camden 1971)★★★, *Elvis Sings Hits From His Movies, Volume 1* (RCA Camden 1972)★★★, *Burning Love And Hits From His Movies, Volume 2* (RCA Camden 1972)★★★, *Separate Ways* (RCA Camden 1973)★★★, *Elvis - A Legendary Performer, Volume 1* (RCA 1974)★★★★, *Hits Of The 70s* (RCA 1974)★★★, *Pure Gold* (RCA 1975)★★★, *Easy Come Easy Go* (RCA Camden 1975)★★★, *The U.S. Male* (RCA Camden 1975)★★★, *Elvis Presley's Greatest Hits* 7-LP box set (Readers Digest 1975)★★★, *Pictures Of Elvis* (RCA Starcall 1975)★★, *Elvis - A Legendary Performer, Volume 2* (RCA 1976)★★★★, *Sun Sessions* (RCA 1976)★★★★★, *Elvis In Demand* (RCA 1977)★★★, *The Elvis Tapes* interview disc (Redwood 1977)★★, *He Walks Beside Me* (RCA 1978)★★★, *Elvis Sings For Children And Grownups Too!* (RCA 1978)★★★, *Elvis - A Canadian Tribute* (RCA 1978)★★★, *The '56 Sessions, Volume 1* (RCA 1978)★★★★, *Elvis' 40 Greatest* (RCA 1978)★★★★★, *Elvis - A Legendary Performer, Volume 3* (RCA 1979)★★★★, *Our Memories Of Elvis* (RCA 1979)★★★, *Our Memories Of Elvis Volume 2* (RCA 1979)★★★, *The '56 Sessions, Volume 2* (RCA 1979)★★★★, *Elvis Presley Sings Leiber And Stoller* (RCA 1979)★★★★, *Elvis - A Legendary Performer, Volume 4* (RCA 1980)★★★★, *Elvis Aaron Presley* 8-LP box set (RCA 1980)★★★, *This Is Elvis* (RCA 1981)★★★, *Elvis - Greatest Hits, Volume 1* (RCA 1981)★★, *The Elvis Medley* (RCA 1982)★★★, *I Was The One* (RCA 1983)★★★, *Elvis' Golden Records, Volume 5* (RCA 1984)★★★★, *Elvis: A Golden Celebration* 6-LP box set (RCA 1984)★★★, *Rocker* (RCA 1984)★★★★, *Reconsider Baby* (RCA 1985)★★★★, *A Valentine Gift For You* (RCA 1985)★★★, *Always On My Mind* (RCA 1985)★★★★, *Return Of The Rocker* (RCA 1986)★★★, *The Number One Hits* (RCA 1987)★★★★★, *The Top Ten Hits* (RCA 1987)★★★★, *The Complete Sun Sessions* (RCA 1987)★★★★★, *Essential Elvis* (RCA 1988)★★★★, *Stereo '57 (Essential Elvis Volume 2)* (RCA 1988)★★★★, *Known Only To Him: Elvis Gospel: 1957-1971* (RCA 1989)★★★★, *Hits Like Never Before: Essential Elvis, Volume 3* (RCA 1990)★★★, *Collector's Gold* (RCA 1991)★★★★, *The King Of Rock 'n' Roll: The Complete '50s

Masters* 5-CD box set (RCA 1992)★★★★★, *From Nashville To Memphis: The Essential '60s Masters* 5-CD box set (RCA 1993)★★★★★, *Amazing Grace: His Greatest Sacred Songs* (RCA 1994)★★★★, *Heart And Soul* (RCA 1995)★★, *Walk A Mile In My Shoes: The Essential '70s Masters* 5-CD box set (RCA 1995)★★★★, *Presley - The All Time Greats* (RCA 1996)★★★★, *Great Country Songs* (RCA 1997)★★★, *Platinum - A Life In Music* 4-CD box set (RCA 1997)★★★★.

● VIDEOS: *Elvis On Tour* (MGM/UA 1984), *Elvis Presley In Concert* (Mountain Films 1986), *68 Comeback Special* (Virgin Vision 1986), *One Night With You* (Virgin Vision 1986), *Aloha From Hawaii* (Virgin Vision 1986), *'56 In the Beginning* (Virgin Vision 1987), *Memories* (Vestron Music Video 1987), *This Is Elvis* (Warner Home Video 1988), *Graceland* (Video Gems 1988), *Great Performances Volume 1* (Buena Vista 1990), *Great Performances Volume 2* (Buena Vista 1990), *Young Elvis* (Channel 5 1990), *Sun Days With Elvis* (MMG Video 1991), *Elvis: A Portrait By His Friends* (Qube Pictures 1991), *The Lost Performances* (BMG 1992), *Private Elvis* (1993), *Elvis In Hollywood* (1993), *The Alternate Aloha Concert* (Lightyear 1996), *Elvis 56 - The Video* (BMG 1996), *Elvis - That's The Way It Is* (1996), *Private Moments* (Telstar 1997), *The Great Performance* (Wienerworld 1997), *The Legend Lives On* (Real Entertainment 1997), *Collapse Of The Kingdom* (Real Entertainment 1997), *The King Comes Back* (Real Entertainment 1997), *Wild In Hollywood* (Real Entertainment 1997), *Rocket Ride To Stardom* (Real Entertainment 1997), *Elvis: All The Kings Men* (Real Entertainment 1997), *NBC T.V. Special* (Lightyear 1997).

● FURTHER READING: *I Called Him Babe: Elvis Presley's Nurse Remembers*, Marian J. Cocke. *The Three Loves Of Elvis Presley: The True Story Of The Presley Legend*, Robert Holmes. *A Century Of Elvis*, Albert Hand. *The Elvis They Dig*, Albert Hand. *Operation Elvis*, Alan Levy. *The Elvis Presley Pocket Handbook*, Albert Hand. *All Elvis: An Unofficial Biography Of The 'King Of Discs'*, Philip Buckle. *The Elvis Presley Encyclopedia*, Roy Barlow. *Elvis: A Biography*, Jerry Hopkins. *Meet Elvis Presley*, Favius Friedman *Elvis Presley*, Paula Taylor. *Elvis*, Jerry Hopkins. *The Elvis Presley Scrapbook 1935-1977*, James Robert Paris. *Elvis And The Colonel*, May Mann. *Recording Sessions 1954-1974*, Ernst Jorgensen and Erik Rasmussen. *Elvis Presley: An Illustrated Biography*, W.A. Harbinson. *Elvis: The Films And Career Of Elvis Presley*, Steven Zmijewsky and Boris Zmijewsky. *Presley Nation*, Spencer Leigh. *Elvis*, Peter Jones. *Presley: Entertainer Of The Century*, Antony James. *Elvis And His Secret*, Maria Gripe. *On Stage, Elvis Presley*, Kathleen Bowman. *The Elvis Presley American Discography*, Ron Barry. *Elvis: What Happened*, Red West, Sonny West and Dave Hebler. *Elvis: Tribute To The King Of Rock*, Dick Tatham. *Elvis Presley*, Todd Slaughter. *Elvis: Recording Sessions*, Ernst Jorgensen, Erick Rasmussen and Johnny Mikkelsen. *The Life And Death Of Elvis Presley*, W.A. Harbinson. *Elvis: Lonely Star At The Top*, David Hanna. *Elvis In His Own Words*, Mick Farren and Pearce Marchbank. *Twenty Years Of Elvis: The Session File*, Colin Escott and Martin Hawkins. *Starring Elvis*, James W. Bowser. *My Life With Elvis*, Becky Yancey and Cliff Lindecker. *The Real Elvis: A Good Old Boy*, Vince Staten. *The Elvis Presley Trivia Quiz Book*, Helen Rosenbaum. *A Presley Speaks*, Vester Presley. *The Graceland Gates*, Harold Lloyd. *The Boy Who Dared To Rock: The Definitive Elvis*, Paul

Lichter. *Eine Illustrierte Dokumentation*, Bernd King and Heinz Plehn. *Elvis Presley Speaks*, Hans Holzer. *Elvis: The Legend Lives! One Year Later*, Martin A. Grove. *Private Elvis*, Diego Cortez. *Bill Adler's Love Letters To Elvis*, Bill Adler. *Elvis: His Life And Times In Poetry And Lines*, Joan Buchanan West. *Elvis '56: In The Beginning*, Alfred Wertheimer. *Elvis Presley: An Illustrated Biography*, Rainer Wallraf and Heinz Plehn. *Even Elvis*, Mary Ann Thornton. *Elvis: Images & Fancies*, Jac L. Tharpe. *Elvis In Concert*, John Reggero. *Elvis Presley: A Study In Music*, Robert Matthew-Walker. *Elvis; Portrait Of A Friend*, Marty Lacker, Patsy Lacker and Leslie E. Smith. *Elvis Is That You?*, Holly Hatcher. *Elvis: Newly Discovered Drawings Of Elvis Presley*, Betty Harper. *Trying To Get To You: The Story Of Elvis Presley*, Valerie Harms. *Love Of Elvis*, Bruce Hamilton and Michael L. Liben. *To Elvis With Love*, Lena Canada. *The Truth About Elvis*, Jess Stearn. *Elvis: We Love You Tender*, Dee Presley, David Rick and Billy Stanley. *Presleyana*, Jerry Osborne and Bruce Hamilton. *Elvis: The Final Years*, Jerry Hopkins. *When Elvis Died*, Nancy Gregory and Joseph. *All About Elvis*, Fred L. Worth and Steve D. Tamerius. *Elvis Presley: A Reference Guide And Discography*, John A. Whisle. *The Illustrated Discography*, Martin Hawkins and Colin Escott. *Elvis: Legend Of Love*, Marie Greenfield. *Elvis Presley: King Of Rock 'N' Roll*, Richard Wooton. *The Complete Elvis*, Martin Torgoff. *Elvis Special 1982*, Todd Slaughter. *Elvis*, Dave Marsh. *Up And Down With Elvis Presley*, Marge Crumbaker with Gabe Tucker. *Elvis For The Record*, Maureen Covey. *Elvis: The Complete Illustrated Record*, Roy Carr and Mick Farren. *Elvis Collectables*, Rosalind Cranor. *Jailhouse Rock: The Bootleg Records Of Elvis Presley 1970*, Lee Cotten and Howard A. DeWitt. *Elvis The Soldier*, Rex and Elisabeth Mansfield. *All Shook Up: Elvis Day-By-Day, 1954-1977*, Lee Cotten. *Elvis*, John Townson, Gordon Minto and George Richardson. *Priscilla, Elvis & Me*, Michael Edwards. *Elvis On The Road To Stardom: 1955-1956*, Jim Black. *Return To Sender*, Howard F. Banney. *Elvis: His Life From A To Z*, Fred L. Worth and Steve D. Tamerius. *Elvis And The Colonel*, Dirk Vallenga with Mick Farren. *Elvis: My Brother*, Bill Stanley with George Erikson. *Long Lonely Highway: 1950's Elvis Scrapbook*, Ger J. Rijff. *Elvis In Hollywood*, Gerry McLafferty. *Reconsider Baby: Definitive Elvis Sessionography*, E. Jorgensen. *Elvis '69, The Return*, Joseph A. Tunzi. *The Death Of Elvis: What Really Happened*, Charles C. Thompson and James P. Cole. *Elvis For Beginners*, Jill Pearlman. *Elvis, The Cool King*, Bob Morel and Jan Van Gestel. *The Elvis Presley Scrapbooks 1955-1965*, Peter Haining (ed.). *The Boy Who Would Be King. An Intimate Portrait Of Elvis Presley By His Cousin*, Earl Greenwood and Kathleen Tracy. *Elvis: The Last 24 Hours*, Albert Goldman. *The Elvis Files*, Gail Brewer-Giorgio. *Elvis, My Dad*, David Adler and Ernest Andrews. *The Elvis Reader: Texts And Sources On The King Of Rock 'n' Roll*, Kevin Quain (ed.). *Elvis Bootlegs Buyer's Guide, Pts 1 & 2*, Tommy Robinson. *Elvis: The Music Lives On - The Recording Sessions 1954-1976*, Richard Peters. *The King Forever*, no author listed. *Dead Elvis: A Chronicle Of A Cultural Obsession*, Greil Marcus. *Elvis People: Cult Of The King*, Ted Harrison. *In Search Of The King*, Craig Gelfand, Lynn Blocker-Krantz and Rogerio Noguera. *Aren Med Elvis*, Roger Ersson and Lennart Svedberg. *Elvis And Gladys*, Elaine Dundy. *King And I: Little Gallery of Elvis Impersonators*, Kent Barker and Karin Pritikin. *Elvis Sessions: The Recorded Music Of Elvis Aron Presley 1953-1977*, Joseph A. Tunzi. *Elvis: The Sun Years*, Howard A. DeWitt. *Elvis In Germany: The Missing Years*, Andreas Schroer. *Graceland: The Living Legend Of Elvis Presley*, Chet Flippo. *Elvis: The Secret Files*, John Parker. *The Life And Cuisine Of Elvis Presley*, David Adler. *Last Train To Memphis: The Rise Of Elvis Presley*, Peter Guralnick. *In His Own Words*, Mick Farren. *Elvis: Murdered By The Mob*, John Parker. *The Complete Guide To The Music Of...*, John Robertson. *Elvis's Man Friday*, Gene Smith. *The Hitchhiker's Guide To Elvis*, Mick Farren. *Elvis, The Lost Photographs 1948-1969*, Joseph Tunzi and O'Neal. *Elvis Aaron Presley: Revelations From The Memphis Mafia*, Alanna Nash. *The Elvis Encyclopaedia*, David E. Stanley. *E: Reflections On The Birth Of The Elvis Faith*, John E. Strausbaugh. *Elvis Meets The Beatles: The Untold Story Of Their Entangled Lives*, Chris Hutchins and Peter Thompson. *Elvis, Highway 51 South, Memphis, Tennessee*, Joseph A. Tunzi. *Elvis In The Army*, William J. Taylor Jr. *Everything Elvis*, Pauline Bartel. *Elvis In Wonderland*, Bob Jope. *Elvis: Memories And Memorabilia*, Richard Bushkin. *Elvis Sessions II: The Recorded Music Of Elvis Aron Presley 1953-1977*, Joseph A. Tunzi. *The Ultimate Album Cover Book*, Paul Dowling. *The King Of The Road*, Robert Gordon. *That's Alright, Elvis*, Scotty Moore and James Dickerson. *Raised On Rock: Growing Up At Graceland*, David A. Stanley and Mark Bego. *Elvis: In The Twilight Of Memory*, June Juanico. *The Rise And Fall And Rise Of Elvis*, Aubrey Dillon-Malone. *In Search Of Elvis: Music, Race, Art, Religion*, Vernon Chadwick (editor). *The Complete Idiot's Guide To Elvis*, Frank Coffey. *The Elvis Encyclopedia: An Impartial Guide To The Films Of Elvis*, Eric Braun. *Essential Elvis*, Peter Silverton.

● FILMS: *Love Me Tender* (1956), *Loving You* (1957), *Jailhouse Rock* (1957), *King Creole* (1958), *G.I. Blues* (1960), *Flaming Star* (1960), *Wild In The Country* (1961), *Blue Hawaii* (1961), *Kid Galahad* (1962), *Girls Girls Girls* (1962), *Follow That Dream* (1962), *It Happened At The World's Fair* (1963), *Fun In Acapulco* (1963), *Roustabout* (1964), *Viva Las Vegas* (1964), *Kissin' Cousins* (1964), *Tickle Me* (1965), *Harem Scarum a.k.a. Harem Holiday* (1965), *Girl Happy* (1965), *Spinout* (1966), *Paradise Hawaiian Style* (1966), *Frankie And Johnny* (1966), *Easy Come Easy Go* (1967), *Clambake* (1967), *Live A Little Love A Little* (1968), *Speedway* (1968), *Stay Away Joe* (1968), *Double Trouble* (1968), *The Trouble With Girls* (1969), *Charro!* (1969), *Change Of Habit* (1969), *This Is Elvis* compilation (1981).

PRESTON, ROBERT

b. Robert Preston Meservey, 8 June 1918, Newton Highlands, Massachusetts, USA, d. 21 March 1987, Santa Barbara, California, USA. An actor and singer, Preston had already enjoyed a busy, but undistinguished career in Hollywood for nearly 20 years when he landed the role of a lifetime on Broadway in *The Music Man* (1957). He grew up in Hollywood, and spent several of his teenage years in the theatre before signing for Paramount and making his first movie, *King Of Alcatraz*, in 1938. From then, until 1942, he made some 15 films, including *Union Pacific*, *Beau Geste*, *Typhoon*, *Moon Over Burma*, *Northwest Mounted Police*, and *This Gun For Hire* (1942). After serving in the US Army Air Force during World War II, Preston resumed his film career in features such as *The Macomber Affair*, *Tulsa* and *When I*

Grow Up, until 1951 when he moved to New York. He appeared on Broadway in a number of straight plays including *Twentieth Century*, *The Tender Trap* and *Janus*, and was out of town in Philadelphia with *Boy Meets Girl* when he was asked to audition for *The Music Man*. His portrayal of the likeable con man, Harold Hill, who travels to small US towns such as Iowa, selling band instruments (which never materialize) to parents for their children to play, made Preston a gilt-edged Broadway star. Meredith Willson's fine score featured numbers such as 'Seventy-Six Trombones', ''Til There Was You', and Preston's *tour de force*, 'Ya Got Trouble'. He won the Tony Award for best actor in a musical, and stayed with the show for over two years. After being virtually ignored during initial casting, he recreated the part in the 1962 film version. Cary Grant was one of the actors to whom the role was offered, and he reportedly said: 'Not only won't I play it, but unless Robert Preston plays it, I won't even go see it.' After appearing in several more straight parts, Preston returned to the musical stage in 1964 with *Ben Franklin In Paris*, but, unlike the large onstage floating balloon in which Preston rode, the show did not really take off. Much more satisfying was *I Do! I Do!*, a two-hander with Mary Martin for which Preston won another Tony. His final Broadway musical appearance came in 1974 with *Mack And Mabel*, which, despite a splendid Jerry Herman score, only lasted for six weeks. During the 50s and 60s he had continued to make films, and in the 70s and early 80s he appeared in several more, including the musical *Mame* (1973), with Lucille Ball, and *S.O.B.* and *Victor/Victoria* (1982), both with Julie Andrews. He also starred in several television movies, including the highly regarded *Finnegan Begin Again*, a poignant story of the love of an older man for a young woman played by Mary Tyler Moore. Preston died of lung cancer in 1987, and in the same year was awarded a special posthumous Tony, the Lawrence Langner Memorial Award for Distinguished Lifetime Achievement in the American Theatre.

PRICE, LLOYD

b. 9 March 1933, Kenner, Louisiana, USA. Price, who launched his career in the early 50s performing rocking R&B, New Orleans-style, was - like his Crescent City compatriot Fats Domino - made for the rock 'n' roll era. He did not have to modify his approach at all to become a rock 'n' roll hit-maker in the late 50s. Price formed his own band in New Orleans in 1949 and in 1952 was signed with the Los Angeles-based Specialty Records, who made a practice of recording New Orleans artists. His first hit, 'Lawdy Miss Clawdy' (US R&B number 1, 1952), established his career in the R&B field and he followed with four more Top 10 hits. Military service intervened and took Price out of action from 1954-56. On returning to civilian life he settled in Washington, DC, and set up a record company with Harold Logan. Price regained his place on the chart in 1957 with 'Just Because' (US R&B number 3 and pop Top 30). Signed to ABC-Paramount, the company transformed their R&B veteran into a rock 'n' roll hit-maker for the new teen market. He and Logan revamped an old blues, 'Stack-O-Lee', that had been a hit for Ma Rainey in the 20s, and made it one of his biggest successes (US R&B and pop number 1, 1959). In the UK, it entered the Top 10. Price's chart career peaked in 1959, with such hits as 'Where Were You (On Our Wedding

Day)' (US R&B number 4 and pop Top 30), 'Personality' (US R&B number 1 and pop number 2) and 'I'm Gonna Get Married' (US R&B number 1 and pop number 3), all of which were similarly successful in the UK. The hits continued, to a lesser extent, the following year with 'Lady Luck' (US R&B number 3 and pop Top 20) and 'Question' (US R&B number 5 and number 19 pop). Three years later Price resurfaced on the Double-L label (owned by Price and Logan), briefly making an impact on the emerging soul market with his reworking of jazz standards 'Misty' (US R&B number 11 and pop Top 30) and 'Bill Bailey' (US R&B Top 40 and pop Top 100 as 'Billy Baby'). Double-L also released Wilson Pickett's first solo sides, and in the late 60s Price began another label called Turntable for which Howard Tate, among others, recorded. Price's last chart record was in 1976 on the LPG label, a label he formed in partnership with the notorious boxing promoter Don King.

● ALBUMS: *Lloyd Price* (Specialty 1959)★★★★, *The Exciting Lloyd Price* (ABC-Paramount 1959)★★★★, *Mr. Personality* (ABC-Paramount 1959)★★★★, *Mr. Personality Sings The Blues* (ABC-Paramount 1960)★★★★, *The Fantastic Lloyd Price* (ABC-Paramount 1960)★★★, *Lloyd Price Sings The Million Sellers* (ABC-Paramount 1961)★★★, *Cookin' With Lloyd Price* (ABC-Paramount 1961)★★, *The Lloyd Price Orchestra* (Double-L 1963)★★, *Misty* (Double-L 1963)★★, *Lloyd Swings For Sammy* (Monument 1965)★★, *Lloyd Price Now* (Jad 1969)★★, *To The Roots And Back* (1972)★★, *The Nominee* (1978)★★.

● COMPILATIONS: *Mr. Personality's Big 15* (ABC-Paramount 1960)★★★★, *The Best Of Lloyd Price* (1970)★★★★, *Lloyd Price's 16 Greatest Hits* (ABC 1972)★★★★, *Original Hits* (1972)★★★, *The ABC Collection* (ABC 1976)★★★★, *Mr. Personality Revisited* (Charly 1983)★★★, *Lloyd Price* (Specialty 1986)★★★, *Personality Plus* (Specialty 1986)★★★, *Walkin' The Track* (Specialty 1986)★★, *Lawdy!* (Specialty 1991)★★★, *Stagger Lee & All His Other Greatest Hits* (1993)★★★★, *Greatest Hits* (MCA 1995)★★★★.

PRIDE, DICKIE

b. Richard Knellar, Thornton Heath, England. Pride, a former Royal College of Church Music chorister and trainee stonemason, was 'discovered' in 1958 singing rock 'n' roll in a London pub by Russ Conway who recommended him to both EMI producer Norrie Paramor and pop svengali Larry Parnes. Groomed and given a *nom de théâtre*, the diminutive youth's voice rather than his face was his fortune - though his onstage convulsions earned him the nickname 'The Sheik Of Shake'. The first that Britain at large saw of him was on ITV's *Oh Boy!*, promoting his 1959 cover version of Little Richard's 'Slippin' And Slidin'.' While his third single, 'Primrose Lane', touched the Top 30, the failure of later singles contradicted any claims that Pride was realistically a potential rival to Cliff Richard. Nevertheless, he was still impressing audiences in 1960 when he recorded a creditable album of Tin Pan Alley chestnuts with Ted Heath's orchestra. This ploy might have set him on the road of the 'all round entertainer' had not his dabbling with amphetamines alienated him from Parnes, and precipitated a fall from grace that found him delivering coal and nursing debilities related to the drug abuse that sent him to an early grave.

● ALBUMS: *Pride Without Prejudice* (Columbia 1960)★★.

PRIMA, LOUIS

b. 7 December 1911, New Orleans, Louisiana, USA, d. 24 August 1978, New Orleans, Louisiana, USA. A trumpeter, bandleader, singer, and composer, Prima was the son of Italian immigrant parents. He was educated at Jesuit High School, and studied the violin for several years under Hemmersback, before switching to the trumpet. At the age of 17, inspired by jazz greats such as Louis Armstrong and King Oliver, he gained his first job as a singer/trumpeter in a New Orleans theatre - his elder brother, Leon, also played trumpet at a local nightspot. For a time in the early 30s Prima worked with Red Nichols, before forming his own seven-piece New Orleans Gang, with its signature tune, 'Way Down Yonder In New Orleans', who recorded more than 70 titles in New York for various labels from 1934-39. Several of them made the US Hit Parade, including 'The Lady In Red', 'In A Little Gypsy Tea Room' and 'The Goose Hangs High'. His sidemen during this period included Georg Brunis (trombone), Claude Thornhill (piano), George Van Eps (guitar), Artie Shapiro (bass), Eddie Miller (reeds), Ray Bauduc (drums), Sidney Arodin (clarinet), Frank Pinero (piano), Frank Frederico (guitar), Oscar Bradley (drums), and Pee Wee Russell (clarinet). By this stage, Prima was also composing songs, and one of them, 'Sing, Sing, Sing', when developed by Benny Goodman, became a smash hit for the 'King Of Swing', and remains a Swing Era classic. Over the years, Prima wrote or co-wrote many other numbers, including 'Robin Hood', which was successful for Les Brown in 1945, and the 1947 Jo Stafford hit, 'A Sunday Kind Of Love', along with 'Alone', 'Little Boy Blew His Top', 'Marguerita', 'New Aulins', 'Angelina', 'Where Have We Met Before?', 'Brooklyn Boogie', 'Boogie In The Bronx', 'Bridget O'Brien', 'Boogie In Chicago', 'It's The Rhythm In Me', 'Sing A Spell', 'It's A Southern Holiday' and 'Rhythm On The Radio'. His collaborators included Jack Loman, Dave Franklin, Milton Kabak, Bob Miketta, Barbara Belle, Anita Leonard, and Stan Rhodes. After making an good impression on his feature film debut in the Bing Crosby movie musical *Rhythm On The Range* (1936), Prima continued to have relatively small, but telling roles in a number of other movies, notably *Rose Of Washington Square* (1939), in which he enhanced Alice Faye's rendering of 'I'm Just Wild About Harry' with his ebullient and exciting trumpet accompaniment. By this time he had his own big band which he fronted with great showmanship and panache. It had had 40s hits with 'Angelina', 'Bell-Bottom Trousers' (vocal: Lily Ann Carol), and 'Civilization (Bongo, Bongo, Bongo)', an amusing novelty from the 1947 Broadway revue *Angel In The Wings*. In 1948, Prima began working with the poker-faced singer Keely Smith, and, after having a US hit in 1950 with their joint composition 'Oh, Babe!', they were married two years later. During the next decade they were recognized as one of the hottest nightclub acts in the USA, and became known as 'The Wildest Show In Las Vegas'. Prima's inspired clowning and zany vocals delivered in a fractured Italian dialect, coupled with Smith's cool image and classy singing, were augmented by tenor saxophonist Sam Butera and his group, the Witnesses. A typical performance was filmed at Lake Tahoe in 1957, and released under the title of *The Wildest*, and they reassembled in 1959 for the feature *Hey Boy! Hey Girl!* Prima and Smith were awarded Grammys in 1958 for their inimitable reading of the Harold Arlen-Johnny Mercer standard,

'That Old Black Magic'. In 1958 Prima was briefly in the UK Top 30 with Carl Sigman and Peter de Rose's likeable 'Buona Sera', and two years later made the US singles and albums charts with the instrumental 'Wonderland By Night'. Other Top 40 albums included *Las Vega-Prima Style* and *Hey Boy!, Hey Girl!* In 1961, while still at the height of their fame - and having recently signed a multi-million dollar contract with the Desert Inn, Las Vegas - the couple were divorced. Prima and Butera subsequently attempted to cash in on the then-popular dance fad by appearing in the movie *Twist All Night*, which sank without a trace, in spite (or because) of items such as 'When The Saints Go Twistin' In'. Far more lasting was Prima's contribution in 1967 to *The Jungle Book*, the Walt Disney Studio's first cartoon feature for four years, which went on to gross around $26 million. Prima provided the voice of hip orang-utan King Louie, and sang the film's hit song, 'I Wanna Be Like You'. In later years he mostly confined himself to performing with a small group at venues such as the Sands Hotel, Las Vegas, and in 1975 underwent surgery for the removal of a brain tumour. He never recovered from the operation, and remained in a coma until his death nearly three years later in a New Orleans nursing home.

● ALBUMS: *A Nite On 42nd Street* (50s)★★★, *One Night Stand With Louis Prima Volumes 1 & 2* (50s)★★★, *Louis Prima At Frank Dailey's Terrace Room* (Mercury 1953)★★, *Swings* (Capitol 1955)★★★, *The Wildest* (Capitol 1956)★★★, *Call Of The Wildest* (Capitol 1957)★★★, *The Wildest Show At Tahoe* (Capitol 1957)★★★, with Keely Smith *Las Vegas-Prima Style* (Capitol 1958)★★★★, *Jump, Jive An' Wail* (Capitol 1958)★★★, with Smith *Hey Boy! Hey Girl!* film soundtrack (Capitol 1959)★★★★, with Smith *Louis And Keely!* (Dot 1959)★★★, *Strictly Prima* (Capitol 1959)★★★, with Smith *Senior Prom* (1959)★★★, with Sam Butera *The Continental Twist* (Capitol 60s)★★★, with Smith *Together* (Dot 1960)★★★, *Plays Pretty Music Prima Style* (Dot 1960)★★★, with Smith *On Stage* (Dot 1960)★★★, *Wonderland By Night* (Dot 1961)★★★★, *Blue Moon* (Dot 1961)★★★, with Smith *Return Of The Wildest* (Dot 1961)★★★, *The Wildest Comes Home* (Capitol 1962)★★★, *Doin' The Twist* (Dot 1962)★★★, *Lake Tahoe Prima Style* (Capitol 1963)★★★, *Plays Pretty For The People* (1964)★★★, *Plays And Sings* (Hamilton 1965)★★★, *On Broadway* (United Artists 1967)★★, with Jimmie Lunceford *Lunceford And Prima-1945* (Aircheck 1979)★★★, *Live From Las Vegas* (Jazz Band 1988)★★, *Angelina* (Big Band Era 1989)★★★.
● COMPILATIONS: *His Greatest Hits* (Dot 1960)★★★★, with Keely Smith *Hits* (Capitol 1961)★★★★, *Best Of Louis Prima* (MFP 1985)★★★, *Just A Gigolo 1945-50* (Bandstand 1988)★★★, *Capitol Collectors Series* (Capitol 1991)★★★★.
● FILMS: *Rhythm On The Range* (1936), *The Star Reporter In Hollywood* (1936), *Swing It* (1936), *Vitaphone Varieté* (1936), *You Can't Have Everything* (1937), *Manhattan Merry-Go-Round* (1937), *Start Cheering* (1938), *Swing Cat's Jamboree* (1938), *Rose Of Washington Square* (1939), *New Orleans Blues* (1943), *Rhythm Masters* (1948), *The Wildest* (1957), *Senior Prom* (1958), *Hey Boy! Hey Girl!* (1959), *Twist All Night* (1961), voice only *The Man Called Flintstone* (1966), voice only *The Jungle Book* (1967), *Rafferty And The Gold Dust Twins* (1974).

PRISONAIRES

As their name suggests, this doo-wop group were formed in 1940 while each member was in the State Penitentiary, Tennessee, USA. The founding member was second tenor Ed Thurman, and he took on Johnny Bragg (lead), John Drue (first tenor), William Stuart (baritone and guitar) and Marcell Sanders (bass). The group was paraded around a variety of receptions and civic functions as demonstration of the jail's enlightened rehabilitation programme, where they played a mix of blues, gospel and pop songs under armed guard. Edwards then arranged for two talent scouts from Sam Phillips' Sun Records to see the group. They were subsequently driven down to Memphis in June 1953 to record a song written by Bragg and fellow inmate Robert Riley, 'Just Walkin' In The Rain'. The record took hold first on radio and then became a major seller, moving over 250,000 copies, despite a competing version from Johnny Ray that sold eight times that amount. Still, the Prisonaires had arrived, and found themselves in demand for a series of television and concert appearances. They gradually became high-status figures in Tennessee, and never betrayed the trust placed in them by trying to escape their guards on their numerous forays outside the prison (on one occasion they were said to have lost their escorts but nevertheless travelled back to the prison under their own guidance). A second single followed in August 1953, the highly spiritual 'My God Is Real', followed by 'I Know' and its autobiographical b-side, 'A Prisoner's Prayer'. While recording it they made the acquaintance of Elvis Presley, who later visited them in prison. By now some of his colleagues had become eligible for parole, so Bragg formed a new version of the band titled the Sunbeams with Hal Hebb, Willy Wilson, Al Brooks and Henry 'Dishrag' Jones. This group lasted only until 1955, when the group was retitled the Marigolds and had a number 8 R&B chart success with 'Rollin' Stone'. However, by 1956 Bragg had been released and he recorded a series of singles under his own name for Decca Records. He was then arrested for 'parole violation' in 1960 when found in the back seat of a car with a white woman (his wife). His penalty was to return to prison for an incredible six and a half years. Despite this second injustice, Bragg put together another version of the Prisonaires with new inmates, but they never recorded again. On release, he worked in a cemetery.
● COMPILATIONS: *Five Beats Behind Bars* (Charly 1978)★★★.

PRYOR, SNOOKY

b. James Edward Pryor, 15 September 1921, Lambert, Mississippi, USA. As a child he became drawn to the harmonica after watching an albino player, John Blissett, together with his friend Jimmy Rogers. When he was 13 he saw Rice Miller (Sonny Boy Williamson number 2) play. After settling in Chicago in 1945 after US Army service, Pryor joined the Maxwell Street group of blues singers which included Johnny Young, Floyd Jones and Moody Jones, with whom he recorded in 1948. Their records were harbingers of the amplified down-home sound of post-war Chicago blues, although at this time Pryor's singing and harmonica were heavily influenced by John Lee 'Sonny Boy' Williamson. Pryor made his first record, 'Telephone Blues', with guitarist Moody Jones in 1949. There were later singles for J.O.B. ('Boogy Fool', 1950), Parrot (1953), Blue Lake (1954) and Vee

Jay Records ('Someone To Love Me', 1956). During the 50s Pryor also frequently toured the south. After making the dance novelty 'Boogie Twist', Pryor left the music business in 1963 but returned in the early 70s, touring and recording in Europe in 1973. A 1974 album was made with a New Orleans rhythm section including guitarist Justin Adams. In recent years he has benefited from the revived interest in blues, recording his 1992 album for Texas label Antone's, which has to date resulted in regular new albums, notably his 1997 release *Mind Your Own Business*.
● ALBUMS: *Snooky Pryor* (Flyright 1969)★★, *Snooky Pryor And The Country Blues* (1973)★★★, *Do It If You Want To* (1973)★★★, *Homesick James And Snooky Pryor* (Caroline 1974)★★★, *Shake Your Boogie* (Big Bear 1979)★★★, *Too Cool To Move* (Antone's 1992)★★, with Johnny Shines *Back To The Country* (Black Pig 1993)★★★, *In This Mess Up To My Chest* (Antone's 1994)★★★, *Mind Your Own Business* (Antone's 1997)★★★★.
● COMPILATIONS: *Snooky Pryor - 1947 To 1960s* (Flyright 1990)★★★.

QUARRYMEN

John Lennon went to the Quarry Bank High School in Liverpool and his first group, a skiffle band, was formed in March 1957. The initial line-up was John Lennon (guitar, vocals), Eric Griffiths (guitar), Rod Davis (banjo), Colin Hanton (drums), Pete Shotton (washboard) and Bill Smith (tea chest bass). Their repertoire included skiffle favourites, 'Lost John' and 'Cumberland Gap', and a few rock 'n' roll songs. Lennon was introduced to Paul McCartney by a common friend, Ivan Vaughan, at St. Peter's church fete in Woolton on 6 July 1957. McCartney told Lennon the correct words to 'Come Go With Me' and became a Quarryman. McCartney brought George Harrison into the group and in June 1958, they recorded 'That'll Be The Day' and 'In Spite Of All The Danger' at Percy Phillips' recording studio in Kensington, Liverpool, the line-up including John Duff Lowe (piano) and Len Garry (tea chest bass). The tracks were released on the Beatles' *Anthology 1* along with some rehearsal tapes from 1960. Although the Quarrymen did not play many bookings, they had a residency at the Casbah, the club owned by Mona Best, Pete's mother. In October 1959, the Quarrymen disbanded over an argument about fees, but

Lennon, McCartney and Harrison stuck together, becoming Johnny And The Moondogs, then the Beatals, the Silver Beatles and, of course, the Beatles. In recent years, former Quarrymen have appeared at Beatles Conventions and Pete Shotton, a friend of John Lennon, has written a memoir, *John Lennon: In My Life*. Pianist John Duff Lowe, now a member of the Four Pennies, used the group as the nucleus for *Open For Engagements*, which also included Rod Davis. Five former Quarrymen were together at the celebrations for the fortieth anniversary of the Cavern in January 1997.
● ALBUMS: *Open For Engagements* (Kewbank 1994)★★.

RABINOWITZ, HARRY

b. 26 March 1916, Johannesburg, South Africa. Trained as a classical pianist, Rabinowitz was educated at Athlone High School and Witwatersrand University and made his first radio broadcast in 1933. After service with the South African Army, he studied composition and conducting, and moved to London in 1946 to continue his studies at the Guildhall School of Music. He played the piano on several popular BBC radio programmes, including *Variety Bandbox*, and spent some time as house pianist at EMI Records. His first conducting jobs were with the show *Golden City* (1950), followed by four ice spectaculars at London's Empress Hall, and as musical director for Alan Jay Lerner and Frederick Loewe's 1953 hit, *Paint Your Wagon*. In the same year he joined the BBC staff and was conductor of the BBC Revue Orchestra until 1960, working on programmes such as *Take It From Here*, *Henry Hall's Guest Night*, *Variety Playhouse* and *Just Fancy*. He also featured as a pianist on *Piano Playtime*, *Rendezvous* and *Midday Music Hall*. In 1960, he moved to BBC Television as Head Of Music for Light Entertainment, and was responsible for programmes such as the *Val Doonican Show*, *Michael Bentine Show*, *Billy Cotton Band Show* and *Not Only But Also*, featuring Peter Cook and Dudley Moore. Rabinowitz moved to the rival London Weekend Television as Head of Music in 1968, and during the next nine years his projects included *Black Beauty*, *Upstairs, Downstairs* and several David Frost programmes. He also composed many themes to successful television programmes such *The Agatha Christie Hour* and *Love For Lydia*, which was nominated for an Ivor Novello Award in 1977. In the same year he won the Television And Radio Industries Council Celebrity Award for 'Best Television Theme Music Of The Year' for his music to *Reilly, Ace Of Spies*. Since returning to freelance work in 1977, Rabinowitz has been musical director for many feature films, such as *The Greek Tycoon* (1978), *Mon Oncle D'Amerique* (1980), *Chariots Of Fire* (1981), *Time Bandits* (1981), *Heat And Dust* (1982), *Maurice* (1987), *Queen Of Hearts* (1989), *Music Box* (1989), *Lord Of The Flies* (1990) and *The Ballad Of The Sad Cafe* (1990). In the early 80s, he conducted the first six weeks of the London runs of Andrew Lloyd Webber's *Cats* and *Song And Dance*, and travelled to the USA to conduct the Los Angeles Philharmonic Orchestra in concerts at the Hollywood Bowl. In the UK, he frequently conducts the Royal Philharmonic, the London Symphony, and the London Concert Orchestras. In 1977, he was awarded an MBE for services to music.

RADIO LUXEMBOURG

The Compagnie Luxembourgeoise de Radiodiffusion was set up in 1931 to broadcast in German and French and two years later began Sunday broadcasts in English on 208 metres medium wave. Until 1939, programmes of dance music were punctuated with commercials. Sponsored shows included *The Palmolive Hour* and *The Ovaltineys*. After World War II, the English service was broadcast daily and most of its programming consisted of records, although the station broadcast a Top 20 compiled from sheet music sales until 1959. Until the arrival of pirate radio ships in 1964, Radio Luxembourg's evening shows were the most important source of pop music broadcasting for British listeners. While the BBC Light Programme devoted only a few hours a week to record shows, Luxembourg played new releases for six hours a night. Beginning with Teddy Johnson (1948) and Pete Murray (1950), virtually every disc jockey from that era had a show on Radio Luxembourg. Among those who made their broadcasting debut there were Jimmy Young, Alan Freeman and Jimmy Saville, who made his first broadcast in 1957 and hosted the *Teen And Twenty Disc Club*. For a period, a *Fab 208* magazine was also published. From 1946-68, record companies paid for 15-minute shows on the station, plugging their latest releases. These were pre-recorded in London by name disc jockeys such as Young, Kent Walton, Barry Aldis, Ray Orchard and Saville. In 1968, Radio Luxembourg abolished these slots in favour of 'mixed' programmes and the sponsored plays were spread throughout the schedule. In 1971, the station became 'all live' with every show presented by disc jockeys based in Luxembourg itself. By that time, strong competition from BBC Radio 1, and after 1973, from Capital Radio and other UK-based commercial stations, was affecting Luxembourg's listening figures. At the end of 1991, the English-language service was moved from 208 metres to a satellite waveband and was reorganized. By then, however, the company had set up Atlantic 252, a highly successful long-wave pop station based in Ireland but transmitting to the western side of Britain. 'Lux', as it was known, had a huge part to play in every UK 60s pop fan's life, in spite of the maddening fade-in and fade-out owing to poor reception, and the disc jockeys' habit of often only playing part of the record (presumably because of the programme's sponsor).

RAELETTES

This vocal group was formed in the USA around Margie Hendrix, and was previously known as the Cookies, whose R&B backing voices appeared on numerous 50s sessions and inspired the new group's inception. Founded to provide responsive vocals for singer Ray Charles, this female trio provided the launching pad for several careers. Merry Clayton, Mable John, Minnie Riperton, Clydie King and Estella Yarbrough were all members at some point, although Hendrix provided a long-serving constant. The Raelettes did have several minor hits via Charles's Tangerine label, but their frequently changing personnel denied them a more constructive recording career. Hendrix, however, who had had early solo exposure on the Lamp label, also recorded on her own in the 60s, for Tangerine, Mercury and Sound Stage 7.

● ALBUMS: *Souled Out* (Tangerine 1969)★★★, *Yesterday, Today And Tomorrow* (Tangerine 1972)★★.

● FILMS: *Blues for Lovers* aka *Ballad In Blue* (1964).

RAINBOWS

R&B vocal group the Rainbows were formed in the early 50s in Washington, DC, USA, by John Berry (lead and second tenor), Ronald 'Poosie' Miles (lead and second tenor), Henry 'Shorty' Womble (first tenor; ex-Serenaders), James 'Sally' Nolan (baritone) and Frank 'Jake' Hardy (bass; also ex-Serenaders). They were signed by Bobby Robinson of Red Robin Records in 1955 after unsuccessfully auditioning a year earlier. 'Mary Lee', their debut, followed in June, and proved popular both in New York and Boston (where it was licensed to Pilgrim Records). After a young Marvin Gaye and soul star Billy Stewart had sung with the group, Henry Womble's impending college career meant the group had a vacancy; it was filled by two new members, Don Covay and Chester Simmons. However, only two further Rainbows singles emerged. 'Shirley' and 'Minnie' continued their use of female names as titles. By 1957 the group had broken up, allowing Nolan and Simmons to join with Gaye and Reese Palmer to form the Marquees before becoming the new Moonglows. A new Rainbows was formed in 1961 with Miles now joined by Duval Potter (tenor), Joe Walls (tenor), Layton McDonald (baritone) and Victor English (bass). Two singles were released in 1963, 'I Know' and 'It Wouldn't Be Right'. Neither charted and the group folded once more with members scattering in various directions. Covay became a major songwriting talent. Simmons worked for the Reflection Sound studio before joining Reese in 70s group Choice Of Color. The other members retired from the music industry.

RAINWATER, MARVIN

b. Marvin Karlton Percy, 2 July 1925, Wichita, Kansas, USA. A big-voiced, rockabilly singer-songwriter, who is a quarter Cherokee Indian (using his mother's maiden name on stage), Percy became a regular on Red Foley's *Ozark Mountain Jubilee* in the early 50s. After being spotted on Arthur Godfrey's Talent Scouts television show in the mid-50s, he was signed to Coral. The first of his two singles for them, 'I Gotta Go Get My Baby', became a hit for the label when their top act Teresa Brewer covered his record. Rainwater then joined MGM and his second release, the self-composed 'Gonna Find Me A Bluebird' in 1957, gave him his only US Top 40 hit. Later that year a duet with Connie Francis (before her string of hits), 'Majesty Of Love', graced the US Top 100. In 1958, another of his songs, 'Whole Lotta Woman', which only reached number 60 in his homeland,

topped the UK chart, and his UK-recorded follow-up, 'I Dig You Baby', also entered the British Top 20. He later recorded without success for Warwick, Warner Brothers, United Artists, Wesco, his own label Brave, as well as UK labels Philips, Sonet and Westwood. In subsequent years, the man who performed in full American Indian regalia has continued to play the rockabilly and country circuits on both sides of the Atlantic.

● ALBUMS: *Songs By Marvin Rainwater* (MGM 1957)★★★, *Marvin Rainwater Sings With A Beat* (MGM 1958)★★★★, *Gonna Find Me A Bluebird* (MGM 1962)★★★, *Marvin Rainwater* (Crown 1974)★★★, *Marvin Rainwater & Mike Cowdery* (Hoky 1981)★★.

● COMPILATIONS: *Rockin' Rollin' Rainwater* (Bear Family 1982)★★★, *Classic Recordings* (Bear Family 1992)★★★★, *Whole Lotta Woman* (Bear Family 1994)★★★★.

RAITT, JOHN

b. John Emmett Raitt, 19 January 1917, Santa Ana, California, USA. An actor and singer with a fine baritone voice, Raitt sang in light opera and concerts before playing the lead in a Chicago production of *Oklahoma!* (1944). In the following year he made his Broadway debut, playing Billy Bigelow, and introducing immortal songs such as 'If I Loved You' and 'Soliloquy', in Richard Rodgers and Oscar Hammerstein II's magificent *Carousel*. Three years later, he appeared on Broadway again in the short-lived and 'unconventional' *Magdelana*. This was followed in 1952 by the 'whimsical' *Three Wishes For Jamie*, which was 'too treacly' to run for long. *Carnival In Flanders* (1953), despite a score by Johnny Burke and Jerry Van Heusen that contained 'Here's That Rainy Day', provided less than a week's employment, but his next job, as the factory superintendent in *The Pajama Game* (1954), lasted nearly two and a half years. Raitt's spirited and sensitive renditions of Richard Adler and Jerry Ross's 'There Once Was A Man' and 'Small Talk' (both with Janis Paige), plus 'Hey There', a duet with a dictaphone machine, made sufficient impact in Hollywood for him to be cast opposite Doris Day in the 1957 film version, despite his being a complete newcomer to the big screen. In the 50s and 60s Raitt appeared frequently on US television, and in 1960 toured with the satirical musical *Destry Rides Again*. In the spring of 1966 he recreated his original role in a New York Music Theater revival of *Carousel* and, later in the year, dwelt for a brief spell amid the 'newly created folk songs' of *A Joyful Noise*. Thereafter, Raitt devoted much of his time to touring, and in 1975 was back on Broadway, along with Patricia Munsell, Tammy Grimes, Larry Kert, Lillian Gish and Cyril Ritchard, in *A Musical Jubilee*, a 'potpourri' claiming to demonstrate the development of the American musical. By that time, his daughter, Bonnie Raitt, was gaining recognition as one of the best female singer/guitarists of the 70s and 80s. John Raitt himself continued to be active, and in 1992 he received an Ovation Award in Hollywood for services to the Los Angeles theatre scene. A year later he was inducted into New York's Theater Hall Of Fame, and celebrated the 50th anniversary of *Oklahoma!* by singing the show's title song on the stage of the St. James Theatre in New York (the theatre in which *Oklahoma!* first opened in 1943) prior to a performance of a very different kind of musical - *The Who's Tommy*.

● ALBUMS: *Highlights Of Broadway* (Capitol 1955)★★★★,

Mediterranean Magic (Capitol 1956)★★★, *Under Open Skies* (Capitol 1958)★★★, *Songs The Kids Brought Home* (Capitol 1959)★★★, with Bonnie Raitt *Broadway Legend* (Angel 1995)★★★★, and many Original Cast recordings.

RASPBERRY, RAYMOND
b. 1930, USA, d. 20 October 1995, Los Angeles, California, USA. After working as a pianist with several of the most prominent gospel stars, including Mahalia Jackson, Wynona Carr and the Clara Ward Singers, in 1954 Raspberry formed his own group, the Raspberry Singers. One of the first all-male gospel choirs, they frequently recorded in Spanish. They eventually disbanded in 1966 when Raspberry moved to New York, where he worked as a songwriter. His compositions include staples of the gospel repertoire including 'I'll Let Nothing Separate Me From The Love Of God', 'Touch Somebody's Life' and 'I Want To Be More Like Jesus'. In 1971 he moved to Los Angeles where he founded a new Raspberry Singers with an all-female line up. He died in 1995 while receiving dialysis treatment.

RAVENS
An African-American vocal group from New York City, New York, USA. Formed in 1945, the Ravens are considered the first of the 'bird groups' and their success was highly influential in ushering in an avalanche of vocal groups in the post-World War II R&B revolution. The original members were Ollie Jones (tenor), Leonard Puzey (tenor), Warren Suttles (baritone) and Jimmy Ricks (bass). After Maithe Marshall replaced Jones in 1946, the Ravens featured two leads, Ricks, who used his outstanding bass with terrific rhythmic bounce on the mid-tempo tunes, and Marshall, whose soaring falsetto tenor lent great poignancy to the ballads. The group also used with great effectiveness the switchover lead between Marshall and Ricks, which gave the Ravens a unique sound until it was widely imitated by other vocal ensembles. The Ravens first recorded for the Hub label in 1946, but only after they signed with National did they reach the charts, with the Ricks-led 'Write Me A Letter' (number 5 R&B) in 1948. Memorable recordings by the group at this time also included the Marshall-led songs 'September Song' and 'Searching For Love'. Their 1948 hit versions of 'Silent Night' (number 8 R&B) and 'White Christmas' (number 9 R&B) paved the way for later R&B vocal groups to interpret Christmas standards with an R&B flavour (the Ravens' vocal arrangement of 'White Christmas' was lifted for Clyde McPhatter And The Drifters' version from 1955). The Ravens' last chart record was in 1952 on Mercury with 'Rock Me All Night Long' (number 4 R&B). The group's last notable recording was 'Give Me A Simple Pray' in 1955 on the Argo label. With Ricks' departure for a solo career in 1956 the group faded from the scene.
● COMPILATIONS: *The Ravens* (Harlem Hit Parade 1973)★★★, *The Greatest Group Of Them All* (Savoy 1978)★★★★, *Old Man River* (Savoy Jazz 1985)★★★.

RAY, JOHNNIE
b. 10 January 1927, Dallas, Oregon, USA, d. 24 February 1990, Los Angeles, California, USA. Known at various times in his career as the Prince of Wails, the Nabob of Sob and the Howling Success because of his highly emotional singing and apparent ability to cry at will, Ray is rated an important influence in the development of 50s and early 60s popular music. Of North American Indian origin, he became deaf in his right ear at the age of 12, which caused him to wear a hearing-aid throughout his career. He was heavily influenced by gospel and R&B music and performed in bars and clubs around Detroit in the late 40s, singing to his own piano accompaniment. Signed by Columbia Records in 1951, his first two releases were on their small OKeh label, usually reserved for black artists. His first record, 'Whiskey And Gin', was followed by 'Cry'. Unsophisticated, full of anguish, despair and a good deal of sobbing, it shocked a pop world accustomed to male singers crooning in front of big bands, and streaked to the top of the US charts, complete with Ray's own composition, 'The Little White Cloud That Cried', on the b-side. 'Cry' became his 'identity' song, and a multi-million-seller.

Ray was then transferred to the Columbia label, and during the next couple of years, he had several massive US hits including 'Please Mr Sun', 'Here Am I - Broken Hearted', 'Walkin' My Baby Back Home' and 'Somebody Stole My Gal'. His stage performances, with their overt sexuality and hysterical audience reaction, made him *persona non grata* to parents of teenagers worldwide. For a few years during the 50s, he enjoyed phenomenal success, revolutionizing popular music and symbolizing teenagers' frustrations and desires. Always acknowledging his gospel roots, Ray recorded several tracks associated with black artists, including the Drifters' R&B hit 'Such a Night' (1954), which was banned on several US radio stations, and 'Just Walkin' In the Rain' (1956), which climbed to number 2 in the US charts, and was originally recorded by the Prisonaires. By contrast, in 1954, he played a young singer who decides to become a priest in Irving Berlin's musical film *There's No Business Like Show Business*. Ray sang the gospel-styled 'If You Believe' and 'Alexander's Ragtime Band'. During the late 50s in the USA, rumours were rife concerning his possible homosexuality and drug-taking, and as a result he became more popular abroad than at home. In the UK, in person and on record, he had been a favourite since 1952. Three of his US hits reached UK number 1, including 'Yes Tonight Josephine' (1957). Other UK successes included 'Faith Can Move Mountains', 'Hey There' and 'Look Homeward Angel'. Ray also duetted with Doris Day ('Ma Says Pa Says', 'Full Time Job', 'Let's Walk That-Away') and Frankie Laine ('Good Evening Friends'). In the early 60s, suffering from financial problems and alcoholism, and left behind as the musical climate rapidly changed, he turned to cabaret in the USA. During the 70s he began to revive his career, leaning heavily on his old material for its nostalgic appeal. Always in demand in the UK, he was headlining there until the late 80s. His last performance is said to have been in his hometown on 7 October 1989, and he died of liver failure a few months later. As to his influence, one writer concluded: 'Ray was the link between Frank Sinatra and Elvis Presley, re-creating the bobby-sox mayhem that elevated "The Voice" while anticipating the sexual chaos that accompanied Presley.'
● ALBUMS: *Johnnie Ray* (Columbia 1951)★★★, *At The London Palladium* (Philips 1954)★★, *I Cry For You* (Columbia 1955)★★★, *Johnnie Ray* (Epic 1955)★★★, *The Voice Of Your Choice* (Philips 1955)★★★, *Johnnie Ray Sings The Big Beat* (Columbia 1957)★★★★, *Johnnie Ray At The Desert Inn In Las Vegas* (Columbia 1959)★★★, *A Sinner Am*

I (Philips 1959)★★, *'Til Morning* (Columbia 1959)★★, *Johnnie Ray On The Trail* (Columbia 1959)★★, *I Cry For You* (1960)★★, *Johnnie Ray* (Liberty 1962)★★, *Yesterday, Today And Tomorrow* (Celebrity 1980)★★, *Yesterday - The London Sessions 1976* (1993)★★.
● COMPILATIONS: *Showcase Of Hits* (Philips 1958)★★★★, *Johnnie Ray's Greatest Hits* (Columbia 1959)★★★★, *The Best Of Johnny Ray* (Realm 1966)★★★★, *An American Legend* (Columbia 1978)★★★★, *Portrait Of A Song Stylist* (Masterpiece 1989)★★★★, *Greatest Hits* (Pickwick 1991)★★★.
● FURTHER READING: *The Johnnie Ray Story*, Ray Sonin.

RAYBURN, MARGIE

b. Madera, California, USA. Her first significant professional experience was as vocalist for the Ray Anthony Orchestra. She later sang with Gene Autry and as a member of the Sunnysiders, on their sole Top 20 hit, 'Hey, Mr. Banjo', in 1955. Going solo after the Sunnysiders' fortunes dimmed, Rayburn released 'I'm Available', written by Dave Burgess, later of the Champs, for Liberty Records, eventually peaking at number 9 in the *Billboard* pop charts in 1957. She was unable to follow the single with another hit and gave up her recording career by the mid-60s.

REDHEAD

Composer Albert Hague and veteran lyricist and librettist Dorothy Fields came together for the first time to write the score for this musical, which opened at the 46th Street Theatre in New York on 5 February 1959. Fields, together with her brother, Herbert, and their fellow authors, Sydney Sheldon and David Shaw, came up with what was an unusual subject for a Broadway musical - a murder mystery. Set in Victorian London at around the time of the Jack the Ripper killings, the story has Essie Whimple (Gwen Verdon) and Tom Baxter (Richard Kiley) chasing suspects around various parts of the metropolis, including a waxworks museum bearing a remarkable resemblance to Madame Tussaud's emporium. Hague and Fields' score is not considered to be remarkable, but any show that contains such engaging songs as 'I Feel Merely Marvellous', 'The Right Finger Of My Right Hand' and 'Look Who's In Love', merits serious consideration. Add to those Verdon's music hall version of 'Erbie Fitch's Twitch', and several other bright numbers, including 'I'm Back In Circulation', The Uncle Sam Rag', 'My Girl Is Just Enough Woman For Me' and 'We Loves Ya, Jimmy', and it was not all bad news. The Tony Awards committee certainly did not think so, and their kudos went to Verdon, Kiley and Hague, along with others for best musical, libretto, and Bob Fosse's brilliant choreography. The public gave the show their vote, too, and it ran for well over a year, a total of 452 performances.

REED, JIMMY

b. Mathis James Reed, 6 September 1925, Leland, Mississippi, USA, d. 29 August 1976, Oakland, California, USA. Jimmy Reed was a true original: he sang in a lazy mush-mouthed ramble, played limited, if instantly recognizable, harmonica, and even more minimal guitar. He produced a series of hits in the 50s that made him the most successful blues singer of the era. He was born into a large sharecropping family and spent his early years on Mr.

Johnny Collier's plantation situated near Dunleith, Mississippi. Here, he formed a childhood friendship with Eddie Taylor which was to have a marked effect on his later career. Reed sang in church and learned rudimentary guitar along with Taylor, but while the latter progressed Reed never became more than basically competent on the instrument. He left school in 1939 and found work farming around Duncan and Meltonia, Mississippi. Around 1943-44 he left the south to find work in Chicago where opportunities abounded due to the war effort. He was drafted in 1944 and served out his time in the US Navy. Discharged in 1945 he returned briefly to Mississippi before gravitating north once more to the Chicago area. Working in the steel mills, Reed gigged around in his leisure time with a friend named Willie Joe Duncan, who played a one-string guitar, or Diddley-bow. He also re-established contact with Eddie Taylor who had similarly moved north to try his luck. This led to Reed's becoming known on the local club scene and after appearances with John and Grace Brim, he secured a recording contract with Vee Jay Records in 1953. His initial sessions, though highly regarded by collectors, produced no hits and Vee Jay were considering dropping him from their roster when in 1955 'You Don't Have To Go' took off. From then on, his success was phenomenal as a string of hits such as 'Ain't That Lovin' You Baby', 'You've Got Me Dizzy', 'Bright Lights Big City', 'I'm Gonna Get My Baby' and 'Honest I Do' carried him through to the close of the decade. Many of these timeless blues numbers were adopted by every white R&B beat group during the early 60s. Two of his songs are now standards and are often used as rousing encores by name bands; 'Baby What You Do You Want Me To Do' closed the Byrds' and Closer Than Most's live performances for many years and 'Big Boss Man' is arguably the most performed song of its kind - sung by the Merseybeats, Pretty Things, Grateful Dead and countless blues artists. Much of the credit for this success must be attributed to his friend Eddie Taylor, who played on most of Reed's sessions, and his wife, Mama Reed, who wrote many of his songs and even sat behind him in the studio reciting the lyrics into his forgetful ear as he sang. On some recordings her participation is audible. Reed's songs had little to do with the traditional blues, but they were eminently danceable and despite employing the basic blues line-up of harmonica, guitars and drums were generally classed as R&B. His hits were 'crossovers', appealing to whites as well as blacks. Perhaps this contributed to his continuing success as the blues entered its post-rock 'n' roll hard times. In his later days at Vee Jay, various gimmicks were tried, such as dubbing an album's worth of 12-string guitar solos over his backing tracks, faking live performances and introducing a commentary between album cuts; none were too successful in reviving his flagging sales. To counter the positive elements in his life, Reed was continually undermined by his own unreliability, illness (he was an epileptic) and a propensity towards the bottle. He visited Europe in the early 60s, by which time it was obvious that all was not well with him. He was supremely unreliable and prone to appear on stage drunk. By the mid-60s his career was in the hands of the controversial Al Smith and his recordings were appearing on the Bluesway label. Inactive much of the time due to illness, Reed seemed on the road to recovery and further success, having gained control over his drink problem. Ironically, he died soon afterwards of respiratory failure, and was buried in Chicago. Reed is an important figure who has influenced countless artists through his songs. Steve Miller recorded *Living In The 20th Century* with a segment of Reed songs and dedicated the album to him. The Rolling Stones, Pretty Things and the Grateful Dead also acknowledge a considerable debt to him.

● ALBUMS: *I'm Jimmy Reed* (Vee Jay 1958)★★★, *Rockin' With Reed* (Vee Jay 1959)★★★★, *Found Love* (Vee Jay 1960)★★★★, *Now Appearing* (Vee Jay 1960)★★★★, *At Carnegie Hall* (Vee Jay 1961)★★★, *Just Jimmy Reed* (Vee Jay 1962)★★★★, *T'ain't No Big Thing…But He Is!* (Vee Jay 1963)★★★, *The Best Of The Blues* (Vee Jay 1963)★★★, *The 12-String Guitar Blues* (Vee Jay 1963)★★★★, *Jimmy Reed At Soul City* (Vee Jay 1964)★★★, *The Legend, The Man* (Vee Jay 1965)★★★, *The New Jimmy Reed Album* (Bluesway 1967)★★★, *Soulin'* (Bluesway 1967)★★★, *Big Boss Man* (Bluesway 1968)★★★, *Down In Virginia* (Bluesway 1969)★★★, *As Jimmy Is* (Roker 1970)★★★, *Let The Bossman Speak!* (Blues On Blues 1971)★★★.

● COMPILATIONS: *The Best Of Jimmy Reed* (Vee Jay 1962)★★★★, *More Of The Best Of Jimmy Reed* (Vee Jay 1964)★★★★, *The Soulful Sound Of Jimmy Reed* (Upfront 1970)★★★, *I Ain't From Chicago* (Bluesway 1973)★★★, *The Ultimate Jimmy Reed* (Bluesway 1973)★★★★, *Cold Chills* (Antilles 1976)★★★, *Jimmy Reed Is Back* (Roots 1980)★★★, *Hard Walkin' Hanna* (Versatile 1980)★★★, *Greatest Hits* (Hollywood 1992)★★★, *Speak The Lyrics To Me, Mama Reed* (Vee Jay 1993)★★★, *Cry Before I Go* (Drive Archive 1995)★★★, *The Classic Recordings Volumes 1-3* (Tomato/Rhino 1995)★★★★, *Big Legged Woman* (Collectables 1996)★★★★.

REGAN, JOAN

b. 19 January 1928, Romford, Essex, England. A popular singer in the UK during the 50s and early 60s, with a particularly glamorous image, it was after working at various jobs, including one as a photographer's re-toucher, that Regan first made an impression on the music scene in 1953. Her private recordings of 'Too Young' and 'I'll Walk Alone' gained her a contract with Decca Records, partly because she was thought to have a 'Vera Lynn sound'. Her first releases, 'Till I Waltz Again With You' and 'I'll Always Be Thinking Of You', were followed by 'Ricochet', on which she was backed by Ronnie Aldrich's Squadronaires. It made the UK Top 10, and led to the nationwide fame she achieved when she became the resident singer on producer Richard Afton's television series *Quite Contrary*, followed later by four series of her own *Be My Guest* programmes. After being knocked out by a descending safety curtain during her first appearance in variety, she developed her act to include effective impressions of artists such as Gracie Fields, Judy Garland, and actress Anna Neagle, to whom Regan bore a remarkable facial resemblance. During the late 50s and early 60s, Regan appeared in several shows at the London Palladium, including *We're Having A Ball* with Max Bygraves; *Stars In Your Eyes* with Russ Conway, Cliff Richard, Edmund Hockridge and Billy Dainty; in pantomime with Frankie Vaughan and Jimmy Edwards; and several Royal Command Performances. Her other record hits, through to 1961, included 'Someone Else's Roses', 'If I Give My Heart To You', 'Prize Of Gold', 'Open Up Your Heart', 'May You Always', 'Happy Anniversary', 'Papa Loves Mama', 'One Of The

Lucky Ones', 'Must Be Santa' and 'Wait For Me' (with the Johnston Brothers). She also recorded several duets, such as 'Seven And A Half Cents'/'Good Evening Friends' with Max Bygraves, 'Cleo And Me-O' with Dickie Valentine, and 'Open Up Your Heart' with her son, Rusty. In July 1957 Regan married Harry Claff, the joint general manager and box office manager of the London Palladium. In November, the *Daily Herald* reported that she was to have a baby in February of the following year - seven months after the wedding. After receiving 'abusive and wounding letters from people who were personally unknown to her', Regan successfully sued the newspaper for libel, and her daughter was born in April. In 1963, she was involved in a far more serious court case, when her husband was sentenced to five years' imprisonment for 'frauds on his employers involving £62,000'. Regan, who had known nothing about the deceptions, suffered a nervous breakdown, and divorced him later on the grounds of adultery. She resumed work later, and in 1968 married a doctor, Martin Cowan, eventually settling in Florida, USA. In 1984 she slipped in the shower, hit her head on the tiles, and suffered a brain haemorrhage. After an emergency operation she was left paralyzed and speechless. Her recovery, which entailed much physical and speech therapy, was aided by her miming to her old records. In 1987, some of those tracks, together with others by various 'Stars Of The Fifties', including Dickie Valentine, Lita Roza and Jimmy Young, were issued on the double album *Unchained Melodies*. In the same year, while on holiday in the UK, Regan was invited by her old accompanist, Russ Conway, to sing on stage again. Such was the response, that she has become a familiar figure in UK shows in the 90s.

● ALBUMS: *The Girl Next Door* (Decca 1955)★★★, *Just Joan* (Decca 1957)★★★★, with Edmund Hockridge *Joan And Ted* (Pye-Nixa 1961)★★.

● COMPILATIONS: *The World Of Joan Regan* (Decca 1976)★★★★, *Joan Regan Collection* (Nectar 1989)★★★★.

REYNOLDS, DEBBIE

b. Mary Frances Reynolds, 1 April 1932, El Paso, Texas, USA. A popular actress and singer, particularly in movies. After moving to California in 1940 she became a majorette and played French horn with the Burbank Youth Orchestra. It was there she was spotted by talent scouts at a Miss Burbank competition in 1948. She quickly became a leading light in film musicals such as *The Daughter Of Rosie O'Grady* (1950), *Three Little Words* (as 'Boop-Boop-A-Doop' girl Helen Kane), *Two Weeks With Love*, *Singin' In The Rain* (perhaps her most memorable role), *Skirts Ahoy!*, *I Love Melvin*, *The Affairs Of Dobie Gillis*, *Athena*, *Give A Girl A Break*, *Hit The Deck*, *The Tender Trap* (comedy with music), *Bundle Of Joy*, *Meet Me In Las Vegas*, *Say One For Me*, *Pepe* and *The Unsinkable Molly Brown* (1964, Oscar nomination). In 1951 she recorded her first million-selling single, 'Abba Daba Honeymoon' (from the film *Two Weeks With Love*), on which she duetted with Carleton Carpenter. She also went to the top of the US charts in 1957 with the million-selling 'Tammy' (from *Tammy And The Bachelor*). She married the singer and actor Eddie Fisher in September 1955, and their daughter Carrie has since become an established actress and writer. They divorced in 1959 when Fisher married Elizabeth Taylor. In 1966 Reynolds appeared in *The Singing Nun* (a fictionalized story about Soeur Sourire), and three years later starred in her own television series, *Debbie*. As her film career declined, she made an acclaimed Broadway debut in the 1973 revival of the much-loved American musical *Irene*, and appeared in her own nightclub revue. In later years, she survived severe financial problems when her second husband's business failed, and she and Carrie were estranged after Carrie's hard-hitting novel, *Postcards From The Edge*, which was supposedly based on their lives together, was filmed in 1990. Always the trouper, she bounced right back, launching two keep-fit videos, and headlining at venues such as Harrah's in Reno, and Caesar's Palace in Las Vegas, often in the company of her former film co-stars, such as Harve Presnell (*The Unsinkable Molly Brown*) and Donald O'Connor (*Singin' In The Rain*). In 1993 she opened the Debbie Reynolds Hotel on the fringe of the Las Vegas Strip, where she presents her two-hour autobiographical one-woman show, which contains often bawdy impressions of Zsa Zsa Gabor, Mae West and Barbra Streisand. The complex also houses Reynolds' museum of Hollywood memorabilia.

● ALBUMS: *Debbie Reynolds* (Dot 1959)★★★, *Am I That Easy To Forget* (Dot 1960)★★★ *Fine & Dandy* (Dot 1960)★★, *From Debbie With Love* (Dot 1960)★★, *Tammy* (Dot 1963)★★★, *Raising A Ruckus* (Metro 1965)★★★, *Debbie* (Jasmine 1985)★★, and film soundtrack recordings.
● FURTHER READING: *Debbie - My Life*, Debbie Reynolds with David Patrick Columba.
● FILMS: *June Bride* (1948), *Three Little Words* (1950), *Two Weeks With Love* (1950), *The Daughter Of Rosie O'Grady* (1950), *Mr. Imperium* (1951), *Singin' In The Rain* (1952), *Skirts Ahoy!* (1952), *Give A Girl A Break* (1953), *The Affairs Of Dobie Gillis* (1953), *I Love Melvin* (1953), *Susan Slept Here* (1954), *Athena* (1954), *The Tender Trap* (1955), *Hit The Deck* (1955), *Bundle Of Joy* (1956), *The Catered Affair* (1956), *Meet Me In Las Vegas* (1956), *Tammy And The Bachelor* (1957), *This Happy Feeling* (1958), *It Started With A Kiss* (1959), *The Mating Game* (1959), *Say One For Me* (1959), *Pepe* (1960), *The Rat Race* (1960), *The Gazebo* (1960), *The Pleasure Of His Company* (1961), *The Second Time Around* (1961), *How The West Was Won* (1962), *My Six Loves* (1963), *Mary, Mary* (1963), *The Unsinkable Molly Brown* (1964), *Goodbye Charlie* (1964), *The Singing Nun* (1966), *Divorce American Style* (1967), *How Sweet It Is* (1968), *What's The Matter With Helen?* (1971), *Charlottes's Web* (1973), *That's Entertainment!* (1974), *The Bodyguard* (1992), *Heaven And Earth* (1993), *Mother* (1994), *That's Entertainment! III* (1994).

REYNOLDS, JODY

b. 3 December 1938, Denver, Colorado, USA. Reynolds grew up in Oklahoma and formed his first band, the Storms, in 1952. He played guitar in the group and worked various jobs until he could make a living playing music. In 1958 the band went to Los Angeles, where they were signed to the new Demon label. The label did not use the Storms but did record Reynolds, backed with a number of professional session musicians on his 1958 single 'Endless Sleep' (covered in the UK by Marty Wilde), a song Reynolds had written with George Brown (credited under the pseudonym Delores Nance). The song reached number 5 and became one of the first of the so-called 'death rock' hits of the 50s and 60s (others in that category included 'Tell Laura I Love Her', 'Terry', 'Teen Angel' and 'Leader Of The Pack'). Reynolds made the charts once more with 'Fire Of Love' (also in

1958), but none of his subsequent recordings for Demon, Smash or other labels charted. Reynolds continued to perform with the Storms for much of the 60s, but by the 70s had retired to a non-musical career. His only album was a 1978 set on the Tru-Gems label including a remake of his only hit.
● ALBUMS: *Endless Sleep* (Tru-Gems 1978)★★.

RICHARD, CLIFF

b. Harry Roger Webb, 14 October 1940, Lucknow, India. One of the most popular and enduring talents in the history of UK showbusiness, Richard began his career as a rock 'n' roll performer in 1957. His fascination for Elvis Presley encouraged him to join a skiffle group and several months later he teamed up with drummer Terry Smart and guitarist Ken Payne to form the Drifters. They played at various clubs in the Cheshunt/Hoddesdon area of Hertfordshire before descending on the famous 2I's coffee bar in London's Soho. There, they were approached by lead guitarist Ian Samwell and developed their act as a quartet. In 1958, they secured their big break in the unlikely setting of a Saturday morning talent show at the Gaumont cinema in Shepherd's Bush. It was there that the senatorial theatrical agent George Ganyou recognized Richard's sexual appeal and singing abilities and duly financed the recording of a demonstration tape of 'Breathless' and 'Lawdy Miss Clawdy'. A copy reached the hands of EMI producer Norrie Paramor who was impressed enough to grant the ensemble an audition. Initially, he intended to record Richard as a solo artist backed by an orchestra, but the persuasive performer insisted upon retaining his own backing group. With the assistance of a couple of session musicians, the unit recorded the American teen ballad 'Schoolboy Crush' as a projected first single. An acetate of the recording was paraded around Tin Pan Alley and came to the attention of the influential television producer Jack Good. It was not the juvenile 'Schoolboy Crush' that captured his attention, however, but the Ian Samwell b-side 'Move It'. Good reacted with characteristically manic enthusiasm when he heard the disc, rightly recognizing that it sounded like nothing else in the history of UK pop. The distinctive riff and unaffected vocal seemed authentically American, completely at odds with the mannered material that usually emanated from British recording studios. With Good's ceaseless promotion, which included a full-page review in the music paper *Disc*, Richard's debut was eagerly anticipated and swiftly rose to number 2 in the UK charts. Meanwhile, the star made his debut on Good's television showcase *Oh Boy!*, and rapidly replaced Marty Wilde as Britain's premier rock 'n' roll talent. The low-key role offered to the Drifters persuaded Samwell to leave the group to become a professional songwriter, and by the end of 1958 a new line-up emerged featuring Hank B. Marvin and Bruce Welch. Before long, they changed their name to the Shadows, in order to avoid confusion with the black American R&B group, the Drifters. Meanwhile, Richard consolidated his position in the rock 'n' roll pantheon, even outraging critics in true Elvis Presley fashion. The *New Musical Express* denounced his 'violent, hip-swinging' and 'crude exhibitionism' and pontificated: 'Tommy Steele became Britain's teenage idol without resorting to this form of indecent, short-sighted vulgarity'. Critical mortification had little effect on the screaming female fans who responded to the singer's boyish sexuality with increasing intensity.

1959 was a decisive year for Richard and a firm indicator of his longevity as a performer. With management shake-ups, shifts in national musical taste and some distinctly average singles his career could easily have been curtailed, but instead he matured and transcended his Presley-like beginnings. A recording of Lionel Bart's 'Living Doll' provided him with a massive UK number 1 and three months later he returned to the top with the plaintive 'Travellin' Light'. He also starred in two films, within 12 months. *Serious Charge*, a non-musical drama, was banned in some areas as it dealt with the controversial subject of homosexual blackmail. The Wolf Mankowitz-directed *Expresso Bongo*, in which Richard played the delightfully named Bongo Herbert, was a cinematic pop landmark, brilliantly evoking the rapacious world of Tin Pan Alley. It remains one of the most revealing and humorous films ever made on the music business and proved an interesting vehicle for Richard's varied talents. From 1960 onwards Richard's career progressed along more traditional lines leading to acceptance as a middle-of-the-road entertainer. Varied hits such as the breezy, chart-topping 'Please Don't Tease', the rock 'n' rolling 'Nine Times Out Of Ten' and reflective 'Theme For A Dream' demonstrated his range, and in 1962 he hit a new peak with 'The Young Ones'. A glorious pop anthem to youth, with some striking guitar work from Hank Marvin, the song proved one of his most memorable number 1 hits. The film of the same name was a charming period piece, with a strong cast and fine score. It broke box office records and spawned a series of similar movies from its star, who was clearly following Elvis Presley's cinematic excursions as a means of extending his audience. Unlike the King, however, Richard supplemented his frequent movie commitments with tours, summer seasons, regular television slots and even pantomime appearances. The run of UK Top 10 hits continued uninterrupted until as late as mid-1965. Although the showbiz glitz had brought a certain aural homogeneity to the material, the catchiness of songs such as 'Bachelor Boy', 'Summer Holiday', 'On The Beach' and 'I Could Easily Fall' was undeniable. These were neatly, if predictably, complemented by ballad releases such as 'Constantly', 'The Twelfth Of Never' and 'The Minute You're Gone'. The formula looked likely to be rendered redundant by the British beat boom, but Richard expertly rode that wave, even improving his selection of material along the way. He bravely, although relatively unsuccessfully, covered a Rolling Stones song, 'Blue Turns To Grey', before again hitting top form with the beautifully melodic 'Visions'. During 1966, he had almost retired after converting to fundamentalist Christianity, but elected to use his singing career as a positive expression of his faith. The sparkling 'In The Country' and gorgeously evocative 'The Day I Met Marie' displayed the old strengths to the full, but in the swiftly changing cultural climate of the late 60s, Richard's hold on the pop charts could no longer be guaranteed. The 1968 Eurovision Song Contest offered him a chance of further glory, but the jury placed him a close second with the 'oom-pah-pah'-sounding 'Congratulations'. The song was nevertheless a consummate Eurovision performance and proved one of the biggest UK number 1s of the year. Immediately thereafter, Richard's chart progress declined and his choice of material proved at best desultory. Although there were a couple of solid entries, Raymond Froggatt's 'Big Ship' and a superb duet with Hank Marvin,

'Throw Down A Line', Richard seemed a likely contender for Variety as the decade closed.

The first half of the 70s saw him in a musical rut. The chirpy but insubstantial 'Goodbye Sam, Hello Samantha' was a Top 10 hit in 1970 and heralded a notable decline. A second shot at the Eurovision Song Contest with 'Power To All Our Friends' brought his only other Top 10 success of the period and it was widely assumed that his chart career was over. However, in 1976 there was a surprise resurgence in his career when Bruce Welch of the Shadows was assigned to produce his colleague. The sessions resulted in the bestselling album *I'm Nearly Famous*, which included two major hits, 'Miss You Nights' and 'Devil Woman'. The latter was notable for its decidedly un-Christian imagery and the fact that it gave Richard a rare US chart success. Although Welch remained at the controls for two more albums, time again looked as although it would kill off Richard's perennial chart success. A string of meagre singles culminated in the dull 'Green Light', which stalled at number 57, his lowest chart placing since he started singing. Coincidentally, his backing musicians, Terry Britten and Alan Tarney, had moved into songwriting and production at this point and encouraged him to adopt a more contemporary sound on the album *Rock 'N' Roll Juvenile*. The most startling breakthrough, however, was the attendant single 'We Don't Talk Anymore', written by Tarney and produced by Welch. An exceptional pop record, the song gave Richard his first UK number 1 hit in over a decade and also reached the Top 10 in the USA. The 'new' Richard sound, so refreshing after some of his staid offerings in the late 70s, brought further well-arranged hits, such as 'Carrie' and 'Wired For Sound', and ensured that he was a chart regular throughout the 80s.

Although he resisted the temptation to try anything radical, there were subtle changes in his musical approach. One feature of his talent that emerged during the 80s was a remarkable facility as a duettist. Collaborations with Olivia Newton-John, Phil Everly, Sarah Brightman, Sheila Walsh, Elton John and Van Morrison added a completely new dimension to his career. It was something of a belated shock to realize that Richard may be one of the finest harmony singers working in the field of popular music. His perfectly enunciated vocals and the smooth texture of his voice have the power to complement work that he might not usually tackle alone. The possibility of his collaborating with an artist even further from his sphere than Van Morrison remains a tantalizing challenge. Throughout his four decades in the pop charts, Richard has displayed a valiant longevity. He parodied one of his earliest hits with comedy quartet the Young Ones and registered yet another number 1; he appeared in the stage musicals *Time* and *Heathcliff*; he sang religious songs on gospel tours; he sued the *New Musical Express* for an appallingly libellous review, far more vicious than their acerbic comments back in 1958; he was decorated by the Queen; and he celebrated his 50th birthday with a move into social commentary with the anti-war hit 'From A Distance'. Richard was nominated to appear at the celebrations in 1995 for VE day, appearing with Vera Lynn, and has now been adopted as her male equivalent. It was no surprise, therefore, to learn that he was to be knighted for his services to popular music in May 1995. His most recent album, *Songs From Heathcliff*, was drawn from the John Farrar and Tim Rice production of *Heathcliff*. And so he goes on - Sir Cliff

Richard has outlasted every musical trend of the past four decades with a sincerity and commitment that may well be unmatched in his field. He is British pop's most celebrated survivor.

● ALBUMS: *Cliff* (Columbia 1959)★★★, *Cliff Sings* (Columbia 1959)★★★★, *Me And My Shadows* (Columbia 1960)★★★★, *Listen To Cliff* (Columbia 1961)★★★, *21 Today* (Columbia 1961)★★★, *The Young Ones* (Columbia 1961)★★★, *32 Minutes And 17 Seconds With Cliff Richard* (Columbia 1962)★★★★, *Summer Holiday* (Columbia 1963)★★★, *Cliff's Hit Album* (Columbia 1963)★★★★, *When In Spain* (Columbia 1963)★★★, *Wonderful Life* (Columbia 1964)★★★, *Aladdin And His Wonderful Lamp* (Columbia 1964)★★★, *Cliff Richard* (Columbia 1965)★★★, *More Hits By Cliff* (Columbia 1965)★★★, *When In Rome* (Columbia 1965)★★, *Love Is Forever* (Columbia 1965)★★★, *Kinda Latin* (Columbia 1966)★★★, *Finders Keepers* (Columbia 1966)★★, *Cinderella* (Columbia 1967)★★, *Don't Stop Me Now* (Columbia 1967)★★★, *Good News* (Columbia 1967)★★★, *Cliff In Japan* (Columbia 1968)★★★, *Two A Penny* (Columbia 1968)★★★, *Established 1958* (Columbia 1968)★★★, *Sincerely Cliff* (Columbia 1969)★★★, *It'll Be Me* (Regal Starline 1969)★★★, *Cliff 'Live' At The Talk Of The Town* (Regal Starline 1970)★★★, *All My Love* (MFP 1970)★★★, *About That Man* (Columbia 1970)★★★, *Tracks 'N' Grooves* (Columbia 1970)★★★, *His Land* (Columbia 1970)★★★, *Cliff's Hit Album* stereo reissue of 1963 album (EMI 1971)★★★★, *Take Me High* (EMI 1973)★★★, *Help It Along* (EMI 1974)★★★, *The 31st Of February Street* (EMI 1974)★★★, *Everybody Needs Someone* (MFP 1975)★★★, *I'm Nearly Famous* (EMI 1976)★★★, *Cliff Live* (MFP 1976)★★★, *Every Face Tells A Story* (EMI 1977)★★★, *Small Corners* (EMI 1977)★★★, *Green Light* (EMI 1978)★★★, *Thank You Very Much* (EMI 1979)★★★, *Rock 'N' Roll Juvenile* (EMI 1979)★★★, *Rock On With Cliff* (MFP 1980)★★★, *Listen To Cliff* (MFP 1980)★★★, *I'm No Hero* (EMI 1980)★★★, *Love Songs* (EMI 1981)★★★, *Wired For Sound* (EMI 1981)★★★, *Now You See Me, Now You Don't* (EMI 1982)★★★, *Dressed For The Occasion* (EMI 1983)★★★, *Silver* (EMI 1983)★★★, *Cliff In The 60s* (MFP 1984)★★★, *Cliff And The Shadows* (EMI 1984)★★★, *Thank You Very Much* (MFP 1984)★★★, *The Rock Connection* (EMI 1984)★★★, *Walking In The Light* (Myrrh 1985)★★★, *Time* (EMI 1986)★★★, *Hymns And Inspirational Songs* (Word 1986)★★★, *Always Guaranteed* (EMI 1987)★★★, *Stronger* (EMI 1989)★★★, *From A Distance ...The Event* (EMI 1990)★★★, *Together With Cliff* (EMI 1991)★★★, *The Album* (EMI 1993)★★★, *Songs From Heathcliff* (EMI 1995)★★★.

● COMPILATIONS: *The Best Of Cliff* (Columbia 1969)★★★★, *The Best Of Cliff Volume 2* (Columbia 1972)★★★★, *The Cliff Richard Story* 6-LP box set (WRC 1972)★★★, *40 Golden Greats* (EMI 1979)★★★★, *The Cliff Richard Songbook* 6-LP box set (WRC 1980)★★★, *Private Collection 1979-1988* (EMI 1988)★★★, *20 Original Greats* (EMI 1989)★★★, *The Hit List* (EMI 1994)★★★★, *At The Movies 1959-1974* (EMI 1996)★★★, *The Rock 'N' Roll Years 1958-1963* 4-CD box set (EMI 1997)★★★.

● VIDEOS: *Two A Penny* (1978), *The Video Connection* (PMI 1984), *Together* (PMI 1984), *Thank You Very Much* (Thorn-EMI 1984), *Rock In Australia* (PMI 1986), *We Don't Talk Anymore* (Gold Rushes 1987), *Video EP* (PMI 1988), *The Young Ones* (1988), *Summer Holiday* (1988), *Wonderful Life* (1988), *Take Me High* (Warner Home Video 1988), *Private Collection* (PMI 1988), *Always Guaranteed* (PMI 1988), *Live And Guaranteed* (PMI 1989), *From A Distance . . . The Event Volumes 1 and 2* (PMI 1990), *Together With Cliff Richard* (PMI 1991), *Expresso Bongo* (1992), *Cliff-When The Music Stops* (1993), *Access All Areas* (1993), *The Story So Far* (1993), *The Hit List* (PMI 1995), *The Hit List Live* (PMI 1995), *Finders Keepers* (1996), *Cliff At The Movies* (1996).

● FURTHER READING: *Driftin' With Cliff Richard: The Inside Story Of What Really Happens On Tour*, Jet Harris and Royston Ellis. *Cliff, The Baron Of Beat*, Jack Sutter. *It's Great To Be Young*, Cliff Richard. *Me And My Shadows*, Cliff Richard. *Top Pops*, Cliff Richard. *Cliff Around The Clock*, Bob Ferrier. *The Wonderful World Of Cliff Richard*, Bob Ferrier. *Questions: Cliff Answering Reader And Fan Queries*, Cliff Richard. *The Way I See It*, Cliff Richard. *The Cliff Richard Story*, George Tremlett. *New Singer, New Song: The Cliff Richard Story*, David Winter. *Which One's Cliff?*, Cliff Richard with Bill Latham. *Happy Christmas From Cliff*, Cliff Richard. *Cliff In His Own Words*, Kevin St. John. *Cliff*, Patrick Doncaster and Tony Jasper. *Cliff Richard*, John Tobler. *Silver Cliff: A 25 Year Journal 1958-1983*, Tony Jasper. *Cliff Richard, Single-Minded*, no author listed. *Cliff Richard: The Complete Recording Sessions, 1958-1990*, Peter Lewry and Nigel Goodall. *Cliff: A Biography*, Tony Jasper. *Cliff Richard, The Complete Chronicle*, Mike Read, Nigel Goodall and Peter Lewry. *Cliff Richard: The Autobiography*, Steve Turner. *Ultimate Cliff*, Peter Lewry and Nigel Goodall.

● FILMS: *Serious Charge* (1959), *Expresso Bongo* (1960), *The Young Ones* (1961), *Summer Holiday* (1962), *Wonderful Life* (1964), *Thunderbirds Are Go!* (1966), *Finders Keepers* (1966), *Two A Penny* (1968), *Take Me High* (1973).

RIDDLE, NELSON

b. Nelson Smock Riddle, 1 June 1921, Oradell, New Jersey, USA, d. 6 October 1985. After studying piano, Riddle took up the trombone when in his early teens, and in the late 30s played in a number of big bands, including those led by Jerry Wald, Charlie Spivak, Tommy Dorsey and Bob Crosby. After a stint in the army, he settled in California and studied arranging with Mario Castelnuovo-Tedesco and conducting with Victor Bay. In the late 40s Riddle joined NBC, but was lured to Capitol Records and registered immediately with a driving arrangement of 'Blacksmith Blues' for Ella Mae Morse. He confirmed his outstanding ability when he began to arrange and conduct for recordings by Nat 'King' Cole and Frank Sinatra. Among these were some of Cole's most engaging and memorable sides, such as 'Unforgettable', 'Somewhere Along The Way' and 'Ballerina', along with a good many of his bestselling albums. Riddle also worked with Sinatra on his important early Capitol albums, such as *Songs For Young Lovers, Swng Easy, Songs For Swingin' Lovers, In the Wee Small Hours*, and many other later ones. In addition, he served as musical director on most of the singer's popular television specials. To a considerable extent, Riddle's easy swinging charts, with their echoes of the big band music of an earlier era (and the distinctive solos of George Roberts on trombone and Harry Edison on trumpet), were of considerable importance in re-establishing Sinatra as a major star of popular music. Riddle also worked extensively with Ella Fitzgerald on *Ella Swings Brightly With Nelson*, and the highly acclaimed *Songbook* series. Other artists to benefit from the distinctive Riddle touch were Judy Garland (*Judy*), Rosemary Clooney (*Rosie Solves The Swinging Riddle*), Sammy Davis Jnr. (*That's Entertainment*), Eddie Fisher (*Games That Lovers Play*), Jack Jones (*There's Love*), Peggy Lee (*Jump For Joy*), Dean Martin (*This Time I'm Swinging*), Johnny Mathis (*I'll Buy You A Star*), Antonio Carlos Jobim (*The Brazilian Mood*), Shirley Bassey (*Let's Face The Music*), Dinah Shore (*Yes Indeed*) and many more. In 1954, Riddle had some success with 'Brother John', adapted from the French song 'Frère Jacques', and in the following year, his instrumental version of 'Lisbon Antigua' topped the US chart. He also made some fine, non-vocal albums, which contrasted the lush ballads of *The Tender Touch* and *The Joy Of Living* with the up-tempo exuberance of *Hey ... Let Yourself Go* and *C'mon ... Get Happy*. Although under contract to Capitol at the time, he is usually credited with conducting and arranging another label's *Phil Silvers Swings Bugle Calls For Big Band*, which contained Riddle compositions (with US Army/Sgt. Bilko connotations) such as 'Chow, A Can Of Cow And Thou' and 'The Eagle Screams'. Another unusual record item was *Sing A Song With Riddle*, a set of genuine Riddle arrangements, complete with sheet music, and an invitation to the listener to become the featured vocalist. From the mid-50s Riddle was also active in television and feature films: he wrote the theme for the long-running series *Route 66*, and received Oscar nominations for his background scores for the movies *Li'l Abner*, *Can-Can*, *Robin And The Seven Hoods* and *Paint Your Wagon*, and won an Academy Award in 1974 for his music for *The Great Gatsby*. Among his other film credits were *The Pajama Game*, *St. Louis Blues*, *Merry Andrew* and several Sinatra movies such as *The Joker Is Wild* and *Pal Joey*. After attempting retirement, Riddle made an unexpected and hugely successful comeback in the early 80s, when he recorded three albums with Linda Ronstadt: *What's New*, *Lush Life* and *For Sentimental Reasons*. A gentle, self-effacing man, he was in poor health for some years before he died. Riddle was probably the finest arranger/leader of modern times, always having the edge and always guaranteeing quality with whomever he worked. He was as reliable and luxurious as a Mont Blanc pen and a Mercedes car.

● ALBUMS: *Oklahoma!* (Capitol 1955)★★★, *Moonglow* (Capitol 1955)★★★, *Lisbon Antigua* (Capitol 1956)★★★, *Hey ... Let Yourself Go!* (Capitol 1957)★★★, *The Tender Touch* (Capitol 1957)★★★, *Conducts Johnny Concho* (Capitol 1957)★★★, *C'mon ... Get Happy!* (Capitol 1958)★★★, *Gold Record* (Capitol 1958)★★★, *Pal Joey* film soundtrack (Capitol 1958)★★★, *Sea Of Dreams* (Capitol 1958)★★★, *The Girl Most Likely* film soundtrack (Capitol 1958)★★★, *Merry Andrew* film soundtrack (Capitol 1959)★★★, *Sing A Song With Riddle* (Capitol 1959)★★★, *The Joy Of Living* (Capitol 1959)★★★, *Can-Can* film soundtrack (Capitol 1960)★★★, *Love Tide* (Capitol 1961)★★★, *The Gay Life* (Capitol 1961)★★★, *Tenderloin* (Capitol 1961)★★★, *Magic Moments* (Capitol 1962)★★★, *Route 66 And Other Great TV Themes* (Capitol 1962)★★★, *Love Is Just A Game Of Poker* (Capitol 1962)★★★, *Come Blow Your Horn* film soundtrack (1962)★★★, *Lolita* film soundtrack (MCA 1962)★★★, *British Columbia Suite* (1963)★★★, *Paris When It Sizzles* film soundtrack (Reprise 1963)★★★, *Robin And the Seven Hoods* film soundtrack (Reprise 1964)★★★, *Hits Of 1964* (Reprise 1964)★★★, *A Rage To Live* film soundtrack (United Artists

1965)★★★, *Harlow* film soundtrack (Warners 1965)★★★, *Great Music, Great Films, Great Sounds* (Reprise 1965)★★★, *Batman* (20th Century-Fox 1966)★★★, *Music For Wives And Lovers* (United Artists 1967)★★★, *El Dorado* film soundtrack (Columbia 1967)★★★, *How To Succeed In Business Without Really Trying* film soundtrack (United Artists 1967)★★★, *Bright And The Beautiful* (1967)★★★, *Riddle Of Today* (1968)★★★, *The Today Sound Of Nelson Riddle* (Sunset 1969)★★★, *Nat - An Orchestral Portrait* (Columbia 1969)★★★, *The Look Of Love* (Bulldog 1970)★★★, *On A Clear Day You Can See Forever* film soundtrack (Columbia 1970)★★★, *Nelson Riddle Conducts The 101 Strings* (Marble Arch 1970)★★★, *Communication* (MPS 1972)★★★, *Changing Colours* (MPS 1972)★★★, *Vivé Legrand!* (Daybreak 1973)★★★, *The Great Gatsby* (Paramount 1974)★★★, *Romance Fire And Fancy* (Intersound 1983)★★★.

● COMPILATIONS: *The Silver Collection* (Polydor 1985)★★★, *The Capitol Years* (Capitol 1993)★★★.

RIVERA, CHITA

b. Dolores Conchita Figueroa del Rivero, 23 January 1933, Washington, DC, USA. A vivacious singer, dancer, and actress - an exciting and explosive performer - Rivera was born to Puerto Rican parents and grew up in the Bronx. She started dancing when she was seven, and from the age of 11, trained for a career in classical ballet. After studying at the New York City Ballet via a scholarship from choreographer George Balanchine, in 1952 she turned from classical dance and joined the chorus of *Call Me Madam* on Broadway. Further chorus work in *Guys And Dolls* and *Can-Can* was followed by appearances in *Shoestring Revue*, *Seventh Heaven*, and *Mr. Wonderful* (1956). She rocketed to stardom in 1957 as Anita in *West Side Story*, and stopped the show nightly by singing and dancing herself into a frenzy to the whooping rhythms of 'America'. She caused even more of a sensation when *West Side Story* opened in London on 12 December 1958; it is still regarded by many as the most exciting first night of the post-war years. Two years later she was back on Broadway as Dick Van Dyke's secretary Rose, in the first successful rock 'n' roll musical, *Bye Bye Birdie*, and she recreated her role in London in the following year. A musical adaptation of the *The Prisoner Of Zenda* (1963), in which she starred with Alfred Drake, folded before it reached New York, but a year later, Rivera was acclaimed for her role as a gypsy princess in *Bajour* on Broadway. In the late 60s, she toured in various productions including *Sweet Charity*, and also appeared in the 1969 film version with Shirley MacLaine. After more national tours in the early 70s in musicals such as *Jacques Brel Is Alive And Well And Living In Paris* and *Kiss, Me Kate*, in addition to several straight roles, she co-starred with Gwen Verdon in the 'sinfully seductive' *Chicago* (1975). John Kander and Fred Ebb wrote the score, and they also devised and developed Chita Rivera's cabaret act, which included a number called 'Losing', a reference to the number of Tony Award nominations she had received. She gained one more nomination for her performance in *Bring Back Birdie* (1981), which closed after only four nights, and *Merlin* (1983) was also unsuccessful. Rivera was finally awarded the coveted Tony - and a Drama Desk Award - when she co-starred with Liza Minnelli in *The Rink* (1984), another of Kander and Ebb's projects. Shortly afterwards, she was

was involved in a serious car accident which 'mangled my leg from the knee down'. After having 12 bolts inserted in the bones, she was back on Broadway, along with Leslie Uggams, Dorothy Loudon, and others, in *Jerry's Girls*, a tribute to the composer Jerry Herman. During the rest of the 80s, she performed in cabaret and continued to tour in America and other countries including the UK. In 1988/9, she joined the Radio City Music Hall Rockettes in a national tour of *Can-Can* that lasted for over a year. In 1991, she was inducted into New York's Theatre Hall Of Fame, along with Kander and Ebb. She was subsequently widely applauded - and won London *Evening Standard* and Tony Awards - for her outstanding dual performance as the movie star Aurora and the Spider Woman in Kander and Ebb's musical *Kiss Of the Spider Woman*. After 749 performances in Toronto, London and New York, in November 1994 she set out on the show's two-year road tour of North America. Her outstanding contribution to the musical theatre was recognized in the early 90s by the Drama Desk's Annual Achievement Award, and the first annual Bandai Musical Award for Excellence in Broadway Theatre.

ROBBINS, JEROME

b. Jerome Rabinowitz, 11 October 1918, New York, USA. An important director, choreographer and dancer, Robbins began his career with the celebrated Ballet Theatre in New York, and subsequently appeared as a dancer on Broadway in shows such as *Great Lady*, *The Straw Hat Revue* and *Stars In Your Eyes*. In 1944, he and composer Leonard Bernstein conceived a short ballet, *Fancy Free*, which, with the participation of Betty Comden and Adolph Green, evolved into the musical *On The Town* - and Robbins was off and running (or rather, dancing). During the 40s and early 50s he was constantly acclaimed for his stylish and original choreography for shows such as *Billion Dollar Baby* (1945), *High Button Shoes* (Tony Award), *Look Ma, I'm Dancing*, *Miss Liberty*, *Call Me Madam*, *The King And I* and *Two's Company* (1952). From then on, he also served as the director on series of notable productions: *The Pajama Game*, *Peter Pan*, *Bells Are Ringing*, *West Side Story* (Tony Award), *Gypsy*, *A Funny Thing Happened On The Way To The Forum*, *Funny Girl* and *Fiddler On The Roof*. For the last-named show, one of his greatest achievements, he won Tony Awards as choreographer and director. He and Robert Wise were also awarded Oscars when they co-directed the film version of *West Side Story* in 1961. After working on the London productions of *Funny Girl* and *Fiddler On The Roof* in 1966 and 1967, Robbins turned away from the Broadway musical theatre and announced that he was devoting his life to ballet. He returned to the popular field in February 1989 to direct a celebratory revue of his work entitled *Jerome Robbins' Broadway*. In a season that was so bereft of original musicals that *Kenny Loggins On Broadway* and *Barry Manilow At The Gershwin* were catagorized as such, this reminder of Broadway's glory days was greeted with relief and rejoicing (and six Tony Awards). It featured extended sequences from *West Side Story* and *Fiddler On The Roof*, along with other delights such as the gloriously incongruous 'You Gotta Have A Gimmick' from *Gypsy*, and the famous Keystone Cops chase from *High Button Shoes*, all sandwiched between excerpts from Robbins' first hit, *On The Town*, which opened and closed the show. An enormously expensive investment

at $8 million, the show reportedly lost around half of that, even though it ran for 538 performances.

ROBERTS, PADDY

b. 1910, South Africa, d. September 1975, England. A songwriter, pianist and singer, Roberts' early education took place in England. He subsequently attended university in South Africa before joining a law practice. Intent on becoming a songwriter, he returned to the UK where he had some success in the late 30s with songs such as 'Angel Of The Great White Way' (written with Elton Box, Desmond Cox and Don Pelosi), and 'Horsey, Horsey' (with Box, Cox and Ralph Butler) which became popular for Jack Jackson, Billy Cotton and Henry Hall. During World War II Roberts flew with the RAF, and when peace came he became an airline captain on BOAC Constellations. Subsequently, he returned to songwriting, and during the 50s, had several UK chart hits, including 'The Book' (David Whitfield), 'Heart Of A Man' (Frankie Vaughan), 'Lay Down Your Arms' (Anne Shelton), 'Meet Me On The Corner' (Max Bygraves), 'Pickin' A Chicken' (Eve Boswell); and 'Evermore', 'Softly, Softly' (number 1) and 'You Are My First Love' (the last three sung by Ruby Murray). The latter song was featured in the British musical film *It's Great To Be Young*, and Roberts wrote several other movie songs, including 'In Love For The Very First Time' (for *An Alligator Named Daisy*, starring Diana Dors) and the title number to *The Good Companions*. His other 50s compositions included 'Johnny Is The Boy For Me', 'It's A Boy', 'That Dear Old Gentleman', 'Send For Me' and 'The Three Galleons (Las Tres Carabelas)'. Most of the aforementioned songs were written in collaboration with others, such as Hans Gottwald, C.A. Rossi, Geoffrey Parsons, Peggy Cochran, Jack Woodman, Gerry Levine, Ake Gerhard, Leon Land, Peter Hart, Garfield De Mortimer, Derek Bernfield, Augusto Alguego, G. Moreu and Lester Powell. However, towards the end of the decade, he was beginning to write unaided more and more frequently, and during the 60s he included several of his own, often wry, witty and sophisticated, numbers in an accomplished cabaret act. Probably the best-known of these is 'The Ballad Of Bethnal Green', which enjoyed a good deal of airplay, but there were many others too, including 'The Belle Of Barking Creek', 'The Big Dee-Jay', 'Follow Me', 'Country Girl', 'I Love Mary', 'The Tattooed Lady', 'What's All This Fuss About Love?', 'The Lavender Cowboy' and 'Don't Upset The Little Kiddywinks'. Paddy Roberts won several Ivor Novello Awards, and held high office in the Performing Right Society and the Song Writers Guild.

● ALBUMS: *Paddy Roberts At The Blue Angel* (Decca 1961)★★.

● COMPILATIONS: *Best Of Paddy Roberts* (MFP 1968)★★★.

ROBERTSON, JEANNIE

b. Regina Christina Robertson, 1908, Aberdeen, Scotland, d. March 1975. This Scottish traditional singer was the youngest of five children of Donald Robertson and Maria Stewart. Her parents were both from tinker families, who would travel in caravans, selling goods from house to house during the summer, and then spend the winter living in Aberdeen. It was from her mother that Jeannie learned much of her repertoire. Robertson was 'discovered' in Aberdeen by Hamish Henderson in 1953, when it was apparent that she possessed an outstanding voice and capacity for story-telling. Riverside Records, in the USA, were the first to offer a recording contact to Robertson. The recordings were made by Bill Leader, in April 1956, and featured a guitar accompaniment by the late Josh MacRae. *Songs Of A Scots Tinker Lady* was re-released in the UK in 1965 by Topic Records and retitled *Jeannie Robertson*. They also removed the accompanying guitar tracks. A series of EPs were issued in 1959 by Collector Records that included *The Gallowa' Hills*, *The Twa Brothers*, *I Know Where I'm Going* and *Jeannie's Merry Muse*. Robertson was awarded the MBE in 1968 for her services to traditional music, and continued singing up to her death in 1975.

● ALBUMS: *Songs Of A Scots Tinker Lady* (Riverside 1956)★★★, *Lord Donald* (1959)★★★★, *The Cuckoo's Nest* (1960)★★★ *Jeannie Robertson, The World's Greatest Folksinger* (Prestige International 1961)★★★, *Scotch Folk Songs* (Prestige International 1963)★★★.

ROBINS

An R&B vocal group from Los Angeles, California, USA, formed in 1947. The original members were 'Ty' Terrell Leonard, twins Billy and Roy Richard and Bobby Nunn. The group recorded some tracks for Aladdin before they hooked up with bandleader Johnny Otis in 1949, when they won second place at a talent contest at his club, The Barrelhouse. Their first chart record, in 1950 for Savoy Records, was the mid-tempo 'If It's So, Baby' (number 10 R&B), recorded with the Johnny Otis Orchestra. Its excellent ballad b-side, 'If I Didn't Love You So', received much more airplay in many areas. Otis also used the Robins to back his young prodigy, Little Esther, on the hit 'Double Crossing Blues' in 1950. The Savoy recordings were made in a bluesy modulated style of the period and did nothing to set apart the Robins from other groups. During 1950-52 the group recorded for Modern, RPM (as the Nic Nacs), and Recorded In Hollywood without notable success. In 1953 the Robins, with the addition of tenor lead Grady Chapman, were signed to RCA and came under the production aegis of the up-and-coming songwriting team of Leiber And Stoller. Jerry Leiber and Mike Stoller began radically to transform the Robins into a proto-rock 'n' roll group with an exuberant beat-infected sound. No hits resulted on RCA, but in 1954, with a move to Leiber and Stoller's own Spark label, and with Carl Gardner having replaced Grady Chapman, the Robins found success with 'Riot In Cell Block No. 9'. The song, which used the menacing bass of Richard Berry and machine-gun sound-effects, was one of the most controversial records of 1954. It sold well in California and a few other locales but failed to chart nationally because of poor distribution. The group successfully followed it with another regional hit, 'Framed' (1954), and in 1955 hit with 'Smokey Joe's Cafe'. Fast-rising independent Atlantic Records took notice of sales in California and assumed distribution, making it a national hit (number 10 R&B) on their Atco subsidiary. The Robins, however, split up, with Gardner and Nunn joining with Billy Guy and Leon Hughes to form the Coasters to record for Atlantic. Under the aegis of producers Jerry Leiber and Mike Stoller, the Coasters flourished. The Robins - with newcomer H.B. Barnum and with returning Grady Chapman - continued to record, on the Whippet and other labels, albeit unsuccessfully, until breaking up some time in the early 60s.

● ALBUMS: *Rock 'N' Roll With The Robins* (Whippet 1958)★★★.
● COMPILATIONS: *The Best Of The Robins* collects their Whippet recordings (GNP-Crescendo 1975)★★★, *The Roots Of Rock 'N Roll* collects their Savoy recordings (Savoy Jazz 1987)★★★.

ROCK 'N ROLL STAGE SHOW - BILL HALEY AND HIS COMETS ★★★★

Although this 1956 album features studio recordings, it offers some indication of what Bill Haley And His Comets sounded like on stage. Haley led a showband who just happened to find fame with rock 'n' roll, and upon securing this success, he was keen that the Comets should demonstrate their versatility as a band, and not focus on Haley himself as the centre of attention. There are instrumentals on this release, notably 'Rudy's Rock', featuring Rudy Pompilli's sax, 'Goofin' Around', featuring Franny Beecher's lead guitar, and an old-style vocal number, 'Hey Then, There Now', with the Comets, who shortly afterwards left for the Jodimars. Accordionist Johnny Grande took the lead vocal on 'A Rockin' Little Tune' and steel guitarist Billy Williamson performed lead vocals on 'Tonight's The Night' and 'Hide And Seek'. It all served to give the impression that Bill Haley was merely making a guest appearance on his own record. The album reached number 18 in the US album chart.
● TRACKS: *Calling All Comets; Rockin' Through The Rye; A Rockin' Little Tune; Hide And Seek; Hey Then, There Now; Goofin' Around; Hook, Line And Sinker; Rudy's Rock; Choo Choo Ch'boogie; Blue Comet Blues; Hot Dog, Buddy Buddy; Tonight's The Night*.

ROCK 'N' ROLL REVUE

Jazz and R&B performers were at the fore of this 1956 film, despite its grossly misleading title. Also known as *Harlem Rock 'n' Roll*, it was shot at New York's fabled Apollo Theatre. Lionel Hampton, Duke Ellington and Nat 'King' Cole headed a star-studded cast that also featured the Clovers, Joe Turner and Ruth Brown. Shot in sepia-inspired yellow and brown - known as Wondercolour - the film captures several performers at their peak and provides a fascinating insight into several acts inspiring, although not recording, rock 'n' roll. Curiously, the portion featuring Dinah Washington was cut from the UK print, but *Rock 'n' Roll Revue* remains a highly interesting feature.

ROCK AROUND THE CLOCK

Fred Sears directed this 1956 second feature, inspired by the reaction generated by Bill Haley And The Comets' contribution to *The Blackboard Jungle*. Although not seen on-screen, the group's recording of 'Rock Around The Clock' had been heard over the opening credits, provoking riots in cinemas. The same occurred when this film was screened, prompting several local authorities to ban it from municipal screens. The first feature wholly devoted to rock 'n' roll music, *Rock Around The Clock* cast Haley's group as a small-town act that a bank manager tries to turn into a national attraction, despite the efforts of a booking agent to sabotage his plans. The Comets naturally provide the lion's share of the material, including 'Rock A Beatin' Boogie', 'See You Later Alligator' and the title track. The Platters, Little Richard and Freddie Bell And His Bellboys are among the other acts included, as is disc jockey Alan Freed in the first of a string of roles in rock 'n' roll films. Although hardly innovatory in terms of plot or acting, for better or worse, *Rock Around The Clock* opened the doors for celluloid pop.

ROCK AROUND THE CLOCK - BILL HALEY AND HIS COMETS ★★★★

Bill Haley was not an overnight success; he had been working as a country performer since the 40s and 'Rock Around The Clock' was his 28th single. He had even recorded rock 'n' roll in the past, but it was 'Rock Around The Clock', used in the film *The Blackboard Jungle*, that became an international teenage anthem. The only thing Haley dropped was his yodel - somewhat reluctantly, as he had been a champion yodeller in Indiana. Featuring on this 1956 album, 'Shake, Rattle And Roll' was an expurgated version of a R&B hit by Big Joe Turner. Haley's perception of his audience can also be discerned from 'ABC Boogie', which, like many of his songs, seems intent on teaching his audience to spell. *Rock Around The Clock* reached number 12 in the USA and number 34 in the UK.

● TRACKS: *Rock Around The Clock*; *Shake, Rattle And Roll*; *ABC Boogie*; *Thirteen Women*; *Razzle-dazzle*; *Two Hound Dogs*; *Dim, Dim The Lights*; *Happy Baby*; *Birth Of The Boogie*; *Mambo Rock*; *Burn That Candle*; *Rock-a-beatin' Boogie*.

ROCK ROCK ROCK

Manifestly another formula 'quickie' made to cash in on rock 'n' roll, *Rock Rock Rock* nonetheless contains several points of interest to pop historians. This 1957 film, reportedly shot in two weeks, starred Tuesday Weld as the girl-friend of an aspiring entrepreneur who organizes a concert. Famed disc jockey Alan Freed makes an obligatory appearance - herein leading an 18-piece band - but *Rock Rock Rock* is notable for the acts it enshrines. Frankie Lymon And The Teenagers offer the memorable 'I'm Not A Juvenile Delinquent', while doo-wop acts the Flamingos and Moonglows perform 'Would I Be Crying' and 'Over And Over Again', respectively. Chuck Berry makes his celluloid debut with 'You Can't Catch Me' and vibrant rockabilly act the Johnny Burnette Trio roar through 'Lonesome Train' in what was their only appearance on film. LaVern Baker, the Three Chuckles and the Bowties are among the others on offer. Ms. Weld contributes 'I Never Had A Sweetheart' and 'Little Blue Wren', but her 'voice' was provided by the then-unknown Connie Francis. Much of the material aired in *Rock Rock Rock* was released by the Chess label, who advertised the set as the first rock soundtrack album. Although failing to break new ground as far as plot and style were concerned, the film showcases several seminal acts at the height of their creative powers.

ROCK-A-BYE BABY

Frank Tashlin, who directed the seminal rock film *The Girl Can't Help It*, took charge of this 1958 feature. It starred comedian Jerry Lewis, former partner of Dean Martin, who excelled in zany, 'misfit' roles, notably *The Nutty Professor*. In *Rock-A-Bye Baby* he plays a nanny, responsible for a film star's triplets, who finds time to satirize rock 'n' roll and US television. The film is largely forgettable, although Lewis does perform a duet, 'In The Land Of La La La', with his 12-year old son, Gary. In the following decade, Gary Lewis became a pop star in his own right as leader of Gary Lewis And The Playboys, who enjoyed a number 1 US hit with 'This Diamond Ring', following it with six further Top 10 entries.

ROCKABILLY

The derivation of the term rockabilly comes from the classification US trade papers employed to identify rock 'n' roll music that originated in rural (hillbilly) areas. Only later in the 50s did it come to symbolize a specific type of music - generally, basic rock 'n' roll mixed with country and bluegrass roots, with an emphasis on acoustic instruments. Elvis Presley is widely cited as its main popularizer, but Dale Hawkins and Carl Perkins are better examples of artists who remained within the tradition. Country artists such as Roy Orbison and Johnny Cash also flourished from a starting point in rockabilly, but many of the 'true' rockabilly stars remained largely anonymous, except to their devotees in the USA and UK. The Beatles recorded Perkins' 'Matchbox' and 'Honey Don't', but rockabilly never truly escaped its public perception of being 'backward' music. Chart success was rare - though Hank Mizell's 'Jungle Rock' did reach number 3 in the UK charts in 1976. Typically, this came many years after its initial recording, and its popularity was largely prompted by the proliferation of 'Teddy Boy' rocker cults during the period. Ironically, the Teds' sworn enemies, punk rockers, would flock to see the Clash perform updated rockabilly material such as 'Brand New Cadillac', while in America the Cramps created a similar hybrid. It took New York trio the Stray Cats to bring about a popular revival of the form in the early 80s, accompanied by UK bands Matchbox and the Polecats. By the late 80s and early 90s, labels such as Ace Records had begun to repackage rare 45s from the golden era of rockabilly as further evidence of the form's overlooked musical vitality.

ROCKETONES

The Rocketones were an R&B group started at Junior High School in Brooklyn, New York, USA. Bill Witt (lead), Allen Days (first tenor), Ronald Johnson (second tenor), Harold Chapman (baritone) and Arthur Blackman (bass) originally titled themselves the Avalons, and practised hard to perfect their vocal blend. After numerous attempts the group finally found a sympathetic hearing at Melba Records, who signed the band in 1956. However, it took some time before their sole single, 'Mexico'/'Dee I', was released, and when it was they discovered Melba Records' boss Marty Croft had credited the band as the Rocketones. With its distinctive bull-fighting intro, 'Mexico' proved popular on New York radio, but was never followed up. Both Days and Johnson were later drafted while Witt joined the Paragons. The Rocketones' solitary recording is now something of a legend in doo-wop nostalgia circles.

RODGERS, JIMMIE

b. James Frederick Rodgers, 18 September 1933, Camus, Washington, USA. After being taught by his mother, the young Rodgers successfully auditioned for the Arthur Godfrey talent show and impressed Luigi Creatore and Hugo Peretti who signed him to their recently formed Roulette Records. Rodgers' creamy, effortless voice and blend of folk-tinged pop appealed to a post-war middle America, and over the next decade he made the *Billboard* singles chart 25 times. He never, however, topped his debut, 'Honeycomb', which stayed at number 1 for four weeks in 1957 (number 30 in the UK). His early successes included 'Kisses Sweeter Than Wine' a Top 3 hit in 1957 which vied with Frankie Vaughan in the UK for the best position (Rodgers number 7, Vaughan number 8). One of Rodgers' most memorable songs was the innocent but catchy 'English Country Garden', which, although it became his biggest UK hit (reaching the Top 5 in 1962), did not appear to warrant an American release, possibly because of its parochial title. Rodgers was the victim of a serious mugging in 1967 that left him with a fractured skull. Although he eventually returned to performing full-time, his career had lost its momentum. He was still singing professionally in the late 80s.

● ALBUMS: *Jimmie Rodgers* (Roulette 1957)★★★, *The Long Hot Summer* film soundtrack (Roulette 1958)★★, *Number One Ballads* (Roulette 1958)★★★, *Sings Folk Songs* (Roulette 1958)★★★★, *His Golden Year* (Roulette 1959)★★★, *TV Favorites* (Roulette 1959)★★★, *Twilight On The Trail* (Roulette 1959)★★★, *It's Christmas Once Again* (Roulette 1959)★★★, *When The Spirit Moves You* (Roulette 1960)★★★, *At Home With Jimmie Rodgers* (Roulette 1960)★★★, *The Folk Song World Of Jimmie Rodgers* (Roulette 1961)★★★★, *15 Million Sellers* (Roulette 1962)★★★, *Folk Songs* (Roulette 1963)★★★★, *Its Over* (Dot 1966)★★★, *Child Of Clay* (A&M 1968)★★, *Windmills Of Your Mind* (A&M 1969)★★, *This Is Jimmie Rodgers* (1987)★★.

● COMPILATIONS: *The Best Of Jimmie Rodgers Folk Songs* (Roulette 1961)★★★, *Best Of Jimmie Rodgers* (MCA 1988)★★★, *Kisses Sweeter Than Wine* (Pickwick 1988)★★★.

RODGERS, RICHARD

b. 28 June 1902, Hammells Station, Arverne, Long Island, USA, d. 30 December 1979, New York, USA. One of the all-time great composers for the musical theatre, Rodgers was raised in a comfortable middle-class family and developed an early love of music. Encouraged by his parents, he was able to pick out a tune on the piano at the age of four, and wrote his first songs, 'Campfire Days' and 'Auto Show Girl' (lyric: David Dyrenforth), when he was 14. Many years later, when he was asked what he had done before he began composing music, he is supposed to have said: 'I was a baby.' In 1919, Rodgers was introduced to the lyricist Lorenz Hart, and they collaborated on the scores for two well-received Columbia University Varsity shows, *Fly With Me* and *You'll Never Know*, and on songs for other productions, such as the Broadway musicals *A Lonely Romeo* (1919, 'Any Old Place With You') and *Poor Little Ritz Girl* (1920). The early 20s presented few further opportunities, and a frustrated Rodgers was contemplating taking a job as a wholesaler in the baby-wear business, when, in 1925, he and Hart were asked to write the score for a benefit show in aid of the Theatre Guild, the prestigious theatrical production organization. The resulting revue, *The Garrick Gaieties*, was so successful that it began a commercial run that lasted for 211 performances. Rodgers and Hart's lively and amusing score included the charming 'Sentimental Me' as well as one of their most enduring standards, 'Manhattan'. A second edition of the *Gaieties* in 1926, featured another of the songwriters' brightest and inventive numbers, 'Mountain Greenery', which was associated in later years with the distinguished jazz singer Mel Tormé. From this point, Rodgers and Hart were off and running, and during the next few years, wrote some of their most romantic and innovative songs for a series of musical shows that met with varying degrees of success. They included *Dearest Enemy* (1925, 'Here In My Arms'), *The Girl Friend* (1926, 'The Blue Room', 'The Girl Friend'), *Lido Lady* (London 1926, 'Try Again Tomorrow'), *Peggy-Ann* (1926, 'Where's That Rainbow?', 'A Tree In The Park'), *Betsy* (a 39 performance flop in 1926, 'This Funny World'), *One Dam Thing After Another* (London 1927, 'My Heart Stood Still'), *A Connecticut Yankee* (1927, 'Thou Swell', 'On A Desert Island With Thee!', 'Nothing's Wrong'), *She's My Baby* (1928, 'You're What I Need'), *Present Arms!* (1928, 'You Took Advantage Of Me', 'A Kiss For Cinderella'), *Chee-Chee* (a 31-performance flop in 1928, 'Better Be Good to Me'), *Lady Fingers* (1929, 'I Love You More Than Yesterday'), *Spring Is Here* (1929, 'With A Song In My Heart', 'Why Can't I?', 'Baby's Awake Now'), *Heads Up!* (1929, 'A Ship Without A Sail'), *Simple Simon* ('Ten Cents A Dance', 'He Was Too Good To Me'), and *Ever Green* (London 1930, 'Dancing On The Ceiling', 'No Place But Home', 'The Colour Of Her Eyes'). When the team wrote the optimistic 'I've Got Five Dollars' for Ann Sothern and Jack Whiting to sing in *America's Sweetheart* in 1931, the USA was in the middle of the Depression. Although more than 20 new musicals were being produced each season on Broadway, Rodgers and Hart's previous five shows had been relatively unsuccessful, and they spent much of the early 30s in Hollywood writing some memorable songs for early film musicals such as *The Hot Heiress* (1931, 'You're The Cats'), *Love Me Tonight* (1932, 'Isn't It Romantic?', 'Mimi', 'Lover'), *The Phantom President* (1932, 'Give Her A Kiss'), *Hallelujah, I'm A Bum* (1933, 'You Are Too Beautiful'), *Hollywood Party* (1934, 'Hello'), *Nana* (1934, 'That's Love'), and *Mississippi* (1935, 'It's Easy To Remember', 'Soon', 'Down By The River'). They also contributed a song called 'The Bad In Every Man' (previously known as 'Prayer') to the Oscar-winning screen thriller *Manhattan Melodrama*. After Hart wrote a new lyric, it was retitled 'Blue Moon', and became one of their biggest hits. That song, alongside many of their other successful numbers, was featured in the 1948 biopic *Words And Music*, in which Rodgers was played by Tom Drake and Hart by Mickey Rooney.

Rodgers and Hart returned to New York in 1935, and embarked on a body of work that surpassed even their previous achievements. *Jumbo* (1935), with a score containing three outstanding numbers, 'My Romance', 'Little Girl Blue' and 'The Most Beautiful Girl In The World', was followed by the splendid *On Your Toes* (1936, 'Glad To Be Unhappy', 'There's A Small Hotel', 'Too Good For The Average Man', 'Slaughter On Tenth Avenue'), *Babes In Arms* (1937, 'I Wish I Were In Love Again', 'The Lady Is A Tramp', 'My Funny Valentine', 'Where Or When', 'Johnny One Note'), *I'd Rather Be Right* (1937, 'Have You Met Miss Jones?'), *I Married An Angel* (1938, 'Spring Is Here', 'I Married An Angel', 'At The Roxy Music Hall'), *The Boys From Syracuse* (1938, 'Falling In Love With Love', 'This Can't Be Love', 'Sing For Your Supper', 'You Have Cast Your Shadow On The Sea'), *Too Many Girls* (1939, 'I Didn't Know What Time It Was', 'Give It Back To The Indians', 'I Like To Recognize The Tune', 'You're Nearer'), *Higher And Higher* (1940, 'It Never Entered My

Mind'), *Pal Joey* ('Bewitched', 'I Could Write A Book', 'Den Of Iniquity') and *By Jupiter* (1942, 'Wait Till You See Her', 'Nobody's Heart', 'Careless Rhapsody'). *Pal Joey*, in particular, was regarded as a landmark in Broadway history, partly because it was the first musical in which the leading character, played by Gene Kelly, was a villain - an anti-hero. Rodgers and Hart's final work together was probably on the songs for a revised production of their 1927 hit, *A Connecticut Yankee*, which contained the witty 'To Keep My Love Alive'. By the time that show opened on 3 November 1943, Hart's physical condition, which had been worsening for several years, had deteriorated to such an extent that he was unable to work, and he died some two weeks later.

In the previous year, Rodgers had been asked by the Theatre Guild to write the score for what eventually became *Oklahoma!* (1943). With Hart unavailable, he began a collaboration with Oscar Hammerstein II that produced some of the biggest blockbusters in the (pre-Andrew Lloyd Webber) history of the musical theatre. Marvellous songs such as 'Oh, What A Beautiful Mornin'', 'People Will Say We're In Love', 'The Surrey With The Fringe On Top', and the rousing title number, were cleverly integrated into the story, and *Oklahoma!* won a special Pulitzer Prize, and ran for 2,212 performances in New York. Next came the magnificent *Carousel* (1945, 'If I Loved You', 'June Is Bustin' Out All Over', 'What's The Use Of Wond'rin'', 'You'll Never Walk Alone', 'Soliloquy'), which is often regarded as Rodgers and Hammerstein's best score. Also in 1945, the partners wrote their only original film score for the highly popular *State Fair*, which featured the exuberant 'It's A Grand Night For Singing' and the lovely ballad 'It Might As Well Be Spring'. Back on Broadway, the uncharacteristic *Allegro* (1947, 'A Fellow Needs A Girl', 'The Gentleman Is A Dope'), complete with its Greek chorus, was a disappointment. However, there were more triumphs just around the corner in the shape of *South Pacific* (1949, 'I'm Gonna Wash That Man Right Outa My Hair', 'Bali Ha'i', 'Some Enchanted Evening', 'This Nearly Was Mine', 'There Is Nothin' Like A Dame'), which ran for nearly five years and won the Pulitzer Prize for Drama, and *The King And I* (1951, 'Hello, Young Lovers', 'I Have Dreamed', 'Shall We Dance?', 'We Kiss In A Shadow', 'Getting To Know You').

In 1952, Richard Rodgers wrote the music for the NBC documentary television series *Victory At Sea*, for which he was awarded the US Navy's Distinguished Public Service Medal. A musical theme from one of the episodes entitled 'Beyond The Southern Cross', attracted a great deal of interest, and Rodgers used it, with a lyric by Hammerstein, as a part of the score for their next Broadway show, *Me And Juliet* (1953). The song was called 'No Other Love', and featured again in television and stage versions of *Cinderella*. Neither *Me And Juliet*, or Rodgers and Hammerstein's Broadway follow-up, *Pipe Dream* (1955, 'All At Once You Love Her', 'The Next Time It Happens'), are considered to be among their best work. Nor, for that matter, is *Flower Drum Song* ('I Enjoy Being A Girl', 'Sunday', 'Love, Look Away'), but the show did endure for 602 performances, and was still running when the final Rodgers and Hammerstein smash hit, *The Sound Of Music* ('Climb Ev'ry Mountain', 'Edelweiss', 'Do-Re-Mi', 'My Favourite Things', 'The Sound Of Music') opened in November 1959 and ran for nearly three and a half years in New York, and more than five and a half in London. The

film versions of this and several other Rodgers and Hammerstein shows were among the highest-grossing movie musicals of the 50s and 60s. Less than a year after *The Sound Of Music* opened, Hammerstein was dead. Rodgers subsequently contributed five new songs (music and lyrics) to the 1962 remake of *State Fair*, and wrote the complete score for the Broadway musical *No Strings* ('The Sweetest Sounds'), which ran for 580 performances. For his work on that show he won a Tony Award for Outstanding Composer, and a Grammy for the Original Cast album. From then on, apart from providing both words and music for a US television adaptation of *Androcles And The Lion* (1967), starring Noël Coward and Norman Wisdom, for the remainder of his career Rodgers worked with established lyricists. These included Stephen Sondheim (in 1965 for *Do I Hear A Waltz?*, 'We're Gonna Be All Right', 'Do I Hear A Waltz'), Martin Charnin (in 1970 for *Two By Two*, 'I Do Not Know A Day I Did Not Love You'), Sheldon Harnick (in 1976 for *Rex*), and Martin Charnin (in 1979 for *I Remember Mama*). When he was working on the last two shows, which were both dismal failures at the box office, Rodgers was a sick man, and he died in December 1979. The emotionally uplifting and often witty and sophisticated melodies he left behind - written in collaboration with two supremely gifted, but temperamentally opposite partners - played an important part in the development of American's own indigenous popular music, and in the acceptance of the musical as an important and respected art form. His honours included special Tonys in 1962 and 1972, a Trustee Grammy Award, and the 1979 Lawrence Langner Award for Distinguished Lifetime Achievement in the Theatre. In 1993, on the 50th anniversary of the birth of his second momentous partnership, a celebratory revue entitled *A Grand Night For Singing*, which was crammed with Rodgers and Hammerstein's songs, was presented in New York.

Richard Rodgers' elder daughter, Mary Rodgers (b. 11 January 1931, New York, USA), enjoyed substantial success in the musical theatre with her music for *Once Upon A Mattress* (1959). Earlier, she had studied harmony and counterpoint and written numerous songs for children's records. Rodgers collaborated with lyricist and librettist Marshall Barer on *Once Upon A Mattress*, which was based on the fairytale *The Princess And The Pea*. It ran for 216 performances off-Broadway, and a further 244 at Broadway's Alvin Theatre. Her next effort on Broadway was a musical about the Peace Corps, *Hot Spot* (1963), which had lyrics by Martin Charnin. It folded rapidly, in spite of the presence in the cast of Judy Holliday. Rodgers worked with Barer again in 1966 on *The Mad Show*, which was inspired by the immensely popular *Mad* magazine. The *Mad Show* stayed at the New Theatre, off-Broadway, for 871 performances, and included one song that Rodgers wrote with Stephen Sondheim, entitled 'The Boy From', which mocked the worldwide bossa nova hit, 'The Girl From Ipanema'. In 1978 Rodgers contributed material to the New York musical *Working*, along with others such as Stephen Schwartz, and has also been involved with several projects that were not developed. One that was developed, however, was *The Griffin And The Minor Canon*, which was described as 'a folk tale about the bonding friendship between the last griffin on earth and a minor church official in a small French village.' It had a book by Wendy Kesselman and lyrics by Ellen Fitzhugh, and was presented at Stockbridge, Massachusetts, in August 1988. Over the years, Rodgers has also written several children's books, including the classic teen novel *Freaky Friday*. She later adapted it into a movie and a children's musical. In 1993, the revue *Hey, Love: The Songs Of Mary Rodgers*, played at Eighty-Eight's in New York. The show, named after a song from *Hot Spot*, was conceived and directed by Richard Maltby Jnr. It contained some of his lyrics, and those of Martin Charnin, Marshall Barer, John Forster, Stephen Sondheim and William Shakespeare.

● ALBUMS: *Mary Martin Sings Richard Rodgers Plays* (1958)★★★.

● FURTHER READING: *Musical Stages: His Autobiography*, Richard Rodgers. *With A Song In His Heart*, David Ewen. *The Rodgers And Hammerstein Story*, Stanley Green. *Rodgers And Hart: Bewitched, Bothered And Bedevilled*, S. Marx and J. Clayton. *The Sound Of Their Music: The Story Of Rodgers And Hammerstein*, Frederick Nolan.

ROGERS, ROY

b. Leonard Franklin Slye, 5 November 1911, Cincinnati, Ohio, USA. Rogers worked on the west coast picking fruit and, after several singing jobs, he formed the Sons Of The Pioneers in 1933. They performed in many Western films, and, as a result of Republic's dispute with Gene Autry, Rogers received his first starring role, playing a singing congressman in the 1938 film *Under Western Skies*. When he and John Wayne jumped off a cliff in *Dark Command*, Hollywood's treatment of horses was severely questioned, which led to the formation of the Society for Prevention of Cruelty to Animals. In 1946 his wife died shortly after giving birth to their son, Roy Jnr. On 31 December 1947 he married an actress he met on the set of the film *The Cowboy And The Senorita*, Dale Evans. His films include *King Of The Cowboys*, *Son Of Paleface* with Bob Hope and Jane Russell, and *Hollywood Canteen*, in which he sang 'Don't Fence Me In'. Rogers' four-legged friend, Trigger ('the smartest horse in the movies'), had been ridden by Olivia de Havilland in *The Adventures Of Robin Hood* and cost Rogers $2,500. His films and television series (100 shows between 1951 and 1957) also featured a lovable, toothless and fearless old-timer, George 'Gabby' Hayes. They featured no sex and little violence (he would wing the baddies in black hats), and his wholesome image found favour when he toured UK theatres in the 50s. High prices are now paid for Roy Rogers memorabilia, whether it be cut-out dolls, thermos flasks or holster sets. Rogers' records include 'Blue Shadows On The Trail', 'These Are The Good Old Days', a tribute to the past, 'Hoppy, Gene And Me' and 'Ride, Concrete Cowboy, Ride' from the film *Smokey And The Bandit 2*. His palomino Trigger died in 1965 at the age of 33 and was stuffed and mounted, as referred to in Jimmy Webb's song 'P.F. Sloan'. Rogers became a successful businessman with a chain of restaurants, and he and Evans confined their appearances to religious ones. He made his first film in 16 years in 1975, *Mackintosh And T.J.*, while his son, Roy Rogers Jnr., made an album, *Dusty*, in 1983. Don McLean recorded Rogers' famous signature tune, 'Happy Trails', and Rogers revived it with Randy Travis in 1990. San Francisco rock band the Quicksilver Messenger Service used Rogers' *Happy Trails* as the title of their album in 1968 as well as recording the song as the closing track. Rogers was elected to the Country Music

Hall Of Fame in 1988, having already gained entry as part of the Sons Of The Pioneers in 1980. He returned to the US country chart with his album *Tribute* in 1991, which included guest appearances from contemporary country performers. Clint Black helped to revitalize his career, the first time Rogers had accepted help from a man in a black hat. In 1992, a feature-length documentary entitled *Roy Rogers, King Of The Cowboys*, was shown at the Rotterdam Film Festival, and in the same year Rogers was reported to have signed a contract with Republic Pictures that involved an animated film based on Hollywood's most famous 'good guy'.

● ALBUMS: *Roy Rogers Souvenir Album* 10-inch album (RCA Victor 1952)★★★, with Spade Cooley *Skip To My Lou And Other Square Dances* (1952)★★★, *Roy Rogers Roundup* (1952)★★★★, with Dale Evans *Hymns Of Faith* 10-inch album (RCA Victor 1954)★★, with Evans *Sweet Hour Of Prayer* (RCA Victor 1957)★★, with Evans *Roy Rogers And Dale Evans' Song Wagon* (Golden 1958)★★★, with Evans *16 Great Songs Of The Old West* (Golden 1958)★★★, with Evans *Jesus Loves Me* (RCA Victor 1959)★★, with Evans *The Bible Tells Me So* (Capitol 1962)★★, with The Sons Of The Pioneers *Pacos Bill* (RCA Camden 1964)★★★★, *Lore Of The West (And Favorite Western Songs For Growing Boys And Girls)* (RCA Camden 1966)★★★, with Evans *Christmas Is Always* (Capitol 1967)★★, *Peter Cottontail And His Friends* (RCA Camden 1968)★★★, *The Country Side Of Roy Rogers* (Capitol 1970)★★★, *A Man From Duck Run* (Capitol 1971)★★★, *Take A Little Love And Pass It On* (Capitol 1972)★★★, with Evans *In The Sweet Bye And Bye* (Word 1973)★★★, *Happy Trails To You* (20th Century 1975)★★★★, with Evans *The Good Life* (Word 1977)★★★, with The Sons Of The Pioneers *King Of The Cowboys* (1983)★★★★, *Roy Rogers* (Columbia 1984)★★★, with Evans, Roy Rogers Jnr. *Many Happy Trails* (1984)★★★, *The Republic Years* (1985)★★★, *Tribute* (RCA 1991)★★★.

● COMPILATIONS: *Roll On Texas Moon* (Bear Family 1986)★★★, *The Best Of Roy Rogers* (Curb 1990)★★★, *Country Music Hall Of Fame* (MCA 1992)★★★, with Evans *Peace In The Valley* (Pair 1996)★★★.

● FURTHER READING: *Roy Rogers: King Of The Cowboys*, Georgia Morris and Mark Pollard.

ROME, HAROLD

b. 27 May 1908, Hartford, Connecticut, USA, d. 26 October 1993, New York, USA. While still attending school Rome played piano in local dance bands and was already writing music. Despite this early interest in music, he went on to study architecture and law at Yale. In 1934 he practised as an architect in New York City, but studied piano and composition in his spare time. This was a fortunate decision because by the following year, with work opportunities diminishing with the Depression, he was obliged to turn more and more to his second string activity for support. Much of the music Rome was writing at this time was socially conscious and was thus of little interest to Tin Pan Alley. Nevertheless, he was engaged to write a revue for the International Garment Workers' Union. To everyone's surprise, the revue, *Pins And Needles* (1937), staged for members of the union, became a popular success and one song, 'Sunday In The Park', established a life outside of the show. Rome was now much sought-after, although his next show displayed similarly political concerns. This was *Sing Out The News* (1939) and, once again, there was a universally accepted hit song, 'F.D.R. Jones'. In the early 40s Rome wrote songs for several revues and shows, but it was not until after the end of World War II that he had his first major success. This was *Call Me Mister* (1946), from which came 'South America, Take It Away'. More revues followed until his first fully fledged musical show, *Wish You Were Here*, in 1952. Two years later he wrote *Fanny*, his most popular Broadway show, which included 'Love Is A Very Light Thing'. This was followed by *Destry Rides Again* (1959) and *I Can Get It For You Wholesale* (1962), in which Barbra Streisand made her Broadway debut. In the mid-60s Rome showed that the social conscience that had marked his early work was still intact when he wrote *The Zulu And The Zayda* (1965), which dealt with racial and religious intolerance. In 1970 he wrote *Scarlett*, based upon the novel *Gone With The Wind*, for a Japanese production in Tokyo. More than with any other American composer in the field of mainstream popular music, Rome's work consistently demonstrated an awareness of social issues, often to the extent that it kept him from the massive successes enjoyed by many of his contemporaries. He was also a gifted painter and a dedicated art collector.

RONALD AND RUBY

Ronald was teenage singer Lee Morris and Ruby was Beverly Ross (b. 1939, New Jersey, USA), his singing partner. Ross, who had already penned a hit for Bill Haley And His Comets ('Dim, Dim The Lights'), wrote a song in 1958 called 'Lollipop' and the pair, renamed Ronald and Ruby by their manager, recorded it for RCA-Victor. The irritating repeated lyric 'lollipop, lollipop ooh lolly lolly lolly' was hummed by millions over the next few months. The Chordettes immediately covered the song for Cadence Records, and that group's version outsold Ronald And Ruby's; the pair's rendition reached number 20 in the US charts while the Chordettes' made it to number 2 (in the UK the Mudlarks took it to number 2). Ross went on to become a successful songwriter; among her credits were Roy Orbison's 'Candy Man', Lesley Gore's 'Judy's Turn To Cry' and the Earls' 'Remember Then'. Ronald And Ruby never recorded an album and the act disintegrated after their initial hit.

ROS, EDMUNDO

b. 7 December 1910, Port Of Spain, Trinidad. The leader of one of the most popular - if not the most popular - Latin American band in the UK for many years, spent his early life in Venezuela, before attending the Military Academy at Caracas, where, via the Academy's band, he became interested in music and learned to play the euphonium or 'bombardin'. Despite harbouring ambitions to study criminal law, he travelled to the UK in 1937 and studied composition and harmony at the Royal Academy of Music. Although he recorded with jazzman Fats Waller in 1938, Ros mainly sang and served as a percussionist with various Latin-styled bands, including one led by pianist Don Marino Barretto. He formed his own five-piece unit, Rumba With Ros, in 1940, and for the next 35 years, played and recorded with groups such as Ros's Rumba Romeos, his Rumba Band, and Edmundo Ros and his Orchestra. After making his London debut at the New Cosmos Club and St. Regis Hotel, he played all the smartest nightspots, including the Bagatelle, before opening his own Edmundo Ros Club, on the site of

the Coconut Grove, in 1949. By then, with his gently rhythmic style and engaging vocals, he was enormously popular with the public generally, and a favourite of London's high society and some members of the Royal Family. Earlier in his career, he had decided that the best way to introduce complex Latin rhythms to his audiences would be to apply them to popular and familiar songs, and throughout the 40s and 50s, on radio and records, he had great success with numbers such as 'Enjoy Yourself', 'Melodie D'Amour', 'Tico, Tico', 'I Got The Sun In The Morning', 'South America, Take It Away', 'I'm Crazy For You', 'Her Bathing Suit Never Got Wet', 'The Coffee Song', 'No Can Do', 'The Maharajah Of Magador', his theme, 'The Cuban Love Song', and especially 'The Wedding Samba', which was also a hit in the USA in 1949, although he was not allowed to perform there because of Musicians' Union regulations. His music was in demand in many other parts of the world too, particularly in Japan. In the early 60s, he collaborated on an album with Ted Heath that exploited the relatively new stereo recording process. The shift in musical tastes during the decade affected Ros's standing but he played on into the 70s. Disillusioned with the business, he disbanded in 1975, and, so he says, destroyed most of the bands' arrangements, keeping just one set in case he received an offer he could not refuse. He retired to Spain, emerging occasionally for events such as his 80th birthday celebrations in 1990, and to introduce a series of record programmes for BBC Radio in 1992. Two years later, he joined another veteran musical personality, Stanley Black, in a 'Latin Reunion' at London's Royal Festival Hall. Often the butt of jokes by the musical élite, he was gently satirized by the Bonzo Dog Doo-Dah Band in 'Look Out There's A Monster Coming'.

● ALBUMS: *Calypsos* (Decca 1956)★★★, *Mambos* (Decca 1956)★★★, *Rhythms Of The South* (Decca 1957)★★★, *Calypso Man* (Decca 1958)★★★, *Perfect For Dancing* (Decca 1958)★★★, *Ros On Broadway* (Decca 1959)★★★, *Hollywood Cha Cha Cha* (Decca 1959)★★★, *Bongos From The South* (Decca 1961)★★★, *Dance Again* (Decca 1962)★★★, *Sing And Dance With Edmundo Ros* (Decca 1963)★★★, with Ted Heath *Heath Versus Ros* (Phase 4 1964)★★★, with Heath *Heath Versus Ros, Round Two* (Phase 4 1967)★★, *This Is My World* (Decca 1972)★★★, *Ros Remembers* (Decca 1974)★★★, *Edmundo Ros Today* (Decca 1978)★★★, *Latin Favourites* (Gold Crown 1979)★★★, *Latin Song And Dance Men* (Pye 1980)★★★, *Music For The Millions* (Decca 1983)★★★, *Strings Latino* (London 1985)★★★, *Cuban Love Song* (1985)★★★, *Latin Magic* (London 1987)★★★, *Edmundo Ros & His Rumba Band, 1939-1941* (1992)★★★.

ROSENMAN, LEONARD

b. 7 September 1924, Brooklyn, New York, USA. A composer and arranger for films and television, who only studied music seriously after serving in the US Air Force during World War II. His first film score, *East Of Eden* (1955), was followed in the same year by another James Dean vehicle, *Rebel Without A Cause*. Rosenman's other 50s scores included dramas such as *Bombers B-52*, *Edge Of The City*, *The Young Stranger*, *Lafayett Escadrille*, *Pork Chop Hill* and *The Savage Eye*. After providing music for more in the same genre in the 60s, such as *The Rise And Fall Of Legs Diamond*, *The Bramble Bush*, *The Chapman Report*, *A Covenant With Death* and

Hellfighters, plus essays into science-fiction with *Countdown* and *Fantastic Voyage*, Rosenman received much critical acclaim for his score to *A Man Called Horse* and *Beneath The Planet Of The Apes* (1970). He also scored two 'Apes' sequels. During the 70s Rosenman received two Academy Awards for his adaptation of the scores to *Barry Lyndon* (1975) and *Bound For Glory* (1976). Rosenman's original background scores around that time included *Birch Interval*, *The Car*, *Race With The Devil*, *Prophecy*, *Promises In The Dark* and the animated feature *The Lord Of The Rings*. In the 80s and early 90s, apart from the occasional feature film such as *Hide In Plain Sight*, *Making Love*, *Cross Creek* (Oscar nomination), *Robocop 2*, *Heart Of The Stag* and *Ambition* (1992), Rosenman wrote more and more for television, although he still managed to score the occasional big feature, such as *The Jazz Singer* and *Star Trek IV: The Voyage Home*. Rosenman's music for television included *Stranger On The Run*, *Shadow Over Elveron*, *Any Second Now*, *Banyon*, *Vanished*, *In Broad Daylight*, *The Bravos*, *The Cat Creature*, *The Phantom Of Hollywood*, *Nakia*, *Lanigan's Rabbi*, *Kingston: The Power Play*, *The Possessed*, *Friendly Fire*, *City In Fear*, *The Wall*, *Murder In Texas*, *Celebrity* (mini-series), *Heartsounds*, *First Steps*, *Promised A Miracle*, *Where Pigeons Go To Die*, the popular series *The Defenders*, *Marcus Welby MD*, its sequel, *The Return Of Marcus Welby MD* and the telefilm *Keeper Of The City* (1991). Rosenman has also composed several classical works.

ROTENBERG, JUNE

b. *c*.1926, Philadelphia, Pennsylvania, USA. Encouraged in her interest in music, she was thought to be taking piano lessons but was, in fact, taking lessons on the bass. By the time her ruse was detected she had gained enough proficiency to stay with the instrument, becoming one of very few female bass players in any kind of music. In fact, although trained in classical music, and later a jazz player of distinction, Rotenberg played in many musical forms, including classical, throughout her career. In New York from the early 40s, she met and sat in with many fine jazz musicians including Ben Webster, Lester Young and Mary Lou Williams. She played and recorded in a trio led by Williams, with Bridget O'Flynn on drums. She also played in a trio with O'Flynn led by Beryl Booker. In the mid- to late 40s Rotenberg was splitting her musical time between long spells with the St. Louis Symphony Orchestra and after-hours sessions with Art Tatum. During the 50s she spent some time in Europe, mostly playing classical music but with the occasional jazz session in Parisian clubs. She played at festivals centred upon the playing of the renowned classical cellist Pablo Casals. Eventually, Rotenberg began spending most of her time in New York, playing in studios and in Broadway pit orchestras. Despite her status, she still found it necessary to prove herself; she told Sally Placksin, 'to be treated as an equal, you better be very good.'

ROTONDO, NUNZIO

b. 1924, Palestrina, Italy. A gifted child, Rotondo studied music, first playing piano, then trumpet. In the late 40s he was leader of a small jazz group and in those years and into the early 50s regularly supported visiting American jazzmen including Louis Armstrong. He also played with Bill Coleman, Roy Eldridge and others from the jazz main-stream, but by the early 50s he was taking heed of bop, leading and co-leading several boppish bands in company with fellow nationals such as Gil Cuppini and Romano Mussolini. During the 60s he was active with many forward-thinking musicians, among them Albert Mangelsdorff, Gato Barbieri and Mal Waldron. In the early 70s he was co-leader of a band with Franco D'Andrea. After a period outside music he resumed performing in the early 80s. A lyrical player with a strong melodic sense, Rotondo also composes in a contemporary style.

● ALBUMS: with others *IIIrd Festival Del Jazz Del San Remo* (Carish 1958)★★.

ROYAL TEENS

Formed in 1956 in Bergen County, New Jersey, USA, the Royal Teens are remembered primarily for the 1958 rock 'n' roll novelty number 'Short Shorts'. The group was originally a quartet called the Royal Tones, including pianist Bob Gaudio, saxophonist Bill Crandall, bassist Billy Dalton and drummer Tom Austin. Influenced by black music, the group worked as back-up band to travelling R&B artists, and Gaudio and Austin had written an instrumental dance song as a warm-up for their stage show. Adding the lyrics, 'Who wears short shorts? We wear short shorts', the song was heard by an executive of ABC-Paramount Records, who signed the group; the single hit number 3 in the USA. At that time Crandall was replaced by Larry Quagliano and Dalton also left, to be replaced by Al Kooper. Joe Villa, formerly of the doo-wop group the Three Friends, was added as vocalist, making the group a quintet. The group scored one further chart single for ABC and one for Capitol Records before starting to disintegrate in 1960. Although some members continued with the unit until 1965, recording for such labels as Mighty, All New, Jubilee, Blue Jay and Swan, there was no further success. Gaudio went on to become a founding member of the Four Seasons and a top producer. Kooper later formed the Blues Project and Blood, Sweat And Tears. The Royal Teens never recorded an album.

ROYAL WEDDING

Inspired by the wedding of Princess Elizabeth to Philip Mountbatten in 1947, this film, which was released by MGM four years later in 1951, was also loosely based on the experiences of one of its stars, Fred Astaire. In 1928, he and his sister Adele appeared in the London production of the stage musical *Funny Face*. They were fêted by the city's fashionable high society, and, eventually, Adele broke up their double act and married Lord Charles Cavendish in 1932. Alan Jay Lerner's screenplay for *Royal Wedding* also concerns a brother and sister dance team, Tom and Ellen Bowen (Astaire and Jane Powell), who take their hit Broadway show, *Every Night At Seven*, to the British capital where Ellen marries Lord John Brindale (Peter Lawford) and gives up her showbusiness career. Tom also finds happiness in London with a music hall performer (played by Sarah Churchill, daughter of Britain's new Prime Minister in 1951), and all three couples (including Elizabeth and Philip) are married on the same November day. Burton Lane (music) and Alan Jay Lerner (lyrics) wrote the score which contained one of the longest song titles ever: 'How Could You Believe Me When I Said I Love You When You Know I've Been A Liar All My Life.' That number provided a humorous, no-punches-pulled, knockabout duet for Astaire and Powell, a young and up-and-coming singer-actress who surprised many people with her all-round versatility in this film. She also had the tender 'Too Late Now' and 'Open Your Eyes', while Fred, amazingly innovative as usual, danced with a hat stand in 'Sunday Jumps', and appeared to dance on the floor, walls and ceiling of a room filled with furniture, accompanied by 'You're All The World To Me'. Illustrated lectures have since been given as to how that last feat was accomplished. Nick Castle (with uncredited assistance from Astaire) was responsible for the choreography. The rest of the score included 'I Left My Hat In Haiti', 'Open Your Eyes', 'Ev'ry Night At Seven', 'The Happiest Day Of My Life' and 'What A Lovely Day For A Wedding'. Stanley Donen directed the film, which was photographed in Technicolor and retitled *Wedding Bells* when it was released in the UK.

ROZA, LITA

b. 1926, Liverpool, England. A popular singer, particularly during the 50s, whose name is forever associated with the renowned Ted Heath Orchestra. At the age of 12 she appeared in a Christmas pantomime in Norwich, and when she was 15, took part in the revue *Black Velvet*, which starred top UK comedian Ted Ray. After working outside showbusiness for a while, she became the resident vocalist at the New York restaurant in the northern seaside resort of Southport. By the time she was 17, she had joined Harry Roy's Band for a tour of the Middle East, and then sang with Art Thompson's group at London's Embassy Club. Later, she toured with Edmundo Ros before moving to the USA, where she stayed until 1950. On her return to the UK, Roza successfully auditioned for Ted Heath by singing on one of his popular London Palladium Swing Concerts, and was allocated the middle stool, between Dickie Valentine and Dennis Lotis. During her stay of over four years with Heath, she recorded both with his band and in her own right. In 1951 she had a big hit with Irving Gordon's 'Allentown Jail', followed by other successful sides, such as 'High Noon', 'Half As Much', 'Walkin' to Missouri', 'I Went To Your Wedding', 'Why Don't You Believe Me' and 'Hi-Lili, Hi-Lo'. In 1953 she topped the UK chart with Bob Merrill's novelty '(How Much Is) That Doggie In The Window', a cover version of Patti Page's enormous US hit. Her other chart entries included 'Hey There', the big ballad from *The Pajama Game*, which was also successful in the UK for Rosemary Clooney, Sammy Davis Jnr. and Johnnie Ray, and, finally, 'Jimmy Unknown'. She also sang 'A Tear Fell' on *All Star Hit Parade*, a single record that also featured songs by Joan Regan, David Whitfield, Dennis Lotis, Winifred Atwell and Dave King. When Roza left Heath, she toured the UK variety circuit and appeared extensively on radio and television in shows such as *Off The Record*, *The Jack Jackson Show*, *Saturday Spectacular*, *Music Shop* and the top pop music programmes, *6.5 Special* and *Oh Boy!*; she also featured in the ITV series *The Ted Heath Story*. She recorded several albums, including one entitled *Drinka Lita Roza Day* (presumably a play on the television advertising slogan 'Drinka Pinta Milka Day'), but eventually became yet another victim of the rapidly changing musical climate. In later years she has made television and concert appearances with her contemporaries, celebrating the good times of years gone by, and was one of the 'Four Stars Of The 50s', along with Jimmy Young, Dickie Valentine and Joan Regan, on the double album *Unchained Melodies*.

● ALBUMS: *Presenting Lita Roza* (Decca 1954)★★★, *Love Is The Answer* (Decca 1957)★★★★, *The Night Is Young* (Decca 1957)★★★, *Between The Devil And The Deep Blue Sea* (Decca 1958)★★★, *Me On A Carousel* (Pye 1959)★★★, *Drinka Lita Roza Day* (Pye 1960)★★, *Love Songs For Night People* (Ember 1964)★★, *You're Driving Me Crazy* (President 1983)★★, *Somewhere, Somehow, Someday* (C5 1990)★★.

● COMPILATIONS: includes performances with Dennis Lotis and the Ted Heath Orchestra *Lita Roza* (1977)★★★.

ROZSA, MIKLOS

b. 18 April 1907, Budapest, Hungary, d. 27 July 1995. An important composer for films from the early 30s until the early 80s, who had an equally distinguished career in the world of classical music, Rozsa began to play the piano at the age of five and soon added the violin to his studies. He gave his first public performance when he was seven, playing a movement from a Mozart violin concerto and conducting a children's orchestra in Haydn's 'Toy Symphony'. In his teens Rozsa attended Leipzig University and, during his four years there, completed his first serious compositions. His big breakthrough came in 1934 with his 'Theme, Variations, And Finale (Opus 13)'. A year later he moved to London to write a ballet, and was invited to compose the music for Alexandra Korda's film *Knight Without Armour*, starring Robert Donat and Marlene Dietrich. The successful outcome marked the beginning of Rozsa's five-year association with Korda, which, in the late 30s, produced *The Squeaker*, *The Divorce Of Lady X*, *The Spy In Black* and *The Four Feathers*. In 1940, Rozsa went to Hollywood to finish work on *The Thief Of Baghdad* and then scored *Sundown* and *The Jungle Book*. All three films gained him Oscar nominations, and together with *The Four Feathers*, were designated as his 'Oriental' period. Rozsa was nominated again, for *Lydia*, before Korda shut down London Films for the duration of World War II. Rozsa moved to Paramount where he provided the 'stark, powerful, dissonant score' for 'the archetypal film noir of the 40s', Billy Wilder's *Double Indemnity* (1944), followed by other Wilder movies such as *Five Graves To Cairo* and *The Lost Weekend* (1945). In the latter, Rozsa introduced a new instrument, the theremin, 'an ideal accompaniment to torture'. It was one of around 10 'psychological' movies with which Rozsa was involved during his career. Another, in the same year, was Alfred Hitchcock's *Spellbound*, for which Rozsa won his first Academy Award for a 'bleak and exciting' score. In the late 40s, besides Paramount, Rozsa worked mostly for United Artists and Universal on films such as *Because Of Him*, *The Strange Love Of Martha Ivers*, *The Killers* (Burt Lancaster's first movie), *The Red House*, *The Macomber Affair*, *Brute Force*, *The Naked City* (with Frank Skinner) and *A Double Life* (1947), for which he won another Oscar. At the end of the decade Rozsa began to work for MGM, and embarked on his 'religious and historical epic' period, with monumental scores for *Quo Vadis*, *Ivanhoe*, *Julius Caesar*, *Knights Of The Round Table*, *Valley Of The Kings* and *Ben Hur* (1959 - his third Academy Award, and his last major assignment for MGM). Rozsa pursued the epic into the 60s with the blockbusters *King Of Kings* and *El Cid* (1961), both of which were made in Spain. By no means all of Rozsa's scores in the 50s and 60s were of such gigantic proportions; he also provided the

music for movies with a wide variety of subjects, such as *The Asphalt Jungle*, *Crisis*, *The Story Of Three Loves*, *Moonfleet*, *Tribute To A Bad Man*, *Bhowani Junction*, *Lust For Life*, *Something Of Value*, *The World, The Flesh And The Devil*, *The V.I.P's*, *The Power*, *The Green Berets*, and many more. In 1970 Rozsa made his last film with Billy Wilder, *The Private Life Of Sherlock Holmes*, and played a cameo role as a ballet conductor. His other 70s film music included *The Golden Voyage Of Sinbad*, *The Secret Files Of J. Edgar Hoover*, *Fedora*, *The Last Embrace*, *Time After Time* and *Providence*, described as his 'most inspiring project for years'. Somewhat ironically, during the 70s and 80s, when the demand for elaborate orchestral movie scores had declined, to be replaced by a montage of pop records, renewed interest in Rozsa's earlier classic film works caused record companies to make new recordings of his scores. In 1981, Rozsa's music for *Eye Of The Needle*, suggested, for some, shades of Korda's *The Spy In Black* over 40 years earlier, and *Dead Men Don't Wear Plaid* (1982), a parody of the 40s film noir which included footage from classics of the genre, found Rozsa writing music for scenes that he had originally scored many years previously. Even though he was partially paralyzed by a stroke in 1982, he continued to compose classical works and, on his 80th birthday, was presented with a Golden Soundtrack Award by ASCAP. The anniversary was declared 'Miklos Rozsa Day' in Los Angeles, and the composer was presented with greetings from President Reagan, Queen Elizabeth, and other luminaries such as Margaret Thatcher and Pope John Paul II. Later in 1987 Rozsa was the guest of honour at a gala charity concert of his music given by the Royal Philharmonic Orchestra at London's Royal Festival Hall.
● ALBUMS: *Miklos Rozsa Conducts His Great Film Music* (Polydor 1975)★★★★, *Spellbound-The Classic Film Scores Of Miklos Rozsa* (RCA 1975)★★★★, *Miklos Rozsa Conducting The Royal Philharmonic Orchestra* (Polydor 1976)★★★.
● FURTHER READING: *Miklos Rozsa: A Sketch Of His Life And Work*, C. Palmer. *Double Life: The Autobiography Of Miklos Rozsa*, Miklos Rozsa.

RUSSO, BILL

b. 25 June 1928, Chicago, Illinois, USA. After studies in arranging, Russo wrote for Lennie Tristano and occasionally played trombone. One of the earliest musicians to lead a rehearsal band, his experimental style came to the attention of Stan Kenton in the early 50s. In the mid-50s he concentrated on performing with a small group but by the end of the decade was again involved in writing for larger jazz ensembles. He was also active as a teacher and this combination of work continued on throughout the 60s and early 70s. After spending some time in film and television work he returned to teaching in the 80s. He remains one of the more interesting writers for the large modern jazz orchestra.
● ALBUMS: *A Recital In New American Music* 10-inch album (Dee Gee 1952)★★, with Shelly Manne *Deep People* (Savoy 1955)★★★, *Bill Russo Plus The Hans Koller Ensemble* (1955)★★, *Bill Russo And The New Jazz Group, Hanover* (1955)★★★★, *The World Of Alcina* (Atlantic 1956)★★★, *School Of Rebellion* (Roulette 1960)★★★, *The Seven Deadly Sins* (Roulette 1960)★★, *Suite No. 1 Opus 5 & Suite No. 2 Opus 8* (1962)★★★, *Bill Russo On The Air In London* (1963)★★★, *Bill Russo And The London Jazz Orchestra* (1964)★★★.

RUTHERFORD, RUDY

b. Elman Rutherford, 1912, Detroit, Michigan, USA. Rutherford played alto and baritone saxophones and clarinet in various local bands until joining Lionel Hampton in 1943. He played baritone in the band and also with Count Basie whom he joined in 1944. He went into this band as replacement for baritone saxophonist Jack Washington, and when Washington returned he stayed on, switching to alto. In 1947 he left to play with Teddy Buckner and thereafter played in several bands, including a return spell with Basie, and also led his own groups. The return to Basie coincided with the leader's brief period with a small band in the early 50s, with Rutherford again playing baritone and doubling on his other instruments. In the 50s he was with Wilbur De Paris and Roger 'Ram' Ramirez and also worked with Chuck Berry. In the 60s he was with Buddy Tate and during the early 70s he played with Earl 'Fatha' Hines. As a section player, Rutherford's work was solid without being especially notable. As a clarinet soloist, however, he played with verve and distinction while his baritone playing had a lightness of touch and fluidity.
● ALBUMS: with Count Basie *The Jubilee Alternatives* (Hep 1943-44)★★★★, with Wilbur De Paris *Over And Over Again* (Atlantic 1959-60)★★★, with Earl 'Fatha' Hines *Swingin' Away* (Black Lion 1973)★★★.

RYDELL, BOBBY

b. Robert Ridarelli, 26 April 1942, Philadelphia, Pennsylvania, USA. Probably the most musically talented of the late 50s Philadelphia school of clean-cut teen-idols, Rydell first performed in public as a drummer at the age of seven. At nine he debuted on Paul Whiteman's *Teen Club* amateur television show and was the show's regular drummer for three years. He attended the same boys club as Fabian and Frankie Avalon, formed a duo with Avalon in 1954 and shortly afterwards, they both joined local group Rocco And The Saints. After several rejections from labels, he recorded his first solo single 'Fatty Fatty' for his manager's Veko label. In 1958 he joined Cameo-Parkway and his fourth release for that label, 'Kissin' Time' (which owed something to 'Sweet Little Sixteen'), became the first of his 18 US Top 40 hits over the next four years. The photogenic pop/rock singer's best-known transatlantic hits are 'Wild One', 'Sway' and 'Volare' (only two years after the song first topped the charts) all in 1960 and 'Forget Him', a song written and produced in Britain by Tony Hatch in 1963. Rydell, whose ambition was always to be an all-round entertainer, starred in the movie *Bye Bye Birdie* and quickly, and initially successfully, moved into the cabaret circuit. The arrival of the British groups in 1964 was the final nail in his chart coffin. He later recorded without success for Capitol, Reprise, RCA, Perception and Pickwick International. Rydell has continued to work the club and oldies circuit and had some recognition for his role in rock when the high school in the hit 70s musical *Grease* was named after him. He returned to the studio in 1995 to re-record all his greatest hits as *The Best Of Bobby Rydell*.
● ALBUMS: *We Got Love* (Cameo 1959)★★★, *Bobby Sings* (Cameo 1960)★★, *Bobby Rydell Salutes The Great Ones* (Cameo 1961)★★, *Rydell At The Copa* (Cameo 1961)★★, *Bobby Rydell/Chubby Checker* (Cameo-Parkway 1961)★★★, *Bye Bye Birdie* (Cameo 1963)★★, *Wild Wood Days* (Cameo

1963)★★, *The Top Hits Of 1963* (Cameo 1964)★★, *Forget Him* (Cameo 1964)★★.
● COMPILATIONS: *Bobby's Biggest Hits* (Cameo 1961)★★★, *All The Hits* (Cameo 1962)★★★, *Biggest Hits, Volume 2* (Cameo 1962)★★, *16 Golden Hits* (Cameo 1965)★★, *Greatest Hits* (1993)★★, *Best Of Bobby Rydell* (K-Tel 1995)★★.
● FILMS: *Because They're Young* (1960).

SANDS, TOMMY

b. 27 August 1937, Chicago, Illinois, USA. Tommy Sands' father was a pianist, and his mother was Grace Lou Dixon, a singer with the Art Keassel Band. He sang in a local folk music television series, *Lady Of The Mountain*, when he was only five years old, and made his first recording, 'Love Pains', on Freedom in 1949, when aged only 12. In 1952, with help from his new manager, Colonel Tom Parker, he joined RCA Records as a country artist. In the early and mid-50s Sands played many country shows including some with Hank Williams, Elvis Presley and Johnny Cash. His big break came when he secured the role of a rock 'n' roll star in NBC's *The Singing Idol*, a part that was originally offered to Elvis Presley. The show was a smash hit, and its main song, 'Teen-Age Crush', attracted over half a million advance orders and shot to number 2 in the US charts. The television show was snapped up by Hollywood and was adapted to become Sands' first film, *Sing, Boy, Sing* (1958). The first of his five albums on Capitol Records, *Steady Date With Tommy Sands*, and *Sing Boy Sing* both made the US Top 20, and he was tipped by some as likely to replace Presley. However, of his other eight singles that charted, only 'Goin' Steady' made the US Top 40 in 1957. That same year in the UK he was the subject of BBC Television's *This Is Your Life*. He made a string of films including *Mardi Gras* with Pat Boone, *Love In A Goldfish Bowl* with Fabian, *Babes In Toyland* with Annette, the star-studded *The Longest Day*, and *None But The Brave* with his father-in-law Frank Sinatra (he was married to Nancy Sinatra from 1960-65). Together with his group the Raiders (aka the Sharks), which included the future top session drummer Hal Blaine, he later recorded on ABC, Paramount, Imperial and Liberty without further chart success. In the late 60s he moved to Hawaii and opened a club. He tried to make a comeback between 1974 and 1979, and again in 1987. He played his first UK dates in 1990.
● ALBUMS: *Steady Date With Tommy Sands* (Capitol

1957)★★★, *Sing, Boy, Sing* film soundtrack (Capitol 1958)★★, *Sands Storm* (Capitol 1959)★★★, *Teenage Rock* (1959)★★★, *This Thing Called Love* (Capitol 1959)★★★, *When I'm Thinking Of You* (Capitol 1960)★★★, *Sands At The Sands* (Capitol 1960)★★★, *Dream Of Me* (Capitol 1961)★★★, *The Parent Trap* film soundtrack (1961)★★, *Babes In Toyland* film soundtrack (1961)★★, *Blue Ribbon Baby* (Revival 1987)★★, *Down By Bendy's Lane* (Green Linnet 1988)★★, *Beyond The Shadows* (1992)★★.
● COMPILATIONS: *The Worryin' Kind* (Bear Family 1992)★★★.
● FILMS: *Sing Boy Sing* (1957), *Mardi Gras* (1958), *Love In A Goldfish Bowl* (1959), *Babes In Toyland* (1960), *The Longest Day* (1962), *None But The Brave* (1965).

SATCHMO THE GREAT

Made for television by Ed Murrow, this 1956 film follows Louis Armstrong on a tour of Europe and Africa. Intercut with scenes of live performance by Armstrong And His All Stars, and their reception, often by tens of thousands of well-wishers, at airports, are interviews with Armstrong. Although one of the finest and most respected journalists of his, or any other, era, Murrow's questions are sometimes a shade naïve, but Armstrong takes it all in his stride. The film ends with a New York concert performance of 'St Louis Blues' in which Armstrong and his men are joined by Leonard Bernstein and the New York Philharmonic to play to a capacity audience that includes W.C. Handy. One moving moment shows Handy, then over 80, removing his hat to take his handkerchief from his head to mop a tear from his blind eyes. The All Stars featured are Trummy Young, Edmond Hall, Billy Kyle, Jack Lesberg and Barrett Deems with singer Velma Middleton.

SAUTER, EDDIE

b. 2 December 1914, New York City, New York, USA, d. 21 April 1981. After studying arranging and composition at the Juilliard School of Music, Sauter became staff arranger for Red Norvo. In 1939, after four years with Norvo, he free-lanced, writing charts for several prominent big bands, including Artie Shaw's, Woody Herman's and Tommy Dorsey's. He made his greatest impact with Benny Goodman, for whom he wrote 'Clarinet A La King' in the early 40s. He later worked for Ray McKinley where, unusually for an arranger at that time (or any other), he was given prominent billing. While hospitalized with tuberculosis Sauter began corresponding with Bill Finegan and in 1952 the two arrangers formed their own orchestra. The resulting 21-piece band was conceived as a studio band, but its records, which included the joyous 'The Doodletown Fifers' and the irresistible 'Midnight Sleigh Ride' were so popular that they took it on the road. In 1957, Sauter became musical director of the South-West German Radio Big Band in Baden-Baden. He later worked with Stan Getz, the New York Saxophone Quartet and in films and television.
● ALBUMS: all by Sauter-Finegan Orchestra *New Directions In Music* 10-inch album (RCA Victor 1953)★★★★, *Inside Sauter-Finegan* (RCA Victor 1954)★★★, *The Sound Of Sauter-Finegen* (RCA Victor 1954)★★★, *Sons Of Sauter-Finegan* (RCA Victor 1955)★★★, *Concert Jazz* (RCA Victor 1955)★★★, *New Directions In Music* (RCA Victor 1956)★★★★★, *Adventure In Time* (RCA Victor 1956)★★★,

Under Analysis (RCA Victor 1957)★★★, *One Night Stand With The Sauter-Finegan Orchestra* (RCA Victor 1957)★★★, *Straight Down The Middle* (RCA Victor 1957)★★★, *Inside Sauter-Finegan Revisited* (RCA Victor 1961)★★★, *Sleigh Ride* (RCA Victor 1961)★★★★, *The Return Of The Doodletown Fifers* (Capitol 1985)★★★.

SCOTT, BOBBY

b. 29 January 1937, New York City, New York, USA, d. 5 November 1990, New York City, New York, USA. Scott was a pianist, singer, composer, arranger, teacher and record producer. He also played several other instruments such as cello, bass, vibes, accordion and clarinet, but was mainly known for his jazz piano work and vocals. He attended Dorothea Anderson Follette's School of Music, and then in 1949 studied composition with Edward Moritz, a former pupil of Claude Debussy. Despite his early classical training, Scott turned to jazz in his teens, and played with small bands led by the likes of Louis Prima, Tony Scott and Gene Krupa, with whom he cut some sides for Verve Records. From 1954, he recorded under his own name for labels such as Bethlehem, Savoy, Atlantic and ABC, and in 1956 had a US Top 20 hit with 'Chain Gang', written by Sol Quasha and Hank Yakus (not the Sam Cooke song). In 1960, Scott wrote the title theme for Shelagh Delaney's play *A Taste Of Honey*, which became popular for pianist Martin Denny and, when Ric Marlow added a lyric, for Tony Bennett. It was also included on the Beatles' first album (UK). The song won a Grammy in 1962, and three more when Herb Alpert took it into the US Top 10 in 1965. In the early 60s Scott was the musical director for Dick Haymes for a time, and, as a pianist, arranger and record producer for Mercury Records, also maintained a close working relationship with Quincy Jones. Scott played piano on most of Jones's Mercury albums, and accompanied Tania Vega and John Lee Hooker on Jones's soundtrack music for the film *The Color Purple* (1986). As a producer, Scott supervised sessions for important artists such as Aretha Franklin, Marvin Gaye, Bobby Darin, Harry Belafonte and Sarah Vaughan. He discovered and recorded guitarist/vocalist Perry Miller, who changed his name to Jesse Colin Young, and he is also credited with taking singer Bobby Hebb back to Mercury, although Scott left the label before Hebb released his biggest hit, 'Sunny', in 1966. Scott's compositions included 'He Ain't Heavy, He's My Brother' (written with Bob Russell), a hit for Neil Diamond in 1970 and a UK number 1 for the Hollies that same year and later in 1988, when it featured impressively in a UK television commercial for Miller Lite Lager; 'Where Are You Going?' (with Danny Meehan), sung by Joe Butler in the film *Joe* (1970); and 'Slaves (Don't You Know My Name?)', performed by Dionne Warwick in the movie *Slaves* (1969). Scott also composed incidental music for the play *Dinny And The Witches*, and several pieces for harp and string trios, including 'The Giacometti Variations', so-called because it was part-used as a radio advertisement for the Giacometti Exhibition held at the New York Museum of Modern Art. His compositions for guitar included 'Solitude Book' and 'The Book Of Hours', the latter recorded with Brazilian guitarist Carlos Barbosa-Lima. *For Sentimental Reasons* displayed Scott simply as an accomplished pianist, who also sang. He died of lung cancer in 1990.
● ALBUMS: *The Jazz Keyboard Of Bobby Scott* (1953)★★★,

Great Scott 10-inch album (Bethlehem 1954)★★★ *The Compositions Of Bobby Scott, Volume 1* 10-inch album (Bethlehem 1954)★★, *The Compositions Of Bobby Scott, Volume 2* 10-inch album (Bethlehem 1954)★★, *The Compositions Of Bobby Scott* (Bethlehem 1955)★★, *Scott Free* (ABC-Paramount 1956)★★★, *Bobby Scott And Two Horns* (ABC-Paramount 1957)★★★, *Bobby Scott Sings The Best Of Lerner And Loewe* (Verve 1958)★★★, *Serenade - Bobby Scott, Pianist* (Verve 1959)★★★, *Bobby Scott Plays The Music Of Leonard Bernstein* (Verve 1959)★★★, *Bobby Scott With Friends* (1960)★★★, *The Complete Musician* (Atlantic 1960)★★★, *A Taste Of Honey* (Atlantic 1960)★★, *Joyful Noises* (Mercury 1962)★★★, *When The Feeling Hits You* (Mercury 1963)★★★, *108 Pounds Of Heartache* (Mercury 1963)★★, *I Had A Ball* (Mercury 1964)★★★, *For Sentimental Reasons* (Music Masters 1990)★★★.

SCOTT, JACK

b. Jack Scafone Jnr., 24 January 1936, Windsor, Ontario, Canada. This distinctive, deep-voiced rock 'n' roll and ballad singer-songwriter moved to Michigan at the age of 10 and fronted the Southern Drifters from 1954. He signed to ABC Records in 1957 and his first release was the rocker 'Baby She's Gone'. Scott joined Carlton in 1958 and had a transatlantic Top 10 hit with his double-sided debut for the label 'My True Love'/'Leroy'. Always backed on records by session vocal group the Chantones, he had a further seven US Top 40 successes over the next two years, including the Top 10 hits 'Goodbye Baby' in 1958, 'What In The World's Come Over You' (a UK Top 20 hit) and 'Burning Bridges' both in 1960 (the latter two released on Top Rank). He achieved a couple of minor hits on Capitol in 1961 and later recorded on various labels including Groove, Guaranteed, RCA, Jubilee, GRT, Dot (where he notched up a country hit in 1974) and Ponie. He remains a top-drawing act on the rock 'n' roll club circuit around the world.
● ALBUMS: *Jack Scott* (Carlton 1958)★★★, *What Am I Living For* (Carlton 1959)★★★, *I Remember Hank Williams* (Top Rank 1960)★★★, *What In The World's Come Over You?* (Top Rank 1960)★★★, *The Spirit Moves Me* (Top Rank 1961)★★★, *Burning Bridges* (Capitol 1964)★★, *Scott On Groove* (Bear Family 1980)★★, *Greaseball* (Bison Bop 1985)★★.
● COMPILATIONS: *Grizzly Bear* (Charly 1986)★★★, *Capitol Collectors Series* (Capitol 1991)★★★.

SCOTT, LITTLE JIMMY

b. James Victor Scott, 17 July 1925, Cleveland, Ohio, USA. An influential figure to popular singers as stylistically diverse as Nancy Wilson, Ray Charles, and Frankie Valli, the highly acclaimed balladeer 'Little' Jimmy Scott nevertheless found it extremely difficult to transcend his enduring cult status. Revered by only the most knowledgeable of jazz aficionados, it was not until quite recently that Scott was able to mount a successful comeback after suffering decades of undeserved obscurity. His wavering, ethereal contralto vocal range, much closer in pitch to that of a woman than a man, was a result of a rare hereditary condition called Kallmann's Syndrome, which restricted Scott's height to 4 feet 11 inches until he was in his mid-30s (when he suddenly grew to an unprecedented 5 feet 7 inches), blocked his sexual development, and stopped his voice from lowering into a conventional masculine register - thereby creating one of the most unusual and stunning vocal deliveries in post-war music history. He was one of 10 children, all of whom sang along heartily to their mother Justine's spirited piano playing at Hagar's Universal Spiritual Church in Cleveland. After her death (she was struck down while pushing her daughter out of the way of a speeding car), Scott was raised in various foster homes from the age of 13. While in his teens, he ushered at Cleveland's Metropolitan Theater, where he heard the bands of Buddy Johnson, Erskine Hawkins and Lucky Millinder. He received his first chance to sing in front of an audience in Meadsville, Pennsylvania, in the mid-40s, backed by jazz saxophone legends Ben Webster and Lester Young. Scott toured from 1945 to 1949 with shake dancer Estelle 'Caledonia' Young. Comedian Redd Foxx, actor Ralph Cooper, and heavyweight boxing champion Joe Louis helped the promising young singer to gain a job in 1948 at the Baby Grand nightclub on 125th Street in New York City. Scott joined Lionel Hampton's band the next year, with whom he made his debut recordings. In 1950, he sang the hit 'Everybody's Somebody's Fool' on Decca Records as Hampton's featured vocalist (the song reached number 6 on *Billboard*'s R&B charts). Scott was also spotlighted vocally on 'I Wish I Knew', a popular but non-charting 1950 Decca side credited to the Lionel Hampton Quintet that featured Doug Duke's organ accompaniment, and 'I've Been A Fool'. Scott soon left Hampton's band to join forces with New Orleans R&B mainstay Paul Gayten's band (which also featured vocalist Annie Laurie) in 1951. Scott made some live recordings for Fred Mendelsohn's Regal label that year with Gayten's band (trumpeter John Hunt, tenor saxophonist Ray Abrams, baritone saxophonist Pee Wee Numa-Moore, pianist Teddy Brannon, bassist Thomas Legange, and drummer Wesley Landis) that were captured for posterity at Rip's Playhouse, a New Orleans nightspot. Those long-buried tapes belatedly saw the light of day in 1991 on a Specialty Records disc. Mendelsohn sold Scott's contract to Teddy Reig and Jack Hook's Roost Records, where he recorded 16 further tracks under his own name (including his first classic rendition of 'The Masquerade Is Over') before signing with Herman Lubinsky's larger Savoy label in 1955. Four ballad-heavy sessions were held that year for Savoy, surrounding Scott with top-notch bandsmen including pianist/arranger Howard Biggs, saxophonist Budd Johnson, guitarists Mundell Lowe, George Barnes, and Everett Barksdale, bassist Charles Mingus, and drummer Kenny Clarke. Scott was unhappy with the skimpy financial rewards he received while under contract to the Newark, New Jersey-based Savoy (more dates ensued in 1956 and 1958). Nevertheless, under Mendelsohn's astute supervision, Scott did manage to create numerous classic ballads for the company despite the fiscal discord. 'When Did You Leave Heaven', 'Imagination', and the bluesy 'Don't Cry Baby' are among Scott's finest performances for Savoy. Although his early years were artistically enriching, Scott's offstage existence was apparently another matter. The singer endured multiple divorces and suffered from a reported drinking problem. Scott temporarily switched over to Syd Nathan's King Records in 1957 for a dozen sides supervised by Henry Glover before returning to Savoy in 1960 for one more session. Finally, in 1962, Scott received what appeared to be his big break: a contract with Ray Charles's

fledgling Tangerine label. With Marty Paich and Gerald Wilson supplying lush arrangements and Charles himself deftly handling the keyboards, the resulting album, *Falling in Love is Wonderful*, would have most likely boosted Scott's national profile considerably. Unfortunately, Lubinsky quashed the set's distribution shortly after its release, claiming that Scott remained under contract to Savoy. In 1969, Atlantic Records producer Joel Dorn recorded an album with Scott, *The Source*, with arrangements by Arif Mardin and sporting a varied set that included 'Day By Day', 'This Love Of Mine', and 'Exodus', but it failed to further Scott's fortunes. He returned to Savoy one last time in 1975 for a Mendelsohn-produced album that made little impact. For a lengthy period prior to his triumphant return to live performance in 1985 (which was spurred by the urging of his fourth wife, Earlene), Scott toiled as a shipping clerk at Cleveland's Sheraton Hotel, forgotten by all but his most loyal fans. Scott has engineered quite an amazing comeback in the years since. In 1992, his Blue Horizon album *All The Way* (listed as being by Jimmy Scott, with no reference to his height) found him backed by an all-star jazz aggregation that included saxophonist David 'Fathead' Newman, pianist Kenny Barron, bassist Ron Carter, and drummer Grady Tate and string arrangements by Johnny Mandel. Scott followed it in 1994 with another set for Sire/Blue Horizon, *Dream*. Jimmy Scott's reputation as a unique vocal master is assured, but his status definitely has not come easily.

● ALBUMS: *Very Truly Yours* (Savoy 1955)★★★, *The Fabulous Little Jimmy Scott* reissued as *The Fabulous Songs Of Jimmy Scott* (Savoy 1959)★★★, *Falling In Love Is Wonderful* (Tangerine 1962)★★★, *If You Only Knew* (Savoy 1963)★★★, *The Source* (Atlantic 1969)★★, *Can't We Begin Again* (Savoy 1975)★★, *Little Jimmy Scott* (Savoy Jazz 1984)★★★, *All Over Again* (Savoy Jazz 1985)★★★, *Regal Records: Live In New Orleans!* (Specialty 1991)★★★, *All The Way* (Blue Horizon 1992)★★★, *Lost And Found* (Rhino/Atlantic 1993)★★★, *Dream* (Sire/Blue Horizon 1994)★★★, *All Over Again* (Denon/Savoy Jazz 1994)★★★.

SEEGER, PETE

b. 3 May 1919, New York City, New York, USA. Educated at Harvard University, he is the brother of Peggy Seeger and half-brother of Mike Seeger. Pete Seeger's mother was a violin teacher, and his father a renowned musicologist. While still young, Pete Seeger learned to play banjo and ukulele, and shortly afterwards he developed his interest in American folk music. Seeger took his banjo round the country, playing and learning songs from the workers and farmers. He served in the US Army during World War II. In addition to being a member of the Weavers from 1949-58, he had earlier been in a group called the Almanac Singers. The group included Woody Guthrie, Lee Hays and Millard Lampell. The Almanac Singers had frequently given free performances to union meetings and strikers' demonstrations. Despite such apparent diversions, Seeger maintained a successfully high profile in his own solo career. The era of McCarthyism put a blight on many live performances, owing to the right-wing political paranoia that existed at the time. It was in 1948 that Seeger was blacklisted and had to appear before the House of Un-American Activities Committee for his alleged communist sympathies. This did not stop Seeger from performing sell-out concerts abroad and speaking out on a wide range of civil rights and environmental issues. He became known for popularizing songs such as 'Little Boxes', 'Where Have All The Flowers Gone' and 'We Shall Overcome'. In more recent times Seeger also performed and recorded with Arlo Guthrie. Seeger was also involved with the Clearwater Sloop project on the Hudson River, attempting to publicize the threat of pollution. He has always worked and campaigned for civil rights, peace and equality, and has never compromised his ideals.

By the mid-70s, Seeger had released in excess of 50 albums, several of which were instructional records for banjo playing. In addition to these albums Seeger has appeared on the work of many other artists providing either vocal or instrumental back-up. The 1993 release *Live At Newport* consisted of previously unreleased recordings made at the Newport Folk Festival between 1963 and 1965. After a gap of 14 years in releasing a new album Seeger was aided and produced by Paul Winter on *Pete* in 1996. Seeger is one of the most important figures in the development of free speech and humanitarian causes through folk music.

● ALBUMS: with the Almanac Singers *Songs For John Doe* (Keynote/Almanac 1941)★★★, with the Almanac Singers *Talking Union And Other Union Songs* (Keynote 1941)★★★, with the Almanac Singers *Sod Buster Ballads, Deep Sea Shanties* (General Records 1941)★★★, with the Almanac Singers *Dear Mr. President* (Keynote 1942)★★★, *Songs Of The Lincoln Bridge* (Asch 1943)★★★, *Songs For Political Action* (CIO-Political Action Commitee 1946)★★★, *Bawdy Ballads And Real Sad Songs* (Charter 1947)★★★, *Darling Corey* (Folkways 1950)★★★★, *Lonesome Valley* (Folkways 1951)★★★, *Songs To Grow On* (Folkways 1952)★★★, *Lincoln Bridge* (Stinson 1953)★★★, *A Pete Seeger Concert* (Stinson 1953)★★★, *American Folk Songs For Children* (Folkways 1953)★★★, *Pete Seeger Sampler* (Folkways 1954)★★★, *Goofing-Off Suite* (Folkways 1954)★★★, *How To Play The Five String Banjo* (Folkways 1954)★, *Frontier Ballads, Volume 1* (Folkways 1954)★★★★, *Frontier Ballads, Volume 2* (Folkways 1954)★★★★, *Birds, Beasts, Bugs And Little Fishes* (Folkways 1954)★★★, *The Folksinger's Guitar Guide* (1955)★★, *Bantu Choral Folk Songs* (Folkways 1955)★★★★, *Folk Songs Of Four Continents* (Folkways 1955)★★★, *With Voices Together We Sing* (Folkways 1956)★★★, *American Industrial Ballads* (Folkways 1956)★★★, *Love Songs For Friends And Foes* (Folkways 1956)★★★, *American Ballads* (Folkways 1957)★★★★, *American Favorite Ballads, Volume 1* (Folkways 1957)★★★★, *Gazette With Pete Seeger, Volume 1* (1958)★★★, *Sleep Time* (1958)★★★, *Pete Seeger And Sonny Terry At Carnegie Hall* (Folkways 1958)★★★, *Song And Play Time With Pete Seeger* (1958)★★★, *Folk Songs For Young People* (Folkways 1959)★★★, *American Favorite Ballads, Volume 2* (Folkways 1959)★★★, *Sing Out! Hootenanny* (Folkways 1959)★★★, *Hootenanny Tonight* (1959)★★★, *Folk Festival At Newport, Volume 1* (1959)★★★, *Pete Seeger In Concert Volumes. 1 & 2* (Folkways 1959)★★★, with Mike Seeger, Rev. Larry Eisenberg *American Playparties* (Folkways 1959)★★★, with Frank Hamilton *Nonesuch* (1959)★★★, *Old Time Fiddle Tunes* (Folkways 1960)★★★, *American Favorite Ballads, Volume 3* (Folkways 1960)★★★, *Songs Of The Civil War* (1960)★★★★, *Champlain Valley Songs* (Folkways 1960)★★★, *With Memphis Slim And Willie Dixon At The Village Gate, Volume 1* (Folkways 1960)★★★★,

Rainbow Quest (Folkways 1960)★★★, *Sing Out With Pete* (1961)★★★, *American Favorite Ballads, Volume 4* (Folkways 1961)★★★, *Gazette, Volume 2* (1961)★★★, *Pete Seeger: Story Songs* (Columbia 1961)★★★, *At The Village Gate, Volume 2* (Folkways 1962)★★★★, *American Favorite Ballads, Volume 5* (Folkways 1962)★★★, *In Person At The Bitter End* (Columbia 1962)★★★, *American Game And Activity Songs For Children* (Folkways 1962)★★★, *The Bitter And The Sweet* (1963)★★★, *Pete Seeger, Children's Concert At Town Hall* (Columbia 1963)★★★, *Broadside Ballads, Volume 1* (Folkways 1963)★★★, *We Shall Overcome* (Columbia 1963)★★★, *Little Boxes And Other Broadsides* (Verve/Folkways 1963)★★★, *The Story Of The Nativity* (Folkways 1963)★★★, *In Concert, Volume 2 (St. Pancras Town Hall)* recorded 1959 (1964)★★★, *Freight Train* (1964)★★★★, *Songs Of Struggle And Protest 1930 - 1950* (Folkways 1964)★★★, *Broadside Ballads, Volume 2* (Folkways 1965)★★★, *Pete Seeger And Big Bill Broonzy In Concert* (Verve/Folkways 1965)★★★★, *Strangers And Cousins* (1965)★★★, *The Pete Seeger Box* (1965)★★★★, *WNEW's Story Of The Sea* (Folkways 1965)★★★, *Pete Seeger On Campus* (Verve/Folkways 1965)★★★, *I Can See A New Day* (1965)★★★, *God Bless The Grass* (1966)★★★, *Dangerous Songs!?* (1966)★★★, *Pete Seeger Sings Woody Guthrie* (Folkways 1967)★★★★, *Waist Deep In The Big Muddy* (Columbia 1967)★★★, *Traditional Christmas Carols* (Folkways 1967)★★, *Pete Seeger Sings Leadbelly* (Folkways 1968)★★★, *American Folksongs For Children* (1968)★★★, *Pete Seeger Sings And Answers Questions At The Ford Hall Forum In Boston* (Broadside 1968)★★★, *Where Have All The Flowers Gone* (1969)★★★, *Pete Seeger Now* (1969)★★★, *Young Vs. Old* (Columbia 1971)★★★, *Rainbow Race* (1973)★★★, *America's Balladeer* (Everest/Olympic 1973)★★★, *Banks Of Marble* (Folkways 1974)★★★, *Pete Seeger And Brother Kirk Visit Sesame Street* (1974)★, with Arlo Guthrie *Together In Concert* (Reprise 1975)★★, with Ed Renehan *Fifty Sail On Newburgh Bay* (1976)★★★, *Tribute To Leadbelly* (1977)★★★, *Circles And Seasons* (Warners 1979)★★★, with Arlo Guthrie *Precious Friend* (Warners 1982)★★★, *We Shall Overcome: The Complete Carnegie Hall Concert* (Columbia 1989)★★★, *Pete Seeger Singalong: Sanders Theater, 1980* (Smithsonian/Folkways/Rounder 1991)★★★, *Pete Seeger Live At Newport* (1993)★★★, *Pete 50s* recordings (Living Music 1996)★★★.

● COMPILATIONS: *Pete Seeger's Greatest Hits* (Columbia 1967)★★★★, *The World Of Pete Seeger* (Columbia 1972)★★★, *The Essential Pete Seeger* (Vanguard 1978)★★★, *Greatest Hits* (Ember 1984)★★★, *Live At The Royal Festival Hall* (1986)★★★, *Can't You See This System's Rotten Through And Through* (Greenwich Village 1986)★★★, *A Link In The Chain* (Columbia/Legacy 1998)★★★★, various artists *Where Have All The Flowers Gone: The Songs Of Pete Seeger* (Appleseed 1998)★★★.

● FURTHER READING: *How Can I Keep From Singing*, David King Dunaway. *The Foolish Frog*, Pete Seeger. *How Can I Keep From Singing?*, David King Dunaway. *Everbody Says Freedom*, Bob Reiser. *Carry It On!: History In Song And Pictures Of The Working Men & Women Of America*, Pete Seeger and Bob Reiser. *Where Have All The Flowers Gone?*, Pete Seeger. *Incompleat Folksinger*, Jo Metcalf Schwartz.

● FILMS: *Alice's Restaurant* (1969).

SEVEN BRIDES FOR SEVEN BROTHERS

Adapted from Stephen Vincent Benet's short story *The Sobbin' Women*, which was 'inspired' by Plutach's *Rape Of The Sabine Women*, this film was released by MGM in 1954 and, somewhat surprisingly, went on to become one of the most successful screen musicals of the decade. Frances Goodrich, Albert Hackett, and Dorothy Kingsley wrote the screenplay, which told of Adam Pontipee (Howard Keel), who leaves his six scruffy brothers to the squalor of their farmhouse in Oregon (*c*.1850s) to go in search of a hard-working wife. He finds her in the shape of Milly (Jane Powell), and their subsequent life together, during which Milly successfully advises the slovenly sextet on how to live and love, makes for an endearing and entertaining film. Her first 'lesson' is 'Goin' Co'tin', just one of the many musical highlights in Gene De Paul and Johnny Mercer's spirited and exuberant score. Others included the optimistic 'Bless Your Beautiful Hide' (Keel), 'Wonderful, Wonderful Day' (Powell), 'When You're In Love' (Powell-Keel), 'Sobbin' Women' (Keel-brothers), 'June Bride' (Powell-brides), and 'Spring, Spring, Spring' (Powell-brothers-brides). The six virile brothers, named by their god-fearing mother as Benjamin, Caleb, Daniel, Ephram, Frankincense and Gideon, were played by Russ Tamblyn, Tommy Rall, Marc Platt, Jeff Richards, Matt Mattox and Jacques d'Amboise. In the end, they all find their brides (Virginia Gibson, Julie Newmeyer, Betty Carr, Nancy Kilgas, Norma Doggett and Rita Kilmonis) by somewhat unconventional methods, after displaying exceptionally brilliant dancing skills in the contrasting languorous 'Lonesome Polecat' and spectacular 'barn-raising' scenes. The choreography for those, and the rest of the innovative dance numbers, was designed by Michael Kidd. Saul Chaplin and Adolph Deutsch won Academy Awards for 'scoring of a musical picture'. Stanley Donen directed with style and vigour. George Folsey was responsible for the breathtakingly beautiful photography in Amsco and CinemaScope. This film is considered by many to be among the all-time great musicals, but a 1982 stage version was not welcomed in New York and folded after five performances. Four years later, a West End production fared a little better.

SEVILLE, DAVID

b. Ross Bagdasarian, 27 January 1919, Fresno, California, USA, d. 16 January 1972. This singer-songwriter, conductor and actor is best remembered as the creator of the Chipmunks. He first appeared on Broadway in the late 30s and was drafted to Britain during the war. His first musical success came in 1951 when a song he had co-written a decade earlier, 'Come On-A My House', topped the chart in a version by Rosemary Clooney. He recorded on Coral in 1951 and joined Mercury Records two years later. Seville made the UK Top 20 in 1956 under the name Alfi And Harry with 'The Trouble With Harry' (inspired by the film of the same name, in which he appeared), and he was successful again later that year with 'Armen's Theme' (inspired not by his Armenian descent but by his wife, singer Kay Armen). His biggest 'solo' hit came in 1958 with the transatlantic novelty smash 'Witch Doctor', which topped the US chart. He extended the idea of a speeded-up voice (as used on that hit) to produce a trio that he called the Chipmunks. They sold millions of records and had a top-rated cartoon televi-sion show before he retired them in 1967. After his death in 1972, his son Ross Jnr. brought back the Chipmunks and they have since enjoyed more success on both sides of the Atlantic.
● ALBUMS: *The Music Of David Seville* (Liberty 1957)★★★, *The Witch Doctor* (Liberty 1958)★★★.

SHAKE, RATTLE AND ROLL

Taking its title from a bestselling single by Bill Haley And The Comets, this 1956 'B' film attempted to capitalize on rock 'n' roll. In a plot that would quickly become overused, conservative adults attempt to ban the new music, but are challenged to a television trial by teenagers. R&B singer Joe Turner performs 'Lipstick, Powder And Paint' and 'Feelin' Happy', and Fats Domino adds 'Ain't That A Shame', 'Honey Chile' and 'I'm In Love Again'; otherwise, *Shake, Rattle And Roll* is largely forgettable. Clumsily scripted hip parlance - 'dig', 'dad', 'man' and 'the most' - renders the youths' arguments laughable, while the use of subtitles as translation verges on spiteful. It is difficult to imagine the motives behind director Edward Cahn's ideas, but the final sensation is of a film desperate to exploit a genre while apparently at the same time belittling it and its adherents.

SHARON, RALPH

b. 17 September 1923, London, England. Sharon came to prominence as pianist with the Ted Heath band in the years immediately after World War II. He also played, and sometimes recorded, with British bop musicians of the late 40s, including Ronnie Scott and Victor Feldman. In the early 50s he moved to the USA, became an American citizen, and continued to play piano in a variety of settings, frequently in distinguished company. He also established a reputation as a sympathetic accompanist to singers, notably Tony Bennett and Chris Connor. On one of his albums with Bennett, Sharon wrote arrangements for the Count Basie band, playing piano on most tracks, while on another album, three decades later, he arranged songs by Irving Berlin for his own small group, with added guests who included George Benson, Dexter Gordon and Dizzy Gillespie. Sharon's habitual diffidence has kept him hidden from the spotlight he clearly deserves. Among his early American recordings were some with his wife, the singer Sue Ryan. In the mid-90s he was regularly on the world's stages accompanying Tony Bennett.
● ALBUMS: *The Ralph Sharon Sextet i* (1955)★★★, *The Ralph Sharon Trio* (Bethlehem 1956)★★★, *Mr & Mrs Jazz* (Fresh Sounds 1956)★★, *The Ralph Sharon Sextet ii* (1957)★★★, *The Ralph Sharon Quartet* (1958)★★★, with Tony Bennett *Bennett/Basie* (1959)★★★, *Ralph Sharon With The Rolena Carter Chorale* (1962)★★★, *Do I Hear A Waltz* (Columbia 1965)★★★, with Bennett *Bennett/Berlin* (1987)★★★★, *The Magic Of George Gershwin* (Horatio Nelson 1988)★★★★, *The Magic Of Irving Berlin* (Horatio Nelson 1989)★★★★, *The Magic Of Cole Porter* (Horatio Nelson 1989)★★★★, *Portrait Of Harold* (DRG 1996)★★★.

SHELTON, ANNE

b. Patricia Sibley, 10 November 1923, Dulwich, London, England, d. 31 July 1994, East Sussex, England. One of the most important and popular of UK popular singers, Anne Shelton came to prominence as the 'Forces sweetheart' during World War II and remained a fondly regarded figure thereafter. She made her first BBC radio broadcast on 30 May 1940 in *Monday Night At Eight*, in which she sang 'Let The Curtain Come Down'. Her performance was heard by top UK bandleader Bert Ambrose, who signed her to sing with his band, and with whom she appeared on radio in *School Uniform*. Her own radio show, *Introducing Anne*, aimed mainly at British troops in the North African Desert, ran for four years, and she co-hosted *Calling Malta* with comedy actor Ronald Shiner; the programme was the only link with British troops on the island during the air bombardment and siege during the early months of 1942. In that same year, Shelton started her recording career, and in 1944 had an enormous hit with her signature tune, 'Lili Marlene', a German song that was equally popular with the armed forces of 'both sides', and to which UK songwriter Tommie Connor added an English lyric. Also in 1944, she was one of the UK 'guest' vocalists who sang in concerts and on broadcasts with the American Band of the Supreme Allied Command and the American Band of the Allied Expeditionary Force, directed by Glenn Miller. Shelton also worked on radio with Bing Crosby. She appeared in several films, a mixture of musicals and comedies, including *Miss London Ltd.*, *Bees In Paradise*, and *King Arthur Was A Gentleman* (each starring diminutive comedian Arthur Askey) and *Come Dance With Me* (with comedians Derek Roy and Max Wall).

After the war, she toured the UK variety circuit, and in 1949 updated her wartime hit by recording 'The Wedding Of Lilli Marlene'. In the same year she had two US hits with 'Be Mine' and 'Galway Bay', and in 1951, became the first British artist to tour the USA coast to coast, staying there for almost a year. In the UK she appeared extensively on radio and television during the 50s, and had several successful records, including 'I Remember The Cornfields', 'My Yiddishe Momma', 'Once In A While', ' I'm Praying To St. Christopher', 'Arrivederci Darling', 'Seven Days', 'Lay Down Your Arms' (a Swedish song with an English lyric by Paddy Roberts, which spent several weeks at the top of the UK chart), and 'Village Of Bernadette'. Her last chart entry, in 1961, was 'Sailor', a song of Austrian origin, which was a UK number 1 for Petula Clark. Albums around this time included *The Shelton Sound*, which contained impressive readings of standards such as 'Happiness Is Just A Thing Called Joe', 'Tangerine' and 'I'll Never Smile Again'. Throughout her career she worked with the cream of musical directors, including Percy Faith, Wally Stott, Stanley Black, George Melachrino, Frank Cordell, Ken Mackintosh, Robert Farnon, Reg Owen, David Rose, Jerry Gray and many more.

In later years Shelton continued to feature on television and tour various parts of the world, including the UK, Europe, USA and Hong Kong. In 1978 she appeared in cabaret when 1,200 US veterans revisited the the D-Day Normandy beaches, and in the following year, performed one of her most popular 40s songs, 'I'll Be Seeing You', in John Schlesinger's film *Yanks*, which starred Richard Gere. In 1980 she sang 'You'll Never Know' for the Queen Mother on the occasion of her 80th birthday, and during the rest of the decade took part in charity and reunion affairs in aid of the British Legion and British Services organizations. These included occasions such as the 40th anniversary of D-Day,

when she sang on UK television with a contemporary 'Glenn Miller' Band, and the 50th anniversary of the start of World War II. Anne Shelton also held the important post of Entertainments Officer for the Not Forgotten Association, which looks after disabled ex-servicemen and women from as far back as World War I. In 1990 she was awarded the OBE for services to the Association, and in the same year, her husband, Lieutenant Commander David Reid, died. They had met when she was only 17 years of age.

● ALBUMS: *Favourites Volumes 1 & 2* (Decca 1952)★★★★, *The Shelton Sound* (Philips 1958)★★★, *Songs From Her Heart* (Philips 1959)★★★, *Anne Shelton Showcase* (Philips 1961)★★★, *Anne* (Ace Of Clubs 1962)★★★, *Captivating Anne* (Encore 1962)★★★, *A Souvenir Of Ireland* (Philips 1962)★★★, *My Heart Sings* (Wing 1967)★★★, *Irish Singalong* (Fontana 1968)★★, *The World Of Anne Shelton* (Decca 1971)★★★★, *I'll Be Seeing You* (Decca 1977)★★★, *I'll Be There* (Decca 1977)★★★, *Anne Shelton's Sentimental Journey* (President 1982)★★★, *Sing It Again, Anne* (President 1983)★★, *Anne Shelton Sings With Ambrose And His Orchestra* (Recollections 1984)★★★, *Wartime Memories* (EMI 1993)★★★★, with Ambrose And His Orchestra *Let There Be Love* (1994)★★★, *Lili Marlene* (ASV Living Era 1995)★★★.

● COMPILATIONS: *The Anne Shelton Collection* (Encore 1979)★★★, *The Magic Of Anne Shelton* (MFP 1984)★★★, *EMI Years* (Capitol 1990)★★★★.

SHEPHERD SISTERS

A quartet consisting of sisters Martha, Mary Lou, Gayle and Judy Shepherd, this group is best remembered for the 1957 Top 20 hit 'Alone (Why Must I Be Alone)'. Hailing from Middletown, Ohio, USA, the girls sang in four-part harmony and were originally called the La-La Quartet when a booking agent discovered them. They were signed to the small Melba Records with no success. The label's owner, Morty Craft, next gave the sisters a song he had written, 'Alone', which he placed on his Lance label. The single, an upbeat, if melancholy, number, reached number 18 in the US chart and number 14 in the UK. The Shepherd Sisters recorded further singles for such labels as MGM and United Artists without any luck. 'Alone' was later covered by the Four Seasons, who had a moderate hit with it in the 60s.

SHIRLEY AND LEE

New Orleans-based duo Shirley Goodman (b. 19 June 1936, New Orleans, Louisiana, USA) and Leonard Lee (b. 29 June 1936, d. 23 October 1976) began recording together in 1952. Billed as the Sweethearts Of The Blues, they enjoyed a series of US R&B hits, including 'I'm Gone' (1952) and 'Feel So Good' (1955), marked by the juxtaposition between Shirley's shrill, childlike intonation and Lee's bluesy counterpart. In 1956 they crossed over into the US pop Top 20 with 'Let The Good Times Roll', a charming, infectious performance, written and arranged by Lee. The song became the first million-seller for the Aladdin label and is now regarded as an R&B standard. Shirley And Lee enjoyed minor hits with 'I Feel Good' (1956) and 'When I Saw You' (1957), before parting company in 1963. Shirley moved to the west coast, where she appeared on sessions for producer Harold Battiste and Dr. John, while Lee pursued a low-key solo career. His death in 1976 paradoxically coincided with Goodman's new-

found popularity as leader of Shirley And Company.
● ALBUMS: *Let The Good Times Roll* (Aladdin 1956)★★★, *Let The Good Times Roll* (Imperial 1962)★★★.
● COMPILATIONS: *Legendary Masters Shirley & Lee* (EMI 1974)★★★, *Happy Days* (Manhattan 1980)★★, *Respectfully Yours* (Manhattan 1980)★★, *The Best Of Shirley & Lee* (Ace 1982)★★★.

SHORE, DINAH

b. Frances Rose Shore, 1 March 1917, Winchester, Tennessee, USA, d. 24 February 1994, Los Angeles, California, USA. One of her country's most enduring all-round entertainers, Shore staked her first claim to fame while still at school, on Nashville radio. Further broadcasting and theatre engagements in New York soon followed. She recorded with Xaviar Cugat and Ben Bernie, and sang on some of Cugat's early 40s hits, such as 'The Breeze And I', 'Whatever Happened To You?', 'The Rhumba-Cardi' and 'Quierme Mucho (Yours)', initially under the name Dinah Shaw. Shore was one of the first vocalists to break free from the big bands (she had been rejected at auditions for Benny Goodman and Tommy Dorsey) and become a star in her own right. She became extremely popular on radio, and made her solo recording debut in 1939. Her smoky, low-pitched voice was especially attractive on slow ballads, and from 1940-57 she had a string of some 80 US chart hits, including 'Yes, My Darling Daughter', 'Jim', 'Blues In The Night', 'Skylark', 'You'd Be So Nice To Come Home To', 'Murder, He Says', 'Candy', 'Laughing On The Outside (Crying On The Inside)', 'All That Glitters Is Not Gold', 'Doin' What Comes Natur'lly', 'You Keep Coming Back Like A Song', 'I Wish I Didn't Love You So', 'You Do', 'Baby, It's Cold Outside' (with Buddy Clark), 'Dear Hearts And Gentle People', 'My Heart Cries For You', 'A Penny A Kiss', 'Sweet Violets', and number 1s with 'I'll Walk Alone', 'The Gypsy', 'Anniversary Song' and 'Buttons And Bows'.

She made a number of film appearances, including *Thank Your Lucky Stars* (1943), *Up In Arms* (1944), *Follow The Boys* (1944), *Belle Of The Yukon* (1945), *Till The Clouds Roll By* (1946) and *Aaron Slick From Punkin Crick* (1952). She also lent her voice to two Walt Disney animated features, *Make Mine Music* (1946) and *Fun And Fancy Free* (1957), and was last seen on the big screen in the George Burns comedy *Oh God!* (1977), and Robert Altman's quirky political satire *H.E.A.L.T.H.* (1979). In 1951 Shore began appearing regularly on television, making several spectaculars. Later, it was her continuing success on the small screen that brought about a career change when she became host on a highly rated daytime talk show, a role she maintained into the 80s. Her popularity on television barely declined throughout this period, and she won no less than 10 Emmys in all. The late 80s saw her performing on stage once more, though she returned to the television format for *Conversation With Dinah*, which ran from 1989-91.
● ALBUMS: *Dinah Shore Sings* 10-inch album (Columbia 1949)★★★, *Reminiscing* 10-inch album (Columbia 1949)★★★, *Bongo/Land Of The Lost* (Columbia 1950)★★, *Call Me Madam* 10-inch album (RCA Victor 1950)★★, *The King And I* 10-inch album (RCA Victor 1951)★★★, *Two Tickets To Broadway* 10-inch album (RCA Victor 1951)★★★, *Aaron Slick From Punkin Crick* film soundtrack (RCA Victor 1952)★★, *Dinah Shore Sings The Blues* 10-inch album (RCA

Victor 1953)★★★, with Buddy Clark *'SWonderful* (1953)★★★★, *The Dinah Shore TV Show* 10-inch album (RCA Victor 1954)★★, *Holding Hands At Midnight* (RCA Victor 1955)★★★, *Bouquet Of Blues* (RCA Victor 1956)★★★, *Moments Like These* (RCA Victor 1957)★★★, *Buttons And Bows* (1959)★★★★, *Dinah, Yes Indeed!* (Capitol 1959)★★★, with André Previn *Dinah Sings, Previn Plays* (Capitol 1960)★★★, *Lavender Blue* (Capitol 1960)★★★, with the Red Norvo Quintet *Dinah Sings Some Blues With Red* (Capitol 1960)★★★★, *Dinah, Down Home!* (Capitol 1962)★★★, *Fabulous Hits Newly Recorded* (Capitol 1962)★★★, *Lower Basin St. Revisted* (1965)★★★, *Make The World Go Away* (1987)★★★, *Oh Lonesome Me* (1988)★★★.
● COMPILATIONS: *Best Of Dinah Shore* (RCA 1981)★★★, *'Deed I Do (1942-1952)* (Hep Jazz 1988)★★★, *Dinah Shore's Greatest Hits* (Capitol 1988)★★★★, *The Capitol Years* (Capitol 1989)★★★★.
● FURTHER READING: *Dinah!*, B. Cassidy.
● FILMS: *Thank Your Lucky Stars* (1943), *Up In Arms* (1944), *Follow The Boys* (1944), *Belle Of The Yukon* (1945), *Till The Clouds Roll By* (1946), *Make Mine Music* (1946), *Aaron Slick From Punkin Crick* (1952), *Fun And Fancy Free* (1957), *Oh God!* (1977), *H.E.A.L.T.H.* (1979).

SHORT, BOBBY

b. Robert Waltrip, 15 September 1926, Danville, Illinois, USA. A self-taught pianist, Short worked in vaudeville as a child and sang in clubs and on radio in Chicago. In mid-1937 he went to New York where he played and sang for audiences unprepared for smart-suited sophistication from a pre-teenager. Short went back to school, but, influenced by the stylish performances of such nightclub artistes as Hildegarde, he continued to hone his act. When he returned to showbusiness he toured extensively, eventually spending some time on the west coast. By the early 50s he had matured into a sophisticated singer-pianist. Whether in Los Angeles, New York or Paris, he played the most exclusive nightclubs, establishing a reputation as a witty purveyor of songs. His vocal range is limited, and accordingly he sings with engaging restraint. His club appearances over the years at such places as the Café Carlyle and 21, have earned him a loyal following.
● ALBUMS: *Bobby Short Loves Cole Porter* (Atlantic 1952)★★★, *Songs By Bobby Short* (Atlantic 1955)★★★, *Bobby Short* (Atlantic 1956)★★★, *Speaking Of Love* (Atlantic 1958)★★★, *Sing Me A Swing Song* (Atlantic 1958)★★★, *The Mad Twenties* (Atlantic 1959)★★, *On The East Side* (Atlantic 1960)★★, *Songs Of New York Live At The Cafe Carlyle* (Telarc 1995)★★★★.
● FURTHER READING: *Black And White Baby*, Bobby Short. *The Life And Times Of A Saloon Slinger*, Bobby Short with Robert Mackintosh.

SIGNATURES

Formed in 1954 at the Servicemen's Center in Seattle, Washington, USA, the Signatures featured Cathi Hayes (lead), Lee Humes (tenor), Ruth Alcivar (alto), Jerry Hayes (baritone) and Bob Alcivar (bass). Their style, as well as being made notable by the presence of two female singers, was also distinguished by a pronounced lean towards jazz as well as doo-wop. They were also proficient on several instruments: Cathi Hayes (vibes), Ruth Alcivar (drums), Humes (bass), Bob Alcivar (piano) and Jerry Hayes (guitar). Their first major performance came in front of a big-band jazz ensemble created by local disc jockey Norm Bobrow, and thereafter, they continued to feature prominently on the jazz circuit. After a year of such pursuits the Hayes siblings were replaced by Bunny Phillips on lead, and multi-instrumentalist and former Four Freshmen member Hal Kratzsch as bass singer. Their recording debut came in July 1956, when an album was recorded for Whippet Records. The resulting collection sold steadily, as did the accompanying single 'Julie Is Her Name'. Engagements at prestigious New York jazz nightclubs followed, where Count Basie became a fan. He encouraged Morris Levy of Roulette Records to sign the still young band, but they stayed instead with an earlier mentor, Stan Kenton, who brought them to Warner Brothers Records. A second album attracted further good notices, and was used as the launch pad for coast to coast tours playing with prestigious jazz artists including Dizzy Gillespie. Phillips was replaced on lead by Dottie Dunn just as the album was released, and Don Purdy also stepped in for Humes. Their next project was a tribute album to Duke Ellington and Billy Strayhorn, but this was never completed. Instead, they issued *Prepared To Flip* before appearing at the Playboy Jazz Festival in Chicago. However, the advent of rock 'n' roll in the 60s proved to be their nemesis, and after several more tours they finally folded. Most of the ex-members retired to day jobs, though Cathi Hayes recorded a solo jazz album. Bob Alcivar and his wife Ruth moved to Los Angeles where he still works as a film composer and she as a painter.

● ALBUMS: *The Signatures, Their Voices And Instruments* (Whippet 1956)★★★, *The Signatures Sign In* (Warners 1959)★★★, *The Signatures - Prepared To Flip* (Warners 1959)★★★.

SILHOUETTES

Formed in 1956 in Philadelphia, Pennsylvania, USA, the Silhouettes recorded one of the classics of the doo-wop era of rock 'n' roll, 'Get A Job'. The song was written by tenor Rick Lewis when he was in the US Army, stationed in Germany. Upon returning home, Lewis joined a singing group called the Parakeets. He left them to front a band called the Gospel Tornadoes, comprising lead singer Bill Horton, bass singer Raymond Edwards and baritone Earl Beal. When the gospel group changed to secular music, it took on a new name, the Thunderbirds. A disc jockey, Kae Williams, signed the group to his own Junior Records in 1958 and 'Get A Job' was recorded as the b-side to the ballad 'I'm Lonely'. The group's name was changed to the Silhouettes and the record was released on the larger Ember label. 'Get A Job' received more attention than the ballad side and ultimately found its way to number 1 in the USA, becoming, in time, one of the best-known up-tempo doo-wop records. The nonsense phrase 'sha-na-na-na', part of its lyric, was borrowed in the late 60s by the rock 'n' roll revival group Sha Na Na. The Silhouettes recorded a number of follow-ups but never again returned to the charts. With numerous personnel changes, the group managed to stay afloat until 1968. Four original members reunited in 1980 and were still working the revival circuit in the early 90s.

● ALBUMS: *The Original And New Silhouettes - '58-'68 Get A Job* (1968)★★★.

SILK STOCKINGS (STAGE MUSICAL)

Cole Porter's final Broadway show was based on the 1939 film *Ninotchka*, which starred Greta Garbo. During the out-of-town try-outs, Abe Burrows' name was added to those of librettists George S. Kaufman and Leueen McGrath, and Kaufman was replaced as director by Cy Feur. *Silk Stockings* opened at the Imperial Theatre in New York on 24 February 1955. In this musical version of the by now familiar story, Ninotchka (Hildegarde Neff) is seduced by a glib Hollywood talent agent, Steve Canfield (Don Ameche), who is trying to persuade a famous Russian composer, Peter Ilyich Boroff (Philip Sterling), to expand his 'Ode To A Tractor' into the score for a ritzy movie version of *War And Peace*. The score was not top-drawer Porter by any means, but there were some worthwhile numbers, especially the gorgeous ballad 'All Of You', the amusing and contemporary 'Stereophonic Sound', and several more varied and entertaining items including 'Paris Loves Lovers', 'Without Love', 'It's A Chemical Reaction, That's All', 'Too Bad', 'Silk Stockings', 'The Red Blues', 'As On The Seasons We Sail', 'Satin And Silk', 'Josephine' and 'Siberia'. The show enjoyed a run of 478 performances and was filmed in 1957 with Fred Astaire and Cyd Charisse.

SILK STOCKINGS (FILM MUSICAL)

Two years after *Silk Stockings* began its successful run on Broadway, MGM released this screen version which reunited Fred Astaire with one of his most thrilling dancing partners, Cyd Charisse. Leonard Gershe and Leonard Spigelgass's screenplay was adapted from the show's libretto, which itself was based on the 1939 Greta Garbo movie *Ninotchka* and a story by Melchior Lengyel. The plot concerns a beautiful Russian emissary, Nina (Ninotchka), played by Charisse, who eventually falls for an American businessman (Astaire) after being sent to the USA in an effort to discover why three previous 'comrades' have failed to retrieve a Russian composer who is believed to be contemplating defection to the West. However, by then, the trio of messengers, Jules Munshin, Peter Lorre and Joseph Buloff, are themselves well on the way to capitulating to the capitalist way of life. Most of Cole Porter's songs from the stage show were retained and two new ones, 'Fated To Be Mated' and 'The Ritz Roll And Rock', added. The dancing, predictably, was 'out of this world', and Astaire was his usual charming vocal self on numbers such as 'All Of You', 'Paris Loves Lovers' and 'It's A Chemical Reaction, That's All' (with Charisse, dubbed by Carole Richards), and 'Stereophonic Sound' (with Janis Paige). Other numbers included 'Too Bad', 'Silk Stockings', 'Satin And Silk', 'Without Love', 'Josephine' and 'The Red Blues'. After helping themselves to generous portions of Western liquid hospitality, the three reluctant Reds, Munshin, Lorre and Buloff, are hilarious as they muse - musically - on the subject of 'Siberia'. *Silk Stockings*, which turned out to be Fred Astaire's last musical film (apart from the generally unsatisfactory *Finian's Rainbow*, made when he was nearly 70), was a fine affair. The choreographers were Hermes Pan and Eugene Loring (with Astaire, as usual, uncredited) and the director was Rouben Mamoulian. The musical director was André Previn, and the film was photographed in Metrocolor and Cinemascope.

SIMEONE, HARRY, CHORALE

b. 9 May 1911, Newark, New Jersey, USA. An arranger, conductor and composer, Simeone studied at the Juilliard School of Music, before working for CBS, where he was spotted by bandleader Fred Waring. He took him onto his staff as an arranger in 1939, and from there Simeone moved to Hollywood and worked for Paramount with the legendary composer-conductor Victor Young on several Bing Crosby movies, including *Here Come The Waves* and the 'Road' series with Hope and Lamour. In 1945 he rejoined Waring and became the editor of Waring's *Shawnee Press*. From 1952-59 he served as the conductor and chorale arranger for the popular weekly *Firestone Hour* on television. In 1958 Simeone released the chorale album *Sing We Now Of Christmas*, a collection of sacred songs and carols. It also contained 'The Little Drummer Boy', written by Simeone with Henry Onorati and Katherine Davis. The tune was taken from the Spanish song 'Tabolilleros'. Issued as a single, the Harry Simeone Chorale version entered the US charts each December for five consecutive years, from 1958-62. In the UK Top 20 there were additional versions by the Beverley Sisters and Michael Flanders in 1959, and in 1972 the songs was again successful in Britain in a version by the Pipes And Drums And Military Band Of The Royal Scots Guards. In 1970, estimated sales from some 150 versions were in the order of 25 million. The original *Sing We Now Of Christmas* was retitled *The Little Drummer Boy* in 1963, and remained in catalogues throughout the 80s.

● ALBUMS: *Sing We Now Of Christmas* aka *The Little Drummer Boy* (20th Century Fox 1958)★★★.

SINATRA, FRANK

b. Francis Albert Sinatra, 12 December 1915, Hoboken, New Jersey, USA. After working for a time in the office of a local newspaper, *The Jersey Observer*, Frank Sinatra decided to pursue a career as a singer. Already an admirer of Bing Crosby, he was impelled to pursue this course after attending a 1933 Crosby concert, and sang whenever and wherever he could, working locally in clubs and bars. Then, in 1935 he entered a popular US radio talent show, *Major Bowes Amateur Hour*. Also on the show was a singing trio, and the four young men found themselves teamed together by the no-nonsense promoter. The ad-hoc teaming worked, and the group, renamed 'The Hoboken Four', won first prize. Resulting from this came a succession of concert dates with the Major Bowes travelling show, along with club and occasional radio dates. By 1938 Sinatra was singing on several shows on each of a half-dozen radio stations, sometimes for expenses - often for nothing. The experience and, especially, the exposure were vital if he was to be recognized. Among the bands with which he performed was one led by songwriter Harold Arlen but in 1939, shortly after he married his childhood sweetheart, Nancy Barbato, he was heard and hired by Harry James, who had only recently formed his own big band. James recognized Sinatra's talent from the beginning and also identified the source of his determination to succeed, his massive self-confidence and powerful ego. During their brief association, James remarked to an interviewer, 'His name is Sinatra, and he considers himself the greatest vocalist in the business. Get that! No one's even heard of him! He's never had a hit record, and he looks like a wet rag, but he says he's the greatest.' In 1939 and early 1940 Sinatra made a number of records with James and began to develop a small following. His records with James included 'My Buddy' and 'All Or Nothing At All'.

In 1940 Sinatra was approached with an offer by Tommy Dorsey, then leading one of the most popular swing era bands. Only some six months had expired on Sinatra's two-year contract with James, who must have realized he was parting with a potential goldmine, but he was a generous-spirited man and let the singer go. Sinatra had many successful records with Dorsey including 'Polka Dots And Moonbeams', 'Imagination', 'Fools Rush In', 'I'll Never Smile Again', 'The One I Love', 'Violets For Your Furs', 'How About You?' and 'In The Blue Of Evening', some of which became fixtures in his repertoire. One record from this period became a major hit a few years later when the USA entered World War II. This song, recorded at Sinatra's second session with Dorsey in February 1940, was 'I'll Be Seeing You', and its lyric gained a special significance for servicemen, and the women they had left behind. Sinatra's popularity with the young female population, achieved despite, or perhaps because of, his gangling, unheroic and rather vulnerable appearance, prompted him to leave Dorsey and begin a solo career. In spite of the tough line taken by Dorsey over the remaining half of his five-year contract (Dorsey allegedly settled for 43% of the singer's gross over the next 10 years), Sinatra quit. Within months his decision proved to be right. He had become the idol of hordes of teenage girls, his public appearances were sell-outs and his records jostled with one another for hit status. In the early 40s he had appeared in a handful of films as Dorsey's vocalist, but by the middle of the decade he began appearing in feature films as an actor-singer. These included lightweight if enjoyable fare such as *Higher And Higher* (1944), *Anchors Aweigh* (1945), *It Happened In Brooklyn* (1947), *The Kissing Bandit* (1948) and *Double Dynamite* (1951). By the 50s, however, Sinatra's career was in trouble; both as a singer and actor, he appeared to have reached the end of the road. His acting had suffered in part from the quality of material he was offered, and had accepted. Nevertheless, it was his film career that was the first to recover when he landed the role of Angelo Maggio in *From Here To Eternity* (1953) for which he won an Academy Award as Best Supporting Actor. Thereafter, he was taken seriously as an actor even if he was rarely given the same standard of role or achieved the same quality of performance. He continued to make films, usually in straight acting roles, but occasionally in musicals. Among the former were *The Man With The Golden Arm* (1955), one of the roles that matched his breakthrough performance as Maggio, *Johnny Concho* (1956), *Kings Go Forth* (1958), *A Hole In The Head* (1959), *The Manchurian Candidate* (1962), *Von Ryan's Express* (1965), *Assault On A Queen* (1966), *Tony Rome* (1967) and *The Detective* (1968). His musicals included *Guys And Dolls* (1955), *High Society* (1956), *Pal Joey* (1957), *The Joker Is Wild* (1957), *Can-Can* (1960) and *Robin And The 7 Hoods* (1964). Later, he appeared in an above average television movie, *Contract On Cherry Street* (1977), and *The First Deadly Sin* (1980).

Soon after his Oscar-winning appearance in *From Here To Eternity*, Sinatra made a comeback as a recording artist. He had been recording for Columbia, where he fell out of step when changes were made to the company's musical policy, and in 1953 he was signed by Capitol Records. Sinatra's first session at Capitol was arranged and conducted by Axel Stordahl whom Sinatra had known in the Dorsey band. For the next session, however, he was teamed with Nelson Riddle. Sinatra had heard the results of earlier recording sessions made by Nat 'King' Cole at Capitol on which Riddle had collaborated. Sinatra was deeply impressed by the results and some sources suggest that on joining Capitol he had asked for Riddle. The results of this partnership set Sinatra's singing career firmly in the spotlight. Over the next few years classic albums such as *Songs For Young Lovers*, *This Is Sinatra*, *A Swingin' Affair*, *Come Fly With Me*, *Swing Easy*, *In The Wee Small Hours* and the exceptional *Songs For Swingin' Lovers* set standards for popular singers that have rarely been equalled and almost never surpassed. The two men were intensely aware of one another's talents and although critics were unanimous in their praise of Riddle, the arranger was unassumingly diffident, declaring that it was the singer's 'great talent that put him back on top'. For all Riddle's modesty, there can be little doubt that the arranger encouraged Sinatra's latent feeling for jazz, which helped to create the relaxed yet superbly swinging atmosphere that epitomized their work together. On his albums for Capitol, his own label Reprise, and other labels, sometimes with Riddle, other times with Robert Farnon, Neal Hefti, Gordon Jenkins, Quincy Jones, Billy May or Stordahl, Sinatra built upon his penchant for the best in American popular song, displaying a deep understanding of the wishes of composer and lyricist. Fans old and new bought his albums in their tens of thousands and several reached the top in the *Billboard* charts. The 1955 album *In The Wee Small Hours* was in the charts for 29 weeks, reaching number 2; the following year's *Songs For Swingin' Lovers* charted for 66 weeks, also reaching the second spot. *Come Fly With Me*, from 1958, spent 71 weeks in the charts, reaching number 1, and other top positions were attained by 1958's *Only The Lonely* (120 weeks), 1960's *Nice 'N' Easy* (86 weeks), and in 1966, *Strangers In The Night* (73) weeks. The title song from this latter album also made number 1 in *Billboard*'s singles charts, as did the following year's 'Something Stupid' on which he duetted with his daughter, Nancy Sinatra. At a time in popular music's history when ballads were not the most appealing form, and singers were usually in groups and getting younger by the minute, these represented no mean achievements for a middle-aged solo singer making a comeback. The secret of this late success lay in Sinatra's superior technical ability, his wealth of experience, his abiding love for the material with which he worked and the invariably high standards of professionalism he brought to his recordings and public performances. During his stint with Dorsey, the singer had taken a marked professional interest in the bandleader's trombone playing. He consciously learned breath control, in particular circular breathing, and the use of dynamics from Dorsey. Additionally, he employed Dorsey's legato style, which aided the smooth phrasing of his best ballad work. Complementing this, Sinatra's enjoyment of jazz and the company of jazz musicians prompted him to adopt jazz phrasing, which greatly enhanced his rhythmic style. More than any other popular singer of his or previous generations, Sinatra learned the value of delayed phrasing and singing behind the beat, and he and his arrangers invariably found exactly the right tempo. His relaxed rhythmic style contrasted strikingly with the stiffer-sounding singers

who preceded him. Even Crosby, whose popularity Sinatra eventually surpassed, later accommodated some of Sinatra's stylistic devices. (Crosby's habitual lazy-sounding style was of a different order from Sinatra's and until late in his career he never fully shook off his 2/4 style, while Sinatra, almost from the start, was completely comfortable with the 4/4 beat of swing.)

Sinatra's revived career brought him more attention even than in his heyday as the bobby-soxers' idol. Much of the interest was intrusive and led to frequently acrimonious and sometimes violent clashes with reporters. With much of what is written about him stemming from a decidedly ambivalent view, the picture of the man behind the voice is often confused. Undoubtedly, his private persona is multi-faceted. He has been described by acquaintances as quick-tempered, pugnacious, sometimes vicious and capable of extreme verbal cruelty, and he has often displayed serious lack of judgement in the company he has kept. In marked contrast, others have categorically declared him to be enormously generous to friends in need and to individuals and organizations he believes can benefit from his personal or financial support. His political stance has changed dramatically over the years and here again his judgement seems to be flawed. At first a Democrat, he supported Roosevelt and later Kennedy with enormous enthusiasm. His ties with the Kennedy clan were close, and not always for the best of reasons. Sinatra was unceremoniously dropped by the Kennedys following allegations that he had introduced to John Kennedy a woman who became simultaneously the mistress of the President of the United States and a leading figure in the Mafia. Sinatra then became a Republican and lent his support as fund-raiser and campaigner to Richard Nixon and Ronald Reagan, apparently oblivious to their serious flaws.

An immensely rich man, with interests in industry, real estate, recording companies, and film and television production, Sinatra chose to continue working, making frequent comebacks and presenting a never-ending succession of 'farewell' concerts, which, as time passed, became less like concerts and more like major events in contemporary popular culture. He continued to attract adoring audiences and in the late 80s and early 90s, despite being in his mid- to late seventies, could command staggering fees for personal appearances. In 1992, a two-part television biography, *Sinatra*, was transmitted in the USA, produced by Tina Sinatra, and starring Philip Casnoff in the leading role. Almost inevitably, it topped the weekly ratings. In 1993 Capitol Records re-signed Sinatra after 30 years with Reprise Records and announced a new album as 'the recording event of the decade'. *Duets* was a brilliant piece of marketing: it had Sinatra teamed with a varied all-star cast, including Aretha Franklin, Carly Simon, Barbra Streisand, Tony Bennett, Natalie Cole, Kenny G. and U2's Bono. A subsequent volume, *Duets II*, featuring artists such as Stevie Wonder, Antonio Carlos Jobim, Chrissie Hynde, Willie Nelson, Lena Horne, Gladys Knight and Patti LaBelle, was released in 1994. However, rumours of ill health persisted through 1996 and 1997, and although it was not confirmed, Alzheimer's disease was cited as the most likely condition.

When an assessment has to be made of his life, it is not the money or the worship of his fans that matters; neither is it the mixed quality of his film career and the uncertainties surrounding his personal characteristics and shortcomings. What really matters is that in his treatment of the classics from the Great American Songbook, Sinatra has made a unique contribution to 20th-century popular music. Despite an occasional lapse, when carefully crafted lyrics have been replaced with his own inimitable (yet all too often badly imitated) phrases, over several decades he fashioned countless timeless performances. There are some songs that, however many singers may have recorded them before or since Sinatra, or will record them in the future, have become inextricably linked with his name: 'I'll Walk Alone', 'It Could Happen To You', 'I'll Never Smile Again', 'Violets For Your Furs', 'How About You?', 'Jeepers Creepers', 'All Of Me', 'Taking A Chance On Love', 'Just One Of Those Things', 'My Funny Valentine', 'They Can't Take That Away From Me', 'I Get A Kick Out Of You', 'You Make Me Feel So Young', 'Old Devil Moon', 'The Girl Next Door', 'My One And Only Love', 'Three Coins In The Fountain', 'Love And Marriage', 'Swingin' Down The Lane', 'Come Fly With Me', 'Fly Me To The Moon', 'The Tender Trap', 'Chicago', 'New York, New York', 'Let Me Try Again', 'Night And Day', 'Here's That Rainy Day', 'Strangers In The Night', 'I Thought About You', 'Lady Is A Tramp', 'Anything Goes', 'All The Way', 'One For My Baby' and 'I've Got You Under My Skin'. Not all these songs are major examples of the songwriters' art, yet even on lesser material, of which 'My Way' is a notable example, he provides a patina of quality the songs and their writers may not deserve and that no one else could have supplied. Since the 70s Sinatra's voice has shown serious signs of decay. The pleasing baritone had given way to a worn and slightly rusting replica of what it once had been. Nevertheless, he sang on, adjusting to the changes in his voice and, as often as not, still creating exemplary performances of many of his favourite songs. In these twilight years he was especially effective in the easy-swinging mid-tempo he had always preferred and that concealed the inevitable vocal deterioration wrought by time.

In assessing Sinatra's place in popular music it is very easy to slip into hyperbole. After all, through dedication to his craft and his indisputable love for the songs he sang, Sinatra became the greatest exponent of a form of music that he helped to turn into an art form. In so doing, he became an icon of popular culture, a huge achievement for a skinny kid from Hoboken. Writing in the *Observer*, when Sinatra's retirement was thought, mistakenly, to be imminent, music critic Benny Green observed: 'What few people, apart from musicians, have never seemed to grasp is that he is not simply the best popular singer of his generation . . . but the culminating point in an evolutionary process which has refined the art of interpreting words set to music. Nor is there even the remotest possibility that he will have a successor. Sinatra was the result of a fusing of a set of historical circumstances which can never be repeated.' Sinatra himself has never publicly spoken of his work in such glowing terms, choosing instead to describe himself simply as a 'saloon singer'. Deep in his heart, however, Sinatra must know that Green's judgement is the more accurate and it is one that will long be echoed by countless millions of fans all around the world. Musically at least, it is a world better for the care that Frank Sinatra has lavished upon its popular songs.

● ALBUMS: *The Voice Of Frank Sinatra* 10-inch album (Columbia 1949)★★★, *Christmas Songs By Frank Sinatra* 10-inch album (Columbia 1950)★★★, *Frankly Sentimental* 10-inch album (Columbia 1951)★★★, *Songs By Sinatra, Volume 1* 10-inch album (Columbia 1951)★★★, *Dedicated To You* 10-inch album (Columbia 1952)★★★, *Sing And Dance With Frank Sinatra* 10-inch album (Columbia 1953)★★★, *I've Got A Crush On You* 10-inch album (Columbia 1954)★★★, *Songs For Young Lovers* 10-inch album (Capitol 1954)★★★★, *Swing Easy* 10-inch album (Capitol 1954)★★★★★, *In The Wee Small Hours* (Capitol 1955)★★★★★, *Songs For Swingin' Lovers!* (Capitol 1956)★★★★★, *High Society* film soundtrack (Capitol 1956)★★★★, *Frank Sinatra Conducts Tone Poems Of Colour* (Capitol 1956)★★★, *Close To You* (Capitol 1957)★★★★, *A Swingin' Affair!* (Capitol 1957)★★★★★, *Where Are You?* (Capitol 1957)★★★★, *Pal Joey* film soundtrack (Capitol 1957)★★★, *A Jolly Christmas From Frank Sinatra* (Capitol 1957)★★★, *Come Fly With Me* (Capitol 1958)★★★★★, *Frank Sinatra Sings For Only The Lonely* (Capitol 1958)★★★★★, *Come Dance With Me!* (Capitol 1959)★★★★★, *No One Cares* (Capitol 1959)★★★★, *Can-Can* film soundtrack (Capitol 1960)★★, *Nice 'N' Easy* (Capitol 1960)★★★★★, *Sinatra's Swinging Session!!!* (Capitol 1961)★★★★, *Ring-A-Ding Ding!* (Reprise 1961)★★★★, *Sinatra Swings* aka *Swing Along With Me* (Reprise 1961)★★★★, *Come Swing With Me!* (Capitol 1961)★★★★, *I Remember Tommy ...* (Reprise 1961)★★★, *Sinatra And Strings* (Reprise 1962)★★★★, *Point Of No Return* (Capitol 1962)★★★★, *Sinatra And Swingin' Brass* (Reprise 1962)★★★★★, *All Alone* (Reprise 1962)★★★★, with Count Basie *Sinatra-Basie* (Reprise 1963)★★★, *The Concert Sinatra* (Reprise 1963)★★★★★, *Sinatra's Sinatra* (Reprise 1963)★★★, *Days Of Wine And Roses, Moon River, And Other Academy Award Winners* (Reprise 1964)★★★, with Bing Crosby, Fred Waring *America I Hear You Singing* (Reprise 1964)★★, with Basie *It Might As Well Be Swing* (Reprise 1964)★★★, *Softly As I Leave You* (Reprise 1964)★★★, *Sinatra '65* (Reprise 1965)★★★, *September Of My Years* (Reprise 1965)★★★★★, *My Kind Of Broadway* (Reprise 1965)★★★, *Moonlight Sinatra* (Reprise 1965)★★★★, *A Man And His Music* (Reprise 1965)★★★★, *Strangers In The Night* (Reprise 1966)★★★, with Basie *Sinatra At The Sands* (Reprise 1966)★★★★, *That's Life* (Reprise 1966)★★★, with Antonio Carlos Jobim *Francis Albert Sinatra And Antonio Carlos Jobim* (Reprise 1967)★★★★, *Frank Sinatra (The World We Knew)* (Reprise 1967)★★, with Duke Ellington *Francis A. And Edward K.* (Reprise 1968)★★★, *Cycles* (Reprise 1968)★★★, *The Sinatra Family Wish You A Merry Christmas* (Reprise 1968)★★, *My Way* (Reprise 1969)★★★, *A Man Alone And Other Songs By Rod McKuen* (Reprise 1969)★★, *Watertown* (Reprise 1970)★★, with Antonio Carlos Jobim *Sinatra And Company* (Reprise 1971)★★★, *Ol' Blue Eyes Is Back* (Reprise 1973)★★★, *Some Nice Things I've Missed* (Reprise 1974)★★, *Sinatra - The Main Event Live* (Reprise 1974)★★★, *Trilogy: Past, Present, Future* (Reprise 1980)★★★, *She Shot Me Down* (Reprise 1981)★★, *LA Is My Lady* (Qwest 1984)★★, *Duets* (Capitol 1993)★★, *Sinatra And Sextet: Live In Paris* (Reprise 1994)★★★, *From Hoboken NJ To The White House* (1994)★★★, with Dean Martin *A Swingin' Night At The Sabre Room* (1994)★★★, *Old Gold Shows 1946* (1994)★★★, *Duets II* (Capitol 1994)★★.

● COMPILATIONS: *Frankie* (Columbia 1955)★★★, *That Old Feeling* (Columbia 1956)★★★, *This Is Sinatra!* (Capitol

1957)★★★★, *Adventures Of The Heart* (Columbia 1957)★★★, *This Is Sinatra, Volume 2* (Capitol 1958)★★★★, *The Frank Sinatra Story In Music* (Columbia 1958)★★★★, *Look To Your Heart* (Capitol 1958)★★★, *Put Your Dreams Away* (Columbia 1958)★★★, *Love Is A Kick* (Columbia 1958)★★★, *The Broadway Kick* (Columbia 1959)★★★, *Come Back To Sorrento* (Columbia 1959)★★★, *Reflections* (Columbia 1959)★★★, *All The Way* (Capitol 1961)★★★★, *Sinatra Sings ... Of Love And Things* (Capitol 1962)★★★★, *Tell Her You Love Her* (Capitol 1963)★★★, *Sinatra: A Man And His Music (1960-65)* (Reprise 1965)★★★★★, *The Essential Frank Sinatra, Volumes 1-3* (Columbia 1966)★★★★, *The Movie Songs (1954-60)* (Capitol 1967)★★★, *Greatest Hits - The Early Years* (Columbia 1967)★★★, *Frank Sinatra In Hollywood 1943-1949* (Columbia 1968)★★★, *Frank Sinatra's Greatest Hits!* (Reprise 1968)★★★★, *Frank Sinatra's Greatest Hits, Vol. 2* (Reprise 1972)★★★★, *The Dorsey/Sinatra Sessions, 1940-42* (RCA 1972)★★★★, *Round # 1* (Capitol 1974)★★★, *The Best Of Ol' Blue Eyes* (Reprise 1975)★★★★, *Classics* (Columbia 1977)★★★★, *Portrait Of Sinatra (400 Songs From The Life Of A Man)* (Reprise 1977)★★★★, *20 Golden Greats* (Capitol 1978)★★★★, *The Rare Sinatra* (Capitol 1978)★★★, *Screen Sinatra* (Capitol 1980)★★★, *20 Classic Tracks* (MFP 1981)★★★★, *The Dorsey/Sinatra Radio Years* (RCA 1983)★★★★, *Lena Horne And Frank Sinatra* (Astan 1984)★★★, *The Capitol Years* 20-LP box set (Capitol 1985)★★★, *Collection* (Castle 1986)★★★, *Now Is The Hour* (Castle 1986)★★★, *All-Time Classics* (Pair 1986)★★★★, *The Voice: The Columbia Years (1943-1952)* 6-LP box set (Columbia 1986)★★★★, *Sinatra: The Radio Years 1939 - 1955* (Meteor 1987)★★★, *Hello Young Lovers* (Columbia 1987)★★★, *Tommy Dorsey/Frank Sinatra All-Time Greatest Hits, Volumes 1-4* (RCA 1988-90)★★★★, *Sinatra Rarities* (Columbia 1988)★★★, *Rare Recordings 1935-70* (Sandy Hook 1989)★★★, *Capitol Collectors Series* (Capitol 1990)★★★★, *The Capitol Years* 3-CD box set (Capitol 1990)★★★★, *The Reprise Collection* 4-CD box set (Reprise 1990)★★★★, *Sinatra Reprise - The Very Good Years* (Reprise 1991)★★★★, *Gold Collection* (1993)★★★, *Sings The Songs Of Cahn And Styne* (1993)★★★★, *This Is Frank Sinatra 1953-57* (1994)★★★★, with Tommy Dorsey *The Song Is You* 5-CD box set (Columbia 1994)★★★★, *The Soundtrack Sessions* (Bravura 1994)★★★, *Two From Sinatra* (Capitol 1995)★★★, *The Columbia Years* (Sony 1995)★★★★, *Sinatra 80th: Live In Concert* (EMI 1995)★★★, *All The Best* 2-CD (EMI 1995)★★★★, *Swing And Dance With Frank Sinatra* (Legacy 1996)★★★★, *Sinatra Sings Rodgers And Hammerstein* (Legacy 1996)★★★, *The Complete Capitol Singles Collection* 4-CD box set (Capitol 1996)★★★★★, *My Way: The Best Of Frank Sinatra* (Reprise 1997)★★★.
● VIDEOS: *Old Blue Eyes* (World Of Video 1988), *A Man And His Music (1965)* (Braveworld 1990), *A Man And His Music Part II (1966)* (Braveworld 1990), *A Man And His Music + Ella + Jobim (1967)* (Braveworld 1990), *Francis Albert Sinatra Does His Thing (1968)* (Braveworld 1990), *Sinatra (1969)* (Braveworld 1990), *Sinatra In Concert: Royal Festival Hall (1970)* (Braveworld 1990), *Ol' Blue Eyes Is Back (1973)* (Braveworld 1990), *The Main Event: Madison Square Garden (1974)* (Braveworld 1990), *Sinatra And Friends (1977)* (Braveworld 1990), *Sinatra: The First 40 Years (1979)* (Braveworld 1990), *Sinatra: The Man And His Music (1981)*

(Braveworld 1990), *Concert For The Americas (1982)* (Braveworld 1990), *Sinatra In Japan (1985)* (Braveworld 1990), *His Way* (Polygram 1995), *My Way* (VCI 1997).
● FURTHER READING: *The Voice: The Story Of An American Phenomenon*, E.J. Kahn. *Sinatra And His Rat Pack: A Biography*, Richard Gehman. *Sinatra*, Robin Douglas-Home. *Sinatra: Retreat Of The Romantic*, Arnold Shaw. *The Films Of Frank Sinatra*, Gene Ringold. *Sinatra And The Great Song Stylists*, Ken Barnes. *Songs By Sinatra, 1939-1970*, Brian Hainsworth. *Frank Sinatra*, Paula Taylor. *On Stage: Frank Sinatra*, Harriet Lake. *Frank Sinatra*, Anthony Scaduto. *The Sinatra File: Part One*, John Ridgway. *Sinatra: An Unauthorized Biography*, Earl Wilson. *The Sinatra File: Part Two*, John Ridgway. *Sinatra*, Alan Frank. *The Revised Complete Sinatra: Discography, Filmography And Television Appearances*, Albert I. Lonstein. *Frank Sinatra*, John Howlett. *Sinatra In His Own Words*, Frank Sinatra. *The Frank Sinatra Scrapbook: His Life And Times In Words And Pictures*, Richard Peters. *Frank Sinatra: My Father*, Nancy Sinatra. *His Way: The Unauthorized Biography Of Frank Sinatra*, Kitty Kelly. *Frank Sinatra*, Jessica Hodge. *Frank Sinatra: A Complete Recording History*, Richard W. Ackelson. *The Recording Artistry Of Francis Albert Sinatra 1939-1992* , Ed O'Brien and Scott P. Sayers. *Frank Sinatra Reader: Seven Decades Of American Popular Music*, Steven Petkov and Leonard Mustazza (eds.). *Sinatra! The Song Is You: A Singer's Art*, Will Friedwald. *Sinatra: His Life And Times*, Fred Dellar.
● FILMS: *Major Bowes' Amateur Theatre Of The Air (1935)*, *Las Vegas Nights (1941)*, *Ship Ahoy (1942)*, *Reveille With Beverley (1943)*, *Higher And Higher (1943)*, *Step Lively (1944)*, *The Road To Victory (1944)*, *The House I Live In (1945)*, *Anchors Aweigh (1945)*, *The All Star Bond Rally (1945)*, *Till The Clouds Roll By (1946)*, *It Happened In Brooklyn (1947)*, *The Miracle Of The Bells (1948)*, *The Kissing Bandit (1948)*, *Take Me Out To The Ball Game (1949)*, *On The Town (1949)*, *Double Dynamite (1951)*, *Meet Danny Wilson (1952)*, *From Here To Eternity (1953)*, *Suddenly (1954)*, *Young At Heart (1955)*, *Not As A Stranger (1955)*, *The Tender Trap (1955)*, *Guys And Dolls (1955)*, *The Man With The Golden Arm (1955)*, *Meet Me In Las Vegas* cameo (1956), *Johnny Concho (1956)*, *High Society (1956)*, *Around The World In 80 Days* cameo (1956), *The Pride And The Passion (1957)*, *The Joker Is Wild (1957)*, *Pal Joey (1957)*, *Kings Go Forth (1958)*, *Some Came Running (1958)*, *A Hole In The Head (1959)*, *Invitation To Monte Carlo* travelogue (1959), *Never So Few (1959)*, *Can-Can (1960)*, *Ocean's Eleven (1960)*, *Pepe* cameo (1960), *The Devil At 4 O'Clock (1961)*, *Sergeants 3 (1962)*, *The Road To Hong Kong* cameo (1962), *The Manchurian Candidate (1962)*, *Sinatra In Israel (1962)*, *The List Of Adrian Messenger (1963)*, *Come Blow Your Horn (1963)*, *4 For Texas (1963)*, *Robin And The 7 Hoods (1964)*, *None But The Brave (1965)*, *Von Ryan's Express (1965)*, *Marriage On The Rocks (1965)*, *The Oscar* cameo (1966), *Cast A Giant Shadow (1966)*, *Assault On A Queen (1966)*, *The Naked Runner (1967)*, *Tony Rome (1967)*, *The Detective (1968)*, *Lady In Cement (1968)*, *Dirty Dingus Magee (1970)*, *That's Entertainment!* on-screen narrator (1974), *Contract On Cherry Street (1977)*, *The First Deadly Sin (1980)*, *Cannonball Run II (1984)*, *Who Framed Roger Rabbit?* voice of Singing Sword (1988), *Listen Up: The Lives Of Quincy Jones (1990)*.

SINGERS UNLIMITED

This vocal quartet originally started life as an extension of jazz band the Hi-Lo's. From that prominent 50s band came Don Shelton, who decided to form Singers Unlimited after the Hi-Lo's broke up in 1964. After retreating to Chicago, Illinois, USA, where he worked on a series of television commercials, he enlisted fellow Hi-Lo's veteran Eugene Thomas Puerling to join him in the city in 1967. The group was formed with the addition of Len Dresslar (ex-J's) and Bonnie Herman, with the express intention of recording commercials in the doo-wop/vocal group idiom. Shelton's connections in the industry ensured the group was able to exploit the market successfully, and lucrative work rolled in. However, the 30-second snatches of songs hardly satisfied their artistic ambitions, and when they found themselves with studio time left over after one session they recorded a take on the Beatles' 'Fool On The Hill'. Through visiting jazz pianist Oscar Peterson, the demo of the a cappella recording was passed to MPS Records. As a consequence the Singers Unlimited, as the group had christened themselves, found themselves with their own recording contract. An album of standards followed in 1972, with more John Lennon/Paul McCartney compositions, plus material plucked from Joni Mitchell's back catalogue, all performed in a technically precise but spirited doo-wop/a cappella idiom. While it hardly set the pop charts alight, the collection did receive one notable accolade, the German Record Grand Prix of 1973. A steady stream of albums has continued to be issued ever since to a loyal following, the best of which were on Verve Records in the mid-80s.

● ALBUMS: *A Cappella* (MPS 1972)★★★, *Eventide* (MPS 1978)★★★.

● COMPILATIONS: *A Cappella 1* (Polygram 1991)★★★.

SINGIN' IN THE RAIN

Regarded by many as the most entertaining film musical of all time, this MGM classic was released in 1952. Betty Comden and Adolph Green's witty screenplay parodies that momentous and painful period in Hollywood movie history when talkies took over from silent pictures. Don Lockwood (Gene Kelly) and Lina Lamont (Jean Hagen) are Monumental Studio's brightest silent stars. Lockwood, encouraged by his ex-dancing partner Cosmo Brown (Donald O'Connor), has no problem making the transition, while Lina's voice is so squeaky and sharp it could break glass. Luckily, aspiring actress Kathy Selden (Debbie Reynolds) pops out of a giant cake and provides a dubbing service - and Kelly's love interest. The team's first attempt at a sound film is a total disaster, but Kelly and O'Connor turn it into a musical, and, at the triumphant premiere, Reynolds is revealed as the hidden starlet, while Hagen is hilariously disgraced. *Singin' In The Rain* is indeed one of the greatest film musicals of all time, and its comedy exists apart from, and within, the musical numbers. The scenes poking fun at the changeover to sound are very effective, particularly when irate director Roscoe Dexter (Douglas Fowley) is attempting to place Hagen's microphone in a strategic position, desperate to find a place on the set ('It's in the bush!') or on her person where a consistent level of sound can be obtained. Most of the score consisted of a collection of songs written by Arthur Freed and Nacio Herb Brown for early MGM musicals, and every one of them is performed brilliantly. O'Connor is marvellously athletic and funny on 'Make 'Em Laugh' (most critics noted the similarities with Cole Porter's 'Be A Clown'), and on two duets with Kelly, 'Fit As A Fiddle' (Al Goodhart-Al Hoffman) and 'Moses Supposes' (Roger Edens-Comden-Green). Reynolds joins both of them for the uplifting 'Good Morning', and then, just with Kelly, milks the lovely 'You Were Meant For Me' for all its worth. Other highlights include the spectacular 'Broadway Ballet' which is presented as part of the film within a film featuring Cyd Charisse and Kelly, and 'All I Do Is Dream Of You', 'Beautiful Girl', 'I've Got A Feelin' You're Foolin'', 'Should I' and 'Would You?'. However, the moment from the film people always remember, and the clip that most frequently crops up in nostalgia programmes, is the one in which Kelly splashes around in the teeming rain, viewed by a rather bemused and soaking-wet policeman, creating a truly memorable moment from a memorable film. The film was photographed in Technicolor by Harold Rosson and produced by Arthur Freed's MGM unit; the director-choreographers were Gene Kelly and Stanley Donen.

In 1983 Comden and Green adapted the film into a stage musical that ran at the London Palladium for over three years, breaking all theatre records. It starred Tommy Steele (who also directed), Roy Castle, Sarah Payne and Danielle Carson, and featured several additional songs. A 1985 Broadway production failed to recover its costs. Ten years later, Steele directed a highly successful UK revival tour, with Paul Nicholas in the leading role.

SINGS FOR ONLY THE LONELY - FRANK SINATRA ★★★★★

Asked to reveal the mood of this album prior to its release in 1958, Frank Sinatra (tongue-in-cheek) said: 'Put it this way - we discarded "Gloomy Sunday" [the 'suicide' song] because it was too swingin'!' Bleak, it certainly is, but with the singer at the height of his powers, singing a classy set of saloon songs, superbly arranged and conducted by Nelson Riddle, this is still the number 1 album of all time for many a Sinatra aficionado. Even into the 90s Sinatra was compelled to include one of the tracks, 'One For My Baby', complete with its distinctive piano introduction, in every concert performance. The album's cover, with its sad clown-face picture, won a Grammy Award, and it also topped the US album charts, reaching number 5 in the UK.

● TRACKS: *Only The Lonely; Angel Eyes; What's New?; It's A Lonesome Old Town; Willow Weep For Me; Good-bye; Blues In The Night; Guess I'll Hang My Tears Out To Dry; Ebb Tide; Spring Is Here; Gone With The Wind; One For My Baby.*

6.5 SPECIAL

BBC Television's *6.5 Special*, so-called after the time it was screened, was one of the first British attempts at a pop-based television show. The opening 'train' credits are fixed in the mind of a generation of rock music aficionados. Producer Jack Good used informal camera angles and unconventional methods to invest the show with a sense of spontaneity and movement, and although staid in comparison with its immediate successors, *Oh Boy* and *Boy Meets Girl*, *6.5 Special* began to link music's aural excitement with complementary visual effects. The show's success inspired this 1957 feature, which simply repeated the formula for the big screen. In keeping with its television counterpart, the film contained many acts of questionable quality, including MOR-styled singers Dickie Valentine, Petula Clark and Joan Regan. Comperes Pete Murray and Josephine Douglas did introduce a handful of home-grown, but polite, rock 'n' roll acts, Jim Dale, the King Brothers and the kilt-wearing Jackie Dennis, but their contributions were overtly sanitized. One of the brightest moments was provided by skiffle king Lonnie Donegan, while studio house band Don Lang And His Frantic Five injected a measure of pulse into the proceedings. Better still were the superb John Barry Seven, but *6.5 Special* is recalled for the doors it opened, rather than this film. It does, however, document the sterile nature of British 50s pop and helps to explain why Good later left for the USA.

SKIP AND FLIP

This US pop duo, Skip Battin (b. Clyde Battin, 2 February 1934, Galipolis, Ohio, USA) and Flip (b. Gary S. Paxton, Mesa, Arizona, USA), met while attending the University of Arizona in the late 50s. Once known as the Rockabillies, they recorded on Rev as the Pledges and then as Gary & Clyde. Time Records picked up their Rev master, 'Why Not Confess'/'Johnny Risk', and then moved them to its Brent label, with the more distinctive name Skip And Flip. Their recording of Paxton's song 'It Was I' entered the US Top 20 in 1959 and the follow-up, 'Fancy Nancy', also charted. Their next release, a revival of Marvin And Johnny's R&B hit 'Cherry Pie' made the Top 20 but proved to be their last chart entry together. Paxton has since recorded under several names (including the chart-topping Hollywood Argyles) for many labels. He has also had hits as a producer and label owner, including the two-time charter 'Monster Mash', by Bobby 'Boris' Pickett. Paxton went into country music in the 70s and is now a noted personality in the gospel music world. Battin recorded on Indigo, May, Groove, Audicon and Signpost and played in the Byrds, New Riders Of The Purple Sage and the Flying Burrito Brothers.

SKYLARKS

This vocal group was formed in 1942 when four army servicemen in Panama started touring together. The group consisted of Bob Sprague (first tenor), Harry Gedicke (second tenor), Harry Shuman (baritone) and George Becker (lead). When the war ended the group returned to Detroit, Michigan, where Gilda Maiken joined as lead singer. Band leader Woody Herman invited the group to join his orchestra and they made their debut recording with Herman in 1946 with 'Stars Fell On Alabama'. While in New York the Herman Orchestra broke up, but the Skylarks then met Bing Crosby, with whom they recorded two singles, 'Ko Ko Mo Indiana' and 'Chaperone'. Afterwards they joined Jimmy Dorsey's orchestra and made several recordings for MGM before that orchestra broke up too. Undeterred, they moved to California where they were hired by the bandleader and trumpet player Harry James. With trombonist Russ Morgan, the Skylarks had two number 1 singles with 'Crusin' Down The River' and 'Forever And Ever'. Following this they played live with Frank Sinatra, Danny Kaye, Dinah Shore, Dean Martin and others, although by this time only Maiken and Becker remained of the original formation. The replacements for Gedicke, Shuman and Sprague were Joe Hamilton, Earl Brown and Jackie Gershwin. In the 50s the

Skylarks signed a new contract with RCA Records and reached number 28 with 'I Had The Craziest Dream', taken from the film *Springtime In The Rockies*. Jackie Gershwin replaced Carol Lombard as lead. From the 50s television shows of Danny Kaye and Dinah Shore they progressed to Sonny And Cher's 60s shows. The band finally broke up in 1979 with a farewell appearance at the Hollywood Palladium.

SLADE, JULIAN

b. 28 May 1930, London, England. A composer, lyricist, librettist and pianist, Slade began to write when he was at Cambridge University, and his first two musicals, *The Meringue* and *Lady May*, were presented by the Cambridge Amateur Dramatic Club. He then went to the Bristol Old Vic Theatre School, and in 1952 was invited by Denis Carey to join the company as a minor role actor and musical director. In the same year he composed the music for a highly successful version of Sheridan's *The Duenna*, and it was at Bristol that he met Dorothy Reynolds, a leading actress, who collaborated with him on libretto and lyrics. Their long association began with *Christmas In King Street* and *The Merry Gentlemen*, written for the Theatre Royal, Bristol, and then, in 1954, *Salad Days*, which transferred to the Vaudeville Theatre in London. It continued to delight audiences until 1960, becoming the longest-running British musical of its era. Slade played the piano in the pit for the first 18 months, while onstage, a magic piano in a London park caused passers-by to dance uncontrollably. The piece was typical Slade - a simple plot and inconsequential humour, accompanied by charming, hummable songs, such as 'We Said We Wouldn't Look Back', 'I Sit In The Sun', 'It's Easy To Sing', 'The Time Of My Life' and 'Cleopatra'. In 1956, *The Comedy Of Errors*, a comic operetta adapted from Shakespeare's play, for which Slade wrote the music, played a season at the Arts Theatre. It had originally been performed on BBC Television two years earlier. In 1957, Slade and Reynolds wrote *Free As Air*, which lasted for over a year. This was succeeded by *Follow That Girl*, *Hooray For Daisy* and *Wildest Dreams*, which even contained a 'rock' number. However, these shows seemed out of place in the theatre of the 'angry young men'. 'Our shows went well out of town, but London didn't seem to want them', Slade recalled. *Vanity Fair*, with lyrics by Roger Miller, faded after 70 performances at the Queen's Theatre, and Slade's first solo effort, *Nutmeg And Ginger* (1963), based on Francis Beaumont's 1609 comedy, *The Knight Of The Burning Pestle*, did not play the West End. Neither did some of the others, such as *The Pursuit Of Love* and *Out Of Bounds* (1973), although *Trelawney* (1972) stayed at the Prince of Wales Theatre for over six months. Slade received his warmest reviews for that show, the last time London saw his work until 1991, when a revival of his *Nutmeg And Ginger* opened to enthusiastic reviews on the Fringe, at the Orange Tree Theatre in Richmond, Surrey, England.

SLIM WHITMAN FAVORITES - SLIM WHITMAN ★★★★

This 1956 album remains a classic of its time, despite the cover portrait of Slim Whitman, which is even worse than Bob Dylan's 'Self-Portrait'. Nevertheless, long-playing records were still a novelty in 1956, so the fans were grateful for anything (Bob Dylan had no similar excuse). This collection included the original versions of Whitman's chief successes, 'Indian Love Call' and 'Rose Marie', both from the operetta *Rose Marie*. Whitman's yodelling on 'Love Song Of The Waterfall' still sounds remarkable and the combination of his tenor voice with Hoot Rains' steel guitar created many memorable tracks. According to Whitman, Paul McCartney was so impressed at seeing him play the guitar left-handed in the 50s at the Liverpool Empire that he followed his style, but Whitman is a southpaw guitarist, having lost part of a finger in an accident.

● TRACKS: *Beautiful Dreamer; I Went To Your Wedding; Marjie; I Remember You; Carolina Moon; Oh My Darlin (I Love You); Just An Echo In The Valley; If I Had My Life To Live Over; Silver Haired Daddy Of Mine; Ghost Riders In The Sky; Edelweiss; Take Good Care Of Her; Secret Love; Can't Help Falling In Love; When You Wore A Tulip; You Are My Sunshine; Rose Marie; Mr. Songman; Goodbye Little Darlin' Goodbye; Where Did Yesterday Go?; Indian Love Call; Love Song Of The Waterfall.*

SMITH, HUEY 'PIANO'

b. 26 January 1934, New Orleans, Louisiana, USA. Pianist Smith drew his pulsating style from a variety of musical sources, including the boogie-woogie of Albert Ammons and jazz of Jelly Roll Morton. Having served in bands led by Earl King and Eddie 'Guitar Slim' Jones, Smith became a respected session musician before embarking on an independent recording career. Leading his own group, the Clowns, which at its peak included Gerry Hall, Eugene Francis, Billy Roosevelt and vocalist Bobby Marchan, he achieved two million-selling singles in 1957 with 'Rockin' Pneumonia And The Boogie Woogie Flu' and 'Don't You Just Know It'. Both releases showcased classic New Orleans rhythms as well as the leader's vibrant, percussive technique. The pianist was also featured on 'Sea Cruise', a 1959 smash for Frankie Ford, whose speeded-up vocal was overdubbed onto an existing Clowns tape. However, despite other excellent releases, Huey Smith did not enjoy another substantial hit and, having become a Jehovah's Witness, forsook music in favour of preaching.

● ALBUMS: *Having A Good Time* (Imperial 1959)★★★, *For Dancing* (Imperial 1961)★★, *T'was The Night Before Christmas* (Imperial 1962)★★, *Rock 'N' Roll Revival* (Imperial 1963)★★★.

● COMPILATIONS: *Rockin' Pneumonia And The Boogie Woogie Flu* (1965)★★★, *Huey 'Piano' Smith's Rock And Roll Revival* (1974)★★★, *Rockin' Pneumonia And The Boogie Woogie Flu* different from previous entry (Ace 1979)★★★, *Rockin' And Jivin'* (Charly 1981)★★★, *The Imperial Sides 1960/1961* (Pathe Marconi 1984)★★★, *Somewhere There's Honey For The Grizzly* (Ace 1984)★★★, *Serious Clownin' - The History Of Huey 'Piano' Smith And The Clowns* (Rhino 1986)★★★★, *Pitta Pattin'* (Charly 1987)★★★.

SMITH, KEELY

b. Dorothy Smith, 9 March 1932, Norfolk, Virginia, USA. Smith was a jazzy singer who worked with her husband, bandleader Louis Prima. She made her professional debut in 1950, joining Prima three years later. As well as her solo spots with the big band, she frequently duetted with Prima on stylized versions of well-known songs. In 1958, one of

these, Johnny Mercer and Harold Arlen's 'That Old Black Magic' became a surprise US Top 20 hit. The duo followed up with the minor successes 'I've Got You Under My Skin' and 'Bei Mir Bist Du Schoen', a revival of the 1937 Andrews Sisters hit. Smith appeared with Prima in the movie *Hey Boy, Hey Girl* (1959), singing 'Fever', and she also sang on the soundtrack of *Thunder Road* (1958). In the early 60s, Smith separated from Prima and signed to Reprise, where her musical director was Nelson Riddle. In 1965, she had Top 20 hits in the UK with an album of Beatles compositions and a version of 'You're Breaking My Heart'.

● ALBUMS: *I Wish You Love* (Capitol 1957)★★, with Louis Prima *Las Vegas-Prima Style* (Capitol 1958)★★★★, *Politely!* (Capitol 1958)★★★★, with Prima *Hey Boy! Hey Girl!* film soundtrack (Capitol 1959)★★★★, with Prima *Louis And Keely!* (Dot 1959)★★★, with Prima *Senior Prom* (1959)★★★, *Swingin' Pretty* (Capitol 1959)★★★, with Prima *Together* (Dot 1960)★★★, with Prima *On Stage* (Dot 1960)★★★, *Be My Love* (Dot 1960)★★★, *Swing, You Lovers* (Dot 1960)★★★, with Prima *Return Of The Wildest* (Dot 1961)★★★, *Dearly Beloved* (Dot 1961)★★★, *A Keely Christmas* (Dot 1961)★★, *Twist With Keely Smith* (Dot 1962)★★, *Because You're Mine* (Dot 1962)★★★, *Cherokeely Swings* (Dot 1962)★★, *What Kind Of Fool Am I* (Dot 1962)★★★, *Little Girl Blue, Little Girl New* (Reprise 1963)★★★, *The Lennon-McCartney Songbook* (Reprise 1964)★★, *The Intimate Keely Smith* (Reprise 1964)★★★, *That Old Black Magic* (Reprise 1965)★★★.

● COMPILATIONS: with Louis Prima *Hits* (Capitol 1961)★★★★, *Spotlight On Keely Smith* (Capitol 1995)★★★★.

SNOW, HANK

b. Clarence Eugene Snow, 9 May 1914, Brooklyn, near Liverpool, Nova Scotia, Canada. After his parents divorced when he was eight years old, Snow spent four unhappy years with his grandmother, finally running away to rejoin his mother when she remarried. However, he was cruelly mistreated by his stepfather, which prompted him to abscond again. Though only 12 years old, he went to sea and spent the next four years working on fishing boats in the Atlantic where, on several occasions, he almost lost his life. An early interest in music, gained from his mother who had been a pianist for silent films, led him to sing for fellow crew members. On his return home, he worked wherever he could but at the same time seeking a singing career. He gained great inspiration listening to his mother's recordings of Jimmie Rodgers, and, acquiring a cheap guitar, he practised Rodgers' blue yodel, guitar playing and delivery, and set out to emulate his idol. He began to sing locally and eventually, through the help of Cecil Landry, the station announcer and chief engineer, he obtained a weekly unpaid spot on CHNS Halifax on a programme called *Down On The Farm*, where he became known as 'Clarence Snow and his Guitar' and 'The Cowboy Blue Yodeller'. It was Landry who, in 1934, first suggested the name of Hank, since he thought the boy needed a good western name. Snow became a talented guitarist and in the following years always played lead guitar for his own recordings. He met and married his wife Minnie in 1936 and the couple struggled to overcome financial hardship; eventually through sponsorship, he was given a programme on the network *Canadian Farm Hour*. In

October 1936, by now known as 'Hank the Yodelling Ranger', he persuaded Hugh Joseph of RCA Victor, Montreal, to allow him to record two of his own songs, 'Lonesome Blue Yodel' and 'The Prisoned Cowboy'. This marked the start of a recording career destined to become the longest that any one country artist ever spent with the same record company. Rodgers' influence remained with him and when Snow's only son was born in 1937, he was named Jimmie Rodgers Snow. In 1944, after further recordings and regular work in Canada, and having become 'Hank The Singing Ranger' (owing to the fact that as his voice deepened he found he could no longer yodel), he extended his career to the USA. He played various venues, including the *Wheeling Jamboree*, and worked in Hollywood, usually appearing with his performing horse, Shawnee. However, the anticipated breakthrough did not materialize; RCA, New York informed him that they could not record him until he was known in America, but eventually they relented and in 1949 his recording of 'Brand On My Heart' brought him success in Texas. In December 1949, he achieved his first minor country chart hit with 'Marriage Vow'. At the recommendation of fellow Jimmie Rodgers devotee Ernest Tubb, he made his debut on the *Grand Ole Opry* in January 1950; he did not make a great impression and seriously considered abandoning thoughts of a career in the USA. This idea was forgotten when his self-penned million-seller, 'I'm Moving On', established him for all time. It spent 44 weeks on the US country charts, 21 at number 1 and even reached number 27 on the US pop charts. In the late 40s, Snow worked on tours with Hank Williams, later stating, 'I found Hank to be a fine person but the stories about him have been blown completely out of proportion. Take it from me, Hank Williams was okay'. Williams can be heard introducing Snow on the 1977 *A Tribute To Hank Williams*. Snow formed a booking agency with Colonel Tom Parker and in 1954, they were responsible for Elvis Presley's only *Opry* performance. Presley sang 'Blue Moon Of Kentucky', but failed to make any impression on the audience that night. Parker, to Snow's chagrin, took over Presley's management, but Presley recorded material associated with Snow, including 'A Fool Such As I', 'Old Shep' and later, 'I'm Movin' On'. 'I don't mean to brag but Elvis was a big fan of mine and he was always sitting around singing my songs', says Snow. After his initial breakthrough, Snow became an internationally famous star whose records sold in their millions, and between 1950 and 1980, he amassed 85 country chart hits. Further number 1 records were 'The Golden Rocket', 'I Don't Hurt Anymore', 'Let Me Go, Lover', 'Hello Love' and the tongue-twisting 'I've Been Everywhere'. The last, which gave him his second million-seller, was an Australian song originally naming Australian towns, but Snow requested that the writer change it to appeal to Americans. He was later proud to state he recorded it on the sixth take, in spite of the fact that there were 93 place names to memorize. Hank Snow's penchant for wearing a toupee that does not always appear to fit correctly has at times caused mirth, and many people believe he deliberately emphasizes it. Legend has it that, as a joke for the audience, one night on stage his fiddler player removed it with his bow and, understandably, received instant dismissal from his boss. Some album sleeves clearly show the toupee; others, such as *My Nova Scotia Home*, are most beautiful designs, while the noose on *Songs Of Tragedy*

easily makes it one of the most remembered. It is generally assumed that the character played by Henry Gibson in Robert Altman's controversial 1975 film *Nashville* was modelled on Snow. Over the years his melodic voice, perfect diction and distinctive guitar playing make his recordings immediately identifiable, and his band, the Rainbow Ranch Boys, has always contained some of country music's finest musicians. His songwriting gained him election to the Nashville Songwriters' International Hall Of Fame in 1978 and the following year he was inducted into the Country Music Hall Of Fame, the plaque rightly proclaiming him as one of country music's most influential entertainers. In 1981, after a 45-year association, he parted company from RCA, stating it was 'because I would not record the type of things that are going today'. Snow has not recorded since, feeling that 'I have done everything in the recording line that was possible'. He resisted over-commercializing country music during his long career and says of the modern scene that '80% of today's would be country music is a joke and not fit to listen to - suggestive material and a lot of it you can't even understand the words, just a lot of loud music'. Snow has played in many countries all over the world, being a particular favourite in the UK. An ability to handle all types of material has led to him being classed as one of the most versatile country artists in the music's history. In memory of his own unhappy childhood, he set up a foundation in Nashville to help abused children. He rarely tours now but maintains his regular *Opry* appearances and is still readily recognizable by his flamboyant stage costumes, which have been his hallmark over the years.

● ALBUMS: *Hank Snow Sings* 10-inch album (RCA Victor 1952)★★★★, *Country Classics* 10-inch album (RCA Victor 1952)★★★★, *Hank Snow Salutes Jimmie Rodgers* 10-inch album (RCA Victor 1953)★★★★, *Country Guitar* 10-inch album (RCA Victor 1954)★★★, *Just Keep A-Moving* (RCA Victor 1955)★★★★, *Old Doc Brown & Other Narrations* (RCA Victor 1955)★★★, *Country & Western Jamboree* (RCA Victor 1957)★★★, *Hank Snow Sings Sacred Songs* (RCA Victor 1958)★★, *The Hank Snow E-Z Method of Spanish Guitar* (School Of Music 1958)★, *When Tragedy Struck* (RCA Victor 1958)★★★, *Hank Snow Sings Jimmie Rodgers Songs* (RCA Victor 1959)★★★★, *The Singing Ranger* (RCA Victor 1959)★★★, *Hank Snow's Souvenirs* (RCA Victor 1961)★★★, *Big Country Hits (Songs I Hadn't Recorded Till Now)* (RCA Victor 1961)★★★, *The Southern Cannonball* (RCA Victor 1961)★★★★, *One & Only Hank Snow* (RCA Camden 1962)★★★, with Anita Carter *Together Again* (RCA Victor 1962)★★★, *Railroad Man* (RCA Victor 1963)★★★★, *I've Been Everywhere* (RCA Victor 1963)★★★★, *The Last Ride* (RCA Camden 1963)★★★, *More Hank Snow Souvenirs* (RCA Victor 1964)★★★, *Old & Great Songs by Hank Snow* (RCA Camden 1964)★★★, *Songs Of Tragedy* (RCA Victor 1964)★★★, with Chet Atkins *Reminiscing* (RCA Victor 1964)★★★, *Gloryland March* (RCA Victor 1965)★★★, *Heartbreak Trail - A Tribute To The Sons Of The Pioneers* (RCA Victor 1965)★★★, *The Highest Bidder And Other Favorites* (RCA Camden 1965)★★★, *Your Favorite Country Hits* (RCA Victor 1965)★★★, *Gospel Train* (RCA Victor 1966)★★★, *The Guitar Stylings Of Hank Snow* (RCA Victor 1966)★★, *This Is My Story* (RCA Victor 1966)★★★, *Gospel Stylings* (RCA Victor 1966)★★, *Travelin' Blues* (RCA Camden 1966)★★★, *Spanish Fireball* (RCA Victor 1967)★★, *My*

Early Country Favorites (RCA Camden 1967)★★★, *Snow In Hawaii* (RCA Victor 1967)★★★, *Christmas With Hank Snow* (RCA Victor 1967)★★★, *My Nova Scotia Home* i (RCA Victor 1967)★★★, *My Nova Scotia Home* ii (RCA Victor 1968)★★★, *Lonely And Heartsick* (RCA Victor 1968)★★★, *Somewhere Along Life's Highway* (RCA Victor 1968)★★★, *Tales of The Yukon* (RCA Victor 1968)★★★, *I Went To Your Wedding* (RCA Victor 1969)★★★, *Snow In All Seasons* (RCA Victor 1969)★★★, *Hits Covered By Snow* (RCA Victor 1969)★★★, *Cure For The Blues* (RCA Victor 1970)★★★, *Hank Snow Sings In Memory Of Jimmie Rodgers* (RCA Victor 1970)★★★★, *Memories Are Made Of This* (RCA Victor 1970)★★★, with Chet Atkins *C.B. Atkins & C.E. Snow By Special Request* (RCA Victor 1970)★★★, *Wreck Of The Old 97* (RCA Camden 1971)★★★, *Award Winners* (RCA Victor 1971)★★★, *Tracks & Trains* (RCA Victor 1971)★★★, *Lonesome Whistle* (RCA Victor 1972)★★★, *The Jimmie Rodgers Story* (RCA Victor 1972)★★★★, *Legend Of Old Doc Brown* (RCA Victor 1972)★★★, *Snowbird* (RCA Victor 1973)★★★, *When My Blue Moon Turns To Gold Again* (RCA Victor 1973)★★★, *Grand Ole Opry Favorites* (RCA Victor 1973)★★★, *Hello Love* (RCA Victor 1974)★★★, *I'm Moving On* (RCA Victor 1974)★★★, *Now Is The Hour - For Me To Sing To My Friends In New Zealand* (RCA Victor 1974)★★★, *That's You And Me* (RCA Victor 1974)★★★, *You're Easy To Love* (RCA Victor 1975)★★★, *All About Trains* one side Jimmie Rodgers (RCA Victor 1975)★★★★, with Rodgers *Live From Evangel Temple* (1976)★★★, *#104 - Still Movin' On* (RCA Victor 1977)★★★, *Living Legend* (RCA Victor 1978)★★★, *Mysterious Lady* (RCA Victor 1979)★★★, *Instrumentally Yours* (RCA Victor 1979)★★★, with Kelly Foxton *Lovingly Yours* (1980)★★★, *By Request* (RCA Victor 1981)★★★, with Foxton *Win Some, Lose Some, Lonesome* (1981)★★★, with Willie Nelson *Brand On My Heart* (Columbia 1985)★★★.
● COMPILATIONS: *The Best Of Hank Snow* (RCA Victor 1966)★★★, *Hits, Hits & More Hits* (RCA Victor 1968)★★★, *Hank Snow, The Singing Ranger Volume 1 (1949-1953)* box set (Bear Family 1989)★★★★, *Hank Snow, The Singing Ranger Volume 2 (1953-1958)* 4-CD box set (Bear Family 1990)★★★★, *Hank Snow, The Thesaurus Transcriptions (1950-1956)* 5-CD box set (Bear Family 1991)★★★★, *Hank Snow, The Singing Ranger Volume 3 (1958-1969)* 12-CD box set (Bear Family 1992)★★★★, *The Yodelling Ranger 1936-47* 5-CD box set (Bear Family 1993)★★★★, *The Singing Ranger Volume 4* 9-CD box set (Bear Family 1994)★★★★, *My Early Country Favorites* (RCA Camden 1996)★★★, *The Essential Hank Snow* (RCA 1997)★★★★.
● FURTHER READING: *The Hank Snow Story*, Hank Snow with Jack Ownby and Bob Burris.

SOLITAIRES

From Harlem, New York, USA, the Solitaires, like no other vocal group of the 50s, sang lushly harmonized doo-wop with a dreamy romantic feeling, and rank as one of the great groups of the 50s. Formed in 1953, the group originally comprised veterans of the doo-wop scene and consisted of lead Herman Curtis (ex-Vocaleers), tenor Buzzy Willis and bass Pat Gaston (both ex-Crows), tenor/guitarist Monte Owens and baritone Bobby Baylor (both of whom had recorded with the Mellomoods), and pianist Bobby Williams. They signed

with Hy Weiss's Old Town label in 1954, and with Curtis's haunting falsetto on 'Wonder Why', 'Blue Valentine', 'Please Remember My Heart' and 'I Don't Stand A Ghost Of A Chance', the group quickly established themselves locally, if not nationally. Their deep, yet crisp and clean, R&B sound set a standard for other groups. Curtis left in 1955 and, with the wonderfully flavourful tenor of new recruit Milton Love, the group entered their most commercially successful period. With such great records as 'The Wedding' (1955), 'The Angels Sang' (1956), 'You've Sin' (1956) and 'Walking Along' (1957), the latter covered by the Diamonds, they became a rock 'n' roll phenomenon. By the time the Solitaires left Old Town in 1960, however, they had metamorphosed into a Coasters-sounding group, and by the time of their last recording in 1964 personnel changes had left little that was recognizable from the classic group. In the following decades, various ensembles of the Solitaires would appear on revival shows.
● COMPILATIONS: *Walking Along With* (Ace 1992)★★★.

SONGS FOR SWINGING LOVERS - FRANK SINATRA ★★★★★

Songs For Swinging Lovers, released in 1956, is, for most fans and critics, the best Sinatra album and unquestionably his most perfect work. No album could claim to encapsulate high-quality 50s pop more than this. Quite aside from his graceful vocals, the orchestral arrangements are immaculate and fresh over 40 years later. The band, conducted by Nelson Riddle, gave Sinatra such space and freedom that he was able to make already established songs his own. The 15 songs contained on this record should serve to educate élitists that pop music has to swing before it rocks, and nobody should be too coy to have this indispensable record in their collection. In spite of its artistic achievement, the album failed to top the US charts, peaking at number 2, and reached number 8 in the UK.
● TRACKS: *You Make Me Feel So Young; It Happened In Monterey; You're Getting To Be A Habit With Me; You Brought A New Kind of Love To Me; Too Marvellous For Words; Old Devil Moon; Pennies From Heaven; Love Is Here To Stay; I've Got You Under My Skin; I Thought About You; We'll Be Together Again; Makin' Whoopee; Swingin' Down The Lane; Anything Goes; How About You.*

SONGS OUR DADDY TAUGHT US - THE EVERLY BROTHERS ★★★

In 1959, Don and Phil Everly walked right back to the songs of their youth for this delightful set of 12 plaintive, old-time melodies. They had been regular performers in their parents' radio show and this tribute to their father, Ike, was performed with warmth and affection. The only accompaniment came from Don's guitar and Floyd Chance's stand-up bass, prompting Chance to remark, 'Damn. You would put me on an album where every one of my notes can be heard.' Their hit single 'Take A Message To Mary' continued the mood of the album, and to this day, the Everlys continue to perform the same songs, usually 'Long Time Gone' and 'Barbara Allen'.
● TRACKS: *Roving Gambler; Down In The Willow Green; Long Time Gone; Lightning Express; That Silver Haired Daddy Of Mine; Who's Gonna Shoe Your Pretty Little Feet?; Barbara Allen; Oh So Many Years; I'm Here To Get My Baby Out Of*

Jail; Rockin' Alone In My Old Rockin' Chair; Kentucky; Put My Little Shoes Away.

SOUL STIRRERS

One of gospel's renowned vocal groups, the Soul Stirrers first performed in the early 30s, but their ascendancy began the following decade under the leadership of Rebert H. Harris. Eschewing the accustomed quartet format, Harris introduced the notion of a fifth member, a featured vocalist, thus infusing a greater flexibility without undermining traditional four-part harmonies. Harris left the group in 1950, tiring of what he perceived as non-spiritual influences. His replacement was Sam Cooke, late of the Highway QCs, a singer already groomed as a likely successor by Soul Stirrer baritone R.B. Robinson. This particular line-up was completed by Silas Roy Crain (b. 1911, Texas, USA, d. 14 September 1996), Jesse J. Farley, T.L. Bruster and Paul Foster (d. 20 August 1995), although Bob King replaced Bruster in 1953. Cooke's silky delivery brought the group an even wider appeal, while his compositions, including 'Nearer To Thee' and 'Touch The Hem Of His Garment', anticipated the styles he would follow on embracing secular music in 1956. Cooke's replacement, Johnnie Taylor, was also drawn from the ranks of the Highway QCs. The newcomer bore an obvious debt to the former singer as the group's work on Cooke's Sar label attested. Taylor also embarked on a solo career, but the Stirrers continued to record throughout the 60s with Willie Rogers, Martin Jacox and Richard Miles assuming the lead role in turn. Like the Staple Singers before them, the veteran group latterly began to include material regarded as inspirational (for example 'Let It Be'), as opposed to strictly religious. In the late 80s and early 90s UK Ace released a series of fine CD reissues of Specialty material, chiefly featuring Sam Cooke as lead singer.

● ALBUMS: with Sam Cooke *The Soul Stirrers Featuring Sam Cooke* (Specialty 1959)★★★★, with Cooke *The Wonderful World Of Sam Cooke* (Keen 1965)★★★, *Going Back To The Lord Again* (Specialty 1972)★★★, *Strength, Power And Love* (1974)★★★, *Tribute To Sam Cooke* (Chess/MCA 1986)★★★, *Resting Easy* (Chess/MCA 1986)★★★, *In The Beginning* (1989)★★★, with Cooke *Sam Cooke With The Soul Stirrers* (Specialty 1991)★★★★, *The Soul Stirrers Featuring R.H. Harris Shine On Me* (Ace 1992)★★★, *Jesus Gave Me Water* (Ace 1993)★★★, *Heaven Is My Home* (Ace 1993)★★★, *The Last Mile Of The Way* (Ace 1994)★★.

SOUND OF MILES DAVIS, THE

Produced and directed by the same team responsible for *The Sound Of Jazz* (Robert Herridge and Jack Smight), this 1959 film was originally entitled *Theater For A Song*. Davis is presented with his quintet (John Coltrane, Wynton Kelly, Paul Chambers and Jimmy Cobb) and also with Gil Evans And His Orchestra. The performance captures Davis in eloquent form and the contributions from the other musicians on hand help to make this an important filmed record of one of the music's most important figures.

SOUND OF MUSIC, THE

Even before its Broadway opening at the Lunt-Fontanne Theatre on 16 November 1959, *The Sound Of Music* was set to become a financial success. Advance sales exceeded three million dollars and with numerous touring versions, best-selling albums and a blockbuster film, it made a fortune for its composers, Richard Rodgers and Oscar Hammerstein II. The show had a strong narrative book, by Howard Lindsey and Russel Crouse, that was based upon the real-life story of Maria Rainer, her marriage to George von Trapp and her relationship with his family of singing youngsters. The family's evasion of capture by the Nazis during World War II gave the story a tense dramatic core and the fact that the family became professional singers meant that music and song blended well into the narrative, even if, at times, there seemed to be rather more sentiment than reality would have allowed. Starring Mary Martin as Maria, Theodore Bikel and Patricia Neway, the show was filled with songs that became very popular, including the title song, 'Do-Re-Mi', 'My Favorite Things', 'Edelweiss', 'So Long, Farewell', 'Sixteen Going On Seventeen', 'How Can Love Survive?', 'Maria', 'The Lonely Goatherd', and 'Climb Ev'ry Mountain'. Sentimental or not, it is hard to imagine that at the time he was working on this show, Hammerstein was a sick man; less than a year after the Broadway opening he was dead. *The Sound Of Music* played for 1,443 performances, and won Tony Awards for best musical (tied with *Fiorello!*), actress (Martin), featured actress (Neway), musical director (Frederick Dvonch), and scenic design (Oliver Smith). Jean Bayliss and Roger Dann headed the cast of the 1961 London production, which surpassed the original and ran for 2,385 performances. New York revivals included one in 1967 at the City Centre, and another in 1990, presented by the New York City Opera, in which the ex-chart-topper Debby Boone played Maria. London audiences saw the show again in 1992 when it was presented at Sadlers Wells, with Liz Robertson and Christopher Cazenove. The 1965 film version, which starred Julie Andrews, won three Oscars and spawned one of the bestselling soundtrack albums of all time.

SOUTH PACIFIC

This immensely successful screen version of Richard Rodgers and Oscar Hammerstein's 1949 Broadway hit musical was released by 20th Century-Fox in 1958. Paul Osborn's screenplay, which was adapted from the stage production and James A. Michener's *Tales Of The South Pacific*, told the story of life on a South Sea island that is temporarily occupied by American troops during World War II. Two love stories run in parallel: that between the mature, sophisticated French planter, Emile de Becque (Rossano Brazzi), and a young nurse, Nellie Forbush (Mitzi Gaynor); and the other, which involves Lt. Joe Cable (John Kerr) and Liat (France Nuyen), the Polynesian daughter of Bloody Mary (Juanita Hall). Some felt that Oscar Hammerstein and Joshua Logan, who wrote the original libretto, fudged the 'racial issue' by allowing Cable to be killed in action so that he could not marry Liat. On the other hand, Nellie, after much personal torment and heart-searching, found herself able to accept de Becque's ethnic children from a previous marriage. The supporting cast was excellent, with Ray Walston outstanding as Luther Billis. Early on in the film he led a group of fellow marines in the rousing, but poignant, 'There Is Nothing Like A Dame', one of the songs in Rodgers and Hammerstein's marvellous score that came from Broadway intact - with the addition of one other number, 'My Girl Back Home', which had been written, but not used, for the 1949 show. The remainder of the film's much-loved songs were 'Dites-moi', 'A Cockeyed Optimist', 'Twin Soliloquies', 'Some Enchanted Evening', 'Bloody Mary', 'Bali Ha'i', 'I'm Gonna Wash That Man Right Outa My Hair', 'A Wonderful Guy', 'Younger Than Springtime', 'Happy Talk', 'Honey Bun', 'Carefully Taught' and 'This Nearly Was Mine'. The singing voices of Rossano Brazzi, John Kerr, and Juanita Hall were dubbed by Giorgio Tozzi, Bill Lee, and Muriel Smith, respectively. The choreographer was LeRoy Prinz, and Joshua Logan directed, as he had done on Broadway. *South Pacific* was photographed by Leon Shamroy in Technicolor and the Todd-AO wide-screen process. There was a good deal of adverse criticism regarding the use of colour filters in the various musical sequences. The soundtrack album proved to be one of the bestsellers of all time, spending an unprecedented (to date) total of 115 weeks at the top of the UK chart, and 31 weeks at number 1 in the USA.

SOUTHERN, JERI

b. Genevieve Hering, 5 August 1926, Royal, Nebraska, USA, d. 4 August 1991, Los Angeles, California, USA. A warm, 'smokey' voiced, jazz-influenced singer/pianist, Southern studied at the Notre Dame Academy, Omaha, and later played piano at the local Blackstone Hotel. After touring with a US Navy recruiting show, where she began singing, she worked at several venues in Chicago in the late 40s. These included the Hi Note Club, where she supported stars such as Anita O'Day. After obtaining a nightly spot on television, Southern was signed to Decca Records and had US Top 30 hits with 'You Better Go Now' (1951) and 'Joey' (1954). Her wistful version of 'When I Fall In Love' established her as a favourite in the UK, where she also had a Top 30 hit with 'Fire Down Below' (1957). She then switched to the Capitol label and made the highly acclaimed *Jeri Southern Meets Cole Porter*, which featured a set of humorous arrangements by Billy May, including a 20s setting of 'Don't Look At Me That Way'. One of her many album releases, *When I Fall In Love*, which was released by MCA Records in 1984, contained several numbers closely identified with Southern including 'An Occasional Man'. She retired from performing in the mid-60s to become a vocal and piano coach for professional artists. She subsequently moved to Hollywood, and worked on arrangements with the film music composer Hugo Friedhofer, and later, cared for him. She also published a book, *Interpreting Popular Music At The Keyboard*. Her last public performance was at the Vine Street Bar And Grill in Los Angeles, where she was persuaded by Anita O'Day to emerge from the audience and play a medley of Jerome Kern songs. She died of pneumonia six months later.
● ALBUMS: *Intimate Songs* 10-inch album (Decca 1954)★★★, *Southern Style* (Decca 1955)★★★, *You Better Go Now* (Decca 1956)★★★, *When Your Heart's On Fire* (Decca 1956)★★★, *Jeri Southern Gently Jumps* (Decca 1957)★★★, *Prelude To A Kiss* (Decca 1958)★★★, *Southern Breeze* (Roulette 1958)★★★, *Southern Hospitality* (Decca 1958)★★★, *Jeri Southern Meets Cole Porter* (Capitol 1959)★★★★, *Coffee, Cigarettes And Memories* (Capitol 1959)★★★, *Jeri Southern Meets Johnny Smith* (Roulette 1959)★★★, *At The Crescendo* (Capitol 1960)★★, *You Better Go Now* (Official 1989)★★★.
● COMPILATIONS: *When I Fall In Love* (MCA 1984)★★★.

● FURTHER READING: *Interpreting Popular Music At The Keyboard*, Jeri Southern.

SPANIELS

This vocal ensemble was formed in 1952 in Gary, Indiana, USA. The Spaniels were universally recognized as one of the great R&B vocal harmony groups of the 50s, whose magnificent body of work was not truly reflected in their moderate chart success. The group originally consisted of Roosevelt High students James 'Pookie' Hudson (lead), Ernest Warren (first tenor), Opal Courtney (baritone), Willis C. Jackson (baritone) and Gerald Gregory (bass). In 1953 the quintet enjoyed an R&B Top 10 hit with 'Baby, It's You', but the following year achieved their biggest success when 'Goodnite Sweetheart, Goodnite' reached the US pop Top 30 despite competition from an opportunistic pop-style version by the McGuire Sisters. The Spaniels' delicate doo-wop harmonies turned this ballad into one of the era's best-loved performances, with the song's emotional pull outweighing its intrinsic simplicity. The Spaniels in 1955 followed with two fine regional hits, 'Let's Make Up' and 'You Painted Pictures'. The Spaniels reorganized in 1956, and Hudson and Gregory were augmented by James Cochran (baritone), Carl Rainge (tenor) and Don Porter (second tenor). Top recordings by this group included 'You Gave Me Peace Of Mind' (1956), 'Everyone's Laughing' (number 13 R&B 1957) and 'I Lost You' (1958). Another reorganization in 1960, in which Hudson and Gregory brought in Andy McGruder, Billy Cary and Ernest Warren, yielded the group's last hit, 'I Know' (US R&B number 23 in 1960). Hudson went solo in 1961, but formed a soul-styled Spaniels group in 1969 that brought 'Fairy Tales' to the charts in 1970.
● ALBUMS: *Goodnite, It's Time To Go* (Vee Jay 1958)★★★, *The Spaniels* (Vee Jay 1960)★★★, *Spaniels* (Calla 1968)★★★.
● COMPILATIONS: *Hits Of The Spaniels* (1971)★★★, *Great Googley Moo!* (Charly 1981)★★★, *16 Soulful Serenades* (1984)★★★, *Stormy Weather* (Charly 1986)★★★, *Play It Cool* (Charly 1990)★★★★, *40th Anniversary 1953-1993* (1993)★★★.

SPECIALTY RECORDS

Formed in 1946 in Los Angeles, California, USA, by Art Rupe, originally from Pittsburgh, Pennsylvania, Specialty Records gave rise to some of the most powerful early R&B and rock 'n' roll performers, particularly Little Richard. Rupe had briefly run the small-time label Juke Box Records, and with money earned there, launched Specialty. Among the label's first signings were blues singers Percy Mayfield and Joe Liggins. He also signed gospel artists including the Soul Stirrers. In 1952 Rupe expanded his artist roster beyond the west coast and signed New Orleans R&B singer Lloyd Price, who was the label's greatest success up to that time with his number 1 R&B hit 'Lawdy Miss Clawdy'. Other New Orleans acts on Specialty included Art Neville and Ernie K-Doe. In 1955, Rupe signed Little Richard (Penniman), who became the label's greatest success and one of the pioneers of early rock 'n' roll. All of Little Richard's hits, including 'Tutti Frutti', 'Good Golly Miss Molly' and 'Lucille', were on the Specialty label. Other Specialty rock 'n' roll/R&B artists included Larry Williams and Don And Dewey. The label was wound down during the 60s, but later revived in the 80s by

Beverly Rupe, daughter of Art, who launched a reissue campaign making much of the classic Specialty material available once more.

● COMPILATIONS: *The Specialty Story* 5-CD box set (Specialty 1994)★★★★.

SQUIRES, DOROTHY

b. Edna May Squires, 25 March 1918, Llanelli, Dyfed, Wales, d. 14 April 1998. A dynamic, dramatic and highly emotional singer, who retained an army of fans throughout a career spanning over many decades. At her 'live' performances, especially during the 70s, the audience were there not just to be entertained, but also to pay homage. At the age of 18 she moved to London to become a singer, and worked at the Burlington Club, where she was discovered by American pianist and bandleader Charlie Kunz. She sang with his band at the Casani Club, and made her first radio broadcast from there. In 1938 she joined songwriter Billy Reid And His Orchestra, beginning a partnership that lasted until 1951, when she left to concentrate on a solo career. In between, she recorded many of Reid's songs, such as 'The Gypsy', 'It's A Pity To Say Goodnight', 'A Tree In A Meadow' and 'When China Boy Meets China Girl'. During the 40s Reid and Squires teamed up to become one of the most successful double acts on the UK variety circuit, and she made frequent appearances on BBC Radio's *Melody Lane*, *Band Parade*, *Variety Fanfare* and *Henry Hall's Guest Night*.

In 1953 Squires had a UK chart hit with one of Reid's biggest hit songs, 'I'm Walking Behind You' and, in the same year, married the young actor Roger Moore. They settled in California for most of the 50s, sometimes playing cabaret engagements. After the couple's acrimonious split in 1961, Squires made the UK Top 30 in collaboration with personality pianist Russ Conway, with her own composition 'Say It With Flowers'. She also became the first British artist to play London's Talk Of The Town. In 1968, after several unfruitful years, she financed her own album, *Say It With Flowers*, for President Records. This was followed by a version of the Stevie Wonder hit 'For Once In My Life', along with 'Till' and 'My Way' (an anthem which fitted her as perfectly as it did Frank Sinatra). During 1970, her version spent nearly six months in the UK chart, and inspired her to hire the London Palladium for a sell-out comeback concert, which she played to an ecstatic reception; a double album was released on Decca.

In the 70s Squires was headlining again throughout the UK, in concerts and cabaret, and also returned to the USA to play New York's Carnegie Hall. She hired the Palladium again in 1974 for a concert in memory of Billy Reid, and in 1979 released another double album, *With All My Heart*. During the 80s she became semi-retired, giving a few concerts, one of which became *We Clowns - Live At The Dominion* (1984), on her own Esban label; she also released *Three Beautiful Words Of Love* on Conifer. Squires' career was bathed in controversy and she became one of the most notoriously prolific libel litigants in showbusiness history. In 1989 she was evicted from her 17-bedroom Thames-side mansion that had once belonged to the celebrated actress Lily Langtry, and in 1995 her home was reportedly under threat once again. During the early 90s, Squires continued to perform occasionally and in 1991 she released *The Best Of The EMI Years*, a 20-track compilation of her work with Billy Reid, some of

her own compositions, and several of the other recordings she made for Columbia during the early 60s.

● ALBUMS: *Dorothy Squires Sings Billy Reid* (Nixa 1958)★★★, *Say It With Flowers* (President 1968)★★★, *This Is My Life* (Ace Of Clubs 1967)★★★, *Reflections* (Marble Arch 1968)★★★, *Seasons Of Dorothy Squires* (President 1969)★★★, with Dennis Lotis *Cheese And Wine* (Pye 1973)★★★, *London Palladium* (EMI 1973)★★★, *Live At The Theatre Royal Drury Lane* (Pye 1974)★★★, *Rain, Rain Go Away* (Decca 1977)★★★, *Golden Hour Presents Dorothy Squires* (Golden Hour 1977)★★★, *With All My Heart* (Decca 1979)★★★, *We Clowns - Live At The Dominion* (Esban 1984)★★★, *Three Beautiful Words Of Love* (Conifer 1988)★★★.

● COMPILATIONS: *The Best Of The EMI Years* (EMI 1991)★★★, *Best Of* (1994)★★★.

STAFFORD, JO

b. 12 November 1920, Coalinga, near Fresno, California, USA. Although the birth date above is the one that has been accepted for some time, the alternative year of 1917 is given in the booklet accompanying the 1991 CD in the Capitol *Collectors Series*. One of the most popular female singers of the 40s and 50s, while still at high school Stafford studied serious music with the intention of pursuing a career as a classical soprano. After five years of intensive work, she abandoned the idea and joined her two older sisters in their country music act, but later left to freelance on radio with the seven-man vocal group the Pied Pipers. In 1939, after appearing on radio with Tommy Dorsey, they reduced the group to a quartet and joined Dorsey permanently. A large part of their appeal was Stafford's pure, almost academic tone, her distinctive vocal timbre and the complete lack of vibrato, which provided a rock-steady lead. While with Dorsey she had solo success with 'Little Man With A Candy Cigar', 'Manhattan Serenade' and a 12-inch disc of 'For You'. She also duetted with Dorsey arranger Sy Oliver on his own composition, 'Yes Indeed'. When the Pipers left Dorsey in 1942 and started recording for Capitol Records, Stafford was soon out on her own as one of the top stars of the 40s. She stayed with the label until 1950, having hits such as 'Candy' (with Johnny Mercer), 'That's For Me', 'Serenade Of The Bells', 'Some Enchanted Evening' and 'Tennessee Waltz'. There were also several duets with Gordon MacRae, including 'My Darling, My Darling' from the Broadway musical *Where's Charley*, and 'Whispering Hope', an old religious song also recorded by Pat Boone. In 1950 she switched to Columbia Records, immediately having further success with 'Make Love To Me', 'Shrimp Boats', 'Keep It A Secret', 'Jambalaya' and her biggest seller, 'You Belong To Me'. Just as important as the singles were a series of high-class albums of standards scored by her husband, ex-Dorsey arranger Paul Weston, who had become her musical alter-ego. Her reputation in some quarters as being a purely academic singer was given the lie on two notable occasions. The first was when she recorded pseudonymously as the lunatic Cinderella G. Stump on Red Ingle and the Natural Seven's 1947 comedy hit 'Temptation'; and the second was a decade later when, with her husband, she made a series of albums as 'Jonathan And Darlene Edwards', in which they wickedly sent up amateur pianists and singers. In 1959 Stafford retired from public performing, but recorded until the mid-60s, sometimes for Frank Sinatra's Reprise Records. Dissatisfied with their former recording companies' neglect of their output, Stafford and Weston acquired the rights themselves and released them on their own Corinthian label.

● ALBUMS: *American Folk Songs* 10-inch album (Capitol 1950)★★, with Gordon MacRae *Songs Of Faith* 10-inch album (Capitol 1950)★★, *Autumn In New York* 10-inch album (Capitol 1950)★★, *As You Desire Me* 10-inch album (Columbia 1952)★★★, with MacRae *Sunday Evening Songs* 10-inch album (Capitol 1953)★★★, *Broadways Best* 10-inch album (Columbia 1953)★★★, *Starring Jo Stafford* 10-inch album (Capitol 1953)★★★, with MacRae *Memory Songs* (Capitol 1954)★★★, with Frankie Laine *Musical Portrait Of New Orleans* (Columbia 1954)★★, *Garden Of Prayers* 10-inch album (Columbia 1954)★★, *My Heart's In The Highlands* 10-inch album (Columbia 1954)★, *Soft And Sentimental* 10-inch album (Columbia 1955)★★★, *A Gal Named Jo* (Columbia 1956)★★★, *Happy Holiday* (Columbia 1956)★★, *Ski Trails* (Columbia 1956)★★★, *Once Over Lightly* (Columbia 1957)★★★, *Songs Of Scotland* (Columbia 1957)★, *Swingin' Down Broadway* (Columbia 1958)★★★, *I'll Be Seeing You* (Columbia 1959)★★★, *Ballad Of The Blues* (Columbia 1959)★★★, *Jo + Jazz* (Columbia 1960)★★★, *Jo + Blues* (Columbia 1961)★★★, *Jo + Broadway* (Columbia 1961)★★★, *Songs Of Faith Hope And Love* (Columbia 1961)★★★, with MacRae *Whispering Hope* (Capitol 1962)★★★, with MacRae *Peace In The Valley* (Capitol 1963)★★, with MacRae *Old Rugged Cross* (Capitol 1963)★★★, *Sweet Hour Of Prayer* (1964)★★, *Joyful Season* (1964)★★, *Getting Sentimental Over Tommy Dorsey* (Reprise 1964)★★★, *Do I Hear A Waltz?* (Dot 1965)★★★, *This Is Jo Stafford* (Dot 1966)★★★, *G.I. Joe - Songs Of World War II* (Corinthian 1979)★★★, *Broadway Revisited - Romantic Ballads From The Theater* (Corinthian 1983)★★★, *Fan Favorites Through The Years* (Corinthian 1984)★★★, *International Hits* (Corinthian 1988)★★★.

As Jonathan And Darlene Edwards *Sing Along With Jonathan And Darlene Edwards - Only The Chorus Is For Real* (Columbia 1959)★★★, *Jonathan And Darlene's Original Masterpiece* (Columbia 1960)★★★, *Jonathan And Darlene Edwards In Paris* (Columbia 1960)★★★.

● COMPILATIONS: *Jo Stafford's Greatest Hits* (Columbia 1959)★★★★, *Jo Stafford Showcase* (Columbia 1960)★★★★, *The Hits Of Jo Stafford* (Columbia 1963)★★★★, *Jo Stafford's Greatest Hits - Best On Columbia* (Columbia 1977)★★★★, *Hits Of Jo Stafford* (MFP 1984)★★★★, *Stars Of The 50s* (EMI 1984)★★★★, *Introducing Jo Stafford* (Capitol 1987)★★★, *Capitol Collectors Series* (Capitol 1991)★★★★, *The Very Best Of ...* (Parade 1995)★★, *The Jo Stafford Story* (Jasmine 1997)★★★★.

STAPLETON, CYRIL

b. 31 December 1914, Nottingham, England, d. 25 February 1974. Stapleton played the violin at the age of 11, and served in pit orchestras for silent movies before joining Henry Hall as a violinist in the early 30s. By 1939, and the outbreak of World War II, he had moved on to working under Billy Ternent, via Jack Payne, and married impressionist Beryl Orde. He joined the Royal Air Force, initially as an air-gunner, later conducting the RAF Symphony Orchestra at the Potsdam Summit Conference. At the end of the war he formed a band to play at Fisher's Restaurant in London's

New Bond Street. In the late 40s, the band, plus strings, was featured on BBC radio programmes such as *Hit Parade* and *Golden Slipper*. In the 50s he became known as the UK's 'Mr. Music' when he became the leader of the all-star BBC Show Band which made its first broadcast on the Light Programme on 2 October 1952, and was featured three nights a week thereafter. He led the band for five years, playing host to star US artists such as Frank Sinatra and Nat 'King' Cole, along with residents Janie Marlow and the Stargazers vocal group. With his own band he had a string of UK chart hits for Decca Records from 1955-57, including 'Elephant Tango', 'Blue Star' (theme from the US television series *The Medics*), 'The Italian Theme', 'The Happy Whistler' and 'Forgotten Dreams'. In the USA Stapleton made the Top 30 with 'The Children's Marching Song' (from the film *The Inn Of The Sixth Happiness*) which, along with 'Blue Star', sold a million copies. In the early 60s Stapleton was resident band leader at the Lyceum Ballroom in the Strand, London. One of his early protégés was a 14-year-old dancer by the name of Jeff Dexter, who achieved notoriety as a disc jockey and compere of numerous rock festivals and concerts in the 60s and 70s, and became the manager of the 70s soft rock band America. In 1966 the Stapleton band moved to Pye Records, where Stapleton later became A&R controller and an independent producer, masterminding the multi-million-selling *Singalong* series of albums by Max Bygraves. In the last few years of his life Stapleton began to tour with a big band, attempting to recreate the sounds of his heyday.

● ALBUMS: *Songs Of The Golden West* (Decca 1958)★★★, *Music For Dancing In The Dark* (Decca 1958)★★★, *Just For You* (Decca 1959)★★★, *Italy After Dark* (Decca 1959)★★★, *New York After Dark* (Decca 1959)★★★, *Come 'N' Get It* (Decca 1959)★★★, *Big Hits From Broadway* (Decca 1960)★★★, with Don Rendell *All-Time Big Band Hits* (Decca 1960)★★★, with his Concert Orchestra *'Congress Dances'* (Decca 1960)★★★, with Brian Johnson, Ray Merrell, Joy Worth *'Gigi' And 'South Pacific'* (Decca 1960)★★★, *Great Movie Hits* (Decca 1960)★★★, *Great Movie Hits, Volume 2* (Decca 1961)★★★, *Top Pop Instrumentals* (Decca 1961)★★★, *Songs You Won't Forget* (Decca 1962)★★★, *My Fair Lady/King And I* (Eclipse 1969)★★★.

● COMPILATIONS: *The Big Band's Back* (Golden Hour 1974)★★★, *Golden Hour Of Strict Tempo* (Golden Hour 1974)★★★.

STAR IS BORN, A

Over the years, several films have attempted to strip the veneer of glamour from Hollywood, the film capital of the world, and expose the sadness and bitterness that sometimes lay beneath. *Sunset Boulevard* (1950) is, perhaps, the prime example of the genre, and, more recently, *The Player* (1992) dwelt on the greed and double-dealing inherent in the movie business. Adela Rogers St. John's original story, which eventually evolved into the 1954 Warner Brothers musical picture *A Star Is Born*, first came to the screen in 1932 under the title of *What Price Hollywood?*. Five years later, it was adapted for an Academy Award-winning dramatic film enti-tled *A Star Is Born*, which had a story by William A. Wellman, a screenplay by Dorothy Parker, Alan Campbell and Robert Carson, and starred Janet Gaynor and Fredric March. Moss Hart's superbly crafted screenplay for the 1954 musical version, which stayed fairly close to the plot of the previous film, tells of Norman Maine (James Mason), a has-been movie actor, whose temperamental and brutish behaviour results in him being ostracized from Hollywood studios and society. While taking solace in the bottle, he is forced to become dependent on his wife, Esther Blodgett (professional name Vicki Lester), played by Judy Garland. Mainly through his influence (and her talent), she becomes a big star herself. Eventually, unable to cope with life at the bottom of the barrel, he drowns himself. Garland was outstanding throughout - this was probably her greatest film role - and Mason, who is said to have been the fifth choice for the part, was wonderful, too. Charles Bickford, as the studio head who is reluctant to let Maine go, and Jack Carson, in the role of the studio's publicity chief who is only too glad to be rid of him, featured in a fine supporting cast, along with Lucy Marlow, Grady Sutton, Tommy Noonan, Amanda Blake, Irving Bacon and James Brown. Harold Arlen and Ira Gershwin wrote most of the songs, including the compelling 'The Man That Got Away', 'Gotta Have Me Go With You', 'Someone At Last', 'It's A New World' and two that were cut because of the film's excessive length, 'Lose That Long Face' and 'Here's What I'm Here For'. The remainder were 'Swanee' (George Gershwin-Irving Caesar), and 'Born In A Trunk' (Leonard Gershe-Roger Edens) which effectively topped and tailed a medley of old songs. The choreographer was Richard Barstow, and the film was produced by Sidney Luft (at that time Garland's husband), directed by George Cukor, and photographed in Technicolor and CinemaScope. One of the all-time great film musicals, *A Star Is Born* was re-released in the 80s complete with the two songs that were cut from the original print, and with some other scenes restored.

In the 1976 remake of *A Star Is Born*, starring Barbra Streisand and Kris Kristofferson, screenwriters John Gregory Dunne, Frank Pierson and Joan Didion set their new plot in the world of rock music, with an appropriate score that included such numbers as 'Lost Inside Of You' (Streisand-Leon Russell), 'I Believe In Love' (Kenny Loggins-Alan And Marilyn Bergman), 'Queen Bee' (Rupert Holmes) and 'The Woman In The Moon' (Paul Williams-Kenny Ascher). Streisand and Williams also collaborated on 'Love Theme (Evergreen)', which won an Academy Award and topped the US chart. The film was released by Warner Brothers and photographed in Metrocolor and Panavision. The director was Frank Pierson, and *A Star Is Born* (Mark III) was a smash hit, grossing nearly $40 million in the USA and Canada alone.

● FURTHER READING: *The Making Of The 1954 Movie And Its 1983 Reconstruction*, Ronald Haver.

STARGAZERS

Formed in 1949, they developed into Britain's most popular vocal group in the early 50s. The original line-up consisted of Dick James, Cliff Adams, Marie Benson, Fred Datcheler and Ronnie Milne. They first attracted attention on radio programmes such as *The Derek Roy Show* and *The Family Hour*, later moving to *Top Score*, the *Goon Show* and *Take It From Here*. The Stargazers began recording towards the end of 1949, working for a variety of labels, including Decca, HMV, Columbia and Polygon, backing artists such as Steve Conway and Benny Lee, and later, Dennis Lotis and Jimmy

Young. Their own releases included 'Me And My Imagination', 'Red Silken Stockings', 'A-Round The Corner' and 'Sugarbush'. In April 1953, they became the first British act to reach number 1 in the infant *New Musical Express* chart, with 'Broken Wings'. Amost a year later, they hit the top spot again, with Meredith Willson's 'I See The Moon'. They continued to record into the late 50s, and made the UK chart with 'Happy Wanderer', 'Somebody', 'Crazy Otto Rag', 'Close The Door', 'Twenty Tiny Fingers' and 'Hot Diggity' (1956). They worked constantly in radio, and their own series, *The Stargazers' Music Shop*, opened for business on Radio Luxembourg in 1952, crossing to the BBC nearly five years later. The group also had a regular slot on the BBC's *Show Band Show* with Cyril Stapleton, and toured the UK variety circuit.

Their first permanent personnel change came in 1953, when David Carey replaced Ronnie Milne. Milne emigrated to Canada and took up a post in the Canadian Army, training young musicians. Two years later, the group appeared in the Royal Variety Performance, and, in the same year, Eula Parker took over from her fellow Australian, Marie Benson, who embarked on a solo career, armed with a two-year contract with Philips Records. Parker herself was later succeeded by June Marlow. After being replaced by Bob Brown, Dick James, the Stargazers' original leader, had solo hits with 'Robin Hood' and 'Garden Of Eden' before becoming a successful music publisher and the proprietor of DJM Records. Cliff Adams went on to devise the radio programme *Sing Something Simple* in 1959, and he and his Singers have remained with the show ever since. Fred Datcheler became a member of the Polka Dots, a vocal group bearing some resemblance to the Hi-Lo's. Datcheler's son, Clark, was a founder-member of the 80s vocal/instrumental band Johnny Hates Jazz.

● ALBUMS: *Make It Soon* (Decca 1955)★★, *South Of The Border* (Decca 1960)★★★.

STARR, KAY

b. Katherine LaVerne Starks, 21 July 1922, Dougherty, Oklahoma, USA. While she was still a child, Starr's family moved to Dallas, Texas, where she made her professional debut on local radio before she had left school. In 1939 she was hired briefly by Glenn Miller when his regular singer, Marion Hutton, was sick. Starr made records with Miller, but was soon on the move. She spent brief spells with the bands of Bob Crosby and Joe Venuti, and attracted most attention during her mid-40s stint with Charlie Barnet. Among the records she made with Barnet was 'Share Croppin' Blues', which was modestly successful. However, the record sold well enough to interest Capitol Records, and, from 1948-54, she had a string of hits with the label, including 'So Tired', 'Hoop-Dee-Doo', 'Bonaparte's Retreat', 'I'll Never Be Free', 'Oh, Babe!', 'Come On-Aa My House', 'Wheel Of Fortune' (US number 1 1952), 'Comes A-Long A-Love' (UK number 1 1952), 'Side By Side', 'Half A Photograph', 'Allez-Vous-En', 'Changing Partners', 'The Man Upstairs', 'If You Love Me (Really Love Me)' and 'Am I A Toy Or A Treasure?'. In 1955 she switched to RCA Records, and went straight to the top of the charts in the USA and UK with 'Rock And Roll Waltz'. Her last singles hit to date was 'My Heart Reminds Me' (1957). Starr sang with controlled power and a strong emotional undertow, which made her an appealing live performer. In the 60s she became a regular attraction at venues such as Harrah's, Reno, and, as recently as the late 80s, she returned there, and also played New York clubs as a solo attraction and as part of nostalgia packages such as *3 Girls 3* (with Helen O'Connell and Margaret Whiting), and *4 Girls 4* (then joined by Kaye Ballard). In the spring of 1993, she joined Pat Boone, another popular 50s survivor, on *The April Love Tour* of the UK.

● ALBUMS: *Songs By Starr* 10-inch album (Capitol 1950)★★, *Kay Starr Style* 10-inch album (Capitol 1953)★★★, *The Hits Of Kay Starr* 10-inch album (Capitol 1953)★★★, *In A Blue Mood* (Capitol 1955)★★★, *The One And Only Kay Starr* (RCA Victor 1955)★★★, *Swingin' With The Starr* (Liberty 1956)★★★, with Erroll Garner *Singin' Kay Starr, Swingin' Erroll Garner* (Modern 1956)★★★, *Blue Starr* (RCA Victor 1957)★★★, *Them There Eyes* (Rondo-lette 1958)★★, *Movin'* (Capitol 1959)★★★, *Rockin' With Kay* (RCA Victor 1959)★★, *I Hear The Word* (RCA Victor 1959)★★★, *Just Plain Country* (1959)★, *Losers Weepers* (Capitol 1960)★★★, *One More Time* (Capitol 1960)★★★, *Movin' On Broadway* (Capitol 1960)★★★, *Jazz Singer* (Capitol 1960)★★★, *I Cry By Night* (Capitol 1962)★★★, *Fabulous Favorites* (Capitol 1964)★★★, *Tears And Heartaches* (Capitol 1966)★★, *When The Lights Go On Again* (ABC 1968)★★, with Count Basie *How About This* (Paramount 1969)★★.

● COMPILATIONS: *All Starr Hits* (Capitol 1961)★★★, *Pure Gold* (RCA 1981)★★★, with Bob Crosby *Suddenly It's 1939* (Giants Of Jazz 1985)★★★, *1947: Kay Starr* (Hindsight 1986)★★★, *Wheel Of Fortune And Other Hits* (Capitol 1989)★★★, *Capitol Collectors Series* (Capitol 1991)★★★.

STATON, DAKOTA

b. Aliyah Rabia, 3 June 1931, Pittsburgh, Pennsylvania, USA. After singing in clubs in a style modelled on that of such diverse artists as Dinah Washington and Sarah Vaughan, Staton began to attract wider attention in the mid-50s. She extended her repertoire to include popular songs, R&B, soul and gospel and made a number of successful record albums. In the mid-60s she took up residence in the UK and Europe, but was back in the USA early in the following decade. She is at her best with mainstream jazz accompaniment, whether a big band, such as Manny Albam's or Kurt Edelhagen's, or a small group, such as those led by George Shearing and Jonah Jones. Staton's R&B material is less attractive, often performed at feverish tempos and with a deliberate coarsening of her powerful voice.

● ALBUMS: *The Late, Late Show* (Capitol 1957)★★★★, *In The Night* (Capitol 1958)★★★, *Dynamic!* (Capitol 1958)★★★, *Crazy He Calls Me* (Capitol 1959)★★★, *Time To Swing* (Capitol 1959)★★★, *More Than The Most* (Capitol 1959)★★★, *Ballads And The Blues* (Capitol 1960)★★★, *Softly* (Capitol 1960)★★★, *Round Midnight* (Capitol 1961)★★★, *Dakota Staton At Storyville* (Capitol 1961)★★★, *From Dakota With Love* (United Artists 1963)★★★, *Live And Swinging* (United Artists 1963)★★★★, *Dakota Staton With Strings* (United Artists 1964)★★★, with Richard 'Groove' Holmes *Let Me Off Uptown* (1972)★★★, *Dakota Staton With The Manny Albam Big Band* (1973)★★★, *Darling, Please Save Your Love* (1992)★★★.

STEELE, TOMMY

b. Thomas Hicks, 17 December 1936, Bermondsey, London, England. After serving as a merchant seaman, Hicks formed a skiffle trio called the Cavemen, with Lionel Bart and Mike Pratt, before being discovered by entrepreneur John Kennedy in the 2I's coffee bar in Soho, London. A name change to Tommy Steele followed, and after an appearance at London's Condor Club, the boy was introduced to manager Larry Parnes. From that point, his rise to stardom was meteoric. Using the old 'working-class boy makes good' angle, Kennedy launched the chirpy cockney in the unlikely setting of a debutante's ball. Class-conscious Fleet Street lapped up the idea of Steele as the 'Deb's delight' and took him to their hearts. His debut single, 'Rock With The Caveman', was an immediate Top 20 hit and although the follow-up, 'Doomsday Rock'/'Elevator Rock', failed to chart, the management was unfazed. Their confidence was rewarded when Steele hit number 1 in the UK charts with a cover version of Guy Mitchell's 'Singing The Blues' in January 1957. By this point, he was Britain's first and premier rock 'n' roll singer and, without resorting to sexual suggestiveness, provoked mass teenage hysteria unseen since the days of Johnnie Ray. At one stage, he had four songs in the Top 30, although he never restricted himself to pure rock 'n' roll. A minor role in the film *Kill Me Tomorrow* led to an autobiographical musical, *The Tommy Steele Story*, which also spawned a book of the same title. For a time, Steele combined the twin roles of rock 'n' roller and family entertainer, but his original persona faded towards the end of the 50s. Further movie success in *The Duke Wore Jeans* (1958) and *Tommy The Toreador* (1959) effectively redefined his image. His rocking days closed with cover versions of Ritchie Valens' 'Come On Let's Go' and Freddy Cannon's 'Tallahassee Lassie'. The decade ended with the novelty 'Little White Bull', after which it was farewell to rock 'n' roll. After appearing on several variety bills during the late 50s, Steele sampled the 'legit' side of showbusiness in 1960 when he played Tony Lumpkin in *She Stoops To Conquer* at the Old Vic, and he was back in straight theatre again in 1969, in the role of Truffaldino in *The Servant Of Two Masters* at the Queen's Theatre. In the years between those two plays, he experienced some of the highlights of his career. In 1963, he starred as Arthur Kipps in the stage musical *Half A Sixpence*, which ran for 18 months in the West End before transferring to Broadway in 1965. Steele recreated the role in the 1967 film version. A year later, he appeared in another major musical movie, *Finian's Rainbow*, with Fred Astaire and Petula Clark. His other films included *Touch It Light*, *It's All Happening*, *The Happiest Millionaire* and *Where's Jack?*. In 1974, Steele made one of his rare television appearances in the autobiographical *My Life, My Song*, and appeared at the London Palladium in the musical *Hans Andersen*. He also starred in the revival three years later. In 1979/80 his one-man show was resident at London's Prince of Wales Theatre for a record 60 weeks - the Variety Club Of Great Britain made him their Entertainer Of The Year. He was also awarded the OBE. Steele was back at the Palladium again in 1983 and 1989, heading the cast of the highly popular *Singin' In The Rain*, which he also directed. In the latter capacity he tried - too late as it transpired - to save impresario Harold Fielding's *Ziegfeld* (1988) from becoming a spectacular flop. Fielding had originally cast Steele in *Half A Sixpence* some 25 years earlier. Off-stage in the 80s, Steele published a thriller called *The Final Run*, had one of his paintings exhibited at the Royal Academy, was commissioned by Liverpool City Council to fashion a bronze statue of 'Eleanor Rigby' as a tribute to the Beatles, and composed two musical pieces, 'A Portrait Of Pablo' and 'Rock Suite - An Elderly Person's Guide To Rock'. After *Hans Andersen* and *Singin' In The Rain*, the third, and least successful of Steele's stage adaptations of memorable musical movies, was *Some Like It Hot* (1992). A hybrid of Billy Wilder's classic film, and the Broadway stage musical *Sugar* (1972), it received derisory reviews ('The show's hero is Mr Steele's dentist'), and staggered along for three months in the West End on the strength of its star's undoubted box-office appeal. In 1993, Steele was presented with the Hans Andersen Award at the Danish Embassy in London, and two years later he received the Bernard Delfont Award from the Variety Club of Great Britain for his 'outstanding contribution to show business'. By that time, Tommy Steele was back on the road again with 'A Dazzling New Song & Dance Spectacular' entitled *What A Show!*.

● ALBUMS: *The Tommy Steele Stage Show* 10-inch album (Decca 1957)★★★, *The Tommy Steele Story* 10-inch album (Decca 1957)★★★★, *Stars Of 6.05* (Decca 1958)★★★, *The Duke Wore Jeans* film soundtrack (Decca 1958)★★, *Tommy The Toreador* film soundtrack (1959)★★★, *Light Up The Sky* (1959)★★★, stage cast *Cinderella* (1959)★★★, *Get Happy With Tommy* (Decca 1960)★★★, *It's All Happening* (Decca 1962)★★★, London stage cast *Half A Sixpence* (Decca 1963)★★★, *So This Is Broadway* (1964)★★★, *Everything's Coming Up Broadway* (1967)★★★, *The Happiest Millionaire* (1967)★★, *My Life My Song* (Buena Vista 1974)★★★, London stage cast *Hans Andersen* (Decca 1978)★★★, with Sally Ann Howes *Harold Fielding's Hans Andersen* (1985)★★★.

● COMPILATIONS: *The Happy World Of Tommy Steele* (Decca 1969)★★★, *The World Of Tommy Steele, Volume 2* (Decca 1971)★★★, *Focus On Tommy Steele* (Decca 1977)★★★, *The Family Album* (Ronco 1979)★★★, *The Tommy Steele Story* (Decca 1981)★★★, *20 Greatest Hits* (Spot 1983)★★★, *Tommy Steele And The Steelmen - The Rock 'N' Roll Years* (See For Miles 1988)★★★, *Very Best Of Tommy Steele* (Pickwick 1991)★★★, *The EP Collection* (See For Miles 1992)★★★, *Handful Of Songs* (1993)★★★.

● FILMS: *Kill Me Tomorrow* (1955), *The Tommy Steele Story* (1957), *The Duke Wore Jeans* (1959), *Light Up The Sky* (1959), *Tommy The Toreador* (1960), *It's All Happening* (1962), *The Happiest Millionaire* (1967), *Half A Sixpence* (1967), *Finian's Rainbow* (1968), *Where's Jack?* (1969).

● FURTHER READING: *Tommy Steele: The Facts About A Teenage Idol And An Inside Picture Of Show Business*, John Kennedy.

STONE, KIRBY, FOUR

This vocal quartet comprised Kirby Stone (b. 27 April 1918, New York, USA), Eddie Hall, Larry Foster and Mike Gardner. They had a hip brand of humour and a distinctive, upbeat, swinging style. Originally an instrumental quintet, the group became a vocal foursome before making a name for themselves in nightclubs and local television shows. They came to prominence in 1958 with an appearance on the *Ed Sullivan Show*, which led to a contract with Columbia Records, and the release of *Man, I Flipped ... When I Heard The Kirby Stone Four*. It was a mixture of standards and special material written by Stone and Gardner. Their programme included 'Juke Box Dream', a vehicle for Foster's uncanny vocal impressions. In the same year they also had a Top 30 single with their original version of 'Baubles, Bangles And Beads', from the musical *Kismet*. The accompanying album reached the US Top 20. Among their other album releases, *Guys And Dolls (Like Today)* (1962) included a 'liberetto-ture' (a combination of libretto and overture) by Kirby Stone and the group's frequent arranger and conductor, Dick Hyman, as an attempt to present the Abe Burrows/Jo Swerling/Frank Loesser masterpiece as a 'show for the ear alone'. Stone added some extra lyrics for his 'guys', who were augmented by the 'dolls' - a female vocal chorus - plus a 25-piece orchestra that included such luminaries as Alvino Rey, Shelly Manne and Al Klink. Subsequently, the Kirby Stone Four continued to flourish, and went forward, armed with this common credo: 'A pox on all harmonica players, nightclub owners named Rocky, and juveniles who win contests by playing 'Lady Of Spain' on white accordions.'

● ALBUMS: *Man, I Flipped ... When I Heard The Kirby Stone Four* (Columbia 1958)★★★★, *Baubles, Bangles And Beads* (Columbia 1958)★★★★, *The "Go" Sound Of The Kirby Stone Four* (Columbia 1959)★★★, *The Kirby Stone Touch* (Columbia 1959)★★★, *The Kirby Stone Four At The Playboy Club* (Columbia 1960)★★★, *Guys And Dolls (Like Today)* (Columbia 1962)★★★.

STORM, GALE

b. Josephine Cottle, 5 April 1922, Bloomington, Texas, USA. A dynamic singer who came to fame mainly through covering the hits of others, Storm arrived in Hollywood in 1939 after winning a Gateway To Hollywood contest in her home state. She was soon working for the Universal and RKO studios, though she ultimately achieved popularity playing Margie Albright in *My Little Margie* (1952-54), a television series. By 1955, she was recording for Randy Wood's Dot label, reaching the US Top 5 with her cover version of Smiley Lewis's 'I Hear You Knocking', followed by 'Teen Age Prayer', 'Memories Are Made Of This' (both 1955), 'Why Do Fools Fall In Love?', 'Ivory Tower' (both 1956) and 'Dark Moon' (1957). During 1956-59, she had her own 125-segment television series which was considered a precursor for *Love Boat*. By the late 70s, Storm was living in the San Fernando Valley, but still working with local theatre companies. In 1987 Storm was appearing on the west coast with two other veterans, Betty Garrett and Sheree North, in Terry Kingsley-Smith's comedy *Breaking Up The Act*.

● ALBUMS: *Gale Storm* (Dot 1956)★★★, *Sentimental Me* (Dot 1956)★★★, *Softly And Tenderly* (Dot 1959)★★★, *Gale Storm Sings* (Dot 1959)★★★.

● COMPILATIONS: *Gale Storm Hits* (Dot 1958)★★★, *Dark Moon: The Best Of ...* (Varese Sarabande 1995)★★★.

STRITCH, ELAINE

b. 2 February 1925, Detroit, Michigan, USA. A highly individual actress and singer, Stritch has been called caustic, sardonic, witty, tough, and much else besides. She is said to have sung for the first time on stage in the Long Island revue *The Shape Of Things!*, in June 1947, and a few months later she introduced 'Civilization (Bongo, Bongo, Bongo)' on

Broadway, in another revue, *Angels In The Wings*. Stritch subsequently understudied Ethel Merman in Irving Berlin's hit musical *Call Me Madam*, and played Merman's role of ambassador Sally Adams in the 1952/3 US tour. Also in 1952, she was Melba Snyder in a revival of *Pal Joey* at the Broadhurst Theatre, and gave a memorable reading of the amusing 'Zip'. During the remainder of the 50s, Stritch appeared on Broadway in short-lived versions of *On Your Toes* and *Goldilocks*, and in 1961, sang 'Why Do The Wrong People Travel?', among other songs, in Noël Coward's *Sail Away*. In the following year she went with the latter show to London. Although she starred as Vera Charles in the US tour of *Mame*, and appeared in a US television version of the legendary revue *Pins And Needles*, Stritch did not appear on Broadway again until *Company* (1970), the show that brought her cult status. The television programme documenting the agonies involved in recording its Original Cast album, particularly the sequence in which a weary Stritch struggles to lay down a Stephen Sondheim-pleasing version of 'The Ladies Who Lunch', proved to be riveting viewing, and was eventually released on videotape and laser disc. After starring in the 1972 London production of *Company*, Stritch lived in England for about 10 years, appearing in various plays, and co-starring with Donald Sinden in the top-rated television series *Two's Company*. In 1985, she returned in triumph to New York for the two-performance *Follies In Concert* at the Lincoln Centre. She played Hattie, and very nearly stopped the show with her sensational rendering of 'Broadway Baby'. In the early 90s, she was back at the Lincoln Center with the original cast of *Company* for benefit concerts, made her cabaret debut at New York's Rainbow and Stars, and played the role of Parthy in the 1994 Tony Award-winning revival of *Show Boat* on Broadway. Her accomplished musical career has run in parallel with a distinguished career in the straight theatre.

● ALBUMS: *Stritch* (Dolphin 1955)★★★, Original and Studio Cast recordings.

STUDENT PRINCE, THE

Mario Lanza walked out on MGM producer Joe Pasternak before filming had even started on Sigmund Romberg and Dorothy Donnelly's epic operetta, which eventually reached the screen in 1954. Fortunately for all concerned, Lanza had recorded all the songs before he left, so it was simply a matter of matching his voice to the performing style of Edmund Purdom, the British actor chosen to co-star with Ann Blyth in this tale located in old Heidelberg. Set in the late 1800s, Sonia Levien and William Ludwig's screenplay, which was based on Donnelly's Broadway libretto and Wilhelm Meyer-Forster's play, told the familiar story of the brief romance between the Student Prince, Karl Franz (Purdom), and the waitress, Kathy (Blyth), to the accompaniment of immortal songs from the 1924 hit stage production, such as 'Serenade', 'Deep In My Heart, Dear', 'Drinking Song', 'Come Boys, Let's All Be Gay Boys' and 'Golden Days'. To these were added three new ones by Nicholas Brodszky and Paul Francis Webster, 'I Walk With God', Summertime In Heidelberg' and 'Beloved'. Louis Calhern, S.Z. Sakall, Edmund Gwenn, John Williams, Evelyn Vardon, Richard Anderson and John Hoyt were among those taking part in this lavish production which was expertly photographed in Ansco Color and CinemaScope by Paul Vogel and directed by

Richard Thorpe. An earlier, silent film of *The Student Prince*, directed by Ernst Lubitsch and starring Ramon Navarro and Norma Shearer, was released in 1927.

STYNE, JULE

b. Julius Kerwin Stein, 31 December 1905, London, England, d. 20 September 1994, New York, USA. A highly distinguished composer for the musical theatre, films and Tin Pan Alley, Styne spent his early life in the east London district of Bethnal Green, where his father ran a butter and eggs store. He used to do Harry Lauder impressions, and when he was five, he was taken by his parents to see the great entertainer at the London Hippodrome. He climbed up on stage, and Lauder lent him his crook and encouraged him to sing 'She's My Daisy'. Something of a child prodigy, he was a competent pianist even before he emigrated with his family to the USA at the age of eight. They settled in Chicago, and Styne studied harmony and composition, and played with the Chicago Symphony Orchestra, but had to abandon a classical career because 'my hands were too small - my span was inadequate'. While he was still at high school, Styne played the piano at burlesque houses, and composed his first two songs, 'The Guy In the Polka-Dot Tie' and 'The Moth And The Flame'. After graduating, he worked in nightclubs and for various pick-up groups, and in 1927, had a hit with the catchy 'Sunday' (written with Ned Miller, Chester Conn and Bennie Kreuger). In the late 20s, Styne was a member of Ben Pollack's big-time Chicago Band, which at various times included legendary names such as Benny Goodman, Glenn Miller and Charlie Spivak. By 1932, he had formed his own band, which played at the nightclubs and speakeasies in Chicago. During the 30s he moved to Hollywood, via New York, and worked as a vocal coach at 20th Century Fox ('I taught Shirley Temple and Alice Faye how to sing!'), and wrote some songs for low-budget movies such as *Hold That Co-Ed* (1938, 'Limpy Dimp' with Sidney Clare and Nick Castle). He transferred to Republic Studios, the home of Gene Autry and Roy Rogers, and continued to contribute to shoestring productions such as *Hit Parade Of 1941* ('Who Am I?', with Walter Bullock), *Melody Ranch*, *Rookies On Parade* and *Angels With Broken Wings*. On loan to Paramount, Styne teamed with Frank Loesser for 'I Don't Want To Walk Without You' and 'I Said No', which were featured in the Eddie Bracken movie *Sweater Girl* (1942). The former number was an enormous wartime hit, particularly for Harry James and his Orchestra, with a vocal by Helen Forrest. While at Republic, Styne met lyricist Sammy Cahn, and during the 40s they collaborated on numerous appealing songs, mostly for films, including 'I've Heard That Song Before', 'Five Minutes More', 'Victory Polka', 'Poor Little Rhode Island', 'Saturday Night (Is The Loneliest Night Of The Week)', 'Zuyder Zee', 'Guess I'll Hang My Tears Out To Dry' (from the 1944 flop musical *Glad To See You*), 'Anywhere', 'Can't You Read Between The Lines?', 'When The One You Love (Simply Won't Come Back)', 'I've Never Forgotten', 'The Things We Did Last Summer', 'Let It Snow! Let It Snow! Let It Snow!', 'I Gotta Gal I Love In North And South Dakota', 'It's Been A Long, Long Time', 'Ev'ry Day I Love You (Just A Little Bit More)', 'I'm In Love', 'It's Magic', 'It's You Or No One', 'Put 'Em In A Box (Tie It With A Ribbon And Throw 'Em In the Deep Blue Sea' (the last three were from Doris Day's first movie, *Romance On The High Seas*),

'Give Me A Song With A Beautiful Melody' and 'It's A Great Feeling' (1949). During that period, Styne also collaborated with others, including Herb Magidson ('Barrelhouse Bessie From Basin Street' and 'Conchita, Marquita, Lolita, Pepita, Rosita, Juanita Lopez') and Walter Bishop ('Bop! Goes My Heart'). Many of those songs were immensely successful for Frank Sinatra, and Styne and Cahn wrote the scores for three of the singer's most successful films of the 40s, *Step Lively* ('As Long As There's Music', 'Come Out, Wherever You Are', 'Some Other Time'), *Anchors Aweigh* ('The Charm Of You', 'I Fall In Love Too Easily', 'I Begged Her'), and *It Happened In Brooklyn* ('It's The Same Old Dream', 'Time After Time', 'I Believe', 'The Brooklyn Bridge'). Sinatra also introduced Styne and Cahn's Oscar-winning 'Three Coins In The Fountain' in 1954. Some years before that, Styne and Cahn had moved to New York to work on the score for the stage musical *High Button Shoes* ('Papa, Won't You Dance With Me', 'I Still Get Jealous', 'Can't You Just See Yourself?'). It starred Phil Silvers and Nanette Fabray, and ran for 727 performances. After returning briefly to Hollywood, at the age of 44 Styne embarked on an illustrious Broadway career, composing the music for a string of mostly highly successful shows, including *Gentlemen Prefer Blondes* (1949, 'Diamonds Are A Girl's Best Friend', 'Bye, Bye, Baby'), *Two On The Aisle* (1951, 'Hold Me-Hold Me-Hold Me', 'If You Hadn't But You Did'), *Hazel Flagg* (1953, 'Ev'ry Street's A Boulevard', 'How do you Speak To An Angel?'), *Peter Pan* (1954, 'Never Never Land', 'Distant Melody'), *Wake Up Darling* (1956, a five-performance flop, 'L'il Ol' You And L'il Ol' Me'), *Bells Are Ringing* (1956, 'Just In Time', 'The Party's Over', 'Long Before I Knew You'), *Say, Darling* (1958, 'Dance Only With Me'), *Gypsy* (1959, 'Small World', 'Everything's Coming Up Roses', 'Rose's Turn', 'All I Need Is The Girl'), *Do Re Mi* (1960, 'Make Someone Happy', 'Fireworks'), *Subways Are For Sleeping* (1961, 'I Just Can't Wait', 'Comes Once In A Lifetime', 'Be A Santa'), *Funny Girl* (1964, 'The Music That Makes Me Dance', 'Sadie, Sadie', 'People', 'Don't Rain On My Parade'), *Fade Out-Fade In* (1964, 'You Mustn't Feel Discouraged'), *Hallelujah, Baby!* (1967, 'My Own Morning', 'Now's The Time'), *Darling Of The Day* (1968, 'Let's See What Happens', 'That Something Extra Special'), *Look To The Lilies* (1970, 'I! Yes, Me! That's Who!'), *Prettybelle* (1971, closed out of town), *Sugar* (1972, 'It's Always Love', 'We Could Be Close' [revised for London as *Some Like It Hot* in 1992]), *Lorelei* (1974, a revised version of *Gentlemen Prefer Blondes*), *Hellzapoppin'!* (1976, closed out of town, 'Only One To A Customer'), *Bar Mitzvah Boy* (London 1978, 'You Wouldn't Be You', 'The Sun Shines Out Of Your Eyes', 'Where The Music Is Coming From'), *One Night Stand* (1980, closed during previews, 'Too Old To Be So Young', 'Long Way From Home'), *Pieces Of Eight* (1985, closed during regional try-out in Canada), and *The Red Shoes* (1993, closed after three days). Styne's chief collaborators for Broadway were Betty Comden and Adolph Green, and he also worked with Leo Robin, E.Y 'Yip' Harburg, Sammy Cahn and Bob Hilliard, among others. His two longest-running (and legendary) shows were written with Bob Merrill (*Funny Girl*) and Stephen Sondheim (*Gypsy*). Styne also co-produced several musicals, and composed the scores for television specials, and films such as *West Point Story*, *Two Tickets To Broadway* and *My Sister Eileen*.

One of the most talented, and prolific ('I believe in perspira-tion - not inspiration') all-round songwriters in the history of American popular music, Styne won many awards and honours, and was inducted into the Songwriters Hall of Fame and the Theatre Hall of Fame. Several artists have devoted complete albums to his songs, and in 1995, *Everything's Coming Up Roses-The Overtures Of Jule Styne*, played by the National Symphony Orchestra conducted by Jack Everly, was released. ASCAP's memorial tribute to Styne in February of that year included a Stephen Sondheim lyric that ran: 'Jule/You never took things cooly/Your syntax was unduly/Unruly/But Jule/I love you truly.'

● ALBUMS: *My Name Is Jule* (United Artists 1958)★★, with Michael Feinstein *Michael Feinstein Sings The Jule Styne Songbook* (Elektra Nonesuch 1991)★★★.

● FURTHER READING: *Jule*, Theodore Taylor.

SULTANS

The Sultans trace their origins to Omaha, Nebraska, USA gospel group the Echoes Of Joy, formed by 11-year-old Eugene McDaniels in 1946. This troupe then became the Five Echoes with the addition of brothers Willie and Gene Barnes (both on lead), James Farmer (baritone), Rosenwald Alexander (tenor) and Jimmy Mims (bass). The latter pair were soon replaced by Wesley Devereaux and Richard Beasley, respectively. Devereaux was actually the son of blues singer Wynonie Harris. Farmer's uncle owned a local record shop and the Showcase nightclub, which became the Five Echoes' semi-official home. This was 1953, at which time the group changed name to the Sultans and upped their tempo from gospel to R&B. Their first recordings took place shortly thereafter, for the Houston-based Duke Records label. Released in June, 'Good Thing Baby' was backed by a cover version of Rudy Vallee's 1932 hit 'How Deep Is The Ocean', but failed to make any impression. Johnny Otis, who had brought the Sultans to Duke, then took them on tour, before the release of their second single, 'I Cried My Heart Out'. Like 1954's 'Boppin' With The Mambo', it floundered. Dissatisfied with their label's promotion, the group found a new contract with King Records in Cincinnati, but were forced to change their name to the Admirals to break out of their existing contract. The Admirals debuted with 'Oh Yes', before a cover version of the Five Keys' 'Close Your Eyes'. It was to be their final single, though they did back other New York artists, including Robert 'Bubber' Johnson and Kathy Ryan, on record. The Admirals retreated to Omaha and back to their old name, the Sultans. Two singles for original home Duke Records followed, 'If I Could Tell' and 'My Love Is So High'. However, when Farmer enlisted there seemed little point in continuing the group. Willie Barnes went on to record solo for United Artists Records as Bobby Barnes. His brother, Gene (as Eugene Barnes was now called), also worked solo, finding significant early 60s success with Liberty Records ('A Hundred Pounds Of Clay' reaching number 3 in the *Billboard* charts). He also wrote a number 1 single for Roberta Flack ('Feel Like Makin' Love'). The Sultans then re-formed for a well-received appearance at Ronnie I's Collectors Group Concert Volume 3.

SUMAC, YMA

b. Emperatriz Chavarri, 10 September 1927, Ichocan, Peru. A flamboyant singer, of striking appearance, who was the subject of a series of publicity campaigns designed to shroud her origins in mystery: was she an Inca princess, one of the chosen 'Golden Virgins'? Or a Brooklyn housewife named Amy Camus (Yma Sumac spelt backwards)? Whatever the doubts as to her heritage, what was abundantly genuine was her four octave range, ascending from 'female baritone, through lyric soprano, to high coloratura'. Reportedly, she was the sixth child of an Indian mother and a mixed Indian and Spanish father, and was raised a Quechuan. After performing in local Indian festivals, she moved with her family to Lima, and joined the Compania Peruana de Arte, a group of 46 Indian dancers, singers and musicians. In 1942, Sumac married the Compania's leader, musician and composer Moises Vivanco, and four years later, travelled to New York with him and her cousin, Cholita Rivero, as the Inca Taqui Trio. In the late 40s the Trio played nightclubs such as New York's Blue Angel, and appeared on radio programmes and Arthur Godfrey's television show. Other work included an eight-week tour of the Borscht Circuit in the Catskill mountains. Signed for Capitol Records, her first album, *Voice Of Xtabay*, was released in 1950. It featured Sumac 'imitating birds and kettledrums, and singing a selection of strangely compelling songs, such as "Chant Of The Chosen Maidens" and "Virgin Of The Sun God", which were written for her by Moises Vivanco, and based on ancient Peruvian folk music'. With only the advantage of minimum publicity (at first), and the notorious 'phony biography', the 10-inch album sold half a million copies 'overnight'. It was followed by several more in the same vein, and led to an enormously successful concert appearance at the Hollywood Bowl. In 1951, Sumac made her Broadway debut in the short-lived musical *Flahooley*, singing three songs written for her by Vivanco 'with no lyrics and no real relevance to the story'. During the 50s she continued to be popular, playing Carnegie Hall, the Roxy Theatre with Danny Kaye, Las Vegas nightclubs and concert tours of South America and Europe. She also appeared in the film *Secret Of The Incas* (1954), with Charlton Heston and Robert Young. By the end of the decade she was beginning to be regarded by some as *passé*, and, eventually, as a 'nostalgic camp icon'. She retired in the early 60s, but is reported to have performed in 1975 at the Chateau Madrid club in Manhattan. In 1987 she hit the comeback trail with a three-week engagement at New York's Ballroom, and a year later, gained favourable reviews in Los Angeles for 'charming and frequently breathtaking performance'. In her set she featured well-known Latin songs such as 'La Molina' as well as the ethereal material 'that I recorded for Capitol 2,000 years ago!'. In 1992, a German documentary film, *Yma Sumac: Hollywood's Inca Princess*, mapped out her exotic career, and attempted to examine her remarkable range with the aid of computer technology. The lady herself declined to co-operate with the venture, thereby leaving the mystery, and the legend, intact.

● ALBUMS: *Voice Of Xtabay* 10-inch album (Capitol 1950)★★★, with various artists *Flahooley* 10-inch album (Capitol 1951), *Legend Of The Sun Virgin* 10-inch album (Capitol 1951)★★★, *Presenting Yma Sumac/Early Recordings* 10-inch album (Coral 1952)★★★, *Inca Taqui* 10-inch album (Capitol 1953)★★, *Mambo!* 10-inch album (Capitol 1954)★★★★, *Legend Of The Jivaro* (Capitol 1957)★★★, *Feugo Del Andes* (Capitol 1959)★★★ *Live In Concert* (1961)★★, *Miracles* (London 1972)★★★.

● FILMS: *Secret Of The Incas* (1954).

SUN RECORDS

The Sun Record Company was founded in Memphis, Tennessee, in February 1952. It evolved out of the Memphis Recording Service, a small studio installed two years earlier by Sam Phillips, a former disc jockey on stations WMSL and WREC. Although early work often consisted of social occasions, Phillips' ambitions focused on an untapped local blues market. Completed masters were leased to a variety of independent outlets, including Chess, Duke and RPM, in the process launching the careers of B.B. King, Howlin' Wolf and Bobby Bland. The Sun label was the natural extension of this success and its early reputation for superior R&B was established with hits by Rufus Thomas ('Bear Cat') and 'Little' Junior Parker ('Feelin' Good'). In 1954 Phillips began recording country music, and the confluence of these two styles resulted in rockabilly. Its most vocal proponent was Elvis Presley, signed by Phillips that year, who completed five exceptional singles for the label before joining RCA Victor. Presley's recordings, which included 'That's Alright Mama', 'Good Rockin' Tonight' and 'Mystery Train', featured Scotty Moore on guitar and Bill Black on bass, whose sparse, economical support enhanced the singer's unfettered delivery. The crisp production defined Sun rockabilly, a sound the singer was unable to recapture following his move to a major label. Although many commentators questioned Phillips' decision, he retorted that he could now develop the careers of Carl Perkins and Johnny Cash. The former's exemplary releases included 'Blue Suede Shoes' (Sun's first national pop hit), 'Matchbox' and 'Boppin' The Blues', but a near-fatal car crash undermined his progress. His mantle was taken up by other rockabilly singers - Warren Smith, Sonny Burgess and Billy Lee Riley - but these lesser acts failed to establish a consistent career. Roy Orbison and Charlie Rich enjoyed limited success on Sun, but found greater acclaim elsewhere. The aforementioned Cash then became Sun's most commercial property and he enjoyed several hits, including 'I Walk The Line' (1957), 'Ballad Of A Teenage Queen' and 'Guess Things Happen That Way' (both 1958), thus emphasizing the label's country heritage. Four million-sellers - 'Whole Lotta Shakin' Goin' On', 'Great Balls Of Fire', 'Breathless' and 'High School Confidential' - by the exuberant Jerry Lee Lewis, closed a highly productive decade, but the same singer's rapid fall from grace, coupled with the loss of Cash and Perkins, proved hard to surmount. Sun's simple, rhythmic sound - the only device used to enhance a performance was echo - now proved anachronistic, yet a move to new, larger premises in 1960 paradoxically meant it was lost forever. The label was never Phillips' sole business investment; radio stations, mining and the Holiday Inn Hotel chain vied for his attention, while new record companies, Hi and Stax, seemed better able to capture the changing Memphis music scene. Paradoxically, this allowed Sun's achievements to remain untarnished and thus its legend is still undiminished. On 1 July 1969, Sam Phillips sold the entire company to country music entrepreneur Shelby Singleton who, with the able assistance of British licensees Charly Records, have completed a series of judicious repackages.

● COMPILATIONS: *The Roots Of Rock Volumes 1-13* (Sun 1977)★★★, *Sun Golden Hits* (Sun 1981)★★★, *The Sun Box* (1982)★★★★, *Sun: The Blues* 9-LP box set (Sun 1985)★★★, *The Sun Country Years* 11-LP box set (Bear Family

1987)★★★★, *Sun: The Rocking Years* 12-LP box set (Charly 1987)★★★★, *The Sound Of Sun* (1988)★★★, *The Sun Story Volumes 1 & 2* (1991)★★★★, *The Very Best Of Sun Rock 'N' Roll* (1991)★★★, *The Sun Singles Collection Volume 1* 4-CD box set (Bear Family 1995)★★★.
● FURTHER READING: *Sun Records*, Colin Escott and Martin Hawkins.

SUNSHINE, MONTY

b. 8 April 1928, London, England. After teaching himself to play clarinet, Sunshine became involved in the UK trad jazz scene of the late 40s. He was a founder-member of the Crane River Jazz Band and later teamed up with Chris Barber to form a co-operative group. For a while this band was under the nominal leadership of Ken Colyer, but later reverted to its original democratic status. Sunshine was featured on several records, notably 'Petite Fleur', and helped the band to establish a reputation as one of the best of the UK trad outfits. In 1960 he left Barber to form his own band which, while retaining a high level of popularity for a number of years, never equalled the success of the Barber/Sunshine band. However, Sunshine established a name in Europe, especially in Germany. In the 70s he had occasional reunions with the re-formed Crane River Jazz Band and with Barber. Although a proponent of New Orleans jazz, Sunshine's playing style has always favoured the full, romantic sound of musicians such as Sidney Bechet and Barney Bigard. In the 80s he was often on tour as a solo artist, still popular with the audience he had known from his earliest days in the business.
● ALBUMS: *A Taste Of Sunshine* (DJM 1976)★★★, *Magic Is The Moonlight* (Telefunken 1978)★★★, *Sunshine In London* (Black Lion 1979)★★★, *On Sunday* (Wam 1987)★★★.
● COMPILATIONS: *Monty Sunshine And The Crane River Jazz Band, 1950-53* (Dormouse 1988)★★★, *Gotta Travel On* (Timeless 1992)★★★.

SWAN SILVERTONES

This vocal quartet was formed in 1938 in West Virginia, USA, by four coalminers, Claude Jeter (lead), Eddie Boroughas, John Myles and Leroy Watkins. The Swan in their name refers to their early sponsors, the Swan Bakery. Their first sessions were recorded for King Records in Cincinnati in 1946. At this time Henry Brossard (bass) and Soloman Womack (joint lead) joined. The line-up changed frequently throughout the late 40s, with Reverend Percell Perkins, Reverend Robert Crenshaw and Roosevelt Payne all joining at various points. Paul Owens, formerly of the Nightingales and Dixie Hummingbirds, also joined the group. Although their recording career (for Specialty Records) was sparser than more celebrated gospel/R&B groups, the Silvertones continued to tour and appear on radio. William Connor of the Trumpeteers replaced Brossard in 1955, though by the time the group moved to Vee Jay Records in 1959, Louis Johnson had joined as third lead. Claude Jeter became a minister in 1963, after which the group lost much of its momentum. Various singers flitted in and out of the group, and the only remaining original member, John Miles, retired in 1978. The same year former members reunited to play a one-off concert in Chicago.

SWANN, DONALD

b. Donald Ibrahim Swann, 30 September 1923, Llanelli, Wales, d. 23 March 1994, London, England. Swann was the progeny of a union between a Russian doctor and Turkoman nurse who fled St. Petersburg, Russia, during the Revolution. He attended school at Westminster where he proved a popular member of the revue team alongside Michael Flanders (see Flanders And Swann) and stage manager and future UK MP Tony Benn, before beginning studies at Oxford University. While working with the Friends' Ambulance Unit he visited Greece, whose serenity and sense of community, greatly influenced his music. However, he soon returned to London to contribute material to West End revues, linking again with Michael Flanders. Both were soon buoyed by the success of ventures such as *Penny Plain* (1951), *Airs On A Shoestring* (1953) and *Fresh Airs* (1956). However, it was their own two-man show, *At The Drop Of A Hat*, that propelled them to nationwide fame after it opened on New Year's Eve in 1956. A massive hit, the show ran for over two years in London, before playing on Broadway and touring the USA and Canada. It was followed in 1963 by *At The Drop Of Another Hat*. However, Swann grew discontented with the endless cycle of engagements and touring that followed, leading to the dissolution of his first marriage. He remained in his house in Battersea, collaborating with Flanders on an album of animal songs for children, and scoring adaptations of the works of his friends C.S. Lewis and J.R.R. Tolkien. He also composed music as a backdrop to his favourite poet, Emily Dickinson, and formed less succesful partnerships with John Amis, Frank Topping, Ian Wallace and Lili Malandraki, following the death of Flanders in 1975. Fortunately, he was able to complete his autobiography with the help of second wife Alison Smith before he succumbed to cancer at the age of 70. At that time he was also working on material for a new revue, *Swann Amongst The Sirens*, based on his wartime experiences in Greece (to have been staged by the Cherub Theatre Company).
● FURTHER READING: *Swann's Way: A Life In Song*.

SWEET BEAT

This low-budget 1959 British film was produced by Jeff Kruger who co-owned London's fabled Flamingo nightclub and subsequently operated the Ember label. It starred Julie Amber as a beauty queen-turned-singer who is offered a lucrative spot in a New York venue by a promoter seeking sexual favours in return. The title song was performed by Tony Crombie who, as leader of Tony Crombie And His Rockets, was one of the first UK musicians to embrace nascent rock 'n' roll earlier in the decade. Fred Parris And His Satins, Cindy Mann, Jeri Lee and Lee Allen And His Band were among the other acts featured in a film that promptly sank with little trace.

TAKE ME ALONG

Bob Merrill, the composer and lyricist for a host of pop hits during the 50s, wrote his first Broadway score in 1957 for *New Girl In Town*, a musical adaptation of Eugene O'Neill's classic drama *Anna Christie*. Two years later, for *Take Me Along*, he tackled another of the playwright's works, but one with a much lighter theme - *Ah, Wilderness!* It opened at the Shubert Theatre in New York on 22 October 1959 with a strong cast that was headed by a legendary Hollywood leading man of the 30s and 40s, Walter Pidgeon, and Jackie Gleason, whose main claim to fame at that time was as a comedian on US television. Joseph Stein and Robert Russell wrote the book, which was set in the homely town of Centerville, Connecticut, in 1910. Pidgeon plays Ned Miller, the publisher of the local newspaper, and the father of Richard, whose adolescent problems with his girlfriend, Muriel Macomber (Susan Luckey) and the devil drink, are resolved when he enters the hallowed halls of Yale University. The sub-plot concerns Sid Davis (Jackie Gleason), a far more serious drinker, who would like to settle down with Ned's sister, Lily (Eileen Herlie), but has to sober up before she will accept him. Pidgeon and Gleason duetted on the the lively 'Take Me Along', and the rest of Merrill's score, which has been described as 'wistful and enchanting', included 'I Would Die', 'Staying Young', 'I Get Embarrassed', 'Sid Ol' Kid', 'We're Home', 'Promise Me A Rose', 'Nine O'Clock' and 'But Yours'. Pidgeon and Gleason were both nominated for the Tony Award for best actor, and Gleason won for the most satisfying stage role of his career. He was succeeded during the show's run of 448 performances by William Bendix, a movie tough-guy with a heart of gold. *Take Me Along* returned to Broadway during the 1984/5 season, which, according to experienced Broadway watchers, was one of the worst in living memory. The climate was not right for the show's warm and charming approach, and it closed after only one performance.

TARHEEL SLIM

b. Alden Bunn, 24 September 1924, Bailey, North Carolina, USA, d. 21 August 1977. Tarheel Slim was a blues, gospel and doo-wop singer and guitarist who took his sobriquet from the popular nickname of North Carolina - Tarheel State. Bunn learned guitar at the age of 12 and sang in church by the age of 20. He began working with the Gospel Four following World War II and then joined the Selah Jubilee Singers, with whom he first recorded, in the late 40s. As the gospel group could not record secular music, they also worked under the names the Four Barons and the Larks, recording the R&B hits 'Eyesight To The Blind' and 'Little Side Car' for Apollo Records in 1951. Bunn recorded under his real name for Apollo and also with the group the Wheels in 1956 on

Premium Records. That was followed by a partnership with his wife as the Lovers for Lamp Records in 1958. They then recorded for the Fire label as Tarheel Slim And Little Ann, a name they kept until 1962. After a spell outside the music business, Slim returned in 1970, when he recorded for Trix Records, an association that lasted until his death.
● ALBUMS: *Lock Me In Your Heart* (1989)★★★, *No Time At All* (Trix 1994)★★★.

TARRIERS

Formed *c.*1954, the Tarriers are remembered for two primary reasons: their 1956 US Top 5 recording of 'The Banana Boat Song' and the fact that one of the group members was Alan Arkin, who went on to become a highly successful actor. The folk group was put together by Erik Darling (b. 25 September 1933, Baltimore, Maryland, USA), who was influenced by the folk revivalists of the day. After performing briefly with a large troupe of vocalists, Darling hooked up with Arkin (b. 26 March 1934, Brooklyn, New York) and Bob Carey as the Tunetellers. The group changed its name to the Tarriers and wrote and recorded 'The Banana Boat Song' to capitalize on the calypso music craze then sweeping the USA. Simultaneously, they recorded a similar song called 'Cindy, Oh Cindy' with singer Vince Martin. Both singles were released on Glory Records, 'Cindy' reaching number 9 and 'The Banana Boat Song' number 4. The Tarriers never again made the charts, however, and the original trio dissolved two years later. Darling joined the Weavers and later formed the Rooftop Singers; Arkin began his acting career and Carey kept a Tarriers group in existence until 1964.
● ALBUMS: *The Tarriers* (Glory 1958)★★★, *Hard Travelin'* (United Artists 1959)★★★★, *Tell The World About This* (Atlantic 1960)★★★, *The Tarriers* (Decca 1962)★★★, *The Original Tarriers* (Kapp 1963)★★★, *Gather 'Round* (Decca 1964)★★.

TATUM, ART

b. 13 October 1909, Toledo, Ohio, USA, d. 5 November 1956. Born into a musical family, Tatum was handicapped from birth by impaired sight. Blind in one eye and only partially sighted in the other, he nevertheless studied piano formally and learned to read music. By his mid-teens he was playing professionally in Toledo. He played briefly in the Speed Webb band, but was mostly active as a soloist or in small groups working in clubs and playing on radio. He was heard by singer Adelaide Hall, who took him on the road as her accompanist. With Hall he travelled to New York in 1932 and the following year made his first recordings. He spent the next few years playing clubs in Cleveland and Chicago, but in 1937 was back in New York, where he established his reputation as a major figure in jazz circles. He toured the USA and also played in the UK. In the early 40s he formed a trio with bassist Slam Stewart and guitarist Tiny Grimes which became extremely popular. For the next decade Tatum toured extensively, performing throughout North America. In the early 50s he was signed by Norman Granz who recorded him in a series of remarkable performances, both as soloist (*The Solo Masterpieces*) and in a small group context with Benny Carter, Buddy De Franco, Roy Eldridge, Lionel Hampton, Ben Webster and others (*The Group Masterpieces*). A matchless virtuoso performer, Tatum's impact on the New York jazz scene in the early 30s had extensive repercussions. Even Fats Waller, an acknowledged master and someone Tatum had listened to on record in his own formative years, was aware of the phenomenal talent of the newcomer, reputedly declaring onstage - when he spotted Tatum in the audience - 'God is in the house tonight'. Tatum's dazzling extemporizations on themes from jazz and the classics, but mostly from the popular songbook, became bywords and set standards few of his successors matched and none surpassed. Capable of breathtaking runs, interspersed with striking single notes and sometimes unexpected chords, he developed a unique solo style. His powerful left-hand figures tipped a hat in the direction of stride while he simultaneously explored the limits of an orthodox keyboard like no other pianist in jazz (and few elsewhere). A playful habit of quoting from other melodies, a technique that in unskilled hands can be merely irritating, was developed into a singular stylistic device. Unlike some virtuoso performers, Tatum never sacrificed feeling and swing for effect. Although he continued to develop throughout his career, it is hard to discover any recorded evidence that he was never poised and polished. His prodigious talent allowed him to achieve extraordinary recording successes: his solo sessions for Granz were mostly completed in two days - 69 tracks, all but three needing only one take. Ray Spencer, whose studies of the artist are extensive, has commented that Tatum achieved such a remarkable work rate through constant 'refining and honing down after each performance until an ideal version remained needing no further adjustments'. While this is clearly the case, Tatum's performances never suggest a man merely going through the motions. Everything he did sounded fresh and vital, as if minted especially for the occasion in hand. Although he remains a major figure in jazz piano, Tatum is often overlooked in the cataloguing of those who affected the course of the music. He appears to stand to one side of the developing thrust of jazz, yet his creativity and the manner in which he explored harmonic complexities and unusual chord sequences influenced many musicians, including Bud Powell and Herbie Hancock, and especially non-pianists, among whom can be listed Charlie Parker and John Coltrane.

● ALBUMS: *Art Tatum Trio* (Dial 1950)★★★, *Art Tatum* (Asch 1950)★★★★, *Art Tatum Piano Solos* (Brunswick 1950)★★★★, *Encores* (Capitol 1951)★★★★, *Art Tatum Trio* (Folkways 1951)★★★★, *Gene Norman Concert At Shrine Auditorium, May 1949* (Columbia 1952)★★★★, *Piano Solo Private Sessions* (1952)★★★★, *Here's Art Tatum* (Brunswick 1954)★★★★, *An Art Tatum Concert* reissued as *The Tatum Touch* (Columbia 1954)★★★★, *Presenting The Art Tatum Trio* (Verve 1961)★★★★.

● COMPILATIONS: *The Genius Of Art Tatum Volumes 1-11* (Clef/Verve 1954-57)★★★★, *The Complete Pablo Solo Masterpieces Volumes 1-12* 1953-56 recordings (Pablo 1978)★★★★, *The Tatum Group Masterpieces Vols 1-9* 1955-56 recordings (Pablo 1978)★★★★,*The Chronological Art Tatum* (1932-34)★★★★, *The Chronological Art Tatum* (1934-40)★★★★, *Pure Genius* (1934-45)★★★★, *The Standard Sessions* (1935-43)★★★★, *Get Happy!* (1938-39)★★★★, *Pieces Of Eight* (1939-55)★★★★, with Les Paul *Together* (early 40s)★★★★, *The Complete Trio Sessions With Tiny Grimes And Slam Stewart Vols 1 & 2* (1944)★★★★, *Moods* (1944-55)★★★★, *Pieces Of Eight* (1945-55)★★★★, *The*

Complete Capitol Recordings (1949-52)★★★, *Art Tatum On The Air* (Aircheck 1978)★★★★, *The V Discs 1944-46* recordings (Black Lion 1979)★★★★, *20th Century Piano Genius* (Emarcy 1987)★★★★, *Complete Art Tatum Volumes 1 & 2* (Capitol 1990)★★★★, *Complete Brunswick And Decca Sessions 1932-41* (Affinity 1993)★★★★, *20th Century Piano Genius* (Verve 1996)★★★★.

● FURTHER READING: *Art Tatum, A Guide To His Recorded Music*, Arnold Laubich. *Too Marvellous For Words: The Life And Genius Of*, James Lester.

TAYLOR, VINCE

b. *c.*1940, d. 1991. One of the first and most authentic British rock 'n' rollers, Taylor was virtually ignored by his native Britons but managed to make a decent living in France, where he spent most of his life. He started out in 1958 backed by his Playboys, who comprised Tony Harvey (guitar), Tony Sheridan (guitar, vocals), Brian 'Licorice' Locking (bass) and Brian Bennett (drums). They appeared regularly on the pioneering UK television rock show *Oh Boy!* and released a cover version of a Charlie Rich song, 'Right Behind You Baby', on Parlophone. A second single in 1959, 'Brand New Cadillac', penned by Taylor, ranks alongside Ian Samwell's 'Move It' as one of *the* authentic British rock records. The Clash would later contribute a version that restored it to the UK rock tradition. The band split in early 1959 (Locking and Bennett moved to various bands, including the Shadows, and Sheridan went to Hamburg where he worked with the fledgling Beatles) and Taylor assembled a new backing band with Harvey plus Alan LeClaire on piano, Johnny Vance on bass, and Bobby Woodman on drums. This line-up of the Playboys also backed Screaming Lord Sutch in 1960. Taylor toured with Sutch, Keith Kelly and Lance Fortune on a '2 I's (coffee bar)' package tour. Around the Summer of 1961 Harvey joined Nero And The Gladiators, the rest of the Playboys went to France to back Johnny Hallyday, and Taylor followed their trail, becoming a minor celebrity in the process. He continued to record throughout the 60s, 70s and 80s, mostly doing cover versions of rock 'n' roll classics.

● ALBUMS: *Le Rock C'est Ça!* (1961)★★★, *Vince* (1965)★★★, *Alive, Well & Rocking In Paris* (1972)★★, *Cadillac* (1975)★★, *Live 1977* (1979)★★, *Luv* (1980)★★★, *Bien Compris* (1987)★★★, *Black Leather Rebel* (1993)★★★, *Vince Live At The Olympia* (Big Beat 1997)★★.

● COMPILATIONS: *The Early Sides* (Big Beat 1997)★★★.

TEDDY BEARS

Were it not for the fact that Phil Spector began as a member of the Teddy Bears, this one-hit-wonder trio would most likely be a minor footnote in the history of rock. Spector moved to the USA with his family at the age of nine following the suicide of his father, whose tombstone bore the legend 'To know him is to love him'. While in high school in Los Angeles, Spector sang at talent shows and assembled a group called the Sleepwalkers. He formed the Teddy Bears with singers Marshall Leib, Annette Kleinbard and Harvey Goldstein (who left the group shortly after its formation), after graduating from high school in June 1958. The group recorded a demo of Spector's composition 'Don't You Worry, My Little Pet', which Dore Records released. For the b-side, Spector's 'To Know Him Is To Love Him' was recorded and it

was that side which caught the ear of the public, rising to number 1 in the US charts in late 1958. Following that success, the group signed with the larger Imperial Records and recorded an album (which is very rare and valuable today) as well as further singles. No more were hits and the group disbanded after Kleinbard was seriously injured in a 1960 car accident. The striking 'To Know Him Is To Love Him' became a standard, and was later successfully revived by Peter And Gordon in 1965. The later career of Phil Spector has been well documented. Kleinbard, after her recovery, changed her name to Carol Connors and became a successful songwriter including 'Hey Little Cobra' for the Rip Chords, Vicki Lawrence's 'The Night The Lights Went Out In Georgia', and music for numerous films including two of the *Rocky* series. Marshall Leib joined the group the Hollywood Argyles, played guitar on some Duane Eddy records and produced records by the Everly Brothers and others.
● ALBUMS: *The Teddy Bears Sing!* (Imperial 1959)★★.

TEEN QUEENS
This R&B duo of Betty and Rosie Collins came from Los Angeles, California, USA. Their entry into the recording business and signing to RPM Records in 1955 was facilitated by their older brother, Aaron Collins of the Jacks/Cadets, who recorded for the same company. The youthful amateurishness of the singing on their one hit, 'Eddie My Love' (number 2 R&B and number 14 pop), probably helped to make the record a hit in 1956. It was one of the first records specifically to direct its appeal to teenagers. It was the era of the cover record, and both the Fontane Sisters and the Chordettes also took the song high on the pop charts, but it is the Teen Queens' version that endures. The duo could not follow up with a hit, despite recording some excellent material over the years. Moves to RCA in 1958 and Antler in 1960 did not help and the duo broke up in 1961.
● ALBUMS: *Eddie My Love* (RPM 1956)★★★, *The Teen Queens* (1963)★★★.
● COMPILATIONS: *Rock Everybody* (Ace 1986)★★★.

THE "CHIRPING" CRICKETS - THE CRICKETS ★★★★
Another great classic, from 1957, that failed to chart on either side of the Atlantic, the Crickets credit on the cover may have deterred purchasers who did not realize that this featured Mr Holly. The tracks speak for themselves, timeless rock 'n' roll songs that still take some beating; 'Maybe Baby', 'That'll Be The Day' and 'Oh Boy' were the main hit singles, but the inclusion of 'Not Fade Away', 'It's Too late' and 'Send Me Some Lovin'' makes this collection essential. The cover is a priceless timepiece from the days before real graphic designers were used, where a wonderful false sky has been dropped in behind four men who look like senior citizens posing uncomfortably with guitars.
● TRACKS: *Oh Boy*; *Not Fade Away*; *You've Got Love*; *Maybe Baby*; *It's Too Late*; *Tell Me How*; *That'll Be The Day*; *I'm Looking For Someone To Love*; *An Empty Cup (And A Broken Date)*; *Send Me Some Lovin'*; *Last Night*; *Rock Me My Baby*.

THE BUDDY HOLLY STORY - BUDDY HOLLY ★★★★★
Few other artists exercised as profound an influence in such a short space of time as Buddy Holly. His death robbed pop

of a performer adept both as a solo act and as leader of his group, the Crickets. He wrote, or co-wrote, most of his own material at a time when many singers relied on outside material, and his sparse, but effective, guitar style proved highly influential, particularly on British beat groups. *The Buddy Holly Story*, from 1959, abounds with songs now indisputably pop classics and confirms Holly's status as a major figure. The Beatles, Tex-Mex music and the singer-songwriter genre each owe Holly a debt, which in itself is a lasting tribute to the quality of his work. The album peaked at number 2 in the UK chart and number 11 in the USA.
● TRACKS: *Raining In My Heart*; *Early In The Morning*; *Peggy Sue*; *Maybe Baby*; *Everyday*; *Rave On*; *That'll Be The Day*; *Heartbeat*; *Think It Over*; *Oh Boy*; *It's So Easy*; *It Doesn't Matter Any More*.

THE DIAMONDS - THE DIAMONDS ★★★★
The Diamonds, invariably dressed in dinner jackets and bow ties, had such overblown vocal arrangements that one might question whether their rock 'n' roll was serious or a parody. Indeed, their version of the Gladiolas' 'Little Darlin'' could have passed for one of Stan Freberg's fun-filled records and Elvis Presley later used it as a comedy number in stage appearances. Nevertheless, the Diamonds were a top rock 'n' roll group and this 1957 album contains such doo-wop favourites as 'The Stroll' (actually, a slow dance), 'A Thousand Miles Away' and 'Daddy Cool'.
● TRACKS: *The Stroll*; *You Baby You*; *Ev'ry Night About This Time*; *Ka-Ding-Dong*; *A Thousand Miles Away*; *Ev'ry Minute Of The Day*; *Little Darlin'*; *Faithful And True*; *Straight Skirts*; *Silhouettes*; *Passion Flower*; *Daddy Cool*.

THE FABULOUS - LITTLE RICHARD ★★★★★
Little Richard's third album captured a singer building on his own acknowledged style. He had forged a reputation based on undiluted R&B, typified on such expressive recordings as 'Tutti Frutti', 'Long Tall Sally' and 'Good Golly Miss Molly'. *The Fabulous* offered a wider musical perspective, although there was no denying the frantic fervour surrounding his readings of 'Kansas City' and 'Whole Lotta Shakin' Goin' On'. Such performances contrast with the more conciliatory 'Directly From My Heart', but the opportunity to broaden musical horizons suggested by this set was never fully taken up. In 1957 Richard denounced his work and joined the church, but although he later reversed that decision, this 1958 album closed his most creative period.
● TRACKS: *Shake A Hand*; *Chicken Little Baby*; *All Night Long*; *The Most I Can Offer*; *Lonesome And Blue*; *Wonderin'*; *Whole Lotta Shakin' Goin' On*; *She Knows How To Rock*; *Kansas City*; *Directly From My Heart*; *Maybe I'm Right*; *Early One Morning*; *I'm Just A Lonely Guy*.

THE GEORGE AND IRA GERSHWIN SONGBOOK - ELLA FITZGERALD ★★★★★
The paradox surrounding Ella Fitzgerald's prominence in the history of jazz singing and her lack of emotional intensity is much less apparent on this 1959 album. George Gershwin's affinity with jazz, and the corresponding delight jazz musicians took in performing his material, allowed the singer to fly with the music. As for brother Ira's lyrics, they

received their due as cheerful, tender and always delightful examples of the lyricist's art. The *Songbook* series remains one of Fitzgerald's major contributions to American popular music, and this, in particular, is one of the best of the bunch.
● TRACKS: including *Sam And Delilah; But Not For Me; My One And Only; Let's Call The Whole Thing Off; I've Got Beginners Luck; Lady Be Good; Nice Work If You Can Get It; Things Are Looking Up; Just Another Rhumba; How Long Has This Been Going On; S'Wonderful; Man I Love; That Certain Feeling; By Strauss; Who Cares; Someone To Watch Over Me; Real American Folk Song; They All Laughed; Looking For A Boy; My Cousin From Milwaukee; Somebody From Somewhere; Foggy Day; Clap Yo' Hands; For You, For Me, Forever More; Stiff Upper Lip; Strike Up The Band; Soon; I've Got A Crush On You; Bidin' My Time; Aren't You Kind Of Glad We Did; Of Thee I Sing; Half It Dearie Blues; I Was Doing It Right; He Loves And She Loves; Love Is Sweeping The Country; Treat Me Rough; Love Is Here To Stay; Slap That Bass; Isn't It A Pity; Shall We Dance.*

THE KINGSTON TRIO AT LARGE ▪ THE KINGSTON TRIO ★★★★

As if to prove a point, this was the second album by the Trio that went to number 1 in the USA in the same year (1959). Back in post-McCarthy America, the folk song had been far less complicated and more immediate. This was an era when right-on students and town dwellers began to look to folk as a focal point for social comment. Recreators such as the Kingstons opened up folk to an ever-expanding audience. With albums like this, folk for 'pop thinkers' was being created and a whole movement had its foundations in back-to-basics, quickly formulated recordings. *The Kingston Trio At Large* remains a credit to its genre.
● TRACKS: *MTA; All My Sorrows; Blew Ye Winds; Carey, Carey; The Seine; I Bowled; Good News; Getaway John; The Long Black Rifle; Early Mornin'; Scarlet Ribbons (For Her Hair); Remember The Alamo.*

THE MUSIC MAN ▪ ORIGINAL BROADWAY CAST ★★★★

Meredith Willson's charming and amusing score benefited from early stereo ('also available in regular monophonic', according to the sleeve), and inspired singing performances, especially from Robert Preston and Barbara Cook. The latter's thrilling voice is particularly effective on 'Goodnight, My Someone' and 'Till There Was You', and Preston has a ball with his *tour de force*, 'Ya Got Trouble'. It all added up to a spell of 123 weeks in the US Top 40, 12 of them at number 1, and the 1958 Grammy award for best Original Cast album.
● TRACKS: *Overture & Rock Island; Iowa Stubborn; Ya Got Trouble; Piano Lesson; Goodnight, My Someone; Seventy-six Trombones; Sincere; Sadder But Wiser Girl For Me; Pick-a-little, Take-a-little & Goodnight Ladies; Marian The Librarian; My White Knight; Wells Fargo Wagon; It's You; Shipoopi; Lida Rose & Will I Ever Tell You; Gary, Indiana; Till There Was You; Finale.*

THE PAJAMA GAME ▪ ORIGINAL BROADWAY CAST ★★★★

Broadway newcomers Richard Adler and Jerry Ross wrote the marvellous score for this show, which ran for well over 1,000 performances in New York. Few could have foreseen that the subject of a strike in a pyjama factory would produce great songs such as 'Hey, There', 'I'm Not At All In Love', 'Small Talk' and 'Hernando's Hideaway'. That fine singer John Raitt leads the cast, which also includes Janis Paige, Carol Haney and Eddie Foy Jnr. Every track, whether witty, romantic, or downright hilarious, is appealing on this enduring and memorable album from 1955.
● TRACKS: *Overture; The Pajama Game; Racing With The Clock; A New Town Is A Blue Town; I'm Not At All In Love; I'll Never Be Jealous Again; Hey, There; Her Is; Once A Year Day; Small Talk; There Once Was A Man; Steam Heat; Think Of The Time I Save; Hernando's Hideaway; Seven And A Half Cents; Finale.*

THERE'S NO BUSINESS LIKE SHOW BUSINESS

Incongruous is perhaps an appropriate word to describe the casting of the 'Nabob of Sob', pop singer Johnnie Ray, in this film, which was one of the last of the truly lavish screen musicals and was released by 20th Century-Fox in 1955. Ray plays one of the Donahues, a vaudeville act consisting of his brother and sister (Mitzi Gaynor and Donald O'Connor) and their parents (Dan Dailey and Ethel Merman). Ray even manages to induce a few of his trademark tears, although in this instance they swell up in the eyes of his proud old Mom and Dad after he has announced his decision to become a priest. That scene, and his strangulated version of 'If You Believe', one of the two new songs in Irving Berlin's otherwise entertaining score, should surely have won someone a bad-taste Oscar. Instead, the only whiff of an Academy Award was the nomination for Lamar Trotti's story (adapted for the screen by Henry and Phoebe Ephron). It deals with the triumphs and crises experienced by the family group, and O'Connor's initially ill-fated love affair with a cabaret singer played by Marilyn Monroe. After spending some time in the US Navy 'growing up', O'Connor joins the rest of the clan for the finale and a rousing version of the title song. Before going away to sea, he has some of the best numbers, singing and dancing delightfully in 'A Man Chases A Girl (Until She Catches Him)' and (with Gaynor and Monroe) 'Lazy'. He also adopted a Scottish accent for his part in a spectacular setting of 'Alexander's Ragtime Band'. Gaynor gave the number a touch of the Parisian, Merman was gamely Germanic, and Johnnie Ray . . . well, his intended articulation was unclear. Other highlights of the film were Monroe's sizzling versions of 'Heat Wave' and 'After You Get What You Want You Don't Want It', and Merman and Dailey's 'Play A Simple Melody', 'A Pretty Girl Is Like A Melody', 'Let's Have Another Cup Of Coffee' and 'You'd Be Surprised'. Jack Cole, who had worked with Monroe on *Gentlemen Prefer Blondes* two years earlier, staged her dances, and the remainder of the film's spirited routines were choreographed by Robert Alton. Sol C. Siegel was the producer, and it was directed by Walter Lang. The impressive DeLuxe Color and CinemaScope photography was by Leon Shamroy.

THIELE, BOB

b. 1922, Brooklyn, New York, USA, d. 30 January 1996, New York City, New York, USA. Thiele was one of the most important and prolific jazz and pop producers in US popular music. A teenage jazz fan, Thiele joined the US Decca company after World War II and produced Teresa Brewer and the

McGuire Sisters. He became head of A&R for Coral Records in 1958. There he supervised hundreds of records including hits by Jackie Wilson, as well as licensing Buddy Holly material from Norman Petty. In 1961, Thiele set up the Impulse! jazz label with Creed Taylor. Over the rest of the decade he signed and recorded many of the greatest names in the 'new wave' jazz scene, including John Coltrane, Charles Mingus, Dizzy Gillespie, Sonny Rollins, Archie Shepp and Albert Ayler. His biggest hit, however, was with Louis Armstrong's 'What A Wonderful World', which he co-wrote with George David Weiss. Thiele's first independent label had been Signature, during the brief life of which he had released jazz-and-poetry records by beat-poet Jack Kerouac and jazz pianist Art Hodes. In 1969 he set up the Flying Dutchman label with Bernard 'Pretty' Purdie as musical director. Among its signings were Gil Scott-Heron and Lonnie Liston Smith, whose records Thiele continued to produce until the late 80s. He married Teresa Brewer in 1972, some 20 years after he first recorded her. After Flying Dutchman was closed down, Bob returned to freelance production but in 1983 he founded Dr. Jazz, a company devoted to mainstream jazz from the orchestras of Duke Ellington and Count Basie as well as Brewer. In 1988, Dr. Jazz was sold to CBS but Thiele returned three years later, launching Red Baron Records with albums from Brewer and McCoy Tyner. He died of kidney failure.

● FURTHER READING: *What A Wonderful World*, Bob Golden.

THIS IS FATS DOMINO - FATS DOMINO ★★★★

Despite the cheap appearance of the cover, this is one of the most potent rock 'n' roll albums of the 50s. Domino's revival of Louis Armstrong's 'Blueberry Hill' was so successful that most people now regard it as Domino's own song. That, and other classics, feature on this 1957 release, which reached number 19 in the US album chart. Domino and his producer Dave Bartholomew wrote straightforward, conversational rock 'n' roll songs, including 'Ain't It A Shame', now known as 'Ain't That A Shame'. (Pat Boone, an graduate in English, originally objected to covering a song with the word 'Ain't' in the title.) 'Blue Monday', which Domino sang in *The Girl Can't Help It*. He also mocked himself in 'The Fat Man's Hop', begging the question of why there was so much controversy when Elvis Presley put on weight; Fats Domino always looked the same and was much heavier than Presley.

● TRACKS: *Blueberry Hill; Honey Chile; What's The Reason I'm Not Pleasing You; Blue Monday; So Long; La La; Troubles Of My Own; You Done Me Wrong; Reeling And Rocking; The Fat Man's Hop; Poor Poor Me; Trust In Me.*

THREE CHUCKLES

Formed in Brooklyn, New York, USA, vocal/instrumental doo-wop group the Three Chuckles took their name from the fact that they began life as a comedy troupe. Tommy Romano (tenor and guitar) and Russ Gilberto (lead vocals and bass guitar) met while playing baseball, and soon added accordion player Phil Benti. After lengthy touring, Benti departed, and they took on 15-year-old Teddy Randazzo as replacement. After further local concerts the group were spotted at a bowling alley in Detroit in 1953 by Ray Gayhan. Through him they secured a recording contract with Great

Lakes Records' subsidiary, Boulevard Records. Two songs were recorded, 'At Last You Understand' and 'Runaround', the latter written for them by Cirino Colacrais. It was this side that caused all the interest, and significant local airplay led to the band being snapped up for wider distribution by RCA Records. 'Runaround' subsequently peaked at number 20 in the *Billboard* charts, going on to sell over a million copies. The Three Chuckles used this exposure to secure prestigious television slots on shows hosted by Perry Como, Steve Allen and others, before being recruited by disc jockey Alan Freed for his 1955 movie, *Rock, Rock, Rock*, in which Romano played the male lead. A second celluloid appearance came in 1958 with *The Girl Can't Help It*, before the group retired to the studio to complete their first album. This was a steady seller, but their success on the singles front had now declined, with only 'Times Two, I Love You' and 'And The Angels Sing', the latter part of a new contract with Vik Records, making the charts. Randazzo then left for a solo career (subsequently writing hits for Little Anthony And The Imperials), and although he was replaced by Jackie Farrell, no further Three Chuckles recordings were issued.

● ALBUMS: *The Three Chuckles* (RCA 1958)★★.

THREEPENNY OPERA, THE

A dramatic play with music by Kurt Weill, and a book and lyrics by Bertolt Brecht, this three-act production was first presented at the Theatre am Schiffbauerdam in Berlin on 31 August 1928 under the title of *Die Dreigroschenoper*. That was 200 years after the show on which it was based, *The Beggar's Opera* by John Gay, was first seen in London. *The Threepenny Opera* had its first English language production on Broadway in 1933, and then returned to New York in 1954. This revised version, with an English book and lyrics by Marc Blitzstein, opened off-Broadway at the Theatre de Lys on 10 March, and ran for just three months. Public demand caused it to return in September 1955, and this time it stayed for an incredible 2,706 performances. The cynical and satirical tale of morality that had seemed so appropriate, yet futile, in the Germany of the 20s, remained the same, with its familiar characters including the outlaw Macheath, otherwise known as Mack the Knife (Scott Merrill), his wife Polly Peachum (Jo Sullivan), the police chief's daughter Lucy Brown (Beatrice Arthur), and Jenny Diver, the whore, played by Lotte Lenya (Weill's widow), the actress who had created the role in Germany. The score included 'The Ballad Of Mack The Knife', 'Love Song', 'Army Song', 'Pirate Jenny', 'Tango-Ballad', 'Useless Song', 'Ballad Of The Easy Life', 'Barbara Song', 'Solomon Song' and 'Instead-Of-Song'. During the show's extremely long run, many well-known actors and actresses took part, including Charlotte Rae, James Mitchell, Jerry Orbach, Carole Cook, Nancy Andrews, and Edward Asner. The English actress Georgia Brown played Lucy for a time, and she recreated her role, along with Bill Owen, Daphne Anderson, Lisa Lee, Eric Pohlmann and Warren Mitchell for the 1956 London production, which ran for 140 performances. Thirty years later in March 1986, a UK National Theatre production starred Tim Curry. A new adaptation of the piece, by Ralph Manheim and John Willett, spent 10 months on Broadway in 1976, and yet another version, billed as *3 Penny Opera* and translated by Michael Feingold, gave 65 performances at the Lunt-Fontanne Theatre in November 1989. Perhaps in an attempt to attract a different kind of audience, the cast for that production included rock star Sting as Macheath, along with popular singers Maureen McGovern and Kim Criswell. A 1994 London revival at the Donmar Warehouse, starring Tom Hollander and Sharon Small as Macheath and Polly Peachum, was set in the year 2001. Several film versions have been released, notably in 1931 with Lotte Lenya, and in 1964 with Hildegarde Neff and Curt Jurgens. The show is best remembered by many people for one song - 'Mack the Knife' (originally entitled 'Moriat'). It was introduced by Lotte Lenya in the tinkly Victorian-style of most of the show's music, and became successful in 1956 in the USA for several artists including the Dick Hyman Trio, Richard Hayman with Jan August, Lawrence Welk, Louis Armstrong and Billy Vaughn. Three years later the song became a massive number 1 hit on both sides of the Atlantic in a superb swinging version by Bobby Darin. Shortly afterwards, Ella Fitzgerald made a popular recording, and in 1984, yet another version, by the vocal-instrumental group King Kurt, entered the UK chart.

TIME OUT · DAVE BRUBECK ★★★★★

Second only to *Jazz Samba* by Stan Getz as the most commercially successful jazz record of all time (it even contained a single for the pop charts, Paul Desmond's magnificent 'Take Five'), Brubeck popularized jazz and offered it as an alternative to Bobby Vee. This 1959 album sold by the trunkload, reaching number 2 in the USA and number 11 in the UK, and made Brubeck a popular star. Those jazz critics who shunned him for becoming too commercial should eat their words, as this is a monumental album showcasing the finest modern jazz. 'Blue Rondo A La Turk' and 'Kathy's Waltz' demonstrate this man's graceful, nonchalant class.
● TRACKS: *Blue Rondo A La Turk*; *Strange Meadow Lark*; *Take Five*; *Three To Get Ready*; *Kathy's Waltz*; *Everybody's Jumpin'*; *Pick Up Sticks*.

TIOMKIN, DIMITRI

b. 10 May 1894, St. Petersburg, Russia, d. 11 November 1979, London, England. An important composer of film music from the 30s through to the 60s. After being coached in music by his mother as a small child, Tiomkin later studied at the St. Petersburg Conservatory. He worked as a professional musician, playing on the concert platform and as a pianist in silent-movie theatres, before moving to Berlin in 1921 to continue his studies. He gave numerous concert performances in Europe as a soloist, and duetting with another pianist. In 1925 he made his first visit to the USA, and returned in 1930 when his wife, a ballet dancer and choreographer, was hired to work on some Hollywood films. Tiomkin was also engaged to write music for films, and was soon in great demand. His first major film score was for *Alice In Wonderland* (1933). By now an American citizen, Tiomkin quickly became one of the most successful and prolific film composers, writing scores and incidental music in the late 30s, 40s and 50s for films such *Lost Horizon*, *The Great Waltz*, *You Can't Take It With You*, *Lucky Partners*, *The Westerner*, *Meet John Doe*, *The Corsican Brothers*, *Twin Beds*, *A Gentleman After Dark*, *The Moon And Sixpence*, *Unknown Guest*, *The Bridge Of San Luis Rey*, *The Imposter*, *Forever Yours*, *Dillinger*, *Pardon My Past*, *Duel In The Sun*, *The Dark Mirror*, *Whistle Stop*, *The Long Night*, *It's A Wonderful Life*, *Red River*, *So This Is New York*, *Champion*, *Home Of The Brave*, *Cyrano De Bergerac*, *Champagne For Caesar*, *Strangers On A Train*, *Bugles In The Afternoon*, *High Noon* (1952, Oscars for best score and title song with lyric by Ned Washington), *The Big Sky*, *The Four Poster*, *Angel Face*, *The Steel Trap*, *Return To Paradise*, *The High And The Mighty* (1954, another Oscar), *Dial M For Murder*, *Blowing In the Wind*, *Take The High Ground*, *Land Of The Pharaohs*, *Giant*, *Friendly Persuasion*, *Wild Is The Wind*, *Search For Paradise*, *Gun Fight At The O.K Corral*, *The Old Man And The Sea* (1958, his fourth Oscar) and *Rio Bravo* (1959). In the late 50s Tiomkin composed the theme music for the popular television series *Rawhide*, and throughout the 60s provided scores for some of the most popular and spectacular movies of the decade, including *The Alamo*, *The Sundowners*, *The Unforgiven*, *The Guns Of Navarone*, *Town Without Pity*, *55 Days At Peking*, *The Fall Of The Roman Empire*, *Circus World*, *36 Hours*, *The War Wagon* and *Great Catherine*. Among the songs that came from these and other films were 'Friendly Persuasion (Thee I Love)' and 'The Green Leaves Of Summer' (both with lyrics by Paul Francis Webster) and 'Wild Is The Wind' and 'Strange Are The Ways Of Love' (with Washington). He also worked as executive producer on the Russian film *Tchaikowsky* (1970), arranging the music of the film's subject. After moving to London in the 70s, Tiomkin died there in 1979.
● COMPILATIONS: *Lost Horizon-The Classic Film Scores Of Dimitri Tiomkin* (RCA 1976)★★★★.

TOMLINSON, ERNEST

b. 19 September 1924, Rawtenstall, Lancashire, England. A prolific writer with boundless energy, Tomlinson has been one of the major figures in British light music during the second half of the twentieth century. Delayed by war service in the RAF, his musical career began as a staff arranger for a London publisher after graduating in 1947 with a degree of Bachelor of Music for composition. Tomlinson was soon in demand for radio, television, stage and recording commitments, providing numerous arrangements as well as, occasionally, his own compositions - the first was broadcast in 1949. Many of his own works were first heard with his Ernest Tomlinson Light Orchestra (formed in 1955), and his 'Little Serenade' (1955) was destined to become a light music standard. Later the same year his work for the radio play *The Story Of Cinderella* finally allowed him to become a full-time freelance composer. His north country roots explain Tomlinson's love of brass bands and choirs, and he has been active in both these areas. 'An English Overture' was originally conceived for brass band, but it transferred well to full orchestra. Of special importance have been his suites of 'English Folk-Songs' - the first was in 1949 (receiving the first performance at the English Folk-Dance and Song Society's New Year Festival at London's Royal Albert Hall in January 1950), and the second suite followed in 1977. Many of the individual movements have become recognized in their own right, with wonderful titles such as 'Dick's Maggot', 'Jenny Pluck Pears', 'Woodicock' and 'Love-in-a-Mist'. Other popular works include 'Concert Jig' (from the 'Silverthorn Suite'), 'Kielder Water', 'Comedy Overture', 'Mediterranean Suite', 'English Pageant Suite', the 'Light Music Suite' (1971) and 'Passepied'. Tomlinson has been a tireless worker for his profession, serving in various capacities with the Light Music Society, the Composers' Guild of

Great Britain and the Performing Rights Society. He is the recipient of the Composers' Guild Award (1965) and two Ivor Novello Awards (1970 and 1975). In 1984 he founded The Library Of Light Orchestral Music which is housed in a huge barn at his farmhouse in Lancashire, and contains over 10,000 scores, many of which would have been otherwise lost.

● ALBUMS: *British Light Music - Ernest Tomlinson Volume 1* (Marco Polo 1992)★★★★, *British Light Music - Ernest Tomlinson Volume 2* (Marco Polo 1994)★★★★.

TOMMY STEELE STORY, THE

Former merchant seaman Tommy Hicks was discovered while performing in Soho's legendary 2 I's coffee bar. Renamed by manager Larry Parnes, Tommy Steele became Britain's first bona fide rock 'n' roll star with two 1956 hit singles, 'Rock With The Caveman' and 'Singing The Blues', the latter of which was a chart-topper. Although touted as the antidote to Elvis Presley, it was quickly clear that Steele lacked sex appeal or sultry menace, offering instead a clean-cut, boy-next-door image, ripe for his subsequent mutation into all-round entertainer. For many years he remained a peculiarly British institution; indeed, the film was retitled *Rock Around The World* for the USA. Steele was an unknown quantity there and his name had little significance. Released in 1957, *The Tommy Steele Story* retold the artist's rise from rags to riches, while offering a glimpse of music popular in the UK during this transitional period. The influence of jazz on rock 'n' roll was acknowledged by an appearance by Humphrey Lyttelton's band, while the concurrent skiffle craze allowed for the inclusion of Chas McDevitt's Skiffle Group, who, with Nancy Whiskey, were high in the UK charts with the memorable 'Freight Train'. Chris O'Brien's Caribbeans and Tommy Etie's Calypso Band reflected London's nascent interest in West Indian music, yet the film's lacklustre style and pace meant that its symbolism was greater than the audio/visual experience. Indeed, its star's appeal was already undergoing a transformation by the time *The Tommy Steele Story* reached the cinema. His last rock 'n' roll hit, 'Tallahassie Lassie', was succeeded by 'Little White Bull' from the singer's 1959 feature, *Tommy The Toreador*. His mutation into a peculiarly adult attraction was all but complete, and was finally accomplished with Steele's subsequent role in *Half A Sixpence*.

TONY AWARDS

The Antoinette Perry Awards, America's most prestigious theatrical awards - the equivalent to the Hollywood Oscars - were inaugurated in 1947. Their fascinating history began during World War I when an obsure playwright, Rachel Crothers, and a few other women, organized theatre people to sell Liberty Bonds and run a canteen for servicemen in Times Square. In 1939 Crothers and her voluntary workers, including an actress-director named Antoinette Perry, surfaced again and formed the American Theatre Wing War Service. The Wing founded two famous institutions: the Stage Door Canteen, where stars of stage, screen and radio served coffee and doughnuts and entertained visiting service personnel, and which was immortalized in the 1943 film of the same name; and the annual award given in memory of Antoinette Perry's pioneering work both for women and young people in the theatre, and for the

American Theatre Wing itself, which still organizes the Awards. As an example, in 1993 the nominations for the 19 categories were selected by an independent committee of 12 theatre professionals, and they in turn were voted on by 670 theatre professionals and journalists. In that year the specific musical sections consisted of best musical, book, original score, performance by a leading actor, leading actress, featured actor, and featured actress; and best direction and choreography. Musical productions could also win in the best scenic, costume, and lighting design categories, and the best revival of a play or musical. In most years one or more special Tonys are awarded for outstanding service to the theatre, and in 1993 one of these celebrated the 50th anniversary of Richard Rodgers and Oscar Hammerstein II's *Oklahoma!*. Over the years the Award itself has taken many forms. The current honour is in the shape of a Tony Medallion, the product of a Stage Designer's Union competition won by Herman Rose in 1950. An annual live television audience of some 10 million watch the ceremony, the outcome of which often means the difference between success and failure on Broadway.

● FURTHER READING: *The Tony Award Book*, Lee Alan Morrow. *The Tony Award*, Crown Publishers USA.

TORMÉ, MEL

b. 13 September 1925, Chicago, Illinois, USA. A child prodigy, Tormé first sang on radio as a toddler and while still in his teens was performing as a singer, pianist, drummer and dancer. He was also composing songs and wrote arrangements for the band led by Chico Marx. He acted on radio and in films and in addition to singing solo led his own vocal group, the Mel-Tones. In this last capacity he recorded with Artie Shaw, enjoying a hit with 'Sunny Side Of The Street'. By the 50s he was established as one of the leading song stylists, performing the great standards and often working with a jazz backing, notably with the Marty Paich Dek-tette on albums such as *Lulu's Back In Town*. He headlined concert packages across the USA and in Europe, appeared on television, often producing his own shows, and always delivering performances of impeccable professionalism. He continued in such a vein throughout the 60s and 70s, making many fine albums of superior popular music, on several of which he was accompanied by jazzmen. Among these were Shorty Rogers ('*Round Midnight*), Al Porcino (*Live At The Maisonette*), Buddy Rich (*Together Again - For The First Time*), Gerry Mulligan (*Mel Tormé And Friends*) and Rob McConnell (*Mel Tormé With Rob McConnell And The Boss Brass*). Of all his musical collaborations, however, the best and most satisfying has been a long series of concerts and radio and television shows, many of which were issued on record, with George Shearing. Among these albums are *An Evening At Charlie's*, *An Elegant Evening*, *A Vintage Year* and *Mel And George "Do" World War II*.

In the early 90s Tormé was still drawing rave reviews for records and personal appearances, with Shearing, at festivals in California and the Channel Islands, and with Bill Berry's big band at the Hollywood Bowl. As a songwriter Tormé has several hundred compositions to his credit, of which the best-known by far is 'The Christmas Song' (written with Robert Wells), first recorded by Nat 'King' Cole. As a performer, Tormé often features himself on drums - for many years he used a drum kit that was formerly the property of

Gene Krupa - and he plays with unforced swing. As a singer, Tormé's work is touched with elegant charm. His voice, with the characteristic huskiness that earned him the sobriquet 'The Velvet Fog', has deepened over the years and by the early 90s still retained all the qualities of his youth, not least remarkable pitch and vocal control. In his choice of material he has never shown anything other than perfect taste and his repertoire is an object lesson in musical quality. The fact that he also writes almost all the arrangements of the songs he sings adds to his status as a major figure in the story of American popular song. Tormé suffered a stroke during 1996 and it is not yet known whether this will curtail his career.

● ALBUMS: *California Suite* 10-inch album (Capitol 1950)★★★, *Songs* 10-inch album (MGM 1952)★★★, *Musical Sounds Are The Best Songs* (Coral 1955)★★★, *It's A Blue World* (Bethlehem 1955)★★★★, with Marty Paich *Mel Tormé With The Marty Paich Dek-tette* (Bethlehem 1956)★★★★, *Gene Norman Presents Mel Torme Live At The Crescendo* (Coral 1956)★★★★, *Lulu's Back In Town* (1957)★★★, *Mel Tormé Sings Astaire* (Bethlehem 1957)★★★, *'Round Midnight* i (1957)★★★, with Paich *Tormé* (Verve 1958)★★★, with Paich *Prelude To A Kiss* (Tops 1958)★★★, *Songs For Any Taste* (Bethlehem 1959)★★★, *Olé Tormé - Mel Tormé Goes South Of The Border With Billy May* (Verve 1959)★★★★, with Paich *Back In Town* (Verve 1959)★★★, with Paich *Mel Tormé Swings Schubert Alley* (Verve 1960)★★★★, *Swingin' On The Moon* (Verve 1960)★★★★, *I Dig The Duke, I Dig The Count* (Verve 1960)★★★★, *Mel Tormé Sings* (Strand 1960)★★★, with Margaret Whiting *Broadway Right Now!* (Verve 1961)★★★, *'Round Midnight* ii (1961)★★★, *Mel Tormé At The Red Hill Inn* (Atlantic 1962)★★★, *Comin' Home Baby* (Atlantic 1962)★★★, *Sunday In New York* (Atlantic 1963)★★★★, *I Wished On The Moon* (Metro 1965)★★★, *That's All; A Lush Romantic Album* (Columbia 1965)★★★, *Mel Tormé Right Now* (Columbia 1966)★★★, *A Day In The Life Of Bonnie And Clyde* (Liberty 1968)★★★, *Live At The Maisonette* (1974)★★★, *Tormé A New Album* (Paddlewheel 1978)★★★★, with Buddy Rich *Together Again - For The First Time* (RCA 1978)★★★, *Mel Tormé And Friends* (Finesse 1981)★★★, *Encore At Marty's, New York* (1982)★★★, with George Shearing *An Evening At Charlie's* (Concord Jazz 1983)★★★, with Shearing *An Elegant Evening* (Concord Jazz 1985)★★★, *Mel Tormé With Rob McConnell And The Boss Brass* (Concord Jazz 1986)★★★, with Shearing *A Vintage Year* (Concord Jazz 1987)★★★, with Paich *Reunion* (Concord Jazz 1988)★★★★, with Paich *In Concert Tokyo* (Concord Jazz 1989)★★★★, *Night At The Concord Pavilion* (Concord Jazz 1990)★★★★, with Shearing *Mel And George 'Do' World War II* (Concord Jazz 1991)★★★, *In Hollywood* 1954 recording (1992)★★★, *Live At Fujitsu - Concord Jazz Festival 1992* (1992)★★★, *Christmas Songs* (Telarc 1992)★★, with Cleo Laine *Nothing Without You* (1993)★★★★, *A Tribute To Bing Crosby* (Concord 1994)★★★, *Velvet & Brass* (Concord 1995)★★★★, *A&E - An Evening With Mel Tormé* (Concord 1996)★★★★.

● COMPILATIONS: *Verve's Choice The Best Of Mel Tormé* (Verve 1964)★★★, *Walkman Jazz* 1958-61 recordings (Verve 1990)★★★, *Capitol Years* (Capitol 1992)★★★, *The Magic Of ...* (Music Club 1995)★★★, *The Mel Tormé Collection: 1944-1985* 4-CD box set (Rhino 1996)★★★★.

● FURTHER READING: all by Mel Tormé *The Other Side Of*

The Rainbow-With Judy Garland On The Dawn Patrol. It Wasn't All Velvet: An Autobiography. My Singing Teachers.
● FILMS: *Girl's Town* aka *The Innocent And The Damned* (1959).

TRADITION RECORDS

Before the emergence of Tradition Records in the 50s, American folk and blues had often been poorly recorded and packaged. Tradition changed all that, establishing a catalogue of fine recordings that also engaged with flamenco, Irish and jazz music. Arguably Tradition's most pivotal release was Odetta's *Sings Ballads & Blues*, which was later cited by Bob Dylan as 'the first thing that turned me on to folk singing'. Lightnin' Hopkins released two groundbreaking live albums, *Autobiography In Blues* and *Country Blues*, for the label, drawn from a Houston, Texas performance in 1959. 'Big' Bill Broonzy's *Treat Me Right* was also recorded live in Paris in 1951, and the label was additionally responsible for the first release of Lead Belly sessions conducted in New York between 1943 and 1944. Irish folk legends Liam Clancy and Tommy Makem also recorded their first album, *The Lark In The Morning*, for Tradition. Other artists on the roster included Carlos Montoya, Errol Garner, Woody Herman and Coleman Hawkins. A series of reissues in 1996 on the Rykodisc Records label helped to reinstate Tradition's role in the emergence of popular music.

TRAVIS, MERLE

b. Merle Robert Travis, 29 November 1917, Rosewood, Kentucky, USA, d. 20 October 1983, Tahlequah, Oklahoma, USA. He was the son of a tobacco farmer but by the time Travis was four years old, the family had moved to Ebenezer, Kentucky, and his father was working down the mines. Travis's father often remarked, 'Another day older and deeper in debt', a phrase his son used in 'Sixteen Tons'. His father played the banjo, but Travis preferred the guitar. He befriended two coalminers, Mose Reger and Ike Everly, the father of the Everly Brothers, who demonstrated how to use the thumb for the bass strings while playing the melody on treble strings. Travis hitched around the country, busking where he could, and in 1935, he joined the Tennessee Tomcats and from there, went to a better-known country group, Clayton McMichen's Georgia Wildcats. In 1937 he became a member of the Drifting Pioneers, who performed on WLW Cincinnati. In 1943 he recorded for the local King label, recording a solo as Bob McCarthy and a duet with Grandpa Jones as the Shepherd Brothers. He and Jones did many radio shows together and many years later, recreated that atmosphere for an album. Travis, Jones and the Delmore Brothers also worked as a gospel quartet, the Browns Ferry Four. After war service in the marines, he settled in California and worked with artists such as Tex Ritter. Travis's arrangement of 'Muskrat' for Ritter was later developed into a hit single for the Everly Brothers.

He played with several bands, becoming one of the first to appreciate that a guitar could be a lead instrument, and he had success as a solo artist for the newly formed Capitol Records with 'Cincinnati Lou', 'No Vacancy', 'Divorce Me C.O.D.', 'Missouri' and a US country number 1, 'So Round, So Firm, So Fully Packed'. He co-wrote Capitol's first million-seller, 'Smoke, Smoke, Smoke That Cigarette' with Tex Williams, who recorded it. Burl Ives and Josh White were spearheading a craze for folk music, so Capitol producer Lee Gillette asked Travis for a 78 rpm album set of Kentucky folk songs. 'I don't know any', said Travis. 'Then write some', was the reply. His eight-song *Folk Songs Of Our Hills*, included 'Nine Pound Hammer' (a rewritten folk song), 'Dark As A Dungeon' and 'Sixteen Tons', with spoken introductions about the coalmining locale. Although Travis maintained that 'Sixteen Tons' was a 'fun song', it dealt with the exploitation of miners in the company store. It won a gold record for Tennessee Ernie Ford in 1955 and was parodied by Spike Jones as 'Sixteen Tacos' and by Max Bygraves as 'Seventeen Tons'. Travis himself was also enjoying a country hit with a revival of 'Wildwood Flower' with Hank Thompson, and he won acclaim for his portrayal of a young GI in the 1954 film *From Here To Eternity*, in which he sang 'Re-enlistment Blues'. Travis's *Walkin' The Strings* is a highly regarded album of acoustic guitar solos. His style influenced Doc Watson, who named his son after him, and Chet Atkins, who did the same with his daughter.

In 1948 he devised a solid-body electric guitar, which was built for him by Paul Bigsby and developed by Leo Fender. 'I got the idea from a steel guitar,' he said, 'I wanted the same sustainability of notes, and I came up with a solid-body electric guitar with the keys all on one side.' Travis had an entertaining stage act in which he would mimic animals on his guitars. He was a good cartoonist and he worked as a scriptwriter on Johnny Cash's television shows. He took part in the Nitty Gritty Dirt Band's tribute to country music, *Will The Circle Be Unbroken?*, and was one of the Texas Playboys in the Clint Eastwood film *Honkytonk Man*. Travis was elected to the Country Music Hall Of Fame in 1977 but his drug addiction and alcoholism made him unreliable and wrecked his private life. Says Tennessee Ernie Ford, 'Merle Travis was one of the most talented men I ever met. He could write songs that would knock your hat off, but he was a chronic alcoholic and when those binges would come, there was nothing we could do about it.' Travis died in October 1983. A posthumous album of blues songs played on 12-string guitar, *Rough, Rowdy And Blue*, included a tune from his mentor, Mose Reger, 'Merry Christmas, Pretty Baby'. His friend and fellow guitarist Joe Maphis wrote a tribute, 'Me And Ol' Merle', which concluded, 'We liked good whiskey and we loved the pretty girls, And we loved them guitars - Me and Ol' Merle.'
● ALBUMS: *Folk Songs Of The Hills* 10-inch album (Capitol 1947)★★★, *The Merle Travis Guitar* (Capitol 1956)★★★, *Back Home* expanded reissue of *Folk Songs Of The Hills* (Capitol 1957)★★★, *Walkin' The Strings* (Capitol 1960)★★★★, *Travis!* (Capitol 1962)★★★, *Songs Of The Coal Mines* (Capitol 1963)★★★, with Joe Maphis *Two Guitar Greats* (Capitol 1964)★★★, with Johnny Bond *Great Songs Of The Delmore Brothers* (Capitol 1969)★★★, *Strictly Guitar* (Capitol 1969)★★★★, with Chet Atkins *The Atkins-Travis Traveling Show* (RCA Victor 1975)★★★, with Maphis *Country Guitar Giants* (CHM 1979)★★★, *Light Singin' And Heavy Pickin'* (1980)★★★, *Guitar Standards* (1980)★★★, *Travis Pickin'* (CMH 1981)★★★, with Mac Wiseman *The Clayton McMichen Story* (CHM 1982)★★★, with Grandpa Jones *Merle And Grandpa's Farm And Home Hour* (1985)★★★, *Rough, Rowdy And Blue* (CMH 1985)★★★.
● COMPILATIONS: *The Best Of Merle Travis* (Capitol 1967)★★★, *The Merle Travis Story* (CMH 1979)★★★★, *The Best Of Merle Travis* (Rhino 1990)★★★, *The Radio Shows 1944-1949* (Country Routes 1991)★★★, *Capitol Country Music Classics* (Capitol 1993)★★★.
● FURTHER READING: *In Search Of My Father*, Pat Travis Eatherly.

TRENIER TWINS

b. 14 July 1919, Mobile, Alabama, USA. Cliff (d. 2 March 1983) and Claude Trenier formed their first band, the Alabama State Collegians, in college during the 30s and took it on the road after graduating in 1941. Claude left in 1943 to replace Dan Grissom as ballad singer with Jimmie Lunceford's Orchestra, and Cliff joined him the following year. Claude also sang on sessions headed by Barney Bigard and Charles Mingus in 1946. After going solo in 1947 with their own small group, which included Don Hill on alto saxophone and Gene Gilbeaux on piano, they began recording for Mercury, going on to record for Chord (1949), London (1950), OKeh/Epic (1951-55), RCA's Vik subsidiary (1956), Brunswick (1957) and Dot (1958). After becoming the visual act of the early rock 'n' roll era and inspiring clones such as the Comets and the Bellboys, the Treniers appeared in several major rock 'n' roll movies (notably *Don't Knock The Rock* and *The Girl Can't Help It*) and visited Europe in 1958, where they were the support act on the ill-fated Jerry Lee Lewis tour. Increasingly becoming a supper-club act in the 60s, they made albums for Hermitage, TT and their own Mobile Records. Cliff died in 1983, but Claude is still active and continues to lead the Treniers with older brother Buddy, nephew Skip and Don Hill on alto saxophone.
● ALBUMS: *Go! Go! Go! The Treniers On TV* (OKeh/Epic 1955)★★, *The Treniers Souvenir Album* (Dot 1958)★★★, *After Hours With The Fabulous Treniers* (Hermitage 1962)★★★, *The Treniers By The Sea* (1962)★★, *Popcorn Man* (60s)★★★, *Live And Wild At The Flamingo* (70s)★★, *The Fabulous Treniers* (70s)★★, *Those Crazy Treniers* (70s)★★★, *Rockin' Is Our Bizness* (Edsel 1983)★★★, *You're Killin' Me* (Mr R&B 1985)★★★, *Hey Sister Lucy* (Bear Family 1988)★★★, *Cool It Baby* (Bear Family 1988)★★★.

TRENT, BRUCE

b. William Butters, 21 August 1912, St. Helier, Jersey, d. 19 November 1995, Burgh Heath, Surrey, England. An actor and singer with a fine, baritone voice and matinée idol good looks, Trent was one of the British theatre's most popular romantic leading men in the 40s and 50s. After singing with local dance groups, in the late 30s he spent two years touring the UK with Jack Hylton's famous show band, before joining Jack Payne's new BBC orchestra in 1940. He left Payne in 1942 in order to co-star with Frances Day, Arthur Riscoe, Jackie Hunter and Bud Flanagan in Cole Porter's musical *Du Barry Was A Lady* at His Majesty's Theatre in London. Trent subsequently returned to the West End, and then toured, in *The Student Prince*, before joining the army and entertaining the troops in the company of the Stars In Battledress. He was also a guest artist, along with Dorothy Carless, on a BBC broadcast with Glenn Miller's Band of the AEF. After the war, Trent took over the leading roles in *Carissima* (1948) and *Brigadoon* (1950), as well as starring in London in *Rainbow Square* (1951), *Wish You Were Here* (1953) and *The Burning Boat* (1955, Royal Court Theatre). He also toured in various other productions, including *Lilac Time, Good-Night Vienna* and *The Desert Song*. In 1958, Trent joined the all-star cast of Tommy Steele, Jimmy Edwards, Yana, and Ted Durante, in Richard Rodgers and Oscar Hammerstein II's lavish *Cinderella* at the Coliseum. As the dashing Prince, he sang the show's big ballad, 'No Other Love', and duetted with Yana on the equally splendid 'Do I Love You Because You're Beautiful?'. In later years he continued to tour in numerous revivals, both at home and abroad, notably as Arthur in *Camelot* in 1966. He also participated in re-recordings of favourite musicals, and was a regular broadcaster on BBC light music programmes. After retiring in the 70s, he worked tirelessly for the Grand Order of Water Rats charity.

TROUP, BOBBY

b. 18 October 1918, Harrisburg, Pennsylvania, USA. After studying extensively, including taking a degree in economics, Troup turned to songwriting and singing to his own piano accompaniment. In 1941 he was hired by Tommy Dorsey, but was drafted the same year. After five years in the US Navy, where he wrote scores for several shows, he settled in Los Angeles. He played nightclubs, married Julie London and formed a jazz trio. He began making films, gaining small acting roles and sometimes playing piano and singing. Among these films were *The Duchess Of Idaho* (1950), *The Five Pennies* (1959) and *The Gene Krupa Story* (1960). Troup wrote scores for several films, including *The Girl Can't Help It* (1956), for which he also contributed the title song, and *Man Of The West* (1958). Among his other songs are 'Daddy', '(Get Your Kicks On) Route 66', 'Baby, Baby, All The Time', both of which were recorded by Nat 'King' Cole, and 'The Meaning Of The Blues'; he also wrote the lyrics for 'Free And Easy' and 'Girl Talk'. By the early 60s Troup's acting career was in good shape; he had leading roles in several films and also appeared on television in *Acapulco*, for which he wrote the background music. In the 60s and on through the 70s he took leading roles in such television movies as *Dragnet* (1966) and *Benny And Barney: Las Vegas Undercover* (1976). He also acted in *Emergency!* (1971) and its spin-off series, in which Julie London appeared. His 80s film roles included *M*A*S*H* (1981). Not surprisingly, given the number of acting roles he has been offered over the years, this area of Troup's work has tended to overshadow his music. In some respects this is a pity because, although an eclectic piano player, Troup sings with an engaging simplicity, and a dedication to the intentions of the lyricist seldom displayed by many more famous performers.

● ALBUMS: *Bobby* 10-inch album (Capitol 1953)★★★, *Bobby Troup* 10-inch album (Capitol 1955)★★★, *The Distinctive Style Of Bobby Troup* (Bethlehem 1955)★★★, *Bobby Troup With Bob Enevoldson And His Orchestra* (Liberty 1955)★★, *Bobby Troup Sings Johnny Mercer* (Bethlehem 1955)★★★, *Do Re Mi* (Liberty 1957)★★, *Bobby Swings Tenderly* (Mode 1957)★★★, *In A Class Beyond Compare* (1957)★★★, *Here's To My Lady* (Liberty 1958)★★, *Bobby Troup And His Jazz All-Stars* (RCA Victor 1959)★★.

TUCKER, LUTHER

b. 20 January 1936, Memphis, Tennessee, USA, d. 17 June 1993, San Rafael, California, USA. Tucker moved to Chicago, Illinois, at the age of nine and was probably best known as one of Little Walter's backing guitarists both on stage and on record in the 50s. He was heavily influenced by his mother

who played piano and guitar, but Tucker started playing guitar himself after hearing Robert Lockwood Jr. Lockwood became his mentor, together with his mother. He also worked with other musicians such as J.T. Brown, Junior Wells, Muddy Waters and Sonny Boy 'Rice Miller' Williamson in the same decade. Tucker remained an in-demand backing guitarist and recorded with numerous blues artists, including James Cotton, Otis Rush and John Lee Hooker. He settled in California in 1969 and occasionally led a group under his own name. He was known for the speed of his playing and recorded in his own right for Messaround and Paris Albums. He lived in the Netherlands for some years but later returned to live in California. Tucker died in 1993 from a heart attack.

● COMPILATIONS: *Blue Bay* three tracks only (1976)★★, *San Francisco Blues Festival European Sessions* three tracks only (1980)★★, *Sad Hours* (Antone's 1994)★★★, with the Ford Blues Band *Luther Tucker And The Ford Blues Band* (Cross Cut 1995)★★★.

UNCLE CYP AND AUNT SAP

A popular husband-and-wife comedy duo, Uncle Cyp (b. Laurence Lemarr Brasfield, 1 March 1888, Smithville, Mississippi, USA, d. 6 September 1966, Raymondsville, Texas, USA) and Aunt Sap (b. Neva Inez Fisher Greevi, 14 March 1889, Luther, Michigan, USA, d. 19 March 1980, Raymondsville, Texas, USA) married *circa* 1906 and put together a comedy act that featured a rustic couple. Brasfield initially played a country hayseed character known as Boob, which became Cyprus, and eventually they adopted the names of Uncle Cyp and Aunt Sap. They first worked on various tent and vaudeville shows, including the Bisbee Comedians, all over the USA, before they became regulars on the original *Ozark Jubilee*, when it was formed. They were the only act to play on the show from its beginning until it closed in 1961, whereupon they retired from showbusiness. Brasfield, who died of lung cancer in 1966, was an elder brother of *Grand Ole Opry* comedian Rod Brasfield, who at one time worked with him on the vaudeville circuit.

VALANCE, RICKY

b. David Spencer, c.1939, Ynytsdou, South Wales. After singing in local clubs for a couple of years, Valance was discovered by an A&R representative from EMI Records and placed in the hands of producer Norrie Paramor. At the first recording session, Valance was given the chance of covering Ray Peterson's US hit, 'Tell Laura I Love Her'. A wonderfully enunciated reading was rewarded with a number 1 hit in September 1960, thanks to airplay on Radio Luxembourg, but none of Valance's follow-ups, including 'Movin' Away', 'Jimmy's Girl', 'Bobby' and 'Try To Forget Her', created any interest, and even with a move to Decca Records the dismal 'Six Boys' flopped. He continues playing clubs and the revival circuit.

VALE, JERRY

b. Genaro Louis Vitaliano, 8 July 1932, Bronx, New York, USA. A popular singer, especially of ballads, with several chart hits to his credit during the 50s and 60s, Vale had studied piano and worked as a shoeshine boy while still at school. Later, he was employed in an electrical component factory, and sang in his spare time. After winning a talent contest at the Club del Rio, he stayed there for over a year, and then, while performing at the Enchanted Room in New York, he was spotted by Guy Mitchell, who recommended him to Columbia Records' A&R manager, Mitch Miller. His first chart entry for the label, 'You Can Never Give Me Back My Heart' (1953), on which he was accompanied by Percy Faith And His Orchestra, was followed by 'Two Purple Shadows', 'I Live Each Day', 'Innamorata' and 'You Don't Know Me' (1956). Despite the 60s beat boom, Vale registered in the bestsellers lists with singles such as 'Have You Looked Into Your Heart?' (1964), and entered the US Top 40 album chart six times between 1963 and 1966. He continued to be popular in clubs and on television during the 70s and 80s, and, in 1988, was the guest of honour at a Friars Club dinner, held to celebrate his long and successful career. Vale wound up the proceedings by singing a few favourites, including his signature tune, 'Al Di La', the winner of the San Remo Song Festival in 1961.

● ALBUMS: *I Remember Buddy* (Columbia 1958)★★, *I Remember Russ* (1958)★★, *Same Old Moon* (1959)★★, *I Have But One Heart* (Columbia 1962)★★★, *Arrivederci Roma* (Columbia 1963)★★★★, *Language Of Love* (Columbia 1963)★★★, *Till The End Of Time* (Columbia 1964)★★★★, *Be My Love* (Columbia 1964)★★★★, *Moonlight Becomes You* (Columbia 1965)★★★, *Have You Looked Into Your Heart* (Columbia 1965)★★★, *Standing Ovations* (Columbia 1965)★★★, *There Goes My Heart* (Columbia 1965)★★★, *Everybody Loves Somebody* (Columbia 1966)★★★, *Great Moments On Broadway* (Columbia 1966)★★★, *It's Magic* (Columbia 1966)★★★, *The Impossible Dream* (Columbia 1967)★★★, *Time Alone Will Tell* (Columbia 1967)★★★, *You Don't Have To Say You Love Me* (Columbia 1968)★★★, *This Guy's In Love With You* (Columbia 1968)★★★, *Till* (Columbia 1969)★★★, *Where's The Playground Susie?* (Columbia 1969)★★, *With Love Jerry Vale* (Columbia 1969)★★, *Jerry Vale Sings 16 Greatest Hits Of The 60s* (Columbia 1970)★★, *Let It Be* (Columbia 1970)★★, *Jerry Vale Sings The Great Hits Of Nat King Cole* (Columbia 1972)★★.

● COMPILATIONS: *Greatest Hits* (Columbia 1960)★★★, *More Greatest Hits* (Columbia 1967)★★★.

VALENS, RITCHIE

b. Richard Steve Valenzuela, 13 May 1941, Pacoima, Los Angeles, California, USA, d. 3 February 1959, Iowa, USA. Valens was the first major Hispanic-American rock star, the artist who popularized the classic 50s hit 'La Bamba'. He grew up in the city of Pacoima, California, and was raised in poverty. His parents separated when he was a child and Valens lived with his father until the latter's death in 1951. Afterwards he lived with his mother and brothers and sisters, but occasionally they stayed with other relatives who introduced him to traditional Mexican music. He also enjoyed cowboy songs by Roy Rogers and Gene Autry and began playing in junior high school. It was while attending school that Valens was first exposed to R&B music and rock 'n' roll. In 1956 he joined the Silhouettes (not the group that recorded 'Get A Job'), who performed at record hops in the San Fernando Valley area. Valens also performed solo and was heard by Bob Keane of Del-Fi Records, who took him into Gold Star Studios to record several songs. (Keane also shortened the singer's name from Valenzuela to Valens and added the 't' to Richie.) A session band including Earl Palmer (drums), Carol Kaye (guitar), Red Collendar (stand-up bass), Ernie Freeman (piano) and Rene Hall (guitar) played behind Valens (who also played guitar). Their first single, the Valens original 'Come On, Let's Go', reached number 42 in the USA, and following its release the singer went on an 11-city US tour. In October 1958 the single 'Donna'/'La Bamba' was issued. Contrary to popular belief it was actually the ballad 'Donna', written by Valens about his high school friend Donna Ludwig, that was the bigger hit, reaching number 2. 'La Bamba', the b-side, only reached number 22 in the USA but has proved to be the more fondly remembered song. 'La Bamba' was a traditional huapango song from the Vera Cruz region of eastern Mexico, performed as early as World War II, and sung at weddings. (A huapango is a Mexican song consisting of nonsense verses, the meaning of the lyrics often known only to the composer.) Valens was reportedly reluctant to record the song, fearing its Spanish lyrics would not catch on with American record buyers. Following the record's release, Valens again went on tour, performing in California, Hawaii and on the *American Bandstand* show in Philadelphia. It was during the winter part of the tour that Valens and his fellow performers met their fate, choosing to charter a small aeroplane rather than ride to the next concert site in a bus whose heater had broken. It was on 3 February 1959 when he, Buddy Holly and the Big Bopper were killed in an aeroplane crash following a concert in Clear Lake, Iowa. In the wake of Valens' death, several further singles were issued, only two of which - 'That's My

Little Suzie' and 'Little Girl' - were minor chart hits. Three albums - *Ritchie Valens, Ritchie* and *Ritchie Valens In Concert At Pacoima Junior High* - were released from sessions recorded for Del-Fi and at a performance for Valens' classmates. Valens' status grew in the years following his death, culminating in the 1987 film *La Bamba*, a dramatized version of Valens' brief life and stardom. His songs have been covered by several artists, including the Hispanic-American group Los Lobos, who supervised the film's music and recorded 'La Bamba'. Their version, ironically, went to number 1 in 1987, outperforming Valens' original chart position.

● ALBUMS: *Ritchie Valens* (Del Fi 1959)★★★, *Ritchie* (Del Fi 1959)★★★★, *Ritchie Valens In Concert At Pacoima Junior High* (Del Fi 1960)★★★.

● COMPILATIONS: *His Greatest Hits* (Del Fi 1963)★★★★, *His Greatest Hits Volume 2* (Del Fi 1965)★★, *I Remember Ritchie Valens* (President 1967)★★★, *The Best Of Richie Valens* (Rhino 1987)★★★, *The Ritchie Valens Story* (Ace 1993)★★★★, *The Very Best Of Ritchie Valens* (Music Club 1995)★★★.

● FURTHER READING: *Ritchie Valens: The First Latino Rocker*, Beverly Mendheim. *Ritchie Valens 1941-1959: 30th Anniversary Memorial Series No 2*, Alan Clark.

● FILMS: *Go Johnny Go* (1958).

VALENTINE, DICKIE

b. Richard Brice, 4 November 1929, London, England, d. 6 May 1971, Wales. An extremely popular singer in the UK during the 50s. At the age of three, Valentine appeared in the Jack Hulbert/Cicely Courtneidge comedy film *Jack's The Boy*. Later, as a backstage assistant at Her Majesty's Theatre in London, he became the protégé of Canadian stage star Bill O'Connor, who sent him for singing tuition. After playing the club circuit as a singer/impressionist he made his debut with the successful Ted Heath band in a broadcast from Aeolian Hall. Initially, Heath featured him as a straight ballad vocalist, but later allowed him to display his range of impressions, including those of Mario Lanza, Nat 'King' Cole, Billy Daniels and an accurate parody of Johnnie Ray. Good-looking, with dark, curly hair and a rich melodic voice, Valentine became Britain's number one band singer, a heart-throb who set the teenagers screaming. In 1952 he recorded 'Never' (from the Mitzi Gaynor movie *Golden Girl*) and 'Lorelei' for Melodisc Records. In the following year he signed for Decca, and throughout the 50s produced a string of Top 20 hits, including 'Broken Wings', 'Endless', 'Mr Sandman', 'A Blossom Fell', 'I Wonder', 'Old Pianna Rag', 'Christmas Island', 'Venus', and two number 1 hits, 'Finger Of Suspicion' and 'Christmas Alphabet'. In 1959 he again made the Top 20 with 'One More Sunrise (Morgen)' for Pye, but groups rather than solo singers soon came to dominate the charts, and Valentine described his own 'Rock 'N' Roll Party' as 'the biggest clanger I have dropped'. At the height of his career he appeared on American television with a performance on the *Ed Sullivan Show*, and headlined at theatres where he had once been employed backstage. After the record hits dried up, he remained a firm favourite on the British club circuit, and while returning from one such engagement in Wales, died in a car crash in 1971.

● ALBUMS: *Presenting* (Decca 1954)★★★, *Here Is Dickie Valentine* (Decca 1955)★★★, *Over My Shoulder* (Decca 1956)★★★★, *With Vocal Refrain By* (Decca 1958)★★★, *Dickie* (Ace Of Clubs 1961)★★★, *At The Talk Of The Town* (Philips 1967)★★★, *My Favourite Songs* (1993)★★★, with Lita Roza, Dennis Lotis, Joan Regan *Dickie Valentine & Friends* (1993)★★★.

● COMPILATIONS: *The World Of Dickie Valentine* (Decca 1981)★★★, *The Very Best Of Dickie Valentine* (Decca 1984)★★★, *The Voice* (President 1989)★★★, *The Best Of ...* (Soundwaves 1994).

VALENTINES

From Harlem, New York, USA, the original members of this vocal group were lead Richard Barrett, tenor Raymond Briggs, second tenor Carl Hogan, baritone Mickey Francis and bass Ronnie Bright. (Hogan was replaced by Donald Razor in 1954, who in turn was replaced by Eddie Edgehill in 1955, who, in full circle, was replaced by Hogan in 1957.) The Valentines typified the New York City doo-wop sound. The group's first record, 'Tonight Kathleen' (1954), recorded for Hy Weiss's Old Town label, established the group locally. The following year the Valentines joined George Goldner's Rama label where they achieved a string of hits. The group had success with the up-tempo 'Lily Maebelle', followed by their biggest hit, 'The Woo Woo Train' (1956). Also recorded that year was the splendid ballad 'Nature's Creation'. The Valentines made their last record in 1957. Barrett was becoming more involved in the backroom aspect of the recording industry, having discovered and brought Frankie Lymon And The Teenagers to Goldner and also having begun regular production duties with the Chantels. Bright later joined the Cadillacs and was the bass player on Johnny Cymbal's 'Mr. Bassman'.

● COMPILATIONS: *The Best Of The Valentines* (Collectables 1991)★★★.

VALINO, JOE

b. 9 March 1929, Philadelphia, Pennsylvania, USA. A pop-jazz vocalist in the mode of Frank Sinatra, Valino belongs to a breed of pop singers who were generally swept away in the late 50s with the advent of rock 'n' roll. His one hit, 'Garden Of Eden', was a pop confection, but it had enough teen-appeal to reach many of the same buyers of rock 'n' roll in 1956. He had minor success in the UK as well with the song, which went to number 23. As a youngster, Valino was proficient at piano and guitar as well as at singing, and by the age of 13 was on the road touring. He sang in several bands, notably those of Charlie Ventura and Woody Herman, before beginning his recording career in 1950 on the Philadelphia-based Gotham label. He was thwarted in gaining his first hit with 'Learnin' The Blues' in 1955 when it was covered by Frank Sinatra. He moved to Los Angeles in the 60s and acted in several motion pictures, notably *The Commitment* (1976).

● ALBUMS: *Sinner Or Saint* (1967)★★, *Atlantic City To MacArthur Park* (1968)★★★.

VAN HEUSEN, JIMMY

b. Edward Chester Babcock, 26 January 1913, Syracuse, New York, USA, d. 6 February 1990, Rancho Mirage, California, USA. Van Heusen was an extremely popular and prolific composer from the late 30s through to the 60s, particularly for movies. He was an affable, high-living, fun-loving character. His main collaborators were lyricists Johnny Burke and Sammy Cahn. While still at high school, Van Heusen worked at a local radio station, playing piano and singing. He changed his name to Van Heusen, after the famous shirt manufacturer. In the early 30s he studied piano and composition at Syracuse University, and met Jerry Arlen, son of composer Harold Arlen. Arlen Snr. gave Van Heusen the opportunity to write for Harlem's *Cotton Club Revues*.

His big break came in 1938 when bandleader Jimmy Dorsey wrote a lyric to Van Heusen's tune for 'It's The Dreamer In Me'. Ironically, the song was a big hit for rival bandleader Harry James. In the same year Van Heusen started working with lyricist Eddie DeLange. Their songs included 'Deep In A Dream', 'All This And Heaven Too', 'Heaven Can Wait' (a number 1 hit for Glen Gray), 'This Is Madness' and 'Shake Down The Stars' (a hit for Glenn Miller). In 1939 they wrote the score for the Broadway musical *Swingin' The Dream*, a jazzy treatment of Shakespeare's *A Midsummer Night's Dream*. Despite the presence in the cast of the all-star Benny Goodman Sextet, Louis Armstrong, Maxine Sullivan, and the Deep River Boys, plus the song 'Darn That Dream', the show folded after only 13 performances. In 1940 Van Heusen was placed under contract to Paramount Pictures, and began his association with Johnny Burke. Their first songs together included 'Polka Dots And Moonbeams' and 'Imagination', both hits for the Tommy Dorsey Orchestra, with vocals by Frank Sinatra, who was to have an enormous effect on Van Heusen's later career. After contributing to the Fred Allen-Jack Benny comedy film *Love Thy Neighbor* (1940), Van Heusen and Burke supplied songs for 16 Bing Crosby films through to 1953, including 'It's Always You' (*Road To Zanzibar*), 'Road To Morocco', 'Moonlight Becomes You' (*Road To Morocco*), 'Sunday, Monday Or Always' (*Dixie*), 'Swinging On A Star' (which won the 1944 Academy Award, from the film *Going My Way*), 'Aren't You Glad You're You?' (*The Bells Of St Mary's*), 'Personality' (*Road To Utopia*), 'But Beautiful', 'You Don't Have To Know The Language', 'Experience' (*Road To Rio*), 'If You Stub Your Toe On the Moon', 'Busy Doing Nothing' (*A Connecticut Yankee In King Arthur's Court*) and 'Sunshine Cake' (*Riding High*). Besides working on other films, Van Heusen and Burke also wrote the score for the 1953 Broadway musical *Carnival In Flanders*, which contained the songs 'Here's That Rainy Day' and 'It's An Old Spanish Custom'. Other Van Heusen songs during this period include 'Oh, You Crazy Moon', 'Suddenly It's Spring' and 'Like Someone In Love' (all with Burke). The last song received a memorable delivery from Frank Sinatra on his first album, *Songs For Young Lovers*, in 1953, as did 'I Thought About You', on Sinatra's *Songs For Swinging Lovers*. Van Heusen also wrote, along with comedian Phil Silvers, one of Sinatra's special songs, dedicated to his daughter, 'Nancy (With The Laughing Face)'. When Burke became seriously ill in 1954 and was unable to work for two years, Van Heusen began a collaboration with Sammy Cahn. Cahn had recently ended his partnership with Jule Styne in style by winning an Oscar for their title song to the film *Three Coins In The Fountain* (1954). The new team had immediate success with another film title song, for the 1955 Sinatra comedy, *The Tender Trap*, and then won Academy Awards for their songs in two more Sinatra movies: 'All The Way' (from the Joe E. Lewis biopic, *The Joker Is Wild*) in 1957, and 'High Hopes' (from *A Hole In The Head*) in 1959. They also contributed songs to several other Sinatra movies, including

'Ain't That A Kick In The Head' (*Ocean's 11*), 'My Kind Of Town', 'Style' (*Robin And The Seven Hoods*), the title songs to *A Pocketful Of Miracles*, *Come Blow Your Horn* and several of Sinatra's bestselling albums, such as *Come Fly With Me*, *Only The Lonely*, *Come Dance With Me*, *No One Cares*, *Ring-A-Ding-Ding* and *September Of My Years*. Van Heusen and Cahn also produced their successful *Timex* television series (1959-60). They won their third Academy Award in 1963 for 'Call Me Irresponsible', from the film *Papa's Delicate Condition*, and contributed songs to many other movies, including 'The Second Time Around' (*High Time*), and the title songs for *Say One For Me*, *Where Love Has Gone*, *Thoroughly Modern Millie* and *Star!*.

The duo also supplied the songs for a musical version of Thornton Wilder's classic play *Our Town*, which included 'Love And Marriage' and 'The Impatient Years'. They wrote the scores for two Broadway musicals, *Skyscraper* in 1965 ('Everybody Has The Right To Be Wrong', 'I'll Only Miss Her When I Think Of Her') and *Walking Happy* in 1966, starring UK comedian Norman Wisdom. From then on, Van Heusen concentrated on his other interests such as music publishing (he had formed a company with Johnny Burke in 1944), photography, flying his own aeroplanes and helicopters, and collecting rare manuscripts by classical composers. He continued to make television appearances, especially on tribute shows for composers. He died in 1990, after a long illness.

VANCE, DICK

b. Richard Thomas Vance, 28 November 1915, Mayfield, Kentucky, USA, d. July 1985. Vance took up the trumpet after first playing the violin. He played professionally with various bands in Cleveland, where he was raised, and in the north-east. His first name-band engagement came in 1934 when he joined Lillian Armstrong, and he then played with Willie Bryant and others before joining Fletcher Henderson in 1936. In 1939 he joined Chick Webb shortly before the leader's death and stayed on with the band under Ella Fitzgerald. By this time Vance was writing arrangements extensively and during the 40s this activity took precedence over his playing. His arrangements, meanwhile, were being performed by bands led by Cab Calloway, Redman, Harry James and Earl 'Fatha' Hines. In the early 50s he played in and wrote arrangements for Duke Ellington's orchestra. In the mid-50s he formed his own band, occasionally sharing leadership with Taft Jordan, with which he played several residencies including one at the Savoy Ballroom in Harlem. He also played on numerous recording sessions with many leaders. A competent player, Vance's most important contribution to jazz and, in particular, to big band jazz, was his talent for arranging.

● ALBUMS: with Fletcher Henderson *Sextet* (Alamac 1950)★★★★, as arranger *Ellington '55* (Capitol 1953)★★★★, with the Henderson All Stars *The Big Reunion* (Jazztone 1957)★★★.

VAUGHAN, FRANKIE

b. Frank Abelson, 3 February 1928, Liverpool, England. While studying at Leeds College of Art, Vaughan's vocal performance at a college revue earned him a week's trial at the Kingston Empire music hall. Warmly received, he went on to play the UK variety circuit, developing a stylish act with trademarks that included a top hat and cane, a particularly athletic side kick, and his theme song 'Give Me The Moonlight' (Albert Von Tilzer-Lew Brown). His Russian-born maternal grandmother inspired his stage name by always referring to him as her 'Number Vorn' grandchild. After registering strongly in pre-chart days with 'That Old Piano Roll Blues', 'Daddy's Little Girl', 'Look At That Girl', and 'Hey, Joe', during the mid to late 50s Vaughan was consistently in the UK Top 30 with hits such as 'Istanbul (Not Constantinople)', 'Happy Days And Lonely Nights', 'Tweedle Dee', 'Seventeen', 'My Boy Flat Top', 'Green Door', 'Garden Of Eden' (number 1), 'Man On Fire'/'Wanderin' Eyes', 'Gotta Have Something In the Bank Frank' (with the Kaye Sisters), 'Kisses Sweeter Than Wine', 'Can't Get Along Without You'/'We Are Not Alone', 'Kewpie Doll', 'Wonderful Things', 'Am I Wasting My Time On You', 'That's My Doll', 'Come Softly To Me' (with the Kaye Sisters), 'The Heart Of A Man' and 'Walkin' Tall'.

In spite of the burgeoning beat boom, he continued to flourish in the 60s with 'What More Do You Want', 'Kookie Little Paradise', 'Milord', 'Tower Of Strength' (number 1), 'Don't Stop Twist', 'Loop-De-Loop', 'Hey Mama', 'Hello Dolly', 'There Must Be A Way', 'So Tired' and 'Nevertheless' (1968). With his matinée idol looks he seemed a natural for films, and made his debut in 1956 in the Arthur Askey comedy *Ramsbottom Rides Again*. This was followed by a highly acclaimed straight role in *These Dangerous Years*, and a musical frolic with the normally staid Anna Neagle in *The Lady Is A Square*. Other screen appearances included *Wonderful Things! Heart Of A Man* with Anne Heywood, Tony Britton and Anthony Newley, and *It's All Over Town*, a pop extravaganza in which he was joined by then-current favourites such as Acker Bilk, the Bachelors, the Springfields, and the Hollies. In the early 60s, Vaughan began to experience real success in America, in nightclubs and on television. He was playing his second season in Las Vegas when he was chosen to star with Marilyn Monroe and Yves Montand in the 20th Century-Fox picture *Let's Make Love*. Although he gave a creditable performance, especially when he duetted with Monroe on Sammy Cahn and Jimmy Van Heusen's 'Incurably Romantic', his disaffection with Hollywood ensured that a US film career was not pursued. At home, however, he had become an extremely well-established performer, headlining at the London Palladium and enjoying lucrative summer season work, appealing consistently to mainly family audiences. In 1985, he was an unexpected choice to replace James Laurenson as the belligerent Broadway producer Julian Marsh in the West End hit musical *42nd Street*. A one-year run in the show ended with ill health and some acrimony. His career-long efforts for the benefit of young people, partly through the assignment of record royalties to bodies such as the National Association of Boys' Clubs, was recognized with an OBE in 1965. He was honoured further in 1993, when the Queen appointed him as the Deputy Lord Lieutenant of Buckinghamshire. In the preceding year he had undergone a life-saving operation to replace a ruptured main artery in his heart. However, in 1994, when he was in cabaret at London's Café Royal, the legendary side-kick was still (gingerly) in evidence.

● ALBUMS: *Happy Go Lucky* (Philips 1957)★★★, *Showcase* (Philips 1958)★★★, *At The London Palladium* (Philips 1959)★★★, *Let Me Sing And I'm Happy* (Philips 1961)★★★, *Warm Feeling* (Philips 1961)★★★, *Songbook* (1967)★★★,

There Must Be A Way (Columbia 1967)★★★, *Double Exposure* (Columbia 1971)★★★, *Frankie* (Columbia 1973)★★★, *Frankie Vaughan's Sing Song* (One Up 1973)★★★, *Sincerely Yours, Frankie Vaughan* (Pye 1975)★★★, *Sings* (Columbia 1975)★★★, *Someone Who Cares* (Pye 1976)★★, *Seasons For Lovers* (Pye 1977)★★★, *Moonlight And Love Songs* (SRT 1979)★★, *Time After Time* (Hour Of Pleasure 1986)★★★.

● COMPILATIONS: *The Very Best Of Frankie Vaughan* (EMI 1975)★★★, *Spotlight On Frankie Vaughan* (Philips 1975)★★★, *100 Golden Greats* (Ronco 1977)★★★, *Golden Hour Presents* (Golden Hour 1978)★★★, *Greatest Hits* (Spot 1983)★★★, *Love Hits And High Kicks* (Creole 1985)★★★, *Music Maestro Please* (PRT 1986)★★★, *The Best Of The EMI Years* (EMI 1990)★★★, *The Essential Recordings 1955-65* (1993)★★★.

VAUGHAN, MALCOLM

b. Abercynon, Mid Glamorgan, Wales. A popular ballad singer with a strong tenor voice, Vaughan first made an impression in the early 50s as the 'singing straight man' in a double act with comedian Kenny Earle. They were touring the UK variety circuit when Vaughan was spotted by EMI Records' recording manager Wally Ridley. In 1955, Vaughan had his first Top 10 hit on the HMV label with 'Every Day Of My Life', which stayed in the chart for four months. Several other hits followed, through to 1959, including 'With Your Love', 'St. Therese Of The Roses', 'The World Is Mine', 'Chapel Of The Roses', 'My Special Angel', 'To Be Loved', 'More Than Ever (Come Prima)' and 'Wait For Me'. His UK television appearances included *Sunday Night At The London Palladium, Startime, Saturday Spectacular, Music Shop, Melody Dances* and *The Jack Jackson Show*. After surviving the initial onslaught of rock 'n' roll, Vaughan's recording career suffered, along with so many others of his style, in the face of the 60s beat boom. In the early part of the decade he still retained an association with Earle, although with variety on the wane, clubs and cabaret were the main showplaces. In 1990, *Malcolm Vaughan: The EMI Years* provided a reminder that he was still a popular nightclub attraction in the north of England.

● ALBUMS: *Hello, Malcolm Vaughan* (HMV 1959)★★★.

● COMPILATIONS: *The Best Of Malcolm Vaughan* (One Up 1974)★★★, *The Very Best Of Malcolm Vaughan - 16 Favourites Of The 50s* (MFP 1984)★★★, *Malcolm Vaughan: The EMI Years* (EMI 1990)★★★.

VAUGHAN, SARAH

b. Sarah Lois Vaughan, 27 March 1924, Newark, New Jersey, USA, d. 3 April 1990. Although she was not born into an especially musical home environment (her father was a carpenter and her mother worked in a laundry), the young Sarah Vaughan had plenty of contact with music-making. As well as taking piano lessons for nearly 10 years, she sang in her church choir and became the organist at the age of 12. Her obvious talent for singing won her an amateur contest at Harlem's Apollo Theater in 1942, and opportunities for a musical career quickly appeared. Spotted by Billy Eckstine, who was at the time singing in Earl Hines' big band, she was invited to join Hines' band as a female vocalist and second pianist in 1943. Eckstine had been sufficiently impressed by Vaughan to give her a place in his own band, formed a year later. It was here that she met fellow band members and pioneers of modern jazz Charlie Parker and Dizzy Gillespie. Recording with Eckstine's band in 1945, full as it was of modern stylists, gave her a fundamental understanding of the new music that characterized her entire career.

After leaving Eckstine, she spent a very short time with John Kirby's band, and then decided to perform under her own name. In 1947 she married trumpeter George Treadwell, whom she had met at the Cafe Society. Recognizing his wife's huge potential, Treadwell became her manager, as she began a decade of prolific recording and worldwide tours. She began by recording with Miles Davis in 1950, and then produced a torrent of albums in either a popular vein for Mercury Records, or more jazz-oriented material for their subsidiary label EmArcy. On the EmArcy recordings she appeared with Clifford Brown, Cannonball Adderley and members of the Count Basie band; these remain some of her most satisfying work. By the 60s, as Vaughan rose to stardom, her jazz activity decreased slightly, and the emphasis remained on commercial, orchestra-backed recordings. It was not until the 70s that she began to perform and record with jazz musicians again on a regular basis. Vaughan performed at the 1974 Monterey Jazz Festival and made an album in 1978 with a quartet consisting of Oscar Peterson, Joe Pass, Ray Brown, and Louie Bellson. The following year she recorded her *Duke Ellington Song Book One*, on which a large number of top jazz players appeared, including Zoot Sims, Frank Foster, Frank Wess, J.J. Johnson, and Joe Pass. In 1980 she appeared in a much-heralded concert at Carnegie Hall, and returned to the Apollo where her career had begun, to sing with Eckstine who had encouraged her at that early stage. They worked the Apollo Theater in a show recorded and broadcast by NBC-TV. She recorded an album of Latin tunes in 1987, and around this time appeared in another televised concert, billed as *Sass And Brass*. With a rhythm section featuring Herbie Hancock, Ron Carter, and Billy Higgins, as well as a collection of trumpeters including Dizzy Gillespie, Don Cherry, Maynard Ferguson, and Chuck Mangione, she proved herself still a musical force to be reckoned with. Tragically, she died of lung cancer in April 1990. Sarah Vaughan won the *Esquire* New Star poll in 1945, the *Downbeat* poll (1947-52) and the *Metronome* poll (1948-52). She also sang at the White House as early as 1965; Vaughan's name was synonymous with jazz singing for two generations. Gifted with an extraordinary range and perfect intonation, she would also subtly control the quality of her voice to aid the interpretation of a song, juxtaposing phrases sung in a soft and warm tone with others in a harsh, nasal vibrato or throaty growl. Her knowledge of bebop, gained during her time with Eckstine's band, enabled her to incorporate modern passing tones into her sung lines, advancing the harmonic side of her work beyond that of her contemporaries. Her recordings will continue to influence vocalists for many years to come. Vaughan probably ranks as a close second only to Ella Fitzgerald in terms of influence, vocal range and sheer, consistent brilliance.

● ALBUMS: *Sarah Vaughan* 10-inch album (Columbia 1950)★★★★ reissued as *Sarah Vaughan In Hi-Fi* (Columbia 1956), *Sarah Vaughan Sings* 10-inch album (MGM 1951)★★★, *Tenderly* 10-inch album (MGM 1952)★★★, *Early Sarah* 10-inch album (Allegro 1953)★★, *Sarah Vaughan* (Allegro 1954)★★, *Lullaby Of Birdland* (1954)★★★, *Sarah Vaughan With Clifford Brown* (EmArcy 1954)★★★, *My Kinda Love* (MGM 1955)★★★, *After Hours With Sarah Vaughan* (Columbia 1955)★★★, *Sarah Vaughan Sings With John Kirby* 10-inch album (Riverside 1955)★★★, *Divine Sarah* 10-inch album (Mercury 1955)★★★, *Great Songs From Hit Shows* (Mercury 1956)★★★, *Sarah Vaughan In The Land Of Hi Fi* (EmArcy 1956)★★★★, *Sarah Vaughan At The Blue Note* (Mercury 1956)★★★, *Linger Awhile* (Columbia 1956)★★★★, *Sassy* (EmArcy 1956)★★★★, *Sarah Vaughan Sings George Gershwin* (Mercury 1957)★★★★, *Images* reissued as *Swinging Easy* (EmArcy 1957)★★★, *The Rodgers And Hart Songbook* (EmArcy 1957)★★★★, *Wonderful Sarah* (Mercury 1957)★★★★, *In A Romantic Mood* (Mercury 1957)★★★★, *Sarah Vaughan Concert* (Concord 1957)★★★, *Close To You* (Mercury 1957)★★★, *Sarah Vaughan And Billy Eckstine Sing The Best Of Irving Berlin* (Mercury 1958)★★★★, *Vaughan And Violins* (Mercury 1958)★★★, *Sarah Vaughan And Her Trio At Mr. Kelly's* (EmArcy 1958)★★★, *After Hours At The London House* (Mercury 1958)★★★, *Vaughan And Violins* (Mercury 1958)★★★★, *Tenderly* (Lion 1958)★★, *Sarah Vaughan And Her Trio At Mr Kelly's* (Mercury 1958)★★★, *Great Songs From Hit Shows Volume 1 & 2* (Mercury 1958)★★★, *Sarah Vaughan Sings George Gershwin Volumes 1 & 2* (Mercury 1958)★★★★, *No Count Sarah* (Mercury 1959)★★★, with Eckstine *Billy And Sarah* (Lion 1959)★★★, *Songs Of Broadway* (1959)★★★, *The Magic Of Sarah Vaughan* (Mercury 1959)★★★, *Misty* (EmArcy 1959)★★★★, *Dreamy* (Roulette 1960)★★★, *The Divine Sarah Vaughan* (Mercury 1960)★★★★, *Count Basie/Sarah Vaughan* (1960)★★★, *Divine One* (Roulette 1960)★★★, *My Heart Sings* (Mercury 1961)★★★, *After Hours* (Roulette 1961)★★★★, *You're Mine, You* (Roulette 1962)★★★, *Snowbound* (Roulette 1962)★★★, *The Explosive Side Of Sarah* (Roulette 1962)★★★, *Star Eyes* (Roulette 1963)★★★, *Sassy Swings The Tivoli* (Mercury 1963)★★★, *Vaughan With Voices* (Mercury 1964)★★★, *Viva Vaughan* (Mercury 1964)★★★, with Dinah Washington, Joe Williams *We Three* (1964)★★★, *The Lonely Hours* (Roulette 1964)★★★, *The World Of Sarah Vaughan* (Roulette 1964)★★★, *Sweet 'N' Sassy* (Roulette 1964)★★★, *Sarah Sings Soulfully* (Roulette 1965)★★★, *Sarah Plus Two* (Roulette 1965)★★★, *Sarah Vaughan Sings The Mancini Songbook* (Mercury 1965)★★★★, *The Pop Artistry Of Sarah Vaughan* (Mercury 1966)★★★, *New Scene* (Mercury 1966)★★★, *Sassy Swings Again* (Mercury 1967)★★★, *I'm Through With Love* (Xtra 1970)★★★, with Michel Legrand *Sarah Vaughan/Michel Legrand* (Mainstream 1972)★★★★, *Feelin' Good* (Mainstream 1973)★★★, *The Summer Knows* (Mainstream 1973)★★★, *Live In Japan* (Mainstream 1974)★★★, *A Time In My Life* (Mainstream 1974)★★★, *Sarah Vaughan And The Jimmy Rowles Quintet* (Mainstream 1975)★★★, *More Sarah Vaughan - Live In Japan* (Mainstream 1976)★★★, with Oscar Peterson, Joe Pass, Ray Brown, Louie Bellson *How Long Has This Been Going On?* (Pablo Jazz 1978)★★★, *Live At Ronnie Scott's* (Pye/Ronnie Scott's 1978)★★★, *Send In The Clowns* (Pablo Jazz 1978)★★★, *Duke Ellington Song Book One* (Pablo Jazz 1979)★★★, *I Love Brazil* (Pablo Today 1979)★★★, *Duke Ellington Song Book Two* (Pablo Jazz 1981)★★★, *Songs Of The Beatles* (Atlantic 1981)★★★, with Barney Kessel, Joe Comfort *The Two Sounds Of Sarah* (Vogue Jazz 1981)★★★, *Copacabana* (Pablo Jazz

1981)★★★, *Crazy And Mixed Up* (Pablo Jazz 1982)★★★, *O, Some Brasileiro De* (RCA 1984)★★★.

● COMPILATIONS: *Sarah Vaughan's Golden Hits* (Mercury 1967)★★★★, *Recorded Live* (EmArcy 1977)★★★★, with Billy Eckstine (coupled with a Dinah Washington and Brook Benton collection) *Passing Strangers* (Mercury 1978)★★★, shared with Billie Holiday, Ella Fitzgerald and Lena Horne *Billie, Ella, Lena, Sarah!* (Columbia 1980)★★★★, *Spotlight On Sarah Vaughan* (PRT 1984)★★★, *The Sarah Vaughan Collection* (Deja Vu 1985)★★★★, *The Rodgers And Hart Songbook* (Pablo Jazz 1985)★★★★, *The Best Of Sarah Vaughan - Walkman Series* (Verve 1987)★★★★, *The Complete Sarah Vaughan On Mercury Vols 1-3 18-CD box sets* (Mercury 1988)★★★★★, *The Singles Sessions* (Capitol/Blue Note 1991)★★★★, *16 Greatest Hits* (1993)★★★★, *The Divine One* (1993)★★★★.

● VIDEOS: *Sass And Brass* (Excalibur 1990), *The Divine One* (1993).

● FURTHER READING: *Sassy - The Life Of Sarah Vaughan*, Leslie Gourse.

VAUGHN, BILLY

b. Richard Vaughn, 12 April 1931, Glasgow, Kentucky, USA, d. 26 September 1991, Escondido, California, USA. An extremely successful orchestra leader, arranger and musical director during the 50s and early 60s. In 1952, singing baritone and playing piano, he formed the Hilltoppers vocal quartet, with Jimmy Sacca, Seymour Speigelman and Don McGuire. They had a string of US hits through to 1957, commencing in August 1952 with Vaughn's composition 'Trying', and in the following year with the million-selling 'P.S I Love You'. When Vaughn left the group in 1955 to become musical director for Dot Records, the other three members continued together until the early 60s, when they too accepted jobs with Dot. Throughout the 50s, Vaughn contributed significantly to the label's chart success, particularly with his arrangements for the somewhat antiseptic 'cover-versions' of rock 'n' roll and R&B hits, especially those by black artists, who were unacceptable to some sections of the US audience. Most of the Fontane Sisters' hits, which were backed by Vaughn's Orchestra, were cover versions, including their million-seller, 'Hearts Of Stone', which was first released by the R&B group Otis Williams And The Charms. Others such examples included Gale Storm's cover version of Smiley Lewis's 'I Hear You Knocking', written by Dave Bartholomew and Pearl King, and several Pat Boone hits, including another Bartholomew number, 'Ain't That A Shame', originally released by the co-writer of the song, Fats Domino. Several of Vaughn's own instrumental hits were in the same vein; his first, 'Melody Of Love' (1954), was also successful for Frank Sinatra and Ray Anthony, the Four Aces and David Carroll. 'The Shifting Whispering Sands (Parts 1 & 2)' (with narration by Ken Nordine) was a hit for country singer Rusty Draper, and the classic 'Raunchy' was a million-seller for Sun Records' musical director, Bill Justis.

Vaughn's other US Top 20 chart entries included 'When The Lilacs Bloom Again', 'Look For A Star' and German-born orchestra leader Bert Kaempfert's 'A Swingin' Safari'. Vaughn was very popular in Germany; his versions of 'Wheels', 'La Paloma', and a revival of the 1937 song 'Sail Along Silv'ry Moon', reputedly sold a million copies in that country alone. From 1958-70 Vaughn was ever-present in the US album

charts with 36 titles entering the Top 200, including the 1960 number 1, *Theme From A Summer Place*. Having been one of the most successful orchestra leaders during the rock 'n' roll era, Vaughn seemed unable to recreate that level of success in the face of the 60s beat boom. Ironically, his last single of any significance, in 1966, was a cover version of the Beatles' 'Michelle'.

● ALBUMS: *Sail Along Silv'ry Moon* (Dot 1958)★★★, *Billy Vaughn Plays The Million Sellers* (Dot 1958)★★★, *Christmas Carols* (Dot 1958)★★, *Billy Vaughn Plays* (Dot 1959)★★, *Blue Hawaii* (Dot 1959)★★★, *Golden Saxophones* (Dot 1959)★★★, *Theme From A Summer Place* (Dot 1960)★★★★, *Look For A Star* (Dot 1960)★★★, *Theme From The Sundowners* (Dot 1960)★★★★, *Orange Blossom Special And Wheels* (Dot 1961)★★, *Golden Waltzes* (Dot 1961)★★★, *Berlin Melody* (Dot 1961)★★★, *Greatest String Band Hits* (Dot 1962)★★★, *Chapel By The Sea* (Dot 1962)★★, *A Swingin' Safari* (Dot 1962)★★★★, *1962's Greatest Hits* (Dot 1963)★★★, *Sukiyaki And 11 Hawaiian Hits* (Dot 1963)★★, *Number 1 Hits, Volume 1* (Dot 1963)★★★, *Blue Velvet And 1963's Great Hits* (Dot 1963)★★★, *Forever* (Dot 1964)★★★, *Another Hit Album!* (Dot 1964)★★★, *Pearly Shells* (Dot 1964)★★, *Mexican Pearls* (Dot 1965)★★, *Moon Over Naples* (Dot 1965)★★★, *Michelle* (Dot 1966)★★★, *Great Country Hits* (Dot 1966)★★, *Alfie* (Dot 1966)★★★★, *Sweet Maria* (Dot 1967)★★★, *That's Life And Pineapple Market* (Dot 1967)★★★, *Josephine* (Dot 1967)★★★, *I Love You* (Dot 1967)★★★, *Ode To Billy Joe* (Dot 1967)★★, *A Current Set Of Standards* (Dot 1968)★★★, *As Requested* (Dot 1968)★★★, *Quietly Wild* (Dot 1969)★★, *The Windmills Of Your Mind* (Dot 1969)★★★, *True Grit* (Dot 1970)★★★, *Winter World Of Love* (Dot 1970)★★★.

● COMPILATIONS: *Golden Hits/The Best Of Billy Vaughn* (Dot 1967)★★★, *The Best Of Billy Vaughn* (MFP 1974)★★★, *Moonlight Serenade* (Lotus 1979)★★★, *Melody Of Love* (Varese Sarabande 1994)★★★.

VELOURS

From New York, USA, the Velours - featuring the wonderfully expressive lead of Jerome Ramos, whose halting and vibrato-laden vocal style was one of the most intriguing in doo-wop - were one of the most impressive groups of the doo-wop era. Other members included Charles Moffett, John Pearson, Don Haywoode, John Cheatdom and pianist Calvin Hayes. The group first recorded for Baton, although nothing was released, but in 1957 they joined Onyx and success followed. Among their songs, 'Can I Come Over Tonight?', 'This Could Be The Night' and 'Romeo' particularly impress. After some unsuccessful singles for Studio and Gone, the Velours broke up in the early 60s. In 1965 four members of the group - Don Haywoode, Jerome Ramos, John Cheatdom and Richie Pitts regrouped. In 1967 they toured the UK and were told when they arrived that they would be appearing as the 'Fabulous Temptations'. The following year, with new member Richie Pitts, they began recording as the Fantastics with far greater success than they had ever achieved as the Velours.

VERDON, GWEN

b. Gwyneth Evelyn Verdon, 13 January 1926, Culver City, California, USA. A vivacious, red-headed dancer, actress and singer, Verdon can be funny or tender, sassy or seductive, depending on the music and the mood. She studied dancing from an early age, and, after assisting the notable choreographer Jack Cole on *Magdalena* (1948), made her first appearance on Broadway two years later in *Alive And Kicking*. However, it was Cole Porter's *Can-Can* that made her a star in 1953. Her thrilling performance as the (very) high-kicking Claudine gained her a Tony Award, and she won another two years later for her portrayal of the bewitching Lola in *Damn Yankees* ('Two Lost Souls', 'Whatever Lola Wants [Lola Gets]', 'Who's Got The Pain'), a show that was brilliantly choreographed by her future husband, Bob Fosse. He restaged his innovative dance sequences for the 1958 film version, for which, instead of casting an already established film star, Verdon was invited to reprise her Broadway role. From then on, Fosse choreographed and/or directed all Verdon's shows. In 1957 she played Anna Christie in *New Girl In Town* ('Ven I Valse', 'On The Farm', 'It's Good To Be Alive', 'If That Was Love'), a musical adaptation of Eugene O'Neill's 1921 play, and on this occasion she shared the Tony with fellow cast member Thelma Ritter - the first time there had been a Tony-tie. In 1959, Verdon won outright - and for the last time (so far) - when she starred with Richard Kiley in *Redhead*. After that, Broadway audiences had to wait another seven years before they saw Verdon on the musical stage, but the wait was more than worthwhile. In *Sweet Charity* (1966) she played a dancehall hostess with a heart of gold who yearns for marriage and roses round the door. Cy Coleman and Dorothy Fields provided her with some lovely songs, including 'If My Friends Could See Me Now' and 'There's Gotta Be Something Better Than This'. Verdon's final Broadway musical (to date) was *Chicago* (1975), a razzle-dazzle affair set in the roaring 20s, full of hoods and Chita Rivera. In more recent times she has turned once more to films. She had appeared in several during the 50s, including *On The Riviera, Meet Me After The Show, David And Bathsheba, The Merry Widow, The I Don't Care Girl, The Farmer Takes A Wife*, as well as *Damn Yankees*. In 1983, she played a choreographer in the television movie *Legs*, and had several other good roles in big-screen features such as *The Cotton Club, Cocoon, Nadine, Cocoon-The Return* and *Alice* (1990). In 1992 she donated a substantial amount of material documenting her own career and that of her late husband, Bob Fosse (he died in 1987), to the Library of Congress. A year later, Gwen Verdon received the 1993 New Dramatists Lifetime Achievment Award at a ceremony in which fellow Broadway legends such as Richard Adler, Chita Rivera, Cy Coleman, John Kander, and Fred Ebb, gathered to pay tribute.

VERRELL, RONNIE

b. 21 February 1926, Rochester, Kent, England. While playing in a boy's club band Verrell heard a professional drummer and immediately decided this was what he wanted to do. Seeing and hearing Gene Krupa in a film confirmed his ambition. In 1939 he took one lesson from Max Abrams, the noted British drummer and teacher, but was too impatient to take further lessons. Thereafter, he taught himself and was given his first chance to play in public in Wales, where he had been evacuated when the bombing of London began. On his return to Kent he joined the Claude Giddings band in Gillingham. The outfit was well known for the quality of its young musicians, who included Tommy Whittle and pianist

Arthur Greenslade, who later worked with Vic Lewis and Shirley Bassey. Verrell also played with Carl Barriteau and the Londonaires band which was briefly popular in Germany. In 1948 Verrell auditioned for the Ted Heath band when Jack Parnell was considering moving on.

He failed the audition but was hired instead by Cyril Stapleton. Three years later Parnell finally left Heath, and was replaced briefly by Basil Kirchin before Verrell took over the drum chair. This was the time when the Heath band reached its peak and as cracks appeared in the UK Musicians Union ban on visiting Americans, Heath was one of the first to tour the USA (on a reciprocal arrangement that brought Stan Kenton to the UK). The Heath band was part of a package that included June Christy, the Four Freshmen and Nat 'King' Cole and it culminated in a concert at Carnegie Hall. The band was a huge success and many of the individual musicians, Verrell among them, attracted favourable attention from critics and fans alike. Apart from the US tour, Verrell was with the Heath band on its Australasian tour. During his stint with the band Verrell was partly responsible for at least two of their chart successes in the UK. His solo feature on 'Skin Deep' helped the record reach number 9 in 1954, and his lithely swinging backing assisted 'Swingin' Shepherd Blues' to its number 3 spot in 1958.

The band also had a Top 20 album success in 1962 with *Big Band Percussion*. After leaving Heath, Verrell worked extensively in television studio bands, among them the house band at ATV which was directed by Parnell. Subsequently, Verrell played in the Syd Lawrence band but continued to be active on television where he gained a kind of anonymous fame as 'Animal', the drummer on *The Muppet Show*. In the late 80s Verrell began playing occasionally with the Pizza Express All Stars in London and made infrequent appearances backing visiting American jazzmen, including Buddy Tate and Clark Terry. He also played in the recreated Ted Heath band led by Don Lusher. In the 90s he continued to divide his time between studio and jazz work. A solid dance-band drummer and excellent timekeeper, Verrell was also explosive when it mattered and his work with the Heath band remains a high spot in the story of big band drumming in the UK.

● ALBUMS: with Ted Heath *Ted Heath At Carnegie Hall* (London 1957)★★★, with Heath *Big Band Percussion* (Decca 1962)★★★.

VINCENT, GENE

b. Eugene Vincent Craddock, 11 February 1935, Norfolk, Virginia, USA, d. 12 October 1971. One of the original bad boys of rock 'n' roll, the self-destructive Vincent was involved in a motorcycle crash in 1955 and his left leg was permanently damaged. Discharged from the US Navy, he began appearing on country music radio and came under the wing of disc jockey 'Sheriff' Tex Davis, who supervised his recording of a demo of 'Be-Bop A-Lula'. In May 1956, the track was re-recorded at Capitol Records's Nashville studio, with backing by the Blue Caps. The original line-up comprised Cliff Gallup (lead guitar), Jack Neal (upright bass), Willie Williams (acoustic guitar) and Dickie Harrell (drums). Weeks later, 'Be-Bop-A-Lula' stormed the charts, temporarily providing Capitol with their own version of Elvis Presley. The strength of the single lay in Vincent's engaging vocal and the loping guitar runs of the influential Gallup.

Vincent's image was brooding, inarticulate and menacing and with such rock 'n' roll authenticity he was not easily marketable in the USA. His second single, 'Race With The Devil', failed to chart in his homeland, but proved successful in the UK, where he attracted a devoted following. Dogged by bad advice and often unsuitable material, Vincent rapidly lost the impetus that had thrust him to the centrestage as a rock 'n' roll icon. Even an appearance in the movie *The Girl Can't Help It* failed to arrest his commercial decline. A respite was offered by the million-selling 'Lotta Love', but line-up changes in the Blue Caps and a multitude of personal problems were conspiring against him. His damaged leg perpetually threatened to end his singing career and renewed injuries resulted in the limb being supported by a metal brace. Vincent's alcoholism and buccaneering road life made him a liability to promoters and by the late 50s, his career seemed in ruins. He relocated to England, where Jack Good exacerbated his rebel image by dressing him in black leather and encouraging the star to accentuate his limp.

Although he failed to retrieve past glories on record, he toured frequently and survived the car crash that killed Eddie Cochran. Thereafter, he appeared regularly in the UK and France, having come under the wing of the notoriously proprietorial manager Don Arden. Increasingly redundant during the beat group era, his lifestyle grew more erratic and uncontrollable and alcoholism made him a bloated and pathetic figure. A comeback album of sorts, *I'm Back And I'm Proud*, lacked sufficient punch to revitalize his career and he continued playing with pick-up groups, churning out his old repertoire. He often railed against old friends and grew increasingly disillusioned about the state of his career. Still regarded as a legend of rock 'n' roll and a true original, he seemed frustratingly stuck in a time warp and lacked any sense of a career pattern. The often intolerable pain he suffered due to his festering leg merely exacerbated his alcoholism, which in turn devastated his health. On 12 October 1971, his abused body finally succumbed to a fatal seizure and rock 'n' roll lost one of its genuinely great rebellious spirits.

● ALBUMS: *Bluejean Bop!* (Capitol 1956)★★★★, *Gene Vincent And The Blue Caps* (Capitol 1957)★★★, *Gene Vincent Rocks! And The Bluecaps Roll* (Capitol 1958)★★★, *A Gene Vincent Record Date* (Capitol 1958)★★★, *Sounds Like Gene Vincent* (Capitol 1959)★★★, *Crazy Times!* (Capitol 1960)★★★, *The Crazy Beat Of Gene Vincent* (Capitol 1963)★★★, *Shakin' Up A Storm* (Columbia 1964)★★★, *Bird Doggin'* reissued as *Ain't That Too Much* (London 1967)★★★, *Gene Vincent* (London 1967)★★, *I'm Back And I'm Proud* reissued as *The Bop They Couldn't Stop* (Dandelion 1970)★★, *If Only You Could See Me Today* UK title *The Day The World Turned Blue* US title (Kama Sutra 1971)★★.

● COMPILATIONS: *The Best Of Gene Vincent* (Capitol 1967)★★★, *The Best Of Gene Vincent Volume 2* (Capitol 1968)★★★, *Gene Vincent's Greatest* (Capitol 1969)★★★, *Pioneers Of Rock Volume One* (Regal Starline 1972)★★★, *The King Of Fools* (Regal Starline 1974)★★★, *The Bop That Just Won't Stop* (Capitol 1974)★★★, *Greatest Hits* (Capitol 1977)★★★, *Greatest Hits Volume 2* (Capitol 1979)★★★, *Rock On With Gene Vincent* (MFP 1980)★★★, *The Gene Vincent Singles Album* (Capitol 1981)★★★, *Dressed In Black* (Magnum Force 1982)★★★, *Gene Vincent's Greatest Hits* (Fame 1982)★★★, *From LA To 'Frisco* (Magnum Force 1983)★★★, *For Collectors Only* (Magnum Force 1984)★★★, *Forever Gene Vincent* (Rollin' Rock 1984)★★★, *Born To Be A Rolling Stone* (Topline 1985)★★★, *Gene Vincent: The Capitol Years* 10-LP box set (Charly 1987)★★★★, *Into The Seventies* (See For Miles 1988)★★★, *The EP Collection* (See For Miles 1989)★★★, *The Gene Vincent Box Set* 6-CD box set (EMI 1990)★★★★, *His 30 Original Hits* (Entertainers 1992)★★★, *Rebel Heart Volume 1* (Magnum 1992)★★★, *Be-Bop-A-Lula* (Charly 1993)★★★, *Ain't That Too Much: The Complete Challenge Sessions* (Hollowbody/Sundazed 1994)★★★, *Rebel Heart Volume 2* (Magnum 1995)★★, *Rebel Heart Volume 3* (Magnum 1996)★★, *500 Miles* (Camden 1998)★★★.

● FURTHER READING: *Wild Cat: A Tribute To Gene Vincent*, Eddie Muir. *Gene Vincent & The Blue Caps*, Rob Finnis and Bob Dunham. *I Remember Gene Vincent*, Alan Vince. *Gene Vincent: The Screaming End*, Alan Clark. *The Day The World Turned Blue*, Britt Hagerty. *Gene Vincent: A Discography*, Derek Henderson.

● FILMS: *The Girl Can't Help It* (1956), *Hot Rod Gang* aka *Fury Unleashed* (1958), *It's Trad, Dad* aka *Ring-A-Ding Rhythm* (1962).

VIPERS SKIFFLE GROUP

Formed in 1956, the group consisted of various members, including Wally Whyton (b. 23 September 1929, London, England, d. 23 January 1997, London, England), Tommy Steele, Hank Marvin, Jet Harris and Bruce Welch. It grew out of the 'frothy coffee' scene, centred at the 2I's coffee bar in London's Soho district in the late 50s. Whyton was the musical brains, and with Bill Varley, wrote the group's first hit, 'Don't You Rock Me Daddy-O', which was even more successful for the 'King Of Skiffle', Lonnie Donegan. After having their 'cleaned up' version of 'Maggie May' banned by the BBC, the Vipers had two other UK chart entries in 1957 - 'Cumberland Gap' and 'Streamline Train'. However, the whole skiffle craze was short-lived, and before long Steele had become an 'all-round entertainer', Marvin, Harris and Welch had formed the Shadows, via the Drifters, and Whyton had carved out a career as a singer and broadcaster on radio programmes such as *Country Meets Folk* and *Country Club*, having previously hosted a number of UK children's television shows, one of which featured the glove-puppet Pussy Cat Willum. In 1960, the Vipers sang 11 songs in the musical play *Mr. Burke M.P.* at London's Mermaid Theatre. Whyton also played the part of 'The Commentator'.

● ALBUMS: *Coffee Bar Session* (Parlophone 1957)★★.
● COMPILATIONS: *Coffee Bar Sessions* (Rollercoaster 1986)★★.

VISCOUNTS

When three disgruntled members of the Morton Fraser Harmonica Gang decided to leave the variety theatres and join the English rock 'n' roll live circuit, the Viscounts were born. Gordon Mills (b. 1935, Madras, India, d. 29 July 1986, Los Angeles, California, USA), Don Paul and Ronnie Wells, were not only harmonica champions, but excellent harmony singers, whose tireless professionalism was in great demand on the debilitating package tours put together by UK promoters such as Larry Parnes. The Viscounts specialized in all-purpose backing vocals, comedy routines and parodic impressions of other acts. They released several singles before charting with the standard 'Short'nin' Bread' in 1960. They registered in the chart again the following year with the number 21 hit cover version of Barry Mann's 'Who Put The Bomp?'. Mills, however, was looking beyond the group and, after writing hits for Johnny Kidd And The Pirates and Cliff Richard, became a full-time composer and later, manager. He was briefly replaced by former Parnes discovery Johnny Gentle, but by 1964 the Viscounts had decided to split. Wells remained on the periphery of the pop scene and recorded for Mills' MAM label under the name Darren Wells. Don Paul later teamed up with Tony Stratton-Smith as co-manager of Paddy, Klaus And Gibson.

VOCALEERS

The original members of this vocal group from Harlem, New York, USA, were Joe Duncan (lead), Herman Curtis (first tenor), William Walker (second tenor), Melvin Walton (baritone) and Teddy Williams (bass). One of the pioneering groups of the R&B era, the Vocaleers' great hit, 'Is It A Dream?' (number 4 R&B, 1953), became a part of the repertoires of a myriad of street-corner groups across the country. The group was formed in 1951 and the following year signed with Bobby Robinson's Red Robin label. Their first release was the ballad 'Be True', which established the group's sound of Duncan's plaintive lead answered by Curtis's falsetto, and earned the group local notices. Williams left the unit at this time and was replaced with Lamar Cooper. The Vocaleers made their last record in 1954, after Herman Curtis was replaced with Joe Powell; Curtis joined the Solitaires. The Vocaleers, with slightly different personnel, reunited in the late 50s, but after a few uninteresting records they disbanded for good in 1961.
● COMPILATIONS: *Is It A Dream?* (Relic 1992)★★★.

VOICE MASTERS

An R&B vocal group from Detroit, Michigan, USA. The members were lead Ty Hunter, Lamont Dozier (b. 16 June 1941, Detroit, USA), David Ruffin (b. 18 January 1941, Meridian, Mississippi, USA, d. 1 June 1991), Walter Gaines and Crathman Spencer. The group was representative of the transitional era from doo-wop to the soul sounds of the Motown label. By the time of their formation in 1959, the Voice Masters were almost all veterans of the Detroit doo-wop scene, Hunter and Dozier having been in the Romeos and Spencer and Gaines having been in the Five Jets. The Voice Masters first recorded for the Anna label, owned by Berry Gordy's sister, Anna Gordy. Only one of their four releases for the label during 1959/60 was heard outside the confines of Detroit, 'Everything About You' (number 18 R&B) in 1960. In an attempt by Anna to promote Hunter as a solo artist, the record was also released under Hunter's name alone. Hunter went on to record for Check-mate, recording the gorgeous 'Memories' in 1961 and having a hit with 'Lonely Baby (number 22 R&B) in 1962, both with backing from the Voice Masters. He moved to Chess in 1963 but was not able to sustain any success. Spencer, Gaines and Hunter all eventually became a part of the late 60s Motown group the Originals. Hunter died in 1981. Ruffin went on to join the Temptations, and later developed a solo recording career.

VOXPOPPERS

Little is known about this group who had one US chart single, 'Wishing For Your Love', in 1958 before returning to obscurity. The group was a quintet (including saxophone, accordion, guitar, bass and drums) from New York City, and had earlier recorded both instrumentals and vocal ballads for such labels as Poplar and Amp-3. They cut 'Wishing For Your Love', written by Sampson Horton, for the latter label and when it received airplay, the larger Mercury Records picked up distribution and the single reached the US Top 20. They continued to record for Mercury and Warwick Records but disappeared from the scene before long.

WAKELY, JIMMY

b. Clarence Wakely, 16 February 1914, near Mineola, Arkansas, USA, d. 25 September 1982, Mission Hills, California, USA. Wakely's family relocated to Oklahoma when he was child, moving several times as they struggled to make a living, usually by sharecropping. He gave himself the name of Jimmy and attended High School at Cowden, Oklahoma, where he learned to play the guitar and piano and worked on various projects, until, after winning a local radio talent contest, he became a musician. In 1937, he married and moved to Oklahoma City, where he first worked as the pianist with a local band and appeared in a medicine show, before he was given a spot on WKY with Jack Cheney and Scotty Harrel as the Bell Boys (Cheney was soon replaced by Johnny Bond). In 1940, as the Jimmy Wakely Trio, they were hired by Gene Autry to appear on his CBS *Melody Ranch* radio show in Hollywood. He worked with Autry for two years, at one time being known as the Melody Kid, before leaving to form his own band, which at times included Merle Travis, Cliffie Stone and Spade Cooley. Wakely made his film debut in 1939, in the Roy Rogers B-movie western *Saga Of Death Valley*, and went on to appear in support roles (sometimes with his trio) in many films and with many other cowboy stars. In 1944, he starred in *Song Of The Range* and between then and 1949, when he made *Lawless Code*, he starred in almost 30 Monogram films. He became so popular as a cowboy actor that, in 1948, he was voted the number 4 cowboy star after Rogers, Autry and Charles Starrett. He made his first appearance in the US country charts in 1944 with his Decca recording of 'I'm Sending You Red Roses'. In 1948, recording for Capitol, he charted two country number 1 hits - 'One Has My Name,

The Other Has My Heart' (which held the top spot for 11 weeks and remained in the country charts for 32, as well as being a national US Top 10 hit) and 'I Love You So Much It Hurts'. In 1949, he had even more success with solo hits including 'I Wish I Had A Nickel' and 'Someday You'll Call My Name', plus several duet hits with Margaret Whiting, including their million-selling recording of Floyd Tillman's song 'Slipping Around', which was a country and pop number 1. At this time, Wakely's popularity was such that, in *Billboard*'s nationwide poll, he was voted America's third most popular singer behind Perry Como and Frankie Laine - edging Bing Crosby into fourth place. Wakely and Whiting followed it with several more Top 10 country and pop hits, including 'I'll Never Slip Around Again' and 'A Bushel And A Peck'. Strangely, after his 1951 solo Top 10 hits 'My Heart Cries For You' (a UK pop hit for Guy Mitchell), 'Beautiful Brown Eyes' and a further duet with Margaret Whiting, entitled 'I Don't Want To Be Free', Wakely never made the country charts again. During the late 40s and the 50s, he toured extensively throughout the USA, the Pacific, the Far East, Korea and Alaska, sometimes appearing with Bob Hope. Musical tastes changed with the advent of Hank Williams and other country singers, and the cowboy song and image lost much of its appeal. Wakely, however, hosted his own network radio show from 1952-58 and in 1961 he co-hosted a network television series with another silver-screen cowboy, Tex Ritter. During the 60s and throughout much of the 70s, he was still a popular entertainer, mainly performing on the west coast (he made his home in Los Angeles) or playing the club circuits of Las Vegas and Reno with his family show, which featured his children Johnny and Linda. He had formed his own Shasta label in the late 50s and in the 70s, he subsequently recorded a great deal of material on that label. In 1971, he was elected to the Nashville Songwriters' Association International Hall Of Fame. Jimmy Wakely died, after a prolonged illness, in September 1982.

● ALBUMS: *Songs Of The West* (Capitol 1954)★★★★, *Christmas On The Range* (Capitol 1954)★★, *Santa Fe Trail* (Decca 1956)★★★★, *Enter And Rest And Pray* (Decca 1957)★★★, *Country Million Sellers* (Shasta 1959)★★★, *Merry Christmas* (Shasta 1959)★★, *Jimmy Wakely Sings* (Shasta 1960)★★★, *Slipping Around* (Dot 1966)★★★, *Christmas With Jimmy Wakely* (Dot 1966)★★, with Margaret Whiting *I'll Never Slip Around Again* (Hilltop 1967)★★★, *Show Me The Way* (1968)★★★, *Heartaches* (Decca 1969)★★★, *Here's Jimmy Wakely* (Vocalion 1969)★★★, *Lonesome Guitar Man* (60s)★★★, *Big Country Songs* (Vocalion 1970)★★★, *Now And Then* (Decca 1970)★★★, *Jimmy Wakely Country* (1971)★★★, *Blue Shadows* (Shasta 1973)★★★, *Family Show* (Shasta 1973)★★, *The Wakely Way With Country Hits* (Shasta 1974)★★★, *Jimmy Wakely* (Shasta 1974)★★★, *On Stage Volume 1* (1974)★★, *Western Swing And Pretty Things* (Shasta 1975)★★★, *The Gentle Touch* (Shasta 1975)★★★, *The Jimmy Wakely CBS Radio Show* (1975)★★★, *Jimmy Wakely Country* (Shasta 1975)★★★, *Singing Cowboy* (Shasta 1975)★★★, *An Old Fashioned Christmas* (Shasta 1976)★★, *A Tribute To Bob Wills* (Shasta 1976)★★★, *Precious Memories* (Shasta 1976)★★★, *Moments To Remember* (Shasta 1977)★★★, *Reflections* (Shasta 1977)★★★.

● COMPILATIONS: *Vintage Collection* (Capitol 1996)★★★★.

● FURTHER READING: *See Ya Up There, Baby - A Biography*, Linda Lee Wakely.

WALKER, T-BONE

b. Aaron Thibeaux Walker, 28 May 1910, Linden, Texas, USA, d. 16 March 1975, Los Angeles, California, USA. Walker, whose T-Bone acronym is a corruption of his middle name, was raised in Dallas where his parents operated an 'open house' to all the touring blues musicians. During his childhood, Walker was brought into contact with artists such as Blind Lemon Jefferson, and in fact he became Jefferson's 'eyes' around the streets of Dallas whenever the blind musician was in town. Inspired by the more sophisticated blues and singing style of pianist Leroy Carr, Walker took up the guitar, and began performing himself. During the mid-20s he toured Texas as a musician/comedian/dancer with Dr. Breeding's Big B Tonic Show, before joining a travelling revue led by singer Ida Cox. By 1929 he had made a solitary country blues record for Columbia Records as 'Oak Cliff T-Bone'. His recording career may very well have started and finished there, had he not travelled to Oklahoma City and met Chuck Richardson, the man who was teaching young Charlie Christian (a boyhood friend of Walker's) to play single string solos on the new electrified instrument - 'T-Bone' began his instruction alongside Christian that same day. Developing his act as a singer and dancer in the style of Cab Calloway (with whose band he toured for a week in 1930 as first prize in a talent contest), Walker was introduced to the slick world of jazz and big band swing. He moved to Los Angeles in 1934 and obtained a job with 'Big' Jim Wynn's band in Little Harlem. Walker's popularity steadily grew throughout the late 30s and in 1940 he took a job with Les Hite's Orchestra. His amplified guitar, still a novelty, brought a distinctive touch to the ensemble's overall sound while an undoubted showmanship increased the attention lavished upon the artist. Upon arriving in New York with Hite, Varsity Records recorded the orchestra, and Walker's feature, 'T-Bone Blues', became a great success - although Frank Pasley and not 'T-Bone' played the electric guitar accompaniment. Leaving Hite, upon his return to California, Walker co-led a band with Big Jim Wynn at the top Los Angeles nightspots, honing his provocative act which included playing the guitar behind his head while doing the splits - a sense of showmanship that would later influence Chuck Berry and Jimi Hendrix.

In 1942-44 Walker recorded for Capitol Records with Freddie Slack's band. Slack repaid the compliment by supporting Walker on the first release under the guitarist's name. The two tracks, 'Mean Old World' and 'I Got A Break Baby', rapidly became standards for the next generation of electric blues guitarists. During 1945-46 Walker was in Chicago, starring at the Rhumboogie Club with Milt Larkins' or Marl Young's Orchestras (Young's band accompanied Walker on the recordings he made in Chicago for the club's own Rhumboogie label and for disc jockey Al Benson's Swingmaster Records). Upon his return to the west coast, Walker was in great demand, both in concert and with his new records released on the Black & White label and its jazz subsidiary Comet (1946-47 - later purchased and released by Capitol Records). These included classics such as 'I'm Gonna Find My Baby', 'T-Bone Shuffle' and 'Call It Stormy Monday'. The latter melancholic ballad, also known as 'Stormy

Monday' and 'Stormy Monday Blues', has since been the subject of numerous interpretations by artists as disparate as Chris Farlowe, Bobby Bland and the Allman Brothers.

In the late 40s the second musician's union ban and a heavy touring schedule with his old partner Big Jim Wynn prevented Walker from recording, but in 1950 he secured a four-year contract with Imperial Records where he demonstrated a harder, funkier style of blues, with sessions utilizing T.J. Fowler's band in Detroit and Dave Bartholomew's band in New Orleans, as well as his own working unit from Los Angeles. These experiments continued after moving to Atlantic Records from 1955-59, where he teamed up with blues harmonica player Junior Wells in Chicago and modern jazz guitarist Barney Kessel in Los Angeles. Although nominally versed in blues, Walker often sought the accompaniment of jazz musicians who allowed free rein for the guitarist's fluid style. He continued to record prolifically throughout the early 50s, but gradually eased such strictures in favour of regular concert appearances. He visited Europe on several occasions and performed successfully at many large-scale jazz and blues festivals. Later albums, including *The Truth* and *Funky Town*, showcased a virtually undiminished talent, still capable of incisive playing. However, by the early 70s his powers were diminished through ill health, and at personal appearances he often played piano instead of his guitar. In 1974 he suffered a severe stroke from which he never made a recovery. T-Bone Walker died of bronchial pneumonia on 16 March 1975, his reputation as a giant of blues music assured.

● ALBUMS: *Classics In Jazz* (Capitol 1953)★★★, *T-Bone Walker* i (1956)★★★★, *Sings The Blues* (Imperial 1959)★★★★, *T-Bone Blues* (Atlantic 1960)★★★★, *Singing The Blues* (Imperial 1960)★★★, *I Get So Weary* (Imperial 1961)★★★★, *The Great Blues, Vocals And Guitar* (1963)★★★★, *T-Bone Walker* ii (Capitol 1964)★★★★, *I Want A Little Girl* (Delmark 1967)★★★, *Stormy Monday Blues* (Wet Soul 1967)★★★★, *The Truth* (Brunswick 1968)★★★, *Blue Rocks* (1968)★★★, *Funky Town* (Bluesway 1968)★★★, *Feeling The Blues* (B&B 1969)★★★, *Very Rare* (Reprise 1973)★★★, *Dirty Mistreater* (1973)★★★, *Good Feelin'* 1968 recording (Polydor 1982)★★★, *Hot Leftovers* (Pathé Marconi 1985)★★★, *Low Down Blues* (Charly 1986)★★★★, with 'Big' Joe Turner *Bosses Of The Blues* (Bluebird 1989)★★★.

● COMPILATIONS: *The Blues Of T-Bone Walker* (1965)★★★★, *Classics Of Modern Blues* (Blue Note 1975)★★★★, *Stormy Monday Blues* (Charly 1978)★★★★, *T-Bone Jumps Again* (Charly 1980)★★★, *Plain Ole Blues* (Charly 1982)★★★, *The Natural Blues* (Charly 1983)★★★, *Collection - T-Bone Walker* (Déjà Vu 1985)★★★, *I Don't Be Jivin'* (Bear Family 1987)★★★, *The Inventor Of The Electric Guitar Blues* (Blues Boy 1987)★★★★, *The Bluesway Sessions* (Charly 1988)★★★★, *The Talkin' Guitar* (Blues Encore 1990)★★★, *The Hustle Is On: Imperial Sessions, Volume 1* (Sequel 1990)★★★★, *The Complete 1940 - 1954 Recordings Of T-Bone Walker* (Mosaic 1990)★★★★, *The Complete Imperial Recordings, 1950-54* (EMI 1991)★★★★, *T-Bone Blues* recorded 1955-57 (Sequel 1994)★★★★, *The Complete Capitol Black And White Recordings* 3-CD set (Capitol 1995)★★★★.

● FURTHER READING: *Stormy Monday*, Helen Oakly Dance.

WALLIS, BOB

b. 3 June 1934, Bridlington, Yorkshire, England. Wallis started his first band in Bridlington in 1950, which lasted right through to 1957. Later he joined Papa Bue's Viking Jazz Band (1956), Diz Disley's Jazz Band (1957) and, briefly, Acker Bilk's Band (1958). From 1958 he had his own Storyville Jazzmen who were very popular throughout the 'trad' boom of the late 50s. His own trumpet playing and singing forcefully reflected the influence of Henry 'Red' Allen. He had two minor UK hits with 'I'm Shy Mary Ellen I'm Shy' (1961, number 44) and 'Come Along Please' (1962, number 33). Change in popular taste brought the demise of the Storyville Jazzmen but Wallis played with a variety of bands including Monty Sunshine's. He then he moved to Switzerland where he played throughout the 80s.

● ALBUMS: *Everybody Loves Saturday Night* (Top Rank 1960)★★★, *Bob Wallis's Storyville Jazzmen* (Storyville 1973),★★★★ *Live* (Storyville 1975)★★, *Jazz Doctor* (Storyville 1975)★★★, *Doctor Jazz* (Storyville 1988)★★★.

WANDERERS

A pop and jazz vocal group, the Wanderers were formed in 1952 in Harlem, New York, USA, by Alfonso Brown (lead), Robert Yarborough (baritone), Frank Joyner (second tenor) and Shephard Grant (d. 1970; bass). They had already worked under two previous names, the Larks and the Singing Wanderers. Under the latter name they won an amateur talent contest at the Apollo Theatre, before Brown was ejected in favour of Ray Pollard on lead. The group released its first single, 'We Could Find Happiness', in late 1953 on Savoy. Two more sides intended for Savoy were not released, though they were allocated catalogue numbers. By the following year they had moved on to Decca Records where two further singles were issued, 'Say Hey, Willie Mays' and 'The Wrong Party Again'. Presumably due to contractual obligations, these were both credited to their former name, the Singing Wanderers. They did shows with Eartha Kitt and others, and made numerous appearances on television's *The Ed Sullivan Show*. By 1957 the group had signed with Onyx Records for 'Single Of You', but a more permanent association was found with Curb Records (when MGM Records took over Onyx and transferred the group). However, it was not until 1961 that the group first made the charts, with a revision of 'For Your Love', and even this only reached number 93 in the *Billboard* charts. Later singles included one notable ballad in 'Somebody Else's Sweetheart' - the first Hal David and Burt Bacharach composition to be recorded. Despite being an interesting footnote in their career, it also flopped. The Wanderers made one final chart appearance in 1962 with 'There Is No Greater Love', which peaked at number 88 in the US charts. This was their first release after transferring to parent label MGM Records, but its success did not prevent the group from being dropped shortly thereafter. Nevertheless, the Wanderers continued out of contract as a potent live act, until calling a halt to their performances in 1970 when Shephard Grant died.

WARD, BILLY, AND THE DOMINOES

This group was sometimes billed as the Dominoes, or Billy Ward And His Dominoes. Ward (b. 19 September 1921, Los Angeles, California, USA), a songwriter, arranger, singer and pianist, studied music as a child in Los Angeles, and at the age of 14 won a nationwide contest with his composition 'Dejection'. During a spell in the US Army in the early 40s he took up boxing, and continued with the sport when he was released. After working as a sports columnist for the *Transradio Express*, and spending some time with a New York advertising agency, Ward became a vocal coach in his own studio at Carnegie Hall, and founded the Dominoes in 1950. The vocal quintet originally consisted of Clyde McPhatter (b. Clyde Lensley McPhatter, 15 November 1932, Durham, North Carolina, USA, d. 13 June 1972), Charlie White (b. 1930, Washington, DC, USA; second tenor), Joe Lamont (baritone), Bill Brown (bass) and Ward on piano. Ward rarely sang, but over the years, was the only constant member of the group. Important changes in personnel came in 1952 when White was replaced by James Van Loan, and Bill Brown by David McNeil; and in 1953, when Jackie Wilson (b. 9 June 1934, Detroit, Michigan, USA, d. 21 January 1984, New Jersey, USA) took over from McPhatter, who went on to found his own group, the Drifters. Ward originally formed the group as a gospel unit, and as such, they appeared on the *Arthur Godfrey Talent Show*. However, they began singing more blues numbers, and in the early 50s, made the R&B charts with 'Do Something For Me', 'Sixty Minute Man' (written by Ward and regarded by many as the prototype rock 'n' roll record, featuring a scorching lead vocal from McPhatter), 'I Am With You', 'Have Mercy Baby', 'I'd Be Satisfied', 'One Mint Julep', 'That's What You're Doing To Me', 'The Bells', 'Rags To Riches' and 'These Foolish Things'. By 1956, when *Billy Ward And The Dominoes* was released, the group's personnel consisted of Gene Mumford, Milton Merle, Milton Grayson, Cliff Owens and Ward. In the late 50s they had US Top 20 hits with 'St. Therese Of The Roses', 'Deep Purple' and 'Stardust', which sold over a million copies. Afterwards, the recorded hits dried up, but the Dominoes, regarded as one of the important, pioneering R&B vocal groups of the 50s, continued to be a popular US concert attraction throughout the 60s.

● ALBUMS: *Billy Ward And His Dominoes* (Federal 1955)★★★★, *Clyde McPhatter With Billy Ward* (Federal 1956)★★★, *24 Songs* (King 1956)★★★, *Sea Of Glass* (Liberty 1957)★★★, *Yours Forever* (Liberty 1958)★★★, *Pagan Love Song* (Liberty 1959)★★★.

● COMPILATIONS: *Billy Ward And His Dominoes With Clyde McPhatter* (King 1958)★★★★, *Billy Ward & His Dominoes Featuring Clyde McPhatter And Jackie Wilson* (King 1961)★★★★, *The Dominoes Featuring Jackie Wilson* (1977)★★★★, *Have Mercy Baby* (1985)★★★★, *14 Original Hits* (King 1988)★★★★, *21 Original Greatest Hits* (King 1988)★★★★, *Feat* (Sing 1988)★★★, *Sixty Minute Man* (Charly 1991)★★★★.

WARD, CLARA

b. c.1922, Pennsylvania, USA, d. 16 January 1973. Like so many of her contemporaries, Ward gained her first musical experience singing in church. As gospel music began to reach a wider audience, she formed a group, the Clara Ward Singers, that became enormously popular. Featuring such outstanding individuals as Marion Williams, the Ward Singers were a superb act and appealed to audiences both sacred and secular. In the 50s the group was at the height of its power, appearing at the 1957 Newport Jazz Festival and other prestigious venues. Under Ward's direction the group

later broadened its appeal and became very showbiz-orientated. Eventually, as bookings continued to flood in, she formed several groups to sing under the Clara Ward banner. The Singers toured extensively, appearing in the Middle and Far East. In the early 60s, by which time Williams had moved on to form the Stars Of Faith, Ward accepted engagements at the Village Vanguard in New York and in a Las Vegas casino, the latter kind of establishment usually being shunned by gospel singers, for obvious religious reasons. In these unlikely surroundings, Ward was a huge success and her contract was regularly extended.

● ALBUMS: *Gospel Concert* (Vogue 1988)★★★.

WARNER, FRANK AND ANNE

b. 5 April 1903, Selma, Alabama, USA. Guitar and banjo player Frank Warner and his wife Anne were known for their song collecting. Frank went to university in 1921, where he learned a large number of folk songs. Following his degree, he pursued a career with the YMCA, but continued his hobby of singing, and lecturing on folk music. In 1935, he and Anne were married, and together they travelled regularly to rural areas along the US Eastern seaboard, collecting songs and tunes from the area. The two eventually met Frank Proffitt, the son-in-law of musical instrument maker Nathan Hicks. The family lived in the mountains of North Carolina, and it was on the first visit that Proffitt taught the Warners 'Tom Dooley'. Later, in 1939, Frank and Anne travelled to the Adirondacks, and in 1940, to New England, still collecting songs and regional stories. It was only on the later trips that they were able to record some of the material. Proffitt's version of 'Tom Dooley' was included on *Frank Warner Sings American Folk Songs And Ballads*, along with 'He's Got The Whole World In His Hands', which was collected in 1935. Warner has performed all over the USA, and in Britain at colleges and historical societies, singing a great number of the songs he has collected and thus keeping those traditions alive. He even had a part in the 1956 film *Run Of The Arrow*. Anne spent eight years compiling *American Folk Songs From The Anne And Frank Warner Collection*, having started it when she was 70 years old. After a lifetime's commitment to collecting, she died in 1991. Proffitt's albums, recorded for labels such as Elektra and Vanguard, have included sleeve notes written by Anne.

● ALBUMS: *Frank Warner Sings American Folk Songs And Ballads* 10-inch album (Elektra 1952)★★★★, *Songs And Ballads Of America's Wars* 10-inch album (Elektra 1954)★★★, *Our Singing Heritage Volume 3* (1958)★★★, *Come All You Good People* (1976)★★★, *Story Of A Folksong USA* (Folktracks 1979)★★★★.

● FURTHER READING: *Folk Songs And Ballads Of The Eastern Seaboard: From A Collector's Notebook*, Frank Warner. *Traditional American Folk Songs From The Anne And Frank Warner Collection*, Anne Warner.

WASHINGTON, DINAH

b. Ruth Jones, 29 August 1924, Tuscaloosa, Alabama, USA, d. 14 December 1963, Detroit, Michigan, USA. Raised in Chicago, Dinah Washington first sang in church choirs for which she also played piano. She then worked in local clubs, where she was heard by Lionel Hampton, who promptly hired her. She was with Hampton from 1943-46, recording hits with 'Evil Gal Blues', written by Leonard Feather, and

'Salty Papa Blues'. After leaving Hampton she sang R&B, again achieving record success, this time with 'Blow Top Blues' and 'I Told You Yes I Do'. In the following years Washington continued with R&B, but also sang jazz, blues, popular songs of the day, standards, and was a major voice of the burgeoning, but as yet untitled, soul movement. However, her erratic lifestyle caught up with her and she died suddenly at the age of 39. Almost from the start of her career, Washington successfully blended the sacred music of her childhood with the sometimes earthily salacious secularity of the blues. This combination was a potent brew and audiences idolized her, thus helping her towards riches rarely achieved by black artists of her generation. She thoroughly enjoyed her success, spending money indiscriminately on jewellery, cars, furs, drink, drugs and men. She married many times and had countless liaisons. Physically, she appeared to thrive on her excesses, as can be seen from her performance in the film of the 1958 Newport Jazz Festival, *Jazz On A Summer's Day*. She was settling down happily with her seventh husband when she took a lethal combination of pills, probably by accident, after having too much to drink. Washington's voice was rich and she filled everything she sang with heartfelt emotion. Even when the material was not of the highest quality, she could make the most trite of lyrics appear deeply moving. Amongst her popular successes were 'What A Diff'rence A Day Makes', her biggest hit, which reached number 8 in the USA in 1959, and 'September In The Rain', which made number 35 in the UK in 1961. Washington usually sang alone but in the late 50s she recorded some duets with her then husband, Eddie Chamblee. These records enjoyed a measure of success and were followed in 1960 with songs with Brook Benton, notably 'Baby (You Got What It Takes)' and 'A Rockin' Good Way (To Mess Around And Fall In Love)', both of which proved to be enormously popular, reaching numbers 5 and 7, respectively, in the US charts. Washington left a wealth of recorded material, ranging from *The Jazz Sides*, which feature Clark Terry, Jimmy Cleveland, Blue Mitchell and others, to albums of songs by or associated with Fats Waller and Bessie Smith. On these albums, as on almost everything she recorded, Washington lays claim to being one of the major jazz voices, and probably the most versatile of all the singers to have worked in jazz.

● ALBUMS: *Dinah Washington Songs* 10-inch album (Mercury 1950)★★★, *Dynamic Dinah* 10-inch album (Mercury 1951)★★★, *Blazing Ballads* 10-inch album (Mercury 1952)★★★, *After Hours With Miss D* 10-inch album (EmArcy 1954)★★★, *Dinah Jams* (EmArcy 1954)★★★, *For Those In Love* (EmArcy 1955)★★★, *Dinah* (EmArcy 1956)★★★, *In The Land Of Hi Fi* (EmArcy 1956)★★★★, *The Swingin' Miss D* (EmArcy 1956)★★★, *Dinah Washington Sings Fats Waller* (EmArcy 1957)★★★, *Music For A First Love* (Mercury 1957)★★★, *Music For Late Hours* (Mercury 1957)★★★★, *The Best In Blues* (Mercury 1958)★★★, *Dinah Washington Sings Bessie Smith* (EmArcy 1958)★★★, *Newport '58* (EmArcy 1958)★★★★, *The Queen* (Mercury 1959)★★★, *What A Difference A Day Makes!* (Mercury 1959)★★★, *Unforgettable* (Mercury 1960)★★★, *I Concentrate On You* (Mercury 1961)★★★, *For Lonely Lovers* (Mercury 1961)★★★★, *September In The Rain* (Mercury 1961)★★★★, *Tears And Laughter* (Mercury 1962)★★★, *Dinah '62* (Roulette 1962)★★★★, *In Love* (Roulette

1962)★★★, *Drinking Again* (Roulette 1962)★★★, *I Wanna Be Loved* (Mercury 1962)★★★★, *Back To The Blues* (Roulette 1963)★★★, *Dinah '63* (Roulette 1963)★★★.

● COMPILATIONS: with the Quincy Jones Orchestra *This Is My Story, Volume One* (Mercury 1963)★★★★, *This Is My Story, Volume Two* (Mercury 1963)★★★★, *In Tribute* (Roulette 1963)★★★, *The Good Old Days* (Mercury 1963)★★, with Sarah Vaughan, Joe Williams *We Three* (1964)★★★, *Stranger On Earth* (Roulette 1964)★★★, *The Best Of Dinah Washington* (Roulette 1965)★★★, *The Queen And Quincy* (Mercury 1965)★★★, *The Original Queen Of Soul* (Mercury 1969)★★★, *The Jazz Sides* (EmArcy 1976)★★★, *Spotlight On Dinah Washington* (Philips 1977)★★★★, with Brook Benton (coupled with a Sarah Vaughan and Billy Eckstine collection) *The Two Of Us* (Mercury 1978)★★★, *A Slick Chick (On The Mellow Side)* (EmArcy 1983)★★★★, *The Best Of Dinah Washington* (Mercury 1987)★★★★, *The Complete Dinah Washington Volumes 1-14 (1943-55)* (Mercury 1990)★★★, *Best Of Dinah Washington* (Roulette 1992)★★★★, *Mellow Mama* 1945 recording (Delmark 1992)★★★★, *The Dinah Washington Story* (Mercury 1993)★★★★, *First Issue: The Dinah Washington Story, The Original Recordings* 1943-61 recordings (Mercury 1993)★★★★, *Blue Gardenia* (EmArcy/Verve 1995)★★★.

● FURTHER READING: *Queen Of The Blues: A Biography Of Dinah Washington*, James Haskins.

WATTERS, CYRIL

b. 7 February 1907, London, England, d. 24 November 1984, London, England. One of the finest 'back-room boys' in the London music business for many years, Cyril Watters' music was heard by millions, yet his name was known to only a few. Essentially a staff arranger with publishers such as Chappells (working on music by Robert Farnon and others), Watters also wrote over 250 mood music compositions for many London publishers' recorded music libraries, specially for the exclusive use of radio, television and film companies. From this source came his 'Willow Waltz' (used by BBC Television as the signature tune for the television serial *The World Of Tim Frazer*), which won him an Ivor Novello Award in 1960. He also wrote the music for 'White Wedding' which sold over 100,000 copies when recorded by Sheila Southern for HMV in 1962. During the 60s he served as Secretary of the Light Music Society, in which capacity he generously assisted many fellow writers.

WAYNE, THOMAS

b. Thomas Wayne Perkins, 22 July 1940, Battsville, Mississippi, USA, d. 15 August 1971, Tennessee, USA. Wayne was a classic one-hit artist, the younger brother of Luther Perkins, the guitarist who developed and first played the trademark two-string guitar style behind Johnny Cash. Wayne attended Humes High School in Memphis, where a few years earlier the young Elvis Presley had come and gone with little fanfare. There Wayne formed a group called the De-Lons, which was recorded by Scotty Moore, guitarist for Presley, for the Fernwood Records label, which Moore co-owned. That first single did nothing, but Wayne's second single for Fernwood, a weepy ballad titled 'Tragedy', made it to number 5 in the US national chart. The song had renewed life in 1961 as a hit for the Fleetwoods. Wayne recorded for other labels but was unable to follow that hit, although Presley recorded a song he had written, 'The Girl Next Door Went A Walking', in 1960. Wayne eventually moved into production work, but his life was tragically cut short when he was killed in a car collision near Memphis in 1971.

WEAVERS

This US folk group was formed in 1949 by artists with a background of traditional music, and comprised Lee Hays (b. 1914, Little Rock, Arkansas, USA, d. 26 August 1981; vocals, guitar), Fred Hellerman (b. 13 May 1927, New York, USA; vocals, guitar), Ronnie Gilbert (b. vocals) and Pete Seeger (b. 3 May 1919, New York City, New York, USA; vocals, guitar, banjo). Previously, Seeger and Hays had been members of the Almanac Singers with Woody Guthrie. Unlike many similar groups of the time, the Weavers were able to attain commercial acceptance and success, without having to compromise their folk heritage. Virtually all their record releases charted, a precedent for a folk group. They have at times been credited with creating the climate for the post-war folk revival. Many songs became 'standards' as a result of the popularity achieved by the group, in particular, 'Goodnight Irene', which sold one million copies in 1950. Other successful songs were 'Kisses Sweeter Than Wine' and 'On Top Of Old Smokey', the latter remaining at number 1 for three months. Despite Seeger being blacklisted in 1952, and brought before the House of Un-American Activities Committee, the group still sold over four million records during that period. The Weavers disbanded the same year because of personal reasons as well as the pressures brought about by the McCarthy era. The group had lost bookings after being added to the blacklist of left-wing, or even suspected left-wing, sympathizers at the time.

In 1955, their manager Harold Leventhal, persuaded them to reunite for a Christmas concert at Carnegie Hall. Such was the success of the event that they continued to tour internationally for a few more years, while still recording for the Vanguard Records label. At this point, Seeger was still able to combine his role in the group with a successful solo career, but by 1958, he had left the group. He was replaced in fairly quick succession by Erik Darling, then Frank Hamilton and finally Bernie Krause. The Weavers disbanded at the end of 1963, after 15 years together, and capped the event with an anniversary concert at Carnegie Hall. Travelling and personal ambitions were cited as the reasons for the split. After the group left the music scene, there were many who tried to fill their space but none had the same combination of enthusiasm and commitment that had made the Weavers such a popular act. Lee Hays, in his latter years confined to a wheelchair, died after many years of poor health in August 1981. In compliance with Hay's wishes, his ashes were mixed with his garden compost pile! Nine months earlier, the original line-up had joined together to film the documentary *Wasn't That A Time?*, recalling the group's earlier successes.

● ALBUMS: *Folk Songs Of America And Other Lands* 10-inch album (Decca 1951)★★★★, *We Wish You A Merry Christmas* 10-inch album (Decca 1952)★★, *The Weavers At Carnegie Hall* (Vanguard 1957)★★★, *The Weavers On Tour* (Vanguard 1957)★★★, *The Weavers At Home* (Vanguard 1958)★★, *Travelling On With The Weavers* (Vanguard 1959)★★★, *Folk Songs From Around The World* (Decca

1959)★★★, *The Weavers At Carnegie Hall, Volume Two* (Vanguard 1961)★★★, *Almanac* (Vanguard 1963)★★★, *Reunion At Carnegie Hall, 1963* (Vanguard 1964)★★★, *The Weavers' Reunion, Part Two* (Vanguard 1964)★★★, *The Weavers Song Bag* (Vanguard 1967)★★★, *Together Again* (1984)★★★.

● COMPILATIONS: *Greatest Hits* (1957)★★★, *The Best Of The Weavers* (Decca 1959)★★★, *Best Of The Weavers* (Decca 1965)★★★, *The Weavers' Greatest Hits* (Vanguard 1971)★★★, *Weavers Classics* (Vanguard 1987)★★★★, *Wasn't That A Time?* 4-CD box set (Vanguard 1994)★★★.

WEBER, JOAN

b. 1936, Paulsboro, New Jersey, USA, d. 13 May 1981. Joan Weber had a number 1 hit in the USA in January 1955, but was unable to follow up that success. The record was 'Let Me Go Lover', released on Columbia Records. Weber was 18 when she met manager Eddie Joy, who brought her to Charles Randolph Grean (a 'one-hit-wonder' himself in the late 60s), who worked in A&R at the famed Brill Building in New York. Grean gave Weber's demo tape of a song called 'Marionette' to Mitch Miller at Columbia, who signed her to the label. Miller took a song titled 'Let Me Go, Devil' and had it rewritten as 'Let Me Go Lover', which Weber recorded. Performed on the television program *Studio One*, the song became an immediate success, selling half a million copies and reaching the top of the chart in the USA and peaking at number 16 in the UK. Weber had given birth around the time her record was most successful and was unable to spend time promoting her career. Subsequently, she was dropped from Columbia's roster and never had another hit.

WEBSTER, PAUL FRANCIS

b. 20 December 1907, New York City, New York, USA, d. 18 March 1984, Beverly Hills, California, USA. An important lyricist for movie songs from the 40s through to the 60s, Webster was educated at Cornell and New York Universities, but dropped out without graduating, to take a job first as a seaman, and then as a dancing instructor. He developed an interest in lyric writing, and in 1932 had a hit with 'Masquerade' (music by John Jacob Loeb). Among his other songs in the early 30s were 'My Moonlight Madonna' (music by William Scotti), 'Two Cigarettes In The Dark' (with Lew Pollack), and 'Got The Jitters' (Loeb). In 1934, Webster and Pollack were hired to write for films, and it was while he was in Hollywood that Webster collaborated with composer Duke Ellington on *Jump For Joy* ('I Got It Bad (And That Ain't Good)', 'Jump For Joy'), an all-black musical that opened in Los Angeles in 1941. He also had hits in the 40s with 'Lily Of Laguna' (music by Ted Fio Rito), and a succession of songs composed by Hoagy Carmichael, among them, 'Baltimore Oriole', 'The Lamplighter's Serenade', 'Doctor, Lawyer, Indian Chief' and 'Memphis In June'. Several of those numbers were introduced in minor films, but in the 50s and 60s Webster wrote the lyrics for numerous songs and themes that featured in some of the highest-grossing movies of the times. These included *The Great Caruso* (1951, 'The Loveliest Night Of The Year', with Irving Aaronson and Juventino Rosas), *Calamity Jane* (1953, 'Secret Love' (Oscar-winner), 'The Deadwood Stage', 'The Black Hills Of Dakota', with Sammy Fain), *Lucky Me* (1954, 'I Speak To The Stars', with Fain), *Battle Cry* (1955, 'Honey Babe', with Max Steiner),

Marjorie Morningstar (1958, 'A Very Precious Love', with Fain), *The Alamo* (1960, 'The Green Leaves Of Summer', with Dimitri Tiomkin), *55 Days At Peking* (1963, 'So Little Time', with Tiomkin), *The Sandpiper* (1965, 'The Shadow Of Your Smile' (Oscar-winner), with Johnny Mandel) and *Doctor Zhivago* (1965, 'Somewhere My Love (Lara's Theme)', with Maurice Jarre). In addition, Webster collaborated on the immensely popular title themes for several other films, including 'Love Is A Many Splendored Thing' (1955, (Oscar-winner) with Fain), 'Friendly Persuasion (Thee I Love)' (1956, with Tiomkin), 'Anastasia' (1956, with Alfred Newman), 'Giant' (1956, with Tiomkin), 'April Love' (1957, with Fain), 'A Certain Smile' (1958, with Fain), 'Rio Bravo' (1950, with Tiomkin), 'The Guns Of Navarone' (1961, with Tiomkin), 'El Cid' (love theme, 1961, with Miklos Rozsa), and 'Tender Is The Night' (1962, with Fain). He also wrote the lyrics for 'Like Young' (music by André Previn), 'Black Coffee' (with Sonny Burke), which received a memorable rendering from Peggy Lee, and 'The Twelfth Of Never' (Jerry Livingston), a US Top 10 entry for both Johnny Mathis and Donny Osmond. His other collaborators included Henry Mancini, Frank Churchill, Walter Jurrman, and Louis Alter. Apart from his three Academy Awards, Webster was nominated on more than 10 other occasions. Among his honours were ASCAP, Dramatist's Guild, *Photoplay*, Limelight Film Critics, and Grammy Awards. He was elected to the Songwriters Hall of Fame in 1972.

WEEDON, BERT

b. 10 May 1920, London, England. Weedon may be one of the most omnipotent of British electric guitarists, given that fretboard heroes including Jeff Beck and George Harrison, began by positioning as yet uncalloused fingers on taut strings while poring over exercises prescribed in Weedon's best-selling *Play In A Day* and *Play Every Day* manuals. This self-taught guitarist started learning flamenco guitar at the age of 12 before playing in London dance bands. During World War II, he strummed chords in the touring groups of Django Reinhardt and Stéphane Grappelli. With such prestigious experience, he became the featured soloist with Mantovani, Ted Heath and, by the early 50s, Cyril Stapleton's BBC Show Band. By 1956, he was leading his own quartet and had released a debut single, 'Stranger Than Fiction', but only his theme to television's *$64,000 Question* sold even moderately before 1959. That year, his cover version of the Virtues' 'Guitar Boogie Shuffle' made the UK Top 10. Subsequent hit parade entries, however, proved less lucrative than countless record dates for bigger stars. Although he accompanied visiting Americans such as Frank Sinatra, Rosemary Clooney and Nat 'King' Cole - later the subject of a Weedon tribute album - his bread-and-butter was sessions for domestic artists from Dickie Valentine and Alma Cogan to the new breed of Elvis Presley-inspired teen-idols - Tommy Steele, Cliff Richard, Billy Fury, *et al*. Steele won music press popularity polls as Best Guitarist, but the accolade belonged morally to his middle-aged hireling. In the early 60s, Weedon's singles hovered around the lower middle of the Top 40. The most notable of these was 1960's 'Apache' which was eclipsed by the Shadows' version. Although the group was dismissive of his 'Apache', they acknowledged an artistic debt to Weedon by penning 'Mr. Guitar', his last singles chart entry to date. Nevertheless, he

remained in the public eye through a residency on the ITV children's series *Five O' Clock Club* - as well as a remarkable 1964 spot on *Sunday Night At The London Palladium*, on which he showed that he could rock out on his Hofner 'cutaway' as well as anyone. Indeed, it was as a rock 'n' roller that Weedon succeeded seven years later - with *Rockin' At The Roundhouse*, a budget-price album much at odds with the easy listening efforts that sustained him during the 70s. A renewal of interest in guitar instrumentals suddenly placed him at the top of the album chart in 1976 with *22 Golden Guitar Greats*. Nothing since has been as successful - and 1977's *Blue Echoes* was criticized severely in the journal *Guitar*, but - hit or miss - Bert Weedon, ever the professional, continued to record production-line albums throughout his sixth decade. In 1991, Weedon made history by becoming the first instrumentalist to be elected King Rat, the top post in the best-known showbusiness charity organization, the Grand Order of Water Rats.
● ALBUMS: *King Size Guitar* (Top Rank 1960)★★★, *Honky Tonk Guitar* (Top Rank 1961)★★★, *The Romantic Guitar Of Bert Weedon* (Fontana 1970)★★★, *Rockin At The Roundhouse* (Fontana 1971)★★★, *Sweet Sounds* (Contour 1971)★★★, *Bert Weedon Remembers Jim Reeves* (Contour 1973)★★, *The Gentle Guitar Of Bert Weedon* (Contour 1975)★★, *Bert Weedon Remembers Nat 'King' Cole* (Contour 1975)★★, *22 Golden Guitar Greats* (Warwick 1976)★★★, *Let The Good Times Roll* (Warwick 1977)★★★, *Blue Echoes* (Polydor 1977)★★★, *Honky Tonk Guitar Party* (EMI 1977)★★★, *16 Country Guitar Greats* (Polydor 1978)★★★, *40 Guitar Greats* (Pickwick 1979)★★★, *Heart Strings* (Celebrity 1980)★★★, *Dancing Guitars* (1982)★★★, *Guitar Favourites* (Ditto 1983)★★★, *Love Letters* (Everest 1983)★★★, *Mr Guitar* (MFP 1984)★★★, *An Hour Of Bert Weedon* (EMI 1987)★★★, *Once More With Feeling* (Pickwick 1988)★★★.
● COMPILATIONS: *Guitar Gold - 20 Greatest Hits* (Pickwick 1978)★★★.

WEISS BROTHERS

Sam and Hy Weiss formed their Old Town Records label in 1952 on 125th Street, New York City - later moving to Broadway - with Sam as a 'sleeping partner'. He worked full-time for the Old Town Stationery Company, although he had formerly been a sales representative for the Apollo and Jubilee labels, as well as east coast distributor for Exclusive and Modern during the 40s. Hy was the main driving-force, producing records and hunting down such untapped talent as Robert And Johnny, the Harptones, Billy Bland and the Solitaires after the company took off in the mid-50s. Sam left in the late 50s to become a full-time record distributor, but the label carried on in his absence, going from strength to strength with acts such as the Fiestas, Arthur Prysock and Ella Johnson. Hy Weiss sold Old Town to MGM Records in the late 60s, but later repossessed the successful Prysock masters and has since produced several reissues by this, his biggest-selling artist.

WELK, LAWRENCE

b. 11 March 1903, Strasburg, North Dakota, USA, d. 17 May 1992, Santa Monica, California, USA. After achieving a measure of competence on the piano-accordion, Welk formed a dance band in the mid-20s, and soon became immensely popular, with engagements at leading hotels and endless one-night stands on the country's dancehall circuit. The band was widely criticized in the musical press for its lack of imagination and simplistic arrangements, coupled with occasionally elementary playing. Nevertheless, Welk's star continued to rise and his became one of the most successful broadcasting bands in the history of American popular music. Welk called his style 'champagne music' and he made no concessions to changing tastes, firmly believing that he knew exactly what middle-Americans wanted to hear. He must have been right, because he retained his popularity throughout the 30s and 40s, and in 1951 his regular radio shows transferred smoothly to television. For the next four years he had a weekly show from the Aragon Ballroom at Pacific Ocean Park, and in 1955 switched to ABC with even greater success.

In 1961, two of his albums spent the entire year in the charts, with *Calcutta* holding the number 1 spot for 11 weeks. During his unprecedented chart run between 1956 and 1972, no less than 42 albums made the lists. During the early 60s there was always a Welk album in the bestsellers. Also in 1961 he signed a lifetime contract with the Hollywood Palladium and a decade later was still on television, by now syndicated across the North American continent. The band's musical policy, which stood it in such good stead for so many years, had a central core of European music, including waltzes, seasoned with numerous ballads. Although the band's book occasionally hinted that Welk was aware of other forms of music, even jazz, the bland arrangements he used watered down the original so much that it sounded barely any different from the wallpaper music he usually played. The astonishing longevity of the band's popular appeal suggests that, however cynical musicians and critics might have been about him, Welk clearly had his finger much closer to the silent majority's pulse than almost any other bandleader in history. He died of pneumonia, at his home in Santa Monica, California, in 1992.

● ALBUMS: *Lawrence Welk And His Sparkling Strings* (Coral 1955)★★★, *TV Favourites* (Coral 1956)★★★, *Shamrocks And Champagne* (Coral 1956)★★★, *Bubbles In The Wine* (Coral 1956)★★★, *Say It With Music* (Coral 1956)★★★, *Champagne Pops Parade* (Coral 1956)★★★, *Moments To Remember* (Coral 1956)★★★, *Merry Christmas* (Coral 1956)★★★, *Pick-A-Polka!* (Coral 1957)★★★, *Waltz With Lawrence Welk* (Coral 1957)★★★, *Lawrence Welk Plays Dixieland* (Coral 1957)★★★, *Jingle Bells* (Coral 1957)★★★, *Last Date* (Dot 1960)★★★, *Calcutta!* (Dot 1961)★★★, *Yellow Bird* (Dot 1961)★★★, *Moon River* (Dot 1961)★★★, *Silent Night And 13 Other Best Loved Christmas Songs* (Dot 1961)★★★, *Young World* (Dot 1962)★★★, *Baby Elephant Walk And Theme From The Brothers Grimm* (Dot 1962)★★★, *Waltz Time* (Dot 1963)★★★, *1963's Early Hits* (Dot 1963)★★★, *Scarlett O'Hara* (Dot 1963)★★★, *Wonderful! Wonderful!* (Dot 1963)★★★, *Early Hits Of 1964* (Dot 1964)★★★, *A Tribute To The All-Time Greats* (Dot 1964)★★★, *The Lawrence Welk Television Show 10th Anniversary* (Dot 1964)★★★, *The Golden Millions* (Dot 1964)★★★, *My First Of 1965* (Dot 1965)★★★, *Apples And Bananas* (Dot 1965)★★★, with Johnny Hodges *Johnny Hodges With Lawrence Welk's Orchestra* (Dot 1965)★★★, *Today's Great Hits* (Dot 1966)★★★, *Champagne On Broadway* (Dot 1966)★★★, *Winchester Cathedral* (Dot 1966)★★★, *Lawrence Welk's 'Hits Of Our Time'* (Dot

1967)★★★, *Love Is Blue* (Ranwood 1968)★★★, *Memories* (Ranwood 1969)★★★, *Galveston* (Ranwood 1969)★★★, *Lawrence Welk Plays 'I Love You Truly' And Other Songs Of Love* (Ranwood 1969)★★★, *Jean* (Ranwood 1969)★★★, *Candida* (Ranwood 1970)★★★.

● COMPILATIONS: *Golden Hits/The Best Of Lawrence Welk* (Dot 1967)★★★, *Reminiscing* (Ranwood 1972)★★★, *22 All-Time Big Band Favourites* (Ranwood 1989)★★★, *22 All-Time Favourite Waltzes* (Ranwood 1989)★★★, *22 Great Songs For Dancing* (Ranwood 1989)★★★, *22 Of The Greatest Waltzes* (Ranwood 1989)★★★, *Dance To The Big Band Sounds* (Ranwood 1989)★★★, *The Best Of Lawrence Welk* (Ranwood 1989)★★★.

● FURTHER READING: *Wunnerful, Wunnerful*, Lawrence Welk. *Ah-One, Ah-Two: Life With My Musical Family*, Lawrence Welk.

WELSH, ALEX

b. 9 July 1929, Edinburgh, Scotland, d. 25 June 1982. Welsh began his musical career in Scotland playing cornet, and later trumpet, in trad jazz bands. In the early 50s he moved to London and formed a band that quickly became one of the most proficient of its kind. With every chair filled by musicians of great skill and enthusiasm, the Welsh band was a major force in the British trad jazz movement. Eschewing the fancy dress eccentricities and pop music escapades of many of his rivals (although 'Tansy' did reach the UK Top 50 in 1961), Welsh concentrated on creating exciting music that echoed the vitality of the best of Chicago-style Dixieland jazz. Among Welsh's sidemen over the years were Archie Semple, Fred Hunt, Roy Crimmins, Roy Williams, John Barnes, Lennie Hastings and Al Gay. During the 60s and early 70s Welsh toured the UK and Europe, building up a rapturous following, and also made occasional successful sorties to the USA. In common with Chris Barber, Welsh saw the need to maintain a wide repertoire, drawing (as jazz always has) from the best of popular music and thus creating a band that effectively swam in the mainstream. By the mid-70s Welsh's health was poor, but he continued to play for as long as he could. Throughout his career Welsh blew with great exuberance, sometimes sang too and always encouraged his sidemen by his example. Not only popular with audiences, he was also respected and admired by his fellow musicians.

● ALBUMS: *Music Of The Mauve Decade* (1957)★★★, *The Melrose Folio* (1958)★★★, *Alex Welsh In Concert* (Columbia 1961)★★, *Echoes Of Chicago* (1962)★★★, *Strike One* (1966)★★★, *At Home With Alex Welsh* (Dormouse 1967)★★★, *Vintage '69* (1969)★★, *Classic Concert* (Black Lion 1971)★★★★, *An Evening With Alex Welsh, Part 1* (Polydor 1974)★★★, *Dixieland Party* (Black Lion 1975)★★, *If I Had A Talking Picture Of You* (Black Lion 1975)★★★, *The Alex Welsh Showcase, Volume 1* (Black Lion 1976)★★★, *The Alex Welsh Showcase, Volume 2* (Black Lion 1976)★★★, *Alex Welsh In Concert* (Black Lion 1977)★★★, *In A Party Mood* (One-Up 1977)★★★, with Humphrey Lyttelton, Bruce Turner, George Chisholm *Salute To Satchmo* (Black Lion 1979)★★★, *Dixieland To Duke* (Dormouse 1986)★★★★, *Live At The Royal Festival Hall (1954-55)* (Lake 1988)★★★, *Doggin' Around* 1973 recordings (Black Lion 1993)★★★.

WESS, FRANK

b. 4 January 1922, Kansas City, Missouri, USA. Wess started out on alto saxophone, playing in bands in and around Washington, DC, where he was raised. Later, he switched to tenor saxophone and worked briefly in the band led by Blanche Calloway. He developed his musical abilities while on military service and, following his discharge at the end of World War II, he played in the bands of artists such as Billy Eckstine and Lucky Millinder. During this period he began to play the flute. In 1953 he joined the Count Basie band, mostly playing tenor and flute, and becoming a featured attraction with the band both as soloist and as duettist with fellow sideman Frank Foster. In the late 50s Wess reverted to alto saxophone but continued to feature his flute playing, becoming the first major jazz soloist to popularize this instrument and proving in the process that it could be used in a gimmick-free fashion. He left Basie in 1964, thereafter working in studios, leading his own small groups, making records and working in groups such as the New York Jazz Quartet and Dameronia, the band led by Philly Joe Jones. Wess also wrote numerous arrangements, for his own groups and for other bands. In the mid-80s he was briefly with Woody Herman and also continued to lead his own small group and to co-lead a quintet with Foster. In the late 80s and early 90s he was leading a splendid Basie-style big band, which included in its ranks Harry 'Sweets' Edison, Joe Newman, Snooky Young, Al Grey, Benny Powell, Marshal Royal and Billy Mitchell, and which made highly successful appearances in Japan. Albums by this band, *Dear Mr Basie* and *Entre Nous*, showed that Wess had ably assumed the role of big band leader and arranger in the Basie tradition. As a soloist (whichever instrument he uses), Wess plays with uncluttered swing, fashioning his phrases with care and is always polished and highly sophisticated.

● ALBUMS: *Frank Wess Quintet* 10-inch album (Commodore 1952)★★★, *Frank Wess* 10-inch album (Commodore 1952)★★★, *Wess Of The Moon* (Commodore 1954)★★★, *Flutes And Reeds* (Savoy 1955)★★★, *North, South, East...Wess* (Savoy 1956)★★, *I Hear Ya Talkin'* (1959)★★★, *Frank Wess Quartet* (Moodsville 1960)★★, *Southern Comfort* (Prestige 1962)★★★, with Kenny Burrell *Steamin'* (Prestige 1963)★★★, *Yo Ho! Poor You, Little Me* (Prestige 1963)★★★, with Thad Jones *Touche* (Status 1965)★★★, with Coleman Hawkins *Commodore Years* (Atlantic 1973)★★★, with Frank Foster *Two For The Blues* (Pablo Jazz 1983)★★★, with Foster *Frankly Speaking* (Pablo Jazz 1984)★★★, *Dear Mr Basie* (Concord Jazz 1989)★★, *Entre Nous* (Concord Jazz 1990)★★★, *Live At The 1990 Concord Jazz Festival* (Concord Jazz 1991)★★★, *Trombones And Flute* (1992)★★★, *Jazz For Playboys* (1992)★★★.

WEST COAST JAZZ

This was the name given to a style of jazz emanating from the west coast of America in the 50s, much of it played by the (predominantly) white clique of musicians who worked in the Hollywood studios. It took its aesthetic from Miles Davis's *Birth Of The Cool* sessions of 1949, seeking to pin the harmonic adventurousness of bebop into classically influenced arrangements. Critics at the time liked to contrast the cool west coast scene with the fiery hard bop or soul jazz of (black) east coast stars such as Horace Silver and Art Blakey. Still, however useful as a descriptive term for the jazz cre-

ated by the likes of Gerry Mulligan, Art Pepper, Shelly Manne, Bud Shank and Shorty Rogers (and often played at the Lighthouse Club on Hermosa Beach), it rapidly became a restrictive label, and after John Coltrane proved how universal music based on hard bop could be, almost a term of abuse. The 'classical' pretensions of Dave Brubeck - canons and fugues - proved to be a cul-de-sac, but it should be remembered that the strand of free jazz pioneered by Eric Dolphy and Ornette Coleman was initially nurtured on the west coast. Coleman's second album for Contemporary - the quintessential west coast label - had Shelly Manne on drums and Dolphy emerged as part of Chico Hamilton's Quintet (and never forgot Hamilton's typically west coast use of cello). Attention to harmonic subtlety was as important to 60s free jazz as the fire and brimstone of hard bop, and west coast jazz had its own input. In addition, the use of the 'west coast' label to describe the white jazz of the 50s has had the result of obscuring a parallel history of black west coast jazz that not only covers a wider stylistic range and a greater time span but also includes prominent figures such as Gerald Wilson, Wardell Gray, Sonny Criss, Hampton Hawes, Horace Tapscott, Bobby Lee Bradford, John Carter and James Newton.

● FURTHER READING: *Jazz West Coast*, Robert Gordon. *California Cool; West Coast Cover Art*, Graham Marsh and Glyn Callingham.

WEST SIDE STORY

Opening at the Winter Garden Theatre in New York on 26 September 1957, the stage musical *West Side Story* shook audiences with its powerful, even aggressive, score, dancing and storyline. Transposing the *Romeo And Juliet* story to contemporary New York, the plot traced the doomed love affair between a member of one of the immigrant Puerto Rican families and a native-born American. Maria, the Puerto Rican girl, and Tony, her lover, are denied happiness through the conflict between the two sides in the urban gang war. In a fight, Tony kills Maria's brother, Bernardo. Later, Tony, believing that Maria has been killed by Bernardo's friend, Chino, is himself killed. This death stuns the rival gangs, the Puerto Rican 'Sharks' and the American 'Jets'. With music by Leonard Bernstein, lyrics by Stephen Sondheim, a book by Arthur Laurents, and the exciting and dynamic Tony-winning choreography of Jerome Robbins (who had also conceived the idea for the show), *West Side Story* blasted many preconceptions about form and content of American musical comedy. The brilliant 'America' cynically contrasted the difference between the expectations of immigrants and the reality they found in their new homeland (although some later recordings managed to turn it into a paean of praise for the USA). 'Gee, Officer Krupke!' was wickedly funny and realistically disrespectful of authority. Among the songs that had a lighter mood than those that dominated much of the show were 'I Feel Pretty', sung by Carol Lawrence as Maria, 'Maria' sung by Larry Kert as Tony, and 'Tonight', a duet for Maria and Tony. The other songs included 'Something's Coming', 'One Hand, One Heart', 'Cool', 'Somewhere' and 'A Boy Like That', which was sung by Chita Rivera as Anita. Rivera also led the ensemble in 'America'. Critical reaction was good, and word-of-mouth reports ecstatic. The show ran for 732 performances on Broadway and 1,039 in London. There were major New York revivals in 1968 and 1980, and West End audiences saw the show again in 1973, 1984 and 1992. The 1961 screen version starred Natalie Wood, Richard Beymer, Rita Moreno, Russ Tamblyn and George Chakiris. Leonard Bernstein conducted the original full-length score for the first time in 1984, for a recording with opera stars Kiri Te Kanawa and José Carreras. The event, which was filmed and televised, ensured substantial sales for the album. *West Side Story* has also spawned many hit singles in radically different interpretations, from artists as diverse as P.J. Proby ('Somewhere' and 'Maria'), the Nice ('America') and the Pet Shop Boys ('Somewhere').

WESTON, PAUL

b. Paul Wetstein, 12 March 1912, Springfield, Massachusetts, USA, d. 20 September 1996, Santa Monica, California, USA. A leading arranger and conductor, who recorded numerous albums of mood music, and was particularly successful working with female singers such as Lee Wiley, Ella Fitzgerald, Doris Day, Dinah Shore, Kate Smith, Sarah Vaughan, Margaret Whiting, Connee Boswell, Rosemary Clooney, Judy Garland, and Diahann Carroll. Weston first attracted attention arranging for Rudy Vallee in the mid-30s, and made his name during a lengthy spell as one of Tommy Dorsey's staff arrangers after Dorsey had taken over the Joe Haymes band. Among Weston's most notable charts for Dorsey were those featuring Jo Stafford, whom he married in 1952. When Capitol Records were formed in 1943, Weston joined as conductor-arranger, and later became A&R director. Throughout the 40s he served as musical director on various radio shows, and late in the decade began recording mood music, an activity that was boosted by the development of the long-playing record. In 1951 he moved over to Columbia Records, but by the end of the 50s was back at Capitol. The extent of Weston's musicianship is also displayed on a series of records he and Stafford made under the names Jonathan And Darlene Edwards. Stafford's deliberately off-key singing to Weston's out-of-tempo playing is brilliantly executed and the results number among the most hilarious comedy albums ever made. One of them, *Jonathan And Darlene Edwards In Paris*, was awarded a Grammy in 1960. In the 60s and 70s Weston conducted on several top-rated television programmes, starring Danny Kaye and Jonathan Winters. A gifted composer, Weston collaborated on several popular songs, including 'I Should Care' (with Axel Stordahl-Sammy Cahn), 'Day By Day' (Stordahl-Cahn), one of Stafford's biggest hits 'Shrimp Boats' (Paul Mason Howard), 'Autumn In Rome' (Cahn), 'Hey, Mr. Postman' (Don Raye), 'Indiscretion' (Cahn), 'The Gandy Dancers' Ball' (Howard), 'Congratulations' (Sid Robin) and 'No Other Love' (Bob Russell). He also wrote serious works such as 'Mass For Three Voices' and 'Crescent City Suite'. In 1971 Weston received the Trustees Award from the National Academy Of Recording Arts And Science (NARAS) for his 'inspiring and tireless dedication to the Academy's development'. During the 90s, he operated the Corinthian Records label in Beverly Hills, California, formed by himself and Stafford, which released the couple's new recordings and reissued their leased back catalogue. Weston died in September 1996.

● ALBUMS: as Paul Weston And His Orchestra *Crescent City - A Musical Portrait Of New Orleans* (Columbia 1954)★★★★, *Mood For 12* (Columbia 1955)★★★★, *Easy Jazz* (Columbia 1955)★★★, *Solo Mood* (Columbia 1956)★★★, *Cinema Cameos* (Columbia 1956)★★★, *Reflections Of An Indian Boy* (Columbia 1957)★★, *Music For A Rainy Night* (Columbia 1957)★★★, *Moonlight Becomes You* (Columbia 1958)★★★, *The Music Of Jerome Kern* (Columbia 1958)★★★, *Columbia Album Of Romberg* (Columbia 1958)★★★, *Hollywood* (Columbia 1958)★★★, *Carefree* (Capitol 1959)★★★, *Memories That Linger On* (Decca 1959)★★★, *Floatin' Like A Feather* (Capitol 1959)★★★, *Music For Memories* (Capitol 1959)★★★, *Music For Romancing* (Capitol 1959)★★★, *Music For The Fireside* (Capitol 1959)★★★, *Music For Dreaming* (Capitol 1959)★★★, *The Sweet And Swingin'* (Capitol 1960)★★★, *Music For My Love* (Capitol 1961)★★★.

As Jonathan And Darlene Edwards *Sing Along With Jonathan And Darlene Edwards - Only The Chorus Is For Real* (Columbia 1959)★★★, *Jonathan And Darlene's Original Masterpiece* (Columbia 1960)★★★, *Jonathan And Darlene Edwards In Paris* (Columbia 1960)★★★, *Songs For Sheiks And Flappers* (Corinthian 1988)★★, *Darlene Remembers Duke, Jonathan Plays Fats* (Corinthian 1988)★★★.

● COMPILATIONS: *Paul Weston - The Original* (1985)★★★★. With Jo Stafford *Jo And Broadway* (Columbia 1960)★★★, with Stafford *As You Desire Me* (Columbia 1960)★★★, with Stafford *Swingin' Down Broadway* (Columbia 1960)★★★★.

As Jonathan And Darlene Edwards *Jonathan And Darlene's Greatest Hits* (Corinthian 1987)★★★.

WHISKEY, NANCY

b. c.1937, Glasgow, Scotland. Whiskey started her career playing and singing traditional songs but later, during the skiffle music boom in the 50s, she moved south, with her repertoire of Scottish traditional songs. She was given the surname Whiskey having become associated with the song 'The Calton Weaver', whose chorus includes the line 'Whiskey, Whiskey, Nancy Whiskey'. An EP recorded for Topic Records, *Nancy Whiskey Sings*, included the Irish rebel song 'The Bold Fenian Men' on the track listing, but this track did not appear on the record, having been substituted. Her major claim to fame came in 1957, when the Chas McDevitt Skiffle Group, featuring Nancy Whiskey, made the UK Top 5 with 'Freight Train'. They had a degree of success with a subsequent single, 'Greenback Dollar', which made the UK Top 30 the same year. In 1958, Nancy left the group to be replaced by Shirley Douglas, since which time she has occasionally performed as a folk artist; she appeared performing with McDevitt on UK television as recently as 1991.

● FILMS: *The Golden Disc* (1958).

WHITE CHRISTMAS

With this title, the score for this musical just had to be written by Irving Berlin, and a good score it was too. The problem with this film, which was released by Paramount in 1954, lay with the screenplay. It required three men, Norman Krasna, Norman Panama and Melvin Frank, to devise the story about Bob (Captain) Wallace (Bing Crosby) and Phil (Private First Class) Davis (Danny Kaye), who leave the US Army at the end of World War II and form a successful song-and-dance act, which eventually leads to them producing their own shows. After meeting with the Haynes Sisters singing duo (Rosemary Clooney and Vera-Ellen), the quartet end up at a Vermont holiday resort run by the ex-

GIs' former (and much-respected) commanding officer (Dean Jagger). Business is bad owing to the lack of snow, but everything turns out fine when Wallace and Davis organize a benefit show, which - surprise, surprise - ends with the much-needed flakes drifting down while everyone sings 'White Christmas', and Crosby and Kaye are melting into the arms of Clooney and Vera-Ellen, respectively. Irving Berlin 'borrowed' the song from the 1942 Crosby-Fred Astaire film *Holiday Inn*, which was similar in many ways to *White Christmas*. The rest of the songs were a mixture of old and new. One of the most appealing was 'Sisters', in which Crosby and Kaye, waving feather boas and with their trousers rolled up to the knees, parody a typical Haynes Sisters routine. The remainder included 'The Best Things Happen While You're Dancing', 'The Old Man', 'Gee, I Wish I Was Back In The Army', 'Count Your Blessings Instead Of Sheep', 'Love, You Didn't Do Right By Me', 'Blue Skies', 'Choreography', 'Snow', 'What Can You Do With A General', 'I'd Rather See A Minstrel Show' and 'Mandy'. Also in the cast were Mary Wickes, John Brascia, Anne Whitfield, Grady Sutton, Sig Ruman, and the 21-year-old dancer George Chakiris. The dances and musical numbers were staged by Robert Alton and the film was nicely photographed in Technicolor and VistaVision by Loyal Griggs. The director was Michael Curtiz. *White Christmas* proved to be a tremendous box-office success, becoming one of the Top 20 films of the 50s in the USA, and the fifth highest-grossing musical.

WHITFIELD, DAVID

b. 2 February 1925, Hull, Yorkshire, England, d. 15 January 1980, Sydney, Australia. A popular ballad singer in the UK during the 50s, with a tenor voice that proved to be suitable for light opera. After working as a labourer, and singing in local clubs, Whitfield spent some time in the merchant navy before signing to Decca Records and having hits in 1953 with 'Bridge Of Sighs', 'Answer Me' (number 1) and 'Rags To Riches'. He toured the variety circuit, and in 1954 appeared in the *Royal Command Performance* with other pop stars such as Guy Mitchell, Dickie Valentine, and Frankie Laine. Throughout the 50s, he defied the onslaught of rock 'n' roll, and registered strongly in the UK Top 30 with 'The Book', 'Santo Natale', 'Beyond The Stars', 'Mama', 'Ev'rywhere', 'When You Lose The One You Love', 'My September Love', 'My Son John', 'My Unfinished Symphony', 'Adoration Waltz', 'I'll Find You', 'Cry My Heart', 'On The Street Where You Live' and 'The Right To Love'. The extraordinary 'Cara Mia', on which Whitfield was accompanied by Mantovani and his Orchestra, dominated the UK number 1 position for a staggering 10 weeks, and sold over three and a half million copies. The song reached the US Top 10. He also had some success in the USA with 'Smile', originally written for the Charles Chaplin movie *Modern Times* (1936). By the turn of the 60s, singers of Whitfield's style had begun to go out of fashion, and in 1961 he indicated his future direction by releasing *My Heart And I*, a selection of operetta favourites that included 'I Kiss Your Hand, Madame' and 'You Are My Heart's Delight'. Subsequently, he toured abroad, and had sung aboard a Chinese passenger liner on a cruise in the South Pacific Islands, shortly after concluding his tenth tour of Australia, when he died in Sydney. His ashes were later scattered at sea, near to where he was born.
● ALBUMS: *Yours From The Heart* (Decca 1954)★★★, *Whitfield Favourites* (Decca 1958)★★★, *From David With Love* (Decca 1958)★★★, *My Heart And I* (Decca 1960)★★★, *Alone* (Decca 1961)★★★, *Great Songs For Young Lovers* (Decca 1966)★★★, *Hey There, It's David Whitfield* (Philips 1975)★★★.
● COMPILATIONS: *The World Of David Whitfield* (Decca 1969)★★★, *World Of David Whitfied Volume 2* (Decca 1975)★★★, *Focus On David Whitfield* (Decca 1978)★★★, *Greatest Hits* (Decca 1983)★★★, *The Magic Of David Whitfield* (Decca 1986)★★★, *Sings Stage And Screen Favourites* (Pickwick 1989)★★★.
● FURTHER READING: *Cara Mia - The David Whitfield Story*, Alan Britton.

WHITING, MARGARET

b. 22 July 1924, Detroit, Michigan, USA. A popular vocalist in the 40s and 50s, recording dozens of hits for Capitol Records, Whiting was the daughter of Richard Whiting, himself a successful songwriter, and author of, among others, 'On The Good Ship Lollipop', 'The Japanese Sandman' and 'Ain't We Got Fun?'. Margaret began singing as a small child and by the age of seven she was working with Johnny Mercer, the popular songwriter and founder of Capitol Records, for whom her father worked. When Mercer and two partners launched Capitol, Margaret Whiting was one of their first signings. Whiting started recording for the label in 1942, her first major hit being the Mercer-Harold Arlen composition 'That Old Black Magic', as featured singer with Freddie Slack And His Orchestra. That was followed in 1943 by 'Moonlight In Vermont', with Whiting singing as a member of Billy Butterfield's Orchestra, and 'It Might As Well Be Spring', with Paul Weston And His Orchestra, from the film *State Fair*. Whiting first recorded under her own name in late 1945, singing the Jerome Kern-Oscar Hammerstein II composition 'All Through The Day', which became a bestseller in the spring of 1946, and 'In Love In Vain', both of which were featured in the film *Centennial Summer*. Whiting also had hits with songs from the Broadway musicals *St. Louis Woman* and *Call Me Mister* in 1946. Those first recordings under her name were recorded in New York. In late 1946 Whiting returned to California and began recording there, with Jerry Gray And His Orchestra; 'Guilty' and 'Oh, But I Do' were the bestselling fruits of that session. Whiting's hit streak continued in 1948-49. Due to a musician's strike in the USA, orchestral tracks were recorded outside of the country and vocals added in US studios. Whiting supplied vocals to tracks cut by Frank DeVol And His Orchestra, including 'A Tree In The Meadow', a number 1 hit in the summer of 1948, recorded in London. Her next number 1 occurred in 1949 with 'Slippin' Around', one of a series of duet recordings made with country film star Jimmy Wakely. Also during that year, Whiting recorded a duet with Mercer, 'Baby, It's Cold Outside'. In 1950, she had a hit with 'Blind Date', a novelty record she made with Bob Hope and the Billy May Orchestra. Whiting continued recording hits for Capitol into the mid-50s, until her run of hits dried up. She left Capitol in 1958 for Dot Records but achieved only one hit on that label. She switched to Verve Records in 1960 and recorded a number of albums, including one with jazz vocalist Mel Tormé. A brief return to Capitol was followed by a hiatus, after which Whiting signed to London Records in 1966, for whom she recorded her last two charting pop singles. Her recordings continued to appear on the easy listening charts into the 70s. Whiting was still recording in the early 90s, and performing in cabaret and concerts.

● ALBUMS: *South Pacific* 10-inch album (Capitol 1950)★★★, *Margaret Whiting Sings Rodgers And Hart* 10-inch album (Capitol 1950)★★★★, *Songs* 10-inch album (Capitol 1950)★★★, *Love Songs By Margaret Whiting* reissued 1985 (Capitol 1955)★★★, *Margaret Whiting Sings For The Starry-Eyed* (Capitol 1955)★★★, *Goin' Places* (Dot 1957)★★★, *Margaret* (Dot 1958)★★, *Ten Top Hits* (Dot 1960)★★, *Just A Dream* (Dot 1960)★★, *Margaret Whiting Sings The Jerome Kern Songbook* reissued 1987 (Verve 1961)★★★★, with Mel Tormé *Broadway Right Now!* (Verve 1961)★★★, *Past Midnight* (1962)★★, *The Wheel Of Hurt* (London 1967)★★, *Maggie Isn't Margaret Anymore* (1967)★★★, *Pop Country* (1968)★, *The Lady's In Love With You* (Audiophile 1986)★★★, *Come A Little Closer* (Audiophile 1988)★★★, *Too Marvelous For Words* (Audiophile 1988)★★★.

● COMPILATIONS: *Margaret Whiting Great Hits* (Dot 1959)★★★, *Her Greatest Hits* (Contour 1974)★★★, *Capitol Collectors Series* (Capitol 1991)★★★★.

WHITMAN, SLIM

b. Otis Dewey Whitman Jnr., 20 January 1924, Tampa, Florida, USA. As a child, Whitman's stutter was ridiculed by other children and consequently, he left school as soon as he could. Even though his stutter is now cured, he has never cared for public speaking and says little during his stage act. Several members of his family were musical and he became interested in Jimmie Rodgers' recordings when he discovered that he too could yodel. After leaving school, he worked in a meat-packing plant where he lost part of a finger, which, several years later, led to him turning a guitar tutor upside down and learning to play left-handed. He later remarked, 'Paul McCartney saw me in Liverpool and realized that he too could play the guitar left-handed.' Whitman sang at his family's local church, the Church of the Brethren, and it was here, in 1938, that he met the new minister's daughter, Geraldine Crisp. After borrowing $10 from his mother for the license, he married her in 1941. Whitman regards his long-standing marriage as a major ingredient in his success, and he wrote and dedicated a song to her, 'Jerry'. During World War II, he worked as a fitter in a shipyard and then saw action in the US Navy. While on board, he soon realized his talents for entertaining his fellow crew members, but in his first concert, he tempted fate by singing 'When I'm Gone You'll Soon Forget Me'. However, his singing became so popular that the captain blocked his transfer to another ship - fortunately for Whitman, as the other ship was sunk with all hands lost.

After his discharge, he had some success in baseball, but he preferred singing, choosing the name Slim Whitman as a tribute to Wilf Carter (Montana Slim), and often working on radio. He first recorded for RCA Victor at the suggestion of Tom Parker, in 1949. After moderate successes with 'I'm Casting My Lasso Towards The Sky' and 'Birmingham Jail', he moved to Shreveport, Louisiana, so that he could appear each week on the radio show *Louisiana Hayride*. His wife embroidered black shirts for Whitman and the band, which has led him to claim he was the original 'Man In Black'. His steel player, Hoot Rains, developed an identifiable sound,

but it came about by accident: when Rains overshot a note on 'Love Song Of The Waterfall', Whitman decided to retain it as a trademark. Whitman maintained a level-headed attitude towards his career and was working as a postman while his first single for Imperial Records, 'Love Song Of The Waterfall', was selling half a million copies. 'You don't quit on one record,' he says, 'then I had "Indian Love Call" and I decided to go. I was told that if I ever wanted my job back, I could have it'. 'Indian Love Call' came from Rudolph Friml's operetta *Rose Marie*, and in 1955, the song gave Slim Whitman 11 consecutive weeks at the top of the UK charts. 'All I did was throw in a few yodels for good measure,' says Slim, 'and the folks seemed to go for it.' The b-side of 'Indian Love Call', 'China Doll', was a UK hit in its own right, and his other chart records include 'Cattle Call', 'Tumbling Tumbleweeds', 'Serenade' and 'I'll Take You Home Again, Kathleen,' although, astonishingly, he has never topped the US country charts. He says, 'A lot of people think of me as a cowboy because I've sung "Cattle Call" and one or two others. The truth is, I've never been on a horse in my life.' In 1955, Whitman moved back to Florida, which restricted his appearances on the *Grand Ole Opry* because he found the trips too time-consuming. In 1956 Whitman became the first country star to top the bill at the London Palladium. Despite being a light-voiced country balladeer, he was featured in the 1957 rock 'n' roll film *Disc Jockey Jamboree*. He has always taken a moral stance on what he records, refusing, for example, to record 'Almost Persuaded'. He says, 'I'm not a saint. It's just that I've no interest in singing songs about cheating or the boozer'. His popularity in Britain was such that his *25th Anniversary Concert* album was recorded at the Empire Theatre, Liverpool, in March 1973. He had a UK hit in 1974 with 'Happy Anniversary', but United Artists executive Alan Warner decided that his US country albums were unsuitable for the UK market, and that he should record albums of pop standards that could be marketed on television. His 1976 album, *The Very Best Of Slim Whitman*, entered the UK album charts at number 1, and was followed by *Red River Valley* (number 1) and *Home On The Range* (number 2). Whitman then repeated his role as a purveyor of love songs for the middle-aged in the USA. Since 1977, Whitman has toured with his son Byron (b. 1957), who, he says, is matching him 'yodel for yodel', and they have pioneered the double yodel. Of his continued success, constantly playing to full houses, he says, 'I don't know the secret. I guess it's the songs I sing and my friendly attitude. When I say hello, I mean it'. In 1996, Whitman's name was made known to younger audiences in the film *Mars Attacks!* - after failing to destroy the evil, marauding Martian invaders with nuclear strikes, it is discovered that their brains explode upon hearing any Slim Whitman recording.

● ALBUMS: *Slim Whitman Sings And Yodels* 10-inch album (RCA Victor 1954)★★★, *America's Favorite Folk Artist* 10-inch album (Imperial 1954)★★★, *Slim Whitman Favorites* (Imperial 1956)★★★, *Slim Whitman Sings* (Imperial 1957)★★★★, *Slim Whitman Sings* (Imperial 1958)★★★★, *Slim Whitman Sings* (Imperial 1959)★★★★, *Slim Whitman Sings Annie Laurie* (Imperial 1959)★★★, *I'll Walk With God* (Imperial 1960)★★, *First Visit To Britain* (Imperial 1960)★★, *Just Call Me Lonesome* (Imperial 1961)★★★, *Once In A Lifetime* (Imperial 1961)★★★, *Heart Songs And Love Songs* (Imperial 1961)★★★, *I'm A Lonely Wanderer*

(Imperial 1962)★★★, *Yodeling* (Imperial 1963)★★★, *Irish Songs - The Slim Whitman Way* (Imperial 1963)★★, *Love Song Of The Waterfall* (Imperial 1964)★★★★, *Reminiscing* (Imperial 1964)★★★, *More Than Yesterday* (Imperial 1965)★★★, *Forever* (Imperial 1966)★★★, *God's Hand In Mine* (Imperial 1966)★★, *A Travellin' Man* (Imperial 1966)★★★, *A Time For Love* (Imperial 1966)★★★, *A Lonesome Heart* (Sunset 1967)★★★, *Country Memories* (Imperial 1967)★★★, *In Love, The Whitman Way* (Imperial 1968)★★★★, *Unchain Your Heart* (Sunset 1968)★★★, *Happy Street* (Imperial 1968)★★★, *Slim!* (Imperial 1969)★★★, *The Slim Whitman Christmas Album* (Imperial 1969)★★, *Ramblin' Rose* (1970)★★★, *Tomorrow Never Comes* (United Artists 1970)★★★, *Guess Who* aka *Snowbird* (United Artists 1971)★★★, *It's A Sin To Tell A Lie* (United Artists 1971)★★★, *I'll See You When* (United Artists 1973)★★★, *25th Anniversary Concert* (United Artists 1973)★★★, *Happy Anniversary* (United Artists 1974)★★★, *Everything Leads Back To You* (United Artists 1975)★★★, *Home On The Range* (United Artists 1977)★★★, *Red River Valley* (United Artists 1977)★★★, *Ghost Riders In The Sky* (United Artists 1978)★★★, *Till We Meet Again* (United Artists 1980)★★★, *Just For You* (Suffolk 1980)★★★, *Songs I Love To Sing* (Cleveland International 1980)★★★, *Christmas With Slim Whitman* (Cleveland International 1980)★★, *Mr. Songman* (Liberty 1981)★★★, *I'll Be Home For Christmas* (1981)★★, *Angeline* (Epic 1984)★★★, *A Dream Come True - The Rarities Album* (1987)★★★, with Byron Whitman *Magic Moments* (1990)★★★.

● COMPILATIONS: *Country Hits Volume 1* (Imperial 1960)★★★, *All Time Favourites* (Imperial 1964)★★★, *Country Songs, City Hits* (1965)★★★, *Birmingham Jail* (RCA Camden 1966)★★★, *Fifteenth Anniversary* (Imperial 1967)★★★, *The Very Best Of Slim Whitman* (United Artists 1976)★★★, *All My Best* (Suffolk 1979)★★★, *Slim Whitman's 20 Greatest Love Songs* (MFP 1981)★★★, *Slim Whitman: The Collection* (Liberty 1989)★★★, *The Best Of Slim Whitman (1952-1972)* (Rhino 1990)★★★★, *20 Golden Greats* (1992)★★★, *EMI Country Masters: 50 Orginal Tracks* (EMI 1993)★★★, *Love Songs* (MFP 1994)★★★, *Rose Marie: Slim Whitman 1949-1959* 6-CD box set (Bear Family 1996)★★★, *50th Anniversary Collection* (EMI 1997)★★★.

● FURTHER READING: *Mr. Songman - The Slim Whitman Story*, Kenneth L. Gibble.

● FILMS: *Jamboree* aka *Disc Jockey Jamboree* (1957).

WHYTON, WALLY

b. 23 September 1929, London, England, d. 23 January 1997, London, England. Broadcaster and singer Wally Whyton enjoyed a fascinating and varied professional career after initially training as a commercial artist. However, after socializing with Lionel Bart and his first exposure to the jazz records of Louis Armstrong and Bessie Smith, Whyton soon developed ambitions to become a singer. He subsequently formed a skiffle band, the Vipers, with himself on vocals and fellow members Johnny Martyn, Jean Van den Bosch, Tony Tolhurst and John Pilgrim. They established a residency at the 2Is Coffee Bar in New Compton Street, Soho, in 1956. A record contract with Parlophone Records ensued, and the group's second single, 'Don't You Rock Me Daddy-O', entered the UK Top 10 later that year. Their other chart successes were 'Cumberland Gap' and 'Streamline Train' (a version of

'Maggie May' was banned by the BBC), but the skiffle boom quickly faded, although the Vipers remained active until the end of the 50s. During that period several musicians passed through the group's ranks, including future Shadows Hank Marvin, Jet Harris and Tony Meehan. Hoping to concentrate on a career as a folk-singer, Whyton was then diverted into television entertainment when a one-off appearance on a Rolf Harris show led to a permanent spot. Eventually, he hosted his own children's series, *The Five O'Clock Show*, for Rediffusion. Here he introduced the hugely popular glove puppet Pussycat Willum, followed by other creations including Ollie Beak, Joe Crow and Spike McPike. Whyton recorded a series of successful children's albums, but also remained active on the folk scene. Recording for Argo and Phillips Records, he became a regular on BBC Radio, presenting *Folk Room, Strings 'n' Things* and *Junior Choice*. He was then approached to host *Country Meet Folk*, a series where the two complementary musical styles were to be combined. It ran for over six years after originally being devised as a six-week series. He was a natural choice as host when the BBC launched *The Country Club* show in the mid-70s. With his regular visits to Nashville and reports on the Silk Cut Country Music Festival at Wembley, Whyton effectively became 'the voice of country music' in Britain throughout the 70s and 80s. He was still presenting a show for the BBC World Service until a month before his death in January 1997.

WICKMAN, PUTTE

b. Hans-Olof Wickman, 10 September 1924, Borlänge, Sweden. He played clarinet from childhood, emerging in the years after World War II as a distinguished player in the swing era style of Benny Goodman. Soon, however, he began to adapt to the new sounds of bop, and was thus one of very few clarinettists to make the move. By the early 50s he was sufficiently well regarded to be on regular call to support visiting American jazz musicians and he also played with fellow-countryman Lars Gullin. In the 60s he moved into more commercial music, forming a dance band that became successful. In the 70s he returned to jazz, playing with increasing technical mastery as the years passed. His recordings of the 90s demonstrate a sometimes clinical accuracy, although Wickman never fails to swing.

● ALBUMS: *Young, Searching And Swinging* (Phontastic 1945-55)★★, *The Sound Of Surprise* (Dragon 1969)★★★, *Happy New Year!* (Odeon 1973)★★★, *Putte Wickman Quartet Live In Stockholm* (Out 1977)★★, *Mr Clarinet* (Four Leaf Clover 1985)★★★, *In Trombones* (Phontastic 1992)★★★, *In Silhouette* (Phontastic 1994)★★★.

WILDE, MARTY

b. Reginald Leonard Smith, 15 April 1936, London, England. After playing briefly in a skiffle group, this UK rock 'n' roll singer secured a residency at London's Condor Club under the name Reg Patterson. He was spotted by songwriter Lionel Bart, who subsequently informed entrepreneur Larry Parnes. The starmaker was keen to sign the singer and rapidly took over his career. Reg Smith henceforth became Marty Wilde. His Christian name was coined from the sentimental film *Marty*, while the surname was meant to emphasize the wilder side of Smith's nature. Parnes next arranged a recording contract with Philips Records, but Wilde's initial singles, including a reading of Jimmie Rodgers' 'Honeycomb,' failed to chart. Nevertheless, Wilde was promoted vigorously and appeared frequently on BBC Television's pop music programme *6.5 Special*. Extensive media coverage culminated with a hit recording of Jody Reynolds' alluringly morbid 'Endless Sleep' in 1957.

Soon afterwards, Parnes persuaded the influential producer Jack Good to make Wilde the resident star of his new television programme *Oh Boy!*. The arrangement worked well for Wilde until Good objected to his single 'Misery's Child' and vetoed the song. Worse followed when Good effectively replaced Wilde with a new singing star, Cliff Richard. Before long, Richard had taken Wilde's mantle as the UK's premier teen-idol and was enjoying consistent hits. Wilde, meanwhile, was gradually changing his image. After considerable success with such songs as 'Donna', 'Teenager In Love', 'Sea Of Love' and his own composition 'Bad Boy', he veered away from rock 'n' roll. His marriage to Joyce Baker of the Vernons Girls was considered a bad career move at the time, and partly contributed to Wilde's announcement that he would henceforth be specializing in classy, Frank Sinatra-style ballads. For several months he hosted a new pop show, *Boy Meets Girls*, and later starred in the West End production of *Bye Bye Birdie*. Although Parnes was intent on promoting Wilde as an actor, the star was resistant to such a move. His last major success was with a lacklustre version of Bobby Vee's 'Rubber Ball' in 1961.

Later in the decade he recorded for several labels, including a stint as the Wilde Three with his wife Joyce, and future Moody Blues vocalist Justin Hayward. Wilde enjoyed considerable radio play and was unfortunate not to enjoy a belated hit with the catchy 'Abergavenny' in 1969. He also found some success as the writer of hits such as Status Quo's 'Ice In The Sun'. By the 70s, Wilde was managing his son Ricky, who was briefly promoted as Britain's answer to Little Jimmy Osmond. Ricky later achieved success as a songwriter for his sister, Kim Wilde, who would go on to achieve far greater chart fame in the UK and USA than her father. In 1994, Marty Wilde appeared at London's Royal Albert Hall with Brenda Lee, Joe Brown, Eden Kane and John Leyton in the nostalgic *Solid Gold Rock 'N' Roll Show*. In the following year he presented *Coffee Bar Kids*, a BBC Radio 2 documentary programme that examined the origins of rock 'n' roll in Britain.

● ALBUMS: *Wilde About Marty* (Philips 1959)★★★, *Bad Boy* (Epic 1960)★★★, *Showcase* (Philips 1960)★★★, *The Versatile Mr. Wilde* (Philips 1960)★★★, *Diversions* (Philips 1969)★★, *Rock 'N' Roll* (Philips 1970)★★, *Good Rocking - Then And Now* (Philips 1974)★★★.
● COMPILATIONS: *Wild Cat Rocker* (Jan 1981)★★★, *The Hits Of Marty Wilde* (Philips 1984)★★★.

WILDER, ALEC

b. Alexander LaFayette Chew Wilder, 16 February 1907, Rochester, New York, USA, d. 23 December 1980, Gainesville, Florida, USA. A composer of popular ballads, illustrative works, jazz and classical pieces, Wilder attended Collegiate School, New York, and studied privately at the Eastman School of Music. He became an active composer in 1930 when his first popular song, 'All The King's Horses', was interpolated into the Arthur Schwartz and Howard Dietz revue *Three's A Crowd*. Thereafter, he is reputed to have

written several hundred popular songs, including 'Stop That Dancin' Up There', 'It's So Peaceful In The Country', 'J.P. Dooley III' (a jazz piece recorded by Harry James), 'Who Can I Turn To?', 'Soft As Spring', 'Moon And Sand', 'At The Swing Shift Ball', 'While We're Young', 'I'll Be Around', 'The Long Night', 'One More Road', 'All The Cats Join In' (featured by Benny Goodman And His Orchestra in the 1946 Walt Disney cartoon *Make Mine Music*), 'Kalamazoo To Timbuktu', 'Goodbye John', 'Crazy In The Heart', 'Winter Of My Discontent', 'You're Free', 'Is It Always Like This?', 'Summer Is A-Comin' In', and 'April Age'. Artists who have recorded from his popular catalogue include Frank Sinatra, Mabel Mercer, Bing Crosby, Mildred Bailey, Marlene Dietrich, Peggy Lee, Nat 'King' Cole, Jeri Southern, and Anita O'Day.

UK singer Elaine Delmar devoted a complete album, *Elaine Sings Wilder*, to him. Among his serious works were sonatas for flute, tuba and bassoon, a concerto for saxophone and chamber orchestra, quintets and trios for various musical instruments, piano works, four operas, the *Juke Box* ballet, and several unorthodox pieces, such as 'A Debutante's Diary', 'Sea Fugue Mama', 'She'll Be Seven In May', 'Neurotic Goldfish', 'Dance Man Buys A Farm', 'Concerning Etchings', 'Walking Home In The Spring', 'Amorous Poltergeist' and 'The Children Met The Train'. For over 50 years of his life he lived in the Algonquin Hotel, Manhattan, and the Sheraton in Rochester, New York City. His memoir of the period he spent at the Algonquin was unpublished at the time of his death from lung cancer in 1980. Two of his books that did emerge are *Letter I Never Mailed* (1975), a collection of imaginary letters to real people, and *American Popular Song: The Great Innovators 1900-1950* (with James T. Maher) (1972). He hosted a weekly series based on the latter book for the National Public Radio.

● ALBUMS: *Alec Wilder And His Octet* 10-inch album (Mercury 1949)★★★, *Alec Wilder Octet* 10-inch album (Columbia 1951)★★★, *The Music Of Alec Wilder Conducted By Alec Wilder* (Columbia 1974)★★★.
● FURTHER READING: *Alec Wilder And His Friends*, Whitney Balliett.

WILKINS, JOE WILLIE

b. 7 January 1923, Davenport, Mississippi, USA, d. 28 March 1979, Memphis, Tennessee, USA. His reputation as a guitarist higher among his fellow musicians than it is even with those who possessed examples of his work, Wilkins has apologists who maintain that his influence reached further and deeper than is currently recognized. His father Frank bought Joe a guitar when he was 12; he was already proficient on the harmonica. He learned more from Bob Williams, Pat Rhodes and Sam Harris, members of a string band that included his father. Soon he took to the road, working in cottonfields and playing on street corners, earning the name 'Joe Willie The Walking Seeburg'. He encountered Sonny Boy Williamson (Rice Miller) and Robert Lockwood during his travels, trading ideas with the latter. He linked up with them in 1942 in Helena, Arkansas, broadcasting on station KFFA. He was one of the King Biscuit Boys with Williamson, and promoted *Mother's Best* flour alongside Lockwood. He also met and worked with Robert Nighthawk and B.B. King in west Memphis. In Jackson, Mississippi, in 1951, he played on sessions for Williamson and Willie Love, and in Memphis in 1953 was on Albert Williams' session for Sun. He continued to work with Williamson until the latter's death in 1965. During the 70s, despite being hampered by illness, he worked the Memphis area with his own King Biscuit Boys and recorded a single and album.

● ALBUMS: *Goin' In Your Direction* (1991)★★★.

WILLIAMS, ANDY

b. Howard Andrew Williams, 3 December 1928, Wall Lake, Iowa, USA. Williams began his singing career in the local church choir with his three brothers. The quartet became popular on their own radio shows from Cincinnati, Des Moines and Chicago. They backed Bing Crosby on his Oscar-winning 'Swinging On A Star', from the 1944 movie *Going My Way*, and in the same year appeared in the minor musical film *Kansas City Kitty*. In the following year, Andy Williams dubbed Lauren Bacall's singing voice in her first film with Humphrey Bogart, *To Have And Have Not*. From 1947-48 the Williams Brothers worked with top pianist/singer Kay Thompson in nightclubs and on television. Williams went solo in 1952, and featured regularly on Steve Allen's *Tonight Show* for over two years. Signed to the Cadence label, Williams had his first success in 1956 with 'Canadian Sunset', which was followed by a string of Top 20 entries, including 'Butterfly' (number 1), 'I Like Your Kind Of Love' (a duet with Peggy Powers), 'Lips Of Wine', 'Are You Sincere?', 'Promise Me, Love', 'The Hawaiian Wedding Song', 'Lonely Street' and 'The Village Of St. Bernadette'. In 1961, Williams moved to Columbia Records, and had his first big hit for the label with the Doc Pomus/Mort Shuman composition, 'Can't Get Used To Losing You', which went to number 2 in the US charts in 1963. From then, until 1971 when the singles hits dried up, he was in the US Top 20 with 'Hopeless', 'A Fool Never Learns', and '(Where Do I Begin) Love Story'. Williams reached number 4 in the UK in 1973 with Neil Sedaka's 'Solitaire', but it was in the album charts that he found greater success.

By the early 70s it was estimated that he had received 13 worldwide gold disc awards for chart albums such as *Moon River & Other Great Movie Themes*, *Days Of Wine And Roses* (a US number 1), *The Wonderful World Of Andy Williams*, *Dear Heart*, *Born Free*, *Love Andy* (a UK number 1), *Honey*, *Happy Heart*, *Home Loving Man* (another UK number 1) and *Love Story*. The enormous sales were no doubt assisted by his extremely successful weekly variety showcase that ran from 1962-71, and won an Emmy for 'Best Variety Show'. It also gave the Osmond Brothers nationwide exposure. In 1964, Williams made his film debut in *I'd Rather Be Rich*, which starred Maurice Chevalier, Robert Goulet, Sandra Dee and Hermione Gingold. It was a remake of the 1941 comedy *It Started With Eve*, and Williams sang the Jerry Keller/Gloria Shayne number, 'Almost There', which just failed to reach the top of the UK chart in 1965. Despite the lack of consistent television exposure in the late 70s, Williams still sold a remarkable number of albums, particularly in the UK where his *Solitaire*, *The Way We Were*, and *Reflections*, all made the Top 10. In 1984, the album *Greatest Love Classics* featured Williams singing contemporary lyrics to classical themes, accompanied by the Royal Philharmonic Orchestra. In the early 90s, Williams became the first non-country entertainer to build his own theatre along Highway 76's music-theatre-strip in Branson, Missouri. The $8 million

2,000-seater Andy Williams Moon River Theatre is part of a complex that includes a 250-room hotel and restaurant. Williams headlines there himself, and remains one of America's most popular singers, renowned for his smooth vocal texture and relaxed approach. As a stylist, he is the equal of any popular singer from his era.

● ALBUMS: *Andy Williams Sings Steve Allen* (Cadence 1957)★★, *Andy Williams* (Cadence 1958)★★, *Andy Williams Sings Rogers And Hammerstein* (Cadence 1959)★★★, *Lonely Street* (Cadence 1959)★★★, *The Village Of St. Bernadette* (Cadence 1960)★★, *Two Time Winners* (Cadence 1960)★★★, *To You Sweetheart, Aloha* reissued as *Hawaiian Wedding Song* (Cadence 1960)★★, *Under Paris Skies* (Cadence 1961)★★★, *'Danny Boy' And Other Songs I Like To Sing* (Columbia 1962)★★★, *Moon River & Other Great Movie Themes* (Columbia 1962)★★★★, *Warm And Willing* (Columbia 1962)★★★, *Million Seller Songs* (Cadence 1963)★★★, *Days Of Wine And Roses* (Columbia 1963)★★★★, *The Andy Williams Christmas Album* (Columbia 1963)★★★, *The Wonderful World Of Andy Williams* (Columbia 1964)★★★, *The Academy Award Winning 'Call Me Irresponsible'* (Columbia 1964)★★★, *The Great Songs From 'My Fair Lady' And Other Broadway Hits* (Columbia 1964)★★★★, *Dear Heart* (Columbia 1965)★★★★, *Almost There* (Columbia 1965)★★★★, *Can't Get Used To Losing You* (Columbia 1965)★★★★, *Merry Christmas* (Columbia 1965)★★★, *The Shadow Of Your Smile* (Columbia 1966)★★★, *May Each Day* (Columbia 1966)★★★, *In The Arms Of Love* (Columbia 1967)★★★, *Born Free* (Columbia 1967)★★★★, *Love, Andy* (Columbia 1967)★★★★, *Honey* (Columbia 1968)★★★★, *Happy Heart* (Columbia 1969)★★★★, with the Osmonds *Get Together With Andy Williams* (Columbia 1969)★★, *Can't Help Falling In Love* (Columbia 1970)★★★★, *Raindrops Keep Falling On My Head* (Columbia 1970)★★★, *The Andy Williams' Show* (Columbia 1970)★★★, *Home Loving Man* (Columbia 1971)★★★★, *Love Story* (Columbia 1971)★★★, *You've Got A Friend* (Columbia 1971)★★★, *The Impossible Dream* (Columbia 1972)★★★★, *Love Theme From 'The Godfather'* (Columbia 1972)★★★, *A Song For You* (Columbia 1972)★★★, *Alone Again (Naturally)* (Columbia 1972)★★★, *The First Time Ever I Saw Your Face* (Columbia 1973)★★★, *Solitaire* (Columbia 1973)★★★, *The Way We Were* (Columbia 1974)★★★, *You Lay So Easy On My Mind* (Columbia 1974)★★★, *An Evening With Andy Williams, Live In Japan* (Columbia 1975)★★★, *The Other Side Of Me* (Columbia 1975)★★★, *Showstoppers* (Embassy 1977)★★★, *Let's Love While We Can* (Columbia 1980)★★★, *Wedding And Anniversary Album* (Columbia 1981)★★★, with the Royal Philharmonic Orchestra *Greatest Love Classics* (EMI 1984)★★★, *Close Enough For Love* (Warners 1986)★★★.

● COMPILATIONS: *Andy Williams' Best* reissued as *Canadian Sunset* (Cadence 1962)★★★, *Andy Williams' Newest Hits* (Columbia 1966)★★★, *The Andy Williams Sound Of Music* (Columbia 1969)★★★, *Andy Williams' Greatest Hits* (Columbia 1970)★★★, *Andy Williams' Greatest Hits, Volume Two* (Columbia 1973)★★★, *Reflections* (Columbia 1978)★★★, *Great Songs Of The Seventies* (Columbia 1979)★★★, *Great Songs Of The Sixties* (Columbia 1980)★★★, *Collection* (Pickwick 1980)★★★, *The Very Best Of Andy Williams* (Hallmark 1984)★★★, *Andy Williams Collection* (Castle 1987)★★★, *Portrait Of A Song Stylist*

(Masterpiece 1989)★★★, *16 Most Requested Songs* (1993)★★★, *The Best Of Andy Williams* (Columbia 1996)★★★.

WILLIAMS, BIG JOE

b. Joe Lee Williams, 16 October 1903, Crawford, Mississippi, USA, d. 17 December 1982, Macon, Mississippi, USA. Big Joe Williams was one of the most important blues singers to have recorded and also one whose life conforms almost exactly to the stereotyped pattern of how a 'country' blues singer should live. He was of partial Red Indian stock, his father being 'Red Bone' Williams, a part-Cherokee. 'Big Joe' took his musical influences from his mother's family, the Logans. He made the obligatory 'cigar box' instruments as a child and took to the road when his stepfather threw him out around 1918. He later immortalized this antagonist in a song that he was still performing at the end of his long career. Williams' life was one of constant movement as he worked his way around the lumber camps, turpentine farms and juke-joints of the south. Around 1930 he married and settled in St. Louis, Missouri, but still took long sweeps through the country as the rambling habit never left him. This rural audience supported him through the worst of the Depression when he appeared under the name 'Poor Joe'. His known recordings began in 1935 when he recorded six tracks for Bluebird in Chicago. From then on he recorded at every opportunity. He stayed with Bluebird until 1945 before moving to Columbia Records. He formed a loose partnership on many sessions with John Lee 'Sonny Boy' Williamson that has been likened to that of Muddy Waters and Little Walter. In 1952, he worked for Trumpet in Jackson, Mississippi, then went back to Chicago for a session with Vee Jay. Other recordings made for smaller companies are still being discovered. During 1951-52, he also made recordings of other singers at his St. Louis base. Williams found a wider audience when blues came into vogue with young whites in the 60s. He continued to record and tour, adding Europe and Japan to his itinerary. He still used cheap, expendable guitars fixed up by himself with an electrical pick-up and usually festooned with extra machine heads to accommodate nine strings. With his gruff, shouting voice and ringing guitar - not to mention his sometimes uncertain temper - he became a great favourite on the club and concert circuit. He had come full circle and was living in a caravan in Crawford, Mississippi, when he died. The sheer volume of easily accessible albums recorded during his last years tended to obscure just how big a blues talent Williams really was.

● ALBUMS: *Piney Woods Blues* (1958)★★★, *Tough Times* (Fontana 1960)★★★, *Mississippi's Big Joe Williams And His Nine-String Guitar* (Folkways 1962)★★★, *Blues On Highway 49* (Delmark 1962)★★★, *Blues For 9 Strings* (Bluesville 1962)★★★, *Big Joe Williams At Folk City* (Bluesville 1963)★★★, *Studio Blues* (Bluesville 1964)★★★, *Starvin' Chain Blues* (Delmark 1966)★★★, *Classic Delta Blues* (Milestone 1966)★★★, *Back To The Country* (Bounty 1966)★★★, *Hellbound And Heaven Sent* (Folkways 1967)★★★, *Don't You Leave Me Here* (Storyville 1969)★★★, *Big Joe Williams* (Xtra 1969)★★★, *Hand Me Down My Old Walking Stick* (Liberty 1969)★★★, *Crawlin' King Snake* (RCA 1970)★★★, *Legacy Of The Blues, Volume 6* (Sonet 1972)★★★, *Guitar Blues* (Storyville 1973)★★★, *Malvina My*

Sweet Woman (Old Blues 1974)★★★, *Ramblin' Wanderin' Blues* (Storyville 1974)★★★, *Tough Times* (Arhoolie 1981)★★★, *Thinking Of What They Did* (Arhoolie 1981)★★★, *Big Joe Williams 1974* (Arhoolie 1982)★★★.

● COMPILATIONS: *Field Recordings 1973-80* (L&R 1988)★★★, *Complete Recorded Works In Chronological Order Volumes 1 & 2* (Blues Document 1991)★★★, with Luther Huff, Willie Love *Delta Blues - 1951* (1991)★★★, *The Final Years* (Verve 1995)★★★.

WILLIAMS, GENE

b. USA. Gene Williams first entered the entertainment industry as vocalist with the Claude Thornhill Orchestra, before forming his own dance band in 1950 in New York City, New York, USA. The musical sidemen enrolled included Harry Wegbreit, Jack Mootz, Don Josephs, Harry Di Vito, Dick Hoch, Sam Marowitz, Charlie O'Cain, Mickey Folus, Joe Reisman, Teddy Napoleon, Russ Saunders and Mel Zelnick. While Gene Williams himself and Adele Castle were the featured vocalists, Gil Evans, Hubie Wheeler, Chico O'Farrill and Joe Reisman served as the band's arrangers. Their initial contracts came from college dates, before the membership elected to put the group on a more permanent footing. Mixing bebop instrumentals with the smooth style inherited from Williams' time with Claude Thornhill, by 1952 they had secured engagements at such venues as the Glen Island Casino. Thereafter, however, they struggled to make any headway, hamstrung by the reduced air time available to dance bands with the advent of rock 'n' roll.

WILLIAMS, HANK

b. Hiram (misspelt on birth certificate as Hiriam) Williams, 17 September 1923, Georgiana, Alabama, USA, d. 1 January 1953, Virginia, USA. Misspelling notwithstanding, Williams disliked the name and took to calling himself Hank. He was born with a spine defect that troubled him throughout his life, and which was further aggravated after being thrown from a horse when he was 17 years old. Initially, his parents, Lon and Lilly, ran a general store, but Lon later entered a veterans' hospital following a delayed reaction to the horrors he had experienced during World War I. The young Williams was raised by his imposing, resourceful mother, who gave him a cheap guitar when he was seven. He learned chords from an elderly black musician, Teetot (Rufe Payne). Williams later said, 'All the musical training I ever had came from him.' It also explains the strong blues thread that runs through his work. In 1937, Lilly opened a boarding house in Montgomery, Alabama. Williams won a talent contest and formed his own band, the Drifting Cowboys. As clubs were tough, Hank hired a wrestler, Cannonball Nichols, as a bass player, more for protection than musical ability, but he could not be protected from his mother, who handled his bookings and earnings (in truth, Williams was not particularly interested in the money he made). While working for a medicine show, he met Audrey Sheppard and married her in December 1944. Although rivals, both his wife and his mother would thump the pale, lanky singer for his lack of co-operation. Williams was a local celebrity, but on 14 September 1946, he and Audrey went to Nashville, impressing Fred Rose and his son Wesley at the relatively new Acuff-Rose publishers. On 11 December 1946 Williams made his first recordings for the small Sterling label. They included 'Callin' You' and 'When God Comes And Gathers His Jewels'. Fred Rose secured a contract with the more prestigious MGM Records, and he acted as his manager, record producer and, occasionally, co-writer ('Mansion On The Hill', 'Kaw-liga'). Williams' first MGM release, 'Move It On Over', sold several thousand copies. He then joined the prestigious radio show *Louisiana Hayride* in 1948 and was featured on its concert tours. Fred Rose opposed him reviving 'Lovesick Blues', originally recorded by Emmett Miller in 1925, and later a success for Rex Griffin in 1939; nevertheless, he recorded the song, following Miller's and Griffin's playful yodels. 'Lovesick Blues' topped the US country charts for 16 weeks and remained in the listings for almost a year. The *Grand Ole Opry*, although wary of his hard-drinking reputation, invited him to perform 'Lovesick Blues', which led to an unprecedented six encores. He and the Drifting Cowboys became regulars and the publicity enabled them to command $1,000 for concert appearances; they even upstaged comedian and film star Bob Hope. 'Wedding Bells' made number 2, as did a contender for the greatest country single ever released, the poignant 'I'm So Lonesome I Could Cry', backed with the old blues song, 'My Bucket's Got A Hole In It'; the *Opry* sponsors, disapproving of the word 'beer' in the latter song, made Williams sing 'milk' instead. In 1950, he had three country number 1 hits, 'Long Gone Lonesome Blues', 'Why Don't You Love Me?' and 'Moanin' The Blues'. The following year, he had two further chart-toppers with 'Cold, Cold Heart' and 'Hey, Good Lookin'. Another superb double-sided hit, 'Howlin' At The Moon'/'I Can't Help It (If I'm Still In Love With You)', made number 2.

In 1952, Williams went to number 1 with his praise of Cajun food in 'Jambalaya', while 'Half As Much' made number 2. Another well-balanced double-sided hit, 'Settin' The Woods On Fire'/'You Win Again', made number 2. Williams was a showman, often wearing a flashy suit embroidered with sequins and decorated with musical notes. Although MGM studios considered making films with him, nothing materialized. It is arguable that, with his thinning hair, he looked too old, or it may have been that he was just too awkward. His lifestyle was akin to the later spirit of rock 'n' roll; he drank too much, took drugs (admittedly, excessive numbers of painkillers for his back), played with guns, destroyed hotel rooms, threw money out of windows and permanently lived in conflict. His son, Hank Williams Jnr., said, 'I get sick of hearing people tell me how much they loved my daddy. They hated him in Nashville.' Williams' songs articulated the lives and loves of his listeners and he went a stage further by recording melodramatic monologues as Luke The Drifter. They included 'Beyond The Sunset', 'Pictures From Life's Other Side', 'Too Many Parties And Too Many Pals' and 'Men With Broken Hearts'. Although Luke the Drifter's appeal was limited, Fred Rose saw how Williams' other songs could have wide appeal. Country songs had been recorded by pop performers before Williams, but Rose aggressively sought cover versions. Soon Tony Bennett ('Cold, Cold Heart'), Jo Stafford ('Jambalaya') and Joni James ('Your Cheatin' Heart') had gold records. Williams' wife, 'Miss Audrey', also made solo records, but Williams knew her talent was limited. She was frustrated by her own lack of success and many of Williams' songs stemmed from their quarrels. They were divorced on 29 May 1952 and, as Williams regarded possessions as unim-

portant, she was awarded their house and one half of all his future royalties. He did, however, have the sadness of losing custody of his son.

Like any professional show, the *Opry* preferred sober non-descripts to drunk superstars, and on 11 August 1952, Williams was fired and told that he could return when he was sober. However, Williams did not admit to his problem, joking about missing shows and falling off stage. He lost Fred Rose's support, the Drifting Cowboys turned to Ray Price, and, although the *Louisiana Hayride* tolerated his wayward lifestyle, his earnings fell and he was reduced to playing small clubs with pick-up bands. When Williams met the 19-year-old daughter of a policeman, Billie Jean Jones, he said, 'If you ain't married, ol' Hank's gonna marry you.' On 19 October 1952 he did just that - three times. First, before a Justice of the Peace in Minden, Louisiana, and then at two concerts at the New Orleans Municipal Auditorium before several thousand paying guests. The newlyweds spent Christmas with relations in Georgiana, Alabama. His biggest booking for some time was on New Year's Day 1953 with Hawkshaw Hawkins and Homer And Jethro in Canton, Ohio, but because of a blizzard, Williams' plane was cancelled. An 18-year-old taxi driver, Charles Carr, was hired to drive Williams' Cadillac. They set off, Williams having a bottle of whiskey for company. He sank into a deep sleep. A policeman who stopped the car for ignoring speed restrictions remarked, 'That guy looks dead'. Five hours later, Carr discovered that his passenger was indeed dead. Death was officially due to 'severe heart attack with haemorrhage', but alcohol and pills played their part. At the concert that night, the performers sang Williams' 'I Saw The Light' in tribute. An atmospheric stage play, *Hank Williams: The Show He Never Gave*, by Maynard Collins, filmed with Sneezy Waters in the title role, showed what might have happened had Williams arrived that night. Some commentators took Williams' then-current number 1, 'I'll Never Get Out Of This World Alive', as an indication that he knew he had little time left. Chet Atkins, who played 'dead string rhythm' on the record, disagreed: 'All young men of 28 or 29 feel immortal and although he wrote a lot about death, he thought it was something that would happen when he got old.' 20,000 saw Williams' body as it lay in state in an embroidered Nudie suit (designed by Miss Audrey) at the Montgomery Municipal Auditorium. His shrine in Montgomery Oakwood Cemetery is the subject of Steve Young's song, 'Montgomery In The Rain'.

1953 was a remarkable year for his records. 'Kaw-Liga', inspired by a visit to South Alabama and backed by 'Your Cheatin' Heart', went to the top of the chart, and his third consecutive posthumous number 1 was with Hy Heath and Fred Rose's 'Take These Chains From My Heart'. MGM, desperate for fresh material, overdubbed a backing onto demos for 'Weary Blues From Waitin'' and 'Roly Poly' - Hank Williams was the first deceased star to have his recordings altered. Albums of Hank Williams with strings and duets with his son followed. In 1969, Hank Jnr. completed some of his father's scribblings for an album, 'Songs My Father Left Me', the most successful being 'Cajun Baby'. In recent years, Williams and Willie Nelson proved a popular duo with 'I Told A Lie To My Heart', while a battered demo of 'There's A Tear In My Beer', which had been given by Williams to Big Bill Lister to perform, was magically restored with the addition of Hank Williams Jnr.'s voice and, accompanied by an even more ingenious video, sold 250,000 copies.

Hank Williams recorded around 170 different songs between 1946 and 1952, and there are over 230 and around 130 'Tribute to Hank Williams' albums that have also been recorded, not only by country artists, but by artists including Spike Jones, Del Shannon and Hardrock Gunter. The first was 'The Death Of Hank Williams' by disc jockey Jack Cardwell. Other contemporary ones included 'Hank, It Will Never Be The Same Without You' by Ernest Tubb, 'Hank Williams Will Live Forever' by Johnnie And Jack, 'The Life Of Hank Williams' by Hawkshaw Hawkins and 'Hank Williams Meets Jimmie Rodgers' by Virginia Rounders. Most tributes lack inspiration, are too morbid and too reverent, and are recorded by artists who would usually never enter a recording studio. The most pertinent tributes are Moe Bandy's reflective 'Hank Williams, You Wrote My Life', Johnny Cash's jaunty 'The Night Hank Williams Came To Town', Tim Hardin's plaintive 'Tribute To Hank Williams', Kris Kristofferson's rousing 'If You Don't Like Hank Williams' and Emmylou Harris's isolated 'Rollin' And Ramblin''. Hank Williams *is* the Phantom of the *Opry*; his influence on Moe Bandy, George Jones, Vernon Oxford and Boxcar Willie is especially marked. They have all recorded albums of his songs, as have Roy Acuff, Glen Campbell, Floyd Cramer, Don Gibson, Ronnie Hawkins, Roy Orbison, Charley Pride, Jack Scott, Del Shannon and Ernest Tubb. Johnny Cash, Jerry Lee Lewis, Little Richard, Elvis Presley, Linda Ronstadt and Richard Thompson have also appropriated his repertoire. Major UK chart hits include 'Lovesick Blues' by Frank Ifield, 'Take These Chains From My Heart' by Ray Charles, and 'Jambalaya' by the Carpenters. Before Williams was laid to rest, Lilly, Audrey and Billie Jean were squabbling for the rights to Williams' estate. Audrey's name is on his tombstone, and the inaccurate 1964 biopic *Your Cheatin' Heart*, which starred George Hamilton as Hank Williams, miming to Hank Williams Jnr.'s recordings, did not even mention Billie Jean. Both wives performed as Mrs. Hank Williams, and Billie Jean was widowed a second time when Johnny Horton died in 1960. A more recent development has been the claims of Jett Williams, the illegitimate daughter of Williams and country singer Bobbie Jett, who was born three days after his death. The pressures Williams suffered in his life appear to have sharpened his awareness and heightened his creative powers. His compact, aching songs flow seamlessly and few have improved upon his own emotional performances. His plaque in the Country Music Hall Of Fame states: 'The simple beautiful melodies and straightforward plaintive stories in his lyrics of life as he knew it will never die.'

● ALBUMS: *Hank Williams Sings* 10-inch album (MGM 1951)★★★★, *Moanin' The Blues* (MGM 1952/56)★★★★, *Hank Williams Memorial Album* (MGM 1953/55)★★★★, *Hank Williams as Luke The Drifter* overdubbed as *Beyond The Sunset* MGM 1963 (MGM 1953/55)★★★, *Honky Tonkin'* (MGM 1954/57)★★★, *I Saw The Light* (MGM 1954/56)★★★, *Ramblin' Man* (MGM 1954/55)★★★, *Sing Me A Blue Song* (MGM 1957)★★★, *The Immortal Hank Williams* overdubbed as *First Last And Always* MGM 1969 (MGM 1958)★★★, *The Unforgettable Hank Williams* overdubbed MGM 1968 (MGM 1959)★★★, *Lonesome Sound Of Hank Williams* (MGM 1960)★★★, *Wait For The Light To Shine* overdubbed MGM 1968 (MGM 1960)★★★, *Let Me Sing A Blue Song* overdubbed 1968 (MGM 1961)★★★, *Wanderin' Around* overdubbed 1968 (MGM 1961)★★★, *I'm Blue Inside* overdubbed MGM 1968 (MGM 1961)★★★, *The Spirit Of Hank Williams* overdubbed MGM 1969 (MGM 1961)★★★, *On Stage-Live Volume 1* (MGM 1962)★★★, *On Stage Volume II* (MGM 1963)★★★, *Lost Highways & Other Folk Ballads* (MGM 1964)★★★, *Father And Son* overdubbed (MGM 1965)★★★, *Kawliga And Other Humerous Songs* some overdubbed (MGM 1965)★★★, *Hank Williams With Strings* overdubbed (MGM 1966)★★★, *Hank Williams, Hank Williams Jr. Again* (MGM 1966)★★★, *Movin' On - Luke The Drifter* overdubbed (MGM 1966)★★★, *Mr & Mrs Hank Williams (With Audrey)* (Metro 1966)★★★, *More Hank Williams And Strings* (MGM 1967)★★★, *I Won't Be Home No More* overdubbed (MGM 1967)★★★, *Hank Williams And Strings, Volume III* (MGM 1968)★★★, *In The Beginning* (MGM 1968)★★★, *Life To Legend Hank Williams* (MGM 1970)★★★, *The Last Picture Show Film Soundtrack* (MGM 1971)★★★, *Hank Williams/Hank Williams Jr. Legend In Story And Song* (MGM 1973)★★★, *Hank Williams/Hank Williams Jr. Insights In Story And Song* (MGM 1974)★★★, *A Home In Heaven* (MGM 1975)★★★, *Live At The Grand Ole Opry* (MGM 1976)★★★★, *Hank Williams And The Drifting Cowboys On Radio* (Golden Country 1982)★★★★, *Early Country Live Volume 1 (Hank Williams On Radio Shows Plus Others)* (ACM 1983)★★★★, *Rare Takes And Radio Cuts* (Polydor 1984)★★★, *Early Country Live Volume 2 (Hank Williams On Radio Shows)* (ACM 1984)★★★★, *Early Country Music Live Volume 3 (Hank Williams On Radio Shows* (ACM 1985)★★★★, *Just Me And My Guitar* (CMF 1985)★★★, *Hank Williams - The First Recordings* (CMF 1985)★★★★, *Hank Williams - On The Air* (Polydor 1985)★★★, *Hank Williams: I Ain't Got Nothin' But Time December 1946-August 1947* (Polydor 1985)★★★★, *Hank Williams: Lovesick Blues - August 1947-December 1948* (Polydor 1985)★★★★, *Hank Williams: Lost Highway - December 1948-March 1949* (Polydor 1986)★★★, *Hank Williams: I'm So Lonesome I Could Cry - March 1949-August 1949* (Polydor 1986)★★★★, *Hank Williams: Long Gone Lonesome Blues - August 1949-December 1950* (Polydor 1987)★★★★, *Hank Williams: Hey, Good Lookin' - December 1950-July 1951* (Polydor 1987)★★★★, *Hank Williams: Let's Turn Back The Years, July 1951-June 1952* (Polydor 1987)★★★★, *Hank Williams: I Won't Be Home No More, June 1952-September 1952* (Polydor 1987)★★★★, *There's Nothing As Sweet As My Baby* (Mount Olive 1988)★★★, *Hank Williams - Jambalaya* (Creative Sounds 1992)★★★, *Health And Happiness Shows* (Mercury 1993)★★★, *Alone And Forsaken* (Mercury 1995)★★★, *Three Hanks, Men With Broken Hearts* (Curb 1996)★★★.

● COMPILATIONS: *Greatest Hits* (Polydor 1963)★★★, *The Very Best Of Hank Williams* (Polydor 1963)★★★, *24 Of Hank Williams' Greatest Hits* (MGM 1970)★★★★, *24 Greatest Hits, Volume 2* (Polydor 1976)★★, *40 Greatest Hits* (Polydor 1978)★★★★, *The Collectors' Edition* 8-LP box set of Polydor albums listed above (Polydor 1987)★★★★★, *Rare Demos: First To Last* (CMF 1990)★★★, *The Original Singles Collection Plus* 3-CD box set (Polydor 1990)★★★★★, *Low Down Blues* (Polygram 1996)★★★.

● VIDEOS: *The Hank Williams Story* (1994).

● FURTHER READING: *Sing A Sad Song: The Life Of Hank*

Williams, Roger M. Williams. *Hank Williams: From Life To Legend*, Jerry Rivers. *I Saw The Light: The Gospel Life Of Hank Williams*, Al Bock. *Hank Williams: Country Music's Tragic King*, Jay Caress. *The First Outlaw: Hank Williams*, Jim Arp. *Your Cheating Heart, A Biography Of Hank Williams*, Chet Flippo. *Hank Williams: A Bio-Bibliography*, George William Koon. *Still In Love With You: The Story Of Hank And Audrey Williams*, Lycrecia Williams and Dale Vinicur. *Ain't Nothin' As Sweet As My Baby: The Story Of Hank Williams' Lost Daughter*, Jett Williams. *Hank Williams: The Complete Lyrics*, Don Cusic. *The Life And Times Of Hank Williams*, Arnold Rogers and Bruce Gidoll. *Hank Williams: The Biography*, Colin Escott.

HANK WILLIAMS SINGS - HANK WILLIAMS ★★★★

Like one Hank Williams album and you will like all of them, and in 1951, this 10-inch album was the very first. All Williams' trademarks feature in these eight songs: devotion to one's mother, loveless marriages (his own is reflected in 'A House Without Love'), the deep religious convictions of the southern states and the problems of living up to those beliefs. Numerous interpretations have turned 'I Saw The Light' into a standard and far too many musicians have followed Williams down that 'Lost Highway'.
● TRACKS: *A House Without Love; Wedding Bells; The Mansion On The Hill; Wealth Won't Save Your Soul; I Saw The Light; Six More Miles To The Graveyard; Lost Highway; I've Just Told Mama Goodbye*.

WILLIAMS, LARRY

b. 10 May 1935, New Orleans, Louisiana, USA, d. 2 January 1980, Los Angeles, California, USA. Williams recorded a handful of raucous rock 'n' roll songs for Specialty Records that later influenced, among others, John Lennon. Williams learned to play the piano while in New Orleans, and moved to Oakland, California, with his family while in his teens. There he joined a group called the Lemon Drops. In 1954, while visiting his old home-town of New Orleans, he met and was hired as a pianist by Lloyd Price, who recorded for Specialty. Price introduced Williams to producer Robert 'Bumps' Blackwell. At that time Specialty head Art Rupe signed Williams. His first record was a cover version of Price's 'Just Because', which reached number 11 on the R&B chart for Williams and number 3 for Price. Backed by fellow Specialty artist Little Richard's band, Williams recorded his own 'Short Fat Fannie', which reached number 1 in the R&B chart and number 5 in the pop chart during 1957. To follow up his song about a fat girl, Williams next recorded one about a skinny girl, 'Bony Moronie', which was almost as big a hit. Williams had one final chart single for Specialty the following year, 'Dizzy, Miss Lizzy', which reached number 69 (it was later covered by the Beatles, with Lennon singing - they also covered 'Slow Down' and 'Bad Boy', while Lennon later recorded 'Bony Moronie' and 'Just Because', providing Williams with a steady royalties income until his death). A number of singles and an album were issued by Specialty up to 1959, none of which were hits. In that year, he was arrested for selling drugs and sent to jail, causing Specialty to drop him and his career to fade. He recorded later for Chess Records, Mercury Records and for Island Records and Decca Records in the mid-60s, by which time he was

working with Johnny 'Guitar' Watson. In 1966 Williams became a producer for OKeh Records and recorded an album with Watson for that label. He was virtually inactive between 1967 and 1979, at which point he recorded a funk album for Fantasy Records. In January 1980, Williams was found in his Los Angeles home with a gunshot wound in the head, judged to be self-inflicted, although it was rumoured that Williams was murdered owing to his involvement with drugs and, reportedly, prostitution.
● ALBUMS: *Here's Larry Williams* (Specialty 1959)★★★★, *Larry Williams* (Chess 1961)★★★, *Live* (1965)★★★, *The Larry Williams Show* (1965)★★★, with Johnny 'Guitar' Watson *Two For The Price Of One* (OKeh 1967)★★★★, *That Larry Williams* (Fantasy 1979)★★.
● COMPILATIONS: *Greatest Hits* (OKeh 1967)★★★★, *Dizzy Miss Lizzy* (Ace 1985)★★★, *Unreleased Larry Williams* (Specialty 1986)★★★, *Hocus Pocus* (Specialty 1986)★★★, *Alacazam* (Ace 1987)★★★, *Slow Down* (Specialty 1987)★★★, *The Best Of Larry Williams* (Ace 1988)★★★★, *Bad Boy* (Specialty 1989)★★★★, *Fabulous Larry Williams* (Ace 1991)★★★.

WILLIAMS, OTIS, AND THE CHARMS

This US R&B vocal group came from Cincinnati, Ohio, and was formed in 1953. Like the Jacks/Cadets for Modern records in Los Angeles, the Charms for King served as the 'house group' who were available to cover the latest hits. Similarly, the group had some of their hits covered, such as 'Hearts Of Stone' by the Fontane Sisters, 'Two Hearts' by Pat Boone and 'Ivory Tower' by Cathy Carr. They first recorded for the Miami-based Rockin' label in 1953, but later in the year, the Cincinnati-based King purchased Rockin' and also the Charms' contract. Their membership at the time of the Charms' joining King was Otis Williams (b. 2 June 1936, Cincinnati, Ohio, USA; lead), Rolland Bradley (tenor), Donald Peak (tenor), Joe Penn (tenor/baritone) and Richard Parker (bass). The group had a zestful approach that made them a rock 'n' roll act, and they first had success with a Jewels cover version, 'Hearts Of Stone' (US R&B number 1 and pop number 15 in 1954), a Five Keys cover version 'Ling Ting Tong' (US R&B number 5 and pop number 26 in 1955), and an original, 'Two Hearts' (US R&B number 8 in 1955). Williams lost the Charms in 1955, but carried on with a new group, appropriately called 'New Group', which included besides Williams, Rollie Willis (tenor), Larry Graves (baritone) and Chuck Barksdale (bass, later to join the Dells). This group took the name 'Charms' in 1956, and soon replaced Graves and Barksdale with Matt Williams and Winfred Gregory, respectively, and added Lonnie Carter (tenor). This group hit with two more cover versions - 'Ivory Tower' (US R&B number 5 and pop number 11 in 1956) and 'United' (US R&B number 5 in 1957), the group's last hit. After the Charms broke up in the early 60s, Otis Williams went on to pursue a solo career in C&W music and even recorded a surprisingly good album in that genre.
● ALBUMS: *Their All Time Hits* (Deluxe 1957)★★★, *This Is Otis Williams And The Charms* (King 1959)★★★, as Otis Williams And The Midnight Cowboys *Otis Williams And the Midnight Cowboys* (Stop 1971)★★★.
● COMPILATIONS: *Otis Williams And His Charms Sing Their All-Time Hits* (King/Gusto 1978)★★★, *16 Original Greatest Hits* (King 1988)★★★.

WILLIAMSON, SONNY BOY 'RICE MILLER'

b. Aleck/Alex Ford, 5 December 1899, Glendora, Mississippi, USA. d. 25 May 1965, Helena, Arkansas, USA. Being a man who would never compromise a good story by affording undue attention to veracity, and mischievous to boot, Sonny Boy's own various accounts of his life were never to be trusted and led to much confusion. Often referred to as 'Sonny Boy Williamson II' he was, in fact, older than John Lee 'Sonny Boy' Williamson, whose name, and associated glory, he appropriated some time in the late 30s or early 40s. Why he felt the need to do so is odd in light of the fact that he owed John Lee Williamson nothing in terms of style or ability, and alongside the latter and Little Walter Jacobs, was one of the most innovatory and influential exponents of the blues harmonica. He was the illegitimate child of Millie Ford, but he took to using his stepfather's name and by common association became 'Rice Miller'. He mastered his chosen instrument (he could also play guitar and drums) early in his life and seems to have taken to the road as soon as he was able, relying on his skill for a livelihood. His wanderings throughout the south brought him into contact with many blues artists. The list includes Robert Johnson, Robert Lockwood, Elmore James and Howlin' Wolf, whose half sister, Mary, he married in the 30s.

During this period Williamson used many names, working as 'Little Boy Blue', Willie Williamson, Willie Williams and Willie Miller (after his brother) and known to his friends as 'Foots' because of his habit of razoring his shoes, no matter how new they might be, to make them comfortable. He was cashing in on the popularity of John Lee Williamson (safely out of the way in Chicago) when he secured a job broadcasting over KFFA radio out of Helena on the *King Biscuit Show* in 1941. The show was heard all over the south and made Williamson famous. He continued to travel but now sought radio stations to advertise his activities. In the early 50s he recorded for Lillian McMurray's Trumpet label in Jackson, Mississippi, along with friends Willie Love and Elmore James. His work on this label includes many outstanding performances, with 'Mighty Long Time' being perhaps the greatest of all. On the strength of his increased popularity he extended his area of work and began to appear in the bars of Detroit, where he worked with Baby Boy Warren, and in Chicago (John Lee Williamson was dead by this time).

He began his career with Chess Records of Chicago in 1955 with his hit 'Don't Start Me Talkin'' and became a mainstay of the label almost until his death. In 1963, he took Europe by storm as a result of his appearances with the AFBF. His impressive appearance - tall and stooped in his famous grey/blue suit (quartered like a jester's doublet) and sporting a bowler hat and umbrella, along with his hooded eyes and goatee beard - hypnotized audiences as he weaved back and forth, snapping his fingers and clicking his tongue in a display of perfect rhythmic control. His skill on the harmonica was augmented by many tricks of showmanship such as playing two instruments at once (one with his large and plastic nose) or holding the harp end in his mouth and manoeuvring it with his tongue. If Europe took to him, Williamson seems to have enjoyed Europe: he stayed after the tour had ended and played his way around the burgeoning blues clubs, travelling as far as Poland. He recorded for the Storyville label in Denmark and with Chris Barber in Britain, then returned to mainland Europe, often stating his intention to take up permanent residence. He never lived to see the days when Chess tried to convert their roster of blues singers into pop stars by uniting them with the most unlikely material and musical support, but in earlier days he had been quite happy to follow a similar route, by recording with such groups as the Yardbirds and the Animals, and a jazz band led by Brian Auger. Some of these efforts stand up better than others but Williamson did not care - as long as he was paid. Despite moving around extensively, he still maintained a home in the USA with his second wife Mattie Lee Gordon. He was back in Helena, appearing on the *King Biscuit Show* once more, when he died in his sleep in 1965. Apart from his skill as a harmonica player and singer Sonny Boy Williamson was also a 'character' and anecdotes about him are legendary, both among the blues fraternity and his fans in Europe. If he was difficult, contentious, and unreliable, he was also a charming man who played upon his reputation as an evil, dangerous, hard-living blues troubadour. His music reveals that he was also capable of being both sensitive and humorous. He will always remain something of a conundrum, but as an artist his stature is recognized and his fame deserved.

● ALBUMS: *Down And Out Blues* (Checker 1959)★★★★, *Portraits In Blues Volume 4* (Storyville 1964)★★★★, *The Real Folk Blues* (Checker 1965)★★★★, *In Memoriam* (Chess 1965)★★★, *More Real Folk Blues* (Checker 1966)★★★, *Sonny Boy Williamson And The Yardbirds* (Mercury 1966)★★, *Bummer Road* (Chess 1969)★★★, *One Way Out* (MCA 1976)★★★, *The Animals With Sonny Boy Williamson* 1963 recording (Charly 1982)★★★, *King Biscuit Time* (Arhoolie 1989)★★★, *Goin' In Your Direction* (Trumpet 1992)★★★, *The EP Collection* (See For Miles 1994)★★★★.

WILLIS, CHUCK

b. 31 January 1928, Atlanta, Georgia, USA, d. 10 April 1958. R&B singer Willis made his recording debut in 1951. The following year he reached number 2 in the black music charts with 'My Story', the first of several hits the artist enjoyed while signed to the renowned OKeh label. In 1956 Willis had his first hit for Atlantic Records when 'It's Too Late' reached the US R&B Top 3, and the following year he topped the same chart with the compulsive 'C.C. Rider'. In April 1958, the singer succumbed to peritonitis, in the wake of which his posthumous single, 'What Am I Living For', sold in excess of one million copies. The ironically titled b-side, 'I'm Gonna Hang Up My Rock 'N' Roll Shoes', also reached the R&B Top 10, and despite his brief life and career, Willis remained an influential stylist in the development of R&B. He composed many of his best-known recordings, and cover versions by acts as disparate as Derek And The Dominos, the Animals, Buddy Holly, Jerry Lee Lewis, the Band, Ted Taylor and Otis Redding are a tribute to their longevity.

● ALBUMS: *Chuck Willis Wails The Blues* (Epic 1958)★★★, *The King Of The Stroll* (Atlantic 1958)★★★.
● COMPILATIONS: *Tribute To Chuck Willis* (Epic 1960)★★★, *I Remember Chuck Willis* (Atlantic 1963)★★★, *His Greatest Recordings* (Atlantic 1971)★★★, *Chuck Willis - My Story* (Official 1980)★★★, *Keep A Drivin'* (Charly 1984)★★★, *Be Good Or Be Gone* (Edsel 1986)★★★.

WILLOWS

A New York doo-wop group formed in 1953 as the Five Willows, this quintet is best remembered for the up-tempo rocker 'Church Bells May Ring', a song that still enjoys airplay on US nostalgia-orientated radio stations. The group consisted of Tony Middleton, brothers Ralph and Joe Martin, Richie Davis and John Steele. Relying on bass singer Steele's vocal acrobatics to give them an identity, they were signed to small labels Allen and Pee-Dee before recording one single for Herald, and finally, their hit for Melba. The shuffle 'Church Bells May Ring' was released in early 1956 and the chimes on the track were played by a then unknown Neil Sedaka. The Willows continued to record for such labels as Club, Eldorado, Gone and Heidi, and the group finally retired in 1965. They recorded no albums, but their one hit, which peaked at number 62 pop and number 11 on the R&B charts, is featured on numerous anthologies.

WILLS, BOB

b. James Robert Wills, 6 March 1905, on a farm near Kosse, Limestone County, Texas, USA, d. 13 May 1975, Fort Worth, Texas, USA. The eldest of the ten children of John Thompkins Wills and Emmaline (Foley), Bob was a sickly child and there were fears that he would not survive his early years. His father, known locally as Uncle John, was a skilled fiddler, and later taught his son Bob to play the mandolin so that he could accompany his father's playing; however, initially Bob showed no great interest in music. In 1913, the Wills family relocated to Memphis, Texas. Bob rode his donkey behind the family wagon and the 500-mile journey took over two months. John and Bob played for farm dances along the way to raise money for food and it was at one of these dances that Bob first became interested in music played by black families, featuring trumpet and guitar. When he was 10 years old, much to his father's relief, he took up the fiddle and made his first solo public appearance. On one occasion, his father failed to appear to play at a dance, and in spite of knowing only six fiddle tunes for dancing, he kept playing alone (his father eventually arrived at 2 a.m., too drunk to play). John Wills was successful as a farmer and by 1921, he had moved to a 600-acre ranch/farm near Oxbow Crossing, which remained their home until 1931. The family continued to play for local functions; it was suggested that the Wills family, which by 1926 included nine children, produced more music than cotton. Realizing the farm could not sustain them all, in 1924, Bob moved to Amarillo where, by working on building sites and as a shoeshine boy, he made enough money to buy himself a fiddle. He then found work playing for dances on Saturday nights and made his first radio broadcasts on Amarillo's two radio stations, KGRS and WDAG. A year later, he returned home driving a Model T Ford, which enabled him to travel around playing. In 1926, he married for the first time and leased a farm, but after a crop failure in 1927, he and his wife moved to Amarillo and he gave up farming for good. He moved to Fort Worth where, sometimes in blackface, he found work in a Medicine Show. Here he met guitarist Herman Arnspiger and the two men began to appear as the Wills Family Band. They played for dances, did comedy routines and in November 1929, they recorded for Brunswick in Dallas, although the two songs were not released. In 1930, the duo became a quartet when Milton Brown and his brother Durwood joined as vocalist and guitarist, respectively, although Durwood was at the time still at school (Milton Brown later became famous with his own band, the Musical Brownies). They found regular work playing for dances, at times adding banjoist Frank Barnes, and played on KTAT and KFJZ where the assistant programme director of the latter station, Alton Strickland, would five years later became Wills' pianist. In 1930, Wills' band were sponsored on WBAP by the Aladdin Lamp Company (they appeared as the Aladdin Laddies), and also gained a residency at the Crystal Springs dancehall in Fort Worth. In January 1931, through the sponsorship of the Burrus Mill and Elevator Company and billed as the Light Crust Doughboys, he and the band began to advertise Light Crust Flour on KFJZ. After two weeks, in spite of their popularity with the listeners, the President of Burrus Mill, Mr. Wilbert Lee O'Daniel (later a US Senator and Governor of Texas) sacked them, because he considered their music was too hillbilly. KFJZ kept them on air without a sponsor and Wills succeeded in getting O'Daniel to resume sponsorship and pay the band as well, although for a time all members had to work a 40-hour week in the mill. Their popularity grew and soon the programme was being heard over all the south-west, even reaching as far as Oklahoma City. The band recorded for RCA Victor in 1932, the only recordings made by Wills with the Light Crust Doughboys. The same year, vocalist Thomas Elmer Duncan replaced Milton Brown. In 1933, after differences of opinion and occasional drinking sprees that saw him miss shows, Wills was sacked by O'Daniel. He moved to Waco, assembled a band that included his brother, Johnnie Lee Wills, and Duncan, and for the first time, he called his band the Playboys; he also added 'formerly the Light Crust Doughboys' (he found himself in lawsuits from O'Daniel for using the name, but eventually the courts found in his favour). He then moved to Oklahoma City, where he began to call his band the Texas Playboys, but O'Daniel stopped his programme by promising the radio station he would put on the *Burrus Mill Show* in Oklahoma if they did not broadcast Wills' band. Wills moved to KVOO Tulsa, where in February 1934, Bob Wills And The Texas Playboys finally began to broadcast and this time O'Daniel's attempts to stop them failed.

In 1935, the group made their first, historic studio recordings. The band consisted of twelve musicians, namely Bob Wills (fiddle), Tommy Duncan (vocals, piano), Johnnie Lee Wills (tenor banjo), Son Lansford (bass), Herman Arnspiger (guitar), Sleepy Johnson (guitar), Jesse Ashlock (fiddle), Art Baines (fiddle, trombone), Smokey Dacus (drums), Robert McNally (saxophone), Al Stricklin (piano) and Leon McAuliffe (steel guitar). Wills stayed in Tulsa and during the late 30s, he continued to shape his band; changes in personnel saw the arrival of guitarist Eldon Shamblin and saxophonist Joe Ferguson. In 1936, Leon McAuliffe first recorded his 'Steel Guitar Rag'. Wills made further recording sessions in Chicago (1936) and Dallas (1937 and 1938). When he recorded in Saginaw, Texas, in April 1940, his band numbered 18 musicians - more than the big bands of the period such as Glenn Miller, Benny Goodman and the Dorseys were using. It was at this session that he recorded his million-selling version of 'New San Antonio Rose', the (Tommy Duncan) vocal version of his 1935 fiddle tune, previously known as 'Spanish Two Step'. This version differed from his original fiddle one in that it featured only reeds and brass and was played in the swing style as used by the big bands of the time (over the years the song has usually been referred to as simply 'San Antonio Rose'). Wills was by this time one of the top-selling recording artists in the USA. In 1939, the demand was such that Wills decided for the first time to run a second band, which was led by his brother Johnnie Lee and also included his younger brother Luke Wills. Although successful with his music, Bob Wills was far from successful in marriage. He had troubles at times with excessive drinking and a fondness for the ladies. He was divorced in 1935 and married and divorced a second time in 1936. In 1938, he married again but once more was divorced within the year, and though he persuaded this wife to remarry him, they were divorced for the second time in 1939. He married again in July 1939, only to be divorced (yet again!) in June 1941.

In 1940, he appeared with Tex Ritter in the film *Take Me Back To Oklahoma*, even duetting with Ritter on the title track, and the following year, with his full band, he featured in the film *Go West Young Man*. In 1942, Duncan left for military service (he rejoined on discharge) but Wills maintained a band containing 15 instruments, although only four were stringed. He recorded in Hollywood and made eight B-movie westerns with Russell Hayden. He was also married that year to Betty Anderson, a girl 18 years his junior and this time, in spite of his drinking, the marriage lasted until his death. After the filming was completed, more band members left for the US Army and Wills moved to Tulsa, finally disbanding the group in December 1942. He enlisted himself, but was discharged in July 1943. He moved to California, re-formed a band and returned to the film studios. Wills never liked Hollywood but he loved the cowboy image. He spent lavishly on horses, harnesses and dress for himself and was a popular figure on his favourite stallion, Punkin, around the California rodeo circuit. He bought a ranch in the San Joaquin Valley and stocked it with horses and a dairy herd 'just to keep my father busy'. At one stage in 1944, his band consisted of 22 instruments and 2 vocalists, but he never recorded with this unit. Duncan left in 1947 to form his own band, probably because he had tired of having to take responsibility for fronting the band when Wills failed to appear as a result of excessive drinking sprees. During 1944-45, Wills had US country and pop chart hits with 'New San Antonio Rose', 'We Might As Well Forget It' and 'You're From Texas'. He also had country number 1 hits with such war songs as 'Smoke On The Water', 'Stars And Stripes At Iwo Jima', 'Silver Dew On The Blue Grass Tonight' and 'White Cross At Okinawa'. In 1946, his 'New Spanish Two-Step' topped the country charts for 16 weeks as well as having Top 20 pop success. Wills left Columbia Records in 1947 to record for MGM Records and in 1950, he recorded his classic 'Faded Love' - a composition that he and his father wrote with some words added by brother Billy Jack Wills. He toured extensively and relocated to Dallas, where he invested heavily in a dancehall that he called Bob Wills' Ranch House. Due to unscrupulous advisers and accountants, he soon found himself heavily in debt. Faced with jail, he sold his Bob Wills Music Company and accidentally with it, the ownership of 'San Antonio Rose'. For two years, he struggled to raise funds; he ran two bands - one played at the Ranch House and he toured with the other. In January 1952,

he finally sold the Ranch House to a Jack Ruby - a name then unknown outside Dallas, but later internationally known following the assassination of Lee Harvey Oswald (in turn, killer of President John F. Kennedy). Throughout the 50s, he recorded and toured extensively and several times moved his base of operations. Wills continued to experiment but the influence of television began to affect the dancehalls; tastes had changed and he never recaptured the earlier successes. He recorded in Nashville for the first time in 1955, and again in 1956, but most of his recordings were made in California. In 1959, he appeared at the Golden Nugget in Las Vegas but still missed a few shows through his drinking. He was reunited with Tommy Duncan, and during the period of 1960/1 they recorded over 40 sides for Liberty Records. In 1962, he suffered a heart attack but in 1963, he was back, even though he had sold his band to Carl Johnson. He suffered a further heart attack in 1964 and when he recovered sufficiently to work again, he always acted as a frontman for other bands. Between 1963 and 1969, he recorded almost 100 sides for either Liberty, Longhorn or Kapp Records. He was elected to the Country Music Hall Of Fame in 1968.

After an appearance on 30 May 1969, he suffered a stroke and was rushed to hospital where he underwent two major operations. The stroke left him paralyzed on his right side and hospitalized for months. In 1970, he moved to Tulsa and in 1971 underwent surgery for a kidney complaint, but suffered a stroke on the left side a few hours after the operation. Months later, he recovered sufficiently to talk and to use his left arm, even telling people that he would play again. Country star Merle Haggard admired Wills and in 1970, he recorded his album *Tribute To The Best Damn Fiddle Player In The World (Or My Salute To Bob Wills)*, which actually featured some of the Texas Playboys. Wills was unable to attend the recordings but in 1971, he was reunited with 10 of his old Texas Playboys at Haggard's house, near Bakersfield, and watched and listened as recordings were made. In 1973, he made a few appearances, at one even holding his fiddle while Hoyle Nix used the bow. He travelled to Dallas to attend a recording session of the Texas Playboys and on 3 December even included a few of his famous yells and 'hollers' as the band recorded some of his hits. During the night, he suffered a further stroke and remained unconscious for almost 18 months until his death from pneumonia on 13 May 1975. He was buried in Memorial Park, Tulsa, a city that saw most of the glory days of Bob Wills' western swing music. It could never be said that he copied any other style - he devised his own, as the words of his song said, 'Deep within my heart lies a melody'. His long-time friend, steel guitarist Leon McAuliffe, who, though 12 years younger than Wills, had retired from the music scene, summed things up when he said, 'My desire wore out before my body, Bob never did wear out at this. His body wore out before his desire did'. There have been other bands that played the music but none that ever matched the instrumental integration or the wide variation in the styles and music of Bob Wills. His habit of uttering spasmodic high-pitched shouts during the playing of numbers, such as his famed 'Ah haaa', originated from the days when, as a young boy, he performed with his father at ranch dances in Texas. His father (and the cowboys) used similar loud cries at points when the music or the whiskey moved them to feel that something was special. As Waylon Jennings sang, 'When you're down in Austin, Bob Wills is still the King'.

● ALBUMS: *Bob Wills Round-Up* 10-inch album (Columbia 1949)★★★, *Ranch House Favorites* 10-inch album (MGM 1951)★★★, *Old Time Favorites By Bob Wills & His Texas Playboys 1* (Antone's 1953)★★★, *Old Time Favorites By Bob Wills & His Texas Playboys 2* (Antone's 1953)★★★, *Dance-O-Rama No: 2* (Decca 1955)★★★, *Ranch House Favorites* ii (MGM 1956)★★★, *Bob Wills Special* (Harmony 1957)★★★, *Bob Wills & His Texas Playboys* (Decca 1957)★★★, *Western Swing In Hi-Fi* (1957)★★★, with Tommy Duncan *Together Again* (Liberty 1960)★★★, with Tommy Duncan *Bob Wills & Tommy Duncan* (Liberty 1961)★★★, *Living Legend - Bob Wills & His Texas Playboys* (Liberty 1961)★★★, *Mr Words & Mr Music* (Liberty 1961)★★★, *Bob Wills Sings And Plays* (Liberty 1963)★★★, *Best Of Bob Wills & His Texas Playboys - Original Recordings* (Harmony 1963)★★★★, *My Keepsake Album* (Longhorn 1965)★★★, *The Great Bob Wills* (Harmony 1965)★★★, *San Antonio Rose/Steel Guitar Rag* (Starday 1965)★★★, *Western Swing Band* (Vocalion 1965)★★★, with Leon Rausch *From The Heart Of Texas* (Kapp 1966)★★★, *King Of Western Swing* (Kapp 1967)★★★, *Bob Wills* (Metro 1967)★★★, *Here's That Man Again* (Kapp 1968)★★★★, *Plays The Greatest String Band Hits* (Kapp 1969)★★★, *A Country Walk* (Sunset 1969)★★★, *Time Changes Everything* (Kapp 1969)★★★, *The Living Legend* (Kapp 1969)★★★, *Bob Wills Special* (Harmony 1969)★★★, *The Bob Wills Story* (Starday 1970)★★★, *Bob Wills In Person* (Kapp 1970)★★★, *A Tribute To Bob Wills* (MGM 1971)★★★, *The History Of Bob Wills & The Texas Playboys* (MGM 1973)★★★, *The Best Of Bob Wills* (MCA 1973), *For The Last Time* (United Artists 1974)★★★★, *Bob Wills & His Texas Playboys In Concert* (Capitol 1976)★★★, *I Love People* (1976)★★★, *Lonestar Rag* (1979)★★★, *Faded Love* (1981)★★★, *31st Street Blues* (1981)★★★, *The San Antonio Rose Story* (1982)★★★, *Texas Fiddle & Milk Cow Blues* (1982)★★★, *Heaven, Hell Or Houston* (1983)★★★, *Swing Hi! Swing Lo!* (1993)★★★.

● COMPILATIONS: with Tommy Duncan *Legendary Masters - Bob Wills & Tommy Duncan* (United Artists 1971)★★★★, *The Bob Wills Anthology* (Columbia 1973)★★★★, *The Legendary Bob Wills* (Columbia 1975)★★★, *The Tiffany Transcriptions 1945-1948* (Lariat 1977)★★★, *The Tiffany Transcriptions* (Tishomingo 1978)★★★, *The Rare Presto Transcriptions Volumes 1 - 5* German releases (Outlaw 1981-1985)★★★, *Columbia Historic Edition* (Columbia 1982)★★★, *The Tiffany Transcriptions Volumes 1 - 9* (Kaleidoscope 1983-1988, reissued by Rhino in the 1990s)★★★, *The Golden Era* (Columbia 1987)★★★, *Fiddle* (CMF 1987)★★★, *Anthology 1935-1973* (Rhino 1991)★★★★, *Country Music Hall Of Fame Series* (MCA 1992)★★★★, *The Essential Bob Wills And His Texas Playboys 1935-47* (Columbia 1992)★★★★, *The Longhorn Recordings* (Bear Family 1993)★★★, *Classic Western Swing* (Rhino 1994)★★★, *Encore* 3-CD box set (Liberty 1994)★★★★.

● FURTHER READING: *San Antonio Rose, The Life and Music of Bob Wills*, Charles R.Townsend. *The Life Of Bob Wills, The King Of Western Swing*, Jimmy Latham. *My Years With Bob Wills*, Al Stricklin. *Hubbin' It, The Life Of Bob Wills*, Ruth Sheldon.

WILSON, JACKIE

b. 9 June 1934, Detroit, Michigan, USA, d. 21 January 1984, New Jersey, USA. When parental pressure thwarted his boxing ambitions, Wilson took to singing in small local clubs. He sang with the Thrillers (a predecessor group to the Royals) and recorded some solo tracks for Dizzy Gillespie's Dee Gee label as Sonny Wilson, before replacing Clyde McPhatter in Billy Ward And The Dominoes. Wilson joined this notable group in 1953, but embarked on a solo career four years later with Brunswick Records. His first single for that label was the exuberant 'Reet Petite', a comparative failure in the USA where it crept to a lowly pop position and missed the R&B lists altogether. In the UK, however, it soared to number 6, thereby establishing Wilson in the minds of the British pop-purchasing audience. 'Reet Petite' had been written by Berry Gordy and Tyran Carlo (Roquel 'Billy' Davis), who went on to compose several of Wilson's subsequent releases, including the hits 'Lonely Teardrops' (1958), 'That's Why (I Love You So)' (1959) and 'I'll Be Satisfied' (1959).

In 1960, Wilson enjoyed two R&B number 1 hits with 'Doggin' Around' and 'A Woman, A Lover, A Friend'. His musical direction then grew increasingly erratic, veering from mainstream to pseudo-opera. There were still obvious highlights such as 'Baby Workout' (1963), 'Squeeze Her Please Her' (1964), 'No Pity (In The Naked City)' (1965), but all too often his wonderfully fluid voice was wasted on cursory, quickly dated material. The artist's live appearances, however, remained both exciting and dramatic, capable of inspiring the ecstasy his sometimes facile recordings belied. Wilson's career was rejuvenated in 1966. Abandoning his New York recording base, he moved to Chicago, where he worked with producer Carl Davis. He offered a more consistent empathy and 'Whispers (Gettin' Louder)' (1966), '(Your Love Keeps Lifting Me) Higher And Higher' (1967) and the sublime 'I Get The Sweetest Feeling' (1968) stand among his finest recordings. However, it did not last; 'This Love Is Real (I Can Feel Those Vibrations)' (1970) proved to be Wilson's last Top 10 R&B entry, by which time his work was influenced by trends rather than setting them. In September 1975, while touring with the Dick Clark revue, Wilson suffered a near-fatal heart attack onstage at New Jersey's Latin Casino. He struck his head on falling and the resulting brain damage left him comatose. He remained hospitalized until his death on 21 January 1984.

Wilson's career remains a puzzle; he never did join Berry Gordy's Motown empire, despite their early collaboration and friendship. Instead, the singer's legacy was flawed - dazzling in places, disappointing in others. Immortalized in the Van Morrison song 'Jackie Wilson Said', which was also a UK Top 5 hit for Dexys Midnight Runners in 1982, his name has remained in the public's eye. Fate provided a final twist in 1987, when an imaginative video (which some claimed belittled the singer's memory), using plasticine animation, propelled 'Reet Petite' to number 1 in the UK charts. He was inducted into the Rock And Roll Hall Of Fame the same year.

● ALBUMS: *He's So Fine* (Brunswick 1958)★★★, *Lonely Teardrops* (Brunswick 1959)★★★★, *Doggin' Around* (Brunswick 1959)★★★, *So Much* (Brunswick 1960)★★★, *Night* (Brunswick 1960)★★★, *Jackie Wilson Sings The Blues* (Brunswick 1960)★★★★, *A Woman A Lover A Friend* (Brunswick 1961)★★★★, *Try A Little Tenderness*

(Brunswick 1961)★★★, *You Ain't Heard Nothing Yet* (Brunswick 1961)★★★, *By Special Request* (Brunswick 1961)★★★, *Body And Soul* (Brunswick 1962)★★★, *Jackie Wilson At The Copa* (Brunswick 1962)★★★, *Jackie Wilson Sings The World's Greatest Melodies* (Brunswick 1962)★★★, *Baby Workout* (Brunswick 1963)★★★★, *Merry Christmas* (Brunswick 1963)★★, with Linda Hopkins *Shake A Hand* (Brunswick 1963)★★, *Somethin' Else* (Brunswick 1964)★★★★, *Soul Time* (Brunswick 1965)★★★★, *Spotlight On Jackie Wilson* (Brunswick 1965)★★★, *Soul Galore* (Brunswick 1966)★★★, *Whispers* (Brunswick 1967)★★★, *Higher And Higher* (Brunswick 1967)★★★★, with Count Basie *Manufacturers Of Soul* (Brunswick 1968)★★★, with Basie *Too Much* (1968)★★★, *I Get The Sweetest Feeling* (Brunswick 1968)★★★★, *Do Your Thing* (Brunswick 1970)★★★, *This Love Is Real* (Brunswick 1970)★★★, *You Got Me Walking* (Brunswick 1971)★★, *Beautiful Day* (Brunswick 1973)★★, *Nowstalgia* (Brunswick 1974)★★, *Nobody But You* (Brunswick 1976)★★.
● COMPILATIONS: *My Golden Favourites* (Brunswick 1960)★★★, *My Golden Favourites - Volume 2* (Brunswick 1964)★★★, *Jackie Wilson's Greatest Hits* (Brunswick 1969)★★★, *It's All Part Of Love* (Brunswick 1969)★★★, *Jackie Wilson: S.R.O.* (1982)★★★, *Classic Jackie Wilson* (Skratch 1984)★★★, *Reet Petite* (Ace 1985)★★★★, *The Soul Years* (Kent 1985)★★★★, *The Soul Years Volume 2* (Kent 1986)★★★, *Higher And Higher* i (Kent 1986)★★★, *Through The Years* (Rhino 1987)★★★, *The Very Best Of Jackie Wilson* (Ace 1987)★★★, *Mr Excitement!* 3-CD box set (Rhino 1992)★★★★, *Higher And Higher* ii (1993)★★★, *The Dynamic Jackie Wilson* (1993)★★★★, *The Chicago Years Volume 1* (1993)★★★★, *Original Hits* (1993)★★★★, *The Jackie Wilson Hit Story Volume1* (1993)★★★★, *The Jackie Wilson Hit Story Volume 2* (1993)★★★, *The Very Best Of Jackie Wilson* (Rhino 1994)★★★★, *A Portrait Of Jackie Wilson* (Essential Gold/Pickwick 1995)★★★★, *Higher And Higher* (Rhino 1995)★★★★.
● FURTHER READING: *Lonely Teardrops: The Jackie Wilson Story*, Tony Douglas.
● FILMS: *Go Johnny Go* (1958).

WILSON, JULIE

b. Julia May Wilson, 21 October 1924, Omaha, Nebraska, USA. An actress and singer, Wilson is acknowledged as one of the greatest interpreters of standard popular songs in the world of cabaret. Her sophisticated image, with a figure-hugging gown, and a gardenia tucked into her swept-back gleaming black hair, is a reminder of a bygone era. She started young, being voted 'Miss Nebraska' when she was only 17. A year later, she joined the chorus of a touring edition of the *Earl Carroll's Vanities* which was passing through Omaha, and ended up in New York. From there, she moved to a Miami nightclub, doing a solo act five shows a night. It was in Miami that she believes she learnt how to control an audience with the occasional aggressive 'drop-dead bitchy' remark. Next stop was Los Angeles where she won a contest on Mickey Rooney's radio show. The prize was a two-week engagement at Hollywood's top nightclub, the Mocambo. Soon afterwards she was offered the part of Lois Lane in the touring version of the musical *Kiss Me, Kate*, and in 1951 recreated the role at the London Coliseum. She stayed in London for nearly four years, appearing in various shows,

including *Bet Your Life* (1952), and undergoing voice training at RADA. Back in the USA, during the remainder of the 50s and throughout most of the 60s, Wilson took over roles on Broadway in *The Pajama Game* and *Kismet*, played in various regional productions, returned to London for *Bells Are Ringing*, and did some television work, including the soap opera *The Secret Storm*. In the 1969/70 Broadway season she appeared in two flop musicals, and subsequently played several cabaret engagements at New York's Brothers and Sisters club, as well as continuing to tour. In the mid-70s she went into semi-retirement in order to look after her ailing parents in Omaha. She returned to the New York cabaret scene with an evening of Cole Porter songs at Michael's Pub in 1984. Since then, she has attracted excellent reviews in two otherwise unsuccessful New York musicals, *Legs Diamond* (1988) and *Hannah...1939* (1990), recorded several superb albums, as well as, in critic Clive Barnes' words, 'putting over a torch song with the sultry heat of a flame thrower' in cabaret. There was great rejoicing at nightspots around the world when in 1993, along with her long-time accompanist William Roy, she celebrated her 50 years in showbusiness.
● ALBUMS: *Love* (Dolphin 1956)★★★, *This Could Be The Night* film soundtrack (MGM 1957)★★, *My Old Flame* (Vik 1957)★★★, *Julie Wilson At The St. Regis* (Vik 1957)★★★, *Meet Julie Wilson* (Cameo 1960)★★★, with Kay Stevens, Connie Russell, Cara Williams *Playgirls* (Warners 1964)★★★, *Jimmy* Broadway Cast (RCA Victor 1969)★★, *Julie Wilson At Brothers And Sisters* (Arden 1974)★★★, *Bet Your Life* London Cast reissue (Blue Pear *c.*80s)★★★, *Sings The Kurt Weill Songbook* (DRG 1987)★★★★, *Sings The Stephen Sondheim Songbook* (DRG 1987)★★★★, *Legs Diamond* Broadway Cast (RCA Victor 1988)★★★, *Hannah...1939* off-Broadway Cast (1990)★★★, *Sings The Cole Porter Songbook* (DRG 1989)★★★★, *Sings The Harold Arlen Songbook* (DRG 1990)★★★★, *Live From The Russian Tea Room* (Cabaret Records 1993)★★★, and Ben Bagley recordings.
● FILMS: *The Strange One* (1957), *This Could Be The Night* (1957).

WILSON, SANDY

b. Alexander Galbraith Wilson, 19 May 1924, Sale, Cheshire, England. A composer, lyricist and author, Wilson studied at Harrow and Oxford University, where he wrote and appeared in many undergraduate productions. He began to make his mark in the West End by contributing songs to revues such as *Slings And Arrows* (1948) and *Oranges And Lemons* (1949). In 1950 he provided the lyrics for a provincial production of Michael Pertwee's musical play *Caprice*, and then was the author and composer of *See You Later* (1951) and *See You Again* (1952). His big break came in 1953 when he was asked to write the book, music and lyrics for *The Boy Friend*, a light-hearted spoof of the musical comedies of the 20s. The delightful score included 'I Could Be Happy With You', 'A Room In Bloomsbury', 'Won't You Charleston With Me?', 'It's Never Too Late To Fall In Love', 'Fancy Forgetting', and the lively title song. After starting its life as an hour-long entertainment at the tiny Player's Theatre, in London, *The Boy Friend* moved first to the Embassy Theatre, where it was expanded, before finally transferring to Wyndhams's Theatre in the West End on 14 January 1954. It ran for over five years, and Julie Andrews made her New York stage debut in the Broadway production, which lasted for over a year. The show has subsequently been produced in many countries throughout the world, and enjoyed revivals in New York (1958) and London (1967 and 1993). The 1971 film version was directed by Ken Russell, and starred Twiggy, Christopher Gable, Moyra Fraser and Tommy Tune. As well as *The Boy Friend*, Sandy Wilson has been the composer and/or author and lyricist of some of the most civilized and enjoyable shows (British or otherwise) ever to play the West End. They included *The Buccaneer* (1955), *Valmouth* (1958), *Pieces Of Eight* (1959), *Call It Love* (1960), *Divorce Me, Darling!* (1965), *As Dorothy Parker Once Said* (1966), *Sandy Wilson Thanks The Ladies* (in which he also appeared, 1971), *His Monkey Wife* (1971), *The Clapham Wonder* (1978) and *Aladdin* (1979).

● FURTHER READING: all by Sandy Wilson *This Is Sylvia*. *The Boy Friend*. *I Could Be Happy: His Autobiography*. *Ivor* (a biography of Ivor Novello). *The Roaring Twenties*.

WISDOM, NORMAN

b. 4 February 1915, Paddington, London, England. A slapstick comedian, singer and straight actor, Wisdom has been a much-loved entertainer for four decades in the UK, not to mention other such unlikely places as Russia, China, and - more recently - Albania. He broke into films in 1953 with *Trouble In Store*, and during the remainder of the 50s, had a string of box-office smashes with *One Good Turn*, *Man Of The Moment*, *Up In The World*, *Just My Luck*, *The Square Peg* and *Follow A Star*. Dressed in his famous tight-fitting Gump suit, he was usually accompanied by straight man Jerry Desmonde, and, more often than not, portrayed the little man battling against the odds, eventually overcoming prejudice and snobbery, to win justice and his inevitably pretty sweetheart. He nearly always sang in his films, and his theme song, 'Don't Laugh At Me', which he co-wrote with June Tremayne, was a number 3 hit in 1954 on EMI/Columbia. He also made the Top 20 in 1957 with a version of the Five Keys' 'Wisdom Of A Fool'. In 1958, Wisdom appeared in the London production of *Where's Charley?*, a musical based on Brandon Thomas's classic farce, *Charley's Aunt*. Frank Loesser's score included 'Once In Love With Amy' and 'My Darling, My Darling', and the show ran for 18 months. In 1965, he played the lead in Leslie Bricusse and Anthony Newley's musical *The Roar Of The Greasepaint - The Smell Of The Crowd*, which toured UK provincial theatres. He was not considered sufficiently well-known in the USA to play the part on Broadway, but did make his New York debut in the following year, when he starred in *Walking Happy*, a musical version of *Hobson's Choice* with a score by Sammy Cahn and Jimmy Van Heusen. Wisdom also appeared on US television in the role of Androcles, with Noël Coward as Julius Caesar, in Richard Rodgers' musical adaptation of Bernard Shaw's *Androcles And The Lion*. His feature films during the 60s included *On the Beat*, *A Stitch In Time*, and *The Night They Raided Minsky's* with Jason Robards and Britt Ekland. Thanks to television re-runs of his films he is regarded with warm affection by many sections of the British public, and can still pack theatres, although, like many showbusiness veterans, he is not called on to appear much on television. In his heyday, he made two celebrated 'live' one-hour appearances on *Sunday Night At The London Palladium* in the company of Bruce Forsyth, which are con-

sidered to be classics of their kind. In 1992, with the UK rapidly running out of traditional funnymen (Benny Hill and Frankie Howerd both died in that year), Wisdom experienced something of a renaissance when he played the role of a gangster in the movie *Double X*, starred in a radio series, *Robbing Hood*, released the album *A World Of Wisdom*, completed a sell-out tour of the UK, and published his autobiography. In the following year he celebrated 50 years in showbusiness, and was still performing regularly. In 1995, he toured Albania as a guest of the Minister of Culture. Apparently, whereas the country's state censors banned most American and British films with their 'Marxist messages', Wisdom, in his customary role as 'the plucky proletarian', was considered politically and morally inoffensive. He was given the freedom of the capital, Tirana, met President Sali Berisha, attended several rallies in his honour, and gave a 90-minute television performance.

● ALBUMS: *I Would Like To Put On Record* (1956)★★★, *Where's Charley?* stage production (1958)★★, *Walking Happy* Broadway Cast (1966)★★★, *Androcles And The Lion* (1967)★★.

● COMPILATIONS: *A World Of Wisdom* (Decca 1992)★★★.

● FURTHER READING: *Trouble In Store*, Richard Dacre. *Don't Laugh At Me*, Norman Wisdom.

WISH YOU WERE HERE

In the early 50s, when Broadway audiences were enjoying such lavish musicals as *Call Me Madam*, *The King And I*, *Can-Can* and *Kismet*, *Wish You Were Here* went one better than all of them, and splashed out on a real swimming pool that was built into the stage. Perhaps the show's director, producer, choreographer, and co-librettist Joshua Logan still had fond watery memories of his association with the enormously successful *South Pacific* a few years earlier. In any event, the pool attracted a good deal of early publicity, as did a record of the title song by Eddie Fisher which soared to the top of the US chart just three weeks after the show opened at the Imperial Theatre on 25 June 1952. The story, which was adapted by Joshua Logan and Arthur Kober from Kober's 1937 play, *Having A Wonderful Time*, is set in Camp Karefree, a Jewish adult summer vacation resort in the Catskill Mountains. Teddy Stern (Patricia Marand) loses interest in her mature boyfriend, Herbert Fabricant (Harry Clark), when the young, suave and slinky waiter-cum-dancer Chick Miller (Jack Cassidy) sweeps her off her feet. It is all perfectly legal because, back home in New York, Chick is actually a law student. As well as the title number, which also became a hit for Jane Froman and Guy Lombardo, Harold Rome's amusing and tuneful score contained another appealing ballad, 'Where Did The Night Go', along with 'Tripping The Light Fantastic', 'Could Be', 'Ballad Of A Social Director', 'Mix And Mingle', 'Camp Kare-Free', 'Summer Afternoon', 'Shopping Around', 'Don José Of Far Rockaway' and 'Flattery'. *Wish You Were Here* was a warm and friendly show, so it was not surprising that it ran for nearly a year and a half, a total of 598 performances. The 1953 London production, with Bruce Trent, Shani Wallis, Elizabeth Larner and Dickie Henderson, stayed at the Casino Theatre (complete with swimming pool) for eight months. (The 1987 British film of the same name that starred Emily Lloyd and Tom Bell, is in no way related to this musical production.)

WITH A SONG IN MY HEART

Susan Hayward gave an outstanding performance in this 1952 20th Century-Fox film which was based on the life of the popular singer Jane Froman. There was hardly a dry eye in the house as producer Lamar Trotti's screenplay traced Froman's brave fight back to the top following a terrible air crash during World War II that left her confined to a wheelchair. David Wayne was fine as her mentor and husband, and so was Thelma Ritter, who played her hard-bitten nurse and companion. The 22-year-old Robert Wagner had a small but effective role as a shell-shocked young airman, and also in the strong supporting cast were Rory Calhoun, Richard Allan, Una Merkel, Helen Wescott, Leif Erikson, Max Showalter and Lyle Talbot. It was Jane Froman's own voice that was heard on the soundtrack singing a marvellous selection of songs, many of which were particularly associated with her. There were especially endearing versions of 'With A Song In My Heart' (Richard Rodgers-Lorenz Hart), 'I'll Walk Alone' (Jule Styne-Sammy Cahn), 'I'm Through With Love' (Gus Kahn-Matty Malneck-Fud Livingstone) and 'They're Either Too Young Or Too Old' (Frank Loesser), along with excellent readings of 'Embraceable You' (George and Ira Gershwin), 'It's A Good Day' (Peggy Lee-Dave Barbour), 'Indiana' (James Hanley-Ballard MacDonald), 'Blue Moon' (Rodgers-Hart), 'Deep In The Heart Of Texas' (Don Swander-June Hershey), 'Tea For Two' (Vincent Youmans-Irving Caesar), 'That Old Feeling' (Lew Brown-Sammy Fain), and several more. Musical director Alfred Newman won an Oscar for his scoring. Billy Daniels staged the dance numbers and the impressive Technicolor photography was by Leon Shamroy. Walter Lang directed what was certainly one of the best films of its kind.

WITHERSPOON, JIMMY

b. 8 August 1923, Gurdon, Arkansas, USA, d. 18 September 1997. Witherspoon crossed over into rock, jazz and R&B territory, but his deep and mellow voice placed him ultimately as a fine blues singer. He sang in his local Baptist church from the age of seven. From 1941-43 he was in the Merchant Marines and, during stopovers in Calcutta, he found himself singing the blues with a band led by Teddy Weatherford. In 1944, he replaced Walter Brown in the Jay McShann band at Vallejo, California, and toured with it for the next four years. In 1949 he had his first hit, 'Tain't Nobody's Business If I Do', which stayed on the *Billboard* chart for 34 weeks. Other recordings at the time with bands led by Jimmy 'Maxwell Street' Davis are fine examples of rollicking west coast R&B (collected as *Who's Been Jivin' You*). Witherspoon's popularity as an R&B singer faded during the course of the 50s, but he made a great impression on jazz listeners at the Monterey Jazz Festival in October 1959, performing with a group that included Ben Webster. Other collaborations with jazz artists included *Some Of My Best Friends Are The Blues*, with horns and strings arranged and conducted by Benny Golson, and a guest performance on Jon Hendricks' *Evolution Of The Blues Song*. He won the *Downbeat* critics' poll as a 'new star' in 1961. Frequent tours of Europe followed, beginning in 1961 with a Buck Clayton group and later with Coleman Hawkins, Roy Eldridge, Earl Hines and Woody Herman. He also did community work, including singing in prisons. In the early 70s he gave up touring for a sedentary job as a blues disc jockey on the radio station KMET in Los Angeles, but resumed active music thanks to the encouragement of Eric Burdon. During his touring with Burdon he introduced a young Robben Ford as his guitarist and toured Japan and the Far East. In 1974 his 'Love Is A Five Letter Word' was a hit, though some fans regretted his neglect of the blues. A record with the Savoy Sultans in 1980 was a spirited attempt to recall a bygone era. *The Blues, The Whole Blues And Nothin' But The Blues* was the first album release for Mike Vernon's new label Indigo. Witherspoon has been revered by generations during different eras, and his name was often cited as a major influence during the 60s beat boom; his work is destined to endure.

● ALBUMS: *New Orleans Blues* (1956)★★★, *Goin' To Kansas City Blues* (RCA Victor 1957)★★★★, with Eddie Vinson *Battle Of The Blues, Volume 3* (1959)★★★, *At The Monterey Jazz Festival* (Hifi 1959)★★★★, with Gerry Mulligan *Mulligan With Witherspoon* (1959)★★★, *Jimmy Witherspoon* (Crown 1959)★★★, *Feelin' The Spirit* (Hifi 1959)★★★★, *Jimmy Witherspoon At The Renaissance* (Hifi 1959)★★★, *Singin' The Blues* reissued as *There's Good Rockin' Tonight* (World Pacific 1959)★★★★, *Jimmy Witherspoon Sings The Blues* (Crown 1960)★★★, *Spoon* (Reprise 1961)★★★, *Hey, Mrs. Jones* (Reprise 1962)★★★, *Roots* (Reprise 1962)★★★, *Baby, Baby, Baby* (Prestige 1963)★★★, *Evenin' Blues* (Prestige 1964)★★★, *Goin' To Chicago Blues* (Prestige 1964)★★★, *Blues Around The Clock* (1964)★★★, *Blue Spoon* (Prestige 1964)★★★, *Some Of My Best Friends Are The Blues* (Prestige 1964)★★★, *Take This Hammer* (Constellation 1964)★★★, *Blues For Spoon And Groove* (Surrey 1965)★★★, *Spoon In London* (Prestige 1965)★★★, *Blues Point Of View* (Verve 1967)★★★, with Jack McDuff *The Blues Is Now* (Verve 1967)★★★, *Blues For Easy Livers* (Prestige 1967)★★★, *A Spoonful Of Soul* (Verve 1968)★★★, *The Blues Singer* (Stateside 1969)★★★, *Back Door Blues* (Polydor 1969)★★★, *Hunh!* (1970)★★★, *Handbags & Gladrags* (Probe 1970)★★★, *Blues Singer* (Stateside 1970)★★★, with Eric Burdon *Guilty!* (United Artists 1971)★★★, *Ain't Nobody's Business* (Polydor 1974)★★★, *Love Is A Five Letter Word* (Capitol 1975)★★★, *Jimmy Witherspoon And Ben Webster (That's Jazz)* (Warners 1977)★★★, with New Savoy Sultans *Sings The Blues* (Muse 1980)★★★, with Buck Clayton *Live In Paris, Big Blues* (Vogue 1981)★★★, *Call My Baby* (1991)★★★, *The Blues, The Whole Blues And Nothin' But The Blues* (Indigo 1992)★★★, with Robben Ford *Live At The Notodden Blues Festival* (1993)★★★★, *Spoon's Blues* (Stony Plain 1995)★★★, with Howard Scott *American Blues* (Avenue/Rhino 1995)★★★, with Robben Ford *Ain't Nothin' New But The Blues* 1977 recording (AIM 1996)★★★★, with Robben Ford *Live At The Mint* (On The Spot 1996)★★★, *Spoonful* (ARG Jazz 1997)★★★.

● COMPILATIONS: *The Best Of Jimmy Witherspoon* (Prestige 1969)★★★★, *Never Knew This Kind Of Hurt Before: The Bluesway Sessions* 1969-71 recordings (Charly 1988)★★★, *Meets The Jazz Giants* 1959 recordings (1989)★★★, *Blowin' In From Kansas* (Ace 1991)★★★★, *Jimmy Witherspoon & Jay McShann* 40s recordings (1992)★★★.

WOOLEY, SHEB

b. Shelby F. Wooley, 10 April 1921, near Erick, Oklahoma, USA. Wooley, who is part Cherokee Indian, grew up on the family farm, learned to ride as a child and rode in rodeos as a teenager. His father traded a shotgun for Sheb's first guitar and while still at high school, he formed a country band that played at dances and on local radio. After leaving school, he found work on an oilfield as a welder, but soon tired of this work and moved to Nashville. He appeared on the WLAC and WSM radio stations and recorded for the Bullet label. In 1946, he relocated to Fort Worth, where until 1949, he became the frontman for a major show on WBAP, sponsored by Calumet Baking Powder. He then moved to Los Angeles, where he signed with MGM Records and with thoughts of a film career, he also attended the Jack Koslyn School of Acting. In 1949, he had his first screen role (as a heavy) in the Errol Flynn film *Rocky Mountain*. In 1952, he made a memorable appearance as Ben Miller, the killer plotting to gun down Gary Cooper in the classic western *High Noon*. During the 50s, he appeared in several other films including *Little Big Horn* (1951), *Distant Drums* (1951), *Man Without A Star* (1955), *Giant* (1956) and *Rio Bravo* (1959). He is also well remembered for his performances as Pete Nolan in the television series *Rawhide*, which ran from 1958-65 (he also wrote some scripts for the series). During his career, he appeared in over 40 films.

Other artists began to record songs he had written and in 1953, Hank Snow had a big hit with 'When Mexican Joe Met Jole Blon' - a parody of two hit songs. In 1958, his novelty number, 'Purple People Eater', became a million-seller and even reached number 12 in the UK pop charts. He based the song on a schoolboy joke that he had heard from Don Robertson's son and initially, MGM did not consider it to be worth releasing. Further US pop successes included 'Sweet Chile'. He first appeared in the US country charts in 1962, when another novelty number, 'That's My Pa', became a number 1. It was intended that Wooley should record 'Don't Go Near The Indians' but due to film commitments Rex Allen's version was released before he could record it. Wooley jokingly told MGM that he would write a sequel and came up with the comedy parody 'Don't Go Near The Eskimos'. He developed an alter-ego drunken character, whom he called Ben Colder, and in this guise, he recorded and charted it and other humorous parodies of pop/country hits, including 'Almost Persuaded No. 2', 'Harper Valley PTA (Later That Same Day)' and 'Fifteen Beers (Years) Ago'. (The name Ben Colder was the selection made by MGM from the three alternatives that Wooley offered. The other two were Ben Freezin and Klon Dyke.) He had some further minor hits with serious recordings, including 'Blue Guitar' and 'Tie A Tiger Down'. In 1969, he joined the CBS network *Hee Haw* country show, remaining with it for several years, and also wrote the theme music.

Throughout the 60s and 70s, he maintained a busy touring schedule, appearing all over the USA and overseas. In 1968, Ben Colder was voted Comedian of the Year by the Country Music Association. He cut back his work during the 80s and although he has remained a popular entertainer, he has had no chart entries since 1971. Over the years, the parodies by the drunken Ben Colder have proved more popular than his serious recordings and have certainly accounted for the majority of his record sales.
● ALBUMS: as Sheb Wooley *Sheb Wooley* (MGM 1956)★★★, *Songs From The Days Of Rawhide* (MGM 1961)★★★, *That's My Pa & That's My Ma* (MGM 1962)★★★★, *Tales Of How The West Was Won* (MGM 1963)★★★★, *It's A Big Land* (MGM 1965)★★★, *Warm & Wooley* (MGM 1969)★★★. As Ben Colder *Spoofing The Big Ones* (MGM 1962)★★★, *Ben Colder* (MGM 1963)★★★, *Big Ben Strikes Again* (MGM 1966)★★★★, *Wine Women & Song* (MGM 1967)★★★, *Harper Valley PTA & Other Parodies Of Top Ten Hits* (MGM 1968)★★★, *Have One On Ben Colder* (1969)★★, *Big Ben Colder Wild Again* (1970)★★★, *Ben Colder* (1970)★★★, *Live & Loaded At Sam Houston Coliseum* (1971)★★★, *Wacky World Of Ben Colder* (1973)★★★.
● COMPILATIONS: as Sheb Wooley *The Very Best Of Sheb Wooley* (MGM 1965)★★★★, *Country Boogie Wild And Wooley (1948-55)* (1984)★★★, *Blue Guitar* (Bear Family 1985)★★★. As Ben Colder *The Best Of Ben Colder* (MGM 1968)★★★, *Golden Hits* (Gusto 1979)★★★.

WRAY, LINK

b. 1930, Fort Bragg, North Carolina, USA. Guitarist Wray formed his first group in 1942, but his musical ambitions were thwarted by his induction into the US Army. He subsequently formed the Wraymen with Shorty Horton (bass) and Doug Wray (drums), and enjoyed a million-seller in 1958 with 'Rumble', a pioneering instrumental on which the artist's frenzied style and distorted tone invoked a gang-fight. The single incurred bans both on technical grounds and on account of its subject matter, but is now recognized as one of pop's most innovative releases, and includes the Who's Pete Townshend as a vociferous proponent. Wray achieved another gold disc for 'Rawhide' (1959), but ensuing releases, including 'Jack The Ripper' (1960), 'The Sweeper' (1963) and 'Batman Theme' (1965), failed to match this success.

He continued to record, using a home-made three-track studio built in a converted chicken shack, and a 1971 album, *Link Wray*, was the subject of critical acclaim. It drew heavily on the artist's country roots - he is part-Shawnee Indian - yet was still imbued with the primitive atmosphere of his early work. Renewed interest in Wray resulted in several archive releases, while contemporary recordings, although of interest, failed to match the promise of his initial 'rediscovery' collection. In the late 70s the guitarist forged a fruitful partnership with new-wave rockabilly singer Robert Gordon, before resurrecting a solo career the following decade. Wray's primeval sound is echoed in the work of the Cramps and many other more contemporary groups. He is particularly respected in the UK where his influence on 'trash' guitar groups, notably the Stingrays and Milkshakes, has been considerable. In 1997 he made a new album with UK's Ace Records, having been previously associated with their Chiswick label. 'Rumble On The Docks' is vintage Link Wray and worth the price of the CD alone.
● ALBUMS: *Link Wray And The Raymen* (Epic 1959)★★★★, *Jack The Ripper* (Swan 1963)★★★, *Great Guitar Hits* (Vermillion 1963)★★★, *Link Wray Sings And Plays Guitar* (Vermillion 1964)★★★, *Yesterday And Today* (Record Factory 1969)★★★, *Link Wray* (Polydor 1971)★★★, *Be What You Want To Be* (Polydor 1973)★★★, *The Link Wray Rumble* (Polydor 1974)★★★, *Interstate 10* (Virgin 1975)★★★, *Stuck In Gear* (Virgin 1976)★★★, with Robert Gordon *Robert Gordon With Link Wray* (Private Stock 1977)★★★, with Gordon *Fresh Fish Special* (Private Stock 1978)★★★, *Bullshot* (Charisma 1979)★★★, *Live At The Paradiso* (Magnum Force 1980)★★★, *Live In '85* (Big Beat

1986)★★★, *Indian Child* (Creation 1993)★★★, *Shadowman* (Ace 1997)★★★.

● COMPILATIONS: *There's Good Rockin' Tonight* (Union Pacific 1971)★★★, *Beans And Fatback* (Virgin 1973)★★★, *Rockin' And Handclappin'* (Epic 1973)★★★, *Rock 'N' Roll Rumble* (Charly 1974)★★★★, *Early Recordings* reissue of *Jack The Ripper* (Chiswick 1978)★★★★, *Link Wray: Good Rocking' Tonight* (Chiswick 1983)★★★★, *Link Wray And The Wraymen* (Edsel 1985)★★★★, *Growlin' Guitar* (Ace 1987)★★★, *Mr. Guitar* (Norton 1995)★★★.

● VIDEOS: *Link Wray: The Rumble Man* (Visionary 1996).

WRIGHT, CAROL SUE

b. 1945, Nashville, Tennessee, USA. The youngest of the three children of Kitty Wells and Johnnie Wright, she began to sing with her parents from an early age. In December 1955, standing on a chair to reach the microphone, Wright duetted with her mother when she recorded their well-known version of 'How Far Is Heaven?'. In the late 50s, she sang with her sister, Ruby Wright, as the Wright Sisters, recording under the production of Chet Atkins for the Cadence label, who saw them as the female version of the label's popular Everly Brothers. She toured for a time with the family show but eventually, with no desire to pursue a singing career, she restricted her appearances and devoted her time to raising her own family. In the 80s, she and sister Ruby ran the family Museum and Tourist attraction in Nashville.

YANA

b. Pamela Guard, 16 February 1932, Romford, Essex, England, d. 21 November 1989, London, England. A popular singer in the UK during the 50s and 60s, Yana became a model while still in her teens, before being 'discovered' when singing at a private party at London's Astor club. This led to engagements at several top nightspots, and a contract with Columbia Records. In the 50s her single releases included sultry renderings of 'Small Talk', 'Something Happened To My Heart', 'Climb Up The Wall', 'If You Don't Love Me', 'I Miss You, Mama', 'I Need You Now' and 'Mr Wonderful'. Her glamorous image made her a natural for television, and she was given her own BBC series in 1956. Later, following the advent of ITV, she appeared regularly on *Sunday Night At The London Palladium*. In 1958, Yana starred in Richard Rodgers and Oscar Hammerstein II's *Cinderella* at

the London Coliseum: her solo numbers in the show and on the Original Cast album were 'In My Own Little Corner' and 'A Lovely Night', and she duetted with Tommy Steele ('When You're Driving Through The Moonlight'), Betty Marsden ('Impossible') and Bruce Trent ('Do I Love You?' and 'Ten Minutes Ago'). Two years later she was back in the West End with Norman Wisdom in the London Palladium's longest-running pantomime, *Turn Again Whittington*. She was something of a pantomime 'specialist', and throughout the 60s and into the 70s, was one of Britain's leading principal boys. It is probably not a coincidence that the second of her three marriages was to the actor Alan Curtis, who is renowned for his performances of the 'Demon King' and other 'nasty' pantomime characters, although he is probably better known in the 90s for his PA work at important cricket matches. In her heyday Yana toured abroad, including the Middle East, and she appeared on several US variety shows hosted by Bob Hope and Ed Sullivan. She also played small roles in the British films *Zarak*, with Victor Mature and Michael Wilding, and *Cockleshell Heroes*, an early Anthony Newley feature. Her last performance is said to have been as the 'Good Fairy' in *The Wizard Of Oz* at an English provincial theatre in 1983. She died of throat cancer six years later.

YOUNG AT HEART

Adapted by Julius J. Epstein and Lenore Coffee from Fannie Hurst's novel *Sister Act*, and the 1938 Claude Rains-John Garfield movie *The Four Daughters*, this 1954 Warner Brothers release provided a glimpse of the American suburban family viewed through the proverbial rose-coloured spectacles. The story concerns three sisters (one was dropped from the original), played by Doris Day, Dorothy Malone and Elizabeth Fraser, who live with their music teacher father (Robert Keith) and crusty aunt (Ethel Barrymore). Day is engaged to budding songwriter Gig Young, but one day, old chip-on-the-shoulder Frank Sinatra turns up on the doorstep and ruins the whole arrangement. Day marries Sinatra, but his career prospects remain at zero (the people 'upstairs' never give him a break), and one dark, snowy night he attempts to 'take the easy way out'. His will to live is rekindled when his wife tells him they are about to become a threesome. Perhaps because of the film's sentimental character, the Sinatra-Day combination failed to work as well as might have been expected, although, individually, they had some satisfying moments. At the time, both were probably at the peak of their vocal powers, and a collection of engaging songs gave them ample chance to shine - Day with such as 'Hold Me In Your Arms' (Ray Heindorf-Charles Henderson-Don Pippin) and the more upbeat 'Ready, Willing And Able' (Floyd Huddleston-Al Rinker-Dick Gleason), and Sinatra on 'Someone To Watch Over Me' (George and Ira Gershwin), 'Just One Of Those Things' (Cole Porter) and 'One For My Baby' (Harold Arlen-Johnny Mercer). Sinatra sings a number of these while working in a local 'joint' for what he calls 'tips on a plate'. Other numbers included 'You, My Love' (Mack Gordon-Jimmy Van Heusen), 'There's A Rising Moon (For Every Falling Star)' (Paul Francis Webster-Sammy Fain) and 'Young At Heart' (Carolyn Leigh-Johnny Richards). Photographed in Warnercolor and directed by Gordon Douglas, this was the kind of film that - at the time - made audiences feel warm all over.

YOUNG, FARON

b. 25 February 1932, Shreveport, Louisiana, USA, d. 10 December 1996, Nashville, Tennessee, USA. Young was raised on the farm his father bought just outside Shreveport and learned to play the guitar and sing country songs as a boy. Greatly influenced by Hank Williams (in his early days he was something of a soundalike) and while still at school, he formed a country band and began to establish a local reputation as an entertainer. In 1950, he gave up his college studies to accept an offer of a professional career and joined radio station KWKH, where he soon became a member of the prestigious *Louisiana Hayride* show and found other work in the nightclubs and honky tonks. He became friends with Webb Pierce and for a time toured with him as a vocalist with Pierce's band. In 1951, he made his first recordings for the Gotham label with Tillman Franks and his band, and achieved minor success with 'Have I Waited Too Long' and 'Tattle Tale Eyes' before he joined Capitol Records. In the summer of 1952, Faron was dating a girl called Billie Jean Jones, when she attracted the attention of Hank Williams. He persuaded Faron to arrange a double date, which resulted in Williams threatening him with a pistol and claiming Jones for himself. Young backed off and Billie Jean became the second Mrs. Hank Williams. In 1953, Young formed his own band, moved to Nashville, where he became a member of the *Grand Ole Opry* and gained his first US country chart hit with a self-penned song called 'Goin' Steady'. His career was interrupted when, because of the Korean War, he was drafted into the army. Although interrupted by this, his career certainly benefited from the exposure he received after winning an army talent competition. This led to him touring the world entertaining US forces, as well as appearing on recruiting shows that were networked to hundreds of radio stations. Young returned to Nashville in November 1954 and resumed his career, gaining his first US country number 1 the following year with 'Live Fast, Love Hard, Die Young'. This established him beyond any doubt as a major recording star, and between 1955 and 1969 he amassed a total of 63 US country chart hits, of which 46 made the Top 20. He developed the knack of picking the best material by other writers and had a number 2 hit with Don Gibson's 'Sweet Dreams' and further number 1s with Roy Drusky's songs 'Alone With You' and 'Country Girl'. In 1961, he recorded 'Hello Walls', thereby making the song one of the first Willie Nelson compositions to be recorded by a major artist. It reached number 1 in the US country charts, also became a Top 20 US pop hit and was Young's first million-seller.

In 1956, his popularity as a singer earned him a role in the film *Hidden Guns*. This led to his own nickname of The Young Sheriff and his band being called the Country Deputies (at one time Roger Miller was a member of the band). In later years he became the Singing Sheriff before, as he once suggested, someone queried his age and started asking 'What's he trying to prove?' After the initial success with this easily forgettable B-movie western, he made further film appearances over the years including *Daniel Boone, Stampede, Raiders Of Old California, Country Music Holiday, A Gun And A Gavel, Road To Nashville* and *That's Country*. He left Capitol for Mercury in 1962, immediately charting with 'The Yellow Bandanna', 'You'll Drive Me Back' and a fine duet recording with Margie Singleton of 'Keeping Up With

The Joneses'. In 1965, he had a US country Top 10 hit with 'Walk Tall', a song that had been a UK pop hit for Val Doonican the previous year. Young quit the *Opry* in the mid-60s, finding, like several other artists, that it was not only difficult keeping up with the expected number of Saturday night appearances but also that he lost many other lucrative bookings. After the success of 'Hello Walls', he perhaps unintentionally tended to look for further pop chart hits, and in consequence, his recordings, at times, became less countrified in their arrangements. He soon returned to his country roots, usually choosing his favourite twin fiddle backings. Young easily maintained his popularity throughout the 60s and 70s and toured extensively in the USA and made several visits to Europe, where he performed in the UK, France and Germany. He appeared on all the major network television shows but seemed to have little interest in having his own regular series. At times he has not endeared himself to some of his fellow performers with his imitations of their acts. In the 70s he was still a major star, with a series of Top 10 US country hits including 'Step Aside', 'Leavin' And Saying Goodbye', 'This Little Girl Of Mine' and 'Just What I Had In Mind'. 'It's Four In The Morning', another country number 1, had crossover success and also gave him a second million-seller. It also became his only UK pop chart success, peaking at number 3 during a 23-week chart run. He left Mercury Records in 1979 and briefly joined MCA. In 1988, he joined Step One Records and 'Stop And Take The Time', a minor hit, became country chart entry number 85. Over the years, he became involved in several business interests and, with the exception of heavy losses in the 60s (in respect of investments to convert an old baseball stadium into a stock-car racing track in Nashville), he was very successful. Young became involved in publishing companies, a recording studio, and a booking agency, plus co-ownership of *Music City News* newspaper. He was always noted for very plain speaking and has incurred the wrath of the establishment on several occasions for his outspoken views. A suggested association with Patsy Cline led to various stories of his dalliances and whether correct or not, it may well be that he revelled in the publicity they caused. In September 1972, he gained unwanted publicity by his reaction to an incident at a show. At a time when 'This Little Girl Of Mine' was a hit for him, he invited six-year-old Nora Jo Catlett to join him on stage in Clarksville, West Virginia. She refused, whereupon Young swore at the audience, stormed off stage, grabbed the child and spanked her repeatedly (the child collected autographs and had been told by her mother not to approach the stage but to wait near the front until Young finished his act). The child's father swore out a warrant for his arrest and after pleading guilty to a charge of assault, he was fined $35. The following year a civil action claiming $200,000 was filed. In his defence, Young claimed the child spat in his face. Eventually, almost two years later, the Catlett family were awarded only $3400. He has been involved in various actions, once stating, 'I am not an alcoholic, I'm a drunk', and on one occasion, he shot out the light fittings of a Nashville bar. He is reputed to have had affairs with many women while supposedly remaining happily married. In 1987, after 34 years of marriage, his wife finally obtained a divorce on the grounds of physical abuse. She claimed that he had threatened her and their 16-year-old daughter with a gun and often shot holes in the kitchen ceiling. A fair and concise summary was offered in 1980 by Bob Allen, who parodied Young's hit song in his article entitled 'Live Fast, Love Hard And Keep On Cussin'. Faron Young is one of country music's greatest legends, while remaining relatively unknown to many. Paddy MacAloon of Prefab Sprout paid tribute to him when he wrote the beautiful 'Faron Young' on the group's *Steve McQueen* album. Until his death in 1996 he was semi-retired but still made concert performances as well as guest appearances on the *Opry*.

● ALBUMS: *Sweethearts Or Strangers* (Capitol 1957)★★★, *The Object Of My Affection* (Capitol 1958)★★★, *My Garden Of Prayer* (Capitol 1959)★★, *This Is Faron Young* (Capitol 1959)★★★★, *Talk About Hits* (Capitol 1959)★★★, *Sings The Best Of Faron Young* (Capitol 1960)★★★, *Hello Walls* (Capitol 1961)★★★, *The Young Approach* (Capitol 1961)★★★, *This Is Faron* (Mercury 1963)★★★★, *Faron Young Aims At The West* (Mercury 1963)★★★, *Country Dance Favorites* (Mercury 1964)★★★★, *Story Songs For Country Folks* (Mercury 1964)★★★★, *Story Songs Of Mountains And Valleys* (Mercury 1964)★★★★, *Memory Lane* (Capitol 1965)★★★, *Falling In Love* (Capitol 1965)★★★, *Pen And Paper* (Mercury 1965)★★★, *Faron Young* (Hilltop 1966)★★★, *Faron Young Sings The Best Of Jim Reeves* (Mercury 1966)★★★, *If You Ain' t Lovin', You Ain't Livin'* (Capitol 1966)★★★, *It's A Great Life* (Tower 1966)★★★, *Unmitigated Gall* (Mercury 1967)★★★, *Here's Faron Young* (Mercury 1968)★★★, *I'll Be Yours* (Hilltop 1968)★★★, *This Is Faron Young* (Merc   ury 1968)★★★, *Just Out Of Reach* (Mercury 1968)★★★, *The World Of Faron Young* (Mercury 1968)★★★★, *I've Got Precious Memories* (Mercury 1969)★★★, *Wine Me Up* (Mercury 1969)★★★★, *20 Hits Over The Years* (Mercury 1969)★★★★, *Occasional Wife/If I Ever Fall In Love With A Honky Tonk Girl* (Mercury 1970)★★★, *Leavin' And Sayin' Goodbye* (Mercury 1971)★★★, *Step Aside* (Mercury 1971)★★★, *It's Four In The Morning* (Mercury 1972)★★★, *This Little Girl Of Mine* (Mercury 1972)★★★, *This Time The Hurtin's On Me* (Mercury 1973)★★★, *Just What I Had In Mind* (Mercury 1973)★★★, *Some Kind Of Woman* (Mercury 1974)★★★, *A Man And His Music* (Mercury 1975)★★★★, *I'd Just Be Fool Enough* (Mercury 1976)★★★, *That Young Feelin'* (Mercury 1977)★★★, *Chapter Two* (1979)★★★, *Free And Easy* (MCA 1980)★★★, *The Young Sheriff (1955-1956 Radio Broadcasts)* (1981)★★★★, *The Sheriff* (Allegiance 1984)★★, with Jerry Lee Lewis, Webb Pierce, Mel Tillis *Four Legends* (1985)★★★, *Here's To You* (Step One 1988)★★★, *Country Christmas* (1990)★★, with Ray Price *Memories That Last* (1992)★★★.

● COMPILATIONS: *All-Time Great Hits* (Capitol 1963)★★★★, *Capitol Country Classics* (Capitol 1980)★★★, *Greatest Hits Volumes 1, 2 & 3* (1988)★★★★, *All Time Greatest Hits* (Curb 1990)★★★, *The Capitol Years 1952 - 1962 5-CD box set* (Bear Family 1992)★★★★, *Live Fast, Love Hard: Original Capitol Recordings, 1952-1962* (CMF 1995)★★★★, *All American Country* (Spectrum 1997)★★★★.

YOUNG, JIMMY

b. Leslie Ronald Young, 21 September 1923, Cinderford, Gloucestershire, England. A popular ballad singer in the UK during the 50s, Young carved out a new career for himself in

broadcasting when rock 'n' roll took over in the latter part of the decade. The son of a miner, he was an excellent boxer and rugby player, but turned down an offer of a professional career with top rugby league club Wigan. Always keen on music, he was taught to play the piano by his mother, and received professional voice training. He worked as a baker and an electrician before joining the Royal Air Force in 1939. After demobilization he intended to train as a teacher, but was spotted, singing at a sports club, by BBC producer George Innes. He made his first broadcast two weeks later, and subsequently toured the UK variety circuit. From 1951 he had several successful records on the small Polygon label, including 'My Love And Devotion', 'Because Of You' and 'Too Young'. In January 1953, two months after the first UK singles chart appeared in the *New Musical Express*, Young had a hit with 'Faith Can Move Mountains' for his new label, Decca, and followed that with 'Eternally (Terry's Theme)', from the Charles Chaplin film *Limelight*. In 1955, Young became the first UK artist to top the *NME* chart with successive releases. The first, 'Unchained Melody', made the top spot in spite of intense competition from Al Hibbler, Les Baxter and Liberace. The second, the title song from the movie *The Man From Laramie*, and another 1955 hit, 'Someone On My Mind', clinched Young's position as the UK's second biggest-selling artist of the year - after Ruby Murray. Following further 50s hits, including 'Chain Gang', 'The Wayward Wind', 'Rich Man Poor Man', 'More' and 'Round And Round', Young switched to EMI's Columbia label in the early 60s, and had some success with a recording of Charles and Henry Tobias's 1929 song 'Miss You', and a re-recording of 'Unchained Melody'. In 1960, he introduced BBC Radio's popular record request programme, *Housewives' Choice*, for two weeks. It was the start of a new career that has lasted more than 30 years, initially as a conventional disc jockey and compere, and then, from 1967, as host of his own daily BBC morning radio show. This mixes records with consumer information, discussions on current affairs, and talks with figures in the public eye. He has interviewed every Chancellor and Prime Minister since 1963. For his radio work on the programme, he was awarded the OBE, and later, the CBE. In 1992, for *The Jimmy Young Story*, a silver anniversary celebration of his radio show, Young was interviewed by another distinguished broadcaster, David Frost.

● ALBUMS: *T.T.T.J.Y.S.* (Polydor 1974)★★★, *Too Young* (PRT 1981)★★★, *The Ballymena Cowboy* (1987)★★★.

● COMPILATIONS: *The World Of Jimmy Young* (Decca 1969)★★★★, *This Is Jimmy Young* (EMI 1980)★★★, *What A Wonderful World* (Flashback 1985)★★★.

● FURTHER READING: *J.Y.: The Autobiography Of Jimmy Young*, Jimmy.Young.

YOUNG, VICTOR

b. 8 August 1900, Chicago, Illinois, USA, d. 11 November 1956, Palm Springs, California, USA. A violinist, conductor, bandleader, arranger and composer, Young is said to have been responsible for over 300 film scores and themes. He studied at the Warsaw Conservatory in 1910 before joining the Warsaw Philharmonic as a violinist, and touring Europe. He returned to the USA at the outbreak of World War I, and later, in the early 20s, toured as a concert violinist, and then became a concert master in theatre orchestras. On 'defecting' to popular music, he served for a while as vio-

linist-arranger with the popular pianist-bandleader Ted Fio Rito. During the 30s, Young worked a great deal on radio, conducting for many artists including Al Jolson, Don Ameche and Smith Ballew. He also started recording with his own orchestra, and had a string of hits from 1931-54, including 'Gems From "The Band Wagon"', 'The Last Round-Up', 'Who's Afraid Of The Big Bad Wolf', 'The Old Spinning Wheel', 'This Little Piggie Went To Market' (featuring Jimmy Dorsey, Bunny Berigan and Joe Venuti), 'Flirtation Walk', 'Ev'ry Day', 'Way Back Home', 'About A Quarter To Nine' and 'She's A Latin From Manhattan' (both from the Jolson movie *Go Into Your Dance*), 'It's A Sin To Tell A Lie', 'Mona Lisa', 'The Third Man Theme', 'Ruby', 'Limelight Theme', and 'The High And The Mighty'. He also provided the orchestral accompaniments for other artists, such as Dick Powell, Eddie Cantor, Deanna Durbin, Helen Forrest, Frances Langford, trumpet virtuoso Rafael Mendez, Cliff Edwards, the Boswell Sisters, and western movies singer Rex Allen. Most notably, it was Young's orchestra that backed Judy Garland on her record of 'Over The Rainbow', the Oscar-winning song from the legendary 1939 film *The Wizard Of Oz*. He also backed Bing Crosby on two of his million-sellers: 'Too-Ra-Loo-Ra-Loo-Ral (That's An Irish Lullaby)', from *Going My Way* (the 'Best Picture' of 1944), and British doctor Arthur Colahan's somewhat unconventional song, 'Galway Bay' (1948). Young's extremely successful and prolific career as a film composer, musical director, conductor, and arranger, began in the early 30s with Paramount. Some of his best-known film works included *Wells Fargo* (1937), *Swing High, Swing Low* (1937), *Breaking The Ice* (1938), *Golden Boy* (1939), *Man Of Conquest* (1939), *Arizona* (1940), *I Wanted Wings* (1941), *Hold Back The Dawn* (1941), *Flying Tigers* (1942), *Silver Queen* (1942), *The Glass Key* (1942), *Take A Letter, Darling* (1942), *For Whom The Bell Tolls* (1943), *The Uninvited* (1944), *Samson And Delilah* (1949), *Rio Grande* (1950), *Scaramouche* (1952), *The Greatest Show On Earth* (1952), *Shane* (1953) and *Three Coins In The Fountain* (1954). In 1956, Young was awarded a posthumous Academy Award for his score for Mike Todd's spectacular film *Around The World In Eighty Days*. His record of the title song made the US charts in 1957, and had a vocal version by Bing Crosby on the b-side. He also wrote some television themes, including 'Blue Star' for the US *Medic* series, and contributed music to two minor Broadway shows, *Pardon Our French* (1950) and *Seventh Heaven* (1955). Young's popular songs were written mostly with lyricist Ned Washington. These included 'Can't We Talk It Over?', 'A Hundred Years From Today' (from the revue *Blackbirds Of 1933/34*), and three beautiful and enduring ballads: 'A Ghost Of A Chance' (co-writer, Bing Crosby), 'Stella By Starlight' and 'My Foolish Heart' (film title song). Young's other lyricists included Will J. Harris ('Sweet Sue'), Wayne King, Haven Gillespie, and Egbert Van Alstyne ('Beautiful Love'), Sam M. Lewis ('Street Of Dreams'), Edward Heyman ('When I Fall In Love' and 'Love Letters') and Sammy Cahn (the film title song, 'Written On The Wind'). Young also wrote 'Golden Earrings' with the songwriting team of Jay Livingston and Ray Evans.
● ALBUMS: *April In Paris* (c.50s)★★★, *Cinema Rhapsodies* (c.50s)★★★, *Gypsy Magic* (c.50s)★★, *Imagination* (c.50s)★★★, *Night Music* (c.50s)★★★, *Pearls On Velvet* (c.50s)★★, *Themes From 'For Whom The Bell Tolls' And 'Golden Earrings'* (c.50s)★★★, *Valentino Tangos* (c.50s)★★, *Hollywood Rhapsodies* (c.50s)★★★, *Around The World In 80 Days* film soundtrack (1957)★★★★, *Forever Young* (1959)★★★, *Love Themes From Hollywood* (1959)★★★, *Wizard Of Oz/Pinocchio* (Ace Of Hearts/Decca 1966)★★, *The Quiet Man/Samson And Delilah* film soundtracks (Varese International 1979)★★★.

YUKL, JOE

b. Joseph Yukl, 5 March 1909, New York, USA, d. March 1981. After first playing violin he switched to trombone and played in college dance bands. In New York in the 20s he joined the staff of CBS Records but also appeared from time to time on record with jazzmen such as Red Nichols and Tommy and Jimmy Dorsey. In the 30s he was with Joe Haymes and Jimmy Dorsey, also playing dates and sometimes recording with a wide range of popular and jazz artists, including Bing Crosby, Louis Armstrong, Frankie Trumbauer and Ted Fio Rito. By this time he had relocated to the west coast where he again worked in studios. He continued these activities into the 40s and 50s, playing jazz dates with Wingy Manone and others. He also played on soundtracks or appeared in at least two motion pictures: *Rhythm Inn* (1951), which also featured Manone, Pete Daily and Barrett Deems, and *The Glenn Miller Story* (1953). In the latter film, together with Murray McEachern, he both coached and ghosted for James Stewart in his role as Miller. Yukl played with skill and a pleasing sound.

INDEX

AMERICAN POETRY:
THE NINETEENTH CENTURY

VOLUME TWO

AMERICAN POETRY:
THE NINETEENTH CENTURY

VOLUME TWO
Herman Melville to Trumbull Stickney
American Indian Poetry
Folk Songs and Spirituals

THE LIBRARY OF AMERICA

The paper used in this publication meets the
minimum requirements of the American National Standard for
Information Sciences—Permanence of Paper for Printed
Library Materials, ANSI Z39.48—1984.

Distributed to the trade in the United States
by Penguin Books USA Inc
and in Canada by Penguin Books Canada Ltd.

Library of Congress Catalog Number: 93–10702
For cataloging information, see end of Index.
ISBN 0–940450–78–X

Second Printing
.   The Library of America—67

Manufactured in the United States of America

JOHN HOLLANDER
SELECTED THE CONTENTS AND WROTE
THE NOTES FOR THIS VOLUME

This volume has been published with grants from the National Endowment for the Humanities and the Lila Wallace-Reader's Digest Fund.

Contents

HERMAN MELVILLE

(1819–1891)

Song from *Mardi*

Like the fish of the bright and twittering fin,
   Bright fish! diving deep as high soars the lark,
So, far, far, far, doth the maiden swim,
   Wild song, wild light, in still ocean's dark.

"The ribs and terrors in the whale"

The ribs and terrors in the whale,
   Arched over me a dismal gloom,
While all God's sun-lit waves rolled by,
   And left me deepening down to doom.

I saw the opening maw of hell,
   With endless pains and sorrows there;
Which none but they that feel can tell—
   Oh, I was plunging to despair.

In black distress, I called my God,
   When I could scarce believe him mine,
He bowed his ear to my complaints—
   No more the whale did me confine.

With speed he flew to my relief,
   As on a radiant dolphin borne;
Awful, yet bright, as lightning shone
   The face of my Deliverer God.

My song for ever shall record
   That terrible, that joyful hour;
I give the glory to my God,
   His all the mercy and the power.

The Portent

(*1859*)

Hanging from the beam,
  Slowly swaying (such the law),
Gaunt the shadow on your green,
  Shenandoah!
The cut is on the crown
(Lo, John Brown),
And the stabs shall heal no more.

Hidden in the cap
  Is the anguish none can draw;
So your future veils its face,
  Shenandoah!
But the streaming beard is shown
(Weird John Brown),
The meteor of the war.

Misgivings

(*1860*)

When ocean-clouds over inland hills
  Sweep storming in late autumn brown,
And horror the sodden valley fills,
  And the spire falls crashing in the town,
I muse upon my country's ills—
The tempest bursting from the waste of Time
On the world's fairest hope linked with man's foulest crime.

Nature's dark side is heeded now—
  (Ah! optimist-cheer disheartened flown)—
A child may read the moody brow
  Of yon black mountain lone.
With shouts the torrents down the gorges go,
  And storms are formed behind the storm we feel:
The hemlock shakes in the rafter, the oak in the driving keel.

The Conflict of Convictions

(1860 – 1)

On starry heights
   A bugle wails the long recall;
Derision stirs the deep abyss,
   Heaven's ominous silence over all.
Return, return, O eager Hope,
   And face man's latter fall.
Events, they make the dreamers quail;
Satan's old age is strong and hale,
A disciplined captain, gray in skill,
And Raphael a white enthusiast still;
Dashed aims, whereat Christ's martyrs pale,
Shall Mammon's slaves fulfill?

> *(Dismantle the fort,*
> *Cut down the fleet —*
> *Battle no more shall be!*
> *While the fields for fight in æons to come*
> *Congeal beneath the sea.)*

The terrors of truth and dart of death
   To faith alike are vain;
Though comets, gone a thousand years,
      Return again,
Patient she stands—she can no more—
And waits, nor heeds she waxes hoar.

> *(At a stony gate,*
> *A statue of stone,*
> *Weed overgrown —*
> *Long 'twill wait!)*

But God his former mind retains,
   Confirms his old decree;
The generations are inured to pains,

And strong Necessity
Surges, and heaps Time's strand with wrecks.
   The People spread like a weedy grass,
   The thing they will they bring to pass,
And prosper to the apoplex.
The rout it herds around the heart,
   The ghost is yielded in the gloom;
Kings wag their heads—Now save thyself
   Who wouldst rebuild the world in bloom.

> *(Tide-mark*
> *And top of the ages' strife,*
> *Verge where they called the world to come,*
> *The last advance of life —*
> *Ha ha, the rust on the Iron Dome!)*

Nay, but revere the hid event;
   In the cloud a sword is girded on,
I mark a twinkling in the tent
   Of Michael the warrior one.
Senior wisdom suits not now,
The light is on the youthful brow.

> *(Ay, in caves the miner see:*
> *His forehead bears a taper dim;*
> *Darkness so he feebly braves*
> *Which foldeth him!)*

But He who rules is old—is old:
Ah! faith is warm, but heaven with age is cold.

> *(Ho ho, ho ho,*
> *The cloistered doubt*
> *Of olden times*
> *Is blurted out!)*

The Ancient of Days forever is young,
    Forever the scheme of Nature thrives;
I know a wind in purpose strong—
    It spins *against* the way it drives.
What if the gulfs their slimed foundations bare?
So deep must the stones be hurled
Whereon the throes of ages rear
The final empire and the happier world.

> (*The poor old Past,*
> *The Future's slave,*
> *She drudged through pain and crime*
> *To bring about the blissful Prime,*
> *Then—perished.* There's *a grave!*)

    Power unanointed may come—
Dominion (unsought by the free)
    And the Iron Dome,
Stronger for stress and strain,
Fling her huge shadow athwart the main;
But the Founders' dream shall flee.
Age after age shall be
As age after age has been,
(From man's changeless heart their way they win);
And death be busy with all who strive—
Death, with silent negative.

> YEA AND NAY—
> EACH HATH HIS SAY;
> BUT GOD HE KEEPS THE MIDDLE WAY.
> NONE WAS BY
> WHEN HE SPREAD THE SKY;
> WISDOM IS VAIN, AND PROPHESY.

The Temeraire

*(Supposed to have been suggested to an Englishman of the old order
by the fight of the Monitor and Merrimac)*

The gloomy hulls, in armor grim,
　Like clouds o'er moors have met,
And prove that oak, and iron, and man
　Are tough in fibre yet.

But Splendors wane. The sea-fight yields
　No front of old display;
The garniture, emblazonment,
　And heraldry all decay.

Towering afar in parting light,
　The fleets like Albion's forelands shine—
The full-sailed fleets, the shrouded show
　Of Ships-of-the-Line.

　　　　The fighting Temeraire,
　　　　　Built of a thousand trees,
　　　　Lunging out her lightnings,
　　　　　And beetling o'er the seas—
　　　　O Ship, how brave and fair,
　　　　　That fought so oft and well,
　　　　On open decks you manned the gun
　　　　　　　Armorial.
　　　　What cheerings did you share,
　　　　　Impulsive in the van,
　　　　When down upon leagued France and Spain
　　　　　We English ran—
　　　　The freshet at your bowsprit
　　　　　Like the foam upon the can.
　　　　Bickering, your colors
　　　　　Licked up the Spanish air,
　　　　You flapped with flames of battle-flags—
　　　　　Your challenge, Temeraire!

The rear ones of our fleet
  They yearned to share your place,
Still vying with the Victory
  Throughout that earnest race—
The Victory, whose Admiral,
  With orders nobly won,
Shone in the globe of the battle glow—
  The angel in that sun.
Parallel in story,
  Lo, the stately pair,
As late in grapple ranging,
  The foe between them there—
When four great hulls lay tiered,
And the fiery tempest cleared,
And your prizes twain appeared,
        Temeraire!

But Trafalgar' is over now,
  The quarter-deck undone;
The carved and castled navies fire
  Their evening-gun.
O, Titan Temeraire,
  Your stern-lights fade away;
Your bulwarks to the years must yield,
  And heart-of-oak decay.
A pigmy steam-tug tows you,
  Gigantic, to the shore—
Dismantled of your guns and spars,
  And sweeping wings of war.
The rivets clinch the iron-clads,
  Men learn a deadlier lore;
But Fame has nailed your battle-flags—
  Your ghost it sails before:
O, the navies old and oaken,
  O, the Temeraire no more!

A Utilitarian View of the Monitor's Fight

Plain be the phrase, yet apt the verse,
    More ponderous than nimble;
For since grimed War here laid aside
His Orient pomp, 'twould ill befit
        Overmuch to ply
    The rhyme's barbaric cymbal.

Hail to victory without the gaud
    Of glory; zeal that needs no fans
Of banners; plain mechanic power
Plied cogently in War now placed—
        Where War belongs—
    Among the trades and artisans.

Yet this was battle, and intense—
    Beyond the strife of fleets heroic;
Deadlier, closer, calm 'mid storm;
No passion; all went on by crank,
        Pivot, and screw,
    And calculations of caloric.

Needless to dwell; the story's known.
    The ringing of those plates on plates
Still ringeth round the world—
The clangor of that blacksmiths' fray.
        The anvil-din
    Resounds this message from the Fates:

War yet shall be, and to the end;
    But war-paint shows the streaks of weather;
War yet shall be, but warriors
Are now but operatives; War's made
        Less grand than Peace,
    And a singe runs through lace and feather.

Shiloh

A Requiem

(APRIL, 1862)

Skimming lightly, wheeling still,
    The swallows fly low
Over the field in clouded days,
    The forest-field of Shiloh—
Over the field where April rain
Solaced the parched ones stretched in pain
Through the pause of night
That followed the Sunday fight
    Around the church of Shiloh—
The church so lone, the log-built one,
That echoed to many a parting groan
        And natural prayer
    Of dying foemen mingled there—
Foemen at morn, but friends at eve—
    Fame or country least their care:
(What like a bullet can undeceive!)
    But now they lie low,
While over them the swallows skim,
    And all is hushed at Shiloh.

Malvern Hill

(JULY, 1862)

Ye elms that wave on Malvern Hill
    In prime of morn and May,
Recall ye how McClellan's men
        Here stood at bay?
While deep within yon forest dim
    Our rigid comrades lay—
Some with the cartridge in their mouth,
Others with fixed arms lifted South—
        Invoking so
The cypress glades? Ah wilds of woe!

The spires of Richmond, late beheld
   Through rifts in musket-haze,
Were closed from view in clouds of dust
     On leaf-walled ways,
Where streamed our wagons in caravan;
   And the Seven Nights and Days
Of march and fast, retreat and fight,
Pinched our grimed faces to ghastly plight—
     Does the elm wood
Recall the haggard beards of blood?

The battle-smoked flag, with stars eclipsed,
   We followed (it never fell!)—
In silence husbanded our strength—
     Received their yell;
Till on this slope we patient turned
   With cannon ordered well;
Reverse we proved was not defeat;
But ah, the sod what thousands meet!—
     Does Malvern Wood
Bethink itself, and muse and brood?

> *We elms of Malvern Hill*
>   *Remember every thing;*
> *But sap the twig will fill:*
> *Wag the world how it will,*
>   *Leaves must be green in Spring.*

The House-top

A Night Piece

(JULY, 1863)

No sleep. The sultriness pervades the air
And binds the brain—a dense oppression, such
As tawny tigers feel in matted shades,
Vexing their blood and making apt for ravage.
Beneath the stars the roofy desert spreads
Vacant as Libya. All is hushed near by.

Yet fitfully from far breaks a mixed surf
Of muffled sound, the Atheist roar of riot.
Yonder, where parching Sirius set in drought,
Balefully glares red Arson—there—and there.
The Town is taken by its rats—ship-rats
And rats of the wharves. All civil charms
And priestly spells which late held hearts in awe—
Fear-bound, subjected to a better sway
Than sway of self; these like a dream dissolve,
And man rebounds whole æons back in nature.
Hail to the low dull rumble, dull and dead,
And ponderous drag that shakes the wall.
Wise Draco comes, deep in the midnight roll
Of black artillery; he comes, though late;
In code corroborating Calvin's creed
And cynic tyrannies of honest kings;
He comes, nor parlies; and the Town, redeemed,
Gives thanks devout; nor, being thankful, heeds
The grimy slur on the Republic's faith implied,
Which holds that Man is naturally good,
And—more—is Nature's Roman, never to be scourged.

The Swamp Angel

There is a coal-black Angel
    With a thick Afric lip,
And he dwells (like the hunted and harried)
    In a swamp where the green frogs dip.
But his face is against a City
    Which is over a bay of the sea,
And he breathes with a breath that is blastment,
    And dooms by a far decree.

By night there is fear in the City,
    Through the darkness a star soareth on;
There's a scream that screams up to the zenith,
    Then the poise of a meteor lone—
Lighting far the pale fright of the faces,

And downward the coming is seen;
Then the rush, and the burst, and the havoc,
    And wails and shrieks between.

It comes like the thief in the gloaming;
    It comes, and none may foretell
The place of the coming—the glaring;
    They live in a sleepless spell
That wizens, and withers, and whitens;
    It ages the young, and the bloom
Of the maiden is ashes of roses—
    The Swamp Angel broods in his gloom.

Swift is his messengers' going,
    But slowly he saps their halls,
As if by delay deluding
    They move from their crumbling walls
Farther and farther away;
    But the Angel sends after and after,
By night with the flame of his ray—
    By night with the voice of his screaming—
Sends after them, stone by stone,
    And farther walls fall, farther portals,
And weed follows weed through the Town.

Is this the proud City? the scorner
    Which never would yield the ground?
Which mocked at the coal-black Angel?
    The cup of despair goes round.
Vainly she calls upon Michael
    (The white man's seraph was he),
For Michael has fled from his tower
    To the Angel over the sea.

Who weeps for the woeful City
    Let him weep for our guilty kind;
Who joys at her wild despairing—
    Christ, the Forgiver, convert his mind.

"The Coming Storm"

A Picture by S. R. Gifford, and owned by E. B.
Included in the N. A. Exhibition, April, 1865

All feeling hearts must feel for him
   Who felt this picture. Presage dim—
Dim inklings from the shadowy sphere
   Fixed him and fascinated here.

A demon-cloud like the mountain one
   Burst on a spirit as mild
As this urned lake, the home of shades.
   But Shakspeare's pensive child

Never the lines had lightly scanned,
   Steeped in fable, steeped in fate;
The Hamlet in his heart was 'ware,
   Such hearts can antedate.

No utter surprise can come to him
   Who reaches Shakspeare's core;
That which we seek and shun is there—
   Man's final lore.

"Formerly a Slave"

An idealized Portrait, by E. Vedder,
in the Spring Exhibition of the National Academy, 1865

The sufferance of her race is shown,
   And restrospect of life,
Which now too late deliverance dawns upon;
   Yet is she not at strife.

Her children's children they shall know
   The good withheld from her;
And so her reverie takes prophetic cheer—
   In spirit she sees the stir

Far down the depth of thousand years,
   And marks the revel shine;
Her dusky face is lit with sober light,
   Sibylline, yet benign.

The Apparition

(*A Retrospect*)

Convulsions came; and, where the field
   Long slept in pastoral green,
A goblin-mountain was upheaved
(Sure the scared sense was all deceived),
Marl-glen and slag-ravine.

The unreserve of Ill was there,
   The clinkers in her last retreat;
But, ere the eye could take it in,
Or mind could comprehension win,
   It sunk!—and at our feet.

So, then, Solidity's a crust—
   The core of fire below;
All may go well for many a year,
But who can think without a fear
   Of horrors that happen so?

America

I

Where the wings of a sunny Dome expand
I saw a Banner in gladsome air—
Starry, like Berenice's Hair—
Afloat in broadened bravery there;
With undulating long-drawn flow,
As rolled Brazilian billows go

Voluminously o'er the Line.
The Land reposed in peace below;
    The children in their glee
Were folded to the exulting heart
    Of young Maternity.

II

Later, and it streamed in fight
    When tempest mingled with the fray,
And over the spear-point of the shaft
    I saw the ambiguous lightning play.
Valor with Valor strove, and died:
Fierce was Despair, and cruel was Pride;
And the lorn Mother speechless stood,
Pale at the fury of her brood.

III

Yet later, and the silk did wind
            Her fair cold form;
Little availed the shining shroud,
    Though ruddy in hue, to cheer or warm.
A watcher looked upon her low, and said—
She sleeps, but sleeps, she is not dead.
    But in that sleep contortion showed
The terror of the vision there—
    A silent vision unavowed,
Revealing earth's foundation bare,
    And Gorgon in her hidden place.
It was a thing of fear to see
    So foul a dream upon so fair a face,
And the dreamer lying in that starry shroud.

IV

But from the trance she sudden broke—
    The trance, or death into promoted life;
At her feet a shivered yoke,
    And in her aspect turned to heaven
    No trace of passion or of strife—

A clear calm look. It spake of pain,
But such as purifies from stain—
Sharp pangs that never come again—
   And triumph repressed by knowledge meet,
Power dedicate, and hope grown wise,
   And youth matured for age's seat—
Law on her brow and empire in her eyes.
   So she, with graver air and lifted flag;
While the shadow, chased by light,
Fled along the far-drawn height,
   And left her on the crag.

A Requiem

for Soldiers lost in Ocean Transports

When, after storms that woodlands rue,
   To valleys comes atoning dawn,
The robins blithe their orchard-sports renew;
   And meadow-larks, no more withdrawn,
Caroling fly in the languid blue;
The while, from many a hid recess,
Alert to partake the blessedness,
The pouring mites their airy dance pursue.
   So, after ocean's ghastly gales,
When laughing light of hoyden morning breaks,
      Every finny hider wakes—
   From vaults profound swims up with glittering scales;
   Through the delightsome sea he sails,
With shoals of shining tiny things
Frolic on every wave that flings
   Against the prow its showery spray;
All creatures joying in the morn,
Save them forever from joyance torn,
   Whose bark was lost where now the dolphins play;
Save them that by the fabled shore,
   Down the pale stream are washed away,
Far to the reef of bones are borne;
   And never revisits them the light,

Nor sight of long-sought land and pilot more;
  Nor heed they now the lone bird's flight
Round the lone spar where mid-sea surges pour.

from *Clarel: A Poem and Pilgrimage in the Holy Land*

The Hostel

In chamber low and scored by time,
Masonry old, late washed with lime—
Much like a tomb new-cut in stone;
Elbow on knee, and brow sustained
All motionless on sidelong hand,
A student sits, and broods alone.
  The small deep casement sheds a ray
Which tells that in the Holy Town
It is the passing of the day—
The Vigil of Epiphany.
Beside him in the narrow cell
His luggage lies unpacked; thereon
The dust lies, and on him as well—
The dust of travel. But anon
His face he lifts—in feature fine,
Yet pale, and all but feminine
But for the eye and serious brow—
Then rises, paces to and fro,
And pauses, saying, "Other cheer
Than that anticipated here,
By me the learner, now I find.
Theology, art thou so blind?
What means this naturalistic knell
In lieu of Siloh's oracle
Which here should murmur? Snatched from grace,
And waylaid in the holy place!
Not thus it was but yesterday
Off Jaffa on the clear blue sea;
Nor thus, my heart, it was with thee
Landing amid the shouts and spray;

Nor thus when mounted, full equipped,
Out through the vaulted gate we slipped
Beyond the walls where gardens bright
With bloom and blossom cheered the sight.
    "The plain we crossed. In afternoon,
How like our early autumn bland—
So softly tempered for a boon—
The breath of Sharon's prairie land!
And was it, yes, her titled Rose,
That scarlet poppy oft at hand?
Then Ramleh gleamed, the sail-white town
At even. There I watched day close
From the fair tower, the suburb one:
Seaward and dazing set the sun:
Inland I turned me toward the wall
Of Ephraim, stretched in purple pall.
Romance of mountains! But in end
What change the near approach could lend.
    "The start this morning—gun and lance
Against the quarter-moon's low tide;
The thieves' huts where we hushed the ride;
Chill day-break in the lorn advance;
In stony strait the scorch of noon,
Thrown off by crags, reminding one
Of those hot paynims whose fierce hands
Flung showers of Afric's fiery sands
In face of that crusader-king,
Louis, to wither so his wing;
And, at the last, aloft for goal,
Like the ice-bastions round the Pole,
Thy blank, blank towers, Jerusalem!"

    Again he droops, with brow on hand.
But, starting up, "Why, well I knew
Salem to be no Samarcand;
'Twas scarce surprise; and yet first view
Brings this eclipse. Needs be my soul,
Purged by the desert's subtle air
From bookish vapors, now is heir
To nature's influx of control;

Comes likewise now to consciousness
Of the true import of that press
Of inklings which in travel late
Through Latin lands, did vex my state,
And somehow seemed clandestine. Ah!
These under-formings in the mind,
Banked corals which ascend from far,
But little heed men that they wind
Unseen, unheard—till lo, the reef—
The reef and breaker, wreck and grief.
But here unlearning, how to me
Opes the expanse of time's vast sea!
Yes, I am young, but Asia old.
The books, the books not all have told.
    "And, for the rest, the facile chat
Of overweenings—what was that
The grave one said in Jaffa lane
Whom there I met, my countryman,
But new-returned from travel here;
Some word of mine provoked the strain;
His meaning now begins to clear:
Let me go over it again:—
    "Our New World's worldly wit so shrewd
Lacks the Semitic reverent mood,
Unworldly—hardly may confer
Fitness for just interpreter
Of Palestine. Forego the state
Of local minds inveterate,
Tied to one poor and casual form.
To avoid the deep saves not from storm.
    "Those things he said, and added more;
No clear authenticated lore
I deemed. But now, need now confess
My cultivated narrowness,
Though scarce indeed of sort he meant?
'Tis the uprooting of content!"
    So he, the student. 'Twas a mind,
Earnest by nature, long confined
Apart like Vesta in a grove
Collegiate, but let to rove

At last abroad among mankind,
And here in end confronted so
By the true genius, friend or foe,
And actual visage of a place
Before but dreamed of in the glow
Of fancy's spiritual grace.

    Further his meditations aim,
Reverting to his different frame
Bygone. And then: "Can faith remove
Her light, because of late no plea
I've lifted to her source above?"
Dropping thereat upon the knee,
His lips he parted; but the word
Against the utterance demurred
And failed him. With infirm intent
He sought the house-top. Set of sun:
His feet upon the yet warm stone,
He, Clarel, by the coping leant,
In silent gaze. The mountain town,
A walled and battlemented one,
With houseless suburbs front and rear,
And flanks built up from steeps severe,
Saddles and turrets the ascent—
Tower which rides the elephant.
Hence large the view. There where he stood,
Was Acra's upper neighborhood.
The circling hills he saw, with one
Excelling, ample in its crown,
Making the uplifted city low
By contrast—Olivet. The flow
Of eventide was at full brim;
Overlooked, the houses sloped from him—
Terraced or domed, unchimnied, gray,
All stone—a moor of roofs. No play
Of life; no smoke went up, no sound
Except low hum, and that half drowned.

    The inn abutted on the pool
Named Hezekiah's, a sunken court
Where silence and seclusion rule,
Hemmed round by walls of nature's sort,

Base to stone structures seeming one
E'en with the steeps they stand upon.
   As a three-decker's stern-lights peer
Down on the oily wake below,
Upon the sleek dark waters here
The inn's small lattices bestow
A rearward glance. And here and there
In flaws the languid evening air
Stirs the dull weeds adust, which trail
In festoons from the crag, and veil
The ancient fissures, overtopped
By the tall convent of the Copt,
Built like a light-house o'er the main.
   Blind arches showed in walls of wane,
Sealed windows, portals masoned fast,
And terraces where nothing passed
By parapets all dumb. No tarn
Among the Kaatskills, high above
Farm-house and stack, last lichened barn
And log-bridge rotting in remove—
More lonesome looks than this dead pool
In town where living creatures rule.
   Not here the spell might he undo;
The strangeness haunted him and grew.
   But twilight closes. He descends
And toward the inner court he wends.

Part I: Jerusalem, Canto 1

The Recluse

Ere yet they win that verge and line,
Reveal the stranger. Name him—Vine.
His home to tell—kin, tribe, estate—
Would naught avail. Alighting grow,
As on the tree the mistletoe,
All gifts unique. In seeds of fate
Borne on the winds these emigrate
And graft the stock.
                    Vine's manner shy

A clog, a hindrance might imply;
A lack of parlor-wont. But grace
Which is in substance deep and grain
May, peradventure, well pass by
The polish of veneer. No trace
Of passion's soil or lucre's stain,
Though life was now half ferried o'er.
If use he served not, but forbore—
Such indolence might still but pine
In dearth of rich incentive high:
Apollo slave in Mammon's mine?
Better Admetus' shepherd lie.

    A charm of subtle virtue shed
A personal influence coveted,
Whose source was difficult to tell
As ever was that perfumed spell
Of Paradise-flowers invisible
Which angels round Cecilia bred.

    A saint then do we here unfold?
Nay, the ripe flush, Venetian mould
Evinced no nature saintly fine,
But blood like swart Vesuvian wine.
What cooled the current? Under cheer
Of opulent softness, reigned austere
Control of self. Flesh, but scarce pride,
Was curbed: desire was mortified;
But less indeed by moral sway
Than doubt if happiness thro' clay
Be reachable. No sackclothed man;
Howbeit, in sort Carthusian
Tho' born a Sybarite. And yet
Not beauty might he all forget,
The beauty of the world, and charm:
He prized it tho' it scarce might warm.

    Like to the nunnery's denizen
His virgin soul communed with men
But thro' the wicket. Was it clear
This coyness bordered not on fear—
Fear or an apprehensive sense?
Not wholly seemed it diffidence

Recluse. Nor less did strangely wind
Ambiguous elfishness behind
All that: an Ariel unknown.
It seemed his very speech in tone
Betrayed disuse. Thronged streets astir
To Vine but ampler cloisters were.
Cloisters? No monk he was, allow;
But gleamed the richer for the shade
About him, as in sombre glade
Of Virgil's wood the Sibyl's Golden Bough.

Part I: Jerusalem, Canto 29

Of Mortmain

"Our friend there—he's a little queer,"
To Rolfe said Derwent riding on;
"Beshrew me, there is in his tone
Naught of your new world's chanticleer.
Who's the eccentric? can you say?"
  "Partly; but 'tis at second hand.
At the Black Jew's I met with one
Who, in response to my demand,
Did in a strange disclosure run
Respecting him."—"Repeat it, pray."—
And Rolfe complied. But here receive
Less the details of narrative
Than what the drift and import may convey.

  A Swede he was—illicit son
Of noble lady, after-wed,
Who, for a cause over which be thrown
Charity of oblivion dead,—
Bore little love, but rather hate,
Even practiced to ensnare his state.
His father, while not owning, yet
In part discharged the natural debt
Of duty; gave him liberal lore
And timely income; but no more.
  Thus isolated, what to bind

But the vague bond of human kind?
The north he left, to Paris came—
Paris, the nurse of many a flame
Evil and good. This son of earth,
This Psalmanazer, made a hearth
In warm desires and schemes for man:
Even *he* was an Arcadian.
Peace and good will was his acclaim—
If not in words, yet in the aim:
Peace, peace on earth: that note he thrilled,
But scarce in way the cherubs trilled
To Bethlehem and the shepherd band.
Yet much his theory could tell;
And he expounded it so well,
Disciples came. He took his stand.

   Europe was in a decade dim:
Upon the future's trembling rim
The comet hovered. His a league
Of frank debate and close intrigue:
Plot, proselyte, appeal, denounce—
Conspirator, pamphleteer, at once,
And prophet. Wear and tear and jar
He met with coffee and cigar:
These kept awake the man and mood
And dream. That uncreated Good
He sought, whose absence is the cause
Of creeds and Atheists, mobs and laws.
Precocities of heart outran
The immaturities of brain.

   Along with each superior mind
The vain, foolhardy, worthless, blind,
With Judases, are nothing loath
To clasp pledged hands and take the oath
Of aim, the which, if just, demands
Strong hearts, brows deep, and priestly hands.
Experience with her sharper touch
Stung Mortmain: Why, if men prove such,
Dote I? love theory overmuch?
Yea, also, whither will advance
This Revolution sprung in France

So many years ago? where end?
That current takes me. Whither tend?
Come, thou who makest such hot haste
To forge the future—weigh the past.
    Such frame he knew. And timed event
Cogent a further question lent:
Wouldst meddle with the state? Well, mount
Thy guns; how many men dost count?
Besides, there's more that here belongs:
Be many questionable wrongs:
By yet more questionable war,
Prophet of peace, these wouldst thou bar?
The world's not new, nor new thy plea.
Tho' even shouldst thou triumph, see,
Prose overtakes the victor's songs:
Victorious right may need redress:
No failure like a harsh success.
Yea, ponder well the historic page:
Of all who, fired with noble rage,
Have warred for right without reprieve,
How many spanned the wings immense
Of Satan's muster, or could cheat
His cunning tactics of retreat
And ambuscade? Oh, now dispense!
The world is portioned out, believe:
The good have but a patch at best,
The wise their corner; for the rest—
Malice divides with ignorance.
And what is stable? find one boon
That is not lackey to the moon
Of fate. The flood ebbs out—the ebb
Floods back; the incessant shuttle shifts
And flies, and weaves and tears the web.
Turn, turn thee to the proof that sifts:
What if the kings in Forty-eight
Fled like the gods? even as the gods
Shall do, return they made; and sate
And fortified their strong abodes;
And, to confirm them there in state,
Contrived new slogans, apt to please—

Pan and the tribal unities.
Behind all this still works some power
Unknowable, thou'lt yet adore.
That steers the world, not man. States drive;
The crazy rafts with billows strive.—
Go, go—absolve thee. Join that band
That wash them with the desert sand
For lack of water. In the dust
Of wisdom sit thee down, and rust.

So mused he—solitary pined.
Tho' his apostolate had thrown
New prospects ope to Adam's kind,
And fame had trumped him far and free—
Now drop he did—a clod unknown;
Nay, rather, he would not disown
Oblivion's volunteer to be;
Like those new-world discoverers bold
Ending in stony convent cold,
Or dying hermits; as if they,
Chastised to Micah's mind austere,
Remorseful felt that ampler sway
Their lead had given for old career
Of human nature.
                        But this man
No cloister sought. He, under ban
Of strange repentance and last dearth,
Roved the gray places of the earth.
And what seemed most his heart to wring
Was some unrenderable thing:
'Twas not his bastardy, nor bale
Medean in his mother pale,
Nor thwarted aims of high design;
But deeper—deep as nature's mine.
Tho' frequent among kind he sate
Tranquil enough to hold debate,
His moods he had, mad fitful ones,
Prolonged or brief, outbursts or moans;
And at such times would hiss or cry:

"Fair Circe—goddess of the sty!"
More frequent this: "Mock worse than wrong:
The Syren's kiss—the Fury's thong!"

  Such he. Tho' scarce as such portrayed
In full by Rolfe, yet Derwent said
At close: "There's none so far astray,
Detached, abandoned, as might seem,
As to exclude the hope, the dream
Of fair redemption. One fine day
I saw at sea, by bit of deck—
Weedy—adrift from far away—
The dolphin in his gambol light
Through showery spray, arch into sight:
He flung a rainbow o'er that wreck."

Part II: The Wilderness, Canto 4

Concerning Hebrews

As by the wood drifts thistle-down
And settles on soft mosses fair,
Stillness was wafted, dropped and sown;
Which stillness Vine, with timorous air
Of virgin tact, thus brake upon,
Nor with chance hint: "One can't forbear
Thinking that Margoth is—a *Jew*."
  Hereat, as for response, they view
The priest.
              "And, well, why me?" he cried;
"With one consent why turn to *me*?
Am I professional? Nay, free!
I grant that here by Judah's side
Queerly it jars with frame implied
To list this geologic Jew
His way Jehovah's world construe:
In Gentile 'twould not seem so odd.
But here may preconceptions thrall?
Be many Hebrews we recall
Whose contrast with the breastplate bright

Of Aaron flushed in altar-light,
And Horeb's Moses, rock and rod,
Or closeted alone with God,
Quite equals Margoth's in its way:
At home we meet them every day.
The Houndsditch clothesman scarce would seem
Akin to seers. For one, I deem
Jew banker, merchant, statesman—these,
With artist, actress known to fame,
All strenuous in each Gentile aim,
Are Nature's off-hand witnesses
There's nothing mystic in her reign:
Your Jew's like wheat from Pharaoh's tomb:
Sow it in England, what will come?
The weird old seed yields market grain."

   Pleased by his wit while some recline,
A smile uncertain lighted Vine,
But died away.
                "Jews share the change,"
Derwent proceeded: "Range, they range—
In liberal sciences they roam;
They're leavened, and it works, believe;
Signs are, and such as scarce deceive:
From Holland, that historic home
Of erudite Israel, many a tome
Talmudic, shipped is over sea
For antiquarian rubbish."
                        "Rest!"
Cried Rolfe; "e'en that indeed may be,
Nor less the Jew keep fealty
To ancient rites. Aaron's gemmed vest
Will long outlive Genevan cloth—
Nothing in Time's old camphor-chest
So little subject to the moth.
But Rabbis have their troublers too.
Nay, if thro' dusty stalls we look,
Haply we disinter to view
More than one bold freethinking Jew
That in his day with vigor shook
Faith's leaning tower."

            "Which stood the throe,"
Here Derwent in appendix: "look,
Faith's leaning tower was founded so:
Faith leaned from the beginning; yes,
If slant, she holds her steadfastness."
    "May be;" and paused: "but wherefore clog?—
Uriel Acosta, he was one
Who troubled much the synagogue—
Recanted then, and dropped undone:
A suicide. There's Heine, too,
(In lineage crossed by blood of Jew,)
Pale jester, to whom life was yet
A tragic farce; whose wild death-rattle,
In which all voids and hollows met,
Desperately maintained the battle
Betwixt the dirge and castanet.
But him leave to his Paris stone
And rail, and friendly wreath thereon.
Recall those Hebrews, which of old
Sharing some doubts we moderns rue,
Would fain Eclectic comfort fold
By grafting slips from Plato's palm
On Moses' melancholy yew:
But did they sprout? So *we* seek balm
By kindred graftings. Is that true?"
    "Why ask? But see: there lived a Jew—
No Alexandrine Greekish one—
You know him—Moses Mendelssohn."
    "Is't him you cite? True spirit staid,
He, though his honest heart was scourged
By doubt Judaic, never laid
His burden at Christ's door; he urged—
'Admit the mounting flames enfold
My basement; wisely shall my feet
The attic win, for safe retreat?' "
    "And *he* said that? Poor man, he's cold.
But was not this that Mendelssohn
Whose Hebrew kinswoman's Hebrew son,
Baptized to Christian, worthily won
The good name of Neander so?"

"If that link were, well might one urge
From such example, thy strange flow,
Conviction! Breaking habit's tether,
Sincerest minds will yet diverge
Like chance-clouds scattered by mere weather;
Nor less at one point still they meet:
The self-hood keep they pure and sweet."

"But Margoth," in reminder here
Breathed Vine, as if while yet the ray
Lit Rolfe, to try his further cheer:
"But Margoth!"
                    "He, poor sheep astray,
The Levitic cipher quite erased,
On what vile pig-weed hath he grazed.
Not his Spinosa's starry brow
(A non-conformer, ye'll allow),
A lion in brain, in life a lamb,
Sinless recluse of Amsterdam;
Who, in the obscure and humble lane,
Such strangers seemed to entertain
As sat by tent beneath the tree
On Mamre's plain—mysterious three,
The informing guests of Abraham.
But no, it had but ill beseemed
If God's own angels so could list
To visit one, Pan's Atheist.
That high intelligence but dreamed—
Above delusion's vulgar plain
Deluded still. The erring twain,
Spinosa and poor Margoth here,
Both Jews, which in dissent do vary:
In these what parted poles appear—
The blind man and the visionary."
"And whose the eye that sees aright,
If any?" Clarel eager asked.
Aside Rolfe turned as overtasked;
And none responded. 'Twas like night
Descending from the seats of light,
Or seeming thence to fall. But here

Sedate a kindly tempered look
Private and confidential spoke
From Derwent's eyes, Clarel to cheer:
Take heart; something to fit thy youth
Instill I may, some saving truth—
Not best just now to volunteer.
    Thought Clarel: Pray, and what wouldst prove?
Thy faith an over-easy glove.

    Meanwhile Vine had relapsed. They saw
In silence the heart's shadow draw—
Rich shadow, such as gardens keep
In bower aside, where glow-worms peep
In evening over the virgin bed
Where dark-green periwinkles sleep—
Their bud the Violet of the Dead.

Part II: The Wilderness, Canto 22

The Inscription

While yet Rolfe's foot in stirrup stood,
Ere the light vault that wins the seat,
Derwent was heard: "What's this we meet?
A Cross? and—if one could but spell—
Inscription Sinaitic? Well,
Mortmain is nigh—*his* crazy freak;
Whose else? A closer view I'll seek;
I'll climb."
            In moving there aside
The rock's turned brow he had espied;
In rear this rock hung o'er the waste
And Nehemiah in sleep embraced
Below. The forepart gloomed Lot's wave
So nigh, the tide the base did lave.
Above, the sea-face smooth was worn
Through long attrition of that grit
Which on the waste of winds is borne.
And on the tablet high of it—
Traced in dull chalk, such as is found

Accessible in upper ground—
Big there between two scrawls, below
And over—a cross; three stars in row
Upright, two more for thwarting limb
Which drooped oblique.
                              At Derwent's cry
The rest drew near; and every eye
Marked the device.—Thy passion's whim,
Wild Swede, mused Vine in silent heart.
"Looks like the *Southern Cross* to me,"
Said Clarel; "so 'tis down in chart."
"And so," said Rolfe, " 'tis set in sky—
Though error slight of place prevail
In midmost star here chalked. At sea,
Bound for Peru, when south ye sail,
Startling that novel cluster strange
Peers up from low; then as ye range
Cape-ward still further, brightly higher
And higher the stranger doth aspire,
'Till off the Horn, when at full hight
Ye slack your gaze as chilly grows the night.
But Derwent—see!"
                              The priest having gained
Convenient lodge the text below,
They called: "What's that in curve contained
Above the stars? Read: we would know."
"Runs thus: *By one who wails the loss,*
This altar to the Slanting Cross."
"Ha! under that?" "Some crow's-foot scrawl."
"Decipher, quick! we're waiting all."
"Patience: for ere one try rehearse,
 'Twere well to make it out. 'Tis verse."
"Verse, say you? Read." " 'Tis mystical:

    " 'Emblazoned bleak in austral skies—
        A heaven remote, whose starry swarm
        Like Science lights but cannot warm—
        Translated Cross, hast thou withdrawn,
        Dim paling too at every dawn,

With symbols vain once counted wise,
And gods declined to heraldries?
Estranged, estranged: can friend prove so?
Aloft, aloof, a frigid sign:
How far removed, thou Tree divine,
Whose tender fruit did reach so low—
Love apples of New-Paradise!
About the wide Australian sea
The planted nations yet to be—
When, ages hence, they lift their eyes,
Tell, what shall they retain of thee?
But class thee with Orion's sword?
In constellations unadored,
Christ and the Giant equal prize?
The atheist cycles—*must* they be?
Fomentors as forefathers we?'

"Mad, mad enough," the priest here cried,
 Down slipping by the shelving brinks;
"But 'tis not Mortmain," and he sighed.
 "Not Mortmain?" Rolfe exclaimed. "Methinks,"
The priest, " 'tis hardly in his vein."
"How? fraught with feeling is the strain?
His heart's not ballasted with stone—
He's crank." "Well, well, e'en let us own
That Mortmain, Mortmain is the man.
We've then a pledge here at a glance
Our comrade's met with no mischance.
Soon he'll rejoin us." "There, amen!"
"But now to wake Nehemiah in den
Behind here.—But kind Clarel goes.
Strange how he naps nor trouble knows
Under the crag's impending block,
Nor fears its fall, nor recks of shock."

 Anon they mount; and much advance
Upon that chalked significance.
The student harks, and weighs each word,
Intent, he being newly stirred.

But tarries Margoth? Yes, behind
He lingers. He placards his mind:
Scaling the crag he rudely scores
With the same chalk (how here abused!)
Left by the other, after used,
A sledge or hammer huge as Thor's;
A legend lending—this, to wit:
*"I, Science, I whose gain's thy loss,
I slanted thee, thou Slanting Cross."*
    But sun and rain, and wind, with grit
Driving, these haste to cancel it.

Part II: The Wilderness, Canto 31

Afterward

"Seedsmen of old Saturn's land,
  Love and peace went hand in hand,
    And sowed the Era Golden!

"Golden time for man and mead:
  Title none, nor title-deed,
    Nor any slave, nor Soldan.

"Venus burned both large and bright,
  Honey-moon from night to night,
    Nor bride, nor groom waxed olden.

"Big the tears, but ruddy ones,
  Crushed from grapes in vats and tuns
    Of vineyards green and golden!

"Sweet to sour did never sue,
  None repented ardor true—
    Those years did so embolden.

"Glum Don Graveairs slunk in den:
  Frankly roved the gods with men
    In gracious talk and golden.

"Thrill it, cymbals of my rhyme,
  Power was love, and love in prime,
    Nor revel to toil beholden.

"Back, come back, good age, and reign,
  Goodly age, and long remain—
    Saturnian Age, the Golden!"

The masquer gone, by stairs that climb,
In seemly sort, the friars withdrew;
And, waiting that, the Islesman threw
His couplets of the Arcadian time,
Then turning on the pilgrims: "Hoo!

  "The bird of Paradise don't like owls:
  A handful of acorns after the cowls!"

But Clarel, bantered by the song,
Sad questioned, if in frames of thought
And feeling, there be right and wrong;
Whether the lesson Joel taught
Confute what from the marble's caught
In sylvan sculpture—Bacchant, Faun,
Or shapes more lax by Titian drawn.
Such counter natures in mankind—
Mole, bird, not more unlike we find:
Instincts adverse, nor less how true
Each to itself. What clew, what clew?

Part III: Mar Saba, Canto 20

The Medallion

In Saba, as by one consent,
Frequent the pilgrims single went;
So, parting with his young compeer,
And breaking fast without delay,
For more restorative and cheer,
Good Derwent lightly strolled away
Within this monkish capital.

Chapels and oratories all,
And shrines in coves of gilded gloom;
The kitchen, too, and pantler's room—
Naught came amiss.
                          Anear the church
He drew unto a kind of porch
Such as next some old minsters be,
An inner porch (named *Galilee*
In parlance of the times gone by),
A place for discipline and grief.
And here his tarry had been brief
But for a shield of marble nigh,
Set in the living rock: a stone
In low relief, where well was shown,
Before an altar under sky,
A man in armor, visor down,
Enlocked complete in panoply,
Uplifting reverent a crown
In invocation.
                          This armed man
In corselet showed the dinted plate,
And dread streaks down the thigh-piece ran;
But the bright helm inviolate
Seemed raised above the battle-zone—
Cherubic with a rare device;
Perch for the Bird-of-Paradise.
A victor seemed he, without pride
Of victory, or joy in fame:
'Twas reverence, and naught beside,
Unless it might that shadow claim
Which comes of trial. Yes, the art
So cunning was, that it in part
By fair expressiveness of grace
Atoned even for the visored face.

    Long time becharmed here Derwent stood,
Charmed by the marble's quiet mood
Of beauty, more than by its tone
Of earnestness, though these were one

In that good piece. Yes, long he fed
Ere yet the eye was lower led
To trace the inscription underrun:

    O fair and friendly manifested Spirit!
        Before thine altar dear
    Let me recount the marvel of the story
        Fulfilled in tribute here.

    In battle waged where all was fraudful silence,
        Foul battle against odds,
    Disarmed, I, fall'n and trampled, prayed: Death, succor!
        Come, Death: thy hand is God's!

    A pale hand noiseless from the turf responded,
        Riving the turf and stone:
    It raised, re-armed me, sword and golden armor,
        And waved me warring on.

    O fairest, friendliest, and ever holy—
        O Love, dissuading fate—
    To thee, to thee the rescuer, thee sainted,
        The crown I dedicate:

    To thee I dedicate the crown, a guerdon
        The winner may not wear;
    His wound re-opens, and he goes to haven:
        Spirit! befriend him there.

  "A hero, and shall he repine?
'Tis not Achilles;" and straightway
He felt the charm in sort decline;
And, turning, saw a votary gray:
"Good brother, tell: make this thing clear:
Who set this up?" " 'Twas long ago,
Yes, long before I harbored here,
Long centuries, they say." "Why, no!
So bright it looks, 'tis recent, sure.
Who set it up?" "A count turned monk."

"What count?" "His name he did abjure
  For Lazarus, and ever shrunk
  From aught of his life's history:
  Yon slab tells all or nothing, see.
  But this I've heard; that when the stone
  Hither was brought from Cyprus fair
  (Some happy sculptors flourished there
  When Venice ruled), he said to one:
  'They've made the knight too rich appear—
  Too rich in helm.' He set it here
  In Saba as securest place,
  For a memorial of grace
  To outlast him, and many a year."

Part III: Mar Saba, Canto 22

The Pillow

When rule and era passed away
With old Sylvanus (stories say),
The oracles adrift were hurled,
And ocean moaned about the world,
And wandering voices without name
At sea to sailors did proclaim,
Pan, Pan is dead!
          Such fables old—
From man's deep nature are they rolled,
Pained and perplexed—awed, overawed
By sense of change? But never word
Aërial by mortal heard,
Rumors that vast eclipse, if slow,
Whose passage yet we undergo,
Emerging on an age untried.
If not all oracles be dead,
The upstart ones the old deride:
Parrots replace the sibyls fled—
By rote repeat in lilting pride:

Lodged in power, enlarged in all,
Man achieves his last exemption—
Hopes no heaven, but fears no fall,
King in time, nor needs redemption.

They hymn. But these who cloistral dwell
In Bethlehem here, and share faith's spell
Meekly, and keep her tenor mild—
What know they of a world beguiled?
Or, knowing, they but know too well.

Buzzed thoughts! To Rolfe they came in doze
(His brain like ocean's murmuring shell)
Between the dream and slumber's light repose.

Part IV: Bethlehem, Canto 8

Symphonies

Meanwhile with Vine there, Clarel stood
Aside in friendly neighborhood,
And felt a flattering pleasure stir
At words—nor in equivocal tone
Freakish, or leaving to infer,
Such as beforetime he had known—
Breathed now by that exceptional one
In unconstraint:
        " 'Tis very much
The cold fastidious heart to touch
This way; nor is it mere address
That so could move one's silver chord.
How he transfigured Ungar's sword!
Delusive is this earnestness
Which holds him in its passion pale—
Tenant of melancholy's dale
Of mirage? To interpret him,
Perhaps it needs a swallow-skim
Over distant time. Migrate with me
Across the years, across the sea.—

How like a Poor Clare in her cheer
(Grave Sister of his order sad)
Showed nature to that Cordelier
Who, roving in the Mexic glade,
Saw in a bud of happy dower
Whose stalk entwined the tropic tree,
Emblems of Christ's last agony:
In anthers, style, and fibers torn,
The five wounds, nails, and crown of thorn;
And named it so the passion-flower.
What beauty in that sad conceit!
Such charm, the title still we meet.
Our guide, methinks, where'er he turns
For him this passion-flower burns;
And all the world is elegy.
A green knoll is to you and me
But pastoral, and little more:
To him 'tis even Calvary
Where feeds the Lamb. This passion-flower—
But list!"
    Hid organ-pipes unclose
A timid rill of slender sound,
Which gains in volume—grows, and flows
Gladsome in amplitude of bound.
Low murmurs creep. From either side
Tenor and treble interpose,
And talk across the expanding tide:
Debate, which in confusion merges—
Din and clamor, discord's hight:
Countering surges—pæans—dirges—
Mocks, and laughter light.
  But rolled in long ground-swell persistent,
A tone, an under-tone assails
And overpowers all near and distant;
Earnest and sternest, it prevails.
  Then terror, horror—wind and rain—
Accents of undetermined fear,
And voices as in shipwreck drear:
A sea, a sea of spirits in pain!

The suppliant cries decrease—
The voices in their ferment cease:
One wave rolls over all and whelms to peace.

But hark—oh, hark!
Whence, whence this stir, this whirr of wings?
Numbers numberless convening—
Harps and child-like carolings
In happy holiday of meaning:

To God be glory in the hight,
  For tidings glad we bring;
Good will to men, and peace on earth
  We children-cherubs sing!

To God be glory in the depth,
  As in the hight be praise;
He who shall break the gates of death
  A babe in manger rays.

Ye people all in every land,
  Embrace, embrace, be kin:
Immanuel's born in Bethlehem,
  And gracious years begin!

It dies; and, half around the heavenly sphere,
Like silvery lances lightly touched aloft—
Like Northern Lights appealing to the ear,
An elfin melody chimes low and soft.
That also dies, that last strange fairy-thrill:
Slowly it dies away, and all is sweetly still.

Part IV: Bethlehem, Canto 15

Dirge

Stay, Death. Not mine the Christus-wand
Wherewith to charge thee and command:
I plead. Most gently hold the hand
Of her thou leadest far away;

Fear thou to let her naked feet
Tread ashes—but let mosses sweet
Her footing tempt, where'er ye stray.
Shun Orcus; win the moonlit land
Belulled—the silent meadows lone,
Where never any leaf is blown
From lily-stem in Azrael's hand.
There, till her love rejoin her lowly
(Pensive, a shade, but all her own)
On honey feed her, wild and holy;
Or trance her with thy choicest charm.
And if, ere yet the lover's free,
Some added dusk thy rule decree—
That shadow only let it be
Thrown in the moon-glade by the palm.

Part IV: Bethlehem, Canto 31

Easter

BUT ON THE THIRD DAY CHRIST AROSE;
And, in the town He knew, the rite
Commemorative eager goes
Before the hour. Upon the night
Between the week's last day and first,
No more the Stabat is dispersed
Or Tenebræ. And when the day,
The Easter, falls in calendar
The same to Latin and the array
Of all schismatics from afar—
Armenians, Greeks from many a shore—
Syrians, Copts—profusely pour
The hymns: 'tis like the choric gush
Of torrents Alpine when they rush
To swell the anthem of the spring.
   That year was now. Throughout the fane,
Floor, and arcades in double ring
About the gala of THE TOMB,
Blazing with lights, behung with bloom—
What child-like thousands roll the strain,

The hallelujah after pain,
Which in all tongues of Christendom
Still through the ages has rehearsed
That Best, the outcome of the Worst.
　　Nor blame them who by lavish rite
Thus greet the pale victorious Son,
Since Nature times the same delight,
And rises with the Emerging One;
Her passion-week, her winter mood
She slips, with crape from off the Rood.
　　In soft rich shadow under dome,
With gems and robes repletely fine,
The priests like birds Brazilian shine:
And moving tapers charm the sight,
Enkindling the curled incense-fume:
A dancing ray, Auroral light.

　　Burn on the hours, and meet the day.
The morn invites; the suburbs call
The concourse to come forth—this way!
Out from the gate by Stephen's wall,
They issue, dot the hills, and stray
In bands, like sheep among the rocks;
And the Good Shepherd in the heaven,
To whom the charge of these is given,
The Christ, ah! counts He there His flocks?
　　But they, at each suburban shrine,
Grateful adore that Friend benign;
Though chapel now and cross divine
Too frequent show neglected; nay,
For charities of early rains
Rim them about with vernal stains,
Forerunners of maturer May,
When those red flowers, which so can please,
(*Christ's-Blood-Drops* named—anemones),
Spot Ephraim and the mountain-way.
　　But heart bereft is unrepaid
Though Thammuz' spring in Thammuz' glade
Invite; then how in Joel's glen?
What if dyed shawl and bodice gay

Make bright the black dell? what if they
In distance clear diminished be
To seeming cherries dropped on pall
Borne graveward under laden tree?
The cheer, so human, might not call
The maiden up; *Christ is arisen:*
But Ruth, may Ruth so burst the prison?

The rite supreme being ended now,
Their confluence here the nations part:
Homeward the tides of pilgrims flow,
By contrast making the walled town
Like a depopulated mart;
More like some kirk on week-day lone,
On whose void benches broodeth still
The brown light from November hill.

But though the freshet quite be gone—
Sluggish, life's wonted stream flows on.

Part IV: Bethlehem, Canto 33

Via Crucis

Some leading thoroughfares of man
In wood-path, track, or trail began;
Though threading heart of proudest town,
They follow in controlling grade
A hint or dictate, nature's own,
By man, as by the brute, obeyed.

Within Jerusalem a lane,
Narrow, nor less an artery main
(Though little knoweth it of din),
In part suggests such origin.
The restoration or repair,
Successive through long ages there,
Of city upon city tumbled,
Might scarce divert that thoroughfare,
Whose hill abideth yet unhumbled

Above the valley-side it meets.
Pronounce its name, this natural street's:
The *Via Crucis*—even the way
Tradition claims to be the one
Trod on that Friday far away
By Him our pure exemplar shown.

    'Tis Whitsun-tide. From paths without,
Through Stephen's gate—by many a vein
Convergent brought within this lane,
Ere sun-down shut the loiterer out—
As 'twere a frieze, behold the train!
Bowed water-carriers; Jews with staves;
Infirm gray monks; over-loaded slaves;
Turk soldiers—young, with home-sick eyes;
A Bey, bereaved through luxuries;
Strangers and exiles; Moslem dames
Long-veiled in monumental white,
Dumb from the mounds which memory claims;
A half-starved vagrant Edomite;
Sore-footed Arab girls, which toil
Depressed under heap of garden-spoil;
The patient ass with panniered urn;
Sour camels humped by heaven and man,
Whose languid necks through habit turn
For ease—for ease they hardly gain.
In varied forms of fate they wend—
Or man or animal, 'tis one:
Cross-bearers all, alike they tend
And follow, slowly follow on.

    But, lagging after, who is he
Called early every hope to test,
And now, at close of rarer quest,
Finds so much more the heavier tree?
From slopes whence even Echo's gone,
Wending, he murmurs in low tone:
"They wire the world—far under sea
They talk; but never comes to me
A message from beneath the stone."

Dusked Olivet he leaves behind,
And, taking now a slender wynd,
Vanishes in the obscurer town.

Part IV: Bethlehem, Canto 34

Epilogue

If Luther's day expand to Darwin's year,
Shall that exclude the hope—foreclose the fear?

   Unmoved by all the claims our times avow,
The ancient Sphinx still keeps the porch of shade;
And comes Despair, whom not her calm may cow,
And coldly on that adamantine brow
Scrawls undeterred his bitter pasquinade.
But Faith (who from the scrawl indignant turns)
With blood warm oozing from her wounded trust,
Inscribes even on her shards of broken urns
The sign o' the cross—*the spirit above the dust!*

   Yea, ape and angel, strife and old debate—
The harps of heaven and dreary gongs of hell;
Science the feud can only aggravate—
No umpire she betwixt the chimes and knell:
The running battle of the star and clod
Shall run forever—if there be no God.

   Degrees we know, unknown in days before;
The light is greater, hence the shadow more;
And tantalized and apprehensive Man
Appealing—Wherefore ripen us to pain?
Seems there the spokesman of dumb Nature's train.
   But through such strange illusions have they passed
Who in life's pilgrimage have baffled striven—
Even death may prove unreal at the last,
And stoics be astounded into heaven.

   Then keep thy heart, though yet but ill-resigned—
Clarel, thy heart, the issues there but mind;

That like the crocus budding through the snow—
That like a swimmer rising from the deep—
That like a burning secret which doth go
Even from the bosom that would hoard and keep;
Emerge thou mayst from the last whelming sea,
And prove that death but routs life into victory.

Part IV: Bethlehem, Canto 35

from *John Marr*

Since as in night's deck-watch ye show,
Why, lads, so silent here to me,
Your watchmate of times long ago?

Once, for all the darkling sea,
You your voices raised how clearly,
Striking in when tempest sung;
Hoisting up the storm-sail cheerly,
Life is storm:—let storm! you rung.
Taking things as fated merely,
Child-like though the world ye spanned;
Nor holding unto life too dearly,
Ye who held your lives in hand:
Skimmers, who on oceans four
Petrels were, and larks ashore.

O, not from memory lightly flung,
Forgot, like strains no more availing,
The heart to music haughtier strung;
Nay, frequent near me, never staling,
Whose good feeling kept ye young.
Like tides that enter creek or stream,
Ye come, ye visit me; or seem
Swimming out from seas of faces,
Alien myriads memory traces,
To enfold me in a dream!

I yearn as ye. But rafts that strain,
Parted, shall they lock again?

Twined we were, entwined, then riven,
Ever to new embracements driven,
Shifting gulf-weed of the main!
And how if one here shift no more,
Lodged by the flinging surge ashore?

Nor less, as now, in eve's decline,
Your shadowy fellowship is mine.
Ye float around me, form and feature:—
Tattooings, ear-rings, love-locks curled;
Barbarians of man's simpler nature,
Unworldly servers of the world.
Yea, present all, and dear to me,
Though shades, or scouring China's sea.

Whither, whither, merchant-sailors,
Whitherward now in roaring gales?
Competing still, ye huntsman-whalers,
In leviathan's wake what boat prevails?
And man-of-war's men, whereaway?
If now no dinned drum beat to quarters
On the wilds of midnight waters—
Foemen looming through the spray;
Do yet your gangway lanterns, streaming,
Vainly strive to pierce below,
When, tilted from the slant plank gleaming,
A brother you see to darkness go?

But, gunmates lashed in shotted canvas,
If where long watch-below ye keep,
Never the shrill *"All hands up hammocks!"*
Breaks the spell that charms your sleep;
And summoning trumps might vainly call,
And booming guns implore—
A beat, a heart-beat musters all,
One heart-beat at heart-core.
It musters. But to clasp, retain;
To see you at the halyards main—
To hear your chorus once again!

Tom Deadlight

(*1810*)

During a tempest encountered homeward-bound from the Mediterranean, a grizzled petty-officer, one of the two captains of the fore-
castle, dying at night in his hammock, swung in the *sick-bay* under
the tiered gun-decks of the British *Dreadnaught*, 98, wandering in
his mind, though with glimpses of sanity, and starting up at whiles,
sings by snatches his good-bye and last injunctions to two messmates
his watchers, one of whom fans the fevered tar with the flap of his
old sou'-wester.

Some names and phrases, with here and there a line, or part of
one; these, in his aberration wrested into incoherency from their
original connection and import, he involuntarily derives, as he does
the measure, from a famous old sea-ditty, whose cadences, long rife,
and now humming in the collapsing brain, attune the last flutterings
of distempered thought: —

Farewell and adieu to you noble hearties, —
    Farewell and adieu to you ladies of Spain,
For I've received orders for to sail for the Deadman,
    But hope with the grand fleet to see you again.

I have hove my ship to, with main-top-sail aback, boys;
    I have hove my ship to, for to strike soundings clear —
The black scud a' flying; but by God's blessing dam'me,
    Right up the Channel for the Deadman I'll steer.

I have worried through the waters that are callèd the
        Doldrums,
    And growled at Sargasso that clogs while ye grope —
Blast my eyes, but the light-ship is hid by the mist, lads: —
    Flying-Dutchman — oddsbobbs — off the Cape of Good
        Hope!

But what's this I feel that is fanning my cheek, Matt?
    The white goney's wing? — how she rolls! — 'tis the
        Cape! —
Give my kit to the mess, Jock, for kin none is mine, none;
    And tell *Holy Joe* to avast with the crape.

Dead-reckoning, says *Joe*, it w'ont do to go by;
   But they doused all the glims, Matt, in sky t'other night.
Dead-reckoning is good for to sail for the Deadman;
   And Tom Deadlight he thinks it may reckon near right.

The signal!—it streams for the grand fleet to anchor.
   The Captains—the trumpets—the hullabaloo!
Stand by for blue-blazes, and mind your shank-painters,
   For the Lord High Admiral he's squinting at you!

But give me my *tot*, Matt, before I roll over;
   Jock, let's have your flipper, it's good for to feel;
And do'nt sew me up without *baccy* in mouth, boys,
   And do'nt blubber like lubbers when I turn up my keel.

The Haglets

By chapel bare, with walls sea-beat,
The lichened urns in wilds are lost
About a carved memorial stone
That shows, decayed and coral-mossed,
A form recumbent, swords at feet,
Trophies at head, and kelp for a winding sheet.

I invoke thy ghost, neglected fane,
Washed by the waters' long lament;
I adjure the recumbent effigy
To tell the cenotaph's intent—
Reveal why fagotted swords are at feet,
Why trophies appear and weeds are the winding sheet.

———

By open ports the Admiral sits,
And shares repose with guns that tell
Of power that smote the arm'd Plate Fleet
Whose sinking flag-ship's colors fell;
But over the Admiral floats in light
His squadron's flag, the red-cross Flag of the White.

The eddying waters whirl astern,
The prow, a seedsman, sows the spray;
With bellying sails and buckling spars
The black hull leaves a Milky Way:
Her timbers thrill, her batteries roll,
She revelling speeds exulting with pennon at pole.
    But ah, for standards captive trailed
For all their scutcheoned castles' pride—
Castilian towers that dominate Spain,
Naples, and either Ind beside;
Those haughty towers, armorial ones,
Rue the salute from the Admiral's dens of guns.

Ensigns and arms in trophy brave—
Braver for many a rent and scar,
The captor's naval hall bedeck,
Spoil that insures an earldom's star—
Toledoes great, grand draperies too,
Spain's steel and silk, and splendors from Peru.
    But crippled part in splintering fight,
The vanquished flying the victor's flags,
With prize-crews, under convoy-guns,
Heavy the fleet from Opher drags—
The Admiral crowding sail ahead,
Foremost with news who foremost in conflict sped.
    But out from cloistral gallery dim,
In early night his glance is thrown;
He marks the vague reserve of heaven,
He feels the touch of ocean lone;
Then turns, in frame part undermined,
Nor notes the shadowing wings that fan behind.

There, peaked and gray, three haglets fly,
And follow, follow fast in wake
Where slides the cabin-lustre shy,
And sharks from man a glamour take,
Seething along the line of light
In lane that endless rules the war-ship's flight.
    The sea-fowl here whose hearts none know,
They followed late the flag-ship quelled

(As now the victor one) and long
Above her gurgling grave, shrill held
With screams their wheeling rites—then sped
Direct in silence where the victor led.
   Now winds less fleet, but fairer, blow,
A ripple laps the coppered side,
While phosphor sparks make ocean gleam
Like camps lit up in triumph wide;
With lights and tinkling cymbals meet
Acclaiming seas the advancing conqueror greet.

But who a flattering tide may trust,
Or favoring breeze, or aught in end?—
Careening under startling blasts
The sheeted towers of sails impend;
While, gathering bale, behind is bred
A livid storm-bow, like a rainbow dead.
   At trumpet-call the topmen spring;
And, urged by after-call in stress,
Yet other tribes of tars ascend
The rigging's howling wilderness;
But ere yard-ends alert they win,
Hell rules in heaven with hurricane-fire and din.
   The spars, athwart at spiry height,
Like quaking Lima's crosses rock;
Like bees the clustering sailors cling
Against the shrouds, or take the shock
Flat on the swept yard-arms aslant
Dipped like the wheeling condor's pinions gaunt.

A lull! and tongues of languid flame
Lick every boom and lambent show
Electric 'gainst each face aloft;
The herds of clouds with bellowings go:
The black ship rears—beset—harassed,
Then plunges far with luminous antlers vast.
   In trim betimes they turn from land,
Some shivered sails and spars they stow:
One watch, dismissed, they troll the can,
While loud the billow thumps the bow—

Vies with the fist that smites the board
Obstreperous at each reveller's jovial word.
  Of royal oak by storms confirmed,
The tested hull her lineage shows;
Vainly the plungings whelm her prow—
She rallies, rears, she sturdier grows;
Each shot-hole plugged, each storm-sail home,
With batteries housed she rams the watery dome.

Dim seen adrift through driving scud,
The wan moon shows in plight forlorn;
Then, pinched in visage, fades and fades
Like to the faces drowned at morn,
When deeps engulfed the flag-ship's crew
And, shrilling round, the inscrutable haglets flew.
  And still they fly, nor now they cry,
But constant fan a second wake,
Unflagging pinions ply and ply,
Abreast their course intent they take;
Their silence marks a stable mood,
They patient keep their eager neighborhood.
  Plumed with a smoke, a confluent sea,
Heaved in a combing pyramid full,
Spent at its climax, in collapse
Down headlong thundering stuns the hull:
The trophy drops; but, reared again,
Shows Mars' high-altar and contemns the main.

Rebuilt it stands, the brag of arms,
Transferred in site—no thought of where
The sensitive needle keeps its place,
And starts, disturbed, a quiverer there;
The helmsman rubs the clouded glass—
Peers in, but lets the trembling portent pass.
  Let pass as well his shipmates do
(Whose dream of power no tremors jar)
Fears for the fleet convoyed astern:
"Our flag they fly, they share our star;
Spain's galleons great in hull are stout:
Manned by our men—like us they'll ride it out."

To-night's the night that ends the week—
Ends day and week and month and year:
A four-fold imminent flickering time,
For now the midnight draws anear:
Eight bells! and passing-bells they be—
The Old Year fades, the Old Year dies at sea.

He launched them well. But shall the New
Redeem the pledge the Old Year made,
Or prove a self-asserting heir?
But healthy hearts few qualms invade:
By shot-chests grouped in bays 'tween guns
The gossips chat, the grizzled, sea-beat ones.
    And boyish dreams some graybeards blab:
"To sea, my lads, we go no more
Who share the Acapulco prize;
We'll all night in, and bang the door;
Our ingots red shall yield us bliss:
Lads, golden years begin to-night with this!"
    Released from deck, yet waiting call,
Glazed caps and coats baptized in storm,
A watch of Laced Sleeves round the board
Draw near in heart to keep them warm:
"Sweethearts and wives!" clink, clink, they meet,
And, quaffing, dip in wine their beards of sleet.

"Ay, let the star-light stay withdrawn,
So here her hearth-light memory fling,
So in this wine-light cheer be born,
And honor's fellowship weld our ring—
Honor! our Admiral's aim foretold:
A tomb or a trophy, and lo, 'tis a trophy and gold!"
    But he, a unit, sole in rank,
Apart needs keep his lonely state,
The sentry at his guarded door
Mute as by vault the sculptured Fate;
Belted he sits in drowsy light,
And, hatted, nods—the Admiral of the White.
    He dozes, aged with watches passed—

Years, years of pacing to and fro;
He dozes, nor attends the stir
In bullioned standards rustling low,
Nor minds the blades whose secret thrill
Perverts overhead the magnet's Polar will;—

Less heeds the shadowing three that ply
And follow, follow fast in wake,
Untiring wing and lidless eye—
Abreast their course intent they take;
Or sigh or sing, they hold for good
The unvarying flight and fixed inveterate mood.
  In dream at last his dozings merge,
In dream he reaps his victory's fruit:
The Flags-o'-the-Blue, the Flags-o'-the-Red,
Dipped flags of his country's fleets salute
His Flag-o'-the-White in harbor proud—
But why should it blench? Why turn to a painted shroud?
  The hungry seas they hound the hull,
The sharks they dog the haglets' flight;
With one consent the winds, the waves
In hunt with fins and wings unite,
While drear the harps in cordage sound
Remindful wails for old Armadas drowned.

Ha—yonder! are they Northern Lights?
Or signals flashed to warn or ward?
Yea, signals lanced in breakers high;
But doom on warning follows hard:
While yet they veer in hope to shun,
They strike! and thumps of hull and heart are one.
  But beating hearts a drum-beat calls,
And prompt the men to quarters go;
Discipline, curbing nature, rules—
Heroic makes who duty know:
They execute the trump's command,
Or in peremptory places wait and stand.
  Yet cast about in blind amaze—
As through their watery shroud they peer:

"We tacked from land: then how betrayed?
Have currents swerved us—snared us here?"
None heed the blades that clash in place
Under lamps dashed down that lit the magnet's case.

Ah, what may live, who mighty swim,
Or boat-crew reach that shore forbid,
Or cable span? Must victors drown—
Perish, even as the vanquished did?
Man keeps from man the stifled moan;
They shouldering stand, yet each in heart how lone.
   Some heaven invoke; but rings of reefs
Prayer and despair alike deride
In dance of breakers forked or peaked,
Pale maniacs of the maddened tide;
While, strenuous yet some end to earn,
The haglets spin, though now no more astern.
   Like shuttles hurrying in the looms
Aloft through rigging frayed they ply—
Cross and recross—weave and inweave,
Then lock the web with clinching cry
Over the seas on seas that clasp
The weltering wreck where gurgling ends the gasp.

Ah, for the Plate-Fleet trophy now,
The victor's voucher, flags and arms;
Never they'll hang in Abbey old
And take Time's dust with a holier palms;
Nor less content, in liquid night,
Their captor sleeps—the Admiral of the White.

         Imbedded deep with shells
         And drifted treasure deep,
         Forever he sinks deeper in
         Unfathomable sleep—
         His cannon round him thrown,
         His sailors at his feet,
         The wizard sea enchanting them
         Where never haglets beat.

On nights when meteors play,
And light the breakers' dance,
The Oreads from the caves
With silvery elves advance;
And up from ocean stream,
And down from heaven far,
The rays that blend in dream
The abysm and the star.

The Man-of-War Hawk

Yon black man-of-war hawk that wheels in the light
O'er the black ship's white sky-s'l, sunned cloud to the sight,
Have we low-flyers wings to ascend to his height?

No arrow can reach him; nor thought can attain
To the placid supreme in the sweep of his reign.

The Tuft of Kelp

All dripping in tangles green,
　Cast up by a lonely sea,
If purer for that, O Weed,
　Bitterer, too, are ye?

The Maldive Shark

About the Shark, phlegmatical one,
Pale sot of the Maldive sea,
The sleek little pilot-fish, azure and slim,
How alert in attendance be.
From his saw-pit of mouth, from his charnel of maw
They have nothing of harm to dread,

But liquidly glide on his ghastly flank
Or before his Gorgonian head;
Or lurk in the port of serrated teeth
In white triple tiers of glittering gates,
And there find a haven when peril's abroad,
An asylum in jaws of the Fates!

They are friends; and friendly they guide him to prey,
Yet never partake of the treat—
Eyes and brains to the dotard lethargic and dull,
Pale ravener of horrible meat.

To Ned

Where is the world we roved, Ned Bunn?
    Hollows thereof lay rich in shade
By voyagers old inviolate thrown
    Ere Paul Pry cruised with Pelf and Trade.
To us old lads some thoughts come home
Who roamed a world young lads no more shall roam.

Nor less the satiate year impends
    When, wearying of routine-resorts,
The pleasure-hunter shall break loose,
    Ned, for our Pantheistic ports:—
Marquesas and glenned isles that be
Authentic Edens in a Pagan sea.

The charm of scenes untried shall lure,
    And, Ned, a legend urge the flight—
The Typee-truants under stars
    Unknown to Shakespere's *Midsummer-Night*;
And man, if lost to Saturn's Age,
Yet feeling life no Syrian pilgrimage.

But, tell, shall he the tourist find
    Our isles the same in violet-glow
Enamoring us what years and years—

Ah, Ned, what years and years ago!
Well, Adam advances, smart in pace,
But scarce by violets that advance you trace.

But we, in anchor-watches calm,
   The Indian Psyche's languor won,
And, musing, breathed primeval balm
   From Edens ere yet over-run;
Marvelling mild if mortal twice,
Here and hereafter, touch a Paradise.

The Berg

(A Dream)

I saw a Ship of martial build
(Her standards set, her brave apparel on)
Directed as by madness mere
Against a stolid Iceberg steer,
Nor budge it, though the infatuate Ship went down.
The impact made huge ice-cubes fall
Sullen, in tons that crashed the deck;
But that one avalanche was all—
No other movement save the foundering wreck.

Along the spurs of ridges pale
Not any slenderest shaft and frail,
A prism over glass-green gorges lone,
Toppled; nor lace of traceries fine,
Nor pendant drops in grot or mine
Were jarred, when the stunned Ship went down.

Nor sole the gulls in cloud that wheeled
Circling one snow-flanked peak afar,
But nearer fowl the floes that skimmed
And crystal beaches, felt no jar.
No thrill transmitted stirred the lock
Of jack-straw needle-ice at base;
Towers undermined by waves—the block

Atilt impending—kept their place.
Seals, dozing sleek on sliddery ledges
Slipt never, when by loftier edges,
Through very inertia overthrown,
The impetuous Ship in bafflement went down.

Hard Berg (methought) so cold, so vast,
With mortal damps self-overcast;
Exhaling still thy dankish breath—
Adrift dissolving, bound for death;
Though lumpish thou, a lumbering one—
A lumbering lubbard loitering slow,
Impingers rue thee and go down,
Sounding thy precipice below,
Nor stir the slimy slug that sprawls
Along thy dense stolidity of walls.

Timoleon

(394 B. C.)

I

If more than once, as annals tell,
Through blood without compunction spilt,
An egotist arch rule has snatched,
And stamped the seizure with his sabre's hilt,
    And, legalised by lawyers, stood;
Shall the good heart whose patriot fire
Leaps to a deed of startling note,
Do it, then flinch? Shall good in weak expire?
    Needs goodness lack the evil grit
That stares down censorship and ban,
And dumbfounds saintlier ones with this—
God's will's avouched in each successful man?
    Or, put it, where dread stress inspires
A virtue beyond man's standard rate,
Seems virtue there a strain forbid—
Transcendence such as shares transgression's fate?

If so, and wan eclipse ensue,
Yet glory await emergence won,
Is that high Providence, or Chance?
And proved it which with thee, Timoleon?
    O, crowned with laurel twined with thorn,
Not rash thy life's cross-tide I stem,
But reck the problem rolled in pang
And reach and dare to touch thy garment's hem.

II

When Argos and Cleone strove
Against free Corinth's claim or right,
Two brothers battled for her well:
A footman one, and one a mounted knight.
    Apart in place, each braved the brunt
Till the rash cavalryman, alone,
Was wrecked against the enemy's files,
His bayard crippled, and he maimed and thrown.
    Timoleon, at Timophanes' need,
Makes for the rescue through the fray,
Covers him with his shield, and takes
The darts and furious odds and fights at bay;
    Till, wrought to pallor of passion dumb,
Stark terrors of death around he throws,
Warding his brother from the field
Spite failing friends dispersed and rallying foes.
    Here might he rest, in claim rest here,
Rest, and a Phidian form remain;
But life halts never, life must on,
And take with term prolonged some scar or stain.
    Yes, life must on. And latent germs
Time's seasons wake in mead and man;
And brothers, playfellows in youth,
Develop into variance wide in span.

III

Timophanes was his mother's pride—
Her pride, her pet, even all to her
Who slackly on Timoleon looked.

Scarce *he* (she mused) may proud affection stir.
　He saved my darling, gossips tell:
If so, 'twas service, yea, and fair;
But instinct ruled, and duty bade,
In service such, a henchman e'en might share.
　When boys they were I helped the bent;
I made the junior feel his place,
Subserve the senior, love him, too;
And sooth he does, and that's his saving grace.
　But me the meek one never can serve,
Not he, he lacks the quality keen
To make the mother through the son
An envied dame of power, a social queen.
　But thou, my first-born, thou art I
In sex translated; joyed, I scan
My features, mine, expressed in thee;
Thou art what I would be were I a man.
　My brave Timophanes, 'tis thou
Who yet the world's fore-front shalt win,
For thine the urgent resolute way,
Self pushing panoplied self through thick and thin.
　Nor here maternal insight erred:
Forsworn, with heart that did not wince
At slaying men who kept their vows,
Her darling strides to power, and reigns—a Prince.

IV

　Because of just heart and humane,
Profound the hate Timoleon knew
For crimes of pride and men-of-prey
And impious deeds that perjurous upstarts do;
　And Corinth loved he, and in way
Old Scotia's clansman loved his clan.
Devotion one with ties how dear,
And passion that late to make the rescue ran.
　But crime and kin—the terrorised town,
The silent, acquiescent mother—
Revulsion racks the filial heart,
The loyal son, the patriot true, the brother.

In evil visions of the night
He sees the lictors of the gods,
Giant ministers of righteousness,
Their *fasces* threatened by the Furies' rods.
  But undeterred he wills to act,
Resolved thereon though Ate rise;
He heeds the voice whose mandate calls,
Or seems to call, peremptory from the skies.

V

  Nor less but by approaches mild,
And trying each prudential art,
The just one first advances him
In parley with a flushed intemperate heart.
  The brother first he seeks—alone,
And pleads; but is with laughter met;
Then comes he, in accord with two,
And these adjure the tyrant and beset;
  Whose merriment gives place to rage:
"Go," stamping, "what to me is Right?
I am the Wrong, and lo, I reign,
And testily intolerant too in might";
  And glooms on his mute brother pale,
Who goes aside; with muffled face
He sobs the predetermined word,
And Right in Corinth reassumes its place.

VI

  But on his robe, ah, whose the blood?
And craven ones their eyes avert,
And heavy is a mother's ban,
And dismal faces of the fools can hurt.
  The whispering-gallery of the world,
Where each breathed slur runs wheeling wide,
Eddies a false perverted truth,
Inveterate turning still on fratricide.
  The time was Plato's. Wandering lights
Confirmed the atheist's standing star;
As now, no sanction Virtue knew

For deeds that on prescriptive morals jar.
    Reaction took misgiving's tone,
Infecting conscience, till betrayed
To doubt the irrevocable doom
Herself had authorised when undismayed.
    Within perturbed Timoleon here
Such deeps were bared as when the sea
Convulsed, vacates its shoreward bed,
And Nature's last reserves show nakedly.
    He falters. And from Hades' glens
By night insidious tones implore—
Why suffer? hither come, and be
What Phocion is who feeleth man no more.
    But, won from that, his mood elects
To live—to live in wilding place;
For years self-outcast, he but meets
In shades his playfellow's reproachful face.
    Estranged through one transcendent deed
From common membership in mart,
In severance he is like a head
Pale after battle trunkless found apart.

VII

    But flood-tide comes though long the ebb,
Nor patience bides with passion long;
Like sightless orbs his thoughts are rolled
Arraigning heaven as compromised in wrong:
    "To second causes why appeal?
Vain parleying here with fellow-clods.
To *you*, Arch Principals, I rear
My quarrel, for this quarrel is with gods.
    "Shall just men long to quit your world?
It is aspersion of your reign;
Your marbles in the temple stand—
Yourselves as stony, and invoked in vain?"
Ah, bear with *one* quite overborne,
Olympians, if he chide ye now;
Magnanimous be even though he rail
And hard against ye set the bleaching brow.—

"If conscience doubt, she'll next recant.
What basis then? O, tell at last,
Are earnest natures staggering here
But fatherless shadows from no substance cast?
  "Yea, *are* ye, gods? Then ye, 'tis ye
Should show what touch of tie ye may,
Since ye too, if not wrung, are wronged
By grievous misconceptions of your sway.
  "But deign, some little sign be given—
Low thunder in your tranquil skies;
Me reassure, nor let me be
Like a lone dog that for a master cries."

VIII

  Men's moods, as frames, must yield to years,
And turns the world in fickle ways:
Corinth recalls Timoleon—ay,
And plumes him forth, but yet with schooling phrase.
  On Sicily's fields, through arduous wars,
A peace he won whose rainbow spanned
The isle redeemed; and he was hailed
Deliverer of that fair colonial land.
  And Corinth clapt: Absolved, and more!
Justice in long arrears is thine:
Not slayer of thy brother, no,
But saviour of the state, Jove's soldier, man divine.
  Eager for thee thy City waits:
Return! with bays we dress your door.
But he, the isle's loved guest, reposed,
And never for Corinth left the adopted shore.

After the Pleasure Party

LINES TRACED
UNDER AN IMAGE OF
AMOR THREATENING

Fear me, virgin whosoever
Taking pride from love exempt,
    Fear me, slighted. Never, never
Brave me, nor my fury tempt:
Downy wings, but wroth they beat
Tempest even in reason's seat.

Behind the house the upland falls
With many an odorous tree—
White marbles gleaming through green halls—
Terrace by terrace, down and down,
And meets the star-lit Mediterranean Sea.

'Tis Paradise. In such an hour
Some pangs that rend might take release.
Nor less perturbed who keeps this bower
Of balm, nor finds balsamic peace?
From whom the passionate words in vent
After long revery's discontent?

"Tired of the homeless deep,
Look how their flight yon hurrying billows urge
    Hitherward but to reap
Passive repulse from the iron-bound verge!
Insensate, can they never know
'Tis mad to wreck the impulsion so?

"An art of memory is, they tell:
But to forget! forget the glade
Wherein Fate sprung Love's ambuscade,
To flout pale years of cloistral life
And flush me in this sensuous strife.
'Tis Vesta struck with Sappho's smart.

No fable her delirious leap:
With more of cause in desperate heart,
Myself could take it—but to sleep!

    "Now first I feel, what all may ween,
That soon or late, if faded e'en,
One's sex asserts itself. Desire,
The dear desire through love to sway,
Is like the Geysers that aspire—
Through cold obstruction win their fervid way.
But baffled here—to take disdain,
To feel rule's instinct, yet not reign;
To dote, to come to this drear shame—
Hence the winged blaze that sweeps my soul
Like prairie-fires that spurn control,
Where withering weeds incense the flame.

    "And kept I long heaven's watch for this,
Contemning love, for this, even this?
O terrace chill in Northern air,
O reaching ranging tube I placed
Against yon skies, and fable chased
Till, fool, I hailed for sister there
Starred Cassiopea in Golden Chair.
In dream I throned me, nor I saw
In cell the idiot crowned with straw.

    "And yet, ah yet, scarce ill I reigned,
Through self-illusion self-sustained,
When now—enlightened, undeceived—
What gain I, barrenly bereaved!
Than this can be yet lower decline—
Envy and spleen, can these be mine?

    "The peasant-girl demure that trod
Beside our wheels that climbed the way,
And bore along a blossoming rod
That looked the sceptre of May-Day—
On her—to fire this petty hell,
His softened glance how moistly fell!

The cheat! on briers her buds were strung;
And wiles peeped forth from mien how meek.
The innocent bare-foot! young, so young!
To girls, strong man's a novice weak.
To tell such beads! And more remain,
Sad rosary of belittling pain.

  "When after lunch and sallies gay
Like the Decameron folk we lay
In sylvan groups; and I——let be!
O, dreams he, can he dream that one
Because not roseate feels no sun?
The plain lone bramble thrills with Spring
As much as vines that grapes shall bring.

  "Me now fair studies charm no more.
Shall great thoughts writ, or high themes sung
Damask wan cheeks—unlock his arm
About some radiant ninny flung?
How glad, with all my starry lore,
I'd buy the veriest wanton's rose
Would but my bee therein repose.

  "Could I remake me! or set free
This sexless bound in sex, then plunge
Deeper than Sappho, in a lunge
Piercing Pan's paramount mystery!
For, Nature, in no shallow surge
Against thee either sex may urge,
Why hast thou made us but in halves—
Co-relatives? This makes us slaves.
If these co-relatives never meet
Self-hood itself seems incomplete.
And such the dicing of blind fate
Few matching halves here meet and mate.
What Cosmic jest or Anarch blunder
The human integral clove asunder
And shied the fractions through life's gate?

"Ye stars that long your votary knew
Rapt in her vigil, see me here!
Whither is gone the spell ye threw
When rose before me Cassiopea?
Usurped on by love's stronger reign—
But, lo, your very selves do wane:
Light breaks—truth breaks! Silvered no more,
But chilled by dawn that brings the gale
Shivers yon bramble above the vale,
And disillusion opens all the shore."

One knows not if Urania yet
The pleasure-party may forget;
Or whether she lived down the strain
Of turbulent heart and rebel brain;
For Amor so resents a slight,
And hers had been such haught disdain,
He long may wreak his boyish spite,
And boy-like, little reck the pain.

One knows not, no. But late in Rome
(For queens discrowned a congruous home)
Entering Albani's porch she stood
Fixed by an antique pagan stone
Colossal carved. No anchorite seer,
Not Thomas à Kempis, monk austere,
Religious more are in their tone;
Yet far, how far from Christian heart
That form august of heathen Art.
Swayed by its influence, long she stood,
Till surged emotion seething down,
She rallied and this mood she won:

"Languid in frame for me,
To-day by Mary's convent-shrine,
Touched by her picture's moving plea
In that poor nerveless hour of mine,
I mused—A wanderer still must grieve.
Half I resolved to kneel and believe,

Believe and submit, the veil take on.
But thee, arm'd Virgin! less benign,
Thee now I invoke, thou mightier one.
Helmeted woman—if such term
Befit thee, far from strife
Of that which makes the sexual feud
And clogs the aspirant life—
O self-reliant, strong and free,
Thou in whom power and peace unite,
Transcender! raise me up to thee,
Raise me and arm me!"

                         Fond appeal.
For never passion peace shall bring,
Nor Art inanimate for long
Inspire. Nothing may help or heal
While Amor incensed remembers wrong.
Vindictive, not himself he'll spare;
For scope to give his vengeance play
Himself he'll blaspheme and betray.

Then for Urania, virgins everywhere,
O pray! Example take too, and have care.

The Ravaged Villa

In shards the sylvan vases lie,
   Their links of dance undone,
And brambles wither by thy brim,
   Choked Fountain of the Sun!
The spider in the laurel spins,
   The weed exiles the flower:
And, flung to kiln, Apollo's bust
   Makes lime for Mammon's tower.

Monody

To have known him, to have loved him,
    After loneness long;
And then to be estranged in life,
    And neither in the wrong;
And now for death to set his seal—
    Ease me, a little ease, my song!

By wintry hills his hermit-mound
    The sheeted snow-drifts drape,
And houseless there the snow-bird flits
    Beneath the fir-tree's crape:
Glazed now with ice the cloistral vine
    That hid the shyest grape.

The Bench of Boors

In bed I muse on Teniers' boors,
Embrowned and beery losels all:
    A wakeful brain
    Elaborates pain:
Within low doors the slugs of boors
Laze and yawn, and doze again.

In dreams they doze, the drowsy boors,
Their hazy hovel warm and small:
    Thought's ampler bound
    But chill is found:
Within low doors the basking boors
Snugly hug the ember-mound.

Sleepless, I see the slumberous boors
Their blurred eyes blink, their eyelids fall:
    Thought's eager sight
    Aches—overbright!
Within low doors the boozy boors
Cat-naps take in pipe-bowl light.

Art

In placid hours well-pleased we dream
Of many a brave unbodied scheme.
But form to lend, pulsed life create,
What unlike things must meet and mate:
A flame to melt—a wind to freeze;
Sad patience—joyous energies;
Humility—yet pride and scorn;
Instinct and study; love and hate;
Audacity—reverence. These must mate,
And fuse with Jacob's mystic heart,
To wrestle with the angel—Art.

Shelley's Vision

Wandering late by morning seas
When my heart with pain was low—
Hate the censor pelted me—
Deject I saw my shadow go.

In elf-caprice of bitter tone
I too would pelt the pelted one:
At my shadow I cast a stone.

When lo, upon that sun-lit ground
I saw the quivering phantom take
The likeness of Saint Stephen crowned:
Then did self-reverence awake.

Fragments of a Lost Gnostic Poem
of the 12th Century

*   *   *   *

Found a family, build a state,
The pledged event is still the same:
Matter in end will never abate
His ancient brutal claim.

*   *   *   *

Indolence is heaven's ally here,
And energy the child of hell:
The Good Man pouring from his pitcher clear
But brims the poisoned well.

Venice

With Pantheist energy of will
The little craftsman of the Coral Sea
Strenuous in the blue abyss,
Up-builds his marvellous gallery
     And long arcade,
Erections freaked with many a fringe
     Of marble garlandry,
Evincing what a worm can do.

Laborious in a shallower wave,
     Advanced in kindred art,
A prouder agent proved Pan's might
When Venice rose in reefs of palaces.

In a Bye-Canal

A swoon of noon, a trance of tide,
The hushed siesta brooding wide
   Like calms far off Peru;
No floating wayfarer in sight,
Dumb noon, and haunted like the night
   When Jael the wiled one slew.

A languid impulse from the oar
Plied by my indolent gondolier
Tinkles against a palace hoar,
   And, hark, response I hear!
A lattice clicks; and, lo, I see,
Between the slats, mute summoning me,
What loveliest eyes of scintillation,
What basilisk glance of conjuration!

   Fronted I have, part taken the span
Of portents in nature and peril in man.
I have swum—I have been
'Twixt the whale's black flukes and the white shark's fin;
The enemy's desert have wandered in,
And there have turned, have turned and scanned,
Following me how noiselessly,
Envy and Slander, lepers hand in hand.
All this. But at the latticed eye—
"Hey! Gondolier, you sleep, my man;
Wake up!" And, shooting by, we ran;
The while I mused, This, surely, now,
Confutes the Naturalists, allow!
Sirens, true sirens verily be,
Sirens, waylayers in the sea.

Well, wooed by these same deadly misses,
   Is it shame to run?
No! flee them did divine Ulysses,
   Brave, wise, and Venus' son.

In a Church of Padua

   In vaulted place where shadows flit,
An upright sombre box you see:
A door, but fast, and lattice none.
But punctured holes minutely small
In lateral silver panel square
Above a kneeling-board without,
Suggest an aim if not declare.

Who bendeth here the tremulous knee
No glimpse may get of him within,
And he immured may hardly see
The soul confessing there the sin;
Nor yields the low-sieved voice a tone
Whereby the murmurer may be known.

Dread diving-bell! In thee inurned
What hollows the priest must sound,
Descending into consciences
    Where more is hid than found.

The Archipelago

Sail before the morning breeze
The Sporads through and Cyclades,
They look like isles of absentees—
                Gone whither?

You bless Apollo's cheering ray,
But Delos, his own isle, to-day
Not e'en a Selkirk there to pray
                God friend me!

Scarce lone these groups, scarce lone and bare,
When Theseus roved a Raleigh there,
Each isle a small Virginia fair—
                Unravished.

Nor less, though havoc fell they rue,
They still retain, in outline true,
Their grace of form when earth was new
                And primal.

But beauty clear, the frame's as yet,
Never shall make one quite forget
Thy picture, Pan, therein once set—
                Life's revel!

'Tis Polynesia reft of palms,
Seaward no valley breathes her balms—
Not such as musk thy rings of calms,
                    Marquesas!

Rose Window

The preacher took from *Solomon's Song*
Four words for text with mystery rife—
The Rose of Sharon,—figuring Him
The Resurrection and the Life;
And, pointing many an urn in view,
How honied a homily he drew.

There, in the slumberous afternoon,
Through minster gray, in lullaby rolled
The hummed metheglin charged with swoon.
Drowsy, my decorous hands I fold
Till sleep overtakes with dream for boon.

I saw an Angel with a Rose
Come out of Morning's garden-gate,
And lamp-like hold the Rose aloft.
He entered a sepulchral Strait.
I followed. And I saw the Rose
Shed dappled dawn upon the dead;
The shrouds and mort-cloths all were lit
To plaids and chequered tartans red.

I woke. The great Rose-Window high,
A mullioned wheel in gable set,
Suffused with rich and soft in dye
Where Iris and Aurora met;
Aslant in sheaf of rays it threw
From all its foliate round of panes
Transfiguring light on dingy stains,
While danced the motes in dusty pew.

The Rose Farmer

Coming through the rye:
Hereof the rural poet whistles;
But who the flute will try
At *scrambling through the thistles!*
Nor less upon some roseate way
Emerge the prickly passage may.

But we who after ragged scrambles
Through fate's blessed thorns and brambles
Come unto our roses late—
Aright to manage the estate,
This indeed it well may task us
Quite inexperienced as we be
In aught but thickets that unmasque us
Of man's ennobling drapery.

Indigence is a plain estate:
Riches imply the complicate.
What peevish pestering wants surprise,
What bothering ambitions rise!
Then, too, Fate loans a lot luxurious
At such hard cent-per-cent usurious!
Mammon, never meek as Moses,
Gouty, mattressed on moss-roses,
A crumpled rose-leaf makes him furious.
Allow, as one's purveyor here
Of sweet content of Christian cheer,
"Vile Pelf" we overestimate.
Howbeit, a rose-farm nigh Damascus
Would Dives change at even rate
For Lazarus' snow-farm in Alaskus?

But chat recalls me: I return.—
A friend, whose shadow has decreased,
For whom they reared a turbaned urn,
A corpulent grandee of the East,
Whose kind good will to me began
When I against his Rhamadan

Prepared a *chowder* for his feast,
Well, dying, he remembered me:
A brave bequest, a farm in fee
Forever consecrate to roses,
And laved by streams that sacred are,
Pharpar and twin-born Abana,
Which last the pleasure-ground incloses,
At least winds half-way roundabout—
That garden to caress, no doubt.

But, ah, the stewardship it poses!
Every hour the bloom, the bliss
Upbraid me that I am remiss.
For still I dally,—I delay,—
Long do hesitate, and say,
"Of fifty thousand Damask Roses,—
(For my rose-farm no great matter),—
Shall I make me heaps of posies,
Or some crystal drops of Attar?
To smell or sell or for a boon
Quick you cull a rose and easy;
But Attar is not got so soon,
Demanding more than gesture breezy.
Yet this same Attar, I suppose,
Long time will last, outlive indeed
The rightful sceptre of the rose
And coronations of the weed.

Sauntering, plunged in this debate,
And somewhat leaning to elect
The thing most easy to effect,
I chanced upon a Persian late,
A sort of gentleman-rose-farmer
On knees beside his garden-gate
Telling his beads, just like a palmer.
Beads? coins, I meant. Each golden one
Upon a wire of silver run;
And every time a coin he told
His brow he raised and eyes he rolled
Devout in grateful orison.

Surely, methought, this pious man,
A florist too, will solve my doubt.
Saluting him, I straight began:
"Decide, I pray, a dubious matter,—"
And put the Roses and the Attar.

Whereat the roses near and far—
For all his garden was a lawn
Of roses thick as daisies are
In meads from smoky towns withdrawn—
They turned their heads like ladies, when
They hear themselves discussed by men.
But he, he swerved a wrinkled face,
Elderly, yet with ruddy trace—
Tinged doubly by warm flushings thrown
From sunset's roses and his own;
And, after scanning me and sounding,
"And you? an older man than I?
Late come you with your sage propounding:
Allah! your time has long gone by."—
"Indeed, Sir, but so ruled the fate
I came unto my roses late.
What then? these gray hairs but disguise,
Since down in heart youth never dies—
O, sharpened by the long delay,
I'm eager for my roses quite;
But first would settle this prime matter—
Touching the Roses and the Attar:
I fear to err there; set me right."

Meseemed his purs'd eyes grateful twinkled
Hearing of veteran youth unwrinkled,
Himself being old. But now the answer
Direct came, like a charging lancer:
"Attar? go ask the Parsee yonder.
Lean as a rake with his distilling,
Cancel his debts, scarce worth a shilling!
How he exists I frequent wonder.
No neighbor loves him: sweet endeavor
Will get a nosegay from him never;

No, nor even your ducats will;
A very save-all for his still!
Of *me,* however, all speak well;
You see, my little coins I tell;
I give away, but more I sell.
In mossy pots, or bound in posies,
Always a market for my roses.
But attar, why, it comes so dear
Tis far from popular, that's clear.
I flourish, I; yon heavens they bless me,
My darlings cluster to caress me."
At that fond sentence overheard,
Methought his rose-seraglio stirred.
But further he: "Yon Parsee lours
Headsman and Blue Beard of the flowers.
In virgin flush of efflorescence
When buds their bosoms just disclose,
To get a mummified quintessence
He scimeters the living rose!
I grant, against my different way,
Something, and specious, one might say.
Ay, pluck a rose in dew Auroral,
For buttonette to please the sight,—
The dawn's bloom and the bloom but floral,
Why, what a race with them in flight!
Quick, too, the redolence it stales.
And yet you have the brief delight,
And yet the next morn's bud avails;
And on in sequence."
                    Came that close,
And, lo, in each flushed garden-bed,
What agitation! every rose
Bridling aloft the passionate head!
But *what* it was that angered here,—
Just *why* the high resentment shown,
Pray ask of her who'll hint it clear—
A Mormon's first-wife making moan.
But he, rose-farmer, long time versed
In roses husbanded by him,

Letting a glance upon them skim,
Followed his thread and more rehearsed.
And, waxing now a trifle warm:
"This evanescence is the charm!
And most it wins the spirits that be
Celestial, Sir. It comes to me
It was this fleeting charm in show
That lured the sons of God below,
Tired out with perpetuity
Of heaven's own seventh heaven aglow;
Not Eve's fair daughters, Sir; nay, nay,
Less fugitive in charm are they:
It was the rose." As this he said
So flattering in imputation,—
Angelic sweethearts overhead,
Even seraphs paying them adoration,—
Each rose, as favoring the whim
Grave nodded,—as attesting him.

"But now, Sir, for your urgent matter.
Every way—for wise employment,
Repute and profit, health, enjoyment,
I am for roses—*sink* the Attar!"

And hereupon the downright man
To tell his rosary re-began.
And never a rose in all the garden
Blushed deeper there to hear their warden
So forcefully express his mind.
Methought they even seemed to laugh—
True ladies, who, in temper kind,
Will pardon aught, though unrefined,
Sincerely vouched in their behalf.

Discreet, in second thought's immersion
I wended from this prosperous Persian
Who, verily, seemed in life rewarded
For sapient prudence not amiss,
Nor transcendental essence hoarded

In hope of quintessential bliss:
No, never with painstaking throes
Essays to crystallize the rose.

But here arrest the loom—the line.
Though damask be your precious stuff,
Spin it not out too superfine:
The flower of a subject is enough.

L'ENVOI

Rosy dawns the morning Syrian,
   Youthful as in years of Noah:
    Why then aging at three-score?
Do moths infest your mantle Tyrian?
    Shake it out where the sun-beams pour
Time, Amigo, does but masque us—
    Boys in gray wigs, young at core.
Look, what damsels of Damascus,
    Roses, lure to Pharpar's shore!
Sigh not—Age, dull tranquilizer,
    And arid years that filed before,
For flowers unfit us. Nay, be wiser:
    Wiser in relish, if sedate
    Come gray-beards to their roses late.

Pontoosuce

Crowning a bluff where gleams the lake below,
Some pillared pines in well-spaced order stand
And like an open temple show.
And here in best of seasons bland,
Autumnal noon-tide, I look out
From dusk arcades on sunshine all about.

Beyond the Lake, in upland cheer
Fields, pastoral fields, and barns appear,
They skirt the hills where lonely roads
Revealed in links through tiers of woods

Wind up to indistinct abodes
And faery-peopled neighborhoods;
While further fainter mountains keep
Hazed in romance impenetrably deep.

Look, corn in stacks, on many a farm,
And orchards ripe in languorous charm,
As dreamy Nature, feeling sure
Of all her genial labor done,
And the last mellow fruitage won,
Would idle out her term mature;
Reposing like a thing reclined
In kinship with man's meditative mind.

For me, within the brown arcade—
Rich life, methought; sweet here in shade
And pleasant abroad in air!—But, nay,
A counter thought intrusive played,
A thought as old as thought itself,
And who shall lay it on the shelf!—
I felt the beauty bless the day
In opulence of autumn's dower;
But evanescence will not stay!
A year ago was such an hour
As this, which but foreruns the blast
Shall sweep these live leaves to the dead leaves past.

All dies!—
                    I stood in revery long.
Then, to forget death's ancient wrong,
I turned me in the brown arcade,
And there by chance in lateral glade
I saw low tawny mounds in lines
Relics of trunks of stately pines
Ranked erst in colonnades where, lo!
Erect succeeding pillars show!

All dies! and not alone
The aspiring trees and men and grass;
The poet's forms of beauty pass,

And noblest deeds they are undone.
Even truth itself decays, and lo,
From truth's sad ashes fraud and falsehood grow.
All dies!
The workman dies, and, after him, the work;
Like to these pines whose graves I trace,
Statue and statuary fall upon their face:
In very amaranths the worm doth lurk,
Even stars, Chaldæans say, have left their place.
Andes and Apalachee tell
Of havoc ere our Adam fell,
And present Nature as a moss doth show
On the ruins of the Nature of the æons of long ago.

But look—and hark!
                    Adown the glade,
Where light and shadow sport at will,
Who cometh vocal, and arrayed
As in the first pale tints of morn—
So pure, rose-clear, and fresh and chill!
Some ground-pine sprigs her brow adorn,
The earthy rootlets tangled clinging.
Over tufts of moss which dead things made,
Under vital twigs which danced or swayed,
Along she floats, and lightly singing:

"Dies, all dies!
The grass it dies, but in vernal rain
Up it springs and it lives again;
Over and over, again and again
It lives, it dies and it lives again.
Who sighs that all dies?
Summer and winter, and pleasure and pain
And everything everywhere in God's reign,
They end, and anon they begin again:
Wane and wax, wax and wane:
Over and over and over amain
End, ever end, and begin again—
End, ever end, and forever and ever begin again!"
She ceased, and nearer slid, and hung

In dewy guise; then softlier sung:
"Since light and shade are equal set
And all revolves, nor more ye know;
Ah, why should tears the pale cheek fret
For aught that waneth here below.
Let go, let go!"

With that, her warm lips thrilled me through,
She kissed me, while her chaplet cold
Its rootlets brushed against my brow
With all their humid clinging mould.
She vanished, leaving fragrant breath
And warmth and chill of wedded life and death.

Billy in the Darbies

Good of the chaplain to enter Lone Bay
And down on his marrowbones here and pray
For the likes just o' me, Billy Budd.—But, look:
Through the port comes the moonshine astray!
It tips the guard's cutlass and silvers this nook;
But 'twill die in the dawning of Billy's last day.
A jewel-block they'll make of me tomorrow,
Pendant pearl from the yardarm-end
Like the eardrop I gave to Bristol Molly—
O, 'tis me, not the sentence they'll suspend.
Ay, ay, all is up; and I must up too,
Early in the morning, aloft from alow.
On an empty stomach now never it would do.
They'll give me a nibble—bit o' biscuit ere I go.
Sure, a messmate will reach me the last parting cup;
But, turning heads away from the hoist and the belay,
Heaven knows who will have the running of me up!
No pipe to those halyards.—But aren't it all sham?
A blur's in my eyes; it is dreaming that I am.
A hatchet to my hawser? All adrift to go?
The drum roll to grog, and Billy never know?
But Donald he has promised to stand by the plank;

So I'll shake a friendly hand ere I sink.
But—no! It is dead then I'll be, come to think.
I remember Taff the Welshman when he sank.
And his cheek it was like the bidding pink.
But me they'll lash in hammock, drop me deep.
Fathoms down, fathoms down, how I'll dream fast asleep.
I feel it stealing now. Sentry, are you there?
Just ease these darbies at the wrist,
And roll me over fair!
I am sleepy, and the oozy weeds about me twist.

HENRY HOWARD BROWNELL

(1820–1872)

Suspiria Noctis

Reading, and reading—little is the gain
  Long dwelling with the minds of dead men leaves.
List rather to the melancholy rain,
               Drop—dropping from the eaves.

Still the old tale—how hardly worth the telling!
  Hark to the wind!—again that mournful sound,
That, all night long, around this lonely dwelling,
               Moans like a dying hound.

The Battle Summers

Again the glory of the days!
  Once more the dreamy sunshine fills
  Noon after noon,—and all the hills
Lie soft and dim in autumn haze.

And lovely lie these meadows low
  In the slant sun—and quiet broods
  Above the splendor of the woods
All touched with autumn's tenderest glow.

The trees stand marshalled, clan by clan,
  A bannered army, far and near—
  (Mark how yon fiery maples rear
Their crimson colors in the van!)

Methinks, these ancient haunts among,
  A fuller life informs the fall—
  The crows in council sit and call,
The quail through stubble leads her young.

The woodcock whirrs by bush and brake,
　　The partridge plies his cedar-search —
　　(Old Andy says the trout and perch
Are larger now, in stream and lake.)

O'er the brown leaves, the forest floor,
　　With nut and acorn scantly strewed,
　　The small red people of the wood
Are out to seek their winter store.

To-day they gather, each and all,
　　To take their last of autumn suns —
　　E'en the gray squirrel lithely runs
Along the mossy pasture wall.

By marsh and brook, by copse and hill,
　　To their old quiet haunts repair
　　The feeble things of earth and air,
And feed and flutter at their will.

The feet that roved this woodland round,
　　The hands that scared the timid race,
　　Now mingle in a mightier chase,
Or mould on that great Hunting-Ground.

Strange calm and peace! — ah, who could deem,
　　By this still glen, this lone hill-side,
　　How three long summers, in their pride,
Have smiled above that awful Dream? —

Have ever woven a braver green,
　　And ever arched a lovelier blue
　　Yet nature, in her every hue,
Took color from the dread Unseen.

The haze of Indian Summer seemed
　　Borne from far fields of sulphury breath —
　　A subtile atmosphere of death
Was ever round us as we dreamed.

The horizon's dim heat-lightning played
    Like small-arms, still, through nights of drouth,
    And the low thunder of the south
Was dull and distant cannonade.

To us the glory or the gray
    Had still a stranger, stormier dye,
    Remembering how we watched the sky
Of many a waning battle day,

O'er many a field of loss or fame—
    How Shiloh's eve to ashes turned,
    And how Manassas' sunset burned
Incarnadine of blood and flame.

And how, in thunder, day by day,
    The hot sky hanging over all,
    Beneath that sullen, lurid pall,
The Week of Battles rolled away!

Give me my legions!—so, in grief,
    Like him of Rome, our Father cried—
    (A Nation's Flower lay down and died
In yon fell shade!)—ah, hapless chief—

Too late we learned thy star!—o'erta'en,
    (Of error or of fate o'erharsh,)
    Like Varus, in the fatal marsh
Where skill and valor all were vain!

All vain—Fair Oaks and Seven Pines!
    A deeper hue than dying Fall
    May lend, is yours!——yet over all
The mild Virginian autumn shines.

And still a Nation's Heart o'erhung
    The iron echoes pealed afar,
    Along a thousand leagues of war
The battle thunders tossed and flung.

Till, when our fortunes paled the most,
   And Hope had half forgot to wave
   Her banner o'er the wearied brave—
A morning saw the traitor host

Rolled back o'er red Potomac's wave,
   And the Great River burst his way!—
   And all on that dear Summer's Day
Day that our fathers died and gave.

Rest in thy calm, Eternal Right!
   For thee, though levin-scarred and torn,
   Through flame and death shall still be borne
The Red, the Azure, and the White.

We pass—we sink like summer's snow—
   Yet on the mighty Cause shall move,
   Though every field a Cannæ prove,
And every pass a Roncesvaux.

Though every summer burn anew
   A battle-summer—though each day
   We name a new Aceldama,
Or some dry Golgotha re-dew.

And thou, in lonely dream withdrawn!
   What dost thou, while in tempest dies
   The long drear Night, and all the skies
Are red with Freedom's fiery Dawn!

Behold, thy summer days are o'er—
   Yet dearer, lovelier these that fall
   Wrapped in red autumn's flag, than all
The green and glory gone before.

'Twas well to sing by stream and sod,
   And they there were that loved thy lays—
   But lo, where, 'neath yon battle-haze,
Thy brothers bare the breast for God!

Reck not of waning force nor breath—
  Some little aid may yet be thine,
  Some honor to the All-Divine,—
To-day, where, by yon River of Death,

His stars on Rosecrans look down—
  Or, on the morrow, by moat and wall,
  Once more when the Great Admiral
Thunders on traitor fleet and town.

O wearied heart! O darkening eye!
  (How long to hope and trust untrue!)
  What in the hurly can ye do?
Little, 'tis like—yet we can die.

ALICE CARY

(1820–1871)

The Sea-Side Cave

*"A bird of the air shall carry the voice, and that
which hath wings shall tell the matter."*

At the dead of night by the side of the Sea
I met my gray-haired enemy,—
The glittering light of his serpent eye
Was all I had to see him by.

At the dead of night, and stormy weather
We went into a cave together,—
Into a cave by the side of the Sea,
And—he never came out with me!

The flower that up through the April mould
Comes like a miser dragging his gold,
Never made spot of earth so bright
As was the ground in the cave that night.

Dead of night, and stormy weather!
Who should see us going together
Under the black and dripping stone
Of the cave from whence I came alone!

Next day as my boy sat on my knee
He picked the gray hairs off from me,
And told with eyes brimful of fear
How a bird in the meadow near

Over her clay-built nest had spread
Sticks and leaves all bloody red,
Brought from a cave by the side of the Sea
Where some murdered man must be.

To Solitude

I am weary of the working,
   Weary of the long day's heat;
To thy comfortable bosom,
   Wilt thou take me, spirit sweet?

Weary of the long, blind struggle
   For a pathway bright and high,—
Weary of the dimly dying
   Hopes that never quite all die.

Weary searching a bad cipher
   For a good that must be meant;
Discontent with being weary,—
   Weary with my discontent.

I am weary of the trusting
   Where my trusts but torments prove;
Wilt thou keep faith with me? wilt thou
   Be my true and tender love?

I am weary drifting, driving
   Like a helmless bark at sea;
Kindly, comfortable spirit,
   Wilt thou give thyself to me?

Give thy birds to sing me sonnets?
   Give thy winds my cheeks to kiss?
And thy mossy rocks to stand for
   The memorials of our bliss?

I in reverence will hold thee,
   Never vexed with jealous ills,
Though thy wild and wimpling waters
   Wind about a thousand hills.

Autumn

Shorter and shorter now the twilight clips
   The days, as through the sunset gates they crowd,
And Summer from her golden collar slips
   And strays through stubble-fields, and moans aloud,

Save when by fits the warmer air deceives,
   And, stealing hopeful to some sheltered bower,
She lies on pillows of the yellow leaves,
   And tries the old tunes over for an hour.

The wind, whose tender whisper in the May
   Set all the young blooms listening through th' grove,
Sits rustling in the faded boughs to-day
   And makes his cold and unsuccessful love.

The rose has taken off her tire of red—
   The mullein-stalk its yellow stars have lost,
And the proud meadow-pink hangs down her head
   Against earth's chilly bosom, witched with frost.

The robin, that was busy all the June,
   Before the sun had kissed the topmost bough,
Catching our hearts up in his golden tune,
   Has given place to the brown cricket now.

The very cock crows lonesomely at morn—
   Each flag and fern the shrinking stream divides—
Uneasy cattle low, and lambs forlorn
   Creep to their strawy sheds with nettled sides.

Shut up the door: who loves me must not look
   Upon the withered world, but haste to bring
His lighted candle, and his story-book,
   And live with me the poetry of Spring.

Katrina on the Porch

A Bit of Turner Put into Words

An old, old house by the side of the sea,
   And never a picture poet would paint;
   But I hold the woman above the saint,
And the light of the hearth is more to me
   Than shimmer of air-built castle.

It fits as it grew to the landscape there—
   One hardly feels as he stands aloof
   Where the sandstone ends, and the red slate roof
Juts over the window, low and square,
   That looks on the wild sea-water.

From the top of the hill so green and high
   There slopeth a level of golden moss,
   That bars of scarlet and amber cross,
And rolling out to the further sky
   Is the world of wild sea-water.

Some starved grape-vineyards round about—
   A zigzag road cut deep with ruts—
   A little cluster of fishers' huts,
And the black sand scalloping in and out
   'Twixt th' land and th' wild sea-water.

Gray fragments of some border towers,
   Flat, pellmell on a circling mound,
   With a furrow deeply worn all round
By the feet of children through the flowers,
   And all by the wild sea-water.

And there, from the silvery break o' th' day
   Till the evening purple drops to the land,
   She sits with her cheek like a rose in her hand,
And her sad and wistful eyes one way—
   The way of the wild sea-water.

And there, from night till the yellowing morn
　　Falls over the huts and th' scallops of sand—
　　A tangle of curls like a torch in her hand—
She sits and maketh her moan so lorn,
　　With the moan of the wild sea-water.

Only a study for homely eyes,
　　And never a picture poet would paint;
　　But I hold the woman above the saint,
And the light of the humblest hearth I prize
　　O'er the luminous air-built castle.

The West Country

Have you been in our wild west country? then
　　You have often had to pass
Its cabins lying like birds' nests in
　　The wild green prairie grass.

Have you seen the women forget their wheels
　　As they sat at the door to spin—
Have you seen the darning fall away
　　From their fingers worn and thin,

As they asked you news of the villages
　　Where they were used to be,
Gay girls at work in the factories
　　With their lovers gone to sea!

Ah, have you thought of the bravery
　　That no loud praise provokes—
Of the tragedies acted in the lives
　　Of poor, hard-working folks!

Of the little more, and the little more
    Of hardship which they press
Upon their own tired hands to make
    The toil for the children less:

And not in vain; for many a lad
    Born to rough work and ways,
Strips off his ragged coat, and makes
    Men clothe him with their praise.

JOHN HENRY HOPKINS, JR.

(1820–1891)

Three Kings of Orient

We Three Kings of Orient are,
Bearing gifts we traverse afar,
    Field and fountain,
    Moor and mountain,
Following yonder Star.

           O Star of Wonder, Star of Night,
           Star with Royal Beauty bright,
           Westward leading,
           Still proceeding,
           Guide us to Thy perfect Light.

GASPARD.

Born a KING on Bethlehem plain,
GOLD I bring to crown Him again,
    King for ever,
    Ceasing never
Over us all to reign.

Chorus

MELCHIOR.

FRANKINCENSE to offer have I,
Incense owns a Deity nigh:
    Prayer and praising
    All men raising,
Worship Him GOD on High.

Chorus

BALTHAZAR.

MYRRH is mine; its bitter perfume
Breathes a life of gathering gloom;—
    Sorrowing, sighing,
    Bleeding, dying,
Sealed in the stone-cold tomb.

Chorus

Glorious now behold Him arise,
KING, and GOD, and SACRIFICE;
    Heav'n sings Hallelujah:
    Hallelujah the earth replies.

Chorus

FREDERICK GODDARD TUCKERMAN

(1821–1873)

Sonnets

I.

The starry flower, the flower-like stars that fade
And brighten with the daylight and the dark,—
The bluet in the green I faintly mark,
And glimmering crags with laurel overlaid,
Even to the Lord of light, the Lamp of shade,
Shine one to me,—the least, still glorious made
As crownèd moon, or heaven's great hierarch.
And, so, dim grassy flower, and night-lit spark,
Still move me on and upward for the True;
Seeking through change, growth, death, in new and old.
The full in few, the statelier in the less,
With patient pain; always remembering this,—
His hand, who touched the sod with showers of gold,
Stippled Orion on the midnight blue.

II.

And so, as this great sphere (now turning slow
Up to the light from that abyss of stars,
Now wheeling into gloom through sunset bars)—
With all its elements of form and flow,
And life in life; where crowned, yet blind, must go
The sensible king,—is but an Unity
Compressed of motes impossible to know;
Which worldlike yet in deep analogy,
Have distance, march, dimension, and degree;
So the round earth—which we the world do call—
Is but a grain in that that mightiest swells,
Whereof the stars of light are particles,
As ultimate atoms of one infinite Ball,
On which God moves, and treads beneath his feet the All!

The Question

How shall I array my love?
How should I arrange my fair?
Leave her standing white and silent
In the richness of her hair?
Motion silent, beauty bare
In the glory of her hair?
Or, for place and drapery,
Ravage land, and sack the sea?

Or from darkest summer sky,
When the white belts, riding high,
Cut the clear like ribs of pearl,
On the eastern upland's curl,
In the time of dusk and dew
Tear away a breadth of blue?
Touched from twilight's rosy bars,
With each twinkling tuft of stars,
And, shaking out the glints of gold,
Catch her softly from the cold?—
Catch, and lift her to the cloud,
Where to crown her, passing proud,
Gliding, glistening woods of June,
Reach the rain-ring from the moon?

Or—to fold her warmer-wise—
Let me try, in garb and guise
Gathered from this mortal globe;
Roll her beauty in a robe
Of the Persian lilach stain,
Purple, dim with filigrane;
Belted-in with rarer red
Than India's leaf ere figurèd,
Put a crown upon her head!
Then to lead her, high and cold,
Where, from a step of silver rolled
A crimson floweth on the floor;
Like a river riding o'er

Pearl, and priceless marbles bright,—
Onyx, myrrhine, marcasite,
And jasper green!—nor these alone,
But the famed Phengites stone,—
And leading upward to the throne.
Prop and pillar, roof and rise,
All ashake with drops and dyes,
And the diamond's precious eyes;
And she, as if a sudden storm
Had fallen upon her face and form;
Diamonds like raindrops rare,
Pearls like hailstones in her hair;
In the lamplight's ruddy stream,
Jewels crossed with jewels gleam
On jewels, jewel-circled there;
While, round her wrists and ankles bare,
Gems of jewels glimpse and gaze,—
Hyacinth, rose-stone, idocrase.

Or she stealeth, soft arrayed
Like a white Hæmonian maid
Winding under cypress shade;
Cedar shade, and paths of green,
With porch and pillar, white between;
Amaranth eyes do mine behold,
Hair like the pale marigold:
Dreamily she seems to me
Hero, or Herodice!
With a sidelong motion sweet,
Thoro' flowers she draws her feet;
This way now the ripples come,—
Shower myrtles, myrrh, and gum,
With heliochryse and ámomum!

Ah! not so, New England's flower!
Separate must her beauty be
From stars of old mythology,—
Priestesses, or Chrysophoræ,
Nor fairy garb, nor kingly dower,

May fit her in her radiant hour;
Free and bold her steps must flow,
All men see her come and go;
At her feet the planet lies,
Day and night are in her eyes,
Over her the star-flag strewn:
Lo! she standeth there alone,
Pride, in her dark glances, king!
Love, her cheek rose-colouring;
In a garden all her own,
Lo! she standeth, crownèd on
With rare roses, round her drawn
Texture like the webs of dawn
On the rose-beds lingering,
While my heart to her I bring;
Heart and garden all her own—
What, in truth, cares such a one,
Though my arm could round her throw
Gleam of gods, or crowns bestow?
Or though the old gods could confer
All godlike gifts and grace on her?
The young Medusa's locks divine,
Pelops' shoulder eburnine,
Lips that drew the Ismenean bees,
Tears of the Heliades,
Dropped into shimmering shells that be
About the indraught of the sea.
The river-riches of the sphere,
All that the dark sea-bottoms bear,
The wide earth's green convexity,
The inexhaustible blue sky,
Hold not a prize, so proud, so high,
That it could grace her, gay or grand,
By garden-gale and rose-breath fanned;
Or as to-night I saw her stand,
Lovely in the meadow-land,
With a clover in her hand.

from *Sonnets, First Series*

VII

Dank fens of cedar; hemlock-branches gray
With tress and trail of mosses wringing-wet;
Beds of the black pitch-pine in dead leaves set
Whose wasted red has wasted to white away;
Remnants of rain, and droppings of decay,—
Why hold ye so my heart, nor dimly let
Through your deep leaves the light of yesterday,
The faded glimmer of a sunshine set?
Is it that in your darkness, shut from strife,
The bread of tears becomes the bread of life?
Far from the roar of day, beneath your boughs
Fresh griefs beat tranquilly, and loves and vows
Grow green in your gray shadows, dearer far
Even than all lovely lights, and roses, are?

VIII

As when, down some broad River dropping, we,
Day after day, behold the assuming shores
Sink and grow dim, as the great Water-course
Pushes his banks apart and seeks the sea;
Benches of pines, high shelf and balcony,
To flats of willow and low sycamores
Subsiding, till, where'er the wave we see,
Himself is his horizon utterly:
So fades the portion of our early world.
Still on the ambit hangs the purple air;
Yet, while we lean to read the secret there,
The stream that by green shore-sides plashed and purled
Expands; the mountains melt to vapors rare,
And life alone circles out flat and bare.

X

An upper chamber in a darkened house,
Where, ere his footsteps reached ripe manhood's brink,
Terror and anguish were his cup to drink,—
I cannot rid the thought, nor hold it close;
But dimly dream upon that man alone;—
Now though the autumn clouds most softly pass;
The cricket chides beneath the doorstep stone,
And greener than the season grows the grass.
Nor can I drop my lids, nor shade my brows,
But there he stands beside the lifted sash;
And, with a swooning of the heart, I think
Where the black shingles slope to meet the boughs,
And—shattered on the roof like smallest snows—
The tiny petals of the mountain-ash.

XXII

The morning comes; not slow, with reddening gold,
But wildly driven, with windy shower, and sway
As though the wind would blow the dark away!
Voices of wail, of misery multifold,
Wake with the light, and its harsh glare obey;
And yet I walk betimes this day of spring,
Still my own private portion reckoning,
Not to compute, though every tear be told.
Oh, might I on the gale my sorrow fling!
But sweep, sweep on, wild blast! who bids thee stay?
Across the stormy headlands shriek and sing;
And, earlier than the daytime, bring the day
To pouring eyes, half-quenched with watery sight,
And breaking hearts that hate the morning light!

from *Sonnets, Second Series*

VII

His heart was in his garden; but his brain
Wandered at will among the fiery stars:
Bards, heroes, prophets, Homers, Hamilcars,
With many angels, stood, his eye to gain;
The devils, too, were his familiars.
And yet the cunning florist held his eyes
Close to the ground,—a tulip-bulb his prize,—
And talked of tan and bone-dust, cutworms, grubs,
As though all Nature held no higher strain;
Or, if he spoke of Art, he made the theme
Flow through box-borders, turf, and flower-tubs;
Or, like a garden-engine's, steered the stream,—
Now spouted rainbows to the silent skies;
Now kept it flat, and raked the walks and shrubs.

XVI

Under the mountain, as when first I knew
Its low dark roof, and chimney creeper-twined,
The red house stands; and yet my footsteps find
Vague in the walks, waste balm and feverfew.
But they are gone: no soft-eyed sisters trip
Across the porch or lintels; where, behind,
The mother sat,—sat knitting with pursed lip.
The house stands vacant in its green recess,
Absent of beauty as a broken heart;
The wild rain enters; and the sunset wind
Sighs in the chambers of their loveliness,
Or shakes the pane; and in the silent noons,
The glass falls from the window, part by part,
And ringeth faintly in the grassy stones.

XVII

Roll on, sad world! not Mercury or Mars
Could swifter speed, or slower, round the sun,
Than in this year of variance thou hast done
For me. Yet pain, fear, heart-break, woes, and wars
Have natural limit; from his dread eclipse
The swift sun hastens, and the night debars
The day, but to bring in the day more bright;
The flowers renew their odorous fellowships;
The moon runs round and round; the slow earth dips,
True to her poise, and lifts; the planet-stars
Roll and return from circle to ellipse;
The day is dull and soft, the eave-trough drips;
And yet I know the splendour of the light
Will break anon: look! where the gray is white!

XVIII

And Change, with hurried hand, has swept these scenes:
The woods have fallen; across the meadow-lot
The hunter's trail and trap-path is forgot;
And fire has drunk the swamps of evergreens!
Yet for a moment let my fancy plant
These autumn hills again,—the wild dove's haunt,
The wild deer's walk. In golden umbrage shut,
The Indian river runs, Quonecktacut!
Here, but a lifetime back, where falls to-night
Behind the curtained pane a sheltered light
On buds of rose, or vase of violet
Aloft upon the marble mantel set,—
Here, in the forest-heart, hung blackening
The wolf-bait on the bush beside the spring.

XXIII

Some truths may pierce the spirit's deeper gloom,
Yet shine unapprehended: grand, remote,
We bow before their strength, yet feel them not;

When some low promise of the life to come,
Blessing the mourner, holds the heart indeed,
A leading lamp that all may reach and read!
Nor reck those lights, so distant over us,
Sublime, but helpless to the spirit's need
As the night-stars in heaven's vault! yet, thus,
Though the great asterisms mount and burn
In inaccessible glory,—this, its height
Has reached; but lingers on till light return,
Low in the sky, like frosty Sirius,
To snap and sparkle through the winter's night.

XXIX

How oft in schoolboy-days, from the school's sway
Have I run forth to Nature as to a friend,—
With some pretext of o'erwrought sight, to spend
My school-time in green meadows far away!
Careless of summoning bell, or clocks that strike,
I marked with flowers the minutes of my day:
For still the eye that shrank from hated hours,
Dazzled with decimal and dividend,
Knew each bleached alder-root that plashed across
The bubbling brook, and every mass of moss;
Could tell the month, too, by the vervain-spike,—
How far the ring of purple tiny flowers
Had climbed; just starting, may-be, with the May,
Half-high, or tapering off at Summer's end.

XXX

Yet, even 'mid merry boyhood's tricks and scapes,
Early my heart a deeper lesson learnt;
Wandering alone by many a mile of burnt
Black woodside, that but the snow-flake decks and drapes.
And I have stood beneath Canadian sky,
In utter solitudes, where the cricket's cry
Appals the heart, and fear takes visible shapes;
And on Long Island's void and isolate capes

Heard the sea break like iron bars: and still,
In all, I seemed to hear the same deep dirge;
Borne in the wind, the insect's tiny trill,
And crash and jangle of the shaking surge;
And knew not what they meant,—prophetic woe?
Dim bodings, wherefore? Now, indeed, I know!

from *Sonnets, Third Series*

IV

Thin little leaves of wood fern, ribbed and toothed,
Long curved sail needles of the green pitch pine,
With common sandgrass, skirt the horizon line,
And over these the incorruptible blue!
Here let me gently lie and softly view
All world asperities, lightly touched and smoothed
As by his gracious hand, the great Bestower.
What though the year be late? some colors run
Yet through the dry, some links of melody.
Still let me be, by such, assuaged and soothed
And happier made, as when, our schoolday done,
We hunted on from flower to frosty flower,
Tattered and dim, the last red butterfly,
Or the old grasshopper molasses-mouthed.

V

How well do I recall that walk in state
Across the Common, by the paths we knew:
Myself in silver badge and riband blue,
My little sister with her book and slate;
The elm tree by the Pond, the fence of wood,
The burial place that at the corner stood
Where once we crossed, through the forbidden grate,
The stones that grudg'd us way, the graveside weed,
The ominous wind that turned us half about.
Smit by the flying drops, at what a speed

Across the paths, unblessed and unforgiven
We hurried homeward when the day was late
And heard, with awe that left no place for doubt,
God's anger mutter in the darkened heaven.

X

Sometimes I walk where the deep water dips
Against the land. Or on where fancy drives
I walk and muse aloud, like one who strives
To tell his half-shaped thought with stumbling lips,
And view the ocean sea, the ocean ships,
With joyless heart: still but myself I find
And restless phantoms of my restless mind:
Only the moaning of my wandering words,
Only the wailing of the wheeling plover,
And this high rock beneath whose base the sea
Has wormed long caverns, like my tears in me:
And hard like this I stand, and beaten and blind,
This desolate rock with lichens rusted over,
Hoar with salt-sleet and chalkings of the birds.

from *Sonnets, Fourth Series*

VI

And two I knew, an old man and a boy,
Alternate helpers: for their day was spent
In gathering forest bark; and when they went
Late home, the elder did his time employ
To teach the other and tell him what he knew
Of history, myth, or mathematics hard,
In hours of night and, when the night was dark,
Showed him Job's Coffin, and the Golden Yard,
Showed the nine moonstars in the moonless blue,
And the great Circle of the Bestiary;

So that the child grew up to love the sky
And, in the woods beyond the hemlock bark,
To heed the intricate moss that o'er it grew,
The shadowy flower all wet with all-day dew.

VII

But war his overturning trumpet blew.
And in that scattering blast, the knot was rent
That held them: one his faint steps northward bent,
The younger the blind lot of battle drew;
And all seemed well, no cause for tears or joy;
But tidings came, or else, of these in lieu,
A written word: a hand, though rough to see,
The old man loved, for he had taught the boy.
At length all ceased: the last one *was* the last;
But still he read and with a fond belief
Weighed each, as 'twere to find some link or clue.
It never came, — but days the old man passed
Pondering upon the letters wistfully,
Silent, and with the fiery eye of grief.

VIII

Nor strange it is, to us who walk in bonds
Of flesh and time, if virtue's self awhile
Gleam dull like sunless ice; whilst graceful guile—
Blood-flecked like hamatite or diamonds
With a red inward spark—to reconcile
Beauty and evil seems and corresponds
So well with good that the mind joys to have
Full wider jet and scope: nor swings and sleeps
Forever in one cradle wearily
Like those vast weeds that off d'Acunha's isle
Wash with the surf and flap their mighty fronds
Mournfully to the dipping of the wave,
Yet cannot be disrupted from their deeps
By the whole heave and settle of the sea.

from *Sonnets, Fifth Series*

XV

Let me give something!—though my spring be done,
Give to the children, ere their summertime:
Though stirred with grief, like rain let fall my rhyme
And tell of one whose aim was much, of one
Whose strife was this: that in his thought should be
Some power of wind, some drenching of the sea,
Some drift of stars across a darkling coast,
Imagination, insight, memory, awe,
And dear New England nature first and last,—
Whose end was high, whose work was well-begun:
Of one who from his window looked and saw
His little hemlocks in the morning sun,
And while he gazed, into his heart almost
The peace that passeth understanding passed.

XVI

Let me give something!—as the years unfold,
Some faint fruition, though not much, my most:
Perhaps a monument of labor lost.
But thou, who givest all things, give not me
To sink in silence, seared with early cold,
Frost-burnt and blackened, but quick fire for frost!
As once I saw at a houseside, a tree
Struck scarlet by the lightning, utterly
To its last limb and twig: so strange it seemed,
I stopped to think if this indeed were May,
And were those windflowers? or had I dreamed?
But there it stood, close by the cottage eaves,
Red-ripened to the heart: shedding its leaves
And autumn sadness on the dim spring day.

The Cricket

I

The humming bee purrs softly o'er his flower;
  From lawn and thicket
The dogday locust singeth in the sun
  From hour to hour:
Each has his bard, and thou, ere day be done,
  Shalt have no wrong.
So bright that murmur mid the insect crowd,
Muffled and lost in bottom-grass, or loud
  By pale and picket:
Shall I not take to help me in my song
  A little cooing cricket?

II

The afternoon is sleepy; let us lie
Beneath these branches whilst the burdened brook,
Muttering and moaning to himself, goes by;
And mark our minstrel's carol whilst we look
Toward the faint horizon swooning blue.
  Or in a garden bower,
Trellised and trammeled with deep drapery
  Of hanging green,
  Light glimmering through—
There let the dull hop be,
Let bloom, with poppy's dark refreshing flower:
Let the dead fragrance round our temples beat,
Stunning the sense to slumber, whilst between
The falling water and fluttering wind
  Mingle and meet,
  Murmur and mix,
No few faint pipings from the glades behind,
  Or alder-thicks:
But louder as the day declines,
From tingling tassel, blade, and sheath,
Rising from nets of river vines,
  Winrows and ricks,

Above, beneath,
At every breath,
At hand, around, illimitably
Rising and falling like the sea,
   Acres of cricks!

III

Dear to the child who hears thy rustling voice
Cease at his footstep, though he hears thee still,
Cease and resume with vibrance crisp and shrill,
Thou sittest in the sunshine to rejoice.
Night lover too; bringer of all things dark
And rest and silence; yet thou bringest to me
Always that burthen of the unresting Sea,
The moaning cliffs, the low rocks blackly stark;
These upland inland fields no more I view,
But the long flat seaside beach, the wild seamew,
   And the overturning wave!
Thou bringest too, dim accents from the grave
To him who walketh when the day is dim,
Dreaming of those who dream no more of him,
With edged remembrances of joy and pain;
And heyday looks and laughter come again:
Forms that in happy sunshine lie and leap,
With faces where but now a gap must be,
Renunciations, and partitions deep
And perfect tears, and crowning vacancy!
And to thy poet at the twilight's hush,
No chirping touch of lips with laugh and blush,
But wringing arms, hearts wild with love and woe,
Closed eyes, and kisses that would not let go!

IV

So wert thou loved in that old graceful time
   When Greece was fair,
While god and hero hearkened to thy chime;
   Softly astir
Where the long grasses fringed Caÿster's lip;
Long-drawn, with glimmering sails of swan and ship,

And ship and swan;
    Or where
    Reedy Eurotas ran.
Did that low warble teach thy tender flute
    Xenaphyle?
Its breathings mild? say! did the grasshopper
Sit golden in thy purple hair
    O Psammathe?
    Or wert thou mute,
Grieving for Pan amid the alders there?
And by the water and along the hill
That thirsty tinkle in the herbage still,
Though the lost forest wailed to horns of Arcady?

                              v

Like the Enchanter old—
Who sought mid the dead water's weeds and scum
For evil growths beneath the moonbeam cold,
    Or mandrake or dorcynium;
And touched the leaf that opened both his ears,
So that articulate voices now he hears
In cry of beast, or bird, or insect's hum,—
Might I but find thy knowledge in thy song!
    That twittering tongue,
Ancient as light, returning like the years.
    So might I be,
Unwise to sing, thy true interpreter
Through denser stillness and in sounder dark,
Than ere thy notes have pierced to harrow me.
    So might I stir
    The world to hark
    To thee my lord and lawgiver,
    And cease my quest:
Content to bring thy wisdom to the world;
Content to gain at last some low applause,
    Now low, now lost
Like thine from mossy stone, amid the stems and straws,
    Or garden gravemound tricked and dressed—
    Powdered and pearled

By stealing frost—
In dusky rainbow beauty of euphorbias!
For larger would be less indeed, and like
The ceaseless simmer in the summer grass
To him who toileth in the windy field,
    Or where the sunbeams strike,
Naught in innumerable numerousness.
    So might I much possess,
    So much must yield;
But failing this, the dell and grassy dike,
The water and the waste shall still be dear,
And all the pleasant plots and places
    Where thou hast sung, and I have hung
    To ignorantly hear.
Then Cricket, sing thy song! or answer mine!
Thine whispers blame, but mine has naught but praises.
It matters not. Behold! the autumn goes,
    The shadow grows,
The moments take hold of eternity;
Even while we stop to wrangle or repine
    Our lives are gone—
    Like thinnest mist,
Like yon escaping color in the tree;
Rejoice! rejoice! whilst yet the hours exist—
Rejoice or mourn, and let the world swing on
Unmoved by cricket song of thee or me.

MARIA WHITE LOWELL

(1821–1853)

Rouen

Place de la Pucelle

Here blooms the legend fed with time and chance,
Fresh as the morning, though in centuries old;
The whitest lily in the shield of France,
        With heart of virgin gold.

Along this square she moved, sweet Joan of Arc,
With face more pallid than a day-lit star,
Half seen, half doubted, while before her dark
        Stretched the array of war.

Swift furled the battle-smoke of lying breath
From off her path, as if a wind had blown,
And showed no faithless king, but righteous death
        On the low, wooden throne.

He would reward her; she who meekly wore
Alike her gilded mail and peasant gown,
Meekly received one earthly honor more,—
        The formless, fiery crown.

A white dove trembled up the heated air,
And in the opening zenith found its goal;
Soft as a downward feather fell a prayer
        For each repentant soul.

An Opium Fantasy

Soft hangs the opiate in the brain,
And lulling soothes the edge of pain,
Till harshest sound, far off or near,
Sings floating in its mellow sphere.

What wakes me from my heavy dream?
        Or am I still asleep?
Those long and soft vibrations seem
        A slumberous charm to keep.

The graceful play, a moment stopped,
        Distance again unrolls,
Like silver balls, that, softly dropped,
        Ring into golden bowls.

I question of the poppies red,
        The fairy flaunting band,
While I a weed, with drooping head,
        Within their phalanx stand.

"Some airy one, with scarlet cap,
        The name unfold to me
Of this new minstrel, who can lap
        Sleep in his melody?"

Bright grew their scarlet-kerchiefed heads,
        As freshening winds had blown,
And from their gently swaying beds
        They sang in undertone,

"Oh he is but a little owl,
        The smallest of his kin,
Who sits beneath the midnight's cowl,
        And makes this airy din."

"Deceitful tongues, of fiery tints,
    Far more than this you know,—
That he is your enchanted prince,
    Doomed as an owl to go;

"Nor his fond play for years hath stopped,
    But nightly he unrolls
His silver balls, that, softly dropped,
    Ring into golden bowls."

JAMES MONROE WHITFIELD

(1822–1871)

America

America, it is to thee,
Thou boasted land of liberty,—
It is to thee I raise my song,
Thou land of blood, and crime, and wrong.
It is to thee, my native land,
From whence has issued many a band
To tear the black man from his soil,
And force him here to delve and toil;
Chained on your blood-bemoistened sod,
Cringing beneath a tyrant's rod,
Stripped of those rights which Nature's God
    Bequeathed to all the human race,
Bound to a petty tyrant's nod,
    Because he wears a paler face.
Was it for this, that freedom's fires
Were kindled by your patriot sires?
Was it for this, they shed their blood,
On hill and plain, on field and flood?
Was it for this, that wealth and life
Were staked upon that desperate strife,
Which drenched this land for seven long years
With blood of men, and women's tears?
When black and white fought side by side,
    Upon the well-contested field,—
Turned back the fierce opposing tide,
    And made the proud invader yield—
When, wounded, side by side they lay,
    And heard with joy the proud hurrah
From their victorious comrades say
    That they had waged successful war,
The thought ne'er entered in their brains
That they endured those toils and pains,
To forge fresh fetters, heavier chains

For their own children, in whose veins
Should flow that patriotic blood,
So freely shed on field and flood.
Oh no; they fought, as they believed,
    For the inherent rights of man;
But mark, how they have been deceived
    By slavery's accursed plan.
They never thought, when thus they shed
    Their heart's best blood, in freedom's cause,
That their own sons would live in dread,
    Under unjust, oppressive laws:
That those who quietly enjoyed
    The rights for which they fought and fell,
Could be the framers of a code,
    That would disgrace the fiends of hell!
Could they have looked, with prophet's ken,
    Down to the present evil time,
    Seen free-born men, uncharged with crime,
Consigned unto a slaver's pen,—
Or thrust into a prison cell,
With thieves and murderers to dwell—
While that same flag whose stripes and stars
Had been their guide through freedom's wars
As proudly waved above the pen
Of dealers in the souls of men!
Or could the shades of all the dead,
    Who fell beneath that starry flag,
Visit the scenes where they once bled,
    On hill and plain, on vale and crag,
By peaceful brook, or ocean's strand,
    By inland lake, or dark green wood,
Where'er the soil of this wide land
    Was moistened by their patriot blood,—
And then survey the country o'er,
    From north to south, from east to west,
And hear the agonizing cry
Ascending up to God on high,
From western wilds to ocean's shore,
    The fervent prayer of the oppressed;
The cry of helpless infancy

Torn from the parent's fond caress
By some base tool of tyranny,
    And doomed to woe and wretchedness;
The indignant wail of fiery youth,
    Its noble aspirations crushed,
Its generous zeal, its love of truth,
    Trampled by tyrants in the dust;
The aerial piles which fancy reared,
    And hopes too bright to be enjoyed,
Have passed and left his young heart seared,
    And all its dreams of bliss destroyed.
The shriek of virgin purity,
    Doomed to some libertine's embrace,
Should rouse the strongest sympathy
    Of each one of the human race;
And weak old age, oppressed with care,
    As he reviews the scene of strife,
Puts up to God a fervent prayer,
    To close his dark and troubled life.
The cry of fathers, mothers, wives,
    Severed from all their hearts hold dear,
And doomed to spend their wretched lives
    In gloom, and doubt, and hate, and fear:
And manhood, too, with soul of fire,
And arm of strength, and smothered ire,
Stands pondering with brow of gloom,
Upon his dark unhappy doom,
Whether to plunge in battle's strife,
And buy his freedom with his life,
And with stout heart and weapon strong,
Pay back the tyrant wrong for wrong,
Or wait the promised time of God,
    When his Almighty ire shall wake,
And smite the oppressor in his wrath,
And hurl red ruin in his path,
And with the terrors of his rod,
    Cause adamantine hearts to quake.
Here Christian writhes in bondage still,
    Beneath his brother Christian's rod,
And pastors trample down at will,

The image of the living God.
While prayers go up in lofty strains,
   And pealing hymns ascend to heaven,
The captive, toiling in his chains,
   With tortured limbs and bosom riven,
Raises his fettered hand on high,
   And in the accents of despair,
To him who rules both earth and sky,
   Puts up a sad, a fervent prayer,
To free him from the awful blast
   Of slavery's bitter galling shame—
Although his portion should be cast
   With demons in eternal flame!
Almighty God! 't is this they call
   The land of liberty and law;
Part of its sons in baser thrall
   Than Babylon or Egypt saw—
Worse scenes of rapine, lust and shame,
   Than Babylonian ever knew,
Are perpetrated in the name
   Of God, the holy, just, and true;
And darker doom than Egypt felt,
May yet repay this nation's guilt.
Almighty God! thy aid impart,
And fire anew each faltering heart,
And strengthen every patriot's hand,
Who aims to save our native land.
We do not come before thy throne,
   With carnal weapons drenched in gore,
Although our blood has freely flown,
   In adding to the tyrant's store.
Father! before thy throne we come,
   Not in the panoply of war,
With pealing trump, and rolling drum,
   And cannon booming loud and far;
Striving in blood to wash out blood,
   Through wrong to seek redress for wrong;
For while thou 'rt holy, just and good,
   The battle is not to the strong;
But in the sacred name of peace,

Of justice, virtue, love and truth,
We pray, and never mean to cease,
   Till weak old age and fiery youth
In freedom's cause their voices raise,
And burst the bonds of every slave;
Till, north and south, and east and west,
The wrongs we bear shall be redressed.

To A. H.

I just had turned the classic page,
   With ancient lore and wisdom fraught,
Which many a hoary-headed sage
   Had stamped with never-dying thought;
And many a bard of lofty mind,
   With measured lay and tuneful lyre,
And strains too grand for human kind,
   All pregnant with celestial fire—
In notes majestic, loud and long,
Had poured the volumed tide of song.
Here Egypt's sages, skilled of yore
   In Isis' dark mysterious rites,
Unvailed their find of mystic lore
   To eager Grecian neophytes.
And as I sadly musing sat,
   Thinking on ages long gone by,
The Pantheon arose in state,
   And passed before my fancy's eye.
Juno's majestic mien was there,
   And Venus' beauteous form and face,
Diana, modest, chaste, and fair,
   Hebe, adorned with youthful grace,
Ceres, with sheaves and plenteous horn,
   Minerva, with high wisdom crowned,
Aurora, radiant as the morn,
   Whose smiles shed light on all around;
The Graces, sisterhood divine,
   Prepared to charm each mortal sense,

And last of all, the immortal Nine,
    With music, verse, and eloquence,—
Naiads and Nymphs, a numerous train,
Came thronging through the ample fane.
Peris, from eastern regions came,
    Bearing aloft the sacred fire,
Which Zoroaster, son of flame,
    Kindled on Mithra's ancient pyre.
The dark-eyed maids who wait to greet
    The Moslem brave in Paradise,
Forsook awhile their blissful seat,
    And left the region of the skies,
The palm of beauty to dispute
With sovereign Jove's immortal suit.
And as I sat, entranced, amazed,
    With radiant beauty circled round,
Thy form, high o'er the rest upraised,
    Appeared, with brighter splendor crowned,
And every eye was turned on thee,
    Of Houri, Peri, Goddess, Grace,
As, bright in peerless majesty,
    You mounted to the highest place.
Juno resigned her crown to thee,
    Venus her zone of love unbound,
While haughty Pallas bowed the knee,
    And laid her armor on the ground.
The Muses, also, owned thee queen
    Of music, eloquence, and verse,
And tuned their lyres and harps, I ween,
    Thy matchless praises to rehearse.
The Peri owned thy dazzling eye
    Might kindle far a brighter fire
Than that which erst blazed to the sky,
    On many an oriental pyre,
There lighting up with ray divine,
The ancient Gheber's fiery shrine.
The Houris owned that could thy charms
    Be viewed from regions of the skies,
'T would tempt the faithful from their arms,
    And all the joys of Paradise;

Or were the Prophet's self on earth,
   And but a glimpse of thee were given,
He'd own one smile of thine were worth
   All pleasures of his highest Heaven;
And from the Moslem creed erase
   That portion so unjustly given,
Which shuts one half the human race
   Forever from the joys of Heaven.
And all the bright Olympic train,
Finding the contest waged in vain,
And that each boasted Deity
Was far eclipsed in charms by thee,
Fled from the scene where all their charms,
   The power of wisdom, beauty, grace,
Had prostrate sunk beneath the arms
   Of one who, though of mortal race,
In her own person did combine
All of the attributes divine
Which Grecian fancy erst did trace
In Nymph, in Goddess, or in Grace;
And ne'er did eastern poet tell,
'Mid all the fabled sprites that dwell
On earth, in water, or in air,
Of aught that could with thee compare—
Of mortal, or immortal kind,
In grace of person and of mind:
For in thy presence pleasures grow.
   And brightest glories round thee move,
Whether it be with men below,
   Or seraphs in the realms above
And when thy spirit shall return
   Back to that Heaven from whence it came,
Angels and seraphs, in their turn,
   Shall join to celebrate thy name,
And spread through Heaven as well as earth,
The story of thy matchless worth.

THOMAS BUCHANAN READ

(1822–1872)

Sheridan's Ride

Up from the South at break of day,
Bringing to Winchester fresh dismay,
  The affrighted air with a shudder bore,
  Like a herald in haste, to the chieftain's door,
  The terrible grumble, and rumble, and roar,
  Telling the battle was on once more,
And Sheridan twenty miles away.

And wider still those billows of war,
Thundered along the horizon's bar;
And louder yet into Winchester rolled
The roar of that red sea uncontrolled,
Making the blood of the listener cold,
As he thought of the stake in that fiery fray,
And Sheridan twenty miles away.

But there is a road from Winchester town,
A good broad highway leading down;
And there, through the flush of the morning light,
A steed as black as the steeds of night,
Was seen to pass, as with eagle flight,
As if he knew the terrible need;
He stretched away with his utmost speed;
Hills rose and fell; but his heart was gay,
With Sheridan fifteen miles away.

Still sprung from those swift hoofs, thundering South,
The dust, like smoke from the cannon's mouth;
Or the trail of a comet, sweeping faster and faster,
Foreboding to traitors the doom of disaster.
The heart of the steed, and the heart of the master
Were beating like prisoners assaulting their walls,
Impatient to be where the battle-field calls;

Every nerve of the charger was strained to full play,
With Sheridan only ten miles away.

Under his spurning feet the road
Like an arrowy Alpine river flowed,
And the landscape sped away behind
Like an ocean flying before the wind,
And the steed, like a bark fed with furnace ire,
Swept on, with his wild eye full of fire.
But lo! he is nearing his heart's desire;
He is snuffing the smoke of the roaring fray,
With Sheridan only five miles away.

The first that the general saw were the groups
Of stragglers, and then the retreating troops,
What was done? what to do? a glance told him both,
Then striking his spurs, with a terrible oath,
He dashed down the line, 'mid a storm of huzzas,
And the wave of retreat checked its course there, because
The sight of the master compelled it to pause.
With foam and with dust, the black charger was gray;
By the flash of his eye, and the red nostril's play,
He seemed to the whole great army to say,
"I have brought you Sheridan all the way
From Winchester, down to save the day!"

Hurrah! hurrah for Sheridan!
Hurrah! hurrah for horse and man!
And when their statues are placed on high,
Under the dome of the Union sky,
The American soldiers' Temple of Fame;
There with the glorious general's name,
Be it said, in letters both bold and bright,
    "Here is the steed that saved the day,
By carrying Sheridan into the fight,
    From Winchester, twenty miles away!"

GEORGE HENRY BOKER

(1823–1890)

from *Sonnets: A Sequence on Profane Love*

Farewell once more,—and yet again farewell!
I cannot quit thee. On thy lips I press
A parting kiss. I cease from my caress;
Slowly I loose thy waist; the troubled swell
Of thy fair bosom, with the sighs that tell
Thy own emotion, falls from me. I bless
Thy downcast head; upon each lustrous tress
Rest my poor hands, as if some sacred spell
Were in my benediction. Then I try
A sudden parting. Ah! how whirls my brain!
How pang crowds pang; how pain leaps over pain!
My purpose falters; o'er my senses fly
Oblivious clouds; and then—I know not why—
Lo! I am hanging on thy lips again!

———

The leaden eyelids of wan twilight close
Upon the sun; and now the misty dew
Trails its wet skirts across the glades, and through
The tangled grasses of the meadow goes,
Shaking a drop in every open rose,
In every lily's cup; Yon dreary yew
Alone looks darker for the tears that strew
Its dusky leaves, and deeper shadow throws,
And closer gathers; as if it would sit
As one who, mourning, wraps his mantle tight,
And huddles nearer to the dismal sight
Of some lost love; so yonder tree seems knit
Fast to the grave beneath; my heart takes flight,
To that lone yew, and cowers under it.

If she should give me all I ask of her,
The virgin treasures of her modest love;
If lip to lip in eager frenzy clove,
And limb with limb should palpitate and stir
In that wild struggle whose delights confer
A rapture which the jealous gods above
Envy and long for as they coldly move
Through votive fumes of spice and burning myrrh;
Yea, were her beauty thus securely mine,
Forever waiting at my beck and call,
I lord and master of her all in all;
Yet at that weakness I would fret and pine
Which makes exhausted nature trip and fall
Just at the point where it becomes divine.

As stands a statue on its pedestal,
Amidst the storms of civil mutiny,
With an unchanged and high serenity,
Though Caesar's self be toppled to his fall;
So stands my faith in thee amidst the brawl
Within my heart—the woeful tragedy
Of passions that conspire for mastery
Above the power that holds their rage in thrall.
Image of comfort! Lustrous as the star
That crests the morning, and as virgin pure,
All is not lost if thou wilt but endure!
If through the dust and turmoil of this war,
I may behold thee, stately and secure,
Brooding on things unearthly and afar.

My darling's features, painted by the light;
As in the convex of a mirror, see
Her face diminished so fantastically
It scarcely hints her lovely self aright.
Away, poor mockery! My outraged sight

Turns from the fraud you perpetrate on me;
This is no transcript, but a forgery,
As far from semblance as is black from white.
Breathe, smile, blush, kiss me! Murmur in my ear
The things we know—we only! and give heed
To this deep sigh and this descending tear,
Ere from my senses you can win the meed
Of faith, to make your doubtful title clear,
And so convince me you are she indeed.

———————

Ah, lute, how well I know each tone of thee,
From shrillest treble unto solemn bass,
The power of every fret, the time and place
Where falls each finger tipped with melody!
Full well I know the sounds that come and flee,
The chords that swell, and part, and interlace,
Lending the whole one long united grace—
That regnant rhythm of thorough harmony.
Shell of my fancy, in my arms awake!
Exchange thy torpor for the vivid smart
Of sentient life! With joy and sorrow shake!
Throb with a soul which of herself is part!
Mimic her phrases! Feign, for pity's sake,
That thou art she now nestling o'er my heart!

"Blood, blood! The lines of every printed sheet"

Blood, blood! The lines of every printed sheet
  Through their dark arteries reek with running gore;
    At hearth, at board, before the household door,
    'T is the sole subject with which neighbors meet.
  Girls at the feast, and children in the street,
    Prattle of horrors; flash their little store
    Of simple jests against the cannon's roar,
    As if mere slaughter kept existence sweet.
  O, heaven, I quail at the familiar way

This fool, the world, disports his jingling cap;
  Murdering or dying with one grin agap!
Our very Love comes draggled from the fray,
  Smiling at victory, scowling at mishap,
  With gory Death companioned and at play.

"Oh! craven, craven! while my brothers fall"

Oh! craven, craven! while my brothers fall,
  Like grass before the mower, in the fight,
  I, easy vassal to my own delight,
  Am bound with flowers, a far too willing thrall.
Day after day along the streets I crawl,
  Shamed in my manhood, reddening at the sight
  Of every soldier who upholds the right
  With no more motive than his country's call.
I love thee more than honor; ay, above
  That simple duty, conscience-plain and clear
  To dullest minds, whose summons all men hear.
Yet as I blush and loiter, who should move
  In the grand marches, I cannot but fear
  That thou wilt scorn me for my very love.

"Brave comrade, answer! When you joined the war"

Brave comrade, answer! When you joined the war,
  What left you? "Wife and children, wealth and friends,
  A storied home whose ancient roof-tree bends
  Above such thoughts as love tells o'er and o'er."
Had you no pang or struggle? "Yes; I bore
  Such pain on parting as at hell's gate rends
  The entering soul, when from its grasp ascends
  The last faint virtue which on earth it wore."
You loved your home, your kindred, children, wife;
  You loathed yet plunged into war's bloody whirl!—
  What urged you? "Duty! Something more than life.
That which made Abraham bare the priestly knife,
  And Isaac kneel, or that young Hebrew girl
  Who sought her father coming from the strife."

JAMES MATHEWES LEGARÉ

(1823–1859)

To a Lily

Go bow thy head in gentle spite,
Thou lily white.
For she who spies thee waving here,
With thee in beauty can compare
As day with night.

Soft are thy leaves and white: Her arms
Boast whiter charms.
Thy stem prone bent with loveliness
Of maiden grace possesseth less:
Therein she charms.

Thou in thy lake dost see
Thyself: So she
Beholds her image in her eyes
Reflected. Thus did Venus rise
From out the sea.

Inconsolate, bloom not again
Thou rival vain
Of her whose charms have thine outdone:
Whose purity might spot the sun,
And make thy leaf a stain.

Tallulah

Recollect thou, in thunder
How TALLULAH spoke to thee,
When thy little face with wonder
Lifted upwards, rocks asunder
Riven, shattered,
Black and battered,
Thou aloft didst see?

Downward stalking through TEMPESTA,
Did a giant shape appear.
All the waters leaping after
Hound-like, with their thunder-laughter
Shook the valley
Teocalli,
Hill-top bleak and bare.

Vast and ponderous, of granite,
Cloud enwrapt his features were.
In his great calm eyes emotion
Glimmered none; and like an ocean
Billowy, tangled,
Foam bespangled
Backward streamed his hair.

On his brow like dandelions
Nodded pines: the solid floor
Rocked and reeled beneath his treading,
Black on high a tempest spreading,
Pregnant, passive,
As with massive
Portal, closed the corridor.

Frighted, sobbing, clinging to me
In an agony of dread,
Sawest thou this form tremendous
Striding down the steep stupendous
With the torrent:
Night abhorrent
Closing overhead.

Then my heart dissembling courage,
That thine own so loudly beat.
Comfort thee, I said, poor trembler:
Providence is no dissembler.
Higher power
Guards each flower
Blooming at thy feet.

Flushed and tearful from my bosom
Thereat thou did'st lift thy face.
Blue and wide thy eyes resplendent,
Turned upon the phantom pendent,
Whose huge shadow
Overshadowed
All the gloomy place.

Back revolving into granite,
Foam and fall and nodding pine,
Sank the phantom. Slantwise driven
Through the storm-cloud rent and riven,
Sunshine glittered
And there twittered—
Birds in every vine

Then sonorous from the chasm
Pealed a voice distinct and loud:
'Innocence and God-reliance
Set all evil at defiance.
Maiden, by these,
(As by snow, trees,)
Evil heads are bowed.'

GEORGE BOYER VASHON

(1824–1878)

Vincent Ogé

There is, at times, an evening sky—
  The twilight's gift—of sombre hue,
All checkered wild and gorgeously
  With streaks of crimson, gold and blue;—
A sky that strikes the soul with awe,
  And, though not brilliant as the sheen,
Which in the east at morn we saw,
  Is far more glorious, I ween;—
So glorious that, when night hath come
And shrouded it in deepest gloom,
We turn aside with inward pain
And pray to see that sky again.
Such sight is like the struggle made
When freedom bids unbare the blade,
And calls from every mountain-glen—
  From every hill—from every plain,
Her chosen ones to stand like men,
  And cleanse their souls from every stain
Which wretches, steeped in crime and blood,
Have cast upon the form of God.
Though peace like morning's golden hue,
  With blooming groves and waving fields,
Is mildly pleasing to the view,
  And all the blessings that it yields
Are fondly welcomed by the breast
  Which finds delight in passion's rest,
That breast with joy foregoes them all,
While listening to Freedom's call.
Though red the carnage,—though the strife
Be filled with groans of parting life,—
Though battle's dark, ensanguined skies
Give echo but to agonies—
  To shrieks of wild despairing,—

136

We willingly repress a sigh—
Nay, gaze with rapture in our eye,
Whilst "FREEDOM!" is the rally-cry
    That calls to deeds of daring.
*   *   *   *   *   *   *   *
The waves dash brightly on thy shore,
    Fair island of the southern seas!
As bright in joy as when of yore
    They gladly hailed the Genoese,—
That daring soul who gave to Spain
A world—last trophy of her reign!
Basking in beauty, thou dost seem
A vision in a poet's dream!
Thou look'st as though thou claim'st not birth
With sea and sky and other earth,
That smile around thee but to show
Thy beauty in a brighter glow,—
That are unto thee as the foil
    Artistic hands have featly set
Around Golconda's radiant spoil,
    To grace some lofty coronet,—
A foil which serves to make the gem
The glory of that diadem!
*   *   *   *   *   *   *   *
If Eden claimed a favored haunt,
    Most hallowed of that blessed ground,
Where tempting fiend with guileful taunt
    A resting-place would ne'er have found,—
As shadowing it well might seek
    The loveliest home in that fair isle,
Which in its radiance seemed to speak
    As to the charmed doth Beauty's smile,
That whispers of a thousand things
For which words find no picturings.
Like to the gifted Greek who strove
    To paint a crowning work of art,
And form his ideal Queen of Love,
    By choosing from each grace a part,
Blending them in one beauteous whole,
To charm the eye, transfix the soul,

And hold it in enraptured fires,
Such as a dream of heaven inspires,—
So seem the glad waves to have sought
    From every place its richest treasure,
And borne it to that lovely spot,
    To found thereon a home of pleasure;—
A home where balmy airs might float
    Through spicy bower and orange grove;
Where bright-winged birds might turn the note
    Which tells of pure and constant love;
Where earthquake stay its demon force,
And hurricane its wrathful course;
Where nymph and fairy find a home,
And foot of spoiler never come.

*   *   *   *   *   *   *   *

And Ogé stands mid this array
    Of matchless beauty, but his brow
Is brightened not by pleasure's play;
    He stands unmoved—nay, saddened now,
As doth the lorn and mateless bird
That constant mourns, whilst all unheard,
The breezes freighted with the strains
Of other songsters sweep the plain,—
That ne'er breathes forth a joyous note,
Though odors on the zephyrs float—
The tribute of a thousand bowers,
Rich in their store of fragrant flowers.
Yet Ogé's was a mind that joyed
    With nature in her every mood,
Whether in sunshine unalloyed
    With darkness, or in tempest rude
And, by the dashing waterfall,
    Or by the gently flowing river,
Or listening to the thunder's call,
    He'd joy away his life forever.
But ah! life is a changeful thing,
    And pleasures swiftly pass away,
And we may turn, with shuddering,
    From what we sighed for yesterday.
The guest, at banquet-table spread

With choicest viands, shakes with dread,
Nor heeds the goblet bright and fair,
Nor tastes the dainties rich and rare,
Nor bids his eye with pleasure trace
The wreathed flowers that deck the place,
If he but knows there is a draught
Among the cordials, that, if quaffed,
Will send swift poison through his veins.
  So Ogé seems; nor does his eye
With pleasure view the flowery plains,
  The bounding sea, the spangled sky,
As, in the short and soft twilight,
  The stars peep brightly forth in heaven,
And hasten to the realms of night,
  As handmaids of the Even.

   *   *   *   *   *   *   *   *

The loud shouts from the distant town,
  Joined in with nature's gladsome lay;
The lights went glancing up and down,
  Riv'ling the stars—nay, seemed as they
  Could stoop to claim, in their high home,
    A sympathy with things of earth,
  And had from their bright mansions come,
    To join them in their festal mirth.
For the land of the Gaul had arose in its might,
And swept by as the wind of a wild, wintry night;
And the dreamings of greatness—the phantoms of power,
Had passed in its breath like the things of an hour.
Like the violet vapors that brilliantly play
Round the glass of the chemist, then vanish away,
The visions of grandeur which dazzlingly shone,
Had gleamed for a time, and all suddenly gone.
And the fabric of ages—the glory of kings,
Accounted most sacred mid sanctified things,
Reared up by the hero, preserved by the sage,
And drawn out in rich hues on the chronicler's page,
Had sunk in the blast, and in ruins lay spread,
While the altar of freedom was reared in its stead.
And a spark from that shrine in the free-roving breeze,
Had crossed from fair France to that isle of the seas;

And a flame was there kindled which fitfully shone
Mid the shout of the free, and the dark captive's groan;
As, mid contrary breezes, a torch-light will play,
Now streaming up brightly—now dying away.

    *   *   *   *   *   *   *   *

  The reptile slumbers in the stone,
    Nor dream we of his pent abode;
  The heart conceals the anguished groan,
    With all the poignant griefs that goad
        The brain to madness;
  Within the hushed volcano's breast,
    The molten fires of ruin lie;—
  Thus human passions seem at rest,
    And on the brow serene and high,
        Appears no sadness.
But still the fires are raging there,
Of vengeance, hatred, and despair;
And when they burst, they wildly pour
  Their lava flood of woe and fear,
And in one short—one little hour,
  Avenge the wrongs of many a year.

    *   *   *   *   *   *   *

And Ogé standeth in his hall;
  But now he standeth not alone;—
A brother's there, and friends; and all
  Are kindred spirits with his own;
For mind will join with kindred mind,
As matter's with its like combined.
They speak of wrongs they had received—
Of freemen, of their rights bereaved;
And as they pondered o'er the thought
Which in their minds so madly wrought,
Their eyes gleamed as the lightning's flash,
Their words seemed as the torrent's dash
That falleth, with a low, deep sound,
Into some dark abyss profound,—
A sullen sound that threatens more
Than other torrents' louder roar.
Ah! they had borne well as they might,
  Such wrongs as freemen ill can bear;

And they had urged both day and night,
　　In fitting words, a freeman's prayer;
And when the heart is filled with grief,
　　For wrongs of all true souls accurst,
In action it must seek relief,
　　Or else, o'ercharged, it can but burst.
Why blame we them, if they oft spake
Words that were fitted to awake
The soul's high hopes—its noblest parts—
The slumbering passions of brave hearts,
And send them as the simoom's breath,
Upon a work of woe and death?
And woman's voice is heard amid
　　The accents of that warrior train;
And when has woman's voice e'er bid,
　　And man could from its hest refrain?
Hers is the power o'er his soul
　　That's never wielded by another,
And she doth claim this soft control
　　As sister, mistress, wife, or mother.
So sweetly doth her soft voice float
　　O'er hearts by guilt or anguish riven,
It seemeth as a magic note
　　Struck from earth's harps by hands of heaven.
And there's the mother of Ogé,
　　Who with firm voice, and steady heart,
And look unaltered, well can play
　　The Spartan mother's hardy part;
And send her sons to battle-fields,
　　And bid them come in triumph home,
Or stretched upon their bloody shields,
　　Rather than bear the bondman's doom.
"Go forth," she said, "to victory;
Or else, go bravely forth to die!
Go forth to fields where glory floats
In every trumpet's cheering notes!
Go forth, to where a freeman's death
Glares in each cannon's fiery breath!
Go forth and triumph o'er the foe;
Or failing that, with pleasure go

To molder on the battle-plain,
Freed ever from the tyrant's chain!
But if your hearts should craven prove,
Forgetful of your zeal—your love
For rights and franchises of men,
My heart will break; but even then,
Whilst bidding life and earth adieu,
This be the prayer I'll breathe for you:
'Passing from guilt to misery,
May this for aye your portion be,—
A life, dragged out beneath the rod—
An end, abhorred of man and God—
As monument, the chains you nurse—
As epitaph, your mother's curse!' "

 * * * * * * * *

A thousand hearts are breathing high,
And voices shouting "Victory!"
  Which soon will hush in death;
  The trumpet clang of joy that speaks,
  Will soon be drowned in the shrieks
   Of the wounded's stifling breath,
  The tyrant's plume in dust lies low—
  Th' oppressed has triumphed o'er his foe.
 But ah! the lull in the furious blast
 May whisper not of ruin past;
 It may tell of the tempest hurrying on,
 To complete the work the blast begun.
With the voice of a Syren, it may whisp'ringly tell
 Of a moment of hope in the deluge of rain;
And the shout of the free heart may rapt'rously swell,
 While the tyrant is gath'ring his power again.
Though the balm of the leech may soften the smart,
 It never can turn the swift barb from its aim;
And thus the resolve of the true freeman's heart
 May not keep back his fall, though it free it from shame.
Though the hearts of those heroes all well could accord
With freedom's most noble and loftiest word;
Their virtuous strength availeth them nought
With the power and skill that the tyrant brought.
Gray veterans trained in many a field

Where the fate of nations with blood was sealed,
In Italia's vales—on the shores of the Rhine—
Where the plains of fair France give birth to the vine—
Where the Tagus, the Ebro, go dancing along,
Made glad in their course by the Muleteer's song—
All these were poured down in the pride of their might,
On the land of Ogé, in that terrible fight.
Ah! dire was the conflict, and many the slain,
Who slept the last sleep on that red battle-plain!
The flash of the cannon o'er valley and height
Danced like the swift fires of a northern night,
Or the quivering glare which leaps forth as a token
That the King of the Storm from his cloud-throne has
       spoken.
And oh! to those heroes how welcome the fate
Of Sparta's brave sons in Thermopylæ's strait;
With what ardor of soul they then would have given
Their last look at earth for a long glance at heaven!
Their lives to their country—their backs to the sod—
Their heart's blood to the sword, and their souls to their
       God!
But alas! although many lie silent and slain,
More blest are they far than those clanking the chain,
In the hold of the tyrant, debarred from the day;—
And among these sad captives is Vincent Ogé!

  * * * * * * * *

  Another day's bright sun has risen,
  And shines upon the insurgent's prison;
  Another night has slowly passed,
  And Ogé smiles, for 'tis the last
  He'll droop beneath the tyrant's power—
  The galling chains! Another hour,
  And answering to the jailor's call,
  He stands within the Judgment Hall.
  They've gathered there;—they who have pressed
  Their fangs into the soul distressed,
  To pain its passage to the tomb
  With mock'ry of a legal doom.
  They've gathered there;—they who have stood
  Firmly and fast in hour of blood,—

Who've seen the lights of hope all die,
As stars fade from a morning sky,—
They've gathered there, in that dark hour—
The latest of the tyrant's power,—
An hour that speaketh of the day
Which never more shall pass away,—
The glorious day beyond the grave,
Which knows no master—owns no slave.
And there, too, are the rack—the wheel—
The torturing screw—the piercing steel,—
Grim powers of death all crusted o'er
With other victims' clotted gore.
Frowning they stand, and in their cold,
Silent solemnity, unfold
The strong one's triumph o'er the weak—
The awful groan—the anguished shriek—
The unconscious mutt'rings of despair—
The strained eyeball's idiot stare—
The hopeless clench—the quiv'ring frame—
The martyr's death—the despot's shame.
The rack—the tyrant—victim,—all
Are gathered in that Judgment Hall.
Draw we the veil, for 'tis a sight
But friends can gaze on with delight.
The sunbeams on the rack that play,
For sudden terror flit away
From this dread work of war and death,
As angels do with quickened breath,
From some dark deed of deepest sin,
Ere they have drunk its spirit in.

*   *   *   *   *   *   *   *

No mighty host with banners flying,
  Seems fiercer to a conquered foe,
Than did those gallant heroes dying,
  To those who gloated o'er their woe;—
Grim tigers, who have seized their prey,
Then turn and shrink abashed away;
And, coming back and crouching nigh,

Quail 'neath the flashing of the eye,
Which tells that though the life has started,
The will to strike has not departed.

*   *   *   *   *   *   *   *

Sad was your fate, heroic band!
Yet mourn we not, for yours' the stand
Which will secure to you a fame,
That never dieth, and a name
That will, in coming ages, be
A signal word for Liberty.
Upon the slave's o'erclouded sky,
   Your gallant actions traced the bow,
Which whispered of deliv'rance nigh—
   The meed of one decisive blow.
Thy coming fame, Ogé! is sure;
Thy name with that of L'Ouverture,
And all the noble souls that stood
With both of you, in times of blood,
Will live to be the tyrant's fear—
Will live, the sinking soul to cheer!

CHARLES GODFREY LELAND

(1824–1903)

Ballad

By Hans Breitmann

Der noble Ritter Hugo
    Von Schwillensaufenstein,
Rode out mit shpeer and helmet,
    Und he coom to de panks of de Rhine.

Und oop dere rose a meer-maid,
    Vot hadn't got nodings on,
Und she say, "Oh, Ritter Hugo,
    Vhere you goes mit yourself alone?"

And he says, "I rides in de creenwood,
    Mit helmet und mit shpeer,
Till I cooms into em Gasthaus,
    Und dere I trinks some beer."

Und den outsphoke de maiden
    Vot hadn't got nodings on:
"I tont dink mooch of beoplesh
    Dat goes mit demselfs alone.

"You'd petter coom down in de wasser,
    Vhere dere's heaps of dings to see,
Und hafe a shplendid tinner
    Und drafel along mit me.

"Dere you sees de fisch a schwimmin',
    Und you catches dem efery one:"—
So sang dis wasser maiden
    Vot hadn't got nodings on.

"Dere ish drunks all full mit money
 In ships dat vent down of old;
Und you helpsh yourself, by dunder!
 To shimmerin' crowns of gold.

"Shoost look at dese shpoons und vatches!
 Shoost see dese diamant rings!
Coom down and fill your bockets,
 Und I'll giss you like efery dings.

"Vot you vantsh mit your schnapps und lager?
 Coom down into der Rhine!
Der ish pottles der Kaiser Charlemagne
 Vonce filled mit gold-red wine!"

Dat fetched him—he shtood all shpell pound;
 She pooled his coat-tails down,
She drawed him oonder der wasser,
 De maiden mit nodings on.

Wein Geist

I stoompled oud ov a dafern,
 Berauscht mit a gallon of wein,
Und I rooshed along de strassen,
 Like a derriple Eberschwein.

Und like a lordly boar-big,
 I doomplet de soper folk;
Und I trowed a shtone droo a shdreed lamp
 Und bot' of de classes I proke.

Und a gal vent roonin' bast me,
 Like a vild coose on de vings,
Boot I gatch her for all her skreechin',
 Und giss her like efery dings.

Und denn mit an board und a parell,
   I blay de horse-viddle a biece,
Dill de neighbours shkreem "deat'!" und "murder!"
   Und holler aloudt "bolice!"

Und vhen der crim night wæchter
   Says all of dis foon moost shtop,
I oop mit mein oomberella,
   Und schlog him ober de kop.

I leaf him like tead on de bavemend,
   Und roosh droo a darklin' lane,
Dill moonlighd und tisdand musik,
   Pring me roundt to my soul again.

Und I sits all oonder de linden,
   De hearts-leaf linden dree;
Und I dink of de quick gevanisht lofe
   Dat vent like de vind from me.
Und I voonders in mine dipsyhood,
   If a damsel or dream vas she!

Dis life is all a lindens
   Mit holes dat show de plue,
Und pedween de finite pranches
   Cooms Himmel-light shinin' troo.

De blaetter are raushlin' o'er me,
   Und efery leaf ish a fay,
Und dey vait dill de windsbraut comet,
   To pear dem in Fall afay.

Denn I coomed to a rock py der rifer,
   Vhere a stein ish of harpe form,
—Jahrdausand in, oud, it standet'—
   Und nopody blays but de shtorm.

Here, vonce on a dimes, a vitches,
   Soom melodies here peginned,
De harpe ward all zu steine,
   Die melodie ward zu wind.

Und so mit dis tox-i-gation,
   Vitch hardens de outer Me;
Ueber stein and schwein, de weine
   Shdill harps oud a melodie.

Boot deeper de Ur-lied ringet',
   Ober stein und wein und svines,
Dill it endeth vhere all peginnet,
   Und alles wird ewig zu eins,
In de dipsy, treamless sloomper
   Vhich units de Nichts und Seyns.

Und im Mondenlicht it moormoors,
   Und it burns by waken wein,
In Mädchenlieb or Schnapsenrausch
   Das Absolut ist dein.

from *Hans Breitmann as a Politician: III*

Pardt De Virst.
The Author Asserts the Vast Intellectual Superiority
of Germans to Americans.

There's a liddle fact in hishdory vitch few hafe oondershtand,
Dat de Deutschers are, *de jure*, de owners of dis land,
Und I brides mineself oonshpeak-barly dat I foorst make
   be-known,
De primordial cause dat Columbus vas derivet from Cologne.

For ash his name vas Colon, it fisiply does shine,
Dat his Eldern are geboren been in Co-logne on der Rhein,
Und Colonia peing a colony, it sehr bemerkbar ist,
Dat Columbus in America was der firster colonist.

Und ash Columbus ish a tofe, id ish wort de drople to mark,
Dat an bidgeon foorst tiscofer land a-vlyin' from de ark;
Und shtill wider—in de peginnin', mitout de leastest toubt,
A tofe vas vly ofer de wassers und pring de vorldt herout.

Ash mein goot oldt teacher Der Kreutzer to me tid ofden
     shbeak,
De mythus of name rebeats itself—vitch see in his
     "Symbolik,"
So also de name America, if we a liddle look,
Vas coom from der oldt king Emerich in de Deutsche
     Heldenbuch.

Und id vas from dat fery Heldenbuch—how voonderful
     it ron,
Dat I shdole de Song of Hildebrand, or der Vater und der
     Sohn,
Und dishtripude it to Breitemann for a reason vitch now ish
     plain,
Dat dis Sagen Cyclus full-endet, pring me round to der
     Hans again.

Dese laws of un-endly un-winding ish so teep and broad and
     tall,
Dat nopody boot a Deutscher hafe a het to versteh dem at
     all,
Und should I write mine dinks all out, I tont peliefe inteed,
Dat I mineself vould versteh de half of dis here Breitmann's
     Lied.

Ash der Hegel say of his system—dat only von man's knew,
Vot der tyfel id meant—und he couldn't tell—und der Jean
     Paul Richter, too,
Who saidt: "Gott knows I meant somedings vhen foorst dis
     buch I writ,
Boot Gott only wise vot das buch means now—for I hafe
     forgotten it!"

Und all of dis be-wises so blain ash de face on your nose,
Dat der Deutscher hafe efen more intellects dan he himself
    soopose,
Und his tifference mit de over-again vorldt, as I really do
    soospect,
Ish dat oder volk hafe more *soopose*—und lesser intellect.

Yet oop-righty I confess it—mitout ashkin' vhy or vhence,
Dere ish also dimes vhen Amerigans hafe shown sharp-
    pointet sense,
Und a fery outsigned exemple of genius in dis line,
Vas dishblayed in dis elegdion py Mishder Hiram Twine.

Breitmann in Paris

"*Recessit in Franciam.*"

"*Et affectu pectoris,*
Et toto gestu corporis,
Et scholares maxime,
Qui festa colunt optime."

      —CARMINA BURANA, 13TH CENTURY.

Der teufel's los in Bal Mabille,
    Dere's hell-fire in de air,
De fiddlers can't blay noding else
    Boot Orphée aux Enfers:
Vot makes de beoples howl mit shoy?
    Da capo—bravo!—bis!!
It's a Deutscher aus Amerikà:
    Hans Breitmann in Paris.

Dere's silber toughts vot might hafe peen,
    Dere's golden deeds vot *must*:
Der Hans ish come to Frankenland
    On one eternal bust.
Der same old rowdy Argonaut
    Vot hoont de same oldt vleece,
A hafin all de foon dere ish—
    Der Breitmann in Paris.

Mit a gal on eider shoulder
    A holdin py his beard,
He tantz de Cancan, sacrament!
    Dill all das Volk vas skeered.
Like a roarin hippopotamos,
    Mit a kangarunic shoomp,
Dey feared he'd smash de Catacombs,
    Each dime der Breitmann bump.

De pretty liddle cocodettes
    Lofe efery dings ish new,
"D'ou vient il donc ce grand M'sieu?
    O sacré nom de Dieu!"
In fain dey kicks deir veet on high,
    And sky like vlyin geese,
Dey can not kick de hat afay
    From Breitmann in Paris.

O vhere vas id der Breitmann life?
    Oopon de Rond Point gay,
Vot shdreet lie shoost pehind his house?
    La rue de Rabelais.
Aroundt de corner Harper's shtands
    Vhere Yankee drinks dey mill,
Vhile shdraight ahet, agross de shdreet,
    Dere lies de Bal Mabille.

Id's all along de Elysées,
    Id's oop de Boulevarce,
He's sampled all de weinshops,
    Und he's vinked at efery garçe.
Dou schveet plack-silken Gabrielle,
    O let me learn from dee,
If 'tis in lofe—or absinthe drunks,
    Dat dis wild ghost may pe?

Und dou may'st kneel in Notre Dame,
    Und veep avay dy sin,
Vhile I go vight at Barriere balls,
    Oontil mine poots cave in;

Boot if ve pray, or if ve sin—
   Vhile nodings ish refuse,
'Tis all de same in Paris here,
   So long ash *l'on s'amuse.*

O life, mein dear, at pest or vorst,
   Ish boot a vancy ball,
Its cratest shoy a vild *gallop*,
   Vhere madness goferns all.
Und should dey toorn ids gas-light off,
   Und nefer leafe a shbark,
Sdill I'd find my vay to Heafen—or—
   Dy lips, lofe, in de dark.

O crown your het mit roses, lofe!
   O keep a liddel sprung!
Oonendless wisdom ish but dis:
   To go it vhile you 're yung!
Und Age vas nefer coom to him,
   To him Spring plooms afresh,
Who finds a livin' spirit in
   Der Teufel und der Flesh.

PHOEBE CARY

(1824–1871)

Samuel Brown

It was many and many a year ago,
    In a dwelling down in town,
That a fellow there lived whom you may know,
    By the name of Samuel Brown;
And this fellow he lived with no other thought
    Than to our house to come down.

I was a child, and he was a child,
    In that dwelling down in town,
But we loved with a love that was more than love,
    I and my Samuel Brown,—
With a love that the ladies coveted,
    Me and Samuel Brown.

And this was the reason that, long ago,
    To that dwelling down in town,
A girl came out of her carriage, courting
    My beautiful Samuel Brown;
So that her high-bred kinsman came
    And bore away Samuel Brown,
And shut him up in a dwelling-house,
    In a street quite up in town.

The ladies not half so happy up there,
    Went envying me and Brown;
Yes! that was the reason, (as all men know,
    In this dwelling down in town,)
That the girl came out of the carriage by night,
    Coquetting and getting my Samuel Brown.

But our love is more artful by far than the love
    Of those who are older than we,—
    Of many far wiser than we,—

And neither the girls that are living above,
    Nor the girls that are down in town,
Can ever dissever my soul from the soul
    Of the beautiful Samuel Brown.

For the morn never shines without bringing me lines
    From my beautiful Samuel Brown;
And the night 's never dark, but I sit in the park
    With my beautiful Samuel Brown.
And often by day, I walk down in Broadway,
With my darling, my darling, my life and my stay,
    To our dwelling down in town,
To our house in the street down town.

Granny's House

Comrades, leave me here a little, while as yet 't is early morn,
Leave me here, and when you want me, sound upon the
        dinner-horn.
'T is the place, and all about it, as of old, the rat and mouse
Very loudly squeak and nibble, running over Granny's
        house; —
Granny's house, with all its cupboards, and its rooms as neat
        as wax,
And its chairs of wood unpainted, where the old cats rubbed
        their backs.
Many a night from yonder garret window, ere I went to
        rest,
Did I see the cows and horses come in slowly from the west;
Many a night I saw the chickens, flying upward through the
        trees,
Roosting on the sleety branches, when I thought their feet
        would freeze;
Here about the garden wandered, nourishing a youth
        sublime
With the beans, and sweet potatoes, and the melons which
        were prime;

When the pumpkin-vines behind me with their precious fruit
    reposed,
When I clung about the pear-tree, for the promise that it
    closed,
When I dipt into the dinner far as human eye could see,
Saw the vision of the pie, and all the dessert that would be.
In the spring a fuller crimson comes upon the robin's breast;
In the spring the noisy pullet gets herself another nest;
In the spring a livelier spirit makes the ladies' tongues more
    glib;
In the spring a young boy's fancy lightly hatches up a fib.
Then her cheek was plump and fatter than should be for one
    so old,
And she eyed my every motion, with a mute intent to scold.
And I said, My worthy Granny, now I speak the truth to
    thee, —
Better believe it, — I have eaten all the apples from one tree.
On her kindling cheek and forehead came a color and a
    light,
As I have seen the rosy red flashing in the northern night;
And she turned, — her fist was shaken at the coolness of the
    lie;
She was mad, and I could see it, by the snapping of her eye,
Saying I have hid my feelings, fearing they should do thee
    wrong, —
Saying, "I shall whip you, Sammy, whipping, I shall go it
    strong!"
She took me up and turned me pretty roughly, when she'd
    done,
And every time she shook me, I tried to jerk and run;
She took off my little coat, and struck again with all her
    might,
And before another minute I was free and out of sight.
Many a morning, just to tease her, did I tell her stories yet,
Though her whisper made me tingle, when she told me
    what I'd get;
Many an evening did I see her where the willow sprouts
    grew thick,
And I rushed away from Granny at the touching of her
    stick.

O my Granny, old and ugly, O my Granny's hateful deeds,
O the empty, empty garret, O the garden gone to weeds,
Crosser than all fancy fathoms, crosser than all songs have
       sung,
I was puppet to your threat, and servile to your shrewish
       tongue,
Is it well to wish thee happy, having seen thy whip decline
On a boy with lower shoulders, and a narrower back, than
       mine?
Hark, my merry comrades call me, sounding on the dinner-
       horn,—
They to whom my Granny's whippings were a target for
       their scorn;
Shall it not be scorn to me to harp on such a mouldered
       string?
I am shamed through all my nature to have loved the mean
       old thing;
Weakness to be wroth with weakness! woman's pleasure,
       woman's spite,
Nature made them quicker motions, a considerable sight.
Woman is the lesser man, and all thy whippings matched
       with mine
Are as moonlight unto sunlight, and as water unto wine.
Here at least when I was little, something, O, for some
       retreat
Deep in yonder crowded city where my life began to beat,
Where one winter fell my father, slipping off a keg of lard,
I was left a trampled orphan, and my case was pretty hard.
Or to burst all links of habit, and to wander far and fleet,
On from farm-house unto farm-house till I found my Uncle
       Pete,
Larger sheds and barns, and newer, and a better
       neighborhood,
Greater breadth of field and woodland, and an orchard just
       as good.
Never comes my Granny, never cuts her willow switches
       there;
Boys are safe at Uncle Peter's, I'll bet you what you dare.
Hangs the heavy fruited pear-tree: you may eat just what
       you like.

'T is a sort of little Eden, about two miles off the pike.
There, methinks, would be enjoyment, more than being
    quite so near
To the place where even in manhood I almost shake with
    fear.
There the passions, cramped no longer, shall have scope and
    breathing space.
I will 'scape that savage woman, she shall never rear my race;
Iron-jointed, supple-sinewed, they shall dive and they shall
    run;
She has caught me like a wild goat, but she shall not catch
    my son.
He shall whistle to the dog, and get the books from off the
    shelf,
Not, with blinded eyesight, cutting ugly whips to whip
    himself.
Fool again, the dream of fancy! no, I don't believe it's bliss,
But I'm certain Uncle Peter's is a better place than this.
Let them herd with narrow foreheads, vacant of all glorious
    gains,
Like the horses in the stables, like the sheep that crop the
    lanes;
Let them mate with dirty cousins, — what to me were style
    or rank,
I the heir of twenty acres, and some money in the bank?
Not in vain the distance beckons, forward let us urge our
    load,
Let our cart-wheels spin till sun-down, ringing down the
    grooves of road;
Through the white dust of the turnpike she can't see to give
    us chase:
Better seven years at uncle's, than fourteen at Granny's
    place.
O, I see the blessed promise of my spirit hath not set!
If we once get in the wagon, we will circumvent her yet.
Howsoever these things, be a long farewell to Granny's
    farm:
Not for me she'll cut the willows, not at me she'll shake her
    arm.

Comes a vapor from the margin, blackening over heath and
     holt,
Cramming all the blast before it,—guess it holds a
     thunderbolt:
Wish 't would fall on Granny's house, with rain, or hail, or
     fire, or snow,
Let me get my horses started Uncle Peteward, and I'll go.

"The Day Is Done"

The day is done, and darkness
    From the wing of night is loosed,
As a feather is wafted downward
    From a chicken going to roost.

I see the lights of the baker
    Gleam through the rain and mist,
And a feeling of sadness comes o'er me,
    That I cannot well resist.

A feeling of sadness and *longing*,
    That is not like being sick,
And resembles sorrow only
    As a brick-bat resembles a brick.

Come, get for me some supper,—
    A good and regular meal,
That shall soothe this restless feeling,
    And banish the pain I feel.

Not from the pastry baker's,
    Not from the shops for cake,
I would n't give a farthing
    For all that they can make.

For, like the soup at dinner,
    Such things would but suggest
Some dishes more substantial,
    And to-night I want the best.

Go to some honest butcher,
  Whose beef is fresh and nice
As any they have in the city,
  And get a liberal slice.

Such things through days of labor,
  And nights devoid of ease,
For sad and desperate feelings
  Are wonderful remedies.

They have an astonishing power
  To aid and reinforce,
And come like the "Finally, brethren,"
  That follows a long discourse.

Then get me a tender sirloin
  From off the bench or hook,
And lend to its sterling goodness
  The science of the cook.

And the night shall be filled with comfort,
  And the cares with which it begun
Shall fold up their blankets like Indians,
  And silently cut and run.

Jacob

He dwelt among "apartments let,"
  About five stories high;
A man I thought that none would get,
  And very few would try.

A boulder, by a larger stone
  Half hidden in the mud,
Fair as a man when only one
  Is in the neighborhood.

He lived unknown, and few could tell
   When Jacob was not free;
But he has got a wife,—and O!
   The difference to me!

"When Lovely Woman"

When lovely woman wants a favor,
   And finds, too late, that man wont bend,
What earthly circumstance can save her
   From disappointment in the end?

The only way to bring him over,
   The last experiment to try,
Whether a husband or a lover,
   If he have feeling, is, to cry!

Advice Gratis to Certain Women

By a Woman

O, my strong-minded sisters, aspiring to vote,
And to row with your brothers, all in the same boat,
When you come out to speak to the public your mind,
Leave your tricks, and your airs, and your graces behind!

For instance, when you by the world would be seen
As reporter, or editor (first-class, I mean),
I think—just to come to the point in one line—
What you write will be finer, if 'tis not too fine.

Pray, don't let the thread of your subject be strung
With "golden," and "shimmer," "sweet," "filter," and
     "flung;"
Nor compel, by your style, all your readers to guess
You've been looking up words Webster marks *obs.*

And another thing: whatever else you may say,
Do keep personalities out of the way;
Don't try every sentence to make people see
What a dear, charming creature the writer must be!

Leave out affectations and pretty appeals;
Don't "drag yourself in by the neck and the heels,"
Your dear little boots, and your gloves; and take heed,
Nor pull your curls over men's eyes while they read.

Don't mistake me; I mean that the public's not home,
You must do as the Romans do, when you're in Rome;
I would have you be womanly, while you are wise;
'Tis the weak and the womanish tricks I despise.

On the other hand: don't write and dress in such styles
As astonish the natives, and frighten the isles;
Do look, on the platform, so folks in the show
Needn't ask, "Which are lions, and which tigers?" you
          know!

'Tis a good thing to write, and to rule in the state,
But to be a true, womanly woman is great:
And if ever you come to be that, 'twill be when
You can cease to be babies, nor try to be men!

BAYARD TAYLOR

(1825–1878)

from *The Echo Club*

Night the Second:
All or Nothing

Whoso answers my questions
   Knoweth more than me;
Hunger is but knowledge
   In a less degree:
Prophet, priest, and poet
   Oft prevaricate,
And the surest sentence
   Hath the greatest weight.

When upon my gaiters
   Drops the morning dew,
Somewhat of Life's riddle
   Soaks my spirit through.
I am buskined by the goddess
   Of Monadnock's crest,
And my wings extended
   Touch the East and West.

Or ever coal was hardened
   In the cells of earth,
Or flowed the founts of Bourbon,
   Lo! I had my birth.
I am crowned coeval
   With the Saurian eggs,
And my fancy firmly
   Stands on its own legs.

Wouldst thou know the secret
   Of the barberry-bush,
Catch the slippery whistle

Of the moulting thrush,
Dance upon the mushrooms,
Dive beneath the sea,
Or anything else remarkable,
Thou must follow me!

Night the Sixth:
Hadramaut

The grand conglomerate hills of Araby
    That stand empanoplied in utmost thought,
With dazzling ramparts front the Indian sea,
            Down there in Hadramaut.

The sunshine smashes in the doors of morn
    And leaves them open; there the vibrant calm
Of life magniloquent pervades forlorn
            The giant fronds of palm.

The cockatoo upon the upas screams;
    The armadillo fluctuates o'er the hill;
And like a flag, incarnadined in dreams,
            All crimsonly I thrill!

There have iconoclasts no power to harm,
    So, folded grandly in translucent mist,
I let the light stream down my jasper arm,
            And o'er my opal fist.

An Adamite of old, primeval Earth,
    I see the Sphinx upon the porphyry shore,
Deprived of utterance ages ere her birth,
            As I am,—only more!

Who shall ensnare me with invested gold,
    Or paper symbols, backed like malachite?
Let gaunt reformers objurgate and scold,
            I gorge me with delight.

I do not yearn for what I covet most;
  I give the winds the passionate gifts I sought;
And slumber fiercely on the torrid coast,
      Down there in Hadramaut!

Night the Eighth:
Camerados

Everywhere, everywhere, following me;
Taking me by the buttonhole, pulling off my boots, hustling
      me with the elbows;
Sitting down with me to clams and the chowder-kettle;
Plunging naked at my side into the sleek, irascible surges;
Soothing me with the strain that I neither permit nor
      prohibit;
Flocking this way and that, reverent, eager, orotund,
      irrepressible;
Denser than sycamore leaves when the north-winds are
      scouring Paumanok;
What can I do to restrain them? Nothing, verily nothing.
Everywhere, everywhere, crying aloud for me;
Crying, I hear; and I satisfy them out of my nature;
And he that comes at the end of the feast shall find
      something over.
Whatever they want I give; though it be something else,
      they shall have it.
Drunkard, leper, Tammanyite, small-pox and cholera patient,
      shoddy, and codfish millionnaire,
And the beautiful young men, and the beautiful young
      women, all the same,
Crowding, hundreds of thousands, cosmical multitudes,
Buss me and hang on my hips and lean up to my shoulders,
Everywhere listening to my yawp and glad whenever they
      hear it;
Everywhere saying, say it, Walt, we believe it:
Everywhere, everywhere.

Bedouin Song

From the Desert I come to thee
   On a stallion shod with fire;
And the winds are left behind
   In the speed of my desire.
Under thy window I stand,
   And the midnight hears my cry:
I love thee, I love but thee,
   With a love that shall not die
         Till the sun grows cold,
         And the stars are old,
         And the leaves of the Judgment
            Book unfold!

Look from thy window and see
   My passion and my pain;
I lie on the sands below,
   And I faint in thy disdain.
Let the night-winds touch thy brow
   With the heat of my burning sigh,
And melt thee to hear the vow
   Of a love that shall not die
         Till the sun grows cold,
         And the stars are old,
         And the leaves of the Judgment
            Book unfold!

My steps are nightly driven,
   By the fever in my breast,
To hear from thy lattice breathed
   The word that shall give me rest.
Open the door of thy heart,
   And open thy chamber door,
And my kisses shall teach thy lips
   The love that shall fade no more
         Till the sun grows cold,
         And the stars are old,
         And the leaves of the Judgment
            Book unfold!

FRANCES ELLEN WATKINS HARPER

(1825–1911)

The Slave Mother

Heard you that shriek? It rose
　　So wildly on the air,
It seem'd as if a burden'd heart
　　Was breaking in despair.

Saw you those hands so sadly clasped—
　　The bowed and feeble head—
The shuddering of that fragile form—
　　That look of grief and dread?

Saw you the sad, imploring eye?
　　Its every glance was pain,
As if a storm of agony
　　Were sweeping through the brain.

She is a mother pale with fear,
　　Her boy clings to her side,
And in her kyrtle vainly tries
　　His trembling form to hide.

He is not hers, although she bore
　　For him a mother's pains;
He is not hers, although her blood
　　Is coursing through his veins!

He is not hers, for cruel hands
　　May rudely tear apart
The only wreath of household love
　　That binds her breaking heart.

His love has been a joyous light
   That o'er her pathway smiled,
A fountain gushing ever new,
   Amid life's desert wild.

His lightest word has been a tone
   Of music round her heart,
Their lives a streamlet blent in one—
   Oh, Father! must they part?

Bible Defence of Slavery

Take sackcloth of the darkest dye,
   And shroud the pulpits round!
Servants of Him that cannot lie,
   Sit mourning on the ground.

Let holy horror blanch each cheek,
   Pale every brow with fears;
And rocks and stones, if ye could speak,
   Ye well might melt to tears!

Let sorrow breathe in every tone,
   In every strain ye raise;
Insult not God's majestic throne
   With th' mockery of praise.

A "reverend" man, whose light should be
   The guide of age and youth,
Brings to the shrine of Slavery
   The sacrifice of truth!

For the direst wrong by man imposed,
   Since Sodom's fearful cry,
The word of life has been unclos'd,
   To give your God the lie.

Oh! when ye pray for heathen lands,
   And plead for their dark shores,
Remember Slavery's cruel hands
   Make heathens at your doors!

The Slave Auction

The sale began—young girls were there,
   Defenceless in their wretchedness,
Whose stifled sobs of deep despair
   Revealed their anguish and distress.

And mothers stood, with streaming eyes,
   And saw their dearest children sold;
Unheeded rose their bitter cries,
   While tyrants barter'd them for gold.

And woman, with her love and truth—
   For these in sable forms may dwell—
Gaz'd on the husband of her youth,
   With anguish none may paint or tell.

And men, whose sole crime was their hue,
   The impress of their Maker's hand,
And frail and shrinking children too,
   Were gathered in that mournful band.

Ye who have laid your lov'd to rest,
   And wept above their lifeless clay,
Know not the anguish of that breast,
   Whose lov'd are rudely torn away.

Ye may not know how desolate
   Are bosoms rudely forced to part,
And how a dull and heavy weight
   Will press the life-drops from the heart.

Lines

At the Portals of the Future,
    Full of madness, guilt and gloom,
Stood the hateful form of Slavery,
    Crying, Give, Oh! give me room—

Room to smite the earth with cursing,
    Room to scatter, rend and slay,
From the trembling mother's bosom
    Room to tear her child away;

Room to trample on the manhood
    Of the country far and wide;
Room to spread o'er every Eden
    Slavery's scorching lava-tide.

Pale and trembling stood the Future,
    Quailing 'neath his frown of hate,
As he grasped with bloody clutches
    The great keys of Doom and Fate.

In his hand he held a banner
    All festooned with blood and tears:
'Twas a fearful ensign, woven
    With the grief and wrong of years.

On his brow he wore a helmet
    Decked with strange and cruel art;
Every jewel was a life-drop
    Wrung from some poor broken heart.

Though her cheek was pale and anxious,
    Yet, with look and brow sublime,
By the pale and trembling Future
    Stood the Crisis of our time.

And from many a throbbing bosom
  Came the words in fear and gloom,
Tell us, Oh! thou coming Crisis,
  What shall be our country's doom?

Shall the wings of dark destruction
  Brood and hover o'er our land,
Till we trace the steps of ruin
  By their blight, from strand to strand?

STEPHEN FOSTER

(1826–1864)

Old Folks at Home

Way down upon de Swanee ribber,
Far, far away,
Dere's wha my heart is turning ebber,
Dere's wha de old folks stay.
All up and down de whole creation,
Sadly I roam,
Still longing for de old plantation,
And for de old folks at home.

> *All de world am sad and dreary,*
> *Ebry where I roam,*
> *Oh! darkeys how my heart grows weary,*
> *Far from de old folks at home.*

All round de little farm I wandered
When I was young,
Den many happy days I squandered,
Many de songs I sung.
When I was playing wid my brudder
Happy was I—.
Oh! take me to my kind old mudder,
Dere let me live and die.

Chorus

One little hut among de bushes,
One dat I love,
Still sadly to my mem'ry rushes,
No matter where I rove
When will I see de bees a humming
All round de comb?
When will I hear de banjo tumming
Down in my good old home?

Chorus

My Old Kentucky Home, Good-Night!

The sun shines bright in the old Kentucky home,
'Tis summer, the darkies are gay,
The corn top's ripe and the meadow's in the bloom
While the birds make music all the day.
The young folks roll on the little cabin floor,
All merry, all happy and bright:
By'n by Hard Times comes a knocking at the door,
Then my old Kentucky Home, good night!

Weep no more, my lady, oh! weep no more to-day!
We will sing one song
For the old Kentucky Home,
For the old Kentucky Home, far away.

They hunt no more for the possum and the coon
On the meadow, the hill and the shore,
They sing no more by the glimmer of the moon,
On the bench by the old cabin door.
The day goes by like a shadow o'er the heart,
With sorrow where all was delight:
The time has come when the darkies have to part,
Then my old Kentucky Home, good-night!

Chorus

The head must bow and the back will have to bend,
Wherever the darkey may go:
A few more days, and the trouble all will end
In the field where the sugar-canes grow.
A few more days for to tote the weary load,
No matter 'twill never be light,
A few more days till we totter on the road,
Then my old Kentucky Home, good-night!

Chorus

Jeanie with the Light Brown Hair

I dream of Jeanie with the light brown hair,
Borne, like a vapor, on the summer air;
I see her tripping where the bright streams play,
Happy as the daisies that dance on her way.
Many were the wild notes her merry voice would pour,
Many were the blithe birds that warbled them o'er:
Oh! I dream of Jeanie with the light brown hair,
Floating, like a vapor, on the soft summer air.

I long for Jeanie with the daydawn smile,
Radiant in gladness, warm with winning guile;
I hear her melodies, like joys gone by,
Sighing round my heart o'er the fond hopes that die: —
Sighing like the night wind and sobbing like the rain, —
Wailing for the lost one that comes not again:
Oh! I long for Jeanie, and my heart bows low,
Never more to find her where the bright waters flow.

I sigh for Jeanie, but her light form strayed
Far from the fond hearts round her native glade;
Her smiles have vanished and her sweet songs flown,
Flitting like the dreams that have cheered us and gone.
Now the nodding wild flowers may wither on the shore
While her gentle fingers will cull them no more:
Oh! I sigh for Jeanie with the light brown hair,
Floating, like a vapor, on the soft summer air.

Susanna

I come from Alabama with my Banjo on my knee—
I'se gwine to Lou'siana my true lub for to see.
It rain'd all night de day I left, de wedder it was dry;
The sun so hot I froze to def— Susanna, dont you cry.

> *Oh! Susanna, do not cry for me;*
> *I come from Alabama,*
> *Wid my Banjo on my knee.*

I jump'd aboard the telegraph and trabbled down de ribber,
De lectrick fluid magnified, and kill'd five hundred Nigga.
De bulgine bust and de hoss ran off, I really thought I'd die;
I shut my eyes to hold my bref— Susanna dont you cry.

Chorus

I had a dream de udder night, when ebry ting was still;
I thought I saw Susanna dear, a coming down de hill,
De buckweat cake was in her mouf, de tear was in her eye,
I says, I'se coming from de souf,— Susanna dont you cry.

Chorus

ROBERT LOWRY

(1826–1899)

Beautiful River

*"And he showed me a pure River of Water of Life, clear as crystal,
proceeding out of the Throne of God and of the Lamb."*
    —REV. xxii. 1.

Shall we gather at the river
    Where bright angel feet have trod;
With its crystal tide forever
    Flowing by the throne of God?

> *Yes, we'll gather at the river,*
>   *The beautiful, the beautiful river —*
> *Gather with the saints at the river*
>   *That flows by the throne of God.*

On the margin of the river,
    Washing up its silver spray,
We will walk and worship ever,
    All the happy, golden day.

Chorus

On the bosom of the river,
    Where the Saviour-king we own,
We shall meet, and sorrow never
    'Neath the glory of the throne.

Chorus

Ere we reach the shining river,
    Lay we every burden down;
Grace our spirits will deliver,
    And provide a robe and crown.

Chorus

At the smiling of the river,
   Rippling with the Saviour's face,
Saints, whom death will never sever,
   Lift their songs of saving grace.

Chorus

Soon we'll reach the shining river,
   Soon our pilgrimage will cease,
Soon our happy hearts will quiver
   With the melody of peace.

Chorus

ROSE TERRY COOKE

(1827–1892)

Blue-Beard's Closet

Fasten the chamber!
Hide the red key;
Cover the portal,
That eyes may not see.
Get thee to market,
To wedding and prayer;
Labor or revel,
The chamber is there!

In comes a stranger—
"Thy pictures how fine,
Titian or Guido,
Whose is the sign?"
Looks he behind them?
Ah! have a care!
"Here is a finer."
The chamber is there!

Fair spreads the banquet,
Rich the array;
See the bright torches
Mimicking day;
When harp and viol
Thrill the soft air,
Comes a light whisper:
The chamber is there!

Marble and painting,
Jasper and gold,
Purple from Tyrus,
Fold upon fold,
Blossoms and jewels,

Thy palace prepare:
Pale grows the monarch;
The chamber is there!

Once it was open
As shore to the sea;
White were the turrets,
Goodly to see;
All through the casements
Flowed the sweet air;
Now it is darkness;
The chamber is there!

Silence and horror
Brood on the walls;
Through every crevice
A little voice calls:
"Quicken, mad footsteps,
On pavement and stair;
Look not behind thee,
The chamber is there!"

Out of the gateway,
Through the wide world,
Into the tempest
Beaten and hurled,
Vain is thy wandering,
Sure thy despair,
Flying or staying,
The chamber is there!

Arachne

I watch her in the corner there,
As, restless, bold, and unafraid,
She slips and floats along the air
Till all her subtile house is made.

Her home, her bed, her daily food
All from that hidden store she draws;
She fashions it and knows it good,
By instinct's strong and sacred laws.

No tenuous threads to weave her nest,
She seeks and gathers there or here;
But spins it from her faithful breast,
Renewing still, till leaves are sere.

Then, worn with toil, and tired of life,
In vain her shining traps are set.
Her frost hath hushed the insect strife
And gilded flies her charm forget.

But swinging in the snares she spun,
She sways to every wintry wind:
Her joy, her toil, her errand done,
Her corse the sport of storms unkind.

Poor sister of the spinster clan!
I too from out my store within
My daily life and living plan,
My home, my rest, my pleasure spin.

I know thy heart when heartless hands
Sweep all that hard-earned web away:
Destroy its pearled and glittering bands,
And leave thee homeless by the way.

I know thy peace when all is done.
Each anchored thread, each tiny knot,
Soft shining in the autumn sun;
A sheltered, silent, tranquil lot.

I know what thou hast never known,
—Sad presage to a soul allowed;—
That not for life I spin, alone.
But day by day I spin my shroud.

FRANCIS MILES FINCH

(1827–1907)

The Blue and the Gray

*"The women of Columbus, Mississippi, animated by nobler
sentiments than are many of their sisters, have shown themselves
impartial in their offerings made to the memory of the dead.
They strewed flowers alike on the graves of the Confederate and
of the National soldiers."*

—NEW YORK TRIBUNE.

By the flow of the inland river,
  Whence the fleets of iron have fled,
Where the blades of the grave-grass quiver,
  Asleep are the ranks of the dead;—
    Under the sod and the dew,
      Waiting the judgment day;—
    Under the one, the Blue;
      Under the other, the Gray.

These in the robings of glory,
  Those in the gloom of defeat,
All with the battle-blood gory,
  In the dusk of eternity meet;—
    Under the sod and the dew,
      Waiting the judgment day;—
    Under the laurel, the Blue;
      Under the willow, the Gray.

From the silence of sorrowful hours
  The desolate mourners go,
Lovingly laden with flowers
  Alike for the friend and the foe;—
    Under the sod and the dew,
      Waiting the judgment day;—
    Under the roses, the Blue;
      Under the lilies, the Gray.

So with an equal splendor
   The morning sun-rays fall,
With a touch, impartially tender,
   On the blossoms blooming for all;
      Under the sod and the dew,
         Waiting the judgment day;—
      Broidered with gold, the Blue;
         Mellowed with gold, the Gray.

So, when the Summer calleth,
   On forest and field of grain
With an equal murmur falleth
   The cooling drip of the rain;—
      Under the sod and the dew,
         Waiting the judgment day;—
      Wet with the rain, the Blue;
         Wet with the rain, the Gray.

Sadly, but not with upbraiding,
   The generous deed was done;
In the storm of the years that are fading,
   No braver battle was won;—
      Under the sod and the dew,
         Waiting the judgment day;—
      Under the blossoms, the Blue,
         Under the garlands, the Gray.

No more shall the war-cry sever,
   Or the winding rivers be red;
They banish our anger forever
   When they laurel the graves of our dead!
      Under the sod and the dew,
         Waiting the judgment day;—
      Love and tears for the Blue,
         Tears and love for the Gray.

JOHN ROLLIN RIDGE

(1827–1867)

Mount Shasta

Behold the dread Mt. Shasta, where it stands
Imperial midst the lesser heights, and, like
Some mighty unimpassioned mind, companionless
And cold. The storms of Heaven may beat in wrath
Against it, but it stands in unpolluted
Grandeur still; and from the rolling mists upheaves
Its tower of pride e'en purer than before.
The wintry showers and white-winged tempests leave
Their frozen tributes on its brow, and it
Doth make of them an everlasting crown.
Thus doth it, day by day and age by age,
Defy each stroke of time: still rising highest
Into Heaven!
Aspiring to the eagle's cloudless height,
No human foot has stained its snowy side;
No human breath has dimmed the icy mirror which
It holds unto the moon and stars and sov'reign sun.
We may not grow familiar with the secrets
Of its hoary top, whereon the Genius
Of that mountain builds his glorious throne!
Far lifted in the boundless blue, he doth
Encircle, with his gaze supreme, the broad
Dominions of the West, which lie beneath
His feet, in pictures of sublime repose
No artist ever drew. He sees the tall
Gigantic hills arise in silentness
And peace, and in the long review of distance
Range themselves in order grand. He sees the sunlight
Play upon the golden streams which through the valleys
Glide. He hears the music of the great and solemn sea,
And overlooks the huge old western wall
To view the birth-place of undying Melody!

Itself all light, save when some loftiest cloud
Doth for a while embrace its cold forbidding
Form, that monarch mountain casts its mighty
Shadow down upon the crownless peaks below,
That, like inferior minds to some great
Spirit, stand in strong contrasted littleness!
All through the long and Summery months of our
Most tranquil year, it points its icy shaft
On high, to catch the dazzling beams that fall
In showers of splendor round that crystal cone,
And roll in floods of far magnificence
Away from that lone, vast Reflector in
The dome of Heaven.
Still watchful of the fertile
Vale and undulating plains below, the grass
Grows greener in its shade, and sweeter bloom
The flowers. Strong purifier! From its snowy
Side the breezes cool are wafted to the "peaceful
Homes of men," who shelter at its feet, and love
To gaze upon its honored form, aye standing
There the guarantee of health and happiness.
Well might it win communities so blest
To loftier feelings and to nobler thoughts—
The great material symbol of eternal
Things! And well I ween, in after years, how
In the middle of his furrowed track the plowman
In some sultry hour will pause, and wiping
From his brow the dusty sweat, with reverence
Gaze upon that hoary peak. The herdsman
Oft will rein his charger in the plain, and drink
Into his inmost soul the calm sublimity;
And little children, playing on the green, shall
Cease their sport, and, turning to that mountain
Old, shall of their mother ask: "Who made it?"
And she shall answer,— "GOD!"

And well this Golden State shall thrive, if like
Its own Mt. Shasta, Sovereign Law shall lift
Itself in purer atmosphere—so high
That human feeling, human passion at its base

Shall lie subdued; e'en pity's tears shall on
Its summit freeze; to warm it e'en the sunlight
Of deep sympathy shall fail:
Its pure administration shall be like
The snow immaculate upon that mountain's brow!

A Cherokee Love Song

Oh come with me by moonlight, love,
   And let us seek the river's shore;
My light canoe awaits thee, love,
   The sweetest burden e'er it bore!

The soft, low winds are whispering there
   Of human beauty, human love,
And with approving faces, too,
   The stars are shining from above.

Come place thy small white hand in mine,
   My boat is 'neath those willow trees,
And with my practised arm, the oar
   Will ask no favor from the breeze.

Now, now we're on the waters, love,
   Alone upon the murmuring tide—
Alone! but why should we regret,
   If there were none on earth beside?

What matters it, if all were gone?
   Thy bird-like voice could yet beguile,
And earth were heaven's substitute,
   If thou were left to make it smile!

Oh, mark how soft the dipping oar,
   That silent cleaves the yielding blue—
Oh list, the low, sweet melody
   Of waves that beat our vessel too!

Oh, look to heaven, how pure it seems,
   No cloud to dim, no blot, no stain,
And say—if we refuse to love,
   Ought we to hope or smile again?

That island green, with roses gemmed,
   Let's seek it, love—how sweet a spot?
Then let the hours of night speed on,
   We live to love—it matters not!

The Rainy Season in California

The rains have come, the winds are shrill,
   Dark clouds are trailing near the ground;
The mists have clothed each naked hill,
   And all is sad and drear around.

The swollen torrents rapid rush,
   Far down the mountain gorges deep;
Now, falling o'er the jagged rocks,
   They thunder through the hollows steep.

Now, in a basin boiling round,
   They dance in maddest music high,
Or, with a sudden leap or bound,
   Dash on like bolts of destiny.

From mountain's side to mountain's side,
   The chasms vast in vapors lost,
Seem like a sea of darkness wide,
   Which fancy dreams can ne'er be crost.

Far off the loftier mountains stand,
   Calm, saint-like in their robes of white,
Like heaven-descended spirits grand
   Who fill the darkness with their light.

Black clouds are rolling round their feet,
   And ever strive to higher climb,
But still their mists dissolve in rain,
   And reach not to that height sublime.

Gone are the birds with sunny days,
   But flowers shall cheer us in their room,
And shrubs that pined in summer rays
   Shall top their leafy boughs with bloom.

The grass grows green upon the hills,
   (Now wrapt in thickly fallen clouds),
Which tall and beautiful shall rise
   When they have cast their wintry shrouds.

Then wandering through their thousand vales,
   Each flowery bordered path shall lead
To gardens wild, where nature's hand
   Hath nurtured all with kindly heed.

Her own voluptuous couch is spread
   Beneath the curtains of the sky,
And on her soft and flowery bed
   The night looks down with loving eye.

But Fancy paints the scene too fast,
   For thus she always loves to leave
The bitter present or the past,
   And rainbows from the future weave.

Lo! night upon my musings here,
   With rapid, stealthy foot hath crept
Unheard amid the sullen sounds
   Which o'er my head have lately swept.

The pouring rain upon the roof,
   The winds in wild careering bands,
Seem bent to see if tempest proof
   The building on its basis stands.

The fiend of this dark night and storm
   Stands howling at my very door—
I dread to see her haggard form
   Break in and pass the threshold o'er.

But hold your own my trusty door!
   Yield not an inch to's utmost might,
Nor let the hellish wild uproar
   That reigns without come in to-night.

It stands—my lonely candle burns,
   The single light for miles around;
Reminding me of some last hope
   That still will light life's gloom profound.

Howl on ye elemental sprites,
   And mutter forth your curses deep,
The anarchy that others frights,
   Shall rock me soundly into sleep.

For, oh, I love to slumber 'neath
   The tempest's wrathful melody,
And dream all night that on its wings
   My soul enchanted soareth free.

The Stolen White Girl

The prairies are broad, and the woodlands are wide
And proud on his steed the wild half-breed may ride,
With the belt round his waist and the knife at his side,
And no white man may claim his beautiful bride.

Though he stole her away from the land of the whites,
Pursuit is in vain, for her bosom delights
In the love that she bears the dark-eyed, the proud,
Whose glance is like starlight beneath a night-cloud.

Far down in the depths of the forest they'll stray,
Where the shadows like night are lingering all day;
Where the flowers are springing up wild at their feet,
And the voices of birds in the branches are sweet.

Together they'll roam by the streamlets that run,
O'ershadowed at times then meeting the sun—
The streamlets that soften their varying tune,
As up the blue heavens calm wanders the moon!

The contrast between them is pleasing and rare;
Her sweet eye of blue, and her soft silken hair,
Her beautiful waist, and her bosom of white
That heaves to the touch with a sense of delight;

His form more majestic and darker his brow,
Where the sun has imparted its liveliest glow—
An eye that grows brighter with passion's true fire,
As he looks on his loved one with earnest desire.

Oh, never let Sorrow's cloud darken their fate,
The girl of the "pale face," her Indian mate!
But deep in the forest of shadows and flowers,
Let Happiness smile, as she wings their sweet hours.

from *California*

And shall we view these miracles and more
Which mind and muscle never wrought before,
Without remembrance in these latter years,
Of those brave men, those hardy Pioneers,
Who led the way for Science, Art, and Law,
'Mid dangers their successors never saw,
And countless hardships that they never knew?
The famed and unfamed heroes tried and true,
Who crowded into months or days the deeds
Of years, and of young empire sowed the seeds?

Amid the mass there here and there appears
Some reverend head, majestic as a seer's—
Arising from the rest like snow-crowned peak,
Around whose brow the whitening tempests break!
These are the Pioneers of Pioneers,
Those elder heroes in the fight, who, years
And years agone, did drive the wild beast back
To plant their homes where late he left the track.
They're sinking, one by one, like pines that long
Have braved, erect, the howling winters strong,
To fall at last midst stillest peace profound,
And wake the woods with wonder at the sound.
Shall these old heroes be forgot? Not so,
For, while they yet survive Time's downward flow,
I see a rescuing hand stretched forth to save
The good, the true, from dark Oblivion's grave.
'T is woman's hand that thus would snatch from night
Those honored names far worthier of the light,
And them transmit to shine on History's scroll
When that gray sage his records shall unroll.
And yet some whom the weeping muse laments,
Have their unwrit but lasting monuments.
Such is that Peak which bears brave Lassen's name—
A fit memorial of the grandest fame;
For it shall stand while crowns and laurels fail,
And Time strews men like leaves upon the gale.

JOHN TOWNSEND TROWBRIDGE

(1827–1916)

An Idyl of Harvest Time

Swift cloud, swift light, now dark, now bright, across the
    landscape played;
And, spotted as a leopard's side in chasing sun and shade,
To far dim heights and purple vales the upland rolled away,
Where the soft, warm haze of summer days on all the
    distance lay.

From shorn and hoary harvest-fields to barn and bristling
    stack,
The wagon bore its beetling loads, or clattered empty back;
The leaning oxen clashed their horns and swayed along the
    road,
And the old house-dog lolled beside, in the shadow of the
    load.

The children played among the sheaves, the hawk went
    sailing over,
The yellow-bird was on the bough, the bee was on the
    clover,
While at my easel by the oak I sketched, and sketched in
    vain: —
Could I but group those harvesters, paint sunshine on the
    grain!

While everywhere, in the golden air, the soul of beauty
    swims,
It will not guide my feeble touch, nor light the hand that
    limns.
(The load moves on—that cloud is gone! I must keep down
    the glare
Of sunshine on my stubble-land. Those boys are my
    despair!)

My fancies flit away at last, and wander like the gleams
Of shifting light along the hills, and drift away in dreams;
Till, coming round the farm-house porch and down the
      shady lane,
A form is seen, half hid, between the stooks of shaggy grain.

Beside my easel, at the oak, I wait to see her pass.
'T is luncheon-time: the harvesters are resting on the grass.
I watch her coming to the gap, and envy Master Ben
Who meets her there, and helps to bear her basket to the
      men.

In the flushed farmer's welcoming smile, there beams a
      father's pride.
More quiet grows, more redly glows, the shy youth by his
      side:
In the soft passion of his look, and in her kind, bright
      glance,
I learn a little mystery, I read a sweet romance.

With pewter mug, and old brown jug, she laughing kneels:
      I hear
The liquid ripple of her lisp, with the gurgle of the beer.
That native grace, that charming face, those glances coy and
      sweet,
Ben, with the basket, grinning near—my grouping is
      complete!

The picture grows, the landscape flows, and heart and fancy
      burn,—
The figures start beneath my brush! (So you the rule may
      learn:
Let thought be thrilled with sympathy, right touch and tone
      to give,
And mix your colors with heart's blood, to make the canvas
      live.)

All this was half a year ago: I find the sketch to-day,—
Faulty and crude enough, no doubt, but it wafts my soul
      away!

I tack it to the wall, and lo! despite the winter's gloom,
It makes a little spot of sun and summer in my room.

Again the swift cloud-shadow sweeps across the stooks of
     rye;
The cricket trills, the locust shrills, the hawk goes sailing by;
The yellow-bird is on the bough, the bee is on the thistle,
The quail is near—"Ha hoyt!"—I hear his almost human
     whistle!

Recollections of "Lalla Rookh"

Read at the Moore Banquet in Boston, May 27, 1879

When we were farm-boys, years ago,
  I dare not tell how many,
When, strange to say, the fairest day
  Was often dark and rainy;

No work, no school, no weeds to pull,
  No picking up potatoes,
No copy-page to fill with blots,
  With little o's or great O's;

But jokes and stories in the barn
  Made quiet fun and frolic;
Draughts, fox-and-geese, and games like these,
  Quite simple and bucolic;

Naught else to do, but just to braid
  A lash, or sing and whittle,
Or go, perhaps, and set our traps,
  If it "held up" a little;

On one of those fine days, for which
  We boys were always wishing,
Too wet to sow, or plant, or hoe,
  Just right to go a fishing,—

I found, not what I went to seek,
   In the old farmhouse gable,—
Nor line, nor hook, but just a book
   That lay there on the table,

Beside my sister's candlestick
   (The wick burned to the socket);
A handy book to take to bed,
   Or carry in one's pocket.

I tipped the dainty cover back,
   With little thought of finding
Anything half so bright within
   The red morocco binding;

And let by chance my careless glance
   Range over song and story;
When from between the magic leaves
   There streamed a sudden glory,—

As from a store of sunlit gems,
   Pellucid and prismatic,—
That edged with gleams the rough old beams,
   And filled the raftered attic.

I stopped to read; I took no heed
   Of time or place, or whether
The window-pane was streaked with rain,
   Or bright with clearing weather.

Of chore-time or of supper-time
   I had no thought or feeling;
If calves were bleating to be fed,
   Or hungry pigs were squealing.

The tangled web of tale and rhyme,
   Enraptured, I unraveled;
By caravan, through Hindostan,
   Toward gay Cashmere, I traveled.

Before the gate of Paradise
  I pleaded with the Peri;
And even of queer old Fadladeen
  I somehow did not weary;

Until a voice called out below:
  "Come, boys! the rain is over!
It's time to bring the cattle home!
  The lambs are in the clover!"

My dream took flight; but day or night,
  It came again, and lingered.
I kept the treasure in my coat,
  And many a time I fingered

Its golden leaves among the sheaves
  In the long harvest nooning;
Or in my room, till fell the gloom,
  And low boughs let the moon in.

About me beamed another world,
  Refulgent, oriental;
Life all aglow with poetry,
  Or sweetly sentimental.

My hands were filled with common tasks,
  My head with rare romances;
My old straw hat was bursting out
  With light locks and bright fancies.

In field or wood, my thoughts threw off
  The old prosaic trammels;
The sheep were grazing antelopes,
  The cows, a train of camels.

Under the shady apple-boughs,
  The book was my companion;
And while I read, the orchard spread
  One mighty branching banyan.

To mango-trees or almond-groves
   Were changed the plums and quinces.
I was the poet, Feramorz,
   And had, of course, my Princess.

The well-curb was her canopied,
   Rich palanquin; at twilight,
'T was her pavilion overhead,
   And not my garret skylight.

Ah, Lalla Rookh! O charmèd book!
   First love, in manhood slighted!
To-day we rarely turn the page
   In which our youth delighted.

Moore stands upon our shelves to-day,
   I fear a trifle dusty;
With Scott, beneath a cobweb wreath,
   And Byron, somewhat musty.

But though his orient cloth-of-gold
   Is hardly now the fashion,
His tender melodies will live
   While human hearts have passion.

The centuries roll; but he has left,
   Beside the ceaseless river,
Some flowers of rhyme untouched by Time,
   And songs that sing forever.

Circumstance

Stalking before the lords of life, one came,
   A Titan shape! But often he will crawl,
   Their most subservient, helpful, humble thrall;
Swift as the light, or sluggish, laggard, lame;
Stony-eyed archer, launching without aim
   Arrows and lightnings, heedless how they fall, —

Blind Circumstance, that makes or baffles all,
Happiness, length of days, power, riches, fame.
Could we but take each wingèd chance aright!
    A timely word let fall, a wind-blown germ,
        May crown our glebe with many a golden sheaf;
A thought may touch and edge our life with light,
    Fill all its sphere, as yonder crescent worm
        Brightens upon the old moon's dusky leaf.

The Old Lobsterman

Cape Arundel, Kennebunkport, Maine

Just back from a beach of sand and shells,
    And shingle the tides leave oozy and dank,
Summer and winter the old man dwells
    In his low brown house on the river bank.
Tempest and sea-fog sweep the hoar
And wrinkled sand-drifts round his door,
Where often I see him sit, as gray
And weather-beaten and lonely as they.

Coarse grasses wave on the arid swells
    In the wind; and two bright poplar-trees
Seem hung all over with silver bells
    That tinkle and twinkle in sun and breeze.
All else is desolate sand and stone:
And here the old lobsterman lives alone:
Nor other companionship has he
But to sit in his house and gaze at the sea.

A furlong or more away to the south,
    On the bar beyond the huge sea-walls
That keep the channel and guard its mouth,
    The high, curved billow whitens and falls;
And the racing tides through the granite gate,
On their wild errands that will not wait,
Forever, unresting, to and fro,
Course with impetuous ebb and flow.

They bury the barnacled ledge, and make
   Into every inlet and crooked creek,
And flood the flats with a shining lake,
   Which the proud ship plows with foam at her beak:
The ships go up to yonder town,
Or over the sea their hulls sink down,
And many a pleasure pinnace rides
On the restless backs of the rushing tides.

I try to fathom the gazer's dreams,
   But little I gain from his gruff replies;
Far off, far off the spirit seems,
   As he looks at me with those strange gray eyes;
Never a hail from the shipwrecked heart!
Mysterious oceans seem to part
The desolate man from all his kind—
The Selkirk of his lonely mind.

He has growls for me when I bring him back
   My unused bait—his way to thank;
And a good shrill curse for the fishing-smack
   That jams his dory against the bank;
But never a word of love to give
For love,—ah! how can he bear to live?
I marvel, and make my own heart ache
With thinking how his must sometimes break.

Solace he finds in the sea, no doubt.
   To catch the ebb he is up and away.
I see him silently pushing out
   On the broad bright gleam at break of day;
And watch his lessening dory toss
On the purple crests as he pulls across,
Round reefs where silvery surges leap,
And meets the dawn on the rosy deep.

His soul, is it open to sea and sky?
   His spirit, alive to sound and sight?
What wondrous tints on the water lie—
   Wild, wavering, liquid realm of light!

Between two glories looms the shape
Of the wood-crested, cool green cape,
Sloping all round to foam-laced ledge,
And cavern and cove, at the bright sea's edge.

He makes for the floats that mark the spots,
   And rises and falls on the sweeping swells,
Ships oars, and pulls his lobster-pots,
   And tumbles the tangled claws and shells
In the leaky bottom; and bails his skiff;
While the slow waves thunder along the cliff,
And foam far away where sun and mist
Edge all the region with amethyst.

I watch him, and fancy how, a boy,
   Round these same reefs, in the rising sun,
He rowed and rocked, and shouted for joy,
   As over the boat-side one by one
He lifted and launched his lobster-traps,
And reckoned his gains, and dreamed, perhaps,
Of a future as glorious, vast and bright
As the ocean, unrolled in the morning light.

He quitted his skiff for a merchant-ship;
   Was sailor-boy, mate,—gained skill and command;
And brought home once from a fortunate trip
   A wife he had found in a foreign land:
So the story is told: then settled down
With the nabobs of his native town,—
Jolly old skippers, bluff and hale,
Who owned the bottoms they used to sail.

Does he sometimes now, in his loneliness,
   Live over again that happy time,
Beguile his poverty and distress
   With pictures of his prosperous prime?
Does ever, at dusk, a fond young bride
Start forth and sit by the old man's side;
Children frolic, and friends look in;
With all the blessings that might have been?

Yet might not be! The same sad day
  Saw wife and babe to the churchyard borne;
And he sailed away, he sailed away,—
  For that is the sailor's way to mourn.
And ever, 't is said, as he sailed and sailed,
Heart grew reckless and fortune failed,
Till old age drifted him back to shore,
To his hut and his lobster-pots once more.

The house is empty, the board is bare;
  His dish he scours, his jacket he mends;
And now 't is the dory that needs repair;
  He fishes; his lobster-traps he tends;
And, rowing at nightfall many a mile,
Brings floodwood home to his winter pile;
Then his fire 's to kindle, and supper to cook;
The storm his music, his thoughts his book.

He sleeps, he wakes; and this is his life.
  Nor kindred nor friend in all the earth;
Nor laughter of child, nor gossip of wife;
  Not even a cat to his silent hearth!
Only the sand-hills, wrinkled and hoar,
Bask in the sunset, round his door,
Where now I can see him sit, as gray
And weather-beaten and lonely as they.

HENRY TIMROD

(1828–1867)

Dreams

Who first said "false as dreams?" Not one who saw
  Into the wild and wondrous world they sway;
No thinker who hath read their mystic law;
  No Poet who hath weaved them in his lay.

Else had he known that through the human breast
  Cross and recross a thousand fleeting gleams,
That, passed unnoticed in the day's unrest,
  Come out at night, like stars, in shining dreams;

That minds too busy or to dull to mark
  The dim suggestions of the noisier hours,
By dreams in the deep silence of the dark,
  Are roused at midnight with their folded powers.

Like that old fount beneath Dodona's oaks,
  That, dry and voiceless in the garish noon,
When the calm night arose with modest looks,
  Caught with full wave the sparkle of the moon.

If, now and then, a ghastly shape glide in,
  And fright us with its horrid gloom or glee,
It is the ghost of some forgotten sin
  We failed to exorcise on bended knee.

And that sweet face which only yesternight
  Came to thy solace, dreamer (did'st thou read
The blessing in its eyes of tearful light?)
  Was but the spirit of some gentle deed.

Each has its lesson; for our dreams in sooth,
  Come they in shape of demons, gods, or elves,
Are allegories with deep hearts of truth
  That tell us solemn secrets of ourselves.

Retirement

My gentle friend! I hold no creed so false
As that which dares to teach that we are born
For battle only, and that in this life
The soul, if it would burn with starlike power,
Must needs forsooth be kindled by the sparks
Struck from the shock of clashing human hearts.
There is a wisdom that grows up in strife,
And one—I like it best—that sits at home
And learns its lessons of a thoughtful ease.
So come! a lonely house awaits thee!—there
Nor praise, nor blame shall reach us, save what love
Of knowledge for itself shall wake at times
In our own bosoms; come! and we will build
A wall of quiet thought, and gentle books,
Betwixt us and the hard and bitter world.
Sometimes—for we need not be anchorites—
A distant friend shall cheer us through the Post
Or some gazette—of course no partisan—
Shall bring us pleasant news of pleasant things,
Then twisted into graceful allumettes,
Each ancient joke shall blaze with genuine flame
To light our pipes and candles; but to wars,
Whether of words or weapons, we shall be
Deaf—so we twain shall pass away the time
Ev'n as a pair of happy lovers, who,
Alone, within some quiet garden-nook,
With a clear night of stars above their heads,
Just hear, betwixt their kisses and their talk,
The tumult of a tempest rolling through
A chain of neighboring mountains; they awhile
Pause to admire a flash that only shows
The smile upon their faces, but, full soon,
Turn with a quick, glad impulse, and perhaps
A conscious wile that brings them closer yet,
To dally with their own fond hearts, and play
With the sweet flowers that blossom at their feet.

Ethnogenesis

Written during the meeting of the first Southern Congress,
at Montgomery, February, 1861.

I.

Hath not the morning dawned with added light?
And will not evening call another star
Out of the infinite regions of the night,
To mark this day in Heaven? At last, we are
A nation among nations; and the world
Shall soon behold in many a distant port
        Another Flag unfurled!
Now, come what may, whose favor need we court?
And, under God, whose thunder need we fear?
        Thank Him who placed us here
Beneath so kind a sky—the very sun
Takes part with us; and on our errands run
All breezes of the ocean; dew and rain
Do noiseless battle for us; and the Year,
And all the gentle daughters in her train,
March in our ranks, and in our service wield
        Long spears of golden grain!
A yellow blossom as her fairy shield,
June flings her azure banner to the wind,
    While in the order of their birth
Her sisters pass, and many an ample field
Grows white beneath their steps, till now, behold
        Its endless sheets unfold
THE SNOW OF SOUTHERN SUMMERS! Let the earth
Rejoice! beneath those fleeces soft and warm
        Our happy land shall sleep
        In a repose as deep
    As if we lay intrenched behind
Whole leagues of Russian ice and Arctic storm!

II.

And what if, mad with wrongs themselves have wrought,
     In their own treachery caught,
     By their own fears made bold,
     And leagued with him of old,
Who long since in the limits of the North
Set up his evil throne, and warred with God—
What if, both mad and blinded in their rage,
Our foes should fling us down their mortal gage,
And with a hostile step profane our sod!
We shall not shrink, my brothers, but go forth
To meet them, marshalled by the Lord of Hosts,
And overshadowed by the mighty ghosts
Of Moultrie and of Eutaw—who shall foil
Auxiliars such as these? Nor these alone,
     But every stock and stone
     Shall help us: but the very soil,
And all the generous wealth it gives to toil,
And all for which we love our noble land,
Shall fight beside, and through us, sea and strand,
     The heart of woman, and her hand,
Tree, fruit, and flower, and every influence,
     Gentle, or grave, or grand;
     The winds in our defence
Shall seem to blow; to us the hills shall lend
     Their firmness and their calm;
And in our stiffened sinews we shall blend
     The strength of pine and palm!

III.

Nor would we shun the battle-ground,
     Though weak as we are strong;
Call up the clashing elements around,
     And test the right and wrong!
On one side, creeds that dare to teach
What Christ and Paul refrained to preach;
Codes built upon a broken pledge,
And Charity that whets a poniard's edge;
Fair schemes that leave the neighboring poor

To starve and shiver at the schemer's door,
While in the world's most liberal ranks enrolled,
He turns some vast philanthropy to gold;
Religion, taking every mortal form
But that a pure and Christian faith makes warm,
Where not to vile fanatic passion urged,
Or not in vague philosophies submerged,
Repulsive with all Pharisaic leaven,
And making laws to stay the laws of Heaven!
And on the other, scorn of sordid gain,
Unblemished honor, truth without a stain,
Faith, justice, reverence, charitable wealth,
And, for the poor and humble, laws which give,
Not the mean right to buy the right to live,
          But life, and home, and health!
To doubt the end were want of trust in God,
          Who, if he has decreed
     That we must pass a redder sea
Than that which rang to Miriam's holy glee,
          Will surely raise at need
          A Moses with his rod!

                    IV.

But let our fears—if fears we have—be still,
And turn us to the future! Could we climb
Some mighty Alp, and view the coming time,
We should indeed behold a sight to fill
          Our eyes with happy tears!
Not for the glories which a hundred years
Shall bring us; not for lands from sea to sea,
And wealth, and power, and peace, though these shall be;
But for the distant peoples we shall bless,
And the hushed murmurs of a world's distress:
For, to give labor to the poor,
          The whole sad planet o'er,
And save from want and crime the humblest door,
Is one among the many ends for which
          God makes us great and rich!
The hour perchance is not yet wholly ripe

When all shall own it, but the type
Whereby we shall be known in every land
Is that vast gulf which laves our Southern strand,
And through the cold, untempered ocean pours
Its genial streams, that far off Arctic shores
May sometimes catch upon the softened breeze
Strange tropic warmth and hints of summer seas.

"I know not why, but all this weary day"

I know not why, but all this weary day,
(Suggested by no definite grief or pain)
Sad fancies have been flitting through my brain
Now it has been a vessel losing way,
Rounding a stormy headland, now a gray
Dull waste of clouds above a wintry main;
And then, a banner, drooping in the rain,
And meadows beaten into bloody clay.
Strolling at random with this shadowy woe
At heart, I chanced to wander hither! Lo!
A league of desolate marsh-land, with its bush,
Hot grasses in a noisome, tide-left bed,
And faint, warm airs, that nestle in the hush,
Like whispers round the body of the dead!

The Cotton Boll

While I recline
At ease beneath
This immemorial pine,
Small sphere!
(By dusky fingers brought this morning here
And shown with boastful smiles),
I turn thy cloven sheath,
Through which the soft white fibres peer,
That, with their gossamer bands,
Unite, like love, the sea-divided lands,

And slowly, thread by thread,
Draw forth the folded strands,
Than which the trembling line,
By whose frail help yon startled spider fled
Down the tall spear-grass from his swinging bed,
Is scarce more fine;
And as the tangled skein
Unravels in my hands,
Betwixt me and the noonday light,
A veil seems lifted, and for miles and miles
The landscape broadens on my sight,
As, in the little boll, there lurked a spell
Like that which, in the ocean shell,
With mystic sound,
Breaks down the narrow walls that hem us round,
And turns some city lane
Into the restless main,
With all his capes and isles!

Yonder bird
Which floats, as if at rest,
In those blue tracts above the thunder, where
No vapors cloud the stainless air,
And never sound is heard,
Unless at such rare time
When, from the City of the Blest,
Rings down some golden chime,
Sees not from his high place
So vast a cirque of summer space
As widens round me in one mighty field,
Which, rimmed by seas and sands,
Doth hail its earliest daylight in the beams
Of gray Atlantic dawns;
And, broad as realms made up of many lands,
Is lost afar
Behind the crimson hills and purple lawns
Of sunset, among plains which roll their streams
Against the Evening Star!
And lo!
To the remotest point of sight,

Although I gaze upon no waste of snow,
The endless field is white;
And the whole landscape glows,
For many a shining league away,
With such accumulated light
As Polar lands would flash beneath a tropic day!
Nor lack there (for the vision grows,
And the small charm within my hands—
More potent even than the fabled one,
Which oped whatever golden mystery
Lay hid in fairy wood or magic vale,
The curious ointment of the Arabian tale—
Beyond all mortal sense
Doth stretch my sight's horizon, and I see
Beneath its simple influence,
As if, with Uriel's crown,
I stood in some great temple of the Sun,
And looked, as Uriel, down)!
Nor lack there pastures rich and fields all green
With all the common gifts of God,
For temperate airs and torrid sheen
Weave Edens of the sod;
Through lands which look one sea of billowy gold
Broad rivers wind their devious ways;
A hundred isles in their embraces fold
A hundred luminous bays;
And through yon purple haze
Vast mountains lift their plumed peaks cloud-crowned;
And, save where up their sides the ploughman creeps,
An unhewn forest girds them grandly round,
In whose dark shades a future navy sleeps!
Ye Stars, which though unseen, yet with me gaze
Upon this loveliest fragment of the earth!
Thou Sun, that kindlest all thy gentlest rays
Above it, as to light a favorite hearth!
Ye Clouds, that in your temples in the West
See nothing brighter than its humblest flowers!
And, you, ye Winds, that on the ocean's breast
Are kissed to coolness ere ye reach its bowers!
Bear witness with me in my song of praise,

And tell the world that, since the world began,
No fairer land hath fired a poet's lays,
Or given a home to man!

But these are charms already widely blown!
His be the meed whose pencil's trace
Hath touched our very swamps with grace,
And round whose tuneful way
All Southern laurels bloom;
The Poet of "The Woodlands," unto whom
Alike are known
The flute's low breathing and the trumpet's tone,
And the soft west-wind's sighs;
But who shall utter all the debt,
O, Land! wherein all powers are met
That bind a people's heart,
The world doth owe thee at this day,
And which it never can repay,
Yet scarcely deigns to own!
Where sleeps the poet who shall fitly sing
The source wherefrom doth spring
That mighty commerce which, confined
To the mean channels of no selfish mart,
Goes out to every shore
Of this broad earth, and throngs the sea with ships
That bear no thunders; hushes hungry lips
In alien lands;
Joins with a delicate web remotest strands;
And gladdening rich and poor,
Doth gild Parisian domes,
Or feed the cottage-smoke of English homes,
And only bounds its blessings by mankind!
In offices like these, thy mission lies,
My Country! and it shall not end
As long as rain shall fall and Heaven bend
In blue above thee; though thy foes be hard
And cruel as their weapons, it shall guard
Thy hearth-stones as a bulwark; make thee great
In white and bloodless state;
And, haply, as the years increase—

Still working through its humbler reach
With that large wisdom which the ages teach—

Revive the half-dead dream of universal peace!
As men who labor in that mine
Of Cornwall, hollowed out beneath the bed
Of ocean, when a storm rolls overhead,
Hear the dull booming of the world of brine
Above them, and a mighty muffled roar
Of winds and waters, yet toil calmly on,
And split the rock, and pile the massive ore,
Or carve a niche, or shape the arched roof;
So I, as calmly, weave my woof
Of song, chanting the days to come,
Unsilenced, though the quiet summer air
Stirs with the bruit of battles, and each dawn
Wakes from its starry silence to the hum
Of many gathering armies. Still,
In that we sometimes hear,
Upon the Northern winds the voice of woe
Not wholly drowned in triumph, though I know
The end must crown us, and a few brief years
Dry all our tears,
I may not sing too gladly. To Thy will
Resigned, O Lord! we cannot all forget
That there is much even Victory must regret.
And, therefore, not too long
From the great burthen of our country's wrong
Delay our just release!
And, if it may be, save
These sacred fields of peace
From stain of patriot or of hostile blood!
Oh, help us Lord! to roll the crimson flood
Back on its course, and, while our banners wing
Northward, strike with us! till the Goth shall cling
To his own blasted altar-stones, and crave
Mercy; and we shall grant it, and dictate
The lenient future of his fate
There, where some rotting ships and crumbling quays
Shall one day mark the Port which ruled the Western seas.

La Belle Juive

Is it because your sable hair
Is folded over brows that wear
At times a too imperial air;

Or is it that the thoughts which rise
In those dark orbs do seek disguise
Beneath the lids of Eastern eyes;

That choose whatever pose or place
May chance to please, in you I trace
The noblest women of your race?

The crowd is sauntering at its ease,
And humming like a hive of bees—
You take your seat and touch the keys.

I do not hear the giddy throng;
The sea avenges Israel's wrong,
And on the wind floats Miriam's song!

You join me with a stately grace;
Music to Poesy gives place;
Some grand emotion lights your face.

At once I stand by Mizpeh's walls:
With smiles the martyred daughter falls,
And desolate are Mizpeh's halls!

Intrusive babblers come between;
With calm, pale brow and lofty mien,
You thread the circle like a queen!

Then sweeps the royal Esther by;
The deep devotion in her eye
Is looking "If I die, I die!"

You stroll the garden's flowery walks;
The plants to me are grainless stalks,
And Ruth to old Naomi talks.

Adopted child of Judah's creed,
Like Judah's daughters true at need,
I see you mid the alien seed.

I watch afar the gleaner sweet;
I wake like Boaz in the wheat,
And find you lying at my feet!

My feet! Oh! if the spell that lures
My heart through all these dreams endures,
How soon shall I be stretched at yours!

Carolina

I.

The despot treads thy sacred sands,
Thy pines give shelter to his bands,
Thy sons stand by with idle hands,
                    Carolina!
He breathes at ease thy airs of balm,
He scorns the lances of thy palm;
Oh! who shall break thy craven calm,
                    Carolina!
Thy ancient fame is growing dim,
A spot is on thy garment's rim,
Give to the winds thy battle hymn,
                    Carolina!

II.

Call on thy children of the hill,
Wake swamp and river, coast and rill,
Rouse all thy strength and all thy skill,
                    Carolina!

Cite wealth and science, trade and art,
Touch with thy fire the cautious mart,
And pour thee through the people's heart,
    Carolina!
Till even the coward spurns his fears,
And all thy fields and fens and meres,
Shall bristle like thy palm with spears,
    Carolina!

III.

Hold up the glories of thy dead;
Say how thy elder children bled,
And point to Eutaw's battle-bed,
    Carolina!
Tell how the patriot's soul was tried,
And what his dauntless breast defied;
How Rutledge ruled and Laurens died,
    Carolina!
Cry! till thy summons, heard at last,
Shall fall like Marion's bugle blast
Re-echoed from the haunted Past,
    Carolina!

IV.

I hear a murmur as of waves
That grope their way through sunless caves,
Like bodies struggling in their graves,
    Carolina!
And now it deepens; slow and grand
It swells, as rolling to the land
An ocean broke upon the strand,
    Carolina!
Shout! let it reach the startled Huns!
And roar with all thy festal guns!
It is the answer of thy sons,
    Carolina!

V.

They will not wait to hear thee call;
From Sachem's head to Sumter's wall
Resounds the voice of hut and hall,
                    Carolina!
No! thou hast not a stain they say,
Or none save what the battle-day
Shall wash in seas of blood away,
                    Carolina!
Thy skirts indeed the foe may part,
Thy robe be pierced with sword and dart,
They shall not touch thy noble heart,
                    Carolina!

VI.

Ere thou shalt own the tyrant's thrall
Ten times ten thousand men must fall;
Thy corpse may hearken to his call,
                    Carolina!
When by thy bier in mournful throngs
The women chant thy mortal wrongs,
'T will be their own funereal songs,
                    Carolina!
From thy dead breast by ruffians trod
No helpless child shall look to God;
All shall be safe beneath thy sod,
                    Carolina!

VII.

Girt with such wills to do and bear,
Assured in right, and mailed in prayer,
Thou wilt not bow thee to despair,
                    Carolina!

Throw thy bold banner to the breeze!
Front with thy ranks the threatening seas
Like thine own proud armorial trees,
                    Carolina!
Fling down thy gauntlet to the Huns,
And roar the challenge from thy guns;
Then leave the future to thy sons,
                    Carolina!

Charleston

Calm as that second summer which precedes
    The first fall of the snow,
In the broad sunlight of heroic deeds,
    The City bides the foe.

As yet, behind their ramparts stern and proud,
    Her bolted thunders sleep—
Dark Sumter, like a battlemented cloud,
    Looms o'er the solemn deep.

No Calpe frowns from lofty cliff or scar
    To guard the holy strand;
But Moultrie holds in leash her dogs of war
    Above the level sand.

And down the dunes a thousand guns lie couched,
    Unseen, beside the flood—
Like tigers in some Orient jungle crouched
    That wait and watch for blood.

Meanwhile, through streets still echoing with trade,
    Walk grave and thoughtful men,
Whose hands may one day wield the patriot's blade
    As lightly as the pen.

And maidens, with such eyes as would grow dim
   Over a bleeding hound,
Seem each one to have caught the strength of him
   Whose sword she sadly bound.

Thus girt without and garrisoned at home,
   Day patient following day,
Old Charleston looks from roof, and spire, and dome,
   Across her tranquil bay.

Ships, through a hundred foes, from Saxon lands
   And spicy Indian ports,
Bring Saxon steel and iron to her hands,
   And summer to her courts.

But still, along yon dim Atlantic line,
   The only hostile smoke
Creeps like a harmless mist above the brine,
   From some frail, floating oak.

Shall the spring dawn, and she still clad in smiles,
   And with an unscathed brow,
Rest in the strong arms of her palm-crowned isles,
   As fair and free as now?

We know not; in the temple of the Fates
   God has inscribed her doom;
And, all untroubled in her faith, she waits
   The triumph or the tomb.

Christmas

How grace this hallowed day?
Shall happy bells, from yonder ancient spire,
Send their glad greetings to each Christmas fire
Round which the children play?

Alas! for many a moon,
That tongueless tower hath cleaved the Sabbath air,
Mute as an obelisk of ice aglare
    Beneath an Arctic noon.

Shame to the foes that drown
Our psalms of worship with their impious drum,
The sweetest chimes in all the land lie dumb
    In some far rustic town.

There, let us think, they keep,
Of the dead Yules which here beside the sea
They've ushered in with old-world, English glee,
    Some echoes in their sleep.

How shall we grace the day?
With feast, and song, and dance, and antique sports,
And shout of happy children in the courts,
    And tales of ghost and fay?

Is there indeed a door,
Where the old pastimes, with their lawful noise,
And all the merry round of Christmas joys,
    Could enter as of yore?

Would not some pallid face
Look in upon the banquet, calling up
Dread shapes of battle in the wassail cup,
    And trouble all the place?

How could we bear the mirth,
While some loved reveller of a year ago
Keeps his mute Christmas now beneath the snow,
    In cold Virginian earth?

How shall we grace the day?
Ah! let the thought that on this holy morn
The Prince of Peace—the Prince of Peace was born,
    Employ us, while we pray!

Pray for the peace which long
Hath left this tortured land, and haply now
Holds its white court on some far mountain's brow,
There hardly safe from wrong.

Let every sacred fane
Call its sad votaries to the shrine of God,
And, with the cloister and the tented sod,
Join in one solemn strain!

With pomp of Roman form,
With the grave ritual brought from England's shore,
And with the simple faith which asks no more
Than that the heart he warm!

He, who till time shall cease,
Will watch that earth, where once, not all in vain,
He died to give us peace, may not disdain
A prayer whose theme is—peace.

Perhaps ere yet the spring
Hath died into the summer, over all
The land, the peace of His vast love shall fall
Like some protecting wing.

Oh ponder what it means!
Oh turn the rapturous thought in every way!
Oh give the vision and the fancy play,
And shape the coming scenes!

Peace in the quiet dales,
Made rankly fertile by the blood of men;
Peace in the woodland, and the lonely glen,
Peace in the peopled vales!

Peace in the crowded town,
Peace in a thousand fields of waving grain,
Peace in the highway and the flowery lane,
Peace on the wind-swept down!

Peace on the farthest seas,
Peace in our sheltered bays and ample streams,
Peace wheresoe'er our starry garland gleams,
     And peace in every breeze!

Peace on the whirring marts,
Peace where the scholar thinks, the hunter roams,
Peace, God of Peace! peace, peace, in all our homes,
     And peace in all our hearts!

Lines

Sleep sweetly in your humble graves,
     Sleep martyrs of a fallen cause!—
Though yet no marble column craves
     The pilgrim here to pause.

In seeds of laurels in the earth,
     The garlands of your fame are sown;
And, somewhere, waiting for its birth,
     The shaft is in the stone.

Meanwhile, your sisters for the years
     Which hold in trust your storied tombs,
Bring all they now can give you—tears,
     And these memorial blooms.

Small tributes, but your shades will smile
     As proudly on those wreaths to-day,
As when some cannon-moulded pile
     Shall overlook this Bay.

Stoop angels hither from the skies!
     There is no holier spot of ground,
Than where defeated valor lies
     By mourning beauty crowned.

PAUL HAMILTON HAYNE

(1830–1886)

October

The passionate Summer's dead! the sky's a-glow,
　With roseate flushes of matured desire,
The winds at eve are musical and low,
　As sweeping chords of a lamenting lyre,
　Far up among the pillared clouds of fire,
Whose pomp of strange procession upward rolls,
With gorgeous blazonry of pictured folds,
　To celebrate the Summer's past renown;
　Ah, me! how regally the Heavens look down,
O'ershadowing beautiful autumnal woods,
　And harvest fields with hoarded increase brown,
And deep-toned majesty of golden floods,
　That raise their solemn dirges to the sky,
　To swell the purple pomp that floateth by.

On the Occurrence of a Spell of
Arctic Weather in May, 1858

We thought that Winter with his hungry pack
Of hounding Winds had closed his dreary chase,—
For virgin Spring, with arch, triumphant face,
Lightly descending, had strewed o'er his track
Gay flowers that hid the stormy season's wrack.
Vain thought! for, wheeling on his northward path,
And girt by all his hungry Blasts, in wrath
The shrill-voiced Huntsman hurries swiftly back,—
The frightened vernal Zephyrs shrink and die
Through the chilled forest,—the rare blooms expire,—
And Spring herself, too terror-struck to fly,
Seized by the ravening Winds with fury dire,
Dies 'mid the scarlet flowers that round her lie,
Like waning flames of some rich funeral fire!

Charlotte Brontë

Through the deep shadows of the darkening years,
She strove with griefs, which oft were agonies,—
The traitorous Hopes transformed to haunting Fears,
The transient Raptures ending but in sighs:

Till at the last, the life-clouds cleared away,
The future bathed in promise heavenly bright,
She heard a tender voice which seemed to say,
"At evening time, behold! I give thee light!"

For love, true love, her woman's nature yearned,—
And now true Love hath crowned her longing wild,
And all without, and all within her burned
The glory of his Godhead undefiled.

A new world dawned upon her; divine forms
Gleamed in the sunset on her earnest eyes,
And throned above the years which set in storms,
She saw the opening gates of Paradise;

An earthly Eden, freed from earth's alloy;
Across the happy porch her footsteps passed,
When on the very threshold of her joy,
Death's sudden angel blew his trumpet blast:

The gates of light, as that fierce trumpet rang,
Dissolved, like some vain phantom of the air,
And born of desolation deep, outsprang
A passionate cry—the last—of her despair:

"Love! we have been so happy! Must we part?"
Even as she spoke the final darkness came,
To many sorrowing, and one broken heart,
Leaving thenceforth but memory, and—a name!

HELEN HUNT JACKSON

(1830–1885)

My Lighthouses

At westward window of a palace gray,
Which its own secret still so safely keeps
That no man now its builder's name can say,
I lie and idly sun myself to-day,
Dreaming awake far more than one who sleeps,
Serenely glad, although my gladness weeps.

I look across the harbor's misty blue,
And find and lose that magic shifting line
Where sky one shade less blue meets sea, and through
The air I catch one flush as if it knew
Some secret of that meeting, which no sign
Can show to eyes so far and dim as mine.

More ships than I can count build mast by mast
Gay lattice-work with waving green and red
Across my window-panes. The voyage past,
They crowd to anchorage so glad, so fast,
Gliding like ghosts, with noiseless breath and tread,
Mooring like ghosts, with noiseless iron and lead.

"O ships and patient men who fare by sea,"
I stretch my hands and vainly questioning cry,
"Sailed ye from west? How many nights could ye
Tell by the lights just where my dear and free
And lovely land lay sleeping? Passed ye by
Some danger safe, because her fires were nigh?"

Ah me! my selfish yearning thoughts forget
How darkness but a hand's-breadth from the coast
With danger in an evil league is set!
Ah! helpless ships and men more helpless yet,
Who trust the land-lights' short and empty boast;
The lights ye bear aloft and prayers avail ye most.

But I—ah, patient men who fare by sea,
Ye would but smile to hear this empty speech,—
I have such beacon-lights to burn for me,
In that dear west so lovely, new, and free,
That evil league by day, by night, can teach
No spell whose harm my little bark can reach.

No towers of stone uphold those beacon-lights;
No distance hides them, and no storm can shake;
In valleys they light up the darkest nights,
They outshine sunny days on sunny heights;
They blaze from every house where sleep or wake
My own who love me for my own poor sake.

Each thought they think of me lights road of flame
Across the seas; no travel on it tires
My heart. I go if they but speak my name;
From Heaven I should come and go the same,
And find this glow forestalling my desires.
My darlings, do you hear me? Trim the fires!

Poppies on the Wheat

Along Ancona's hills the shimmering heat,
A tropic tide of air with ebb and flow
Bathes all the fields of wheat until they glow
Like flashing seas of green, which toss and beat
Around the vines. The poppies lithe and fleet
Seem running, fiery torchmen, to and fro
To mark the shore.
                   The farmer does not know
That they are there. He walks with heavy feet,
Counting the bread and wine by autumn's gain,
But I,—I smile to think that days remain
Perhaps to me in which, though bread be sweet
No more, and red wine warm my blood in vain,
I shall be glad remembering how the fleet,
Lithe poppies ran like torchmen with the wheat.

October

Bending above the spicy woods which blaze,
Arch skies so blue they flash, and hold the sun
Immeasurably far; the waters run
Too slow, so freighted are the river-ways
With gold of elms and birches from the maze
Of forests. Chestnuts, clicking one by one,
Escape from satin burs; her fringes done,
The gentian spreads them out in sunny days,
And, like late revelers at dawn, the chance
Of one sweet, mad, last hour, all things assail,
And conquering, flush and spin; while, to enhance
The spell, by sunset door, wrapped in a veil
Of red and purple mists, the summer, pale,
Steals back alone for one more song and dance.

Crossed Threads

The silken threads by viewless spinners spun,
Which float so idly on the summer air,
And help to make each summer morning fair,
Shining like silver in the summer sun,
Are caught by wayward breezes, one by one,
And blown to east and west and fastened there,
Weaving on all the roads their sudden snare.
No sign which road doth safest, freest run,
The wingèd insects know, that soar so gay
To meet their death upon each summer day.
How dare we any human deed arraign;
Attempt to reckon any moment's cost;
Or any pathway trust as safe and plain
Because we see not where the threads have crossed?

September

The golden-rod is yellow;
   The corn is turning brown;
The trees in apple orchards
   With fruit are bending down.

The gentian's bluest fringes
   Are curling in the sun;
In dusty pods the milkweed
   Its hidden silk has spun.

The sedges flaunt their harvest,
   In every meadow nook;
And asters by the brook-side
   Make asters in the brook.

From dewy lanes at morning
   The grapes' sweet odors rise;
At noon the roads all flutter
   With yellow butterflies.

By all these lovely tokens
   September days are here,
With summer's best of weather,
   And autumn's best of cheer.

But none of all this beauty
   Which floods the earth and air
Is unto me the secret
   Which makes September fair.

'T is a thing which I remember;
   To name it thrills me yet:
One day of one September
   I never can forget.

Dreams

Mysterious shapes, with wands of joy and pain,
Which seize us unaware in helpless sleep,
And lead us to the houses where we keep
Our secrets hid, well barred by every chain
That we can forge and bind: the crime whose stain
Is slowly fading 'neath the tears we weep;
Dead bliss which, dead, can make our pulses leap—
Oh, cruelty! To make these live again!
They say that death is sleep, and heaven's rest
Ends earth's short day, as, on the last faint gleam
Of sun, our nights shut down, and we are blest.
Let this, then, be of heaven's joy the test,
The proof if heaven be, or only seem,
That we forever choose what we will dream!

Cheyenne Mountain

By easy slope to west as if it had
    No thought, when first its soaring was begun,
    Except to look devoutly to the sun,
It rises, and has risen, until, glad,
With light as with a garment, it is clad,
    Each dawn, before the tardy plains have won
    One ray; and after day has long been done
For us, the light doth cling reluctant, sad
To leave its brow.
                    Beloved mountain, I
Thy worshiper, as thou the sun's, each morn,
    My dawn, before the dawn, receive from thee;
    And think, as thy rose-tinted peaks I see,
That thou wert great when Homer was not born,
And ere thou change all human song shall die!

EMILY DICKINSON

(1830–1886)

Success is counted sweetest
By those who ne'er succeed.
To comprehend a nectar
Requires sorest need.

Not one of all the purple Host
Who took the Flag today
Can tell the definition
So clear of Victory

As he defeated—dying—
On whose forbidden ear
The distant strains of triumph
Burst agonized and clear!

———

Exultation is the going
Of an inland soul to sea,
Past the houses—past the headlands—
Into deep Eternity—

Bred as we, among the mountains,
Can the sailor understand
The divine intoxication
Of the first league out from land?

———

Our lives are Swiss—
So still—so Cool—
Till some odd afternoon
The Alps neglect their Curtains

227

And we look farther on!
Italy stands the other side!
While like a guard between—
The solemn Alps—
The siren Alps
Forever intervene!

———

The Bee is not afraid of me.
I know the Butterfly.
The pretty people in the Woods
Receive me cordially—

The Brooks laugh louder when I come—
The Breezes madder play;
Wherefore mine eye thy silver mists,
Wherefore, Oh Summer's Day?

———

Bring me the sunset in a cup,
Reckon the morning's flagons up
And say how many Dew,
Tell me how far the morning leaps—
Tell me what time the weaver sleeps
Who spun the breadths of blue!

Write me how many notes there be
In the new Robin's ecstasy
Among astonished boughs—
How many trips the Tortoise makes—
How many cups the Bee partakes,
The Debauchee of Dews!

Also, who laid the Rainbow's piers,
Also, who leads the docile spheres
By withes of supple blue?

Whose fingers string the stalactite—
Who counts the wampum of the night
To see that none is due?

Who built this little Alban House
And shut the windows down so close
My spirit cannot see?
Who'll let me out some gala day
With implements to fly away,
Passing Pomposity?

———

These are the days when Birds come back—
A very few—a Bird or two—
To take a backward look.

These are the days when skies resume
The old—old sophistries of June—
A blue and gold mistake.

Oh fraud that cannot cheat the Bee—
Almost thy plausibility
Induces my belief.

Till ranks of seeds their witness bear—
And softly thro' the altered air
Hurries a timid leaf.

Oh Sacrament of summer days,
Oh Last Communion in the Haze—
Permit a child to join.

Thy sacred emblems to partake—
Thy consecrated bread to take
And thine immortal wine!

———

Musicians wrestle everywhere—
All day—among the crowded air
I hear the silver strife—
And—waking—long before the morn—
Such transport breaks upon the town
I think it that "New Life"!

It is not Bird—it has no nest—
Nor "Band"—in brass and scarlet—drest—
Nor Tamborin—nor Man—
It is not Hymn from pulpit read—
The "Morning Stars" the Treble led
On Time's first Afternoon!

Some—say—it is "the Spheres"—at play!
Some say that bright Majority
Of vanished Dames—and Men!
Some—think it service in the place
Where we—with late—celestial face—
Please God—shall Ascertain!

———

A *Wounded* Deer—leaps highest—
I've heard the Hunter tell—
'Tis but the Ecstasy of *death* —
And then the Brake is still!

The *Smitten* Rock that gushes!
The *trampled* Steel that springs!
A Cheek is always redder
Just where the Hectic stings!

Mirth is the Mail of Anguish—
In which it Cautious Arm,
Lest anybody spy the blood
And "you're hurt" exclaim!

———————

As if some little Arctic flower
Upon the polar hem—
Went wandering down the Latitudes
Until it puzzled came
To continents of summer—
To firmaments of sun—
To strange, bright crowds of flowers—
And birds, of foreign tongue!
I say, As if this little flower
To Eden, wandered in—
What then? Why nothing,
Only, your inference therefrom!

———————

"Faith" is a fine invention
When Gentlemen can *see*—
But *Microscopes* are prudent
In an Emergency.

———————

I taste a liquor never brewed—
From Tankards scooped in Pearl—
Not all the Vats upon the Rhine
Yield such an Alcohol!

Inebriate of Air—am I—
And Debauchee of Dew—
Reeling—thro endless summer days—
From inns of Molten Blue—

When "Landlords" turn the drunken Bee
Out of the Foxglove's door—
When Butterflies—renounce their "drams"—
I shall but drink the more!

Till Seraphs swing their snowy Hats—
And Saints—to windows run—
To see the little Tippler
Leaning against the—Sun—

Safe in their Alabaster Chambers—
Untouched by Morning—
And untouched by Noon—
Lie the meek members of the Resurrection—
Rafter of Satin—and Roof of Stone!

Grand go the Years—in the Crescent—above them—
Worlds scoop their Arcs—
And Firmaments—row—
Diadems—drop—and Doges—surrender—
Soundless as dots—on a Disc of Snow—

I like a look of Agony,
Because I know it's true—
Men do not sham Convulsion,
Nor simulate, a Throe—

The Eyes glaze once—and that is Death—
Impossible to feign
The Beads upon the Forehead
By homely Anguish strung.

Wild Nights—Wild Nights!
Were I with thee
Wild Nights should be
Our luxury!

Futile—the Winds—
To a Heart in port—
Done with the Compass—
Done with the Chart!

Rowing in Eden—
Ah, the Sea!
Might I but moor—Tonight—
In Thee!

———————

I shall keep singing!
Birds will pass me
On their way to Yellower Climes—
Each—with a Robin's expectation—
I—with my Redbreast—
And my Rhymes—

Late—when I take my place in summer—
But—I shall bring a fuller tune—
Vespers—are sweeter than Matins—Signor—
Morning—only the seed of Noon—

———————

I can wade Grief—
Whole Pools of it—
I'm used to that—
But the least push of Joy
Breaks up my feet—

And I tip—drunken—
Let no Pebble—smile—
'Twas the New Liquor—
That was all!

Power is only Pain—
Stranded, thro' Discipline,
Till Weights—will hang—
Give Balm—to Giants—
And they'll wilt, like Men—
Give Himmaleh—
They'll Carry—Him!

"Hope" is the thing with feathers—
That perches in the soul—
And sings the tune without the words—
And never stops—at all—

And sweetest—in the Gale—is heard—
And sore must be the storm—
That could abash the little Bird
That kept so many warm—

I've heard it in the chillest land—
And on the strangest Sea—
Yet, never, in Extremity,
It asked a crumb—of Me.

There's a certain Slant of light,
Winter Afternoons—
That oppresses, like the Heft
Of Cathedral Tunes—

Heavenly Hurt, it gives us—
We can find no scar,
But internal difference,
Where the Meanings, are—

None may teach it—Any—
'Tis the Seal Despair—
An imperial affliction
Sent us of the Air—

When it comes, the Landscape listens—
Shadows—hold their breath—
When it goes, 'tis like the Distance
On the look of Death—

———

A single Screw of Flesh
Is all that pins the Soul
That stands for Deity, to Mine,
Upon my side the Veil—

Once witnessed of the Gauze—
Its name is put away
As far from mine, as if no plight
Had printed yesterday,

In tender—solemn Alphabet,
My eyes just turned to see,
When it was smuggled by my sight
Into Eternity—

More Hands—to hold—These are but Two—
One more new-mailed Nerve
Just granted, for the Peril's sake—
Some striding—Giant—Love—

So greater than the Gods can show,
They slink before the Clay,
That not for all their Heaven can boast
Will let its Keepsake — go

———————

I felt a Funeral, in my Brain,
And Mourners to and fro
Kept treading — treading — till it seemed
That Sense was breaking through —

And when they all were seated,
A Service, like a Drum —
Kept beating — beating — till I thought
My Mind was going numb —

And then I heard them lift a Box
And creak across my Soul
With those same Boots of Lead, again,
Then Space — began to toll,

As all the Heavens were a Bell,
And Being, but an Ear,
And I, and Silence, some strange Race
Wrecked, solitary, here —

And then a Plank in Reason, broke,
And I dropped down, and down —
And hit a World, at every plunge,
And Finished knowing — then —

———————

That after Horror — that 'twas *us* —
That passed the mouldering Pier —
Just as the Granite Crumb let go —
Our Savior, by a Hair —

A second more, had dropped too deep
For Fisherman to plumb—
The very profile of the Thought
Puts Recollection numb—

The possibility—to pass
Without a Moment's Bell—
Into Conjecture's presence—
Is like a Face of Steel—
That suddenly looks into ours
With a metallic grin—
The Cordiality of Death—
Who drills his Welcome in—

———

A Clock stopped—
Not the Mantel's—
Geneva's farthest skill
Can't put the puppet bowing—
That just now dangled still—

An awe came on the Trinket!
The Figures hunched, with pain—
Then quivered out of Decimals—
Into Degreeless Noon—

It will not stir for Doctors—
This Pendulum of snow—
This Shopman importunes it—
While cool—concernless No—

Nods from the Gilded pointers—
Nods from the Seconds slim—
Decades of Arrogance between
The Dial life—
And Him—

———————

I'm Nobody! Who are you?
Are you—Nobody—Too?
Then there's a pair of us!
Don't tell! they'd advertise—you know!

How dreary—to be—Somebody!
How public—like a Frog—
To tell one's name—the livelong June—
To an admiring Bog!

———————

I know some lonely Houses off the Road
A Robber'd like the look of—
Wooden barred,
And Windows hanging low,
Inviting to—
A Portico,
Where two could creep—
One—hand the Tools—
The other peep—
To make sure All's Asleep—
Old fashioned eyes—
Not easy to surprise!

How orderly the Kitchen'd look, by night,
With just a Clock—
But they could gag the Tick—
And Mice won't bark—
And so the Walls—don't tell—
None—will—

A pair of Spectacles ajar just stir—
An Almanac's aware—
Was it the Mat—winked,

Or a Nervous Star?
The Moon—slides down the stair,
To see who's there!

There's plunder—where—
Tankard, or Spoon—
Earring—or Stone—
A Watch—Some Ancient Brooch
To match the Grandmama—
Staid sleeping—there—

Day—rattles—too
Stealth's—slow—
The Sun has got as far
As the third Sycamore—
Screams Chanticleer
"Who's there"?

And Echoes—Trains away,
Sneer—"Where"!
While the old Couple, just astir,
Fancy the Sunrise—left the door ajar!

———————

Of Bronze—and Blaze—
The North—Tonight—
So adequate—it forms—
So preconcerted with itself—
So distant—to alarms—
An Unconcern so sovereign
To Universe, or me—
Infects my simple spirit
With Taints of Majesty—
Till I take vaster attitudes—
And strut upon my stem—
Disdaining Men, and Oxygen,
For Arrogance of them—

My Splendors, are Menagerie—
But their Competeless Show
Will entertain the Centuries
When I, am long ago,
An Island in dishonored Grass—
Whom none but Beetles—know.

———————

I got so I could take his name—
Without—Tremendous gain—
That Stop-sensation—on my Soul—
And Thunder—in the Room—

I got so I could walk across
That Angle in the floor,
Where he turned so, and I turned—how—
And all our Sinew tore—

I got so I could stir the Box—
In which his letters grew
Without that forcing, in my breath—
As Staples—driven through—

Could dimly recollect a Grace—
I think, they call it "God"—
Renowned to ease Extremity—
When Formula, had failed—

And shape my Hands—
Petition's way,
Tho' ignorant of a word
That Ordination—utters—

My Business, with the Cloud,
If any Power behind it, be,
Not subject to Despair—
It care, in some remoter way,
For so minute affair
As Misery—
Itself, too vast, for interrupting—more—

———————

I reason, Earth is short—
And Anguish—absolute—
And many hurt,
But, what of that?

I reason, we could die—
The best Vitality
Cannot excel Decay,
But, what of that?

I reason, that in Heaven—
Somehow, it will be even—
Some new Equation, given—
But, what of that?

———————

The Soul selects her own Society—
Then—shuts the Door—
To her divine Majority—
Present no more—

Unmoved—she notes the Chariots—pausing—
At her low Gate—
Unmoved—an Emperor be kneeling
Upon her Mat—

I've known her—from an ample nation—
Choose One—
Then—close the Valves of her attention—
Like Stone—

The Soul's Superior instants
Occur to Her—alone—
When friend—and Earth's occasion
Have infinite withdrawn—

Or She—Herself—ascended
To too remote a Height
For lower Recognition
Than Her Omnipotent—

This Mortal Abolition
Is seldom—but as fair
As Apparition—subject
To Autocratic Air—

Eternity's disclosure
To favorites—a few—
Of the Colossal substance
Of Immortality

I should have been too glad, I see—
Too lifted—for the scant degree
Of Life's penurious Round—
My little Circuit would have shamed
This new Circumference—have blamed—
The homelier time behind.

I should have been too saved—I see—
Too rescued—Fear too dim to me
That I could spell the Prayer
I knew so perfect—yesterday—
That Scalding One—Sabachthani—
Recited fluent—here—

Earth would have been too much—I see—
And Heaven—not enough for me—
I should have had the Joy
Without the Fear—to justify—
The Palm—without the Calvary—
So Savior—Crucify—

Defeat—whets Victory—they say—
The Reefs—in old Gethsemane—
Endear the Coast—beyond!
'Tis Beggars—Banquets—can define—
'Tis Parching—vitalizes Wine—
"Faith" bleats—to understand!

———————

He fumbles at your Soul
As Players at the Keys
Before they drop full Music on—
He stuns you by degrees—
Prepares your brittle Nature
For the Ethereal Blow
By fainter Hammers—further heard—
Then nearer—Then so slow
Your Breath has time to straighten—
Your Brain—to bubble Cool—
Deals—One—imperial—Thunderbolt—
That scalps your naked Soul—

When Winds take Forests in their Paws—
The Universe—is still—

———————

I'll tell you how the Sun rose—
A Ribbon at a time—
The Steeples swam in Amethyst—
The news, like Squirrels, ran—

The Hills untied their Bonnets—
The Bobolinks—begun—
Then I said softly to myself—
"That must have been the Sun"!
But how he set—I know not—
There seemed a purple stile
That little Yellow boys and girls
Were climbing all the while—
Till when they reached the other side,
A Dominie in Gray—
Put gently up the evening Bars—
And led the flock away—

———————

The nearest Dream recedes—unrealized—
The Heaven we chase,
Like the June Bee—before the School Boy,
Invites the Race—
Stoops—to an easy Clover—
Dips—evades—teases—deploys—
Then—to the Royal Clouds
Lifts his light Pinnace—
Heedless of the Boy—
Staring—bewildered—at the mocking sky—
Homesick for steadfast Honey—
Ah, the Bee flies not
That brews that rare variety!

———————

Of all the Sounds despatched abroad,
There's not a Charge to me
Like that old measure in the Boughs—
That phraseless Melody—
The Wind does—working like a Hand,
Whose fingers Comb the Sky—
Then quiver down—with tufts of Tune—
Permitted Gods, and me—

Inheritance, it is, to us—
Beyond the Art to Earn—
Beyond the trait to take away
By Robber, since the Gain
Is gotten not of fingers—
And inner than the Bone—
Hid golden, for the whole of Days,
And even in the Urn,
I cannot vouch the merry Dust
Do not arise and play
In some odd fashion of its own,
Some quainter Holiday,
When Winds go round and round in Bands—
And thrum upon the door,
And Birds take places, overhead,
To bear them Orchestra.

I crave Him grace of Summer Boughs,
If such an Outcast be—
Who never heard that fleshless Chant—
Rise—solemn—on the Tree,
As if some Caravan of Sound
Off Deserts, in the Sky,
Had parted Rank,
Then knit, and swept—
In Seamless Company—

————

There came a Day at Summer's full,
Entirely for me—
I thought that such were for the Saints,
Where Resurrections—be—

The Sun, as common, went abroad,
The flowers, accustomed, blew,
As if no soul the solstice passed
That maketh all things new—

The time was scarce profaned, by speech—
The symbol of a word
Was needless, as at Sacrament,
The Wardrobe—of our Lord—

Each was to each The Sealed Church,
Permitted to commune this—time—
Lest we too awkward show
At Supper of the Lamb.

The Hours slid fast—as Hours will,
Clutched tight, by greedy hands—
So faces on two Decks, look back,
Bound to opposing lands—

And so when all the time had leaked,
Without external sound
Each bound the Other's Crucifix—
We gave no other Bond—

Sufficient troth, that we shall rise—
Deposed—at length, the Grave—
To that new Marriage,
Justified—through Calvaries of Love—

I cannot dance upon my Toes—
No Man instructed me—
But oftentimes, among my mind,
A Glee possesseth me,

That had I Ballet knowledge—
Would put itself abroad
In Pirouette to blanch a Troupe—
Or lay a Prima, mad,

And though I had no Gown of Gauze—
No Ringlet, to my Hair,
Nor hopped to Audiences—like Birds,
One Claw upon the Air,

Nor tossed my shape in Eider Balls,
Nor rolled on wheels of snow
Till I was out of sight, in sound,
The House encore me so—

Nor any know I know the Art
I mention—easy—Here—
Nor any Placard boast me—
It's full as Opera—

————

Before I got my eye put out
I liked as well to see—
As other Creatures, that have Eyes
And know no other way—

But were it told to me—Today—
That I might have the sky
For mine—I tell you that my Heart
Would split, for size of me—

The Meadows—mine—
The Mountains—mine—
All Forests—Stintless Stars—
As much of Noon as I could take
Between my finite eyes—

The Motions of the Dipping Birds—
The Morning's Amber Road—
For mine—to look at when I liked—
The News would strike me dead—

So safer—guess—with just my soul
Upon the Window pane—
Where other Creatures put their eyes—
Incautious—of the Sun—

A Bird came down the Walk—
He did not know I saw—
He bit an Angleworm in halves
And ate the fellow, raw,

And then he drank a Dew
From a convenient Grass—
And then hopped sidewise to the Wall
To let a Beetle pass—

He glanced with rapid eyes
That hurried all around—
They looked like frightened Beads, I thought—
He stirred his Velvet Head

Like one in danger, Cautious,
I offered him a Crumb
And he unrolled his feathers
And rowed him softer home—

Than Oars divide the Ocean,
Too silver for a seam—
Or Butterflies, off Banks of Noon
Leap, plashless as they swim.

'Tis not that Dying hurts us so—
'Tis Living—hurts us more—
But Dying—is a different way—
A Kind behind the Door—

The Southern Custom—of the Bird—
That ere the Frosts are due—
Accepts a better Latitude—
We—are the Birds—that stay.

The Shiverers round Farmers' doors—
For whose reluctant Crumb—
We stipulate—till pitying Snows
Persuade our Feathers Home.

I know that He exists.
Somewhere—in Silence—
He has hid his rare life
From our gross eyes.

'Tis an instant's play.
'Tis a fond Ambush—
Just to make Bliss
Earn her own surprise!

But—should the play
Prove piercing earnest—
Should the glee—glaze—
In Death's—stiff—stare—

Would not the fun
Look too expensive!
Would not the jest—
Have crawled too far!

After great pain, a formal feeling comes—
The Nerves sit ceremonious, like Tombs—
The stiff Heart questions was it He, that bore,
And Yesterday, or Centuries before?

The Feet, mechanical, go round—
Of Ground, or Air, or Ought—
A Wooden way
Regardless grown,
A Quartz contentment, like a stone—

This is the Hour of Lead—
Remembered, if outlived,
As Freezing persons, recollect the Snow—
First—Chill—then Stupor—then the letting go—

I dreaded that first Robin, so,
But He is mastered, now,
I'm some accustomed to Him grown,
He hurts a little, though—

I thought if I could only live
Till that first Shout got by—
Not all Pianos in the Woods
Had power to mangle me—

I dared not meet the Daffodils—
For fear their Yellow Gown
Would pierce me with a fashion
So foreign to my own—

I wished the Grass would hurry—
So—when 'twas time to see—
He'd be too tall, the tallest one
Could stretch—to look at me—

I could not bear the Bees should come,
I wished they'd stay away
In those dim countries where they go,
What word had they, for me?

They're here, though; not a creature failed—
No Blossom stayed away
In gentle deference to me—
The Queen of Calvary—

Each one salutes me, as he goes,
And I, my childish Plumes,
Lift, in bereaved acknowledgment
Of their unthinking Drums—

———

God is a distant—stately Lover—
Woos, as He states us—by His Son—
Verily, a Vicarious Courtship—
"Miles", and "Priscilla", were such an One—

But, lest the Soul—like fair "Priscilla"
Choose the Envoy—and spurn the Groom—
Vouches, with hyperbolic archness—
"Miles", and "John Alden" were Synonym—

———

Dare you see a Soul *at the White Heat*?
Then crouch within the door—
Red—is the Fire's common tint—
But when the vivid Ore
Has vanquished Flame's conditions,
It quivers from the Forge
Without a color, but the light
Of unanointed Blaze.
Least Village has its Blacksmith
Whose Anvil's even ring
Stands symbol for the finer Forge
That soundless tugs—within—
Refining these impatient Ores
With Hammer, and with Blaze
Until the Designated Light
Repudiate the Forge—

A precious—mouldering pleasure—'tis—
To meet an Antique Book—
In just the Dress his Century wore—
A privilege—I think—

His venerable Hand to take—
And warming in our own—
A passage back—or two—to make—
To Times when he—was young—

His quaint opinions—to inspect—
His thought to ascertain
On Themes concern our mutual mind—
The Literature of Man—

What interested Scholars—most—
What Competitions ran—
When Plato—was a Certainty—
And Sophocles—a Man—

When Sappho—was a living Girl—
And Beatrice wore
The Gown that Dante—deified—
Facts Centuries before

He traverses—familiar—
As One should come to Town—
And tell you all your Dreams—were true—
He lived—where Dreams were born—

His presence is Enchantment—
You beg him not to go—
Old Volumes shake their Vellum Heads
And tantalize—just so—

———

Of Course—I prayed—
And did God Care?
He cared as much as on the Air
A Bird—had stamped her foot—
And cried "Give Me"—
My Reason—Life—
I had not had—but for Yourself—
'Twere better Charity
To leave me in the Atom's Tomb—
Merry, and Nought, and gay, and numb—
Than this smart Misery.

———

There's been a Death, in the Opposite House,
As lately as Today—
I know it, by the numb look
Such Houses have—alway—

The Neighbors rustle in and out—
The Doctor—drives away—
A Window opens like a Pod—
Abrupt—mechanically—

Somebody flings a Mattress out—
The Children hurry by—
They wonder if it died—on that—
I used to—when a Boy—

The Minister—goes stiffly in—
As if the House were His—
And He owned all the Mourners—now—
And little Boys—besides—

And then the Milliner—and the Man
Of the Appalling Trade—
To take the measure of the House—

There'll be that Dark Parade—

Of Tassels—and of Coaches—soon—
It's easy as a Sign—
The Intuition of the News—
In just a Country Town—

———

A Visitor in Marl—
Who influences Flowers—
Till they are orderly as Busts—
And Elegant—as Glass—

Who visits in the Night—
And just before the Sun—
Concludes his glistening interview—
Caresses—and is gone—

But whom his fingers touched—
And where his feet have run—
And whatsoever Mouth he kissed—
Is as it had not been—

———

What Soft—Cherubic Creatures—
These Gentlewomen are—
One would as soon assault a Plush—
Or violate a Star—

His Countenance—a Billow—
His Fingers, as He passed
Let go a music—as of tunes
Blown tremulous in Glass—

He visited—still flitting—
Then like a timid Man
Again, He tapped—'twas flurriedly—
And I became alone—

Prayer is the little implement
Through which Men reach
Where Presence—is denied them.
They fling their Speech

By means of it—in God's Ear—
If then He hear—
This sums the Apparatus
Comprised in Prayer—

This is my letter to the World
That never wrote to Me—
The simple News that Nature told—
With tender Majesty

Her Message is committed
To Hands I cannot see—
For love of Her—Sweet—countrymen—
Judge tenderly—of Me

This was a Poet—It is That
Distills amazing sense
From ordinary Meanings—
And Attar so immense

From the familiar species
That perished by the Door—
We wonder it was not Ourselves
Arrested it—before—

Of Pictures, the Discloser—
The Poet—it is He—
Entitles Us—by Contrast—
To ceaseless Poverty—

Of Portion—so unconscious—
The Robbing—could not harm—
Himself—to Him—a Fortune—
Exterior—to Time—

I died for Beauty—but was scarce
Adjusted in the Tomb
When One who died for Truth, was lain
In an adjoining Room—

He questioned softly "Why I failed"?
"For Beauty", I replied—
"And I—for Truth—Themself are One—
We Brethren, are", He said—

And so, as Kinsmen, met a Night—
We talked between the Rooms—
Until the Moss had reached our lips—
And covered up—our names—

The Outer—from the Inner
Derives its Magnitude—
'Tis Duke, or Dwarf, according
As is the Central Mood—

The fine—unvarying Axis
That regulates the Wheel—
Though Spokes—spin—more conspicuous
And fling a dust—the while.

The Inner—paints the Outer—
The Brush without the Hand—
Its Picture publishes—precise—
As is the inner Brand—

On fine—Arterial Canvas—
A Cheek—perchance a Brow—
The Star's whole Secret—in the Lake—
Eyes were not meant to know.

———

I heard a Fly buzz—when I died—
The Stillness in the Room
Was like the Stillness in the Air—
Between the Heaves of Storm—

The Eyes around—had wrung them dry—
And Breaths were gathering firm
For that last Onset—when the King
Be witnessed—in the Room—

I willed my Keepsakes—Signed away
What portion of me be
Assignable—and then it was
There interposed a Fly—

With Blue—uncertain stumbling Buzz—
Between the light—and me—
And then the Windows failed—and then
I could not see to see—

———————

They put Us far apart—
As separate as Sea
And Her unsown Peninsula—
We signified "These see"—

They took away our Eyes—
They thwarted Us with Guns—
"I see Thee" each responded straight
Through Telegraphic Signs—

With Dungeons—They devised—
But through their thickest skill—
And their opaquest Adamant—
Our Souls saw—just as well—

They summoned Us to die—
With sweet alacrity
We stood upon our stapled feet—
Condemned—but just—to see—

Permission to recant—
Permission to forget—
We turned our backs upon the Sun
For perjury of that—

Not Either—noticed Death—
Of Paradise—aware—
Each other's Face—was all the Disc
Each other's setting—saw—

———————

"Why do I love" You, Sir?
Because—
The Wind does not require the Grass
To answer—Wherefore when He pass
She cannot keep Her place.

Because He knows—and
Do not You—
And We know not—
Enough for Us
The Wisdom it be so—

The Lightning—never asked an Eye
Wherefore it shut—when He was by—
Because He knows it cannot speak—
And reasons not contained—
—Of Talk—
There be—preferred by Daintier Folk—

The Sunrise—Sir—compelleth Me—
Because He's Sunrise—and I see—
Therefore—Then—
I love Thee—

———————

This World is not Conclusion.
A Species stands beyond—
Invisible, as Music—
But positive, as Sound—
It beckons, and it baffles—
Philosophy—don't know—
And through a Riddle, at the last—
Sagacity, must go—
To guess it, puzzles scholars—
To gain it, Men have borne
Contempt of Generations
And Crucifixion, shown—
Faith slips—and laughs, and rallies—
Blushes, if any see—

Plucks at a twig of Evidence—
And asks a Vane, the way—
Much Gesture, from the Pulpit—
Strong Hallelujahs roll—
Narcotics cannot still the Tooth
That nibbles at the soul—

———————

At least—to pray—is left—is left—
Oh Jesus—in the Air—
I know not which thy chamber is—
I'm knocking—everywhere—

Thou settest Earthquake in the South—
And Maelstrom, in the Sea—
Say, Jesus Christ of Nazareth—
Hast thou no Arm for Me?

———————

Better—than Music! For I—who heard it—
I was used—to the Birds—before—
This—was different—'Twas Translation—
Of all tunes I knew—and more—

'Twasn't contained—like other stanza—
No one could play it—the second time—
But the Composer—perfect Mozart—
Perish with him—that Keyless Rhyme!

So—Children—told how Brooks in Eden—
Bubbled a better—Melody—
Quaintly infer—Eve's great surrender—
Urging the feet—that would—not—fly—

Children—matured—are wiser—mostly—
Eden—a legend—dimly told—
Eve—and the Anguish—Grandame's story—
But—I was telling a tune—I heard—

Not such a strain—the Church—baptizes—
When the last Saint—goes up the Aisles—
Not such a stanza splits the silence—
When the Redemption strikes her Bells—

Let me not spill—its smallest cadence—
Humming—for promise—when alone—
Humming—until my faint Rehearsal—
Drop into tune—around the Throne—

I would not paint—a picture—
I'd rather be the One
Its bright impossibility
To dwell—delicious—on—
And wonder how the fingers feel
Whose rare—celestial—stir—
Evokes so sweet a Torment—
Such sumptuous—Despair—

I would not talk, like Cornets—
I'd rather be the One
Raised softly to the Ceilings—
And out, and easy on—
Through Villages of Ether—
Myself endued Balloon
By but a lip of Metal—
The pier to my Pontoon—

Nor would I be a Poet—
It's finer—own the Ear—
Enamored—impotent—content—
The License to revere,
A privilege so awful
What would the Dower be,
Had I the Art to stun myself
With Bolts of Melody!

———

I'm ceded—I've stopped being Theirs—
The name They dropped upon my face
With water, in the country church
Is finished using, now,
And They can put it with my Dolls,
My childhood, and the string of spools,
I've finished threading—too—

Baptized, before, without the choice,
But this time, consciously, of Grace—
Unto supremest name—
Called to my Full—The Crescent dropped—
Existence's whole Arc, filled up,
With one small Diadem.

My second Rank—too small the first—
Crowned—Crowing—on my Father's breast—
A half unconscious Queen—
But this time—Adequate—Erect,
With Will to choose, or to reject,
And I choose, just a Crown—

———

It was not Death, for I stood up,
And all the Dead, lie down—
It was not Night, for all the Bells
Put out their Tongues, for Noon.

It was not Frost, for on my Flesh
I felt Siroccos—crawl—
Nor Fire—for just my Marble feet
Could keep a Chancel, cool—

And yet, it tasted, like them all,
The Figures I have seen
Set orderly, for Burial,
Reminded me, of mine—

As if my life were shaven,
And fitted to a frame,
And could not breathe without a key,
And 'twas like Midnight, some—

When everything that ticked—has stopped—
And Space stares all around—
Or Grisly frosts—first Autumn morns,
Repeal the Beating Ground—

But, most, like Chaos—Stopless—cool—
Without a Chance, or Spar—
Or even a Report of Land—
To justify—Despair.

'Twas warm—at first—like Us—
Until there crept upon
A Chill—like frost upon a Glass—
Till all the scene—be gone.

The Forehead copied Stone—
The Fingers grew too cold
To ache—and like a Skater's Brook—
The busy eyes—congealed—

It straightened—that was all—
It crowded Cold to Cold—
It multiplied indifference—
As Pride were all it could—

And even when with Cords—
'Twas lowered, like a Weight—
It made no Signal, nor demurred,
But dropped like Adamant.

———————

I started Early—Took my Dog—
And visited the Sea—
The Mermaids in the Basement
Came out to look at me—

And Frigates—in the Upper Floor
Extended Hempen Hands—
Presuming Me to be a Mouse—
Aground—upon the Sands—

But no Man moved Me—till the Tide
Went past my simple Shoe—
And past my Apron—and my Belt
And past my Bodice—too—

And made as He would eat me up—
As wholly as a Dew
Upon a Dandelion's Sleeve—
And then—I started—too—

And He—He followed—close behind—
I felt His Silver Heel
Upon my Ankle—Then my Shoes
Would overflow with Pearl—

Until We met the Solid Town—
No One He seemed to know—
And bowing—with a Mighty look—
At me—The Sea withdrew—

———————

Mine—by the Right of the White Election!
Mine—by the Royal Seal!
Mine—by the Sign in the Scarlet prison—
Bars—cannot conceal!

Mine—here—in Vision—and in Veto!
Mine—by the Grave's Repeal—
Titled—Confirmed—
Delirious Charter!
Mine—long as Ages steal!

———————

The Heart asks Pleasure—first—
And then—Excuse from Pain—
And then—those little Anodynes
That deaden suffering—

And then—to go to sleep—
And then—if it should be
The will of its Inquisitor
The privilege to die—

———————

The Martyr Poets—did not tell—
But wrought their Pang in syllable—
That when their mortal name be numb—
Their mortal fate—encourage Some—

The Martyr Painters—never spoke—
Bequeathing—rather—to their Work—
That when their conscious fingers cease—
Some seek in Art—the Art of Peace—

———————

I've seen a Dying Eye
Run round and round a Room—
In search of Something—as it seemed—
Then Cloudier become—
And then—obscure with Fog—
And then—be soldered down
Without disclosing what it be
'Twere blessed to have seen—

———

One Crucifixion is recorded—only—
How many be
Is not affirmed of Mathematics—
Or History—

One Calvary—exhibited to Stranger—
As many be
As persons—or Peninsulas—
Gethsemane—

Is but a Province—in the Being's Centre—
Judea—
For Journey—or Crusade's Achieving—
Too near—

Our Lord—indeed—made Compound Witness—
And yet—
There's newer—nearer Crucifixion
Than That—

———

My period had come for Prayer—
No other Art—would do—
My Tactics missed a rudiment—
Creator—Was it you?

God grows above—so those who pray
Horizons—must ascend—
And so I stepped upon the North
To see this Curious Friend—

His House was not—no sign had He—
By Chimney—nor by Door
Could I infer his Residence—
Vast Prairies of Air

Unbroken by a Settler—
Were all that I could see—
Infinitude—Had'st Thou no Face
That I might look on Thee?

The Silence condescended—
Creation stopped—for Me—
But awed beyond my errand—
I worshipped—did not "pray"—

We learned the Whole of Love—
The Alphabet—the Words—
A Chapter—then the mighty Book—
Then—Revelation closed—

But in Each Other's eyes
An Ignorance beheld—
Diviner than the Childhood's—
And each to each, a Child—

Attempted to expound
What Neither—understood—
Alas, that Wisdom is so large—
And Truth—so manifold!

I reckon—when I count at all—
First—Poets—Then the Sun—
Then Summer—Then the Heaven of God—
And then—the List is done—

But, looking back—the First so seems
To Comprehend the Whole—
The Others look a needless Show—
So I write—Poets—All—

Their Summer—lasts a Solid Year—
They can afford a Sun
The East—would deem extravagant—
And if the Further Heaven—

Be Beautiful as they prepare
For Those who worship Them—
It is too difficult a Grace—
To justify the Dream—

———

I gave myself to Him—
And took Himself, for Pay,
The solemn contract of a Life
Was ratified, this way—

The Wealth might disappoint—
Myself a poorer prove
Than this great Purchaser suspect,
The Daily Own—of Love

Depreciate the Vision—
But till the Merchant buy—
Still Fable—in the Isles of Spice—
The subtle Cargoes—lie—

At least—'tis Mutual—Risk—
Some—found it—Mutual Gain—
Sweet Debt of Life—Each Night to owe—
Insolvent—every Noon—

I found the words to every thought
I ever had—but One—
And that—defies me—
As a Hand did try to chalk the Sun

To Races—nurtured in the Dark—
How would your own—begin?
Can Blaze be shown in Cochineal—
Or Noon—in Mazarin?

I like to see it lap the Miles—
And lick the Valleys up—
And stop to feed itself at Tanks—
And then—prodigious step

Around a Pile of Mountains—
And supercilious peer
In Shanties—by the sides of Roads—
And then a Quarry pare

To fit its Ribs
And crawl between
Complaining all the while
In horrid—hooting stanza—
Then chase itself down Hill—

And neigh like Boanerges—
Then—punctual as a Star
Stop—docile and omnipotent
At its own stable door—

What care the Dead, for Chanticleer—
What care the Dead for Day?
'Tis late your Sunrise vex their face—
And Purple Ribaldry—of Morning

Pour as blank on them
As on the Tier of Wall
The Mason builded, yesterday,
And equally as cool—

What care the Dead for Summer?
The Solstice had no Sun
Could waste the Snow before their Gate—
And knew One Bird a Tune—

Could thrill their Mortised Ear
Of all the Birds that be—
This One—beloved of Mankind
Henceforward cherished be—

What care the Dead for Winter?
Themselves as easy freeze—
June Noon—as January Night—
As soon the South—her Breeze

Of Sycamore—or Cinnamon—
Deposit in a Stone
And put a Stone to keep it Warm—
Give Spices—unto Men—

I think I was enchanted
When first a sombre Girl—
I read that Foreign Lady—
The Dark—felt beautiful—

And whether it was noon at night—
Or only Heaven—at Noon—
For very Lunacy of Light
I had not power to tell—

The Bees—became as Butterflies—
The Butterflies—as Swans—
Approached—and spurned the narrow Grass—
And just the meanest Tunes

That Nature murmured to herself
To keep herself in Cheer—
I took for Giants—practising
Titanic Opera—

The Days—to Mighty Metres stept—
The Homeliest—adorned
As if unto a Jubilee
'Twere suddenly confirmed—

I could not have defined the change—
Conversion of the Mind
Like Sanctifying in the Soul—
Is witnessed—not explained—

'Twas a Divine Insanity—
The Danger to be Sane
Should I again experience—
'Tis Antidote to turn—

To Tomes of solid Witchcraft—
Magicians be asleep—
But Magic—hath an Element
Like Deity—to keep—

———————

There is a pain—so utter—
It swallows substance up—
Then covers the Abyss with Trance—
So Memory can step
Around—across—upon it—
As one within a Swoon—
Goes safely—where an open eye—
Would drop Him—Bone by Bone.

———————

They shut me up in Prose—
As when a little Girl
They put me in the Closet—
Because they liked me "still"—

Still! Could themself have peeped—
And seen my Brain—go round—
They might as wise have lodged a Bird
For Treason—in the Pound—

Himself has but to will
And easy as a Star
Abolish his Captivity—
And laugh—No more have I—

———————

Our journey had advanced—
Our feet were almost come
To that odd Fork in Being's Road—
Eternity—by Term—

Our pace took sudden awe—
Our feet—reluctant—led—
Before—were Cities—but Between—
The Forest of the Dead—

Retreat—was out of Hope—
Behind—a Sealed Route—
Eternity's White Flag—Before—
And God—at every Gate—

Glee—The great storm is over—
Four—have recovered the Land—
Forty—gone down together—
Into the boiling Sand—

Ring—for the Scant Salvation—
Toll—for the bonnie Souls—
Neighbor—and friend—and Bridegroom—
Spinning upon the Shoals—

How they will tell the Story—
When Winter shake the Door—
Till the Children urge—
But the Forty—
Did they—come back no more?

Then a softness—suffuse the Story—
And a silence—the Teller's eye—
And the Children—no further question—
And only the Sea—reply—

I asked no other thing—
No other—was denied—
I offered Being—for it—
The Mighty Merchant sneered—

Brazil? He twirled a Button—
Without a glance my way—
"But—Madam—is there nothing else—
That We can show—Today?"

———————

The Tint I cannot take—is best—
The Color too remote
That I could show it in Bazaar—
A Guinea at a sight—

The fine—impalpable Array—
That swaggers on the eye
Like Cleopatra's Company—
Repeated—in the sky—

The Moments of Dominion
That happen on the Soul
And leave it with a Discontent
Too exquisite—to tell—

The eager look—on Landscapes—
As if they just repressed
Some Secret—that was pushing
Like Chariots—in the Vest—

The Pleading of the Summer—
That other Prank—of Snow—
That Cushions Mystery with Tulle,
For fear the Squirrels—know.

Their Graspless manners—mock us—
Until the Cheated Eye
Shuts arrogantly—in the Grave—
Another way—to see—

———————

I watched the Moon around the House
Until upon a Pane—
She stopped—a Traveller's privilege—for Rest—
And there upon

I gazed—as at a stranger—
The Lady in the Town
Doth think no incivility
To lift her Glass—upon—

But never Stranger justified
The Curiosity
Like Mine—for not a Foot—nor Hand—
Nor Formula—had she—

But like a Head—a Guillotine
Slid carelessly away—
Did independent, Amber—
Sustain her in the sky—

Or like a Stemless Flower—
Upheld in rolling Air
By finer Gravitations—
Than bind Philosopher—

No Hunger—had she—nor an Inn—
Her Toilette—to suffice—
Nor Avocation—nor Concern
For little Mysteries

As harass us—like Life—and Death—
And Afterwards—or Nay—
But seemed engrossed to Absolute—
With shining—and the Sky—

The privilege to scrutinize
Was scarce upon my Eyes
When, with a Silver practise—
She vaulted out of Gaze—

And next—I met her on a Cloud—
Myself too far below
To follow her superior Road—
Or its advantage—Blue—

The Brain—is wider than the Sky—
For—put them side by side—
The one the other will contain
With ease—and You—beside—

The Brain is deeper than the sea—
For—hold them—Blue to Blue—
The one the other will absorb—
As Sponges—Buckets—do—

The Brain is just the weight of God—
For—Heft them—Pound for Pound—
And they will differ—if they do—
As Syllable from Sound—

When Bells stop ringing—Church—begins—
The Positive—of Bells—
When Cogs—stop—that's Circumference—
The Ultimate—of Wheels.

My Portion is Defeat—today—
A paler luck than Victory—
Less Paeans—fewer Bells—
The Drums don't follow Me—with tunes—
Defeat—a somewhat slower—means—
More Arduous than Balls—

'Tis populous with Bone and stain—
And Men too straight to stoop again,
And Piles of solid Moan—
And Chips of Blank—in Boyish Eyes—

And scraps of Prayer—
And Death's surprise,
Stamped visible—in Stone—

There's somewhat prouder, over there—
The Trumpets tell it to the Air—
How different Victory
To Him who has it—and the One
Who to have had it, would have been
Contenteder—to die—

I cannot live with You—
It would be Life—
And Life is over there—
Behind the Shelf

The Sexton keeps the Key to—
Putting up
Our Life—His Porcelain—
Like a Cup—

Discarded of the Housewife—
Quaint—or Broke—
A newer Sevres pleases—
Old Ones crack—

I could not die—with You—
For One must wait
To shut the Other's Gaze down—
You—could not—

And I—Could I stand by
And see You—freeze—
Without my Right of Frost—
Death's privilege?

Nor could I rise—with You—
Because Your Face
Would put out Jesus'—
That New Grace

Glow plain—and foreign
On my homesick Eye—
Except that You than He
Shone closer by—

They'd judge Us—How—
For You—served Heaven—You know,
Or sought to—
I could not—

Because You saturated Sight—
And I had no more Eyes
For sordid excellence
As Paradise

And were You lost, I would be—
Though My Name
Rang loudest
On the Heavenly fame—

And were You—saved—
And I—condemned to be
Where You were not—
That self—were Hell to Me—

So We must meet apart—
You there—I—here—
With just the Door ajar
That Oceans are—and Prayer—
And that White Sustenance—
Despair—

Pain—has an Element of Blank—
It cannot recollect
When it begun—or if there were
A time when it was not—

It has no Future—but itself—
Its Infinite contain
Its Past—enlightened to perceive
New Periods—of Pain.

———

A Prison gets to be a friend—
Between its Ponderous face
And Ours—a Kinsmanship express—
And in its narrow Eyes—

We come to look with gratitude
For the appointed Beam
It deal us—stated as our food—
And hungered for—the same—

We learn to know the Planks—
That answer to Our feet—
So miserable a sound—at first—
Nor ever now—so sweet—

As plashing in the Pools—
When Memory was a Boy—
But a Demurer Circuit—
A Geometric Joy—

The Posture of the Key
That interrupt the Day
To Our Endeavor—Not so real
The Cheek of Liberty—

As this Phantasm Steel—
Whose features—Day and Night—
Are present to us—as Our Own—
And as escapeless—quite—

The narrow Round—the Stint—
The slow exchange of Hope—
For something passiver—Content
Too steep for looking up—

The Liberty we knew
Avoided—like a Dream—
Too wide for any Night but Heaven—
If That—indeed—redeem—

———

I dwell in Possibility—
A fairer House than Prose—
More numerous of Windows—
Superior—for Doors—

Of Chambers as the Cedars—
Impregnable of Eye—
And for an Everlasting Roof
The Gambrels of the Sky—

Of Visitors—the fairest—
For Occupation—This—
The spreading wide my narrow Hands
To gather Paradise—

———

One need not be a Chamber—to be Haunted—
One need not be a House—
The Brain has Corridors—surpassing
Material Place—

Far safer, of a Midnight Meeting
External Ghost
Than its interior Confronting—
That Cooler Host.

Far safer, through an Abbey gallop,
The Stones a'chase—
Than Unarmed, one's a'self encounter—
In lonesome Place—

Ourself behind ourself, concealed—
Should startle most—
Assassin hid in our Apartment
Be Horror's least.

The Body—borrows a Revolver—
He bolts the Door—
O'erlooking a superior spectre—
Or More—

The Soul that hath a Guest
Doth seldom go abroad—
Diviner Crowd at Home—
Obliterate the need—

And Courtesy forbid
A Host's departure when
Upon Himself be visiting
The Emperor of Men—

Essential Oils—are wrung—
The Attar from the Rose
Be not expressed by Suns—alone—
It is the gift of Screws—

The General Rose—decay—
But this—in Lady's Drawer
Make Summer—When the Lady lie
In Ceaseless Rosemary—

They say that "Time assuages"—
Time never did assuage—
An actual suffering strengthens
As Sinews do, with age—

Time is a Test of Trouble—
But not a Remedy—
If such it prove, it prove too
There was no Malady—

Victory comes late—
And is held low to freezing lips—
Too rapt with frost
To take it—
How sweet it would have tasted—
Just a Drop—
Was God so economical?
His Table's spread too high for Us—
Unless We dine on tiptoe—
Crumbs—fit such little mouths—
Cherries—suit Robins—
The Eagle's Golden Breakfast strangles—Them—
God keep His Oath to Sparrows—
Who of little Love—know how to starve—

The Sun kept setting—setting—still
No Hue of Afternoon—
Upon the Village I perceived—
From House to House 'twas Noon—

The Dusk kept dropping—dropping—still
No Dew upon the Grass—
But only on my Forehead stopped—
And wandered in my Face—

My Feet kept drowsing—drowsing—still
My fingers were awake—
Yet why so little sound—Myself
Unto my Seeming—make?

How well I knew the Light before—
I could see it now—
'Tis Dying—I am doing—but
I'm not afraid to know—

Their Height in Heaven comforts not—
Their Glory—nought to me—
'Twas best imperfect—as it was—
I'm finite—I can't see—

The House of Supposition—
The Glimmering Frontier that
Skirts the Acres of Perhaps—
To Me—shows insecure—

The Wealth I had—contented me—
If 'twas a meaner size—
Then I had counted it until
It pleased my narrow Eyes—

Better than larger values—
That show however true—
This timid life of Evidence
Keeps pleading—"I don't know."

———————

Publication—is the Auction
Of the Mind of Man—
Poverty—be justifying
For so foul a thing

Possibly—but We—would rather
From Our Garret go
White—Unto the White Creator—
Than invest—Our Snow—

Thought belong to Him who gave it—
Then—to Him Who bear
Its Corporeal illustration—Sell
The Royal Air—

In the Parcel—Be the Merchant
Of the Heavenly Grace—
But reduce no Human Spirit
To Disgrace of Price—

———————

Because I could not stop for Death—
He kindly stopped for me—
The Carriage held but just Ourselves—
And Immortality.

We slowly drove—He knew no haste
And I had put away
My labor and my leisure too,
For His Civility—

We passed the School, where Children strove
At Recess—in the Ring—
We passed the Fields of Gazing Grain—
We passed the Setting Sun—

Or rather—He passed Us—
The Dews drew quivering and chill—
For only Gossamer, my Gown—
My Tippet—only Tulle—

We paused before a House that seemed
A Swelling of the Ground—
The Roof was scarcely visible—
The Cornice—in the Ground—

Since then—'tis Centuries—and yet
Feels shorter than the Day
I first surmised the Horses' Heads
Were toward Eternity—

Behind Me—dips Eternity—
Before Me—Immortality—
Myself—the Term between—
Death but the Drift of Eastern Gray,
Dissolving into Dawn away,
Before the West begin—

'Tis Kingdoms—afterward—they say—
In perfect—pauseless Monarchy—
Whose Prince—is Son of None—
Himself—His Dateless Dynasty—
Himself—Himself diversify—
In Duplicate divine—

'Tis Miracle before Me—then—
'Tis Miracle behind—between—
A Crescent in the Sea—
With Midnight to the North of Her—
And Midnight to the South of Her—
And Maelstrom—in the Sky—

———————

It's easy to invent a Life—
God does it—every Day—
Creation—but the Gambol
Of His Authority—

It's easy to efface it—
The thrifty Deity
Could scarce afford Eternity
To Spontaneity—

The Perished Patterns murmur—
But His Perturbless Plan
Proceed—inserting Here—a Sun—
There—leaving out a Man—

———————

Four Trees—upon a solitary Acre—
Without Design
Or Order, or Apparent Action—
Maintain—

The Sun—upon a Morning meets them—
The Wind—
No nearer Neighbor—have they—
But God—

The Acre gives them—Place—
They—Him—Attention of Passer by—
Of Shadow, or of Squirrel, haply—
Or Boy—

What Deed is Theirs unto the General Nature—
What Plan
They severally—retard—or further—
Unknown—

Renunciation—is a piercing Virtue—
The letting go
A Presence—for an Expectation—
Not now—
The putting out of Eyes—
Just Sunrise—
Lest Day—
Day's Great Progenitor—
Outvie
Renunciation—is the Choosing
Against itself—
Itself to justify
Unto itself—
When larger function—
Make that appear—
Smaller—that Covered Vision—Here—

My Life had stood—a Loaded Gun—
In Corners—till a Day
The Owner passed—identified—
And carried Me away—

And now We roam in Sovereign Woods—
And now We hunt the Doe—
And every time I speak for Him—
The Mountains straight reply—

And do I smile, such cordial light
Upon the Valley glow—
It is as a Vesuvian face
Had let its pleasure through—

And when at Night—Our good Day done—
I guard My Master's Head—
'Tis better than the Eider-Duck's
Deep Pillow—to have shared—

To foe of His—I'm deadly foe—
None stir the second time—
On whom I lay a Yellow Eye—
Or an emphatic Thumb—

Though I than He—may longer live
He longer must—than I—
For I have but the power to kill,
Without—the power to die—

———————

Presentiment—is that long Shadow—on the Lawn—
Indicative that Suns go down—

The Notice to the startled Grass
That Darkness—is about to pass—

———————

On a Columnar Self—
How ample to rely
In Tumult—or Extremity—
How good the Certainty

That Lever cannot pry—
And Wedge cannot divide
Conviction—That Granitic Base—
Though None be on our Side—

Suffice Us—for a Crowd—
Ourself—and Rectitude—
And that Assembly—not far off
From furthest Spirit—God—

———————

A Light exists in Spring
Not present on the Year
At any other period—
When March is scarcely here

A Color stands abroad
On Solitary Fields
That Science cannot overtake
But Human Nature feels.

It waits upon the Lawn,
It shows the furthest Tree
Upon the furthest Slope you know
It almost speaks to you.

Then as Horizons step
Or Noons report away
Without the Formula of sound
It passes and we stay—

A quality of loss
Affecting our Content
As Trade had suddenly encroached
Upon a Sacrament.

———————

The Wind begun to rock the Grass
With threatening Tunes and low—
He threw a Menace at the Earth—
A Menace at the Sky.

The Leaves unhooked themselves from Trees—
And started all abroad
The Dust did scoop itself like Hands
And threw away the Road.

The Wagons quickened on the Streets
The Thunder hurried slow—
The Lightning showed a Yellow Beak
And then a livid Claw.

The Birds put up the Bars to Nests—
The Cattle fled to Barns—
There came one drop of Giant Rain
And then as if the Hands

That held the Dams had parted hold
The Waters Wrecked the Sky,
But overlooked my Father's House—
Just quartering a Tree—

———

The Only News I know
Is Bulletins all Day
From Immortality.

The Only Shows I see—
Tomorrow and Today—
Perchance Eternity—

The Only One I meet
Is God—The Only Street—
Existence—This traversed

If Other News there be—
Or Admirabler Show—
I'll tell it You—

———

Just as He spoke it from his Hands
This Edifice remain—
A Turret more, a Turret less
Dishonor his Design—

According as his skill prefer
It perish, or endure—
Content, soe'er, it ornament
His absent character.

———

Split the Lark—and you'll find the Music—
Bulb after Bulb, in Silver rolled—
Scantily dealt to the Summer Morning
Saved for your Ear when Lutes be old.

Loose the Flood—you shall find it patent—
Gush after Gush, reserved for you—
Scarlet Experiment! Sceptic Thomas!
Now, do you doubt that your Bird was true?

———

A Shade upon the mind there passes
As when on Noon
A Cloud the mighty Sun encloses
Remembering

That some there be too numb to notice
Oh God
Why give if Thou must take away
The Loved?

———

The Poets light but Lamps—
Themselves—go out—
The Wicks they stimulate—
If vital Light

Inhere as do the Suns—
Each Age a Lens
Disseminating their
Circumference—

The Admirations—and Contempts—of time—
Show justest—through an Open Tomb—
The Dying—as it were a Height
Reorganizes Estimate
And what We saw not
We distinguish clear—
And mostly—see not
What We saw before—

'Tis Compound Vision—
Light—enabling Light—
The Finite—furnished
With the Infinite—
Convex—and Concave Witness—
Back—toward Time—
And forward—
Toward the God of Him—

I felt a Cleaving in my Mind—
As if my Brain had split—
I tried to match it—Seam by Seam—
But could not make them fit.

The thought behind, I strove to join
Unto the thought before—
But Sequence ravelled out of Sound
Like Balls—upon a Floor.

Pain—expands the Time—
Ages coil within
The minute Circumference
Of a single Brain—

Pain contracts—the Time—
Occupied with Shot
Gamuts of Eternities
Are as they were not—

The Missing All—prevented Me
From missing minor Things.
If nothing larger than a World's
Departure from a Hinge—
Or Sun's extinction, be observed—
'Twas not so large that I
Could lift my Forehead from my work
For Curiosity.

Far from Love the Heavenly Father
Leads the Chosen Child,
Oftener through Realm of Briar
Than the Meadow mild.

Oftener by the Claw of Dragon
Than the Hand of Friend
Guides the Little One predestined
To the Native Land.

———

There is a Zone whose even Years
No Solstice interrupt—
Whose Sun constructs perpetual Noon
Whose perfect Seasons wait—

Whose Summer set in Summer, till
The Centuries of June
And Centuries of August cease
And Consciousness—is Noon.

———

Further in Summer than the Birds
Pathetic from the Grass
A minor Nation celebrates
Its unobtrusive Mass.

No Ordinance be seen
So gradual the Grace
A pensive Custom it becomes
Enlarging Loneliness.

Antiquest felt at Noon
When August burning low
Arise this spectral Canticle
Repose to typify

Remit as yet no Grace
No Furrow on the Glow
Yet a Druidic Difference
Enhances Nature now

Perception of an object costs
Precise the Object's loss—
Perception in itself a Gain
Replying to its Price—
The Object Absolute—is nought—
Perception sets it fair
And then upbraids a Perfectness
That situates so far—

Title divine—is mine!
The Wife—without the Sign!
Acute Degree—conferred on me—
Empress of Calvary!
Royal—all but the Crown!
Betrothed—without the swoon
God sends us Women—
When you—hold—Garnet to Garnet—
Gold—to Gold—
Born—Bridalled—Shrouded—
In a Day—
Tri Victory
"My Husband"—women say—
Stroking the Melody—
Is *this*—the way?

At Half past Three, a single Bird
Unto a silent Sky
Propounded but a single term
Of cautious melody.

At Half past Four, Experiment
Had subjugated test
And lo, Her silver Principle
Supplanted all the rest.

At Half past Seven, Element
Nor Implement, be seen—
And Place was where the Presence was
Circumference between.

———————

Ended, ere it begun—
The Title was scarcely told
When the Preface perished from Consciousness
The Story, unrevealed—

Had it been mine, to print!
Had it been yours, to read!
That it was not Our privilege
The interdict of God—

———————

My Cocoon tightens—Colors tease—
I'm feeling for the Air—
A dim capacity for Wings
Demeans the Dress I wear—

A power of Butterfly must be—
The Aptitude to fly
Meadows of Majesty implies
And easy Sweeps of Sky—

So I must baffle at the Hint
And cipher at the Sign
And make much blunder, if at last
I take the clue divine—

———

Between the form of Life and Life
The difference is as big
As Liquor at the Lip between
And Liquor in the Jug
The latter—excellent to keep—
But for ecstatic need
The corkless is superior—
I know for I have tried

———

The murmuring of Bees, has ceased
But murmuring of some
Posterior, prophetic,
Has simultaneous come.
The lower metres of the Year
When Nature's laugh is done
The Revelations of the Book
Whose Genesis was June.
Appropriate Creatures to her change
The Typic Mother sends
As Accent fades to interval
With separating Friends
Till what we speculate, has been
And thoughts we will not show
More intimate with us become
Than Persons, that we know.

———

There is another Loneliness
That many die without—
Not want of friend occasions it
Or circumstance of Lot

But nature, sometimes, sometimes thought
And whoso it befall
Is richer than could be revealed
By mortal numeral—

———————

Tell all the Truth but tell it slant—
Success in Circuit lies
Too bright for our infirm Delight
The Truth's superb surprise
As Lightning to the Children eased
With explanation kind
The Truth must dazzle gradually
Or every man be blind—

———————

The Props assist the House
Until the House is built
And then the Props withdraw
And adequate, erect,
The House support itself
And cease to recollect
The Auger and the Carpenter—
Just such a retrospect
Hath the perfected Life—
A past of Plank and Nail
And slowness—then the Scaffolds drop
Affirming it a Soul.

———————

Ourselves we do inter with sweet derision.
The channel of the dust who once achieves
Invalidates the balm of that religion
That doubts as fervently as it believes.

After a hundred years
Nobody knows the Place
Agony that enacted there
Motionless as Peace

Weeds triumphant ranged
Strangers strolled and spelled
At the lone Orthography
Of the Elder Dead

Winds of Summer Fields
Recollect the way—
Instinct picking up the Key
Dropped by memory—

Great Streets of silence led away
To Neighborhoods of Pause—
Here was no Notice—no Dissent
No Universe—no Laws—

By Clocks, 'twas Morning, and for Night
The Bells at Distance called—
But Epoch had no basis here
For Period exhaled.

Somehow myself survived the Night
And entered with the Day—
That it be saved the Saved suffice
Without the Formula.

Henceforth I take my living place
As one commuted led—
A Candidate for Morning Chance
But dated with the Dead.

My Triumph lasted till the Drums
Had left the Dead alone
And then I dropped my Victory
And chastened stole along
To where the finished Faces
Conclusion turned on me
And then I hated Glory
And wished myself were They.

What is to be is best descried
When it has also been—
Could Prospect taste of Retrospect
The tyrannies of Men
Were Tenderer—diviner
The Transitive toward.
A Bayonet's contrition
Is nothing to the Dead.

The Clover's simple Fame
Remembered of the Cow—
Is better than enameled Realms
Of notability.
Renown perceives itself
And that degrades the Flower—
The Daisy that has looked behind
Has compromised its power—

To pile like Thunder to its close
Then crumble grand away
While Everything created hid
This—would be Poetry—

Or Love—the two coeval come—
We both and neither prove—
Experience either and consume—
For None see God and live—

———

There is no Frigate like a Book
To take us Lands away
Nor any Coursers like a Page
Of prancing Poetry—
This Traverse may the poorest take
Without oppress of Toll—
How frugal is the Chariot
That bears the Human soul.

———

Go slow, my soul, to feed thyself
Upon his rare approach—
Go rapid, lest Competing Death
Prevail upon the Coach—
Go timid, should his final eye
Determine thee amiss—
Go boldly—for thou paid'st his price
Redemption—for a Kiss—

———

"Heavenly Father"—take to thee
 The supreme iniquity
 Fashioned by thy candid Hand

In a moment contraband—
Though to trust us—seem to us
More respectful—"We are Dust"—
We apologize to thee
For thine own Duplicity—

A Route of Evanescence
With a revolving Wheel—
A Resonance of Emerald—
A Rush of Cochineal—
And every Blossom on the Bush
Adjusts its tumbled Head—
The mail from Tunis, probably,
An easy Morning's Ride—

One of the ones that Midas touched
Who failed to touch us all
Was that confiding Prodigal
The reeling Oriole—

So drunk he disavows it
With badinage divine—
So dazzling we mistake him
For an alighting Mine—

A Pleader—a Dissembler—
An Epicure—a Thief—
Betimes an Oratorio—
An Ecstasy in chief—

The Jesuit of Orchards
He cheats as he enchants
Of an entire Attar
For his decamping wants—

The splendor of a Burmah
The Meteor of Birds,
Departing like a Pageant
Of Ballads and of Bards—

I never thought that Jason sought
For any Golden Fleece
But then I am a rural man
With thoughts that make for Peace—

But if there were a Jason,
Tradition bear with me
Behold his lost Aggrandizement
Upon the Apple Tree—

———

More than the Grave is closed to me—
The Grave and that Eternity
To which the Grave adheres—
I cling to nowhere till I fall—
The Crash of nothing, yet of all—
How similar appears—

———

How happy is the little Stone
That rambles in the Road alone,
And doesn't care about Careers
And Exigencies never fears—
Whose Coat of elemental Brown
A passing Universe put on,
And independent as the Sun
Associates or glows alone,
Fulfilling absolute Decree
In casual simplicity—

The Moon upon her fluent Route
Defiant of a Road—
The Star's Etruscan Argument
Substantiate a God—

If Aims impel these Astral Ones
The ones allowed to know
Know that which makes them as forgot
As Dawn forgets them—now—

As imperceptibly as Grief
The Summer lapsed away—
Too imperceptible at last
To seem like Perfidy—
A Quietness distilled
As Twilight long begun,
Or Nature spending with herself
Sequestered Afternoon—
The Dusk drew earlier in—
The Morning foreign shone—
A courteous, yet harrowing Grace,
As Guest, that would be gone—
And thus, without a Wing
Or service of a Keel
Our Summer made her light escape
Into the Beautiful.

The Bible is an antique Volume—
Written by faded Men
At the suggestion of Holy Spectres—
Subjects—Bethlehem—
Eden—the ancient Homestead—
Satan—the Brigadier—
Judas—the Great Defaulter—
David—the Troubadour—
Sin—a distinguished Precipice
Others must resist—
Boys that "believe" are very lonesome—
Other Boys are "lost"—
Had but the Tale a warbling Teller—
All the Boys would come—
Orpheus' Sermon captivated—
It did not condemn—

———————

Those—dying then,
Knew where they went—
They went to God's Right Hand—
That Hand is amputated now
And God cannot be found—

The abdication of Belief
Makes the Behavior small—
Better an ignis fatuus
Than no illume at all—

———————

The Clock strikes one that just struck two—
Some schism in the Sum—
A Vagabond for Genesis
Has wrecked the Pendulum—

———

The Spirit lasts—but in what mode—
Below, the Body speaks,
But as the Spirit furnishes—
Apart, it never talks—
The Music in the Violin
Does not emerge alone
But Arm in Arm with Touch, yet Touch
Alone—is not a Tune—
The Spirit lurks within the Flesh
Like Tides within the Sea
That make the Water live, estranged
What would the Either be?
Does that know—now—or does it cease—
That which to this is done,
Resuming at a mutual date
With every future one?
Instinct pursues the Adamant,
Exacting this Reply—
Adversity if it may be, or
Wild Prosperity,
The Rumor's Gate was shut so tight
Before my Mind was sown,
Not even a Prognostic's Push
Could make a Dent thereon—

———

He ate and drank the precious Words—
His Spirit grew robust—
He knew no more that he was poor,
Nor that his frame was Dust—

He danced along the dingy Days
And this Bequest of Wings
Was but a Book—What Liberty
A loosened spirit brings—

There came a Wind like a Bugle—
It quivered through the Grass
And a Green Chill upon the Heat
So ominous did pass
We barred the Windows and the Doors
As from an Emerald Ghost—
The Doom's electric Moccasin
That very instant passed—
On a strange Mob of panting Trees
And Fences fled away
And Rivers where the Houses ran
Those looked that lived—that Day—
The Bell within the steeple wild
The flying tidings told—
How much can come
And much can go,
And yet abide the World!

A Word made Flesh is seldom
And tremblingly partook
Nor then perhaps reported
But have I not mistook
Each one of us has tasted
With ecstasies of stealth
The very food debated
To our specific strength—

A Word that breathes distinctly
Has not the power to die
Cohesive as the Spirit
It may expire if He—
"Made Flesh and dwelt among us"
Could condescension be
Like this consent of Language
This loved Philology.

_____

In Winter in my Room
I came upon a Worm—
Pink, lank and warm—
But as he was a worm
And worms presume
Not quite with him at home—
Secured him by a string
To something neighboring
And went along.

A Trifle afterward
A thing occurred
I'd not believe it if I heard
But state with creeping blood—
A snake with mottles rare
Surveyed my chamber floor
In feature as the worm before
But ringed with power—
The very string with which
I tied him—too
When he was mean and new
That string was there—

I shrank—"How fair you are"!
Propitiation's claw—
"Afraid," he hissed
"Of me"?
"No cordiality"—
He fathomed me—
Then to a Rhythm *Slim*
Secreted in his Form
As Patterns swim
Projected him.

That time I flew
Both eyes his way
Lest he pursue

Nor ever ceased to run
Till in a distant Town
Towns on from mine
I set me down
This was a dream.

———————

A Pit—but Heaven over it—
And Heaven beside, and Heaven abroad,
And yet a Pit—
With Heaven over it.

To stir would be to slip—
To look would be to drop—
To dream—to sap the Prop
That holds my chances up.
Ah! Pit! With Heaven over it!

The depth is all my thought—
I dare not ask my feet—
'Twould start us where we sit
So straight you'd scarce suspect
It was a Pit—with fathoms under it—
Its Circuit just the same.
Seed—summer—tomb—
Whose Doom to whom?

———————

By a departing light
We see acuter, quite,
Than by a wick that stays.
There's something in the flight
That clarifies the sight
And decks the rays.

———

I took one Draught of Life—
I'll tell you what I paid—
Precisely an existence—
The market price, they said.

They weighed me, Dust by Dust—
They balanced Film with Film,
Then handed me my Being's worth—
A single Dram of Heaven!

———

My life closed twice before its close—
It yet remains to see
If Immortality unveil
A third event to me

So huge, so hopeless to conceive
As these that twice befell.
Parting is all we know of heaven,
And all we need of hell.

———

That it will never come again
Is what makes life so sweet.
Believing what we don't believe
Does not exhilarate.

That if it be, it be at best
An ablative estate—
This instigates an appetite
Precisely opposite.

———

This docile one inter
While we who dare to live
Arraign the sunny brevity
That sparkled to the Grave

On her departing span
No wilderness remain
As dauntless in the House of Death
As if it were her own —

———

'Twas here my summer paused
What ripeness after then
To other scene or other soul
My sentence had begun.

To winter to remove
With winter to abide
Go manacle your icicle
Against your Tropic Bride.

———

Experiment escorts us last —
His pungent company
Will not allow an Axiom
An Opportunity

———

Too happy Time dissolves itself
And leaves no remnant by —
'Tis Anguish not a Feather hath
Or too much weight to fly —

The earth has many keys.
Where melody is not
Is the unknown peninsula.
Beauty is nature's fact.

But witness for her land,
And witness for her sea,
The cricket is her utmost
Of elegy to me.

BENJAMIN PAUL BLOOD

(1832–1919)

Late

"Ye cannot enter now."

And shall it ever be again—the joy
That greeted the fond bard when books were few,
And title-pages opened into Heaven?
How swelled the isles of Greece when Homer sung!
How soared the tulip night with loftier bloom,
And poured serener dreams o'er Maro's lay!
E'en thou, sad Harold, of the lonesome string,
Shall lyrist thrill the world again as thou,
The young, the beautiful?—beautiful and broken,
As for the bread of Life! (May the white hands
Of seraphs win thee to the Fatherhouse,
And soothe the sobbing locks, so heavy—heavy
From these Judean hills!)

      Oh, where was Fame
In that red morning when I was, like thee,
Soft-eyed and open-necked to the wild wind—
In love with mine own motions, ere my steps
Forgot the barefoot feel of the clay world?
My days lay open to the universe,
And all night long the clang of their musical gates
Retold the echoes of Apollo's harp,
And Mars his gory shield!—I wooed in vain.
Above my weedy and untitled moors
The mantle of a blooded Moon swept on,
With old regalia strange to me. . . . 'Twas well.
I lacked the builder's skill, the delver's faith;
I lacked the nether compass—maybe more
I lacked the central fire, the reckless poise
Of the born-drunken and the autocrat,
That breathe the courage of the soul's farewells.

But manhood came, nor yet her trumpet spoke—
And Disillusion mocked the arts of Art . . .
I saw the One of all things—branching trees
That fork the bird-nests, as the branching rivers
That fork the nests of men—and saw, beyond,
The field transcend the One, where tangent spirits
Would leave to slaves all spheric harmonies—
Till knowledge fells the last man as the first.

How long Redemption waits!—For they are gone—
The rosebloom of my youth, the tireless limbs,
The velvet-pointed lips that beauty wooed
With long, mute kisses in the hooded night,
Or on the spongy mead when sodden June
Gushed milk in the rank-sprouting grass, and blood
Hot, fitful, fateful, through the yearning arms,
And to the throbbing heart.—Could I forget!
Throw off this sorry wisdom, and inch deep
Besmear my wrinkles—young by torchlight yet!
Then leap to the arena!—who should know
The smiling athlete had a grewsome cheek,
Until the lamps were lowering?—Late, oh, late!
The westering pathos glooms the fervent hours.
Again my gray gull lifts against the nightfall,
And takes the damp leagues with a shoreless eye.

from *The Bride of the Iconoclast*

Stop!—Gaze thro' this hushed gallery! The air
Is beat by wild-limbed statues: how they glow
With life and action! from their blocks they rear,
As ye turn towards them, but they stop e'en so—
They will not if ye watch them! Soft doth flow
A rosy light around the marble nude,
Giving vitality. The walls do show
Full many a landscape, old and dim-subdued,
Of battle, wood and wild, and breathless solitude.

Ye wake the spirits of the startled walls,
Tread ne'er so softly, as on either hand
We mount to chambers thro' o'erarching halls,
Far more voluptuous—no whit less grand,
Where all that Art for Luxury hath plann'd,
On which unwearièd the eye may feast—
Purple, and gold, and velvets weltering bland,
Sleeps in the heavy splendor of the East;
And taste, which hath disposed, hath all things' worth
      increased.

Nought jars the harmony that fills the eye!
Advantage nought of furniture could more!
And lo! yon curtains, of th' old Tyrian dye,
Melt day's plain sunlight to the rose of love,
Deep'ning in richness every ridge and groove
Of carvèd wainscot, mirrors, picture-frames
With tasselled cordage, carpets whereon rove
The feet unheard, caskets, and things whose names
I doubt the artist knew—strange mechanism of games.

Spend not thy gaze on th' ornamental bits
Of ivory carved, and ebony, and pearl,
Or wilt thou so bemarvel thy five wits
With cunning, quaintest whimsies in the worl',
Thou wilt e'en cry 'have done!' amid the whirl.—
But oh! the pictures—curious, old, and rare—
What wight could pass them, but a foolish churl?
Hath each some precious meaning, wise and fair,
Or tells some truth of life, as old as Pain and Prayer.

Mark thou this portrait! As about we rove,
Forever rolleth its deep gaze at thee?
And thee in preference?—I nought can prove—
Yet true is 't, ever doth it gaze on me:
And so say all men who this picture see.
Perchance this scripture doth th' intent exhale:
WITH EVERY CONSCIENCE DEALETH DEITY.
BUT ONE EXPERIENCE DOTH ONE SOUL AVAIL.
THOU FEEL'ST THE EYE ON THEE. THOU CANST PROVE
      NO MAN'S TALE.——

Here is a tropic mountain, standing lone.
His rounded summit hath a scalp of snow;
But down his side go wander: every zone,
From torrid verdure up to th' icy glow,
Is belted on him, with his fruits also,
And plants and animals.—'Tis little worth;
Yet hath it truth in 't, tho' it hath no mo':
A tropic mountain models half the earth:—
And from this odd conceit the picture got its birth.—

With haunted atmosphere—no winds astir
Round dreaming ruins hushed upon the sand—
Wrecked tombs and temples of the days that were,
Far, tent-like piles, and solid sphynxes bland—
Hangs monstrous Egypt, old, mysterious land—
A faded, slumbrous picture. Hath gone down
The smoky sun: all things seem at a stand,
Save where, all-solemnly, to ocean boun',
Nilus turns sad away from yon poor gipsy town.—

Here is a whirlpool. On its cycling throat
The wilted billows are with fear uncurled.
Pale ships lean hastening from it, but they float
Still closer: some on th' water tiers are whirled;
Some down, 'neath skies of dizzy trouble hurled;
While none may tell them, if that tunnelled stream
Cascades the hissing rocks of Netherworld,
Or lifts its victim—past that horrid dream—
Thro' brine of other zones, where fairer suns shall beam.

These be Life-vessels, on the Pool of Death.
Fast, faster glide they, till the cycles drear
Grow swift monotony, and not the breath
Of worldly hurricane a wave can rear;
And far around the sky is full of fear,
And solemn clouds of tribulation frown,
Tho' tinged with hope! But penitence a tear
Drops o'er the dubious oblivion,—
And, with few flags half-mast, the fated barks go down.—

from Canto II, ii

ELIZABETH AKERS ALLEN

(1832—1911)

Rock Me to Sleep

Backward, turn backward, O Time, in your flight,
Make me a child again just for to-night!
Mother, come back from the echoless shore,
Take me again to your heart as of yore;
Kiss from my forehead the furrows of care,
Smooth the few silver threads out of my hair;
Over my slumbers your loving watch keep;—
Rock me to sleep, mother,—rock me to sleep!

Backward, flow backward, O tide of the years!
I am so weary of toil and of tears,—
Toil without recompense, tears all in vain,—
Take them, and give me my childhood again!
I have grown weary of dust and decay,—
Weary of flinging my soul-wealth away;
Weary of sowing for others to reap;—
Rock me to sleep, mother,—rock me to sleep!

Tired of the hollow, the base, the untrue,
Mother, O mother, my heart calls for you!
Many a summer the grass has grown green,
Blossomed and faded, our faces between:
Yet, with strong yearning and passionate pain,
Long I to-night for your presence again.
Come from the silence so long and so deep;—
Rock me to sleep, mother,—rock me to sleep!

Over my heart, in the days that are flown,
No love like mother-love ever has shone;
No other worship abides and endures,—
Faithful, unselfish, and patient like yours:
None like a mother can charm away pain

From the sick soul and the world-weary brain.
Slumber's soft calms o'er my heavy lids creep;—
Rock me to sleep, mother,—rock me to sleep!

Come, let your brown hair, just lighted with gold,
Fall on your shoulders again as of old;
Let it drop over my forehead to-night,
Shading my faint eyes away from the light;
For with its sunny-edged shadows once more
Haply will throng the sweet visions of yore;
Lovingly, softly, its bright billows sweep;—
Rock me to sleep, mother,—rock me to sleep!

Mother, dear mother, the years have been long
Since I last listened your lullaby song:
Sing, then, and unto my soul it shall seem
Womanhood's years have been only a dream.
Clasped to your heart in a loving embrace,
With your light lashes just sweeping my face,
Never hereafter to wake or to weep;—
Rock me to sleep, mother,—rock me to sleep!

HENRY CLAY WORK

(1832–1884)

Kingdom Coming

Say, darkeys, hab you seen de massa,
Wid de muffstash on his face,
Go long de road some time dis mornin',
Like he gwine to leab de place?
He seen a smoke, was up de ribber,
Whar de Linkum gumboats lay;
He took his hat, an' lef berry sudden,
An' I spec he's run away!

> *De massa run? ha, ha!*
> *De darkey stay? ho, ho!*
> *It mus' be now de kingdom comin',*
> *An' de year ob Jubilo!*

He six foot one way, two foot tudder,
An' he weigh tree hundred pound,
His coat so big, he couldn't pay de tailor,
An' it won't go half way round.
He drill so much dey call him Cap'an,
An' he get so drefful tann'd,
I spec he try an' fool dem Yankees
For to tink he's contraband.

Chorus

De darkeys feel so lonesome libing
In de loghouse on de lawn,
Dey move dar tings to massa's parlor
For to keep it while he's gone.
Dar's wine an' cider in de kitchen,
An' de darkeys dey'll hab some;
I spose dey'll all be cornfiscated
When de Linkum sojers come.

Chorus

De oberseer he make us trouble,
An' he dribe us round a spell;
We lock him up in de smokehouse cellar,
Wid de key trown in de well.
De whip is lost, de han'cuff broken,
But de massa'll hab his pay;
He's ole enough, big enough, ought to known better
Dan to went an' run away.

Chorus

Marching Through Georgia

Bring the good old bugle, boys! we'll sing another song—
Sing it with a spirit that will start the world along—
Sing it as we used to sing it, fifty thousand strong,
While we were marching through Georgia.

> *"Hurrah! Hurrah! we bring the Jubilee!*
> *Hurrah! Hurrah! the flag that makes you free!"*
> *So we sang the chorus from Atlanta to the sea,*
> *While we were marching through Georgia.*

How the darkeys shouted when they heard the joyful
　　　sound!
How the turkeys gobbled which our commissary found!
How the sweet potatoes even started from the ground,
While we were marching through Georgia.

Chorus

Yes, and there were Union men who wept with joyful tears,
When they saw the honor'd flag they had not seen for years;
Hardly could they be restrained from breaking forth in
　　　cheers,
While we were marching through Georgia.

Chorus

"Sherman's dashing Yankee boys will never reach the coast!"
So the saucy rebels said, and 'twas a handsome boast,
Had they not forgot, alas! to reckon with the host,
While we were marching through Georgia.

Chorus

So we made a thoroughfare for Freedom and her train,
Sixty miles in latitude—three hundred to the main;
Treason fled before us, for resistance was in vain,
While we were marching through Georgia.

Chorus

"Come Home, Father!"

*'Tis the
Song of little Mary,
Standing at the bar-room door,
While the shameful midnight revel
Rages wildly as before.*

Father, dear father, come home with me now!
The clock in the steeple strikes one;
You said you were coming right home from the shop,
As soon as your day's work was done.
Our fire has gone out—our house is all dark—
And mother's been watching since tea,
With poor brother Benny so sick in her arms,
And no one to help her but me.
Come home! come home! come home!
Please, father, *dear* father, come home.

> *Hear the sweet voice of the child
> Which the night-winds repeat as they roam!
> Oh who could resist this most plaintive of prayers?
> "Please, father, dear father, come home!"*

Father, dear father, come home with me now!
The clock in the steeple strikes two;
The night has grown colder, and Benny is worse—
But he has been calling for you.
Indeed he is worse—Ma says he will die,
Perhaps before morning shall dawn;
And this is the message she sent me to bring—
"Come quickly, or he will be gone."
Come home! come home! come home!
Please, father, *dear* father, come home.

Chorus

Father, dear father, come home with me now!
The clock in the steeple strikes three;
The house is so lonely—the hours are so long
For poor weeping mother and me.
Yes, we are alone—poor Benny is dead,
And gone with the angels of light;
And these were the very last words that he said—
"I want to kiss Papa good night."
Come home! come home! come home!
Please, father, *dear* father, come home.

Chorus

EDMUND CLARENCE STEDMAN

(1833–1908)

Prelude to *An American Anthology*

I saw the constellated matin choir
Then when they sang together in the dawn,—
The morning stars of this first rounded day
Hesperian, hundred-houred, that ending leaves
Youth's fillet still upon the New World's brow;
Then when they sang together,—sang for joy
Of mount and wood and cataract, and stretch
Of keen-aired vasty reaches happy-homed,—
I heard the stately hymning, saw their light
Resolve in flame that evil long inwrought
With what was else the goodliest demain
Of freedom warded by the ancient sea;
So sang they, rose they, to meridian,
And westering down the firmament led on
Cluster and train of younger celebrants
That beaconed as they might, by adverse skies
Shrouded, but stayed not nor discomfited,—
Of whom how many, and how dear, alas,
The voices stilled mid-orbit, stars eclipsed
Long ere the hour of setting; yet in turn
Others oncoming shine, nor fail to chant
New anthems, yet not alien, for the time
Goes not out darkling nor of music mute
To the next age,—that quickened now awaits
Their heralding, their more impassioned song.

JOHN JAMES PIATT

(1835–1917)

Farther

Far-off a young State rises, full of might:
  I paint its brave escutcheon. Near at hand
  See the log cabin in the rough clearing stand;
A woman by its door, with steadfast sight,
Trustful, looks Westward, where, uplifted bright,
  Some city's Apparition, weird and grand,
  In dazzling quiet fronts the lonely land,
With vast and marvelous structures wrought of light,
Motionless on the burning cloud afar: —
  The haunting vision of a time to be,
After the heroic age is ended here,
Built on the boundless, still horizon's bar
  By the low sun, his gorgeous prophecy
Lighting the doorway of the pioneer!

To the Statue on the Capitol

Looking Eastward at Dawn

What sunken splendor in the Eastern skies
  Seest thou, O Watcher, from thy lifted place? —
Thine old Atlantic dream is in thine eyes,
  But the new Western morning on thy face.

Beholdest thou, in reäpparent light,
  Thy lost Republics? They were visions, fled.
Their ghosts in ruin'd cities walk by night—
  It is no resurrection of their dead.

But look, behind thee, where in sunshine lie
  Thy boundless fields of harvest in the West,
Whose savage garments from thy shoulders fly,
  Whose eagle clings in sunrise to thy crest!

Fires in Illinois

How bright this weird autumnal eve—
    While the wild twilight clings around,
Clothing the grasses every-where,
    With scarce a dream of sound!

The high horizon's northern line,
    With many a silent-leaping spire,
Seems a dark shore—a sea of flame—
    Quick, crawling waves of fire!

I stand in dusky solitude,
    October breathing low and chill,
And watch the far-off blaze that leaps
    At the wind's wayward will.

These boundless fields, behold, once more,
    Sea-like in vanish'd summers stir;
From vanish'd autumns comes the Fire—
    A lone, bright harvester!

I see wide terror lit before—
    Wild steeds, fierce herds of bison here,
And, blown before the flying flame,
    The flying-footed deer!

Long trains (with shaken bells, that moved
    Along red twilights sinking slow)
Whose wheels grew weary on their way,
    Far westward, long ago;

Lone wagons bivouack'd in the blaze,
    That, long ago, stream'd wildly past;
Faces from that bright solitude
    In the hot gleam aghast!

A glare of faces like a dream,
    No history after or before,
Inside the horizon with the flames,
    The flames—nobody more!

That vision vanishes in me,
    Sudden and swift and fierce and bright;
Another gentler vision fills
    The solitude, to-night:

The horizon lightens every-where,
    The sunshine rocks on windy maize;
Hark, every-where are busy men,
    And children at their plays!

Far church-spires twinkle at the sun,
    From villages of quiet born,
And, far and near, and every-where,
    Homes stand amid the corn.

No longer driven by wind, the Fire
    Makes all the vast horizon glow,
But, numberless as the stars above,
    The windows shine below!

My Shadow's Stature

Whene'er, in morning airs, I walk abroad,
Breasting upon the hills the buoyant wind,
Up from the vale my shadow climbs behind,
An earth-born giant climbing toward his god;
Against the sun, on heights before untrod,
I stand: faint glorified, but undefined,
Far down the slope in misty meadows blind,
I see my ghostly follower slowly plod.
"O stature of my shade," I muse and sigh,
"How great art thou, how small am I the while!"
Then the vague giant blandly answers, "True,
But though thou art small thy head is in the sky,
Crown'd with the sun and all the Heaven's smile—
My head is in the shade and valley too."

Taking the Night-Train

A tremulous word, a lingering hand, the burning
  Of restless passion smoldering—so we part;
Ah, slowly from the dark the world is turning
  When midnight stars shine in a heavy heart.

The streets are lighted, and the myriad faces
  Move through the gaslight, and the homesick feet
Pass by me, homeless; sweet and close embraces
  Charm many a threshold—laughs and kisses sweet.

From great hotels the stranger throng is streaming,
  The hurrying wheels in many a street are loud;
Within the depot, in the gaslight gleaming,
  A glare of faces, stands the waiting crowd.

The whistle screams; the wheels are rumbling slowly,
  The path before us glides into the light:
Behind, the city sinks in silence wholly;
  The panting engine leaps into the night.

I seem to see each street a mystery growing,
  In mist of dreamland—vague, forgotten air:
Does no sweet soul, awakened, feel me going?
  Loves no dear heart, in dreams, to keep me there?

AUGUSTA COOPER BRISTOL

(1835–1910)

Night

I stood and watched the still, mysterious Night,
Steal from her shadowy caverns in the East,
To work her deep enchantments on the world.
Her black veil floated down the silent glens,
While her dark sandalled feet, with noiseless tread,
Moved to a secret harmony. Along
The brows of the majestic hills, she strung
Her glorious diamonds so stealthily,
It never marred their dreams; and in the deep,
Cool thickets of the wood, where scarce the Day
Could reach the dim retreat, her dusky hand
Pinned on the breast of the exhaling flower,
A glittering gem; while all the tangled ferns
And forest lace-work, as she moved along,
Grew moist and shining.

                    Who would e'er have guessed,
The queenly Night would deign to stoop and love
A little flower! And yet, with all her stealth,
I saw her press her damp and cooling lip
Upon the feverish bosom of a Rose;
At which a watchful bird poured sudden forth
A love-sick song, of sweet and saddest strain.

Upon the ivied rocks, and rugged crags
On which the ocean billows break, she hung
Her sombre mantle; and the gray old sea
That had been high in tumult all the day,
Became so mesmerized beneath her wiles,
He seemed a mere reflection of herself.
The billows sank into a dimpled sleep;
Only the little tide-waves glided up
To kiss the blackness of the airy robe
That floated o'er them.

Long I stood and watched
The mystic, spell-like influence of Night;
Till o'er the eastern hills, came up the first
Faint glories of the crown that Phœbus wears.
And soon, the Earth, surprised to see the work
That Night had wrought, began to glow and blush,
Like maidens, conscious of the glance of Love.
While she,—the dark Enchantress,—like to one
Who decorates her bower with all things fair,
Wherewith to please her lover, but yet flees
At his approaching step,—at the first gleam
That lit the zenith from the Day-god's eye,
Fled timid o'er the distant western hills.

The Crime of the Ages

1861

Poet, write!
Not of a purpose dark and dire,
That souls of evil fashion,
Nor the power that nerves the assassin's hand,
In the white heat of his passion:
But let thy rhyme,
Through every clime,
A burthen bear of this one crime:
Let the world draw in a shuddering breath,
O'er the crime that aims at a nation's death!

Minstrel, sing!
Not in affection's dulcet tone,
Or with sound of a soft recorder:
Strike not thy harp to a strain arranged
In measured, harmonic order:
But loud and strong
The tones prolong,
That thunder of a Nation's wrong;
Let a sound of war in thy notes appear,
Till the world opes wide a startled ear!

Soldier, fight!
Thou hast a patriot's throbbing pulse,
And future history's pages,
Shall tell of the blood so freely shed
To redeem "the crime of the ages."
    Well may'st thou fight
    For Truth and Right,
And teach a rebel foe thy might!
Let a loyal heart, and undaunted will,
Show the world we are a Nation still!

Prophet, speak!
Speak for the children of martyred sires,
An offspring the most ungrateful!
Warn them of Justice hurrying on,
To punish a deed so hateful!
    O read with thy
    Prophetic eye,
The omens of our troubled sky!
What is the picture beyond the gloom?
New life, new birth, or a Nation's tomb?

ADAH ISAACS MENKEN

(1835? – 1868)

Judith

"Repent, or I will come unto thee quickly, and will fight thee with the sword of my mouth."

—REVELATION ii. 16.

I.

Ashkelon is not cut off with the remnant of a valley.
Baldness dwells not upon Gaza.
The field of the valley is mine, and it is clothed in verdure.
The steepness of Baal-perazim is mine;
And the Philistines spread themselves in the valley of
Rephaim.
They shall yet be delivered into my hands.
For the God of Battles has gone before me!
The sword of the mouth shall smite them to dust.
I have slept in the darkness—
But the seventh angel woke me, and giving me a sword of
flame, points to the blood-ribbed cloud, that lifts his reeking
head above the mountain.
Thus am I the prophet.
I see the dawn that heralds to my waiting soul the advent
of power.

   Power that will unseal the thunders!
   Power that will give voice to graves!
    Graves of the living;
    Graves of the dying;
    Graves of the sinning;
    Graves of the loving;
    Graves of despairing;
And oh! graves of the deserted!
These shall speak, each as their voices shall be loosed.
And the day is dawning.

II.

Stand back, ye Philistines!

Practice what ye preach to me;

I heed ye not, for I know ye all.

Ye are living burning lies, and profanation to the garments which with stately steps ye sweep your marble palaces.

Your palaces of Sin, around which the damning evidence of guilt hangs like a reeking vapor.

Stand back!

I would pass up the golden road of the world.

A place in the ranks awaits me.

I know that ye are hedged on the borders of my path.

Lie and tremble, for ye well know that I hold with iron grasp the battle axe.

Creep back to your dark tents in the valley.

Slouch back to your haunts of crime.

Ye do not know me, neither do ye see me.

But the sword of the mouth is unsealed, and ye coil yourselves in slime and bitterness at my feet.

I mix your jeweled heads, and your gleaming eyes, and your hissing tongues with the dust.

My garments shall bear no mark of ye.

When I shall return this sword to the angel, your foul blood will not stain its edge.

It will glimmer with the light of truth, and the strong arm shall rest.

III.

Stand back!

I am no Magdalene waiting to kiss the hem of your garment.

It is mid-day.

See ye not what is written on my forehead?

I am Judith!

I wait for the head of my Holofernes!

Ere the last tremble of the conscious death-agony shall have shuddered, I will show it to ye with the long black hair clinging to the glazed eyes, and the great mouth opened in search of voice, and the strong throat all hot and reeking

with blood, that will thrill me with wild unspeakable joy as it courses down my bare body and dabbles my cold feet!

My sensuous soul will quake with the burden of so much bliss.

Oh, what wild passionate kisses will I draw up from that bleeding mouth!

I will strangle this pallid throat of mine on the sweet blood!

I will revel in my passion.

At midnight I will feast on it in the darkness.

For it was that which thrilled its crimson tides of reckless passion through the blue veins of my life, and made them leap up in the wild sweetness of Love and agony of Revenge!

I am starving for this feast.

Oh forget not that I am Judith!

And I know where sleeps Holofernes.

MARK TWAIN

(1835–1910)

Ode to Stephen Dowling Bots, Dec'd.

And did young Stephen sicken,
    And did young Stephen die?
And did the sad hearts thicken,
    And did the mourners cry?

No; such was not the fate of
    Young Stephen Dowling Bots;
Though sad hearts round him thickened,
    'Twas not from sickness' shots.

No whooping-cough did rack his frame,
    Nor measles drear, with spots;
Not these impaired the sacred name
    Of Stephen Dowling Bots.

Despised love struck not with woe
    That head of curly knots,
Nor stomach troubles laid him low,
    Young Stephen Dowling Bots.

O no. Then list with tearful eye,
    Whilst I his fate do tell.
His soul did from this cold world fly,
    By falling down a well.

They got him out and emptied him;
    Alas it was too late;
His spirit was gone for to sport aloft
    In the realms of the good and great.

PHILLIPS BROOKS

(1835–1893)

O Little Town of Bethlehem

O little town of Bethlehem!
    How still we see thee lie,
Above thy deep and dreamless sleep,
    The silent stars go by;
Yet in thy dark streets shineth
    The Everlasting light;
The hopes and fears of all the years,
    Are met in thee tonight.

For Christ is born of Mary,
    And gathered all above,
While mortals sleep the angels keep
    Their watch of wondering love.
O morning stars together
    Proclaim the holy birth!
And praises sing to God the King,
    And peace to men on earth.

How silently, how silently,
    The wondrous gift is given;
So God imparts to human hearts
    The blessings of his heaven.
No ear may hear his coming,
    But in this world of sin,
Where meek souls will receive him still,
    The dear Christ enters in.

O holy child of Bethlehem!
    Descend to us, we pray,
Cast out our sin and enter in,
    Be born in us to-day.
We hear the Christmas angels,
    The great glad tidings tell,
O, come to us, abide with us,
    Our Lord Emmanuel!

BRET HARTE

(1836–1902)

Plain Language from Truthful James

Table Mountain, 1870

Which I wish to remark,—
    And my language is plain,—
That for ways that are dark
    And for tricks that are vain,
The heathen Chinee is peculiar.
    Which the same I would rise to explain.

Ah Sin was his name;
    And I shall not deny
In regard to the same
    What that name might imply,
But his smile it was pensive and childlike,
    As I frequent remarked to Bill Nye.

It was August the third;
    And quite soft was the skies;
Which it might be inferred
    That Ah Sin was likewise;
Yet he played it that day upon William
    And me in a way I despise.

Which we had a small game,
    And Ah Sin took a hand:
It was Euchre. The same
    He did not understand;
But he smiled as he sat by the table,
    With the smile that was childlike and bland.

Yet the cards they were stocked
    In a way that I grieve,
And my feelings were shocked

At the state of Nye's sleeve:
Which was stuffed full of aces and bowers,
    And the same with intent to deceive.

But the hands that were played
    By that heathen Chinee,
And the points that he made,
    Were quite frightful to see,—
Till at last he put down a right bower,
    Which the same Nye had dealt unto me.

Then I looked up at Nye,
    And he gazed upon me;
And he rose with a sigh,
    And said, "Can this be?
We are ruined by Chinese cheap labor,"—
    And he went for that heathen Chinee.

In the scene that ensued
    I did not take a hand,
But the floor it was strewed
    Like the leaves on the strand
With the cards that Ah Sin had been hiding,
    In the game "he did not understand."

In his sleeves, which were long,
    He had twenty-four jacks,—
Which was coming it strong,
    Yet I state but the facts;
And we found on his nails, which were taper,
    What is frequent in tapers,—that's wax.

Which is why I remark,
    And my language is plain,
That for ways that are dark,
    And for tricks that are vain,
The heathen Chinee is peculiar,—
    Which the same I am free to maintain.

California Madrigal

on the Approach of Spring

Oh come, my beloved! from thy winter abode,
From thy home on the Yuba, thy ranch overflowed:
For the waters have fallen, the winter has fled,
And the river once more has returned to its bed.

Oh, mark how the spring in its beauty is near!
How the fences and tules once more re-appear!
How soft lies the mud on the banks of yon slough
By the hole in the levee the waters broke through!

All Nature, dear Chloris, is blooming to greet
The glance of your eye, and the tread of your feet;
For the trails are all open, the roads are all free,
And the highwayman's whistle is heard on the lea.

Again swings the lash on the high mountain trail,
And the pipe of the packer is scenting the gale;
The oath and the jest ringing high o'er the plain,
Where the smut is not always confined to the grain.

Once more glares the sunlight on awning and roof,
Once more the red clay's pulverized by the hoof,
Once more the dust powders the "outsides" with red,
Once more at the station the whiskey is spread.

Then fly with me, love, ere the summer's begun,
And the mercury mounts to one hundred and one;
Ere the grass now so green shall be withered and sear,
In the spring that obtains but one month in the year.

Mrs. Judge Jenkins

[Being the Only Genuine Sequel to "Maud Muller."]

Maud Muller, all that summer day,
Raked the meadow sweet with hay;

Yet, looking down the distant lane,
She hoped the judge would come again.

But when he came, with smile and bow,
Maud only blushed, and stammered, "Ha-ow?"

And spoke of her "pa," and wondered whether
He'd give consent they should wed together.

Old Muller burst in tears, and then
Begged that the judge would lend him "ten;"

For trade was dull, and wages low,
And the "craps," this year, were somewhat slow.

And ere the languid summer died,
Sweet Maud became the judge's bride.

But, on the day that they were mated,
Maud's brother Bob was intoxicated;

And Maud's relations, twelve in all,
Were very drunk at the judge's hall.

And when the summer came again,
The young bride bore him babies twain.

And the judge was blest, but thought it strange
That bearing children made such a change:

For Maud grew broad and red and stout;
And the waist that his arm once clasped about

Was more than he now could span. And he
Sighed as he pondered, ruefully,

How that which in Maud was native grace
In Mrs. Jenkins was out of place;

And thought of the twins, and wished that they
Looked less like the man who raked the hay

On Muller's farm, and dreamed with pain
Of the day he wandered down the lane.

And, looking down that dreary track,
He half regretted that he came back.

For, had he waited, he might have wed
Some maiden fair and thoroughbred;

For there be women fair as she,
Whose verbs and nouns do more agree.

Alas for maiden! alas for judge!
And the sentimental,—that's one-half "fudge;"

For Maud soon thought the judge a bore,
With all his learning and all his lore.

And the judge would have bartered Maud's fair face
For more refinement and social grace.

If, of all words of tongue and pen,
The saddest are, "It might have been,"

More sad are these we daily see:
"It is, but hadn't ought to be."

Truthful James to the Editor

in the Modoc War
1873

Which it is not my style
    To produce needless pain
By statements that rile,
    Or that go 'gin the grain,
But here's Captain Jack still a livin', and Nye
    has no skelp on his brain!

On that Caucasian head
    There is no crown of hair.
It has gone, it has fled!
    And Echo sez "where?"
And I asks, "Is this Nation a White Man's,
    and is generally things on the square?"

She was known in the camp
    As "Nye's other squaw,"
And folks of that stamp
    Hez no rights in the Law,
But is treacherous, sinful, and slimy, as Nye
    might hev well known before.

But she said that she knew
    Where the Injins was hid,
And the statement was true,
    For it seemed that she did;
Since she led William where he was covered
    by seventeen Modocs, and—slid!

Then they reached for his hair;
    But Nye sez, "By the Law
Of Nations, forbear!
    I surrenders,—no more:
And I looks to be treated, you hear me?—as
    a pris'ner, a pris'ner of war!"

But Captain Jack rose
        And he sez "It's too thin.
Such statements as those
        It's too late to begin.
There's a *Modoc indictment* agin you, O Pale-
        face, and you're goin' in!

        "You stole Schonchin's squaw
                In the year 'sixty-two;
        It was in 'sixty-four
                That Long Jack you went through,
And you burned Nasty Jim's rancheria and
        his wives and his pappooses too.

        "This gun in my hand
                Was sold me by you
        'Gainst the law of the land,
                And I grieves it is true!"
And he buried his face in his blanket and
        wept as he hid it from view.

        "But you're tried and condemned,
                And skelping's your doom,"
        And he paused and he hemmed,—
                But why this resume?
He was skelped 'gainst the custom of Nations,
        and cut off like a rose in its bloom.

        So I asks without guile,
                And I trusts not in vain,
        If this is the style
                That is going to obtain,—
If here's Captain Jack still a-livin, and Nye
        with no skelp on his brain?

What the Bullet Sang

O joy of creation
           To be!
O rapture to fly
           And be free!
Be the battle lost or won,
   Though its smoke shall hide the sun,
I shall find my love — The one
           Born for me!

I shall know him where he stands,
           All alone,
With the power in his hands
           Not o'erthrown;
I shall know him by his face,
   By his god-like front and grace;
I shall hold him for a space,
           All my own!

It is he — O my love!
           So bold!
It is I — All thy love
           Foretold!
It is I. O love what bliss!
   Dost thou answer to my kiss?
Oh! sweetheart, what is this!
           Lieth there so cold!

Chicago

(October 10, 1871.)

Blackened and bleeding, helpless, panting, prone,
On the charred fragments of her shattered throne
Lies she who stood but yesterday alone.

Queen of the West! by some enchanter taught
To lift the glory of Aladdin's court,
Then lose the spell that all that wonder wrought.

Like her own prairies by some chance seed sown,
Like her own prairies in one brief day grown,
Like her own prairies in one fierce night mown.

She lifts her voice, and in her pleading call
We hear the cry of Macedon to Paul—
The cry for help that makes her kin to all.

But haply with wan fingers may she feel
The silver cup hid in the proffered meal—
The gifts her kinship and our loves reveal.

SARAH MORGAN PIATT

(1836–1919)

Giving Back the Flower

So, because you chose to follow me into the subtle sadness
    of night,
    And to stand in the half-set moon with the weird fall-light
      on your glimmering hair,
Till your presence hid all of the earth and all of the sky from
    my sight,
    And to give me a little scarlet bud, that was dying of
      frost, to wear,

Say, must you taunt me forever, forever? You looked at my
    hand and you knew
    That I was the slave of the Ring, while you were as free as
      the wind is free.
When I saw your corpse in your coffin, I flung back your
    flower to you;
    It was all of yours that I ever had; you must keep it,
      and—keep from me.

Ah? so God is your witness. Has God, then, no world to
    look after but ours?
    May He not have been searching for that wild star, with
      the trailing plumage, that flew
Far over a part of our darkness while we were there by the
    freezing flowers,
    Or else brightening some planet's luminous rings, instead
      of thinking of you?

Or, if He was near us at all, do you think that He would sit
    listening there
    Because you sang "Hear me, Norma," to a woman in
      jewels and lace,
While, so close to us, down in another street, in the wet,
    unlighted air,

There were children crying for bread and fire, and mothers
    who questioned His grace?

Or perhaps He had gone to the ghastly field where the fight
    had been that day,
  To number the bloody stabs that were there, to look at
    and judge the dead;
Or else to the place full of fever and moans where the
    wretched wounded lay;
  At least I do not believe that He cares to remember a
    word that you said.

So take back your flower, I tell you—of its sweetness I now
    have no need;
  Yes, take back your flower down into the stillness and
    mystery to keep;
When you wake I will take it, and God, then, perhaps will
    witness indeed,
  But go, now, and tell Death he must watch you, and not
    let you walk in your sleep.

WILLIAM DEAN HOWELLS

(1837–1920)

Forlorn

I.

Red roses, in the slender vases burning,
  Breathed all upon the air, —
The passion and the tenderness and yearning,
  The waiting and the doubting and despair.

II.

Still with the music of her voice was haunted,
  Through all its charméd rhymes,
The open book of such a one as chanted
  The things he dreamed in old, old summer-times.

III.

The silvern chords of the piano trembled
  Still with the music wrung
From them; the silence of the room dissembled
  The closes of the songs that she had sung.

IV.

The languor of the crimson shawl's abasement, —
  Lying without a stir
Upon the floor, — the absence at the casement,
  The solitude and hush were full of her.

V.

Without, and going from the room, and never
  Departing, did depart
Her steps; and one that came too late forever
  Felt them go heavy o'er his broken heart.

VI.

And, sitting in the house's desolation,
    He could not bear the gloom,
The vanishing encounter and evasion
    Of things that were and were not in the room.

VII.

Through midnight streets he followed fleeting visions
    Of faces and of forms;
He heard old tendernesses and derisions
    Amid the sobs and cries of midnight storms.

VIII.

By midnight lamps, and from the darkness under
    That lamps made at their feet,
He saw sweet eyes peer out in innocent wonder,
    And sadly follow after him down the street.

IX.

The noonday crowds their restlessness obtruded
    Between him and his quest;
At unseen corners jostled and eluded,
    Against his hand her silken robes were pressed.

X.

Doors closed upon her; out of garret casements
    He knew she looked at him;
In splendid mansions and in squalid basements,
    Upon the walls he saw her shadow swim.

XI.

From rapid carriages she gleamed upon him,
    Whirling away from sight;
From all the hopelessness of search she won him
    Back to the dull and lonesome house at night.

XII.

Full early into dark the twilights saddened
    Within its closéd doors;
The echoes, with the clock's monotony maddened,
    Leaped loud in welcome from the hollow floors;

XIII.

But gusts that blew all day with solemn laughter
    From wide-mouthed chimney-places,
And the strange noises between roof and rafter,
    The wainscot clamor, and the scampering races

XIV.

Of mice that chased each other through the chambers,
    And up and down the stair,
And rioted among the ashen embers,
    And left their frolic footprints everywhere,—

XV.

Were hushed to hear his heavy tread ascending
    The broad steps, one by one,
And toward the solitary chamber tending,
    Where the dim phantom of his hope alone

XVI.

Rose up to meet him, with his growing nearer,
    Eager for his embrace,
And moved, and melted into the white mirror,
    And stared at him with his own haggard face.

XVII.

But, turning, he was 'ware *her* looks beheld him
    Out of the mirror white;
And at the window yearning arms she held him,
    Out of the vague and sombre fold of night.

XVIII.

Sometimes she stood behind him, looking over
    His shoulder as he read;
Sometimes he felt her shadowy presence hover
    Above his dreamful sleep, beside his bed;

XIX.

And rising from his sleep, her shadowy presence
    Followed his light descent
Of the long stair; her shadowy evanescence
    Through all the whispering rooms before him went.

XX.

Upon the earthy draught of cellars blowing
    His shivering lamp-flame blue,
Amid the damp and chill, he felt her flowing
    Around him from the doors he entered through.

XXI.

The spiders wove their webs upon the ceiling;
    The bat clung to the wall;
The dry leaves through the open transom stealing,
    Skated and danced adown the empty hall.

XXII.

About him closed the utter desolation,
    About him closed the gloom;
The vanishing encounter and evasion
    Of things that were and were not in the room

XXIII.

Vexed him forever; and his life forever
    Immured and desolate,
Beating itself, with desperate endeavor,
    But bruised itself, against the round of fate.

XXIV.

The roses, in their slender vases burning,
  Were quenchéd long before;
A dust was on the rhymes of love and yearning;
  The shawl was like a shroud upon the floor.

XXV.

Her music from the thrilling chords had perished;
  The stillness was not moved
With memories of cadences long cherished,
  The closes of the songs that she had loved.

XXVI.

But not the less he felt her presence never
  Out of the room depart;
Over the threshold, not the less, forever
  He felt her going on his broken heart.

The Empty House

The wet trees hung above the walks
  Purple with damps and earthish stains,
  And strewn by moody, absent rains
With rose-leaves from the wild-grown stalks.

Unmown, in heavy, tangled swaths,
  The ripe June-grass is wanton blown;
  Snails slime the untrodden threshold-stone;
Along the sills hang drowsy moths.

Down the blank visage of the wall,
  Where many a wavering trace appears,
  Like a forgotten trace of tears,
From swollen eaves the slow drops crawl.

Where everything was wide before,
   The curious wind, that comes and goes,
   Finds all the latticed windows close,
Secret and close the bolted door.

And with the shrewd and curious wind,
   That in the archéd doorway cries,
   And at the bolted portal tries,
And harks and listens at the blind,—

Forever lurks my thought about,
   And in the ghostly middle-night
   Finds all the hidden windows bright,
And sees the guests go in and out,

And lingers till the pallid dawn,
   And feels the mystery deeper there
   In silent, gust-swept chambers, bare,
With all the midnight revel gone;

But wanders through the lonesome rooms,
   Where harsh the astonished cricket calls,
   And, from the hollows of the walls
Vanishing, start unshapen glooms;

And lingers yet, and cannot come
   Out of the drear and desolate place,
   So full of ruin's solemn grace,
And haunted with the ghost of home.

The Royal Portraits

(at Ludwigshof)

I.

Confronting each other the pictures stare
   Into each other's sleepless eyes;
   And the daylight into the darkness dies,

From year to year in the palace there:
 But they watch and guard that no device
Take either one of them unaware.

Their majesties the king and the queen,
 The parents of the reigning prince:
 Both put off royalty many years since,
With life and the gifts that have always been
 Given to kings from God, to evince
His sense of the mighty over the mean.

I cannot say that I like the face
 Of the king; it is something fat and red;
 And the neck that lifts the royal head
Is thick and coarse; and a scanty grace
 Dwells in the dull blue eyes that are laid
Sullenly on the queen in her place.

He must have been a king in his day
 'T were well to pleasure in work and sport:
 One of the heaven-anointed sort
Who ruled his people with iron sway,
 And knew that, through good and evil report,
God meant him to rule and them to obey.

There are many other likenesses
 Of the king in his royal palace there;
 You find him depicted everywhere, —
In his robes of state, in his hunting-dress,
 In his flowing wig, in his powdered hair, —
A king in all of them, none the less;

But most himself in this on the wall
 Over against his consort, whose
 Laces, and hoops, and high-heeled shoes
Make her the finest lady of all
 The queens or courtly dames you choose,
In the ancestral portrait hall.

A glorious blonde: a luxury
  Of luring blue and wanton gold,
  Of blanchéd rose and crimson bold,
Of lines that flow voluptuously
  In tender, languorous curves to fold
Her form in perfect symmetry.

She might have been false. Of her withered dust
  There scarcely would be enough to write
  Her guilt in now; and the dead have a right
To our lenient doubt if not to our trust:
  So if the truth cannot make her white,
Let us be as merciful as we—must.

II.

The queen died first, the queen died young,
  But the king was very old when he died,
  Rotten with license, and lust, and pride;
And the usual Virtues came and hung
  Their cypress wreaths on his tomb, and wide
Throughout his kingdom his praise was sung.

How the queen died is not certainly known,
  And faithful subjects are all forbid
  To speak of the murder which some one did
One night while she slept in the dark alone:
  History keeps the story hid,
And Fear only tells it in undertone.

Up from your startled feet aloof,
  In the famous Echo-Room, with a bound
  Leaps the echo, and round and round
Beating itself against the roof,—
  A horrible, gasping, shuddering sound,—
Dies ere its terror can utter proof

Of that it knows. A door is fast,
  And none is suffered to enter there.
  His sacred majesty could not bear

To look at it toward the last,
   As he grew very old. It opened where
The queen died young so many years past.

III.

How the queen died is not certainly known;
   But in the palace's solitude
   A harking dread and horror brood,
And a silence, as if a mortal groan
   Had been hushed the moment before, and would
Break forth again when you were gone.

The present king has never dwelt
   In the desolate palace. From year to year
   In the wide and stately garden drear
The snows and the snowy blossoms melt
   Unheeded, and a ghastly fear
Through all the shivering leaves is felt.

By night the gathering shadows creep
   Along the dusk and hollow halls,
   And the slumber-broken palace calls
With stifled moans from its nightmare sleep;
   And then the ghostly moonlight falls
Athwart the darkness brown and deep.

At early dawn the light wind sighs,
   And through the desert garden blows
   The wasted sweetness of the rose;
At noon the feverish sunshine lies
   Sick in the walks. But at evening's close,
When the last, long rays to the windows rise,

And with many a blood-red, wrathful streak
   Pierce through the twilight glooms that blur
   His cruel vigilance and her
Regard, they light fierce looks that wreak
   A hopeless hate that cannot stir,
A voiceless hate that cannot speak

In the awful calm of the sleepless eyes;
   And as if she saw her murderer glare
   On her face, and he the white despair
Of his victim kindle in wild surmise,
   Confronted the conscious pictures stare,—
And their secret back into darkness dies.

In Earliest Spring

Tossing his mane of snows in wildest eddies and tangles,
   Lion-like, March cometh in, hoarse, with tempestuous
      breath,
Through all the moaning chimneys, and thwart all the
      hollows and angles
   Round the shuddering house, threating of winter and
      death.

But in my heart I feel the life of the wood and the
      meadow
   Thrilling the pulses that own kindred with fibres
      that lift
Bud and blade to the sunward, within the inscrutable
      shadow,
   Deep in the oak's chill core, under the gathering drift.

Nay, to earth's life in mine some prescience, or dream, or
      desire
   (How shall I name it aright?) comes for a moment and
      goes,—
Rapture of life ineffable, perfect,—as if in the brier,
   Leafless there by my door, trembled a sense of
      the rose.

November

Impression

A weft of leafless spray
Woven fine against the gray
Of the autumnal day,
And blurred along those ghostly garden tops
Clusters of berries crimson as the drops
That my heart bleeds when I remember
How often, in how many a far November,
Of childhood and my children's childhood I was glad,
With the wild rapture of the Fall,
Of all the beauty, and of all
The ruin, now so intolerably sad.

FORCEYTHE WILLSON

(1837–1867)

The Estray

"Now tell me, my merry woodman,
    Why standest so aghast?"
"My lord!—'t was a beautiful creature
    That hath but just gone past!"

"A creature—what kind of a creature?"
    "Nay now, but I do not know!"
"Humph—what did it make you think of?"
    "The sunshine on the snow."

"I shall overtake my horse then:"
    The woodman opened his eye:—
The gold fell all around him,
    And a rainbow spanned the sky.

To Hersa

Maiden, there is something more
Than raiment to adore:
Thou must have more than a dress,
More than any mode or mould,
More than mortal loveliness,
To captivate the cold.

Bow the knightly when they bow,
To a star behind the brow:
Not to marble, not to dust;
    But to that which warms them:
Not to contour nor to bust;
    But to that which forms them:
Not to languid lid nor lash,
Satin fold nor purple sash;

But unto the living flash
So mysteriously hid
Under lash and under lid.

But—vanity of vanities,—
If the red-rose in a young cheek, lies,
    Fatal disguise!
For the most terrible lances
Of the True, true Knight,
Are his bold eyebeams;
And every time that he opens his eyes,
The Falsehood that he looks on, dies.

If the heavenly light be latent,
It can need no earthly patent.
      Unbeholden unto art,
      Fashion or lore,
      Scrip or store,
      Earth or ore,
      Be thy heart,
Which was music from the start,
Music, music to the core.

Music, which, though voiceless,
Can create
Both form and fate,
As Petrarch could a sonnet.
That, taking flesh upon it,
Spirit-noiseless,
Doth the same inform and fill
With a Music sweeter still,—
Lives, and breathes, and palpitates,
Moves, and moulds, and animates,
And sleeps not from its duty
Till the maid in whom 't is pent,
From a mortal rudiment,
From the earth-cell
  And the love-cell
By the birth-spell
  And the love-spell,
Come to beauty.

Beauty is music mute,
Music's flower and fruit,
          Music's lute:
Music's lute be thou,
Maiden of the starry brow,
(Keep thy heart true to know how!)
A Lute which he alone,
As all in good time shall be shown,
Shall prove and thereby make his own,
Who is god enough to play upon it.

Happy, happy maid is she
Who is wedded unto Truth!
Thou shalt know him, when he comes,
          (Welcome youth!)
Not by any din of drums,
Nor the vantage of his airs;
Neither by his crown,
Nor his gown,
Nor by anything he wears.
He shall only well-known be,
By the holy Harmony
That his coming makes in thee!

In State

I.

O Keeper of the Sacred Key,
And the Great Seal of Destiny,
Whose eye is the blue canopy,
Look down upon the warring world, and tell us what the
          end will be.

"Lo, through the wintry atmosphere,
On the white bosom of the sphere,
A cluster of five lakes appear;
And all the land looks like a couch, or warrior's shield, or
          sheeted bier.

"And on that vast and hollow field,
With both lips closed and both eyes sealed,
A mighty Figure is revealed,—
Stretched at full length, and stiff and stark, as in the hollow
of a shield.

"The winds have tied the drifted snow
Around the face and chin; and lo,
The sceptred Giants come and go,
And shake their shadowy crowns and say: "We always feared
it would be so!"

"She came of an heroic race:
A giant's strength, a maiden's grace,
Like two in one seem to embrace,
And match, and blend, and thorough-blend, in her colossal
form and face.

"Where can her dazzling falchion be?
One hand is fallen in the sea;
The Gulf-Stream drifts it far and free;
And in that hand her shining brand gleams from the depths
resplendently.

"And by the other, in its rest,
The starry banner of the West
Is clasped forever to her breast;
And of her silver helmet, lo, a soaring eagle is the crest.

"And on her brow, a softened light,
As of a star concealed from sight
By some thin veil of fleecy white,—
Or of the rising moon behind the rainy vapors of the night.

"The Sisterhood that was so sweet,
The Starry System sphered complete,
Which the mazed Orient used to greet,
The Four and Thirty fallen Stars glimmer and glitter at her
feet.

"And over her,—and over all,
For panoply and coronal,—
The mighty Immemorial,
And everlasting Canopy and starry Arch and Shield of All."

II.

"Three cold, bright moons have marched and wheeled;
And the white cerement that revealed
A Figure stretched upon a Shield,
Is turned to verdure; and the Land is now one mighty
        Battle-Field.

"And lo, the children which she bred,
And more than all else cherishéd,
To make them true in heart and head,
Stand face to face, as mortal foes, with their swords crossed
        above the dead.

"Each hath a mighty stroke and stride:
One true—the more that he is tried;
The other dark and evil-eyed;—
And by the hand of one of them, his own dear mother
        surely died!

"A stealthy step—a gleam of hell,—
It is the simple truth to tell,—
The Son stabbed and the Mother fell:
And so she lies, all mute and pale, and pure and irreproachable!

"And then the battle-trumpet blew;
And the true brother sprang and drew
His blade to smite the traitor through;
And so they clashed above the bier, and the Night sweated
        bloody dew.

"And all their children, far and wide,
That are so greatly multiplied,
Rise up in frensy and divide;

And choosing, each whom he will serve, unsheathe the
    sword and take their side.

"And in the low sun's bloodshot rays,
Portentous of the coming days,
The Two great Oceans blush and blaze,
With the emergent continent between them, wrapt in
    crimson haze.

"Now whichsoever stand or fall,
As God is great and man is small,
The Truth shall triumph over all,—
Forever and forevermore, the Truth shall triumph over all!"

III.

"I see the champion sword-strokes flash;
I see them fall and hear them clash;
I hear the murderous engines crash;
I see a brother stoop to loose a foeman-brother's bloody
    sash.

"I see the torn and mangled corse,
The dead and dying heaped in scores,
The headless rider by his horse,
The wounded captive bayoneted through and through
    without remorse.

"I hear the dying sufferer cry,
With his crushed face turned to the sky,
I see him crawl in agony
To the foul pool, and bow his head into its bloody slime and
    die.

"I see the assassin crouch and fire,
I see his victim fall—expire;
I see the murderer creeping nigher
To strip the dead: He turns the head: The face! The son
    beholds his sire!

"I hear the curses and the thanks;
I see the mad charge on the flanks,
The rents—the gaps—the broken ranks,—
The vanquished squadrons driven headlong down the river's
    bridgeless banks.

"I see the death-gripe on the plain,
The grappling monsters on the main,
The tens of thousands that are slain,
And all the speechless suffering and agony of heart and
    brain.

"I see the dark and bloody spots,
The crowded rooms and crowded cots,
The bleaching bones, the battle-blots,—
And writ on many a nameless grave, a legend of forget-me-
    nots.

"I see the gorgéd prison-den,
The dead line and the pent-up pen,
The thousands quartered in the fen,
The living-deaths of skin and bone that were the goodly
    shapes of men.

"And still the bloody Dew must fall!
And His great Darkness with the Pall
Of His dread Judgment cover all,
Till the Dead Nation rise Transformed by Truth to triumph
    over all!"

"And last—and last I see—The Deed."

Thus saith the Keeper of the Key,
And the Great Seal of Destiny,
Whose Eye is the blue canopy,
And leaves the Pall of His great Darkness over all the Land
    and Sea.

JOAQUIN MILLER

(1837–1913)

Sierras

Like fragments of an uncompleted world,
  From icy bleak Alaska, white with spray,
To where the peaks of Darien lie curled
  In clouds, the broken lands loom bold and gray.
  The seamen nearing San Francisco Bay,
Forget the compass here; with sturdy hand
  They seize the wheel, look up, then bravely lay
The ship to shore by snowy peaks that stand
The stern and proud patrician fathers of the land.

They stand, white stairs of heaven—stand, a line
  Of climbing, endless, and eternal white.
They look upon the far and flashing brine,
  Upon the boundless plains, the broken height
  Of Kamiakin's battlements. The flight
Of time is underneath their untopped towers.
  They seem to push aside the moon at night,
To jostle and unloose the stars. The flowers
Of Heaven fall about their brows in shining showers.

They stand, a line of lifted snowy isles,
  High held above a tossed and tumbled sea—
A sea of wood in wild unmeasured miles:
  White pyramids of Faith, where man is free;
  White monuments of Hope, that yet shall be
The mounts of matchless and immortal song. . . .
  I look far down the hollow days; I see
The bearded prophets, simple-souled and strong,
That fill the hills and thrill with song the heeding throng.

Serene and satisfied! supreme! white, lone
  As God, they loom above cloud-banners furled;
They look as cold as kings upon a throne:

The mantling wings of night are crushed and curled
   As feathers curl. The elements are hurled
From off their bosoms, and are bidden go,
   Like evil spirits, to an under-world.
They stretch from Cariboo to Mexico,
A line of battle-tents in everlasting snow.

Africa

   Oh! she is very old. I lay,
Made dumb with awe and wonderment,
Beneath a palm before my tent,
With idle and discouraged hands,
Not many days ago, on sands
Of awful, silent Africa.
Long gazing on her ghostly shades,
That lift their bare arms in the air,
I lay. I mused where story fades
From her dark brow and found her fair.

   A slave, and old, within her veins
There runs that warm, forbidden blood
That no man dares to dignify
In elevated song. The chains
That held her race but yesterday
Hold still the hands of men. Forbid
Is Ethiop. The turbid flood
Of prejudice lies stagnant still,
And all the world is tainted. Will
And wit lie broken as a lance
Against the brazen mailèd face
Of old opinion. None advance,
Steel-clad and glad, to the attack,
With trumpet and with song. Look back!
Beneath yon pyramids lie hid
The histories of her great race. . . .
Old Nilus rolls right sullen by,

With all his secrets. Who shall say:
My father rear'd a pyramid;
My brother clipp'd the dragon's wings;
My mother was Semiramis?
Yea, harps strike idly out of place;
Men sing of savage Saxon kings
New-born and known but yesterday,
And Norman blood presumes to say. . . .

   Nay, ye who boast ancestral name
And vaunt deeds dignified by time
Must not despise her. Who hath worn
Since time began a face that is
So all-enduring, old like this—
A face like Africa's? Behold!
The Sphinx is Africa. The bond
Of silence is upon her. Old
And white with tombs, and rent and shorn;
With raiment wet with tears, and torn,
And trampled on, yet all untamed;
All naked now, yet not ashamed,—
The mistress of the young world's prime,
Whose obelisks still laugh at Time,
And lift to heaven her fair name,
Sleeps satisfied upon her fame.

   Beyond the Sphinx, and still beyond,
Beyond the tawny desert-tomb
Of Time; beyond tradition, loom
And lift ghostlike from out the gloom
Her thousand cities, battle-torn
And grey with story and with Time.
Her humblest ruins are sublime;
Her thrones with mosses overborne
Make velvets for the feet of Time.

   She points a hand and cries: "Go read
The letter'd obelisks that lord
Old Rome, and know my name and deed.

My archives these, and plunder'd when
I had grown weary of all men."
We turn to these; we cry: "Abhorr'd
Old Sphinx, behold, we cannot read!"

In Père La Chaise

I.

An avenue of tombs! I stand before
The tomb of Abelard and Eloise.
A long, a dark bent line of cypress trees
Leads past and on to other shrines; but o'er
This tomb the boughs hang darkest and most dense,
Like leaning mourners clad in black. The sense
Of awe oppresses you. This solitude
Means more than common sorrow. Down the wood
Still lovers pass, then pause, then turn again,
And weep like silent, unobtrusive rain.

II.

'Tis but a simple, antique tomb that kneels
As one that weeps above the broken clay.
'Tis stained with storms, 'tis eaten well away,
Nor half the old-new story now reveals
Of heart that held beyond the tomb to heart.
But oh, it tells of love! And that true page
Is more in this cold, hard, commercial age,
When love is calmly counted some lost art,
Than all man's mighty monuments of war
Or archives vast of art and science are.

III.

Here poets pause and dream a listless hour;
Here silly pilgrims stoop and kiss the clay;
Here sweetest maidens leave a cross or flower,
While vandals bear the tomb in bits away.

The ancient stone is scarred with name and scrawl
Of many tender fools. But over all,
And high above all other scrawls, is writ
One simple thing, most touching and most fit.
Some pitying soul has tiptoed high above,
And with a nail has scrawled but this: "O Love!"

IV.

O Love! . . . I turn; I climb the hill of tombs,
Where sleeps the "bravest of the brave," below,
His bed of scarlet blooms in zone of snow—
No cross nor sign, save this red bed of blooms,
I see grand tombs to France's lesser dead,—
Colossal steeds, white pyramids, still red
At base with blood, still torn with shot and shell,
To testify that here the Commune fell:
And yet I turn once more from all of these,
And stand before the tomb of Eloise.

At Our Golden Gate

At our gate he groaneth, groaneth,
Chafes as chained, and chafes all day;
As leashed greyhound moaneth, moaneth,
When the master keeps away.
Men have seen him steal in lowly,
Lick the island's feet and face,
Lift a cold wet nose up slowly,
Then turn empty to his place:
Empty, idle, hungered, waiting
For some hero, dauntless-souled,
Glory-loving, pleasure-hating,
Minted in God's ancient mold.

What ship yonder stealing, stealing,
Pirate-like, as if ashamed?
Black men, brown men, red, revealing—
Not one white man to be named!

What flag yonder, proud, defiant,
Topmast, saucy, and sea blown?
Tall ships lordly and reliant—
All flags yonder save our own!
Surged atop yon half-world water
Once a tuneful tall ship ran;
Ran the storm king, too, and caught her,
Caught and laughed as laughs a man:

Laughed and held her, and so holden,
Holden high, foam-crest and free
As famed harper, hoar and olden,
Held his great harp on his knee.
Then his fingers wildly flinging
Through chords, ropes—such symphony
As if some wild Wagner singing—
Some wild Wagner of the sea!
Sang he of such poor cowed weaklings,
Cowed, weak landsmen such as we.
While ten thousand storied sea kings
Foam-white, storm-blown, sat the sea.

Oh, for England's old sea thunder!
Oh, for England's bold sea men,
When we banged her over, under
And she banged us back again!
Better old time strife and stresses,
Cloud top't towers, walls, distrust;
Better wars than lazinesses,
Better loot than wine and lust!
Give us seas? Why, we have oceans!
Give us manhood, sea men, men!
Give us deeds, loves, hates, emotions!
Else give back these seas again.

Columbus

Behind him lay the gray Azores,
  Behind the Gates of Hercules;
Before him not the ghost of shores,
  Before him only shoreless seas.
The good mate said: "Now must we pray,
  For lo! the very stars are gone.
Brave Adm'r'l, speak; what shall I say?"
  "Why, say: 'Sail on! sail on! and on!' "

"My men grow mutinous day by day;
  My men grow ghastly wan and weak."
The stout mate thought of home; a spray
  Of salt wave washed his swarthy cheek.
"What shall I say, brave Adm'r'l, say,
  If we sight naught but seas at dawn?"
"Why, you shall say at break of day:
  'Sail on! sail on! sail on! and on!' "

They sailed and sailed, as winds might blow,
  Until at last the blanched mate said:
"Why, now not even God would know
  Should I and all my men fall dead.
These very winds forget their way,
  For God from these dread seas is gone.
Now speak, brave Adm'r'l; speak and say——"
  He said: "Sail on! sail on! and on!"

They sailed. They sailed. Then spake the mate:
  "This mad sea shows its teeth to-night.
He curls his lip, he lies in wait,
  With lifted teeth, as if to bite!
Brave Adm'r'l, say but one good word;
  What shall we do when hope is gone?"
The words leapt as a leaping sword:
  "Sail on! sail on! sail on! and on!"

Then, pale and worn, he kept his deck,
    And peered through darkness. Ah, that night
Of all dark nights! And then a speck—
    A light! A light! A light! A light!
It grew, a starlit flag unfurled!
    It grew to be Time's burst of dawn.
He gained a world; he gave that world
    Its grandest lesson: "On! sail on!"

ABRAM JOSEPH RYAN

(1838–1886)

Lines

Respectfully Inscribed to the Ladies' Memorial Association
of Fredericksburg, Va.

Gather the sacred dust
  Of the warriors tried and true,
Who bore the Flag of our nation's trust,
And fell in a cause as great as just,
  And died for me and you.

Wherever the brave have died
  They should not rest apart;
Living they struggled side by side—
Why should the hand of Death divide
  A single heart from heart?

Gather them, each and all,
  From the Private to the Chief;
Came they from cabin or lordly hall,
Over their dust let the fresh tears fall
  Of a nation's holy grief.

No matter whence they came—
  Dear is their lifeless clay—
Whether unknown or known to fame,
Their cause and country were the same—
  They died—and wore the Gray.

Gather the corpses strown
  O'er many a battle plain—
From many a grave that lies so lone,
Without a name and without a stone—
  Gather the Southern slain.

And the dead shall meet the dead,
   While the living o'er them weep;
For the men whom Lee and Stonewall led,
And the hearts that once together bled,
   Should now together sleep.

WILLIAM REED HUNTINGTON

(1838–1909)

The Cold Meteorite

While through our air thy kindling course was run
   A momentary glory filled the night;
    The envious stars shone fainter, for thy light
Garnered the wealth of all their fires in one.
Ah, short-lived splendor! journey ill-begun!
   Half-buried in the Earth that broke thy flight,
    No longer in thy broidered raiment dight,
Here liest thou dishonored, cold, undone.
"Nay, critic mine, far better 't is to die
   "The death that flashes gladness, than alone,
"In frigid dignity, to live on high;
    "Better in burning sacrifice be thrown
"Against the world to perish, than the sky
    "To circle endlessly a barren stone."

Lowlands

As one who goes from holding converse sweet
   In cloistered walls with great ones of the past,
   And steps, enwrapt in visions high and vast,
To meet his fellows in the noisy street;
So we, descending from the mountain's height,
   Feel strange discordance in the world below.
   Is this the calm that there enchanted so?
It cannot be that we beheld aright.
But courage! not for ever on the mount;
   Far oftener in the valley must we move;
   The things that lie about us learn to love,
And for the work allotted us account;
   Content if, now and then, we track above
The tumbling waters to their placid fount.

From Green Mountain

I.

Two seas our eyes beheld—one dark, one light;
    And one above the other; for a screen
    Of billowy cloud lay, level-poised, between
Ocean and sky, in undulation white
As snows of Zembla. Half-way up the height
    That caps Mount Désert, spell-bound by the scene,
    We stood and marvelled. Had there ever been,
Since Israel's pilgrim march, so weird a sight?
Meanwhile the sailors, beating to and fro
    On shadowed waters, dreamed not of the still,
    Pellucid beauty of that upper day;
Their captive eyes saw only from below,
    While we, from our sheer lookout on the hill,
    Scanned either level, happier-placed than they.

II.

Brief our advantage; presently the sun,
    Nearing the noon-mark, gathered all his might,
    And smote those vapors till they broke in flight;
Not hastily, for panic there was none,
But with slow movement Eastward, one by one,
    The cloud battalions drifted from our sight,
    Till everywhere, from verge to verge, was light;
And those below saw clear, as we had done.
God shows enfranchised spirits, such as thine,
    Dear friend, dear brother, who beside me stood
    That morning on the mount, both sides of things;
The dim, the bright; the earthly, the divine.
    Spirits in shadow see but one. Oh, would
    The days were born of which the Sibyl sings!

JOHN HAY

(1838–1905)

Jim Bludso,

Of the Prairie Belle

Wall, no! I can't tell whar he lives,
　　Becase he don't live, you see;
Leastways, he's got out of the habit
　　Of livin' like you and me.
Whar have you been for the last three year
　　That you haven't heard folks tell
How Jimmy Bludso passed in his checks
　　The night of the Prairie Belle?

He weren't no saint,—them engineers
　　Is all pretty much alike,—
One wife in Natchez-under-the-Hill
　　And another one here, in Pike;
A keerless man in his talk was Jim,
　　And an awkward hand in a row,
But he never flunked, and he never lied,—
　　I reckon he never knowed how.

And this was all the religion he had,—
　　To treat his engine well;
Never be passed on the river
　　To mind the pilot's bell;
And if ever the Prairie Belle took fire,—
　　A thousand times he swore,
He'd hold her nozzle agin the bank
　　Till the last soul got ashore.

All boats has their day on the Mississip,
　　And her day come at last,—
The Movastar was a better boat,
　　But the Belle she *wouldn't* be passed.

And so she come tearin' along that night—
    The oldest craft on the line—
With a nigger squat on her safety-valve,
    And her furnace crammed, rosin and pine.

The fire bust out as she clared the bar,
    And burnt a hole in the night,
And quick as a flash she turned, and made
    For that willer-bank on the right.
There was runnin' and cursin', but Jim yelled out,
    Over all the infernal roar,
"I'll hold her nozzle agin the bank
    Till the last galoot's ashore."

Through the hot, black breath of the burnin' boat
    Jim Bludso's voice was heard,
And they all had trust in his cussedness,
    And knowed he would keep his word.
And, sure's you're born, they all got off
    Afore the smokestacks fell,—
And Bludso's ghost went up alone
    In the smoke of the Prairie Belle.

He weren't no saint,—but at jedgment
    I'd run my chance with Jim,
'Longside of some pious gentlemen
    That wouldn't shook hands with him.
He seen his duty, a dead-sure thing,—
    And went for it thar and then;
And Christ ain't a going to be too hard
    On a man that died for men.

HENRY ADAMS

(1838–1918)

Buddha and Brahma

To John Hay

The Buddha, known to men by many names—
Siddartha, Sakya Muni, Blessed One,—
Sat in the forest, as had been his wont
These many years since he attained perfection;
In silent thought, abstraction, purity,
His eyes fixed on the Lotus in his hand,
He meditated on the perfect Life,
While his disciples, sitting round him, waited
His words of teaching, every syllable
More and more precious as the Master gently
Warned them how near was come his day of parting.
In silence, as the Master gave example,
They meditated on the Path and Law,
Till one, Malunka, looking up and speaking,
Said to the Buddha: "O Omniscient One,
Teach us, if such be in the Perfect Way,
Whether the World exists eternally."

The Buddha made no answer, and in silence
All the disciples bent their contemplation
On the perfection of the Eight-fold Way,
Until Malunka spoke again: "O Master,
What answer shall we offer to the Brahman
Who asks us if our Master holds the World
To be, or not, Eternal?"
                              Still the Buddha sat
As though he heard not, contemplating
The pure white Lotus in his sacred hand,
Till a third time Malunka questioned him:
"Lord of the World, we know not what we ask;
We fear to teach what thou hast not made pure."

Then gently, still in silence, lost in thought,
The Buddha raised the Lotus in his hand,
His eyes bent downward, fixed upon the flower.
No more! A moment so he held it only,
Then his hand sank into its former rest.

Long the disciples pondered on the lesson.
Much they discussed its mystery and meaning,
Each finding something he could make his own,
Some hope or danger in the Noble Way,
Some guide or warning to the Perfect Life.
Among them sat the last of the disciples,
Listening and pondering, silently and still;
And when the scholars found no certain meaning
In Buddha's answer to Malunka's prayer,
The young man pondered: I will seek my father,
The wisest man of all men in the world,
And he with one word will reveal this secret,
And make me in an instant reach the light
Which these in many years have not attained
Though guided by the Buddha and the Law.

So the boy sought his father—an old man
Famous for human wisdom, subtle counsel,
Boldness in action, recklessness in war—
Gautama's friend, the Rajah of Mogadha.
No follower of Buddha, but a Brahman,
Devoted first to Vishnu, then to caste,
He made no sign of anger or remonstrance
When his son left him at Siddartha's bidding
To take the vows of poverty and prayer—
If Vishnu willed it, let his will be done!

The Rajah sat at evening in his palace,
Deep in the solitude of his own thought,
When silently the young man entering
Crouched at a distance, waiting till his father
Should give some sign of favor. Then he spoke:
"Father, you are wise! I come to ask you
A secret meaning none of us can read;

For, when Malunka three times asked the Master
Whether the world was or was not eternal,
Siddartha for a moment lifted up
The Lotus, and kept silence."

The Rajah pondered long, with darkened features,
As though in doubt increasing. Then he said:
"Reflect, my son! The Master had not meant
This last and deepest lesson to be learned
From any but himself—by any means
But silent thought, abstraction, purity,
The living spirit of his Eight-fold Way,
The jewels of his Lotus. Least of all
Had he, whose first and easiest lesson taught
The nothingness of caste, intended you
To seek out me, a Warrior, Kshatriya,
Knowing no duties but to caste and sword,
To teach the Buddha and unveil his shrine.
My teaching is not his; mine not his way;
You quit your Master when you question me."

Silent they sat, and long. Then slowly spoke
The younger: "Father, you are wise.
I must have Wisdom." "Not so, my son.
Old men are often fools, but young men always.
Your duty is to act; leave thought to us."
The younger sat in patience, eyes cast down,
Voice low and gentle as the Master taught;
But still repeated the same prayer: "You are wise;
I must have wisdom. Life for me is thought,
But, were it action, how, in youth or age,
Can man act wisely, leaving thought aside?"

The Rajah made no answer, but almost
His mouth seemed curving to a sudden smile
That hardened to a frown; and then he spoke:
"If Vishnu wills it, let his will be done!
The child sees jewels on his father's sword,
And cries until he gets it for a plaything.
He cannot use it but to wound himself;

Its perfect workmanship wakes no delight;
Its jewels are for him but common glass;
The sword means nothing that the child can know;
But when at last the child has grown to man,
Has learned the beauty of the weapon's art,
And proved its purpose on the necks of men,
Still must he tell himself, as I tell you:
Use it, but ask no questions! *Think not! Strike!*
This counsel you reject, for you want wisdom.
So be it! Yet I swear to you in truth
That all my wisdom lies in these three words.

"You ask Gautama's meaning, for you know
That since his birth, his thoughts and acts alike
Have been to me a mirror, clearer far
Than to himself, for no man sees himself.
With the solemnity of youth, you ask
Of me, on whom the charm of childhood still
Works greater miracles than magicians know,
To tell, as though it were a juggler's trick
The secret meaning which himself but now
Could tell you only by a mystic sign,
The symbol of a symbol—so far-thought,
So vague and vast and intricate its scope.
And I, whom you compel to speak for him,
Must give his thought through mine, for his
Passes your powers—yours and all your school.

"Your Master, Sakya Muni, Gautama,
Is, like myself and you, a Kshatriya,
And in our youths we both, like you, rebelled
Against the priesthood and their laws of caste.
We sought new paths, desperate to find escape
Out of the jungle that the priests had made.
Gautama found a path. You follow it.
I found none, and I stay here, in the jungle,
Content to tolerate what I cannot mend.
I blame not him or you, but would you know
Gautama's meaning, you must fathom mine.
He failed to cope with life; renounced its cares;

Fled to the forest, and attained the End,
Reaching the End by sacrificing life.
You know both End and Path. You, too, attain.
I could not. Ten years older, I;
Already trained to rule, to fight, to scheme,
To strive for objects that I dared not tell,
Not for myself alone, but for us all;
Had I thrown down my sword, and fled my throne,
Not all the hermits, priests, and saints of Ind,
Buddhist or Brahman, could have saved our heads
From rolling in the dirt; for Rajahs know
A quicker than the Eight-fold Noble Way
To help their scholars to attain the End.
Renounce I could not, and could not reform.
How could I battle with the Brahman priests,
Or free the people from the yoke of caste,
When, with the utmost aid that priests could give,
And willing service from each caste in turn,
I saved but barely both my throne and them.

"So came it that our paths were separate,
And his led up to so supreme a height
That from its summit he can now look down
And see where still the jungle stifles me.
Yet was our starting-point the same, and though
We now seem worlds apart—hold fast to this!—
The Starting-point must be the End-point too!
You know the Veda, and need not be taught
The first and last idea of all true knowledge:
One single spirit from which all things spring;
One thought containing all thoughts possible;
Not merely those that we, in our thin reason,
Hold to be true, but all their opposites;
For Brahma is Beginning, Middle, End,
Matter and Mind, Time, Space, Form, Life and Death.
The Universal has no limit. Thought
Travelling in constant circles, round and round,
Must ever pass through endless contradictions,
Returning on itself at last, till lost
In silence.

"This is the Veda, as you know,
The alphabet of all philosophy,
For he who cannot or who dares not grasp
And follow this necessity of Brahma,
Is but a fool and weakling; and must perish
Among the follies of his own reflection.

"Your Master, you, and I, and all wise men,
Have one sole purpose which we never lose:
Through different paths we each seek to attain,
Sooner or later, as our paths allow,
A perfect union with the single Spirit.
Gautama's way is best, but all are good.
He breaks a path at once to what he seeks.
By silence and absorption he unites
His soul with the great soul from which it started.
But we, who cannot fly the world, must seek
To live two separate lives; one, in the world
Which we must ever seem to treat as real;
The other in ourselves, behind a veil
Not to be raised without disturbing both.

"The Rajah is an instrument of Brahma,
No more, no less, than sunshine, lightning, rain;
And when he meets resistance in his path,
And when his sword falls on a victim's neck,
It strikes as strikes the lightning—as it must;
Rending its way through darkness to the point
It needs must seek, by no choice of its own.
Thus in the life of Ruler, Warrior, Master,
The wise man knows his wisdom has no place,
And when most wise, we act by rule and law,
Talk to conceal our thought, and think
Only within the range of daily need,
Ruling our subjects while ourselves rebel,
Death always on our lips and in our act.

"This is the jungle in which we must stay,
According to the teachings of the Master,
Never can we attain the Perfect Life.

Yet in this world of selfishness and striving
The wise man lives as deeply sunk in silence,
As conscious of the Perfect Life he covets,
As any recluse in his forest shadows,
As any Yogi in his mystic trances.
We need no Noble Way to teach us Freedom
Amid the clamor of a world of slaves.
We need no Lotus to love purity
Where life is else corruption.

"So read Siddartha's secret! He has taught
A certain pathway to attain the End;
And best and simplest yet devised by man,
Yet still so hard that every energy
Must be devoted to its sacred law.
Then, when Malunka turns to ask for knowledge,
Would seek what lies beyond the Path he teaches,
What distant horizon transcends his own,
He bids you look in silence on the Lotus.
For you, he means no more. For me, this meaning
Points back and forward to that common goal
From which all paths diverge; to which,
All paths must tend—Brahma, the only Truth!

"Gautama tells me my way too is good;
Life, Time, Space, Thought, the World, the Universe
End where they first begin, in one sole Thought
Of Purity in Silence."

JAMES RYDER RANDALL

(1839–1908)

Maryland

The despot's heel is on thy shore,
    Maryland!
His torch is at thy temple door,
    Maryland!
Avenge the patriotic gore
That flecked the streets of Baltimore,
And be the battle-queen of yore,
    Maryland! My Maryland!

Hark to a wand'ring son's appeal,
    Maryland!
My mother State! to thee I kneel,
    Maryland!
For life and death, for woe and weal,
Thy peerless chivalry reveal,
And gird thy beauteous limbs with steel,
    Maryland! My Maryland!

Thou wilt not cower in the dust,
    Maryland!
Thy beaming sword shall never rust,
    Maryland!
Remember Carroll's sacred trust,
Remember Howard's warlike thrust—
And all thy slumberers with the just,
    Maryland! My Maryland!

Come! 'tis the red dawn of the day,
    Maryland!
Come! with thy panoplied array,
    Maryland!
With Ringgold's spirit for the fray,

With Watson's blood at Monterey,
With fearless Lowe and dashing May,
    Maryland! My Maryland!

Come! for thy shield is bright and strong,
    Maryland!
Come! for thy dalliance does thee wrong,
    Maryland!
Come! to thine own heroic throng,
That stalks with Liberty along,
And give a new *Key* to thy song,
    Maryland! My Maryland!

Dear Mother! burst the tyrant's chain,
    Maryland!
Virginia should not call in vain,
    Maryland!
She meets her sisters on the plain—
"*Sic semper,*" 'tis the proud refrain,
That baffles minions back amain,
    Maryland!
Arise, in majesty again,
    Maryland! My Maryland!

I see the blush upon thy cheek,
    Maryland!
But thou wast ever bravely meek,
    Maryland!
But lo! there surges forth a shriek
From hill to hill, from creek to creek—
Potomac calls to Chesapeake,
    Maryland! My Maryland!

Thou wilt not yield the Vandal toll,
    Maryland!
Thou wilt not crook to his control,
    Maryland!
Better the fire upon thee roll,

Better the blade, the shot, the bowl,
Than crucifixion of the soul,
    Maryland! My Maryland!

I hear the distant thunder-hum,
    Maryland!
The Old Line's bugle, fife and drum,
    Maryland!
She is not dead, nor deaf, nor dumb—
Huzza! she spurns the Northern scum!
She breathes—she burns! she'll come! she'll come!
    Maryland! My Maryland!

CONSTANCE FENIMORE WOOLSON

(1840–1894)

Love Unexpressed

The sweetest notes among the human heart-strings
    Are dull with rust;
The sweetest chords, adjusted by the angels,
    Are clogged with dust;
We pipe and pipe again our dreary music
    Upon the self-same strains,
While sounds of crime, and fear, and desolation,
    Come back in sad refrains.

On through the world we go, an army marching
    With listening ears,
Each longing, sighing, for the heavenly music
    He never hears;
Each longing, sighing, for a word of comfort,
    A word of tender praise,
A word of love, to cheer the endless journey
    Of earth's hard, busy days.

They love us, and we know it; this suffices
    For reason's share.
Why should they pause to give that love expression
    With gentle care?
Why should they pause? But still our hearts are aching
    With all the gnawing pain
Of hungry love that longs to hear the music,
    And longs and longs in vain.

We love them, and they know it; if we falter,
    With fingers numb,
Among the unused strings of love's expression,
    The notes are dumb.

We shrink within ourselves in voiceless sorrow,
    Leaving the words unsaid,
And, side by side with those we love the dearest,
    In silence on we tread.

Thus on we tread, and thus each heart in silence
    Its fate fulfils,
Waiting and hoping for the heavenly music
    Beyond the distant hills.
The only difference of the love in heaven
    From love on earth below
Is: Here we love and know not how to tell it,
    And there we all shall know.

The Florida Beach

Our drift-wood fire burns drowsily,
    The fog hangs low afar,
A thousand sea-birds fearlessly
    Hover above the bar;
Our boat is drawn far up the strand,
    Beyond the tide's long reach;
Like a fringe to the dark green winter land,
    Shines the silvery Florida beach.

Behind, the broad pine barrens lie
    Without a path or trail,
Before, the ocean meets the sky
    Without a rock or sail.
We call across to Africa,
    As a poet called to Spain:
A murmur of "Antony! Antony!"
    The waves bring back in refrain.

Far to the south the beach shines on,
    Dotted with giant shells;
Coral sprays from the white reef won,
    Radiate spiny cells;

Glass-like creatures that ride the waves,
   With azure sail and oar,
And wide-mouthed things from the deep sea caves
   That melt away on the shore.

Wild ducks gaze as we pass along:
   They have not learned to fear;
The mocking-bird keeps on his song
   In the low palmetto near;
The sluggish stream from the everglade
   Shows the alligator's track,
And the sea is broken in light and shade
   With the heave of the dolphin's back.

The Spanish light-house stands in haze:
   The keeper trims his light;
No sail he sees through the long, long days,
   No sail through the still, still night;
But ships that pass far out at sea,
   Along the warm Gulf Stream,
From Cuba and tropic Carribee,
   Keep watch for his distant gleam.

Alone, alone we wander on,
   In the southern winter day.
Through the dreamy veil the fog has spun
   The world seems far away;
The tide comes in—the birds fly low,
   As if to catch our speech.
Ah, Destiny! Why must we ever go
   Away from the Florida beach?

Detroit River

Thou brimming river, full, how full
Thou sweepest by thy even banks!
E'en one drop more, thou must o'erflow
The velvet land, where pluméd ranks

Of inland grains come calmly down
To the smooth edge, and dip their feet
Within thy still dark-flowing tide,
Where, almost brushed in passing, glide
The dark hulls of the freshwater fleet.

Sweep on, O river, past the green—
The indolent Canadian farms
With low thatched house and old-time mill
Stretch down to meet thy clasping arms;
The grey small churches lift on high
Their crosses, and the long watch keep
Over the deep-grassed churchyards where
'Mong sunken tombstones clustered there,
The old French *habitans* lie asleep.

Insouciant French! your fathers sailed
These Lakes as Kings;—but now their claims
From Gaspé Bay to far La Pointe,
Live only in the Gallic names
They gave;—sweet echoes from the past,
Chiming from cliff and strait and bay,
Mixed with the vowelled Indian tongue,
And fainter, fainter, fainter rung,—
Till now forgotten,—dying away.

Sweep on, O river. Thou dost bind
The mighty Lakes with thy soft sheen
Of silver water; Huron's blue,
And dark Superior, and the green
Of Michigan do come to thee,
And flow where thou dost say, thy shore
Doth feel their coolness hasting by,—
But haste not, river;—stay where I
Love thee, remember thee, evermore.

EDWARD ROWLAND SILL

(1841–1887)

The Fool's Prayer

The royal feast was done; the King
  Sought some new sport to banish care,
And to his jester cried: "Sir Fool,
  Kneel now, and make for us a prayer!"

The jester doffed his cap and bells,
  And stood the mocking court before;
They could not see the bitter smile
  Behind the painted grin he wore.

He bowed his head, and bent his knee
  Upon the monarch's silken stool;
His pleading voice arose: "O Lord,
  Be merciful to me, a fool!

"No pity, Lord, could change the heart
  From red with wrong to white as wool;
The rod must heal the sin; but Lord,
  Be merciful to me, a fool!

" 'Tis not by guilt the onward sweep
  Of truth and right, O Lord, we stay;
'Tis by our follies that so long
  We hold the earth from heaven away.

"These clumsy feet, still in the mire,
  Go crushing blossoms without end;
These hard, well-meaning hands we thrust
  Among the heart-strings of a friend.

"The ill-timed truth we might have kept—
  Who knows how sharp it pierced and stung?
The word we had not sense to say—
  Who knows how grandly it had rung?

"Our faults no tenderness should ask,
    The chastening stripes must cleanse them all;
But for our blunders—oh, in shame
    Before the eyes of heaven we fall.

"Earth bears no balsam for mistakes;
    Men crown the knave, and scourge the tool
That did his will; but Thou, O Lord,
    Be merciful to me, a fool!"

The room was hushed; in silence rose
    The King, and sought his gardens cool,
And walked apart, and murmured low,
    "Be merciful to me, a fool!"

Opportunity

This I beheld, or dreamed it in a dream:—
There spread a cloud of dust along a plain;
And underneath the cloud, or in it, raged
A furious battle, and men yelled, and swords
Shocked upon swords and shields. A prince's banner
Wavered, then staggered backward, hemmed by foes.
A craven hung along the battle's edge,
And thought, "Had I a sword of keener steel—
That blue blade that the king's son bears,—but this
Blunt thing—!" he snapt and flung it from his hand,
And lowering crept away and left the field.
Then came the king's son, wounded, sore bestead,
And weaponless, and saw the broken sword,
Hilt-buried in the dry and trodden sand,
And ran and snatched it, and with battle-shout
Lifted afresh he hewed his enemy down,
And saved a great cause that heroic day.

Truth at Last

Does a man ever give up hope, I wonder,—
Face the grim fact, seeing it clear as day?
When Bennen saw the snow slip, heard its thunder
Low, louder, roaring round him, felt the speed
Grow swifter as the avalanche hurled downward,
Did he for just one heart-throb—did he indeed
Know with all certainty, as they swept onward,
There was the end, where the crag dropped away?
Or did he think, even till they plunged and fell,
Some miracle would stop them? Nay, they tell
That he turned round, face forward, calm and pale,
Stretching his arms out toward his native vale
As if in mute, unspeakable farewell,
And so went down.—'T is something, if at last,
Though only for a flash, a man may see
Clear-eyed the future as he sees the past,
From doubt, or fear, or hope's illusion free.

California Winter

This is not winter: where is the crisp air,
And snow upon the roof, and frozen ponds,
And the star-fire that tips the icicle?

Here blooms the late rose, pale and odorless;
And the vague fragrance in the garden walks
Is but a doubtful dream of mignonette.
In some smooth spot, under a sleeping oak
That has not dreamed of such a thing as spring,
The ground has stolen a kiss from the cool sun
And thrilled a little, and the tender grass
Has sprung untimely, for these great bright days,
Staring upon it, will not let it live.
The sky is blue, and 't is a goodly time,
And the round, barren hillsides tempt the feet;

But 't is not winter: such as seems to man
What June is to the roses, sending floods
Of life and color through the tingling veins.

   It is a land without a fireside. Far
Is the old home, where, even this very night,
Roars the great chimney with its glorious fire,
And old friends look into each other's eyes
Quietly, for each knows the other's trust.

   Heaven is not far away such winter nights:
The big white stars are sparkling in the east,
And glitter in the gaze of solemn eyes;
For many things have faded with the flowers,
And many things their resurrection wait;
Earth like a sepulchre is sealed with frost,
And Morn and Even beside the silent door
Sit watching, and their soft and folded wings
Are white with feathery snow.

               Yet even here
We are not quite forgotten by the Hours,
Could human eyes but see the beautiful
Save through the glamour of a memory.
Soon comes the strong south wind, and shouts aloud
Its jubilant anthem. Soon the singing rain
Comes from warm seas, and in its skyey tent
Enwraps the drowsy world. And when, some night,
Its flowing folds invisibly withdraw,
Lo! the new life in all created things.
The azure mountains and the ocean gates
Against the lovely sky stand clean and clear
As a new purpose in the wiser soul.

CHARLES EDWARD CARRYL

(1841–1920)

A Nautical Ballad

A capital ship for an ocean trip
    Was "The Walloping Window-blind;"
No gale that blew dismayed her crew
    Or troubled the captain's mind.
The man at the wheel was taught to feel
    Contempt for the wildest blow,
And it often appeared, when the weather had cleared,
    That he'd been in his bunk below.

The boatswain's mate was very sedate,
    Yet fond of amusement, too;
And he played hop-scotch with the starboard watch,
    While the captain tickled the crew.
And the gunner we had was apparently mad,
    For he sat on the after-rail,
And fired salutes with the captain's boots,
    In the teeth of the booming gale.

The captain sat in a commodore's hat,
    And dined, in a royal way,
On toasted pigs and pickles and figs
    And gummery bread, each day.
But the cook was Dutch, and behaved as such;
    For the food that he gave the crew
Was a number of tons of hot-cross buns,
    Chopped up with sugar and glue.

And we all felt ill as mariners will,
    On a diet that's cheap and rude;
And we shivered and shook as we dipped the cook
    In a tub of his gluesome food.
Then nautical pride we laid aside,

And we cast the vessel ashore
On the Gulliby Isles, where the Poohpooh smiles,
   And the Anagazanders roar.

Composed of sand was that favored land,
   And trimmed with cinnamon straws;
And pink and blue was the pleasing hue
   Of the Tickletoeteaser's claws.
And we sat on the edge of a sandy ledge
   And shot at the whistling bee;
And the Binnacle-bats wore water-proof hats
   As they danced in the sounding sea.

On rubagub bark, from dawn to dark,
   We fed, till we all had grown
Uncommonly shrunk,—when a Chinese junk
   Came by from the torriby zone.
She was stubby and square, but we didn't much care,
   And we cheerily put to sea;
And we left the crew of the junk to chew
   The bark of the rubagub tree.

SIDNEY LANIER

(1842–1881)

Hymns of the Marshes

Sunrise

In my sleep I was fain of their fellowship, fain
    Of the live-oak, the marsh, and the main.
The little green leaves would not let me alone in my sleep;
Up-breathed from the marshes, a message of range and of
              sweep,
Interwoven with wafture of wild sea-liberties, drifting,
   Came through the lapped leaves sifting, sifting,
     Came to the gates of sleep.
  Then my thoughts, in the dark of the dungeon-keep
Of the Castle of Captives hid in the City of Sleep,
   Upstarted, by twos and by threes assembling:
    The gates of sleep fell a-trembling
Like as the lips of a lady that forth falter *yes*,
    Shaken with happiness:
    The gates of sleep stood wide.

I have waked, I have come, my beloved! I might not abide:
I have come ere the dawn, O beloved, my live-oaks, to hide
    In your gospelling glooms,—to be
As a lover in heaven, the marsh my marsh and the sea my
          sea.

  Tell me, sweet burly-bark'd, man-bodied Tree
  That mine arms in the dark are embracing, dost know
  From what fount are these tears at thy feet which flow?
They rise not from reason, but deeper inconsequent deeps.
    Reason's not one that weeps.
    What logic of greeting lies
Betwixt dear over-beautiful trees and the rain of the eyes?

O cunning green leaves, little masters! like as ye gloss
All the dull-tissued dark with your luminous darks that
           emboss
   The vague blackness of night into pattern and plan,
               So,
  (But would I could know, but would I could know,)
With your question embroid'ring the dark of the question of
           man, —
So, with your silences purfling this silence of man
While his cry to the dead for some knowledge is under the
           ban,
     Under the ban, —
     So, ye have wrought me
Designs on the night of our knowledge, — yea, ye have
           taught me,
               So,
  That haply we know somewhat more than we know.

  Ye lispers, whisperers, singers in storms,
  Ye consciences murmuring faiths under forms,
  Ye ministers meet for each passion that grieves,
  Friendly, sisterly, sweetheart leaves,
  Oh, rain me down from your darks that contain me
  Wisdoms ye winnow from winds that pain me, —
  Sift down tremors of sweet-within-sweet
  That advise me of more than they bring, — repeat
  Me the woods-smell that swiftly but now brought breath
  From the heaven-side bank of the river of death, —
  Teach me the terms of silence, — preach me
  The passion of patience, — sift me, — impeach me, —
      And there, oh there
As ye hang with your myriad palms upturned in the air,
    Pray me a myriad prayer.

    My gossip, the owl, — is it thou
  That out of the leaves of the low-hanging bough,
    As I pass to the beach, art stirred?
    Dumb woods, have ye uttered a bird?

       *   *   *   *   *

Reverend Marsh, low-couched along the sea,
  Old chemist, rapt in alchymy,
    Distilling silence, — lo,
That which our father-age had died to know —
The menstruum that dissolves all matter — thou
Hast found it: for this silence, filling now
The globèd clarity of receiving space,
This solves us all: man, matter, doubt, disgrace,
    Death, love, sin, sanity,
Must in yon silence's clear solution lie.
Too clear! That crystal nothing who'll peruse?
The blackest night could bring us brighter news.
  Yet precious qualities of silence haunt
  Round these vast margins, ministrant.
Oh, if thy soul's at latter gasp for space,
With trying to breathe no bigger than thy race
Just to be fellow'd, when that thou hast found
No man with room, or grace, enough of bound
To entertain that New thou tell'st, thou art, —
'Tis here, 'tis here, thou canst unhand thy heart
  And breathe it free, and breathe it free,
By rangy marsh, in lone sea-liberty.

The tide's at full: the marsh with flooded streams
Glimmers, a limpid labyrinth of dreams.
Each winding creek in grave entrancement lies,
A rhapsody of morning-stars. The skies
  Shine scant with one forked galaxy, —
The marsh brags ten: looped on his breast they lie.

    Oh, what if a sound should be made!
    Oh, what if a bound should be laid
To this bow-and-string tension of beauty and silence
          a-spring, —
To the bend of beauty the bow, or the hold of silence the
          string!
I fear me, I fear me yon dome of diaphanous gleam
  Will break as a bubble o'er-blown in a dream, —
Yon dome of too-tenuous tissues of space and of night,
  Over-weighted with stars, over-freighted with light,

Over-sated with beauty and silence, will seem
　　But a bubble that broke in a dream,
　If a bound of degree to this grace be laid,
　　Or a sound or a motion made.

But no: it is made: list! somewhere,—mystery, where?
　　　　　In the leaves? in the air?
　　　In my heart? is a motion made:
'Tis a motion of dawn, like a flicker of shade on shade.
In the leaves, 'tis palpable: low multitudinous stirring
Upwinds through the woods; the little ones, softly
　　　　　conferring,
Have settled, my lord's to be looked for; so; they are still;
　But the air and my heart and the earth are a-thrill,—
And look where the wild duck sails round the bend of the
　　　　　river,—
　　And look where a passionate shiver
　　Expectant is bending the blades
Of the marsh-grass in serial shimmers and shades,—
And invisible wings, fast fleeting, fast fleeting,
　　　　　　Are beating
The dark overhead as my heart beats,—and steady and free
　Is the ebb-tide flowing from marsh to sea
　　　　(Run home, little streams,
　　With your lapfulls of stars and dreams);—
　And a sailor unseen is hoisting a-peak,
　For list, down the inshore curve of the creek
　　How merrily flutters the sail,—
　And lo, in the east! Will the East unveil?
　The East is unveiled, the East hath confessed
A flush: 'tis dead; 'tis alive: 'tis dead, ere the West
Was aware of it: nay, 'tis abiding, 'tis unwithdrawn:
　　Have a care, sweet Heaven! 'Tis Dawn.

　　　　　*　　*　　*　　*　　*

Now a dream of a flame through that dream of a flush is
　　　　　uprolled:
To the zenith ascending, a dome of undazzling gold
Is builded, in shape as a bee-hive, from out of the sea:
The hive is of gold undazzling, but oh, the Bee,

The star-fed Bee, the build-fire Bee,
—Of dazzling gold is the great Sun-Bee
That shall flash from the hive-hole over the sea.

Yet now the dew-drop, now the morning gray,
Shall live their little lucid sober day
Ere with the sun their souls exhale away.
Now in each pettiest personal sphere of dew
The summ'd morn shines complete as in the blue
Big dew-drop of all heaven: with these lit shrines
O'er-silvered to the farthest sea-confines,
The sacramental marsh one pious plain
Of worship lies. Peace to the ante-reign
Of Mary Morning, blissful mother mild,
Minded of nought but peace, and of a Child.

Not slower than Majesty moves, for a mean and a
                    measure
Of motion,—not faster than dateless Olympian leisure
Might pace with unblown ample garments from pleasure to
                    pleasure,—
The wave-serrate sea-rim sinks, unjarring, unreeling,
    Forever revealing, revealing, revealing,
Edgewise, bladewise, halfwise, wholewise,—'tis done!
            Good-morrow, lord Sun!
    With several voice, with ascription one,
    The woods and the marsh and the sea and my soul
Unto thee, whence the glittering stream of all morrows
                    doth roll,
Cry good and past-good and most heavenly morrow, lord
            Sun.

O Artisan born in the purple,—Workman Heat,—
Parter of passionate atoms that travail to meet
And be mixed in the death-cold oneness,—innermost Guest
At the marriage of elements,—fellow of publicans,—blest
King in the blouse of flame, that loiterest o'er
The idle skies yet laborest fast evermore—

            *   *   *   *   *

Thou, in the fine forge-thunder, thou, in the beat
Of the heart of a man, thou Motive,—Laborer Heat:
Yea, Artist, thou, of whose art yon sea's all news,
With his inshore greens and manifold mid-sea blues,
Pearl-glint, shell-tint, ancientest perfectest hues
    Ever shaming the maidens,—lily and rose
    Confess thee, and each mild flame that glows
In the clarified virginal bosoms of stones that shine,
         It is thine, it is thine:
Thou chemist of storms, whether driving the winds a-swirl
Or a-flicker the subtiler essences polar that whirl
In the magnet earth,—yea, thou with a storm for a heart,
Rent with debate, many-spotted with question, part
From part oft sundered, yet ever a globèd light,
Yet ever the artist, ever more large and bright
Than the eye of a man may avail of:—manifold One,
I must pass from thy face, I must pass from the face of the
         Sun:
Old Want is awake and agog, every wrinkle a-frown;
The worker must pass to his work in the terrible town:
But I fear not, nay, and I fear not the thing to be done;
    I am strong with the strength of my lord the Sun:
How dark, how dark soever the race that must needs be run,
         I am lit with the Sun.

    Oh, never the mast-high run of the seas
         Of traffic shall hide thee,
Never the hell-colored smoke of the factories
           Hide thee,
Never the reek of the time's fen-polities
           Hide thee,
And ever my heart through the night shall with knowledge
         abide thee,
And ever by day shall my spirit, as one that hath tried thee,
Labor, at leisure, in art,—till yonder beside thee
    My soul shall float, friend Sun,
       The day being done.

The Cloud

Sail on, sail on, fair cousin Cloud;
Oh, loiter hither from the sea.
  Still-eyed and shadow-brow'd,
Steal off from yon far-drifting crowd,
And come and brood upon the marsh with me.

Yon laboring low horizon-smoke,
Yon stringent sail, toil not for thee
  Nor me: did heaven's stroke
The whole deep with drown'd commerce choke,
No pitiless tease of risk or bottomry

Would to thy rainy office close
Thy will, or lock mine eyes from tears
  Part wept for traders'-woes,
Part for that ventures mean as those
In issue bind such sovereign hopes and fears.

Stern Cloud, thy downward countenance stares
Blank on the blank-faced marsh, and thou
  Mindest of dark affairs;
Thy substance seems a warp of cares;
Like late wounds run the wrinkles on thy brow.

Well may'st thou pause, and gloom, and stare,
A visible conscience; I arraign
  Thee, criminal Cloud, of rare
Contempts on Mercy, Right, and Prayer,
Of murders, arsons, thefts, of nameless stain.

Yet though life's logic grow as gray
As thou, my soul's not in eclipse.
  Cold Cloud, but yesterday
Thy lightning slew a child at play,
And then a priest with prayers upon his lips

For his enemies, and then a bright
Lady that did but ope the door

Upon the stormy night
To let a beggar in,—strange spite,—
And then thy sulky rain refused to pour

Till thy quick torch a barn had burned
Where twelve months' store of victual lay
    A widow's sons had earned,
Which done, thy floods of rain returned,—
The river raped their little herd away.

What myriad righteous errands high
Thy flames *might* run on! In that hour
    Thou slewest the child, oh why
Not rather slay Calamity,
Breeder of Pain and Doubt, infernal Power?

Or why not plunge thy blades about
Some maggot politician throng
    Swarming to parcel out
The body of a land, and rout
The maw-conventicle, and ungorge Wrong?

> *What the cloud doeth,*
> *The Lord knoweth,*
> *The cloud knoweth not.*
> *What the artist doeth,*
> *The Lord knoweth;*
> *Knoweth the artist not?*

Well-answered! O dear artists, ye
—Whether in forms of curve or hue
    Or tone, your gospels be—
Say wrong, *This work is not of me,*
But God: it is not true, it is not true.

Awful is Art, because 'tis free.
The artist trembles o'er his plan,
    Where men his Self must see.
Who made a song or picture, he
Did it, and not another, God nor man.

My Lord is large, my Lord is strong:
Giving, He gave: my me is mine.
    How poor, how strange, how wrong,
To dream He wrote the little song
I made to Him with love's unforced design!

Oh, not as clouds dim laws have plann'd
To strike down Good and fight for Ill,
    Oh, not as harps that stand
In the wind and sound the wind's command:
Each artist—gift of terror!—owns his will.

For thee, Cloud,—if thou spend thine all
Upon the South's o'er-brimming sea
    That needs thee not; or crawl
To the dry provinces, and fall
Till every convert clod shall give to thee

Green worship; if thou grow or fade,
Bring mad delight or misery,
    Fly east or west, be made
Snow, hail, rain, wind, grass, rose, light, shade;—
What is it all to thee? There is no thee.

Pass, kinsman Cloud, now fair and mild:
Discharge the will that's not thine own.
    I work in freedom wild,
But work, as plays a little child,
Sure of the Father, Self, and Love, alone.

Marsh Song—At Sunset

Over the monstrous shambling sea,
    Over the Caliban sea,
Bright Ariel-cloud, thou lingerest:
Oh wait, oh wait, in the warm red West,—
    Thy Prospero I'll be.

Over the humped and fishy sea,
    Over the Caliban sea,

O cloud in the West, like a thought in the heart
Of pardon, loose thy wing and start,
  And do a grace for me.

Over the huge and huddling sea,
  Over the Caliban sea,
Bring hither my brother Antonio,—Man,—
My injurer: night breaks the ban;
  Brother, I pardon thee.

The Marshes of Glynn

Glooms of the live-oaks, beautiful-braided and woven
With intricate shades of the vines that myriad-cloven
 Clamber the forks of the multiform boughs,—
   Emerald twilights,—
   Virginal shy lights,
Wrought of the leaves to allure to the whisper of vows,
When lovers pace timidly down through the green
    colonnades
 Of the dim sweet woods, of the dear dark woods,
  Of the heavenly woods and glades,
That run to the radiant marginal sand-beach within
  The wide sea-marshes of Glynn;—

 Beautiful glooms, soft dusks in the noon-day fire,—
 Wildwood privacies, closets of lone desire,
Chamber from chamber parted with wavering arras of
    leaves,—
Cells for the passionate pleasure of prayer to the soul that
    grieves,
 Pure with a sense of the passing of saints through the
    wood,
 Cool for the dutiful weighing of ill with good;—

O braided dusks of the oak and woven shades of the vine,
While the riotous noon-day sun of the June-day long did
    shine,
Ye held me fast in your heart and I held you fast in mine;

But now when the noon is no more, and riot is rest,
And the sun is a-wait at the ponderous gate of the West,
And the slant yellow beam down the wood-aisle doth
seem
Like a lane into heaven that leads from a dream, —
Ay, now, when my soul all day hath drunken the soul of the
oak,
And my heart is at ease from men, and the wearisome sound
of the stroke
Of the scythe of time and the trowel of trade is low,
And belief overmasters doubt, and I know that I know,
And my spirit is grown to a lordly great compass within,
That the length and the breadth and the sweep of the
marshes of Glynn
Will work me no fear like the fear they have wrought me
of yore
When length was fatigue, and when breadth was but
bitterness sore,
And when terror and shrinking and dreary unnamable
pain
Drew over me out of the merciless miles of the plain, —
Oh, now, unafraid, I am fain to face
The vast sweet visage of space.
To the edge of the wood I am drawn, I am drawn,
Where the gray beach glimmering runs, as a belt of the
dawn,
For a mete and a mark
To the forest-dark: —
So:
Affable live-oak, leaning low, —
Thus — with your favor — soft, with a reverent hand,
(Not lightly touching your person, Lord of the land!)
Bending your beauty aside, with a step I stand
On the firm-packed sand,
Free
By a world of marsh that borders a world of sea.
Sinuous southward and sinuous northward the
shimmering band
Of the sand-beach fastens the fringe of the marsh to the
folds of the land.

Inward and outward to northward and southward the beach-
        lines linger and curl
As a silver-wrought garment that clings to and follows the
        firm sweet limbs of a girl.
    Vanishing, swerving, evermore curving again into sight,
    Softly the sand-beach wavers away to a dim gray looping
        of light.
    And what if behind me to westward the wall of the woods
        stands high?
    The world lies east: how ample, the marsh and the sea and
        the sky!
    A league and a league of marsh-grass, waist-high, broad in
        the blade,
    Green, and all of a height, and unflecked with a light or a
        shade,
        Stretch leisurely off, in a pleasant plain,
        To the terminal blue of the main.

    Oh, what is abroad in the marsh and the terminal sea?
        Somehow my soul seems suddenly free
    From the weighing of fate and the sad discussion of sin,
    By the length and the breadth and the sweep of the
        marshes of Glynn.
Ye marshes, how candid and simple and nothing-
        withholding and free
Ye publish yourselves to the sky and offer yourselves to the
        sea!
Tolerant plains, that suffer the sea and the rains and the sun,
Ye spread and span like the catholic man who hath mightily
        won
    God out of knowledge and good out of infinite pain
    And sight out of blindness and purity out of a stain.

    As the marsh-hen secretly builds on the watery sod,
    Behold I will build me a nest on the greatness of God:
    I will fly in the greatness of God as the marsh-hen flies
    In the freedom that fills all the space 'twixt the marsh and
        the skies:
    By so many roots as the marsh-grass sends in the sod
    I will heartily lay me a-hold on the greatness of God:

Oh, like to the greatness of God is the greatness within
The range of the marshes, the liberal marshes of Glynn.

And the sea lends large, as the marsh: lo, out of his plenty
        the sea
    Pours fast: full soon the time of the flood-tide must be:
        Look how the grace of the sea doth go
    About and about through the intricate channels that flow
        Here and there,
            Everywhere,
Till his waters have flooded the uttermost creeks and the
        low-lying lanes,
    And the marsh is meshed with a million veins,
    That like as with rosy and silvery essences flow
        In the rose-and-silver evening glow.
            Farewell, my lord Sun!
    The creeks overflow: a thousand rivulets run
    'Twixt the roots of the sod; the blades of the marsh-grass
        stir;
Passeth a hurrying sound of wings that westward whirr;
Passeth, and all is still; and the currents cease to run;
        And the sea and the marsh are one.

    How still the plains of the waters be!
    The tide is in his ecstasy.
    The tide is at his highest height:
        And it is night.

And now from the Vast of the Lord will the waters of
        sleep
    Roll in on the souls of men,
    But who will reveal to our waking ken
    The forms that swim and the shapes that creep
        Under the waters of sleep?
And I would I could know what swimmeth below when the
        tide comes in
On the length and the breadth of the marvellous marshes of
        Glynn.

"Who made thee thy last spring doublet"

Who made thee thy last spring doublet, Cavalier Earth,
That sat so trim to the curve of thy manful girth
       As thou wert a-riding?—'Twas he.—
Who brought thee, Ship, straight over the surly sea,
     Forging steadily, westward steadily,
     Sails hilarious, sea-current readily
       Serving?—He:
     Out of two caldrons of air and sea
He wrought me the trade-wind that faithfully blew me,
Set me the sea-tide that servant-wise drew me,
     Forging steadily, westward steadily,
       Over the surly sea.

Clover

Inscribed to the Memory of John Keats

Dear uplands, Chester's favorable fields,
My large unjealous Loves, many yet one—
A grave good-morrow to your Graces, all,
Fair tilth and fruitful seasons!
                Lo, how still!
The midmorn empties you of men, save me;
Speak to your lover, meadows! None can hear.
I lie as lies yon placid Brandywine,
Holding the hills and heavens in my heart
For contemplation.
            'Tis a perfect hour.
From founts of dawn the fluent autumn day
Has rippled as a brook right pleasantly
Half-way to noon; but now with widening turn
Makes pause, in lucent meditation locked,
And rounds into a silver pool of morn,
Bottom'd with clover-fields. My heart just hears
Eight lingering strokes of some far village-bell,
That speak the hour so inward-voiced, meseems
Time's conscience has but whispered him eight hints

Of revolution. Reigns that mild surcease
That stills the middle of each rural morn—
When nimble noises that with sunrise ran
About the farms have sunk again to rest;
When Tom no more across the horse-lot calls
To sleepy Dick, nor Dick husk-voiced upbraids
The sway-back'd roan for stamping on his foot
With sulphurous oath and kick in flank, what time
The cart-chain clinks across the slanting shaft,
And, kitchenward, the rattling bucket plumps
Souse down the well, where quivering ducks quack loud,
And Susan Cook is singing.
                                    Up the sky
The hesitating moon slow trembles on,
Faint as a new-washed soul but lately up
From out a buried body. Far about,
A hundred slopes in hundred fantasies
Most ravishingly run, so smooth of curve
That I but seem to see the fluent plain
Rise toward a rain of clover-bloom, as lakes
Pout gentle mounds of plashment up to meet
Big shower-drops. Now the little winds, as bees,
Bowing the blooms come wandering where I lie
Mixt soul and body with the clover-tufts,
Light on my spirit, give from wing and thigh
Rich pollens and divine sweet irritants
To every nerve, and freshly make report
Of inmost Nature's secret autumn-thought
Unto some soul of sense within my frame
That owns each cognizance of the outlying five,
And sees, hears, tastes, smells, touches, all in one.

Tell me, dear Clover (since my soul is thine,
Since I am fain give study all the day,
To make thy ways my ways, thy service mine,
To seek me out thy God, my God to be,
And die from out myself to live in thee)—
Now, Cousin Clover, tell me in mine ear:
Go'st thou to market with thy pink and green?
Of what avail, this color and this grace?

Wert thou but squat of stem and brindle-brown,
Still careless herds would feed. A poet, thou:
What worth, what worth, the whole of all thine art?
Three-Leaves, instruct me! I am sick of price.

Framed in the arching of two clover-stems
Where-through I gaze from off my hill, afar,
The spacious fields from me to Heaven take on
Tremors of change and new significance
To th' eye, as to the ear a simple tale
Begins to hint a parable's sense beneath.
The prospect widens, cuts all bounds of blue
Where horizontal limits bend, and spreads
Into a curious-hill'd and curious-valley'd Vast,
Endless before, behind, around; which seems
Th' incalculable Up-and-Down of Time
Made plain before mine eyes. The clover-stems
Still cover all the space; but now they bear,
For clover-blooms, fair, stately heads of men
With poets' faces heartsome, dear and pale—
Sweet visages of all the souls of time
Whose loving service to the world has been
In the artist's way expressed and bodied. Oh,
In arms' reach, here be Dante, Keats, Chopin,
Raphael, Lucretius, Omar, Angelo,
Beethoven, Chaucer, Schubert, Shakspere, Bach,
And Buddha (sweetest masters! Let me lay
These arms this once, this humble once, about
Your reverend necks—the most containing clasp,
For all in all, this world e'er saw!), and there,
Yet further on, bright throngs unnamable
Of workers worshipful, nobilities
In the Court of Gentle Service, silent men,
Dwellers in woods, brooders on helpful art,
And all the press of them, the fair, the large,
That wrought with beauty.
                          Lo, what bulk is here?
Now comes the Course-of-things, shaped like an Ox,
Slow browsing, o'er my hillside, ponderously—
The huge-brawned, tame, and workful Course-of-things,

That hath his grass, if earth be round or flat,
And hath his grass, if empires plunge in pain
Or faiths flash out. This cool, unasking Ox
Comes browsing o'er my hills and vales of Time,
And thrusts me out his tongue, and curls it, sharp
And sicklewise, about my poets' heads,
And twists them in, all—Dante, Keats, Chopin,
Raphael, Lucretius, Omar, Angelo,
Beethoven, Chaucer, Schubert, Shakspere, Bach,
And Buddha, in one sheaf—and champs and chews,
With slanty-churning jaws, and swallows down;
Then slowly plants a mighty forefoot out,
And makes advance to futureward, one inch.
So: they have played their part.
                              And to this end?
This, God? This, troublous-breeding Earth? This, Sun
Of hot, quick pains? To this no-end that ends,
These Masters wrought, and wept, and sweated blood,
And burned, and loved, and ached with public shame,
And found no friends to breathe their loves to, save
Woods and wet pillows? This was all? This Ox?
"Nay," quoth a sum of voices in mine ear,
"God's clover, we, and feed His Course-of-things;
The pasture is God's pasture; systems strange
Of food and fiberment He hath, whereby
The general brawn is built for plans of His
To quality precise. Kinsman, learn this:
The artist's market is the heart of man;
The artist's price, some little good of man.
Tease not thy vision with vain search for ends.
The End of Means is art that works by love.
The End of Ends . . . in God's Beginning's lost."

The Waving of the Corn

Ploughman, whose gnarly hand yet kindly wheeled
  Thy plough to ring this solitary tree
    With clover, whose round plat, reserved a-field,

In cool green radius twice my length may be—
   Scanting the corn thy furrows else might yield,
To pleasure August, bees, fair thoughts, and me,
    That here come oft together—daily I,
     Stretched prone in summer's mortal ecstasy,
Do stir with thanks to thee, as stirs this morn
      With waving of the corn.

   Unseen, the farmer's boy from round the hill
Whistles a snatch that seeks his soul unsought,
   And fills some time with tune, howbeit shrill;
The cricket tells straight on his simple thought—
   Nay, 'tis the cricket's way of being still;
The peddler bee drones in, and gossips naught;
    Far down the wood, a one-desiring dove
    Times me the beating of the heart of love:
And these be all the sounds that mix, each morn,
      With waving of the corn.

   From here to where the louder passions dwell,
Green leagues of hilly separation roll:
   Trade ends where yon far clover ridges swell.
Ye terrible Towns, ne'er claim the trembling soul
   That, craftless all to buy or hoard or sell,
From out your deadly complex quarrel stole
    To company with large amiable trees,
    Suck honey summer with unjealous bees,
And take Time's strokes as softly as this morn
      Takes waving of the corn.

Song of the Chattahoochee

   Out of the hills of Habersham,
    Down the valleys of Hall,
I hurry amain to reach the plain,
Run the rapid and leap the fall,
Split at the rock and together again,
Accept my bed, or narrow or wide,

And flee from folly on every side
With a lover's pain to attain the plain
    Far from the hills of Habersham,
    Far from the valleys of Hall.

    All down the hills of Habersham,
    All through the valleys of Hall,
The rushes cried *Abide, abide,*
The willful waterweeds held me thrall,
The laving laurel turned my tide,
The ferns and the fondling grass said *Stay,*
The dewberry dipped for to work delay,
And the little reeds sighed *Abide, abide,*
    Here in the hills of Habersham,
    Here in the valleys of Hall.

    High o'er the hills of Habersham,
    Veiling the valleys of Hall,
The hickory told me manifold
Fair tales of shade, the poplar tall
Wrought me her shadowy self to hold,
The chestnut, the oak, the walnut, the pine,
Overleaning, with flickering meaning and sign,
Said, *Pass not, so cold, these manifold*
    Deep shades of the hills of Habersham,
    These glades in the valleys of Hall.

    And oft in the hills of Habersham,
    And oft in the valleys of Hall,
The white quartz shone, and the smooth brook-stone
Did bar me of passage with friendly brawl,
And many a luminous jewel lone
—Crystals clear or a-cloud with mist,
Ruby, garnet and amethyst—
Made lures with the lights of streaming stone
    In the clefts of the hills of Habersham,
    In the beds of the valleys of Hall.

    But oh, not the hills of Habersham,
    And oh, not the valleys of Hall

Avail: I am fain for to water the plain.
Downward the voices of Duty call—
Downward, to toil and be mixed with the main,
The dry fields burn, and the mills are to turn,
And a myriad flowers mortally yearn,
And the lordly main from beyond the plain
     Calls o'er the hills of Habersham,
     Calls through the valleys of Hall.

From the Flats

    What heartache—ne'er a hill!
Inexorable, vapid, vague, and chill
The drear sand-levels drain my spirit low.
With one poor word they tell me all they know;
Whereat their stupid tongues, to tease my pain,
Do drawl it o'er again and o'er again.
They hurt my heart with griefs I cannot name:
    Always the same, the same.

    Nature hath no surprise,
No ambuscade of beauty 'gainst mine eyes
From brake or lurking dell or deep defile;
No humors, frolic forms—this mile, that mile;
No rich reserves or happy-valley hopes
Beyond the bends of roads, the distant slopes.
Her fancy fails, her wild is all run tame:
    Ever the same, the same.

    Oh, might I through these tears
But glimpse some hill my Georgia high uprears,
Where white the quartz and pink the pebble shine,
The hickory heavenward strives, the muscadine
Swings o'er the slope, the oak's far-falling shade
Darkens the dogwood in the bottom glade,
And down the hollow from a ferny nook
    Bright leaps a living brook!

The Mocking Bird

Superb and sole, upon a plumèd spray
　　That o'er the general leafage boldly grew,
　　He summ'd the woods in song; or typic drew
The watch of hungry hawks, the lone dismay
Of languid doves when long their lovers stray,
　　And all birds' passion-plays that sprinkle dew
　　At morn in brake or bosky avenue.
Whate'er birds did or dreamed, this bird could say.
Then down he shot, bounced airily along
The sward, twitched-in a grasshopper, made song
　　Midflight, perched, primped, and to his art again.
　　Sweet Science, this large riddle read me plain:
　　　　How may the death of that dull insect be
　　　　The life of yon trim Shakspere on the tree?

from *Street Cries*

To Richard Wagner

I saw a sky of stars that rolled in grime.
　　All glory twinkled through some sweat of fight.
From each tall chimney of the roaring time
　　That shot his fire far up the sooty night
Mixt fuels—Labor's Right and Labor's Crime—
　　Sent upward throb on throb of scarlet light
Till huge hot blushes in the heavens blent
With golden hues of Trade's high firmament.

Fierce burned the furnaces; yet all seemed well.
　　Hope dreamed rich music in the rattling mills.
"Ye foundries, ye shall cast my church a bell,"
　　Loud cried the Future from the farthest hills:
"Ye groaning forces, crack me every shell
　　Of customs, old constraints, and narrow ills:
Thou, lithe Invention, wake and pry and guess,
Till thy deft mind invents me Happiness."

And I beheld high scaffoldings of creeds
   Crumbling from round Religion's perfect Fane:
And a vast noise of rights, wrongs, powers, needs,
   —Cries of new Faiths that called "This Way is plain,"
—Grindings of upper against lower greeds—
   —Fond sighs for old things, shouts for new,—did reign
Below that stream of golden fire that broke,
Mottled with red, above the seas of smoke.

Hark! Gay fanfares from horns of old Romance
   Strike through the clouds of clamor: who be these
That, paired in rich processional, advance
   From darkness o'er the murk mad factories
Into yon flaming road, and sink, strange Ministrants!
   Sheer down to earth, with many minstrelsies
And motions fine, and mix about the scene
And fill the Time with forms of ancient mien?

Bright ladies and brave knights of Fatherland;
   Sad mariners, no harbor e'er may hold;
A swan soft floating tow'rds a tragic strand;
   Dim ghosts, of earth, air, water, fire, steel, gold,
Wind, grief, and love; a lewd and lurking band
   Of Powers—dark Conspiracy, Cunning cold,
Gray Sorcery; magic cloaks and rings and rods;
Valkyries, heroes, Rhinemaids, giants, gods!

     *   *   *   *   *

O Wagner, westward bring thy heavenly art.
   No trifler thou: Siegfried and Wotan be
Names for big ballads of the modern heart.
   Thine ears hear deeper than thine eyes can see.
Voice of the monstrous mill, the shouting mart,
   Not less of airy cloud and wave and tree,
Thou, thou, if even to thyself unknown,
Hast power to say the Time in terms of tone.

A Ballad of Trees and the Master

Into the woods my Master went,
   Clean forspent, forspent.
Into the woods my Master came,
   Forspent with love and shame.
But the olives they were not blind to Him,
The little gray leaves were kind to Him:
The thorn-tree had a mind to Him
   When into the woods He came.

Out of the woods my Master went,
   And He was well content.
Out of the woods my Master came,
   Content with death and shame.
When Death and Shame would woo Him last,
From under the trees they drew Him last:
'Twas on a tree they slew Him—last
   When out of the woods He came.

The Raven Days

I.

Our hearths are gone out, and our hearts are broken,
   And but the ghosts of homes to us remain,
And ghostly eyes and hollow sighs give token
   From friend to friend of an unspoken pain.

II.

O, Raven Days, dark Raven Days of sorrow,
   Bring to us, in your whetted ivory beaks,
Some sign out of the far land of To-morrow,
   Some strip of sea-green dawn, some orange streaks.

III.

Ye float in dusky files, forever croaking—
    Ye chill our manhood with your dreary shade.
Pale, in the dark, not even God invoking,
    We lie in chains, too weak to be afraid.

IV.

O, Raven Days, dark Raven Days of sorrow,
    Will ever any warm light come again?
Will ever the lit mountains of To-morrow
    Begin to gleam across the mournful plain?

The Dying Words of Jackson

"Order A. P. Hill to prepare for battle."
"Tell Major Hawks to advance the Commissary train."
"Let us cross the river and rest in the shade."

The stars of Night contain the glittering Day,
And rain his glory down with sweeter grace
Upon the dark World's grand, enchanted face
    All loth to turn away.

And so the Day, about to yield his breath,
Utters the Stars unto the listening Night
To stand for burning fare-thee-wells of light
    Said on the verge of death.

O hero-life that lit us like the Sun!
O hero-words that glittered like the Stars
And stood and shone above the gloomy wars
    When the hero-life was done!

The Phantoms of a battle came to dwell
I' the fitful vision of his dying eyes—
Yet even in battle-dreams, he sends supplies
    To those he loved so well.

His army stands in battle-line arrayed:
His couriers fly: all's done—now God decide!
And not till then saw he the Other Side
    Or would accept the Shade.

Thou Land whose Sun is gone, thy Stars remain!
Still shine the words that miniature his deeds—
O Thrice-Beloved, where'er thy great heart bleeds,
    Solace hast thou for pain!

The Revenge of Hamish

It was three slim does and a ten-tined buck in the bracken
    lay;
  And all of a sudden the sinister smell of a man,
  Awaft on a wind-shift, wavered and ran
Down the hill-side and sifted along through the bracken and
    passed that way.

Then Nan got a-tremble at nostril; she was the daintiest doe;
  In the print of her velvet flank on the velvet fern
  She reared, and rounded her ears in turn.
Then the buck leapt up, and his head as a king's to a crown
    did go

Full high in the breeze, and he stood as if Death had the
    form of a deer;
  And the two slim does full lazily stretching arose,
  For their day-dream slowlier came to a close,
Till they woke and were still, breath-bound with waiting and
    wonder and fear.

Then Alan the huntsman sprang over the hillock, the hounds
    shot by,
  The does and the ten-tined buck made a marvellous bound,
  The hounds swept after with never a sound,
But Alan loud winded his horn, in sign that the quarry was
    nigh.

For at dawn of that day proud Maclean of Lochbuy to the
    hunt had waxed wild,
  And he cursed at old Alan till Alan fared off with the
    hounds
For to drive him the deer to the lower glen-grounds:
"I will kill a red deer," quoth Maclean, "in the sight of the
    wife and the child."

So gayly he paced with the wife and the child to his chosen
    stand;
  But he hurried tall Hamish the henchman ahead: "Go
    turn,"—
  Cried Maclean—"if the deer seek to cross to the burn,
Do thou turn them to me: nor fail, lest thy back be red as
    thy hand."

Now hard-fortuned Hamish, half blown of his breath with
    the height of the hill,
  Was white in the face when the ten-tined buck and the
    does
  Drew leaping to burn-ward; huskily rose
His shouts, and his nether lip twitched, and his legs were
    o'er-weak for his will.

So the deer darted lightly by Hamish and bounded away to
    the burn.
  But Maclean never bating his watch tarried waiting below
  Still Hamish hung heavy with fear for to go
All the space of an hour; then he went, and his face was
    greenish and stern,

And his eye sat back in the socket, and shrunken the eyeballs
    shone,
  As withdrawn from a vision of deeds it were shame to see.
  "Now, now, grim henchman, what is't with thee?"
Brake Maclean, and his wrath rose red as a beacon the wind
    hath upblown.

"Three does and a ten-tined buck made out," spoke Hamish,
      full mild,
    "And I ran for to turn, but my breath it was blown, and
          they passed;
    I was weak, for ye called ere I broke me my fast."
Cried Maclean: "Now a ten-tined buck in the sight of the
      wife and the child

I had killed if the gluttonous kern had not wrought me a
      snail's own wrong!"
    Then he sounded, and down came kinsmen and clansmen
          all:
    "Ten blows, for ten tine, on his back let fall,
And reckon no stroke if the blood follow not at the bite of
      thong!"

So Hamish made bare, and took him his strokes; at the last
      he smiled.
    "Now I'll to the burn," quoth Maclean, "for it still may
          be,
    If a slimmer-paunched henchman will hurry with me,
I shall kill me the ten-tined buck for a gift to the wife and
      the child!"

Then the clansmen departed, by this path and that; and
      over the hill
    Sped Maclean with an outward wrath for an inward
          shame;
    And that place of the lashing full quiet became;
And the wife and the child stood sad; and bloody-backed
      Hamish sat still.

But look! red Hamish has risen; quick about and about
      turns he.
    "There is none betwixt me and the crag-top!" he screams
          under breath.
    Then, livid as Lazarus lately from death,
He snatches the child from the mother, and clambers the
      crag toward the sea.

Now the mother drops breath; she is dumb, and her heart
      goes dead for a space,
  Till the motherhood, mistress of death, shrieks, shrieks
      through the glen,
  And that place of the lashing is live with men,
And Maclean, and the gillie that told him, dash up in a
      desperate race.

Not a breath's time for asking; an eye-glance reveals all the
      tale untold.
  They follow mad Hamish afar up the crag toward the sea,
  And the lady cries: "Clansmen, run for a fee! —
Yon castle and lands to the two first hands that shall hook
      him and hold

Fast Hamish back from the brink!"—and ever she flies up
      the steep,
  And the clansmen pant, and they sweat, and they jostle
      and strain.
  But, mother, 'tis vain; but, father, 'tis vain;
Stern Hamish stands bold on the brink, and dangles the
      child o'er the deep.

Now a faintness falls on the men that run, and they all stand
      still.
  And the wife prays Hamish as if he were God, on her
      knees,
  Crying: "Hamish! O Hamish! but please, but please
For to spare him!" and Hamish still dangles the child, with a
      wavering will.

On a sudden he turns; with a sea-hawk scream, and a gibe,
      and a song,
  Cries: "So; I will spare ye the child if, in sight of ye all,
  Ten blows on Maclean's bare back shall fall,
And ye reckon no stroke if the blood follow not at the bite
      of the thong!"

Then Maclean he set hardly his tooth to his lip that his
    tooth was red,
  Breathed short for a space, said: "Nay, but it never shall
    be!
  Let me hurl off the damnable hound in the sea!"
But the wife: "Can Hamish go fish us the child from the sea,
    if dead?

Say yea!—Let them lash *me*, Hamish?"—"Nay!"—
    "Husband, the lashing will heal;
  But, oh, who will heal me the bonny sweet bairn in his
    grave?
  Could ye cure me my heart with the death of a knave?
Quick! Love! I will bare thee—so—kneel!" Then Maclean
    'gan slowly to kneel

With never a word, till presently downward he jerked to the
    earth.
  Then the henchman—he that smote Hamish—would
    tremble and lag;
  "Strike, hard!" quoth Hamish, full stern, from the crag;
Then he struck him, and "One!" sang Hamish, and danced
    with the child in his mirth.

And no man spake beside Hamish; he counted each stroke
    with a song.
  When the last stroke fell, then he moved him a pace down
    the height,
  And he held forth the child in the heartaching sight
Of the mother, and looked all pitiful grave, as repenting a
    wrong.

And there as the motherly arms stretched out with the
    thanksgiving prayer—
  And there as the mother crept up with a fearful swift pace,
  Till her finger nigh felt of the bairnie's face—
In a flash fierce Hamish turned round and lifted the child in
    the air,

And sprang with the child in his arms from the horrible
       height in the sea,
   Shrill screeching, "Revenge!" in the wind-rush; and pallid
       Maclean,
   Age-feeble with anger and impotent pain,
Crawled up on the crag, and lay flat, and locked hold of
       dead roots of a tree—

And gazed hungrily o'er, and the blood from his back drip-
       dripped in the brine,
   And a sea-hawk flung down a skeleton fish as he flew,
   And the mother stared white on the waste of blue,
And the wind drove a cloud to seaward, and the sun began
       to shine.

AMBROSE BIERCE

(1842–1914?)

Alone

In contact, lo! the flint and steel,
By spark and flame, the thought reveal
That he the metal, she the stone,
Had cherished secretly alone.

Body-Snatcher

"One night," a doctor said, "last fall,
I and my comrades, four in all,
    When visiting a grave-yard stood
Within the shadow of a wall.

"While waiting for the moon to sink
We saw a wild hyena slink
    About a new-made grave, and then
Begin to excavate its brink!

"Shocked by the horrid act, we made
A sally from our ambuscade,
    And, falling on the unholy beast,
Dispatched him with a pick and spade."

Corporal

Fiercely the battle raged and, sad to tell,
Our corporal heroically fell!
Fame from her height looked down upon the brawl
And said: "He had n't very far to fall."

Egotist

Megaceph, chosen to serve the State
In the halls of legislative debate,
One day with all his credentials came
To the capitol's door and announced his name.
The doorkeeper looked, with a comical twist
Of the face, at the eminent egotist,
And said: "Go away, for we settle here
All manner of questions, knotty and queer,
And we cannot have, when the speaker demands
To be told how every member stands,
A man who to all things under the sky
Assents by eternally voting 'I'."

Elegy

The cur foretells the knell of parting day;
    The loafing herd winds slowly o'er the lea;
The wise man homeward plods; I only stay
    To fiddle-faddle in a minor key.

Freedom

Freedom, as every schoolboy knows,
    Once shrieked as Kosciusko fell;
On every wind, indeed, that blows
    I hear her yell.

She screams whenever monarchs meet,
    And parliaments as well,
To bind the chains about her feet
    And toll her knell.

And when the sovereign people cast
    The votes they cannot spell,
Upon the lung-impested blast
    Her clamors swell.

For all to whom the power's given
　　To sway or to compel,
Among themselves apportion heaven
　　And give her hell.

Gorgon

Who looked upon her awful brow.
We dig them out of ruins now,
And swear that workmanship so bad
Proves all the ancient sculptors mad.

Hypochondriasis

Some heaps of trash upon a vacant lot
Where long the village rubbish had been shot
Displayed a sign among the stuff and stumps—
"Hypochondriasis." It meant The Dumps.

Lead

Hail, holy Lead!—of human feuds the great
　　And universal arbiter; endowed
　　With penetration to pierce any cloud
Fogging the field of controversial hate,
And with a swift, inevitable, straight,
　　Searching precision find the unavowed
　　But vital point. Thy judgment, when allowed
By the chirurgeon, settles the debate.
O useful metal!—were it not for thee
　　We'd grapple one another's ears alway:
But when we hear thee buzzing like a bee
　　We, like old Muhlenberg, "care not to stay."
And when the quick have run away like pullets
Jack Satan smelts the dead to make new bullets.

Nose

There's a man with a Nose,
And wherever he goes
The people run from him and shout:
"No cotton have we
For our ears if so be
He blow that interminous snout!"

So the lawyers applied
For injunction. "Denied,"
Said the Judge: "the defendant prefixion,
Whate'er it portend,
Appears to transcend
The bounds of this court's jurisdiction."

Orthography

A spelling reformer indicted
For fudge was before the court cicted.
The judge said: "Enough—
His candle we'll snough,
And his sepulchre shall not be whicted."

Prospect

Blow, blow, ye spicy breezes—
O'er Ceylon blow your breath,
Where every prospect pleases,
Save only that of death.

Rimer

The rimer quenches his unheeded fires,
The sound surceases and the sense expires.
Then the domestic dog, to east and west,
Expounds the passions burning in his breast.
The rising moon o'er that enchanted land
Pauses to hear and yearns to understand.

Safety-Clutch

Once I seen a human ruin
    In a elevator-well,
And his members was bestrewin'
    All the place where he had fell.

And I says, apostrophisin'
    That uncommon woful wreck:
"Your position's so surprisin'
    That I tremble for your neck!"

Then that ruin, smilin' sadly
    And impressive, up and spoke:
"Well, I wouldn't tremble badly,
    For it's been a fortnight broke."

Then, for further comprehension
    Of his attitude, he begs
I will focus my attention
    On his various arms and legs—

How they all are contumacious;
    Where they each, respective, lie;
How one trotter proves ungracious,
    T'other one an *alibi*.

These particulars is mentioned
    For to show his dismal state,
Which I wasn't first intentioned
    To specifical relate.

None is worser to be dreaded
    That I ever have heard tell
Than the gent's who there was spreaded
    In that elevator-well.

Now this tale is allegoric—
    It is figurative all,
For the well is metaphoric
    And the feller didn't fall.

I opine it isn't moral
    For a writer-man to cheat,
And despise to wear a laurel
    As was gotten by deceit.

For 'tis Politics intended
    By the elevator, mind,
It will boost a person splendid
    If his talent is the kind.

Col. Bryan had the talent
    (For the busted man is him)
And it shot him up right gallant
    Till his head begun to swim.

Then the rope it broke above him
    And he painful come to earth
Where there's nobody to love him
    For his detrimented worth.

Though he's livin' none would know him,
    Or at leastwise not as such.
Moral of this woful poem:
    Frequent oil your safety-clutch.

The Passing Show

I.

I know not if it was a dream. I viewed
A city where the restless multitude,
  Between the eastern and the western deep
Had reared gigantic fabrics, strong and rude.

Colossal palaces crowned every height;
Towers from valleys climbed into the light;
  O'er dwellings at their feet, great golden domes
Hung in the blue, barbarically bright.

But now, new-glimmering to-east, the day
Touched the black masses with a grace of gray,
  Dim spires of temples to the nation's God
Studding high spaces of the wide survey.

Well did the roofs their solemn secret keep
Of life and death stayed by the truce of sleep,
  Yet whispered of an hour when sleepers wake,
The fool to hope afresh, the wise to weep.

The gardens greened upon the builded hills
Above the tethered thunders of the mills
  With sleeping wheels unstirred to service yet
By the tamed torrents and the quickened rills.

A hewn acclivity, reprieved a space,
Looked on the builder's blocks about his base
  And bared his wounded breast in sign to say:
"Strike! 't is my destiny to lodge your race.

" 'T was but a breath ago the mammoth browsed
  Upon my slopes, and in my caves I housed
    Your shaggy fathers in their nakedness,
While on their foeman's offal they caroused."

Ships from afar afforested the bay,
Within their huge and chambered bodies lay
    The wealth of continents; and merrily sailed
The hardy argosies to far Cathay.

Beside the city of the living spread—
Strange fellowship!—the city of the dead;
    And much I wondered what its humble folk,
To see how bravely they were housed, had said.

Noting how firm their habitations stood,
Broad-based and free of perishable wood—
    How deep in granite and how high in brass
The names were wrought of eminent and good,

I said: "When gold or power is their aim,
The smile of beauty or the wage of shame,
    Men dwell in cities; to this place they fare
When they would conquer an abiding fame."

From the red East the sun—a solemn rite—
Crowned with a flame the cross upon a height
    Above the dead; and then with all his strength
Struck the great city all aroar with light!

II.

I know not if it was a dream. I came
Unto a land where something seemed the same
    That I had known as 't were but yesterday,
But what it was I could not rightly name.

It was a strange and melancholy land,
Silent and desolate. On either hand
    Lay waters of a sea that seemed as dead,
And dead above it seemed the hills to stand.

Grayed all with age, those lonely hills—ah me,
How worn and weary they appeared to be!
  Between their feet long dusty fissures clove
The plain in aimless windings to the sea.

One hill there was which, parted from the rest,
Stood where the eastern water curved a-west.
  Silent and passionless it stood. I thought
I saw a scar upon its giant breast.

The sun with sullen and portentous gleam
Hung like a menace on the sea's extreme;
  Nor the dead waters, nor the far, bleak bars
Of cloud were conscious of his failing beam.

It was a dismal and a dreadful sight,
That desert in its cold, uncanny light;
  No soul but I alone to mark the fear
And imminence of everlasting night!

All presages and prophecies of doom
Glimmered and babbled in the ghastly gloom,
  And in the midst of that accursèd scene
A wolf sat howling on a broken tomb.

To the Bartholdi Statue

O Liberty, God-gifted—
  Young and immortal maid—
In your high hand uplifted,
  The torch declares your trade.

Its crimson menace, flaming
  Upon the sea and shore,
Is, trumpet-like, proclaiming
  That Law shall be no more.

Austere incendiary,
  We're blinking in the light;
Where is your customary
  Grenade of dynamite?

Where are your staves and switches
  For men of gentle birth?
Your mask and dirk for riches?
  Your chains for wit and worth?

Perhaps, you've brought the halters
  You used in the old days,
When round religion's altars
  You stabled Cromwell's bays?

Behind you, unsuspected,
  Have you the axe, fair wench,
Wherewith you once collected
  A poll-tax from the French?

America salutes you—
  Preparing to disgorge.
Take everything that suits you,
  And marry Henry George.

The Statesmen

How blest the land that counts among
  Her sons so many good and wise,
To execute great feats of tongue
  When troubles rise.

Behold them mounting every stump
  Our liberty by speech to guard.
Observe their courage—see them jump
  And come down hard!

"Walk up, walk up!" each cries aloud,
    "And learn from me what you must do
To turn aside the thunder cloud,
        The earthquake too.

"Beware the wiles of yonder quack
    Who stuffs the ears of all that pass.
I—I alone can show that black
        Is white as grass."

They shout through all the day and break
    The silence of the night as well,
They'd make—I wish they'd *go* and make—
        Of Heaven a Hell.

A advocates free silver, B
    Free trade and C free banking laws.
Free board, clothes, lodging would from me
        Win warm applause.

Lo, D lifts up his voice: "You see
    The single tax on land would fall
On all alike." More evenly
        No tax at all.

"With paper money" bellows E
    "We'll all be rich as lords." No doubt—
And richest of the lot will be
        The chap without.

As many "cures" as addle wits
    Who know not what the ailment is!
Meanwhile the patient foams and spits
        Like a gin fizz.

Alas, poor Body Politic,
    Your fate is all too clearly read:
To be not altogether quick,
        Nor very dead.

You take your exercise in squirms,
  Your rest in fainting fits between.
'T is plain that your disorder's worms—
      Worms fat and lean.

Worm Capital, Worm Labor dwell
  Within your maw and muscle's scope.
Their quarrels make your life a Hell,
      Your death a hope.

God send you find not such an end
  To ills however sharp and huge!
God send you convalesce! God send
      You vermifuge.

RICHARD WATSON GILDER

(1844–1909)

The Sonnet

(In Answer to a Question.)

What is a sonnet? 'T is the pearly shell
   That murmurs of the far-off murmuring sea;
   A precious jewel carved most curiously;
   It is a little picture painted well.
What is a sonnet? 'T is the tear that fell
   From a great poet's hidden ecstasy;
   A two-edged sword, a star, a song—ah me!
   Sometimes a heavy-tolling funeral bell.
This was the flame that shook with Dante's breath;
   The solemn organ whereon Milton played,
   And the clear glass where Shakespeare's shadow falls:
A sea this is—beware who ventureth!
   For like a fjord the narrow floor is laid
   Deep as mid-ocean to the sheer mountain walls.

On the Bay

This watery vague how vast! This misty globe,
Seen from this center where the ferry plies,—
It plies, but seems to poise in middle air,—
Soft gray below gray heavens, and in the west
A rose-gray memory of the sunken sun;
And, where gray water touches grayer sky,
A band of darker gray pricked out with lights,—
A diamond-twinkling circlet bounding all;
And where the statue looms, a quenchless star;
And where the lighthouse, a red, pulsing flame;
While the great bridge its starry diadem
Shows through the gray, itself in grayness lost!

An Hour in a Studio

Each picture was a painted memory
Of the far plains he loved, and of their life
Weird, mystical, dark, inarticulate, —
And cities hidden high against the blue,
Whose sky-hung steps one Indian could guard.
The enchanted Mesa there its fated wall
Lifted, and all its story lived again, —
How, in the happy planting time, the strong
Went down to push the seeds into the sand,
Leaving the old and sick. Then reeled the world
And toppled to the plain the perilous path.
Death climbed another way to them who stayed.
He showed us pictured thirst, a dreadful sight;
And many tales he told that might have come, —
Brought by some planet-wanderer, —fresh from Mars,
Or from the silver deserts of the moon.

But I remember better than all else
One night he told of in that land of fright, —
The love-songs swarthy men sang to their herds
On the high plains to keep the beasts in heart;
Piercing the silence one keen tenor voice
Singing "Ai nostri monti" clear and high:
Instead of stakes and fences round about
They circled them with music in the night.

GEORGE WASHINGTON CABLE

(1844–1925)

Creole Slave Songs

Belle Layotte

> *I done been 'roun' to evvy spot*
> *Don't foun' nair match fo' sweet Layotte.*

I done hunt all dis settle*ment*
All de way 'roun' fum Pierre Soniat';
Never see yalla gal w'at kin
'Gin to lay 'longside sweet Layotte.

> *I done been, etc.*

I yeh dey talk 'bout 'Loïse gal—
Loïse, w'at b'long to Pierre Soniat';
I see her, but she can't biggin
Stan' up 'longside my sweet Layotte.

> *I done been, etc.*

I been meet up wid John Bayou,
Say to him, "John Bayou, my son,
Yalla gal nevva meet yo' view
Got a face lak dat chahmin' one!"

> *I done been, etc.*

The Song of Cayetano's Circus

Dass Cap'm Cayetano,
    W'at comin' fum Havano,
Wid 'is monkey' an' 'is nag'!
An' one man w'at dance in bag,
An' mans dance on dey han'—cut shine'
An' gallop hoss sem time drink wine!
An' b'u'ful young missy dah beside,
Ridin' 'dout air sadd' aw brid'e;
To tell h-all dat—he cann' be tole.
Man teck a sword an' swall' 'im whole!
Beas'es? ev'y sawt o' figgah!
Dat show ain't fo' no common niggah!
Dey don' got deh no po' white cuss'—
Sunbu'nt back!—to holla an' fuss.
Dass ladies fine, and gennymuns gran',
Fetchin' dey chilluns dah—all han'!
    Fo' see Cayetano,
    W'at come fum Havano
Wid 'is monkey' an' 'is nag'!

"The English muskets went bim! bim!"

The English muskets went bim! bim!
Kentucky rifles went zim! zim!
I said to myself, save your skin!
I scampered along the water's edge;
When I got back it was day-break.
Mistress flew into a passion;
She had me whipped at the 'four stakes,'
Because I didn't stay with master;
But the 'four stakes' for me is better than
A musket shot from an Englishman.

The Dirge of St. Malo

Alas! young men, come, make lament
For poor St. Malo in distress!
They chased, they hunted him with dogs,
They fired at him with a gun,

They hauled him from the cypress swamp.
His arms they tied behind his back,
They tied his hands in front of him;
They tied him to a horse's tail,
They dragged him up into the town.
Before those grand Cabildo men
They charged that he had made a plot
To cut the throats of all the whites.
They asked him who his comrades were;
Poor St. Malo said not a word!
The judge his sentence read to him,
And then they raised the gallows-tree.
They drew the horse—the cart moved off—
And left St. Malo hanging there.
The sun was up an hour high
When on the Levee he was hung;
They left his body swinging there,
For carrion crows to feed upon.

Criole Candjo

One day one young Creole candio,
Mo' fineh dan sho nuf white beau,
    Kip all de time meckin' free—
    "Swithawt, meck merrie wid me."
"Naw, sah, I dawn't want meck merrie, me.
Naw, sah, I dawn't want meck merrie."

I go teck walk in wood close by;
But Creole tek' sem road, and try
    All time, all time, to meck free—

"Swithawt, meck merrie wid me."
"Naw, sah, I dawn't want meck merrie, me.
Naw, sah, I dawn't want meck merrie."

But him slide roun' an' roun' dis chile,
Tell, jis' fo' sheck 'im off lill while,
    Me, I was bleedze fo' say, "Shoo!
    If I'll meck merrie wid you?
O, yass, I ziss leave meck merrie me;
Yass, seh, I ziss leave meck merrie."

You-alls w'at laugh at me so well,
I wish you'd knowed dat Creole swell,
    Wid all 'is swit, smilin' trick'.
    'Pon my soul! you'd done say, quick,
"O, yass, I ziss leave meck merrie, me;
Yass, seh, I ziss leave meck merrie."

JOHN BANISTER TABB

(1845–1909)

The Bridge

Where, as a lordly dream,
Glides the deep-winding stream
    For evermore,
Calm, as in conscious strength,
Bends thy majestic length,
    From shore to shore.

Life, in its fevered heat,
Surges, with pulsing feet,
    Restless, above;
Doomed, in its anxious flow,
Like the strong tide below,
    Onward to move.

Strange is the motley throng!
Hearts yet untaught of wrong,
    Thoughtless of pain,
Mingle with souls accurs'd,
Sands in a desert thirst—
    Clouds without rain.

While o'er thee and below
Swift the twin currents flow,
    Thy form serene,
Still as the shades that sleep,
On the reflecting deep
    Arches between.

O, teach thy power to me,
Calm mid all storm to be,
    And evermore,
Over Time's restless tide,
World-weary feet to guide
    From shore to shore!

Echoes

Where of old, responsive
  As the wind and foam,
Rose the joyous echoes,
  Desolate I roam,
Nor find one lingering sound to hail the wanderer home.

Silence, long unbroken,
  Break thy rigid spell!
Free the fairy captives
  Of the mountain dell,
If yet in veiling mist the mimic minions dwell.

Children of the distance,
  Shall I call in vain?
From your slumbers waking,
  Speak to me again
As erst in childhood woke your soft Æolian strain!

Hark! the wavy chorus,
  Faint and far away,
Like a dream returning
  In the light of day,—
Too fond to flee; alas! too timorous to stay!

Hints of heavenly voices,
  Tone for silvery tone,
Move in rarer measures
  Than to us are known,
Still wooing hence to worlds beyond the shadowy zone.

Pausing, still they linger
  As in love's delay,
With sibyllic omen
  Seeming thus to say;
"Of all the vanished Past, we Echoes only stay!"

Evolution

Out of the dusk a shadow,
   Then, a spark;
Out of the cloud a silence,
   Then, a lark;
Out of the heart a rapture,
   Then, a pain;
Out of the dead, cold ashes,
   Life again.

Milton

So fair thy vision that the night
Abided with thee, lest the light,
A flaming sword before thine eyes,
Had shut thee out from Paradise.

Whisper

Close cleaving unto Silence, into sound
   She ventures as a timorous child from land,
Still glancing, at each wary step, around,
   Lest suddenly she lose her sister's hand.

The Shadow

O Shadow, in thy fleeting form I see
The friend of fortune that once clung to me.
In flattering light, thy constancy is shown;
In darkness, thou wilt leave me all alone.

A Winter Twilight

Blood-shotten through the bleak gigantic trees
   The sunset, o'er a wilderness of snow,
   Startles the wolfish winds that wilder grow
As hunger mocks their howling miseries.
In every skulking shadow Fancy sees
   The menace of an undiscovered foe—
   A sullen footstep, treacherous and slow,
That comes, or into deeper darkness flees.

Nor Day nor Night, in Time's eternal round
   Whereof the tides are telling, e'er hath passed
This Isthmus-hour—this dim, mysterious land
   That sets their lives asunder—where up-cast
Their earliest and their latest waves resound,
   As each, alternate, nears or leaves the strand.

Echo

O famished Prodigal, in vain—
Thy portion spent—thou seek'st again
     Thy father's door;
His all with latest sigh bequeathed
To thee the wanderer—he breathed,
     Alas! no more.

The Mid-Day Moon

Behold, whatever wind prevail,
Slow westering, a phantom sail—
The lonely soul of Yesterday—
Unpiloted, pursues her way.

Tenebræ

Whate'er my darkness be,
'T is not, O Lord, of Thee:
The light is Thine alone;
The shadows, all my own.

The Sisters

The waves forever move;
The hills forever rest:
Yet each the heavens approve,
And Love alike hath blessed
A Martha's household care,
A Mary's cloistered prayer.

EMMA LAZARUS

(1849–1887)

from *Phantasies*

(After Robert Schumann)

I. Evening.

Rest, beauty, stillness: not a waif of cloud
From gray-blue east sheer to the yellow west—
No film of mist the utmost slopes to shroud.

The earth lies grave, by quiet airs caressed,
And shepherdeth her shadows, but each stream,
Free to the sky, is by that glow possessed,

And traileth with the splendors of a dream
Athwart the dusky land. Uplift thine eyes!
Unbroken by a vapor or a gleam,

The vast clear reach of mild, wan twilight skies.
But look again, and lo, the evening star!
Against the pale tints black the slim elms rise,

The earth exhales sweet odors nigh and far,
And from the heavens fine influences fall.
Familiar things stand not for what they are:

What they suggest, foreshadow, or recall
The spirit is alert to apprehend,
Imparting somewhat of herself to all.

Labor and thought and care are at an end:
The soul is filled with gracious reveries,
And with her mood soft sounds and colors blend;

For simplest sounds ring forth like melodies
In this weird-lighted air—the monotone
Of some far bell, the distant farmyard cries,

A barking dog, the thin, persistent drone
Of crickets, and the lessening call of birds.
The apparition of yon star alone

Breaks on the sense like music. Beyond words
The peace that floods the soul, for night is here,
And Beauty still is guide and harbinger.

Echoes

Late-born and woman-souled I dare not hope,
The freshness of the elder lays, the might
Of manly, modern passion shall alight
Upon my Muse's lips, nor may I cope
(Who veiled and screened by womanhood must grope)
With the world's strong-armed warriors and recite
The dangers, wounds, and triumphs of the fight;
Twanging the full-stringed lyre through all its scope.
But if thou ever in some lake-floored cave
O'erbrowed by rocks, a wild voice wooed and heard,
Answering at once from heaven and earth and wave,
Lending elf-music to thy harshest word,
Misprize thou not these echoes that belong
To one in love with solitude and song.

The New Colossus

Not like the brazen giant of Greek fame,
With conquering limbs astride from land to land;
Here at our sea-washed, sunset gates shall stand
A mighty woman with a torch, whose flame
Is the imprisoned lightning, and her name

Mother of Exiles. From her beacon-hand
Glows world-wide welcome; her mild eyes command
The air-bridged harbor that twin cities frame.
"Keep, ancient lands, your storied pomp!" cries she
With silent lips. "Give me your tired, your poor,
Your huddled masses yearning to breathe free,
The wretched refuse of your teeming shore.
Send these, the homeless, tempest-tost to me,
I lift my lamp beside the golden door!"

Venus of the Louvre

Down the long hall she glistens like a star,
The foam-born mother of Love, transfixed to stone,
Yet none the less immortal, breathing on.
Time's brutal hand hath maimed but could not mar.
When first the enthralled enchantress from afar
Dazzled mine eyes, I saw not her alone,
Serenely poised on her world-worshipped throne,
As when she guided once her dove-drawn car,—
But at her feet a pale, death-stricken Jew,
Her life adorer, sobbed farewell to love.
Here *Heine* wept! Here still he weeps anew,
Nor ever shall his shadow lift or move,
While mourns one ardent heart, one poet-brain,
For vanished Hellas and Hebraic pain.

The Cranes of Ibycus

There was a man who watched the river flow
Past the huge town, one gray November day.
Round him in narrow high-piled streets at play
The boys made merry as they saw him go,
Murmuring half-loud, with eyes upon the stream,
The immortal screed he held within his hand.
For he was walking in an April land

With Faust and Helen. Shadowy as a dream
Was the prose-world, the river and the town.
Wild joy possessed him; through enchanted skies
He saw the cranes of Ibycus swoop down.
He closed the page, he lifted up his eyes,
Lo—a black line of birds in wavering thread
Bore him the greetings of the deathless dead!

The South

Night, and beneath star-blazoned summer skies
   Behold the Spirit of the musky South,
A creole with still-burning, languid eyes,
   Voluptuous limbs and incense-breathing mouth:
      Swathed in spun gauze is she,
From fibres of her own anana tree.

Within these sumptuous woods she lies at ease,
   By rich night-breezes, dewy cool, caressed:
'Twixt cypresses and slim palmetto trees,
   Like to the golden oriole's hanging nest,
      Her airy hammock swings,
And through the dark her mocking-bird yet sings.

How beautiful she is! A tulip-wreath
   Twines round her shadowy, free-floating hair:
Young, weary, passionate, and sad as death,
   Dark visions haunt for her the vacant air,
      While movelessly she lies
With lithe, lax, folded hands and heavy eyes.

Full well knows she how wide and fair extend
   Her groves bright-flowered, her tangled everglades,
Majestic streams that indolently wend
   Through lush savanna or dense forest shades,
      Where the brown buzzard flies
To broad bayous 'neath hazy-golden skies.

Hers is the savage splendor of the swamp,
   With pomp of scarlet and of purple bloom,
Where blow warm, furtive breezes faint and damp,
   Strange insects whir, and stalking bitterns boom—
       Where from stale waters dead
Oft looms the great-jawed alligator's head.

Her wealth, her beauty, and the blight on these,—
   Of all she is aware: luxuriant woods,
Fresh, living, sunlit, in her dream she sees;
   And ever midst those verdant solitudes
       The soldier's wooden cross,
O'ergrown by creeping tendrils and rank moss.

Was hers a dream of empire? was it sin?
   And is it well that all was borne in vain?
She knows no more than one who slow doth win,
   After fierce fever, conscious life again,
       Too tired, too weak, too sad,
By the new light to be or stirred or glad.

From rich sea-islands fringing her green shore,
   From broad plantations where swart freemen bend
Bronzed backs in willing labor, from her store
   Of golden fruit, from stream, from town, ascend
       Life-currents of pure health:
Her aims shall be subserved with boundless wealth.

Yet now how listless and how still she lies,
   Like some half-savage, dusky Indian queen,
Rocked in her hammock 'neath her native skies,
   With the pathetic, passive, broken mien
       Of one who, sorely proved,
Great-souled, hath suffered much and much hath loved!

But look! along the wide-branched, dewy glade
   Glimmers the dawn: the light palmetto-trees
And cypresses reissue from the shade,
   And *she* hath wakened. Through clear air she sees
       The pledge, the brightening ray,
And leaps from dreams to hail the coming day.

Long Island Sound

I see it as it looked one afternoon
In August,—by a fresh soft breeze o'erblown.
The swiftness of the tide, the light thereon,
A far-off sail, white as a crescent moon.
The shining waters with pale currents strewn,
The quiet fishing-smacks, the Eastern cove,
The semi-circle of its dark, green grove.
The luminous grasses, and the merry sun
In the grave sky; the sparkle far and wide,
Laughter of unseen children, cheerful chirp
Of crickets, and low lisp of rippling tide,
Light summer clouds fantastical as sleep
Changing unnoted while I gazed thereon.
All these fair sounds and sights I made my own.

City Visions

I.

As the blind Milton's memory of light,
The deaf Beethoven's phantasy of tone,
Wrought joys for them surpassing all things known
In our restricted sphere of sound and sight,—
So while the glaring streets of brick and stone
Vex with heat, noise, and dust from morn till night,
I will give rein to Fancy, taking flight
From dismal now and here, and dwell alone
With new-enfranchised senses. All day long,
Think ye 't is I, who sit 'twixt darkened walls,
While ye chase beauty over land and sea?
Uplift on wings of some rare poet's song,
Where the wide billow laughs and leaps and falls,
I soar cloud-high, free as the winds are free.

II.

Who grasps the substance? who 'mid shadows strays?
He who within some dark-bright wood reclines,
'Twixt sleep and waking, where the needled pines
Have cushioned all his couch with soft brown sprays?
He notes not how the living water shines,
Trembling along the cliff, a flickering haze,
Brimming a wine-bright pool, nor lifts his gaze
To read the ancient wonders and the signs.
Does he possess the actual, or do I,
Who paint on air more than his sense receives,
The glittering pine-tufts with closed eyes behold,
Breathe the strong resinous perfume, see the sky
Quiver like azure flame between the leaves,
And open unseen gates with key of gold?

In Exile

*"Since that day till now our life is one unbroken paradise. We
live a true brotherly life. Every evening after supper we take a
seat under the mighty oak and sing our songs.*
        —Extract from a letter of a Russian refugee in Texas.

Twilight is here, soft breezes bow the grass,
    Day's sounds of various toil break slowly off,
The yoke-freed oxen low, the patient ass
    Dips his dry nostril in the cool, deep trough.
Up from the prairie the tanned herdsmen pass
    With frothy pails, guiding with voices rough
Their udder-lightened kine. Fresh smells of earth,
The rich, black furrows of the glebe send forth.

After the Southern day of heavy toil,
    How good to lie, with limbs relaxed, brows bare
To evening's fan, and watch the smoke-wreaths coil
    Up from one's pipe-stem through the rayless air.
So deem these unused tillers of the soil,
    Who stretched beneath the shadowing oak-tree, stare
Peacefully on the star-unfolding skies,
And name their life unbroken paradise.

The hounded stag that has escaped the pack,
   And pants at ease within a thick-leaved dell;
The unimprisoned bird that finds the track
   Through sun-bathed space, to where his fellows
      dwell;
The martyr, granted respite from the rack,
   The death-doomed victim pardoned from his cell,—
Such only know the joy these exiles gain,—
Life's sharpest rapture is surcease of pain.

Strange faces theirs, wherethrough the Orient sun
   Gleams from the eyes and glows athwart the skin.
Grave lines of studious thought and purpose run
   From curl-crowned forehead to dark-bearded chin.
And over all the seal is stamped thereon
   Of anguish branded by a world of sin,
In fire and blood through ages on their name,
Their seal of glory and the Gentiles' shame.

Freedom to love the law that Moses brought,
   To sing the songs of David, and to think
The thoughts Gabirol to Spinoza taught,
   Freedom to dig the common earth, to drink
The universal air—for this they sought
   Refuge o'er wave and continent, to link
Egypt with Texas in their mystic chain,
And truth's perpetual lamp forbid to wane.

Hark! through the quiet evening air, their song
   Floats forth with wild sweet rhythm and glad refrain.
They sing the conquest of the spirit strong,
   The soul that wrests the victory from pain;
The noble joys of manhood that belong
   To comrades and to brothers. In their strain
Rustle of palms and Eastern streams one hears,
And the broad prairie melts in mist of tears.

1492

Thou two-faced year, Mother of Change and Fate,
Didst weep when Spain cast forth with flaming sword,
The children of the prophets of the Lord,
Prince, priest, and people, spurned by zealot hate.
Hounded from sea to sea, from state to state,
The West refused them, and the East abhorred.
No anchorage the known world could afford,
Close-locked was every port, barred every gate.

Then smiling, thou unveil'dst, O two-faced year,
A virgin world where doors of sunset part,
Saying, "Ho, all who weary, enter here!
There falls each ancient barrier that the art
Of race or creed or rank devised, to rear
Grim bulwarked hatred between heart and heart!"

SARAH ORNE JEWETT

(1849–1909)

At Home from Church

The lilacs lift in generous bloom
   Their plumes of dear old-fashioned flowers;
Their fragrance fills the still old house
   Where left alone I count the hours.

High in the apple-trees the bees
   Are humming, busy in the sun,—
An idle robin cries for rain
   But once or twice and then is done.

The Sunday-morning quiet holds
   In heavy slumber all the street,
While from the church, just out of sight
   Behind the elms, comes slow and sweet

The organ's drone, the voices faint
   That sing the quaint long-meter hymn—
I somehow feel as if shut out
   From some mysterious temple, dim

And beautiful with blue and red
   And golden lights from windows high,
Where angels in the shadows stand
   And earth seems very near the sky.

The day-dream fades—and so I try
   Again to catch the tune that brings
No thought of temple nor of priest,
   But only of a voice that sings.

A Country Boy in Winter

The wind may blow the snow about,
    For all I care, says Jack,
And I don't mind how cold it grows,
    For then the ice won't crack.
Old folks may shiver all day long,
    But I shall never freeze;
What cares a jolly boy like me
    For winter days like these?

Far down the long snow-covered hills
    It is such fun to coast,
So clear the road! the fastest sled
    There is in school I boast.
The paint is pretty well worn off,
    But then I take the lead;
A dandy sled's a loiterer,
    And I go in for speed.

When I go home at supper-time,
    Ki! but my cheeks are red!
They burn and sting like anything;
    I'm cross until I'm fed.
You ought to see the biscuit go,
    I am so hungry then;
And old Aunt Polly says that boys
    Eat twice as much as men.

There's always something I can do
    To pass the time away;
The dark comes quick in winter-time —
    A short and stormy day
And when I give my mind to it,
    It's just as father says,
I almost do a man's work now,
    And help him many ways.

I shall be glad when I grow up
    And get all through with school,
I'll show them by-and-by that I
    Was not meant for a fool.
I'll take the crops off this old farm,
    I'll do the best I can.
A jolly boy like me won't be
    A dolt when he's a man.

I like to hear the old horse neigh
    Just as I come in sight,
The oxen poke me with their horns
    To get their hay at night.
Somehow the creatures seem like friends,
    And like to see me come.
Some fellows talk about New York,
    But I shall stay at home.

A Caged Bird

High at the window in her cage
    The old canary flits and sings,
Nor sees across the curtain pass
    The shadow of a swallow's wings.

A poor deceit and copy, this,
    Of larger lives that mark their span,
Unreckoning of wider worlds
    Or gifts that Heaven keeps for man.

She gathers piteous bits and shreds,
    This solitary, mateless thing,
To patient build again the nest
    So rudely scattered spring by spring;

And sings her brief, unlistened songs,
    Her dreams of bird life wild and free,
Yet never beats her prison bars
    At sound of song from bush or tree.

But in my busiest hours I pause,
    Held by a sense of urgent speech,
Bewildered by that spark-like soul,
    Able my very soul to reach.

She will be heard; she chirps me loud,
    When I forget those gravest cares,
Her small provision to supply,
    Clear water or her seedsman's wares.

She begs me now for that chief joy
    The round great world is made to grow,—
Her wisp of greenness. Hear her chide,
    Because my answering thought is slow!

What can my life seem like to her?
    A dull, unpunctual service mine;
Stupid before her eager call,
    Her flitting steps, her insight fine.

To open wide thy prison door,
    Poor friend, would give thee to thy foes;
And yet a plaintive note I hear,
    As if to tell how slowly goes

The time of thy long prisoning.
    Bird! does some promise keep thee sane?
Will there be better days for thee?
    Will thy soul too know life again?

Ah, none of us have more than this:
    If one true friend green leaves can reach
From out some fairer, wider place,
    And understand our wistful speech!

The Widows' House

[At Bethlehem, Pennsylvania]

What of this house with massive walls
    And small-paned windows, gay with blooms?
A quaint and ancient aspect falls
    Like pallid sunshine through the rooms.

Not this new country's rush and haste
    Could breed, one thinks, so still a life;
Here is the old Moravian home,
    A placid foe of worldly strife.

For this roof covers, night and day,
    The widowed women poor and old,
The mated without mates, who say
    Their light is out, their story told.

To these the many mansions seem
    Dear household fires that cannot die;
They wait through separation dark
    An endless union by and by.

Each window has its watcher wan
    To fit the autumn afternoon,
The dropping poplar leaves, the dream
    Of spring that faded all too soon.

Upon the highest window-ledge
    A glowing scarlet flower shines down.
Oh, wistful sisterhood, whose home
    Has sanctified this quiet town!

Oh, hapless household, gather in
    The tired-hearted and the lone!
What broken homes, what sundered love,
    What disappointment you have known!

They count their little wealth of hope
    And spend their waiting days in peace,
What comfort their poor loneliness
    Must find in every soul's release!

And when the wailing trombones go
    Along the street before the dead
In that Moravian custom quaint,
    They smile because a soul has fled.

JAMES WHITCOMB RILEY

(1849–1916)

The Old Swimmin'-Hole

Oh! the old swimmin'-hole! whare the crick so still and deep
Looked like a baby-river that was laying half asleep,
And the gurgle of the worter round the the drift jest below
Sounded like the laugh of something we onc't ust to know
Before we could remember anything but the eyes
Of the angels lookin' out as we left Paradise;
But the merry days of youth is beyond our control,
And it's hard to part ferever with the old swimmin'-hole.

Oh! the old swimmin'-hole! In the happy days of yore,
When I ust to lean above it on the old sickamore,
Oh! it showed me a face in its warm sunny tide
That gazed back at me so gay and glorified,
It made me love myself, as I leaped to caress
My shadder smilin' up at me with such tenderness.
But them days is past and gone, and old Time's tuck his toll
From the old man come back to the old swimmin'-hole.

Oh! the old swimmin'-hole! In the long, lazy days
When the hum-drum of school made so many run-a-ways,
How pleasant was the jurney down the old dusty lane,
Whare the tracks of our bare feet was all printed so plain
You could tell by the dent of the heel and the sole
They was lots o' fun on hands at the old swimmin'-hole.
But the lost joys is past! Let your tears in sorrow roll
Like the rain that ust to dapple up the old swimmin'-hole.

Thare the bullrushes growed, and the cat-tails so tall,
And the sunshine and shadder fell over it all;
And it mottled the worter with amber and gold
Till the glad lilies rocked in the ripples that rolled;
And the snake-feeder's four gauzy wings fluttered by

Like the ghost of a daisy dropped out of the sky,
Or a wownded apple-blossom in the breeze's control,
As it cut acrost some orchard to'rds the old swimmin'-hole.

Oh! the old swimmin'-hole! When I last saw the place,
The scenes was all changed, like the change in my face:
The bridge of the railroad now crosses the spot
Whare the old divin'-log lays sunk and fergot.
And I stray down the banks whare the trees ust to be—
But never again will their shade shelter me!
And I wish in my sorrow I could strip to the soul,
And dive off in my grave like the old swimmin'-hole!

The Days Gone By

O the days gone by! O the days gone by!
The apples in the orchard, and the pathway through the rye;
The chirrup of the robin, and the whistle of the quail
As he piped across the meadows sweet as any nightingale;
When the bloom was on the clover, and the blue was in the
        sky,
And my happy heart brimmed over in the days gone by.

In the days gone by, when my naked feet were tripped
By the honey-suckle's tangles where the water-lilies dipped,
And the ripples of the river lipped the moss along the brink
Where the placid-eyed and lazy-footed cattle came to drink,
And the tilting snipe stood fearless of the truant's wayward
        cry
And the splashing of the swimmer, in the days gone by.

O the days gone by! O the days gone by!
The music of the laughing lip, the luster of the eye;
The childish faith in fairies, and Aladdin's magic ring—
The simple, soul-reposing, glad belief in everything,—
When life was like a story, holding neither sob nor sigh,
In the golden olden glory of the days gone by.

When the Frost Is on the Punkin

When the frost is on the punkin and the fodder's in the
    shock,
And you hear the kyouck and gobble of the struttin' turkey-
    cock,
And the clackin' of the guineys, and the cluckin' of the hens,
And the rooster's hallylooyer as he tiptoes on the fence;
O, it's then's the times a feller is a-feelin' at his best,
With the risin' sun to greet him from a night of peaceful
    rest,
As he leaves the house, bareheaded, and goes out to feed the
    stock,
When the frost is on the punkin and the fodder's in the
    shock.

They's something kindo' harty-like about the atmusfere
When the heat of summer's over and the coolin' fall is
    here—
Of course we miss the flowers, and the blossums on the
    trees,
And the mumble of the hummin'-birds and buzzin' of the
    bees;
But the air's so appetizin'; and the landscape through the
    haze
Of a crisp and sunny morning of the airly autumn days
Is a pictur' that no painter has the colorin' to mock—
When the frost is on the punkin and the fodder's in the
    shock.

The husky, rusty russel of the tossels of the corn,
And the raspin' of the tangled leaves, as golden as the morn;
The stubble in the furries—kindo' lonesome-like, but still
A-preachin' sermons to us of the barns they growed to fill;
The strawstack in the medder, and the reaper in the shed;
The hosses in theyr stalls below—the clover overhead!—
O, it sets my hart a-clickin' like the tickin' of a clock,
When the frost is on the punkin and the fodder's in the
    shock!

Then your apples all is gethered, and the ones a feller keeps
Is poured around the celler-floor in red and yeller heaps;
And your cider-makin' 's over, and your wimmern-folks is
          through
With their mince and apple-butter, and theyr souse and
          saussage, too! . . .
I don't know how to tell it—but ef sich a thing could be
As the Angels wantin' boardin', and they'd call around on
          me —
I'd want to 'commodate 'em—all the whole-indurin' flock—
When the frost is on the punkin and the fodder's in the
          shock!

Little Orphant Annie

Little Orphant Annie's come to our house to stay
An' wash the cups and saucers up, and brush the crumbs
          away,
An' shoo the chickens off the porch, an' dust the hearth, an'
          sweep,
An' make the fire, an' bake the bread, an' earn her board-an'-
          keep;
An' all us other children, when the supper things is done,
We set around the kitchen fire an' has the mostest fun
A-list'nin' to the witch tales 'at Annie tells about,
An' the gobble-uns 'at gits you
                    Ef you
                  Don't
                Watch
                    Out!

Onc't they was a little boy wouldn't say his pray'rs—
An' when he went to bed 'at night, away up stairs,
His mammy heerd him holler, an' his daddy heerd him bawl,
An' when they turn't the kivvers down, he wasn't there at
          all!
An' they seeked him in the rafter-room, an' cubby-hole, an'
          press,

An' seeked him up the chimbly-flue, an' ever 'wheres, I
    guess,
But all they ever found was thist his pants an' round-
    about!—
An' the gobble-uns 'll git you
         Ef you
            Don't
               Watch
                  Out!

An' one time a little girl 'ud allus laugh an' grin,
An' make fun of ever' one an' all her blood-an'-kin,
An' onc't when they was "company," an' ole folks was there,
She mocked 'em an' shocked 'em, an' said she didn't care!
An' thist as she kicked her heels, an' turn't to run an' hide,
They was two great big Black Things a-standin' by her side,
An' they snatched her through the ceilin' 'fore she know'd
    what she's about!
An' the gobble-uns 'll git you
         Ef you
            Don't
               Watch
                  Out!

An' little Orphant Annie says, when the blaze is blue,
An' the lampwick sputters, an' the wind goes woo-oo!
An' you hear the crickets quit, an' the moon is gray
An' the lightnin'-bugs in dew is all squenched away,—
You better mind yer parents, and yer teachers fond and dear,
An' churish them 'at loves you, an' dry the orphant's tear,
An' he'p the pore an' needy ones 'at clusters all about,
Er the gobble-uns 'll git you
         Ef you
            Don't
               Watch
                  Out!

EUGENE FIELD

(1850–1895)

The Duel

The gingham dog and the calico cat
Side by side on the table sat;
'T was half-past twelve, and (what do you think!)
Nor one nor t' other had slept a wink!
    The old Dutch clock and the Chinese plate
    Appeared to know as sure as fate
There was going to be a terrible spat.
      (*I was n't there; I simply state*
      What was told to me by the Chinese plate!)

The gingham dog went "bow-wow-wow!"
And the calico cat replied "mee-ow!"
The air was littered, an hour or so,
With bits of gingham and calico,
    While the old Dutch clock in the chimney-place
    Up with its hands before its face,
For it always dreaded a family row!
      (*Now mind: I 'm only telling you*
      What the old Dutch clock declares is true!)

The Chinese plate looked very blue,
And wailed, "Oh, dear! what shall we do!"
But the gingham dog and the calico cat
Wallowed this way and tumbled that,
    Employing every tooth and claw
    In the awfullest way you ever saw —
And, oh! how the gingham and calico flew!
      (*Don't fancy I exaggerate —*
      I got my news from the Chinese plate!)

Next morning, where the two had sat
They found no trace of dog or cat;
And some folks think unto this day

That burglars stole that pair away!
　　But the truth about the cat and pup
　　Is this: they ate each other up!
Now what do you really think of that!
　　(The old Dutch clock it told me so,
　　And that is how I came to know.)

Dutch Lullaby

Wynken, Blynken, and Nod one night
　　Sailed off in a wooden shoe,—
Sailed on a river of misty light
　　Into a sea of dew.
"Where are you going, and what do you wish?"
　　The old moon asked the three.
"We have come to fish for the herring-fish
　　That live in this beautiful sea;
　　Nets of silver and gold have we,"
　　　　　Said Wynken,
　　　　　Blynken,
　　　　　And Nod.

The old moon laughed and sung a song,
　　As they rocked in the wooden shoe,
And the wind that sped them all night long
　　Ruffled the waves of dew;
The little stars were the herring-fish
　　That lived in the beautiful sea.
"Now cast your nets wherever you wish,
　　But never afeard are we!"
　　So cried the stars to the fishermen three,
　　　　　Wynken,
　　　　　Blynken,
　　　　　And Nod.

All night long their nets they threw
   For the fish in the twinkling foam,
Then down from the sky came the wooden shoe,
   Bringing the fishermen home;
'T was all so pretty a sail, it seemed
   As if it could not be;
And some folk thought 't was a dream they'd dreamed
   Of sailing that beautiful sea;
    But I shall name you the fishermen three:
         Wynken,
         Blynken,
         And Nod.

Wynken and Blynken are two little eyes,
   And Nod is a little head,
And the wooden shoe that sailed the skies
   Is a wee one's trundle-bed;
So shut your eyes while Mother sings
   Of wonderful sights that be,
And you shall see the beautiful things
   As you rock on the misty sea
    Where the old shoe rocked the fishermen three,—
         Wynken,
         Blynken,
         And Nod.

ELLA WHEELER WILCOX

(1850–1919)

Friendship After Love

After the fierce midsummer all ablaze
    Has burned itself to ashes, and expires
    In the intensity of its own fires,
There come the mellow, mild, St. Martin days
Crowned with the calm of peace, but sad with haze.
    So after Love has led us, till he tires
    Of his own throes, and torments, and desires,
Comes large-eyed friendship: with a restful gaze,
He beckons us to follow, and across
    Cool verdant vales we wander free from care.
    Is it a touch of frost lies in the air?
Why are we haunted with a sense of loss?
We do not wish the pain back, or the heat;
And yet, and yet, these days are incomplete.

No Classes!

No classes here! Why, that is idle talk.
    The village beau sneers at the country boor;
The importuning mendicants who walk
    Our cities' streets despise the parish poor.

The daily toiler at some noisy loom
    Holds back her garments from the kitchen aid.
Meanwhile the latter leans upon her broom,
    Unconscious of the bow the laundress made.

The grocer's daughter eyes the farmer's lass
    With haughty glances; and the lawyer's wife
Would pay no visits to the trading class,
    If policy were not her creed in life.

The merchant's son nods coldly at the clerk;
   The proud possessor of a pedigree
Ignores the youth whose father rose by work;
   The title-seeking maiden scorns all three.

The aristocracy of blood looks down
   Upon the "nouveau riche"; and in disdain,
The lovers of the intellectual frown
   On both, and worship at the shrine of brain.

"No classes here," the clergyman has said;
   "We are one family." Yet see his rage
And horror when his favorite son would wed
   Some pure and pretty player on the stage.

It is the vain but natural human way
   Of vaunting our weak selves, our pride, our worth!
Not till the long delayed millennial day
   Shall we behold "no classes" on God's earth.

The Sonnet

Alone it stands in Poesy's fair land,
   A temple by the muses set apart;
   A perfect structure of consummate art,
By artists builded and by genius planned.
Beyond the reach of the apprentice hand,
   Beyond the ken of the untutored heart,
   Like a fine carving in a common mart,
Only the favored few will understand.
A *chef-d'œuvre* toiled over with great care,
   Yet which the unseeing careless crowd goes by,
A plainly set, but well-cut solitaire,
An ancient bit of pottery, too rare
   To please or hold aught save the special eye,
These only with the sonnet can compare.

The Engine

Into the gloom of the deep, dark night,
  With panting breath and a startled scream;
Swift as a bird in sudden flight
  Darts this creature of steel and steam.

Awful dangers are lurking nigh,
  Rocks and chasms are near the track,
But straight by the light of its great white eye
  It speeds through the shadows, dense and black.

Terrible thoughts and fierce desires
  Trouble its mad heart many an hour,
Where burn and smoulder the hidden fires,
  Coupled ever with might and power.

It hates, as a wild horse hates the rein,
  The narrow track by vale and hill;
And shrieks with a cry of startled pain,
  And longs to follow its own wild will.

Nothing New

Oh, what am I but an engine, shod
  With muscle and flesh, by the hand of God,
Speeding on through the dense, dark night,
  Guided alone by the soul's white light.

Often and often my mad heart tires,
  And hates its way with a bitter hate,
And longs to follow its own desires,
  And leave the end in the hands of fate.

O, mighty engine of steel and steam;
  O, human engine of blood and bone,
Follow the white light's certain beam—
  There lies safety, and there alone.

The narrow track of fearless truth,
  Lit by the soul's great eye of light,
O passionate heart of restless youth,
  Alone will carry you through the night.

ROSE HARTWICK THORPE

(1850–1939)

Curfew Must Not Ring To-Night

England's sun was slowly setting o'er the hill-tops far away,
Filling all the land with beauty at the close of one sad day;
And its last rays kissed the forehead of a man and maiden
    fair,—
He with steps so slow and weary, she with sunny, floating
    hair:
He with bowed head, sad and thoughtful; she with lips so
    cold and white,
Struggled to keep back the murmur, "Curfew must not ring
    to-night!"

"Sexton," Bessie's white lips faltered, pointing to the prison
    old,
With its walls so tall and gloomy,—moss-grown walls dark,
    damp, and cold,—
"I've a lover in that prison, doomed this very night to die
At the ringing of the curfew, and no earthly help is nigh.
Cromwell will not come till sunset"; and her lips grew
    strangely white
As she spoke in husky whispers, "Curfew must not ring
    to-night!"

"Bessie," calmly spoke the sexton (every word pierced her
    young heart
Like a gleaming death-winged arrow, like a deadly
    poisoned dart),
"Long, long years I've rung the curfew from that gloomy,
    shadowed tower;
Every evening, just at sunset, it has tolled the twilight hour.
I have done my duty ever, tried to do it just and right;
Now I'm old I will not miss it: Curfew bell must ring
    to-night!"

Wild her eyes and pale her features, stern and white her
    thoughtful brow,
And within her heart's deep centre Bessie made a solemn
    vow.
She had listened while the judges read, without a tear or
    sigh,
"At the ringing of the curfew Basil Underwood *must die*."
And her breath came fast and faster, and her eyes grew
    large and bright;
One low murmur, faintly spoken, "Curfew *must not* ring
    to-night!"

She with quick step bounded forward, sprang within the
    old church door,
Left the old man coming, slowly, paths he'd trod so oft
    before.
Not one moment paused the maiden, but, with cheek and
    brow aglow,
Staggered up the gloomy tower where the bell swung to
    and fro;
As she climbed the slimy ladder, on which fell no ray of
    light,
Upward still, her pale lips saying, "Curfew *shall not* ring
    to-night!"

She has reached the topmost ladder; o'er her hangs the
    great, dark bell;
Awful is the gloom beneath her, like the pathway down to
    hell.
See, the ponderous tongue is swinging! 't is the hour of
    curfew now!
And the sight has chilled her bosom, stopped her breath
    and paled her brow.
Shall she let it ring? No, never! Her eyes flash with sudden
    light,
As she springs and grasps it firmly: "Curfew *shall not* ring
    to-night!"

Out she swung, far out; the city seemed a speck of light
      below,
There 'twixt heaven and earth suspended, as the bell swung
      to and fro.
And the sexton at the bell-rope, old and deaf, heard not the
      bell;
Sadly thought that twilight curfew rang young Basil's
      funeral knell.
Still the maiden, clinging firmly, quivering lip and fair face
      white,
Stilled her frightened heart's wild beating: *"Curfew shall not
      ring to-night!"*

It was o'er!—the bell ceased swaying, and the maiden
      stepped once more
Firmly on the damp old ladder, where, for hundred years
      before,
Human foot had not been planted. The brave deed that she
      had done
Should be told long ages after. As the rays of setting sun
Light the sky with golden beauty, aged sires, with heads of
      white,
Tell the children why the curfew did not ring that one sad
      night.

O'er the distant hills comes Cromwell. Bessie sees him, and
      her brow,
Lately white with sickening horror, has no anxious traces
      now.
At his feet she tells her story, shows her hands, all bruised
      and torn;
And her sweet young face, still haggard with the anguish it
      had worn,
Touched his heart with sudden pity, lit his eyes with misty
      light.
"Go! your lover lives," cried Cromwell. "Curfew shall not
      ring to-night!"

Wide they flung the massive portals, led the prisoner forth
      to die,
All his bright young life before him, 'neath the darkening
      English sky.
Bessie came, with flying footsteps, eyes aglow with
      lovelight sweet,
Kneeling on the turf beside him, laid his pardon at his feet.
In his brave, strong arms he clasped her, kissed the face
      upturned and white,
Whispered, "Darling, you have saved me! curfew will not
      ring to-night."

ALBERY ALLSON WHITMAN

(1851–1901)

from *Twasinta's Seminoles,*

or Rape of Florida

Have I not seen the hills of Candahar
Clothed in the fury of a thunder storm,
When Majesty rolled in His cloud-dark car—
Wreathed His dread brow with lightning's livid form,
And with a deluge robed His threat'ning arm!
Not seen, when night fled His terrific feet,
The great deep rose to utter forth alarm,
The hills in dreadful hurry rushed to meet,
And rocking mountains started from their darkened seat!

In happy childhood I have even loved
To sport the wild, and in the front and face
Of dreadest Nature, watch the storm unmoved,
That tore the oak tree from its ancient place
And took the hilltops in its dark embrace;
And then I've loved the pleasing after-view—
The quiet valleys spanned with light and grace—
The watery field, replete with life anew,
And sunset robing earth in love's sublimest hue.

Thus, when afar the wide Bahamas shone,—
In lucent stillness gleamed the sunset sea—
When day's last rim sank like a molten zone,
Emblaz'ning in Omnific heraldry
The far-off crag and latest mountain tree;
Thus, on a stand dividing worlds I've stood,
Till, touched by the dark wand of mystery,
I felt the brow of night, and earth imbued
With dread emotions of a great eternal Good.

Upon the shells by Carribea's wave
I've heard the anthems of the mighty sea;
Heard there the dark pines that their voices gave,
And heard a stream denote its minstrelsy—
How sweet, *all* lonely, was it there to be!
The stars were bright, the moon was up and clear;
But, when I thought of those who once were free,
And came at wonted times to worship there;
The sea's deep voice grew sad and claimed of me a tear!

Oh! sing it in the light of freedom's morn,
Tho' tyrant wars have made the earth a grave;
The good, the great, and true, are, if so, born,
And so with slaves, *chains do not make the slave!*
If high-souled birth be what the mother gave,—
If manly birth, and manly to the core,—
Whate'er the test, the man will he behave!
Crush him to earth and crush him o'er and o'er,
A man he'll rise at last and meet you as before.

Part I, stanzas 15–19

Is manhood less because man's face is black?
Let thunders of the loosened seals reply!
Who shall the rider's restive steed turn back,
Or who withstand the arrows he lets fly,
Between the mountains of eternity?
Genius ride forth! thou gift and torch of heav'n!
The mastery is kindled in thine eye;
To conquest ride! thy bow of strength is giv'n—
The trampled hordes of caste before thee shall be driv'n!

Who is't would beg? What man permission crave
To give his thoughts their scope and rightful reign?
Let him be cursed! a self-manacled slave!
He's a polution to the mind's domain—
A moral garbage scattered on the plain—
An execration of the world!—God's arm
Defend not him! Oh! if there is disdain
To freeze the bosom's every impulse warm,
I crave it for all who to Favor's alm's house swarm.

Shall thunders ask of man what time to beat
The march of clouds? Or oceans beg his leave
To rock their under-worlds? In his dread seat,
Doth Blanc consider him? When did he weave
A mantle for the hurricane, or give
The Rockies leave to hold the dying Sun!—
Sooner all these—sooner an earthquake heave,
And sink earth back where broods oblivion,
Than God-giv'n mind submit for gyves to be put on.

'T is hard to judge if hatred of one's race,
By those who deem themselves superior-born,
Be worse than that quiescence in disgrace,
Which only merits—and *should* only—scorn!
Oh! let me see the negro, night and morn,
Pressing and fighting in, for place and power!
If he a proud escutcheon would adorn,
All earth is place—all time th' auspicious hour,
While heaven leans forth to see, oh! can he quail or cower?

Ah! I abhor his protest and complaint!
His pious looks and patience I despise!
He can't evade the test, disguised as saint,
The manly voice of freedom bids him rise,
And shake himself before Philistine eyes!
And, like a lion roused, no sooner than
A foe dare come, play all his energies,
And court the fray with fury if he can;
For hell itself respects a fearless manly man!

Negro, or Arab, Zulu if one choose,
Unmoved be thou reproached for all but fear!
By the unhindered waters learn to muse,
With nature's liberal voices in thy ear;
Dwell on her nobler aspects that appear,
And make companions of all one may find:
Go rove the mountain forests far and near,
And hear the laughter of the open wind;
Then ask, what earth affords like freedom of the mind!

Be thine the shoulders that may bleed—not wince,
Tho' insolence in power lay on the lash.
Look retribution! court the worst nor flinch,
If thou must meet!—upon the insult gnash!
And let thy kindled courage on him flash;
For whom he can not conquer—dare not kill—
In suff'ring dumb—in manly virtues rash—
Must with respect e'en tyrant bosoms fill,
So godlike is the man who is invincible!

I never was a slave—a robber took
My substance—what of that? The *law* my rights—
And that? I still was free and had my book—
All nature. And I learned from during hights
How silence is majestic, and invites
In admiration far beholding eyes!
And heaven taught me, with her starry nights,
How deepest speech unuttered often lies,
And that Jehovah's lessons mostly he implies.

My birth-place where the scrub-wood thicket grows,
My mother bound, and daily toil my dower;
I envy not the halo title throws
Around the birth of any; place and power
May be but empty phantoms of an hour,—
For me, I find a more enduring bliss:
Rejoicing fields, green woods—the stream—the flower,
To me have speech, and born of God, are his
Interpreters, proclaiming what true greatness is.

Part II, stanzas 4–12

The Lute of Afric's Tribe

When Israel sate by Babel's stream and wept,
The heathen said, "Sing one of Zion's songs;"
But tuneless lay the lyre of those who slept
Where Sharon bloomed and Oreb vigil kept;
For holy song to holy ears belongs.

So, when her iron clutch the Slave power reached,
And sable generations captive held;
When Wrong the gospel of endurance preached;
The lute of Afric's tribe, tho' oft beseeched,
In all its wild, sweet warblings never swelled.

And yet when Freedom's lispings o'er it stole,
Soft as the breath of undefiled morn,
A wand'ring accent from its strings would stroll—
Thus was our Simpson, man of song and soul,
And stalwart energies, to bless us born.

When all our nation's sky was overcast
With rayless clouds of deepening misery,
His soaring vision mounted thro' the blast,
And from behind its gloom approaching fast,
Beheld the glorious Sun of Liberty.

He sang exultant: "Let her banner wave!"
And cheering senates, fired by his zeal,
Helped snatch their country from rebellion's grave
Looked through brave tears upon the injured slave,
And raised the battle-arm to break his gyves of steel.

But hushed the bard, his harp no longer sings
The woes and longings of a shackled mind;
For death's cold fingers swept its trembling strings,
And shut the bosom of its murmurings
Forever on the hearing of mankind.

The bird that dips his flight in noonday sun,
May fall, and spread his plumage on the plain;
But when immortal mind its work hath done
On earth, in heaven a nobler work's begun,
And it can never downward turn again.

Of him, whose harp then, lies by death unstrung—
A harp that long his lowly brethren cheered,
May'nt we now say, that, sainted choirs among,
An everlasting theme inspires his tongue,
Where slaves ne'er groan, and death is never feared?

Yes, he is harping on the "Sea of glass,"
Where saints begin, and angels join the strain;
While Spheres in one profound, eternal bass,
Sing thro' their orbs, illumined as they pass,
And constellations catch the long refrain.

from *An Idyll of the South*

I had a dream: Columbia the Great,
    The Arbitress of Nations had prevailed.
From Europe trains crossed bridge-spanned Behrings's Strait
    And ships through Panama from South Seas sailed.
Through atmospheric tubes the mail and freight
    Skimmed hill and dale and loftiest mountains scaled;
Threading the richest cities, on they went,
And in a few hours crossed the continent.

I saw our fleets guarding a hundred seas,
    All with unshotted guns ride proudly home;
I saw the hosts that watch our liberties
    By land afar from bloodless conquest come.
And shouts of welcome then rose on the breeze,
    With bells and whistles in uproarous hum;
And Peace's multitudes went singing, streaming
Through leagues of bunting, and of standards gleaming.

And not a home, a mansion or a hut
    In all the land, but heard the call that day.
From plainsman's ranch and miner's cabin shut
    In forest depths and mountain far away,
The sons of Freedom came, and cities put
    Their millions forth to swell the concourse gay.
It was a jubilee of joy and tears:
Columbia had reigned a thousand years!

The Sphinx of Race Hate looked into the past,
    Unheeded as the cheering throngs went by
In thund'rous unison, a concourse vast,
    Proclaimed the triumphing of Liberty.
The walls of Wrong had gone down at the blast
    Of Truth's oncoming trumpets; Earth and Sky
Attesting the inexorable plan,
That all men shall arise in raising man.

And then I saw that Toil need not sweat blood;
    But be reduced to healthful exercise.
Yet mankind had sufficiency of food,
    That, barring avarice, all had full supplies
For mind and body. Then I understood—
    The State-fixed bounds for corporate Enterprise,
Adjusting all disputes 'twixt Capital
And Labor fairly—Law deciding all.

I saw the children cared for by the State,
    As well as by their parents—that, indeed,
The nation held first claim in all the great
    Concerns of health and training—man's first need.
I saw that man must rule and regulate
    His home by love, and never by a creed:
That health, intelligence, Morality,
Saved in the child, safeguarded Liberty.

And so, no children roamed the streets at will,
    In hungry shoals to swarm the streams of Time;
But wise apprenticeships restrained them till
    They had escaped the snares of early crime,
And reached safe heights of industry and skill;
    And there was not allowed a wedding chime
When there was presence of a known disease,
Hence, no divorces, no adulteries.

I saw a city in the setting sun,
    Superb and vast, that crowned a noble height;
It was the city of the Yellowstone.
    In New World greatness, from its ancient site
Removed—the future's Washington.
    And guarded round, in its unconquered might,
By leagues of fortress, was a populace
Unnumbered, drawn from ev'ry human race.

And then I stood within a stately hall;
    Ten thousand brilliant dancers thronged the floor;
'Twas at the Nation's great Inaugural,
    And there were guests from home and foreign shore—
Statesmen and epauleted warriors tall,
    Churchmen of note, and far-famed men of lore,
All in the sunny light of woman's love,
With airs of valor, like the gods, they move.

On swept the throngs, in eddies whirled and flowed
    Through flow'ry aisles and flag-hung corridors;
On, on, while Fortune's trophies flashed and glowed
    'Neath lamps that on the tessellated floors
Poured floods of light; and strangers proudly strode
    Among admiring groups—the guests of our fair
        shores—
While hid in labyrinths of shrubs and flowers,
Enchanting strains beguiled the fleeting hours.

There from the South I saw the blue-eyed blonde,
    And from the North the Junoesque brunette;
From Hawaii the olive maiden fond,
    The dainty Cuban with her eyes of jet—
And Octoroon whose beauty was beyond
    Description, in a swirl of glory met,
Through mazy depths of flow'rs and lace to stream—
A symphony of lovely forms—My Dream.

Part II: The Southland's Charms
and Freedom's Magnitude,
stanzas 64–74

EDWIN MARKHAM

(1852–1940)

The Man with the Hoe

Written after seeing Millet's World-Famous Painting

> *God made man in His own image,*
> *in the image of God made He him.* —GENESIS.

Bowed by the weight of centuries he leans
Upon his hoe and gazes on the ground,
The emptiness of ages in his face,
And on his back the burden of the world.
Who made him dead to rapture and despair,
A thing that grieves not and that never hopes,
Stolid and stunned, a brother to the ox?
Who loosened and let down this brutal jaw?
Whose was the hand that slanted back this brow?
Whose breath blew out the light within this brain?

Is this the Thing the Lord God made and gave
To have dominion over sea and land;
To trace the stars and search the heavens for power;
To feel the passion of Eternity?
Is this the Dream He dreamed who shaped the suns
And pillared the blue firmament with light?
Down all the stretch of Hell to its last gulf
There is no shape more terrible than this—
More tongued with censure of the world's blind greed—
More filled with signs and portents for the soul—
More fraught with menace to the universe.

What gulfs between him and the seraphim!
Slave of the wheel of labor, what to him
Are Plato and the swing of Pleiades?
What the long reaches of the peaks of song,
The rift of dawn, the reddening of the rose?

Through this dread shape the suffering ages look;
Time's tragedy is in that aching stoop;
Through this dread shape humanity betrayed,
Plundered, profaned and disinherited,
Cries protest to the Judges of the World,
A protest that is also prophecy.

O masters, lords and rulers in all lands,
Is this the handiwork you give to God,
This monstrous thing distorted and soul-quenched?
How will you ever straighten up this shape;
Touch it again with immortality;
Give back the upward looking and the light;
Rebuild in it the music and the dream;
Make right the immemorial infamies,
Perfidious wrongs, immedicable woes?

O masters, lords and rulers in all lands,
How will the Future reckon with this Man?
How answer his brute question in that hour
When whirlwinds of rebellion shake the world?
How will it be with kingdoms and with kings—
With those who shaped him to the thing he is—
When this dumb Terror shall reply to God,
After the silence of the centuries?

A Leaf from the Devil's Jest-Book

Beside the sewing-table chained and bent,
    They stitch for the lady, tyrannous and proud—
    For her a wedding-gown, for them a shroud;
They stitch and stitch, but never mend the rent
Torn in life's golden curtains. Glad Youth went,
    And left them alone with Time; and now if bowed
    With burdens they should sob and cry aloud,—
Wondering, the rich would look from their content.

And so this glimmering life at last recedes
   In unknown, endless depths beyond recall;
And what's the worth of all our ancient creeds,
   If here at the end of ages this is all—
   A white face floating in the whirling ball,
A dead face plashing in the river reeds?

In Death Valley

There came gray stretches of volcanic plains,
Bare, lone and treeless, then a bleak lone hill,
Like to the dolorous hill that Dobell saw.
Around were heaps of ruins piled between
The Burn o' Sorrow and the Water o' Care;
And from the stillness of the down-crushed walls
One pillar rose up dark against the moon.
There was a nameless Presence everywhere;
In the gray soil there was a purple stain,
And the gray reticent rocks were dyed with blood—
Blood of a vast unknown Calamity.
It was the mark of some ancestral grief—
Grief that began before the ancient Flood.

After Reading Shakspere

Blithe Fancy lightly builds with airy hands
   Or on the edges of the darkness peers,
   Breathless and frightened at the Voice she hears:
Imagination (lo! the sky expands)
Travels the blue arch and Cimmerian sands,—
   Homeless on earth, the pilgrim of the spheres,
   The rush of light before the hurrying years,
The Voice that cries in unfamiliar lands.

Men weigh the moons that flood with eerie light
   The dusky vales of Saturn—wood and stream;
But who shall follow on the awful sweep
Of Neptune through the dim and dreadful deep?
Onward he wanders in the unknown night,
And we are shadows moving in a dream.

ERNEST FENOLLOSA

(1853–1908)

from *East and West*

from *The Separated West*

Soul of my inner face, face of my race,
Strong mask of self-assertion, positive,
Firm lip of competition, masculine,
Broad brow of Mercury, quick, cunning, keen,
Fierce eye of Mars with crest of sunlit fringe!
Through nights of Time I mark thy luminous course,
Furrowing rich worlds with prow piratical,
Grafting new shoots on broken racial stems,
Sowing old soils fresh fertilized with blood.
Thou art the sieve of men, whence weaker bulks
Slip through the meshes to oblivion.
Breathe through my blood once more thy feverish glow,
Long chilled by cooling crusts of compromise;
Thou, strong in reciprocity of needs,
Expansive self-willed personality!

Standing upon the vantage-ground of peaks
Kissed by the light of rising Easter dawns,
I mark long lines of shadows surge like ghosts
Waging with noiseless shout their mimic war.
  As some vast wave o'ertopping lunar tides,
Engendered at the bottom of the sea
By stifled monsters wrenched, whose fissured mouths
Feed on her protoplasmic gelatines,
Sweeps on with circling rim, like living discs
Of light from stars long centuries extinct,
Slipping from pole to pole as if a hand
Caressed the tiny surface of this ball; —
So from dark mouths of prehistoric woods
Which once had reared their gloomy palisades
To hail the slow retreat of baffled ice,

Issue chill floods of melting Northern snows,
A wild Teutonic wave of glacial steel
Submerging Roman worlds; with surge of spray
Mocking the lonely sentinels of Alps,
Cresting the faithful bar of Apennines,
Storming the portals of the Pyrenees,
Tainting the sunlit laughter of the Rhine
With eddying crimson shrieks of tortured hearts;—
A flood of human fiends, by furies driven
To quaff the wine of life from lipless skulls,
And doom for slaves fair weeping captive maids
In marts of their own marble palaces.

lines 1–42

   The West provokes the East. The iron arm
Slips off the narrow edges of this world.
Flaxen-haired vandals hunt for zest of blood
The black striped tigers of the Bengalee,
Scaling the slippery crests of Himavats,
Holding the poisoned cup to Mongol lips.
See in last glimpse how unchecked years condense
The forces of destruction.—Miles of wall
Gemmed like enamelled rainbows, gleam of lakes
Shot through fair parks, whose lines of granite bridge
Sweep like the sculptured drapery of a god;
Cresting the hill a dream of jewelled tents
Caught from the mirror of the sunset skies,
Now crystallized in marble terraces,
And gilded pillars, and the arch of roofs
Bright with chromatic coronet of tiles,
And endless treasures of green-hearted bronze,
And blood-red urns, and rare canary sheens
Flashed from a whispering sea of draperies;—
The Summer Palace of the Dragon Throne
Unmatched by all the wonders of the world;—
Now lapped in flame, whose red remorseful lip
Shrinks from the dread repast, pillars of smoke
Bearing earth's funeral wail to weeping stars

For the lost marvel of the centuries; —
Like crumbling glow of Alexandria's tomes
Or shattered fragments of the Parthenon!

lines 161 – 87

The Separated East

O sweet dead artist and seer, O tender prophetic priest,
Draw me aside the curtain that veils the heart of your East.

O wing of the Empress of mountains,
Brood white o'er a world of surprises;
And soar to thy Sun as she rises
From the mazarine arch of her fountains.
For thine islands she dropped in the reeds
As a girdle of emerald beads,
And her rainbow promise of genius spanned
As a bridge for the gods to their chosen land.
And her last pure poet shall sing
Like a farewell note
From a nightingale's throat
Of her peace, through thy roseate window of Spring.

I saw him last in the solemn grove
Where the orange temples of Kásŭga shine,
Feeding the timorous deer that rove
Through her tall, dark, purple pillars of pine,
And marking the pattern of leaves
Which the golden mesh of the willow weaves
On the olive bed of her moss-grown eaves.
And I cried to my painter-sage,
"O spirit lone of a bygone age,
Smiling mid ruin and change,
With faith in the beautiful soul of things,
I would gaze on the jewels thy vision brings
From the calm interior depths of its range.
For I 've flown from my West
Like a desolate bird from a broken nest

To learn thy secret of joy and rest.
Quaff from thy fancy's chalice,
And build me anew the fairy palace
With arches gilded and ceiling pearled
Where dwells the soul of thine Asian world."

Then I thought that his smile grew finer,
As if touched with an insight diviner;
Dear Hogai, my master,
Perched on a wild wistaria stem.
And I marked the light on his mantle's hem
Of a halo pure as a purple aster.
And the cold green blades of a bamboo spear
Pierced to his hand through the atmosphere,
Like the note of a silver bell to the ear.
And his voice came soft as the hymn
Which the snow-clad virgins in cloister dim
Were chanting, with rhythmical sway of limb.
"The past is the seed in the heart of a rose
Whose petalled present shall fade as it blows.
The past is the seed in the soul of man,
The infinite Now of the spirit's span.
For flesh is a flower
That blooms for an hour;
And the soul is the seed
Which determines the breed,
The past in the present
For monarch or peasant.
Eye to eye
'T is ourselves we spy;
For doom or grace
One manifold face;
Life's triumphs and errors
In self-resurrections,
Like endless reflections
From parallel mirrors.

"Now I speed on a charger of wind
To the snow-capped castles of Ind.
Mid statues of Buddha the meek,

Link between Mongol and Greek,
Kanishka haughty and lone
Here lolled on his sculptured throne,
The great Vasubandhu to mark,
Lion-faced patriarch.
Now moss like a pall
Shrouds the ruined wall;
Afar in the desert the tigers call.
One pilgrim alone
From its sandy bed
Is lifting a beautiful Buddha's head.
'O take me, loved of the dragon throne,
Back to thy pious imperial prince;
For ages and ages since
'T was I who carved that form
From the limestone warm.
I 'll show thee where germinate in the soil
A thousand truncated gods for thy spoil.
Gather these Bodhisats,
And battle-scarred features of grim Arhats,
And arrogant alabaster kings
With eyes of jacinth
Dethroned from their plinth,
And the masterful heads of Scythian knights
Scowling in mortal fights
With misshapen elemental things.
And hurry thy laden ship
On a heaven-blessed homeward trip; —
So shall the Northern and Eastern plains
Clap their hands at thy gains.
For the light of unborn states
From these things radiates;
Blood for solution
Of crystal worlds Confucian;
Stars for the final Asian man
Rising in far Japan.
I 'll paint on the wall
Of thy Tartar capital
Blue gods unmoved in everlasting flame,
Vast planetary coils without a name,

Invigorating thrills
From unseen wills.
And spurred by these I shall cast
Black bronze in an infinite mould,
As high as a pine
And as fine
As the patient jeweller carves his gold;
Impersonal types which shall last
As the noblest ideals of the Past.'

*   *   *   *   *   *   *   *

"O crystalline flash at the bar of billows!
 O amethyst gate of the Eastern seas!
 O balmy bosom of soft spring willows!
 O pearly vision of white plum trees!

"O blest Hangchow, I fly to thee now
 As a fluttering dove to her leafy home;
 As the seabirds sweep o'er the spray of the deep
 To the reedy fringe of Sientang's foam.

"Now a mirror of pines thy soft lake shines
 By the dewy breath of the morning kissed.
 And the spouting rills like the blood of the hills
 Are drunk by the passionate lips of the mist.

"In a tangle of leaves with silken sleeves
 Thy poets sing on the terraced beach,
 Where the blue-flagged taverns with mossy eaves
 Are starred by the pink of the blossoming peach.

"Thy ramparts rise with roofs to the skies
 Like a jewelled cluster of golden peaks.
 'Neath the crystal ridge of the arching bridge
 Is the dreamy shade which the boatman seeks.

"While sunbeams play on the rock-hewn way
 To the dizzy heights of his temple's spire,
 Like a spirit roves in mountain groves
 The priestly painter with soul a-fire.

"Nor frost of age shall the saintly sage
 Restrain from the balm of his walk at noon;
 Nor the hem of the night retard the flight
 Of the maiden who bares her breast to the moon.

"In dainty dells where the silver bells
 Of far-off temples caress the breeze,
 Shall nature's child with her locks blown wild
 Her herbs let fall as she falls on her knees.

"For visions come on the noontide hum
 Of soul in the infinite warmth of things,
 The mirror of moods where spirit broods
 With the glory of love on her half-grown wings.

"There knotted pines with their storm-torn lines
 Are stamped with the stress of a passion human;
 And the willow swims on its current of limbs
 Like the yielding heart of a queenly woman.

"And mountains crossed by the track of the frost,
 And rocks that harden with weight of woes,
 And rivers that hide like a sweet, shy bride,
 And thorns which sting in the kiss of a rose,

"And habits that twine in a clinging vine,
 And innocent herons in lotus beds,
 And water that showers the vernal flowers,
 Are the patterns of soul with its rainbow threads.

"And a song of pity is rife in the city;
 And the marts of toil are a revel of mirth;
 And the passion of labor is help to a neighbor
 For the sake of the love God breathes on the earth.

"Let the painter paint a world for a saint!
 Let the poet sing of the realm of the heart!
 Where the spur of duty is the passion for beauty
 There Love is a law, and the Law is an art.

"O crystalline flash at the bar of billows,
  O tremulous secret the pine-trees hum!
  There once was a life like the peace of thy willows,—
  But night shuts down, and my voice is dumb.

                *   *   *   *   *   *   *   *

"Farewell to the dawn in the meadow!
  Farewell to the glint on the dew!
  All hail to the wing of the shadow,
  And a kiss for the curse of the new!
  'T is the flight of the wild goose graven
  On the pale green gold of the West;
  And I wake to the call of the raven.
  Let me sing to the land of my rest!

"O land where the towns are like garden blooms!
  O land where the maids are like peaches!
  O gardens faint with their own perfumes!
  O maidens like waves on the beaches!
  O erratic child Japanese!
  Heir of Mongolian peace,
  Though we know not thy fate hereafter,
  Thank God for thy genuine laughter.
  Bathe in the passing mood of thy mirth
  As in sunlit ether the earth;
  Like the plunging bow of a ship
  In the pools of thy faith still dip;
  And freshen the Asian ideal
  In the cooling floods of the real.

"Not for sages only
  Or hermits lonely
  Blows the bud of truth;
  But for innocent youth,
  Hearts that smile
  With no shadow of guile.
  Let pink-veined pleasure bloom!
  Bliss
  Like the kiss
  Of a summer air,
  Roving it knows not where,

Blessing it cares not whom!
Words
Like the glad good morning of the birds;
Loves
Like the coo of doves;
Soft whispers
As of fair nuns at vespers;
Airs
Pure as a child's first prayers!
Let us dance
To the moon
In a ring of wild flowers!
In a trance
Let us swoon
On the lap of the hours!
Let us fly
Like a lark to the sky!
Let us graze
Like a dove-eyed fawn
On the purple pastures of haze!
Let us leap on the gem-starred lawn
Of the virginal dawn!
Let us gaze
In a pool
In the heart of a dell
Shady and cool;
On the film of that well
See unexpected
Beauty reflected,
The world of art
Like a thing apart; —
Ripples of notes
From wild birds throats,
Blurred outlines
Of the shimmer of pines,
Tangled masses
Of dew-soaked grasses,
Faint perfumes
From the mirrored blooms!
This is thy mission,

O child of transition,
To illumine the gloomy pages
Of later ages.
Retain simplicity
Even to eccentricity,
Prize individuality
As man's divinest quality,
The spontaneity
Of Deity!
Teach them the music fine
In the curve of a perfect line;
Teach them to water their art
With the blood of the heart!

"O happy children of blest Japan,
 Relics of elemental man
 Before souls wilt
 In the parching consciousness of guilt!
 Dance to the tune of thy flutes,
 Or weep at thy pathos of lutes;
 Gather like laughing stars
 Round the course of thy festal cars;
 Light the smoking torch
 O'er the flower-bed in thy porch;
 Hang evergreen
 On the gate at New Year's e'en;
 Love storks and deer
 And all things significant and queer;
 Wine cups of buds like myrtles,
 And the hairy tails of turtles,
 Pigeons feasting on temple crumbs,
 The explosive eloquence of plums;
 Crowds picnicking merry
 In snowy vistas of cherry,
 Where perfumed avalanches
 Slip from the laden branches;
 Leap of the carp
 To strike the wistaria's harp,
 Garlands to deck the brow
 Of the marble cow;

The pleasant croon
Of far secluded priests at noon
Gliding o'er lacquered floors,
Pacing long lines of orange corridors,
Where the dim gold Buddh of the altars
Nods to the hum of their psalters!
In the very incense smoke
Consecrate thy harmless joke;
Banter of paradoxes,
Folk-lore of badgers and foxes;
Fathers of families
Preaching droll homilies;
Children in merry hosts
Frightened by masks of ghosts,
Toasting rice-cakes on winter nights,
Battling with saw-stringed kites,
Sisters and brothers
Basking like kittens in the love of their mothers!

"O mother heart, pierced with keen
Anxieties that banish sleep
For sons who rove on the deep,
Pray to the holy snow-white Queen,
Spirit of Providence
Choosing her throne
On the cold gray stone,
In love intense
Sweeping with inner sense
O'er miles of watery waste,
Rushing in haste
Where cold billows lift monstrous lips
To suck in blasted hulls of ships!
Pray for the golden peace
Of the Buddha of Infinite Light!
Let the importunity cease
Of the Self who knocks in the night!
Make thy choice
Of the low inarticulate voice!
Save the man at thy breast
Who screams

At the sting of the gold in his dreams,
The unholy strife of the West!"

     *   *   *   *   *   *   *   *

O wing of the Empress of mountains!
So sang thy last poet at Kásŭga's fountains.
The chant of the vestals had ceased.
The moon was awake in the East.
The love-locked pine-branches o'er us
Tinkled their bells in sympathetic chorus;
And the willow wept
Where the violet smiled as she slept.
My heart too was swelling
With the tears of a love past telling.
But I said: —
"O blossom of life in a dew-starred bed,
Thou art too sweet for this earth,
Too exquisite to linger;
Like the peace of a blest babe who dies at birth,
Like the agony of tears
When the young mother robbed of its prayed-for years
Kisses the listless finger.
Say, on the feminine curves of thy plain
Rises no rock for a counter-strain?
Are there no trumpets to shriek
In the sleeping ear of the meek?
No comet to threaten the sun?"
Yes, there was one; —
One priest white-robed who seemed to glide
Like a ghost from the rock at my side,
With a smile that pierced like a sword
And a soul-compelling word.
And I heard him say,
As we fell on our knees to pray: —

"The fire of combat flashes
'Neath the grass-grown slopes of the ashes.
The planets are held in their places
By the struggles of mighty races.
Choice souls have forever come

To be trained for their martyrdom
Since the days when Kukai hurled
His dart from the Chinese world.
What can the dreaming people know
Of the tempest surging below,
Of the devils storming the very
Fort of the monastery?
He who would strangle an elf
Must first of all conquer himself;
The true knight
With his own heart fight,
Antagony
Of untold agony!
On no external god relying,
Self-armed, heaven and hell alike defying,
Lonely,
With bare will only,
Biting his bitter blood-stained sod; —
This for the *world*, as for Japan,
This is to be a man!
This is to be a god!"

Fuji at Sunrise

Startling the cool gray depths of morning air
    She throws aside her counterpane of clouds,
    And stands half folded in her silken shrouds
With calm white breast and snowy shoulder bare.
High o'er her head a flush all pink and rare
    Thrills her with foregleam of an unknown bliss,
    A virgin pure who waits the bridal kiss,
Faint with expectant joy she fears to share.
Lo, now he comes, the dazzling prince of day!
    Flings his full glory o'er her radiant breast;
    Enfolds her to the rapture of his rest,
Transfigured in the throbbing of his ray.
O fly, my soul, where love's warm transports are;
And seek eternal bliss in yon pink kindling star!

from *Ode on Reincarnation*

III

Here let me sit, in this empty, cool, terraced hall.
The soft breeze wafts into beautiful curve the thick line of
    incense smoke;
The great boom of Chionin's bell seems to pulse its length.
The great truth flashes on me of sitting just so before!—
Was it when Nobunaga built new towers in the West?
Was she the Lady O-tsu who sang poems at my side?
Or was I some noble believer of the Fujiwara court,
And did Komachi flash for me her matchless songs?
And there are vistas beyond of Indian and Chinese ages
    rolling their beauty and faith into the lap of Kioto!
I feel, I know, that the continuity of that spirit is not
    broken.
Though no lady or priest prays through my lingering soul,
    and these courts seem silent,
Yet is this moment before my death but as the links of sleep
    which bind the jewelled beads of my days.
I feel,—I know—I have lived here, and shall live again!

VIII

I remember an ancient Chinese picture kept over there in
    Daitokuji,
That long low pair of roofs to the North that cut the
    brocaded green of the rice-fields, like gray scissors.
No one but him of the Dragon's Brightness could have
    designed it.
Once it was exhibited to the blind, borrowed for the Art
    Museum of Boston.
It was a world of clouds, as should befit a mystic soul-
    drama;
Far up peered out the wrinkled and unkempt gray face of a
    dead saint.
Awakened by the prayers of floating spirits to behold the
    wonder of his own immediate re-incarnation,
He stared in bewilderment with his hands instinctively
    clasped in prayer.

A simply clad pair, a Chinese husband and wife, stood
      reverently with frames bent slightly forward,
Hands clasped, faces sweetly lifted in gladness, but in
      absence of wonder at the miracle,
Stood ready to receive the soul for which they had prayed.
And lo, walking down the path of the clouds,
A figure like a Chinese nurse, in cap and wadded garment,
But gleaming with unearthly brightness,
Bears to them with careful step on a golden dish, and
      wrapped in a crystal globe,
A little naked crouching babe, the soft casket of the new-old
      soul;
While back of all stands a master spirit, whose very fingers
      are like knots with the currents of power.
Here between two clay tabernacles of the dead and quick
Hovered the soul in the miracle of an immediate passage
Of a saint whose life deserved instant renewal of its self-
      sacrifice, whose continuity of life the world needed.
Yet it is but the perfect type of what in us is only delayed.
It will not be long before these old hands which can do
      hardly more than relight this incense,
Will be bathing in azalea flames on Mount Hiyeizan, and
      patting the mossy grisly face of some wayside Jizo.

JAMES A. BLAND

(1854–1911)

Oh, Dem Golden Slippers!

Oh, my golden slippers am laid away,
Kase I don't 'spect to wear 'em till my weddin' day,
And my long-tail'd coat, dat I loved so well,
I will wear up in de chariot in de morn;
And my long, white robe dat I bought last June,
I'm gwine to git changed kase it fits too soon,
And de ole grey hoss dat I used to drive,
I will hitch him to de chariot in de morn.

> *Oh, dem golden slippers! Oh, dem golden slippers!*
> *Golden slippers I'm gwine to wear, becase dey look so neat;*
> *Oh, dem golden slippers! Oh, dem golden slippers!*
> *Golden slippers Ise gwine to wear, to walk de golden street.*

Oh, my ole banjo hangs on de wall,
Kase it aint been tuned since way last fall,
But de darks all say we will hab a good time,
When we ride up in de chariot in de morn;
Dar's ole Brudder Ben and Sister Luce,
Dey will telegraph de news to Uncle Bacco Juice,
What a great camp-meetin' der will be dat day,
When we ride up in de chariot in de morn.

> *Chorus.*

So, it's good bye, children, I will have to go
Whar de rain don't fall or de wind don't blow,
And yer ulster coats, why, yer will not need,
When yer ride up in de chariot in de morn;
But yer golden slippers must be nice and clean,
And yer age must be just sweet sixteen,
And yer white kid gloves yer will have to wear,
When yer ride up in de chariot in de morn.

> *Chorus.*

Carry Me Back to Old Virginny

Carry me back to old Virginny,
There's where the cotton and the corn and tatoes grow,
There's where the birds warble sweet in the springtime,
There's where the old darkey's heart am long'd to go.
There's where I labor'd so hard for old massa,
Day after day in the field of yellow corn,
No place on earth do I love more sincerely
Than old Virginny, the state where I was born.

Carry me back to old Virginny,
There let me live 'till I wither and decay,
Long by the old Dismal Swamp have I wander'd,
There's where this old darkey's life will pass away.
Massa and missis have long gone before me,
Soon we will meet on that bright and golden shore.
There we'll be happy and free from all sorrow,
There's where we'll meet and we'll never part no more.

LIZETTE WOODWORTH REESE

(1856–1935)

Love, Weeping, Laid This Song

On a Copy of the Iliad Found with the Mummy of a Young Girl

Lo! an old song, yellow with centuries!
    She, she who with her young dust kept it sweet;
    She, in some green court on a carvëd seat,
Read it at dusk fair-paged upon her knees;
And, looking up, saw there, beyond the trees,
    Tall Helen through the darkling shadows fleet;
    And heard, out in the fading river-street,
The roar of battle like the roar of seas.
Love, weeping, laid this song when she was dead
    In that sealed chamber, strange with nard and musk.
        Outliving Egypt, see it here at last.
We touch its leaves: back rush the seasons sped;
    For us, as once for her, in that old dusk,
        Troy trembles like a reed before the blast!

One Night

One lily scented all the dark. It grew
Down the drenched walk a spike of ghostly white.
Fine, sweet, sad noises thrilled the tender night,
From insects couched on blades that dripped with dew.
The road beyond, cleaving the great fields through,
Echoed no footstep; like a streak of light,
The gaunt and blossoming elder gleamed in sight.
The boughs began to quake, and warm winds blew,
And whirled a myriad petals down the air.
An instant, peaked and black the old house stood;
The next, its gables showed a tremulous gray,
Then deepening gold; the next, the world lay bare!
The moon slipped out the leash of the tall wood,
And through the heavenly meadows fled away.

April in Town

Straight from the east the wind blows sharp with rain,
  That just now drove its wild ranks down the street,
  And westward rushed into the sunset sweet.
Spouts brawl, boughs drip and cease and drip again,
Bricks gleam; keen saffron glows each window-pane,
  And every pool beneath the passing feet.
  Innumerable odors fine and fleet
Are blown this way from blossoming lawn and lane.
Wet roofs show black against a tender sky;
  The almond bushes in the lean-fenced square,
    Beaten to the walks, show all their draggled white.
A troop of laborers comes slowly by;
  One bears a daffodil, and seems to bear
    A new-lit candle through the fading light.

In Time of Grief

Dark, thinned, beside the wall of stone,
The box dripped in the air;
Its odor through my house was blown
Into the chamber there.

Remote and yet distinct the scent,
The sole thing of the kind,
As though one spoke a word half meant
That left a sting behind.

I knew not Grief would go from me,
And naught of it be plain,
Except how keen the box can be
After a fall of rain.

A Lyric on the Lyric

This road our blithe-heart elders knew,
    And down it trooped together;
They plucked their reeds from out the dew,
    And piped the morning weather.

Shepherd or gallant, cloak or smock,
    They lead where we do follow;
Hear Colin there among his flock
    To Phyllis in the hollow!

Corinna goes a-Maying yet;
    Phillida's laugh is ringing;
And see Castara, violet
    Of early English singing.

But were these lovers never sad,
    Did not some heart go breaking?
Were youth and cowslips to be had
    Just for the simple taking?

Oh, Sorrow, too, has gone this way,
    And Loss as well as Leisure;
Yet Sorrow lasted for a day,
    And Loss through scarce a measure.

And here Beau Waller stayed to snatch,
    Just at Oblivion's portal,
A single rose that none can match—
    And after grew immortal.

No rain can strip it of its red;
    No gust pelt out its savor;
Though Celia died and he is dead,
    This is the rose he gave her.

What riverside shall grow once more
    The reed bared of dull teaching?
And who shall bring unto our door
    Music instead of preaching?

Yet here forget the evil days;
    Let go the Now and After;
Our blithe-heart elders trooped these ways,
    And filled them full of Laughter!

Death's Guerdon

Secure in death he keeps the hearts he had;
    Two women have forgot the bitter truth;
To one he is but her sweet little lad;
    To one the husband of her youth.

The Lavender Woman

A Market Song

Crooked, like bough the March wind bends wallward across
    the sleet,
Stands she at her blackened stall in the loud market street;
All about her in the sun, full-topped, exceeding sweet,
Lie bundles of gray lavender, a-shrivel in the heat.

What the Vision that is mine, coming over and o'er?
'T is the Dorset levels, aye, behind me and before;
Creeks that slip without a sound from flaggy shore to shore;
Orchards gnarled with spring-times and as gust-bound as of
    yore.

Oh, the panes at sunset burning rich-red as the rose!
Oh, colonial chimneys that the punctual swallow knows!
Land where like a memory the salt scent stays or goes;
Where wealthy is the reaper and right glad is he that sows!

Drips and drips the last June rain, but toward the evenfall
Copper gleam the little pools behind the pear-trees tall;
In a whirl of violet, and the fairest thing of all,
The lavender, the lavender sways by the sagging wall!

.   .   .   .

Fade the levels, the sea-scent, the sheltered garden space;
Town roars all about me, and its roofs are here apace;
Country-sick, with heavy step my homeward road I trace,
Bearing the keen stuff I bought in the loud market-place.

Oh, my heart, why should you break at any thoughts like
          these?
So sooth are they of the old time that they should bring you
          ease;
Of Hester in the lavender and out among the bees,
Clipping the long stalks one by one under the Dorset trees.

KATHARINE LEE BATES

America the Beautiful

O beautiful for spacious skies,
   For amber waves of grain,
For purple mountain majesties
   Above the fruited plain!
     America! America!
   God shed His grace on thee
And crown thy good with brotherhood
   From sea to shining sea!

O beautiful for pilgrim feet,
   Whose stern, impassioned stress
A thoroughfare for freedom beat
   Across the wilderness!
     America! America!
   God mend thine every flaw,
Confirm thy soul in self-control,
   Thy liberty in law!

O beautiful for heroes proved
   In liberating strife,
Who more than self their country loved,
   And mercy more than life!
     America! America!
   May God thy gold refine,
Till all success be nobleness,
   And every gain divine!

O beautiful for patriot dream
   That sees beyond the years
Thine alabaster cities gleam
   Undimmed by human tears!
     America! America!
   God shed His grace on thee
And crown thy good with brotherhood
   From sea to shining sea!

CLINTON SCOLLARD

(1860–1932)

As I Came Down from Lebanon

As I came down from Lebanon,
Came winding, wandering slowly down
Through mountain passes bleak and brown,
The cloudless day was well-nigh done.
The city, like an opal set
In emerald, showed each minaret
Afire with radiant beams of sun,
And glistened orange, fig and lime
Where song-birds made melodious chime,
As I came down from Lebanon.

As I came down from Lebanon,
Like lava in the dying glow,
Through olive orchards far below
I saw the murmuring river run;
And 'neath the wall upon the sand
Swart sheiks from distant Samarcand,
With precious spices they had won,
Lay long and languidly in wait
Till they might pass the guarded gate,
As I came down from Lebanon.

As I came down from Lebanon,
I saw strange men from lands afar
In mosque and square and gay bazaar,
The Magi that the Moslem shun,
And grave Effendi from Stamboul
Who sherbet sipped in corners cool;
And, from the balconies o'errun
With roses, gleamed the eyes of those
Who dwell in still seraglios,
As I came down from Lebanon.

As I came down from Lebanon
The flaming flower of daytime died,
And Night, arrayed as is a bride
Of some great king in garments spun
Of purple and the finest gold,
Outbloomed in glories manifold;
Until the moon, above the dun
And darkening desert, void of shade,
Shone like a keen Damascus blade,
As I came down from Lebanon.

A Bit of Marble

This bit of polished marble—this—
    Was found where Athens proudly rears
Its temple-crowned Acropolis
    So hoar with years.

In antique time some sculptor's hand,
    Deft-turning, carved it fine and small,
A part of base, or column grand,
    Or capital.

Pentelicus' white heart it knew
    Before the chisel fashioned it;
Long ere so fair of form it grew,
    And delicate.

Regarding it, I mind me so
    A song should be, with ardor wrought,—
Cut in the firm Pentelic snow
    Of lofty thought.

HAMLIN GARLAND

(1860–1940)

Indian Summer

At last there came
The sudden fall of frost, when Time
Dreaming through russet September days
Suddenly awoke, and lifting his head, strode
Swiftly forward—made one vast desolating sweep
Of his scythe, then, rapt with the glory
That burned under his feet, fell dreaming again.
And the clouds soared and the crickets sang
In the brief heat of noon; the corn,
So green, grew sere and dry—
    And in the mist the ploughman's team
    Moved silently, as if in dream—
And it was Indian summer on the plain.

In August

From the great trees the locusts cry
In quavering ecstatic duo—a boy
Shouts a wild call—a mourning dove
In the blue distance sobs—the wind
Wanders by, heavy with odors
Of corn and wheat and melon vines;
The trees tremble with delirious joy as the breeze
Greets them, one by one—now the oak,
Now the great sycamore, now the elm.

And the locusts in brazen chorus, cry
Like stricken things, and the ring-dove's note
Sobs on in the dim distance.

On the Mississippi

Through wild and tangled forests
  The broad, unhasting river flows—
   Spotted with rain-drops, gray with night;
    Upon its curving breast there goes
A lonely steamboat's larboard light,
   A blood-red star against the shadowy oaks;
Noiseless as a ghost, through greenish gleam
Of fire-flies, before the boat's wild scream—
     A heron flaps away
     Like silence taking flight.

Fighting Fire

A creeping serrate line of dusty red,
That gnaws its way across a smooth low hill
Toward long ricks of grain.
Silhouetted against the murky light four men,
With spades at back, stride singly
With unhasting resolute action along the hill
From left to right. Against the wall
Of red and purple smoke
Each form leans in sharp outline;
The smell of burning hay fills the train;
Then loosely, amply, as a curtain falls
Swinging in the wind, the smoke shuts down
And all is lost to sight.

Boyish Sleep

And all night long we lie in sleep,
   Too sweet to sigh in, or to dream,
Unnoting how the wild winds sweep,
   Or snow clouds through the darkness stream
Above the trees that moan and sigh
   And clutch with naked hands the sky.
Beneath the checkered counterpane
   We rest the soundlier for the storm;
Its wrath is only lullaby,
   A far off, vast and dim refrain.

HARRIET MONROE

(1860–1936)

To W. S. M.

With a copy of Shelley.

Behold, I send thee to the heights of song,
My brother! Let thine eyes awake as clear
As morning dew, within whose glowing sphere
Is mirrored half a world; and listen long,
Till in thine ears, famished to keenness, throng
The bugles of the soul—till far and near
Silence grows populous, and wind and mere
Are phantom-choked with voices. Then be strong—
Then halt not till thou seest the beacons flare
Souls mad for truth have lit from peak to peak.
Haste on to breathe the intoxicating air—
Wine to the brave and poison to the weak—
Far in the blue where angels' feet have trod,
Where earth is one with heaven, and man with God.

LOUISE IMOGEN GUINEY

(1861—1920)

A Salutation

High-hearted Surrey! I do love your ways,
Venturous, frank, romantic, vehement,
All with inviolate honor sealed and blent,
To the axe-edge that cleft your soldier-bays:
I love your youth, your friendships, whims, and frays;
Your strict, sweet verse, with its imperious bent,
Heard as in dreams from some old harper's tent,
And stirring in the listener's brain for days.
Good father-poet! if to-night there be
At Framlingham none save the north-wind's sighs,
No guard but moonlight's crossed and trailing spears,
Smile yet upon the pilgrim named like me,
Close at your gates, whose fond and weary eyes
Sought not one other down three hundred years!

At a Symphony

Oh, I would have these tongues oracular
Dip into silence, tease no more, let be!
They madden, like some choral of the free
Gusty and sweet against a prison-bar.
To earth the boast that her gold empires are,
The menace of delicious death to me,
Great Undesign, strong as by God's decree,
Piercing the heart with beauty from afar!
Music too winning to the sense forlorn!
Of what angelic lineage was she born,
Bred in what rapture?—These her sires and friends:
Censure, Denial, Gloom, and Hunger's throe.
Praised be the Spirit that thro' thee, Schubert! so
Wrests evil unto wholly heavenly ends.

W. H.

1778 – 1830

Between the wet trees and the sorry steeple,
Keep, Time, in dark Soho, what once was Hazlitt,
Seeker of Truth, and finder oft of Beauty;

Beauty's a sinking light, ah, none too faithful;
But Truth, who leaves so here her spent pursuer,
Forgets not her great pawn: herself shall claim it.

Therefore sleep safe, thou dear and battling spirit,
Safe also on our earth, begetting ever
Some one love worth the ages and the nations!

Nothing falls under to thine eyes eternal.
Sleep safe in dark Soho: the stars are shining,
Titian and Wordsworth live; the People marches.

Open, Time

Open, Time, and let him pass
Shortly where his feet would be!
Like a leaf at Michaelmas
Swooning from the tree,

Ere its hour the manly mind
Trembles in a sure decrease,
Nor the body now can find
Any hold on peace.

Take him, weak and overworn;
Fold about his dying dream
Boyhood, and the April morn,
And the rolling stream:

Weather on a sunny ridge,
Showery weather, far from here;
Under some deep-ivied bridge,
Water rushing clear:

Water quick to cross and part,
(Golden light on silver sound),
Weather that was next his heart
All the world around!

Soon upon his vision break
These, in their remembered blue;
He shall toil no more, but wake
Young, in air he knew.

He has done with roofs and men.
Open, Time, and let him pass,
Vague and innocent again,
Into country grass.

Fog

Like bodiless water passing in a sigh,
Thro' palsied streets the fatal shadows flow,
And in their sharp disastrous undertow
Suck in the morning sun, and all the sky.
The towery vista sinks upon the eye,
As if it heard the Hebrew bugles blow,
Black and dissolved; nor could the founders know
How what was built so bright should daily die.

Thy mood with man's is broken and blent in,
City of Stains! and ache of thought doth drown
The primitive light in which thy life began;
Great as thy dole is, smirchèd with his sin,
Greater and elder yet the love of man
Full in thy look, tho' the dark visor's down.

Strikers in Hyde Park

A woof reversed the fatal shuttles weave,
How slow! but never once they slip the thread.
Hither, upon the Georgian idlers' tread,
Up spacious ways the lindens interleave,
Clouding the royal air since yester-eve,
Come men bereft of time and scant of bread,
Loud, who were dumb, immortal, who were dead,
Thro' the cowed world their kingdom to retrieve.

What ails thee, England? Altar, mart, and grange
Dream of the knife by night; not so, not so
The clear Republic waits the general throe,
Along her noonday mountains' open range.
God be with both! for one is young to know
The other's rote of evil and of change.

The Lights of London

The evenfall, so slow on hills, hath shot
Far down into the valley's cold extreme,
Untimely midnight; spire and roof and stream
Like fleeing spectres, shudder and are not.
The Hampstead hollies, from their sylvan plot
Yet cloudless, lean to watch as in a dream,
From chaos climb with many a sudden gleam,
London, one moment fallen and forgot.

Her booths begin to flare; and gases bright
Prick door and window; all her streets obscure
Sparkle and swarm with nothing true nor sure,
Full as a marsh of mist and winking light;
Heaven thickens over, Heaven that cannot cure
Her tear by day, her fevered smile by night.

In the Reading-Room of the British Museum

Praised be the moon of books! that doth above
A world of men, the fallen Past behold,
And fill the spaces else so void and cold
To make a very heaven again thereof;
As when the sun is set behind a grove,
And faintly unto nether ether rolled,
All night his whiter image and his mould
Grows beautiful with looking on her love.

Thou therefore, moon of so divine a ray,
Lend to our steps both fortitude and light!
Feebly along a venerable way
They climb the infinite, or perish quite;
Nothing are days and deeds to such as they,
While in this liberal house thy face is bright.

Sunday Chimes in the City

Across the bridge, where in the morning blow
The wrinkled tide turns homeward, and is fain
Homeward to drag the black sea-goer's chain,
And the long yards by Dowgate dipping low;
Across dispeopled ways, patient and slow,
Saint Magnus and Saint Dunstan call in vain:
From Wren's forgotten belfries, in the rain,
Down the blank wharves the dropping octaves go.

Forbid not these! Tho' no man heed, they shower
A subtle beauty on the empty hour,
From all their dark throats aching and outblown;
Aye in the prayerless places welcome most,
Like the last gull that up a naked coast
Deploys her white and steady wing, alone.

EDITH WHARTON

(1862–1937)

The Last Giustiniani

O wife, wife, wife! As if the sacred name
Could weary one with saying! Once again
Laying against my brow your lips' soft flame,
Join with me, Sweetest, in love's new refrain,
Since the whole music of my late-found life
Is that we call each other "husband—wife."

And yet, stand back, and let your cloth of gold
Straighten its sumptuous lines from waist to knee,
And, flowing firmly outward, fold on fold,
Invest your slim young form with majesty
As when, in those calm bridal robes arrayed,
You stood beside me, and I was afraid.

I was afraid—O sweetness, whiteness, youth,
Best gift of God, I feared you! I, indeed,
For whom all womanhood has been, forsooth,
Summed up in the sole Virgin of the Creed,
I thought that day our Lady's self stood there
And bound herself to me with vow and prayer.

Ah, yes, that day. I sat, remember well,
Half-crook'd above a missal, and laid in
The gold-leaf slowly; silence in my cell;
The picture, Satan tempting Christ to sin
Upon the mount's blue, pointed pinnacle,
The world outspread beneath as fair as hell—

When suddenly they summoned me. I stood
Abashed before the Abbot, who reclined
Full-bellied in his chair beneath the rood,

And roseate with having lately dined;
And then—I standing there abashed—he said:
"The house of Giustiniani all lie dead."

It scarcely seemed to touch me (I had led
A grated life so long) that oversea
My kinsmen in their knighthood should lie dead,
Nor that this sudden death should set me free,
Me, the last Giustiniani—well, what then?
A monk!—The Giustiniani had been men.

So when the Abbot said: "The State decrees
That you, the latest scion of the house
Which died in vain for Venice overseas,
Should be exempted from your sacred vows,
And straightway, when you leave this cloistered place,
Take wife, and add new honors to the race,"

I hardly heard him—would have crept again
To the warped missal—but he snatched a sword
And girded me, and all the heart of men
Rushed through me, as he laughed and hailed me lord,
And, with my hand upon the hilt, I cried,
"Viva San Marco!" like my kin who died.

But, straightway, when, a new-made knight, I stood
Beneath the bridal arch, and saw you come,
A certain monkish warping of the blood
Ran up and struck the man's heart in me dumb;
I breathed an Ave to our Lady's grace,
And did not dare to look upon your face.

And when we swept the waters side by side,
With timbrelled gladness clashing on the air,
I trembled at your image in the tide,
And warded off the devil with a prayer,
Still seeming in a golden dream to move
Through fiendish labyrinths of forbidden love.

But when they left us, and we stood alone,
I, the last Giustiniani, face to face
With your unvisioned beauty, made my own
In this, the last strange bridal of our race,
And, looking up at last to meet your eyes,
Saw in their depths the star of love arise.

Ah, then the monk's garb shrivelled from my heart,
And left me man to face your womanhood.
Without a prayer to keep our lips apart
I turned about and kissed you where you stood,
And gathering all the gladness of my life
Into a new-found word, I called you "wife!"

Life

Life, like a marble block, is given to all,
A blank, inchoate mass of years and days,
Whence one with ardent chisel swift essays
Some shape of strength or symmetry to call;
One shatters it in bits to mend a wall;
One in a craftier hand the chisel lays,
And one, to wake the mirth in Lesbia's gaze,
Carves it apace in toys fantastical.

But least is he who, with enchanted eyes
Filled with high visions of fair shapes to be,
Muses which god he shall immortalize
In the proud Parian's perpetuity,
Till twilight warns him from the punctual skies
That the night cometh wherein none shall see.

Experience

I

Like Crusoe with the bootless gold we stand
Upon the desert verge of death, and say:
"What shall avail the woes of yesterday
To buy to-morrow's wisdom, in the land
Whose currency is strange unto our hand?
In life's small market they had served to pay
Some late-found rapture, could we but delay
Till Time hath matched our means to our demand."

But otherwise Fate wills it, for, behold,
Our gathered strength of individual pain,
When Time's long alchemy hath made it gold,
Dies with us—hoarded all these years in vain,
Since those that might be heir to it the mould
Renew, and coin themselves new griefs again.

II

O Death, we come full-handed to thy gate,
Rich with strange burden of the mingled years,
Gains and renunciations, mirth and tears,
And love's oblivion, and remembering hate,
Nor know we what compulsion laid such freight
Upon our souls—and shall our hopes and fears
Buy nothing of thee, Death? Behold our wares,
And sell us the one joy for which we wait.
Had we lived longer, like had such for sale,
With the last coin of sorrow purchased cheap,
But now we stand before thy shadowy pale,
And all our longings lie within thy keep—
Death, can it be the years shall naught avail?

"Not so," Death answered, "they shall purchase sleep."

Chartres

I

Immense, august, like some Titanic bloom,
   The mighty choir unfolds its lithic core,
Petalled with panes of azure, gules and or,
   Splendidly lambent in the Gothic gloom,
And stamened with keen flamelets that illume
   The pale high-altar. On the prayer-worn floor,
By worshippers innumerous thronged of yore,
   A few brown crones, familiars of the tomb,
The stranded driftwood of Faith's ebbing sea—
   For these alone the finials fret the skies,
The topmost bosses shake their blossoms free,
   While from the triple portals, with grave eyes,
Tranquil, and fixed upon eternity,
   The cloud of witnesses still testifies.

II

The crimson panes like blood-drops stigmatise
   The western floor. The aisles are mute and cold.
A rigid fetich in her robe of gold,
   The Virgin of the Pillar, with blank eyes,
Enthroned beneath her votive canopies,
   Gathers a meagre remnant to her fold.
The rest is solitude; the church, grown old,
   Stands stark and grey beneath the burning skies.
Well-nigh again its mighty framework grows
   To be a part of nature's self, withdrawn
From hot humanity's impatient woes;
   The floor is ridged like some rude mountain lawn,
And in the east one giant window shows
   The roseate coldness of an Alp at dawn.

Two Backgrounds

I

La Vierge au Donateur

Here by the ample river's argent sweep,
Bosomed in tilth and vintage to her walls,
A tower-crowned Cybele in armoured sleep
The city lies, fat plenty in her halls,
With calm parochial spires that hold in fee
The friendly gables clustered at their base,
And, equipoised o'er tower and market-place,
The Gothic minster's winged immensity;
And in that narrow burgh, with equal mood,
Two placid hearts, to all life's good resigned,
Might, from the altar to the lych-gate, find
Long years of peace and dreamless plenitude.

II

Mona Lisa

Yon strange blue city crowns a scarpèd steep
No mortal foot hath bloodlessly essayed;
Dreams and illusions beacon from its keep,
But at the gate an Angel bares his blade;
And tales are told of those who thought to gain
At dawn its ramparts; but when evening fell
Far off they saw each fading pinnacle
Lit with wild lightnings from the heaven of pain;
Yet there two souls, whom life's perversities
Had mocked with want in plenty, tears in mirth,
Might meet in dreams, ungarmented of earth,
And drain Joy's awful chalice to the lees.

The Tomb of Ilaria Giunigi

Ilaria, thou that wert so fair and dear
That death would fain disown thee, grief made wise
With prophecy thy husband's widowed eyes,
And bade him call the master's art to rear
Thy perfect image on the sculptured bier,
With dreaming lids, hands laid in peaceful guise
Beneath the breast that seems to fall and rise,
And lips that at love's call should answer "Here!"

First-born of the Renascence, when thy soul
Cast the sweet robing of the flesh aside,
Into these lovelier marble limbs it stole,
Regenerate in art's sunrise clear and wide,
As saints who, having kept faith's raiment whole,
Change it above for garments glorified.

An Autumn Sunset

I

Leaguered in fire
The wild black promontories of the coast extend
Their savage silhouettes;
The sun in universal carnage sets,
And, halting higher,
The motionless storm-clouds mass their sullen threats,
Like an advancing mob in sword-points penned,
That, balked, yet stands at bay.
Mid-zenith hangs the fascinated day
In wind-lustrated hollows crystalline,
A wan Valkyrie whose wide pinions shine
Across the ensanguined ruins of the fray,
And in her hand swings high o'erhead,
Above the waste of war,
The silver torch-light of the evening star
Wherewith to search the faces of the dead.

II

Lagooned in gold,
Seem not those jetty promontories rather
The outposts of some ancient land forlorn,
Uncomforted of morn,
Where old oblivions gather,
The melancholy unconsoling fold
Of all things that go utterly to death
And mix no more, no more
With life's perpetually awakening breath?
Shall Time not ferry me to such a shore,
Over such sailless seas,
To walk with hope's slain importunities
In miserable marriage? Nay, shall not
All things be there forgot,
Save the sea's golden barrier and the black
Close-crouching promontories?
Dead to all shames, forgotten of all glories,
Shall I not wander there, a shadow's shade,
A spectre self-destroyed,
So purged of all remembrance and sucked back
Into the primal void,
That should we on that shore phantasmal meet
I should not know the coming of your feet?

JOHN JAY CHAPMAN

(1862–1933)

Bismarck

At midnight, Death dismissed the chancellor
But left the soul of Bismarck on his face.
Titanic, in the peace and power of bronze,
With three red roses loosely in his grasp,
Lies the Constructor. His machinery
Revolving in the wheels of destiny
Rolls onward over him. Alive, inspired,
Vast, intricate, complete, unthinkable,
Nice as a watch and strong as dynamite,
An empire and a whirlwind, on it moves,
While he that set it rolling lies so still.

Unity! Out of chaos, petty courts,
Princelings and potentates—thrift, jealousy,
Weakness, distemper, cowardice, distrust
To build a nation: the material—
The fibres to be twisted: human strands.
One race, one tongue, one instinct. Unify
By banking prejudice and, gaining power,
Attract by vanity, compel by fear.
Arm to the teeth: your friends will love you more,
And we have much to do for Germany.
Organized hatred, that is unity.

Prussia's a unit; Denmark's enmity
Is so much gain, and gives us all the North.
Next: humble Austria, a rapid stroke
That leaves us laurels and a policy.
Now for some chance, some—any fluke or crime
By which a war with France can be brought on:
And, God be glorified, the thing is done.
Organized hatred. That foundation reaches
The very bottom rock of Germany

And out of it the structure rises up
Bristling with arms.

"But you forget the soul,
"The universal shout, the Kaiser's name,
"Fatherland, anthems, the heroic dead,
"The discipline, the courage, the control,
"The glory and the passion and the flame—"
   Are calculated by the captain's eye
   Are used, subdued, like electricity
   Turned on or off, are set to making roads,
   Or building monuments, or writing verse,
   Twitched by the inspired whim of tyranny
   To make that tyranny perpetual
   And kill what intellect it cannot use.

The age is just beginning, yet we see
The fruits of hatred ripen hourly
And Germany's in bondage—muzzled press—
The private mind suppressed, while shade on shade
Is darkening o'er the intellectual sky.
And world-forgotten, outworn crimes and cries
With dungeon tongue accost the citizen
And send him trembling to his family.

Organized hatred. Educated men
Live in habitual scorn of intellect,
Hate France, hate England, hate America.
Talk corporals, talk until Napoleon
(—Who never could subdue the mind of France)
Seems like some harmless passing episode,
Unable to reveal to modern man
What tyranny could compass. Years of this
Will leave a Germany devoid of fire,
Unlettered, unrebellious, impotent,
Nursing the name of German unity
And doing pilgrimage to Bismarck's shrine,
Bismarck the god, who having but one thought,
Wrote it out largely over Germany
But could not stay to read it. Those who can,

Who reap the crop he sowed may count the grains
And every seed a scourge. For on the heart
One or a million, each envenomed throb
Relentlessly records an injury,
While the encrusted nation loses health,
And like a chemical experiment
The crucible gives back its quantities.

The thing this man employed so cleverly
Was poison then, and poison in the end,
And Germany is writhing in its grip.
For Bismarck, Caesar's broker, bought the men.
They paid their liberties and got revenge—
The ancient bargain. But upon a scale
A scope, a consequence, a stretch of time
That made a camp of Europe, and set back
The cultured continent for centuries.
The fear of fire-arms has dwarfed the French
To gibbering lunatics; and Zola's friends
Are all that France can show for common-sense.
Italy's bankrupt, Russia barbarous
Kept so by isolation, and the force,
The only force that can improve the world,
Enlightened public thought in private men,
Is minimized in Europe, till The Powers
Stand over Crete to watch a butchery
And diplomats decide the fate of men.

Bismarck, how much of all lies in thy head
Thought cannot fathom. But, gigantic wreck,
Thou wast the Instrument. And thy huge limbs
Cover nine kingdoms as thou lie'st asleep.

GEORGE SANTAYANA

(1863–1952)

Sonnet III

O world, thou choosest not the better part!
It is not wisdom to be only wise,
And on the inward vision close the eyes,
But it is wisdom to believe the heart.
Columbus found a world, and had no chart,
Save one that faith deciphered in the skies;
To trust the soul's invincible surmise
Was all his science and his only art.
Our knowledge is a torch of smoky pine
That lights the pathway but one step ahead
Across a void of mystery and dread.
Bid, then, the tender light of faith to shine
By which alone the mortal heart is led
Unto the thinking of the thought divine.

Sonnet V

Dreamt I to-day the dream of yesternight,
Sleep ever feigning one evolving theme,—
Of my two lives which should I call the dream?
Which action vanity? which vision sight?
Some greater waking must pronounce aright,
If aught abideth of the things that seem,
And with both currents swell the flooded stream
Into an ocean infinite of light.
Even such a dream I dream, and know full well
My waking passeth like a midnight spell,
But know not if my dreaming breaketh through
Into the deeps of heaven and of hell.
I know but this of all I would I knew:
Truth is a dream, unless my dream is true.

Sonnet XXV

As in the midst of battle there is room
For thoughts of love, and in foul sin for mirth;
As gossips whisper of a trinket's worth
Spied by the death-bed's flickering candle-gloom;
As in the crevices of Caesar's tomb
The sweet herbs flourish on a little earth:
So in this great disaster of our birth
We can be happy, and forget our doom.
For morning, with a ray of tenderest joy
Gilding the iron heaven, hides the truth,
And evening gently woos us to employ
Our grief in idle catches. Such is youth;
Till from that summer's trance we wake, to find
Despair before us, vanity behind.

Sonnet XLIII

The candour of the gods is in thy gaze,
The strength of Dian in thy virgin hand,
Commanding as the goddess might command,
And lead her lovers into higher ways.
Aye, the gods walk among us in these days,
Had we the docile soul to understand;
And me they visit in this joyless land,
To cheer mine exile and receive my praise.
For once, methinks, before the angels fell,
Thou, too, didst follow the celestial seven
Threading in file the meads of asphodel.
And when thou comest, lady, where I dwell,
The place is flooded with the light of heaven
And a lost music I remember well.

Sonnet XLVIII

Of Helen's brothers, one was born to die
And one immortal, who, the fable saith,
Gave to the other that was nigh to death
One half his widowed immortality.
They would have lived and died alternately,
Breathing each other's warm transmuted breath,
Had not high Zeus, who justly ordereth,
Made them twin stars to shine eternally.
My heart was dying when thy flame of youth
Flooded its chambers through my gazing eyes.
My life is now thy beauty and thy truth.
Thou wouldst come down, forsaking paradise
To be my comfort, but by Heaven's ruth
I go to burn beside thee in the skies.

On a Piece of Tapestry

Hold high the woof, dear friends, that we may see
The cunning mixture of its colours rare.
Nothing in nature purposely is fair,—
Her beauties in their freedom disagree;
But here all vivid dyes that garish be,
To that tint mellowed which the sense will bear,
Glow, and not wound the eye that, resting there,
Lingers to feed its gentle ecstasy.
Crimson and purple and all hues of wine,
Saffron and russet, brown and sober green
Are rich the shadowy depths of blue between;
While silver threads with golden intertwine,
To catch the glimmer of a fickle sheen,—
All the long labour of some captive queen.

Before a Statue of Achilles

I

Behold Pelides with his yellow hair,
Proud child of Thetis, hero loved of Jove;
Above the frowning of his brows it wove
A crown of gold, well combed, with Spartan care.
Who might have seen him, sullen, great, and fair,
As with the wrongful world he proudly strove,
And by high deeds his wilder passion shrove,
Mastering love, resentment, and despair.
He knew his end, and Phoebus' arrow sure
He braved for fame immortal and a friend,
Despising life; and we, who know our end,
Know that in our decay he shall endure
And all our children's hearts to grief inure,
With whose first bitter battles his shall blend.

II

Who brought thee forth, immortal vision, who
In Phthia or in Tempe brought thee forth?
Out of the sunlight and the sapful earth
What god the simples of thy spirit drew?
A goddess rose from the green waves, and threw
Her arms about a king, to give thee birth;
A centaur, patron of thy boyish mirth,
Over the meadows in thy footsteps flew.
Now Thessaly forgets thee, and the deep
Thy keeled bark furrowed answers not thy prayer;
But far away new generations keep
Thy laurels fresh; where branching Isis hems
The lawns of Oxford round about, or where
Enchanted Eton sits by pleasant Thames.

III

I gaze on thee as Phidias of old
Or Polyclitus gazed, when first he saw
These hard and shining limbs, without a flaw,

And cast his wonder in heroic mould.
Unhappy me who only may behold,
Nor make immutable and fix in awe
A fair immortal form no worm shall gnaw,
A tempered mind whose faith was never told!
The godlike mien, the lion's lock and eye,
The well-knit sinew, utter a brave heart
Better than many words that part by part
Spell in strange symbols what serene and whole
In nature lives, nor can in marble die.
The perfect body is itself the soul.

Ode V

Of thee the Northman by his beachèd galley
Dreamt, as he watched the never-setting Ursa
And longed for summer and thy light, O sacred
          Mediterranean.

Unseen he loved thee; for the heart within him
Knew earth had gardens where he might be blessed,
Putting away long dreams and aimless, barbarous
          Hunger for battle.

The foretaste of thy langours thawed his bosom;
A great need drove him to thy caverned islands
From the gray, endless reaches of the outer
          Desert of ocean.

He saw thy pillars, saw thy sudden mountains
Wrinkled and stark, and in their crooked gorges,
'Neath peeping pine and cypress, guessed the torrent
          Smothered in flowers.

Thine incense to the sun, thy gathered vapours,
He saw suspended on the flanks of Taurus,
Or veiling the snowed bosom of the virgin
          Sister of Atlas.

He saw the luminous top of wide Olympus,
Fit for the happy gods; he saw the pilgrim
River, with rains of Ethiopia flooding
      Populous Egypt.

And having seen, he loved thee. His racked spirit,
By thy breath tempered and the light that clothes thee,
Forgot the monstrous gods, and made of Nature
      Mistress and mother.

The more should I, O fatal sea, before thee
Of alien words make echoes to thy music;
For I was born where first the rills of Tagus
      Turn to the westward,

And wandering long, alas! have need of drinking
Deep of the patience of thy perfect sadness,
O thou that constant through the change of ages,
      Beautiful ever,

Never wast wholly young and void of sorrows,
Nor ever canst be old, while yet the morning
Kindles thy ripples, or the golden evening
      Dyes thee in purple.

Thee, willing to be tamed but still untamable,
The Roman called his own until he perished,
As now the busy English hover o'er thee,
      Stalwart and noble;

But all is naught to thee, while no harsh winter
Congeals thy fountains, and the blown Sahara
Chokes not with dreadful sand thy deep and placid
      Rock-guarded havens.

Thou carest not what men may tread thy margin;
Nor I, while from some heather-scented headland
I may behold thy beauty, the eternal
      Solace of mortals.

Cape Cod

The low sandy beach and the thin scrub pine,
The wide reach of bay and the long sky line,—
    O, I am far from home!

The salt, salt smell of the thick sea air,
And the smooth round stones that the ebbtides wear,—
    When will the good ship come?

The wretched stumps all charred and burned,
And the deep soft rut where the cartwheel turned,—
    Why is the world so old?

The lapping wave, and the broad gray sky
Where the cawing crows and the slow gulls fly,—
    Where are the dead untold?

The thin, slant willows by the flooded bog,
The huge stranded hulk and the floating log,—
    Sorrow with life began!

And among the dark pines, and along the flat shore,
O the wind, and the wind, for evermore!
    What will become of man?

On an Unfinished Statue

By Michael Angelo in the Bargello,
Called an Apollo or a David

What beauteous form beneath a marble veil
    Awaited in this block the Master's hand?
Could not the magic of his art avail
    To unseal that beauty's tomb and bid it stand?

Alas! the torpid and unwilling mass
    Misknew the sweetness of the mind's control,
And the quick shifting of the winds, alas!
    Denied a body to that flickering soul.

Fair homeless spirit, harbinger of bliss,
   It wooed dead matter that they both might live,
But dreamful earth still slumbered through the kiss
   And missed the blessing heaven stooped to give,

As when Endymion, locked in dullard sleep,
   Endured the gaze of Dian, till she turned
Stung with immortal wrath and doomed to weep
   Her maiden passion ignorantly spurned.

How should the vision stay to guide the hand,
   How should the holy thought and ardour stay,
When the false deeps of all the soul are sand
   And the loose rivets of the spirit clay?

What chisel shaking in the pulse of lust
   Shall find the perfect line, immortal, pure?
What fancy blown by every random gust
   Shall mount the breathless heavens and endure?

Vain was the trance through which a thrill of joy
   Passed for the nonce, when a vague hand, unled,
Half shaped the image of this lovely boy
   And caught the angel's garment as he fled.

Leave, leave, distracted hand, the baffling stone,
   And on that clay, thy fickle heart, begin.
Mould first some steadfast virtue of thine own
   Out of the sodden substance of thy sin.

They who wrought wonders by the Nile of old,
   Bequeathing their immortal part to us,
Cast their own spirit first into the mould
   And were themselves the rock they fashioned thus.

Ever their docile and unwearied eye
   Traced the same ancient pageant to the grave,
And awe made rich their spirit's husbandry
   With the perpetual refluence of its wave,

Till 'twixt the desert and the constant Nile
   Sphinx, pyramid, and awful temple grew,
And the vast gods, self-knowing, learned to smile
   Beneath the sky's unalterable blue.

Long, long ere first the rapt Arcadian swain
   Heard Pan's wild music pulsing through the grove,
His people's shepherds held paternal reign
   Beneath the large benignity of Jove.

Long mused the Delphic sibyl in her cave
   Ere mid his laurels she beheld the god,
And Beauty rose a virgin from the wave
   In lands the foot of Heracles had trod.

Athena reared her consecrated wall,
   Poseidon laid its rocky basement sure,
When Theseus had the monstrous race in thrall
   And made the worship of his people pure.

Long had the stripling stood in silence, veiled,
   Hearing the heroes' legend o'er and o'er,
Long in the keen palaestra striven, nor quailed
   To tame the body to the task it bore,

Ere soul and body, shaped by patient art,
   Walked linkèd with the gods, like friend with friend,
And reason, mirrored in the sage's heart,
   Beheld her purpose and confessed her end.

Mould, then, thyself and let the marble be.
   Look not to frailty for immortal themes,
Nor mock the travail of mortality
   With barren husks and harvesting of dreams.

Echo

Alas, to be
Mortal, and know our sad mortality!
To earth we come
Thinking no evil, deeming we are free:
We gaze too long upon the sky and sea,
This sweet life darkens into mystery,
And we grow dumb.

We can no more
On the compelling wings of rapture soar,
And of no choice
Sing to the gods a hymn unsung before:
Our song, the echo of a storm that's o'er,
A dying ripple on the beaten shore,
But feigns a voice.

STUART MERRILL

(1863–1915)

Ballade of the Chinese Lover

Down the waves of the Yang-tse-Kiang,
  In a gilded barge with saffron sails,
I wooed my Li to the brazen clang
  Of kettledrums, and the weary wails
  Of flutes, whilst under her spangled veils
She would sway her willowy waist, and sing
  Sweet songs that made me dream of the dales
Of Han-Yang, Woo-hoo and far Tchin-Ting.

Past the porcelain towers of Keou-Kang,
  And its peach blooms, loud with nightingales,
We drifted fast, as the dim gongs rang,
  Toward the horizon's purple pales.
  Hark! our hoarse pilot once more hails
The anchored junks, as they swerve and swing,
  Laden with silk and balsam bales
From Han-Yang, Woo-hoo and far Tchin-Ting.

Of nights, when the hour had come to hang
  Our paper lamps to their bamboo rails,
And afar we heard the silvery twang
  Of lutes from the tea fleet's moonlit trails,
  Then, oh my Li of the jasper nails,
As on the shore swooned the winds of spring,
  I lay at thy feet and told thee tales,
Of Han-Yang, Woo-hoo and far Tchin-Ting.

ENVOY.

Loved Princess, ere my fantasy fails,
Farewell, and I'll make thy praises ring
  O'er the Flowery Kingdom's fields and swales,
From Han-Yang, Woo-hoo to far Tchin-Ting.

Ballade of the Outcasts

The Voice of the Men.

We are the Vagabonds that sleep
  In ditches by the midnight ways
Where wolves beneath the gibbets leap:
  Our hands against black Fate we raise
  In lifelong turmoil of affrays,
Until we die, in some dark den,
  The death of dogs that hunger slays:
For we are hated of all men.

The Voice of the Women.

We are the Courtesans that creep
  Beyond the town's lamp-litten haze,
Toward the bridges of the deep:
  We watch the dawn with sinful gaze,
  And dreaming of the golden days
When Jesus hallowed Magdalen,
  We seek death in the river's maze:
For we are hated of all men.

The Voice of the Children.

We are the Innocents that weep,
  While our bones rot with foul decays,
For all the woes that we must reap:
  No mother sings us lulling lays,
  No father o'er our slumber prays,
But forth we fare from den to den
  To filch the death-bread of the strays:
For we are hated by all men.

The Envoy of the Outcasts.

  Beware, O Kings whom Mammon sways,
Lest morrows nearer than ye ken
  With our red flags of battle blaze!
For we are hated of all men.

ERNEST LAWRENCE THAYER

(1863–1940)

Casey at the Bat

A Ballad of the Republic, Sung in the Year 1888

The outlook wasn't brilliant for the Mudville nine that day;
The score stood four to two with but one inning more to
      play.
And then when Cooney died at first, and Barrows did the
      same,
A sickly silence fell upon the patrons of the game.

A straggling few got up to go in deep despair. The rest
Clung to that hope which springs eternal in the human
      breast;
They thought if only Casey could but get a whack at that—
We'd put up even money now with Casey at the bat.

But Flynn preceded Casey, as did also Jimmy Blake,
And the former was a lulu and the latter was a cake;
So upon that stricken multitude grim melancholy sat,
For there seemed but little chance of Casey's getting to the
      bat.

But Flynn let drive a single, to the wonderment of all,
And Blake, the much despis-ed, tore the cover off the ball;
And when the dust had lifted, and the men saw what had
      occurred,
There was Jimmy safe at second and Flynn a-hugging third.

Then from 5,000 throats and more there rose a lusty yell;
It rumbled through the valley, it rattled in the dell;
It knocked upon the mountain and recoiled upon the flat,
For Casey, mighty Casey, was advancing to the bat.

There was ease in Casey's manner as he stepped into his
    place;
There was pride in Casey's bearing and a smile on Casey's
    face.
And when, responding to the cheers, he lightly doffed his
    hat,
No stranger in the crowd could doubt 'twas Casey at the
    bat.

Ten thousand eyes were on him as he rubbed his hands
    with dirt;
Five thousand tongues applauded when he wiped them on
    his shirt.
Then while the writhing pitcher ground the ball into his
    hip,
Defiance gleamed in Casey's eye, a sneer curled Casey's lip.

And now the leather-covered sphere came hurtling through
    the air,
And Casey stood a-watching it in haughty grandeur there.
Close by the sturdy batsman the ball unheeded sped—
"That ain't my style," said Casey. "Strike one," the umpire
    said.

From the benches, black with people, there went up a
    muffled roar,
Like the beating of the storm-waves on a stern and distant
    shore.
"Kill him! Kill the umpire!" shouted some one on the stand;
And it's likely they'd have killed him had not Casey raised
    his hand.

With a smile of Christian charity great Casey's visage
    shone;
He stilled the rising tumult; he bade the game go on;
He signaled to the pitcher, and once more the spheroid
    flew;
But Casey still ignored it, and the umpire said, "Strike
    two."

"Fraud!" cried the maddened thousands, and echo answered
        fraud;
But one scornful look from Casey and the audience was
        awed.
They saw his face grow stern and cold, they saw his
        muscles strain,
And they knew that Casey wouldn't let that ball go by
        again.

The sneer is gone from Casey's lip, his teeth are clinched in
        hate;
He pounds with cruel violence his bat upon the plate.
And now the pitcher holds the ball, and now he lets it go,
And now the air is shattered by the force of Casey's blow.

————

Oh, somewhere in this favored land the sun is shining
        bright;
The band is playing somewhere, and somewhere hearts are
        light,
And somewhere men are laughing, and somewhere children
        shout;
But there is no joy in Mudville—mighty Casey has struck
        out.

RICHARD HOVEY

(1864–1900)

Evening on the Potomac

The fervid breath of our flushed Southern May
Is sweet upon the city's throat and lips,
As a lover's whose tired arm slips
Listlessly over the shoulder of a queen.

Far away
The river melts in the unseen.
Oh, beautiful Girl-City, how she dips
Her feet in the stream
With a touch that is half a kiss and half a dream!
Her face is very fair,
With flowers for smiles and sunlight in her hair.

My westland flower-town, how serene she is!
Here on this hill from which I look at her,
All is still as if a worshipper
Left at some shrine his offering.

Soft winds kiss
My cheek with a slow lingering.
A luring whisper where the laurels stir
Wiles my heart back to woodland-ward again.

But lo,
Across the sky the sunset couriers run,
And I remain
To watch the imperial pageant of the Sun
Mock me, an impotent Cortez here below,
With splendors of its vaster Mexico.

O Eldorado of the templed clouds!
O golden city of the western sky!

Not like the Spaniard would I storm thy gates;
Not like the babe stretch chubby hands and cry
To have thee for a toy; but far from crowds,
Like my Faun brother in the ferny glen,
Peer from the wood's edge while thy glory waits,
And in the darkening thickets plunge again.

A Song by the Shore

"Lose and love" is love's first art;
  So it was with thee and me,
For I first beheld thy heart
  On the night I last saw thee.
Pine-woods and mysteries!
Sea-sands and sorrows!
Hearts fluttered by a breeze
That bodes dark morrows, morrows,—
Bodes dark morrows!

Moonlight in sweet overflow
  Poured upon the earth and sea!
Lovelight with intenser glow
  In the deeps of thee and me!
Clasped hands and silences!
Hearts faint and throbbing!
The weak wind sighing in the trees!
The strong surf sobbing, sobbing,—
The strong surf sobbing!

At Sea

As a brave man faces the foe,
Alone against hundreds, and sees Death grin in his teeth,
But, shutting his lips, fights on to the end
Without speech, without hope, without flinching,—
So, silently, grimly, the steamer
Lurches ahead through the night.

A beacon-light far off,
Twinkling across the waves like a star!
But no star in the dark overhead!
The splash of waters at the prow, and the evil light
Of the death-fires flitting like will-o'-the-wisps beneath! And
      beyond
Silence and night!

I sit by the taffrail,
Alone in the dark and the blown cold mist and the spray,
Feeling myself swept on irresistibly,
Sunk in the night and the sea, and made one with their
      footfall-less onrush,
Letting myself be borne like a spar adrift
Helplessly into the night.

Without fear, without wish,
Insensate save of a dull, crushed ache in my heart,
Careless whither the steamer is going,
Conscious only as in a dream of the wet and the dark
And of a form that looms and fades indistinctly
Everywhere out of the night.

O love, how came I here?
Shall I wake at thy side and smile at my dream?
The dream that grips me so hard that I cannot wake nor
      stir!
O love! O my own love, found but to be lost!
My soul sends over the waters a wild inarticulate cry,
Like a gull's scream heard in the night.

The mist creeps closer. The beacon
Vanishes astern. The sea's monotonous noises
Lapse through the drizzle with a listless, subsiding cadence.
And thou, O love, and the sea throb on in my brain
      together,
While the steamer plunges along,
Butting its way through the night.

The Mocking-Bird

Hear! hear! hear!
Listen! the word
Of the mocking-bird!
Hear! hear! hear!
I will make all clear;
I will let you know
Where the footfalls go
That through the thicket and over the hill
Allure, allure.
How the bird-voice cleaves
Through the weft of leaves
With a leap and a thrill
Like the flash of a weaver's shuttle, swift and sudden and
     sure!

And lo, he is gone—even while I turn
The wisdom of his runes to learn.
He knows the mystery of the wood,
The secret of the solitude;
But he will not tell, he will not tell,
For all he promises so well.

Earth's Lyric

April. You hearken, my fellow,
Old slumberer down in my heart?
There's a whooping of ice in the rivers:
The sap feels a start.

The snow-melted torrents are brawling;
The hills, orange-misted and blue,
Are touched with the voice of the rainbird
Unsullied and new.

The houses of frost are deserted,
Their slumber is broken and done,
And empty and pale are the portals
Awaiting the sun.

The bands of Arcturus are slackened;
Orion goes forth from his place
On the slopes of the night, leading homeward
His hound from the chase.

The Pleiades weary and follow
The dance of the ghostly dawn;
The revel of silence is over;
Earth's lyric comes on.

A golden flute in the cedars,
A silver pipe in the swales,
And the slow large life of the forest
Wells back and prevails.

A breath of the woodland spirit
Has blown out the bubble of spring
To this tenuous hyaline glory
One touch sets a-wing.

Verlaine

Avid of life and love, insatiate vagabond,
With quest too furious for the graal he would have won,
He flung himself at the eternal sky, as one
Wrenching his chains but impotent to burst the bond.

Yet under the revolt, the revel, the despond,
What pools of innocence, what crystal benison!
As through a riven mist that glowers in the sun,
A stretch of God's blue calm glassed in a virgin pond.

Prowler of obscene streets that riot reels along,
And aisles with incense numb and gardens mad with rose,
Monastic cells and dreams of dim brocaded lawns,

Death, which has set the calm of Time upon his song,
Surely upon his soul has kissed the same repose
In some fair heaven the Christ has set apart for Fauns.

Accident in Art

What painter has not with a careless smutch
Accomplished his despair?—one touch revealing
All he had put of life, thought, vigor, feeling,
Into the canvas that without that touch
Showed of his love and labor just so much
Raw pigment, scarce a scrap of soul concealing!
What poet has not found his spirit kneeling
A-sudden at the sound of such or such
Strange verses staring from his manuscript,
Written he knows not how, but which will sound
Like trumpets down the years? So Accident
Itself unmasks the likeness of Intent,
And ever in blind Chance's darkest crypt
The shrine-lamp of God's purposing is found.

MADISON CAWEIN

(1865–1914)

Poetry

Who hath beheld the goddess face to face,
Blind with her beauty, all his days shall go
Climbing lone mountains towards her temple's place,
Weighed with song's sweet, inexorable woe.

The Unimaginative

Each form of beauty 's but the new disguise
Of thoughts more beautiful than forms can be:
Sceptics, who search with unanointed eyes,
Never the Earth's wild fairy-dance shall see.

Music

God-born before the Sons of God, she hurled,
With awful symphonies of flood and fire,
God's name on rocking Chaos—world by world
Flamed as the universe rolled from her lyre.

The Three Elements

They come as couriers of Heaven: their feet
Sonorous-sandaled with majestic awe;
With raiment of swift foam and wind and heat,
Blowing the trumpets of God's wrath and law.

Rome

Above the Circus of the World she sat,
Beautiful and base, a harlot crowned with pride:
Fierce nations, upon whom she sneered and spat,—
Shrieked at her feet and for her pastime died.

On Reading the Life of Haroun Er Reshid

Down all the lanterned Bagdad of our youth
He steals, with golden justice for the poor:
Within his palace—you shall know the truth—
A blood-smeared headsman hides behind each door.

Echo

Dweller in hollow places, hills and rocks,
Daughter of Silence and old Solitude,
Tip-toe she stands within her cave or wood,
Her only life the noises that she mocks.

The Stars

These—the bright symbols of man's hope and fame,
In which he reads his blessing or his curse—
Are syllables with which God speaks His name
In the vast utterance of the universe.

Beauty

High as a star, yet lowly as a flower,
Unknown she takes her unassuming place
At Earth's proud masquerade—the appointed hour
Strikes, and, behold, the marvel of her face.

Mnemosyne

In classic beauty, cold, immaculate,
  A voiceful sculpture, stern and still she stands,
Upon her brow deep-chiselled love and hate,
  That sorrow o'er dead roses in her hands.

The Purple Valleys

Far in the purple valleys of illusion
I see her waiting, like the soul of music,
With deep eyes, lovelier than cerulean pansies,
Shadow and fire, yet merciless as poison;
With red lips, sweeter than Arabian storax,
Yet bitterer than myrrh.—O tears and kisses!
O eyes and lips, that haunt my soul forever!

Again Spring walks transcendent on the mountains:
The woods are hushed: the vales are blue with shadows:
Above the heights, steeped in a thousand splendors,
Like some vast canvas of the gods, hangs burning
The sunset's wild sciography: and slowly
The moon treads heaven's proscenium,—night's stately
White queen of love and tragedy and madness.

Again I know forgotten dreams and longings;
Ideals lost; desires dead and buried
Beside the altar sacrifice erected
Within the heart's high sanctuary. Strangely
Again I know the horror and the rapture,
The utterless awe, the joy akin to anguish,
The terror and the worship of the spirit.

Again I feel her eyes pierce through and through me;
Her deep eyes, lovelier than imperial pansies,
Velvet and flame, through which her fierce will holds me,
Powerless and tame, and draws me on and onward
To sad, unsatisfied and animal yearnings,

Wild, unrestrained—the brute within the human—
To fling me panting on her mouth and bosom.

Again I feel her lips like ice and fire,
Her red lips, odorous as Arabian storax,
Fragrance and fire, within whose kiss destruction
Lies serpent-like. Intoxicating languors
Resistlessly embrace me, soul and body;
And we go drifting, drifting—she is laughing—
Outcasts of God, into the deep's abysm.

Caverns

Written of Colossal Cave, Kentucky

Aisles and abysses; leagues no man explores,
    Of rock that labyrinths and night that drips;
    Where everlasting silence broods, with lips
Of adamant, o'er earthquake-builded floors.
Where forms, such as the Demon-World adores,
    Laborious water carves; whence echo slips
    Wild-tongued o'er pools where petrifaction strips
Her breasts of crystal from which crystal pours.—
Here where primordial fear, the Gorgon, sits
    Staring all life to stone in ghastly mirth,
    I seem to tread, with awe no tongue can tell,—
Beneath vast domes, by torrent-tortured pits,
    'Mid wrecks terrific of the ruined Earth,—
    An ancient causeway of forgotten Hell.

Dead Cities

Out of it all but this remains:—
I was with one who crossed wide chains
Of the Cordilleras, whose peaks
Lock in the wilds of Yucatan,
Chiapas and Honduras. Weeks—

And then a city that no man
Had ever seen; so dim and old,
No chronicle has ever told
The history of men who piled
Its temples and huge teocallis
Among mimosa-blooming valleys;
Or how its altars were defiled
With human blood; whose idols there
With eyes of stone still stand and stare.

So old the moon can only know
How old, since ancient forests grow
On mighty wall and pyramid.
Huge ceïbas, whose trunks were scarred
With ages, and dense yuccas, hid
Fanes 'mid the cacti, scarlet-starred.
I looked upon its paven ways,
And saw it in its kingliest days;
When from the lordly palace one,
A victim, walked with prince and priest,
Who turned brown faces toward the east
In worship of the rising sun:
At night ten hundred temples' spires
On gold burnt everlasting fires.

Uxmal? Palenque? or Copan?
I know not. Only how no man
Had ever seen; and still my soul
Believes it vaster than the three.
Volcanic rock walled in the whole,
Lost in the woods as in some sea.
I only read its hieroglyphs,
Perused its monster monoliths
Of death, gigantic heads; and read
The pictured codex of its fate,
The perished Toltec; while in hate
Mad monkeys cursed me, as if dead
Priests of its past had taken form
To guard its ruined shrines from harm.

Orgie

On nights like this, when bayou and lagoon
   Dream in the moonlight's mystic radiance,
   I seem to walk like one deep in a trance
With old-world myths born of the mist and moon.

Lascivious eyes and mouths of sensual rose
   Smile into mine; and breasts of luring light,
   And tresses streaming golden to the night,
Persuade me onward where the forest glows.

And then it seems along the haunted hills
   There falls a flutter as of beautiful feet,
   As if tempestuous troops of Mænads meet
To drain deep bowls and shout and have their wills.

And then I feel her limbs will be revealed
   Like some great snow-white moth among the trees;
   Her vampire beauty, waiting there to seize
And dance me downward where my doom is sealed.

GELETT BURGESS

(1866–1951)

The Purple Cow

I never saw a PURPLE COW,
I never HOPE to see one;
But I can tell you, anyhow,
I'd rather SEE than BE one!

The Purple Cow: Suite

Ah, yes, I wrote the "Purple Cow"—
I'm Sorry, now, I wrote it;
But I can tell you Anyhow
I'll Kill you if you Quote it!

WILLIAM VAUGHN MOODY

(1869–1910)

Gloucester Moors

A mile behind is Gloucester town
Where the fishing fleets put in,
A mile ahead the land dips down
And the woods and farms begin.
Here, where the moors stretch free
In the high blue afternoon,
Are the marching sun and talking sea,
And the racing winds that wheel and flee
On the flying heels of June.

Jill-o'er-the-ground is purple blue,
Blue is the quaker-maid,
The wild geranium holds its dew
Long in the boulder's shade.
Wax-red hangs the cup
From the huckleberry boughs,
In barberry bells the grey moths sup,
Or where the choke-cherry lifts high up
Sweet bowls for their carouse.

Over the shelf of the sandy cove
Beach-peas blossom late.
By copse and cliff the swallows rove
Each calling to his mate.
Seaward the sea-gulls go,
And the land-birds all are here;
That green-gold flash was a vireo,
And yonder flame where the marsh-flags grow
Was a scarlet tanager.

This earth is not the steadfast place
We landsmen build upon;
From deep to deep she varies pace,

And while she comes is gone.
Beneath my feet I feel
Her smooth bulk heave and dip;
With velvet plunge and soft upreel
She swings and steadies to her keel
Like a gallant, gallant ship.

These summer clouds she sets for sail,
The sun is her masthead light,
She tows the moon like a pinnace frail
Where her phosphor wake churns bright.
Now hid, now looming clear,
On the face of the dangerous blue
The star fleets tack and wheel and veer,
But on, but on does the old earth steer
As if her port she knew.

God, dear God! Does she know her port,
Though she goes so far about?
Or blind astray, does she make her sport
To brazen and chance it out?
I watched when her captains passed:
She were better captainless.
Men in the cabin, before the mast,
But some were reckless and some aghast,
And some sat gorged at mess.

By her battened hatch I leaned and caught
Sounds from the noisome hold,—
Cursing and sighing of souls distraught
And cries too sad to be told.
Then I strove to go down and see;
But they said, "Thou art not of us!"
I turned to those on the deck with me
And cried, "Give help!" But they said, "Let be:
Our ship sails faster thus."

Jill-o'er-the-ground is purple blue,
Blue is the quaker-maid,
The alder-clump where the brook comes through

Breeds cresses in its shade.
To be out of the moiling street
With its swelter and its sin!
Who has given to me this sweet,
And given my brother dust to eat?
And when will his wage come in?

Scattering wide or blown in ranks,
Yellow and white and brown,
Boats and boats from the fishing banks
Come home to Gloucester town.
There is cash to purse and spend,
There are wives to be embraced,
Hearts to borrow and hearts to lend,
And hearts to take and keep to the end,—
O little sails, make haste!

But thou, vast outbound ship of souls,
What harbor town for thee?
What shapes, when thy arriving tolls,
Shall crowd the banks to see?
Shall all the happy shipmates then
Stand singing brotherly?
Or shall a haggard ruthless few
Warp her over and bring her to,
While the many broken souls of men
Fester down in the slaver's pen,
And nothing to say or do?

An Ode in Time of Hesitation

(After seeing at Boston the statue of Robert Gould Shaw, killed while storming Fort Wagner, July 18, 1863, at the head of the first enlisted negro regiment, the 54th Massachusetts.)

I

Before the solemn bronze Saint Gaudens made
To thrill the heedless passer's heart with awe,
And set here in the city's talk and trade

To the good memory of Robert Shaw,
This bright March morn I stand,
And hear the distant spring come up the land;
Knowing that what I hear is not unheard
Of this boy soldier and his negro band,
For all their gaze is fixed so stern ahead,
For all the fatal rhythm of their tread.
The land they died to save from death and shame
Trembles and waits, hearing the spring's great name,
And by her pangs these resolute ghosts are stirred.

II

Through street and mall the tides of people go
Heedless; the trees upon the Common show
No hint of green; but to my listening heart
The still earth doth impart
Assurance of her jubilant emprise,
And it is clear to my long-searching eyes
That love at last has might upon the skies.
The ice is runneled on the little pond;
A telltale patter drips from off the trees;
The air is touched with southland spiceries,
As if but yesterday it tossed the frond
Of pendent mosses where the live-oaks grow
Beyond Virginia and the Carolines,
Or had its will among the fruits and vines
Of aromatic isles asleep beyond
Florida and the Gulf of Mexico.

III

Soon shall the Cape Ann children shout in glee,
Spying the arbutus, spring's dear recluse;
Hill lads at dawn shall hearken the wild goose
Go honking northward over Tennessee;
West from Oswego to Sault Sainte-Marie,
And on to where the Pictured Rocks are hung,
And yonder where, gigantic, willful, young,
Chicago sitteth at the northwest gates,
With restless violent hands and casual tongue

Moulding her mighty fates,
The Lakes shall robe them in ethereal sheen;
And like a larger sea, the vital green
Of springing wheat shall vastly be outflung
Over Dakota and the prairie states.
By desert people immemorial
On Arizonan mesas shall be done
Dim rites unto the thunder and the sun;
Nor shall the primal gods lack sacrifice
More splendid, when the white Sierras call
Unto the Rockies straightway to arise
And dance before the unveiled ark of the year,
Sounding their windy cedars as for shawms,
Unrolling rivers clear
For flutter of broad phylacteries;
While Shasta signals to Alaskan seas
That watch old sluggish glaciers downward creep
To fling their icebergs thundering from the steep,
And Mariposa through the purple calms
Gazes at far Hawaii crowned with palms
Where East and West are met,—
A rich seal on the ocean's bosom set
To say that East and West are twain,
With different loss and gain:
The Lord hath sundered them; let them be sundered yet.

IV

Alas! what sounds are these that come
Sullenly over the Pacific seas,—
Sounds of ignoble battle, striking dumb
The season's half-awakened ecstasies?
Must I be humble, then,
Now when my heart hath need of pride?
Wild love falls on me from these sculptured men;
By loving much the land for which they died
I would be justified.
My spirit was away on pinions wide
To soothe in praise of her its passionate mood
And ease it of its ache of gratitude.

Too sorely heavy is the debt they lay
On me and the companions of my day.
I would remember now
My country's goodliness, make sweet her name.
Alas! what shade art thou
Of sorrow or of blame
Liftest the lyric leafage from her brow,
And pointest a slow finger at her shame?

V

Lies! lies! It cannot be! The wars we wage
Are noble, and our battles still are won
By justice for us, ere we lift the gage.
We have not sold our loftiest heritage.
The proud republic hath not stooped to cheat
And scramble in the market-place of war;
Her forehead weareth yet its solemn star.
Here is her witness: this, her perfect son,
This delicate and proud New England soul
Who leads despisèd men, with just-unshackled feet,
Up the large ways where death and glory meet,
To show all peoples that our shame is done,
That once more we are clean and spirit-whole.

VI

Crouched in the sea fog on the moaning sand
All night he lay, speaking some simple word
From hour to hour to the slow minds that heard,
Holding each poor life gently in his hand
And breathing on the base rejected clay
Till each dark face shone mystical and grand
Against the breaking day;
And lo, the shard the potter cast away
Was grown a fiery chalice crystal-fine
Fulfilled of the divine
Great wine of battle wrath by God's ring-finger stirred.
Then upward, where the shadowy bastion loomed
Huge on the mountain in the wet sea light,

Whence now, and now, infernal flowerage bloomed,
Bloomed, burst, and scattered down its deadly seed, —
They swept, and died like freemen on the height,
Like freemen, and like men of noble breed;
And when the battle fell away at night
By hasty and contemptuous hands were thrust
Obscurely in a common grave with him
The fair-haired keeper of their love and trust.
Now limb doth mingle with dissolvèd limb
In nature's busy old democracy
To flush the mountain laurel when she blows
Sweet by the southern sea,
And heart with crumbled heart climbs in the rose: —
The untaught hearts with the high heart that knew
This mountain fortress for no earthly hold
Of temporal quarrel, but the bastion old
Of spiritual wrong,
Built by an unjust nation sheer and strong,
Expugnable but by a nation's rue
And bowing down before that equal shrine
By all men held divine,
Whereof his band and he were the most holy sign.

VII

O bitter, bitter shade!
Wilt thou not put the scorn
And instant tragic question from thine eyes?
Do thy dark brows yet crave
That swift and angry stave —
Unmeet for this desirous morn —
That I have striven, striven to evade?
Gazing on him, must I not deem they err
Whose careless lips in street and shop aver
As common tidings, deeds to make his cheek
Flush from the bronze, and his dead throat to speak?
Surely some elder singer would arise,
Whose harp hath leave to threaten and to mourn
Above this people when they go astray.
Is Whitman, the strong spirit, overworn?

Has Whittier put his yearning wrath away?
I will not and I dare not yet believe!
Though furtively the sunlight seems to grieve,
And the spring-laden breeze
Out of the gladdening west is sinister
With sounds of nameless battle overseas;
Though when we turn and question in suspense
If these things be indeed after these ways,
And what things are to follow after these,
Our fluent men of place and consequence
Fumble and fill their mouths with hollow phrase,
Or for the end-all of deep arguments
Intone their dull commercial liturgies—
I dare not yet believe! My ears are shut!
I will not hear the thin satiric praise
And muffled laughter of our enemies,
Bidding us never sheathe our valiant sword
Till we have changed our birthright for a gourd
Of wild pulse stolen from a barbarian's hut;
Showing how wise it is to cast away
The symbols of our spiritual sway,
That so our hands with better ease
May wield the driver's whip and grasp the jailer's keys.

VIII

Was it for this our fathers kept the law?
This crown shall crown their struggle and their ruth?
Are we the eagle nation Milton saw
Mewing its mighty youth,
Soon to possess the mountain winds of truth,
And be a swift familiar of the sun
Where aye before God's face his trumpets run?
Or have we but the talons and the maw,
And for the abject likeness of our heart
Shall some less lordly bird be set apart?—
Some gross-billed wader where the swamps are fat?
Some gorger in the sun? Some prowler with the bat?

IX

Ah no!
We have not fallen so.
We are our fathers' sons: let those who lead us know!
'T was only yesterday sick Cuba's cry
Came up the tropic wind, "Now help us, for we die!"
Then Alabama heard,
And rising, pale, to Maine and Idaho
Shouted a burning word.
Proud state with proud impassioned state conferred,
And at the lifting of a hand sprang forth,
East, west, and south, and north,
Beautiful armies. Oh, by the sweet blood and young
Shed on the awful hill slope at San Juan,
By the unforgotten names of eager boys
Who might have tasted girls' love and been stung
With the old mystic joys
And starry griefs, now the spring nights come on,
But that the heart of youth is generous,—
We charge you, ye who lead us,
Breathe on their chivalry no hint of stain!
Turn not their new-world victories to gain!
One least leaf plucked for chaffer from the bays
Of their dear praise,
One jot of their pure conquest put to hire,
The implacable republic will require;
With clamor, in the glare and gaze of noon,
Or subtly, coming as a thief at night,
But surely, very surely, slow or soon
That insult deep we deeply will requite.
Tempt not our weakness, our cupidity!
For save we let the island men go free,
Those baffled and dislaureled ghosts
Will curse us from the lamentable coasts
Where walk the frustrate dead.
The cup of trembling shall be drainèd quite,
Eaten the sour bread of astonishment,
With ashes of the hearth shall be made white
Our hair, and wailing shall be in the tent;

Then on your guiltier head
Shall our intolerable self-disdain
Wreak suddenly its anger and its pain;
For manifest in that disastrous light
We shall discern the right
And do it, tardily.—O ye who lead,
Take heed!
Blindness we may forgive, but baseness we will smite.

Harmonics

This string upon my harp was best beloved:
I thought I knew its secrets through and through;
Till an old man, whose young eyes lightened blue
'Neath his white hair, bent over me and moved
His fingers up and down, and broke the wire
To such a laddered music, rung on rung,
As from the patriarch's pillow skyward sprung
Crowded with wide-flung wings and feet of fire.

O vibrant heart! so metely tuned and strung
That any untaught hand can draw from thee
One clear gold note that makes the tired years young—
What of the time when Love had whispered me
Where slept thy nodes, and my hand pausefully
Gave to the dim harmonics voice and tongue?

The Bracelet of Grass

The opal heart of afternoon
Was clouding on to throbs of storm,
Ashen within the ardent west
The lips of thunder muttered harm,
And as a bubble like to break
Hung heaven's trembling amethyst,
When with the sedge-grass by the lake
I braceleted her wrist.

And when the ribbon grass was tied,
Sad with the happiness we planned,
Palm linked in palm we stood awhile
And watched the raindrops dot the sand;
Until the anger of the breeze
Chid all the lake's bright breathing down,
And ravished all the radiancies
From her deep eyes of brown.

We gazed from shelter on the storm,
And through our hearts swept ghostly pain
To see the shards of day sweep past,
Broken, and none might mend again.
Broken, that none shall ever mend;
Loosened, that none shall ever tie.
O the wind and the wind, will it never end?
O the sweeping past of the ruined sky!

The Departure

I

I sat beside the glassy evening sea,
One foot upon the thin horn of my lyre,
And all its strings of laughter and desire
Crushed in the rank wet grasses heedlessly;
Nor did my dull eyes care to question how
The boat close by had spread its saffron sails,
Nor what might mean the coffers and the bales,
And streaks of new wine on the gilded prow.
Neither was wonder in me when I saw
Fair women step therein, though they were fair
Even to adoration and to awe,
And in the gracious fillets of their hair
Were blossoms from a garden I had known,
Sweet mornings ere the apple buds were blown.

II

One gazed steadfast into the dying west
With lips apart to greet the evening star;
And one with eyes that caught the strife and jar
Of the sea's heart, followed the sunward breast
Of a lone gull; from a slow harp one drew
Blind music like a laugh or like a wail;
And in the uncertain shadow of the sail
One wove a crown of berries and of yew.
Yet even as I said with dull desire,
"All these were mine, and one was mine indeed,"
The smoky music burst into a fire,
And I was left alone in my great need,
One foot upon the thin horn of my lyre
And all its strings crushed in the dripping weed.

EDWIN ARLINGTON ROBINSON

(1869–1935)

The Torrent

I found a torrent falling in a glen
Where the sun's light shone silvered and leaf-split;
The boom, the foam, and the mad flash of it
All made a magic symphony; but when
I thought upon the coming of hard men
To cut those patriarchal trees away,
And turn to gold the silver of that spray,
I shuddered. Yet a gladness now and then
Did wake me to myself till I was glad
In earnest, and was welcoming the time
For screaming saws to sound above the chime
Of idle waters, and for me to know
The jealous visionings that I had had
Were steps to the great place where trees and torrents go.

Aaron Stark

Withal a meagre man was Aaron Stark—
Cursed and unkempt, shrewd, shrivelled, and morose:
A miser was he, with a miser's nose,
And eyes like little dollars in the dark.
His thin, pinched mouth was nothing but a mark;
And when he spoke there came like sullen blows
Through scattered fangs a few snarled words and close,
As if a cur were chary of its bark.

Glad for the murmur of his hard renown,
Year after year he shambled through the town,—
A loveless exile moving with a staff;
And oftentimes there crept into his ears
A sound of alien pity, touched with tears,—
And then (and only then) did Aaron laugh.

Supremacy

There is a drear and lonely tract of hell
From all the common gloom removed afar:
A flat, sad land it is, where shadows are,
Whose lorn estate my verse may never tell.
I walked among them and I knew them well:
Men I had slandered on life's little star
For churls and sluggards; and I knew the scar
Upon their brows of woe ineffable.

But as I went majestic on my way,
Into the dark they vanished, one by one,
Till, with a shaft of God's eternal day,
The dream of all my glory was undone,—
And, with a fool's importunate dismay,
I heard the dead men singing in the sun.

Boston

My northern pines are good enough for me,
But there's a town my memory uprears—
A town that always like a friend appears,
And always in the sunrise by the sea.
And over it, somehow, there seems to be
A downward flash of something new and fierce,
That ever strives to clear, but never clears
The dimness of a charmed antiquity.

I know my Boston is a counterfeit,—
A frameless imitation, all bereft
Of living nearness, noise, and common speech;
But I am glad for every glimpse of it,—
And there it is, plain as a name that's left
In letters by warm hands I cannot reach.

A Poem for Max Nordau

Dun shades quiver down the lone long fallow,
And the scared night shudders at the brown owl's cry;
The bleak reeds rattle as the winds whirl by,
And frayed leaves flutter through the clumped shrubs callow.

Chill dews clinging on the low cold mallow
Make a steel-keen shimmer where the spent stems lie;
Dun shades quiver down the lone long fallow,
And the scared night shudders at the brown owl's cry.

Pale stars peering through the clouds' curled shallow
Make a thin still flicker in a foul round sky;
Black damp shadows through the hushed air fly;
The lewd gloom wakens to a moon-sad sallow,
Dun shades quiver down the lone long fallow.

Walt Whitman

The master-songs are ended, and the man
That sang them is a name. And so is God
A name; and so is love, and life, and death,
And everything. — But we, who are too blind
To read what we have written, or what faith
Has written for us, do not understand:
We only blink, and wonder.

Last night it was the song that was the man,
But now it is the man that is the song.
We do not hear him very much to-day; —
His piercing and eternal cadence rings
Too pure for us — too powerfully pure,
Too lovingly triumphant, and too large;
But there are some that hear him, and they know
That he shall sing to-morrow for all men,
And that all time shall listen.

The master-songs are ended?—Rather say
No songs are ended that are ever sung,
And that no names are dead names. When we write
Men's letters on proud marble or on sand,
We write them there forever.

The Children of the Night

For those that never know the light,
    The darkness is a sullen thing;
And they, the Children of the Night,
    Seem lost in Fortune's winnowing.

But some are strong and some are weak,—
    And there's the story. House and home
Are shut from countless hearts that seek
    World-refuge that will never come.

And if there be no other life,
    And if there be no other chance
To weigh their sorrow and their strife
    Than in the scales of circumstance,

'T were better, ere the sun go down
    Upon the first day we embark,
In life's imbittered sea to drown,
    Than sail forever in the dark.

But if there be a soul on earth
    So blinded with its own misuse
Of man's revealed, incessant worth,
    Or worn with anguish, that it views

No light but for a mortal eye,
    No rest but of a mortal sleep,
No God but in a prophet's lie,
    No faith for "honest doubt" to keep;

If there be nothing, good or bad,
   But chaos for a soul to trust,—
God counts it for a soul gone mad,
   And if God be God, He is just.

And if God be God, He is Love;
   And though the Dawn be still so dim,
It shows us we have played enough
   With creeds that make a fiend of Him.

There is one creed, and only one,
   That glorifies God's excellence;
So cherish, that His will be done,
   The common creed of common sense.

It is the crimson, not the gray,
   That charms the twilight of all time;
It is the promise of the day
   That makes the starry sky sublime;

It is the faith within the fear
   That holds us to the life we curse;—
So let us in ourselves revere
   The Self which is the Universe!

Let us, the Children of the Night,
   Put off the cloak that hides the scar!
Let us be Children of the Light,
   And tell the ages what we are!

John Evereldown

"Where are you going to-night, to-night,—
    Where are you going, John Evereldown?
There's never the sign of a star in sight,
    Nor a lamp that's nearer than Tilbury Town.
Why do you stare as a dead man might?
Where are you pointing away from the light?
And where are you going to-night, to-night,—
    Where are you going, John Evereldown?"

"Right through the forest, where none can see,
    There's where I'm going, to Tilbury Town.
The men are asleep,—or awake, may be,—
    But the women are calling John Evereldown.
Ever and ever they call for me,
And while they call can a man be free?
So right through the forest, where none can see,
    There's where I'm going, to Tilbury Town."

"But why are you going so late, so late,—
    Why are you going, John Evereldown?
Though the road be smooth and the path be straight,
    There are two long leagues to Tilbury Town.
Come in by the fire, old man, and wait!
Why do you chatter out there by the gate?
And why are you going so late, so late,—
    Why are you going, John Evereldown?"

"I follow the women wherever they call,—
    That's why I'm going to Tilbury Town.
God knows if I pray to be done with it all,
    But God is no friend to John Evereldown.
So the clouds may come and the rain may fall,
The shadows may creep and the dead men crawl,—
But I follow the women wherever they call,
    And that's why I'm going to Tilbury Town."

Luke Havergal

Go to the western gate, Luke Havergal,—
There where the vines cling crimson on the wall,—
And in the twilight wait for what will come.
The wind will moan, the leaves will whisper some—
Whisper of her, and strike you as they fall;
But go, and if you trust her she will call.
Go to the western gate, Luke Havergal—
Luke Havergal.

No, there is not a dawn in eastern skies
To rift the fiery night that's in your eyes;
But there, where western glooms are gathering,
The dark will end the dark, if anything:
God slays Himself with every leaf that flies,
And hell is more than half of paradise.
No, there is not a dawn in eastern skies—
In eastern skies.

Out of a grave I come to tell you this,—
Out of a grave I come to quench the kiss
That flames upon your forehead with a glow
That blinds you to the way that you must go.
Yes, there is yet one way to where she is,—
Bitter, but one that faith can never miss.
Out of a grave I come to tell you this—
To tell you this.

There is the western gate, Luke Havergal,
There are the crimson leaves upon the wall.
Go,—for the winds are tearing them away,—
Nor think to riddle the dead words they say,
Nor any more to feel them as they fall;
But go! and if you trust her she will call.
There is the western gate, Luke Havergal—
Luke Havergal.

Ballade of Broken Flutes

(To A. T. Schumann.)

In dreams I crossed a barren land,
    A land of ruin, far away;
Around me hung on every hand
    A deathful stillness of decay;
    And silent, as in bleak dismay
That song should thus forsaken be,
    On that forgotten ground there lay
The broken flutes of Arcady.

The forest that was all so grand
    When pipes and tabors had their sway
Stood leafless now, a ghostly band
    Of skeletons in cold array.
    A lonely surge of ancient spray
Told of an unforgetful sea,
    But iron blows had hushed for aye
The broken flutes of Arcady.

No more by summer breezes fanned,
    The place was desolate and gray;
But still my dream was to command
    New life into that shrunken clay.
    I tried it. Yes, you scan to-day,
With uncommiserating glee,
    The songs of one who strove to play
The broken flutes of Arcady.

ENVOY

So, Rock, I join the common fray,
    To fight where Mammon may decree;
And leave, to crumble as they may,
    The broken flutes of Arcady.

The House on the Hill

They are all gone away,
  The House is shut and still,
There is nothing more to say.

Through broken walls and gray
  The winds blow bleak and shrill:
They are all gone away.

Nor is there one to-day
  To speak them good or ill:
There is nothing more to say.

Why is it then we stray
  Around that sunken sill?
They are all gone away,

And our poor fancy-play
  For them is wasted skill:
There is nothing more to say.

There is ruin and decay
  In the House on the Hill:
They are all gone away,
There is nothing more to say.

Richard Cory

Whenever Richard Cory went down town,
We people on the pavement looked at him:
He was a gentleman from sole to crown,
Clean favored, and imperially slim.

And he was always quietly arrayed,
And he was always human when he talked;
But still he fluttered pulses when he said,
"Good-morning," and he glittered when he walked.

And he was rich,—yes, richer than a king,—
And admirably schooled in every grace:
In fine, we thought that he was everything
To make us wish that we were in his place.

So on we worked, and waited for the light,
And went without the meat, and cursed the bread;
And Richard Cory, one calm summer night,
Went home and put a bullet through his head.

The Pity of the Leaves

Vengeful across the cold November moors,
Loud with ancestral shame there came the bleak
Sad wind that shrieked, and answered with a shriek,
Reverberant through lonely corridors.
The old man heard it; and he heard, perforce,
Words out of lips that were no more to speak—
Words of the past that shook the old man's cheek
Like dead, remembered footsteps on old floors.

And then there were the leaves that plagued him so!
The brown, thin leaves that on the stones outside
Skipped with a freezing whisper. Now and then
They stopped, and stayed there—just to let him know
How dead they were; but if the old man cried,
They fluttered off like withered souls of men.

The Clerks

I did not think that I should find them there
When I came back again; but there they stood,
As in the days they dreamed of when young blood
Was in their cheeks and women called them fair.
Be sure, they met me with an ancient air,—
And yes, there was a shop-worn brotherhood
About them; but the men were just as good,
And just as human as they ever were.

And you that ache so much to be sublime,
And you that feed yourselves with your descent,
What comes of all your visions and your fears?—
Poets and kings are but the clerks of Time,
Tiering the same dull webs of discontent,
Clipping the same sad alnage of the years.

Reuben Bright

Because he was a butcher and thereby
Did earn an honest living (and did right),
I would not have you think that Reuben Bright
Was any more a brute than you or I;
For when they told him that his wife must die,
He stared at them, and shook with grief and fright,
And cried like a great baby half that night,
And made the women cry to see him cry.

And after she was dead, and he had paid
The singers and the sexton and the rest,
He packed a lot of things that she had made
Most mournfully away in an old chest
Of hers, and put some chopped-up cedar boughs
In with them, and tore down the slaughter-house.

"Oh for a poet —for a beacon bright"

Oh for a poet—for a beacon bright
To rift this changeless glimmer of dead gray;
To spirit back the Muses, long astray,
And flush Parnassus with a newer light;
To put these little sonnet-men to flight
Who fashion, in a shrewd, mechanic way,
Songs without souls, that flicker for a day,
To vanish in irrevocable night.

What does it mean, this barren age of ours?
Here are the men, the women, and the flowers,
The seasons, and the sunset, as before.
What does it mean? Shall not one bard arise
To wrench one banner from the western skies,
And mark it with his name forevermore?

"*The master and the slave go hand in hand*"

The master and the slave go hand in hand,
Though touch be lost. The poet is a slave,
And there be kings do sorrowfully crave
The joyance that a scullion may command.
But, ah, the sonnet-slave must understand
The mission of his bondage, or the grave
May clasp his bones, or ever he shall save
The perfect word that is the poet's wand!

The sonnet is a crown, whereof the rhymes
Are for Thought's purest gold the jewel-stones;
But shapes and echoes that are never done
Will haunt the workshop, as regret sometimes
Will bring with human yearning to sad thrones
The crash of battles that are never won.

George Crabbe

Give him the darkest inch your shelf allows,
Hide him in lonely garrets, if you will,—
But his hard, human pulse is throbbing still
With the sure strength that fearless truth endows:—

In spite of all fine science disavows,
Of his plain excellence and stubborn skill
There yet remains what fashion cannot kill,
Though years have thinned the laurel from his brows.

Whether or not we read him, we can feel
From time to time the vigor of his name
Against us like a finger for the shame
And emptiness of what our souls reveal
In books that are as altars where we kneel
To consecrate the flicker, not the flame.

Verlaine

Why do you dig like long-clawed scavengers
To touch the covered corpse of him that fled
The uplands for the fens and rioted
Like a sick satyr with doom's worshippers?—
Come!—let the grass grow there; and leave his verse
To tell the story of the life he led.
Let the man go: let the dead flesh be dead,
And let the worms be its biographers.

Song sloughs away the sin to find redress
In art's complete remembrance: nothing clings
For long but laurel to the stricken brow
That felt the Muse's finger; nothing less
Than hell's fulfilment of the end of things
Can blot the star that shines on Paris now.

Cliff Klingenhagen

Cliff Klingenhagen had me in to dine
With him one day; and after soup and meat,
And all the other things there were to eat,
Cliff took two glasses and filled one with wine
And one with wormwood. Then, without a sign
For me to choose at all, he took the draught
Of bitterness himself, and lightly quaffed
It off, and said the other one was mine.

And when I asked him what the deuce he meant
By doing that, he only looked at me
And grinned, and said it was a way of his.
And though I know the fellow, I have spent
Long time a-wondering when I shall be
As happy as Cliff Klingenhagen is.

STEPHEN CRANE

(1871–1900)

from *The Black Riders and Other Lines*

I

Black riders came from the sea.
There was clang and clang of spear and shield,
And clash and clash of hoof and heel,
Wild shouts and the wave of hair
In the rush upon the wind:
Thus the ride of sin.

III

In the desert
I saw a creature, naked, bestial,
Who, squatting upon the ground,
Held his heart in his hands,
And ate of it.
I said, "Is it good, friend?"
"It is bitter—bitter," he answered;
"But I like it
"Because it is bitter,
"And because it is my heart."

IX

I stood upon a high place,
And saw, below, many devils
Running, leaping,
And carousing in sin.
One looked up, grinning,
And said, "Comrade! Brother!"

X

Should the wide world roll away
Leaving black terror
Limitless night,
Nor God, nor man, nor place to stand
Would be to me essential
If thou and thy white arms were there
And the fall to doom a long way.

XXIV

I saw a man pursuing the horizon;
Round and round they sped.
I was disturbed at this;
I accosted the man.
"It is futile," I said,
"You can never——"

"You lie," he cried,
And ran on.

XXV

Behold, the grave of a wicked man,
And near it, a stern spirit.

There came a drooping maid with violets,
But the spirit grasped her arm.
"No flowers for him," he said.
The maid wept:
"Ah, I loved him."
But the spirit, grim and frowning:
"No flowers for him."

Now, this is it——
If the spirit was just,
Why did the maid weep?

XXVI

There was set before me a mighty hill,
And long days I climbed
Through regions of snow.
When I had before me the summit-view,
It seemed that my labor
Had been to see gardens
Lying at impossible distances.

XXVII

A youth in apparel that glittered
Went to walk in a grim forest.
There he met an assassin
Attired all in garb of old days;
He, scowling through the thickets,
And dagger poised quivering,
Rushed upon the youth.
"Sir," said this latter,
"I am enchanted, believe me,
"To die, thus,
"In this medieval fashion,
"According to the best legends;
"Ah, what joy!"
Then took he the wound, smiling,
And died, content.

LVI

A man feared that he might find an assassin;
Another that he might find a victim.
One was more wise than the other.

LXV

Once, I knew a fine song,
—It is true, believe me,—
It was all of birds,

And I held them in a basket;
When I opened the wicket,
Heavens! They all flew away.
I cried, "Come back, little thoughts!"
But they only laughed.
They flew on
Until they were as sand
Thrown between me and the sky.

LXVI

If I should cast off this tattered coat,
And go free into the mighty sky;
If I should find nothing there
But a vast blue,
Echoless, ignorant,—
What then?

LXVII

God lay dead in Heaven;
Angels sang the hymn of the end;
Purple winds went moaning,
Their wings drip-dripping
With blood
That fell upon the earth.
It, groaning thing,
Turned black and sank.
Then from the far caverns
Of dead sins
Came monsters, livid with desire.
They fought,
Wrangled over the world,
A morsel.
But of all sadness this was sad,—
A woman's arms tried to shield
The head of a sleeping man
From the jaws of the final beast.

from *War Is Kind*

Do not weep, maiden, for war is kind.
Because your lover threw wild hands toward the sky
And the affrighted steed ran on alone,
Do not weep.
War is kind.

> Hoarse, booming drums of the regiment
> Little souls who thirst for fight,
> These men were born to drill and die
> The unexplained glory flies above them
> Great is the battle-god, great, and his kingdom——
> A field where a thousand corpses lie.

Do not weep, babe, for war is kind.
Because your father tumbled in the yellow trenches,
Raged at his breast, gulped and died,
Do not weep.
War is kind.

> Swift, blazing flag of the regiment
> Eagle with crest of red and gold,
> These men were born to drill and die
> Point for them the virtue of slaughter
> Make plain to them the excellence of killing
> And a field where a thousand corpses lie.

Mother whose heart hung humble as a button
On the bright splendid shroud of your son,
Do not weep.
War is kind.

———

> A little ink more or less!
> It surely can't matter?
> Even the sky and the opulent sea,
> The plains and the hills, aloof,
> Hear the uproar of all these books.
> But it is only a little ink more or less.

What?
You define me God with these trinkets?
Can my misery meal on an ordered walking
Of surpliced numbskulls?
And a fanfare of lights?
Or even upon the measured pulpiting
Of the familiar false and true?
Is this God?
Where, then, is hell?
Show me some bastard mushroom
Sprung from a pollution of blood.
It is better.

Where is God?

———————

I explain the silvered passing of a ship at night
The sweep of each sad lost wave
The dwindling boom of the steel thing's striving
The little cry of a man to a man
A shadow falling across the greyer night
And the sinking of the small star.

Then the waste, the far waste of waters
And the soft lashing of black waves
For long and in loneliness.

Remember, thou, oh ship of love
Thou leavest a far waste of waters
And the soft lashing of black waves
For long and in loneliness.

———————

A newspaper is a collection of half-injustices
Which, bawled by boys from mile to mile,
Spreads its curious opinion
To a million merciful and sneering men,
While families cuddle the joys of the fireside

When spurred by tale of dire lone agony.
A newspaper is a court
Where every one is kindly and unfairly tried
By a squalor of honest men.
A newspaper is a market
Where wisdom sells its freedom
And melons are crowned by the crowd.
A newspaper is a game
Where his error scores the player victory
While another's skill wins death.
A newspaper is a symbol;
It is fetless life's chronicle,
A collection of loud tales
Concentrating eternal stupidities,
That in remote ages lived unhaltered,
Roaming through a fenceless world.

———————

The wayfarer
Perceiving the pathway to truth
Was struck with astonishment.
It was thickly grown with weeds.
"Ha," he said,
"I see that none has passed here
"In a long time."
Later he saw that each weed
Was a singular knife.
"Well," he mumbled at last,
"Doubtless there are other roads."

———————

A man said to the universe:
"Sir, I exist!"
"However," replied the universe,
"The fact has not created in me
"A sense of obligation."

———————

Each small gleam was a voice
—A lantern voice—
In little songs of carmine, violet, green, gold.
A chorus of colors came over the water;
The wondrous leaf-shadow no longer wavered,
No pines crooned on the hills
The blue night was elsewhere a silence
When the chorus of colors came over the water,
Little songs of carmine, violet, green, gold.

Small glowing pebbles
Thrown on the dark plane of evening
Sing good ballads of God
And eternity, with soul's rest.
Little priests, little holy fathers
None can doubt the truth of your hymning
When the marvelous chorus comes over the water
Songs of carmine, violet, green, gold.

Ah, God, the way your little finger moved
As you thrust a bare arm backward
And made play with your hair
And a comb, a silly gilt comb
Ah, God—that I should suffer
Because of the way a little finger moved.

"Little birds of the night"

Little birds of the night
Aye, they have much to tell
Perching there in rows
Blinking at me with their serious eyes
Recounting of flowers they have seen and loved
Of meadows and groves of the distance
And pale sands at the foot of the sea
And breezes that fly in the leaves.
They are vast in experience
These little birds that come in the night

"There is a grey thing that lives in the tree-tops"

There is a grey thing that lives in the tree-tops
None know the horror of its sight
Save those who meet death in the wilderness
But one is enabled to see
To see branches move at its passing
To hear at times the wail of black laughter
And to come often upon mystic places
Places where the thing has just been.

"A man adrift on a slim spar"

A man adrift on a slim spar
A horizon smaller than the rim of a bottle
Tented waves rearing lashy dark points
The near whine of froth in circles.
                                        God is cold.

The incessant raise and swing of the sea
And growl after growl of crest
The sinkings, green, seething, endless
The upheaval half-completed.
                                        God is cold.

The seas are in the hollow of Thy Hand;
Oceans may be turned to a spray
Raining down through the stars
Because of a gesture of pity toward a babe.
Oceans may become grey ashes,
Die with a long moan and a roar
Amid the tumult of the fishes
And the cries of the ships,
Because The Hand beckons the mice.

A horizon smaller than a doomed assassin's cap,
Inky, surging tumults
A reeling, drunken sky and no sky
A pale hand sliding from a polished spar.
                    God is cold.

The puff of a coat imprisoning air.
A face kissing the water-death
A weary slow sway of a lost hand
And the sea, the moving sea, the sea.
                    God is cold.

"Unwind my riddle"

Unwind my riddle.
Cruel as hawks the hours fly,
Wounded men seldom come home to die,
The hard waves see an arm flung high,
Scorn hits strong because of a lie,
Yet there exists a mystic tie.
Unwind my riddle.

"A naked woman and a dead dwarf"

A naked woman and a dead dwarf;
Wealth and indifference.
Poor dwarf!
Reigning with foolish kings
And dying mid bells and wine
Ending with a desperate comic palaver
While before thee and after thee
Endures the eternal clown—
—The eternal clown—
A naked woman.

PAUL LAURENCE DUNBAR

(1872–1906)

Accountability

Folks aint got no right to censuah uthah folks about dey
    habits;
Him dat giv de squir'ls de bushtails made de bobtails fu' de
    rabbits.
Him dat built de grea' big mountains hollered out de little
    valleys,
Him dat made de streets an' driveways wasn't shamed to
    make de alleys.

We is all constructed diff'rent, d'ain't no two of us de same;
We can't he'p ouah likes an' dislikes, ef we'se bad we ain't to
    blame.
Ef we'se good, we needn't show off, case you bet it ain't
    ouah doin'
We gits into su'ttain channels dat we jes caint he'p pu'suin'.

But we all fits into places dat no othah ones cud fill
An' we does the things we has to, big er little, good er ill.
John cain't tek de place o' Henry, Su an' Sally ain't alike;
Bass ain't nuthin' like a suckah, chub ain't nuthin' like a
    pike.

When you come to think about it, how it's all planned out
    it's splendid.
Nuthin's done er evah happens, 'dout hit's somefin' dat's
    intended;
Don't keer whut you does, you has to, an' hit sholy beats de
    dickens,—
Viney go put on de kittle, I got one o' mastah's chickens.

The Mystery

I was not; now I am—a few days hence,
I shall not be; I fain would look before
And after, but can neither do; some Pow'r
Or lack of pow'r says "no" to all I would.
I stand upon a wide and sunless plain,
Nor chart nor steel to guide my steps aright.
Whene'er, o'ercoming fear, I dare to move,
I grope without direction and by chance.
Some feign to hear a voice and feel a hand
That draws them ever upward thro' the gloom.
But I—I hear no voice and touch no hand,
Tho' oft thro' silence infinite, I list,
And strain my hearing to supernal sounds;
Tho' oft thro' fateful darkness do I reach,
And stretch my hand to find that other hand.
I question of th' eternal bending skies
That seem to neighbor with the novice earth;
But they roll on and daily shut their eyes
On me, as I one day shall do on them,
And tell me not the secret that I ask.

Song of Summer

Dis is gospel weathah sho'—
    Hills is sawt o' hazy.
Meddahs level ez a flo'
    Callin' to de lazy.
Sky all white wif streaks o' blue,
    Sunshine softly gleamin',
D'ain't no wuk hit's right to do,
    Nothin' 's right but dreamin'.

Dreamin' by de rivah side
    Wif de watahs glist'nin',
Feelin' good an' satisfied
    Ez you lay a-list'nin'

To the little nakid boys
    Splashin' in de watah,
Hollerin' fu' to spress deir joys
    Jes' lak youngsters ought to.

Squir'l a-tippin' on his toes,
    So 's to hide an' view you;
Whole flocks o' camp-meetin' crows
    Shoutin' hallelujah.
Peckahwood erpon de tree
    Tappin' lak a hammah;
Jaybird chattin' wif a bee,
    Tryin' to teach him grammah.

Breeze is blowin' wif perfume,
    Jes' enough to tease you;
Hollyhocks is all in bloom,
    Smellin' fu' to please you.
Go 'way, folks, an' let me 'lone,
    Times is gettin' dearah—
Summah 's settin' on de th'one,
    An' I'm a-layin' neah huh!

A Summer's Night

The night is dewy as a maiden's mouth,
    The skies are bright as are a maiden's eyes,
    Soft as a maiden's breath, the wind that flies
Up from the perfumed bosom of the South.
Like sentinels, the pines stand in the park;
    And hither hastening like rakes that roam,
    With lamps to light their wayward footsteps home,
The fire-flies come stagg'ring down the dark.

We Wear the Mask

We wear the mask that grins and lies,
It hides our cheeks and shades our eyes—
This debt we pay to human guile;
With torn and bleeding hearts we smile
And mouth with myriad subtleties,

Why should the world be over-wise,
In counting all our tears and sighs?
Nay, let them only see us, while
    We wear the mask.

We smile, but oh great Christ, our cries
To Thee from tortured souls arise.
We sing, but oh the clay is vile
Beneath our feet, and long the mile,
But let the world dream otherwise,
    We wear the mask!

Compensation

Because I had loved so deeply,
    Because I had loved so long,
God in His great compassion
    Gave me the gift of song.

Because I have loved so vainly,
    And sung with such faltering breath,
The Master in infinite mercy
    Offers the boon of Death.

When Malindy Sings

G'way an' quit dat noise, Miss Lucy—
    Put dat music book away;
What's de use to keep on tryin'?
    Ef you practise twell you 're gray,

You cain't sta't no notes a-flyin'
　　Lak de ones dat rants and rings
F'om de kitchen to de big woods
　　When Malindy sings.

You ain't got de nachel o'gans
　　Fu' to make de soun' come right,
You ain't got de tu'ns an' twistin's
　　Fu' to make it sweet an' light.
Tell you one thing now, Miss Lucy,
　　An' I'm tellin' you fu' true,
When hit comes to raal right singin',
　　'T ain't no easy thing to do.

Easy 'nough fu' folks to hollah,
　　Lookin' at de lines an' dots,
When dey ain't no one kin sence it,
　　An' de chune comes in, in spots;
But fu' real melojous music,
　　Dat jes' strikes yo' hea't and clings,
Jes' you stan' an' listen wif me
　　When Malindy sings.

Ain't you nevah hyeahd Malindy?
　　Blessed soul, tek up de cross!
Look hyeah, ain't you jokin', honey?
　　Well, you don't know whut you los'.
Y' ought to hyeah dat gal a-wa'blin',
　　Robins, la'ks, an' all dem things,
Heish dey moufs an' hides dey faces
　　When Malindy sings.

Fiddlin' man jes' stop his fiddlin',
　　Lay his fiddle on de she'f;
Mockin'-bird quit tryin' to whistle,
　　'Cause he jes' so shamed hisse'f.
Folks a-playin' on de banjo
　　Draps dey fingahs on de strings—
Bless yo' soul—fu'gits to move 'em,
　　When Malindy sings.

She jes' spreads huh mouf and hollahs,
    "Come to Jesus," twell you hyeah
Sinnahs' tremblin' steps and voices,
    Timid-lak a-drawin' neah;
Den she tu'ns to "Rock of Ages,"
    Simply to de cross she clings,
An' you fin' yo' teahs a-drappin'
    When Malindy sings.

Who dat says dat humble praises
    Wif de Master nevah counts?
Heish yo' mouf, I hyeah dat music,
    Ez hit rises up an' mounts—
Floatin' by de hills an' valleys,
    Way above dis buryin' sod,
Ez hit makes its way in glory
    To de very gates of God!

Oh, hit 's sweetah dan de music
    Of an edicated band;
An' hit 's dearah dan de battle's
    Song o' triumph in de lan'.
It seems holier dan evenin'
    When de solemn chu'ch bell rings,
Ez I sit an' ca'mly listen
    While Malindy sings.

Towsah, stop dat ba'kin', hyeah me!
    Mandy, mek dat chile keep still;
Don't you hyeah de echoes callin'
    F'om de valley to de hill?
Let me listen, I can hyeah it,
    Th'oo de bresh of angel's wings,
Sof' an' sweet, "Swing Low, Sweet Chariot,"
    Ez Malindy sings.

Little Brown Baby

Little brown baby wif spa'klin' eyes,
  Come to yo' pappy an' set on his knee.
What you been doin', suh—makin' san' pies?
  Look at dat bib—you's ez du'ty ez me.
Look at dat mouf—dat's merlasses, I bet;
  Come hyeah, Maria, an' wipe off his han's.
Bees gwine to ketch you an' eat you up yit,
  Bein' so sticky an sweet—goodness lan's!

Little brown baby wif spa'klin' eyes,
  Who's pappy's darlin' an' who's pappy's chile?
Who is it all de day nevah once tries
  Fu' to be cross, er once loses dat smile?
Whah did you git dem teef? My, you's a scamp!
  Whah did dat dimple come f'om in yo' chin?
Pappy do' know you—I b'lieves you's a tramp;
  Mammy, dis hyeah's some ol' straggler got in!

Let's th'ow him outen de do' in de san',
  We do' want stragglers a-layin' 'roun' hyeah;
Let's gin him 'way to de big buggah-man;
  I know he's hidin' erroun' hyeah right neah.
Buggah-man, buggah-man, come in de do',
  Hyeah's a bad boy you kin have fu' to eat.
Mammy an' pappy do' want him no mo',
  Swaller him down f'om his haid to his feet!

Dah, now, I t'ought dat you'd hug me up close.
  Go back, ol' buggah, you sha'n't have dis boy.
He ain't no tramp, ner no straggler, of co'se;
  He's pappy's pa'dner an' playmate an' joy.
Come to you' pallet now—go to yo' res';
  Wisht you could allus know ease an' cleah skies;
Wisht you could stay jes' a chile on my breas'—
  Little brown baby wif spa'klin' eyes!

A Negro Love Song

Seen my lady home las' night,
  Jump back, honey, jump back.
Hel' huh han' an' sque'z it tight,
  Jump back, honey, jump back.
Hyeahd huh sigh a little sigh,
Seen a light gleam f'om huh eye,
An' a smile go flittin' by —
  Jump back, honey, jump back.

Hyeahd de win' blow thoo de pine,
  Jump back, honey, jump back.
Mockin'-bird was singin' fine,
  Jump back, honey, jump back.
An' my hea't was beatin' so,
When I reached my lady's do',
Dat I could n't ba' to go —
  Jump back, honey, jump back.

Put my ahm aroun' huh wais',
  Jump back, honey, jump back.
Raised huh lips an' took a tase,
  Jump back, honey, jump back.
Love me, honey, love me true?
Love me well ez I love you?
An' she answe'd, " 'Cose I do" —
  Jump back, honey, jump back.

Ere Sleep Comes Down to Soothe the Weary Eyes

Ere sleep comes down to soothe the weary eyes,
  Which all the day with ceaseless care have sought
The magic gold which from the seeker flies;
  Ere dreams put on the gown and cap of thought,
And make the waking world a world of lies, —
  Of lies most palpable, uncouth, forlorn,
That say life's full of aches and tears and sighs, —
  Oh, how with more than dreams the soul is torn,
Ere sleep comes down to soothe the weary eyes.

Ere sleep comes down to soothe the weary eyes,
    How all the griefs and heartaches we have known
Come up like pois'nous vapors that arise
    From some base witch's caldron, when the crone,
To work some potent spell, her magic plies.
    The past which held its share of bitter pain,
Whose ghost we prayed that Time might exorcise,
    Comes up, is lived and suffered o'er again,
Ere sleep comes down to soothe the weary eyes.

Ere sleep comes down to soothe the weary eyes,
    What phantoms fill the dimly lighted room;
What ghostly shades in awe-creating guise
    Are bodied forth within the teeming gloom.
What echoes faint of sad and soul-sick cries,
    And pangs of vague inexplicable pain
That pay the spirit's ceaseless enterprise,
    Come thronging through the chambers of the brain,
Ere sleep comes down to soothe the weary eyes.

Ere sleep comes down to soothe the weary eyes,
    Where ranges forth the spirit far and free?
Through what strange realms and unfamiliar skies
    Tends her far course to lands of mystery?
To lands unspeakable—beyond surmise,
    Where shapes unknowable to being spring,
Till, faint of wing, the Fancy fails and dies
    Much wearied with the spirit's journeying,
Ere sleep comes down to soothe the weary eyes.

Ere sleep comes down to soothe the weary eyes,
    How questioneth the soul that other soul,—
The inner sense which neither cheats nor lies,
    But self exposes unto self, a scroll
Full writ with all life's acts unwise or wise,
    In characters indelible and known;
So, trembling with the shock of sad surprise,
    The soul doth view its awful self alone,
Ere sleep comes down to soothe the weary eyes.

When sleep comes down to seal the weary eyes,
    The last dear sleep whose soft embrace is balm,
And whom sad sorrow teaches us to prize
    For kissing all our passions into calm,
Ah, then, no more we heed the sad world's cries,
    Or seek to probe th' eternal mystery,
Or fret our souls at long-withheld replies,
    At glooms through which our visions cannot see,
When sleep comes down to seal the weary eyes.

The Colored Soldiers

If the muse were mine to tempt it
    And my feeble voice were strong,
If my tongue were trained to measures,
    I would sing a stirring song.
I would sing a song heroic
    Of those noble sons of Ham,
Of the gallant colored soldiers
    Who fought for Uncle Sam!

In the early days you scorned them,
    And with many a flip and flout
Said "These battles are the white man's,
    And the whites will fight them out."
Up the hills you fought and faltered,
    In the vales you strove and bled,
While your ears still heard the thunder
    Of the foes' advancing tread.

Then distress fell on the nation,
    And the flag was drooping low;
Should the dust pollute your banner?
    No! the nation shouted, No!
So when War, in savage triumph,
    Spread abroad his funeral pall—
Then you called the colored soldiers,
    And they answered to your call.

And like hounds unleashed and eager
   For the life blood of the prey,
Sprung they forth and bore them bravely
   In the thickest of the fray.
And where'er the fight was hottest,
   Where the bullets fastest fell,
There they pressed unblanched and fearless
   At the very mouth of hell.

Ah, they rallied to the standard
   To uphold it by their might;
None were stronger in the labors,
   None were braver in the fight.
From the blazing breach of Wagner
   To the plains of Olustee,
They were foremost in the fight
   Of the battles of the free.

And at Pillow! God have mercy
   On the deeds committed there,
And the souls of those poor victims
   Sent to Thee without a prayer.
Let the fulness of Thy pity
   O'er the hot wrought spirits sway
Of the gallant colored soldiers
   Who fell fighting on that day!

Yes, the Blacks enjoy their freedom,
   And they won it dearly, too;
For the life blood of their thousands
   Did the southern fields bedew.
In the darkness of their bondage,
   In the depths of slavery's night,
Their muskets flashed the dawning,
   And they fought their way to light.

They were comrades then and brothers,
    Are they more or less to-day?
They were good to stop a bullet
    And to front the fearful fray.
They were citizens and soldiers,
    When rebellion raised its head;
And the traits that made them worthy,—
    Ah! those virtues are not dead.

They have shared your nightly vigils,
    They have shared your daily toil;
And their blood with yours commingling
    Has enriched the Southern soil.
They have slept and marched and suffered
    'Neath the same dark skies as you,
They have met as fierce a foeman,
    And have been as brave and true.

And their deeds shall find a record
    In the registry of Fame;
For their blood has cleansed completely
    Every blot of Slavery's shame.
So all honor and all glory
    To those noble sons of Ham—
The gallant colored soldiers
    Who fought for Uncle Sam!

Sympathy

I know what the caged bird feels, alas!
    When the sun is bright on the upland slopes;
When the wind stirs soft through the springing grass,
And the river flows like a stream of glass;
    When the first bird sings and the first bud opes,
And the faint perfume from its chalice steals—
I know what the caged bird feels!

I know why the caged bird beats his wing
   Till its blood is red on the cruel bars;
For he must fly back to his perch and cling
When he fain would be on the bough a-swing;
   And a pain still throbs in the old, old scars
And they pulse again with a keener sting—
I know why he beats his wing!

I know why the caged bird sings, ah me,
   When his wing is bruised and his bosom sore,—
When he beats his bars and he would be free;
It is not a carol of joy or glee,
   But a prayer that he sends from his heart's deep core,
But a plea, that upward to Heaven he flings—
I know why the caged bird sings!

An Ante-Bellum Sermon

We is gathahed hyeah, my brothahs,
   In dis howlin' wildaness,
Fu' to speak some words of comfo't
   To each othah in distress.
An' we chooses fu' ouah subjic'
   Dis—we'll 'splain it by an' by;
"An' de Lawd said, 'Moses, Moses,'
   An' de man said, 'Hyeah am I.'"

Now ole Pher'oh, down in Egypt,
   Was de wuss man evah bo'n,
An' he had de Hebrew chillun
   Down dah wukin' in his co'n;
'T well de Lawd got tiahed o' his foolin',
   An' sez he: "I'll let him know—
Look hyeah, Moses, go tell Pher'oh
   Fu' to let dem chillun go."

"An' ef he refuse to do it,
    I will make him rue de houah,
Fu' I 'll empty down on Egypt
    All de vials of my powah."
Yes, he did—an' Pher'oh's ahmy
    Was n't wuth a ha'f a dime;
Fu' de Lawd will he'p his chillun,
    You kin trust him evah time.

An' yo' enemies may 'sail you
    In de back an' in de front;
But de Lawd is all aroun' you,
    Fu' to ba' de battle's brunt.
Dey kin fo'ge yo' chains an' shackles
    F'om de mountains to de sea;
But de Lawd will sen' some Moses
    Fu' to set his chillun free.

An' de lan' shall hyeah his thundah,
    Lak a blas' f'om Gab'el's ho'n,
Fu' de Lawd of hosts is mighty
    When he girds his ahmor on.
But fu' feah some one mistakes me,
    I will pause right hyeah to say,
Dat I 'm still a-preachin' ancient,
    I ain't talkin' 'bout to-day.

But I tell you, fellah christuns,
    Things 'll happen mighty strange;
Now, de Lawd done dis fu' Isrul,
    An' his ways don't nevah change,
An' de love he showed to Isrul
    Was n't all on Isrul spent;
Now don't run an' tell yo' mastahs
    Dat I 's preachin' discontent.

'Cause I is n't; I 'se a-judgin'
    Bible people by deir ac's;
I 'se a-givin' you de Scriptuah,
    I 'se a-handin' you de fac's.

Cose ole Pher'oh b'lieved in slav'ry,
    But de Lawd he let him see,
Dat de people he put bref in,—
    Evah mothah's son was free.

An' dahs othahs thinks lak Pher'oh,
    But dey calls de Scriptuah liar,
Fu' de Bible says "a servant
    Is a-worthy of his hire."
An' you cain't git roun' nor thoo dat,
    An' you cain't git ovah it,
Fu' whatevah place you git in,
    Dis hyeah Bible too'll fit.

So you see de Lawd's intention,
    Evah sence de worl' began,
Was dat His almighty freedom
    Should belong to evah man,
But I think it would be bettah,
    Ef I'd pause agin to say,
Dat I'm talkin' 'bout ouah freedom
    In a Bibleistic way.

But de Moses is a-comin',
    An' he's comin', suah and fas'
We kin hyeah his feet a-trompin',
    We kin hyeah his trumpit blas'.
But I want to wa'n you people,
    Don't you git too brigity;
An' don't you git to braggin'
    'Bout dese things, you wait an' see.

But when Moses wif his powah
    Comes an' sets us chillun free,
We will praise de gracious Mastah
    Dat has gin us liberty;
An' we'll shout ouah halleluyahs,
    On dat mighty reck'nin' day,
When we'se reco'nised ez citiz'—
    Huh uh! Chillun, let us pray!

Signs of the Times

Air a-gittin' cool an' coolah,
 Frost a-comin' in de night,
Hicka' nuts an' wa'nuts fallin',
 Possum keepin' out o' sight.
Tu'key struttin' in de ba'nya'd,
 Nary step so proud ez his;
Keep on struttin', Mistah Tu'key,
 Yo' do' know whut time it is.

Cidah press commence a-squeakin'
 Eatin' apples sto'ed away,
Chillun swa'min' 'roun' lak ho'nets,
 Huntin' aigs ermung de hay.
Mistah Tu'key keep on gobblin'
 At de geese a-flyin' souf,
Oomph! dat bird do' know whut 's comin';
 Ef he did he 'd shet his mouf.

Pumpkin gittin' good an' yallah
 Mek me open up my eyes;
Seems lak it 's a-lookin' at me
 Jes' a-la'in' dah sayin' "Pies."
Tu'key gobbler gwine 'roun' blowin',
 Gwine 'roun' gibbin' sass an' slack;
Keep on talkin', Mistah Tu'key,
 You ain't seed no almanac.

Fa'mer walkin' th'oo de ba'nya'd
 Seein' how things is comin' on,
Sees ef all de fowls is fatt'nin'—
 Good times comin' sho 's you bo'n,
Hyeahs dat tu'key gobbler braggin',
 Den his face break in a smile—
Nebbah min', you sassy rascal,
 He 's gwine nab you atter while.

Choppin' suet in de kitchen,
    Stonin' raisins in de hall,
Beef a-cookin' fu' de mince meat,
    Spices groun'—I smell 'em all.
Look hyeah, Tu'key, stop dat gobblin',
    You ain' luned de sense ob feah,
You ol' fool, yo' naik's in dangah,
    Do' you know Thanksgibbin's hyeah?

ALEXANDER L. POSEY

(1873–1908)

Song of the Oktahutchee

Far, far, far are my silver waters drawn;
  The hills embrace me, loth to let me go;
The maidens think me fair to look upon,
  And trees lean over, glad to hear me flow.
Thro' field and valley, green because of me,
I wander, wander to the distant sea.

Thro' lonely places and thro' crowded ways,
  Thro' noise of strife and thro' the solitude,
And on thro' cloudy days and sunny days,
  I journey till I meet, in sisterhood,
The broad Canadian, red with the sunset,
Now calm, now raging in a mighty fret!

On either hand, in a grand colonnade,
  The cottonwoods rise in the azure sky,
And purple mountains cast a purple shade
  As I, now grave, now laughing, pass them by;
The birds of air dip bright wings in my tide,
In sunny reaches where I noiseless glide.

O'er sandy reaches with rocks and mussel-shells,
  Blue over spacious beds of amber sand,
By hanging cliffs, by glens where echo dwells—
  Elusive spirit of the shadow-land—
Forever blest and blessing do I go,
A-wid'ning in the morning's roseate glow.

Tho' I sing my song in a minor key,
  Broad lands and fair attest the good I do;
Tho' I carry no white sails to the sea,
  Towns nestle in the vales I wander thro';
And quails are whistling in the waving grain,
And herds are scattered o'er the verdant plain.

July

The air without has taken fever;
Fast I feel the beating of its pulse.
The leaves are twisted on the maple,
In the corn the autumn's premature;
The weary butterfly hangs waiting
For a breath to waft him thither at
The touch, but falls, like truth unheeded,
Into dust-blown grass and hollyhocks.

The air without is blinding dusty;
Cool I feel the breezes blow; I see
The sunlight, crowded on the porch, grow
Smaller till absorbed in shadow; and
The far blue hills are changed to gray, and
Twilight lingers in the woods between;
And now I hear the shower dancing
In the cornfield and the thirsty grass.

Midsummer

I see the millet combing gold
    From summer sun,
In hussar caps, all day;
    And brown quails run
Far down the dusty way,
    Fly up and whistle from the wold;

Sweet delusions on the mountains,
    Of hounds in chase,
        Beguiling every care
    Of life apace,
        Though only fevered air
That trembles, and dies in mounting.

Autumn

In the dreamy silence
Of the afternoon, a
Cloth of gold is woven
Over wood and prairie;
And the jaybird, newly
Fallen from the heaven,
Scatters cordial greetings,
And the air is filled with
Scarlet leaves, that, dropping,
Rise again, as ever,
With a useless sigh for
Rest—and it is Autumn.

Nightfall

As evening splendors fade
  From yonder sky afar,
The Night pins on her dark
  Robe with a large bright star,
And the new moon hangs like
  A high-thrown scimitar.
Vague in the mystic room
  This side the paling west,
The Tulledegas loom
  In an eternal rest,
And one by one the lamps are lit
  In the dome of the Infinite.

GEORGE CABOT LODGE

(1873–1909)

Tuckanuck, I

I am content to live the patient day:
    The wind sea-laden loiters to the land
    And on the glittering gold of naked sand
    The eternity of blue sea pales to spray.
In such a world we have no need to pray;
    The holy voices of the sea and air
    Are sacramental, like a mighty prayer
    In which the earth has dreamed its tears away.
We row across the waters' fluent gold
    And age seems blessèd, for the world is old.
    Softly we take from Nature's open palm
The dower of the sunset and the sky,
    And dream an Eastern dream, starred by the cry
    Of sea-birds homing through the mighty calm.

Pastoral

Slopes of the sun and vine, and thou dark stream,
    Thou minstrel of the forest-gloom, whose roll
Is like the passing of a natural dream
    Through depths of patient sleep
    To lend endurance to the taxèd soul.
    The cruel life beneath the cruel noon,
Where men are quenched like dewdrops in the sun,
    Where haggard women reach to God and weep,
Never corrodes thy silent solitude;
But where thy sheer, green shadows shoreward creep
    Through the slow afternoon,
The battle lost, the poem half-begun,
Are chaplets that the hymning dawn-stars keep
To grace the splendid hope our youth imbued.

The twilight flowers close
And down the shadow falls a timid star;
                    Afar
The sigh and silence of a changing wind,
    The perfume of a dying rose—
Beyond the senses and beyond the mind
    Dimly we hear a graver music grow,—
    Peace! Peace! the world is tuneful of her woes:
    With man's despair the richer chord impearled
Is infinite of grief; we in the world
    Hear scattered discord, nor the broad full flow
Of song until, waxed greater than the whole,
    Wide, from their slumber's mystery, unclose
The vision-laden eyelids of the soul.

Fall

Nay, be content—our door that opens wide
    On whitened fields this autumn dawn, all furred
    With silver imagery, the sudden bird
That soothes the crystal air, the windless tide
Of light across the world from roof to floor—
    Thy heart can ask no more.
The fringed horizon of the pines
    Is delicate with frore,
And holds our world within its shadow shore,
Our world where beauty fresh with dewy wines
    Sits naked at our door.
Thine eyes in mine! The vineyard's dusky bloom,
    The garnered grain, are gifts of autumn's mirth;
And now, while softly through the forest gloom
    The warm awakening of the good wet earth
Suspires through the dawn, we need not fear
    The ceaseless pageantry of death and birth,
The swallow's passing with the changing year.
    Our souls could say, "Perfection was and is;
    Death comes like slumber,"—if to-morrow's sun
Should find us fallen with the summer's rose.

This moment stolen from the centuries,
This foretaste of the soul's oblivion
We hold and cherish, and because of this
Are life and death made perfect, and thy woes
Turn lyric through the glory we have won.
The morning flower that drew its petals close
And slept the cold night through is now unfurled
To catch the breathless moment; big and sane
Our autumn day forsakes the gates of rose,
And like a lion shakes its golden mane
    And leaps upon the world.

On an Æolian Harp

Lure of the night's dædalian sea-born breath,
    Wild as the heart's uncomprehended dole,
    Strange as the grieving of a mighty soul
    Touched with the lyric woe of life and death.
Phraser of world-wide monotones that toll
    Like far enormous bells from sky to sky,
    Voice of the vaster solitudes that lie
    With life's solution past the mind's control.
The golden eyes of long-forgotten days,
    The dolorous memory of simple things,
    Sadden thy lapsing chords:—the present pays
The past's arrears of sorrow, and they seem
    To wake a sense, among thy weeping strings,
    Of other lives, like some unceasing dream.

"Strong saturation of sea! O widely flown"

Strong saturation of sea! O widely flown,
    Far winds of fall, your litanies of pain
    Moan like the music of a wild refrain
    Heard thro' the midnight of a feudal town!
Young night is lipped with jasper where the blown
    Burden of evening lights intensely wane,

And, shuddering seaward from the tawny plain,
  Vague fold on fold the enormous dark comes down.
Gusty and fervid as the sleepless sea
  The passionate fancies of a formless fear
  Spring in my nervous brain like monstrous flowers;
The night, the wind-chant work their will of me,
  And thoughts like death-bells echoing far and near,
  Toll for life's lost, irrevocable hours.

Lower New York

I

Before Dawn

Time has no spectacle more stern and strange;
  Life has no sleep so dense as that which lies
  On walls and windows, blank as sightless eyes,
  On court and prison, warehouse and exchange.
Earth has no silence such as fills the range
  Of streets left bare beneath the haughty skies:—
  Of unremembered human miseries
  Churned without purpose in the trough of change.
For here where day by day the tide-race rolls
  Of sordid greed and passions mean and blind,
  Here is a vast necropolis of souls!
And life, that waits as with suspended breath,
  Weary and still, here seems more dead than death,
  Aimless and empty as an idiot's mind.

II

At Dawn

Here is the dawn a hopeless thing to see:
  Sordid and pale as is the face of one
  Who sinks exhausted in oblivion
  After a night of deep debauchery.
Here, as the light reveals relentlessly

All that the soul has lost and greed has won,
Scarce we believe that somewhere now the sun
Dawns overseas in stainless majesty.
Yet the day comes!—ghastly and harsh and thin
Down the cold street; and now, from far away,
We hear a vast and sullen rumor run,
As of the tides of ocean turning in . . .
And know, for yet another human day,
The world's dull, dreadful labor is begun!

TRUMBULL STICKNEY

(1874–1904)

In Ampezzo

Only once more and not again—the larches
Shake to the wind their echo, "Not again,"—
We see, below the sky that over-arches
Heavy and blue, the plain

Between Tofana lying and Cristallo
In meadowy earths above the ringing stream:
Whence interchangeably desire may follow,
Hesitant as in dream,

At sunset, south, by lilac promontories
Under green skies to Italy, or forth
By calms of morning beyond Lavinores
Tyrolward and to north:

As now, this last of latter days, when over
The brownish field by peasants are undone
Some widths of grass, some plots of mountain clover
Under the autumn sun,

With honey-warm perfume that risen lingers
In mazes of low heat, or takes the air,
Passing delicious as a woman's fingers
Passing amid the hair;

When scythes are swishing and the mower's muscle
Spans a repeated crescent to and fro,
Or in dry stalks of corn the sickles rustle,
Tangle, detach and go,

Far thro' the wide blue day and greening meadow
Whose blots of amber beaded are with sheaves,
Whereover pallidly a cloud-shadow
Deadens the earth and leaves:

Whilst high around and near, their heads of iron
Sunken in sky whose azure overlights
Ravine and edges, stand the gray and maron
Desolate Dolomites,—

And older than decay from the small summit
Unfolds a stream of pebbly wreckage down
Under the suns of midday, like some comet
Struck into gravel stone.

Faintly across this gold and amethystine
September, images of summer fade;
And gentle dreams now freshen on the pristine
Viols, awhile unplayed,

Of many a place where lovingly we wander,
More dearly held that quickly we forsake,—
A pine by sullen coasts, an oleander
Reddening on the lake.

And there, each year with more familiar motion,
From many a bird and windy forestries,
Or along shaking fringes of the ocean
Vapours of music rise.

From many easts the morning gives her splendour;
The shadows fill with colours we forget;
Remembered tints at evening grow tender,
Tarnished with violet.

Let us away! soon sheets of winter metal
On this discoloured mountain-land will close,
While elsewhere Spring-time weaves a crimson petal,
Builds and perfumes a rose.

Away! for here the mountain sinks in gravel.
Let us forget the unhappy site with change,
And go, if only happiness be travel
After the new and strange:—

Unless 't were better to be very single,
To follow some diviner monotone,
And in all beauties, where ourselves commingle,
Love but a love, but one,

Across this shadowy minute of our living,
What time our hearts so magically sing,
To meditate our fever, simply giving
All in a little thing?

Just as here, past yon dumb and melancholy
Sameness of ruin, while the mountains ail,
Summer and sunset-coloured autumn slowly
Dissipate down the vale;

And all these lines along the sky that measure,
Sorapis and the rocks of Mezzodì
Crumble by foamy miles into the azure
Mediterranean sea:

Whereas to-day at sunrise, under brambles,
A league above the moss and dying pines
I picked this little—in my hand that trembles—
Parcel of columbines.

Mnemosyne

It's autumn in the country I remember.

How warm a wind blew here about the ways!
And shadows on the hillside lay to slumber
During the long sun-sweetened summer-days.

It's cold abroad the country I remember.

The swallows veering skimmed the golden grain
At midday with a wing aslant and limber;
And yellow cattle browsed upon the plain.

It's empty down the country I remember.

I had a sister lovely in my sight:
Her hair was dark, her eyes were very sombre;
We sang together in the woods at night.

It's lonely in the country I remember.

The babble of our children fills my ears,
And on our hearth I stare the perished ember
To flames that show all starry thro' my tears.

It's dark about the country I remember.

There are the mountains where I lived. The path
Is slushed with cattle-tracks and fallen timber,
The stumps are twisted by the tempests' wrath.

But that I knew these places are my own,
I'd ask how came such wretchedness to cumber
The earth, and I to people it alone.

It rains across the country I remember.

Eride, V

Now in the palace gardens warm with age,
On lawn and flower-bed this afternoon
The thin November-coloured foliage
Just as last year unfastens lilting down,

And round the terrace in gray attitude
The very statues are becoming sere
With long presentiment of solitude.
Most of the life that I have lived is here,

Here by the path and autumn's earthy grass
And chestnuts standing down the breadths of sky:
Indeed I know not how it came to pass,
The life I lived here so unhappily.

Yet blessing over all! I do not care
What wormwood I have ate to cups of gall;
I care not what despairs are buried there
Under the ground, no, I care not at all.

Nay, if the heart have beaten, let it break!
I have not loved and lived but only this
Betwixt my birth and grave. Dear Spirit, take
The gratitude that pains, so deep it is.

When Spring shall be again, and at your door
You stand to feel the mellower evening wind,
Remember if you will my heart is pure,
Perfectly pure and altogether kind;

That not an aftercry of all our strife
Troubles the love I give you and the faith:
Say to yourself that at the ends of life
My arms are open to you, life and death. —

How much it aches to linger in these things!
I thought the perfect end of love was peace
Over the long-forgiven sufferings.
But something else, I know not what it is,

The words that came so nearly and then not,
The vanity, the error of the whole,
The strong cross-purpose, oh, I know not what
Cries dreadfully in the distracted soul.

The evening fills the garden, hardly red;
And autumn goes away, like one alone.
Would I were with the leaves that thread by thread
Soften to soil, I would that I were one.

"You say, Columbus with his argosies"

You say, Columbus with his argosies
Who rash and greedy took the screaming main
And vanished out before the hurricane
Into the sunset after merchandise,
Then under western palms with simple eyes
Trafficked and robbed and triumphed home again:
You say this is the glory of the brain
And human life no other use than this?
I then do answering say to you: The line
Of wizards and of saviours, keeping trust
In that which made them pensive and divine,
Passes before us like a cloud of dust.
What were they? Actors, ill and mad with wine,
And all their language babble and disgust.

On Rodin's "L'Illusion, Sœur d'Icare"

She started up from where the lizard lies
Among the grasses' dewy hair, and flew
Thro' leagues of lower air until the blue
Was thin and pale and fair as Echo is.
Crying she made her upward flight. Her cries
Were naught, and naught made answer to her view.
The air lay in the light and slowly grew
A marvel of white void in her eyes.
She cried: her throat was dead. Deliriously
She looked, and lo! the Sun in master mirth
Glowed sharp, huge, cruel. Then brake her noble eye.
She fell, her white wings rocking down the abyss,
A ghost of ecstasy, backward to earth,
And shattered all her beauty in a kiss.

On Some Shells Found Inland

These are my murmur-laden shells that keep
A fresh voice tho' the years be very gray.
The wave that washed their lips and tuned their lay
Is gone, gone with the faded ocean sweep,
The royal tide, gray ebb and sunken neap
And purple midday,—gone! To this hot clay
Must sing my shells, where yet the primal day,
Its roar and rhythm and splendour will not sleep.
What hand shall join them to their proper sea
If all be gone? Shall they forever feel
Glories undone and worlds that cannot be?—
'Twere mercy to stamp out this agèd wrong,
Dash them to earth and crunch them with the heel
And make a dust of their seraphic song.

"Live blindly and upon the hour"

Live blindly and upon the hour. The Lord,
Who was the Future, died full long ago.
Knowledge which is the Past is folly. Go,
Poor child, and be not to thyself abhorred.
Around thine earth sun-wingèd winds do blow
And planets roll; a meteor draws his sword;
The rainbow breaks his seven-coloured chord
And the long strips of river-silver flow:
Awake! Give thyself to the lovely hours.
Drinking their lips, catch thou the dream in flight
About their fragile hairs' aërial gold.
Thou art divine, thou livest,—as of old
Apollo springing naked to the light,
And all his island shivered into flowers.

"Be still. The Hanging Gardens were a dream"

Be still. The Hanging Gardens were a dream
That over Persian roses flew to kiss
The curlèd lashes of Semiramis.
Troy never was, nor green Skamander stream.
Provence and Troubadour are merest lies.
The glorious hair of Venice was a beam
Made within Titian's eye. The sunsets seem,
The world is very old and nothing is.
Be still. Thou foolish thing, thou canst not wake,
Nor thy tears wedge thy soldered lids apart,
But patter in the darkness of thy heart.
Thy brain is plagued. Thou art a frighted owl
Blind with the light of life thou'ldst not forsake,
And Error loves and nourishes thy soul.

On the Concert

When first this canvas felt Giorgione's hand,
From out his soul's intensity he drew
In lines most acrid yet superbly few
A man,—a soul, whose water at command
Of pain had stiffened to ice, whom grief had banned,
Till music even and harmony's rich dew
Fell fruitless. Poised, defiant and calm he threw
To the earth that wronged him his life's reprimand.
Yet, as he drew, a wind mellow with dole
Of past life as of sea-coast pine did rise
And warm the rigour of the painter's soul.
For his tear-moistened fingers warmed the frore
Hard colours of the cheek, and in the eyes
Set the large stare of Sorrow's Nevermore.

"*The melancholy year is dead with rain*"

The melancholy year is dead with rain.
Drop after drop on every branch pursues.
From far away beyond the drizzled flues
A twilight saddens to the window pane.
And dimly thro' the chambers of the brain,
From place to place and gently touching, moves
My one and irrecoverable love's
Dear and lost shape one other time again.
So in the last of autumn for a day
Summer or summer's memory returns.
So in a mountain desolation burns
Some rich belated flower, and with the gray
Sick weather, in the world of rotting ferns
From out the dreadful stones it dies away.

"*As a sad man, when evenings grayer grow*"

As a sad man, when evenings grayer grow,
Desires his violin, and call to call
Tunes with unhappy heart the interval;
Then after prelude, suffering his bow,
Along the crying strings his fingers fall
To some persuasion born of long ago,
While mixed in higher melodies the low
Dull song of his life's heard no more at all:
So with thy picture I alone devise,
Passing on thy uncoloured face the tone
Of memory's autumnal paradise;
And all myself for yearning weary lies
Fallen to but thy shadow, near upon
The void motion of eternities.

"He said: 'If in his image I was made"

He said: "If in his image I was made,
I am his equal and across the land
We two should make our journey hand in hand
Like brothers dignified and unafraid."
And God that day was walking in the shade.
To whom he said: "The world is idly planned,
We cross each other, let us understand
Thou who thou art, I who I am," he said.
Darkness came down. And all that night was heard
Tremendous clamour and the broken roar
Of things in turmoil driven down before.
Then silence. Morning broke, and sang a bird.
He lay upon the earth, his bosom stirred;
But God was seen no longer any more.

Lakeward

'Twill soon be sunrise. Down the valley waiting
Far over slope and mountain-height the firs
Undulate dull and furry under the beating
　　　　Heaven of autumn stars.

To westward yet the summits hang in slumber
Like frozen smoke; there, growing wheel on wheel,
As 'twere an upward wind of rose and amber
　　　　Goes up the sky of steel;

And indistinguishable thro' the valley
An endless murmur freshens as of bees,—
The stream that gathering torrents frantically
　　　　Churns away thro' the trees.—

Mountains, farewell! Into your crystal winter
To linger on unworlded and alone
And feel the glaciers of your bosom enter
　　　　One and another my own,

And on the snow that falling edges nearer
To lose my very shade,—'t were well, 't were done
Had I not in me the soul of a wayfarer!
    No, let me wander down

The road that, as the boulders higher and higher
Go narrower each to each and hold the gloom,
Follows like me the waters' loud desire
    Of a sun-sweetened home.

And as I pass, methinks once more the Titan
From in the bosom of the humid rocks,
Where yet his aged eyes grow vague and whiten
    Weary and wet his locks,

Gazes away upon this brightened weather
As asking it in reason and in rhyme
How long shall mountain iron and ice together
    Hold against summer-time.

Long, surely! long, perhaps! but not for ever.
Now here across the buried road and field,
Torn from the dizzy flanks up there that quiver,
    Down to the plain and spilled

In sand and wreckage lies the avalanche's
Dead mass under the sun, and not a sound!—
The morning grows and from the rich pine-branches
    Shadows make blue the ground.

To wander south! Already here the grasses
Feather and glint across the sunny air.
It's warmer. Up the road a peasant passes
    Brown-skinned and dark of hair.

Some of an autumn glamour on the highway
Softens the dust, and yonder I have seen
Catching the sunlight something in the byway
    Else than an evergreen,

And weeds along the ditch are parching.—Sudden
Once more from either side the ranges draw
Near each to each; beneath struggle and madden
        Down in the foamy flaw

The waters, and, a span across, the boulders
Stand to the burning heaven upright and cold.
Then drawing lengthily along their shoulders
        Vapours of white and gold

Blow from the lowland upward; all the gloaming
Quivers with violet; here in the wedge
The tunnelled road goes narrow and outcoming
        Stealthily on the edge

Lies free. The outlines have a gentle meaning.
Willows and clematis, foliage and grain!
And the last mountain falls in terraces to the greening
        Infinite autumn plain.

O further southward, down the brooks and valley, on
And past the lazy farms and orchards, on!
It smells of hay, and thro' the long Italian
        Flowerful afternoon

Sodden with sunlight, green and gold, the country
Suspends her fruit and stretches ripe and still
Between the clumsy fig and silver plane-tree
        Circled, from hill to hill

And down the vale along the running river:
The vale, the river and the hills, that take
The perfect south and here at last for ever
        Merge into thee, O Lake!—

Sunset-enamoured in the autumnal hours!
When large and westering his heavy rays
Fall from the vineyards and the garden-flowers
        Hazily o'er thy face,

And colouring thy bosom with a lover's
Warm and quick lips and hesitating hand,
He murmurs to thee while the twilight hovers
    Lilac about the strand,

Thou, mid the grape-hung terraces low-levelled,
Lookest into the green and crimson sky
With swimming eyes and auburn hair dishevelled,
    Radiant in ecstasy.—

'Tis evening. In the open blueness stretches
A feathery lawn of light from moon to shore,
And a boat-load of labourers homeward plashes,
    Singing "Amor, Amor."

Pandora's Songs
from Prometheus Pyrphoros

As a poplar feels the sun's enfolding kiss,
And softly alone on the quiet plain
Yields to him all her silver trellises,
A ghost of green in the golden rain,
And trembles lightly thro' the shining air
Nearly unseen and melting in sky
Save for a shadow on the grasses there:
So over the earth and world am I.
The lips of Gods and mortals in a dream
Have lain on my lips of a summer night:
They fade like images down-stream,
But I have remained behind the light.
I give the giver more than that he sought,
And more than I give am I, much more:
As words are to an everlasting thought,
So less than the mother the child she bore.

––––––––––

Before my eyes they come and go;
The shadows on my dreaming face

Move to and fro,
Yet I look further over larger ways.
For pity is not of that nor this,
And kindness stretches out her arm
On all that is,
To keep the grass-blade and the star from harm.
She kisses every dying wave
Into the sweetness of her trust,
And stoops to save
The bird that sank from heaven into dust.—
The battle hurtles long and loud
Between the mountains and the sea;
The yellow cloud
Crashes the woods in sunder tree by tree,
And struggling over land and main
The generations masterful
With greed and pain
Scatter upon the turf a brother's skull:
I walk the places where they drove
And sing my song where all is cursed.
Then, for my love,
The child will play again, the flower burst.

———

Many who have only dreamed of me
Have grown unhappy and lost their years.
They gather the daisies thoughtfully,
Then throw them away and burst in tears.
Their eyes are filled—for they looked so long—
With the sunset-light of my aureole;
Their lips will quiver to utter song,
And the spring lies swelling under their soul.
For their hand in a woman's hand is laid
And between a woman's breasts their brow.
For a while they feel no longer afraid
With the sky above and the earth below:
But never the whole and the fulness come.
Their eyes are blind with another light.
They walk through echoes and have no home,
Like shadows waving upon the night.

———

As an immortal nightingale
I sing behind the summer sky
Thro' leaves of starlight gold and pale
That shiver with my melody,
Along the wake of the full-moon
Far on to oceans, and beyond
Where the horizons vanish down
In darkness clear as diamond.

———

My dew is everywhere
    Where things are;
I fall and flutter and fare,
    Leaving a star
By the roads of earth, in the far
    Paths of the air.

Mine is the milk to charm
    In a mother's breast,
Sweet with her pain and warm
    With her rest,
The life that asks for a nest
    In her arm;

And mine is the violet
    That so lies
In the evening of her wet
    Sorrowful eyes.
For another thing may rise,
    But her youth has set.

Nothing is less with me,
    Nothing is lost.
For I smile on the earth and sea,
    On the infinite host
Of the dead and the living, and most
    On the yet-to-be.

———

My soul of sunset every human day
In long sad colours on the evening dwells
And gives her solemn violet away
Over the quiet endlessness of hills.

Mild and gold burns from cloud to cloud, above
The obscurer fields, my pity for an hour;
And then life goes to sleep within my love,
The world is drawn together as a flower.

Labour at last within the soul is peace,
And faithful pain after a certain while
Like other things will strengthen and increase
And colour at the last into a smile. —

Rest in my bosom till thy day be due,
Until my day be finished at sunrise,
And I behold thee glittering thro' the blue
And playing in the sunset of my eyes.

"And, the last day being come, Man stood alone"

And, the last day being come, Man stood alone
Ere sunrise on the world's dismantled verge,
Awaiting how from everywhere should urge
The Coming of the Lord. And, behold, none

Did come, — but indistinct from every realm
Of earth and air and water, growing more
And louder, shriller, heavier, a roar
Up the dun atmosphere did overwhelm

His ears; and as he looked affrighted round
Every manner of beast innumerable
All thro' the shadows crying grew, until
The wailing was like grass upon the ground.

Asudden then within his human side
Their anguish, since the goad he wielded first,
And, since he gave them not to drink, their thirst,
Darted compressed and vital.—As he died,

Low in the East now lighting gorgeously
He saw the last sea-serpent iris-mailed
Which, with a spear transfixèd, yet availed
To pluck the sun down into the dead sea.

At Sainte-Marguerite

The gray tide flows and flounders in the rocks
Along the crannies up the swollen sand.
Far out the reefs lie naked—dunes and blocks
Low in the watery wind. A shaft of land
Going to sea thins out the western strand.

It rains, and all along and always gulls
Career sea-screaming in and weather-glossed.
It blows here, pushing round the cliff; in lulls
Within the humid stone a motion lost
Ekes out the flurried heart-beat of the coast.

It blows and rains a pale and whirling mist
This summer morning. I that hither came—
Was it to pluck this savage from the schist,
This crazy yellowish bloom without a name,
With leathern blade and tortured wiry frame?

Why here alone, away, the forehead pricked
With dripping salt and fingers damp with brine,
Before the offal and the derelict
And where the hungry sea-wolves howl and whine
Live human hours? now that the columbine

Stands somewhere shaded near the fields that fall
Great starry sheaves of the delighted year,
And globing rosy on the garden wall
The peach and apricot and soon the pear
Drip in the teasing hand their sugared tear.

Inland a little way the summer lies.
Inland a little and but yesterday
I saw the weary teams, I heard the cries
Of sicklemen across the fallen hay,
And buried in the sunburned stacks I lay

Tasting the straws and tossing, laughing soft
Into the sky's great eyes of gold and blue
And nodding to the breezy leaves aloft
Over the harvest's mellow residue.
But sudden then—then strangely dark it grew.

How good it is, before the dreary flow
Of cloud and water, here to lie alone
And in this desolation to let go
Down the ravine one with another, down
Across the surf to linger or to drown

The loves that none can give and none receive,
The fearful asking and the small retort,
The life to dream of and the dream to live!
Very much more is nothing than a part,
Nothing at all and darkness in the heart.

I would my manhood now were like the sea.—
Thou at high-tide, when compassing the land
Thou find'st the issue short, questioningly
A moment poised, thy floods then down the strand
Sink without rancour, sink without command,

Sink of themselves in peace without despair,
And turn as still the calm horizon turns,
Till they repose little by little nowhere
And the long light unfathomable burns
Clear from the zenith stars to the sea-ferns.

Thou art thy Priest, thy Victim and thy God.
Thy life is bulwarked with a thread of foam,
And of the sky, the mountains and the sod
Thou askest nothing, evermore at home
In thy own self's perennial masterdom.

An Athenian Garden

The burned and dusty garden said:
"My leaves are echoes, and thy earth
Is packed with footsteps of the dead.

"The strength of spring-time brought to birth
Some needles on the crooked fir,—
A rose, a laurel—little worth.

"Come here, ye dreaming souls that err
Among the immortals of the grave:
My summer is your sepulchre.

"On earth what darker voices rave
Than now this sea-breeze, driving dust
And whirling radiance wave on wave,

"With lulls so fearful thro' the gust
That on the shapeless flower-bed
Like timber splits the yellow crust.

"O thirsty, thirsty are the dead,
Still thirsty, ever unallayed.
Where is no water, bring no bread."

I then had almost answer made,
When round the path in pleasure drew
Three golden children to the shade.

They stirred the dust with pail and hoe.
Then did the littlest from his fears
Come up and with his eyes of blue

Give me some berries seriously.
And as he turned to his brother, I
Looked after him thro' happy tears.

Sonnets from Greece

Sunium

These are the strings of the Ægean lyre
Across the sky and sea in glory hung:
Columns of white thro' which the wind has flung
The clouds and stars, and drawn the rain and fire.
Their flutings now to fill the notes' desire
Are strained and dubious, yet in music young
They cast their full-blown answer far along
To where in sea the island hills expire.
How bravely from the quarry's earthen gloom
In snow they rose amid the blue to stand
Melodious and alone on Sunium!
They shall not wither back into the land.
The sun that harps them with his golden hand
Doth slowly with his hand of gold consume.

Mt. Lykaion

Alone on Lykaion since man hath been
Stand on the height two columns, where at rest
Two eagles hewn of gold sit looking East
Forever; and the sun goes up between.
Far down around the mountain's oval green
An order keeps the falling stones abreast.
Below within the chaos last and least
A river like a curl of light is seen.
Beyond the river lies the even sea,

Beyond the sea another ghost of sky,—
O God, support the sickness of my eye
Lest the far space and long antiquity
Suck out my heart, and on this awful ground
The great wind kill my little shell with sound.

Near Helikon

By such an all-embalming summer day
As sweetens now among the mountain pines
Down to the cornland yonder and the vines,
To where the sky and sea are mixed in gray,
How do all things together take their way
Harmonious to the harvest, bringing wines
And bread and light and whatsoe'er combines
In the large wreath to make it round and gay.
To me my troubled life doth now appear
Like scarce distinguishable summits hung
Around the blue horizon: places where
Not even a traveller purposeth to steer,—
Whereof a migrant bird in passing sung,
And the girl closed her window not to hear.

Eleusis

Here for a thousand years processional
Winding around the Eleusinian bay,
The world with drooping eyes has made her way
By stair and portal to the sombre Hall.
As then the litanies antiphonal
Obscurely through the pillars sang away,
It dawned, and in the shaft of sudden day
Demeter smiling gave her bread to all.
They drew as waves out of a twilight main,
Long genuflecting multitudes, to feed
With God upon the sacramental grain.
And lo, the temple veil was rent in twain;
But thro' the rift their choirs in silver train
Still passing out rehearsed the human creed.

Mt. Ida

I

I long desired to see, I now have seen.
Yonder the heavenly everlasting bride
Draws the white shadows to her virgin side,
Ida, whom long ago God made his Queen.
The daylight weakens to a fearful sheen;
The mountains slumber seaward sanctified,
And cloudy shafts of bluish vapour hide
The places where a sky and world have been.
O Ida, snowy bride that God espoused
Unto that day that never wholly is,
Whiten thou the horizon of my eyes,
That when the momentary sea aroused
Flows up in earthquake, still thou mayest rise
Sacred above the quivering Cyclades.

II

Art thou still veiled, and ne'er before my sight
At sunset, as I yearn to see thee most,
Wilt thou appear in crimson robes and lost,
Aloft the crystal vapours of the night?
Is it the rule of all things infinite
To trail across remoteness and in clouds
The glory of their sacerdotal shrouds,
And shade with evening their eternal light?
O travellers abroad the mortal plain
On weary beasts of burden overta'en
By the unspeakable hours, I say: Press on.
For tho' a little part be hardly seen,
Hope spangles out the rest, and while ye strain
Another cloud already, look, is gone.

III

As now my ship at midday passes out
Into the lonely circles of the sea,
Thou o'er thy southern island loftily
Vague in the light appearest like a thought.
Over the blazing waves my vessel caught
Continues more into infinity:
And, as adoring I look after thee,
My eyes see white and in thy place is nought.
In the decline and speed of human things
When time drags on the dreamer by the hand
Like an unwilling child and reprobate,
It is enough if on the parting sings
The certain voice he could not understand—
It is enough, it is not yet too late.

Six O'Clock

Now burst above the city's cold twilight
The piercing whistles and the tower-clocks:
For day is done. Along the frozen docks
The workmen set their ragged shirts aright.
Thro' factory doors a stream of dingy light
Follows the scrimmage as it quickly flocks
To hut and home among the snow's gray blocks.—
I love you, human labourers. Good-night!
Good-night to all the blackened arms that ache!
Good-night to every sick and sweated brow,
To the poor girl that strength and love forsake,
To the poor boy who can no more! I vow
The victim soon shall shudder at the stake
And fall in blood: we bring him even now.

"The Autumn's done; they have the golden corn in"

The Autumn's done; they have the golden corn in,
Clover and fern from either slope are gone,
The peaks high up in the crystalline morning
    Glister of gray and roan.

These pitiless two hours of midday hotter
Than from the [   ] of a furnace, flare
The very shadows like a sunken water,
    Leaving but sunlight there,

Till eve: and in the valley that expires
A quick chill wind seizes the duskiness,
While, on the summits lighting, sunset fires
    Kindle in Sorapis.

One of these days I know, just as they sadden
Spangling awhile the rose and yellow sky,
You'll go away and watch the country gladden
    Softly to Italy.

There, take this ring of gold—and when your fancy
Glides by to songs under the autumn moon
Where like unfurling silks of necromancy
    Lies out the white lagoon,

Throw it away, that it be mine no longer.
Italian, give it back to Italy,
I will not have thy Past about me stronger
    Than what is yet to be.

Nay, hurry home to sleep. The ferns are rigid
With hoar, and dark and denser hangs the mist;
It freezes and the stars quaver in frigid
    Heaven of amethyst.

Down thro' San Vito and the land Cadore,
To which—when closed the pestered city gate—
The dying Titian strained, homeward from glory,
  Home from eternal fate;

Down where the outlines have a softer meaning—
Willow and clematis, the fruit and grain;
And the last mountain height sinks greening
  Into the golden plain,—

To Venice. There the October days purpureal
Fall down to earth from Heaven wearily,—
And wounded at the last, insatiate Uriel
  Dies on the flaming sea.—

One of these days you'll leave me in the mountains,
For I go Northward, not to see this year
Gold Italy and her wind-silvered plantains,
  But there the sad and sere—

I go elsewhere. . . .

"Here in the North I chase an old despair"

Here in the North I chase an old despair
And study Error which is Life within.
I hear old voices, and the city din,
The heart-and-hammer beat of common care.
And dusk outside and cold, the sky and air
Are miserable as unforgiven sin
Round the sick foliage, rotting, stiffly thin.
One more day dies which never yet was fair.
Then may I take your letter and console
The bloodless temper of my life, to learn
How down Maggiore the superb gold soul
And marvel of Italian sunset turn
A velvet violet deep within the shoal,
And the high vineyard lies like purple fern.

On Sandro's Flora

She is not happy as the Poets say,
And passing thro' her garden paradise
She scatters the divine wet flower that dies
For so much gathered in the luscious day.
Behind, the rioting Satyr has his play,
A wind lays near the Graces' draperies,
And the sweet Earth with inattentive eyes
Mildly remembers toward the growing day.
Her lips would sing but, fearing hazard, press
The music inward where her breath is caught.
She dances to an under-melting stream.
But dubious of this utter happiness
She dulls her simple ecstasy with thought,
And lacking Summer doubts herself a Dream.

from *Dramatic Fragments*

V

Sir, say no more.
Within me 't is as if
The green and climbing eyesight of a cat
Crawled near my mind's poor birds.

IX

I hear a river thro' the valley wander
Whose water runs, the song alone remaining.
A rainbow stands and summer passes under.

AMERICAN INDIAN POETRY

The Song of the Lenape Warriors
Going Against the Enemy

(*Delaware*)

O poor me!
Who am going out to fight the enemy,
And know not whether I shall return again,
To enjoy the embraces of my children
And my wife.
O poor creature!
Whose life is not in his own hands,
Who has no power over his own body,
But tries to do his duty
For the welfare of his nation.
O! thou Great Spirit above!
Take pity on my children
And on my wife!
Prevent their mourning on my account!
Grant that I may be successful in this attempt—
That I may slay my enemy,
And bring home the trophies of war
To my dear family and friends,
That we may rejoice together.
O! take pity on me!
Give me strength and courage to meet my enemy,
Suffer me to return again to my children,
To my wife
And to my relations!
Take pity on me and preserve my life
And I will make to thee a sacrifice.

John Heckewelder, *An Account of the History, Manners, and Customs of the Indian Nations Who Once Inhabited Pennsylvania and the Neighbouring States,* 1819.

Two Cherokee Songs of Friendship

Song the first.

A friend you resemble.
Chorus: Yai, ne, noo, way. E,noo,way,hā.

Song the second.

Brothers I think we are.
Chorus: Yai, ne, noo, way. E,noo,way,hā.

> Samuel L. Mitchill, "Letter from Samuel L. Mitchill,
> of New York, to Samuel M. Burnside," *Transactions
> and Collections of the American Antiquarian Society,* 1820.

Specimens of Indian Songs

(*Miami*)

I will kill—I will kill—the Big Knives, I will kill.

————

I will go and get my friends—I will go and get my
friends—I am anxious to see my enemies. A clear sky
is my friend, and it is him I am seeking.

> Lewis Cass, "Indian Customs,"
> *The Columbian Star,* April 1822.

Music and Poetry of the Indians

(*Ojibwa*)

Song for the Metai,
or for Medicine Hunting

 Now I hear it, my friends, of the Metai, who are sitting about me.

 Who makes this river flow? The Spirit, he makes this river flow.

 Look at me well, my friends; examine me, and let us understand that we are all companions.

 Who maketh to walk about, the social people? A bird maketh to walk about the social people.

 I fly about, and if any where I see an animal, I can shoot him.

 I shoot your heart; I hit your heart, oh animal, your heart, I hit your heart.

 I make myself look like fire.

 I am able to call water from above, from beneath, and from around.

I cause to look like the dead, a man I did.
I cause to look like the dead, a woman I did.
I cause to look like the dead, a child I did.

I am such, I am such, my friends; any animal, any
     animal, my friends, I hit him right, my
     friends.

Song for the Metai Only

I walk about in the night time.

I hear your mouth, you are an ill spirit.

Now I come up out of the ground; I am wild cat.

Behold! I am wild cat; I am glad to see you all wild
     cats.

I am a spirit; what I have I give to you in your
     body.

Your own tongue kills you; you have too much
     tongue.

Song for Medicine Hunting —
Rarely for the Metai

 I wished to be born, I was born, and after I was
born I made all spirits.

 I created the spirits.

 He sat down Na-na-bush; his fire burns forever.

 Notwithstanding you speak evil of me, from above
are my friends, my friends.

 I can use many kinds of wood to make a bear
unable to walk.

 Of you I think, that you use the We-nis-ze-bug-
gone, I think this of you.

 That which I take is blood, that which I take.

 Now I have something to eat.

 I cover my head, sitting down to sleep, ye spirits.

 I fill my kettle for the spirit.

Long ago, in the old time, since I laid myself down,
    ye are spirits.

 I open you for a bear, I open you.

 That is a Spirit which comes both from above and
    below.

 I am he that giveth success, because all spirits help
    me.

 The feather, the feather; it is the thing, the feather.

 Who is a spirit? He that walketh with the serpent,
    walking on the ground; he is a spirit.

 Now they will eat something, my women; now I tell
    them they will eat.

 This yellow ochre, I will try it.

 Now I wish to try my bird; sometimes I used to try,
    and sometimes it used to be something.

 I can kill any animal, because the loud-speaking
    thunder helps me; I can kill any animal.

 I take a bear, his heart I take.

A rattle snake makes a noise on the poles of my
      lodge; he makes a noise.

 To a Shawnee, the four sticks used in this song
      belonged. When struck together they were
      heard all over the country.

 I come up from below; I come down from above; I
      see the spirit; I see beavers.

 I can make an east wind come and pass over the
      ground.

 Thus have I sat down, and the earth above and
      below has listened to me sitting here.

 I make to crawl, a bear, I make to crawl.

*A Narrative of the Captivity and Adventures of John Tanner
During Thirty Years Residence Among the Indians in the
Interior of North America,* Edwin S. James, editor, 1830.

Hoatchunk' Narwoanar,
or Winnebago War Song

I am not to be trifled with, &c.
Friends! a man walks thro' this village.

Who shall dare to sport with me?
Friends! 'tis a warrior chief you see.

Who shall dare contend with me?
Friends! 'tis the chief of chiefs you see.

Caleb Atwater, *Remarks Made on a Tour to Prairie
du Chien; Thence to Washington City, in 1829,* 1831.

Medicine Song of an Indian Lover

(*Ojibwa*)

I.

Who, maiden, makes this river flow?
The Spirit—he makes its ripples glow—
But I have a charm that can make thee, dear,
Steal o'er the wave to thy lover here.

II.

Who, maiden, makes this river flow?
The Spirit—he makes its ripples glow—
Yet every blush that my love would hide,
Is mirror'd for me in the tell-tale tide.

III.

And though thou shouldst sleep on the farthest isle,
Round which these dimpling waters smile—
Yet I have a charm that can make thee, dear,
Steal over the wave to thy lover here.

Charles Fenno Hoffman, *Wild Scenes in
the Forest and Prairie,* 1839.

from *War Dance*

(*Iowa*)

Eh-Ros-ka, The Warrior's Dance

O-ta-pa!
> Why run you from us when you
> Are the most powerful?
> But it was not you,

O-ta-pa!
> It was your body that run,
> It was your body, O-ta-pa!
> It was your body that run.

Wa-Sissica, The War Song

> How-a! How-a!

O-ta-pa!
> I am proud of being at home!
> I am proud, O-ta-pa! I am proud
> I am at home—my enemy run
> I am proud, I am proud, O-ta-pa!

The Approaching Dance

O-ta-pa!
> I am creeping on your track,
> Keep on your guard, O-ta-pa!
> Or I will hop on your back,
> I will hop on you, I will hop on you.

> Stand back, my friends, I see them
> The enemies are here, I see them!
> They are in a good place,
> Don't move, I see them!

Ha-Kon-E-Crase, The Eagle Dance

It's me—I am a War Eagle!
The wind is strong, but I am an Eagle!
I am not ashamed—no, I am not,
The twisting Eagle's quill is on my head.
I see my enemy below me!
I am an Eagle, a War Eagle!

George Catlin, *The Fourteen Ioway Indians,* 1844.

The Loon Upon the Lake

(*Ojibwa*)

I looked across the water,
    I bent o'er it and listened,
I thought it was my lover,
    My true lover's paddle glistened.
Joyous thus his light canoe would the silver ripples wake.—
But no!—it is the loon alone—the loon upon the lake.
Ah me! it is the loon alone—the loon upon the lake.

    I see the fallen maple
        Where he stood, his red scarf waving,
    Though waters nearly bury
        Boughs they then were newly laving.
I hear his last farewell, as it echoed from the brake.—
But no, it is the loon alone—the loon upon the lake,
Ah me! it is the loon alone—the loon upon the lake.

Charles Fenno Hoffman, in Henry Rowe Schoolcraft,
Oneóta, or Characteristics of the Red Race of America, 1845.

Death Song

(*Ojibwa*)

Under the centre of the sky,
I utter my baim wä wä.

Every day, thou star!
I gaze at you.

The half of the day
I abide—gazing
Ye warlike birds.

They fly round the circuit of the sky.
The birds—circling
Round half the circuit of the sky.

They cross the enemy's line
The birds.

The high gods
My praise
They sound.

Full happy—I
To lie on the battle-field
Over the enemy's line.

> Henry Rowe Schoolcraft, *Oneóta, or Characteristics of the Red Race of America,* 1845.

George Copway's Dream Song

(*Ojibwa*)

It is I who travel in the winds,
It is I who whisper in the breeze,
    I shake the trees,
    I shake the earth,
I trouble the waters on every land.

> George Copway, *Life, History, and Travels of Kah-Ge-Ga-Gah-Bowh,* 1847.

Meda Songs

(Ojibwa)

 The Great Spirit's lodge—you have heard of it. I
    will enter it.

 I have always loved that that I seek. I go into the
    new green leaf lodge.

 I shall give you a share, my friend.

 I go into the bath—I blow my brother strong.

 I wish to wear this, my father—my friend.

 What! my life, my single tree!—we dance around
    you.

 I wish to see them appear—that that has grown—I
    wish them to appear.

 What are you saying, you mee dá man? This—this
    is the meda bone.

 My kite's skin is fluttering.

All round the circle of the sky I hear the Spirit's
voice.

 The Wabeno tree—it dances.

 How rings aloud the drum-stick's sound.

 I walk upon half of the sky.

 I sound all round the sky, that they can hear me.

 You shall hear the sound of my Ta-wa-e-gun.

 Do you understand my drum?

 I sing the raven that has brave feathers.

 I am the crow—I am the crow—his skin is my
body.

 I wish to go into your lodge—I go into your lodge.

Henry Rowe Schoolcraft, *Information Respecting
the History, Condition, and Prospects of the
Indian Tribes of the United States,* vol. 1, 1851.

Prophetic Powers

(*Ojibwa*)

1.

At the place of light—
At the end of the sky—
I (the Great Spirit)
Come and hang
      Bright sign.

2.

Lo! with the sound of my voice,
(The prophet's voice)
I make my sacred lodge to shake—
(By unseen hands my lodge to shake,)
      My sacred lodge.

3.

Haih! the white bird of omen,
He flies around the clouds and skies—
(He sees,—unuttered sight!)
Around the clouds and skies—
By his bright eyes I see—I see—I know.

Henry Rowe Schoolcraft, *Information Respecting the History, Condition, and Prospects of the Indian Tribes of the United States,* vol. 1, 1851.

Chants to the Deity

(*Ojibwa*)

1.

I am the living body of the Great Spirit above,
(The Great Spirit, the Ever-living Spirit above,)
The living body of the Great Spirit,
(Whom all must heed.)
      Heh! heh! heh! heh!

2.

I am the Great Spirit of the sky,
The overshadowing power.
I illumine earth,
I illumine heaven.
     Way, ho! ho! ho! ho!

3.

Ah say! what Spirit, or Body, is this Body?
(That fills the world around,
Speak man!) ah say!
What Spirit, or Body, is this Body?
     Way, ho! ho! ho! ho!

Henry Rowe Schoolcraft, *Information Respecting the History, Condition, and Prospects of the Indian Tribes of the United States,* vol. i, 1851.

Song of the Owl

(*Ojibwa*)

The owl, —
  Au
The owl
  Au
The great black
Owl
  Au
Hi! a! haa!

Henry Wadsworth Longfellow, letter to Ferdinand Freiligrath, January 11, 1856; adapted from Henry Rowe Schoolcraft, *Information Respecting the History, Condition, and Prospects of the Indian Tribes of the United States,* vol. i, 1851.

Magic Song

(Ojibwa)

I walk about in the night.
I that walk along—'tis I.

I hear your mouth.
You that are a spirit.

Now I come out of the ground,
I that am a lynx.

See! I am a lynx;
Do you like my looks?

Henry Rowe Schoolcraft, *Information Respecting
the History, Condition, and Prospects of
the Indian Tribes of the United States,* vol. 2, 1852.

Hawk Chant of the Saginaws

(Ojibwa)

The hawks turn their heads nimbly round;
They turn to look back on their flight.
The spirits of sun-place have whispered them words,
They fly with their messages swift,
They look as they fearfully go,
They look to the farthermost end of the world,
Their eyes glancing bright, and their beaks boding harm.

Henry Rowe Schoolcraft, *Information Respecting
the History, Condition, and Prospects of
the Indian Tribes of the United States,* vol. 3, 1853.

Love Song

(*Ojibwa*)

I will walk into some one's dwelling,

I will walk into somebody's home.

My sweetheart, into thy home
I will walk, in the night.

My sweetheart, in the winter
I shall walk into your abode.

This night I will walk into your lodge.

Henry Rowe Schoolcraft, *Information Respecting
the History, Condition, and Prospects of
the Indian Tribes of the United States,* vol. 5, 1855.

War Songs

(*Ojibwa*)

I.

From the south they come,
The birds, the warlike birds, with sounding wings.

I wish to change myself
To the body of that swift bird.

I throw away my body in the strife.

II.

The warrior speaks to the war-bird, and says:
    From time to time, I dwell in a bird.
The bird says to him:
    I answer you, my son-in-law.

Henry Rowe Schoolcraft, *Information Respecting
the History, Condition, and Prospects of
the Indian Tribes of the United States,* vol. 5, 1855.

Corn Song

(Ojibwa)

Crooked ear, crooked ear,
Walker at night.

Stop, little old man,
And take not to flight.

Crooked ear, crooked ear,
Stand up strong,
Little old crooked man,
I'll give you a song.

Henry Rowe Schoolcraft, *Information Respecting the History, Condition, and Prospects of the Indian Tribes of the United States,* vol. 5, 1855.

Chant to the Fire-Fly

(Ojibwa)

Fire-fly, fire-fly, light me to bed.
Come, come, little insect of light,
You are my candle, and light me to go.

Henry Rowe Schoolcraft, *Information Respecting the History, Condition, and Prospects of the Indian Tribes of the United States,* vol. 5, 1855.

Minnetare Songs

(Hidatsa)

from *New Moon Ceremonies*

The buffalo are coming. We will feed and feast. We wish to be fortunate and we expect it.

———

I want the robes, the skins of the game animals, the meat of the game animals. Bring them to me. Let us enjoy ourselves.

———

Spring from the earth, food for our children. Give us good health. Let us grow up, and become ripe.

———

If the clouds come good, our tobacco will grow. We will be happy.

Song of the Weasel

We wish a drove of weasels transmuted into horses.

Song of the Pheasant

My child, I do this for you. I give this to you.

Song of the Elk

Bring them to me. Bring them to me. Bring them to me.

Song of the Bear

Make my heart as powerful as your own. Lead me to conquer.

Song of the White Man

Yellow Eyes, look at me and look for me. Let me see.

Song of the Gun

What we charge upon. Eat them for us.

Song of the Bald Eagle

We want what is real. We want what is real. Don't deceive us.

Leslie A. White, ed., *Lewis Henry Morgan:*
The Indian Journals, 1859–62, 1959.

Song for a Fallen Warrior

(*Blackfeet*)

O my son, farewell!
You have gone beyond the great river,
Your spirit is on the other side of the Sand Buttes;
I will not see you for a hundred winters;
You will scalp the enemy in the green prairie,
Beyond the great river.
When the warriors of the Blackfeet meet,
When they smoke the medicine-pipe and dance the
     war-dance,
They will ask, "Where is Isthumaka?—
Where is the bravest of the Mannikappi?"
He fell on the war-path.
     Mai-ram-bo, mai-ram-bo.

Many scalps will be taken for your death;
The Crows will lose many horses;
Their women will weep for their braves,
They will curse the spirit of Isthumaka.

O my son! I will come to you
And make moccasins for the war-path,
As I did when you struck the lodge
Of the "Horse-Guard" with the tomahawk.
Farewell, my son! I will see you
Beyond the broad river.
   Mai-ram-bo, mai-ram-bo.

John Mason Browne, "Indian Medicine,"
Atlantic Monthly, 1866.

War Songs

(*Sioux*)

I have cast in here a soul,
I have cast in here a soul,
I have cast in here a buffalo soul;
I have cast in here a soul.

———

I make my way with my face covered,
I make my way with my face covered;
The people are buffaloes;
I make my way with my face covered.

———

Night now passes along,
Night now passes along;
It passes along with a thunder bird;
Night now passes along.

———

Whose sacred road lies plainly,
Whose sacred road lies plainly;
The sacred road of day lies plainly.

———

Ojibwa, hurry along!
Ojibwa, get out of the way!
We're coming there again.

———

Ojibwa, hallo!
Tell your older brother
You're too slow.

———

Terrifying all I journey,
Terrifying all I journey;
By the *Toon-kan'* at the North,
Terrifying all I journey.

———

Something I've killed, and I lift up my voice,
Something I've killed, and I lift up my voice;
The northern buffalo I've killed, and I lift up my voice;
Something I've killed, and I lift up my voice.

Alfred Longley Riggs, "Dakota Songs and Music,"
in Stephen Return Riggs, *Tah'-koo Wah-kan';
or, The Gospel Among the Dakotas,* 1869.

Songs of the Sacred Mysteries

(*Sioux*)

In the home of mysterious life I lie;
In the home of mysterious life I lie;
In the home of mystery, may I grow into mystery;
In the home of mysterious life I lie.

———

Shooting an arrow, I come;
Shooting an arrow, I come;
In the east my father sings for me:—I come,
Shooting an arrow, I come.

———

Having those, may I come;
Having those four souls, may I make my camp-fires.

The day that is determined for me;
May it come earthward.

I have four souls;
Holy boy! I give them to thee.

Sun-gazer, where have you gone?
Behold your friend!

The day to see thee;
May it come.

Encrowned with glory,
I come forth resplendent.

Sounding Cloud, my friend!
Do you want water?

———

I sing to a Spirit;
This is the Thunder.

———

Lo! a cloud is let down from above!
Father! shall I fly upon it?

———

Across the lake mysteriously I lie;
Across the lake mysteriously I lie;
That, decoying some soul, I may eat him alive.
So may it be.

———

This wakan' I whirled,
This wakan' I whirled,
This house I levelled.

This wakan' I whirled,
This house I levelled,
This wakan' I whirled.

———

Grandfather made me mysterious medicine;
        That is true.
Being of mystery, grown in the water,
        He gave it to me.
To grandfather's face wave the imploring hand;
Holding a quadruped, wave the imploring hand.

———

In red down he made it for me;
In red down he made it for me;
He of the water, he of the mysterious countenance,
        Gave it to me,
        Grandfather!

Alfred Longley Riggs, "Dakota Songs and Music,"
in Stephen Return Riggs, *Tah'-koo Wah-kan'*;
or, The Gospel Among the Dakotas, 1869.

Southern Paiute Poetry

The Earthquake

In that land, in that land,
    In that glittering land;
Far away, far away,
    The mountain was shaken with pain.

Sunset Clouds

The red clouds of sunset are drifting
Like down on the peaks of the mountain.

Eagle's Tears

At morn the eagle will cry,
  On the farther shore of the sea,
And a rainbow will be in the sky.

The Red Ant

The little red ant
  Descended the hill
With one arrow only.

A Paradox

The crest of the mountain
  Forever remains,
  Forever remains,
Though rocks continually fall.

> John Wesley Powell, *Report of Explorations in 1873*
> *of the Colorado of the West and its Tributaries,* 1874.

Songs and Chants

(Southern Paiute)

The Home of the River

The edge of the sky
Is the home of the river

Song of the Mountain Sheep

My curved horns
Like a necklace stand

(*Untitled*)

As feathers are drifted
So is the foam in the Colorado
Where the creeks run in

My Love

In yonder distant glen
Perchance she's cutting reeds

A Morning Walk

Over the land over the land
I walked at morn
Singing and trembling with cold

Winter Song

The feathers of the reed
Are lying on the ground
And the quails are perched on the pines

The Tobacco Plant

The tobacco plant is standing
Where the babbling water runs
On the side of the mountain

Our Song

Our song will enter
That distant land
That gleaming land
That gleaming land
And roll the lake in waves

Music

Over the land at night
Slowly the music floats

The Traveller's Rest

In the red valley I sleep
On my way to a far distant land

The Trout

In the blue water
The trout wags its tail

The Spirit

The spirit
Is swaying and singing

The Storm Creek

Along the land
A-down the gulch
The mountain stream
The feathery mountain stream

The Pines

The lofty pines
The tops of the lofty pines
The lofty pines
Are swaying with the winds

The Desert

The land is hungry
The ants are starving

The Storm Crown

It rains on the mountains
It rains on the mountains
A white crown encircles the mountain

The Blue Bird

At the foot of the cliff
On the face of the cliff
The blue bird sings

The Kai-nu-shuk

Through the cleft of the rock
In the land far away
The water was dashed from the mountain

The Mountain Peak

On the peak of the mountain
The eagle is dancing,
The tempest is roaring

The Storm

The sky will fall
The red water eddies

Cave Lake Song

The twilight has a home
And the black fish has a home

The Rattlesnake

In the stony land
Near by a rock
With head erect you crawled along

A Dream

Upon the Un-kar-tu-wan-an
I quiver, I quiver
Suspended from the mountain

(Untitled)

It is smokey on the cliffs
We dance in the smoke

(Untitled)

The morning is leaking out
The coyote wolf
Is calling, is calling

(Untitled)

The blue water in
The Mountain cañon
The grizzly bear on the mountain
Is digging

(Untitled)

The grass, on the Mountain
Moves in the Mountain Breeze

(*Untitled*)

The red water of the Mountain Stream
In the summer time
The rills are singing

(*Untitled*)

On the bushes
The Blossoms are hanging

(*Untitled*)

The blue water rolls on the Mountain

The Song of the Wichits

What is it
What is it
What is it

(*Untitled*)

In the pines on the sides
Of the Mountains
The Blue wind sighs

(*Untitled*)

Rainwater at the foot of mountain
Rainwater singing

Don D. Fowler and Catherine S. Fowler, eds.,
*Anthropology of the Numa: John Wesley Powell's
Manuscripts on the Numic Peoples of
Western North America, 1868–1880,* 1971.

from *Sacred Songs of the Konkau*

Red Cloud's Song
(*Heard by the mother of Oan-koi'-tu-peh*)

I am the Red Cloud.
My father formed me out of the sky.
I sing among the mountain flowers.
I sing among the flowering chamize of the mountains.
I sing in the mountains like the *wēk'-wēk*.
I sing among the rocks like the *wēk'-wēk*.
In the morning I cry in the mountains.
In the morning I walk the path.
I cry to the morning stars.

The Acorn Song

The acorns come down from heaven.
I plant the short acorns in the valley.
I plant the long acorns in the valley.
I sprout, I, the black-oak acorn, sprout, I sprout.

Ki-u-nad'-dis-si's Song

I am the only one, the only one left.
An old man, I carry the gambling-board; an old man, I sing
    the gambling song.
The roots I eat of the valley.
The pepper-ball is round.
The water trickles, trickles.
The water-leaves grow along the river bank.
I rub the hands, I wiggle the tail.
I am a doctor, I am a doctor.

Stephen Powers, "Tribes of California,"
Contributions to North American Ethnology, 1877.

Soldier's Song

(*Sioux*)

Over the earth I come;
Over the earth I come;
  A soldier I come;
Over the earth I am a ghost.

Stephen Return Riggs, trans.
"Narrative of Paul Mazakootemane,"
Collections of the Minnesota Historical Society, 1880.

from *Ancient Rites of the Condoling Council*

(*Iroquois*)

TEHKARIHHOKEN!
Continue to listen!
Thou who wert ruler,
  HAYENWATHA!
Continue to listen!
Thou who wert ruler,
  SHADEKARIHWADE!
That was the roll of you,
You who were joined in the work,
You who completed the work,
The Great League.

Continue to listen!
Thou who wert ruler,
  SHARENHHOWANE!
Continue to listen!
Thou who wert ruler,
  TEHYONHEGHKWEN!
Continue to listen!
Thou who wert ruler,
  OWENHEGHKOHNA!
That was the roll of you,

You who were joined in the work,
You who completed the work,
The Great League.

Continue to listen!
Thou who wert ruler,
     TEHHENNAGHKARIHNE!
Continue to listen!
Thou who wert ruler,
     AGHSTAWENSERONTTHA!
Continue to listen!
Thou who wert ruler,
     SHAGHSKOHAROWANE!
That was the roll of you,
You who were joined in the work,
You who completed the work,
The Great League.

Ye two were principals,
Father and son,
Ye two completed the work,
The Great League.
Ye two aided each other,
Ye two founded the House.
Now, therefore, hearken!
Thou who wert ruler,
     ODATSEGHDEH!
Continue to listen!
Thou who wert ruler,
     KAHNONKWENYAH!
Continue to listen!
Thou who wert ruler,
     TEHYOHHAKWENDEH!
That was the roll of you,
You who were joined in the work,
You who completed the work,
The Great League.

Continue to listen!
Thou who wert ruler,

SHONONGHSESEH!
Continue to listen!
Thou who wert ruler,
      THONAEGHKENAH!
Continue to listen!
Thou who wert ruler,
      HAHTYADONNENTHA!
That was the roll of you,
You who were joined in the work,
You who completed the work,
The Great League.

Continue to listen!
Thou who wert ruler,
      TEHWAHTAHONTENYONK!
Continue to listen!
Thou who wert ruler,
      KAHNYADAGHSHAYEN!
Continue to listen!
Thou who wert ruler,
      HONWATSHADONNEH!
That was the roll of you,
You who were joined in the work,
You who completed the work,
The Great League.

These were his uncles:
Now hearken!
Thou who wert ruler,
      WATHADOTARHO:
Continue to listen!
These were the cousins:
Thou who wert ruler,
      ONEHSEAGHHEN!
Continue to listen!
Thou who wert ruler,
      TEHHATKAHDONS!
Continue to listen!
These were as brothers thenceforth:
Thou who wert ruler,

SKANIADAJIWAK:
Continue to listen!
Thou who wert ruler,
    AWEAKENYAT!
Continue to listen!
Thou who wert ruler,
    TEHAYATKWAYEN!
That was the roll of you!

Then his son:
He is the great Wolf.
There were combined
The many minds!
    HONONWIREHDONH!
That was the roll of you.

These were his uncles,
Of the two clans:
    KAWENENSEAGHTONH!
    HAHHIHHONH!
That was the roll of them!

These were as brothers thenceforth:
    HOHYUNHNYENNIH!
    SHOTEHGWASEH!
    SHAHKOHKENNEH!
This was the roll of you.

This befell
In ancient times.
They had their children,
Those the two clans.
He the high chief,
    SAHHAHWIH!
This put away the clouds:
He was a war chief;
He was a high chief—
Acting in either office:
    SKAHNAHWAHTIH!
This was the roll of you!

Then his son,
   TAHKAHENHYUNH!
With his brother,
   JIHNONTAHWEHHEH.
This was the roll of you!

   KAHTAHGWAHJIH!
   SHONYUNHWESH!
   HAHTYAHSENHNEH!
This was the roll of you!

Then they who are brothers:
   TEHYUHENHYUNHKOH!
   TEHYUHTOHWEHGWIH!
   TYAWENHHEHTHONH!
This was the roll of you.

   HAHTONHTAHHEHHAH!
   TESHKAHHEA!
This was the roll of you!

Then his uncle,
   SKAHNYAHTEIHYUH!
With his cousin,
   SHAHTEHKAHENHYESH.
This was the roll of you!

   SAHTYEHNAHWAHT!
With his cousin,
   SHAKENHJOHNAH!
This was the roll of you!

   KAHNOHKAIH!
With his cousin,—then
   NISHAHYEHNENHHAH!
This was the roll of you!

Then, in later times,
They made additions
To the great mansion.

These were at the doorway,
They who were cousins,
These two guarded the doorway:
    KANONHKEHIHTAWIH!
With his cousin,
    TYUHNINHOHKAWENH!
This was the roll of you!

Now we are dejected
In our minds.

Horatio Hale, *The Iroquois Book of Rites*, 1883.

Chant from the Iroquois Book of Rites

(*Onondaga*)

Woe! Woe!
Hearken ye!
We are diminished!
    Woe! Woe!
The cleared land has become a thicket.
    Woe! Woe!
The clear places are deserted.
    Woe!
They are in their graves—
They who established it—
    Woe!
The great League.
Yet they declared
It should endure—
The great League.
    Woe!
Their work has grown old.
    Woe!
Thus we are become miserable.

Horatio Hale, *The Iroquois Book of Rites*, 1883.

Hunter's Song

(Hitchiti)

Somewhere the deer lies on the ground, I think; I walk
          about.
     Awake, arise, stand up!
It is raising up its head, I believe; I walk about.
     Awake, arise, stand up!
It attempts to rise, I believe; I walk about.
     Awake, arise, stand up!
Slowly it raises its body, I think; I walk about.
     Awake, arise, stand up!
It has now risen on its feet, I presume; I walk about.
     Awake, arise, stand up!

Albert S. Gatschet, A Migration
Legend of the Creek Indians, 1884.

The Song of the Stars

(Passamaquoddy)

We are the stars which sing,
We sing with our light;
We are the birds of fire,
We fly over the sky.
Our light is a voice;
We make a road for spirits,
For the spirits to pass over.
Among us are three hunters
Who chase a bear;
There never was a time
When they were not hunting.
We look down on the mountains.
This is the Song of the Stars.

Charles Godfrey Leland, *The Algonquin Legends of
New England; or, Myths and Folk Lore of the Micmac,
Passamaquoddy, and Penobscot Tribes,* 1884.

from *The Walam Olum, or Red Score,*
of the Lenâpé

(*Delaware*)

I.

 At first, in that place, at all times, above the earth,

 On the earth, was an extended fog, and there the
great Manito was.

 At first, forever, lost in space, everywhere, the great
Manito was.

 He made the extended land and sky.

 He made the sun, the moon, the stars.

 He made them all to move evenly.

 Then the wind blew violently, and it cleared, and
the water flowed off far and strong.

 And groups of islands grew newly, and there
remained.

 Anew spoke the great Manito, a manito to manitos,

 To beings, mortals, souls and all,

And ever after he was a manito to men, and their
    grandfather.

He gave the first mother, the mother of beings.

He gave the fish, he gave the turtles, he gave the
    beasts, he gave the birds.

But an evil Manito made evil beings only, monsters,

He made the flies, he made the gnats.

All beings were then friendly.

Truly the manitos were active and kindly

To those very first men, and to those first mothers;
    fetched them wives,

And fetched them food, when first they desired it.

All had cheerful knowledge, all had leisure, all
    thought in gladness.

But very secretly an evil being, a mighty magician,
    came on earth,

And with him brought badness, quarreling,
    unhappiness,

Brought bad weather, brought sickness, brought
          death.

 All this took place of old on the earth, beyond the
          great tide-water, at the first.

II.

 Long ago there was a mighty snake, and beings evil
          to men.

 This mighty snake hated those who were there and
          greatly disquieted those whom he hated.

 They both did harm, they both injured each other,
          both were not in peace.

 Driven from their homes they fought with this
          murderer.

 The mighty snake firmly resolved to harm the men.

 He brought three persons, he brought a monster, he
          brought a rushing water.

Between the hills the water rushed and rushed,
          dashing through and through, destroying
          much.

Nanabush, the Strong White One, grandfather of
          beings, grandfather of men, was on the Turtle
          Island.

There he was walking and creating, as he passed by and created the turtle.

 Beings and men all go forth, they walk in the floods and shallow waters, down stream thither to the Turtle Island.

 There were many monster fishes, which ate some of them.

 The Manito daughter, coming, helped with her canoe, helped all, as they came and came.

 And also Nanabush, Nanabush, the grandfather of all, the grandfather of beings, the grandfather of men, the grandfather of the turtle.

 The men then were together on the turtle, like to turtles.

 Frightened on the turtle, they prayed on the turtle that what was spoiled should be restored.

 The water ran off, the earth dried, the lakes were at rest, all was silent, and the mighty snake departed.

III.

After the rushing waters had subsided the Lenape of the turtle were close together, in hollow houses, living together there.

It freezes where they abode, it snows where they abode, it storms where they abode, it is cold where they abode.

 At this northern place they speak favorably of mild, cool lands, with many deer and buffaloes.

 As they journeyed, some being strong, some rich, they separated into house-builders and hunters;

 The strongest, the most united, the purest, were the hunters.

 The hunters showed themselves at the north, at the east, at the south, at the west.

 In that ancient country, in that northern country, in that turtle country, the best of the Lenape were the Turtle men.

 All the cabin fires of that land were disquieted, and all said to their priest, "Let us go."

 To the Snake land to the east they went forth, going away, earnestly grieving.

 Split asunder, weak, trembling, their land burned, they went, torn and broken, to the Snake Island.

Those from the north being free, without care, went
forth from the land of snow, in different
directions.

The fathers of the Bald Eagle and the White Wolf
remain along the sea, rich in fish and muscles.

Floating up the streams in their canoes, our fathers
were rich, they were in the light, when they
were at those islands.

Head Beaver and Big Bird said,
"Let us go to Snake Island," they said.

All say they will go along to destroy all the land.

Those of the north agreed,
Those of the east agreed.
Over the water, the frozen sea,
They went to enjoy it.

On the wonderful, slippery water,
On the stone-hard water all went,
On the great Tidal Sea, the muscle-bearing sea.

Ten thousand at night,
All in one night,
To the Snake Island, to the east, at night,
They walk and walk, all of them.

The men from the north, the east, the south,
The Eagle clan, the Beaver clan, the Wolf clan,
The best men, the rich men, the head men,
Those with wives, those with daughters, those with
    dogs,

They all come, they tarry at the land of the spruce
    pines;
Those from the west come with hesitation,
Esteeming highly their old home at the Turtle land.

Daniel Garrison Brinton, *The Lenâpé and
Their Legends; with the Complete Text
and Symbols of the Walam Olum,* 1885.

from *The Mountain Chant*

(*Navajo*)

First Song of the Thunder

Thonah! Thonah!
There is a voice above,
The voice of the thunder.
Within the dark cloud,
Again and again it sounds,
Thonah! Thonah!

Thonah! Thonah!
There is a voice below;
The voice of the grasshopper.
Among the plants,
Again and again it sounds,
Thonah! Thonah!

Twelfth Song of the Thunder

The voice that beautifies the land!
The voice above,
The voice of the thunder
Within the dark cloud
Again and again it sounds,
The voice that beautifies the land.

The voice that beautifies the land!
The voice below,
The voice of the grasshopper
Among the plants
Again and again it sounds,
The voice that beautifies the land.

Sixth Song of the Holy Young Men

There's a god on each side.
Now the Holy Young Man
Is the god on top of the black mountain,
With his black notched stick,
The implement of his dance, his magic wand.

There's a god on each side.
Now the Holy Young Woman
Is the god on top of the blue mountain,
With her blue notched stick,
The implement of her dance, her magic wand.

Twelfth Song of the Holy Young Men

There lie the black mountains;
There lie the black sticks;
There lie my sacrifices.

There lie the blue mountains;
There lie the blue sticks;
There lie my sacrifices.

One of the Awl Songs

The Maid Who Becomes a Bear walks far around
On the black mountains, she walks far around.
Far spreads the land. It seems not far to her.
Far spreads the land. It seems not dim to her.

The Holy Young Woman walks far around
On the blue mountains, she walks far around.
Far spreads the land. It seems not far to her.
Far spreads the land. It seems not dim to her.

Last Song of the Exploding Stick

Maid Who Becomes a Bear sought the gods and found
  them;
On the high mountain peaks she sought the gods and found
  them;
Truly with my sacrifice she sought the gods and found them.
Somebody doubts it, so I have heard.

Holy Young Woman sought the gods and found them;
On the summits of the clouds she sought the gods and
  found them;
Truly with my sacrifice she sought the gods and found them.
Somebody doubts it, so I have heard.

Last Daylight Song

Lullaby, lullaby.
It is daybreak. Lullaby.
Now comes the Daylight Boy. Lullaby.
Now it is day. Lullaby.
Now comes the Daylight Girl. Lullaby.

Washington Matthews, "The Mountain Chant:
A Navajo Ceremony," *Fifth Annual Report
of the Bureau of Ethnology*, 1887.

Summer Song

(*Eskimo*)

Aya!
Ayaya, it is beautiful, beautiful it is out-doors when the
     summer comes at last.
Ayaya, ayaya, aya!

Ayaya, it is beautiful, beautiful it is out-doors when the
     reindeer begin to come,
Ayaya, ayaya, aya!

Ayaya, when the roaring river rushes from the hills in
     summer.
Ayaya, ayaya, aya!

Ayaya, there is no reason for me to be mournful when the
     gulls cease crying.
Ayaya, ayaya, aya!

Ayaya, plenty of meat I shall have and plenty codfish.
Ayaya, ayaya, aya!

Ayaya, it is beautiful, beautiful it is out-doors when the
     summer comes at last.
Ayaya, ayaya, aya!

Franz Boas, "Poetry and Music of Some
North American Tribes," *Science,* 1887.

Chinook Songs

Whose sweetheart is very drunk?
My sweetheart is very drunk!
You do not like me,
You do not like me,
You do not like me!
I know you.

———

I cry always.
Far away is my country now.

———

Because my relations are dead,
When the steamboat leaves, I cry.

———

Good-bye, barkeeper! I am going now to-day.
Come! give me a full cocktail.

———

Ya, always I long
For my husband in California.

———

Very unhappy I was
With my wife,
In Victoria.
Nobody
Said good-day to us
In Victoria.

———

Good-bye, oh my dear Charlie!
When you take a wife,
Don't forget me.

———

What is Billy doing now?
He is going to the beerhouse.
The American says: Get out of the way!
He goes and cries aloud.

———

Kittie Apples is very unhappy
This winter.
Who will take her away?
The steamboat Hope.

———

I am very glad
When the steamboat comes here.
I think I shall cry
When the steamboat leaves.

———

A white man is now your husband, Mary.
Ha, cast me off thus!
I do not care now.
Ya aya aya.

———

Aya, aya!
I have seen
Sitka your country.
Never mind, if I die
Now soon.

———

I don't care
If you desert me.
Many pretty boys are in the town.
Soon I shall take another one.
That is not hard for me!

Franz Boas, "Chinook Songs,"
Journal of American Folk-Lore, 1888.

Pawnee War-Song

Let us see, is this real,
Let us see, is this real,
Let us see, is this real,
Let us see, is this real,
This life I am living?
Ye gods, who dwell everywhere,
Let us see, is this real,
This life I am living?

Daniel Garrison Brinton, *Essays of an Americanist,* 1890.

Incantation Songs of the Klamath Lake People

Introductory song

I sing, I sing, I sing.

Song, reference unknown

Blown off! the plume-crest has disappeared from me!

Song of the wind

Who, I wonder, is blowing out of my mouth?
The disease is emanating from my mouth.

The conjurer's song

What do I remove from my mouth?
The disease I extract from my mouth.
What is the thing I take out?
It is the disease I am taking out.

Song of the woodchuck
I am descending into the ground.

Little girl's song
In quill-fringed buckskin dressed,
In porcupine-fringed buckskin dressed.

Song of the washpálaks-fox
Long and slim I am, long and slim I am.

Song of the fire-mantle
In fire-flames I am enveloped.

Song of the tuákish-crane
I stand upon the rim of my nest.

Song of the blind medicine-girl
I search the ground with my hands, find there the feathers of
the yellow hammer and devour them.

Another song of the same
Quick! make ye eyes for me!

Bird's song
As a head only, I roll around.

Song, reference unknown
What am I? what am I?

Song, reference unknown
This round thing I hold in my hand.

Song of the long-tailed black marten
I the black marten, I travel around this land.

Song of the skunk
In the north wind I dance around, tail spread, festive and
  gay.

Chorus song
What do I suck out? The disease I am sucking out.

Song of the boards
Lumber-boards are rattling.

Song of the lizard
Lo! thus I the lizard stick my head out.

Song, reference unknown
The north wind has followed me.

Song of the black mouse
Through what do I pass with my paws?
My paws glide over the hair of the disease.

Song of the washpálaks-fox
Crazed I am wandering.

Song of the weasel
I am squealing, I am squalling.

Song of the dog
I the dog am straying,
In the north wind I am straying.

Song, reference unknown
The storm gust dashes right on me.

Song, reference unknown
Heavy hailstones I possess.

Song, reference unknown
I am shivering! the wind blows down on me!

Song of the bug
I the bug, I bite and suck.

Song of the mink
I am swimming out while the south wind blows.

Song of the young silver-fox
The young red fox I follow up.

The incantation sings
I the song I am walking here.

Fox's song

I am blowing air from my flanks.

Song of the tuákish-crane

Tuánχî, tuánχî, tuánχî, tuánχî . . . . . nû.

Songs, forming refrains to song above

a-ahahíya, a-aha-a-ahíya
a nû hé-e-i, a nû hé-e-i

Song of the disease

What thing do I blow around?
The disease I am blowing around in the air.

Song of the grizzly bear's cub

On the mountain top I am peeping out,
Of the grizzly bear I am the child.

Song of the female wolf

I, the she-wolf, am rolling against a tree.

Spoken by the conjurer while manipulating

Netá, netá . . . . hahayí-ía
Nenû', nenû'. . . . . . hahayí-ía

Song of the tchiwitítikaga-bird

Fearfully the wind blows underneath here.

Song of the blind girl

In the fog I am straying blind,
All over the earth I am wandering.

Song of the water-bug

Ádshi ádshi tcháya, ádshi ádshi tcháya

Song of the grizzly bear

I am scratching up the ground.

Song of the little gray tchikass-bird

I am wafted off from the mountain.

Song of the skō'ks or spirit

Reduced to mere bones, I rattle through the air.

Sung by the disease, found to live in water

Breath I am emitting.

Song of the grizzly bear

I have five water springs and all my springs are dry.

Song of the black snake

I the black-spotted snake am hanging here.

Conjurer's own song

I, the earth, am resounding like the roll of thunder.

Bird's song

I flutter along the ground while walking.

Song of the grizzly bear

Yaínalam shulúyualsh

Woman's song

Painted I am on the body,
I, a woman, am painted black.

Song of the weasel

Fooling, fooling I run around.

Song of the gray fox

Everything I can devour.

Conjurer's song

What is coming out of my mouth?
Black substance is hanging down from my mouth.

Song, reference unknown

Fog followed drifting after me.

Song of the turtle

Which game did you play with me?

Albert S. Gatschet, "The Klamath Indians
of Southwestern Oregon," *Contributions
to North American Ethnology*, 1890.

Incantations of Modoc Conjurers

Shkō'ks or spirit's incantation

I am singing to the heavens above.

Another of the same

I am sliding, slipping, sliding,
Towards that wretched land, towards that burning region, to
    remain there.

Another of the same

What was it? what was it? It was he, it was himself!

Song of the dry water-spring

Indeed my spring has dried up.

Song of the old frog

I, the decrepit she-frog, sit down here by the water spring.

Song of the wind

I the wind am blowing,
Everywhere I am blowing,
In the skies I am blowing.

Song of the five female elks

The knife lying at the end of the knife range.

Song of the fisher, a species of otter

Why then do you pursue me so? You flutter and beat your
    wings.

Young otter's song

The otter's offspring, I plunged into the water,
When I emerged from it, the ground blazed up,
The earth was shaken to its foundations.

Weasel's song

I the weasel am starting;
On the soil I draw my circles;
I the weasel I travel in circles.

Song of the weasel

In the spirit-land I blew out from me the heart of the
    skō'ksh.

Mink's song

I the mink am starting off.

Song of the woodpecker

The woodpecker, I am sticking fast,
    Upwards looking I stick to the tree-stump;
The woodpecker, I am sticking fast,
    Downwards I look, and hold myself.

Horned owl's song

I possess the horned owl's sharp vision; my roof-ladder is of
    speckled wood.

Spider's incantation

I the spider am going up; upwards I travel.

Patient's song

I am singing my Earth song.

Another of the same

Now my heart has returned.

Another of the same

Now it has turned!

Another of the same

After I had arrived in the spirit land the Earth wept and
cried.

Albert S. Gatschet, "The Klamath Indians of Southwestern
Oregon," *Contributions to North American Ethnology,* 1890.

Medicine Songs

(*Omaha*)

From here do I send,
From here do I send,
From here do I send,
I send.

Thus, the water to send, I'm enjoined,
Therefore do I send,
Thus, from here do I send,
Therefore do I send.

The pool of water, they proclaim,
The pool of water, they proclaim,
Yield to his entreaties, they declare they will,
The pool of water, they proclaim, sending their voices to me.

Francis La Flesche, "The Omaha Buffalo Medicine-Men,"
Journal of American Folk-Lore, 1890.

The Thanksgivings

(*Iroquois*)

We who are here present thank the Great Spirit that we are
here to praise Him.

We thank Him that He has created men and women, and
ordered that these beings shall always be living to
multiply the earth.

We thank Him for making the earth and giving these beings
its products to live on.

We thank Him for the water that comes out of the earth and
runs for our lands.

We thank Him for all the animals on the earth.

We thank Him for certain timbers that grow and have fluids
coming from them for us all.

We thank Him for the branches of the trees that grow
shadows for our shelter.

We thank Him for the beings that come from the west, the
thunder and lightning that water the earth.

We thank Him for the light which we call our oldest
brother, the sun that works for our good.

We thank Him for all the fruits that grow on the trees and
vines.

We thank Him for his goodness in making the forests, and
thank all its trees.

We thank Him for the darkness that gives us rest, and for
    the kind Being of the darkness that gives us light, the
    moon.
We thank Him for the bright spots in the skies that give us
    signs, the stars.
We give Him thanks for our supporters, who have charge of
    our harvests.
We give thanks that the voice of the Great Spirit can still be
    heard through the words of Ga-ne-o-di-o.
We thank the Great Spirit that we have the privilege of this
    pleasant occasion.
We give thanks for the persons who can sing the Great
    Spirit's music, and hope they will be privileged to
    continue in his faith.
We thank the Great Spirit for all the persons who perform
    the ceremonies on this occasion.

Harriet Maxwell Converse, *Journal of American Folk-Lore,* 1891.

Imploration for Clear Weather

(Ojibwa)

 I swing the spirit like a child.

 The sky is what I am telling you about.

 We have lost the sky.

 I am helping you.

 I have made an error.

I am using my heart.

 What are you saying to me, and I am "in my senses"?

 The spirit wolf.

 I do not know where I am going.

 I depend on the clear sky.

 I give you the other village, spirit that you are.

 The thunder is heavy.

 We are talking to one another.

W. J. Hoffman, "The Midē'wiwin or
'Grand Medicine Society' of the Ojibwa,"
Seventh Annual Report of the Bureau of Ethnology, 1891.

Prayer Upon Cutting Down the Sacred Tree

(*Sioux*)

We are making a good world, we are making a good day.
My friends, look at me; I am making medicine.
I hope you will have a happy life.
Great Spirit! you promised me a bull robe.
Who is our friend? The Lightning is our friend.
Who is our friend? The Lightning is our friend.

Who is our friend? The Thunder is our friend.
Who is our friend? The Thunder is our friend.
Who is our friend? The Bull is our friend.

John G. Bourke, "Religion of the
Apache Indians," *Folk-lore,* 1891.

A Rain Song of the Shu'-wi Chai'än (Snake Society)

(*Sia*)

Priest of the spruce of the north, send all your people to
    work for us;
Priest of the pine of the west, send all your people to work
    for us;
Priest of the oak of the south, send all your people to work
    for us;
Priest of the aspen of the east, send all your people to work
    for us;
Priest of the cedar of the zenith, send all your people to
    work for us;
Priest of the oak of the nadir, send all your people to work
    for us.

Matilda Coxe Stevenson, "The Sia,"
*Eleventh Annual Report of the
Bureau of American Ethnology,* 1894.

A Rain Song of the Quer'ränna Chai'än

(*Sia*)

White floating clouds. Clouds like the plains come and water the earth. Sun embrace the earth that she may be fruitful.
Moon, lion of the north, bear of the west, badger of the
south, wolf of the east, eagle of the heavens, shrew of the
earth, elder war hero, younger war hero, warriors of the six
mountains of the world, intercede with the cloud people

for us, that they may water the earth. Medicine bowl, cloud
bowl, and water vase give us your hearts, that the earth may
be watered. I make the ancient road of meal, that my song
may pass straight over it—the ancient road. White shell bead
woman who lives where the sun goes down, mother whirlwind, father Sûs'sĭstĭnnako, mother Ya'ya, creator of good
thoughts, yellow woman of the north, blue woman of the
west, red woman of the south, white woman of the east,
slightly yellow woman of the zenith, and dark woman of the
nadir, I ask your intercession with the cloud people.

Matilda Coxe Stevenson, "The Sia,"
*Eleventh Annual Report of the
Bureau of American Ethnology,* 1894.

Eskimo Songs

Utitia'q's Song

Aja, I am joyful; this is good!
Aja, there is nothing but ice around me, that is good!
Aja, I am joyful; this is good!
My country is nothing but slush, that is good!
Aja, I am joyful; this is good!
Aja, when, indeed, will this end? this is good!
I am tired of watching and waking, this is good!

Oxaitoq's Song

Inland, inland, inland, inland.
I am walking long inland, inland.
Nobody loves me, she is the greatest of all, I walk inland.
They love me only on account of the things I obtain for
        them.
They love me only on account of the food I obtain for them.

Franz Boas, "Eskimo Tales and Songs,"
Journal of American Folk-Lore, 1894–97.

from *The Hardening of the World,*
and the First Settlement of Men

(*Zuni*)

That the earth be made safer for men, and more stable,
Let us shelter the land where our children be resting,
Yea! the depths and the valleys beyond shall be sheltered
By the shade of our cloud-shield! Let us lay to its circle
Our firebolts of thunder, aimed to all the four regions,
Then smite with our arrows of lightning from under.
Lo! the earth shall heave upward and downward with
          thunder!
Lo! fire shall belch outward and burn the world over,
And floods of hot water shall seethe swift before it!
Lo! smoke of earth-stenches shall blacken the daylight
And deaden the senses of them else escaping
And lessen the number of fierce preying monsters!
That earth be made safer for men, and more stable.

> Frank Hamilton Cushing, "Outlines of Zuñi
> Creation Myths," *Thirteenth Annual Report
> of the Bureau of American Ethnology,* 1896.

from *The Generation of the Seeds,*
or the Origin of Corn

(*Zuni*)

Lo! ye children of men and the Mother,
Ye Brothers of Seed,
Elder, younger,
Behold the *seed plants of all seeds!*
The grass-seeds ye planted, in secret,
Were seen of the stars and the regions,
Are shown in the forms of these tassels!
The plumes that ye planted beside them
Were felt in the far away spaces,
Are shown in the forms of their leaf-blades!
But the seed that ye see growing from them,

Is the gift of my seven bright maidens,
The stars of the house of my children!
Look well, that ye cherish their persons,
Nor change ye the gift of their being,—
As fertile of flesh for all men
To the bearing of children for men,—
Lest ye lose them, to seek them in vain!
Be ye brothers ye people, and people;
Be ye happy ye Priests of the Corn!
Lo! the seed of all seed-plants is born!

Frank Hamilton Cushing, "Outlines of Zuñi
Creation Myths," *Thirteenth Annual Report
of the Bureau of American Ethnology,* 1896.

Ghost-Dance Songs

Songs of the Arapaho

My children, when at first I liked the whites,
My children, when at first I liked the whites,
I gave them fruits,
I gave them fruits.

———

My father, my father,
While he was taking me around,
While he was taking me around,
He turned into a moose,
He turned into a moose.

———

Father, now I am singing it—*Hi'ni'ni!*
Father, now I am singing it—*Hi'ni'ni!*
That loudest song of all,

That loudest song of all—
That resounding song —*Hi'ni'ni!*
That resounding song —*Hi'ni'ni!*

———

Our father, the Whirlwind,
Our father, the Whirlwind,
Now wears the headdress of crow feathers,
Now wears the headdress of crow feathers.

———

I circle around—
I circle around
The boundaries of the earth,
The boundaries of the earth—
Wearing the long wing feathers as I fly,
Wearing the long wing feathers as I fly.

———

My children, my children,
Look! the earth is about to move,
Look! the earth is about to move.
My father tells me so,
My father tells me so.

———

My father, my father—
I am looking at him,
I am looking at him.
He is beginning to turn into a bird,
He is beginning to turn into a bird.

———

The rock, the rock,
I am standing upon it,
I am standing upon it.
By its means I saw our father,
By its means I saw our father.

———

My children, my children,
I am about to hum,
I am about to hum.
My children, my children.

———

Father, have pity on me,
Father, have pity on me;
I am crying for thirst,
I am crying for thirst;
All is gone—I have nothing to eat,
All is gone—I have nothing to eat.

———

The crow has called me,
The crow has called me.
When the crow came for me,
When the crow came for me,
I heard him,
I heard him.

———

The crow is circling above me,
The crow is circling above me,
The crow having come for me,
The crow having come for me.

———

I hear everything,
I hear everything.
I am the crow,
I am the crow.

———

There is a good river,
There is a good river,
Where there is no timber—

Where there is no timber—
But thunder-berries are there,
But thunder-berries are there.

———

My children, my children,
I am flying about the earth,
I am flying about the earth.
I am a bird, my children,
I am a bird, my children,
Says the father,
Says the father.

———

My father, I am poor,
My father, I am poor.
Our father is about to take pity on me,
Our father is about to take pity on me.
Our father is about to make me fly around,
Our father is about to make me fly around.

———

I am going around the sweat-house,
I am going around the sweat-house.
The shell lies upon the mound,
The shell lies upon the mound.

———

My children, my children,
It is I who wear the morning star on my head,
It is I who wear the morning star on my head;
I show it to my children,
I show it to my children,
Says the father,
Says the father.

———

Father, the Morning Star!
Father, the Morning Star!
Look on us, we have danced until daylight,

Look on us, we have danced until daylight.
Take pity on us—*Hi'i'i'!*
Take pity on us—*Hi'i'i'!*

———

Thus says our father, the Crow,
Thus says our father, the Crow.
Go around five times more—
Go around five times more—
Says the father,
Says the father.

Songs of the Paiute

The snow lies there—*ro'răni'!*
The snow lies there—*ro'răni'!*
The snow lies there—*ro'răni'!*
The snow lies there—*ro'răni'!*
The Milky Way lies there,
The Milky Way lies there.

———

A slender antelope, a slender antelope,
A slender antelope, a slender antelope,
He is wallowing upon the ground,
He is wallowing upon the ground,
He is wallowing upon the ground,
He is wallowing upon the ground.

———

The black rock, the black rock,
The black rock, the black rock,
The rock is broken, the rock is broken,
The rock is broken, the rock is broken.

———

The wind stirs the willows,
The wind stirs the willows,
The wind stirs the willows,

The wind stirs the grasses,
The wind stirs the grasses,
The wind stirs the grasses.

———

Fog! Fog!
Lightning! Lightning!
Whirlwind! Whirlwind!

———

The whirlwind! The whirlwind!
The whirlwind! The whirlwind!
The snowy earth comes gliding, the snowy earth comes
    gliding;
The snowy earth comes gliding, the snowy earth comes
    gliding.

———

There is dust from the whirlwind,
There is dust from the whirlwind,
There is dust from the whirlwind.
The whirlwind on the mountain,
The whirlwind on the mountain,
The whirlwind on the mountain.

———

The rocks are ringing,
The rocks are ringing,
The rocks are ringing.
They are ringing in the mountains,
They are ringing in the mountains,
They are ringing in the mountains.

———

The cottonwoods are growing tall,
The cottonwoods are growing tall,
The cottonwoods are growing tall.

They are growing tall and verdant,
They are growing tall and verdant,
They are growing tall and verdant.

Songs of the Sioux

Who think you comes there?
Who think you comes there?
Is it someone looking for his mother?
Is it someone looking for his mother?
Says the father,
Says the father.

———

I love my children—*Ye'ye'*!
I love my children—*Ye'ye'*!
You shall grow to be a nation—*Ye'ye'*!
You shall grow to be a nation—*Ye'ye'*!
Says the father, says the father.
Haye'ye' Eyayo'yo'! Haye'ye' E'yayo'yo'!

———

Mother, come home; mother, come home.
My little brother goes about always crying,
My little brother goes about always crying.
Mother, come home; mother, come home.

———

Now they are about to chase the buffalo,
Now they are about to chase the buffalo,
Grandmother, give me back my bow,
Grandmother, give me back my bow,
The father says so, the father says so.

———

The whole world is coming,
A nation is coming, a nation is coming,
The Eagle has brought the message to the tribe.
The father says so, the father says so.

Over the whole earth they are coming.
The buffalo are coming, the buffalo are coming,
The Crow has brought the message to the tribe,
The father says so, the father says so.

———

It is I who make these sacred things,
Says the father, says the father.
It is I who make the sacred shirt,
Says the father, says the father.
It is I who made the pipe,
Says the father, says the father.

Songs of the Kiowa

The father will descend,
The father will descend.
The earth will tremble,
The earth will tremble.
Everybody will arise,
Everybody will arise.
Stretch out your hands,
Stretch out your hands.

———

The spirit army is approaching,
The spirit army is approaching,
The whole world is moving onward,
The whole world is moving onward.
See! Everybody is standing watching,
See! Everybody is standing watching.
Let us all pray,
Let us all pray.

———

My father has much pity for us,
My father has much pity for us.
I hold out my hands toward him and cry,

I hold out my hands toward him and cry.
In my poverty I hold out my hands toward him and cry,
In my poverty I hold out my hands toward him and cry.

———

That wind, that wind
Shakes my tipi, shakes my tipi,
And sings a song for me,
And sings a song for me.

———

God has had pity on us,
God has had pity on us.
Jesus has taken pity on us,
Jesus has taken pity on us.
He teaches me a song,
He teaches me a song.
My song is a good one,
My song is a good one.

James Mooney, "The Ghost-Dance Religion and
the Sioux Outbreak of 1890," *Fourteenth Annual
Report of the Bureau of American Ethnology*, 1896.

Songs of the Kwakiutl Indians

A Girl's Song

When I am grown up I shall go and stoop digging clams.
When I am grown up I shall go and splash in the water
    digging clams.
When I am grown up I shall stoop down digging clams.
When I am grown up I shall go picking berries.

Love Song

Like pain of fire runs down my body my love to you, my
    dear!
Like pain runs down my body my love to you, my dear!
Just as sickness is my love to you, my dear.
Just as a boil pains me my love to you, my dear.
Just as fire burns me my love to you, my dear.
I am thinking of what you said to me.
I am thinking of the love you bear me.
I am afraid of your love, my dear.
O pain! o pain!
Oh, where is my true love going, my dear?
Oh, they say she will be taken away far from here. She will
    leave me, my true love, my dear.
My body feels numb on account of what I said, my true
    love, my dear.
Good bye, my true love, my dear.

Warsong of the Kwakiutl

I am the thunder of my tribe.
I am the seamonster of my tribe.
I am the earthquake of my tribe.
When I start to fly the thunder resounds through the world.
When I am maddened, the voice of the seabear resounds
    through the world.

Franz Boas, "Songs of the Kwakiutl Indians,"
Internationales Archiv für Ethnographie, 1896.

Dances and Songs of the Winter Ceremonial

(Kwakiutl)

Hā'mats'a Song Composed About Fifty Years Ago

Food will be given to me, food will be given to me, because
    I obtained this magic treasure.
I am swallowing food alive; I eat living men.
I swallow wealth; I swallow the wealth that my father is
    giving away.

Hā'mats'a Song of the Lau'itsîs

I went all around the world to find food.
I went all around the world to find human flesh.
I went all around the world to find human heads.
I went all around the world to find corpses.

Hā'mats'a Song of the Koskimo

You will be known all over the world; you will be known all
    over the world, as far as the edge of the world, you
    great one who safely returned from the spirits.
You will be known all over the world; you will be known all
    over the world, as far as the edge of the world. You
    went to BaxbakuālanuXsī'waē, and there you ate first
    dried human flesh.
You were led to his cannibal pole in the place of honor of
    his house, and his house is our world.
You were led to his cannibal pole, which is the milky way of
    our world.
You were led to his cannibal pole at the right-hand side of
    our world.

Hā′mats′a Song, La′Lasiqoala

Truly! He goes around the whole world, the great hā′mats′a,
      looking for food everywhere, the great hā′mats′a, on
      both sides of the world.
Truly! He wants to eat plenty, the great hā′mats′a. He is
      trying to eat all himself, the great hā′mats′a, but he
      did not reach the food that he was going to obtain at
      the edge of the world.
He wants to eat with both hands, the great hā′mats′a, at the
      house of the one who is trying to eat all himself all
      over the world; but he did not reach the coppers that
      he was going to obtain at the edge of the world.

K·î′nqalaLala Song

The sounds of the winter dance are heard wherever you are,
      great one.
Hā′mats′a cries are heard wherever you are, great one.
You went right up to the raven, and the sound of fighting
      ravens is heard wherever you are.
You went right up to the shutting mouth, and the sound of
      the hō′Xhok·ᵘ is heard wherever you are.
You went right up to him who carries one corpse on each
      arm for you.

Song of a Bear Dancer Named Walas Nā′nē (Great Bear)

How shall we hide from the bear that is moving all around
      the world?
Let us crawl underground! Let us cover our backs with dirt
      that the great terrible bear from the north end of our
      world may not find us.

Song for Pacifying the Excited Nū′LmaL

Great is the fury of these supernatural ones.
He will carry men away on his arms and torment them.
He will devour them skin and bones, crushing flesh and
      bones with his teeth.

Song of Nū'LmaL, La'Lasiqoala

Oh wonder! He is making a turmoil on the earth.
Oh wonder! He makes the noises of falling objects on the earth.
Oh wonder! He makes the noise of breaking objects on the earth.

Song of a Salmon Dancer

The salmon came to search for a dancer.
He came and put his supernatural power into him.
You have supernatural power. Therefore the chief of the salmon came from beyond the ocean. The people praise you, for they cannot carry the weight of your wealth.

Ku'nXulaL, Thunder Bird Dance

You are swooping down from heaven, pouncing upon a whole tribe.
You are swooping down from heaven, burning villages, killing everything before you, and the remains of the tribes are like a rest of your food, great thunder bird; great thunderer of our world.
You are swooping down from heaven, going from one tribe to the other. You seize with your talons the chiefs of the tribes.

Song of the Ia'k·îm

The great Ia'k·îm will rise from below.
He makes the sea boil, the great Ia'k·îm. We are afraid.
He will upheave the seas, the great Ia'k·îm. We shall be afraid.
He will throw blankets from out of the sea, the great Ia'k·îm.
He will distribute blankets among all tribes, the great Ia'k·îm.
We fear him, the great Ia'k·îm.

Song of the Ghost Dancer

I went down to the under world with the chief of the
    ghosts. Therefore I have supernatural power.
The chief of the ghosts made me dance. Therefore I have
    supernatural power.
He put a beautiful ornament on to my forehead. Therefore I
    have supernatural power.

A Song of the Ghost Dancer of the La'ʟasiqoala

You sent us everything from out of the under world, ghosts!
    who take away man's senses.
You heard that we were hungry, ghosts! who take away
    man's senses.
We shall receive plenty from you, ghosts! who take away
    man's senses.

A Song of the Tsʼēʼkʼois

Keep silent the sacred voices which we hear proceeding from
    your body.
Everybody knows your name. Keep your sacred whistles
    quiet.
Everybody knows your name, great healer!

Franz Boas, "The Social Organization and
the Secret Societies of the Kwakiutl Indians,"
Report of the U.S. National Museum, 1897.

Kūʼsiut Song

(Bella Coola)

My child perished like the sky when it broke.
Go to Sʼaʟwalōʼsɛm of the sky, my child!
Gladden my heart, my child!
Sit down in the mouth of the sky, my child!

Franz Boas, "The Mythology of the
Bella Coola Indians," *Memoirs of the
American Museum of Natural History,* 1898.

Songs of Spirits

(*Wintun*)

Lightning's Song

I bear the sucker-torch to the western tree-ridge.
Look at me first born and greatest.

The Song of Olelbis

I am great above. I tan the black cloud there.

Song of Hau (*Red Fox*)

On the stone ridge east I go.
On the white road I, Hau, crouching go.
I, Hau, whistle on the road of stars.

Song of Waida Werris (*the Polar Star*)

The circuit of earth which you see,
The scattering of stars in the sky which you see,
All that is the place for my hair.

Jeremiah Curtin, *Creation Myths of Primitive
America in Relation to the Religious History
and Mental Development of Mankind*, 1898.

Captive's Song

(*Omaha*)

Where can I go
That I might live forever?
Where can I go
That I might live forever?

The old fathers have gone to the spirit-land,
    Where can I go
    That we might live together?

Fannie Reed Giffen, Oo-Mah-Ha
Ta-Wa-Tha (Omaha City), 1898.

Songs from the Great Feast to the Dead

(Eskimo)

We will sing a song.
We will go down the current.
The waves will rise;
The waves will fall.
The dogs will growl at us.

———

Come, my brother,
Return to us again;
We wait for you;
Come, brother, come.

Our mother, come back to us.
Return once more.

Return, our father;
We wait for you;
Come back to us,
And we, who are lonely,
Will give you food.

———

Oh, my brother, come back to me,
    Ai-yă-yă-yai.
Come back, my brother, I am lonely,
    Ai-yă-yă-yai.

My brother come back and we
  Will give you a small present,
    Ai-yă-yă-yai-yae-yai, etc.

———

My children, where are you?
    Ai-yă-yă-yai.
Come back to us, our children,
  We are lonely and sad.
    Ai-yă-yă-yai.
For our children are gone,
  While those of our friends remain.
    Ai-yă-yă-yai.
Come back, nephew, come back, we miss you;
    Ai-yă-yă-yai.
Come back to us, our lost ones,
  We have presents for you,
    Ai-yă-yă-yai.

Edward William Nelson, "The Eskimo About
Bering Strait," *Eighteenth Annual Report of
the Bureau of American Ethnology,* 1899.

The Mocking-Bird's Song

(*Tigua*)

Rain, people, rain!
The rain is all around us.
It is going to come pouring down,
And the summer will be fair to see,
The mocking-bird has said so.

Alice C. Fletcher, *Indian Story and
Song from North America,* 1900.

Song of an Old Gray Wolf

(Cheyenne)

The world is large and wide and long.
A great many wolves have been in the world.
But I alone have been all over the world.
To-day I am so old that at last my old age is over.

Alfred Kroeber, "Cheyenne Tales,"
Journal of American Folk-Lore, 1900.

The Wizard's Chant

(Passamaquoddy)

I sit and beat the wizard's magic drum;
And by its mystic sound I call the beasts.
From mountain lair and forest nook they throng;
E'en mighty storms obey the dreadful sound.

I sit and beat the wizard's magic drum;
The storm and thunder answer when it calls.
Aplasemwesit, mighty whirlwind, stops
To hearken to the mystic sound I make.

I sit and beat the wizard's magic drum;
And Chibela'kwe, night-air spirit, flies
To hearken to the mystic sound I make;
And old Wu'cho'sen, storm-bird of the North,
Rests his great pinions, causing calm to reign,
To hearken to the mystic sound I make.

I sit and beat the wizard's magic drum;
And Lumpeguin, who dwells beneath the wave,
Arises to the surface struck with awe,
To hearken to the mystic sound I make.

E'en Atwuskniges, armed with axe of stone,
Will cease his endless chopping, and be still
To hearken to the mystic sound I make.

I sit and beat the wizard's magic drum;
And Appodumken, with his long, red hair,
Ariseth from the depths, and draweth near
To hearken to the mystic sound I make.

The lightning, thunder, storm and forest sprite,
The whirlwind, gale, and spirit of the deep,
The Chibela'kwe, loathly night-air ghost,
All come together, and with reverent mien
Will hearken to the mystic sound I make.

Charles Godfrey Leland and John Dyneley Prince,
Kulóskap the Master and Other Algonkin Poems, 1902.

from *The Night Chant*

(*Navajo*)

Tsĕ'ni Gisĭ'n, or Song in the Rock

I.

In the House of the Red Rock,
There I enter;
Half way in, I am come.
The corn-plants shake.

II.

In the House of Blue Water,
There I enter;
Half way in, I am come.
The plants shake.

Last Tsĕ'ni Gisĭ'n, or Song in the Rock

I.

At the Red Rock House it grows,
There the giant corn-plant grows,
With ears on either side it grows,
With its ruddy silk it grows,
Ripening in one day it grows,
Greatly multiplying grows.

II.

At Blue Water House it grows,
There the giant squash-vine grows,
With fruit on either side it grows,
With its yellow blossom grows,
Ripening in one night it grows,
Greatly multiplying grows.

Prayer of First Dancers

In Tse'gíhi,
In the house made of the dawn,
In the house made of the evening twilight,
In the house made of the dark cloud,
In the house made of the he-rain,
In the house made of the dark mist,
In the house made of the she-rain,
In the house made of pollen,
In the house made of grasshoppers,
Where the dark mist curtains the doorway,
The path to which is on the rainbow,
Where the zigzag lightning stands high on top,
Where the he-rain stands high on top,
Oh, male divinity!
With your moccasins of dark cloud, come to us.
With your leggings of dark cloud, come to us.
With your shirt of dark cloud, come to us.
With your head-dress of dark cloud, come to us.

With your mind enveloped in dark cloud, come to us.
With the dark thunder above you, come to us soaring.
With the shapen cloud at your feet, come to us soaring.
With the far darkness made of the dark cloud over your
          head, come to us soaring.
With the far darkness made of the he-rain over your head,
          come to us soaring.
With the far darkness made of the dark mist over your head,
          come to us soaring.
With the far darkness made of the she-rain over your head,
          come to us soaring.
With the zigzag lightning flung out on high over your head,
          come to us soaring.
With the rainbow hanging high over your head, come to us
          soaring.
With the far darkness made of the dark cloud on the ends of
          your wings, come to us soaring.
With the far darkness made of the he-rain on the ends of
          your wings, come to us soaring.
With the far darkness made of the dark mist on the ends of
          your wings, come to us soaring.
With the far darkness made of the she-rain on the ends of
          your wings, come to us soaring.
With the zigzag lightning flung out on high on the ends of
          your wings, come to us soaring.
With the rainbow hanging high on the ends of your wings,
          come to us soaring.
With the near darkness made of the dark cloud, of the
          he-rain, of the dark mist and of the she-rain, come
          to us.
With the darkness on the earth, come to us.
With these I wish the foam floating on the flowing water
          over the roots of the great corn.
I have made your sacrifice.
I have prepared a smoke for you.
My feet restore for me.
My limbs restore for me.
My body restore for me.
My mind restore for me.
My voice restore for me.

To-day, take out your spell for me.
To-day, take away your spell for me.
Away from me you have taken it.
Far off from me it is taken.
Far off you have done it.
Happily I recover.
Happily my interior becomes cool.
Happily my eyes regain their power.
Happily my head becomes cool.
Happily my limbs regain their power.
Happily I hear again.
Happily for me the spell is taken off.
Happily I walk.
Impervious to pain, I walk.
Feeling light within, I walk.
With lively feelings, I walk.
Happily abundant dark clouds I desire.
Happily abundant dark mists I desire.
Happily abundant passing showers I desire.
Happily an abundance of vegetation I desire.
Happily an abundance of pollen I desire.
Happily abundant dew I desire.
Happily may fair white corn, to the ends of the earth, come
　　　with you.
Happily may fair yellow corn, to the ends of the earth, come
　　　with you.
Happily may fair blue corn, to the ends of the earth, come
　　　with you.
Happily may fair corn of all kinds, to the ends of the earth,
　　　come with you.
Happily may fair plants of all kinds, to the ends of the earth,
　　　come with you.
Happily may fair goods of all kinds, to the ends of the earth,
　　　come with you.
Happily may fair jewels of all kinds, to the ends of the earth,
　　　come with you.
With these before you, happily may they come with you.
With these behind you, happily may they come with you.
With these below you, happily may they come with you.
With these above you, happily may they come with you.

With these all around you, happily may they come with you.
Thus happily you accomplish your tasks.
Happily the old men will regard you.
Happily the old women will regard you.
Happily the young men will regard you.
Happily the young women will regard you.
Happily the boys will regard you.
Happily the girls will regard you.
Happily the children will regard you.
Happily the chiefs will regard you.
Happily, as they scatter in different directions, they will
    regard you.
Happily, as they approach their homes, they will regard you.
Happily may their roads home be on the trail of pollen.
Happily may they all get back.
In beauty I walk.
With beauty before me, I walk.
With beauty behind me, I walk.
With beauty below me, I walk.
With beauty above me, I walk.
With beauty all around me, I walk.
It is finished again in beauty,
It is finished in beauty,
It is finished in beauty,
It is finished in beauty.

Atsá'lei Song

I.

The corn comes up, the rain descends,
The corn-plant comes therewith.
The rain descends, the corn comes up,
The child-rain comes therewith.

II.

The corn comes up, the rain descends,
Vegetation comes therewith.
The rain descends, the corn comes up,
The pollen comes therewith.

Song of the Stricken Twins

From the white plain where stands the water,
          From there we come,
Bereft of eyes, one bears another.
          From there we come.
Bereft of limbs, one bears another.
          From there we come.
Where healing herbs grow by the waters,
          From there we come.
With these your eyes you shall recover.
          From there we come.
With these your limbs you shall recover.
          From there we come.

From meadows green where ponds are scattered,
          From there we come.
Bereft of limbs, one bears another.
          From there we come.
Bereft of eyes, one bears another.
          From there we come.
By ponds where healing herbs are growing,
          From there we come.
With these your limbs you shall recover.
          From there we come.
With these your eyes you shall recover.
          From there we come.

Washington Matthews, "The Night Chant,
a Navaho Ceremony," *Memoirs of the
American Museum of Natural History*, 1902.

from *The Hako*

(*Pawnee*)

from *Mother Corn Assumes Leadership*

I

Mother with the life-giving power now comes,
Stepping out of far distant days she comes,
Days wherein to our fathers gave she food;
As to them, so now unto us she gives,
Thus she will to our children faithful be.
Mother with the life-giving power now comes!

II

Mother with the life-giving power is here.
Stepping out of far distant days she comes.
Now she forward moves, leading as we walk
Toward the future, where blessings she will give,
Gifts for which we have prayed granting to us.
Mother with the life-giving power is here!

Song to the Trees and Streams

I

Dark against the sky yonder distant line
Lies before us. Trees we see, long the line of trees,
Bending, swaying in the breeze.

II

Bright with flashing light yonder distant line
Runs before us, swiftly runs, swift the river runs,
Winding, flowing o'er the land.

III

Hark! Oh hark! A sound, yonder distant sound
Comes to greet us, singing comes, soft the river's song,
Rippling gently 'neath the trees.

Song of the Promise of the Buffalo

I

Clouds of dust arise, rolling up from earth,
Spreading onward; herds are there.
Speeding on before,
Going straight where we must journey.

II

What are those we see moving in the dust?
This way coming from the herd;
Buffalo and calf!
Food they promise for the Children.

Alice C. Fletcher, "The Hako: A Pawnee
Ceremony," *Twenty-second Annual Report
of the Bureau of American Ethnology,* 1904.

from *History Myth of the Coming of the A'shiwi as Narrated by ⁺Kiäklo*

(*Zuni*)

Following their road of exit, they stooped over and came
    out.
They walked this way.
They came to the gaming-stick spring.
They came to the gaming-ring spring.
They came to the Ne'wekwe baton spring.
They came to the spring with prayer plume standing.
They came to the cat-tail place.

They came to the moss spring.
They came to the muddy spring.
They came to the sun-ray spring.
They came to the spring by many aspens.
They came to shell place.
They came to dragon-fly place.
They came to flower place.
They came to the place of trees with drooping limbs.
They came to fish spring.
They came to young-squash spring.
They came to listening spring.

*   *   *

We come this way. We come to a large lake; here we get up
        and move on. We come to a valley with watercress in
        the middle; here we get up and move on.
We come to the stealing place; here we get up and move on.
We come to houses built in mesa walls; here we get up and
        move on.
We come to the last of a row of springs; here we get up and
        move on.
We come to the middle of a row of springs; here we get up
        and move on.
We come again to the middle of a row of springs; here we
        get up and move on.
We come to the house of Ko'loowisi; here we get up and
        move on.
We come to watercress place; here we get up and move on.
We come to a small spring; here we get up and move on.
We come to a spring in a hollow place in a mound, hidden
        by tall bending grasses; here we get up and move on.
We come to ashes spring; here we get up and move on.
We come to high-grass spring; here we get up and move on.
We come to rainbow spring; here we get up and move on.
We come to place of the Sha'läko; here we get up and move
        on.
We come to the place with many springs; here we get up
        and move on.
We come to moss place; here we get up and move on.

We come to stone-lodged-in-a-cleft place; here we get up
    and move on.
We come to stone-picture place; here we get up and move
    on.
We come to poison-oak place; here we get up and move on.
We come to a spring in a mesa wall; here we get up and
    move on.
We come to rush place; here we get up and move on.
We come to a place of bad-smelling water; here we get up
    and move on.
We come to the place of sack of meal hanging; here we get
    up and move on.
We come to the blue-jay spring; here we get up and move
    on.
We come to Corn mountain; here we get up and move on.
We come to the spring at the base of the mesa; here we get
    up and move on.
We come to the ant-entering place; here we get up and
    move on.
We come to vulva spring; here we get up and move on.
We come to a spring high in the mountain; here we get up
    and move on.
We come to Apache spring; here we get up and move on.
We come to coyote spring; here we get up and move on.
We come to salt place; here we get up and move on.
We come to a place with fumes like burning sulphur; here
    we get up and move on.
We come to ant place; here we get up and move on.
We come to the Middle place.

Matilda Coxe Stevenson, "The Zuñi Indians: Their
Mythology, Esoteric Fraternities, and Ceremonies,"
*Twenty-third Annual Report of the
Bureau of American Ethnology,* 1904.

Invocation to the U'wannami

(*Zuni*)

I

Come you, ascend the ladder; all come in; all sit down.
We were poor, poor, poor, poor, poor, poor,
When we came to this world through the poor place,
Where the body of water dried for our passing.
Banked up clouds cover the earth.
All come four times with your showers,
Descend to the base of the ladder and stand still;
Bring your showers and great rains.
All, all come, all ascend, all come in, all sit down.

(*The above stanza is repeated four times.*)

II

I throw out to you my sacred meal that you may all come.
Hold your gaming-stick; throw it forward; all come.
Hold your gaming-ring; throw it forward; all come.
All come out and give us your showers and great rains; all
        come,
That the seeds may be strong and come up, that all seed
        plants may come up and be strong.
Come you that all trees and seeds may come up and be
        strong.
Come you hither; all come.

III

Cover my earth mother four times with many flowers.
Let the heavens be covered with the banked up clouds.
Let the earth be covered with fog; cover the earth with
        rains.
Great waters, rains, cover the earth. Lightning cover the
        earth.
Let thunder be heard over the earth; let thunder be heard;
Let thunder be heard over the six regions of the earth.

IV

Rain-makers, come out from all roads that great rivers may
        cover the earth;
That stones may be moved by the torrents;
That trees may be uprooted and moved by the torrents.
Great rain-makers, come out from all roads, carry the sands
        of our earth mother of the place.
Cover the earth with her heart, that all seeds may develop,
That my children may have all things to eat and be happy;
That the people of the outlying villages may all laugh and be
        happy;
That the growing children may all have things to eat and be
        happy.
This way our great father ꞌkĭa꞉Ꞌĕttonĕ wishes you to come.
This way our great mother chuꞋĕttonĕ wishes you to come;
That we may have all kinds of seeds and all things good;
That we may inhale the sacred breath of life;
That our fathers ꞌkĭaꞋĕttowe and our mothers chuꞋettowe
        may bring us happy days.
Let our children live and be happy.
Send us the good south winds.
Send us your breath over the lakes that our great world may
        be made beautiful and our people may live.

V

There, far off, my Sun Father arises, ascends the ladder,
        comes forth from his place.
May all complete the road of life, may all grow old.
May the children inhale more of the sacred breath of life.
May all my children have corn that they may complete the
        road of life.
Here sit down; here remain; we give you our best thoughts.
Hasten over the meal road; we are jealous of you.
We inhale the sacred breath through our prayer plumes.

Matilda Coxe Stevenson, "The Zuñi Indians: Their
Mythology, Esoteric Fraternities, and Ceremonies,"
*Twenty-third Annual Report of the
Bureau of American Ethnology,* 1904.

FOLK SONGS
AND
SPIRITUALS

Blow Your Trumpet, Gabriel

De talles' tree in Paradise,
De Christian call de tree of life;
    And I hope dat trump might blow me home
    To de new Jerusalem.
Blow your trumpet, Gabriel,
Blow louder, louder;
    And I hope dat trump might blow me home
    To de new Jerusalem.

Paul and Silas, bound in jail,
Sing God's praise both night and day;
    And I hope dat trump might blow me home
    To de new Jerusalem.
Blow your trumpet, Gabriel,
Blow louder, louder;
    And I hope dat trump might blow me home
    To de new Jerusalem.

Buffalo Gals

As I was lumb'ring down de street,
    down de street,
    down de street,
A handsome gal I chanc'd to meet;
Oh! she was fair to view.

    Buffalo gals, cant you come out tonight?
        cant you come out tonight?
        cant you come out tonight?
    Buffalo gals, cant you come out tonight?
    And dance by de light ob de moon.

I ax'd her would she hab some talk,
                 hab some talk,
                 hab some talk,
Her feet cover'd up de whole sidewalk
As she stood close by me.

I ax'd her would she hab a dance,
                 hab a dance,
                 hab a dance,
I taught dat I might get a chance,
To shake a foot wid her.

I'd like to make dat gal my wife,
                 gal my wife,
                 gal my wife,
I'd be happy all my life,
If I had her by me.

The Cowboy's Lament

As I walked out in the streets of Laredo,
As I walked out in Laredo one day,
I spied a poor cowboy wrapped up in white linen,
Wrapped up in white linen as cold as the clay.

"Oh, beat the drum slowly and play the fife lowly,
Play the Dead March as you carry me along;
Take me to the green valley, there lay the sod o'er me,
For I'm a young cowboy and I know I've done wrong.

"I see by your outfit that you are a cowboy,"
These words he did say as I boldly stepped by.
"Come sit down beside me and hear my sad story;
I was shot in the breast and I know I must die.

"Let sixteen gamblers come handle my coffin,
Let sixteen cowboys come sing me a song.
Take me to the graveyard and lay the sod o'er me,
For I'm a poor cowboy and I know I've done wrong.

"My friends and relations, they live in the Nation,
  They know not where their boy has gone.
  He first came to Texas and hired to a ranchman,
  Oh, I'm a young cowboy and I know I've done wrong.

"Go write a letter to my gray-haired mother,
  And carry the same to my sister so dear;
  But not a word of this shall you mention
  When a crowd gathers round you my story to hear.

"Then beat your drum lowly and play your fife slowly,
  Beat the Dead March as you carry me along;
  We all love our cowboys so young and so handsome,
  We all love our cowboys although they've done wrong.

"There is another more dear than a sister,
  She'll bitterly weep when she hears I am gone.
  There is another who will win her affections,
  For I'm a young cowboy and they say I've done wrong.

"Go gather around you a crowd of young cowboys,
  And tell them the story of this my sad fate;
  Tell one and the other before they go further
  To stop their wild roving before 'tis too late.

"Oh muffle your drums, then play your fifes merrily;
  Play the Dead March as you go along.
  And fire your guns right over my coffin;
  There goes an unfortunate boy to his home.

"It was once in the saddle I used to go dashing,
  It was once in the saddle I used to go gay;
  First to the dram-house, then to the card-house,
  Got shot in the breast, I am dying to-day.

"Got six jolly cowboys to carry my coffin;
  Get six pretty maidens to bear up my pall.
  Put bunches of roses all over my coffin,
  Put roses to deaden the clods as they fall.

"Then swing your rope slowly and rattle your spurs lowly,
  And give a wild whoop as you carry me along;
  And in the grave throw me and roll the sod o'er me,
  For I'm a young cowboy and I know I've done wrong.

"Go bring me a cup, a cup of cold water,
  To cool my parched lips," the cowboy said;
  Before I turned, the spirit had left him
  And gone to its Giver,—the cowboy was dead.

We beat the drum slowly and played the fife lowly,
  And bitterly wept as we bore him along;
  For we all loved our comrade, so brave, young, and
        handsome,
  We all loved our comrade although he'd done wrong.

Cripple Creek

I got a gal at the head of the creek,
  Go up to see her 'bout the middle of the week,
  Kiss her on the mouth, just as sweet as any wine,
  Wraps herself around me like a sweet pertater vine.

  Goin' up Cripple Creek, goin' in a run,
  Goin' up Cripple Creek to have a little fun.
  Goin' up Cripple Creek, goin' in a whirl,
  Goin' up Cripple Creek to see my girl.

Girls on the Cripple Creek 'bout half grown,
  Jump on a boy like a dog on a bone.
  Roll my britches up to my knees,
  I'll wade old Cripple Creek when I please.

Cripple Creek's wide and Cripple Creek's deep,
  I'll wade old Cripple Creek afore I sleep,
  Roads are rocky and the hillside's muddy
  And I'm so drunk that I can't stand study.

Cumberland Gap

Lay down, boys, and take a little nap,
Lay down, boys, and take a little nap,
Lay down, boys, and take a little nap,
Fourteen miles to Cumberland Gap.

Lay down, boys, an' take a little nap,
They're all raisin' Hell in Cumberland Gap.

The first white man in Cumberland Gap,
Was Doctor Walker, an English chap.

Daniel Boone on Pinnacle Rock,
He killed Indians with an old flintlock.

Cumberland Gap is a noted place,
Three kinds of water to wash your face.

Cumberland Gap with its cliff and rocks,
Home of the panther, bear, and fox.

September mornin' in Sixty-two,
Morgan's Yankees all withdrew.

They spiked Long Tom on the mountain top,
And over the cliffs they let him drop.

They burned the hay, the meal, and the meat,
And left the rebels nothing to eat.

Braxton Bragg with his rebel band,
He run George Morgan to the blue-grass land.

The rebels now will give a little yell,
They'll scare the niggers all to Hell.

Ol' Aunt Dinah, ef you don't keer,
Leave my little jug settin' right here.

Ef it's not here when I come back,
I'll raise Hell in Cumberland Gap.

Ol' Aunt Dinah took a little spell,
Broke my little jug all to Hell.

I've got a woman in Cumberland Gap,
She's got a boy that calls me "pap."

Me an' my wife an' my wife's gran'pap,
All raise Hell in Cumberland Gap.

Lay down, boys, an' take a little nap,
Lay down, boys, an' take a little nap,
Lay down, boys, an' take a little nap,
Fourteen miles to the Cumberland Gap.

The Days of '49

Here you see old Tom Moore
    A relic of bygone days,
A bummer too they call me now,
    But what care I for praise
For my heart is filled with woe,
    And I often grieve and pine,
For the days of old, the days of gold,
    The days of '49.

> *For the days of gold, the days of old,*
> *the days of '49.*

I had comrades then a saucy set,
    They were rough I must confess
But staunch and brave, as true as steel,
    Like hunters from the west;
But they like many another fish,
    Have now run out of line;
But like good old bricks they stood the kicks,
    Of the days of '49.

There was Monte Pete, I'll ne'er forget
   The luck that he always had,
He'd deal for you both night and day,
   Or as long as you had a scad.
One night a pistol laid him out,
   'Twas his last lay out in fine,
It caught Pete sure, right bang in the door,
   In the days of '49.

There was another chap from New Orleans,
   Big Reuben was his name,
On the plaza there with a sardine box
   He opened a faro game,
He dealt so fair that a millionaire
   He became in course of time,
Till death stept in and called the turn
   In the days of '49.

There was Kentuck Bill, one of the boys
   Who was always in for a game;
No matter whether he lost or won,
   To him 'twas all the same,
He'd ante a slug; he'd pass the buck;
   He'd go for a hat full blind.
In the game of death Bill lost his breath
   In the days of '49.

There was New York Jake, the butcher boy,
   So fond of getting tight;
Whenever Jake got full of gin
   He was looking for a fight.
One night he ran against a knife
   In the hands of old Bob Kline
And over Jake we had a wake
   In the days of '49.

There was North Carolina Jess, a hard old case,
    Who never would repent.
Jess was never known to miss a meal,
    Or ever pay a cent.
But poor old Jess like all the rest,
    To death did at last resign,
And in his bloom he went up the flume
    In the days of '49.

There was Rackensack Jim who could out roar
    A buffalo bull you bet,
He roared all night; he roared all day;
    He may be roaring yet.
One night he fell in prospect hole,
    'Twas a roaring bad design,
And in that hole Jim roared out his soul
    In the days of '49.

Of all the comrades I had then
    There's none left now but me,
And the only thing I'm fitting for
    Is a Senator to be;
The people cry as I pass by,
    "There goes a traveling sign;
That's old Tom Moore, a bummer sure,
    Of the days of '49."

Since that time how things have changed
    In this land of liberty,
Darkies didn't vote nor plead in court
    Nor rule this country,
But the Chinese question, the worst of all
    In those days did not shine,
For the country was right and the boys all white
    In the days of '49.

Deep River

Deep river,
My home is over Jordan,
Deep river,
Lord, I want to cross over into camp ground,
Lord, I want to cross over into camp ground,
Lord, I want to cross over into camp ground,
Lord, I want to cross over into camp ground.

Oh, don't you want to go to that Gospel feast,
That promis'd land where all is peace?

I'll go into heaven, and take my seat,
Cast my crown at Jesus' feet.

Oh, when I get to heav'n, I'll walk all about,
There's nobody there for to turn me out.

Dere's No Hidin' Place Down Dere

Dere's no hidin' place down dere,
Dere's no hidin' place down dere,
Oh I went to de rock to hide my face,
De rock cried out, "No hidin' place,"
Dere's no hidin' place down dere.

Oh de rock cried, "I'm burnin' too,"
Oh de rock cried, "I'm burnin' too,"
Oh de rock cried out I'm burnin' too,
I want a go to hebben as well as you,
Dere's no hidin' place down dere.

Oh de sinner man he gambled an' fell,
Oh de sinner man he gambled, an' fell,
Oh de sinner man gambled, he gambled an' fell;
He wanted to go to hebben, but he had to go to hell
Dere's no hidin' place down dere.

Didn't My Lord Deliver Daniel

Didn't my Lord deliver Daniel,
D'liver Daniel, d'liver Daniel,
Didn't my Lord deliver Daniel,
And why not a every man?

He deliver'd Daniel from the lion's den,
Jonah from the belly of the whale,
And the Hebrew children from the fiery furnace,
And why not every man?

The moon run down in a purple-stream,
The sun forbear to shine,
And every star disappear,
King Jesus shall be mine.

The wind blows East, and the wind blows West,
It blows like the judgment day,
And every poor soul that never did pray,
'll be glad to pray, that day.

I set my foot on the Gospel ship,
And the ship it begin to sail,
It landed me over on Canaan's shore,
And I'll never come back any more.

Down in the Valley

Down in the valley, valley so low,
Hang your head over, hear the wind blow.
    Hear the wind blow, love, hear the wind blow,
    Hang your head over, hear the wind blow.

If you don't love me, love whom you please,
But throw your arms round me, give my heart ease.
    Give my heart ease, dear, give my heart ease.
    Throw your arms round me, give my heart ease.

Down in the valley, walking between,
Telling our story, here's what it sings:
    Here's what it sings, dear, here's what it sings,
    Telling our story, here's what it sings:

Roses of sunshine, vi'lets of dew,
Angels in heaven knows I love you,
    Knows I love you, dear, knows I love you,
    Angels in heaven knows I love you.

Build me a castle forty feet high,
So I can see her as she goes by,
    As she goes by, dear, as she goes by,
    So I can see her as she goes by.

Bird in a cage, love, bird in a cage,
Dying for freedom, ever a slave;
    Ever a slave, dear, ever a slave,
    Dying for freedom, ever a slave.

Write me a letter, send it by mail,
And back it in care of the Birmingham jail.
    Birmingham jail, love, Birmingham jail,
    And back it in care of the Birmingham jail.

Ev'ry Time I Feel the Spirit

Ev'ry time I feel the Spirit
Moving in my heart I will pray.

Upon the mountain my Lord spoke,
Out His mouth came fire and smoke.

All around me looks so shine,
Ask my Lord if all was mine.

Jordan river is chilly and cold,
Chills the body but not the soul.

Ezekiel Saw de Wheel

Ezekiel saw de wheel,
'Way up in de middle ob de air,
Ezekiel saw de wheel,
'Way in de middle ob de air;
An' de little wheel run by faith,
An' de big wheel run by de grace ob God,
'Tis a wheel in a wheel,
'Way in de middle ob de air.

Some go to church fo' to sing an' shout,
'Way in de middle ob de air;
Befo' six months dey are all turned out,
'Way in de middle ob de air.

Let me tell you what a hypocrit'll do,
'Way in de middle ob de air;
He'll talk 'bout me an' he'll talk 'bout yo',
'Way in de middle ob de air.

One o' dese days, 'bout twelve o'clock,
'Way in de middle ob de air;
Dis ole worl' gwine reel an' rock,
'Way in de middle ob de air.

Frankie and Albert

Frankie was a good woman,
Ev'rybody knows,
She spent a hundred dollars
For to buy her man some clothes.
    He was her man,
    But he done her wrong.

Frankie went a-walkin'
Did not go for fun,
Underneath her little red petticoat
She had Albert's forty-one.
    Gonna kill her man
    For doin' her wrong.

Frankie went to the barroom
Ordered her a glass of beer,
Says to the bartender,
"Has my lovin' man been here?
    He's my man,
    But he's doin' me wrong."

"I will not tell you no story,
I will not tell you no lie,—
Albert left here about an hour ago
With a gal named Alice Fly.
    He's your man,
    But he's doin' you wrong."

Frankie went by the house,
She did not give no 'larm,
She looked in through the window glass
And saw Albert in the woman's arms.
    He was her man, Lawd,
    Doin' her wrong.

When Albert, he saw Frankie,
For the backdoor, he did scoot,
Frankie drew that forty-four,

Went —*rooty-toot-toot-toot-toot!*
    She shot her man,
    For doin' her wrong.

First time she shot him, he staggered,
Next time she shot him, he fell,
Third time she shot him, O Lawdy,
There was a new man's face in hell.
    She killed her man,
    For doin' her wrong.

When Frankie, she shot Albert,
He fell all in a knot,
Cryin', "O Mrs. Johnson,
See where your son is shot.
    She's killed your son,
    The only one.

"O turn me over doctor,
Turn me over slow,
I got a bullet in my lef' han' side,
Great God, is hurtin' me so.
    I was her man,
    But I done her wrong."

Frankie went to Mrs. Johnson,
Fell down on her knees,
Cryin' "O Mrs. Johnson,
Will you forgive me please?
    I kilt your son,
    The onlies' one."

"I will forgive you Frankie,
I will forgive you not,
You shot my lovin' Albert,
The only support I'm got.
    Kilt my son,
    The only one."

Poor boy, poor boy,
Poor boy, poor boy.
Done gone, done gone,
Done gone, done gone.

Frankie went to the graveyard,
Fell down on her knees, —
"Speak one word, Albert,
And give my heart some ease.
        You was my man,
        But you done me wrong."

A rubber tir'ed buggy,
A decorated hack
Took po' Albert to the graveyard
But it didn't bring him back.
        He was her man,
        But he done her wrong.

Poor boy, poor boy,
Poor boy, poor boy.
Done gone, done gone,
Done gone, done gone.

Frankie looked down Main street,
Far as she could see,
All she could hear was a two string bow,
Playin' *Nearer My God to Thee,*
        All over town,
        Po' Albert's dead.

Frankie said to the sheriff,
"What do you think it'll be?"
The sheriff said, "It looks jest like
Murder in the first degree,
        He was your man,
        But you shot him down."

It was not murder in the first degree,
Nor murder in the third,
A woman simply dropped her man,
Like a hunter dropped a bird.
  She shot her man,
  For doin' her wrong.

Last time I saw Frankie
She was sittin' in the 'lectric chair,
Waitin' for to go and meet her God
With the sweat drippin' outa her hair.
  He was her man
  But he done her wrong.

  Poor gal, poor gal,
  Poor gal, poor gal.
  Done gone, done gone,
  Done gone, done gone.

Free at Last

Free at last, free at last;
I thank God I'm free at last;
Free at last, free at last,
I thank God I'm free at last,
O free at last.

'Way down yonder in the grave-yard walk,
I thank God I'm free at last,
Me and my Jesus goin' to meet and talk,
I thank God I'm free at last,
O free at last.

On-a my knees when the light pass'd by,
I thank God I'm free at last,
Tho't my soul would rise and fly,
I thank God I'm free at last,
O free at last.

Some of these mornings, bright and fair,
I thank God I'm free at last,
Goin' meet King Jesus in the air,
I thank God I'm free at last,
O free at last.

Got a Home in That Rock

I've got a home in a-that Rock,
Don't you see? Don't you see?
I've got a home in a-that Rock,
Don't you see? Don't you see?
Between the earth and sky,
Thought I heard my Saviour cry,
I've got a home in a-that Rock,
Don't you see?

Poor old Laz'rus, poor as I,
Don't you see? Don't you see?
Poor old Laz'rus, poor as I,
Don't you see? Don't you see?
Poor old Laz'rus, poor as I
When he died had a home on high.
He had a home in a-that Rock,
Don't you see?

Rich man, Dives, lived so well,
Don't you see? Don't you see?
Rich man, Dives, lived so well,
Don't you see? Don't you see?
Rich man, Dives, lived so well,
When he died he found a home in hell,
Had no home in that Rock,
Don't you see?

God gave Noah the Rainbow sign,
Don't you see? Don't you see?
God gave Noah the Rainbow sign,

Don't you see? Don't you see?
God gave Noah the Rainbow sign,
No more water but fire next time,
Better get a home in that Rock,
Don't you see?

He Never Said a Mumblin' Word

O they took my blessed Lawd,
Blessed Lawd, Blessed Lawd,
O they took my blessed Lawd,
An' He never said a mumblin' word,
Not a word, not a word, not a word.

O they lead Him to Pilate's bar,
Pilate's bar, Pilate's bar,
O they lead Him to Pilate's bar,
An' He never said a mumblin' word,
Not a word, not a word, not a word.

O they bound Him with a purple cord,
Purple cord, purple cord,
O they bound Him with a purple cord,
An' He never said a mumblin' word,
Not a word, not a word, not a word.

O they plaited Him a crown o' thorn,
Crown o' thorn, crown o' thorn,
O they plaited Him a crown o' thorn,
An' He never said a mumblin' word,
Not a word, not a word, not a word.

O they put it on His head,
On His head, on His head,
O they put it on His head,
An' He never said a mumblin' word,
Not a word, not a word, not a word.

An' the blood come streamin' down,
Streamin' down, streamin' down,
O the blood come streamin' down,
An' He never said a mumblin' word,
Not a word, not a word, not a word.

An' they judged Him all night long,
All night long, all night long,
Yes they judged Him all night long,
An' He never said a mumblin' word,
Not a word, not a word, not a word.

An' they whipped Him up the hill,
Up the hill, up the hill,
O they whipped Him up the hill,
An' He never said a mumblin' word,
Not a word, not a word, not a word.

Then they nailed Him to the cross,
To the cross, to the cross,
Yes they nailed Him to the cross,
An' He never said a mumblin' word,
Not a word, not a word, not a word.

An' the blood come tricklin' down,
Tricklin' down, tricklin' down,
O the blood come tricklin' down,
An' He never said a mumblin' word,
Not a word, not a word, not a word.

An' the stars refused to shine,
'Fused to shine, 'fused to shine,
Yes the stars refused to shine,
An' He never said a mumblin' word,
Not a word, not a word, not a word.

O wasn't that a pity an' a shame,
Pity an' a shame, pity an' a shame?
O wasn't that a pity an' a shame?
An' He never said a mumblin' word,
Not a word, not a word, not a word.

A Home on the Range

Oh, give me a home where the buffalo roam,
Where the deer and the antelope play,
Where seldom is heard a discouraging word
And the skies are not cloudy all day.

Home, home on the range,
Where the deer and the antelope play;
Where seldom is heard a discouraging word
And the skies are not cloudy all day.

Where the air is so pure, the zephyrs so free,
The breezes so balmy and light,
That I would not exchange my home on the range
For all of the cities so bright.

The red man was pressed from this part of the West,
He's likely no more to return
To the banks of Red River where seldom if ever
Their flickering camp-fires burn.

How often at night when the heavens are bright
With the light of the glittering stars,
Have I stood here amazed and asked as I gazed
If their glory exceeds that of ours.

Oh, I love these wild flowers in this dear land of ours,
The curlew I love to hear scream,
And I love the white rocks and the antelope flocks
That graze on the mountain-tops green.

Oh, give me a land where the bright diamond sand
Flows leisurely down to the stream;
Where the graceful white swan goes gliding along
Like a maid in a heavenly dream.

Then I would not exchange my home on the range,
Where the deer and the antelope play;
Where seldom is heard a discouraging word
And the skies are not cloudy all day.

Home, home on the range,
Where the deer and the antelope play;
Where seldom is heard a discouraging word
And the skies are not cloudy all day.

I Know Moon-Rise

I know moon-rise, I know star-rise,
 Lay dis body down.
I walk in de moonlight, I walk in de starlight,
 To lay dis body down.
I 'll walk in de graveyard, I 'll walk through de
  graveyard,
 To lay dis body down.
I 'll lie in de grave and stretch out my arms;
 Lay dis body down.
I go to de judgment in de evenin' of de day,
 When I lay dis body down;
And my soul and your soul will meet in de day
 When I lay dis body down.

Jesse James

Jesse James was a lad that killed many a man,
He robbed the Danville train;
But that dirty little coward that shot Mr. Howard,
Has laid Jesse James in his grave.
It was little Robert Ford, that dirty little coward;
I wonder how does he feel;
For he ate of Jesse's bread and slept in Jesse's bed,
Then laid Jesse James in his grave.

 Poor Jesse had a wife, to mourn for his life,
 Children they were brave;
 But that dirty little coward, that shot Mr. Howard
 Has laid Jesse James in his grave.

It was with his brother Frank, he robbed the Gallatin bank,
And carried the money from the town;
It was at this very place they had a little chase,
For they shot Capt. Sheets to the ground.
They went to a crossing not very far from there,
And there they did the same,
With the agent on his knees he delivered up the keys
To the outlaws Frank and Jesse James.

It was on a Wednesday night, the moon was shining bright,
They robbed the Danville train;
The people they did say for many miles away,
It was robbed by Frank and Jesse James.
It was on Saturday night, the moon was shining bright,
Talking with his family brave,
Robert Ford came along like a thief in the night,
And he laid Jesse James in his grave.

The people held their breath when they heard of Jesse's
        death,
And wondered however he came to die.
It was one of the gang called little Robert Ford,
He shot Jesse James on the sly.
This song was made by Billy LaShade,
As soon as the news did arrive;
He said there's no man with the law in his hand
Can take Jesse James alive.

Jim Crack Corn

or the Blue Tail Fly

When I was young I us'd to wait
On Massa and hand him de plate;
Pass down de bottle when he git dry,
And bresh away de blue tail fly.

Jim crack corn I don't care,
Jim crack corn I don't care,
Jim crack corn I don't care,
Ole Massa gone away.

Den arter dinner massa sleep,
He bid dis niggar vigil keep;
An' when he gwine to shut his eye,
He tell me watch de blue tail fly.

An' when he ride in de arternoon,
I foller wid a hickory broom;
De poney being berry shy,
When bitten by de blue tail fly.

One day he rode aroun' de farm,
De flies so numerous dey did swarm;
One chance to bite 'im on the thigh,
De debble take dat blue tail fly.

De poney run, he jump an' pitch,
An' tumble massa in de ditch;
He died, an' de jury wonder'd why
De virdic was de blue tail fly.

Dey laid 'im under a 'simmon tree,
His epitaph am dar to see:
'Beneath dis stone I'm forced to lie,
All by de means ob de blue tail fly.

Ole massa gone, now let 'im rest,
Dey say all tings am for de best;
I nebber forget till de day I die,
Ole massa an' dat blue tail fly.

John Brown's Body

John Brown's body lies a-mould'ring in the grave,
John Brown's body lies a-mould'ring in the grave,
John Brown's body lies a-mould'ring in the grave,
    His soul is marching on.

Glory, glory, hallelujah!
Glory, glory, hallelujah!
Glory, glory, hallelujah!
His soul is marching on!

The stars of heaven are looking kindly down,
    On the grave of old John Brown.

He's gone to be a soldier in the army of the Lord,
    His soul is marching on.

John Brown died that the slave might be free,
    But his soul goes marching on.

He captured Harper's Ferry with his nineteen men so true,
And he frightened old Virginia till she trembled through
        and through;
They hung him for a traitor, themselves the traitor crew,
    But his soul goes marching on.

John Brown's knapsack is strapped to his back,
    His soul is marching on.

His pet lambs will meet on the way,
    And they'll go marching on.

They will hang Jeff Davis on a sour apple tree,
    As they go marching on.

Now has come the glorious jubilee,
    When all mankind are free.

John Hardy

John Hardy was a desp'rate little man,
He carried two guns ev'ry day,
He shot down a man on the West Virginia line,
You oughta seen John Hardy gettin' away, poor boy,
You oughta seen John Hardy gettin' away.

John Hardy stood at the gamblin' table,
Didn't have no int'rest in the game,
Up stepped a yellow gal and threw a dollar down,
Said, "Deal John Hardy in the game, poor boy,
Deal John Hardy in the game."

John Hardy took that yellow gal's money,
And then he began to play,
Said, "The man that wins my yellow gal's dollar,
I'll lay him in his lonesome grave, poor boy,
I'll lay him in his lonesome grave.

John Hardy drew to a four-card straight,
And the Chinaman drew to a pair,
John failed to catch and the Chinaman won,
And he left him sitting dead in his chair, poor boy,
And he left him sitting dead in his chair.

John started to catch that East-bound train,
So dark he could not see,
Up stepped the police and took him by the arm,
Said, "Johnny come and go with me, poor boy,
Johnny come and go with me."

John Hardy's father came to him,
Come for to go his bail;
No bail was allowed for a murderin' man,
So they shoved John Hardy back in jail, poor boy,
So they shoved John Hardy back in jail.

They took John Hardy to his hangin' ground,
The hung him there to die,

And the very last word I heard him say—
"My forty gun never told a lie, poor boy,
My forty gun never told a lie.

"I've been to the East, I've been to the West,
I've travelled this wide world around,
I've been to the river and I've been baptised
And now I'm on my hangin' ground, poor boy,
And now I'm on my hangin' ground."

John Hardy had a loving little wife,
And children she had three,
But he cared no more for his wife and his child,
Than he did for the rocks in the sea, poor boy,
Than he did for the rocks in the sea.

John Henry

John Henry was a little baby,
Sittin' on his mamy's knee,
Said, "The Big Bend tunnel on the C. & O. road
Gonna be the death of me,
Lawd, Lawd, gonna be the death of me."

John Henry was a little baby,
Sittin' on his daddy's knee,
Point his finger at a little piece of steel,
"That's gonna be the death of me,
Lawd, Lawd, that's gonna be the death of me."

John Henry had a little woman
And her name was Mary Magdelene,
She would go to the tunnel and sing for John
Jes' to hear John Henry's hammer ring,
Lawd, Lawd, jes' to hear John Henry's hammer ring.

John Henry had a little woman
And her name was Polly Anne,

John Henry took sick and he had to go to bed,
Polly Anne drove steel like a man,
Lawd, Lawd, Polly Anne drove steel like a man.

Cap'n says to John Henry,
"Gonna bring me a steam drill 'round,
Gonna take that steam drill out on the job,
Gonna whop that steel on down,
Lawd, Lawd, gonna whop that steel on down."

John Henry told his cap'n,
Said, "A man ain't nothin' but a man,
And befo' I'd let that steam drill beat me down
I'd die with this hammer in my hand,
Lawd, Lawd, I'd die with the hammer in my hand."

Sun were hot and burnin',
Weren't no breeze atall,
Sweat ran down like water down a hill,
That day John let his hammer fall,
Lawd, Lawd, that day John let his hammer fall.

White man told John Henry,
"Nigger, damn yo' soul,
You may beat dis steam and drill of mine,—
When the rocks in the mountains turn to gold,
Lawd, Lawd, when the rocks in the mountains turn to
        gold."

John Henry said to his shaker,
"Shaker, why don't you sing?
I'm throwin' twelve pounds from my hips on down,
Jes' lissen to the cold steel ring,
Lawd, Lawd, jes' lissen to the cold steel ring."

O, the cap'n told John Henry,
"I b'lieve this mountain's sinkin' in."
John Henry said to his cap'n, O my!
"It's my hammer just a-hossin' in the wind,
Lawd, Lawd, it's my hammer just a-hossin' in the wind."

John Henry told his shaker,
"Shaker, you better pray,
For, if I miss this six-foot steel,
Tomorrow be yo' buryin' day,
Lawd, Lawd, tomorrow be yo' buryin' day."

John Henry told his captain,
"Looky yonder what I see—
Yo' drill's done broke an' yo' hole's done choke,
An' you can't drive steel like me,
Lawd, Lawd, an' you can't drive steel like me."

John Henry was hammerin' on the mountain,
An' his hammer was strikin' fire,
He drove so hard till he broke his pore heart,
An' he lied down his hammer an' he died,
Lawd, Lawd, an' he lied down his hammer an' he died.

They took John Henry to the graveyard
An' they buried him in the sand
An' ev'ry locomotive come roarin' by,
Says, "There lays a steel drivin' man,
Lawd, Lawd, says, "There lays a steel drivin' man."

John Henry had a little woman,
An' the dress she wore was blue,
She went walkin' down the track and she never looked back,
Said, "John Henry, I've been true to you,
Lawd, Lawd, John Henry, I've been true to you."

"Now who's gonna shoe your little feetses?
An' who's gonna glove your hands?
An' who's gonna kiss yo' red, rosy lips?
An' who's gonna be your man,
Lawd, Lawd, who's gonna be your man?"

"O my mama's gonna shoe my little feetses,
An' my papa's gonna gloves my little hands,
And my sister's gonna kiss my red, rosy lips,
An' I don' need no man,
Lawd, Lawd, an' I don' need no man."

"Johnny come down de hollow"

Johnny come down de hollow.
Oh hollow!
Johnny come down de hollow.
Oh hollow!
De nigger-trader got me.
Oh hollow!
De speculator bought me.
Oh hollow!
I'm sold for silver dollars.
Oh hollow!
Boys, go catch de pony.
Oh hollow!
Bring him round de corner.
Oh hollow!
I'm goin' away to Georgia.
Oh hollow!
Boys, good-by forever!
Oh hollow!

Joshua Fit de Battle ob Jerico

Joshua fit de battle ob Jerico,
Jerico, Jerico,
Joshua fit de battle ob Jerico,
An' de walls come tumblin' down.

You may talk about yo' king ob Gideon,
You may talk about yo' man ob Saul,
Dere's none like good ole Joshua
At de battle ob Jerico.

Up to de walls ob Jerico,
He marched with spear in han'
"Go blow dem ram horns" Joshua cried,
"Kase de battle am in my han'."

Den de lam'ram sheep horns begin to blow,
Trumpets begin to soun',
Joshua commanded the chillen to shout,
An' de walls come tumblin' down.

Dat mornin' Joshua fit de battle ob Jerico,
Jerico, Jerico,
Joshua fit de battle ob Jerico,
An' de walls come tumblin' down.

Let My People Go

A Song of the "Contrabands"

When Israel was in Egypt's land,
  O let my people go!
Oppressed so hard they could not stand,
  O let my people go!

> O go down, Moses
> Away down to Egypt's land,
> And tell King Pharaoh,
> To let my people go!

Thus saith the Lord, bold Moses said,
  O let my people go!
If not, I'll smite your first born dead,
  O let my people go!

No more shall they in bondage toil,
  O let my people go!
Let them come out with Egypt's spoil,
  O let my people go!

Then Israel out of Egypt came,
  O let my people go!
And left the proud oppressive land,
  O let my people go!

O 'twas a dark and dismal night,
    O let my people go!
When Moses led the Israelites,
    O let my people go!

'Twas good old Moses, and Aaron, too,
    O let my people go!
'Twas they that led the armies through,
    O let my people go!

The Lord told Moses what to do,
    O let my people go!
To lead the children of Israel through,
    O let my people go!

O come along Moses, you'll not get lost,
    O let my people go!
Stretch out your rod and come across,
    O let my people go!

As Israel stood by the water side,
    O let my people go!
At the command of God it did divide,
    O let my people go!

When they had reached the other shore,
    O let my people go!
They sang a song of triumph o'er,
    O let my people go!

Pharaoh said he would go across,
    O let my people go!
But Pharaoh and his host were lost,
    O let my people go!

O Moses, the cloud shall cleave the way,
    O let my people go!
A fire by night, a shade by day,
    O let my people go!

You'll not get lost in the wilderness,
   O let my people go!
With a lighted candle in your breast,
   O let my people go!

Jordan shall stand up like a wall,
   O let my people go!
And the walls of Jericho shall fall,
   O let my people go!

Your foe shall not before you stand,
   O let my people go!
And you'll possess fair Canaan's land,
   O let my people go!

'Twas just about in harvest time,
   O let my people go!
When Joshua led his host Divine,
   O let my people go!

O let us all from bondage flee,
   O let my people go!
And let us all in Christ be free,
   O let my people go!

We need not always weep and mourn,
   O let my people go!
And wear these Slavery chains forlorn,
   O let my people go!

This world's a wilderness of woe,
   O let my people go!
O let us on to Canaan go,
   O let my people go!

What a beautiful morning that will be!
   O let my people go!
When time breaks up in eternity,
   O let my people go!

Lonesome Valley

You got to walk that lonesome valley,
You got to go there by yourself,
Ain't nobody here can go there for you,
You got to go there by yourself.

If you cannot preach like Peter,
If you cannot pray like Paul,
You can tell the love of Jesus,
You can say he died for all.

Your mother's got to walk that lonesome valley,
She's got to go there by herself,
Ain't nobody else can go there for her,
She's got to go there by herself.

Your father's got to walk that lonesome valley,
He's got to go there by himself,
Ain't nobody else can go there for him,
He's got to go there by himself.

Your brother's got to walk that lonesome valley,
He's got to go there by himself,
Ain't nobody else can go there for him,
He's got to go there by himself.

Lord, Remember Me!

O do, Lord, remember me!
  O do, Lord, remember me!
O, do remember me, until de year roll round!
  Do, Lord, remember me!

If you want to die like Jesus died,
  Lay in de grave,
You would fold your arms and close your eyes
  And die wid a free good will.

For Death is a simple ting,
  And he go from door to door,
And he knock down some, and he cripple up some,
  And he leave some here to pray.

O do, Lord, remember me!
  O do, Lord, remember me!
My old fader 's gone till de year roll round;
  Do, Lord, remember me!

Low Bridge, Everybody Down

or Fifteen Years on the Erie Canal

I've got an old mule and her name is Sal,
Fifteen years on the Erie Canal,
She's a good old worker and a good old pal,
Fifteen years on the Erie Canal.
We've hauled some barges in our day,
Filled with lumber, coal and hay—
And every inch of the way I know
From Albany to Buffalo.

> *Low bridge, everybody down,*
> *Low bridge! We're coming to a town!*
> *You can always tell your neighbor, you can always tell*
>   *your pal*
> *If you've every navigated on the Erie Canal.*

We'd better look around for a job, Old Gal,
Fifteen years on the Erie Canal.
You bet your life I wouldn't part with Sal,
Fifteen years on the Erie Canal.
Giddap there, Gal, we've passed that lock,
We'll make Rome 'fore six o'clock—
So one more trip and then we'll go
Right straight back to Buffalo.

Low bridge, everybody down;
Low bridge, I've got the finest mule in town.
Once a man named Mike McGintey tried to put over Sal,
Now he's way down at the bottom of the Erie Canal.

Oh! where would I be if I lost my pal?
Fifteen years on the Erie Canal,
Oh, I'd like to see a mule as good as Sal,
Fifteen years on the Erie Canal.
A friend of mine once got her sore,
Now he's got a broken jaw,
'Cause she let fly with her iron toe
And knocked him in to Buffalo.

Low bridge, everybody down;
Low bridge, I've got the finest mule in town.
If you're looking for trouble, better stay away,
She's the only fighting donkey on the Erie Canal.

I don't have to call when I want my Sal,
Fifteen years on the Erie Canal,
She trots from the stall like a good old gal,
Fifteen years on the Erie Canal.
I eat my meals with Sal each day,
I eat beef and she eats hay,
She ain't so slow if you want to know,
She put the "Buff" in Buffalo.

Low bridge, everybody down;
Low bridge, I've got the finest mule in town.
Eats a bale of hay for dinner, and on top of that my Sal
Tries to drink up all the water in the Erie Canal.

You'll soon hear them sing all about my gal,
Fifteen years on the Erie Canal,
It's a darned fine ditty 'bout my darn fool Sal,
Fifteen years on the Erie Canal.
Oh, any band will play it soon,
Darned fool words and darned fool tune;
You'll hear it sung everywhere you go,
From Mexico to Buffalo.

Low bridge, everybody down;
Low bridge, I've got the finest mule in town.
She's a perfect, perfect lady, and she blushes like a gal
If she hears you sing about her and the Erie Canal.

Many Thousand Gone

No more auction block for me,
No more, no more;
No more auction block for me,
Many thousand gone.

No more peck o' corn for me,
No more, no more;
No more peck o' corn for me,
Many thousand gone.

No more driver's lash for me,
No more, no more;
No more driver's lash for me,
Many thousand gone.

No more pint o' salt for me,
No more, no more;
No more pint o' salt for me,
Many thousand gone.

No more hundred lash for me,
No more, no more;
No more hundred lash for me,
Many thousand gone.

No more mistress' call for me,
No more, no more;
No more mistress' call for me,
Many thousand gone.

Michael Row the Boat Ashore

Michael row de boat ashore,
Hallelujah!

Michael boat a gospel boat,
Hallelujah!

I wonder where my mudder deh,
Hallelujah!

See my mudder on de rock gwine home,
Hallelujah!

On de rock gwine home in Jesus' name,
Hallelujah!

Michael boat a music boat,
Hallelujah!

Gabriel blow de trumpet horn,
Hallelujah!

O you mind your boastin' talk,
Hallelujah!

Boastin' talk will sink your soul,
Hallelujah!

Brudder, lend a helpin' hand,
Hallelujah!

Sister, help for trim dat boat,
Hallelujah!

Jordan stream is wide and deep,
Hallelujah!

Jesus stand on t' oder side,
Hallelujah!

I wonder if my maussa deh,
Hallelujah!

My fader gone to unknown land,
Hallelujah!

O de Lord he plant his garden deh,
Hallelujah!

He raise de fruit for you to eat,
Hallelujah!

He dat eat shall neber die,
Hallelujah!

When de riber overflow,
Hallelujah!

O poor sinner, how you land?
Hallelujah!

Riber run and darkness comin',
Hallelujah!

Sinner row to save your soul,
Hallelujah!

My Lord, What a Morning

My Lord, what a morning,
My Lord, what a morning,
My Lord, what a morning,
When de stars begin to fall.

You'll hear de trumpet sound,
  To wake de nations underground,
Look in my God's right hand,
  When de stars begin to fall.
You'll hear de sinner moan,

To wake de nations underground,
Look in my God's right hand,
When de stars begin to fall.

You'll hear de Christians shout,
To wake de nations underground,
Look in my God's right hand,
When de stars begin to fall.
You'll hear de angels sing,
To wake de nations underground,
Look in my God's right hand,
When de stars begin to fall.

You'll see my Jesus come,
To wake de nations underground,
Look in my God's right hand,
When de stars begin to fall.
His chariot wheels roll round,
To wake de nations underground,
Look in my God's right hand,
When de stars begin to fall.

Nobody Knows the Trouble I've Had

Nobody knows de trouble I've had,
Nobody knows but Jesus,
Nobody knows de trouble I've had,
Glory hallelu!

One morning I was a-walking down, O yes, Lord!
I saw some berries a-hanging down, O yes, Lord!

I pick de berry and I suck de juice, O yes, Lord!
Just as sweet as the honey in de comb, O yes, Lord!

Sometimes I'm up, sometimes I'm down, O yes, Lord!
Sometimes I'm almost on de groun', O yes, Lord!

What make ole Satan hate me so? O yes, Lord!
Because he got me once and he let me go, O yes, Lord!

Oh My Darling Clementine

In a cabin, in a canon,
An excavation for a mine;
Dwelt a miner, a Forty-niner,
And his daughter Clementine.

> *Oh my darling, oh my darling,*
> *Oh my darling Clementine,*
> *You are lost and gone forever,*
> *Drefful sorry, Clementine.*

She drove her ducklets, to the river,
Ev'ry morning just at nine;
She stubb'd her toe against a sliver,
And fell into the foaming brine.

I saw her lips above the water,
Blowing bubbles soft and fine;
Alas for me, I was no swimmer,
And so I lost my Clementine.

Old Joe Clark

I would not go to old Joe's house,
Tell you the reason why,
I can't get around his garden spot,
For tearing down all his rye.

> *Round and round all, old Joe Clark,*
> *Round and round, I say,*
> *He'll foller me ten thousand miles,*
> *To hear my fiddle play.*

Old Joe's got an old red cow,
I know her by the bell.
If she ever gits in my cornfield,
I'll shoot her shore as Hell.

> *Round and round all, old Joe Clark,*
> *Round and round, I say,*
> *Round and round, old Joe Clark,*
> *I ain't got long to stay.*

I went up to old Joe's house,
Old Joe wasn't at home;
I eat up all of his ham meat
And throwed away the bone.

> *Fare you well, old Joe Clark,*
> *Good-by, Betty Brown,*
> *Fare you well, old Joe Clark,*
> *Fare you well, I'm gone.*

I went down to old Joe Clark's,
Old Joe wasn't at home;
Jumped in bed with old Joe's wife
And broke her tucking comb.

I won't go down to old Joe's house,
I've told you here before;
He fed me in a hog-trough
And I won't go there any more.

Sixteen horses in my team,
And the leaders, they are blind;
And every time the sun goes down,
There's a pretty gal on my mind.

Eighteen miles of mountain road
And fifteen miles of sand;
If I ever travel this road again,
I'll be a married man.

Never got no money,
Got no place to stay,
Got no place to lay my head,
Chicken's a-crowin' for day.

I wish I was an apple
A-hanging on yonder's tree—
Ev'ry time a pretty gal passed
She'd take a bite of me.

Wish I was a sugar tree,
Standing in the middle of some town—
Ev'ry time a pretty gal passed,
I'd shake some sugar down.

Wish I had a nickel,
Wish I had a dime,
Wish I had a pretty lil gal,
For to kiss her an' call her mine.

Wish I was in Tennessee,
Settin' in a big armcheer,
One arm round my whisky jug,
The other round my dear.

I climbed up the oak tree,
She climbed up the gum;
Never saw a pretty lil gal,
But what I liked her some.

When I was a little girl
I used to play with toys;
But now I am a bigger girl
I'd rather play with boys.

When I was a little boy
I used to want a knife;
But now I am a bigger boy
All I want is a wife.

Old-Time Religion

Give me that old-time religion,
Give me that old-time religion,
Give me that old-time religion,
It's good enough for me.

It was good for our fathers,
It was good for our fathers,
It was good for our fathers,
It's good enough for me.

It was good for our mothers,
It was good for our mothers,
It was good for our mothers,
It's good enough for me.

It was good for Paul and Silas,
It was good for Paul and Silas,
It was good for Paul and Silas,
It's good enough for me.

It makes you love ev'rybody,
It makes you love ev'rybody,
It makes you love ev'rybody,
It's good enough for me.

It makes you love the Bible,
It makes you love the Bible,
It makes you love the Bible,
It's good enough for me.

It will do when you are dying,
It will do when you are dying,
It will do when you are dying,
It's good enough for me.

It will take us all to heaven,
It will take us all to heaven,
It will take us all to heaven,
It's good enough for me.

One More River

O, Jordan bank was a great old bank!
   Dere ain't but one more river to cross.
We have some valiant soldier here,
   Dere ain't but one more river to cross.
O, Jordan stream will never run dry,
   Dere ain't but one more river to cross.
Dere 's a hill on my leff, and he catch on my right,
   Dere ain't but one more river to cross.

Poor Naomi

Come all good people, I'd have you draw near,
A sorrowful story you quickly shall hear;
A story I'll tell you about N'omi Wise,
How she was deluded by Lewis's lies.

He promised to marry and use me quite well;
But conduct contrary I sadly must tell,
He promised to meet me at Adams's spring;
He promised me marriage and many fine things.

Still nothing he gave, but yet flattered the case.
He says we'll be married and have no disgrace,
Come get up behind me, we'll go up to town,
And there we'll be married, in union be bound.

I got up behind him and straightway did go
To the banks of Deep river where the water did flow;
He says now Naomi, I'll tell you my mind,
Intend here to drown you and leave you behind.

O pity your infant and spare me my life;
Let me go rejected and be not your wife;
No pity, no pity, this monster did cry;
In Deep river's bottom your body shall lie.

The wretch then did choke her, as we understand,
And threw her in the river below the milldam;
Be it murder or treason, O! what a great crime,
To drown poor Naomi and leave her behind.

Naomi was missing they all did well know,
And hunting for her to the river did go;
And there found her floating on the water so deep,
Which caused all the people to sigh and to weep.

The neighbors were sent for to see the great sight,
While she lay floating all that long night;
So early next morning the inquest was held;
The jury correctly the murder did tell.

Red River Valley

From this valley they say you are going,
We will miss your bright eyes and sweet smile,
For they say you are taking the sunshine
That brightens our pathway awhile.

> *Come and sit by my side if you love me,*
> *Do not hasten to bid me adieu,*
> *But remember the Red River Valley*
> *And the girl that has loved you so true.*

For a long time I have been waiting
For those dear words you never would say,
But at last all my fond hopes have vanished,
For they say you are going away.

Won't you think of the valley you're leaving?
Oh how lonely, how sad it will be.
Oh think of the fond heart you're breaking,
And the grief you are causing me to see?

From this valley they say you are going;
When you go, may your darling go too?
Would you leave her behind unprotected
When she loves no other but you?

I have promised you, darling, that never
Will a word from my lips cause you pain;
And my life,—it will be yours forever
If you only will love me again.

Must the past with its joys be blighted
By the future of sorrow and pain,
And the vows that was spoken be slighted?
Don't you think you can love me again?

As you go to your home by the ocean,
May you never forget those sweet hours,
That we spent in Red River Valley,
And the love we exchanged 'mid the flowers.

There never could be such a longing
In the heart of a pure maiden's breast,
That dwells in the heart you are breaking
As I wait in my home in the West.

And the dark maiden's prayer for her lover
To the Spirit that rules over the world;
May his pathway be ever in sunshine,
Is the prayer of the Red River girl.

Roll, Jordan, Roll

My brudder sittin' on de tree of life,
An' he yearde when Jordan roll;
  Roll, Jordan,
  Roll, Jordan,
  Roll, Jordan, roll!
 O march de angel march,
 O march de angel march;
 O my soul arise in Heaven, Lord,
 For to yearde when Jordan roll.

Little chil'en, learn to fear de Lord,
And let your days be long;
  Roll, Jordan,
  Roll, Jordan,
  Roll, Jordan, roll!
 O march de angel march,
 O march de angel march;
 O my soul arise in Heaven, Lord,
 For to yearde when Jordan roll.

O, let no false nor spiteful word
Be found upon your tongue;
  Roll, Jordan,
  Roll, Jordan,
  Roll, Jordan, roll!
 O march de angel march,
 O march de angel march;
 O my soul arise in Heaven, Lord,
 For to yearde when Jordan roll.

Rye Whisky

I'll eat when I'm hungry, I'll drink when I'm dry;
If the hard times don't kill me, I'll live till I die.

 Rye whisky, rye whisky, rye whisky, I cry,
 If you don't give me rye whisky, I surely will die.

I'll tune up my fiddle, and I'll rosin my bow,
And make myself welcome wherever I go.

Beefsteak when I'm hungry, red liquor when I'm dry,
Greenbacks when I'm hard up, and religion when I die.

They say I drink whisky; my money's my own,
All them that don't like me can leave me alone.

Sometimes I drink whisky, sometimes I drink rum,
Sometimes I drink brandy, at other times none.

But if I get boozy, my whisky's my own,
And them that don't like me can leave me alone.

Jack o' diamonds, jack o' diamonds, I know you of old,
You've robbed my poor pockets of silver and gold.

Oh, whisky, you villain, you've been my downfall;
You've kicked me, you've cuffed me, but I love you for all.

If the ocean was whisky and I was a duck
I'd dive to the bottom and get one sweet suck.

But the ocean ain't whisky and I ain't a duck,
So we'll round up the cattle and then we'll get drunk.

Sweet milk when I'm hungry, rye whisky when I'm dry,
If a tree don't fall on me, I'll live till I die.

I'll buy my own whisky, I'll make my own stew;
If I get drunk, madam, it's nothing to you.

I'll drink my own whisky, I'll drink my own wine;
Some ten thousand bottles I've killed in my time.

I'll drink and I'll gamble, my money's my own,
And them that don't like me can leave me alone.

My foot in the stirrup, my bridle in my hand,
A-courting fair Mollie, to marry if I can.

My foot's in my stirrup, my bridle's in my hand;
I'm leaving sweet Mollie, the fairest in the land.

Her parents don't like me, they say I'm too poor;
They say I'm unworthy to enter her door.

I've no wife to quarrel, no babies to bawl;
The best way of living is no wife at all.

Way up on Clinch Mountain I wander alone;
I'm as drunk as the devil. Oh, let me alone.

You may boast of your knowledge, and brag of your sense,
'Twill be all forgotten a hundred years hence.

Shady Grove

Shady grove, my true love,
Shady grove I know,
Shady grove, my true love,
I'm bound for the shady grove.

Peaches in the summertime,
Apples in the fall,
If I can't get the girl I love,
Won't have none at all.

Once I was a little boy,
Playin' in the sand,
Now I am a great big boy,
I think myself a man.

When I wus a little boy,
I wanted a whittlin' knife;
Now I am a great big boy
An' I want a little wife.

Wish I had a banjo string,
Made of golden twine,
And every tune I'd pick on it—
Is 'I wish that girl were mine.'

Some come here to fiddle en dance,
Some come here to tarry,
Somes come here to fiddle en dance,
I come here to marry.

Ev'ry night when I go home,
My wife, I try to please her,
The more I try, the worse she gets,
Damned if I don't leave her.

> *Shady grove, my little love,*
> *Shady grove, my darlin',*
> *Shady grove, my little love*
> *Goin' back to Harlan.*

Fly around, my blue-eyed girl,
Fly around, my daisy,
Fly around, my blue-eyed girl,
Nearly drive me crazy.

The very next time I go that road
And it don't look so dark and grazy,
The very next time I come that road
I'll stop and see my daisy.

I once had a mulie cow,
Mulie when she's born,
Took a jay-bird forty year
To fly from horn to horn.

Shenandoah

Missouri, she's a mighty river.
   Away, you rolling river.
The redskins' camp lies on its borders
   Ah ha I'm bound away, 'cross the wide Missouri.

The white man loved the Indian maiden,
   Away, you rolling river.
With notions his canoe was laden.
   Ah ha I'm bound away, 'cross the wide Missouri.

"O, Shenandoah, I love your daughter,"
   Away, you rolling river.
"I'll take her 'cross yon rolling water."
   Ah ha I'm bound away, 'cross the wide Missouri.

The chief disdained the trader's dollars;
   Away, you rolling river.
"My daughter never you shall follow."
   Ah ha I'm bound away, 'cross the wide Missouri.

At last there came a Yankee skipper,
   Away, you rolling river.
He winked his eye, and he tipped his flipper.
   Ah ha I'm bound away, 'cross the wide Missouri.

He sold the chief that fire-water,
   Away, you rolling river.
And 'cross the river he stole his daughter.
   Ah ha I'm bound away, 'cross the wide Missouri.

"O, Shenandoah, I long to hear you,"
   Away, you rolling river.
"Across that wide and rolling river."
   Ah ha I'm bound away, 'cross the wide Missouri.

Simple Gifts

'Tis the gift to be simple, 'tis the gift to be free,
'Tis the gift to come down where we ought to be,
And when we find ourselves in the place just right,
'Twill be in the valley of love and delight.
When true simplicity is gain'd,
To bow and to bend we shan't be asham'd,
To turn, turn will be our delight
'Till by turning, turning we come round right.

Sometimes I Feel Like a Motherless Child

Sometimes I feel like a motherless child,
Sometimes I feel like a motherless child,
Sometimes I feel like a motherless child,
A long ways from home,
A long ways from home.
True believer.
A long ways from home,
A long ways from home.

Ef this was judgment day,
Ef this was judgment day,
Ef this was judgment day,
Eb'ry little soul would pray,
Eb'ry little soul would pray.
True believer.
Eb'ry little soul would pray,
Eb'ry little soul would pray.

Sometimes I feel like I'm almos' gone,
Sometimes I feel like I'm almos' gone,
Sometimes I feel like I'm almos' gone,
Way up in de Hebbenly lan',
Way up in de Hebbenly lan'.
True believer.
Way up in de Hebbenly lan',
Way up in de Hebbenly lan'.

Stackalee

Come all you sporty fellows,
And listen unto me,
I will tell to you the awful tale
Of that bad man Stackalee,
    That bad, that bad man Stackalee.

The night was dark and stormy,
And the rain came pouring down;
There was nary a police
In that part of town.
    That bad, that bad man Stackalee.

It was on this dark and
Cold stormy night
That Billy Lyons and Stackalee
They had that awful fight.
    That bad, that bad man Stackalee.

Billy Lyons on the sidewalk
Dropped his razor from his hand;
In front of him a-shootin'
Old Stackalee did stand,
    That bad, that bad man Stackalee.

"O Stackalee, O Stackalee,
Please spare my life,
For I have got two babies
And a darling little wife."
    That bad, that bad man Stackalee.

"I care not for your babies
Nor your darling little wife;
You dun ruint my Stetson hat,
And I am bound to have your life."
    That bad, that bad man Stackalee.

Then he leaned down right close
And put that gun agin Billy's breast,

And fired two shots so close to him
They sot fire to his vest,
    That bad, that bad man Stackalee.

Down Walker Street
Old Stackalee did run,
Holding in his right hand
That smoking forty-one,
    That bad, that bad man Stackalee.

He run into Ben Scott's saloon
And before the bar did stand,
Saying, "Take my pistol, bar boy,
I dun killed another man."
    That bad, that bad man Stackalee.

Ben Scott sent for the police
And they came on the run;
The bar boy up and told them
What old Stackalee dun done,
    That bad, that bad man Stackalee.

Says a police to the Sergeant,
"Now what do you think of that!
Old Stackalee shot Billy Lyons
About a damned old hat,
    That bad, that bad man Stackalee."

Says the Captain to the police,
"Just keep still as any mouse,
And we will sure catch old Stackalee
At his woman's house,
    That bad, that bad man Stackalee."

Two police in the alley
Hiding behind a tree;
Two more out in the front yard
For to catch old Stackalee,
    That bad, that bad man Stackalee.

A man run up the alley,
Splashing through the mud;
He run right up against that tree
Where them two police stood—
  That bad, that bad man Stackalee.

"Your name is Henry Wells,
But they call you Stackalee;
You are my prisoner;
Come and go with me."
  That bad, that bad man Stackalee.

"My name's not Stackalee,
Nor is it Henry Wells;
I am not your prisoner
You go get someone else."
  That bad, that bad man Stackalee.

They put the handcuffs on him
And took him to the jail,
And there they put him in a cell
And wouldn't take no bail,
  That bad, that bad man Stackalee.

Mrs. Stackalee,
When she heard the awful news,
Was sitting in the bedroom
A-taking off her shoes.
  That bad, that bad man Stackalee.

She rushed down to the jailhouse
And fell upon her knees,
"I'll give ten thousand dollars
Just to get the jailor's keys."
  That bad, that bad man Stackalee.

Next morning in the jailhouse,
Old Stackalee in bed,
A turnkey came and told him
That Billy Lyons was dead.
  That bad, that bad man Stackalee.

Then they took him into court
To have him make his plea,
The judge says, "Are you guilty?"
"I is," says Stackalee,
    That bad, that bad man Stackalee.

"I cannot sleep,
Neither can I eat,
Since I shot poor Billy Lyons
Down in Walker Street."
    That bad, that bad man Stackalee.

The judge put on the black cap,
His voice was stern and cold;
"I sentences you to be hanged—
The Lord have mercy on your soul."
    That bad, that bad man Stackalee.

Now all you sporty fellows
That have listened to my tale,
Do not shoot another man
Or they'll hang you in the jail,
    Like they did that bad man Stackalee.

Starving to Death on a Government Claim

or The Lane County Bachelor

Frank Baker's my name, and a bachelor I am;
I'm keeping old batch on an elegant plan.
You'll find me out west in the county of Lane—
I'm starving to death on a government claim.
My house, it is built of the natural soil;
The walls are erected according to Hoyle.
The roof has no pitch, but is level and plain,
And I always get wet when it happens to rain.
    Hurrah for Lane County, the land of the free,

The home of the grasshopper, bedbug and flea.
I'll sing loud its praises and tell of its fame
While starving to death on a government claim.

My clothes, they are ragged; my language is rough;
My bread is case-hardened both solid and tough.
The dough is scattered all over the room,
And the floor, it gets scared at the sight of a broom.
My dishes are scattered all over the bed;
They are covered with sorghum and Government bread.
Still I have a good time and live at my ease
On common sop-sorghum, old bacon, and grease.
    Then come to Lane County. Here is a home for you all
    Where the winds never cease and the rains never fall,
    And the sun never sets but will always remain
    Till it burns you all up on a Government claim.

How happy I feel when I crawl into bed,
And a rattlesnake rattles a tune at my head,
And the gay little centipede, void of all fear,
Crawls over my neck and down into my ear,
And the little bed bugs so cheerful and bright,
They keep me a-laughing two-thirds of the night,
And the gay little flea with sharp tacks in his toes
Plays "why don't you catch me" all over my nose.
    Hurrah for Lane County, hurrah for the West,
    Where farmers and laborers are ever at rest,
    For there's nothing to do but to sweetly remain
    And starve like a man on a Government claim.

How happy am I on my government claim,
For I've nothing to lose nor I've nothing to gain.
I've nothing to eat, and I've nothing to wear,
And nothing from nothing is honest and fair.
Oh, it is here I am solid and here I will stay,
For my money is all gone and I can't get away.
There is nothing that makes a man hard and profane
Like starving to death on a Government claim.

Hurrah for Lane County, where blizzards arise,
Where the winds never cease and the flea never dies.
Come join in the chorus and sing of its fame,
You poor hungry hoboes that's starved on the claim.

No, don't get discouraged, you poor hungry men,
For we are all here as free as a pig in a pen.
Just stick to your homestead and battle the fleas
And look to your Maker to send you a breeze.
Now, all you claim holders, I hope you will stay
And chew your hardtack till you are toothless and grey;
But, as for myself, I'll no longer remain
And starve like a dog on a Government claim.
Farewell to Lane County, farewell to the West.
I'll travel back East to the girl I love best.
I'll stop in Topeka and get me a wife,
And there shall I stay the rest of my life.

The State of Arkansas

My name is Stanford Barnes, I come from Nobleville
        town;
I've traveled this wide world over, I've traveled this wide
        world round.
I've met with ups and downs of life, but better days I've
        saw;
But I've never knew what mis'ry were till I came to
        Arkansas.

I landed in St. Louis with ten dollars and no more;
I read the daily papers till both my eyes were sore;
I read the evening papers till at last I saw
Ten thousand men were wanted in the state of Arkansas.

I wiped my eyes with great surprise when I read this grateful
        news,
And straightway off I started to see the agent, Billy Hughes.
I handed him five dollars though it gave my heart a shock;
I was soon on the railway bound for the city of Little Rock.

I started off one morning at a quarter after five,
I started from St. Louis half dead and half alive;
I bought me a quart of whisky my misery to thaw;
I got as drunk as a biled owl when I left for old Arkansas.

I landed in Fort Smith one sultry Sunday afternoon;
It was in the month of May, the early month of June,
Up stepped a walking skeleton with a long and lantern jaw,
Invited me to his hotel, "the best in Arkansas."

There met me at the depot this seedy-looking chap,
With a ragged coat and britches and an old and greasy cap.
Says he, "Good morning, gentlemen, the morning's rather
        raw,
On yonder hill stands my hotel, the best in Arkansas."

I started off next morning to catch the morning train;
He says to me: "You'd better work. I have some land to
        drain.
I'll pay you fifty cents a day, your board, washing and all—
You'll find yourself a different man when you leave old
        Arkansas."

I met with good connections and started for the camp,
Where every accommodation was fitted for the tramp;
I slept beside the fire without tent or bed or straw,
As I worked upon the railroad in the state of Arkansas.

I worked six weeks for the son-of-a-gun, Jesse Howard was
        his name,
He was six feet seven in his stocking feet and taller than any
        crane.
His hair hung down in strings over his long and lantern jaw,
He was the photograph of all the gents who live in
        Arkansas.

He fed me on corn-dodgers as hard as any rock,
Until my teeth began to loosen and my knees began to
      knock;
I got so thin on sass'fras tea I could hide behind a straw,
And indeed I was a different man when I left old Arkansas.

I started out next morning at a quarter after five;
I staggered into a saloon, half dead and half alive;
I called for liquor merrily, I called for whisky raw;
I jumped the train for Chicago and good-by to Arkansas.

Farewell to swamp angels, canebrakes and chills;
Farewell to sage and sass'fras, and corn-dodger pills;
If I ever see this land again, I'll give to you my paw,
It will be through a telescope from here to Arkansas.

Steal Away

> Steal away, steal away, steal away to Jesus!
> Steal away, steal away home,
> I hain't got long to stay here.

My Lord calls me,
   He calls me by the thunder;
The trumpet sounds it in my soul:
   I hain't got long to stay here.

Green trees are bending,
   Poor sinners stand trembling;
The trumpet sounds it in my soul:
   I hain't got long to stay here.

My Lord calls me,
   He calls me by the lightning;
The trumpet sounds it in my soul:
   I hain't got long to stay here.

Tombstones are bursting,
    Poor sinners stand trembling;
The trumpet sounds it in my soul:
    I hain't got long to stay here.

Sweet Betsey from Pike

Oh, don't you remember Sweet Betsey from Pike,
Who crossed the big mountains with her lover, Ike;
With two yoke of cattle, a large yellow dog,
A tall Shanghai rooster, and one spotted hog.

> *Tooral lal looral lal looral lal la la,*
> *Tooral lal looral lal looral lal la la.*

One evening quite early they camped on the Platte,
'Twas nearby the road on a green shady flat,
Where Betsey, sore-footed, lay down to repose—
With wonder Ike gazed on that Pike County rose.

Their wagons broke down with a terrible crash,
And out on the prairie rolled all kinds of trash;
A few little baby clothes done up with care—
'Twas rather suspicious, though all on the square.

The shanghai ran off and their cattle all died;
That morning the last piece of bacon was fried;
Poor Ike was discouraged and Betsey got mad,
The dog drooped his tail and got wondrously sad.

They stopped at Salt Lake to inquire the way,
When Brigham declared that sweet Betsey should stay;
But Betsey got frightened and ran like a deer,
While Brigham stood pawing the ground like a steer.

They soon reached the desert, where Betsey gave out,
And down in the sand she lay rolling about;
While Ike, half distracted, looked on with surprise,
Saying, "Betsey, get up, you'll get sand in your eyes."

Sweet Betsey got up in a great deal of pain,
Declared she'd go back to Pike County again;
But Ike gave a sigh, and they fondly embraced,
And they traveled along with his arm round her waist.

They suddenly stopped on a very high hill,
With wonder they looked upon old Placerville;
Ike sighed when he said, and he cast his eyes down,
"Sweet Betsey, my darling, we've got to Hangtown."

Long Ike and Sweet Betsey attended a dance;
Ike wore a pair of his Pike County pants;
Sweet Betsey was covered with ribbons and rings;
Says Ike, "You're and angel, but where are your wings?"

A miner said, "Betsey, will you dance with me?"
"I will that, old hoss, if you don't make too free;
But don't dance me hard; do you want to know why?
Dog on you! I'm chock full of strong alkali!"

This Pike County couple got married of course;
And Ike became jealous—obtained a divorce;
Sweet Betsey, well satisfied, said with a shout,
"Good-by, you big lummux, I'm glad you backed out!"

Swing Low, Sweet Chariot

Swing low, sweet chariot,
Coming for to carry me home,
Swing low, sweet chariot,
Coming for to carry me home.

I looked over Jordan, and what did I see,
Coming for to carry me home?
A band of angels coming after me,
Coming for to carry me home.

If you get there before I do,
Coming for to carry me home,
Tell all my friends I'm coming too,
Coming for to carry me home.

The brightest day that ever I saw,
Coming for to carry me home,
When Jesus wash'd my sins away,
Coming for to carry me home.

I'm sometimes up and sometimes down,
Coming for to carry me home,
But still my soul feels heavenly bound,
Coming for to carry me home.

"We raise de wheat"

We raise de wheat,
Dey gib us de corn;
We bake de bread,
Dey gib us de cruss;
We aif de meal,
Dey gib us de huss;
We peal de meat,
Dey gib us de skin,
And dat's de way
Dey takes us in.
We skim de pot,
Dey gib us the liquor,
And say dat's good enough for nigger.
  Walk over! walk over!
  Tom butter and de fat;
  Poor nigger you can't get over dat;
              Walk over!

Were You There?

Were you there when they crucified my Lord? (were you
    there?)
Were you there when they crucified my Lord?
Oh! Sometimes it causes me to tremble, tremble, tremble.
Were you there when they crucified my Lord?

Were you there when they nailed Him to the tree? (to the
    tree?)
Were you there when they nailed Him to the tree?
Oh! Sometimes it causes me to tremble, tremble, tremble.
Were you there when they nailed Him to the tree?

Were you there when they pierced Him in the side? (in the
    side?)
Were you there when they pierced Him in the side?
Oh! Sometimes it causes me to tremble, tremble, tremble.
Were you there when they pierced Him in the side?

Were you there when the sun refused to shine? (were you
    there?)
Were you there when the sun refused to shine?
Oh! Sometimes it causes me to tremble, tremble, tremble.
Were you there when the sun refused to shine?

Were you there when they laid Him in the tomb? (in the
    tomb?)
Were you there when they laid Him in the tomb?
Oh! Sometimes it causes me to tremble, tremble, tremble.
Were you there when they laid Him in the tomb?

What Yo' Gwine t' Do
When de Lamp Burn Down?

Oh, po' sinner,
Now is yo' time
Oh, po' sinner
What yo' gwine to do when de lamp burn down?

Oh, de lamp burn down an' yo' cannot see;
  What yo' gwine t' do when de lamp burn down?
Oh, de lamp burn down an' yo' cannot see;
  What yo' gwine t' do when de lamp burn down?

Ezekiel saw dat wheel o' time;
  What yo' gwine t' do when de lamp burn down?
An' ev'ry spoke was of human kind;
  What yo' gwine t' do when de lamp burn down?

God made man an' He made him out o' clay,
  What yo' gwine t' do when de lamp burn down?
An' put him on de earth, but not to stay;
  What yo' gwine t' do when de lamp burn down?

Dey cast ole Daniel in de lion's den;
  What yo' gwine t' do when de lamp burn down?
An' Jesus locked de lion's jaw;
  What yo' gwine t' do when de lamp burn down?

Ole Satan's mad an' I am glad;
  What yo' gwine t' do when de lamp burn down?
He miss one soul he thought he had,
  What yo' gwine t' do when de lamp burn down?

Ole Satan's a liar an' a conjurer too;
  What yo' gwine t' do when de lamp burn down?
If yo' don't mind, he slip in on yo'
  What yo' gwine t' do when de lamp burn down?

Whoopee Ti Yi Yo, Git Along Little Dogies

As I walked out one morning for pleasure,
I spied a cow-puncher all riding alone;
His hat was throwed back and his spurs was a jingling,
As he approached me a-singin' this song,

> *Whoopee ti yi yo, git along little dogies,*
> *It's your misfortune, and none of my own.*
> *Whoopee ti yi yo, git along little dogies,*
> *For you know Wyoming will be your new home.*

Early in the spring we round up the dogies,
Mark and brand and bob off their tails;
Round up our horses, load up the chuck-wagon,
Then throw the dogies upon the trail.

It's whooping and yelling and driving the dogies;
Oh how I wish you would go on;
It's whooping and punching and go on little dogies,
For you know Wyoming will be your new home.

Some boys goes up the trail for pleasure,
But that's where you get it most awfully wrong;
For you haven't any idea the trouble they give us
While we go driving them all along.

When the night comes on and we hold them on the
        bedground,
These little dogies that roll on so slow;
Roll up the herd and cut out the strays,
And roll the little dogies that never rolled before.

Your mother she was raised way down in Texas,
Where the jimson weed and sand-burrs grow;
Now we'll fill you up on prickly pear and cholla
Till you are ready for the trail to Idaho.

Oh, you'll be soup for Uncle Sam's Injuns;
"It's beef, heap beef," I hear them cry.
Git along, git along, git along little dogies,
You're going to be beef steers by and by.

Working on the Railway

In eighteen hundred and forty-one
I put my corduroy breeches on,
I put my corduroy breeches on,
To work upon the railway.

For-o-my-or-o-my-or-o-my-ay,
For-o-my-or-o-my-or-o-my-ay,
For-o-my-or-o-my-or-o-my-ay,
To work upon the railway.

In eighteen hundred and forty-two
I left the old world for the new,
The emigrationists put me through,
To work upon the railway.

In eighteen hundred and forty-three,
'Twas first I met sweet Biddy McGee,
And an iligant wife she's been to me
While working on the railway.

In eighteen hundred and forty-four,
It left me where I was before;
Bad cess to luck that brought me o'er
To work upon the railway.

In eighteen hundred and forty-five,
Dan O'Connell was then alive,
And Teddy McGuinness to my surprise
Was working on the railway.

In eighteen hundred and forty-six,
I got meself in the divils' own fix
For callin' some gents a parcel o' micks,
As works upon the railway.

In eighteen hundred and forty-seven,
Sweet Biddy McGee has gone to heaven,
If she left one child she left eleven
To work upon the railway.

In eighteen hundred and forty-eight,
I learned to take my whiskey straight.
'Tis a beautiful drink and can't be bate
For working on the railway.

In eighteen hundred and fifty-two,
My earthly career is almost through,
And there's nothing on earth that I can do
But work upon the railway.

In eighteen hundred and fifty-three,
The imps and the divil they took me
To work upon the machinery
In the Sub-terranean Railway.

CHRONOLOGY

BIOGRAPHICAL NOTES

NOTE ON THE TEXTS

NOTES

INDEXES

Chronology

1800   The Library of Congress established.

1801   Washington Allston begins art studies at the Royal Academy in London, under tutelage of Benjamin West. The New York *Evening Post* founded as Federalist newspaper by Alexander Hamilton, under editorship of William Coleman. *The Port Folio* (1801–27) founded by Joseph Dennie under pseudonym "Oliver Oldschool" (early contributors include Charles Brockden Brown and Royall Tyler).

1802   *The Boston Weekly Magazine* (later *The Emerald*) begins publication under the editorship of Samuel Gilbert and Thomas Dean of Boston, publishing some poetry along with fiction and theatrical reviews.

1803   Phineas Adams founds *The Monthly Anthology and Boston Review* (1803–11); after six months Adams succeeded as editor by the Rev. William Emerson, father of Ralph Waldo Emerson (contributors will include Washington Allston, William Cullen Bryant, Daniel Webster, and Joseph Story).

1804   Joel Barlow returns to America after 17 years in Europe. The Anthology Club (associated with the *The Monthly Anthology* and devoted to raising standards of American literature) founded in Boston.

1805   Joel Barlow publishes *Prospectus of a National Institution to be Established in the United States*, proposal for a national institute devoted to artistic and scientific research. The Boston Athenaeum (which eventually encompasses a library, a museum, and a laboratory) founded by members of the Anthology Club. At age 13, John Howard Payne publishes theatrical paper *The Thespian Mirror* (1805–06) in New York City. Samuel Woodworth publishes juvenile paper *The Fly* (1805–06), to which John Howard Payne contributes. In Rome, Washington Allston spends time with the visiting Washington Irving.

1806   John Howard Payne's *Thespian Mirror* attracts notice of
        William Coleman, editor of New York *Evening Post*;
        through Coleman's efforts Payne gains reputation as prod-
        igy and becomes acquainted with New York literary and
        theatrical circles; his play *Julia, or The Wanderer* produced
        in New York. In Rome, Washington Allston forms close
        friendship with Samuel Taylor Coleridge.

1807   Joel Barlow publishes *The Columbiad*, an extensive rework-
        ing of his epic *The Vision of Columbus* (1787). James Kirke
        Paulding collaborates with Washington Irving and Irving's
        brother William on *Salmagundi*. John Howard Payne
        issues first number of literary magazine *The Pastime*
        (1807–08), most of which he writes himself.

        Joel Barlow: *The Columbiad*.

1808   At his father's urging, William Cullen Bryant publishes
        The Embargo, an anti-Jeffersonian poetic satire written at
        age 13. Washington Allston returns to the U.S. to marry
        Ann Channing, sister of William Ellery Channing. Con-
        vention of the Universalists of New England publishes
        Hymns Composed by Different Authors, containing only
        American hymns (written by Hosea Ballou, Abner
        Kneeland, and Edward Turner).

        William Cullen Bryant: *The Embargo*.

1809   John Howard Payne makes acting debut in New York
        City. The Scottish poet Thomas Campbell publishes *Ger-
        trude of Wyoming*, narrative poem about a Pennsylvania
        Indian massacre.

        Philip Freneau: *Poems Written and Published During
          the American Revolutionary War*.
        Samuel Woodworth: *New-Haven*.

1810   Washington Allston reads a long poem (possibly "The
        Sylphs of the Seasons") at the Phi Beta Kappa Society of
        Harvard.

1811   Joel Barlow appointed by President Madison to negotiate
        trade agreement with France.

        Samuel Woodworth: *Beasts at Law*.

1812   Joel Barlow writes "Advice to a Raven in Russia" while in
         Vilna (now Vilnius, Lithuania) on diplomatic mission;
         caught up in Napoleon's retreat from Russia, contracts
         pneumonia and dies December 24 in a village near Cra-
         cow, Poland. American Antiquarian Society founded in
         Worcester, Massachusetts, by Isaiah Thomas.

         John Pierpont: *The Portrait*.
         Samuel Woodworth: *Quarter-Day*.

1813   Joseph Rodman Drake meets Fitz-Greene Halleck in New
         York. John Howard Payne settles in England. *The Analectic
         Magazine* (1813–21) begins publication in Philadelphia un-
         der editorship of Washington Irving; contributors include
         James Kirke Paulding and Gulian Verplanck.

         Washington Allston: *The Sylphs of the Seasons*.

1814   After being detained by the British during bombardment
         of Baltimore on September 14, Francis Scott Key writes
         "The Star-Spangled Banner"; the poem, published a few
         days later in *The Baltimore American*, achieves nationwide
         popularity. John Neal and John Pierpont open dry goods
         franchises in Baltimore, Boston, and Charleston; business
         fails within two years.

         Francis Scott Key: "The Star-Spangled Banner."

1815   *The North American Review* begins publication under edi-
         torship of William Tudor. Edward Coote Pinkney com-
         missioned as midshipman in U.S. Navy (serves until 1822).

         Philip Freneau: *A Collection of Poems on American Affairs*.
         John Howard Payne: *Lispings of the Muse*.
         Lydia Huntley Sigourney: *Moral Pieces in Prose and Verse*.
         Samuel Worcester: *Christian Psalmody*.

1816   John Pierpont publishes long poem *Airs of Palestine*. Jo-
         seph Rodman Drake writes fairy fantasy "The Culprit
         Fay" (poem not published until 14 years after his death).
         The Delphian Club founded in Baltimore; members in-
         clude John Neal, John Pierpont, Tobias Watkins, Francis
         Scott Key, and Samuel Woodworth; Neal serves as editor
         of the club's literary organ *The Portico* (1816–18).

         John Pierpont: *Airs of Palestine*.

1817   William Cullen Bryant's "Thanatopsis" and "Lines" (later retitled "Inscription for the Entrance to a Wood") sent by the poet's father (without Bryant's knowledge) to *The North American Review*; on publication there, the poems attract wide attention. Jared Sparks replaces William Tudor as editor of *North American Review*.

Manoah Bodman: *An Oration on Death*.
William Cullen Bryant: "Thanatopsis."

1818   Edward Tyrrel Channing becomes editor of *The North American Review*, with Richard Henry Dana as assistant; Dana contributes reviews of Irving, Hazlitt, and Washington Allston. Joseph Rodman Drake tours Europe with his wife. Washington Allston returns to United States, after five-year residence in England, settling in Boston.

William Cullen Bryant: "To a Waterfowl."
John Neal: *Battle of Niagara*.
James Kirke Paulding: *The Backwoodsman*.
Samuel Woodworth: "The Bucket."

1819   In the New York *Evening Post*, Joseph Rodman Drake and Fitz-Greene Halleck publish "The Croaker Papers," anonymous series of satirical poems of New York life. Edward Everett replaces Edward Tyrrel Channing as editor of *The North American Review*; Richard Henry Dana resigns from staff of the *Review*. John Pierpont becomes minister of the Hollis Street Church in Boston. Thomas Cole emigrates with family from Liverpool to America.

Joseph Rodman Drake and Fitz-Greene Halleck: "The Croaker Papers."
Fitz-Greene Halleck: *Fanny*.
John Neal: *Otho*.
Richard Henry Wilde: "The Lament of the Captive."

1820   John Neal resigns from Delphian Club. John Howard Payne imprisoned for debt in London. Joseph Rodman Drake dies in September in New York City.

Maria Gowen Brooks: *Judith, Esther, and Other Poems*.
James Wallis Eastburn and Robert C. Sands: *Yamoyden*.

1821   William Cullen Bryant reads "The Ages" to Phi Beta Kappa Society at Harvard. Richard Henry Dana founds

The Idle Man (1821–22); contributors include Bryant and Washington Allston. *The Saturday Evening Post* begins weekly publication in Philadelphia (early contributors include Edgar Allan Poe, Nathaniel Parker Willis, and James Fenimore Cooper). James Gates Percival publishes first verse collection, containing long poem "Prometheus."

Richard Henry Dana: "The Dying Raven."
Fitz-Greene Halleck: "On the Death of Joseph
    Rodman Drake."
James Gates Percival: *Poems.*

1822   William Cullen Bryant publishes first collection of verse. Fitz-Greene Halleck tours Europe. In New York City, the Bread and Cheese Club becomes informal gathering place for writers and artists including Bryant, Halleck, Thomas Cole, James Fenimore Cooper, and Asher B. Durand. The anthology *Specimens of the American Poets* published in London. Clement Moore reads "A Visit from St. Nicholas" to his family. Henry Rowe Schoolcraft appointed government agent for Indian affairs in the Great Lakes region, based at Sault Ste. Marie.

William Cullen Bryant: *Poems.*
Philip Freneau: "On the Civilization of the Western
    Aboriginal Country."
Fitz-Greene Halleck: "Alnwick Castle."
James Gates Percival: *Clio I*; *Clio II*; *Prometheus
    Part II with Other Poems.*
Lydia Huntley Sigourney: *Traits of the Aborigines.*
Carlos Wilcox: *The Age of Benevolence.*

1823   Clement Moore's "A Visit from St. Nicholas" published (without Moore's knowledge) in *The Troy Sentinel*. John Howard Payne writes "Home, Sweet Home" for the operetta *Clari*; song becomes immediate success. Maria Gowen Brooks moves to Cuba; begins epic poem *Zophiël, or the Bride of Seven*. George Pope Morris founds *The New-York Mirror and Ladies' Literary Gazette* (1823–57); Samuel Woodworth serves as editor for a year before being replaced by Morris (later editors include Nathaniel Parker Willis, Charles Fenno Hoffman, and Epes Sargent). John Neal challenged to a duel by Edward Coote Pinkney because of a satiric passage about Pinkney's father in Neal's novel *Randolph*; Neal begins four-year stay in England.

Clement Moore: "A Visit from St. Nicholas."
John Howard Payne: "Home, Sweet Home."
James Gates Percival: *Poems*.

1824   John Neal, in London, publishes survey of 135 American authors in *Blackwood's Magazine*. Thomas Cole, studying at Philadelphia Academy of Fine Arts, publishes poems in *The Saturday Evening Post*. Theophilus Parsons founds *The United States Literary Gazette* (1824–26) in Boston (contributors include William Cullen Bryant, Henry Wadsworth Longfellow, James Gates Percival, and Richard Henry Dana).

1825   William Cullen Bryant becomes co-editor of short-lived *New York Review and Athenaeum Magazine*, publishing among other work Fitz-Greene Halleck's "Marco Bozzaris"; delivers series of lectures on poetry to the American Athenaeum Society. Maria Gowen Brooks publishes the first canto of her epic poem *Zophiël, or the Bride of Seven*; begins correspondence with Robert Southey. Thomas Cole established as landscape painter in New York City. Henry D. Gilpin edits *The Atlantic Souvenir* (1825–31), first series of "gift book" anthologies designed as Christmas or New Year's presents (contributors include James Gates Percival, Lydia Maria Child, and James Kirke Paulding). Henry Wadsworth Longfellow and Nathaniel Hawthorne graduate from Bowdoin College.

William Cullen Bryant: "Forest Hymn."
Fitz-Greene Halleck: "Marco Bozzaris."
Edward Coote Pinkney: *Poems*.

1826   William Lloyd Garrison publishes poetry by John Greenleaf Whittier in Newburyport *Free Press*; Garrison visits Whittier at his family's farm in East Haverhill, and the two become close friends. With Charles Folsom, William Cullen Bryant co-edits *United States Review and Literary Gazette* (1826–27), merger of *United States Literary Gazette* and *New York Review and Athenaeum Magazine*. *The Casket* (renamed *Graham's Magazine* in 1841) begins publication under editorship of Samuel C. Atkinson.

Samuel Woodworth: *Melodies, Duets, Songs, and Ballads*.

1827   William Cullen Bryant, Robert Sands, and Gulian Verplanck publish *The Talisman*, first of three annual gift

books. Bryant delivers lectures on mythology at National Academy of the Arts of Design (series repeated in 1828, 1829, and 1831). John Neal returns from England to the U.S.; settles in Portland, Maine.

Richard Henry Dana: *The Buccaneer*.
Fitz-Greene Halleck: *Alnwick Castle, with Other Poems*.
James Gates Percival: *Clio No. III*.
Edgar Allan Poe: *Tamerlane and Other Poems*.
William Gilmore Simms: *Lyrical and Other Poems*; *Early Lays*.
Nathaniel Parker Willis: *Sketches*.

1828   Three poems by George Moses Horton, a North Carolina slave, published in *Lancaster Gazette* (Massachusetts). John Neal becomes editor of the Portland (Maine) *Yankee* (1828–29); publishes work by Edgar Allan Poe, John Greenleaf Whittier, and Henry Wadsworth Longfellow. William Gilmore Simms edits *Southern Literary Gazette* (1828–29). Edward Coote Pinkney dies in April in Baltimore, at age 26.

Fitz-Greene Halleck: "Red Jacket."
Carlos Wilcox: *Remains*.

1829   William Cullen Bryant becomes editor of the New York *Evening Post* upon the death of William Coleman. George Moses Horton's *The Hope of Liberty* published in unsuccessful attempt to subsidize purchase of the poet's freedom from slavery. After three years abroad, Henry Wadsworth Longfellow begins tenure teaching modern languages at Bowdoin College. Ralph Waldo Emerson becomes minister of Second Church of Boston. Thomas Cole leaves for three-year European visit; Bryant writes "To an American Painter, Departing for Europe." Samuel Kettell publishes *Specimens of American Poetry*, a comprehensive three-volume anthology of work from the 17th century onward. Nathaniel Parker Willis founds *The American Monthly Magazine* (1829–31), writing most of it himself. John Greenleaf Whittier edits *The American Manufacturer*, political paper in which he publishes many of his early poems.

George Moses Horton: *The Hope of Liberty*.
Samuel Kettell (editor): *Specimens of American Poetry*.

Edgar Allan Poe: *Al Aaraaf, Tamerlane, and Other Poems*.
William Gilmore Simms: *The Vision of Cortes, Cain,
   and Other Poems*.
Nathaniel Parker Willis: *Fugitive Poetry*.

1830   In Hartford, Connecticut, John Greenleaf Whittier edits
       The New England Weekly Review (1830–32), contributing
       many poems, articles, and sketches; forms friendship with
       Lydia Huntley Sigourney. Editor Edwin James appends
       translations of Ojibwa ritual songs to *A Narrative of the
       Captivity and Adventures of John Tanner*.

       Samuel Henry Dickson: "I Sigh for the Land of the
          Cypress and Pine."
       Oliver Wendell Holmes: "Old Ironsides."
       George Pope Morris: "The Oak" ("Woodman, Spare
          That Tree!").

1831   Maria Gowen Brooks visits Robert Southey in England.
       As foreign correspondent for *New-York Mirror*, Nathaniel
       Parker Willis sets out on four years of travel in Europe and
       Middle East.

       Edgar Allan Poe: *Poems*.
       John Greenleaf Whittier: *Legends of New-England
          in Prose and Verse*.

1832   William Cullen Bryant publishes first major collection of
       his work; meets with President Andrew Jackson and vari-
       ous members of his cabinet in Washington; on tour of
       Illinois prairie, sees ancient Indian mounds. Ralph Waldo
       Emerson resigns ministry and sails to Europe. Fitz-Greene
       Halleck goes to work as confidential clerk for John Jacob
       Astor. Fanny Kemble tours America with her father's the-
       atrical company. John Howard Payne returns penniless
       from Europe. William Davis Ticknor and John Allen
       found publishing house Allen and Ticknor in Boston
       (Allen leaves company after two years). Philip Freneau
       dies in December in blizzard near his home at Mount
       Pleasant, New Jersey.

       John Quincy Adams: *Dermot MacMorrogh; or,
          the Conquest of Ireland*.
       William Cullen Bryant: *Poems*.

Thomas Holley Chivers: *The Path of Sorrow, or the Lament of Youth*.
Thomas Hastings and Lowell Mason: *Spiritual Songs for Social Worship*.

1833   Maria Gowen Brooks' *Zophiël* published in England by Robert Southey. *The Knickerbocker* (1833–65) begins publication in New York under editorship of Charles Fenno Hoffman (contributors include Longfellow, Irving, Willis, Paulding, Halleck, Whittier, Holmes, and Bryant). William Gilmore Simms travels to New York; forms friendships with William Cullen Bryant and publisher Evert Duyckinck. Charles Fenno Hoffman travels in the West, 1833–34. Ralph Waldo Emerson travels in Italy, France, and England, meeting Walter Savage Landor, John Stuart Mill, Thomas Carlyle, Samuel Taylor Coleridge, and William Wordsworth. Henry Wadsworth Longfellow publishes translation of *Coplas por la muerte de su padre* by 15th-century Spanish poet Jorge Manrique.

Maria Gowen Brooks: *Zophiël, or the Bride of Seven*.
Richard Henry Dana: *Poems and Prose Writings*.

1834   Ralph Waldo Emerson settles in Concord. Bronson Alcott founds Masonic Temple School in Boston. John Greenleaf Whittier elected as Whig to Massachusetts legislature. Fanny Kemble marries Pierce Mease Butler in Philadelphia; retires from stage. *Southern Literary Messenger* (1834–64) begins publication in Richmond under editorship of James A. Heath, replaced the following year by Thomas W. White (contributors include Edgar Allan Poe, Richard Henry Wilde, Nathaniel Parker Willis, Lydia Huntley Sigourney, Philip Pendleton Cooke, and William Gilmore Simms). *The Ladies' Companion* (1834–44) begins publication in New York under editorship of William Snowden (contributors include Poe, Simms, Willis, Henry Wadsworth Longfellow, and James Kirke Paulding). Following newspaper controversy over authorship of Richard Henry Wilde's "The Lament of the Captive" (first published anonymously in 1819), Wilde acknowledges the poem as his.

Thomas Hastings: *The Mother's Nursery Songs*.
Lydia Huntley Sigourney: *Poems*.

1835   Henry Wadsworth Longfellow appointed Smith Professor
            of Modern Languages at Harvard; travels to Europe for
            year of further study; in Heidelberg, Germany, meets and
            spends much time with William Cullen Bryant. *The West-
            ern Messenger* (1835–41) begins publication in Cincinnati
            under editorship of Ephraim Peabody, subsequently re-
            placed by James Freeman Clarke (1836–39) and William
            Henry Channing (1840–41); initially associated closely
            with Unitarianism, the *Messenger*'s contributors include
            Ralph Waldo Emerson, Margaret Fuller, Jones Very,
            Christopher Pearse Cranch, William Ellery Channing,
            Charles Timothy Brooks, Theodore Parker, Elizabeth Pea-
            body, and Francis Parkman. Daniel K. Whitaker founds
            The Southern Literary Journal (1835–38) in Charleston, with
            William Gilmore Simms as chief contributor. Edgar Allan
            Poe works as editor on *Southern Literary Messenger*, con-
            tributing poems, stories, and reviews. Charles Fenno Hoff-
            man assumes editorship of *American Monthly Magazine*,
            1835–37. Joseph Rodman Drake's *The Culprit Fay* (edited
            by daughter Janet Halleck Drake) published 14 years after
            Drake's death. Christopher Pearse Cranch begins career as
            Unitarian minister. Traveling in Georgia, John Howard
            Payne meets John Ross, head of Cherokee Nation, and so-
            licits information on Cherokee history for prospective lit-
            erary magazine; arrested with Ross by Georgia militia,
            charged with abolitionism, and jailed for 13 days; writes
            newspaper account complaining of ill-treatment. John
            Pierpont travels to Holy Land. In England, Nathaniel
            Parker Willis attacked by Harriet Martineau and Frederick
            Marryat for journalistic indiscretion in publishing private
            conversations. James Gates Percival begins seven-year ser-
            vice as state geologist of Connecticut. Richard Henry
            Wilde settles in Florence; studies Dante and Italian lyric
            poets.

            Joseph Rodman Drake: *The Culprit Fay*.
            Nathaniel Parker Willis: *Melanie and Other Poems*.

1836   In *Southern Literary Messenger*, Edgar Allan Poe attacks in-
            flated reputation of Joseph Rodman Drake and Fitz-
            Greene Halleck: "That we have among us poets of the
            loftiest order we believe—but we do *not* believe that these
            poets are Drake and Halleck." Bronson Alcott publishes
            first volume of *Conversations with Children on the Gospels*;

Margaret Fuller works briefly as Alcott's assistant at his Temple School (1836–37), replacing Elizabeth Peabody. Fuller meets Ralph Waldo Emerson; spends three weeks as guest in his household. Emerson and Henry David Thoreau develop close friendship. In *The American Nations*, Constantine Rafinesque publishes translation of what he claims to be Leni-Lenâpé (Delaware) tribal chronicle "Walam Olum" with "the songs annexed thereto in the original language." Thomas Cole completes series of paintings "The Course of Empire."

Oliver Wendell Holmes: *Poems*.
Richard Henry Wilde: "To the Mocking Bird."

1837   The first issue of *The Gentleman's Magazine*, later *Burton's Gentleman's Magazine* (1837–40), appears in Philadelphia under editorship of William E. Burton (contributors include Edgar Allan Poe and Thomas Dunn English). *United States Magazine and Democratic Review* (1837–55) begins publication under editorship of John L. O'Sullivan and Samuel D. Langtree (contributors in early years include Poe, James Russell Lowell, John Greenleaf Whittier, William Gilmore Simms, and Bayard Taylor). At Lac-qui-parle mission, Stephen Return Riggs and his wife, Mary Ann, begin study of Sioux language. Charles Fenno Hoffman edits *The New-York Book of Poetry*, containing first book publication of Clement Moore's "A Visit from St. Nicholas." James Kirke Paulding appointed Secretary of the Navy by Martin Van Buren.

Thomas Holley Chivers: *Nacoochee*.
Charles Fenno Hoffman (editor): *The New-York Book of Poetry*.

1838   Following intense religious experience, Jones Very's sanity is questioned; he is forced to resign from Harvard Divinity School, and is briefly committed to McLean Asylum in Somerville, Massachusetts. Ralph Waldo Emerson delivers controversial address at Harvard Divinity School. Walt Whitman founds *The Long Islander* (1838–39). John Greenleaf Whittier becomes editor of *The Pennsylvania Freeman* (1838–40); in May, Pennyslvania Hall in Philadelphia is burned by anti-abolitionist mob, destroying Whittier's editorial office in the process. Oliver Wendell

Holmes becomes professor of anatomy and physiology at Dartmouth. Richard Henry Dana delivers lectures on Shakespeare in Providence, Rhode Island. Fanny Kemble begins six-month stay at her husband's Georgia plantation.

Josiah D. Canning: *Poems*.
Henry Wadsworth Longfellow: "A Psalm of Life."
John Greenleaf Whittier: *Poems*.

1839   Henry Wadsworth Longfellow publishes first verse collection, *Voices of the Night*, and romance *Hyperion*. Twenty-seven sonnets by Jones Very published by James Freeman Clarke in *The Western Messenger*, followed by *Essays and Poems* (prepared with the assistance of Ralph Waldo Emerson). Margaret Fuller initiates series of "conversations" in Boston, educational experiment (continued until 1844) intended to provide "a point of union to well-educated and thinking women, in a city which, with great pretensions to mental refinement, boasts, at present, nothing of the kind"; she interviews Washington Allston in connection with exhibit of his paintings in Boston. Bronson Alcott forced to close Masonic Temple School after charges of heterodoxy lead to decreased enrollment and severe indebtedness. Richard Henry Dana lectures on Shakespeare in Boston. George Graham takes over editorship of *The Casket*, eventually renaming it (in 1841) *Graham's Magazine*; turns it into important literary magazine (contributors include Edgar Allan Poe, James Russell Lowell, Lydia Huntley Sigourney, William Cullen Bryant, Thomas Buchanan Read, George Pope Morris, Henry Wadsworth Longfellow, Charles Fenno Hoffman, Fanny Osgood, and James Fenimore Cooper). *Littell's Living Age* founded under editorship of Eliakim Littell; contributors include Poe, Emerson, Fitz-Greene Halleck, and Nathaniel Parker Willis. *The Liberty Bell* (published irregularly between 1839 and 1857), abolitionist gift book, begins publication under editorship of Maria Weston Chapman and her sisters Anne Warren and Caroline (contributors include Emerson, Fuller, Longfellow, Lydia Maria Child, Frederick Douglass, James Russell Lowell, and Maria White Lowell). Henry Rowe Schoolcraft's *Algic Researches* is published, first major study of American Indian folklore. Herman Melville sails to Liverpool as crew member of trading ship *St. Lawrence*. Henry David Thoreau and his

brother John make 13-day trip on the Concord and Merrimack rivers.

Henry Wadsworth Longfellow: *Voices of the Night*.
Jones Very: *Essays and Poems*.

1840   Ralph Waldo Emerson and Margaret Fuller bring out first
issue of *The Dial* (1840–44) with Fuller as editor (other
contributors will include Henry David Thoreau, Christopher Pearse Cranch, Bronson Alcott, George Ripley, Theodore Parker, and Elizabeth Peabody). Cornelius Mathews
and Evert Duyckinck found *Arcturus* (1840–42) in New
York (contributors include Henry Wadsworth Longfellow,
Nathaniel Hawthorne, and James Russell Lowell). *The
Union Magazine* (1847–52) begins publication, edited by
Caroline M. Kirkland and others (contributors include
Lowell, Longfellow, Nathaniel Parker Willis, Lydia Huntley Sigourney, Charles Fenno Hoffman, and Fanny Osgood). Edgar Allan Poe writes to Thomas Holley Chivers,
then in New York, in effort to solicit funding for Poe's
prospective *Penn Magazine* (never published). John
Howard Payne travels from Washington with John Ross to
the latter's home in Indian Territory (later Oklahoma);
meets Sequoya, creator of Cherokee alphabet. Christopher
Pearse Cranch meets Ralph Waldo Emerson in Boston.
Lydia Huntley Sigourney travels to Europe, where she
meets William Wordsworth and Thomas Carlyle.

William Cullen Bryant (editor): *Selections from the
    American Poets*.
Philip Pendleton Cooke: "Florence Vane."

1841   Cooperative community Brook Farm, offshoot of Transcendental Club, established near West Roxbury, Massachusetts, by George Ripley and others; residents include
Nathaniel Hawthorne, George William Curtis, and
Charles Anderson Dana. Edgar Allan Poe becomes literary
editor of *Graham's Magazine*. Ephraim George Squier
founds *The Poet's Magazine* in Albany. William Cullen
Bryant and Thomas Cole go on walking tour of the
Catskills. Lydia Maria Child moves to New York to assume editorship of *The National Anti-Slavery Standard* (remains as editor until 1844). Dismissed from position as
Indian agent in Sault Ste. Marie, Henry Rowe Schoolcraft

moves to New York City. Herman Melville sails for South
Seas on whaling ship *Acushnet*.

Ralph Waldo Emerson: *Essays*.
Henry Wadsworth Longfellow: *Ballads and Other Poems*.
James Russell Lowell: *A Year's Life*.
Cornelius Mathews: *Wakondah: The Master of Life*.
Lydia Huntley Sigourney: *Pocahontas and Other Poems*;
      Poems, Religious and Elegiac.

1842   Charles Dickens visits the United States and meets
            William Cullen Bryant, Richard Henry Dana, Sr. and Jr.,
            Fitz-Greene Halleck, Cornelius Mathews, Edgar Allan
            Poe, and other literary figures. John Greenleaf Whittier
            runs for Congress as Liberty Party candidate. Ralph Waldo
            Emerson succeeds Margaret Fuller as editor of *The Dial*.
            Poe resigns from *Graham's Magazine*, complaining of
            inadequate compensation. Daniel K. Whitaker founds
            Southern Quarterly Review (1842–57). *Arcturus* absorbed
            into *Boston Miscellany of Literature and Fashion* (1842–43)
            under editorship of Nathan Hale, Jr. (contributors include
            Poe, James Russell Lowell, Cornelius Mathews, and Evert
            Duyckinck). Nathaniel Hawthorne settles in Concord
            with his wife, Sophia Peabody. With financial assistance
            from Emerson, Bronson Alcott travels to England; meets
            Thomas Carlyle. William Ellery Channing marries Ellen
            Fuller, sister of Margaret Fuller; settles in Concord.
            William Cullen Bryant visits William Gilmore Simms in
            Florida. John Howard Payne appointed American consul
            at Tunis by President John Tyler. Herman Melville deserts
            whaling ship *Acushnet* in the Marquesas.

            Charles Timothy Brooks (editor and translator): *Songs
                and Ballads*.
            William Cullen Bryant: *The Fountain and Other Poems*.
            Christopher Pearse Cranch (translator): *The Aeneid*.
            Rufus Griswold (editor): *The Poets and Poetry of America*.
            Henry Wadsworth Longfellow: *Poems on Slavery*.

1843   Bronson Alcott attempts to establish utopian community
            at Fruitlands, a farm near Harvard, Massachusetts (ex-
            periment abandoned in 1845). James Russell Lowell and
            Robert Carter found short-lived magazine *The Pioneer*
            (January–June); contributors include Jones Very, William

Wetmore Story, John Neal, John Greenleaf Whittier, and Edgar Allan Poe ("The Rationale of Verse"). Poe lectures on "Poets and Poetry of America." Ralph Waldo Emerson completes translation of Dante's *La Vita Nuova*. Henry David Thoreau's translation of Aeschylus' *Prometheus Bound* and *Seven Against Thebes* published in *The Dial*. Daniel Decatur Emmett's Virginia Minstrels make debut at Bowery Amphitheatre in New York City. James T. Fields admitted as junior partner of Ticknor and Company. Washington Allston dies in Cambridge, Massachusetts.

William Ellery Channing: *Poems*.
Thomas Dunn English: "Ben Bolt."
Henry Wadsworth Longfellow: *The Spanish Student*.
Cornelius Mathews: *Poems on Man in His Various Aspects under the American Republic*.
James Gates Percival: *The Dream of a Day, and Other Poems*.
John Pierpont: *Anti-Slavery Poems*.
John Greenleaf Whittier: *Lays of My Home and Other Poems*.
Nathaniel Parker Willis: *Poems of Passion*.

1844   Margaret Fuller moves to New York, upon invitation of Horace Greeley to become book reviewer for *New-York Daily Tribune*; during three-year residence, immerses herself in literary life, meeting writers and critics including Edgar Allan Poe, Lydia Maria Child, Anne Lynch, William Gilmore Simms, Evert Duyckinck, Cornelius Mathews, and Christopher Pearse Cranch. James Russell Lowell marries Maria White. At 19, Bayard Taylor publishes first collection of poetry and begins two years of travel in Europe as foreign correspondent for *The Saturday Evening Post* and other papers. Whittier asks Longfellow to run for Congress as candidate of the abolitionist Liberty Party; Longfellow turns down the offer, stating, "I am not a member of any society, and fight under no single banner . . . Partizan warfare becomes too violent—too vindictive for my taste." William Cullen Bryant builds new residence, Springbank, in Roslyn, New York. Translations of Pindar by Henry David Thoreau published in *The Dial*.

William Cullen Bryant: *The White Footed Deer and Other Poems*.

Christopher Pearse Cranch: *Poems*.
Samuel Henry Dickson: *Poems*.
Ralph Waldo Emerson: *Essays: Second Series*.
Fanny Kemble: *Poems*.
Clement Moore: *Poems*.
Bayard Taylor: *Ximena, or The Battle of the Sierra Morena*.
Dan Emmit's Original Banjo Melodies (including
   "The Blue-Tail Fly").

1845   Edgar Allan Poe's "The Raven" published in the *New-York
Mirror*. Poe becomes editor of the *Broadway Journal*
(1845–46); other contributors include Richard Henry
Dana, Lydia Maria Child, Thomas Dunn English, Margaret Fuller, and William Gilmore Simms. In the *Journal's*
pages, Poe resumes attacks on Longfellow (begun in *Burton's Gentleman's Magazine* and New York *Evening Mirror*),
charging him with plagiarism. Longfellow, in response to
the *Journal's* attacks, remarks in letter to James Russell
Lowell: "I have had nothing to do with the discussion,
and shall have nothing to do with it; as I consider, with
you, life too precious to be wasted in street brawls." Poe
meets Evert Duyckinck (who selects 12 stories for *Tales*,
published in July) and is visited at *Broadway Journal* office
by Walt Whitman. Thomas Holley Chivers arrives in New
York to arrange for publication of *The Lost Pleiad*; meets
Poe; Poe reviews Chivers' book favorably in the *Broadway
Journal*. Critical discussion of Poe's work published in
leading French literary journal *La Revue des Deux Mondes*.
James Russell Lowell writes editorials for abolitionist
paper *The Pennsylvania Freeman*. William Gilmore Simms
edits *The Southern and Western Monthly Magazine and Review* (January–December), writing most of it himself;
other contributors include Thomas Holley Chivers, James
Mathewes Legaré, Albert Pike, Caroline Lee Hentz, and
Evert Duyckinck. George Ripley edits Fourierist journal
The Harbinger (1845–49); contributors include Christopher Pearse Cranch, James Russell Lowell, Thomas Wentworth Higginson, Horace Greeley, John Greenleaf
Whittier, and William Wetmore Story. Thomas Dunn English edits short-lived magazine *The Aristidean*, to which
Poe and Whitman contribute. After years of conflict with
his congregation over his temperance and anti-slavery
views, John Pierpont resigns ministry of Hollis Street Uni-
tarian Church in Boston. William Cullen Bryant sails for

Europe; meets Thomas Moore and Leigh Hunt. William Wetmore Story commissioned to sculpt memorial to his late father, the Supreme Court justice Joseph Story. Fanny Kemble, separated from husband Pierce Butler, returns to London. Henry David Thoreau begins 26-month residence at Walden Pond. Maria Gowen Brooks dies in November in Cuba. Henry Rowe Schoolcraft publishes examples of Ojibwa poetry in *Oneóta; or, Characteristics of the Red Race of America.*

Thomas Holley Chivers: *The Lost Pleiad.*
George Moses Horton: *The Poetical Works of George M. Horton, the Colored Bard of North Carolina.*
James Russell Lowell: *Conversations on Some of the Old Poets.*
Edgar Allan Poe: *The Raven and Other Poems.*
Henry Rowe Schoolcraft: *Oneóta; or, Characteristics of the Red Race of America.*

1846   Margaret Fuller departs for Europe as foreign correspondent for the *New-York Tribune.* In *Godey's Lady's Book*, Poe publishes series of sketches of "The Literati of New York City"; Thomas Dunn English, incensed at description of him, attacks Poe's character in *Evening Mirror*; Poe successfully sues for damages. Poe moves with family to cottage in Fordham, New York. Walt Whitman works for Brooklyn *Daily Eagle. The National Press* begins publication under editorship of George Pope Morris and Nathaniel Parker Willis; name changes within the year to *The Home Journal* (1846–1901). Christopher Pearse Cranch travels to Italy; forms close friendship with Robert and Elizabeth Barrett Browning.

Ralph Waldo Emerson: *Poems.*
Frances Sargent Osgood: *Poems.*
William Gilmore Simms: *Areytos; or, Songs of the South.*
John Greenleaf Whittier: *Voices of Freedom.*

1847   Oliver Wendell Holmes becomes professor of anatomy and physiology at Harvard Medical School. John Greenleaf Whittier becomes an editor of *The National Era* (remains until 1860). *The Literary World* (1847–53) begins weekly publication in New York under editorship of Evert Duyckinck (temporarily replaced by Charles Fenno Hoffman, May 1847–September 1848); contributors include

Charles Timothy Brooks, James Kirke Paulding, and William Gilmore Simms. Herman Melville marries Elizabeth Shaw and moves to New York City. Edgar Allan Poe's young wife, Virginia, dies of tuberculosis. Ralph Waldo Emerson visits England; meets with Thomas Carlyle, Charles Dickens, William Wordsworth, and Alfred Tennyson. Richard Henry Wilde dies in September in New Orleans.

Henry Howard Brownell: *Poems*.
Philip Pendleton Cooke: *Froissart Ballads and Other Poems*.
William Ellery Channing: *Conversations in Rome between
    an Artist, a Catholic, and a Critic*; *Poems: Second Series*.
Fitz-Greene Halleck: *Works*.
Henry Wadsworth Longfellow: *Evangeline*.
Edgar Allan Poe: *Eureka: A Prose Poem*.
Epes Sargent: *Songs of the Sea with Other Poems*.
William Wetmore Story: *Poems*.
A Collection of Millenial Hymns, Shaker hymnal.

1848   In a single year, James Russell Lowell publishes four important books of poetry. Edgar Allan Poe delivers "The Poetic Principle" as lecture in Providence, Rhode Island. Poe meets Sarah Helen Whitman; proposes marriage to her; engagement is broken off after three months. George Boyer Vashon becomes first black lawyer in the state of New York. Walt Whitman founds *Brooklyn Freeman* (1848–49). Bayard Taylor becomes literary editor of *New-York Tribune* under Horace Greeley's editorship. Charles Godfrey Leland briefly caught up in revolutionary struggle in Paris. Ralph Waldo Emerson, also in Paris, meets Alexis de Tocqueville. Thomas Cole dies in February in Catskill, New York; eulogized by William Cullen Bryant at New York's Academy of Music.

John Quincy Adams: *Poems of Religion and Society*.
George Henry Boker: *A Lesson of Life*.
Stephen Foster: *Songs of the Sable Harmonists*.
Rufus Griswold (editor): *The Female Poets of America*.
James Mathewes Legaré: *Orta-Undis and Other Poems*.
James Russell Lowell: *The Biglow Papers*; *A Fable for
    Critics*; *The Vision of Sir Launfal*; *Poems: Second Series*.
William Gilmore Simms: *Lays of the Palmetto*.
Music of the Ethiopian Serenaders (including "Buffalo
    Gals").

1849   Edgar Allan Poe dies after being found delirious on Balti-
        more street. Longfellow writes to a correspondent: "What
        a melancholy death is that of Mr. Poe, a man so richly
        endowed with genius! . . . The harshness of his criti-
        cisms, I have never attributed to anything but the irrita-
        tion of a sensitive nature chafed by some indefinite sense
        of wrong." Rufus Griswold writes damaging obituary of
        Poe for *New-York Tribune*. Asher B. Durand paints "Kin-
        dred Spirits," double portrait of William Cullen Bryant
        and Thomas Cole in the Catskills. Bryant travels to Cuba
        in the early part of the year, then sails for Europe in June.
        Bayard Taylor reports on California gold rush for *New-
        York Tribune*. Josiah Gilbert Holland becomes assistant
        editor of *The Springfield Republican* in Massachusetts.
        William Gilmore Simms takes over editorship of *Southern
        Quarterly Review*. Ticknor and Company changes imprint
        to Ticknor, Reed and Fields. Henry Rowe Schoolcraft re-
        ceives U.S. government commission to compile survey of
        American Indians (published in six volumes as *History,
        Condition and Prospects of the Indian Tribes of the United
        States*, 1851–57). Margaret Fuller, involved in Italian revo-
        lution, flees from Rome to Italian mountain village with
        the Marchese Ossoli and their child after the fall of the
        Roman republic. Following recurrent attacks of mental ill-
        ness, Charles Fenno Hoffman confined to Harrisburg
        (Pennsylvania) Insane Asylum (remains there until his
        death in 1884).

        William Ellery Channing: *The Woodman and Other Poems*.
        Stephen Foster: *Foster's Ethiopian Melodies*.
        Henry Wadsworth Longfellow: *The Seaside and
            the Fireside*.
        Edgar Allan Poe: "Annabel Lee"; "The Bells."
        William Gilmore Simms: *The Cassique of Accabee*.
        Bayard Taylor: *Rhymes of Travel, Ballads, and Poems*.
        Henry David Thoreau: *A Week on the Concord and
            Merrimack Rivers*.
        John Greenleaf Whittier: *Poems*.

1850   John Greenleaf Whittier writes "Ichabod" to protest
        Daniel Webster's support of Fugitive Slave Law. Return-
        ing from Europe, Margaret Fuller dies on July 19 with
        husband and son in shipwreck off Fire Island; at Ralph
        Waldo Emerson's request, Henry David Thoreau goes to

site of wreck to search for her effects and manuscripts. Thomas Holley Chivers, charged by Jedediah Hunt with imitating Poe and others, responds: "Poe stole every thing that is worthy any thing from me . . . Poe stole all his *Raven* from me; but was the greatest Poetical Critic that ever existed." Rufus Griswold publishes edition of the works of Poe, altering some letters included in it, and further attacks Poe's character in attached "Memoir." Nathaniel Hawthorne settles in Lenox, Massachusetts, and forms friendship with Herman Melville, who had recently published highly favorable review of Hawthorne's short stories. Alice Cary travels from Ohio to New England and meets John Greenleaf Whittier; later in the year moves to New York City, joined by her sisters Phoebe and Elmina. Bayard Taylor reads Phi Beta Kappa poem at Harvard; wins prize offered by P. T. Barnum for poem to be sung by celebrated Swedish singer Jenny Lind on her appearance at New York's Castle Garden. In Washington, with John Howard Payne in the audience, Jenny Lind sings "Home, Sweet Home." *Harper's New Monthly Magazine* founded under editorship of Henry J. Raymond. Rufus Griswold edits *International Weekly Miscellany* (1850–52), assisted by Charles Godfrey Leland; contributors include Bayard Taylor, Alice Cary, Constance Fenimore Woolson, Nathaniel Hawthorne, and William Gilmore Simms. Philip Pendleton Cooke dies in January in Martinsburg, Virginia, at age 33.

Washington Allston: *Lectures on Art, and Poems* (edited by Richard Henry Dana).
Alice and Phoebe Cary: *Poems*.
Thomas Holley Chivers: *Eonchs of Ruby*.
William H. C. Hosmer: *Indian Traditions and Songs*; *Legends of the Senecas*.
William Gilmore Simms: *The City of the Silent*.
John Greenleaf Whittier: *Songs of Labor*; "Ichabod!"

1851   Bayard Taylor departs for two years of travel in Egypt, Abyssinia, the Middle East, India, China, and Japan.

Stephen Foster: "Old Folks at Home."
Henry Wadsworth Longfellow: *The Golden Legend*.
Herman Melville: *Moby-Dick*.
Bayard Taylor: *A Book of Romances, Lyrics, and Songs*.

1852   On visit to U.S., William Makepeace Thackeray meets
        Henry Wadsworth Longfellow, Christopher Pearse
        Cranch, Richard Henry Dana, Oliver Wendell Holmes,
        and James Russell Lowell. John James Piatt and William
        Dean Howells become friends while working on the staff
        of *The Ohio State Journal*. *The Golden Era* (1852–94)
        founded in San Francisco under editorship of J. Macdon-
        ough Foard and Rollin M. Daggett; contributors include
        John Rollin Ridge, Bret Harte, Mark Twain, and Adah
        Isaacs Menken. At the New-York Historical Society, with
        Daniel Webster presiding, William Cullen Bryant eulo-
        gizes James Fenimore Cooper, who had died at end of
        1851. John Howard Payne dies in April in Tunis while serv-
        ing as American consul. Poems of Margaret Fuller in-
        cluded in posthumous *The Memoirs of Margaret Fuller
        Ossoli*. Charles Baudelaire publishes the first of his critical
        studies of Edgar Allan Poe.

        Josiah D. Canning: *The Harp and Plow.*
        Alice Cary: *Lyra and Other Poems.*
        Edmund Hamilton Sears: "It Came Upon the Midnight
            Clear."
        A Sacred Repository of Anthems and Hymns (Shaker
            hymnal).

1853   Nathaniel Hawthorne sails to Liverpool to serve as U.S.
        consul; Henry Wadsworth Longfellow gives him a fare-
        well dinner where guests include Ralph Waldo Emerson,
        James Russell Lowell, and Charles Eliot Norton. Bronson
        Alcott embarks on first of his lecture tours in the West.
        Putnam's Monthly Magazine begins publication under edi-
        torship of Charles F. Briggs, with early contributions
        from Longfellow, Lowell, Henry David Thoreau, Herman
        Melville, Fitz-James O'Brien, and Bayard Taylor. Maria
        White Lowell dies in October.

        Charles Timothy Brooks: *Songs of Field and Flood*;
            (translator) *German Lyrics.*
        Thomas Holley Chivers: *Memoralia*; *Virginalia*; *Atlanta.*
        Stephen Foster: "My Old Kentucky Home."
        William Gilmore Simms: *Poems: Descriptive, Legendary,
            and Contemplative.*
        James Monroe Whitfield: *America and Other Poems.*
        Sarah Helen Whitman: *Hours of Life and Other Poems.*
        John Greenleaf Whittier: *The Chapel of the Hermits.*

1854   Frances Ellen Watkins Harper works for Underground
            Railroad. James T. Fields enters into full partnership with
            William Davis Ticknor; authors published under their im-
            print, Ticknor & Fields, include Longfellow, Emerson,
            Holmes, Lowell, Hawthorne, Thoreau, Harriet Beecher
            Stowe, Bayard Taylor, and Julia Ward Howe. Bret Harte
            moves from New York to California.

            Benjamin Paul Blood: *The Bride of the Iconoclast*.
            Phoebe Cary: *Poems and Parodies*.
            Stephen Foster: "Jeanie with the Light Brown Hair."
            Frances Ellen Watkins Harper: *Poems on Miscellaneous
                Subjects*.
            Bayard Taylor: *Poems of the Orient*.
            Henry David Thoreau: *Walden*.
            George Boyer Vashon: "Vincent Ogé."

1855   Walt Whitman publishes *Leaves of Grass* at his own ex-
            pense; Ralph Waldo Emerson writes to him upon receiv-
            ing it, "I give you joy of your free & brave thought . . . I
            greet you at the beginning of a great career, which yet
            must have had a long foreground somewhere, for such a
            start." James Russell Lowell succeeds Longfellow as pro-
            fessor of Romance languages and literature at Harvard;
            arranges for posthumous publication of *The Poems of
            Maria Lowell*; delivers lectures on English poets at Lowell
            Institute of Boston. Henry Wadsworth Longfellow pub-
            lishes *The Song of Hiawatha*; sends copy to Henry Rowe
            Schoolcraft, writing: "Without your books I could not
            have written mine." During visit to England, Frederick
            Goddard Tuckerman is guest at Alfred Tennyson's home
            on Isle of Wight. Evert and George Duyckinck publish
            Cyclopaedia of American Literature, containing biographical
            sketches of many poets.

            George Henry Boker: *Francesca da Rimini*.
            Alice Cary: *Poems*.
            Thomas Dunn English: *Poems*.
            Paul Hamilton Hayne: *Poems*.
            Henry Wadsworth Longfellow: *The Song of Hiawatha*.
            Maria White Lowell: *Poems*.
            Bayard Taylor: *Poems of Home and Travel*.
            Walt Whitman: *Leaves of Grass*.

1856   Bronson Alcott and Henry David Thoreau visit Walt Whitman in Brooklyn (Thoreau afterward writes of Whitman: "He occasionally suggests something a little more than human. You can't confound him with the other inhabitants of Brooklyn or New York"). William Gilmore Simms begins series of pro-slavery lectures in New York; forced to cancel tour after hostile public reaction in Buffalo and Rochester. William Makepeace Thackeray, on visit to New York, forms friendship with Bayard Taylor; later in the year Taylor visits Alexander von Humboldt in Berlin. Giving up law for career as artist, William Wetmore Story settles in Rome. Herman Melville sets out on voyage to Europe and the Holy Land; in Liverpool in November meets briefly with Nathaniel Hawthorne. James Gates Percival dies in May at Hazel Green, Wisconsin.

George Henry Boker: *Plays and Poems*.
Charles Timothy Brooks (translator): *Faust*.
George Clark (editor): *The Harp of Freedom*
    (abolitionist songbook).
Walt Whitman: *Leaves of Grass* (second enlarged edition).
John Greenleaf Whittier: *The Panorama and Other Poems*.

1857   *Atlantic Monthly* begins publication under editorship of James Russell Lowell; early contributors include Ralph Waldo Emerson, Henry Wadsworth Longfellow, John Greenleaf Whittier, Harriet Beecher Stowe, Rose Terry Cooke, and Thomas Wentworth Higginson; Oliver Wendell Holmes' series "The Autocrat of the Breakfast-Table" is widely popular. Paul Hamilton Hayne edits *Russell's Magazine* (1857–60) in Charleston, an outgrowth of literary circle centered on John Russell's bookstore; contributors include William Gilmore Simms, Henry Timrod, and Samuel Henry Dickson. *Harper's Weekly* begins publication with Theodore Sedgwick as editor (subsequent editors include George William Curtis, Carl Schurz, and John Kendrick Bangs). Charles Godfrey Leland publishes first Hans Breitmann poems in *Graham's Magazine*. Henry David Thoreau meets John Brown. William Cullen Bryant sails for Europe. Herman Melville keeps journal of his travels in the Holy Land, material later to be used in *Clarel*.

Paul Hamilton Hayne: *Sonnets and Other Poems*.

1858   In Florence, William Cullen Bryant meets Nathaniel Haw-
            thorne while staying with Robert Browning; also spends
            time with Walter Savage Landor. Thomas Holley Chivers
            dies in December in Decatur, Georgia.

            Josiah Gilbert Holland: *Bitter-Sweet*.
            Oliver Wendell Holmes: *The Autocrat of the
               Breakfast-Table*.
            Henry Wadsworth Longfellow: *The Courtship of Miles
               Standish*.
            John A. Stone: *Put's Golden Songster* (including
               "Sweet Betsey from Pike").

1859   Henry David Thoreau speaks in Concord, Boston, and
            Worcester in defense of John Brown; aids fugitive member
            of Brown's party in his escape to Canada. *Vanity Fair*
            (1859–63) begins publication under editorship of William
            Allan Stephens, an outgrowth of bohemian circle fre-
            quenting Pfaff's beer cellar in New York; contributors in-
            clude Thomas Bailey Aldrich, Charles Godfrey Leland,
            Fitz-James O'Brien, Ada Clare, Edmund Clarence Sted-
            man, and Fitz Hugh Ludlow.

            Daniel Decatur Emmett: "Dixie's Land" ("Dixie").

1860   In February, William Cullen Bryant introduces Abraham
            Lincoln at Cooper Union, New York. Walt Whitman
            meets in Boston with Ralph Waldo Emerson, who urges
            him to tone down sexual elements of "Children of Adam"
            poems in new third edition of *Leaves of Grass*. Sarah Helen
            Whitman defends Poe's reputation in *Edgar Poe and His
            Critics*. William Dean Howells publishes campaign biogra-
            phy of Lincoln. On visit to Concord, Howells meets
            Emerson, Hawthorne, Lowell, and Holmes. Charles God-
            frey Leland takes over editorship of *Vanity Fair*, 1860–61.
            Moncure Daniel Conway publishes *The Dial* in Cincin-
            nati; contributors include Emerson, Howells, and Frank-
            lin Sanborn; it fails after a year. As editorialist for *The
            Northern Californian* (Arcata, California), Bret Harte pro-
            tests massacre of Wiyot Indians at Humboldt Bay.

            Elizabeth Akers Allen: "Rock Me to Sleep."
            Stephen Foster: "Old Black Joe."
            Paul Hamilton Hayne: *Avolio*.

William Dean Howells and John James Piatt: *Poems of Two Friends*.
Thomas Buchanan Read: *Complete Poetical Works*.
Edmund Clarence Stedman: *Poems Lyrical and Idyllic*.
Henry Timrod: *Poems*.
Frederick Goddard Tuckerman: *Poems*.
John Greenleaf Whittier: *Home Ballads, Poems and Lyrics*.

1861   John Hay travels to Washington as Abraham Lincoln's assistant private secretary. George Henry Boker founds Union League of Philadelphia. William Dean Howells appointed American consul in Venice. Edmund Clarence Stedman works as Civil War correspondent for New York *World*. John Banister Tabb travels to England to help arrange transport of supplies to Confederacy. Henry Adams, as London correspondent of *New York Times*, reports British reaction to Civil War. Ambrose Bierce joins 9th Indiana Infantry Regiment of Union Army. Edward Rowland Sill delivers acclaimed commencement poem at Yale. Charles Godfrey Leland edits *The Knickerbocker*, 1861–62; during his term writes most material himself, but also publishes work by William Dean Howells, Thomas Bailey Aldrich, Fitz Hugh Ludlow, and Fitz-James O'Brien. Henry David Thoreau travels to Minnesota; visits Lower Sioux Agency at Redwood. John James Piatt and Sarah Morgan Bryan married in Louisville, Kentucky. On July 9 Henry Wadsworth Longfellow's wife, Fanny, is fatally burned when burning sealing wax sets her dress on fire; Longfellow, attempting to save her, also burned severely. Adah Isaacs Menken gives her first performance in title role of *Mazeppa* in Albany, New York. Spiritual "Let My People Go " published in *The National Anti-Slavery Standard* under title "The Contrabands' Freedom Hymn." First printed version of "John Brown's Body."

Rose Terry Cooke: *Poems*.
Henry Wadsworth Longfellow: "Paul Revere's Ride."
James Ryder Randall: "Maryland, My Maryland."
Henry Timrod: "Ethnogenesis."
Henry Clay Work: "Kingdom Coming."

1862   Walt Whitman works in army hospitals in New York. William Cullen Bryant meets with Abraham Lincoln. Abram Joseph Ryan joins Confederate Army as unofficial

chaplain. On leave from his regiment, Henry Timrod works as Civil War correspondent for *Charleston Mercury*; soon is forced to withdraw from service because of poor health. Henry Howard Brownell accepts position as acting ensign under Admiral David Farragut, who is impressed by Brownell's nautical poetry. Bayard Taylor travels to St. Petersburg as secretary of American legation. Emily Dickinson in the course of the year writes over 360 poems; in April, encloses four poems in a letter to Thomas Wentworth Higginson. Henry David Thoreau dies in Concord; Emerson delivers address at his funeral.

Oliver Wendell Holmes: *Songs in Many Keys*.
Julia Ward Howe: "The Battle Hymn of the Republic."
Thomas Buchanan Read: *The Wagoner of the Alleghanies*.
Bayard Taylor: *The Poet's Journal*.

1863   Offices of New York *Evening Post* attacked by draft rioters. Walt Whitman settles in Washington, D.C., where he serves as volunteer nurse in military hospitals, caring for both Union and Confederate wounded; supports himself by working in Army Paymaster's office. Revised edition of Frederick Goddard Tuckerman's *Poems* published in London. Performing in San Francisco, Adah Isaacs Menken meets Bret Harte and other local literary figures.

Henry Wadsworth Longfellow: *Tales of a Wayside Inn*.

1864   Sidney Lanier captured on Confederate blockade runner and imprisoned for four months in Maryland. John Banister Tabb taken prisoner by Union forces; meets Lanier in prison. James Russell Lowell begins tenure as co-editor (with Charles Eliot Norton) of *The North American Review*. Henry Timrod becomes associate editor of *The Daily South Carolinian*. New York's Century Club celebrates 70th birthday of William Cullen Bryant. Adah Isaacs Menken opens as Mazeppa in Virginia City (where she meets Mark Twain) and in London (where she meets Charles Dickens and Charles Reade). Stephen Foster dies in January in Bellevue Hospital, New York City. Nathaniel Hawthorne dies in May in Concord. Henry Rowe Schoolcraft dies in December in Washington, D.C.

George Henry Boker: *Poems of the War*.
Henry Howard Brownell: *Lyrics of a Day, or Newspaper Poems*.
Robert Lowry: "Beautiful River" ("Shall We Gather at the River").
Edmund Clarence Stedman: *Alice of Monmouth*.
John Greenleaf Whittier: *In War Time and Other Poems*.

1865   Henry Timrod reduced to poverty by burning of Columbia, South Carolina, by Sherman's army. George Moses Horton escapes from slavery and reaches Sherman's army in Raleigh, North Carolina; publishes final collection of poems, *Naked Genius*. At Harvard ceremony on July 21, James Russell Lowell reads ode commemorating Harvard students who fought in the Civil War. Helen Hunt Jackson meets Thomas Wentworth Higginson; with his encouragement begins to publish poetry and prose. Walt Whitman works briefly as clerk in Department of Interior; dismissed, allegedly because of official disapproval of his poetry. Opening in Paris, Adah Isaacs Menken meets George Sand and Théophile Gautier. Lydia Huntley Sigourney dies in June in Hartford, Connecticut.

George Moses Horton: *Naked Genius*.
J. N. Plotts (editor): *Poetical Tributes to the Memory of Abraham Lincoln*.
Thomas Buchanan Read: *A Summer Story, Sheridan's Ride, and Other Poems*.
Walt Whitman: *Drum-Taps*; *Sequel to Drum Taps*.
Henry Clay Work: "Marching Through Georgia."

1866   Herman Melville begins 19-year tenure as District Inspector of Customs in New York. William Cullen Bryant travels in Spain and in Italy (where he meets with Garibaldi). Joaquin Miller elected county judge in Canyon City, Oregon. *The Galaxy* (1866–78) founded under editorship of William C. Church and Francis P. Church; contributors include Mark Twain, Henry James, Walt Whitman, Sidney Lanier, Emma Lazarus, Bayard Taylor, and Edmund Clarence Stedman. Bret Harte edits *Outcroppings*, anthology of California poets. Adah Isaacs Menken opens in Paris in *Les Pirates de la Savane*; meets Aléxandre Dumas.

Henry Howard Brownell: *War Lyrics and Other Poems*.
Alice Cary: *Ballads, Lyrics and Hymns*.

Herman Melville: *Battle-Pieces and Aspects of the War*.
John James Piatt: *Poems in Sunshine and Firelight*.
Thomas Buchanan Read: *Poetical Works*.
Abram Joseph Ryan: "Lines" ("Gather the sacred dust").
Bayard Taylor: *The Picture of St. John*.
John Greenleaf Whittier: *Snow-Bound*.

1867   William Francis Allen, Charles Pickard Ware, and Lucy
McKim Garrison publish *Slave Songs of the United States*,
first important collection of spirituals. "Negro Spirituals,"
by Thomas Wentworth Higginson, appears in *Atlantic
Monthly*. Richard Henry Wilde's *Hesperia* published 20
years after his death. In London, Adah Isaacs Menken
meets Dante Gabriel Rossetti and Algernon Swinburne.
Nathaniel Parker Willis dies in January at home near
Tarrytown, New York; at funeral, pallbearers include
Richard Henry Dana, Henry Wadsworth Longfellow, Oliver
Wendell Holmes, and James Russell Lowell. Henry
Timrod dies in October in Columbia, South Carolina.
Fitz-Greene Halleck dies in November in Guilford, Con-
necticut.

John Burroughs: *Notes on Walt Whitman as Poet and Person*.
Ralph Waldo Emerson: *May-Day and Other Pieces*.
Francis Miles Finch: "The Blue and the Gray."
Emma Lazarus: *Poems and Translations*.
James Russell Lowell: *The Biglow Papers (Second Series)*.
Henry Wadsworth Longfellow: *Flower-de-Luce*;
    (translator) *The Divine Comedy*.
John James Piatt: *Western Windows and Other Poems*.
William Gilmore Simms (editor): *War Poetry of the South*.
John Greenleaf Whittier: *The Tent on the Beach*.
Richard Henry Wilde: *Hesperia*.
Forceythe Willson: *The Old Sergeant, and Other Poems*.

1868   Bret Harte becomes first editor of San Francisco journal
The Overland Monthly; under his editorship (1868–70)
contributors include Mark Twain, Ina Coolbrith, Clarence
King, and Charles Warren Stoddard. Adah Isaacs Menken
dies in August in Paris; collected poems, *Infelicia*, published days after her death. John Wesley Powell begins collecting data, including song texts and myths, for ethnographic study of Ute and Southern Paiute tribes (works
on project for 12 years, but never publishes findings).

Julia Ward Howe helps found New England Woman Suffrage Association. John M. Brown publishes "Songs of the Slave" in *Lippincott's Magazine*.

Benjamin Paul Blood: *The Colonnades*.
Augusta Cooper Bristol: *Poems*.
Phillips Brooks: "O Little Town of Bethlehem."
Alice Cary: *The Lover's Diary*.
Fitz-Greene Halleck: *Poetical Writings* (including
    first authorized book publication of "The Croakers"
    by Drake and Halleck).
Henry Wadsworth Longfellow: *The New-England
    Tragedies*.
Adah Isaacs Menken: *Infelicia*.
Joaquin Miller: *Specimens*.
John Rollin Ridge: *Poems*.
Edward Rowland Sill: *The Hermitage and Other Poems*.
William Wetmore Story: *Graffiti d'Italia*.

1869   William Cullen Bryant delivers commemorative address
              on Fitz-Greene Halleck at New-York Historical Society.
              Richard Watson Gilder edits *Hours at Home* (1869–70).
              Stephen Return Riggs includes translations of Sioux
              poetry in *Tah'-koo Wah-kan'; or, The Gospel Among the
              Dakotas*.

              George Henry Boker: *Königsmark, The Legend of the
                  Hounds, and Other Poems*.
              Phoebe Cary: *Poems of Faith, Hope and Love*.
              Frances Ellen Watkins Harper: *Moses: A Story of the Nile*.
              James Russell Lowell: *Under the Willows*.
              Edmund Clarence Stedman: *The Blameless Prince*.
              John Townsend Trowbridge: *The Vagabonds and
                  Other Poems*.
              John Greenleaf Whittier: *Among the Hills*.

1870   Bret Harte's "Plain Language from Truthful James" (also
              known as "The Heathen Chinee"), published in *The Over-
              land Monthly*, becomes enormously popular and is re-
              printed in many other papers. Josiah Gilbert Holland
              becomes founding editor of *Scribner's Monthly*, assisted by
              Richard Watson Gilder; contributors include Gilder,
              Helen Hunt Jackson, George Washington Cable, Emma
              Lazarus, and Joaquin Miller. Joaquin Miller travels to

England. Bayard Taylor publishes first installment of translation of *Faust*. Henry Adams assumes editorship of *The North American Review*. William Gilmore Simms dies in June in Columbia, South Carolina.

William Cullen Bryant (translator): *The Iliad*.
Bret Harte: "Plain Language from Truthful James."
Helen Hunt Jackson: *Verses*.
James Russell Lowell: *The Cathedral*.
Bayard Taylor (translator): *Faust*.
Rose Hartwick Thorpe: "Curfew Must Not Ring
    To-Night."
George Boyer Vashon: "Ode on the Proclamation
    of the Fifteenth Amendment."

1871   William Dean Howells succeeds James T. Fields as editor of *Atlantic Monthly*. George Henry Boker appointed minister to Turkey. Alice and Phoebe Cary die within five months of each other. Julia Ward Howe becomes president of Woman's International Peace Association. Bret Harte visits William Dean Howells and Ralph Waldo Emerson in Concord.

William Cullen Bryant: (translator) *The Odyssey*; (editor) *A Library of Poetry and Song*.
William Ellery Channing: *The Wanderer: A Colloquial Poem*.
Bret Harte: *East and West Poems*.
Frances Ellen Watkins Harper: *Poems*.
John Hay: *Pike County Ballads*.
Emma Lazarus: *Admetus and Other Poems*.
Charles Godfrey Leland: *The Breitmann Ballads*.
Henry Wadsworth Longfellow: *The Divine Tragedy*.
Joaquin Miller: *Pacific Poems*; *Songs of the Sierras*.
Walt Whitman: *Passage to India*.

1872   William Cullen Bryant travels in the Bahamas, Cuba, and Mexico; received with honor by President Juárez of Mexico. George Henry Boker and Charles Godfrey Leland meet Ralph Waldo Emerson while traveling in Egypt. Stéphane Mallarmé publishes the first of his translations of Poe's poetry.

Francis Ellen Watkins Harper: *Sketches of Southern Life*.
Bret Harte: *Poetical Works*; *Echoes of the Foot-Hills*.

Paul Hamilton Hayne: *Legends and Lyrics*.
Josiah Gilbert Holland: *The Marble Prophecy*.
Charles Godfrey Leland: *The Music Lesson of Confucius;
    and Other Poems*.
Henry Wadsworth Longfellow: *Christus, a Mystery*.
Theodore Seward: *Jubilee Songs: As Sung by the Jubilee
    Singers of Fisk University*.
Bayard Taylor: *The Masque of the Gods*.
Celia Thaxter: *Poems*.
Ella Wheeler Wilcox: *Drops of Water*.

1873   Paul Hamilton Hayne edits posthumous edition of Henry
        Timrod's poetry. Sidney Lanier becomes first flutist of
        Peabody Orchestra, Baltimore. Walt Whitman suffers
        stroke. Frederick Goddard Tuckerman dies in May at his
        home in Greenfield, Massachusetts.

        William Ellery Channing: *Thoreau, the Poet-Naturalist*.
        Paul Hamilton Hayne: *The Mountain of the Lovers*.
        William Dean Howells: *Poems*.
        Joaquin Miller: *Songs of the Sun-Lands*.
        Edmund Clarence Stedman: *The Poetical Works
            of Edmund Clarence Stedman*.
        Bayard Taylor: *Lars: A Pastoral of Norway*.
        Henry Timrod: *Poems*.
        Ella Wheeler Wilcox: *Shells*.

1874   Ralph Waldo Emerson omits both Whitman and Poe from
        his poetry anthology *Parnassus*. Edward Rowland Sill as-
        sumes chair of English at Berkeley. Richard Watson Gilder
        marries Helena de Kay, granddaughter of Joseph Rodman
        Drake. Benjamin Paul Blood sends his treatise on nitrous
        oxide, *The Anaesthetic Revelation and the Gist of Philosophy*,
        to William James and Alfred Tennyson. "O Little Town of
        Bethlehem" (written in 1868) published in *The Church
        Porch*. Text of murder ballad "Poor Naomi" published in
        Greensboro (North Carolina) *Patriot*.

        James A. Bland: "Carry Me Back to Old Virginny."
        Paul Bliss: *Gospel Songs*.
        Christopher Pearse Cranch: *Satan: A Libretto*.
        Ralph Waldo Emerson (editor): *Parnassus*.
        Thomas P. Fenner: *Cabin and Plantation Songs: as Sung
            by the Hampton Students*.

Henry Wadsworth Longfellow: *The Hanging of the Crane*.
Sarah Morgan Piatt: *A Voyage to the Fortunate Isles*.
G. D. Pike: *The Jubilee Singers of Fisk University*.
Bayard Taylor: *The Prophet*.

1875   George Henry Boker appointed minister to Russia. Helen
        Hunt Jackson settles in Colorado Springs, Colorado. Walt
        Whitman attends unveiling of monument to Edgar Allan
        Poe in Baltimore.

        Christopher Pearse Cranch: *The Bird and the Bell*.
        Richard Watson Gilder: *The New Day*.
        Oliver Wendell Holmes: *Songs of Many Seasons*.
        Edward King: *Negro Songs and Singers*.
        J.B.T. Marsh: *The Story of the Jubilee Singers: With
            Their Songs*.
        John Townsend Trowbridge: *The Emigrant's Story
            and Other Poems*.
        John Greenleaf Whittier: *Hazel-Blossoms*.
        Ella Wheeler Wilcox: *Maurine*.

1876   Bayard Taylor commissioned to write "Centennial Hymn"
        commemorating Declaration of Independence. Emma
        Lazarus visits Ralph Waldo Emerson in Concord. On
        visit to the United States, Emperor Dom Pedro of Brazil
        meets with Longfellow, Whittier, Bryant, and other liter-
        ary figures.

        Ralph Waldo Emerson: *Selected Poems*.
        Brewster Higley: "Home on the Range."
        Charles Godfrey Leland: *Pidgin-English Sing-Song; or,
            Songs and Stories in the China-English Dialect*.
        Henry Wadsworth Longfellow (editor): *Poems of Places*
            (31 volumes, 1876–79).
        Herman Melville: *Clarel: A Poem and Pilgrimage in the
            Holy Land*.
        Bayard Taylor: *The Echo Club and Other Literary
            Diversions*.
        Walt Whitman: *Leaves of Grass* (Centennial Edition).

1877   In Baltimore, Sara Sigourney Rice publishes *Edgar Allan
        Poe: A Memorial Volume*, including Stéphane Mallarmé's
        sonnet "Le tombeau d'Edgar Poe" and tributes by John
        Greenleaf Whittier, Alfred Tennyson, Algernon Swin-

burne, and others. William Cullen Bryant delivers address at unveiling of statue of Fitz-Greene Halleck in New York's Central Park. John Greenleaf Whittier's 70th birthday celebrated at dinner given by *Atlantic Monthly* in Boston, attended by Emerson, Longfellow, Holmes, Howells, Cranch, Trowbridge, Higginson, and others; humorous speech by Mark Twain regarded as in poor taste by many in attendance; Twain later apologizes. James Russell Lowell appointed minister to Spain (1877–80) by Rutherford B. Hayes. In *Kokomo Dispatch*, James Whitcomb Riley publishes parody "Leonainie" as newly discovered poem by Poe. Stephen Powers publishes translations of California Indian poetry in *Tribes of California*. John Wesley Powell hires Albert S. Gatschet as philologist for Geographical and Geological Survey of the Rocky Mountain Region.

Oliver Wendell Holmes: *Poetical Works*.
Sidney Lanier: *Poems*.
Sarah Morgan Piatt: *That New World*.
Edmund Clarence Stedman: *Hawthorne and Other Poems*.
Albery Allson Whitman: *Not a Man and Yet a Man*.
Constance Fenimore Woolson: *Two Women: 1862*.

1878   Ernest Fenollosa goes to Japan to teach at Imperial University in Tokyo. Bret Harte appointed U.S. consul at Krefeld, Germany. John Hay appointed assistant secretary of state by Rutherford B. Hayes. James A. Bland joins Georgia Minstrels, first all-black minstrel troupe. William Cullen Bryant dies in June in New York City, from a fall following ceremonies for unveiling of Mazzini statue in Central Park. George Boyer Vashon dies in October in Rodney, Mississippi. Bayard Taylor, arriving to assume post as U.S. minister, dies in December in Berlin; body brought back to lie in state in New York's City Hall.

Richard Watson Gilder: *The Poet and His Master*.
Henry Wadsworth Longfellow: *Kéramos and Other Poems*.
Sarah Morgan Piatt: *A Woman's Poems*.

1879   James Whitcomb Riley joins staff of *The Indianapolis Journal*. The Bureau of Ethnology (later the Bureau of American Ethnology) created by Congress; first director is John Wesley Powell. Bureau sends first anthropological expedition to Zuni Pueblo, led by James Stevenson, Matilda

Coxe Stevenson, and Frank Hamilton Cushing. The Jubilee Singers of Fisk University visit John Greenleaf Whittier at his home in Amesbury, New Hampshire. Sidney Lanier becomes lecturer in English at Johns Hopkins. Richard Henry Dana dies in February in Cambridge, Massachusetts.

James A. Bland: "Oh, Dem Golden Slippers."
John James Piatt: *Poems of House and Home.*
Abram Joseph Ryan: *Father Ryan's Poems.*
Celia Thaxter: *Drift-Weed.*

1880   James Russell Lowell appointed minister to Great Britain (1880–85). Augusta Cooper Bristol attends International Convention of Freethinkers in Brussels. Jones Very dies in May in Salem, Massachusetts.

Thomas Dunn English: *American Ballads.*
Sidney Lanier: *The Science of English Verse.*
Henry Wadsworth Longfellow: *Ultima Thule.*

1881   Richard Watson Gilder becomes editor of *Scribner's Monthly*, renamed *The Century*; contributors include William Dean Howells, Mark Twain, George Washington Cable, Paul Laurence Dunbar, and John Hay. Ambrose Bierce becomes editor of *The Wasp* (San Francisco). Walt Whitman visits Ralph Waldo Emerson in Concord. Alice Fletcher begins fieldwork on Omaha reservation. James A. Bland tours England with Minstrel Carnival of Genuine Colored Minstrels. Sidney Lanier dies in September at Lynn, North Carolina, at age 39.

A. Bronson Alcott: *An Autobiographical Poem.*
Oliver Wendell Holmes: *Poetical Works.*
Emma Lazarus: *Poems and Ballads of Heine.*
John James Piatt: *Idyls and Lyrics of the Ohio Valley.*
John Townsend Trowbridge: *A Home Idyl and Other Poems.*

1882   Oscar Wilde makes lecture tour of U.S.; visits Walt Whitman in Camden; meets Oliver Wendell Holmes, Julia Ward Howe, Henry Wadsworth Longfellow, Charles Eliot Norton, and Joaquin Miller. Helen Hunt Jackson appointed special federal commissioner to investigate condition of Mission Indians in California. Daniel Garrison

Brinton publishes first titles in his *Library of Aboriginal American Literature* (eight volumes appear before series is discontinued in 1890). James Whitcomb Riley gives first of many reading tours of the U.S. Richard Watson Gilder helps found the Authors' Club. John James Piatt appointed American consul at Cork, Ireland. Henry Wadsworth Longfellow dies in March in Cambridge, Massachusetts. Ralph Waldo Emerson dies in April in Concord.

A. Bronson Alcott: *Sonnets and Canzonets.*
George Henry Boker: *The Book of the Dead.*
Paul Hamilton Hayne: *Collected Poems.*
Emma Lazarus: *Songs of a Semite.*

1883   Eugene Field joins staff of *The Chicago Morning News.* William Reed Huntington begins tenure as rector of Grace Church, New York.

Daniel Garrison Brinton: *Aboriginal American Authors and Their Productions.*
Horatio Hale: *The Iroquois Book of Rites.*
Henry Wadsworth Longfellow: *Michael Angelo.*
William Wells Newell: *Games and Songs of American Children.*
James Whitcomb Riley: *The Old Swimmin'-Hole.*
Edward Rowland Sill: *The Venus of Milo and Other Poems.*
Ella Wheeler Wilcox: *Poems of Passion.*

1884   John Banister Tabb ordained as Roman Catholic priest. Longfellow commemorated by a bust in Westminster Abbey, the first American poet so honored.

Daniel Garrison Brinton: *The Lenâpé and Their Legends.*
Helen Hunt Jackson: *Easter Bells; Pansies and Orchids.*
Louise Imogen Guiney: *Songs at the Start.*
Charles Godfrey Leland: *The Algonquin Legends of New England.*
Percy Montrose: "Oh My Darling Clementine."
Clinton Scollard: *Pictures in Song.*
Albery Allson Whitman: *The Rape of Florida* (reprinted 1885 as *Twasinta's Seminoles*).

1885   Bret Harte settles permanently in London. James Mooney meets John Wesley Powell and is given post with Bureau

of Ethnology. Katharine Lee Bates appointed professor of English at Wellesley. Edmund Clarence Stedman publishes critical study *Poets of America*. Helen Hunt Jackson dies in August in San Francisco.

Charles Timothy Brooks: *Poems, Original and Translated*.
Charles Edward Carryl: *Davy and the Goblin*.
James Russell Lowell: *Under the Old Elm*.

1886   "The New Colossus" by Emma Lazarus recited at dedi-
cation of Statue of Liberty. William Dean Howells and Stuart Merrill separately take up defense of anarchist demonstrators condemned to death in connection with Haymarket riot in Chicago. George Washington Cable publishes translations of Creole slave songs in *The Cen-tury*. Jules Laforgue's translations of three Walt Whitman poems appear in French periodical *La Vogue*. Henry Adams tours Japan with John La Farge. The German anthropologist Franz Boas does first fieldwork on Northwest Coast, spending time among the Kwakiutl, Bella Coola, and Tsimshian; afterward settles in U.S. Emily Dickinson dies in May in Amherst, Massachusetts.

George Henry Boker: *Sonnets*.
William Ellery Channing: *John Brown and the Heroes of Harper's Ferry*.
Emma Lazarus: "The New Colossus."
Sarah Morgan Piatt: *Selected Poems*.
Clinton Scollard: *With Reed and Lyre*.

1887   James Whitcomb Riley introduced by James Russell Low-
ell at triumphant poetry reading at Chickering Hall, New York City. Stuart Merrill publishes first book, *Les Gammes*, in French (as all but one of his subsequent volumes will be); meets Walt Whitman in New York City and presents him with copies of Jules Laforgue's Whitman translations. Richard Hovey meets Bliss Carman. *Scribner's Magazine* begins publication under editorship of Edward L. Burlin-game; contributors include Edith Wharton, Sarah Orne Jewett, Eugene Field, and James Whitcomb Riley. Madi-son Cawein's first book favorably reviewed by William Dean Howells in *Harper's*. Joaquin Miller settles in Oak-land, California. Emma Lazarus dies in November at age 38 in New York City.

Katharine Lee Bates: *The College Beautiful*.
Madison Cawein: *Blooms of the Berry*.
Richard Watson Gilder: *The Celestial Passion*.
Louise Imogen Guiney: *The White Sail and Other Poems*.
Washington Matthews: *The Mountain Chant:
    A Navajo Ceremony*.
Stuart Merrill: *Les Gammes*.
Lizette Woodworth Reese: *A Branch of May*.
James Whitcomb Riley: *Afterwhiles*.
Rose Hartwick Thorpe: *Ringing Ballads*.
Comic and Popular Songs, Sung by Robert Jones (including
    earliest printed version of "Jesse James").

1888   In Japan, Ernest Fenollosa appointed director of newly
        opened Tokyo Fine Arts Academy and Imperial Museum.
        In Paris, Stéphane Mallarmé collects his prose translations
        of Edgar Allan Poe's poetry. Bronson Alcott dies in March
        in Concord, Massachusetts.

        Madison Cawein: *The Triumph of Music*.
        Rose Terry Cooke: *Poems*.
        James Owen Dorsey: *Osage Traditions*.
        James Russell Lowell: *Heartsease and Rue*.
        Stéphane Mallarmé: *Les Poèmes d'Edgar Poe: Traductions
            en Prose*.
        Herman Melville: *John Marr and Other Sailors*.
        James Whitcomb Riley: *Pipes o' Pan at Zekesbury*.
        Clinton Scollard: *Old and New World Lyrics*.
        Ernest Lawrence Thayer: "Casey at the Bat."
        Ella Wheeler Wilcox: *Poems of Pleasure*.

1889   Edmund Clarence Stedman begins publication of ten-
        volume *Library of American Literature*. George Santayana
        joins philosophy faculty at Harvard.

        Eugene Field: *A Little Book of Western Verse*.
        Emma Lazarus: *The Poems of Emma Lazarus*.

1890   First collection of poetry by Emily Dickinson published,
        edited by Thomas Wentworth Higginson and Mabel
        Loomis Todd. Ernest Fenollosa returns to America to be-
        come curator of Oriental department of Boston Museum
        of Fine Arts. Stuart Merrill publishes only English-
        language volume, *Pastels in Prose* (translations of contem-

porary French writers), with preface by William Dean Howells. In London, on his way back to France, Merrill meets Oscar Wilde. Henry Adams and John La Farge travel in the Pacific and Asia. James Mooney collects Ghost Dance songs in South Dakota. George Henry Boker dies in January in Philadelphia.

Madison Cawein: *Lyrics and Idyls*.
Emily Dickinson: *Poems*.
Albert S. Gatschet: *The Klamath Indians of Southwestern Oregon*.
John Hay: *Poems*.
Stuart Merrill: *Pastels in Prose*.
James Whitcomb Riley: *Rhymes of Childhood*.
John Greenleaf Whittier: *At Sundown*.

1891   Walt Whitman publishes last poems in *Goodbye, My Fancy* and final "deathbed" edition of *Leaves of Grass*. Stuart Merrill publishes *Les Fastes*; settles permanently in Paris, where he becomes manager of the Théâtre d'Art. Ernest Fenollosa meets painter Arthur Dow and works with him to introduce Asian art to American students. Richard Hovey publishes *Launcelot and Guenevere*, first volume of projected verse-drama cycle on Arthurian themes. James Russell Lowell dies in August in Cambridge, Massachusetts. Herman Melville dies in September in New York City.

Emily Dickinson: *Poems: Second Series*.
W. J. Hoffman: *The Mide'wiwin or "Grand Medicine Society" of the Ojibwa*.
Richard Hovey: *Launcelot and Guenevere*.
Herman Melville: *Timoleon*.
Stuart Merrill: *Les Fastes*.
James Mooney: *Sacred Formulas of the Cherokees*.
Lizette Woodworth Reese: *A Handful of Lavendar*.
Walt Whitman: *Goodbye, My Fancy*; *Leaves of Grass* (final edition).

1892   Ernest Fenollosa reads "East and West" to Phi Beta Kappa Society at Harvard. Harriet Monroe commissioned to write "The Columbian Ode" for dedication of World's Columbian Exposition in Chicago. Paul Laurence Dunbar invited to join Western Association of Writers in Dayton, Ohio. Christopher Pearse Cranch dies in January in Cam-

bridge, Massachusetts. Walt Whitman dies in March in Camden, New Jersey. John Greenleaf Whittier dies in September in Hampton Falls, New Hampshire.

Eugene Field: *Second Book of Verse*.
Harriet Monroe: *Valeria and Other Poems*.
James Whitcomb Riley: *Green Fields and Running Brooks*.
Clinton Scollard: *Songs of Sunrise Lands*.

1893   World's Columbian Exposition ("The White City") opens in Chicago, including influential displays of modern architecture and technology, and first major American exhibit of Japanese art and architecture; visitors include Henry Adams (who writes "the mental excitement and disturbance have upset my usual balance so much that I am not yet quite willing to trust myself to talk or write on the subject"), Mark Twain, Ernest Fenollosa, Edwin Markham, Hamlin Garland, Theodore Dreiser, Katharine Lee Bates, and Richard Watson Gilder; Paul Laurence Dunbar employed by Frederick Douglass at Haiti Building; Albery Allson Whitman reads poem "The Freedman's Triumphant Song" to audience including Douglass and Dunbar; Franz Boas supervises exhibit on physical anthropology.

Ambrose Bierce: *Black Beetles in Amber*.
Madison Cawein: *Red Leaves and Roses*.
Paul Laurence Dunbar: *Oak and Ivy*.
Ernest Fenollosa: *East and West, The Discovery of America and Other Poems*.
Alice Fletcher and Francis La Flesche: *A Study of Omaha Indian Music*.
Hamlin Garland: *Prairie Songs*.
Louise Imogen Guiney: *A Roadside Harp*.
Richard Hovey: *Seaward*.
Harriet Monroe: *The Columbian Ode*.
John Banister Tabb: *An Octave to Mary*.

1894   Robert Frost's poem "My Butterfly" appears in *The Independent* (New York); Frost arranges private printing of *Twilight* in an edition of only two copies. In San Francisco, Gelett Burgess edits *Wave*. Constance Fenimore Woolson dies in January in a fall from her balcony in Venice. Oliver Wendell Holmes dies in October in Cambridge, Massachusetts.

Thomas Dunn English: *Select Poems of Dr. Thomas Dunn English.*
Richard Hovey and Bliss Carman: *Songs from Vagabondia.*
Sarah Morgan Piatt: *Collected Poems.*
George Santayana: *Sonnets and Other Verses.*
Matilda Coxe Stevenson: *The Sia.*
John Banister Tabb: *Poems.*

1895   William Dean Howells writes glowing review of Paul Laurence Dunbar's *Majors and Minors*; Dunbar becomes well-known. In San Francisco, Gelett Burgess assumes editorship of *The Lark* (1895–97), associated with literary group Les Jeunes. In Paris, George Cabot Lodge and Trumbull Stickney study at the Sorbonne; Richard Hovey meets Stéphane Mallarmé and other members of symbolist movement. Louise Imogen Guiney travels in England; forms friendshp with Lionel Johnson.

Henry Adams: "Buddha and Brahma."
Katharine Lee Bates: "America the Beautiful."
Augusta Cooper Bristol: *The Web of Life.*
James Edwin Campbell: *Echoes from the Cabin and Elsewhere.*
Stephen Crane: *The Black Riders and Other Lines.*
Paul Laurence Dunbar: *Majors and Minors.*
Louise Imogen Guiney: *Nine Sonnets Written at Oxford.*
Sadakichi Hartmann: *Conversations with Walt Whitman.*
Stuart Merrill: *Petits Poèmes d'Automne.*
James Whitcomb Riley: *The Days Gone By.*

1896   On a visit to Paris, Henry Adams taken by George Cabot Lodge to hear singer Yvette Guilbert; in London, Adams attends dinner hosted by John Hay, whose guests include Henry James, Bret Harte, and John Singer Sargent. Stephen Crane shipwrecked en route to Cuba to report on revolution.

Franz Boas: "Songs of the Kwakiutl Indians."
Madison Cawein: *The Garden of Dreams.*
Ina Coolbrith: *Songs of the Golden Gate.*
Frank Hamilton Cushing: *Outlines of Zuñi Creation Myths.*
Emily Dickinson: *Poems: Third Series.*
Paul Laurence Dunbar: *Lyrics of Lowly Life.*
Richard Hovey and Bliss Carman: *More Songs from Vagabondia.*

James Mooney: *The Ghost-Dance Religion and the Sioux Outbreak of 1890.*
Lizette Woodworth Reese: *A Quiet Road.*
Edwin Arlington Robinson: *The Torrent and the Night Before.*

1897   John Hay appointed ambassador to Great Britain by William McKinley. Paul Laurence Dunbar goes on reading tour of England. Following divorce scandal in Boston, Ernest Fenollosa returns to Japan with second wife, Mary McNeill. Louise Imogen Guiney publishes edition of Irish poet James Clarence Mangan. First printed version of the spiritual "Were You There When They Crucified My Lord?" appears in *The Journal of American Folklore.*

Franz Boas: *The Social Organization and the Secret Societies of the Kwakiutl Indians.*
Gelett Burgess: "The Purple Cow."
Washington Matthews: *Navaho Legends.*
Joaquin Miller: *Complete Poetical Works.*
John James Piatt: *Odes in Ohio.*
Edwin Arlington Robinson: *Children of the Night.*
John Banister Tabb: *Lyrics.*

1898   Carl Sandburg goes to Puerto Rico as soldier in Spanish-American War; George Cabot Lodge enlists in navy, participates in American capture of Ponce, Puerto Rico; Stephen Crane reports on fighting in Cuba for *New York World* and *New York Journal*. English translations of Yiddish poems by New York poet Morris Rosenfeld published in *Songs of the Ghetto*. John Hay appointed Secretary of State by William McKinley.

John Jay Chapman: "Bismarck"; *Emerson and Other Essays.*
Jeremiah Curtin: *Creation Myths of Primitive America.*
Louise Imogen Guiney: *England and Yesterday.*
Richard Hovey: *Along the Trail*; *The Birth of Galahad.*
George Cabot Lodge: *The Song of the Wave.*
Edgar Lee Masters: *A Book of Verses.*
Morris Rosenfeld: *Songs of the Ghetto.*

1899   Edwin Markham's "The Man with the Hoe," published in *The San Francisco Examiner* in January, makes him instant celebrity; his collection *The Man with the Hoe and Other*

Poems becomes bestseller. Edwin Arlington Robinson moves to New York City. Alfred L. Kroeber does fieldwork among the Arapaho, Ute, Northern Shoshone, and Bannock.

Stephen Crane: *War Is Kind*.
Paul Laurence Dunbar: *Lyrics of the Hearthside*.
John Comfort Fillmore: *The Harmonic Structure of Indian Music*.
Louise Imogen Guiney: *The Martyrs' Idyl and Shorter Poems*.
Richard Hovey: *Taliesin: A Masque*.
William Reed Huntington: *Sonnets and a Dream*.
Edwin Markham: *The Man with the Hoe and Other Poems*.
Edward William Nelson: *The Eskimo About Bering Strait*.
Lizette Woodworth Reese: "Tears."
George Santayana: *Lucifer: A Theological Tragedy*.

1900   Trumbull Stickney's verse drama "Prometheus Pyrphoros" appears in *Harvard Monthly*. John Jay Chapman suffers nervous breakdown. Robert Frost farms in New Hampshire. Richard Hovey dies in February in New York City. Stephen Crane dies in June in Germany.

Gelett Burgess: *Goops and How To Be Them*.
Alice Fletcher: *Indian Story and Song from North America*.
Edwin Markham: "Lincoln, the Man of the People."
Stuart Merrill: *Les Quatre Saisons*.
William Vaughn Moody: *The Masque of Judgment*.
Edmund Clarence Stedman (editor): *An American Anthology, 1787–1899*.
Ridgely Torrence: *The House of a Hundred Lights*.
George Santayana: *Interpretations of Poetry and Religion*.
Trumbull Stickney: "Prometheus Pyrphoros."

Biographical Notes

HENRY ADAMS (February 16, 1838–March 27, 1918) b. Boston, Massachusetts. Third son of Abigail Brooks and Charles Francis Adams; grandson of John Quincy Adams, at whose home he was a frequent summer visitor; great-grandson of John Adams. Graduated Harvard 1858; studied law in Berlin and Dresden until 1860; traveled in Austria and Italy, publishing Italian travel letters in *Boston Daily Courier*. After father's reelection to Congress in 1860, accompanied him to Washington to serve as his secretary; Washington correspondent for *Boston Daily Advertiser*. Father appointed minister to Great Britain in 1861; served as his secretary until 1868. As London correspondent of *New York Times* (1861–62), reported British reaction to Civil War; traveled on Continent with mother and other family members; published scholarly articles. Returned to Washington in 1868 to work as journalist and to lobby for reform; attacked spoils system and campaigned for free trade and establishment of civil service. Appointed assistant professor of history at Harvard (1870–77); assumed editorship of *North American Review* (1870–76). On travels in Far West formed friendship with Clarence King of United States Geological Survey. Married Marion (Clover) Hooper in June 1872; they made wedding journey to England, the Continent, and Egypt. Published biography *The Life of Albert Gallatin* (1879). Formed friendships with Senator James D. Cameron, his wife Elizabeth, and John Hay. With Hay, his wife Clara, and Clarence King, the Adamses formed salon "The Five of Hearts." Traveled in Europe to research detailed history of Jefferson and Madison administrations. *Democracy*, fictional attack on Washington corruption, published anonymously in 1880, followed by biography *John Randolph* (1882) and another novel, *Esther* (1884). Wife committed suicide in December 1885. The following spring made four-month tour of Japan with artist John La Farge; met Ernest Fenollosa. *History of the United States during the Administrations of Thomas Jefferson and James Madison* published 1889–91. Traveled (1890–91) with La Farge in South Pacific, meeting Robert Louis Stevenson in Samoa; made other journeys to Cuba and Mexico. Lived mostly in Europe between 1897 and 1900, and afterwards spent part of most years in Europe. *Mont Saint Michel and Chartres* (1904) and *The Education of Henry Adams* (1907) published in private editions; *The Life of George Cabot Lodge* appeared 1911. Trade edition of *Mont Saint Michel and Chartres* enjoyed wide success. Died in Washington. *The Education of Henry Adams* awarded Pulitzer Prize posthumously the following year.

ELIZABETH AKERS ALLEN (October 9, 1832–August 7, 1911) b. Elizabeth Chase in Strong, Maine. Daughter of Mercy Fenno Barton and Thomas Chase (a lawyer). Mother died when she was a child, and she was sent to live with relatives in Farmington, Maine. Began to write at age 15 under pen name "Florence Percy." In 1851 married Marshall Taylor, son of Presbyterian minister; marriage soon ended in divorce after Taylor left her and their daughter

and moved to California. Moved to Portland, Maine, and became assistant editor of *Portland Transcript*; published collection of poems, *Forest Buds* (1855). Contributed to *Atlantic Monthly* from 1858. Traveled in Europe, 1859–60, sending letters to the *Transcript* and *Boston Evening Gazette*. The poem "Rock Me to Sleep" appeared in *Saturday Evening Post* in 1860; was set to music by Ernest Leslie and became enormously popular, but controversy over authorship (with Alexander M. W. Ball and others claiming to have written it) ensued. Married sculptor Benjamin Paul Akers, whom she had met in Rome, in 1860; he was already seriously ill with tuberculosis and died the following year after the couple had moved to Philadelphia; their daughter died in infancy. Akers resumed editorial position in Portland. In 1863 took a clerkship in Washington, D.C., where she also worked in hospitals with wounded soldiers. In 1865 married E. M. Allen, a lumber merchant. In 1866 a second collection of poetry published, including "Rock Me to Sleep"; her authorship of the poem was finally vindicated in *The New York Times* in 1867. Lived with her husband in Richmond, Virginia, 1866–73; returned to Maine to become literary editor of Portland *Daily Advertiser*. In 1882 moved with her husband to Tuckahoe, New York. Published many volumes of verse, including *Queen Catherine's Rose* (1885), *The Silver Bridge* (1886), *The High-Top Sweeting* (1891), *The Ballad of the Bronx* (1901), and *The Sunset Song* (1902).

KATHARINE LEE BATES   (August 12, 1859–March 28, 1929)   b. Falmouth, Massachusetts. Youngest of five children of Cornelia Frances Lee and William Bates, a Congregational minister who died a month after her birth. Family moved to Grantville (now Wellesley), Massachusetts, where Bates attended local schools. Graduated Wellesley College in 1880. Taught high school in Natick, Massachusetts, and at girls' preparatory schools near Wellesley. In 1885 returned to Wellesley as English instructor and remained there 40 years, becoming the guiding force of Wellesley's English department. In 1893 published *The English Religious Drama* and was invited to lecture on the subject at Colorado College; en route, visited World's Columbian Exhibition in Chicago; at Colorado College, met Hamlin Garland and Woodrow Wilson. Early in her stay, after an outing to Pike's Peak in a prairie wagon, wrote "America the Beautiful." Poem published in *The Congregationalist* on July 4, 1895; set to melody based on "Materna" by Samuel Augustus Ward; revised versions appeared in 1904 and 1911. Verse collections included *The College Beautiful* (1887), *America the Beautiful* (1911), *The Retinue* (1918), *Yellow Clover* (1922), *The Pilgrim Ship* (1926), and *America the Dream* (1930). Also published fictional works *Rose and Thorn* (1888) and *Hermit Island* (1891); other prose including critical survey *American Literature* (1898) and travel books *Spanish Highways and By-Ways* (1900) and *From Gretna Green to Land's End* (1907); and poetry and plays for children including *Sunshine and Other Verses for Children* (1890), *Fairy Gold* (1916), and *Little Robin Stay-Behind* (1923).

AMBROSE BIERCE   (June 24, 1842–January 11, 1914?)   b. Ambrose Gwinnett Bierce on farm near Horse Cave Creek, Ohio. Son of Laura Sherwood

and Marcus Aurelius Bierce; one of many children of poor but well-read farm family; received limited education at home and at high school in Warsaw, Indiana. Attended Kentucky Military Institute, 1859–60. Enlisted in 9th Indiana Infantry in 1861; fought at Shiloh, Murfreesboro, Chattanooga, and Franklin; wounded at Kenesaw Mountain. After the war, served for a time as custodian of captured and abandoned property in Selma, Alabama. Accompanied General W. B. Hazen on tour of northwestern army posts. Joined brother Albert in San Francisco, working with him at the U.S. sub-treasury. Contributed journalism to *The Californian*, *The Golden Era*, *Overland Monthly*, and *San Francisco News Letter and California Advertiser* (of which he became editor in 1868). Married Mary Ellen (Mollie) Day in 1871; they had two sons and one daughter. Lived in England (where his associates included W. S. Gilbert) and in France, 1872–75. Worked on editorial staff of *Fun*; wrote two issues of *The Lantern* (a periodical subsidized by exiled Empress Eugenie); contributed to *Figaro* and *Hood's Comic Annual*. Collected mordantly humorous sketches in three volumes, *The Fiend's Delight* (1873), *Nuggets and Dust Panned Out in California* (1873), and *Cobwebs from an Empty Skull* (1874), all published under pseudonym "Dod Grile." Returning to San Francisco in 1875, wrote for *The Argonaut*. In 1880 worked as general agent for Black Hills Placer Mining Company in Dakota Territory. Edited *The Wasp*, 1881–86. From 1887, columnist and editor for William Randolph Hearst's *Examiner*. Literary associates at this time included George Sterling and Herman Scheffauer. A volume of short stories, *Tales of Soldiers and Civilians*, was printed in 1891 (but not published until 1892, simultaneously with the English edition, *In the Midst of Life*), followed by *The Monk and the Hangman's Daughter* (1892), a medieval story adapted from translation by G. A. Danziger of German work by Richard Voss, *Black Beetles in Amber* (1892), a collection of satirical verse, and *Can Such Things Be?* (1893), a volume of supernatural tales. In January 1896 sent to Washington by Hearst to head lobby opposing congressional approval of Collis Huntington's Funding Bill for Central and Southern Pacific railroads. Bill defeated, largely through Bierce's efforts. Began writing for Hearst's *New York Journal*. In November 1896 returned to San Francisco. Moved permanently to Washington in 1899. On payroll of *New York Journal*, but his material also appeared in *New York American* and *San Francisco Examiner*. Son Leigh died of pneumonia in 1901. In 1906 began writing for *Cosmopolitan*, which took over his salary in 1906. Later books included *Fantastic Fables* (1899); *Shapes of Clay* (1903), a poetry collection; *The Cynic's Word Book*, a sardonic lexicon interspersed with pseudonymous poems (later retitled *The Devil's Dictionary*); *The Shadow on the Dial* (1909); and *Write It Right* (1909), a manual of style. *Collected Works* published in 12 volumes (1909–12). Divorced from his wife in 1905. After settling his affairs, disappeared into Mexico in 1913, writing to a friend: "If you hear of my being stood up against a Mexican stone wall and shot to rags please know that I think it a pretty good way to depart this life." Joined Pancho Villa's forces as an observer and died under mysterious circumstances, almost certainly at the battle of Ojinaga.

JAMES A. BLAND (October 22, 1854–May 5, 1911) b. Flushing, New York; lived in Philadelphia during childhood. His mother was a free black from Wilmington, Delaware; his father, Allen Bland, also free-born, was the first black examiner in the U.S. Patent Office in Washington, D.C. Learned to play banjo and, by age 14, worked as musician in local clubs and hotels, performing popular songs of the day; within a year, began to compose his own songs. Graduated high school in Washington; studied briefly at Howard University, but soon neglected college work to study musical composition privately. Became acquainted with future U.S. Marine Band leader John Philip Sousa, who later used some of Bland's melodies in his band arrangements. Met minstrel celebrity George Primrose at Ford's Theatre in 1874, performing for him newly written song "Carry Me Back to Old Virginny"; Primrose premiered the song with his minstrel show in Baltimore. In 1878 joined the Georgia Minstrels, first successful all-black minstrel group (founded as Callender's Original and Georgia Minstrels in 1865). Performed "Carry Me Back to Old Virginny" with the troupe; other successful songs included "Oh, Dem Golden Slippers" (of which 100,000 copies were sold by 1880), "In the Evening by the Moonlight," "In the Morning by the Bright Light," and "De Golden Wedding"; said to have written as many as 600 songs during his career. Troupe evolved into large-scale show, the Minstrel Carnival of Genuine Colored Minstrels; played Niblo's Garden in New York City in 1879; toured England in 1881. Bland remained in Europe as successful solo performer until 1901, occasionally returning to the U.S.; known as "The Idol of the Music Halls"; gave command performance before Queen Victoria and the Prince of Wales. In 1910 returned destitute to Washington, D.C.; found a job in the law office of an old friend, William Silence; wrote musical *The Sporting Girl*, but realized only $250 on words and music. Moved to Philadelphia where he made unsuccessful effort to renew career as stage performer; died of tuberculosis.

BENJAMIN PAUL BLOOD (November 21, 1832–January 15, 1919) b. Amsterdam, New York, where he was a lifelong resident. Son of Mary Stanton and John Blood; descended on mother's side from *Mayflower* pilgrim John Howland, on father's from 18th-century Irish immigrant. Attended Amsterdam Academy and Union College; inherited family farm. Married twice, to Mary E. Sayles (who died in 1893) and Harriet A. Lefferts. Early writings included *The Philosophy of Justice Between God and Man* (1851), an unorthodox Christian treatise; *The Bride of the Iconoclast* (1854), a narrative poem in Spenserian stanzas, written before age 21; *Optimism, the Lesson of the Ages* (1860), an essay in theological speculation; *Napoleon I: A Historical Lecture* (1863); and *The Colonnades* (1868), a philosophical epic in blank verse. After being administered nitrous oxide in a dentist's office, underwent mystical experience; repeated the experience at frequent intervals, expounding philosophical conclusions from it in *The Anaesthetic Revelation and the Gist of Philosophy* (1874). Sent book to a number of American and European writers, leading to correspondence with William James and Alfred Tennyson. (James later com-

mented on *The Anaesthetic Revelation*: "It fascinated me so 'weirdly' that I am conscious of its having been one of the stepping-stones of my thinking ever since," and went on to publish in 1910 "A Pluralistic Mystic," an article praising Blood.) In 1886 the *Journal of Speculative Philosophy* published some of his writings as "Philosophical Reveries," and eight poems appeared in *Scribner's Magazine* between 1892 and 1904; most of his other works were privately printed and distributed. Other writings included *The Flaw in Supremacy: A Sketch of the Nature, Process and Status of Philosophy, as Inferring the Miracle of Nature, the Contingency of History, the Equation of Reason and Unreason, &c., &c.* (1893), and the posthumously published *Pluriverse* (1920), in which he criticized his earlier monism in favor of a pluralistic philosophy. His uncollected poems were gathered in *Heirlooms: A Book of Poems* (1924).

GEORGE HENRY BOKER (October 6, 1823–January 2, 1890) b. Philadelphia, Pennsylvania, son of Charles Boker, wealthy banker. Attended College of New Jersey (now Princeton), graduating in 1842. Relative and boyhood companion Charles Godfrey Leland described Boker in his youth as "quite familiar, in a refined and gentlemanly way, with all the dissipations of Philadelphia and New York." In 1844 married Julia Mandeville Riggs, with whom, after a brief European tour, he settled in Philadelphia; they had one son, George. Abandoned study of law to pursue career as verse dramatist and lyric poet. In 1848 published first poetry collection, *A Lesson of Life*, and completed *Calaynos*, a blank verse tragedy set in medieval Spain; successful London production in 1849 led to American premiere in 1851. Other plays included *Anne Boleyn* (1850, unproduced); *The Betrothal* (1850), romance of medieval Italy; *The World a Mask* (1851), social satire set in England; *The Widow's Marriage*, unproduced blank verse comedy; *Leonor de Guzman* (1853), heroic tragedy; and his greatest success, the verse play *Francesca da Rimini* (1855), which continued to be revived into the 20th century. Stopped writing for theater after failure of *The Bankrupt* in 1855. In 1856 collected chief writings in *Plays and Poems*. Father's death the following year embroiled him in legal and financial difficulties; forced to defend father's reputation from lingering charges of financial malfeasance in his conduct at the Girard Bank. Around this time, wrote (but withheld from publication) *The Book of the Dead*, a volume of poetry inspired by his ultimately successful struggle to vindicate his father's name. During Civil War, patriotic activities included founding Union League of Philadelphia (of which he was secretary, 1861–71). Wrote much poetry inspired by the conflict, gathered in *Poems of the War* (1864); another volume of poetry, *Königsmark, The Legend of the Hounds, and Other Poems* appeared 1869. In postwar period literary associates included Leland, Richard Henry Stoddard, William Gilmore Simms, and Paul Hamilton Hayne. Appointed by Ulysses S. Grant as minister to Turkey, 1871–75; helped restore diplomatic relations with Ottoman government. On trip to Egypt with Leland in 1872, met Ralph Waldo Emerson at Misraim. In 1875 named minister to Russia; served with distinction until recalled by Hayes administration in 1878. Returned to Philadelphia, where he received many honors; devoted himself to

improvement of city's park system. Encouraged by successful revival of *Francesca da Rimini* in 1882 to resume literary career, wrote unproduced dramatic adaptation of *The Last Days of Pompeii* (entitled in successive versions *Nydia* and *Glaucus*), and published *The Book of the Dead* (1882) and *Sonnets* (1886).

AUGUSTA COOPER BRISTOL (April 17, 1835–May 9, 1910) b. Croydon, New Hampshire; educated at Kimball Union Academy. In 1850 became a teacher. Married Louis Bristol in 1866. Published three volumes of poetry: *Poems* (1868), *The Web of Life* (1895), and *A Spray of Cosmos* (1904). Known primarily as lecturer and writer on social and philosophical issues; published a number of lectures in pamphlet form, including *The Relation of the Maternal Function to the Woman's Intellect* (1876), *The Philosophy of Art* (1878), *Science and Its Relations to Human Character* (1878), and *The Present Phase of Woman's Advancement* (1880); these and other lectures posthumously collected in *The Present Phase of Women's Advancement and Other Addresses* (1916). Went to France in 1880 to study Equitable Association of Labor and Capital at Guise; later that year attended International Convention of Freethinkers in Brussels. Elected state lecturer by Patrons of Husbandry (a vehicle for the National Grange movement, an organization of farmers and agricultural workers) in New Jersey; after 1884, traveled in this capacity throughout the country. Died in Vineland, New Jersey.

PHILLIPS BROOKS (December 13, 1835–January 23, 1893) b. Boston, Massachusetts. Son of Mary Phillips and William Gray Brooks; ancestors on mother's side included founders of Phillips Exeter Academy, Phillips Andover Academy, and Andover Theological Seminary; father was a Boston businessman. Early education at Boston Latin School. Graduated Harvard 1855; studied theology at seminary in Alexandria, Virginia; ordained Episcopal priest in 1859; became rector of Church of the Advent in Philadelphia in 1859, then of Church of the Holy Trinity in Philadelphia in 1862. Drew attention for eloquence of prayer delivered at Harvard Commemoration for Civil War dead in 1865. Wrote "O Little Town of Bethlehem" for his Sunday school; first performed publicly Christmas 1868. In 1869 became rector of Trinity Church in Boston. Invited to preach at Westminister Abbey and before Queen Victoria at Windsor in 1880, the first American so honored. Elected bishop in 1891. Publications included *Lectures on Preaching* (1877), *Sermons* (1878), *The Influence of Jesus* (1879), *Baptism and Confirmation* (1880), *The Candle of the Lord* (1881), and *The Light of the World* (1890), *Essays and Addresses* (1892), and the posthumous volumes *New Starts in Life* (1896) and *The Law of Growth* (1902).

HENRY HOWARD BROWNELL (February 6, 1820–October 31, 1872) b. Providence, Rhode Island. Son of Lucia de Wolf and Dr. Pardon Brownell; nephew of Episcopalian bishop Thomas Church Brownell. Graduated Washington College (now Trinity) in Hartford, Connecticut, 1841; taught briefly in Mobile, Alabama, before returning to Hartford to study law; admitted to bar

1844. Turned to writing career, publishing *Poems* (1847), *The People's Book of Ancient History* (1851), *The Discoverers, Pioneers and Settlers of North and South America* (1853), and *Ephemerson* (1855). In 1862 wrote poem based on Admiral Farragut's "General Orders" to his fleet in the attack on New Orleans; published in various newspapers, poem came to attention of Farragut, who corresponded with Brownell and (supposedly in response to Brownell's expressed desire to witness a naval battle) offered him position as acting ensign on flagship *Hartford*. Wrote descriptive poems about a number of naval engagements that he witnessed, including battle of Mobile Bay. War poems, published as *Lyrics of a Day, or Newspaper Poems*, earned admiration of Oliver Wendell Holmes, who called Brownell "Our Battle Laureate." Accompanied Farragut as secretary on cruises to European ports, 1865–68. Final volume of poetry, *War Lyrics and Other Poems*, appeared in 1866.

GELETT BURGESS (January 30, 1866–September 18, 1951) b. Boston, Massachusetts. Son of Caroline Brooks and Thomas Harvey Burgess; given name Frank Gelett Burgess. Graduated Massachusetts Institute of Technology with engineering degree in 1887. Worked for three years as draftsman for Southern Pacific Railroad; in 1890 became instructor in topographical drawing at University of California at Berkeley. In 1894 named editor of San Francisco society magazine *Wave*; associated with literary group known as Les Jeunes; close friend of Frank Norris. Edited literary magazine *The Lark* (1895–97), where he published humorous drawings and celebrated four-line poem "The Purple Cow." Moved in 1897 to New York City; married actress Estelle Loomis in 1914. Lived in Paris during World War I. Published *The Heart Line* (1907), a novel of San Francisco, but was best known for long series of comic writings and drawings including *Goops and How to Be Them* (1900); *Are You a Bromide? Or, The Sulphitic Theory* (1907); *Blue Goops and Red* (1909); *Burgess Unabridged: A New Dictionary of Words You Have Always Needed* (1914), which coined among other neologisms the word "blurb"; *The Goop Encyclopaedia* (1915); *Why Men Hate Women* (1927); *Look Eleven Years Younger* (1937); *Ladies in Boxes* (1942); and *New Goops: How to Know Them* (1951). Died in Carmel, California.

GEORGE WASHINGTON CABLE (October 12, 1844–January 31, 1925) b. New Orleans, Louisiana. Son of Rebecca Boardman (a New Englander) and George W. Cable (a businessman from an old Virginia slaveholding family). Schooling ended at age 14 due to father's death; thereafter worked to support family. Family left New Orleans in 1863 during Union occupation. Joined 4th Mississippi Cavalry and saw much fighting; was wounded twice. Pursued intense course of self-education, teaching himself French, Latin, and mathematics. At war's end worked briefly as surveyor; contracted malaria and was ill for two years. Married Louise S. Bartlett in 1869; they had seven children. In 1870 began to write columns, articles, and poems for *New Orleans Picayune*; left paper the following year after a quarrel with management. Worked as bookkeeper for firm of cotton factors; eventually resumed writing for *Pic-*

ayune, under different management. Contributed fiction, in part based on research in New Orleans city archives, to *Scribner's Monthly*; stories collected in *Old Creole Days* (1879). Devoted himself full-time to writing; literary reputation furthered by historical novel *The Grandissimes* (1880). Historical study *The Creoles of Louisiana* (1884) and political essays (in defense of freedmen's rights, election reform, prison reform, and other causes) collected in *The Silent South* (1885) met with much local opposition; left New Orleans in 1885 and settled in Northampton, Massachusetts. Gave lectures and readings nationwide; toured with Mark Twain 1884–85; published translations of Creole slave songs in *The Century* in 1886. Continued to address political issues in *The Negro Question* (1888) and *The Southern Struggle for Pure Government* (1890). Later fiction included *Dr. Sevier* (1885), *Bonaventure* (1888), *Strange True Stories of Louisiana* (1889), *Strong Hearts* (1899), *Bylow Hill* (1902), *Posson Jone and Père Raphael* (1909), *Gideon's Band* (1914), *The Flower of the Chapdelaines* (1918), and *Lovers of Louisiana* (1918). First wife, Louise, died in 1904; married Eva C. Stevenson in 1906; after her death in 1923, married Hanna Cowing. Died in St. Petersburg, Florida.

CHARLES EDWARD CARRYL (December 30, 1841–July 3, 1920) b. New York City. Son of Nathan Taylor Carryl. Early education in New York City and at Irving Institute, Tarrytown. Career as officer and director in railroad corporation flourished during the 1860s. Married Mary Wetmore in 1869; they had two children, Constance and Guy (who later became known as writer of fiction, verse, and journalism). In 1874, became member of New York Stock Exchange, retaining seat until 1908; published *The Stock Exchange Primer* in 1882. In his forties began writing juvenile fantasies interspersed with verse in the manner of Lewis Carroll, of which the first was the highly successful *Davy and the Goblin* (1885). Later publications included children's story *The Admiral's Caravan* (1892); *The River Syndicate*, sole attempt at adult fiction (1899); and *Charades by an Idle Man* (1911).

ALICE CARY (April 26, 1820–February 12, 1871) b. Miami Valley, Ohio, near Cincinnati. Daughter of Elizabeth Jessup and Robert Cary (an early settler of Cincinnati). Raised on family farm, the fourth of nine children; received limited education at home. Mother died of tuberculosis in 1835; father remarried two years later; unhappy relationship with stepmother. In 1838, published first poem in Cincinnati newspaper, and continued to make unpaid contributions to periodicals for next decade; began to attract attention with sketches published under pseudonym "Patty Lee" in *The National Era*. Represented (along with her sister Phoebe) in Rufus Griswold's *Female Poets of America* (1848); Edgar Allan Poe praised her contribution "Pictures of Memory" as "the noblest in the book"; visited in Cincinnati by Horace Greeley. *Poems of Alice and Phoebe Cary* published in 1850. Later that year, made a trip to New England and met John Greenleaf Whittier, who had repeatedly invited them (he later commemorated the visit in his poem "The Singer"). Moved to New York in the autumn of 1850; joined the following

year by Phoebe and their younger sister Elmina; Alice and Phoebe supported themselves by literary work. Alice published fiction and verse in many periodicals including *Harper's*, *Putnam's*, and *Atlantic Monthly*. Enjoyed success with sketches based on home life in Ohio, collected in *Clovernook* (1852–53) and *Clovernook Children* (1854); other prose works included *Hagar: A Story of Today* (1852), *Married, Not Mated* (1856), *Pictures of Country Life* (1859), and *The Bishop's Son* (1867). A second verse collection, *Lyra and Other Poems* (1852), was followed by *Poems* (1855), *Ballads, Lyrics and Hymns* (1866), and *The Lover's Diary* (1868). In 1856 the Cary sisters bought a house on 20th Street, and their Sunday evening receptions became a highlight of literary and artistic circles, frequented by such figures as Horace Greeley, Bayard Taylor, John Greenleaf Whittier, Thomas Bailey Aldrich, George Ripley, Elizabeth Cady Stanton, and P. T. Barnum. In addition to literary work, was first president of women's club Sorosis; active in many social causes, including abolition and women's rights; with Phoebe, briefly assisted Susan B. Anthony in editing suffrage paper *The Revolution*. Died after many years as an invalid during which she was cared for by Phoebe. *The Last Poems of Alice and Phoebe Cary*, edited by Mary Clemmer Ames, appeared in 1873.

PHOEBE CARY (September 4, 1824–July 31, 1871) b. Miami Valley, Ohio. Younger sister of Alice Cary; educated at home, as was her sister. Contributed to 1850 collection *Poems of Alice and Phoebe Cary*. After moving New York in 1851 to join Alice, assumed most domestic responsibilities and took care of Alice, who was often in ill health; with Alice, presided over renowned weekly salon; close friendship with P. T. Barnum. Published two volumes of poems independently of her sister, *Poems and Parodies* (1854) and *Poems of Faith, Hope and Love* (1869). With Alice, briefly assisted Susan B. Anthony in editing suffrage paper *The Revolution*. Assisted C. F. Deems in editing *Hymns for All Christians* in 1869. Celebrated as wit; also known for religious verse. Published tribute to Alice, "Light," after the latter's death in early 1871; died five months after her sister. Her late work was collected in *The Last Poems of Alice and Phoebe Cary* (1873), edited by Mary Clemmer Ames.

MADISON CAWEIN (March 23, 1865–December 8, 1914) b. Louisville, Kentucky. Full name Madison Julius Cawein; father William Cawein, a German of Huguenot ancestry who arrived in America in the 1840s, was a herbalist and maker of patent medicines; mother Christiana Stelsly, whose parents were German immigrants, was a spiritualist who believed herself endowed with mediumistic gifts. Apart from three years in New Albany, Indiana, as an adolescent, lived all his life in Louisville. Following graduation in 1886 from local high school, worked for six years as cashier in local pool hall, which was also center for legal off-track betting. At 22 published first collection of poetry, *Blooms of the Berry* (1887). Book was reviewed favorably by William Dean Howells in *Harper's Monthly*; Cawein dedicated second volume, *The Triumph of Music* (1888), to Howells. Supporting himself through real estate and stock market speculation, published 36 volumes of poetry, including *Ascolon of Gaul*

(1889), *Lyrics and Idyls* (1890), *Days and Dreams* (1891), *Red Leaves and Roses* (1893), *The Garden of Dreams* (1896), *Idyllic Monologues* (1898), *Weeds by the Wall* (1901), *A Voice on the Wind* (1902), *Vale of Tempe* (1905), *The Message of the Lilies* (1913), and *Minions of the Moon* (1913). Much of his poetry made use of detailed knowledge of Kentucky natural history. Maintained literary friendships with Edwin Arlington Robinson, Henry van Dyke, and James Whitcomb Riley; received belated recognition when Edmund Gosse prepared British collection of his work, *Kentucky Poems*, in 1902. In 1903 married Gertrude Foster McKelvey; they had one son, Preston. Suffered heavy financial losses in San Francisco earthquake in 1906. Five-volume illustrated edition of his work, *The Poems of Madison Cawein*, appeared in 1907. Died as a result of apoplectic attack in which he fell and hit his head on bathtub railing.

JOHN JAY CHAPMAN (March 2, 1862–November 4, 1933) b. New York, New York. Son of Eleanor Jay and Henry Grafton Chapman. Graduated Harvard 1885; attended Harvard Law School. In 1887 deliberately burned left hand (necessitating amputation) as self-punishment for having beaten another young man in fit of misguided jealousy after he had shown attention to Minna Timmins of Boston. Married Minna in 1889, and settled in New York; she died in 1897, shortly after birth of their third son. Involved in political opposition to Tammany Hall as member of City Reform Club, founded by Theodore Roosevelt. Published first book, *Emerson and Other Essays*, in 1898, followed by political writings collected in *Causes and Consequences* (1898) and *Practical Agitation* (1900). Broke with Theodore Roosevelt when Roosevelt repudiated Independent candidacy in favor of Republican nomination for New York governorship. Ended law practice in 1898. In April 1898 married second wife, Elizabeth Chanler of New York; son Chanler born 1900; shortly thereafter Chapman suffered serious mental breakdown and spent years recuperating, chiefly at Chanler family estate in Barrytown, New York, where he lived much of the time after 1905. In 1912 held public prayer meeting in Coatesville, Pennsylvania, on first anniversary of the lynching of a black man there. Wrote literary criticism, essays, and translations, as well as plays and poems. Friend of Owen Wister. Later publications included *Four Plays for Children* (1908), plays *The Maid's Forgiveness* (1908), *A Sausage from Bologna* (1909), and *Benedict Arnold, A Play for a Greek Theatre* (1911), *Learning and Other Essays* (1911), *Neptune's Isle* (1912), *William Lloyd Garrison* (1913), poetry collection *Homeric Scenes* (1914), *Memories and Milestones* (1915), *Deutschland über Alles* (1915), *Notes on Religion* (1915), *Greek Genius and Other Essays* (1915), *Songs and Poems* (1919), *A Glance Toward Shakespeare* (1922), and *Letters and Religion* (1924). Son Victor, a pilot in the Lafayette Escadrille, was the first American aviator to die in World War I. In later years adopted conservative positions, including militant opposition to Roman Catholic influence in American life and politics.

ROSE TERRY COOKE (February 17, 1827–July 18, 1892) b. West Hartford, Connecticut. Elder of two daughters of Anne Hurlbut and Henry Wadsworth

Terry. At age six, moved with family into the Wadsworth mansion, owned by paternal grandmother, in Hartford. Educated Hartford Female Seminary, graduating 1843; officially joined Congregational Church. Taught briefly in Hartford and then for four years at a Presbyterian church school in Burlington, New Jersey, where she also worked as governess for the minister's family. In 1848, received inheritance from a great uncle, which enabled her to devote herself to writing poetry and fiction, and to establish a home in Hartford. In 1852, began publishing poems in the *New-York Tribune*, where Charles A. Dana was editor. Beginning in 1855—though earlier stories may have appeared pseudonymously—Cooke published short stories in various periodicals, including *Harper's*, *Putnam's*, *The Galaxy*, and *Atlantic Monthly*, whose inaugural issue in November 1857 carried her story "Sally Parson's Duty." In the late 1850s, after her sister Alice fell ill, reared her two children. *Poems*, first verse collection, published 1861. In April 1873 married Rollin H. Cooke, a widower (with two children) 16 years younger than her. Moved to Winsted, Connecticut, where she continued to write and where husband worked in a bank. Writing helped support the family, which suffered financial setbacks as result of husband's and father-in-law's business failures. Close friend of Harriet Prescott Spofford and James T. and Annie Fields; work admired by William Dean Howells. Wrote two adult novels, *Happy Dodd* (1878) and *Steadfast* (1889), and one novel for children, *No* (1886). Many of her stories collected in *Somebody's Neighbors* (1881), *Root-Bound and Other Sketches* (1885), *The Sphinx's Children and Other People's* (1886), and *Huckleberries Gathered from New England Hills* (1891). Invited to read her poetry at Smith College commencement exercises in 1881; *Poems*, an expanded collection, published 1888. Family moved again in 1887 to Pittsfield, Massachusetts. Cooke died after suffering several serious bouts of influenza.

STEPHEN CRANE (November 1, 1871–June 5, 1900) b. Newark, New Jersey. Youngest of 14 children of Mary Helen Peck and the Rev. Jonathan Townley Crane (who died in 1880). Early education at Hudson River Institute, Claverack, New York. In 1890–91, studied at Lafayette College and Syracuse University; left school to become a writer, working first as journalist; met Hamlin Garland. Mother died 1891; Crane established base in New York City. Wrote articles, poems, stories, and the novella *Maggie: A Girl of the Streets* (privately printed 1893), which won the admiration of Garland, who drew it to the attention of William Dean Howells. *The Red Badge of Courage* appeared in abridged form as a syndicated newspaper serial in 1894; revised extensively by Crane before book publication in October 1895; became a best-seller and established his reputation as a writer. Published revised version of *Maggie* (1896), novels *George's Mother* (1896) and *The Third Violet* (1897); collection of stories, *The Little Regiment and Other Episodes of the American Civil War* (1896); poetry collected in *The Black Riders and Other Lines* (1895) and *War Is Kind* (1899). As syndicated newswriter, traveled to Mexico and the American West in 1895. In 1896, traveled by way of Florida to cover Cuban Revolution; met Cora Howorth Steward, proprietor of Hotel de Dream in

Jacksonville. Shipwrecked in January 1897 off Florida coast (incident became basis for story "The Open Boat"). Traveled to Greece (where he was joined by Cora) to cover Greek-Turkish War; he and Cora traveled to England as husband and wife in 1897; friends in England included Joseph Conrad, Henry James, Ford Madox Ford, Harold Frederic, and H. G. Wells. Went to Cuba in 1898 to cover Spanish-American War. In 1899 Crane and Cora returned to England where they rented ancient manor house Brede Place in Sussex. Continued to publish articles, stories, and poems despite ill health; last publications included *The Open Boat and Other Tales of Adventure* (1898), *Active Service* (1899), *The Monster and Other Stories* (1899), and *Whilomville Stories* (1900). Died of tuberculosis at sanatorium in the Black Forest, Germany.

EMILY DICKINSON (December 10, 1830–May 15, 1886) b. Emily Elizabeth Dickinson in Amherst, Massachusetts. Second of three children of Emily Norcross and Edward Dickinson (prominent lawyer who later served as state senator and national congressman); paternal grandfather Samuel Fowler Dickinson was a founder of Amherst College; siblings were older brother William Austin and younger sister Lavinia. Educated at Amherst Academy, 1840–46. In 1844 spent a month in Boston with mother's sister Lavinia to recover from ill health and depression following death of friend Sophia Holland. Attended Mount Holyoke Female Seminary in South Hadley, Massachusetts, 1847–48. Returned to family home, the Homestead, and lived there permanently, rarely leaving except for trips to Washington (where her father was serving a term in Congress) and Philadelphia in 1855 and in 1864–65 to Boston and Concord (where she spent seven months undergoing treatment for eye problems). Resisted the influence of local religious revivals in which other family members and friends (including Lavinia, Austin, and Austin's future wife Susan Gilbert) became involved. Cultivated intense intellectual friendships with several men including Benjamin F. Newton (a law clerk in her father's office) and the Rev. Charles Wadsworth (with whom she appears to have had close personal relationship). Composed over 1,700 brief lyrics, most intensively in the years 1859–65; only a few were published, primarily in the *Springfield Daily Republican*, during her lifetime (most without her consent and in heavily edited form). In 1858 she began binding her poems into what her editor Mabel Loomis Todd later termed "fascicles": homemade booklets made from folded stationery paper stitched together with thread. In April 1862, initiated literary correspondence with Thomas Wentworth Higginson, whom she knew only through his work in *Atlantic Monthly* (first letter began: "Are you too deeply occupied to say if my Verse is alive?"). They continued to write to each other for more than 20 years; he discouraged her from publishing her work; she received several visits from Higginson in the 1870s. Small circle of friends to whom she occasionally showed poems included Samuel Bowles, Josiah Gilbert Holland and his wife Elizabeth (with whom she had a long correspondence), and Helen Hunt Jackson. Close relationship with Judge Otis Lord, with whom she corresponded extensively. Brother Austin married Susan Gilbert in 1856, and they settled in the house

next door to the Homestead, the Evergreens. Father died in 1874, and mother's health declined. In later years rarely left house. Fell ill in June 1884, and never fully recovered; Helen Hunt Jackson asked to be made her literary executor, but died before Dickinson, in 1885. After her death, sister Lavinia found 40 fascicles of poems, along with many unstitched and loose pages, and with Mabel Loomis Todd, Higginson helped prepare *Poems by Emily Dickinson* (1890) and *Poems: Second Series* (1891); *Poems: Third Series*, edited by Todd, appeared in 1896.

PAUL LAURENCE DUNBAR (June 27, 1872–February 9, 1906) b. Dayton, Ohio. Only child of former Kentucky slaves Matilda Murphy and Joshua Dunbar. Father had escaped to Canada before Civil War, in which he served with Massachusetts 55th Regiment; mother had two son from a previous marriage. Parents separated shortly after Dunbar's birth and divorced in 1876; he remained with mother, a laundry worker, who taught him to read and encouraged his literary efforts. Educated at Dayton's public schools; graduated in 1891 from Central High School, where he was editor of the school paper, class poet, and only black member of his class. Wrote poetry from early age; first published poem appeared in *Dayton Herald* in 1888; while still in high school founded short-lived newspaper *The Dayton Tattler*, printed by classmate and future aviator Orville Wright. Worked as elevator operator in Dayton while continuing to publish poems and stories in local newspapers. In 1892 invited by former teacher Helen Truesdale to address Western Association of Writers; asked to become member. After newspaper accounts of his poetry, received letter of encouragement from James Whitcomb Riley. Published chapbook *Oak and Ivy* (1893) at his own expense; book sold well enough to reimburse printing costs. Found work as page at Dayton courthouse; received encouragement from white patrons James Newton Matthews, Charles A. Thatcher, and Henry A. Tobey; gave paid public readings of his work. Employed by Frederick Douglass in 1893 as clerk at Haiti Building of World's Columbian Exposition in Chicago; in Chicago met wide circle of black writers and activists including Angelina Grimké, Ida B. Wells, James Campbell, and composer Will Marion Cook. Work began to appear in *The Century*, *The New York Times*, and other leading publications. Second book, *Majors and Minors* (1895), praised in *Harper's* by William Dean Howells, who called Dunbar "the only man of pure African blood and of American civilization to feel the negro life aesthetically and express it lyrically." Howells' review made Dunbar suddenly famous. Signed with Pond Lecture Bureau and through Pond's efforts secured contract with Dodd, Mead for next collection, *Lyrics of Lowly Life* (1896), which sold well. Went to England in February 1897 on reading tour; major reading in London set up by Americam ambassador John Hay. Returned to U.S. after six months and in 1897 moved to Washington, D.C., to assume post as reading room clerk at Library of Congress. In March 1898 married poet and teacher Alice Ruth Moore, with whom he had corresponded for a number of years. Published short story collection *Folks from Dixie* (1898) and first novel, *The Uncalled* (1898). Literary success made it

possible for him to resign job at library; gave numerous readings; also contributed lyrics and librettos to musical comedies. Had busy social life in Washington; involved in fundraising for Hampton Institute; appeared in Boston with W.E.B. DuBois and Booker T. Washington at benefit for Tuskegee Institute. Received honorary degree from Atlanta University in 1899. On reading tour to promote *Lyrics of the Hearthside* (1899), contracted pneumonia; diagnosed with tuberculosis; health problems compounded by heavy drinking. Settled briefly in Harmon, Colorado, to recuperate. Continued to give public readings and produced further novels (*The Love of Landy*, 1900, *The Fanatics*, 1901, and *The Sport of the Gods*, 1902), story collections *The Strength of Gideon and Other Stories*, 1900, *In Old Plantation Days*, 1903, and *The Heart of Happy Hollow*, 1904), and volumes of verse (*Lyrics of Love and Laughter*, 1903, and *Lyrics of Sunshine and Shadow*, 1905). In 1900 stayed with James Weldon Johnson in Jacksonville, Florida, while recovering from physical breakdown. Separated from wife in 1902; after leaving Washington spent time in New York and Chicago before returning in 1903 to spend final years in Dayton, living with his mother in a house that he had built for her.

ERNEST FENOLLOSA (February 18, 1853–September 21, 1908) b. Salem, Massachusetts. His father, Manuel Francisco Ciriaco Fenollosa, a Spanish musician who arrived in the United States in 1838 and eventually settled in Salem, Massachusetts; taught piano and married one of his pupils, Mary Silsbee, daughter of prominent mercantile family. Fenollosa attended Harvard and studied work of Hegel and Herbert Spencer with enthusiasm. Graduated first in class of 1874, and was class poet; awarded fellowship enabling him to continue studies at Cambridge University in England, where he specialized in philosophy and, briefly, divinity. Shifted studies to art in 1877, attending newly founded school at Boston Museum of Fine Arts. Married Lizzie Goodhue Millett in June 1878; they had a son and a daughter. Under arrangement made by Edward Sylvester Morse, went to Japan in 1878, remaining there for 12 years, for the first eight of which he taught political economy, philosophy, and logic at Imperial University in Tokyo. In close association with Japanese artist Kano Hogai, encouraged preservation and cultivation of traditional Japanese art practices imperiled by Westernization. With Morse and wealthy Bostonian collector William Sturgis Bigelow, traveled throughout the country examining pottery, sculpture, and paintings; with Bigelow's patronage amassed collection of East Asian art (ultimately sold to Boston Museum of Fine Arts). Befriended Percival Lowell, who arrived in Japan in 1883, and Henry Adams and John La Farge, who arrived in 1886. In 1886, on behalf of Japanese government, traveled in Europe and America with Okakura Kakuzō (later author of *The Book of Tea*) surveying Western methods of art education. Became manager of Tokyo Fine Arts Academy and Imperial Museum when they opened in 1888. Under tutelage of Sakurai Keitoku Ajari of Homyōin Temple in Kyoto, converted to Tendai sect of Buddhism. Emperor awarded him Fourth and Third Class Orders of the Rising Sun and Third Class Order of the Sacred Mirror. Fenollosa returned to America in 1890 to become

curator of Oriental department of Boston Museum of Fine Arts. In 1891 met painter and printmaker Arthur Dow and introduced him to Asian art, working with him to develop methods of teaching Asian artistic principles to Western students. In 1892 read poem "East and West," to Phi Beta Kappa Society at Harvard; only published volume of poetry, *East and West: The Discovery of America and Other Poems*, appeared 1893. Represented Japan at World's Columbian Exposition in Chicago in 1893; curated major exhibition of Japanese prints at Boston Museum of Fine Arts in 1894. Divorced wife Lizzie in 1895 and shortly thereafter married Mary McNeill, scandalizing Boston society; relocated briefly to New York before returning by way of Europe to Japan, where Mary converted to Tendai Buddhism. Study of Japanese woodblock art, *The Masters of Ukioye*, published 1896. Resumed teaching career in 1897 as professor of English literature at Imperial Normal School of Tokyo. During second Japanese sojourn, made extensive notes on Chinese poetry and Japanese Noh drama. Placed in financial difficulties by lawsuit with first wife over property settlement. Returned to U.S. in 1900; wrote on Oriental religion, art, and literature, and lectured widely. Helped Charles L. Freer develop Japanese art collection now housed in Freer Gallery of Art, Washington, D.C. Died following a stroke while on a visit to London. Working from her husband's "rough pencil draft" (written in three months in 1906), Mary Fenollosa edited two-volume *Epochs of Chinese and Japanese Art* (1911), and appointed Ezra Pound as executor of Fenollosa's notes and unpublished translations, which Pound edited and amplified in *Cathay* (1915), *Certain Noble Plays of Japan* (1916), '*Noh*'; *or, Accomplishment, a Study of the Classical Stage of Japan* (1916), and *The Chinese Written Character as a Medium for Poetry* (1936).

EUGENE FIELD (September 2, 1850–November 4, 1895) b. St. Louis, Missouri. Father, Roswell Field, a native of Vermont, served as legal counsel for Dred Scott; mother, Frances Reed, died when Field was six years old. Field and brother Roswell Jr. (later a journalist and author who sometimes collaborated with his brother) cared for by cousin Mary Field French in Amherst, Massachusetts. Attended private school in Massachusetts and (briefly) Williams College, Knox College, and the University of Missouri (where he won a prize for oratory in 1872); did not obtain degree. Father died in 1869; in 1872, having received an $8,000 advance on inheritance from father's estate, went to Europe with friend Edgar Comstock; spent much of his inheritance there. Returning the following year, married Edgar Comstock's 16-year-old sister Julia Sutherland Comstock, of St. Joseph, Missouri; they had eight children. Devoted himself to newspaper work, serving as editor on *St. Joseph Gazette*, *St. Louis Journal*, *Kansas City Times*, and *Denver Tribune*. Joined Chicago *Morning News* (later *Record*) in 1883; remained there for rest of life, contributing daily column "Sharps and Flats," which often featured his own verse. Well-known for pranks and practical jokes, some literary, such as attributing his own poems to celebrated public figures. Spent 14 months in Europe, 1889–90, for health reasons, while continuing to write his column. In

later years devoted himself to book-collecting (left unfinished a prose work entitled *The Love Affairs of a Bibliomaniac*) and, with his brother, to translations of Horace's poetry, collected in *Echoes from the Sabine Farm* (1892). Poetry (some written in a variety of dialects, and much of it originally published in newspapers) collected in *A Little Book of Western Verse* (1889), *Second Book of Verse* (1892), and *With Trumpet and Drum* (1892). Other publications, many of them collections of newspaper sketches, included *The Tribune Primer* (1882), *A Little Book of Profitable Tales* (1890), and *The Holy Cross and Other Tales* (1893). Died in his sleep of heart failure. A ten-volume collected edition of his work was published posthumously in 1896.

FRANCIS MILES FINCH (June 9, 1827–July 31, 1907) b. Ithaca, New York. Son of Tryphena Farling and Miles Finch, a merchant. Educated Ithaca Academy; graduated Yale 1849. At Yale edited *Yale Literary Magazine* and was class poet; continued to write poetry at intervals for rest of life. Admitted to bar in Ithaca and began practicing law with success. In 1853 married Elizabeth Brooke of Philadelphia. Poem "The Blue and the Gray" first published in *Atlantic Monthly* in 1867; widely reprinted, it earned him celebrity as poet. Served as district tax collector during Grant's first administration. In 1880 appointed to fill vacancy as associate judge of New York Court of Appeals, and then elected to 14-year term, serving until retirement from bench in 1895. Close friend of Ezra Cornell; active as trustee in founding of Cornell University; served as lecturer in law, dean, and ultimately professor of legal history. In 1899 became president of New York State Bar Association. Of his literary career, he commented: "My whole life as a lawyer has been a battle against literary longings. I have kept the most earnest part of my nature in chains. I fear I have done it so long as to make full liberty dangerous to me." Late in life edited collected poems, published posthumously as *The Blue and the Gray and Other Verses* (1909).

STEPHEN FOSTER (July 4, 1826–January 13, 1864) b. Stephen Collins Foster in Pittsburgh, Pennsylvania. Ninth of ten children of Eliza Clayland Tomlinson and merchant William Barclay Foster. Educated Allegheny Academy (Allegheny, Pennsylvania), and Athens Academy (Tioga Point, Pennsylvania). Briefly attended Jefferson College (Canonsburg, Pennsylvania) in July 1841; education continued in Pittsburgh by tutors. Began to compose at an early age; published first song, "Open Thy Lattice, Love" in 1844. Family, objecting to musical career, sent him to Cincinnati in 1846 to work as bookkeeper for brother Dunning Foster. A number of his songs were published in *Songs of the Sable Harmonists* (1848) and *Foster's Ethiopian Melodies* (1849). In 1850, success of his songs (including "Louisiana Belle," "O Susannah," "Uncle Ned," and "Away Down South") led him to return home to Pittsburgh and devote himself exclusively to music. Later that year, married Jane Denny McDowell of Pittsburgh; daughter Marion born April 1851. Songs popularized by Christy's Minstrels, Campbell Minstrels, and New Orleans Serenaders; in 1851 sold exclusive pre-publication performance rights to E. P. Christy, in-

augurating profitable business arrangement for both parties. During 1850s, produced series of popular songs including "De Camptown Races" (1850), "Ring De Banjo" (1851), "The Old Folks at Home" (1851), "Massa's in de Cold Ground" (1852), "My Old Kentucky Home" (1853), "Old Dog Tray" (1853), "Jeanie with the Light Brown Hair" (1854), and "Come Where My Love Lies Dreaming" (1855). Thereafter productivity and popularity fell off; final minstrel hit was "Old Black Joe" (1860). Foster moved to New York with family in 1860; marital troubles led, by 1862, to a separation, with Jane and Marion living in Lewistown, Pennsylvania. Foster composed prolifically, but without recapturing former success; drank heavily and was reduced to poverty. Lived his last days in a Bowery hotel; died in Bellevue Hospital from wounds received when he fell in his hotel room, lacerating neck and face.

HAMLIN GARLAND (September 14, 1860 – March 4, 1940) b. Hannibal Hamlin Garland, on farm near New Salem, Wisconsin. Son of Isabelle McClintock and Richard H. Garland. Worked with father on succession of family farms in Wisconsin, Iowa, and Dakota Territory. Graduated Cedar Valley Seminary (Osage, Iowa) 1881. Worked as itinerant carpenter and handyman; taught school briefly in Illinois, 1882–83. Homesteaded in Dakotas, 1883–84; earned enough to move to Boston, where he engaged in intensive studies at Boston Public Library; also taught at Boston School of Oratory (1884–91) and wrote book reviews for Boston papers. Introduced himself to William Dean Howells, who became close friend. Trips back home to Iowa and Dakota Territory in the late 1880s led to *Main-Travelled Roads* (1891), collection of realistic stories drawing on midwestern experiences (writing defended publicly by Howells: "If anyone is still at a loss to account for that uprising of the farmers in the West, let him read *Main-Travelled Roads*"). Met the young Stephen Crane and gave him literary encouragement. Became ardent partisan of single-tax economic theories of Henry George (with whom he formed close friendship) and campaigned for Populist party in election of 1892. Four novels published in 1892—*Jason Edwards*, *A Member of the Third House*, *A Spoil of Office*, and *A Little Norsk*—followed by poetry collection *Prairie Songs* (1893) and another volume of Middle Border stories, *Prairie Folks* (1893). Moved to Chicago in 1893; associates there included realist novelist Henry Blake Fuller (who later satirized Garland in short story "The Downfall of Abner Joyce") and sculptor Lorado Taft. Active in many causes and movements: organized Central Art Association; campaigned for women's rights, conservation, and fair treatment for American Indians; pursued interest in spiritualism. Published *Crumbling Idols: Twelve Essays on Art* (1894), novel *Rose of Dutcher's Coolly* (1895), biography *Ulysses S. Grant* (1898), and *The Trail of the Goldseekers* (1899), an account of travels in Canada and Alaska. Married Zuline Taft (sister of Lorado Taft) in 1899; they had two daughters. Made first trip to England in 1899 and cultivated many literary acquaintances there. Realism of early fiction replaced by more romantic tone in series of popular novels including *The Spirit of Sweetwater* (1898), *The Captain of the Gray-Horse Troop* (1902), *The Light of the Star* (1904), and *The Forester's Daughter* (1914);

treated spiritualist themes in novels *The Tyranny of the Dark* (1905), *The Shadow World* (1908), and *Victor Ollnee's Discipline* (1911). Moved to New York City in 1916. Consulted by friend Theodore Roosevelt on federal policy toward American Indians; stories on Indian themes collected in *The Book of the American Indian* (1923). In later years wrote series of volumes of autobiography and family history, of which the most successful were *A Son of the Middle Border* (1917) and *A Daughter of the Middle Border* (1922), for which he won the Pulitzer Prize. *Roadside Meetings* (1930) initiated series of literary memoirs based on diaries. Moved in 1930 to Los Angeles, California. Later poems collected in *Iowa, O Iowa!* (1935); occult studies summarized in *Forty Years of Psychic Research* (1940) and *The Mystery of the Buried Crosses* (1939).

RICHARD WATSON GILDER   (February 8, 1844 – November 18, 1909)   b. Bordentown, New Jersey. Son of Jane Nutt and William Henry Gilder, Methodist minister who conducted Belle Vue Female Seminary in Bordentown. In Gilder's early years, family moved often, as father served as teacher or minister in Flushing, New York, in Redding and Fair Haven, Connecticut, and in Yonkers, New York. They returned to Bordentown at outbreak of Civil War, during which Gilder joined 1st Philadelphia Artillery, a company formed to defend Harrisburg, but did not see much active service; formed friendship with Charles Godfrey Leland. After father's death in 1864, worked as railroad paymaster and later as reporter for *Newark Daily Advertiser*; with R. Newton Crane founded *Newark Morning Register* in 1868. In 1869 became editor of *Hours at Home*, and upon its merger into *Scribner's Monthly* in 1870 became assistant editor of *Scribner's Monthly* under Josiah G. Holland. Helen Hunt (later Helen Hunt Jackson) introduced him to Helena de Kay (granddaughter of poet Joseph Rodman Drake), whom he married in 1874; they had five children. Gilder's love poems to Helena (originally published in *Scribner's*) were collected in *The New Day* (1875). The Gilders' Manhattan homes (off Union Square and Washington Square), and their Massachusetts summer homes on Buzzards Bay and in the Berkshires, became important centers of cultural life; guests included Henry James, John La Farge, Augustus Saint-Gaudens, Stanford White, Helena Modjeska, Joseph Jefferson, Walt Whitman, Rudyard Kipling, Edmund Clarence Stedman, Thomas Bailey Aldrich, Mark Twain, and Grover Cleveland (who became a close friend). Involved in foundation of Society of American Artists (1877) and Authors' Club (1882). In 1879 the Gilders traveled in Europe for a year; in France, Gilder formed links with Provençal poets including Frédéric Mistral; in England renewed friendship with George MacDonald whom he had met earlier in the U.S. Following the resignation in 1881 of Holland (who died later the same year), Gilder assumed full editorship of the magazine, now renamed *The Century*; while he was editor, contributors included Henry James, Mark Twain, William Dean Howells, George Washington Cable, John Hay and Hamlin Garland. Campaigned for civil service reform; participated in founding of Anti-Spoils League in 1893. Became increasingly involved in New York civic affairs; as chairman of state commission investigating tenement buildings, exposed

unsafe conditions in tenements owned by Corporation of Trinity Church; campaigned against Tammany Hall corruption. Traveled in Europe and the Holy Land, 1894–95. Published 16 volumes of verse, including *The Poet and His Master* (1878), *The Celestial Passion* (1887), *The Great Remembrance and Other Poems* (1893), *In Palestine and Other Poems* (1898), *In the Heights* (1905), *A Book of Music* (1906), *The Fire Divine* (1907), and *Poems* (1908). Also published books about Abraham Lincoln and Grover Cleveland. In later years awarded honorary degrees by Yale, Princeton, Harvard, and several other institutions.

LOUISE IMOGEN GUINEY (January 7, 1861–November 2, 1920) b. Boston, Massachusetts. Daughter of Janet Margaret Doyle and Patrick Robert Guiney, a Civil War brigadier general who later practiced law. Raised as Roman Catholic. Father died in 1877. Graduated in 1879 from Elmhurst Academy at Convent of Sacred Heart in Providence, Rhode Island; moved with her mother to Auburndale, Massachusetts. First poetry collection, *Songs at the Start*, published 1884, followed by essays in *Goose-Quill Papers* (1885); work praised by Oliver Wendell Holmes and Richard Watson Gilder. Second collection, *The White Sail and Other Poems*, appeared in 1887. Wrote children's stories collected in *Brownies and Bogles* (1888). With mother, made long visit to England, 1889–91. *The Crust of Society*, adaptation of *Le Demi-Monde* by Aléxandre Dumas fils, produced in Boston and New York in 1892. *A Roadside Harp* (1893) was considered by Guiney and her contemporaries to be her most important collection of poems; essays on English literature collected in *A Little English Gallery* (1894), followed by story collection *Lovers' Saint Ruth's and Three Other Tales* (1895) and privately printed *Nine Sonnets Written at Oxford* (1895). Contributed poems to close friend Alice Brown's study of Robert Louis Stevenson, 1895. Postmistress of Auburndale, 1894–97; endured opposition and boycotts from residents hostile to Roman Catholicism. Made walking tour of England and Wales in the summer of 1895 (forming friendship with English poet Lionel Johnson). Associated with Fred Holland Day and Herbert Copeland in publication of fine editions, under whose Copeland and Day imprint a number of her works appeared. Magazine articles collected in *Patrins* (1897); edited *James Clarence Mangan: His Selected Poems* (1897). English edition of selected poems published as *England and Yesterday: A Book of Short Poems* (1898); *The Martyrs' Idyl and Shorter Poems* (1899) consisted largely of revisions of earlier work. In 1899 took job as cataloguer at Boston Public Library. Traveled again to England with her aunt in 1901, settling in Oxford. Prepared editions of various English literary works by authors including Henry Vaughan, Katherine Philips, and Thomas Stanley; published *Robert Emmet* (1904), biography of Irish nationalist, and *Blessed Edmund Campion* (1908), study of Elizabethan Catholic martyr. Wrote little poetry in later years; *Happy Ending* (1909, enlarged 1927) was her final selection of the poems she wished to preserve. Edited *Some Poems of Lionel Johnson, Newly Selected* (1912). Devoted much scholarly work to projected edition of Henry Vaughan and anthology of English Catholic poetry (neither project was com-

pleted by her, although the anthology eventually appeared, co-edited by
Geoffrey Bliss, as *Recusant Poets* in 1938). Returned to Boston in 1909 to care
for her mother, who died the following spring, after which Guiney returned
permanently to England. Later years marked by poverty, deafness, and increasing ill health.

FRANCES ELLEN WATKINS HARPER   (September 24, 1825–February 22,
1911)   b. Baltimore, Maryland. Parents were free blacks; given name Frances
Ellen Watkins; she was orphaned at early age. Attended school run by uncle,
the Rev. William Watkins (a frequent contributor to *The Liberator*). Found
work in a bookshop in Baltimore. Published collection of poetry, *Forest
Leaves* (1845), of which no copies are known to be extant. In 1850 took position teaching sewing at Union Seminary, near Columbus, Ohio, a school for
free blacks founded by the African Methodist Episcopal Church. Two years
later left for Little York, Pennsylvania, where she obtained another teaching
position. Met black abolitionist William Grant Still, who became close friend;
in 1854 moved to Philadelphia and became active in anti-slavery movement,
working under Still's direction for Underground Railroad. *Poems on Miscellaneous Subjects* (1854), published with a preface by William Lloyd Garrison,
enjoyed wide circulation and went through several editions. Lectured widely,
1854–60, initially for Maine Antislavery Society, and then throughout New
England, in Canada, and in western states. Her poems, stories, lectures, and
speeches published regularly in abolitionist press. Married widower Fenton
Harper (who had three children) in 1860 and settled in Columbus, Ohio;
they had a daughter, Mary. After husband's death in 1864, resumed career as
lecturer and organizer; toured South frequently in late 1860s and early 1870s.
Published two volumes of narrative poetry, *Moses: A Story of the Nile* (1869;
expanded 1889; later incorporated in *Idylls of the Bible*, 1901) and *Sketches of
Southern Life* (1872), as well as the verse collection *Poems* (1871). In 1871 settled
permanently in Philadelphia. Founder and assistant superintendent of a
YMCA Sabbath School from 1872. Active in many political and social organi-
zations in later years, including American Association of Education of Col-
ored Youth (of which she became director in 1894), Women's Christian
Temperance Union, American Woman Suffrage Association, and American
Equal Rights Association; associates included Frederick Douglass, Ida Wells
Barnett, Harriet Tubman, Susan B. Anthony, and Elizabeth Cady Stanton.
Novel *Iola Leroy, or Shadows Uplifted* published in 1892; later poetry collected
in *Atlanta Offering* (1895). Addressed World Congress of Representative
Women in 1893 at World's Columbian Exposition in Chicago. In 1896 helped
found National Association of Colored Women, of which she became vice-
president the following year.

BRET HARTE   (August 25, 1836–May 5, 1902)   b. Francis Brett Harte in
Albany, New York. Son of Elizabeth Rebecca Ostrander and Henry Harte;
paternal grandfather, Bernard Hart, was prominent Jewish merchant of New
York. Father was a teacher and lecturer whose lack of success led to family's

frequently moving. During Harte's childhood, family lived in six different northeastern cities, settling, after father's death in 1845, in New York City, where Harte attended school until age 13. Left school and worked as lawyer's assistant and in counting-house, becoming self-supporting by age 15. In 1853, mother moved to California and married Andrew Williams, who became mayor of Oakland; with his younger sister Margaret, Harte joined her there the following year. For several years drifted in northern California, working at various minor jobs including druggist's assistant, tutor, and stage coach guard. Moved in 1858 to Union (now Arcata), on Humboldt Bay, where he received training as printer on local newspaper, *The Northern Californian*; soon began contributing articles and poems. Local response to his editorial protest in *Northern Californian* against "indiscriminate massacre" of 60 Wiyot Indians on Gunther's Island in February 1860 forced him to leave Arcata. Moved to San Francisco; worked as typesetter for *The Golden Era* and contributed many items to paper including column "Town and Table Talk" and first major short story, "The Work on Red Mountain." Cultivated personal connections with San Francisco society, notably with Jessie Frémont (wife of General John C. Frémont) and minister Thomas Starr King; obtained job as clerk in surveyor-general's office. Married Anna Griswold of New York in 1862; they had four children (born between 1865 and 1875). The following year switched to job in new U.S. Mint, where he worked for six years. Edited local poetry anthology *Outcroppings* (1866); published collections of prose sketches, *The Lost Galleon and Other Tales* (1867) and *Condensed Novels and Other Papers* (1867). Appointed editor of *Overland Monthly* in 1868, attracting national attention with his short stories "The Luck of Roaring Camp" (1868) and "The Outcasts of Poker Flat" (1869). Publication in 1870 of humorous poem "Plain Language from Truthful James" and collection *The Luck of Roaring Camp and Other Sketches* made him world-famous (although Harte described poem as "the worst I ever wrote"). Friends in San Francisco included Mark Twain, Charles Warren Stoddard, Ambrose Bierce, Ina Coolbrith, and Adah Isaacs Menken. Declined offers of employment as professor of literature at the University of California and as editor of Chicago *Lakeside Monthly*. Relocated to the East in 1871; spent a week in Boston with William Dean Howells; settled (after intervals in New York City and Newport, Rhode Island) in Morristown, New Jersey. Lived increasingly separately from wife and children. Given lucrative exclusive contract with *Atlantic Monthly*, but contributions found little favor. Continued to publish fiction, including *Mrs. Skaggs's Husbands* (1873), *Tales of the Argonauts* (1875), *Gabriel Conroy* (1876), and *The Story of a Mine* (1877); wrote plays *Two Men of Sandy Bar* (1876) and, in collaboration with Mark Twain, *Ah Sin* (1877), but these enjoyed slight success; verse collected in *East and West Poems* (1871), *Poetical Works* (1872), *Echoes of the Foot-Hills* (1872), and other volumes. Fell into debt; lectured widely beginning in the early 1870s; unsuccessfully tried to launch magazine in Washington, D.C. Accepted appointment by Rutherford B. Hayes to American consulate in Krefeld, Prussia, and went to Germany alone in July 1878; while officially serving there, spent much time in London. In London

acquaintances included Henry James, George Du Maurier, Thomas Hardy; formed close friendship with Arthur and Marguerite Van de Velde, with whom he frequently stayed. Appointed in 1880 to U.S. consulate in Glasgow; dismissed in 1885 for inattention to duty. Settled permanently in London, living with the Van de Veldes; wrote prolifically, supporting himself entirely by writing after loss of consular job. Later publications included *Flip and Other Stories* (1882), *On the Frontier* (1884), *By Shore and Sedge* (1885), *Maruja* (1885), *The Queen of the Pirate Isle* (1886), *The Heritage of Dedlow Marsh and Other Tales* (1889), *In a Hollow of the Hills* (1895), *Tales of Trail and Town* (1898), and many other works. Wife Anna came to England (where their son Frank had settled five years earlier) in 1898; they saw each other occasionally but never again lived together.

JOHN HAY (October 8, 1838–July 1, 1905)   b. Salem, Indiana. One of six children of Helen Leonard and Dr. Charles Hay, a country doctor; family settled eventually in Spunky Point (now Warsaw), Illinois. Studied at a private school in Pittsfield, Illinois, and at a college in Springfield, Illinois. Graduated Brown University 1858, and returned to Springfield to study law in uncle Milton Hay's law office; made acquaintance of Abraham Lincoln, whose office was next door. Campaigned for Lincoln in 1860 and traveled to Washington in 1861 as his assistant private secretary; remained close to Lincoln through Civil War years, keeping a detailed diary. Served as military aide from 1864 under Generals Hunter and Gillmore, attaining rank of colonel. Following war, appointed first secretary to American legation in Paris, 1865–67; during this period devoted himself to writing occasional verse and prose. After brief return to America, went abroad again to serve successively as chargé d'affaires in Vienna (1867–68) and legation secretary in Madrid (1868–70). Returned to America intending career in journalism; became editorial writer for *New-York Tribune* under Horace Greeley; published popular dialect ballads "Little Breeches" and "Jim Bludso" in the *Tribune*. Volume of Spanish reminiscences, *Castilian Days* (1871), followed by collection of dialect poems, *Pike County Ballads and Other Pieces* (1871). Married Clara Louise Stone of Cleveland, Ohio, in February 1874; they had two daughters and a son. Abandoned journalism and settled in Cleveland as business partner of wealthy father-in-law Amasa Stone. Served as Assistant Secretary of State under Rutherford B. Hayes, 1879–81. In Washington began close friendship with Henry Adams; they built adjoining houses and formed nexus of intellectual group including Clarence King and Henry Cabot Lodge. Returned to *New-York Tribune* as temporary editor-in-chief, 1881–82. Political novel *The Bread-Winners*, an attack on labor unions, published anonymously in 1884. In collaboration with John Nicolay (friend from Springfield who was another of Lincoln's secretaries) worked on *Abraham Lincoln: A History*, serialized over a four-year period in *The Century*, and published in ten volumes in 1890. *Poems* (1890) contained little new work. During 1890s spent much time traveling in Europe. Was close adviser of William McKinley, who appointed him ambassador to Great Britain in 1897. Involved in diplomatic maneuvering relating

to Spanish-American War and annexation of Philippines, which he enthusiastically supported. In 1898, despite ill health, appointed Secretary of State by McKinley; instrumental in promulgating Open Door policy in China. Retained post during administrations of Theodore Roosevelt, but was less active in determining policy. Among first seven members elected to American Academy of Arts and Letters in 1904. *Addresses* collected posthumously in 1906; *Complete Poetical Works* published 1916.

PAUL HAMILTON HAYNE (January 1, 1830–July 6, 1886) b. Charleston, South Carolina, of distinguished family; son of Emily McElhenny and naval lieutenant Paul Hamilton Hayne; descendant of Revolutionary War hero Colonel Isaac Hayne. Father died of yellow fever at sea when Hayne was not yet two; raised by mother and by uncle Robert Young Hayne, governor of South Carolina and previously a U.S. senator. At Christopher Cotes' Classical School in Charleston, formed enduring friendship with Henry Timrod. First poem published in *Charleston Courier* in 1845; continued to contribute verse to magazines including *Southern Literary Messenger*, *Southern Literary Gazette*, and *Graham's Magazine*. Graduated College of Charleston in 1850. Studied law with prominent attorney James L. Petigru; admitted to bar 1852. Married Mary Middleton Michel in 1852 (their son William was born in 1856). Worked as assistant editor and then editor of *Southern Literary Gazette*, 1852–54. A member, with William Gilmore Simms, of group of Southern writers who gathered at John Russell's bookstore in Charleston; edited *Russell's Magazine*, 1857–60. First collections of verse—*Poems* (1855), *Sonnets and Other Poems* (1857), and *Avolio: A Legend of the Island of Cos* (1860)—won praise from Holmes, Bryant, and Longfellow. Served as aide-de-camp to South Carolina governor Francis Pickens for four months in 1861–62; fell ill and was removed from active service; wrote martial lyrics in defense of Southern cause. Home destroyed in the war. Moved in July 1865 to small farm Copse Hill near Groveton, Georgia. Eked out a living writing for newspapers and magazines; also did editorial work for the *Atlanta Sun*, *Charleston News*, and other periodicals. Later collections of poetry included *Legends and Lyrics* (1872) and *The Mountain of the Lovers* (1873); *Collected Poems* published 1882. Edited posthumous edition of the poetry of Timrod in 1873.

JOHN HENRY HOPKINS, JR. (October 28, 1820–August 13, 1891) b. Pittsburgh, Pennsylvania. One of 13 children of Melusina Muller and John Henry Hopkins, a prominent lawyer; after conversion experience, father became member of Trinity Episcopal Church, was elected rector in 1823, and soon achieved full clerical standing. Family moved to Cambridge, Massachusetts, in 1831, and the following year to Burlington, Vermont, where father became Episcopal Bishop of Vermont. Hopkins graduated University of Vermont in 1839; served as tutor in Savannah, Georgia, 1842–44; graduated New York General Theological Seminary in 1850, and in the same year was ordained Episcopal deacon. In 1853 founded *The Church Journal*, which he edited until 1868. Active in foundation of dioceses of Pittsburgh in 1865, and

of Albany and Long Island in 1868. Ordained priest in 1872; served as rector in Plattsburgh, New York (1872–76) and Williamsport, Pennsylvania (1876–87). Published biography of father in 1873; other writings included *Carols, Hymns and Songs* (1863), *The Canticles Noted* (1866), and *Poems by the Wayside* (1883). Died at the home of a friend near Hudson, New York.

RICHARD HOVEY (May 4, 1864–February 24, 1900) b. Normal, Illinois. Son of Harriette Farnham Spofford, an educator, and Charles Edward Hovey, a Civil War general and former president of Normal University of Illinois who later practiced law. Grew up in North Amherst, Massachusetts, and in Washington, D.C. Before college, educated mostly at home by mother. First book, *Poems*, published privately in 1880. Graduated Dartmouth (where he wrote song "Men of Dartmouth") in 1885. Studied art at Art Students' League of Washington, and theology at General Theological Seminary of Episcopal Church in New York City; contemplated taking orders, but did not complete training. In summer 1887 met Canadian poet Bliss Carman and artist Thomas Buford Meteyard, with whom he made walking tour of New England; in Scituate, Massachusetts, met Thomas William Parsons, poet and translator of Dante, whom he regarded as mentor. Corresponded intensively with novelist Amelie Rives, 1888–89. Gave lectures in philosophy, 1888–89, at Thomas Davidson's school in Farmington, Connecticut. In 1890 met Henriette Knapp Russell, wife of actor Edmund Russell and popular proponent of physical training system Delsartism (during stay in London, her friends included Oscar Wilde, James McNeill Whistler, and Madame Blavatsky); began affair with her. Under influence of Sidney Lanier's *The Science of English Verse*, published essays on poetry and poetic technique in *The Independent*, 1891–94. Undertook multi-part verse drama on Arthurian themes titled *Poem in Dramas*; first volume published as *Launcelot and Guenevere* (1891). Went to Europe with Mrs. Russell in 1891; traveled by himself in France, settling in Giverny. Joined Mrs. Russell in Tours; their son Julian born February 1892. Returned to U.S., leaving son in care of foster mother; visited Bliss Carman in Nova Scotia. Elegy on death of Thomas William Parsons, *Seaward*, published in book form in 1893. In collaboration with Carman, and with Meteyard as book designer, wrote *Songs from Vagabondia* (1894), which achieved enormous popularity. Married Mrs. Russell, recently divorced, in January 1894; worked sporadically as actor; in May the couple sailed for Europe. Worked on translations of Belgian symbolist playwright Maurice Maeterlinck (published *The Plays of Maurice Maeterlinck*, 1894–96); after a year in London went to France in June 1895; met Stéphane Mallarmé and other members of symbolist movement; reunited with son Julian. Returned to U.S. in 1896; settled in New York City. Published another volume with Carman, *More Songs from Vagabondia* (1896), and further installments of poetic drama cycle, *The Birth of Galahad* (1898) and *Taliesin: A Masque* (1899); poetry collected in *Along the Trail* (1898), which included poems in support of Spanish-American War. Began lectureship at Barnard College in 1899. After several years of ill health, died following minor intestinal operation when blood clot lodged in

his heart. Posthumously published work included *Last Songs from Vagabondia* (1901), another collaboration with Carman; *The Holy Graal and Other Fragments* (1907), further pieces of Arthurian drama cycle; *To the End of the Trail* (1908); and *Dartmouth Lyrics* (1924).

WILLIAM DEAN HOWELLS (March 1, 1837–May 10, 1920) b. Martins Ferry, Ohio. Son of Mary Dean and William Cooper Howells (a Welsh-born printer and publisher with wide political and philosophical interests). Little formal schooling; assisted father (who had bought a newspaper in Hamilton, Ohio) as typesetter. Published first poem in 1852 in *Ohio State Journal*, for which father was reporter, and for which Howells himself worked as a typesetter; while working there, formed friendship with John James Piatt. Relocated with family to Jefferson, Ohio; maintained rigorous course of self-education while working full time as printer for *Ashtabula Sentinel*, a newspaper with abolitionist sympathies edited by his father. Periodic nervous collapses led to failure as editor of *Cincinnati Gazette*. Became city editor and columnist of *Ohio State Journal* in 1858. Published poems, stories, and reviews in *Atlantic Monthly*, *National Era*, *Dial*, and other periodicals; first book, verse collection *Poems of Two Friends* (written in collaboration with John James Piatt), published 1860. Wrote Lincoln campaign biography, using proceeds to travel East where he met literary figures including James Russell Lowell, James T. Fields, Oliver Wendell Homes, Nathaniel Hawthorne, Ralph Waldo Emerson, and Henry David Thoreau. Appointed U.S. consul in Venice (1861–64), where he studied Italian, Dante, and Venetian art. Married Elinor Mead in Paris in 1862; they had two daughters and a son. Resigning consulship, briefly joined staff of *The Nation* in New York before moving to Cambridge to serve as assistant editor of *Atlantic Monthly*. Formed close friendships with Mark Twain and William and Henry James. In 1871 succeeded James T. Fields as editor of *Atlantic Monthly*. Published first novel, *Their Wedding Journey* (1871), followed by, among other titles, *A Chance Acquaintance* (1873), *Poems* (1873), *A Foregone Conclusion* (1874), *The Lady of the Aroostook* (1879), and *The Undiscovered Country* (1880). Resigned *Atlantic* editorship in 1881 to write full time; moved to Boston. Later novels included *Dr. Breen's Practice* (1881), *A Modern Instance* (1882), *The Rise of Silas Lapham* (1885), *Indian Summer* (1886), *The Minister's Charge* (1886), *April Hopes* (1887), *Annie Kilburn* (1888), *A Hazard of New Fortunes* (1890), utopian novel *A Traveler from Altruria* (1894), *The Landlord at Lion's Head* (1897), *The Story of a Play* (1898), *The Kentons* (1902), and *The Son of Royal Langbrith* (1904). Increasingly involved in radical social causes; pleaded for clemency for anarchists unjustly convicted of murder following Haymarket riot of 1887. Older daughter Winifred died in 1889. Contributed regular "Editor's Study" column to *Harper's Monthly*, 1886–92; moved to New York to edit *Cosmopolitan*, but resigned after conflict with its owner over his political views. Encouraged many younger writers including Stephen Crane, Paul Laurence Dunbar, Henry Blake Fuller, Abraham Cahan, and Stuart Merrill. Elected first president

of American Academy of Arts and Letters in 1908; traveled frequently in Europe. Died of pneumonia in New York.

WILLIAM REED HUNTINGTON (September 20, 1838–July 26, 1909) b. Lowell, Massachusetts. Son of Hannah Hinckley and Elisha Huntington, prominent physician and public official. Graduated Harvard, where he was class poet, in 1859. Studied for Episcopal ministry; ordained 1861; accepted position as assistant minister of Emmanuel Church; in 1862 became rector of All Saints Church, Worcester, Massachusetts, and served in that capacity for 21 years. Married Theresa Reynolds in 1863. Read Phi Beta Kappa poem at Harvard in 1870. From 1883, as rector of Grace Church, was a leading figure in the religious and cultural life of New York City. Worked on revised version of Book of Common Prayer (published 1892); interest in church architecture led to involvement with building of Cathedral of St. John the Divine in New York City, of which he was a trustee for 22 years, and where a memorial chapel was dedicated to him. His religious and ecclesiastical ideas were outlined in many works, including *The Church-Idea* (1870), *Conditional Immortality* (1878), *The Causes of the Soul* (1891), *The Peace of the Church* (1891), *Popular Misconceptions of the Episcopal Church* (1891), *The Spiritual House* (1895), *A National Church* (1898), and *Briefs on Religion* (1902). Published two volumes of memoirs, *Twenty Years of a Massachusetts Rectorship* (1883) and *Twenty Years of a New York Rectorship* (1903). Poems collected in *Sonnets and a Dream* in 1899 (second edition 1903).

HELEN HUNT JACKSON (October 15, 1830–August 12, 1885) b. Helen Maria Fiske in Amherst, Massachusetts. Father Nathan W. Fiske taught classics and moral philosophy at Amherst College; when she was 14, her mother, Deborah Vinal, died of consumption. Educated at Ipswich Female Academy in Massachusetts and Abbott Brothers school in New York City. Early friend and schoolmate of Emily Dickinson, with whom she retained lifelong ties. In 1852 married Edward B. Hunt, officer of army corps of engineers; he died in 1863 while testing a submarine device. Of their two sons, one died in infancy, the other in 1865. Moved to Newport, Rhode Island, where she became acquainted with Thomas Wentworth Higginson. With his encouragement, began to contribute poetry and prose to *New York Independent*, *Hearth and Home*, *Scribner's Monthly*, and other periodicals, some of them pieces based on travels in Europe from 1868 to 1870. Most of these writings were published anonymously, under pseudonuym "Saxe Holm," or identified only with initials "H. H."; she continued this practice for much of her career. Writing was well received; first collection of poetry, *Verses*, appeared in 1870, and over the next decade she published a variety of sketches, essays, and fiction including *Bits of Travel* (1872), *Bits of Talk About Home Matters* (1873), the poem *The Story of Boon* (1874), *Mercy Philbrick's Choice* (1876), *Hetty's Strange History* (1877), *Bits of Travel at Home* (1878), and a novel for children, *Nelly's Silver Mine* (1878). Traveled West for her health in 1872; while wintering in Colorado Springs met banker and railroad

manager William S. Jackson, whom she married in 1875, settling permanently in Colorado Springs. Developed deep interest in American Indians and in 1881 published *A Century of Dishonor*, influential account of U.S. government mistreatment and deception; sent a copy to every member of Congress at her own expense. In 1882 appointed U.S. Special Commissioner to investigate condition of Mission Indians of California; aside from official report, recorded impressions in *Glimpses of California and the Missions* (1883). Disappointment at inaction in response to her report prompted writing of *Ramona* (1884), popular novel about girl of mixed Indian and Scottish blood set against backdrop of American incursions into Spanish California. Two collections of poetry, *Easter Bells* and *Pansies and Orchids*, also appeared in 1884. Other late publications included three books of cat stories for children, *Letters from a Cat* (1879), *Mammy Tittleback and Family: A Story of Seventeen Cats* (1881), and *The Hunter Cats of Connorloa* (1884); *The Training of Children* (1882), and posthumously published volumes *Zeph* (1885), *Glimpses of Three Coasts* (1886), *Sonnets and Lyrics* (1886), and *Between Whiles* (1887). Soon after publication of *Ramona*, broke her hip in fall that left her crippled; traveled to San Francisco to recuperate, and died there of cancer. Emily Dickinson wrote on learning of her death, "Helen of Troy will die, but Helen of Colorado, never. Dear friend, can you walk, were the last words that I wrote her. Dear friend, I can fly—her immortal reply."

SARAH ORNE JEWETT (September 3, 1849–June 24, 1909) b. Theodora Sarah Orne Jewett in South Berwick, Maine. Daughter of Caroline Frances Perry and Theodore Jewett, wealthy physician, professor of medicine, and president of Maine Medical Society. Father's patients included fishermen and farmers whose lives she later described. Graduated from Berwick Academy in 1866. First published story appeared in *Flag of Our Union* in 1868; contributed many children's stories to periodicals including *Riverside* and *Our Young Folks*. Series of stories of Maine village life, published in *Atlantic Monthly* with enthusiastic support of its editor William Dean Howells, appeared in book form as *Deephaven* in 1877, achieving considerable success. Children's stories collected in *Play Days* (1878). Father died in 1878. Continued to live and write in South Berwick, but traveled frequently to Boston and New York. As friend of James T. Fields (publisher of *Atlantic Monthly*) and his wife Annie Adams Fields, became part of Boston literary circle including Oliver Wendell Holmes, John Greenleaf Whittier, James Russell Lowell, Harriet Beecher Stowe, and Thomas Bailey Aldrich. Published further collections and sketches—*Old Friends and New* (1879), *Country By-Ways* (1881), *The Mate of the Daylight and Friends Ashore* (1883)—and novel *A Country Doctor* (1884), whose title character was modeled on her father. Following death of James T. Fields in 1881, became close companion of Annie Fields, living with her for much of every year in Boston and Manchester-by-the-Sea, and traveling with her in Europe, Florida, and the Caribbean. On trips to Europe met Christina Rossetti, Alfred Tennyson, Matthew Arnold, George Du Maurier, Henry James, and Rudyard Kipling. Another novel, *A*

Marsh Island (1885), was followed by the collections *A White Heron* (1886), *The King of Folly Island and Other People* (1888), *Strangers and Wayfarers* (1890), *Tales of New England* (1890), *A Native of Winby* (1893), and *The Life of Nancy* (1895) and popular history *The Story of the Normans* (1887). *The Country of the Pointed Firs* (1896), based on experiences in the Boothbay Harbor region of Maine, was acclaimed by many as her best book; additional stories dealing with the fictional town of Dunnet Landing were published in *The Queen's Twin and Other Stories* (1899). *The Tory Lover*, a novel of the American Revolution, appeared in 1901. Received honorary degree in literature from Bowdoin in 1901, the first woman so honored. Thrown from a carriage in 1902; suffered spinal damage and stopped writing. In later years formed friendship with Willa Cather. Died in her South Berwick home of a cerebral hemorrhage. Poems appeared posthumously in *Verses* (1916).

SIDNEY LANIER (February 3, 1842–September 7, 1881)   b. Macon, Georgia. Son of Mary Jane Anderson and Robert Sampson Lanier, a lawyer. As a child showed precocious musical ability. Graduated Oglethorpe University in Milledgeville, Georgia, in 1860; plans for further study interrupted by outbreak of war. Joined Macon Volunteers in July 1861; the following year fought in Seven Days' Battle near Richmond, Virginia; served as mounted scout along James River, 1863–64. In 1864 captured aboard blockade runner (on which he served as signal officer) and imprisoned for four months at Point Lookout, Maryland. Health deteriorated in prison; contracted tuberculosis. Released February 1865; worked as hotel clerk in Montgomery, Alabama, then as teacher and law clerk in father's office. In 1867 married Mary Day (with whom he had four sons) and published novel *Tiger-Lilies*, based on war experiences. Admitted to Georgia bar in 1869 and practiced for a time in father's law office. Although frequently hindered by chronic tuberculosis (he wrote to Bayard Taylor that "pretty much the whole of life has been merely not dying"), was eventually able to make career in music and poetry. In 1873 named first flutist of the Peabody Orchestra, Baltimore; devoted much study to history of Elizabethan music. Published first poem in *Lippincott's* in 1874. Although only one volume of poetry published during lifetime (*Poems*, 1877), his work appeared in a number of magazines; gained considerable reputation as poet and critic. From 1879 until his death two years later at age 39, lectured on English verse at Johns Hopkins. Wrote series of retellings of medieval tales for children—*The Boy's Froissart* (1879), *The Boy's King Arthur* (1880), *The Boy's Mabinogion* (1881), and *The Boy's Percy* (1882), as well as popular travel guide *Florida: Its Scenery, Climate, and History* (1875). Major critical work, *The Science of English Verse*, appeared in 1880. Died at Lynn, in mountains of North Carolina, where he had gone to recover health. Collected poems, edited by his wife, appeared posthumously in 1884, along with further critical work: *The English Novel* (1883), *Music and Poetry* (1898), and *Shakspere and His Forerunners* (1902).

EMMA LAZARUS (July 22, 1849–November 19, 1887) b. New York City. Daughter of Esther Nathan and Moses Lazarus; father, a wealthy sugar merchant, came from Sephardic family that had been in America at least since 18th century; mother was of German descent; family spent summers in Newport, Rhode Island. Educated by private tutors; little religious training; learned German, French, and Italian at an early age. *Poems and Translations* (1867), published at her father's expense, contained work written between ages 14 and 16. Ralph Waldo Emerson, to whom she sent a copy, wrote to her in February 1868 and they met briefly in April; in an extended correspondence, he served as literary mentor, reading and commenting on her poetry. Also received encouragement from Thomas Wentworth Higginson and Edmund Clarence Stedman; corresponded with naturalist John Burroughs. Second collection, *Admetus and Other Poems*, published 1871; contributed poems frequently to *Lippincott's, Scribner's, The Galaxy, The Century*, and other leading periodicals. Disappointed when Emerson failed to include any of her work in his 1874 anthology *Parnassus*, but made amicable visit to him in Concord in 1876. Published historical novel *Alide: An Episode in Goethe's Life* (1874) and *The Spagnoletto* (1876), verse drama about 17th-century painter Jose de Ribera. Translations of Heine collected in *Poems and Ballads of Heine* (1881); also translated (from German versions) medieval Hebrew poetry of Yehudah HaLevi, Solomon Ibn Gabirol, and Moses Ben Ezra. In response to Russian pogroms of early 1880s, and deeply impressed by 1881 visit (with Reform rabbi Gustav Gottheil) to immigration center at Ward's Island, became prominent worker for Jewish causes; organized refugee relief and contributed articles on Jewish subjects to *The Century*; wrote weekly column "An Epistle to the Hebrews" for *The American Hebrew*, 1882–83 (collected in book form in 1900); in 1882 article espoused creation of a Jewish homeland in Palestine, although not for American Jews; instrumental in founding of Hebrew Technical Institute. In 1882 published *Songs of a Semite*, which included "The Dance of Death," verse drama (based on a work by German writer Richard Reinhard) about 14th-century massacre of German Jews; dedicated "Dance of Death" to George Eliot, whose *Daniel Deronda* she credited with "elevating and ennobling the spirit of Jewish nationality." Wrote sonnet "The New Colossus" in support of fund-raising campaign to build pedestal for Statue of Liberty (poem recited in 1886 at statue's dedication; final lines later embossed on pedestal). Traveled to England and France in 1883; met Robert Browning and William Morris. Ill with cancer, made long visit to Europe, 1885–87; visited the Netherlands, France, and Italy; died less than three months after return to U.S. "By the Waters of Babylon," sequence of prose poems, published in *The Century* in 1887. A posthumous two-volume edition of her works, *The Poems of Emma Lazarus*, edited by sisters Mary and Annie, appeared in 1889.

JAMES MATHEWES LEGARÉ (November 26, 1823–May 30, 1859) b. Charleston, South Carolina. Son of Mary Doughty Mathews and John D.

Legaré. Of Huguenot descent on father's side; third cousin of South Carolina statesman Hugh Swinton Legaré. Father edited a farm journal, briefly kept a hotel, and eventually opened an agricultural supply store. Attended College of Charleston, graduating 1841, and St. Mary's College in Baltimore. Eulogized Hugh Swinton Legaré's death in June 1843 in poem "On the Death of a Kinsman." Worked in law office of James L. Petigru in Charleston; wrote poetry; painted (as he would continue to do throughout his life). Fabricated evidence of noble origins of Legaré family, but hoax was exposed in newspapers. Suffered first of recurrent lung hemorrhages. Had his poetry and fiction published by William Gilmore Simms in various periodicals; John James Audubon, an acquaintance of his father, offered to help find a publisher for his poetry. Moved with family in 1846 to Aiken in the South Carolina midlands; father declared bankruptcy two years later. Contributed writing to *The Opal*, *Southern Literary Messenger*, the Athens (Georgia) *Weekly Gazette*, *The Literary World*, *Graham's Magazine*, and *The Knickerbocker*. Briefly ran school; taught drawing in Augusta, Georgia, and elsewhere. Initiated long correspondence with Henry Wadsworth Longfellow. Verse collection *Orta-Undis* (1848) published by William D. Ticknor of Boston. Formally confirmed as Episcopalian in 1848. Married Anne C. Andrews in 1850; settled in Aiken. Traveled to New York in 1851, meeting Rufus Griswold and Evert Duyckinck. Served as postmaster of Aiken, 1852–53. Set up a laboratory where he worked for years on a variety of inventions, several of which were eventually patented; most successful were experiments in furniture made from plastic fibers derived from chemically treated cotton; exhibited inventions and paintings at Charleston Industrial Institute in 1856 and 1857. Died of tuberculosis.

CHARLES GODFREY LELAND (August 15, 1824 – March 20, 1903)   b. Philadelphia, Pennsylvania. Son of Charlotte Godfrey and Charles Leland, a prosperous merchant. Friend from an early age of George Henry Boker, whose father and Leland's were business partners; schoolmate of George McClellan. Early education in Philadelphia (where his teachers included Bronson Alcott, whom he later described as "the most eccentric man who ever took it on himself to train and form the youthful mind") and at Jamaica Plains, Massachusetts. Voracious reader throughout childhood; deeply affected by early reading of Rabelais, of which he later said: "It seems to me now as if it were the great event of my life." Graduated College of New Jersey (later Princeton) in 1845; after graduating, traveled in France and Italy before continuing studies in Heidelberg, Munich, and Paris for two years, 1846–48; became fluent in German; met poet and occultist Justinus Kerner; in 1848 participated briefly in revolutionary upheavals in Paris. Returned to Philadelphia; studied law; admitted to bar, but by 1853 left profession to pursue career in journalism. Contributed book reviews to *Union Magazine* (1849); in New York, assisted Rufus Griswold on *The International Magazine* (1850–52) and on P. T. Barnum's *Illustrated News* (1853). Became staffer on Philadelphia *Evening Bulletin*. Early publications included *Meister Karl's Sketch-Book* (1855), a collection of essays and sketches; *The Poetry and Mystery of Dreams* (1855); and a trans-

lation of Heinrich Heine's *Pictures of Travel* (1856). Friends included William Makepeace Thackeray, Lola Montez, Bayard Taylor, and Ole Bull. Married Eliza Belle Fisher in 1856. Briefly edited *Graham's Magazine*, where in May 1857 he published first of his enormously popular Hans Breitmann poems in German dialect. Contributed many articles to *Appleton's Cyclopaedia* (1858–63) under editorship of George Ripley and Charles A. Dana; worked as an editor for *New York Times*; edited *Vanity Fair* (1860–61) and *The Knickerbocker* (1861–62). In 1862 became editor of *The Continental Monthly* (1862–63) in Boston; claimed to have popularized term "emancipation" as alternative to controversial "abolition." Published *Sunshine in Thought* (1862), *The Art of Conversation, or Hints for Self-Education* (1863), and political satire *The Book of Copperheads* (1863). Served in Philadelphia artillery company during Gettysburg campaign, although he saw little action; formed friendship with fellow soldier Richard Watson Gilder. At close of war, traveled in the West and speculated briefly in coal and petroleum. Became managing editor of Philadephia *Press* in 1866. Partly through influence of James Russell Lowell, awarded honorary M.A. by Harvard in 1867. Upon the death of his father in 1869, was able to give up newspaper work and travel in Europe; eventually settled in London for a decade. Acquaintances in London included Bret Harte, George Eliot, George Henry Lewes, and publisher Nicolas Trübner. *The Breitmann Ballads* (which enjoyed extraordinary popularity in England) were collected in book form in 1871, followed by books on wide variety of topics: *The Music Lesson of Confucius; and Other Poems* (1872), *Egyptian Sketch-Book* (1873), *The English Gypsies and Their Language* (1873), *Fu-Sang, or the Discovery of America by Chinese Buddhist Priests in the Fifth Century* (1875), *English Gypsy Songs* (1875, with Janet Tuckey and Edward H. Palmer), children's book *Johnnykin and the Goblins* (1876), *Pidgin-English Sing-Song; or, Songs and Stories in the China-English Dialect* (1876), *Abraham Lincoln* (1879), *The Minor Arts; Porcelain Painting, Wood-Carving, Stencilling, Modelling, Mosaic Work, Etc.* (1880), *The Gypsies* (1883), *The Algonquin Legends of New England* (1884), *A Dictionary of Slang* (1889, with Albert Barrere), *Etruscan-Roman Remains in Popular Tradition* (1892), *Memoirs* (1893), *Legends of Florence* (1895–96), *The Unpublished Legends of Virgil* (1901), and, in collaboration with John Dyneley Prince, *Kulóskap the Master and Other Algonkin Poems* (1902). Traveled in Egypt with George Henry Boker in 1872. With Walter Besant founded the Rabelais Club. Developed interest in industrial arts education; returned to Philadelphia to promote the idea and wrote a number of manuals. Returned to London in 1884; in later years spent much time in Florence, where he died.

GEORGE CABOT LODGE (October 10, 1873–August 21, 1909) b. Boston, Massachusetts. Son of Anna Cabot Mills Davis and politician and author Henry Cabot Lodge; reared at father's house in Nahant, Massachusetts. In childhood knew Henry Adams, Edith Wharton, John Hay, Theodore Roosevelt, and other members of parents' circle. Graduated Harvard 1895. Continued studies in Romance languages at the Sorbonne in 1895–96, in

company with close friend Trumbull Stickney. Began to publish poetry in *Scribner's, Harper's,* and other magazines. Briefly returned to Europe in 1897 to study German and philosophy at the University of Berlin. Introduced to Buddhist practices and beliefs by family friend William Sturgis Bigelow. In 1897 went to work in Washington as father's secretary. First book, *The Song of the Wave,* appeared in 1898; saw active service that year in Spanish-American War, participating in capture of Ponce, Puerto Rico. Became interested in "Conservative Christian Anarchy," philosophical position developed with friends Henry Adams and Trumbull Stickney. Verse collected in *Poems 1899–1902* (1902). In 1900 married Elizabeth (Matilda) Frelinghuysen Davis, with whom he had two sons and a daughter. In succeeding years published *Cain, a Drama* (1904), *The Great Adventure* (1905), *Herakles* (1908), and post-humously published *The Soul's Inheritance* (1909). Died following an attack of ptomaine poisoning.

MARIA WHITE LOWELL (July 8, 1821–October 27, 1853) b. Watertown, Massachusetts. Fourth of nine children of Anna Maria Howard and Abijah White; sister of William Abijah White, who became close friend of James Russell Lowell at Harvard; given name Anna Maria White. Although family was not Catholic, she was sent (as were the daughters of many prominent Protestant families) for primary education to the Ursuline Convent on Mt. Benedict in Charlestown, Massachusetts, where she was among the students forced to flee when the convent was burned by an anti-Catholic mob in August 1834. Later participated in Margaret Fuller's "conversations" (pioneering experiment in women's education), 1839–44. During this period became dedicated to abolitionism and the temperance movement. Became engaged to James Russell Lowell in 1840. Published poetry in third and last number of Lowell's magazine *The Pioneer* (1843); later contributed verse to *The Child's Friend, Putnam's Magazine, The Knickerbocker,* and to anti-slavery "gift books." Married Lowell in 1844. Support for abolitionism deeply influenced husband; with him, she assisted numerous fugitive slaves. Of their four children, three died in early childhood: Blanche in 1847, Rose in 1849, and Walter in Rome in 1852; only Mabel (b. 1847) survived to adulthood. Traveled with family to Italy in July 1851, remaining until fall of 1852. Health had been frail for years; died at Elmwood, the Lowell house in Cambridge, after protracted illness. Following her death, Lowell arranged for private publication of *The Poems of Maria Lowell* (1855), containing 20 poems.

ROBERT LOWRY (March 12, 1826–November 23, 1899) b. Philadelphia, Pennsylvania. In 1843 joined First Baptist Church after experiencing religious conversion. Enrolled in 1848 at University of Lewisburg, Lewisburg, Pennsylvania (now Bucknell University); graduated 1854. Entered Baptist ministry. Served as pastor in West Chester, Pennsylvania (1854–58); in New York City (1858–61); in Brooklyn, New York (1861–69). In 1869 joined faculty of University of Lewisburg, serving also as chancellor of the university; served concurrently as pastor in Lewisburg. In 1875 moved to Plainfield, New Jersey, and

the following year became pastor of the Park Avenue Baptist Church there, holding the position until 1885; served as president of New Jersey Baptist School Union, 1880–86. Wrote many hymns; most famous, "Beautiful River" (also known as "Shall We Gather at the River"), was written in 1864 during epidemic in Brooklyn and published in collection *Bright Jewels for the Sunday School* (1869). Edited many other collections of religious music devoted in large part to his own songs, including *Chapel Melodies* (1868), *Pure Gold for the Sunday School* (1871), *Hymn Service* (1871), *Royal Diadem for the Sunday School* (1873), *Temple Anthems for the Service of the Sanctuary* (1873), *The Tidal Wave* (1874), *Brightest and Best* (1875), *Welcome Tidings* (1877), *Fountain of Song* (1877), *Chautauqua Carols* (1878), *Gospel Hymn and Tune Book* (1879), *Good as Gold* (1880), *Our Glad Hosanna* (1882), *Joyful Lays* (1884), and *The Glad Refrain for the Sunday School* (1886). Died in Plainfield, leaving a widow, Mary Runyon Lowry, and three sons.

EDWIN MARKHAM (April 23, 1852–March 7, 1940) b. Charles Edward Anson Markham in Oregon City, Oregon Territory. Sixth child of Elizabeth Winchell Markham (wife of Samuel Barzillai Markham, from whom she was separated and who was probably not Markham's father). Grew up on isolated ranch in Suisun, California (between Sacramento and San Francisco); raised by his mother, a member of Campbellite sect Disciples of Christ, who discouraged his interest in literature and treated him severely. Ran away from home for several months in 1867. Attended California College in Vacaville, earning teacher's certificate in 1870; moved with mother (who continued to live with him until her death) to San Jose, where he attended California State Normal School, 1871–72; continued studies at Christian College, Campbellite school in Santa Rosa, 1873–74. Taught high school in Coloma. Married Annie Cox in 1875. Around 1878 became adherent of spiritualist ideas of Thomas Lake Harris, of whose Brotherhood of the New Life he became a nonresident member. Became county superintendent of schools at Placerville in 1879. Began publishing poems in local newspapers; developed interest in socialism and became involved in Grange movement. Affair with Placerville physician Dr. Elizabeth Senter led to divorce from wife Annie in 1884. Forced to give up school position in 1886 because of affair with Caroline E. Bailey, whom he married in 1887; she left him not long after their marriage. Poetry published in *Scribner's* and *The Century*; awarded prize by *The Magazine of Poetry*. Worked as school principal in Hayward (1889) and, from 1890, at Tompkins Observation School of the University of California in Oakland. Mother died in 1891. Formed friendships with Ambrose Bierce, Jack London, and Frank Norris; met Hamlin Garland in 1893 at World's Columbian Exposition in Chicago. Married teacher Anna Catherine Murphy in 1898; their son Virgil was born the following year. Publication of "The Man with the Hoe" in *San Francisco Examiner* in January 1899 made him famous; poem was translated into many languages, and *The Man with the Hoe and Other Poems* (1899) became best seller; family moved to New York City. Commissioned by Republican Club of New York to write Lincoln tribute, published in successful second collec-

tion, *Lincoln and Other Poems* (1901). Became regular contributor of news-paper articles on progressive themes to Hearst syndicate. Retired to Staten Island, New York; Sunday salons at his home were regularly attended by literary figures including Theodore Dreiser, Upton Sinclair, Vachel Lindsay, Edwin Arlington Robinson, and Joyce Kilmer. Following death of Thomas Lake Harris in 1906, worked for years on uncompleted official biography. Founded Poetry Society of America in 1910; published influential anthology of new poets, *The Younger Choir* (1910); frequently went on lecture tours. Campaigned against child labor and contributed to the volume *Children in Bondage* (1914). Continued to publish poetry regularly, collecting his verse in *The Shoes of Happiness* (1915), *Gates of Paradise* (1920), *New Poems: Eighty Songs at Eighty* (1932), and *The Star of Araby* (1937). Eightieth birthday celebrated at massive ceremony at Carnegie Hall in 1932. Disabled by stroke in 1938 while on tour to Mexico; died of pneumonia two years later.

HERMAN MELVILLE   (August 1, 1819–September 28, 1891)   b. New York City. Son of Maria Gansevoort (daughter of American Revolutionary hero General Peter Gansevoort) and Allan Melvill (importer and merchant). Father's business failed in financial panic of 1830; family forced to move to Albany; father died January 1832. Educated sporadically at various schools in New York City and in upstate New York. Worked successively as bank clerk, on uncle's farm, as bookkeeper and clerk in brother's fur business, and as teacher in school near Pittsfield, Massachusetts. In 1839 published journalistic sketches as "Fragments from a Writing Desk"; sailed from New York to Liverpool and back as crew member of trading ship *St. Lawrence*. Worked briefly as teacher. Sailed for South Seas on whaling ship *Acushnet* in January 1841; in July 1842 deserted with shipmate Richard Tobias Greene at Nuku Hiva in the Marquesas. After month in Taipi valley, sailed on Australian whaling ship *Lucy Ann*, but was sent ashore at Tahiti as mutineer; escaped and explored Tahiti with friend John B. Troy. Sailed from Tahiti to Hawaii on Nantucket whaling ship *Charles and Henry*; worked at various jobs in Hono-lulu. In 1843 enlisted in U.S. Navy in Honolulu; sailed to Boston on frigate *United States*; discharged October 1844. Returned to family and worked on *Typee*, fictionalized account of Marquesan experiences, published with great success in 1846; sequel *Omoo* appeared the following year. Married Elizabeth Shaw, daughter of Massachusetts Chief Justice Lemuel Shaw, in August 1847; moved to New York City; they had four children. Published further fiction, *Mardi* (1849), *Redburn* (1849), and *White-Jacket* (1850). Made four-month trip to London and the Continent, 1849–50. In 1850 met Nathaniel Hawthorne, whose work he had previously reviewed; purchased farm Arrowhead near Pittsfield. *Moby-Dick* published 1851; its indifferent reception followed by fail-ure of *Pierre, or The Ambiguities* (1852); failed to recoup reputation with *Israel Potter* (1855) and *The Piazza Tales* (1856). Family gravely concerned about health and mental stability, as Melville suffered recurrent depression. With father-in-law's financial help made year-long trip to Europe and Holy Land; briefly visited Hawthorne in Liverpool; returned to New York 1857. Last pub-

lished work of fiction, *The Confidence-Man*, appeared in 1857. Between 1857 and 1860 lectured on travels in Rome and the South Seas without success. In 1861 traveled to Washington, D.C., hoping to procure a consular appointment, but failed. Left Pittsfield permanently for New York City in 1863. Visited the front in Virginia in 1864; collection of Civil War poems, *Battle-Pieces and Aspects of the War*, published in 1866. In December of the same year appointed deputy inspector of customs at port of New York. Oldest son Malcolm died of self-inflicted gunshot wound in September 1867. Long poem *Clarel: A Poem and a Pilgrimage*, based on experiences in Holy Land, published at uncle's expense in 1876. Resigned position as customs inspector in 1885; son Stanwix died in San Francisco the following year. In final years published two small books of poetry in limited private editions, *John Marr and Other Sailors* (1888) and *Timoleon* (1891). Left *Billy Budd, Sailor* in manuscript (first published 1924), along with a number of poems.

ADAH ISAACS MENKEN (June 15, 1835?–August 10, 1868) probably b. Memphis, Tennessee. Menken's origins have long been disputed; she herself gave various accounts of her parentage and place of birth, and later biographers have claimed that she was Jewish or mulatto. Recent research suggests that her parents Richard and Catherine McCord were of Irish origin, and that her given name was Ada McCord. Her father probably died in 1842, after which her mother married Josiah Campbell and moved to New Orleans. At age fifteen said to have given public readings of Shakespeare in Texas; published some poetry. Married musician Alexander Isaac Menken (whose father was a prosperous Cincinnati merchant) in Texas in 1856; claimed Jewish parentage, and received instruction in Judaism from Rabbi Isaac M. Wise, editor of *The Cincinnati Israelite*. Made first stage appearances in Shreveport and New Orleans around 1857; appeared in Cincinnati and Dayton in 1858; made New York City debut in 1859. Published poems and articles in *Cincinnati Israelite*, 1857–59, and *New York Sunday Mercury*, 1860–61. Following break-up of marriage to Menken in July 1859, was married to prizefighter John C. Heenan (known as "The Benicia Boy") in September of the same year. Friendly in New York with Ada Clare, Walt Whitman, Fitz-James O'Brien, and others associated with Charlie Pfaff's beer cellar. Toured in play based on life of Lola Montez. Became world-famous for her ride across stage strapped to the back of a horse in the dramatic version of Byron's "Mazeppa"; first performed the role in June 1861 in Albany, New York; toured frequently, billed as "The World's Delight." Abandoned by Heenan amid public speculation about the legitimacy of her divorce from Menken. Married humorist Robert Henry Newell (known by pseudonym "Orpheus C. Kerr") in September 1862. Traveled with Newell to San Francisco, where she performed in August 1863; met Bret Harte, Charles Farrar Browne ("Artemus Ward"), and other literary figures; divorced Newell. Played Virginia City in March 1864; met Mark Twain. In London (where she opened in *Mazeppa* in October 1864) her salon became a fixture of London society; met Charles Dickens and Charles Reade. Traveled to Paris, where she met Théophile Gautier and

George Sand. In Britain again, opened in *The Children of the Sun* in Glasgow and toured England in the role. Returned to New York in March 1866 to be with lover James Paul Barkley, whom she had met while abroad; acted in New York City and on tour of U.S.; married Barkley in August 1866, but couple separated after three days when Menken departed for Europe; never saw Barkley again (he died the following year). Gave birth to a son in November, of whom Barkley was father; child died in infancy. In Paris, acted in *Les Pirates de la Savane*; notorious for affair with elderly novelist Aléxandre Dumas; photographs of the two of them together circulated widely. Appeared in Vienna in spring of 1867. Returned to London, where she became acquainted with Dante Gabriel Rossetti; in autumn of 1867 apparently had affair with Algernon Charles Swinburne. Gave final performance at Sadler's Wells Theatre in London in August 1868; returned to France but was too ill to perform. Visitors during her last illness included Thomas Buchanan Read and Henry Wadsworth Longfellow. Collected poetry in *Infelicia*, dedicated to Charles Dickens (published days after her death). Died in Paris of cancer.

STUART MERRILL (August 1, 1863–December 1, 1915) b. Stuart Fitz-Randolph Merrill in Hempstead, New York. One of three sons of Emma Fitz-Randolph Laing and George Merrill (a lawyer). In 1866 his father was appointed counselor to the American legation in Paris. Attended boarding school in Vanves, a suburb of Paris, 1875–79; afterward studied at Lycée Fontaines in Paris, where Mallarmé was a teacher of English and classmates included future literary figures René Ghil, Ephraim Mikhael, and Pierre Quillard; graduated in 1884. After family's return to New York, studied law at Columbia. First book, *Les Gammes*, written in French; published in Paris in 1887. Met Walt Whitman in April 1887 in New York City, and presented him with copies of translations that the French poet Jules Laforgue had published of several Whitman poems. Interested in economic ideas of Henry George; defended anarchists sentenced to death in 1886 following Haymarket riot. Father died 1888; with mother, returned to Europe; in London, formed close friendship with Oscar Wilde. *Pastels in Prose* (1890), his only English-language volume (with preface by William Dean Howells), contained translations of Baudelaire, Mallarmé, Huysmans, Villiers de l'Isle Adam, Judith Gautier, Aloysius Bertrand, and other French writers. Returned to New York in 1890, remaining only five months. Returned to Paris in May 1891. Became a manager of the Théâtre d'Art. Apartment on Quai Bourbon became meeting place for writers and artists including Paul Verlaine, Alfred Jarry, Emile Verhaeren, and Guillaume Apollinaire; regular guest at Tuesday evening salon of Stéphane Mallarmé; later had a house at Marlotte in the forest of Fontainebleau. Closely associated with French symbolist school; later volumes of poetry, all written in French, included *Les Fastes* (1891), *Petits Poèmes d'Automne* (1895), *Les Quatre Saisons* (1900), and *Une Voix dans la Foule* (1909); poetry collected in 1897 in *Poèmes 1887–1897*. He contributed to many French periodicals including *La Bazoche*, *Le Décadent*, *Le Scapin*, *Ecrits pour*

l'art, *Le Mercure de France*, *La Plume*, and *L'Ermitage*. In Brussels in 1908 married 18-year-old Claire Rion; they settled at Versailles, where he died. *Prose et Vers* published posthumously in 1925.

JOAQUIN MILLER (September 8, 1837–February 17, 1913) b. Cincinnatus Hiner (later spelled Heine) Miller in Liberty, Indiana. Son of Margaret De Witt and Hulings Miller, a Quaker schoolteacher. Family moved from place to place, west along Oregon Trail, settling in early 1853 near what would later be Eugene, Oregon. In 1854, Miller left home and began wandering existence in northern California. Worked as miner and as a cook in mining camps; spent time among Indians near Mount Shasta, and had a daughter, Cali-Shasta, with a woman of the band; involved in several skirmishes among Indians, miners, and soldiers. Returned to Oregon, attending newly opened Columbia College in Eugene, 1858–59. Traveled again to California, where he was briefly jailed for horse theft in July 1859; escaped with cell-mate and again lived with Indians. Studied law in Portland, Oregon, in 1860. Briefly practiced law in Oro Fino, Idaho, before buying interest in a pony express service, riding routes in Idaho, Oregon, and Washington in 1861 and 1862. Used profits from pony express to buy interest in *Democratic-Register* of Eugene in 1862; the same year, the paper was suppressed by federal authorities for supporting Confederacy. Married Theresa Dyer (an aspiring poet who wrote under the name Minnie Myrtle) in September 1862 after brief courtship; they had two children. Edited short-lived *Eugene City Review* under pseudonym "De Weiver" (1862–63). Moved to Canyon City, Oregon, in 1863, where he practiced law; led attack against hostile Indians in 1864, and served as judge of county court, 1866–69. Published two collections of poetry, *Specimens* (1868) and *Joaquin et al* (1869), the title of the latter taken from Miller's poem on Mexican bandit Joaquin Murrietta, whose name he would adopt as his own in 1870. Conducted unsuccessful campaign for Supreme Court Justice in Oregon. After divorce from wife in 1870, custody of children granted to Miller's mother-in-law. In 1870, traveled to San Francisco where he met Bret Harte, Ina Coolbrith, Ambrose Bierce, and other literary figures. Later the same year, traveled to Great Britain, where privately printed *Pacific Poems* (1871) and manners and costume (sombrero, boots, spurs, and buckskin) gained him fame as "frontier poet"; British publisher issued *Songs of the Sierras* (1871) with success. Returned to U.S. in fall of 1871 to find that his popularity did not extend there; traveled in and outside of America, eventually returning to Europe in 1873; stayed chiefly in England and Italy; returned to New York in 1875. Enjoyed some success as playwright with *Forty-Nine* (1882); *The Danites in the Sierras* (first staged 1877; published 1882), a dramatization of his 1875 novel *First Fam'lies of the Sierras*; and *Tally-Ho!* (1883, with music by John Philip Sousa). Published many volumes of verse, including *Songs of the Sun-Lands* (1873), *The Ship in the Desert* (1875), *Songs of Italy* (1878), *Songs of Far-Away Lands* (1878), and *Songs of the Mexican Seas* (1887), and a wide range of prose works, including several novels and the fictionalized memoir *Life Amongst the Modocs* (1873). In 1879, married second wife, hotel heiress Abigail

Leland, and settled in New York; they had one daughter, Juanita. First wife, Minnie, died while visiting Miller in New York in 1882. In 1883, moved to Washington, D.C., where he and wife separated, Abigail returning to New York. Returned to San Francisco in 1886, accepting position as editor of *The Golden Era*; in 1887 settled in Oakland on an estate he named The Hights; established a fruit orchard, and planted thousands of trees. Resigned position at *Golden Era* late in 1887. Toured as lecturer in early 1890s, also occasionally working as journalist. Traveled to Klondike as correspondent for Hearst papers, 1897–98; toured briefly with vaudeville show, 1898–99; traveled to China to cover Boxer Rebellion in 1900. *Complete Poetical Works* appeared in London in 1897 (American edition 1900; revised, 1902). Later volumes of poetry included *Chants for the Boer* (1900), *As it Was in the Beginning* (1903), *Light: A Narrative Poem* (1907), and *Panama: Union of the Oceans* (1912). During later years, daughters Maud and Cali-Shasta and her mother lived with him at The Hights; Miller outlived them all. In February 1911, his second wife and their daughter moved to The Hights to care for Miller, whose health was in decline. Died at The Hights.

HARRIET MONROE (December 23, 1860–September 26, 1936) b. Chicago, Illinois. Daughter of Martha Mitchell and Henry Stanton Monroe, a prosperous lawyer; family's resources severely curtailed as result of Chicago fire of 1876. Graduated from Convent of the Visitation in Georgetown, D.C., in 1879. Returned to live with family in Chicago. Initiated correspondence with Robert Louis Stevenson in 1886; spent summer of 1887 in New York City with mother and sister; met Stevenson. During winter of 1888–89 lived in New York City with sister; frequently attended Sunday evening gatherings at home of Edmund Clarence Stedman, where she met William Dean Howells, Richard Watson Gilder, Elizabeth and Richard Henry Stoddard, and other literary figures; wrote dramatic criticism for the *Herald Tribune*. Returned to Chicago and in 1890 began writing art criticism for *Chicago Tribune*. In 1890 and again in 1897 toured Europe and met literary and artistic figures including Henry James, Aubrey Beardsley, James McNeill Whistler, Thomas Hardy, and Alice Meynell. Associates in Chicago included Albert Pinkham Ryder and Henry Blake Fuller. First collection, *Valeria and Other Poems*, privately printed in 1892. Applied for and received $1,000 commission to write poem for World's Columbian Exposition in Chicago; poem recited by five thousand voices at dedication ceremony in 1892; published as *The Columbian Ode* (1893). In 1896 published biography of brother-in-law John Wellborn Root, the architect who had been one of the chief designers of the Columbian Exposition. *The Passing Show: Five Modern Plays in Verse* appeared in 1903. Worked as freelance journalist; resumed job as art critic for *Chicago Tribune*, 1909–14. Long poem *The Dance of Seasons* published in 1911. With help of close friend Hobart Chatfield-Taylor raised money to launch *Poetry: A Magazine of Verse*; first issue published September 1912. Contributors during Monroe's editorship included Ezra Pound (who served as London editor), Wallace Stevens, William Butler Yeats, William Carlos Williams, Robert Frost, T. S.

Eliot, H.D., Marianne Moore, Hart Crane, Vachel Lindsay, Edgar Lee Masters, Amy Lowell, Carl Sandburg, Langston Hughes, Louis Zukofsky, Basil Bunting, Kenneth Rexroth, W. H. Auden, and many others. Verse collection *You and I* published 1914. With Alice Corbin Henderson (assistant editor of *Poetry*) edited anthology *The New Poetry: An Anthology of Twentieth-Century Verse in English* (1917). *The Difference and Other Poems* (1924) followed by essay collection *Poets and Their Art* (1926); poetry collected in *Chosen Poems: A Selection from My Books of Verse* (1935). In later years traveled in Mexico and Asia. Died of cerebral hemorrhage in Arequipa, Peru, while returning from literary conference in Buenos Aires, Argentina. Autobiography published posthumously as *A Poet's Life: Seventy Years in a Changing World* (1938).

WILLIAM VAUGHN MOODY (July 8, 1869–October 17, 1910) b. Spencer, Indiana. Son of Henriette Emily Stoy (descendant of early Indiana pioneer family) and Francis Burdette Moody (former steamboat captain). Unsuccessful in business in Spencer, father moved family to New Albany, Indiana, in 1870, where he worked as secretary of an iron works. Father died in 1884, mother in 1886. Graduated Riverview Academy, Poughkeepsie, New York, in 1889, having tutored to support himself. Worked his way through Harvard, which he entered in 1889 on a $400 scholarship. Published verse in *Harvard Advocate* and *Harvard Monthly* (for which he also served as editor); came under influence of George Santayana, then a young instructor. College friends included Robert Herrick, Robert Morss Lovett, Phillip Henry Savage, and other aspiring writers. Spent senior year in Europe, supporting himself as private tutor, 1892–93. Graduated Harvard 1893; continued studies there, completing thesis on Sir Philip Sidney and receiving M.A. in 1894; stayed on as instructor for a year. Taught at University of Chicago (1895–1907), first as English instructor and then as assistant professor. First book, verse drama *The Masque of Judgment* (1900), followed by *Poems* (1901), which included "Ode in the Time of Hesitation," already published in *Atlantic Monthly* the year before. Poetry praised by Harriet Monroe and Edwin Arlington Robinson. *The Fire-Bringer*, second in intended triptych of verse dramas, appeared 1904. Publication of textbook *A First View of English Literature* (1905), written with friend Robert Morss Lovett, enabled him to travel in West and in Europe before settling in New York City. Friends included Edwin Arlington Robinson, Ridgely Torrence, Josephine Peabody, Percy MacKaye, and Edmund Clarence Stedman. Prose drama *A Sabine Woman* produced in Chicago in 1906 and opened on Broadway under new title *The Great Divide* the same year, enjoying a successful run and critical acclaim. Traveled in the spring of 1907 with Ridgely Torrence in North Africa, Spain, and Italy. In 1908 awarded honorary degree at Yale, and elected to American Academy of Arts and Letters. Married Harriet Brainard (divorcée who had been his lover since 1901) in 1909; diagnosed with brain tumor soon afterward. Next play, *The Faith Healer* (1909), failed on Broadway. Traveled to Santa Barbara, California, to Chicago, and to Colorado Springs in effort to regain health. Wrote beginning of third verse drama, *The Death of Eve*, but died at Colorado Springs before it could be completed.

Two-volume edition of works published posthumously as *The Poems and Plays of William Vaughn Moody* (1912).

JOHN JAMES PIATT (March 1, 1835–February 16, 1917) b. James' Mills (later Milton), Indiana. Son of Emily Scott and John Bear Piatt; on father's side of French Huguenot descent. Raised in Columbus, Ohio; later attended Capital University and Kenyon College. As apprentice printer working for *Ohio State Journal* met William Dean Howells in 1852, and the two became close friends. Became editor of *Louisville Journal* shortly after the paper published some of his poetry in 1857. With Howells, published collaborative volume *Poems of Two Friends* (1860). Married poet Sarah Morgan Bryan, herself a contributor to *Louisville Journal*, in 1861; the couple settled in Washington, D.C., where Piatt worked as clerk in Treasury Department until 1867; they had seven children, of whom three sons and a daughter survived to adulthood. In Washington, befriended Walt Whitman. Frequently collaborated with wife in writing poetry; results were published in *Nests at Washington* (1864) and *The Children Out-of-Doors* (1885). Returned to editorial work for *Cincinnati Chronicle* (1867–69) and *Cincinnati Commercial* (1869–78); concurrently served as librarian of U.S. House of Representatives (1871–75), dividing time between Cincinnati and Washington. Appointed U.S. consul in Cork, Ireland (1882–93); became friend of Edmund Gosse, Jean Ingelow, Austin Dobson, Alice Meynell, and others. Afterward retired to North Bend, Ohio; continued to write and work as editor. Piatt's verse collections included *Poems in Sunshine and Firelight* (1866), *Western Windows and Other Poems* (1867), *Poems of House and Home* (1879), *Idyls and Lyrics of the Ohio Valley* (1881), *A Book of Gold, and Other Sonnets* (1889), and *Odes in Ohio and Other Poems* (1897). Disabled by carriage accident several years before his death.

SARAH MORGAN PIATT (August 11, 1836–December 22, 1919) b. Sarah Morgan Bryan in Lexington, Kentucky. Daughter of Mary Spiers and Talbot Nelson Bryan; grandfather Morgan Bryan was brother-in-law of Daniel Boone and an early settler of Kentucky. Family moved to Versailles, Kentucky, in 1839; mother died in 1844; raised by various relatives and family friends. Graduated Henry Female College in New Castle, Kentucky. Published poetry in Galveston (Texas) *News* and *Louisville Journal* (where editor George D. Prentice encouraged her writing). In June 1861 married John James Piatt; lived successively in Washington, D.C., North Bend, Ohio, and in Cork, Ireland, where Piatt was U.S. consul; they had seven children, of whom three died in childhood. Published many volumes of verse (two of them in collaboration with her husband), including *A Voyage to the Fortunate Isles* (1874), *That New World* (1877), *A Woman's Poems* (1878), *Selected Poems* (1886), *Child's World Ballads* (1887), *An Irish Wild-Flower* (1891), and *An Enchanted Castle* (1893); two-volume collected edition of her poems published 1894. On returning to the United States in 1893, lived in North Bend, Ohio, until husband's death in 1917, after which she lived with son Cecil Piatt in Caldwell, New Jersey.

ALEXANDER L. POSEY (August 3, 1873–May 27, 1908) b. near Eufaula, Indian Territory (present day McIntosh County, Oklahoma). One of 12 children of Chickasaw-Creek woman who took English name Nancy Phillips and Lewis Henderson (Hence) Posey (rancher and, later, law enforcement officer of Scotch-Irish descent who claimed to be one-sixteenth Creek). By his own account, spoke little English before age 14. In 1890 enrolled at Indian University at Bacone (near Muskogee, Oklahoma); first poems and prose sketches published in faculty newspaper, where he worked as typesetter. Graduated 1895; elected in the same year to the Creek national legislature; served on many councils and delegations. In 1896, appointed superintendent of Creek Orphanage, Okmulgee, Oklahoma. Married Minnie Harris (of Fayetteville, Arkansas) in May, 1896; they had two children. In early 1898, settled on a farm near Stidham, Oklahoma; appointed administrator of Creek national high schools at Eufaula and Wetumka. Edited *The Indian Journal* (1902–03) at Eufaula, to which he contributed "Fus Fixico Letters," sketches in English-Creek dialect satirizing white injustices to Indians; in 1903, became joint editor of *Muskogee Times*. Became fieldworker for Dawes Commission in 1904, enrolling tribal members in government land-allotment program under Dawes Act. Served as secretary of constitutional convention held in 1905 at Muskogee for proposed Indian state of Sequoyah. Prospered as real estate agent. Shortly before his death resumed editorship of *Indian Journal*; drowned while trying to cross the North Canadian (Creek name Oktahutche) River, Oklahoma, in a small boat. *The Poems of Alexander Lawrence Posey* published posthumously by his wife in 1910.

JAMES RYDER RANDALL (January 1, 1839–January 14, 1908) b. Baltimore, Maryland. Son of Ruth Hooper and John Randall, a wealthy merchant; on mother's side, great-great-grandson of René Leblanc, Acadian notary who figures in Longfellow's *Evangeline*. At age ten entered Georgetown College; due to illness left before graduating; traveled in West Indies. On his return worked as printer in Baltimore and shipping clerk in New Orleans. In 1860 appointed professor of English and classics at Poydras College, Creole school in Louisiana. On reading of violence attending passage of 6th Massachusetts Regiment through Baltimore in April 1861, wrote "Maryland, My Maryland." Published in New Orleans *Delta* of April 26, poem quickly achieved popularity throughout the South; set to music (to a tune adapted from the German "Tannenbaum"), became quasi-official battle song of Confederacy. Enlisted in Confederate Army, but ill health caused him to be mustered out almost immediately. In 1866 married Katherine Hammond; they had eight children. Became associate editor of Augusta (Georgia) *Constitutionalist*, and later worked for various other periodicals including Baltimore *Catholic Mirror* and New Orleans *Morning Star*. Served for a time as secretary to several Georgia politicians in Washington, D.C., also acting as correspondent for the Augusta *Chronicle*. Honored by state of Maryland in 1907 on occasion of Jamestown Exposition; collected poems not published until two years after his death.

THOMAS BUCHANAN READ (March 12, 1822–May 11, 1872) b. Chester County, Pennsylvania. After father's death, apprenticed to a tailor; ran away to Philadelphia, where he learned trade of cigar-making. In 1837 went to Cincinnati where he lived with a married sister; supported himself by rolling cigars and painting canal boats. Hired by sculptor Shobal Vail Clevenger (from whom he learned rudiments of sculpting) to chisel engravings on tombstones. Learned trade of sign painter; received sporadic education; published poems in local newspapers. Moved to Dayton, Ohio, where he did theatrical work. Returned to Cincinnati and through generosity of Nicholas Longworth was able to open studio as portrait painter; in 1840, painted portrait of William Henry Harrison, then campaigning for presidency. Moved from town to town, working as portrait painter and sign painter, sometimes giving public entertainments, and occasionally working as cigar-maker. Moved in 1841 to New York and within the year to Boston, where he opened a studio. Befriended Henry Wadsworth Longfellow and Washington Allston. Married Mary J. Pratt (of Gambier, Ohio) in 1843; they had three children. Published poems in Boston *Courier*. Settled in Philadelphia in 1846. Verse collected in *Poems* (1847), *Lays and Ballads* (1849), *The New Pastoral* (1855), *The House by the Sea* (1855), *Sylvia; or, The Last Shepherd* (1857), *Rural Poems* (1857), and other volumes. Visited Europe in 1850; settled in Florence in 1853. In 1855, wife and a daughter died of cholera; Read returned to U.S., and the following year married Harriet Denison Butler (of Northampton, Massachusetts). Spent much time in Philadelphia, Boston, Cincinnati, as well as abroad. During Civil War gave lectures and readings of his war poetry to benefit soldiers; served on the staff of Union general Lew Wallace. Three-volume *Poetical Works* published in 1866. In final years (after 1866) lived mainly in Rome. Painted mythological subjects and portraits of Elizabeth Barrett Browning, Henry Wadsworth Longfellow, and others; also worked occasionally as sculptor, making bust of Sheridan. Later volumes of verse include *The Wagoner of the Alleghanies* (1862), *A Summer Story, Sheridan's Ride, and Other Poems* (1865), and *Good Samaritans* (1867). Died of pneumonia while on a visit to the United States.

LIZETTE WOODWORTH REESE (January 9, 1856–December 17, 1935) b. Huntingdon (now Waverly), Maryland, a suburb of Baltimore. One of four daughters of Louisa Gabler (of German birth) and David Reese (who later served as Confederate soldier). After graduating Eastern High School she became a teacher and continued to teach at various public and private schools in the Baltimore area; taught English at Western High School, 1901–21. Published first poem, "The Deserted House," in *The Southern Magazine* in 1874; first collection of verse, *A Branch of May*, appeared in 1887. Her work was praised by Edmund Clarence Stedman, with whom she formed a close friendship. Her next collection, *A Handful of Lavender* (1891), incorporated the poems of the previous volume with 43 new ones; followed by *A Quiet Road* (1896), *A Wayside Lute* (1909), and *Spicewood* (1920). Sonnet "Tears," published in *Scribner's* in 1899, became widely known. Retired from teaching in

1921. After retirement published verse collections *Wild Cherry* (1923), *Selected Poems* (1926), *Little Henrietta* (1927), *White April* (1930), *Pastures* (1933), and two volumes of prose memoirs, *A Victorian Village* (1920) and *The York Road* (1931). Narrative poem *The Old House in the Country* (1936) and unfinished novel *Worleys* (1936) appeared posthumously.

JOHN ROLLIN RIDGE (March 18, 1827–October 5, 1867) b. in Cherokee Nation near Rome, Georgia. Son of John Ridge and grandson of Major Ridge, Cherokee leaders who helped negotiate 1835 Treaty of New Echota ceding Cherokee lands to the U.S.; mother Sarah Bird Northrup (whom his father met while attending school in Connecticut) was white. Ridge was 11 at time of forced removal of Cherokee to Indian Territory (now Oklahoma). On June 22, 1839, father and grandfather were murdered in retaliation for their involvement with loss of Cherokee lands. Mother moved with children to Fayetteville, Arkansas, where Ridge was educated; briefly attended school in Great Barrington, Massachusetts, but soon returned to Fayetteville, studying Latin and Greek with a missionary to the Cherokee. About 1849 Ridge killed a Cherokee (allegedly in self-defense) who had attacked him as result of the old grievance against his family; fled to Missouri. In 1850, rather than stand trial in Cherokee Nation, emigrated to California with the Gold Rush, leaving a wife, Elizabeth Wilson, and daughter in Arkansas. Worked as miner and trader; in 1853 became deputy clerk, auditor, and recorder in Yuba County, California. Became journalist, writing poems and articles for *Golden Era* and *Hesperian* under pseudonym "Yellow Bird" (literal translation of his Cherokee name Chees-qua-ta-law-ny); sent for family, settling in Marysville, California, and later in San Francisco. In 1854 published *Life and Adventures of Joaquin Murieta*, novel based on life of Mexican bandit. Edited *Sacramento Bee* in 1857, *California Express* in 1857–58, and *San Francisco Herald* in 1861–63. During Civil War, wrote in support of the Confederacy (with which the Cherokee were allied). After the war, headed one of two rival Cherokee delegations sent to Washington to negotiate peace treaty with federal government; unsuccessfully attempted to gain legal division of the tribe along lines of longstanding political feud that had claimed the lives of his father and grandfather. Returned to California, where he died. *Poems* published posthumously in 1868, although most of the poems were written when he was in his teens.

JAMES WHITCOMB RILEY (October 7, 1849–July 22, 1916) b. Greenfield, Indiana. Son of Elizabeth Marine and Reuben A. Riley (a lawyer and state legislator who later served as Union cavalry captain). Educated at home and at local schools; briefly attended Greenfield Academy in 1870. After leaving school, worked as shoe-store clerk, Bible salesman, house painter. Began publishing poems in local papers in 1870. Started sign-painting business in 1871. From 1872–74, toured Midwest as member of medicine show and as itinerant sign painter; gave solo performances as humorist, 1874–76. Worked briefly in father's law office. Resumed touring in 1876, with Wizard Oil Company medicine show. In 1877 worked as assistant to the editor of *The Anderson*

Democrat. In literary hoax, passed off poem "Leonainie" (published in *Kokomo Dispatch* in August 1877) as newly discovered poem by Poe. Regularly contributed poems and sketches to the *Indianapolis Journal*, and in 1879, settling permanently in Indianapolis, joined *Journal* staff as poet and humorist. Humorous verses in Hoosier dialect, written under pseudonym "Benj. F. Johnson, of Boone," became popular and were collected in *The Old Swimmin'-Hole and 'Leven More Poems* (1883). Collection of prose sketches *The Boss Girl* (1885) followed by another volume of verse, *Afterwhiles* (1887). Following successful reading in Boston in 1882, frequently made reading tours of U.S. After 1886 sometimes shared platform with humorist "Bill" Nye; introduced by James Russell Lowell at highly successful 1887 reading at Chickering Hall, New York City, under auspices of International Copyright League. Literary associates included Joel Chandler Harris, George Washington Cable, and Bliss Carman. While continuing as staff writer for *Indianapolis Journal*, continued to publish poetry regularly in collections including *Old-Fashioned Roses* (1888), *Pipes o' Pan at Zekesbury* (1888), *Rhymes of Childhood* (1890), *Green Fields and Running Brooks* (1892), *Poems Here at Home* (1893), *Armazindy* (1894), *A Child World* (1896), *The Rubaiyat of Doc Sifers* (1897), *Home-Folks* (1900), *The Book of Joyous Children* (1902). In addition, due to Riley's wide popularity, earlier work was frequently reissued in illustrated gift editions. Retired from *Indianapolis Journal* in 1888. Visited Scotland and England in 1891. Verse drama *The Flying Islands of the Night* appeared in 1891 but was not well received. Gave final reading tour in 1903. Received numerous honorary degrees; elected to American Academy of Arts and Letters in 1911. Six-volume edition of *The Complete Works of James Whitcomb Riley* was published 1913. Weakened by series of strokes in later years.

EDWIN ARLINGTON ROBINSON (December 22, 1869–April 6, 1935) b. Head Tide, Maine. Son of Mary Elizabeth Palmer and Edward Robinson; descendant of Anne Bradstreet. Grew up in Gardiner, Maine. Studied at Harvard (1891–93); published poems in *Harvard Advocate*. Worked in Boston and Gardiner for a number of years while devoting himself to poetry. Published *The Torrent and the Night Before* (1896) at own expense; it was followed the next year by *The Children of the Night*. In 1899 worked as confidential clerk to Harvard president Charles W. Eliot before moving in October to New York City. Held variety of jobs, including work as time checker for construction of IRT subway in New York City, 1903–04; began to drink heavily. Encouraged by Edmund Clarence Stedman, who anthologized a number of his poems; introduced by Stedman to poet Ridgely Torrence, who became a close friend; renewed friendship with Harvard acquaintance William Vaughn Moody. Published *Captain Craig* (1902); the book's reviews were poor, although Robinson was defended by Trumbull Stickney in *The Harvard Monthly*: "The honesty and simplicity of his mind, the pathos and kindness of his heart, above all the humor with which his imagination is lighted up continually, have made me begin life over again and feel once more that poetry is part of it, nay the truth of it." Robinson continued to live in obscurity until Presi-

dent Theodore Roosevelt, an admirer of his poetry, offered him job in New York custom house, where he worked from 1905 to 1909. *The Town Down the River* (1910), dedicated to Roosevelt, and *The Man Against the Sky* (1916) gained him wider attention as poet; also published plays *Van Zorn* (1914) and *The Porcupine* (1915). From 1911 spent summers at MacDowell Colony in Peterborough, New Hampshire; assisted, beginning in 1916, by financial stipend donated anonymously by friends. *Merlin* (1917) was first of triptych of book-length Arthurian poems, followed by *Lancelot* (1920) and *Tristram* (1927). Won three Pulitzer Prizes, for *Collected Poems* (1921), *The Man Who Died Twice* (1924), and *Tristram*, whose popular success gave Robinson financial security. Other late books of poetry included *The Three Taverns* (1920), *Avon's Harvest* (1921), *Roman Bartholow* (1923), *Dionysus in Doubt* (1925), *Cavender's House* (1929), *The Glory of the Nightingales* (1930), *Matthias at the Door* (1931), *Talifer* (1933), *Amaranth* (1934), and *King Jasper* (1935). Robinson traveled to England in 1923, his sole trip abroad.

ABRAM JOSEPH RYAN (February 5, 1838–April 22, 1886) b. Hagerstown, Maryland. Parents Mary Coughlin and Matthew Ryan were recent immigrants from Clonmell, Ireland. Family moved to the West in the early 1840s, settling in St. Louis, Missouri, where father eventually opened a general store. Attended Christian Brothers Cathedral school in St. Louis (1853–54); took vows in November 1856. Studied theology at Niagara University, Niagara, New York (1858–59). Ordained September 1860 in St. Vincent's Church, St. Louis. Taught theology at Niagara University and at diocesan seminary in Cape Girardeau, Missouri. In 1862 joined Confederate Army as unofficial chaplain (having been rejected in application for commission); ministered to smallpox victims at Gratiot Prison in New Orleans; wrote two elegies for brother killed in April 1863 while fighting for Confederacy. After the war, edited Catholic newspapers *The Pacificator* and *The Banner of the South* in Augusta, Georgia, and *The Star* in New Orleans. Lived briefly in Mississippi and formed friendship with family of Jefferson Davis; later served as priest in Tennessee, Georgia, and Alabama. During Reconstruction remained spokesman for Confederacy, expressing continuing loyalty to the cause in poems published throughout the 1870s (became known as "The Poet-Priest of the Confederacy"); poems collected in *Father Ryan's Poems* (1879) and *Poems, Patriotic, Religious, and Miscellaneous* (1880); also published devotional work *A Crown for Our Queen* (1882). Lectured in United States, Canada, and Mexico, often as part of fundraising effort for Southern war orphans and widows, and for victims of epidemics. Died at Convent of St. Bonifacius in Louisville, Kentucky.

GEORGE SANTAYANA (December 16, 1863–September 26, 1952) b. Madrid, Spain. Son of Josefina Borras de Santayana (widow of American businessman George Sturgis) and Augustin Ruiz de Santayana; christened Jorge Ruiz de Santayana y Borras. Mother separated from second husband when Santayana was five, and moved to Boston; raised by father in Avila,

Spain, until age eight, when they rejoined mother in Boston; father returned permanently to Spain in 1873. Studied at Boston Latin School. Graduated from Harvard 1886, having co-edited the *Harvard Lampoon* (with Ernest Lawrence Thayer and others). Studied in Germany before returning to Harvard for Ph.D. in philosophy, awarded in 1889. Became member of Harvard philosophy faculty (where colleagues included William James and Josiah Royce) and full professor in 1907. Students included T. S. Eliot and Wallace Stevens. Early works included *Sonnets and Other Verses* (1894), first important philosophical work *The Sense of Beauty* (1896), verse play *Lucifer: A Theological Tragedy* (1899), *Interpretations of Poetry and Religion* (1900), and another poetry collection, *The Hermit of Carmel* (1901). *The Life of Reason*, a five-volume study of reason in relation to common sense, society, religion, art, and science, appeared 1905–06; *Three Philosophical Poets*, study of Lucretius, Dante, and Goethe, published 1910. Remained at Harvard until 1912; retired to live off small inheritance from mother, who had died earlier that year. Lived in England and Paris before settling in Rome in 1925. In *Scepticism and Animal Faith* (1923) undertook to reexamine foundations of his philosophy; elaborated on new interpretation in four-volume *The Realms of Being* (1927–40). *Poems, Selected by the Author and Revised* published in London in 1922 (American edition, 1923). Published many other works including *The Genteel Tradition at Bay* (1931) and *The Last Puritan* (1935), a novel about the lingering influence of Calvinism, which became an unexpected bestseller. Autobiography *Persons and Places* appeared in three volumes between 1944 and 1953. During World War II, took refuge in English convent in Rome, remaining there until his death.

CLINTON SCOLLARD (September 18, 1860–November 19, 1932) b. Clinton, New York. Graduated from Hamilton College 1881; graduate studies at Harvard and Cambridge; formed early friendships with Bliss Carman, Frank Dempster Sherman, Edmund Gosse, Austin Dobson, and Andrew Lang. After traveling in the Near East, became professor of English at Hamilton, remaining there until 1896. Beginning with first verse collections *Pictures in Song* (1884) and *With Reed and Lyre* (1886), published over 40 volumes of poetry, fiction, and essays. Frequent travels were reflected in works such as *Old and New World Lyrics* (1888), *Songs of Sunrise Lands* (1892), and *Italy in Arms and Other Poems* (1915). Wrote *A Southern Flight* (1905) in collaboration with close friend Frank Dempster Sherman, to whose memory he dedicated *Elegy in Autumn* (1917). Married Georgia Brown in 1890; in 1924 they were divorced, and he married poet Jessie B. Rittenhouse. Died at his home in Kent, Connecticut.

EDWARD ROWLAND SILL (April 29, 1841–February 27, 1887) b. Windsor, Connecticut. Son of Elizabeth Newberry Rowland and Theodore Sill, a physician. After death by drowning of older brother when he was six and death of mother when he was eleven, moved with father to Cleveland. Father died in 1853 shortly after opening office there. Attended Phillips Exeter Academy

for two years; returned to Ohio, where he lived with uncle Elisha Noyes Sill in Cuyahoga Falls, and attended Western Reserve Preparatory School for a year and a half. Attended Yale, where he was an editor of *Yale Literary Magazine* and author of class poem. After graduating from Yale in 1861, traveled to California by sea for his health. Worked as postal clerk in Sacramento and at bank in Folsom; desultorily studied law and medicine. Went back East in 1866, stopping in Cuyahoga Falls where in February 1867 he married cousin Elizabeth Newberry Sill (daughter of Elisha Noyes Sill). Briefly attended Harvard Divinity School in spring and summer of 1867 before deciding against ministerial career. (He wrote to correspondent, "On religion, I doubt your ever agreeing with me that the church is a great fraud and nuisance. I am convinced it is doing infinitely more harm than good, every day and week.") Moved to New York, working as journalist for *New York Evening Mail* and as teacher in Brooklyn. In 1868 published *The Hermitage and Other Poems*, only volume of verse publicly distributed in his lifetime. Settled again in Ohio in 1868; served two years as superintendent of schools in Cuyahoga Falls before moving in 1871 to California; taught high school in Oakland. From 1874 to 1882, occupied chair of English at University of California at Berkeley; revolutionized curriculum and pedagogy in his department; acquired reputation as one of the great teachers of his generation. Continued to publish poems in magazines. Retired from teaching in 1882; privately published a second book of poems, *The Venus of Milo* (1883); returned to father-in-law's home in Ohio. Became frequent contributor to *The Century*, *Atlantic Monthly*, *Overland Monthly*, and other journals. Health poor in final years; died unexpectedly in a Cleveland hospital, from syncope following a minor operation.

EDMUND CLARENCE STEDMAN (October 8, 1833–January 18, 1908) b. Hartford, Connecticut. Son of Elizabeth C. Dodge (later known as poet and essayist under the name Elizabeth C. D. Stedman Kinney) and Edmund B. Stedman (merchant and army officer). Father died when he was two; raised for next several years on grandfather's farm in Plainfield, New Jersey, passing afterward into care of uncle James B. Stedman in Norwich, Connecticut. Entered Yale 1849, but was expelled in his junior year for "irregularities" and disorderly conduct. Studied law for a time; became part owner of *Norwich Tribunal*. Married Laura Hyde Woodworth in 1853; they had two sons. Dissolved partnership at *Norwich Tribune* and became part owner of *Mountain County Herald* in Winsted, Connecticut, in 1854. Moved to New York in 1855; became partner in clockmaking concern; business failed and Stedman took work as real estate broker. Lived with wife in cooperative "Unitary Home" on East 14th Street. Satirical poem about a society wedding (1859) won him literary reputation furthered by other poems, including "Honest Abe of the West," campaign song for Lincoln. Formed friendships with Bayard Taylor, Richard Henry Stoddard, and Thomas Bailey Aldrich. In 1860 joined staff of New York *World*, and published first collection of verse, *Poems Lyrical and Idyllic*. Based in Washington during early years of Civil War as correspondent

for *World*; often traveled with troops. Assumed position in U.S. attorney general's office in 1862. The following year, returned to New York and entered world of finance with much success, forming his own brokerage company in 1864, and eventually holding a seat on the New York Stock Exchange. Continued to publish volumes of poetry, including *Alice of Monmouth* (1864), *The Blameless Prince* (1869), *Favorite Poems* (1877), *Hawthorne and Other Poems* (1877), and *Lyrics and Idylls* (1879); editions of *Poetical Works of Edmund Clarence Stedman* appeared in 1873 and 1884. First major work of criticism, *Victorian Poets*, appeared in 1875; published pioneering critical study *Poets of America* in 1885. Encouraged many young writers, including Hamlin Garland, Constance Fenimore Woolson, Emma Lazarus, Edwin Arlington Robinson, Ridgely Torrence, Richard Hovey, Lizette Woodworth Reese, Harriet Monroe, William Vaughn Moody, and others. Highly regarded as editor, particularly of American literature; edited 11-volume *A Library of American Literature from the Earliest Settlement to the Present Times* (1889–90); ten-volume edition of the works of Poe co-edited with George Woodberry; *A Victorian Anthology* (1897); and *An American Anthology, 1787–1899* (1900), a major survey of American poetry. Active in wide range of artistic and literary institutions; served as president of American Academy of Arts and Letters (1904–07). Suffered heart attack in 1899, and the following year resigned seat on Stock Exchange.

TRUMBULL STICKNEY (June 20, 1874–October 11, 1904) b. Joseph Trumbull Stickney in Geneva, Switzerland. Son of Harriet Champion Trumbull and Austin Stickney (classics professor). Family lived mostly in Europe; visited U.S. when Stickney was five and nine. Early education at home with father; attended preparatory school in Somerset, England, at age 12, after which the family lived in New York for two years. In 1890, following another stay in Europe, returned to U.S. and entered Harvard in 1891. Worked on *Harvard Monthly*, to which he contributed many poems (would continue to publish almost exclusively in the *Monthly* for the rest of his life); friends included George Cabot Lodge, William Vaughn Moody, Robert Morss Lovett, and George Santayana; graduated 1895. Spent summer of 1895 with family in Germany; began studies at Sorbonne in Paris. Close friendship with George Cabot Lodge, also resident there. Henry Adams, another friend, wrote of the days when he would "totter about with Joe Stickney, talking Greek philosophy or recent poetry." Had close relationship with Adams' friend Mrs. Elizabeth Cameron. Verse drama "Prometheus Pyrphoros" published in *Harvard Monthly* in 1900; poetry collection *Dramatic Verses* appeared in limited edition in 1902. Studied Sanskrit and collaborated with Sylvain Levi on French translation of *Bhagavad-Gita* (not published until 1938). In 1903 was first American to receive doctorate in literature from Sorbonne; thesis on Greek poetry published as *Les Sentences dans la Poésie Grecque d'Homère à Euripides* (1903). Traveled for three months in Greece in the summer of 1903 before returning to America to teach Greek language and literature at Harvard. Worked on uncompleted translation of Aeschylus' *The Persians*; favorably reviewed Edwin Arlington Robinson's *Captain Craig* for *Harvard Monthly*. Diagnosed with

brain tumor in 1904; became blind but continued to write during last months of life. Lodge wrote of Stickney's last days: "He was thirty years old—by far the most promising man I have known, his best work still and surely to come. Under the terrible test of a mortal disease his mind and character rose to higher levels than they had ever touched before." *The Poems of Trumbull Stickney*, edited by Lodge, Moody, and John Ellerton Lodge, published posthumously in 1905.

JOHN BANISTER TABB (March 22, 1845–November 19, 1909) b. at family estate The Forest in Amelia County, Virginia. Son of Marianna Bertrand Archer and Thomas Yelverton Tabb; family of local distinction, with connections to Washington and Randolph families. Educated at home by private tutors. At outbreak of Civil War, unable to enlist due to poor eyesight; with Major B. F. Ficklin, went to England in 1861 to help arrange transport of supplies to Confederacy. Returning to Charleston, served on blockade runner *Robert E. Lee*, but was not present at its capture in 1863. The following year taken prisoner on board the blockade runner *Siren*, and imprisoned at Point Lookout, Maryland; formed friendship with fellow prisoner Sidney Lanier. Following release in 1865, briefly studied music in Baltimore, intending to become concert pianist, but turned toward religion under influence of Episcopal priest Alfred Curtis. Taught at St. Paul's School in Baltimore and Racine College in Wisconsin. In 1872 formally converted to Roman Catholicism. Entered St. Charles' College in Ellicott City, Maryland, graduating 1875; taught at St. Peter's School, Richmond, and at St. Charles' College. In 1881 attended St. Mary's Seminary, Baltimore, where he completed theological studies; ordained 1884. Became lifelong English teacher at St. Charles' College; students included poet George Sterling. Wrote poetry for many years before private publication of first volume in 1882; first book followed by *An Octave to Mary* (1893) and *Poems* (1894), the latter going through 17 printings. Popularity of poetry sustained by subsequent collections: *Lyrics* (1897), *Later Lyrics* (1902), *The Rosary in Rhyme* (1904), *Quips and Quiddities* (1907), and *A Selection from the Verses of John B. Tabb* (1907), edited by Alice Meynell. Also published several volumes of humorous verse. Suffered from progressive blindness in later years; forced to retire from teaching in 1907. After his death additional collections *Later Poems* (1910) and *The Poetry of Father Tabb* (1928) appeared.

BAYARD TAYLOR (January 11, 1825–December 19, 1878) b. Kennett Square, Pennsylvania. Son of Rebecca Way and Joseph Taylor (a merchant who later turned to farming); of German and English descent on both sides. Raised in rural Quaker household; educated locally. At 17 apprenticed himself to printer of West Chester *Village Record*. With assistance of Rufus Griswold (then editor of *Graham's Magazine*) published first collection of poetry, *Ximena, or The Battle of the Sierra Morena* (1844) by subscription. Received backing of *Saturday Evening Post*, *United States Gazette*, and *New-York Tribune* for series of articles on Europe, and set out in 1844 on two-

year European journey. Travel account *Views A-Foot: or, Europe Seen with Knapsack and Staff* (1846) went through many editions and made him best-known traveler of the day. After year as proprietor and editor of Phoenix-ville (Pennsylvania) *Pioneer*, returned to New York to work as journalist for *The Literary World* and for Horace Greeley's *New-York Tribune* (whose literary department he ran from 1848 on). Published further collection of poetry, *Rhymes of Travel, Ballads and Poems* (1849). Sent by *Tribune* to California in 1849 to report on Gold Rush; returned by way of Mexico and published *Eldorado, or Adventures in the Path of Empire* (1850), another popular travel book. Delivered Phi Beta Kappa poem at Harvard (1850); given prize by P. T. Barnum for best lyric to be sung by Jenny Lind at New York's Castle Garden. In October 1850 married Mary Agnew, a woman from his hometown in Pennsylvania, although she was seriously ill; she died two months after wedding. Published *A Book of Romances, Lyrics, and Songs* (1851) and, with George Ripley, edited *The Hand-book of Literature and the Fine Arts* (1852). In August 1851 embarked on two years of travel in Africa and Asia; journey took him to Egypt, Abyssinia, the Sudan, Syria, Palestine, Turkey, India, China, and Japan (where he joined Commodore Perry's expedition as master's mate); wrote up adventures in *A Journey to Central Africa* (1854), *The Lands of the Saracen* (1855), and *A Visit to India, China, and Japan, in the Year 1853* (1855). Published best-received verse collection, *Poems of the Orient* (1854), followed by *Poems of Home and Travel* (1855); compiled *The Cyclopaedia of Modern Travel* (1856); went on lecture tours throughout the U.S. In 1856 set off for Europe, producing *Northern Travel* (1858), *Travels in Greece and Russia* (1859), and *At Home and Abroad* (1859–62). In 1857 married Marie Hansen (daughter of a Danish astronomer) in Gotha, Saxony; they had a daughter, Lilian. Returning to the U.S., retired to family farm in Pennsylvania, where he built country home Cedarcroft. Served as Civil War correspondent for *Tribune*; in 1862 went to Russia as secretary of legation in St. Petersburg. Published several novels, including *Hannah Thurston* (1863), *John Godfrey's Fortunes* (1864), *The Story of Kennett* (1866), and *Joseph and His Friend* (1870), and further volumes of poetry, including *The Poet's Journal* (1862), *The Poems of Bayard Taylor* (1864), *The Picture of St. John* (1866), *The Masque of the Gods* (1872), *Lars: A Pastoral of Norway* (1873), *The Prophet* (1874), and *The Echo Club and Other Literary Diversions* (1876). Close friend of many leading writers, including Henry Wadsworth Longfellow, John Greenleaf Whittier, Oliver Wendell Holmes, George Henry Boker, and Charles Godfrey Leland. In the 1860s devoted himself primarily to complete translation of Goethe's *Faust*, which appeared in two volumes in 1870–71. Continued to travel frequently, visiting Germany, Italy, Egypt, and Iceland; later travel books included *Colorado: A Summer Trip* (1867), *Byways of Europe* (1869), and *Egypt and Iceland in the Year 1874* (1874). Gave lectures at Cornell on German literature in 1870; repeated lectures in New York and elsewhere. In 1878 sent to Germany as American minister; died shortly after his arrival in Berlin. *Studies in German Literature* published posthumously in 1879.

ERNEST LAWRENCE THAYER (August 14, 1863–August 21, 1940) b. Lawrence, Massachusetts. Son of Ellen Darling and Edward Davis Thayer, a prominent woolen manufacturer. Attended Harvard, where he studied with William James and developed lifelong interest in philosophy; co-editor of Harvard *Lampoon* with George Santayana (who later recalled Thayer as "a man apart . . . his wit was not so much jocular as Mercutio-like, curious and whimsical, as if he saw the broken edges of things that appear whole"); other college friends included William Randolph Hearst. Graduated Harvard 1885; moved to San Francisco the following year, joining staff of San Francisco *Examiner*, to which he regularly contributed humorous columns and verse. Returned to Worcester, Massachusetts, late in 1887, but continued to contribute to the *Examiner*, which published "Casey at the Bat" on June 3, 1888, under his usual byline "Phin." After 1888, Thayer worked in his father's woolen business for about eight years. Subsequently spent much time abroad; settled in Santa Barbara, California, in 1912, residing there until his death. Studied philosophy on his own; wrote essays but did not publish them. In 1913 married Rosalind Buel Hammett. "Casey at the Bat" widely popularized by comedian De Wolf Hopper in readings throughout the country; Thayer's authorship not publicly established until 1909, when *The Bookman* published an authorized version.

ROSE HARTWICK THORPE (July 18, 1850–July 19, 1939) b. Mishawaka, Indiana. Daughter of Mary Louisa Wight and William Morris Hartwick (a tailor). Family moved to Kansas and eventually settled in Litchfield, Michigan, in 1860; received public education, graduating high school in 1868. "Curfew Must Not Ring To-Night," written when she was in her teens, appeared in Detroit *Commercial Advertiser* in 1870 and achieved wide popularity; illustrated edition published 1882. In 1871 married Edmund C. Thorpe, a carriage maker and writer of German dialect verse; they had two daughters. Contributed regularly to *Youth's Companion*, *St. Nicholas*, *Wide Awake*, and other periodicals. Husband Edmund's business failed in 1881, and Thorpe took work editing Sunday school papers in Chicago. After Edmund developed tuberculosis, family moved to San Antonio, Texas, and, in 1886, to Pacific Beach, California. Verse collected in *The Yule Log* (1881), *Temperance Poems* (1887), and *Ringing Ballads* (1887); *The Poetical Works of Rose Hartwick Thorpe* appeared in 1912. Other publications included children's books *Fred's Dark Days* (1881), *The Fenton Family* (1884), *Nina Bruce* (1886), and *The Chester Girls* (1887). Edmund died in 1916; thereafter Thorpe worked for woman suffrage, the YWCA, and the Women's Club of San Diego.

HENRY TIMROD (December 8, 1828–October 7, 1867) b. Charleston, South Carolina. Son of Thyrza Prince (of English and Swiss descent) and William Timrod (bookbinder who had published a volume of poetry in 1814); grandfather Heinrich Dimroth was German immigrant. Father served in Seminole War in 1836; died in 1838; family lived in relative poverty. Attended Christopher Cotes' Classical School in Charleston; established friendships

with poet Paul Hamilton Hayne and classicist Basil Gildersleeve. Studied at University of Georgia in Athens, 1845–46; briefly studied law in office of James L. Petigru; worked as private tutor on various plantations in the Carolinas. Contributed to *Southern Literary Messenger*, *Southern Literary Gazette*, and other magazines and newspapers. As member of literary group associated with Russell's Bookstore in Charleston, received encouragement from William Gilmore Simms; regularly contributed poetry and critical articles (including influential essay "Literature in the South") to *Russell's Magazine* (1857–60). First collection, *Poems*, published by Ticknor and Fields in 1860. Ardent supporter of Southern cause; wrote "Ethnogenesis" in February 1861 to herald birth of Confederacy. Enlisted briefly in militia company in July 1861, but was discharged due to health. Reenlisted in 1862 and served briefly as regimental clerk, and then, while on leave, as war correspondent for *The Charleston Mercury*, in which capacity he witnessed the retreat from Shiloh. Suffering from tuberculosis, once again discharged from service in December 1862. Settled in Columbia, South Carolina, in 1864; worked as associate editor of *The Daily South Carolinian* (in which a benefactor had bought him a part interest). Married Katie Goodwin in February 1864; their infant son Willie died the following year. Lost home and possessions when Sherman's army burned Columbia in February 1865; reduced to extreme poverty. Wrote ode sung at Confederate memorial services at Charleston's Magnolia Cemetery in June 1866. Health failed rapidly; died of tuberculosis after suffering severe hemorrhages of the lungs. Paul Hamilton Hayne edited *The Poems of Henry Timrod* (1873).

JOHN TOWNSEND TROWBRIDGE (September 18, 1827–February 12, 1916) b. Ogden, New York. Son of Rebecca Willey and Windsor Stone Trowbridge. Largely self-educated; published poetry in *The Rochester Republican* when he was 16. Studied at Lockport Academy (1844–45); taught briefly at district schools in northwestern Illinois and in Lockport, New York. Went to New York City in 1847 to pursue writing career; with help of Mordecai Manuel Noah, published stories in *Dollar Magazine* and elsewhere. In 1848 settled in Boston; worked as editor of *Yankee Nation* and, in 1850, of Boston *Sentinel*, for which he wrote controversial editorial opposing Fugitive Slave Act. Published first novel, *Father Brighthopes*, in 1853. Married Cornelia Warren in 1860, with whom he had two children; she died in 1864. Moved to Arlington, Massachusetts, in 1865. Married Sarah Adelaide Newton in 1873; they had three children. Produced some 40 volumes of fiction (much of it for children), poetry, plays, and other writing. Fiction included anti-slavery novels *Neighbor Jackwood* (1857) and *Cudjo's Cave* (1864), and *Coupon Bonds* (1866), popular novella of mercenary New England family which he dramatized in 1876. Verse collections included *The Vagabonds and Other Poems* (1869), *The Emigrant's Story and Other Poems* (1875), and *A Home Idyl and Other Poems* (1881). Published *The South: A Tour of Its Battlefields and Ruined Cities* in 1866. As editor of *Our Young Folks* (1865–73), published work by Charles Dickens, Harriet Beecher Stowe, Bayard Taylor, Rose Terry Cooke, and Louisa May

Alcott. Friends included Walt Whitman, Oliver Wendell Holmes, and Henry Wadsworth Longfellow. In 1903 published collected verse, *The Poetical Works of John Townsend Trowbridge*, and autobiography, *My Own Story*.

FREDERICK GODDARD TUCKERMAN   (August 10, 1821–May 14, 1873)   b. Boston, Massachusetts. Son of Sophia May and Edward Tuckerman, a Boston merchant and importer. Younger brother of botanist Edward Tuckerman; cousin of art critic Henry Theodore Tuckerman. Attended preparatory school of Episcopal bishop John Henry Hopkins and Boston Latin School; entered Harvard 1837; was tutored for a brief period by Jones Very, but left due to eye trouble in 1838. The following year, reentered Harvard, this time in the Law School, from which he graduated in 1842; admitted to Suffolk County bar in 1844. Married Hannah Lucinda Jones of Greenfield, Massachusetts, on June 17, 1847; they had two sons and a daughter. Settled in Greenfield; abandoned law practice to devote himself to study of literature, botany, meteorology, and astronomy; published astronomical observations; recognized as authority on local flora. In 1850 began contributing poems to magazines, eventually publishing in *Atlantic Monthly*, *Putnam's*, and *Littel's Living Age*. Traveled twice to Europe, in the summer of 1851 and in 1854–55; formed close friendship with Alfred Tennyson, with whom he stayed on the Isle of Wight in 1855. Wife Hannah died in May 1857, following the birth of her third child. *Poems* privately printed in 1860; Ticknor & Fields published an edition of the book in 1864. Lived reclusively following wife's death.

MARK TWAIN   (November 30, 1835–April 21, 1910)   b. Samuel Langhorne Clemens in Florida, Missouri. Third of four children of John Marshall Clemens and Jane Lampton. At age four moved with family to Mississippi River port village Hannibal, Missouri, where father worked unsuccessfully as storekeeper and farmer. Educated locally; after father's death in 1847 worked as apprentice printer. From 1851 published sketches and squibs in papers published by his brother Orion and elsewhere. Worked as journeyman printer (1853–57) in St. Louis, New York, Philadelphia, and elsewhere. In 1857 became cub pilot on Mississippi riverboat; granted pilot's license in 1859; continued to work on river until traffic disrupted by outbreak of Civil War. Accompanied brother Orion (newly appointed Secretary to Nevada Territory) to Carson City, serving as Orion's secretary, speculating in mining stocks, and prospecting; contributed writing to newspapers in Keokuk, Iowa, and Carson City and Virginia City, Nevada. First used pseudonym "Mark Twain" in 1863. In San Francisco contributed to *The Golden Era* and *The Californian*, and began to publish work in eastern publications such as *The Mercury*, the New York *Saturday Press*, and *Harper's*; reported on five-month trip to Sandwich Islands (Hawaii) for Sacramento *Union*. Achieved reputation as public lecturer and humorist. In 1867 sailed on first American cruise ship, the *Quaker City*, for tour of Europe and the Holy Land; published first collection, *The Celebrated Jumping Frog of Calaveras County and Other Sketches*. Account of *Quaker City* tour published with great success as

The Innocents Abroad (1869). In 1870 married Livy Langdon, with whom he had four children (one of whom died in infancy); settled in Hartford, Connecticut, the following year. *Roughing It*, based on his western experiences, published in 1872. From 1873 traveled frequently with family in Europe, sometimes for years at a time. *The Gilded Age* (1873), written in collaboration with Charles Dudley Warner, followed by novels and travel books including *The Adventures of Tom Sawyer* (1876), *A Tramp Abroad* (1880), *The Prince and the Pauper* (1882), *Life on the Mississippi* (1883), *Adventures of Huckleberry Finn* (1885), *A Connecticut Yankee in King Arthur's Court* (1889), *The American Claimant* (1892), *Tom Sawyer Abroad* (1892), *The Tragedy of Pudd'nhead Wilson* (1894), *Tom Sawyer, Detective* (1895), *Personal Recollections of Joan of Arc* (1896), and *Following the Equator* (1897), based on around-the-world tour, 1895–96. Close literary associates included William Dean Howells, George Washington Cable, and Richard Watson Gilder. Business investments, including establishment of a publishing house (Charles L. Webster & Company) and development of a typesetting machine, led to heavy financial losses. Daughter Susy died in 1896, and wife, Livy, in 1904; daughter Jean suffered from epilepsy and died in 1909. Many later writings, pessimistic treatments of religion and society, remained unpublished; published *What Is Man?* privately and anonymously in 1906. Final years spent at home Stormfield near Redding, Connecticut. *The Mysterious Stranger*, left unfinished, was published posthumously in 1916.

GEORGE BOYER VASHON (July 25, 1824–October 5, 1878) b. Carlisle, Pennsylvania. Father was abolitionist John Bethune Vashon. Family moved to Pittsburgh in 1829; Vashon attended local schools, and became secretary in 1838 of first Juvenile Anti-Slavery Society in America. At 16 entered Oberlin College and in 1844 was its first black recipient of bachelor of arts degree. While still in college taught school in Chillicothe, Ohio, where his students included John Mercer Langston (later dean of Howard Law School and U.S. minister to Haiti). Returned to Pittsburgh after graduation; studied law under Judge Walter Forward. In 1847 application to take bar examination was denied; legal attempts to challenge denial rejected on grounds that as a person of color he was not a citizen. Left Pennsylvania for Haiti; on the way, took bar examination in New York City, and in January 1848 became first black lawyer in the state. Taught college in Port-au-Prince, Haiti, for two and a half years. Upon return to U.S., settled in Syracuse, New York, in 1850, where he practiced law for four years. In 1853, composed "Vincent Ogé," long poem on the hero of the Haitian insurrection of 1790–91. Professor of belles lettres and mathematics at New York Central College in McGrawville, New York, 1854–57. Returned to Pittsburgh and married Susan Paul Smith in 1857; they had seven children. Taught and served as principal in black public schools (1858–63) and taught at Avery College (1864–68); first black to teach at Howard University (1867–68). Contributor to *The Anglo-African Review* and *The New Era*; later writings included articles on black citizenship, history of Nile River, literature, and astronomy, as well as poems "A Life-Day"

(1864) and "Ode on the Proclamation of the Fifteenth Amendment" (1870). Briefly associated in 1867 as attorney with the Freedmen's Bureau in Washington, D.C. In 1869 served as delegate at national convention of Colored Men of America, of whose executive committee he became a member in 1870. Final teaching position, beginning in 1874, believed to have been at Alcorn University in Rodney, Mississippi, where he died of yellow fever.

EDITH WHARTON (January 24, 1862–August 11, 1937) b. Edith Newbold Jones in New York City. Daughter of Lucretia Stevens Rhinelander and George Frederic Jones; parents belonged to old and socially prominent families, with wealth derived from Manhattan landholdings. Family moved to Europe in 1866 following depression in real estate values, and lived successively in England, Italy, France, and Germany. Returned with family to U.S. in 1872, dividing time between New York and Newport, Rhode Island. Educated at home; read extensively in father's library. Private edition of poems published at mother's expense in 1878; one poem published by William Dean Howells in *Atlantic Monthly*. Engagement to Henry Stevens, son of prominent family, broken off by fiancé's family after two years. In 1885 married Edward Wharton, a Harvard graduate interested mainly in outdoor life who lived on an annuity. The Whartons traveled for several months every year in Europe, mostly Italy. In 1889 published poems in *Scribner's, Harper's,* and *Century Magazine*; soon began publishing short stories. Bought New York town house and Newport estate; studied art and interior decoration. With architect Ogden Codman wrote *The Decoration of Houses*, published 1897. Suffered mental and physical breakdown in 1898, followed by "rest cure" under supervision of Dr. S. Weir Mitchell. Settled in Washington, D.C., for four months in 1899, and began close friendship with Walter Berry; short story collection *The Greater Inclination* published to great success in the same year; traveled extensively in Europe. In 1901 bought property in Lenox, Massachusetts, and had large house, The Mount, built there. Published second story collection *Crucial Instances* (1901) and historical novel *The Valley of Decision* (1902). Urged by Henry James to abandon historical subject matter for contemporary material: "*Do New York!* The 1st-hand account is precious." Met Theodore Roosevelt, beginning long friendship. Moved into The Mount. Husband suffered first of series of nervous collapses in 1902. Divided time between Lenox and Europe; toured Sussex with Henry James; at The Mount, house guests included Brooks Adams and George Cabot Lodge. *The House of Mirth* appeared 1905 and was highly successful; adapted for the stage by Wharton and Clyde Fitch. Continued to publish fiction including *Madame de Treymes* (1907), *The Fruit of the Tree* (1907), *Ethan Frome* (1911), *The Reef* (1912), and *The Custom of the Country* (1913). Poems collected in *Artemis to Actaeon* (1909) and *Twelve Poems* (1926). Enjoyed brilliant social life in England and France; friends included Paul Bourget, Howard Sturgis, Percy Lubbock, Henry Adams, and Bernhard Berenson. In 1908 began affair with journalist William Morton Fullerton. The following year, husband admitted embezzling money from Wharton's trust funds; she was granted a divorce in

1913 on grounds of adultery. Traveled in North Africa and Spain in 1914. Following outbreak of World War I, established American Hostels for Refugees; made repeated visits to front; organized Children of Flanders Rescue Committee. Edited *The Book of the Homeless* in 1916 to raise money for refugees, and in the same year was made Chevalier of the Legion of Honor. Bought house in village of St. Brice-sous-Forêt outside Paris. Later fiction included *Summer* (1917), *The Marne* (1918), *The Age of Innocence* (1920), *The Old Maid* (1921), *The Glimpses of the Moon* (1922), *A Son at the Front* (1923), *The Mother's Recompense* (1925), *The Children* (1928), *Hudson River Bracketed* (1929), and *The Gods Arrive* (1932). In 1923 became first woman to receive honorary doctorate of letters from Yale. Autobiography *A Backward Glance* published 1934. Suffered a stroke in June 1937 and died two months later at St. Brice.

JAMES MONROE WHITFIELD (April 10, 1822–April 23, 1871) b. Exeter, New Hampshire. Parents were free blacks about whom little is known. Educated in public grammar schools in Exeter. In 1838, prepared paper for Cleveland convention urging black settlement on borders of California; active thereafter in plans for black emigration and colonization; associates in the 1850s included black nationalists James T. Holly and Martin R. Delany. After a short stay in Boston, relocated in 1839 to Buffalo, New York, working as barber. During late 1840s and 1850s, contributed poems to *The North Star* and *Frederick Douglass' Paper*; verse collection *America and Other Poems* published in Buffalo in 1853. Achieved wide recognition for work with National Emigration Conventions in Cleveland in 1854 and 1856; engaged in controversy with Frederick Douglass over merits of black separatism and emigration; believed to have traveled in 1859 to Central America to investigate possibility of purchasing land there for colonization. Returned to San Francisco in 1861 and, within a year, abandoned emigrationist activities. Worked as barber for remainder of life, mostly in California but also in Oregon, Idaho, and Nevada. Engaged in Masonic activity, serving as grand master of Prince Hall Masons in California (1864–69) and establishing lodge in Virginia City, Nevada. Active (1869–70) in Elko, Nevada, Republican Club. Later writings included 400-line "Poem Written for the Celebration of President Lincoln's Emancipation Proclamation," and letters and verse contributed to *San Francisco Elevator* and *Pacific Appeal*. Died of heart disease in San Francisco.

ALBERY ALLSON WHITMAN (May 30, 1851–June 29, 1901) b. in slavery on a farm near Mumfordville, Kentucky. Mother died in 1862, father in 1863; Whitman became free in 1863. Worked in Kentucky and Ohio as farm laborer, in plough shop, and as railroad construction worker. Attended school for a short period before teaching at Carysville, Ohio, and in Kentucky near his home. Resumed education about 1870, studying for six months at Wilberforce University under Bishop Daniel Alexander Payne, the university's president. First book, *Essays on the Ten Plagues and Miscellaneous Poems*, apparently published in 1871, but no copies are known to be extant; long poem *Leelah*

Misled published 1873. By 1877 became pastor of African Methodist Episcopal church in Springfield, Ohio; worked as general financial agent for Wilberforce University. Resigned position at Wilberforce in 1878, then led congregations in Ohio, Kansas, Texas, and Georgia. Published narrative poem *Not a Man and Yet a Man* in 1877, and *The Rape of Florida*, narrative in Spenserian stanzas, in 1884 (revised edition published in 1885 as *Twasinta's Seminoles*). Poetry collected in 1890 under title *Twasinta's Seminoles; Not a Man and Yet a Man; Drifted Leaves: A Collection of Poems*. He and wife, Caddie, had three daughters, Essie, Mable, and Alberta, who later became vaudeville team the Whitman Sisters. In late 1880s, suffering ill health, moved from Midwest to South; served as pastor at St. Philip's African Methodist Episcopal church in Savannah, Georgia; transferred to Allen Temple in Atlanta. In 1893 at World's Columbian Exposition read poem "The Freedman's Triumphant Song" to audience including Frederick Douglass and Paul Laurence Dunbar. Final poetic work, *An Idyll of the South*, appeared in two volumes in 1901. Contracted pneumonia on visit to Alliston, Alabama; died at his home in Atlanta.

ELLA WHEELER WILCOX (November 5, 1850–October 31, 1919) b. Johnstown Centre, Wisconsin. Daughter of Sarah Pratt and Marius Hartwell Wheeler, a teacher of music and dance; parents originally from Vermont. Educated in public schools and (in 1867–68) at University of Wisconsin. Wrote poems, essays, and fiction from an early age, beginning to publish in magazines in her teens; by age 18 was helping to support family with income from writing. Verse collected in *Drops of Water* (1872), *Shells* (1873), and *Maurine* (1875). Achieved notoriety when *Poems of Passion* (1883) was initially rejected by Jansen & McClurg of Chicago on grounds of immorality. Married Robert M. Wilcox, a silversmith, in 1884, and settled with him in Meriden, Connecticut; only child, a son, died shortly after birth in 1887. The couple spent winters in New York City and (after 1891) summers in Short Beach, Connecticut; they traveled widely in Europe and Asia, and developed a deep interest in theosophy and mediumistic séances. Wilcox continued to published many volumes of poetry, including *Poems of Pleasure* (1888), *Poems of Power* (1901), *Poems of Sentiment* (1906), and *Poems of Problems* (1914); for some years wrote daily poem for newspaper syndicate. Also published a novel, *Mal Moulée* (1885), and two autobiographies, *The Story of a Literary Career* (1905) and *The Worlds and I* (1918). During World War I toured army camps in France reciting poems and lecturing on sexual problems; fell ill and returned to United States; died in Short Beach.

FORCEYTHE WILLSON (April 10, 1837–February 2, 1867) b. Byron Forceythe Willson in Little Genesee, New York. Son of Hiram Willson (teacher who served as local postmaster and operated lumber business). In 1846 moved with family on raft down Allegheny and Ohio rivers; lived in Covington, Kentucky, where his father founded common school system; family settled in New Albany, Indiana, where father died in 1859 leaving comfortable income to family. Studied at Antioch College and then at Harvard,

until failing health forced him to withdraw without taking degree. Returned to Kentucky, where he wrote pro-Union editorials for the Louisville *Journal*; also published poems there, of which "The Old Sergeant" became well-known. In 1863 married Elizabeth Conwell Smith, also a poet. Settled in Cambridge, Massachusetts, 1864–66, to supervise his younger brother's education at Harvard. Literary acquaintances included Oliver Wendell Holmes, Henry Wadsworth Longfellow, and William Dean Howells. Developed interest in spiritualism. *The Old Sergeant and Other Poems* appeared in 1867. Died in Alfred, New York.

CONSTANCE FENIMORE WOOLSON   (March 5, 1840–January 24, 1894)   b. Claremont, New Hampshire. Daughter of Hannah Cooper Pomeroy and Charles Jarvis Woolson (stove manufacturer); great-niece of James Fenimore Cooper. Following scarlet fever epidemic in which three of her sisters died, family moved to Cleveland, Ohio, during winter of 1840–41. After early education at Cleveland Female Seminary, sent to Madame Chegary's School in New York, returning to Cleveland following graduation in 1858. Began to write as early as 1862, and devoted herself to it full-time following move to New York after father's death in 1869. In 1870 began to contribute prose sketches, fiction, and verse to *Harper's*, *Atlantic Monthly*, *Lippincott's*, and other periodicals. First volume was children's book *The Old Stone House* (1872), published under pseudonym "Anne March." From 1873 to 1879 spent winters in the Carolinas and Florida in the company of her ailing mother, with St. Augustine as her base. In Florida met Edmund Clarence Stedman, with whom she formed close literary friendship; became friend of South Carolina poet Paul Hamilton Hayne. Published criticism, travel sketches, memoirs, and verse, including book-length poem *Two Women: 1862* (1877), but was best known for fiction, including story collections *Castle Nowhere: Lake Country Sketches* (1875) and *Rodman the Keeper: Southern Sketches* (1880) and novels *Anne* (1883), *For the Major* (1883), *East Angels* (1886), *Jupiter Lights* (1889), and *Horace Chase* (1894). Following mother's death in 1879, moved to Europe, living in England for several years, but ultimately spending most of her time in Italy; visited Greece and Egypt in 1889–90. Met Henry James in Florence in 1880 and they became close friends. Suffered increasingly from deafness and periods of depression. During bout of influenza, died in Venice in fall from balcony. Two further volumes of short fiction were published after her death: *The Front Yard and Other Italian Stories* (1895) and *Dorothy and Other Italian Stories* (1896).

HENRY CLAY WORK   (October 1, 1832–June 8, 1884)   b. Middletown, Connecticut. Son of Aurelia and Alanson Work. Family moved to Quincy, Illinois, when Work was three years old. In 1841 his father, an active abolitionist, was sentenced to prison in Missouri for his role (as agent of Underground Railroad) in helping fugitive slaves escape. Following father's release in 1845, family returned to Middletown. Received common-school education; apprenticed to a printer; studied harmony in spare time. From 1854 worked as

printer in Chicago, while continuing to write songs. First success was "We're Coming, Sister Mary," written for Christy Minstrels. Became popular as songwriter during Civil War, under contract to music publishers Root & Cady; successful topical songs included "Kingdom Coming," "Marching Through Georgia," "Babylon Is Fallen," and "Wake, Nicodemus!" Other songs included "Lily Dale," "My Grandfather's Clock," and the temperance ballad "Father, Come Home!" (featured in play *Ten Nights in a Barroom*). Married in the early 1860s; had three children; wife later suffered from mental illness. Went to Europe in 1865. Relocated to Philadelphia, after publisher was ruined (and plates to Work's songs destroyed) in 1871 Chicago fire; invested savings from songwriting in 150-acre fruit farm in Vineland, New Jersey, which failed. In 1875 returned to Chicago following reestablishment of Root & Cady; enjoyed continued success as songwriter. Was also an inventor; patented a knitting machine, a walking doll, and a rotary engine. Died in Hartford, Connecticut.

Biographical Notes: 19TH-*Century Versions of American Indian Poetry*

CALEB ATWATER (December 25, 1778 – March 13, 1867) b. North Adams, Massachusetts. Son of Rachel Parker and Ebenezer Atwater (carpenter). Mother died when he was five years old; brought up by neighboring family. Graduated Williams College 1804; opened school for young women in New York City. Became Presbyterian minister; later admitted to bar. First wife, Diana Lawrence, died within a year of their marriage; married for second time to Belinda Butler in 1811. In 1815, moved West after business failure, settling in Circleville, Ohio. Practiced law and studied local earthworks and antiquities; results of researches summarized in 1820 paper to American Antiquarian Society, "Description of Antiquities Discovered in the State of Ohio and Other Western States." In 1821 elected to state legislature; worked to promote Ohio Canal Bill and other state-funded public works, and to provide Ohio with public education system. Published *Remarks Made on a Tour to Prairie du Chien* (1831, reprinted in 1850 as *The Indians of the Northwest*), describing Winnebago and other Indians of Prairie du Chien, Wisconsin. As one of three commissioners appointed by President Jackson, helped negotiate large land cessions from Ojibwa, Ottawa, Potawatomi, and Winnebago to U.S. government. Early writings collected in 1833 as *The Writings of Caleb Atwater*; in 1838 published *A History of the State of Ohio, Natural and Civil* and in 1841 *Essay on Education*.

FRANZ BOAS (July 9, 1858 – December 21, 1942) b. Minden, Westphalian Prussia. Educated at universities of Heidelberg, Bonn, and Kiel; trained as

physicist and geographer. Member of German expedition to Arctic, 1883–84; exposure to Eskimo life in Baffinland shifted his interests to ethnology. Traveled to Pacific Northwest in 1886 where he made first studies of Kwakiutl and other tribes; settled in U.S. as editor of *Science*. Joined faculty of Clark University in Worcester, Massachusetts, in 1888; supervised exhibit of physical anthropology for Chicago Columbian Exposition of 1893. In 1896 became first professor of anthropology at Columbia University, creating influential department of which he remained head until his retirement in 1936; students included Ruth Benedict, Ruth Bunzel, Zora Neale Hurston, Alfred Kroeber, Robert Lowie, Margaret Mead, Edward Sapir, and John R. Swanton. Served as curator of anthropology at American Museum of Natural History, 1901–05. Systematic research methods and opposition to 19th-century theories of race transformed fields of anthropology and linguistics; continued field work on Northwest coast until 1931. In final years, active in opposing Nazi theories of race. His many publications included *The Central Eskimo* (1888), *The Social Organization and the Secret Societies of the Kwakiutl Indians* (1897), *The Mythology of the Bella Coola Indians* (1898), *The Kwakiutl of Vancouver Island* (1909), *The Mind of Primitive Man* (1911), *Tsimshian Mythology* (1916), *Ethnology of the Kwakiutl* (1921), *Primitive Art* (1927), *Anthropology and Modern Life* (1928), *The Religion of the Kwakiutl Indians* (1930), and *Race, Language and Culture* (1940). Edited *Handbook of American Indian Languages* (1911).

JOHN GREGORY BOURKE (June 23, 1846–June 8, 1896) b. Philadelphia, Pennsylvania. Son of Anna Morton and Edward Bourke, emigrants from Galway, Ireland. Studied foreign languages with a Jesuit priest. In 1862 (misrepresenting age as 18) joined 15th Pennsylvania Cavalry, serving with it until the end of the Civil War; won Medal of Honor at battle of Stone's River, Tennessee (Murfreesboro). Appointed to U.S. Military Academy at West Point; commissioned 1869 as second lieutenant of 3rd U.S. Cavalry. Served as aide to Gen. George Crook, 1871–83. Stationed at Fort Craig, New Mexico, and Fort Grant, Arizona; transferred with Crook in 1875 to the Department of the Platte; returned with him to the Southwest in 1882. Participated in campaigns against Apache, Cheyenne, and Nez Percé; military career recounted in *An Apache Campaign in the Sierra Madre* (1886), *Mackenzie's Last Fight with the Cheyennes* (1890), and *On the Border with Crook* (1891). From 1891 commanded troop of 3rd Cavalry at Fort McIntosh and Fort Ringgold, Texas; later stationed at Fort Ethan Allen, Vermont. Ethnographic studies of Indians included *The Snake Dance of the Moquis of Arizona* (1884), *The Medicine-Men of the Apache* (1892), and a series of papers for *American Anthropologist*. Also wrote *Scatalogic Rites of All Nations* (1891). President of American Folk-Lore Society, 1896.

DANIEL GARRISON BRINTON (May 13, 1837–July 31, 1899) b. Thornbury, Pennsylvania. Son of Ann Garrison and Lewis Brinton. Graduated Yale College in 1858. First published work, *Notes on the Floridian Peninsula, its Literary History, Indian Tribes, and Antiquities*, appeared in 1859. Received medical

degree from Jefferson Medical College, Philadephia, 1860; spent a year in further study at Heidelberg and Paris. Practiced medicine in West Chester, Pennsylvania. In 1862 became surgeon in Union Army; served at battles of Chancellorsville and Gettysburg; suffered sunstroke in 1863 and was restricted to work at army hospital in Quincy, Illinois. After leaving the army in 1865 married Sarah Tillson; resumed medical practice in West Chester. Moved to Philadelphia in 1867 to work on staff of *The Medical and Surgical Reporter*, of which he became editor in 1874. Professor of ethnology and archaeology at Academy of Natural Sciences in Philadelphia, 1884–86; in 1886 professor of American linguistics and archaeology at University of Pennsylvania. Retired from medicine in 1887 to devote himself to research. In the eight volumes of his Library of Aboriginal American Literature (1882–90) was first to undertake systematic publication of translations of American Indian texts. Anthropological studies included *The Myths of the New World* (1868), *American Hero-Myths* (1882), *Aboriginal American Authors and Their Productions* (1883), *The Lenâpé and Their Legends* (1884), *A Lenâpé-English Dictionary* (1888, with A. S. Anthony), *Essays of an Americanist* (1890), *The American Race* (1891), and *Religions of Primitive Peoples* (1897). Also published many briefer linguistic and archaeological papers; literary studies of Robert Browning, Alfred Tennyson, and Walt Whitman; and poetry including the verse drama *Maria Candelaria* (1897). President of American Folk-Lore Society (1890) and American Association for the Advancement of Science (1894).

LEWIS CASS (October 9, 1782–June 17, 1866) b. Exeter, New Hampshire. Son of Mary Gilman and Jonathan Cass. Graduated Phillips Exeter Academy in 1799. Moved with family to Wilmington, Delaware, in 1799; taught school there briefly. Settled in 1801 on a farm near Zanesville, Ohio; studied law in Marietta, Ohio, and was admitted to the bar in 1802. Served in Ohio state legislature (1806) and as U.S. marshal in Ohio, 1807–12. Served under William Hull and William Henry Harrison in War of 1812; promoted to brigadier general; fought under Harrison against Indian forces led by Tecumseh. Served as governor of Michigan Territory, 1813–31. While governor won praise for peaceful handling of Indian affairs. Undertook study of Indians, circulating questionnaire published as *Inquiries Respecting the History, Traditions, Languages, Manners, Customs, Religion, &c. of the Indians, Living Within the United States* (1823); findings summarized in "Indians of North America," published in *North American Review* in 1826. Responsible for appointment of Henry Rowe Schoolcraft as Indian agent for Lake Superior tribes (1822) and superintendent of Indian affairs for Michigan (1836). In 1831 appointed Secretary of War under Andrew Jackson; supported and implemented Jackson's policy of Indian removal; defended policy in essay "Removal of the Indians" in *North American Review*. Appointed U.S. minister to France, 1836–42; published *France: Its King, Court and Government* (1840); opposed British efforts to suppress slave-trade by searching and seizing American vessels, and resigned after public dispute with Secretary of State Daniel Webster over his intervention in treaty negotiations concerning the issue. Served as senator for

Michigan, 1845–48; supported annexation of Texas, U.S. claim to Oregon Territory, and Mexican War. Ran for president as Democrat in 1848, but was defeated by Whig Zachary Taylor. Served again in Senate, 1849–57, where he vigorously supported Compromise of 1850. Appointed Secretary of State by James Buchanan, 1857; resigned in 1860 to protest Buchanan's inaction on secession of South Carolina. Retired to Detroit.

GEORGE CATLIN (July 26, 1796–December 23, 1872) b. Wilkes-Barre, Pennsylvania. One of 15 children of Polly Sutton and Putnam Catlin (lawyer and prosperous farmer). Studied law in Litchfield, Connecticut, 1817–18; practiced law in Lucerne, Pennsylvania. Moved to Philadelphia, 1821–25; taught himself to paint and pursued career as portraitist; elected in 1824 to Pennsylvania Academy of Fine Arts. Moved to New York City in 1827; married Clara Gregory of Albany in 1828; they had a son and three daughters. Developed interest in American Indians; painted portrait of Red Jacket in 1826 and in fall of 1828 painted portraits of Winnebago delegates touring the East. Traveled to St. Louis in 1831, where he was welcomed by William Clark (of the Lewis and Clark expedition), superintendent of Indian affairs for western tribes; attended tribal council in Prairie du Chien, Wisconsin; in St. Louis painted portrait of defeated Sauk chief Black Hawk. In 1832 traveled extensively in West; in Nebraska Territory spent time among Oto, Omaha, Missouri, and Pawnee. Sailed in the spring of 1832 up Missouri by steamboat to the mouth of the Yellowstone; executed hundreds of paintings of Sioux, Blackfeet, Assiniboin, Ojibwa, Crow, Plains Cree, and Mandan subjects; returned to St. Louis in fall of 1832. Studied Indians of Southeast and Texas (1834); traveled up Mississippi to Wisconsin and Iowa (1835); returning to North in 1836, visited Winnebago and Menominee and explored pipestone quarry in southwest Minnesota (red stone used for sacred pipes named "catlinite" after him); visited Yuchi and Seminole prisoners in South Carolina in 1837, painting portrait of war chief Osceola. Created over 500 oil paintings and gathered large collection of artifacts; toured eastern U.S. exhibiting them as "Catlin's Indian Gallery." Traveled to Europe, where he exhibited paintings, artifacts, and visiting groups of Iowa and Ojibwa in London and Paris (Paris exhibition attended by George Sand, Eugène Delacroix, and Charles Baudelaire). Profusely illustrated account of travels published in two volumes as *Letters and Notes on the Manners, Customs, and Conditions of the North American Indians* (1841), followed by *Catlin's North American Indian Portfolio* (1844). European experiences recounted in *Catlin's Notes of Eight Years' Travel and Residence in Europe* (1848). Wife Clara died in Paris in 1845, son George two years later. Failed in repeated efforts to sell collection of paintings to U.S. government; purchase, although backed by Daniel Webster and William Clark, blocked in 1852 by Southern politicians associated with policy of Indian removal; reliability of Catlin's writings called into question by Henry Rowe Schoolcraft and others. Forced in 1852 to sell contents of Indian Gallery to Philadephia collector Joseph Harrison in settlement of debts (artifacts and many paintings destroyed by poor warehouse storage; collection eventually

donated to Smithsonian). After 1853 made journeys on U.S. Pacific Coast and in South America. During 1860s resided much of the time in Brussels, Belgium. Later publications included *Life amongst the Indians* (1861); *The Lifted and Subsided Rocks of America* (1870), exposition of geological theories; *Last Rambles Amongst the Indians of the Rocky Mountains and the Andes* (1867), account of final travels; and *O-Kee-Pa: A Religious Ceremony; and Other Customs of the Mandans* (1867), record of Mandan ceremony witnessed in 1830s. Returned in 1871 to New York City; died in Jersey City, New Jersey.

HARRIET MAXWELL CONVERSE (1836–November 18, 1903) b. Elmira, New York. Daughter of Marie Purdy and Thomas Maxwell, a New York assemblyman and congressman. In 1861, after death of first husband, married Frank Buchanan Converse, inventor and musician. After five years of travel in Asia, Africa, and Europe, took up residence in New York. Published collection of poetry, *Sheaves* (1882); contributed regularly to periodicals in America and Great Britain. Beginning in early 1880s, devoted herself to study of Indians of New York; in 1885 adopted into Snipe Clan on Cattaraugus Reservation in western New York. Helped defeat legislation unfavorable to the Iroquois in 1891, and was made legal member of Iroquois Nation. Collected artifacts for New York State Museum, the Peabody, and American Museum of Natural History. *Myths and Legends of the New York State Iroquois* published posthumously in 1908.

GEORGE COPWAY (1818?–1869) b. near mouth of Trent River, Ontario, Canada. Member of Ojibwa (or Mississauga) band living near Rice Lake, north of Lake Ontario; given name Kah-ge-ga-gah-bowh (Standing Firm). Received traditional Ojibwa upbringing. Parents converted to Methodism by missionaries led by half-blood Ojibwa preacher Peter Jones; father adopted name John Copway; joined Methodists at mother's urging shortly before her death in 1830. Studied at Methodist school at Rice Lake. In 1834, went to work at Methodist mission at Lake Superior; became Methodist preacher; with other Ojibwa converts, established mission at Ottawa Lake. Sent to study at Ebenezer Manual Labor School near Jacksonville, Illinois, in 1837; graduated 1839. Visited Chicago, New York, Boston, and other cities. In Upper Canada met Elizabeth Howell, daughter of English farmer Henry Howell; they married June 1840 (of their five children, only one, a daughter born in 1860, lived to adulthood). The couple worked for two years at Upper Mississippi missions, returning to Canada in 1842. Elected vice-president of Grand Council of the Methodist Ojibwas of Canada West, 1845; accused of misappropriating funds; further accused of embezzling tribal monies at Rice Lake; briefly imprisoned in Toronto; expelled from Methodist ministry. With wife Elizabeth, traveled to the East; published memoir *The Life, History, and Travels of Kah-ge-ga-gah-bowh (George Copway)* (1847); the book sold well. Lectured successfully along Atlantic seaboard; in 1848 announced proposal for Indian territory in present-day South Dakota to be named "Kahgega"; submitted proposal to Congress as "Organization

of a New Indian Territory, East of the Missouri River" (1850); solicited statements of support from William Cullen Bryant, Washington Irving, and James Fenimore Cooper; became acquainted with Francis Parkman and Henry Wadsworth Longfellow. Attended peace congress in Frankfurt, Germany; recounted journey in *Running Sketches of Men and Places* (1850); also published *Traditional History and Characteristic Sketches of the Ojibway Nation* (1851) and short-lived newspaper, *Copway's American Indian* (1851). Allied himself briefly with nativist Know-Nothing movement, joining New York chapter of the Order of United Americans in 1852. Lived in New York City in increasing poverty; occasionally lectured. During Civil War collected a bounty for enlisting Canadian Indians in Union Army. Advertised services as healer in Detroit in late 1860s; returned to Canada in 1868. Wife and daughter left him to live near her relatives. Spent final days at Sulpician mission in Quebec; announced conversion to Roman Catholicism shortly before death.

JEREMIAH CURTIN (September 6, 1840?–December 14, 1906) b. Greenfield, Wisconsin. Son of Ellen Furlong and David Curtin. Studied at Carroll College in Waukesha, Wisconsin, Phillips Exeter, and Harvard, from which he graduated in 1863. Through acquaintance with Russian naval officers visiting America, invited to visit Russia; appointed assistant secretary of U.S. legation; remained in Russia until 1870. Studied various languages in Eastern Europe and Asia (was said to know as many as 70 languages and dialects). Collected folklore in the British Isles. Married Alma Cordelle in 1872. Worked for the Bureau of Ethnology under John Wesley Powell collecting American Indian languages, 1883–91. Published translations of works by Henryk Sienkiewicz, Alexei Tolstoy, and other Slavic writers. Extensive publications in the field of folklore included *Myths and Folk-Tales of the Russians, Western Slavs, and Magyars* (1890), *Myths and Folk-Lore of Ireland* (1890), *Hero-Tales of Ireland* (1894), *Tales of the Fairies and of the Ghost World* (1895), *Creation Myths of Primitive America* (1898), *A Journey in Southern Siberia* (1909), *Myths of the Modocs* (1912), *Fairy Tales of Eastern Europe* (1914), *Seneca Fiction, Legends and Myths* (1918, edited by J. N. B. Hewitt), *Wonder Tales from Russia* (1921), and *Seneca Indian Myths* (1923).

FRANK HAMILTON CUSHING (July 22, 1857–April 10, 1900) b. North East, Pennsylvania. Son of Sarah Ann Harding and Thomas Cushing, a doctor. When he was three, family moved to Barre Center, New York. Studied natural science briefly at Cornell University. Hired in 1875 as a research assistant by the Smithsonian, and conducted several archaeological digs; presented papers before Anthropological Society of Washington. Oversaw ethnological exhibit at Centennial Exposition of 1876. In 1879, appointed to Bureau of Ethnology by John Wesley Powell. Spent five years studying the Zuni in New Mexico; admitted to Bow Priesthood and given Zuni name Tenatsali (Medicine Flower). Explored archaeological sites in Salt River Valley, Arizona, and Key Marco, Florida. Publications included "My Adventures

in Zuñi" (1882–83), *Zuñi Fetiches* (1883), *A Study of Pueblo Pottery* (1886), *Outlines of Zuñi Creation Myths* (1896), *Exploration of Ancient Key Dwellers' Remains of the Gulf Coast of Florida* (1896), and the posthumously published *Zuñi Folk Tales* (1901) and *Zuñi Breadstuff* (1920).

JOHN COMFORT FILLMORE (February 4, 1843–August 14, 1898) b. on a farm in New London County, Connecticut. Attended Oberlin College, 1862–65, studying organ and piano under George W. Steele; continued musical studies in Leipzig. Returned to the United States in 1867; taught instrumental music at Oberlin for a year; became professor of music at Ripon College, Wisconsin, 1868–78. Taught at the Milwaukee College for Women for six years, and in 1884 founded and became director of the Milwaukee Music School. Published books on musical history and theory including *Pianoforte Music: Its History* (1883), *New Lessons in Harmony* (1887), *On the Value of Certain Modern Theories* (1887), and *Lessons in Musical History* (1888). Traveled extensively among American Indian tribes transcribing tribal calls and songs. Collaborated with anthropologist Alice Fletcher and her adopted son Francis La Flesche on *A Study of Omaha Indian Music*, published in 1893. In 1895 left the Milwaukee Music School and moved with his wife and two sons to Pomona College, Claremont, California, where he taught for the rest of his life. Died in Taftville, Connecticut. *The Harmonic Structure of Indian Music* published posthumously in 1899.

ALICE CUNNINGHAM FLETCHER (March 15, 1838–April 6, 1923) b. Havana, Cuba, where her parents were temporarily residing. Attended New York private schools. Traveled in Europe as a young woman; lectured for temperance, anti-tobacco, and women's rights movements, as well as on anthropological topics. Met Frederic W. Putnam and Lewis Henry Morgan. In 1879, met Suzette (Bright Eyes) and Francis La Flesche (whom she eventually adopted as her son) of Omaha tribe; visited Omaha reservation in 1881. Drafted petition in support of land allotment to individual Indian landowners; campaign led to passage of Omaha Act of 1882, which served as prototype for broader Dawes Severalty Act of 1887. Oversaw allotment of small farming plots among Omaha (1883–84), Winnebago (1887–89), and Nez Percé (1890–93). Officially joined Peabody Museum as assistant in 1886; first woman with paid academic appointment at Harvard. In 1891 received fellowship to work as collector and scholar. Produced important early studies of American Indian music and religious ceremonies, especially among the Omaha, Pawnee, and Dakota Sioux; publications included *Indian Ceremonies* (1884), *A Study of Omaha Indian Music* (1893), *Indian Story and Song from North America* (1900), *The Hako: A Pawnee Ceremony* (1904), *The Omaha Tribe* (1911, with Francis La Flesche), and *Indian Games and Dances with Native Songs* (1915). In 1903 served as president of American Anthropological Society of Washington, and in 1905 as president of American Folk-Lore Society. Died at her home in Washington.

ALBERT SAMUEL GATSCHET (October 3, 1832–March 16, 1907) b. Saint Beatenberg, Switzerland. Son of Mary Ziegler and minister Karl Albert Gatschet. Educated at schools of Neuchâtel and Bern; entered University of Bern 1852; completed linguistic and theological studies at University of Berlin, where he specialized in Greek language and doctrinal criticism. Wrote for literary and scientific journals in Bern for several years before immigrating to New York in 1868, where he worked as writer and teacher. Interest in American Indian languages originated in 1872, when he was asked to compare vocabularies collected from a geographical survey of the Southwest. Hired in 1877 by John Wesley Powell as philologist for Rocky Mountain Geological Survey; did field work among various tribes in California and Oregon, including the Klamath and Modoc. Member of the Bureau of Ethnology from its organization in 1879 to his retirement in 1905; studied scores of languages of southeastern U.S. and Gulf of Mexico; on visits to the Catawba in South Carolina, and the Biloxi and Tunica of Louisiana and Mississippi, uncovered linguistic relation between these and the Sioux. In addition to vast archival collection, published work included *A Migration Legend of the Creek Indians* (two volumes, 1884 and 1888), and *The Klamath Indians of Southwestern Oregon* (1890). Did much work with Indian delegates and students in Washington. Married at age 70 in 1892. Poor health forced abandonment of final project, a comparative study of Algonquian languages; retired from Bureau in 1905. Died in Washington, D.C.

HORATIO HALE (May 3, 1817–December 28, 1896) b. Horatio Emmons Hale in Newport, New Hampshire. Son of Sarah Josepha Buell (as Sarah Josepha Hale, successful editor and poet, author of "Mary Had a Little Lamb") and David Hale (lawyer). Took early interest in songs and stories of Indians of Maine, New York, and Canada; at age 17 published *Remarks on the Language of the St. John's or Wlastukweek Indians, with a Penobscot Vocabulary.* After graduating Harvard College in 1837, joined U.S. Exploring Expedition under Charles Wilkes as philologist; circumnavigated the world, 1838–42, collecting and comparing vocabularies of indigenous peoples. Published summary of his researches in 1846 as volume six of the expedition's official report, *Ethnography and Philology*; pioneered use of comparative linguistic analysis to reconstruct prehistoric migrations of Polynesians. Married in 1854; admitted to bar in Chicago in 1855. In 1856 opened law practice in Clinton, frontier village in Canada. Established close contacts with Iroquois and Algonquin tribes; discovered 18th-century manuscripts in Mohawk and Onondaga translated in *The Iroquois Book of Rites* (1883). Other publications included *The Tutelo Tribe and Language* (1883), *Hiawatha and the Iroquois Confederation* (1885), *An International Idiom: A Manual of the Oregon Trade Language, or "Chinook Jargon" (1890)*, and "The Fall of Hochelega" (1893). Despite relative isolation from contemporary scientific and academic communities, retained active ties with other ethnologists, and organizations such as American Association for the Advancement of Science and American Folk-Lore Society (of

which he served as president in 1893). Honored after his death in mortuary services by Iroquois nations and Algonquian tribes.

JOHN HECKEWELDER (March 12, 1743–January 31, 1823) b. John Gottlieb Ernestus Heckewelder in Bedford, England. Son of the Rev. David Heckewelder, Moravian minister. Family moved with other Moravian colonists to settlement at Bethlehem, Pennsylvania, in 1754. Worked at Moravian settlement near Nazareth, Pennsylvania; apprenticed to a cedar cooper. In 1762 joined evangelist Christian Frederick Post in trying to establish mission on Muskingum River in Ohio Territory; attempt interrupted by outbreak of Pontiac war. (Mission, Gnadenhütten, subsequently established by Post and David Zeisberger.) From 1771 served as missionary to converted Delaware in Ohio Territory, initially as assistant to Zeisberger; ordained deacon in 1778. Married Sarah Ohneberg in 1780 in Nazareth, Pennsylvania. Arrested in 1781 by British forces and accused of spying for Americans; summoned repeatedly to Detroit by British commander to defend himself against charges; in his absence a massacre of Moravian Indians occurred. Temporarily resettled the mission in Michigan, and returned to Bethlehem in 1786 because of his wife's failing health. Helped negotiate treaties with various tribes of the Old Northwest, 1792–93. Published *Johann Heckewälders Reise von Bethlehem in Pensilvanien bis zum Wabashfluss* (1797, English translation 1888). Returned to Ohio Territory in 1799, and as agent for Society for Propagating the Gospel surveyed distribution of lands to Christian Indians. After retiring to Bethlehem in 1810, wrote pioneering studies *An Account of the History, Manners, and Customs of the Indian Nations, Who Once Inhabited Pennsylvania and the Neighbouring States* (1819) and *A Narrative of the Mission of the United Brethren Among the Delaware and Mohegan Indians* (1820). Other writings, published posthumously, included glossaries, maps, and journals.

CHARLES FENNO HOFFMAN (February 7, 1806–June 7, 1884) b. New York City. Son of Maria Fenno and Josiah Ogden Hoffman (prominent lawyer). Right leg amputated following accident at age 11. Studied at Columbia College, 1821–23, without graduating; studied law in Albany with Harmanus Bleecker; admitted to New York bar in 1827. With Charles King, co-edited *New York American*, 1830–33; was editor of the first issues of *The Knickerbocker* (1833); early literary associates in New York included William Cullen Bryant, Nathaniel P. Willis, Fitz-Greene Halleck, James Kirke Paulding, Robert Sands, and Gulian Verplanck (Hoffman's uncle). Made western tour, 1833–34, visiting Pittsburgh, Detroit, Chicago, Prairie du Chien, Wisconsin Territory, and St. Louis; journey recounted in *A Winter in the West* (1835). On his return to New York, assumed editorship of *American Monthly Magazine*, 1835–37 and *New-York Mirror* (1837). Journalistic sketches collected in *Wild Scenes in the Forest and Prairie* (1839). Briefly served as associate editor of *The New Yorker* under Horace Greeley before assuming patronage jobs as third chief clerk (1841–43) and deputy surveyor (1843–44) for New York Customs

Authority. Published a novel, *Greyslaer: A Romance of the Mohawk* (1840), based on 1828 Beauchamp-Sharp murder case, and three collections of verse: *The Vigil of Faith* (1842), *The Echo* (1844), and *Love's Calendar, Lays of the Hudson, and Other Poems* (1847); also edited anthology *The New-York Book of Poetry* (1837). At request of Henry Rowe Schoolcraft, made verse adaptations of Ojibwa oral poetry printed in Schoolcraft's *Oneóta; or Characteristics of the Red Race of America* (1845). Acquainted with Edgar Allan Poe, Herman Melville, Evert Duyckinck, Rufus Griswold, and other New York literary figures. Editorship of New York *Literary World* (1847–49) interrupted by attack of mental illness. After brief hospitalization, accepted clerkship in State Department; boarded in Washington, D.C., with family of Henry Rowe Schoolcraft; proposed marriage to Schoolcraft's daughter Jane. Following recurrence of mental illness, hospitalized again; ultimately confined to Harrisburg (Pennsylvania) Insane Asylum in 1849, where he remained for the rest of his life.

W. J. HOFFMAN (May 30, 1846–November 8, 1899) b. Walter James Hoffman at Weidasville, Pennsylvania. Graduated Jefferson Medical College, Philadelphia, in 1866. Practiced medicine in Reading, Pennsylvania, until outbreak of Franco-Prussian War in 1870 when he was commissioned as surgeon in the Prussian Army. On return to U.S. appointed acting assistant surgeon in U.S. Army; detailed as naturalist to Wheeler Survey during explorations in Arizona and Nevada. In 1872 served as surgeon of Northern Pacific Railroad survey. Became member of Hayden Survey of 1876 as ethnologist and mineralogist; appointed assistant ethnologist at Bureau of Ethnology at its inception in 1879. Author of *The Midē'wiwin or "Grand Medicine Society" of the Ojibwa* (1891), *The Beginnings of Writing* (1895), *The Menomini Indians* (1896), and *The Graphic Art of the Eskimos* (1897). Served as U.S. consul in Mannheim, Germany.

EDWIN JAMES (August 27, 1797–October 28, 1861) b. Weybridge, Vermont. Youngest of 13 children of Mary Emmes and Daniel James. Graduated Middlebury College in 1816; studied botany, geology, and medicine in Albany, New York. Accompanied 1820 expedition of Major Stephen H. Long to explore country between Mississippi and Rocky Mountains; reached summit of Pike's Peak (named James Peak by Long); explored Arkansas, Red, and Canadian rivers. Summarized findings in *Account of an Expedition from Pittsburgh to the Rocky Mountains* (1822–23). Became a U.S. army surgeon in 1823; subsequently stationed at forts Crawford, Mackinac, and Brady. In April 1827 married Clarissa Rogers; they had one son. Studied Indian languages and published various translations, grammars, and studies; with John Tanner (a former captive among the Ojibwa) wrote *A Narrative of the Captivity and Adventures of John Tanner* (1830); with Tanner made first Ojibwa translation of complete New Testament (1833). Resigned from army in 1833; helped edit *Temperance Herald and Journal* in Albany. Served as sub-agent for Potawatomi at Old Council Bluffs, Nebraska, 1837–38. Settled as farmer at Rock Spring, near Burlington, Iowa. Was an ardent abolitionist and assisted in the escape of fugitive slaves.

ALFRED L. KROEBER (June 11, 1876–October 5, 1960) b. Hoboken, New Jersey. Graduated Columbia University 1896, and went on to take his M.A. (1897) and Ph.D. (1901) there, studying under Franz Boas. Did first fieldwork starting in 1899 among the Arapaho, Ute, Northern Shoshone, and Bannock. Established anthropology department at University of California at Berkeley in 1901; subsequent field work concentrated on California Indians; also made expeditions to New Mexico (1915–20), Mexico (1924 and 1930), and Peru (1925, 1926, 1942). Instrumental in initiating and guiding 50-volume series, University of California Publications in American Archaeology and Ethnology (1903–60); founded Museum of Anthropology at Berkeley; helped found American Anthropological Association, of which he was president in 1917. His publications included *Anthropology* (1923), *Handbook of the Indians of California* (1925), *Three Centuries of Women's Dress Fashions* (1940, with Jane Richardson), *Peruvian Archaeology in 1942* (1944), *Configurations of Culture Growth* (1944), *A Mohave Historical Epic* (1951), *Style and Civilizations* (1957), and *Sparkman Grammar of Luiseno* (1960, with G. Grace). *A Roster of Civilizations and Culture* appeared posthumously in 1962.

FRANCIS LA FLESCHE (December 25, 1857–September 5, 1932) b. Omaha, Nebraska. Son of "Chief Joseph" La Flesche (Omaha leader who was half French and half Omaha) and an Omaha mother. Educated at Presbyterian Mission School in Bellevue, Nebraska; also participated in traditional Omaha ceremonies and dances. Became chief collaborator and interpreter for Alice Cunningham Fletcher, who adopted him as her son. Joined staff of Senate Committee on Indian Affairs in Washington, D.C.; attended National University School of Law, earning law degree in 1893. Published account of his education, *The Middle Five: Indian Boys at School* (1900). Hired for Bureau of Ethnology by Frederick W. Hodge; worked there 1903–29. Twice married. *The Omaha Tribe* (1911, with Alice Fletcher) summarized 25 years of research. Other publications included *The Osage Tribe* (1921–30) and *Dictionary of the Osage Language* (1932). Retired to Omaha community in Macy, Nebraska. *War Ceremony and Peace Ceremony of the Osage Indians* appeared posthumously in 1939.

CHARLES GODFREY LELAND See page 898.

HENRY WADSWORTH LONGFELLOW See page 1011, *American Poetry: The Nineteeth Century*, vol. I.

WASHINGTON MATTHEWS (July 17, 1843–April 29, 1905) b. Killiney, County Dublin, Ireland. Son of Anna Burke and Dr. Nicholas Blayney Matthews. His mother died when he was an infant and his father moved to America, settling in Dubuque, Iowa. Studied at University of Iowa, receiving his medical degree in 1864. Joined army, and served as post surgeon at forts in Montana and North Dakota, 1865–72. Learned Hidatsa; may have had a son by daughter of a Hidatsa chief. Married Caroline Wotherspoon in 1877. Sta-

tioned at Fort Wingate, New Mexico, 1880–84; worked at Army Medical Museum in Washington, D.C., 1884–90; again at Fort Wingate until his retirement in 1894. President of American Folk-Lore Society, 1895. Made extensive studies in Navajo language and culture, as well as in physical anthropology. Publications included *Grammar and Dictionary of the Language of the Hidatsa* (1873–74), *Ethnography and Philology of the Hidatsa Indians* (1877), *The Mountain Chant: A Navajo Ceremony* (1887), *Navaho Legends* (1897), and *The Night Chant* (1902).

SAMUEL LATHAM MITCHILL (August 20, 1764–September 7, 1831) b. North Hempstead, New York. Son of Mary Latham and Robert Mitchill, both Quakers. Studied in New York City with Dr. Samuel Bard; obtained M.D. degree at University of Edinburgh, 1783–86. Practiced medicine in New York. Was among commissioners negotiating land purchases in western New York with the Six Nations in 1788; member of New York state legislature, 1791 and 1798. Appointed professor of natural history, chemistry, and agriculture at Columbia College, 1792; also professor of botany, 1793–95. With Edward Miller and Elihu H. Smith, founded *The Medical Repository* in 1797. Married Catherine Akerly Cock in 1799; they had no children. Promoted chemical theories of Antoine Lavoisier; published *Explanation of the Synopsis of Chemical Nomenclature and Arrangement* (1801). Resigned professorship at Columbia to serve as congressman (1801–04), senator (1804–09), and congressman again (1810–13). Held chair as professor of chemistry at newly founded College of Physicians and Surgeons in New York, 1807–20; thereafter served as professor of botany. Resigned with colleagues in 1826 to found short-lived Rutgers Medical College, 1826–30. Served as physician to New York Hospital; was a founder of New York Literary and Philosophical Society (1814) and of the Lyceum of Natural History (1817). Published many works on wide range of subjects, including *The Life, Exploits, and Precepts of Tammany, the Famous Indian Chief* (1795) and *A Discourse on the Character and Services of Thomas Jefferson* (1826).

JAMES MOONEY (February 10, 1861–December 22, 1921) b. Richmond, Indiana. Son of Ellen Devlin and James Mooney, Irish immigrants; father died shortly after Mooney's birth. At age 12 determined to learn names and locations of every American Indian tribe. In 1879, without attending college, took job as typesetter and staff writer at *Richmond Palladium*. Active in American branch of National Irish Land League. Began independently to amass ethnographic and linguistic information on American Indians. In 1885 met John Wesley Powell, director of U.S. Geological Survey and of Bureau of American Ethnology; hired by Powell to work for Bureau, remained there for the rest of his life. Did his first fieldwork among Eastern Cherokee, 1885–90. Late in 1890 began investigation of ghost-dance religion in South Dakota and elsewhere; within a year met its messiah, Wovoka, and participated in its ceremonies. From 1894 on spent much time among Plains tribes including the Kiowa, Kiowa-Apache, Arapaho, and Cheyenne, with intermittent visits to

the Eastern Cherokee, to Mexico and the Southwest, and to Washington, D.C., to publish his work. Married Ione Lee Gaut in 1897; they had six children. Studied peyote religion, attending peyote ceremonies, and in 1918 helped charter the Native American Church, centered on peyote sacrament. Final years hampered by ill-health and political controversy over his criticisms of government Indian policy and defense of peyotism. Publications included *Sacred Formulas of the Cherokees* (1891), *The Siouan Tribes of the East* (1894), *The Ghost Dance Religion and the Sioux Outbreak of 1890* (1896), *Calendar History of the Kiowa Indians* (1898), *Myths of the Cherokee* (1900), and *The Cheyenne Indians* (1908); contributed over 500 articles to Frederick W. Hodge's *Handbook of American Indians North of Mexico* (1907–10); many of his field notes remain unpublished, including uncompleted studies of Kiowa heraldry and the peyote religion. Died in Washington, D.C. His extensive study of American Indian population before European contact was edited and revised by John R. Swanton and published as *The Aboriginal Population of America North of Mexico* (1928); texts collected in his fieldwork among the East Cherokee were published in *The Swimmer Manuscript: Cherokee Sacred Formulas and Medicinal Prescriptions* (1932).

LEWIS HENRY MORGAN   (November 21, 1818–December 17, 1881)   b. near Aurora, New York. One of eight children of Harriet Steele and Jedediah Morgan, prosperous farmers. Educated at Cayuga Academy in Aurora, New York, and Union College, from which he graduated in 1840. Read law; admitted to bar 1842. In Aurora, founded literary club the Gordian Knot (later the Grand Order of the Iroquois) which aimed to "encourage a kinder feeling towards the Indian" and incorporated elements of Iroquois ceremony. Moved to Rochester, New York, in 1844, opening law practice. Pursuing Iroquois researches, met Seneca Ely S. Parker, with whom he collaborated in visiting reservations and collecting ethnographic information. Research summarized in *League of the Ho-dé-no-sau-nee, or Iroquois* (1851). Married cousin Mary Elizabeth Steele in 1851. Visited Michigan in 1858; struck by similarities between Seneca and Ojibwa kinship systems; began systematic study of kinship patterns; published early findings in "Laws of Consanguinity and Descent of the Iroquois" (1859). Continued research in western field trips, 1859–62; kept extensive journals of his travels. Gave up law practice but continued to work as attorney for mining and railroad companies in Michigan; detailed study of beavers in Michigan published as *The American Beaver and His Works* (1868). Developed kinship theories in *Systems of Consanguinity and Affinity of the Human Family* (1870), *Ancient Society* (1877), and *Houses and House-Life of the American Aborigines* (1881). Served in New York state assembly (1861–68) and senate (1868–69); elected in 1875 to National Academy of Sciences; president of American Association for the Advancement of Science, 1879. Died in Rochester.

EDWARD WILLIAM NELSON   (May 8, 1855–May 19, 1934)   b. Amoskeag, New Hampshire. Eldest of two sons of Nancy Martha Wells and William

Nelson. During Civil War sent to live with grandparents in Adirondack Mountains; father killed in war; mother moved with children to Chicago, where she started successful dressmaking business. Attended public schools; studied briefly at Northwestern University; taught in Dalton, Illinois. In 1872 went on field trip with Edward D. Cope and Samuel Garman to collect natural specimens in Wyoming, Utah, and Nevada. Studied biology at Johns Hopkins, 1876; training cut short by opportunity offered by Spencer Baird of the Smithsonian Institution to undertake field work in Alaska; took up residence at weather station at St. Michael, on Norton Bay, 1877–81; made large collection of artifacts. Upon return, health collapsed and he went to live in Southwest during long convalescence; explored Verde River Valley ruins in Arizona. Over next decade prepared reports of Alaskan field work; results published in *Report upon Natural History Collections Made in Alaska Between the Years 1877 and 1881* (1887) and *The Eskimo About Bering Strait* (1899). In 1892 undertook natural history field work in Mexico for Department of Agriculture, and continued to work frequently in Mexico over the next 14 years; described many newly discovered animal species. Later publications included *Revision of the Squirrels of Mexico and Central America* (1899), *The Rabbits of North America* (1909), and *Wild Animals of North America* (1918). Chief of Bureau of Biological Survey of Department of Agriculture, 1916–27; negotiated treaty protecting migratory birds with Great Britain. Retired in 1927.

JOHN WESLEY POWELL (March 24, 1834–September 23, 1902) b. Mt. Morris, New York. Son of Mary Dean and Joseph Powell, English immigrants; father was a Methodist preacher. Family moved frequently, living successively in Ohio, Wisconsin, and Illinois. Studied sporadically at Methodist school in Wheaton, Illinois, and later at Illinois College (in Jacksonville, Illinois), Oberlin, and Wheaton College; he took no degree. Early interest in botany led to his joining Illinois State Natural History Society in 1854, of which he was later elected secretary. Enlisted in army upon outbreak of Civil War; commissioned captain of artillery company which he recruited; lost right arm at battle of Shiloh in 1862; later rose to rank of major of artillery. Married cousin Emma Dean in 1862; they had a daughter. After discharge from army in 1865, became professor of geology at Illinois Wesleyan College in Bloomington; later served as lecturer and museum curator at Illinois Normal University. Organized natural science expeditions in Colorado. Met Ute bands near the White River, 1868–69, and gradually acquired knowledge of Ute and Southern Paiute languages; continued to gather ethnographic information over next several years. In May 1869 led party of 11 men on journey by boat through canyons of the Green and Colorado rivers; emerged from Grand Canyon in August. Conducted further explorations in 1871, 1874, and 1875; results summarized in *Explorations of the Colorado River of the West and Its Tributaries* (1875). Served as director of second division of U.S. Geological Survey of the Rocky Mountain Region, 1875–79, and as overall director, 1880–94; inaugurated series of bulletins, monographs, and atlases, as well as ethnographic studies (beginning in 1877), *Contributions to*

North American Ethnology. Directed acquisition of Indian materials for 1876 Philadelphia International Exposition. Undertook comparison of Indian vocabularies gathered by Smithsonian Institution; summarized findings in *Introduction to the Study of Indian Languages* (1877); studies of water and irrigation problems of the West published in *Report on the Lands of the Arid Region of the United States* (1878). From 1879 was director of the newly established Bureau of Ethnology (later Bureau of American Ethnology) under the Smithsonian; oversaw ethnological and linguistic researches of James Mooney, Jeremiah Curtin, James Owen Dorsey, Albert Gatschet, and many others; inaugurated series of annual reports (beginning in 1881) and bulletins (beginning in 1887). Linguistic research summarized in *Indian Linguistic Families of America North of Mexico* (1891). Held title of director until his death, although failing health forced his retirement from active duties. Published philosophical study *Truth and Error, or the Science of Intellection* in 1898. Died at his summer home in Haven, Maine.

STEPHEN POWERS (July 20, 1840–April 2, 1904) b. Waterford, Ohio. Graduated University of Michigan in 1863. Worked as war correspondent for *Cincinnati Commercial* during Civil War. Traveled in Europe in 1866–67, reporting for *The New York Times*, *The Nation*, and other publications. In January 1869 undertook walking trip across the United States, reaching San Francisco in November. Published an account of his journey in *Afoot and Alone: A Walk from Sea to Sea* (1872). In the summers of 1871 and 1872 devoted himself to the study of California Indians, producing articles that were published serially in *Overland Monthly*, 1872–75. Arranged with John Wesley Powell, director of the Department of Interior's Geographical and Geological Survey of the Rocky Mountain Region, to publish his Indian articles in book form as *Tribes of California* (1877). Left California in 1875 to live on family farm in Ohio. Appointed by Powell as a commissioner to collect California Indian artifacts for the Centennial Exhibition of 1876; returned to California, 1875–76. Later published on agricultural topics. Died in Jacksonville, Florida.

JOHN DYNELEY PRINCE (April 17, 1868–1945) b. New York City. Son of Anne Maria Morris and John Dyneley Prince. Graduated Columbia 1888; studied subsequently at University of Berlin (1889–90) and Johns Hopkins, where he received his Ph.D. in 1892. Married Adeline Loomis in 1889. Accompanied University of Pennsylvania archaeological expedition to Babylonian sites, 1888–89. Professor of Semitic languages at New York University, 1892–1902; later professor of Semitic languages (1902–15) and Slavonic languages (1915–21) and East European languages (1933–37) at Columbia University. Published many articles on Passamaquoddy, Natick, and Pequot tribes; collaborated with Charles Godfrey Leland on *Kulóskap the Master and Other Algonkin Poems* (1902); *Passamaquoddy Texts* published 1921. Other publications included *Mene, Mene, Tekel, Upharsin* (1893), *A Critical Commentary on the Book of Daniel* (1899), *Materials for a Sumerian Lexicon* (1908), *Assyrian*

Primer (1909), and *Fragments from Babel* (1939). Served in New Jersey assembly (1906, 1908–09) and the New Jersey senate (1912), and as acting governor of New Jersey in 1912. Appointed ambassador to Denmark by Warren G. Harding in 1921; ambassador to Yugoslavia, 1926–33.

ALFRED LONGLEY RIGGS (December 6, 1837–1916) b. at Lac-qui-parle mission in Minnesota. Eldest of nine children of Stephen Return Riggs. Graduated Knox College in Galesburg, Illinois, in 1858; attended Theological Seminary of Chicago, 1860–62. Married Mary Buel Hatch in June 1863; they had five children. Established Congregational mission to Sioux at Santee Agency, Nebraska, in 1870. Founded Santee Normal Training School, Indian boarding school in which instruction was conducted in Dakota language; edited school newspapers *Iapi Oaye* (in Dakota) and *The Word Carrier* (in English) from 1877.

STEPHEN RETURN RIGGS (March 23, 1812–August 24, 1883) b. Steubenville, Ohio. Son of Anna Baird and Stephen Riggs. Educated at the Latin School of Ripley, Ohio, Jefferson College, and Western Theological Seminary in Alleghany, Ohio. Spent a year preaching in Hawley, Massachusetts, where he married Mary Ann Longley in February 1837. Later that year traveled with Mary to Congregational mission at Lac-qui-parle on the Minnesota River to begin work among Wahpeton Sioux. Stationed at Traverse des Sioux (1843–46) before returning to Lac-qui-parle to run the mission; at Hazelwood, 1854–62, established mission near Santee Agency under the name of the Hazelwood Republic. Became leading authority on Siouan languages, in which (with the aid of other missionaries including Jedidiah Stevens, Gideon Pond, and Thomas Williamson) he published numerous Scripture translations, primers, and hymnals; for Smithsonian prepared *Grammar and Dictionary of the Dakota Language* (1852). Following Santee uprising of 1862, served as chaplain and interpreter for military expedition against them. Settled in 1865 in Beloit, Wisconsin; organized mission and school among Santee Sioux prisoners at Davenport, Iowa. Early mission years recounted in *Tah'-koo Wah-kan'; or, The Gospel Among the Dakotas* (1869), which also contained ethnographic description. Wife Mary died in 1869; organized mission at Sisseton agency in 1870; in 1872 married Annie Baker Ackley. Continued work of translation, culminating in *Dakota Wowapi Wakan: The Holy Bible in the Language of the Dakotas* (1879), much of which was his work; edited Sioux-language newspaper *Iapi Oaye*, 1873–83. Published second memoir, *Mary and I: Forty Years with the Sioux* (1880), along with numerous articles. His *Dakota-English Dictionary* (1890) and *Dakota Grammar, Texts and Ethnography* (1893), both edited by J. Owen Dorsey, were published posthumously.

HENRY ROWE SCHOOLCRAFT (March 28, 1793–December 10, 1864) b. Albany County, New York. Son of Margaret Rowe and Lawrence Schoolcraft (glassmaker). Studied at public school in Hamilton, New York, Union Col-

lege, and Middlebury College, where he specialized in geology and mineralogy. Made journey of mineralogical observation in southern Missouri and Arkansas, 1817–18, described in *A View of the Lead Mines of Missouri* (1819). In 1820 served as geologist on Lewis Cass expedition to Upper Mississippi and Lake Superior, publishing *Narrative Journal of Travels through the Northwestern Regions of the United States* (1821). With help of Cass and John C. Calhoun, appointed Indian agent for tribes of Lake Superior region in 1822; the following year married Jane Johnston, a half-blood Ojibwa who had been educated in Europe, granddaughter of Ojibwa chief Waboojeeg. Served in Michigan territorial legislature, 1828–32. Helped found Historical Society of Michigan (1828) and Algic Society of Detroit (1832). Participated in expedition in 1832 that led to what he erroneously believed to be the source of the Mississippi, described in *Narrative of an Expedition through the Upper Mississippi to Itasca Lake, the Actual Source of the Mississippi* (1834). Served as superintendent of Indian affairs for Michigan, 1836–41. Negotiated treaties, including treaty of March 28, 1836, in which the Ojibwa ceded major portion of their territory to the United States. First major study of Ojibwa culture, *Algic Researches* (1839), published in two volumes. Dismissed from position as superintendent for alleged profiteering; moved to New York City. Wife Jane died in 1842; visited Europe. Conducted census of New York Indians in 1845. Further memoirs and compilations of American Indian material appeared as *Notes on the Iroquois* (1842), *Oneóta; or, Characteristics of the Red Race of America* (1845), and *Personal Memoirs of Thirty Years with the Indian Tribes* (1851); also published poem on Indian themes, *Alhalla; or, the Lord of Talladega* (1843). Married in 1847 to Mary Howard of North Carolina. Won congressional funding in 1847 for large-scale survey of American Indians (although most of his material related specifically to the Ojibwa); published in elaborate six-volume edition, illustrated by Seth Eastman and others, as *Historical and Statistical Information Respecting the History, Condition, and Prospects of the Indian Tribes of the United States* (1851–57). Following success of Longfellow's *Song of Hiawatha* (1855), based in large part on Schoolcraft's early work, reissued *Algic Researches* as *The Myth of Hiawatha* (1856). In final years suffered from severe rheumatism. Died in Washington, D.C.

MATILDA COXE STEVENSON (May 12, 1849–June 24, 1915) b. San Augustine, Texas. Raised in Washington, D.C., and educated at Miss Annable's Academy in Philadelphia; intended to become a mineralogist. In 1872 married James Stevenson of U.S. Geological Survey of the Territories, and from 1879 on collaborated with him on his trips to Zuni Pueblo; became expert on domestic rituals from which men were traditionally excluded. In 1887 published *The Religious Life of the Zuñi Child*. Founded Women's Anthropological Society of Washington in 1885. Continued her work after husband's death in 1888; assigned to Bureau of Ethnology in 1889, first woman to be paid as government anthropologist. Conducted studies among the Hopi in 1881; the Sia between 1890 and 1891; and the Taos and Tewa Indians between 1904 and 1910. Work among the Zuni resulted in *The Zuñi Indians: Their Mythology,*

Esoteric Fraternities, and Ceremonies (1904). Poor health forced her to return to Washington, D.C., where she died.

JOHN TANNER (1780?–1847?) Son of Kentucky pioneer family; captured by raiding party in 1789; held prisoner at Ojibwa-Ottawa village of Saginaw for two years; traded to Ottawa woman who adopted him as son. Lived as Indian in Ojibwa country for 30 years; married and raised family. From around 1820 moved between Indian and white society. Settled at Sault Sainte Marie, working as government interpreter. *A Narrative of the Captivity and Adventures of John Tanner,* edited and co-written by Edwin James, was published in 1830; worked with James on complete Ojibwa translation of New Testament published in 1833. Disappeared in 1846 after being suspected of murdering James Schoolcraft, brother of Henry Rowe Schoolcraft; according to local rumor, was murdered by the actual killer of Schoolcraft, a soldier reported to have made a deathbed confession.

Note on the Texts

The choice of text for each of the poems selected for inclusion in this volume has been made on the basis of a study of its textual history and a comparison of editions printed within the author's lifetime, along with relevant manuscripts, periodical appearances, contemporary anthologies, and posthumous editions. In general, each text is from the earliest book edition prepared with the author's participation; revised editions are sometimes followed, in light of the degree of authorial supervision and the stage of the writer's career at which the revisions were made, but the preference has been for the authorially approved book version closest to the date of composition. For some popular poems widely disseminated in periodicals, however, the early periodical versions have been preferred; for example, Ernest Lawrence Thayer's late revisions to "Casey at the Bat" in his collected poems have been rejected in favor of the earlier version published in *The San Francisco Examiner*.

Two categories of poems, "19th-Century Versions of American Indian Poetry" and "Folk Songs and Spirituals," are placed in separate sections at the end because the dates of original composition of these pieces are so uncertain that placing them chronologically in the body of the anthology is not feasible. The texts chosen for "19th-Century Versions of American Indian Poetry" are translations or adaptations of American Indian material collected under a variety of circumstances, the details of which in many cases are unknown. Some of these versions have been published in different forms, reflecting alterations made by subsequent editors; the goal in this volume has been to locate the version closest to the transcription of the work from its original language. (Exceptions have been made in a few cases; for example, Daniel Garrison Brinton's translation of Constantine Rafinesque's transcription of *The Walam Olum* has been preferred to Rafinesque's own translation in view of Brinton's greater linguistic expertise, and Henry Wadsworth Longfellow's modification of a Henry Rowe Schoolcraft translation has been included for its literary interest.) In reprinting these texts no attempt has been made to duplicate material that accompanied some of them in their original contexts, such as original-language texts, interlinear commentary, and bracketed glosses (although some of this material will be found in the notes to this volume). For the selections of "Folk Songs and Spirituals," versions have been chosen on the basis both of publication date and of completeness; thus, later versions have sometimes been preferred to earlier ones that are fragmentary or atypical.

The following is a list of the sources of the texts included in this volume, listed alphabetically by the authors of the poems; the sources for "19th-Century Versions of American Indian Poetry" and "Spirituals and Folk Songs" are listed separately.

Henry Adams. Buddha and Brahma: *The Yale Review*, October 1915.

Elizabeth Akers Allen. Rock Me to Sleep: *Poems* (Boston: Ticknor & Fields, 1866).

Katharine Lee Bates. America the Beautiful: *America the Beautiful and Other Poems* (New York: Thomas Y. Crowell, 1911).

Ambrose Bierce. Alone; Body-Snatcher; Corporal; Egotist; Elegy; Freedom; Gorgon; Hypochondriasis; Lead: *The Cynic's Word Book* (New York: Doubleday & Co., 1906). Nose; Orthography; Prospect; Rimer; Safety-Clutch; The Passing Show; To the Bartholdi Statue; The Statesmen: *The Collected Works of Ambrose Bierce* (Neale Publishing, 1910–11).

James A. Bland. Oh, Dem Golden Slippers!; Carry Me Back to Old Virginny: Boston: John F. Perry & Co., 1879.

Benjamin Paul Blood. Late: *Scribner's*, vol. XXVII, no. 3, 1900. *from* The Bride of the Iconoclast: Canto II, ii: *The Bride of the Iconoclast* (Boston and Cambridge: James Munroe & Co., 1854).

George Henry Boker. *from* Sonnets: A Sequence on Profane Love: Edward Sculley Bradley (ed.), *Sonnets: A Sequence on Profane Love* (Philadelphia: University of Pennsylvania Press, 1929); published with permission of the Manuscripts Division, Department of Rare Books and Special Collections, Princeton University Libraries. "Blood, blood! The lines of every printed sheet"; "Oh! craven, craven! while my brothers fall"; "Brave comrade, answer! When you joined the war": *Poems of the War* (Boston: Ticknor & Fields, 1864).

Augusta Cooper Bristol. Night; The Crime of the Ages: *Poems* (Boston: Adams & Co., 1868).

Phillips Brooks. O Little Town of Bethlehem: *The Church Porch* (New York, 1874).

Henry Howard Brownell. Suspiria Noctis: *Lyrics of a Day* (Hartford, Connecticut: Press of Case, Lockwood, & Co., 1863). The Battle Summers: *Lyrics of a Day* (New York: Carleton, 1864).

Gelett Burgess. The Purple Cow: *The Purple Cow!* (San Francisco: Doxey, 1895). The Purple Cow: Suite: *The Lark*, no. 24, April 1897.

George Washington Cable. Creole Slave Songs: George Washington Cable, "The Dance in Place Congo" and "Creole Slave Songs," *The Century*, February and April 1886.

Charles Edward Carryl. A Nautical Ballad: *Davy and the Goblin* (Boston: Ticknor & Fields, 1885).

Alice Cary. The Sea-Side Cave, To Solitude: *Ballads, Lyrics and Hymns* (Hurd & Houghton, 1866). Autumn; Katrina on the Porch; The West Country: *The Last Poems of Alice Cary* (Hurd & Houghton, 1873).

Phoebe Cary. Samuel Brown; Granny's House; "The Day Is Done"; Jacob; "When Lovely Woman": *Poems and Parodies* (Boston: Ticknor, Reed & Fields, 1854). Advice Gratis to Certain Women: M. C. Ames, *A Memorial of the Life of Alice and Phoebe Cary* (New York: Hurd & Houghton, 1874).

Madison Cawein. Poetry; The Unimaginative; Music; The Three Elements; Rome; On Reading the Life of Haroun Er Reshid: *Poems of Nature and Love* (New York: G. P. Putnam's Sons, 1893). Echo; Caverns: *Weeds by the Wall* (Louisville: J. P. Morton, 1901). The Stars; Beauty; The Purple Valleys: *Myth and Romance* (New York: G. P. Putnam's Sons, 1899). Mnemosyne: *Triumph of Music* (Louisville: J. P. Morton, 1888). Dead Cities; Orgie: *Kentucky Poems* (London: G. Richards, 1902).

John Jay Chapman. Bismarck: *Mid-Summer Supplement to the Nursery*, 1898.

Rose Terry Cooke. Bluebeard's Closet: *Poems* (Boston: Ticknor & Fields, 1861). Arachne: *Poems* (New York: Gottsberger, 1888).

Stephen Crane. *from* The Black Riders; *from* War Is Kind; "There is a grey thing that lives in the tree-tops"; "A man adrift on a slim spar"; "A naked woman and a dead dwarf"; "Little birds of the night"; "Unwind my riddle": Fredson Bowers (ed.), *The Works of Stephen Crane, Volume X: Poems and Literary Remains* (Charlottesville: University Press of Virginia, 1975). Reprinted by permission of the University Press of Virginia.

Emily Dickinson. The texts of all poems are from Thomas H. Johnson (ed.), *The Complete Poems of Emily Dickinson* (Cambridge: The Belknap Press of Harvard University Press, 1951). By courtesy of the following publishers: Harvard University Press (reprinted by permission of the publishers and the Trustees of Amherst College from Thomas H. Johnson, ed., *The Poems of Emily Dickinson* [Cambridge, Mass.: The Belknap Press of Harvard University Press]; copyright © 1951, 1955, 1983 by the President and Fellows of Harvard College); Houghton Mifflin Company (from Martha Dickinson Bianchi, ed., *Life and Letters of Emily Dickinson*, copyright © 1924 by Martha Dickinson Bianchi; copyright renewed 1952 by Alfred Leete Hampson; reprinted by permission of Houghton Mifflin Company; all rights reserved; and from Martha Dickinson Bianchi, ed., *Emily Dickinson Face to Face*; copyright © 1932 by Martha Dickinson Bianchi; copyright renewed 1960 by Alfred Leete Hampson; reprinted by permission of Houghton Mifflin Company; all rights reserved; and Little, Brown and Company (from Thomas H. Johnson, ed., *The Complete Poems of Emily Dickinson*; copyright © 1929, 1935 by Martha Dickinson Bianchi; copyright renewed 1957, 1963 by Mary L. Hampson; by permission of Little, Brown and Company).

Paul Laurence Dunbar. Accountability; The Mystery; A Summer's Night; We Wear the Mask: *Majors and Minors* (Toledo, Ohio: Hadley & Hadley, 1895). Song of Summer; When Malindy Sings; A Negro Love Song; Ere Sleep Comes Down to Soothe the Weary Eyes; The Colored Soldiers; An Ante-Bellum Sermon; Signs of the Times: *Lyrics of Lowly Life* (New York: Dodd, Mead & Co., 1897). Little Brown Baby; Sympathy: *Lyrics of the Hearthside*

(New York: Dodd, Mead & Co., 1899). Compensation: *Lyrics of Sunshine and Shadow*, (New York: Dodd, Mead & Co., 1905).

Ernest Fenollosa. *from* East and West; Fuji at Sunrise: *East and West* (New York: Thomas Y. Crowell & Co., 1893). *from* Ode on Reincarnation: Akiko Murakata, "Ernest F. Fenollosa's 'Ode on Reincarnation,'" *Harvard Library Bulletin*, January 1973.

Eugene Field. The Duel: *Love-Songs of Childhood* (New York: Scribner's, 1894). Dutch Lullaby: *A Little Book of Western Verse* (New York: Scribner's, 1891).

Francis Miles Finch. The Blue and the Gray: *Atlantic Monthly*, September 1867.

Stephen Foster. Old Folks at Home: *Ethiopian Melody as Sung by Christy's Minstrels* (New York: Firth, Pond & Co., 1851). My Old Kentucky Home, Good-Night!: *Foster's Plantation Melodies*, No. 20 (New York: Firth, Pond & Co., 1853). Jeanie with the Light Brown Hair: *Foster's Melodies*, No. 26 (New York: Firth, Pond & Co., 1854). Oh! Susanna: *Songs of the Sable Harmonists* (Louisville: W.C. Peters & Co., 1848).

Hamlin Garland. Indian Summer; In August; On the Mississippi; Fighting Fire; Boyish Sleep: *Prairie Songs* (Chicago: Stone & Kimball, 1893).

Richard Watson Gilder. The Sonnet: *The Poet and His Master and Other Poems* (New York: Scribner's, 1878). On the Bay: *The Great Remembrance and Other Poems* (New York: The Century Co., 1893). An Hour in a Studio: *In Palestine and Other Poems* (New York: The Century Co., 1898).

Louise Imogen Guiney. A Salutation: *The White Sail and Other Poems* (Boston: Ticknor & Co., 1887). At a Symphony: *The White Sail and Other Poems* (Boston: Ticknor & Co., 1887). W.H. 1778–1830; Open, Time; Fog; Strikers in Hyde Park; The Lights of London; In the Reading-Room of the British Museum; Sunday Chimes in the City: *A Roadside Harp* (Boston, New York: Houghton, Mifflin, 1893).

Frances Ellen Watkins Harper. The Slave Mother; Bible Defence of Slavery; The Slave Auction: *Poems on Miscellaneous Subjects* (Boston: J.B. Yerrington & Sons, 1854). Lines: "At the portals of the future": *Poems on Miscellaneous Subjects*, Tenth Thousand (Philadelphia: Merrihew & Thompson, 1857).

Bret Harte. Plain Language from Truthful James: *Poems* (Boston: Fields, Osgood & Co., 1871). California Madrigal; Mrs. Judge Jenkins: *East and West* (Boston: James R. Osgood & Co., 1871). Truthful James to the Editor: *Echoes of the Foothills* (Boston: James R. Osgood & Co., 1875). What the Bullet Sang: *Harper's Weekly*, August 26, 1876. Chicago: *Every Saturday*, October 28, 1871.

John Hay. Jim Bludso, of the Prairie Belle: *Pike County Ballads and Other Pieces* (Boston: James R. Osgood & Co., 1871).

Paul Hamilton Hayne. October: *Poems* (Boston: Ticknor & Fields, 1855). Sonnet on the Occurrence of a Spell of Arctic Weather; Charlotte Brontë: *Avolio; a Legend of the Isle of Cos, with Poems Lyrical, Miscellaneous, and Dramatic* (Boston: Ticknor & Fields, 1860).

John Henry Hopkins, Jr. Three Kings of Orient: *Carols, Hymns and Songs* (New York: Church Book Depository, 1863).

Richard Hovey. Evening on the Potomac; A Song by the Shore; At Sea: Richard Hovey and Bliss Carman, *Songs from Vagabondia* (Boston: Copeland & Day, 1894). The Mocking-Bird; Earth's Lyric; Verlaine; Accident in Art: Richard Hovey and Bliss Carman, *More Songs from Vagabondia* (Boston: Copeland & Day, 1896).

William Dean Howells. Forlorn; The Empty House; The Royal Portraits; In Earliest Spring: *Poems* (Boston: James R. Osgood & Co., 1873). November: *Stops of Various Quills* (New York: Harper & Brothers, 1895).

William Reed Huntington. The Cold Meteorite; Lowlands; From Green Mountain: *Sonnets and a Dream* (New York: Marion Press, 1899).

Helen Hunt Jackson. My Lighthouses; Poppies on the Wheat; October: *Verses* (Boston: Fields, Osgood & Co., 1870). Crossed Threads; September: *Sonnets and Lyrics* (Boston: Roberts Brothers, 1886). Dreams: *The Christian Union*, July 24, 1884. Cheyenne Mountain: *The Independent*, July 31, 1879 (New York).

Sarah Orne Jewett. At Home from Church: *Sunday Afternoon*, June 1879. A Country Boy in Winter: *Harper's Young People*, January 24, 1882. A Caged Bird: *Atlantic Monthly*, June 1887. The Widows' House: *Verses* (Boston: Merrymount Press, 1916).

Sidney Lanier. Hymns of the Marshes; Clover; The Waving of the Corn; Song of the Chattahootchee; From the Flats; The Mocking Bird; *from* Street Cries: To Richard Wagner; A Ballad of Trees and the Master; The Dying Words of Jackson; The Revenge of Hamish: Charles R. Anderson (ed.), *The Works of Sidney Lanier (Centennial Edition)* (Baltimore: Johns Hopkins University Press, 1945). The Raven Days: *New Eclectic*, IV, February 1869.

Emma Lazarus. *from* Phantasies (After Robert Schumann); Echoes; The New Colossus; Venus of the Louvre; The Cranes of Ibycus; The South; Long Island Sound; City Visions; In Exile; 1492: *The Poems of Emma Lazarus* (Boston: Houghton, Mifflin, 1888).

James Mathewes Legaré. To a Lily; Tallulah: *Orta-Undis and Other Poems* (Boston: W. D. Ticknor, 1848).

Charles Godfrey Leland. Ballad: *Hans Breitmann's Party* (Philadelphia: T. B. Peterson & Brothers, 1868). Wein Geist; Hans Breitmann as a Politician—Section III: The Author Asserts the Vast Intellectual Superiority of Germans to Americans; Breitmann in Paris: *The Breitmann Ballads* (London: Trübner & Co., 1871).

George Cabot Lodge. Tuckanuck, I; Pastoral; Fall; On an Æolian Harp: *The Song of the Wave and Other Poems* (New York: Charles Scribner's Sons, 1898). "Strong saturation of sea! O widely flown": *Poems, 1899–1902* (New York: Cameron, Blake & Co., 1902). Lower New York: *Atlantic Monthly*, March 1906.

Maria White Lowell. Rouen, Place de la Pucelle: *Putnam's Monthly Magazine*, November 1853. An Opium Fantasy: *Poems of Maria Lowell* (Cambridge: Privately Printed, 1855).

Robert Lowry. Beautiful River: Robert Lowry (ed.): *Bright Jewels for the Sunday School* (New York: Biglow & Main, 1869).

Edwin Markham. The Man with the Hoe; A Leaf from the Devil's Jest-Book; In Death Valley; After Reading Shakspere: *The Man with the Hoe and Other Poems* (New York: Doubleday & McClure, 1899).

Herman Melville. Song from *Mardi*: Harrison Hayford, et al. (eds.), *The Writings of Herman Melville: Mardi* (Northwestern-Newberry, 1970). "The ribs and terrors in the whale": Harrison Hayford, et al. (eds.), *The Writings of Herman Melville: Moby-Dick* (Northwestern-Newberry, 1988). The Portent; Misgivings; The Conflict of Convictions; The Temeraire; A Utilitarian View of the Monitor's Fight; Shiloh: A Requiem; Malvern Hill; The House-top: A Night Piece; The Swamp Angel; "The Coming Storm"; "Formerly a Slave"; The Apparition; America; A Requiem: for Soldiers Lost in Ocean Transports; John Marr; Tom Deadlight; The Haglets; The Man-of-War Hawk; The Tuft of Kelp; The Maldive Shark; To Ned; The Berg; Timoleon; After the Pleasure Party; The Ravaged Villa; Monody; The Bench of Boors; Art; Shelley's Vision; Fragments of a Lost Gnostic Poem of the 12th Century; Venice; In a Bye Canal; In a Church of Padua; The Archipelago: Robert Ryan, et al. (eds.), *The Writings of Herman Melville: Published Poems* (Northwestern-Newberry, not yet published). *from* Clarel: Harrison Hayford, et al. (eds.), *The Writings of Herman Melville: Clarel* (Northwestern-Newberry, 1991). Rose Window; The Rose Farmer; Pontoosuce: Harrison Hayford, et al. (eds.), *The Writings of Herman Melville: Billy Budd and Other Late Manuscripts* (Northwestern-Newberry, not yet published). Billy in the Darbies: Harrison Hayford and Merton M. Sealts, Jr., eds., *Billy Budd, Sailor* (Chicago: University of Chicago Press, 1962).

Adah Isaacs Menken. Judith: *Infelicia* (London: Hotten, 1868).

Stuart Merrill. Ballade of the Chinese Lover: *Munsey's Weekly*, March 16, 1889. Ballade of the Outcasts: *The Nationalist: A Monthly Magazine*, Vol. 1, June 1889.

Joaquin Miller. Sierras: *The Overland Monthly*, April 1873. Africa: *Songs of Far-Away Lands* (London: Longmans, 1878). In Père La Chaise: *Songs of Italy* (Boston: Roberts Brothers, 1878). At Our Golden Gate: *The Complete Poetical Works of Joaquin Miller* (San Francisco: Whitaker & Ray, 1897). Columbus: *Songs of the Soul* (San Francisco: Whitaker & Ray. 1896).

Harriet Monroe. To W. S. M.: With a copy of Shelley: *Valeria and Other Poems* (Chicago: A. C. McClurg & Co., 1892).

William Vaughn Moody. Gloucester Moors; An Ode in Time of Hesitation; Harmonics; The Bracelet of Grass; The Departure: *Poems* (Boston, New York: Houghton Mifflin, 1901).

John James Piatt. Farther; To the Statue on the Capitol: *Landmarks and Other Poems* (New York: Hurd & Houghton, 1872). Fires in Illinois: *Poems of Sunshine and Firelight* (Cincinnati: R. W. Carroll, 1866). My Shadow's Stature: *Poems of John James Piatt* (Cincinnati: R. W. Carroll, 1868). Taking the Night-Train: John James Piatt (ed.), *American Poetry and Art* (Cincinnati: W. E. Dibble, 1880).

Sarah Morgan Piatt. Taking Back the Flower: *The Galaxy*, February 1867.

Alexander L. Posey. Song of the Oktahutchee; July; Midsummer; Autumn; Nightfall: *The Poems of Alexander Lawrence Posey* (Topeka: Crane, 1910).

James Ryder Randall. Maryland: New Orleans *Daily Delta*, May 5, 1861.

Thomas Buchanan Read. Sheridan's Ride: *A Summer Story, Sheridan's Ride, and Other Poems* (Philadelphia: J. B. Lippincott, 1865).

Lizette Woodworth Reese. Love, Weeping, Laid This Song; One Night; April in Town: *A Handful of Lavender* (Boston, New York: Houghton Mifflin, 1891). In Time of Grief; A Lyric on the Lyric; Death's Guerdon; The Lavender Woman: *A Quiet Road* (Boston, New York: Houghton Mifflin, 1896).

John Rollin Ridge. Mount Shasta; A Cherokee Love Song; The Rainy Season in California; The Stolen White Girl; *from* California: *Poems* (San Francisco: Henry Payot & Co., 1868).

James Whitcomb Riley. The Old Swimmin'-Hole; When the Frost Is on the Punkin: *The Old Swimmin'-hole and 'Leven More Poems* (Indianapolis: George C. Hitt & Co., 1883). The Days Gone By; Little Orphant Annie: *Old Fashioned Roses* (London: Longmans, Green, 1888).

Edwin Arlington Robinson. The Torrent; Supremacy; Boston; The Children of the Night; John Evereldown; Luke Havergal; Ballade of Broken Flutes; The House on the Hill; Richard Cory; The Pity of the Leaves; Reuben Bright; "Oh for a poet—for a beacon bright"; "The master and the slave go hand in hand"; Cliff Klingenhagen: *Children of the Night* (Boston: Richard G. Badger & Co., 1897). Aaron Stark; A Poem for Max Nordau; Walt Whitman; The Clerks; George Crabbe; Verlaine: *The Torrent and the Night Before* (Cambridge, Massachusetts: Riverside Press, 1897).

Abram Joseph Ryan. Lines: Richmond *Dispatch*, December 22, 1866.

George Santayana. Sonnet III: "O world, thou choosest not the better part!"; Sonnet V: "Dreamt I to-day the dream of yesternight"; Sonnet XXV: "As in the midst of battle there is room"; Sonnet XLIII: "The candour of the gods is in thy gaze"; Sonnet XLVIII: "Of Helen's brothers, one was born to die"; On a Piece of Tapestry; Before a Statue of Achilles; Ode V: "Of thee the Northman by his beached galley"; Cape Cod; On an Unfinished Statue; Echo: William G. Holzberger (ed.), *The Complete Poems of George Santayana* (Lewisburg: Bucknell University Press, 1979). Reprinted by permission.

Clinton Scollard. As I Came Down from Lebanon: *With Reed and Lyre* (Boston: D. Lothrop & Co., 1886). A Bit of Marble: *Old and New World Lyrics* (New York: Frederick A. Stokes & Brother, 1888).

Edward Rowland Sill. The Fool's Prayer; Opportunity: *The Venus of Milo and Other Poems* (Berkeley: Bacon & Co., 1883). Truth At Last: *Poems* (Boston, New York: Houghton Mifflin, 1887). California Winter: *The Hermitage* (Boston, New York: Houghton Mifflin, 1889).

Edmund Clarence Stedman. Prelude to *An American Anthology*: Edmund Clarence Stedman (ed.), *An American Anthology* (Boston, New York: Houghton Mifflin, 1900).

Trumbull Stickney. In Ampezzo; Mnemosyne; Eride, V: "Now in the palace gardens warm with age"; "You say, Columbus with his argosies"; On Rodin's "L'Illusion, Sœur d'Icare"; On Some Shells Found Inland; "Live blindly and upon the hour"; "Be still. The Hanging Gardens were a dream"; On the Concert; "The melancholy year is dead with rain"; "As a sad man, when evenings grayer grow"; "He said: ' If in his image I was made' "; Lakeward; Pandora's Songs from *Prometheus Pyrphoro: Dramatic Verses* (Boston: Charles E. Goodspeed, 1902). "And, the last day being come, Man stood alone"; At Sainte-Marguerite; An Athenian Garden; *from* Sonnets from Greece; Six O'Clock; "The Autumn's done; they have the golden corn in"; *from* Dramatic Fragments: *Poems of Trumbull Stickney* (Boston, New York: Houghton Mifflin, 1905). "Here in the North I chase an old despair"; On Sandro's Flora: Amberys R. Whittle (ed.), *Poems of Trumbull Stickney* (New York: Farrar, Straus & Giroux: 1972).

John Banister Tabb. The Bridge: *Poems* (Baltimore, 1882). Echoes; Evolution; Milton; Whisper; The Shadow; A Winter Twilight: *Poems* (Boston: Copeland & Day, 1894). Echo: *Lyrics* (Boston: Copeland & Day, 1897). The Mid-Day Moon; Tenebrae; The Sisters: *Lyrics*, 5th edition (Boston: Copeland & Day, 1900).

Bayard Taylor. Bedouin Song: *Poems of the Orient* (Boston: Ticknor & Fields, 1855). *from* The Echo Club: *The Echo Club and Other Literary Diversions* (Boston: J. R. Osgood & Co., 1876).

Ernest Lawrence Thayer. Casey at the Bat: *The San Francisco Examiner*, June 3, 1888.

Rose Hartwick Thorpe. Curfew Must Not Ring To-Night: *Ringing Ballads* (Boston: D. Lothrop, 1887).

Henry Timrod. Dreams; Ethnogenesis; The Cotton Boll; La Belle Juive; Carolina; Charleston; Christmas: Unpublished proof sheets, courtesy of the Charleston Library Society, Charleston, South Carolina. Retirement: *Poems* (Boston: Ticknor & Fields, 1860). "I know not why, but all this weary day": Charleston *Mercury*, October 7, 1861. Lines: "Sleep sweetly in your humble graves": Charleston *Daily Courier*, July 23, 1866.

John Townsend Trowbridge. An Idyl of Harvest Time; Recollections of "Lalla Rookh"; Circumstance; The Old Lobsterman: *A Home Idyll and Other Poems* (Boston: Houghton, Mifflin & Co., 1881).

Frederick Goddard Tuckerman. Sonnets; The Question; *from* Sonnets, First Series; *from* Sonnets, Second Series: *Poems* (Boston: John Wilson & Son, 1860). *from* Sonnets, Third Series; *from* Sonnets, Fourth Series; *from* Sonnets, Fifth Series; The Cricket: N. Scott Momaday (ed.), *The Complete Poems of Frederick Goddard Tuckerman* (New York: Oxford University Press, 1965). Copyright © 1965 by Oxford University Press, Inc.; reprinted with permission. (Sonnets, Fourth and Fifth Series originally published by Alfred A. Knopf, 1931.)

Mark Twain. Ode to Stephen Dowling Bots, Dec'd.: *Adventures of Huckleberry Finn* (New York: Charles L. Webster, 1885).

George Boyer Vashon. Vincent Ogé: Julia Griffiths (ed.), *Autographs of Freedom*, vol. 2 (Auburn, New York: Alden, Beardsley, & Co., 1854).

Edith Wharton. The Last Giustiniani: *Scribner's Magazine*, October 1889. Life: *Scribner's Magazine*, June 1894. Experience; Chartres; Two Backgrounds; The Tomb of Ilaria Giunigi; An Autumn Sunset: *Artemis to Acteaon and Other Verse* (New York: Charles Scribner's Sons, 1909).

James Monroe Whitfield. America; To A. H.: *America and Other Poems* (Buffalo, New York: J. S. Leavitt, 1853).

Albery Allson Whitman. *from* Twasinta's Seminoles: *Twasinta's Seminoles, or Rape of Florida* (St. Louis: Nixon-Jones, 1885). *from* Not a Man and Yet a Man: *Not a Man, and Yet a Man* (Springfield, Ohio: Republic Printing Co., 1877). *from* An Idyll of the South: *An Idyll of the South* (New York: Metaphysical Publishing Co., 1901).

Ella Wheeler Wilcox. Friendship After Love: *Poems of Passion* (Chicago: Belford, Clark, 1883). No Classes!: *Poems of Pleasure* (New York, Chicago: Belford, Clark, 1888). The Sonnet; The Engine; Nothing New: *Maurine and Other Poems* (Chicago: Jansen, McClurg & Co., 1882).

Forceythe Willson. The Estray; To Hersa; In State: *The Old Sergeant, and Other Poems* (Boston: Ticknor & Fields, 1867).

Constance Fenimore Woolson. Love Unexpressed: *Appleton's Journal* 7, March 9, 1872. The Florida Beach: *Galaxy* 18, October 1874. Detroit River: Clare Benedict, *Constance Fenimore Woolson*, n.d. (London: Ellis).

Henry Clay Work. Kingdom Coming: Sheet music (Chicago: Root & Cady, 1862). Marching Through Georgia: Sheet music (Chicago: Root & Cady, 1865). "Come Home, Father!": Sheet music (Chicago: Root & Cady, 1864).

19TH-CENTURY VERSIONS OF AMERICAN INDIAN POETRY

The Song of the Lenâpé Warriors Going Against the Enemy: John Heckewelder, "An Account of the History, Manners, and Customs of the Indian Nations Who Once Inhabited Pennsylvania and the Neighbouring States," *Transactions of the American Philosophical Society* (Philadelphia, 1819).

Two Cherokee Songs of Friendship: Samuel L. Mitchill, "Letter from Samuel L. Mitchill, of New York, to Samuel M. Burnside," *Transactions and Collections of the American Antiquarian Society*, 1820.

Specimens of Indian Songs (Miami): Lewis Cass, "Indian Customs," *The Columbian Star*, April 1822.

Music and Poetry of the Indians (Ojibwa): Edwin S. James, editor, *A Narrative of the Captivity and Adventures of John Tanner During Thirty Years Residence Among the Indians in the Interior of North America* (New York: G. & H. & C. Carvill, 1830).

Hoatchunk' Narwoanar, or Winnebago War Song: Caleb Atwater, *Remarks Made on a Tour to Prairie du Chien; Thence to Washington City* (Columbus, Ohio: Isaac N. Whiting, 1831).

Medicine Song of a Lover (Ojibwa): Charles Fenno Hoffman, *Wild Scenes in the Forest and Prairie* (London: R. Bentley, 1839).

from War Dance (Iowa): George Catlin, *Fourteen Ioway Indians: Key to their Various Dances, Games, Ceremonies, Songs, Religion, Superstitions, Costumes, Weapons, etc., etc.* (London: W. S. Johnson, 1844).

The Loon Upon the Lake (Ojibwa); Death Song (Ojibwa): Henry Rowe Schoolcraft, *Oneóta, or Characteristics of the Red Race of America* (New York: Wiley & Putnam, 1845).

George Copway's Dream Song (Ojibwa): George Copway, *Life, Letters and Travels of Kah-Ge-Ga-Gah-Bowh* (Albany: Weed and Parson, 1847).

Meda Songs (Ojibwa); Prophetic Powers (Ojibwa); Chants to the Deity (Ojibwa): Henry Rowe Schoolcraft, *Information Respecting History, Condition, and Prospects of the Indian Tribes of the United States*, vol. 1 (Philadelphia: Lippincott, Grambo, 1851–57).

Song of the Owl (Ojibwa): Henry Wadsworth Longfellow, letter to Ferdinand Freiligrath, January 1856; adapted from Henry Rowe Schoolcraft, *Information Respecting History, Condition, and Prospects of the Indian Tribes of the United States*, vol. 1 (Philadephia: Lippincott, Grambo, 1851–57); cited in Andrew Hilen (ed.), *The Letters of Henry Wadsworth Longfellow*, vol. III (Cambridge, Massachusetts: The Belknap Press of Harvard University Press, 1972); copyright © 1972 by the President and Fellows of Harvard College; reprinted by permission of the publishers.

Magic Song (Ojibwa): Henry Rowe Schoolcraft, *Information Respecting History, Condition, and Prospects of the Indian Tribes of the United States*, vol. 2 (Philadelphia: Lippincott, Grambo, 1851–57).

Hawk Chant of the Saginaws (Ojibwa): Henry Rowe Schoolcraft, *Information Respecting History, Condition, and Prospects of the Indian Tribes of the United States*, vol. 3 (Philadelphia: Lippincott, Grambo, 1851–57).

Love Song (Ojibwa); War Songs (Ojibwa); Corn Song (Ojibwa); Chant to the Fire-Fly (Ojibwa): Henry Rowe Schoolcraft, *Information Respecting History, Conditions, and Prospects of the Indian Tribes of the United States*, vol. 5 (Philadelphia: Lippincott, Grambo, 1851–57).

Minnetare Songs (Hidatsa): Leslie A. White (ed.), *Lewis Henry Morgan: The Indian Journals, 1859–62* (Ann Arbor: University of Michigan Press, 1959).

Song for a Fallen Warrior (Blackfeet): John Mason Browne, "Indian Medicine," *Atlantic Monthly*, 1866.

War Songs (Sioux); Songs of the Sacred Mysteries (Sioux): Alfred Longley Riggs, "Dakota Songs and Music," in Stephen Return Riggs, *Tah'-koo Wah-kan'; or, The Gospel Among the Dakotas* (Boston: Congregational Publishing Society, 1869).

Southern Paiute Poetry: John Wesley Powell, *Report of Explorations in 1873 of the Colorado of the West and its Tributaries* (Washington: Government Printing Office, 1874).

Songs and Chants (Southern Paiute): Smithsonian Contributions to Anthropology (Number 14), Don D. Fowler and Catherine S. Fowler, eds., *An-

thropology of the Numa: John Wesley Powell's Manuscripts on the Numic Peoples of Western North America, 1868–1880 (Washington: Smithsonian Institution Press, 1971).

from Sacred Songs of the Konkau: Stephen Powers, "Tribes of California," *Contributions to North American Ethnology*, 1877.

Soldier's Song (Sioux): Stephen Return Riggs, trans., "Narrative of Paul Mazakootemane," *Collections of the Minnesota Historical Society*, 1880.

from Ancient Rites of the Condoling Council (Iroquois); Chant from The Iroquois Book of Rites (Onondaga): Horatio Hale, *The Iroquois Book of Rites* (Philadephia: D. G. Brinton, 1883).

Hunter's Song (Hitchiti): Albert S. Gatschet, *A Migration Legend of the Creek Indians* (Philadelphia: D. G. Brinton, 1884–88).

The Song of the Stars (Passamaquoddy): Charles Godfrey Leland, *The Algonquin Legends of New England; or, Myths and Folk Lore of the Micmac, Passamaquoddy, and Penobscot Tribes* (Boston: Houghton, Mifflin, 1884).

from The Walam Olum, or Red Score (Delaware): Daniel Garrison Brinton, *The Lenâpé and Their Legends; with the Complete Text and Symbols of the Walam Olum* (Philadelphia: D. G. Brinton, 1885).

from The Mountain Chant (Navajo): Washington Matthews, "The Mountain Chant: A Navajo Ceremony," *Fifth Annual Report of the Bureau of Ethnology*, 1887.

Summer Song (Eskimo): Franz Boas, "Poetry and Music of Some North American Tribes," *Science*, 1887.

Chinook Songs: Franz Boas, "Chinook Songs," *Journal of American Folk-Lore*, 1888.

Pawnee War-Song: Daniel Garrison Brinton, *Essays of an Americanist* (Philadelphia: Porter & Coates, 1890).

Incantation Songs of the Klamath People; Incantations of Modoc Conjurers: Albert S. Gatschet, "The Klamath Indians of Southwestern Oregon," *Contributions to North American Ethnology*, 1890.

Medicine Songs (Omaha): Francis La Flesche, "The Omaha Buffalo Medicine-Men," *Journal of American Folk-Lore*, 1890.

The Thanksgivings (Iroquois): Harriet Maxwell Converse, *Journal of American Folk-Lore*, 1891.

Imploration for Clear Weather (Ojibwa): W. J. Hoffman, "The Mide'wiwin or 'Grand Medicine Society' of the Ojibwa," *Seventh Annual Report of the Bureau of Ethnology*, 1891.

Prayer Upon Cutting Down the Sacred Tree (Sioux): John G. Bourke, "Religion of the Apache Indians," *Folk-lore*, 1891.

A Rain Song of the Shu'-wi Chai'än (Snake Society) (Sia); A Rain Song of the Quer'ränna Chai'än (Sia): Matilda Coxe Stevenson, "The Sia," *Eleventh Annual Report of the Bureau of American Ethnology*, 1894.

Eskimo Songs: Franz Boas, "Eskimo Tales and Songs," *Journal of American Folk-Lore*, 1894–97.

from The Hardening of the World (Zuni); *from* The Generation of the Seed of Seeds, or the Origin of Corn (Zuni): Frank Hamilton Cushing, "Out-

lines of Zuñi Creation Myths," *Thirteenth Annual Report of the Bureau of American Ethnology*, 1896.

Ghost-Dance Songs: James Mooney, "The Ghost-Dance Religion and the Sioux Outbreak of 1890," *Fourteenth Annual Report of the Bureau of American Ethnology*, 1896.

Songs of the Kwakiutl Indians: Franz Boas, "Songs of the Kwakiutl Indians," *Internationales Archiv für Ethnographie*, 1896.

Dances and Songs of the Winter Ceremonial (Kwakiutl): Franz Boas, "The Social Organization and the Secret Societies of the Kwakiutl Indians," *Report of the U.S. National Museum* (Washington Government Printing Office, 1897).

Kū'siut Song (Bella Coola): Franz Boas, "The Mythology of the Bella Coola Indians," *Memoirs of the American Museum of Natural History*, 1898.

Songs of Spirits (Wintun): Jeremiah Curtin, *Creation Myths of Primitive America in Relation to the Religious History and Mental Development of Mankind* (Boston: Little, Brown, 1898).

Captive's Song (Omaha): Fannie Reed Giffen, *Oo-Mah-Ha Ta-Wa-Tha (Omaha City)* (Lincoln, Nebraska: By the authors, 1898).

Songs from the Great Feast to the Dead (Eskimo): Edward William Nelson, "The Eskimo About Bering Strait," *Eighteenth Annual Report of the Bureau of American Ethnology*, 1899.

The Mocking-Bird's Song (Tigua): Alice C. Fletcher, *Indian Story and Song from North America* (Boston: Small, Maynard, 1900).

Song of a Gray Wolf (Cheyenne): Alfred Kroeber, "Cheyenne Tales," *Journal of American Folk-Lore*, 1900.

The Wizard's Chant (Passamaquoddy): Charles Godfrey Leland and John Dyneley Prince, *Kulóskap the Master and Other Algonkin Poems* (New York: Funk & Wagnalls, 1902).

from The Night Chant: Washington Matthews, "The Night Chant, a Navaho Ceremony," *Memoirs of the American Museum of Natural History*, 1902.

from The Hako (Pawnee): Alice C. Fletcher, "The Hako: A Pawnee Ceremony," *Twenty-second Annual Report of the Bureau of American Ethnology*, 1904.

from History Myth of the Coming of the A'shiwi as Narrated by 'Kiäklo (Zuni); Invocation to the U'wannami (Zuni): Matilda Coxe Stevenson, "The Zuñi Indians: Their Mythology, Esoteric Fraternities, and Ceremonies," *Twenty-third Annual Report of the Bureau of American Ethnology*, 1904.

FOLK SONGS AND SPIRITUALS

Blow Your Trumpet, Gabriel; Michael Row the Boat Ashore; Nobody Knows the Trouble I've Had; Roll, Jordan, Roll: William Francis Allen, et al. (eds.), *Slave Songs of the United States* (New York: A. Simpson & Co., 1867).

Buffalo Gals: *Music of the Ethiopian Serenaders* (New York: William Hall & Son, 1848).

The Cowboy's Lament; A Home on the Range; Whoopee Ti Yi Yo, Git Along Little Dogies: Alan Lomax (ed.), *Cowboy Songs and Other Frontier Ballads* (New York: Sturgis & Walton, 1910).

Cripple Creek; Shady Grove: Alan Lomax (ed.), *Folk Songs of North America* (New York: Doubleday, 1960).

Cumberland Gap (collected, adapted, and arranged by John A. Lomax and Alan Lomax; TRO—copyright © 1934 [renewed] Ludlow Music, Inc., New York, N.Y.; used by permission); John Brown's Body (collected, adapted, and arranged by John A. Lomax and Alan Lomax; TRO—copyright © 1934 [renewed] Ludlow Music, Inc., New York, N.Y.; used by permission); Low Bridge, Everybody Down; Old Joe Clark (collected, adapted, and arranged by John A. Lomax and Alan Lomax; TRO—copyright © 1934 [renewed] Ludlow Music, Inc., New York, N.Y.; used by permission): John A. Lomax and Alan Lomax (eds.), *American Ballads and Folk Songs* (New York: Macmillan, 1934).

The Days of '49 (San Francisco: Sherman & Hyde, 1876); transcribed in Richard Dwyer, et al. (eds.), *The Songs of the Gold Rush* (Berkeley: University of California Press, 1964); copyright © 1964 The Regents of the University of California.

Deep River: J. B. T. Marsh, *The Story of the Jubilee Singers* (Boston: Houghton, Osgood & Co., 1880).

Dere's No Hidin' Place Down Dere; Joshua Fit de Battle ob Jerico: James Weldon Johnson and J. Rosamond Johnson, *The Book of American Negro Spirituals.* Copyright 1925, 1926 by The Viking Press, Inc., renewed 1953 by Lawrence Brown, 1953, © 1954 by Grace Nail Johnson and J. Rosamond Johnson. Used by permission of Viking Penguin, a division of Penguin Books USA Inc.

Didn't My Lord Deliver Daniel; Many Thousand Gone; Old Time Religion; Steal Away; Swing Low, Sweet Chariot: Theodore Frelinghuysen Seward (ed.), *Jubilee Songs: As Sung by the Jubilee Singers of Fisk University* (New York: Biglow, Main & Co., 1872).

Down in the Valley (collected, adapted, and arranged by John A. Lomax and Alan Lomax; TRO—copyright 1934 [renewed] Ludlow Music, Inc., New York, N.Y., used by permission); Frankie and Albert (collected, adapted, and arranged by John A. Lomax and Alan Lomax; TRO—copyright 1934 [renewed] Ludlow Music, Inc., New York, N.Y., used by permission); John Hardy (collected, adapted, and arranged by John A. Lomax and Alan Lomax; TRO—copyright 1934 [renewed] Ludlow Music, Inc., New York, N.Y., used by permission); John Henry (collected, adapted, and arranged by John A. Lomax and Alan Lomax; TRO—copyright 1934 [renewed] Ludlow Music, Inc., New York, N.Y., used by permission); Lonesome Valley (collected, adapted, and arranged by John A. Lomax and Alan Lomax; TRO—copyright 1947 [renewed] Ludlow Music, Inc., New York, N.Y., used by permission): John A. Lomax and Alan Lomax (eds.), *Folk Song: U.S.A.* (New York: Meredith Press, 1947).

Ev'ry Time I Feel the Spirit; Ezekiel Saw de Wheel: Thomas P. Fenner (ed.), *Religious Folk Songs of the Negro* (Hampton, Virginia: Hampton Institute, 1909).

Free At Last; Got a Home in That Rock: John Wesley Work (ed.), *Folk Songs of the American Negro* (Nashville: Work Brothers, 1907).

He Never Said a Mumblin' Word: R. Emmett Kennedy, editor, *Mellows: A Chronicle of Unknown Singers* (New York: Albert & Charles Boni, 1925).

I Know Moon-Rise; Lord, Remember Me; One More River: Thomas Wentworth Higginson, "Negro Spirituals," *Atlantic Monthly*, June 1867.

Jesse James: *Comic and Popular Songs, Sung by Robert Jones*, 1887.

Jim Crack Corn, or the Blue Tail Fly: Sheet music, Baltimore: F. D. Benteen, 1846.

"Johnny come down de hollow": William Cullen Bryant, letter to the New York *Evening Post*, March 29, 1843.

Let My People Go: *The National Anti-Slavery Standard*, December 21, 1861.

My Lord, What a Morning: Thomas P. Fenner, "Cabin and Plantation Songs," in Mary Frances Armstrong, *Hampton and Its Students* (Hampton, Virginia: Hampton Institute, 1874).

Oh My Darling Clementine: Sheet music, Boston: Oliver Ditson & Co., 1884.

Poor Naomi: *The Patriot*, Greensboro, North Carolina, April 1874.

Red River Valley: Carl Sandburg, *The American Songbag*, copyright 1927 by Harcourt Brace & Company and renewed 1955 by Carl Sandburg, reprinted by permission of the publisher.

Rye Whisky (collected, adapted and arranged by John A. Lomax and Alan Lomax; TRO—copyright © 1938 [renewed] Ludlow Music, Inc., New York, N.Y.; used by permission); The State of Arkansas (collected, adapted and arranged by John A. Lomax and Alan Lomax, TRO—copyright © 1938 [renewed] Ludlow Music, Inc., New York, N.Y.; used by permission): John A. Lomax and Alan Lomax (eds.), *Cowboy Songs and Other Frontier Ballads* (New York: Macmillan, 1938).

Shenandoah: W.B. Whall, *Ships, Sea Songs, and Shanties* (Glasgow: James Brown & Son, 1910).

Simple Gifts: Edward Deming Andrews, *The Gift To Be Simple* (New York: J. J. Augustin, 1940), reprinted courtesy Dover Publications, Inc., New York.

Sometimes I Feel Like a Motherless Child; What Yo' Gwine to Do When De Lamp Burn Down?: Thomas P. Fenner (ed.), *Cabin and Plantation Songs* (Hampton, Virginia: Hampton Institute, 1901).

Stackalee: Sigmund Spaeth, *Weep Some More, My Lady* (New York: Doubleday, Page & Co., 1927).

Starving to Death on a Government Claim: Manuscript, March 8, 1891; transcribed in Richard Lingenfelter et al. (eds.), *Songs of the American West* (Berkeley: University of California Press, 1968); copyright © 1968 The Regents of the University of California.

Sweet Betsey from Pike: *Put's Golden Songster* (San Francisco: Appleton & Co., 1858).

"We raise de wheat": Frederick Douglass, *My Bondage and My Freedom* (New York and Auburn: Miller, Orton & Mulligan, 1855).

Were You There?: John Wesley Work Sr., *New Jubilee Songs* (Nashville, Tennessee: Press of Fisk University, 1902).

Working on the Railway: Lockwood Honore, *Popular College Songs* (Cincinnati: J. Church, 1891).

The following is a list of pages where a stanza break coincides with the foot of the page (except where such breaks are apparent from the regular stanzaic structure of the poem): 33, 38, 45, 56, 68, 73, 74, 78, 183, 236, 239, 244, 248, 249, 254, 255, 257, 276, 278, 281, 285, 296, 301, 303, 317, 332, 363, 383, 387, 403, 497, 498, 520, 583, 588, 594, 595, 596, 597, 598, 604, 608, 621, 695.

This volume presents the texts listed here without change except for the correction of typographical errors, but it does not attempt to reproduce features of their typographic design. For untitled poems, the first line is used as a title. The following is a list of typographical errors in the source texts that have been corrected, cited by page and line number: 92.6, he; 104.3, Dark; 329.2, wierd; 341.23, packs; 390.6, touch; 390.31, maryland!; 489.12, quiesence; 543.16, Prinelings; 544.4, [comma missing]; 557.7, aflrays; 558.25, Johnnie; 613.7, over-wise.; 661.7, Whom; 670.16, Loon; 688.18, fail; 694.24, great; 774.19, him; 779.16, blu; 782.24, me.; 786.3, comanded; 799.5, I'ts. Error corrected second printing: 758.9, might a *(LOA)*.

Notes

In the notes below, the reference numbers denote page and line of this volume (the line count includes titles). No note is made for material included in standard desk-reference books, such as *Webster's Ninth New Collegiate Dictionary* or *Webster's Biographical Dictionary*. References to the Bible have been keyed to the King James Version.

1.3   Song from *Mardi*] Sung by the poet Yoomy in Chapter 88: "Then Yoomy, before buried in a reverie, burst forth with a verse, sudden as a jet from a Geyser."

1.8   "*The ribs . . . whale*"] Read from the pulpit by Father Mapple before his sermon in Chapter 9 of *Moby-Dick*.

3.1   *The Conflict of Convictions*] "The gloomy lull of the early part of the winter of 1860–1, seeming big with final disaster to our institutions, affected some minds that believed them to constitute one of the great hopes of mankind, much as the eclipse which came over the promise of the first French Revolution affected kindred natures, throwing them for the time into doubts and misgivings universal."—Melville's note.

3.8–14   fall . . . Mammon] Cf. Milton's *Paradise Lost*, in which the characters Satan, Raphael (an angel), and Mammon (a fallen angel) appear.

4.14   *Iron Dome*] The new dome of the Capitol (built over the older wooden dome), begun in 1856 and completed in 1865.

5.1   Ancient of Days] God, as described in the vision in Daniel 7:9.

6.1   *The Temeraire*] "The *Temeraire*, that storied ship of the old English fleet, and the subject of the well-known painting by Turner, commends itself to the mind seeking for some one craft to stand for the poetic ideal of those great historic wooden war-ships, whose gradual displacement is lamented by none more than by regularly educated navy officers, and of all nations."—Melville's note. *Temeraire*, which figured prominently in the British victory over the French and Spanish fleet at Trafalgar in 1805, was broken up in 1838; J.M.W. Turner's *The "Fighting Temeraire" Tugged to Her Last Berth To Be Broken Up* (1838) shows her being towed off by a steamboat.

6.3   *Monitor and Merrimac*] The ironclad Union vessel *Monitor*, which had a revolving gun turret, fought an inconclusive engagement on March 9, 1862, with the Confederate ironclad *Virginia* (which had been built using the salvaged hull of the Union ship *Merrimack*). It was the first battle in naval history between ironclad ships.

6.23   Armorial] "Some of the cannon of old times, especially the brass ones, unlike the more effective ordnance of the present day, were cast in

shapes which Cellini might have designed, were gracefully enchased, generally with the arms of the country. A few of them—field-pieces—captured in our earlier wars, are preserved in arsenals and navy-yards."—Melville's note.

7.5   Victory, whose Admiral]   H.M.S. *Victory* was Vice Admiral Horatio Nelson's flagship at the battle of Trafalgar (October 21, 1805).

9.1   *Shiloh*]   A fierce battle was fought near Shiloh Church in southern Tennessee on April 6 and 7, 1862; the combined Union and Confederate losses were over 23,000.

9.23   *Malvern Hill*]   In the last engagement of the Seven Days' Battles, Confederate general Robert E. Lee attacked the retreating Army of the Potomac at Malvern Hill, Virginia, on July 1, 1862. The attack was defeated by massed Union artillery, and the Confederates lost over 5,000 men.

9.31   with the cartridge in their mouth]   Killed while loading their weapons. The gunpowder used in Civil War muzzle-loading rifles and muskets was contained in paper cartridges; soldiers loaded by biting off the end of the cartridge, pouring the powder down the barrel of the gun, and then ramming the ball down onto the powder.

10.6   Seven Nights and Days]   During the Seven Days' Battles, fought outside of Richmond between June 25 and July 1, 1862, Lee succeeded in driving Major General George B. McClellan's forces away from the Confederate capital.

10.26   *The House-top*]   " 'I dare not write the horrible and inconceivable atrocities committed,' says Froissart, in alluding to the remarkable sedition in France during his time. The like may be hinted of some proceedings of the draft-rioters."—Melville's note. More than 100 persons were killed in rioting that broke out in New York City on July 13, 1863, after federal authorities began to draft men under the 1863 Conscription Act. Mobs lynched blacks, attacked Republican newspaper offices, and burned down the Colored Orphans Asylum before the riots were suppressed on July 16.

11.3   parching Sirius]   The brightest star in the constellation Canis Major, Sirius (or the Dog Star) was a token of summer heat to the Greeks and Romans.

11.13   Draco]   Athenian legislator who, according to tradition, codified the Athenian law around 621 B.C., prescribing the death penalty for most offenses.

11.22   *The Swamp Angel*]   "The great Parrott gun, planted in the marshes of James Island, and employed in the prolonged, though at times intermitted

bombardment of Charleston, was known among our soldiers as the Swamp Angel."—Melville's note.

12.27   Michael] "St. Michael's, characterized by its venerable tower, was the historic and aristocratic church of the town."—Melville's note.

13.2   *by S. R. Gifford*] By Robert Swain Gifford (1840–1905), not Sanford R. Gifford.

13.2   *E. B.*] Edwin Booth, Shakespearian actor and brother of John Wilkes Booth.

13.3   *N. A.*] The National Academy of Design in New York City.

13.20   *"Formerly a Slave"*] Elihu Vedder's (1836–1923) painting was listed in the exhibition catalogue as "Jane Jackson, formerly a slave . . ."

14.26   Berenice's Hair] The constellation Coma Berenices.

17.4   *Clarel*] The four-part poem, in 150 cantos running to nearly 18,000 lines, recounts the pilgrimage through the Holy Land of Clarel, an American divinity student struggling with a loss of faith.

17.30   Siloh's oracle] The pool of Siloam in Jerusalem, site of Jesus' miraculous healing of a blind man; also, "Siloa's brook that flow'd/ Fast by the Oracle of God" (Milton, *Paradise Lost*, I.11).

18.9   titled Rose] The "rose of Sharon" in Song of Solomon 2:1.

18.11–13   Ramleh . . . tower] Or Ramla, a city about 25 miles northwest of Jerusalem; the tower is an ancient minaret.

18.16   Ephraim] Mountains north of Jerusalem.

18.26–28   Flung . . . Louis] In the Crusades of 1270 led by Louis IX of France, the Moors defending Carthage were reported to have thrown hot sand into the desert winds so that it would be blown at the Crusaders' army.

18.34   Salem] A religious and poetic usage for Jerusalem.

20.26   Acra's] Then the Christian quarter of Jerusalem.

20.30   Olivet] The Mount of Olives in Jerusalem.

20.37–38   pool . . . Hezekiah's] Cf. 2 Kings 20:20.

21.30   Vine] A middle-aged American who is one of Clarel's fellow pilgrims. He is described in I, 29, 31–39.

22.12   Admetus' shepherd] Apollo served as shepherd to King Admetus of Thessaly after being banished from Olympus for killing the Cyclopes.

22.18   Cecilia] St. Cecilia, patron saint of music.

22.30 Carthusian] The Carthusians are one of the strictest monastic orders of Roman Catholicism.

23.10 Sibyl's Golden Bough] The Golden Bough in Book VI of the *Aeneid*, to which the Cumaean Sibyl directs Aeneas, with instructions to seize it for help in getting to the underworld.

23.12 *Mortmain*] A Swedish revolutionist involved in the 1848 uprising who was later disillusioned.

23.14 Rolfe . . . Derwent] Rolfe is an American intellectual, adventurer, and traveler; Derwent is an Anglican priest.

23.19 Black Jew's] Abdon, the innkeeper in Jerusalem, a black Jew from India, perhaps from Cochin on the southwest coast.

24.5 Psalmanazer] George Psalmanazar (c. 1679–1763), pseudonym of an unidentified French impostor who successfully passed himself off as a native of Formosa.

24.8 *Peace . . . will*] Cf. Luke 2:14.

24.16 a decade dim] The 1840s.

25.35 Forty-eight] 1848, the year of revolutionary uprisings throughout Europe.

27.23 Margoth] A Jewish geologist encountered earlier in Jerusalem.

27.36–28.1 breastplate . . . Aaron] Described in Exodus 28.

28.6 Houndsditch] A street in Stepney, a Jewish section of the East End of London.

28.32 Genevan cloth] Clerical cloth from John Calvin's city.

29.7 Uriel Acosta] Jewish religious thinker (c. 1585–1640) who attacked orthodox doctrine and rabbinic authority. Born in Portugal and raised as a Roman Catholic, he later embraced Judaism and fled to Amsterdam, where his unorthodox writings brought him into conflict with both the Jewish community and the Dutch civil authorities.

29.40 Neander] Johann Neander (1789–1850), German historian and Christian theologian of Jewish parentage; he changed his name from Mendel (not Mendelssohn) at age 17 when he was baptized.

30.22 Mamre's plain] Where Abraham and Sarah receive three visitors, one of whom informs them that they will have a son (Genesis 18:1–15).

31.29 Nehemiah] Another of the pilgrims, an old American of an evangelical and millenarian disposition.

31.30 Lot's wave] The Dead Sea; its Arabic name is Bahr Lut (Sea of Lot). In Genesis 19:24, Sodom and Gomorrah are consumed by fire and

brimstone; the Dead Sea was said to occupy the plain on which they had stood.

34.13   *Afterward*] This song concludes a masque, enacted before the pilgrims in a ravine outside the Greek Orthodox monastery at Mar Saba, on a holy day.

34.14   Saturn's land] Saturn was said to rule the world in the Golden Age.

36.3   pantler's] Butler's.

38.17   Sylvanus] Roman forest god, said to have been banished along with the other pagan gods in the dawn of Christianity.

38.22   *Pan . . . dead!*] The story that a voice called out to one of the sailors on shipboard during the reign of Tiberius was first told by Plutarch in his essay on "Why the Oracles Ceased to Give Answers."

39.27   Ungar] A mercenary former Confederate officer who joins the pilgrims at Mar Saba.

40.1   Poor Clare] One of the Second Order of St. Francis, called Poor Clares.

40.3   Cordelier] French name for a member of the Franciscan order of Recollects.

41.28   *Dirge*] Narrator's interjection as the pilgrims reenter Jerusalem at dawn on Ash Wednesday.

42.4   Orcus] Roman underworld god, identified with Pluto and Hades.

42.7   Azrael's] The angel who, in both Judaic and Islamic tradition, separates the soul from the body at death.

42.23   Stabat] The medieval hymn "Stabat Mater Dolorosa" ("The mother stood sorrowfully"), ascribed to Jacopone da Todi.

43.37   Thammuz'] Or Tammuz; Sumerian, Babylonian, and Assyrian fertility god whose resurrection was celebrated each spring.

43.38   Joel's glen] The valley of decision, or Jehoshaphat, in Joel 3:2–16.

44.7   Ruth] Clarel's beloved, whom he meets in Jerusalem before setting out; she dies while he is away on his pilgrimage.

44.19   *Via Crucis*] "Way of the Cross": the Via Dolorosa, the road in Jerusalem taken by Jesus from the place of judgment to Calvary.

45.36–37   "They wire . . . talk;] A telegraph cable was laid across the Atlantic in 1858 and used for a few weeks; a permanent transatlantic connection was first achieved in 1866.

46.2   wynd] A narrow street or passageway.

47.8   *John Marr*]   As described in a long prose passage that introduces the poem, John Marr is a retired sailor living as a carpenter in a prairie town, and suffering from a sense of isolation from the townspeople who know nothing of the sea: "So limited unavoidably was the mental reach, and by consequence the range of sympathy, in this particular band of domestic emigrants, hereditary tillers of the soil, that the ocean, but a hearsay to their fathers, had now through yet deeper inland removal become to themselves little more than a rumor traditional and vague." Marr muses on his former shipmates, as on his dead wife and child: "He invokes these visionary ones,—striving, as it were, to get into verbal communion with them, or, under yet stronger illusion, reproaching them for their silence."

49.14   famous old sea-ditty]   "Farewell and adieu to you Spanish ladies, / Farewell and adieu to you ladies of Spain, / For we've received orders to sail for old England, / And we hope in a short time to see you again."

49.19   the Deadman]   Dedman Point, near Plymouth.

50.7   blue-blazes]   Those of a Bengal light, a torch used for signaling at night.

50.7   shank-painters]   Short ropes or chains for fixing anchors to a ship's side.

50.13   *Haglets*]   Hacklets or kittiwakes, small gulls.

50.28   Plate Fleet]   The fleet that annually brought the product of American silver mines to Spain.

51.22   Opher]   Usually Ophir; in the Old Testament, a place rich in gold, precious stones, and other treasure; the precise location is unknown.

58.12   Ned Bunn]   One of Melville's pseudonyms for his sailing companion Richard Tobias Greene, the "Toby" of his novel *Typee*, with whom he deserted the whaler *Acushnet* in 1842 in the Marquesas.

60.16   *Timoleon*]   Greek statesman and general (died c. 337 B.C.), known for his defiance of tyrants; his life is recounted by Plutarch, the source for Melville's poem.

61.10   Argos and Cleone]   The latter is also called Cleonoe; these cities were at war with Corinth, c. 368–66 B.C.

61.18   Timophanes]   Timoleon's rash older brother whose life Timoleon saved in battle. Timophanes declared himself tyrant of Corinth, and, ignoring his brother's pleas, was finally assassinated while (as in Plutarch's account) Timoleon, who was effectively an accomplice, stood by weeping.

63.6   Ate]   Greek goddess of discord.

63.33–34   false . . . fratricide] Some accounts claim that Timoleon himself committed the murder.

64.13   Phocion] Athenian general (c. 402–318 B.C.) executed on a false charge of treason.

68.8   Decameron folk] In Boccaccio's 14th-century work, the seven ladies and three gentlemen who leave plague-ridden Florence for villas outside and tell each other a hundred stories on ten summer days.

69.11   Urania] A female astronomer, named after the Muse of Astronomy and also after Milton's muse of *Paradise Lost*.

69.21   Albani's porch] The porch of the Villa Albani in Rome (now Villa Torlonia), containing an important collection of classical sculpture.

70.2   arm'd Virgin] Athena.

71.15   Teniers'] David Teniers the Younger (1610–90), Flemish genre painter.

72.11–12   Jacob's . . . angel] Genesis 32:24–32.

72.13   *Shelley's Vision*] Presumably a reference to an episode of Shelley's last days when, it is reported, he saw a shadowy vision of himself that inquired of him: "Are you satisfied?" The incident was first described by Thomas Medwin in his *Life of P. B. Shelley* (1847).

72.23   Saint Stephen] First Christian martyr, stoned to death (Acts, chapters 6–7).

73.32   Jael] In Judges 4, Jael kills the defeated Canaanite general Sisera in her tent by driving a tent-peg through his skull.

75.11   *Archipelago*] The Aegean.

76.8   *Rose of Sharon*] "I am the rose of Sharon and the lily of the valleys" (Song of Solomon 2:1).

77.2   *Coming through the rye*] Cf. Robert Burns's air "Comin' thro' the rye, poor body, / Comin' thro' the rye."

77.29   Dives] A name given to the rich man in the parable of Lazarus the beggar in Luke 16:19–31; from "dives," Latin for "rich," as used in the Vulgate Bible.

78.6   Pharpar . . . Abana] In 2 Kings 5:12, Naaman the Syrian captain, told by the prophet Elisha to wash seven times in the Jordan to cure his leprosy, protests: "*Are* not Abana and Pharpar, rivers of Damascus, better than all the waters of Israel?"

82.23   *Pontoosuce*] Lake Pontoosuc, north of Pittsfield, Massachusetts.

85.13   *Billy in the Darbies*] At the end of Melville's *Billy Budd, Sailor*, after the hero has been hanged for the killing of Claggart, his shipmates "made

some lines which, after circulating among the shipboard crews for a while, finally got rudely printed at Portsmouth as a ballad. The title given to it was the sailor's." Darbies are handcuffs.

85.20   jewel-block]   Pulley at the end of the fore and main topsail yards on a square-rigged ship.

87.3   *Suspiria Noctis*]   "Sighs of the night."

89.10   Shiloh]   See note 9.1.

89.11   Manassas]   Manassas Junction, Virginia, about 30 miles from Washington. Civil War battles fought near the junction on July 21, 1861, and August 29–30, 1862, were generally known in the South as the first and second battles of Manassas, and in the North as the first and second battles of Bull Run. Both were Confederate victories.

89.16   Week of Battles]   See note 10.6.

89.25   Fair Oaks and Seven Pines]   Fair Oaks and Seven Pines, Virginia, about seven miles from Richmond; scene of a battle (May 31–June 1, 1862) in which McClellan defeated the Confederates under J. E. Johnston.

90.15   Cannæ]   In Apulia, Italy; the site of Hannibal's overwhelming victory in 216 B.C. over the Romans.

90.16   Roncesvaux]   Or Roncesvalles; mountain pass in the Pyrenees where in 778 the entire rearguard of Charlemagne's army was killed in a battle with Arabs.

90.19   Aceldama]   The potter's field said to have been south of Jerusalem, and purchased for the price of Judas Iscariot's bribe; the name means "field of blood" (cf. Acts 1:15–19).

91.4   River of Death]   Chickamauga Creek in northern Georgia, where the Confederates defeated Union forces commanded by Major General William Rosecrans, September 19–20, 1863.

91.7   the Great Admiral]   Rear Admiral John Dahlgren, who attempted in 1863 to seize Charleston Harbor from the Confederates.

92.4–5   *"A bird . . . matter."*]   Ecclesiastes 10:20.

102.4   Phengites]   Selenite, a stone much valued in the past for its beauty and for its supposed supernatural qualities.

102.20   Hæmonian]   Haemonia, or Aemonia, was an early name of Thessaly.

102.27   Hero]   A priestess of Aphrodite whose lover, Leander, drowned while swimming the Hellespont to meet her.

102.32   heliochryse]   "Sun-gold": a bright yellow flower.

102.32   ámomum]   Indian spice-plant.

102.36   Chrysophoræ]   "Gold-appareled women."

103.23   Pelops' . . . eburnine]   The ivory shoulder given Pelops by Zeus had the power, if touched, to heal any complaint or disorder.

103.25   Heliades]   Daughters of the Sun, sisters of Phaeton whose tears at his death turned into drops of amber.

107.24   Quonecktacut]   The Connecticut River.

110.29   Job's . . . Yard]   Job's Coffin is the constellation Delphinus; the Golden Yard is Orion's belt.

110.31   Circle of the Bestiary]   The zodiac.

111.30   d'Acunha's isle]   Tristan da Cunha in the South Atlantic.

114.36   Caÿster's]   Ancient name for a river in Asia Minor, now called Kucuk Menderes River (Turkey); Ephesus was near its mouth.

115.3   Eurotas]   A river in Laconia in Greece.

117.4   *Place de la Pucelle*]   Joan of Arc was burned in Rouen in 1431 at the Place du Vieux-Marché, just above the Place de la Pucelle.

125.36   Gheber]   Or Gabar; a term formerly applied to the Zoroastrians who remained in Iran following the Arab Muslim conquest.

127.3   *Sheridan's Ride*]   On October 19, 1864, Confederate troops under Lieutenant General Jubal A. Early attacked Union forces at Cedar Creek, Virginia, and drove them from their positions. Major General Philip Henry Sheridan, who was returning to his command from a conference in Washington, received news of the battle in Winchester, Virginia, and rode to the front on his horse Rienzi, rallying stragglers and directing a successful counterattack.

132.34   young Hebrew girl]   Jephthah's daughter, in Judges 11.

134.1   *Tallulah*]   A waterfall in Rabun County in northeastern Georgia; the name is Cherokee in origin.

134.14   Teocalli]   Aztec word for "temple," formerly sometimes applied broadly to other American Indian structures.

136.3   *Vincent Ogé*]   In the original edition, this poem was prefaced by the following note: "Fragments of a poem hitherto unpublished, upon a revolt of the free persons of color, in the island of St. Domingo (now Hayti), in the years 1790–1." Jacques Vincent Ogé (1750–91) was executed at Cap-Français after an unsuccessful attempt to emancipate Haitian slaves.

146.5   Ritter]   Knight.

146.6   Schwillensaufenstein]   Comic place name suggesting drunkenness.

146.15   Gasthaus]   Inn.

146.21   wasser]   Water.

147.17   *Wein Geist*]   "Wine Spirit."

147.19   Berauscht]   Drunk.

147.21   Eberschwein]   Wild boar.

148.23   blaetter]   Leaves.

148.25   windsbraut]   Strong gust of wind.

148.29   Jahrdausand]   Millennium.

149.3–4   De harpe . . . wind;]   "The harp turned to stone, the tune to wind."

149.7   stein and schwein]   Stone and boar.

149.9   Ur-lied]   Primal song.

149.12   Und alles . . . eins]   "And all becomes one."

149.15   Mondenlicht]   Moonlight.

149.17–18   In Mädchenlieb . . . ist dein]   "In the love of a girl or drunken fit, the Absolute is yours."

149.30   sehr bemerkbar ist]   Is very remarkable.

150.1   tofe]   Dove.

150.8   "Symbolik,"]   Theological or other religious symbolism.

150.11   Heldenbuch]   Book of Heroes.

150.14   Hildebrand]   Hero of Old High German epic.

150.14–15   Vater . . . Sohn]   The father and the son.

150.18   Sagen Cyclus full-endet]   Tale-cycle completed.

150.25   versteh]   Understand.

150.26   Lied]   Song.

151.10   outsigned]   Excellent (from a literal translation of the German *ausgezeichnet*).

151.13   *"Recessit in Franciam."*]   "He retreats to France": from the medieval Latin scholar's song, *"Huc usque, me miseram,"* *Carmina Burana* no. 126.

151.14–17   *"Et affectu . . . optime."*]   "All must play the harp / and produce the good old songs / and the beating heart / and the body's every gesture / and most of all, scholars / who best love a festival": Lines 3–8 of *"Tempus hoc lititie,"* *Carmina Burana* no. 216.

151.19   Der teufel's los]   "The devil's loose."

151.19   Bal Mabille]   A public dance-hall.

151.22   Orphée aux Enfers]   "Orpheus in the Underworld" (1858), operetta by Jacques Offenbach, which includes the famous "Can-Can" dance music.

151.29   Frankenland]   France.

152.9   cocodettes]   Tarts.

152.11–12   "D'ou vient . . . Dieu!"]   "Where is this great gentleman from? O holy name of God!"

152.18–20   Rond Point . . . Rabelais]   Grand circle on the Champs Elysées in Paris, between the Place de la Concorde and what is now the Etoile, near the rue de Rabelais.

152.28   garçe]   Girl.

152.35   Barriere balls]   Parisian dance halls.

153.4   l'on s'amuse]   "A good time is had."

153.7   gallop]   Galop.

153.20   Teufel]   Devil.

154.3   Samuel Brown]   A parody of Poe's "Annabel Lee" (see American Poetry: The Nineteenth Century, Volume One, p. 550).

155.13   Granny's House]   A parody of Tennyson's "Locksley Hall."

159.8   "The Day Is Done"]   A parody of Longfellow's poem of the same name (see American Poetry: The Nineteenth Century, Volume One, p. 383).

160.21   Jacob]   A parody of Wordsworth's "Lucy" poem: "She dwelt among the untrodden ways / Beside the springs of Dove."

161.5   "When Lovely Woman"]   A parody of Oliver Goldsmith's song from She Stoops to Conquer (1773): "When lovely woman stoops to folly."

163.5   All or Nothing]   A parody of Emerson.

164.7   Hadramaut]   A self-parody by Taylor.

165.6   Camerados]   A parody of Whitman.

175.11   bulgine]   Steam locomotive.

178.3   Blue Beard's Closet]   In the popular tale as told by Charles Perrault, Blue Beard, a man of great wealth, has murdered several of his wives and hidden their bodies in a locked chamber.

178.14   Guido]   Guido Reni (1575–1642), Italian painter.

179.28   Arachne]   Greek for spider.

190.23   Peak . . . Lassen's name]   Mt. Lassen, at the southern end of the Cascade Range, named for the pioneer Peter Lassen (1800–59).

193.9   "*Lalla Rookh*"]   Thomas Moore's 1817 work, consisting of four Oriental tales in verse linked by a prose romance.

195.3   Fadladeen]   The grand chamberlain of the harem in *Lalla Rookh*.

196.3   Feramorz]   The poet (a Sultan in disguise) in *Lalla Rookh*.

201.16   Dodona]   The site in Epirus of the oldest Greek oracle, where a grove of oak trees sometimes delivered the oracles.

203.1   *Ethnogenesis*]   The genesis or beginnings of a race. The Southern Congress (or Convention) in Montgomery, Alabama, was attended by delegates from South Carolina, Georgia, Florida, Alabama, Mississippi, and Louisiana; they met on February 4, 1861, adopted a provisional constitution for the Confederate States of America, and unanimously elected Jefferson Davis as provisional president.

204.14   Moultrie]   Colonel William Moultrie built a fort on Sullivan's Island off Charleston, South Carolina, and successfully defended it against a British naval attack on June 28, 1776; it was later named after him.

204.14   Eutaw]   The battle of Eutaw Springs, South Carolina, September 8, 1781, later celebrated in William Gilmore Simms' novel *Eutaw* (1856).

209.9   The Poet of "The Woodlands"]   William Gilmore Simms, who lived on the plantation "Woodlands" in South Carolina.

211.15–16   The sea . . . Miriam's song!]   Cf. Exodus 15:19–21.

211.20   Mizpeh's]   The home of Jephthah in Gilead (Judges 11).

212.8   I wake like Boaz]   Cf. Ruth 3:7–8.

213.12   Eutaw]   See note 204.14.

213.16   Rutledge]   John Rutledge (1739–1800), president of South Carolina General Assembly (1776–78), then governor (1779–81) and Supreme Court justice.

213.16   Laurens]   John Laurens (1754–82), South Carolina Continental Army officer and diplomat, killed in South Carolina in one of the last skirmishes of the Revolutionary War.

214.3   Sachem's head]   In North Carolina.

215.18   Calpe]   An old name for Gibraltar.

219.9   *Lines*]   *The Courier*, in which this version of the poem was originally published, identifies it as having been written "for the late ceremonial coronation of the Confederate graves at Magnolia."

221.26   "*Love! . . . part?*"]   Hayne notes: "These words, or words to this effect, were the last which Charlotte Brontë uttered." The novelist's last

words are given in Mrs. Gaskell's *Life of Charlotte Brontë* (1857) as: "Oh, I am not going to die, am I? He will not separate us, we have been so happy."

222.3   *My Lighthouses*]   The poem is dated "Genoa, November 30."

234.10   Himmaleh]   The Himalayas.

242.27   Sabachthani]   "Eloi, Eloi, lama sabachthani?" (Aramaic): "My God, my God, why has thou forsaken me?" (Mark 15:34).

246.28   Prima]   Prima Ballerina.

251.12   "Miles", and "Priscilla"]   In Longfellow's "The Courtship of Miles Standish," Priscilla Mullins chooses Miles Standish's surrogate suitor, John Alden.

252.18   Beatrice]   Beatrice Portinari (1266–90), the muse of Dante's *La Vita Nuova* and allegorized in the *Divine Comedy*.

273.12   Mazarin]   Usually "mazarine": a deep, rich blue.

273.26   Boanerges]   James and John, sons of Zebedee, called "sons of thunder" (Mark 3:17).

295.15   Sceptic Thomas]   "Doubting" Thomas (John 20:24–29).

311.30   "Made Flesh . . . us"]   John 1:14.

317.4   "*Ye cannot enter now*"]   Alfred Tennyson, "Guinevere," l. 168.

317.11   sad Harold, . . . string]   Cf. Byron, *Childe Harold's Pilgrimage*, Canto I, stanza XIII: "He seized his harp, which he at times could string, / And strike, albeit with untaught melody, / When deemed he no strange ear was listening."

324.11   *Marching Through Georgia*]   Sherman's army left Atlanta on November 16, 1864, and entered Savannah on December 21.

325.12   "*Come Home, Father!*"]   This song was featured in the temperance play *Ten Nights in a Barroom*, frequently performed from around 1864.

327.3   Prelude]   This poem served as the introduction to Stedman's anthology of American poetry, published in 1900; the "choir" in the first line is comprised of the voices of all the poets included.

328.18   *Statue on the Capitol*]   *Columbia, the Goddess of Liberty* (or *Armed Liberty*) by Thomas Crawford (1814–57) stands 19.5 feet high, surmounting the Capitol's dome, her right hand holding a sheathed sword and her left

resting on a shield and holding an olive branch. Her helmet is topped with eagles' plumes. The piece was installed in 1863 during the Civil War.

335.3   *Judith*]   The story of the slaying of the Philistine chief Holofernes by Judith of Bethulia is recounted in the apocryphal book of Judith.

335.8−9   Ashkelon . . . Gaza]   Cf. Jeremiah 47:5. Ashkelon and Gaza were two of the five principal cities of the Philistines.

335.11−13   Baal-perazim . . . Rephaim]   Sites of victories of David over the Philistines in 2 Samuel 5:18−25.

335.18   the seventh angel]   Cf. Revelation 10:7−11.

338.3   *Ode . . . Dec'd.*]   One of the verse "tributes" by Emmeline Grangerford in Chapter XVII of *Adventures of Huckleberry Finn*.

339.9   Everlasting light]   Cf. Isaiah 60:19−20.

340.16   Bill Nye]   Pseudonym of Edgar Wilson Nye (1850−96), popular humorist and lecturer.

341.2   bowers]   Two jacks—of trumps, and of the same color—in the game of euchre.

341.23   twenty-four jacks]   "Jacks" was erroneously printed in the first edition as "packs," and the error has been repeated in many subsequent editions.

342.21   "outsides"]   Outside passengers on stage coaches.

343.2   *the Only . . . Muller."*]   See Whittier's poem, *American Poetry: The Nineteenth Century, Volume One*, p. 458.

345.2   *Modoc War*]   Fought in 1872−73 against Modoc Indians resisting confinement on a reservation in Oregon.

345.8   Captain Jack]   Kintpuash (1837?−1873), called "captain" because of his fondness for brass buttons and military ornaments, was a leader of the Modoc and a claimant to the chieftanship held by Schonchin. He was hanged for killing General Edward R. S. Canby under a flag of truce.

346.7   Schonchin]   Modoc chieftain.

348.2   *October 10, 1871*]   The great Chicago Fire burned from October 8−10, 1871.

348.13   cry of Macedon to Paul]   Cf. Acts 16:9.

369.17   Kamiakin's]   Kamiak Butte, Washington.

370.5   Cariboo]   Mountain range in Canada, west of the Rockies.

372.5   *Père La Chaise*]   The Père Lachaise cemetery in Paris, where many
celebrated people were buried after 1804.

372.8   tomb . . . Eloise]   The monument to Abelard and Heloise (d. 1141
and 1163).

373.9   "bravest . . . brave"]   Marshal Ney (1769–1815), called the "bravest
of the brave" by Napoleon Bonaparte; he was executed for treason by the
restored Bourbon regime following the battle of Waterloo.

373.15   Commune fell]   One of the last Communard strongholds to fall,
the cemetery was captured by troops of the Versailles government after bitter
fighting on May 27, 1871.

373.18   *Our Golden Gate*]   The strait forming the entrance to San Francisco Bay was so named by Frémont in 1846; the "our" differentiates it from
the Golden Gate of Constantinople.

375.3   Gates of Hercules]   More commonly, "Pillars of Hercules"; the
Rock of Gibraltar and Jebel Musa, in Ceuta, Morocco, both at the eastern
end of the Strait of Gibraltar.

380.7   Zembla]   Nova Zembla (or Novaya Zemlya), two Russian islands
in the Arctic northeast of Archangel.

380.8   Mount Désert]   Island off the coast of Maine.

380.31   days . . . Sibyl sings]   The Cumaean Sibyl, in Virgil's Fourth
Eclogue.

381.16   Pike]   Pike county, Illinois.

383.3–4   *Buddha . . . Hay*]   Adams described the origin of the poem in a
letter to John Hay:

                                                        "26 April, 1895.

My Dear John:
    Once La Farge and I, on our rambles, stopped for an hour to meditate
under the sacred Bo-tree of Buddha in the ruined and deserted city of Anu-
radjapura in the jungle of Ceylon; and, then, resuming our course, we presently found ourselves on the quiet bosom of the Indian Ocean. Perhaps I was
a little bored by the calm of the tropical sea, or perhaps it was the greater
calm of Buddha that bored me. At all events I amused a tedious day or two
by jotting down in a note-book the lines which you profess to want. They are
yours. Do not let them go further.

                                            Ever affectionately,
                                            HENRY ADAMS."

The narrative of "Buddha and Brahma" is derived from an anecdote from *Questions of King Milinda*, as it appeared in F. Max Muller's *Natural Religion*.

383.6   Sakya Muni]   A name for the Buddha, literally "sage of the Sakya" (the Sakya were the tribe Gautama Siddhartha, the Buddha, was born into).

383.24   Eight-fold Way]   The Eight-fold Path of Buddhism, comprising right views, right intention, right speech, right conduct, right livelihood, right effort, right mindfulness, and right concentration.

384.24   Mogadha]   Magadha, an ancient kingdom in northern India and the region in which Buddhism originated.

385.15   Kshatriya]   The warrior or ruling caste into which the Buddha had also been born.

390.8–9   patriotic gore . . . Baltimore]   Twelve citizens of Baltimore were killed by soldiers of the 6th Massachusetts Regiment on April 19, 1861, after a pro-secessionist mob attacked the regiment as it marched through the city.

390.24   Carroll's]   Charles Carroll of Carrollton (1736–1832), signer of the Declaration of Independence.

390.25   Howard's]   John Eager Howard (1752–1827), officer in the American Revolution who was severely wounded at the battle of Eutaw Springs; he later served as governor of Maryland.

390.32   Ringgold's]   Major Samuel Ringgold of Maryland (1800–46), army officer who fought the Seminoles in Florida and was killed at the battle of Palo Alto in the Mexican War.

391.1   Watson's]   Colonel William Watson (1808–46), a Marylander and leader of the "Baltimore Battalion" in the Mexican War; he died at the siege of Monterey.

391.2   May]   Captain Charles Augustus May (1819–64), born in Washington, D.C., commanded cavalry under Zachary Taylor at the Mexican War battles of Palo Alto, Resaca de la Palma, Monterey, and Buena Vista.

391.10   *Key*]   Francis Scott Key, author of "The Star-Spangled Banner," was a Marylander; see biographical sketch in *American Poetry: The Nineteenth Century, Volume One*, p. 1009.

391.17   *"Sic semper",*]   In full, *sic semper tyrannis*: "thus be it ever to tyrants," motto of the state of Virginia.

396.17   Gaspé Bay]   Bay at the easternmost end of the Gaspé Peninsula, Quebec, Canada.

396.17   La Pointe]   Fishing village in northern Wisconsin, on an island in Lake Superior; the French established a fortified trading post there in 1693.

399.4   Bennen] Johann Joseph Bennen, a renowned Swiss Alpine guide killed in an avalanche.

409.11   bottomry] In maritime law, a contract in which a ship is pledged as security in return for a loan; if the ship sinks, the lender loses his money.

412.6   Antonio] Prospero's antagonistic brother in Shakespeare's *The Tempest*.

412.9   *Glynn*] Glynn County, Georgia; the marshes are near the coastal town of Brunswick.

416.16   Chester] County in southeastern Pennsylvania.

420.29–30   Habersham . . . Hall] The Chattahoochee River rises in Habersham and Hall counties in northeast Georgia.

426.11   *Jackson*] Confederate Lieutenant General Thomas J. ("Stonewall") Jackson, who died at Guiney Station, Virginia, on May 10, 1863, eight days after being accidentally shot by his own men during the battle of Chancellorsville.

427.9   *The Revenge of Hamish*] Taken from an episode in Chapter III of *Macleod of Dare* by Scottish novelist William Black (1841–98) that had appeared in *Harper's Magazine*.

434.2   Megaceph] Greek: "large (or swelled) head."

434.15–16   The cur . . . lea] A parody of the opening quatrain of Gray's "Elegy Written in a Country Churchyard" (1750): "The curfew tolls the knell of parting day, / The lowing herd winds slowly o'er the lea, / The plowman homeward plods his weary way, / And leaves the world to darkness and to me."

435.27   We, like old Muhlenberg, "care not to stay."] Cf. William Augustus Muhlenberg's (1796–1877) lyric "I Would Not Live Alway": "I would not live alway: I ask not to stay / Where storm after storm rises dark o'er the way."

441.21   *Bartholdi Statue*] Frédéric-Auguste Bartholdi's "Liberty Lighting Up the World," popularly known as "The Statue of Liberty," unveiled in 1886 in New York Harbor.

443.18   single tax on land] As advocated by the economist Henry George (1839–1897).

446.23   "Ai nostri monti"] "*Ai nostri monti ritorneremo / L'antera pace vi godremo*" ("We will return to our mountains; the peace of old we will enjoy there"): duet in the last act of Verdi's *Il Trovatore* (1853).

457.26   brazen giant] The Colossus of Rhodes, one of the Seven Wonders of the World.

458.10   *Venus . . . Louvre*]   The Venus de Milo.

458.25   *Cranes of Ibycus*]   According to a story told of the Greek lyric poet Ibycus (second half of 6th century B.C.), as he was being murdered by robbers near Corinth, he called on a flock of cranes flying overhead to bear witness. Later, one of the murderers, seeing some cranes, burst out, "These are the cranes that are conscious of the death of Ibycus" and the assassins were caught.

463.20   Gabirol]   11th-century Jewish poet and philosopher of Spain.

487.3   *Twasinta's Seminoles*]   A narrative poem in 251 Spenserian stanzas set against the background of the Seminole wars (1816–42); Twasinta is the Seminole chief in the poem.

491.1   *The Lute of Afric's Tribe*]   The poem is dedicated "To the memory of Dr. J. McSimpson, a colored Author of Anti-Slavery Ballads."

491.2–3   When Israel . . . songs]   Cf. Psalm 137:1–3.

496.4   *Millet's World-Famous Painting*]   *L'Homme a la houe* (1862) by Jean François Millet (1814–75).

498.10   hill that Dobell saw]   English poet Sydney Dobell (1824–74) wrote of war's "great grave upon the hill of blood" in "The Common Grave" (in *Sonnets of War*, 1855, a volume of poems on the Crimean War).

501.18   Himavats]   Himalayas.

502.6   sweet . . . seer]   "Kano Hogai, into whose mouth I put the following summary of Eastern life, was the greatest Japanese painter of recent times, a genius whose penetration to the heart of early oriental ideals seemed like special inspiration. He was for years one of my dearest friends, and in Japanese art my most valued teacher. I have represented him as the reincarnate spirit of oriental art. His death in 1888 was a national calamity." —Fenollosa's note.

502.21   Kásŭga shrine]   "The ancient city of Nara, the capital of Japan in the eighth century, still glories in a grove of mighty pines and cedars which sweep away for a mile to the Eastern mountains, sheltering the dainty buildings of the great Shinto temple, Kásŭga . . . There in the spring and summer of 1886 I spent with Hogai many weeks in delightful study."—from Fenollosa's note.

504.4   Vasubandhu]   "Vasubandhu, the greatest follower of Nagarjuna, and one of the most important patriarchs in the line of esoteric transmission, was a man whose extraordinary spiritual and intellectual endowments enabled him largely to mould the subsequent course of Northern Buddhism, much as St. Paul did that of Christianity. He is the author of numerous works which remain today a cornerstone of Japanese Buddhism."—from Fenollosa's note.

504.19–20   Bodhisats . . . Arhats]   "These are the titles of two degrees in Buddhist saintship. The Arhat, in Northern Buddhism, is one who has attained only subjective purification by withdrawing from the world. He bears marks of the severity of his ascetic discipline. A Bodhisattwa is one who, through the passion of divine love for men, has mingled with the evil of the world and overcome it, thus winning a leadership in the overshadowing army of the good. He is represented as of beautiful face and heavenly mien."—Fenollosa's note.

505.15–18   Hangchow . . . Sientang]   "I have chosen from the several periods of Chinese culture that most typically artistic one of the later Sung Dynasty, whose idealistic outburst of Buddhist illumination in the twelfth century rendered its capital, Hangchow, a birthplace of inspired forms . . . It lay a few miles inland, between the Sientang Estuary and the beautiful 'Western Lake,' surrounded by groves and picturesque mountains, among whose nooks and crags grew mossy temples and secluded villas, where worked the artists, poets, statesmen, and philosophers of that golden age."—from Fenollosa's note.

512.2   Kukai]   "Kukai, or Kobo Daishi, one of the three great founders of Esoteric Buddhism in Japan, spent many years of his youth in study at a famous Chinese monastery. About to return to his native country early in the ninth century, he meditated long concerning the site of his projected temple. Leaving the decision to the powers of heaven, he is said to have thrown his vagra, or metal mace, into the air in the direction of Japan, whither it was borne by divine means, and lodged in a tall tree on the top of Koya mountain."—from Fenollosa's note.

513.6   Chionin's bell]   The bell of Chion-in, temple of the Jodo sect in Kyoto, cast in 1636, is the largest of its kind in Japan, measuring 18 feet in diameter and weighing 74 tons.

513.8   Nobunaga]   Oda Nobunaga (1534–82), general whose victories resulted in the partial reunification of Japan.

513.9   Lady O-tsu]   Princess Oku, seventh-century poet whose work appears in the anthology *Manyoshu*, the oldest extant collection of poetry.

513.10   Fujiwara]   The Fujiwara were the most powerful family in Japan from the ninth to the twelfth century.

513.11   Komachi]   Ono no Komachi (fl. 833–857), legendary beauty and poet.

513.23   Daitokuji]   Buddhist temple in Kyoto.

514.22   Mount Hiyeizan]   Mt. Hiei, near Kyoto.

514.23 Jizo.] A Bodhisattva, the guardian of travelers and children, frequently depicted in Japanese roadside shrines.

519.10 Corinna] In Robert Herrick's (1868–1938) poem "Corinna's Going A-Maying."

519.12 Castara] Muse of William Habington's *Castara* (1634).

519.22–24 Beau Waller . . . rose] Edmund Waller; the poem invoked is his song "Go, Lovely Rose."

525.20 Pentelicus'] Mountain in Greece, from which was quarried the marble used for the Parthenon.

529.3 *W. S. M.*] W. S. Monroe, the poet's younger brother.

530.4 Surrey] The poet, soldier, and courtier Henry Howard (1517?–47), Earl of Surrey, was beheaded for treason.

530.13 Framlingham] Town and parish in east central Suffolk; Surrey was reburied there with a monument completed in 1614.

534.20 Dowgate] Dowgate Hill, a street in London below Southwark Bridge.

534.22 Saint Magnus . . . Dunstan] London churches: Saint Magnus the Martyr, noted for its low tower and cupola, built by Christopher Wren in 1676, and Saint Dunstan's in the East with tower and steeple (added in 1699) by Wren.

539.1 *Chartres*] The Cathedral of Notre-Dame (consecrated 1260) at Chartres, France.

539.16 cloud of witnesses] Cf. Hebrews 12:1.

541.1 *Tomb . . . Giunigi*] Jacope della Quercia's tomb of Ilaria del Carretto (d. 1405), wife of Paolo Giunigi, is in the Cathedral of San Martino at Lucca, Italy.

543.26 Denmark's enmity] Prussia and Austria defeated Denmark in 1864, leading to their joint annexation of Schleswig-Holstein. The two duchies were ceded to Prussia in 1866 after the Austro-Prussian War.

543.28 humble Austria . . . stroke] The Austro-Prussian War of 1866 lasted seven weeks and ended in the defeat of Austria.

545.18 Zola's friends] Supporters of Emile Zola, who came to the defense of Captain Alfred Dreyfus, a Jewish staff officer wrongfully convicted of spying for Germany and sentenced to life imprisonment, in the open letter "J'Accuse" (1898); Zola was subsequently convicted of libel and sentenced to a year in prison, but escaped to England.

545.24–25 The Powers . . . Crete] Fighting between Christians and Muslims in Crete claimed thousands of lives in 1896–97, with both Christian

insurgents and Turkish troops committing atrocities. Six European powers (Great Britain, France, Italy, Germany, Austria-Hungary, Russia) eventually imposed a settlement removing Turkish troops and giving Crete autonomy within the Ottoman Empire.

548.2   Helen's brothers] The Dioscuri, Castor and Pollux.

549.3–4   Pelides . . . Thetis] Achilles; the name Pelides means "son of Peleius," king of Phthiotis in Thessaly; Achilles' mother was the sea-deity Thetis.

549.19   Phthia] A region in Thessaly, in northern Greece.

552.21   *Bargello*] Thirteenth-century Floretine palace celebrated for its art collection.

556.4   Yang-tse Kiang] Yangtse (Yangzi) River.

556.11   Han-Yang . . . Tchin-Ting] Han-Yang is a town on the Yangtese, in east central Hupeh province; Woo-hoo, or Wa-hu, is a former treaty port on the Yangtse, and Tchin-Ting, or Cheng-ting (Zhegding), is located in what is now Hebei province.

556.12   Keou-Kang] Chiu-chiang (Jiujiang), river-port on the Yangtse, downriver from Han-Yang; a center for porcelain export.

569.18   sciography] Sciagraphy, in drawing, is the art of delineating shadows (i.e., shading).

574.14   quaker-maid] Bluet.

577.34   Pictured Rocks] Cliffs along the southern shore of Lake Superior in the Upper Peninsula of Michigan.

588.1   *Max Nordau*] The poem is written in satiric response to the Hungarian writer's attack in *Degeneration* (1892–93) on what he considered to be decadent poetry.

593.2   A. T. SCHUMANN] Alanson Tucker Schumann, homeopathic doctor and poet, a neighbor of Robinson's in his hometown of Gardiner, Maine.

620.13   Wagner] Fort Wagner, on Morris Island near Charleston, where the 54th Massachusetts Regiment, commanded by Col. Robert Shaw, lost 272 of its 650 men during an unsuccessful assault on July 18, 1863.

620.14   Olustee] Village in North Florida where, on February 20, 1864, Union forces were defeated on February 20, 1864, in what is sometimes called the battle of Ocean Pond. Three out of the eight Union regiments engaged were made up of black soldiers.

620.17   Pillow] Dozens of black soldiers were killed after surrendering at Fort Pillow, Tennessee, on April 12, 1864, by Confederate troops commanded by Nathan Bedford Forrest.

627.3   *Oktahutchee*]   The North Canadian River in Oklahoma.

629.23   Tulledegas]   The Talladega Mountains in east central Alabama.

630.3   *Tuckanuck*]   Island near Nantucket, where Lodge spent many summers.

635.3   *Ampezzo*]   In the Dolomite Alps of northern Italy. The place names are all local; Cristallo is a mountain peak, as is Sorapis.

640.16   *Rodin's . . . Icare"*]   Rodin's marble piece is called *L'Illusion, fille d'Icare* (Illusion, the Daughter of Icarus).

642.5   Skamander]   River rising near Mt. Ida and Troy, and flowing into the Hellespont; the Turkish name is Kucuk Menderes River.

642.16   *the Concert*]   This painting in the Pitti Palace in Florence is now ascribed to Titian.

647.13   *Pandora's Songs*]   These songs are sung by Pandora in Stickney's verse-play *Prometheus Pyrphoros* (Prometheus the Fire-bearer).

651.9   *Sainte-Marguerite*]   A town on the seacoast near St. Nazaire in the Loire-Atlantique.

654.8   *Sunium*]   Ancient name for Sounion (also called Colonna), cape southeast of Athens; on its summit is a many-pillared temple of Poseidon.

654.23   *Mt. Lykaion*]   A mountain in Arcadia in the northern Peloponnesus said to have been sacred to Zeus; also spelled Lycaeus. The columns mentioned in the poem are not extant, and ancient accounts of them are based on hearsay.

658.13   Sorapis]   See note 635.3.

659.1   San Vito]   Town not far from Vicenza in the Veneto.

659.1   Cadore]   Titian's birthplace, on the river Piave.

660.1   *Sandro's Flora*]   In Sandro Botticelli's painting *La Primavera*.

19TH-CENTURY VERSIONS OF AMERICAN INDIAN POETRY

Unless otherwise indicated, material in quotation marks in the following notes is taken from the accompanying commentary in the source text. Where possible, tribal designations are given in the form adopted by the *Handbook of North American Indians* (Washington: Smithsonian Institution, 1978–   ). In a few cases, due to the lack of more specific information in the source texts, anachronistic terms have been used.

661.3–4   *The Song . . . Enemy*]   John Heckewelder describes the performance of this song as follows: "They sing it in short lines or sentences, not always the whole at one time, but most generally in detached parts, as time

permits and as the occasion or their feelings prompt them. Their accent is very pathetic, and the whole, in their language, produces considerable effect."

662.1   *Two Cherokee Songs*] Mitchill introduces these translations as follows: "These consist of but one sentence each, with a chorus. Nothing of length seems to exist among them. They repeat the song and the chorus until they are tired.—The words of both were written for me, by Mr. Hicks, a Cherokee of the half blood, with his own hand, both original and version, on the twentyfirst of December, 1805, in the presence of colonel Benjamin Hawkins, colonel R. J. Meigs, general Daniel Smith, of Tennessee, general Stephen R. Bradley, of Vermont, and Double Head, the famous warriour."

662.13   the Big Knives] White Americans.

662.14   I will go . . . friends] "The manner in which these words are sung cannot be described to the reader.—There is a strong expiration of the breath at the commencement of each sentence, and a sudden elevation of the voice at the termination. The Chief, as he passes, looks every person sternly in the face. Those who are disposed to join the expedition exclaim *Yeh, Yeh, Yeh,* with a powerful tone of voice; and this exclamation is continually repeated during the whole ceremony. It is, if I may so speak, the evidence of their enlistment. Those who are silent decline the invitation."

662.15   A clear sky] "[A] metaphorical expression [which] conveys to an Indian the same ideas which are conveyed to us by the words good fortune."

663.1–2   *Music . . . Indians*] The pictographs that accompany the text are described as follows: "These rude pictures are carved on a flat piece of wood, and serve to suggest to the minds of those who have learned the songs, the ideas, and their order of succession; the words are not variable, but a man must be taught them, otherwise, though from an inspection of the figure he might comprehend the idea, he would not know what to sing." The interlinear commentary on text and pictographs is reproduced in the notes which follow.

663.3   *Metai*] The midewiwin or medicine society of the Ojibwa.

663.5   Now I hear] "This, and the three following, are sung by the principal chief of the Metai, to the beat of his bwoin ah-keek, or drum. The lines from the sides of the head of the figure indicate hearing."

663.7   Who makes this river] "The second figure is intended to represent a river, and a beaver swimming down it."

663.9   Look at me] "This translation is by no means literal. The words express the boastful claims of a man, who sets himself up for the best and most skilful in the fraternity."

663.11   Who maketh] "By the bird, the medicine man means himself; he says, that his voice has called the people together. . . . The two lines drawn

across, between this figure and the next, indicate that here the dancing is to commence."

663.13   I fly about] "This figure of a bird, (probably an eagle or hawk,) seems intended to indicate the wakefulness of the senses, and the activity required to ensure success in hunting. The figure of the moose, which immediately follows, reminding the singer of the cunning and extreme shyness of that animal, the most difficult of all to kill."

663.15   I shoot your heart] "This apostrophe is mere boasting, and is sung with much gesticulation and grimace."

663.17   I make . . . fire] "This is a medicine man, disguised in the skin of a bear. The small parallelogram, under the bear, signifies fire, and they, by some composition of gunpowder, or other means, contrive to give the appearance of fire to the mouth and eyes of the bear skin, in which they go about the village late at night, bent on deeds of mischief, oftentimes of blood. We learn how mischievous are these superstitions, when we are informed, that they are the principal men of the Metai, who thus wander about the villages, in the disguise of a bear, to wreak their hatred on a sleeping rival, or their malice on an unsuspecting adversary. But the customs of the Indians require of any one who may see a medicine man on one of these excursions, to take his life immediately, and whoever does so is accounted guiltless."

663.18   I am able to call water] "Here the medicine man boasts of his power over the elements, and his ability to do injury or benefit. The segment of a circle with dots in it, represents water, and the two short lines touching the head of the figure, indicate that he can draw it to him."

664.1   I cause . . . the dead] "The lines drawn across the face of this figure, indicate poverty, distress, and sickness; the person is supposed to have suffered from the displeasure of the medicine man. Such is the religion of the Indians! Its boast is to put into the hands of the devout, supernatural means, by which he may wreak vengeance on his enemies, whether weak or powerful, whether they be found among the foes of his tribe, or the people of his own village. This Metai, so much valued and revered by them, seems to be only the instrument, in the hands of the crafty, for keeping in subjection the weak and the credulous, which may readily be supposed to be the greater part of the people."

664.4   I am such] "This boast of certain success in hunting, is another method by which he hopes to elevate himself in the estimation of his hearers. Having told them that he has the power to put them all to death, he goes on to speak of his infallible success in hunting, which will always enable him to be a valuable friend to such as are careful to secure his good will."

664.8   I walk about] "This first figure represents the wild cat, to whom, on account of his vigilance, the medicines for the cure of diseases were committed. The meaning probably is, that to those who have the shrewdness, the

watchfulness, and intelligence of the wild cat, is entrusted the knowledge of those powerful remedies, which, in the opinion of the Indians, not only control life, and avail to the restoration of health, but give an almost unlimited power over animals and birds."

664.9   I hear your mouth]   "The wild cat, (or the sensible and intelligent medicine man,) is always awake; or if he seems to sleep, by means of the supernatural powers of his medicine, he becomes acquainted with all that passes around him. If one man speaks evil of another, to bring sickness upon him, the wild cat hears and knows it; but confident in his own superior strength, he disregards it. At the bar they begin to dance. The lines from the mouth of the human figure, represent the speeches of the evil minded and malicious."

664.10   Now I come up]   "I am the master of the wild cats; and having heard your talk, I come up out of the ground to see what you do. This man, it appears, claims superiority over other medicine men, and now rouses himself to attend to what is passing. The bar across the neck of the figure representing the wild cat, indicates that he is just coming out of the earth."

664.11   Behold! I am wild cat]   "This figure, with open eyes and erect ears, denotes earnestness and attention."

664.13   I am a spirit]   "This is the figure of a medicine man, with his pah-gah-ko-gun-un, or the instrument with which he beats his drum, in his hand. He appears to be boasting of his own powers."

664.15   Your own tongue]   "This is addressed to the malicious man, and the slanderer, one who speaks evil of others. His crooked and double speech goes out of his mouth, but is changed to an arrow in his hand, and turned against himself; his own body bears the marks of injuries he would have inflicted on others. The lines across the chest are the traces of misfortune, brought on him by the indulgence of his own malicious disposition. In the songs and addresses of some of the most esteemed chiefs, or persons, who may be considered in some measure set apart from the Metai, are many attempts to convey and enforce moral instruction, or rather the inculcation of those opinions and actions which constitute the virtues of savage life."

665.5   I created the spirits]   "The figures in the commencement of this long and much esteemed religious song, represent Na-na-bush, the intercessor, the nephew of mankind. They seem designed to carry back the thoughts towards the beginning of time, and have a manifest allusion to a period when this mysterious and powerful being exercised a wish to assume the form of a man. In the second figure he is represented as holding a rattlesnake in his hand, and he calls himself the creator of the mani-toge. The Indians calling invisible and spiritual beings by the same name which they give to the lowest class of reptiles, it is doubtful whether Na-na-bush here claims to have cre-

ated intelligences superior to man, or only reptiles, and other small creatures, which they commonly call Mani-toag."

665.6   He sat down Na-na-bush]   "This figure appears to be descriptive of the first assumption by Na-na-bush of his office, as the friend and patron of men. He is represented as taking a seat on the ground. Fire, with the northern Indians, is the emblem of peace, happiness, and abundance. When one band goes against another, they go, according to their language, to put out the fire of their enemies; therefore, it is probable that in speaking of the perpetual fire of Na-na-bush, it is only intended to allude to his great power, and the permanence of his independence and happiness."

665.7   Notwithstanding you speak evil]   "The fourth figure, which, in the original, is a priapus, indicates that a man takes up the discourse. The circle about his head but descending no lower than his shoulders, shows that his help and his protection are from above, and in the strength thus derived he is able to defy those who speak evil of him, or seek, by the powers of their medicines, to break his life."

665.9   I can use . . . wood]   "The business of hunting is one of the first importance to the Indians, consequently, it finds a place in his devotions; indeed, devotion itself having apparently no object beyond the wants and weaknesses of this life, relief in times of hunger, is one of the most important blessings they ever ask for in their prayers. Accordingly, their young men are directed never to use these songs, or to have recourse to the medicine hunt, except in times of the extremest need."

665.11   Of you I think]   "The common spicy wintergreen, a stalk of which this figure is intended to represent, is much valued as a medicine by the Indians."

665.13   That which I take is blood]   "Here is the figure of a bear lying dead on the ground, and a hand is thrust into the body, to take out some of the blood. The instruction communicated probably is, that when the prayers offered in the preparation for the medicine hunt have been answered, and an animal killed, offerings should be immediately made, by taking some of the blood in the hand, and pouring it on the ground; or, as is more commonly done, by throwing a handful of it towards each of the cardinal points."

665.14   Now I have something to eat]   "This figure is that of a lean and hungry man, who, having asked for food, has been heard, and is now proceeding to allay his hunger."

665.15   I cover my head]   "The figure is that of a man, probably designed to be represented in a recumbent position, and drawing his blanket over him. His prayer having been answered, his wants supplied, he declares to the spirits his intention to take repose."

665.16   I fill my kettle]   "This is the hunter's lodge, and the kettle hanging in it contains the heart of the animal killed in the medicine hunt, of which

none but a man and a hunter must venture to taste. Should a woman or a dog even touch this heart, or the blood of the animal, sudden death, or lingering sickness, would follow it. This effect, as well as the dark colour which the Indians say the skin of the females assumes, in instances of the violation of this rule, they attribute to the effect of the medicine applied by the hunter to the heart of the Me-ze-nin-ne-shah. They point out instances of women, formerly distinguished among them for beauty, and particularly for the fairness of the skin, who, by eating of the heart, or touching the blood of an animal killed in medicine hunting, have not only lost that enviable distinction, but have become disgusting and frightful objects, the skin being blackened and covered with ulcers."

666.1   Long ago, in the old time] "This is the figure of a snake running over the ground; but some are of the opinion that the delineation should be different, namely, an old woman lying down in the middle of the ground. A new speaker is here introduced, which is the mythological personage Me-suk-kum-me-go-kwa, the grand mother of mankind, to whom Na-na-bush gave in keeping, for the use of his uncles and aunts, all roots and plants, and other medicines, derived from the earth. She received, at the same time, especial direction never to leave home, and always to surrender to men the treasures deposited in her bosom, when they should be, in a suitable manner, demanded of her. Hence it is, that the medicine men make an address to Me-suk-kum-me-go-kwa, whenever they take any thing from the earth, which is to be used as medicine."

666.3   I open you for a bear] "Me-suk-kum-me-go-kwa speaks to one of the medicines whose power she had just acknowledged, by calling them spirits, and says, I disclose, or reveal you for a bear, or to enable the hunter to kill a bear."

666.4   That is a Spirit] "Here they begin to dance."

666.8   The feather, the feather] "It sometimes happens that the hunter has wandered far from his lodge, and has neither birch bark on which to delineate his Me-zen-ne-neens, nor o-num-nu, or other powerful medicine, to apply to its heart. In these cases he takes some of the ashes of his fire, and spreading it on a smooth place, he traces in it the figure of the animal; he then takes a feather and sticks it in the ashes, and on this he places the same reliance as on the more common method of treating the Me-zen-ne-neens."

666.9   Who is a spirit?] "This figure is nearly the same as is given to Na-na-bush, in the beginning of the song, and an allusion is probably intended to the time when this interpreter between mankind and the Supreme Spirit, the Creator of all things, was driven from the presence of his father, to dwell with the meanest things of this world. The allusions in the traditionary fables of the Algonkins, to the quarrel between Na-na-bush and the Great Spirit, are frequent, and cannot fail to remind any one of the most important of the doctrines of the christian religion. It can scarce be doubted that, from

some source or other, these people have derived some obscure conceptions of the incarnation and mediatorial office of the second person in the Divine Trinity."

666.11   Now they will eat] "This figure, with open mouth and distended belly, seems to speak the language of human thanksgiving, and gratitude for favors conferred by a superior power."

666.13   This yellow ochre] "The o-num-mun, a yellowish earth, which they find in many places, and which is particularly abundant on one of the branches of the Illinois River . . . is a medicine to which they attribute great power. It is a little sack of this which is disproportionately represented in the hand of the figure."

666.14   Now I wish to try my bird] "The figure is that of a bird's skin, in which his medicine is contained, and it is that, and not the skin itself, he wishes to try."

666.16   I can kill any animal] "This large bird, whose open mouth indicates the power of his voice, is not one who inhabits the earth, or is ever seen; he lives in the clouds, and his voice is the thunder. He is more commonly called a-nim-me- kee, but here ke-kaun; our loud sounding medicine is strong to give us wind or rain, or whatever state of the air may be needful to ensure success in the hunt."

666.18   I take a bear] "The allusion is here to the observances respecting the heart and blood of animals killed in medicine hunting, and the sacrifices to be made in the event of success."

667.1   A rattle snake] "The jealousy of rival hunters is a frequent cause of quarrels and troubles among the Indians. This man boasts that the rattle snake, which always gives notice when danger is near, is on the poles of his lodge, and no evil can come near him without his being informed of it. His life is guarded by a superior power, and he fears not what his enemies can do to him."

667.3   To a Shawnee] "This is the figure of a man holding in his left hand the four nah-o-bah-e-gun-nun, or sticks, on which this song was recorded, and the authorship is claimed by a Shawnee, from whom the Ojibbeways acknowledge to have received it; and here, it is probable, the performance originally concluded. The remaining figures appear to have been added from other songs."

667.6   I come up from below] "The design of this figure is to suggest to the mind, that the spirit, to whom prayers in the medicine hunting are addressed, not only knows where animals are on the surface of the ground, but that so great is his power, he can create them where they did not before exist,

to supply the wants of those that pray unto him, and can cause them to come up out of the earth."

667.8   I can make an east wind] "This is sung four times, the north, the west, and the south winds being each, in turn, substituted for the east wind here spoken of. The meaning is, that the spirit has power to give a wind in any direction that may be necessary for the success of the hunter; that he controls all the changes of the atmosphere, and will overrule them in such a manner as to ensure the success of those whose medicine is strong; in other words, whose prayer is effectual. They must therefore regard neither the wind nor the sky, but go forward in confidence of success. The idea of the circle in this figure, into which the winds are represented as rushing, is derived from the apparent form of the visible horizon; the Indians neither know, nor will they believe that the form of the earth is globular."

667.10   Thus I have sat down] "This is again the figure of Na-na-bush, sitting on the earth, in the same attitude in which he is represented in the first part of the performance. The meaning is, that all who join in these devotional exercises must, throughout their continuance, which is for the greater part of the night, retain immoveably the same attitude, and give a serious attention to the performer, who must observe the same rule; and when all is finished, he, without uttering a word to any of those about him, rises and walks out of the lodge."

667.12   I make to crawl] "Probably the meaning is, that by these observances, and by this prayer, the hunter may cause to crawl (kill) a bear, or any animal. It is to be observed, that a bear is never, in these songs, called by the common name, but always che-mahn-duk."

668.1   *Hoatchunk' Narwoanar*] Atwater obtained the words of this song "through Mr. Kinzey, the sub agent, at fort Winnebago," and saw it performed at Prairie du Chien, Wisconsin, in the summer of 1829. He writes: "The notes for the drum are struck short and abruptly, and the first and every alternate note in a bar, is sounded loud and strong; the intermediate ones lightly.

"When this tragedy was acted, the actors were so painted as to show with great effect every wound which they had ever received in battle. BROKEN ARM who had been severely wounded in the attack on Fort Meigs, in the late war, was particularly conspicuous. The wound was so painted, and the blood which ran from it, was so well represented by the painter, as to look like the reality itself. At a short distance from him on a first view, I thought he had recently been badly wounded."

668.11   *Medicine Song . . . Lover*] Hoffman describes the circumstances in which he first heard this song as follows: "The fumes of the inebriating weed [tobacco] very soon began to act upon the excitable system of White-plume, and he regaled us with a number of songs, which were anything but musical. There was but one of them that appeared to me to have any thing poetical,

either in sentiment or imagery, to recommend it. It was a *Mezi-nee-neence*, or 'Medicine Song,' of a lover, in which he is supposed to have some magical power of knowing the secret thoughts of his mistress, and being able to charm her to him from any distance."

669.1   *War Dance*]   Catlin accompanied a group of 14 Iowa Indians on a tour of Great Britain, Ireland, and France between 1844 and 1846. The group gave a number of public performances, including one for King Louis Philippe. Jeffrey Doraway, "a mulatto," acted as their interpreter.

669.3   *Eh-Ros-Ka, The Warrior's Dance*]   "The song in this dance seems to be addressed to the body of an enemy, from its name, Eh-Ros-Ka, meaning the body, or the tribe or war party, rather than an individual, although the beginning of the song is addressed to an individual chief or warrior of the enemies party."

669.12   *Wa-Sissica, The War Song*]   "[S]ung for the last part of [The Warrior's Dance] . . . like this, the various parts of the war dance are accompanied with boasts and threats upon an enemy to whom the songs are usually addressed."

669.19   *The Approaching Dance*]   "The Approaching Dance is also a spirited part of the *War Dance*, in which the dancers are by their gestures, exhibiting the mode of advancing upon an enemy, by hunting out and following up the track, discovering the enemy, and preparing for the attack. . . ."

670.1   *Ha-Kon-E-Crase, The Eagle Dance*]   "The Eagle Dance, (or as they call it) the 'soaring eagle' is one of the most pleasing of their dances, and forms a part of the war dance.

"In this beautiful dance each dancer imagines himself a soaring eagle, and as they dance forward from behind the musicians, they take the positions of the eagles, heading against the wind, and looking down, preparing to make the swoop on their prey below them; the wind seems too strong for them, and they fall back, and repeatedly advance forward, imitating the chattering of that bird, with the whistles carried in their hands, whilst they sing."

671.1   *Death Song*]   Schoolcraft writes of an early version of this song that it was "taken from Tsheetsheegwyung, a young Chippewa warrior, of *La Pointe*, in Lake Superior, and translated by Mr. George Johnston" (*Travels in the Central Portions of the Mississippi Valley* (1825)). In *Oneóta*, he adds: "These stanzas have all been actually sung on warlike occasions, and repeated in my hearing. They have been gleaned from the traditional songs of the Chippewas of the north, whose villages extend through the region of lake Superior, and to the utmost sources of the Mississippi. Those bands are the hereditary foes of their western neighbours, the Dacotahs or Sioux, who are generally called by them, by way of distinction, Na do wä′ sees, that is to say, OUR

ENEMIES. The allusions in the song are exclusively to them. In writing the original, I omit the chorus, as it is not susceptible of translation. . . ."

671.23   *George Copway's Dream Song*]   This song, for which Copway gives no title, comes in the middle of his account of a dream he had at the age of twelve: "Myself and others were sleeping far from the wigwam, near a large pine. I saw, in my dream, a person coming from the east; he approached, walking on the air: he looked down upon me, and said, 'Is this where you are?' I said 'yes.' 'Do you see this pine?' 'Yes, I see it.' 'It is a great and high tree.' I observed that the tree was lofty, reaching towards the heavens. Its branches extended over land and water, and its roots were very deep. 'Look on it while I sing, yes, gaze upon the tree.' He sang, and pointed to the tree; it commenced waving its top; the earth about its roots heaved up, and the waters roared and tossed from one side of their beds to the other. As soon as he stopped singing, and let fall his hands, every thing became perfectly still and quiet. 'Now,' said he, 'sing the words which I have sung.' . . . While singing, I heard the winds whistle, saw the tree waving its top, the earth heaving, heard the waters roaring, because they were all troubled and agitated. Then said he, 'I am from the rising of the sun, I will come and see you again. You will not see me often; but you will hear me speak.' Thus spoke the spirit, and then turned away towards the road from which he had come. I told my father of my dream, and after hearing all, he said, 'My son, *the god of the winds* is kind to you; the aged tree, I hope, may indicate long life; the wind may indicate that you will travel much; the water you saw, and the winds, will carry your canoe safely through the waves.' "

672.1   *Meda*]   "The idea of the sacred word Meda . . . is a subtile and all-pervading Principle of Power (whether good, or merely *great* power is not established by any allusions) which is to be propitiated by, or acted on, through certain animals, plants, or mere objects of art, and thus brought under the control of the Meda-man, or necromancer. He exhibits to the initiates and the members of his lodge fraternity a series of boasting and symbolic declamations. This ceremony is called a medicine ceremony, and the lodge a medicine lodge. But the word mus-ké-ke, or medicine, does not occur in it, nor is there any allusion to the healing art, except in a single instance . . . The operators are not mus-ke-ke-win-in-ee, or physicians, but Meda-win-in-ee, that is Meda-men. They assemble, not to teach the art of healing, but the art of supplicating spirits. They do not rely on physical, but on supernatural power."

672.3   The Great Spirit's lodge]   "While this is sung . . . each member of the society holds up one hand in a beseeching manner. All stand, without dancing. The drum is not struck during this introductory chant." The figure represents "a medicine lodge filled with the presence of the Great Spirit, who, it is affirmed, came down with wings, to instruct the Indians in these ceremonies."

672.5 I have always loved] The figure represents "a candidate for admission crowned with feathers, and holding, suspended to his arm, an otter-skin pouch, with the wind represented as gushing out of one end."

672.7 I shall give you] The figure represents "a man holding a dish in his hand, and decorated with magic feathers on his wrists, indicating his character as the master of the feast."

672.8 I go into the bath] The figure represents "a lodge apart from that in which the meda-men are assembled, having a vapor-bath within it. . . . The six heavy marks at the top of the lodge indicate the stream escaping from the bath."

672.9 I wish to wear this] The figures represent "the arm of the priest, or master of ceremonies, who conducts the candidate," and "the goods, or presents given, as a fee of admission, by the novitiate."

672.10 What! my life, my single tree!] The figure represents "a meda-tree. The recurved projection from the trunk denotes the root that supplies the medicine."

672.12 I wish to see them appear] The figure represents "a stuffed crane-skin, employed as a medicine-bag. By shaking this in the dance, plovers and other small birds are made, by a sleight-of-hand trickery, to jump out of it."

672.14 What are you saying] The figure represents "an arrow in the supposed circle of the sky."

672.16 My kite's skin is fluttering.] The figure represents "the Ka kaik, a species of small hawk, swift of wing, and capable of flying high into the sky. The skin of this bird is worn round the necks of warriors going into battle."

673.1 All round the circle] The figure represents "the sky, or celestial hemisphere, with the symbol of the Great Spirit looking over it. A Manito's arm is raised up from the earth in a supplicating posture. Birds of good omen are believed to be in the sky."

673.3 The Wabeno tree—it dances.] The figure represents "a meda-tree. The idea represented is a tree animated by magic or spiritual power."

673.4 How rings aloud] The figure represents "a stick used to beat the Ta-wa-e-gun or drum."

673.5 I walk upon half of the sky] The figure represents "half of the celestial hemisphere—an Indian walking upon it. The idea symbolized is the sun pursuing his diurnal course till noon."

673.6   I sound all round the sky]   The figure represents "the Great Spirit filling all space with his beams, and enlightening the world by the halo of his head. He is here depicted as the god of thunder and lightning."

673.7   You shall hear the sound]   The figure represents "The Ta-wa-e-gun, or single-headed drum."

673.8   Do you understand my drum?]   The figure represents "the Ta-wa-e-gonse, or tambourine, ornamented with feathers, and a wing, indicative of its being prepared for sacred use."

673.9   I sing the raven]   The figure represents "a raven. The skin and feathers of this bird are worn as head ornaments."

673.10   I am the crow]   The figure represents "a crow, the wings and head of which are worn as a head-dress."

673.12   I wish to go . . . lodge]   The figure represents "a medicine lodge. A leader or master of the Meda society, standing with his drum-stick raised, and holding in his hands the clouds and the celestial hemisphere."

674.1   *Prophetic Powers*]   An example of the Jeesukáwin or "sacred prophetic art" of the Ojibwa, this song was composed by Catherine Wabose, a one-time Ojibwa prophetess originally from Chegoimegon, on Lake Superior, and translated by Jane Schoolcraft, Henry Rowe Schoolcraft's wife. Born around 1810 with the name Ogee-wy-ahn-oqut-o-kwa, Wabose converted to Christianity after her second marriage, and thus felt able to relate her songs, traditionally held in secret. Of "Prophetic Powers," Schoolcraft writes: "It is a peculiarity observed in this and other instances of the kind, that the words of these chants are never repeated by the natives without the tune or air, which was full of intonation, and uttered in so hollow or suspended, or inhaled a voice, that it would require a practiced composer to note it down. The chorus is not less peculiarly fixed, and some of its guttural tones are startling."

675.16   *Song of the Owl*]   Adapted from one of Henry Rowe Schoolcraft's translations of Ojibwa "Wabeno Songs" and enclosed in a letter (January 11, 1856) to Longfellow's German translator Ferdinand Freiligrath regarding *The Song of Hiawatha* and the Finnish meter which it adopts. In the letter Longfellow notes that "*parallelism* belongs to Indian poetry as well as to Finnish, and not only belongs to it, but in like manner is the 'rule and law of it.' . . . Inclosed you will find some specimens."

676.3   I walk about in the night]   "A Lynx."

676.5   I hear your mouth]   "A human figure, denoting bad speeches from a medicine-man."

676.7   Now I come out of the ground]   "A Lynx. He is represented as just having emerged from the ground. The bar across the neck denoted this. The lynx is a symbol of a first-rate Meda-man—one deeply versed in the medical mysteries."

676.9   See! I am a lynx] "The Lynx—a symbol of the Meda."

676.14   *Hawk Chant of the Saginaws*] Attributed by Schoolcraft to James Riley. The Saginaw were a band of the Ojibwa.

677.13   *War Songs*] "The following specimens, which have been derived from actors in the depths of the forest, consist of independent songs, or stanzas, each of which is sung by a different or by the same warrior, while the [war] dance is in progress. The words have been taken down from a young Chippewa warrior of lake Superior, of the name of Che che-gwy-ung."

678.1   *Corn Song*] The discovery of a crooked ear of corn, according to Schoolcraft, was taken as "a symbol of a thief in the cornfield" and "is considered as the image of an old man stooping as he enters the lot."

678.14   *Chant to the Fire-Fly*] Attributed to "the Indian Children."

679.1   *Minnetare Songs*] Morgan heard these songs in June 1862 near Fort Benton, Montana. They were translated for him by Robert Meldrum, a fur trader of Scottish descent who had been made a chief of the Crow in 1830 and according to Morgan preferred the Crow language to English. The first five songs were sung by the Minnetare chief, Boo-a-she-pish-ish (Black Fish), also known as Dah-pee-to-a-push (Nose of the Bear); Morgan does not name the other singers. All of the songs, according to what Meldrum told Morgan, were "devotions to the Great Spirit to make them live long and happy." Each song belonged to a medicine bag which bore "a special and absolute property" and was highly valued ("it is not uncommon to give a horse for a bag").

679.3   *New Moon Ceremonies*] "At the new moon there is a general meeting of the medicine men called by those who have provided the corn, sugar, and coffee, bread, meat, and any kind of fruit or berries which they gather themselves, and collect for a feast on this occasion. As soon as they come together they commence singing . . . Very often they all join in the song but the song is led by the one who holds the rattle. When this is done he hands the rattle to the next and he leads a second song in which all join, and so on around. Each is a sort of prayer asking for a particular favor."

679.4   The buffalo are coming] "It is a regular song, the words being in a sort of monotone."

679.13   *Song of the Weasel*] "It is the song of the weasel, but relates to the horse into which he changes himself."

679.15   *Song of the Pheasant*] "The principal part of this song is an imitation of the strutting of the pheasant, his manner of carrying his head, and some other peculiarities."

679.17   *Song of the Elk*] "It is supposed that the elk in their whistling are courting, and in singing the song of the elk they are doing the same thing. The elk invokes the Great Spirit in their place. [The song] is asking of the

Great Spirit matrimonial favors. The song of the elk for this reason brings a large price."

679.19   *Song of the Bear*]   "In this song they imitate the motion of the bear in walking and running as they sing. This song relates to war. They do not invoke the aid of the Great Spirit but ask the bear to do it for them."

680.1   *Song of the White Man*]   "They think the white man has great influence with Great Spirit, and this song is often used. The word or the purport of the syllables is, Yellow Eyes, look at me and look for me. Let me see. They call the white man 'yellow eyes.' This is strictly their name for the French. They call the Americans 'Long Knives.' "

680.9   *Song for a Fallen Warrior*]   "The curiosity of some may be attracted by the following rude and literal translation of the song of a Blackfoot woman to the spirit of her son, who was killed on his first war-party. The words were written down at the time and are not in any respect changed or smoothed."

681.12   I have cast . . . soul]   "This is a song of the 'circle dance,' and is a war incantation. It is sung by the officiating priest, as he concocts his war magic in a hole in the earth, while the chorus dances in a circle around him."

681.14   a buffalo soul]   " 'Buffalo' is here the poetic term for man."

681.16   I make . . . face covered]   An "armor song," of which Riggs writes: "It is a vision of the night. The four black spirits have come to the aspiring war-leader, and he dreams. He sees the enemy an easy prey, like herded buffaloes, while he, with 'covered face,' goes disguised and protected."

681.20   Night now passes along]   "Another vision of the war-leader, by which he attests his divine commission to lead on the war-path. The four black spirits have come up, and black Night appears with a thunder bird in her mouth."

681.24   Whose sacred road lies plainly]   "The war-leader has another revelation, and sees the mysterious or wakan' war-path as plain as day before him; and, with such credentials, he goes forth to gather recruits."

682.7   Terrifying all I journey]   "In the next song, we may suppose the warrior prepared for his campaign, and, as it were, mustering and parading his forces, physical and spiritual."

682.9   the *Toon-kan'* at the North]   "The great lingam, or stone god of the North."

682.11   Something I've killed]   "Now the war party returns, having been successful; and this is the warrior's song . . . Here we have a double metaphor; for the 'northern buffalo' means a black bear, but 'black bear' means a man. The 'lifting up the voice' is a mourning for the slain enemy; for the

successful warriors must paint themselves black, and go dressed as though they had lost their best friend."

682.18   *Songs of the Sacred Mysteries*]   "The whole ritual of their worship is chanted, whether engaged in by the single devotee or the sacred assembly."

682.20   In the home of mysterious life]   "The seeker after divine inspiration, having hung up in his tepee something embodying wakan' or mysterious power, utters his prayer in this song."

682.26   my father]   "*Ta-koo-shkan-shkan'*, the *motion god.*"

683.1   Having those, may I come]   Riggs offers the following commentary on this sun-dance song, which he refers to as "the song of Sounding Cloud": "Of this song, verses 1 and 2 are his prayer to his god. He prays (verse 1) that he may take four scalps, and return safely; and (verse 2) that the appointed day may soon be revealed to him. The sun-god now looks down in favor upon his suppliant, and rewards his devotion. He promises (verse 3) to give four of the enemy into his hand, and recognizes him as now wakan', (Holy boy!) and as henceforth belonging to the mystic circle of the gods. With this assurance of divine acceptance, the devotee claims (verse 4) relationship with the sun-bird himself. Like him, he is henceforth the companion of his god. He, too, has looked upon his face, and lives. Now the night comes on, and its weary, painful hours wear by. Hardly can the dancer, fevered and faint, keep time with the hollow-sounding drum and shrill rattles. But dawn begins to break, and the chorus utter, as their prayer in his behalf, verse 5,—that the god may again look upon him in favor. The sun hears the prayer of the watchers, and now (verse 6) bursts forth, crowned with mysterious splendors, re-animating the flagging powers of his servant. However, as the midday beams again beat down upon the wretched dancer, his sufferings are inexpressible. But now the chorus, instead of cheering him up, in order to make the final test of his fortitude, calls out to him, faint with fasting and dancing, and all on fire with a burning thirst and his torturing wounds,— 'Sounding Cloud, my friend! Do you want water?' "

683.15   I sing to a Spirit]   "This is properly a war song. The warrior has commenced with the thunder, and the four black spirits of the night have told him that he will kill an enemy. For this he sings this song of praise."

683.17   Lo! a cloud is let down]   "In this it would seem that, as the god rolls his cloud-chariot across the sky, almost touching the earth, the enthusiast deems it a messenger of the Deity to himself, and perhaps sent to bear him into the high realm of mystery."

683.19   Across the lake]   "The next four songs belong to the ritual of the society of the sacred dance, of which order *Oon-ktay'-he*, god of water and earth, is the patron god." In the second song, the god "sings out of the

whirlwind and thunder storm." The third and fourth are sung "in praise of their 'mystery sack.' "

684.4   Grandfather]   The god.

684.8   wave the imploring hand]   "Not the literal rendering of the Dakota words . . . which are 'Stroke the face of my grandfather;' but, used with reference to the Deity, it signifies a stroking motion of the hand towards the face of the god, expressive of adoration and entreaty."

684.9   quadruped]   "The 'quadruped' is the wakan' or mystery 'sack,' often made of the skin of some four-footed animal, with the head and claws retained."

684.10   red down]   "Swan's down, dyed red, is a sacred article, and used continually in their worship as an offering to the gods, and as an ornament of consecrated articles, such as the weapons and feathers of the warrior. It is much delighted in by the gods, who are said to wear it largely."

685.16   *Songs and Chants*]   Powell obtained these songs between 1871 and 1873 among the Kaibab band of the Paiute in northwestern Arizona, possibly from Wa-ai'-wints (whom Powell describes as its "poet"), and Chaur-ru-um-pik, a chief.

685.18   *The Home of the River*]   "Chaur-ru-um-pik in explanation of this song says that the river comes from the sky and returns by way of the horizon."

688.20   *Cave Lake*]   Probably a small body of water by that name in upper Kanab Canyon. The pool lies in an overhanging alcove in the sandstone wall of the cliff.

689.5   *A Dream*]   "The poet said that he had a dream while sleeping on Un-kar-tu-waid-an, a mountain in northern Arizona, that he fell over the cliff and caught by his hand, and hung there trembling with fright. On awakening, he composed the above."

690.9   The blue . . . Mountain]   In Powell's manuscript, the line is glossed: "(meaning the clouds are rolling on the Mountain)."

690.10   *Wichits*]   Small birds, possibly a species of titmouse.

690.20   Rainwater singing]   Powell offers "making a noise" as an alternate translation.

691.1   *Sacred Songs of the Konkau*]   Powers heard these songs at the Round Valley Reservation, Mendocino County, California, in 1871 or 1872.

691.4   *Oan-koip'-tu-peh*]   "The Invincible," son of Red Cloud (Yang-wi'-a-kan-ūh), a being in Konkow mythology who fathers Oan-koi'-tu-peh by Ki-u-nad'-dis-si's daughter.

691.8   *wēk'-wēk*]   Kingfisher.

691.13 *The Acorn Song*] "In the acorn song . . . it will be observed that it appears to be spoken by two different persons. The first three verses are attributed by some Indians to Oankoitupeh, and by others to the Red Cloud. The latter would seem to be more poetically correct. Then the last line is evidently spoken by the acorn personified. I have grouped both these together, and called it all the acorn song, but the Indians sing them somewhat confusedly, as indeed they do the other songs more or less. It required a great deal of patient labor to construct order out of their chaos; and even now I am not always positive, for some Indians will attribute a given verse to one of the personages and others to another. Besides that, the interpretation is sometimes a little uncertain, principally, I think, for the reason that a number of the words either belong to an occult, priestly language, or are so antiquated that the modern Indians, in the absence of most of their old men and prophets, are unable to agree absolutely on their meaning."

691.19 *Ki-u-nad'-dis-si*] An ancient chief who lost most of his tribe in gambling; grandfather of Oan-koi'-tu-peh.

692.1 *Soldier's Song*] From a narrative written in Dakota in 1869 by Paul Mazakootemane and translated by Riggs. Mazakootemane, who had converted to Christianity in 1856, attempted in 1862 to negotiate the return of a group of captives from the Dakota. Upon the breakdown of these negotiations, as they departed, the Dakota warriors sang this song; Mazakootemane writes "I disliked it very much."

692.10 *Ancient Rites . . . Council*] Hale prepared this translation in 1879 from an 1832 copy of a manuscript supposed to have been written in the mid-18th century by a Mohawk chief known as David of Schoharie. He was assisted by Chief John "Smoke" Johnson, of the Reserve of the Six Nations near Brantford, Ontario, who explained the meaning of the archaic text in modern Mohawk, and by his son, Chief George H. M. Johnson, and the Rev. Isaac Bearfoot, who provided translations into English.

697.11 *Chant . . . Rites*] Hale found this hymn in an Onondaga manuscript book at "Onondaga Castle" (the Onondaga reservation) in September, 1880. The book had been copied by one of Hale's interpreters, Daniel La Fort, from a manuscript of chief Abram La Fort, his father, who may have been copying from an earlier manuscript. The hymn was originally written as prose. Albert Cusick, another of Hale's interpreters, assured Hale it was traditionally sung—he "chanted a few staves of it, after the native fashion." Hale describes the song as "a sort of cento or compilation, in the Onondaga dialect, of passages from various portions of the Canienga Book of Rites."

698.1 *Hunter's Song*] Gatschet obtained this song from Judge G. W. Stidham, a leading citizen of the Creek Nation and an organizer of the pro-Confederate "United Nations of the Indian Territory."

699.1 *The Walam Olum, . . . Lenâpé*] The *Walam Olum* was first published by the botanist Constantine Samuel Rafinesque (1783–1840) in his

book *The American Nations* (1836). Rafinesque asserted that he had obtained in 1820 from "the late Dr. Ward, of Indiana," who has never been satisfactorily identified, "some of the original Wallam-Olum (painted record) of the Linapi Tribe of Wapihani or White River," but was unable to interpret the pictographs; and that in 1822 "were obtained from another individual the songs annexed thereto in the original language; but no one could be found by me able to translate them." The manuscript with the transcribed songs "was inexplicable till a deep study of the Linapi enabled me to translate them." The text remained controversial, and has been regarded as fraudulent by many scholars. In the commentary accompanying his 1885 retranslation, Daniel Garrison Brinton raises the possibility that Rafinesque may have forged the work, but concludes: "It is a genuine native production, which was repeated orally to some one indifferently conversant with the Delaware language, who wrote it down to the best of his ability. In its present form it can, as a whole, lay no claim either to antiquity, or to purity of linguistic form. Yet, as an authentic modern version, slightly colored by European teachings, of the ancient tribal traditions, it is well worth preservation . . ."

705.13   *The Mountain Chant*]   The Navajo Mountain Chant (*dsilyídje qaçàl*, or "chant towards (a place) within the mountains") was part of a winter healing ceremony of nine days duration. Performed by the shamans of the tribe at the request of an ill person's family, the ceremony was also intended to aid the tribe as a whole, especially in bringing rain and a plentiful harvest. Hundreds of songs were associated with the ceremony, certain sets of which—"songs of sequence"—were sung only in a specific order. Washington Matthews observed the ceremony on a number of occasions over many years, but specifically describes one held at Niqotlízi (Hard Earth) on the Navajo Reservation in New Mexico, beginning (with the fifth day) on October 24, 1884. Matthews comments as follows on his translations:

"Some songs are self-explanatory or readily understood, but the greater number cannot be comprehended without a full knowledge of the mythology and of the symbolism to which they refer; they merely hint at mythic conceptions. Many contain archaic expressions, for which the shaman can assign a meaning, but whose etymology cannot now be learned; and some embody obsolete words whose meaning is lost even to the priesthood. There are many vocables known to be meaningless and recited merely to fill out the rhythm or to give a dignified length to the song. For the same reasons a meaningless syllable is often added or a significant syllable duplicated."

707.10   *Last Song . . . Stick*]   "These songs are accompanied, in beating the drum, with a peculiar sharp strike like a sudden outburst or explosion. Hence, they say, the name, Tsinéilçòï Bigin."

708.1   *Summer Song*]   Boas writes: "we had arrived [1883–84] on the coast of Davis Strait, and struck a track that led to the Eskimo village. No white man had ever visited this part of the coast, and, the men being out hunting, the women and children, who had frequently heard of the *Kadlu-*

nait ('the whites'), rushed out of the huts when they saw the sledge coming with an unknown dog-team and an unknown driver. When they discovered him to be a white man, their excitement reached the highest pitch, and they burst out in a wild dance and chorus, singing the joyful song of summer. This song was the most popular one at the time. It was composed by an Eskimo living farther north, 'Snowwind' (*Kenningnang*) by name, and had spread rapidly over all the settlements."

709.1   *Chinook Songs*]   Boas collected these songs in British Columbia in 1886. He writes: "The Indians are at present in the habit of living part of the year in Victoria, Vancouver, or New Westminster, working in various trades: in saw-mills and canneries, on wharves, as sailors, etc. In the fall they go to Puget Sound hop-picking. At these places members of numerous tribes gather, who use Chinook as a means of communication." The Chinook Jargon, or Oregon Trade Language, a trade lingua franca used on the Northwest Coast, combined elements of indigenous languages, English, and French.

711.1   *Pawnee War-Song*]   Brinton obtained this song from John Brown Dunbar (1841–1914), a schoolteacher and philologist whose father, John Dunbar, had been a missionary among the Pawnee.

711.11   *Incantation Songs*]   Gatschet collected these texts in the fall of 1877 at the Klamath Reservation in Oregon. He writes: "This long series of shamanic songs in use on the Williamson River was obtained from *Mary*, a young pupil of the boarding school of Indian children at the Klamath agency. When living among the Indians on the Williamson River she had heard all these songs very frequently, and in an interesting evening entertainment she faithfully reproduced the manipulations of the male and female conjurers upon a little rag baby lying on the floor on a bed made up of old blankets, the figure representing some poor suffering Indian patient.

"On the day following these incantations were dictated, translated and explained to me by *Minnie Froeben*. [Froeben, born about 1860 to a Klamath mother and a French father, was an assistant to the matron of the Klamath agency school at the time of Gatschet's interviews.]

"Each of these song-lines is sung many times by the conjurer, then *repeated* by the chorus a dozen times or more. The chorus varies the melody somewhat each time, but this musical variation is so slight and insignificant that the general impression of monotony is not dispelled by it.

"The animal or object of nature to which the conjurer attributes each of the song-lines was not remembered in every instance. Where this reference was obtained, it was added at the head of the song or song-line. The animals mentioned in these songs are all supposed to have been sent out by the conjurer to look out for the whereabouts of the *personified* disease, from which the patient is suffering, and whatever the conjurer sings about the animals refers to what he sees them doing while on their errand. . . . The conjurer sometimes diversifies his songs, all of which are sung in the *minor* keys, by

inserting spoken words relating to the condition of the patient and the effects of his treatments. . . .

"Many Indians do not understand these songs, which contain many archaic forms and words, and the conjurers themselves are generally loth to give their meaning, even if they should understand them. Some songs are of a stereotypic application in the treatment of all or of the majority of maladies. A close familiarity with the habits of animals of the forest manifests itself throughout, as well as in the mythic tales.

"The translations added by me are not literal; they render the meaning of the songs in a free and paraphrastic manner. . . ."

712.3   *Little girl's song*]   "On grand occasions young women were in the habit of dressing in buckskin robes, fringed with porcupine quills. In a myth the bull-frog was reported to wear constantly this kind of dress."

712.6   *washpálaks*]   Vulpes velox.

712.10   *Song . . . tuákish-crane*]   "This is called the tuáksham shuinō'tkish or incantation sung by the crane itself through the mouth of the conjurer."

712.12   *Song of the blind medicine-girl*]   "The feathers of the yellow hammer are worn on neck as an ornament."

713.8   *Chorus song*]   "This pretty song is chanted by the choristers while the kíuks [medicine man] feigns to suck out of the body the tiny object which is supposed to have caused the disease, and before he gets it out."

713.12   *Song of the lizard*]   "Alludes to a peculiar nodding observed in lizards when running out of their holes and stopping at the issue."

713.16   *Song of the black mouse*]   "This song, with a beautiful melody, is the [song of] a mouse species with pig-like proboscis."

714.1   *Song of the weasel*]   "The weasel is squealing, because hunters have caught or trapped it."

714.6   *Song, reference unknown*]   "Probably refers to one of those birds to whom the power is attributed to bring about storms, fog, snow, or any change of the weather."

714.12   *Song of the bug*]   "This bug, perhaps a scarabee, bites the skin to suck out the disease from the wound."

715.1   *Fox's song*]   "This song is said to allude to the circumstance that one fox's howl seems to sound like the cries of many foxes howling together."

715.4   Tuánχî]   "I am crying."

715.8   *Song of the disease*] "The *personified* disease spreads the germs of sickness through the atmosphere."

716.8   *Song of the little gray tchikass-bird*] "Speaks of a fog drifting away from the mountains and turning into a cloud, which is drifting also."

716.10   *Song of skō'ks or spirit*] "The bones of a dead person's skeleton are supposed to rattle against each other, the spirit being here identified with the skeleton."

716.18   *Conjurer's own song*] "This is sung when water is poured over the patient. A more literal translation would be: 'I am resounding within the ground.'"

717.4   Yaînalam shulúyualsh] "Round, cylindric or globiform objects standing in a row on a mountain. The den of the grizzly bear is supposed to be in the mountains or on a mountain top. My informants did not know what the objects were which stood in a series, but if any religious notions were connected with them, we may compare the three sacred rocks standing on a mountain top in Peruvian mythology. . . ."

718.1   *Incantations of the Modoc Conjurers*] Gatschet obtained this song from Toby Riddle, a Modoc woman born in 1842; she served as interpreter to the Peace Commission in the Modoc War of 1873.

718.2   *Shkō'ks or spirit's incantation*] "Sung by a 'doctoress' who has sent out into the air a deceased person's spirit to search after the disease of her patient."

718.4   *Another of the same*] "Rime, alliteration and assonance are combined in this interesting song, which is said to be sung by female conjurers. A spirit is sent underground to prospect for the disease. A tripartite division of the song-line is found in none of the other incantations obtained."

718.8   *Another of the same*] "The conjurer asks the returning spirit: 'what did you find to be the cause of the disease, when going below the ground?' The answer is: 'he was the cause of it'; *he* is some subterranean deity, or genius, probably Múnatalkni."

718.10   *Song of the dry water-spring*] "Probably attributed to a grizzly bear."

718.12   *Song of the old frog*] "The frog is prospecting for the disease around and within the water."

718.14   *Song of the wind*] "The wind, while entrusted with the search for the disease, is blowing through the skies and sweeping over the earth."

718.18   *Song of the five female elks*] "The mythic elks which sang this were said to be endowed with human faculties."

719.1   *Song of the fisher*]   "This is an incantation which would seem to proceed rather from a duck or goose beating its wings while chasing another, than from a fisher. First line Modoc, second, Klamath Lake."

719.4   *Young otter's song*]   "The animal had found the *disease* in the water and chased it out to the shore; when there it set the shore on fire and the ground was shaken up under its destructive, ravaging steps."

719.12   *Song of the weasel*]   "The weasel, returning from its errand, reports to the conjurer, that having found the cause of the patient's disease to be a wicked skû'ks's heart, this was brought by the weasel to the spirit land and breathed out, to be left there."

719.17   *Song of the woodpecker*]   "The kíuks [medicine man] had sent the red headed woodpecker to prospect for his patient's disease in the atmosphere. Alliteration and assonance in profusion."

719.23   I possess . . . vision]   "*Meaning*: My eyes are well fitted for the discovery of the patient's disease, hovering in the air, for they are acute, being those of the owl; I am just stepping up my lodge-ladder, the speckled bark of a tree, on the search for the disease. Alliteration is a prominent feature in this incantation."

720.1   *Spider's incantation*]   "Sent by the conjurer, the spider goes up in a web to prospect for the disease."

720.3   *Patient's song*]   "On falling sick, a spirit orders the patient to sing and repeat this Earth-song line for hours."

720.6   Now my heart has returned]   " 'I have recovered the use of my senses.' "

720.14   *Medicine Songs*]   La Flesche, recalling these songs from an episode of his Omaha childhood, describes the scene of their performance as follows: "[The medicine-man] started his song at the top of his voice, which the other doctors, twenty or thirty in number, picked up and sang in unison, with such volume that one would imagine it could have been heard many miles. In the midst of the chorus of voices rose the shrill sound of the bone whistle accompaniment, imitating the call of an eagle. After the doctor had started the song, he put the bits of root into his mouth . . . [and] slowly approached the [injured] boy, bellowing and pawing the earth, after the manner of an angry buffalo at bay."

720.20   Thus, the water to send]   "The meaning is, Because I am commanded, or instructed (by the buffalo vision), to send the water (the medicine) from this distance, therefore I do so."

721.1   The pool of water]   "The composer of this song is said to have seen in a vision a number of buffalo attending one of their number who was wounded. The vision was given to the man to reveal to him the secret of a healing potion. The first two lines mean that the attending buffalo, the doc-

tors, have indicated a pool of water in a buffalo wallow as the place where the wounded one shall be treated; the third line, that they assent to the entreaties of the injured animal to be taken to the water, that his wounds may be healed in it. . . . As all the words that the visionary animals uttered were directed to the dreamer's ears, the last line of the song is intended to convey this meaning. The round pool of water they proclaim sending this way; that is, their voices to me."

721.7   *The Thanksgivings*] Converse attended the three-day Iroquois Green Corn Festival in September, 1890, at the Cattaraugus Reservation, New York. "The Thanksgivings" comes from a part of this festival called the Great Feather Dance.

721.19   certain timbers . . . fluids] "Referring to the maple."

722.6   our supporters] "Three sisters of great beauty, who delight to dwell in the companionship of each other as the spiritual guardians of the corn, the beans, and the squash. These vegetables, the staple food of the red man, are supposed to be in the special care of the Great Spirit, who, in the growing season, sends these 'supporters' to abide in the fields and protect them from the ravages of blight or frost. These guardians are clothed in the leaves of their respective plants, and, though invisible, are faithful and vigilant."

722.9   Ga-ne-o-di-o] Handsome Lake, prophet of the Longhouse religion.

722.18   *Imploration for Clear Weather*] Hoffman obtained this set of songs between 1887 and 1889 at the Red Lake and White Earth reservations in Minnesota. The songs were originally recorded in pictographic form by Sikas′sigĕ, a Midē′ priest, on a birch-bark scroll "made in imitation of one in the possession of his father, Baiĕ′dzĭk, one of the leading Midē′ at Mille Lacs, Minnesota." Sung by a Midē′ priest in order to dispel rain-clouds, each song in the set was "repeated an indefinite number of times, and after being repeated once or twice . . . sung also by the others as an accompaniment."

722.20   I swing . . . child] "The Midē′ Spirit, showing magic lines radiating from his body. The Midē′ claims to be able to receive special favor."

722.21   The sky . . . about] "The sky and the earth united by a pathway of possible rain."

722.22   We have lost the sky] "Clouds obscure the sky, and the arm of the Midē′ is reaching up into it for its favor of clear weather."

722.23   I am helping you] "The Otter-skin Midē′ sack is held up to influence the Otter Spirit to aid them."

722.24   I have made an error] "The Otter-skin Midē′ sack has failed to produce the desired effect."

723.1   I am using my heart]   "Refers to sincerity of motives in practice of Midē′ ceremony."

723.4   The spirit wolf]   "One of the malevolent spirits who is opposed to having the ceremony is assisting the evil man′idōs in causing the sky to be overcast."

723.5   I do not . . . going]   "The Midē′ is in doubt whether to proceed or not in the performance of initiation."

723.6   I depend on the clear sky]   "To have the ceremony go on. Arm reaching toward the sky for help."

723.7   I give you the other village]   "That rain should fall anywhere but upon the assemblage and Mid′wigân."

723.8   The thunder is heavy]   "The Thunder Bird, who causes the rain."

723.9   We are talking to one another]   "The Midē′ communes with Ki′tshi Man′idō; he is shown near the sky; his horns denoting superior wisdom and power, while the lines from the mouth signify speech."

723.13   *the Sacred Tree*]   "For the sun dance."

724.1   Who is our friend?]   "The hands of the 'medicine-men' were here extended, palms toward the sky, but not joined."

724.3   The Bull]   The buffalo.

724.23   *A Rain Song of the Quer′ränna Chai′än*]   Part of the Rain Ceremonial of the Quer′ränna Society, this song "call[ed] upon the cloud people to gather to water the earth." Its performance took over an hour.

725.6   father Sûs′sĭstĭnnako]   In Sia mythology, the creator, a spider.

725.15   *Utitia′q's Song*]   "This song," Boas writes, "was composed by a young man named Utitiaq, who went adrift on the ice when sealing, and did not reach the shore until after a week of hardships and privations." It was obtained in the Cumberland Sound area between 1883 and 1884. Utitiaq (also spelled Utityak) was the nephew of Kenningnang (Snowwind), composer of "Summer Song."

725.23   *Oxaitoq's Song*]   "This song," Boas notes, "was composed by Oxaitoq, who, believing himself offended by some people, left the village and went on a long hunting trip inland. In the solitude of the mountains he gave vent to his feelings by this song."

726.1–2   *The Hardening . . . Men*]   Addressed by the elder to the younger of the "Beloved Twain," twins who figure prominently in Zuni cre-

ation mythology. In Cushing's translation this speech begins in prose: "Brother, behold!"

726.21–22   *The Generation . . . Corn*]   Addressed by Paíyatuma (the God of Dew) to the people.

727.14   *Ghost-Dance Songs*]   "The great underlying principle of the Ghost dance doctrine is that the time will come when the whole Indian race, living and dead, will be reunited upon a regenerated earth, to live a life of aboriginal happiness, forever free from death, disease, and misery. On this foundation each tribe has built a structure from its own mythology, and each apostle and believer has filled in the details according to his own mental capacity or ideas of happiness, with such additions as come to him from the trance . . . The differences of interpretation are precisely such as we find in Christianity, with its hundreds of sects and innumerable shades of individual opinion. The white race, being alien and secondary and hardly real, has no part in this scheme of aboriginal regeneration, and will be left behind with the other things of earth that have served their temporary purpose, or else will cease entirely to exist.

"There is no limit to the number of these songs, as every trance at every dance produces a new one, the trance subject after regaining consciousness embodying his experience in the spirit world in the form of a song, which is sung at the next dance and succeeding performances until superseded by other songs originating in the same way. Thus, a single dance may easily result in twenty or thirty new songs. While songs are thus born and die, certain ones which appeal especially to the Indian heart . . . live and are perpetuated. There are also with each tribe certain songs which are a regular part of the ceremonial, as the opening song and the closing song, which are repeated at every dance. Of these the closing song is the most important and permanent. In some cases certain songs constitute a regular series, detailing the experiences of the same person in successive trance visions."

727.16   My children . . . the whites]   "In his trance vision of the other world," Mooney says of Nawat (Left Hand), the southern Arapaho chief who composed this song, "the father showed him extensive orchards, telling him that in the beginning all these things had been given to the whites, but that hereafter they would be given to his children, the Indians."

727.20   My father, my father]   "This song relates the trance experience of Waqui'si or 'Ugly Face Woman.' In his vision of the spirit world he went into a large Arapaho camp, where he met his dead father, who took him around to the various tipis to meet others of his departed friends. While they were thus going about, a change came o'er the spirit of his dream, as so often happens in this fevered mental condition, and instead of his father he found a moose standing by his side. Such transformations are frequently noted in the Ghost-dance songs."

727.25   Father]   "A term of reverential affection, about equivalent to 'our father' in the Lord's prayer."

728.4   Our father, the Whirlwind]   "In this song the Whirlwind, personified, wears on his head the two crow feathers, by which the dancers are to be borne upward to the new spirit world."

728.8   I circle around—]   "This song probably refers to the Thunderbird [a mythological being whose flapping wings made the sound of thunder]. There is an energetic swing to the tune that makes it a favorite."

728.14   My children, my children]   "In this song the dreamer tells his friends, on the authority of the messiah, that the predicted spiritual new earth is about to start to come over and cover up this old world. It was also taught, as appears in the messiah's letter, that at the moment of contact this world would tremble as in an earthquake."

728.19   My father, my father]   "According to the story of the author, his father is transformed into a bird even while he looks at him. The song is sung in quick time to hasten the trance."

728.24   The rock, the rock]   "This is one of the old songs now obsolete, and its meaning is not clear. It may mean simply that the author of it climbed a rock in order to be able to see farther, but it is more likely that it contains some mythic reference."

729.1   My children, my children]   "The author of this song saw her children in the other world playing with the *hätiku'tha*, or hummer. On going home after awaking from her trance, she made the toy and carried it with her to the next dance and twirled it in the air while singing the song."

729.5   Father, have pity on me]   "This is the most pathetic of the Ghostdance songs. It is sung to a plaintive tune, sometimes with tears rolling down the cheeks of the dancers as the words would bring up thoughts of their present miserable and dependent condition. It may be considered the Indian paraphrase of the Lord's prayer."

729.11   The crow]   "The sacred bird of the Ghost dance, being revered as the messenger from the spirit world because its color is symbolic of death and the shadow land . . . The crow is depicted on the shirts, leggings, and moccasins of the Ghost dancers, and its feathers are worn on their heads, and whenever it is possible to kill one, the skin is stuffed as in life and carried in the dance."

729.17   The crow is circling above me]   "The author of this song, in his trance vision, saw circling above his head a crow, the messenger from the spirit world, to conduct him to his friends who had gone before. The song is a favorite one, and is sung with a quick forcible tune when the excitement

begins to grow more intense, in order to hasten the trances, the idea conveyed to the dancers being that their spirit friends are close at hand."

729.21   I hear everything]   "This is another song expressive of the omniscience of the crow, which, as their messenger from the spirit world, hears and knows everything, both on this earth and in the shadow land. The tune is one of the prettiest of all the ghost songs."

729.25   There is a good river]   "This song refers to a trance vision in which the dreamer found his people camped by a good, i.e., perennial, river, fringed with abundant bushes or small trees of the *baa-ni'bin* or 'thunderberry.'"

730.4   My children, my children]   "In this song the messiah, addressing his children, is represented as a bird (crow?) flying about the whole earth, symbolic of his omniscience."

730.11   My father, I am poor]   "This song refers to the present impoverished condition of the Indians, and to their hope that he is now about to take pity on them and remove them from this dying world to the new earth above; the feathers worn on their heads in the dance being expected to act as wings . . . to enable them to fly to the upper regions."

730.17   I am going to the sweat-house]   "The maker of this song saw in his vision a sweat-house with a white shell lying upon the mound in front, where a buffalo skull is usually placed. The song evidently refers to some interesting religious ceremony, but was heard only once, and from a young man who could give no fuller explanation."

730.21   My children, my children]   "This beautiful song originated among the northern Arapaho, and is a favorite north and south. In it the messiah is supposed to be addressing his children. There is a rhythmic swing to the vocalic syllables that makes the tune particularly pleasing, and the imagery of thought expressed is poetry itself."

730.28   Father, the Morning Star]   "This song is sung about daylight, just before the closing song, after the dancers have danced all night and are now ready to quit and go home."

731.4   Thus says our father, the Crow]   "This is the closing song of the dance since the return of the great delegation of southern Arapaho and Cheyenne who visited the messiah in August, 1891. . . . [When it is finished,] they unclasp hands, wave their blankets in the air to fan away all evil influences, and go down to the river to bathe, the men in one place and the women in another. After bathing, they resume their clothing and disperse to their various camps, and the Ghost dance is over."

731.11   The snow lies there—*ro'răni'!*]   "This is one of the favorite songs of the Paiute Ghost dance. The tune has a plaintive but rather pleasing effect, although inferior to the tunes of most of the ghost songs of the prairie tribes.

The words as they stand are very simple, but convey a good deal of meaning to the Indian. It must be remembered that the dance is held in the open air at night, with the stars shining down on the wide-extending plain walled in by the giant sierras, fringed at the base with dark pines, and with their peaks white with eternal snows. Under such circumstances this song of the snow lying white upon the mountains, and the Milky Way stretching across the clear sky, brings up to the Paiute the same patriotic home love that comes from lyrics of singing birds and leafy trees and still waters to the people of more favored regions. In the mythology of the Paiute, as of many other tribes, the Milky Way is the road of the dead to the spirit world. *Ro'răni'* serves merely to fill in the meter."

731.27   the willows] *Wai'va,* "the sand grass or wild millet of Nevada (*Oryzopsis membranacea*), the seeds of which are ground by the Paiute and boiled into mush for food."

732.4   Fog! Fog!] "This song is an invocation of elemental forces. It was composed by an old woman, who left the circle of dancers and stood in the center of the ring while singing it."

732.7   The whirlwind! The whirlwind!] "This song may possibly refer to the doctrine of the new earth, here represented as white with snow, advancing swiftly, driven by a whirlwind. Such an idea occurs several times in Arapaho songs."

732.19   The rocks are ringing] "This song was explained to refer to the roaring of a storm among the rocks in the mountains."

732.25   The cottonwoods are growing tall] "This song seems to refer to the return to spring. Throughout the arid region of the west the cottonwood skirting the borders of the streams is one of the most conspicuous features of the landscape."

733.5   Who think you comes there?] "In this the singer tells how he was greeted by his former friend upon entering the spirit world, to which he had gone in search of his mother."

733.17   Mother, come home] "This touching song was a favorite among the Sioux. It was composed by a young woman who saw her dead mother in the other world, and on waking out of her trance vision implores the mother to come back to them again, as her little brother is forever crying after her."

733.21   Now they . . . buffalo] "The author of this song, in his trance vision of the spirit world, sees his old-time friends about to start on a buffalo hunt, and calls to his grandmother to give him back his bow, so that he may join them. The form, 'give it back to me,' is intended to show how far remote is the old life of the Indians, before they used the guns and other things of

the white man. The last line has no particular connection with the rest, except as a common refrain of the ghost songs."

733.26   The whole world is coming] "This fine song summarizes the whole hope of the Ghost dance—the return of the buffalo and the departed dead, the message being brought to the people by the sacred birds, the Eagle and the Crow."

733.28   The Eagle] "The war eagle, from which feathers are procured for war bonnets."

734.5   It is I . . . sacred things] "This song refers to the sacred pipe and the ghost shirt . . . which was supposed to make the wearer invulnerable."

734.12   The father will descend] "This is a summary of Ghost-dance doctrine, closing with an invocation to all present to stretch out their hands toward the west and pray to the Father to hasten his coming."

735.4   That wind, that wind] "To the familiar this little song brings up pleasant memories of the prairie camp when the wind is whistling through the tipi poles and blowing the flaps about, while inside the fire burns bright and the song and the game go round."

735.8   God has had pity on us] "In their confounding of aboriginal and Christian ideas the Kiowa frequently call the Indian messiah 'Jesus,' having learned the latter as a sacred name through the whites."

736.23   seabear] "A fabulous sea monster."

737.1   Dances . . . Ceremonial] Referred to as ts'ē'ts'aēqa (literally, "the secrets"), the winter ceremonial of the Kwakiutl saw the transformation of the Kwakiutl clan system into one of hereditary secret societies, each governed by a particular spirit. The dances of the ceremonial were thought to bring back from the realm of the presiding spirit of the secret society, in a possessed state, one of its young members; its songs were meant to restore him or her to sanity. Boas wrote:

"Each . . . member of a society has his own songs. They open with a burden which varies according to the society to which they belong. This burden is sung in order to indicate the tune. Then follow the words, which, however, are interspersed with repetitions of the burden. The words are called 'the walk of the song' . . . Each song is accompanied by beating of time with batons, and by a drum. The beating is sometimes so loud that it almost drowns the song."

737.3   Hā'mats'a Song] "The presents given away at the time of the initiation of the hā'mats'a and at his later dances are said to be swallowed by him. The song means, therefore, that through his ecstasy his father was compelled to give away much wealth." A hā'mats'a is a cannibal.

737.9   Lau'itsîs] A Kwakiutl-speaking tribe.

737.14   *Hā'mats'a Song of the Koskimo*]   Boas writes, "This song was sung for a youth who had taken the place of another one who had died. Therefore the song says that he safely returned from the spirits." The Koskimo are a Kwakiutl-speaking tribe.

737.20   BaxbakuālanuXsT'waē]   One of the guardian spirits presiding over the winter ceremonial, a "cannibal living on the mountains who is always in pursuit of man." Those who encountered him might become *hā'mats'a* or *kₐî'nqalaɹala* (one who procures human flesh for the hā'mats'a).

738.1   *La'ɹasiqoala*]   "Those on the ocean": a Kwakiutl-speaking tribe.

738.13   *Kₐî'nqalaɹala Song*]   "The girl who danced this kₐî'nqalaɹala was a prostitute in her tribe. She is scourged in this song. The composer meant by the eagle down and the piles of red stones the young men who came in crowds to her house."

738.20   ho'Xhokᵘ]   "Shutting mouth."

738.23   *Song of a Bear Dancer*]   The bear dancers, Boas writes, "are perhaps the most dreaded helpers of the hā'mats'a, as it is their duty, in conjunction with the nū'ɹmaɹ, to punish all transgressions of laws referring to the privileges of the hā'mats'a, or to the winter ceremonial in general . . . The dances consist in violent motions of the body, imitating the actions of a bear who sits on his haunches. Every now and then the dancer growls and scratches the ground with his paws."

738.29   *Nū'ɹmaɹ*]   Boas refers to these as "fool dancers." Messengers and helpers of the hā'mats'a, they would "turn to the right instead of to the left . . . break canoes, houses, kettles . . . in short, act the madman in every way."

739.7   *Song of a Salmon Dancer*]   "The novice," Boas writes, "disappears and stays in the woods several months. When he is brought back, the people hide all the eagle down, the symbol of wealth, but put it on when he enters, indicating that the salmon brings affluence . . . His dance is intended to imitate the motions of the jumping salmon."

739.24   *Ia'kₐîm*]   A water monster who obstructs rivers, endangers lakes and the sea, and swallows canoes.

740.1   *Song of the Ghost Dancer*]   "Elaborate preparations are made for this dance. During the days preceding it the members of the seal society hold close watch that nobody enters the dancing house in which they remain assembled. Then a ditch is dug behind the fire, and speaking tubes made of kelp are laid under the house so as to terminate in the fire. The ghost dancer appears, led by a rope . . . He goes around the fire four times, summoning the ghosts. After he has made the fourth circuit he slowly disappears in the ditch near the fire. The people try to hold him by the rope, but apparently he sinks out of reach. Then many voices are heard coming from out of the

fire—actually the voices of people hidden in the bedrooms who speak through the kelp tubes. It is announced that the ghosts have taken the dancer away, who will return after a certain number of days. When the time of his return is at hand, another dance is held. A carving representing a ghost is seen to rise from out of the ground carrying the dancer."

740.15   *Ts'ē'k'ois*] The ts'ē'k'ois, Boas writes, is a being who is believed to have "many birds in his stomach, the voices of which are heard constantly. He holds small whistles in his mouth, which he exchanges from time to time, and thus produces the various sounds."

740.24   *Kū'siut Song*] This song—part of the *kū'siut* or religious winter ceremonial of the Bella Coola—refers to an episode in Bella Coola mythology in which the sky, fed too much firewood, "broke." *S'aLwalō'sEm* was the only piece to remain intact; the "mouth of the sky" was a permanent opening in the sky created after the disaster to prevent its recurrence.

741.1   *Songs of Spirits*] Curtin obtained these songs sometime between 1884 and 1888 in Redding, California, from a Wintun named Norel-putis.

741.6   *Olelbis*] The primary deity of the Wintun.

741.15   All that is the place for my hair] "Hair in Indian mythology, as in other mythologies, is the equivalent of rays of light when connected with the sun and with planet luminaries."

741.19   *Captive's Song*] The "Captive's Song" is taken from a story translated by Dr. Susan Picotte from the Omaha of her mother, Waoo-winchtcha. According to the narrative it was originally sung sometime before 1854 by Nettle (Sha-nug-a-hi), an Omaha Indian being held for the murder of a Frenchman.

742.6   *Songs . . . Dead*] Nelson observed this five-day ceremony at Razbinsky, Alaska (on the lower Yukon) in January 1881. Referred to as *ûkh'-tă* or *I'-lĭ-g'ĭ* (literally, "throwing away") among the Ikogmut Eskimo, and held infrequently, it was attended by people from villages many miles away who brought offerings for their dead relations.

742.8   We will sing a song] Sung on the second day of the feast, this song was "intended to describe the dangers and difficulties of a journey."

742.13   Come, my brother] Nelson refers to this as a "song of invitation to the shades"; each mourner was supposed to invoke the relative he or she was honoring.

742.24   Oh my brother come back] "A small stick, attached to the end of a line, was dropped through the smoke hole in the roof. One of the women feast givers who was sitting below caught hold of it and began to draw in the

line. As she did this she sang a slow-measured song, keeping time to the motions she made in hauling in the cord. It was very mournful."

743.4   My children, where are you?] "One very old woman, on the end of whose line an arrow was tied, began a song as she drew in the line and was joined by her husband. Both were very old, and their quavering voices united in a sad wail for their lost ones. . . . This song had a wild, mournful harmony, and was sung with an earnestness that made it seem like a requiem for the dead."

743.20   *The Mocking-Bird's Song*] According to Fletcher, this song was taken down by John Comfort Fillmore from a Tigua girl of the pueblo of Isleta, New Mexico.

744.1   *Song of a Gray Wolf*] This song arises in the course of a short narrative, as follows: "Some men were travelling. As they came near a river, and entered the timber, they heard some one singing. [Song quoted.] The men found an old gray wolf, so feeble that he was unable to move, and hungering. They fed him. When he was satisfied, the wolf said: 'I will give you my life. You will live on this world your full lives. You will go all over the world, and have success in war. You will live free from danger and sickness, until your old age is passed.' The wolf also told them to get up before sunrise, if they were to have his life. It is said that if a wolf or coyote sleeps until the sun, he dies at once."

744.9   *The Wizard's Chant*] Translated by John Dyneley Prince.

745.1   Atwuskniges] "An invisible being who occasionally fells trees with a single blow of his stone axe. This accounted for the fall of an apparently healthy tree."

745.15   *Night Chant*] The Night Chant is a nine-day healing ceremony, "performed only during the frost weather, in the late autumn and the winter months,— at the season when the snakes are hibernating." Matthews's sources for these texts included *Hatáli* Natlói ("Smiling Chanter") and *Hatáli* Něz ("Tall Chanter").

745.17   *Tsě'ni Gisǐ'n*] "There is little doubt that some special mythical explanation for this song exists, but none has been obtained . . . The Blue Water House is said to be a pond or lake below the Red Rock House; but the name may be introduced here for the sake of antithesis."

746.1   *Last Tse'ni Gisǐ'n*] "While the two yéi [gods] have gone to resume the garb of ordinary mortals, the patient . . . washes himself all over with the [lotion] which the chanter has prepared in the wicker bowl. The patient also drinks some of this lotion. While washing is in progress the chanter, joined usually by four others, sings a song."

746.16   *Prayer of First Dancers*] "This prayer is addressed to a mythic thunder-bird, hence the reference to wings; but the bird is spoken of as a

male divinity, and is supposed to dwell with other yéi at Tse'gíhi (see note 746.17). The prayer is said at the beginning of work, on the last night of the [night chant]. The shaman speaks it, verse by verse, as it is here recorded, and one of the atsá'lei or first dancers, repeats it, verse by verse, after him."

746.17   Tse'gíhi] "North of the San Juan River, in Colorado and Utah, are a number of cañons abounding in ruined cliff-dwellings. Tse'gíhi is one of these cañons; but the author does not know which. It is often mentioned in the myths as the house of numerous yéi or gods who dwelt in the cliff-houses in ancient days. They are thought to still abide there unseen."

749.26   Atsá'lei Song] "Although it consists mostly of meaningless sylla-bles, [this song] is perhaps the most important of the whole ceremony. The singers are drilled long and thoroughly in private before they are allowed to sing in public. It is said that if a single syllable is omitted or misplaced, the ceremony terminates at once; all the preceding work of nine days is consid-ered valueless and the participants and spectators may return, at once, to their homes. Visiting chanters, and others who know the song well, having sung it at other celebrations of the rite, listen attentively and, if they note an error, proclaim it."

750.1   Song of the Stricken Twins] From a myth-text entitled by Matthews "The Stricken Twins" which accounts for the origins of the songs and obser-vances of a "variant of the ceremony of the night chant." Matthews writes: "The singers are supposed to express the idea that they have traveled all over the land from high green mountain tops to low desert plains searching for remedies and have been vainly promising each others that such remedies would be found."

751.1   Hako] Fletcher obtained these texts between 1898 and 1901 from Tahirussawichi, an elder member of the Chaui band of the Pawnee who acted as the Ku'rahus or "leader of the ceremony." For her translations Fletcher relied heavily on the assistance of James R. Murie, an American-educated Pawnee to whom she refers as her collaborator. Hako refers broadly to "all the articles which belong to the ceremony." Suggesting, in Tahirussawichi's words, "the breathing, vibrating tones from the wooden mouth [of a drum]," the term is used because in the course of the ceremony "everything speaks." "With the Hako," he explains, "we are praying for the gift of life, of strength, of plenty, and of peace." Nearly one hundred songs were associated with the ceremony—which could be held in any season—each with an in-variable place in its elaborate structure.

751.3   Mother Corn Assumes Leadership] Sung by six men (the Ku'rahus or "leader of the ceremony," his assistant, two doctors, a chief, and a second chief), each stanza of this song was repeated four times.

751.5   Mother . . . now comes,] Tahirussawichi explains: "As we sing this song we remember that Mother Earth is very old. She is everywhere, she knows all men, she gave life to our fathers, she gives life to us, and she will

give life to our children. The ear of corn represents venerable Mother Earth, and also the authority given by the powers above."

751.12   Mother . . . is here] Tahirussawichi, Fletcher's informant, explains: "As we sing we think that Mother breathing forth life, who has come out of the past, has now started to lead us on the journey we are to take and to the fulfillment of our desire that children may be given us, that generations may not fail in the future, and that the tie may be made strong between the Father and the Son."

751.18   *Song to the Trees and Streams*] From the second part of the fifth ritual of the Hako. Tahirussawichi comments: "As we are led by the supernatural power in Mother Corn we must address with song every object we meet, because Tira'wa ['the father of all'] is in all things. Everything we come to as we travel can give us help, and send help by us to the Children."

752.5   *Song of the Promise*] From the second part of the fifth ritual of the Hako. "While we were traveling," Fletcher's informant explains, "we sometimes saw a great cloud of dust rising in the distance. When we saw this cloud rolling up from the earth we knew that is was caused by a herd of buffalo running away from us toward the land of the Children.
    "Sometimes a cow and a calf would separate from the herd and come nearer us. We were taught to be mindful of all that we saw upon the journey, for these sights meant the promise of plenty of food for the Children."

752.19   *the A'shiwi*] "The people, the reference being to the Zunis only."

752.20   *'Kiäklo*] An ancestral god appointed to teach the Zuni of their coming to this world.

752.27   Ne'wekwe] "Galaxy fraternity."

753.11   listening spring] "The expression has reference to the hearing of voices in the depths of the water."

753.25   Ko'loowisi] "Plumed serpent."

753.33   the Sha'läko] "Giant couriers of the rain-makers."

753.35   the place with many springs] "Named by the Spaniards Ojo Caliente."

754.3   stone-picture place] "Rocks with pictographs."

754.13   blue-jay spring] "So named from the blue jays gathering about the spring to drink."

754.15   the base of the mesa] "Corn mountain."

754.19   vulva spring] "So named because the rock from which the water flows resembles the vulva."

754.22   Apache spring]   "So named because it resembles certain springs of
the Apaches. 'Kĩaki'ma is another name for this spring, which is near a ruin
of the same name."

755.1   *Invocation to the U'wannami*]   Stevenson heard this invocation in
the winter of 1896 at the Zuni pueblo. Continuing "all night . . . in low,
weird, yet musical tones," it was addressed to the u'wannami (rain-making
deities) by a rain-priest and his assistants; it was associated with a sacred
arrangement of fetishes and elaborate painting in corn meal and pollen, all
meant to bring rain.

755.8   Banked up clouds]   "Cumuli . . . The varying forms of the clouds
are significant to the Zuni mind. Cirrus clouds tell that the u'wannami are
passing about for pleasure. Cumulus and nimbus clouds indicate that the
u'wannami will water the earth."

755.12   All, all . . . sit down]   "At these words the A'shiwanni [rain
priests] sprinkle meal up the line of fetishes, symbolic of the rain-makers
passing over the meal line."

756.8   Cover the earth with her heart]   "Reference to rains. The unexpressed idea is, water is the heart and life of the earth."

756.13   This way]   "Reference to the spirits of the rain-makers passing
over the meal line to the et'tone."

756.18   our fathers . . . chu'ĕttowe]   Refers to the most sacred fetishes of
the Zuni, the ĕt'towe in their dual aspect. Both ĕt'towe consisted of a number of hollow reeds sealed with clay or cotton, and were thought to have
been brought from the underworld by the first rain priests. The first contained water and a small toad, *Bufo punctatus*; the second contained all the
edible seeds known to the Zunis.

FOLK SONGS AND SPIRITUALS

757.4   *Blow Your Trumpet, Gabriel*]   Collected by Charles Pickard Ware in
the Port Royal Islands, Georgia.

757.21   *Buffalo Gals*]   The song now generally known as "Buffalo Gals"
was first composed as "Lubly Fan, Will You Cum Out To Night?" (copyrighted in 1844) by Cool White, and performed with great success by his
blackface minstrel troupe The Virginia Serenaders in the years before the
Civil War. In different parts of the United States the song became known
under a variety of titles, including "Bowery Gals," "Louisiana Gals," and
"Pittsburgh Gals." As "Buffalo Gals" (referring to Buffalo, New York) it was
copyrighted in 1848 as a song of the Ethiopian Serenaders, with no author
indicated.

758.16   *The Cowboy's Lament*]   The origins of "The Cowboy's Lament"
can be traced to British broadside ballads of the 18th century taking the form

of a deathbed confession and lamentation for a life of dissipation; examples include "The Unfortunate Rake," "The Trooper Cut Down in His Prime," "The Bad Girl's Lament," and many others. The earliest printed version of "The Cowboy's Lament" appeared in N. Howard Thorp, *Songs of the Cowboys* (Estancia, New Mexico, 1908), although this omits a number of familiar elements present in the 1910 Alan Lomax version reprinted here. Some elements of the song later became part of "St. James Infirmary" and other similar variants.

762.13   *The Days of '49*]   The song's authorship is attributed to Charley Rhodes, who died in 1877.

769.1   *Frankie and Albert*]   Although some writers have dated this song back as far as the 1850s, there are no known versions in print before the 20th century; the first known publication of the music was a variation of the familiar melody under the title of "He Done Me Wrong," written and composed by Hughie Cannon and copyrighted 1904 by Howly, Dresser Co., New York. The John Lomax version printed here was gathered from a Texas source in 1909. The transformation of "Albert" into "Johnny" occurred in the 20th century.

776.1   *A Home on the Range*]   The original version of "A Home on the Range" was written by Brewster Higley (1823–1911); the earliest extant published version appeared under the title "Western Home" in 1876 in the *Kirwin (Kansas) Chief*, accompanied with a headnote stating that the poem "was written by B. Higley, of Beaver Creek, Smith County, Kansas, and first published in the KIRWIN CHIEF, March 21st, 1874." Higley's version, which did not become widely known until the song's authorship was investigated as a result of an infringement of copyright suit in 1934, differs in a number of respects from the more familiar folk adaptation collected in John A. Lomax's *Cowboy Songs* in 1910. The Higley version follows:

> Oh, give me a home where the buffalo roam,
>   Where the deer and the antelope play,
> Where never is heard a discouraging word
>   And the sky is not clouded all day.
>
> *A home, a home where the deer and the antelope play,*
>   *Where seldom is heard a discouraging word*
>   *And the sky is not clouded all day.*
>
> Oh, give me a gale of the Solomon vale,
>   Where the life streams with buoyancy flow,
> On the banks of the Beaver, where seldom if ever
>   Any poisonous herbage doth grow.
>
> Oh, give me land where the bright diamond sand
>   Throws its light from the glittering streams,
> Where glideth along the graceful white swan,
>   Like a maid in a heavenly dream.

I love the wild flowers in this bright land of ours;
   I love the wild curlew's shrill scream,
The bluffs and white rocks and antelope flocks
   That graze on the hillsides so green.

How often at night, when the heavens were bright
   With the light of the glittering stars,
Have I stood here amazed and asked as I gazed
   If their glory exceeds this of ours.

The air is so pure and the breezes so free,
   The zephyrs so balmy and light,
I would not exchange my home here to range
   Forever is azures so bright.

777.19   *Jesse James*] This earliest known printed version of the ballad appeared five years after the shooting of Jesse James by Robert Ford on April 3, 1882.

778.22   Billy LaShade] Other known variants of the song identify its composer as "Billy Gashade."

778.26–27   *Jim Crack . . . Fly*] The song apparently formed part of the repertoire of Daniel Decatur Emmett's Virginia Minstrels; it was published in *Old Dan Emmit's Original Banjo Melodies* (second series) (Boston: Keith's, 1844), but it is not known whether Emmett actually composed it. The version printed was published in 1846 by F. D. Benteen of Baltimore, with no author credited; it contains the chorus "Jim crack corn I don't care," missing from the Emmett version.

780.1   *John Brown's Body*] The song is believed to have originated in the spring of 1861 among the 2nd Battalion, Boston Light Infantry, stationed at Fort Warren near Boston. James E. Greenleaf, the leader of the battalion's choral society, arranged for its publication that year by the publisher C. S. Hall in a version that differs in a number of respects from the later text reprinted here.

781.1   *John Hardy*] The actual John Hardy on whose criminal career the song is based was executed in January 1894, in Welch, McDowell County, West Virginia.

785.1   *"Johnny come down de hollow"*] The song was collected by William Cullen Bryant on a visit to a South Carolina plantation in 1843. In a letter to the New York *Evening Post* he introduced it as follows: "The light-wood fire was made, and the negroes dropped in from the neighboring plantations, singing as they came. The driver of the plantation, a colored man, brought out baskets of corn in the husk, and piled it in a heap; and the negroes began to strip the husks from the ears, singing with great glee as they worked, keeping time to the music, and now and then throwing in a joke and an extravagant burst of laughter. The songs were generally of a comic character;

but one of them was set to a singularly wild and plaintive air, which some of our musicians would do well to reduce to notation. These are the words."

793.1   *Michael Row the Boat Ashore*]   Collected by Charles Pickard Ware in the Port Royal Islands, Georgia.

795.20   *Nobody Knows the Trouble I've Had*]   Collected in Charleston, South Carolina, by William Francis Allen, who noted in *Slave Songs of the United States* (1867): "This song was a favorite in the colored schools of Charleston in 1865; it has since that time spread to the Sea Islands."

796.5   *Oh, My Darling Clementine*]   In the original sheet music (Boston: Oliver Ditson & Co., 1884) the author is identified as Percy Montrose, of whom nothing further is known.

796.22   *Old Joe Clark*]   This dance-call song exists in a very wide variety of versions, frequently incorporating stanzas from other songs.

800.10   *Poor Naomi*]   The ballad was collected by the Rev. Braxton Craven, president of Randolph College, North Carolina, and published under the pseudonym Charles Vernon in the Greensboro (N.C.) *Patriot* in April 1874.

803.29   *Rye Whisky*]   Variants of this song are frequently known under the title "Jack O' Diamonds."

808.1   *Simple Gifts*]   This Shaker hymn exists in various manuscript versions, and is believed to have been composed in the late 1840s.

812.21   *Starving . . . Claim*]   The manuscript of this version is dated March 8, 1891. The song is designed to be sung to the tune of "The Irish Washerwoman."

817.5   *Sweet Betsey from Pike*]   The song was written by the prospector John A. Stone, who published it under the pseudonym "Old Put" in his 1858 collection *Put's Golden Songster*.

819.13   *"We raise de wheat"*]   The song is cited by Frederick Douglass in *My Bondage and My Freedom* (1855); Douglass comments, "This is not a bad summary of the palpable injustice and fraud of slavery, giving—as it does—to the lazy and idle, the comforts which God designed should be given solely to the honest laborer."

823.1   *Working on the Railway*]   The song is also widely known under the title "Paddy Works on the Erie."

Index of Titles and First Lines

Index of Poets

CATALOGING INFORMATION

American poetry : the nineteenth century.
  edited by John Hollander.

  (The Library of America : 66–67)
  Contents: v. 1. Freneau to Whitman — v. 2. Melville
to Stickney. American Indian poetry. Folk songs & spirituals.
  1. American poetry—19th century. I. Series.
ISBN 0–940450–60–7 (v. 1). — ISBN 0–940450–78–X (v. 2)
PS607.A56   1993   93-10702
811'308—dc20

THE LIBRARY OF AMERICA SERIES

*This book is set in 10 point Linotron Galliard,
a face designed for photocomposition by Matthew Carter
and based on the sixteenth-century face Granjon. The paper
is acid-free Ecusta Nyalite and meets the requirements for permanence of the American National Standards Institute. The binding
material is Brillianta, a 100% woven rayon cloth made by
Van Heek-Scholco Textielfabrieken, Holland. The composition is by Haddon Craftsmen, Inc., and The
Clarinda Company. Printing and binding
by R. R. Donnelley & Sons Company.
Designed by Bruce Campbell.*